THE
ALL ENGLAND
LAW REPORTS

Incorporating the

| LAW TIMES | LAW JOURNAL |
| REPORTS | REPORTS |

1968
VOLUME 1

Consulting Editor for Taxation Cases

CYRIL KING, Q.C.

Bencher of the Middle Temple

Editor

J. T. EDGERLEY

of the Inner Temple and Lincoln's Inn, Barrister-at-Law

LONDON
BUTTERWORTHS

ENGLAND:	BUTTERWORTH & CO. (PUBLISHERS) LTD. LONDON: 88 Kingsway, W.C.2
AUSTRALIA:	BUTTERWORTH & CO. (AUSTRALIA) LTD. SYDNEY: 20 Loftus Street MELBOURNE: 473 Bourke Street BRISBANE: 240 Queen Street
CANADA:	BUTTERWORTH & CO. (CANADA) LTD. TORONTO: 14 Curity Avenue, 16
NEW ZEALAND:	BUTTERWORTH & CO. (NEW ZEALAND) LTD. WELLINGTON: 49/51 Ballance Street AUCKLAND: 35 High Street
SOUTH AFRICA:	BUTTERWORTH & CO. (SOUTH AFRICA) LTD. DURBAN: 33/35 Beach Grove

Printed in Great Britain by R. J. Acford, Ltd., Industrial Estate, Chichester, Sussex.

REPORTERS

CITATION

These reports are cited thus:

[1968] 1 All E.R.

REFERENCES

These reports contain references, which follow after the headnotes, to the following major works of legal reference described in the manner indicated below—

HALSBURY'S LAWS OF ENGLAND, SIMONDS EDITION

The reference 2 HALSBURY'S LAWS (3rd Edn.) 20, para. 48, refers to paragraph 48 on page 20 of Volume 2 of the third edition of Halsbury's Laws of England, of which Viscount Simonds is Editor-in-Chief.

HALSBURY'S STATUTES OF ENGLAND, SECOND EDITION

The reference 26 HALSBURY'S STATUTES (2nd Edn.) 138, refers to page 138 of Volume 26 of the second edition of Halsbury's Statutes.

ENGLISH AND EMPIRE DIGEST

References are to the "Blue-Band" volumes of the Digest, and to the Continuation Volumes of the "Blue-Band" or replacement volumes.

The reference 31 DIGEST (Repl.) 244, *3794*, refers to case No. 3794 on page 244 of Digest Replacement Volume 31.

The reference DIGEST (Cont. Vol. B) 287, *7540b*, refers to case No. 7540b on page 287 of Digest Continuation Volume B.

HALSBURY'S STATUTORY INSTRUMENTS

The reference 12 HALSBURY'S STATUTORY INSTRUMENTS 124, refers to page 124 of Volume 12 of Halsbury's Statutory Instruments, first edition.

A reference to a volume as " 1st Re-issue " refers to the first re-issue of the appropriate volume of Halsbury's Statutory Instruments; references to subsequent re-issues are similar.

ENCYCLOPAEDIA OF FORMS AND PRECEDENTS

The reference 15 ENCY. FORMS & PRECEDENTS (3rd Edn.) 938, Form 231, refers to Form 231 on page 938 of Volume 15 of the third edition, and the reference 7 ENCY. FORMS & PRECEDENTS (4th Edn.) 247, Form 12, refers to Form 12 on page 247 of Volume 7 of the fourth edition, of the Encyclopaedia of Forms and Precedents.

CASES REPORTED

IN VOLUME 1

INDEX

x

CASES NOTED

STATUTES, ETC., NOTED

COMMONWEALTH AND OTHER TERRITORIES

RULES

REGULATIONS

WORDS AND PHRASES

CORRIGENDA

[1968] 1 All E.R.
- p. 163.   LORD ADVOCATE *v.* RELIANT TOOL CO.   Counsel for the appellant: read " *G. Slynn* " instead of " *G. Flynn* ".
- p. 251.   CROSS *v.* BRITISH IRON, STEEL AND KINDRED TRADES ASSOCIATION.   Lines H. 4, 5: delete the words " the plaintiff's claim against the second defendants,".   In fact the writ was never served on the firm referred to as the second defendants.
- p. 472.   Re HOLT'S SETTLEMENT.   Line B. 4: for " age of thirty " read " age of twenty-five ".
- p. 474.   Re HOLT'S SETTLEMENT.   Last line: for " inserting " read " averting ".   Line D. 1, delete " the " immediately before " provides ".
- p. 657.   THE ANNIE HAY.   Line F: for the words " Act of 1954 " substitute " Act of 1894 ".
- p. 934.   R. *v.* OVENELL.   Line D. 5: after " police officers " insert asterisk and add footnote " * Consider with this r. 6 of the Judges' Rules [1964] 1 All E.R. at p. 239 ".
- p. 1104.   Re C. L.   Line G: for " 1967 " read " 1968 ".

Motion.   A

The plaintiffs, Calabar Properties, Ltd., issued a writ on June 14, 1967, against Seagull Autos, Ltd. and Varsity Filling Stations, Ltd., claiming as against the first defendants the relief stated in paras. (i)-(vi) next mentioned. (i) Possession of all those premises forming the lower ground floor of the building known as Clare Court, Judd Street, St. Pancras, in the county of London demised to the first defendants by the plaintiffs by a lease made on Mar. 13, 1966, between   B the plaintiffs and the first defendants and the second defendants, the latter being guarantors of the performance by the first defendants of all the tenant's covenants contained in the lease. (ii) £1,875 rent or alternatively mesne profits to the date of the writ. (iii) Mesne profits from the date of writ till the possession of the premises should be delivered to the plaintiffs. (iv) Without prejudice to any of the foregoing—(a) an injunction ordering the first defendants forthwith C to remove the posters and boardings erected or caused to be erected by these defendants on and around the entrance to the premises; (b) an injunction restraining these defendants, their servants or agents, from affixing or exhibiting or permitting to be fixed on or exhibited to, upon, or from any part of the demised premises, any name plate, placard, poster flags, sign or advertisement except those which were already affixed to the premises at the time of the granting D of the lease, and were referred to in the first schedule to the lease, save as should be approved in writing by the plaintiffs and by any local or other authority whose consent might be required; (c) an injunction ordering the first defendants to remove all petrol pumps by them erected or caused to be erected on the premises without the previous licence in writing of the plaintiffs and in particular the petrol tank referred to in the plaintiffs' letter to these defendants dated Feb. 28, E 1967; (d) an injunction ordering the first defendants to remove any additional or other building or erection made by them or procured by them to be made on the premises and ordering these defendants to restore the premises to the condition of the same before they were interfered with by the defendants or on their orders by additions thereto or by cutting or injuring or altering or defacing the walls, timbers, roofs, or ceilings of the premises; (e) an injunction restraining F the defendants, their servants or agents from carrying on upon any part of the premises, any trade, profession, or business except the business solely of a private garage; (f) an injunction restraining the defendants, their servants, or agents from advertising by way of posters, or hoardings on or around the entrance to or in the premises or otherwise advertising the sale at the premises of fuel for taxicabs and any other vehicles used for public hire, and (g) an injunction G restraining these defendants, their servants or agents from doing or permitting to be done on the premises or any part thereof any act or thing which might be or become a nuisance or annoyance to the tenants of Clare Court, of which the premises constitute part, in particular by keeping open the premises for the purpose of business with the public during the hours 10 p.m. to 8 a.m. (v) Damages for breach of covenant. (vi) Damages for nuisance. The plaintiffs' H claim against the second defendants was for an indemnity.

This was a motion by notice dated Sept. 21, 1967, by the plaintiffs claiming injunctions* in the terms of (iv) excluding (d). The facts are set out in the judgment.

J. Hunter for the plaintiffs.
G. N. Butler for the defendants.   I

BUCKLEY, J.: The writ in the action was issued on June 14, 1967, and by that writ the plaintiffs claim possession of certain premises forming the lower ground floor of a block of flats known as Clare Court, Judd Street, St. Pancras, demised to the first defendants by the plaintiffs by a lease of Mar. 13, 1966. There is a further claim for rent, or, alternatively, mesne profits to the date of the writ, mesne profits from the date of the writ to possession, and, by para. 4 in

_____
* The injunctions claimed in the notice of motion were not expressed to be interlocutory.

THE
ALL ENGLAND
LAW REPORTS

INCORPORATING THE

LAW TIMES REPORTS

AND THE

LAW JOURNAL REPORTS

CALABAR PROPERTIES, LTD. *v.* SEAGULL AUTOS, LTD AND ANOTHER.

D [CHANCERY DIVISION (Buckley, J.), October 27, 1967.]

Landlord and Tenant—Lease—Forfeiture—Writ issued by landlord claiming possession and mesne profits—Injunctions to restrain breaches of covenant also claimed, without prejudice to claim for possession—Motion for injunctions—Whether writ an unequivocal demand for possession constituting election to determine term—Whether plaintiff entitled to ask for relief by

E *way of injunction on footing that covenant in lease still subsisted.*

The plaintiffs issued a writ claiming possession of premises that they had demised to the first defendant. They further claimed rent to the date of the writ or, alternatively, mesne profits to that date, and mesne profits until possession. They also claimed, without prejudice to the foregoing, injunc-

F tions restraining the defendants from doing certain acts, which apparently would be in breach of covenants in the lease. The plaintiffs then moved pending trial for the injunctions. The defendants objected that as the plaintiffs were claiming possession, they were not at the same time entitled to relief on the footing that the lease still subsisted.

Held: the injunctions claimed, being expressly sought without prejudice to the claim for possession, were in the nature of an alternative claim; accord-

G ingly the plaintiffs had not, by issuing their writ, made an unequivocal demand for possession operating as a final election to determine the lease, and it would be open to them at the trial to proceed on the basis that the lease remained on foot, with the consequence that the defendants' objection failed (see p. 5, letter B, post).

Moore v. *Ullcoats Mining Co., Ltd.* ([1908] 1 Ch. 575) followed.

Wheeler v. *Keeble (1914), Ltd.* ([1920] 1 Ch. 57) distinguished.

H [As to what amounts to forfeiture of the term under a proviso for re-entry, see 23 HALSBURY'S LAWS (3rd Edn.) 670, para. 1395; and for cases on the subject, see 31 DIGEST (Repl.) 528-530, *6504-6525*.

As to interlocutory injunctions in such circumstances, see 21 HALSBURY'S LAWS (3rd Edn.) 344, para. 716.]

I Cases referred to:

Birch v. *Wright*, [1775-1802] All E.R. Rep. 41; (1786), 1 Term Rep. 378; 99 E.R. 1148; 31 Digest (Repl.) 312, *4499*.

Jones v. *Carter*, (1846), 15 M. & W. 718; 153 E.R. 1040; 31 Digest (Repl.) 530, *6527*.

Moore v. *Ullcoats Mining Co., Ltd.*, [1908] 1 Ch. 575; 77 L.J.Ch. 282; 97 L.T. 845; 31 Digest (Repl.) 529, *6523*.

Wheeler v. *Keeble (1914), Ltd.*, [1920] 1 Ch. 57; 88 L.J.Ch. 554; sub nom. *Wheeler* v. *Hitchings*, 121 L.T. 636; 31 Digest (Repl.) 530, *6524*.

A the indorsement on the writ they claim, expressly without prejudice to any of the foregoing claims to which I have already referred, injunctions restraining the defendants from doing certain things which, I understand, would be in breach of covenants contained in the lease.

It is said by the defendants that in these circumstances the plaintiffs, having claimed possession, are not at the same time entitled to claim relief on the footing

B that the lease is still subsisting.   Reliance is placed on a decision of YOUNGER, J., in *Wheeler* v. *Keeble (1914), Ltd.* (1).   In that case the plaintiffs issued a writ in which they claimed possession of property as against the defendants, damages for breach of covenants contained in the lease and an interim injunction and costs.   It does not appear from the report what the nature of the interim injunction was.   It was held that the issue of the writ to recover possession was

C an unequivocal determination of the lease on the part of the plaintiffs and that it was not open to them to move for an injunction on the footing that the lease was still subsisting and, accordingly, the motion for interlocutory relief by way of injunction was dismissed.   YOUNGER, J., in the course of his judgment said (2):

D
"In my opinion, there can be no question that the writ on its true construction amounts to an unqualified election on the part of the plaintiffs to determine the lease.   All the relief claimed by the writ subsequent to the claim for possession is subsidiary to that relief and claim for possession."

He referred to various authorities including *Jones* v. *Carter* (3) in which the judgment of the court was delivered by PARKE, B., and *Birch* v. *Wright* (4), a

E decision of ASHURST, J.   Later he said (5):

"In my opinion therefore the plaintiffs are not entitled to obtain the injunction which they ask by simply referring to the terms of the lease.   If they are entitled to an injunction at all it must be apart from the terms of the lease and solely in respect of their own interest in the premises and of some irreparable injury which may be sustained by them through the acts of the

F
defendants on the plaintiffs' own property in case those acts are allowed to continue."

That decision proceeded on the view of the judge that the writ amounted to an unequivocal election on the part of the plaintiffs to determine the lease.   He took that view because he considered that the claim indorsed on the writ was

G such, and that all the relief claimed subsequent to the claim for possession was subsidiary to that claim.

On the other hand, I have been referred to a decision of WARRINGTON, J., as he then was, in *Moore* v. *Ullcoats Mining Co., Ltd.* (6).   This case was among the authorities cited to YOUNGER, J., in *Wheeler* v. *Keeble (1914), Ltd.* (1), but was not specifically dealt with by the judge in any way in the course of his

H judgment.   In *Moore* v. *Ullcoats Mining Co., Ltd.* (6) the plaintiff was the freehold reversioner of property subject to a mining lease.   The lease contained covenants by the lessees to work the mine properly and not to do any act which might occasion loss or damage to the mine, and to keep correct maps and plans, and to allow inspection by the lessor and his agents of such maps and plans. There was a covenant by the lessees to permit the lessor and his agents to inspect

I the property, and a proviso that on default by the lessees in performing or observing any of the covenants, the lessor might re-enter and thereupon the lease should be determined.   The lessor had died in January, 1907, and on Apr. 26, 1907, the lessees refused to allow inspection by the lessor's executors' agent.   The executors gave written notice purporting to determine the lease and demanded possession.

---

(1) [1920] 1 Ch. 57.   (2) [1920] 1 Ch. at p. 62.
(3) (1846), 15 M. & W. 718.   (4) [1775-1802] All E.R. Rep. 41.
(5) [1920] 1 Ch. at pp. 63, 64.   (6) [1908] 1 Ch. 575.

On May 4 they issued a writ by which they claimed recovery of possession of the A
mine, mesne profits and an injunction to restrain the defendants, their servants
or agents from further working the mine so as to hazard, endanger or occasion
loss or damage to the mines or the works therein.   They also asked for an order
that the defendants permit inspection and for a receiver, damages and costs.
Those proceedings were, in fact, discontinued two days later because the plaintiffs
were anxious to get additional relief and for that purpose they issued a new writ, B
having obtained leave to join other causes of action.   They then moved for
an injunction to restrain the defendants from working the mines so as to
endanger them, adopting the language of the covenant in that behalf in the lease.
WARRINGTON, J., in the course of his judgment, said (7):

> " Now two questions arise; the first is—is the writ issued on May 4 a
> re-entry within the words of the proviso for re-entry or equivalent to a   C
> re-entry?   I think that it is now settled that under a proviso for re-entry,
> such as the one in the present case, a writ claiming possession simpliciter, and
> any further relief which is incidental to a claim for possession, would be
> equivalent to a re-entry, and if this writ is to be regarded as a writ of that
> nature, then there has been a sufficient re-entry within the meaning of the   D
> covenant, and the lease is terminated."

There he is putting what YOUNGER, J., considered to be the position in *Wheeler*
v. *Keeble (1914), Ltd.* (8) a claim for possession and for incidental relief and
nothing more.   WARRINGTON, J., went on (9):

> " The question I have to determine on this part of the case is this: is this
> writ an unequivocal claim for possession, a claim by which both parties are   E
> bound?   It is argued on behalf of the plaintiffs that claims 3 and 4 of the
> writ must be read as claims for interlocutory relief only, and that not only
> is an opposite construction a wrong construction to put upon them, but it is
> so impossible a construction that it is quite absurd to suppose that those
> claims can have any such meaning.   I think the real question that I have
> to consider is whether this writ is in such a form that it would not have been   F
> open to the plaintiffs thereafter, if they had considered that their most
> convenient course, to ask for relief on the footing of the lease being in
> existence, and to abandon their claim for possession.   I think I am bound
> to come to the conclusion that this writ is equivocal, and that it is a writ to
> which the plaintiffs, had they been so minded, might have given a meaning
> contrary to that which they now contend is the only meaning which could be   G
> given to it."

The plaintiffs, it will be appreciated, were contending that the issue of the writ
of May 4 had had the effect of determining the lease.   The judge thought that
was not so for the reasons indicated in the passage which I have just read.   He
held, having regard to the form of the proviso for re-entry, actual re-entry or   H
its equivalent (the issue of a writ claiming possession simpliciter) was necessary
in order to determine the lease, and that the notices which the lessor's executors
had given were ineffectual for that purpose.   He also held that the claim in the
writ for possession was inconsistent with the claim for an injunction, and that
the writ was not therefore an unequivocal demand for possession so as to operate
as a final election by the executors to determine the lease.   I
In the present case therefore I have to consider whether this is an action in
which the relief claimed is of the kind with which YOUNGER, J., had to deal
or whether it is relief of a kind which falls within WARRINGTON, J.'s judgment.
I have already said what the relief claimed here is.   The injunctions which are

---

(7) [1908] 1 Ch. at p. 584.
(8) [1920] 1 Ch. 57.
(9) [1908] 1 Ch. at pp. 584, 585.

A claimed are injunctions of a permanent nature. They are injunctions founded on breach of covenants contained in the lease; they are claims, it is true, without prejudice to the claim for possession. Those words seem to make it clear that the claim for an injunction is not an ancillary claim to the claim for possession. On the contrary, it is an alternative claim which is put forward, but put forward in such a way as not to prejudice the claim for possession.

B In my judgment, the relief which is claimed in this action is such that it cannot be said that the landlords have unequivocally decided to determine the lease and seek relief solely on the footing that the lease has come to an end. It would be open to them at the trial of the action to abandon their claim for possession and proceed with their claim for relief on the footing that the lease is still on foot. Accordingly, I think that the case is one which falls within the reasoning of C *Moore* v. *Ullcoats Mining Co., Ltd.* (10) and not within *Wheeler* v. *Keeble (1914), Ltd.* (11) and the preliminary point fails.

Solicitors: *George Mitchell, Colman & Co.* (for the plaintiffs); *Stringer & Stringer* (for the defendants).

[*Reported by* JENIFER SANDELL, *Barrister-at-Law.*]

D ———————

Re NATIONAL UNION OF RAILWAYMEN'S RULES.
NATIONAL UNION OF RAILWAYMEN *v.* REGISTRY OF FRIENDLY SOCIETIES.

E [CHANCERY DIVISION (Pennycuick, J.), November 16, 1967.]

Trade Union—Rules—Alteration—Property of union—Investment of union's funds to be held by trustees of union, of whom there were to be three—Alteration of rules with a view to establishing nominee company controlled by trustees to hold investments—Separation of functions—Alteration of rules invalid as contravening Trade Union Act, 1871 (34 & 35 Vict. c. 31), s. 8.

F The plaintiff, the National Union of Railwaymen, was a registered trade union with assets of great value. It was regulated by rules. Rule 8 provided that the funds and property of the union should be held by the trustees of the union, that there should be three trustees of the funds of the union and they should have power on the direction of the finance committee to invest any moneys in their hands belonging to the union in the names of the G trustees. Difficulties were experienced on changes of trustees as the union held a great number of investments and these had to be transferred on the appointment of each new trustee. With the object of reducing the administrative burden and costs and yet enabling the trustees to retain physical control of the investments, it was proposed to establish a company limited by guarantee, of which the individual trustees would be members and directors, and for the company to hold the union's investments, and to alter H r. 8 accordingly. At the union's annual general meeting a resolution was passed altering the rules so far as necessary to permit the proposal to be effected. On application for registration of the alteration of the rules, the Registrar of Friendly Societies declined to register the proposed alteration on the ground that it was contrary to the provisions of s. 8* of the Trade I Union Act, 1871, which required that the property of a trade union should be vested in all the trustees for the time being of the union and should be under the control of such, i.e., the same, trustees.

Held: the alteration contravened s. 8 by providing for a separation of functions in that the investments would be vested in the nominee company but the control of them would be in the individual trustees; accordingly

———————
(10) [1908] 1 Ch. 575.
(11) [1920] 1 Ch. 57.
* Section 8, so far as material, is set out at p. 7, letters E to G, post.

the alteration was not valid and should not be registered (see p. 8, letters A **A**
and G, post).

[**Editorial Note.** Power is conferred by statute for the Public Trustee to
act as custodian trustee (s. 4 of the Public Trustee Act, 1906) and to hold investments of a registered trade union (War Loan (Supplemental Provisions) Act, 1915,
s. 8 (26 HALSBURY'S STATUTES, 2nd Edn., 33 and 22 ibid., 1153).

As to the vesting of union's property in trustees, see 38 HALSBURY'S LAWS **B**
(3rd Edn.) 387, 388, para. 666; and for cases on trustees and officers, see 45
DIGEST (Repl.) 547, *1247-1249.*

For the Trade Union Act, 1871, s. 8, s. 9, s. 14, Sch. 1, see 25 HALSBURY'S
STATUTES (2nd Edn.) 1248, 1252, 1256.]

Case referred to:
    Pilkington Brothers, Ltd. Workmen's Pension Fund, Re, [1953] 2 All E.R. 816; **C**
        [1953] 1 W.L.R. 1084; 25 Digest (Repl.) 321, *100.*

Adjourned Summons.

This was an application by originating summons dated Apr. 10, 1967, by the
plaintiff, the National Union of Railwaymen, for a declaration that the alteration
of its rules made by resolution no. 132 passed at the annual general meeting of **D**
the union held on July 4 to 15, 1966, was a valid alteration of the rules, and
ought to be registered under the Trade Union Acts, 1871 to 1964. The defendant
was the Registry of Friendly Societies.   The facts are set out in the judgment.

The cases noted below* were cited during the argument in addition to that
referred to in the judgment.

    G. B. H. Dillon, Q.C., and *T. L. G. Cullen* for the union. **E**
    J. P. Warner for the Registry of Friendly Societies.

    PENNYCUICK, J.: The National Union of Railwaymen, to which I will
refer as " the union ", is a registered trade union, with a large membership and
assets of great value.   It is regulated by rules which so far as are now material
include the following:

Rule 8 **F**

" 2. The funds, property, and effects of the union shall be held in trust
by the trustees of the union.   3. There shall be three trustees of the funds
of the union . . . 17. (*a*) The trustees shall have power on the direction of the
finance committee, but, subject as hereinafter expressed, to invest any
moneys in their hands belonging to the union in the names of the trustees,
in or upon . . ." **G**

Clause 17 (*a*) then sets out a long list of authorised investments.

As appears from an affidavit filed in support of the summons by Mr. Greene,
the general secretary of the union, considerable difficulties have been experienced
on changes of trustees by reason of the union's holding a great number of investments, and of these having to be transferred on the appointment of each new **H**
trustee.   On the last occasion transfers of something over two hundred
investments had to be made.   Mr. Greene goes on:

" Accordingly, with the object of reducing the administrative burden and
the costs involved, but so as to enable the trustees to retain physical control
of the investments, the executive committee of the union resolved in
December, 1965, to instruct me to take necessary steps to draw up the **I**
documents to establish a nominee company controlled by the trustees to hold
the union's investments, other than freehold and leasehold land and any
mortgages thereof, and also to prepare any necessary alteration to the rules
of the union . . . The union was advised that certain alterations to r. 8

---

* *Lowe* v. *Dorling & Son,* [1906] 2 K.B. 772; *Osborne* v. *Amalgamated Society of
Railway Servants,* [1911-13] All E.R. Rep. 102; [1911] 1 Ch. 540; *Kirkness (Inspector of
Taxes)* v. *John Hudson & Co., Ltd.,* [1955] 2 All E.R. 345; [1955] A.C. 696; *Bonsor* v.
Musicians' Union, [1955] 3 All E.R. 518 ; [1956] A.C. 104.

A   would be required and, accordingly, the executive committee having agreed
the proposed alterations, duly gave notice that the proposed alterations
to r. 8, together with other alterations to the rules would, on their recommendation, be put to the annual general meeting of the union held on
July 4 to 15, 1966."

B   At that annual general meeting a resolution was duly passed in the following
terms:

"Rule 8, cl. 2, line 2: After 'by' insert 'or under the control of';
cl. 17 (a), line 4: After 'of' insert 'or under the control of'; cl. 17: Add
new sub-cl. (g): 'The union may establish or promote a nominee company
incorporated under the Companies Act, 1948, or any statutory re-enactment
or replacement thereof and under the control of the trustees for the purpose
C   of holding such of the investments or other property of the union as the
finance committee shall from time to time direct'."

The proposal is to establish a company limited by guarantee of which the
individual trustees will be the members and directors and for that company to
act as the holding trustee of the union's investments. The individual trustees
D   will continue to act as the managing trustees. Counsel who appeared for the
registry accepted that this is a practical and sensible proposal and that no
abuse is likely to arise in practice in the case of this union. The registry,
however, felt bound to take, and did most properly take, the objection to the
proposed amendment that the amendment is contrary to the provisions of s. 8
of the Trade Union Act, 1871. Section 8 is in these terms:

E   "All real and personal estate whatsoever belonging to any trade union
registered under this Act shall be vested in the trustees for the time being of
the trade union appointed as provided by this Act, for the use and benefit
of such trade union and the members thereof, and the real or personal
estate of any branch of a trade union shall be vested in the trustees of
such branch, [and there is then interpolated by the Trade Union Act
F   Amendment Act, 1876, these words: 'or of the trustees of the trade union,
if the rules of the trade union so provide'. Section 8 continues:] and be
under the control of such trustees, their respective executors or administrators, according to their respective claims and interests, and upon the
death or removal of any such trustees the same shall vest in the succeeding
trustees for the same estate and interest as the former trustees had therein,
G   and subject to the same trusts, without any conveyance or assignment whatsoever, save and except in the case of stocks and securities in the public
funds of Great Britain and Ireland, which shall be transferred into the names
of such new trustees . . ."

I pause to mention that in practice public companies refuse to act on that auto-
matic vesting provision and require that transfers shall be executed and lodged.
H   Section 14 of the Act of 1871 provides:

"With respect to the rules of a trade union registered under this Act,
the following provisions shall have effect: (1) The rules of every such trade
union shall contain provisions in respect of the several matters mentioned
in Sch. 1 to this Act."

I   Schedule 1 contains the following paragraph:

"4. A provision for the appointment and removal of a general committee
of management, of a trustee or trustees, treasurer, and other officers."

The objection taken by the registry is that s. 8 requires that the property of a
trade union shall be vested in the trustees for the time being of the union, i.e., all
the trustees, and shall be under the control of such trustees, i.e., the same trustees.
I see no answer to this objection. The words, and, in particular, the link through
the word "such" are quite unambiguous. It follows that a provision for

division of functions contravenes the section. The effect of such provision in A
the present case would be that the union's property would be vested in one trustee,
i.e., the nominee company, while the control of those investments would be under
the control not of such trustee but of the individual trustees.

Counsel for the union, cited authorities on the juridical character of a trade
union, and pointed out that the explanation of the requirements of s. 8 is that
a trade union is not an incorporated body. He then contended that s. 8 is B
designed only for that purpose and is not directed to prohibiting a division of
functions. That may well be so but, unfortunately, the section does in terms
require that the two functions shall be exercised by the same trustees.

Counsel for the union pointed out that under the general law a trust instrument
may lawfully provide for division of functions, and if it does so provide the
functions may be divided accordingly. Again, that is so. He then goes on to C
contend that the rules of the union corresponding to the trust instrument may
lawfully provide for division of functions. That would be so if one had to
consider nothing but the ordinary general law, but, unfortunately, in the case of a
trade union the general law, in the shape of s. 8, does unequivocally preclude such
division.

Counsel for the union relied on *Pilkington Brothers, Ltd. Workmen's Pension* D
Fund (1). What was decided there was, however, wholly different, namely,
that under the corresponding provisions of the Friendly Societies Act, 1896,
a corporation might be appointed as a trustee. There was no question there of
division of functions and the court was not concerned with the difficulty with
which I am confronted in this case.

Counsel for the union contended that one should not apply to s. 8 the maxim E
expressio unius est exclusio alterius. I do not altogether follow this contention.
Section 8 is a mandatory provision that the property of the union shall be
vested and controlled in a certain manner. Such a provision clearly does exclude
any other manner of vesting and control, not by virtue of the maxim but from
its very nature.

Counsel for the union referred to s. 9 of the Act of 1871 which provides: F

" The trustees of any trade union registered under this Act, or any other
officer of such trade union who may be authorised so to do by the rules
thereof, are hereby empowered to bring or defend, or cause to be brought or
defended, any action . . .",

etc. touching the property of the union. I do not get any help from that section G
as regards the construction of s. 8.

I find myself reluctantly compelled not to make the declaration asked by
the summons. For the reasons which I have given, the alteration made was
not a valid alteration of the rules and it ought not to be registered. In deference
to an argument addressed to me by counsel for the registrar, I should perhaps
say, without pursuing the point, that s. 8 appears to me perfectly unambiguous H
so that no light can properly be thrown on it by substantive legislation.

Application dismissed.

Solicitors: *Pattinson & Brewer* (for the union); *Treasury Solicitor.*

[*Reported by* JENIFER SANDELL, *Barrister-at-Law.*]

I

---

(1) [1953] 2 All E.R. 816.

A R. *v*. INDUSTRIAL INJURIES COMMISSIONER, *Ex parte* CABLE.

[COURT OF APPEAL, CIVIL DIVISION (Lord Denning, M.R., Willmer and Davies, L.JJ.), October 19, 20, November 14, 1967.]

Industrial Injury—Disablement benefit—Assessment of degree of disability— Greater disability than normal by reason of physical condition at date of
B *assessment—Combination of causes—Loss of left eye due to accident and defect of vision in right eye due to disease, not to accident—Whether defect of vision in right eye was to be taken into consideration to increase assessment— National Insurance (Industrial Injuries) Act 1965 (c. 52), Sch. 4, para. 1 (b) —National Insurance (Industrial Injuries) (Benefit) Regulations 1964 (S.I. 1964 No. 504) reg. 2 (3) (a).*

C As a result of an industrial accident in March, 1962, the applicant lost his left eye. After the accident but before the date of assessment, which was on Aug. 21, 1964, he contracted a disease of his right eye which seriously impaired the vision of that eye. This disease was not directly attributable to the previous industrial accident, but was a result of the combination of the accident and the subsequent disease. In consequence the appellant was nearly
D blind. The Industrial Injuries Tribunal, affirming the decision of the Medical Appeal Tribunal, decided that in assessing disablement the right eye should be disregarded and accordingly rejected the appellant's claim that, pursuant to reg. 2 (3) (a)* of the National Insurance (Industrial Injuries) (Benefit) Regulations 1964, the assessment of his loss of faculty should be adjusted upwards. On appeal from refusal of certiorari to the tribunal,

E **Held:** since the appellant's physical condition of near-blindness at the date of assessment (Aug. 21, 1964) was the result of a combination of two causes, viz., the accident and the disease, it was a result of each of those causes; accordingly the appellant was entitled under reg. 2 (3) (a) to have the assessment of the loss of faculty (forty per cent. for loss of the left eye) adjusted upwards to such extent as was reasonable (see p. 11, letters F and
F G, p. 14, letters E and G, and p. 16 letters A and D, post).

Decision of the DIVISIONAL COURT ([1967] 2 All E.R. 119) reversed.

[As to disablement benefit, see 27 HALSBURY'S LAWS (3rd Edn.) 824, 825, paras. 1451, 1452.

For the National Insurance (Industrial Injuries) Act 1965, Sch. 4, see 45 HALSBURY'S STATUTES (2nd Edn.) 1179.

G For the National Insurance (Industrial Injuries) (Benefit) Regulations 1964, reg. 2, see 15 HALSBURY'S STATUTORY INSTRUMENTS (Second Re-Issue) 370.]

Case referred to:

Minister of Pensions v. *Chennell,* [1946] 2 All E.R. 719; [1947] K.B. 250; [1947] L.J.R. 700; 176 L.T. 164; 17 Digest (Repl.) 486, *307*.

H **Appeal.**

This was an appeal by William James Cable from a decision of the Divisional Court of the Queen's Bench Division dated Mar. 9, 1967, and reported [1967] 2 All E.R. 119, dismissing his application for an order of certiorari to quash a decision dated May 11, 1966, made by a tribunal (G. OWEN GEORGE, ESQ., and J. S. WATSON, ESQ., Q.C., deputy commissioners; SIR ROBERT MICKLETHWAIT,
I Q.C., commissioner dissenting), whereby the tribunal dismissed the appeal of the appellant from a decision of a Medical Appeal Tribunal dated Aug. 21, 1964. The facts are summarised in the judgment of LORD DENNING, M.R., and fully set out in the report of the proceedings before the Divisional Court†.

D. J. Turner-Samuels for the applicant.
Nigel Bridge for the respondent.

Cur. adv. vult.

---

* Regulation 2 (3) (a), so far as material, is set out at p. 11, letter D, post.
† See [1967] 2 All E.R. at p. 120.

Nov. 14. The following judgments were read.   A

LORD DENNING, M.R.: The appellant, Mr. Cable is a furnace-worker. On Mar. 23, 1962, a crucible burst. Molten metal escaped and burned his face, eyes, neck and arms. In December, 1962 his left eye had to be removed. This was the result of the accident; but he could see well with his remaining right eye. In July, 1963 his good right eye failed him. He could only see large objects with it.   B That was not due to the accident, but to a disease contracted after the accident. It was nothing to do with his employment. In consequence he was rendered very nearly blind.

On Aug. 21, 1964, the case came before the Medical Appeal Tribunal for the assessment of his disablement benefit. That is an important date—*the date of assessment.* The question that arose was how was his disablement benefit to be   C assessed? Was he only entitled to benefit in respect of his lost left eye taken alone? Or was the disease in his right eye (which happened subsequently) to be taken into account so as to increase his benefit? The Medical Appeal Tribunal held that the left eye alone qualified for benefit, and the right eye was to be disregarded. They assessed the disablement at forty per cent. for life. The appellant appealed to the Industrial Injuries Tribunal. The majority held that the right eye was to   D be disregarded and affirmed the award at forty per cent. SIR ROBERT MICKLE-THWAIT, Q.C., the commissioner, dissented. He thought that regard could be had to the right eye so as to give him somewhat more than forty per cent. The Divisional Court (1) upheld the majority. The appellant appeals to this court.

The matter depends on the true interpretation of the National Insurance (Industrial Injuries) Act, 1946 (now consolidated in the National Insurance   E (Industrial Injuries) Act 1965) and the benefit regulations (2) made thereunder. They constitute, as DIPLOCK, L.J., said (3), " a self-contained code dealing with the right to benefit ". They form part of the important programme of legislation which, twenty years ago, brought in the welfare state: and I would not wish to be unduly critical of the drafting. It has served the country well. But recent cases have shown up the blemishes. The judges have been at their wits end to   F know what some of the provisions mean. There have been acute differences of opinion among them. If the judges find this difficulty, I can imagine how impossible it must be for those who have to apply them. These are, for the most part, not lawyers, but medical men and civil servants. No wonder they have developed their own peculiar terms, such as " connexion factor " and the like, which they may understand but no-one else does. It would be a good thing if   G time could be found to remedy the blemishes.

Turning to this particular case, many of the statutory requirements are obviously satisfied. When the crucible burst, there was an " accident ". When the appellant was burned in the face and eyes, he suffered a " personal injury " by accident arising out of and in the course of his employment. As a result of that accident and injury, he suffered from " loss of faculty ", namely, the loss of his   H left eye. As a result of that loss of faculty, he incurred a " disability ", namely, he could only see with one eye. So long as he retained a good right eye, his " resulting disablement " was to be assessed at forty per cent., being the scheduled percentage for " loss of one eye, without complications, the other being normal " (see reg. 2 (2) and Sch. 2 thereunder). After the right eye became diseased, the extent of the disablement was to be assessed in accordance with the   I principles stated in Sch. 4 to the Act of 1965 and reg. 2 (3) of the National

---

(1) [1967] 2 All E.R. 119; [1967] 2 Q.B. 429.
(2) National Insurance (Industrial Injuries) (Benefit) Regulations 1964 (S.I. 1964 No. 504) as now amended; see 15 HALSBURY'S STATUTORY INSTRUMENTS (Second Re-Issue) 369. The regulations came into force on Apr. 13, 1964. They continue in effect by virtue of s. 87 (1) of the Act of 1965.
(3) [1967] 2 All E.R. at p. 121; [1967] 2 Q.B. at p. 437.

A   Insurance (Industrial Injuries) (Benefit) Regulations 1964 (4). I will not set out all those provisions, but will go through them and apply them to this case.

First, under Sch. 4, para. 1 (*a*) to the Act of 1965, the medical tribunal must take his *mental and physical condition at the date of assessment,* and see what disabilities (however and whenever caused) which he then suffers as compared with a normal person. In this case they find that he is nearly blind, having lost

B   his left eye and having very defective vision in his right eye.

Second, under para. 1 (*b*) the medical tribunal must (*subject to the regulations*) exclude those disabilities (both pre-accident and post-accident) which have nothing to do with the accident. That means that, subject to the regulations, they ought to exclude altogether the disability due to the defective right eye and assess his disablement at forty per cent.

C   Third, the regulations (5) come into play and are given overriding force so as to modify or alter para. 1 (*b*). Regulation 2 (3) (*a*) provides that:

> " Where as a result of the relevant accident, the claimant has suffered [the loss of one eye] but—(*a*) *as a result of that injury* the claimant may be expected, having regard to his *physical and mental condition at the date of*
D   *assessment* . . . to be subject to greater disabilities than would normally be incurred as a result of such an injury; . . . the loss of faculty suffered by the claimant as a result of [the loss of one eye] shall be assessed at [forty per cent.] *subject to such adjustment as may be reasonable in the circumstances of the case.*"

Applying that reg. 2 (3) (*a*), it seems clear to me that *at the date of assessment*

E   (Aug. 21, 1964) the appellant was subject to greater disabilities than would normally be incurred as a result of the loss of an eye. He was at that date nearly blind. That would not normally be the result of losing one eye; but was this blindness " a result of that injury "? I think it was. His blindness was the result of two causes: (i) the loss of the left eye; (ii) the disease in the right eye. If only one of those causes had taken place, he would be able to see well with one eye;

F   but the two causes combined to make him nearly blind. When two causes co-operate to produce a disability, it is a result of each and both of those causes, see the illustration which I gave in *Minister of Pensions* v. *Chennell* (6), heads 2 and 3. Put quite simply, it is this: as a result of losing his left eye, he is now nearly blind, whereas he would not otherwise have been; for, although he has a defective right eye, he could, apart from the accident, have seen well with his left eye.

G   In my opinion, therefore, the case comes precisely within reg. 2 (3) (*a*). The tribunal ought to have assessed the loss of faculty at forty per cent. and adjusted it upwards to such extent as was reasonable in the circumstances of the case, having regard to his greater disabilities at the date of assessment. This view is supported by the special provisions as to " paired organs " in reg. 2 (5). If the claimant had a defective right eye *before* the accident, and then lost his left eye in

H   the accident, his total blindness would be treated as having been incurred as a result of the accident. His disability would be assessed at one hundred per cent. Regulation 2 (5) (*a*) of the regulations of 1964 would override para. 1 (*b*) (i) of Sch. 4 to the Act of 1965. If the claimant had slightly injured his left eye in the accident (resulting in ten per cent. disablement) and afterwards had lost his right eye by a disease unconnected with his employment (forty per cent.), his total

I   disabilities in both eyes would be treated as having been incurred as a result of the accident, but he would be limited to one-half of the total percentage. Regulation 2 (5) (*b*) would apply to increase the ten per cent. to twenty-five per cent. It would override para. 1 (*b*) (ii) of Sch. 4 to the Act of 1965. Counsel for the

---

(4) S.I. 1964 No. 504. The regulations have been amended by S.I. 1965 Nos. 36 and 1804 and by S.I. 1966 No. 338 (which, inter alia, amends reg. 2), but none of the amendments appear material to the decision.

(5) I.e., those mentioned in footnote (2).

(6) [1946] 2 All E.R. 719 at pp. 721, 722; [1947] K.B. 250 at pp. 254, 255.

respondent argued that these provisions as to " paired organs " showed that **A** reg. 2 (3) (*a*) was very limited in its operation; but counsel for the appellant gave the correct answer when he pointed out that reg. 2 (5) (*b*) only applies when it needs to be invoked so as to *increase* an assessment (see reg. 2 (6)). It leaves reg. 2 (3) (*a*) free to operate in other cases, such as the present, where there is no increase under reg. 2 (5) (*b*).

Counsel for the respondent, explained to us the meaning of the phrase **B** " connexion factor " which is used in the ministry. It means the factor which occurs when two disabilities connected together result in a greater total disability than each taken separately. He said that, when a pre-accident disability was followed by an industrial accident, the man was given the benefit of the " connexion factor " under Sch. 4, para. 1 (*b*) (i): but that, when the industrial accident came first and was followed by a subsequent non-industrial disability, **C** the claimant did not get the benefit of the " connexion factor " under Sch. 4, para. 1 (*b*) (ii). This is no doubt true and it was accepted by DIPLOCK, L.J., in the Divisional Court (7). Counsel for the respondent submitted that those provisions of the paragraphs created a " statutory chain of causation " which was not affected by reg. 2 (3): and this argument was accepted by the Divisional Court (8). I am afraid that I cannot take the same view. The words of the **D** regulations are expressly given priority over the paragraphs (9). In my opinion reg. 2 (3) (*a*) prevails over para. 1 (*b*) (ii) of Sch. 4 to the Act of 1965.

I find myself, therefore, in agreement with SIR ROBERT MICKELTHWAIT, Q.C. (10). I would allow this appeal and remit the case to the tribunal so that they can apply reg. 2 (3) (*a*) and make " such adjustment as may be reasonable in the circumstances of the case ". In other words, they are not limited to assessing **E** the appellant's disabilities at forty per cent. but may increase the award to a reasonable figure.

WILLMER, L.J.: I have found this an exceedingly difficult and baffling case, and I confess that both during and since the argument my view has varied more than once. In the end I have come to the conclusion, in agreement with LORD DENNING, M.R., that the Divisional Court (11) came to a wrong conclusion **F** and that the appeal should be allowed. My difficulty has been caused by the obscurity of the regulations (12) which we have had to construe, when read in conjunction with the terms of the enabling Act. It is a melancholy commentary on these regulations that the three judges of this court have reached a conclusion as to the meaning of the relevant regulation diametrically opposed to that reached by the three judges of the Divisional Court (13), and that the members **G** of the tribunal were themselves divided. I regard it as deplorable that in a matter which so vitally affects the lives and welfare of working men and women there should be so much obscurity and so much room for doubt. I venture to express the hope that, whatever else may result from this appeal, it may lead to some revision of the regulations so as to express their meaning with greater clarity.

I refrain from attempting any detailed analysis of the scheme of the National **H** Insurance (Industrial Injuries) Act 1965, since this has been lucidly explained in the judgment of DIPLOCK, L.J., (14) in a manner which is accepted as correct by both parties. I pass at once, therefore, to the question raised by the appeal, which concerns the assessment of the disablement benefit to which the claimant is entitled.

It is common ground that the appellant's disablement arose from the loss of his **I**

---

(7) [1967] 2 All E.R. at p. 122; [1967] 2 Q.B. at p. 439.
(8) [1967] 2 All E.R. 119, see at p. 124, letter C; [1967] 2 Q.B. 429.
(9) See paras. 1 (*b*), 2 of Sch. 4 and p. 13, letter E, post.
(10) He dissented from the decision of the tribunal; see [1967] 2 All E.R. at p. 120.
(11) [1967] 2 All E.R. 119; [1967] 2 Q.B. 429.
(12) National Insurance (Industrial Injuries) (Benefit) Regulations 1964 (S.I. 1964 No. 504).
(13) [1967] 2 All E.R. at p. 121, 122; [1967] 2 Q.B. at pp. 436-439.
(14) [1967] 2 All E.R. 119; [1967] 2 Q.B. 429.

A left eye (the " relevant loss of faculty ") resulting from an injury received (the " relevant injury ") in consequence of an accident at work (the " relevant accident "). By para. 1 of Sch. 4 to the Act of 1965 the extent of disablement is to be assessed by reference to the disabilities incurred by the appellant as a result of the relevant loss of faculty. Paragraph 1 (*a*) goes on to provide that

B ". . . the disabilities to be taken into account shall be all disabilities . . . to which the claimant may be expected, having regard to his physical and mental condition at the date of the assessment, to be subject . . . as compared with a person of the same age and sex whose physical and mental condition is normal."

At the date of the assessment in the present case the disabilities to which the claimant was subject were (i) the loss of his left eye (the relevant loss of faculty),
C and (ii) an impairment of the right eye. He would not have been subject to the latter disability but for a disease contracted after, and not directly attributable to, the relevant accident. To such a state of affairs para. 1 (*b*) is directly relevant. It provides as follows:

"any such disability shall be treated as having been incurred as a result of the relevant loss of faculty except that, subject to the provisions of any
D regulations made under para. 2 of this Schedule, it shall not be so treated in so far as the claimant . . . (ii) would not have been subject thereto but for some injury or disease received or contracted after, and not directly attributable to, [the relevant] accident."

It is conceded that if this provision stood alone, having regard to its clear and unambiguous terms, this appeal, and the appellant's application for certiorari,
E must necessarily fail.

It will be seen, however, that para. 1 (*b*) is expressed to be subject to any regulations made under para. 2. By para. 2 provision may be made by regulations for further defining the principles on which the extent of disablement is to be assessed. It is common ground that this provision empowers the Minister to modify by regulation the express terms of the Act of 1965, and it is accepted that
F para. 1 (*b*) is to be read as subject to any such regulation. It is further accepted that some at least of the regulations that have been made do have the effect of modifying the provisions of that paragraph. This is notably so in the case of reg. 2 (5) of the National Insurance (Industrial Injuries) (Benefit) Regulations 1964, which deals with disbursement in respect of one of two paired organs, and which has the effect of modifying in favour of the claimant the provisions of para. 1 (*b*) of
G the Schedule. In the present case, however, the appellant does not seek to rely on that regulation, since it is clear that in the particular circumstances of the case it would not have the effect of increasing the disablement benefit to which he is already entitled under Sch. 2 of the regulations for the loss of his one eye, viz., forty per cent.

H The appellant's case is based on reg. 2 (3), which, it is contended, entitles him to have the assessment of his disablement adjusted in his favour, having regard to the greater disabilities to which he is subject in view of the supervening impairment of his right eye. This regulation provides:

"Where as a result of the relevant accident, the claimant has suffered an injury specified in the said Sch. 2, but—(*a*) as a result of that injury the
I claimant may be expected, having regard to his physical and mental condition at the date of the assessment in respect thereof, to be subject to greater disabilities than would normally be incurred as a result of such an injury . . . the loss of faculty suffered by the claimant as a result of such injury shall be assessed by reference to the degree of disablement set against such injury in column 2 of the said Sch. 2 subject to such adjustment as may be reasonable in the circumstances of the case."

The appellant's case is that because of the impairment of his right eye he is plainly subject to greater disabilities as the result of the loss of his left eye than would normally be incurred as a result of that injury. He is, therefore, entitled to have A the assessment of his disablement adjusted in his favour regardless of the provisions of para. 1 (*b*) of Sch. 4 to the Act of 1965. For where there is a conflict between that paragraph and any regulation made under the power conferred by para. 2, the regulation must prevail.

For the Minister, on the other hand, it is contended that reg. 2 (3) does not apply. That regulation, it is argued, is not dealing with questions of causation, B but merely confers power to adjust the assessment of quantum in special cases (of which this is not one), where no question of causation is involved. Questions of causation, it is said, are dealt with by para. 1 of Sch. 4 to the Act of 1965, sub-para. (*b*) of which lays down what has been described as a " statutory chain of causation " (15). By this it is specifically provided that a disability to which the claimant would not have been subject but for some disease contracted after, C and not directly attributable to, the accident, is *not* to be treated as having been incurred as a result of the relevant loss of faculty. Reliance is also placed on reg. 1 (2), which provides that expressions used in the regulations are to have the same meaning as in the Act (now the Act of 1965 (16)). If, therefore, reg. 2 (3) were intended to abrogate or modify this statutory chain of causation, it was to be expected that this intention would be expressed in clear and unambiguous D language.

I certainly feel the force of this argument, all the more so having regard to what I have already said about the obscurity of the regulation. On the whole, however, I have come to the conclusion, not without hesitation, that reg. 2 (3) is sufficiently clear, and that it does have the effect contended for on behalf of the appellant. It is plain that because of the condition of his right eye, the appellant E was at the date of the assessment, and is now, subject to greater disabilities than would normally be incurred as a result of the loss of his left eye. This means that the loss of his left eye is of greater consequence to the claimant than it would have been had his right eye remained normal. Giving effect to the ordinary sense of the words used in the regulation, it seems to me that *as a result of the loss of his left eye*, the appellant is subject to greater disabilities than would normally be F incurred as a result thereof. If that is right, then plainly reg. 2 (3) applies to this case, and has the effect of entitling the appellant, notwithstanding the provisions of para. 1 (*b*) of Sch. 4 to the Act of 1965, to rely on the impairment of his right eye as increasing the disability from which he suffers as a result of the loss of his left eye. He is, therefore, entitled to ask for an upward adjustment of the degree of disablement appropriate to the loss of the left eye as prescribed by Sch. 2 to G the regulations of 1964.

It is with reluctance and hesitation that I differ from the view expressed by the experienced judges of the Divisional Court (17); but I venture, with all respect, to criticise the reasoning by which they reached their conclusion. DIPLOCK, L.J., having quoted the relevant part of reg. 2 (3), said (18):

" In order to determine whether the conditions specified in reg. 2 (3) (*a*) H are satisfied, it is necessary first to make a comparison between the disabilities to which the claimant may be expected to be subject *as a result of the injury suffered by him as a result of the relevant accident* and the disabilities which would normally be incurred as a result of that injury."

So far I wholly agree; but DIPLOCK, L.J., then went on (18):

" It is, therefore, necessary to consider each disability separately in order I to determine whether or not it was incurred by the claimant as a result of the injury suffered by him as a result of the relevant accident."

With all respect, this seems to me to be a complete non sequitur, and moreover

(15) See [1967] 2 All E.R. at p. 121, letter F; [1967] 2 Q.B. at p. 437.
(16) See National Insurance (Industrial Injuries) Act 1965, s. 87 (2).
(17) [1967] 2 All E.R. 119; [1967] 2 Q.B. 429.
(18) [1967] 2 All E.R. at p. 123; [1967] 2 Q.B. at pp. 440, 441.

A betrays a failure to have regard to the special circumstances of this particular case. If the supervening disease had been one affecting a different part of the body, not relevant to the eyesight, I would agree that any disability resulting therefrom would have to be considered separately from the disability resulting from the loss of the eye. But it is of the essence of the present case that the disabilities of the appellant are closely connected, in that they affect each of his two eyes and
B react on each other. The disease of the right eye renders the loss of the left eye so much the more serious; and the loss of the left eye in turn magnifies the gravity of the impairment of the right eye. In the circumstances of this case it is quite unreal to consider the disability in respect of each eye in isolation. I can see nothing in the provisions of reg. 2 (3) which would require the tribunal to do so, and in my judgment the Divisional Court (19) misdirected themselves in approach-
C ing the question in this way. Since this was the basis on which the Divisional Court (19) founded their conclusion, it follows that in my view the judgment appealed from cannot stand. In these circumstances I agree that the appeal should be allowed.

      DAVIES, L.J.: In the first place I would wholeheartedly associate myself with the observations which have been made by my lords as to the complication
D and obscurity of the language which falls to be construed by the court in this case. In the light of the differing opinions of those who have had to consider the matter, it is impossible to imagine how an injured workman, or indeed his trade union representatives or advisers, could form any reliable view as to his rights under the statute and regulations.

      It is fundamental, in my opinion, to bear in mind throughout the case that the
E provisions of the statute (now Sch. 4 to the National Insurance (Industrial Injuries) Act 1965) are expressly made subject to the provisions of the regulations. The provisions of para. 1 (*b*) of Sch. 4 are " subject to the provisions of any regulations made under para. 2 of this Schedule ". Regulation 2 (1) of the National Insurance (Industrial Injuries) (Benefit) Regulations 1964, provides that

F   " s. 12 (2) of the Act (20) (general principles relating to the assessment of the extent of disablement) shall have effect subject to the provisions of these regulations."

It must be taken, therefore, that if in fact there is any conflict between the Schedule and the regulations, then the latter must prevail.

      By s. 12 (1) of the Act of 1965 a claimant is entitled to disablement benefit if he
G suffers as a result of the relevant accident from loss of a physical or mental faculty with resulting disablement. Paragraph 1 (*a*) of Sch. 4 may be summarised as providing that in the first instance all disabilities at the date of assessment shall be taken into account. Paragraph 1 (*b*) provides that any such disability shall be treated as having been incurred as a result of the relevant loss of faculty, but excludes what may be called (i) pre-accident disease or injury and (ii) post-
H accident disease or injury. What, of course, is submitted for the Crown in the present case is that the condition of the appellant's right eye, being admittedly quite unconnected with the accident in which he lost his left eye, must be excluded from consideration, for Sch. 4 expressly provides that the disability of the right eye shall not be treated as having been incurred as a result of the relevant loss of faculty. If Sch. 4 stood alone and without reg. 2 (3), this might well have been
I the position.

      That regulation has already been quoted, and I forbear to repeat it; but in my view it applies to the present case. Here the appellant has suffered a relevant accident and as a result has suffered a relevant injury, namely, the loss of his left eye; and it is only in respect of that that he is entitled to disablement benefit. Having regard, however, to his physical condition at the date of assessment, namely, the supervening defect of the right eye, he may be expected to be subject

---

    (19) [1967] 2 All E.R. 119; [1967] 2 Q.B. 429.
    (20) I.e., the National Insurance (Industrial Injuries) Act, 1946, now replaced by para. 1 of Sch. 4 to the National Insurance (Industrial Injuries) Act 1965.

to greater disabilities than would normally be incurred as a result of the loss of A a left eye. Therefore the loss of faculty suffered by the appellant as a result of the loss of his left eye has to be assessed in accordance with the scale, but subject to such adjustment as may be reasonable in the circumstances of the case. There is really, in my judgment, no escape from this conclusion. The Medical Board or Medical Appeal Tribunal are, by the concluding words of reg. 2 (3), given a wide discretion. They are not to grant disablement benefit for the disease of the right B eye; for that did not result from the accident or injury. In assessing the disablement benefit in respect of the left eye, however, they are to consider whether the disablement resulting from the loss of the left eye would in the light of his then condition be greater than it would normally be. I agree with counsel for the appellant that reg. 2 (3) (a) is a special scaling up provision for such circumstances, just as reg. 2 (3) (b) is, conversely, a scaling down provision.   C

I hope that it would not be doing an injustice to the argument of counsel for the respondent to say that it falls into two main parts. His main submission is that the appellant's case is in flat contradiction of para. 1 (b) (ii) of Sch. 4, and that to take into consideration in the assessment the condition of the appellant's right eye would be to compensate him for something which was not the result of the accident resulting in injury resulting in loss of faculty resulting in disable- D ment. For the reasons which I have indicated, that, in my view, is not so. The disablement benefit is and remains benefit in respect of the loss of the left eye; but it is benefit not for a normal one-eyed man but for an abnormal one-eyed man, albeit the abnormality developed after and not in consequence of the accident.

Secondly, there was pressed on the court the fact that the appellant's contention might appear to give rise to serious anomalies. That might well be so, as E SIR ROBERT MICKLETHWAIT, Q.C., admitted in his dissenting opinion. Perhaps the most obvious one adverted to by counsel for the respondent was that which might arise under reg. 2 (5). That deals with paired organs; and the present case is, of course, a paired organ case. What is said is that under reg. 2 (5) (b) if the claimant having lost his left eye, which entitles him to forty per cent., subsequently, due to non-industrial causes as here, develops a serious defect in the F right eye to the extent of say forty per cent., he would only be entitled to one-half of the total of eighty per cent., i.e., forty per cent.; but if the claimant be right, he may well be entitled to something more than forty per cent., for example the sixty per cent. suggested by SIR ROBERT MICKLETHWAIT, Q.C. Indeed it is pointed out that even if the supervening non-industrial event resulted in the complete loss of the right eye, the claimant would only, under this regulation, be G entitled to one-half of one hundred per cent. Counsel for the appellant replies that reg. 2 (6) makes it clear that reg. 2 (5) only applies to cases where it would increase the assessment to which the claimant would otherwise be entitled and not to the converse case.

It was also suggested that if the construction of reg. 2 (3) for which the appellant contends is correct, this might open the door to a flood of claims for upward H reviews of disablement benefit already made, in cases where some non-industrial disease or injury has supervened. All that I would say about that contention is that, if that be so, be it so.

At the end of it all, the case comes down to the construction of reg. 2 (3) (a). On this I agree with my lords and SIR ROBERT MICKLETHWAIT, Q.C. If this result does not commend itself to the Minister and his advisers, as I gather it I does not, then it should not be beyond their power so to alter the regulations as to make their meaning clear to all. I agree that the appeal should be allowed.

Appeal allowed; certiorari granted. Leave to appeal to the House of Lords granted.

Solicitors: *W. H. Thompson* (for the appellant); *Solicitor, Ministry of Social Security* (for the respondent).

[*Reported by* F. GUTTMAN, ESQ., *Barrister-at-Law.*]

A   ADLAM *v.* THE LAW SOCIETY.

[CHANCERY DIVISION (Pennycuick, J.), November 8, 1967.]

*Solicitor—Articled clerk—Qualification for solicitor to take—Continuous practice
for five years—Solicitor in practice for more than five years but taking out
practising certificate after Dec. 15 on four occasions in the five years—*
B   *Whether solicitor had been in continuous practice for five years for the purposes
of Solicitors Act,* 1957 (5 & 6 *Eliz.* 2 c. 27), *s.* 41 (1).

On four occasions in five periods of twelve months from 1961-62 to 1965-66
the plaintiff solicitor, who began practising in 1960, took out his practising
certificate late, that is to say, it was issued to him after Dec. 15 in the
relevant year and so was not retrospective to the expiry day, Nov. 16, of the
C   immediately preceding certificate. The plaintiff practised as a solicitor
throughout. In 1966 he wished to take an articled clerk and forwarded the
articles of clerkship to the Law Society for registration. On the question
whether the plaintiff on Nov. 21, 1966, had been in continuous practice as a
solicitor for a period of five years, as was required by s. 41 (1)* of the Solicitors
Act, 1957, if he were to be entitled to take an articled clerk,

D   **Held:** the plaintiff had not been continuously in practice for a period
of five years as required by s. 41 (1), because in the years when his practising
certificate was issued after Dec. 15 he had not been qualified lawfully to act
as a solicitor during intervals between the dates of his practising certificates
and the last preceding Nov. 16, so that there had been breaks in the continuity of lawful practising in four of the five twelve-month-periods in
E   question (see p. 19, letter H, post).

[**Editorial Note.** The issue date and the expiry date of practising certificates
have been altered by s. 4 of the Solicitors Act 1965 (45 HALSBURY'S STATUTES,
2nd Edn., 1518); but it is thought that this has no effect on the principle decided
in the present case. Section 4 was brought into operation on July 28, 1966, by
the Solicitors Act 1965 (Commencement No. 2) Order 1966, S.I. 1966 No. 862.
F   As to qualifications of clerks and principals for entry into articles, see 36
HALSBURY'S LAWS (3rd Edn.) 23, 24, para. 36, and as to registration of articles,
see ibid., p. 25, para. 38; and for cases as to registration of articles of clerkship,
see 43 DIGEST (Repl.) 25, *14-22.*

For the Solicitors Act, 1957, s. 1, s. 9, s. 10, s. 41, see 37 HALSBURY'S STATUTES
(2nd Edn.) 1055, 1062, 1063, 1088.]

G   **Adjourned Summons.**

This was an application by originating summons dated July 12, 1967, by the
plaintiff, Gordon Leonard Adlam, for the determination of the question whether
on Nov. 21, 1966, he had been in continuous practice as a solicitor for a period
of five years as required by s. 41 (1) of the Solicitors Act, 1957. The defendants
were the Law Society. The facts are set out in the judgment.

H   *Paul V. Baker* for the plaintiff.

J. W. Brunyate for the defendants.

PENNYCUICK, J.: The facts of this case are not in dispute; they are
set out in Mr. Adlam's affidavit. His first practising certificate was issued on
Mar. 7, 1960. Since that date he has practised continuously as a solicitor, first
I   as an assistant to another firm and, later, on his own account. I used the word
" continuously ", but, unfortunately, that word requires qualification, for
reasons which I will mention in a moment. Mr. Adlam has, on four occasions,
been late in taking out his annual practising certificate; particulars are set out
in his affidavit; the effect is that in each of the four years in question he did not
take out his practising certificate until after the month's period of grace allowed
under the Solicitors Act, 1957, and that, in the event, he was, for a relatively
short period in each of those four years, carrying on his practice as a solicitor

---

* Section 41, so far as material, is set out at p. 18, letter D, post.

without having a practising certificate in force. Perhaps I should read the **A** particulars of the dates as given by Mr. Adlam. During the years 1959-60 to 1965-66 inclusive, the Solicitors Act, 1957, was in force and the relevant date for taking out a certificate in each year was Nov. 16. Disregarding the first year in which he commenced his practice, he was in time in 1960-61; in 1961-62 the certificate was issued on Dec. 20; in 1962-63, on Jan. 18; in 1963-64 he was in time; in 1964-65, the certificate was issued on Dec. 18; and, in 1965-66, **B** on Dec. 17. So, therefore, there was only one year out of the last five in which he was in time, and one year the certificate was issued after the month of December.

Mr. Adlam was minded, in 1966, to take a Mr. Simon Sik On Ip as an articled clerk, and the articles of clerkship are exhibited. Thereupon, he forwarded the articles to the Law Society for registration, under art. 9 of the Students Regula- **C** tions, 1962. The Law Society, however, objected to the articles on the ground that Mr. Adlam was not eligible to take an articled clerk having regard to the provisions of s. 41 of the Act of 1957. Section 41 is in these terms:

" (1) No solicitor who has not at some time been in continuous practice as a solicitor for a period of five years shall, without the special leave in writing of the society, take any articled clerk . . . (4) If any solicitor takes or **D** has an articled clerk in contravention of any of the foregoing provisions of this section, the society may of its own motion discharge the articles of that clerk upon such terms, including terms as to return of premium, as the society thinks fit."

Now pausing at that stage, it is clear that a solicitor, in order to be entitled to **E** take an articled clerk under that section, must have been in fact in practice continuously for a period of five years. It is also, to my mind, clear that he must have been lawfully in practice for the same continuous period. It is impossible to treat a solicitor as having been in continuous practice for a five year period if, during any part of that five year period, his practice was unlawful. That brings me back to s. 1 of the Act of 1957, which is in these terms: **F**

" No person shall be qualified to act as a solicitor unless—(a) he has been admitted as a solicitor; and (b) his name is for the time being on the roll; and (c) he has in force a certificate issued by the society in accordance with the provisions of this Part of this Act authorising him to practise as a solicitor (in this Act referred to as a ' practising certificate '); . . ."

I need not read the rest of the section. **G**

There is no suggestion that Mr. Adlam does not fulfil the first and second requirements, but, as regards para. (c), it is said, on behalf of the Law Society, that during the periods, in the four years to which I have referred, in which he had no practising certificate, he was not qualified to act as a solicitor.

Before giving my own view on that point, I should refer to s. 9 and s. 10 of the Act of 1957, which contain provisions as to the issue of a practising certificate. **H** Section 9 provides:

" (1) Not less than fourteen days before a solicitor applies for a practising certificate, he shall attend at the society's hall, either in person or by his agent, and deliver a written declaration in such form as the society may by regulations made with the concurrence of the Lord Chancellor, the Lord Chief Justice and the Master of the Rolls prescribe—(a) specifying the **I** applicant's full name, place or places of business and date of admission; and (b) containing such other particulars as the society may by such regula- tions as aforesaid prescribe; and (c) signed by the applicant personally: . . ."

Then there is a proviso, which I need not read; and there are provisions for registration and for false statements. Section 10 reads:

" (1) Application for a practising certificate shall be made in person at the

A   society's hall either by the applicant or by his agent and, subject to the
provisions of the two next following sections, if the society is satisfied that
the name of the applicant is on the roll and that he is not for the time being
suspended from practice and that the requirements of sub-s. (1) of the
last foregoing section have been complied with, the society shall thereupon
deliver a practising certificate in such form as the society may by regulations
B   made with the concurrence of the Lord Chancellor, the Lord Chief Justice
and the Master of the Rolls prescribe.

" (2) Every practising certificate issued after Nov. 15 and before Dec. 16
in any year shall bear the date of Nov. 16 in that year, and every other
practising certificate shall bear the date of the day on which it is issued.

" (3) Every practising certificate shall have effect from the beginning of
C   the day of which it bears the date, and that date shall be entered by the
society on the roll.

" (4) Every practising certificate shall expire at the end of Nov. 15 next
after it is issued . . ."

I should mention at this stage that those provisions have, for the years 1966-67
onwards been superseded by the Solicitors Act 1965.   For present purposes, it
D   is sufficient to look at the Act of 1957, which covers practically the whole of the
relevant period.

The effect of s. 9 is that a solicitor must deliver his declaration one month
before a practising certificate can be issued to him.   If the certificate is issued
within one month of Nov. 16, then it bears date Nov. 16; and s. 10 (3) makes it
clear that the practising certificate has retrospective operation as from that date.
E   On the other hand, a certificate issued after that one month does not have any
retrospective operation, so that where the declaration is not delivered in such
time as to enable the practising certificate to be issued before Dec. 16, the effect
is that the solicitor in question has been practising without a practising
certificate as from Nov. 15 until the date when the practising certificate is in
fact issued.   Turning back to s. 1, the result is this, that so long as the practising
F   certificate is issued within what one may call the one month's period of grace,
it operates retrospectively, so that the solicitor is treated as having been continuously qualified to act as a solicitor.   On the other hand, where the certificate
is issued after the end of the period of grace, the solicitor has been acting as a
solicitor while not qualified so to act during the period between the expiry of the
last certificate and the issue of the new certificate.   In other words, during that
G   period, although he has been practising, in fact he has been practising unlawfully.

Applying the statutory provisions to the present case, the conclusion, to my
mind, is inescapable, that during a relatively short period in each of the four
years in question, Mr. Adlam, although he was practising in fact as a solicitor,
was not practising lawfully as such and it is quite impossible to say, as a matter
of construction, that he was, during these short periods, in practice as a solicitor,
H   within the meaning of s. 41 of the Act of 1957.   That means, of course, that
he cannot make out the continuous period required by s. 41.   It is a period of
five years, with short breaks in four of the years.

Counsel, who appeared for Mr. Adlam, pointed out—and, no doubt, it is right—
that the object of s. 41 is to ensure that an articled clerk has, during the period of
his articles, a competent master.   On the other hand, that object is ensured by
I   a provision in certain terms and the court is bound to construe those terms
according to their natural meaning.

Counsel for Mr. Adlam said that one is entitled to take a broad view of the
matter and say that, read in their context, the requirements are sufficiently
satisfied if one can show that the solicitor was in continuous practice in fact for
five years and that during most of that time he was duly covered by a practising
certificate and that, during such gaps as there may have been, he showed at
least an intention to take out a certificate.   I do not think that it is open to me,
on the wording of the section, to accept that submission.

A It is worth while to point out that under s. 41 (1) the Law Society has a dispensing power which is conveyed by the words " without the special leave in writing of the society ".   I mention that point because otherwise it would seem that there was a very real hardship on a solicitor who, for some reason such as illness or forgetfulness, was a few days late in taking out his practising certificate. However, there is that dispensing power.

B That really concludes the matter. It may seem hard on Mr. Adlam, who had been for three out of the four years, only a few days out of the period of grace. That is entirely a matter for the Law Society in the exercise of its discretion. So far as the court is concerned, I feel bound to answer the question raised by the summons in the negative.   *Declaration accordingly.*

C Solicitors: *Philip Conway, Thomas & Co.* (for the plaintiff); *Hempsons* (for the defendants).   [*Reported by* JENIFER SANDELL, *Barrister-at-Law.*]

Re L.

[COURT OF APPEAL, CIVIL DIVISION (Lord Denning, M.R., Willmer and Davies, L.JJ.), October 17, 18, 19, November 15, 1967.]

D *Divorce—Custody—Paternity of child in issue—Custodial jurisdiction—Power of judge in Divorce Division to order blood test—Whether guardian ad litem's consent was necessary—Matrimonial Causes Act 1965 (c. 72) s. 33 s. 34.*

The husband and wife were married in 1947. Since 1956 the wife had been committing adultery with the party cited, unknown to the husband. In 1958 a child was born to her. In December, 1963, the wife petitioned

E for divorce. In May, 1964, the husband filed an answer alleging adultery by the wife with the party cited. Both the petition and the answer contained prayers for the custody of the child. In October, 1964, the wife left the husband, taking the child with her. In March, 1965, the husband first became aware that he might not be the father of the child. In July, 1965,

F a decree nisi was made at the hearing of the case undefended on the husband's answer, and an issue of the paternity of the child was directed. The wife and the party cited then admitted that they had committed adultery since 1956. The adult parties to the issue desired that the child's blood group should be ascertained, and each of the adults was willing to submit to serological examination. The Official Solicitor, as guardian ad litem of the child, did not consent to an order for the child's blood group to be taken.

G On appeal from an order that the child's blood grouping should be ascertained, the order being made under the court's custodial jurisdiction,

Held: (i) a judge of the Divorce Division, when exercising his custodial jurisdiction (see p. 34, letters D and F, post), had the same jurisdiction as a judge of the Chancery Division in wardship proceedings, and so had power to order an infant to be subjected to a blood group test, notwithstanding

H that the guardian ad litem did not consent; in the circumstances of the present case the order for arrangements to be made to take the child's blood test was in the best interests of the child and should stand (see p. 25, letter G, p. 27, letters C and H, p. 32, letters D and G, and p. 35, letter B, post).

R. v. *Gyngall* ([1893] 2 Q.B. 232) applied.

I *Hyde* v. *Hyde* ((1888), 13 P.D. 166) not applied.

(ii) submission to a blood group test could not be ordered under s. 33 or s. 34 of the Matrimonial Causes Act 1965 (see p. 26, letter F, p. 33, letter F, and p. 34, letter F, post).

W. v. *W.* (*No. 4*) ([1963] 2 All E.R. 841) applied.

Decision of ORMROD, J. ([1967] 2 All E.R. 1110) affirmed.

[Editorial Note. It was accepted by the parties on appeal apparently without argument, that there was not jurisdiction to order the blood group test on the

Dictum of LORD DENNING, M.R., at P. 25, *applied in* B.R.B. *v.* J.B. [1968] 2 All E.R. 1023.

A paternity issue (see p. 28, letter B, p. 34, letters D and F, post; cf., p. 25, letter G, post). The jurisdiction to order a child to be subjected to a blood test is the court's jurisdiction, and not that of the guardian ad litem, so that the court's decision must prevail despite absence of consent from a guardian ad litem (see e.g., p. 27, letter A, and p. 32, letter D, post).

B Under Item X of the Law Commission's First Programme the commission are considering the whole question of blood tests in paternity issues and whether it will be right to amend the law to enable the courts to order parties to undergo blood tests. This consideration is pursuant to the suggestion of the judges of the Probate, Divorce and Admiralty Division made at the beginning of 1966.

As to orders for custody of children in matrimonial suits, see 12 HALSBURY's LAWS (3rd Edn.) 392, para. 868.

C As to the position of a guardian ad litem for infants, see 21 HALSBURY's LAWS (3rd Edn.) 324, para. 680.

As to the Official Solicitor as guardian ad litem of infants, see 9 HALSBURY's LAWS (3rd Edn.) 434, 435, para. 998.

For the Supreme Court of Judicature (Consolidation) Act, 1925, s. 4 (4), s. 43 as amended, see 5 HALSBURY's STATUTES (2nd Edn.) 342 and 18 ibid., p. 480.

D For the Matrimonial Causes Act 1965 s. 33, s. 34, s. 46, see 45 HALSBURY's STATUTES (2nd Edn.) 490, 491, 504.]

Cases referred to:

Birchall, Re, Wilson v. Birchall, (1880), 16 Ch.D. 41; 44 L.T. 113; 28 Digest (Repl.) 701, 2104.

E Blyth v. Blyth, [1966] 1 All E.R. 524; [1966] A.C. 643; [1966] 2 W.L.R. 634; Digest (Cont. Vol. B) 360, 3344a.

Hall v. Hall, [1963] 2 All E.R. 140; [1963] P. 378; [1963] 2 W.L.R. 1054; Digest (Cont. Vol. A) 933, 2152b.

Hyde v. Hyde, (1888), 13 P.D. 166; 57 L.J.P. 89; 59 L.T. 529; 27 Digest (Repl.) 525, 4679.

F MacGowan v. Middleton, (1883), 11 Q.B.D. 464; 52 L.J.Q.B. 355; 40 Digest (Repl.) 443, 314.

Official Solicitor v. K., [1963] 3 All E.R. 191; [1965] A.C. 201; [1963] 3 W.L.R. 408; Digest (Cont. Vol. A) 933, 2149b.

R. v. Gyngall, [1893] 2 Q.B. 232; sub nom. Re Gyngall, 62 L.J.Q.B. 559; 57 J.P. 773; sub nom. R. v. Gyngall, Re Hausherr (otherwise Austen), 69 L.T. 481; 28 Digest (Repl.) 485, 25.

G R. v. R., (1967), 111 Sol. Jo. 413.

Rhodes v. Swithenbank, (1889), 22 Q.B.D. 577; 58 L.J.Q.B. 287; 60 L.T. 856; 28 Digest (Repl.) 700, 2097.

S. (an infant), Re, [1967] 1 All E.R. 202; [1967] 1 W.L.R. 396.

Salt v. Cooper, [1874-80] All E.R. Rep. 1204; (1880), 16 Ch.D. 544; 50 L.J.Ch. 529; 43 L.T. 682; 16 Digest (Repl.) 197, 864.

H Sheaf Brook, The, [1926] P. 61; 95 L.J.P. 113; 134 L.T. 534; 1 Digest (Repl.) 176, 613.

Spence, Re, (1847), 2 Ph. 247; 16 L.J.Ch. 309; 9 L.T.O.S. 241; 41 E.R. 937; 28 Digest (Repl.) 630, 1314.

W. v. W. (otherwise L.), [1912] P. 78; 81 L.J.P. 29; 27 Digest (Repl.) 275, 2204.

W. v. W. (No. 4), [1963] 2 All E.R. 386, sub nom. W. v. W. [1964] P. 67; I [1963] 3 W.L.R. 540; affd. C.A., [1963] 2 All E.R. 841; sub nom. W. v. W., [1964] P. at p. 72; [1963] 3 W.L.R. 540; Digest (Cont. Vol. A) 703, 2267a.

Wellesley v. Duke of Beaufort, (1827), 2 Russ. 1; 38 E.R. 236; affd. H.L., sub nom. Wellesley v. Wellesley, [1824-34] All E.R. Rep. 189; 4 E.R. 1078; 18 Digest (Repl.) 620, 1239.

Appeal.

This was an appeal by the Official Solicitor as guardian ad litem for the infant girl from an order of ORMROD, J., dated June 1, 1967, and reported [1967] 2 All E.R. 1110, ordering that arrangements should be made for a blood group

test of the infant to be taken.   The facts are set out in the judgment of LORD A
DENNING, M.R.

The authority and cases noted below* were cited during the argument in
addition to those referred to in the judgments.

J. P. Comyn, Q.C., and Bruce Holroyd Pearce for the Official Solicitor as
guardian ad litem for the child.

Joseph Jackson, Q.C., and Margaret Booth for the husband.   B

R. J. A. Temple, Q.C., and Gerald Kidner for the wife.

Cur. adv. vult.

November 15.   The following judgments were read.

LORD DENNING, M.R.: The husband and wife were married on Nov. 22,
1947: and a son was born to them in 1948.   The husband was a van driver with
one firm.   The wife went out to work for another firm.   In 1956 at her work C
she met the party cited.   He was a married man.   From 1956 onwards she had
intercourse regularly with the party cited and she also had intercourse regularly
with the husband.   She conceived and bore a child, a girl, on Feb. 8, 1958.   She
herself did not know which of the men was the father of the child.   It might
have been either of them, for aught she knew; but she let the husband believe
it was his child.   He knew nothing about her affair with the party cited.   He re- D
garded the baby girl as his child and she was brought up as one of the family.   In
1963, when the little girl was aged five, the husband himself formed a relationship
with another woman and told the wife that he wanted a divorce.   On hearing
this, the wife herself on Dec. 5, 1963, presented a petition for divorce on the
ground of her husband's adultery.   On May 1, 1964, the husband filed an answer
denying that he had committed adultery and alleging that the wife had com- E
mitted adultery with the party cited from 1956.   In October, 1964, the wife
left the home and took the little girl with her.   She went to live with the party
cited.   At that stage she and the party cited made confessions admitting adultery
but saying that it only started in January, 1964.   Later on (in a magistrates'
court) the party cited admitted that he had committed adultery with the wife
since 1956 and he asserted that he was the father of the little girl.   Afterwards F
the wife abandoned her petition against the husband, and the husband obtained
a decree nisi against her.   This was granted on July 9, 1965.

As soon as the wife and the party cited admitted adultery from 1956, it became
obvious that there was a serious question as to who was the father of the little
girl.   Was he the husband?   Or the party cited?   It might be either.   There
were two important factors to consider.   One was the presumption of legitimacy. G
The other was the taking of blood tests.   I will deal with them in turn.

1.   *Presumption of legitimacy.*

The presumption of legitimacy goes back for centuries, long before blood tests.
In order to decide the paternity of a child, the court in those days had to rely on
circumstantial evidence.   Illegitimacy was a grave stigma; and carried severe
penalties on the child.   So the courts raised a presumption of legitimacy.   When H
a married woman bore a child, her husband was presumed to be the father
unless the contrary was proved.   The presumption was so strong that it could
not be rebutted except by proof beyond reasonable doubt that the husband was
not the father.   That was often unjust to a husband whose wife had committed
adultery.   The burden on him is not so heavy nowadays.   In divorce cases the   I

---

* CROSS ON EVIDENCE (2nd Edn.), p. 42; *Harrison* v. *Harrison*, (1842), 4 Moo. P.C.
196; *Re Agar-Ellis, Agar-Ellis* v. *Lascelles*, (1883), 24 Ch.D. 317; *Russian Commercial
and Industrial Bank* v. *British Bank for Foreign Trade*, [1921] All E.R. Rep. 329; [1921]
2 A.C. 438; *Andrews* v. *Andrews and Sullivan*, [1958] 2 All E.R. 305; [1958] P. 217;
Re Andrews (infants), [1958] 2 All E.R. 308; [1958] Ch. 665; *Whitehall* v. *Whitehall*,
1957 S.C. 252; *B.* v. *B.*, [1961] 2 All E.R. 396; *Shelton* v. *Shelton*, (1965), 109 Sol. Jo.
393; *H.* v. *H.* (*H. by his guardian, intervening*), [1966] 1 All E.R. 356; *B.* v. *A.-G.*
(*B. intervening*), [1966] 2 All E.R. 145, n.; *Stocker (by her next friend)* v. *Stocker (otherwise
Woodruff, by her guardian)*, [1966] 2 All E.R. 147; *H.* v. *H.*, [1966] 3 All E.R. 560;
Tirran v. *Tirran*, (1966), unreported.

A presumption can be rebutted by showing, on the preponderance of probabilities, that the husband could not be the father (see *Blyth* v. *Blyth* (1)). Logically the position should be the same in legitimacy proceedings or in any proceedings where paternity is in issue. It would be absurd to have a different result in a divorce case from other cases, so that a child would be found legitimate in one and illegitimate in another. Moreover, there is not nearly the same stigma on

B illegitimacy as there used to be. It can be, and often is, cured by subsequent marriage of the parents. Even when the parents do not marry, the penalties on the child have been largely removed. The sins of the fathers are no longer visited on the children. In this new situation I think that we are at liberty to reconsider the presumption of legitimacy. I am prepared to hold that it can be rebutted on the balance of probabilities. Even so, however, it still has to be

C rebutted; and the question is, how far it can be done by blood tests.

2.   *Blood Tests.*

Blood tests are a modern development. Medical science is able to put the blood of individuals into definite groups; and by examining the blood of a given man and a child, the medical men can tell whether the man could or could not be the father of the child. They cannot say positively of any man that he *is* the

D father; but they can say positively that a given man *cannot* be the father, because the blood groups of him and the child are so different. The science has achieved such a degree of accuracy that, when a man is in truth not the father of a child, and desires to prove it, there is at least a seventy per cent. chance, if blood tests are taken, that the doctors can prove positively that he is not the father. In some cases the chance is even higher. As, for instance, when, as in

E the present case, we know that one or other of two given men is the father, there is a ninety per cent. chance that the doctors can say positively that one of them is *not* the father, with the irresistible inference that the other man *is* the father.

3.   *The course of investigation.*

In the present case, on making the decree nisi, the judge ordered an issue to be

F tried as to the paternity of the child. On Dec. 1, 1965, the Official Solicitor was appointed guardian ad litem of the child. That issue was heard by ORMROD, J., (2) on June 28, 1966. A blood test would obviously have been most helpful, but none had been taken. The Official Solicitor would not consent to the child's blood being tested. In the circumstances the presumption of legitimacy seemed to be applicable. It looked as if the judge was bound to decide, according to

G that presumption, that the husband was the father; but the judge was reluctant so to hold. He thought that a blood test might show the true paternity; and he was not inclined to rest on a legal presumption when the truth could be satisfactorily ascertained. He thought that, in custody proceedings, if not on a paternity issue, he might have power to order a blood test. So he adjourned the paternity issue pending custody proceedings. Meanwhile he made the decree

H of divorce absolute under the provisions of s. 33 (2) of the Matrimonial Causes Act 1965.

So proceedings were taken to decide who should have the custody of the child and also questions of access. On these issues it is very desirable to know which of the men is the father. If the husband is the father, he will have an irresistible claim to access and maybe to custody; whereas if he is not the father, he will

I drop out altogether. All three of the adults—the woman and the two men— are anxious to have it decided which of the men is the father. Each of them has already had his blood tested. The medical men say that, if the child's blood is tested, they may be able to say with complete certainty which of the men is the father. There is a ninety per cent. chance that they will be able to establish it beyond a doubt; but, in the absence of a blood test of the child, they cannot say which of the men is the father. Either of them may be the father. The chances

(1) [1966] 1 All E.R. 524 at p. 535; [1966] A.C. 643 at p. 667.
(2) [1967] 2 All E.R. 1126, n.

are equal. Nevertheless, although all three of the adults agree, the Official   A
Solicitor, as the guardian ad litem of the child, does not agree that she should
have a blood test. He says that the court should decide the case according to
the presumption of legitimacy and should hold that the husband is the father,
and give him access on that footing.

I would pause a moment to point out the strange consequences which would
follow from this contention. If the judge held, applying the presumption of   B
legitimacy, that the husband was the father then, as soon as the litigation is
ended, the Official Solicitor will no longer be guardian ad litem of the child. The
mother will be able to take the child quite freely to a doctor and ask him to
test the child's blood. The doctor may then say, with complete certainty, that
the other man is the father and that the husband is not. As soon as that is done,
this court would give leave to appeal out of time and reverse the judge's finding.   C
Similarly, if the mother had taken the child for a blood test *before* the Official
Solicitor had been appointed. There was nothing to stop her doing so. That
blood test might have shown with complete certainty which of the men was the
father; and the evidence would have been accepted by the court. It would be
odd if the Official Solicitor could interpose his own authority to prevent it being
available now.   D

Nevertheless, despite these strange consequences, we have to decide the
question: can the court order a test to be taken of the child's blood in the absence
of consent by the Official Solicitor, and, indeed, in the face of his opposition?

The Court of Chancery.

Counsel for the husband put his argument on the broad ground that the old
Court of Chancery would have had the power to order a blood test on an infant;   E
that the High Court had inherited that power; and that it could now be exercised
by a judge of the Divorce Division.

Counsel for the infant admitted that, if the little girl had been a ward of court,
a judge of the Chancery Division would have power to order a blood test, if it
was in the best interests of the child. He agreed that a Chancery judge had
power to order a surgical operation or a psychiatric examination on a ward: F
see *Re S. (an infant)* (3). So also he could order a blood test; but counsel for
the infant submitted that this power was confined to judges of the Chancery
Division exercising their wardship jurisdiction, and did not extend to judges of
the Divorce Division exercising their custodial or other jurisdiction.

I think that counsel takes altogether too limited a view of the jurisdiction
of the Court of Chancery. It derives from the right and duty of the Crown as   G
parens patriae to take care of those who are not able to take care of themselves.
The Crown delegated this power to the Lord Chancellor, who exercised it in his
Court of Chancery. In the ordinary way he only exercised it when there was
property to be applied for the infant (see *Wellesley* v. *Duke of Beaufort* (4)).
The child was usually made a ward of court, and thereafter no important step
in the child's life could be taken without the court's consent; but that was only   H
machinery. Even if there was no property and the child was not a ward of court,
nevertheless the Court of Chancery had power to interfere for the protection of
the infant by making whatever order might be appropriate. That was made
clear by LORD COTTENHAM, L.C., in *Re Spence* (5), where the infants were not
wards and there was no property. LORD COTTENHAM, L.C., said (6):

I
" I have no doubt about the jurisdiction. The cases in which this court
interferes on behalf of infants are not confined to those in which there is
property . . . This court interferes for the protection of infants, qua infants,
by virtue of the prerogative which belongs to the Crown as parens patriae,
and the exercise of which is delegated to the Great Seal."

This wide jurisdiction of the old Court of Chancery is now vested in the High

(3) [1967] 1 All E.R. 202.   (4) (1827), 2 Russ. 1 at pp. 20, 21.
(5) (1847), 2 Ph. 247.   (6) (1847), 2 Ph. at p. 251.

A Court of Justice and can be exercised by any judge of the High Court. As a matter of convenience, the jurisdiction is exercised by making the child a ward of court and putting it under the care of a judge of the Chancery Division; but that is only machinery. If a question arises as to the welfare of a child before any judge of the High Court, he can make such order as may be appropriate in the circumstances. He need not send the case over to a Chancery judge. Nor

B need he adjourn the case for the child to be made a ward of court. He can deal with it himself. That is fully established by *R.* v. *Gyngall* (7). Speaking of the Supreme Court of Judicature Act, 1873, LORD ESHER, M.R., said (8):

> ". . . the Act in effect provides that, if a person proceeds in the Queen's Bench Division under the common law jurisdiction, and it turns out that the case raises questions to which the Chancery jurisdiction is applicable,

C > the Queen's Bench Division judges are not to send the suitor to a Chancery court, but are to exercise the Chancery jurisdiction themselves."

What LORD ESHER, M.R., there said about the Queen's Bench Division and the Queen's Bench judges is equally true of the Divorce Division and the Divorce judges. If a Divorce judge has to decide what is best in the interests of a child, be it a question as to schools, medical treatment or anything else, he need not—

D and does not—send the case over to a Chancery judge. He deals with it himself. So also if a question arises whether it should have a blood test. He need not adjourn it for the child to be made a ward of court. He need not send it to a Chancery judge. He can deal with it himself.

 I ought to say that in 1888 there was a case of *Hyde* v. *Hyde* (9), where it was held that the divorce court had not so wide a jurisdiction as the Court of Chancery

E in respect of infants. That case cannot, however, stand with the later case of *R.* v. *Gyngall* (7) and should not be regarded as authority.

 I must also mention the cases where a child has been made a ward of court before the application comes before the the Divorce judge. That does not take away the jurisdiction of the Divorce judge (see *Hall* v. *Hall* (10)). He can make such order as he thinks fit for the welfare of the child, but he will take steps to

F ensure that there is no conflict by arranging with the Chancery judge which of them should deal with any particular aspect of the case.

 I hold, therefore, that in proceedings relating to the custody of a child, any judge of the High Court can order a test to be taken of the child's blood. So also in a paternity issue, or any proceedings where it is in the best interests of the child to have its paternity settled one way or the other, the court can order

G a blood test. Even in a petition for divorce on the ground of adultery, the judge can in my view order a blood test on the child, for there too the child is vitally affected by the outcome.

Submission on s. 33 of the Matrimonial Causes Act 1965.

 Counsel for the husband submitted that the divorce court had jurisdiction to order a blood test in aid of its duty under s. 33 of the Matrimonial Causes Act

H 1965. Under that section the divorce court has to be satisfied " as respects every relevant child " that proper arrangements have been made for his care and upbringing. In order to carry out that duty, the court must know whether the child is a " relevant child "; and that, says counsel for the husband, may involve a blood test.

I " Relevant child " is defined in s. 46 as a child who is: (a) a child of both parties to the marriage in question; or (b) a child of one party to the marriage who has been accepted as one of the family by the other party. The word " accepted " in that definition was considered in *R.* v. *R.* (11). A cuckold husband had had a child foisted on him by his unfaithful wife. She deceived him into thinking that it was his child when it was not. As soon as he discovered the truth, he disowned the child. PARK, J., held that he had not

---

(7) [1893] 2 Q.B. 232. (8) [1893] 2 Q.B. at p. 239. (9) (1888), 13 P.D. 166.
(10) [1963] 2 All E.R. 140; [1963] P. 378.   (11) (1967), 111 Sol. Jo. 413.

" accepted " the child. " Acceptance " involved consent with knowledge of   A
the material facts, viz., that it was not his child.   That seems to me a correct
decision.   It would not be fair to make the husband pay maintenance for a child
which was not his, seeing that he had been deceived about it.

If the decision in *R. v. R.* (12) be correct, it follows that the court in the present
case, in order to determine whether the child is a " relevant child " must find
out which is the men is her father.   The court, says counsel for the husband,   B
cannot do its duty by the child until that is ascertained.   It cannot see whether
proper arrangements have been made unless it can say which man is to pay for
her maintenance, and so forth.   So it should be able to order a blood test for the
purpose.

Submission on s. 34 of the Matrimonial Causes Act 1965.

Counsel for the wife submitted that the divorce court has power to order a   C
blood test under s. 34 of the Act of 1965.   Under that section the court may
make such order as it thinks just " for " the custody, maintenance and education
of any relevant child.   The previous sections said that the court might make an
order " with respect to " the custody, etc.   No valid distinction can be drawn
between the words " for " and " with respect to ", and it was accepted that they
cover the same ground.   D

Counsel for the wife urged that these words are wide enough to enable the court
to ask for a blood test to be made of the child.   Blood relationship is, he said, a
basic factor in determining custody and maintenance.   An order for a blood test
is an order " for " or " with respect to " custody and maintenance, and is within
the wide words of the statute.

Effect of the sections.   E

Both counsel for the husband and counsel for the wife felt bound to concede
that, under these sections, the court could not order an adult to submit to a
blood test.   A blood test which involves the insertion of a needle is an assault,
unless consented to.   It would need express statutory authority to require an
adult to submit to it; see *W. v. W. (No. 4)* (13).   If these sections do not authorise   F
the court to order an adult to have his blood tested, I do not see that they
authorise the court to make such an order in the case of an infant.   A test of
the child's blood would be useless unless there were tests of the adults also.
But I would say this.   If an adult unreasonably refuses to have a blood test, or to
allow a child to have one, I think that it is open to the court in any civil proceedings (no matter whether it be a paternity issue or an affiliation summons,
or a custody proceeding) to treat his refusal as evidence against him, and may   G
draw an inference therefrom adverse to him.   This is simply common sense.   It
is in keeping with the rule that in a nullity case, if a party refuses to be medically
examined, the court may infer that some impediment exists pointing to incapacity
(see *W. v. W. (otherwise L.)* (14)).   Moreover, being a rule of evidence, it applies
not only to the High Court but also to the magistrates' court, and to any court of   H
the land.

Guardian ad litem.

Counsel for the Official Solicitor submitted that the Official Solicitor as guardian
ad litem was the representative of the child; and it was his responsibility and
his alone to decide whether the child should be subjected to a blood test.   If he
refused to consent to it, the court could not, he said, overrule his decision.   I

I think that this contention mistakes the position of a guardian ad litem.   He
has not the custody of the child.   He does not stand in loco parentis.   All he
does is to represent the child in the conduct of the suit.   His decisions do not
rest in his unfettered discretion.   He must on occasion seek the approval of the
court, as for instance if he makes a compromise on behalf of the infant.   Likewise, if the court thinks that the child should go to a particular school or have a

(12) (1967), 111 Sol. Jo. 413.   (13) [1963] 2 All E.R. 841; [1964] P. 67.
(14) [1912] P. 78.

A surgical operation, the guardian cannot say " Nay ". So also if the court thinks that the child should have a blood test. The guardian should seek the ruling of the court on the matter and abide by its decision.

Discretion.

In this case the Official Solicitor obtained medical advice suggesting that it would not be right to disturb the little girl. She is at the moment happy with
B her mother and the party cited, whom she calls " Daddy ". If a blood test should prove that the husband is the father, it would, says the doctor, be most upsetting for her. He suggests that the blood test be left till she is much older and can decide for herself.

The judge thought otherwise (15). He was quite satisfied that it was in the best interests, not only of the child but of all the three adults, that the paternity
C should be settled now. I entirely agree.

Conclusion.

In my opinion, therefore, the judge rightly made an order that the Official Solicitor should make arrangements for the child to have a blood test. I would dismiss this appeal.

D   **WILLMER, L.J.:** Two questions have been raised by this appeal, viz., (i) whether the judge exercising divorce jurisdiction has power, in the face of a refusal of consent by the Official Solicitor acting as guardian ad litem of the child, to order that a test be carried out to ascertain the child's blood group for the purpose of determining her paternity; and (ii) whether, if such power exists, the court in its discretion ought, in all the circumstances of this case, to order such
E a test to be carried out. The judge (16) decided that he had such power, and in his discretion directed that the test be carried out, subject to the three adult parties first submitting themselves to a similar test and providing samples of their blood. The Official Solicitor now appeals to this court.

It will be convenient to deal with the second question first, and I can do this quite shortly. I am abundantly satisfied that, if the power exists, it ought in
F the special circumstances of this case to be exercised. All three of the adult parties have at all times been willing to submit themselves to such a test, and since the hearing before the learned judge have in fact done so. We are informed that as a result of the tests already so carried out there is a ninety per cent. chance of conclusively determining the child's paternity if a similar test of her blood is carried out. In the absence of such a test it will be virtually impossible
G for the court to determine which of the two men concerned is the actual father of the child, and it will, therefore, be necessary to fall back on the presumption of legitimacy, which is as likely to be wrong as right. I agree with the view of the learned judge (17) that, assuming there is power to order the test, it would be absurd for the court not to take advantage of the means which modern science has provided of possibly determining the child's paternity for certain. All three
H of the adult parties are genuinely anxious to know which of the two men is really the father of the child, and it would clearly be to their advantage that they should know. I think that it would also be to the advantage of the child that she should know who her father is. It is true that the learned judge had before him a report from a child psychiatrist, in which the view was expressed that to subject the child to a blood test might cause her a serious emotional disturbance, especially
I if the result of the test were to show that the husband, and not the party cited, is her true father. This report, however, was carefully considered by the judge (18), who came to a clear conclusion that the objections put forward by the psychiatrist were outweighed by the advantage to the child of knowing who her real father is. This was very much a matter for the judge, but I am bound to say that I wholly agree with him. From the point of view of the court, which is now faced with the task of deciding questions of custody and access, it is vital to

(15) [1967] 2 All E.R. 1110 at p. 1125.   (16) [1967] 2 All E.R. 1110.
(17) [1967] 2 All E.R. at p. 1122 et seq.   (18) [1967] 2 All E.R. at p. 1125.

know, if this can be scientifically ascertained, which of the two men is the real   A
father of the child.

The question whether a judge exercising divorce jurisdiction has the power,
without the consent of the guardian ad litem, to order that a child who is a party
to the suit shall be subjected to a blood test is in my view one of great difficulty
and of no little public importance. It is now established that in a suit between
husband and wife relating to the paternity of a child, the court has no power to   B
compel either party to submit to a blood test, and still less to direct that the
child's blood be tested. So much was decided in *W.* v. *W.* (*No. 4*) (19), a decision
which both parties accept and which, being a decision of this court, is in any
event binding on us. The judge in the present case, when the matter first came
before him on the issue of paternity in June, 1966 (20), took the view that in
the proceedings then before him he had no power, in face of the Official Solicitor's   C
refusal to consent on behalf of the child, to order that she be subjected to a blood
test. He indicated that in the circumstances, if he were to proceed to judgment
straight away, he would be bound to give effect to the presumption of legitimacy
and to declare that the child was the child of the husband and the wife. He
expressed the view, however, that when the questions of custody and access arose
for decision, as they were bound to do, the court in the exercise of its custodial   D
jurisdiction might well be endowed with wider powers than in ordinary litigation
inter partes, including power to order the child to be subjected to a blood test
even in the absence of consent on the part of the guardian ad litem. It would be
absurd, he thought, if on the paternity issue he were to pronounce that the child
was the child of the husband and the wife, and afterwards, when the questions
of custody and access came before him, he were to find, on scientific evidence   E
as to the result of a blood test, that the child was after all the child of the party
cited. He therefore adjourned the hearing to enable full argument to be addressed
to him on the powers of the court in its custodial jurisdiction. It was in that
context that he ultimately came to deliver the judgment appealed from.

The question which has to be decided, therefore, is whether in a case where,
as here, the child has been made a party to the ligation, a judge of the Divorce   F
Division, exercising his custodial jurisdiction, has the power to order that the
child be subjected to a blood test in the absence of consent on the part of the
guardian ad litem. The argument on behalf of the husband and the wife, in
support of the contention that such power exists, fell into two parts. In the first
place it was argued that, pursuant to s. 24 (7) of the Supreme Court of Judicature
Act, 1873, now re-enacted by s. 43 of the Supreme Court of Judicature (Consoli-   G
dation) Act, 1925, a judge of the Divorce Division, as a judge of the High Court,
is clothed with all the powers of a judge of the Chancery Division exercising his
parental jurisdiction in wardship proceedings. Secondly, it was contended that
the statutory powers conferred on the High Court in the exercise of its divorce
jurisdiction were sufficiently wide to include power, in a proper case, to order that
a child be subjected to a blood test, and reliance was placed particularly on s. 33   H
and s. 34 of the Matrimonial Causes Act 1965.

Dealing with the first and wider point, it was admitted on behalf of the Official
Solicitor that a judge of the Chancery Division exercising his wardship jurisdiction probably has the power to order a blood test, in the same way as he would
have power to order a psychiatric examination or a surgical operation. It was
submitted that it did not by any means follow that a judge exercising divorce   I
jurisdiction has the same power. It was argued that, while any judge of the High
Court has the *power* to make an order within the competence of any division,
he must first be clothed with the appropriate *jurisdiction*. Jurisdiction in divorce
being wholly the creature of statute, a divorce judge is limited to the jurisdiction
conferred by the Matrimonial Causes Acts, and this does not include the wardship
jurisdiction inherited by the High Court from the old Court of Chancery.
Wardship jurisdiction, it was contended, can only be exercised in properly

---

(19) [1963] 2 All E.R. 841; [1964] P. 67.   (20) [1967] 2 All E.R. 1126, n.

A constituted proceedings, i.e., by first taking the appropriate steps to make the child a ward of court. If this were not so, the power expressly conferred on a divorce judge by the concluding words of s. 34 (1) of the Matrimonial Causes Act 1965, to

B " direct that proper proceedings be taken for placing the child under the protection of the court "

would be quite meaningless. This is a power inherited from the original Matrimonial Causes Act, 1857, and, notwithstanding the enactment of the Judicature Acts, preserved in subsequent Matrimonial Causes Acts down to 1965. The protection of the court there referred to, it was argued, can only mean the protection afforded by wardship proceedings, and the presence of this provision

C in the Act of 1965 must, therefore amount to a statutory recognition that a judge exercising divorce jurisdiction is not himself clothed with wardship jurisdiction.

The argument for the Official Solicitor was further supported by reference to the decision of this court in *Hyde* v. *Hyde* (21), in which all three members of the court expressed the view that s. 35 of the Matrimonial Causes Act, 1857 (the forerunner of s. 34 of the Act of 1965), did not enable the court by its order

D to make children wards of the Divorce Division (see per COTTON, L.J. (22), per BOWEN, L.J. (23), and per FRY, L.J. (24)). The words of FRY, L.J., are of special significance. Referring to s. 35 of the Act of 1857, he said (24):

" ... I think that the section itself shows it was not intended by the legislature to clothe the Court of Probate with as wide a jurisdiction as the Court of Chancery had in respect of infants, because it enables the Court

E of Divorce and Matrimonial Causes, if it see fit, to direct proceedings to be taken for placing the children under the protection of the Court of Chancery."

The argument on the other side was based largely on s. 43 of the Supreme Court of Judicature (Consolidation) Act, 1925, re-enacting s. 24 (7) of the Act of 1873. Section 43 provides:

F " The High Court and the Court of Appeal respectively, in the exercise of the jurisdiction vested in them by this Act, shall, in every cause or matter pending before the court, grant, either absolutely or on such terms and conditions as the court thinks just, all such remedies whatsoever as any of the parties thereto may appear to be entitled to in respect of any legal or equitable claim properly brought forward by them in the cause or matter,

G so that, as far as possible, all matters in controversy between the parties may be completely and finally determined, and all multiplicity of legal proceedings concerning any of those matters avoided."

Reference should also be made to s. 4 (4) of the Act of 1925, which was added by s. 6 of the Administration of Justice Act, 1928, whereby it is provided:

H " Without prejudice to the provisions of this Act relating to the distribution of business in the High Court, all jurisdiction vested in the High Court under this Act shall belong to all the divisions alike."

From the earliest days it was held that the purpose and effect of the Supreme Court of Judicature Act, 1873, was to avoid multiplicity of proceedings and to enable every division of the High Court to apply every remedy available to any

I of the pre-existing courts. The authorities in support of this proposition are collected in the notes on p. 856 of Vol. 2 of THE SUPREME COURT PRACTICE 1967. We were referred in particular to *Salt* v. *Cooper* (25), and *MacGowan* v. *Middleton* (26). In the former case SIR GEORGE JESSEL, M.R., after quoting s. 24 (7) of the Act of 1873, said (27):

---

(21) (1888), 13 P.D. 166.   (22) (1888), 13 P.D. at p. 174.
(23) (1888), 13 P.D. at p. 176.   (24) (1888), 13 P.D. at p. 178.
(25) [1874-80] All E.R. Rep. 1204; (1880), 16 Ch.D. 544.
(26) (1883), 11 Q.B.D. 464.   (27) (1880), 16 Ch.D. at p. 550.

"Those are very large terms. The clause clearly applies to any remedy A
whatever; for it says the court shall grant ' all such remedies whatsoever.' "

In the latter case SIR BALIOL BRETT, M.R., said (28):

"This principle was acted upon, not only by JAMES, L.J., but also by SIR
GEORGE JESSEL, M.R., himself, who had much the same mind as JAMES, L.J.,
and like him, was determined to sweep away every kind of technicality."
  B

The authority most relevant to the present case, however, is *R.* v. *Gyngall* (29),
where it was expressly held by this court that the judges of the Queen's Bench
Division were clothed with the paternal jurisdiction derived from the old Court
of Chancery in wardship proceedings. The case arose out of habeas corpus
proceedings, and LORD ESHER, M.R., after referring to the common law jurisdiction, said (30):
  C

"But there was another and an absolutely different and distinguishable
jurisdiction, which has been exercised by the Court of Chancery from time
immemorial. That was not a jurisdiction to determine rights as between a
parent and a stranger, or as between a parent and a child. It was a paternal
jurisdiction, a judicially administrative jurisdiction, in virtue of which the
Chancery Court was put to act on behalf of the Crown, as being the guardian D
of all infants, in the place of a parent, and as if it were the parent of the
child, thus superseding the natural guardianship of the parent. The present
case arises after the Judicature Act, and the proceedings are in the Queen's
Bench Division. The effect of that Act is, as I have often said, not to invent
a new jurisdiction or to create new rights, but to alter the mode of procedure;
and, there having been before two independent jurisdictions, one common law E
and the other equity, the Act in effect provides that, if a person proceeds
in the Queen's Bench Division under the common law jurisdiction, and it
turns out that the case raises questions to which the Chancery jurisdiction
is applicable, the Queen's Bench Division judges are not to send the suitor
to a Chancery Court, but are to exercise the Chancery jurisdiction themselves.
If such a case as this had arisen before the Judicature Act, the Queen's Bench F
judges, not finding any such misconduct as would affect the parent's right,
would have been bound to say that, as between the parent and the person
who had the custody of the child, the right to the custody of the child
belonged to the parent; but, if they had seen that, although there was nothing
to limit the right of the parent as against the other person, there were circumstances calling for the exercise of the Chancery jurisdiction, they might G
have stayed their hands and given time for an application to be made to the
Court of Chancery to exercise its authority in the matter. Under the
Judicature Act, the Queen's Bench Division judges are not to do that, but are
to exercise the Chancery jurisdiction themselves. In the present case I do not
think that the mother has been guilty of any misconduct which as between
her and other people has derogated from her right to the custody of the H
child. Under these circumstances, I do not think that the judges of the
Queen's Bench Division assumed to exercise the common law jurisdiction.
I think that they rightly assumed to exercise the other and independent
jurisdiction, viz., that of the Court of Chancery. The existence of that
jurisdiction is beyond dispute."

A little later he added (31):
  I

"'This court interferes for the protection of *infants*, qua infants, by virtue
of the prerogative which belongs to the Crown as parens patriae, and the
exercise of which is delegated to the Great Seal'."

(28) (1883), 11 Q.B.D. at p. 468.
(29) [1893] 2 Q.B. 232.
(30) [1893] 2 Q.B. at pp. 239, 240.
(31) (1893) 2 Q.B. at p. 240, citing per LORD COTTENHAM, L.C., in *Re Spence*, (1847),
2 Ph. at p. 252.

A   In the same case KAY, L.J., said (32):

  " The court is not since the Act in the difficulty in which courts of common law formerly were when such an application was made to them. They are not bound to refer the matter to a Chancery Court, but can exercise the parental jurisdiction of the Court of Chancery themselves."

B   The decision in R. v. Gyngall (33) was referred to without disapproval by the House of Lords in Official Solicitor v. K. (34), and LORD HODSON, it may be said, expressly approved it. He said (35):

  " I would add that there can now be no doubt that there is no difference in the jurisdiction exercised by the various divisions of the High Court. It so happens that most of these cases are now dealt with in the Probate, C   Divorce and Admiralty Division . . . Since the Supreme Court of Judicature Act, 1873 the practice of the Chancery Division has prevailed and there is no difference in the manner in which this jurisdiction is exercised whether in the Chancery Division or the Queen's Bench Division or the Probate, Divorce and Admiralty Division. This I think has been clear at least since the decision of the Court of Appeal in R. v. Gyngall (33) on appeal from the D   Divisional Court of the Queen's Bench Division."

  The decision in Hyde v. Hyde (36) was not cited to the Court of Appeal in R. v. Gyngall (33). I agree with the submission made to us that the two cases are not easily distinguishable. In Hyde v. Hyde (36), according to the report, there was no more than a passing reference in argument to the Supreme Court of Judicature Act, 1873, and no reference at all to the authorities to which I have E   referred as to the purpose and effect of that Act. Faced with this apparent conflict between the two decisions of this court, I have no doubt that the decision which we ought to follow is that in R. v. Gyngall (33), particularly having regard to the measure of approval which that decision has received from the House of Lords. If there is any room for doubt, I think that that doubt must be resolved in favour of the respondents having regard to the provisions of s. 4 (4) of the F   Act of 1925. That subsection was added to the Act of 1925 in order to get over the decision of this court in The Sheaf Brook (37). In that case an action in personam had been commenced in the Probate, Divorce and Admiralty Division against shipowners in respect of damage to cargo. By s. 22 of the Supreme Court of Judicature (Consolidation) Act, 1925, Admiralty jurisdiction in respect of such a claim did not exist where the shipowners were domiciled in England, G   as were the defendants in that case. On a summons to transfer the action to the King's Bench Division, LORD MERRIVALE, P., held that the action could be retained in the Probate, Divorce and Admiralty Division. That, however, was held by this court to be a wrong exercise of discretion, since s. 58 (2) of the Act of 1925 did not give the court any discretion to retain a cause in respect of which the statute expressly provided that the division had no jurisdiction (my italics). This H   was precisely the sort of situation that could have arisen in the present case if the learned judge had held that he had no power to exercise the jurisdiction commonly exercised by the Chancery judges in wardship proceedings. Parliament evidently felt that the decision of the Court of Appeal was contrary to the intention of the Act of 1925, since they very quickly amended the Act by adding s. 4 (4).

  For these reasons I have come to the conclusion that the learned judge was I   right when he held (38) that in the circumstances of this case he was clothed with the same jurisdiction as is exercised by the judges of the Chancery Division sitting in wardship proceedings. It is conceded that in wardship proceedings a judge would probably have power to order a child to be subjected to a blood test.

---

(32) [1893] 2 Q.B. at pp. 248, 249.   (33) [1893] 2 Q.B. 232.
(34) [1963] 3 All E.R. 191; [1965] A.C. 201.
(35) [1963] 3 All E.R. at p. 207; [1965] A.C. at p. 235.
(36) (1888), 13 P.D. 166.   (37) [1926] P. 61.
(38) [1967] 2 All E.R. at p. 1117.

But the question is raised whether he ought to make such an order in the absence   A
of consent on the part of the Official Solicitor as the child's guardian ad litem.
On the one side it is said that the guardian ad litem is not only the child's legal
adviser for all purposes of the litigation to which the child is a party, but also
represents the child in the sense of speaking for her with an adult voice. It is for
the guardian ad litem, and only for him, to decide whether the suit should be
compromised, and the court is not entitled to overrule his decision (see *Re Birchall*,   B
Wilson v. *Birchall* (39)). It is also for the guardian ad litem, and only for him,
to decide whether the child should give evidence—and here the child is in effect
being invited to provide evidence by furnishing a sample of her blood. Against
this it is said on the other side that the guardian ad litem is in no sense the
custodian of the child, his function being limited to the actual conduct of the
litigation. Reliance is place on *Rhodes* v. *Swithenbank* (40), where the guardian's   C
purported waiver of the infant's right of appeal was overruled as not being for
the benefit of the infant, and it was held that such waiver was a matter beyond
the ordinary conduct of the action.

After weighing carefully these rival contentions, I have come to the conclusion
that the learned judge was right in holding (41) that where he is exercising the
ancient parental jurisdiction it is for the judge, and not for the guardian ad litem,   D
to decide whether the child is to be subjected to a blood test, or indeed to any
other form of medical examination. No judge will make an order for such an
examination unless he has first decided that it will be for the benefit of the child.
Where he has so decided, his decision must prevail notwithstanding the absence of
consent on the part of the guardian ad litem. During the argument some attempt
was made to draw a distinction between a medical examination for therapeutic   E
purposes and a similar examination for what were described as " forensic "
purposes, i.e., for the purpose of furnishing evidence. Assuming that an examination of the latter kind is undertaken for the purpose of furnishing evidence
which is likely to be for the benefit of the child, I can see no reason for distinguishing it from an examination undertaken for purely therapeutic purposes. In
this connexion I venture to express my agreement with the remarks made by   F
CROSS, J., in *Re S.* (*an infant*) (42), which were quoted (41) by the judge in the
course of his judgment in the present case. It is true that CROSS, J.'s, remarks
were directed primarily to psychiatric examinations, but I can see little, if any,
distinction in principle between such an examination and an examination for
the purpose of blood-grouping the child.

For these reasons, I think that the learned judge was right in holding (43) that,   G
in the circumstances of this case, he was, pursuant to the Judicature Acts, clothed
with the jurisdiction of a judge in wardship proceedings, and that in the exercise
of that jurisdiction he had the power, notwithstanding the absence of consent
on the part of the Official Solicitor, to make the order which he did that the child
be subjected to a blood-grouping test.

This conclusion renders it strictly unnecessary to express any decided view with   H
regard to the alternative grounds on which it is sought to support the judge's
judgment. Since, however, we have had the benefit of hearing a full argument
with regard to these alternative grounds, it is right that I should deal briefly with
them, if only to say that I am by no means persuaded that there is any substance
in them. In the first place, reliance was placed on s. 33 (1) of the Matrimonial
Causes Act 1965, which provides that the court shall not make absolute a decree   I
of divorce, unless it is satisfied as respects any relevant child under sixteen, (a)
that arrangements for his care and upbringing have been made and are satisfactory or are the best that can be devised in the circumstances, or (b) that it is
impracticable to make any such arrangements. By the definition contained in

---

(39) (1880), 16 Ch.D. 41.   (40) (1889), 22 Q.B.D. 577.
(41) [1967] 2 All E.R. at p. 1121.   (42) [1967] 1 All E.R. at p. 209.
          (43) [1967] 2 All E.R. at pp. 1116, 1117.

A s. 46 (1) of the Act of 1965, the expression " relevant child " includes not only a child of both parties to the marriage, but also a child of one party to the marriage who has been accepted as one of the family by the other party. The child here in question, even if not the child of the husband, may be said prima facie to have been accepted by him as one of the family. It has, however, been held by PARK, J., in R. v. R. (44), that acceptance depends on consent to receive the child as one

B of the family, and that such consent must be shown to have been given with knowledge of the material facts. In the present case the husband did not know, and in the absence of a blood test could not know, all the material facts, e.g., the true paternity of the child. Unless it is ascertained who is the father of the child, therefore, it cannot be known whether this is a " relevant child ", and the court is consequently in no position to discharge the duty laid on it by s. 33 of the Act

C of 1965. If the court has such a duty it must, it is argued, be endowed with the power to discharge that duty, including the power in a proper case to order that a blood test be made.

I do not find it necessary to express any opinion on the question whether R. v. R. (44) was rightly decided, for in my view the argument addressed to us fails on other grounds. I do not accept that s. 33 of the Act of 1965 lays on the

D court any such duty as is contended for. As I read the section, the duty is laid on the party seeking to have the decree made absolute to satisfy the court with regard to the arrangements for the child. I do not think that the section requires the court to act in an inquisitorial capacity. If the party seeking relief does not satisfy the court, he simply does not get his decree made absolute. Where Parliament intended that the court should be under a duty to inquire, express

E provision to that effect was made—see, for instance, s. 5 (1) of the Act of 1965. If that be right, the whole foundation for the argument addressed to us disappears. Even if, contrary to my view, s. 33 does place the court under some duty to inquire, I do not accept that it follows, in the absense of express provision, that it must be endowed with power to order a blood test in the absence of consent on the part of the party affected. I do not think, therefore, that the argument based on s. 33

F of the Act of 1965 can succeed.

The other argument advanced in support of the judge's conclusion was based on s. 34 (1) of the Act of 1965. By that section the court is empowered to ". . . make such order as it thinks just *for* the custody, maintenance and education of any relevant child . . ." The words used in the corresponding section of the Matrimonial Causes Act, 1857, were " such provision . . . as it may deem just and proper

G *with respect to* the custody, maintenance, and education of the children . . .", and similar expressions were used in all the subsequent Acts preceding the Act of 1965. Since the Act of 1965 is expressed to be a consolidating Act, it is to be presumed that no change of substance was intended by the alteration of the wording, and that the expression " for the custody " is to be construed as having the same meaning as the expression " with respect to the custody ", as enacted in

H the previous Acts. So far I am not disposed to disagree. What is argued, however, is that this means that the court is empowered to make any order which can be said to be in any way ancillary to the questions of custody, access, etc. Since both parties in this case base their claims in respect of custody and access on their alleged blood relationship, it is vital for the court to be able to decide this determining factor. It must, therefore, be endowed with the power to make any

I order which will assist in the determination of this question, which is essentially a question " with respect to " custody. Consequently s. 34 of the Act of 1965 should be construed as conferring on the court power in a proper case to order a blood test to be made, if this is necessary for the determination of any question with respect to custody.

I find myself unable to accept this argument. In my judgment, if Parliament had intended to confer on the court a statutory power to order a blood test as

(44) (1967), 111 Sol. Jo. 413.

against a non-consenting party, it would have said so in express terms. Moreover, A
if the argument were well founded, two consequences would follow. One is that
the Divorce court must always have had such a power ever since 1857, which
nobody has ever previously suggested. The other, and more important, consequence is that the same power would have to be held to have been conferred
on magistrates' courts, since the same, or substantially the same, expression is
used in defining the powers of such courts both in the Guardianship of Infants B
Act, 1886, and in the Matrimonial Proceedings (Magistrates' Courts) Act, 1960.
I cannot think that Parliament ever intended any such consequence.

For these reasons, I do not feel disposed to accept the alternative arguments
addressed to us in support of the judge's conclusion. In my view, however, his
judgment should be affirmed on the ground on which he based it, and on that
ground I would dismiss this appeal.   C

Since preparing this judgment I have had the advantage of reading the judgment which has now been delivered by LORD DENNING, M.R. Having regard to
what has been said by him, I think it right to add two further observations. First,
I confine my judgment with regard to the court's power to order a test of a child's
blood to cases arising, as this case does, within the court's custodial jurisdiction.
I am not, as at present advised, prepared to hold that such a power exists in a D
paternity issue, and still less on a petition for divorce on the ground of adultery.
So to hold would in my judgment be contrary to the decision of this court in
W. v. W. (No. 4) (45). Secondly, I am not, as at present advised, prepared to hold
that the presumption of legitimacy can be rebutted on a mere balance of probabilities. The question does not arise in the present case, at any rate at the
present stage, and we have not had the advantage of hearing any argument with E
regard to what may be the appropriate standard of proof in legitimacy.

DAVIES, L.J.: There have now been three judgments in this case, those of
ORMROD, J. (46), and of my lords, LORD DENNING, M.R., and WILLMER, L.J.
I respectfully agree with the conclusions which have been reached, and the reasoning on which they were based, though I concur with the two reservations made F
by WILLMER, L.J., as to the judgment of LORD DENNING, M.R. In those circumstances no purpose would be served by any repetition of the considerations
which have been so fully and clearly set out by my lords, and I propose to add
but little.

As things now stand, the three adults concerned have been blood-tested and in
consequence there is a ninety per cent. chance that, if the child's blood is tested, G
it will be possible to say with certainty which of the two men is not her father.
In these circumstances it would not only be absurd but quite wrong to allow this
important question to be decided simply on the basis of the presumption of
legitimacy, when it is possible by modern scientific methods to obtain positive
evidence such as, in days when the presumption prevailed, could never have been
available. To oust this evidence at the present stage of these proceedings would H
be particularly strange, as has been pointed out, when one reflects that the mother
could, without objection, have had the child's blood tested before the Official
Solicitor came into the matter and could also do so in the future when the Official
Solicitor becomes functus officio.

It would be equally undesirable for this matter to be adjourned for the child
to be made a ward of court. To take that course would indeed be to create the I
multiplicity of proceedings which s. 43 of the Supreme Court of Judicature
(Consolidation) Act, 1925, is designed to prevent. Counsel for the Official Solicitor
does not dispute that, if that course were taken, the Chancery judge would have
power to make the order which was made by ORMROD, J. (47) though I gather that
he hopes that the Chancery judge would not do so.

(45) [1963] 2 All E.R. 841; [1964] P. 67.
(46) [1967] 2 All E.R. 1110.
(47) [1967] 2 All E.R. at p. 1126

A   One cannot help feeling that to some extent the argument for, and the stand taken up by, the Official Solicitor is based on a misapprehension of his position and function as guardian ad litem. As such he is in no sense a custodial or tutelary guardian. That function is pro tempore in the court, whether the Divorce Division or the Chancery Division. It is always to be remembered that a guardian ad litem is by no means necessarily the Official Solicitor; he might well be a
B   private person.

It is said, however, that, on a strict interpretation of his duties, the guardian ad litem has a right to decide whether or not the infant, or other person under a disability, should give evidence, and that to compel this child to give a sample of her blood is in a sense to compel her to provide evidence. I do not agree that, even on this point, the views of the guardian could in all circumstances prevail. Suppose
C   that in custody proceedings in the Divorce Division the judge were to express the intention of interviewing the child, as, of course, sometimes happens. Such an interview amounts, of course, to the giving of evidence by the child, albeit unsworn; but it would be an astonishing proposition that in such a case the guardian ad litem could prevent the judge from interviewing the child.

Another anomaly which arises from counsel for the infant's argument is that
D   while submitting that a divorce judge cannot overrule the guardian ad litem's refusal to permit a blood test, yet he concedes that the judge could overrule the guardian's permission for such a test to be made.

Finally, I confess that for some time the arguments on behalf of the husband and the wife based on s. 33 and s. 34 of the Matrimonial Causes Act 1965, assuming as I do, that the decision of PARK, J., in R. v. R., (48), was correct, presented con-
E   siderable attraction. For in such circumstances a blood test such as has been ordered in the present case might be all important in deciding whether a particular child was a " relevant child " within the meaning of the Act of 1965. For the reasons given by my lords, however, it would not be right to hold that those provisions of the Act of 1965 are wide enough to give jurisdiction to make the order now in question.
F   I agree with the judgments delivered and that, accordingly, this appeal fails.

Appeal dismissed. Leave to appeal to the House of Lords refused.

Solicitors: *Official Solicitor*; *Lipson, Rumney & Co.* for the husband); *Breeze, Benton & Co.* (for the wife).

G   [*Reported by* F. GUTTMAN, ESQ., *Barrister-at-Law.*]

H

I

(48) (1967), 111 Sol. Jo. 413.

A

Re PENTON'S SETTLEMENTS.
HUMPHREYS v. BIRCH-REYNARDSON AND OTHERS.

[CHANCERY DIVISION (Ungoed-Thomas, J.), October 4, 5, 6, 10, 11, 1967.]

*Settlement—Life interest—Surrender—Power to surrender determinable life
interest in vested share of child or issue in favour of child or issue—Appointment by life tenant to grandchildren " upon attaining " thirty or surviving
twenty-one years from date of appointment—Proviso creating gifts over—
Whether interests appointed were vested subject to being divested or were
contingent interests—Rule in* Phipps v. Ackers*—Surrender of life interest
to trustees to intent that it be extinguished and funds held on trust as if life
tenant were dead—Whether surrender was within the power to surrender or
whether the life interest was forfeited.*

B

C

The appointor was life tenant of a share of funds settled in 1907. Her
life interest was determinable on alienation (as provided in cl. 5), other than
a surrender in accordance with cl. 9. Clause 9 of the settlement provided
that it should be lawful for the appointor to surrender her life interest
" in the vested share of any child or other issue " of hers " in the trust   D
fund in favour of such child or other issue so as to bring such share into
possession ". One of the appointor's daughters had three children, who
would respectively attain thirty years of age in 1982, 1984 and 1986. By
deed of appointment dated Mar. 6, 1965, the appointor appointed (cl. 2)
that the trustees should stand possessed of a certain share of the trust
fund on trust for the children of her daughter on attaining the age of thirty   E
years or surviving twenty-one years from the date of the appointment,
whichever should be the sooner, in equal shares as tenants in common
absolutely. This was followed by a proviso that in the event of any of the
grandchildren dying before attaining a vested interest, leaving a child or
children surviving, the share which such beneficiary would have taken had
he or she attained a vested interest should be held on trust for any such   F
child or children living twenty-one years from the date of the appointment
and, if more than one, in equal shares absolutely. By cl. 4 the appointor
assigned and surrendered her life interest to the trustees to the intent that
it should be merged and extinguished and that the trustees should hold
the trust fund on the trusts appointed to take effect after the appointor's
death. If the interests of the grandchildren of the appointor were con-   G
tingent, the assignment and surrender of the appointor's life interest by
the deed of appointment would not have been in accordance with cl. 9 of the
settlement and so would not have been excepted from cl. 5, with the consequence that the appointor's life interest would have been forfeited. On the
questions whether the grandchildren had vested interests liable to be divested
or had contingent interests, and whether the surrender was in favour of   H
the grandchildren within cl. 9,

Held: the appointment and surrender were effective and no forfeiture
was incurred for the following reasons—

(i) the principle on which the rule of construction, known as the rule
in *Phipps* v. *Ackers**, was founded was based on intention ascertained as a
matter of construction by reading together the prior gift and the gift over   I
and ascertaining whether they indicated an intention that the prior donee
should take, subject only to the subsequent contingency being satisfied
(see p. 43, letters F and G, post); although this rule of construction would yield
to a contrary intention, yet on the true construction of the will and the
deed of appointment, particularly cl. 2 of the deed, the intention shown
accorded with the application of the rule in *Phipps* v. *Ackers*, and the

---

* (1842), 9 Cl. & Fin. 583. The rule is stated at p. 42, letter H, post.

A   grandchildren obtained, under the deed of appointment, interests that were
     vested subject to being divested (see p. 46, letters A and H, post).

         Phipps v. *Ackers* ((1842), 9 Cl. & Fin. 583) applied; *Finch* v. *Lane* ((1870),
     L.R. 10 Eq. 501) followed.

         (ii) the surrender was a surrender in favour of each grandchild of the
     appointor within cl. 9 although it was made to the trustees, and, as it had
B   the effect of accelerating their immediately succeeding interests and bringing
     them into possession, it was a surrender within cl. 9 of the settlement,
     notwithstanding that the grandchildren's vested interests were liable to be
     divested (see p. 48, letter G, post).

         Dicta of HARMAN, J., in *Re Young's Settlement Trusts* ([1959] 2 All E.R.
     at p. 80) and of EVE, J., in *Re Master's Settlement* ([1911] 1 Ch. at p. 325)
C   applied.

     [As to the rule in *Phipps* v. *Ackers*, see 39 HALSBURY'S LAWS (3rd Edn.)
     1124, 1125, para. 1660; as to contingent gifts over, see ibid., 1127, 1128, para.
     1664; and for cases on the subject, see 49 DIGEST (Repl.) 974-979, *9154-9187*.]

     Cases referred to:
D   *Bromfield* v. *Crowder*, (1805), 1 Bos. & P.N.R. 313; 127 E.R. 483; 49 Digest
             (Repl.) 974, *9156*.
     Doe d. Willis v. *Martin*, [1775-1802] All E.R. Rep. 343; (1790), 4 Term Rep.
             39; 100 E.R. 882; 37 Digest (Repl.) 342, *859*.
     Edwards v. *Hammond*, (1684), 3 Lev. 132; 1 Bos. & P. 324, n.; 83 E.R. 614;
             49 Digest (Repl.) 968, *9120*.
E   *Finch* v. *Lane*, (1870), L.R. 10 Eq. 501; 49 Digest (Repl.) 982, *9207*.
     Heath, Re, Public Trustee v. *Heath*, [1935] All E.R. Rep. 677; [1936] Ch. 259;
             105 L.J.Ch. 29; 154 L.T. 536; 49 Digest (Repl.) 1037, *9711*.
     Kilpatrick's Policies Trusts, Re, Kilpatrick v. *Inland Revenue Comrs.*, [1965]
             2 All E.R. 673; [1966] Ch. 730; [1965] 2 W.L.R. 1346; *affd.* C.A.,
             [1966] 2 All E.R. 149; [1966] Ch. at p. 747; [1966] 2 W.L.R. at p. 1360;
F   Digest (Cont. Vol. B) 245, *137a*.
     Lambert v. *Thwaites*, [1861-73] All E.R. Rep. 252; (1866), L.R. 2 Eq. 151;
             35 L.J.Ch. 406; 14 L.T. 159; 37 Digest (Repl.) 343, *864*.
     Master's Settlement, Re Master v. *Master*, [1911] 1 Ch. 321; 80 L.J.Ch. 190;
             103 L.T. 899; 37 Digest (Repl.) 342, *857*.
     Phipps v. *Ackers*, (1842), 9 Cl. & Fin. 583; 8 E.R. 539; 49 Digest (Repl.)
G   975, *9163*.
     Young's Settlement Trusts, Re, Royal Exchange Assurance v. *Taylor-Young*,
             [1959] 2 All E.R. 74; [1959] 1 W.L.R. 457; Digest (Cont. Vol. A)
             1320, *1038a*.

     Adjourned Summons.

H   This was an application by originating summons dated Mar. 14, 1967, as
     amended on May 3, 1967, by the plaintiff, Dame Dorothy Grace Humphreys,
     who claimed to be interested beneficially in the property subject to the trusts
     of the eleven various instruments subsequently mentioned, for the determination
     of several questions, which included the following questions. Whether on the
     true construction of two appointments and surrenders dated Mar. 6, 1965,
I   hereinafter mentioned and in the events which had happened: (i) the invest-
     ments and cash mentioned in the second schedule to one appointment surrender
     and release dated Mar. 6, 1965, and the assets from time to time representing
     the same (the Birch-Reynardson appointed share) and the income thereof were
     held (a) on the trusts appointed by the last mentioned appointment surrender
     and release to take effect after the plaintiff's death; or (b) on trust during the
     life of the plaintiff to apply the annual income thereof in accordance with the
     terms of the discretionary trust limited by cl. 5 of the settlement at June 10,
     1907, to take effect if the trust to pay income to the plaintiff therein contained

should fail or determine in her lifetime and subject thereto on the trusts A
mentioned in alternative (a) of this present question, or (c) on some other and
if so what trusts; (ii) the investments and cash mentioned in the second schedule
to the other appointment surrender and release dated Mar. 6, 1965, and the
assets from time to time representing the same (the Colvile appointment share)
and the income thereof were held (a) on the trusts appointed by the last mentioned
appointment, surrender and release to take effect after the plaintiff's death; B
or (b) on trust during the life of the plaintiff to apply the annual income thereof
in accordance with the terms of the said discretionary trust limited by cl. 5 of
the settlement of June 10, 1907, thereto to take effect if the trust to pay income
to the plaintiff therein contained should fail to determine in her lifetime and
subject thereto on the trusts mentioned in alternative (a) of this present question,
or (c) on some other, and if so what trusts.   C
     There were fourteen defendants and eleven instruments.   These instruments
were—(i) and (ii) settlements dated June 10, 1907, and June 15, 1907; (iii) to
(vii) deeds of covenant and settlement dated Dec. 18, 1915, Dec. 20, 1915, Dec.
22, 1915, Dec. 28, 1915 and Dec. 29, 1915; (viii) a deed of appointment and
surrender dated Mar. 20, 1964, and ((ix) to ((xi)) appointments, surrenders and
releases, one dated Mar. 4, 1965, and two dated Mar. 6, 1965.   The first defen- D
dant, Pamela Matnika Birch-Reynardson, claimed to be interested beneficially
in the property subject to the trusts of the eleven instruments or part of that
property; the second defendant, Janet Camilla Colvile claimed to be beneficially
interested similarly under the eleven instruments; the third defendant Owen
Thomas Humphreys (claimed to be similarly interested beneficially) and was a
trustee of all the property comprised in the settlements (i) to (vii) inclusive E
except the property comprised in one appointment, surrender and release of
Mar. 6, 1965.   The fourth to sixth defendants were the infant children of
Mrs. Birch-Reynardson.   The seventh, eight and fourteenth defendants were
the infant children of Mrs. Colvile.   The ninth defendant, Walter Ogilvy, was a
trustee of all the property comprised in the settlements (i) to (vii) inclusive
except the property comprised in the two deeds of appointment, surrender F
and release dated Mar. 6, 1965.   The tenth to thirteenth defendants were trustees
of various of the instruments.

C. J. Slade, Q.C., and P. M. F. Horsfield for the plaintiff.
Martin Nourse for the first to eighth and fourteenth defendants.
R. Cozens-Hardy Horne for the ninth to thirteenth defendants.
                                                                                G
     UNGOED-THOMAS, J.: In this case the settlement, despite a provision
in the settlement for forfeiture on attempted alienation, authorised the life
tenant to surrender her life interest in the vested share of any issue of hers in
favour of such issue so as to bring such share into possession. The question now
raised is whether the purported surrender of her life interest was valid.
     The surrender was purported to be made to trustees to the intent that the life H
interest should be merged and extinguished and that the trustees should hold the
trust fund on the trust which she appointed to take effect on her death, namely,
for grandchildren on surviving twenty-one years in equal shares absolutely from
the date of the surrender, with a gift over of such grandchild's share on trust for
such grandchild's children in the event of a grandchild dying before attaining a
vested interest leaving a child surviving.   I
     Substantial funds are involved and the question raised is material both for
income tax and estate duty purposes. The Inland Revenue and Estate Duty Office
have been invited to be represented before me, but, being apparently satisfied
that the case would be properly argued, they have, very understandably, not
wished to avail themselves of that invitation.
     The case has been argued with great ability on all sides, and the case which the
Crown would be interested to press has been most fully and vigorously pressed.
     The settlement was made on June 10, 1907, by Frederick Thomas Penton, the

A settlor, who died in 1929. The plaintiff is his daughter, Lady Humphreys, and all the defendants, except two, who are trustees, are his issue. There were later instruments referred to in the summons, which added funds which were amalgamated with the funds of the settlement. The trusts were to divide the trust fund into three shares for the settlor's three younger children. Each child's share was settled on the child for life, and, in case of that child being a daughter, on protected

B life interest, with, (i) power to appoint in favour of issue and subject thereto to the life tenant's children at twenty-one, or being female being married, subject to a hotch pot provision; (ii) power to appoint income to a surviving spouse for life; (iii) power to surrender the life interest in a vested share of any issue in the trust fund in favour of such issue so as to bring such share into possession.

Before coming to the terms of the settlement I will indicate the state of the

C settlor's family. He had four children, the eldest a son, with whom we are not concerned. The three younger children were a son, Cyril Frederick, who died in 1960, leaving a son who had attained full age and with whose share we are not concerned; the second younger child was a daughter, Kathleen Winifred, now Mrs. Ogilvy, who is some seventy-seven years of age and childless, and we are not, in this question, concerned with her share either; the third of the three

D younger children was Dorothy Grace, Lady Humphreys, the plaintiff in this case. She is now some seventy-six years of age and she has had three children: first, Pamela, who married Mr. Birch-Reynardson, and they have three children, Juliet, Clare and Thomas, all of whom are infants; secondly, a daughter, Janet, who married a Mr. Colvile, and has three children, all infants; and thirdly, a son, Owen Thomas. Lady Humphreys exercised the power of appointment in favour

E of issue and purported to exercise the surrender to which I have referred. The power of appointment and corresponding surrender was by one instrument exercised in favour of the Birch-Reynardson grandchildren, and by another instrument was exercised in favour of the Colvile grandchildren. It is with those appointments and surrenders that we are concerned in this case.

I now come to the terms of the settlement. The settlor assigned various policy

F moneys and investments to trustees, who, of course, were party to the settlement, on trust (and I read now from clause 3 of the settlement):

". . . for such of the said three younger children of the said Frederick Thomas Penton as attain the age of twenty-one or being female marry under that age and if more than one in equal shares but so that each child's share shall be retained by the trustees and held upon the trusts and with and sub-

G ject to the powers and provisions hereinafter declared and contained concerning the same."

Clause 5 provides:

" The trustees shall pay the annual income of the share of each of the said daughters of the said Frederick Thomas Penton Kathleen Winifred

H Penton and Dorothy Grace Penton in the trust fund to such daughter for her life (to be for her separate use without power of anticipation during any coverture) or until she does or attempts to do or suffers any act or thing or any event happens (other than a surrender of her life interest under the provisions of cl. 9 hereof or an advance under the power of advancement hereinafter contained) whereby if the same income were payable to her

I absolutely for her life she would be deprived of the right to receive the same or any part thereof in any of which cases as well as on her death whichever first happens the trust hereinbefore declared for payment to her of the said income is to determine And if the trust aforesaid should fail or determine in her lifetime then UPON TRUST during the residue of her life to apply the annual income of her share for the maintenance and support or otherwise for the benefit of all or any one or more exclusively of the others or other of her and any husband and issue of hers for the time being in existence as the trustees in their sole discretion without being liable to account for the

A exercise of such discretion think fit or if there should be no such husband or issue in existence then for the maintenance and support or otherwise for the benefit of all or any one or more exclusively of the others or other of her and the person or persons who would if she were actually dead be for the time being entitled to her share or the income thereof as the trustees in their sole discretion without being liable to account as aforesaid think fit And after the death of such daughter the capital and income of her share or so much thereof B as shall not have been paid or applied under any trust or power affecting the same shall be held UPON the like trusts for the benefit of the issue of such daughter as are by the last preceding clause declared concerning the capital and income of the share of the said Cyril Frederick Penton in the trust fund after his death in the same manner in all respects as if such trusts were herein repeated with the substitution of the name of such daughter for the C name of the said Cyril Frederick Penton."

The trusts to the issue of Cyril, after his death, appear in the preceding cl. 4, where it says that after the death of Cyril his share should be held in trust

". . . for all or any one or more exclusively of the others or other of the issue of the said Cyril Frederick Penton whether children or remoter issue at D such time and if more than one in such shares and with such gifts over and such provisions for maintenance advancement and otherwise at the discretion of any person or persons and generally in such manner for the benefit of such issue or some or one of them as the said Cyril Frederick Penton shall by deed recoverable or irrecoverable or by Will or Codicil appoint but so that under any appointment a child shall not except by way of advancement take a E vested interest before attaining the age of twenty-one or being female marrying under that age And in default of and until and subject to any such appointment IN TRUST for all or any the children or child of the said Cyril Frederick Penton who attain the age of twenty-one or being female marry under that age and if more than one in equal shares PROVIDED ALWAYS that no child who or whose issue takes any part of the share of the said Cyril F Frederick Penton in the trust fund shall in the absence of any discretion (sic) by him to the contrary take any share of the unappointed part without bringing the part appointed to him or her or to his or her issue into hotchpot . . ."

Then cl. 6 provides:

" If the trusts hereinbefore declared concerning the share of any of the G said three younger children . . ."

should fail or determine, one moiety of such share should accrue on the trusts concerning the original share of such child; and the other moiety should be transferred to the settlement trustees of an indenture of Feb. 13, 1907, being a re-settlement by the settlor of the Penton Estate, Clerkenwell. Clause 7 provides: " It shall be lawful for each of the said younger children . . ." to appoint in favour H of a surviving husband for life any part of the annual income of such child's share.

I shall read cl. 8 in full because it is material on a question of construction which arises, so that I shall refer to it later. It reads:

" It shall be lawful for the trustees to raise any part or parts not exceeding I in the whole a moiety of the capital of any share to which any minor shall or if of full age being a male or of full age or married being a female would for the time being be entitled in the capital of the trust fund whether in possession or in reversion or expectancy under these presents and to pay or apply the same for his or her advancement or benefit as the trustees shall think fit PROVIDED that no such advancement shall be made during the existence of any prior life or other interest or interests whether vested or contingent without the consent in writing of the person or persons entitled thereto."

A The material words there, for purposes of construction, are "vested or contingent". Clause 9 reads (and this is the crucial clause in this document):

"It shall be lawful for each of the said younger children of the said Frederick Thomas Penton notwithstanding the restraint on anticipation or any other restriction hereinbefore imposed upon him or her to surrender his
B or her life interest in the vested share of any child or other issue of his or hers in the trust fund in favour of such child or other issue so as to bring such share into possession."

Lady Humphreys made various appointments under the power conferred on her by the settlement and purported to surrender her life interest in the fund so appointed. As I have indicated, we are concerned with two only of such appoint-
C ments, namely the two deeds of appointment and surrender, both of Mar. 6, 1965, being documents marked (x) and (xi) in the heading of the summons, the first being an appointment to the Birch-Reynardson grandchildren of Lady Humphreys, and the other being an appointment to the Colvile grandchildren of Lady Humphreys. It is common ground that although there are differences between these two appointments and surrender, yet those differences have not been relied on for making any distinction between the appointments and
D surrender before me and so, I shall confine myself to the consideration of the Birch-Reynardson appointment and surrender.

By that appointment and surrender, Lady Humphreys appointed part of the trust fund to the three existing Birch-Reynardson grandchildren, whose names I have given, on attaining thirty years or surviving twenty-one years from the date of the appointment, whichever is the earlier, equally and absolutely, with a
E gift over in the event of any child dying before attaining a vested interest leaving children. Then Lady Humphreys surrendered her life interest to the trustees in the appointed assets.

The appointment is indisputably valid, but the question is whether the surrender was within the terms of cl. 9 of the settlement. The deed of appointment, surrender and release was made, of course, between Lady Humphreys on
F the one hand and the trustees of the 1907 settlement on the other hand. Amongst other things, it recited that there had been three children born of the marriage of Lady Humphreys' daughter Pamela to Mr. Birch-Reynardson, namely, those whom I have already named, Juliet, Clare and Thomas. And it gives the dates of their birth. What is material is that their thirtieth birthdays will take place on Mar. 20, 1982, June 29, 1984 and Oct. 8, 1986. Then, after reciting that Lady
G Humphreys is desirous of making the appointment thereinafter contained, and to release her life interest in the funds thereby appointed, she first released the power to appoint for the benefit of the husband and then provided, by cl. 2, which is one of the two crucial clauses, as follows:

"In exercise of the power for this purpose vested in her by the settlements
H and of every other power enabling her the appointor hereby irrevocably appoints that subject to her life interest therein under the settlements the trustees shall stand possessed of the investments and cash mentioned in the said Sch. 2 hereto representing a one-third share of the investments and cash comprising the appointer's share UPON TRUST for the beneficiaries upon attaining the age of thirty years or surviving twenty-one years from the date hereof whichever shall be the sooner in equal shares as tenants in common
I absolutely PROVIDED that in the event of any of the beneficiaries dying before attaining a vested interest leaving a child or children him or her surviving the trustees shall stand possessed of the share which such beneficiary would have taken had he or she attained a vested interest upon trust for any such child or children who shall be living twenty-one years from the date hereof and if more than one in equal shares absolutely."

So the grandchildren had not, and still have not, attained the age of thirty years or survived twenty-one years from the date of the appointment.

Clause 4 provides (which is the other crucial clause):   A

" The appointor HEREBY ASSIGNS AND SURRENDERS unto the trustees ALL THAT the life interest of the appointor in the said investments and cash mentioned in Sch. 2 hereto and the income thereof to the intent that as from the date hereof such life interest shall be merged and extinguished and that the trustees shall henceforth subject to any future appointment by the appointor hold the said investments and cash upon the trusts hereinbefore   B appointed to take effect after the appointor's death."

The only observation that I need make on that clause at this moment is that the words " subject to any future appointment by the appointor " are, clearly, inapplicable, because the appointment was an irrevocable appointment. The only difference in the Colvile appointment, as I have mentioned, is that the appointment was in favour not only of existing grandchildren but also future grand-   C children. So it comes about that Lady Humphreys and her grandchildren are interested to argue in favour of the surrender being valid and Lady Humphreys' children make common cause with their children, Lady Humphreys' grand-children, although it might be against their immediate financial interest to do so. The trustees of the settlement represent unborn issue of Lady Humphreys, who   D would be objects of the discretionary trust that would arise if the surrender were invalid. Therefore, they are interested to argue that the surrender is not a valid surrender and that Lady Humphreys has, by attempting to make that surrender, incurred a forfeiture in accordance with the provisions of the settlement. They thus, incidentally, but inevitably, argue also in the interests of the Inland Revenue and the Estate Duty Office.

The first question which arises is whether the grandchildren's interests under   E Lady Humphreys' appointment are vested interests liable to be divested, as Lady Humphreys says, or contingent interests, as the trustees claim. If the interests are vested interests liable to be divested, then the question arises whether the surrender satisfies the requirements of cl. 9, that the surrender is of a life interest in the vested share of any child or other issue of his or hers in the trust fund in favour of such child or other issue so as to bring such share into possession.   F If the trustees succeed on the first question and it is held therefore that the grand-children's interests under the appointment are contingent interests, there is no possibility of arguing that the surrender is authorised by cl. 9; and it follows indisputably that there has been a forfeiture of Lady Humphreys' interest. So I will take these two submissions in order.

It is argued for Lady Humphreys that her submission that the grandchildren's   G interests are vested interests liable to be divested, is established primarily in accordance with the rule in *Phipps* v. *Ackers* (1). The rule in *Phipps* v. *Ackers* (1), as extended in later cases, at any rate so far as relevant to this case, is that if there is a gift to individuals or a class if or when they attain a specified age or survive a specified time or person and there is a gift over on failure to attain that age or so survive or on such occurrence and some further occurrence such as that   H they leave children, the interests of such individuals or class are not contingent on attaining that age or so surviving, but are vested subject to being divested if they die under that age or do not so survive. The rule applies to a mixed fund and to pure personality as well as to realty (see *Phipps* v. *Ackers* (1), *Bromfield* v. *Crowder* (2), *Re Heath, Public Trustee* v. *Heath* (3) and *Re Kilpatrick's Policies Trusts, Kilpatrick* v. *Inland Revenue Comrs.* (4)).   I

I understand there to be no dispute about the rule as so stated, but there is dispute as to the principle on which it is based and its application to this case. For Lady Humphreys, it is submitted that the rule is a rule of construction to give effect to intention ascertained by the construction of the document as a whole.

(1) (1842), 9 Cl. & Fin. 583.   (2) (1805), 1 Bos. & P.N.R. 313.
(3) [1935] All E.R. Rep. 677; [1936] Ch. 259.
(4) [1965] 2 All E.R. 673; [1966] Ch. 730; *on appeal*, [1966] 2 All E.R. 149; [1966] Ch. at p. 747.

A For the trustees, it is submitted that the rule is designed to dispose of income where, if the gift were treated as contingent instead of vested and liable to be divested, there would be no effective disposition of the income, and that, therefore, it does not apply where, as here, there is a prior interest in possession to absorb the current income. It appears that support for the trustees' contention can be found in the origin and history of this rule. Thus, Cross, J., in *Re*

B *Kilpatrick's Policies Trusts* (5), conveniently reviews the history as follows:

" If A. gives property to B. if B. attains a certain age or fulfils some other condition, it is natural to suppose that A. would wish B., on fulfilling the condition, to receive any income derived from the property since the date of the gift. The obvious way for effect to be given to this intention is for income to be accumulated to abide the event; but in the case of dispositions

C of real property this solution was impossible under the old law, since it would not permit the ownership of the freehold to be in abeyance pending the contingency. Therefore, the rents would pass to the heir or residuary devisee or, in the case of an inter vivos disposition, would revert to the grantor. In order to avoid this result and to give effect to the presumed intention of the testator or grantor, the common law courts seized on any excuse to construe

D dispositions of realty as creating vested interests liable to be divested rather than contingent interests."

Then Cross, J., pointed out (5) that subsequently the rule ceased to be limited to dispositions of mere realty, which he stated was the origin of the rule, but applied to dispositions of realty and personalty combined, and to dispositions of personalty alone, where, of course, its application was not needed, in accordance

E with the explanation given of the origin of the rule, and, as Cross, J., said (5) a little later, the reasons which formed the original justification for the rule were in fact no longer operative.

The motive or reason for introducing the rule originally has to be distinguished from the principle of law on which the rule is founded, and that principle is, even from early times, not based on or limited to the need to dispose of otherwise

F undisposed of income, but is based on intention ascertained as a matter of construction. Further—and this is crucial—an examination of cases clearly reveals that that intention is ascertained, not by reference to the non-disposal of income which would arise before the contingency occurred if the gift were treated as contingent, but by reference to the gift over being dependent on that contingency not occurring. The contingency applicable to the prior gift and the gift over are

G the counterparts of each other, hinging on the same event. When read together, as they should be, as a matter of construction, they indicate an intention that the prior donee should take, subject only to the subsequent contingency of the gift over being satisfied.

In *Phipps* v. *Ackers* (6) the Case submitted for the opinion of the judges was as follows (7):

H
" ' A.B. being seised in fee simple of certain lands and hereditaments at W., by his will duly executed and attested for passing real estates by devise, gave all his real estates at W. to his godson, G.H.A., when and so soon as he should attain his age of twenty-one years; but in case his said godson should die under the age of twenty-one years, then the testator directed that his said estate at W. should sink into and form part of his residuary real estate: and

I by his said will he gave all the residue of his real estates to J.C., subject to various limitations and provisions affecting the same. The testator continued seised in fee simple of the said lands and hereditaments at W. until his death, and he died without revoking or altering his will, leaving his godson G.H.A. an infant of the age of twelve years. The opinion of the judges is desired as to what estate G.H.A. took in the estate at W.' "

(5) [1965] 2 All E.R. at p. 678; [1966] Ch. at p. 738.
(6) (1842), 9 Cl. & Fin. 583.   (7) (1842), 9 Cl. & Fin. at p. 590.

The part of the opinion to which I wish to refer was as follows (8):   A

" The second class of cases [we need not concern ourselves with the first class] goes on the principle that the subsequent gift over in the event of the devisee dying under twenty-one, sufficiently shows the meaning of the testator to have been that the first devisee should take whatever interest the party claiming under the devise over is not entitled to, which of course gives him the immediate interest, subject only to the chance of its being divested   B on a future contingency. Whether the doctrine on which this second class of cases has rested was originally altogether satisfactory, is a point which we need not discuss. It is sufficient to say that it clearly has been established and recognised as a settled rule of construction, not only in the courts below but also in your lordships' House, and that rule appears to us clearly to govern the case put to us by your lordships: in conformity with which rule, there-   C fore, we beg leave to state, that on the question put to us, we are of opinion that G.H.A., on the decease of the testator, took an estate in fee simple in the lands and hereditaments at W., subject to be divested in the event of his dying under twenty-one and without issue."

There, the question was clearly treated as a matter of construction, and the   D construction was clearly decided with reference to the terms of the gift over and not with reference to any disposal or non-disposal of income before the prior estate arose.

In *Bromfield* v. *Crowder* (9), the headnote reads as follows:

" Testator devised to A. for life, and after her death to B. for life, and at the decease of A. and B., or the survivor, gave all his real estate to C. if he   E should live to attain twenty-one; but in case he should die before that age, and D. should survive him, in that case to D. if he should live to attain twenty-one, but not otherwise; but in case both C. and D. should die before either of them should attain twenty-one, then to E. in fee. Held that C. took a vested remainder."

Sir James Mansfield, C.J., said (10):   F

" All the testator's real estate is given to the plaintiff immediately on the death of the preceding devisees, if he live to attain twenty-one; if he die before twenty-one, and his brother Charles Bromfield survive, then the testator gives his real estate to the said Charles Bromfield, if he live to attain twenty-one, but not otherwise. If both die under twenty-one, then he gives it to his godson, John Vale, in fee. The plaintiff was under twenty-one   G at the time of the death of the surviving devisee, and the question is whether he took any and what estate in the freehold or copyhold premises. There does not appear to us to be any distinction between the freehold and copyhold. In fact, this is an immediate devise to the plaintiff, to take place on the death of the two preceding devisees. If so, we must either break in upon the terms of the will, or give them effect. In the latter case, there is an end of all argument   H about the word ' if '. There is nothing in the will to prove that the testator meant the plaintiff not to take a vested estate unless he survived twenty-one. Indeed the true sense of the thing is, that the devisor meant him to take it as an immediate devise in himself, but that it was to go over in the event of his dying under twenty-one. It must be admitted that according to repeated decisions, no precise words are necessary to constitute a condition precedent   I in wills. They must be construed according to the intention of the parties; and it would be absurd, considering the various circumstances under which wills are made, to require particular terms to express particular meanings. The apparent intention, as collected from the whole will, must always control particular expressions. Now the fairest construction that can be put upon this

---

(8) (1842), 9 Cl. & Fin. at pp. 591, 592.   (9) (1805), 1 Bos. & P.N.R. 313.
(10) (1805), 1 Bos. & P.N.R. at pp. 324-326.

A   will, independent of authority, is, that the plaintiff took an immediate
vested estate on the death of the preceding devisees, with a condition
subsequent. With respect to the cases, that of *Edwards* v. *Hammond* (11) is
on all fours with the present. The circumstance of the devise over being to a
stranger makes no difference; for it is clear that the testator meant no one to
take his estate unless in the event of the plaintiff dying under twenty-one.

B   *Edwards* v. *Hammond* (11) is neither opposed nor weakened by any case. No
doubt the general meaning of the word ' if ' implies a condition precedent,
unless it be controlled by other words. But, in this case, there is a variance
between the expression and the meaning, and the case of *Edwards* v. *Hammond* (11) sanctions us in giving effect to the latter. On these grounds, we are
of opinion that the estate vested in the plaintiff on the death of the preceding

C   devisees; and the expression, ' all my estate ', is so general as to pass an
estate in fee. Besides, it would be an absurdity on the face of the will, to
construe it only an estate for life."

There, again, the matter is dealt with as a matter of construction.

   I come to the modern case of *Re Kilpatrick's Policies Trusts* (12), where the
principle is stated by Russell, L.J. He said (13):

D

   " I have no doubt that the principle applied in *Phipps* v. *Ackers* (14)
applies to this case, notwithstanding that the subject-matter is personalty.
If that principle had its origin in an anxiety to preserve contingent
remainders, I do not think that that can be regarded as its sole justification.
It seems to me to be quite sensible to construe what appear at first sight to be

E   two contingent dispositions as in substance an absolute gift to the first taker
defeasible in favour of the substitute takers on a contingency: as it has
been put, the intention is then and there to give the whole property to A.
except to the extent to which it is effectively given to B."

There again, in line with *Phipps* v. *Ackers* (14) the matter is treated as a matter
of construction turning on the terms of the gift over and not on the disposal or

F   non-disposal of any income before the prior estate arose.

   Finally, I come to *Finch* v. *Lane* (15), which seems to me to cover this case.
The headnote states:

   " By a will the testator gave real and personal estate to M.H., her heirs,
executors, administrators, and assigns absolutely, if she should be living at
the death of the testator's wife."

G

The wife, as appears from the statement of fact just below the headnote, was
given a life interest. Then the headnote goes on—

   ". . . but in case M.H. should die in the life-time of the testator's wife
without leaving issue her surviving, then over. Held, that M.H. took an
absolute interest, liable to be divested only in the event of her death in the

H   life-time of the testator's widow without leaving issue."

Lord Romilly, M.R., in a very short judgment, stated (16):

   " I think that the testator intended to give to Mary Ann Houlton an
absolute interest, with an executory gift over in the event of her dying
without issue. The case is governed by *Phipps* v. *Ackers* (14). The event on

I   which the gift over was to take effect has not happened, but there is no
intestacy, and consequently the plaintiffs are entitled."

---

(11) (1684), 3 Lev. 132.
(12) [1966] 2 All E.R. 149; [1966] Ch. 730.
(13) [1966] 2 All E.R. at p. 156; [1966] Ch. at p. 767.
(14) (1842), 9 Cl. & Fin. 583.
(15) (1870), L.R. 10 Eq. 501.
(16) (1870), L.R. 10 Eq. at p. 503.

So, in that case *Phipps* v. *Ackers* (17) was applied to a gift in terms of prima facie   A
contingency, although a life interest preceded that gift.

With respect, it seems to me that this application of the *Phipps* v. *Ackers* (17)
principle is, clearly, correct. So, on the only words that so far have been considered, I would conclude that the rule in *Phipps* v. *Ackers* (17) applied in this
case and that, accordingly, under the appointment the grandchildren take a
vested interest subject to being divested. But, as this is a rule of construction,   B
it yields to a sufficiently indicated contrary intention. What then is the bearing
that other words have in this case on the application of the rule in *Phipps* v.
Ackers (17)?

So I turn to cl. 2 of the deed of appointment and surrender. First, the gift on
trust for the beneficiaries on attaining a certain age is not at any rate as strongly
contingent as if the words had been " if they attained " the specified age.   C
Secondly, the events, that is, attaining thirty or surviving twenty-one years, are
not alternative events suggesting a generally applicable contingency, but specified
events separately applicable to each named child, the date of whose birth is given
in the recital and, therefore, perhaps, it is easier to read the gift to them as not
being contingent. Thirdly, the phrase " in equal shares as tenants in common "
is the phrase used to describe the portions in which the three children are to take   D
and not the phrase " if more than one as tenants in common ". This goes some
little way to suggest that each child has a share from the date of the deed and this
consideration is, perhaps, the stronger because it contrasts with the wording at
the end of the proviso to cl. 2, namely, ". . . upon trust for any such child or
children who shall be living twenty-one years from the date hereof and if more
than one in equal shares absolutely." Fourthly, in the proviso, the words ". . . the   E
trustees shall stand possessed of the share which such beneficiary would have
taken had he or she attained a vested interest . . ." suggest that the beneficiary
attaining a vested interest would have taken possession and, therefore, that there
was an interest before taking possession, and that " vested " here means vested
in possession. Fifthly, " vested " in the proviso must mean indefeasibly vested
and not just vested in interest. If the grandchildren's interest is vested subject   F
to being divested, then it is nonsense to talk of their dying before attaining a
vested interest unless " vested interest " there means indefeasibly vested. Moreover if this interest is contingent, again, on satisfying the contingency, their
interest would be indefeasibly vested. It would, therefore, be unsustainable to
rely on the word " vested " in the proviso as meaning vested interest in order to
establish that the prior interest is contingent, since the vesting to which it in fact   G
refers is vested indefeasibly. Sixthly, the *Phipps* v. *Ackers* (17) principle is based
on intention gathered from the substantive dispositions of the will. The intention
so gathered from the substance is strong enough to prevail even over such a word
of contingency as " if ". I, for my part, fail to see why it should not likewise
prevail over such a more ambiguous word, at any rate in its context in the present
deed, as " vested ".   H

I, therefore, conclude that Lady Humphreys succeeds on her first submission
and that the interests which the grandchildren obtained under the appointment
are vested interests subject to being divested.

So I come to the second question, namely, whether such an interest conferred
by the appointment is within the authority to surrender conferred by cl. 9 of the
1907 settlement. This raises four subsidiary questions.   I

First, did the grandchildren living at the date of the appointment each have a
vested share, within the meaning of cl. 9? The trustees submit that " vested "
in cl. 9 is limited to indefeasibly vested, that is, such a share that, on surrender,
each of the grandchildren has an absolute interest in possession. For Lady
Humphreys, it is submitted that it includes a share which is vested subject to
being divested.

_____

(17) (1842), 9 Cl. & Fin. 583.

A   Assuming that *Phipps* v. *Ackers* (18) applies, as I have held, the effect of the appointment was to give each grandchild under the Birch-Reynardson appointment a vested and defeasible interest in one-third of the investments and cash mentioned in Sch. 2.

Reference was made to s. 32 of the Trustee Act, 1925, (19) where a person is described as entitled to capital or a share thereof though what he has is a vested B interest in remainder subject to defeasance, and proviso (a) refers to a vested share in a context wide enough to include a person with a vested though defeasible interest in remainder. This, of course, is a statute, but it does show the statutory usage of relevant terms.

Clause 9 is an exemption from the forfeiture clause, as shown by cl. 5, to which I have referred. So there is no cause for interpreting it strictly with a view to C avoiding a forfeiture. When I turn to the preceding cl. 8, it is seen that the word " vested " to which I called attention when reading the clause, is used in the proviso in contradistinction to " contingent " and in a sense covering both indefeasibly and defeasibly vested.

I see no reason for limiting the meaning of vested to indefeasibly vested, and it seems to me, as a matter of construction, that the correct conclusion is that each D grandchild had on appointment immediately before the surrender, in the order contemplated by the deed of appointment and surrender, a vested share within cl. 9.

The second subsidiary question that arises is, did Lady Humphreys surrender her life interest in such a vested share in favour of each such grandchild, within the meaning of cl. 9? Surrender was considered in *Re Young's Settlement Trusts,* E *Royal Exchange Assurance* v. *Taylor Young* (20) by HARMAN, J. He quoted (21) COKE ON LITTLETON as saying (22): " *Surrender* . . . properly is a yielding up an estate for life or years to him that hath an immediate estate in reversion or remainder . . ." Then, a little earlier in his judgment, HARMAN, J., said (21):

F   " The second alternative is that . . . Harold . . ., in surrendering his interest in income, must be taken to have surrendered to those next interested, with the result that his two children take the income between them, defeasible in favour of issue pending the date of distribution. I prefer the second alternative."

So a surrender is the yielding up an estate to him with an immediate estate in reversion or remainder. It operates so that the immediately following estate G takes effect, and if the immediately following estate is vested, whether defeasible or indefeasible, it is an immediate estate. It appears that " immediate estate " means capable of taking effect in possession at once if all the prior interests are removed. The right to surrender is reasonably limited under cl. 9 so as to be exercisable in favour of those with vested shares so as to take effect immediately when the prior life interest is extinguished and merged by surrender, H but not otherwise. The line is thus drawn reasonably by cl. 9 between vested and contingent interests. As was submitted, contingent interests are not suitable subject matter for surrender, particularly in a document of 1907, before the Property Acts, which, subject to prior interests, made current income available to those with contingent interests. They are not immediate estates, within the quotation from COKE ON LITTLETON, and surrender would leave doubts as to the I disposition of the released income, because contingent interests do not always carry the immediate income.

Is then the surrender nevertheless in favour of each such grandchild? First, it is said that surrender to trustees cannot be surrender in favour of issue, but, as

---

(18) (1842), 9 Cl. & Fin. 583.
(19) For s. 32 of the Trustee Act, 1925, see 26 HALSBURY'S STATUTES (2nd Edn.) 99.
(20) [1959] 2 All E.R. 74.
(21) [1959] 2 All E.R. at p. 80.
(22) (18th Edn.), p. 337b, sect. 636.

trustees are the means through which the donor's favour is vested in the bene- **A**
ficiary, the favour is nonetheless in favour of the beneficiary because it is vested
through the means of trustees.

Secondly, it is said that the advantage of surrender must be limited to issue
only and that here the grandchildren's vested interest might be divested in favour
of persons who include strangers. Clause 9, in terms, does not require that the
surrender should be in favour of issue exclusively and to the exclusion of any **B**
possible interest that might contingently arise in defeasance of the issues'
interests. In my view, the surrender is, in substance, in favour of issue within
the meaning and intention of cl. 9, and I shall expand this view when dealing
with the next question that arises.

That question is, did the surrender bring such share into possession? This
involves the question whether a share can be said to fall into possession although **C**
the owner of it is not at once indefeasibly entitled to capital, i.e. can a defeasibly
vested share ever be said to be in possession? Lady Humphreys submits that it
can. The trustees submit the contrary. For the trustees, it was submitted that
the surrender was limited to ensure a distribution of capital, but I find no such
limitation in any authority brought to my notice. It appears to me that the
cl. 9 power is not limited to enable capital to be distributed, as the trustees suggest, **D**
but may enable a life tenant to surrender her interest so that any immediately
succeeding interest in capital, whether defeasible or indefeasible, will be
accelerated and brought into possession.

In *Re Master's Settlement, Master* v. *Master* (23), Eve, J., said:

"In my opinion, the argument on behalf of the children ought to prevail:
their interests in the settled fund are vested interests subject to being divested **E**
by the exercise of the power (*Doe d. Willis* v. *Martin* (24); *Lambert* v. *Thwaites*
(25)): and although the existence of the power necessarily precludes the
immediate division of the capital, I cannot see any principle on which the
same result should follow in the case of the current income. Until the right
to receive this is intercepted by the donee of the power I think the trustees are
bound to pay it to those in whom the capital by which it is produced is for **F**
the time being vested."

There, it treats the persons who had an interest subject to being divested as being
persons in whom the capital was for the time being vested.

Accordingly, it seems to me that in this case Lady Humphreys has surrendered
her life interest in favour of her grandchildren in such a manner that their **G**
immediately succeeding interests in vested capital have been accelerated and
brought into possession even though those interests are liable to be divested by
reason of the occurrence of a subsequent contingency. The overall conclusion,
therefore, is that the surrender is an effective surrender and, consequently, that
no forfeiture has been incurred.

Declaration accordingly. **H**

Solicitors: *Macfarlanes* (for all parties).

[*Reported by* Jacqueline Metcalfe, *Barrister-at-Law.*]

I

---

(23) [1911] 1 Ch. 321 at p. 325.
(24) [1775-1802] All E.R. Rep. 343.
(25) [1861-73] All E.R. Rep. 252; (1866), L.R. 2 Eq. 151.

A   Re FLYNN (deceased).   FLYNN v. FLYNN.

[CHANCERY DIVISION (Megarry, J.), November 8, 9, 10, 13.]

Domicile—Abandonment of domicile of choice—Intention—Standard of proof—
Whether absence of intention to return sufficed or positive intention not to
return had to be established.

B   Given a person's physical departure from the country of his domicile of
choice, the ending of his intention to return there, as distinct from the
forming of any positive intention not to return there, is sufficient to bring
to an end that domicile, with the consequence that his domicile of origin
revives until ousted by the subsequent acquisition of another domicile of
choice; and the standard of proof of abandonment of a domicile of choice is
C   the standard of a balance of probabilities not lightly inferred (see p. 58,
letters E and H, p. 59, letters H and I, p. 61, letter H, and p. 62, letter B,
post).

Dictum of LORD HATHERLEY, L.C., in *Udny* v. *Udny* ((1869), L.R. 1 Sc. &
Div. at p. 450) applied.

[Editorial Note. Although the law on the question whether, when a testator
D   who has acquired a domicile of choice departs from the country of that domicile,
it is necessary, for the purpose of establishing abandonment of the domicile, to
show that he had a positive intention not to return, or whether it suffices to show
absence of intention on his part to return, was decided in the present case in the
way stated above, yet on the facts the court concluded that the testator had
formed a positive intention after 1952 not to return to California, which was the
E   country where he had acquired a domicile of choice by August, 1942 (see p. 59,
letter B, post).

As to abandonment of domicile of choice, see 7 HALSBURY'S LAWS (3rd Edn.)
17, 18, para. 32; and for cases on change of domicile, see 11 DIGEST (Repl.)
326-334, *21-27*; 328-331, *30-52*.]

Cases referred to:

F   *Evans, Re, National Provincial Bank, Ltd.* v. *Evans,* [1947] Ch. 695; [1948]
L.J.R. 498; 177 L.T. 585; 11 Digest (Repl.) 358, *270*.
Fuld (decd.) (No. 3), In the estate of, Hartley v. *Fuld (Fuld intervening),* [1965]
3 All E.R. 776; [1966] 2 W.L.R. 717; Digest (Cont. Vol. B) 126, *666a*.
Indian Chief, The, (1801), 3 Ch. Rob. 12; 11 Digest (Repl.) 361, *296*.
King v. *Foxwell,* (1876), 3 Ch.D. 518; 45 L.J.Ch. 693; 11 Digest (Repl.)
G   330, *48*.
Marrett, Re, Chalmers v. *Wingfield,* [1886-90] All E.R. Rep. 816; (1887), 36
Ch.D. 400; 57 L.T. 896; 11 Digest (Repl.) 329, *40*.
Udny v. *Udny,* (1869), L.R. 1 Sc. & Div. 441; 11 Digest (Repl.) 326, *22*.

Administration Action.

By originating summons dated Mar. 20, 1964, to which Theodore Thomson
H   Flynn, his wife Morelle Flynn, and Justin Merton Golenbock (executors of the
will of Errol Flynn, deceased) were defendants, the plaintiff Patricia Wymore
Flynn, the testator's widow and an executrix of his will, claimed an account of
his debts and administration of his estate. Probate of the will of the testator
was granted on Mar. 19, 1964, to the plaintiff, and double probate thereof was
granted on May 11, 1964, to Mr. Golenbock. By an order dated Dec. 3, 1964,
I   made in both actions on summonses issued by each plaintiff an administration
order was made in respect of the testator's estate, his widow admitting assets,
and it was ordered that all further proceedings in the second action should be
stayed. The administration order directed an inquiry where the testator was
domiciled at the time of his death. None of the other inquiries and accounts
directed by the administration order, save the account of what was due to
creditors, was to be prosecuted without the leave of the judge. The question
of the testator's domicile thus came before the court pursuant to the inquiry so
directed.

J. W. Mills, Q.C., and *P. G. Clough* for the plaintiff.   A
P. R. Oliver, Q.C., and *J. A. R. Finlay* for the third defendant.

Cur. adv. vult.

Nov. 13. **MEGARRY, J.**, read the following judgment: Errol Flynn was a
film actor whose performances gave pleasure to many millions. On June 20, 1909,
he was born in Hobart, Tasmania; and on Oct. 14, 1959, he died in Vancouver,   B
British Columbia. When he was seventeen he was expelled from school in Sydney;
and in the next thirty-three years he lived a life which was full, lusty, restless
and colourful. In his career, in his three marriages, in his friendships, in his
quarrels, and in bed with the many women he took there, he lived with zest and
irregularity. The lives of film stars are not cast in the ordinary mould; and
in some respects Errol Flynn's was more stellar than most. When he died, he   C
posed the only question that I have to decide: Where was he domiciled at the
date of his death?

This question has arisen because some of his assets are in England and his two
executors disagree as to his domicile. On Dec. 3, 1964, PENNYCUICK, J., made a
full administration order, directing certain accounts and enquiries to be taken
and made. One of these enquiries was as to his domicile; and the importance   D
of this is at least in part based on the fact that the debts recoverable out of the
English assets appear to differ substantially according to the domicile. On
Feb. 8, 1967, UNGOED-THOMAS, J., gave certain directions as to the evidence to
be adduced on this issue.

Of those directions I need mention only one. During the last year and a half of
his life, Errol (as I shall call him) wrote an autobiography which in England was   E
published shortly after his death under the title of " My Wicked Wicked Ways ".
He wrote this in collaboration with an American journalist and author named
Earl Conrad, who spent some ten weeks with Errol in the Titchfield Hotel,
Port Antonio, Jamaica in the autumn of 1958 working on the book. One direction
given by UNGOED-THOMAS, J., related to this book. It was that the book was to
be admitted as evidence subject to Mr. Conrad verifying the statements in the   F
book made by Errol; and this Mr. Conrad duly did.

I have been referred to a number of specific passages in the book and I have
also looked through it as a whole. Errol would, I think, have been the last
person to claim that it was a serious study. It is plainly a book intended to
entertain and to sell; and I do not doubt that it has done both. I am not covertly
suggesting that what is said in the book is untrue; but truth is many-sided, and   G
a wrong impression is perhaps more often conveyed by what is omitted than by
what is said. Nor is it unknown that in the telling a story intended to entertain
should grow and be refined. The resemblance between a tombstone and an
autobiography may not be very close; but just as in lapidary inscriptions a man
is not upon oath, so may autobiographies, even though verified by the oath of a
collaborator, fail accurately to convey the truth, the whole truth and nothing   H
but the truth, as the author knows it. Accordingly I accept the book both as
giving a general impression of an unusual man and as containing the self-portrait
which Errol wished the public to see. I accept it as containing many true statements of fact and intention, even if at times these are somewhat flamboyant and
highly coloured. I would not, however, accept it in toto without corroboration.
As a sexual athlete Errol may in truth have achieved Olympic standards;   I
but the evident probability that this was part of the public image which the
book was intended to foster (an image perhaps accentuated rather than weakened
by his overt denials) inevitably induces reservations in the reader. On the other
hand, in many matters there seems to be no reason for not accepting the substance
of what is said, subject to due allowance being made for the style and nature of
the publication and for the frailties inherent in the human recollections of a man
who had lived a life such as his. At least in the sphere of intention and state of
mind, an autobiography written near the end of a man's life may be of assistance

A in resolving discrepancies between statements of intention which he is alleged to have made to different people at different times; and I do not forget the perils which lie in seeking too zealously for consistency of statement and fixity of intention in one so mercurial as he.

The issue of domicile was argued before me in chambers during the latter part of last week, and I have adjourned the case into open court for judgment. The

B plaintiff, Mrs. Patricia Wymore Flynn, is Errol's widow. She was his third wife and is one of the two executors appointed by Errol's last will, made in New York and dated Apr. 27, 1954. This will was prepared for him by the third defendant, a Mr. Justin Merton Golenbock, who is an attorney-at-law practising in the State and City of New York. In broad terms, counsel for the plaintiff con- tended for Jamaica as Errol's domicile of choice, or failing that Tasmania as his

C domicile of origin. Counsel for the third defendant, on the other hand, contended for either California or New York, each as Errol's domicile of choice. I am indebted to them for their assistance; and as the case was argued in chambers, it may be convenient if I state that in addition to the other authorities which will be cited in this judgment, I was referred to the authorities noted below (1). I do not think that I need say anything about these save that it seems possible

D that the headnote to *King* v. *Foxwell* (2) may be misleading. It begins with the words—" In order to change his domicile of origin, a man must . . ." Reading what SIR GEORGE JESSEL, M.R., said in its context, I do not find anything which supports the notion that a man may change his domicile of origin so as to replace it by another, different, domicile of origin. If the headnote began—" In order to change his domicile from that of his domicile of origin, a man must . . ."—this

E possibility of misunderstanding would be removed.

With the evidence in the form directed by UNGOED-THOMAS, J., I am satisfied, subject to one qualification, that the evidence now before me suffices to determine the issue and that it is unnecessary to direct further enquiries. In one sense there is no end to the evidence that may be adduced; for the whole of a man's life and all that he has said and done, however trivial, may be prayed in aid in

F determining what his intention was at any given moment of time. The state of a man's mind may be as much a fact as the state of his digestion; but, as HARMAN, L.J., is reputed to have observed, " the doctors know precious little about the one and the judges know nothing about the other ". The difficulty is as old as the Year Books and the celebrated dictum of BRIAN, C.J., in 1477, uttered in theological terms which have waned in fashion: " Le Diable n'ad

G conusance de l'entent de home" (3). All that the court can do is to draw infer- ences from what has been said and done; and in doing this, too much detail may stultify.

The one qualification that I make is in relation to Errol's domicile of origin. This, of course, is determined by the domicile of Errol's father when Errol was born in Hobart on June 20, 1909. His birth was registered there on July 31,

H 1909. The Registrar of Births described his father as " Lecturer in Biology ", and his father's affidavit filed on Nov. 23, 1965, describes his own position thus:

" I was born in Coraki, New South Wales, Australia on Oct. 11, 1883, of parents born and domiciled in New South Wales where I lived during my infancy. I graduated from Sydney University in 1906 and in 1908 I married

I the second defendant. In 1909 I left New South Wales to take up a lecture- ship in the biology faculty of the University of Tasmania in Hobart and in 1911 I was appointed Ralston Professor of Biology at the same university.

(1) *Bell* v. *Kennedy*, (1868), L.R. 1 Sc. & Div. 307; *Re Craignish*, [1892] 3 Ch. 180; *Douglas* v. *Douglas*, (1871), L.R. 12 Eq. 617; *Gatty* v. *A.-G.*, [1951] P. 444; *Harrison* v. *Harrison*, [1953] 1 W.L.R. 865; *Henderson* v. *Henderson*, [1965] 1 All E.R. 179; [1967] P. 77; *King* v. *Foxwell*, (1876), 3 Ch.D. 518; *Moorhouse* v. *Lord*, (1863), 10 H.L. Cas. 272; *Winans* v. *A.-G.*, [1904-07] All E.R. Rep. 410 [1904] A.C. 287.
(2) (1876), 3 Ch.D. 518.
(3) Year Book, 17 Edw. 4, Easter, fo. 2, pl. 2.

I held the Ralston professorship until 1931 and between 1909 and 1931 I   A
had my home in Tasmania, although I was engaged in research work at
London University between 1920 and 1924 and again from about the middle
of 1930 to about the middle of 1931."

As counsel for the third defendant pointed out, it seems that Professor Flynn
went from New South Wales to Hobart only shortly before Errol's birth, and   B
there is nothing to show what the state of mind of Professor Flynn was or had
been then. Did he go to Hobart intending to make his home there and acquire
a domicile of choice in Tasmania before Errol was born; or did he take up his
lectureship without the animus manendi necessary for the acquisition of a
domicile of choice, and form that intention only after Errol's birth? The probability, I think, is that Errol's domicile of origin was Tasmanian; but I see no   C
reason to rely on mere probability when it seems so likely that the point may easily
be resolved. Professor Flynn, though no longer young, is happily still living;
and I have little doubt that even at this distance of time he can remember the
circumstances of so important an event as his first teaching appointment. I
accept counsel for the plaintiff's suggestion that the matter may be dealt with
by referring the point back to the master in chambers if it becomes necessary to   D
decide it. In view of Professor Flynn's age and the possibility that, whatever
my decision, the point may hereafter become material, I direct that such an
affidavit be obtained and filed in any event. I do not at this stage refer the point
back to chambers.

If Errol's domicile of origin was Tasmanian, then it was clearly his domicile
of origin in truth and in substance, and not merely in law; for he spent the first   E
eleven years of his life in Hobart with his parents and Hobart must have been
the first real home he ever had. I say this because, of course, domicile of origin
may sometimes be a purely technical concept, with no foundation in substance.
A legitimate child automatically takes as his domicile of origin the domicile which,
at the moment of his birth, is his father's domicile. Thus a father may leave his
wife enceinte and go to make a new home in a new country before sending for   F
his wife and child to join him. They may never come; yet that child will have
as his domicile of origin a country which he has never seen and has no real connection with. There are many authorities which establish that a domicile of
origin is more durable and more difficult to change than a domicile of choice;
and it is trite law in England (though not in most jurisdictions in the United
States of America) that if one domicile of choice is abandoned without another   G
being acquired, the domicile of origin revives. During the course of the argument
I enquired whether this doctrine extended to what I may call a purely technical
domicile of origin or whether it is confined to a domicile of origin which is bot-
tomed in reality; and it did not appear that there was authority on the point.
The facts of this case make it unnecessary for me to explore this possibility;
and I obey the high authority which proclaims that it is the duty of a judge to   H
send forth into the world not doubts, but decisions.

The main events of Errol's life are conveniently summarised in two exhibits,
DHAN. 19 and PTT. 2, exhibited to the affidavits of the Hon. David Henry
Arthur Nicolson and Mr. Philip Temple respectively and filed on behalf of the
plaintiff and the third defendant respectively. Exhibit DHAN. 19 covers the
whole of Errol's life in outline whereas PTT. 2 covers the last seven years of his   I
life in some detail. Mr. Nicolson is a partner in the firm of solicitors acting for
the plaintiff; Mr. Temple is an attorney-at-law in the firm in New York in which
the third defendant is a partner. I accept both these documents for what they
purport to be, namely, convenient summaries. As I observed during argument,
exhibit PTT. 2 has in places a somewhat tendentious aspect. Thus on the last
page the word " live " (in phrases such as " living at " or " lives in ") is reserved
exclusively for places in New York, in apposition to which it appears five times;
other places, including Jamaica (which of course is a rival to New York on the

A issue of domicile) attract only phrases such as " goes to " or " in ". I have discounted exhibit PTT. 2 accordingly.

From these documents and the other evidence I find that the course of Errol's life after his first eleven years was as follows. From eleven to fifteen he was at school in London, when Professor Flynn was engaged in research at University College, London. The family (including Errol) returned to Hobart in 1924, and **B** Errol was sent to school in Sydney, New South Wales, where he remained for two years. In his father's words, as a boy, Errol " revealed an adventurous and impetuous spirit which was responsible for the premature termination of his school life "; and, he adds, " in adult life he remained impetuous and irresponsible being seemingly incapable of settling down in any one place. His emotional relationships with women were numerous but not enduring, and although he **C** achieved great success as a film actor in Hollywood, California, for some years his manner and scale of living were such that he never managed to conserve his very substantial earnings ".

His boyhood ended, Errol spent some seven years of his adolescence and his early manhood wandering in Australasia and the Pacific, with a substantial period in New Guinea. He spent much time on his yacht and indulged the love **D** of the sea which never deserted him. In 1931, Professor Flynn was appointed Professor of Zoology at Queen's University, Belfast and left Hobart for good; and in Belfast he remained until he retired in 1947. Errol ultimately came to the United Kingdom in 1933, and apart from some periods with his parents in Belfast he was principally engaged in a repertory theatrical company in Northampton, where he spent some eighteen months. He also had some parts in plays **E** at the Malvern Festival and in the West End of London. In 1935, when he was twenty-five or twenty-six, Warner Brothers offered him a six months' contract in Hollywood. He accepted this; and the career which was to engage him for the rest of his life had begun.

On the Atlantic crossing he met an established film star known as Lili Damita. In June, 1935, he married her in Yuma, Arizona, and for some eight years their **F** tempestuous marriage endured. Until 1938, Errol lived in Hollywood, more or less together with his wife. He spent part of 1938 as a war correspondent in Spain, partly to escape her. Later in the year he returned and in New York was temporarily reconciled to his wife. After a cruise in the Caribbean together they returned to Hollywood, but lived apart. Even in the act of living apart Errol was not as other men; for he and his wife, though in separate establish- **G** ments, came together from time to time: and on May 10, 1941, their son was born. During that year he had a house built for him to his own design, Mulholland House (or Mulholland Farm, as his notepaper described it); this was at No. 7,740 Mulholland Drive, Hollywood, and it became his home, though not his wife's. In August, 1942, he became a naturalised citizen of the United States of America.

H In my judgment, by this time Errol had acquired a domicile of choice in California. So far as he ever settled anywhere he had settled there. His home, his work, his new nationality, his life in the film world, his wife (in law, though only intermittently in fact) and his only child, were all there; and Hollywood has never been deficient in what was then, as always, one of Errol's great interests in life, namely, a generous pool of available pulchritude.

I On Apr. 6, 1942, a few months before Errol was naturalised, his wife obtained an interlocutory judgment for divorce from him in the Superior Court of the State of California; and a year later, on Apr. 7, 1943, a final judgment of divorce was granted providing for substantial periodical payments to his former wife for alimony and child support. On Sept. 14, 1944, he married his second wife, Nora Eddington. This from the start was a marriage after Errol's fashion. The ceremony was performed by proxy in Mexico; he also bought a separate house for her in Hollywood, so that from the outset they never lived together in any save an intermittent sexual sense. Her stepmother acted as Errol's housekeeper

in Mulholland House, and man and wife met each other from time to time by A
arrangement. Of this second marriage, two daughters were born, one in January,
1945, and the other in March, 1947.

Meanwhile the war had ended and Errol had bought the yacht Zaca, which was
to be his for the rest of his life. On a cruise in her in 1946 or 1947, bad weather
made him put into Jamaica; and at once he fell in love with the island. Indeed,
this was perhaps the most enduring love of his life; and counsel for the third B
defendant made no attempt to dispute the indisputable, but fully acknowledged
it. Almost at once Errol began buying property in Jamaica. He bought Navy
Island, in the harbour of Port Antonio on the north-east coast of the Island, and
on Feb. 11, 1947, wrote a glowing letter to his parents about the " dream spot "
that he had bought and urging them to come to it and " live like kings ". He
was not forgetful of the return that the island could bring from crops, sheep, C
cattle and chickens; but nobody could read his letter as being dominated by
economics. Later that year he bought a larger estate, the Boston Estate, for
£33,000; and on Sept. 22, 1947, he again wrote to his father a letter of enthusiasm,
which obviously related to a visit which his parents were to make to Jamaica.
Shortly afterwards his parents in fact came to Jamaica; and for ten years they
lived on Errol's property there, in Boston Great House. His father helped to D
manage Errol's estates in Jamaica, which included two houses and various
outbuildings and were substantial in extent. Professor Flynn put them at some
2,300 acres; Errol (at p. 344 of his book) at five thousand acres.

On Mar. 27, 1950, the Superior Court of the State of California established as a
foreign judgment in the State a judgment of divorce between Errol and his
second wife, given in the neighbouring State of Nevada on an unspecified date; E
this no doubt was in obedience to the " full faith and credit " clause of the
Constitution of the United States of America, Art. IV, s. 1. Six months later,
on Oct. 23, 1950, he married his third wife, the plaintiff, in a civil ceremony
in Monte Carlo; but he was still making films in Hollywood and elsewhere
for Warner Brothers. In June he made a film for the company in England,
leaving Mulholland House in the care of his housekeepers. Not long after F
this, in 1952, he quarrelled with Warner Brothers and his contract with them
was terminated by mutual consent. He went with the plaintiff to Italy and
made a film called " Cross Swords " for his own and another company; and
he was by then fully aware of the tax advantages under the United States law
for those who resided outside the United States for seventeen out of any eighteen
consecutive months. He then began the production in Northern Italy of a G
film called " William Tell ", in which he sank much of his own money; but
this production ran out of funds (owing, he says in his book, to the default of
his business associates). Much of 1953 and some of 1954 was spent first in making
part of this film and then in unsuccessful attempts to raise the money needed to
complete it; and he and his wife spent much time in Rome. At about this time
an income tax assessment for over eight hundred thousand dollars was made H
on him by the United States authorities; and he ascribes this to malversation
by a former business manager of his, who had just died.

At this stage Errol's financial position was indeed precarious. He no longer had
a salary from Warner Brothers; much, if not most, of his own money was tied
up in the incomplete " William Tell "; and he faced a heavy claim for income tax
in the United States of America. Further troubles were to follow: for his first I
wife had claims against him for arrears of payments for alimony and child
support, which ultimately led to her purchasing Mulholland House in a fore-
closure sale on Nov. 18, 1954. A year later the time during which Errol could
redeem the house expired; and after negotiations during 1955 an agreement
between Errol and his first wife made on Feb. 16, 1956, settled her claims. Under
this agreement he relinquished all claims to the house but became entitled to
keep certain items of personal property and furnishings (then stored in warehouses in Los Angeles) which his third wife, the plaintiff, selected. Meanwhile,

A   on Christmas Day, 1953, Errol had a daughter by the plaintiff in Rome. He was now doing sporadic work on films and television in New York, Brazil and elsewhere; but much of his time was spent cruising and living in the Mediterranean and Caribbean. From Mar. 14 to Apr. 26, 1954, he and his wife and daughter were living on his estate in Boston House, in the suite which he had reserved for himself there. On this I prefer the evidence of his father, who was there, to the evidence

B   of the third defendant and Mr. Temple, who were not. During that visit Errol sold the Titchfield Hotel in Jamaica, which he had bought many years before; and as part of the transaction of sale he reserved the right to free room and board whenever he chose to stay at the hotel. During that period, on Apr. 18, Errol and the plaintiff had their daughter baptised at St. Mark's Church, Boston, in Jamaica.

C   On Apr. 27, 1954, the day after he left Jamaica, Errol executed his will in New York. It is in American form to the extent that the phrase " in the event that " is used throughout as a substitute for " if ". It begins by stating that he is a citizen of the United States of America, " presently residing in and domiciled in the Republic of Italy ". Nobody, however, attaches much weight to this recital of domicile; and I attach none. He had no settled home in Italy, and

D   apart from the wonderful setting he had for " William Tell " in Courmayeur at the head of the Aosta Valley in Northern Italy, hard up under the Alps, I can find nothing to give him any enduring interest in living in that country. The recital is at least consistent with his desire to mitigate his liability for further income tax in the United States of America; and I accept the third defendant's statement on this point in para. 9 (8) (a) of his first affidavit. Nor, may I add, do I attach

E   the least importance to the recital in the Monaco Register of Acts of Marriage that on Errol's marriage to the plaintiff on Oct. 23, 1950, he was " demeurent et domicilié à Monaco ". They were at the time living on his yacht, the Zaca; and any confidence in the accuracy of this entry in the register is sapped by the statement in the same document that Errol's parents were " domiciliés à Mulholland (États Unis D'Amérique) ". Even if " Mulholland, U.S.A." were a

F   sufficient and accurate address, Errol's parents had for some years been living thousands of miles away in Jamaica. Statements of this kind, made for an immediate and limited purpose, and sometimes with the attention of all concerned directed mainly to other matters, cannot be expected always to reflect the ultimate verities.

    Between April, 1954, and the final agreement with his first wife on Feb. 16,

G   1956, Errol's life was mainly one of films and television. He was in New York, England, Rome, Paris, North Africa, Monte Carlo, England again, back in Monte Carlo, Barcelona, back in England, Palma, New York again, Palma and France, back in New York once more and then, in January, 1956, in Hollywood. After that he returned to England, and after two days in the U.S.A. he made a film in Cuba. Then he came back to England and some while later returned to Palma.

H   During this period, Errol began to encounter difficulties with his passport and his nationality. Subject to certain qualifications the law was that a naturalised United States citizen lost his nationality if he had " a continuous residence for five years in any other foreign state or states ": United States Code, Title 8, ch. 12, s. 1484. The United States passport authorities naturally concerned themselves with this provision, and renewals of passports were limited so as to

I   reflect it. The upshot of various negotiations with the authorities, conducted by Errol and the third defendant, was that in order to preserve his nationality Errol had to return to the United States of America not later than Oct. 1, 1957. If the thoughts of income tax impelled Errol abroad, thoughts of nationality drew him back to the United States. The international pattern exhibited by the first nine months of 1957 was thus not continued into the last three.

    From the beginning of 1957 until the end of September, Errol had continued in films, television and other activities, going to New York, the western parts of the United States, Mexico, Dominica, New York, Washington, France, Palma,

West Berlin, Palma, France, Palma, New York, Dominica, France, Palma and A
England. On Oct. 1 he was back in New York staying in Mr. Huntington Hartford's apartment; soon he went to California again for film and television work,
staying at the Huntington Hartford estates in Los Angeles.   By then his marriage
to his third wife, the plaintiff, was in difficulties. The year 1957 had also seen a
change in Jamaica, for after ten years there his parents had returned to England,
leaving behind them some of their furniture, books and other possessions in B
Boston Great House on his estate.

The year 1958 opened with a stage play by Mr. Huntington Hartford, *The
Master of Thornfield*, with Errol rehearsing it in New York and then taking
part in try-out performances in Detroit and Cincinnati. He then left the play
and returned to films. He spent some three months in the spring in filming in
Africa on a temporary passport and then a month in Paris for further filming. C
He next went to Jamaica for some ten weeks (including the months of August
and September); he went with Mr. Earl Conrad, both of them staying at the
Titchfield Hotel: and for some three weeks of that period his sister, Mrs. Warner,
was there too. He had wanted to stay at his own house, Boston Great House;
but that had been left by his parents over a year before, and was not in a suitable
state for occupation. During this period in Jamaica, he was working on his auto- D
biography with Mr. Conrad, who was his collaborator; and while he was there
Boston Great House was burned down. On this, I prefer the evidence of Mr.
Conrad and Mrs. Warner, who were there, to that of the third defendant who was
not, but says that the house was burned down in the previous year. In addition
to his work on his book he was actively engaged in finding a suitable site for a
house which he wished to build for himself. Boston Great House was to be for E
his parents, whom he hoped would return to Jamaica.

After a month or six weeks in New York, Errol went to Cuba for six weeks,
returning to New York on Jan. 10, 1959, and staying in an apartment there
until in February he went back to Cuba to make a film. While in Cuba he was
seeking to arrange for his furniture to be sent from California to Jamaica; to
this I shall return. After some three months in Cuba he had a few days in New F
York and a few more in Miami, and then went back to his property in Jamaica
for a month or so during May or June. He next spent six weeks in New York
and over a month in California rehearsing for the " Red Shelton Show ", in which
he duly appeared. On Oct. 10, he went to Vancouver to arrange the sale of his
yacht Zaca, and four days later he died suddenly.

On these facts, the first question is whether Errol ever lost the Californian G
domicile of choice which in my judgment he had acquired by August, 1942. There
is no dispute that this domicile could be lost either by abandonment or by the
acquisition of a new domicile of choice; but a curious point has arisen as to the
intention required for abandonment. Given the necessary factor of a physical
departure from the country of domicile, is it necessary to demonstrate that the
departure was animo non revertendi, or does it suffice if it was sine animo rever- H
tendi?   In other words, is it necessary to establish a positive intention not to
return to reside in the country, or will it suffice if there is a merely negative
absence of any intention to continue residing there?   No doubt in the great
majority of cases it will make no difference; but sometimes it may. A devoted
daughter who has looked after her aged mother for many years may, when her
mother dies and the family home is sold, leave England in order to tour the I
world and make up her mind whether to settle elsewhere or whether to return to
England. It cannot be said that she leaves animo non revertendi; but she leaves
sine animo revertendi. Has she abandoned her English domicile?

The point has been argued before me at some length, and although on the
facts of this case as they appear to me I do not think that it makes much difference which test is applied, I think that I should express my views on the point.
The books and the authorities speak with divided voice. DICEY and MORRIS
ON THE CONFLICT OF LAWS (8th Edn., 1967) in r. 10 (1) lays down the less stringent

A   rule; the statement is that " a person abandons a domicile of choice in a country by ceasing to reside there and by ceasing to intend to reside there permanently or indefinitely, and not otherwise." This repeats the rule as it was in the 7th Edn. of DICEY, p. 112, where it appeared for the first time as a rule, constructed out of the material contained in the commentary in the 6th Edn. to r. 8 in that edition. On the other hand, there appears to be much support for the more

B   stringent version. Thus CHESHIRE'S PRIVATE INTERNATIONAL LAW (7th Edn. 1965) p. 162 seems to support it. This states:

> " Since a domicile of choice is voluntarily acquired animo et facto, so it is extinguishable in the same manner, i.e., merely by a removal from the country animo non revertendi and even without acquiring a fresh domicile."

C   Then 7 HALSBURY'S LAWS OF ENGLAND (3rd Edn.), in the part contributed by WYNN-PARRY, J., and Mr. MCMASTER, seems also to support it. At p. 17, para. 32, it is stated that

> " A domicile of choice continues until it is abandoned; it may be retained by residence alone, although an intention to abandon it has been formed, or by an intention to return, although the residence has been temporarily

D   interrupted. It is divested only when the country of domicile has been actually abandoned with the intention of abandoning it for ever, and this process is the exact converse of the process of its acquisition."

Some of the cases are in this form. Thus in *Re Marrett, Chalmers* v. *Wingfield* (4), COTTON, L.J., said that

E   > ". . . in order to lose the domicile of choice once acquired, it is not only necessary that a man should be dissatisfied with his domicile of choice, and form an intention to leave it, but he must have left it, with the intention of leaving it permanently."

Again, in *In the Estate of Fuld* (*decd.*) (*No. 3*), *Hartley* v. *Fuld* (*Fuld intervening*) (5), SCARMAN, J., speaks of a man leaving the territory of his domicile (it was there a

F   domicile of origin) " with the intention of never returning ", a phrase which I think must be read sub modo and as relating merely to an intention of never returning to live there, as distinct from returning on a visit. Even so, this supports the more stringent rule. In the next sentence of the judgment however, the judge speaks of a man abandoning a domicil of choice in a country " because he no longer intends to reside there indefinitely "; and this supports the less stringent

G   rule.

I turn to the leading case of *Udny* v. *Udny* (6). There the language used fluctuates. LORD HATHERLEY, L.C., spoke of (7) " the intention not to return " and (8) " the intention to abandon the new domicil " and also of the animus being (9) " that of never returning ". Yet, he quoted (10), apparently with approval, the phrase used by SIR WILLIAM SCOTT in *The Indian Chief* (11), of a man putting

H   himself in motion " bona fide to quit the country sine animo revertendi ". LORD CHELMSFORD (12) repeated the same phrase immediately after referring to a person carrying out his intention " by removing animo non revertendi ". In appraising the facts of the case (13) he spoke of Colonel Udny giving up his house in London and returning to Boulogne " where he remained for nine years without any apparent intention of again taking up residence in England ". LORD

I   WESTBURY (14) took as an illustration a man domiciled in Holland who " quits Holland, declaring that he will never return to it again ". When he considered the facts of the case, he spoke of Colonel Udny (15) " leaving London in a manner

---

(4) [1886-90] All E.R. Rep. 816 at p. 818; (1887), 36 Ch.D. 400 at p. 407.
(5) [1966] 2 W.L.R. 717 at p. 725.   (6) (1869), L.R. 1 Sc. & Div. 441.
(7) (1869), L.R. 1 Sc. & Div. at p. 448.   (8) (1869), L.R. 1 Sc. & Div. at p. 450.
(9) (1869), L.R. 1 Sc. & Div. at p. 452.   (10) (1869), L.R. 1 Sc. & Div. at p. 451.
(11) (1801), 3 Ch. Rob. 12 at p. 21.   (12) (1869), L.R. 1 Sc. & Div. at p. 454.
(13) (1869), L.R. 1 Sc. & Div. at p. 456.   (14) (1869), L.R. 1 Sc. & Div. at p. 459.
           (15) (1869), L.R. 1 Sc. & Div. at p. 460.

which removes all doubt of his ever intending to return there for the purpose of   **A**
residence ".

So far as mere words are concerned, the cases are inconclusive. As I have said, in most cases it will not matter which test is applied, and where this is the case the different phrases may have been used interchangeably. Any case in which there is a departure animo non revertendi will be a fortiori; and the facts of *Udny* v. *Udny* (16) certainly did not require a decision on the point. But I think that   **B** *Udny* v. *Udny* (16) nevertheless establishes a principle by which the true rule may be determined. LORD HATHERLEY, L.C., said (17):

> " It seems reasonable to say that if the choice of a new abode and actual settlement there constitutes a change of the original domicile, then the exact converse of such a procedure, viz., the intention to abandon the new   **C** domicile, and an actual abandonment of it, ought to be equally effective to destroy the new domicile. That which may be acquired may surely be abandoned, and though a man cannot, for civil reasons, be left without a domicile, no such difficulty arises if it be simply held that the original domicile revives."

Acquisition and abandonment are correlatives; in LORD WESTBURY's words (18),   **D** " Domicile of choice, as it is gained animo et facto, so it may be put an end to in the same manner ". When animus and factum are each no more, domicile perishes also; for there is nothing to sustain it. If a man has already departed from the country, his domicile of choice there will continue so long as he has the necessary animus. When he no longer has this, in my judgment his domicile of choice is at an end, for it has been abandoned; and this is so even   **E** if his intention of returning has merely withered away and he has not formed any positive intention never to return to live in the country. In short, the death of the old intention suffices, without the birth of any new intention. In this way abandonment dovetails in with acquisition. It follows that in my view the true rule is correctly stated in DICEY AND MORRIS ON THE CONFLICT OF LAWS (8th Edn., 1967) r. 10 (1).   **F**

In considering the evidence of abandonment I bear in mind the words of WYNN-PARRY, J., in *Re Evans, National Provincial Bank, Ltd.* v. *Evans* (19). In order to establish the abandonment of a domicile of choice, he said, " it is essential to demonstrate that abandonment by unequivocal intention and act." Many acts and declarations are indeed equivocal; and evidence which establishes that a man was or might have been in two minds does not show an unequivocal   **G** intention.

I have also to bear in mind the standard of proof required; it is not questioned that the burden of proof lies on those who assent that a change of domicile has taken place. In *In the Estate of Fuld (decd.) (No. 3)* (20), which I have already cited, SCARMAN, J., had to consider the abandonment of a domicile established by a domicile of origin; and he rejected any requirement of proof beyond reasonable   **H** doubt. The standard of proof is, I think, the civil standard of a balance of probabilities, subject to the overriding consideration (which I borrow from the judgment of SCARMAN, J.) that so serious a matter as the acquisition of a domicile of choice (or for that matter, I think, the abandonment of a domicile) is " not to be lightly inferred from slight indications or casual words ".

With these consideration in mind, I feel no doubt that Errol's Californian   **I** domicile of choice persisted until 1952, but that at some time thereafter it ended. After the breach with Warner Brothers in 1952, he left California and did not return to it, at any rate for any substantial period, until 1956. During these four

---

(16) (1869), L.R. 1 Sc. & Div. 441.
(17) (1869), L.R. 1 Sc. & Div. at p. 450.
(18) (1869), L.R. 1 Sc. & Div. at p. 458.
(19) [1947] Ch. 695 at p. 707.
(20) [1966] 2 W.L.R. at p. 726.

A   years he was in monetary difficulties and anxious to escape the financial clutches of his third wife, who was still in California. He may indeed have retained some indefinite idea of returning to California one day when he had resolved his difficulties; for he seems to have made no effort to dispose of his house there. But after his first wife had purchased his house on Nov. 18, 1954, and then a year later the time for redeeming it had expired, his last real link with California

B   had gone. The final settlement with his first wife on Feb. 16, 1956, seems to have made it possible for him to return to California without peril from her; but thereafter his only substantial visits to California seem to have been for film and television work. I think that during those years an absence of any intention to return to California as a home had ripened into a positive intention not to return to California. Certainly this was so a year or two later. The third defendant

C   deals with the matter in his affidavit; he states:

> " Upon the testator's return to the United States in 1957, it became necessary for him to adopt a permanent place of residence in the United States. The testator informed me that he had decided that he would not return to California because of the fact that he and Mrs. Flynn had already become estranged [I pause there to say that " Mrs. Flynn " there plainly

D   means the plaintiff in this case, Errol's third wife]. California is a so-called ' community property ' State in which a wife is entitled to share one-half in all of a spouse's earnings and the testator was concerned that were he to go back to California, he would increase his financial problems with his estranged wife. In addition, the testator was concerned, and he so informed me, that were he to return to California, he would be in jeopardy by reason of the

E   number of creditors which he had in California."

The third defendant goes on: " Accordingly, the testator, as he informed me, determined in October, 1957, to adopt New York as his residence and domicil ": to that last sentence I shall have to return shortly. Mr. Barry Mahon, who was Errol's personal business agent and manager from 1952 or 1953, and a film

F   producer, also refers to the matter. He says:

> " During the latter part of 1957, after he had returned to the United States, the decedent told me that New York was *the* most likely place to make his home. He was separated from his wife, Patrice Wymore Flynn, and their daughter and did not want to suffer under the California community property law."

G   Mr. Earl Conrad was emphatic in his evidence; he said:

> " The only place he ever specified as being totally anathema to him was Hollywood which he hated and viewed only as a necessary evil in making pictures and making money."

Accordingly, in my judgment Errol abandoned his Californian domicile at some

H   time in the period 1952 to 1956. If the mere absence of any *animus revertendi* suffices (as I think it does), I hold that the change occurred when he left Warner Brothers and went to Italy, and this seems to have been in October, 1952. If, contrary to my opinion, a positive intention not to return is requisite, I think that intention was formed when he heard of his first wife taking his house in November, 1954. Whichever the date, his domicile of origin, which in all prob-

I   ability was Tasmanian but might, as I have mentioned, have been in New South Wales, thereupon revived.

Did Errol thereafter obtain a domicile of choice, and if so, where? Counsel for the third defendant contended for New York and prayed in aid the third defendant's evidence in particular. I do not think that this contention is right. Apart from a short subtenancy of an apartment in New York which he had in the spring of 1959, he seems to have spent his time there in a variety of hotels, or staying in Mr. Huntington Hartford's apartment there. His visits all seem to have been connected with actual or prospective appearances on television, the stage or films

and, of course, obtaining advice from the third defendant. There is nothing A
which suggests to me that Errol ever had any present intention of a permanent
or indefinite residence in New York. To Mr. Mahon he spoke prospectively:

"During the latter part of 1957, after he had returned to the United States,
the decedent told me that New York was *the* most likely place to make his
home."

B

True, there is the declaration which the third defendant says that Errol made to
him in October, 1957; but one must remember the circumstances in which this
was made. The third defendant was acting for Errol in the negotiations with the
authorities over his passport and citizenship; and whatever Errol's true intentions were, he could not afford to embarrass the third defendant with the knowledge that he meant to live in neither California nor New York nor any other C
part of the United States. I accept that Errol made this declaration but I nevertheless, without disregarding it altogether, treat it with great caution, standing
as it does with little or no extraneous indication of intention to support it. In
this approach I adopt the attitude which SCARMAN, J., took towards a declaration
made by Mr. Fuld to the tax authorities in *In the Estate of Fuld* (decd.) (*No. 3*) (21).
I think that Mr. Conrad is right when he said, speaking of a period nearly a D
year later:

"To the best of my knowledge and belief the testator had no intention of
ever living permanently in the United States or in England. He regarded
New York City as a place that for him spelled violent living and which he
hated and from which he was always in a hurry to depart."

E

I bear in mind, of course, that Mr. Conrad is a wholly independent witness.
Accordingly, I hold that Errol never became domiciled in the State of New York.
    I turn, then, to Jamaica. Errol's love for the island has not been questioned
and is, I think, unquestionable. Yet he made his first acquisitions there when he
was, as I have held, still domiciled in California; and counsel for the third
defendant has pointed to a number of passages in the evidence which indicate F
that Errol regarded his estate there as an investment, a holiday home and a place
for his ultimate retirement. I think that in this counsel is probably right; but
I do not think that it is the whole picture. For it is possible for property acquired
for these purposes nevertheless also to become the owner's present home at
some later date. The question is whether that is what happened here.
    Counsel for the third defendant has very properly emphasised the limited G
periods of time which Errol actually spent in Jamaica. In the last two years of
his life, he was there for some ten weeks in the late summer and early autumn of
1958, and again for a month in the summer of 1959. I agree that such visits
are consonant with holiday visits and with the inspection and management of
his property as an investment. But during this period two events occurred on
which counsel for the plaintiff strongly relied. First, Errol embarked on the H
building of a house on his Jamaican estate. It was no ordinary house, but one
which the architect, Mr. Tamminga, designed on Errol's instructions to meet
his detailed requirements on matters such as the siting of his bedroom and the
swimming pool, and the provision of a storage vault with humidity control for
Errol's films. The final plan of the house was dated Jan. 23, 1959, and Errol
personally guaranteed the cost up to sixty-five thousand dollars, though technically the house was owned by a company. When he died, this house was still in I
course of erection. Secondly, in the spring of 1959 Errol was trying to have some
furniture and effects of his still in California sent to Jamaica. Counsel for the
third defendant stresses that Errol's motive was to get the furniture and effects
out of the potential clutches of his third wife, the plaintiff. "Now is the time
to spring all this stuff ", wrote Errol in a letter dated Mar. 30, 1959. There is, I

(21) [1966] 2 W.L.R. at p. 731.

A think much force in this. But human motives are often complex, rather than single and undivided. The motive for getting the furniture out of California may well have been this; but the fact remains that the furniture was to go to Errol in Jamaica, and not into storage elsewhere.

   It seems to me that Errol had gradually come more and more to treat his property in Jamaica as his home as well as an investment, a holiday home and a
B place to retire to. By 1958, the greater part of his possessions were concentrated there. Much was at Boston Great House. His sister, Mrs. Warner, says:

   " My brother kept a considerable amount of personal property and effects at Boston Great House against the time when he would have his permanent home in Jamaica. In the guest room at that house there were stored clothes
C belonging to both his wife and himself. A part of the furniture and furnishings at Boston Great House also belonged to my brother and in the locked storage rooms under the house he kept his deep-sea fishing equipment, saddles, much wine and imported tin goods. Also belonging to him at Boston Great House were many pictures, books and some nice old things he had picked up abroad and which he thought would suit a home in Jamaica and which
D he was keeping there for that purpose. One incident I remember vividly is that at one time around the end of 1957 or the early part of 1958 one of the crates in his house broke open revealing an old copper measuring vessel. Rather than to leave such an easily stolen article unguarded, I brought it back to Washington, D.C. with me. When I told my brother what I had done he was quite put out and told me that he would expect me to bring it
E back to him in Jamaica when his house was built. On many occasions my brother told me that he planned to settle permanently in Jamaica and to spend the rest of his life there. He said he loved everything about that island from the first moment he saw it. In the summer of 1958 he told me he was making all the necessary arrangements to move to Jamaica permanently and that the balance of his furniture and his personal property that was
F not already in Jamaica was being crated to be shipped there. My brother also discussed plans with me to erect guest cottages for his family on his estate at Boston, Port Antonio, so that they could visit him. He also told me that he ultimately wanted to be buried in Boston Church in Port Antonio. My brother loved the outdoor informal life. He disliked cities where he had to dress and, as before stated, he did not care for hotels. He told me he had no
G intention of ever living in California or New York; in fact, he said he loathed New York City and the life there. I also knew that my brother had many tax problems in the United States which kept him out of that country."

   His father's evidence is similar; and in Mr. Conrad's expressive phrase " legally, spiritually, actually he viewed Jamaica as his place, his home, his spot ".
H The totality of the evidence satisfies me that probably by August, 1958, and certainly by the time of his last arrival in May or June, 1959, Jamaica had become Errol's home and that he was domiciled there. His Jamaican domicile thereupon ousted his domicile of origin. His work might continue to take him to many parts of the world for long periods; but Jamaica had become his centre of gravity. What at first, while he was still domiciled in California, may merely have
I been an investment, a dearly loved holiday resort and possibly a place of future retirement had in addition, when he had abandoned his Californian domicile, become his permanent home. Indeed, it would have been strange if, loving the place as he did, Errol had not regarded it as his home when he had no other, and was making and putting into effect such expensive plans for erecting a house there to his exact specification. Why should he shrink from treating as his present home a place which he loved and which had long been his holiday resort and perhaps the home to which he would in time retire? His professional engagements might be relied upon to keep him in the United States for sufficient periods

to satisfy the authorities in regard to his nationality and his passport; and in **A** Jamaica he could have all this, and haven too. During his absences he may well have intended to let his new house to visitors as the third defendant says. That, however, is in no way inconsistent with its being his home, but might well be an economic recognition of the life he was leading and the state of his finances.

Accordingly I answer the inquiry by saying that the time of his death Errol was domiciled in Jamaica. **B**

Solicitors: *Clifford-Turner & Co.* (for the plaintiff); *Harbottle & Lewis* (for the third defendant).

[*Reported by* R. W. FARRIN, ESQ., *Barrister-at-Law.*]

C

COLESHILL AND DISTRICT INVESTMENT CO., LTD. v. MINISTER OF HOUSING AND LOCAL GOVERNMENT AND ANOTHER.

D

[QUEEN'S BENCH DIVISION (Lord Parker, C.J., Widgery and Chapman, JJ.), November 24, 1967.]

Town and Country Planning—Development—" Building, engineering, mining or other operations "—Removal of spoil banked against blast walls of ammuni- **E** *tion magazine—Demolition of walls—Town and Country Planning Act, 1962 (10 & 11 Eliz. 2 c. 38), s. 12 (1).*

The appellants, having acquired a disused ammunition magazine, removed the protective banks of rubble and soil outside its blast walls, leaving them cleared. The work, which was a comparatively small job of removing some cubic yards of spoil, was done by a mechanical excavator and lorries. Plan- **F** ning permission had not been obtained. The appellants proposed also to demolish the cleared blast walls of the magazine. On appeal under the Town and Country Planning Act, 1962, s. 180 (to quash an enforcement notice in respect of removing the banks) and s. 181 (against a decision that planning permission was required to demolish the cleared walls),

Held: (i) the removal of the embankments, being a simple and compara- **G** tively small operation, was not a building operation nor an engineering operation nor a mining operation within s. 12 (1)* of the Town and Country Planning Act, 1962, neither was it an " other operation " within s. 12 (1), for that description was to be construed ejusdem generis; accordingly the removal of the banks did not amount to development (see p. 65, letter I, to p. 66, letter A, and p. 66, letters A, C and H, post). **H**

(ii) the demolition of the cleared blast walls was not a building, engineering or mining operation, nor was it an " other operation " within s. 12 (1), and thus it would not be development (see p. 66, letter F, post).

Per CURIAM: the creation of an eye-sore is not in itself development capable of restraint under the Act of 1962 (see p. 66, letter D, post).

Appeal allowed. **I**

[As to what constitutes development, see 37 HALSBURY'S LAWS (3rd Edn.) 259-263, para. 366; and for cases on the subject, see 45 DIGEST (Repl.) 325-327, *6-13.*

For the Town and Country Planning Act, 1962, s. 12 (1), s. 43, s. 180, and s. 181, see 42 HALSBURY'S STATUTES (2nd Edn.) 975, 1013, 1147, 1148.]

---

* Section 12 (1) is set out at p. 65, letter C, post.

Reversed. C.A., post p. 945.

A Case referred to:

Cheshire County Council v. Woodward, [1962] 1 All E.R. 517; [1962] 2 Q.B. 126; [1962] 2 W.L.R. 636; 126 J.P. 186; 45 Digest (Repl.) 326, 10.

Appeal.

B The appellants, Coleshill and District Investment Co., Ltd., appealed by notice of appeal dated June 12, 1967, against two decisions of the Minister of Housing and Local Government. The first decision, appeal from which lay under s. 180 of the Town and Country Planning Act, 1962, was given by letter dated May 16, 1967, referring to the report of an inspector who had held a local inquiry into the appellants' appeal against an enforcement notice served by the Meriden Rural District Council, acting on behalf of the Warwickshire County Council, C alleging the carrying out of development without the grant of planning permission by the removal of soil forming the embankments and coverings to ammunition magazines, which had materially affected the external appearance of the magazines. The appeal against the enforcement notice was under s. 46 (1) (c) and (d) of the Act of 1962. The Minister directed a variation in the words of the enforcement notice but subject thereto, upheld it and refused planning permission for the development to which it related and dismissed the appeal. D By another letter dated May 16, 1967, the Minister referred to the appellants' appeal against the failure of the rural district council, acting on behalf of the county council, to give within the prescribed period a valid decision on the appellants' application under s. 43 of the Act of 1962 to determine whether an application for planning permission was required for the carrying out of works E at the former ammunition depot, Meriden Road, Hampton-in-Arden; these works included removal of the blast walls. The Minister accepted the council's view that the blast walls formed part of the buildings and that the removal of the blast walls would constitute an alteration of the buildings and that it would materially affect the external appearance of the buildings. The Minister determined that the removal of the blast wall, and certain other works proposed, F would severally constitute or involve development of the land and that application for planning permission was required.

The appellants appealed from these two decisions of the Minister, and sought orders that the enforcement notice might be quashed, or that the appeal against it might be remitted to the Minister with a direction to quash the notice; and that it might be declared that the removal of the blast walls did not constitute or involve development on the land, or that the matter might be remitted to G the Minister for re-hearing with the opinion of the court to the like effect. The grounds of appeal included the following—(a) that what was assumed in the enforcement notice to be development did not constitute development; (b) that the removal of soil, bricks, rubble and ash making up the embankments that were the subject of the enforcement notice was not an engineering operation; H (c) that the removal of the blast walls did not constitute or involve development, and (d) that the demolition of the magazines or some part thereof was not development.

The case noted below* was cited during the argument in addition to that referred to in the judgment of WIDGERY, J.

I *S. Goldblatt* for the appellants.
Nigel Bridge for the Minister.
A. E. Holdsworth for the local authority.

WIDGERY, J., delivered the first judgment at the invitation of LORD PARKER, C.J.: These are two appeals brought against two decisions of the Minister of Housing and Local Government, each decision being dated May 16,

---

* *London County Council v. Marks and Spencers, Ltd.*, [1953] 1 All E.R. 1095; [1963] A.C. 535.

1967.   Both appeals have one vital point in common, and it will suffice for the A
moment if I deal with the appeal under s. 180 (1) of the Town and Country
Planning Act, 1962, which was an appeal to the Minister against an enforcement
notice served by the local planning authority.

The facts of the case are not in dispute and can be taken from the findings of
the inspector who conducted the inquiry into the appeal against the enforcement
notice.   He found that on this site there are six buildings about eleven feet to B
thirteen feet high of the character associated with an ammunition magazine.
Around these buildings and for protective purposes, in the course of their original
use there were erected concrete blast walls about nine feet high and about four
feet from the edge of the building.   These concrete blast walls were embanked
on their outer side by soil, brick rubble and other material of that kind, and the
inspector finds that these embankments extended to about eight to ten feet C
from the base of the walls and were banked up so as to reach nearly the top of the
wall.   By the time these matters arose the embankments had all grown over
with green vegetation, which no doubt tended to prevent them from being the
eye-sore that they would otherwise have been.

The appellants, Coleshill & District Investment Co., Ltd. acquired this land
in 1964 and were minded to take advantage of the undoubted storage use which D
attached to the buildings as such.   Having no need to use the buildings for the
storage of ammunition and, therefore, having no need to employ the blast walls
and embankments, they were minded to take them down.   They applied for a
determination of the planning authority that this could be done without planning
permission, and it is that application which is the subject of the second appeal.
Not waiting for the decision, however, the appellants proceeded with the work. E
The work was done by means of a mechanical excavator, which loaded the
spoil into lorries.   At the time when the enforcement notice was served they had
removed the embankment behind the blast walls, but the blast walls were
themselves still in situ.

The enforcement notice was dated Mar. 30, 1966; nothing turns on its formal
parts.   The development complained of and the actions required are con- F
veniently set out in the schedules to the notice, and the development complained
of is thus described:

" The removal of the soil forming the embankments and coverings to the
magazines situated on the land described herein which has materially
affected the external appearance of the said magazines."
                                                                          G

There were technical objections to the precise language used, and the Minister
in the course of his decisions in this case directed an amendment of the enforcement notice so as to make it read: " The removal of the embankments to the
magazines situated on the land described herein . . .", and the question which
the Minister had to decide and which comes before this court is whether those H
physical acts carried out in that context amounted to development under the
Town and Country Planning Act, 1962.

The Minister's decision in dealing with this aspect of the case is as follows:

" The [local authority] maintained that the blast walls and the embankments were an integral part of each of the buildings.   This latter view is
accepted as the correct one in this case.   The blast walls surrounding the I
inner buildings cannot be regarded simply as means of enclosures.   They
were erected as essential features of the structures as erected and without
them the inner buildings would have been ineffective for the use for which
magazines were built.   The soil and other materials (ash, rubble, etc.)
which formed the embankments to the walls were similarly parts of the
magazines which description is regarded as covering also the explosive
stores.   The Minister's decision in 1962 that the premises had a use within

A   class X of the Town and Country Planning (Use Classes) Order, 1960 (1), which is a use as a warehouse or repository for any purposes, does not affect this situation."

Then, if I may interpolate, somewhat as an afterthought the Minister adds: " The removal of the embankments was an engineering operation clearly falling into s. 12 (1) of the Act."

B   The real question, as I see it, is whether the Minister was right in thinking that this operation so clearly fell within the terms of the section.   One goes to s. 12, which is substantially in the form in which it has existed since the original Town and Country Planning Act, 1947, was passed.   Subsection (1) is in these terms:

C   " In this Act, except where the context otherwise requires, ' development ', subject to the following provisions of this section, means the carrying out of building, engineering, mining or other operations in, on, over or under land, or the making of any material change in the use of any buildings or other land."

Some additional guidance as to the meaning of that subsection is to be found in
D   the definition section, s. 221, in which " building operations " are said to include

" rebuilding operations, structural alterations of or additions to buildings, and other operations normally undertaken by a person carrying on business as a builder."

" Engineering operations " are defined as including " the formation or laying
E   out of means of access to highways ".

In my judgment, the proper way to approach this problem is to ask oneself whether the activity complained of does or does not fall within the words of s. 12 (1) of the Act of 1962.   If it does fall within those words, then unquestionably the enforcement notice was justified because there is nothing else in the Act of 1962 which would make enforcement action inappropriate.   On the
F   other hand, if the activities do not fall within that subsection, that is an end of the matter and the Minister's decision must be wrong.

I think, with respect, that the Minister has somewhat misled himself in this case by the attention which he has given to the question whether these blast walls and embankments did or did not form part of a building, namely, the original magazine.   Once one embarks on that kind of inquiry there arises the
G   fascinating problem whether demolition of a building is a " building operation "; and that can be even further refined by asking whether demolition of part of a building is a building operation.   These questions, which have exercised the minds of those concerned with this legislation for years, do not to my mind arise if one takes the simple and straightforward approach to this problem: were these activities within the meaning of the section or not?

H   In my judgment, they were clearly not building operations.   Not only do they fail to qualify as operations normally entrusted to a builder, but no one using the phrase " building operations " in its ordinary sense would conceivably regard this simple removal of soil as being within that term.   Equally, as it seems to me, no one would describe them as " engineering operations ".   It is, of course, true that earth-moving on the grand scale which requires the intervention,
I   supervision and planning of qualified engineers may well qualify as an engineering operation; but this little job of shifting a few cubic yards of soil with a digger and a lorry is not, in my judgment, an operation of a kind which could ever be dignified with the title of an engineering operation.   It clearly is not a mining operation. One then has to consider the concluding words of the phrase: " other operations in, on, over or under land ".   It is not disputed that the reference to " other operations " there must be construed ejusdem generis with building, engineering

---

(1) S.I. 1950 No. 1131.

and mining; and, without attempting to define the genus in detail, it seems **A** clear to me that it is restricted to operations of the scale, complexity and difficulty which require a builder or an engineer or some mining expert.

I would not attempt in this case further to define the meaning of s. 12 (1), save to point to the serious practical risk that, unless some restriction of the kind which seems to me appropriate in this phrase is employed, we shall very soon reach the stage when the householder who goes to turn over his lawn and **B** sow potatoes will have to obtain planning permission because it is an operation in, on, over or under land.

LORD PARKER, C.J., in giving judgment in an earlier case of *Cheshire County Council* v. *Woodward* (2), observed that the operations contemplated there must change the physical character of the land. I respectfully adopt that view. However one looks at this case, it seems to me quite impossible, giving the words **C** their ordinary meaning, to say that this simple little activity could come within the terms employed. Therefore, in my view, the complexities considered by the Minister and elaborated in argument before this court do not arise.

I think that the real trouble in this case springs from the fact that the creation of an eye-sore is not in itself development capable of restraint under the Act of 1962. I have the utmost sympathy with the planning authority in seeking to **D** prevent this particular piece of country from being despoiled by the removal of the embankments which undoubtedly screened the unpleasantness which lay beyond. Since the creation of an eye-sore is not in itself development, however, the planning authority cannot control the activities complained of here under the Act of 1962 unless they can bring themselves within s. 12, which, for the reasons I have given, I am satisfied that they cannot. **E**

It follows from that that the Minister, in my judgment, erred in regard to the appeal under s. 180 and I would send that matter back to him for reconsideration in the light of the opinion which I have expressed.

So far as the appeal under s. 181 is concerned, the only difference there is that the application for a determination extends, not only to the removal of the soil embankments, but also to the blast walls themselves. What I have said **F** on the earlier appeal, in my judgment, is sufficient to cover this aspect of the case as well. If someone has a wall, a free-standing wall, on his land, in his garden or as the case may be, and all he seeks to do is to knock down that wall, I find it extremely difficult to say that that is a building, engineering, mining or other operation on land sufficient to come within the terms of the section.

In my judgment, therefore, the same consideration applies to the second appeal, **G** and I would send that matter back to the Minister also with a similar comment.

CHAPMAN, J.: I agree with the judgment which has just been given.

LORD PARKER, C.J.: I also agree.

Appeal allowed. **H**

Solicitors: *Keene, Marsland & Co.*, agents for *Tompkins & Co.*, Birmingham (for the appellants); *Solicitor, Ministry of Housing and Local Government; Sharpe, Pritchard & Co.* (for the local authority).

[*Reported by* ELLEN B. SOLOMONS, *Barrister-at-Law.*]

I

---

(2) [1962] 1 All E.R. 517 at p. 518; [1962] 2 Q.B. 126 at p. 133.

ULRICH v. ULRICH AND FELTON.

[COURT OF APPEAL, CIVIL DIVISION (Lord Denning, M.R., Diplock and Edmund Davies, L.JJ.), November 3, 6, 7, 1967.]

Husband and Wife—Property—Matrimonial home—Purchase before marriage —Wife contributing cash and husband procuring mortgage—Conveyance to husband alone—Both spouses at work and contributing to common fund for household expenses—Equity of redemption of house held beneficially for them as tenants in common equally.

Variation of Settlement (Matrimonial Causes)—Ante-nuptial settlement—House purchased before marriage to provide matrimonial home—Contribution by wife towards purchase price—Conveyance into the name of the husband alone —Divorce on ground of wife's adultery—One child of marriage—Variations of wife's beneficial interest in half share, so as to make provision for child— Variation not punitive—Matrimonial Causes Act 1965 (c. 72) s. 17 (1).

In 1957, before their marriage, the parties bought a bungalow; the wife contributed £415 15s. and the husband obtained a mortgage for the rest of the cost, the amount of the mortgage being about £2,000. The bungalow was conveyed to the husband alone; it was intended to be and became their matrimonial home. After their marriage in September, 1957, both husband and wife continued in work, their joint earnings being used for household expenses. In 1960 a son was born and the wife then ceased work so that she could look after him. Later she resumed some work. The husband and wife had central heating put into the house, the cost being added to the mortgage. In 1966 the wife committed adultery. The husband left the home. The wife and the child remained there. On Mar. 6, 1967, the husband obtained a divorce on the ground of the wife's adultery. It was agreed that the matrimonial home had to be sold. The expected value of the equity of redemption was about £2,600. The breakdown of the marriage was due to the wife's conduct.

Held: (i) moneys contributed before marriage with a view to setting up the matrimonial home were in the same position as moneys contributed after marriage, and accordingly, after the marriage took place, the husband and wife were entitled in equity to the house (viz., to its proceeds of sale) in equal shares as tenants in common (see p. 69, letter I, p. 70, letter F, p. 72, letter I, and p. 73, letter G, post).

(ii) (a) the acquisition of the matrimonial home constituted an ante-nuptial settlement, which there was jurisdiction to vary under s. 17 (1)* of the Matrimonial Causes Act 1964 (see p. 70, letter H, and p. 73, letters B and G, post).

(b) neither the powers under sub-s. (1) nor those under sub-s. (2) of s. 17 of the Act of 1965 would be exercised to punish a party to the marriage, but the court would make such variation of the ante-nuptial settlement as would be fair; in the present case the husband should have his half share of the proceeds of the equity of redemption of the house and the wife's half share should be put into trust in whole or in part for the child of the marriage, the matter being remitted for decision of the proportion so to be put into trust (see p. 71, letters D and H, p. 73, letters F and G, and p. 74, letter B, post).

Matheson v. *Matheson and Hartley* ([1935] All E.R. Rep. 414) and *Moy* v. *Moy and White* ([1961] 2 All E.R. 204) applied.

Appeal allowed on (i) and (ii) (b).

[As to the determination of rights to property as between husband and wife, see 19 HALSBURY'S LAWS (3rd Edn.) 900, 901, para. 1492; and for cases on beneficial ownership of the matrimonial home, see DIGEST (Cont. Vol. A) 692-695, *2130a-2130f.*

---

* Section 17 (1), so far as material, is set out at p. 70, letter H, post.

As to the meaning of settlement for the purposes of s. 17 of the Matrimonial **A**
Causes Act 1965, see 12 HALSBURY's LAWS (3rd Edn.) 451, para. 1015; and for
cases on the subject, see 27 DIGEST (Repl.) 645-649, *6089-6112*.
For the Married Women's Property Act, 1882, s. 17, see 11 HALSBURY's
STATUTES (2nd Edn.) 804.
For the Matrimonial Causes Act 1965 s. 17, see 45 HALSBURY's STATUTES
(2nd Edn.) 470.]   **B**

Cases referred to:
  Bedson v. *Bedson*, [1965] 3 All E.R. 307; [1965] 2 Q.B. 666; [1965] 3 W.L.R.
      891; Digest (Cont. Vol. B) 349, *2130fa.*
  Bull v. *Bull*, [1955] 1 All E.R. 253; [1955] 1 Q.B. 234; [1955] 2 W.L.R. 78;
      38 Digest (Repl.) 827, *398.*
  Cook v. *Cook*, [1962] 2 All E.R. 811; [1962] P. 235; [1962] 3 W.L.R. 441;   **C**
      Digest (Cont. Vol. A) 799, *6101b.*
  Fribance v. *Fribance*, [1957] 1 All E.R. 357; [1957] 1 W.L.R. 384; Digest
      (Cont. Vol. A) 693, *2130ab.*
  March v. *March and Palumbo*, [1861-73] All E.R. Rep. 522; (1867), L.R. 1
      P. & D. 440; 36 L.J.P. & M. 65; 16 L.T. 366; 27 Digest (Repl.) 641,   **D**
      6032.
  Matheson v. *Matheson and Hartley*, [1935] All E.R. Rep. 414; [1935] P. 171;
      104 L.J.P. 59; 153 L.T. 299; 27 Digest (Repl.) 652, *6139.*
  Moy v. *Moy and White*, [1961] 2 All E.R. 204; [1961] 1 W.L.R. 552; Digest
      (Cont. Vol. A) 796, *5993a.*

Appeal.   **E**
This was an appeal by the wife from an order made by BAKER, J., on July 7,
1967, declaring that there was a trust and the beneficial interest in the proceeds
in respect of the property (viz., the matrimonial home, No. 12 Blenheim Park
Close, Leigh-on-Sea, Essex) after the sale thereof, and after payment of the
charges on the said property, should be apportioned as to four-fifths thereof
to the husband and as to one fifth thereof to the wife. The facts are set out   **F**
in the judgment of LORD DENNING, M.R.

Joseph Jackson, Q.C., and *R. R. Russell* for the wife.
P. N. Garland for the husband.

LORD DENNING, M.R.: This is an unusual case about a matrimonial
home. It is unusual because the parties bought the house before their marriage. **G**
The question is whether that makes any difference.
About April, 1957, the parties became engaged to be married. They planned
to get their own home. It was then a plot of land with a bungalow to be built on
it. It was No. 12, Blenheim Park Close, Leigh-on-Sea in Essex. The wife had some
savings: she had about £100 in cash and £300 or more in national saving certificates. She put up that sum of savings, in all £415 15s, in April and June,   **H**
1957 before they were married. That was used to pay the deposit on the house
and the costs and charges, and so forth. The rest of the money, some £2,000,
was raised on mortgage. The husband did not put up any cash for the house.
He was employed by Shell, who gave their employees special facilities for house
loans. The conveyance was taken in his name on July 5, 1957, whilst they were
still engaged to be married, and the mortgage on it was in his name and payable **I**
by him. The result was that some £415 was put up by the wife in cash and there
was a mortgage in the husband's name. In addition he bought some of the
furniture with his savings.
On Sept. 14, 1957, they married and went into the bungalow. Both husband
and wife went out to work and the earnings of each of them were used for the
household expenses. A son David was born some three years later on June 6,
1960. Whilst he was a baby, the wife stayed at home to look after him. When he
was three years old or so, she went out to work again, but not full-time. She used

A to go round as an agent on commission selling cosmetics, which brought in about £2 a week. Whilst they were married they did the usual things that husband and wife do. For instance, they had central heating put in. They could not pay for it in cash, so it was added to the mortgage, some £300. The wife had some money £100 or £200, from a legacy. She put that into the pool to meet expenditure on the house and so forth, as husbands and wives do.

B   Unfortunately, in 1966 the wife got entangled with another man, the postman. In consequence, the husband decided not to stay in the house any longer. On Feb. 14, 1966, he left the matrimonial home. The wife and son remained there. He brought proceedings for divorce on the ground of her adultery. She disputed it, saying that he was guilty of cruelty. It was heard by Baker, J. On Mar. 6, 1967, he found that the wife was the guilty party; she had been guilty of adultery:

C the husband had not been cruel at all. So he made a decree nisi. We have not had the transcript of his judgment, but the judge summarised it in this way:

> " I remember the case very well. The husband forgave the wife's adultery on one occasion and tried to make the marriage work for the sake of the child. Really if ever there was a case where the wife brought the marriage to an end, this was it."

D
So the marriage came to an end. A decree absolute has since been pronounced.
    Now the question arises as to the matrimonial home. Both sides acknowledge that it must be sold. At present prices it can be sold at a considerable profit over the original outlay. We are told that the anticipated price is some £4,600. The mortgage outstanding is nearly £2,000. So the equity, that is the realisable

E profit, is some £2,600. It is a windfall. The question is: What is to happen to the profit on resale? The judge thought it should be divided one-fifth to the wife and four-fifths to the husband. In that way the wife would receive back approximately the money she put in, £400 or £500, and the husband would have the rest, £2,000 or so. Now the wife appeals to this court. We are told that her association with the co-respondent, the postman, has come to an end and she is

F not going to marry him. She goes out to work earning money herself. So she is a woman on her own, going out to work, having the child at home. An order has been made whereby the husband pays £2 10s. a week to the wife for the maintenance of the child. Meanwhile he has kept up the mortgage payments pending sale of the house.
    The first point is this: what is the law about money put up before marriage

G so as to acquire the home? It was submitted to the judge that it was just the same as any case where two strangers (not husband and wife) put up money to buy a house. If the conveyance is taken in the name of one, there is a resulting trust for the two of them, in the proportions in which they contributed. Just like the case of *Bull* v. *Bull*, (1) where there was a mother and son, each of whom contributed money. It was held that, although the property was in the name of the son, there

H was a resulting trust in proportion to their contributions. So here the judge thought that, as the wife had contributed some £500, and the husband contributed £2,000 by way of the mortgage, that there was a resulting trust as to one-fifth and four-fifths.
    I am afraid that I cannot agree with the judge's view. In the first place, I think that money contributed by a man and woman *before* marriage, with a view

I to setting up a matrimonial home, are in the same position as moneys contributed by them *after* marriage. They are contributed to the purchase of property which is intended to be a family asset. When the marriage takes place, it becomes a joint asset belonging to both in equal shares. Such is the position, at any rate, if and when the marriage takes place. It might be very different if there was no marriage at all. If the marriage never took place, the whole thing might have to be cancelled. There would probably in those circumstances be a resulting trust in the proportions in which they contributed. When the marriage takes place as

---

(1) [1955] 1 All E.R. 253; [1955] 1 Q.B. 234.

contemplated, however, I am satisfied that the moneys stand in the same position **A**
as moneys contributed after the marriage. I would repeat at this stage what I
said in *Fribance* v. *Fribance* (2), in regard to family assets. These are

"the things intended to be a continuing provision for them during their
joint lives, such as the matrimonial home and the furniture in it. When
these are acquired by their joint efforts during the marriage [or, I would add,
before it] the parties do not give a thought to future separation. They do not **B**
contemplate divorce. They contemplate living in the house and using the
furniture together for the rest of their lives. They buy the house and
furniture out of their available resources without worrying too much as to
whom it belongs. The reason is plain. So long as they are living together, it
does not matter which of them does the saving and which does the paying,
or which of them goes out to work or which looks after the home . . . The title **C**
to the family assets does not depend on the mere chance of which way round it
was. It does not depend on how they happened to allocate their earnings
and their expenditure . . . the product should belong to them jointly. It
belongs to them in equal shares."

This case stands on a par with all the marriage cases. Although the house stood **D**
in the name of the husband only, nevertheless they were equitable tenants in
common, each being entitled to a half share.

In the second place, I differ from the judge about the mortgage. He regarded
the husband as having put up £2,000 in cash, and to be the same as if he had
saved the £2,000 or it had been given to him by his father or a relative. I do not
regard money on mortgage as equal to a cash contribution. When the house is **E**
subject to a mortgage, the family asset is the equity of redemption in the property. That is the asset to which they are entitled in equal shares. Neither can
turn the other out. Neither can sell without the consent of the other. Nor can
one party sell his interest separately so as to enable the purchaser to turn the
other out (see *Bedson* v. *Bedson*, (3)). If, however, there is a sale by the consent
of both, or by order of the court, then the realisable proceeds (after discharge **F**
of the mortgage) belong to both equally. I hold, therefore, that during the
marriage the husband and wife were equitable tenants in common in the house in
equal shares.

This brings me to the next point. The husband says that it was an ante-nuptial
settlement, and, now that they are divorced, it should be varied so as to give him
the major share. It is plain to my mind that the acquisition of the matrimonial **G**
home was an ante-nuptial settlement. If they had acquired it after marriage for
the benefit of the family, it would be a post-nuptial settlement (see *Cook* v. *Cook*, (4)).
Likewise this house, acquired before marriage by their joint efforts, was an ante-
nuptial settlement. It follows that the court has power to vary that settlement
under s. 17 (1) of the Matrimonial Causes Act 1965, which provides that

"The court may, after granting a decree of divorce—(a) inquire into the **H**
existence of ante-nuptial or post-nuptial settlements made on the parties
whose marriage is the subject of the decree; and (b) make such orders as the
court thinks fit as respects the application, for the benefit of the children of
the marriage or the parties to the marriage, of the whole or any part of the
property settled: . . . "

I think this case falls exactly within that provision so that the court has a **I**
discretion to vary the settlement.

We were referred also to s. 17 (2), which applies when a wife is divorced for
adultery, desertion or cruelty. If she is entitled to any property, either in possession or reversion, the court may make an order or such settlement as it thinks

(2) [1957] 1 All E.R. 357 at pp. 359,360.
(3) [1965] 3 All E.R. 307; [1965] 2 Q.B. 666.
(4) [1962] 2 All E.R. 811; [1962] P. 235.

A reasonable for the benefit of the innocent party and the children. That section can be invoked where a guilty wife has separate property of her own. It need not be invoked when the property is the subject of an ante-nuptial settlement or post-nuptial settlement, for s. 17 (1) gives the court all necessary power. In either case the court has a wide discretion to do what is fair in the circumstances of the case between the parties.

B In exercising its powers under s. 17 (2), the court will have regard to these considerations:

First—

"The section is not penal. It is not intended to be used as a punishment of a guilty wife, or even as a punishment indirectly through her, of the co-respondent:" (see *Matheson* v. *Matheson and Hartley*, (5) per BUCKNILL, J.).

C Second—

"... the object of the court was to try to ascertain and make good the pecuniary damage caused by the wife's adultery: the court will look at the probable pecuniary position which the husband, the wife and the issue of the marriage would have enjoyed if the marriage had not been dissolved:"

D (see *Moy* v. *Moy and White* (6), per HOLROYD PEARCE, L.J.).

Likewise under s. 17 (1) the court will not use its power to vary so as to punish either of the parties. It will try to do what is fair. If a wife, after her divorce, marries a rich man, the court might give her less and the husband more. Whereas if she is without means, she might be given more, and regard must be had to the children. The situations that may arise are so infinitely various that the only thing for the court is to do what is fair in the circumstances.

E On this part of the case the judge said that if there was an ante-nuptial settlement under which the parties shared equally, he would vary the settlement by saying that three-tenths of the wife's half share (leaving her with two-tenths) should be settled on the husband. He declined to settle anything on the child. He preferred to give the three-tenths to the husband, saying that that fact could be taken into consideration in deciding what maintenance the husband had to contribute for the upkeep of the child. I am afraid that I do not agree with that way of doing it. If the whole or part of the wife's share is to go to the child, it should be settled directly on the child and not given to the husband.

F In these circumstances the court must consider the matter afresh. The legal position is this: the husband and wife were tenants in common sharing equally, but there is a power in the court to vary so as to do what is fair in the circumstances. I think that the husband should have the whole of his half share. The wife's half share should be applied for the child, or part for the child and part for the wife. This court has not the material to decide exactly how the wife's share should be allocated: and unless the parties agree, the case must be remitted to

G the judge for him to decide. I would, therefore, allow the appeal, declare that the parties were equitable tenants in common in equal shares and (unless the parties agree) remit the matter to the judge as to the wife's share so that he should say whether the whole should be put on trust for the child or some part of it to her and some part on trust for the child. I would allow the appeal accordingly.

H **DIPLOCK, L.J.:** I agree. The first task of the court, whether under s. 17 of the Married Women's Property Act, 1882, or s. 17 of the Matrimonial Causes Act 1965, is to ascertain what are the interests of the spouses in property of all kinds. Their interest may be joint or common or it may be the sole interest of either party. Under the Married Women's Property Act, 1882 the court has no power to vary sole proprietary interests. As respects joint or common interests, it may make such order as it thinks fit to enable the parties to obtain the benefit

I

---

(5) [1935] All E.R. Rep. 414 at p. 416; [1935] P. 171 at p. 175.
(6) [1961] 2 All E.R. 204 at p. 205.

of their respective interests in the changed circumstances, generally the break-up **A**
of the marriage, but save to this extent, it cannot vary those interests.

Under the Matrimonial Causes Act 1965 s. 17 (2), it can order a settlement of
the sole proprietary interest of a guilty wife for the benefit of a child of the
marriage or for the benefit of the innocent party. Under s. 17 (1) it can vary the
interests of either party in property in which they have a joint or common
interest. **B**

In the present case the judge was exercising powers under s. 17 of the Matrimonial Causes Act 1965. The language of both subsections, which have a long
legislative ancestry, is more appropriate to marriages among the property-
owning classes of the nineteenth century than to marriages between the ordinary
young couples of today. When these young people pool their savings to buy and
equip a home or to acquire any other family asset, they do not think of this as **C**
an " ante-nuptial " or " post-nuptial " settlement, or give their minds to legalistic
technicalities of " advancement " and " resulting trusts ". Nor do they normally
agree explicitly what their equitable interests in the family asset shall be if death,
divorce or separation parts them. Where there is no explicit agreement, the
court's first task is to infer from their conduct in relation to the property what their
common intention would have been had they put it into words before matrimonial **D**
differences arose between them. In the common case today, of which the present
is a typical example, neither party to the marriage has inherited capital, both are
earning their living before marriage, the wife intends to continue to do so until
they start having children. They pool their savings to buy a house on mortgage
in the husband's name or in joint names and to furnish and equip it as the family
home. They meet the expenses of its upkeep and improvement and the payments **E**
of instalments on the mortgage out of the family income, to which the wife
contributes so long as she is earning. In such a case, the prima facie inference
from their conduct is that their common intention is that the house, furniture and
equipment should be family assets in which each is entitled to an equal share.
Conduct and inferred common intention combined constitute a " settlement " of
the family assets within the meaning of s. 17 of the Matrimonial Causes Act 1965: **F**
" ante-nuptial " so far as the assets are acquired before the marriage: " post-
nuptial " so far as acquired afterwards.

The conduct of the parties may give rise to some other inference as to their
common intention. In particular, their respective contributions to the acquisition
of the asset and to its upkeep or improvement, so far as they are not met out of
the current earnings of either or both parties which would otherwise be used for **G**
household expenditure by them both, may show that their intention was that the
respective interests of husband and wife should be in some different proportion
then equality. In the present case the judge drew such an inference from the fact
that the wife contributed her savings, in cash amounting to some £400, while the
husband assumed liability for repayment of the £2,000 mortgage debt. He treated
the liability of the husband as equivalent to a cash contribution and inferred **H**
that the husband's share was four times that of the wife. This ignores the
economic realities of modern mortgages of owner-occupied dwellinghouses.
Without the house the husband was not worth £2,000. The mortgagees' security
for that capital sum was the house which the husband could not have acquired
without his wife's contribution to its price. The husband's credit-worthiness was
relevant to his ability to meet the periodical instalments out of his earnings which **I**
would otherwise have been available for the general household expenditure from
which his wife too would have benefited.

There is nothing here to displace the inference, in my view, of equal shares
in this " family asset ". For many years past, with the continual rise in the value
of house property, the family home which is being purchased on mortgage repayable by instalments paid out of the earnings of the husband or husband and
wife is the principal family asset to the acquisition of which both contribute
by foregoing household luxuries or needs for which the money devoted to the

A instalments would otherwise have been available. Where this is so, the husband's theoretical sole liability for the capital amount of the mortgage debt does not displace any inference which would otherwise arise from the fact that the spouses pooled their savings to provide the cash required for its original acquisition.

I accordingly agree with LORD DENNING, M.R., that the judge was right in holding that there was an ante-nuptial settlement of the house, but in error in

B finding that the interest in the house was not in equal shares.

This does not, however, dispose of the appeal because the judge had discretion to vary the ante-nuptial settlement found to exist. Although the statute does not expressly impose fetters on the discretion of the judge to vary existing ante-nuptial or post-nuptial settlements or to order new settlements of separate property of a spouse in favour of a child of the marriage or innocent party to the

C divorce, a long line of authority dating back one hundred years to *March* v. *March and Palumbo* (7), during the course of which comparable provisions have been successively re-enacted, has laid it down that the power to alter property rights in favour of a spouse should not be exercised in order to punish a guilty party but only to compensate an innocent party for pecuniary loss sustained as a result of the break-up of the marriage. Here there is no relevant pecuniary loss. The

D husband had a half share in the house which was worth the present market value of the property, less the outstanding mortgage debt. The house is no longer the matrimonial home. It can be sold and the value of his interest realised. To give him more at the expense of the wife would be to penalise the wife for her matrimonial offence and not to compensate the husband for his pecuniary loss.

So far, therefore, as the judge ordered that four-fifths and not one-half of the

E expected proceeds of sale should vest in the husband, I think that his order was wrong and should be set aside.

As LORD DENNING, M.R., has pointed out, however, there is a third member of the family who would have benefited from this asset so long as it was the family home, that is the child. I agree that this court has not sufficient factual material to determine whether or not it would be in the child's interest that any or some

F part of the wife's share should be settled on the child, and I, accordingly, agree in allowing the appeal to the extent that LORD DENNING has proposed and remitting the case to the judge to determine the question of whether the child's interest requires that any portion of the wife's share should be settled on it, and, if so, on what terms.

G   EDMUND DAVIES, L.J.: I agree and seek to deal very shortly with only one further point. After referring to those authorities which lay down that, in varying an ante-nuptial or post-nuptial settlement, the object of the court must be to make good the pecuniary damage caused to the innocent party by the matrimonial offence and not by way of punishment of the guilty party (see, for example, *Moy* v. *Moy and White* (8)). BAKER, J., said:

H   " I think the husband has indeed suffered a loss by reason of this wife's conduct. He has lost his wife and he is left unable to get back that which he contributed. I think that it is only justice and fair that he should have back what he initially contributed and that the wife should have back what she contributed."

I   If that be the correct formula, the judge himself did not apply it. He went on to hold that, after the sale of the matrimonial home (which has doubled in value since it was bought in 1957), there must be deducted from its selling-price the amount due on the mortgage and the costs of the sale, and that the balance then remaining must be divided as to one-fifth to the wife and four-fifths to the husband. Although it might be said that thereby the wife would recover her initial contribution, the husband would undoubtedly acquire by that process substantially

(7) [1861-73] All E.R. Rep. 522; (1867), L.R. 1 P. & D. 440.
(8) [1961] 2 All E.R. 204.

more than ". . . what he initially contributed ". That contribution consisted **A** very largely of his undertaking the mortgage liability, and that liability will ex concessis already have been discharged before the capital sum to be divided is arrived at. Accordingly, over and above a discharge of that liability, the husband would (on the judge's formula) also acquire roughly four-fifths of the profit attributable solely to the enhanced market value of the matrimonial home.

The division decided on by the judge, therefore, could not, in any event, be **B** allowed to stand; but, for the reasons already stated by my lords, I do not regard the " initial contribution " approach as correct on the facts of this case. In its stead, in my judgment the order proposed is the one which is right and just in all the circumstances.

I would, accordingly, allow the appeal and remit the case to the learned judge.

Appeal allowed: case remitted. **C**

Solicitors: *Vizard, Oldham, Crowder & Cash* agents for *F. T. Fisher & Lang*, Southend-on-Sea (for the wife); *Kingsford, Dorman & Co.*, (for the husband).

[*Reported by* F. GUTTMAN, ESQ., *Barrister-at-Law.*]

D

R. *v.* CLEAR.

[COURT OF APPEAL, CRIMINAL DIVISION (Sellers, L.J., John Stephenson and James, JJ.), November 6, 10, 1967.]

Criminal Law—Demanding money with menaces—Menaces—Intent—Larceny Act, 1916 (6 & 7 Geo. 5 c. 50), *s.* 30. **E**

In 1963 a lorry of which the appellant, an employee of a company, was the driver, and its load were stolen. The appellant reported to the managing director that he had left the loaded lorry for a short time near his home, having set the alarm system and having taken with him the ignition key and the key of the alarm system. The company claimed against their insurers. In 1966 the appellant was served with a subpoena to give evidence in an **F** action by the owners of the goods against the company. The appellant then visited the managing director on several occasions and, in effect, made demand for £300 threatening to withhold or change his evidence that care had been taken of the lorry and its contents by setting the burglar alarm. There was no evidence that the managing director had any interest in the company other than as managing director. After the appellant's third visit the manag- **G** ing director communicated with the police concerning the appellant's conduct. On appeal by the appellant against conviction of demanding money with menaces contrary to s. 30* of the Larceny Act, 1916,

Held: (i) words or conduct were menaces for the purposes of s. 30 of the Larceny Act, 1916, if they were such as were likely to operate on the mind of a person of ordinary courage and firmness so as to make him accede un- **H** willingly to the demand; the intent of an accused which had to be established for the purposes of an offence against s. 30 was an intent to steal, and that intent must accompany the demand, but it was not essential to prove that the intended victim of the demand must himself have been alarmed by the threats held out to him (see p. 80, letters E and G, post).

R. v. *Walton and Ogden* ((1863), Le. & Ca. 288) criticised. **I**

(ii) in the circumstances of the present case there was evidence proper to be left to the jury and the conviction should stand (see p. 80, letters H and I, post).

[As to demanding money with menaces, see 10 HALSBURY'S LAWS (3rd Edn.) 799, para. 1544; and for cases on the subject, see 15 DIGEST (Repl.) 1122-1125, *11,194-11,218.*

---

* Section 30, so far as material, is set out at p. 75, letter F, post.

A   For the Larceny Act, 1916, s. 30, see 5 HALSBURY'S STATUTES (2nd Edn.)
1030.]
      Cases referred to:
        R. v. *Boyle and Merchant*, [1914-15] All E.R. Rep. 553; [1914] 3 K.B. 339;
             83 L.J.K.B. 1801; 111 L.T. 638; 78 J.P. 290; 10 Cr. App. Rep. 180;
             15 Digest (Repl.) 1123, *11,204*.
B   *R.* v. *Collister and Warhurst*, (1955), 39 Cr. App. Rep. 100.
        R. v. *Tomlinson*, [1895-99] All E.R. Rep. 879; [1895] 1 Q.B. 706; 64 L.J.M.C.
             97; 72 L.T. 155; 15 Digest (Repl.) 1123, *11,200*.
        R. v. *Walton and Ogden*, (1863), Le. & Ca. 288; 32 L.J.M.C. 79; 7 L.T. 754;
             27 J.P. 165; 9 Cox, C.C. 268; 169 E.R. 1399; 15 Digest (Repl.) 1119,
             11,138.

C   **Appeal and application.**
      This was an appeal by Thomas Walter Clear against his conviction at the Central
Criminal Court on June 13, 1967, before JUDGE GILLIS, Q.C., and a jury, of demanding with menaces with intent to steal, contrary to s. 30 of the Larceny Act,
1916.   He was fined £150, or in default four months' imprisonment, and he
applied for leave to appeal against conviction and sentence. The facts are set out
D   in the judgment of the court.
      The authority and the case noted below* were cited during the argument in
addition to those referred to in the judgment of the court.
      T. S. G. Baker for the appellant.
      H. J. Leonard for the Crown.

                                                              Cur. adv. vult.
E
      Nov. 10. **SELLERS, L.J.,** read the following judgment of the court: The
appellant was convicted at the Central Criminal Court on June 13, 1967, of
demanding money, contrary to s. 30 of the Larceny Act, 1916. That section
provides:
      " Every person who with menaces or by force demands of any person
F   anything capable of being stolen with intent to steal the same shall be
      guilty of felony . . ."
      This section is of the same effect, though slightly different in form and wording,
to s. 45 of the Larceny Act, 1861, which was the statute in force when *R.* v. *Walton
and Ogden* (1) was decided in 1863. This decision was relied on before JUDGE
GILLIS, Q.C., by counsel for the appellant as establishing the correct direction
G   to the jury, but, after full argument, the learned judge declined to follow the
submission. The main contention in this appeal is that the learned judge was
wrong in law in ruling, and subsequently directing the jury, that it was immaterial under s. 30 whether or not the menace had any effect on the mind of the
person to whom it was addressed, contrary, it was submitted, to the decision in
R. v. *Walton and Ogden* (1). The further grounds of appeal will be indicated later.
H   The facts were these. They are taken from the summing-up and were not in
dispute. In 1963 the appellant was employed by D. & C. Carriers, Ltd., whose
business included the carriage of goods. In February, 1963, the appellant was
driving one of the company's lorries containing a load valued at about £3,000.
He left the loaded lorry somewhere near his home, to which he went, and on his
return the lorry with its contents had gone and the goods were stolen and not
I   recovered. The appellant informed the managing director, Mr. Chapman, of
the occurence and assured him that the alarm system on the lorry had been set
before he left the loaded lorry, and that he had locked it and had taken with him
both the ignition key and the alarm key. Shortly after that the appellant left
the company's employment. It would appear that the owners of the lost goods,
or persons interested in them, claimed for their loss against D. & C. Carriers, Ltd.

      * ARCHBOLD'S CRIMINAL PLEADING EVIDENCE AND PRACTICE (36th Edn.) paras.
1871, 1877, 1891; *R.* v. *Moran*, [1952] 1 All E.R. 803n.
      (1) (1863), Le. & Ca. 288.

The company was insured, and the claim and the conduct of the litigation were   A
dealt with by the insurers. On Aug. 31, 1966, a Mr. Richardson acting on behalf
of the defendants in an action which had been brought by the goods owners
against the carriers served a subpoena on the appellant requiring him to attend
the High Court to give evidence. This took place in a public house, and Mr.
Richardson stated in evidence that, when he asked the appellant for a statement,
this conversation ensued (and I read from the summing-up):   B

> " ' I am not going to make any statement until I have seen Joe Chapman.'
> ' Who is he? ' enquired Mr. Richardson. ' He is the boss at D. & C. Carriers.
> I must say the right thing. Joe Chapman is worth a couple of hundred
> quid.' And then he went on to indicate to Mr. Richardson that he would see
> Mr. Chapman and then telephone Mr. Richardson concerning any possible
> statement. Mr. Richardson's reaction, you may think, is not unimportant.   C
> He said he did not know what [the appellant] was talking about, but he
> would make a report to the solicitors. When cross-examined Mr. Richardson
> told counsel that [the appellant] was not prepared to say anything to him
> until he had seen Mr. Chapman. He was sure that the words used were ' a
> couple of hundred ', and as you will observe, [the appellant] has not gone
> into the witness box to challenge, or deny the version given by Mr.   D
> Richardson."

Following that the appellant did see Mr. Chapman on several occasions. The
appellant telephoned him and told him that he had had the subpoena and that
it was about the lorry. Mr. Chapman said that he knew nothing about it, and
suggested that the appellant went to see him. On the first occasion Mr. Chapman   E
repeated that he knew nothing about the matter and said that he would telephone
the insurers. The appellant said that he would let Mr. Chapman know when he
heard any more. On a second visit the appellant asked if Mr. Chapman had heard
anything from the insurance company. Mr. Chapman said that he had learnt
that the appellant had been served with a subpoena. The appellant asked
" What is to be done about it? ", to which Mr. Chapman replied that, until he   F
heard further from the insurance broker, he could not do anymore about it. On a
third visit the appellant asked again whether Mr. Chapman had heard anything
from the insurance company. Mr. Chapman's evidence of the further conversation
was not challenged by any evidence to the contrary by the appellant. The
appellant said: " You know this is going to cost you a lot of money ", to which
Mr. Chapman replied: " Well, I know it can't cost me anything because I am   G
insured." The conversation did not end there; the appellant said: " It is going
to cost you money. I can alter my statement." Mr. Chapman reminded him:
" You can't do that, you have already given a statement to the police." Then
the appellant said: " It will cost you about £300." " What for? ", asked Mr.
Chapman. " It would be better than to pay £3,000 ", said the appellant. Mr.
Chapman said that he would think it over and talk it over with his son. Before   H
the appellant came a fourth time Mr. Chapman had communicated with the
police. On this occasion the appellant asked if Mr. Chapman had made up his
mind. Mr. Chapman said: " I don't like this nonsense ", but asked the appellant
how he wanted to be paid. The appellant said by £150 now and the other £150
when it finished. The appellant said again that he could change his statement.
Mr. Chapman added words to the effect that it did not matter to him whether he   I
did so. " We had insured. We could not do any more. We had nothing at all to
lose if he changed his evidence." By Oct. 27, 1966, Mr. Chapman had drawn £150
from the bank and the appellant was asked to count the money contained
in an envelope, Mr. Chapman saying: " I hope this is all right." The appellant
said: " That's all right ", and put the money in his pocket. On an inquiry by
Mr. Chapman how he would know that he would act in the right way, the appellant
said: " I'm acting on my word of honour " or " You can rely on my word of
honour ", and apparently the appellant gave a receipt for the £150 " in advance

A of services to the insurance co.". In cross-examination, Mr. Chapman said that he got in touch with the police as soon as there was a request for money and that he knew that the police would get the money back right away on the day when he had handed it over. The police had installed a listening device in Mr. Chapman's office on the last occasion, and a detective-sergeant in an adjoining room heard this conversation before the money was handed over: Mr. Chapman: "About

B this money. Are you sure when you get it from me you won't just go to the other side? " The appellant: "I will give you my word of honour. I will say the truth what originally happened at the first." " What will you say if I give it to you? " Answer: "Exactly as before, that the burglar alarm was on and I left it for ten minutes, that I took the vehicle from here and left it outside the house for ten minutes."

C It was on that evidence that the prosecution alleged that the appellant had made a demand with menaces with an intent to steal, contrary to s. 30. It is unlikely that the appellant at the outset had thought of insurance or at any time of the effect of subrogation, but some of the jury may have appreciated Mr. Chapman and D. & C. Carriers, Co., Ltd.'s position. The appellant made express reference to the burglar alarm being on and he may have thought that that might

D be an important factor for the defendants in resisting the claim.

Turning now to the ingredients of the offence, there was no doubt a demand made by the appellant for money from Mr. Chapman and the summing-up in that respect was not challenged. A demand may be implicit or explicit. The argument before the trial judge and on this appeal has been in relation to the other two vital elements in the offence, a demand with menaces and with an intent

E to steal the money. It was not suggested, and could not be, that there was a right or justification in claiming £300 to give evidence and the jury were entitled to hold, notwithstanding that there were no express words, that the appellant was threatening either to withhold his evidence that care had been taken of the lorry and its contents, or to give evidence to the contrary and that it would be detrimental to the defence of the action in which D. & C. Carriers Co., Ltd. as

F well as the insurers were interested. Mr. Chapman himself may have been at no financial loss. No evidence was given of his interest in the company save as managing director. On these two matters the summing-up was as follows:

" Secondly, it has to be proved that the demand was accompanied and made by means of menaces. The word ' menace ' or ' menaces ' may not be

G so frequently in use in our modern language as the word ' threats '. Substantially it means, you may no doubt think, the same thing and the menace or threat that has to be proved must amount to such a menace as is calculated, as is likely, to operate upon, to work upon, to have effect upon, the mind of a person, ordinary person, of ordinarily firm mind. As one of the learned counsel indicated in the course of his submissions to you, some persons may be easily

H alarmed, other persons are so constituted as not to be moved by an alarm which might well unsettle another. The test of the menaces must be your answer to the question ' Were the menaces such—if any are proved—that they were likely to operate on a person ordinarily firm and courageous minded? ' It is not essential, as I understand the law, that it has to be proved, in order for this offence to be established, that an intended victim of the de-

I mand must in fact himself have been frightened or menaced or alarmed by the threats or menaces held out to him . . . the prosecution have got to prove to you in regard to this offence that there was an intention in the mind of the [appellant] to alarm Mr. Chapman in this case so as to cause him to yield to the request or demand for the payment of money. You must be careful not to confuse the state of the mind of the accused man with the state of the mind of the alleged victim. What has to be proved in regard to the accused is, among other matters, that he had an intention to alarm his victim and to alarm him by means of the menaces which would have affected the mind of a person of ordinary firm courage and character. Whether it A affected the mind of the alleged victim or not is not an essential matter. In some cases it might; in some cases, if the proposed victim were of strong character, or for other reasons, there would have been no effect upon him. It is essential, when you consider what would be the effect on the mind of a person of ordinary firm courage, first to put such a person in the position revealed by the facts of this case. Members of the jury, the essential element B of this charge likewise is that it has to be proved by the prosecution that the intention of the accused when he made the demand with menaces, if you find that he so made such a demand, was with an intent to steal a sum of money. Intention is a state of mind. It cannot be touched as a physical thing like the hand, it cannot be seen, it cannot be heard; but it is much a fact to be proved as any other fact in the case."   C

The submissions of the appellant before the trial judge were that there was no sufficient evidence of menaces to go to the jury and, consequently, on appeal no sufficient evidence to support the verdict of guilty.

It was submitted first that the correct direction to the jury should have been in accordance with the headnote in *R. v. Walton and Ogden* (2) and that, in failing to apply it, there had been a misdirection by the trial judge; that on such a D direction there was no evidence to go to the jury as Mr. Chapman was not intimidated or influenced by any menaces or threats; and, second, that, even if the trial judge's statement of the law was accepted, what the appellant said and did was not making a demand with menaces, as no reasonable and fair-minded man in the situation in which Mr. Chapman found himself would have been intimidated or influenced to hand over the money involuntarily. It was contended that, E although the menaces need not necessarily be of duress or of personal violence and may be of injury to person or property, they should not be trivial but of some gravity. The headnote to *R. v. Walton and Ogden* (2) is as follows:

" In order to constitute the offence of demanding property with menaces, within the meaning of the 24 & 25 Vict. c. 69 [the Larceny Act, 1861], s. 45, the menaces must cause such alarm as to unsettle the mind of the person on F whom it operates and take away from his acts that element of free, voluntary action which alone constitutes consent. Where the menaces are not necessarily of a character to excite such alarm, it becomes a question for the jury whether they were made under such circumstances of intimidation as to have that effect. Where, therefore, a prisoner had obtained money by threatening to execute a distress warrant which he had no authority to do, G and the judge directed the jury, as a matter of law, that the conduct of the prisoner constituted a menace within the statute, the court quashed the conviction."

The judgment of the court was delivered by WILDE, B., and I take two extracts (3):

" Where then is the proper limit to the operation of this section? It is H to be found in the words ' with intent to steal '. There is no other restriction expressed. Nothing is said about ' violence ' in conjunction with menaces, still less of violence to the person as distinct from violence to property. There is no express limit, except in the words ' with intent to steal '. Now, a demand of money with intent to steal, if successful, must amount to stealing . . . If a man is induced to part with property through fear or alarm, he is I no longer acting as a free agent, and is no longer capable of the consent above referred to. And accordingly, in the cases cited in argument, the threatened violence, whether to persons or property, was of a character to produce in a reasonable man some degree of alarm or bodily fear. The degree of such alarm may vary in different cases. The essential matter is that it be of a nature and extent to unsettle the mind of the person on whom it operates, and take away from his acts that element of free, voluntary action which alone constitutes consent. Now, to apply this principle to the

(2) (1863), Le. & Ca. 288.   (3) (1863), Le. & Ca. at p.p 297, 298.

A present case, a threat or menace to execute a distress warrant is not necessarily of a character to excite either fear or alarm. On the other hand, the
   menace may be made with such gesture and demeanour, or with such
   unnecessarily violent acts, or under such circumstances of intimidation as to
   have that effect. And this should be decided by the jury. Now, in this
   case there was evidence very proper to be left to the jury to raise the above
B question. But the chairman left no such question to them, and directed
   them as a matter of law that the conduct of the prisoners (if believed)
   constituted a menace within the statute. Our judgment that this conviction
   cannot be sustained, is founded entirely on this ground."

   That decision is certainly an authority for the proposition that the question of
   whether the conduct of an accused constitutes a menace within the section is a
C matter to be left to the jury. It is expressly not a decision on any other ground.
   It is at least doubtful whether the headnote accurately reflects the judgment.
   WILDE, B., had used the words (4):

      " the threatened violence . . . was of a character to produce in a reasonable
   man some degree of alarm or bodily fear."

   The later words refer to the threat being " of a nature and extent to unsettle the
D mind of the person on whom it operates ", not to its actually having that effect
   and unsettling his mind. In *R.* v. *Tomlinson* (5), a case under s. 44 of the Larceny
   Act, 1861 (demanding money with menaces), LORD RUSSELL OF KILLOWEN, C.J.,
   cited *R.* v. *Walton and Ogden* (6) as follows (7):

      " There the prisoner had obtained money by threatening to execute a
   distress warrant, which he had no authority to do, and the jury were directed,
E as a matter of law, that the conduct of the prisoner constituted a menace
   within the statute. The Court for Crown Cases Reserved, however, quashed
   the conviction on the ground that it was not for the judge to do more than
   lay down the principle upon which the jury ought to proceed in considering
   whether the threat which had been used there was or was not within the
   statute, and that it was not for him to say as a matter of law that it did
F amount to a menace within the statute. The court further held that he
   ought to have told the jury that the question was whether or not the threat
   or words used, which were said to amount to a threat, was such as would
   naturally unsettle the mind of the person on whom it operates, and cause
   him to act in a way in which he would not otherwise act."

   At the end of his judgment, WILLS, J., said (8):
G
      " With regard to the doctrine that the threat must be of a nature to
   operate on a man of reasonably sound or ordinarily firm mind, I only desire
   to say that it ought, in my judgment, to receive a liberal construction in
   practice; otherwise great injustice may be done, for persons who are thus
   practised upon are not as a rule of average firmness; but I quite appreciate
   the fact that the threat must not be one that ought to influence nobody."
H
   In *R.* v. *Boyle and Merchant* (9), the Court of Criminal Appeal held that a
   threat to injure property may be a menace within s. 45 of the Act of 1861. In the
   course of a reserved judgment of the court, LORD READING, C.J., referred to
   R. v. *Walton and Ogden* (6) and to *R.* v. *Tomlinson* (5), and said (10):

      " We think it would be unwise to attempt to lay down any exhaustive
I definition of the words of the section. The degree of fear or alarm which a
   threat may be calculated to produce upon the mind of the person on whom
   it is intended to operate may vary in different cases and in different circumstances. A threat to injure a man's property may be more serious to him
   and have greater effect upon his mind than a threat of physical violence.

---

(4) (1863), Le. & Ca. at p. 298.
(5) [1895-99] All E.R. Rep. 879; [1895] 1 Q.B. 706.   (6) (1863), Le. & Ca. 288.
(7) [1895-99] All E.R. Rep. at p. 881; [1895] 1 Q.B. at p. 709.
(8) [1895] 1 Q.B. at p. 710.   (9) [1914-15] All E.R. Rep. 553; [1914] 3 K.B. 339.
      (10) [1914-15] All E.R. Rep. at p. 556; [1914] 3 K.B. at pp. 344, 345.

When there is evidence of such a threat as is calculated to operate upon the   A
mind of a person of ordinarily firm mind, and the jury have been properly
directed, it is for them to determine whether in fact the conduct of the
accused has brought them within the section, and whether in the particular
case the ' menace ' is established. If the threat is of such a character that
it is not calculated to deprive any person of reasonably sound and ordinarily
firm mind of the free and voluntary action of his mind, it would not be a   B
menace within the meaning of the section. In our judgment, when a man,
with intent to steal, threatens either to do violence to the person of another,
or to commit acts calculated to injure the property or character of another,
it is a menace within the meaning of the section."

In R. v. *Collister and Warhurst* (11), there is an ambiguity in the direction of the
trial judge as the case is reported and there is nothing in the judgment of the   C
Court of Criminal Appeal which clearly supports the appellant's contention.
RUSSELL ON CRIME (12th Edn. pp. 874-877) and other recognised text books
have not accepted the headnote to R. v. *Walton and Ogden* (12) as a correct
statement of the law.

In our opinion, the offence under s. 30 relates to the acts and the intent of
the accused. The intent to steal must be derived from the whole of the circum-   D
stances.   Words or conduct which would not intimidate or influence anyone to
respond to the demand would not be menaces and might negative any intent to
steal, but threats and conduct of such a nature and extent that the mind of an
ordinary person of normal stability and courage might be influenced or made
apprehensive so as to accede unwillingly to the demand would be sufficient for
a jury's consideration. The demand must be accompanied both by menaces   E
and by an intent to steal, and there is no intent to steal unless there is an intent
to take without the true consent of the person to whom the demand is made.
But there can be such an intent without that person being in fact deprived of
" that element of free, voluntary action which alone constitutes consent " in the
words used by WILDE, B., in R. v. *Walton and Ogden* (13).   There may be special
circumstances unknown to an accused which would make the threats innocuous   F
and unavailing for the accused's demand, but such circumstances would have no
bearing on the accused's state of mind and of his intention. If an accused knew
that what he threatened would have no effect on the victim it might be different.
We are of opinion that the learned judge stated the law correctly in the summing-
up and that the submission to the contrary fails.

The evidence of the appellant's conduct is of an unusual character. The   G
appellant must have thought that he could get £200 or £300 out of Mr. Chapman
by threatening to change his evidence, and he still persisted when he knew the
lost goods or the liability, therefore, were the subject of insurance. Mr. Chapman
himself was sufficiently affected to go to the police and inform them of the demand
of the appellant. We think that there was evidence properly to be left to the
jury's consideration and, therefore, the second ground of appeal fails also. There   H
was a further submission that the summing-up did not go far enough in explaining
that any threat must be such as to unsettle the mind of an ordinary person to
whom the threat and demand were made so as to take away his freedom of
action. These precise words perhaps were not used, but we are of opinion that
the tenor of the learned judge's direction was to that effect.

We dismiss the appeal against conviction. The application for leave to appeal   I
against sentence was not proceeded with and is refused.

Appeal dismissed.   Application refused.

Solicitors: *Wallace Bogan & Co.* (for the appellant);   *Director of Public
Prosecutions* (for the Crown).

[*Reported by* N. P. METCALFE, ESQ., *Barrister-at-Law.*]

---

(11) (1955), 39 Cr. App. Rep. 100.   (12) (1863), Le. & Ca. 288.
                    (13) (1863), Le. & Ca. at p. 298.

A

WOOLWORTHS, LTD. v. STIRLING HENRY, LTD.

[PRIVY COUNCIL (Viscount Dilhorne, Lord Hodson, Lord Guest, Lord Wilberforce and Sir Alfred North), July 5, 10, 11, 12, November 29, 1967.]

B
Privy Council—Australia—New South Wales—Appeal—Findings of fact— Trial judge sitting without jury—Whether appeal lay only on questions of law or to direct trial de novo—Supreme Court Procedure Act (N.S.W.) 1900-57, s. 5—Order in Council Regulating Appeals (N.S.W.) S.R. & O. 1909 No. 1521.

In an action by the respondents against the appellants the parties consented to trial by judge without a jury pursuant to s. 3 (1) of the Supreme
C
Court Procedure Act (N.S.W.) 1900-57. Section 5 (1) of the Act provided: "Subject to the provisions of this section the verdict or finding of any judge sitting without a jury on the trial or assessment of any issue of fact or amount of damages or compensation pursuant to this Act shall be of the like force and effect in all respects as the verdict or finding of a jury". Judgment was directed to be entered pursuant to s. 5 (2); and by that
D
enactment the entry had effect in all respects as the signing of judgment. On appeal the respondents contended that by virtue of s. 5 (1) the Board could not alter the findings of fact made by the trial judge (with the consequence that the appeal must be dismissed) but could only entertain questions of law and error.

Held: (i) by an Order in Council of 1909 (S.R. & O. 1909 No. 1521) an
E
appeal lay as of right from any judgment of the Supreme Court of New South Wales where the matter in dispute was of the value of £500 sterling or upwards, and the Board's power to hear the appeal could not be restricted by the provisions of an Act of the State's legislature dealing with procedure in the Supreme Court of New South Wales (see p. 83, letter G, post).

Riley v. *Nelson* ((1965), 39 A.L.J.R. 389) distinguished.
F
(ii) whilst it was generally desirable that the procedure provided in the Supreme Court Procedure Act, 1900-57 should first have been followed, it was not a condition precedent to the exercise of the unfettered right of appeal given by the Order in Council (see p. 83, letter I, post).

Appeal allowed.

G
[As to appeals to the Judicial Committee as of right from States of Australia, see 5 HALSBURY'S LAWS (3rd Edn.) 685, para. 1462; and for cases on the subject, see 8 DIGEST (Repl.) 830-832, *831-842*.]

Cases referred to:

Australia & New Zealand Bank, Ltd. v. *Ateliers de Constructions Electriques de Charleroi*, [1967] 1 A.C. 86; [1966] 2 W.L.R. 1216; Digest (Cont. Vol.
H
B) 8, *375a*.

Hazeldell, Ltd. v. *The Commonwealth*, (1924), 34 C.L.R. 442.

Riley v. *Nelson*, (1965), 39 A.L.J.R. 389.

Wagon Mound (No. 2), The, Overseas Tankship (U.K.), Ltd. v. *Miller S.S. Co. Pty., Ltd.*, [1966] 2 All E.R. 709; [1967] 1 A.C. 617; [1966] 3 W.L.R. 498; Digest (Cont. Vol. B) 555, *185b*.

I
Appeal.

This was an appeal by Woolworths, Ltd. from a judgment of the Supreme Court of New South Wales (COLLINS, J., sitting in the Commercial Causes jurisdiction without a jury) dated Feb. 15, 1966, entered in favour of the respondents, Stirling Henry, Ltd., against the appellants in the sum of $66,000. The action was brought by the respondents, Stirling Henry, Ltd., for damages for breach of contract. There was no appeal from the judgment to the Supreme Court of New South Wales such as was provided for in s. 5 of the Supreme Court Procedure Act, 1900-57, the relevant provisions of which are set out at p. 82, letter F,

E

post. The appeal to the Judicial Committee was brought by virtue of the A
jurisdiction conferred by the Order in Council regulating Appeals to [Her]
Majesty in Council from the Supreme Court of the State of New South Wales*.
The respondents cross-appealed. The matter is reported only on the right of
the Judicial Committee to review the facts on appeal. The respondents pleaded,
in their case on the appellant's appeal, that the finding of fact of a judge trying
an action in the Supreme Court of New South Wales without a jury was the B
the equivalent in all respects of the verdict of a jury, and that, therefore, the
findings of fact could not be reviewed by the Board†.

    C. L. D. Meares, Q.C. (of the New South Wales Bar) and *D. R. M. Henry*
for the appellants.

    G. J. Samuels, Q.C., and *K. R. Handley* (both of the New South Wales Bar) C
for the respondents.

    VISCOUNT DILHORNE having reviewed the facts and the factors
leading to the conclusion of the trial judge that the appellants had broken
the agreement by failing to offer market prices to the respondents, and having
stated that in the opinion of the Board there was no evidence that the appellants
had so failed and no proof of a breach of the agreement, continued: The respon- D
dents contended that the findings of fact of COLLINS, J., could not be reviewed in
this appeal and that the Board could only entertain questions of law and of error.
In support of this contention they relied on the provisions of the Supreme Court
Procedure Act, 1900-57, of New South Wales. Section 3 (1) of that Act reads
as follows:

    " In any action by consent of both parties the whole or any one or more E
    of the issues of fact in question may be tried, or the amount of any damages
    or compensation may be assessed by a judge without a jury."

It was pursuant to this provision that this action was tried by COLLINS, J.,
without a jury. Section 5 (1) is in the following terms:

    " Subject to the provisions of this section the verdict or finding of any F
    judge sitting without a jury on the trial or assessment of any issue of fact
    or amount of damages or compensation pursuant to this Act shall be of the
    like force and effect in all respects as the verdict or finding of a jury."

Prior to 1924, as ISAACS, A.C.J., pointed out in *Hazeldell, Ltd.* v. *The Common-* G
wealth (1), the Supreme Court could, where the action had been tried by a judge
without a jury pursuant to s. 3 (1), set aside the findings of the judge as wrong
in law or direct one of their number to sit alone and commence the whole proceedings de novo and decide on the facts again, but he said (2)

    " the one course that a reasonable man would think obvious, where
    the materials are present, the law prevents them from taking, namely to say
    what appears to them to be the proper conclusion upon the facts." H

No doubt it was as a result of these observations that the Act was amended in
1924. The words " Subject to the provisions of this section " were inserted in
sub-s. (1) and, inter alia, the following subsections were added:

---

    * Rule 2 of the Order in Council, so far as relevant, provides: Subject to the pro- I
visions of these rules, an appeal shall lie:—(a) as of right, from any final judgment of
the court, where the matter in dispute on the appeal amounts to or is of the value of
£500 sterling or upwards, or where the appeal involves, directly or indirectly, some
claim or question to or respecting property or some civil right amounting to or of the
value of £500 sterling or upwards; and . . ." The term " court " means the Full Court
or a single judge sitting as the Supreme Court of New South Wales; and the term
" appeal " means appeal to Her Majesty in Council.
    † Reliance was placed on *Riley* v. *Nelson* ((1965), 39 A.L.J.R. 389).
    (1) (1924), 34 C.L.R. 442 at p. 448.
    (2) (1924), 34 C.L.R. at p. 448.

A   " (2) Nothing in this section shall authorise judgment to be signed on the verdict or finding, but judgment may be directed to be entered as provided in this section, and the entry shall have the like force and effect in all respects as the signing of judgment.

" (3) The court may direct judgment to be entered for any or either party, and for that purpose the court may be held and its jurisdiction exercised by
B   the judge, and either at or after the trial.

" (5) Any judgment directed by the judge to be entered under the provisions of this section shall, unless there is an appeal as provided in this section against the judgment, have the same force and effect in all respects as a judgment of the court.

" (6) Any party may appeal to the court against any judgment so directed
C   by the judge to be entered.

" (7) The appeal shall be by way of rehearing, and on appeal the court shall
" (*a*) have the powers and duties of the judge as to amendment or otherwise, including the power to make findings of fact and to assess damages or compensation.

" (*b*) . . .
D   " (9) The court may on the appeal give any judgment and make any order which ought to have been given or made in the first instance . . ."

These amendments reduced considerably the effect of sub-s. (1). Provided that there was an appeal from the judgment directed to be entered, the case could be reviewed by the Supreme Court by way of re-hearing. In *Riley* v.
E   *Nelson* (3) it was held that where there had been an appeal to the Supreme Court under s. 5 on an appeal from the Supreme Court to the High Court of Australia, the High Court had the same powers as the Supreme Court, but unless there was such an appeal to the Supreme Court the findings of the trial judge could not be disturbed.

The respondents contended that, as there had been no appeal in the manner
F   provided for in s. 5, the findings of the trial judge could not be altered and consequently this appeal must be dismissed.

Their lordships are unable to accept this contention. Appeals to the Privy Council are governed by an Order in Council made in 1909 (4). That provides, inter alia, that an appeal lies as of right from any judgment of the Supreme Court of New South Wales where the matter in dispute in the appeal amounts to or is of the value of £500 sterling or upwards.
G   This is an appeal from a judgment entered pursuant to s. 5. The entry is to have the like force and effect as the signing of judgment (s. 5 (2)). Their lordships' power to hear the appeal cannot in their view be restricted by the provisions of an Act passed by the state legislature dealing with procedure in the Supreme Court of New South Wales.

While it is generally desirable that procedures such as those contained in the
H   Supreme Court Procedure Act should be followed before there is an appeal to the Privy Council, it is not the case that appeals from judgments based on findings of a judge sitting without a jury will not be entertained unless that is done. In *The Wagon Mound* (*No. 2*), *Overseas Tankship* (*U.K.*), *Ltd.* v. *Miller S.S. Co., Pty., Ltd.* (5) and *Australia & New Zealand Bank, Ltd.* v. *Ateliers de Constructions Electriques de Charleroi* (6) issues of fact were decided by the Board on appeal
I   from a judge sitting alone. In their lordships' opinion it cannot be regarded as a condition precedent to the exercise of the unfettered right of appeal given by the Order in Council that the procedure provided in the Supreme Court Procedure Act should first have been followed.

---

(3) (1965), 39 A.L.J.R. 389.
(4) S.R. & O. 1909 No. 1521.
(5) [1966] 2 All E.R. 709; [1967] 1 A.C. 617.
(6) [1967] 1 A.C. 86.

For the reasons stated their lordships are of the opinion that this appeal A
should be allowed with costs and it follows that the cross-appeal must be
dismissed with costs and they will humbly so advise Her Majesty.

Appeal allowed.

Solicitors: *Oswald Hickson, Collier & Co.* (for the appellants); *Linklaters &*
Paines (for the respondents).   B

[*Reported by* KATHLEEN J. H. O'BRIEN, *Barrister-at-Law.*]

DUNCAN *v.* LONDON BOROUGH OF LAMBETH.   C

[QUEEN'S BENCH DIVISION (Donaldson, J.), November 2, 10, 1967.]

Limitation of Action—When time begins to run—Actions of tort—Disability—
Infant—Child in care of local authority—Whether in custody of parent—
Limitation Act, 1939 (2 & 3 Geo. 6 c. 21), s. 22 (2) (b)—Law Reform (Limita-
tion of Actions &c.) Act, 1954 (2 & 3 Eliz. 2 c. 36), s. 2 (2).   D

London Local Government—Transfer of liabilities—Children's home transferred
from London County Council to London borough—Whether liability for
personal injury to child transferred—London Government Act 1963 (c. 33),
s. 84—London Authorities (Property etc.) Order 1964 (S.I. 1964 No. 1464)
art. 11.

The plaintiff was born in February, 1951, and in March, 1954, was   E
received into the care of the London County Council on the application
of her father, under the provisions of s. 1 of the Children Act, 1948. Thereafter she resided in a home provided by the council under s. 15 of the Act
of 1948, and was visited regularly there by her father, with whom she
sometimes spent week-ends. In October, 1958, she suffered an accident   F
alleged to be due to the negligence or breach of statutory duty of the
council employee who controlled the home. In September, 1962, the
plaintiff ceased to be in care and returned to live with her father. Under
s. 47 of the London Government Act 1963, the London Borough of Lambeth
assumed the functions of a children's authority for its own area under the
Children Act, 1948. Under s. 84* of the Act of 1963, the Minister made
the London Authorities (Property etc.) Order 1964, by art. 11† of which   G
any property held by the London County Council for the purposes of
specified functions and all liabilities attaching to the Council in respect
of the property were transferred to such body as should be agreed between
the " relevant councils ". By an agreement under art. 11 the school and
children's home in which the plaintiff had formerly been resident were
transferred to the London Borough of Lambeth. These premises were not   H
within the boundaries of the borough, nor were the places at which the
plaintiff's father had been resident at any material time. The school and
home continued to receive children in the care of authorities other than
the London Borough of Lambeth. On Aug. 12, 1965, the plaintiff, through
her father as next friend, began an action against the London Borough of
Lambeth claiming damages for personal injuries, the causes of action   I
pleaded being negligence and breach of statutory duty under s. 15 of the
Children Act, 1948.

Held: (i) the transfer to the London Borough of Lambeth under art. 11
of the Order of 1964 was a transfer of property and liabilities attaching to
the property, but was not a transfer of the functions of the children's

---

* Section 84, so far as material, is set out at p. 87, letter I, post.
† Article 11, so far as material, is set out at p. 88, letter E, post.

A   authority and did not transfer to the London Borough of Lambeth the alleged liabilities for negligence and breach of statutory duty on which the plaintiff relied (see p. 88, letter H, and p. 89, letter A, post).

(ii) the plaintiff, having been taken into the care of the London County Council under s. 1 of the Children Act, 1948, some 4½ years before the accident and having remained in care at the time of the accident was not in the

B   custody of a parent at that time for the purposes of s. 22 (2) (b)* of the Limitation Act, 1939, as amended by the Law Reform (Limitation of Actions etc.) Act, 1954, although her father was visiting her regularly; accordingly the plaintiff's claim was not statute barred (see p. 92, letter G, and p. 93, letter D, post).

C   [As to the extension of the time of limitation for bringing personal injury actions where the plaintiff is an infant, see 24 HALSBURY'S LAWS (3rd Edn.), 294, para. 583 text and note (a).

For the Limitation Act, 1939, s. 22, see 13 HALSBURY'S STATUTES (2nd Edn.), 1183; and for the London Government Act 1963, s. 84, see 43 HALSBURY'S STATUTES (2nd Edn.), 763.]

D   Cases referred to:

Brook v. Hoar, [1967] 3 All E,R. 395; [1967] 1 W.L.R. 1336.

Kirby v. Leather, [1965] 2 All E.R. 441; [1965] 2 Q.B. 367; [1965] 2 W.L.R. 1318; compromised, H.L., [1965] 3 All E.R. 927; [1965] 1 W.L.R. 1489; Digest (Cont. Vol. B) 498, 338Aa.

Woodward v. Mayor of Hastings, [1944] 2 All E.R. 119; [1944] K.B. 671;

E   171 L.T. 231; revsd. C.A., [1944] 2 All E.R. 565; [1945] K.B. 174; 114 L.J.K.B. 211; 172 L.T. 16; 109 J.P. 41; 38 Digest (Repl.) 113, 791.

Special Case.

In this action preliminary points of law were raised by a Special Case stated pursuant to an order made under R.S.C., Ord. 33, r. 3. The points for the determination of the court and the facts stated in Special Case are set out in

F   the judgment at p. 86, letters H to I, and letters A to H, post, respectively.

Marven Everett, Q.C., and A. Lipfriend for the plaintiff.
John D. Stocker, Q.C., and M. Stuart-Smith for the defendants.

Cur. adv. vult.

G   Nov. 10.   **DONALDSON, J.,** read the following judgment: In the month of October, 1958, a collision occurred between the plaintiff, then aged 7½, and a large bowl of hot soup, as a result of which she suffered severe injuries. At that time the plaintiff was living in a children's home maintained by the London County Council and the bowl of soup was being carried by a servant or agent of the council.

H   By a writ dated Aug. 12, 1965, the plaintiff, suing by her father and next friend, claimed damages for personal injuries, alleging that the accident was caused by the breach of statutory duty and/or negligence of the London County Council, its servant or agent. The London County Council having been by then dissolved, the plaintiff sued the London Borough of Lambeth as the statutory legatee of the relevant liabilities of the London County Council.

I   The matter comes before me for decision of two preliminary points of law stated in the form of a special case, pursuant to an order made under R.S.C., Ord. 33, r. 3. These two points are as follows: (1) whether the liability of the London County Council, if any, to the plaintiff was transferred to the defendant council as from Apr. 1, 1965, and (2) whether the plaintiff's cause of action, if any, is statute barred. Both these questions are of some interest and neither is easily answered.

The special case is in these terms (omitting the introductory words):

---

* Section 22, so far as material, is set out at p. 89, letters C to E, post.

" (1) The plaintiff herein was born on Feb. 18, 1951. By an order dated   A
May 8, 1961, in proceedings in connexion with the divorce by the next
friend of the plaintiff's mother, custody of the plaintiff was granted to the
next friend.

" (2) In about March, 1954, on the application of the next friend then
residing at 171, Southgate Road, N.1, the plaintiff was received into the
care of the London County Council under s. 1 of the Children Act, 1948,   B
and from about that date until about September, 1962, resided at Shirley
Oaks School, Croydon in the county of Surrey, a home provided and maintained by the London County Council under the provisions of the said Act.

" (3) At the said home the children resident thereat lived in separate
' cottages ' and in October, 1958, the plaintiff resided at Fern Cottage
which was under the control of one Gallagher, a servant or agent of the   C
London County Council.

" (4) In about October, 1958, the plaintiff, then about 7½ years old, collided
with the said servant or agent of the London County Council, who was then
carrying a large bowl of hot soup which was spilled over the plaintiff and she
suffered injuries.

" (5) The plaintiff remained in the care of the London County Council   D
until about September, 1962, when she left the said home, since which date
she has resided with Dennis Leslie Bernard Duncan her father and next
friend herein at 98, Seymour Avenue, London, N.17.

" (6) Throughout the time that the plaintiff was in the care of the London
County Council at the said home, both before and after the said accident,
the plaintiff was regularly visited by the next friend and spent most bank   E
holidays and some weekends with him.

" (7) None of the following places is within the area of the London Borough
of Lambeth as defined in the London Government Act 1963: (a) 171,
Southgate Road, N.1, (b) The Shirley Oaks School, Croydon, which is in the
area of the London Borough of Croydon, and (c) 98, Seymour Avenue,
London, N.17. Mr. Gallagher left the employment of the London County   F
Council in 1960 and has never been employed by the Borough of Lambeth.

" (8) The London Borough of Lambeth assumed the functions of a
children's authority under the Children Act, 1948, as respects the borough
pursuant to s. 47 of the London Government Act, 1963. The plaintiff has
at no time resided within the area of the London Borough of Lambeth.

" (9) Pursuant to art. 11 of the London Authorities (Property etc.)   G
Order 1964 (1), and an agreement made thereunder the Shirley Oaks School
was transferred to and vested in the London Borough of Lambeth.

" (10) There are now and have been since Apr. 1, 1965, children resident
at the Shirley Oaks School who are in the care of London boroughs other than
the London Borough of Lambeth pursuant to their respective functions
under the Children Act, 1948.   H

" (11) The writ in this action was issued on Aug. 12, 1965.

" (12) The question for the opinion of the court is whether the liability
of the London County Council if any, to the plaintiff for the injuries suffered
by her in the said accident in October, 1958, were transferred to the defendants as from Apr. 1, 1965, and whether the plaintiff's cause of action, if any,
is statute barred.   I

" (13) If the court shall be of the opinion either that the said liability
was not transferred to the defendants or that the said cause of action, if
any, is statute barred, then judgment to be given for the defendants with the
costs of the action to be agreed or taxed.

" (14) If the court shall be of the opinion that the said liability was
transferred to the defendants and that the plaintiff's cause of action, if any,

(1) S.I. 1964 No. 1464.

A   is not statute barred, then the action shall continue and that the costs of and relating to this special case be the costs in cause."

Has any liability of the London County Council been transferred to the defendants? Shirley Oaks School, Croydon, was maintained by the London County Council pursuant to the duty imposed on them by s. 15 of the Children Act, 1948, to provide, equip and maintain homes for the accommodation of children

B   in their care. The administration of the homes was subject to the Administration of Children's Homes Regulations, 1951 (2), made by the then Home Secretary, under powers contained in s. 15 (4) of the Act of 1948. Regulation 1 provided:

" The administering authority shall make arrangement for every home . . . to be conducted in such a manner and on such principles as are calculated

C   to secure the well being of the children in the home."

The plaintiff alleges negligence at common law and breaches of the statutory duty imposed by s. 15 of the Act of 1948 and by reg. 1 in the following terms (I quote from para. 5 of the statement of claim):

" The said accident was caused by the negligence and/or breach of statutory duty of the servants or agents of the London County Council and in con-

D   sequence thereof the plaintiff was injured and suffered damage. [Then particulars are given] The London County Council were negligent and/or in breach of their statutory duty in that their servants or agents: (a) spilled hot soup over the plaintiff; (b) failed to have sufficient regard to the fact that the children in the said cottage ran or might run along the corridors thereat; (c) carried hot soup along the said corridor when the said children

E   might run along the said corridor; (d) failed to carry the said soup in a closed container; (e) failed to carry the said soup on a trolley or some other similar vehicle; (f) failed to provide a serving hatch from the kitchen at the said cottage to the dining room; (g) the said Mr. Gallagher pulled the plaintiff's clothes from her immediately after the said accident thereby tearing the skin from her neck, arm and chest; (h) in the premises failed properly to

F   provide equip and maintain the said home contrary to s. 15 of the said Act; (i) in the premises failed to conduct the said school in such a manner as was calculated to secure the well being of the plaintiff contrary to reg. 1 of the Administration of Children's Homes Regulations, 1951."

For present purposes, I shall assume that the matters alleged from para. (a)

G   to para. (g) can amount to breaches of statutory duty as alleged in para. (h) and para. (i) although this may well be debatable. I must also assume that these allegations are made out and that the London County Council was according liable to the plaintiff. How then did this liability come to be transferred to the defendants? The statutory last will and testament of the London County Council is contained in the London Government Act 1963. Section 1 and s. 47 of, and

H   Sch. 1 to, the Act of 1963 created the new London Borough of Lambeth, having the functions under the Children Act, 1948, of a county borough council as respects the administrative area formerly comprising the Metropolitan Borough of Lambeth and part of the Metropolitan Borough of Wandsworth. Section 84 (1) empowered the Minister by order to make

" . . . such incidental, consequential, transitional or supplementary

I   provision as may appear to him—(a) to be necessary or proper for the general or any particular purposes of this Act or in consequence of any of the provisions thereof or for giving full effect thereto; . . ."

Section 84 (2) provided that:

" Any such order may in particular include provision—(a) with respect to the transfer and management or custody of property (whether real or personal) and the transfer of rights and liabilities . . ."

(2) S.I. 1951 No. 1217.

In quoting these sections, both here and elsewhere, I am omitting immaterial **A** words.

The Minister acting under the powers conferred by s. 84 of the Act of 1963 made the London Authorities (Property etc.) Order 1964, and the London Authorities (Children) Order 1965 (3).

The plaintiff contends that the liability relied on in the action was transferred from the London County Council to the defendants by art. 11 of the **B** order of 1964. The defendants contend primarily that it was transferred to the Greater London Council by art. 16 of that order. They do however reserve the argument that this case reveals a lacuna in the transfer arrangements. Such a lacuna, if it exists, could be filled by the Minister making a further order under s. 84 of the Act of 1963.

For present purposes all that I have to decide is whether or not the liability **C** was transferred to the defendants. The scheme of the order of 1964 involved a series of articles transferring various types of property with a sweeping-up provision headed " Residual transfer of property etc." contained in art. 16. Paragraph 1 of this article incorporates art. 12 (1) by reference and thus excludes from its operation any property or liability transferred by art. 11, the article on which the plaintiff relies. As the defendants do not have to satisfy me that **D** the liability was transferred to the Greater London Council but only that it was not transferred to them, it will suffice if I merely record that, if it was transferred to the Greater London Council, it was transferred under paras. (2) (*a*) and (*c*) of art. 16.

I therefore turn to art. 11. The operative part of the article relied on by the plaintiff is para. 2, which provides that: **E**

" Any property held or allocated by the London County Council . . . for the purposes of the specified functions and all liabilities attaching to such council in respect of any such property shall by virtue of this order be transferred to and vest in or attach to such body as may be agreed between the relevant councils."

F

The expression " specified functions " is defined so as to include the functions specified in s. 15 of the Children Act, 1948, and, as is stated in para. 9 of the Special Case, an agreement was made pursuant to art. 11, transferring Shirley Oaks School to the defendants from the London County Council. It is therefore quite clear that the school or home was effectively transferred to the defendants from the London County Council together with " all liabilities attaching to such **G** council in respect of any such property".

The problem thus resolves itself into one of whether the liability alleged by the plaintiff or, if on a true analysis there is more than one head of liability, whether any of the liabilities can be said to have attached to the London County Council in respect of the property transferred. The crucial point, as I see it, is that the property transferred is the school or home and not the function of a **H** children's authority under s. 15 of the Act of 1948 or under the Administration of Children's Homes Regulations, 1951, either in relation to that home or at all. In other words, art. 11 is concerned with the effecting of transfers of real property and chattels and of liabilities in respect of that property and those chattels. The liability or liabilities relied on by the plaintiff do not fall within that category. This conclusion is fatal to the plaintiff. **I**

It is arguable that art. 16 is similarly limited, bearing in mind that the order as a whole appears to be dealing with real property, chattels and funds; but the limiting words " property and all liabilities in respect of any such property " do not occur in art. 16. Had the plaintiff still been in the care of the London County Council immediately before its dissolution on Apr. 1, 1965, she could perhaps have relied on art. 6 and art. 16 of the order of 1965, which deals with

(3) S.I. 1965 No. 554.

A the transfer of functions and not property, but in fact she ceased to be in the care of the London County Council in September, 1962.

Accordingly, I conclude that the plaintiff has sued the wrong defendant.

Is the plaintiff's claim statute barred? The plaintiff's right of action accrued on a date in or about the month of October, 1958, when the soup was spilled. The damages claimed by her for negligence and breach of duty consist of damages

B in respect of personal injuries to herself. Accordingly the claim was barred in or about October, 1961, by the operation of s. 2 (1) of the Limitation Act, 1939, as amended by the Law Reform (Limitation of Actions, etc.) Act, 1954, unless the plaintiff can bring herself within the provisions of s. 22 of the Act of 1939 as amended by the Act of 1954.

Section 22 as amended, so far as is material to this case, provides as follows:

C " Extension of limitation period in case of disability. (1) If on the date when any right of action accrued for which a period of limitation is provided by this Act, the person to whom it accrued was under a disability, the action may be brought at any time before the expiration of three years . . . from the date when the person ceased to be under a disability . . . notwith-standing that the period of limitation has expired . . . (2) In the case of

D actions for damages for negligence . . . or breach of duty . . . where the damages claimed by the plaintiff for the negligence . . . or breach of duty consist of or include damages in respect of personal injuries to any person . . . (*b*) this section shall not apply unless the plaintiff proves that the person under the disability was not, at the time when the right of action accrued to him, in the custody of a parent."

E The wording of para. (*b*) above appears to have come from para. (*d*) from the proviso to s. 22 of the Act of 1939. That paragraph applied to claims against public authorities by plaintiffs under a disability, but is no longer applicable following the repeal of s. 21 of the Act of 1939 by s. 1 of the Act of 1954. The plaintiff is still under the disability of infancy. Accordingly she is entitled

F to bring this action, notwithstanding that the accident occurred over nine years ago, if, but only if, she proves that when the soup was spilled and the right of action accrued she was not in the custody of a parent.

The facts relevant to this issue are agreed and are stated in the Special Case but it may be useful to summarise them as follows: (i) The plaintiff was born on Feb. 18, 1951, and was about 7½ years old on the day of the accident; she was 14½ years old when the writ was issued. (ii) In about March, 1954, the

G plaintiff was received into the care of the London County Council under s. 1 of the Children Act, 1948, on the application of her father and remained in the care of the London County Council until about September, 1962. (iii) The accident happened in about October, 1958. (iv) Whilst the plaintiff was in the care of the London County Council, she lived at a home provided and maintained by the London County Council under the provisions of the Children Act, 1948,

H and was regularly visited by her father and spent most bank holidays and some weekends with him.

On these facts and the inferences to be drawn from them counsel for the plaintiff contended that the plaintiff was not in the custody of her father at the time of the accident, whilst counsel for the defendants contended that she was. Which is right depends primarily on the meaning to be attributed to the words

I " in the custody of a parent " in s. 22 of the Limitation Act, 1939.

So far as I know these words have only been considered in three reported cases. The first was *Woodward* v. *Mayor of Hastings* (4). The infant plaintiff lived at home with his mother and was involved in an accident when attending a day school. His father served as a writer in the Royal Navy, but came home on leave from time to time. HALLETT, J., said (5):

---

(4) [1944] 2 All E.R. 119; [1944] K.B. 671.
(5) [1944] K.B. at p. 676; [1944] 2 All E.R. at p. 122.

"I think that he was in the custody of his father, although the care of   A
his father, if one wants to draw a distinction, was limited to such care as the
father could give on leave and by postal and similar communications. Even
if I were satisfied that the infant plaintiff were not in the custody of his father,
he has certainly failed to satisfy me that he was not in the custody of his
mother. It seems to me plain that he was in the custody of his father or
mother, or, in other words, that he was in the custody of a parent."   B

The second case is *Kirby* v. *Leather* (6). The plaintiff, who was aged twenty-
four, suffered from the disability of unsoundness of mind as a result of a motor
accident. He spent some months in hospital and was then allowed to go home
because his mother was able to look after him. LORD DENNING, M.R., said (7):

"I can understand this proviso in relation to an infant, but I find it   C
difficult to understand it in relation to a grown man or woman over twenty-
one years of age. It is hardly ever appropriate to speak of a grown-up
person as being in the 'custody' of his or her parent. If he is of unsound mind,
he may be tended or cared for by his parent, but he is not in his parent's
custody. In any case, however, to my mind this young man, David Kirby,
was not in the custody of his mother at the time when the right of action   D
accrued to him. He was not in her custody on May 15, 1959, or at any time
on that day. He was on his own in the custody of no one. Shortly after the
accident he was in the care of the hospital authorities. His mother visited
him in hospital that evening, but he was not in her custody. The proviso
therefore does not apply."

DANCKWERTS, L.J., said (8):   E

"'The custody of a parent': what a strange conception that is in regard
to a capable young man of twenty-four years and over. This is such an
extraordinary provision that at times it seemed to me that the draftsman
must have been of unsound mind. Of course that is absurd. The same
provision has been repeated in the Law Reform (Limitation of Actions, &c.)
Act, 1954, and the Limitation Act 1963. We must strain ourselves to give   F
it a sensible meaning. The idea behind this provision is, I suppose, that
the parent in such a case will be capable of taking proceedings as the next
friend of the person in question. A man of adult age is not in the custody
of anybody—not even of his wife. The mere fact that his daily wants are
looked after by his mother, or that he is given a place in his father's business,
does not mean that he is in the custody of either parent, and did not mean   G
that, even in Victorian days. The phrase must have some other meaning.
The idea of custody of an infant is, of course, clear enough. Even in the
case of a ward of court, custody, or at least care and control, is given to
someone, and under the children legislation a local authority may take a
child into its care and control. In the case of an adult, however, even in the
case of a person of unsound mind, the phrase has no sensible meaning. More-   H
over, it would not be reasonable to suppose that a weak-minded person
living with his parents or parent was more able to begin legal proceedings
than a person of unsound mind in respect of whose property a receiver
had been appointed by the court or some such person living in a home for
mental patients. Such persons are well able to begin legal proceedings, even
for the purpose of divorcing an unfaithful wife or husband, under an order   I
of the Court of Protection. Giving the most careful and reasonable consideration that I can to the provisions of the material proviso, I can only
conclude that the draftsman must have had in mind the case of a harmless
imbecile or mongol, who could be expected to be actually in the custody of his

(6) [1965] 2 All E.R. 441; [1965] 2 Q.B. 367.
(7) [1965] 2 All E.R. at p. 443; [1965] 2 Q.B. at p. 383.
(8) [1965] 2 All E.R. at p. 445; [1965] 2 Q.B. at p. 385.

A   parents. That is plainly not the present case. Accordingly, on this point also I agree with the learned judge and LORD DENNING, M.R. I am clear that David Kirby was not, at the time when the right of action accrued to him, in the custody of a parent, in this case his widowed mother. I agree, therefore, that the plaintiff's claim is not barred by the statutes of limitations."

B   The last of the three cases is *Brook* v. *Hoar* (9). There the infant plaintiff was aged eighteen when he was injured in a motor accident. He earned his own living and was of so independent a disposition that his father said of him that from the age of seventeen he was a young lodger. For the plaintiff it was submitted that only a child who by reason of years or financial resources is dependent on parents with whom he is living, one or other of whom is in fact able to exercise C   control over him, is in the custody of a parent for the purposes of s. 22. For the defendant it was submitted that the law grants certain rights to and imposes certain obligations on the parent and infant which result collectively in placing the infant in the custody of a parent until his majority. MELFORD STEVENSON, J., said (10):

D   " I think that the rights and obligations of a parent towards his child are quite distinct from the concept of custody, which arises from the circumstances in which parents and child find themselves or from the order of a competent court. It is apparent from the language of s. 21 (2) (*b*) of the Act of 1954 that the possibility of an infant not being in the custody of a parent is contemplated, and I see no reason to assume that this possibility can only arise when both parents are dead.

E   " Counsel for the defendants has examined the disabilities from which an infant suffers during minority. For example, his incapacity to marry without his parents' consent, or the permission of a court, and his contractual incapacity and his inability to obtain a passport without parental permission; but I do not think that any of these disabilities support the view that there is a status or condition of custody from which the infant cannot escape F   until he is twenty-one. I, therefore, come to the conclusion that the question whether an infant is in the custody of a parent is a question of fact which has to be determined on the available evidence.

" I do not attempt any definition or even description of custody for the purpose of the subsection under consideration in a case where custody has not been granted to a parent by an order of a court, but I think that an G   essential characteristic of such custody is the right to control the infant's life, coupled with the capacity to exercise that control, whether arising from economic circumstances or otherwise. I am satisfied in this case that from the age of seventeen at the latest this plaintiff enjoyed complete economic independence from both his parents and freedom to live as and where he chose. I accept his father's description of him as ' a young lodger '. The H   circumstances attending his acquisition of the motor-cycle involved in the accident in my opinion demonstrates that no effective parental control over the plaintiff was in fact exercised. The father consulted the plaintiff's solicitor at a time when the plaintiff was immobilised in hospital and could not take any such step himself.

" It is also, I think, of some importance that when the father was invited I   to make an application for legal aid with a view to commencing an action as next friend of the plaintiff he was unwilling to do so, and neglected reminders from the plaintiff's solicitors as to the necessity of making an application for legal aid. It may therefore be said that the father failed to perform what might be regarded as a duty of a parent in whose custody an infant was. I therefore find that this plaintiff has proved that he was not

(9) [1967] 3 All E.R. 395.
(10) [1967] 3 All E.R. at p. 398.

at the date when the cause of action arose in the custody of a parent and   **A**
this claim is not statute barred."

The right of a parent to the custody of a child of the marriage is a familiar
concept in the context of matrimonial disputes. It may well be right that a parent
has custody of his or her children in this sense until the child reaches the age
of twenty-one, subject only to the vicissitudes of death, the orders of courts   **B**
and the resolutions of local authorities; see for example s. 2 of the Children
Act, 1948. In this sense the infant plaintiff was undoubtedly at all times in the
custody of her father. However I do not think that this is the sense in which
the word is used in s. 22 of the Limitation Act, 1939, for two reasons. First,
the meaning to be attributed to the word must be appropriate not only to the
disability of infancy but also to that of unsoundness of mind, and in the latter   **C**
context the primary meaning of the word has a quite different connotation,
namely, a deprivation of liberty. Secondly, it must be appropriate to parents
as defined by s. 31 of the Act of 1939, namely, father, mother, step-father,
step-mother, grandfather and grandmother; but certainly in the sense contended for by the defendants the word " custody " is quite inappropriate to
grandparents and step-parents. What then does the phrase mean? The mischief   **D**
at which the Limitation Acts are aimed is the harrassment of persons by stale
claims at the suit of those who have slept on their rights. The exceptions to the
general rule are designed to define the categories of claimants whose failure to
prosecute their claims cannot clearly be regarded as unreasonable in all the
circumstances. Prima facie a person suffering from a disability, including that
of infancy, comes within this category. An exception is then made in relation to   **E**
those who stand in a particular relationship to their parents as defined in the
Acts, such relationship being described as that of custody. In my judgment
that relationship exists and the person under a disability, the claimant, is in the
custody of a parent within the meaning of the section if at the relevant time,
the circumstances of the parent and of the claimant are such that in relation to
one another the average reasonable parent so circumstanced could be expected   **F**
to take such action to prosecute or assist in the prosecution of the claim as he
could be expected to take if the claim were his own.

I derive some slight additional support for this view of the meaning of the
phrase from the fact that the word " parent " is defined by reference to the
Fatal Accidents Act, 1846, whereunder actions may be brought by parents
for the benefit of children.
                                                                                    G
Applying this test, I am satisfied that the plaintiff was not in the custody
of her father at the time of the accident and it is not suggested that she is in the
custody of any other parent. The plaintiff had been taken into the care of the
London County Council some 4½ years before the accident and it follows from
the wording of s. 1 of the Children Act, 1948, that at this time and at all material
times thereafter the father was prevented by some circumstance from providing   **H**
for the proper accommodation, maintenance and upbringing of the plaintiff,
and that it was in the interests of the plaintiff that she should be taken into care.
The situation is thus radically different from that of a child who attends a
boarding school or who lives with relations while her parents are abroad. I
take full account of the fact that the father was a regular visitor of the child
as indicating affection for the child and a desire to keep in touch with her against   **I**
the day when he could make a home for her, but that day did not come for
over eight years. However, the average reasonable father who has been forced
to entrust the physical and moral welfare of his child to the care of a local
authority would I think be surprised to be told that it remained his duty to
safeguard the child's legal rights. This, if he thought about the matter at all,
he would regard as being a matter for action or at least advice to him by the
local authority. These matters must be judged by the standards of the times
and in 1954 the concept that the local authority knows best was by no means

A in its infancy, particularly in local authority circles. The London County Council and its successor authority should not complain if I ascribe a similar approach to the hypothetical reasonable parent.

Before leaving this point I should like to express the hope that the Law Commission will look at this aspect of the limitation of actions. I find the meaning of the phrase " custody of a parent " obscure in this context and I do not think **B** that I am alone in this. At the same time consideration might be given to the provision that the only relevant time is that when the right of action arose. Circumstances then may be radically different from those existing during the remainder of the relevant period of limitation. A child who is in the custody of his or her parents at the time when the right of action arose may well cease to be in such custody as a result of the death of the parents or otherwise before **C** any action on the child's behalf could reasonably be expected to have been taken. Again a child who is not in the custody of parents at the relevant time, as a result of a court order perhaps of an interim nature, may well be restored to their custody long before the period of limitation expires. In the circumstances it may be thought that a more appropriate provision would be that time should not run so long as the specified circumstances existed. This approach is not **D** without precedent in the context of limitation of actions; see s. 14 of the Limitation (Enemies and War Prisoners) Act, 1945.

It follows from my decision that the liability was not transferred to the defendants but that the claim, if any, is not statute barred: that in accordance with para. 13 of the Special Case judgment should be given for the defendants with costs. I am very loth to take any such action and will not do so if I have **E** any discretion in the matter. The court has ample power under R.S.C., Ord. 15, r. 6, to ensure that the rights of the infant plaintiff are not frustrated by technicalities whilst preserving the rights of the defendants. To that end the court could order the joinder of whatever may be the body, if any, to which the liabilities of the London County Council were transferred, and the defendants could then be dismissed from the action with an appropriate order as to costs. Good govern-**F** ment and administration require, and I am sure that the Minister and the local authorities would wish, that any right of the infant plaintiff against the London County Council should not be dissolved with the London County Council. The proper course for me to adopt, as I see the justice of the matter, is to adjourn this case to enable the defendant, the Greater London Council and any other local authority which may be concerned to agree on which is the proper defendant. **G** If this cannot be agreed, it would be open to the Minister to make a further order under s. 84 of the London Government Act 1963 to determine the matter. The action could then continue against the proper defendants, which might of course by reason of a new order under s. 84 be the present defendants.

Adjournment accordingly.

H   Solicitors: *Carters* (for the plaintiff); *Town Clerk, London Borough of Lambeth* (for the defendants).

[*Reported by* MARY COLTON, *Barrister-at-Law.*]

A

R. v. SELVEY.

[VACATIONAL COURT OF APPEAL, CRIMINAL DIVISION (Lord Denning, M.R., Widgery and MacKenna, JJ.), September 27, November 10, 1967.]

Criminal Law—Evidence—Character of accused—Imputation on character of prosecution witness—Discretion—Whether cross-examination of accused as to previous convictions should be allowed—Whether general rule to exclude such evidence where defence necessarily involved such imputations—Criminal Evidence Act, 1898 (61 & 62 Vict. c. 36), s. 1, proviso (f) (ii).

The appellant was charged with buggery with a young man. The young man had complained to the police shortly after the alleged offence had been committed. At the trial of the appellant his defence proceeded on the basis that the young man was a male prostitute soliciting the appellant, an innocent man. The appellant gave evidence that the complainant had offered for money to have sexual connection with the appellant, and that the complainant said that he had sexual connection with another man that day for money. The trial judge at his own instance ruled, in the absence of the jury, that the appellant could be cross-examined as to his previous convictions involving indecency. These convictions were put to the appellant in cross-examination. He refused either to admit or to deny them. In summing-up the trial judge treated that as tantamount to an admission. On appeal against conviction,

Held: (i) an accused could be cross-examined as to previous convictions not only when the nature or conduct of his defence unnecessarily involved imputations on the character of the witnesses for the prosecution, but also when it necessarily involved such imputations, and there was no general rule that in the latter type of case the discretion of the court under s. 1 proviso (f) (ii)* of the Criminal Evidence Act, 1898, should be exercised to exclude the evidence of previous convictions; in the present case the trial judge had rightly exercised his discretion, for the jury were entitled, having regard to the defence raised, to know the credit of the appellant whose evidence impugned the complainant's character (see p. 97, letters D and H, and p. 98, letters C and E, post).

R. v. Hudson ([1912] 2 K.B. 464) applied.

Dictum in *R. v. Flynn* ([1961] 3 All E.R. at p. 63) not applied and decision explained.

Dictum of DEVLIN, J., in *R. v. Cook* ([1959] 2 All E.R. at p. 101) applied.

(ii) the jury were entitled to treat the appellant's attitude in cross-examination on his previous convictions as tantamount to an admission; and there has been no miscarriage of justice (see p. 98, letter F, post).

Appeal dismissed.

[As to cross-examination of defendant as to character, see 10 HALSBURY'S LAWS (3rd Edn.) 450, para. 828, text and note (*b*); and for cases on the subject, see 14 DIGEST (Repl.) 511-513, *4942-4968*, and 515-518, *4987-5016.*

For the Criminal Evidence Act, 1898, s. 1, see 9 HALSBURY'S STATUTES (2nd Edn.) 613.]

Cases referred to:
R. v. *Clark*, [1955] 3 All E.R. 29; [1955] 2 Q.B. 469; [1955] 3 W.L.R. 313; 119 J.P. 531; 39 Cr. App. Rep. 120; 14 Digest (Repl.) 517, *5010.*
R. v. *Cook*, [1959] 2 All E.R. 97; [1959] 2 Q.B. 340; [1959] 2 W.L.R. 616; 123 J.P. 271; 43 Cr. App. Rep. 138; Digest (Cont. Vol. A) 374, *4942a.*

B

C

D

E

F

G

H

I

* Section 1, proviso (*f*), so far as material, provides: " A person charged and called as a witness in pursuance of this Act shall not be asked, and if asked shall not be required to answer, any question tending to show that he has committed or been convicted of . . . any offence other than that wherewith he is then charged . . . unless . . . (ii) . . . the nature or conduct of the defence is such as to involve imputations on the character of the prosecutor or the witnesses for the prosecution; . . ."

Affirmed. H.L. [1968] 2 All E.R. 497.

A   *R.* v. *Flynn,* [1961] 3 All E.R. 58; [1963] 1 Q.B. 729; [1961] 3 W.L.R. 907;
         125 J.P. 539; 45 Cr. App. Rep. 286; Digest (Cont. Vol. A) 376, *5016a.*
     R. v. *Hudson,* [1912] 2 K.B. 464; 81 L.J.K.B. 861; 107 L.T. 31; 76 J.P. 421;
         7 Cr. App. Rep. 256; 14 Digest (Repl.) 512, *4961.*
     R. v. *Jenkins,* (1945), 114 L.J.K.B. 425; 173 L.T. 311; 110 J.P. 86; 31 Cr.
         App. Rep. 1; 14 Digest (Repl.) 512, *4950.*
B   *R.* v. *Ondras,* [1962] Crim. L.R. 543.
     R. v. *Sargvon,* [1967] Crim. L.R. 479.
     Ward v. *James,* [1965] 1 All E.R. 563; [1966] 1 Q.B. 273; [1965] 2 W.L.R.
         455; Digest (Cont. Vol. B) 219, *783a.*

     Appeal.
     This was an appeal by Wilfred George Selvey against his conviction at Notting-
C   ham Assizes on Mar. 21, 1967, before STABLE, J., and a jury of buggery. He
     was sentenced to four years' imprisonment. The main grounds of appeal were
     that the appellant's previous convictions were wrongly allowed to be put to him
     in evidence and, also that the previous convictions were put in evidence without
     having been proved. The facts are set out in the judgment of the court.

D   *R. A. D. Payne* for the appellant.
     J. J. Deave for the Crown.

                                                              Cur. adv. vult.

     Nov. 10.   **LORD DENNING, M.R.,** read the following judgment of the
     court: The facts are distasteful. It happened in Lincoln in January, 1967.
E   On a Thursday at about half-past three in the afternoon, a young man aged
     twenty-one came out of a lodging-house. He stopped a policeman on a bike. He
     told the policeman that a man in the lodging-house had forced him on to the
     bed and interfered sexually with him. Two police officers went with the young
     man to the lodging-house. They found a man of fifty in bed. It was the
     appellant. The young man said: " That's him " and went out of the room and
F   waited outside. The police officers told the appellant of the complaint and
     cautioned him. According to the police officers, the appellant replied: " Well,
     you've got to prove it, haven't you? " According to the appellant, he said:
     " I don't know what you are talking about." The police officers asked him to
     come to the station. He got up and went with them. The young man was a
     little ahead of them. The appellant asked the police officers: " Is that the
G   fellow who is making the complaint? " The police officer said " Yes ". The
     appellant said: " I've never seen him before in my life ", but almost at once
     he retracted saying: " Oh yes, I have, I've seen him once." At the police
     station the appellant refused to answer any questions. He said: " I'm not
     saying anything. I am not going to help you blokes. I am thinking about
     myself and that is all I am saying." The police officers went back to the appel-
H   lant's room. They found two photographs of naked men. They were under
     some books on a table near the bed. The police officers also arranged for the
     young man to be medically examined. A doctor examined him at twenty to
     seven that evening. He found clear indications that the young man had been
     sexually assaulted within a few hours previously. That was ample corroboration
     of the young man's story. So the appellant was charged. At the committal
I   proceedings he learnt for the first time that the police had found the photographs
     and of the medical findings. He was sent to trial at assizes.
     Before the trial the police officers looked up the appellant's record. It was
     not, of course, admissible in evidence, but it told its own story. He had been
     convicted a number of times of theft and dishonesty and had served sentences of
     imprisonment. These were of no particular relevance. He had other convic-
     tions which showed him to be a homosexual. There were five convictions for
     indecency. In 1956 he had indecently assaulted two small boys of six and eight
     years of age in a cinema and was sentenced to twelve months. In 1960 he

indecently assaulted another small boy of eight in a cinema and was sentenced **A**
to six months.   A month or two later he indecently assaulted a boy of eleven in
a cinema and was sentenced to six months.   In the next year, 1961, he enticed
boys into a public lavatory, and was convicted of persistently soliciting for
immoral purposes and was sentenced to two years.   In 1964 he offered two
fifteen-year-old boys ten shillings to go for a walk with him.   He was convicted
of persistently importuning male persons, and was sentenced to six months.   **B**
None of these convictions was, however, admissible in evidence unless he did
something to let them in.   Before the trial, as we have said, the appellant refused
to say anything; but at the trial he had to meet a formidable case against him.
There was not only the evidence of the young man himself, but also the photographs and the medical evidence.   He did it by turning the tables on the young
man, alleging that he was the offending party.   As to the photographs, the   **C**
appellant said that he had never had the photographs in his room; leaving
the jury to infer that they had been " planted " in his room by someone else.
His counsel suggested to the young man in cross-examination that he had brought
them: but the young man denied it.   As to the medical evidence, the appellant
said that the young man must have been sexually interfered with by someone
else that afternoon, but not by him, the appellant.   He said that the young man   **D**
asked him for £1 and told the appellant that " he was prepared to go on the
bed.   He told me that he had already been with a person and that he had given
him £1 ", meaning that " he had earned a pound by going with a fellow and having
sexual connections ".   The appellant said he rejected the offer, saying: " No,
I am not interested."

After the appellant had given evidence, the judge turned to him and said: **E**

" You are asking the jury, are you not, to disbelieve this young man
because, as you say, he told you he had been b . . . . that day and b . . . . by
somebody else?   (A) That is correct.   (Q) You are asking the jury to
disbelieve him because he is that sort of young man?   (A) Yes."

Thereupon the judge turned to counsel for the prosecution and said: " Mr. Deave,   **F**
perhaps we might have a discussion in the absence of the jury."

The jury retired: and after discussion the judge ruled that the appellant could
be cross-examined on his previous convictions on sexual matters.   The appellant
was cross-examined on them.   Each one of them was put to him, but he refused
to admit or deny them.   He merely said: " I don't know ", or " I am not
speaking ".   When the judge came to sum up, he treated the appellant's attitude   **G**
as tantamount to an admission.   He said to the jury:

" You would have been in a perfectly hopeless position, if you had to
try this case with the idea that that young man was a sort of male prostitute,
carrying about filthy photographs on him, and the man in the dock was a
man, so far as you knew, of unblemished character.   It is obvious you
would have had a perfectly false picture before you."   **H**

After a half-an-hour's retirement the jury found him guilty and the judge in
passing sentence said: " While you are about you are a public menace to young
people.   You must go to prison for four years."   Now with the leave of the
single judge, the appellant appeals to this court.

The principal point raised in the appeal is that the judge ought to have shut   **I**
out these previous convictions.   Here he not only permitted the cross-examination.   He himself suggested it.   This, it is said, was wrong.   In support of this
argument, much reliance was placed on the case in 1961 of *R.* v. *Flynn* (1) when
it was said that where

" . . . the very nature of the defence necessarily involves an imputation
against a prosecution witness or witnesses, the discretion should, in the

---

(1) [1961] 3 All E.R. 58 at p. 63; [1963] 1 Q.B. 729 at p. 737.

A   opinion of this court, be as a general rule exercised in favour of the accused, that is to say, the evidence as to his character or criminal record should be excluded."

Now we quite agree that, if there be any " general rule " such as to control the exercise of the judge's discretion, then it would apply in this case. It is plain that the nature of the defence necessarily involved imputations against the young man who was a witness for the prosecution. The defence of the appellant made out that the young man was a homosexual who carried indecent photographs about with him, a young man who had previously that afternoon allowed himself to be sexually interfered with for money, and was offering to allow the appellant also to interfere with him sexually, again for money. It was necessary for the appellant to make these imputations in order to make good his defence. It would be hopeless for him simply to deny the charge. No jury would have accepted his blank denial unless he put forward something to account for the photographs and the medical evidence. He had to describe all that happened in the room that afternoon. It was all one occasion: and he, in his defence, was entitled to give his account of it. We are of opinion, however, that there is no " general rule " such as to control the judge's discretion. It would be an unwarranted gloss on the words of the statute which gives the judge a discretion to permit such cross-examination when

" the nature or conduct of the defence is such as to involve imputations on the character of the prosecutor or the witnesses for the prosecution ",

see s. 1, proviso (*f*) (ii) of the Criminal Evidence Act, 1898. Soon after the statute was passed, some of the judges expressed the opinion that the accused was not to be cross-examined except when he gratuitously or unnecessarily attacked the character of a witness for the prosecution. It was suggested that there was a " general rule " that cross-examination was not permissible when the defence necessarily involved imputations against the prosecution witnesses. In 1912, however, in the leading case of *R.* v. *Hudson* (2) the full court consisting of LORD ALVERSTONE, C.J., BRAY, A.T., LAWRENCE, PICKFORD and AVORY, JJ., rejected the suggestion of any such " general rule ". They said that (3)

" . . . the words of the section ' unless the nature or conduct of the defence is such as to involve imputations ' etc. must receive their ordinary and natural interpretation, and it is not legitimate to qualify them by adding or inserting the words ' unnecessarily,' or ' unjustifiably,' or ' for purposes other than that of developing the defence,' or other similar words."

It follows that the accused can be cross-examined as to his record, not only when the nature or conduct of the defence *unnecessarily* involves imputations on the character of the witnesses for the prosecution, but also when it *necessarily* involves them, as indeed it did in *R.* v. *Hudson* (2) itself. A bank book had been stolen. It was found in Hudson's pocket. His defence was that the bank book had been stolen by two of the witnesses for the prosecution, and that they had " planted " it on him by putting it into his pocket. That defence necessarily involved imputations on the witnesses for the prosecution. Nevertheless, it was held that, by making the allegations against them, he was liable to be cross-examined as to his previous convictions: and that he was properly so cross-examined. We cannot think that in *R.* v. *Flynn* (4), the court meant to resurrect the " general rule " which was so decisively rejected in *R.* v. *Hudson* (2). It cannot have intended to fetter the discretion of the judge by a " general rule ", seeing that by the statute it is unfettered. This has been pointed out repeatedly, particularly by LORD PARKER, C.J., in *R.* v. *Ondras* (5) and by DIPLOCK, L.J.,

(2) [1912] 2 K.B. 464.
(3) [1912] 2 K.B. at pp. 470, 471.
(4) [1961] 3 All E.R. 58; [1963] 1 Q.B. 729.
(5) [1962] Crim. L.R. 543.

in R. v. *Sargvon* (6).   The most that the court can have done in R. v. *Flynn* (7)   **A**
—and the most that it was entitled to do—was to point out the considerations
which the judge should bear in mind in exercising the discretion (see *Ward* v.
James (8)).   We think that the correct proposition to be deduced from R. v.
Flynn (7) is this.   The fact that the attack on a prosecution witness is necessary
to the proper conduct of the defence is a consideration to which the judge will
have regard when exercising his discretion; but it is not the only consideration.   **B**
Amother important consideration is that which was given by DEVLIN, J., giving
the judgment of the full court in R. v. *Cook* (9):

" If there is a real issue about the conduct of an important witness which
the jury will have inevitably have to settle in order to arrive at their verdict,
then as SINGLETON, J., put it in R. v. *Jenkins* (10) and LORD GODDARD, C.J.,
repeated in R. v. *Clark* (11), the jury is entitled to know the credit of the   **C**
man on whose evidence the witness's character is being impugned."

In the present case we think that that consideration mentioned by DEVLIN, J.,
was of overriding importance.   When the appellant made these grave imputations against the young man—alleging that he was a male prostitute soliciting
the innocent appellant—it would have been most unfair that the jury should be
left in the dark about the appellant's own character.   It is all very well to lay   **D**
down rules to shield an accused; but they should not be carried so far as to
aid a guilty man to escape.   The trial of a criminal case must be fair to both
sides—to the prosecution as well as to the defence—and fairness to the prosecution
means that, if the accused man makes imputations against the character of the
witnesses for the prosecution, he can be cross-examined about his own character.
We hold, therefore, that the judge was quite right to allow the appellant to be   **E**
cross-examined about his previous convictions for indecency.   When he was
cross-examined, however, the appellant refused to admit or deny his convictions.
When they were put to him, he said: " I don't know " or " I'm not speaking ".
It is said that thereupon the prosecution ought to have asked for an adjournment
to prove his convictions strictly, or alternatively, the judge ought to have warned
the jury that they had not been proved.   We do not think so.   The jury were   **F**
quite entitled to treat his attitude as tantamount to an admission.   We go
further.   Even if the judge ought to have warned the jury about it, we are clear
that there was no miscarriage of justice.   No one can doubt that the appellant
had in fact been convicted of these previous offences.   When the appellant said:
" I don't know ", the judge intervened in robust fashion: " Nonsense, you know
perfectly well."   After the jury had returned their verdict, and the convictions   **G**
were read out once again, he did not dispute them.   We would not allow him to
escape by taking up the obstinate attitude " I'm not speaking ".   If there was
any irregularity, we would apply the proviso and affirm the conviction.   We
would dismiss this appeal.

Appeal dismissed.   The court certified under s. 1 of the Administration of Justice   **H**
Act, 1960, that a point of law of general public importance was involved, viz. (1) if
the making of the imputation is necessary for the proper development of the defence,
is cross-examination permitted under s. 1, proviso (f) (ii) of the Criminal Evidence
Act, 1898?   If so, (2) is there a general rule as to the exercise of the judge's discretion as
stated in R. v. Flynn (7)?   *But the court refused leave to appeal to the House of Lords.*

Solicitors: *Registrar of Criminal Appeals* (for the appellant); H. B. *Hodgson*,   **I**
Town Clerk, Lincoln (for the Crown).

[*Reported by* N. P. METCALFE, ESQ., *Barrister-at-Law*.]

(6) [1967] Crim. L.R. 479.   (7) [1961] 3 All E.R. 58; [1963] 1 Q.B. 729.
(8) [1965] 1 All E.R. 563 at p. 571; [1966] 1 Q.B. 273 at p. 295.
(9) [1959] 2 All E.R. 97 at p. 101; [1959] 2 Q.B. 340 at p. 348.
(10) [1945] 114 L.J.K.B. 425 at p. 431.
(11) [1955] 3 All E.R. 29 at p. 34; [1955] 2 Q.B. 469 at p. 478.

A   R. *v.* AUBREY-FLETCHER, *Ex parte* ROSS-MUNRO.

[QUEEN'S BENCH DIVISION (Lord Parker, C.J., Salmon, L.J., and Widgery, J.),
        November 7, 8, 10, 1967.]

Extradition—Committal—Offence for which accused committed same as that for
    which accused was surrendered by foreign state—Depositions not be to
    examined but evidence of deponents taken—Whether magistrate entitled to
B   *hear further evidence—Extradition Act, 1870 (33 & 34 Vict. c. 52), s. 19.*

The applicant was surrendered by France pursuant to extradition
proceedings and was brought before the respondent metropolitan magistrate
with a view to committal. Six offences of forgery were alleged in the warrant,
and the charges on which committal was sought were the same charges.
The metropolitan magistrate did not examine the depositions, but heard the
C   testimony of the witnesses who had made the depositions. This testimony
differed somewhat from the evidence contained in the depositions, and the
magistrate intimated that he did not think that a sufficiently strong case
had been made out for committal. The prosecution obtained an adjournment
and then tendered further evidence from a banker in Zurich to the effect that
the alleged forged documents had led to a large sum of money being handed
D   to the applicant. Objection was taken to this evidence, reliance being placed
on s. 19* of the Extradition Act, 1870. On application for mandamus to
examine (in effect) the depositions and for prohibition from receiving or considering evidence relating to facts other than the facts on which the surrender
of the applicant was grounded,

E   **Held:** (i) s. 19 of the Extradition Act, 1870, was not directed to procedure
or evidence but to jurisdiction; accordingly, provided that the crimes with
which the applicant was charged were the offences for which he was surrendered, he could be committed for trial in accordance with the ordinary procedure and laws of England and an order for prohibition to exclude the further
evidence tendered would be refused (see p. 102, letters A, D, G and I, and p.
F   103, letter E, post).

(ii) the metropolitan magistrate was right, in the present case, as the
offences charged were the same as those on which the accused had been
surrendered, in not looking at the depositions; accordingly an order of
mandamus would be refused (see p. 102, letter H, and p. 103, letters D and E,
post).

G   *R. v. Corrigan* ([1931] 1 K.B. 527) distinguished.

[As to the extradition of offenders from foreign states, see 16 HALSBURY'S
LAWS (3rd Edn.) 582, 583, paras. 1208, 1209, 1210; and for cases on the subject,
see 24 DIGEST (Repl.) 1009, *150-153.*

For the Extradition Act, 1870, s. 19, see 9 HALSBURY'S STATUTES (2nd Edn.)
887.]

H   Case referred to:

R. v. Corrigan, [1931] 1 K.B. 527; 100 L.J.K.B. 55; 144 L.T. 187; 32 Cr.
        App. Rep. 106; 24 Digest (Repl.) 1009, *152.*

Motion for mandamus and prohibition.

The applicant, James Alistair Ross-Munro, applied by motion for an order of
mandamus directed to JOHN AUBREY-FLETCHER, ESQ., the metropolitan magis-
I   trate before whom the committal proceedings were being conducted, requiring
him to examine the documents relating to the extradition of the applicant with
a view to ascertaining the facts on which his surrender was grounded, and for
orders prohibiting the said metropolitan magistrate from proceeding with the
said proceedings until he had examined those documents in order to ascertain
the facts on which the applicant's surrender was grounded, and from receiving
and/or considering evidence relating to facts other than the facts on which the
surrender of the applicant was grounded. The facts are set out in the judgment
of LORD PARKER, C.J.

---

* Section 19 is set out at p. 101, letter A, post.

Sebag Shaw, Q.C., and *R. D. L. Du Cann* for the applicant.   A
Paul Wrightson, Q.C., and *H. C. Pownall* for the respondent.

LORD PARKER, C.J.: In these proceedings counsel moves on behalf of one James Alastair Ross-Munro, first for an order of mandamus directed to JOHN AUBREY-FLETCHER, ESQ., the metropolitan magistrate, requiring him to examine the documents relating to the extradition of the applicant with a view B to ascertaining the facts on which his surrender was grounded; secondly for an order prohibiting the metropolitan magistrate from proceeding with the committal proceedings until he has examined those documents, and also from receiving and from considering evidence relating to facts other than the facts on which the surrender of the applicant was grounded. Let me say at once that the real relief as I understand the point is the last which I have mentioned, namely a C prohibition from receiving or considering evidence relating to facts other than the facts on which the surrender of the applicant was grounded.

The short facts here were that extradition proceedings were commenced for the return to this country of the applicant from France. The warrant alleged six offences in two batches of three, in each case that he forged a valuable security, namely a cable transfer; secondly that with intent to defraud he uttered that D forged document; and thirdly with intent to defraud he caused the sum involved to be transferred on a forged instrument knowing the same to be forged. The warrant was supported by depositions, which disclose that a company called S.A. Industrial Suppliers, Ltd. from time to time issued request transfers to their bankers to transfer money to companies abroad. Those transfers had to be signed by a director and the secretary of the company, and the request transfers E would have attached to them invoices so that the director and secretary could see what the documents related to before signing the request transfer. The evidence in the depositions was that two transfers of very large sums of money, in each case over £55,000, had been prepared by the applicant, who was head of the accounts department, the transfers had been signed in blank by the director and purported later to have been signed by the secretary. The secretary, looking F at the signature said that the signature appeared to be his, but for various reasons in regard to the manner in which the request transfer had been drawn up, he felt that it was not his signature. The case, therefore, was one of opportunity and grave suspicion in that the applicant, within a day or two of this, absented himself for a holiday and never returned. It was on that sort of evidence that the foreign state, France, surrendered the applicant to this country. He was then G brought before the metropolitan magistrate with a view to committal. The matter came before the magistrate on Sept. 2 and 11 and again on Sept. 18, 1967. The charges on which the magistrate was asked to commit were the very same charges that were the subject of the extradition proceedings, and I assume that the warrant in the extradition proceedings was before the magistrate. Evidence was then called in the form of witnesses who had deposed in the extradition proceedings, and H having heard that evidence, which varied somewhat from the evidence in the depositions, the magistrate indicated that he did not think that a sufficiently strong case had been made out for committal. At that point the prosecution asked for an adjournment, and, when the matter came before the magistrate again on Oct. 17, the prosecution tendered further evidence. It is unnecessary to go through it in detail, but one of the witnesses whom they desired to call was a banker I from Zurich who gave evidence that these cable transfers had resulted in money coming forward to an account at his bank in the name of Viscotal, and that the applicant in person turned up with what I take it purported to be general authority of Viscotal, and was handed personally many hundreds of thousands of dollars representing the proceeds of these cable transfers. Objection was at once taken by the applicant's representative, and in fact as the witness was only here for a short time, his evidence was given de bene esse.

The point involved here is a novel one in so far as no previous decision appears

A to have been given on the point. It depends on the true construction of s. 19 of
the Extradition Act, 1870; that section reads:

" Where, in pursuance of any arragement with a foreign state, any person
accused or convicted of any crime which, if committed in England, would
be one of the crimes described in Sch. 1 to this Act is surrendered by that
foreign state, such person shall not, until he has been restored or had an
B opportunity of returning to such foreign state, be triable or tried for any
offence committed prior to the surrender in any part of Her Majesty's
dominions other than such of the said crimes as may be proved by the facts
on which the surrender is grounded."

It is convenient at once to state that that section is complementary to s. 3 (2)
C of the Act of 1870 which deals with the case of a fugitive criminal, that is the
foreigner, when he is surrendered by this country to the foreign state, and there
it is provided that he

" . . . shall not be surrendered to a foreign state unless provision is made by
the law of that state, or by arrangement that the fugitive criminal shall not,
until he has been restored or had an opportunity of returning to Her
D Majesty's dominions, be detained or tried in that foreign state for any offence
committed prior to his surrender other than the extradition crime proved by
the facts on which the surrender is grounded."

The argument for the applicant is put very concisely by counsel in this form:
that the person concerned who is surrendered to this country cannot be committed
and put in peril of conviction on any facts other than those put forward to secure
E his surrender. Be it observed that the argument is not that all the magistrate
can do is to look at the evidence in the depositions and the surrender documents,
and to decide whether to commit or not on that evidence alone. Indeed that would
be quite an untenable proposition, if only because the legislation would have
stated that if that were the intention. The way it is put, however, is this, that
one must look at the surrender documents, not merely the warrant, but the
F depositions, to see what the " facts " were that the evidence and the depositions
dealt with. It is conceded that once one finds these facts, it is right and proper
to supplement the evidence by calling further evidence so long as it relates to
these facts. A typical illustration would be a corroborative witness, but where,
as here, the evidence sought to be put in is as to facts which were not specifically
dealt with in the depositions, then it is said that evidence is inadmissible.

G As I said, this is a novel point and for my part, if it be right, it has an alarming
consequence. It would mean that not only is this a restriction on the procedure
on committal, a restriction on the receiving of evidence, but indeed logically it
would affect the trial, because no evidence would be admissible at the trial unless
it was in regard to facts raised in the surrender documents. Another alarming
consequence would be that if, when the person concerned arrives in this country
H after being surrendered by the foreign state, he is arrested, cautioned and
questioned by a police officer, evidence of what he said, whether for him or against
him, would be quite inadmissible. In my judgment Parliament cannot have
intended any such thing in this section. Two things are quite clear, as it seems to
me, one that this section is designed to prevent a man from being tried after his
surrender for a crime other than that for which he has been extradited. That
I is putting the matter quite generally, because as the case of *R.* v. *Corrigan*, (1)
shows, it may be that a committal can take place for, let me say, fraudulent
conversion when the crime alleged in the warrant was false pretences or vice-
versa. Broadly speaking, however, the object is to ascertain the type of crime
for which he can be tried in this country after surrender. The words which have
to be construed are words intended to define and describe that crime for which
he can be committed and tried.

(1) [1931] 1 K.B. 527.

Secondly, as it seems to me, the section is not in any way intended to interfere A
with the ordinary procedures and laws of evidence in this country whether in
committal proceedings or at the trial. Indeed, it is to be observed that this is
the only section in the Extradition Act, 1870, which is dealing with surrender by
a foreign state of someone to this country. The Act of 1870, apart from the
section, is dealing with what are referred to as fugitive criminals who are defined
as persons accused or convicted of an extradition crime committed within the B
jurisdiction of a foreign state, and who are in, or are suspected of being in, some
part of Her Majesty's dominions. All the sections of the Act of 1870 except
s. 19 are dealing with that position, and lay down an elaborate code of procedure
dealing with what is to happen in this country in deciding whether this country
will extradite a fugitive criminal. Section 19, as I have said, is alone dealing with
the converse position, and is something which by treaty would clearly have to C
be provided for to set out the reciprocal position. That being so, and bearing
in mind that this is defining a particular crime for which he can be charged,
it seems to me that the words must be read, if capable of being read, as merely
meaning that provided the crime for which he is charged is based on the same
allegations as the crime set out in the warrant, once he is in this country he can
be dealt with on committal and on trial according to the ordinary procedure and D
laws of this country. It is, I am quite satisfied, in no sense intended to be a
restriction, for instance, on the evidence which can be called in this country,
whether it be in the committal proceedings or in the trial itself.

One comes, therefore, to the important words which have to be construed,
namely that he may only be tried in this country " for such of the said crimes as
may be proved by the facts on which the surrender is grounded ". Admittedly E
they are not easy words to construe; in the first place " proved " cannot mean
" proved " as ordinarily understood. Proof will only arise if and when the
accused is committed, and the matter is dealt with by a jury. " Proved " cannot
there mean proved in the ordinary sense of the word. In the second place " facts "
are clearly not the same as " evidence ". In my judgment the words, however,
are capable of being read and should be read as meaning such of the crimes as may F
be disclosed by the facts alleged in the extradition proceedings. Here the facts
that were alleged were that this man had forged these two cable transfers, had
uttered these two cable transfers, had caused money to be transferred on those
cable transfers, and the depositions described the manner in which it was alleged
that these facts were carried out. In those circumstances I, for my part, can see
no reason whatsoever why further evidence in support of those facts and those G
crimes cannot be called before the magistrate in the committal proceedings, or
indeed at the trial itself.

I would only add that in my judgment the magistrate must, as I see it, have at
any rate the warrant in the extradition proceedings before him, because he must
be certain that he is not being asked to commit for a crime other than that on
which the extradition proceedings were founded. Save in regard to that, however, H
I think that the magistrate was quite right in refusing to look at the depositions;
they are not evidence in our courts, it must be for the prosecution to call, as they
did, the witnesses who deposed, and in my judgment the magistrate was quite
right in agreeing to admit the further evidence which the prosecution desired to
call. Accordingly I would dismiss this application.   I

SALMON, L.J.: I entirely agree. In my judgment s. 19 of the Extradition
Act, 1870, is in no way concerned with procedure but solely with jurisdiction.
It does not seek to limit or prescribe the evidence which may be called at a criminal
trial. It is concerned solely with the type of crime for which our courts have the
power to try a man who has been extradited to this country. The clear object of
the section is to prevent, for example, a man who has been surrendered on a
warrant charging him with forgery, being tried in this country for a murder that

A he is alleged to have committed before the surrender. When, as in this case, the man who has been surrendered is being charged in this country with the very offences in respect of which the warrant was issued, and for the trial of which he was surrendered by the foreign country, it seems to me that it would be putting a very strained, artificial and indeed ridiculous construction on s. 19, to interpret it in the sense suggested by counsel for the applicant. It might mean that these

B courts would have no power to try the man for the very crime in respect of which he was extradited, or at any rate that most material evidence might be excluded. I entirely agree with LORD PARKER, C.J., that the last few words of the section are not very easy to construe. Whatever may be their exact meaning, it seems to me fairly plain that when, as in the present case, a man has been surrendered for forgery, the fact on which the decision of a foreign court to surrender him is

C grounded must be that he dishonestly made or altered the document in question. Obviously, I think, the foreign court decided that he should be surrendered so that those facts should be investigated in our courts to see whether he was guilty of the type of offence with which he was charged. It may well be that in cases such as *R.* v. *Corrigan*, (2) where a man is charged after extradition with an offence which is different from the offence in the warrant, it will be necessary to look at

D the surrender documents to see whether the facts on which the surrender was grounded were such that they might constitute the offence with which it is proposed to charge him. Where, however, as here, the charge which is preferred in this country is the very charge in respect of which he has been extradited, the very charge which the foreign court has surrendered him to this country to meet, it becomes entirely unnecessary in my view even to consider the surrender

E documents. I agree that this application should be dismissed.

WIDGERY, J.: I agree with both judgments and have nothing to add.

Application refused.

Leave to appeal to the House of Lords refused, but the court certified under
F *s. 1 of the Administration of Justice Act, 1960, that a point of law of general public importance was involved, viz., " whether in committal proceedings in respect of the charge on which the applicant was surrendered it was open to the prosecution to lead evidence of facts other than those deposed to in the surrender documents ".*

Solicitors: *Kingsley, Napley & Co.* (for the applicant); *Director of Public Prosecutions* (for the respondent).
G

[*Reported by* BRIAN POCOCK, ESQ., *Barrister-at-Law.*]

H

I

(2) [1931] 1 K.B. 527.

A

UNITED DOMINIONS TRUST (COMMERCIAL), LTD.
v. EAGLE AIRCRAFT SERVICES, LTD.
UNITED DOMINIONS TRUST (COMMERCIAL), LTD.
v. EAGLE AVIATION, LTD.

[COURT OF APPEAL, CIVIL DIVISION (Lord Denning, M.R., Diplock and Edmund B
Davies, L.JJ.), October 24, 25, 26, 1967.]

*Hire-Purchase—Recourse agreement—Obligation to re-purchase goods if hire-
purchase agreement terminated—Implied term that party required to repurchase should be so required within a reasonable time after termination
of the hire-purchase agreement—Hire-purchase of aircraft—Three months a
reasonable period after termination of hire-purchase agreement within which* C
*to call for re-purchase—Call to re-purchase made subsequently—No obliga-
tion to re-purchase—Unilateral contracts and synallagmatic* contracts
distinguished.*

The defendants sold two aircraft to the plaintiff finance company, who
let them, on a hire-purchase agreement, to O., Ltd., the price being payable
by monthly instalments over a period of 2½ years. By a recourse agreement D
the defendants agreed with the plaintiff company that " if for any reason
whatsoever the hire-purchase agreement should be terminated by either
party before the whole amount payable thereunder had been paid [the
defendants] would, when called on to so do, forthwith re-purchase from
[the plaintiff company] the aircraft at a price equal to the balance outstanding of the hire-purchase price, plus certain expenses. By one of four E
provisos, the plaintiffs (whether or not they called on the defendants to
re-purchase the aircraft) were " to notify [the defendants] within seven days
of each and every default made by O., Ltd. in payment of hire rentals ".
O., Ltd. defaulted on their instalments in August, 1960, but the plaintiff
company did not notify the defendants until October, 1960. In November,
1960, the defendants wrote to the plaintiff company claiming that as a result F
they were under no obligation to re-purchase the aircraft. In December,
1960, a compulsory winding-up order was made against O., Ltd., and the
plaintiff company gave them notice terminating the hire-purchase agreement. In May, 1961, the plaintiff company called on the defendants to repurchase the aircraft which the defendants refused to do. The plaintiff G
company claimed damages.

Held: the defendants were not liable to re-purchase the aircraft nor
liable in damages for not having re-purchased them, because—

(i) the agreement to re-purchase was a unilateral contract* which did not
become binding on both sides until certain conditions precedent had been
fulfilled, or (per DIPLOCK, L.J.) until certain events had occurred (see p. 107,
letter D, p. 110, letters A and C, and p. 111, letter I, post); and H

(ii) it was to be implied in the recourse agreement that any call on the
defendants to re-purchase should be made within a reasonable time after
the termination of the hire-purchase agreement, and (per LORD DENNING,
M.R. and EDMUND DAVIES, L.J.) this implied the term was a condition
precedent; in the circumstances a reasonable time was three months, and,
as longer than that had elapsed before the plaintiff company called on the I
defendants to re-purchase, no obligation on the defendants to re-purchase
the aircraft arose (see p. 107, letter I, p. 108, letter E, p. 111, letters A
and B, and p. 112, letters C and F, post).

---

* For the distinction between unilateral and synallagmatic contracts, see p. 108,
letters H and I, and p. 109, letters A, C and D, post. The meanings attributed to the
word " synallagmatic " in the Oxford Dictionary include " reciprocally binding "; cf.,
also, p. 108, note (8), post.

A   *Hong Kong Fir Shipping Co., Ltd.* v. *Kawasaki Kisen Kaisha, Ltd.,*
([1962] 1 All E.R. 474) considered.
Appeal allowed.

[As to guarantees of hire-purchase agreements, see 19 HALSBURY'S LAWS
(3rd Edn.) 525, para. 844.]

B Cases referred to:
Carlill v. *Carbolic Smoke Ball Co.,* [1891-94] All E.R. Rep. 127; [1893]
1 Q.B. 256; 62 L.J.Q.B. 257; 67 L.T. 837; 57 J.P. 325; 12 Digest
(Repl.) 59, *323.*
Finch v. *Underwood,* (1876), 2 Ch.D. 310; 45 L.J.Ch. 522; 34 L.T. 779;
31 Digest (Repl.) 78, *2320.*
C *Hare* v. *Nicoll,* [1966] 1 All E.R. 285; [1966] 2 Q.B. 130; [1966] 2 W.L.R.
411; Digest (Cont. Vol. B) 665, *300a.*
Hong Kong Fir Shipping Co., Ltd. v. *Kawasaki Kisen Kaisha, Ltd.,* [1962]
1 All E.R. 474; [1962] 2 Q.B. 26; [1962] 2 W.L.R. 474; 41 Digest
(Repl.) 363, *1553.*
Jones v. *Gibbons,* (1853), 8 Exch. 920; 22 L.J.Ex. 347; 155 E.R. 1626; 12
D   Digest (Repl.) 343, *2658.*
West Country Cleaners (Falmouth), Ltd. v. *Saly,* [1966] 3 All E.R. 210; [1966]
1 W.L.R. 1485; Digest (Cont. Vol. B) 476, *2288a.*
Weston v. *Collins,* (1865), 34 L.J.Ch. 353; 12 L.T. 4; 29 J.P. 409; 40 Digest
(Repl.) 315, *2601.*

Appeal.
E   This was an appeal by the defendants from a judgment of WIDGERY, J.,
dated Mar. 17, 1967, whereby it was adjudged that there should be judgment
for the plaintiffs against the defendants in two consolidated actions for damages
for breach of a recourse agreement, the damages to be assessed by a master.

Desmond Ackner, Q.C., and *P. E. Webster, Q.C.,* for the defendants.
F   *Leonard Lewis* for the plaintiffs.

LORD DENNING, M.R.: This is a hire-purchase case but, oddly enough,
it does not concern motor cars. It concerns aircraft. Otherwise it is of the usual
pattern. In 1959 the defendants, Eagle Aircraft Services, Ltd. (to whom I
refer as " Eagle "), owned a Viking aircraft. Orion Airways, Ltd. (to whom
I refer as " Orion ") wanted to acquire it; but they had not got the money
G   to pay cash for it. So they acquired it on hire-purchase terms through the
the plaintiffs, a finance company called United Dominions Trust (Commercial),
Ltd. (to whom I refer as " U.D.T."). Eagle sold the aircraft to U.D.T. for
£20,000. U.D.T. let it out on hire-purchase to Orion. The total hire-purchase
price was £22,231, payable by monthly instalments over 2½ years. U.D.T.
asked Eagle to sign a recourse agreement; and Eagle did so in the form of a
H   repurchase agreement. The repurchase agreement was signed on June 8, 1959.
Under it Eagle agreed with U.D.T.

" that if for any reason whatsoever the said hire-purchase agreement
should be terminated by either party before the whole amount payable
thereunder ... has been paid, we will, when called upon to do so, forthwith
I   repurchase from you the said aircraft ... at a price equal to the balance
outstanding [of the hire-purchase price], plus any expenses reasonably
incurred by you in recovering possession of the same ... "

There were four provisos:

"... provided always (a) that when we have thus repurchased the aircraft you will if called upon to do so at our expense assign to us the benefit
of any rights still subsisting against the hirer under the said agreement."
I omit (b). Then (c) is a clause about insurance:

" That at all times while our liability to repurchase the said aircraft   A
remains outstanding you will keep insured . . . the said aircraft."

Proviso (d) is important:

" That you [i.e., U.D.T.] will (whether or not you call upon us to repurchase the said aircraft) notifiy us within seven days of each and every
default made by Orion Airways, Ltd. in payment of hire rentals."   B

All went well in the first year. Orion operated the Viking and kept up the
monthly instalments. It was a summer trade. The Vikings were used during
the summer on charter flights for holidays and tours; but during the winter
they were out of service being overhauled. In 1960, Orion got into difficulties.
They could not pay the May and June instalments on the due dates. U.D.T.
allowed them time to pay. Orion agreed to make double payments in July   C
and August, 1960; but they did not keep their promise. They paid the July
instalment late. They never paid the August and September instalments. They
got more and more into arrear. Now comes the important point. U.D.T. did not
tell Eagle of those defaults at that time. They did not notify Eagle within
seven days as required by proviso (d) of the agreement. It was not until Oct. 4,
1960, that U.D.T. told Eagle about the defaults, that is, some two months later. D
Eagle were upset about this. On Oct. 19, 1960, they complained that they should
have been advised as soon as the default occurred. They telephoned showing
that they were very upset about it. Eventually, on Nov. 28, 1960, Eagle wrote
to U.D.T. saying:

" We have now been advised by [our solicitors] that, as you have failed
to notify us in accordance with sub-cl. 1 (d) . . . within seven days of each   E
and every default by Orion Airways, Ltd. in payment of hire rentals, we
are released from our obligations under this agreement."

That was a clear claim that they were under no obligation to repurchase·
U.D.T. did not contradict them. They replied merely saying that the letter
was receiving their attention; but it never did receive attention, or, at any rate,   F
they never wrote further to Eagle about it. Things got worse with Orion. On
Dec. 5, 1960, a compulsory winding-up order was made against them. On Dec.
15, 1960, U.D.T. gave notice to Orion terminating the hire-purchase agreement.
That is an important date because, under the repurchase agreement, on the
termination, U.D.T. were entitled, subject to proviso (d), to call on Eagle to
repurchase. U.D.T. did not tell Eagle that they had terminated the hire-purchase   G
agreement. They did not at that stage call on Eagle to repurchase. Nearly five
months went by before they told Eagle about it. Meanwhile, after termination
of the hire-purchase agreement, U.D.T. tried to find the aircraft. They found
it towards the end of December, 1960, at Hurn Airport. It was in the possession
of a company called Airwork Services, Ltd. It was being dismantled and overhauled. Airwork Services, Ltd. claimed a lien on it. They said that some £3,000   H
was owing to them for work done on this aircraft. U.D.T. entered into negotiations with Airwork Services, Ltd. about this lien. In April, 1961, they agreed
to pay off the amount due. In addition, they ordered further work to be done
by Airwork Services, Ltd. so as to make the aircraft airworthy. U.D.T. did
not tell Eagle anything about these negotiations. Eventually, however, on
May 4, 1961, at a meeting, U.D.T. called on Eagle to repurchase. Eagle refused.   I
They said that they were not under any obligation to repurchase. U.D.T. then
tried to sell the aircraft; but they did not succeed, because the aircraft was of
little use. A great deal of work had been done on it, nevertheless it was sold for
scrap value. U.D.T. now sue Eagle for damages.

Eagle took two points. First, that U.D.T. had not notified them of Orion's
default within seven days, as required by proviso (d). Second, that U.D.T.
had not called on them to repurchase within a reasonable time. WIDGERY, J.,
rejected both those contentions. The case seems to have been argued before

A him on the footing that the repurchase undertaking was a bilateral contract with obligations binding on each side. So he applied the usual tests to see whether a term of the contract was a " condition " or a " warranty ", or the more familiar test nowadays (and, I think, the better test) whether the breach went to the root of the contract so as to discharge the other party; see *Hong Kong Fir Shipping Co., Ltd.* v. *Kawasaki Kisen Kaisha, Ltd.* (1), per Diplock,

B L.J. The judge, applying those tests, held, first, that the obligation to notify within seven days, although expressed as a " proviso ", was not truly a " condition " and that a failure to comply with it did not discharge Eagle from their obligation to repurchase; and, secondly, that there was an implied term that U.D.T. would call on Eagle within a reasonable time to repurchase, but that, nevertheless, time was not of the essence of the matter and that Eagle ought

C to have given notice to make it so; and that, as Eagle had not given such notice, U.D.T. were entitled still to call on Eagle to repurchase.

Before us the case has been argued quite differently, or, at all events, with different emphasis. It has been shown, quite correctly, that the agreement to repurchase was not an ordinary bilateral contract. It was a unilateral contract of a kind which does not become binding on both sides until a condition precedent

D has been performed. It is like a lease in which the lessee is given an option to renew the lease for a further term. Such a lessee usually covenants to keep the premises in repair during the term; and he is given an option to renew if he gives notice six months before the end of the term and duly performs all the covenants to repair. In order to exercise the option, the lessee must give the notice in the specified time and he must fulfil the covenants to repair accord-

E ing to their terms. He is not entitled to excuse himself by saying that the want of repair is trifling. The cases start with the judgment of Lord Westbury, L.C., in *Weston* v. *Collins* (2), and go on to the judgment of James, L.J., in *Finch* v. *Underwood* (3) (which was followed in *Hare* v. *Nicoll* (4)), and *West Country Cleaners (Falmouth), Ltd.* v. *Saly* (5). In point of legal analysis, the grant of an option in such cases is an irrevocable offer (being supported by consideration

F so that it cannot be revoked). In order to be turned into a binding contract, the offer must be accepted in exact compliance with its terms. The acceptance must correspond with the offer.

Applying that principle here, Eagle made an irrevocable offer to repurchase the aircraft provided that certain conditions precedent were fulfilled. First, the hire-purchase agreement must be terminated. That was done on Dec. 15, 1960.

G Secondly, it was said that notification of default was a condition precedent. Proviso (d) said:

"That you will (whether or not you call upon us to repurchase the said aircraft) notify us within seven days of each and every default made by [Orion] in payment of hire rentals."

H I am inclined to think that that was a condition precedent rather like a covenant to repair in a lease which is both an obligation during the term and also a condition precedent to a renewal. This provisio (d) was not the sort of thing from which damages would ordinarily flow, but Eagle inserted it for their protection so that they could take commercial measures to try and neutralise the effects of any default. If it was a condition precedent, it clearly was not fulfilled. That

I was the ground on which Eagle, on Nov. 28, 1960, claimed to be discharged from their obligations. I think that it was probably a good ground. I do not, however, put my judgment on this second condition. I think that there was a third condition precedent, namely, that U.D.T. must call on Eagle to repurchase *within a reasonable time* after the termination of the hire-purchase agreement on Dec. 15, 1960. Counsel for U.D.T. disputed the third condition. He said that the words

---

(1) [1962] 1 All E.R. 474 at pp. 487, 488, 489; [1962] 2 Q.B. 26 at pp. 69, 72.
(2) (1865), 12 L.T. 4.   (3) (1876), 2 Ch.D. 310.
(4) [1966] 1 All E.R. 285; [1966] 2 Q.B. 130.   (5) [1966] 3 All E.R. 210.

"within a reasonable time" were not to be implied. I am quite satisfied, as A
the judge was, that they should be. It would be absurd to suppose that U.D.T.
could wait for twelve months or more, and let the aircraft go to rack and ruin,
and afterwards still call on Eagle to repurchase. They must call on Eagle within
a reasonable time.

Counsel for U.D.T. next said that Eagle ought to have given notice to U.D.T.
before calling off the deal. He cited *Jones* v. *Gibbons* (6); but that was an B
entirely different case on the words delivery " as required ". It has no application here. If U.D.T. wished to call on Eagle to repurchase, they ought to have
done so within a reasonable time. There was no obligation on Eagle to give any
notice to U.D.T. Eagle could not be expected to give any notice when they
did not know that U.D.T. had terminated the hiring.

Finally, counsel for U.D.T. argued that a reasonable time had not expired. C
U.D.T. were entitled, he said, to ascertain the amount of the lien, and to discharge it, and to put the aircraft into an airworthy condition. A reasonable
time, he said, would not expire until all that was done. The judge considered
all those circumstances, and held that three months was a reasonable time.
I am inclined to think that, in assessing a reasonable time, the discharge of the
lien was not a relevant circumstance, because, after all, Eagle had to pay any D
expenses reasonably incurred in recovering possession. Howsoever that may be,
a reasonable time has always got to be considered in regard to the actual
circumstances. I am quite satisfied that the judge was right in holding that
a reasonable time would be three months, and not more. Nearly five months
expired here from Dec. 15, 1960, to May 4, 1961. That was far too long. It
follows that the condition precedent has not been fulfilled. So U.D.T. cannot E
call on Eagle to repurchase.

This case was not put before the judge in its true legal setting. I think it
plain that the obligation to repurchase never came into being unless the conditions precedent were fulfilled. One of them at least was not fulfilled. Eagle
are not liable. Similarly with the other aircraft, for it is exactly the same position.
I would allow the appeal and give judgment for the defendants.   F

DIPLOCK, L.J.: In *Hong Kong Fir Shipping Co., Ltd.* v. *Kawaski Kisen
Kaisha, Ltd.* (7), a decision of this court on which the judge relied, I was careful
to restrict my own observations to synallagmatic contracts. The insertion of
this qualifying adjective was widely thought to be a typical example of gratuitous
philological exhibitionism; but the present appeal does turn on the difference G
in legal character between contracts which are synallagmatic (a term which I
prefer to bilateral, for there may be more than two parties), and contracts which
are not synallagmatic but only unilateral, an expression which, like synallagmatic, I have borrowed from French law (Code Civil, art. 1102 and art. 1103) (8).
Under contracts of the former kind, each party undertakes to the other party
to do or to refrain from doing something, and, in the event of his failure to perform H
his undertaking, the law provides the other party with a remedy. The remedy of
the other party may be limited to recovering monetary compensation for any
loss which he has sustained as a result of the failure, without relieving him from
his own obligation to do that which he himself has undertaken to do and has
not yet done, or to continue to refrain from doing that which he himself has undertaken to refrain from doing. It may, in addition, entitle him, if he so elects, I
to be released from any further obligation to do or to refrain from doing anything. The *Hong Kong Fir* case (7) was concerned with the principles applicable
in determining what kind of failure by one party to a synallagmatic contract

---

(6) (1853), 8 Exch. 920.   (7) [1962] 1 All E.R. 474; [1962] 2 Q.B. 26.
(8) The terms of these provide: " Art. 1102. Le contrat est *synallagmatique* ou
bilatéral lorsque les contractants s'obligent réciproquement les uns envers les autres.
" Art. 1103. Il est *unilatéral* lorsque'une ou plusieurs personnes sont obligées envers
une ou plusieurs autres, sans que de la part de ces dernières il y ait d'engagement."

A to perform his undertaking releases the other party from an obligation, which ex hypothesi has already come into existence, to continue to perform the undertaking given by him in the contract. The mutual obligations of parties to a synallagmatic contract may be subject to conditions precedent, that is to say, they may not arise until a described event has occurred; but the event must not be one which one party can prevent from occurring, for if it is, it leaves

B that party free to decide whether or not he will enter into any obligations to the other party at all. The obligations under the contract lack that mutuality which is an essential characteristic of a synallagmatic contract.

Under contracts which are only unilateral—which I have elsewhere described as " if " contracts—one party, whom I will call " the promisor ", undertakes to do or to refrain from doing something on his part if another party, " the

C promisee ", does or refrains from doing something, but the promisee does not himself undertake to do or to refrain from doing that thing. The commonest contracts of this kind in English law are options for good consideration to buy or to sell or to grant or take a lease, competitions for prizes, and such contracts as that discussed in *Carlill* v. *Carbolic Smoke Ball Co.* (9). A unilateral contract does not give rise to any immediate obligation on the part of either party to do

D or to refrain from doing anything except possibly an obligation on the part of the promisor to refrain from putting it out of his power to perform his undertaking in the future. This apart, a unilateral contract may never give rise to any obligation on the part of the promisor; it will only do so on the occurrence of the event specified in the contract, viz., the doing (or refraining from doing) by the promisee of a particular thing. It never gives rise, however, to any

E obligation on the promisee to bring about the event by doing or refraining from doing that particular thing. Indeed, a unilateral contract of itself never gives rise to any obligation on the promisee to do or to refrain from doing anything. In its simplest form (e.g., " If you pay the entrance fee and win the race, I will pay you £100 "), no obligations on the part of the promisee result from it at all. But in its more complex and more usual form, as in an option,

F the promisor's undertaking may be to enter into a synallagmatic contract with the promisee on the occurance of the event specified in the unilateral contract, and in that case the event so specified must be, or at least include, the communication by the promisee to the promisor of the promisee's acceptance of his obligations under the synallagmatic contract. By entering into the subsequent synallagmatic contract on the occurrence of the specified event, the promisor

G discharges his obligation under the unilateral contract and accepts new obligations under the synallagmatic contract. Any obligations of the promisee arise, not out of the unilateral contract, but out of the subsequent synallagmatic contract into which he was not obliged to enter but has chosen to do so.

Two consequences follow from this. The first is that there is no room for any inquiry whether any act done by the promisee in purported performance of a

H unilateral contract amounts to a breach of warranty or a breach of condition on his part, for he is under no obligation to do or to refrain from doing any act at all. The second is that, as respects the promisor, the initial inquiry is whether the event, which under the unilateral contract gives rise to obligations on the part of the promisor, has occurred. To that inquiry the answer can only be a simple " Yes " or " No ". The event must be identified by its description in

I the unilateral contract; but if what has occurred does not comply with that description, there is an end of the matter. It is not for the court to ascribe any different consequences to non-compliance with one part of the description of the event than to any other part if the parties by their contract have not done so. See the cases about options: *Weston* v. *Collins* (10); *Hare* v. *Nicoll*, (11).

(9) [1891-94] All E.R. Rep. 127; [1893] 1 Q.B. 256.
(10) (1865), 12 L.T. 4.
(11) [1966] 1 All E.R. 285; [1966] 2 Q.B. 130.

For the inquiry here is: " What have the parties agreed to do? "—not " What   A
are the consequences of their having failed to do what they have agreed to do? "
as it was in the *Hong Kong Fir* case (12). Such an inquiry cannot arise under
a unilateral contract unless and until the event giving rise to the promisor's
obligations has occurred.

While, for simplicity in analysing the relevant differences in legal character,
I have spoken of synallagmatic and unilateral or " if " *contracts*, it would be   B
more accurate to speak of synallagmatic and unilateral obligations, for obligations of these two different kinds are often contained in a single agreement,
as where a lease contains an option for renewal.

In the present case the obligation, for breach of which the defendants
(" Eagle ") have been sued by the plaintiffs (" U.D.T."), is an obligation to
enter into a synallagmatic contract with U.D.T. to buy the aircraft at a specified   C
price. This is clearly unilateral because the description of the event on which
this obligation arises includes U.D.T.'s calling on Eagle to buy the aircraft. The
description of the event further includes the prior determination of the hire-
purchase agreement between U.D.T. and Orion Airways, Ltd. (" Orion ") before
the whole amount payable thereunder for rent for the whole period of hire has
been paid. Eagle's undertaking to buy the aircraft on the occurrence of this   D
event is expressed to be subject to four provisos. Prima facie, as a matter of
construction, one would expect the provisos to do no more than qualify either
the description of the event or Eagle's obligations arising on the occurrence
of the event. It is clear, however, that proviso (a) deals solely with matters
arising after the occurrence of the event. It does not qualify Eagle's obligations
arising on the occurrence of the event, but imposes on U.D.T. a unilateral   E
obligation to assign to Eagle their rights against Orion if called on to do so by
Eagle. Proviso (b) does qualify the description of the event. Proviso (c) is
ambiguous. It deals with the period before Eagle buy the aircraft and is capable
of being a qualification of the description of the event, viz., the aircraft must,
at the time when Eagle are called on to purchase it, be one which had at all
times since the date of the agreement been covered by insurance. It is equally   F
capable of constituting a synallagmatic obligation on the part of U.D.T. to
insure the aircraft or to cause it to be kept insured; but if the latter is, as I
think that it is, the true construction, there was no breach by U.D.T. Proviso (d),
which was not compiled with, also deals with the period before Eagle buy the
aircraft. For my part, I agree with the learned judge in thinking that this
proviso, having regard particularly to the words in parenthesis, cannot be   G
construed otherwise than as a synallagmatic obligation on the part of U.D.T.
to notify Eagle during that period of any default by Orion in payment of hire
rentals. If U.D.T.'s admitted breach of that synallagmatic obligation were the
only ground of defence, it would be necessary to consider whether Eagle's
remedy for that breach was limited, as the learned judge held, to the recovery
of monetary compensation for any loss caused by the breach, or whether it   H
also entitled them to be released from any further obligation to buy the
aircraft as they purported to elect.

This question falls to be determined on the principles laid down in the *Hong
Kong Fir* case (12), and it was these principles that the learned judge applied.
I am not persuaded that he reached the wrong conclusion, but I do not find
it necessary to go further into the matter, for I think that Eagle have a good   I
defence on their second ground. It is, in my view, beyond rational controversy
that the words

> " if for any reason whatsoever the said hire-purchase agreement should
> be terminated by either party before the whole amount payable thereunder
> by way of rent for the full period of hire therein provided for has been
> paid . . . "

---

(12) [1962] 1 All E.R. 474; [1962] 2 Q.B. 26.

A   and the words " when called upon to do so " are descriptive of the event on the occurrence of which Eagle's unilateral obligation to buy the aircraft arises and that they are nothing more. I agree with LORD DENNING, M.R., and the learned judge that, by necessary implication, there must be incorporated in the description of the event that Eagle shall be called on to buy the aircraft within a reasonable time of the termination of the hire-purchase agreement.

B   It is commercially inconceivable that they should have bound themselves until the Greek Kalends to buy at a fixed price an obsolescent chattel whose value would diminish with the passage of time. I see no reason to differ from the learned judge's finding that, in all the circumstances of this case, including the lien on the aircraft, if that be relevant, and the liquidation of Orion, a reasonable time had expired before May 4, 1961, when U.D.T. first called on Eagle

C   to buy the aircraft.   Accordingly, the event giving rise to Eagle's unilateral obligation to buy the aircraft has not occurred and never can occur. There is no obligation; there can be no breach. The action must fail.

With regard to counsel for U.D.T.'s subsidiary arguments, I need say no more than I agree entirely with the judgment of LORD DENNING, M.R.

The learned judge, however, went on to consider whether the failure of U.D.T.

D   to call on Eagle to buy the aircraft within a reasonable time was the kind of breach by U.D.T. of an obligation on their part which entitled Eagle to be released from their obligations; but the need for this inquiry never arose. There was no breach by U.D.T. of any obligation in respect of calling on Eagle to buy the aircraft; for there was no obligation on U.D.T. to call on Eagle to buy the aircraft within a reasonable time or at all. It is only right to say, however, that

E   the argument before the learned judge does not appear to have been on the same lines as that which has so greatly assisted me in this court. In particular, his attention was not drawn to the cases about options to which I have referred.

I, too, would allow this appeal.

EDMUND DAVIES, L.J.:   I also agree that the appeal in these con-

F   solidated actions must be allowed.   The learned trial judge proceeded on the basis that the negotiations between the parties, culminating in the document of June 8, 1959, brought into existence a bilateral contract whereby the defendants (" Eagle ") undertook the repurchase of two aircraft from the plaintiffs (" U.D.T.") if for any reason the hire-purchase agreements entered into between U.D.T. and Orion Airwork, Ltd. (" Orion ") were terminated before all pay-

G   ments thereunder had been made.   As, even on that view, there were terms which trammelled the right of U.D.T. to call on Eagle to repurchase, he thereafter embarked on an enquiry (identical with that undertaken by this court in *Hong Kong Fir Shipping Co., Ltd.* v. *Kawasaki Kisen Kaisha, Ltd.*, (13)) whether those terms were so fundamental that their non-observance could be said to have frustrated the contractual object. Arriving at the conclusion that they

H   were not, the learned judge held that their non-observance could (at most) give rise only to a claim for damages at the instance of Eagle.

In my judgment, that was a wrong approach. As I view it, the proper interpretation and effect of the document is that (as counsel for Eagle submitted) Eagle thereby made an irrevocable offer to repurchase the two aircraft subject to compliance by U.D.T. with one or more conditions precedent. In the light

I   of such decisions as *Weston* v. *Collins* (14), *Hare* v. *Nicoll* (15), and *West Country Cleaners (Falmouth), Ltd.* v. *Saly* (16), cited to this court but unfortunately not to the trial judge, it is nothing to the point for U.D.T. to urge, as they have done, that little or no benefit could enure to Eagle by compliance with those terms.

---

(13) [1962] 1 All E.R. 474; [1962] 2 Q.B. 26.
(14) (1865), 12 L.T. 4.
(15) [1966] 1 All E.R. 285; [1966] 2 Q.B. 130.
(16) [1966] 3 All E.R. 210.

Nor, conversely, would it be material to show that no detriment resulted to **A** Eagle from non-observance by U.D.T. of such conditions. As JAMES, L.J., said in *Finch* v. *Underwood* (17), where a tenant in breach of his covenant to repair was refused a renewal of his lease:

"he [the tenant] is not entitled to excuse himself by saying that the want of repair is trifling. The answer to that is, ' No matter; your bargain **B** was to leave the property in thorough repair '. If he has not fulfilled his legal bargain . . . he cannot sustain his claim for a lease."

Strict compliance with the conditions was essential if U.D.T. chose to exercise their right to call on Eagle to repurchase. That compliance being absent, the obligation of Eagle to repurchase never came into existence. I find no room for doubt that the irrevocable offer of Eagle to re-purchase was conditional on **C** U.D.T. calling on them so to do within a reasonable time of the termination of their hire-purchase contract with Orion. They allowed a period of some five months (from Dec. 15, 1960, to May 5, 1961) to elapse between those two events. Did they thereby unreasonably delay? The learned judge, holding that three months was a reasonable time for the purpose, considered that they did.

Was three months a reasonable time to allow for this purpose? The answer **D** to that question depends, as always, on all the circumstances. In addition to those which have already been referred to by my lords, I think it not immaterial to observe (a) that, notwithstanding that by their letter of Nov. 28, 1960, Eagle made it quite clear they regarded themselves as released from any obligation to repurchase, no protest against or rejection of their attitude ever emerged from U.D.T.; and (b) that when, on Dec. 15, 1960, U.D.T. terminated their hire- **E** purchase agreement with Orion, they refrained (quite contrary to their usual practice) from giving Eagle any notification of that termination. In my judgment, when these and the other circumstances are comprehensively regarded, there are no grounds for rejecting three months, calculated from the date of termination of the hire-purchase agreements, as a reasonable time within which U.D.T. must call on Eagle to repurchase if they desired them so to do. That they failed **F** to do, and the obligation to repurchase, therefore, never arose.

To my way of thinking, greater difficulty arises in relation to the question whether proviso (d) in the document of June 8, 1959, also created a condition precedent, though I am at present inclined to adopt the view expressed by LORD DENNING, M.R., as to the effect of that proviso. Such doubts as I have on that matter, however, need not now be resolved, having regard to the con- **G** clusion to which I have come on the first point. In the light of that conclusion, I concur in holding that this appeal must be allowed.

Appeal allowed. Leave to appeal to the House of Lords refused.

Solicitors: *Lee, Bolton & Lee* agents for *Ashton Hill & Co.*, Nottingham (for the defendants); *Edwin Coe & Calder Woods* (for the plaintiffs). **H**

[*Reported by* F. GUTTMAN, ESQ., *Barrister-at-Law.*]

I

---

(17) (1876), 2 Ch.D. at p. 315.

A

ARUNA MILLS, LTD. v. DHANRAJMAL GOBINDRAM.

[QUEEN'S BENCH DIVISION (Donaldson, J.), November 13, 14, 22, 1967.]

Arbitration—Award—Remission—Legal representation not allowed on arbitration appeal leading to award—Remission for further finding of fact.

B *Money—Currency—Rate of exchange—Damages—Sale of goods—C.i.f. contract containing provision for incidence of revaluation of currency—Devaluation taking place after failure of sellers to ship on agreed date—Whether buyers entitled to recover as damages for breach of contract the amount of the contractual increase in price consequent on devaluation.*

By a c.i.f. contract made in Bombay between Indian nationals the sellers
C agreed to ship cotton by May 31, 1966, for a price expressed in rupees, the contract providing for the buyers to bear any difference in the rate of exchange prevailing on the date of the contract and the date of payment. The contract was subject to the rules and regulations of the Liverpool Cotton Association, Ltd. and to English law. Under these rules disputes were subject to arbitration with a right of appeal, the appeal being by way of re-
D hearing, neither party being allowed legal representation. In breach of contract the sellers failed to ship the goods until June 27. The rupee was revalued on June 6. The buyers, having accepted delivery and paid a price increased in accordance with the revaluation, claimed the amount of the increase as damages for breach of contract. There was no finding in the award on arbitration appeal under the rules whether, if the goods had been
E shipped on May 31, 1966, the documents would have been tendered to the buyers before June 5.

Held: (i) assuming that in the ordinary course of events shipment on May 31 would have resulted in the necessary documents being tendered to the buyers on or before June 5, there would have been causal connexion between the breach of contract and the loss due to revaluation, and on that
F basis the buyers were entitled to recover the amount of the increase in the purchase price as damages for the sellers' breach of contract by failure to ship the goods by May 31, as the contract showed that the parties had contemplated the possibility that late delivery was liable to result in loss to the buyers through revaluation of the rupee (see p. 118, letter F, and p. 120, letters A and D, post).

G *Victoria Laundry (Windsor), Ltd.* v. *Newman Industries, Ltd.* ([1949] 1 All E.R. 997) applied.

The Heron II ([1967] 3 All E.R. 686) considered.

(ii) as the parties were denied legal representation on the arbitration appeal, the award would be remitted for a finding whether, if the goods had been shipped on or before May 31 (viz., on a day when there was a ship
H available on which they could have been shipped), the documents of title would have been tendered to the buyers on or before June 5, with the consequence that the buyers would in the ordinary course of events have avoided paying the enhanced price (see p. 118, letter E, p. 119, letter B, p. 120, letter I, and p. 121, letter A, post).

Per CURIAM: changes in the relative value of currencies are irrelevant.
I if they occur after the date as at which damages fall to be assessed and are usually to be disregarded if they occur on or before this date, either because the loss flowing from the revaluation has no causal connexion with the breach of contract or because such a loss is not within the assumed contemplation of the parties (see p. 120, letter C, post).

[As to damages involving foreign currency, see 11 HALSBURY'S LAWS (3rd Edn.)
306, 307, para. 497, and 27 ibid., p. 6, para. 4; and for cases on the subject, see
17 DIGEST (Repl.) 173, 174, *681-690.* See also the general statement regarding

Dictum of DONALDSON J at 120 applied in BARCLAYS BANK v LEVIN BROS [1976] 3 All ER 900

conversion of damages in foreign currency in *Re United Railways of the Havana* **A**
and Regla Warehouses, Ltd. ([1960] 2 All E.R. at p. 334, letters C, D).

As to remission of an arbitration award, see 2 HALSBURY'S LAWS (3rd Edn.)
56, para. 121.]

Cases referred to:

Celia (Owners) v. *Volturno (Owners)*, [1921] All E.R. Rep. 110; [1921] 2 A.C.
544; 90 L.J.P. 385; 126 L.T. 1; 17 Digest (Repl.) 173, *685.*   **B**

Di Ferdinando v. *Simon, Smits & Co.*, [1920] All E.R. Rep. 347; [1920] 3 K.B.
409; 89 L.J.K.B. 1039; 124 L.T. 117; 17 Digest (Repl.) 173, *686.*

Hadley v. *Baxendale*, [1843-60] All E.R. Rep. 461; (1854), 9 Exch. 341; 23
L.J.Ex. 179; 23 L.T.O.S. 69; 17 Digest (Repl.) 91, *99.*

Heron II, The, Koufos v. *C. Czarnikow, Ltd.*, [1967] 3 All E.R. 686; [1967]
3 W.L.R. 1491.   **C**

Parana, The, (1877), 2 P.D. 118; 36 L.T. 388; 41 Digest (Repl.) 388, *1752.*

Sinason-Teicher Inter-American Grain Corpn. v. *Oilcakes & Oilseeds Trading
Co., Ltd.*, [1954] 2 All E.R. 497; [1954] 1 W.L.R. 935; *affd.* C.A.,
[1954] 3 All E.R. 469; [1954] 1 W.L.R. 1394; 39 Digest (Repl.) 732,
2118.

Victoria Laundry (Windsor), Ltd. v. *Newman Industries, Ltd.*, [1949] 1 All E.R. **D**
997; [1949] 2 K.B. 528; 17 Digest (Repl.) 92, *100.*

Interim award in form of Special Case*.

This was an award stated by the directors of the Liverpool Cotton Association,
Ltd., on an appeal against the award in an arbitration conducted under
the association's rules. The dispute arose out of a contract in writing, dated **E**
Mar. 9, 1966, whereby the sellers (the respondents, Dhanrajmal Gobindram)
sold to the buyers (the appellants, Aruna Mills, Ltd.) two hundred bales of Sudan
cotton. Among other clauses, the contract contained cl. 7 and cl. 8, which were
as follows:—

" 7. The goods are to be imported from foreign countries and the exchange
rate on the date of the contract is calculated in rupee currency while fixing **F**
the price mentioned in the contract. The buyers agree to bear and pay
to the sellers the difference if any in the exchange rate prevailing on the
date of the contract and on the date when the full price is paid.

" 8. Disputes regarding this contract shall be subject to the rules and
regulations of the Liverpool Cotton Association, Ltd., and shall be referred
to the said Liverpool Cotton Association, Ltd., for arbitration."   **G**

The facts and the questions for determination are set out in the judgment.

H. A. P. Fisher, Q.C., and *R. L. Ward* for the buyers.
A. H. M. Evans for the sellers.

Cur. adv. vult.

Nov. 22.   **DONALDSON, J.**, read the following judgment: This dispute **H**
stems from the revaluation of the Indian rupee in terms of sterling and of Sudanese
currency on June 6, 1966. The sellers had agreed to sell to the buyers two
hundred tons of Sudan cotton c.i.f. Bombay at a price of Rs. 393.68 per quintal.
The contract contained a clause providing for a variation in the price should
the prevailing rate of exchange vary between the date of the contract and the
date when the price was paid. The Indian rupee was revalued between these **I**
dates. However, the buyers contend that they should not have been required to
pay an increased price, because the sellers were in breach of contract in failing
to ship and deliver in such time as would, in the event, have enabled them to
pay for the goods before the revaluation and thus at the lower price.

The contract was made in Bombay between Indian nationals, but is subject

---

* The correctness of this description was questioned (see p. 115, letter C, post), but
the directors referred to it as " this our interim award ".

A to the rules and regulations of the Liverpool Cotton Association, Ltd. and to English law. These rules provide for the settlement of disputes by arbitration. If either party is dissatisfied with the award of the arbitrators or umpire, he has a right of appeal to the directors of the Liverpool Cotton Association, Ltd. Such an appeal is in the nature of a re-hearing. Neither party may be legally represented, but it is clear that the directors have access to legal advice. The

B buyers exercised their right of appeal in this case and the matter comes before the court in the form of an award by the directors. In passing I would remark that the settlement of commercial disputes between foreign nationals is a traditional service provided by the trade associations of this country and by the commercial court. The extent to which it is used suggests that it fulfils a useful purpose, and it is clear that it constitutes a not unimportant invisible export.

C There is some doubt whether this award is properly described as an interim award in the form of a Special Case or as a consultative award or whether it is in truth a hybrid, but the label does not matter. The award makes certain findings and submits two questions of law for the opinion of the court. It requests the court to consider these questions and to remit the award to the directors in order that they may make a final award in the light of the court's

D answers to the questions. It also awards that the buyers pay the costs of the award. Finally it adopts the usual and convenient course of making a final award to take effect if for any reason the questions are not answered by the court. It is not entirely clear to me whether the directors intend that the buyers shall pay the costs of the award in any event or whether they intend only that the buyers shall pay these costs as an interim measure and without prejudice to

E which party shall ultimately bear them. I trust that the latter is the case, for it is manifestly unfair that the right of any party to an arbitration to seek the assistance of the court on the decision of questions of law should be fettered by the knowledge that, whether or not he is right, he will have to pay the costs of obtaining that assistance.

F Let me now turn to the questions of law. These fall to be considered in the light of the findings contained in para. 2 of the award which are as follows:

" (2) So far as they are questions of fact we find and so far as they are question of law we decide subject to the opinion of the court upon the said specific questions of law set out in cl. (3) hereof (a) By contract No. SUD/1/65-66 dated Bombay Mar. 9, 1966 and made between the sellers and

G buyers "

—and then they set out the summary of the contract including cl. 7, which is the relevant clause, and cl. 8, which is the arbitration clause, and record that they have annexed the contract to the award.

Then it goes on:

H " (b) Both parties reside and carry on business in India. The buyers are one of the Arvind Group of Mills of Ahmedabad and the sellers carry on business in Bombay.

" (c) The price stated for the cotton in question in the confirmation memo. dated Mar. 9, 1966, is—' Rupees 1400 per candy of 784 lbs. c.i.f. Bombay '. This price is the exact equivalent of the price as stated in the

I contract taking one quintal as being 220.46 lbs.

" (d) On Mar. 25, 1966, the buyers wrote to the sellers a letter . . . In this letter the buyers wrote:—' (5) The import licences that will be issued will expire on May 31, 1966, and there will be no grace period against the licences that will be issued. Therefore you may advise your shippers to definitely ship the cotton on or before May 31, 1966.'

" (e) By this letter buyers and sellers agreed to extend the time for shipment beyond Apr. 30, 1966, to May 31, 1966, and the parties before us agreed that this was the effect of the said letter.

" (f) On Apr. 19, 1966, import licence No. P/Au/1260481 for two hundred   **A**
bales of 180 kgms. each of Sudan cotton was granted and the sellers on
Apr. 21, 1966, wrote to the buyers advising them that they had received
notice of the import licence number, enquiring whether the buyers wished
the sellers to cover ' forward exchange in respect of this import ' and remind-
ing the buyers that according to the terms of the contract ' any difference
in exchange at the time of negotiation of documents is to be for buyers'   **B**
account' . . .

" (g) To this letter there is no evidence that the buyers made any reply.

" (h) The validity of the import licence which would have expired on
May 31 was extended by order of the textile commissioner to June 30, 1966,
by a circular dated May 13, 1966. This was common knowledge to both
parties at this last mentioned date.   **C**

" (i) On June 6, 1966, the Indian rupee was devalued. The rate of
exchange at the date of the contract as appears from the confirmation
memo. of Mar. 9 above referred to was 1s. $5\frac{15}{16}$d. per rupee. The rate
changed on June 6 to 21 rupees to £1 sterling which is the equivalent of
$11\frac{9}{21}$d. per rupee.

"(j) On June 17, 1966, the buyers wrote to the sellers pointing out that to   **D**
date there had been no shipment advice and continuing ' as the cotton has
not been shipped in terms of the contract please note that we shall have no
liability to pay an additional amount on account of devaluation of rupee'
. . .

" (k) To this letter the sellers made no written reply.

" (l) It was admitted before us that the buyers were in great need of the   **E**
cotton the subject matter of the contract and that at no time had they any
intention of repudiating the contract.

" (m) On June 27, 1966, the cotton the subject matter of the contract
was in fact shipped on board the ' Leipzig ' at Port Sudan.

" (n) When the requisite documents were tendered to the buyers they took
them up after some delay and paid the contract price including the increase   **F**
in price brought about by the devaluation of the rupee but they paid this
additional sum, viz., 82,084.81 rupees, merely as a deposit subject to
arbitration on the footing that had timely shipment been made they would
not have had to pay this addition to the price.

" (o) The parties before us stated that they had agreed the amounts
of any damage which would or might become payable by either party to the   **G**
other under any award to be made by us, so that the dispute between them
was limited before us to questions of liability only; that is to say whether
the buyers' contention that the sellers' delay in shipment justified the buyers
in refusing to pay any such additional sum in rupees resulting from the said
devaluation, notwithstanding cl. 7 of the contract and whether the buyers
delay in paying the price had led to increased expenses borne in the first place   **H**
by the sellers which ought to be borne by the buyers.

" (p) The buyers' delay in paying the said price after tender of documents
was not more than was reasonable in the circumstances."

Counsel was instructed by the buyers to tell me that they had not agreed before
the directors that the effect of the letter of Mar. 25, 1966, was to extend the time
of shipment beyond Apr. 30, 1966, until May 31, 1966. (See finding (2) (f).)   **I**
However, he did not ask me to construe the letter in any different sense and
nothing turns on the point. Paragraph (2) (o) reflects something in the nature
of a counterclaim by the sellers for expenses consequent on delay in payment
by the buyers. This was argued before the directors, but was not pursued
before me in view of the finding in para. (2) (p). Both parties were agreed that
para. (2) (o) was not to be construed as an agreement that the solution to the
dispute between the parties must necessarily be an award in favour of the buyers
for Rs. 82,084.81 (or its sterling equivalent) or else an award in favour of the

A   sellers that nothing was payable to the buyers.   The agreement referred to in that paragraph was intended, so I was told, simply to confine the argument to principles, leaving the monetary result to be worked out thereafter.

The questions of law submitted by the award are set out in para. (3) in the following terms:

B   "1.   Whether, in a contract of sale in which time is of the essence, the buyers having agreed to bear and pay to the sellers the difference (if any) in the exchange rate prevailing on the date of contract and on the date when the full price is paid, and performance is delayed by reason of the sellers' breach of contract in failing to ship in time so that the currency is devalued after the agreed date of shipment and payment but before actual shipment and payment such loss is to be borne by the buyers or by the sellers?   2.   Whether, upon a true construction of the contract and upon the facts as stated, the sellers are liable in damages for failing to ship in accordance with the terms of the contract."

C

The parties having considered these questions contended that they could usefully be re-phrased as follows:

D   "(i) Whether on the facts as found and on the true construction of the contract, the sellers were in breach of contract by reason of the fact that the goods were not shipped within the shipment period provided by the contract. (ii) If yes, whether the buyers (not having elected to accept such breach as a repudiation) were by virtue of cl. 7 of the contract liable to pay to the sellers the difference in the exchange rate prevailing on the date of the contract and on the date when the full price was paid.   (iii) If yes, whether the buyers are entitled to recover from the sellers as damages for the said breach of contract the difference so payable."

E

Bearing in mind that the conditional final award of the directors takes effect if, inter alia "the court for any reason does not see fit to answer the said questions", F   it may be more satisfactory if I answer both the original and the revised questions.

The first matter for decision is whether the sellers were in breach of contract in failing to ship the goods or to procure their shipment on or before May 31, 1966. Counsel for the sellers, drew attention to the fact that there was no finding to this effect, but I regard this as a question of law or of mixed fact and law on which no finding by the directors is necessary.   The sellers' argument was that para. 5 G   of the letter of Mar. 25, 1966, properly construed and giving full weight to the word "Therefore" in the last sentence, constitutes an agreement or a promise or a promissory representation that cotton shipped within the period permitted by the import licences as extended from time to time would be accepted by the buyers as a due fulfilment of their obligations under the contract.

I cannot so construe that letter.   The contract itself required the goods to be H   shipped on or before Apr. 30, 1966, and required the buyers to provide such licence as might be necessary to enable cotton so shipped to be imported.   Stipulations in a c.i.f. contract of sale as to the time and place of shipment are ordinarily conditions of the contract, a breach of which entitles the buyer to refuse to accept the documents when presented (KENNEDY'S C.I.F. CONTRACTS (3rd Edn.) p. 30). The importance of such a stipulation and the strictness with which it is construed I   are not altered by the fact that a buyer is obliged or chooses to accept documents relating to goods shipped out of time.   Against this background para. (5) of the letter of Mar. 25, 1966, can legitimately be construed as varying the contract, or at all events as entitling the sellers to treat the contract as varied, to the extent of permitting shipment up to and including May 31, 1966.   The language is, however, wholly inept to constitute an invitation to the sellers to ship the goods at any time during the period of validity of the licence, irrespective of the extent to which this period might thereafter be extended by a third party, namely the textile commissioner.

I therefore decide that the sellers were in breach of the contract of sale in failing **A**
to ship the goods or procure their shipment on or before May 31, 1966. In
reaching this conclusion I have not overlooked the fact that a seller can perform
his duties under a classic c.i.f. contract not only by shipping goods or by procuring their shipmeht, but also by buying goods which are already afloat. In
the present case the sellers did not in fact buy goods afloat and tender documents
relating thereto to the buyers, even if the terms of this contract permitted them **B**
to do so, which is not free from doubt.

What is the consequence of this breach of contract? Counsel for the buyers
frankly conceded that the effect of the buyers' accepting the goods is that the
contract terms as to the payment of the price continue in full force and effect,
notwithstanding that the period for shipment and the correlative period for
tendering the documents had expired. This is plainly right. Accordingly, a **C**
revaluation of the rupee having taken place between the date of the contract
and the date when the full price fell to be paid, the buyers were obliged to pay
an enhanced price, subject to any right of set-off. This leads me to what is the
kernel of the dispute between the parties, namely whether the buyers, having
paid an enhanced price, can recover the difference between the original price
and the enhanced price as damages for breach of contract by the sellers. **D**

Counsel for the buyers submits that, subject to his clients proving a causal
connexion between the late shipment and delivery and the fact that payment
was made after the date of the revaluation, the buyers are entitled to recover a
sum equal to this difference of price as damages for breach of contract and
could have resisted payment on the ground that they had a set-off.

I can dispose briefly of the problem of causation. The sellers were entitled **E**
to ship on any date up to and including May 31, 1966, and they would then tender
a bill of lading. It was their duty to tender this bill of lading to the buyers
as soon after shipment as was commercially practicable, but there is no finding
on whether if the goods had been shipped on May 31, 1966, the documents would,
in the ordinary course of events, have been tendered to the buyers on or before
June 5, 1966. If the answer is that they would have been so tendered, the **F**
buyers have established the necessary causal connexion between the breach and
the loss, i.e., the payment of an enhanced price. If the answer is that the
documents would not have been so tendered, the buyers have not established the
causal connexion and their claim fails.

It is the duty of parties to an arbitration who desire to raise questions of law
for the decision of the court to make plain to the arbitrators all the points on **G**
which they wish the facts to be found for the purpose of arguing the questions of
law. (See *Sinason-Teicher Inter-American Grain Corpn.* v. *Oilcakes & Oilseeds
Trading Co., Ltd.* (1).) The court is reluctant to remit an award for further
findings of fact where there has been a failure by the parties in this respect,
because remission adds considerably to the cost of the proceedings and creates
delay. However, this reluctance is much reduced if the parties are prevented **H**
by the rules of the arbitration from being represented by lawyers, as it is unreasonable to expect the parties themselves to appreciate all the points which are or
may be relevant. I can well understand the Liverpool Cotton Association, Ltd.,
considering that the assistance of lawyers is irrelevant to the decision of a dispute
which turns solely on matters of quality or description, there being no dispute
as to the legal rights and duties of the parties. However, once any question of **I**
law creeps into the dispute, the position is quite different. The assistance of
lawyers may then save both time and expense. Members of trade associations
are fully entitled to agree that their rules shall forbid all legal representation at
arbitrations conducted in accordance with those rules, but I venture to think that
they are most unwise to do so. Contrary to popular belief, lawyers do not
regard it as any part of their duty either to their client or to the tribunal to make

---

(1) [1954] 2 All E.R. 497 at p. 503.

A   confusion worse confounded.   On the contrary, they can and do bring their
professional expertise to bear on the problem of crystallising the issues, thus
saving time and money to all concerned, whilst at the same time ensuring a just
result in accordance with law.

As there is no finding on this essential point and as the buyers were denied
legal representation, the award will be remitted for such a finding if the buyers'
B   contention is otherwise correct.

Counsel for the sellers submits that the buyers rightly paid the enhanced price
and can recover no part of it.   He supports this submission on the following
three grounds.   (a) The contract expressly provides that, in the circumstances
which have arisen, the buyers shall bear and pay the difference in the exchange
rate.   The buyers having accepted the goods are bound by all the terms of the
C   contract.   If they can recover the difference as damages, they are not bearing it
and if they can exercise a right of set-off, they are neither bearing nor paying it.
(b) The loss relied on is too remote as a matter of law to be recoverable.   (c) The
buyers could have avoided this loss and should have done so in the discharge of
their duty to mitigate the damage which they suffered.

Turning now to the wording of the contract, I do not consider that this is any
D   impediment to the buyers' claim.   The parties in using the words " bear and pay "
were providing for what was to happen in the performance of the contract and not
in its breach.   Full effect is given to these words if, as is conceded, they require
the effect of the change in the rate of exchange to be borne by payment of an
enhanced price, but without prejudice to any claim for damages.   This claim for
damages is of a like amount in the present case, but would be of a different
E   amount if some other and additional element of loss flowed from the breach.   The
mere fact that the rules of law relating to set-off and the avoidance of circuity
of action might have enabled the buyers to refuse payment of the enhanced price
does not involve a failure to give effect to the bargain which the parties made.

With regard to remoteness of loss, until recently it could fairly be said that,
subject to the decision in *The Parana* (2), the law on remoteness of damage in
F   contract had been codified by the decision in *Hadley* v. *Baxendale* (3), as explained
in the classic judgment delivered by ASQUITH, L.J., in *Victoria Laundry* (*Windsor*),
Ltd. v. *Newman Industries, Ltd.* (4).   Now the House of Lords in *The Heron II* (5)
has held that *The Parana* (2) is not to be considered as an exception.   In the
course of the speeches their lordships expressed varying degrees of enthusiasm
for the *Victoria Laundry* decision (6); but, subject to two possible qualifications,
G   it seems to me to remain unimpaired as the classic authority on the topic.   These
two qualifications are as follows.   First, reference in the judgment to a loss being
" reasonably foreseeable " should perhaps be taken as referring to the loss having
been within " actual or assumed contemplation " (see the speech of LORD REID
(7)).   Second, the phrase " liable to result " is not correctly paraphrased by the
use of the expression " on the cards ", but conveys the relevant shade of likeli-
H   hood by its own wording (LORD HODSON (8)) or when defined (as it was in proposition (6) in the *Victoria Laundry* case (9)) as indicating that a loss is a " serious
possibility " or " real danger " (see LORD PEARCE (10) and LORD UPJOHN (11)),
words which amongst others had the approval of LORD MORRIS OF BORTH-Y-
GEST (12).

In the present case it is clear that the parties actually contemplated the
I   possibility of revaluation during the period between the date of the contract and
the date of payment for the goods as being a sufficiently serious possibility or

(2) (1877), 2 P.D. 118.   (3) [1843-60] All E.R. Rep. 461;   (1854), 9 Exch. 341.
(4) [1949] 1 All E.R. 997 at pp. 1002, 1003;   [1949] 2 K.B. 528 at pp. 539, 540.
(5) [1967] 3 All E.R. 686.   (6) [1949] 1 All E.R. 997;   [1949] 2 K.B. 528.
(7) [1967] 3 All E.R. at pp. 694-696.   (8) [1967] 3 All E.R. at p. 708.
(9) [1949] 1 All E.R. at pp. 1003;   [1949] 2 K.B. at p. 540.
(10) [1967] 3 All E.R. at p. 711.   (11) [1967] 3 All E.R. at p. 717.
          (12) [1967] 3 All E.R. at p. 701.

real danger to justify their making express provision for that eventuality. In **A** the circumstances they must be assumed to have contemplated that late delivery was "liable to result" (within the meaning explained above) in the buyers' suffering a loss by the payment of an enhanced price.

Counsel for the sellers has, however, another string to his bow in relation to remoteness, for he submits that whatever may be the general rule and its application to this case, there is a special rule that losses resulting from revaluation of **B** currencies are always too remote in law to be recoverable and he relied on *Di Fernando* v. *Simon, Smits & Co.* (13) and *Celia (Owners)* v. *Volturno (Owners)* (14). I do not think that there is any such rule. The true rule is that changes in the relative value of currencies are irrelevant if they occur after the date as at which damages fall to be assessed and are usually to be disregarded if they occur on or before this date, either because the loss flowing from the revaluation has no causal **C** connexion with the breach of contract or because such a loss is not within the assumed contemplation of the parties. Since this case was argued, there has been a revaluation of sterling, which is irrelevant to computation of damages. This case therefore illustrates both the general rule and the exception.

Accordingly I hold that the loss relied on is not too remote in law. In doing so I should perhaps mention that, in the light of the terms of the contract, I do **D** not think that I am impeded in so holding by the absence of any finding of fact as to the likelihood of revaluation.

Dealing with the question of failure to mitigate, the submission that the buyers could and should have avoided the loss is based on the letter from the sellers dated Apr. 21, 1966, in which they inquired whether the buyer wished them "to cover forward exchange in respect of this import". Counsel for the sellers **E** says that if this offer had been accepted, the buyers would in the event have suffered no loss and that they should have accepted it either then or when the sellers were first in breach of contract. I think that there may be a number of answers to this ingenious contention, but perhaps two will suffice. First, the result of entering into a contract for the forward purchase of foreign currency would not have been to eliminate the loss, but to make a collateral profit, which **F** seems to me to be quite a different matter. Second, the sellers could themselves equally well have entered into such a contract at their own expense and in those circumstances I do not see why there should be any duty on the buyers to do so at their expense.

For the reasons set out previously I answer the various questions as follows:

Award question 1: Subject to any right of set-off, the loss is initially to **G** be borne by the buyers, but they may have a cross-claim in damages. Award question 2: If the buyers would in the ordinary course of events have avoided payment of the enhanced price if the goods had been shipped on or before May 31, 1966, the sellers are liable in damages.

Parties' question (i): Yes. Parties' question (ii): Yes, subject to a right of set-off. Parties' question (iii): Yes, subject to proof of causation— **H** see answer to award question 2. [For these questions, see p. 117, letters B to E, ante.]

The award will be remitted to the directors of the Liverpool Cotton Association, Ltd., in order that they may find, if necessary after hearing further evidence, whether the buyers would in the ordinary course of events have avoided the **I** payment of the enhanced price if the goods had been shipped on or before May 31, 1966.

Fisher, Q.C.: in the inquiry into causation which your lordship has indicated that the directors of the Liverpool Cotton Association, Ltd., will have to make, it may be the wish of the buyers to contend that it is relevant to enquire when the last ship before May 31 was available.

(13) [1920] All E.R. Rep. 347 ; [1920] 3 K.B. 409.
(14) [1921] All E.R. Rep. 110; [1921] 2 A.C. 544.

A   **DONALDSON, J.:** I will amend what I have said to explain that when I said that if the goods had been shipped on or before May 31, I meant a date on which they could have been shipped. It was implicit in what I said that it was assumed to be possible to ship on May 31. If the latest date for shipment, because there was no other ship, was May 30, then plainly the question can be answered only on the footing of a shipment on May 30.

B   *Award remitted.*

Solicitors: *Laces & Co.*, Liverpool (for the buyers); *Weightman, Pedder & Co.*, Liverpool (for the sellers).

                                                [*Reported by* MARY COLTON, *Barrister-at-Law.*]

C

GARTSIDE AND ANOTHER v. INLAND REVENUE COMMISSIONERS.

[HOUSE OF LORDS (Lord Reid, Lord Morris of Borth-y-Gest, Lord Hodson, Lord Guest and Lord Wilberforce), October 3, 4, 5, 9, 10 11, 12, 16, 17,
D   December 13, 1967.]

*Estate Duty—Determination of life interest—Discretionary trust—Accumulation of surplus income—Advancement determining discretionary trust in sums advanced—Meaning of " interest " and of " interest in possession "—
Objects of discretionary trust not entitled individually or collectively to
E   receive the whole or part of trust income—Whether any determination of interest rendering estate duty leviable on sums advanced—Finance Act, 1894 (57 & 58 Vict. c. 30), s. 2 (1) (b)—Finance Act, 1940 (3 & 4 Geo. 6 c. 29), s. 43 (1) as amended by Finance Act, 1950 (14 Geo. 6 c. 15), s. 43 (1), Sch. 7, Pt. 1.*

Under the will of a testator who died on Jan. 8, 1941, the trustees held one quarter of his residuary estate on trust that during his son's life they should pay or apply the whole or such part of the income as they thought
F   fit towards the maintenance, support or benefit of his son and his son's wife and children or any of them (" the discretionary beneficiaries "), and should accumulate and invest any surplus income to the intent that the accumulations should be added to the quarter share. The trustees had power to resort to the accumulations at any time during the son's life and to use them for the maintenance, support or benefit of the discretionary
G   beneficiaries. After the son's death, the one quarter share was to be held for such of his children as should attain twenty-one or, if daughters, marry. Under these trusts the discretionary beneficiaries did not have at any time the right to receive any of the income. The only sums which the trustees paid out during the accumulation period were £786 for the benefit of the testator's son and £50 for his wife in 1961; the balance of the income was
H   accumulated. On Jan. 2, 1962, a few days before the period of permissible accumulation ended, the trustees in exercise of a power of advancement conferred by the will executed two deeds poll, whereby they declared that certain investments should be held on trust for each of the twin sons of the testator's son, who were then about seventeen years of age. There were at that time four discretionary beneficiaries only, the testator's
I   son, his wife and their twin sons. The testator's son died on May 8, 1963. The aggregate value of the advancements was then about £47,000. The Crown claimed that estate duty was payable on the advanced sums under s. 43 (1)* of the Finance Act, 1940.

Held: no " interest " had been determined, after becoming an interest in possession, by reason of the advances made on Jan. 2, 1962, and accordingly s. 43 (1) did not apply and estate duty was not exigible for the following reasons—

---

* Section 43 (1), so far as relevant, is printed at p. 124, letters D to G, post.

Applied in and dicta of LORD REID at 129 applied in Re WEIR [1970] 1 All ER 297

Distinguished in PEARSON v IR COMRS [1979] 1 All ER 273

(i) neither individually nor collectively were the discretionary bene-   A
ficiaries entitled in any year to receive any part of the trust income and,
accordingly, they, as objects of the discretionary trust, did not have interests
extending to the whole or any part of the income of the one quarter fund
and thus did not have interests in the fund within s. 2 (1) (b) of the Finance
Act, 1894, nor interests in possession within s. 43 (1) of the Finance Act, 1940
(see p. 128, letter C, p. 129, letter H, p. 131, letters H and I, and p. 133,   B
letter H, post).

(ii) (per LORD WILBERFORCE, LORD HODSON concurring) when the
advances were made, with the consequence that the trust for the accumulation of surplus income was determined (to the extent of the sums advanced),
there was no determination of any interest in possession within s. 43 (1)
of the Finance Act, 1940, because the contingent interests of the testator's   C
grandchildren (the twin sons) in the accumulations when added to capital
were interests in expectancy as distinct from interests in possession, and the
discretionary power to apply accumulations for the discretionary beneficiaries did not confer on any beneficiary any " interest " for the purposes
of s. 2 (1) (b) of the Finance Act, 1894, or of s. 43 (1) of the Act of 1940
(see p. 136, letter H, p. 137, letter A, and p. 131, letter I, post).   D

A.-G. v. Heywood ((1887), 19 Q.B.D. 326 and A.-G. v. Farrell ([1931]
1 K.B. 81) considered.

Burrell v. A.-G. ([1936] 3 All E.R. 758) explained and distinguished.

Per LORD REID, LORD MORRIS OF BORTH-Y-GEST and LORD GUEST concurring: an " interest in possession " (within s. 43 (1) of the Act of 1940)
means an interest which entitles a person to claim now whatever is the   E
subject of his interest (see p. 128, letter E, and p. 131, letters H and I, post).

Decision of the COURT OF APPEAL ([1967] 2 All E.R. 173) reversed.

[As to interests ceasing on death, see 15 HALSBURY'S LAWS (3rd Edn.) 13, 14,
para. 22; as to settlements with reservations, see ibid., p. 23, Para. 42; and for
cases on these subjects, see 21 DIGEST (Repl.) 17-22, 57-77, 29-32, 105-118.   F
For the Finance Act, 1894, s. 2 (1) (b), see 9 HALSBURY'S STATUTES (2nd Edn.)
350; and for the Finance Act, 1940, s. 43, as amended, see 29 ibid., 183.]

Cases referred to:

A.-G. v. Farrell, [1931] 1 K.B. 81; 99 L.J.K.B. 605; 143 L.T. 639; 21 Digest
    (Repl.) 29, 108.

A.-G. v. Heywood, (1887), 19 Q.B.D. 326; 56 L.J.Q.B. 572; 57 L.T. 271;   G
    21 Digest (Repl.) 29, 107.

A.-G. v. Power, [1906] 2 I.R. 272; 21 Digest (Repl.) 33, *40.

A.-G. of Ceylon v. Arunachalam Chettiar (No. 1), [1957] A.C. 513; [1957]
    3 W.L.R. 293; 21 Digest (Repl.) 50, *74.

Burrell v. A.-G., [1936] 3 All E.R. 758; [1937] A.C. 286; 106 L.J.K.B. 134;
    156 L.T. 36; 21 Digest (Repl.) 12, 39.   H

Comr. of Stamp Duties v. Livingston, [1964] 3 All E.R. 692; [1965] A.C. 694;
    [1964] 3 W.L.R. 963; [1965] A.L.R. 803; Digest (Cont. Vol. B) 247,
    *258a.

Coutts & Co. v. Inland Revenue Comrs., [1953] 1 All E.R. 418; [1953] A.C. 267;
    [1953] 2 W.L.R. 364; 21 Digest (Repl.) 21, 74.

Cowley (Earl) v. Inland Revenue Comrs., [1895-99] All E.R. Rep. 1181; [1899]   I
    A.C. 198; 68 L.J.Q.B. 435; 80 L.T. 361; 21 Digest (Repl.) 11, 36.

Public Trustee v. Inland Revenue Comrs., [1960] 1 All E.R. 1; [1960] A.C. 398;
    [1960] 2 W.L.R. 203; 21 Digest (Repl.) 18, 58.

Public Trustee v. Inland Revenue Comrs., [1966] 1 All E.R. 76; sub nom.
    Re Kirkwood, Public Trustee v. Inland Revenue Comrs., [1966] A.C. 520;
    [1966] 2 W.L.R. 136; Digest (Cont. Vol. B) 243, 39a.

Ralli Brothers, Ltd. v. Inland Revenue Comrs., [1966] 1 All E.R. 65; [1966]
    A.C. 483; [1966] 2 W.L.R. 119; Digest (Cont. Vol. B) 243, 56a.

A *Scott v. Inland Revenue Comrs.*, [1936] 3 All E.R. 752; [1937] A.C. 174; 106
  L.J.Ch. 36; 156 L.T. 33; 21 Digest (Repl.) 12, *38.*
  Skinner v. *A.-G., Re White*, [1938] 2 All E.R. 691; [1939] Ch. 131; *affd.*, H.L.,
  [1939] 3 All E.R. 787; [1940] A.C. 350; 108 L.J.Ch. 330; 161 L.T. 169;
  21 Digest (Repl.) 40, *157.*

 Appeal.

B This was an appeal by the appellants as trustees of the will of Thomas Edmund
Gartside (the testator) from an order of the Court of Appeal (LORD DENNING,
M.R., HARMAN and SALMON, L.JJ.) dated Mar. 2, 1967, and reported [1967]
2 All E.R. 173, reversing an order of the Chancery Division (UNGOED-THOMAS, J.)
dated May 27, 1966, and reported [1966] 3 All E.R. 89, declaring that estate
duty was not payable on the death of the testator's son, John Travis Gartside,
C on May 8, 1963, in respect of sums advanced by the trustees to his twin sons from
a one-quarter share of a residuary trust fund. The share was bequeathed by
the trustees on trusts including a discretionary trust of income for the benefit
of the testator's son, his wife and children, during his life-time, and thereafter,
trusts of capital in favour of the son's children at twenty-one. The testator's
son married once only, and there were two children only of the marriage, who were
D twin sons born on Jan. 5, 1945. The testator's will conferred a power of advancement in favour of each of the deceased's children extending to one half of the
share of the child. By deed poll dated Jan. 2, 1962, the trustees of the testator's
will exercised the power of advancement in favour of the twin sons, one by
each deed, contingently on the beneficiary attaining twenty-one. The investments comprised in each deed formed part of the capital of the one-quarter share,
E but no investment or cash so comprised represented accumulations of income.
By virtue of s. 164 of the Law of Property Act, 1925, the trust for accumulation
of surplus income came to an end on Jan. 7, 1962, on the expiration of twenty-one
years from the death of the testator.

 G. A. Rink, Q.C., and *P. W. E. Taylor* for the trustees.

 H. E. Francis, Q.C., and *J. P. Warner* for the Crown.
F
 Their lordships took time for consideration.

 Dec. 13. The following opinions were delivered.

 LORD REID: My Lords, Thomas Gartside, the testator, died in January,
1941. He left four children and this case is concerned with the share of his
 estate which he bequeathed for the benefit of his son John and his family. With
G regard to that share he provided that it should be held by his trustees:

  " Upon trust during the lifetime of my son John Travis Gartside to pay
  or apply the whole or such part as my trustees shall in their absolute and
  uncontrolled discretion think fit of the income of such fourth share for or
  towards the maintenance support or otherwise for the benefit of my said
  son John Travis Gartside or during his life for his wife or children (if any)
H or any one or more exclusively of the other or others of them in such manner
  in all respects as my trustees shall in their absolute and uncontrolled discretion without being liable to account think fit and shall accumulate the
  surplus (if any) of the said income by investing the same and the resulting
  income thereof in manner hereinafter mentioned. To the intent that the
  accumulations shall be added to the fourth share and follow the destination
I thereof with power nevertheless for my trustees at any time to resort to the
  accumulations of any preceding year and apply the same for the maintenance
  support and benefit of my said son John Travis Gartside or (during his life)
  any wife or children of his or any one or more of them."

When the testator died John was unmarried. The next year he married and he
had two sons, twins, born on Jan. 5, 1945. His wife and two sons survived
during the period relevant to this case. John died on May 8, 1963, and the
present case raised the question whether estate duty is payable on his death in

respect of sums which the testator's trustees had advanced to his twin sons A
prior to his death.   From the testator's death until 1960 his trustees accumulated
the whole income of John's share by virtue of the provision which I have already
quoted.   In 1961 they paid out of income sums of £786 for the benefit of John and
of £50 for the benefit of his wife and accumulated the balance.   By Jan. 1, 1962,
the total accumulated income amounted to about £55,000.   On Jan. 2, 1962,
when the twin sons were nearly seventeen years of age the trustees by virtue of a B
power to advance, executed two deeds poll whereby they declared that certain
investments should be held in trust for each of the twin sons if he attained the
age of twenty-one years.   These two advances together amounted to nearly
half the trust funds, apart from the accumulations, and they were worth about
£47,000 at the date of John's death.

It is admitted that estate duty was payable on John's death on the whole of C
these trust funds, including the accumulations, with the exception of the £47,000
which had been advanced to his twin sons.   The Crown claim that estate duty
is also payable on this sum under the provisions of s. 43 (1) of the Finance Act,
1940.   That subsection, as amended, provides:

"43.—(1) Subject to the provisions of this section, where an interest   D
limited to cease on a death has been disposed of or has determined, whether
by surrender, assurance, divesting, forfeiture or in any other manner (except
by the expiration of a fixed period at the expiration of which the interest was
limited to cease), whether wholly or partly, and whether for value or not,
after becoming an interest in possession, and the disposition or determination
(or any of them if there are more than one) is not excepted by sub-s. (2) of   E
this section, then—(a) if, had there been no disposition or determination as
aforesaid of that interest and no disposition of any interest expectant upon
or subject to that interest, the property in which the interest subsisted would
have passed on the death under s. 1 of the Finance Act, 1894, that property
shall be deemed by virtue of this section to be included as to the whole
thereof in the property passing on the death; or (b) if, had there been no dis-   F
position or determination as aforesaid of that interest and no disposition of
any interest expectant upon or subject to that interest, the property in
which the interest subsisted would have been deemed by virtue of para. (b)
of sub-s. (1) of s. 2 of the said Act to be included to a particular extent in the
property passing on the death, the property in which the interest subsisted
shall be deemed by virtue of this section to be included to that extent in the   G
property passing on the death."

The case for the Crown is that by making these advances the trustees determined
an interest or interests limited to cease on the death of John and that such interest
or interests had before that date become interests in possession.   Until the
trustees advanced these funds they were bound under the testator's will to H
decide, from time to time as income accrued, whether and to what extent that
income should be applied for the benefit of John, his wife and his two sons or
any of them.   After the advances had been made they were no longer entitled to
deal with the income from the advanced funds in that way.   If the advances
had not been made the trustees would still have been bound from time to time to
decide whether to exercise that discretion until the death of John, when other   I
trust provisions would have come into operation.   The argument for the Crown
was that the duty of the trustees to exercise that discretion from time to time gave
to each of John, his wife and his two sons an interest in the fund, that that
interest extended to the whole fund because the trustees could at any time have
given the whole of the income from it to any one of them, and that these interests
were interests in possession.   They say that it is immaterial whether or not
the trustees ever at any time in fact gave to any of these beneficiaries any sum
or other benefit: they each had interests in possession of the whole fund even if

A none of them ever received anything from it. If that were right then the section would apply.

The trustees argued that a person's right to require trustees of a discretionary trust to consider from time to time whether or not to apply the whole or some part of the income of the trust funds for his benefit is not an interest, and in any event is not an interest in possession, in the whole fund or in any part of it within

B the meaning of this section.

So the first and main question in this appeal is what is the meaning of the word " interest " in this section. The Act of 1940 provides that it has to be construed as one with the Finance Act, 1894, and the two most closely allied provisions of the latter Act are s. 2 (1) (*b*) and s. 7 (7). It seems clear that the word " interest " must have the same meaning in these three provisions. The word

C " interest ", as an ordinary word of the English language, is capable of having many meanings, and it is equally clear that in these provisions its meaning cannot be limited by any technicality of English law. Not only do these provisions also apply to Scotland, but they may have to be applied where duty is claimed in respect of an interest under deeds which have to be construed under the laws of other countries. That does not mean, however, that everything which

D the man in the street might call an interest is covered by the word " interest " in these sections. A man might say that a son and heir has an interest in his father's property to which he might reasonably expect to succeed; but one can discard that meaning: the son not only has no right in or over his father's property but he has no right to prevent his father from dissipating it. The Crown admit that, to be an interest under these provisions, it must give to the holder of it some

E right.

Then take the next step. A person who has a contingent right to some benefit from a trust fund in some future event, has a present right to prevent the trustees from dissipating the fund; but that right is not an interest in possession separate from and in addition to his contingent interest. That is made clear by the decision in *Coutts & Co.* v. *Inland Revenue Comrs.* (1). There beneficiairies had

F a right to require trustees to make payments of the premiums necessary to keep up a life insurance policy. When the person insured died that right of course ceased because no more premiums were payable. This House rejected the contention that this right to control the actions of the trustees was an interest, the cesser of which on the death gave rise to a claim for estate duty. LORD PORTER said (2): " I cannot think that in any ordinary sense the interest is the

G right to have the premiums paid." But the Crown's argument is that there is a distinction between such a right and a right to require trustees to consider whether to exercise a discretion in favour of the particular beneficiary.

Before I go farther I must examine s. 2 (1) (*b*) and s. 7 (7) of the Act of 1894, which are as follows:

H " 2. (1) Property passing on the death of the deceased shall be deemed to include the property following, that is to say: (*a*) . . . (*b*) Property in which the deceased or any other person had an interest, ceasing on the death of the deceased, to the extent to which a benefit accrues or arises by the cesser of such interest; but exclusive of property the interest in which of the deceased or other person was only an interest as holder of an office, or recipient of the benefits of a charity, or as a corporation sole;

I " 7. . . . (7) The value of the benefit accruing or arising from the cesser of an interest ceasing on the death of the deceased shall—(*a*) if the interest extended to the whole income of the property, be the principal value of that property; and (*b*) if the interest extended to less than the whole income of the property, be the principal value of an addition to the property equal to the income to which the interest extended."

---

(1) [1953] 1 All E.R. 418; [1953] A.C. 267.
(2) [1953] 1 All E.R. at p. 420, letter F; [1953] A.C. at p. 279.

The first thing that strikes one is that these provisions must have been intended   A
to be coterminous.   Section 2 (1) (b) (read in conjunction with s. 1) only makes
the cesser of an interest the cause of liability for estate duty " to the extent to
which a benefit accrues or arises " by the cesser;   and s. 7 (7) directs (3) how
the " benefit accruing or arising from the cesser " shall be valued.   On any
ordinary principle or method of construction I would infer that s. 2 (1) (b) is
only intended to apply to those " interests " the cesser of which causes " a benefit   B
to accrue or arise " and therefore creates a liability to pay estate duty.   Why
should s. 2 (1) (b) have set out to deal with any other kind of right?   There is
nowhere any definition of the word " interest ":   one must infer its meaning from
the context.   The subsection plainly applies to every kind of right the cesser
of which does cause a benefit to accrue or arise, but I find nothing to indicate that
it can have been intended to apply or must be held to apply to any right or any   C
kind of right the cesser of which does not have that result.   To find what is
meant by a benefit accruing or arising one must turn to s. 7 (7) for again there
is no definition of this phrase.   It appears to me to be obvious that s. 7 (7) was
intended to provide a method for valuing every benefit accruing or arising from
any cesser of an interest within the meaning of s. 2 (1) (b), and it is implicit in
s. 7 (7) that every right which is an " interest " within the scope of these pro-   D
visions must " extend " either to the whole or to a part of the income of the
property in which the right gave to its owner the " interest ".   The scheme
appears to me to be perfectly clear.   If the deceased or any other person had a
right which " extended " (whatever that may mean) to the whole or to any
part of the income of any property and that right ceased on the death of the
deceased, then estate duty is to be due to an amount to be determined by s. 7 (7).   E
If the right of the deceased or other person did not " extend " to any part of
the income then it was not an interest within the meaning of these provisions.
It appears to have been assumed in some cases that a right can be an " interest "
within the meaning of s. 2 (1) (b) although its cesser does not cause any benefit
to accrue or arise, or that it is sufficient that the cesser causes some benefit to
accrue or arise although the interest does not " extend " to any part of the   F
income of any property.   I can find nothing either in the words or in the apparent
purpose of these provisions to justify such an extension of the meaning of the
word " interest " in s. 2 (1) (b).   It may well be that the word " interest " in
other provisions of the Act of 1894 has a different or wider meaning, but I must
return to that.

Next comes the question of what is meant by an interest " extending " to the   G
whole or a part of the income of certain property.   Normally that must mean
that the owner of the interest is entitled to receive that income.   In that case,
apart from the method of valuation of the interest, those provisions are in line
with the general scheme of the Act of 1894.   On the cesser of that interest,
someone else will become entitled to receive the income accruing from and
after the cesser.   So the right to receive the income will change hands, and that   H
is what happens when the property itself passes under s. 1.

The Crown seek to attach a much wider meaning to the word " extend ".
They argue that each one of the objects of a discretionary trust, who may be
numerous, has an interest extending to the whole income of the trust fund because
the trustees could if they choose give the whole income to any one of the objects.
If there are a dozen objects of the trust then there would be twelve different   I
interests each extending to the same income.   But they do not take that argument to its logical conclusion, for if they are right I see no escape from the
conclusion that when any one of the twelve dies his interest ceases and there is
therefore a cesser of an interest which extended to the whole income.   That
would at once bring s. 2 (1) (b) and s. 7 (7) into operation, and estate duty would
have to be paid on the whole trust fund;   and the same would happen on the
death of another, and of a third, and of a fourth object before the end of the

(3) Section 7 (7) is printed at p. 125, letter I, ante.

A discretionary trust. So in the course of a few years estate duty would have to be paid on the whole trust fund as many times as there were deaths of objects of the discretionary trust, even if those objects who had died had never in fact received anything, the trustees having throughout exercised their discretion in favour of other objects of the trust who had survived. That would be a monstrous result which could never have been intended. In fact the Crown have
B never tried to claim estate duty when one of several objects of a discretionary trust dies, but that is not relevant in determining what is the true meaning of the word " extend ". If giving an extended meaning to a word in an Act, and particularly in a taxing Act, leads to a wholly unreasonable result, that is a very strong indication that the word was not intended to have that extended meaning; and the strength of that indication cannot be diminished by the fact
C that the revenue authorities have chosen to refrain from collecting tax which, if their view of the law is right, they are entitled to exact.

There are in some of the cases indications of a view that, while each of the objects of a discretionary trust has an interest in the trust fund, this interest does not extend to the whole or any part of the interest accruing from the fund. On the other hand all the objects together have a single class or group interest which
D does extend to the whole interest of the fund. Counsel for the Crown in a clear and well reasoned argument expressly declined to adopt that view, and I think that he was well advised in taking that course. Where a number of persons are members of a company or other incorporation which has a separate legal personality, the incorporation can of course have a single right different from the rights of any of its members. Otherwise two or more persons cannot have a single
E right, unless they hold it jointly or in common. Clearly objects of a discretionary trust do not have that: they each have individual rights: they are in competition with each other and what the trustees give to one is his alone.

I think that this idea of a group or class right must have arisen in this way. Where the trustees are bound to distribute the whole income among the discretionary beneficiairies and have no power to retain any part of it or use any part
F of it for any other purposes, you cannot tell what any one of the beneficiaries will receive until the trustees have exercised their discretion. But you can say with absolute certainty that the individual rights of the beneficiaries when added up or taken together will extend to the whole income. You can have an equation $x+y+z=100$, although you do not yet know the value of x or y or z. And that may lead to important results where the trust is of that character. But that is
G not this case.

There was also an intermediate argument that, although an object of a discretionary trust has an interest in the whole of the trust fund, he does not have any interest in either the whole or any part of the income accruing from the fund. That argument is too subtle for me to understand it. No object of a discretionary trust has, as such, any legal right to or in the capital. His sole
H interest, if it be an " interest " within the scope of these provisions, is with regard to the income: he can require the trustees to exercise, bona fide, their discretion how it shall be distributed, and he can take and enjoy whatever part of the income the trustees choose to give him. I cannot see any ground for holding that he can have any " interest " in the capital if he has no interest in the income. As I have already explained, his right to prevent misappropriation of the capital is
I not a separate interest.

There is one other matter which I think throws light on these provisions. It may be that in 1894 discretionary trusts were not so common that the draftsman of the legislation must have had them in mind. But provisions authorising trustees to apply the whole or a part of the trust income for the maintenance of an infant who had a contingent but not a vested right to capital were extremely common. In such a case the infant (or his guardian) had a present right to make a claim for payment for maintenance and a right to require the trustees to exercise bona fide their discretion whether or to what extent they would apply trust income for

that purpose. If, as the Crown contend, the right of an object of a discretionary A
trust to have the trustees consider his case is an " interest " within the meaning
of these provisions, what about the similar right of an infant with regard to
maintenance? The Crown do not contend that such an infant has any " interest ",
and the draftsman and Parliament cannot possibly have intended that these
provisions should apply on the death of such an infant before majority. The
only distinction, however, which counsel for the Crown was able to suggest was B
that trustees are bound to consider the position of discretionary objects without
waiting for the objects to make a claim, whereas trustees are not bound to consider whether any sum should be applied towards the maintenance of an infant
until a claim is made. That is a very narrow distinction and cannot in my view
justify a conclusion that objects of a discretionary trust have " interests " in
the trust fund but that an infant which has a claim for maintenance has not.   C

In my judgment an examination of the relevant provisions of this legislation
leads to the clear conclusion that objects of a discretionary trust do not have
interests extending to the whole or any part of the income of the trust fund and
it must follow that they do not have interests in the fund within the meaning of
s. 2 (1) (b). When one comes to s. 43 of the Act of 1940, a fortiori they do not
have interests in possession. It does not seem to me to be a reasonable method D
of construction to say first that you must disregard technicalities when considering what " interest " means and then with regard to the rest of the phrase
" in possession " introduce the technicality that any interest which is not " in
expectancy " must be an interest " in possession ". To have an interest in
possession does not merely mean that you possess the interest. You also possess
an interest in expectancy for you may be able to assign it and you can rely on it E
to prevent the trustees from dissipating the trust fund. " In possession " must
mean that your interest enables you to claim now whatever may be the subject
of the interest. For instance, if it is the current income from a certain fund your
claim may yield nothing if there is no income, but your claim is a valid claim,
and if there is any income you are entitled to get it; but a right to require trustees
to consider whether they will pay you something does not enable you to claim F
anything. If the trustees do decide to pay you something, you do not get it by
reason of having the right to have your case considered: you get it only because
the trustees have decided to give it to you. Even if I had thought that objects
of discretionary trusts have interests, I would not find any good reason for
holding that they have interests in possession.

So it is now necessary to consider whether I am in any way precluded by G
authority from giving effect to these views. The Crown relied principally on four
cases in this House and I have not found in any of the other cases cited in argument any very illuminating discussion of the meaning of the word " interest " in
s. 2 (1) (b) or of the phrase " interest in possession " in the Act of 1940.

In *Scott* v. *Inland Revenue Comrs.* (4) before the relevant death

> " The persons beneficially interested in the income of the property . . .   H
> were . . . the various persons who were objects of the discretionary trust
> and the person who might ultimately benefit by the accumulations and
> discharge of incumbrances "

(per LORD RUSSELL OF KILLOWEN (5)).

After the death, the seventh Earl Cadogan became entitled to receive the whole I
income. If the seventh Earl had not been one of the objects of the discretionary
trust, it would seem that the property which yielded the income passed on the
death. Enjoyment of the income changed hands on the death. It was held that
the fact that he had been one of those objects made no difference. I do not
think it useful to examine LORD RUSSELL'S phraseology because no question
was raised under s. 2 (1) (b); but, if one does look at it, he said in the passage

---

(4) [1936] 3 All E.R. 752; [1937] A.C. 174.
(5) [1936] 3 All E.R. at p. 755; [1937] A.C. at p. 181.

A which I have quoted that the objects of the discretionary trust " were beneficially
interested in the income of the property ". He did not invent the idea of a group
right: he must have meant that each object was beneficially interested in the
income. But I think that he would have been extremely surprised if he had been
told that it necessarily followed that each object had an interest extending to the
whole income so that on the death of any one of the objects there was a cesser of
B an interest extending to the whole income within the meaning of s. 2 (1) (*b*) and
s. 7 (7). Confusion will generally result if one tries to apply language adequate for
the point under discussion to a problem which was not in the mind of the speaker
—however eminent may have been the person who used the language. I do not
regard this case as a compelling authority on the present question.

In *Burrell* v. *A.-G.* (6) there was a discretionary trust and a provision that any
C surplus income not used for that purpose was to be carried forward and could be
used for the reduction of capital charges. Lord Russell of Killowen, however,
said (7):

"In my opinion the state of affairs which prevailed at Harry's death is
sufficient to show that the beneficial interest of the heir-at-law and next of
kin in the property was microscopic . . . their interest is so minute and so
D remote that it may for our present purpose be ignored."

So the case was decided on the footing that the trustees were to devote the whole
income to making payments to one or more of the discretionary objects. That
seems to me to be what Lord Russell meant when he said with regard to the
objects of the discretionary trust (8):

E "It is true that no one of them could claim to be beneficially interested
in any defined share of, or to any defined extent in, the property; but the
six together constituted the only people who could, while Harry was alive,
obtain any benefit from the property or have any beneficial enjoyment of the
property."

He then said that those who became interested after the death of Harry were a
F new group becoming interested under a new trust and fulfilling a new qualification
as a condition of membership. So he held that the title to the beneficial interest
in the property as a whole changed hands on the death notwithstanding that
some of the members of the two groups were the same persons. That this case is
no direct authority on the construction of s. 2 (1) (*b*) is shown by the fact that the
Court of Appeal had relied on that section but their order was varied in this
G House so as to strike that out.

Counsel for the Crown put his case so high as to argue that these cases show
that, whenever there is a primary discretionary trust followed by a direction to
deal with any surplus not paid to the discretionary objects by accumulation or
otherwise, the court must disregard any such direction and treat the case as if
the trustees had been directed to divide the whole income among the discretionary
H objects. I can find no basis and no rational justification for any such artificial
rule. The present case must be decided in accordance with the fact that neither
individually nor collectively were the objects of this discretionary trust entitled
in any year to receive any part of the trust income: that is shown by the fact that
in only one out of twenty years did any of them receive any part of the income.

Then it was argued that, although the construction and effect of s. 2 (1) (*b*)
I was not considered in this House in either of these cases, the effect of the decision
in *Public Trustee* v. *Inland Revenue Comrs.* (9) was to make them in some way
authorities on the proper construction of that section. I do not think that this
decision had any such effect. What the case did was to decide

". . . that s. 1 and s. 2 are not mutually exclusive and that the excepting

(6) [1936] 3 All E.R. 758; [1937] A.C. 286.
(7) [1936] 3 All E.R. at pp. 763, 764; [1937] A.C. at p. 299.
(8) [1936] 3 All E.R. at p. 764; [1937] A.C. at p. 300.
(9) [1960] 1 All E.R. 1; [1960] A.C. 398.

words in s. 2 (1) (*b*) are operative in regard to property which falls within   **A**
that subsection even though that property may fall also within the wide words
of s. 1 "
(per VISCOUNT SIMONDS (10)). We are not bound by the decision nor do I think
that we are bound by the reasoning to hold that in every case of settled property
where there is a passing of the property there must also be the cesser of an
interest within the meaning of s. 2 (1) (*b*). It could only be on that footing that **B**
earlier cases where it was decided that there was a passing under s. 1 must
now be regarded as authorities on the scope and meaning of s. 2 (1) (*b*);
but the case (11) is relevant here in another way. If I take the view that for a
long time there has been considerable misunderstanding with regard to s. 2 (1) (*b*),
I need not hesitate to say so because this House in that case removed a much more
fundamental and long standing misunderstanding than any with which we have to **C**
deal in the present case. I can repeat the words of LORD RADCLIFFE (12):

" I can only say that, at the end of the day, I am relieved to find that we
are not constrained by any authority to impose upon ourselves a construction
of taxing provisions which seems to me as much contrary to the plain meaning
of the Act as it would be frivolously capricious in its result."
  D
Here I would only omit the word " frivolously ".
Next I must deal with *Ralli Brothers* v. *Inland Revenue Comrs.* (13) and *Public
Trustee* v. *Inland Revenue Comrs.* (14). In the *Ralli* case (13) both s. 2 (1) (*b*)
and s. 43 were considered, but I do not think that any of the observations regarding these provisions throws any light on the questions now before the House.
The matters for decision with regard to these provisions do not arise in this case. **E**
The *Public Trustee* case (14), however, does require fuller examination. There
was a settlement under which the income went to a discretionary class until the
death of the testator's daughter : she was a member of that class. On her death
her son, John, became entitled to the fund. In 1961 John assigned to the trustees
the income until 1968. His mother was still alive so he could only effectively
assign any income which might accrue after his mother's death and before 1968. **F**
The trustees were to apply this income for the same discretionary trust as that
which then existed but, of course, the objects could not be the same because the
mother would have dropped out before this new trust could take effect. The
mother died a few days after John had made this assignment. So what happened
on her death was that the discretionary trust under the original settlement then
came to an end and the new discretionary trust set up by John took effect. It **G**
was held that the property passed under s. 1 because on the death there was a
passing of the right to the income to a new trust set up by a new settlor for the
benefit of a new class of discretionary objects. There was little said about s. 2 (1)
(*b*). My noble and learned friend, LORD GUEST, merely said (15):

" It thus follows that the beneficial interest ceased on the mother's death
for the benefit of a class different from that group which had the beneficial **H**
interest before the death, in which case there would be a passing under
s. 2 (1) (*b*)."
LORD MORTON OF HENRYTON said (16) that if the share did not pass under s. 1

". . . class A had an interest in the Kirkwood share which ceased on the
death of Mrs. Pattisson, and on her death a benefit accrued to Class B to the
extent of the whole of the share. The property passing on the death of Mrs. **I**
Pattisson must, therefore, be ' deemed to include ' the Kirkwood share and
the case falls within s. 2 (1) (*b*) of the same Act."

---

(10) [1960] 1 All E.R. at p. 9, letter D; [1960] A.C. at p. 416.
(11) [1960] 1 All E.R. 1; [1960] A.C. 398.
(12) [1960] 1 All E.R. at p. 10, letter C; [1960] A.C. at p. 417.
(13) [1966] 1 All E.R. 65; [1966] A.C. 483.
(14) [1966] 1 All E.R. 76; [1966] A.C. 520.
(15) [1966] 1 All E.R. at p. 82, letter D; [1966] A.C. at pp. 544, 545.
(16) [1966] 1 All E.R. at p. 83, letter B; [1966] A.C. at p. 546.

A LORD UPJOHN (17) dealt with the matter at somewhat greater length, but he was under a misapprehension as to the discretionary trust; he thought that there was a power to accumulate any surplus income, but that power in the original settlement had come to an end before the relevant period. He accepted the view of the Crown that there is no claim for duty when one member falls out of a class of discretionary objects. I cannot read the speeches in that case as showing that

B this House came to any clear decision as to the meaning of the word " interest " in s. 2 (1) (b).

Then the Crown founded on two decisions on the meaning of the word " interest " in a different provision, which was obviously passed to deal with a different problem. The Customs and Inland Revenue Act, 1881, required certain property to be brought in although it had ceased to belong to the deceased at the date of

C his death. This included the case where a settlor in making a settlement had reserved an interest in the settled property. In A.-G. v. Heywood (18) the settlor had provided that the trustees had a discretion to apply the trust income for the benefit of himself his wife and children or any one or more of them. It was, I think, rightly decided that he had reserved an interest within the meaning of that provision. It is always proper to construe an ambiguous word or phrase in light

D of the mischief which the provision is obviously designed to prevent, and in light of the reasonableness of the consequences which follow from giving it a particular construction. Here, if " interest " were given a narrow or technical meaning it would be very easy to defeat the obvious purpose of the provision by setting up a discretionary trust and choosing trustees who might be expected to exercise their discretion in favour of the settlor. On the other hand no unreasonable

E consequences would follow if the word were given a wider meaning, so as to include possible benefit that would come to the settlor in a certain event—in the event of the trustees deciding that he should have the whole or part of the income.

If so vague a word as "interest" is used in different Acts dealing with different problems, there is only, in my view, a slender presumption that it has the same meaning in both; where they are dealing with the same problem the presumption

F is very much stronger. There is here the special feature that the Act of 1894, by s. 2 (1) (c), picks up and slightly amends that provision in the Act of 1881; but I see no reason why there should be any strong inference from that fact that, when the Act of 1894 goes on to deal with quite a different problem, the word " interest " must be given the same meaning as it had in the Act of 1881. In the absence of good reason to the contrary one would attach the same meaning; but

G the reasons which I have stated for giving a different meaning to the word in s. 2 (1) (b) and s. 7 (7) appear to me greatly to outweigh any presumption which there might otherwise be for adopting the same meaning. The Crown also founded on A.-G. v. Farrell (19), but that case does not appear to me to throw any additional light on the present question.

I would allow this appeal.

H   **LORD MORRIS OF BORTH-Y-GEST:** My Lords, I have had the advantage of reading the opinion of my noble and learned friend, LORD REID. I agree with it, and would allow the appeal.

LORD HODSON: My Lords, I have had the advantage of reading the opinion of my noble and learned friend, LORD WILBERFORCE. I agree with it,

I and would allow the appeal.

LORD GUEST: My Lords, I have had the opportunity of reading the speech of my noble and learned friend, LORD REID. I agree with it and would allow the appeal.

LORD WILBERFORCE: My Lords, the testator, Thomas Edward Gartside, by his will dated Feb. 8, 1934, gave one-quarter of his residuary estate to

---

(17) [1966] 1 All E.R. at p. 83; [1966] A.C. at p. 546.
(18) (1887), 19 Q.B.D. 326.   (19) [1931] 1 K.B. 81.

his trustees on trusts during the life of his son John Travis Gartside to pay or A
apply the whole or such part of the income as his trustees should in their absolute
and uncontrolled discretion think fit for or towards the maintenance support or
benefit of his said son or the son's wife or children and to accumulate any surplus
income. The trustees had power to resort to the accumulations at any time during
the son's life and to use them for the maintenance etc., of the same class of persons.
After the death of John Travis Gartside the share was to be held for such of his B
children as should attain twenty-one or, if daughters, marry. There was a power of
advancement in favour of any grandchild up to one-half of his or her presumptive
or vested share.

The testator died on Jan. 8, 1941, so that the period of permissible accumulation came to an end on Jan. 7, 1962. On Jan. 2, 1962, just before the termination
of that period, the trustees made advances to the twin sons of John Travis C
Gartside, then aged seventeen, out of the capital of the one-fourth share, of a
value of about £23,500 each. On May 8, 1963, John Travis Gartside died.

The Crown claims estate duty on his death on the advanced funds under s. 43
of the Finance Act, 1940. The conditions laid down by that section for a charge
of estate duty are stated in the words—

" where an interest limited to cease on a death has been disposed of or   D
has determined . . . after becoming an interest in possession;".

It is relevant to add that paras. (a) and (b) of sub-s. (1) proceed to deal separately
with the cases where (a) if the interest had not been determined the property
in which the interest subsisted would have passed on the death under s.1 of the
Finance Act, 1894, and (b) if, on the same hypothesis, that property would have E
been deemed by virtue of s. 2 (1) (b) of the Finance Act, 1894, to be included to a
particular extent in the property passing on the death, imposing a total or partial
charge as the case may be.

The decision in this appeal turns on the meaning of the words " interest " and
" interest in possession ". In the courts below it was generally accepted, following
certain authorities, that the beneficiaries had " interests "; the debate was, in F
the main, concentrated on the question whether they had " interests in possession "; but the prior question is whether they had " interests " at all and to that
I now turn.

At the relevant date, i.e., just before the death of John Travis Gartside, the
potential beneficiaries under the discretionary trusts (for convenience called " the
discretionary beneficiaries ") were four, namely, John Travis Gartside himself, G
his wife and his two sons. Under the trusts of income which applied during his
life, no one of these beneficiaries had any right to receive any income. The trustees
had an absolute discretion to distribute or to withhold distribution of the income
of any year, and, as regards any income that they decided to distribute, to give all
or none of it to any one beneficiary. Any undistributed income had, during the
permissible period, to be accumulated, i.e., added to capital. The accumulations H
so made could subsequently be distributed in the same way as current income—
no beneficiary having any right to any such distribution—and subject to this
power were held by the trustees on trusts under which the two grandchildren had
contingent interests only.

I have said that no one of the discretionary beneficiaries had at the relevant time
any right to receive any income, but this is not the whole of the matter. It is also I
necessary to appreciate that the discretionary beneficiaries taken together had
no right to receive any or, a fortiori, all of the income. Two of them were infants,
but even if they had been of age they could not, with their parents, have called
on the trustees to pay them the income of any year; the reason being that the
trustees had power to accumulate so much as they did not distribute, which might
be the whole, for the possible benefit of persons unborn. To describe them as
" the only people who could during the relevant period obtain any benefit from
the property or have any beneficial enjoyment of it " may be misleading, unless

A one bears in mind that, singly or collectively, they had no right in any year to receive a penny.

I can now consider the language of s. 43 of the Finance Act, 1940. Subsection (1) starts by referring to an " interest " limited to cease on a death but neither this section nor any section of definition, whether in the Finance Act, 1940, or in the Finance Act, 1894, gives any guidance as to the meaning of this word.

B Some limit is placed on the scope of the enquiry by the later words " after becoming an interest in possession ": these suggest, if not compel, the conclusion that the " interests " with which the subsection is dealing are such as are capable of being described as " interests in possession ". Whatever exactly that means, it is safe, I think, to say that " interests in possession " are, in this legislation, contrasted with " interests in expectancy ": so that one may say this of the

C " interests " with which the subsection is concerned, that one would expect these to fit within this classification. I return later to this point.

This is not all the guidance one may get as to the meaning of " interest ". Section 43 of the Finance Act, 1940, is to be construed together with the Finance Act, 1894. Both its structure and its language are related to those of the earlier Act. The parent provision in the Finance Act, 1894, is evidently s. 2 (1) (*b*),

D which deals with interests ceasing on the death, and there cannot be any doubt that " interest limited to cease on a death " in s. 43 must refer to the same kind of interest: in s. 2 (1) (*b*) the interest has ceased, in s. 43 it was limited to cease but has not done so because some event or action has prevented this result.

What, then, can one say of " interest " as used in s. 2 (1) (*b*)? Two indications are given. The first is in the subsection itself which says that the property is

E deemed to pass " to the extent to which a benefit accrues or arises " by the cesser of the interest. We are concerned here with a taxing Act, and if one thing is necessary about taxes it is that the amount of them should be ascertained with precision. The subsection must, then, contemplate that some definite portion of the property should be ascertainable when an interest ceases. The second indication is given by s. 7 (7) which deals precisely with this point; it reads:

F
" 7.—(7) The value of the benefit accruing or arising from the cesser of an interest ceasing on the death of the deceased shall—

" (*a*) if the interest extended to the whole income of the property, be the principal value of that property; and

" (*b*) if the interest extended to less than the whole income of the property,

G be the principal value of an addition to the property equal to the income to which the interest extended."

This shows that, for the cesser of an interest to give rise to a charge for duty, it must be possible to say of the interest that it extended to the whole income, or to a definite part of the income. This notion of definite extension is, in my

H opinion, vital to the understanding and working of s. 2 (1) (*b*) and consequently of s. 43 of the Act of 1940.

It must follow that the discretionary beneficiaries under the settlement had no " interest " within the meaning of the section; no single member of this class had any right to any income: even if one considers them collectively they had no right to any income because the trustees could accumulate the whole of it. This

I makes it unnecessary and indeed otiose to consider whether the discretionary beneficiaries had " interests in possession ", but the use of these words in the subsection do provide a cross check as to the meaning of " interest ". As is well illustrated by the judgments in the courts below, it is exceedingly difficult to fit the rights of the discretionary beneficiaries either into the category of " interests in possession " or into its statutory counterpart " interests in expectancy ": to say that as it is not one it must be the other is not a very satisfactory solution (the categories though mutually exclusive need not be exhaustive), especially if this technique can be used—as it has been used by the courts below—either way.

Rather, the difficulty of giving either answer endorses the conclusion that this is A
not an " interest ", within the meaning of this section at all.

So much as regards the discretionary beneficiaries. Before I deal with the
position of the accumulation beneficiaries I must deal with some arguments presented to us. The Crown sought to establish that a wide meaning should be
attributed to the word " interest ", wide enough to include the interest of a
beneficiary under a discretionary trust, by three main arguments. First, it was B
said that the expression " interest " itself is one of complete generality: in the
context of the estate duty legislation it should be given a popular rather than a
conveyancing meaning. Secondly, when one analyses a beneficiary's rights under
a discretionary trust, the conclusion must be that he has an interest even in a
technical legal sense of the word. Thirdly, the point was said to be settled by
authority, in particular by two decisions, *A.-G.* v. *Heywood* (20) and *A.-G.* v. C
Farrell (21). These arguments were substantially accepted by the Court of
Appeal (22), but I do not find them persuasive.

1. It can be accepted that " interest " is capable of a very wide and general
meaning; but the wide spectrum that it covers make it all the more necessary,
if precise conclusions are to be founded on its use, to place it in a setting: VISCOUNT
RADCLIFFE, delivering the Board's judgment in *Comr. of Stamp Duties* v. *Living-* D
ston (23), shows how this word has to do duty in several quite different legal
contexts to express rights of very different characters, and that to transfer a
meaning from one context to another may breed confusion.

No doubt in a certain sense a beneficiary under a discretionary trust has an
" interest ": the nature of it may, sufficiently for the purpose, be spelt out by
saying that he has a right to be considered as a potential recipient of benefit E
by the trustees and a right to have his interest protected by a court of equity.
Certainly that is so, and when it is said that he has a right to have the trustees
exercise their discretion " fairly " or " reasonably " or " properly " that indicates
clearly enough that some objective consideration (not stated explicitly in declaring the discretionary trust, but latent in it) must be applied by the trustees
and that the right is more than a mere spes. But that does not mean that he has F
an interest which is capable of being taxed by reference to its extent in the trust
fund's income: it may be a right with some degree of concreteness or solidity,
one which attracts the protection of a court of equity, yet it may still lack the
necessary quality of definable extent which must exist before it can be taxed.
This may be illustrated by reference to the decision in *Skinner* v. *A.-G.* (24) on
which the Crown relied. Whatever may be the correct explanation of that case, G
the existence of the element of extent was clearly apparent. In the present case
its absence is equally noticeable, so that merely to show that " interest " in
s. 2 (1) (*b*) has a " popular " meaning—as SIR WILFRID GREENE, M.R., described
it in the Court of Appeal sub nom. *Re White, Skinner* v. *A.-G.* (25)—fails to meet
the critical difficulty in the Crown's way.

LORD DENNING, M.R., and SALMON, L.J., in the Court of Appeal (22) were H
persuaded by an argument which was suggested to meet this difficulty. The
beneficiary's right, it was claimed, is analogous to that of a competitor in a
beauty competition; she has a right to be considered for the prize: if she is
excluded, she can be awarded damages which a jury can assess. The analogy
was inevitably left at some distance, because it could hardly be suggested that a
charge for estate duty could be assessed by any similar procedure: and it is clear I
enough that it fails at the critical point, namely, of establishing that a person
with a chance of success has an interest, in more than the broadest popular
sense, *in the fund.*

---

(20) (1887), 19 Q.B.D. 326.   (21) [1931] 1 K.B. 81.
(22) [1967] 2 All E.R. 173.
(23) [1964] 3 All E.R. 692 at p. 699; [1965] A.C. 694 at p. 712.
(24) [1939] 3 All E.R. 787; [1940] A.C. 350.
(25) [1938] 2 All E.R. 691 at p. 695, letter C; [1939] Ch. 131 at p. 140.

A   2. Returning to the nature of the beneficiary's right, the Crown is met with the difficulty that as a matter of long established acceptance, and also of authoritative decision (*A.-G. of Ceylon* v. *Arunachalam Chettiar* (*No. 1*) (26) per VISCOUNT SIMONDS) no charge for duty arises when one of a discretionary class dies. LORD DENNING, M.R., regarded this as a special rule whose rationale was unsatisfactory and which should not be extended, and SALMON, L.J., said that it was difficult

B   to understand. I do not so regard it: it seems to me an inevitable and necessary, and I am tempted to add reasonable, consequence of the method of taxation laid down by s. 2 (1) (*b*) and s. 7 (7) of the Finance Act, 1894. This was in fact the ground on which it was put by LORD SIMONDS, when he said (27):

C   " ' I find it impossible to conceive of a basis of valuation which, in relation to such an " interest ", would conform to the scheme prescribed by s. 17 (6) ' "

(corresponding to s. 7 (7) of the Finance Act, 1894). If, however, as seems indisputable, the exemption from duty which arises in such cases as these, arises directly from the legislative scheme, it becomes a task of great difficulty for the Crown to suggest a definition of interest which, omitting the exempted case, will cover the present situation. No formulation suggested in argument was in fact

D   able to achieve this.

3. I now come to the decision in *A.-G.* v. *Heywood* (28) and *A.-G.* v. *Farrell* (29). *A.-G.* v. *Heywood* (28) was decided in 1887 on s. 38 (2) (*c*) of the Customs and Inland Revenue Act, 1881, when what was levied, was a stamp duty on property included in an account. The 1881 Act defined various categories of property to be included in an account, viz., property included in a gift made within three months of the death, property held on joint tenancy, and (under para. (*c*)) settled property

E   in which a limited interest was reserved to the settlor or over which the settlor reserved a power of revocation. *A.-G.* v. *Heywood* (28) was concerned with a voluntary settlement, under which the trustees had a discretion to apply income, during the settlor's life, for a class including the settlor, and it was held by a Divisional Court that s. 38 (2) (*c*) applied. The judgment of WILLS, J., contains

F   the following passage (30):

" The word ' interest ' is capable of different meanings, according to the context in which it is used or the subject-matter to which it is applied. If the contention for the defendants is right nobody has any interest in the property settled, and yet the whole fund was to be held for the benefit of three classes of persons—the husband, the wife, and the children; and the sum of

G   the benefits conferred on all these three classes taken together, being the sum of three nothings amounts to nothing, whereas, on the other hand, it must necessarily comprehend the whole interest in the fund. This is simply a reductio ad absurdum. The application of the word ' interest ' is not confined to a vested or a necessarily contingent interest. The Act was meant to cast a wider net than such a construction would imply."

H   When this decision was followed in *A.-G.* v. *Farrell* (29) s. 38 (2) (*c*) of the Act of 1881 (as amended in 1889) had been incorporated by the unhappy technique of reference into s. 2 (1) (*c*) of the Finance Act, 1894—" as if therein enacted ". This case, too, was concerned with a settlement which contained a discretionary trust of income for the settlor and other persons. The Court of Appeal, not without hesitation, held that duty was payable and that *A.-G.* v. *Heywood* (28) ought to be

I   followed. LORD HANWORTH, M.R. (31), expressed himself as unwilling to dissent from a case which had stood for so long and been acted upon: GREER, L.J. (32), considered that but for *A.-G.* v. *Heywood* (28) the case would have presented great

(26) [1957] A.C. 513.
(27) [1957] A.C. at p. 539. VISCOUNT SIMONDS was quoting the words of GRATIAEN, J., in the Supreme Court (1953), 55 C.N.L.R. 481 at pp. 493, 494.
(28) (1887), 19 Q.B.D. 326.   (29) [1931] 1 K.B. 81.
(30) (1887), 19 Q.B.D. at p. 331.   (31) [1931] 1 K.B. at p. 97.
(32) [1931] 1 K.B. at p. 100.

difficulty. ROMER, L.J. (33), both applied and approved the previous decision. **A**
The trustees invited your lordships to overrule these cases. The Crown supported
them and urged that they should be treated as governing the meaning of
" interest " in the present case. I see no need to take either course. Perhaps
A.-G. v. *Farrell* (34) could have been decided the other way on the ground that
once s. 38 (2) (*c*) had been embodied in the Finance Act, 1894, s. 2 (1), the word
" interest " in the earlier section should be given a meaning similar to that which it **B**
bears in para. (*b*) and (*d*), each of which involved the conception of extent. But
this was not done and one can appreciate why not. For s. 38 (2) (*c*) is concerned,
broadly, with the case of persons who settle their property yet wish to benefit
from it so long as they live. To tax them in such a case is perfectly understandable,
however large or small the reserved benefit may be and whether it is defined in
extent or undefined. No definition is necessary, because the measure of the charge **C**
is the whole value of the property. So naturally no reference is made to " extent "
—the mere fact of reservation is enough, I think, therefore, that the decisions in
principle are acceptable; but this is the other limb—acceptance of them does not
carry the present case. In s. 2 (1) (*b*) of the Finance Act, 1894 (and the same is
true of s. 2 (1) (*d*)) a duty is imposed the quantum of which is related to the extent
of the interest, and I see no difficulty in saying that the element of extent is **D**
relevant under the two sections but not under the third: the distinction is both
made in the language and is necessary if the tax is to work.

Before leaving the subject of discretionary trusts I must consider one further
point. When one object of a discretionary class dies, there is no charge for duty:
the same must follow (under s. 43 of the Finance Act, 1940), if the interest of one
object is disposed of or determined (if that can be done). But there is also the **E**
case of a " closed class ", i.e., a class of discretionary objects, no one of whom is
entitled to any income, but who between them can claim to be entitled, in each
year, to the whole. It may well be possible to apply s. 2 (1) (*b*) of the Finance Act,
1894, or s. 43 of the Finance Act, 1940 (as the case may be) to such a situation, as
some of their lordships who decided the recent appeal in *Public Trustee* v. *Inland
Revenue Comrs.* (35) suggest. I do not find it necessary to pursue this particular **F**
argument, since we are not concerned with a closed class.

I now consider the position as regards the surplus income in each year, i.e.,
the amount of income not distributed among the discretionary class. There is no
difficulty here; in the first place (one may call this the primary trust) this income
had to be added to capital and held on trusts under which the testator's grandchildren had contingent interests. In the second place (one may call this the **G**
secondary trust) the trustees had power to resort to any accumulations and to
apply them as income, i.e., to distribute them between the discretionary beneficiaries. The interest of the accumulation beneficiaries under the primary trust
was, in the terminology of the Finance Act, 1894, an interest in expectancy (as
contrasted with an interest in possession): the discretionary beneficiaries under **H**
the secondary trust had, for the reasons already given, no " interest " at all. So
it is impossible to say that when, by the advances, the trust for accumulation
of the surplus income was, pro tanto, determined, there was any determination
within the section. In the Court of Appeal (36), HARMAN, L.J. (37), while accepting that the rights of the accumulation beneficiaries taken by themselves were in
expectancy and that those of the discretionary beneficiaries, taken by themselves, **I**
were not such that duty would be chargeable, came to the conclusion that taking
all the rights together, an interest in possession could be found. " Somebody ",
he said (38), " must have an interest in possession ". I would, respectfully, agree

---

(33) [1931] 1 K.B. at pp. 103, 104.   (34) [1931] 1 K.B. 81.
(35) [1966] 1 All E.R. 76; [1966] A.C. 520.   (36) [1967] 2 All E.R. 173.
(37) [1967] 2 All E.R. at p. 180, letter A.
(38) [1967] 2 All E.R. at p. 180, letter C.

A with his judgment but for the latter point: for, at any rate for the purposes of estate duty, cases may exist where, at the relevant time, no " interest in possession " can be found: one such is where the whole income is being validly accumulated for the benefit of persons with contingent interests. That, in fact, is this case and the fact that it is so prevents the section from attaching.

B Finally, I must now say something of certain authorities. First, there are two cases in this House the authority of which was invoked by the Crown: these are *Scott* v. *Inland Revenue Comrs.* (39) and *Burrell* v. *A.-G.* (40). In each of these cases income was held on trust for a class of discretionary beneficiaries who, singly and collectively, had no right to receive any income in any year. In *Scott's* case (39) the surplus income, during the relevant life (of the sixth Earl Cadogan) was to be accumulated and applied in the discharge of debts or incumbrances
C affecting the estates and subject thereto as capital money. The capital of the estate was held on trust for a person (the seventh Earl Cadogan) who had an interest in expectancy. It was held that on the death of the sixth Earl the property as a whole passed under s. 1 of the Finance Act, 1894.

In *Burrell's* case (40) the trusts were more elaborate and cannot accurately be described except by repeating in full the analysis of LORD RUSSELL
D OF KILLOWEN (41). However, but for one complicating factor, the case would be a simple one, as it was then regarded by this House and has since been regarded, namely, as a case where before the relevant death the income was held for a discretionary class (" A ") and after the death for a distinct but overlapping discretionary class (" B ") in neither case either any individual, nor the class
E collectively, having a right to any, or the whole, income. The decision was that in such a case there was a passing of the property under s. 1. The complicating factor was that if, and only if, the whole income was not distributed to class A, or to class B, or applied by the trustees in paying off certain portions actually charged and other portions which might be charged or in paying off capital charges, there might, at a date in the future (i.e. when all possible allowancers
F were dead or the entail barred) be an ultimate trust for the heir-in-law or next-of-kin of the testator. This consideration was relied on by the taxpayer to support an argument that there was no passing, because the whole estate legal and equitable remained in the heir-at-law and next-of-kin except to the extent that the trustees decided to distribute. It is not surprising that this argument did not succeed. LORD RUSSELL OF KILLOWEN (42) disposes of it by showing how remote in time
G and also in reality (" so remote and so minute ") the interest was, and called it " microscopic ". I cannot regard the position of the heir-at-law or next-of-kin as other than a special factor which neither had any bearing on the decision of *Burrell's* case (40) nor any relevance by analogy to the present. This matter apart, the nature of the two decisions is clear. They were both decisions on a
H passing within s. 1 of the Finance Act, 1894, on the footing that the property as a whole changed hands, and, if so, neither the decisions, nor any phrases in which the unavoidable word " interest " was used can be used as authority that the discretionary class in either case, or any member of it, or aggregate of any other persons had an " interest " within s. 2 (1) (*b*). Counsel for the Crown sought to adapt them for this purpose. The argument was they they were decided at a time
I when (following LORD MACNAGHTEN's opinion in *Earl Cowley* v. *Inland Revenue Comrs.* (43)) s. 1 and s. 2 of the Finance Act, 1894, were thought to be mutually exclusive, so that a case could only come within one of the subsections of s. 2

(39) [1936] 3 All E.R. 752; [1937] A.C. 174.
(40) [1936] 3 All E.R. 758; [1937] A.C. 286.
(41) [1936] 3 All E.R. at p. 759 et seq.; [1937] A.C. at p. 293 et seq.
(42) [1936] 3 All E.R. at pp. 763, 764; [1937] A.C. at p. 299.
(43) [1895-99] All E.R. Rep. 1181 at p. 1187; [1899] A.C. 198 at p. 210.

if it did not fall within s. 1. This House having now in *Public Trustee* v. *Inland* A *Revenue Comrs*. (44), departed from this view of the matter and having held that s. 2 is definitive of s. 1 by " exclusion and inclusion ", *Scott's* case (45) and *Burrell's* case (46) must, it was said, now be regarded as decisions under s. 2 (1) (*b*) and so as decisions that an " interest " or " interests " existed. I find this argument totally unacceptable. I know of no principle by which an expressed ratio decidendi can be converted into another ratio decidendi merely because (if such B is the case) the first is founded on a principle which has been superseded by a new principle which would support the second. One cannot have authority by translation. The impossibility indeed of such a process is shown by the fact that in *Burrell's* case (46) not only did LORD RUSSELL OF KILLOWEN (47) expressly decide that the case fell not within s. 2 (1) (*b*) but within s. 1, but this House rescinded the order of the Court of Appeal which was based on the former section and C restored that of FINLAY, J., which was based on the latter. It may be permissible, or even necessary, if a case similar to *Burrell's* case (46) arises for decision, to consider whether, after *Public Trustee* v. *Inland Revenue Comrs*. (44) the new decision should be put on the same or on another ground: what one cannot do is to force on those who gave the decision of the House of 1937 reasoning which they did not accept.　　　　D

The remaining authority is that of *A.-G.* v. *Power* (48). I need say no more of this case than that I agree with the analysis of it by UNGOED-THOMAS, J. (49), and with his observations (50) that it shows that the Crown's contention in the present case would involve the consequence that duty could be claimed on the death under twenty-one of an infant contingently entitled, if there was a discretionary power of maintenance, a conclusion for which the Crown did not E contend.

I would allow the appeal and restore the judgment of UNGOED-THOMAS, J. (51).

Appeal allowed.

Solicitors: *Gregory, Rowcliffe & Co.*, agents for *John Taylor & Co.*, Blackburn (for the trustees); *Solicitor of Inland Revenue*.　　　　F

[*Reported by* KATHLEEN J. H. O'BRIEN, *Barrister-at-Law*.]

G

H

I

---

(44) [1960] 1 All E.R. 1; [1960] A.C. 398.
(45) [1936] 3 All E.R. 752; [1937] A.C. 174.
(46) [1936] 3 All E.R. 758; [1937] A.C. 286.
(47) [1936] 3 All E.R. at pp. 765, 766; [1937] A.C. at pp. 302, 303.
(48) [1906] 2 I.R. 272.
(49) [1966] 3 All E.R. 89 at pp. 98, 99; [1967] Ch. 543 at pp. 563, 565.
(50) [1966] 3 All E.R. at p. 104, letter E; [1967] Ch. at p. 522.
(51) [1966] 3 All E.R. 89; [1967] Ch. 543.

A

CRICKITT *v.* KURSAAL CASINO, LTD. (No. 2) AND OTHERS.

[HOUSE OF LORDS (Viscount Dilhorne, Lord MacDermott, Lord Guest, Lord Wilberforce and Lord Pearson), November 7, 8, 9, December 19, 1967.]

B
Gaming—Lawful and unlawful gaming—Clubs—Roulette—Odds favouring bank —Bank available to be taken by any player—Whether gaming so conducted that chances equally favourable to all players—Inference of knowledge of director other than managing director—Offences by company and others— Betting, Gaming and Lotteries Act 1963 (c. 2), s. 32 (1) (a) (ii), (4), s. 53 (1).

C
Roulette, using a wheel which included a zero and numbers from one to thirty-six, was played at the respondent company's casino over a period of some five and a half months* in 1966. Owing to the presence of the zero the chances at each spin of the wheel were more favourable to the bank than to other players; e.g., on a player's staking that the ball would come to rest in any of the first eighteen numbers, the bank would have nineteen chances against his eighteen owing to the chance that the ball would come to rest in zero. Thus the game was inherently a game of unequal chances.

D
Any player who wished to take the bank could do so, however, on informing the chef-de-table or other club employee supervising the gaming at the roulette table, of the maximum amount for which the player was prepared to be liable on any spin of the wheel and on satifying the chef-de-table that the player had that amount of money. Stakes sought to be laid by other players would then be regulated so as to ensure that the maximum potential

E
liability of the bank did not exceed the sum that the player holding the bank was prepared to risk. Players were aware of this option, but in five and a half months the bank was taken only twice by players. The company, its managing director and manager, were convicted by the justices of unlawful gaming contrary to s. 32 (4)† of the Betting, Gaming and Lotteries Act 1963. Another director, who had been a director throughout the three months

F
covered by the charges was convicted under s. 32 (4) taken with s. 53 (1)‡, and the secretary of the company was convicted of aiding and abetting the offence against s. 32 (4). On appeal from an order of the Divisional Court quashing the convictions,

Held: (i) the gaming was unlawful gaming and offences under s. 32 (4) of the Betting, Gaming and Lotteries Act 1963 were established, for the

G
following reasons—

(a) although the company's offer to allow a player to hold the bank was genuine and accordingly was a factor to be taken into account in determining whether the game was so conducted that the chances were equally favourable to all players, yet, if in practice the offer were almost never taken, the fact that it was made had little weight; on the facts of the present case

H
the offer did not convert the gaming, which was one wherein the chances were inherently unequal, into gaming so conducted that the chances were equally favourable to all players, for the company had enjoyed the bank's advantage throughout virtually the whole period of five and a half months during which the game was played with the offer being made (see p. 145, letters E to H, and p. 141, letters B to D, post).

I

---

* This period is the period from Apr. 7, 1966, when new rules were adopted to try to comply with a previous decision, *Kursaal Casino, Ltd.* v. *Crickitt* ([1966] 2 All E.R. 639).

† Section 32 (4) of the Act of 1963 provides, so far as is material—" If any gaming takes place on any premises—(*a*) which is . . . unlawful gaming; . . . any person concerned in the organisation or management of the gaming . . . who . . . (i) allowed the premises to be used for the purposes of gaming . . . shall be guilty of an offence . . .".

‡ Section 53 (1), so far as relevant, is printed at p. 146, letter H, post.

Principle stated by SACHS, J., in *Kursaal Casino, Ltd.* v. *Crickitt (No. 1)*   A
([1966] 2 All E.R. at p. 642, letter G) approved.

(b) moreover there would be no gaming unless some players were electing
not to take the bank, and, as between them and the bank, inequality of
chances must result (see p. 146, letter B, and p. 141, letters B to D, post).

(ii) the magistrates were entitled to infer from the fact that there had
been systematic gaming for the three months during which the other   B
director had been a director that there had been neglect of duty on her
part with the consequence that she was rightly convicted by virtue of s. 53 (1)
of an offence against s. 32 (4) of the Act of 1963 (see p. 147, letter A, post).

(iii) there was no evidence of the secretary having aided and abetted
other accused, and his conviction would accordingly not be restored (see
p. 147, letter B, post).   C

Decision of the DIVISIONAL COURT (sub nom. *Kursaal Casino, Ltd.* v.
Crickitt (No. 2), [1967] 3 All E.R. 360) reversed.

[Editorial Note.   If passed into law, the Gaming Bill, as presented to
Parliament on Dec. 19, 1967, will repeal s. 32 to s. 39 of the Betting, Gaming
and Lotteries Act 1963.
As to lawful and unlawful gaming, see SUPPLEMENT to 18 HALSBURY'S LAWS   D
(3rd Edn.) title, GAMING AND WAGERING, para. 369A, 2; and for cases on the
subject, see 25 DIGEST (Repl.) 448-450, *292-302*.

For the Betting, Gaming and Lotteries Act 1963, s. 32, see 43 HALSBURY'S
STATUTES (2nd Edn.) 343.]

Cases referred to: E
Alan (J. M.) (Merchandising), Ltd. v. *Cloke*, [1963] 2 All E.R. 258; [1963]
2 Q.B. 340; [1963] 2 W.L.R. 899; 61 L.G.R. 304; Digest (Cont.
Vol. A) 621, *291b*.
Casino Club (Bolton), Ltd. v. *Parr*, (1966), 64 L.G.R. 155; Digest (Cont. Vol.
B) 318, *287c*.
Kelland v. *Raymond*, [1964] 1 All E.R. 564; [1964] 2 Q.B. 108; [1964] 2   F
W.L.R. 662; 128 J.P. 254; 62 L.G.R. 272; Digest (Cont. Vol. B)
319, *291d*.
Kursaal Casino, Ltd. v. *Crickitt (No. 1)*, [1966] 2 All E.R. 639; [1966] 1 W.L.R.
960; 130 J.P. 301; Digest (Cont. Vol. B) 318, *287d*.
Mills v. *MacKinnon*, [1964] 1 All E.R. 155; [1964] 2 Q.B. 96; [1964] 2 W.L.R.
363; 128 J.P. 185; 62 L.G.R. 168; Digest (Cont. Vol. B) 318, *291c*.   G
Quinn v. *MacKinnon*, [1963] 1 All E.R. 570; [1963] 1 Q.B. 874; [1963]
2 W.L.R. 391; 127 J.P. 222; 61 L.G.R. 219; Digest (Cont. Vol. A)
621, *291a*.

Appeal.
This was an appeal from a judgment of the Divisional Court of the Queen's   H
Bench Division (LORD PARKER, C.J., WINN, L.J., and WIDGERY, J.), dated July
10, 1967, and reported [1967] 3 All E.R. 360, allowing an appeal on a Case Stated
by the justices for the county borough of Southend-on-Sea in respect of their
adjudication as a magistrates' court sitting at Southend on Dec. 1 and Dec. 2,
1966. The respondent company, Kursaal Casino, Ltd., was convicted on informations laid down by the appellant, Jack Hammond Crickitt, of being concerned   I
in the management of unlawful gaming to wit, roulette, contrary to s. 32 (4)
of the Betting, Gaming and Lotteries Act 1963. Eight other respondents were
also convicted on informations of committing offences which arose out of that
unlawful gaming. Fines totalling £130 were imposed by the justices on the
company; £190 on the managing director; £125 on the other director; £110
on the secretary; £150 on the manager, and £10 each on the other respondents.
The relevant facts found in the Case Stated and the opinion of the justices are
set out in the opinion of LORD PEARSON.

A   *J. H. Buzzard* and *M. D. L. Worsley* for the appellant.
Sebag Shaw, Q.C., and *William Denny* for the respondents.

Their Lordships took time for consideration.

Dec. 19.   The following opinions were delivered.

B   **VISCOUNT DILHORNE:** My Lords, I do not wish to add anything to what my noble and learned friend, Lord Pearson, has said in his speech, with which I entirely agree. In my opinion this appeal should be allowed.

LORD MacDERMOTT: My Lords, I have had the advantage of reading the opinion prepared by my noble and learned friend, Lord Pearson. I fully agree with his conclusions and reasoning and have only to add that I would,
C   allow the appeal and restore the convictions, under s. 32 (4) of the Betting Gaming and Lotteries Act 1963, of the company, the managing director, the other director and the manager.

LORD GUEST: My Lords, I have had the advantage of reading the speech of my noble and learned friend, Lord Pearson. I agree with it and have nothing to add.
D

LORD WILBERFORCE: My Lords, I have had the advantage of reading the speech of my noble and learned friend, Lord Pearson. I agree with it.

LORD PEARSON: My Lords, this appeal relates to the playing of roulette at the casino of the respondent company (to whom I will refer as " the company "),
E   the roulette wheel being of the ordinary kind on which there is a zero as well as the numbers one to thirty-six. It is not disputed that at each spin of the wheel the chances are more favourable to the holder of the bank than to the other players, and that this disparity of chances is caused by the presence of the zero. The details of the playing are not stated, but I think that a very simple example under typical rules might be this: suppose that a player stakes £1 at evens on
F   what is in effect a bet with the holder of the bank that the ball will come to rest on one of the first eighteen numbers: if he wins, he gains £1; if he loses, he forfeits his £1 stake: he had eighteen chances in his favour, but owing to the presence of the zero he has eighteen plus one chances against him. Although this disparity of chances is referred to in the Case Stated as " the theoretical mathematical advantage to the holder of the bank ", it must have great practical importance for any casino company making profits wholly or mainly by holding
G   the bank and winning money from the other players in the course of the gaming. If there were no disparity of chances, the casino company would not on the average win money from the other players and so would not make profits out of the gaming. It is of assistance in considering the main question at issue in this appeal to bear in mind that roulette, played with a board which includes a
H   zero, is inherently and naturally a game of unequal chances.

The Betting, Gaming and Lotteries Act 1963, is a consolidating Act, and s. 32 to s. 39 of that Act are in substance identical with s. 16 to s. 22 of the Betting and Gaming Act, 1960. The Act of 1960 legalised gaming so long as it complied with certain conditions. Section 32 (1) and (2) of the Act of 1963 provides as follows:—

I   " (1) Subject to the provisions of this Act, any gaming shall be lawful if but only if, it is conducted in accordance with the following conditions, that is to say—(*a*) that either—(i) the chances in the game are equally favourable to all the players; or (ii) the gaming is so conducted that the chances therein are equally favourable to all the players; and (*b*) that no money or money's worth which any of the players puts down as stakes, or pays by way of losses, or exchanges for tokens used in playing the game, is disposed of otherwise than by payment to a player as winnings; and (*c*) that no other payment in money or money's worth is required for a person to take part in the gaming.

" (2) If in any proceedings under this section evidence is adduced that   A
gaming took place on any premises and either—(a) that the game was, or
was a variant of or of a similar nature to, a game which is capable of being
played in accordance with the ordinary rules thereof in such a manner that
the chances therein are not equally favourable to all the players, and that
ten or more persons were present at the gaming; or (b) that a payment
of money or money's worth was required in order to obtain access to the   B
premises, then, subject to s. 36 of this Act, it shall be held that the gaming
was unlawful gaming unless it is proved that the gaming was conducted in
accordance with the conditions set out in sub-s. (1) of this section."

Section 36, which relaxes the requirements of s. 32 (1) (c) in the case of gaming
carried on as an activity of a club, does not affect any issue in the present case
and need not be set out. Section 55 includes the following definitions: C

" ' game of chance ' includes a game of chance and skill combined and a
pretended game of chance or of chance and skill combined, but does not
include any athletic game or sport; ' gaming ' means the playing of a game
of chance for winnings in money or money's worth; ' player ', in relation
to a game of chance, includes any person taking part in the game against
whom other persons taking part in the game stake, play or bet."   D

A question was raised in the course of the argument whether the expression a
" game of chance " in the definitions and in s. 32 refers to that which takes place
on a particular occasion or to the type of game, e.g., roulette. A decision on
this question is not required for the present case and might affect other cases
which are not before your lordships. (See *Quinn* v. *Mackinnon* (1); *Allan J. M.*   E
(Merchandising) Ltd. v. *Cloke* (2); *Mills* v. *Mackinnon* (3); and *Kelland* v. *Ray-*
mond (4).) It is sufficient for the present case to say that playing roulette for
money is " gaming ". A single spin of the wheel, if players stake on it, is, in
itself gaming, but is usually only a small part of the gaming at a session, if the
series of spins of the wheel be regarded as continuous gaming.

The operation of s. 32 (1) (a) (ii) and sub-s. (2) can be illustrated by a simple   F
example. Suppose the game that is played is in other respects the same as roulette,
but the zero is eliminated, either by using a wheel that has no zero or by a rule
that if on any spin the ball comes to rest on zero that spin does not count. Then
the game is a variant of roulette, and the defendant has the burden of proving
compliance with the conditions set out in sub-s. (1), but, as the chances are equal
owing to the elimination of the zero, he will be able to discharge that burden
so far as the condition set out in sub-s. (1) (a) is concerned. That is only an   G
example, and there might perhaps be other ways of complying with s. 32 (1) (a) (ii).

It will be convenient, before coming to the facts of the present case, to refer
to the previous prosecution and conviction of the company for unlawful gaming
by playing roulette in the first *Kursaal* case (*Kursaal Casino, Ltd.* v. *Crickitt*
(*No. 1*) (5)). The game being played was ordinary roulette with the zero, and
the odds in favour of the bank ranged from three per cent. to eleven per cent.   H
according to the combination of numbers on which a player had staked. There
was, however, a special arrangement with regard to the holding of the bank.
The croupier was in attendance at the roulette table for a period of half an
hour and, before commencing his first spin, he announced " the bank is up for
option ", thereby giving any of the assembled persons an opportunity of acting
as banker. At the end of each half-hour session the croupier at the table changed   I
and a new croupier took over and the same procedure was adopted. At any time
after the spin any of the assembled players could take the bank if he desired
to do so and could show that he was able to meet his financial commitments
should the bank lose whilst in his possession. Members were aware of this.

(1) [1963] 1 All E.R. 570;   [1963] 1 Q.B. 874.
(2) [1963] 2 All E.R. 258;   [1963] 2 Q.B. 340.
(3) [1964] 1 All E.R. 155;   [1964] 2 Q.B. 96.
(4) [1964] 1 All E.R. 564;   [1964] 2 Q.B. 108.   (5) [1966] 2 All E.R. 639.

A It was not contended by the Crown that this was not genuine. If two persons claimed the bank at the same time, the manager of the club was available to act as arbitrator. If none of the other assembled players wished to take over the bank it would be taken over by a croupier on behalf of the company. On only one evening during the eighteen months that the club had been in existence had a person other than a croupier acting on behalf of the company taken the bank

B and that occasion was not one of the dates laid in the information. The magistrates having convicted the company of unlawful gaming, there was an appeal to the Divisional Court of the Queen's Bench Division (6). SACHS, J., delivered the first judgment (7), and VEALE, J. (8) and LORD PARKER, C.J., (8) agreed with the judgment. SACHS, J. (9) cited from his judgment in the *Bolton* case (*Casino Club (Bolton), Ltd.* v. *Parr* (10)) this passage (11):

C " I would only emphasise that in this case there has not been explored, nor has there been a need to explore, the question as to at what stage and in what circumstances the fact that the proprietors of a club (or some person with the approval of the proprietors) so consistently held the bank for such a high proportion of the gaming sessions over a sufficient period

D might cause the court to hold that on the realities of the case the conduct of the game on that ground alone falls within the mischief of one or other of the provisions of s. 32. That is a matter which may well fall for consideration on some future occasion."

SACHS, J., then (12) went on to apply that principle or method of approach to the facts of the case before him (the first *Kursaal* case), (6) contrasting the

E theoretical or " paper " position with the realities and setting out the factor to be taken into account (12). He said (13):

" Whether an offer of the bank is such that it is genuine in the sense that in relation to those normally playing it is so capable of attracting acceptances and so likely to attract them as to cause the gaming to be so conducted that the chances therein are equally favourable to all players

F (I would emphasise the words ' all players '), is to my mind a question of fact and degree "

He then referred to the finding of the magistrates that (14)

" . . . an offer could only be deemed to be genuine if it was capable of acceptance and there was no evidence that the financial status of most of the

G members of the club would make it possible for them to be able to accept the offer under any circumstances."

He then said (15):

" It appears to me that the magistrates were correctly directing their minds on the relevant point, and that here is a finding of fact that the option offered was not a genuine one within the meaning of that word as

H above indicated. That can be a valid finding, however true it may have been, that if some exceptional player had come along who could have passed the means test, he would have been allowed to accept the offer and take his turn at the bank."

At the end of his judgment he expressly reserved the question whether the

I offer of the option would, but for the factors which he had set out, have brought the appellants within the protection of sub-s. (*a*) (ii).

In my opinion, the principle or method of approach suggested by SACHS, J. in the *Bolton* case (11) was correct, and it was correctly applied in the first

(6) [1966] 2 All E.R. 639.   (7) [1966] 2 All E.R. at p. 640.
(8) [1966] 2 All E.R. at p. 643.   (9) [1966] 2 All E.R. at p. 642, letter A.
(10) (1966), 64 L.G.R. 155.   (11) (1966), 64 L.G.R. at p. 167.
(12) [1966] 2 All E.R. at p. 642.   (13) [1966] 2 All E.R. at p. 642, letter G.
(14) [1966] 2 All E.R. at p. 642, letter I.   (15) [1966] 2 All E.R. at p. 643, letter A.

Kursaal case (16) to the special facts of that case. The first *Kursaal* case (16) is, **A**
however, distinguishable from the present case, because the company have now
modified their system so as to take it outside the ratio decidendi of the first
Kursaal case (16), which was that the offer was not " genuine " in the sense there
indicated, because most of the players would not have sufficient financial resources
to accept the bank or to " pass the means test ".

The facts of the present case relevant to the main issue are set out in paras. 2   **B**
and 3 of the Case Stated. The passages in para. 3 which show the modifications
made in the system since the first *Kursaal* case (16) are these:

" (i) Subsequent to the decision in " (the first *Kursaal* case (16)) " the club
made a genuine effort to comply therewith and amended its rules to take
effect from Apr. 7, 1966, copies of which amended rules were sent to members
and were available at the club premises and were known to members . . .   **C**
(v) Any player who wished to take the bank would be required to inform
the chef-de-table, or other person employed by the club then supervising
the gaming at the roulette table, of the maximum amount for which he was
prepared to be liable on any spin of the wheel and this would be done before
any stakes were placed. He also had to satisfy the chef-de-table that he had
that amount of money. The chef-de-table or other person supervising would   **D**
then control and regulate the amounts and types of stakes sought to be laid
by the other players so that at no time did the maximum potential liability
of the bank exceed the sum previously stated by the holder of the bank. This
system was capable of operation and could be used to limit the maximum
potential liability of the bank to the amount of the minimum stake 2s. 0d.,
although in such a case the types of stake which could be made would be   **E**
considerably limited. The players were aware of their right to limit their
maximum potential liability to an amount of their choosing and were aware
and accepted as part of the rules of playing roulette at the club that when
such maximum potential liability was limited to a very small one, the
types of stake which might be laid would be limited as might also their
amount. There was no express rule governing the length of time for which   **F**
any one player might hold the bank in the event of two or more desiring to
take it from the club, but this would be arranged equitably by the chef-
de-table . . . (viii) Although players were aware of the theoretical mathematical advantage to the holder of the bank and that they could if they
wished take the bank themselves and limit their maximum potential liability
as they chose, it appeared from the evidence of those members who were   **G**
called on behalf of the company that they did not wish to hold the bank,
preferring to bet on their own ideas of what number or combination of
numbers was likely to succeed. If any other player did not wish to take
the bank it was taken by a croupier on behalf of the company. During
the period from Apr. 7, 1966, until Sept. 17, 1966, the bank was taken by
players, other than a croupier on behalf of the company, on two occasions   **H**
neither of which was on any of the dates laid in the said informations. On
one such occasion the player held the bank for about ten spins and limited
his maximum liability to £40. On the second occasion another player took
the bank for three or four spins and limited such liability to £10."

The opinions of the magistrates relevant to the main issue are set out in para. 14   **I**
of the Case Stated as follows:

" (i) that the offer of the bank in accordance with the new rules did not
render the chances in the game equally favourable to all the players; (ii)
that the gaming was not so conducted that the chances therein were equally
favourable to all the players . . . (v) that the offer of the bank was made and
was capable of being accepted by any player."

---

(16) [1966] 2 All E.R. 639.

A The magistrates therefore convicted the company and other accused of offences involving unlawful gaming.

The Divisional Court (17) on appeal took a different view, allowing the appeal and quashing the convictions. Winn, L.J., (18) gave the first judgment and I think the essence of his decision was that (19)

B ". . . where the advantage which the banker's turn affords is made equally available realistically to any player, that eliminates and evens out the inequality which is present in the playing of any single game, represented by one spin of the roulette wheel."

Widgery, J., agreed (20), but expressed some concern whether it was in the circumstances possible to say that the offer was a realistic one. Lord Parker,
C C.J. (20), agreed with both judgments. The Divisional Court gave leave to appeal to your lordships' House, certifying as the point of law of general public importance the following (21):

". . . in gaming in which there is a bank and which is played according to rules under which the chances are more favourable to the bank than to the other players, does the genuine and realistic offer of the bank to, and
D which is capable of being accepted by, any of the players who wish to take it render the chances in the gaming equally favourable to all the players therein in compliance with s. 32 (1) (*a*) (ii) of the Betting, Gaming and Lotteries Act 1963."

I entirely agree with the magistrates and the Divisional Court (17) that the
E respondents' offer to allow any other player to hold the bank was and is genuine. If the offer is accepted, the acceptance will be honoured and the accepting player will be allowed to hold the bank.

There is, however, a further enquiry to be made what happens in fact in the actual playing of the game. The word "realistic" does not sufficiently define the issue: it is aimed in the right direction, but does not quite hit the
F target. The right enquiry is whether the offer, which may also be called the option or the opportunity, for any player to hold the bank, is in practice effective to convert a game, which is naturally one of unequal chances, into a game where the chances are equal. One must ask what happens in fact. Do the players play on equal terms, or does one player in the game as it is actually played have an advantage over the others? The offer or option or opportunity
G for any player to hold the bank is a relevant factor to be taken into account in considering whether the gaming is so conducted that the chances therein are equally favourable to all the players; if in practice the offer or option or opportunity is almost never accepted or exercised or taken, the weight to be assigned to this factor is almost nothing. In the present case the contrast between the "paper" position and the realities is substantially no less prominent than it
H was in the first *Kursaal* case (22). In this case the offer was accepted only twice in the period of nearly five-and-a-half months. Thus, the company were holding the bank and enjoying the banker's advantage for virtually the whole of that period. It seems to me that the conclusion is irresistible that the gaming was not so conducted that the chances therein were equally favourable to all the players. I agree with the opinions of the magistrates and would restore their
I decision on the main issue.

It would not be satisfactory, however, to rest the decision solely on the particular facts of this case. There is in ordinary roulette, where the zero is not

---

(17) [1967] 3 All E.R. 360.
(18) [1967] 3 All E.R. at p. 361.
(19) [1967] 3 All E.R. at p. 366, letter B.
(20) [1967] 3 All E.R. at p. 366.
(21) [1967] 3 All E.R. at p. 366, letter H.
(22) [1966] 2 All E.R. 639.

eliminated, a fundamental inequality of chances which is present at every spin **A** of the wheel and has far-reaching effects, of which examples can be given:

" (i) The company take the bank whenever no other player wishes to hold it, and so the company gain an advantage. There is no obligation or arrangement for the company ever to play against the bank, and so the company's advantage is not eliminated or evened out by any countervailing **B** disadvantage. It is true that any other player could elect to play only when he holds the bank and not at any other time, but if every player so elected there would be no gaming and so the gaming must take place on the basis that the players are not all so electing and an inequality of chances must result.

" (ii) Any player can come to the roulette table and participate in the game **C** for one spin, or two or three or four spins, and then leave the table or otherwise refrain from further participation in the game. While he is participating he is either holding the bank, or he is not. If he holds the bank, he has an advantage over the other players; if he does not hold the bank, he is at a disadvantage in relation to the holder of the bank—and as he ceases to participate in the gaming, there is no opportunity for rectifying or offsetting **D** or evening out the advantage or disadvantage."

I am thinking only of roulette. Different considerations might apply to a game in which the bank passes from player to player in the ordinary course of play.

Finally, I would say on this main issue, using a homely phrase, that a casino company cannot have the best of both worlds. They cannot both so conduct the gaming that the chances are equally favourable to all the players, including **E** the casino company, and also retain the advantage in the playing which they (the casino company) need to have if they are to win on the average from the other players and so make a profit from the gaming.

There are some minor issues relating to the details of the convictions. These were, with the approval of your lordships, dealt with shortly in the argument of the appeal. The submissions were in substance confined to the principal **F** offence under s. 32 (4) of the Act of 1963 as committed or alleged to have been committed by the company, its managing director, another director, the secretary and the manager. Counsel for the appellant were willing that the convictions under the Licensing Act 1964, relating to unlawful gaming in licensed premises, should not be considered, and I think that they were adopting a similar attitude with regard to the convictions of the chef-de-table and the three croupiers. **G** At any rate, as these convictions were not considered, or not fully considered, in the argument, it would not be right for your lordships to restore them, but there is no implied criticism of the informations having been laid or of the convictions having been entered.

Section 32 (4) of the Act of 1963 provides, so far as is material for this case, that if there is unlawful gaming any person concerned in the organisation or **H** management of the gaming shall be guilty of an offence. Section 53 (1) of the Act of 1963 provides that:

" Where an offence under this Act committed by a body corporate is proved to have been committed with the consent or connivance of, or to have been attributable to any neglect on the part of, any director, manager, secretary or other similar officer of the body corporate . . . he, as well as the **I** body corporate, shall be guilty of that offence . . ."

There cannot be any doubt that the company and the managing director and the manager were concerned in the management of the gaming. Their convictions under s. 32 (4) should be restored.

The other director charged under this s. 32 (4) was convicted under it by virtue of s. 53 (1). The prosecution argument before the magistrates was that, since there had been systematic gaming for at least the three months covered

A by the summonses and this accused person had been a director of the company
which owned the club in which the gaming was carried on, such systematic
gaming could only have been carried on as a result of some neglect of duty
on her part. The magistrates accepted this argument and held that there was
a case to answer and ultimately convicted. In my opinion, there was good
ground for the inference that was drawn, and the conviction was right and
B should be restored.

The secretary was not held to have been concerned in the management of
the unlawful gaming and was not convicted by virtue of s. 53 (1), but he was
convicted of aiding and abetting the other accused in the commission of their
offences under s. 32 (4). Whether or not he might properly have been convicted
on some other ground, I think that there was no evidence or at any rate no
C sufficient evidence (23) of his having so aided and abetted and that his conviction should not be restored.

Accordingly, I would allow the appeal and would restore the convictions of
the company, the managing director, the other director and the manager under
s. 32 (4) of the Act of 1963 and the fines imposed in respect of those convictions.
Also I would set aside the Divisional Court's order as to costs and would direct
D that those respondents (the company, the managing director, the other director
and the manager) do pay the present appellant's costs of the appeal to the
Divisional Court (24). I would make no order as to the costs of the appeal to
your lordships' House.

Appeal allowed.

E Solicitors: *Sharpe, Pritchard & Co.* (for the appellant); *Nelson Mitchell &
Williams,* Southend-on-Sea (for the respondents).

[*Reported by* KATHLEEN J. H. O'BRIEN, *Barrister-at-Law.*]

F

G

H

I

(23) It was found in the Case Stated that on Sept. 17, 1966, a night when the police
entered the club, the secretary arrived at the club after the police had entered. The
justices accepted, in relation to the secretary, the same argument as that put before,
and accepted by, them in relation to the director who was not the managing director.
In regard to both of these respondents the justices accepted evidence of a croupier,
who stated that he had seen each of them at the club premises on one or two occasions,
though he could not say whether before or after introduction of the new roulette rules
in April, 1966; he had not seen either of them at the gaming tables.
(24) [1967] 3 All E.R. 360.

Re HOLMDEN'S SETTLEMENT TRUSTS.   A

INLAND REVENUE COMMISSIONERS *v.* HOLMDEN

AND OTHERS.

[HOUSE OF LORDS (Lord Reid, Lord Morris of Borth-y-Gest, Lord Hodson, Lord
Guest and Lord Wilberforce), October 18, 19, 23, December 13, 1967.]

B

Estate Duty—Determination of life interest—Discretionary trust for class limited
to cease on death of widow—Variation by order of court extending period
of trust until death of widow or twenty-one years from date of order, whichever
was longer—Death of widow within three years after order—Whether order
operated to determine interest of class—Whether estate duty chargeable on
trust fund on death of widow—Finance Act, 1940 (3 & 4 Geo. 6 c. 29), s. 43 (1),   C
as amended by Finance Act, 1950 (14 Geo. 6 c. 15), s. 43, Sch. 7, Pt. 1.

Trust and Trustee—Variation of trusts by the court—Effect of order of court
approving arrangement—Variation taking effect by virtue of consents of
beneficiaries—Variation of Trusts Act, 1958 (6 & 7 Eliz. 2 c. 53), s. 1 (1).

After the death of a settlor, who died in 1945, the trust fund was held
on discretionary trusts, as to income, to pay or apply the whole or the   D
part of the income, as the trustees thought fit, for the benefit of the settlor's
widow, their two children and any grandchildren. Prior to the settlor's
death any income not so paid or applied had been accumulated, but after
his death the income became part of his estate. On Jan. 12, 1960, the court
approved, under s. 1 of the Variation of Trusts Act, 1958, an arrangement
whereby the discretionary trust of income should have effect during the life   E
of the widow or for twenty-one years from Jan. 12, 1960, whichever should
be the longer period. The widow died on Dec. 22, 1962. On appeal from a
decision that estate duty was not payable in respect of the settled funds
on the death of the widow, it being assumed for the purposes of the present
decision that the interest of an object of a discretionary trust could be an
interest in possession for the purposes of s. 43 (1)* of the Finance Act, 1940,   F

Held: estate duty was not exigible on the widow's death for the following
reasons—

(i) (per LORD REID and LORD WILBERFORCE) although the effect of the
arrangement was to substitute a new trust for income as from Jan. 12, 1960,
and (per LORD REID) to terminate the prior income trust, yet this was not a
disposal or determination for the purposes of s. 43 (1) of the Finance Act,   G
1940, as none of the beneficiaries whose interests were concerned lost
anything thereby, so that any disposal or determination was not one in favour
of any other person (see p. 151, letters E and H, p. 159, letter H, and p. 161,
letter F, post).

(ii) (per LORD MORRIS OF BORTH-Y-GEST, LORD HODSON and LORD GUEST)
the effect of the arrangement was to vary the period of the discretionary
trust of income as from Jan. 12, 1960, with the consequence that there was   H
no determination of the income trust but it became a trust continuing until
Jan. 12, 1981, and no new trust began on the widow's death, which, as she was
one only of the class of discretionary objects, did not result in the passing of
the trust property; further, even if there had been a termination of the
income trust by virtue of the arrangement, it was not a disposal or determination within s. 43 (1) of the Finance Act, 1940, since it was not in favour of   I
some other person than those who were beneficiaries prior to the arrangement
(see p. 152, letters C and G, p. 153, letters D and I, p. 155, letter D, p. 156,
letter H, and p. 157, letters B and F, post).

Public Trustee v. *Inland Revenue Comrs.* ([1966] 1 All E.R. 76) distinguished.

Per LORD REID and LORD WILBERFORCE: the arrangement approved
by the court under the Variation of Trusts Act, 1958, s. 1 took effect because

---

* Section 43 (1) is printed at p. 155, letter H, post.

A   each beneficiary had consented to the arrangement, not because the court
had made the variation, the court's order merely conferring consent on behalf
of beneficiaries who were not in a position to give their consent themselves (see p. 151, letter B, and p. 159, letter E, post, cf., p. 155, letter F,
post).

Decision of the Court of Appeal ([1966] 2 All E.R. 661) affirmed.

B
[As to the determination of life interests leading to estate duty becoming
chargeable, see 15 HALSBURY'S LAWS (3rd Edn.) 15, para. 25; and for cases on
interests in property limited to cease on death, see 21 DIGEST (Repl.) 17-22,
57-77.

As to the binding effect of reasons for decisions of courts, see 22 HALSBURY'S
C   LAWS (3rd Edn.) 797, para. 1682.

For the Finance Act, 1894, s. 1, s. 2, s. 22, see 9 HALSBURY'S STATUTES (2nd
Edn.) 348, 350, 382.

For the Finance Act, 1940, s. 43 (1), as amended, see 29 HALSBURY'S STATUTES
(2nd Edn.) 183.]

Cases referred to:
D   A.-G. of Ceylon v. Arunachalam Chettiar (No. 1), [1957] A.C. 513; [1957]
3 W.L.R. 293; 21 Digest (Repl.) 50, *74.
Chapman v. Chapman, [1954] 1 All E.R. 798; [1954] A.C. 429; [1954] 2
W.L.R. 723; 47 Digest (Repl.) 329, 2973.
Gartside v. Inland Revenue Comrs., [1966] 3 All E.R. 89; [1966] 3 W.L.R. 759;
revsd. H.L., ante, p. 121.
E   Public Trustee v. Inland Revenue Comrs., [1966] 1 All E.R. 76; sub nom. Re
Kirkwood, Public Trustee v. Inland Revenue Comrs., [1966] A.C. 520;
[1966] 2 W.L.R. 136; Digest (Cont. Vol. B) 243, 39a.
Ralli Brothers, Ltd. v. Inland Revenue Comrs., [1966] 1 All E.R. 65; [1966]
A.C. 483; [1966] 2 W.L.R. 119; revsg. sub nom. Re Ralli's Settlement,
Ralli Brothers, Ltd. v. Inland Revenue Comrs., [1964] 3 All E.R. 780;
F   [1965] Ch. 286; [1964] 3 W.L.R. 1240; Digest (Cont. Vol. B) 243, 56a.

Appeal.

This was an appeal from an order of the Court of Appeal (HARMAN and RUSSELL,
L.JJ.; LORD DENNING, M.R., dissenting) dated May 12, 1966, and reported
[1966] 2 All E.R. 661, affirming an order of the Chancery Division (PENNYCUICK,
J.) dated June 15, 1964, and reported [1965] 1 All E.R. 744, made on an originat-
G   ing summons issued by the respondents under s. 3 of the Administration of
Justice (Miscellaneous Provisions) Act, 1933.   The order of PENNYCUICK, J.,
declared that on the true construction of a settlement dated Dec. 28, 1927, made
between Sir Osborn George Holmden, Dame Mary Mildred Holmden and another
and an order dated Jan. 12, 1960, made by DANCKWERTS, J., entitled " In the
matter of the trusts for settlement dated Dec. 28, 1927, and made between Sir
H   Osborn George Holmden and others and in the matter of the Variation of Trusts
Act, 1958 (1959 H. 2593) " the trust funds vested in the respondents to this
appeal as trustees of the settlement did not become liable to estate duty on the
death of Dame Mary Mildred Holmden on Dec. 22, 1962.

Arthur Bagnall, Q.C., and J. P. Warner for the Crown.

J. A. Brightman, Q.C., and S. W. Templeman, Q.C., for the respondents.

I   Their Lordships took time for consideration.

Dec. 13. The following opinions were delivered.

LORD REID: My Lords, it has long been notorious that the estate duty
legislation can cause great injustice or hardship in many cases.   An individual
who is well advised can often take action during his life which will diminish tax
liability on his death.   Before 1958, however, no such action was possible with
regard to trust funds, except in the unlikely case where all who had vested or

contingent rights were of full age: then they could combine to require immediate **A**
payment of the fund or alter the trust purposes. By the Variation of Trusts
Act, 1958, it became possible to make application to the court. Generally all of full
age combined to put forward an arrangement and, if it was otherwise unobjection-
able, the court could approve the arrangement on behalf of minor beneficiaries
and of unborn persons who might become beneficiaries if the arrangement was for
their benefit. An arrangement which would avoid large payments of estate duty **B**
could hardly fail to be for the benefit of such infant and potential beneficiaries.

In the present case an arrangement was approved by the court in 1960. The
original settlement was made by the settlor, Sir Osborn Holmden, in 1927.
He died in 1945, survived by his widow and two children. The position after
his death was that the trustees had power during the life of the widow to pay
or apply the whole or such part of the income of the trust fund as they should **C**
in their uncontrolled discretion think fit for the benefit of the widow, the children
and any grandchildren or any of them. A provision in the settlement for the
accumulation of any surplus income not so paid or applied came to an end at the
death of the settlor and thereafter any surplus was not disposed of by the settlement but belonged to the settlor's estate. On the death of the widow the discretionary trust came to an end and, subject to a power of appointment given to **D**
the widow, half of the fund was to be held in trust for each child and his or her
family.

It was obvious that, if no alteration was made, estate duty would be payable
on the death of the widow. It is not disputed that the purpose of the arrangement
was to alter the trust purposes so that there should be no passing of the property
on the death of the widow. The arrangement provided that as from Jan. 12, 1960, **E**
the date of the order of the court, the discretionary trusts of income should have
effect during the life of the widow or the period of twenty-one years from that
date whichever should be the longer. The arrangement also altered the rights of
the children and grandchildren to receive the capital at the end of the twenty-one
year period. The widow died in 1962.

Estate duty is claimed on the ground that as regards rights to income the **F**
arrangement did not come into operation until the death of the widow; but
in my opinion the whole arrangement did come into operation in 1960. I can
see no ground at all for the Crown's argument that until the death of the widow
the original settlement continued unaltered: the plain meaning of the arrangement is that the whole of it came into operation at once. So the discretionary
trust set out in the arrangement came into operation in 1960 and continued in **G**
operation until after the widow's death. The only change at the widow's death
was that one of the objects of the discretionary trust dropped out and admittedly
such a change does not involve any liability for estate duty.

The Crown also found on s. 43 of the Finance Act, 1940. [HIS LORDSHIP read
s. 43 (1) which is set out at p. 155, letter **H**, post, and continued:] Let me assume
for the moment that the rights under the settlement of the objects of the dis- **H**
cretionary trust were interests or an interest in possession within the meaning
of this section. The question then is whether such interests were " determined "
by the coming into operation of the arrangement. If they were, and the other
express or implied requirements of the section are satisfied, then the trust fund
must be deemed to have passed on the death of the widow.

There are two ways of looking at the effect of the arrangement. One is that it **I**
merely amended or varied the original settlement by writing into cl. 2 (a) the
alternative period of twenty-one years from 1960: otherwise that clause remained
unaltered. If that is an adequate statement of the effect of the arrangement, then
there was no determination of the clause or of the " interest limited to cease "
on the death of the widow which it contained. All that happened was that an
alternative period of duration of the interest was added, and in the event which
happened, the death of the widow within the twenty-one years, the alternative
period prevailed.

A   The other way of looking at the effect of the arrangement raises the question what was the true nature of the arrangement. Under the Variation of Trusts Act, 1958, the court does not itself amend or vary the trusts of the original settlement. The beneficiaries are not bound by variations because the court has made the variation. Each beneficiary is bound because he has consented to the variation. If he was not of full age when the arrangement was made, he is bound

B   because the court was authorised by the Act of 1958 to approve of it on his behalf and did so by making an order. If he was of full age and did not in fact consent, he is not affected by the order of the court and he is not bound. So the arrangement must be regarded as an arrangement made by the beneficiaries themselves. The court merely acted on behalf of or as representing those beneficiaries who were not in a position to give their own consent and approval.

C   So we have an alteration of the settlement which was not made by the settlor or by the court as being empowered to make it, but which was made by the beneficiaries quite independently of the settlor or of any power, express or implied, given or deemed to have been given by him. Is it possible in those circumstances to say that, when the agreement of the beneficiaries alters the settlement, it merely amends the settlement? Or is the true position that, in so far as the

D   arrangement alters the provisions of the settlement, it brings to an end or " determines " those provisions and substitutes for them new provisions arranged by the beneficiaries? Here the settlor gave interests limited to cease on his widow's death: the beneficiaries substituted interests which probably would not and in fact did not cease on her death. I do not find the point at all easy, but I have come to be of opinion that the effect of the arrangement was to determine the interest

E   provided by the settlor which was limited to cease on the widow's death and to substitute a different interest which was so limited that it might or might not cease on her death.

That, however, is not an end of the matter. It is said that there cannot be a determination within the meaning of this section unless those who previously had the interests which have been determined lose something by reason of the

F   determination. If I had to decide this point I would not find it easy. There are arguments both ways; but in my view the point was decided by this House in *Ralli Brothers, Ltd.* v. *Inland Revenue Comrs.* (1). Lord Upjohn said (2) with regard to s. 43:

> " Subsection (2) of that section makes it clear beyond doubt there must be a determination or disposal in favour of some other party for the section to
G   have any effect and here there was none."

That interpretation was accepted by the majority of the noble lords engaged in the case, and I see no good reason for re-opening the question. In the present case none of the beneficiaries whose interests were determined lost anything thereby and the determination was not in favour of any other person. So s. 43 has no application and, therefore, I am of opinion that this appeal should be
H   dismissed.

LORD MORRIS OF BORTH-Y-GEST: My Lords, by the order of the court made on Jan. 12, 1960, approval was given to the arrangement which was scheduled to the order. The approval of the court was given on behalf of all infant and unborn persons interested under the trusts of the settlement. Those parties to

I   the originating summons before the court who were not under any incapacity expressed their consent to the arrangement. The court gave its approval on behalf of the infant and unborn persons by virtue of the power given to the court by the Variation of Trusts Act, 1958. That was " An Act to extend the jurisdiction of courts of law to vary trusts in the interests of beneficiaries and sanction dealings with trust property ". The power may be exercised in respect of any arrangement varying or revoking all or any of the trusts arising under any will, settlement or

_____

(1) [1966] 1 All E.R. 65; [1966] A.C. 483.
(2) [1966] 1 All E.R. at p. 69, letter C; [1966] A.C. at p. 509.

other disposition or enlarging the powers of the trustees of managing or **A**
administering any of the property subject to the trusts.

The first question now arising concerns the effect of the arrangement which
was made and approved. This I regard as a question of construction. In my
view, the effect of cll. 2 and 3 of the arrangement was that as from Jan. 12, 1960,
the provisions of cl. 2 (a) of the settlement were varied in one respect. The period
of the discretionary trusts was varied. Those trusts were to have had effect (as **B**
was then known) during the life of Lady Holmden. The variation was that they
were to have effect during the life of Lady Holmden or until Jan. 12, 1981,
whichever of those periods should be the longer. In my view, the result was that
there was one single discretionary trust which would have effect (subject to cl. 6)
during the trust period as varied. The variation became effective as from the
date of the order of the court. The destination of any income which, after the **C**
death of the settlor, was not applied among the discretionary objects, was not
affected. No new discretionary trusts were to begin on Lady Holmden's death.
As from Jan. 12, 1960, it was arranged that the discretionary trusts would continue during the newly agreed period. Lady Holmden was one of the objects
of the discretionary trust but her death (when it occurred on Dec. 22, 1962) was
no more than the dropping of one of the lives within the discretionary class and **D**
did not result in a passing of property under the provisions of the Finance Act,
1894.

The question then arises whether the provisions of s. 43 of the Finance Act,
1940, are applicable. Was there an " interest " (or were there interests) limited
to cease on a death which had been disposed of or had determined? Was such
" interest " (or were such interests) " in possession "? **E**

Even if it could be said that there was an interest in possession limited to cease
on a death, I cannot think that there is any ground for saying that the interest
of the discretionary class under the settlement trusts had been " disposed of ".
There was nothing like an assignment. There was no new receiving hand. The
effect of the arrangement was not to get rid of the discretionary trust but to
preserve it for a longer period. This circumstance makes it equally difficult to **F**
say that the discretionary trust was in some manner (either by surrender, assurance, divesting, forfeiture or in some other manner) " determined ". The arrangement of Jan. 12, 1960, did not bring about the ending of the discretionary trust;
it brought about its prolongation. In my opinion, the arrangement did not
either dispose of or determine an interest limited to cease on a death, even if it be
assumed that there was such an interest within the meaning of s. 43. Furthermore, **G**
I consider that in the context of the section what is contemplated is a disposition
or determination in favour of some other party. Though sub-s. (2) is an exception
subsection, the references in para. (a) to " . . . the person becoming entitled by
virtue of or upon the disposition or determination " and to " the person who
immediately before the disposition or determination had the interest. . ." seem to
me to be references to the kind of disposition or determination with which the **H**
section as a whole is dealing. Being of this opinion I find it unnecessary to express
a view in this case on the question whether there was an interest in possession
limited to cease on a death.

I would dismiss the appeal.

LORD HODSON: My Lords, the questions argued on this appeal were two. **I**
First: was the trust fund—which passed on the death of Lady Holmden liable
to estate duty under s. 2 (1) (b) of the Finance Act, 1894?

Second: since the trust fund was property in which the beneficiaries under the
discretionary trust declared by cl. 2 (a) of the settlement of Dec. 28, 1927, made
by the late Sir Osborn Holmden, had an interest limited to cease on the death of
Lady Holmden, was it disposed of or determined by the arrangement made on
Jan. 12, 1960, so as to make estate duty exigible under s. 43 (1) of the Finance
Act, 1940, as amended?

A   The first question depends on the construction of the arrangement and in particular of cl. 3 thereof which reads:

" 3. The discretionary trusts of income declared by cl. 2 (a) of the settlement shall have effect during the life of Lady Holmden or the period of twenty-one years from the operative date whichever shall be the longer . . ."

B   The operative date was the date of the approval of the arrangement by the court pursuant on the provisions of the Variation of Trusts Act, 1958, viz., Jan. 12, 1960.

The contention of the Crown is that on the true construction of the order the settlement trusts continued until the death of the widow and were then succeeded by new trusts under the 1960 arrangement so that there was a passing of property under s. 2 (1) (b) of the Act of 1894 as in *Public Trustee* v. *Inland Revenue* C   *Comrs.* (3).

In my opinion, the effect of the arrangement varying the settlement was, as HARMAN, L.J., pointed out (4), to re-write the settlement from the date of the order in the terms proposed and approved by the court. Clause 2 (a) of the settlement which sets up the discretionary trust must then be read as taking effect, not only during the life of the widow, but from twenty-one years from D   the date of the order, if she died before that period expired, as she did. There was no passing within the meaning of s. 2 (1) (b) on Lady Holmden's death for that was only the dropping of one of the lives in the discretionary trust, this interest being of no ascertainable value under s. 7 (7) of the Finance Act, 1894.

Second: if s. 2 (1) (b) is out of the picture, is duty payable under s. 43 of the Act of 1940? In order to bring this section into operation there must be a disposition E   or determination of an interest. I am, again, in agreement with HARMAN, L.J. (5), of opinion that the effect of the order was neither to dispose of nor to determine the discretionary trust. The order enlarged or extended the trust and did not bring it to an end.

The scheme of the Variation of Trusts Act, 1958, provides for the continuation of the old settlement as if the original settlor were himself a living party and the F   giving effect to proposals by whomsoever made

". . . varying or revoking all or any of the trusts, or enlarging the powers of the trustees of managing or administering any of the property subject to the trusts . . ."

(See s. 1 (1) of the Variation of Trusts Act, 1958.)

G   The intervention of the court under the Variation of Trusts Act, 1958 approving the arrangement which had been proposed did not prevent the continued existence of the settlement made by the settlor notwithstanding the variations which flow from the arrangement. As counsel for the respondents puts it in his argument, the settlor in making the settlement made it subject to any legislative hazards. This particular Act is only one example of such a hazard.

H   There is a further difficulty in the way of the application of s. 43 of the Act of 1940 which, in my opinion, is conclusive. Assuming that there is a relevant interest the whole language of s. 43 (1) is consistent with a shifting of the interest to another person for the benefit of that other, rather than with the adding to that interest some additional benefit derived from the same source. Here none of the beneficiaries lost anything and the disposal was not in favour of any other I   person. I appreciate the force of the opinion expressed by LORD DENNING, M.R. (6), that this is a charging section and is not necessarily to be controlled in its interpretation by the exceptions which are contained in the succeeding subsection, namely, s. 43 (2); nevertheless I think that the respondents are supported in their argument by the undoubted fact that the exceptions are all dealing with determination or disposal in favour of some other person. I conclude that this was the kind

(3) [1966] 1 All E.R. 76; [1966] A.C. 520.
(4) [1966] 2 All E.R. 661 at p. 668, letter H; [1966] Ch. 511 at p. 533.
(5) [1966] 2 All E.R. at p. 669, letter E; [1966] Ch. at p. 534.
(6) [1966] 2 All E.R. at p. 667, letter C; [1966] Ch. at p. 530.

of determination or disposal with which the whole section is concerned and that **A**
the language of s. 43 (1) by itself does not carry with it the claim for duty for which
the Crown contends. In other words " dispose " and " determine " have the same
meaning in both subsections.

It would appear that in the case of the owner of a life interest acquiring an
absolute interest in remainder expectant on his life interest in property no duty is
in practice claimed by the Crown. I cannot understand the reason for this unless **B**
the construction of the subsection contended for by the taxpayer is correct;
for I do not accept the Crown's contention that in such a case there is a sublimation of the life interest into one interest without a merger in the sense of a
drowning of one interest in the other.

This construction of s. 43 was adopted by RUSSELL, L.J., in *In re Ralli's
Settlement, Ralli Brothers, Ltd.* v. *Inland Revenue Comrs.* (7) and by my noble and **C**
learned friend, LORD UPJOHN (8), with whom three of your lordships agreed in
the House in the same case. Whether the opinion expressed was necessary to the
decision of that case or not, I would adhere to it after hearing the argument
addressed to your lordships in this case.

I would dismiss the appeal.

LORD GUEST: My Lords, by a settlement made on Dec. 28, 1927, **D**
the settlor, Sir Osborn Holmden, appointed discretionary trusts (by cl. 2 (a) of the
settlement) in relation to the income of the trust fund, during the lives of the
settlor and of his wife and the life of the survivor, in favour of Lady Holmden,
his son and daughter and their issue, with a direction to accumulate the surplus
income which might be distributed among the discretionary objects and, so
far as not distributed, to be added to capital. The settlor died on Apr. 16, 1945. **E**

An order was made under the Variation of Trusts Act, 1958, on Jan. 12, 1966,
by DANCKWERTS, J., in the Chancery Division approving of an arrangement
varying the trusts of the settlement. The parties to the application included all
the living beneficiaries under the settlement and the trustees. Clauses 2 and 3
of the arrangement were in the following terms:
F
" 2. As from the operative date the settlement shall have effect subject
to the variations which are hereinafter set forth.

" 3. The discretionary trusts of income declared by clause 2 (a) of the
settlement shall have effect during the life of Lady Holmden or the period of
twenty-one years from the operative date whichever shall be the longer
(hereinafter called ' the trust period ')."
G
It is not necessary for the present purpose to refer to the other provisions in the
arrangement varying the settlement. Lady Holmden died on Dec. 22, 1962.

On an originating summons in the Chancery Division, PENNYCUICK, J., held
(9) that the trust fund did not become liable to estate duty on the death of
Lady Holmden. The Court of Appeal (10) by a majority (LORD DENNING, M.R.,
dissenting) (11) confirmed that decision. It is not necessary to refer to the opinion **H**
of PENNYCUICK, J., (9) as his decision has been overtaken by the judgment of
this House in *Ralli Brothers, Ltd.* v. *Inland Revenue Comrs.* (12) and *Public
Trustee* v. *Inland Revenue Comrs.* (13). The opinions of the House were not
available at the time when the judgment was given.

The argument for the Crown was presented in the form of a dilemma. It was
said that on the death of Lady Holmden the discretionary trust of the settlement **I**
came to an end and was succeeded by a new discretionary trust under the
arrangement until Jan. 12, 1981; in which case it was said that estate duty was

---

(7) [1964] 3 All E.R. 780 at p. 795; [1965] Ch. 286 at p. 333.
(8) [1966] 1 All E.R. at p. 69; [1966] A.C. at pp. 509, 510.
(9) [1965] 1 All E.R. 744.
(10) [1966] 2 All E.R. 661; [1966] Ch. 511.
(11) [1966] 2 All E.R. at p. 664; [1966] Ch. at p. 526.
(12) [1966] 1 All E.R. 65; [1966] A.C. 483.
(13) [1966] 1 All E.R. 76; [1966] A.C. 520.

A payable on the death of Lady Holmden under s. 1 or s. 2 (1) (*b*) of the Finance Act, 1894. If that was not the effect of the arrangement, then it was argued that the old discretionary trust determined on Jan. 12, 1960, the date of the order approving the arrangement, and a new discretionary trust arose; in which case it was said that the trust fund was liable to estate duty under s. 43 of the Finance Act, 1940.

B The argument for the Crown depends on the proper construction of the settlement and of the deed of arrangement. I have no doubt that the majority of the Court of Appeal (14) were right in holding that as from the operative date in the arrangement, Jan. 12, 1960, the old settlement was varied so far as affecting this case to the effect that the term of the discretionary trust extended until the date of Lady Holmden's death or until Jan. 12, 1981, whichever was the later, just as C if the original settlement had contained the variation. There was not, as Lord Denning, M.R., held, (15) a continuance of the old settlement until Lady Holmden's death to be succeeded on her death by a new discretionary trust. There was, at the date of Lady Holmden's death, a single discretionary trust operating from the date of the settlement until Jan. 12, 1981. Upon the death of Lady Holmden the only change which took place was the dropping of one life from D the class of discretionary objects: otherwise the trust continued unimpaired, the fund was the same and the beneficiaries were the same.

The Crown argued that the effect of the settlement and of the arrangement was to create a charge to duty as occurred in *Public Trustee* v. *Inland Revenue Comrs.*, (16) but in that case the reversioner was the only party to the variation and he could only assign his interest after his mother's death. He could not assign any E income prior to his mother's death which was dealt with by the settlement. The effect was that a different interest arose on the death resulting in a passing under s. 1 of the Finance Act, 1894. In the present case all the beneficiaries were parties to the arrangement either by themselves or through the approval of the court under s. 1 of the Variation of Trusts Act, 1958. At the date of the arrangement they could competently deal with the whole income in which they were F beneficially interested. Under the arrangement the income was dealt with in such a way that on the death of Lady Holmden the same trusts continued, the only difference being the dropping of one life. If this be so, the case is within the ratio of the concession by the Crown that the dropping of one life from the objects of a discretionary trust does not result in a passing under s. 1 (see *A.-G. of Ceylon* v. *Arunachalam Chettiar* (*No. 1*) (17)).

G I turn now to what has been described as the other horn of the dilemma. The dilemma argument is seldom a satisfactory ground of decision and, in my view, in this case there is no true dilemma. To enable the Crown to succeed on this point the Crown must bring this case within s. 43 of the Finance Act, 1940, which is in the following terms (18):

H " 43.—(1) Subject to the provisions of this section, where an interest limited to cease on a death has been disposed of or has determined, whether by surrender, assurance, divesting, forfeiture or in any other manner (except by the expiration of a fixed period at the expiration of which the interest was limited to cease), whether wholly or partly, and whether for value or not, after becoming an interest in possession, and the disposition or determination (or any of them if there are more than one) is not excepted by sub-s. I (2) of this section, then—(a) if, had there been no disposition or determination as aforesaid of that interest and no disposition of any interest expectant upon or subject to that interest, the property in which the interest subsisted would

(14) [1966] 2 All E.R. 661; [1966] Ch. 511.
(15) [1966] 2 All E.R. at pp. 665, 666; [1966] Ch. at pp. 528, 529.
(16) [1966] 1 All E.R. 76; [1966] A.C. 520.
(17) [1957] A.C. 513.
(18) Section 43 (1) is printed as amended by the Finance Act, 1950, s. 43; see Part 2 of Sch. 7 to the latter Act (29 Halsbury's Statutes, 2nd Edn., 183).

have passed on the death under s. 1 of the Finance Act, 1894, that property   **A**
shall be deemed by virtue of this section to be included as to the whole thereof
in the property passing on the death; or (b) if, had there been no disposition
or determination as aforesaid of that interest and no disposition of any interest
expectant upon or subject to that interest, the property in which the interest
subsisted would have been deemed by virtue of para. (b) of sub-s. (1) of s. 2
of the said Act to be included to a particular extent in the property passing   **B**
on the death, the property in which the interest subsisted shall be deemed by
virtue of this section to be included to that extent in the property passing
on the death."

The Crown argued that as from the operative date, Jan. 12, 1960, the life interest
under the settlement determined after becoming an interest in possession and that
the trust fund was deemed to pass under s. 1 of the Finance Act, 1894.   **C**

Before dealing with this argument, it is necessary to dispose of one preliminary
point. This involves the proper construction of the Variation of Trusts Act, 1958.
This Act of which the long title reads " An Act to extend the jurisdiction of courts
of law to vary trusts in the interest of beneficiaries and sanction dealings with
trust property " provides as follows:

" 1.—(1) Where property, whether real or personal, is held on trusts arising,   **D**
whether before or after the passing of this Act, under any will, settlement
or other disposition, the court may if it thinks fit by order approve on behalf
of—(a) any person having directly or indirectly, an interest, whether vested
or contingent, under the trusts who by reason of infancy or other incapacity
is incapable of assenting, or . . . (c) any person unborn, . . . any arrangement
(by whomsoever proposed, and whether or not there is any other person   **E**
beneficially interested who is capable of assenting thereto) varying or
revoking all or any of the trusts, or enlarging the powers of the trustees of
managing or administering any of the property subject to the trusts:
" Provided that except by virtue of para. (d) of this subsection the court
shall not approve an arrangement on behalf of any person unless the carrying
out thereof would be for the benefit of that person."   **F**

The Act followed closely on a decision of the House in *Chapman* v. *Chapman*,
(19) where the House refused to extend the jurisdiction of the Chancery Division
in varying settlements beyond the cases mentioned by LORD ASQUITH OF
BISHOPSTONE (20).   The power of the court under the Act of 1958 is to approve
of an arrangement inter alia " varying or revoking the trusts ". It must be a   **G**
matter of construction in each case whether the arrangement in question varies
or revokes the trusts. While there may be cases where an arrangement revokes the
trust, I have no doubt in the present case that the arrangement merely varied
the original trust by inserting an extended terminal date for the exercise of the
discretionary powers. The question thus arises whether this variation was, within
the meaning of s. 43, a determination of the life interest of the discretionary   **H**
beneficiaries under the settlement. A variation might have the effect of determining the life interests, but, with respect to those who hold the opposite view, I
do not consider that the approval by the court of an arrangement under the
Act of 1958 necessarily determines any pre-existing life interest. It was argued
that because the order of the court was the approval of an arrangement by the
beneficiaries, this was a new trust and that the previous beneficial interests were   **I**
determined. In other words, the arrangement was contractual, effecting a compromise by the beneficiaries, approved of by the court for a re-settlement of
the trust fund. In my view, however, the arrangment merely varies the trusts to
the extent already stated. Section 1 of the Act of 1958 enabled the court to give
approval to an arrangement on behalf of such persons as were unable by incapacity
or otherwise to give their approval. The court thus supplied the capacity which

A the incapax lacked. This arrangement did not, in my view, create a new trust, but merely varied the old settlement.

Turning next to the construction of s. 43, the effect of the arrangement was not, in my view, to determine the life interests but to enlarge them so that the terminal date was extended. It would be a misuse of language to say that the interest " determined " when all that happened was that the beneficial interests **B** were increased. The life interests under the settlement did not come to an end or cease to exist after Jan. 12, 1960. They continued for a period up to Jan. 12, 1981, if Lady Holmden pre-deceased that date. This must be the only logical justification for the view of the Crown that where the life tenant acquires the reversion there is no charge to duty under s. 43. Alternative justifications put forward by the Crown for the alleged concession were, in my view, not substanti-**C** ated. It is no concession at all; it is the logical result of a proper construction of s. 43.

If the beneficial interest did not determine under s. 43 it is unnecessary to consider the further point which was raised in *Ralli Brothers, Ltd.* v. *Inland Revenue Comrs.* (21) by Lord Upjohn where he said (22):

D   " Section 43 of the Finance Act, 1940, can have no possible application for, as I have already said, as a matter of construction the life interest under the 1895 settlement continued until Mrs. Ralli's death and was never determined or disposed of. Subsection (2) of that section makes it clear beyond doubt that there must be a determination or disposal in favour of some other party for the section to have any effect and here there was none."

E A majority of their lordships of which I was one, concurred in his opinion. I remain of the same opinion. To elaborate on Lord Upjohn's opinion, it is only necessary to state that " determination " in sub-s. (1) and sub-s. (2) must be used in the same sense. If a determination under sub-s. (2) requires a determination in favour of some other person, then a determination under sub-s. (1) must equally be in favour of another person. As in this case there was no deter-**F** mination or disposition in favour of another person, s. 43 has, in my opinion, no application.

In view of my opinion as to the construction of s. 43, it is unnecessary to deal with the question whether the interests of the discretionary beneficiaries had become in this case " interests in possession " within the meaning of s. 43. Both parties appeared to leave this question on the decision of the case of *Gartside* **G** v. *Inland Revenue Comrs.*, (23) but as the terms of the two settlements are dissimilar I prefer to reserve my opinion on this point.

Upon the whole matter I would dismiss the appeal.

LORD WILBERFORCE: My lords, in this case the Crown claims estate duty on the death of Lady Holmden under s. 43 of the Finance Act, 1940. This **H** case has some similarity with those previously considered in this House in *Public Trustee* v. *Inland Revenue Comrs.*, (24) and *Ralli Brothers, Ltd.* v. *Inland Revenue Comrs.* (21).

The trusts by virtue of which the property would have passed, if certain transactions in 1960 had not taken place, were established by a settlement dated Dec. 28, 1927, made by Sir Osborn George Holmden, Bt., whose widow Lady Holmden **I** was. Under this settlement a trust fund was, before those transactions, held on discretionary trusts during Lady Holmden's life for a class which comprised Lady Holmden, her children and their issue. The trustees had a discretion as to the amount (if any) of income which they might distribute in any year to any one beneficiary or to the class as a whole. Any surplus not distributed was to be

---

(21) [1966] 1 All E.R. 65; [1966] A.C. 483.
(22) [1966] 1 All E.R. at p. 69, letter B; [1966] A.C. at pp. 509, 510.
(23) Ante p. 121.
(24) [1966] 1 All E.R. 76; [1966] A.C. 520.

accumulated. The capital was to be held after Lady Holmden's death, subject **A** to a special power of appointment exercisable by Lady Holmden, on trusts under which each of her two children George and Mary took life interests in one half with remainders to their respective children. At the relevant date both George and Mary were living; George Holmden had three children, two of whom were infants; Mary Shearer had two, both of full age.

The period of permissible accumulation, as regards surplus income, came to **B** an end on Apr. 16, 1945, when the settlor, Sir Osborn Holmden, died; and thereafter any surplus income not distributed under the discretionary trust became payable to his legal personal representatives as part of his estate. It appears that the persons interested in this estate were Lady Holmden, George Holmden, Mary Shearer and her children.

On Oct. 29, 1959, an originating summons was taken out in the Chancery **C** Division seeking the approval of the court to a variation of the trusts of the settlement under the Variation of Trusts Act, 1958. The application was made by Lady Holmden, and the respondents included all living beneficiaries under the settlement and the trustees. On Jan. 12, 1960, an order was made by which the court approved the arrangement on behalf of all infant and unborn persons interested under the trusts of the settlement. It was recited in the order that all **D** adult beneficiaries had consented to it.

The arrangement was scheduled to the order. After defining " the operative date " as the date of the order, the arrangement provided in paras. (2) and (3) as follows:

" 2. As from the operative date the settlement shall have effect subject to the variations which are hereinafter set forth. **E**

" 3. The discretionary trusts of income declared by cl. 2 (a) of the settlement shall have effect during the life of Lady Holmden or the period of twenty-one years from the operative date whichever shall be the longer (hereinafter called ' the trust period ')."

Paragraphs 4 and 5 of the arrangement contained provisions varying the trusts **F** as to capital, the details of which are not material. Paragraph 6 conferred power on the trustees at any time after Lady Holmden's death by deed to bring the trust period to an end and the trusts as to capital into operation. The remaining paragraphs contained provisions as to other trusts and administrative matters which have no relevance on the present appeal.

Lady Holmden died on Dec. 22, 1962, i.e., during the currency of the trust **G** period, and the question is whether estate duty falls to be paid on her death in respect of the settled funds. The claim for duty is put on two alternative grounds: either that the settlement funds must be deemed to pass under s. 2 (1) (b) of the Finance Act, 1894, on the basis that, notwithstanding the arrangement of 1960 there was a cesser of an interest or interests limited to cease on Lady Holmden's death: or alternatively that, if that is not so, there must have been a disposition **H** or determination of such interest(s) by the arrangement of 1960 so that s. 43 of the Finance Act, 1940, comes into play. The Crown's main argument was that the taxpayer was faced with a dilemma: either the original limited interest continued to exist after 1960, in which case s. 2 (1) (b) applies; or, if it did not continue to exist, it must have been disposed of or determined so as to attract s. 43.

My lords, I cannot accept this method of reasoning. A man is not to be taxed **I** by a dilemma: he must be taxed by a positive provision under which the Crown can satisfactorily show that he is fairly and squarely taxed. There is no presumption in taxing law that two sections, however complementary they appear, are exhaustive: there may always be a no man's land between them which the subject does not have to define but on which he can take his stand. In the present case, and I suspect that this is generally true, at any rate in the field of taxation, the supposed dilemma is not a true one. The original limited interest may not be in existence at the relevant death, and yet it may not have been either disposed of

A or determined within the meaning of the taxing section. That I believe to be the case here.

I proceed, as I venture to think one must, by considering the first limb of the Crown's argument. Did the interest limited to cease on Lady Holmden's death by the settlement continue in existence after the 1960 arrangement? I use the word " interest " in the present discussion to describe the trusts declared by the B settlement during Lady Holmden's life, so that the question relates to those trusts.

On this question the rival views are as follows. The Crown contends that all that was done in 1960 was to add to the existing trusts declared during Lady Holmden's life fresh trusts to operate for an additional period. If this is right, it is clear that this case is indistinguishable in result from *Public Trustee* v. *Inland Revenue Comrs.* (25), and that the Crown must succeed. The respondents contend C that the effect of the arrangement was to bring into existence a new single discretionary trust of income terminating on the death of Lady Holmden or on Jan. 12, 1981, which date should be the later, in which case, on the principle accepted in *A.-G. of Ceylon* v. *Arunachalam Chettiar (No. 1)* (26) no duty would be payable.

I can deal with this issue shortly because I am in complete agreement, as to it, D with the majority of the Court of Appeal (26). If all the beneficiaries under the settlement had been sui juris, they could, in my opinion, have joined together with the trustees and declared different trusts which would supersede those originally contained in the settlement. Those new trusts would operate proprio vigore, by virtue of a self-contained instrument—namely, the deed of arrangement or variation. The original settlement would have lost any force or relevance. E The effect of an order made under the Variation of Trusts Act, 1958, is to make good by act of the court any want of capacity to enter into a binding arrangement of any beneficiary not capable of binding himself and of any beneficiary unborn : the nature and effect of any arrangement so sanctioned is the same as that I have described. So far there is really no dispute : the difference between the Crown and the respondents and between the two views in the Court of Appeal (27) is on F the question whether this is in fact what the arrangement has done. I have set out cll. 2 and 3 (see p. 158, letter E, ante): to my mind, they cannot be read as an affirmation of the trusts of the settlement plus an addition : they can only be read as a true " variation "—the substitution by binding agreement of a new period (the trust period) for the old. One may test this by asking what the trusts as to income were after the arrangement and before Lady Holmden's death : were they G the same as before, or were they different? In my opinion, they were clearly different : the trustees, after 1960, could and should have exercised their discretion as to distribution of income on the basis (theretofore not existing) that the discretion might continue (at least) till 1981—a basis which might materially affect the policy they chose to adopt. I reach the conclusion on this point that a new single trust was created in 1960, extending the previous limited " interest ", H which therefore did not cease on Lady Holmden's death. In this case, the parties have been able, with the assistance of the court, to do what the reversioner alone could not do in the case of *Public Trustee* v. *Inland Revenue Comrs.* (28), so that they succeed where he failed.

The second question is whether the arrangement of 1960 brought about, or was, a disposition or determination of the previous limited interest within the I meaning which those expressions have in s. 43 of the Finance Act, 1940.

It now becomes relevant to ask whether there was an " interest " in the statutory sense to be disposed of or determined. I find some difficulty in answering this question. The argument in this appeal took place after the argument was

---

(25) [1966] 1 All E.R. 76; [1966] A.C. 520.
(26) [1957] A.C. 513.
(27) [1966] 2 All E.R. 661; [1966] Ch. 511.
(28) [1966] 1 All E.R. 76; [1966] A.C. 520.

completed in *Gartside* v. *Inland Revenue Comrs.* (29) but before the decision was A
given in that appeal, so that counsel were unaware of the manner in which the
meaning of " interest " was to be dealt with in this House. The trusts of income
in the Holmden settlement are not identical with those with which the *Gartside*
case (29) was concerned, because in the present case the trust for accumulation
had come to an end and any surplus income had to be distributed to ascertained
persons. This circumstance possibly distinguishes the present case from *Gart-* B
side's (29), but your lordships heard no argument on the point. Being as I am of
opinion that the Crown's case under s. 43 fails on other grounds, I prefer to leave
the question undecided.

The argument that, even assuming that there was a relevant " interest " here,
s. 43 of the Finance Act, 1940, has no application can be put in two ways. The
first, which may for convenience be described as that based on commonsense (I C
am not using this as an argument for its adoption) is to say that the subsection,
when dealing with " dispositions " or " determinations " must surely contemplate
a transaction by which the owner of the limited interest gives up or is deprived
of something : it cannot have been intended to impose a charge where he acquires
something more than he had, or where his " limited " interest is enlarged. The
second, directed perhaps to more sophisticated minds, is to suggest that the D
section as a whole only deals with cases where there is a disposition or determination in favour of some other person : this argument is supported by reference to
s. 43 (2).

In discussion of these arguments reference was made by both sides to the fact
that in practice no duty is claimed under the words we are dealing with when the
owner of a life interest acquires the absolute interest in remainder, expectant E
on his life interest. The respondents say that this practice can only be justified if
the legal position is as it suggested above. The Crown seeks to find some other and
more special support for it which does not involve acceptance of the respondents'
argument.

My lords, I find myself persuaded by the two submissions of the respondents :
these seem to me interrelated and mutually supporting. I think that they F
justify, and that they alone can justify, the practice which I have mentioned.
Purely on sub-s. (1) and considering the whole of its language (" disposed of
or has determined, whether by surrender, assurance, divesting, forfeiture or
in any other manner . . . whether for value or not ") I find it hard to believe that a
duty was to be imposed in cases where the owner of the limited interest acquires,
and adds to that interest, a further interest in the property. I am not in this G
influenced by technical considerations as to merger, nor by the use of meta-
phorical expressions such as " drowning ", or " sublimation " or the recently
criticised " enlargement " : I find it more helpful to consider the purpose of this
enactment. That seems to me fairly clearly to be to bring within the charge
cases where a limited interest, on the cesser of which a charge would otherwise
arise, has been got rid of. The width of the language used in sub-s. (1), which I H
have quoted, finds sufficient justification in the variety of mechanisms which
might be employed in order to achieve this end without making it necessary to
give up this basic conception. That is, moreover, to my mind, confirmed by the
presence of sub-s. (2) which applies the familiar five-year rule accompanied by
total exclusion, fitting enough if the conception is that of parting with or deprivation of an interest, but inappropriate by reference to transactions of acquisition. I
The language, too, of that subsection, by mentioning " the person " seems to
show that it rests on the assumption that, in a transaction to which sub-s. (1)
applies, there is a person who becomes entitled by virtue of or on the disposal
or determination.

It was forcefully pointed out, and this argument is reflected in the judgment
of LORD DENNING, M.R. (30), that sub-s. (2) takes the form of an exception to

(29) Ante p. 121.
(30) [1966] 2 All E.R. at p. 667; [1966] Ch. at p. 531.

A sub-s. (1). It is said that it is faulty reasoning to construe a rule by an exception to it: the presence of an exception in favour of broadly gifts to another made outside five years does not mean that sub-s. (1) is confined to this case: it shows at most that the subsection includes it. With the general proposition I would certainly agree: there is no presumption that an exception and a rule cover the same ground; but after the full examination which was made in argument of

B the antecedents of this legislation, I am persuaded that in this case the exception does do this.

I shall not weary your lordships with an enumeration of the various sections which preceded the Finance Act, 1940. The original provision was s. 38 (2) (a) of the Customs and Inland Revenue Act, 1881: then, after certain decisions, surrenders of life interests were dealt with by the Finance Act, 1900. In s. 11 of

C that Act the charge and the exception were united in the same subsection: the charge only arose, as did the exception, where there was a disposition to or for the benefit of a person entitled to remainder or reversion. Later, cases involving dispositions to companies were covered by the Finance Act, 1930: this, too, in s. 35, referred to dispositions to or for the benefit of a company, and the (then) three-year exemption mentioned *the* company, evidently the company to which

D the disposition had been made. So it appears that up to this time the legislation invariably contemplated a disposition to someone and that the exemption covered part of the same ground. In the Finance Act, 1940, there was a further expansion of the type of disposition, etc., covered, notably by addition of " forfeiture "; the language was generalised so as to include not only persons entitled in remainder or reversion but also companies or individuals who at the time of the disposition

E had no interest in the property, and the exemption was segregated in a distinct subsection. It is always possible that changes of this character are designed to effect changes in substance, but it is for the Crown either to show that the language used clearly achieves this, or, at least, to demonstrate some mischief as revealed in previous decisions, which Parliament must have intended to correct. It did not convince me of either. I think that, as before, sub-s. (1) deals with dispositions

F and determinations which result in some other person (or company) becoming entitled and that sub-s. (2), as before, exempts *those* dispositions or determinations if the stated conditions are complied with.

Lastly there is the practice to which I have referred above: the best that the Crown could do to explain it was to say that, when the reversion is acquired by a life tenant, the life interest is not determined because otherwise there would be

G no basis on which the life tenant would remain entitled to the income during his life. But there is no precision in this proposition unless one adds to it the word " only ", in which case the failure of the argument at once appears. On the other hand, not only does the interpretation of sub-ss. (1) and (2), which the respondents suggest give ample sense and justification for the practice, but the practice itself, so supported, seem to fit logically into the legislative scheme.

H I would add that the opinion which I have just expressed coincides entirely with that which, as I understand it, was accepted after argument by their lordships in the *Ralli* case (31) and with that both originated and (correctly) followed by Russell, L.J., in the Court of Appeal (32).

I would dismiss the appeal.

Appeal dismissed.

I
Solicitors: *Solicitor of Inland Revenue; Macfarlanes* (for the respondents).

[*Reported by* Kathleen J. H. O'Brien, *Barrister-at-Law.*]

---

(31) [1966] 1 All E.R. 65; [1966] A.C. 483.
(32) [1964] 3 All E.R. at p. 791; [1965] Ch. at p. 327.

LORD ADVOCATE *v.* RELIANT TOOL CO.

[HOUSE OF LORDS (Viscount Dilhorne, Lord MacDermott, Lord Guest, Lord Wilberforce and Lord Pearson), November 6, 7, December 19, 1967.]

Selective Employment Tax—Premium—Carrying on part only of an activity specified in the Standard Industrial Classification—Designing—Employers prepared designs of metal-working machine tools for other companies who made the tools and used them to manufacture other products—Whether employers carried on an activity within Heading 332 of the classification, viz., manufacturing metal-working machine tools—Selective Employment Payments Act 1966 (c. 32), s. 1 (2) (a) (i), s. 10 (5).

The respondents were basically designers of metal-working machine tools, and, though they could also make certain tools if required to do so, yet their relevant activity for present purposes was the preparing of designs for machine tools, which manufacturing companies then used in order to make the tools for the purpose of manufacturing other products. The tools so designed were used by the respondents' customers, the manufacturing companies, for making a range of products within Orders III to XVI of the Standard Industrial Classification. By s. 1 (2) (a)* of the Selective Employment Payments Act 1966, an employer who had paid selective employment tax became entitled to payment of selective employment premium, if the employment were in an establishment which was engaged by way of business wholly or partly in activities falling under any of the minimum list headings within Orders III to XVI of the classification. Heading 332† of Order VI included, as part of the description of the activity‡, "manufacturing metal-working machine tools". It was conceded that if the respondents' did not come within that heading, they were not entitled to premium under any other heading. The tribunal found that the designing was a necessary stage in the manufacture, and they held that the respondents were entitled to premium. On appeal,

Held: the tribunal's decision involved no error of law and should stand for the following reasons—

(i) (per VISCOUNT DILHORNE, LORD GUEST and LORD WILBERFORCE) whether the activity of designing a product was an activity separate from that of making the product, or whether the designing formed part of the process of manufacture, was a question of fact for the tribunal to decide (see p. 166, letter D, p. 167, letter G, p. 171, letter I, and p. 173, letters C and G, post); or (per LORD MACDERMOTT) was a mixed question of law and fact, on which the tribunal had found correctly in fact and law (see p. 170, letters A and D, post).

(ii) (per LORD MACDERMOTT; cf., per LORD GUEST and LORD WILBERFORCE) s. 1 (2) (*a*) (i) included activities (in this instance the designing) which constituted a part, though not the whole, of the process involved in the manufacture of metal-working machine tools (see p. 169, letter D, post; cf., p. 171, letter I, p. 174, letters A and D, and p. 167, letter B, post).

(iii) (per LORD PEARSON) the introduction to the Standard Industrial Classification could be taken into account in ascertaining the meaning of the minimum list headings, and, by virtue of so doing, the tribunal's decision that designing machine tools was within Heading 332 was shown to be reasonable and correct (see p. 175, letter F, and p. 176, letter H, post).

(iv) (per LORD MACDERMOTT and LORD GUEST) the respondents' activities were not within Heading 879 (which was not within Orders III to XVI) and, even if they had been, would not have been excluded thereby from

* For s. 1 (2) (*a*) (i) see p. 168, letter B, post.
† Heading 332 is set out at p. 165, letter E, post.
‡ See, e.g., p. 165, letter E, and p. 168, letter F, post.

A   Heading 332, as s. 10 (5) of the Act of 1966 was not exclusive (see p. 169, letter G, and p. 172, letter D, post; cf., p. 166, letter F, post).

Appeal dismissed.

[As to Selective Employment Tax, see Supplement to 33 Halsbury's Laws (3rd Edn.) para. 479A.

B   For the Selective Employment Payments Act 1966 s. 1 (2) (*a*), s. 2, and s. 10 (5), see 46 Halsbury's Statutes (2nd Edn.) 167, 171 and 184.]

Appeal.

This was an appeal against an interlocutor of the First Division of the Court of Session, dated May 12, 1967, refusing an appeal by the Lord Advocate, as representing the Minister of Labour, from a decision of an industrial tribunal

C   in Scotland. On Nov. 18, 1966, the Minister refused an application by the respondents for registration of their business under s. 7 (1) of the Selective Employment Payments Act 1966. The ground of the refusal was that their establishment did not qualify for registration under s. 1 (2) (*a*). On Dec. 12, 1966, the respondents referred the decision to the tribunal. On Feb. 2, 1967, the tribunal entered the decision in favour of the respondents. By appeal dated

D   Feb. 22, 1967, the appellant appealed from the appellant's decision to the Court of Session. The appeal was heard before the Lord President (Lord Clyde), Lord Guthrie, Lord Migdale and Lord Cameron on May 4, 1967, when the appeal was refused.

The Solicitor General for Scotland (Ewan Stewart, Q.C.), D. R. B. Cary, Q.C. (both of the Scottish Bar) and *G. Flynn* for the appellant.

E   *A. M. Johnston, Q.C.,* and *A. M. Grossart* (both of the Scottish Bar) for the respondents.

Their Lordships took time for consideration.

Dec. 19.   The following opinions were delivered.

F   **VISCOUNT DILHORNE:** My lords, s. 1 of the Selective Employment Payments Act 1966, requires the Minister of Labour to refund to certain employers the selective employment tax paid by them and to pay to them premiums in respect of their employees. The employers who are entitled to these refunds and payments are those where the employment is in or carried out from an establishment which comes within s. 1 (2) of the Act of 1966.

G   Section 1 (2) prescribes (inter alia) that the establishment must be one which

" . . . (*a*)—is engaged by way of business wholly or partly in—
" (i) activities falling under any of the minimum list headings shown in Orders III-XVI of the Standard Industrial Classification . . ."

The question which has to be decided in this case is whether or not the respondents' establishment was engaged in any such activity. If it was, then it is

H   agreed that they are entitled to have their establishment entered on the register which the Minister of Labour is by s. 7 of the Act of 1966 required to keep of the establishments coming within s. 1 (2), and entitled to a refund of tax and payment of the premiums.

The Minister of Labour refused to enter their establishment on the register and the respondents then, pursuant to s. 7 (5) of the Act of 1966, required the

I   question to be determined by an Industrial Tribunal. The tribunal which heard their claim unanimously decided that the respondents were

"entitled to selective employment premium, the business being an establishment which satisfies the requirements of s. 1 (2) (*a*) and (*b*) of the Selective Employment Payments Act 1966."

From that decision the Lord Advocate appealed to the Court of Session. On May 12, 1967, the appeal was dismissed. It was a unanimous decision.

The Standard Industrial Classification is a production of the Central Statistical

Office, issued, as its introduction reveals, to promote uniformity and com- **A**
parability in official statistics of the United Kingdom. The introduction states
that it contains 152 Minimum List Headings distinguished by arabic numerals
and that these Minimum List Headings are grouped into twenty-four orders.
The Act of 1966 does not contain, nor does the Standard Industrial Classification
contain, any definition of the meaning to be attached to the words " Minimum
List Heading ". These words appear on the left of each page of the classification **B**
and under them appear the arabic numerals. Order I has the title " Agriculture,
Forestry, Fishing " and appears in the following form:

" ORDER I—AGRICULTURE, FORESTRY, FISHING

Minimum
List
Heading   **C**

001   Agriculture and Horticulture

    1. Farming (not fruit) and stock-rearing

      All types of agricultural holdings, except market gardens and
    holdings used mainly for the production of fruit, flowers or seeds.
    Ancillary activities such as thatching, the retting, scutching and **D**
    combing of flax and the destruction of rabbits and other vermin
    are included.

    2. Agricultural contracting

      Services such as ploughing, harvesting or threshing performed
    for farmers on a contract basis.

    3. Market gardening, fruit, flower, and seed growing **E**

      Agricultural holdings used mainly for the production of vege-
    tables, fruit, flowers or seeds (other than seed potatoes, which are
    included in ' farming and stock-rearing '). Nursery gardens
    producing plants, fruit trees, ornamental trees and shrubs, etc.,
    are included.

002   Forestry **F**

    Planting, replanting and maintenance of woodlands and forests;
    tree felling (except tree felling carried out by sawmilling establish-
    ments); gathering of uncultivated vegetable products such as
    ferns, furze, moss, reeds, etc., from forests and elsewhere.

003   Fishing

    1. Sea fishing **G**

      Sea fishing by net or line; fishing for oysters, lobsters, crabs
    and other shellfish. The whaling industry is included."

    2. Fishing in inland waters

      Fishing in rivers, lakes and canals and the operation of fish farms
    and hatcheries."

  H

Each page of the classification is set out in the same fashion and in the same
appendix to the classification under the heading " Minimum List Heading " the
various numbers are listed.

Section 2 (3) of the Act of 1966 provides that the activities referred to in sub-s.
(2) (a) of the section are

    " (a) activities falling under any of the following minimum list headings **I**
in the Standard Industrial Classification, namely

      (i) heading 003 (which relates to fishing)

      (ii) . . .

      (iii) heading 602 or 603 (which relate to electricity and water supply); and

      (iv) any heading in Order XIX (which relates to transport and
          communication) other than heading 709

      . . .

" (e) activities falling under minimum list heading 001 or 002 . . ."

A and in s. 2 (4) appear the words " activities falling under minimum list heading
703 . . ."

In view of these provisions in the Act of 1966, it might be inferred that the
words " minimum list heading " in s. 1 (2) (*a*) were meant to refer to the arabic
numerals in the classification, as it would seem the words were meant to do
in the classification itself. However, it is not possible to reconcile this interpreta-
B tion with s. 10 (4) and (5) of the Act of 1966 which are in the following terms:

" (4) Where in the case of any minimum list heading in Orders III to
XVI of the Standard Industrial Classification the title of the heading is not
accompanied by a description of the industries or services included therein,
the heading shall be construed as referring only to the manufacture of the
goods specified in that title.

C " (5) Where any minimum list heading in the Standard Industrial
Classification contains express provision that a specified activity is excluded
from or included in that heading . . ."

It is clear from s. 10 (4) that the title of the heading and, where it is accompanied
by a description of the industries, the description of those industries is to be
regarded as covered by the words " Minimum List Heading " and it is clear
D from s. 10 (5) that the small print below the title of the heading forms part of
the " minimum list heading ", for it is only in the small print that one finds a
specified activity included or excluded.

In the light of these provisions, despite what appears in s. 2 (3) and (4) of the
Act of 1966, in my view one must treat all that is printed opposite a set of arabic
numerals as forming part of a minimum list heading.
E The respondents contended that their establishment was engaged by way
of business in activities falling under the following minimum list heading:

" **332.   Metal-Working Machine Tools**
Manufacturing metal-working machine tools . . ."

The tribunal found that the respondents " were basically designers of machines
F and tools, although they could also make certain tools if required to do so ".
It was common ground that the machines and tools they designed could be
described as metal-working machine tools. The tribunal said that the respondents

" did not deal with the general public, but designed machine tools on a
contract basis only for manufacturing companies, such as Rolls Royce,
Singer, Remington, Massey Ferguson and others. Those tools were used
G in the manufacture of a whole range of products falling within various
minimum list headings within Orders III to XVI of the Standard Industrial
Classification."

The word " activities " is frequently used, but is not defined, in the Act of 1966.
It must be given its ordinary natural meaning. The designing of machine tools
is an activity. The question is, is it an activity " falling under " the heading
H containing the words " Manufacturing machine tools "?   " Falling under " is
another expression used in a number of sections in the Act of 1966. It has, in
my opinion, the same meaning as the words " covered by " or " coming within ".

Whether a particular activity falls under a particular heading as forming
part of the activities described in that heading or is to be regarded as a distinct
and separate activity seems to me to be largely if not entirely a question of fact.
I The designing of a ship is an essential preliminary to the building of it, but
would not be regarded as part of the making of the ship. It would be treated
as a distinct activity. So, in this case it was argued that the designing of machine
tools to make certain products did not form part of the manufacture of those
tools.   While it may not be difficult to determine when the process of manufacture of a particular article has been completed, there may be considerable
dispute which an Industrial Tribunal would appear particularly well fitted to
resolve, as to the point when that process began.

The tribunal held that

" The designing was a necessary stage in the manufacture, but it was   A
not the first step, since drawings and specifications of the finished product
had usually to be drawn up by the [respondents'] customers and handed
over to the [respondents]."

If by this sentence the tribunal meant that the production of drawings and
specifications of the finished product was to be regarded as part of the manufac-   B
ture of the machine tools to produce that product. I would have doubted the
correctness of that finding; but I doubt if this is what the tribunal meant.
They were, I think, describing the course of business between the respondents
and their customers. The respondents were told what the machines were required
to do and they designed a tool to do it. If a customer said to a firm, " make me
a tool which will produce this ", it does not seem to me unreasonable to hold   C
that the designing of the tool was part of the process of manufacture. If it is
to be regarded as part of the manufacture when the designing and actual making
take place in the same establishment, it is none the less to be regarded as part
of the manufacturing process if the designing and the making take place in
different establishments.

While in the majority of cases it may be that the activity of designing is to   D
be regarded as a distinct and separate activity from the making or building
of what has been designed, in particular cases a finding that it forms part of the
process of manufacture may be justified. In each case it is, in my view, a question
of fact.

Heading 879, which is in Order XXII, covers consulting engineers, architects,
surveyors, analytical chemists, metallurgists, actuaries, etc., in private practice   E
and s. 10 (5) of the Act of 1966 requires one when determining the activities
falling under any particular heading to have regard to any express provision
of any other heading.

While this heading to which one is required to have regard supports the view
that in the majority of cases designing is to be regarded, as a separate activity
from the making or building of anything, it does not, in my opinion, suffice to   F
show that designing can never properly be regarded as part of a manufacturing
process.

The appellant contended that an activity could not fall under the words
" Manufacturing metal-working machine tools " unless it constituted the whole
process of manufacture and at the end of the process there was a machine tool.
This, in my view, places a very narrow and restrictive interpretation on these   G
words. Ordinarily one would describe anyone making parts of a machine tool
as engaged in the activity of manufacturing machine tools. It was argued that
the making of parts of machine tools would come under heading:

" **349.   Other Mechanical Engineering not elsewhere specified**

. . .

" 3.   Establishments manufacturing machinery parts not elsewhere speci-   H
fied, or undertaking general sub-contract or repair work . . ."

I am by no means sure that the existence of this heading shows that the manufacture of parts of machine tools does not come within heading 332. Minimum
List Heading 381 is entitled " Motor Vehicle Manufacturing ", and the words in
small print show that manufacturing bodies, chassis, chassis frames and other   I
parts of motor vehicles falls under this heading. Assuming that the classification
follows this pattern in classifying industrial establishments, the manufacture
of parts of machine tools comes within heading 332 and not heading 349, for
statistical purposes.

However this may be, the Act of 1966 says (1) that the activity must be one
falling under one of the minimum list headings in Orders III to XVI. If ordinarily

_____

(1) See s. 1 (2) (a), p. 163, letter G, ante.

A   the maker of parts of machine tools is engaged in the manufacture of metal-working machine tools, then for the purposes of s. 2 (1) (*a*) of the Act of 1966 he is to be regarded as engaged in the activity of manufacturing metal-working machine tools.

In my opinion, the contention that an activity does not come within the words " Manufacturing metal-working machine tools ", unless that activity

B   actually produces a machine tool should be rejected.

Assuming that the tribunal could properly have decided that the respondents' activities came within heading 332, it was contended that in this case they had misdirected themselves. They held that the respondents' establishment was:

" engaged by way of business in activities falling under the minimum
list headings 331-335, 349, 352, 362, 363, 365, 381 and 411 and shown in

C   Orders III to XVI of the Standard Industrial Classification and especially
heading 332 (manufacture of metal-working machines tools)."

It was argued that this finding treated the designing of machine tools to produce the articles coming within the headings other than heading 332 as part of the activity of making those articles, and that this was clearly wrong. While I am inclined to think that this contention was well founded and that the making

D   of the articles mentioned in these headings is a separate and distinct activity from the making of the tools to make them, it is not in this case necessary to decide this question.

If the tribunal were wrong in thinking that the respondents' activity came within the other headings, it does not follow that they misdirected themselves when they held that it came within heading 332. The tribunal's decision records

E   that the respondents submitted " that the design work they did was an essential part of the process of manufacture ". The tribunal said:

" We were of opinion that to be ' engaged in the activities of manufacture '
of a product does not mean that one has to take the product through every
stage of its creation, from raw material to finished product. It is sufficient
if one is responsible for any stage in the process of manufacture."

F
This last sentence shows, to my mind, that the tribunal were considering the right question. Then followed a sentence which was much criticised: " In this case, the specialised machine tools could not be made without being designed." It was rightly argued for the appellant that despite the truth of this statement it did not follow that the designing was a necessary stage in the manufacture.

G   This sentence was followed by the following: " The designing was a necessary stage in the manufacture . . ." Reading this part of their decision as a whole and having regard to the respondents' submission as recorded in their decision, there was, in my opinion, a clear finding of fact that the designing in this case did form part of the manufacture. It was for them to determine when the process of manufacture started and what it included and I do not think that there are

H   any grounds on which their finding should be disturbed. The Court of Session unanimously came to the conclusion that it should stand.

In my opinion this appeal should be dismissed with costs.

LORD MacDERMOTT: My Lords, the respondents, the Reliant Tool Co., are employers who have paid selective employment tax, and the question for decision is whether they are entitled to a repayment of that tax plus a premium

I   as provided for by s. 1 (1) of the Selective Employment Payments Act 1966.

The determination of this question depends on the answers to two other questions—First, what is the proper construction of sub-s. (2) (*a*) (i) of that section? Secondly, do the respondents come within the terms of that provision? I shall take these questions in turn, but before doing so it will be convenient to say a word about the respondents' business activities as disclosed in the findings of the tribunal which heard and allowed their claim. They are basically designers of machines and tools. They do not deal with the general public but design machine tools on a contract basis only for manufacturing companies, " such as

Rolls Royce, Singer, Remington, Massey Ferguson and others ". The respondents A
can make certain tools if required to do so, but for the purposes of this case their
relevant activities are the production of designs for machine tools which their
manufacturing customers then use in order to make such tools for the purpose
of producing other articles. It may be assumed that the machine tools designed
by the respondents were for metal-working.

The material part of sub-s. (2) (a) (i) of s. 1 of the Act of 1966 reads as follows: B

"(2) . . . this section applies to any employment in, or carried out from,
an establishment where—
"(a) the establishment is engaged by way of business wholly or partly in—
(i) activities falling under any of the minimum list headings shown
in Orders III to XVI of the Standard Industrial Classification; . . ."

The words "minimum list" have no significance and may be disregarded. The   C
Standard Industrial Classification is an official publication for statistical purposes
which was issued in 1948 and revised in 1958. The only heading in it which is
directly in point in this appeal is that numbered 332, for it was conceded that
if the respondents could not bring their case within that heading they could
not bring it within any other heading. Heading 332 appears in Order VI of the
classification which relates to the manufacturing of "Engineering and Electrical   D
Goods". The number 332 is in a marginal column entitled at the top "Minimum
List Heading". Opposite the number, in heavy type, is the title "Metal-working
Machine Tools" and immediately below this are seven lines of small type which
start off with the words

"Manufacturing metal-working machine tools, including forging machines   E
and hammers, extrusion and other presses, wire-drawing machines and sheet
metal-working machines . . ."

and continue with descriptions of other metal-working machine tools within the
title and of some which are expressly excluded from it.

When sub-s. (2) (a) (i) refers to "minimum list headings" the reference
must, in my opinion, include not only the number and title of each heading   F
but the small type (where there is such) under the title. I think that this follows
from the fact that the small type is obviously descriptive and to some extent
definitive in character; but it also follows from s. 10 (5) of the Act of 1966
which plainly refers to the small type when it says

"Where any minimum list heading . . . contains express provision that a
specified activity is excluded from or included in that heading . . ."   G

On the facts of the present case this view means that the material words of
heading 332 are "Manufacturing metal-working machine tools".

Coming back to sub-s. (2) (a) (i) the words "employment in . . . an establishment" and "the establishment is engaged by way of business wholly or partly"
raise no difficulty. The issue is concerned with the other words of this provision.   H
Is the respondents' establishment "engaged . . . in . . . activities falling under
any of the minimum list headings"?

My lords, I find no reason for denying the words "falling under" their natural
meaning, and would read them as the equivalent of "included in". The interpretation of the word "activities", however, is more open to debate. Is it
restricted—and this I call the narrow construction—so as to mean the totality   I
of activities comprehended in the manufacturing industry, or each of the manufacturing industries, described or deemed to be described in the relevant heading?
In this instance, for example, does it mean the whole course of stages or processes
covered by the phrase "manufacturing metal-working machine tools"? Or,
on the other hand—and this I call the wider construction—does it include not
only what would satisfy the narrow construction but also activities which constitute only a part of the entire manufacturing process? Section 10 (5), with its
reference to "a specified activity" in a heading seems to use the word in the

A   narrow sense in relation to a described manufacturing industry, but I see nothing in this or elsewhere in the statute to justify the conclusion that in s. 1 (2) (*a*) (i) the word is not capable of the wider construction and so of including an activity which is a part but not the whole of the manufacturing process. I think that wider view accords better with the policy of the statute for the selective employment premiums were presumably intended to encourage the manufacture of

B   certain products, and it would be strange to the point of absurdity if the meaning of " activities " were such as to exclude from benefit those who carried through not the whole but an essential part of the production of a listed manufacturing industry. The classification itself shows how composite a thing modern manufacturing can be, with different establishments responsible for the various steps and processes which together produce the finished article, and neither in it,

C   nor in the statute incorporating it, can I discover any trace of an intention to prefer comprehensive activities to those devoted to a part only of the production.

    The appellant, indeed, conceded that " activities " did not mean all the processes which went to the production of the finished article, but submitted that the word must include at least the process or processes that completed the manufacturing. My lords, I cannot accept that view. If the performance

D   of a part of the total process of producing a manufactured article comes within the word " activities " I can see no ground for thinking that a terminal process stands in any special or privileged position. For these reasons I would hold that on its true construction sub-s. (2) (*a*) (i) of s. 1 of the Act of 1966 includes activities which constitute a definite part, though not the whole, of the processes involved in the manufacture of metal-working machine tools.

E   On this construction do the respondents qualify under s. 1 (2)? Here, I would first refer to the appellant's submission that the respondents were excluded from heading 332 because they came within heading 879 which is entitled " Other Professional and Scientific Services " and is outside the parts of the classification incorporated by s. 1 (2) (*a*) (i) of the Act of 1966. In support of this argument reliance was placed on the latter part of s. 10 (5) of the Act which provides:

F   " . . . in determining the activities falling under any particular minimum list heading in the Standard Industrial Classification, regard shall be had to any express provision of any other such heading."

I cannot accede to this submission. Head 879 does not contain any express provision relating to designers and on that account does not seem to attract

G   this part of s. 10 (5). In any event, I very much doubt if the respondents could rightly be regarded as coming within the general terms of this head; and even if they could be so regarded I do not think that that would take them outside head 332 if they were otherwise within it.

    The question then becomes whether the designing of machine tools by the respondents constituted a part of the manufacturing process of such tools so as

H   to amount to " activities " within the meaning of sub-s. (2) (*a*) (i). The tribunal, in addition to the facts already mentioned, found that—1. " In this case, the specialised machine tools could not be made without being designed ", and 2. " The designing was a necessary stage in the manufacture . . ." The tribunal then held that the respondents' establishment was accordingly engaged by way of business in activities within s. 1 (2) (*a*) of the Selective Employment Payments

I   Act, 1966, and that the respondents were therefore entitled under sub-s. (1) of that section.

    My lords, in my opinion, the tribunal had ample material on which to reach the finding, at 1. above, that the machine tools for which the respondents prepared designs—a process requiring high technical skill, knowledge and experience—could not be made without being designed. That, as I see it, was entirely a finding of fact and it must therefore stand. Part 2 of the finding— that the designing was a necessary stage in the manufacture—I take as meaning that the designing work of the respondents was an essential part of the process

of the manufacture of the machine tools to which the designs related. I do not   A
think this can be described as just a question of fact. It is rather a question of
mixed law and fact, for whether a preliminary process, no matter how essential
to a subsequent process of manufacture, can rank as part of the latter process,
may well depend on legal considerations involving the nature of the relationship
between the preliminary and the subsequent processes. An example of this
may be found in the reasoning of the tribunal in this case, for they appear to   B
have reached the conclusion that the respondents were engaged not only in the
process of manufacturing machine tools, but also in the process of manufacturing
the products which those machine tools were used to make. In my opinion,
that further conclusion would be of doubtful validity in law, for the relationship
of the preliminary to the subsequent process in that instance would seem too
remote to support it. The law may not say precisely where a line is to be drawn,   C
but that does not prevent the question whether a given relationship is on one
side of the line or the other from being a question of law.

This brings me to the last and, as I see it, the most difficult branch of the
case. Is what I have referred to as Part 2 of the tribunal's finding bad in law?
I think, reading this finding as I have, that it approaches the line which marks
off what is simply preliminary from what is a part of the manufacturing process,   D
but my conclusion is that the finding lies on the right side of the line, was correct
in law and should not be disturbed. It was based on a relationship between the
preliminary and subsequent processes which was particularly intimate and
direct and not at one or more removes; and it reflected a state of affairs in which
the designs pervaded and were essential to all that followed in the sense that they
informed and controlled the subsequent steps and stages of the manufacture.   E
If this designing had been done by those who made the tools I do not think that it
would have occurred to any one to regard it as a preliminary activity that
was not part and parcel of the process of manufacture, and the situation here
does not seem to me to be materially different.

On these grounds I consider that the conclusions reached by the tribunal
and the First Division were right, and I would therefore dismiss the appeal.   F

LORD GUEST: My Lords the short, but by no means simple, question in
this appeal is whether the respondents are entitled, under s. 1 of the Selective
Employment Payments Act 1966 to a selective employment premium. The
First Division of the Court of Session affirmed a decision by the Industrial
Tribunal that they were so entitled. The employer is qualified to receive a   G
selective employment premium if the employment is in or carried out from any
establishment

" where—(a) the establishment is engaged by way of business wholly or
partly in—(i) activities falling under any of the minimum list headings shown
in Orders III to XVI of the Standard Industrial Classification "

and if certain other conditions which are immaterial are satisfied, (s. 1 (2)).   H

The respondents, as found by the Industrial Tribunal established for the
purposes of the Act of 1966, are

" basically designers of machines and tools, although they could also make
certain tools if required to do so. They did not deal with the general public,
but designed machine tools on a contract basis only for manufacturing
companies, such as Rolls Royce, Singer, Remington, Massey Ferguson and
others. Those tools were used in the manufacture of a whole range of products
falling within various minimum list headings within Orders III to XVI of
the Standard Industrial Classification."

I have found the construction of s. 1 (2) (a) of the Act of 1966 difficult. This
difficulty is accentuated by the fact that the Standard Industrial Classification
was prepared by the Central Statistical Office for an entirely different purpose
from providing the qualification for the selective employment premium. The

A classification is described as industrial, but some of the orders deal with services and not with industries at all. The Standard Industrial Classification contains, under minimum list headings, a number against which, in thick black type, is a heading. The relevant heading in this case is 332 " Metal-Working Machine Tools " and below in smaller type various industries are set out, the relevant one in this case being " Manufacturing metal-working machine tools ". From

B internal evidence in the Act of 1966, particularly s. 10 (4) which refers to the title of the heading " being accompanied by a description of the industries . . . therein ", a minimum list heading in s. 1 (2) (*a*) must consist of the " title " in heavy black type and " a description of the industries " in small type. What is, then, meant by " activities falling under a minimum list heading "? The appellant maintained that the activities were the various industries described in the small type and that

C " falling under" meant textually what came below the title of the minimum list heading. Qualification was therefore strictly limited to the industries described in small type. Thus, in order to qualify for the premium the establishment would have to be engaged by way of business wholly or partly in manufacturing metal-working machine tools. I am unable to give s. 1 (2) (*a*) this restricted meaning. In my view " activities " is not limited to the description of the industries which follows

D the heading but the word must refer to such activities of the applicant company as would fairly come within the industries described in the small type. The industries are classified under various headings but this does not limit the qualification to the particular industry. " Activities " is a word of wider import than industry. The difficulty is that " activities " in the Act of 1966 is used in a loose sense, sometimes referring to what the industry does, as in s. 2 (3) (*b*), and sometimes

E referring to the description of the industries in the heading, as in s. 10 (5); but in my view, " activities " in s. 1 (2) (*a*) must go beyond the mere description of the industry contained in the minimum list heading. The appellant argued that to give " activities " this wide meaning would render s. 1 (2) (*b*), which refers to persons employed " in connexion with such activities ", otiose. I cannot agree. Section 1 (2) (*a*) is dealing with the qualification of the business for the premium

F and s. 1 (2) (*b*) is dealing with the qualification of persons employed in that industry. Moreover if, as I think, the activity must be an essential part of the industry, this is in marked distinction to the wide connotation of " in connexion with " in s. 1 (2) (*b*).

It was on this basis that the First Division proceeded in their construction of s. 1 of the Act of 1966 and I consider that it was correct.

G The appellant argued that the approach of the Industrial Tribunal to s. 1 (2) (*a*) invalidated their decision. It is apparent from their findings and reasons that the tribunal considered that if the activities of the respondents were associated with the production of the final artifact, such as agricultural machinery (heading 331) or textile machinery and accessories (heading 335), this was sufficient to bring them within the qualifying section. I think that this was the wrong approach

H and that the only justification for the respondents' qualification was heading 332 " Metal-working machine tools ". This approach, however, does not, in my view, invalidate their decision. They relied for their decision (inter alia) on heading 332, and the question is ultimately whether there was evidence to justify their finding that the respondents' establishment was engaged by way of business in activities falling under this heading. The tribunal found as a fact that the specialised

I machine tools could not be made without being designed and that designing was a necessary step in the manufacture. From these findings I understand that their view was that the process of manufacture was not limited to the actual making of the article but included preliminary processes such as designing which were essential to the final production of the article. In my view, their approach to the question which they had to determine was correct and their findings justified their decision. We should not, therefore, be entitled in these circumstances to interfere with their decision.

Heading 879 was referred to by the appellant as indicating that services such

as the respondents provide did not come within the activities in heading 332. **A**
Heading 879 could only be relevant if s. 10 (5) applied. Section 10 (5) is in these
terms:

" (5) Where any minimum list heading in the Standard Industrial Classification contains express provision that a specified activity is excluded
from or included in that heading if it is carried on at premises attached to
premises of a specified class, and but for that express provision that activity **B**
would have fallen under that or,· as the case may be, some other minimum
list heading, that express provision shall be deemed to be omitted; but,
save as provided by the foregoing provisions of this sub-section, in determining the activities falling under any particular minimum list heading in
the Standard Industrial Classification, regard shall be had to any express
provision of any other such heading." **C**

Heading 879 nowhere contains an "express provision" that machine tool
designers are excluded. Designers are not included in the classification of the
professional and scientific services in heading 879 (1). In any event all that
s. 10 (5) does is to require that "regard shall be had to any express provision".
It does not make the exclusion decisive. **D**

It was argued for the appellant that the construction of s. 1 (2) (*a*) of the Act
of 1966 by the Court of Session would render the working of the Act of 1966
administratively impracticable. If Parliament uses such imprecise language as
is found in the Selective Employment Payments Act 1966, it must not be surprised
if the result occasions difficulty in administration. Parliament speaks through the
mouth of the statute. If this is the effect of the decision, Parliament has the **E**
remedy in its own hands.

For these reasons I would dismiss the appeal.

LORD WILBERFORCE: My Lords, persons who have paid the selective
employment tax under the Finance Act 1966, are divided into three categories,
first, those who simply pay the tax and have no right of recovery, secondly, those **F**
who are reimbursed the tax that they have paid, thirdly, those who not only
recover the tax but also become entitled to a premium. The conditions on which
payments are made to the second and third categories are laid down in the
Selective Employment Payments Act 1966, and administered by the Ministry of
Labour.

Broadly speaking, the right to recovery and premium depends on whether the **G**
applicant is engaged in manufacture, the intention apparently being to favour
such persons by contrast to those engaged in providing services. The test of
engagement in manufacture is applied, not to individuals or corporate entities, or
enterprises, but to "establishments".

The administration of this scheme involves questions of classification. These
are certain to be multitudinous and delicate, since no one enterprise is organised **H**
exactly like any other, and industrial activities do not readily lend themselves to
precise categorisation. The decision of these questions has, therefore, been
committed to industrial tribunals as fact finding bodies. These are required to
classify establishments by reference to the Standard Industrial Classification, a
list prepared for statistical purposes by the Central Statistical Office. No doubt
this was the best available list at the time, but its uses for a purpose for which it **I**
was not designed must lead to difficulties. In view of its origin it would be a
mistake, in my opinion, to look too closely into its wording for solutions which it
is not adapted to provide. The list, in the relevant orders, contains what are
described as a number of minimum list headings, to each of which is ascribed a
number and a title. Under each title (with a few exceptions) appears a list of
certain activities regarded as covered by the title: but a reading of these shows
that it is not intended to be definitive or exhaustive.

The tribunal, after taking evidence as to the respondents' activities, have found

A that they are entitled to repayment plus premium, so one must first consider what they were entitled to find and then examine their actual findings.

What they are entitled to find is whether the respondents' establishment is engaged by way of business wholly or partly in activities falling under one of the minimum list headings (s. 1 (2) (*a*) (i) of the Act of 1966). There is no difficulty in identifying the establishment. The material minimum list heading is No. 332
B which has as its title " Metal-working Machine Tools ". Under the title there appear a number of activities, the first of which is " Manufacturing metal-working machine tools "; others are of a similar character.

In my opinion, what the tribunal had to find is clear enough: the heading refers to metal-working machine tools: to arrive at an activity (which is what the question relates to) it is necessary to add the word " manufacturing " which
C appears in the descriptive matter following the title. So the question is whether the respondents' activities fall under the heading Manufacturing Metal-Working Machine Tools. The words " fall under the heading " I understand to mean the same as " come within the description ". To answer a question such as this is eminently one for a tribunal of fact. Whatever " manufacturing " may have meant at the time of the handloom or the spinning jenny, now it is often a far-
D reaching process containing many sub-processes and specialised techniques and involving a large number of skilled workers and organisers. It is a wider word than " production ": for there is much to do, much time and money to be spent, many decisions and experiments to be made, before the risk of large sale production is taken. Exactly at what point the preparation for manufacture ends and the process of manufacture begins may often be a matter of opinion. This is for
E the tribunal of fact to decide. The courts should only overrule their findings if satisfied that no reasonable body could find as they have done.

Can one, then, say this of a finding that design of a product is part of, or covered by the description of, or falls under the heading of, manufacture? Can one say this where the object of manufacture is a machine tool? For my part I cannot, any more than I could say that a man who produces a design in the course
F of the manufacture, or a man who, without putting pencil to paper, communicates his idea to the working engineer, is not engaged in the activity of manufacture. It is for the tribunal to draw the line, and I find no reason in grammar or common-sense for saying that they must draw it short of these activities.

I think, then, that the tribunal were entitled to find that the activities of the respondents fall under the relevant heading, and I approach the second question,
G which is to ask whether they have done so without any vitiating misdirection.

The finding gives a description of the nature of the applicants' business. They are basically designers of machines and tools, although they could also make tools. They do not deal with the general public but design machine tools on a contract basis for manufacturing companies. When the tribunal come to apply the relevant section of the Act of 1966 to a business of this type, they first record their opinion
H that in order to be engaged in the activities of manufacture it is not necessary to take the product through every stage of its creation. It is sufficient if one is responsible for any stage in the process of manufacture. This is evidently a decision on construction and so reviewable by a court of law. Then comes the finding of fact that " the specialised machine tools " could not be made without being designed. The designing was a necessary stage in the manufacture. The
I applicants' establishment therefore was engaged in activities falling under the minimum list headings and especially No. 332 (Manufacture of Metal-Working Machine Tools). In relation to this finding the issue of possible misdirection arises.

The appellant attacks the decision on three grounds. First, it was said that the tribunal were wrong in law in their construction of the relevant section and headings. An activity could only be said to fall under a heading if it extended to the entire activity covered by the heading—in this case manufacturing a machine tool, or, as a possible alternative, if it extended to the production of the finished, or end, product. An activity, it was argued, confined to the manufacture of a

part or parts of the manufactured product described in or under the heading A
must be brought (if at all) under some other heading appropriate to cover it by
particular or general description.

I cannot accept this. It may be the case—I do not know—that, for statistical
purposes, manufactures of parts, or certain parts of (say) machine tools are
classified under a different heading from that of manufacturers of machine tools;
but even assuming this, it does not follow that when the standard classification is B
adopted and used for a totally different purpose the tribunal are bound to follow
the same scheme of division.

The headings are grafted into the Selective Employment Payments Act 1966
through a provision containing its special terminology, designed for its special
purpose, and one must interpret them in this new framework. For that purpose,
the guiding words are " activities falling under the minimum list headings " (2), C
words which present the tribunal with a clearly defined test which they can, and
should, apply without being shepherded into statistical compartments. It might
in fact lead to absurd results if, in relation to an enterprise engaged in manufacturing machine tools, but doing so in a number of self-contained establishments, the
tribunal had to seek for headings appropriate to each separate establishment
instead of bring them all under the single heading appropriate to the product. D
In my opinion, the tribunal's construction of the section was correct.

Secondly, it was said that the finding was not clear: " a necessary stage "
was claimed to be ambiguous: it might merely refer to a condition precedent
to the manufacture (such as the erection of a factory or the laying-on of electrical
power) and, if so, this would be a case of misdirection. I do not agree. I think,
and I note that all the learned judges in the Court of Session read the report in E
the same way, that the finding clearly means that the designing is a part and a
necessary part of the manufacture itself: this was how the respondents are
recorded (3) as having put their case " the design work formed an essential part
of the process of manufacture of the machine tool ", and I can have no doubt
that the tribunal regarded their task as being to decide whether this was correct
and that they did so decide. In a later passage indeed they describe the F
respondents (4) as " persons contractually engaged in processes of manufacture ".

Thirdly, it was submitted that the decision showed a confusion of mind between
the manufacture of the machine tools and that of the end product (e.g., aircraft
engines) for which the machine tools were designed. The tribunal could hardly be
blamed if, in applying this confusing legislation, they deviated from perfect
lucidity. After mentioning various headings with which the applicants were G
" associated in a design capacity " the tribunal said immediately after the finding
that the designing was a necessary stage in the manufacture " but it was not the
first step since drawings and specifications of the finished product had usually to
be drawn up by the [respondents'] customers and handed over to the
[respondents] ": they continued with the finding that the respondents (4) were
engaged in activities falling under the headings referred to and especially heading H
332. I understand this passage to be saying that in designing a machine tool for
(say) an aircraft engine or an agricultural implement, the respondents first (as
the first step) had to obtain a drawing of the ultimate product. In itself this is a
mere statement of fact and, indeed, might be relevant as showing the close
relation between the designers and the process of manufacturing the machine
tool. It is possible (and I do not wish so to decide until the case arises) that the
tribunal went too far in finding that this brought the respondents' activities
under a heading appropriate to the ultimate product as well as under that
appropriate to the machine tools: but even if this were so, that would not invalidate their findings as to heading 332 which is clear and self-contained. And I
cannot regard the reference to " the first step " as showing that by " a necessary

(2) Selective Employment Payments Act 1966 s. 1 (2) (a) (i).
(3) I.e., as having put their case before the tribunal.
(4) I.e., the respondents on this appeal; they were applicants before the tribunal.

A stage " they meant something preliminary to manufacture: to me it suggests rather the contrary, that they saw the difference between a preliminary and a part.

I conclude therefore that, the tribunal being entitled to find as they did, there is nothing by way of misdirection or otherwise which vitiates their finding.

B I would only add that if and so far as there are passages in the judgments of the judges in the First Division which, read alone, might suggest that it is enough, for the section to apply, to show that the activities in question are such as are normally carried out by manufacturers, these must, in my opinion, be read together with those which make it clear that the activities must be such as fall within the description of manufacturing activities. I do not think that they intended in these passages or when giving a " wider interpretation " to " activities

C of manufacture " to suggest that activities outside the field of manufacture, even though carried on by the manufacturer as ancillary to the manufacturing process, are within the description, or indeed to do more than exclude a construction which would limit the activities to the whole process, or to all the activities from first to last.

I would dismiss the appeal.

D
LORD PEARSON: My Lords, the question is whether the respondents' establishment which is engaged in the designing of machine tools, has been properly held to be, within the meaning of s. 1 (2) (*a*) (i) of the Selective Employment Payments Act 1966, an establishment

E ". . . engaged by way of business wholly or partly in—(i) activities falling under any of the miminum list headings shown in Orders III to XVI of the Standard Industrial Classification; . . ."

The Standard Industrial Classification referred to in the section is a document which has an introduction. I think that the introduction can properly be taken into account for the purpose of ascertaining (subject to any special qualifications or adaptations provided by the Act of 1966 for the purposes of the Act, e.g., in

F s. 10 (4) and (5)) what is meant by the expressions " minimum list headings ", " activities " and " falling under ".

It appears from para. 9 of the introduction that the adjective " minimum " applies to " list " rather than " headings ". There is a minimum list of headings, evidently for the guidance of statisticians compiling statistics and intended to be the shortest list of headings which will suffice for a proper industrial classification,

G though it might need to be enlarged by the addition of further sub-headings for the purposes of a particular statistical exercise.

Paragraphs 10 and 11 of the introduction show that a heading consists of a distinguishing number, a title and " a brief description of the main industries or services included ". It follows from that language that the description is not necessarily exhaustive: there may be minor or subordinate industries or services

H included under the title and therefore in the heading, though not covered by the " brief description of the main industries or services ". An example of such minor or subordinate industries or services is repair work, of which para. 8 (*c*) of the introduction says:

" Most kinds of repair work are associated with activities which are

I classified either to manufacturing or to distribution and in these cases the underlying principle of classification is that where the bulk of the repair work on goods of any particular type is carried out by manufacturers, any establishments specialising in the repair of these goods are classified to manufacturing. Where, however, most of the repairs are carried out at establishments whose main business is distribution the specialist repair establishments are also classified to distribution."

Section 10 (4) of the Act of 1966 shows that the title of the heading is usually " accompanied by a description of the industries or services included therein ".

The wording of the Act of 1966 closely follows the wording of the Standard **A**
Industrial Classification.

The word " activities " is a word of wide application. It can refer to operations
and processes and, generally, things that people do, but in the Standard Industrial
Classification it refers to what is done in departments of a business rather than
merely by individuals. Paragraph 4 of the introduction states:

  B

> " For the purpose of this classification the unit taken is the ' establishment '.
> An establishment is normally the whole of the premises, such as a farm, a
> mine, a factory or a shop at a particular address. All activities carried on at
> that address (including, for example, departments engaged in selling, bott-
> ling, packing, transport, providing power or manufacturing containers or
> packing for the distribution of the products of the establishment) are **C**
> included. Canteens run by the management are regarded as part of the
> establishment."

The wide meaning of the word " activities " is supported by the language of
para. 8 (c) of the introduction (cited above) and of minimum list heading 001
(Agriculture and Horticulture) Sub-heading 1, which reads as follows:

  D

> " Farming (not fruit) and stock-rearing. All types of agricultural holdings,
> except market gardens and holding used mainly for the production of fruit,
> flowers or seeds. Ancillary activities such as thatching, the retting, scutching
> and combing of flax and the destruction of rabbits and other vermin is
> included."

Section 10 (5) of the Act of 1966 shows that the word " activity " or " activities " **E**
is used in same wide sense in the Act as in the Standard Industrial Classification.

The expression " falling under " is used in s. 1 (2) (a) (i) of the Act of 1966 for
the reason, presumably, that it is the natural word to use in conjunction with
" headings ". The mental picture is of a heading at the top of a page and activities
entered on the page because they fall under the heading. In effect " falling under "
has the same meaning as " coming within " would have. **F**

The relevant heading is numbered 332. Its title is " Metal-working Machine
Tools ". There follows a description, which must, in pursuance of para. 11 of the
introduction, be understood as a " brief description of the main industries or
services included ". I think that for the purposes of this case only the opening
words of the description, viz., " manufacturing metal-working machine tools "
are material. **G**

After this examination of the meanings of the relevant words and phrases, I
think that the question can be stated in this way: does the respondents' activity
of designing machine tools come within the title of heading No. 332 and the
description (understood as a brief description of the main industries and services
included) " manufacturing metal-working machine tools "? The Industrial
Tribunal have said that it does. In my opinion the tribunal's decision was reason- **H**
able and involved no error of law. The Court of Session upheld the tribunal's
decision.

I would dismiss the appeal.

Appeal dismissed.

Solicitors: *Solicitor, Ministry of Labour*, agents for *Shepherd & Wedderburn*,
Edinburgh (for the appellant); *Alan, George & Sacker*, agents for *Levy & M'Rae*,
Glasgow and *Drummond & Reid*, Edinburgh (for the respondents).

[*Reported by* KATHLEEN J. H. O'BRIEN, *Barrister-at-Law.*]

A   PARRY-JONES v. THE LAW SOCIETY AND OTHERS.

[COURT OF APPEAL, CIVIL DIVISION (Lord Denning, M.R., Diplock and Salmon, L.JJ.), November 14, 15, 1967.]

Solicitor—Clients' account—Inspection of books of account, bank pass books, vouchers, etc.—Law Society's power to require solicitor to produce books
B   *for inspection—Legal professional privilege—Solicitors' Accounts Rules, 1945 (S.R. & O. 1944 No. 781); r. 11 (1), (2)—Solicitors Act, 1957 (5 & 6 Eliz. 2 c. 27), s. 29 (1), (2).*

The Law Society, acting under r. 11* of the Solicitors' Accounts Rules, 1945, required the plaintiff solicitor to produce at his office his books of account, bank pass books, statements of accounts, vouchers and other
C   necessary documents relating to his practice at that office for the inspection of the society's investigation accountant. The solicitor brought an action against the society and others claiming an injunction to restrain them from acting on the notices, and claiming that the plaintiff solicitor was entitled to particulars of any complaint or representation made to any of the defendants as to his conduct as a solicitor. The plaintiff solicitor
D   contended that the investigation accountant was not entitled on investigation under s. 29† of the Act of 1957 to inspect privileged documents, relying on s. 46 (6) of the Solicitors Act, 1957. On appeal from an order striking out the statement of claim as showing no cause of action,

Held: (i) the duty of a solicitor to his client not to disclose his client's affairs was a contractual duty implicit in the relationship of solicitor and
E   client, and this obligation was subject to the solicitor's duty to obey the law, viz., in this instance to comply with the Solicitors' Accounts Rules, 1945, r. 11 and to make the disclosure required by that rule; accordingly the statement of claim had been rightly struck out (see p. 178, letters G and H, p. 179, letter C, and p. 180, letters C and H, post).

(ii) the plaintiff was not entitled to see the complaint lodged against
F   him, because (per LORD DENNING, M.R.) the enquiry being whether there was a prima facie case, the rules of natural justice did not apply so as to require notice to be given to the plaintiff of the complaint, and (per DIPLOCK, L.J.) the required inspection was not a judicial nor a quasi-judicial enquiry but was an enquiry which the Council of the Law Society was entitled to make without any instigation (see p. 179, letter G, and p. 180, letters G and
G   H, post).

Wiseman v. *Borneman* ([1967] 3 All E.R. 1045) applied.
Decision of BUCKLEY, J. ([1967] 3 All E.R. 248) affirmed.

[Editorial Note. The terms of r. 11 (1) of the Solicitors' Trust Accounts Rules, 1945, are the same, substantially, as those of r. 11 (1) of the Solicitors' Accounts Rules, 1945; the decision is, accordingly, authority on r. 11 of the
H   trust accounts rules, as well as on r. 11 of the client account rules.

As to the power to require production of a solicitor's books of accounts, etc., see 36 HALSBURY'S LAWS (3rd Edn.) 243, 244, para. 341.

For the Solicitors Act, 1957, s. 29, s. 46, s. 88, see 37 HALSBURY'S STATUTES (2nd Edn.) 1076, 1090, 1127.

For the Solicitors' Accounts Rules, 1945, r. 11, see 20 HALSBURY'S STATUTORY
I   INSTRUMENTS (First Re-Issue) 195, 196; and for the Solicitors' Trust Accounts Rules, 1945, r. 11, see ibid., p. 199.]

Cases referred to:
Tournier v. *National Provincial and Union Bank of England, Ltd.*, [1923] All E.R. Rep. 550; [1924] 1 K.B. 461; 93 L.J.K.B. 449; 130 L.T. 682; 3 Digest (Repl.) 343, *1108.*

---

* Rule 11, so far as material, is set out at p. 179, letter B, post.
† Section 29, so far as material, is set out at p. 178, letter I, post.

H

Wiseman v. *Borneman*, [1967] 3 All E.R. 546; [1967] 3 W.L.R. 1372; *affd.* A
C.A., [1967] 3 All E.R. 1045.

Interlocutory appeal.

This was an appeal by the plaintiff, Aneurin Glanmor Parry-Jones, by notice
dated Aug. 2, 1967, from an order made by BUCKLEY, J., dated July 21, 1967,
whereby it was ordered that the endorsement on the writ issued by the plaintiff
commencing these proceedings should be struck out; the plaintiff sought leave B
to serve a statement of claim and to take all necessary proceedings in the action.

The plaintiff appeared in person.

T. H. Bingham for the defendants.

LORD DENNING, M.R.: For many years now the Law Society have
made rules about clients' money. Every solicitor has to keep his clients' money C
in a separate account relating to clients' money. This has been a very important
safeguard for clients all over the country. Every solicitor has also every year
to engage an accountant to examine his accounts and to give a certificate that
he is complying with the rules. In addition, the council can send down an
accountant of their own choice to make an investigation of the solicitor's books
to see whether he is complying with the rules.   D

On Feb. 9, 1967, and also on Mar. 3, 1967, the Law Society wrote to the plaintiff
requiring him to produce at his office his various books of account for the inspection of Mr. Harden, the Law Society's investigating accountant. As far as we
know, the plaintiff has complied with that request and the investigation has been
held. In the course of it, the plaintiff raised two points of some importance;
and he has brought an action to test the position. The first point is this. He E
says that he is not bound to produce to the accountant a document or information
which is privileged from production. We all know that, as between solicitor
and client, there are two privileges. The first is the privilege relating to legal
proceedings, commonly called legal professional privilege. A solicitor must not
produce or disclose in any legal proceedings any of the communications between
himself and his client without the client's consent. The second privilege arises F
out of the confidence subsisting between solicitor and client similar to the confidence which applies between doctor and patient, banker and customer, accountant and client, and the like. The law implies a term into the contract whereby
a professional man is to keep his client's affairs secret and not to disclose them
to anyone without just cause (see *Tournier* v. *National Provincial Bank, Ltd.* (1)).
This particularly applies in the relationship of solicitor and client. The solicitor G
is not to disclose his client's affairs to anyone at all except under the most special
and exceptional circumstances. In reliance on these principles, the plaintiff
says that the accountant sent by the Law Society should not be allowed to see
documents or information relating to a client's affairs.

We have been into the matter with the help of the plaintiff (who has argued
his case very well on his own behalf) and counsel on behalf of the Law Society. H
In my opinion the contract between solicitor and client must be taken to contain
this implication:—the solicitor must obey the law, and, in particular, he must
comply with the rules made under the authority of statute for the conduct of
the profession. If the rules require him to disclose his client's affairs, then he
must do so. The rules are made under s. 29 of the Solicitors Act, 1957. It
provides: I

" (1) The council shall make rules—(*a*) as to the opening and keeping by
solicitors of accounts at banks for clients' money; (*b*) as to the keeping by
solicitors of accounts containing particulars and information as to moneys
received, held or paid by them for or on account of their clients; and (*c*)
empowering the council to take such action as may be necessary to enable
them to ascertain whether or not the rules are being complied with: . . ."

(1) [1923] All E.R. Rep. 550 at pp. 557, 558; [1924] 1 K.B. 461 at pp. 479-481.

A   All the matters contained in paras. (*a*), (*b*) and (*c*) are clients' matters. The books and accounts contain information as to clients' affairs. By enabling the council to "take such action as may be necessary", the statute imports that rules can be made whereby the council can look into the solicitor's books and supporting documents in order to see that the rules are complied with, even if it does mean disclosing the clients' affairs.

B   Under the statute the council have made r. 11 (1) of the Solicitors' Accounts Rules, 1945, (2) which provides:

> "In order to ascertain whether these rules have been complied with, the council, acting either—(*a*) on their own motion; or (*b*) on a written statement or request transmitted to them by or on behalf of the governing body of a provincial law society or a committee thereof; or (*c*) on a written complaint
>
C   > lodged with them by a third party; may require any solicitor to produce . . . his books . . ."

In my opinion that rule is a valid rule which overrides any privilege or confidence which otherwise might subsist between solicitor and client. It enables the Law Society for the public good to hold an investigation, even if it involves getting

D   information as to clients' affairs; but they and their accountant must themselves respect the obligation of confidence. They must not use it for any purpose except the investigation, and any consequential proceedings. If there should be subsequent application to the disciplinary committee, the information can be used for that purpose. In all other respects the usual rules of legal professional privilege apply (see s. 46 (6) of the Act of 1957).

E   Then the plaintiff raised another point. He said that if the council act under r. 11 (1) (*c*) on a written complaint lodged by a third party, then that complaint should be shown to him, the solicitor. He says he is entitled to know who is making the complaint and the nature of it. Such is required, he says, by natural justice. I would point out that under r. 11 (4) it is provided that,

> "Before instituting an inspection on a written complaint lodged with
F   > them by a third party, the council shall require prima facie evidence that the ground of complaint exists, . . ."

That shows that the council have only to enquire whether there is prima facie evidence. As we held a few days ago in the case of *Wiseman* v. *Borneman* (3), a prima facie case stands on a very different footing from an actual determination. Where the only enquiry is whether there is prima facie evidence, natural justice

G   does not require that the party should be given notice of it. Nor do I think that the solicitor is entitled to know whether the council are acting under paras. (*a*), (*b*) or (*c*) of r. 11 (1). The rule does not require it. The council are entitled to send their accountant to make an investigation without disclosing on which ground they are acting. The solicitor is not entitled to be told the particulars of the complaint.

H   In the result I am of opinion that all the claims which the plaintiff raises by the endorsement on the writ in this action are not well-founded. The judge (4) was quite right to strike it out and dismiss the action.

I would, therefore, dismiss the appeal.

DIPLOCK, L.J.: I agree. I think that this action is obviously mis-
I   conceived. If I did not think so, then I should not think it right to strike it out under the summary procedure.

The foundation of the plaintiff's case is the submission that an inspection of documents under r. 11 of the Solicitors' Accounts Rules, 1945, is in the nature of a judicial proceeding. In my view it is no more in the nature of a judicial proceeding than an inspection by a factory inspector under the Factories Acts

---

(2) S.R. & O. 1944 No. 781.
(3) [1967] 3 All E.R. 1045.
(4) [1967] 3 All E.R. 248.

of factory premises. The result of it may lead to subsequent judicial or quasi-   A
judicial proceedings, but that does not make the enquiry or inspection a judicial
or quasi-judicial proceeding itself.

So far as the plaintiff's point as to privilege is concerned, privilege is irrelevant
when one is not concerned with judicial or quasi-judicial proceedings because,
strictly speaking, privilege refers to a right to withhold from a court, or a tribunal
exercising judicial functions, material which would otherwise be admissible in   B
evidence.   What we are concerned with here is the contractual duty of confidence, generally implied though sometimes expressed, between a solicitor and
client.   Such a duty exists not only between solicitor and client, but, for example,
between banker and customer, doctor and patient, and accountant and client.
Such a duty of confidence is subject to, and overriden by, the duty of any party
to that contract to comply with the law of the land.   If it is the duty of such a   C
party to a contract, whether at common law or under statute, to disclose in
defined circumstances confidential information, then he must do so, and any
express contract to the contrary would be illegal and void.   For example, in the
case of banker and customer, the duty of confidence is subject to the overriding
duty of the banker at common law to disclose and answer questions as to his
customer's affairs when he is asked to give evidence on them in the witness box   D
in a court of law.   I think that similar provisions as to disclosure apply to
doctors under the National Health Acts.   I agree with LORD DENNING, M.R.,
that s. 29 of the Solicitors' Act, 1957, which deals with accounts (the whole of the
material in which consist of information about clients' affairs because it is the
clients' accounts only which are dealt with in this section) and empowers the
council of the Law Society to take such action as may be necessary to enable   E
them to ascertain whether or not the rules are being complied with, necessarily
empowers the council to make rules which entitle the council to override that
privilege.   They have in my view made such a rule in r. 11 of the Solicitors'
Accounts Rules, 1945, and there is accordingly nothing in the first point which
the plaintiff raises.

The second point is that the plaintiff is entitled under the rules of natural justice   F
to see a complaint, if indeed there was a complaint laid against him.   I agree
with LORD DENNING, M.R., that there is nothing in the second point at all.   It
is also founded on the assumption that the inspection is a judicial or quasi-
judicial enquiry.   It is nothing of the sort, and I can see no reason why the
plaintiff should have any right to know what has instigated the Law Society to
make the enquiries which they are entitled to make without any instigation at   G
all.

SALMON, L.J.:   I agree with both the judgments which have been
delivered.

Appeal dismissed.

Solicitors: *Hempsons* (for the defendants).   H

[*Reported by* F. GUTTMAN, ESQ., *Barrister-at-Law.*]

A

Re d'ALTROY'S WILL TRUSTS.
CRANE AND ANOTHER *v.* LOWMAN AND OTHERS.

[CHANCERY DIVISION (Pennycuick, J.), July 4, November 2, 1967.]

B
Will—Life interest—Protective trusts—Bequest of protected life interest in testatrix' residuary estate to deceased daughter's husband for so long as he should remain daughter's widower—Remarriage—Nullity decree obtained by second wife—Residuary estate and income retained by trustees of will—Whether deceased daughter's husband entitled to life interest until marrying again.

A testatrix made a will and codicil under which her residuary estate would
C be held on protective trusts for L. for life so long as he should remain the
widower of A. L. re-married before the testatrix died. After her death on
Feb. 15, 1966, L.'s second wife brought a suit for nullity against him, and a
decree nisi and later a decree absolute were made. The trustees retained the
residuary estate and its income pending determination of the question
whether L. was entitled to a life interest in the residuary estate.

D
Held: the whole estate being in hand, and L. being in the position, in law,
that he had never contracted his second marriage, the income of the residuary
estate was held on protective trusts for him for the remainder of his life or
until he contracted another marriage (see p. 183, letter H, post).

Re Wombwell's Settlement ([1922] All E.R. Rep. 115) and *Re Dewhirst*
([1948] 1 All E.R. 147) followed.

E
Re Eaves ([1939] 4 All E.R. 260) considered.

Per CURIAM: if any part of the estate had been transferred to the next-of-
kin while L.'s second marriage subsisted, they would have been entitled to
hold it free from any interest of L. (see p. 183, letter G, post).

F
[As to consequences of marriage being void or voidable, see 12 HALSBURY'S
LAWS (3rd Edn.) 226-228, para. 424; and for cases on conditions in wills relating
to marriage, see 48 DIGEST (Repl.) 333-335, *2861-2874*.]

Cases referred to:
Dewhirst, Re, Flower v. *Dewhirst*, [1948] 1 All E.R. 147; [1948] Ch. 198; [1948]
    L.J.R. 912; 48 Digest (Repl.) 334, *2871*.
Dredge v. *Dredge* (*otherwise Harrison*), [1947] 1 All E.R. 29; 27 Digest (Repl.)
G   281, *2255*.
Eaves, Re, Eaves v. *Eaves*, [1939] 4 All E.R. 260; [1940] Ch. 109; 109 L.J.Ch.
    97; 162 L.T. 8; 49 Digest (Repl.) 885, *8287*.
Wombwell's Settlement, Re, Clerke v. *Menzies*, [1922] All E.R. Rep. 115; [1922]
    2 Ch. 298; 92 L.J.Ch. 18; 127 L.T. 295; 27 Digest (Repl.) 551, *5016*.

Adjourned Summons.

H
This was an application by originating summons dated Mar. 10, 1967, by the
plaintiffs William David Crane and the National Provincial Bank, Ltd. The
plaintiffs sought the following relief pursuant to R.S.C., Ord. 85, r. 2, namely:
(i) that directions might be given whether the plaintiffs who were the executors
and trustees of the will and codicil of Kate Gertrude d'Altroy deceased (" the
testatrix "), should on the true construction of the will and codicil and in
I the events which happened (a) distribute her residuary estate on the footing that
the first defendant Charles Henry Lowman had no interest therein and that the
same was (in the events which had happened) wholly undisposed of by the will and
codicil; or (omitting (b) which is not material to be set out in this report) (c) take
some other and if so what steps in regard to the residuary estate. (ii) if the capital
of the residuary estate were directed to be retained by the plaintiffs, that directions might be given to them whether the income thereof arising before such
decree absolute should be (a) distributed to the persons entitled to the testatrix'
property undisposed of by the will and codicil or (b) paid to the first defendant

Dictum of PENNYCUICK, J., *at pp.*
182, 183, *applied in* Re RODWELL,
[1969] 3 All E.R. 1363

Charles Henry Lowman, or (c) dealt with in some other and if so what manner. A
The other defendants were Hope Anna Nason, Faith Ellen Reed and Walter
Augustus Scott, who claimed to be entitled to any part of the estate as to which
the testatrix died intestate.   The facts are set out in the judgment.

The cases noted below* were cited during the argument in addition to those
referred to in the judgment.

R. Walker for the plaintiffs.   B
Stella Hydleman for the first defendant.
E. G. Nugee for the next-of-kin.

                                                        Cur. adv. vult.

     Nov. 2.   **PENNYCUICK, J.**: Mrs. Kate Gertrude d'Altroy, to whom I will
refer as " the testatrix ", made her will on Dec. 20, 1961.   At that date she had C
one child living, namely, a daughter, Alice, who was the wife of the first defendant
Charles Henry Lowman.   The testatrix appointed the plaintiffs, William David
Crane and National Provincial Bank, Ltd. as her executors and trustees.   She
settled her residuary estate on trust for her daughter Alice for life, with certain
trusts in reversion.   The daughter Alice died on Mar. 17, 1965.   By a codicil dated
June 11, 1965, the testatrix revoked the reversionary trusts under her will and D
directed that her trustees should pay the whole income of her residuary estate to
Mr. Lowman during his lifetime on protective trusts so long as he should remain
the widower of Alice.

     On Aug. 6, 1965, Mr. Lowman re-married.   The testatrix died on Feb. 15, 1966.
Her will and codicil were proved by the plaintiffs.   Before the death of the
testatrix the plaintiff Mr. Crane had been informed that Charles Henry Lowman E
and his second wife had separated and, at some time after the death of the
testatrix, he had been informed that the second wife was contemplating
proceedings based on nullity; it does not appear, from the evidence, exactly at
what date Mr. Crane communicated this information to the plaintiff bank.   On
Feb. 21, 1967, the second wife presented a petition based on nullity.   The present
originating summons was issued on Mar. 10, 1967.   On June 7, 1967, a decree nisi F
was made on the petition and, on Sept. 11, 1967, the decree was made absolute.
The decree is in the common form and declares the marriage to have been, and to
be, absolutely null and void to all intents and purposes in the law whatsoever by
reason of the incapacity of the respondent to consummate the marriage.

     The plaintiffs have retained the entire capital and income of the residuary
estate pending the decision on this summons.   The remaining defendants are the G
statutory next-of-kin of the testatrix, who are admittedly entitled to the capital
of the residuary estate on the footing of a partial intestacy.   The question that
I am now asked to decide is whether the defendant Mr. Lowman is entitled to a
life interest in the residuary estate for the remainder of his life, or whether, as
the result of his second marriage, the next-of-kin take free of any life interest on
the part of Charles Henry Lowman.   H

     The basic principle of law applicable in this connexion is well established.
Where the parties have been duly married the marriage is, notwithstanding
failure to consummate it, treated as subsisting for all purposes unless and until a
decree absolute is pronounced.   That is to say, the marriage is voidable, but not
void.   Once a decree absolute is pronounced the marriage is not merely
determined, but is treated retrospectively as if it had never been contracted (see

---

* *Turner* v. *Thompson*, [1886-90] All E.R. Rep. 576; (1888), 13 P.D. 37; *Re Gloucester
Municipal Election Petition, 1900 (Tuffley Ward)*, [1901] 1 K.B. 683; *Re Garnett*, [1904-07]
All E.R. Rep. 479; *Inverclyde (otherwise Tripp)* v. *Inverclyde*, [1931] P. 29; *Dodsworth*
v. *Dale*, [1936] 2 All E.R. 440; [1936] 2 K.B. 503; *Re Ames' Settlement*, [1946] 1 All E.R.
689; [1946] Ch. 217; *De Reneville* v. *De Reneville*, [1948] 1 All E.R. 56; [1948] P. 100;
R. v. *Algar*, [1953] 2 All E.R. 1381; [1954] 1 Q.B. 279; *Wiggins* v. *Wiggins (otherwise
Brooks) and Ingram*, [1958] 2 All E.R. 555; *Ross Smith* v. *Ross Smith (otherwise Radford)*,
[1962] 1 All E.R. 344; [1963] A.C. 280.

A *Re Wombwell's Settlement, Clerke* v. *Menzies* (1), per Russell, J.). This retrospective doctrine, derived from the canon law, has often been criticised (see *Re
Eaves, Eaves* v. *Eaves* (2), per Goddard, L.J.); but, however much one may
sympathise with those criticisms, there is no doubt that the doctrine still
represents the law today.

The basic principle stated above has frequently been applied in regard to
B proprietary interests created by reference to matrimonial status. On the one hand,
transactions completed during the subsistence of that status and on the footing
that it subsists, cannot be undone (see *Re Eaves* (3)). On the other hand, when the
decree absolute is pronounced, then, except insofar as the relevant fund has
already been affected, to use a neutral term, by completed transactions, the fund
must be dealt with on the footing that there has never been a marriage (see *Re
C Dewhirst, Flower* v. *Dewhirst* (4)). I will read one passage from the judgment
of Harman, J. (4):

   " It seems to me that there is an apparent difference of judicial views on
this subject, but I think that can be explained in this way. It is one thing to
say that a person is entitled to property or rights after the annulment of the
marriage, but it is quite another thing to upset transactions, completed and
D permanent, entered into while the marriage was current; cf., *Dredge* v. *Dredge
(otherwise Harrison)* (5). There is no doubt that, during that time the whole
world is bound to accept the fact that the ' spouses ' have the status of
married people, and all the results which flow from that necessarily follow.
I need not decide today whether, if the first defendant had claimed the
income during the time between the celebration of her second ' marriage '
E and its annulment, she could have succeeded. At any rate, the decision in
Re Eaves (3) is only that a transaction which was completed in reliance on the
coming into effect of the new status of the plaintiff and within the period
before the dissolution of her second marriage, should not be upset. It may
very well lead to different results according to whether the transaction in
question is before or after the decree."

F
To return to the present case, Mr. Lowman's second marriage was subsisting at
the death of the testatrix and continued to subsist until the decree absolute in
September, 1967. During this period, Mr. Lowman did not possess the qualification for a life interest, that is, that he should remain the widower of Alice.
Equally, the next-of-kin were absolutely entitled to the residuary estate. It
follows that if any part of the estate had been actually transferred to the next-of-
G kin during this period, they would be entitled to hold it free from any interest on
the part of Mr. Lowman. On the other hand, when the decree absolute was
pronounced, Mr. Lowman was placed, in law, in the position that he had
never contracted his second marriage at all. In other words, he has throughout
remained the widower of Alice. The whole estate is in fact still in hand and it
follows, in my judgment, inevitably, that the plaintiffs must now deal with the
H estate in accordance with the terms of the codicil. That is to say, they hold the
income on protective trusts for Mr. Lowman for the remainder of his life or until
he contracts another marriage, and the next-of-kin are only entitled subject to
that life interest.

Counsel for the next-of-kin, has sought to avoid this consequence, and to
distinguish the case of *Re Dewhirst* (6) on the ground that here, apart from
I Mr. Lowman's life interest, the next-of-kin took a vested interest in possession
immediately on the death of the testatrix. That is so. But when the decree was
pronounced their vested interest was divested to the extent of letting in the life

(1) [1922] All E.R. Rep. 115 at p. 117; [1922] 2 Ch. 298 at p. 305.
(2) [1939] 4 All E.R. 260 at p. 267; [1940] Ch. 109 at p. 122.
(3) [1939] 4 All E.R. 260; [1940] Ch. 109.
(4) [1948] 1 All E.R. 147 at p. 151; [1948] Ch. 198 at p. 205.
(5) [1947] 1 All E.R. 29.
(6) [1948] 1 All E.R. 147; [1948] Ch. 198.

interest and I do not see how the plaintiffs can now disregard that life interest. A
Counsel for the next-of-kin contends that for this purpose a vesting in possession
should be treated as tantamount to actual transfer, but this would, I think,
extend the exception from the retrospective operation of the decree beyond
anything that is justified either in principle or on authority. Counsel for the next-
of-kin says that the maxim " equity regards that as done which ought to have
been done " is applicable; but that is a two-edged argument, for once the B
decree has been pronounced it produces the retrospective result that the transfer
ought never to have been made to the next-of-kin. Counsel for the next-of-kin
makes the valid point that unless one looks at vesting rather than actual
transfer, the rights of the beneficiaries depend on the administrative acts of the
trustees. I think this anomaly is inherent in the doctrine, itself anomalous, of
relation back. C

Counsel for the next-of-kin relied on the judgment of SIR WILFRID GREENE,
M.R., in Re Eaves (7) and, in particular, the paragraphs numbered (1), (2) and
(3). I do not think that those paragraphs support his argument. The reasoning
was that in the circumstances mentioned in para. 1, the court would order transfer
of the fund and, equally, that the trustees could safely and properly transfer the
fund without an order of the court. In such circumstances, the transaction could D
not be re-opened. His reasoning is not addressed to the position where there is
neither an actual transfer nor an order of the court and I do not think that it can
be extended by implication so as to cover that position.

If, contrary to my view, the rights of the beneficiaries depend not on what
the trustees in fact did, but on what they ought to have done, a further question
would arise: was the duty of the trustees to make a transfer affected by notice E
either (a) that a decision had been made to take proceedings based on nullity,
or (b) that such proceedings had actually been initiated? Counsel for the next-
of-kin stoutly contended that it would made no difference if, at the date of
death, a decree absolute was expected to be pronounced next day. On the
view which I take, I am not concerned to pursue this point.

That concludes what I have to say on the destination of capital. The summons, F
which was issued before the decree absolute, asks for directions as to capital in
rather different terms. The declaration will be in accordance with the foregoing
judgment.

The summons raises a second question as to the income which has arisen since
the death of the testatrix and has been retained by the trustees. It seems to me
that the same principle is applicable to this income as to the capital. That is to G
say, the income being still in hand, it must now be paid to the beneficiary who
is now known to be properly entitled to it by the retrospective operation of the
decree, i.e., Mr. Lowman. I think that this view is in accordance with the
reasoning in the passage which I have read from the judgment of HARMAN, J.,
Re Dewhirst (8).

Order accordingly. H

Solicitors: Waterhouse & Co., agents for Wells & Hind, Nottingham (for the
plaintiffs); Wegg-Prosser & Co. (for the first defendant); Herbert Oppenheimer,
Nathan & Vandyk (for the next-of-kin).

[Reported by JENIFER SANDELL, Barrister-at-Law.]

I

---

(7) [1939] 4 All E.R. at pp. 262, 263; [1940] Ch. at pp. 114, 115.
(8) [1948] 1 All E.R. at p. 151; [1948] Ch. at p. 205.

A

COOPER *v.* HALL.

[QUEEN'S BENCH DIVISION (Lord Parker, C.J., Widgery and Chapman, JJ.), November 20, 1967.]

Road Traffic—Traffic sign—Parking—London—Restricted street—No yellow line on road to indicate that street was restricted—Car parked in restricted

B
street during prescribed hours—Whether offence committed—Parking Zones (Waiting and Loading Restriction) Order 1966, art. 3 (1), art. 5 (1)—London Government Act 1963 (c. 33), s. 9—Road Traffic Act, 1960 (8 & 9 Eliz. 2 c. 16), s. 34, s. 51 (3), s. 52 (1), (2)—Traffic Signs Regulations and General Directions 1964 (S.I. 1964 No. 1857) direction 6, 26, as amended by Traffic Signs General Directions 1966 (S.I. 1966 No. 489).

C
At about 4.15 p.m. on Mar. 17, 1967, the respondent left his motor car in Dowgate Hill in the City of London, which was a restricted street under art. 3 (1) and art. 5 (1)* of the Parking Zones (Waiting and Loading Restriction) Order 1966, Pt. 1 of Sch. 1, made by the Greater London Council in exercise of powers conferred on them under s. 9 of the London Government Act 1963. By the Traffic Signs Regulations and General Directions 1964

D
direction 6†, signs shown in diagrams 1015 and 1021 " may be placed " on or near a road, or, under direction 26 " may be placed " on a side road, for the purpose of indicating a statutory prohibition or restriction on the waiting of vehicles. These directions were made under s. 51‡ and s. 52‡ of the Road Traffic Act, 1960, which were in permissive terms in regard to the planning of traffic signs. On appeal against acquittal of the respondent on the ground that restriction was not shown by the usual yellow line on the

E
street,

Held: the requirement of directions 6 and 26 set out in Pt. 2 of the Traffic Signs Regulations and General Directions 1964 were permissive, and had not been made mandatory in the Greater London area (unlike the rest of the country); accordingly the absence of the yellow line on Dowgate Hill in the City of London was no defence (see p. 187, letter I, and p. 188,

F
letters E and G, post).

James v. *Cavey* ([1967] 1 All E.R. 1048) distinguished.

Appeal allowed.

[As to the power to make orders relating to the use of parking places in the London traffic area, see 33 HALSBURY'S LAWS (3rd Edn.) 526, para. 896, 529,

G
530, para. 902.

For the Road Traffic Act, 1960, s. 34, s. 51, s. 52, see 40 HALSBURY'S STATUTES (2nd Edn.) 739, 757, 758.

For the London Government Act 1963, s. 9, see 43 HALSBURY'S STATUTES (2nd Edn.) 679.]

Case referred to:

H
James v. *Cavey*, [1967] 1 All E.R. 1048; [1967] 2 W.L.R. 1239.

Case Stated.

This was a Case Stated by ALDERMAN SIR LIONEL DENNY, a justice of the peace for the City of London, in respect of his adjudication as a magistrates' court sitting at the Mansion House Justice Room, whereby he dismissed an information preferred on June 8, 1967, by the appellant against the respondent that between

I
4.10 p.m. and 4.35 p.m. on Mar. 17, 1967, the respondent, during the prescribed hours, did cause a motor car to wait in a restricted street called Dowgate Hill, contrary to art. 3 and art. 5 of the Parking Zones (Waiting and Loading Restriction) Order 1966, Pt. 1 of Sch. 1 to the Greater London Council Traffic Management Order 1966 No. 16, s. 10 of the London Government Act 1963, and s. 34 (4) of the Road Traffic Act, 1960, as amended.

---

* Articles 3 (1) and 5 (1), so far as material, are set out at p. 186, letter H, post.
† Directions 6 and 26, so far as material, are set out at p. 187, letters G and H, post.
‡ Section 51 and s. 52, so far as material, are set out at p. 188, letters B and D, post.

The information was heard on July 17, 1967, and the following facts were **A** found. On Mar. 17, 1967, between 4.10 p.m. and 4.35 p.m. the respondent left his car parked in Dowgate Hill. Dowgate Hill was a restricted street, within a controlled parking zone. The whole of the time for which the respondent's car was left was within the prescribed hours. There were no yellow lines or signs of any sort in Dowgate Hill to give warning that it was a restricted street. On each approach road to the City of London there were signs indicating " Meter **B** Zone " such as that depicted in diagram 806 in Sch. 1 Pt. 4 to the Traffic Signs Regulations and General Directions 1964.

It was contended by the respondent before the magistrate that the Common Council of the City of London (hereinafter referred to as " the Common Council ") by not having the road-marking in Dowgate Hill prescribed by the Minister's regulations and directions for such a street, namely, a single yellow line as **C** depicted in diagram 1017 in Sch. 2 to the Traffic Signs Regulations and General Directions 1964, had accordingly failed to comply with the requirements imposed on the making of the order and a prosecution for an offence under that order failed.

It was contended by the appellant before the magistrate that the Traffic Signs Regulations and General Directions 1964 were permissive only and that neither **D** they nor any other statutory provision made it obligatory on the Common Council as the highway authority to mark such a road as Dowgate Hill with such a yellow line. It was submitted that the car had been left in a restricted street in a controlled parking zone of which in fact warning had been given, and that the offence was complete.

The magistrate was of the opinion that the Traffic Signs and General Directions **E** 1964 applied to the City of London, that direction 28 of these regulations excepted only the need for a plate in a controlled zone and that the wording " lines to be laid " under diagram 1017 in Sch. 2 implied that the lines should be laid to indicate to motorists that waiting was restricted. Accordingly the magistrate interpreted the regulations in favour of the respondent and dismissed the information. The question for the opinion of the High Court was whether the **F** magistrate came to a correct conclusion in law.

C. G. Lea for the appellant.
Jean Henderson for the respondent.

LORD PARKER, C.J.: This is an appeal by way of Case Stated from a decision of one of the aldermen for the City of London sitting at the Mansion **G** House Justice Room, who dismissed an information preferred by the appellant against the respondent that on Mar. 17, 1967, during the prescribed hours he did cause a motor car to wait in a restricted street, viz., Dowgate Hill, contrary to art. 3 and art. 5 of the Parking Zones (Waiting and Loading Restriction) Order 1966. The respondent in fact left his motor car at about 4.15 p.m. on Mar. 17 in Dowgate Hill, which was a restricted street. **H**

The order in question, the Parking Zones (Waiting and Loading Restriction) Order 1966 provides by art. 5 (1) that:

" No person shall cause or permit any vehicle to wait during the prescribed hours in any restricted street except . . .."

The exceptions do not matter. By art. 3 (1): **I**

" ' restricted street ' means any street specified in Sch. 1 and includes any length on either side of any such street."

Dowgate Hill in fact appears in Sch. 1. Pausing there, it is quite clear that the Parking Zones (Waiting and Loading Restriction) Order 1966 was validly made by the Greater London Council pursuant to the powers which they inherited by s. 9 of the London Government Act 1963 from the Minister, whose powers for other than the London Traffic Area are contained in s. 34 of the Road Traffic

A Act, 1960. Accordingly, if there was nothing further, this offence would be made out.

There is one additional fact, however, and that is that the Common Council, who were the highway authority, failed to put, or chose not to put, along the sides of Dowgate Hill the usual yellow line marking the area of restriction. The alderman, was referred to *James* v. *Cavey* (1), and it may be because of that

B decision that he came to the conclusion that the offence was not made out in that this yellow line had not been placed there. The facts in *James* v. *Cavey* (1) arose in another part of the country, not the Greater London Area, and the decision in that case turns on a set of regulations which do not apply in the Greater London Area. They were the Traffic Regulation Orders (Procedure) (England and Wales) Regulations, 1961 (2). Regulation 15 (c) provided that

C the local authority shall:

" (c) Forthwith take all such steps as are reasonably practicable to cause to be erected on or near to the said roads traffic signs in such positions as the local authority may consider to be requisite for the purpose of securing that adequate information as to the effect of the order is given to persons using the said roads: . . ."

D
The authority failed to take the requisite steps for securing that adequate information was given to the users of the road, and in those circumstances this court held that the offence charged had not been made out. That in my judgment has really nothing to do with this case. It is not authority for a general proposition that unless adequate information is given so that the user has full knowledge, he has committed no offence. *James* v. *Cavey* (1) was based on the breach of

E those regulations to which I have referred, which had no application within the City.

Accordingly, in those circumstances counsel for the respondent, who has sought to support the decision in this case, claims that although the Regulations of 1961 to which I have referred did not apply in the City, yet the Traffic Signs Regulations and General Directions 1964 (3) do apply in the City and are man-

F datory. They are clearly made, as stated, under s. 51 and s. 52 of the Road Traffic Act, 1960, s. 51 dealing with traffic signs and s. 52 dealing with the powers and duties of highway authorities as to the placing of traffic signs. When one looks at the directions given (4), the relevant ones are directions 6 and 26, and to a lesser extent 13 and 38, but it will be sufficient to refer to directions 6 and 26. So far as it is relevant, direction 6 provides that:

G
" Signs shown in diagrams . . . 1015 to 1021 . . . may be placed on or near a road only to indicate the effect of an order, regulation, bye-law or notice which prohibits or restricts the use of the road by vehicular traffic."

I refer to the diagrams 1015 to 1021 because the yellow line diagram is 1017. It is to be observed that the direction on its face merely says that the sign 1017

H " may be placed " on a road. Direction 26 (1) provides that:

" The road marking shown in diagram 1017 may be placed on a side of a road only for the purpose of indicating a statutory prohibition or restriction on the waiting of vehicles . . ."

Accordingly on their face those directions are purely permissive.

I Before the magistrate, reference was made to the diagram itself which is scheduled to the regulations, where in referring to diagrams 1015 to 1018 (5) it

---

(1) [1967] 1 All E.R. 1048.
(2) S.I. 1961 No. 485.
(3) S.I. 1964 No. 1857.
(4) The directions are in Part 2 of S.I. 1964 No. 1857, which follows after Sch. 6. Directions 6 and 26 have been amended as from May 16, 1966, by the Traffic Signs General Directions 1966 (S.I. 1966 No. 489), but in a manner not making material difference for the purposes of this report.
(5) The diagrams are in Sch. 2 to S.I. 1964 No. 1857.

says: " Longitudinal lines to be laid near the edge of the carriageway to indicate A
...", which might suggest some mandatory element in the laying of the lines.
However when one looks at the powers under which those apparently permissive
directions are made, one finds that they in turn are dealing with permissive
matters.   Section 51 of the Road Traffic Act, 1960, defines traffic signs, and
then provides that regulations may be made as to " the size, colour and type ",
and so on of such signs " generally or in such circumstances only as may be B
specified in the regulations ".   Section 52 (1), which is dealing with directions,
provides:

> " Subject to and in conformity with such general directions as may be
> given by the Minister and the Secretary of State acting jointly, or such other
> directions as may be given by the appropriate Minister, a highway authority
> may cause or permit traffic signs to be placed on or near the road in their   C
> area."

again a permissive power in the highway authority to erect the traffic signs.
Subsection (2) goes on, however, to provide that:

> " The appropriate Minister may give directions to a highway authority—
> (a) for the placing of a traffic sign of any prescribed type or authorised   D
> character specified in the directions; ..."

In my judgment it is quite clear that the directions here given, directions 6 and 26,
were made under s. 52 (1) providing that the highway authority may erect
traffic signs of the type prescribed.   They are certainly not directions under
sub-s. (2) requiring a highway authority to place a traffic sign of any description,
type or authorised character specified in the direction or for replacing a sign so E
specified.   The truth of the matter, as I see it, is that the Traffic Signs Regulations and General Directions 1964 apply on their face generally to all areas in
this country, but they are purely permissive in character; and, whereas for the
rest of the country there are regulations making them mandatory, so far as the
Greater London area is concerned there are no such regulations.   It is pointed
out that this may produce a chaotic state of affairs, but as I understand it, and F
I am not deciding this matter, the Minister of Transport has power either under
s. 12 (1) of the London Government Act 1963 or under s. 10 (7) of that Act, to
take steps to ensure that the Common Council, if it were thought necessary,
should lay out the yellow line.   In my judgment the magistrate came to a wrong
conclusion.   I would send this case back with a direction to convict.

WIDGERY, J.: I agree.   G

CHAPMAN, J. : I agree.

Appeal allowed.   Case remitted with a direction to convict.

Solicitors: *The Comptroller and City Solicitor* (for the appellant); *Amery-Parkes
& Co.* (for the respondent).   H

[*Reported by* S. A. HATTEEA, *Barrister-at-Law.*]

A

GAINES *v.* W. (an infant).

[QUEEN'S BENCH DIVISION (Lord Parker, C.J., Salmon, L.J., and Widgery, J.), November 2, 1967.]

B

Affiliation—" Single woman "—Mother married and living in same house as husband, though separate and apart from him, at dates of conception and birth of illegitimate child—At the date of the application for affiliation order, the husband had left the matrimonial home—Whether mother entitled to bring affiliation proceedings—Affiliation Proceedings Act, 1957 (5 & 6 Eliz. 2 c. 55), s. 1.

C

A woman who is a single woman at the time when she applies for an affiliation order is entitled under s. 1* of the Affiliation Proceedings Act, 1957, to make the application, and can obtain such an order, notwithstanding that she was not a single woman at the time of the child's birth (see p. 191, letters E and H, post).

D

[As to the meaning of " single woman " for the purposes of taking affiliation proceedings, see 3 HALSBURY'S LAWS (3rd Edn.) 111, para. 172; and for cases on the subject, see 3 DIGEST (Repl.) 442-445, *342-359.*

For the Affiliation Proceedings Act, 1957, s. 1, see 37 HALSBURY'S STATUTES (2nd Edn.) 37; and for s. 4 of the Legitimacy Act, 1959, see 39 ibid., p. 34.]

Cases referred to:

Jones v. *Davies,* [1900-03] All E.R. Rep. 243; [1901] 1 K.B. 118; 70 L.J.Q.B. 38; 83 L.T. 412; 65 J.P. 39; 3 Digest (Repl.) 443, *351.*

E

R. v. *Pilkington,* (1853), 2 E. & B. 546; 21 L.T.O.S. 165; 17 J.P. Jo. 388; 118 E.R. 872; sub nom. *Ex p. Grimes,* 22 L.J.M.C. 153; 3 Digest (Repl.) 443, *350.*

Case Stated.

This was an appeal by way of Case Stated from a decision of a deputy chairman and justices of Inner London Quarter Sessions allowing an appeal by the present

F

respondent, Elizabeth Alice Gaines (herein referred to as " the mother "), against a finding by the stipendiary magistrate at South Western Magistrates' Court in affiliation proceedings brought by her against the present appellant (who was an infant and is herein referred to as " the putative father "). On Jan. 23, 1966, the mother, a married woman, gave birth to an illegitimate child and on May 6, 1966, she preferred a complaint against the putative father that he was the

G

father of that child. The stipendiary magistrate dismissed her complaint. The mother appealed to quarter sessions. Quarter sessions, by order dated Oct. 19, 1966, allowed the appeal, adjudged the putative father to be the father of the child and ordered weekly payments to be made by him for the child's maintenance and education. On appeal to quarter sessions, the following facts, among others, were found. At all material times the mother was a married

H

woman. From about September, 1964, she and her husband occupied separate bedrooms at the matrimonial home. In January, 1966, shortly after the birth of the child, the husband left the matrimonial home and thereafter lived apart from her. From September, 1964, until he left in January, 1966, the mother provided the husband with meals and ordinary services, but no longer treated him as her husband.

I

It was contended before quarter sessions for the mother, among other contentions, that at the time when she preferred her complaint, which was the only material time, she was a single woman within the meaning of s. 1 of the Affiliation Proceedings Act, 1957, and thus was entitled to bring the proceedings. It was contended before quarter sessions for the putative father that on the true construction of s. 1 of the Act of 1957 a complaint could only be made by a woman who was single at the date of the birth of the child. The deputy chairman and

---

* Section 1 is set out at p. 190, letter G, post.

justices were of opinion that whether or not the mother was to be regarded as a A single woman at the date of the birth of the child she was to be so regarded at the date of the complaint, and that accordingly her complaint under s. 1 of the Act of 1957 could be entertained.

D. M. *Cheatle* for the appellant putative father.
C. M. *Smith* for the respondent mother.

B

WIDGERY, J., delivered the first judgment at the invitation of LORD PARKER, C.J.: On Jan. 23, 1966, a child was born to the respondent mother. The justices found that the appellant (the putative father) was the father of the child. I need not go into the details on which they reached that conclusion. At the time when the child was conceived the mother was a married woman living with her husband, and the facts found are that the husband continued to C live in the same house as the mother up to a date a few days following the birth of the child, and I will assume for the purposes of this judgment that the mother was not a " single woman " for the purposes of the affiliation proceedings until her husband left her. Following the husband leaving the house, the mother made an application to the justices, at a time when on any view of the matter she was a single woman, and the question which arises in this case is whether D it is competent for the justices to hear an application by a woman in the position of the mother if, although she was a single woman at the date when she made the application, she was a married woman living with her husband at the date when the child was born. That is initially the question for decision, and in my judgment is really the substantial matter in this court.

When one turns to the legislation, it is helpful to start by looking at the terms E of the Bastardy Laws Amendment Act, 1872, where in s. 3 it is provided:

" Any single woman who may be with child or who may be delivered of a bastard child after the passing of this Act may either before the birth or at any time within twelve months from the birth of such child . . . make application . . . for a summons to be served on . . ."

the putative father. The Act of 1872 was repealed in 1957 and the corresponding F provisions contained in s. 1 of the Affiliation Proceedings Act, 1957, are in these terms:

" A single woman who is with child, or who has been delivered of an illegitimate child, may apply by complaint to a justice of the peace for a summons to be served on the man alleged by her to be the father of the G child."

In my judgment, although the language of the two provisions differs in detail, it is substantially the same. A further amendment to this legislation appears in the Legitimacy Act, 1959, s. 4, which provides:

" An application under s. 1 of the Affiliation Proceedings Act, 1957, may be made by a woman who was a single woman at the date of the birth of the H child whether or not she is a single woman at the time of the application and the reference to a single woman in s. 2 of that Act (which relates to the time within which such application may be made) shall be construed accordingly."

Quarter sessions took the view, construing this legislation, that it was sufficient I to give jurisdiction to the justices if the applicant was a single woman at the date of the application, which in this case the mother clearly was.

Counsel for the putative father submits to this court that the fact that the mother was not a single woman at the date of the birth, if that be the case, is sufficient to prevent the justices from having jurisdiction. There is, in a sense, a somewhat puzzling lack of authority on this simple point. We have been referred to a number of decisions which make it clear that prior at any rate to the Act of 1959 it was necessary for the applicant to be a single woman at the date

A when the application was made. I need refer only to one of these decisions, namely *Jones* v. *Davies* (1), where the brief headnote accurately reflects the decision in these words (2):

" A married woman, who at the date of the application is living with her husband, cannot obtain an order for the affiliation of her bastard child under the Bastardy Laws Amendment Act, 1872, s. 3."

B
In the course of the judgment of KENNEDY, J., there is a reference to the fact that in an earlier case the date of the conception of the child had been put forward as a possible date, but KENNEDY, J., said (3):

" The next case was *Ex p. Grimes* (4), and in that case also at the time of making the application the married woman was living apart from her

C husband. LORD CAMPBELL, C.J., in giving judgment said (5): ' I think . . . that in contemplation of law a married woman living separate from her husband may be within the meaning of the Act, which was passed for the purpose of providing for the support of the child.' It is suggested that if the woman were living apart from her husband at the time of the conception of the child, that would be sufficient to enable her to be treated as a single

D woman under the Act, but no authority has been adduced for that proposition . . ."

Accordingly, the state of authority appears to me to be this. First, it is over-whelmingly clear that prior to the passing of the Act of 1959 the woman had to be single at the date of the application. Secondly, there is no suggestion in the cases to which we have been referred that her state at the date when the child

E was born was a material matter. Against that background one turns to the terms of s. 1 of the Act of 1957, and in my judgment, giving the words their ordinary meaning, the requirement contained in that section is a requirement that the woman should be single at the time when the application is made. Not only does that seem to me to be the proper interpretation of the language, but it also seems fairly good common sense, because the question whether the woman

F ought to receive money for the support of the child must surely depend on her circumstances at the time when she seeks the order. I would think that the construction which I favour complies not only with the language used, but also with the requirements of the situation in practice. If that be right, of course, the effect of s. 4 of the Act of 1959 is merely to supply an alternative relevant date, namely the date of birth, which would be of value to her if she were not a

G single woman at the date of the application, a situation which might arise if she had meanwhile married some man who was not the putative father of the child.

For those reasons I think that the decision which the justices reached as a matter of law on the construction of the section was a correct one. I would dismiss this appeal.

H   **SALMON, L.J.:** I agree.

LORD PARKER, C.J.: I also agree.

Appeal dismissed.

Solicitors: *Robert W. Thompson* (for the appellant); *Warren & Co.* (for the respondent).

I   [*Reported by* PATRICIA JOHNSTON, *Barrister-at-Law.*]

---

(1) [1900-03] All E.R. Rep. 243; [1901] 1 K.B. 118.
(2) [1901] 1 K.B. at p. 118.
(3) [1901] 1 K.B. at p. 122; [1900-03] All E.R. Rep. at p. 246.
(4) (1853), 22 L.J.M.C. 153.
(5) (1853), 22 L.J.M.C. at p. 154.

PIONEER PLASTIC CONTAINERS, LTD. *v.* COMMISSIONERS OF CUSTOMS AND EXCISE (No. 2).

[CHANCERY DIVISION (Pennycuick, J.), November 10, 1967.]

Purchase tax—Chargeable goods—Plastic lids supplied with coffee tins for resealing opened tins—Whether plastic lids were " hardware " or " kitchen-ware " within Group 11—Purchase Tax Act 1963 (c. 9) Sch. 1, Pt. 1, Group 11.

The plaintiff company manufactured plastic lids, which it supplied to J. Lyons & Co., Ltd., for use with the half-pound sealed tins of ground coffee which the latter company sold as part of its trade. The lids fitted the tins, and their purpose was to enable the coffee to be kept fresh after a tin was opened. The lids were supplied in bulk and fitted to the sealed tins before the latter were sold retail. The Commissioners of Customs and Excise contended that the lids were chargeable to purchase tax as being either hardware or kitchen-ware within Group 11* in Pt. 1 of Sch. 1 to the Purchase Tax Act 1963 and chargeable under para. (*a*). Group 11 comprised " furniture, hardware, ironmongery, turnery, table-ware, kitchen-ware and toilet-ware, being articles of a kind used for domestic or office purposes. The plaintiff company sought a declaration that the lids were not chargeable to purchase tax under Group 11,

Held: the plastic lids were not so chargeable because—

(i) the lids did not constitute " hardware ", as that word in its ordinary meaning did not include plastic objects (see p. 194, letter C, post).

(ii) to qualify as " kitchen-ware " an article must have a degree of permanence, and applying the test of durability the lids were not articles of sufficient permanence to qualify as kitchen-ware, for the lids had no element permanence extending beyond the life of the coffee tins (see p. 194, letter H, post).

[As to chargeable goods for purposes of purchase tax, see 33 HALSBURY'S LAWS (3rd Edn.) 224, para. 383; and for cases on purchase tax, see 39 DIGEST (Repl.) 348-351, *822-839.*

For the Purchase Tax Act 1963 s. 2, Sch. 1 Group 11, see 43 HALSBURY'S STATUTES (2nd Edn.) 1016, 1061.]

Case referred to:

Pioneer Plastic Containers, Ltd. v. Comrs. of Customs and Excise, [1967] 1 All E.R. 1053; [1967] Ch. 597; [1967] 2 W.L.R. 1085.

Action.

This was an action brought by the plaintiff company, Pioneer Plastic Containers, Ltd., by writ issued on Apr. 26, 1966, against the Commissioners of Customs and Excise for a declaration that the plastic lids manufactured and sold by the plaintiff company to J. Lyons & Co., Ltd., were not (and never had been) chargeable goods within Group 11 (*a*) of Pt. 1 of Sch. 1, to the Purchase Tax Act 1963. The facts are set out in the judgment.

The cases noted below† were cited during the argument in addition to the case referred to in the judgment.

D. ·C. Potter for the plaintiff company.

J. P. Warner for the commissioners.

PENNYCUICK, J.: The relevant facts are set out in para. 3 of the amended statement of claim, and, as para. 3 is admitted, I cannot do better than read it. It is in these terms:

---

* Group 11, so far as material, is set out at p. 193, letter G, post.

† A.-G. v. Milliwatt, Ltd., [1948] 1 All E.R. 331; Customs and Excise Comrs. v. E. Keil & Co., Ltd., [1951] 1 K.B. 469; Comrs. of Customs and Excise v. H. G. Kewley, Ltd., [1965] 1 All E.R. 929.

A   " In the course of its trade the plaintiff manufactures and supplies to J. Lyons & Co., Ltd. a plastic lid. J. Lyons & Co., Ltd. fits these lids to the half-pound sealed tins of pure ground coffee which it sells as part of its trade. The purpose of the lid is to enable the coffee to be kept fresh after the tin has been opened. The lid is specifically designed to fit the tin in which the coffee is sold and for this purpose only. The lid is embossed with the

B following words: ' Lyons Pure Ground Coffee. Remove plastic lid before opening tin. Re-seal tin with lid to keep your coffee fresh.' The lids are supplied in bulk by the plaintiff to J. Lyons & Co., Ltd. and are fitted by the latter company's staff to the individual tins before the tins are sold through the retail shop. The price of the tin includes the lid for which no separate charge is made."

C Purchase tax is now imposed by the Purchase Tax Act 1963; s. 1 contains the charge of purchase tax and s. 2 (1) is in these terms:

    " Subject to the provisions of this section, the goods which are chargeable goods are those comprised in the Groups listed in Pt. 1 of Sch. 1 to this Act, other than goods which are exempt from all charge to tax under the said Pt. 1: ..."

D Then, under s. 3, tax is chargeable on the wholesale value of goods at the date of the chargeable purchase as prescribed by s. 9, that is, as far as is now material, the purchase of the lids by J. Lyons & Co., Ltd. from the plaintiff company. Schedule 1 contains in Part 1 certain rules; I shall read the first three rules:

    " The list in this Part of this Schedule is to be interpreted in accordance

E with the following rules. 1. Where a group begins with a general description of the goods comprised in the group, the goods mentioned below in the group (including those mentioned under a heading ' Exempt ') comprise only goods falling within the general description. 2. Goods comprised in a heading ' Exempt ' are exempt from all charge to tax. 3. A heading ' Not chargeable under this Group ' is to be taken as excluding the goods referred

F to from any charge to tax under that group (but not other groups), and not as restricting or extending the descriptions of goods to be treated as comprised in the group."

There follows a number of groups, the relevant group for the present purpose being Group 11. That group is expressed as

G   " comprising Furniture, hardware, ironmongery, turnery, table-ware, kitchen-ware and toilet-ware, being articles of a kind used for domestic or office purposes."

Then under the words " Not chargeable under this Group " are:

    " Builders' hardware, sanitary ware and other articles of kinds ordinarily installed by builders as fixtures."

H Under the heading of " Exempt " there are twelve paragraphs, containing a great number of articles. The contention on behalf of the commissioners is that the lids manufactured by the plaintiff company and sold by it to J. Lyons & Co., Ltd. constitute either hardware or kitchen-ware, being articles of a kind used for domestic purposes.

I   In order to answer this question I must first ascertain the meaning of the statutory words according to their ordinary use in the English language and I must then ascertain whether the lids fall within the scope of those words.

That point was well put by BUCKLEY, J., in his judgment on a preliminary application in the present action (1):

    " It seems to me that the question which the court has to decide in this action is partly one of law and partly one of fact. The interpretation of the

_____

(1) I.e., *Pioneer Plastic Containers, Ltd.* v. *Commissioners of Customs and Excise* [1967] 1 All E.R. 1053 at p. 1055; [1967] Ch. 597 at p. 601.

provisions of Purchase Tax Act 1963, is a matter of law pure and simple.   A
The nature of the article, the plastic lid, with which the action is concerned
and the uses for which it is designed and to which it can be put, are questions
of fact."

There is no issue as to the nature of the lid or the use to which it is designed to
be put.
    As regards the word " hardware " I was referred to the definition in the   B
OXFORD ENGLISH DICTIONARY, namely " small ware or goods of metal; ironmongery "; I was also referred to a definition from a later dictionary. I
do not think that in its ordinary meaning the word " hardware " should be treated
as covering plastic objects. Counsel for the commissioners points out that today
plastic has in many respects superseded ironmongery and is certainly sold in   C
some shops to serve the same purposes. I do not, however, think that I ought
to construe " plastic " as included in " hardware ".
    The next relevant expression is " kitchen-ware ". It is clear, and is common
ground, that this expression is confined to ware of such a character as is appropriate for use in a kitchen. Again it is clear, and is common ground, that the
word "kitchen-ware" cannot be intended to cover consumer goods or the mere   D
packaging of consumer goods. It is further common ground—and this is a
point of the first importance—that in order to qualify as kitchen-ware an article
must have some degree of durability.
    Counsel, who appeared for the plaintiff company, used the expression " reason-
ably permanent nature "; and counsel for the commissioners used the expression
" some element of permanence ". Applying this restriction to containers in   E
which consumer goods are sold, it is still common ground, at any rate for the
purpose of the present action (counsel for the commissioners naturally makes
no concession going beyond the purpose of this action) that a container serving
no other purpose than as a container for consumer goods, which will have fully
served that purpose when the goods are used up, does not possess the necessary
element of permanence to qualify as an article of kitchen-ware for the purpose   F
of Group 11. It might well be otherwise where the container is of such a nature
that it will or may continue to serve some enduring purpose after the consumer
goods which it contains have been used up: the question must always be one
of fact and degree depending on the particular circumstances and there may be
borderline cases.
    Applying the test of durability here it is clear that for the purpose of this   G
action the tin itself—that is, the tin containing the coffee—is not an article of
kitchen-ware. The only purpose of the tin is to contain the coffee and when the
coffee has been used up its purpose will be spent. It seems to me to follow
necessarily that the lid is equally not an article of kitchen-ware. The only
purpose of the lid is to serve as a cover for the particular tin, and when the
coffee in the tin has been used up the purpose of the lid, no less than the purpose   H
of the tin, will have been spent. I do not see how the lid can be said to have
any element of durability extending beyond the life of the tin. In this connexion, I do not see that it can make any difference that the lid is manufactured
separately from the tin and sold separately to J. Lyons & Co., Ltd. The purpose
as regards Group 11 must be ascertained by reference to the use to be made of
it by the consumer in his or her kitchen.
    Again—apart from the point that I shall mention next—it can, I think, make   I
no difference that the lid is detachable from the tin in contradistinction to being
fixed to the tin; that circumstance cannot in itself affect the purpose of the
lid.
    In the course of argument counsel for the plaintiff company was rightly much
concerned to meet a contention that the lid being detachable might be put to some
other use. A contention on those lines is adumbrated in para. 2 of the amended
defence in these terms:

A
" The [commissioners] deny that each lid is a part of the tin to which
it is attached. The [commissioners] admit that such lid is not designed to have
independent utility, but do not admit that it cannot have such utility. The
[commissioners] admit that each tin with its lid is disposable after the
contents of the tin have been extracted, but do not admit that the lid must
necessarily be disposed of then."

B
Counsel for the commissioners, however, disclaimed—rightly, as it seems to me—
any contention based on a possible continuing use of the lid after the tin with
which it was sold had been disposed of.

I should perhaps add that the view which I have taken of the scope of the
expression " kitchen-ware " makes it unnecessary to consider further the scope of
the expression " domestic purposes ". If I were wrong on the view that I have
C
taken as to the scope of the word " hardware ", the same result would, I think,
be reached through the requirement that the article must be one of a kind used
for domestic purposes.

The point is a very short one and I do not think that I can usefully add anything. I propose accordingly to make the declaration as asked in the statement
of claim.

D
Declaration accordingly.

Solicitors: *Bartlett & Gluckstein* (for the plaintiff company); *Solicitor,
Customs and Excise.*

[*Reported by* JENIFER SANDELL, *Barrister-at-Law.*]

E

NOTE.

Re ROBERT STEPHEN HOLDINGS, LTD.

F
[CHANCERY DIVISION (Plowman, J.), December 4, 11, 1967.]

*Company—Reduction of capital—Part of a class of shares—Some ordinary shares
to be repaid, but consent of all ordinary shareholders not obtained—Desirability of proceeding by scheme of arrangement—Reduction nevertheless
confirmed—Petition unopposed.*

G
[As to the reduction and return of capital, see 6 HALSBURY'S LAWS (3rd Edn.)
158, 159, paras. 331, 334; and for cases on the subject, see 9 DIGEST (Repl.)
150-153, *876-894*, 164, 165, *973-981.*

For the Companies Act, 1948, s. 206, see 3 HALSBURY'S STATUTES (2nd Edn.)
624.]

Case referred to:

H
British and American Trustee and Finance Corpn. v. *Couper,* [1891-94] All
E.R. Rep. 667; [1894] A.C. 399; 63 L.J.Ch. 425; 70 L.T. 882; 9 Digest
(Repl.) 151, *883.*

Petition.

This was a petition presented by Robert Stephen Holdings, Ltd. asking for
confirmation of the reduction of the capital of the company from £1,250,000
I
to £1,143,500 by the return of capital paid up on 1,065,000 ordinary shares of
2s. each, and the cancellation of those shares pursuant to special resolution
passed at an extraordinary general meeting of the company on Nov. 13, 1967.
The special resolution provided for an increase of capital, after the reduction
took effect, increasing it to £1,250,000 by the creation of 1,065,000 ordinary
shares of 2s. each. The petition was unopposed. The facts are set out in the
judgment.

R. B. S. Instone for the petitioner.

Cur. adv. vult. **A**

Dec. 11.   **PLOWMAN, J.**, read the following judgment: This is a petition for the confirmation of the reduction of the company's capital from £1,250,000 to £1,143,500.   The present capital of the company is divided into six and a half million ordinary shares of 2s. each and six million deferred shares of 2s. each. Of those shares, four million ordinary and all of the deferred shares have been **B** issued and are fully paid.   They rank pari passu for repayment of capital in a winding-up.   All of the deferred shares and all but 1,065,000 of the ordinary shares are held by members of the Rubin family.

The proposed reduction is to be effected by return of capital paid up on the 1,065,000 ordinary shares held outside the Rubin family and cancelling such shares.   This involves a sum of £106,500 which the company proposes to borrow **C** for the purpose.   The Rubin shareholders have all consented to the reduction.

In relation to the shares being repaid, 120 shareholders gave proxies for use at the meeting at which the special resolution for reduction was passed.   Of those 120, 119, representing 788,150 shares, sent in proxies in favour of the reduction; one, representing one thousand shares, sent in a proxy against, but no-one has appeared before me to oppose the petition.   **D**

Counsel for the petitioner referred me to a passage in BUCKLEY ON THE COMPANIES ACTS (13th Edn.), p. 155, where it is stated as follows:

" Subject, however, to the confirmation by the court, which is required, and which is the safeguard of the minority, the question of reducing capital is a domestic one for the decision of the majority, and the Act leaves the company to determine the extent, the mode and the incidence of the reduc- **E** tion and the application of any capital moneys which the reduction may set free.

" A reduction therefore by which capital moneys are to be returned to some or one only and not to all of the shareholders may be resolved upon and confirmed if it be fair and equitable."

F

The cases cited in the footnote in support of this proposition is the case to which counsel for the petitioning company referred me, *British and American Trustee and Finance Corpn.* v. *Couper* (1).   Counsel submitted that a case of fairness had been made out on the facts of this case.   I agree, and propose to confirm the reduction; but I want to add this: in cases where one part of a class of equity shareholders treated differently from another part of the same class the usual **G** practice is, I think, for the company to proceed by way of a scheme of arrangement under s. 206 of the Companies Act, 1948.   It is true that there have been cases in which the court has confirmed a reduction effected by cancelling part of the preference shares without a scheme, but such cases raise different considerations because the maximum entitlement of preference shares is known.   It is also true that there have been cases in which the court has confirmed a reduction effected by cancelling **H** part of the equity shares without a scheme where all the members of the class have consented.   I understand, however, that this is the first time, at any rate since s. 38 of the Companies Act, 1907, which applied the Joint Stock Companies Arrangement Act, 1870, to a company not in the course of winding-up, in which the court has been asked to confirm a reduction effected by paying off part of the equity shares where all the equity shareholders have not consented in the absence of a **I** scheme of arrangement.

Whilst, as I have said, I propose to confirm the reduction in this case, I think it right to express the view that it is desirable in cases like the present to proceed by way of a scheme of arrangement, for although no doubt it is true that a dissentient minority shareholder can come to the court and object to confirmation of a reduction, nevertheless the interests of the minority shareholders are

---

(1) [1891-94] All E.R. Rep. 667; [1894] A.C. 399.

A better protected under s. 206. The weakening of that protection is not, I think, a thing that the court ought to encourage.

I will make the usual order confirming the reduction, approving the minute and giving the usual direction as to advertisement.

Order accordingly.

B Solicitors: *Linklaters & Paines* (for the petitioner).

[*Reported by* JACQUELINE METCALFE, *Barrister-at-Law.*]

C R. *v.* WINSON.

[COURT OF APPEAL, CRIMINAL DIVISION (Lord Parker, C.J., Salmon, L.J., and Widgery, J.), November 10, 1967.]

Licensing—Offences—Knowingly selling liquor in breach of condition of licence—
D *Condition of on-licence for club that liquor should be supplied only to persons who had been members for two days—Delegation by licensee of managerial responsibilities under licence—Club conducted by manager in breach of condition—Whether licensee liable for breach of condition committed in his absence and without his knowledge—Licensing Act 1964 (c. 26), s. 161 (1).*

Applied in HOWKER v ROBINSON [1972] 2 All ER 786

The appellant was a director of a company which owned a discotheque
E club, and was the holder of a justices' on-licence in respect of the club. It was a term of the licence that intoxicating liquor should not be sold to anybody who had been a member of the club for less than forty-eight hours. Two police officers were admitted to the club on three days in January, 1967, on payment of 5s. each and were served with drinks on each occasion without the forty-eight hour waiting period having been observed. At the material
F times the club was being run by a manager appointed by the managing director, not by the appellant, the manager, according to the evidence of the managing director, being responsible for seeing that conditions of the licence were observed. The appellant was convicted of contravening s. 161 (1)* of the Licensing Act 1964. On appeal against conviction the court stated† that it was clear that the manager of the club knew that people were being
G served with liquor who had no business to be served.

Held: the appellant had been rightly convicted, because the doctrine of delegation was applicable to an offence alleged under s. 161 (1) of the Licensing Act 1964, the principle being that a man could not get out of the responsibilities and duties attached to a licence by absenting himself (see p. 204, letter G, post).

H Dicta of LORD REID and LORD EVERSHED in *Vane* v. *Yiannopoullos*, ([1964] 3 All E.R. at pp. 823, 827, respectively) applied; dicta of LORD MORRIS OF BORTH-Y-GEST and LORD DONOVAN (at pp. 830, 832, respectively) not applied.

Per CURIAM: the doctrine of delegation is something quite independent of the principles which come into play when Parliament has created an
I absolute offence, for then the person on whom a duty is thrown is responsible, whether he has delegated or whether he has acted through a servant, regardless of any intent or knowledge. The principle of delegation only comes into play in cases where, though the statute uses words which import knowledge or intent such as " knowingly " or in some other cases " permitting " or " suffering " and the like, it has been held that a man cannot get out of the

---

* Section 161 (1) is set out at p. 199, letter E, post.
† See p. 200, letter D, post.

responsibilities which have been put on him by delegating those   A
responsibilities to another (see p. 202, letter F, post).

Appeal dismissed.

[As to the offence of selling intoxicating liquor contrary to justices' licences,
see SUPPLEMENT to 22 HALSBURY'S LAWS (3rd Edn.), para. 1393; and for cases
on the licensee's knowledge of a sale, see 30 DIGEST (Repl.) 99, *740-743*, 105,   B
770, 771.

As to a master's criminal liability for his servant's acts where the statute makes
knowledge an ingredient of the offence, see 10 HALSBURY'S LAWS (3rd Edn.)
278, 279, para. 516; and for cases on a master's liability where the servant's
act is unauthorised, see 14 DIGEST (Repl.) 42-45, *108-134*.

For the Licensing Act 1964, s. 161, see 44 HALSBURY'S STATUTES (2nd Edn.)   C
617.]

Cases referred to:

Allen v. *Whitehead*, [1929] All E.R. Rep. 13; [1930] 1 K.B. 211; 99 L.J.K.B.
146; 142 L.T. 141; 94 J.P. 17; 30 Digest (Repl.) 105, *770*.

Linnett v. *Metropolitan Police Comr.*, [1946] 1 All E.R. 380; [1946] K.B. 290;
115 L.J.K.B. 513; 174 L.T. 178; 110 J.P. 153; 30 Digest (Repl.) 105,   D
771.

Noble v. *Heatley*, [1967] S.L.T. 26.

Ross v. *Moss*, [1965] 3 All E.R. 145; [1965] 2 Q.B. 396; [1965] 3 W.L.R. 416;
129 J.P. 537; Digest (Cont. Vol. B) 83, *141a*.

Somerset v. *Hart*, (1884), 12 Q.B.D. 360; 53 L.J.M.C. 77; 48 J.P. 327; 25
Digest (Repl.) 461, *348*.   E

Vane v. *Yiannopoullos*, [1964] 2 All E.R. 820; [1964] 2 Q.B. 739; [1964]
2 W.L.R. 1335; *affd.* H.L., [1964] 3 All E.R. 820; [1965] A.C. 486;
[1964] 3 W.L.R. 1218; 129 J.P. 50; Digest (Cont. Vol. B) 465, *743a*.

Appeal.

This was an appeal by Denis Archibald Winson against his conviction on   F
June 2, 1967, at Plymouth City Quarter Sessions on six counts of knowingly
selling intoxicating liquor in a club in contravention of the conditions of a justices'
on-licence contrary to s. 161 (1) of the Licensing Act 1964. The appellant was
fined £25 on each count, making £150 in all, and was ordered to pay £50 towards
the costs of the prosecution. The appeal was by a certificate of the assistant
recorder (ROBERT HUGHES, ESQ.) under s. 3 (*b*) of the Criminal Appeal Act, 1907,   G
viz., on a question of law, whether the doctrine of delegation applied to an
offence under s. 161 (1). The facts are set out in the judgment of the court.

The chain of delegation was as follows. The company of which the appellant
was a director owned the club. The administration of the club was in the hands
of the managing director, a Mr. Hancock. A Mr. James was appointed manager
of the club (which was on the second floor of the premises), and he was formally   H
responsible to a Mr. McBride; but, according to the evidence of the managing
director, Mr. James was solely responsible for the running of the club and it was
his duty to see that conditions of the licence were observed. Mr. McBride had
been the manager of the whole of the premises, but after Mr. James' appointment,
he was in fact the manager of the bowling alleys on the first floor of the premises.
There was also a Mr. Evans, an ex-detective-inspector, whose duties included   I
seeing that licence conditions were observed. The appellant was the director
approved by the board of directors to hold licences and attend to the work
involved in their maintenance. He in fact held licences in respect of three premises,
of which the club was one. When the jury returned at the trial after retiring,
they had not answered a question that had been put for their guidance, viz.,
whether there had been delegation by the appellant of his managerial responsibilities under the licence. The assistant recorder directed the jury that if the
appellant did not have actual knowledge of the breach of conditions (and the

A prosecution did not allege that he had), any delegation must have been to Mr. James. Further, if the jury's answers were that the appellant had not delegated to Mr. James, their verdict must be one of " not guilty ". The jury found the appellant guilty.

The cases noted below* were cited during the argument in addition to those referred to in the judgment of the court.

B *J. G. Marriage* for the appellant.
Arthur Mildon for the Crown.

LORD PARKER, C.J., delivered the following judgment of the court: The appellant was a director of a limited company, or a group of companies, owning clubs in various places. One of those clubs was at Plymouth, and con-
C sisted of a bowling centre and, as we understand it, on the first floor above the bowling centre there was a club. It was run as one of these discotheque clubs, and was known as the Spotlight Discotheque Club. The company of which the appellant was a director had on its board a man called Hancock who was the managing director, and he on behalf of the board appointed managers to the different clubs owned by the company or group of companies. The offences
D alleged were in regard to two police officers who on three days in January, 1967, got into the club on payment of 5s. each; they were admitted without any waiting period at all, and when in the club on each occasion they were served with drinks. It was a term of the justices' licence, which was in the name of the appellant, that no drink should be served to anybody who had not been a member for two days. Accordingly, the service of drinks to these police officers was quite clearly in
E breach of the conditions of the licence held by the appellant. Section 161 (1) of the Licensing Act 1964, is in these terms:

" If the holder of a justices' on-licence knowingly sells or supplies intoxicating liquor to persons to whom he is not permitted by the conditions of the
licence to sell or supply it he shall be guilty of an offence under this section."

The penalty laid down by sub-s. (3) is a heavy one for this type of offence in that
F the offender is liable to imprisonment for a term not exceeding six months or to a fine not exceeding £200 or to both.

The appellant lived at Exeter and it is quite clear, though it does not affect the result of this case, that he took, I was going to say no interest whatever or at any rate little interest, in seeing that the club conformed to the licence which he held. He said that he visited the club on a number of occasions, but he quite clearly
G did not take any great interest. Accordingly, his defence was that he did not " knowingly " sell or supply intoxicating liquors to these police officers. That was admitted by the prosecution, but their case was that he was liable neverthe- less, because he had delegated his duties and responsibilities under the licence to a person who was managing, and in control of, the club. The prosecution went on to say that since the evidence was that, on numbers of occasions people were
H admitted, as these police officers were, in disregard of the terms of the licence, whoever was the manager in control must have known himself that the terms of the licence were being broken, and that alcohol was being sold contrary to the licence. On the last day on which these offences were alleged there was a raid on the premises, and it was found that a Mr. McBride was on the premises, not in the club upstairs but in the bowling centre downstairs, and as soon as the police
I arrived he came on the scene and in answer to questions from the police he admitted that he was the centre manager and gave the police help in the matter. The police in due course interrogated the appellant, who said that Mr. McBride was the centre manager, and in answer to the question " Have you delegated your responsibility as licence-holder to him ", the appellant replied " Yes, Mr. McBride was appointed by the managing director, Mr. Hancock, with the approval

---

* *Cundy* v. *Le Cocq*, [1881-85] All E.R. Rep. 412; (1884), 13 Q.B.D. 207; *Chisholm* v. *Doulton*, (1889), 22 Q.B.D. 736; *Brooks* v. *Mason*, [1902] 2 K.B. 743.

of the board of directors ". Accordingly, the prosecution case as opened was that **A**
the appellant, the holder of the licence, had delegated his responsibilities in
regard to the premises to Mr. McBride, and they alleged that Mr. McBride must
have known what was happening in the club.

A submission was made at the end of the prosecution case that there was no
case to go to the jury; that was overruled and Mr. McBride was called to say,
and he did say, that he had no knowledge of the persons being admitted and **B**
served with liquor contrary to the licence. Not content with that, he went on to
say that, at the material date, he in fact was not the manager of the club because
a Mr. James had been appointed, first as doorman where his responsibility would
be to see who could and who could not be admitted, and later as manager under
him, Mr. McBride. After that Mr. Hancock, the managing director, was called,
and he confirmed that he had written a letter to Mr. James appointing him not **C**
merely as doorman but manager, as it was put, under Mr. McBride of the Spotlight Discotheque Club. He said that he had informed the board as a matter of
courtesy of the appointment, while the appellant went further and in fact said
that not only had it been reported to the board, but that the board of which he
was a member and present on the occasion in question had confirmed and ratified
the appointment. Accordingly, at the end of the appellant's case the prosecution **D**
put their case, or sought to put their case, that the delegation here, if delegation
there was, was by the appellant to Mr. James and not Mr. McBride. In fact,
having regard to what had admittedly happened, it was quite clear that Mr. James
knew full well that people were being served with liquor who had no business to
be served. Objection was taken very naturally by the defence, but the assistant
recorder ruled that, though it was a new case in the sense that a new delegate **E**
was being alleged, nevertheless it was open to the prosecution to do so, and in due
course the appellant was convicted.

In this appeal, counsel for the appellant, to whom the court is indebted for his
argument, has taken a number of points, many of which can be disposed of quite
readily, and it seems convenient to dispose of what I may call the minor points
at the outset. The first of these points is that the assistant recorder was wrong in **F**
ruling that there was a case to go to the jury. At that time, as I have said, the
case was that there had been a delegation to Mr. McBride, and a submission of
no case was made on the basis that the prosecution had not proved that Mr.
McBride knew of these contraventions. In the opinion of this court, the assistant
recorder was perfectly right in leaving it to the jury if, as was thought by the
prosecution, and as the prosecution were invited to think by the appellant's **G**
own statement to the police, Mr. McBride was the manager when it was almost
impossible having regard to the number of contraventions to think that he did
not know of them, and, accordingly, there was matter fit to go to the jury.

The second point that is taken is in regard to the ruling which I have referred
to that the prosecution were entitled to change their case in the sense of substituting Mr. James for Mr. McBride as the alleged delegate. The court has been referred **H**
to various authorities in connexion with this matter (1); each case must depend
on its own facts, and on the facts here the court is quite satisfied that the assistant
recorder was right in ruling as he did. The prosecution case was that there must
have been delegation to somebody to control and manage this club, the appellant
living in Exeter and hardly ever coming to the premises, and, when it was found
that Mr. McBride had ceased to be the manager, they sought to say very naturally **I**
that it was Mr. James. Of course, if the defence were taken by surprise or desired
to call further evidence, maybe the evidence of Mr. James himself, to deny
that he had any knowledge, there would undoubtedly have been an adjournment.
Naturally, however, no adjournment was requested.

The next point concerns a passage in the assistant recorder's summing-up
in dealing with delegation. He put it in this way:

---

(1) See footnote *, p. 199, ante, and the cases referred to in the judgment.

A   " Mr. James was appointed by Mr. Hancock as the doorman and he was the club manager responsible to Mr. McBride and Mr. McBride was responsible to Mr. Hancock and Mr. Hancock if he were responsible to anybody, was responsible to the board."

Counsel for the appellant contends that the assistant recorder ought to have gone on to say that this raised great difficulties in that the knowledge of Mr. James

B would have to be shown to devolve on Mr. McBride and Mr. McBride's knowledge in turn on Mr. Hancock and Mr. Hancock's knowledge in turn on the board. The truth of the matter is, of course, that it was the board that appointed Mr. James, the board acting through Mr. Hancock who appointed Mr. James; his responsibility was to the board itself of which the appellant was a member, though he was under Mr. McBride who was in overall charge of the premises.

C   The next point concerns a matter that occurred after the jury had retired and come back for the second time. They came back with a very sensible question which was:

" Is [the appellant], as a member of the board, equally responsible for the letter confirming the appointment of Mr. James, the manager?"

D The assistant recorder said:

" I think the evidence was this. Mr. Hancock appointed Mr. James by that letter and then he was cross-examined by [counsel for the Crown] and he said that Mr. James's appointment was confirmed by the board. The position was this that when Mr. Hancock wrote that letter he reported it to the board of directors. We do not know whether [the appellant] was at the meeting,

E but the board of directors confirmed the actions of Mr. Hancock."

In fact by a slip that was wrong, because it was the appellant himself who said that the board, he being present, had confirmed and ratified the appointment of Mr. James. There is clearly nothing in that point.

Finally of these that I have referred to as minor points, is the general one that the trial was unsatisfactory and that it would be unsafe to let the verdict

F stand having regard to the fact that the jury appeared to be confused, from their subsequent return into court on two occasions. This was not an easy case from the jury's point of view because they were not left to determine merely the question of guilty or not guilty, but were asked to answer a number of questions, and they were clearly at one time somewhat confused in regard to the questions. The court has considered this point and can see no reason whatever to come to the conclusion

G that the trial was unsatisfactory.

The main point here, which I have left to last, is one of law, the question being whether the doctrine of delegation, which has found its way and remained for some time in English law in the realm of licensing cases, has any application to s. 161 (1) of the Licensing Act 1964. Counsel for the appellant urges that it has no application whatever to that section, and he refers very naturally in support of

H that to the two speeches, first that of Lord Morris of Borth-y-Gest and then that of Lord Donovan in *Vane* v. *Yiannopoullos* (2). Both their lordships in that case, while assuming without deciding that the doctrine of delegation was part of the law of England, decided that it could not apply in the case of what was then s. 22 of the Licensing Act, 1961, which is reproduced in s. 161 of the Act of

I 1964. Those two speeches are undoubtedly very powerful and persuasive authority in his favour. Nevertheless, in the judgment of this court, one has to look deeper into the matter. In that same case it is right to say that Lord Reid and Lord Evershed in their speeches (3) quite clearly were saying that if on the facts of that case there had been delegation, it would apply to s. 22. What had happened in

---

(2) [1964] 3 All E.R. 820 at p. 830, and p. 832, respectively; [1965] A.C. 486 at p. 507 and pp. 511, 512, respectively.

(3) [1964] 3 All E.R. at p. 823 and p. 827 respectively; [1965] A.C. at p. 497 and pp. 503, 504 respectively.

Vane v. *Yiannopoullos* (4) was that the licensee of a restaurant had a justices' **A**
on-licence, which was subject to the condition that intoxicating liquor was to be
sold only to persons ordering meals. Behind his back and without his knowledge,
because he was downstairs or out of the room, a waitress did in fact serve
someone with intoxicating liquor without food. The prosecution urged that,
despite the word " knowingly " in the section, it really in effect was a section
constituting an absolute offence. That was an argument which quite clearly did **B**
not find favour either with the Divisional Court (5) or the House of Lords (4).
The second way in which the prosecution put it was that there had been a delegation by the licensee to the waitress. The Divisional Court (5) had held on the facts
that there was no delegation in that the licensee was running the place himself
and that, through no fault of his own, a servant employed by him contravened
her instructions and acted contrary to the terms of the licence. LORD REID, **C**
LORD EVERSHED and LORD HODSON all affirmed the Divisional Court on that
point, holding that, on the facts, there could not be delegation. LORD REID
and LORD EVERSHED, however, went on to discuss the doctrine of delegation,
and, while not at all happy about the manner in which it had crept into English
law, both considered that it was part of English law and that, it having been
administered in that form ever since the turn of the century at any rate, it was too **D**
late to upset so long standing a practice. As I have said, when one reads the two
speeches, that of LORD REID and LORD EVERSHED, it is quite impossible to come
to any conclusion other than that they were saying that, if on the facts there had
been delegation, then that principle would apply to the section.

Accordingly, it seems to the court that their lordships in *Vane* v. *Yiannopoullos*
(4) were equally divided on this point. It is, therefore, necessary to look a little **E**
further back into the inception of this doctrine. It is to be observed in the
first instance that this doctrine is something quite independent of the principles
which come into play when Parliament has created an absolute offence. When an
absolute offence has been created by Parliament, then the person on whom a
duty is thrown is responsible, whether he has delegated or whether he has acted
through a servant; he is absolutely liable regardless of any intent or knowledge **F**
or mens rea. The principle of delegation comes into play, and only comes into
play, in cases where, though the statute uses words which import knowledge or
intent such as in this case " knowingly " or in some other cases " permitting " or
" suffering " and the like, cases to which knowledge is inherent, nevertheless it has
been held that a man cannot get out of the responsibilities which have been put
on him by delegating those responsibilities to another. **G**

Though not the first case by any means on the subject, the first case to which
attention is drawn is that of *Allen* v. *Whitehead* (6). The offence in question there
was knowingly permitting or suffering prostitutes to meet together on premises,
contrary to s. 44 of the Metropolitan Police Act, 1839. In that case, the occupier
and licensee of a refreshment house did not manage the refreshment house himself
but employed a manager for that purpose. A number of women known to the **H**
manager to be prostitutes resorted to the refreshment house. In that case, as here,
the occupier and licensee said " It was not knowingly on my part, I was not there,
I had appointed a manager ". LORD HEWART, C.J., said this (7):

"... I think that this provision in this statute would be rendered nugatory,
if the contention raised on behalf of this respondent were held to prevail.
That contention was that, as the respondent did not himself manage the **I**
refreshment house, had no personal knowledge that prostitutes met together
and remained therein, had not been negligent in failing to notice these facts,
and had not wilfully closed his eyes to the facts, he could not, in law, be held
responsible."

---

(4) [1964] 3 All E.R. 820; [1965] A.C. 486.
(5) [1964] 2 All E.R. 820; [1964] 2 Q.B. 739.
(6) [1929] All E.R. Rep. 13; [1930] 1 K.B. 211.
(7) [1929] All E.R. Rep. at p. 16; [1930] 1 K.B. at p. 220.

A He went on to say (8):

".... he had transferred to the manager the exercise of discretion in the conduct of the business, and it seems to me that the only reasonable conclusion is, regard being had to the purposes of this Act, that knowledge in the manager was knowledge in the keeper of the house."

B BRANSON, J., put the matter very succinctly. He said (9):

" I agree. The essence of the respondent's case was that he had no personal knowledge of the fact that prostitutes were meeting and remaining upon these premises. It is found that his manager knew, and it is said in *Somerset* v. *Hart* (10), that a man may put another in his position, so as to represent him for the purpose of knowledge. I think that is what the respondent has

C done here, and that consequently his contention fails."

It is just worth referring to *Somerset* v. *Hart* (11) itself, if only because that was decided on the basis that there had been no valid delegation. The offence there concerned gaming, that the licensee of premises had suffered gaming to take place on the premises. In fact he had not delegated the management to anybody else, but a servant of his employed on the premises, without any connivance or

D wilful blindness on the part of the licensee, had suffered gaming to take place. In the course of the argument, LORD COLERIDGE, C.J., said (12):

"How can a man suffer a thing done when he does not know of it? It is true that a man may put another in his position so as to represent him for the purpose of knowledge, but there is no evidence of such delegation here."

E In his judgment, LORD COLERIDGE, C.J., said (13):

" I quite agree that the provisions of an Act which is passed in the interests of public morality and order should receive a reasonably liberal construction. I do not say that proof of actual knowledge on the part of the landlord is necessary. Slight evidence might be sufficient to satisfy the magistrates that the landlord might have known what was taking place if he had pleased,

F but where no actual knowledge is shown there must, as it seems to me, be something to show either that the gaming took place with the knowledge of some person clothed with the landlord's authority, or that there was something like connivance on his part, that he might have known but purposely abstained from knowing."

G Finally, of the more important authorities on this point, there is *Linnett* v. *Metropolitan Police Comr.* (14). The offence there was " knowingly permitting disorderly conduct, contrary to s. 44 of the Metropolitan Police Act, 1839 ". In fact the licensee of the premises had absented himself from the premises and left the control to another man. It was held that, although he, the licensee, had no knowledge, the man he had appointed manager or controller did have knowledge and that, on the principle of delegation, he the licensee, was liable. LORD

H GODDARD, C.J., said (15):

" The point does not, as I say, depend merely on the fact that the relationship of master and servant exists; it depends on the fact that the person who is responsible in law as the keeper of the house, or the licensee of the house if the offence is under the Licensing Act, has chosen to delegate his

I duties, powers and authority to somebody else."

(8) [1929] All E.R. Rep. at p. 16; [1930] 1 K.B. at p. 221.
(9) [1929] All E.R. Rep. at p. 17, [1930] 1 K.B. at pp. 221, 222.
(10) (1884), 12 Q.B.D. 360 at p. 362.
(11) (1884), 12 Q.B.D. 360.
(12) (1884), 12 Q.B.D. at p. 362.
(13) (1884), 12 Q.B.D. at p. 364.
(14) [1946] 1 All E.R. 380; [1946] K.B. 290.
(15) [1946] 1 All E.R. at p. 382; [1946] K.B. at pp. 294, 295.

He went on to refer to *Somerset* v. *Hart* (16) and pointed out that in that case **A** there had been no delegation of control, but that it was merely a case, as indeed was *Vane* v. *Yiannopoullos* (17), of a servant acting behind the back of the licensee. He ended up by saying (18):

" Where there is such delegation [that is true delegation] then the knowledge of the servant or agent becomes that of the master or principal. In this **B**
case there was no relationship of master and servant between the appellant
and Baker. They were joint licensees. If one licensee chooses to say to his
co-licensee, although not his servant: ' We are both licensees and both
keepers of this house, but I am not going to take any part in the management
of this house, I leave the management to you ', he is putting his co-licensee
into his own place to exercise his own powers and duties and he must, therefore, accept responsibility for what is done or known by his co-licensee in that **C**
exercise. That is the principle which underlies all the cases to which I
have referred. I am far from saying, and I do not wish it to be thought
that I am saying, that where a statute provides that in any business a
certain act permitted by the manager shall be an offence on the part of the
manager if it is done with his knowledge, that if that act takes place whilst
the manager himself is carrying on that business and is in charge of that **D**
business but without his knowledge, so that he was powerless to prevent it,
that person necessarily commits the offence. But if the manager chooses
to delegate the carrying on of the business to another, whether or not that
other is his servant, then what that other does or what he knows must be
imputed to the person who put the other into that position.

That is the doctrine of delegation which does form part of our law, and no one in **E**
the House of Lords has said that it does not. I should add that reference was
made to a Scottish case since the decision of the House of Lords in *Vane's* case (17),
that of *Noble* v. *Heatley* (19). The court can get no assistance from that case,
if only because it was a decision that this doctrine of delegation, though as I
said part of the law of England, formed no part of the law of Scotland. **F**
Accordingly, one comes back to the question whether this well established
doctrine applies to s. 161 of the Licensing Act 1964—a matter on which their
lordships in *Vane's* case (17) were divided. This court can see no valid distinction
between the earlier cases, whether they concern prostitutes, drunkenness or
gaming, and the provisions in this section. Parliament must be taken, when
this section was originally introduced in 1961 (20) and continued in 1964, to **G**
know that the doctrine of delegation had been applied in a number of licensing
cases, and that the principle of those cases was that a man cannot get out of the
responsibilities and duties attached to a licence by absenting himself. The position
of course is quite different if he remains in control. It would be only right that he
should not be liable if a servant behind his back did something which contravened
the terms of the licence. If, however, he wholly absents himself leaving some- **H**
body else in control, he cannot claim that what has happened has happened
without his knowledge if the delegate has knowingly carried on in contravention
of the licence. Indeed, with all respect to LORD MORRIS and LORD DONOVAN,
it is difficult to see how s. 22 of the Act of 1961 differs in essential respects from
the sections in other Acts dealt with in the earlier cases. The general principle
in the opinion of this court must be applicable to a licensing case under this **I**
section as it is applicable in the other cases.
Finally, in a recent case since *Vane's* case (17), namely, *Ross* v. *Moss* (21),

---

(16) (1884), 12 Q.B.D. 360.
(17) [1964] 3 All E.R. 820; [1965] A.C. 486.
(18) [1946] K.B. at pp. 295, 296; [1946] 1 All E.R. at pp. **382, 383**.
(19) [1967] S.L.T. 26.
(20) In s. 22 of the Licensing Act, 1961.
(21) [1965] 3 All E.R. 145; [1965] 2 Q.B. 396.

A   while intimating that the matter remained open for argument and decision in the future, I did venture to suggest (22) that in the present state of authority the principle of delegation would seem to apply to an offence against this section.

Accordingly, for the reasons that I have endeavoured to state, this court has come to the conclusion that this appeal fails and must be dismissed.

B   *Appeal dismissed.*

Leave to appeal to the House of Lords granted, the court certifying under s. 1 of the Administration of Justice Act, 1960, that a point of law of general public importance was involved, viz., whether the doctrine of delegation applies to s. 161 of the Licensing Act 1964.

C   Solicitors: *Bond, Pearce, Elliott & Knape,* Plymouth (for the appellant); *Bulcraig & Davis,* agents for *Goodman & Emerson,* Plymouth (for the Crown).

[*Reported by* N. P. METCALFE, ESQ., *Barrister-at-Law.*]

D

WEST MIDLAND BAPTIST (TRUST) ASSOCIATION (INCORPORATED) *v.* BIRMINGHAM CITY CORPORATION.

E   [COURT OF APPEAL, CIVIL DIVISION (Sellers, Salmon and Sachs, L.JJ.), July 4, 5, 6, 10, 11, October 27, 1967.]

Compulsory Purchase—Compensation—Assessment—Date by reference to which compensation is to be assessed—Cost of equivalent reinstatement—Chapel—Deemed notice to treat in 1947—Work of reinstatement first possible in 1961—Whether compensation assessed according to cost at date of notice to treat or
F   *date when work begun—Acquisition of Land (Assessment of Compensation) Act, 1919 (9 & 10 Geo. 5 c. 57), s. 2, r. (5).*

Compulsory Purchase—Compensation—Assessment—Date by reference to which compensation is to be assessed—Value of land acquired—Whether assessed as at date of notice to treat—Acquisition of Land (Assessment of Compensation) Act, 1919 (9 & 10 Geo. 5 c. 57), s. 2, r. (2).

G   *Lands Tribunal—Decisions—Whether previous legal decisions of tribunal binding on it.*

In 1947 a compulsory purchase order providing for the compulsory acquisition of a chapel in Birmingham by the Corporation of the City of Birmingham (the " compensating authority ") was confirmed by the Minister of Town and Country Planning. On Aug. 14, 1947, confirmation of the order was
H   registered in the local land charges register, and thereupon, by virtue of the Town and Country Planning Act, 1944, Sch. 6, Pt. 1, para. 1 (1) and (2), a notice to treat was deemed to have been served on all parties legally entitled thereto. For ten years the compensating authority concentrated on other properties in its redevelopment programme; in 1958 it allocated a new site for the chapel and, allowing for time in preparing plans and obtaining plan-
I   ning permission, the earliest date on which building work on the new chapel might reasonably have been begun was Apr. 30, 1961. It was agreed that the chapel was and would have continued to be devoted to a purpose of such a nature that there was no general demand or market for that purpose and that reinstatement was bona fide intended, with the consequence that compensation for the taking of the chapel fell to be assessed on the basis of the

Affirmed. H.L. [1969] 3 All E.R. 172.

---

(22) [1965] **3** All E.R. at p. 149; [1965] 2 Q.B. at pp. 407, 408.

reasonable cost of equivalent reinstatement under s. 2*, r. (5) of the Acquisi- A
tion of Land (Assessment of Compensation) Act, 1919.   The Lands Tribunal
determined the compensation for the land at £45,000 on the basis of the cost
of reinstatement at the date of the notice to treat in 1947, but found that
it would have been £84,550 if assessed on the basis of cost in 1961, the
earliest time when reinstatement could reasonably have begun.

Held: the compensation should be determined at the cost of reinstatement B
in 1961 when the building work could reasonably have been begun and not
as at the date of the notice to treat in 1947 (thus the compensation under
r. (5) would be the sum of £84,550 not £45,000), for s. 2 of the Acquisition of
Land (Assessment of Compensation) Act, 1919, should not be interpreted so
as to produce injustice, and the concept of cost of reinstatement established
by r. (5) envisaged actual cost (see p. 211, letter H, p. 213, letters A and I, C
p. 218, letter I, p. 220, letter C, and p. 223, letter H, post).

Aston Charities Trust, Ltd. v. *Stepney Borough Council* ((1952), 2 P. & C.R.
289) disapproved.

Dictum of SIR WILLIAM PAGE WOOD, V.-C., in *Penny* v. *Penny* ((1868),
L.R. 5 Eq. at p. 236) not followed.

Per CURIAM: it is doubtful whether open market price prevailing at the D
date of service of the notice to treat forms the correct basis for assessing
compensation for the value of land under r. (2) of s. 2 of the Act of 1919
though (per SELLERS, L.J., this point may not be open to this court, see
p. 210, letter H, post); but even if the court were bound by authority to hold
that such a basis was correct when applying r. (2), the court would decline to
extend the principle to assessment under r. (5) (see p. 214, letter G, p. 217, E
letter F, p. 218, letters E, F and I, p. 223, letter H, and p. 224, letter C, post).

Phoenix Assurance Co. v. *Spooner* ([1905] 2 K.B. 753) and *Re Rowton
Houses, Ltd.'s Leases* ([1966] 3 All E.R. 996) doubted.

Per SACHS, L.J.: if the claimants should have purposely saved money
by allowing disrepair, that should be taken into account against them in
assessing the final sum (see p. 224, letter F, post; cf., p. 212, letter C, post). F

Semble: previous decisions of the Lands Tribunal on points of law should
not be treated by the tribunal as binding when reaching subsequent decisions
(see p. 210, letter F, p. 213, letter C, and p. 222, letter H, post).

Appeal allowed.

[Editorial Note. The Acquisition of Land (Assessment of Compensation)
Act, 1919, s. 2, is now repealed by the Land Compensation Act, 1961, and the G
rules are re-enacted in s. 5.

As to the date at which compensation for the compulsory purchase of land
falls to be assessed, see 10 HALSBURY'S LAWS (3rd Edn.) 93, para. 156, 105, 106,
para. 178; and for cases on the subject, see 11 DIGEST (Repl.) 136, 137, *198-200.*

As to stare decisis in special courts or tribunals, see 22 HALSBURY'S LAWS
(3rd Edn.) 805, para. 1693. H

For the Acquisition of Land (Assessment of Compensation) Act, 1919, s. 2,
see 3 HALSBURY'S STATUTES (2nd Edn.) 977; and for the Land Compensation
Act, 1961, s. 5, see 41 ibid., p. 49.]

Cases referred to:

Aston Charities Trust, Ltd. v. *Stepney Borough Council,* (1952), 2 P. & C.R. 289;
    affd. C.A., [1952] 2 All E.R. 228; [1952] 2 Q.B. 642; 116 J.P. 441; I
    11 Digest (Repl.) 127, *168.*

Bailey v. *Derby Corpn.,* [1965] 1 All E.R. 443; [1965] 1 W.L.R. 213; 124 J.P.
    140; Digest (Cont. Vol. B) 121, *187a.*

Bwllfa and Merthyr Dare Steam Collieries (1891), Ltd. v. *Pontypridd Waterworks
    Co.,* [1900-03] All E.R. Rep. 600; [1903] A.C. 426; 72 L.J.K.B. 805;
    89 L.T. 280; 11 Digest (Repl.) 136, *199.*

---

* Section 2, so far as material, is set out at p. 208, letter I, to p. 209, letter D, post.

A   *Colonial Sugar Refining Co., Ltd.* v. *Melbourne Harbour Trust Comrs.*, [1927] A.C. 343; 96 L.J.P.C. 74; 136 L.T. 709; 44 Digest (Repl.) 297, *1276*.

Grice v. *Dudley Corpn.*, [1957] 2 All E.R. 673; [1958] Ch. 329; [1957] 3 W.L.R. 314; 121 J.P. 466; Digest (Cont. Vol. A) 213, *520a*.

Harvey v. *Crawley Development Corpn.*, [1957] 1 All E.R. 504; [1957] 1 Q.B. 485; [1957] 2 W.L.R. 332; 121 J.P. 166; Digest (Cont. Vol. A) 210,
B   *192b*.

Horn v. *Sunderland Corpn.*, [1941] 1 All E.R. 480; [1941] 2 K.B. 26; 110 L.J.K.B. 353; 165 L.T. 298; 105 J.P. 223; 11 Digest (Repl.) 127, *167*.

Hull & Humber Investment Co., Ltd. v. *Hull Corpn.*, [1965] 1 All E.R. 429; [1965] 2 Q.B. 145; [1965] 2 W.L.R. 161; 129 J.P. 143; Digest (Cont. Vol. B) 122, *826a*.

C   *Inland Revenue Comrs.* v. *Glasgow & South Western Ry. Co.*, (1887), 12 App. Cas. 315; 56 L.J.P.C. 82; 11 Digest (Repl.) 249, *785*.

London County Council v. *Tobin*, [1959] 1 All E.R. 649; [1959] 1 W.L.R. 354; 123 J.P. 250; Digest (Cont. Vol. A) 205, *168a*.

Mercer v. *Liverpool, St. Helens & South Lancashire Ry. Co.*, [1904] A.C. 461; 73 L.J.K.B. 960; 91 L.T. 605; 68 J.P. 533; 11 Digest (Repl.) 289, *1951*.

D   *Penny* v. *Penny*, (1868), L.R. 5 Eq. 227; 37 L.J.Ch. 340; 18 L.T. 13; 11 Digest (Repl.) 136, *198*.

Phoenix Assurance Co. v. *Spooner*, [1905] 2 K.B. 753; 74 L.J.K.B. 792; 93 L.T. 306; 29 Digest (Repl.) 446, *3269*.

Richmond v. *North London Ry. Co.*, (1868), L.R. 5 Eq. 352; *affd.* (1868), 3 Ch. App. 679; 37 L.J.Ch. 886; 33 J.P. 86; 11 Digest (Repl.) 185, *519*.

E   *Ricket* v. *Metropolitan Ry. Co.* (*Directors, etc.*), (1865), 34 L.J.Q.B. 257; *affd.* H.L., (1867), L.R. 2 H.L. 175; 36 L.J.Q.B. 205; 16 L.T. 542; 31 J.P. 484; 11 Digest (Rep.) 150, *281*.

Rowton Houses, Ltd.'s, Leases, Re, Square Grip Reinforcement Co. (*London*), *Ltd.* v. *Rowton Houses, Ltd.*, [1966] 3 All E.R. 996; [1967] Ch. 877; [1967] 2 W.L.R. 160; Digest (Cont. Vol. B) 121, *200a*.

F   *Simpsons Motor Sales* (*London*), *Ltd.* v. *Hendon Corpn.*, [1962] 3 All E.R. 75; [1963] Ch. 57; [1962] 3 W.L.R. 666; *affd.* H.L., [1963] 2 All E.R. 484; [1964] A.C. 1088; [1963] 2 W.L.R. 1187; 127 J.P. 418; Digest (Cont. Vol. A) 655, *135a*.

Tiverton and North Devon Ry. Co. v. *Loosemore*, (1884), 9 App. Cas. 480; 53 L.J.Ch. 812; 50 L.T. 637; 48 J.P. 372; 11 Digest (Repl.) 231, *954*.

G

Case Stated.

The claimants appealed by way of Case Stated to the Court of Appeal against a decision of the Lands Tribunal (ERSKINE SIMES, ESQ., Q.C.) given on Nov. 15, 1966, in which it determined the compensation which was payable for the compulsory acquisition of premises comprising a chapel vested in the claimants and
H   which by agreement was to be assessed under s. 2, r. (5), of the Acquisition of Land (Assessment of Compensation) Act, 1919, on the basis of the reasonable cost of equivalent reinstatement. The tribunal determined that the compensation should be assessed at £50,025 based on prices ruling at Aug. 14, 1947, when notice to treat was deemed to have been served in respect of the premises. The claimants sought an order quashing the tribunal's decision that the compensation
I   amounted to £50,025, and determining that it amounted to £89,575. The grounds of appeal were as follows: (i) that the tribunal was wrong to hold that compensation payable under s. 2, r. (5), was in law to be assessed at prices ruling at the date of notice to treat; (ii) that compensation payable under r. (5) was to be the reasonable cost of equivalent reinstatement; (iii) that compensation payable under r. (5) was to be the cost of reinstatement when such reinstatement reasonably did or could take place; (iv) that any rule that compensation on compulsory purchase was to be assessed as at the date of notice to treat did not apply to a case falling within r. (5); and (v) that the decision of the Lands

Tribunal in *Aston Charities Trust, Ltd.* v. *Stepney Borough Council** should not **A** have been followed and was wrong in law.

D. G. *Widdicombe*, Q.C., and David *Trustram Eve* for the claimants.
K. F. *Goodfellow*, Q.C., and J. D. *James* for the compensating authority.

Cur. adv. vult.

Oct. 27.   The following judgments were read.   **B**

SELLERS, L.J.: The claimants were the owners of the People's Chapel, Great King Street, Birmingham, which was erected in 1887 after the destruction by fire of the original premises of the church, founded in 1848.   Owing to the circumstances which have intervened, the claimants are now in the course of completing a new church to replace the People's Chapel and the only question **C** in the appeal is whether they are entitled to receive from the compensating authority by way of compensation for the old building the reinstatement cost on Apr. 30, 1961, of £89,575, or only the sum of £50,025 which is the amount due on a reinstatement basis on Aug. 14, 1947.   In each of these figures there is included £5,025 which the parties have agreed as the 1961 cost of disturbance, i.e., moving the pews, the organ and other equipment and expenses consequent **D** on the removal, which is provided for under s. 2, r. 6 of the Acquisition of Land (Assessment of Compensation) Act, 1919, cited below.

The church is within an area of 981 acres which the compensating authority as far back as 1946 wished to acquire and redevelop.   The authority took the appropriate steps and on June 26, 1947, a compulsory purchase order was confirmed by the Minister of Town and Country Planning.   On Aug. 14, 1947, this **E** was registered in the local land charges register and accordingly a notice to treat was deemed to have been served on all parties who should be served under s. 18 of the Lands Clauses Consolidation Act, 1845, by reason of the Town and Country Planning Act, 1944, Sch. 6, Pt. 1, para. 1 (1) and (2).

In the first ten years the compensating authority concentrated on the purchase of the slum houses and commenced a redevelopment programme.   The allocation **F** of new sites for the churches had to await the advance of the redevelopment scheme and it was not until April, 1957, that the layout was sent to the churches concerned.   In September, 1958, the compensating authority allocated a new site for the claimants' church, which was accepted in September, 1959.   Thereafter discussions took place on the compensation to be paid, the respective valuers failing to agree on a date for assessing the cost of reinstatement.   Time **G** was necessarily taken in preparing plans and obtaining planning permission and Apr. 30, 1961, has been agreed between the parties as the earliest date on which building work on the new church might reasonably have been begun.

By a vesting declaration the ownership of the People's Chapel vested in the compensating authority on June 24, 1963, since when the claimants have been allowed to remain in possession on the terms that they claim no interest on the **H** compensation and pay no rent.   The compensating authority has been paying instalments of compensation to the claimants from 1966 as the new building progresses in its erection.

The compensation falls to be assessed under s. 2 of the Acquisition of Land (Assessment of Compensation) Act, 1919, and at the present time any question of disputed compensation falls to be determined by the Lands Tribunal, to whom **I** this dispute went and from whom this appeal comes.   Section 2 provides that compensation shall be assessed in accordance with the following rules:

" (1) No allowance shall be made on account of the acquisition being compulsory; (2) the value of land shall, subject as hereinafter provided be taken to be the amount which the land if sold in the open market by a

---

* (1952), 2 P. & C.R. 289; *affirmed on other points* [1952] 2 All E.R. 228.

A   willing seller might be expected to realise: Provided always that the arbitrator shall be entitled to consider all returns and assessments of capital value
for taxation made or acquiesced in by the claimant; (3) the special suitability
or adaptability of the land for any purpose shall not be taken into acccount
if that purpose is a purpose to which it could be applied only in pursuance
of statutory powers, or for which there is no market apart from the special

B   needs of a particular purchaser or the requirements of any Government
department or any local or public authority; Provided that any bona fide
offer for the purchase of the land made before the passing of this Act which
may be brought to the notice of the arbitrator shall be taken into consideration; (4) where the value of the land is increased by reason of the use
thereof or of any premises thereon in a manner which could be restrained by

C   any court, or is contrary to law, or is detrimental to the health of the inmates
of the premises or to the public health, the amount of that increase shall not
be taken into account; (5) where land is, and but for the compulsory acquisition would continue to be, devoted to a purpose of such a nature that there is
no general demand or market for land for that purpose, the compensation
may, if the official arbitrator is satisfied that reinstatement in some other

D   place is bona fide intended, be assessed on the basis of the reasonable cost of
equivalent reinstatement; (6) the provisions of r. (2) shall not affect the
assessment of compensation for disturbance or any other matter not directly
based on the value of land . . ."

It was agreed between the parties that r. (5) was the appropriate rule to be
applied.   The church was, when compulsorily acquired, and would have con-

E   tinued to be but for the acquisition, devoted to a purpose of such a nature that
there was no general demand or market for that purpose.   Reinstatement in
some other place is already in progress and compensation, it is conceded, falls to
be assessed on the basis of the reasonable cost for " equivalent reinstatement".

Whenever rebuilding (which is the commonest form of reinstatement) is contemplated to replace a building which is compulsorily acquired, some delay would

F   appear to be unavoidable.   A new site has to be obtained, frequently from the
acquiring authority in whose control lies the allocation, plans have to be prepared
and approved, authority to build has to be obtained and ultimately a contract
has to be placed for the erection of the substituted building.   Under the most
favourable conditions there must be some delay, measured normally in years
rather than months.   Under less favourable conditions the delays experienced

G   in this case may not be untypical, some fourteen years may go by before the
actual reinstatement can be contemplated.   Whatever may have been the position
in 1845 or even in 1919, when a considerable delay between the date of the
notice to treat and the final assessment of compensation on a reinstatement
basis may not have led to a variation in amount of assessment, or only relatively
small fluctuations up or down whether the calculation was made on the one day

H   or the other, since 1947 the cost of labour and material and the total cost of
building has increased so enormously over relatively short periods that compensation fixed at building rates in one year would prove inadequate to meet the erection
of the same building in the next.   A period of fourteen years between 1947 and
1961 gives the discrepancy revealed in the figures in the present case.

Notwithstanding these unquestionable features the finding of the Lands

I   Tribunal has been in favour of the compensating authority, viz., that the
claimants are only entitled to receive £50,025, being the cost of reinstatement on
Aug. 14, 1947, when the notice to treat is deemed to have been served.   In
arriving at this conclusion the tribunal followed and applied one of its own
decisions in 1952: *Aston Charities Trust, Ltd.* v. *Stepney Borough Council* (1).
That was a decision of J. P. C. DONE, Esq., F.R.I.C.S.   The main issue in the
case was whether, consequent on war damage to a church and its locality, the

(1) (1952), 2 P. & C.R. 289; *affd.* [1952] 2 All E.R. 228; [1952] 2 Q.B. 642.

premises were devoted to purposes which brought them to be assessed for com- **A**
pensation on the basis of r. (5).   This issue was decided in favour of the claimants
and was upheld on appeal (2).   Issue (ii) was stated (3) to be

" whether the expression ' reasonable cost ' in the said r. (5) means the
expense to be incurred at the time of the reinstatement or the cost of such
reinstatement calculated upon the basis of prices ruling at the date of the
service of the notice to treat."   **B**

In that case the notice to treat was dated Feb. 26, 1946, nearly six years earlier
than the date of the tribunal's assessment.   The decision stated (4):

" Issue (ii), however, raises the point as to whether in assessing the cost of
equivalent reinstatement that cost must be calculated by applying the prices
for builders' work ruling at the date of the notice to treat or at the date of   **C**
signature of the contract for the construction of alternative premises.   I do
not think that the claimants are entitled to the cost of reinstatement other
than that calculated at prices ruling at the date of the notice to treat.   I
received no evidence as to why a period of 4¾ years had elapsed between
the date of the notice to treat and that of the reference to this tribunal; but
such delay need not have taken place if either party, being apprehensive as   **D**
to its effects upon their interests, had referred the question of compensation
after the statutory fourteen days.   In my view the proper cost is that
based upon the prices likely to apply to a notional contract for the construction of alternative premises entered into on the date of the notice to treat
even if such contract might be expected to contain a clause for adjustment
of prices during the period of construction.   Some hardship might ensue   **E**
from this, but it is a risk to which both claimants and acquiring authority
are subject, and the obvious method of minimising it is to settle the question
of compensation or refer it without delay."

That decision was strongly attacked before the tribunal and in this court by the
claimants, who submitted that it was arrived at without adequate consideration
and was wrong.   It is not binding on this court and it is questionable whether it   **F**
should have been regarded as binding on the Lands Tribunal, whatever is to be
said of its normal practice of following its own decisions, as the decision was
that of a layman, no doubt a very experienced surveyor, whereas in the present
case the tribunal was a very experienced lawyer.   The claimants submit that
the decision was wrong and rely on the five reasons set out in the decision now
under review.   **G**

In the course of the argument the submission (influenced, I think, by the court)
widened considerably and the question arose whether the date of a notice to treat
should be the date of assessment even under s. 2, r. (2).   I have not felt that this
consideration is open to this court.   It has been too long accepted and applied
that where the value of the land has to be assessed the time for the assessment
is the date of the notice to treat.   This was so under the Lands Clauses Consolida-   **H**
tion Act, 1845, and it has been accepted to be so under the Acquisition of Land
(Assessment of Compensation) Act, 1919.   The authorities, particularly in the
light of present day conditions, do not provide very persuasive reasons for the
conclusion, but in *Penny* v. *Penny* (5) it was stated unequivocally:

" The scheme of the Act I take to be this: that every man's interest shall
be valued, rebus sic stantibus, just as it occurs at the very moment when the   **I**
notice to treat was given."

From that date that does not appear to have been challenged.   It is so stated
and accepted in the textbooks and was expressly repeated in this court by SCOTT,

---

(2) [1952] 2 All E.R. 228; [1952] 2 Q.B. 642.
(3) (1952), 2 P. & C.R. at p. 291.
(4) (1952), 2 P. & C.R. at p. 294.
(5) (1868), L.R. 5 Eq. 227 at p. 236.

A L.J., in *Horn* v. *Sunderland Corpn.* (6). Perhaps an even greater obstacle to a reconsideration of the courts of this long accepted principle is that it was recognised by statute in the Town and Country Planning Act, 1944. The House of Lords may have greater freedom.

The date of the notice to treat establishes the interest to be acquired and the physical state of the land at that time. It does not prevent an owner dealing

B with his property, but he cannot increase the burden of the purchaser. It was submitted on behalf of the compensating authority that, as the established time for assessing the value of the land under r. (2) was the date of the notice to treat, that was also the date of ascertaining the cost of reinstatement under r. (5) and that to hold otherwise would be illogical and inconsistent. If the rule under r. (2) were otherwise (and I am not out of harmony with my brethren in seeing present

C day injustice in the working of the rule), I do not think that anyone would readily hold that the cost of reinstatement ought or even could be fairly ascertained at the date of the notice to treat. It could be based on nothing but conjecture and guesswork. The assessment would have at least to envisage a hypothetical site on which to construct, which might have no resemblance to the site ultimately built on.

D The cost of reinstatement is so different from the " value of land " basis in r. (2) that I see no good reason for applying the decision in respect of r. (2) (or to embrace the position in the Act of 1845 in respect of value) to govern the date of assessment under r. (5). Previous High Court authority does not restrict the freedom of this court in considering the date, in the circumstances of this case, of assessing the cost of reinstatement. The conceptions involved are different.

E In respect of the value of land compensation is met by the price of the land being acquired. There is machinery (which either party can invoke) for it to be ascertained without long delay and it bears interest from the date of its agreement or assessment. It can be obtained and utilised to acquire new premises if so desired. It is not so under r. (5). The claimants submitted, and I agree, that the position under r. (5) is more akin to the type of assessment under r. (6), where

F it has been established that the loss or damage falls to be assessed on the basis of the cost at the time the loss was incurred (*Harvey* v. *Crawley Development Corpn.* (7); *London County Council* v. *Tobin* (8); *Bailey* v. *Derby Corpn.* (9)). Further r. (6) expressly provides that the provisions of r. (2) shall not affect any other matter not directly based on the value of land.

Under r. (5) compensation is not met by the market price which is capable of

G being assessed on any given day, but is dependent on many factors, inevitably involving delays after the notice to treat has been received, as I have earlier pointed out. If an owner cannot reinstate or rebuild on the day of the notice to treat (which he cannot) it is difficult to see how even prima facie that day can be the one for assessing the cost for so doing. When the time comes for incurring the expense, the then cost would appear to be the compensation, for it is irrelevant

H what it would have cost earlier, whether it be more or less. The owner gets his replacement at the earliest date replacement could be obtained, and the cost of the replacement is the measure of his loss. That is the due compensation. The basis of the payment is the cost of the thing acquired, whereas under r. (2) the compensation is based on the value of what is compulsorily taken. The claimants will make no profit out of the transaction if they are paid £89,575 and they will

I not make the loss which the decision of the Lands Tribunal would impose on them.

I do not see what the claimants could have done to avoid the loss. They could not have built before 1961, and at that time they could not have built for less than £89,575. They could not have entered into an effective contract on Aug. 14,

---

(6) [1941] 1 All E.R. 480 at p. 495; [1941] 2 K.B. 26 at p. 48.
(7) [1957] 1 All E.R. 504; [1957] 1 Q.B. 485.
(8) [1959] 1 All ER. 649.
(9) [1965] 1 All E.R. 443.

1947, with any contractor to build in April, 1961, a new church for £50,025 and A that sum is wholly inadequate compensation for them in the circumstances of this case. I find it hard to envisage what MR. DONE's "notional contract" would contain. Here we know the actual cost of rebuilding and there is no conjecture. The circumstances were not in the control of the claimants. They were to some extent in the control of the compensating authority.

What the claimants could have done and may have done after the notice to B treat was to have reduced the expenditure on the upkeep of the fabric of a building which was intended for demolition and prudently could have put the saving on one side towards the new building. If this has been done and if the claimants are entitled to receive the 1961 cost of obtaining a new building, they will have the new building and the saving on the cost of maintenance of the old. As they are only entitled to compensation for what they have lost, it would seem to me C that they ought to give credit for any such saving, as otherwise they would be better off, but no point was made of this.

The compensating authority's counsel relied on the provisions of s. 18 of the Act of 1845 which are still effective. I will assume that they apply where, as here, the notice to treat is deemed to have been served and that it is to be deemed to demand from the claimants "particulars of their estate and interest in such D lands and of the claims made in respect thereof". The documents, if any, were not before us but I do not doubt that the claimants have throughout claimed reinstatement and particulars of their claim could not further be given at that date. I would allow the appeal and find the compensation to be that assessed by the tribunal at £89,575.

E

SALMON, L.J.: The facts have been fully stated by SELLERS, L.J., and I need not repeat them. I would, however, emphasise the following matters. A compulsory purchase order made by the compensating authority was confirmed on June 26, 1947. This order applied to 981 acres of the city of Birmingham and included the chapel owned by the claimants. On Aug. 14, 1947, that order was registered in the local land charges register, and accordingly a notice to treat F under s. 18 of the Lands Clauses Consolidation Act, 1845, was then deemed to have been served inter alios on the claimants in accordance with the provisions of the Town and Country Planning Act, 1944, Sch. 6, Pt. 1, para. 1 (2). At that time it was fully recognised by the compensating authority and the claimants (i) that it would probably be very many years before the compensating authority would acquire the chapel, (ii) that but for the order the claimants' land would G always have continued to be used for the purpose of a chapel, (iii) that there was and would be no general demand or market for land for that purpose, (iv) that reinstatement in some other place was bona fide intended, and accordingly (v) that compensation would fall to be assessed on the basis of the reasonable cost of equivalent reinstatement under s. 2, r. (5), of the Acquisition of Land (Assessment of Compensation) Act, 1919.

H

April 30, 1961, was the date (as agreed between the parties) on which building work on the new chapel might reasonably have been begun. The reasonable cost of reinstating the chapel on a new site in June, 1947 (if such a site had then been available), would have been £45,000. The reasonable cost of reinstating the chapel in April, 1961, was £84,550. The claimants contend that they are entitled to the latter sum plus £5,025, which is agreed between the parties as I proper compensation for disturbance under r. (6) of s. 2 of the Act of 1919, i.e., £89,575 in all. The compensating authority contends that it is liable to pay only £50,025, being the reasonable cost of reinstatement in April, 1947, plus the agreed figure of £5,025.

The determination of the dispute between the parties turns entirely on the true construction of r. (5) which has been read by SELLERS, L.J. In my view, it is plain beyond argument that looking at that rule by itself, "the reasonable cost of reinstatement" is the cost in April, 1961, which was the earliest date on

A which reinstatement could reasonably have been effected. It would be ridiculous and monstrously unjust to hold that compensation must now be assessed on what would have been the reasonable cost of reinstatement in 1947, when no site was available and no reinstatement could have been effected. Unless compelled to do so by direct and binding authority, I would refuse to make any such absurd and unjust finding. There is no reported case dealing with the true construction

B of r. (5) other than *Aston Charities Trust, Ltd.* v. *Stepney Borough Council* (10), decided in the Lands Tribunal by a distinguished surveyor in 1952. That decision is not binding on this court and, in so far as it seeks to lay down any general principle, it is, in my judgment, plainly wrong. The most experienced and learned member of the Lands Tribunal who decided the present case in favour of the compensating authority felt himself bound by the *Aston Charities*

C *Trust* case (10) and referred to "the established practice of the tribunal in following decisions [of its own] given on points of law". For my part, I think that the sooner this practice is discontinued the better. No doubt previous decisions of the tribunal on points of law should be treated by the tribunal with great respect and considered as persuasive authority even when made by a layman; but they should never be treated as binding. It is important that

D such decisions should be most carefully scrutinised and if necessary rejected, particularly in cases such as the present which raise points of law of outstanding importance with far-reaching consequences.

It should be remembered that the law has long recognised as stated by ERLE, C.J., in *Ricket* v. *Metropolitan Ry. Co. (Directors, etc.)* (11), that:

E "The company, claiming to take land by compulsory process, expel the owner from his property, and are bound to compensate him for all the loss caused by the expulsion . . ."

This is the price which the acquiring authority has to pay for what it compulsorily acquires. This principle was reaffirmed by this court in *Horn* v. *Sunderland Corpn.* (12). It must never be forgotten that the price to be paid for the land

F compulsorily acquired is equivalent to compensation for the loss suffered by the party deprived of his land by the compulsory purchase. It is not the value of the land to the party exercising compulsory powers. Section 2 of the Act of 1919 merely sets out the rules (many of them already recognised by the common law) for measuring the price, i.e., the compensation for the loss caused by the expulsion. Broadly, r. (1) abrogated the special allowance which had formerly been added to the price because the land was being acquired compulsorily. Rule (2) stated

G that generally the price should include the value of the land, the value to be taken as the amount the land would fetch if sold on the open market by a willing seller. Rules (3) and (4) stated certain special circumstances which should not be taken into account so as to enhance the price. Rule (5), to which I have already referred, related to cases in which it would be impossible or unfair to apply r. (2). Rule (6) provided for elements of loss caused by expulsion not covered by r. (2)

H or r. (5), e.g., in the present case, the expense of moving the pews and the organ from the old chapel to the new, and of installing them there.

The price or compensation to be paid is always a sum calculated under r. (2) or r. (5) as the case may require, plus any sum that may be due under r. (6). Since it was not reasonably possible for the claimants to build their new chapel until 1961, and their compensation for loss suffered by expulsion falls to be assessed

I on the basis of the reasonable cost of equivalent reinstatement, I do not understand how they can properly be compensated by being paid what it would have cost to reinstate fourteen years earlier—costs having risen by almost one hundred per cent. in the meantime.

It has been suggested that the claimants might have made a claim for compensation at the time of the deemed notice to treat in 1947. This is quite true. The

_____
(10) (1952), 2 P. & C.R. 289; *affd.* [1952] 2 All E.R. 228; [1952] 2 Q.B. 642.
(11) (1865), 34 L.J.Q.B. 257 at p. 261; *affd.* (1867), L.R. 2 H.L. 175.
(12) [1941] 1 All E.R. 480; [1941] 2 K.B. 26.

reason why they did not do so is obvious. In 1947 it was known that reinstatement **A** would most probably be impossible for many years. How many years was then pure guesswork. It was no doubt also then recognised that site and building costs were likely to rise over the years—but by how much was equally guesswork. Accordingly, the difficulties in 1947 of formulating a claim for compensation or of any tribunal then assessing a fair amount for compensation were well nigh insuperable. It would appear that the claimants very sensibly decided not to **B** guess but to wait and postpone making their claim until such time as reinstatement became feasible and they could form a reasonable estimate of what it would in fact cost. The compensating authority too might have taken steps in 1947 to have the amount of compensation assessed. It did not do so, no doubt for excellent reasons. The fact that steps to have the compensation assessed might have been taken by either party in 1947 and that neither party took any such **C** steps does not seem to me to help the compensating authority or to throw any light on the correct basis on which compensation should be assessed. It certainly does not suggest that the basis should be the prices ruling in 1947.

If compensation had been assessed in 1947, on the view I take of r. (5), the very difficult task would have had to be attempted of estimating the reasonable cost of equivalent reinstatement at such date in the future as a suitable site might **D** become available and rebuilding might reasonably be commenced. As it is, it is now unnecessary to guess because the figure is now known, viz., £89,575 inclusive of compensation for disturbance.

In the course of his most interesting and able argument counsel for the compensating authority conceded, as indeed he had to, that to fix compensation on the basis of the 1947 prices would appear to be unreasonable and unjust. He con- **E** tended that nevertheless the tribunal was right in adopting that basis and that this court is bound to uphold the tribunal's decision because of the settled law and practice relating to compensation cases under r. (2). He contended that in such cases the value of the interest in the land falls to be assessed as at the date of the service of the notice to treat, and that, since that is the date at which the value of the interest in the land must be assessed, logically the same date must apply **F** in assessing the costs of equivalent reinstatement under r. (5). I recognise the force of this argument but I cannot accept it. First, I have grave doubts whether the open market prices prevailing at the date of the service of the notice to treat form the correct basis for assessing compensation under r. (2). Secondly, even if I were bound by the authorities to hold that the contention of counsel for the compensating authority was correct in respect of the principles applicable to **G** r. (2) cases, I would refuse to extend the authorities so as to apply those principles to r. (5) cases.

One hundred years ago SIR WILLIAM PAGE WOOD, V.-C., in his judgment in *Penny* v. *Penny* (13), said:

" The scheme of the Act [of 1845] I take to be this: that every man's interest shall be valued rebus sic stantibus, just as it occurs at the very **H** moment when the notice to treat was given."

This sentence, divorced from its context, seems to have been accepted ever since as holy writ and applied in its strict literal sense. It has been endorsed by the courts, see, e.g., *Horn's* case (14) and *Hull & Humber Investment Co., Ltd.* v. *Hull Corpn.* (15). It has been adopted by all the textbooks, see, for example, CRIPPS **I** ON COMPULSORY ACQUISITION OF LAND (11th Edn.) p. 366, and 10 HALSBURY'S LAWS OF ENGLAND (3rd Edn.) at pp. 63, 64, and it has been consistently acted on in practice—a practice which in modern times has produced the most grotesquely unjust results. In the stable days of the mid-Victorian era, fluctuations in prices were not very violent. In modern times, certainly since the end of the last war,

---

(13) (1868), L.R. 5 Eq. at p. 236.
(14) [1941] 1 All E.R. 480; [1941] 2 K.B. 26.
(15) [1965] 1 All E.R. 429; [1965] 2 Q.B. 145.

A there has been very serious inflation; prices have consistently risen at an alarming rate so that site and building costs may well be doubled or even trebled in ten to twenty years. Schemes for compulsory acquisition such as the present nowadays frequently envisage a notice to treat being served ten to twenty years before it is intended to acquire the land. On the strength of what appears to have been a casual observation by Sir William Page Wood, V.-C., in 1867, (16), corporations

B and others have, since the last war, been able to take over land at half and often less than half its true value at the date of its acquisition. The curious thing is that no point of this kind was ever argued nor did it arise for decision and certainly was not decided in *Penny* v. *Penny* (17) nor in any of the cases in which Sir William Page Wood, V.-C.'s dictum was adopted in this court.

In *Penny* v. *Penny* (17), a testator bequeathed the residue of a term of years

C under a lease of a house to his executors on trust to allow his sons to occupy the house so long as they carried on the same business there as they had formerly carried on there with him, they paying a low rent to the executors and the executors paying the rent reserved by the lease. On May 8, 1866, a notice to treat for the premises was served by the Metropolitan Board of Works. This meant that as soon as the board took the house, the sons would no longer be able to

D carry on business there. The executor obtained an award of compensation of some £8,000 on the basis that he was entitled to the whole residue of the term from the date of the service of the notice to treat because the sons would no longer be able to carry on business in the house. The sons obtained an award of compensation of some £4,000 on the basis that the compulsory acquisition prevented them from carrying on business in the house. Not unnaturally, the board objected to

E paying both these sums. Sir William Page Wood, V.-C., decided that they need not do so and that the executor's interest should be valued on the basis of the sons' rights to remain in possession at the low rent which, for but the expropriation, they might well have exercised. In arriving at this decision, the Vice-Chancellor assumed that the date of the notice to treat was the time when the house was about to be taken—as no doubt it was in 1867. He said (18):

F   ". . . I think the valuation ought to be made as at the time when the house was about to be taken, and should be made of the exact interest which the [executors] would at that moment have had, assuming that the house had not been taken . . . As to the value of the interest, it appears to me clear that the [executors'] interest is not to be treated as having been increased through [the expropriation]."

G In other words, the expropriation cannot operate to diminish nor can it be utilised by an owner for the purpose of increasing the value of his interest in the land. This is all that that case decided and that was plainly right. As I have already indicated, no question arose as to what would be the position if the notice to treat was served at a time when the land was not about to be taken

H and on account of long delays there should be a great difference between the value of the land at the date of the service of the notice to treat and its value at the date of the expropriation. Nor did any such question arise in any of the cases in which the dictum of Sir William Page Wood, V.-C. (19), was adopted in this court. I think that Sir William Page Wood, V.-C., who let fall this dictum, and the judges who have since taken it up would be shocked to discover that it has been

I used to establish a practice which nowadays very often enables those exercising statutory powers of expropriation to acquire property at half and sometimes less than half its true value.

It has sometimes been said that the service of a notice to treat creates a quasi-contractual relationship between the parties. This is a somewhat loose expression.

(16) In *Penny* v. *Penny*, (1868), L.R. 5 Eq. at p. 236.
(17) (1868), L.R. 5 Eq. 227.
(18) (1868), L.R. 5 Eq. at p. 235.
(19) In *Penny* v. *Penny*, (1868), L.R. 5 Eq. at pp. 235, 236.

Whatever it may mean, the relationship created by the service of a notice to treat A
certainly differs drastically from the relationship created by a contract of sale,
since service of the notice to treat passes no interest in the land. It is a step
towards expropriation. A landowner who has received a notice to treat cannot
deal with his land so as to increase the burden of compensation to be paid for its
compulsory acquisition but otherwise he has the right to deal with it as he likes,
although there may well be practical difficulties in his doing so (*Mercer* v. *Liver-* B
pool, St. Helens & South Lancashire Ry. Co. (20), per LORD LINDLEY). The notice
to treat confers a legal right on the party serving it to acquire the land on payment
of proper compensation to be assessed if necessary by the appropriate tribunal and
on the owner to have the compensation assessed and paid. It is not until compensation is agreed or assessed that the equitable title in the land passes to the party
who has served the notice to treat. Either party can then—but only then— C
obtain specific performance, the one to have the legal title conveyed to him on
payment of the price, the other to have the price paid on conveying the legal
title (*Grice* v. *Dudley Corpn.* (21); *Simpsons Motor Sales (London), Ltd.* v. *Hendon
Corpn.* (22)). Since the party exercising compulsory powers is bound to compensate the owner for all the loss that he suffers by being deprived of his interest in
the land and being expelled from it (*Ricket* v. *Metropolitan Ry. Co.* (*Directors,* D
etc.) (23), and *Horn's* case (24)), and no interest passes and no expulsion can
occur until immediately after the compensation is agreed or assessed, I do not
understand why the value of the land in r. (2) cases should not be assessed as at
the date when the compensation is agreed or assessed by the appropriate tribunal,
or the land is taken over, whichever is the earlier, for it is not until then that the
equitable title passes and the loss is suffered. To assess compensation on the basis E
of the value of the land at the date of the service of the notice to treat, which
today is often very many years prior to the expulsion, is grossly unfair. And not
only to the owner. In the case of leasehold interests, which are diminishing assets,
an acquiring authority might find itself compelled to pay for the remaining two
years of a lease, what had been its value fourteen years previously when the notice
to treat was served. The owner would thus be compensated for loss of the lease F
for twelve of the years during which he had in fact enjoyed it.

In 1867 it did not matter very much whether one described the date at which the
value was to be assessed as the date of the service of the notice to treat or the date
of the assessment or the date of expropriation. There would be little difference
between these dates, and in those days the value was likely to be much the same
whichever of the dates was chosen. SIR WILLIAM PAGE WOOD, V.-C., rightly G
assumed that in his day, the date of the service of the notice to treat was (25) "the
time when the house was about to be taken ". Today it is not so. Whatever may
have been the position one hundred years ago, it is, in post-war England, as
unreasonable as it is arbitrary to choose the date of the service of the notice to
treat as the date for automatically fixing the value of the expropriated land—and,
as we have seen, it leads to manifest injustice. H

Counsel for the compensating authority has argued that the present practice for
assessing value under r. (2) is not so unfair as it might seem, because the owner
has the right to take steps to have the compensation assessed as soon as he is
served with the notice to treat. No doubt he has such a right but I do not think
that that can be counted against him. After all, we are dealing with compulsory
purchase. An owner may quite naturally, to quote LORD ROMILLY, M.R., in I
Richmond v. *North London Ry. Co.* (26), desire " to keep his land, and not to part
with it for any price, if he can help it ". Why in these circumstances should he

---

(20) [1904] A.C. 461 at p. 465.
(21) [1957] 2 All E.R. 673; [1958] Ch. 329.
(22) [1963] 2 All E.R. 484; [1964] A.C. 1088.
(23) (1865), 34 L.J.Q.B. 257; *affd.* (1867), L.R. 2 H.L. 175.
(24) [1941] 1 All E.R. 480; [1941] 2 K.B. 26.
(25) (1868), L.R. 5 Eq. at p. 235.
(26) (1868), L.R. 5 Eq. 352 at p. 360.

A exercise his right to force the compensating authority to dispossess him? A man condemned to death must no doubt walk to the scaffold on the day fixed for his execution; he is not, however, obliged, even if he had the right, to present himself for execution in advance of that date. After all, he may be reprieved. And so may the owner be reprieved. Sometimes after notice to treat has been served, the acquiring authority decides not to go on or by unreasonable delay is deemed to

B have abandoned its project. (See e.g., *Grice* v. *Dudley Corpn.* (27).) It was decided in *Grice's* case (27), which was approved in the House of Lords in *Simpsons Motor Sales (London), Ltd.* v. *Hendon Corpn.* (28), that an owner's right to force on an assessment of compensation at any time after service of the notice to treat does not prevent a delay on the part of the authority in proceeding to assessment from being so unreasonable as to amount to abandonment. If the fact that the

C owner has not exercised his right to force on the assessment of compensation does not count against him for the purpose of deciding whether there has been abandonment of the notice to treat by delay on the part of the authority, I can see still less reason why it should count against the owner for the purpose of deciding the appropriate date for assessing compensation under r. (2). It can hardly be argued that it is not unfair compulsorily to deprive an owner of his

D property now at half its present value because he could have compelled the acquiring authority to dispossess him many years earlier when the value of the property was half what it now is.

The next point taken by counsel for the compensating authority, was that, even if there is no binding authority to justify the long-established practice of assessing value under r. (2) it has so long been recognised and followed that it is

E now too late to depart from it. I cannot accept this argument. No doubt there have been very many r. (2) cases during the last twenty years in which compensation has been agreed or assessed so as to cause grave injustice. I can see no reason why this state of affairs should be perpetuated. On the contrary, in my view it is now high time that this practice should be changed so that justice may be done.

The last point taken by counsel for the compensating authority was that the

F practice to which I have referred has been recognised and affirmed by the legislature. This, at first sight, is a formidable point, but I am by no means sure that it is valid. Section 57 of the Town and Country Planning Act, 1944 was passed to obviate the injustice of land compulsorily acquired for public purposes being acquired at the depressed prices current during the last war. That section provides that compensation should be

G ". . . ascertained by reference to the prices current at Mar. 31, 1939, on the assumption that the interest had at that date been subsisting as it was in fact subsisting at the time of the notice to treat, and that the land in which the interest subsisted . . . had been at that date in the state in which it in fact was at the time of the service of the notice to treat."

H By 1947 prices had risen far above those current during the war and prior to it. Accordingly, s. 50 of the Town and Country Planning Act, 1947 provided that s. 57 of the Town and Country Planning Act, 1944 should not apply to compensation in respect of a compulsory acquisition of land in pursuance of a notice to treat served after the passing of the Act of 1947. Section 14 and s. 15 of the Town and Country Planning Act 1959 made similar provisions to abrogate 1939 prices in cases where the notice to treat had been served before the date of the passing

I of the Act of 1947 and no effective steps had been taken by either party towards completion of the transaction. Section 15 enabled the person for the time being entitled to the interest in the land in respect of which such a notice had been served, in certain circumstances, to elect that compensation should be assessed as if the original notice to treat had been served on Jan. 1, 1958. Certainly the legislature did not avail itself of the opportunity of including in these statutes any

---

(27) [1957] 2 All E.R. 673.
(28) [1963] 2 All E.R. 484; [1964] A.C. 1088.

provision rescinding the practice that had hitherto prevailed in respect of r. (2)   **A**
cases. No doubt the legislature must be taken to have recognised that the practice
existed—a practice founded on no statutory enactment or decision of the courts,
but merely on obiter dicta pronounced long ago without any consideration of
the problems and injustice to which the practice now gives rise. I do not believe
that these problems or this injustice were even considered by the legislature when
the Town and Country Planning Acts of 1944, 1947 and 1959 were passed or that   **B**
any question then arose whether or not the practice should be retained. The
legislature did no more than recognise the existence of the practice. It did not,
in my view, intend to take away from the courts the power of altering the practice
should the courts conclude that the practice rested only on obiter dicta, had no
legal validity and was, in modern conditions, unjust. Accordingly, I do not think
that we ought to consider any of these Town and Country Planning Acts as giving   **C**
statutory force to the practice which in modern conditions admittedly does cause
grave injustice. This at any rate cannot be said to have been the clear intention
of the legislature and

> ". . . in construing an Act of Parliament, we ought not to put a construction
> on it that would work injustice, or even hardship, or inconvenience, unless
> it is clear that such was the intention of the legislature."   **D**

(*Tiverton and North Devon Ry. Co.* v. *Loosemore* (29), per LORD BLACKBURN).
For the reasons that I have stated, I am far from convinced of the legality of the
practice now adopted for assessing compensation in r. (2) cases or of the correctness of the two decisions at first instance on which counsel for the compensating
authority relies, viz., *Phoenix Assurance Co.* v. *Spooner* (30), and *Re Rowton House,*   **E**
Ltd.'s Leases, Square Grip Reinforcement Co. (London), Ltd. v. *Rowton Houses,*
Ltd. (31). It follows that, in my view, the argument founded on applying the
present r. (2) practice to r. (5) cases cannot prevail.

Even if I were convinced that the principles now adopted for assessing compensation in r. (2) cases is correct, I should not (as I have already indicated at the
beginning of this judgment) extend them to r. (5) cases. In no r. (5) case can   **F**
reinstatement begin on the date of the service of the notice to treat. It cannot
begin until a site has been acquired, tenders obtained and a building contract
signed. All this must necessarily take months and sometimes years. In the present
case everyone recognised that no site would become available and that no rebuilding could reasonably be expected to begin for very many years after 1947,
when the deemed notice to treat was served. It is absurd to suggest that the reas-   **G**
onable cost of equivalent reinstatement, which is the compensation to which the
claimants are entitled for the loss that they have suffered, is to be measured by
1947 site and building prices when reinstatement could not reasonably have been
begun until these prices had nearly doubled in 1961. It is quite true that it is
hardly less absurd and unjust to take a man's land and pay him by way of
compensation only half its value at the date it is taken.   **H**

Counsel for the compensating authority has argued that, if the value of the land
is to be assessed at the market price ruling at the date of the service of the notice
to treat, it is only consistent and logical to assess the cost of reinstatement by
reference to site and building costs ruling on this date. And so it may be. In my
view, however, too great a price can be paid for consistency and logic. Even if
I were obliged (which I do not think I am) to accept the unjust practice in r. (2)   **I**
cases, I would not be prepared in the name of consistency or logic to extend the
practice to r. (5) cases. I would prefer to do justice in one class of case only rather
than in neither. I would accordingly allow the appeal.

---

(29) (1884), 9 App. Cas. 480 at p. 497.
(30) [1905] 2 K.B. 753.
(31) [1966] 3 All E.R. 996; [1967] Ch. 877.

A   **SACHS, L.J.:** This appeal raises an important point as to the interpretation of r. (5) of s. 2 of the Acquisition of Land (Assessment of Compensation) Act, 1919, which sets out the rules for quantifying the compensation payable to large numbers of subjects on their property being taken from them in derogation of their pre-existing rights and against their wishes. Before examining the words of that particular section it is as well to consider what are the general principles
B   applicable to the construction of such provisions in a statute. In the first place there is the classic and much quoted passage in the speech of LORD WARRINGTON OF CLYFFE in *Colonial Sugar Refining Co., Ltd.* v. *Melbourne Harbour Trust Comrs.* (32), when he referred to

". . . the well-known principle that a statute should not be held to take away private rights of property without compensation unless the intention
C   to do so is expressed in clear and unambiguous terms."

Next there is the definition of compensation in the judgment of SCOTT, L.J., in *Horn* v. *Sunderland Corpn.* (33), where he said:

". . . what it gives to the owner compelled to sell is compensation—the right to be put, so far as money can do it, in the same position as if his land
D   had not been taken from him. In other words, he gains the right to receive a money payment not less than the loss imposed on him in the public interest, but, on the other hand, no greater."

That definition, was cited with approval by PEARSON, L.J., in *Hull & Humber Investment Co., Ltd.* v. *Hull Corpn.* (34), and as he there stated: " It is a very simple principle, when certain largely verbal complications have been cleared
E   out of the way ".

Thirdly it is plain that, where (as all too frequently happens) a statute provides for the subject to be paid something materially less than compensation as above defined, it is in truth depriving the subject of compensation in the sense that that word is used in common parlance and as above defined. (That a particular statute may blandly apply the word " compensation " to some payment which no
F   man in his senses would regard as reasonable compensation is not in point). It follows that no statute which provides for compensation to be paid should be construed so as to cause the subject to be paid sums materially less than an amount which conforms to the definition given by SCOTT, L.J., unless the statute clearly compels such a construction.

The foregoing principles were each in turn inevitably conceded by counsel for
G   the compensating authority as being applicable to the Acquisition of Land (Assessment of Compensation) Act, 1919. They are in substance merely sub-heads of a principle mentioned by LORD BLACKBURN in his speech in *Tiverton and North Devon Ry. Co.* v. *Loosemore* (35), viz.:

". . . in construing an Act of Parliament we ought not to put a construction on it that would work injustice, or even hardship, or inconvenience unless it
H   is clear that such was the intention of the legislature."

With that preface it is now convenient to turn to the relevant part of s. 2 of the Act of 1919, an amending (not a consolidating) Act, which for the first time laid down general rules for the assessment of compensation in cases where land was compulsorily acquired. That part reads:

I   " 2. In assessing compensation an official arbitrator shall act in accordance with the following rules: . . . (5) Where land is, and but for the compulsory acquisition would continue to be, devoted to a purpose of such a nature that there is no general demand or market for land for that purpose, the compensation may, if the official arbitrator is satisfied that reinstatement in

(32) [1927] A.C. 343 at p. 359.
(33) [1941] 1 All E.R. at p. 491; [1941] 2 K.B. at p. 42.
(34) [1965] 1 All E.R. at p. 433; [1965] 2 Q.B. at pp. 160, 161.
(35) (1884), 9 App. Cas. at p. 497.

some other place is bona fide intended, be assessed on the basis of the reason-   **A**
able cost of equivalent reinstatement."

It is as well to note at the outset that the opening words of the section refer to
" compensation " and that neither in those words nor in r. (5) do the words
" value of the land " appear. Also to be observed is the use in r. (5) of the word
" may ".

In this appeal the short issue is whether the " cost " means (a) the cost at the   **B**
date of the notice to treat (here a " deemed " notice), at which time there is
normally not the slightest possibility of the necessary work being commenced
because there is no site available, and, a fortiori, no architect's plans for the
reinstatement work, or (b) the cost at the date (agreed as between the parties in
this particular case) at which reinstatement might first reasonably have been
begun.   **C**

As a matter not only of first impression but of any considered approach untrammelled by authority, the second construction is plainly right, and the first
obviously wrong—whatever be the course of building costs between the two dates.
If by the second date the costs have risen, the owner most unjustly does not get
true compensation at all if (a) is accepted, and if they have fallen, the authority
unjustly has to pay too much. So any other view is bound to involve a contra-   **D**
vention of at least one of the principles already stated.

In the face of the manifest cogency of the case against the cost being taken at
the date of the notice to treat, and the absurd injustice of so taking it in the present
case (both of which counsel for the compensating authority clearly felt it difficult
to contest), the submissions for the authority that this court was bound to
decide in favour of the first construction not unnaturally, in the absence of any   **E**
direct authority binding this court on the point in issue, took a lengthy and
devious course which I will later examine; for my part I found the arguments
singularly unconvincing depite the care and erudition with which they were
pressed. By way of convenient shorthand I will for the remainder of this judgment refer to the product of the first construction as the " deemed cost " and the
product of the second as the " actual cost ". To avoid semantics of the type   **F**
faintly raised in argument as to the words " actual cost ", it is as well to mention
the obvious, i.e., that whichever date be the relevant one the tribunal concerned
with the assessment of cost will only occasionally have before it complete evidence
as to what has been paid for all that has to be bought or done and thus in the vast
majority of cases will become involved in considering expert evidence on what
that cost probably will be or probably would have been on that relevant date—   **G**
and will have in the end the normal task of forming an appropriate assessment on
that evidence. If by good fortune it does have before it the best evidence of the
type above referred to, then, to use the words of LORD MACNAGHTEN in *Bwllfa
and Merthyr Dare Steam Collieries (1891), Ltd.* v. *Pontypridd Waterworks Co.* (36):

" If the question goes to arbitration, the arbitrator's duty is to determine   **H**
the amount of compensation payable. In order to enable him to come to a
just and true conclusion it is his duty, I think, to avail himself of all information at hand at the time of making his award, which may be laid before him.
Why should he listen to conjecture on a matter which has become an accom-
plished fact? Why should he guess when he can calculate? With the light
before him, why should he shut his eyes and grope in the dark?"   **I**

Turning now to the agreed facts of the present case, it is as well not only to
state what they are but also to make clear what points are not raised by them,
particularly as the latter could have involved issues which are in this instance
not before this court—though that has not precluded them from being canvassed.
The scheme which resulted in the deemed notice to treat was one propounded by
the compensating authority Birmingham City Council, for a major development

---

(36) [1900-03] All E.R. Rep. 600 a t p. 603; [1903] A.C. 426 at p. 432.

A under the provisions of the Town & Country Planning Act, 1944, which was the subject of what was perhaps euphemistically termed a "purchase order providing for expedited completion". It involved no less than 981 acres.

The relevant order was confirmed on June 26, 1947, and registered in the local land register on Aug. 14, 1947, which thus became the date of the deemed notice to treat (see s. 18 (3) (*b*) of the Act of 1944). It was a vast and progressive scheme
B which, despite the fact that the order provided for expedited completion, all concerned well knew would take many years to complete. Such schemes with similar time lags between the order and completion have for long been a part of the normal town planning scene. It so happens that twenty years later this particular scheme is not yet complete; but whether that particular time lag is or is not abnormal matters not—for the principle involved is no different whether
C the time lags are normally five, fifteen or twenty-five years. So far as the claimants are concerned, the compensating authority—as the church authorities in the relevant area well knew—was not in a position to offer alternative sites for resinstatement of churches during the years which immediately succeeded 1947. Indeed, it was unable to take this essential step (which is one normally taken by local authorities in parallel cases) until 1957, and it was not until
D September, 1958, that a site was allocated to the claimants.

The next, and important, fact is that Apr. 30, 1961, has been specifically agreed between the parties as the date on which reinstatement might reasonably have been begun by the claimants. This date was obviously fixed with due regard to the period that must necessarily elapse between the receipt of notice of allocation of a site and the time work can commence, to give the claimants reasonable time
E for such steps as considering the situation created by the allocation, commissioning an architect, the preparation of plans, the obtaining of planning permits, and the obtaining and examination of estimates and the placing of contracts.

It is to be noted, first, that Apr. 30, 1961, differs from the date, June 24, 1963, when by virtue of a vesting declaration the property in the chapel vested in the compensating authority, and it differs even more from the date at the end
F of 1965 when work on the new chapel actually commenced: in other words, agreement was reached on a point which would otherwise have had to be left to arbitration—the reasonable period which must elapse in the particular case before reinstatement work can start. It is secondly to be noted that this period was about $2\frac{1}{2}$ years, and that presumably some such period would have had to elapse before work started even if an alternative site for the chapel had been available
G on the date of the deemed notice to treat. No suggestion has been made in this case, nor could it have been in view of the agreement as to the facts, that there was some earlier date when the claimants could in practice have commenced work.

Next it is to be observed that this court is dealing with the case of a particular freehold which was agreed to fall within the description of land to which r. (5)
H could apply, and that it is agreed to be a case where the exercise of such discretion as may be embodied in the use of the words "may . . . be assessed" ought correctly to be exercised by making a r. (5) assessment "on the basis of the reasonable cost of reinstatement". These two points need to be emphasised because so much of the argument concerned possible cases of very differing types,
I for instance, leases with but a few years to run. For my part, I found but little assistance from such cases, especially as both parties made their submissions on the basis that the above-mentioned phrase "may" imported a discretion—which clearly might result on some basis other than r. (5) being adopted in some of those cases put forward for academic consideration.

Next there is the particularly important agreement between the parties (set out in para. 8 of the decision of the Lands Tribunal), in these terms:

"The claimants and [compensating authority] agree that the sums set out

below are the total proper amounts of compensation payable by the [com-   A
pensating authority] to the claimants in relation to the dates against which
they are set, namely: Aug. 14, 1947: £50,025; Apr. 30, 1961: £89,575.''

The court was informed by counsel that in each of those sums there was included
£5,025 being a sum calculated at the prices prevailing in 1961 to cover such
expenses as those entailed in the physical removal of chattels (e.g., pews) from
the old chapel to the new one, the removing and re-erecting of the organ, and the   B
issue of pamphlets and literature to the congregation. It follows that the '' proper
amounts of compensation '' for those costs which are in issue before this court (the
calculation of which differs according to whether they should be deemed costs or
actual costs) varies as between £45,000 and £84,550—the increase over the relevant fourteen years being of the order of ninety per cent. How grave would be
the injustice if deemed costs provide the correct measure of compensation could   C
hardly be better illustrated.

Finally it is to be noted in connexion with those two agreed figures that nothing
is said as to whether any percentage of the true cost has been deducted on account
of the age of the original chapel or its state of repair. Agreement having been
reached as to proper amounts payable, there is no need, to my mind, to examine
the submissions made in this court as to whether or not some and, if some, what   D
allowance of this nature should in some and what circumstances be made. It is,
however, clear that, if material deductions were to be made because of the
age of the original buildings, the whole object of r. (5) would be defeated, at
least so far as buildings owned by charities which have no other capital assets
are concerned; and the extinction of the charity would in many cases be ensured
by a rule that was obviously intended to enable them to survive.   E

Once there have been eliminated from consideration those points which are
not before the court, the essential facts of the present case are manifestly as
straightforward as is the issue. The injustice of applying the deemed costs basis is
about as clear as could be, and to hold that it applies would do no credit to the
legislature or indeed to the courts—unless the legislature has made plain an
intention to effect an injustice.   F

How then does the compensating authority put its case for insisting on the
deemed cost basis? No authority was cited from among the decisions of the
High Court of this country or of any parallel courts of Scotland or Northern
Ireland that r. (5) must be construed as relating to deemed costs. Reliance however was placed on a decision in 1952 by a single member of the Lands Tribunal
in *Aston Charities Trust, Ltd.* v. *Stepney Borough Council* (37). It was a briefly   G
expressed decision on what seems not to have been the main issue in the case.
It appears to have been followed in other cases heard by other members of that
tribunal on the basis that they were bound to follow it. It am in full agreement
with what has been said by my lords deprecating the practice of the tribunal
of following without further consideration decisions of its own members; indeed,
I find it difficult to see why all the individual members of that tribunal should   H
invariably and for ever unquestioningly bow the knee to the decisions of any
single one of their colleagues, however distinguished, when even High Court
judges are not bound blindly to follow each other's judgments. Such a practice
can produce unfortunate results.

The *Aston* case (37) not being an authority that in any way binds the High
Court, the compensating authority fell back on an assertion that, having regard   I
to the way r. (2) is applied to cases falling within it, the word '' cost '' in r. (5)
must necessarily be construed as referring to deemed cost. Rule (2), so far as
relevant, reads:

'' The value of land shall, subject as hereinafter provided be taken to be the
amount which the land if sold in the open market by a willing seller might
be expected to realise: . . .''

---

(37) (1952), 2 P. & C.R. 289; *affd.* [1952] 2 All E.R. 228; [1952] 2 Q.B. 642.

A It is undoubtedly the fact for the purposes of r. (2) that the " value of land " has now for many years been assessed as at the date of the notice to treat. Whether the rule that has been followed is one of practice or one of law and whether in either case the rule is binding on this court is a matter to which I will advert later. That this rule has for years produced much manifest injustice is not open to question, and the point for examination is whether the court must so construe

B r. (5) as to produce a parallel injustice. The submission that both rules relate to calculations to be made on the basis of prices ruling at the date of the notice to treat seemed in the end to rest on the following contention. The true objective of s. 2 was to arrive at the value of the land to be acquired by the local authority; all calculations under the relevant rules should be made on the basis of one set of prices; and as r. (2) prices are taken at the date of notice to treat, so must r. (5)

C prices.

The fallacy of that contention lies in the fact that the true objective of s. 2 is to assess proper compensation. Where r. (2) applies, the value of the land referred to in it is not the compensation to be paid; it is only an element—though normally the preponderating element—in the sum payable by way of compensation. In such cases one normally adds two elements together to produce the latter

D sum; one is the value of the land, the other the amount payable under r. (6) for disturbance—an amount calculated on the basis of actual cost and not deemed cost (*London County Council* v. *Tobin* (38) in the Court of Appeal; and *Bailey* v. *Derby Corpn.* (39), in the Court of Appeal). Similarly in pre-1919 cases it is clear that the value of the land acquired was no more than something to which regard had to be had (see s. 63 of the Lands Clauses Consolidation Act, 1845)

E and thus constituted an element in the sum payable by way of compensation but not necessarily the whole of that sum. Once it is appreciated that the value of the land is only an element in the compensation to be paid, the fallacy underlying this much pressed contention of the compensating authority becomes apparent. I would only add that the use of the phrases " value of land " and " price of land " with varying meanings in some authorities may have obscured this otherwise

F manifest point.

Quite apart from such effect as it may have on that contention of the compensating authority the mere fact that r. (6) provides for an actual cost element in compensation (an element applicable to the bulk of what have been in argument styled r. (2) cases, but which in reality are normally r. (2) plus r. (6) cases) makes it to my mind difficult to the point of impossibility to say that there is anything

G illogical or wrong in r. (5) also providing for the actual cost as a basis for compensation. A further and no less formidable point is that r. (2) and r. (5) are concerned with entirely different concepts—the former with value of what is taken away, the latter with the cost of what is to be provided in its place. Why the latter should unnecessarily be so interpreted as to produce injustice I cannot understand; the argument that because r. (2) by present practice does produce in-

H justice and therefore it is wrong to allow r. (5) to work fairly is singularly unattractive. Indeed, so clear is it that r. (5) must refer to actual cost that it is not necessary to fall back on the principle that, if there were an ambiguity in the rule, it must be resolved so as not to produce injustice.

Having regard to these conclusions, it is not strictly necessary for me to pass an opinion on the much canvassed issue whether in r. (2) cases the " value of land "

I be assessed as at the date of notice to treat. Out of deference, however, to the many hours of sustained submissions devoted to this point, it seems proper to say something about it. Such assessments having for many years been so consistently made on that basis, it is clear that a rule to that effect has developed. That the rule regularly works much injustice is clear; but it is not so clear whether the rule is one of practice or of law or in either case whether it has become binding on this court.

(38) [1959] 1 All E.R. 649.
(39) [1965] 1 All E.R. 443.

A close analysis of the authorities shows that it originates from dicta in cases **A**
under the Lands Clauses Consolidation Act, 1845 (in what would now be r. (2)
cases), where the court was not asked to consider an issue as to any difference
between the deemed cost and the actual cost—and where indeed on the facts
it is highly improbable that any such issue could have existed. Moreover, those
dicta originated at a time when it was considered that, under the Lands Consolidation Clauses Act, 1845 procedure, the notice to treat produced for the purposes **B**
of assessment of compensation substantially the same effect as a contract between
the local authoity and the owner of the land.   Whether or not that view was
correct vis-à-vis the procedure under the Act of 1845, it has now been held not to
be correct vis-à-vis the procedure under the Act of 1919 (*Grice v. Dudley Corpn.*
(40), and *Simpsons Motor Sales (London), Ltd.* v. *Hendon Corpn.* (41); and see
also the Court of Appeal report of this case (42)). In those circumstances it is at **C**
least arguable that it is open to this court to review the question whether the value
of land must in law necessarily always be assessed as at the date of notice to
treat. Having had the considerable advantage of reading the judgment of SALMON,
L.J., it is sufficient for me to say that I am in general agreement with the views
which he has expressed on this issue and do not feel able usefully to add anything
save to venture a hope that it is not too late for the courts to remedy the injustices **D**
at present being worked in the name of what in argument was referred to as
" the sacred cow of r. (2) ".

Of the many further points canvassed before this court, I would single out but
one—as to the effect of an owner allowing his property to go into disrepair between
the date of notice to treat and the date the reinstatement can first commence.
The problem of state of repair in relation to the cost of reinstatement must always **E**
exist in r. (5) cases (whatever be the date to which the word " cost " refers)
and has not been put in issue in the present case. I thus merely note that in
relation to that word of paramount importance " compensation ", counsel for
the claimants conceded that, if the claimants in fact save money by purposely
allowing disrepair, that could be taken into general account against them when
assessing the final sum. **F**

In conclusion, it is perhaps apposite to recall that some eighty years ago LORD
HALSBURY, L.C. (see *Inland Revenue Comrs.* v. *Glasgow & South Western Ry.
Co.* (43)) commented on " a whole nomenclature " having been " invented by
gentlemen who devote themselves to the consideration of such questions ", and
went on to say, " we, however, must be guided by what the language of the
legislature is ". **G**

Had he been present in July at the hearing before this court, he might have
added a few words as to the introvert rules of practice built up by those concerned with the assessment of compensation, and emphasised that the duty of
the courts today is the same as it then was. Indeed, it might be no bad thing if
the tribunal concerned with such cases felt able from time to time to take a
reviewing look at rules of practice it has, perhaps under the persuasion of **H**
practitioners, evolved when assessing compensation—with an eye to considering
whether they conform to the intentions of the legislature to provide proper
compensation. I would allow the appeal.

*Appeal allowed. Leave to appeal to the House of Lords granted on terms that the
compensating authority do not seek to disturb the court's order as to costs.*

Solicitors: *Ellis & Fairbairn* (for the claimants); *Town Clerk*, Birmingham **I**
(for the compensating authority).

[*Reported by* F. A. AMIES, ESQ., *Barrister-at-Law.*]

---

(40) [1957] 2 All E.R. 673; [1958] 1 Ch. 329.
(41) [1963] 2 All E.R. at p. 488; [1964] A.C. at p. 1117.
(42) [1962] 3 All E.R. 75 at p. 80; [1963] Ch. 57 at p. 82.
(43) (1887), 12 App. Cas. 315 at p. 321.

A
R. *v.* AREA COMMITTEE No. 14 (LONDON WEST) LEGAL AID AREA, *Ex parte* DHARGALKAR.

[COURT OF APPEAL, CIVIL DIVISION (Lord Denning, M.R., Diplock and Edmund Davies, L.JJ.), November 2, 1967.]

B
Legal Aid—Certificate—Discharge—Assisted person's requiring unreasonable conduct of proceedings causing unjustifiable expense—Solicitor and counsel still acting for assisted person—Discharge under reg. 12 (3) (*b*)—*Whether that or reg.* 12 (2) (*d*) *applicable—Legal Aid (General) Regulations,* 1962 (*S.I.* 1962 *No.* 148), *reg.* 12 (2) (*d*), (3) (*b*).

The applicant obtained two civil aid certificates. On July 5, 1967, the area committee of the legal aid area notified her that they would consider
C
whether these certificates should be discharged under reg. 12 (3) (*b*)* of the Legal Aid (General) Regulations, 1962, on the ground that, in the committee's opinion, the applicant was "requiring the proceedings to be conducted unreasonably so as to incur an unjustifiable expense to the legal aid fund". These words, quoted from the letter, were words that were in reg. 12 (2) (*d*)†, not reg. 12 (3) (*b*). On July 17, 1967, the applicant attended before the
D
area committee and presented her case. On July 18, 1967, the area committee wrote, telling the applicant that they had discharged the certificates. Solicitor and counsel were still acting for the applicant at the time. On application for leave to move for an order of certiorari to quash the area committee's decision,

Held: reg. 12 (3) (*b*) and reg. 12 (2) (*d*) were not mutually exclusive, and,
E
if solicitor and counsel were still acting, a civil aid certificate could be discharged under reg. 12 (3) (*b*) on the ground that the proceedings were being required to be conducted unreasonably so as to cause unjustifiable expense, though if solicitor or counsel were not acting at the time the certificate could be discharged under reg. 12 (2) (*d*) on the same ground; in the present case the applicant had had sufficient notice and the certificates
F
were validly discharged under reg. 12 (3) (*b*) (see p. 227, letters E and I, and p. 228, letters H and I, post).

Appeal dismissed.

[As to the discharge of civil aid certificates by area committees, see 30 HALSBURY'S LAWS (3rd Edn.) 520, 521, paras. 980, 981; and for cases on such certificates, see DIGEST (PRACTICE) (Repl.) 488-491, *1711-1729.*
G
For the Legal Aid (General) Regulations, 1962, reg. 12, see 5 HALSBURY'S STATUTORY INSTRUMENTS (First Re-Issue) 233.]

Appeal.

This was an appeal by the applicant, Jean Dhargalkar, from a decision of the Divisional Court of the Queen's Bench Division, refusing her leave to apply for an order of certiorari to quash decisions of the Area Committee No. 14 (London
H
West) Legal Aid Area made on July 18, 1967, discharging two civil aid certificates granted to the applicant. The grounds of the application for leave to apply for certiorari were as follows:—(A) (i) want of jurisdiction, in that the area committee in discharging the certificates did not purport to act, and did not act, on any one or more of the grounds provided in reg. 12 of the Legal Aid (General) Regulations, 1962; (ii) discharging the certificates when the ground of
I
discharge to which the area committee referred to was applicable only to one certificate; (B) acting without any evidence on which to found decision, and (C) reaching conclusions on the facts without giving the applicant an opportunity to be heard. The facts are set out in the judgment of LORD DENNING, M.R.

J. F. F. Platts-Mills, Q.C., and *L. J. Blom-Cooper* for the applicant.
John K. Wood for the Law Society.

---

* Regulation 12 (3) (*b*), so far as material, is set out at p. 227, letter C, post.
† Regulation 12 (2) (*d*), so far as material, is set out at p. 226, letter I, to p. 227, letter A, post.

LORD DENNING, M.R.: In 1959 the applicant, Mrs. Dhargalkar, was   A
studying social science at the University of Hull. She had an operation for
appendicitis. There were complications which included toxæmia and delirium.
She was sent to a mental health hospital and was there for a few weeks. She
was very upset about her treatment and she sought to bring legal actions. In
the first place, she wanted to bring an action against the persons who caused her
to be sent to a mental home and detained there; but under s. 141 of the Mental   B
Health Act, 1959, she could not bring proceedings against them except by leave
of the court. She applied to ROSKILL, J., for leave but he refused it. She
wished to appeal from his decision to the Court of Appeal. In the second place,
she wanted to bring an action against the surgeon and the hospital authorities
for negligence in performing the operation. She did not need leave for that
action. She could bring it without the leave of the court. She obtained civil   C
aid certificates enabling her to proceed with those two matters. In 1963 she
was given a legal aid certificate in the mental matter enabling her to appeal to
the Court of Appeal from the decision of ROSKILL, J. In 1966 she was given a
civil aid certificate in the negligence matter enabling her to continue an action
against the surgeon and the hospital authorities. She was given a solicitor and
counsel.   D
    The area committee of the legal aid area have recently taken away her legal
aid. They have discharged these two civil aid certificates. Now counsel for
the applicant contends that their action in discharging them is unlawful, and
he applies for an order of certiorari to quash the discharge of them and thus to
restore the certificates. The steps leading to the discharge were these. On
July 5, 1967, the committee wrote to the applicant referring to the civil aid   E
certificates and stating:

    " They have resolved that they should consider whether or not these
    certificates should be discharged under reg. 12 (3) (b) of the Legal Aid (General)
    Regulations, 1962 (1), having regard to the fact that, in the committee's
    opinion, you are requiring the proceedings to be conducted unreasonably
    so as to incur an unjustifiable expense to the legal aid fund."   F

She wrote a letter on July 6, asking for an explanation. The committee replied
on July 10:

    " Your solicitors have reported to the committee that you have failed to
    accept leading counsel's advice which has been explained to you and argued
    about on numerous occasions at conference and that you have persisted in   G
    visiting counsel's chambers and seeking to discuss matters with counsel
    without your solicitor's knowledge or consent."

The committee gave her notice that they would consider the case on July 17.
On that day the applicant attended in person and was given an opportunity of
presenting her case. After hearing her, the committee decided to discharge the
certificates. On July 18, the area secretary wrote telling her that the area   H
committee had discharged the certificates issued to her. Those documents
constitute the record of the proceedings. Counsel for the applicant says that
there is an error of law on the face of the record. He says that the relevant
regulations were not fulfilled. He contends that, although the committee
purported to act under reg. 12 (3) (b), they in fact acted under reg. 12 (2) (d)
and did not fulfil the requirements of that regulation. He points out that her   I
solicitor and counsel were still acting for her at the time. I must refer, therefore,
to these regulations.
    Regulation 12 (2) (d) provides that the appropriate area committee *may*
discharge a certificate

    " where the assisted person's solicitor or counsel has given up the case and
    the area committee are satisfied that the assisted person has required the

(1) S.I. 1962 No. 148.

A claim to be asserted or disputed, or the proceedings to be conducted, unreasonably so as to incur an unjustifiable expense to the fund or has required unreasonably that the claim be continued to be asserted or disputed or the proceedings be continued: . . . ."

Counsel for the applicant says that if you look at the very words of the letter of
B July 5, 1967, you will see they use the very words of reg. 12 (2) (*d*). The letter charges the applicant with " requiring the proceedings to be conducted unreasonably so as to incur an unjustifiable expense to the legal aid fund ". That shows, he says, that the committee are acting under reg. 12 (2) (*d*); and that regulation was not fulfilled because the assisted person's solicitor or counsel has not given up the case as required by that regulation.

C Regulation 12 (3) provides that

" The appropriate area committee *shall* discharge a certificate if— . . . (*b*) as a result of any information coming to their knowledge they consider that the assisted person no longer has reasonable grounds for asserting or disputing the claim or for taking, defending or being a party to the proceedings, or that it is unreasonable in the particular circumstances for him
D to continue to receive legal aid . . ."

The committee say that they acted under that regulation, because they considered that it was unreasonable for the applicant to continue to receive legal aid; and that is why they specified reg. 12 (3) (*b*) in this letter.

If these two regulations were mutually exclusive, I should be in favour of
E counsel for the applicant's argument; but I do not think that they are. There is a very considerable overlap: so much so that the same conduct may be brought under either regulation. Thus, if a person requires the proceedings to be conducted unreasonably so as to cause an unjustifiable expense to be incurred, then, if the solicitor and counsel are still acting, the committee can discharge the certificate under reg. 12 (3) (*b*). But if the solicitor or counsel has given up the
F case, the committee can discharge the certificate under reg. 12 (2) (*d*). In support of this view, I would give as an instance the common case where the defendant has made a very good offer of settlement which the plaintiff (the assisted person) unreasonably refuses to accept. If his own solicitor or counsel thinks that he is being unreasonable, he can give up the case and draw the matter to the attention of the committee, who can discharge the certificate under reg. 12 (2) (*d*);
G but if it is the other side who think that his conduct is unreasonable, in which case they can draw it to the attention of the committee, who can discharge the certificate under reg. 12 (3) (*b*) even though his own solicitor and counsel are still acting.

It is true that the power of the committee under reg. 12 (2) (*d*) is discretionary: whereas under reg. 12 (3) (*b*) it is mandatory. But I do not think too much
H should be made of that difference. Even under reg. 12 (3) (*b*) the committee are given a wide latitude, seeing that its operation depends on what they " consider ".

On the true interpretation of the letter of July 5, 1967, I think that these certificates were discharged under reg. 12 (3) (*b*) and that the applicant was given sufficient notice. It is true that the letter charged her with " requiring
I the proceedings to be conducted unreasonably " (which are the actual words of reg. 12 (2) (*d*)). Nevertheless, those words are apt and suitable also to show that it was " unreasonable in the particular circumstances for [her] to continue to receive legal aid " (which are the words of reg. 12 (3) (*b*)). The subsequent letter of July 10 gave her full particulars of the case against her. It said that she had not accepted legal advice and had caused much difficulty by her behaviour. Those are particular circumstances which may make it unreasonable for her to continue to receive legal aid. In the circumstances I am satisfied that she had sufficient notice of the charge against her. The area committee

acted within their jurisdiction and in accordance with the law.   I see no reason **A**
for interfering with their decision.   This application for certiorari should be
refused.

      DIPLOCK, L.J.: I agree with the judgment which LORD DENNING, M.R.,
has delivered.

      It is quite impossible, reading reg. 12 (2) and (3) of the Legal Aid (General)
Regulations, 1962, to come to the conclusion that reg. 12 (2) (*d*) and reg. 12 (3) (*b*) **B**
are mutually exclusive.   It would make nonsense of the regulation.   It is, at
first sight, curious, that being so, that reg. 12 (2) should in form be permissive,
" the appropriate area committee *may* discharge a certificate ", and reg. 12 (3)
should appear to be mandatory, " the appropriate area committee *shall* discharge
a certificate ".   On the other hand, while that is appropriate so far as reg. 12
(3) (*a*) is concerned, since reg. 12 (3) (*b*) provides if " as a result of any information **C**
coming to their knowledge they consider ", they have, it seems to me, a
discretion under reg. 12 (3) (*b*) which is difficult to distinguish from the discretion
given them by the word " may " in reg. 12 (2).   It seems to me likely that
reg. 12 (2) (*d*) takes the form that it does in view of the provisions of reg. 15 (8)
to (10), which deal with the right of a solicitor or counsel to give up a case.
Regulation 15 (8) provides: **D**

    " Without prejudice to the right of solicitors or counsel to give up a case
    for good reason, any solicitor or counsel may give up an assisted person's
    case if, in *his* opinion, the assisted person has required it to be conducted
    unreasonably so as to incur an unjustifiable expense to the fund or has
    required unreasonably that the case be continued."

That reflects back, of course, to reg. 12 (2) (*d*).   Regulation 15 (9) provides that **E**
when a solicitor or counsel exercises the right, he must make a report to the area
committee.   Regulation 15 (10) makes it plain (again reflecting back, I think,
to reg. 12 (2) (*d*)) that the area committee are not bound by the opinion of the
solicitor or counsel who gave up the case but must make up their own mind on
the matter.   Regulation 15 (10) provides: **F**

    " Where an area committee to whom such report is made do not discharge
    the assisted person's certificate under the provisions of reg. 12, they shall
    require the assisted person to select another solicitor from the appropriate
    panel to act for him . . ."

So that the purpose of reg. 12 (2) (*d*) is that where counsel or solicitor has formed
an opinion that the assisted person has been acting unreasonably in the manner **G**
there described, and has for that reason exercised his right to give up the case,
the area committee must consider the matter and make up their own mind
whether they are satisfied that the assisted person has so acted.

      I cannot commend the drafting of the regulations either for literary style or
for the accuracy of legal drafting; but I think that their meaning is tolerably
clear.   I agree that this application should be dismissed. **H**

      EDMUND DAVIES, L.J.: I agree.   I am satisfied that there can be an
overlap of reg. 12 (2) (*d*) and reg. 12 (3) (*b*) of the Legal Aid (General) Regulations,
1962.   One example of that overlap is where the assisted person requires " the
proceedings to be conducted, unreasonably so as to incur an unjustifiable expense
to the fund ", a set of circumstances which falls under both provisions, even **I**
though those very words do not expressly appear in reg. 12 (3) (*b*).   The proviso
to reg. 12 (3) (*b*) requires that a certificate shall not be discharged until notice
has been served on the assisted person, and, that the person in the present case,
having sought information as to the grounds on which the area committee was
proceeding, it is true that in stating those grounds the committee used the
ipsissima verba of reg. 12 (2) (*d*).   But they did not thereby make the proceedings
themselves other than under reg. 12 (3) (*b*).   I am satisfied that it was under
reg. 12 (3) (*b*) provision that the area committee proceeded.

A   Having had the benefit of both counsel's submissions, I, too, see nothing wrong in the procedure adopted here, and would accordingly dismiss this application.

Application dismissed.   Leave to appeal to the House of Lords refused.

Solicitors: *Ambrose Appelbe* (for the appellant);   *A. M. V. Panton, Area Secretary, No. 14 (London West) Legal Aid Area* (for the Law Society).

B   [*Reported by* F. GUTTMAN, ESQ., *Barrister-at-Law.*]

CHIC FASHIONS (WEST WALES), LTD. *v.* JONES.

C   [COURT OF APPEAL, CIVIL DIVISION (Lord Denning, M.R., Diplock and Salmon, L.JJ.), November 15, 16, December 12, 1967.]

Police—Search warrant—Seizure of goods believed on reasonable grounds to be stolen goods—Goods seized not of manufacture specified in warrant—Constable entered company's premises and seized goods of other manufacture believing on reasonable grounds them to be stolen goods received by an officer or officers of the company—Explanation subsequently made on behalf of company and
D *accepted by police and goods returned—Whether police liable in action for trespass to goods.*

Where police officers, having lawfully entered the premises of a company, have reasonable grounds for believing that goods on the premises are stolen goods and may be relevant evidence for the prosecution of the company's managing director or other responsible officer on a charge of stealing or of
E receiving stolen goods, the police are entitled to seize the goods and to detain them until the prosecution has been heard and determined or so long as reasonable grounds for believing that such a charge will lie and be prosecuted remain (see p. 236, letter G, p. 237, letters D and G, p. 238, letter H, and p. 241, letter D, post).

Crozier v. *Cundey* ((1827), 9 Dow. & Ry. K.B. 224) considered.

F   Police had reasonable grounds for believing that items of clothing in the plaintiff company's shop had been stolen and would be material evidence on a criminal charge against the company or their officers. The police obtained a search warrant in respect of clothing manufactured by a particular manufacturer. They entered the premises and searched. They found items of property which they reasonably believed to be stolen property, but the items were all
G made by other manufacturers than the manufacturer named on the warrant. They seized these goods. The plaintiff company gave an explanation which the police accepted and they returned the goods. In an action by the plaintiff company for damages, the cause of action lying in trespass,

Held: the police were not liable (see p. 237, letter A, p. 239, letter H, and p. 241, letter H, post).

H   Per SALMON, L.J.: I incline to the view that, if a policeman finds property which he reasonably believes to be stolen in the possession of a person whom he has no reasonable grounds to believe to be criminally implicated, the policeman has no common law right to seize the property (see p. 241, letter F, post).

Appeal allowed.

I   [As to a constable's power of entry, and his protection in the execution of warrants, see 30 HALSBURY'S LAWS (3rd Edn.) 130, 131, paras. 209, 210; as to powers of arrest at common law, and as to search warrants, see 10 ibid., 344, para. 636, and pp. 356-358, paras. 652, 653; and for cases on the subject of search and search warrants, see 14 DIGEST (Repl.) 211, 212, *1767-1777.*]

Cases referred to:

Bessell v. *Wilson*, (1853), 1 E. & B. 492, n.; 22 L.J.M.C. 94, 95, n.; 20 L.T.O.S. 233, n.; 118 E.R. 518; 14 Digest (Repl.) 192, *1566.*

Canadian Pacific Wine Co. v. *Tuley*, [1921] 2 A.C. 417; 90 L.J.P.C. 233; **A**
    126 L.T. 78; 46 Digest (Repl.) 375, *181.*

Christie v. *Leachinsky*, [1947] 1 All E.R. 567; [1947] A.C. 573; [1947] L.J.R.
    757; 176 L.T. 443; 111 J.P. 224; 14 Digest (Repl.) 204, *1691.*

Cowles v. *Dunbar and Callow*, (1827), 2 C. & P. 565; 172 E.R. 257; 14 Digest
    (Repl.) 195, *1599.*

Crozier v. *Cundey*, (1827), 6 B. & C. 232; 5 L.J.O.S.M.C. 50; 108 E.R. 439; **B**
    9 Dow. & Ry. K.B. 224; 14 Digest (Repl.) 212, *1773.*

Dillon v. *O'Brien and Davis*, (1887), 16 Cox, C.C. 245; 14 Digest (Repl.) 193,
    *972.

Elias v. *Pasmore*, [1934] All E.R. Rep. 380; [1934] 2 K.B. 164; 103 L.J.K.B.
    223; 150 L.T. 438; 98 J.P. 92; 14 Digest (Repl.) 212, *1776.*

Entick v. *Carrington*, (1765), 2 Wils. 275; 95 E.R. 807; 19 State Tr. 1029; **C**
    14 Digest (Repl.) 211, *1767.*

Fowler v. *Lanning*, [1959] 1 All E.R. 290; [1959] 1 Q.B. 426; [1959] 2 W.L.R.
    241; 46 Digest (Repl.) 416, *593.*

Haynes v. *G. Harwood & Son*, [1934] All E.R. Rep. 103; [1935] 1 K.B. 146;
    104 L.J.K.B. 63; 152 L.T. 121; 36 Digest (Repl.) 151, *795.*

Letang v. *Cooper*, [1964] 2 All E.R. 929; [1965] 1 Q.B. 232; [1964] 3 W.L.R. **D**
    573; Digest (Cont. Vol. B) 498, *146a.*

Price v. *Messenger*, (1800), 2 Bos. & P. 158; 126 E.R. 1213; 38 Digest (Repl.)
    69, *455.*

Pringle v. *Bremner and Stirling*, (1867), 5 Macph. (H. of L.) 55.

Semayne's Case, (1604), 5 Co. Rep. 91a; 15 Digest (Repl.) 978, *9523.*

Six Carpenters' Case, (1610), 8 Co. Rep. 146a; 77 E.R. 695; 18 Digest (Repl.) **E**
    314, *591.*

Sommersett's Case, (1772), 20 State Tr. 1; sub nom. *Somerset* v. *Stewart*, Lofft. 1;
    98 E.R. 499; 45 Digest (Repl.) 387, *44.*

Ward v. *T. E. Hopkins & Son, Ltd. Baker* v. *T. E. Hopkins & Son, Ltd.*, [1959]
    3 All E.R. 225; [1959] 1 W.L.R. 996; Digest (Cont. Vol. A) 1188,
    1016a.   **F**

Wiltshire v. *Barrett*, [1965] 2 All E.R. 271; [1966] 1 Q.B. 312; [1965] 2 W.L.R.
    1195; Digest (Cont. Vol. B) 160, *1691a.*

Appeal.

In an action begun in Carmarthen County Court on Aug. 12, 1966, the plaintiff
company claimed damages against the defendant, John Ronald Jones, who was
Chief Constable of the Carmarthenshire and Cardiganshire Constabulary, for **G**
alleged trespass by police officers of that constabulary at the plaintiffs' shop at
Stepney Street, Llanelly, on the morning of Mar. 31, 1966, when police officers,
under the authority of a search warrant (the terms of which are set out at p. 231,
letter I, to p. 232, letter C, post) entered the premises and after exhaustive search
took away sixty-five items of clothing, which were retained until Apr. 2, 1966,
and were then returned to the plaintiffs' shop. The plaintiffs alleged, by para. **H**
3 of their particulars of claim that the police officers, in disregard of the limitations and authority of the search warrant, wrongfully committed unlawful acts
(whereof particulars were given in (1) to (5) of para. 3) by reason of which they
became and were trespassers on the premises. The parties agreed certain facts
for the purposes of the action, the agreement of facts being summarised at p. 232,
letter H, post. They also agreed that the sole issue on liability for determina- **I**
tion by the court was the issue raised by para. 3 (4) of the particulars of claim
and para. 3 and para. 9 of the amended defence. Paragraph 3 (4) of the
particulars of claim was as follows—

    "[The police officers] took away from the Llanelly branch sixty-five
items of clothing, the property of the plaintiffs, and retained possssion of
the same until the late afternoon of Apr. 2, 1966."

Paragraph 3 and para. 9 of the amended defence were as follows—

A   " 3. It is denied that the police officers or any of them disregarded any
limitations or authority of the warrant as alleged or at all.   It is denied that
the police officers or any of them committed any unlawful acts as alleged
or at all.   It is denied that the police officers became or were at any time
trespassers as alleged or at all.
        " 9. The police officers in taking away and retaining [the clothing] acted
B   reasonably in the execution of the warrant.   Further, or in the alternative
the taking away and retaining were not unlawful acts.   Further or in the
further alternative, in taking away and retaining as aforesaid, the police
officers believed, on reasonable grounds, that the sixty-five items were
stolen goods and would form material evidence on the prosecution of a
criminal charge.

C   Particulars of the grounds of belief pleaded in para. 9 of the defence were set
out in that paragraph.   It was agreed in the agreed facts that the facts alleged
in these particulars were true and that the police officers did so believe on reasonable grounds.   The trial judge found that the plaintiffs had suffered loss as a
result of an unlawful taking away by the police officers of sixty-five items of
clothing and by the retaining of them, and that there should be judgment for
D   the plaintiffs with an inquiry as to damages.   By notice of appeal the defendant
appealed that the judgment should be reversed and that judgment might be
entered for the defendant.   The grounds of the appeal were—(i) that the trial
judge was wrong in law in deciding that taking away by the police officers of
sixty-five items of clothing the property of the plaintiffs and the retaining
thereof was unlawful; and (ii) that on the facts as found or admitted the trial
E   judge was wrong in law in deciding that the defendant by the police officers was
guilty of trespass.

        The cases noted below* were cited during the argument in addition to those
referred to in the judgments.

        W. N. Francis for the defendant.
        S. Goldblatt for the plaintiffs.

F   *Cur. adv. vult.*
        Dec. 12.   The following judgments were read.

        LORD DENNING, M.R.:   In 1965 and 1966 thieves broke into several
shops and factories and stole ladies' clothes valued at £30,000.   The stolen goods
were of various makes, including " Ian Peters ", " Mornessa ", " Mansfield "
G   and " Blanes ".   In March, 1966, the police received information that clothes
of these makes were being sold at certain stores in Cardiff and Llanelly.   These
shops were owned by the plaintiffs, Chic Fashions (West Wales), Ltd., and controlled by the managing director, Mr. Jack Raeburn.   The goods were being
sold at less than trade prices.   On Mar. 26, 1966, an " Ian Peters " garment
was exhibited for sale at the Cardiff branch of the plaintiffs.   Now it so happened
H   that a few weeks earlier the factory of Ian Peters, Ltd., in Leicestershire had been
broken into and goods stolen.   The police suspected that these stolen goods
had found their way to the shops of the plaintiffs.   So they arranged to search
all their shops at one swoop; also Mr. Raeburn's home and his parents' home.
On Mar. 30, 1966, police officers went before the magistrates in the various
towns and obtained search warrants.   A typical example is the search warrant
I   for the shop of the plaintiffs in Llanelly.   It was in these terms:

" IN THE COUNTY OF CARMARTHEN
Petty Sessional Division of LLANELLY
To each and all of the constables of the [said] county
        " INFORMATION has this day been laid before me, the undersigned justice
of the peace, by John Owen Evans of No. 8 Regional Crime Squad that the
following goods, *to wit,*

---

* *Levine* v. *O'Keefe*, [1930] V.L.R. 70;   *R.* v. *Waterfield*, [1963] 3 All E.R. 659;
1964] 1 Q.B. 164.

ladies' coats, skirts and suits, knitwear, jumpers and skirts, the property
of Ian Peters, Ltd.

have lately been feloniously stolen, taken, and carried away out of the
factory at Star Works, Mountsorrel Lane, Rothley, Leicestershire, and
that he hath reasonable cause to suspect, and doth suspect, that the said
goods, or some part thereof, are concealed in the shop of the [plaintiffs]
at Stepney Street, Llanelly, in the said county of Carmarthen.

" You are therefore hereby authorised and commanded forthwith, with
proper assistance, to enter the said shop of the [plaintiffs] in the daytime,
and there diligently search for the said goods, and if the same, or any part
thereof, shall be found upon such search, that you bring the goods so found
before the magistrates' court sitting at the Town Hall, Kidwelly in the said
county to be disposed of and dealt with according to law.

" Dated Mar. 30, 1966.

[Signature]

" Justice of the Peace for the county first aforesaid."

Armed with this warrant, the police on the morning of Mar. 31, 1966, went to
the Llanelly branch of the plaintiffs. As soon as the shop opened at 9 a.m. they
entered and searched the premises. They did not find any garments of " Ian
Peters " make such as were specified in the search warrant; but they found
garments of other makes of the kinds which had been stolen previously, such
as " Mornessa ", " Mansfield " and " Blanes ". These bore signs that the labels
had been removed and they bore prices much less than the trade prices. The
police thought that these were stolen and seized them. There were sixty-five
items altogether which they seized.

The police saw Mr. Raeburn the same day. He said that the goods were
" cabbage ". He explained what this meant. The manufacturers used to
supply cloth to sub-contractors for them to make up a number of garments.
After fulfilling the order, the sub-contractors had surplus cloth left over. They
were allowed to use this surplus cloth for their own benefit and to make up
garments with it for sale, but they had to see that the manufacturers' label was
removed. As the sub-contractors got the surplus cloth for nothing, they could
sell to the retailers at less than manufacturers' prices. Mr. Raeburn's explanation
was accepted by the police. They returned the goods to the shop on Apr. 2,
1966.

The plaintiffs now sue the Chief Constable for damages. To save expense,
the parties have agreed to limit the issue to the question whether the police
officers were justified in taking away and retaining the sixty-five items of clothing.
They have also agreed the following facts:—(i) None of the sixty-five items of
clothing taken away and retained was within the description of the search
warrant issued on Mar. 30, 1966. (ii) None of the said sixty-five items was stolen.
(iii) None of the said sixty-five items was used as evidence on the prosecution of
a criminal charge. (iv) The said sixty-five items were lawfully acquired by the
plaintiffs in the course of their business. (v) In taking away and retaining the
said sixty-five items of clothing, the police officers believed on reasonable grounds
that the said sixty-five items were stolen goods and would form material evidence
on the prosecution of a criminal charge.

It comes to this, therefore. The police officers held a search warrant entitling
them to enter the shop to search for ladies' garments which had been recently
stolen from the factory of Ian Peters, Ltd. When the police entered the shop
and searched it, they found none of the goods that had been stolen from Ian
Peters, Ltd., but they found sixty-five items of clothing, not mentioned in the
warrant, which they believed on reasonable grounds were stolen and would form
material evidence on a criminal charge. The question is: were the police
entitled to seize goods not mentioned in the warrant but which they believed
on reasonable grounds to have been stolen?

A   One might have thought that this question would have been settled long ago; but, strangely enough, there is very little authority on it. Our English law has always had great regard for the integrity of a man's home. In 1604 Lord Coke declared that " every man's house is his castle " (see *Semayne's Case* (1) and Coke, 3 Inst., 73), and his aphorism has come down the centuries. It was given dramatic force by William Pitt, Earl of Chatham, when he declared

B   that:

> " The poorest man may in his cottage bid defiance to all the forces of the Crown. It may be frail—its roof may shake—the wind may blow through it—the storm may enter—the rain may enter—but the King of England cannot enter—all his force dares not cross the threshold of the ruined tenement."

C   See Brougham's Statesmen in the Times of George III, First Series.

Exceptions, however, have had to be made to this principle. They have been made in the public interest. No man's house is to be used as a hiding place for thieves or a receptacle for stolen goods. If there is reasonable ground for believing that there are stolen goods in the house, information can be laid before

D   a magistrate on oath, and the magistrate can then issue a search warrant authorising a constable to enter the house and seize the goods. That case was the only exception permitted by the common law. In no other case was a constable allowed to enter and search a man's house. Even if a constable suspected that counterfeit coins were being made there, or banknotes forged, he could not at common law obtain a search warrant to enter. In the celebrated case of *Entick* v. *Carrington* (2), Lord Halifax, the Secretary of State, issued a

E   warrant authorising a search to be made for seditious papers. It was held to be unlawful. Lord Camden, C.J., said (3):

> ". . . we can safely say there is no law in this country to justify the defendants in what they have done; if there was, it would destroy all the comforts of society: for papers are often the dearest property a man can have. This

F   > case was compared to that of stolen goods; Lord Coke denied the lawfulness of granting warrants to search for stolen goods, 4 Inst. 176, 177, though now it prevails to be law; but in that case the justice and the informer must proceed with great caution; there must be an oath that the party has had his goods stolen, and his strong reason to believe they are concealed in such a place: but if the goods are not found there, he is a trespasser . . ."

G   Since that time further exceptions have been made by statute. In a great many cases now Acts of Parliament permit magistrates to grant search warrants so as to enable the police to enter and see if a house is being used for unlawful purposes, such as coining, betting, and so forth; but with none of these are we concerned today. We have to deal with stolen goods, for which the common law always allowed a search warrant to be granted. There is, to be sure, a

H   statute on the matter (s. 42 of the Larceny Act, 1916), but, so far as concerns stolen goods, it does little more than state the common law. It provides that

> " (1) If it is made to appear by information on oath before a justice of the peace that there is reasonable cause to believe that any person has in his custody or possession or on his premises any property whatsoever, with respect to which any offence against this Act has been committed, the justice

I   > may grant a warrant to search for and seize the same."

That section deals with goods mentioned in the warrant. It does not say whether the constable can seize goods not mentioned in the warrant. To solve this question we must resort to the cases.

At one time the courts held that the constable could seize only those goods

---

(1) (1604), 5 Co. Rep. 91a.
(2) (1765), 2 Wils. 275; 19 State Tr. 1029.
(3) (1765), 2 Wils. at pp. 291, 292.

which answered the description given in the warrant. He had to make sure, **A**
at his peril, that the goods were the very goods in the warrant. If he seized
other goods, not mentioned in the warrant, he was a trespasser in respect of those
goods; and not only so, but he was a trespasser on the land itself, a trespasser
ab initio, in accordance with the doctrine of the *Six Carpenters' Case* (4), which
held that, if a man abuse an authority given by the law, he becomes a trespasser
ab initio.   **B**

If such had remained the law, no constable would be safe in executing a search
warrant. The law as it then stood was a boon to receivers of stolen property
and an impediment to the forces of law and order. So much so, that the judges
gradually altered it. In the year 1800 they held that a constable is entitled to
seize, by virtue of the warrant, any goods which he reasonably believes to be
included in the warrant, even though it should turn out afterwards that his   **C**
belief was mistaken. That is shown by *Price* v. *Messenger* (5). A search warrant
authorised a constable to search Price's shop for a quantity of sugar which had
been " stolen from some ship or vessel lying in the River Thames ". The constable entered the shop and seized some sugar there which Price was selling under
prime cost, and also a bag of nails and two parcels of tea of which no satisfactory
account was given. After enquiries were made, it turned out that they were not **D**
stolen, and all the goods were returned to Price. He then sued the constable
for trespass. It was argued for Price that

" . . . the warrant was to seize stolen sugar, and the officers were bound
at their peril to seize stolen sugar or none at all."

The court rejected this argument. It was held that the constable was not liable   **E**
in respect of the sugar. As to the tea and nails, the constable admitted that
he was not justified in taking them because they were not mentioned in the
warrant; and he suffered judgment by default in respect of them.

In 1827 the judges extended the protection of a constable further. They
held that a constable is entitled to seize, by virtue of the warrant, not only the
goods mentioned in the warrant, but also any other goods which are likely to   **F**
furnish evidence of the *identity* of the stolen goods so as to show that they really
are the goods mentioned in the warrant. This is shown by *Crozier* v. *Cundey* (6).
We were referred only to the report in 6 B. & C. 232, but the facts are more
fully reported in 5 L.J.O.S.M.C. 50, and the arguments and judgment are
much better reported in 9 Dow. & Ry.K.B. 224. Cundey owned one hundred
pounds of cotton copps contained in two packing cases. They were stolen from **G**
him. A search warrant authorised a constable to enter Crozier's house to search
for the " one hundred pounds weight of cotton copps ". The warrant did not
mention the packing cases. The constable found the cotton in packing cases.
He seized not only the cotton but also the packing cases in which it was contained.
Then Cundey told the constable that there were other things of his. Thereupon
he and the constable ransacked the place looking for other things. They rum-   **H**
maged for half an hour and ultimately took away a tin pan and a sieve besides
the cotton. There was no reason for supposing that Crozier had stolen the
things. There had been previous disputes between Crozier and Cundey about
property. Crozier alleged that the seizure of the packing cases, tin pan and
sieve was illegal because they were not mentioned in the warrant and that the
illegality related back so as to make the original entry unlawful. He sued   **I**
Cundey and the constable for trespass (i) for entering the house (trespass
ab initio) and (ii) for seizing the goods. The trial judge nonsuited the plaintiff,
who, being aggrieved, went to the Court of King's Bench, consisting of ABBOTT,
C.J., and BAYLEY, HOLROYD and LITTLEDALE, JJ. They held that the trial
judge was right in rejecting the claim for the seizure of the packing cases, because

(4) (1610), 8 Co. Rep. 146a.
(5) (1800), 2 Bos. & P. 158.
(6) (1827), 6 B. & C. 232.

A   they were likely to furnish evidence of the identity of the cotton copps; but they held that he ought not to have nonsuited the plaintiff in respect of the tin pan and sieve. Abbott, C.J., said (7):

B   " If those articles had from their nature been likely to furnish evidence of the identity of the articles stolen and mentioned in the warrant, I should have been inclined to assent to Mr. Reader's argument, and to think that there might have been reasonable ground for seizing them, though not mentioned in the warrant. But it cannot be contended that the tin pan and the hair sieve were therefore articles likely to furnish such evidence, and I am of opinion that the nonsuit cannot be supported."

C   Before leaving this case, it should be noticed that Crozier failed in his claim for trespass to the house (trespass ab initio). This illustrates the proposition that nowadays, if a constable lawfully enters a house by virtue of a search warrant and seizes the goods mentioned in the warrant, his entry does not become unlawful simply because he unjustifiably seizes other goods. He is liable for trespass in respect of those other goods, but not for trespass to the house (see *Canadian Pacific Wine Co.* v. *Tuley* (8)).

D   In *Crozier* v. *Cundey* (6) seizure of other goods was only allowed so as to prove the *identity* of the stolen goods. The next case goes to allow seizure of other goods so as to prove the *guilt* of the thief or receiver. In 1867 in the House of Lords observations were made from which it may be inferred that a constable may seize other goods not mentioned in the warrant if they afford useful evidence to substantiate the charge for which the warrant was issued. In *Pringle* v.

E   *Bremner and Stirling* (9) a search warrant authorised a constable to search a house for a piece of fuse used in making an explosion. The constable, in searching the house for the piece of fuse, found letters which served to throw light on the perpetrators of the explosion. The constable took possession of them. Lord Chelmsford, L.C., said (10):

F   " Now it may be said (and as the argument has been urged it may be as well to observe upon it) that the constable, having a warrant to search merely for pieces of wood and pieces of a fuse, had no right whatever to go beyond that, to ransack the house (if I may use the expression) and to endeavour to find something which might implicate the pursuer on the charge which was preferred against him. But supposing that in a search which might have been improper originally, there were matters discovered which showed

G   the complicity of the pursuer in a crime, then I think the officers, I can hardly say would have been justified, but would have been excused by the result of their search."

Those are the only cases on search warrants; but the last extension (where a constable may seize other goods which go to prove *guilt*) is supported by the cases on warrants of arrest.   In *Dillon* v. *O'Brien and Davis* (11) John Dillon

H   was said to have taken part in a conspiracy. The magistrates issued a warrant for the arrest of Dillon. The constable who went to effect the arrest found in the house a quantity of banknotes and papers which he thought would be useful evidence. Palles, C.B., said (12):

I   " I, therefore, think that it is clear, and beyond doubt, that, at least in cases of treason and felony, constables (and probably also private persons) are entitled, upon a lawful arrest by them of one charged with treason or felony, to take and detain property found in his possession which will form material evidence in his prosecution for the crime . . . The interest of the State in the person charged being brought to trial in due course necessarily

---

(7) (1827), 9 Dow. & Ry. K.B. 224 at p. 226.
(8) [1921] 2 A.C. 417.
(9) (1867), 5 Macph. (H. of L.) 55.
(10) (1867), 5 Macph. (H. of L.) at p. 60.
(11) (1887), 16 Cox, C.C. 245.
(12) (1887), 16 Cox, C.C. at p. 249.

extends to the preservation of material evidence of his guilt or innocence, **A**
as well as to his custody for the purpose of trial. His custody is of no value
if the law is powerless to prevent the abstraction or destruction of the
evidence, without which a trial would be no more than an empty form."

I must mention, however, *Elias* v. *Pasmore* (13). A man called Hannington
made a speech in Trafalgar Square which was said to be seditious. A warrant
was issued for his arrest. The police went to the headquarters of the movement **B**
and arrested him. They seized also several documents, including a letter signed
" P.C." to a Labour paper. HORRIDGE, J., said (14):

" In my opinion, the seizure of these documents was justified because
they were capable of being and *were used* as evidence in that trial. If I am
right in that view, the original seizure of these documents, though improper **C**
at the time, would, therefore, be excused."

It will be noticed that HORRIDGE, J., relied on the fact that the documents *were*
used in evidence at the trial; but I cannot think that is a necessary condition
to justify their seizure. It may often happen that, on investigation, the prosecution decide not to go on with the case. The seizure must be justified at the
time, irrespective of whether the case goes to trial or not. It cannot be made **D**
lawful or unlawful according to what happens afterwards.

Such are the cases. They contain no broad statement of principle, but
proceed, in our English fashion, from case to case until the principle emerges.
Now the time has come when we must endeavour to state it. We have to
consider, on the one hand, the freedom of the individual. The security of his
home is not to be broken except for the most compelling reason. On the other **E**
hand, we have to consider the interest of society at large in finding out wrong-
doers and repressing crime. In these present times, with the ever-increasing
wickedness there is about, honest citizens must help the police and not hinder
them in their efforts to track down criminals. I look at it in this way. So far
as a man's individual liberty is concerned, the law is settled concerning powers
of arrest. A constable may arrest him and deprive him of his liberty, if he has **F**
reasonable grounds for believing that a felony (now an " arrestable offence ")
has been committed and that he is the man. I see no reason why goods should
be more sacred than persons. In my opinion, when a constable enters a house
by virtue of a search warrant for stolen goods, he may seize not only the goods
which he reasonably believes to be covered by the warrant, but also any other
goods which he believes on reasonable grounds to have been stolen and to be **G**
material evidence on a charge of stealing or receiving against the person in
possession of them or anyone associated with him. Test it this way. Suppose
the constable does not find the goods mentioned in the warrant, but finds other
goods which he reasonably believes to be stolen. Is he to quit the premises
and go back to the magistrate and ask for another search warrant to cover these
other goods? If he went away, I should imagine that, in nine cases out of ten, **H**
by the time when he came back with a warrant, these other goods would have
disappeared. The true owner would not recover them. The evidence of the
crime would have been lost. That would be to favour thieves and to discourage
honest men. Even if it should turn out that the constable was mistaken and
that the other goods were not stolen goods at all, nevertheless, so long as h eacted
reasonably and did not retain them longer than necessary, he is protected. The **I**
lawfulness of his conduct must be judged at the time and not by what happens
afterwards. I know that at one time a man could be made a trespasser ab initio
by the doctrine of relation back; but that is no longer true. The *Six Carpenters'*
Case (15) was a by-product of the old forms of action. Now that they are buried,
it can be interred with their bones.

---

(13) [1934] All E.R. Rep. 380; [1934] 2 K.B. 164.
(14) [1934] All E.R. Rep. at p. 384; [1934] 2 K.B. at p. 173.
(15) (1610), 8 Co. Rep. 146a.

A   In this case, on the agreed facts, the police had reasonable grounds for believing the sixty-five items of clothing to have been stolen and to be material evidence on a criminal charge against the plaintiffs or their officers. So they seized them. On investigation they found out that they were not stolen and they returned them. On the principles which I have stated they are not liable. I would allow this appeal and give judgment to the defendant.

B
     DIPLOCK, L.J.: I need not repeat the facts agreed or proven; they have been stated by Lord Denning, M.R.; but I may mention that the expression " cabbage ", in the sense used by Mr. Raeburn, has respectable antiquity and dates back to the eighteenth century. None of the goods seized turned out to be within the description contained in the search warrant; for none were in fact C   " the property of Ian Peters, Ltd." Their seizure was not authorised by the warrant. Its only relevance is that it made lawful the entry of the police officers on the plaintiffs' premises and their remaining there for the purpose of conducting a search for the goods described in the warrant.

     The question in this appeal, therefore, is whether at common law *today* a police officer, who is lawfully on private property, is entitled without the permis- D   sion of the occupier of the premises to seize and take away goods in the possession of the occupier which he has reasonable grounds to believe are stolen and to detain them as material evidence on a criminal prosecution of the occupier for stealing the goods, or for receiving them knowing them to be stolen, until either such a prosecution is heard and determined or further information discloses that such a prosecution would not be justified.

E   In the present case there was no specific admission that at the time the goods were seized the police officers believed that the plaintiffs, in whose possession they were at the time of seizure, had themselves received the goods knowing them to be stolen. The case was argued before the county court judge on the broader submission by the defendant that it was sufficient justification for the seizure that the police officers had reasonable grounds for believing that the F   goods had been stolen and might be material evidence on the prosecution of a criminal charge against any person, whether that person was the plaintiffs themselves or some third party. The admitted facts, however, made it plain beyond a peradventure that, at the time of the seizure, the police officers had reasonable grounds for believing that the plaintiffs through their responsible officers—in particular, their managing director—had received the goods knowing G   them to be stolen; and I propose to deal with this appeal on that more limited basis. It may well be that there are other considerations which are relevant when police officers, although they have reasonable grounds for believing that goods are stolen, have none for believing that they came otherwise than innocently (which might include purchase in market overt) into the possession of the person in whose possession they are found. On this I deliberately refrain from expressing H   any view.

     What answer does the common law today give to the question I have posed? No direct answer is to be found in any decision of the English courts, ancient or modern. From general observations to be found in various judgments ranging over two centuries to which we have been referred, it is possible to discern where on this matter various judges would have thought the balance I   lay between the inviolability of private property and the pursuit of public weal in a society of the kind in which they lived. It is worth while remembering, however, that until *Sommersett's Case* (16) in 1772 the balance lay in favour of private property in slaves. This was seven years later than *Entick* v. *Carrington* (17), a case to which we have been referred, whose reasoning we have been urged to follow. The society in which we live is not static, nor is the common law, since it comprises those rules which govern men's conduct in contemporary society

---

     (16) (1772), 20 State Trials 1.
     (17) (1765), 2 Wils. 275.

on matters not expressly regulated by legislation. That is why in the question   A
we have to answer I have stressed the word " today ".

The plaintiffs' cause of action for interference to their property in goods lies in
trespass—a cause of action which historically did not necessarily involve blameworthiness on the part of the defendant. The development of the common law
in the last thirty years, however, has tended towards equating civil liability
with conduct which right-minded men in contemporary society would regard as   B
blameworthy (see *Fowler* v. *Lanning* (18) and *Letang* v. *Cooper* (19)) and towards
protecting those who act reasonably in intended performance of what right-
minded men would deem a duty to their fellow men: see *Haynes* v. *G. Harwood
& Son* (20) and *Ward* v. *T. E. Hopkins & Son, Ltd., Baker* v. *T. E. Hopkins & Son,
Ltd.* (21). Today stealing is more widespread than it has ever been since statistics
of crime have been available. Stolen goods can be swiftly carried far from the   C
scene of the theft. Today, unlike the time of *Entick* v. *Carrington* (22), *Price* v.
Messenger (23), and *Crozier* v. *Cundey* (24), there are throughout the country
regular police forces whose officers are charged with the duty of preventing
and detecting crime. The common law has always recognised that the discharge
of this duty may justify some interference with rights of innocent private citizens
who would in other circumstances be entitled to its protection. At common   D
law a constable, even before there were regular police forces, was entitled to
arrest a person whom he had reasonable grounds for believing to have committed
a serious crime (felony). At the time of the arrest the arrestor cannot know that
the arrested person is guilty. The purpose of the arrest is to bring him before
a court so that this issue may be tried. The justification of the arrest does not
depend on the result of the subsequent trial. The reasonable belief of the   E
arrestor at the time of the arrest was a good defence to an action of false imprisonment notwithstanding that it ultimately proved to be unfounded. The balance
between the inviolability of personal liberty and the pursuit of public weal in this
case came down on the side of him who acted reasonably in intended performance of what right-minded men would deem a duty to their fellow men;
the prevention and detection of crime.   F

It may be that well into the nineteenth century when arrest on mesne
process and imprisonment for debt formed part of the ordinary procedure of the
courts, the protection of private property weighed heavier in the scale of social
values than the preservation of human liberty. Some of the language in *Entick*
v. *Carrington* (22) might so suggest. Such is not the case today, however,
and, unless forced to do so by recent binding authority, I decline to accept that a   G
police officer who is unquestionably justified at common law in arresting a
person whom he has reasonable grounds to believe is guilty of receiving stolen
goods, is not likewise justified in the less draconian act of seizing what he, on
reasonable grounds, believes to be the stolen goods in that person's possession.
The purpose of the seizure in such a case is twofold: first, that the goods may
be produced as material evidence on the prosecution of a criminal charge   H
against the person from whom they were seized, and, secondly, that after the
trial they may be restored to their rightful owner, and a similar justification
exists for their detention so long as the detainer has reasonable grounds for
believing that such a charge will lie and that the goods will be material evidence
on its prosecution. I leave aside the question, which does not arise in the
present case, of what constitutes sufficient justification for the seizure and detention if the contemplated criminal charge is not against the person in whose   I
possession the goods were at the time of seizure.

---

(18) [1959] 1 All E.R. 290; [1959] 1 Q.B. 426.
(19) [1964] 2 All E.R. 929; [1965] 1 Q.B. 232.
(20) [1934] All E.R. Rep. 103; [1935] 1 K.B. 146.
(21) [1959] 3 All E.R. 225.
(22) (1765), 2 Wils. 275.
(23) (1800), 2 Bos. & P. 158.
(24) (1827), 6 B. & C. 232.

A   In *Dillon* v. *O'Brien and Davis* (25), an Irish case, the seizure of the goods had been accompanied by the arrest of the person in whose possession the goods were found. The goods in question were not believed to be stolen but to be material evidence on a charge of conspiracy against the person arrested. In the result the person arrested was convicted; but the robust common sense of the reasoning of Palles, C.B., is not so limited in its application. It does not

B   depend for its validity on the contemporaneous arrest of the person in whose possession the goods were found, nor does it depend on his subsequent conviction. The goods of Dillon which were seized were unquestionably his property; the justification of the seizure of the goods was not the assertion of any jus tertii but their intended production as material evidence on the prosecution of a criminal charge against him of conspiracy. Moreover, the same reasoning which leads

C   to the conclusion that in the case of an arrest itself reasonable grounds for belief in guilt at the time of arrest is sufficient justification, though subsequent information or events may show those grounds to be deceptive, leads to the same conclusion in the case of seizure. At common law, with the possible exception of the antiquarian doctrine of trespass ab initio (see *Six Carpenters' Case* (26)), subsequent events do not render unlawful an act which was lawful at the time

D   when it was done, at any rate if those events are not themselves caused by the doer of the act. What application, if any, the rule applied in the *Six Carpenters' Case* (26) has in the modern law of tort, may some day call for re-examination, but it has no relevance to the present case if the original seizure of the goods was lawful.

The county court judge, after a careful review of all the cases cited to him,

E   came to the conclusion that they did not constitute authority for the proposition that seizure of goods could be justified if in the result the goods proved not to have been stolen, but to be in truth the property of the person from whose possession they were taken. I think that he was right in so concluding, but equally these cases are not authority for the converse of that proposition. Neither in *Price* v. *Messenger* (27), nor in *Crozier* v. *Cundey* (28), the cases nearest in their

F   facts to these, was the point which has been argued in this appeal taken. In the former case the defendants had suffered judgment by default in respect of the goods not described in the search warrant. In the latter, in which the facts and arguments are very summarily reported, the argument appears to have been limited to the contention that the seizure of goods not mentioned in the warrant was justified if " they might be serviceable in the investigation of the felony

G   mentioned in the warrant ". This contention was accepted as correct, but it was found that the particular facts in the case did not support it.

The point of law in this appeal thus comes before us in 1967 untrammelled by authority. It is for us to say how in 1967 it should be answered. For my part I, like Lord Denning, M.R., would answer it by allowing this appeal.

H   SALMON, L.J.: It is strange that there is no direct authority on the question which arises for decision on this appeal. It is a narrow question but one of great general importance, namely, whether the common law allows a policeman to seize goods which he finds in the possession or custody of a person if he believes, on reasonable grounds, that that person has stolen the goods or received them knowing them to be stolen. Since undoubtedly such a person can lawfully

I   be arrested (*Cowles* v. *Dunbar and Callow* (29)), it is difficult to discover any sensible reason for conferring immunity from seizure on the goods found on his premises. The production of stolen goods from the possession of an accused often provides most material evidence at his trial. There is certainly no decided case or statutory provision which compels us to find that in the circumstances

(25) (1887), 16 Cox, C.C. 245.
(26) (1610), 8 Co. Rep. 146a.
(27) (1800), 2 Bos. & P. 158.
(28) (1827), 6 B. & C. 232.
(29) (1827), 2 C. & P. 565.

postulated a policeman has no power of seizure, whilst common sense and principle **A**
alike strongly suggest that he must have such a power.

The common law has always been, and I hope and believe always will be, the
jealous guardian of the right of the innocent to go free and also of rights of
property. These rights are perhaps complementary to each other. Today,
however, the first is undoubtedly regarded as of paramount importance. It may
not always have been so. Indeed, the emphasis was at one time different. A **B**
little more than two hundred years ago LORD CAMDEN, C.J., observed:

> " The great end for which men entered into society was to secure their
> property. That right is preserved sacred and incommunicable in all instances
> where it has not been abridged by some public law for the good of the whole."

(See *Entick* v. *Carrington* (30)). This today has an odd ring—both archaic and **C**
incongruous. I cannot be sure how the question which confronts us might
have been answered in the eighteenth or even in the nineteenth century, but I
have no doubt about how it should be answered now. It has often been
stated that the common law is not static. It is a growing organism which
continually adapts itself to meet the changing needs of time. There has never
been a time when the incidence of crime was higher or the need for prevention **D**
of crime greater than it is today. The right of a policeman to arrest a person
whom he believes on reasonable grounds to be guilty of a felony was an invasion
of private liberty. It was an exception which was evolved and gained general
acceptance as a necessary measure for the prevention of crime. No-one can
doubt that it has worked for the benefit of society.

The arrested man must be informed of the offence for which he is arrested **E**
unless the circumstances of his arrest make this obvious. If there proves to be
no evidence to justify his continued detention, he must be immediately released.
Otherwise he must be brought before the magistrates and dealt with as they
direct (*Christie* v. *Leachinsky* (31); *Wiltshire* v. *Barrett* (32)). If the preservation
of law and order requires that a policeman shall have the power to arrest a man
whom he believes on reasonable grounds to be a thief or a receiver, it is difficult **F**
to understand why the policeman should not have the power to seize goods on
that man's premises which the policeman believes on reasonable grounds that
he has stolen or received. If the man's person is not sacrosanct in the eyes of the
law, how can the goods which he is reasonably suspected of having stolen or
received be sacrosanct? Only if the law regards property as more important
than liberty; and I do not accept that it does so. It would be absurd if the **G**
police had the power to arrest a man, but, having failed to catch him, had no
power to seize the goods in his house which they reasonably believed he had
stolen or unlawfully received. There is no doubt that, if they find the goods in
his possession when they arrest him, they may seize the goods (see the observations of LORD CAMPBELL, C.J., in the footnote to *Bessell* v. *Wilson* (33), *Dillon*
v. *O'Brien and Davis* (34) and *Elias* v. *Pasmore* (35)). Suppose the police, **H**
reasonably believing a man has stolen some jewellery, follow him into his house
in order to arrest him. As they enter the front door they see him disappearing
out of the back door, but there on the table is the jewellery. Surely they may
seize it; the fact that he has evaded capture cannot confer any immunity on
him in respect of the stolen goods. He may be captured later and then the fate of
the goods will depend on whether or not he is committed for trial, and, if
committed, whether he is found guilty or not guilty. If the suspected man **I**
disappears, the goods will be preserved until the true owner can be ascertained.

In the present case the warrant was badly drawn. It could have been drawn

---

(30) (1765), 19 State Tr. 1029 at p. 1060.
(31) [1947] 1 All E.R. 567; [1947] A.C. 573.
(32) [1965] 2 All E.R. 271 at p. 276; [1966] 1 Q.B. 312 at pp. 324, 325.
(33) (1853), 20 L.T.O.S. 233, n.
(34) (1887), 16 Cox, C.C. 245.
(35) [1934] All E.R. Rep. 380; [1934] 2 K.B. 164.

A   to protect the defendants, but it did not do so.   It authorised the police to enter
the plaintiffs' Llanelly shop and search for certain goods " the property of
Ian Peters, Ltd.", and, if found, bring them before the magistrates.   The goods
found and seized there were not the property of Ian Peters, Ltd., but of other
manufacturers.   The defendant, therefore, could not rely on the warrant for
the seizure of the goods and it is on wrongful seizure alone that the plaintiffs
B   now rely in this action.   The warrant enabled the police to enter the plaintiffs'
premises.   They were lawfully there.   The question does not arise for decision
and I express no concluded view on it, but in spite of the *Six Carpenters' Case* (36),
I very much doubt whether the seizure of the goods, if wrongful, would have
made the entry on the premises wrongful ab initio.   The general rule is that an
act which is lawful at the time is not to be rendered unlawful afterwards by the
C   doctrine of " relation back " (*Wiltshire* v. *Barrett*, per LORD DENNING, M.R. (37)).
    There is no doubt that the defendant had reasonable grounds to believe and
did believe that the goods found on the plaintiffs' premises were stolen goods
and had been received by Mr. Raeburn, the plaintiffs' alter ego, knowing them
to be stolen.   Similar goods had recently been stolen from the Ian Peters'
factory.   The plaintiffs were not a customer of Ian Peters.   Many of these
D   goods were similar to the goods of Ian Peters, had had their name tags removed,
and were being offered for sale by the plaintiffs at prices below manufacturers'
prices.   Mr. Raeburn was being interviewed by other members of the police
force at about the same time as the plaintiffs' shop was entered and searched and,
unless Mr. Raeburn had given an explanation which the police felt able to accept,
he would no doubt have been detained and charged.   As it was, he went free
E   and the goods were returned.
    On the facts of this case I would hold that the defendant has a good defence
at common law.   I go no further.   In particular I wish to make it plain that
I incline to the view that, if a policeman finds property which he reasonably
believes to be stolen in the possession of a person whom he has no reasonable
grounds to believe is criminally implicated, the policeman has no common law
F   right to seize the property.   If, for example, a policeman is admitted to a house,
and whilst there sees some silver on the sideboard which he reasonably believes
is stolen but which he has no reason to suppose was dishonestly acquired by the
householder, he cannot take it away without the householder's consent.   Nor
do I think that, in practice, magistrates would or should issue a warrant under
s. 42 (1) of the Larceny Act, 1916, enabling the police to enter the house of a
G   respectable citizen and search for and seize stolen goods of which the householder is thought to be innocently in possession after having acquired them in
good faith.
    I agree, however, that on the facts of the present case the plaintiffs' goods were
lawfully seized and the appeal should accordingly be allowed.

                    Appeal allowed.   Leave to appeal to the House of Lords refused.
H
    Solicitors: *Lewin, Gregory, Mead & Sons*, agents for *Richard John*, Cardiff
(for the defendant); *Lewis Cutner & Co.* (for the plaintiffs).

                        [*Reported by* F. GUTTMAN, ESQ., *Barrister-at-Law.*]

I

---

(36) (1610), 8 Co. Rep. 146a.
(37) [1965] 2 All E.R. at p. 275;   [1966] 1 Q.B. at p. 323.

F. v. F.   A

[PROBATE, DIVORCE AND ADMIRALTY DIVISION (Rees, J.), October 30, 31, November 1, 6, 1967.]

Divorce—Adultery—Evidence—Blood groups—Proof by this means beyond reasonable doubt—Standard of proof where child's legitimacy in issue.

The husband and wife were married in 1959. He finally left her on Jan. 14,   B
1961. A child was conceived by the wife in about October, 1960, and was
born to her on June 17, 1961. In divorce proceedings instituted by the
husband in October, 1964, based on adultery by the wife, an issue of the
paternity of the child was directed. Samples of the blood of the husband,
the wife and the child had been taken in September, 1961, and samples were
again taken in June, 1966. These showed that the child's blood contained the   C
Willis " C " factor, which was not present in the blood of the husband or of
the wife. On the medical evidence based on these samples the child was not
the child of the husband but there was a possibility, too remote to be of practical significance, that the Willis " C " factor had appeared in the child's
blood as the result of a mutation. The wife admitted that the child was her
child. It was accepted by the parties that the standard of proof of adultery   D
by the wife, where the consequence of proof would be to bastardise a child
born during wedlock, was proof beyond reasonable doubt*.

Held: on the medical evidence alone, based on the samples of blood, the
court was satisfied beyond reasonable doubt that the wife had committed
adultery in or about October, 1960 (see p. 249, letter A, post).

[As to onus and standard of proof of adultery, see 12 HALSBURY'S LAWS (3rd   E
Edn.) 237, para. 445; and as to proof of adultery by the birth of a child, see
ibid., p. 240, para. 451; and for cases on the subjects, see 27 DIGEST (Repl.)
313, 314, *2620, 2622,* 320, *2670*; and DIGEST (Cont. Vol. B) 360, *3344a* (standard
of proof), and 318-321, *2649-2673* (by birth of child).]

Cases referred to: F
    Blyth v. *Blyth,* [1966] 1 All E.R. 524; [1966] A.C. 643; [1966] 2 W.L.R. 634;
        Digest (Cont. Vol. B) 360, *3344a.*
    Cotton v. *Cotton,* [1954] 2 All E.R. 105; [1954] P. 305; [1954] 2 W.L.R. 947;
        3 Digest (Repl.) 402, *38.*
    Head v. *Head,* (1823), Turn. & R. 138; 37 E.R. 1049; 3 Digest (Repl.) 399, *13.*
    Loveden v. *Loveden,* [1803-13] All E.R. Rep. 339; (1810), 2 Hag. Con. 1;   G
        161 E.R. 648; 27 Digest (Repl.) 315, *2634.*
    Mordaunt v. *Moncreiffe,* [1874-80] All E.R. Rep. 288; (1874), L.R. 2 Sc. & Div.
        374; 43 L.J.P. & M. 49; 30 L.T. 649; 39 J.P. 4; 27 Digest (Repl.)
        457, *3928.*
    Preston-Jones v. *Preston-Jones,* [1951] 1 All E.R. 124; [1951] A.C. 391; 27
        Digest (Repl.) 320, *2670.*   H
    Richards v. *Richards,* [1952] 1 All E.R. 1384; [1952] P. 307; 116 J.P. 358;
        Digest (Cont. Vol. A) 728, *2979a.*
    Turner v. *Turner,* [1961] 3 All E.R. 944; [1962] P. 283; [1961] 3 W.L.R. 1269;
        Digest (Cont. Vol. A) 784, *5581c.*

Petition.

This was a petition, dated Oct. 19, 1964, by a husband for dissolution of   I
marriage on the ground of his wife's adultery as a result of which, as he alleged,
she conceived a child. The wife by her amended answer denied adultery and
alleged expressly that the child was the child of herself and the husband. By
order made on Dec. 7, 1965, an issue of the paternity of the child was directed
to be tried with the trial of the divorce suit. The facts are set out in the judgment. The case is reported only on the question of proof of adultery by blood

---

* See, as regards the standard of proof, p. 247, letters G, et seq., post.

A group tests in circumstances in which it would have the consequence of bastardising a child born during wedlock.

   K. Bruce Campbell, Q.C., and *G. Rodway* for the husband.
   H. E. Hooson, Q.C., and *A. B. Hollis* for the wife.
   L. I. Stanger-Jones for the official solicitor as guardian ad litem of the child.

B   *Cur. adv. vult.*

   Nov. 6.   REES, J., read the following judgment: In this suit the husband seeks a decree of dissolution of his marriage from the wife, alleging against her that she has been guilty of adultery, as a result of which adultery the husband alleges that the wife conceived a child. By an order made by HEWSON, J., on Dec. 7, 1965, an issue as to the paternity of that child was ordered to be tried with the trial of
C the suit. By her answer the wife denies that she was guilty of adultery and alleges expressly that the child is in fact the child of herself and the husband. She alleges that the husband deserted her on Jan. 14, 1961, by leaving the matrimonial home on that day. By his reply the husband denies that he was guilty of desertion, admits that he left the matrimonial home on Jan. 14, 1961, and that he has never since resumed cohabitation with the wife, but alleges that he had just
D cause for doing so by reason of the wife's adultery or alternatively by reason of his belief in that adultery, and that for these reasons he has had just cause for living apart from the wife. There are no children of the family save the child whom I shall refer to as D., who is the child in issue in this suit and in respect of whom I must decide whether it is a child of the husband and whether accordingly the child is a legitimate child of this marriage.

E   The two major issues therefore which I have to try are these: whether the husband has established that his wife has committed adultery, and secondly, whether the wife has established that her husband deserted her. At the outset of the hearing of the case the wife sought leave to amend her answer to seek a decree of dissolution of the marriage in the exercise of the court's discretion notwithstanding adultery committed by her. The application was unopposed
F and leave was given for that amendment.

   These parties separated as I have already stated on Jan. 14, 1961, after the marriage had lasted rather less than thirteen months. At this time the wife was pregnant of the child D., who was born on June 17, 1961. She instituted proceedings by summons in the West Ham magistrates' court alleging that the husband had deserted her. Her complaint was heard on Feb. 8, 1961, and
G the justices found that the husband had deserted her and made an order for the payment by the husband to her of maintenance in the weekly sum of £3. The wife was not represented, but the husband was, and both gave evidence. At this hearing no suggestion was made by or on behalf of the husband that the wife had committed adultery. After the birth of the child the wife, on July 27, 1961, applied for, and was granted, a summons seeking a variation of the order
H made on Feb. 8, 1961, to include the child D. By a letter addressed to the wife and dated Aug. 1, 1961, the husband's solicitors indicated that the husband was denying paternity of the child and invited the wife to give her consent to the taking of blood samples from herself and from the child so that blood grouping tests might be undertaken by a medical specialist. The wife was then unrepresented, but it is common ground that, when the matter came before the justices
I on Aug. 10, 1961, the wife immediately expressed her desire for such a test and the hearing was accordingly adjourned. On Sept. 25, 1961, the wife was informed by the husband's solicitors that the results of the tests showed that in the opinion of the medical specialist the husband was not the father of the child D. born to the wife on June 17, 1961. The husband therefore took out a summons to discharge the order made on Feb. 8, 1961, on the ground that the wife had committed adultery. Both summonses came on for hearing before the West Ham magistrates' court on Jan. 17, 1962, when the justices, finding that adultery had been established, refused to order that maintenance should be paid by the

husband in respect of the child and revoked the order of Feb. 8, 1961. Both A
parties were represented by solicitors and both gave evidence, the only witness
in addition to the parties being the medical specialist, Dr. Alan Grant, who gave
expert evidence as to the results of the blood test. The wife appealed from this
decision to the Divisional Court and the appeal was heard by SIR JOCELYN
SIMON, P., and KARMINSKI, J., on May 7, 1962. The appeal was successful,
the order of the justices being set aside and a re-hearing directed before a fresh B
panel of justices. I have had the considerable advantage of reading the judgment of SIR JOCELYN SIMON, P. That judgment shows that the error into which
the justices had fallen was that they concluded that they could only find in
favour of the wife if they rejected Dr. Alan Grant's expert evidence, and this
they were not prepared to do. SIR JOCELYN SIMON, P., pointed out that, since
Dr. Alan Grant conceded that there was a possibility, however small, that the C
child in question might have been the child of the husband, then if the justices
believed the wife's evidence that she had never committed adultery it was open
to them to find in her favour without rejecting Dr. Alan Grant's evidence.

The case was re-heard before a fresh panel of justices on Sept. 10, 1962. Again
both parties gave evidence, both were represented, and the only witness in
addition to the parties was Dr. Alan Grant. The justices were not satisfied D
that the high standard of proof which is required in cases of adultery involving
the legitimacy of a child had been attained. Accordingly they found in favour
of the wife, dismissed the husband's complaint alleging that the wife had
committed adultery, and made an order for the custody of the child and for
maintenance in favour of the wife and the child. There has been no appeal
from the decision, and the husband has been complying with the order and the E
payment of maintenance to the wife and to this child for the past five years, or so.
The husband's petition in this suit was dated Oct. 19, 1964.

It is important that the history of these earlier proceedings should have been
set out in some detail for a number of reasons. In the first place it is necessary to
bear in mind, when considering the reliability of the evidence given before me,
both by the husband and the wife that each has already previously given evidence F
about a substantial part of the case on no less than three previous occasions.
It must be difficult enough for any person to give an accurate account of events
which happened some six or seven years ago, but I apprehend that the difficulties
may be greatly increased where effort is made to recall what actually happened
as opposed to remembering what the person has said happened in previous
proceedings. When experienced counsel armed with notes of evidence of G
previous trials quite properly cross-examine the parties, it is only to be expected
that witnesses will be caught in contradictions. In these circumstances my
approach to the testimony given before me is to exercise very great caution
before reaching conclusions about the reliability of the witnesses and especially
about their truthfulness. In the second place it has been submitted on behalf
of the wife that the justices' finding in her favour on Sept. 10, 1962, should be H
given considerable weight in her favour when deciding the issues before me.
Although it is true that there was not a positive finding in favour of the wife
(as distinct from a finding that the husband had failed to prove adultery against
her) nevertheless the justices did, so long ago as 1962, consider and reject
the husband's allegation of adultery against her. In any event the basis of
the justices' orders were that the child was the child of the husband and that the I
wife had not committed adultery. I have been usefully referred to the decision
of the Court of Appeal in *Turner* v. *Turner* (1), and in particular to the following
passages from the judgment of HOLROYD PEARCE, L.J., where he said (2):

" The wife, therefore, in this case started on strong ground. She had in
her favour the order of an experienced magistrate made when the evidence

_____

(1) [1961] 3 All E.R. 944; [1962] P. 283.
(2) [1961] 3 All E.R. at pp. 948, 949; [1962] P. at pp. 291, 292.

A   of the parties was still fresh. This, though in no sense conclusive, was prima facie of strong probative value ... Although a wife starts on strong ground, as here, with an order in her favour—an order having the effect of a decree of judicial separation—it is always possible that the Divorce Court will, after hearing the evidence on both sides, conclude that, for some reason, the first court did not have the same advantage for ascertaining the truth

B as the Divorce Court has, and that it was mistaken in its view. On forming a firm opinion on credibility, it may feel itself compelled to disregard the order in her favour. But it must do so with a realisation that the order is prima facie of definite probative value. It should, in my view, remember that against the advantage of a more leisurely and scientific investigation in the Divorce Court must be weighed the advantage of a more con-

C temporary and direct confrontation of the parties and their stories in the magistrates' court before time and reiteration of their stories to their advisers has had its effect. The weight of these respective advantages will, of course, depend on circumstances. If the court does not put the order into the scales on her side at all, the matter is not properly weighed."

  I have accordingly put the decision of the justices on Sept. 10, 1962, into the scales

D in the favour of the wife. I have not felt it right to differ from the findings of the justices on credibility or on the facts save where I have formed a firm and clear view of my own on the material before me. So far as Dr. Alan Grant's expert evidence is concerned (on which no question of credibility, of course, arises) I have felt it right to form my own views, particularly as I accepted his evidence that medical science has developed in such a way since 1962 that he

E is now, in 1967, able to express a more confident opinion than when he gave evidence before the justices in 1962.

  It was submitted by counsel for the husband that the court should regard the finding of the justices on Jan. 17, 1962, in favour of the husband as having even greater weight than that in favour of the wife, on the ground that it amounted to a finding that the justices were then satisfied that the wife had committed

F adultery in spite of the very strong presumption that the child was legitimate. Since, however, the Divisional Court has held that these justices erred in principle in thinking that a finding in favour of the wife involved a rejection of Dr. Alan Grant's evidence, I do not think it would be right to, and I do not, place this finding in the scales in favour of the husband.

  I think that it is useful to state that I have had the considerable advantage

G not enjoyed by the justices of the presence of experienced leading counsel on both sides, who ensured that the evidence of the witnesses was presented and tested with thoroughness and skill.

  I now turn to examine the relevant facts as shortly as I may. I state at the outset that I formed a clear opinion that the evidence of the husband was more reliable than that of the wife. Counsel on each side attacked the credit of the

H opposite party and it will be necessary for me to set out later in the course of this judgment my reasons for the clear opinion which I have formed about the respective reliability of the parties. It is, I think, necessary for me to say that the husband appeared to me to be a very much simpler and less sophisticated person than did his wife. Indeed, if the husband had been more astute and more a man of the world, the trial of this case might have been a good deal simpler than it was.

  [HIS LORDSHIP turned to examine the facts, reviewed the evidence, intimated that he did not believe the wife when she said that adultery had not taken place between the named man and herself between October, 1966, and July, 1967, while the named man was residing in the same house as herself, into which he had moved, and continued:] Before coming to consider the expert medical evidence of Dr. Alan Grant it may be useful to summarise my findings on the evidence thus far. First, throughout the marriage up to the parting the wife had persisted in staying out late in spite of the husband's complaints and in such

circumstances as did in fact, and reasonably, give rise to suspicions in the hus- **A**
band's mind that she might be associating with another man, or men.   Secondly,
that on these occasions she had ample opportunity to commit adultery had she
been minded to do so.   Thirdly, that on her own admissions the wife is a person
who has no special claim to chastity, for she has not felt inhibited from indulging
in sexual intercourse outside wedlock—she did so with two unmarried men (of
whom one is of course her husband) before marriage, and has lived in adultery **B**
with a married man since at least the month of July, 1967.   Fourthly, the
wife has given deliberately untruthful evidence in the respects stated in the
foregoing parts of this judgment, so that I am not prepared to rely on her evidence.
Fifthly, during the relevant time when the child D. was conceived, the wife and
the husband were having regular sexual intercourse together using contraceptive
procedures which made it possible though not probable that the wife might con- **C**
ceive a child by her husband.   It goes without saying that these findings fall
very far short of establishing even the thinnest case of adultery against the wife.
I shall consider hereafter whether they are capable of playing any part at all in
the case against her.

By letter dated Aug. 1, 1961, the husband's solicitors enquired of the wife
whether she was willing to submit herself and the child D. to the taking of blood **D**
samples with a view to carrying out a blood grouping test in conjunction with a
sample taken from the husband. The husband offered to defray the cost involved.
Shortly thereafter the wife readily agreed to the course proposed.   Dr. Alan
Grant accordingly took samples from the parties and the child on Aug. 26,
1961, and he grouped these blood samples under a number of systems including
the Rhesus blood group system.   In the child's blood he found a Willis " C " **E**
factor which was absent from the blood of the husband and the wife. It is perhaps
convenient to record at this stage that further blood samples were taken from the
child and the parties on June 11, 1966, when the same result was found.   On this
occasion portions of the samples were handed to a medical specialist on behalf of
the child.   Dr. Alan Grant grouped these samples under three systems available
in 1966 which were not available in 1961.   These new groupings did not advance **F**
the matter one way or the other.

Accordingly the case against the wife on the basis of the medical evidence
stands or falls on the presence of the Willis " C " factor in the child's blood, which
is absent from the blood of both the husband and the wife.   The only medical
evidence called before me was that of Dr. Alan Grant.   His qualifications, experience, and standing are so high and so well known that I need not give details **G**
in this judgment.   Dr. Alan Grant's opinion was that as there was no dispute
that the child was the child of the wife and neither she nor her husband had that
factor in her or his blood, the husband could not be the father of the child.   He
stated that this opinion was subject to the biological possibility that the Willis " C "
factor might have appeared in the child's blood as the result of a mutation.   A
very great deal of the argument before me turned on the evaluation of that **H**
possibility.   Dr. Alan Grant said that it was clear from the structure of the blood
groups that in the course of evolution mutation had occurred, that for some
twenty years or more he had been feverishly searching for evidence of a mutation
and had found none, and that in his view if the blood of the whole human race
were examined he would expect to find examples of mutations.   It was suggested
to him that an explanation for the failure to find an example of mutation in the
course of twenty years or so was that Dr. Alan Grant himself would only accept as
an example of a mutation an instance established to a standard of scientific
certainty.   It was also suggested to him that his deductions were based on the
examination of only a small sample of the population and that a good deal of the
work had been done on diseased blood.   Dr. Alan Grant was obviously aware of
and had considered these points.   My note of his evidence runs thus in part:

" One can say that these mutations don't occur except in the rarest circumstances by virtue of the number of cases examined without showing

A   exceptions. The families examined so far is a small proportion of the total families. This aspect has been explored to a tremendous extent. We have examined what we say is a fair sample."

Dr. Alan Grant himself referred to the fact in giving evidence before the magistrates in this case in 1962 he had assessed the chances of a mutation occurring as one chance in fifty thousand generations. For reasons which he gave and which

B   I need not repeat, he said that in the light of medical knowledge in 1967 it was more likely to be in the region of one chance in a million generations. When pressed he said that he himself would put the chance of a mutation as much smaller than one in fifty thousand generations but that that assessment was a reasonable point of view. The difficulty of expressing the possibility of a mutation in this way is that Dr. Alan Grant was not himself aware of a single instance of a muta-

C   tion. One or two alleged instances recorded in text books were put to Dr. Alan Grant and he gave reasons, which satisfied me, for his view that these were not instances of a mutation or were instances of the loss—or trans-location—of a blood factor and therefore not strictly relevant to a case such as the present where a fresh factor has appeared. It was also suggested to him that an explanation in the present case might be that the Willis " C " factor could be present in

D   the blood of the husband or the wife but was not apparent on examination because it had been suppressed. I accepted Dr. Alan Grant's view that this possibility was far less likely even than a mutation.

The only medical evidence before me given by a medical witness of high standing satisfied me that though there was a possibility that the Willis " C " factor had appeared in the child's blood as the result of a mutation that possibility was, to

E   quote Dr. Alan Grant's words, " too remote to be of practical significance ". Though he was not aware of any case which he accepted as an example of a mutation having occurred in some twenty years, when pressed he himself valued the chance of it occurring at about one chance in a million generations. Dr. Alan Grant was not prepared to treat the chances of suppression having occurred as being one which affected his assessment in this case and I accept his view.

F   The remaining questions therefore are: first, is that evidence by itself sufficient to establish adultery against the wife? Second, if not, is the burden of proof satisfied by the medical evidence taken together with the whole of the rest of the evidence? In this case a finding of adultery would inevitably have the effect of bastardising the child D. Counsel on both sides agreed that consequently the husband could not succeed unless he succeeded in establishing adultery beyond

G   all reasonable doubt. Counsel for the husband, did not seek to argue that the decision of the House of Lords in *Blyth* v. *Blyth* (3) lowered the standard of proof in a suit involving the legitimacy of a child. Accordingly I approached the issue of adultery on the footing that the burden on the husband is one of strict proof beyond reasonable doubt. It will be sufficient if I cite only some passages from a few of the number of authorities to which I was referred. The duty of the court

H   by statute is to pronounce a decree " if satisfied on the evidence ". These passages illuminate that duty. From *Preston-Jones* v. *Preston-Jones* (4). This is the well-known case in which the evidence was that an interval of 360 days elapsed between intercourse with the husband and the birth of the child to the wife. The legitimacy of the child was an issue. LORD SIMONDS is recorded as having said (5):

I   " Let me first get one difficulty out of the way. A question was raised as to the standard of proof. The result of a finding of adultery in such a case as this is in effect to bastardise the child. That is a matter in which from time out of mind strict proof has been required. That does not mean, however, that a degree of proof is demanded such as in a scientific inquiry

---

(3) [1966] 1 All E.R. 524; [1966] A.C. 643.
(4) [1951] 1 All E.R. 124; [1951] A.C. 391.
(5) [1951] 1 All E.R. at p. 127; [1951] A.C. at pp. 400, 401.

would justify the conclusion that such and such an event is impossible. In this context at least no higher proof of a fact is demanded than that it is established beyond all reasonable doubt: see *Head* v. *Head* (6). To prove that a period of so many days between fruitful coition and the time of conception is in a scientific sense impossible is itself, I suppose, a scientific impossibility. The utmost that a court of law can demand is that it should be established beyond all reasonable doubt that a child conceived so many days after a particular coitus cannot be the result of that coitus. I would add that since writing this opinion I have had the advantage of reading that of my noble and learned friend LORD MACDERMOTT, and concur in what he says on this matter."

LORD MACDERMOTT is reported as having said (7):

"The evidence must, no doubt, be clear and satisfactory, beyond a mere balance of probabilities, and conclusive in the sense that it will satisfy what SIR WILLIAM SCOTT, described in *Loveden* v. *Loveden* (8) as 'the guarded discretion of a reasonable and just man', but these desiderata appear to me entirely consistent with the acceptance and proof beyond reasonable doubt as to the standard required. Such, in my opinion, is the standard required by the statute. If a judge is satisfied beyond reasonable doubt as to the commission of the matrimonial offence relied on by a petitioner as ground for divorce, he must surely be 'satisfied' within the meaning of the enactment, and no less so in cases of adultery where the circumstances are such as to involve the paternity of a child. On the other hand, I am unable to subscribe to the view which, though not propounded here, has had its adherents, namely, that on its true construction the word 'satisfied' is capable of connoting something less than proof beyond reasonable doubt. The jurisdiction in divorce involves the status of the parties and the public interest requires that the marriage bond shall not to be set aside lightly or without strict inquiry. The terms of the statute recognised this plainly, and I think it would be quite out of keeping with the anxious nature of its provisions to hold that the court might be 'satisfied', in respect of a ground for dissolution, with something less than proof beyond reasonable doubt. I should, perhaps, add that I do not base my conclusions as to the appropriate standard of proof on any analogy drawn from the criminal law. I do not think it is possible to say, at any rate since the decision of this House in *Mordaunt* v. *Moncreiffe* (9), that the two jurisdictions are other than distinct. The true reason, as it seems to me, why both accept the same general standard—proof beyond reasonable doubt—lies not in any analogy, but in the gravity and public importance of the issues with which each is concerned."

Counsel instructed by the Official Solicitor, for the child D. invited my particular attention to the case of *Cotton* v. *Cotton* (10). That was a case in which the wife and the husband occupied the same bed at the time when the child in issue was conceived. The husband denied that any sexual intercourse had taken place at the material time, while the wife said it had, though the trial judge found her evidence to be worthless. He nevertheless held the child was legitimate although there was a body of other evidence indicating an adulterous association by the wife including the fact that she herself thought the child was illegitimate. The Court of Appeal refused to interfere with the trial judge's findings. It was, of course, a case decided in 1954 which cried out for blood test evidence. I do not think that I need cite any passages from the judgment of SINGLETON, L.J., in that case.

(6) (1823), Turn. & R. 138.
(7) [1951] 1 All E.R. at p. 138; [1951] A.C. at p. 417.
(8) [1803-13] All E.R. Rep. 339 at p. 340, letter F.
(9) [1874-80] All E.R. Rep. 288; (1874), L.R. 2 Sc. & Div. 374.
(10) [1954] 2 All E.R. 105; [1954] P. 305.

A　　I approach the crucial decision which I must make in the light of the principles enunciated above and with a proper sense of the importance of the issue of the paternity of the child D. and of the issue of adultery to the wife. I am satisfied beyond all reasonable doubt on the medical evidence alone that the wife did commit adultery in about the month of October, 1960, and that consequently the husband is not the father of the child D. If that view were wrong then putting
B the whole of the rest of the evidence which I have summarised earlier in this judgment in the scale in addition to the medical evidence, I would certainly be satisfied beyond reasonable doubt of the wife's adultery and the consequent illegitimacy of the child D.

　　I can deal shortly with the wife's allegation of desertion. The husband has failed to satisfy me that he had such grave and weighty cause in the conduct of his
C wife as justified him in leaving her on Jan. 14, 1961. However, when Dr. Alan Grant's report was available in September, 1961, I am satisfied that the husband had just cause to believe that his wife had committed adultery and for remaining apart from her, and that he continued to be so justified until Sept. 10, 1962, when the magistrates decided that adultery had not been established against her. Three years have not elapsed between that date and the date of the wife's answer
D in this suit. This technical difficulty is of course capable of being disposed of by the necessary leave being given for the filing of a fresh cross-petition. It is common ground that I should approach the issue of the husband's desertion in the light of the wife's adultery on the basis of the principle conveniently stated in *Richards* v. *Richards* (11) in the headnote (12):

E　　" Where a husband deserts his wife and later the wife commits adultery, the wife's adultery terminates the desertion, unless the wife can show that her adultery has had no effect on her husband's conduct. If she can show (i) that he did not know of the adultery, or (ii) that he would never have come back to her again in any event, his desertion continues. If there should be some chance of the husband returning to his wife and her conduct destroys that chance, then the desertion comes to an end when he becomes aware of
F the adultery, because he then has good cause for staying away from his wife."

　　There was a powerful passage in the evidence of the husband of which my note reads thus: " I had no intention of going back. No, I wouldn't go back. I certainly would not change my mind whatever happened." Nevertheless, so much time has passed since 1961 and the husband's feelings have run so high in
G this bitter and protracted suit that I am not satisfied that he is now able to describe what course he would have taken if Dr. Alan Grant's report had indicated that his wife had not committed adultery. The burden of proof being on the wife, she has failed in my view to discharge it; but in any event, even if contrary to my view, desertion for three years had been established, in all the circumstances of this case I do not consider that the discretion of the court should be exercised
H in favour of the wife in respect of her adultery. If it had been necessary to exercise the court's discretion in favour of the husband in respect of any period or periods of desertion by him (which appears to me to be unnecessary since the wife's proved adultery preceded any desertion by the husband) I should have done so without hesitation.

　　As it is, I find adultery established by the husband and that desertion for three
I years has not been established by the wife; I therefore pronounce a decree nisi on the ground of the wife's adultery.

Decree nisi.

　　Solicitors: *John Ramage & Co.* (for the husband); *Daybells* (for the wife); *Official Solicitor.*

[Reported by ALICE BLOOMFIELD, *Barrister-at-Law.]*

---

(11) [1952] 1 All E.R. 1384; [1952] P. 307.
(12) [1952] P. at p. 307.

CROSS v. BRITISH IRON, STEEL AND KINDRED TRADES ASSOCIATION.

[COURT OF APPEAL, CIVIL DIVISION (Lord Denning, M.R., Diplock and Salmon, L.JJ.), November 24, 27, 1967.]

Trade union—Legal assistance—Alleged negligence of union in relation to member's claim for damages—Member's claim investigated and reported to central office by branch secretary in accordance with union's rules—Union's solicitor advised no cause of action—Advice communicated to member— Some two years later member apparently again raised the matter with branch secretary—No warning that any claim would become statute-barred on expiration of three-year period—Whether union in breach of duty.

The plaintiff was a member of the defendant union. Under their rules the union were under a duty to give legal assistance to their members on, among other occasions, the happening of any event which would reasonably appear to entitle the member to claim damages at common law. The rules further provided that the member should notify the branch secretary, and that the branch secretary should immediately forward to the union's central office full particulars on the form provided for the purpose. Any proceedings were to be conducted by the union. On Apr. 22, 1958, the plaintiff sustained an accident at work; he reported it to the branch secretary, who took statements from him and a fellow worker and sent the report to head office together with a covering letter summarising the fellow worker's evidence. The report and letter were put before a competent solicitor of the union who advised*, in effect, that on the evidence before him the plaintiff had no case. The solicitor did not advise that any further enquiries should be made. The plaintiff was informed of that advice and accepted it at the time. Two years later, in 1960 or 1961 before the three-year time limit had expired, the plaintiff raised the matter (as the trial judge inferred) with the branch secretary, but no further information was adduced by the plaintiff, and nothing was done. The plaintiff was not informed that any cause of action of his would be statute-barred three years after the accident. After the three years expired, the plaintiff wrote to the union asking them to look into the matter. In an action by the plaintiff against the union for alleged negligence in relation to the plaintiff's claim for damages the trial judge found that there was no negligence on the part of the union's solicitor in advising as solicitor for the plaintiff, but that the union should have warned the plaintiff when he raised the matter in 1960 or 1961, of the barring of any cause of action by expiration of three years from the date of the accident. On appeal,

Held: the duty imposed by the union's rules was fulfilled by the branch secretary's collecting the particulars and forwarding them to the union's central office and by the union's obtaining the advice of a solicitor whom they reasonably believed to be competent; as no further enquiries were advised, there was no duty on the union to make further enquiries, and when the matter was raised some two years later there remained no duty on the union, in particular, no duty to advise the plaintiff on the three-year time limit for bringing an action (see p. 254, letters E, G and I, p. 255, letter E, and p. 256, letters F and H, post).

Per SALMON, L.J.: on the true construction of the relevant rules the defendant union did not warrant that the solicitor or barrister to whom a matter was referred should perform his duties carefully or skilfully, still less that the legal advice given was right (see p. 255, letter I, post).

Appeal allowed.

---

* On the question whether the solicitor was advising the union or the plaintiff, compare p. 253, letter H, and p. 255, letter H, post.

A   [**Editorial Note.** The present case should be considered with *Buckley* v. *National Union of General and Municipal Workers* ([1967] 3 All E.R. 767) where there was no warning of time running to bar any possible cause of action, but the union was found not to have been negligent nor in breach of duty, in the circumstances and under the rules of that union, in not obtaining legal advice for the plaintiff.

B   As to rules authorising the institution of proceedings and legal aid by a trade union, see 38 HALSBURY's LAWS (3rd Edn.) 360, para. 623; and for cases as to the rules of trade unions, see 45 DIGEST (Repl.) 545, 546, *1230-1238*, and for cases on the liability of trade unions to be sued see ibid., 594-596, *1490-1504*.]

Appeal.

C   By writ issued on Oct. 15, 1964, the plaintiff, Donald Cross, brought an action against the defendant union, and, by the writ as amended on Mar. 14, 1966, adding as second defendants, Russell Jones and Walker, a firm of solicitors, claimed damages for negligence for breach of duty of the defendants or one of them or their servants or agents for failing to exercise proper care in connexion with or about the conduct of the plaintiff's claim for compensation in respect of an accident which occurred on Apr. 22, 1958. The plaintiff was a member of the

D defendant union. On Apr. 22, 1958, he met with an accident in the course of his employment. By his statement of claim he alleged that by virtue of r. 36 of the defendant union's rules it was a term of his contract of membership that he was entitled to legal assistance from the union and that negligently and in breach of union duty the defendant union failed to exercise proper care in the conduct of his claim against his employers in respect of the accident. At the

E trial before JAMES, J., the trial judge found, on May 12, 1967, that the defendant union were in breach of contract with the plaintiff in the following respects, as pleaded in the statement of claim—(i) failing to carry out or cause to be carried out any sufficient investigation into the facts and circumstances of the plaintiff's accident; failing to interview or take statements from all or any of the available witnesses, and concluding in or about May, 1958, that the plaintiff had no cause

F of action against his employers without examining properly or at all the available evidence relevant to the accident. The trial judge further found that the defendant union were in breach of contract, in relation to the period from April, 1960, to April, 1961, of the following respects as alleged as particulars of negligence in the statement of claim, viz. (vi) failing to advise the plaintiff that his claim would become statute-barred on Apr. 22, 1961, and (vii) failing to advise the

G plaintiff properly or at all as to his position in relation to the Limitation Acts or to give him such assistance or advice as would have enabled him to seek the assistance of a solicitor before his claim became statute-barred. There was no plea by the defendant union of fault on the plaintiff's part whereby damages flowing from any breach of contract by the union might have been reduced. The trial judge found that there was no duty on the defendant union to advise the

H plaintiff in 1958 concerning the operation of the Limitation Act, 1939, as distinct from duty to advise on that subject in 1960 and 1961 by informing the plaintiff that if he wished to pursue the claim time was running out under the Act of 1939. The limitation period actually expired with Apr. 21, 1961. In regard to the plaintiff's claim against the second defendants, the solicitors, a member of whose firm, Mr. Walker, advised when the matter was referred to him by the defendant

I union, the trial judge in his judgment said—

> " I do not find any conduct on Mr. Walker's part which fell short of the standard of care demanded of him as solicitor for the defendants. Mr. Walker wrote to [the branch secretary of the defendant union, Mr. Morley] in the matter in a letter of May 9 which reads—' Form 34 has been received by us in this matter. In view of the remarks which you make in your letter of May 6, we do not think that anyone could really be blamed for this accident and it seems to be one of those unfortunate occurrences for which

A

no-one can be blamed '.   Mr. Walker says that his language was deliberately
chosen.   This was not a matter in which he was telling the branch secretary
' There is no claim in law ', nor was he telling the branch secretary ' There
is a good cause of action available to [the plaintiff] '.   He was leaving the
door open for further discussion if [the plaintiff] on being informed of his
view, or if Mr. Morley or a branch committee disputed the view he expressed
on the information placed before him.   Mr. Walker was entitled to assume
that Mr. Morley had obtained the relevant information with his usual
efficiency.   Mr. Morley received the solicitors' letter.   It appears from the
evidence of Mr. Walker and the statement of Mr. Morley in evidence, the latter
knew that if a member was dissatisfied with the decision of the legal department, as the solicitors were called, then the member's observations could
and should be sent to the solicitors and, if the matter could not be resolved
by correspondence, a personal interview with Mr. Walker would be arranged."

B

C

The trial judge gave judgment for the plaintiff against the defendant union for
£200, at which sum he assessed the compensation of the plaintiff for the loss of
his chance of success in an action against his employers if brought in time.

By notice dated June 20, 1967, the defendant union appealed from the judgment of the trial judge, stating the following among other grounds of appeal—
(a) that on the facts the trial judge was wrong in law in finding a breach of
contract; (b) that the trial judge was wrong in law in holding that in 1960 and
1961 the defendant union were in breach of contract in failing to advise the
plaintiff about the Limitation Act, 1939; (c) the trial judge was wrong in finding
that the plaintiff's claim was not properly investigated by the defendant union
and (d) that on the facts the trial judge should have held the defendant union
fulfilled their contract to the plaintiff by consulting and being advised by a
reputable firm of solicitors.

D

E

F. B. Purchas, Q.C., and *A. C. Lauriston* for the defendant union.
S. Terrell, Q.C., and *S. E. Brodie* for the plaintiff.

F

LORD DENNING, M.R.:   The plaintiff, Donald Cross was a member of
the defendant trade union, the British Iron, Steel & Kindred Trades Association.
He sustained an accident on Apr. 22, 1958.   He lost a piece of the third finger
of his right hand.   It was in some way caught between two rails on which he was
working with some other men.   After that accident he gave particulars to the
branch secretary of the union.

G

The question in the case is: did the union do their duty by the plaintiff? The
plaintiff says that they ought to have taken up a claim for him at common law
against his employers, and that they failed to do so in breach of their contractual
obligations to him. He says further that when the three years were running out,
they ought to have advised him that a writ should be issued so as to save the
claim from being statute-barred: but they failed to do so. In consequence, so
he says, he has lost the chance of claiming against his employers at common
law: and having lost that chance, he is entitled to damages. JAMES, J., has so
found. He did not think a great deal of the plaintiff. He said: " Morally he is
not deserving of any damages." But he gave him £200 damages for loss of the
chance. Now the union appeal to this court.

H

This brings me at once to the rules of the trade union. It is accepted by both
sides that the rules form a contract between the union and the members. The
relevant rule is r. 36. It provides for legal assistance. It states that

I

" Any member . . . shall be entitled . . . to receive legal assistance as the
circumstances may require in the following cases, viz:—(a) upon the happening of any event which would entitle or reasonably appear to entitle the
member or his dependants to claim damages at common law, or under the
Fatal Accidents Act, or the National Insurance (Industrial Injuries) Act."

A Such an event clearly happened here. The plaintiff was entitled to claim under one or other of those heads. The rule goes on to provide that on the happening of such an event

B " The member or his representative or anyone on his behalf shall notify his branch secretary thereof within three days of the happening of the said event, and the branch secretary shall immediately thereafter forward to the central office of the association full particulars of the said event on the form provided for that purpose signed by the member or by someone on his behalf. Such notice is additional to any other notice required by these rules in respect of a claim for other benefits, and neglect or failure to comply with this clause may entail forfeiture of benefit under this rule."

C Later on the rule states that:

" The acceptance by the association of liability for assistance under this rule, or for payment of any legal or medical or other expenses, shall be strictly subject to observance by the member or his representative or his dependants, as the case may be, of the following conditions, viz., that the negotiations or legal or other proceedings required in the case shall be wholly

D carried out or instituted or defended by the association, or by its agents employed or retained for that purpose."

In pursuance of that rule the plaintiff told his branch secretary, Mr. Morley, about the accident. Mr. Morley is a very experienced branch secretary who has handled many claims. On Apr. 28, 1958. Mr. Morley took down full particulars on the form provided. It is Form 34. The plaintiff did not actually sign the docu-

E ment himself because of the injury to his hand; but Mr. Morley signed for him. In giving the particulars, the plaintiff gave details of the accident and he described how it happened. Then he was asked this question: " Was it the employer's fault? If so, state why." His answer was: " Rollers were in bad condition." Then the next question: " Was it the fault of a fellow workman? If so, state why and give his name." The plaintiff gave no answer to that question. From which

F it follows that he did not suggest it was the fault of any fellow workman. He was asked to give the names of any witnesses. He gave the names of Mr. Moxon and Mr. Garbutt. Such were the particulars on Form 34.

On getting those particulars, Mr. Morley saw one of the witnesses, Mr. Moxon, and got his account of what had happened. Then on May 6, 1958, Mr. Morley

G sent the form forward, together with a covering letter summarising Mr. Moxon's evidence. He reported Mr. Moxon as saying that:

" The second rail came into contact with the first rail, causing [the plaintiff's] hand to be trapped."

It seems to me that at that stage Mr. Morley had done all that reasonable care required.

H When the form was received at the headquarters of the union it was passed to the legal adviser, Mr. Walker, of the firm of Russell Jones & Walker, solicitors. That was clearly done in pursuance of their contract to give legal assistance: and thenceforward no doubt Mr. Walker was advising the plaintiff but being paid by the defendant union. Now Mr. Walker is himself very knowledgeable on the nature of the work in this industry. He knows exactly how these bars are moved.

I Mr. Walker considered Form 34 and the covering letter. He took the view that the plaintiff's complaint against the employers (about the condition of the rollers) was not well-founded. Their condition could not have played any part in causing the accident. Mr. Walker did not see any basis for a claim at common law. Accordingly, he wrote a letter on May 9, 1958, to the branch secretary, Mr. Morley:

" Form 34 has been received by us in this matter. In view of the remarks which you make in your letter of May 6, we do not think that anyone could

A

really be blamed for this accident, and it seems to be one of those unfortunate occurrences for which no-one can be blamed."

Such was the advice of the experienced solicitor.

Mr. Morley passed on that advice to the plaintiff, who appeared to accept it at the time. So Mr. Morley took no steps to see any other witness or to make any further investigations. Nor did he put the matter again before Mr. Walker. So the matter slept—but it slept uncomfortably so far as the plaintiff was concerned. He says he raised the matter from time to time with Mr. Morley and got no satisfaction. He raised it before the three years had expired, but still Mr. Morley did nothing. In September, 1961, after the three years had expired, the plaintiff, through his wife, wrote a letter to headquarters. He said:

B

"I am writing this letter in hope you will answer it and tell me how I stand in my claim for injuries I received at work, as I cannot get any satisfaction from my branch secretary. I have asked the secretary for my letters concerning my case and he will not give them to me. I would be obliged if you could see into this matter for me. Furthermore I would like to know what I have been kept waiting all this time. If nothing is done this time about it I will go and see a solicitor about it. Would you kindly answer this letter?"

C

D

That was in September, 1961, after the three years had expired; but from that letter the judge inferred that within the three years, the matter had been raised with Mr. Morley and nothing had been done. The judge felt that advice should have been given to the plaintiff that the three years were running out and that he ought to issue his writ.

E

Such being the facts in the case, the question is: what was the duty under the rules? It seems to me that on the true interpretation of these rules, the branch secretary fulfilled his duty by collecting the particulars and sending forward to the central office full particulars on the form. That being done, it was the duty of the defendant union to provide the legal assistance. They did this by passing the papers to the solicitor, Mr. Walker, to advise. Mr. Walker advised that there was no claim and his advice was passed on to the plaintiff. On that being done, the defendant union had done their duty by the plaintiff under the rules. They had afforded legal assistance and advice. It had been given to him quite properly, honestly and carefully by the solicitors. That was all that duty required. The judge said in terms:

F

"I do not find any conduct on Mr. Walker's part which fell short of the standard of care demanded of him as solicitor for the defendants."

G

It would follow, I would add, "as solicitor for [the plaintiff]". There is no cross-notice challenging that finding, and although counsel for the plaintiff at one stage did suggest the possibility of a cross-notice, we did not think it right to allow that at this stage. I am quite satisfied that counsel and those advising him were quite right in not putting in a cross-notice.

H

If Mr. Walker had advised that further enquiries should be made or that an action should be brought, no doubt the defendant union would have come under a duty to act accordingly in pursuing a claim. The control of the proceedings and payment for them would be by the defendant union, but the relationship of solicitor and client would be between the solicitor and the member. Such would be the legal position; but it never reached that stage here because when the solicitor advised that there was no case, the defendant union had fulfilled all their obligations to the plaintiff. I do not see that there were any further obligations on them. It is true that two years later he raised the matter again, but there was then no duty on them to say to him: "Be careful to issue a writ or the Statute of Limitations will run." They had already fulfilled their duty when they had provided legal assistance and it was adverse to the claim.

I

In these circumstances it seems to me the defendant union were in no breach of their duty. I am confirmed in this view by the conduct of the plaintiff himself.

A In the course of his evidence he went so far as to deny the entries in Form 34, and he suggested that Mr. Morley had got them all wrong. He said that he had told Mr. Morley that it was Mr. Moxon's fault. That shows that the plaintiff realised that his case would only be good if he put forward a case of fault against a fellow workman; but he never did so. The judge did not accept the plaintiff's statements. He said: " In some respects his evidence was false to his knowledge."

B When a man gives false evidence to bolster up his case, it usually means that he loses it. I think that the plaintiff has not succeeded in showing any breach of duty by the defendant union. I would allow this appeal and enter judgment for the defendant union.

C DIPLOCK, L.J.: I agree, and I need add very little. The defendant union contracted with the plaintiff that he should receive legal assistance as the circumstances might require, among other cases, on the happening of any event which would entitle him or reasonably appear to entitle him to damages at common law, and various other things. At the first stage, the duty of the defendant union is to obtain for the member legal advice from a person of reasonable skill and experience in legal matters, that is to say, either a solicitor or it may be a barrister.

D In order to obtain that legal assistance and to provide material for it, the rule which LORD DENNING, M.R., has read, makes it incumbent on the member to give notice of an event of the kind that I have described, and to provide full particulars of the said event on the form provided for that purpose signed by the member or someone on his behalf. The branch secretary is required to forward that immediately to the central office, and in my view the branch secretary has no duty in relation to the form otherwise than to obtain it from the member and E forward it to the central office.

If, on that material, advice is given by a qualified lawyer that it discloses no cause of complaint and that advice is transmitted to the member and he acquiesces in it at the time, in my view the duty of the defendant union under the rules to the member is at an end. In this particular case the judge has found, after careful investigation of the matter, that there was no negligence on the part of Mr. F Walker, the solicitor instructed by the defendant union, who in fact gave the advice. In those circumstances I do not think it necessary to reach any final decision on the matter which was canvassed to some extent in argument as to whether the defendant union fulfil their duty by sending on the material which has been provided by the member to a solicitor whom they have instructed and reasonably suppose to be one of reasonable skill and competence, or whether G they warrant to the member that the advice will in fact be given with reasonable skill and competence. I think that that point is a difficult one, because although Mr. Walker in his evidence said that, from the time when he received the member's form, he regarded the plaintiff as his client, it does not appear that it is the practice that the letter of advice written by Mr. Walker is given to the member; and indeed the learned judge has found, for it was refused in this case, that the H member had no right to it. That suggests some difficulty about regarding the member as the client of the solicitor at the time at which the advice is given; but in the present case it is not necessary to resolve that doubt or difficulty, because there is the finding that the solicitor in fact gave this advice with reasonable skill on the information before him. I agree that this appeal should be allowed.

I SALMON, L.J.: I agree, and add a word only out of respect for the judgment of the judge from whose conclusion we are differing.

I incline to the view that on the true construction of r. 36 (1), the defendant union perform their duty in the circumstances there postulated if they make available to their members the legal services of solicitors or barristers whom on reasonable grounds they believe to be reasonably competent, skilful and of good reputation. As at present advised, I do not think that the defendant union warrant that the solicitor or barrister concerned shall perform his duties carefully or skilfully: still less that the legal advice given is right.

When an event happens which would reasonably appear to entitle the member, **A** amongst other things, to claim damages at common law and, therefore, to receive legal assistance under r. 36 (1), there is no doubt that the branch secretary has to obtain from the member, and the member is obliged to supply, if he can, the full particulars of the event. Those particulars are then sent by the branch secretary to the central office to be forwarded to the defendant union's solicitor. In this case that is exactly what occurred. I am not prepared to decide whether **B** in any special circumstances there might be an obligation on the defendant union's officers to look for further information. In the present case the branch secretary, Mr. Morley, certainly did look for further information and he got it from a Mr. Moxon, who was operating the machine which expelled the piece of steel which crushed the plaintiff's finger. He sent forward that information given to him by Mr. Moxon, together with the particulars supplied by the plaintiff, **C** to the defendant union's solicitor, Mr. Walker. Mr. Walker said in evidence that he had ample information in those documents to enable him to come to a conclusion.

The conclusion at which he arrived is expressed in the letter which LORD DENNING, M.R., has read dated May 9, 1958. As I read that letter, and as I have no doubt the defendant union's officials read that letter, it meant (whatever Mr. **D** Walker said he intended it to mean) that there was no prospect of a claim succeeding and there was no necessity to make further enquiries. On receipt of that letter, Mr. Morley communicated its contents to the plaintiff, who at that stage appeared to accept them. The case, as I understand it, against the defendant union is that Mr. Morley was negligent because he did not make any further enquiries. The judge has found that Mr. Walker, in advising as he did, did not fall short of the **E** standard of care demanded of a solicitor. That finding is perhaps not very important if the defendant union do not, as I think they do not, warrant that their solicitor will in fact use reasonable skill and care. In any event, there is no cross-notice in respect of that finding.

The letter from the solicitor is, however, of the greatest importance. I think it would be quite wrong to find that the officers of a union were negligent because **F** they accepted the advice of their solicitor whom they had every reason to believe was competent and careful. They cannot be expected to be any wiser than he was.

That in my view is the end of the case. Some years later in 1960 or 1961 the plaintiff was indicating that he proposed to go to other solicitors, and the judge I think has found (though I cannot agree with him) that at that stage there was an obligation on the defendant union's officials to advise the plaintiff that he had **G** better hurry up as the limitation period was about to expire. It is not, however, suggested that any further information was put before the defendant union's officials by the plaintiff in relation to this accident after they had received and passed on to him what I regard as the categorical advice from their solicitor in May, 1958, to the effect that no action would lie. I do not think that in those circumstances there was any obligation on the defendant union to take any fur- **H** ther action. There are undoubtedly cases in which a defendant union's handling of their member's claim is deserving of criticism and sometimes severe criticism; but this, in my view, is not such a case.

I agree that the appeal succeeds.

Appeal allowed. Action dismissed.

Solicitors: *Russell Jones & Walker* (for the defendant union); *Clutton, Moore & Lavington*, agents for *Doberman, Richardson, Broady & Horsman*, Middlesbrough (for the plaintiff).

[*Reported by* F. GUTTMAN, ESQ., *Barrister-at-Law.*]

A

RODWELL SECURITIES, LTD. v. INLAND REVENUE COMMISSIONERS.

[CHANCERY DIVISION (Pennycuick, J.), November 20, 1967.]

B
Stamp Duty—Transfer of property from one associated company to another—" Beneficial ownership "—Parent company having two wholly-owned subsidiaries—Transfer by one subsidiary to a company that was the wholly-owned subsidiary of the other subsidiary of the parent company—Share capital of transferee not in the beneficial ownership of the parent company—Parent company could be said to have " controlling interest "—Finance Act, 1930 (20 & 21 Geo. 5 c. 28), *s.* 42 (2).

C
A wholly-owned subsidiary of a parent company conveyed land to the wholly-owned subsidiary of another wholly-owned subsidiary of the parent company. The transferee claimed exemption from stamp duty on, so far as relevant, the ground that no less than ninety per cent. of its share capital was in the beneficial ownership of the parent company of the transferor.

Held: the capital of the transferee subsidiary was not in the beneficial

D
ownership of the parent company of the transferor subsidiary; accordingly the exemption from stamp duty on the conveyance of sale under s. 42 (2) of the Finance Act, 1930, was inapplicable (see p. 259, letter G, *post*).

Per CURIAM: the transaction would have been within the exemption if s. 42 (2) had referred to the " controlling interest " instead of " beneficial ownership ", or had included such words as " directly or indirectly " (see

E
p. 259, letter I, to p. 260, letter A, *post*).

Dictum of JENKINS, L.J., in *Parway Estates, Ltd.* v. *Inland Revenue Comrs.* ((1957), 37 A.T.C. at p. 168) applied.

Appeal dismissed.

F
[As to relief from stamp duty on conveyances or transfers on sale between associated companies, see 33 HALSBURY'S LAWS (3rd Edn.) 318, 319, para. 556; and for a case on the subject, see 39 DIGEST (Repl.) 321, *653*.

For the Finance Act, 1930, s. 42 (1), (2), and the Finance Act, 1938, s. 50 (1), see 21 HALSBURY'S STATUTES (2nd Edn.) 959, 1196.]

Cases referred to:

G
British American Tobacco Co., Ltd. v. *Inland Revenue Comrs.*, [1943] 1 All E.R. 13; [1943] A.C. 335; 112 L.J.K.B. 81; 169 L.T. 98; 29 Tax Cas. 49; 28 Digest (Repl.) 376, *1640*.

English Sewing Cotton, Ltd. v. *Inland Revenue Comrs.*, [1947] 1 All E.R. 679; 176 L.T. 481; 28 Digest (Repl.) 445, *1933*.

Parway Estates, Ltd. v. *Inland Revenue Comrs.*, [1958] T.R. 193; 37 A.T.C. 164.

Case Stated.

H
This was a Case Stated by the Commissioners of Inland Revenue pursuant to s. 13 of the Stamp Act, 1891. The question at issue was whether a transfer of registered land, dated Dec. 19, 1963, was exempted from stamp duty under the head of charge " Conveyance or Transfer on Sale " by the provisions of s. 42 of the Finance Act, 1930. The transferor company, Sun Real Estates, Ltd. (hereinafter called " the Sun company "), and the appellant transferee company,

I
Rodwell Securities, Ltd. (hereinafter called " the Securities company ") were both members of a group of companies. The structure of the group, so far as relevant to this case, was in outline as follows. The principal company of the group was a public company, whose name at the date of the transfer was Rodwell London and Provincial Properties, Ltd. (hereinafter called " the London company "); the London company had a number of subsidiaries of which two were the Sun company and a company whose name at the date of the transfer was Rodwell Group, Ltd. (hereinafter called " the Group company ") of which the Securities company was a subsidiary. At the date of the transfer, the

issued share capital of the Sun company consisted of 3,100,000 ordinary shares A
of 2s. each, of which 3,093,997 were held by the London company and the
remaining 6,003 were held as to two thousand by Bernard Myers, as to two
thousand by Sefton Siegmond Myers, as to two thousand by Leonard Woolf,
as to one by Peter Edward Walker, as to one by John Solomon Cohan, and as to
the remaining one by Roderick Hamilton Purves, in each case as nominee for
the London company, which was solely and beneficially entitled thereto. At the B
same date the issued share capital of the Group company consisted of one million
ordinary shares of 5s. each of which 999,999 were held by the London company
and one was held by Bernard Myers as nominee for the London company which
was solely and beneficially entitled thereto. At the same date the issued share
capital of the Securities company consisted of one hundred ordinary shares of
£1 each. Of these, ninety-nine were held by the Group company and one was C
held jointly by Sefton Siegmond Myers and the Group company as nominees for
the Group company which was solely and beneficially entitled thereto.

It was common ground that (a) the effect of the transfer was to convey or
transfer a beneficial interest in property from the Sun company to the Securities
company; (b) the London company, the Sun company, the Group company and
the Securities company were all companies with limited liability; (c) at the date D
of the transfer, not less than ninety per cent. of the issued share capital of each
of the Sun company and the Group company was in the beneficial ownership of
the London company; and (d) at the same date the Group company was the
beneficial owner of not less than ninety per cent. of the issued share capital
of the Securities company.

The Securities company claimed that the transfer should be relieved from duty E
under s. 42 of the Finance Act, 1930, on the ground that the London company
was the beneficial owner of all the shares in the Securities company. The
commissioners, however, were not satisfied that the London company was the
beneficial owner of any of the issued share capital of the Securities company.

The commissioners were therefore of the opinion that the relationship between
the Sun company and the Securities company was not such as to qualify the F
transfer for relief from stamp duty under s. 42 of the Finance Act, 1930.
The commissioners accordingly assessed the transfer to duty in accordance with
Sch. 1 to the Stamp Act, 1891 (as amended), at the rate of 10s. for every £50 on
the amount or value of the consideration. The said consideration consisted of
the cash consideration of £29,320 mentioned in the transfer, and a mortgage
debt of £46,930 chargeable under the provisions of s. 57 of the Stamp Act, 1891, G
together making a total of £76,250. The duty thus assessed was £762 10s.
It was not disputed by the Securities company that if relief under s. 42 of the
Finance Act, 1930, was not available in this case the duty on the transfer was
correctly assessed in that sum.

The Securities company appealed; and the questions for the opinion of the
court were: (i) whether the transfer was chargeable with the ad valorem duty H
assessed by the commissioners, and (ii) if not, with what duty, if any, was it
chargeable.

M. D. Jones for the Securities company.
J. P. Warner for the Crown.

PENNYCUICK, J.: This is an appeal by way of Case Stated against the I
refusal of the Commissioners of Inland Revenue to allow exemption from stamp
duty under the heading " Conveyance or transfer on sale " on a certain transfer.
It is contended on behalf of the appellant company, Rodwell Securities, Ltd.,
to which I will refer as the Securities company, that the transfer is exempted
from duty by s. 42 of the Finance Act, 1930. I will read that section:

" (1) Stamp duty under the heading ' Conveyance or transfer on sale ' in
Sch. 1 to the Stamp Act, 1891 shall not be chargeable on an instrument to
which this section applies . . .

A

" (2) This section applies to any instrument as respects which it is shown to the satisfaction of the Commissioners of Inland Revenue (a) that the effect thereof is to convey or transfer a beneficial interest in property from one company with limited liability to another such company; and (b) that either—(i) one of the companies is beneficial owner of not less than ninety per cent. of the issued share capital of the other company; or (ii) not less

B

than ninety per cent. of the issued share capital of each of the companies is in the beneficial ownership of a third company with limited liability."

The facts in the present case are these. There is a company which was, at the relevant date, known as Rodwell London and Provincial Properties, Ltd. This " London company " had, always at the relevant date, two wholly-owned sub-

C

sidiaries. One was then known as Rodwell Group, Ltd., the Group company, and the other was Sun Real Estates, Ltd., the Sun company. The Securities company was the wholly owned subsidiary of the Group company. The position then was that the London company owned all the shares in the Sun and Group companies and the Group company owned all the shares in the Securities company. On Dec. 19, 1963, the Sun company executed a transfer in favour of the Securities

D

company of a property known as 39-47 Villiers Street, Westminster, in considera-tion of a sum of £29,320. An application was made for exemption from stamp duty under s. 42, and that application was refused.

In order to bring an instrument within the charge of stamp duty, the Revenue must show that the instrument falls fairly and squarely within the terms of the charging provision. Equally, in order to bring an instrument within an exemp-

E

tion from stamp duty, the taxpayer must show that the instrument falls fairly and squarely within the terms of the exempting provision. It is therefore necessary for the appellant in this case to show that the transfer falls within the terms of s. 42. The first condition in that section is that the effect of the instrument shall be to convey or transfer a beneficial interest in property from one company to another, and that condition is undoubtedly satisfied here. The

F

second condition, so far as is now relevant, is that not less than ninety per cent. of the issued share capital of each of the two companies in question shall be in the beneficial ownership of a third company.

In the present case it is in my judgment perfectly clear that the capital of the Securities company is not in the beneficial ownership of the London company. The position is that the London company owns the shares in the Group company,

G

so that the whole of the share capital in the Group company is in the beneficial ownership of the London company. The Group company in turn owns the whole of the shares in the Securities company, so that the whole of the issued share capital in the Securities company is in the beneficial ownership of the Group company. No part of the shares in the Securities company is in the beneficial ownership of the London company.

H

In order to escape from that position, counsel for the Securities company has to get through the company structure and establish that the exempting provision covers the position where one company has the entire interest, to use a neutral term, in another company, through the medium of a subsidiary of the first company of which the second company is in itself in turn a subsidiary. That is a position which it seems to me is not covered by the wording of s. 42. Counsel

I

for the Securities company puts it in this way. He says that the term " beneficial ownership " is not a term of art and falls to be construed liberally; the term " beneficial owner " includes any person having complete control over the disposition of property; and so here the London company has complete control over the disposition of the shares in the Securities company. If the section contained, instead of the expression " beneficial ownership ", the expression " controlling interest ", I apprehend that the present position would be within the exempting section. Again the position would probably be so if the section contained the words " directly or indirectly ". However, the section does not

refer to controlling interest but refers to beneficial ownership, and it does not A
contain the words " directly or indirectly ".

I was referred to a number of cases, none of which, with all respect to counsel
for the Securities company, appeared to come anywhere near bearing out his
proposition. I will, however, refer to two passages in cases which were cited to
me, which appear to me to go in precisely the opposite direction. In *Parway
Estates, Ltd.* v. *Inland Revenue Comrs.* (1) JENKINS, L.J., with whom the other B
lords justices agreed, said this:

> " Then there is a reference to the case of *English Sewing Cotton Co., Ltd.*
> v. *Inland Revenue Comrs.* (2). Speaking for myself, I find it difficult as
> at present advised to derive any assistance from consideration of what the
> ordinary person would understand by the words ' beneficial owner ' in their
> ordinary sense. I am open to conviction, but prima facie it seems to me C
> difficult to ascribe any different meaning to those words than their legal
> meaning, and that little assistance can be derived from speculation as to
> what an ordinary person would take them to mean in their popular sense."

That passage is directly in point here. According to the legal meaning of the
words, a company is not the beneficial owner of the assets of its own subsidiary. D
The legal meaning of the words takes account of the company structure and the
fact that each company is a separate legal person.

The other passage is from the speech of VISCOUNT SIMON, L.C., in *British
American Tobacco Co., Ltd.* v. *Inland Revenue Comrs.* (3), where the House of
Lords was concerned with the expression " controlling interest ". LORD SIMON
said this: E

> " The appellant argues that, in order that one company should have a
> controlling interest in another, it must be the beneficial owner of a requisite
> number of shares in that other company, either registered in its own name
> or in the name of its nominees; and that if company No. 1 owns all the shares
> in company No. 2, which in turn owns all the shares in company No. 3,
> company No. 1 has no interest, controlling or otherwise, in company No. 3. F
> It is true that in such circumstances company No. 1 owns none of the
> assets of company No. 2, and a fortiori owns none of the assets of company
> No. 3 and in that sense neither owns, nor has an interest in, company No. 3.
> But that is to treat the phrase ' controlling interest ' as capable of connoting
> only a proprietary right, that is, an interest in the nature of ownership. The
> word ' interest', however, as pointed out by LAWRENCE, J., is a word of wide G
> connotation, and I think the conception of ' controlling interest ' may well
> cover the relationship of one company towards another, the requisite
> majority of whose shares are, as regards their voting power, subject, whether
> directly or indirectly, to the will and ordering of the first mentioned
> company."
 H
In that passage, LORD SIMON, with whom all the other lords agreed, was drawing
a distinction between controlling interest and ownership, and he makes it clear
that, where there is a chain of controlled companies, the parent company may
very well have a controlling interest right down the line, but does not own any of
the assets of the subsidiaries. So here, although the London company plainly
has a controlling interest in the Securities company, it does not own beneficially I
any of the assets of the Group company, including the shares in the Securities
company.

Counsel for the Securities company made a number of contentions. He said
that to give effect to the intention of the legislature one must break down the
artificial personality of the members of a group of companies. I do not think I

---

(1) (1958), 37 A.T.C. 164 at p. 168.
(2) [1947] 1 All E.R. 679.
(3) [1943], 1 All E.R. 13 at pp. 14, 15; 29 Tax. Cas. 49 at p. 67.

A am obliged or entitled to do that. It is worth observing that where you have a chain of companies it is always possible, by arranging the transfer in a certain way, to obtain the benefit of exemption under the section. The rest of counsel's contentions really amounted in one set of terms or another to the proposition that the expression " beneficial owner " requires, and must be given, a wide and liberal construction. I can answer that only by saying that it seems to me that

B one must construe the expression according to its legal meaning. I do not think that there is anything in the context of the section which requires one to do otherwise.

For the reasons which I have given, it seems to me that the transfer is not within the scope of the exemption under s. 42 and I must accordingly dismiss this appeal.

C   *Appeal dismissed.*

Solicitors: *Stones, Porter & Co.* (for the Securities company); *Solicitor of Inland Revenue.*

[*Reported by* F. A. Amies, Esq., *Barrister-at-Law.*]

D ———————

POOK (Inspector of Taxes) *v.* OWEN.

[Court of Appeal, civil division (Lord Denning, M.R., Diplock and Edmund
E Davies, L.JJ.), November 8, 9, 1967.]

*Income Tax—Income—Emoluments—Perquisites or profits of office or employ-
ment—Travelling expenses—Medical practitioner practising at residence
and also holding part-time appointments at hospital fifteen miles away as
obstetrician and anaesthetist—Emergency cases—Payment of allowance
for travel by car to hospital—Payment irrespective of the method of travel
—Whether emoluments of office—Finance Act, 1956 (4 & 5 Eliz. 2 c. 54),
F Sch. 2, para. 1 (1).*

*Income Tax—Deduction in computing profits—Expenses—Medical practitioner—
General medical practitioner practising at his residence and also holding
part-time appointments at hospital fifteen miles away—Hospital work as
obstetrician and anaesthetist—Emergency cases—Expenses of travel by
G car to and from hospital—Whether expenses deductible—Income Tax Act,
1952 (15 & 16 Geo. 6 & 1 Eliz. 2 c. 10), s. 156, Sch. E, Case I, as
substituted by Finance Act, 1956 (4 & 5 Eliz. 2 c. 54), s. 10 (1), and Sch. 9,
r. 7 to the Act of 1952.*

The taxpayer was a medical practitioner and resided at Fishguard.
He held part-time appointments as obstetrician and anaesthetist at
H Haverfordwest, fifteen miles away. Under his appointments he was on
stand-by duty for emergencies, as an obstetrician one week-end a month,
as an anaesthetist one week-end a month, and on Monday and Friday nights.
He had to be accessible on the telephone at those times, and on receipt of a
telephone call telling him of an emergency he would give instructions
over the telephone to the hospital staff and then usually would set off
I immediately for the hospital by car, although he might advise treatment
on the telephone and await a further report. His responsibility for the
patient began as soon as he received the telephone call. He was paid a
mileage allowance at a fixed rate per mile for journeys between Fishguard
and the hospital irrespective of how he travelled. He was assessed to
income tax under Sch. E on the amounts received for mileage allowance
as being emoluments of his office, and he claimed to deduct from his income
the expenses that he incurred in such travelling to and from the hospital.
Held: (i) the sums received for mileage allowance were emoluments as

defined in para. 1 (1) of Sch. 2* to the Finance Act, 1956, as they were paid   A
irrespective of how the taxpayer travelled and of whether he spent more
or less on travelling and were not, therefore, an indemnification against
losses (see p. 264, letter E, p. 265, letter H, and p. 267, letter E, post).

Fergusson (Surveyor of Taxes) v. *Noble* ((1919), 7 Tax Cas. 176) applied with
approval.

Hochstrasser (Inspector of Taxes) v. *Mayes* ([1959] 3 All E.R. 817)   B
distinguished.

(ii) (LORD DENNING, M.R., dissenting) the expenses incurred by the taxpayer were the result of his living in Fishguard, fifteen miles from the
hospital at Haverfordwest and therefore of circumstances in relation to his
office which were personal to himself and the result of his own volition
(dictum of LORD BLANESBURGH in *Ricketts* v. *Colquhoun (Inspector of Taxes)*   C
([1926] A.C. at pp. 7, 8) applied; and (per DIPLOCK and EDMUND DAVIES,
L.JJ.) it was immaterial that the taxpayer travelled only on emergency
duties, that his duties began when the telephone rang (which did not mean
that his subsequent travelling was on duty as part of the duties of his
office), or that he needed to live in an area accessible to the hospital (*Nolder*
v. *Walters* ((1930), 15 Tax Cas. 380) applied (see p. 266, letters F and H,   D
and p. 267, letters A, G and I, post).

Per LORD DENNING, M.R. (DIPLOCK, L.J., concurring): if the taxpayer
had kept a note of his actual travelling expenses and had been reimbursed
exactly the sums which he had expended, those sums might not have been
emoluments (see p. 264, letter F, and p. 265, letter H, post).

Decision of STAMP, J. ([1967] 2 All E.R. 579) affirmed.   E

[Editorial Note. The position where the medical practitioner held
part-time appointments in conjunction with private practice, with the
consequence that assessments fell to be made under Sch. D and Sch. E, was
considered in *Mitchell* v. *Ross* ([1961] 3 All E.R. 49).

As to what constitutes an emolument of an office or employment under Sch. 2
to the Finance Act, 1956, see 20 HALSBURY'S LAWS (3rd Edn.) 312-314, paras.   F
574-576; and for cases on the subject, see 28 DIGEST (Repl.) 225-237, *971-1040*.

As to deductions in respect of travelling expenses in computing assessable
emoluments, see 20 HALSBURY'S LAWS (3rd Edn.) 327, 328, para. 600; and for
cases on the subject, see 28 DIGEST (Repl.) 242-247, *1059-1099*.

For the Finance Act, 1956, Sch. 2, see 36 HALSBURY'S STATUTES (2nd Edn.)
448.   G

For the Income Tax Act, 1952, s. 156, as amended, see SUPPLEMENT to 31
HALSBURY'S STATUTES (2nd Edn.), para. [158] Amended Texts; and for r. 7
of Sch. 9 to the Act of 1952, see 31 HALSBURY'S STATUTES (2nd Edn.) 524.**]**

Cases referred to:

Fergusson (Surveyor of Taxes) v. *Noble*, 1919 S.C. 534; 7 Tax Cas. 176; 28   H
Digest (Repl.) 237, *565*.

Hochstrasser (Inspector of Taxes) v. *Mayes*, [1959] 3 All E.R. 817; [1960]
A.C. 376; [1960] 2 W.L.R. 63; Digest (Cont. Vol. A) 888, *987*.

Nolder v. *Walters*, (1930), 15 Tax Cas. 380; 28 Digest (Repl.) 244, *1074*.

Ricketts v. *Colquhoun (Inspector of Taxes)*, [1924] 2 K.B. 347; *affd.* C.A.,
[1925] 1 K.B. 725; *affd.* H.L., [1926] A.C. 1; 95 L.J.K.B. 82; 134 L.T.
106; 90 J.P. 9; 10 Tax Cas. 118; 28 Digest (Repl.) 242, *1059*.   I

Appeal.

The taxpayer, Dr. David Norman Howell Owen, appealed to the General
Commissioners of Income Tax for Kemes in Pembrokeshire against the following
assessments made on him under Sch. E to the Income Tax Act, 1952: 1962-63
(additional assessment) employment, etc., £412 plus superannuation disallowed
£39, £451; 1963-64, employment, etc., £1,481, less superannuation £48, £1,433.

---

* Schedule 2, para. 1 (1), so far as material, is set out at p. 267, letter D, post.

A The taxpayer contended before the commissioners: (i) that his duties under his part-time appointments under the South West Wales Hospital Management Committee (which were all connected with emergency cases at the committee's hospital at Haverfordwest) commenced when he received a telephone call from the hospital and that his journeys to and from the hospital were wholly, necessarily and exclusively in the performance of the duties; (ii) that under r. 7

B of Sch. 9 to the Act of 1952 there should be deducted from the emoluments of his appointments assessed on him the costs of journeys made between his residence and the hospital, being £150 for 1962-63 and £123 for 1963-64. The Crown contended before the commissioners that the taxpayer's place of employment during the relevant period was the hospital, that in travelling to and from the hospital he was not performing the duties of his office or employment, and

C that accordingly the expenses of the journeys should not be deducted from the emoluments.

The commissioners decided that the taxpayer's duties commenced at the moment when he was first contacted by the hospital authorities and thereafter his travelling expenses to and from the hospital or to and from an emergency were wholly, exclusively and necessarily incurred or expended in the duties of

D that office. They therefore allowed the appeal and determined the assessments at the agreed figures on that basis of £301 and £1,310. On Mar. 3, 1967, as reported at [1967] 2 All E.R. 579, Stamp, J., allowed the Crown's appeal against that decision, holding that the travelling expenses were not deductible from the taxpayer's emoluments of his appointments as computed for income tax purposes, because they were not money expended " wholly, exclusively and neces-

E sarily in the performance of his duties " under r. 7 of the rules applicable to Sch. E (s. 156) to the Income Tax Act, 1952 (see Sch. 9, r. 7). The taxpayer appealed to the Court of Appeal.

Herbert H. Monroe, Q.C., and *J. R. Cherryman* for the taxpayer.
Heyworth Talbot, Q.C., and *J. R. Phillips* for the Crown.

F **LORD DENNING, M.R.:** The taxpayer, Dr. Owen, is a medical practitioner in Fishguard. He has a part-time appointment at the hospital at Haverfordwest. That is fifteen miles away from Fishguard. His appointment is as an obstetrician and anaesthetist. Under his appointment he is on stand-by duty for emergencies: as an obstetrician one week-end a month: as an anaesthetist one week-end a month, and also on Monday and Friday nights. He has

G got to be accessible by telephone during that time. All his part-time work is concerned with emergency cases at the hospital at Haverfordwest. As soon as he gets a telephone call telling him of an emergency, he gives instructions over the telephone to the hospital staff. For instance, as an obstetrician, he may tell them to prepare the patient for an operation, or to do what is necessary for the patient. Or, as an anaesthetist, he may have to give instructions relating

H to the pre-anaesthetic treatment. After giving instructions he usually sets off immediately to the hospital by car. Sometimes he advises treatment by telephone and then awaits a further report. Sometimes a telephone call is received while he is out on his rounds and he has to deal with the emergency accordingly. His responsibility for the patient begins as soon as he receives the telephone call.

I Now, here is the point. He gets travelling expenses allowed to him at a fixed rate per mile for journeys between Fishguard and the hospital at Haverfordwest. The questions which have been raised in this court are twofold: *First*: Do the moneys paid to him for travelling expenses count as part of his " emoluments " which he has to bring into account for tax? *Second*: If they do count as emoluments, is he allowed to deduct on the other side the like amount (or a greater amount) by reason of the expenses he actually incurs in getting to the hospital?

The commissioners decided that, although the moneys are to be brought into account, nevertheless they are cancelled out immediately because they are

expenses which he has necessarily incurred in carrying out the duties of his   **A**
employment. The commissioners found that the duties of the doctor commenced
at the moment he was first contacted by the hospital authorities, and thereafter his travelling expenses to and from the hospital or to and from an emergency were wholly, exclusively and necessarily incurred or expended in the duties
of that office. So they decided that he was entitled to have his assessments
reduced by reason of his travelling expenses. STAMP, J., reversed that decision (1).   **B**
He thought that the case was indistinguishable from the case of the Recorder of
Portsmouth, *Ricketts* v. *Colquhoun* (*Inspector of Taxes*) (2). He held that the
doctor was not entitled to have the expenses allowed. Now there is an appeal to
this court.

The first point taken by counsel for the taxpayer before us was not taken in the
court below (1). He says that the mileage allowance which was paid to the   **C**
taxpayer ought not to come into account at all as being part of his emoluments.
" Emoluments " are defined in Sch. 2 to the Finance Act, 1956, as including
" all salaries, fees, wages, perquisites and profits whatsoever ". Counsel said
this mileage allowance was not within those words. He referred us to *Hochstrasser* (*Inspector of Taxes*) v. *Mayes* (3), where compensation paid to indemnify
an employee against losses was held not to be profit from his employment.   **D**

The important thing to notice is that this mileage allowance was payable in
any case, no matter how the taxpayer made his way to the hospital. He might
spend *more* than the allowance if he went by a very expensive car. He might
spend *less* than the allowance if he went by bus or by bicycle. Yet he got the
allowance just the same. It seems to me that an allowance which is payable
whether actually incurred or not is properly to be regarded as part of his emolu-   **E**
ments. It is covered by the case of the detective's allowance in *Fergusson*
(*Surveyor of Taxes*) v. *Noble* (4), to which we were referred. It might be otherwise
if the taxpayer had kept a note of his actual expenses and was reimbursed exactly
the sums which he had expended. Those might not be emoluments, but that is
not this case.

This brings me to the second point. Is the taxpayer entitled to deduct his   **F**
actual travelling expenses getting to and from the hospital? This depends on
the wording of r. 7 of Sch. 9 to the Income Tax Act, 1952, which repeats the
words of the Income Tax Act, 1853, when people used horses for their work.
It provides:

> " If the holder of an office or employment of profit is necessarily obliged to
> incur and defray out of the emoluments thereof the expenses of travelling   **G**
> in the performance of the duties of the office or employment, or of keep-
> ing and maintaining a horse to enable him to perform the same, or other-
> wise to expend money wholly, exclusively and necessarily in the perform-
> ance of the said duties, there may be deducted from the emoluments to be
> assessed the expenses so necessarily incurred and defrayed."

Looking at this case apart from authority, I should have thought that the   **H**
expenses of the taxpayer in travelling to and from Fishguard on an emergency
call were expenses which he was " necessarily obliged to incur . . . in the performance of the duties " of his employment. That seems to be so plain as to be
almost beyond argument. The only thing which is cited against this view is an
authority of the House of Lords, *Ricketts* v. *Colquhoun* (*Inspector of Taxes*) (5).
Mr. Ricketts was the Recorder of Portsmouth. He practised at the Bar in Lon-   **I**
don. He went down to Portsmouth every quarter in order to sit as Recorder and
try cases there. He asked to be allowed his railway fare from London to Portsmouth, his hotel expenses and the cost of carrying his tin box to the court.

(1) [1967] 2 All E.R. 579.
(2) [1926] A.C. 1; 10 Tax Cas. 118.
(3) [1959] 3 All E.R. 817; [1960] A.C. 376.
(4) (1919), 7 Tax Cas. 176.
(5) [1926] A.C. 1; 10 Tax Cas. 118.

A   The House of Lords said that he was not to be allowed them. Viscount Cave, L.C., said (6):

> " In order that they may be deductible under this rule from an assessment under Sch. E, they must be expenses which the holder of an office is neces-sarily obliged to incur—that is to say, obliged by the very fact that he holds the office and has to perform its duties—and they must be incurred in —that is, in the course of—the performance of those duties."

B

The House held that it was Mr. Ricketts' own choice that he lived in London and he was not " necessarily obliged " to incur any of those expenses in regard to his office. They were only his expenses as an individual.

That case binds this court in any case which is strictly comparable; but it should not be carried any further than its own particular circumstances. To my
C   mind the position of the taxpayer is quite distinguishable. He is a person whose work is in two places. He is like a Member of Parliament who is in London during the week and goes at the week-end to his constituency. His work is in both places. When he is travelling to and fro, his expenses can be deducted because they are expenses which he is " necessarily obliged to incur " in the course of his
D   office. That was recognised by the Crown in *Ricketts* v. *Colquhoun* (*Inspector of Taxes* (7) and accepted by Rowlatt, J., and in the House of Lords.

So in this case the taxpayer is on duty when he is in his surgery in Fishguard, or when he is out on his rounds, or on a farm delivering a woman of a child. He is on duty—stand-by duty. He takes on the case then and there. He gives directions on the telephone about the treatment to be given. At that moment
E   he is doing his work—performing the duties of his employment—just as much as when he gets to Haverfordwest and administers the anaesthetic. I see no differ-ence between his position and that of the archdeacon. He had to have a horse to take him to the parishes and was allowed the expense of it. So now he has to have a car and is allowed his travelling expenses. Quite generally, when a man is necessarily obliged to travel in the course of his employment, he is entitled to
F   deduct his expenses. In many cases it is a question of degree and, therefore, a question for the commissioners. The commissioners have directed themselves quite properly. They found that

> " his travelling expenses to and from the hospital or to and from an emer-gency were wholly, exclusively and necessarily incurred or expended in the duties of that office."

G   It seems to me on that finding that it was entirely proper for the taxpayer to be allowed his expenses against the assessment. I would allow the appeal.

DIPLOCK, L.J.: As regards the first point taken by counsel for the tax-payer in this court, which was perhaps advisedly not taken in the court below (8), viz., that the mileage allowance was not part of the emoluments of the tax-
H   payer, I agree with what Lord Denning, M.R., has said and have nothing to add.

With regard to the second point, viz., whether this mileage allowance is a deductible expense within r. 7 of Sch. 9 to the Income Tax Act, 1952, I agree with Lord Denning to this extent, that the only thing against the argument of counsel for the taxpayer is a judgment of the House of Lords, one which I should myself be only too happy to overrule if I thought that I had the power to do so.
I   What, of course, is binding on us is the ratio decidendi of their lordships in *Ricketts* v. *Colquhoun* (*Inspector of Taxes*) (9). I would read here a passage from the speech of Lord Blanesburgh which in my view expresses, I regret to say, the ratio decidendi which appealed to their lordships. Dealing with the rule

---

(6) [1926] A.C. at p. 4; 10 Tax Cas. at p. 133.
(7) [1924] 2 K.B. 347 at pp. 350, 351; [1926] A.C. at pp. 4, 5; 10 Tax Cas. at pp. 121, 133.
(8) [1967] 2 All E.R. 579.
(9) [1926] A.C. 1; 10 Tax Cas. 118.

which has, as LORD DENNING has said, gone on for many years—I do not agree, A
however, that the day of the horse is past—LORD BLANESBURGH said this (10):

"Undoubtedly its most striking characteristic is its jealously restricted
language, some of it repeated apparently to heighten its effect. But I am also
struck by this, that, as it seems to me, although undoubtedly less obtru-
sively, the language of the rule points to the expenses with which it is
concerned as being confined to those which each and every occupant of the   B
particular office is necessarily obliged to incur in the performance of its
duties, to expenses imposed upon each holder ex necessitate of his office and
to such expenses only."

I pause to interpose there the observation that the words in the rule are " necessarily obliged ", which are tautologous unless one gives to " necessarily obliged "   C
the meaning which LORD BLANESBURGH gives to it.   LORD BLANESBURGH
went on (11):

"It says: ' If the holder of an office '—the words be it observed are not
' if any holder of an office '—' is obliged to incur expenses in the performance of the duties of the office '—the duties again are not the duties of *his*
office; in other words, the terms employed are strictly, and, I cannot doubt,   D
purposely, not personal but objective.   The deductible expenses do not
extend to those which the holder has to incur mainly and, it may be, only
because of circumstances in relation to his office which are personal to
himself or are the result of his own volition."

The expenses in the form of mileage allowance which the taxpayer seeks to
deduct in this case are the result of his living in Fishguard, some fifteen miles   E
from the hospital where he was employed in Haverfordwest.   It seems to me
that his position is indistinguishable from that of the recorder so far as that
ratio decidendi is concerned.   Counsel for the taxpayer has sought to make
distinctions on three grounds.   First, he says that, unlike the recorder, the
taxpayer was only required to travel in an emergency because he was employed
only for emergency cases.   I do not think that giving a label to the occasions   F
on which he travels as " emergencies " helps one way or the other.   It merely
involves the feature, that he has to travel immediately or very promptly after a
telephone call is received; but that was the position of the airline pilot in
Nolder v. *Walters* (12).

Secondly, it is said that there is a distinction because the taxpayer's duties
commence when the telephone rings.   That is because he may, and sometimes   G
does, give over the telephone some instructions as to what is to be done with
the patient pending his arrival at the hospital where his work as an anaesthetist,
and in this case so far as is relevant as an obstetrician, takes place.   It does not
seem to me that the fact that he gives some advice, it may be, over the telephone before going out to do his job as an anaesthetist or obstetrician at the
hospital, can mean that, while he is travelling, he is travelling on duty as part   H
of the duties of his office.   Indeed, if this were so, I think that, as ROWLATT, J.,
pointed out in the airline pilot's case (13) if the taxpayer drove his car negligently
while travelling to or from the hospital, the hospital would be vicariously responsible for his negligence, and I do not think that anyone would think that that
was the consequence of his office.

Finally, it is pointed out that whereas a recorder may live, as SCRUTTON, L.J.,   I
pointed out (14), four hundred or four miles from his borough, it is a necessary
consequence of this particular employment of the taxpayer that he should live

---

(10) (1925), 10 Tax Cas. at p. 135; [1926] A.C. at p. 7.
(11) (1925), 10 Tax Cas. at p. 135; [1926] A.C. at pp. 7, 8.
(12) (1930), 15 Tax Cas. 380.
(13) I.e., *Nolder* v. *Walters*, (1930), 15 Tax Cas. 380.
(14) I.e., *Ricketts* v. *Colquhoun* (*Inspector of Taxes*), [1925] 1 K.B. 725 at pp. 738;
10 Tax Cas. at p. 130.

A in an area which is accessible to the hospital where he has to carry out his function. Again that feature was a feature of the airline pilot's case (15). It does not seem to me that the fact that holders of an office must necessarily be drawn from a restricted area can make any relevant distinction between this case and *Ricketts* v. *Colquhoun* (*Inspector of Taxes*) (16) or can be brought outside the ratio decidendi of LORD BLANESBURGH which I have read.

B   For my part, therefore, much as I regret to differ in this respect from LORD DENNING, M.R., and much as I regret—though I must declare an interest in this —being unable to overrule the decision in *Ricketts* v. *Colquhoun* (*Inspector of Taxes*) (16) I feel bound to dismiss this appeal.

C   **EDMUND DAVIES, L.J.:** Two questions arise in this appeal. I am aware that in expressing regret that, having regard to the decision in *Ricketts* v. *Colquhoun* (*Inspector of Taxes*) (16) in my judgment both have to be answered adversely to the taxpayer, I am repeating an oft-sung dirge; but my regret is none the less real on that account.

The first question is: do the two sums of £100 and £82 received by the tax-payer in respect of travelling expenses constitute emoluments which have to be taken into consideration when his assessable income falls to be determined?

D Schedule 2 to the Finance Act, 1956, provides that—" . . . the expression 'emoluments' shall *include* all salaries, fees, wages, perquisites and profits whatsoever ". Counsel for the taxpayer in the course of an attractive argument, submitted that what the taxpayer received was reimbursement of his actual expenditure on travelling. We do not know as a matter of fact that this was so, but I am prepared to assume that that was indeed the case. Even so, it seems to

E me, by analogy with *Fergusson* (*Surveyor of Taxes*) v. *Noble* (17) that these two sums must be regarded as emoluments. Indeed, quite apart from authority, and simply applying the ordinary standards of speech, were anyone to ask the taxpayer what the emoluments of his employment were, I think that he would surely reply: " Oh, I get X guineas per visit and my travelling expenses."

F The second question is perhaps a little more difficult: are the taxpayer's actual travelling expenses deductible? The test is provided by r. 7 of Sch. 9 to the Income Tax Act, 1952, which I refrain from quoting in the course of this short judgment because it is already so familiar. Can it be said that the taxpayer's travelling expenses from Fishguard to Haverfordwest were such as he was " necessarily obliged to incur and defray " out of the emoluments of his office? With all respect to the views expressed by LORD DENNING, M.R., I do not see how that

G question can be answered in a manner favourable to the taxpayer. It seems to me nihil ad rem that the duties which he was called on to perform were emer-gency duties or that his responsibility for the patient began at the moment when he answered the telephone call. Both of these features might equally be present were the taxpayer resident in Haverfordwest and able to stroll up the hill to the hospital by the expenditure of nothing except a little shoe leather.

H The car journeys actually performed were, in my judgment, in no sense inherent in the office itself and the expense thereof not such as each and every holder of the office would be " necessarily obliged to incur or defray ". Unfortunately for the taxpayer, he was obliged to incur such expenses if he desired to hold the office while continuing to reside in Fishguard, but that is not the test to be applied. Accordingly, on both points I regret to have to say that I agree with

I DIPLOCK, L.J., in holding that this appeal should be dismissed.

Appeal dismissed. Leave to appeal to the House of Lords granted.

Solicitors: *Le Brasseur & Oakley* (for the taxpayer); *Solicitor of Inland Revenue.*

[*Reported by* F. A. AMIES, ESQ., *Barrister-at-Law.*]

---

(15) I.e., *Nolder* v. *Walters*, (1930), 15 Tax Cas. 380.
(16) [1926] A.C. 1; 10 Tax Cas. 118.   (17) (1919), **7 Tax Cas. 176.**

R. *v.* THOMSON NEWSPAPERS, LTD. AND OTHERS, *Ex parte* ATTORNEY-GENERAL.

[QUEEN'S BENCH DIVISION (Lord Parker, C.J., Widgery and Chapman, JJ.), November 27, 1967.]

Contempt of Court—Publications concerning legal proceedings—Publication of matter likely to prejudice a fair trial—Newspaper published a photograph of an accused, with a derogatory caption, the accused being due to be tried soon—Aspects of seriousness of such contempts—Likelihood of prejudice to fair trial—System designed to avoid contempts was operated by newspaper—Editor unaware of caption before publication—Whether any penalty should be imposed on publishers, printers or editor.

A newspaper, which had a clean record for some 150 years, committed a contempt of court by publishing a photograph of an accused person, who was awaiting trial on a charge under the Race Relations Act 1965, s. 6 (1)*, there being below the photograph a caption which was highly derogatory of him. The charge against the accused was of using at a public meeting words which were threatening, abusive or insulting, being words likely to stir up hatred against a section of the public on grounds of colour. The caption named the accused and stated that he took to politics after an unedifying career as a brothel keeper, procurer and property racketeer. The newspaper operated a reasonable system designed for the avoidance of contempts. The writer of the article had been advised that an article on race relations with a reference to the accused would not necessarily avoid the risk of contempt of court, but the legal adviser was not told of the words of the caption. A barrister, reader of the newspaper for libel, saw the article and approached the author because of the libel risk, but contempt of court was not raised between them nor drawn to the attention of the editor. On the question of penalty to be imposed on the publishers, printers and editor,

Held: (i) the seriousness of contempt of court of such character as this could be judged from two aspects, viz., (a) by the likely prejudice to the fair trial of the accused, and (b) by the culpability of those concerned with committing the contempt, the most serious forms of contempt viewed from these two aspects being respectively (a) where adverse comment was made on an accused as being the accused person at a particular trial, and (b) where the matter was published with the intention of prejudicing a fair trial (see p. 269, letter H, and p. 270, letters A and C, post).

(ii) the contempt in the present case was a serious contempt from the point of view of its likelihood to prejudice a fair trial, and the publishers of the newspaper would be fined £5,000, but no fine would be imposed on the printers, having regard to the relation between the parties, and in the circumstances no penalty would be imposed on the editor, having regard to the system operated to avoid contempts and to the fact that he had no knowledge of the matter that was to be published as the caption (see p. 271, letters A, B and C, post).

[As to contempt of court by publication of articles in a newspaper while criminal proceedings are pending, see 8 HALSBURY'S LAWS (3rd Edn.) 9, 10, para. 12; and for cases on the subject, see 16 DIGEST (Repl.) 25, *191, 192*; 28, 29 *205-234.*

For the Race Relations Act 1965, s. 6 (1), see 45 HALSBURY'S STATUTES (2nd Edn.) 35.]

---

* Section 6 (1) provides: " A person shall be guilty of an offence under this section if, with intent to stir up hatred against any section of the public in Great Britain distinguished by colour, race, or ethnic or national origins—(*a*) he publishes or distributes written matter which is threatening, abusive or insulting; or (*b*) he uses in any public place or at any public meeting words which are threatening, abusive or insulting, being matter or words likely to stir up hatred against that section on grounds of colour, race, or ethnic or national origins."

A   **Motion.**

This was a motion by the Attorney-General by notice dated Nov. 17, 1967, to commit for contempt of court, first, Thomson Newspapers, Ltd., the printers, secondly Times Newspapers, Ltd., the publishers of an article in The Sunday Times on Oct. 29, 1967, and thirdly, Mr. Harold Evans, editor of that newspaper. The motion was in respect of the publication of an article headed " Race Rela-

B   tions " wherein was published a photograph of one Michael Abdul Malik with a caption derogatory of him, while he was an accused awaiting trial on a charge under the Race Relations Act 1965 s. 6 (1) for using at a public meeting words likely to stir up hatred against a section of the public distinguished by colour. The facts are set out in the judgment of the court. At the hearing of the motion the publication was admitted to be a contempt of court.

C   *The Attorney-General* (*Sir Elwyn Jones, Q.C.*) and *Nigel Bridge* for the applicant. *P. H. R. Bristow, Q.C.*, and *M. E. I. Kempster* for the respondents.

LORD PARKER, C.J.: On Oct. 17, 1967, one Michael Abdul Malik appeared at Reading Borough quarter sessions charged with an offence contrary to s. 6 (1) of the Race Relations Act 1965, it being alleged that with intent to stir up hatred

D   against a section of the public in Great Britain distinguished by colour he used at a public meeting words which were threatening, abusive or insulting being words likely to stir up hatred against that section of the public on the grounds of colour. The next day, Oct. 18, the jury were discharged and a new trial was ordered at a date to be fixed; that trial in fact came on on Nov. 8, and on Nov. 9 Malik was convicted and sentenced to twelve months' imprisonment (1). Mean-

E   while, on Oct. 29, there was published in The Sunday Times an article headed " Race Relations " dealing with a number of organisations in this country, one of them being the Racial Adjustment Action Society founded it was said in 1965 and modelled on the exclusive Black Moslem sect in the United States. Underneath that caption was a photograph of Malik, and these words followed:

F   " Michael Abdul Malik, thirty-four, West Indian. Came to U.K. 1960, took to politics after unedifying career as brothel-keeper, procurer and property racketeer. Muddled thinker, but natural flair for self-advertisement."

It is quite clearly and indeed, though not at the outset, it is now frankly admitted to be, a serious contempt of court. That it is a serious contempt of court must be obvious to anyone when one realises that, except in special circumstances, a jury

G   is not entitled to know anything of the prisoner's bad character, if he has a bad character; and to say of a man that he has had an unedifying career as a brothel-keeper, procurer and property racketeer, is undoubtedly something which is likely to prejudice the fair trial of that person before a jury.

Happily, these cases do not come before the court very often and it is as well before considering the case to make a few general observations. In the opinion

H   of this court, the question of the seriousness of a contempt of court can be looked at from two angles: first, the seriousness of the contempt judged by the likely prejudice to the fair trial of an accused, and secondly, the seriousness of the contempt from the point of view of what I may call the culpability of those concerned. No doubt the most serious form of contempt from the point of view

I   of likely prejudice is the sort of case where a photograph is published of an

_____

(1) Malik appealed against conviction and sentence. Judgment on his appeal was given on Dec. 21, 1967, by the Court of Appeal (criminal division). Among the grounds of appeal was danger that Malik had not had a fair trial owing to the matter published in the article in the Sunday Times. The appeal was dismissed. Lord Parker, C.J., delivering the judgment of the court stressed that there was no question of the jury's weighing up Malik's credibility as a witness against that of prosecution witnesses, because when he gave evidence at his trial he admitted using words of the character charged. It was inevitable that the jury must have reached the conclusion that they did reach, and there was thus no possible prejudice affecting the result of the trial.

accused, and adverse comment is made on him as an accused person in a particular A
trial. That would undoubtedly be the most serious form of contempt looked at
from the point of view of likely prejudice. In this case the photograph and the
caption are not in relation to the accused as an accused person in the circumstances
of his trial. To that extent it is perhaps less serious; but very little when one
realises that the photograph and the caption are in relation to the accused's
activity in connexion with race relations, something which itself was a matter B
involved in the trial Accordingly, looked at from this point of view, this was a
very serious contempt

When one begins to look at it from the other angle of culpability, it is only right
to say that the most serious contempts from that point of view are publications
of matter done intentionally with the very object of prejudicing a fair trial. The
court is quite satisfied that there can be no suggestion of that sort in the present C
case. In the course of the argument the court sought to make that clear and
wishes to say so once again. On the other hand if anybody and any newspaper
chooses to make highly derogatory remarks in relation to someone who happens
to be an accused, it is clearly done at their peril, and it is for that reason that
newspapers very properly take elaborate precautions, so far as they can, to see
that they are not culpable in that sense. Here the court is quite satisfied that this D
newspaper, with a clean record of some 150 years, had devised, and the editor,
Mr. Harold Evans, had ensured was operated, an elaborate and reasonable
system to avoid contempts of this sort, or indeed any contempt of court. They
were fully alive to their obligations as a responsible newspaper and devised this
system. At the same time any system is liable to break down owing to the
human element, and undoubtedly it did so in this case. The court feels it only E
right to say where the human element did break down. It broke down primarily,
as it seems to this court, owing to Mr. Marks, who was the author of the article,
failing to realise where it was leading. He was fully aware that there was this
pending trial; he had been to Mr. James Evans, the legal adviser to the newspaper, and in his very frank affidavit Mr. Marks says that Mr. Evans advised
him that the mere article on race relations with a reference to Mr. Malik would F
not necessarily avoid the risk of contempt of court. When one reads Mr. James
Evans' affidavit itself he makes it quite clear that he advised Mr. Marks that to
deal with Mr. Malik's beliefs and attitudes on racial issues would be likely to
depict Mr. Malik as someone likely to have made the speech of which he was
accused in the pending case and that therefore the mere publishing of the article
might involve a risk of contempt. Mr. James Evans was never told of the highly G
derogatory remarks which ultimately found their place under the photograph.

Notwithstanding that clear warning, Mr. Marks never approached Mr. Evans
again, never referred the matter to his superior Mr. Hall, or indeed to the editor,
Mr. Harold Evans. It is true that he had a conversation with the young barrister
who had been given the galley-proofs to read, and Mr. Marks says, in fairness to
the barrister, that it was the barrister who approached him because of the libel H
risk, and Mr. Marks acknowledges that he never drew the attention of Mr. Milmo,
the barrister, to what Mr. James Evans had said as to publishing the article about
race relations at all, in the course of which Mr. Malik's name was mentioned,
much less the derogatory remarks which appeared under the photograph. Here
again, however, Mr. Milmo quite frankly admits, and this is the second instance
of the human element breaking down, that notwithstanding that contempt was I
never mentioned he had it in the back of his mind and admits that he failed to
draw attention to the possibility of contempt.

Those are really the facts as the court finds them, and it becomes necessary then
to consider the question of penalties. It is quite clear, having regard to the
seriousness of this contempt from the point of view of its likelihood to prejudice
a fair trial that the publishers must be penalised. It is not one of the very worst
cases, as I have said; on the other hand it is a serious case and in all the circumstances the court feels that the publishers, Times Newspapers, Ltd., must pay a

A considerable fine. The court sees no reason why, having regard to the relationship between the parties, any separate or further fine should be imposed on Thomson Newspapers, Ltd. So far as Mr. Harold Evans is concerned, he, of course, as editor takes full responsibility. On the other hand, when one is considering the question of penalty one must consider his personal culpability. It is quite clear that he knew nothing about this. It is also quite clear that an editor in his position

B could not possibly be expected to know everything that was happening. It cannot be said that he acted recklessly or turned a blind eye. Indeed, in the opinion of the court he had devised, so far as it is humanly possible, a system which would prevent this sort of thing. In those circumstances, this court has come to the conclusion that it is quite unnecessary to impose a sentence of imprisonment or in the circumstances of this case any penalty whatever on him. It remains,

C therefore, to fix the fine to be paid by Times Newspapers Ltd., and the court in all the circumstances will fix a fine of £5,000.

Order accordingly.

Solicitors: *Director of Public Prosecutions; Theodore Goddard & Co.* (for the respondents).

[*Reported by* S. A. Hatteea, Esq., *Barrister-at-Law.*]

D

IRVIN *v.* IRVIN.

[Probate, Divorce and Admiralty Division (Sir Jocelyn Simon, P., and Stirling, J.), October 10, 11, December 7, 1967.]

E *Magistrates—Husband and wife—Desertion—Resumption of cohabitation— Husband in desertion at time of wife's complaint—Resumption of cohabitation before adjudication on complaint—Simple desertion unaccompanied by disruptive conduct—Return of husband to matrimonial home on advice of solicitor—Husband willing to resume matrimonial relations—Wife's children by former marriage hostile—Whether entitlement of wife to maintenance*

F *by virtue of desertion negatived by husband's return.*

The parties were married in 1964, the wife being a widow with three children by her previous husband. On marriage the husband went to live in the wife's house. He never developed a satisfactory relationship with his step-children, but there was nothing in the evidence to suggest that this was his fault. The youngest child, a girl, C., was very nervous and at times

G needed psychiatric treatment. The wife sometimes slept with her. In May, 1966, following a fracas involving the husband, the wife and the two children who were then living at home, the husband left the wife. This constituted desertion by him. On July 5, 1966, the parties attended before justices on a summons issued by the wife alleging desertion; no evidence was taken and on the same day the husband returned to the matrimonial

H home, telling the wife that he had been advised by his solicitor to do so. Thereafter the wife did his cooking and washing and they shared the same table for meals, but otherwise they had little social contact; they did not sleep together, and the wife slept with C. The children never spoke to the husband. In October, 1966, the justices heard evidence of the wife and the two children on her summons, but the husband did not give evidence.

I In her evidence the wife admitted that the husband had tried to make a go of things with her since his return, though not with her children; she made no complaint against him. The son in evidence said that the husband, in conversation before his return home, had said that he would be boss in the home and that everything would have to be done his way; the son said that he had told the wife of this conversation. The justices found that the husband had not returned home through genuine repentance at leaving the wife nor with a view to making sincere attempts to resume the marriage, that he had not reinstated the wife to her former position and that his

offer to resume matrimonial relations was not such as she could reasonably   A
be expected to accept. The justices found the husband to be in desertion
at the date of their adjudication. On appeal by the husband,

    Held: (i) having regard to the fact that the desertion in May, 1966,
was simple desertion, unaccompanied by disruptive conduct, express
assurances by the husband for the future were not called for, and there had
been a resumption of cohabitation in law since the husband's return on July 5,   B
1966; the main impediment thereafter was the hostility of the children,
and, as it had been the wife's duty to receive the husband back, the justices
could not properly have found on the evidence that the husband was in
desertion at the date of their adjudication or since his return to cohabitation
(see p. 274, letters B, H and I, post).

    (ii) the resumption of cohabitation negatived the cause of complaint   C
arising from the desertion in May, 1966, as a matrimonial order, such as the
wife sought by her summons, was designed to operate prospectively; accordingly, in order to lead to entitlement to such an order, the cause of complaint
must exist not only at the time of the commencement of proceedings but
also at the time of adjudication (see p. 276, letters G and H, post).

    Williams v. *Williams* ([1904] P. 145) explained and applied; *Jones* v.   D
Jones ((1941), 165 L.T. 398) applied.

    Perry v. *Perry* ([1952] 1 All E.R. 1076) considered.

    Appeal allowed.

[As to the termination of desertion by resumption of cohabitation, see 12
HALSBURY'S LAWS (3rd Edn.) 490, 491, para. 1090; and for cases on the subject,
see 27 DIGESST (Repl.) 714, *6812, 6813.*]   E

Cases referred to:

    Jones v. *Jones*, (1941), 165 L.T. 398; 105 J.P. 353; 27 Digest (Repl.) 717, *6841.*

    Perry v. *Perry*, [1952] 1 All E.R. 1076; [1952] P. 203; 116 J.P. 258; Digest
        (Cont. Vol. A) 727, *2976a.*

    Price v. *Price*, [1951] 2 All E.R. 580, n.; [1951] P. 413; 116 J.P. 468, n.;   F
        27 Digest (Repl.) 85, *636.*

    Theobald v. *Theobald*, [1962] 2 All E.R. 863; [1962] 1 W.L.R. 837; 126 J.P.
        377; Digest (Cont. Vol. A) 842, *7023ac.*

    Williams v. *Williams*, [1904] P. 145; 73 L.J.P. 31; 90 L.T. 174; 68 J.P. 188;
        27 Digest (Repl.) 714, *6812.*

Appeal.   G

This was an appeal by the husband against a decision of the Leeds magistrates,
dated Oct. 10, 1966, finding that he had deserted the wife and ordering him to
pay the weekly sum of £2 for her maintenance. The facts are set out in the
judgment of the court.

J. M. Graham for the husband.

L. B. Stephen for the wife.   H

                                                          Cur. adv. vult.

    Dec. 7. **STIRLING, J.,** read the following judgment of the court at
the invitation of SIR JOCELYN SIMON, P.: On Oct. 10, 1966, the Leeds justices
found proved a complaint by a wife, Leah Irvin, that her husband had deserted
her, and ordered that he should pay the weekly sum of £2 for her maintenance.   I
From that order the husband now appeals to this court.

    The parties were married on Jan. 9, 1964. The wife was a widow and had
three children by her previous husband; two sons, Robert then aged twenty,
and Derek aged sixteen, and a girl, Carol, then aged fourteen. On marriage
the husband went to live at his wife's house. Unfortunately, he never developed
a satisfactory relationship with his step-children; but there is nothing in the
notes of evidence to suggest, nor do the justices find, that this was his fault.
As the years passed, this relationship worsened, particularly with Carol. Carol's

A nervous health was precarious; she at some time required psychiatric treatment. The husband and wife had from the time of their marriage shared a bed, but there came a time when the wife started sleeping with Carol two nights a week. There is nothing to challenge the wife's assertion that this was at the husband's suggestion, or at least with his consent. One son, Derek, married and moved away from the home, but Carol and Robert remained in the house. Both were

B hostile to the husband, though probably with different intensity. It must have been a difficult situation for both husband and wife, who had a natural loyalty to her children. It is not surprising that the husband should from time to time have expressed the wish to be alone; but we do not understand this as expressing a desire or intention to separate from his wife. On, probably, May 26, 1966, there was a fracas in which the husband, the wife, Carol and Robert were all

C involved. The following day the husband asked the wife, who had not slept with him that night, if she wanted a separation. She replied " No, not really ". He said, nonetheless, that he was going, and her response to that was to tell him not to be silly. Nevertheless, he left, returning the same day to collect his belongings. This would date his departure as May 27, 1966; and this is the date stated in the complaint. (In her evidence the wife averred that the fracas

D was on June 3, 1966, and her husband's departure on June 4, but we think that the date in the complaint is more likely to be accurate.)

On June 4, 1966, the wife issued a summons alleging desertion. The return date was July 5, 1966. The parties attended before the justices on July 5, 1966, but no evidence was taken. It may be that it was adjourned for want of time. On the same day as this abortive hearing, the husband returned to the matri-

E monial home, telling the wife that he had been advised by his solicitor to do so. The son Derek, giving evidence for his mother, stated that he had had a conversation with his step-father before the latter's return, in which his step-father had said that, when he returned home, as he wished to do, he would be boss in the home, and that everything would have to be done his way. Derek recounted this conversation to his mother. From his return the husband slept in the bed which

F at the outset of the marriage he had shared with his wife. She, however, slept every night with Carol; there is no evidence that this was the husband's wish or at his suggestion. From, we think, the date of his return, neither Robert nor Carol would speak to the husband; and understandably, perhaps, in the circumstances he has not spoken to them. The wife made certain important admissions in evidence; she said that the husband had tried to make a go of

G things with her, although not with the children; but that she had no complaint about him since the date of his return. As regards their general living arrangements after the date of the husband's return, the wife did his cooking, they shared the same table for meals and she did his washing. Otherwise they had little if any social contact; and, as we have said, they did not sleep together. There was no evidence or finding, however, that this degree of estrangement

I was due to the husband, or coincided with his wishes.

These facts, which we have recited at some length, emerged when the parties finally attended before the justices on Oct. 10, 1966, now over a year ago. We have been told by counsel that the same situation prevails in the home today. The facts are to be found solely in the evidence of the wife and her witnesses (the two sons, Robert and Derek), because the husband's solicitor elected to call no evidence and stood on a submission of no case. The justices in substance accepted the evidence of the wife and her witnesses. They found that the husband left the home in May, 1966, intending to break off matrimonial relations. It is accepted by counsel for the husband that it would not be possible to challenge that finding before this court; and we are of opinion that this court should respect it. It follows, therefore, that, in leaving the home in May, 1966, the husband deserted the wife.

The real attack is on the way the justices dealt with subsequent events. In their reasons, the justices say this:

A

" 3. The husband returned to the matrimonial home after a reasonably short absence, but we believe the wife when she states in her evidence that she was told by the husband that his solicitor had advised him to return. We do not believe that the husband returned through genuine repentance at leaving his wife and with a view to making sincere attempts to resume the marriage."

B

We think that this reason is open to the criticism which has been made of it. The husband's departure was what is sometimes called " simple desertion ", that is, was not complicated by acts of disruptive conduct, which might well call for expressions of repentance and assurance for the future. The wife's own evidence negatives, in our view, the finding that the husband was unprepared to make any sincere attempt to resume the marriage. Insofar as the justices seem to have been influenced by the fact that the husband told the wife that he had been advised by his solicitor to return, the decision of the Court of Appeal in *Price* v. *Price* (1) is in point. If the husband was willing to implement his offer to return, his motive was immaterial—whether it was financial or the consequence of legal advice. Of course, the husband must be willing to return as a husband, not merely as a hostile lodger; but, in our judgment, there was no evidence that the husband was not willing to play his full part as a husband if he were allowed to do so.

C

D

The justices' fourth reason for their finding is in substance an amplification of their third; it reads as follows:

" 4. Regardless of the fact that the wife admits she performed certain household duties on the husband's return, we cannot accept that the husband reinstated her to her former position. We accept the wife's evidence when she states that her husband's attitude to the family was no different on his return and although she states that he has tried to ' make a go of it ' with her, she also states that no conversation took place between him and the children. We therefore believe that any offers by the husband to resume matrimonial relations were not made under such circumstances that she could reasonably be expected to accept them."

E

F

Again, we find no evidence that the husband was unwilling to " reinstate the wife to her former position ", had she been willing to be reinstated. It is, we think, obvious from her own evidence and proved conduct that she was not. She did not want him back and regretted the return. The main impediment was the hostility of the children. The wife found herself in a difficult position, and felt that the absence of her husband was the simpler solution. On the evidence that the children refused ever to speak to their step-father on his return, it is inadmissible to hold him responsible for failure to break down the barrier— even if the tension between the husband and his step-children were to be taken against him in judging his relationship with his wife (and we are far from satisfied that it should be).

G

H

In the circumstances, it was the duty of the wife to receive her husband back; and the justices were wrong in holding that the wife could not reasonably be expected to accept his offer. The latter phrase was, indeed, inappropriate; because, unless the justices were prepared to hold that there never was a resumption of cohabitation between husband and wife, the latter did accept his offer and allow him to return. The evidence did not suggest that these two persons have, since July 5, 1966, been living in two separate households under the same roof. Their cohabitation may not be satisfactory; but, in our judgment, it is cohabitation in law. In our judgment, the justices could not properly have found on the evidence that the husband was in desertion at the date of their adjudication, or, indeed, since his return to cohabitation on July 5, 1966.

It was not seriously contended by counsel for the wife that, since July 5, 1966, there have been two separate households. He contended, however, that a spouse

(1) [1951] 2 All E.R. 580, n.; [1951] P. 413.

A guilty of desertion—and he was speaking of simple not constructive desertion—does not terminate such desertion merely by the fact of return. On the facts of this case, he says, the husband must show—and the onus is on him to prove it—that he was, at the date of such offer to return, prepared to make an effort to get on with the children. We cannot agree; a simply deserting husband must merely, as we have said, be prepared to return as a husband; and on the

B facts of this case, we repeat that we do not find evidence that the relationship between the husband and the step-children was inconsistent with his willingness to resume cohabitation with the wife.

There remains one further point. The husband having, as the justices found and as we think, deserted the wife on May 27, 1966, and remained in desertion up to July 5, 1966 (that is, after the date of the summons), could the justices

C properly find desertion proved notwithstanding that the husband and wife were cohabiting at the date of the adjudication? A similar point fell for decision by the Divisional Court in *Williams* v. *Williams* (2). There, the husband left the wife on Aug. 3, 1903. On Aug. 5 she lodged her complaint under the Summary Jurisdiction (Married Women) Act, 1895. On Aug. 14, the justices heard the evidence of the wife and adjourned the hearing until Oct. 28, in the hope of a

D reconciliation and resumption of cohabitation. This in fact took place on Aug. 29, and the parties lived together as man and wife until Sept. 27, when, after some slight quarrel, they took to occupying separate beds, though remaining under the same roof, until the date fixed for the adjourned hearing. The wife then, unbeknown to the husband, went to the justices, stated that her husband had not " lived " with her for a month past and obtained from them a matri-

E monial order on the ground of desertion. On Nov. 3, the husband applied to the justices to rescind the order on the ground that it was made without his knowledge and that there was fresh evidence, namely, condonation, which should have been adduced. (At that time, " fresh evidence " was necessary for the variation or discharge of an order.) The justices, however, held that the husband's only remedy was by appeal to the Divisional Court. That court, consisting of SIR

F FRANCIS JEUNE, P., and GORELL BARNES, J., allowed the appeal. SIR FRANCIS JEUNE, P., held (3) that the offence had been condoned in such a way as " to put an end to the cause of complaint—not by virtue of " s. 7 of the Act of 1895, which did not (since the resumption of cohabitation took place during the course of litigation and before the date of the order) cover the situation, " but by force of law ". GORELL BARNES, J., said (4) that the last clause of s. 7 of

G the Act of 1895:

(" if any married woman upon whose application an order shall have been made under this 'Act . . . shall voluntarily resume cohabitation with her husband . . . such order shall, upon proof thereof, be discharged ")

was really based on the principle that, by resuming cohabitation, the married

I woman condones and puts an end to the cause of complaint. He added (5),

" Therefore, if it is shown that the parties have voluntarily resumed co-habitation, that puts an end to any cause of complaint which the one party had or may have had against the other."

The question arises whether the authority of *Williams* v. *Williams* (2) is nullified by any subsequent statutory provision or by the decision of the Court of Appeal in *Perry* v. *Perry* (6). The only subsequent statutory provisions which could be in question are the Summary Jurisdiction (Separation and Maintenance) Act, 1925, s. 1, and the Matrimonial Proceedings (Magistrates' Courts) Act, 1960, s. 7, which replaced the provision of the Act of 1925. Although s. 1 of the Act of 1925 permitted married women to obtain certain matrimonial orders while still in cohabitation, these were limited to orders on the ground of cruelty and

(2) [1904] P. 145.   (3) [1904] P. at p. 147.
(4) [1904] P. at p. 148.   (5) [1904] P. at pp. 148, 149.
          (6) [1952] 1 All E.R. 1076; [1952] P. 203.

wilful neglect to maintain. Though s. 7 of the Act of 1960 is not expressly so A
limited, in the nature of things a married woman could not, by virtue of the
provision, obtain a matrimonial order based on desertion while still in cohabitation, since cohabitation and desertion are mutually exclusive concepts. Moreover,
the judgments of the court in *Williams* v. *Williams* (7), were founded on a
principle of law whereby resumption of cohabitation blotted out the cause of
complaint, quite apart from any statutory provision. In *Perry* v. *Perry* (8), B
the wife deserted her husband in 1944. The husband visited her from time to
time, and a few isolated acts of sexual intercourse took place between them in
1949 and 1950, as a result of which a child was born. The wife, however, stead-
fastly refused to resume cohabitation; and in 1951 the husband petitioned for
divorce on the ground of desertion. It was held by the Court of Appeal that
desertion as a ground for divorce differs from the other statutory grounds of C
adultery and cruelty, in that the offence founding the cause of action is not
complete until the action is constituted by the presentation of a petition. The
conception of condonation, either in strictness or by analogy, has no application
to the continuing matrimonial offence of desertion as defined in the Matrimonial
Causes Act, 1950, s. 1 (1) (*b*) (now the Matrimonial Causes Act 1965, s. 1 (1)
(*a*) (ii)). The resumption of cohabitation, in the sense of setting up a matrimonial D
home together, accompanied by a common intention to do so, is necessary to
end or interrupt desertion; accordingly, sexual intercourse between a deserted
and a deserting spouse, unaccompanied by the setting up of any such home or
any such intention cannot end or interrupt the state of desertion.

In our judgment, *Williams* v. *Williams* (7) would now be differently phrased
in the light of *Perry* v. *Perry* (8); but we do not think that its authority is E
abrogated thereby. It was cited to the Court of Appeal in that case, and there
is no indication in any of the judgments that it was wrongly decided. It was
pointed out by this court in *Theobald* v. *Theobald* (9), that, if a bona fide offer
to resume cohabitation is made at the trial, it would be idle for the justices to
make an order which would be subject to immediate discharge. The present
case is, of course, a stronger one, since there has been an actual resumption of F
cohabitation and not merely an offer. (See also *Jones* v. *Jones* (10), where it was
held by this court (LORD MERRIMAN, P., and HODSON, J.) that a wife who was in
desertion at the time of the hearing could not obtain an order on the ground
of pre-existing wilful neglect to maintain.) It is, we think, rather on this line of
principle that *Willians* v. *Williams* (7) would today be supported—namely,
that the cause of complaint must be in existence not only at the time of the G
summons but also at the time of adjudication. Adultery or persistent cruelty
which have been condoned, albeit between the issue of the summons and the date
of adjudication, do not satisfy this test; nor does wilful neglect to maintain on
which there has supervened a state of desertion on the part of the complainant
(e.g., by her refusal of an acceptable offer of support in a state of cohabitation)
arising between complaint and adjudication; nor does a state of desertion ter- H
minated by a resumption of cohabitation between summons and adjudication.
The reason for this rule is that a matrimonial order is designed to operate
prospectively: see *Jones* v. *Jones* (10).

For these reasons, we would allow the appeal.

Appeal allowed.

Solicitors: *Ward, Bowie & Co.*, agents for *Barrie Hill & Co.*, Leeds (for the
husband); *Lovell, White & King*, agents for *Denis Lyth*, Leeds (for the wife).

[*Reported by* ALICE BLOOMFIELD, *Barrister-at-Law.*]

---

(7) [1904] P. 145.　　　　　　　　　　(8) [1952] 1 All E.R. 1076; [1952] P. 203.
(9) [1962] 2 All E.R. 863; at p. 864.　　　　(10) (1941), 165 L.T. 398.

A LONDON BOROUGH OF REDBRIDGE *v.* WESTS (ILFORD), LTD.

[QUEEN'S BENCH DIVISION (Lord Parker, C.J., Widgery and Chapman, JJ.), Nov. 28, 29, 1967.]

Shop—Hours of closing—Early closing day—Mixed shop—Supermarket—
Exemption order exempting shop of specified classes from early closing—
B *Commodities sold by supermarket included some of those sold by shops of*
classes specified in order—Whether supermarket was entitled to exemption
from early closing in respect of the sale of commodities sold by shops within
the exemption order—Shops Act, 1950 (14 Geo. 6 c. 28), s. 1, s. 13 (1).

The respondents were occupiers of shop premises where they carried on a multi-store business. On Nov. 1, 1966, the appellant local authority
C made an order under s. 1 (4)* of the Shops Act, 1950, exempting shops of classes specified in the order from the statutory requirement of closing at 1 p.m. on one early closing day in each week. Among other commodities the respondents sold commodities that were sold by shops of the classes specified in the exemption order. After Nov. 1, 1966, the respondents, who had previously closed their shop on Thursday afternoons, kept it open
D solely for the sale of such commodities. The respondents conceded that their store did not fall within any of the classes of shop specified in the exemption order. On appeal against the dismissal of an information against the respondents for failing to close their store not later than 1 p.m. on one week day in each week contrary to s. 1 (1)† of the Shops Act, 1950,

Held: where, as in the present case, a shop was not within a class of
E shop specified in an exemption order, which accordingly did not apply to the shop as a shop, s. 13 (1)‡ of the Shops Act, 1950, applied; and, according to the natural meaning of the words of s. 13 (1), the respondents' multi-store shop was exempted from weekly early closing in respect of the carrying on of trades or business normally carried on by classes of shops specified in the exemption order, viz., it was exempted for selling commodities ordinarily
F sold in the course of such trades or businesses (see p. 280, letter G, p. 281, letter H, and p. 283, letter A, post).

Per LORD PARKER, C.J.: the exemption to which s. 13 (1) of the Act of 1950 refers includes both exemption under s. 1 (4) and exemption under s. 1 (6) of the Act (see p. 281, letter C, post).

Fine Fare, Ltd. v. Aberdare Urban District Council ([1965] 1 All E.R. 679)
G explained.

Appeal dismissed.

[As to closing hours of shops where more than one business is carried on, see 17 HALSBURY'S LAWS (3rd Edn.) 195, para. 320, 199, para. 328; and for cases on the subject, see DIGEST (Cont. Vol. B) 310, 524b.

For the Shops Act, 1950, s. 1, s. 2, s. 8, and s. 13, see 29 HALSBURY'S STATUTES
H (2nd Edn.) 189, 190, 191, 195, 199, and for the Shops (Early Closing Days) Act 1965, see 45 HALSBURY'S STATUTES (2nd Edn.) 377.]

Cases referred to:

Fine Fare, Ltd. v. Aberdare Urban District Council, [1965] 1 All E.R. 679;
[1965] 2 Q.B. 39; [1965] 2 W.L.R. 535; Digest (Cont. Vol. B) 310, 524b.
I
Fine Fare, Ltd. v. Brighton County Borough Council, [1959] 1 All E.R. 476;
[1959] 1 W.L.R. 223; 123 J.P. 197; Digest (Cont. Vol. A) 611, 524a.
Macdonald v. Groundland, 1923 S.C. (J.) 28.
Thomson v. Somerville, 1917 S.C. (J.) 3; 25 L.T. 172; 24 Digest (Repl.) 1109, 169.

---

* Section 1 (4), so far as material, is set out at p. 279, letters E to G, post, and the exemption order is printed, so far as relevant, in the footnote at p. 278, post.
† Section 1 (1) is set out at p. 279, letter C, post.
‡ Section 13 (1) is set out at p. 280, letter A, post.

Case Stated.   A

This was a Case Stated by justices for the North East London Area acting for Beacontree.   On Mar. 21, 1967, an information was preferred by the appellants against the respondents, Wests (Ilford), Ltd. that the respondents, being the occupiers of a certain shop situate at 15/19 Cranbrook Road, Ilford in the London Borough of Redbridge, during the week commencing at midnight on Saturday, Jan. 7, 1967, and ending at midnight on Saturday, Jan. 14, 1967, did fail to   B close the said shop for the serving of customers not later than 1 p.m. on one week day in the said week contrary to s. 1 (1) of the Shops Act, 1950.

The following facts were found.   The respondents operated a multi-store business at their premises at 15/19 Cranbrook Road, Ilford, which was within the area described in the London Borough of Redbridge Early Closing Day Exemption Order 1966*.   The store was in one unit on four floors laid out depart-   C ment by department according to the classes of goods sold.   Before Nov. 1, 1966, the respondents closed the entire store for the serving of customers on Thursday of each week at 1 p.m.   On Nov. 1, 1966, the London Borough of Redbridge Early Closing Day Exemption Order 1966 came into force.   During the week commencing midnight on Jan. 7, 1967, and ending midnight on Jan. 14, 1967, the store was open between the hours of 9 a.m. to 5.30 p.m. on Monday, Tuesday   D and Wednesday, 9 a.m. to 7 p.m. on Friday, and 9 a.m. to 6 p.m. on Saturday.

On Thursday of the said week the store was open for all purposes of the respondents' business there between the hours of 9 a.m. and 1 p.m. and for the sale of drapery, haberdashery, ladies' wear, stationery, carpets, shoes, bedding, underwear, knitwear, hosiery, gloves and furs between the hours of 1 p.m. to 5.30 p.m. Men's and boys' clothing, leather and fancy goods, jewellery, babies' and   E children's wear, millinery and cosmetics were not on sale between the hours of 1 p.m. to 5.30 p.m. on Thursday of the said week and the sections of the store in which those items were then normally sold were roped off from the public. The china and glass department was not roped off but no staff were in attendance. A notice in the prescribed form was displayed in the store entrance denoting the trades for which the shop was not closed on Thursday of the same week.   On a   F normal working day ninety to one hundred staff are employed in the store attending to customers and between the hours of 1 p.m. to 5.30 p.m. on Thursday of the said week about thirty to thirty-five were similarly engaged.   No customer was served with commodities which were outside the provisions of the said order between the hours of 1 p.m. to 5.30 p.m. on Thursday of the said week.

The justices were of opinion that the exemption order applied to the respon-   G dents' shop because it described certain trades carried on in the shop and it was their view that the effect of s. 1 (4) and s. 13 (1) of the Shops Act, 1950, was to exempt the shop from the obligation to be closed on the weekly half-holiday so far as the carrying on of those trades was concerned, provided that the conditions

---

* The order provided, so far as relevant, as follows:—" The Mayor, Aldermen and   H
Burgesses of the London Borough of Redbridge acting by the council of the said borough in pursuance of the powers conferred upon them by the Shops Act, 1950, do hereby order as follows:— . . . (2) This Order applies to all shops of the following classes:—

Bookseller	Farrier
Caravan Dealer	Grocery & Provisions
Carpets & other Floor Coverings	Horticultural Sundries & Plants
Domestic & Electrical Appliances & supplies	Ladies Dress & Ladies Wear
Drapery & Haberdashery	Motor Accessories
Dress Hire	Optical Supplies
Dyers & Cleaners	Photographers & Photographic Supplies
Foot Comfort Aids	Portable Buildings
Footwear & Allied Sundries	Radio & Television
Furniture & Bedding	Stationery
	Trading Stamp Gift Shop

" (3) All shops to which this Order applies are hereby exempted from the provisions of s. 1 (1) of the Shops Act, 1950, as amended by the Shops (Early Closing Days) Act 1965, in regard to closing on one early closing day in each week.

" (4) This order shall come into force on Nov. 1, 1966."

A   prescribed under s. 13 (1) were complied with.   They held that the trades for which the respondents' shop was open for the serving of customers between 1 p.m. and 5.30 p.m. on Jan. 12, 1967, were trades described in the exemption order and as in their view the respondents were complying with the conditions prescribed under s. 13 (1) of the Act, no offence was committed by them.

G. T. Hesketh for the appellants.

B   *Norman C. Tapp*, Q.C., and *J. A. Speed* for the respondents.

LORD PARKER, C.J., having stated the nature of the appeal and having summarised the facts found in the Case Stated, continued: It is necessary to look at a number of provisions of the Shops Act, 1950.   It has been in fact amended in some respects by the Shops (Early Closing Days) Act 1965, but in my judgment

C   it is unnecessary to refer to that Act.   Section 1 (1) of the Shops Act, 1950 provides quite generally that:

" Every shop shall be closed for the serving of customers not later than one o'clock in the afternoon on one week day in every week."

Subsection (2) then goes on to provide that:

D   " The local authority may, by order, fix the day on which a shop is to be so closed . . . and any such order may either fix the same day for all shops, or may fix—(*a*) different days for different classses of shops; . . .

Pausing there, it is only necessary to point out that an order under s. 1 (2) is dealing with classes of shops.   Then by s. 1 (4) it is provided that:

E   " Where the local authority have reason to believe that a majority of the occupiers of shops of any particular class in any area are in favour of being exempted from the provisions of this section, either wholly or by fixing as the closing hour instead of one o'clock some other hour not later than two o'clock, the local authority, unless they consider that the area in question is unreasonably small, shall take steps to ascertain the wishes of such

F   occupiers.

" If the local authority are satisfied that a majority of the occupiers of such shops are in favour of the exemption, or, in the case of a vote being taken, that at least one half of the votes recorded by the occupiers of shops within the area of the class in question are in favour of the exemption, the local authority shall make an order exempting the shops of that class within

G   the area from the provisions of this section either wholly or to such extent as aforesaid."

It is pursuant to s. 1 (4) that the London Borough of Redbridge Early Closing Day Exemption Order 1966 was made.   Again, it is to be observed that an exemption order under sub-s. (4) is dealing with shops of certain classes.   Finally, in passing, it is to be observed that sub-s. (6) goes on to provide that

H   " [Section 1] shall not apply to any shop in which the only trade or business carried on is trade or business of any of the classes mentioned in Sch. 1 to this Act . . ."

Schedule 1 to the Shops Act, 1950, sets out a number of trades or businesses exempted from the provisions as to the weekly half-holiday, and includes the

I   sale of tobacco and smokers' requisites, medicines, periodicals and newspapers, and retail sale of intoxicating liquor and the like.

Section 2 of the Act of 1950 is dealing with the general closing hours, and when one comes to s. 8, provision is made for making what are called closing orders fixing the hours on the several days of the week when all shops of any specified class are to be closed for serving customers.   Finally, one gets to s. 13, which deals with shops where more than one trade or business is carried on.   It is only necessary, I think, for the purposes of this judgment to refer to sub-ss. (1) and (3). Subsection (1) provides that:

A

" Where several trades or businesses are carried on in the same shop, and any of those trades or businesses is of such a nature that, if it were the only trade or business carried on in the shop, the shop would be exempt from the obligation to be closed on the weekly half-holiday, the exemption shall apply to the shop so far as the carrying on of that trade or business is concerned, subject, however, to such conditions as may be prescribed."

That is dealing with exemption. Then sub-s. (3):

B

" Where several trades or businesses are carried on in the same shop and any of those trades or businesses is of such a nature that if it were the only trade or business carried on in the shop a closing order would not apply to the shop, the shop may be kept open for the purposes of that trade and business alone after the closing hour fixed by the closing order, but on such terms and under such conditions as may be specified in the order."

C

Approaching this case apart from authority, it seems to me quite clear, and indeed it is admitted by the respondents, that the London Borough of Redbridge Early Closing Day Exemption Order 1966 applies only to shops of certain classes there set out, and it seems to me that when for instance it says " stationery " it is referring to a shop which can be generally called a stationer's shop. Looked at in that way, it seems to me perfectly clear that the exemption order did not apply directly to this multiple store. It was impossible to say that this multiple store is other than a shop of the class of a multiple store. It certainly could not be described as a stationer's shop, a bookseller's shop, or a shop of any of the classes referred to in the exemption order.

D

The matter does not rest there because one then has to look at s. 13 (1), which I have already read; I will read it again inserting in it one of the exempted classes of shops:

E

" Where several trades or businesses are carried on in the same shop [that is undoubtedly true in the present case] and any of those trades or businesses [and, may I say, stationery] and the [stationery trade or business] is of such a nature that, if it were the only trade or business carried on in the shop, the shop would be exempt from the obligation to be closed on the weekly half-holiday [and stationery, as I have said, is within the exemption order, the] the exemption shall apply to the shop so far as the carrying on of that trade [viz., stationery] is concerned, subject, however, to such conditions as may be prescribed."

F

G

As I have said, approaching this apart from authority, it seems to me perfectly clear that the justices came to a correct decision in deciding that s. 13 (1) entitled these respondents to treat that part of their trade or business dealing with activities coming within the exemption order as falling within that order and therefore as enabling them to keep the part of the shop where those commodities were sold open throughout the week.

H

Cases concerning the Shops Acts are, as has often been said, confusing and difficult, and I would myself like to congratulate the justices in this case, who have not only seen their way through the tangle of the law in this regard, but have attached proper importance, or lack of importance rather, to certain remarks which I am afraid that I made in the case of *Fine Fare, Ltd.* v. *Aberdare Urban District Council* (1).

I

Turning to the authorities, the justices were referred to two Scottish cases, *Thomson* v. *Somerville* (2), and *MacDonald* v. *Groundland* (3), and also to *Fine Fare, Ltd.* v. *Brighton County Borough Council* (4). It is unnecessary to refer to those three cases because they were dealing, not with s. 13, but with the question whether an order either under s. 8 (a closing order) or under s. 1 (2), applied

---

(1) [1965] 1 All E.R. 679; [1965] 2 Q.B. 39.   (2) 1917 S.C. (J.) 3.
(3) 1923 S.C. (J.) 28.   (4) [1959] 1 All E.R. 476.

A   to the particular shop. Indeed, the same is true of *Fine Fare, Ltd.* v. *Aberdare Urban District Council* (5) to which I have already referred. The question there was whether a closing order made under s. 8 applied to a shop of the class to which Fine Fare, Ltd., a supermarket, belonged. It was held, and this is the ratio decidendi of the decision, that the closing order in question there did not apply to the premises of Fine Fare, Ltd.

B   Unfortunately, I then proceeded, perhaps falling into the trap of deciding more than was necessary, to consider s. 13; and s. 13 really did not arise in the case, save in so far as the magistrate seems to have referred to it. I referred first to sub-s. (1), and said that the exempting provision there referred to applied to businesses exempted by s. 1 (6) and Sch. 1. Quite clearly I had not got in mind the possible exemption that might be made, as has been made in this case,

C under s. 1 (4).

  In my judgment it is quite plain that the exemptions in s. 13 (1) cover not only those under s. 1 (6), but also under s. 1 (4). Again, unfortunately, I went on in dealing with s. 13 (3) to suggest that the only operation of that subsection was in regard to some ancillary business carried on in connexion with the main business. In fact there is no warrant for inserting any such words in sub-s. (1)

D or sub-s. (3) of s. 13.

  The justices came to a correct conclusion despite the difficulties and the observations of mine in the last-mentioned case, and accordingly I would dismiss this appeal.

    WIDGERY, J.: I agree with the order proposed, and also with everything
E which has fallen from LORD PARKER, C.J. I would add a few words in regard to the inter-relation between proceedings based on s. 8 of the Shops Act, 1950, and those based on s. 1, and on the inter-relation between the present case and the case of *Fine Fare, Ltd.* v. *Aberdare Urban District Council* (5) to which reference has been made. It is, I think, important to remember that under s. 1 (4) an exemption order can apply only, as my Lord has said, to a class of shops specified
F by the local authority. Whether or not a particular shop enjoys the benefit of the exemption, depends on whether that shop falls into one of the specified classes. If it falls into one of the specified classes it is wholly exempt, that is to say exempt in regard to all its activities. If it fails to fall into one of the specified classes, then it enjoys no such direct exemption under the order at all.

  It is conceded by counsel for the respondents in this case that this large depart-
G ment store did not fall into any of the specified classes in the exemption order, and therefore that it is not exempted as a shop. He has made that perfectly clear from the beginning of his argument, and it follows that the respondents seek to gain no direct advantage from the order at all. The case for the respondents in this court, as it was below, is based simply on the express terms of s. 13 (1) which LORD PARKER, C.J., has read, and the only issue in this case is
H whether we can in the circumstances give those words their plain and simple meaning. If we can, then the effect is to justify what the respondents have done, and to justify the justices' decision in this case.

  The argument against that view, and therefore the argument relied on by the appellants in this case, is based on s. 8 (closing orders) and the authorities on that section. Section 8 is a restrictive section; it is contemplating the making of an order which will restrict the right of a shopkeeper to carry on in accordance
I with the general law, and it is therefore to be contrasted with exemption orders under s. 1 which are enabling orders, giving the shopkeeper rights which he would not otherwise enjoy. Apart from that, however, there is a very great similarity in the proceedings and orders applicable under these two sections. In s. 8 one finds again that the shops concerned are to be specified by reference to a class; again one finds the principle that if a shop is within the class specified then a closing order applies to it and applies to all of it; whereas if the shop is not

---

(5) [1965] 1 All E.R. 679; [1965] 2 Q.B. 39.

within the specified class, the closing order does not apply to it at all. That, A
however, has to be read in the light of s. 13 (3), just as the equivalent provisions
of s. 1 (4) have to be read in the light of s. 13 (1).

What happened in the *Aberdare* case (6) was simply this. The shopkeeper
was a keeper of a supermarket in which a very large range of articles, including
foodstuffs, was sold, and amongst other articles there were sold groceries and
greengroceries. The local authority, the Aberdare Urban District Council, B
made a closing order under s. 8 of the Act of 1950, and one of the trades specified
in the closing order was the trade of a grocer. The trade of a greengrocer was
not specified. The order contained a provision on the lines of s. 13 (3), which in
effect provided that if greengrocery were sold after the closing hours prescribed
for other trades, then certain notices had to be exhibited in the shops. The
shopkeeper, Fine Fare, Ltd., taking the view, however, that this closing order C
had no application to their supermarket at all, proceeded to sell groceries after the
hour specified in the closing order for groceries, and also proceeded to sell greengroceries without exhibiting the notice which the order required. They were
accordingly prosecuted, and it is quite clear, I think, if one reads the report in
full, that the magistrate, having had his attention directed to s. 13 (3), and
having appreciated that that subsection on its face covered precisely the situation D
with which he was concerned, assumed that the closing order could in effect
operate to close the grocery department without closing the greengrocery
department.

This is in fact a fallacy for the reason already given by LORD PARKER, C.J.,
because a closing order cannot directly operate in that piecemeal fashion. The
true answer to the Aberdare situation was that since the supermarket was not E
in any of the specified classes of shop, the closing order did not apply to the
supermarket at all, and since a prosecution based on s. 8 must clearly establish
that the closing order was effective for the particular shop, the prosecution was
doomed to failure before any reference came to be made to s. 13 (3) of the Act
of 1950 at all. Had the supermarket in fact been a two-trade shop only, had
it consisted of a grocery shop with greengroceries as an ancillary or sideline, F
then one can well see that the shop would have fallen within the closing order,
because its main purpose would have been one of the specified trades. Then, as
I see it, it would have been necessary to consider the application of s. 13 (3) in
regard to the ancillary trade of greengroceries. Indeed, it is that fact, namely
the fact that in proceedings based on a closing order the " main purpose " may
become relevant, which has given rise to the argument put before this court by G
counsel for the appellants.

Putting it in my own words, and much abbreviating the submissions made to
us by counsel for the appellants, he is really inviting us to say that just as the
magistrate was wrong in the *Aberdare* case (6) in looking at s. 13 (3) on its face
without regard to the main purpose of the shop, so the justices are wrong in the
present case in looking at s. 13 (1) on its face without reference to the main H
purpose of the shop. His submission is that s. 13 (1) cannot apply unless the
main purpose of the shop is one of the purposes specified in the exemption order.

In my view that argument is ill-founded, because the considerations applicable
to these matters are different by reason of the fact that an exemption order is an
enabling order, and a closing order is a restrictive order. For the reasons which
I have already mentioned, one cannot proceed on a closing order without I
proving the efficacy of the order as applied to the particular shop, and that in
turn leads to considerations of the main purpose of the activities in that shop.

When one is dealing, however, with an exemption order, it is open to the
shopkeeper to do as he has done here and to admit frankly that the exemption
order as such is of no direct benefit to him at all, and then, as I see it, the way

---

(6) [1965] 1 All E.R. 679; [1965] 2 Q.B. 39.

A is clear without restriction to give the words of s. 13 (1) their simple and literal meaning.   That is all the justices did and in my judgment they did so correctly.

CHAPMAN, J.: I agree with both the judgments which have been delivered.   This case turns or falls clearly on the language of s. 13 (1) of the Shops Act, 1950.   If one takes those words in the ordinary and natural meaning,
B they clearly authorise what the respondents were here doing, and no offence was established against the respondents.

Appeal dismissed.   The court certified under s. 1 (2) *of the Administration of Justice Act,* 1960, *that a point of law of general public importance was involved, namely, as to the true construction of s.* 1 (4) *and* (6) *and s.* 13 (1) *of the Shops Act,* 1950; *but the court refused leave to appeal to the House of Lords.*

C Solicitors: *Town Clerk,* Redbridge (for the appellants); *Paisner & Co.* (for the respondents).

[*Reported by* ELLEN B. SOLOMONS, *Barrister-at-Law.*]

D # BOYS *v.* CHAPLIN.

[COURT OF APPEAL, CIVIL DIVISION (Lord Denning, M.R., Lord Upjohn and Diplock, L.J., October 10, 11, 12, December 6, 1967.]

Conflict of Laws—Tort—Damages—Remoteness of damage—Accident in Malta between servicemen normally resident in England but stationed in Malta—
E *Action in England—Whether damages to be assessed in accordance with English or Maltese law.*
Judgment—Judicial decision as authority—Court of Appeal—Interlocutory decision—Court composed of two lord justices—Ratio decidendi not binding on Court of Appeal if wrong.

An interlocutory order made by a Court of Appeal consisting of two
F lord justices is not binding as authority on the Court of Appeal, and the ratio decidendi of the interlocutory order need not be followed by the Court of Appeal subsequently if it is wrong (per LORD DENNING, M.R. and DIPLOCK, L.J., LORD UPJOHN not dissenting; see p. 288, letter I, p. 289, letter B, and p. 296, letter G, post, cf., p. 292, letter G, and p. 293, letter A, post).
Young v. Bristol Aeroplane Co., Ltd. ([1944] 2 All E.R. 293) considered.
G The plaintiff was injured in a motor accident in Malta caused by the negligence of the defendant.   Both the plaintiff and the defendant were British nationals, who were domiciled and normally resident in England, but were serving with British forces stationed in Malta.   The damages recoverable by Maltese law would not have included compensation for pain or suffering; they would have been £53, but, if damages were assessed in
H accordance with English law, they would be £2,250 together with the £53, which in English law would be special damage.
Held (DIPLOCK, L.J., dissenting): the damages should be assessed in accordance with English law for the following reasons—
(i) (per LORD DENNING, M.R.) the law of the country with which the parties had the most significant connexion (viz., the " proper law of the
I tort ") should be applied both in regard to the cause of action and in regard to the measure of damages, and this law was in the circumstances the law of England (see p. 289, letter I, and p. 290, letters E and F, post; cf., p. 294, letter C, post).
Babcock v. Jackson ([1963] 2 Lloyd's Rep. 286) and *Griffith v. United Air Lines, Inc.,* ((1964), 203 Atlantic Reporter (2nd Ser.) 796) applied.
First proposition in *Machado v. Fontes* ([1897] 2 Q.B. 231) not followed.
(ii) (per LORD UPJOHN) there being a cause of action for tort actionable in England according to the test stated by WILLES, J., in *Phillips v. Eyre,*

it followed (cf., on this point, per DIPLOCK, L.J., at p. 296, letter A, and   A
p. 300, letter E, post) that the rules of English law must apply in relation
not only to procedure but also to substantive law, including the measure of
damages, which accordingly, like all questions of remedy, was governed by
the lex fori, viz., in this instance by the law of England (see p. 292, letter I,
p. 293, letter E, and p. 294, letter H, post).

Test in *Phillips* v. *Eyre* ((1870), L.R. 6 Q.B. at pp. 28, 29) and second   B
proposition in *Machado* v. *Fontes* supra (see dictum of LOPES, L.J., in [1897]
2 Q.B. at p. 234, cf., p. 295, letter I, post) applied.

Per DIPLOCK, L.J. (dissenting): where, because the act of the defendant
had been committed abroad, the law to be applied in determining whether
the act was actionable is the lex loci delicti, the first inquiry involved in
the assessment of damages is to be conducted by applying the criteria as   C
to " heads of damage " provided by the lex loci delicti; accordingly the
damages of £2,250 should not be recoverable (see p. 299, letter I, and
p. 302, letter F, post).

Decision of MILMO, J. ([1967] 2 All E.R. 665) affirmed.

[As to the decisions of the Court of Appeal as authority, see 22 HALSBURY'S   D
LAWS (3rd Edn.) 799-801, para. 1687; and for cases on the subject, see 30 DIGEST
(Repl.) 225-227, *689-720.*

The view that an act done abroad, which might give rise to criminal liability
(though not to civil liability) there, would, if actionable in tort had it been done
in England, give rise to civil liability in England was rejected by DIPLOCK, L.J.,
as well as (as is indicated in the headnote) by LORD DENNING, M.R. (see p. 297,   E
letter C, p. 298, letter H, and p. 288, letter E, post).   This view is referred to
in the headnote as the first proposition in *Machado* v. *Fontes*; the second proposition in that case is that, if the act abroad is actionable in tort in England, the
ordinary incidents and remedies ensue according to the law of England.   The
two propositions are stated, for the purposes of the question in issue in regard
to damages in the present case at p. 295, letter H, post.   F

As to the measure of damages for torts committed abroad, see 7 HALSBURY'S
LAWS (3rd Edn.) 86. para. 157; and for cases on the subject, see 11 DIGEST
(Repl.) 449, 450, *878-884.*]

Cases referred to:
    Babcock v. *Jackson*, [1963] 2 Lloyd's Rep. 286.   G
    Baschet v. *London Illustrated Standard Co.*, [1900] 1 Ch. 73;   69 L.J.Ch. 35;
        81 L.T. 509; 13 Digest (Repl.) 102, *439.*
    Canadian National Steamships Co., Ltd. v. *Watson*, [1939] S.C.R. 11.
    Canadian Pacific Ry. Co. v. *Parent*, [1917] A.C. 195; 11 Digest (Repl.) 427,
        369.
    Carr v. *Fracis Times & Co.*, [1902] A.C. 176; 71 L.J.K.B. 361; 85 L.T. 144;   H
        11 Digest (Repl.) 453, *895.*
    Chartered Mercantile Bank of India v. *Netherlands India Steam Navigation
        Co., Ltd.*, (1883), 10 Q.B.D. 521; 52 L.J.Q.B. 220; 48 L.T. 546; 47 J.P.
        260; 11 Digest (Repl.) 450, *881.*
    Daglish v. *Barton*, [1900] 1 Q.B. 284; 68 L.J.Q.B. 1044; 81 L.T. 551; 51
        Digest (Repl.) 691, *2955.*
    D'Almeida Araujo (J.), Lda v. *Sir Frederick Becker & Co., Ltd.*, [1953] 2 All
        E.R. 288; [1953] 2 Q.B. 329; [1953] 3 W.L.R. 57; Digest (Cont.
        Vol. A) 229, *739a.*
    Ekins v. *East-India Co.*, (1717), 1 P. Wms. 395; *affd.*, H.L., (1718), 2 Bro.
        Parl. Cas. 382; 11 Digest (Repl.) 453, *898.*
    Gerard v. *Worth of Paris, Ltd.*, [1936] 2 All E.R. 905; 10 Digest (Repl.) 1081,
        7485.
    Griffith v. *United Air Lines, Inc.*, (1964), 203 Atlantic Reporter (2nd Ser.) 796.

A   *Handel* (*N. V.*), *My. J. Smits Import-Export* v. *English Exporters* (*London*), Ltd., [1955] 2 Lloyd's Rep. 69; *affd.* C.A., [1955] 2 Lloyd's Rep. 317; Digest (Cont. Vol. B) 127, *750c.*

Heron II, The, Koufos v. *C. Czarnikow, Ltd.*, [1967] 3 All E.R. 686; [1967] 3 W.L.R. 1491.

Indermaur v. *Dames*, [1861-73] All E.R. Rep. 15; (1866), L.R. 1 C.P. 274;
B   35 L.J.C.P. 184; 14 L.T. 484; (1867), L.R. 2 C.P. 311; 36 L.J.C.P. 181; 16 L.T. 293; 31 J.P. 390; 36 Digest (Repl.) 46, *246.*

Kohnke v. *Karger*, [1951] 2 All E.R. 179; [1951] 2 K.B. 670; 21 Digest (Repl.) 281, *527.*

Koop v. *Bebb*, (1952), 84 C.L.R. 629; [1952] A.L.R. 37; 25 A.L.J. 610; Digest (Cont. Vol. A) 233, **447a.*

C   *Lancaster Motor Co.* (*London*), *Ltd.* v. *Bremith, Ltd.*, [1941] 2 All E.R. 11; [1941] 1 K.B. 675; 110 L.J.K.B. 398; 165 L.T. 134; 3 Digest (Repl.) 189, **55.*

M'Elroy v. *M'Alistair*, 1949 S.C. 110; 11 Digest (Repl.) 452, **475.*

Machado v. *Fontes*, [1897] 2 Q.B. 231; 66 L.J.Q.B. 542; 76 L.T. 588; 11 Digest (Repl.) 450, *882.*

D   *McLean* v. *Pettigrew*, [1945] S.C.R. 62; 11 Digest (Repl.) 450, **458.*

Mills v. *Jennings*, (1880), 13 Ch.D. 639; *varied*, H.L., sub nom. *Jennings* v. *Mills*, (1881), 6 App. Cas. 698; 51 L.J.Ch. 129; 45 L.T. 593; 35 Digest (Repl.) 400, *964.*

Morris and Stulback v. *Angel*, (1956), 5 D.L.R. (2d) 30; Digest (Cont. Vol. A) 233, **447b.*

E   *Moxham* (*M.*), *The*, (1876), 1 P.D. 107; 46 L.J.P. 17; 34 L.T. 559; 11 Digest (Repl.) 370, *372.*

Naftalin v. *London, Midland and Scottish Ry. Co.*, 1933 S.C. 259; 8 Digest (Repl.) 118, **531.*

Phillips v. *Eyre*, (1870), L.R. 6 Q.B. 1; 10 B. & S. 1004; 40 L.J.Q.B. 28; 22 L.T. 869; 11 Digest (Repl.) 451, *888.*

F   *Scott* v. *Lord Seymour*, (1862), 1 H. & C. 219; 32 L.J. Ex. 61; 8 L.T. 511; 158 E.R. 865; 11 Digest (Repl.) 451, *887.*

Slater v. *Mexican National Railroad Co.*, (1904), 194 U.S. 120.

Tassell v. *Smith*, (1858), 2 De G. & J. 713; 27 L.J.Ch. 694; 32 L.T.O.S. 4; 44 E.R. 1166; 35 Digest (Repl.) 485, *1700.*

Tramontana v. *S.A. Empresa De Viacao Aerea Rio Grandense*, (1965), 350 F.
G   2d 468.

Wynne-Finch v. *Chayter*, [1903] 2 Ch. 475; 72 L.J.Ch. 723; 89 L.T. 123; 51 Digest (Repl.) 690, *2944.*

Young v. *Bristol Aeroplane Co., Ltd.*, [1944] 2 All E.R. 293; [1944] K.B. 718; 113 L.J.K.B. 513; 171 L.T. 113; *affd.* H.L., [1946] 1 All E.R. 98; [1946] A.C. 163; 30 Digest (Repl.) 225, *691.*

H   **Appeal.**

This was an appeal by notice dated Apr. 4, 1967, by the defendant, Richard Meredity MacNair Chaplin from an order of MILMO, J., dated Mar. 22, 1967, whereby he adjudged, in an action brought by the plaintiff, David Malcolm Boys by writ issued on Aug. 23, 1965, that the defendant should pay to the plaintiff the sum of £2,250 general damages and £53 special damages, making a
I   total of £2,303. The proceedings before MILMO, J., are reported in [1967] 2 All E.R. 665. The ground of appeal was that the trial judge was wrong in law in deciding that damages should be awarded in accordance with the law of England instead of the law of Malta, where the accident that was the subject of the action occurred, and accordingly was wrong in awarding to the plaintiff damages in excess of the agreed special damages of £53.

Tudor Evans, Q.C., and *D. J. Hyamson* for the defendant.
Leonard Caplan, Q.C., *J. M. Cope* and *V. C. Kothari* for the plaintiff.

Cur. adv. vult.

Dec. 6.   The following judgments were read.   A

LORD DENNING, M.R.: The plaintiff, David Boys, is a young Englishman whose home is at Surbiton.   When he was sixteen he joined up in the Royal
Air Force on a twelve years' engagement.   On Oct. 6, 1963, when he was twenty-
two, he was stationed in Malta on his duties as a technician in the Royal Air
Force.   His friend, Charles Ducat, who was also stationed in Malta, gave him a   B
ride on the pillion of his motor-cycle.   They were run into by a motor car driven
by the defendant, Richard Chaplin.   He was serving in the Royal Naval Air
Squadron and was also stationed in Malta at the time.   The plaintiff was badly
injured.   He had a fractured skull and was unconscious for three days.   The
right side of his face was crushed.   He was taken to the Royal Naval Hospital
in Malta.   He was there for about six weeks.   Then he was brought back to   C
England on Sept. 19, 1963, and taken to the Royal Air Force Hospital at Wrough-
ton in Wiltshire.   He was there for over six months, until Apr. 7, 1964.   Then
he was an out-patient for two months.   Eventually on June 5, 1964, owing to
his injuries, he was discharged from the Royal Air Force.   He is wholly and
permanently deaf in one ear and his sense of balance has been substantially
impaired.   The right side of his face is partially paralysed and he suffers much   D
from headaches.   Nevertheless, he is able to do good work.   Soon after his discharge
he found employment as an electronics engineer at a good wage; and it is unlikely
that he will suffer any loss of earnings in the future on account of this accident.

The defendant, the driver of the car, is also back in England.   He is stationed
at Culdrose in Cornwall.   In August, 1965, the plaintiff was given legal aid to
sue the defendant and he issued a writ claiming damages.   At first the defendant   E
denied negligence, but later it was admitted.   So the only question is: What
damages should be awarded?   We were told that both vehicles are fully insured
against liability for damages, whatever sum is awarded.   Both are insured
with the same insurance company, an English company.

Now the question arises: what is the law to be applied in the assessment of
damages?   According to the law of England, the plaintiff should be compensated   F
not only for his expenses and money loss, but also for his pain and suffering and
loss of amenities of life.   The figure would be £2,303.   According to the law of
Malta, however, (as found by the judge (1)), the plaintiff should receive only
his expenses and his money loss, and nothing whatever for his pain and suffering
and loss of amenities.   The figure would be £53.   The judge held (2) that the
damages should be assessed according to the law of England, and he awarded   G
the plaintiff £2,303.   The defendant appeals to this court, claiming that the
matter is governed by the law of Malta and that the plaintiff should recover
only £53.

The case throws up one of the most vexed questions in the conflict of laws:
when a wrong is committed abroad, and the injured party seeks redress in
England, what is the law to be applied?   The cases on the subject are legion.   H
So are the writers.   The trend of the authorities is to this effect.   In England,
in general and subject to certain conditions, the courts apply the law of the
place of trial (lex fori).   Canada does the same.   In Scotland, and at one time
in the United States of America, the courts applied the law of the place where
the wrong was committed (lex loci delicti).   In recent cases in the United States
the courts have applied the law of the place which has the most significant
contacts with the matter in dispute (the proper law of the tort, lex propria
delicti).

After considering the authorities, I am of opinion that we should apply the
proper law of the tort, that is, the law of the country with which the parties and the
act done have the most significant connexion.   And once we have decided which
is the correct law to apply, I think that law should be applied, not only to ascertaining whether there is a cause of action, but also to ascertaining the heads

---

(1) [1967] 2 All E.R. 665 at p. 667.   (2) [1967] 2 All E.R. at p. 670.

A of damage that are recoverable and also the measure of damages: for these are matters of substantive law.   They are quite distinct from the mere quantification of damages, which is a matter of procedure for the lex fori.

I will show how the English authorities can be fitted in so as to achieve this result.

Phillips v. *Eyre* (3)

B The leading case in England is *Phillips* v. *Eyre* (3), a decision of the Court of Exchequer Chamber consisting of seven judges.   It is of high authority. It must be read in the light of the facts.   In 1865 there was an insurrection in Jamaica.   The Governor, Edward Eyre, proclaimed martial law and called out the forces to suppress it.   Phillips was arrested in his house, handcuffed, put on board a ship and taken away.   After the insurrection was suppressed,

C the legislative council of Jamaica passed an Act of Indemnity saving Governor Eyre from any liability for what was done in repressing the revolt.   Governor Eyre returned to England.   Phillips also returned and brought an action in these courts for assault and false imprisonment.   Governor Eyre pleaded that the Act of Indemnity was an answer to the action, and his plea was held good. Much of the argument was taken up with a discussion as to whether the Act of

D Indemnity was valid.   It was held to be valid.   Next, the plaintiff said that, even if it was valid and a defence in Jamaica, it could not have extra-territorial effect and take away the right of action in England.   This argument was rejected on the short and simple ground that validity was to be determined by the law of Jamaica: and as the conduct of Governor Eyre could not be questioned in Jamaica, it could not be questioned here.   WILLES, J., laid down the law in

E these words (4):

  "... the civil liability arising out of a wrong derives its birth from the law of the place, and its character [whether it is valid or not] is determined by that law.   Therefore, an act committed abroad, if valid and unquestionable by the law of the place, cannot, so far as civil liability is concerned, be

F drawn in question elsewhere ..."

That principle was quite sufficient to determine *Phillips* v. *Eyre* (3).   After stating it, WILLES, J., went on (5) to formulate two conditions which he said must, *as a general rule*, be fulfilled in order to found a suit in England for a wrong committed abroad.

G " First, the wrong must be of such a character that it would have been actionable if committed in England ... Secondly, the act must not have been justifiable by the law of the place where it was done."

Once those two conditions are fulfilled, the English courts determine the actionability of the wrong according to the law of England, and determine also the heads of damages and the measure of them by English law.   Those two conditions have long been treated as good law.   LORD MACNAGHTEN in the House of Lords

H accepted them as correct (see *Carr* v. *Fracis Times & Co.* (6)).   So have the Supreme Court of Canada (see *Canadian National Steamships Co., Ltd.* v. *Watson* (7) and *McLean* v. *Pettigrew* (8)).   But those conditions are not of universal application.   WILLES, J., was careful to say (4) that " as a general rule " those two conditions must be fulfilled.   Like every general rule, it is subject to exceptions. To some of these I now turn.

I *Machado* v. *Fontes* (9)

The actual decision in *Machado* v. *Fontes* (9) was on a point of pleading.   It would appear that the defendant Fontes published in Brazil a pamphlet that was libellous of the plaintiff Machado.   One would think that the natural place

---

(3) (1870), L.R. 6 Q.B. 1.   (4) (1870), L.R. 6 Q.B. at p. 28.
(5) (1870), L.R. 6 Q.B. at pp. 28, 29.   (6) [1902] A.C. 176 at p. 182.
(7) [1939] S.C.R. 11 at p. 13.   (8) [1945] S.C.R. 62.
                       (9) [1897] 2 Q.B. 231.

for the plaintiff to sue for the libel was in Brazil, the place where the libel was   A
published; but the plaintiff did not sue in Brazil—and for a very good reason.
He could not recover any damages in Brazil.   So he sued in England.   I suppose
that by this time the defendant Fontes was in England and was served here.
At first the defendant Fontes only denied the libel.   Afterwards he sought to
amend his plea by saying that the publication was not actionable in civil proceedings in Brazil (though it might be made the subject of criminal proceedings),   B
or, alternatively, that general damages were not recoverable in Brazil.   The
court, consisting of LOPES and RIGBY, L.JJ., held that the plea was absolutely
bad and ought to be struck out.   If the plea were allowed, it would mean that
a commission would have to go to Brazil to inquire into Brazilian law.   LOPES,
L.J., said (10): ". . . that would be a great waste of time and money ".   So the
case fell to be determined, both as to actionability and as to heads of damage,   C
according to English law (the lex fori) and not by the law of Brazil (the lex loci
delicti).   In coming to this conclusion, the lord justices took the two conditions
stated by WILLES, J., in *Phillips* v. *Eyre* (11) and held that they were fulfilled.
The first condition was fulfilled because the libel was of such a character that it
would have been actionable if committed in England.   The second condition was
fulfilled because it was not justified by the law of Brazil, seeing that it was not   D
an innocent act there but might be made the subject of criminal proceedings.

I think that the court was in error in applying the two conditions so literally.
They treated them as if they were contained in a statute; but if there was ever
to be a case where an exception should be made to the " general rule ", it was
Machado v. *Fontes* (12).   Those two gentlemen were, I suppose, Brazilian citizens.
Their names suggest it.   The libel was in Brazil: and, I suppose, in Portuguese.   E
It was an entirely Brazilian affair.   If the plaintiff could not recover damages in
Brazil, he ought not to be allowed to recover damages in England.   It was a
mere accident that Fontes happened to come here and thus be served with a
writ here.   Suppose that Fontes had not come to England but had gone to
Portugal, to France, or anywhere else.   Can it really be supposed that Machado
could follow Fontes all over the world and choose the forum that suited him   F
best?   It cannot be.   If the libel was not actionable in Brazil, it should not be
actionable in England.   If general damages could not be recovered in Brazil,
they should not be recoverable in England.   At any rate, the two points were
so well arguable that leave should have been given to raise them.

Is Machado v. *Fontes* (12) *binding?*   G

Is *Machado* v. *Fontes* (12) binding on this court?   I do not think so.   It was
an interlocutory appeal, heard by two lord justices only, on the bare question
whether there should be leave to amend or not.   Such questions are dealt with
expeditiously—I might almost say summarily—because they do not usually
raise points of great moment.   On the occasions when they do raise important
points, arrangements are made to have them heard by three judges.   No such   H
arrangements were made in *Machado* v. *Fontes* (12).   It was regarded as a
usual interlocutory appeal, to be disposed of in an hour or two, by two lord
justices only.

I cannot regard such a decision as a binding precedent.   There is no case in
the books where a decision of two lord justices has been held to be binding when
it is afterwards discovered to be wrong.   On the contrary, there are three cases
in which such a decision has been overruled by a court of three or more.   Thus
the decision of the two lord justices in the old Court of Chancery in *Tassell* v.
Smith (13) was overruled by three lord justices in the Court of Appeal in *Mills* v.
Jennings (14).   The decision of two lord justices in an interlocutory matter in
Daglish v. *Barton* (15) was overruled by SIR RICHARD HENN COLLINS, M.R., and

---

(10) [1897] 2 Q.B. at p. 234.   (11) (1870), L.R. 6 Q.B. at pp. 28, 29.
(12) [1897] 2 Q.B. 231.   (13) (1858), 2 De G. & J. 713.
(14) (1880), 13 Ch.D. 639 at p. 648.   (15) [1900] 1 Q.B. 284.

A five lord justices in the Court of Appeal in *Wynne-Finch* v. *Chayter* (16). The decision of two lord justices in an interlocutory matter in *Gerard* v. *Worth of Paris, Ltd.* (17) was overruled by Sir Wilfrid Greene, M.R., and two lord justices in *Lancaster Motor Co. (London), Ltd.* v. *Bremith, Ltd.* (18). I do not think that *Young* v. *Bristol Aeroplane Co., Ltd.* (19) is any authority to the contrary. The court there did not discuss interlocutory appeals heard by two

B lord justices: whereas I think it plain, to anyone who knows how this court works, that they ought not to be regarded as binding when they are afterwards shown to be wrong. It is unnecessary to consider today the position of final decisions of this court: though I foresee the time may come when we have to reconsider the self-imposed limitation stated in *Young's* case (19), especially in view of the recent change in practice in the House of Lords (20).

C   In my opinion, therefore, *Machado* v. *Fontes* (21) is not binding on this court. Test it in this way. Suppose that in the present case the parties involved in the accident had been all Maltese citizens, ordinarily resident in Malta. The injured man would naturally seek his remedy in the courts of Malta. The cause of action and the measure of damages would be governed by that law. Even if by some chance the injured man were able to bring an action in England

D —as he might do if the negligent driver came to England on a visit and was served with a writ here—nevertheless, the rights of the parties would still be governed by the law of Malta. The English courts would apply the law of Malta. The plaintiff would not get a new head of damages by the mere chance that the defendant had happened to come to England. In such a case the reason why English courts apply the law of the place (lex loci delicti) is because

E it is the place with which the whole affair is most significantly connected. It is the proper law of the tort.

The Proper Law of the Tort
      This brings me to the crux of the case. The plaintiff and the defendant were not Maltese citizens resident in Malta. They were two English servicemen stationed in Malta on duty. Does this make any difference? I think it does.

F It goes far to show that English law is the proper law of the tort. They were insured in England by an English company. The plaintiff was brought back for treatment in England, his native land. Quite naturally, he seeks his remedy in the courts of England: and he is enabled to bring his action here, not by any chance visit to England by the defendant, but as of right, because the defendant is regularly here. It is the defendant's home, too, as well as the plaintiff's.

G Why should not the plaintiff bring his action here and have it determined by English law? I see no reason why he should not do so. He gets justice here in that he gets fair compensation. Whereas the law of Malta gives him less than fair compensation. The two conditions stated by Willes, J., in *Phillips* v. *Eyre* (22) are fulfilled. The first is fulfilled because the wrong done in Malta (negligent driving) was of such a character that it would have been actionable

H if committed in England. The second is fulfilled because the act was not justifiable by the law of Malta.

      Seeing that the two conditions are fulfilled, why should we not apply the law of England to the whole case? We have to apply it so as to see whether the wrong was of such a character as to be actionable in England. We should also apply it so as to determine the measure of damages and heads of damage.

I   I know that this means drawing a distinction between a collision in Malta between two Maltese and a collision between two English servicemen; but I am prepared to draw the distinction. It has been drawn by others besides me. Take *Scott* v. *Lord Seymour* (23). Lord Seymour struck Mr. Scott in Naples

---

(16) [1903] 2 Ch. 475 at p. 485.   (17) [1936] 2 All E.R. 905.
(18) [1941] 2 All E.R. 11; [1941] 1 K.B. 675.
(19) [1944] 2 All E.R. 293; [1944] K.B. 718.
(20) See *Note*, [1966] 3 All E.R. 77.   (21) [1897] 2 Q.B. 231.
(22) (1870), L.R. 6 Q.B. at pp. 28, 29.   (23) (1862), 1 H. & C. 219.

and injured him severely. When they got home to England, Mr. Scott sued **A**
Lord Seymour for damages.   It was said that in Naples no-one could bring
an action for damages for assault, and that only criminal proceedings lay.
WIGHTMAN, J., said (24):

> ". . . whatever might be the case as between two Neapolitan subjects,
> or between a Neapolitan and an Englishman, I find no authority for holding
> that, even if Neapolitan law gives no remedy for an assault and battery,   **B**
> however violent and unprovoked, by recovery of damages, that therefore
> a British subject is deprived of his right to damages given by the English
> law against another British subject; "

and WILLES, J., said (25): " I am far from saying that I differ from any part
of the judgment of WIGHTMAN, J."   **C**

These views are echoed in DICEY AND MORRIS ON THE CONFLICT OF LAWS
(8th Edn.), p. 914:

> " If one Englishman assaults another while both are together on a holiday
> or a business trip in Italy, little can be urged in favour of the application of
> Italian law by an English court called upon to decide the question of
> damages."   **D**

We were referred to several Scottish cases where the Scottish judges, insistent as
ever on principle, rigorously apply the law of the place (lex loci delicti) without
exception; but I cannot help noting that this has led to injustice. So much so
that I am not inclined to follow them.

I am of opinion that in these cases we should apply the law of the country
with which the parties and the act done have the most significant connexion.   **E**
This has been called " the proper law of the tort ". It has been done in many
cases recently in the United States, in particular in *Babcock* v. *Jackson* (26),
and *Griffith* v. *United Air Lines, Inc.*, (27). I would do the same here.

On the facts of this case, I think that England is the place with which the
parties and the act done have the most significant connexion. I think that we
should apply the law of England and award the plaintiff £2,303. I would   **F**
dismiss this appeal.

LORD UPJOHN (read by LORD DENNING, M.R.): The facts of this case
can be very briefly stated. On Oct. 6, 1963, the plaintiff, riding pillion on a
motor-scooter in Malta, met with an accident and suffered severe injuries when
the defendant, driving a motor car, collided with him. The plaintiff has sued **G**
the defendant in our courts and the latter at the trial before MILMO, J. (28)
admitted that he drove negligently and is, accordingly, liable in damages to
him. The whole issue in this case is caused by the circumstance that while the
plaintiff had a cause of action in Malta based on the defendant's negligence and
could have successfully sued him there, yet having regard to para. 1088 of the
Civil Code, he could only have recovered, putting it shortly, what we should   **H**
describe as special damages plus certain (as distinct from problematical) future
financial loss (which in this case has been assessed at £53) but nothing for general
damages for pain and suffering or loss of amenity, nor for problematical future
financial loss.

MILMO, J., however, came to the conclusion (29), following the decision of this
court in *Machado* v. *Fontes* (30) that in an English action he was entitled to   **I**
award general damages in accordance with our rules for the assessment of
damages and he awarded him £2,000 in addition to the sum of £53 admittedly
recoverable by the law of Malta. The whole question is whether he was right
to do so.

---

(24) (1862), 1 H. & C. at p. 235.   (25) (1862), 1 H. & C. at p. 236.
(26) [1963] 2 Lloyd's Rep. 286.
(27) (1964), 203 Atlantic Reporter (2nd Ser.) 796.   (28) [1967] 2 All E.R. 665.
(29) [1967] 2 All E.R. at p. 670.   (30) [1897] 2 Q.B. 231.

A   Both plaintiff and defendant are English nationals domiciled and normally resident in this country and both were in Malta in the service of the Crown, though at the time of the accident neither was engaged on duty, so no question of any liability on the part of the Crown arises.

We were referred to the case of *Scott* v. *Lord Seymour* (31), where Wightman, J.,
B   in the Court of Exchequer Chamber expressed the view that if one Englishman assaulted another Englishman while abroad, on their return here the sufferer could sue his assailant without regard to foreign law; that view did not meet with the approval of all of his brethren and I propose to treat the matter as though the plaintiff was a resident domiciled Maltese who had pursued the defendant here.

Counsel for the defendant has argued that in a transitory tort such as negli-
C   gence, all questions of substantive law must be determined by the lex loci delicti and questions of procedure by the lex fori; but he further argued that although the remedy to be granted is normally a question of procedure, yet it is not true that the remedy of damages is necessarily such a question. When considering what kind or head of damage is recoverable (e.g. general damages for pain and suffering), that is a question of principle and should be determined by the lex loci
D   delicti, though quantification or assessment of damages he agrees is a matter for the lex fori. He relies by analogy on the case of *J. D'Almeida Araujo Lda.* v. *Sir Frederick Becker & Co., Ltd.* (32), a case of contract, where Pilcher, J., held that the question of remoteness of damages must be determined by the proper law of the contract, a case to which I shall return.

The foundation of the defendant's argument that all questions of substantive
E   law must depend on the lex loci delicti rests on the case of *Phillips* v. *Eyre* (33), a decision of seven judges sitting in the Exchequer Chamber, the judgment of the court being delivered by Willes, J. Eyre was the Governor of Jamaica at the time of a rebellion there in 1865. He imprisoned Phillips without trial and later the Jamaican legislature passed a retrospective Act indemnifying Eyre from his acts as Governor in suppression of the rebellion. Phillips sued him in this
F   country and a number of points were debated; among them it was said that the Act of the Jamaican legislature could have no extra-territorial effect to protect Eyre from an action in this country for wrongful imprisonment. This point was dealt with by the court; after pointing out that the submission was based on a misconception, Willes, J., said (34):

G   " A right of action, whether it arise from contract governed by the law of the place or wrong, is equally the creature of the law of the place and subordinate thereto. The terms of the contract or the character of the subject matter may show that the parties intended their bargain to be governed by some other law; but, prima facie, it falls under the law of the place where it was made. And in like manner the civil liability arising out of a wrong derives its birth from the law of the place, and its character is deter-
H   mined by that law. Therefore, an act committed abroad, if valid and unquestionable by the law of the place, cannot, so far as civil liability is concerned, be drawn in question elsewhere. . . . In this respect no sound distinction can be suggested between the civil liability in respect of a contract governed by the law of the place and a wrong."

I   All this was directed to showing that the submission that the Indemnity Act could have no extra-territorial effect was without substance, for the Governor's acts took their colour from the law of the place where the alleged wrong was committed; the character of the civil liability must be determined by that law. So that extra-territoriality had nothing to do with it; the Governor's acts must be judged of in the light of the fact that he was immune by the law of Jamaica. But the learned judge was very careful not to say that, that being so, the tortious

(31) (1862), 1 H. & C. at pp. 234, 235.   (32) [1953] 2 All E.R. 288; [1953] 2 Q.B. 329.
(33) (1870), L.R. 6 Q.B. 1.   (34) (1870), L.R. 6 Q.B. at p. 28.

act must be determined by the lex loci delicti. Had that been the view of the court, **A**
it would have been a very short answer and would have been decisive of the issue.
On the contrary, having, so to speak, got rid of the misconceived issue of extra-
territoriality, WILLES, J., went on to consider a different point altogether,
namely, what were the necessary ingredients in an action in England in respect
of a tort committed abroad. After stating that the English courts were said to
be more open to admit actions founded on foreign transactions than other **B**
countries, continued (35):

> "As a general rule, in order to found a suit in England for a wrong alleged
> to have been committed abroad, two conditions must be fulfilled. First,
> the wrong must be of such a character that it would have been actionable
> if committed in England. . . . Secondly, the act must not have been **C**
> justifiable by the law of the place where it was done."

Though the court expressed it to be " a general rule " and, therefore, I suppose
capable of exception, I, for my part, can see nothing in the circumstances of this
case which would justify a departure from that general rule; indeed, the facts
seem to me to support its application in this case.

In the interlocutory appeal of *Machado* v. *Fontes* (36), so much debated before **D**
us, LOPES, L.J., and RIGBY, L.J., held that this test clearly distinguished between
actionability in this country for the tort had it been committed here and un-
justifiability in the place where the alleged wrong was committed, for the court
held that an action for defamation in respect of an alleged libel published in
Brazil (plainly actionable if published here) was actionable here though not
actionable in Brazil by way of civil proceedings but only the subject of criminal **E**
proceedings. So they held that actionability in a civil sense by the lex loci delicti
was not necessary and struck out two pleas in bar by the defendant—(i) that in
Brazil the plaintiff could not maintain legal proceedings against the defendant
in which damages could be recovered; (ii) alternatively, that in Brazil it could
not be a ground of legal proceedings in which the plaintiff could recover general
damages for injury to his credit, character or feelings. LOPES, L.J., said (37): **F**

> " It then follows, directly the right of action is established in this country,
> that the ordinary incidents of that action and the appropriate remedies
> ensue."

However, that decision, as PROFESSOR CHESHIRE has pointed out in his work on
PRIVATE INTERNATIONAL LAW (7th Edn.) pp. 247, 248:
G
> ". . . has been commended, reprobated, reconciled with doctrine, explained,
> doubted, followed by some courts, repudiated by others . . . ,"

though all the criticisms have been directed to the first plea in bar.

The decision, however, in *Phillips* v. *Eyre* (38) was accepted as settling the law
in *The M. Moxham* (39), by a strong court (JAMES, MELLISH and BAGGALLAY,
L.JJ.) and (after *Machado* v. *Fontes* (36)) was approved in terms by LORD **H**
MACNAGHTEN in *Carr* v. *Fracis Times & Co.* (40). For my part I can see no reason
for departing from the perfectly clear test laid down in *Phillips* v. *Eyre* (38).
It is said that the words of WILLES, J., have been treated as though they were
contained in a statute. I cannot understand this argument. The court was laying
down the practical test for actionability in England for a tort committed abroad;
tests for actionability or per contra liability are laid down every day in judge- **I**
made law. The test is either right or wrong, and, as I have already said, I think
that only the House of Lords can say that test is wrong; this court cannot
usefully criticise the test by saying it has been treated (especially in *Machado* v.
Fontes (36)), as though it was contained in a statute where (as I think) it cannot

---

(35) (1870), L.R. 6 Q.B. at pp. 28, 29.   (36) [1897] 2 Q.B. 231.
(37) [1897] 2 Q.B. at p. 234.   (38) (1870), L.R. 6 Q.B. 1.
(39) (1876), 1 P.D. 107.   (40) [1902] A.C. at p. 182.

A   be argued that this case is an exception to the general rule. If this court thought that *Machado* v. *Fontes* (41) was wrongly decided, it could probably review that case because it was an interlocutory appeal heard by two judges, though this court undoubtedly remains bound by the principles of *Young* v. *Bristol Aeroplane Co., Ltd.* (42), notwithstanding some recent relaxation from the binding effect of precedent in the House of Lords, a relaxation which applies only to that House.

B   That, however, is not the real point; that only goes to the question whether this court in that case misinterpreted what was said in *Phillips* v. *Eyre* (43). As a matter of plain English language, I should have thought it was clear that WILLES, J., while recognising that the lex loci delicti provided a fundamental condition to be satisfied, was being very careful to say that the tort did not have to be actionable by the lex loci delicti. As I have already pointed out, it would have

C   been so simple to have said, had the court so intended, that foreign torts were, by the law of England, in an action in this country to be judged by the lex loci delicti and not by the law of England. If we are to say that the major proposition in *Machado* v. *Fontes* (41) namely, that the tort need only be unjustifiable but not necessarily actionable by the lex loci delicti, was wrong, we must in my judgment overrule the test laid down in *Phillips* v. *Eyre* (43), which we have not been invited

D   to do, and only the House of Lords can.

If, therefore, the test is to be read in its ordinary sense, I for my part cannot see how the lex loci delicti can be applicable, for if the only test of actionability is actionability as if the tort were committed in this country, then the rules of English law must surely follow not only in relation to procedure but also in respect of all substantive law, once non-justifiability by the place of the delict is estab-

E   lished; I can see no other principle of law that can be applicable. That, I think, is what LOPES, L.J., was saying in *Machado* v. *Fontes* (44) in the passage which I have quoted.

This aspect of the matter, however, was not canvassed at length before the court, and I must deal, though shortly, with the cogent arguments developed on the footing that in matters of substance the lex loci delicti governed, for in fact

F   there is no issue on that point because having suffered damage, there is no dispute that the plaintiff could have sued for damages for the tort in Malta. So we are really only concerned with the second proposition in *Machado* v. *Fontes* (41). That is directly in point here, for the court negatived any idea that a mere kind or head of damage could be excluded because it was not recoverable by the lex loci delicti. That part of the judgment has never been criticised in any English

G   decision and only by the text writers after PILCHER, J.'s decision in *D'Almeida* (45). LYNSKEY, J., in *Kohnke* v. *Karger* (46) applied English principles of damages in preference to French principles to a motor car accident in France.

Some of the text writers (see DICEY AND MORRIS (8th Edn.) p. 848, CHESHIRE (7th Edn.) p. 603) have referred to a very old case decided in 1717, *Ekins* v. *East India Co.* (47), as establishing that even in tort, the lex loci delicti may be applied

H   to damages. That was a case in trover where a ship was tortiously sold by the defendants' servants in India and damages were assessed by reference to the law of India. The defendant was ordered to pay damages based on the rate of interest obtaining in India, not in obedience to any rule of private international law depending on the locus delicti but because the defendant had employed the proceeds of the tortious sale in India and it was right that he should account

I   accordingly, for money earned a higher rate of interest in India than in this country. That case has nothing whatever to do with the question before this court.

In deciding *D'Almeida* (45), PILCHER, J., applied the proper law of the contract

---

(41) [1897] 2 Q.B. 231.   (42) [1944] 2 All E.R. 293; [1944] K.B. 718.
(43) (1870), L.R. 6 Q.B. 1.   (44) [1897] 2 Q.B. at p. 234.
(45) [1953] 2 All E.R. 288; [1953] 2 Q.B. 329.
(46) [1951] 2 All E.R. 179; [1951] 2 K.B. 670.
(47) (1717), 1 P.Wms. 395.

(Portugal) to a question of remoteness of damage and awarded damages to the   A
plaintiff which would have been too remote by our law of contract. He agreed,
however, that assessment remained a matter for the English courts, a distinction
which McNAIR, J., in *N.V. Handel, My. J. Smits Import-Export* v. *English Ex-porters (London), Ltd.* (48), had some difficulty in appreciating. I have some
sympathy with McNAIR, J., and I think *D'Almeida* (49) may one day require
reconsideration. We are not concerned, however, with contract here and we do   B
not recognise any principle of the " proper law of the tort ", though such a
principle has recently been adopted in certain States of the U.S.A. in place of the
former rule which (in contrast, as I think, to this country) undoubtedly obtained
there of applying the lex loci delicti. (See generally *Babcock* v. *Jackson* (50)
(State of New York); *Griffith* v. *United Air Lines, Inc.* (51) (State of Pennsyl-vania); and *Tramontana* v. *S.A. Empresa* (52) (District of Columbia)). It has   C
not been suggested in argument that our courts should adopt any such principle
which, however convenient in a vast country like the U.S.A. which has fifty
States with no system of law of torts common to all and an enormous network of
internal airlines, would, I think, in this country give rise to much practical
difficulty and, that bugbear of the law, enormous uncertainty in its application.
I would reject any idea that such a principle should be introduced in this country.   D
There is no relevant analogy between the proper law of the contract and a
similar concept in tort, for while contracting parties can choose the law by which
their relationship shall be governed, the victim of a tort cannot; damages too
are assessed on entirely different principles (see *The Heron II, Koufos* v. *C.
Czarnikow, Ltd.* (53)).

Then some reliance was placed on the Scottish cases based on " solatium ";   E
but those cases make it clear that a claim based on solatium is a new, substantial
and entirely separate cause of action which may be vested in a spouse or relation
of the injured party quite independently of the latter's rights, and it cannot be
described as a mere head or kind of damage (see *Naftalin* v. *London, Midland
and Scottish Ry. Co.* (54); *M'Elroy* v. *M'Alistair* (55)). Though these cases dissent
from the first plea in *Machado* v. *Fontes* (56), they throw no doubt on the second.   F

In my view the ordinary rule must apply, namely, that even if, contrary to
my opinion, the lex loci delicti applies to questions of substantive law, all ques-tions of the remedy, both as to its nature and kinds or heads of assessment of
pecuniary damage, must be determined in an English action entirely by English
principles. The contrary would not have been argued at all thirty years ago and
in my view it cannot be so argued successfully today.   G

In *Baschet* v. *London Illustrated Standard Co.* (57), KEKEWICH, J., pointed out
the great difficulty in applying the rules of some other country when dealing
with the nature of the remedy.

The rule that the lex fori must be applied to all questions of the remedy is clear
and simple and gives rise to no difficulty in its application; it does no injustice,
for I cannot see any injustice in claiming damages here of a kind or head which, by   H
some local rule of the locus delicti, is denied to the plaintiff. The difficulties of
trying to apply some foreign rule about damages would be immense. First, the
practical difficulty (pace McNAIR, J. (48)) of distinguishing between the head or
kind of damage on the one hand and mere assessment on the other. Then if the
foreign rule is to be applied, where does it stop? In this case, for example, the
judge has found (58) as a fact that the plaintiff by the law of Malta can only   I
claim his present pecuniary ascertained loss, but if later on as the result of the

(48) [1955] 2 Lloyd's Rep. 69.
(49) [1953] 2 All E.R. 288; [1953] 2 Q.B. 329.
(50) [1963] 2 Lloyd's Rep. 286.
(51) (1964), 203 Atlantic Reporter (2nd Ser.) 796.
(52) (1965), 350 F. 2d. 468.   (53) [1967] 3 All E.R. 686.
(54) 1933 S.C. 259.   (55) 1949 S.C. 110.
(56) [1897] 2 Q.B. 231.   (57) [1900] 1 Ch. 73.
            (58) [1967] 2 All E.R. at p. 667.

A injury he suffers further incapacity, he can make further application for more damages. We have no machinery for that purpose and it is, in my judgment, no answer to say that under our system we reach the same result by giving at once damages for prospective or possible loss in the future; the quantitative result is plaintly quite different.

B The truth is that the two countries concerned may estimate (to use a neutral word) their damages in a different way and on different principles and with different modes and manners of assessment, so that if one starts to apply the foreign law of damages, I cannot see where one can logically stop. This would in some cases give rise to much difficulty. I would stick to the rule that damages must be awarded in accordance with the lex fori. That has the practical advantage that counsel experienced in these matters can give their expert opinion, so helpful

C and sometimes economical to their clients, and so useful in the speedy administration of justice, on matters of payment into court; if the court was bound to administer some different method of awarding damages, this might be very difficult and nearly impossible. For these reasons I would dismiss this appeal.

D **DIPLOCK, L.J.:** The plaintiff was injured in a motor accident in Malta when a motor-scooter on which he was a passenger came into collision with a motor car which was being driven without reasonable care by the defendant.

As a result the plaintiff suffered serious physical injuries and sustained pecuniary loss in the amount of £53. Whether that loss would have been greater had he received medical treatment as a civilian in Malta, there is no evidence to show; but there is a clear finding of fact by the judge (59) that had he sued the defendant

E in Malta, he could have recovered only the £53, for under Maltese law there is no civil liability for physical injuries suffered as a result of the negligent act of another person. If he had sustained no pecuniary loss, he would not have had a right of action against the defendant at all. Whether the defendant was criminally liable for his driving under Maltese law, we do not know.

Both plaintiff and defendant are of British nationality and domiciled in England,

F and the plaintiff chose to sue the defendant not in Malta but in England. Milmo, J. (60), awarded him damages, not only for his pecuniary loss of £53, but also for his physical injuries. The total amount awarded was £2,250 under the latter head.

The question in this case is whether, by choosing England as his forum instead of Malta, where the defendant's act was committed and the plaintiff's injuries sustained, he can recover the additional £2,250.

G Milmo, J. (61) decided this case on the principles to be extracted from an interlocutory judgment of the Court of Appeal in *Machado* v. *Fontes* (62). I think that his analysis (61) of the decision in *Machado* v. *Fontes* (62) was correct and that that judgment was one which was binding on him sitting as he was at first instance. Although the headnotes and the argument as recorded in the three reports of *Machado* v. *Fontes* (62), refer to one proposition only as being the subject of the decision of the court, I think that the judge was right in saying (63)

H that the judgments lay down two propositions, neither of which was obiter, viz.— (i) that an act done outside the territorial jurisdiction of the English courts is nevertheless actionable in an English court if such act (a) would have been actionable if it had been committed in England, and (b) could have been the subject of criminal proceedings against the defendant in the country where the act was committed, although it did not give rise to any civil liability on the part of

I the defendant under the law of that country; and (ii) that where such an act is actionable under proposition (i), the damages recoverable in an action in an English court are to be assessed on the same basis as if the act had been committed in England. It is the second proposition in *Machado* v. *Fontes* (62) which is

(59) [1967] 2 All E.R. at p. 667.
(60) [1967] 2 All E.R. at p. 670.
(61) [1967] 2 All E.R. at p. 668.
(62) [1897] 2 Q.B. 231.
(63) [1967] 2 All E.R. at pp. 668-670.

immediately involved in the present case. But for my part, for reasons which will **A**
appear later, I think that if the first proposition is right, the second must follow.
That may be why the law reporters in 1897 did not think it necessary to single it
out for mention in the headnotes or the argument.

The first question in this appeal is accordingly whether this court is bound to
accept the propositions laid down in *Machado* v. *Fontes* (64) as correct. Unless
we are entitled to re-examine them, there is an end of the appeal.   **B**

The House of Lords in an extra-judicial pronouncement has expressed its
intention of loosening its self-imposed fetters of stare decisis; but this was
expressly stated not to apply to any other courts. Indeed, it is difficult to see
how a pronouncement by the House of Lords which did not form part of the
reasons for judgment in any appeal before it could have any binding effect on
any other court. In the Court of Appeal we are bound by judicial decisions of the **C**
House of Lords, but so far as concerns the binding effect on the Court of Appeal
of its own decisions, our fetters too are self-imposed. Their extent was discussed
in *Young* v. *Bristol Aeroplane Co., Ltd.* (65), and I concede that the decision in
Machado v. *Fontes* (64) does not fall within any of the three exceptions to the
binding effect of decisions of the Court of Appeal on a subsequent Court of
Appeal of co-ordinate jurisdiction which are set out in *Young's* case (65). But **D**
in *Young's* case (65) it was only final judgments of the Court of Appeal which
were under consideration. *Machado* v. *Fontes* (64), was an appeal from an interlocutory order of a judge in chambers, and the order made by the Court of Appeal
was an interlocutory, not a final, judgment. In interlocutory appeals the Court
of Appeal does not usually have the benefit of a reasoned judgment by the judge
against whose order the appeal is brought. The statute constituting the Court of **E**
Appeal treats interlocutory appeals as being in a lower category than final appeals;
the appeal may be heard by two lord justices, as *Machado* v. *Fontes* (64) was,
instead of by three. In practice lengthy and detailed argument in interlocutory
appeals is discouraged. *Machado* v. *Fontes* (64), which raised a question of
fundamental importance in the then almost untilled field of conflict of laws, was
argued and disposed of by extempore judgments within a single day. In practice, **F**
too, appeals to the House of Lords from interlocutory orders of the Court of
Appeal are discouraged and leave to pursue them is seldom obtained. These
differences in practice in interlocutory and final appeals to the Court of Appeal
detract from the weight to be attached to the reasons given for an interlocutory
order of the Court of Appeal. *Young's* case (65), which I loyally, if regretfully,
accept as binding on me, does not, as I think, preclude this court from declining **G**
to follow the ratio decidendi of a previous interlocutory order of the Court of
Appeal if this court thinks that the ratio decidendi was wrong. In the present
state of juristic opinion, I would not extend the doctrine of stare decisis any
further.

I think, therefore, that we are entitled to re-examine the two propositions laid
down by Lopes and Rigby, L.JJ., in *Machado* v. *Fontes* (64) and to form our own **H**
view whether they are correct. The actual question for decision was whether in
an action for damages for the publication in Brazil of a statement defamatory
of the plaintiff, the defendant should be allowed to add to his defence a plea which
the court construed as averring that the publication did not constitute grounds
for a civil action on the part of the plaintiff against the defendant under Brazilian
law, or, alternatively, that if it did, the plaintiff could not recover under Brazilian **I**
law general damages for any injury to his credit, character or feelings. But the
actual decision appears to be based on a concession made by counsel for the
defendant in the course of the hearing that the publication could be the subject
matter of criminal proceedings in Brazil. Both lord justices purported to apply
to that legal situation under the law of Brazil, where the act of publication took
place, the proposition laid down by Willes, J., delivering the judgment of a

(64) [1897] 2 Q.B. 231.
(65) [1944] 2 All E.R. 293; [1944] K.B. 718.

A seven-judge Court of Exchequer Chamber in *Phillips* v. *Eyre* (66), in the second
passage from his judgment which LORD UPJOHN has cited:

B
    " As a general rule, in order to found a suit in England for a wrong alleged
    to have been committed abroad, two conditions must be fulfilled. First, the
    wrong must be of such a character that it would have been actionable if com-
    mitted in England. . . . Secondly, the act must not have been justifiable
    by the law of the place where it was done."

C
It seems to have been the fate of WILLES, J., to have passages in his judgment
taken out of their context and construed as if they were Acts of Parliament (cf.
Indermaur v. *Dames* (67)). At any rate, LOPES and RIGBY, L.JJ., concentrating
on an assumed contrast in that passage between the word " actionable " in the
first condition and the word " justifiable " in the second, reached the conclusion
that WILLES, J., had meant that the second condition was satisfied if the act
complained of could give rise to any liability, whether civil or criminal, on the
part of the defendant under the law of the country where the act was committed.
They overlooked the contrast between the use of the word " wrong " in the first
condition and the word " act " in the second, and having regard to the subject
matter of the decision and the reasoning on which the " general rule " so stated
D was based, this is a much more significant contrast.

    In *Phillips* v. *Eyre* (68) which was decided on demurrer, the acts of the defen-
dant in respect of which the action was brought were done in Jamaica, a self-
governing colony whose legislature had no power to make laws having
extra-territorial effect. The acts complained of ex concessis constituted a " tort "
E under the law of Jamaica at the time they were done. An actionable wrong had
been committed in Jamaica. The only defence which was relevant on the demurrer
was that it was justified ex post facto by an Act of Indemnity passed subsequently
in the legislature of Jamaica. It was argued that this Act, even though effective
to deprive the plaintiff of any right of action in Jamaica, could not have the
extra-territorial effect of destroying the right of action already vested in the
F plaintiff in England. This argument involved the proposition which was supported
by the dicta of WIGHTMAN, J., in *Scott* v. *Lord Seymour* (69), that an act done
abroad could at common law give rise to a right of action in England distinct from
any civil liability incurred by the doer under the law of the country where the
act was done. This proposition, which is one of substantive law, not of conflict
of laws, was rejected by the Court of Exchequer Chamber in the paragraph
G preceding that which I have already cited. WILLES, J., said (70):

    " A right of action whether it arise from contract governed by the law of
    the place or wrong, is equally the creature of the law of the place and
    subordinate thereto . . . the civil liability arising out of a wrong derives its
    birth from the law of the place, and its character is determined by that law."

H
He thus rejects the contention of substantive law that the civil liability which is
enforced by the English courts is anything other than the civil liability arising
under the law of the place where the act was committed. It is to be noted that
in this passage and throughout the judgment " wrong " as a noun is used in the
sense of an act giving rise to civil liability in the place where it is committed.

I
    He then goes on to discuss the limitations on the jurisdiction of the English
courts to entertain what he calls (70) " foreign causes of action " which, in the
context of what has gone before, clearly refers to actions brought to enforce the
civil liability arising under the law of a foreign place from an act done in that
place. This in my view is what he meant by " a suit in England for a wrong
alleged to have been committed abroad " in the passage which was cited in
Machado v. *Fontes* (71) and has been reproduced in LORD UPJOHN's judgment in

---

(66) (1870), L.R. 6 Q.B. at pp. 28, 29.
(67) [1861-73] All E.R. Rep. 15; (1866), L.R. 1 C.P. 274.
(68) (1870), L.R. 6 Q.B. 1.   (69) (1862), 1 H. & C. 219.
(70) (1870), L.R. 6 Q.B. at p. 28.   (71) [1897] 2 Q.B. at p. 233.

this appeal. This is borne out by the terms in which the first condition is **A** expressed (72): " the *wrong* must be of such a character that it would have been actionable if committed in England ", not, it is to be noted, the " act " or the " foreign transaction ". This qualification restricts the English court's jurisdiction to entertain actions to enforce a civil liability arising under the law of a foreign place from an act done in that place; it does not assert the existence of a separate English cause of action arising from an act done in a foreign place which would **B** have been a tort if done in England but does not give rise to any civil liability under the law of the place where it was done; for such an assertion was that which he had rejected in the immediately preceding paragraph.

This first condition states what is strictly a rule of jurisdiction comparable to that whereby English courts decline jurisdiction over actions relating to foreign land to which WILLES, J., also referred (72) in the same passage. It is a rule of **C** public policy that our courts do not hear and determine liability for acts of a kind which are not regarded as giving rise to liability in tort in England, notwithstanding that such acts give rise to civil liability under a foreign system of law and could be the subject of a foreign judgment which would be recognised here.

The second condition is of a rather different character. It does not express what today would be called a rule of " jurisdiction "; but a rule about choice of law. **D** It had been decided in the cases cited in support of it that an act done abroad which did not give rise to any civil liability under the law of the place where it was done (i.e., was not a " wrong " there) did not give rise to any liability in England. In *Phillips* v. *Eyre* (73) itself, however, the acts complained of had been actionable under the law of Jamaica at the time when they were committed but had ceased to be actionable under that law at the time when the action was **E** brought in England by reason of the Jamaican Act of Indemnity. Hence the use of the word " act " instead of " wrong " was appropriate to cover the cases cited, and the use of the phrase " must not have been justifiable " instead of " must have been actionable " was appropriate to cover the ex post facto extinction of a civil liability which had at one time existed. The ratio decidendi of the rule as respects extinguishment under foreign law of a civil liability incurred under that **F** law is later expressed in the following terms (74):

> ". . . if the foreign law extinguishes the right it is a bar in this country equally as if the extinguishment had been by a release of the party, or an act of our own legislature."

In my view *Phillips* v. *Eyre* (73) did lay down the law as BRETT, L.J., formulated **G** it in *Chartered Mercantile Bank of India* v. *Netherlands India Steam Navigation Co., Ltd.* (75), viz.:

> ". . . for any tort committed in a foreign country within its own exclusive jurisdiction an action of tort cannot be maintained in this country unless the cause of action would be a cause of action in that country, and would also be a cause of action in this country," **H**

and the first proposition in *Machado* v. *Fontes* (76) is wrong in so far as it decided that an act committed abroad was actionable in England if it gave rise to criminal, although not to civil, liability under the law of the country where it was committed.

This is not sufficient, however, to dispose of the present appeal. The act committed by the defendant in Malta did give rise to some civil liability on his part to the plaintiff under Maltese law. It is contended that even though the " action- **I** ability " of that act (i.e. the question whether or no there is any right of action in England) is to be determined by the lex loci delicti, recovery of damages is merely the remedy granted by the court for the wrong, and accordingly all questions of assessment of damages are governed by the lex fori, i.e. by English law.

---

(72) (1870), L.R. 6 Q.B. at p. 28.   (73) (1870), L.R. 6 Q.B. 1.
(74) (1870), L.R. 1 Q.B. at p. 29.
(75) (1883), 10 Q.B.D. at pp. 521, 536, 537.
(76) [1897] 2 Q.B. 231.

A   " Actionability " in English law may arise in two different kinds of circumstances. It may arise as a result of the doing of a particular kind of act by the
defendant, irrespective of the consequences of that act to the plaintiff. Breach of
contract and trespass are examples. On the other hand, it may arise as a result
of the particular consequences to the plaintiff of the doing by the defendant of a
particular kind of act. Unless the act has those consequences, it is not actionable.
B Negligence and all other actions for tort derived from trespass on the case are
examples. In France under the Code Civile and in most European countries,
including Malta, nearly all actionable wrongs are in the latter category. It is to
this category of civil liability to which our attention in the present appeal can be
confined.

    The consequences to the plaintiff which make the act of the defendant action-
C able are generally some loss or injury to the plaintiff or his property of a particular
kind or kinds. For instance, in English law the erection of a neighbouring building
may be actionable if it has the consequence that it injures the plaintiff's right to
light to windows on his property. It is not actionable if its only consequence is to
injure the plaintiff's view from his windows. For the consequence of injury to
light, the remedy is monetary compensation. The assessment of the monetary
D equivalent of a loss not directly sustained in money must necessarily be made by
the court before which the remedy is sought and is in this sense decided by the
lex fori. But for the consequences of injury to view, no question of remedy arises,
for injury to view is not a wrong; and if the erection of the building injures both
light and view, compensation cannot be awarded for the injury to view. To include
a sum of money for this in the assessment of damages would be to give a remedy
E for, and thus to treat as " actionable ", a consequence of the defendant's act
which does not give rise to any right of action.

    Turning to negligence, in English law an act done in England without reason-
able care by a defendant which causes the death of a third party is actionable in a
suit brought on behalf of a dependant of the deceased if its consequence is
pecuniary loss to the dependant. It is not actionable if its consequence is only
F injury to the health or happiness of a survivor of the deceased. Where the
consequence of such an act to a dependant of the deceased is both pecuniary loss
and also injury to health or happiness, it is clear law that the court cannot, in its
assessment of damages, award any compensation for these latter kinds of injuries.
The " heads of damage ", as distinct from the " quantification of damages "
sustained under each head, are matters of substantive law on which the decider
G of fact, whether jury or judge, has no discretion to give effect to an idiosyncratic
opinion. For what is compendiously called " assessment of damages " involves
two distinct inquiries. The first is to ascertain what loss or injury of the particular
kind or kinds which make the defendant's act " actionable " were in fact sustained
by the plaintiff as a consequence of the defendant's act. It would be too irrational,
even for English law, if this inquiry were conducted by applying any different
H criteria than those which determine whether the act of the defendant is actionable
at all.   The second inquiry is to estimate what is the appropriate monetary
equivalent of the loss or injury so ascertained. In this inquiry the court cannot
do otherwise than form its own idiosyncratic estimate.

    Where, because the act of the defendant has been committed abroad, the law to be
applied in determining whether the act was actionable at all is the lex loci delicti,
I the first inquiry involved in the assessment of damages is, in my opinion, to be
conducted by applying the criteria as to " heads of damage " provided by the
lex loci delicti:

        ". . . the civil liability arising out of a wrong derives its birth from the law
    of the place, and *its character is determined by that law.*"

The words are those of Willes, J. (77), the italics are mine.

---

(77) In *Phillips* v. *Eyre*, (1870), L.R. 6 Q.B. at p. 28.

This rule as respects damages recoverable for an act committed abroad has **A** been applied in Scotland in a number of cases in which it is only necessary to cite *Naftalin* v. *London, Midland and Scottish Ry. Co.* (78). I find this case indistinguishable from the present case and its reasoning convincing, save in one passage in LORD MURRAY's judgment (79) in which he accepts the first proposition in *Machado* v. *Fontes* (80) as correct, but considers that the second proposition does not follow from the first. For my part, if I were able to accept the camel that **B** English law requires an English court to award damages in respect of an act committed abroad on the same principles as if it had been committed in England when *no* damages at all could be recovered under the lex loci delicti, I could not strain at the gnat that English courts should apply the same principles when some damages could be recovered under the lex loci delicti. To accept the first but to reject the second proposition in *Machado* v. *Fontes* (80) would mean that in the **C** present case, if the plaintiff had sustained *no* pecuniary loss as a result of the accident in Malta, he could have recovered in England full damages for his bodily injuries, whereas if he had also sustained the slightest pecuniary loss, he could not recover in England a single penny of damages for his bodily injuries, which is absurd.

So far as English cases are concerned, there is none reported in which either **D** of the decisions in *Machado* v. *Fontes* (80) have been applied, although it is equally true to say that there is no subsequent reported case which conflicts with them. In *Kohnke* v. *Karger* (81), LYNSKEY, J., applied English law in assessing the damages recoverable in an action for damages caused by the negligent driving by the defendant of a motor car in France. The issue in that case was whether a satisfied judgment for damages sustained by the plaintiff in the same accident against a **E** third party who was not sued in the English proceedings was a bar to a further action in England against the defendant. It was not disputed that the " heads of damage ", for which the defendant incurred civil liability under French law, were the same as those for which he would have incurred liability in English law had the accident occurred in England. Damages for injury to the plaintiff's property, although recoverable under French law in an ordinary civil action in **F** France, were not recoverable in the type of proceedings which the plaintiff had in fact taken, viz. as partie civile in a criminal prosecution of the third party. There was no satisfied judgment against the third party in respect of the plaintiff's cause of action in French law for compensation for this head of damage. Damages for physical injury were also recoverable under French law, but under French procedure damages under this head are not awarded once and for all. A plaintiff **G** may re-open the proceedings and apply for a further award if there should be any subsequent deterioration of his physical condition. A further difference between the practice of the English and the French courts in assessing damages for physical injury was accepted by LYNSKEY, J., on the evidence before him to be that the French courts avowedly took into consideration the social rank of the plaintiff. The effect of the first difference was that the French judgment against the third **H** party did not exhaust the plaintiff's rights under French law to recover compensation for the physical injuries sustained by him in the accident, with the consequence that there was no satisfied final judgment for the whole of her cause of action in France for compensation for this head of damage. That any balance of compensation would not have been recovered in France until her physical condition had actually deteriorated, whereas in England it would be recoverable **I** in anticipation of the physical deterioration, is a mere difference of procedure governed by the lex fori. The second difference is merely one of " quantification of damages ". Neither is a difference between English and French law as to the

(78) 1933 S.C. 259.
(79) 1933 S.C. at p. 274.
(80) [1897] 2 Q.B. 231.
(81) [1951] 2 All E.R. 179; [1951] 2 K.B. 670.

A " actionability " of the consequences of the defendant's negligent act in causing physical injuries to the plaintiff. This decision does not conflict with the rule that " actionability ", including the " heads of damage " as distinct from the " quantification of damages " sustained under those heads, is governed by the lex loci delicti.

The decision in *Machado v. Fontes* (82) has been much criticised by writers on
B private international law. It has, as I have already noted, been rejected in Scotland. It has been coldly received and doubted by the Privy Council in *Canadian Pacific Ry. Co.* v. *Parent* (83), and rejected by the High Court of Australia (*Koop* v. *Bebb* (84)), although it has been applied in the Supreme Court of Canada (*McLean* v. *Pettigrew* (85); *Morris and Stulback* v. *Angel* (86)) so as to evade the consequences in other provinces of an Ontario statute which
C deprived a passenger in a vehicle of any cause of action in negligence against the driver. It has never been accepted in the United States where, until the last few years, the lex loci delicti has been applied (*Slater* v. *Mexican National Railroad Co.*, (87)). In a number of States recently the courts have departed from the lex loci delicti in favour of some other law, generally that of their own State, under a still embryonic and much debated doctrine of " the proper law of the tort ".
D (See *Babcock* v. *Jackson* (88) and *Griffith* v. *United Airlines Inc.* (89), which contains an interesting summary of other cases.) This United States tendency to stray from the lex loci delicti, is not ostensibly, at any rate, in the direction of the lex fori. In all the American cases to which our attention has been drawn, the court where it has applied the law of its own State to a tort committed outside the State has always managed to find some other reason based on sociological
E considerations for doing so. In this connexion it is significant that in the AMERICAN RESTATEMENT (SECOND) CONFLICT OF LAWS (TENTATIVE DRAFT No. 9) 1964, the important factors to be taken into consideration in determining the proper law of the tort are listed as: (a) the place where the injury occurred, (b) the place where the conduct occurred, (c) the domicile, nationality, place of incorporation and place of business of the parties, and (d) the place where the relationship, if
F any, between the parties is centred. The place where suit is brought is not included in the list. In theory, at any rate, the proper law of any tort would be the same in whichever State the plaintiff chose to sue.

In most cases, as in the present case, the injury and the conduct occur in the same place, and factors (a) and (b) point to the lex loci delicti. The novelty of the doctrine lies in the possible displacement of the lex loci delicti by factors
G (c) and (d). These factors are, in my view, irrelevant under the existing English rules of conflict of laws. Apart from the chauvinistic dicta of WIGHTMAN, J., in *Scott* v. *Lord Seymour* (90), cited by LORD DENNING, M.R., which BLACKBURN, J. (91) expressly disapproved, it has never been suggested that a British subject when he goes abroad carries with him as an extra-territorial aura the English—though not apparently the Scottish—law of tort; and any development
H of our rules of conflict of laws in the direction of making civil liability for wrongs dependent on the nationality or, as I suppose WIGHTMAN, J., would have said, had Scotland crossed his mind, the domicile of the wrongdoer or the victim would seem to me to be a retrograde step in the latter half of the twentieth century. Where there exists a special relationship between the doer of the act and the person injured by it, such as carrier and passenger or driver and guest, there may

I
　　(82) [1897] 2 Q.B. 231.
　　(83) [1917] A.C. 195.
　　(84) (1952), 84 C.L.R. 629.
　　(85) [1945] S.C.R. 62.
　　(86) (1956), 5 D.L.R. (2d.) 30.
　　(87) (1904), 194 U.S. 120.
　　(88) [1963] 2 Lloyd's Rep. 286.
　　(89) (1964), 203 Atlantic Reporter (2nd Ser.) 796.
　　(90) (1862), 1 H. & C. at pp. 234, 235.
　　(91) (1862), 1 H. & C. at p. 237.

be a plausible argument in favour of applying the law of the place where that   A
relationship was created, in order to determine the extent of the mutual rights
and obligations of the parties to it. No such relationship existed, however, between
the plaintiff and the defendant in the present case. The only relationship between
them which gave rise to a duty of care owed by the plaintiff to the defendant was
that of temporary physical propinquity on a Maltese road. That relationship
arose in Malta. Factor (d) as well as (a) and (b) pointed to the lex loci delicti   B
in the present case.

My sympathies are naturally with the plaintiff. He suffered serious physical
injuries for which I should like to award him compensation at the defendant's
insurance company's expense; but, with great respect, I cannot find in the special
circumstances relied on by LORD DENNING, M.R., any justification in law for
doing so. Nor do I know of any American case which jettisons the lex loci delicti   C
on such tenuous grounds. That the defendant was stationed in Malta as a member
of the Royal (i.e. British, not English) Navy, of which a Maltese citizen might be
a member, and not as a visitor, does not seem to me to impose on him any higher
duty or greater liability than a visitor to other users of the Maltese roads; nor
does the fact that the plaintiff was a member of the Royal (i.e. British, not
English) Air Force, of which a Maltese citizen might also be a member, appear   D
to me to give him any greater rights than other persons as a user of the Maltese
roads. Whether the plaintiff was insured at all must surely be irrelevant, and I
can see no grounds on which the fact that he has entered into a policy of insurance
against civil liability in Malta with an English insurer instead of a Scottish,
American or Maltese one can alter the rights against the defendant of a stranger
to the contract of insurance. Finally, I cannot accept that his coming to England   E
for treatment after the event which gave rise to the defendant's liability can ex
post facto alter the legal nature of a wrong which was already complete. I am
sorry that we have been unable to agree on the relevant conflicts rule. Lex propria
delicti, lex fori, lex loci delicti; quot judices tot sententiae.

It is found as a fact on the evidence in the present case that under Maltese
law physical injuries sustained by the plaintiff as a result of the defendant's   F
act in Malta do not give rise to any civil liability. In my view the damages of
£2,250 awarded under this head are not recoverable but only the £53 for which
the defendant incurred civil liability under the law of Malta. If it rested with me,
I would allow this appeal accordingly.

Appeal dismissed. Leave to appeal to the House of Lords granted.

G

Solicitors: *Gascoin & Co.* (for the defendant); *Roche, Son & Neale*, agents for
Buss, Cheale & Co., Tunbridge Wells (for the plaintiff).

[*Reported by* F. GUTTMAN, ESQ., *Barrister-at-Law.*]

A

WESTWARD TELEVISION, LTD. *v.* HART (Inspector of Taxes).

[CHANCERY DIVISION (Pennycuick, J.), November 23, 24, 1967.]

Affirmed. C.A. [1968] 3 All E.R. 91.

Income Tax—Relief—Losses—Computation—Carry forward—Loss for initial
B *accounting period—Profits in subsequent years—Assessment for second and third years based on same period, viz., first year's trading—Part of profits of second accounting period apportioned to first year's trading period—Apportioned amount taken into account in reduction of initial loss for each of the second and third years of assessment—Scottish authority followed—Income Tax Act, 1952 (15 & 16 Geo. 6 & 1 Eliz. 2 c. 10), s. 155, s. 342.*

In the accounting period for the first months of its trading, from Aug. 1,
C 1960, to Apr. 28, 1961, the taxpayer company made a loss of £132,107; and in the second, third and fourth years of its trading from Apr. 29, 1961, to Apr. 30, 1964, it made profits respectively of £165,572, £74,735 and £276,583. It was assessed to income tax for the fiscal year to Apr. 5, 1961, at nil on the basis of the loss in its first accounting period; and for the second and third fiscal years the taxpayer company was assessed on the basis of its profits for
D the first twelve months of its trading, viz., at nil. The basis period for these computations (viz., Aug. 1, 1960 to July 31, 1961) included three months (Apr. 29, 1961 to July 31, 1961), to which profit was apportioned from the accounting period Apr. 29, 1961, to Apr. 30, 1962, at £41,393, being approximately one quarter of the year's profits (£165,572). For the third year, 1963-64, the taxpayer company was assessed on its profits for the accounting
E period Apr. 29, 1961 to Apr. 30, 1962, less capital allowances, the result, after setting off the loss remaining from the first year's trading, being again a loss. The taxpayer company was similarly assessed for 1964-65, the ultimate result again being a loss. For 1965-66 the taxpayer company was assessed on its profits for the relevant accounting period (£276,583) less, so far as relevant, the balance of the loss remaining from the first year's trading. On the
F computation* of the Inland Revenue the amount of this remainder of the loss was £9,312, but on the taxpayer company's computation it was £80,886. The difference between the two amounts was due to the first year's loss being treated by the Inland Revenue as absorbed in each of the second and third fiscal years to the extent of £41,393 in each of those years, on the footing that the loss of that amount had been taken into account with profits in a calcula-
G tion under s. 155† of the Income Tax Act, 1952, for the purposes of the carry forward of loss under s. 342 in the basis period (which was the same) for each of the two years 1961-62 and 1962-63.

Held: there being Scottish authority exactly in point, the court should follow it and, therefore, the taxpayer company's loss on the first year must be regarded as reduced in each of the second and third fiscal years by the sum
H of £41,393, i.e., reduced by the amount apportioned under s. 155 to the basis period of assessment (Aug. 1, 1960, to July 31, 1961) from the profits of the second accounting period, which amount was one quarter (in respect of the period Apr. 29, 1961, to July 31, 1961) of those profits, £165,572, viz., £41,393; accordingly the loss remaining to be carried forward under s. 342 to the year 1965-66 was £9,312 not £80,886 (see p. 306, letter I,
I to p. 307, letter A, and p. 309, letter H, post).

---

* The computation is shown at p. 305, letters E to H, post.
† Section 155 provides: " (1) Where in the case of any profits or gains chargeable under Case 1 . . . of Sch. D, it is necessary in order to arrive at the profits or gains or losses of any year of assessment or other period, to divide and apportion to specific periods the profits or gains or losses for any period for which the accounts have been made up, or to aggregate any such profits or gains or losses or any apportioned parts thereof, it shall be lawful to make such a division and apportionment or aggregation. (2) Any apportionment under this section shall be made in proportion to the number of months or fractions of months in the respective periods."

Inland Revenue v. *Adamson* ((1932), 17 Tax Cas. 679) followed.   A

Appeal dismissed.

[As to the carry forward of relief for losses in income tax assessments, see 20 HALSBURY'S LAWS (3rd Edn.) 469, 470, para. 891; and for cases on the subject, see 28 DIGEST (Repl.) 308, *1351, 1352*.

For the Income Tax Act, 1952, s. 155 and s. 342, see 31 HALSBURY'S STATUTES   B
(2nd Edn.) 149 and 328.]

Cases referred to:

Abbott v. *Philbin* (*Inspector of Taxes*), [1959] 3 All E.R. 590; [1960] Ch. 27;
     [1959] 3 W.L.R. 739; 39 Tax Cas. 82; *affd.* H.L., [1960] 2 All E.R. 763;
     [1961] A.C. 352; [1960] 3 W.L.R. 255; 39 Tax Cas. 82; Digest (Cont.
     Vol. A) 890, *1058a*.   C
Inland Revenue v. *Adamson*, 1933 S.C. 23; 17 Tax Cas. 679; 28 Digest (Repl.)
     112, **323*.

Case Stated.

The taxpayer company appealed to the Commissioners for the Special Purposes of the Income Tax Acts against a restriction of relief for the taxpayer company's sixth year of assessment, 1965-66, in respect of a loss sustained in its first account-   D
ing period from Aug. 1, 1960, to Apr. 28, 1961. The relevant loss which the Crown were prepared to allow was £9,312. The loss which the taxpayer company contended it was entitled to be allowed was £80,886. The computation by which these two sums was reached is at p. 305, letters E to H, post.

The taxpayer company was incorporated on Jan. 12, 1960. On Aug. 1, 1960, it commenced the trade of television programme contractors. The results   E
shown by the agreed adjusted profit and loss accounts were as follows—

Period	Profit or Loss
Aug. 1, 1960—Apr. 28, 1961 a loss of	£132,107
Apr. 29, 1961—Apr. 30, 1962 a profit of	£165,572
May 1, 1962—Apr. 30, 1963 a profit of	£74,735
May 1, 1963—Apr. 30, 1964 a profit of	£276,583

F

The taxpayer company's liability to tax under Case 1 of Sch. D for the year 1960-61, being the tax year in which it started its trade, was computed by reference to the profit (if any) for the period Aug. 1, 1960, to Apr. 5, 1961. This was computed on the basis of the taxpayer company's first set of accounts, for the period from the date of incorporation to Apr. 28, 1961, apportioned* on a   G
time basis after disallowing expenditure incurred prior to the commencement of trading. Apart from the loss so computed, the taxpayer company had other income subject to tax for the year 1960-61 amounting to £4,056. It was allowed a claim for repayment of tax on this other income under s. 341 of the Income Tax Act, 1952. It was agreed that the £4,056 fell to be deducted from the losses available to be carried forward and set off against assessable profits of   H
subsequent tax years under s. 342 of the Act of 1952.

For the year 1961-62, which was the second year in which the taxpayer company carried on trade, it was assessed by reference to the profits (if any) of its first twelve months of trading, viz., from Aug. 1, 1960, to July 31, 1961. The parties agreed that the profits for this period should be computed by reference to those of the accounting periods from Aug. 1, 1960, to Apr. 28, 1961, and those   I
from Apr. 29, 1961, to Apr. 30, 1962, apportioned on a time basis. It was agreed that on that basis a loss resulted.

For the year 1962-63 the basis period was determined by s. 127 (2) (*b*)† of the Act of 1952, and in accordance with normal practice the period of twelve months ended July 31, 1961, was adopted. The result on this basis was a loss.

---

* Section 155 of the Income Tax Act, 1952, so far as relevant, is set out in the footnote at p. 303, ante.

† The relevant terms of s. 12 (2) (*b*) and s. 128 are set out at p. 310, letters D and E, post.

A   For the year 1963-64 the taxpayer company was assessed by reference to its accounting period from Apr. 29, 1961, to Apr. 30, 1962. The profit amounted to £165,053, but the tax chargeable was discharged by offset of capital allowances under s. 323 of the Act of 1952. The unrelieved loss derived from the initial trading period was thus carried forward under s. 342 of the Act of 1952. Its amount was in dispute.

B   For the year 1964-65 the taxpayer company was assessed by reference to its accounting period from May 1, 1962, to Apr. 30, 1963. The profits amounted to £74,735 against which were set capital allowances reducing the profits to £35,953. This resulting balance (£35,953) was absorbed by the unrelieved loss carried forward from the first trading period.

C   For the year 1965-66 the taxpayer company was assessed by reference to its accounting period from May 1, 1963, to Apr. 30, 1964. The profits amounted to £276,583, which were reduced by capital allowances to £255,652. The taxpayer company claimed to set against that amount the unrelieved loss carried forward from the initial year of assessment, 1960-61. It was agreed that by virtue of s. 345 of the Act of 1952 there was a further sum of £20,328 which ought to be set against the profits on account of interest paid by the taxpayer

D   company under deduction of tax in the years 1961-62 to 1964-65, the taxpayer company having been assessed to tax on this interest under s. 170. The contentions of the taxpayer company and of the Crown, respectively, in regard to the computation of the amount of the unrelieved loss to be set against the profits of 1965-66 are shown by the table below—

	Taxpayer Company	Revenue
Loss Aug. 1, 1960 to Apr. 28, 1961	£120,895	£132,107
Relieved under s. 341, 1960-61	£4,056	£4,056
	£116,839	£128,051
Relieved 1961-62	——	£41,393
	£116,839	£86,658
Relieved 1962-63	——	£41,393
	£116,839	£45,265
Relieved 1964-65	£35,953	£35,953
	£80,886	£9,312
Add amounts allowable under s. 345	£20,328	£20,328
Available for relief 1965-66	£101,214	£29,640

H   It was contended before the commissioners on behalf of the taxpayer company —(i) that s. 155 of the Act of 1952 was concerned with a process of computation and not with relief, and that, therefore, losses included with profits in a computation made under s. 155 for whatever purpose did not fall to be regarded as relieved pro tanto; (ii) that the computation of amount was according to the taxpayer company's view as stated previously; (iii) alternatively, even if s. 155 could be regarded as affording a measure of relief, the loss incurred by the taxpayer company in 1960-61 could not be regarded as having been relieved both in 1961-62 and in 1962-63, because it formed an element in the computation of the taxpayer company's liability to tax for both years; (iv) that on this alternative basis the amount to be carried forward and set off against the profits of the taxpayer company's trade for 1965-66 was £71,033, and (b) that relief should be granted on the basis contended for under (i) and (ii) above, or, failing that, on the basis contended for under (iii) and (iv) above.

It was contended by the Crown before the commissioners—(a) that losses A
taken into account with profits in a calculation made under s. 155 of the Act of
1952 for the purposes of affording relief to a taxpayer under s. 342 fell to be treated
as relieved pro tanto; (b) that the amount which fell to be carried forward
or set off against the profits or gains for the taxpayer company's trade for 1965-66
was (so far as relevant to the dispute) £9,312; (c) that relief should be granted
accordingly.   This sum of £9,312 did not include the amount allowable under s. B
345; the total relief admitted by the Crown for set off for 1965-66 was £29,640.

The decision of the commissioners so far as necessary is set out at p. 307, letters
B to D, post.   The commissioners determined the claim for losses in the sum
of £29,640.   The taxpayer company accordingly required a case to be stated
for the opinion of the court.   The question of law so stated was whether on
the facts found there was evidence on which the commissioners could properly C
arrive at their decision and whether their determination was correct in law.

Peter Rees for the taxpayer company.
G. B. Graham, Q.C., and J. R. Phillips for the Crown.

PENNYCUICK, J., having stated the nature of the appeal and having D
read s. 127, s. 128 and s. 342 (1) of the Income Tax Act, 1952, as set out subsequently (see p. 310, letters A to F, post) continued: The facts in the present case
are not in dispute and were placed before the Special Commissioners in the form
of an agreed statement.   The facts are basically simple, the only complication
being introduced by the necessity to make apportionments in respect of the
appropriate periods.   The taxpayer company commenced its trade as a tele- E
vision programme contractor on Aug. 1, 1960.   Particulars with regard to its
relevant accounting periods and actual profits and losses for those periods are
as follows: (i) Accounting period Aug. 1, 1960—Apr. 28, 1961—a loss of
£132,107.   (ii) Accounting period Apr. 29, 1961—Apr. 30, 1962—a profit of
£165,572.   (iii) Accounting period May 1, 1962—Apr. 30, 1963—a profit of
£74,735. (iv) Accounting period, May 1, 1963—Apr. 30, 1964—a profit of £276,583. F

Applying the provisions of s. 127 and s. 128 of the Income Tax Act, 1952, to
the corresponding fiscal years, the computed losses and profits are as follows:
1. Fiscal year Aug. 1, 1960—Apr. 5, 1961, a loss of £132,107 scaled down by the
amount apportionable to the period from Apr. 6—Apr. 28, 1961.   2. Fiscal
year ended Apr. 5, 1962, basis period twelve months Aug. 1, 1960—July 31, 1961;
loss for the nine months Aug. 1, 1960—Apr. 28, 1961, £132,107; profit for the G
three months Apr. 29—July 31, 1961, equals one-fourth of the profit for the
year of account Apr. 28, 1961—Apr. 30, 1962, £41,393.   That leaves a balance
of loss of £90,714. 3. Fiscal year ended Apr. 5, 1962, basis period the same as for
fiscal year No. 2, loss the same as for fiscal year No. 2.   4. Fiscal year ended
Apr. 5, 1964, basis period the year of account ended Apr. 30, 1962; profit
£165,572.   The subsequent years follow a regular pattern. H

The present appeal is concerned with the basis on which the loss incurred in the
first fiscal year, i.e., that from Aug. 1, 1960—Apr. 5, 1961, should be carried
forward by way of relief against tax for subsequent years.   The taxpayer company has in fact received substantial reliefs under other heads.   These reliefs
have, of course, to be brought into account in any actual tax calculation, but they
only serve to complicate the issues of principle and I will not mention them again. I
The contention of the taxpayer company is that one takes the loss for 1960-61
and carries it forward year by year until it has been wholly relieved by being
set off against profits which would otherwise be chargeable to tax for the successive years, i.e., the computed profits for each of the years.   The contention of the
revenue is that the loss for 1960-61 must be treated as relieved pro tanto in
1961-62 and 1962-63 to the extent of the one-fourth of the profit for the year of
account ended Apr. 30, 1962, which goes by apportionment into the computation

A of profit or loss for the years 1961-62 and 1962-63 respectively, i.e., £41,393 for each year.

The commissioners gave their decision in these terms:

B " This is an appeal by [the taxpayer company] against the restriction by H.M. inspector of taxes, St. George District . . . to the sum of £29,640 of a claim for relief for the year 1965-66 made under the provisions of Income Tax Act, 1952, s. 342, in respect of a loss sustained by the [taxpayer company] in its first accounting period from Aug. 1, 1960, to Apr. 28, 1961, amounting to £101,214 after taking into account certain relief already granted. The facts in this case are not in dispute and the point at issue is whether losses which are combined with profits in a calculation made under the provisions of s. 155 **C** of the Income Tax Act, 1952, so as to produce a net figure of loss (and consequently *no* assessment) for a basis year of assessment can be said to have been relieved pro tanto to such profits.

" This question has already been canvassed in *Inland Revenue* v. *Adamson* (1), a decision of the Court of Session in Scotland which is binding on us. In our opinion, the facts of that case, though somewhat simpler, cannot **D** really be distinguished from the present case, and following that decision this appeal fails.

" The figures being agreed between the parties we determine the claim for losses in the sum of £29,640."

I will preface my citation of *Inland Revenue* v. *Adamson* (1) by reading a passage from the judgment of LORD EVERSHED, M.R., in *Abbott* v. *Philbin* **E** (*Inspector of Taxes*) (2):

" Those two things the Scottish court has, I think, plainly decided. I ask myself, therefore, having expressed such doubts as I have, with all respect to the learned judge in Scotland, ought this court now to answer those two questions in a precisely opposite sense? We in this court are **F** not bound to follow the decisions of the Court of Session, but the Income Tax Acts . . . apply indifferently both north and south of the border, and, if we were to decide those questions in a sense diametrically opposite to the sense which appealed to the Scottish judges, we should lay down a law for England in respect of this not unimportant matter which was completely opposite to the law which was being applied on exactly the same statutory provisions **G** north of the border. I cannot think that that is right. In a case of a revenue statute of this kind, I think it is the duty of this court, unless there are compelling reasons to the contrary, and while expressing such doubts as we feel we ought to do, to say that we follow the Scottish decision."

I turn now to *Inland Revenue* v. *Adamson* (3). That was decided in the Court of Session, Scotland (First Division), sitting as its Court of Exchequer. The **H** headnote is as follows:

" The respondent commenced business on June 1, 1929. The first accounts of his business were for the period of ten months to Mar. 31, 1930, and showed a loss of £61. His second accounts were for the year to Mar. 31, 1931, and showed a profit of £142. The respondent's income tax liability **I** was computed for the income tax years as follows:
1929-30

Loss for ten months to Mar. 31, 1930	£61
Assessment	Nil

(1) (1932), 17 Tax Cas. 679.
(2) [1959] 3 All E.R. 590 at pp. 600, 601; 39 Tax Cas. 82 at p. 112.
(3) (1932), 17 Tax Cas. 679.

1930-31

Loss for ten months to Mar. 31, 1930	£61
Profit for two months to May 31, 1930, i.e., one sixth of £142	£24
Loss	£37
Assessment	Nil

1931-32

Profit for year to Mar. 31, 1931	£142

" An assessment was made for the year 1931-32 in the sum of £142, against which the inspector of taxes was prepared to agree to a set-off under s. 33 of the Finance Act, 1926, of £37. The respondent claimed that under s. 33 he was entitled to set the losses of £61 and £37, total £98, which he contended were ' computed in like manner as profits and gains under the rules applicable to Cases I and II of Sch. D ', against the assessment of £142. The General Commissioners allowed the claim and reduced the 1931-32 assessment to £44 (£142 less £98).

" Held, that the relief granted by s. 33 extended only to the actual loss sustained which, as computed, was £61, and that relief having been effectively given in 1930-31 to the extent of £24, the amount to be set-off against the 1931-32 assessment was the balance only of £37."

Section 33 was the statutory predecessor of s. 342. It was pointed out in argument (4) that the inspector of taxes contended

" that s. 33 referred to an actual loss sustained in any year and not to a statutory loss computed by reference to the loss actually sustained in the preceding year."

The first opinion was given by the Lord President (LORD CLYDE). He set out fully (5) the facts which, as will have been seen from the headnote, bear a close resemblance to those here. He then proceeded as follows (6):

" It has been seen that, for the purposes of the taxpayer's first year of assessment, there was a computed loss of £61 on his business. Owing to the operation of the somewhat complicated provisions of the Income Tax Acts referred to in the second paragraph of this opinion, this same computed loss of £61 entered again into the ascertainment of the balance of profits and gains for the taxpayer's second year of assessment. The result of this was actually to relieve the taxpayer from any assessment to income tax in his second year. When s. 33 (1) of the Finance Act, 1926, speaks of relief in respect of a loss, what is meant is neither more nor less than relief from assessment in respect of profits which would otherwise have been assessed, and such relief is equally given whether a formal assessment has been delivered to the taxpayer or not. The situation accordingly was that, to the extent of £24 (part of the original loss of £61), the taxpayer was actually given relief from assessment, in his second year of assessment to income tax, in respect of the said original loss of £61; and this was the result of the provisions of the Income Tax Acts. He was, however, still without relief in respect of the balance of the original loss amounting to £37. Under s. 33 (1) of the Finance Act, 1926, he is entitled to claim that this 'portion of the loss for which relief has not been . . . given shall be carried forward ' into the third year of assessment, and ' deducted from or set-off against the amount of profits and gains on which he is assessed under Sch. D in respect of ' his profession for that year. The portion in question amounts to £37,

(4) (1932), 17 Tax Cas. at p. 681.
(5) (1932), 17 Tax Cas. at pp. 682, 683.
(6) (1932), 17 Tax Cas. at p. 684.

A   and the Revenue does not dispute his right to relief to that extent from assessment on his profits for the third year, which amount to £142.   The taxpayer, however, contends that he sustained two losses, one of £61 for the period from June 1, 1929, to Mar. 31, 1930, and another for the period from June 1, 1929, to May 31, 1930, and that, in his third year of assessment, he is entitled to relief in respect of the sum of these duplicated losses, that is

B   to say, in respect of a loss of £61 plus £37, or £98 in all.   This is a preposterous contention.   The section merely secures complete relief in so far as relief has not already been obtained under the provisions of the Income Tax Acts—it does not warrant any claim for a double relief—and I think we should answer the question put to us accordingly."

The other three lords concurred.   I need not read their opinions.

C   I have reached the conclusion, as did the commissioners, that that decision is directly in point in the present case and that I should follow it.   Counsel for the taxpayer company sought to distinguish the present case from the *Adamson* case (7) on two grounds.   First, he pointed out that in the revenue's argument in the *Adamson* case (7) it was contended that s. 33 referred to an actual loss and not to a statutory loss.   In the present case it is rightly conceded by counsel

D   for the Crown that, on the construction of s. 342, " loss " must mean loss computed under the Act of 1952.   In regard to the first year, this is really a distinction without a difference, since the basis of computation for the first year is the actual loss.   Moreover, it is perfectly clear from the speech of the Lord President, which I have read, that he was under no illusion as to the nature of the statutory provisions.   He actually used the expression, " computed loss at

E   £61 ".   The ratio decidendi of the Court of Session as regards the first year is that the loss for that year must somehow be regarded as set-off against the profit element brought by apportionment into the computed income for the second year. I do not, myself, find that an easy conception, but the ratio decidendi corresponds precisely to the contention of the Crown in the present case.   Secondly, counsel for the taxpayer company pointed out that, in the *Adamson* case (7), the taxpayer

F   claimed not only for his loss in the first year, but also for his computed loss in the second year.   No doubt this cumulative claim somewhat bedeviled the taxpayer's case in that it made it less attractive to the court, the Lord President describing it as preposterous, but the fact remains that the court dealt primarily with the claim in respect of the first year and the decision in respect of that year is not dependent on the decision in respect of the second year.   It is

G   worth while to point out that, as counsel for the taxpayer company himself agreed, if his contention here is right, a claim for the second year must in logic at least be open to him.

It seems to me that I ought to follow the decision of the Court of Session in the *Adamson* case (7).   As I am taking that course, I think that it is best to express no view of my own.   Counsel for the taxpayer company developed an extremely

H   interesting argument as to how loss should be dealt with assuming that the case were free from authority.   I will confine myself to saying, and I use these words deliberately in a neutral way, that the argument presented by counsel appeared to me to possess more substance than the Court of Session attributed to the corresponding argument presented to them.   I propose, accordingly, to dismiss this appeal.

I   *Appeal dismissed.*

Solicitors: *Iliffe, Sweet & Phillips* (for the taxpayer company); *Solicitor of Inland Revenue.*

[*Reported by* F. A. AMIES, ESQ., *Barrister-at-Law.*]

NOTE.

The following were read by PENNYCUICK, J., in his judgment in *Westward Television, Ltd.* v. *Hart*, viz., ss. 127 (1), (2), 128 and 342, of the Income Tax Act, 1952, the last-mentioned section being printed as amended by the Finance Act, 1952, s. 27 (1):

" 127 (1) Subject to the provisions of this and the three next following sections, tax shall be charged under Cases I and II of Sch. D on the full amount of the profits or gains of the year preceding the year of assessment.

" (2) Where, in the case of the trade, profession or vocation, an account has or accounts have been made up to a date or dates within the period of three years immediately preceding the year of assessment—(a) if an account was made up to a date within the year preceding the year of assessment and that account was the only account made up to a date in that year and was for a period of one year beginning either at the commencement of the trade, profession or vocation, or at the end of the period on the profits or gains of which the assessment for the last preceding year of assessment was to be computed, the profits or gains of the last year ending on that date shall be taken to be the profits or gains of the year preceding the year of assessment; (b) in any case to which the provisions of para. (a) do not apply, the Commissioners of Inland Revenue shall decide what period of twelve months ending on a date within the year preceding the year of assessment shall be deemed to be the year the profits or gains of which are to be taken to be the profits or gains of the year preceding the year of assessment.

" 128 (1) Where the trade, profession or vocation has been set up and commenced within the year of assessment, the computation of the profits or gains chargeable to tax under Case I or Case II shall be made either on the full amount of the profits or gains arising in the year of assessment or according to the average of such period, not being greater than one year, as the case may require and as may be directed by [an inspector]. (2) Where the trade, profession or vocation has been set up and commenced within the year preceding the year of assessment, the computation of the profits or gains chargeable to tax under Case I or Case II shall be made on the profits or gains for one year from the first setting up thereof.

" 342 (1) Where a person has in any trade, profession or vocation carried on by him, either solely or in partnership, sustained a loss (to be computed in like manner as profits or gains under the provisions of this Act applicable to Cases I and II of Sch. D) in respect of which relief has not been wholly given either under the last preceding section or under any other provision of this Act, he may claim that any portion of the loss for which relief has not been so given shall be carried forward and, as far as may be, deducted from or set off against the amount of profits or gains on which he is assessed under Sch. D in respect of that trade, profession or vocation for [subsequent years of assessment] . . ."

MINISTER OF LABOUR *v.* SOUTHAM NEWS SERVICES OF CANADA.

[QUEEN'S BENCH DIVISION (Lord Parker, C.J., Salmon, L.J., and Widgery, J.), October 19, 1967.]

Selective Employment Tax—Premium—Activity in which establishment engaged —Publishing—Three journalists employed in London by Canadian publishers to collect news for newspapers published in Canada—Whether activities carried on in London fell within minimum list heading No. 486—Smaller activity not shown to be part of a larger activity of publishers—Whether editorial staff of publishers within heading No. 486—Selective Employment Payments Act 1966 (c. 32), s. 1 (2).

A Canadian company, S., Ltd., which published newspapers and magazines in Canada, employed three journalists in Fleet Street, London, to collect news material, which they sent to Canada, where S., Ltd. used such part of it as it chose for publication in Canada. Application was made that the three journalists in Fleet Street were an establishment that qualified under s. 1 (2)* of the Selective Employment Payments Act 1966 and minimum list heading No. 486 of the Standard Industrial Classification for repayment

---

* Section 1 (2), so far as material, is set out at p. 311, letter I, to p. 312, letter A, post.

A   of selective employment tax and for payment of premium. Heading No. 486* specified " printers and publishers . . . of newspapers, magazines . . ." Paragraph (*a*) (i) of s. 1 (2) of the Act of 1966 stipulated that the establishment must be engaged in activities under an appropriate heading, heading No. 486 being such a heading, and para. (*b*) (i) of s. 1 (2) stipulated further that more than half the persons employed in the establishment

B   must be employed " in connexion with " such activities. The Industrial Tribunal found that the Fleet Street activity came within heading No. 486, because it was an activity in connexion with the activity of printing and publishing in Canada. On appeal,

     Held: when considering, for the purposes of s. 1 (2) (*a*) (i) of the Selective Employment Payments Act 1966, an activity in which an establishment

C   was engaged, it was wrong to consider with what that activity was in connexion; the activity carried on in Fleet Street in the present case was a separate activity carried on before any question of printing and publishing the product arose, and accordingly was not within minimum list heading No. 486, with the consequence that employment in the Fleet Street establishment did not qualify under s. 1 (2) for repayment of selective employment

D   tax or for payment of premium (p. 313, letters E and I, and p. 314, letter A, post).

     Per CURIAM: the activity of the editorial staff in Canada would come within the description " publishing " and, together with the activity of actual printing, would come within minimum list heading No. 486 (see p. 313, letter I, post).

E   **Quaere** whether if an activity is part of a larger activity that qualifies for repayment of selective employment tax and payment of premium, it follows that the smaller activity so qualifies (see p. 313, letter G, post).

     Appeal allowed.

     [As to selective employment tax, see SUPPLEMENT TO 33 HALSBURY'S LAWS (3rd Edn.) para. 479A.

F   For the Selective Employment Payments Act 1966, s. 1, see 46 HALSBURY'S STATUTES (2nd Edn.) 167.]

     Appeal.

     This was an appeal by the Minister of Labour from a decision of the Industrial Tribunal dated Feb. 13, 1967, whereby it held that the respondents, Southam News Services of Canada, carrying on busines at 40/43, Fleet Street, was an

G   establishment engaged by way of business wholly or partly in a minimum list heading which qualified under s. 1 of the Selective Employment Payments Act 1966 to repayment of the tax paid and a premium. The case was treated as if the respondents were a Canadian company, Southam Press, Ltd. (see p. 312, letter C, post). The facts are set out in the judgment of LORD PARKER, C.J.

H   *G. Slynn* for the Minister.
     Graham Eyre for the respondents.

     LORD PARKER, C.J.: The relevant provisions of the Selective Employment Payments Act 1966 are first s. 1, whereby under sub-s. (1) an employer who has paid selective employment tax is entitled to repayment of the tax together with a premium in respect of each person in employment to which the section applies. By sub-s. (2) it is then provided that:

     ". . . this section applies to any employment in, or carried out from, an establishment where—

     " (*a*) the establishment is engaged by way of business wholly or partly in—
(i) activities falling under any of the minimum list headings shown in Orders III to XVI of the Standard Industrial Classification . . ."

---

     * Minimum list heading No. 486, so far as material, is set out at p. 312, letter E, post.

It then goes on to provide that even if so far the employer qualifies for repayment   A
and premium, he must fulfil yet a further condition, namely that:

> " (b) more than half of the employed persons employed in any employment
> in, or carried out from, that establishment—(i) are so employed wholly or
> mainly in connexion with such activities, research or training as aforesiad;
> and (ii) are not so employed wholly or mainly in nonqualifying activities,   B
> . . ."

The short facts here were that there is a company in Canada called Southam
Press, Ltd., who carry on the publication of newspapers and magazines.   They
have an office at 40/43 Fleet Street where three journalists are employed, the
junior one acting also as typist and stenographer.   They in fact have chosen
the name for the office of " Southam News Services of Canada ", and, strictly,   C
the applicants to the tribunal and the respondents to this appeal should clearly
be in my judgment Southam Press, Ltd.   However, no point has been taken
on this, and I will treat the matter as if the applicants and the present respondents
here were the Canadian company, Southam Press, Ltd., to which I will refer as
" the company ".   These three journalists in Fleet Street do two things; they
collect news at first hand, and they also extract items from other publications,   D
and the material so collected and extracted is then sent to Canada and such
part of it as is thought right is used by Southam Press, Ltd. in Canada for
publication in Canada.

Those are the short facts of the case, and the contention of the company
before the tribunal was that the activity carried on at the establishment at 40/43
Fleet Street came under the minimum list heading 486 which reads in this form: E

> " Printers and Publishers (including publishers who do not do their own
> printing) of newspapers, magazines, reviews, trade journals, etc. and printers
> of newspapers, etc. working on commission."

The rival contention by the Minister was that the activity of the establishment
in Fleet Street was an activity not of manufacture, but of the rendering of
services, that that activity came under one or other of three headings in Order   F
XXII of the Standard Industrial Classification.   The first suggested heading
under which the activity fell was No. 879, para. 5, which is dealing with " Other
professional and scientific services ", and says:

> " Other.   Artists, authors, composers, playwrights, free lance journalists
> and other professional services not elsewhere specified."

Alternatively it was said that the activity fell under No. 899, para. 6 dealing with   G

> " Trade associations and business services.   Employers associations,
> chambers of commerce and similar business organisations, trade unions;
> advertising and bill posting agencies; typewriting, duplicating, translating,
> employment agencies (not Government) and other similar business services."

Finally, if all else failed, the Minister would say that the activity fell in what   H
one may call the sweeping-up clause, namely para. 9 of heading 899, which is
dealing with other services " All other services not elsewhere specified, including
chimney sweeping, window cleaning etc."

The tribunal in a careful judgment came to the conclusion that the activity
carried on at 40/43 Fleet Street fell under heading No. 486, and therefore (1)
qualified for repayment of tax and premium.   The relevant part of the judgment
is in these terms:

> " We consider in this case that although this organisation has a name it is
> not really a separate organisation of any sort.   It is merely three journalists
> in the employ of [the company] who are stationed in London.   They have

---

(1) Minimum list heading No. 486 comes under Ord. XV of the Standard Industrial
Classification, and thus is within Ord. III to Ord. XVI to which s. 1 (2) (a) (i) of the
Selective Employment Payments Act 1966 refers.

A   for their convenience given themselves a name, which may appear in the telephone book or which will enable people to get in touch with the publishing company in Canada if they have any reason to do so. But in essence what this bureau is, is a collection of three persons employed by the Canadian publishing company. We can see no reason why the employees of a company which is obviously engaged in the printing and publication of newspapers

B   and periodicals, should not be regarded as carrying out part of those activities because the organisation itself is outside the country. We consider that these journalists in the employ of [the company] are carrying on only journalistic work, collection of news and transmission of news to the paper which employs them, are carrying out activities in connexion with the printing and publishing of a newspaper. Their activities fall under heading

C   No. 486.''

I may add that no question arises, or could arise in the present case, as to failure of the company to prove the second condition in regard to the numbers of their employees, in particular because by s. 10 there are excluded from minimum list heading No. 486 those who otherwise would be treated as engaged in non-

D   qualifying activities by reason of being engaged in office work or as editorial staff.

It is clear, when one looks at the judgment of the Industrial Tribunal to which I have referred, that they have found that the activity in Fleet Street was an activity falling under heading No. 486 because it was an activity in connexion with the activity of printing and publishing, which of course was done in the ordinary sense of the word in Canada.

E   In my judgment, in looking at the activity carried on at an establishment, it is wrong to go on to consider with what that activity was in connexion. There are many activities carried out at an establishment which are in connexion with manufacture, and yet, as I see it, could not possibly be said to qualify for repayment of tax and premium. Indeed, counsel for the respondents, to whom the

F   court is indebted for his careful argument, realises that those words are too wide; he would put it in this way, that in considering the activity carried on at an establishment, one is entitled to look at the context, the background, and if one finds that what is being carried on at the establishment is, as he puts it, an integral part of a different and larger activity which qualifies for repayment of tax and premium, then one can say that the activity carried on, in this case at Fleet Street, is part of the larger activity of printing and publishing, and accordingly that the company qualifies for repayment of tax and premium.

For my part I should like to leave open for another case the question whether, if the activity carried on is part of a different activity which qualifies, it can be said that the smaller activity itself qualifies. One can imagine difficult cases where the manufacture of a particular article is carried out at three or four or

I   more factories, all of which are engaged in producing parts or materials for ultimate assembly, and I should like to leave it for decisions in those cases whether it can be said that each of those factories is engaged in business in the activity of producing the final article.

Having said that, I have come to the conclusion nevertheless that the decision of the tribunal was wrong in this case, in that I am not satisfied that the activity carried on at Fleet Street was an integral part, or part of the activity which was carried on by the company in Canada of printing and publishing. As it seems to me, what these journalists were doing was collecting material which would then go forward to Canada, and would come before, presumably, an editorial staff who would decide which, if any, of the information supplied would by published. The activity of that editorial staff would, I think, clearly come within publishing, and therefore together with the activity of actual printing would come under minimum list heading 486. This, however, is an activity which arises before there is any question of printing and publishing, and is a

separate activity, not part of printing and publishing, and accordingly does not A
come under minimum list heading 486. It is, of course, for the respondents to
prove that the activity does come within that minimum list heading, the only
relevant one in my judgment; the respondents fail to do so, and I find it unnecessary to go further and decide under which of the suggested headings by the
Minister the activity of these three journalists falls. In my judgment the tribunal
erred in law, and I would allow this appeal.   B

SALMON, L.J.: I agree.

WIDGERY, J.: I agree.

Appeal allowed.   Leave to appeal to the House of Lords granted.

Solicitors: *Solicitor, Ministry of Labour; Gillhams* (for the respondents).   C

[*Reported by* ELLEN B. SOLOMONS, *Barrister-at-Law.*]

RILEY (Inspector of Taxes) v. COGLAN.

[CHANCERY DIVISION (Ungoed-Thomas, J.), July 14, 1967.]   D

*Income Tax—Income—Professional footballer—Signing-on fee—Paid in con-
sideration of footballer agreeing to serve—Proportionate part recoverable if
footballer unable to play—No mention of relinquishment of amateur status—
Whether fee taxable as an income profit from the employment—Income Tax
Act, 1952 (15 & 16 Geo. 6 & 1 Eliz. 2 c. 10), s. 156, Sch. E, r. 1, as amended
by Finance Act, 1956 (4 & 5 Eliz. 2 c. 54), s. 44 (9) and Sch. 5, Pt. 1.*   E

The respondent taxpayer signed an agreement with a Rugby League
football club to play for that club for payments to be made to him for each
match, their amounts varying with the results of the matches. By an
additional clause at the end of the printed agreement, which provided that in
consideration of £500 to be paid to the taxpayer as to £100 on his signing
professional forms and as to £400 after taking up residence in York, the   F
taxpayer agreed to serve the club for the remainder of his football career, if
the club should so long require his services, or for a period of twelve years,
whichever should be the greater. If, for any cause except incapacity from
injuries received while playing football for the club, the taxpayer should be
unable to serve the club for that period, he was to repay to the club a proportionate part of the £500, which part would be recoverable as liquidated   G
damages.

Held: as the £500 was paid in consideration of the taxpayer agreeing to
serve the club, and a proportionate part was recoverable if he did not play
for the club, the £500 was consideration for his services as employee and was
an income profit; as such it was within the scope of r. 1 of Sch. E, s. 156,
of the Income Tax Act, 1952, and Sch. 9 as amended, and was taxable   H
accordingly (see p. 319, letter I, and p. 320, letters D and H, post).

Dictum of LORD ROMER in *Cameron* v. *Prendergast (Inspector of Taxes)*
([1940] 2 All E.R. at p. 44) applied.

Jarrold (Inspector of Taxes) v. *Boustead* ([1964] 3 All E.R. 76) distinguished
on the facts.

Appeal allowed.

[As to emoluments under Sch. E, see 20 HALSBURY'S LAWS (3rd Edn.) 311-313,
paras. 573, 574 and pp. 324, 325, paras. 593, 594; and for cases on the subject,
of taxable profits derived from employment, see 28 DIGEST (Repl.) 225-237,
971-1040.

As to factors determining whether a receipt is capital or income in the hands
of its recipient, see 20 HALSBURY'S LAWS (3rd Edn.) 12-15, paras. 7, 8; and for
cases on the subject of what constitutes revenue receipts of trade, see 28 DIGEST
(Repl.) 20-38, *78-173.*

A   For the Income Tax Act, 1952, s. 156, see 31 HALSBURY'S STATUTES (2nd Edn.)
149, and for the Finance Act, 1956, s. 44 (9) and Sch. 5, Pt. 1, see 36 ibid., p. 448,
455-457.]

Cases referred to:

    Cameron v. *Prendergast (Inspector of Taxes)*, [1940] 2 All E.R. 35; [1940]
        A.C. 549; 109 L.J.K.B. 486; 162 L.T. 348; 23 Tax Cas. 122; 28
B   Digest (Repl.) 231, *1004.*

    Hochstrasser (Inspector of Taxes) v. *Mayes*, [1958] 1 All E.R. 369; [1959] Ch. 22;
        [1958] 2 W.L.R. 982; *affd.* C.A., [1958] 3 All E.R. 285; [1959] Ch. at
        p. 39; [1958] 3 W.L.R. 215; *affd.* H.L., [1959] 3 All E.R. 817; [1960]
        A.C. 376; [1960] 2 W.L.R. 63; 38 Tax Cas. 673; Digest (Cont. Vol. A)
        888, *987.*

C   *Jarrold (Inspector of Taxes)* v. *Boustead, McInnes (Inspector of Taxes)* v. *Large,*
        McInnes (Inspector of Taxes) v. *Simms*, [1964] 3 All E.R. 76; [1964]
        1 W.L.R. 1357; 41 Tax Cas. 701; Digest (Cont. Vol. B) 411, *1011a.*

    Way v. *Latilla*, [1937] 3 All E.R. 759; 34 Digest (Repl.) 94, *668.*

Appeal.

D   This was an appeal by the Crown from a decision of the General Commissioners
by way of Case Stated and the following is summarised therefrom.

    At a meeting of the Commissioners for the General Purposes of the Income Tax
Acts held on Nov. 3, 1963, Robert Liversay Coglan appealed against an assess-
ment to income tax made on him under the provisions of Sch. E to the Income
Tax Act, 1952. The grounds of appeal as stated on behalf of the taxpayer
E were that the sum of £100 paid on Jan. 26, 1960, to him by the York Football
Club, Ltd. (" the club ") and the sum of £400 paid to him by the club on Sept. 8
1960, were " signing-on fees ", and not remuneration payable in advance and
assessable to income tax under the provisions of Sch. E. An agreement dated
Apr. 16, 1960, between the club and the taxpayer was produced and proved
(hereinafter called " the agreement "), and also a separate unnumbered clause
F attached providing for the payment of £100 or £400 (hereinafter called the
" Additional Clause "). The taxpayer was twenty-nine years of age. From 1952
to 1958 he played for the Furness Rugby Union Football Club and Rugby Union
for the Cumberland and Westmorland County XV. Rugby Union is an amateur
game and a Rugby Union player who becomes a professional playing Rugby
League football cannot subsequently retain his amateur status and is debarred
G from playing most amateur sports; he is debarred from playing in Rugby Union
games. Early in 1960 the taxpayer was approached by the Oldham Rugby League
Football Club to play as a professional for them and a week later by the club, who
made him an offer which he accepted and which was reduced to writing as an
additional clause. On Apr. 16, 1960, the taxpayer signed the agreement*;
shortly after signing the taxpayer applied to the Northern Rugby Football League
H to be registered as a Rugby League player for the club and also signed a form of
consent to be registered as a player by the club.

    The additional clause, so far as relevant, was in the following terms—

I   " The club hereby engages the player and the player in consideration of
    the sum of £500 to be paid to him as follows: £100 on signing professional
    forms, £400 after taking up permanent residence in York (the receipt of
    such first instalment the player hereby acknowledges and further instal-
    ments being paid as set out above) agrees to serve the club for the remainder
    of his football career from the date hereof, if the club shall so long require
    his services, or for a period of twelve years whichever be the greater.

---

    * The agreement was expressed to be made between (1) the secretary, acting pursuant
to resolution and authority on behalf of the club and two members of the committee,
and (2) the respondent taxpayer. It was in fact signed by the secretary, one other
individual and the respondent. The club was defined in the agreement as " the club ",
but was in fact a limited company.

"If for any cause whatsoever except incapacity resulting from injuries   A
received whilst playing football for the club the player shall fail to carry
out the terms of this agreement or be unable to serve the club for the set
period he shall repay the company [sic.] such a proportionate part of the said
sum of £500 as shall be commensurate with the period remaining to be served
by him which said proportionate part shall be recoverable from the player
by way of ascertained and liquidated damages.   B

" The player undertakes not to become a licensee or accept tenancy or
managership of licensed premises or to reside therein without the written
consent of the Board of Directors or until attaining the age of thirty-five.

" In the event of the player gaining his county cap he shall receive the
sum of £100.

" In the event of his gaining full international honours he shall receive   C
the sum of £100."

After signing the agreement the taxpayer was paid the sum of £100 (in pursuance of the additional clause) by the club less £10 3s., which he understood
to be in respect of income tax. Subsequently on taking up permanent residence
in York he was paid by the club the balance of £400 less £104 18s., which again
was understood to be in respect of income tax. The taxpayer stated that the   D
club paid all its players the same salaries for matches played but that some other
clubs paid their professional players larger sums than those paid by the club.
The taxpayer also stated that under the bye-laws of the Rugby Football League
in force at the time of the agreement: (a) the terms of payment must not be by
annual or weekly payments but must be per match only, and (b) a player who
relinquished his amateur status was permitted to receive a signing-on fee from   E
the club with which he first registered as a professional player.

It was contended on behalf of the taxpayer before the commissioners: (i) that
the two sums of £100 and £400 were paid to the taxpayer for the same consideration and were not distinguishable; (ii) that the consideration for the payment
to the taxpayer of the total sum of £500 was the relinquishment of his amateur
status; (iii) that the remuneration for the taxpayer's services to the club was   F
provided for in cl. 4 and cl. 5 of the agreement, and the payment of £500, which
was a capital payment, was an entirely different thing; (iv) that the £500 was a
signing-on fee paid to the taxpayer as such and not remuneration paid in advance
for his services; and (v) that the sums of £100 and £400 should be excluded from
the taxpayer's emoluments for the relevant years.

It was contended on behalf of the Crown before the commissioners: (i) that   G
the sums of £100 and £400 were not payments made to the taxpayer as compensation for loss of amateur status because the additional clause stated such sums
were paid to the taxpayer in consideration of him agreeing to serve the club for
the remainder of his football career, if the club should so long require him or
for a period of twelve years whichever should be the greater; (ii) that the sums
were accordingly renumeration paid in advance to the taxpayer for his services;   H
and (iii) that the sums were properly included in the emoluments of the taxpayer.

The decision of the General Commissioners was as follows: A. The agreement,
excluding the additional clause, clearly provided that the taxpayer would during
only the next (or remainder of the present) playing season of Rugby League
football play that game for the club. The taxpayer's remuneration during such
season, and during that period only, was the sums payable per match as stated
in the agreement. B. The proper construction of the additional clause and the
remaining clauses of the agreement, read as a whole, was that the club could not
have compelled the taxpayer to play the game for the club in any season other
than that envisaged in the agreement because the remuneration of the taxpayer
for playing was neither fixed nor ascertainable from the agreement. Accordingly
the commissioners held that the agreement read as a whole, provided for two
different kinds of payment to the taxpayer namely: (a) salary or wages specified
in the agreement for the playing of Rugby League football during the next, or

A remainder of the then, present playing season only, and (b) a capital lump sum payable under the additional clause, but repayable proportionately by him as ascertained and liquidated damages should he fail or be unable to serve the club for the remainder of his football career. Such capital sum was paid to the taxpayer as an inducement to become a paid professional Rugby League football player and as compensation for the relinquishment by him of the following advantages:

B (i) of his liability to refuse, except on payment of a financial penalty to play for the club during the remainder of his football career; (ii) of his liability to become a licensee or tenant or manager of licensed premises or to reside therein without the written consent of the directors of the club or until attaining the age of thirty-five; and (iii) of his amateur status. The commissioners accordingly allowed the appeal and the Crown appealed to the High Court.

C *J. R. Phillips* for the Crown.
The taxpayer did not appear and was not represented.

UNGOED-THOMAS, J.: This appeal raises the question whether a payment of £500, paid in two instalments of £100 and £400, to a Rugby League football player, was, to use the governing words applicable under Case I of
D Sch. E, " an emolument therefrom ", " therefrom " referring to the taxpayer's employment.
UPJOHN, J., in *Hochstrasser (Inspector of Taxes) v. Mayes* (1), said this:

" In my judgment, the authorities show this, that it is a question to be answered in the light of the particular facts of every case whether or not a particular payment is or is not a profit arising from the employment.
E Disregarding entirely contracts for full consideration in money or money's worth and personal presents, in my judgment not every payment made to an employee is necessarily made to him as a profit arising from his employment. Indeed, in my judgment, the authorities show that, to be a profit arising from the employment the payment must be made in reference to the services the employee renders by virtue of his office, and it must be something
F in the nature of a reward for services past, present or future."

The case went to the House of Lords (2) where VISCOUNT SIMONDS approved (3) of UPJOHN, J.'s statement, with the observation, which does not matter for our purposes, that the word " past " in the passage which I have just quoted " may be open to question ". So the question may be roughly stated as being whether these payments of £100 and £400 were as a reward for services to be
G rendered, or as payments from his employers for something other than those services.

The Case Stated shows that the taxpayer signed an agreement, which is dated Apr. 16, 1960, to which was added an additional clause. The agreement provided in the body of it for payments to the player of sums for each match to be played varying according to whether his side won, drew or lost. It also provided that
H in the event of his being incapacitated the payments should cease and not be payable except in the event of an accident occurring to the player whilst he was engaged in playing or travelling during his service with the club, in which case he would be entitled to certain insurance payments. It appears from the Case Stated that these payments per match were in accordance with the byelaws of the Rugby Football League which provided that a player who relinquished
I his amateur status was permitted to receive a signing-on fee from the club with which he was first registered as a professional player. The claim here is that this £500 was paid as a signing-on fee. A signing-on fee, apart from being a fee which is paid when the player signs on, does not appear to me to constitute of itself a term of art. It refers to a payment which is made on the occasion of his

---

(1) [1958] 1 All E.R. 369 at pp. 374, 375; 38 Tax. Cas. 673 at p. 685.
(2) [1959] 3 All E.R. 817; 38 Tax. Cas. 673.
(3) [1959] 3 All E.R. at p. 821; 38 Tax. Cas. at p. 705.

signing on. To ascertain, for the purposes of the Income Tax Acts, the nature A
of any payment made on such an occasion, it is necessary to consider the terms of
the agreement under which that payment is made.

In the body of the agreement the provision for payment of match fees was
referred to only as payments " during the (next or present) playing season . . ."
The body of the agreement was in printed form and obviously contemplated that
either the word " next " or the words " or present " should be crossed out, but B
that was not in fact done. The agreement did not provide for payments being
made per match after the conclusion of the next or present playing season.
The commissioners say this in their Case Stated:

> " We considered that on the proper construction of the additional clause
> [which I will come to in a moment] and the remaining clauses of the agree-
> ment, read as a whole, the club could not have compelled the [taxpayer] C
> to play the game of Rugby League football for the club in any season other
> than that envisaged in cll. 1 and 4 of the agreement, because the remunera-
> tion of the [taxpayer] for playing was neither fixed nor ascertainable from
> the agreement."

Pausing there, of course, the taxpayer could not have been compelled to play in D
any event because such an agreement is not specifically enforceable. Further,
if, however, what is meant by that reference was that the taxpayer was not
under any obligation by contract to play because the remuneration was not
fixed, then the reference is not correct in law. In accordance with, e.g., LORD
ATKIN's observation in *Way* v. *Latilla* (4), where he refers to such a relationship
between employer and employee as was established by the agreement in this E
case, if the circumstances established showed that payment for services rendered
was to be made by the employer to the employee—and there is no difficulty
whatsoever in arriving at such a conclusion in the circumstances of this case—
there was an implied obligation on the part of the employer to pay reasonable
remuneration for services rendered. As a matter of practice, what would be
expected in such a case as this would doubtless be that, as all the players for this F
particular club were paid at the same rate, the taxpayer would continue to be
paid at the same rate as his fellow players. However that may be, the legal
position would be that he would be entitled to reasonable remuneration. So the
statements which the commissioners made in leading up to their conclusion are
not statements which appear to me to be correct.

I now come to the additional clause. That clause, which is added at the end G
of the printed form, commences with these words: " It is hereby mutually agreed
by and between the parties hereto as follows . . ." As this is a specific agreement between the parties added to the printed form, it is established, in accordance with, e.g., the statements made in 11 HALSBURY's LAWS (3rd Edn.) 415,
para. 671, that the added clause must for obvious reasons be given greater weight
than those of the printed form. The added clause continues in these terms: H

> " The club hereby engages the [taxpayer], and the [taxpayer], in con-
> sideration of the sum of £500, to be paid to him as follows: £100 on signing
> professional forms; £400 after taking up permanent residence in York
> (the receipt of such said first instalment the [taxpayer] hereby acknowledges
> and further instalments being paid as set out above), agrees to serve the club
> for the remainder of his football career from the date hereof, if the club shall
> so long require his services, or for a period of twelve years whichever be the
> greater. If for any cause whatsoever except incapacity resulting from
> injuries received whilst playing football for the club the [taxpayer] shall fail
> to carry out the terms of this agreement or be unable to serve the club for
> the same period he shall repay the company such a proportionate part of the
> said sum of £500 as shall be commensurate with the period remaining to be
> served by him which said proportionate part shall be recoverable from the

(4) [1937] 3 All E.R. 759 at p. 763.

A [taxpayer] by way of ascertained and liquidated damages. The [taxpayer] undertakes not to become a licensee or accept tenancy or managership of licensed premises or to reside therein without the written consent of the board of directors or until attaining the age of thirty-five. In the event of the [taxpayer] gaining his county cap he shall receive the sum of £100. In the event of his gaining full international honours he shall receive a sum of

B £100."

Neither of those events in fact occurred.

The commissioners concluded that the agreement provided for two different kinds of payments to the taxpayer: the match payments to which I have referred and what they call

C " a capital lump sum paid under the additional clause to the [taxpayer], but repayable proportionately by him as ascertained and liquidated damages if he should fail or be unable to serve the club for the remainder of his football career ",

and then the commissioners go on to say:

D " Such capital lump sum was paid to the [taxpayer] as an inducement to become a paid professional Rugby League football player and as compensation for the relinquishment by him of the following advantages: (i) of his liberty to refuse, except on payment of a finanical penalty, to play for the club during the remainder of his football career; (ii) of his liberty to become a licensee or tenant or manager of licensed premises or to reside therein without the written consent of the directors of the club or until attaining

E the age of thirty-five; (iii) of his amateur status."

As I have already indicated there is no power to compel the taxpayer to play. In the event of his not playing he was not to provide for liquidated damages from resources other than those which this agreement itself provided, and the £500 was paid to him subject to the liability to repay a proportionate part if during the course of his career he did not make himself available to play. There-

F fore, the £500 was to be a running payment for his making himself available to serve the club when required to do so. The agreement contains an undertaking by the taxpayer not to become a licensee, in the terms which I have mentioned. That appears in a separate paragraph without any express reference in that paragraph or elsewhere to any part of the £500 in fact being consideration for

G that undertaking. Nor is there any reference in the agreement anywhere to this sum of £500 being in relinquishment of his amateur status. It may conceivably be said that the £100 has a connexion with giving up amateur status, because it is to be paid on signing professional forms, but it is difficult to see that taking up permanent residence in York has any connexion with anything except being available to give service to the club which was his employer. What the

H parties say and what they agree to in respect of this payment of £500 is that,

" The club hereby engages the [taxpayer], and the [taxpayer] in consideration of the sum of £500 [payable as I have indicated] . . . agrees to serve the club for the remainder of his football career from the date hereof . . .",

for the period which is relevant. This seems to me to be an inescapable and perfectly clear agreement on behalf of the taxpayer to agree to serve the club

I in consideration of the sum of £500. What the club was getting, therefore, was his agreement to serve and what the player was getting in return for that was the payment of £500.

In *Cameron* v. *Prendergast (Inspector of Taxes)* (5), Lord Romer, dealing with the case of a director who was paid £45,000 in consideration of his agreeing to continue to serve as a director, said this:

" Was the sum of £45,000 paid to the appellant as the consideration

(5) [1940] 2 All E.R. 35 at p. 44; 23 Tax. Cas. 122 at p. 150.

A

for a promise on his part to continue the performance of his services as a director of the company? If this question be answered in the affirmative, the appeal must fail, for the sum would in that case clearly be part of the ' salaries, fees, wages, perquisites or profits ' from the appellant's office of director within the meaning of the Income Tax Act, 1918, Sch. E, r. 1. It matters not that the sum is a lump sum, payable at once, instead of being spread over a number of years, and depending in no way upon the number of years already spent, or to be spent in the future, by the appellant in the office. Nor does it matter that the sum is so large as to present the appearance of a capital, rather than an income, payment. If a company chooses to pay a director's remuneration in a lump sum, it can, no doubt, lawfully do so, but the sum nevertheless represents income, whatever its amount, and will be taxable as such. Remuneration which, if paid by instalments over a number of years, would be income, is income though paid once and for all in a lump sum, just as much as the capital consideration for a sale, say, of land is capital, even though payable by instalments spread over a number of years.''

B

C

In this case, a fortiori having regard to LORD ROMER'S observation, the payment is income because a proportionate part of the £500 was to be repaid if the taxpayer did not serve the club for a specified time of his playing life: it was thus specifically related to the playing period during which he was to serve the club.

D

To my mind, this case would hardly have engendered hope if it had not been for the decision of the Court of Appeal in *Jarrold (Inspector of Taxes)* v. *Boustead* (6). In that case Rugby League footballers claimed that—and I use a vague term—signing-on fees were not subject to income tax and they succeeded. In one instance, from which the others were not materially different, the provision was that the club would pay the player the sum of £3,000 less income tax on his signing professional forms for the club and it was stated and decided on the facts of that case that the £3,000 was paid as an inducement to give up amateur status. LORD DENNING, M.R., quite clearly based his decision on the principle that this was a payment which, although made by the employer to the employee, yet was not for services as employee. He made this perfectly clear where he said (7):

E

F

" In the course of the argument an illustration was taken by counsel on both sides. Suppose there was a man who was an expert organist but was very fond of playing golf on Sundays. He is asked to become the organist of the parish church for the ensuing seven months at a salary of £10 a month. It is expressly stipulated by this strange parish council that, if he takes up the post, he is to give up Sunday golf for the rest of his life. Thereupon he says that, if he is to give up golf, he wants an extra £500; and they agree to pay it. In such a case the £500 is not a payment for his services as an organist for seven months. It is a payment for relinquishing what he considered to be an advantage to him.''

G

Here however we have a contract whereby the club engages the taxpayer and the taxpayer in consideration of the sum of £500 agrees to serve the club for the remainder of his football career. To my mind that is conclusive and the appeal, in my judgment, succeeds.

Appeal allowed.

Solicitor: *Solicitor of Inland Revenue.*

[*Reported by* PATRICIA JOHNSTON, *Barrister-at-Law.*]

---

(6) [1964] 3 All E.R. 76; 41 Tax. Cas. 701.
(7) [1964] 3 All E.R. at p. 80; 41 Tax Cas. at p. 729.

A

Re TURNER'S WILL TRUSTS.
WESTMINSTER BANK, LTD. *v.* TURNER AND OTHERS.

[CHANCERY DIVISION (Plowman, J.), November 3, 10, 1967.]

Administration of Estates—Ademption—Double portions—Share of residue
B   *adeemed by gifts inter vivos—Residue bequeathed as net fund remaining*
    after payment of testamentary expenses, etc.—Whether gifts should be brought
    into account against net residue after deducting estate duty or against gross
    residue.

A testator made gifts in his lifetime (such gifts being " portions ") to his
son and daughter which, so the court decided, had to be brought into account,
C   by virtue of the rule against double portions, in the distribution of the
testator's residuary estate. The testamentary portions were bequeathed by
the will out of a net fund, viz., what remained of the testator's residuary
estate after payment of, among other things, testamentary expenses. Estate
duty on free personalty was a testamentary expense, and the testator left no
residuary realty. On the question whether the inter vivos gifts should be
D   brought into account in the distribution of the testator's residuary estate
against net value (viz., after estate duty had been paid out of the residuary
estate) or against gross value (viz., adding back the amount of the relevant
estate duty paid),

    Held: the inter vivos gifts should be brought into account against the net
residuary estate after payment of estate duty, because the fund from which
E   the testamentary portions were given was the net residue of the testator's
estate after payment of, among other things, estate duty, so that to add
back the amount of the estate duty would be to treat that amount as part
of the testamentary portions which it was not (see p. 323, letter I, and p. 327,
letter G, post).

    Re Beddington ([1900] 1 Ch. 771) followed.
F   *Re Tollemache* ([1930] W.N. 138) and *Re Slee (decd.)* ([1962] 1 All E.R. 542)
distinguished.

   [As to ademption in relation to testamentary gifts, see 39 HALSBURY'S LAWS
(3rd Edn.) 934, para. 1412; and for cases on the subject, see 48 DIGEST (Repl.)
256-270, *2304-2425*. As to the presumption of satisfaction of legacy by portion,
see 14 HALSBURY'S LAWS (3rd Edn.) 599, 600, para. 1109; and for cases on the
G   subject, see 20 DIGEST (Repl.) 478-480, *1846-1861*.]

Cases referred to:
    Beddington, Re, Micholls v. Samuel, [1900] 1 Ch. 771; 69 L.J.Ch. 374; 82 L.T.
       557; 21 Digest (Repl.) 74, *331.*
    Berry v. Gaukroger, [1900-03] All E.R. Rep. 166; [1903] 2 Ch. 116; 72 L.J.Ch.
       435; 88 L.T. 521; 21 Digest (Repl.) 64, *255.*
I   Crocker, Re, Crocker v. Crocker, [1916] 1 Ch. 25; 85 L.J.Ch. 179; 114 L.T. 61;
       21 Digest (Repl.) 75, *332.*
    Dawson's Will Trusts, Re, National Provincial Bank, Ltd. v. National Council
       of the Y.M.C.A. Inc., [1957] 1 All E.R. 177; [1957] 1 W.L.R. 391; 21
       Digest (Repl.) 119, *611.*
I   Slee (decd.), Re, Midland Bank Executor and Trustee Co., Ltd. v. Slee, [1962]
       1 All E.R. 542; [1962] 1 W.L.R. 496; Digest (Cont. Vol. A) 559, *5463a.*
    Tollemache, Re, Forbes v. Public Trustee, [1930] W.N. 138; 21 Digest (Repl.)
       66, *271.*
    Watson v. Watson, (1864), 33 Beav. 574; 55 E.R. 491; 20 Digest (Repl.) 487,
       1964.

Adjourned Summons.

This was an application by originating summons dated Aug. 24, 1964, as
amended on Oct. 20, 1966, by Westminster Bank, Ltd., the executor of the will

dated Mar. 29, 1930, and codicil dated July 22, 1958, of Horace Bickerton Turner, A
deceased, who died on Feb. 15, 1961, against the following defendants, all of whom
claimed to be beneficiaries under the trusts of the above-mentioned will and
codicil: (i) Charles William Henry Turner, the surviving son of the testator,
(ii) Anthea Helen MacKinnon, the testator's daughter, (iii) Charles Alexander
MacKinnon, (iv) Donald Ian Alasdair MacKinnon and (v) Flora MacKinnon,
the infant children of the second defendant, and (vi) Kathleen Victoria Turner B
the testator's widow.

The summons came before PLOWMAN, J., on Mar. 20, 21, 1967 and Apr. 10,
1967, when various of the questions were disposed of and the remaining questions
were stood over. The summons was restored before PLOWMAN, J., on Nov. 3,
1967. The case is reported only on question 10 of the summons, viz., whether in
calculating the testator's residuary estate for the purposes of bringing into account C
inter vivos gifts against shares of the testator's residuary estate there should be
included any and if so what part of the amount of the estate duty payable on the
death of the testator. The facts and provisions of the will are set out in the
judgment.

W. H. Goodhart for the plaintiffs.   D
J. A. Brightman, Q.C., and J. E. Vinelott for the first defendant.
B. L. Bathurst, Q.C., and E. W. Griffith for the second and sixth defendants.
S. W. Templeman, Q.C., and Martin Nourse for the third, fourth and fifth
defendants.

                                                              Cur. adv. vult.

                                                                               E
Nov. 10. **PLOWMAN, J.,** read the following judgment. The testator,
Horace Bickerton Turner, who died on Feb. 15, 1961, had three children: the
first defendant, whom I will call Charles, the second defendant, whom I will call
Anthea, and a son, Richard, who died in the lifetime of the testator aged twenty-
four and unmarried.

By cl. 9 and cl. 10 of his will, dated Mar. 29, 1930, the testator disposed of his
residuary estate as follows: F

" 9. I DEVISE AND BEQUEATH all the real estate and personal estate
whatsoever and wheresoever of or to which I shall be seised possessed or
entitled at my death or over which I shall then have a general power of
appointment or disposition by will except what I otherwise dispose of by
this my will or any codicil hereto unto and to the use of my trustees their C
heirs executors or administrators respectively according to the nature and
tenure thereof UPON TRUST that my trustees shall sell call in and collect or
otherwise convert into money such parts of the premises as shall not consist
of ready money and shall out of the moneys arising thereby pay my funeral
and testamentary expenses and debts and the legacies given by this my
will or any codicil hereto and the duties on any legacies given free of duty H
by this my will or any codicil hereto and shall stand possessed of the residue
of the said moneys and of the investments for the time being representing the
same (hereinafter referred to as 'my residuary estate') upon the trusts
and subject to the powers and provisions hereinafter contained concerning
the same (that is to say) UPON TRUST to pay the income thereof to my said
wife during her life for her separate use without power of anticipation And
after her death IN TRUST as to both capital and income for my said three
children as follows: as to fifty-one one hundredth parts thereof for said
son Richard Charles Turner (if he shall attain the age of twenty-five years)
absolutely as to thirty-seven one hundredth parts thereof for said son
Charles William Henry Turner (if he shall attain the age of twenty-five years)
absolutely as to twelve one hundredth parts thereof for my said daughter
Anthea Helen Turner (if she shall attain the age of twenty-five years or
marry under that age) upon the trusts hereinafter declared.

A   " 10. If either of my said sons shall die before attaining the age of twenty-five years leaving a child or children . . . but if either of my said sons shall die before attaining the age of twenty-five years and without leaving any such child or if my said daughter shall die before attaining that age and unmarried then the share of residuary estate of my son or daughter so dying shall accrue by way of addition to the shares or share of my said sons or the

B   survivor of them and if more than one in proportion to their original shares so that every such addition to any share shall as from the time of its accruer thereto follow the destination of the share to which it shall be so added and be for all purposes inseparably blended therewith . . ."

The rest of cl. 10 is not material and I need not read it.

C   The testator's widow is still living; and Charles and Anthea have long since attained the age of twenty-five. In the events which have happened, therefore, the testator's residuary estate, subject to the life interest of his widow, is held as to eighty-eight per cent. in trust for Charles and as to twelve per cent. in trust for Anthea, her share being settled by a later provision of the will. I have, on a previous occasion, held that Charles and Anthea have to bring into account in the distribution of the testator's residuary estate, certain gifts made to them

D   by the testator during his lifetime. This decision was an application of the rule against double portions.

The question which now arises is whether the gifts inter vivos have to be brought into account against the gross residuary estate, that is to say, the residuary estate before deduction of estate duty, or against the net residue after deduction of estate duty. Question 10 of the originating summons which raises this question

E   is as follows:

" That it may be determined whether in calculating for the purposes of any account as aforesaid the value of the testator's residuary estate there should be included any and if so what part of the estate duty payable in respect of the death of the testator."

F   If the inter vivos gifts to Anthea have to be brought in against the gross estate, her settled share of residue, on the figures that have been given to me, will be a sum approaching £20,000, while if they have to be brought in against the net residue it will be nil, since her twelve per cent. of the residuary estate is less than the amount of her inter vivos portions. Apart from authority, I should have thought that it was tolerably plain that in the present case the portions have to

G   be brought into account against the net residue.

The question is one of ademption, namely to what extent were the portions given to Charles and Anthea by the testator's will adeemed by the portions which he subsequently gave to them during his lifetime? To answer this question, the first step must be to ascertain the amount or value of each portion given by the will; the next step must be to ascertain the amount or value of the inter vivos

H   portions given to the beneficiary in question; the final step to subtract the latter from the former. The first step necessarily involves deducting from the proceeds of sale of the testator's residuary estate his funeral and testamentary expenses and debts and the legacies given by his will, because it is a percentage of a fund constituted as a result of making those deductions to which Charles and Anthea are each entitled. Estate duty on free personalty is a testamentary expense

I   and the testator left no residuary realty. It is, therefore, plain that the residuary trust fund in which Charles and Anthea participate is a net fund, after payment of estate duty. To add back the amount of the estate duty would be to treat a part of that estate duty as part of the beneficiary's testamentary portion, which it is not. In Anthea's case, since the amount or value of the inter vivos portions was greater than that of her percentage of the net residuary trust fund, the ademption of the gift of the latter was total.

I must, however, now turn to certain cases which were cited during the course of the argument. Counsel for the first defendant, who argued in support of

the prima facie view which I have already expressed, referred first to *Re Bedding-* **A**
ton, Micholls v. *Samuel* (1). That case was concerned with the value to be
attributed, not to the testamentary portion, but to the inter vivos portion.
The headnote reads:

"A testator, within one year of his death, spent £4,000 on the purchase of
a house, which he settled on one of his daughters, and contributed £4,320
towards the purchase of another house for another daughter; the court, **B**
having decided that these gifts must be considered as an ademption pro
tanto of the daughters' shares in the testator's residuary estate, which must
be brought into account. Held, that the amount for which the daughters
were accountable was the sums so advanced, less the amount they were
liable to pay for estate duty by reason of the death of the testator within one
year of the gift." **C**

The terms of the will are stated in the report only in this way (2):

"The testator by his will, dated Mar. 30, 1896, directed his residuary
estate, which was chiefly personalty, to be divided into as many shares as he
had daughters living at his death, or should have predeceased him leaving
a child or children living at his death, and then settled each share on the **D**
daughter for life without power of anticipation, and after her death on her
children in the usual way."

Counsel for the first defendant has obtained, however, a copy of the original
will and from this it appears that the residuary estate which the testator directed
to be divided into shares was a net residue arrived at after deducting funeral
and testamentary expenses, debts and legacies. It is clear, therefore, that **E**
BYRNE, J., accepted the view that it was against this net residue that the amount
or value of the portion had to be brought into account. Inferentially, therefore,
that case supports the view which I have already expressed.

Junior counsel for the third, fourth and fifth defendants, Anthea's infant children, invited me to decline if necessary to follow *Re Beddington* (1), but I see no
reason why I should do that, first because I respectfully agree with it, and **F**
secondly because it has been followed in at least two subsequent cases. The first
of these is *Re Crocker, Crocker* v. *Crocker* (3). The headnote of the report is as
follows:

"A testator who died in 1914 had in his lifetime settled certain stocks on
two of his daughters and their children, and these stocks had depreciated
in value at the time of his death. By his will he gave his residuary estate in **G**
trust for all his children equally, subject to a proviso that for the purposes
of division there should be brought into hotchpot, in respect of each of the
two daughters or her children, the value of the trust funds which he had
settled upon them. It was conceded that under s. 2 (1) (c) and s. 9 (1) of the
Finance Act, 1894, the estate duty payable in respect of the portion of the
settled funds which were settled within three years of the testator's death **H**
must be borne by those funds. Held, that the sum to be brought into account
under the hotchpot clause in respect of all the settled funds was the value of
all the settled funds at the date of settlement (and not at the date of the will)
less the estate duty payable in respect of the funds settled within three
years of the testator's death. *Watson* v. *Watson* (4) and *Re Beddington* (1)
followed." **I**

I need not, I think, concern myself further with the facts of the case, but SARGANT,
J., said this (5):

"I see no reason why I should differ from the decision of BYRNE, J., in
Re Beddington (1), especially as it appears to be a decision which tells in

(1) [1900] 1 Ch. 771.   (2) [1900] 1 Ch. at p. 772.
(3) [1916] 1 Ch. 25.   (4) (1864), 33 Beav. 574.
                        (5) [1916] 1 Ch. at p. 30.

A favour of equality. What decision I should have arrived at without its help
I need not consider."

I read those words in view of certain observations of Vaisey, J., in *Re Dawson's
Will Trusts, National Provincial Bank, Ltd.* v. *National Council of the Y.M.C.A.
Inc.* (6). Vaisey, J., said this (7):

B   " Shortly, I think that the case is in principle covered by the decision of
Byrne, J., in *Re Beddington* (8), in which the headnote is as follows . . . [the
judge read the headnote and continued:—] That decision was approved and
followed by Sargant, J., in *Re Crocker* (9), and I think I also ought to follow
it though I share to some extent the doubts of Sargant, J., as to its correctness."

C Speaking for myself, I should not have regarded the observations of Sargant, J.,
as expressing doubt as to the correctness of *Re Beddington* (8).

The argument on the other side turned on *Re Tollemache, Forbes* v. *Public
Trustee* (10). That case decided that where advances, made out of settled property
more than three years (as it was in those days) before the death of the life tenant,
have to be brought into hotchpot, they must be brought in against the gross fund
D before deducting the estate duty payable on the death of the tenant for life, so
that each beneficiary bears the duty attributable to the proportion of the fund
paid to him on that death. I will read the whole of the judgment of Clauson,
J. (11), which is quite short.

" Clauson, J., said that for the purpose of collection the estate duty
must be treated as imposed upon the whole fund in the hands of the trustees
E at the death of Lady Sudeley. In considering the incidence of the duty, the
question was how it ought to be borne by the several beneficiaries inter se.
The advances having been made more than three years before the death of
Lady Sudeley, each advanced share was, to the extent of the amount
advanced, exempt from the duty. In cases where, as in the present case, the
executors of the deceased were not accountable for the duty on property
F which had passed on the death to beneficiaries in possession, although the
duty would be collected from the trustees, it ought to be borne by and
adjusted between the several beneficiaries according to the amount chargeable in respect of the sums which they received as their shares at the death,
the advanced beneficiaries not paying duty in respect of advances received
at an earlier date: *Berry* v. *Gaukroger* (12). It had been contended that the
G effect of the hotchpot clause was to require the advances to be brought into
account with the net sum after payment of the duty; but that would have
the effect of throwing upon the advanced sums which did not pass on Lady
Sudeley's death part of the duty payable in respect of the residue of the
fund. True, the ultimate division of the fund, after paying the duties, would
not be in equal shares if the advanced shares escaped duty in respect of the
H advances; but the object of the hotchpot clause was to produce equality between beneficiaries in the participation of the fund, and did not aim at
producing equality in shouldering the imposts, the contribution to which
ought not to be different from what it would be if the impost were charged
direct against the beneficiary. The proper mode of distributing the fund was
not by bringing the advanced sums into hotchpot against what remained of
I the fund after deducting the amount of estate duty, a process which would
involve an equal distribution of the duty, but by bringing the advances into
hotchpot against the gross fund before deducting the duty, the effect of
which would be to leave each beneficiary to bear the duty chargeable in
respect of the sum which he received as his share at the death."

(6) [1957] 1 All E.R. 177.   (7) [1957] 1 All E.R. at pp. 180, 181.
(8) [1900] 1 Ch. 771.   (9) [1916] 1 Ch. 25.
(10) [1930] W.N. 138.   (11) [1930] W.N. at p. 139.
        (12) [1900-03] All E.R. Rep. 166; [1903] 2 Ch. 116.

The principle which emerges from that case was stated by CROSS, J., in *Re Slee* (*decd.*), *Midland Bank Executor and Trustee Co., Ltd.* v. *Slee* (13), as follows:

> " CLAUSON, J., decided in *Re Tollemache* (14), that if an advance has been made more than five years before the death of the life tenant, so that it is not itself subject to duty, and the advanced beneficiary has to bring the advance into hotchpot, against a fund which bears its own duty, the advance should be brought into account against the gross fund—that is, the duty which has been paid on the fund is added back."

A similar statement appears in THEOBALD ON WILLS (12th Edn.) para. 2011, where it is stated:

> " But when an advance is made in sufficient time before the relevant death, so that it is not itself subject to duty, and the advanced beneficiary has to bring it into hotchpot against a fund which bears its own duty, the advance is brought in against the gross fund, i.e., the duty which has been paid in the fund is added back."

In my judgment the *Re Tollemache* (14) principle applies and applies only to a case where an advance has to be brought into account against a fund which bears its own duty. In such a case the advanced beneficiary is sharing in a fund encumbered with a charge for duty and must bear a share of that duty; but in the present case the fund with which I am concerned is not one which bears its own duty, it is a fund which does not come into existence until duty has been paid.

Re Slee (*decd.*) (15) is interesting as exhibiting both aspects of the matter. The facts, so far as material, were these. A testatrix had made certain advances more than five years before her death out of a legacy settled by the will of her father. By her own will she directed that these advances and the balance of the settled legacy and certain funds settled on her by her marriage settlement should be brought into hotchpot with her residuary estate after payment of her funeral and testamentary expenses including all estate duty leviable at her death in respect of her residuary estate and debts and legacies. The originating summons raised among other questions the question whether the division of the settled legacy, marriage settlement funds and residuary estate should be considered as constructively made or done before or after payment of the whole or some and what part of the estate duty payable thereout on the testatrix's death. CROSS, J., said this (16):

> " Turning now to the question of duty, I think one must make a distinction between the duties on the residuary estate on the one hand and the duties on the settled legacy and the marriage settlement fund on the other hand. As I have pointed out, the residuary estate as defined by the will is the net fund ascertained after the payment of all duties. In cl. 12 the testatrix speaks of the distribution of the marriage settlement fund and the settled legacy fund and the residuary estate. She has plainly contemplated that the sums will be brought into hotchpot against the net residue so that there can be no question so far as the residue is concerned of adding back any duty. The position with regard to the marriage settlement fund and the settled legacy, however, is quite different. Duty on those funds is not a testamentary expense. It is charged on the funds themselves and ultimately has to be borne by the beneficiaries in the proportions in which they take the fund."

Then comes the reference to *Re Tollemache* (14) which I have already read. CROSS, J., continued (17):

---

(13) [1962] 1 All E.R. 542 at pp. 550, 551.
(14) [1930] W.N. 138.
(15) [1962] 1 All E.R. 542.
(16) [1962] 1 All E.R. at p. 550.
(17) [1962] 1 All E.R. at p. 551.

A "It was suggested that that case was inconsistent with two earlier cases dealing with duty on gifts which had to be brought into hotchpot. The first case is *Re Beddington* (18) and the second is *Re Crocker* (19). Those cases decided that where there is a question of bringing a gift into hotchpot, the gift being itself liable to duty, the amount to be brought into hotchpot is the net benefit to the donee and not the gross amount. It was suggested that it

B was rather odd to value the sums to be brought into hotchpot in that way and at the same time to deal with the duty on the balance of the fund in the way Clauson, J., did in *Re Tollemache* (20). Be that as it may, I think the decision in *Re Tollemache* (20) is binding on me. The only question is whether it can be applied in this case because I am not dealing with a single fund but I am dealing with three funds, one of which, the residuary estate, I have

C decided is a net fund. I cannot see that there is any unsurmountable diffi-culty in applying the *Re Tollemache* (20) decision in the present instance. I think that what one must do is to value the three funds at the date of distribution and add to the marriage settlement fund and the settled legacy the amount of duty which has been paid on them and add in also the advances calculated in the way which I have indicated, divide the total

D between the parties in their respective proportions, debit the advanced beneficiaries with their advances and treat the resultant shares as having come to each of them rateably out of the three funds so that in so far as they come out of the settled legacy or the marriage settlement fund the respective beneficiaries have to bear their share of the duties on those funds."

E *Re Slee* (*decd.*) (21) was, of course, a case where there was an express provision requiring duty free advances to be brought into account against a net fund of residue and is, therefore, distinguishable from the present case.

It was persuasively urged on me that there was really no difference in principle between bringing into account, under the rule against double portions, gifts made by a testator in his lifetime and bringing into hotchpot advances made out of a

F settled fund during the lifetime of the tenant for life. No doubt there are similarities, but the incidence of estate duty is not, in my judgment, necessarily one of them and I cannot accept the view that *Re Tollemache* (20) is decisive of this case.

In my judgment, it is against the net residue that the inter vivos portions have to be brought into account and I may summarise my reasons for this conclusion

G as follows: (i) It accords with the nature of the portions given by the will, which are percentages of the net estate after deduction of estate duty; (ii) It derives support from *Re Beddington* (18); (iii) No case was cited to me in which estate duty was required to be added back to a fund which did not bear its own duty; (iv) *Re Tollemache* (20) is distinguishable, since the court was there concerned with a fund which did bear its own duty.

H Accordingly, I answer question 10 of the originating summons (22) in the negative sense.

Declaration accordingly.

Solicitors: *Trower, Still & Keeling* (for the plaintiffs and the second to sixth defendants); *Official Solicitor.*

I *[Reported by* Jacqueline Metcalfe, *Barrister-at-Law.]*

---

(18) [1900] 1 Ch. 771.
(19) [1916] 1 Ch. 25.
(20) [1930] W.N. 138.
(21) [1962] 1 All E.R. 542.
(22) Question 10 is stated at p. 323, letter F, ante.

GURTNER v. CIRCUIT.

[COURT OF APPEAL, CIVIL DIVISION (Lord Denning, M.R., Diplock and Salmon, L.JJ.), November 21, 22, December 14, 1967.]

Practice—Parties—Adding persons as parties—Action by pedestrian against motor cyclist—Defendant insured but insurance company unknown—Defendant unable to be traced—Whether Motor Insurers' Bureau should be added as a party—R.S.C., Ord. 15, r. 6 (2) (b).

In June, 1961, the plaintiff was severely injured when he was run down by the defendant, who was riding a motor cycle. In June, 1964, the plaintiff issued a writ against the defendant. No steps were taken to serve the writ until June, 1965, when it was discovered that the defendant had gone to Canada about three years previously. The writ was renewed and, in November, 1965, the defendant still not having been traced, the plaintiff's then solicitor wrote to the Motor Insurers' Bureau, who asked an insurance company to investigate the matter, but neither the defendant's insurers nor the defendant were found. There were two further renewals of the writ, the last being in June, 1967, until a date in September, 1967. In June, 1967, the plaintiff obtained an order for substituted service on the defendant c/o the insurance company which the bureau had asked to investigate the matter. In July, 1967, the bureau applied to be added as defendants. On appeal from an order reversing a decision that the bureau should be added as second defendants under R.S.C., Ord. 15, r. 6 (2) (b)*,

Held: (i) the bureau should be added as defendants, on their undertaking to pay any damages that might be awarded to the plaintiff, for the following reasons—

(a) (per LORD DENNING, M.R., SALMON, L.J., concurring) under R.S.C., Ord. 15, r. 6 (2) (b) the court had discretion to add a party to an action if he would be affected in his legal rights or his pocket (in that he would be bound to foot the bill) by the determination of the dispute; and in the present case the bureau would be directly affected in both these ways (see p. 332, letters B, G and H, and p. 338, letter G, post).

Fire, Auto and Marine Insurance Co., Ltd. v. *Greene* ([1964] 2 All E.R. 761) disapproved.

(b) (per DIPLOCK, L.J., SALMON, L.J., concurring) a matter was not effectively " adjudicated upon " within R.S.C., Ord. 15, r. 6 (2) (b) unless all those who would be liable to satisfy the judgment were given an opportunity to be heard; in the present case the bureau were so liable, though they were liable to the Minister of Transport rather than to the plaintiff, and accordingly the court had a discretion to add the bureau as parties, which discretion should be exercised in their favour (see p. 336, letters G and I, to p. 337, letters A and D, and p. 338, letter G, post).

Dictum of DEVLIN, J., in *Amon* v. *Raphael Tuck & Sons, Ltd.* ([1956] 1 All E.R. at p. 287) not applied.

(ii) the order for substituted service had been wrongly made, but as no practical purpose would be served in the circumstances by setting it aside, service would be allowed to stand (see p. 332, letter I, p. 333, letter B, and p. 338, letters B, D and F, post).

(iii) the orders for renewals of the writ should stand because (per LORD DENNING, M.R., SALMON, L.J., concurring) the defendant had been away in Canada and could not be traced so as to be served (see p. 333, letter C, and p. 338, letter F, post) and (per DIPLOCK, L.J., SALMON, L.J., concurring), the bureau not having applied promptly to set the renewal aside, opportunity for ascertaining whether there was adequate explanation why there had

---

* The relevant terms of R.S.C. Ord. 15, r. 6 (2) (b) are at p. 335, letter D, post.

Approved in Re VANDERVELL. [1969] 3 All E.R. 496.

Considered in SETTLEMENT CORPN. v. HOCHSCHILD (NO. 2). [1970] 1 All E.R. 60.

A   been delay in attempting to trace the defendant had been lost (see p. 338, letters A and F, post).

Per DIPLOCK, L.J., SALMON, L.J., concurring: the order adding the bureau as parties should incorporate an express statement that they, as second defendants, should be entitled to exercise all the rights of the first defendant in the action (see p. 337, letter E, and p. 338, letter F, post).

B   Appeal allowed in part.

[**Editorial Note.** It is to be observed that DIPLOCK, L.J., with whose judgment SALMON, L.J., concurred, approved the view that an ordinary insurer could be added as a party to a running down action, if the policy of insurance did not contain a clause giving the insurer a contractual right to conduct the defence

C   in the name of the insured, upholding in this respect the view of JOHN STEPHENSON, J., in *Fire Auto and Marine Insurance Co., Ltd.* v. *Greene* ([1964] 2 All E.R. 761); see p. 336, letter H, post.

As to adding of parties, see 3 HALSBURY'S LAWS (3rd Edn.) 394, 395, para. 735; and for cases on the subject, see DIGEST (Practice) (Repl.) 460-463, *1550-1575*.

As to renewal of a writ, see ibid., p. 303, para. 558; and as to substituted service,

D   see ibid., pp. 321, 322, paras. 585, 586.

As to the Motor Insurers' Bureau, see 22 HALSBURY'S LAWS (3rd Edn.) 382, para. 778.]

Cases referred to:

Amon v. *Raphael Tuck & Sons, Ltd.*, [1956] 1 All E.R. 273; [1956] 1 Q.B. 357; [1956] 2 W.L.R. 372; 50 Digest (Repl.) 452, *1489*.

E   *Battersby* v. *Anglo-American Oil Co., Ltd.*, [1944] 2 All E.R. 387; [1945] K.B. 23; 114 L.J.K.B. 49; 171 L.T. 300; 50 Digest (Repl.) 292, *336*.

Beswick v. *Beswick*, [1967] 2 All E.R. 1197; [1967] 3 W.L.R. 932.

Byrne v. *Brown*, (1889), 22 Q.B.D. 657; 58 L.J.Q.B. 410; 60 L.T. 651; 50 Digest (Repl.) 452, *1490*.

Fire, Auto and Marine Insurance Co., Ltd. v. *Greene*, [1964] 2 All E.R. 761;

F   [1964] 2 Q.B. 687; [1964] 3 W.L.R. 319; Digest (Cont. Vol. B) 463, *3722a*.

Hardy v. *Motor Insurers' Bureau*, [1964] 2 All E.R. 742; [1964] 2 Q.B. 745; [1964] 3 W.L.R. 433; Digest (Cont. Vol. B) 462, *3703a*.

Interlocutory Appeal.

G   This was an appeal by the Motor Insurers' Bureau from an order of CHAPMAN, J., dated Oct. 11, 1967, setting aside orders made by Master RITCHIE on July 14 and July 28, 1967, and ordering that the service of the writ in an action by the plaintiff against the defendant by substituted service on the Royal Insurance Co., Ltd., should stand. Master RITCHIE had ordered (i) that the Motor Insurers' Bureau be added as defendants to the action on their undertaking to satisfy any

H   damages awarded to the plaintiff; (ii) that the orders extending the validity of the writ be set aside; (iii) that the orders for substituted service of the writ be set aside and (iv) that the service of the writ be set aside. By the order dated June 22, 1967, it was ordered that service of a copy of the order and a copy of the writ of summons in the action, by sending the same by pre-paid ordinary post letter, addressed to the defendant John Christopher Circuit at c/o Royal

I   Insurance Co., Ltd., 24/28 Lombard Street, London, E.C.3, should be good and sufficient service of the writ. The grounds of the appeal were as follows: 1. That the order of July 14, 1967, adding the bureau as defendants in the action was made by consent and should not have been set aside. 2. That the order adding the bureau as defendants in the action was in any event correctly made on the evidence, whether the plaintiff did or did not consent thereto. 3. That an order adding the bureau ought to be made under R.S.C., Ord. 15, r. 6 (2) (*b*)—(a) because the obligation of the bureau under the agreement with the Minister of Transport dated June 17, 1946, imposed on the bureau such duties, and gave to the bureau

such an interest in this action, that the bureau was a necessary party to the action; A
(b) because the obligations of the bureau under the agreement were with reference
to the plaintiff's legal obligations and not merely moral obligations; and (c)
because the undertaking which the bureau gave, and was still willing to give, both
to the court and to the plaintiff, made the obligation of the bureau to the plaintiff
a legal obligation and not merely a moral obligation and in any event provided
sufficient justification for the order adding the bureau to the action as defendants. B
4. That there was no sufficient explanation or justification for the delay which had
occurred in the issuing and serving of the writ in the action and that the orders
extending the validity of the writ ought to be set aside whether or not the bureau
were to be added as defendants in the action. 5. That service of the writ on Royal
Insurance Co., Ltd., ought to be set aside since there was no evidence to justify
an order for substituted service and Royal Insurance Co., Ltd., could not either C
inform the defendant of the issue of the writ, or act on his behalf.

R. B. Gibson for the Motor Insurers' Bureau.
The plaintiff appeared in person.

Cur. adv. vult.

Dec. 14. The following judgments were read.

D

LORD DENNING, M.R.: On June 29, 1961, the plaintiff, Frederick
Gurtner, was walking across Robin Hood Way on the Kingston by-pass. He was
run down by a motor cycle and severely injured. His skull was fractured and he
lost his memory. A police officer came up after the accident and took down
particulars. The motor cyclist gave his name and address as John Christopher
Circuit of 45 Alpine Avenue, Tolworth, Surrey. His machine was a 350 cc. E
" Royal Enfield " Bullet, VPG 816. The police officer took also the names and
addresses of three witnesses and noted down the statements made by them. Within five days the motor cyclist, the defendant, gave to the police the details of his
insurance. It was certificate No. 381512 issued by Lloyds Motor Policies; but
the police did not take down the name of the syndicate which had issued the
certificate. Some time later the plaintiff instructed solicitors, Messrs. Beer & Co., F
to act for him. They got particulars from the police, but they do not appear to
have communicated with the defendant at all. They seem to have waited till
the three years' period of limitation had nearly expired. Then, on June 26, 1964,
they issued a writ against the defendant, John Christopher Circuit, of 45 Alpine
Avenue, Tolworth, which was the address given in the police report. It was endorsed with a claim for " damages for personal injuries caused to him by the G
defendant's negligent driving on June 29, 1961 ". It does not appear that Beer &
Co. at that time made any attempt to serve the writ. If they had tried to serve it
in 1964 and called at the address in Tolworth, they would have discovered that
the Circuit family left that address in 1962. The defendant went to Canada and
married out there. Efforts have been made to trace him but without success.

The writ was only valid for the first twelve months from June 26, 1964, to H
June 16, 1965; but Beer & Co. did not try to effect service of the writ till the twelve
months had nearly expired. Then, on June 24, 1965, a process server called at
45, Alpine Avenue, Tolworth, and got no answer. The people next door said that
the defendant had gone to Canada about three years ago. Thereupon, on June 25,
1965, Beer & Co. applied for the renewal of the writ ex parte. It was renewed for
a second twelve months until June 25, 1966. Soon afterwards the plaintiff I
instructed other solicitors, Messrs. Nye & Donne. They obtained a legal aid
certificate and, not being able to find the defendant they wrote on Nov. 8, 1965,
to the Motor Insurers' Bureau; because that bureau does in some circumstances
pay the damages awarded to injured persons. The plaintiff's solicitors gave the
bureau the particulars taken by the police of the insurance of the defendant
(certificate No. 381512 issued by Lloyds Motor Policies) and asked the bureau
if they could trace the insurers involved. The bureau asked the Royal Insurance
Co., Ltd. to investigate the matter, but without success. No-one has been able

A to trace the insurers or the defendant. These investigations took some time. So much so that the second twelve months was near to expiring on June 25, 1966. To safeguard the position, Nye & Donne, on June 23, 1966, applied for the writ to be renewed. It was renewed for a third twelve months until June 24, 1967; but during the third twelve months the plaintiff's legal aid certificate was discharged, and he acted thenceforward in person. The third twelve months was near

B to expiring when, on June 15, 1967, he applied for the writ to be renewed. It was renewed for three months until Sept. 14, 1967.

Now comes an important step. On June 22, 1967, the plaintiff applied for substituted service by serving the writ on the Royal Insurance Co., Ltd. He made in support this affidavit:

C " 1. Affidavit in support of an application for substituted service. 2. I, Frederick Gurtner, medical research scientist of 157, Marine Parade, Brighton, Sussex, make oath and say as follows: 3. As already mentioned in my application for renewal of the aforesaid writ, [the defendant] went to Canada still in 1961, and in spite of repeated endeavours, his present whereabouts cannot be ascertained. 4. With letter of the 3/12/1965, Messrs. Nye & Donne, Brighton, who dealt with this matter, informed me that the Motor Insurers'

D Bureau have passed the matter to the Royal Insurance Co. who would negotiate on their behalf. 5. I ask, therefore, for leave to serve this writ to the Royal Insurance Co. so that the latter may deal with the matter on behalf of the Motor Insurers' Bureau."

On reading that affidavit, Master RITCHIE on June 22, 1967, ordered that service could be effected by sending the writ by ordinary prepaid post addressed to John

E Christopher Circuit, c/o Royal Insurance Co., Ltd., 24/28 Lombard Street, E.C.3. In pursuance of that order, the plaintiff sent the writ in a letter to the defendant at that address. It, of course, never reached him. The Royal Insurance Co., Ltd., did not know his whereabouts any more than anyone else. They had no authority to enter an appearance on his behalf. Nor had the Motor Insurers' Bureau. No-one had any authority to enter an appearance on his behalf. It looked

F as if judgment would go against the defendant by default unless something was done. One may ask: why should anyone worry if judgment did go against the defendant by default? The answer is that the Motor Insurers' Bureau had every reason to worry. They had entered into an agreement with the Minister of Transport by which they promised to pay any judgment against a motorist if it was not satisfied by his insurers within seven days. Faced with this obligation,

G the Bureau were desirous of coming into the proceedings. They wanted to investigate the plaintiff's claim. They had got the statements of one or two witnesses who said that the plaintiff was himself to blame because he ran across the road. So contributory negligence might arise. The bureau also wanted to enquire into the amount of damages in case he claimed too much. He is said to have asked for £20,000 or £30,000. They also wanted to enquire into the order

H for substituted service so as to see if it was rightly made; and also to investigate the renewals of the writ. In order to be able to take these points, the Motor Insurers' Bureau on July 3, 1967, applied to be added as defendants to the action. Master RITCHIE granted the application on their giving an undertaking to satisfy any damages awarded to the plaintiff; but CHAPMAN, J., reversed that decision. He thought that, on the authorities, the Motor Insurer's Bureau could not be

I added as defendants.

The relevant rule is the new R.S.C., Ord. 15, r. 6 (2) (*b*), which provides that the court may order any person to be added as a party

". . . whose presence before the court is necessary to ensure that all matters in dispute in the cause or matter may be effectually and completely determined and adjudicated upon . . ."

That rule is in substantially the same terms as the old R.S.C., Ord. 16, r. 11, and nothing turns on the difference in wording. There were many cases decided on it; but I need not analyse them today. That was done by DEVLIN, J., in *Amon* v. *Raphael Tuck & Sons, Ltd.* (1). He thought that the rule should be given a narrow construction, and his views were followed by JOHN STEPHENSON, J., in *Fire, Auto and Marine Insurance Co., Ltd.* v. *Greene* (2). I am afraid that I do not agree with them. I prefer to give a wide interpretation to the rule, as LORD ESHER, M.R., did in *Byrne* v. *Brown* (3). It seems to me that, when two parties are in dispute in an action at law and the determination of that dispute will directly affect a third person in his legal rights or in his pocket, in that he will be bound to foot the bill, then the court in its discretion may allow him to be added as a party on such terms as it thinks fit. By so doing, the court achieves the object of the rule. It enables all matters in dispute " to be effectually and completely determined and adjudicated upon " between all those directly concerned in the outcome.

I would apply this proposition to the present case. If the Motor Insurers' Bureau are not allowed to come in as a defendant, what will happen? The order for substituted service will go unchallenged. The service on the defendant will be good, even though he knows nothing of the proceedings. He will not enter an appearance. The plaintiff will sign judgment in default of appearance. The judgment will be for damages to be assessed. The master will assess the damages with no-one to oppose. The judgment will be completed for the ascertained sum. The defendant will not pay it. Then the plaintiff will be able to come down on the Motor Insurers' Bureau and call on them to pay because they have made a solemn agreement that they will pay. They made an agreement with the Minister of Transport on June 17, 1946, by cl. 1 of which they agreed that, if a judgment for an injured person against a motorist is not satisfied in full within seven days, the Motor Insurers' Bureau would pay the amount of the judgment to the injured person. The agreement is well known. It is set out in full in a note to *Hardy* v. *Motor Insurers' Bureau* (4). It is true that the injured person was not a party to that agreement between the bureau and the Minister of Transport and he cannot sue in his own name for the benefit of it; but the Minister of Transport can sue for specific performance of it. He can compel the bureau to honour their agreement by paying the injured person (see *Beswick* v. *Beswick* (5)). If the Minister of Transport obtains an order for specific performance, the injured person can enforce it for his own benefit (see per LORD PEARCE (6)). If the Minister of Transport should hesitate to sue, I think that it may be open to the plaintiff to make him a defendant and thus compel performance. It is thus apparent that the Motor Insurers' Bureau are vitally concerned in the outcome of the action. They are directly affected, not only in their legal rights, but also in their pocket. They ought to be allowed to come in as defendants. It would be most unjust if they were bound to stand idly by watching the plaintiff get judgment against the defendant without saying a word when they are the people who have to foot the bill. I think that *Fire, Auto and Marine Insurance Co., Ltd.* v. *Greene* (7) was wrongly decided and should be overruled.

In my opinion, we should make an order allowing the Motor Insurers' Bureau to be added as defendants. They are prepared to undertake to pay any damages that may be awarded. This undertaking should be embodied in the order. On being added, they should be entitled to defend the action and to exercise all the rights of the defendant therein.

Once they are added as defendants, they would be in a position to urge that the order for substituted service was not properly made and should be set aside. It seems to me not to have been properly made. The affidavit in support was

(1) [1956] 1 All E.R. 273; [1956] 1 Q.B. 357.
(2) [1964] 2 All E.R. 761; [1964] 2 Q.B. 687.
(3) (1889), 22 Q.B.D. 657.
(4) [1964] 2 Q.B. 745 at pp. 770-775.
(5) [1967] 2 All E.R. 1197.
(6) [1967] 2 All E.R. at p. 1214.
(7) [1964] 2 All E.R. 761; [1964] 2 Q.B. 687.

A insufficient to warrant the order, for the simple reason that it did not show that the writ was likely to reach the defendant, nor to come to his knowledge. All that it showed was that, if the writ were sent to the Royal Insurance Co., Ltd., it would reach the Motor Insurers' Bureau; but the Motor Insurers' Bureau were not defendants at that time. So that would not suffice. It would be different if the defendant were insured with Royal Insurance Co., Ltd., but that was not

B suggested. In my opinion, therefore, the order for substituted service made on June 22, 1967, could be set aside if that would serve any useful purpose. If there were any possibility of tracing the defendant in Canada, substituted service should be ordered by advertisement; but that seems to be a useless procedure here. The practical course is to allow the order for substituted service to stand without incurring any further costs; and to allow the service to stand.

C   Next, the Motor Insurers' Bureau wish to set aside the renewals of the writ made on June 25, 1965 (for a second twelve months); on June 23, 1966 (for a third twelve months) and on June 15, 1967 (for a further three months). I do not think that those renewals should be set aside. The defendant was away in Canada and could not be traced so as to be served. That is a good reason for renewing a writ. LORD GODDARD said in *Battersby* v. *Anglo-American Oil Co., Ltd.* (8):

D   " The best reason, of course, would be that the defendant has been avoiding service, or *his address is unknown*, and there may well be others."

    Finally, the Motor Insurers' Bureau wish to lodge a counterclaim. They wish to say that, if the defendant is liable, they are exempt. They say that the condition in cl. 5 (1) (A) of their agreement with the Minister of Transport was not fulfilled in that the defendant was an uninsured person; and that they were not given

E notice of the proceedings against him within twenty-four days, as required by that condition. I do not think that there is anything in this point. The defendant showed his certificate of insurance to the police. He was plainly an insured person, even though his insurers cannot now be found. So cl. 5 (1) (A) does not apply. The bureau should not be allowed to put in this counterclaim.

F   I would, therefore, allow the appeal. The Motor Insurers' Bureau should be added as defendants and be entitled to defend the action and to exercise all the rights of the defendant therein. The Motor Insurers' Bureau undertake to pay to the plaintiff any damages that may be awarded against the defendant.

        DIPLOCK, L.J.: This appeal illustrates once again the legal anomalies which result from the method adopted by the Minister of Transport in 1946

G to fill a gap in the protection of third parties injured by negligent driving of motor vehicles provided by the Road Traffic Acts, 1930 and 1934. Under those Acts, although insurance against third party risks was made compulsory and insurers made directly liable to satisfy judgments against their assured, an injured person, although he had recovered judgment against a negligent defendant, could whistle for his money if (a) the defendant was not insured

H at the time of the accident or (b) his policy of insurance was avoided in the circumstances specified in s. 10 (3) of the Act of 1934 for non-disclosure or misrepresentation or (c) his insurer, too, was insolvent. To fill this gap, the insurers transacting compulsory motor vehicle insurance business in Great Britain, acting in agreement with the Minister of Transport, formed a company, the Motor Insurers' Bureau, to assume liability to satisfy judgments of these three

I kinds. Instead, however, of amending the legislation so as to impose on the Motor Insurers' Bureau a statutory liability to the unsatisfied judgment creditor as had been done by the Road Traffic Act, 1934, in respect of the liability of insurers to satisfy judgments against defendants covered by a valid policy of insurance, the matter was dealt with by an agreement of June 17, 1946, between the Minister of Transport and the Motor Insurers' Bureau.

    To this contract, for that is all that it is in law, no unsatisfied judgment creditor

---

(8) [1944] 2 All E.R. 387 at p. 391; [1945] K.B. 23 at p. 32.

is a party.   Although clearly intended by both parties to be for the benefit of   A
such creditors, the Minister did not enter into it otherwise than as a principal.
He was not purporting to act as agent so as to make it capable in law of ratification by those whom it was intended to benefit.   Many of them were not born
at the time when it was made.   The only person entitled to enforce the contract
is the Minister.   I do not doubt that, on the principle accepted by the House
of Lords in *Beswick* v. *Beswick* (9), the Minister could enforce it by obtaining a   B
judgment for specific performance which, once obtained, could be enforced
against the bureau by the unsatisfied judgment creditor in whose favour the order
for specific performance was made; but the Minister is the only party entitled to
bring an action to enforce the contract.   It confers no right of action against
the Motor Insurers' Bureau on any unsatisfied judgment creditor.   Nevertheless,
the courts have on a number of occasions entertained actions by unsatisfied   C
judgment creditors brought against the bureau to enforce on their own behalf
undertakings given by the bureau to the Minister under the contract.   In these
actions, in which the Minister was not joined as a party, the bureau has not
taken the point that the plaintiff was not privy to the contract on which he
has sued.   The court, for its part, has turned a blind eye to this.   Unless the
point is specifically raised, the court is entitled to proceed on the assumption   D
that the bureau has, before action is brought, contracted for good consideration
with the plaintiff to perform the obligations specified in its contract with the
Minister or has by its conduct raised an estoppel which would bar it from relying
on the absence of privity of contract.   This Nelsonian solution, however, cannot
be adopted where a party to the litigation does raise the point that there is no
privity of contract or where, as in the present case, one party is a litigant in   E
person who does not understand the point but in whose interest it is to take it
if it be a valid one.

Under cl. 1 of its contract with the Minister and subject only to the conditions
precedent in cl. 5, the bureau give an unqualified undertaking to pay to the
judgment creditor all sums remaining unpaid after seven days under a judgment
against any person in respect of any liability for negligent driving of a motor   F
vehicle.   The existence and the amount of the bureau's liability, of which the
Minister can obtain an order for specific performance for the benefit of the
unsatisfied judgment creditor, thus depends on the result of an action to which
the bureau is not a necessary party.   Although there may be a good defence
to that action, judgment in it may be obtained by default either collusively—
which is not the case in the present appeal—or because the defendant is unaware   G
of the action or through impecuniosity or for some other reason is not concerned
to resist it; and the damages may be assessed on such evidence as the plaintiff
chooses to tender without being subjected to cross-examination.   Clearly the
bureau have a lively interest, at any rate commercial, in seeing that all proper
defences in that action as respects liability are raised and that all relevant
material which tends to reduce the quantum of damages recoverable is adduced   H
to the court.   We have been informed that, in an attempt to mitigate the injustice
to the bureau of allowing assessment of damages on judgments by default to
proceed without critical scrutiny, it has been the practice of the Queen's Bench
masters, with the acquiescence of plaintiffs, to allow the bureau to be represented
at the hearing of the assessment to cross-examine the plaintiff's witnesses and to
adduce other evidence.   Save, however, with the consent of the plaintiff, this
sensible practice cannot be followed unless the bureau is entitled to be joined as a
party to the action, and, even where the plaintiff does consent, it is desirable that
this formality should be observed—if only to give the bureau a right to appeal
or to resist an appeal by the plaintiff.

In the present action brought by the plaintiff against the defendant in which
the plaintiff is now in a position to obtain, but has not yet recovered, judgment

(9) [1967] 2 All E.R. 1197.

A   by default, the bureau seek to be added as parties in order that they may take
steps which would be available to the defendant to set aside the renewal of the
writ and the order for substituted service of the writ on him, and, if the action
is not dismissed on either of these grounds, to dispute the defendant's liability
on the merits, to raise the defence of contributory negligence, and to dispute
the quantum of damages claimed.   In addition to these steps, which would be
B   available to the defendant, the bureau wish to raise a point which does not
concern that defendant in any way, to wit, that the defendant was an " uninsured
person " and that, since notice of the bringing of the proceedings against him
was not given to the bureau within the time limited by cl. 5 (1) (A) of their
contract with the Minister, the bureau are under no liability to satisfy any
judgment recovered against the defendant in the action.   If the court has any
C   discretion to grant the bureau's application to be added as a party so that they
may take the steps which would be available to the defendant if he wished to
contest his liability, justice clearly requires that the court should do so.   CHAP-
MAN, J., felt that he should follow the decision of JOHN STEPHENSON, J., in *Fire,
Auto and Marine Insurance Co., Ltd.* v. *Greene* (10) and held that there was no
such discretion.

D   The court's powers to order a party to be joined in an existing action are
governed by R.S.C., Ord. 15, r. 6, of which the relevant provisions are:

> " (2) At any stage of the proceedings in any cause or matter the court
> may on such terms as it thinks just and either of its own motion or on
> application . . . (*b*) order any person who ought to have been joined as a
> party or whose presence before the court is necessary to ensure that all
E   > matters in dispute in the cause or matter may be effectually and completely
> determined and adjudicated upon be added as a party . . ."

The bureau are plainly not " a person who ought to have been joined as a party ".
The action is perfectly well constituted without them.   The question is whether,
within the meaning of the rule, the bureau are

F   " a person . . . whose presence before the court is necessary to ensure that
all matters in dispute in the cause or matter may be effectually and completely determined and adjudicated upon . . ."

The *Fire, Auto and Marine* case (10) was an action by an insurance company
for a declaration under s. 207 (3) of the Road Traffic Act, 1960, which replaces
s. 10 (3) of the Act of 1934, that the policy of insurance of the defendant, who
G   was being sued for damages in a running-down action brought by another person,
was void.   If such a declaration were obtained, the bureau would become liable
under their contract with the Minister to satisfy any judgment obtained in the
running-down action against the plaintiff.   The bureau clearly had a commercial
interest in resisting the declaration; but this is not enough.   JOHN STEPHENSON,
J., accepted the analysis of the rule and the many previous decisions under it
H   contained in the exhaustive judgment of DEVLIN, J., in *Amon* v. *Raphael Tuck &
Sons, Ltd.* (11) and took the view that the court had no jurisdiction to add a
party against the will of the plaintiff unless the person seeking to be added was
(12):

> ". . . at least able to show that some legal right enforceable by him against
I   > one of the parties to the action or some legal duty enforceable against him
> by one of the parties to the action will be affected by the result of the action."

DEVLIN, J., in *Amon's* case (11), after analysing the previous decisions which
he thought disclosed conflicting " wider " and " narrower " constructions of the
rule, whose actual wording has varied from time to time but without affecting

---

(10) [1964] 2 All E.R. 761; [1964] 2 Q.B. 687.
(11) [1956] 1 All E.R. 273; [1956] 1 Q.B. 357.
(12) [1964] 2 All E.R. at p. 768; [1964] 2 Q.B. at p. 697.

its substance, finally came down in favour of an even narrower construction A than JOHN STEPHENSON, J. DEVLIN, J., said (13):

" The only reason which makes it *necessary* to make a person a *party* to an action is so that he may be bound by the result of the action, and the question to be settled, therefore, must be a question in the action which cannot be effectually and completely settled unless he is a party."

B

Tested by either of these criteria, the bureau do not qualify for joinder as a party to the present action. Applying DEVLIN, J.'s test, they will be bound by the judgment in the sense that, under their contract with the Minister, they can be compelled by him to satisfy it. Whether they are a party to the action or not, it is not *necessary* to make them a party so that they may be bound. Applying JOHN STEPHENSON, J.'s test, the legal duty owed by the bureau to the Minister C is not enforceable by either party to the action brought by the plaintiff against the defendant.

For my part, I do not think that either test should be treated as comprehensive. Both illustrate the undesirability of propounding general propositions wider than are strictly necessary for the determination of the particular case. The legal position of the Motor Insurers' Bureau, which DEVLIN, J., did not have in D mind in *Amon's* case (14), is unique. They will be bound by the judgment in the plaintiff's action against the defendant in that they will be under a legal obligation to satisfy it; but their legal obligation to satisfy the judgment will not be owed directly to the plaintiff. It will not be enforceable by him. It will be enforceable by the Minister by an order for specific performance in favour of the plaintiff and, if the Minister seeks and obtains such an order, the order E will be enforceable by the plaintiff himself (see *Beswick* v. *Beswick* (15), which was decided after JOHN STEPHENSON, J.'s decision in the *Fire, Auto and Marine* case (16)). The bureau's legal obligation differs from the statutory obligation of an ordinary insurer under s. 207 of the Road Traffic Act, 1960, owed to a judgment creditor in a running-down action to satisfy the judgment obtained against the assured, in that the insurer's legal obligation is directly enforceable F by the plaintiff in the running-down action, whereas the bureau's legal obligation is not enforceable by the plaintiff himself but is enforceable for his benefit by the Minister who is *not* a party to the action. Clearly the rules of natural justice require that a person who is to be bound by a judgment in an action brought against another party and directly liable to the plaintiff on the judgment should be entitled to be heard in the proceedings in which the judgment is sought to be G obtained. A matter in dispute is not, in my view, effectually and completely " *adjudicated upon* " (my italics) unless the rules of natural justice are observed, and all those who will be liable to satisfy the judgment are given an opportunity to be heard. In the case of an ordinary insurer, this does not arise in practice, since the standard terms of a third-party liability policy give to the insurer a contractual right to conduct the defence of the running-down action in the name H of the assured. As I read his judgment in the *Fire, Auto and Marine* case (16), however, JOHN STEPHENSON, J., would have allowed an ordinary insurer to be added as a party to a running-down action if the policy of insurance did not contain such a term; and this, I think, would be right.

For my part, I do not think that the rules of natural justice depend on a technicality as to the procedure by which the liability of a person who is bound I to satisfy the judgment obtained by the plaintiff in the running-down action is enforceable. So long as it is legally enforceable against that person either directly by the plaintiff or indirectly by the Minister for the plaintiff's benefit under such a contract as exists in the present case, the court has jurisdiction

---

(13) [1956] 1 All E.R. at p. 287; [1956] 1 Q.B. at p. 380.
(14) [1956] 1 All E.R. 273; [1956] 1 Q.B. 357.
(15) [1967] 2 All E.R. 1197.
(16) [1964] 2 All E.R. 761; [1964] 2 Q.B. 687.

A to add that person as a party and ought normally to exercise its discretion by granting his application to be added. I think, therefore, that the bureau are entitled to be added as a party to the present action and that to this extent, at any rate, this appeal should be allowed.

Having drawn attention to the undesirability of propounding general propositions, I desire to emphasise that my judgment in the present case is based on the

B special position of the bureau under their contract with the Minister. What reasons influenced the government to adopt this oblique and extra-statutory way of imposing liability on the bureau, despite the legal complications this involves, I do not know. The courts must, however, accept it as it is and try, so far as we are permitted by the rules, to make it work with justice to the bureau as well as to the persons for whose benefit the Minister made the contract.

C Nothing that I have said is intended necessarily to have any wider application than to this unique legal situation resulting from the Minister's contract with the bureau. I prefer to decide other cases on their own different facts when they arise.

The order of the learned master of July 14, 1967, ordering that the bureau be added as defendants, which was set aside by CHAPMAN, J., was made on an

D undertaking of the bureau to satisfy any damages awarded to the plaintiff in respect of the defendant's negligence, but without prejudice to their being able to raise in the action any defence on the question of their liability so to do. The undertaking to the court seems to me to be appropriate in the circumstances. The bureau's contract with the Minister is terminable on notice, but in the present case where the defendant has not appeared and is not likely ever to do so,

E it would, I think, be convenient to incorporate in the order adding the bureau as second defendants to the action, an express statement that they shall be entitled to defend the action and to exercise all the rights of the first defendant therein.

The bureau also desire, however, to raise in the plaintiff's action a counterclaim for a declaration that, even though judgment be recovered by the plaintiff

F against the defendant, they are relieved from liability to satisfy it because the defendant was an uninsured person, and the notice, which, under cl. 5 (1) (A) of their contract with the Minister, is a condition precedent to their liability, was not served. Counsel for the Motor Insurers' Bureau has frankly conceded that the issue to be raised by the proposed counterclaim is one of construction of that contract. I do not think that it would be right to allow him to raise

G it without joining the Minister as defendant to the counterclaim. There may possibly be cases where it would be proper to allow the bureau to raise a counterclaim for a declaration that the conditions precedent in cl. 5 (1) of the contract have not been fulfilled but, if counsel will forgive my saying so, I think that, on the facts of the present case, there is so little merit in the argument which he wishes to advance in the proposed counterclaim that it would not be right to

H increase the costs of the action by permitting its ambit to be extended by the inclusion of the counterclaim.

The bureau also applied to the master for an order setting aside the renewals of the writ, the order for substituted service and the service of the writ pursuant thereto. The master made such orders on July 28, 1967. These orders were not considered on their merits by CHAPMAN, J., since, as a result of his reversal

I of the earlier order adding the bureau as a party in the action, the bureau had in his view no locus standi to apply for them. It is this part of the appeal which has occasioned me most anxiety. The writ was first renewed on June 25, 1965, on an ex parte application by the plaintiff's then solicitors, supported by an affidavit which did not disclose sufficient information to justify the renewal of the writ in accordance with the practice laid down in recent decisions of the court. We now know, however, that the defendant had disappeared and there may have been some good explanation for the apparent delay in the attempt to find him. The bureau were informed on Nov. 8, 1965,

of the date of the accident and of the fact that a writ had been issued.   Had they   A
applied promptly then to be added as defendants and to set aside the renewal
of the writ, such explanation might have been available to the plaintiff.   But
the bureau in fact delayed until July, 1967, by which time the plaintiff had
changed his solicitors, the legal executive of the former solicitors concerned had
left their employment and the opportunity of ascertaining whether there was any
adequate explanation has been lost.   In these special circumstances, I do not   B
think that it would be right to accede at this date to the bureau's application to
set aside the orders for the renewal of the writ.

The order for substituted service obtained on the plaintiff's own affidavit,
for he was then acting in person, was obviously wrong.   There was no possible
reason for serving the defendant at the address of the Royal Insurance Co., Ltd.
In a case like this, however, which must be rare, where there is strong prima facie   C
evidence that the defendant is insured but it is not possible to ascertain the
identity of his insurers, an order for substituted service might properly be made
on the defendant at the address of the Motor Insurers' Bureau.   Such an order,
of course, should not be made except on evidence that all reasonable efforts
have been made by the plaintiff to trace the defendant and effect personal
service.   It is now common ground, however, that the defendant has left this   D
country and that there is no real prospect of tracing him.   In these circumstances,
it would only add unnecessarily to the costs to set aside the service in order
that a further application may be made by the plaintiff for substituted service
on the defendant at the address of the bureau.   Counsel for the Motor Insurers'
Bureau has not really pressed us to do so in the present appeal.   His main
anxiety is lest the impression should be gained that plaintiffs need no longer   E
search diligently for defendants before applying for an order for substituted
service on them at the address of the bureau.   I hope that I have said enough to
make it clear that this is not so.

I would, therefore, allow the appeal against the learned judge's order to the
extent of adding the Motor Insurers' Bureau as defendants to the action on the
terms which I have already indicated.   F

SALMON, L.J.: I agree with both judgments which have been delivered.
I would only add that, in my view, no person would be entitled to sue the Motor
Insurers' Bureau on its contract with the Minister other than the Minister
himself.   He may obtain an order for specific performance in favour of the
persons for whose benefit the contract was made (*Beswick* v. *Beswick* (17)).   G
I do not think, however, that any such person, not being a party to that contract,
can sue on it.   I agree for the reasons stated by my lords, that, in the circumstances of this case, the bureau is entitled to be added as defendants to the
action.

Appeal allowed in part.   H

Solicitors: *L. Bingham & Co.* (for the Motor Insurers' Bureau).

[*Reported by* F. GUTTMAN, ESQ., *Barrister-at-Law.*]

---

(17) [1967] 2 All E.R. 1197.

A

R. *v.* WARN.

Affirmed. H.L. [1968] 2 All E.R. 300.

[COURTS-MARTIAL APPEAL COURT (Winn, L.J., Fenton Atkinson and Browne,
 JJ.), November 20, 1967.]

B *Court-Martial—Civil offence—Consent of Director of Public Prosecutions required
 for institution of proceedings—Gross indecency between males one of whom
 under twenty-one years of age—" Proceedings "—Consent of Director of
 Public Prosecutions not obtained—Whether naval court-martial a nullity—
 Sexual Offences Act, 1956 (3 & 4 Eliz. 2 c. 69), s. 13—Naval Discipline
 Act, 1957 (5 & 6 Eliz. 2 c. 53), s. 42—Sexual Offences Act 1967 (c. 60) s. 8,
 s. 10 (2).*

C Under s. 8* of the Sexual Offences Act 1967, which received the royal
assent and came into force on July 27, 1967, no " proceedings " were to be
instituted, except by or with the consent of the Director of Public Prosecutions, against any man for the offence of gross indecency with another man,
if either of the men were at the time of the commission of the offence under
the age of twenty-one. By letter dated July 31, a naval court-martial was
D convened for the trial of the appellant and another man on a charge under
s. 42† of the Naval Discipline Act, 1957, and s. 13‡ of the Sexual Offences
Act, 1956, of committing on July 15, 1967, an act of gross indecency with
another man. The consent of the Director of Public Prosecutions was
not obtained. The appellant was twenty-five years of age and the other
man concerned was eighteen. On appeal against conviction,

E **Held** (by a majority of the court): accepting that the charge was of an
offence created by s. 42 of the Naval Discipline Act, 1957, so as to become an
offence against that Act, yet the offence so created consisted in being guilty
of a civil offence and since, in the absence of the consent of the Director of
Public Prosecutions, there was not a civil offence by reason of the conduct
charged, the conviction of the s. 42 offence was a nullity and would be
F quashed (see p. 344, letter G, post).

 R. v. *Bates* ([1911] 1 K.B. 964) applied.

 Per CURIAM: caution should be observed in applying *R.* v. *Jennings*
([1956] 3 All E.R. 429) to offences charged at military or air force courts-
martial under s. 70§ of the Army Act or Air Force Act, 1955 (see p. 342,
letter D, post).

G Appeal allowed.

 [As to the liability of a person subject to naval discipline for civil offences,
see 33 HALSBURY'S LAWS (3rd Edn.) 947, para. 1586; and for the comparable
liability of persons subject to military or air force law, see ibid., 1026, para. 1711,
text and note (*r*).

H For the Sexual Offences Act, 1956, s. 13, see 36 HALSBURY'S STATUTES (2nd
Edn.) 223.

---

 * Section 8, so far as material, is printed at p. 340, letter I, post.
 † Section 42, so far as material, provides: " (1) Every person subject to this Act who
is guilty of any civil offence (that is to say any act or omission which is punishable by
the law of England ...) shall be liable on conviction under this Act ... (c) ... (i) to
I such punishment (being a punishment authorised by this Act) as could be imposed on
the offender on conviction before a civil court of the like offence committed in England,
..."
 ‡ Section 13 of the Sexual Offences Act, 1956, provides " It is an offence for a man to
commit an act of gross indecency with another man, whether in public or private, or
to be a party to the commission by a man to an act of gross indecency with another man,
or to procure the commission by a man of an act of gross indecency with another man."
See in regard to this, s. 1 (1) and s. 1 (5) of the Sexual Offence Act 1967.
 § Section 70, so far as material, is set out at p. 342, letter F, post. For s. 70 of the
Air Force Act, 1955, which is in similar terms, mutatis mutandis, see 35 HALSBURY'S
STATUTES (2nd Edn.) 650.

For the Naval Discipline Act, 1957, s. 42, see 37 HALSBURY'S STATUTES (2nd   A
Edn.) 970.]

Cases referred to:

> Cox v. *Army Council*, [1962] 1 All E.R. 880; [1963] A.C. 48; [1962] 2 W.L.R.
> 950; 46 Cr. App. Rep. 258; 39 Digest (Repl.) 411, *294*.
>
> *R.* v. *Bates*, [1911] 1 K.B. 964; 80 L.J.K.B. 507; 104 L.T. 688; 75 J.P. 271;   B
> 6 Cr. App. Rep. 153; 15 Digest (Repl.) 1216, *12,404*.
>
> *R.* v. *Bryant*, [1955] 2 All E.R. 406; [1955] 1 W.L.R. 715; 39 Cr. App. Rep.
> 59; 15 Digest (Repl.) 863, *8298*.
>
> *R.* v. *Jennings*, [1956] 3 All E.R. 429; [1956] 1 W.L.R. 1497; 40 Cr. App. Rep.
> 147; 39 Digest (Repl.) 425, *358*.

Appeal.   C

The appellant, Peter John Warn, a naval rating, was charged that he on
July 15, 1967, committed an act of gross indecency with one Mullin, a man.
The charge was laid under s. 42 of the Naval Discipline Act, 1957, and s. 13 of
the Sexual Offences Act, 1956. He appealed against his conviction on Aug. 15,
1967, by a naval court-martial held at the naval barracks at Portsmouth. Mullin
was eighteen years old at the time of the alleged offence and the appellant was   D
twenty-five. The proceedings were instituted without the consent of the
Director of Public Prosecutions pursuant to s. 8 of the Sexual Offences Act 1967,
which came into force on July 27, 1967.

J. B. R. Hazan for the appellant.
A. F. Waley for the Crown.

  E

WINN, L.J., delivered the following judgment of the court: By leave of
the single judge this appeal is brought against a conviction by naval court-
martial sitting at the naval barracks at Portsmouth on Aug. 15, 1967. The
appellant, Peter John Warn, was then convicted on two charges which had been
presented against him. Evidence was given which, if accepted, established
that he had been guilty of conduct undoubtedly amounting to gross indecency,
in the ordinary meaning of those words, with another man serving with him who   F
was at the time under twenty-one years of age. The appellant himself was
twenty-five and the other man, whose name was Mullin, was eighteen. No
point is taken by counsel for the appellant about admission of the evidence which
was heard by the court-martial. No criticism is made of the summing-up or any
direction given with regard to the evidence or the onus of proof. It is quite
unnecessary for this court to dwell at all on the evidence. It may suffice to   G
say that the official documents relating to the evidence and the charges were
all marked " male eyes only ". The story was a disgusting one and, if the
charges were rightly pressed home to conviction against the appellant as a matter
of law then, there is no ground for interfering with this conviction.

The point which arises is quite a different point. It is a point of general   H
importance and not an easy point, coming up, as it does, as a novel matter,
very soon after the commencement of the Sexual Offences Act 1967, which
received the royal assent on July 27, 1967. I say at once that the view formed
by this court is not unanimous and the decision of the court is the decision of the
majority of the court.

The question may, I think, be shortly stated. It is this. Section 8 of the   I
Sexual Offences Act 1967—which came into force on July 27, whereas the court-
martial in question was convened by circumstantial letter dated July 31, four
days later, was ordered to be held by the Commander-in-Chief on Aug. 3 and
was held on Aug. 15—provides as follows:

> " No proceedings shall be instituted except by or with the consent of the
> Director of Public Prosecutions against any man for the offence of . . .
> gross indecency with, another man, . . . where either of those men was at
> the time of its commission under the age of twenty-one . . ."

A The word " proceedings " in that phrase is not defined by the Act of 1967.   It
does not seem to this court that by the use of that word " proceedings " Parliament can properly be taken to have indicated any intention to restrict its meaning,
and the effect, therefore, of s. 8, to proceedings taken in the civil courts of this
country.   " Proceedings " is a word often used in relation to courts-martial
and a glance at the Naval Discipline Act, 1957, itself shows that in several
B places in the Act of 1957 the word " proceedings " is used in relation to court-
martial cases.   If anything, there is a contrary intention indicated by the
Sexual Offences Act 1967 itself in s. 10 (2), since the latter part of that section
refers specifically to courts-martial ordered or convened before the passing of
the Act.   This court-martial was ordered and convened after the passing of the
Sexual Offences Act 1967.   The latter part of s. 10 (2) provides that the Act shall
C not have effect in relation to an offence where a court-martial for the trial of the
offence has been ordered or convened before the passing of the Act.

A further indication tending to negative any construction of s. 8 in so narrow
a sense as to deprive it of any reference to trials by court-martial is to be found
in s. 7 (2) of the Sexual Offences Act 1967, which refers expressly to any offence
under s. 13 of the Sexual Offences Act, 1956, referring there to a particular
D statute and an offence under a particular statute; indeed there are other references
in the same subsection.   No consent was obtained from the Director of Public
Prosecutions before this court-martial was convened, ordered or opened or at
any stage during the hearing.   Objection was accordingly taken by counsel
appearing for the appellant that the proceedings were for that reason incompe-
tent.   The judge advocate considered the objection, but rejected it in quite
E brief terms.   The objection was taken in these words:

> " Now, under s. 8 of this Act, sir, it specifically provides that no pro-
> ceedings shall be instituted except by or with the consent of the Director
> of Public Prosecutions.   I understand, sir, that that consent has not been
> obtained."

F Reference was made to the relevant dates and the section was read completely
and the objection was rounded off by reference to s. 10 (2) as an indication that
proceedings within the meaning of s. 8 do include courts-martial.   The judge
advocate advised the court:

> " Sir, in my view this is a point of law on which I should advise you, but I
> do not think I need call on the prosecutor to reply in this particular case.
> G My view is that s. 8 of the Act is a purely procedural section and, therefore,
> is not a bar to trial by court-martial under s. 42 of the Naval Discipline Act,
> which is the section of the Act all these charges have been drawn under.
> I, therefore, advise that the trial may be allowed to proceed, sir."

It is quite clear that the opinion has been put forward, particularly by those
H learned editors responsible for editing the Manual of Military Law (11th
Edn. 1965) and the Manual of Air Force Law (4th Edn. 1964), that the decision
in the case of *R.* v. *Jennings* (1) has general application in such a context as this
(2).   *R.* v. *Jennings* (1) related to a charge of careless driving brought against
the appellant in that case for driving a motor car in Germany.   He was charged
under s. 41 (5) of the Army Act, 1955, with a civil offence of driving in circum-
I stances which would have amounted to careless driving contrary to s. 12 of the
Road Traffic Act, 1930, if the driving had been in England.   It was held, that s. 21
of the Road Traffic Act, 1930, which required notice to be given of intended
prosecution within fourteen days of the alleged offence, was only a procedural
section: the court-martial was entitled to convict, although the procedure

(1) [1956] 3 All E.R. 429.
(2) See Manual of Military Law, Part 1 (11th Edn. 1965), p. 356, note (*c*); and
Manual of Air Force Law (4th Edn. 1964), Vol. 1, p. 376, note 9.

specified by that s. 21 of Road Traffic Act, 1930, had not been complied with. **A** In giving the judgment of the court, PILCHER, J., said (3):

" In the opinion of the court, the submission of the Solicitor-General is correct, and s. 21 is a procedural section. Consequently, in spite of the fact that the procedure provided for by that section was not carried out in this case, the court-martial were entitled to convict the appellant in respect of an offence of which he was guilty."

B

It is said by counsel for the Crown in this case, though not as his primary or main submission, that *R.* v. *Jennings* (4) does apply to the present case and that this requirement of the consent of the Director of Public Prosecutions is only a procedural requirement.   The court thinks that it is plain that that submission must be rejected.

C

Caution should be observed in the future by those concerned with these Acts before they apply in any other given case the same reasoning which they have set out in the manuals; for example, a note to s. 70 both of the Army Act 1955, (5) and the Air Force Act 1955, (5), to the effect that the requirement of consent does not apply when a person is charged under this section with committing one of the civil offences to which s. 70 refers, since the offence under s. 70 is an offence **D** against that Act, i.e., the Army Act, 1955 or the Air Force Act, 1955, respectively. The court goes no further than saying that caution should be observed with regard to matters arising under the Army Act and the Air Force Act, not being concerned on this occasion with either of those Acts but only with the Naval Discipline Act, 1957.

Counsel for the Crown's main submission (and I say at once that it seems to the **E** court to be sound) is that s. 42 of the Naval Discipline Act, 1957, is a section which creates offences.   It is an " offence creating section " and in that respect is properly to be compared with s. 70 of the Army Act, 1955, which fell to be considered by the House of Lords in *Cox* v. *Army Council* (6).   Section 70 of the Army Act, 1955, provides that:

" (1) Any person subject to military law who commits a civil offence, **F** whether in the United Kingdom or elsewhere, shall be guilty of an offence against this section. (2) In this Act the expression ' civil offence ' means any act or omission punishable by the law of England or which, if committed in England, would be punishable by that law . . ."

Accepting counsel for the Crown's submission, the court is of the opinion that the proper construction of s. 42 of the Naval Discipline Act, 1957, is that it means **G** that every person subject to naval discipline who is guilty of any civil offence shall be liable on conviction under the Act to the punishments set out.   The proper effect to give to that section is that it makes it an offence against the Naval Discipline Act, 1957, to commit (the offender being himself liable to naval discipline) any civil offence.   " Civil offence " is for this purpose defined by s. 42 (1) of the Act of 1957 as " any act or omission which is punishable by the **H** law of England or would be so punishable if committed in England ".   The appellant was charged with having committed a civil offence when subject to naval discipline.

It does not seem that the rules of procedure for naval courts-martial define with any precision the form in which charges are to be presented.   The court has been referred to the rules (7) made under s. 58 of the Naval Discipline Act, **I** 1957, which provide for severance of charges and provide for amendment of charges: but nothing is found there or elsewhere, so far as this court is aware,

---

(3) [1956] 3 All E.R. at p. 431.
(4) [1956] 3 All E.R. 429.
(5) See footnote (2), p. 341, ante.
(6) [1962] 1 All E.R. 880; [1963] A.C. 48.
(7) See The Naval Courts-Martial (Procedure) Order, 1957 (S.I. 1957 No. 2225), as to severance, para. 2153; as to amending charges, para. 2180.

A　which is comparable in any way with the provisions of the Indictments Act, 1915. As is well known, that Act provides for compliance with the rules contained in Sch. 1 to the Act, and, r. 4, relevant indirectly for the present purposes, provides (8):

B　" (1) A description of the offence charged in an indictment, or where one or more offence is charged . . . (2) . . . shall commence with a statement of the offence charged, called the statement of offence. (3) The statement of offence shall describe the offence shortly in ordinary language, . . . and without necessarily stating all the essential elements of the offence . . . (4) After the statement of the offence, particulars of such offence shall be set out in ordinary language . . ."

C　In the court-martial in respect of which this appeal arises, the charge sheet charged the two accused, the appellant and Mullin, both of H.M.S. Dolphin, persons subject to the Naval Discipline Act, 1957, and at the time of the offences specified in the charges subject to that Act, for that—and then there is a marginal note: " Naval Discipline Act, s. 42, and Sexual Offences Act, 1956, s. 13 "—

D　" On July 15, 1967, at about 00.50, he [the appellant], being a man, did commit an act of gross indecency with John Kevin Mullin, a man."

The second charge is the converse, charging Mullin in respect of indecency with the appellant and the third and fourth charges again are the charges relating to a period some fifteen minutes later.

Those are charges which could be said to be offences against s. 42 of the Naval Discipline Act, 1957, and against s. 13 of the Sexual Offences Act, 1956, or in the E　alternative could be said to be charges of gross indecency of a kind which is a civil offence by force of s. 13 of the Sexual Offences Act, 1956. As it seems to this court, in either form (and really there is nothing but a semantic difference between those two readings of the charge sheet) the charges are charges of gross indecency with a male person, one of the two persons charged being under the age of twenty-one, as the evidence revealed. It may be that until the evidence showed one of F　them to be under twenty-one, s. 8 of the Sexual Offences Act 1967, could not be said to have applied: but s. 8 does provide, in language which seems to the court not to permit of more than one interpretation, that any form of proceedings for gross indecency with another man, one of the two men concerned being under twenty-one, shall not be instituted, or if instituted shall not be brought to conclusion, except with or by the consent of the Director of Public Prosecutions.

G　The fact that s. 42 is an offence creating section, as counsel for the Crown submits and the court accepts, is borne out clearly, in the opinion of the court, by reference to s. 68 of the Naval Discipline Act, 1957, which provides, without reading it in extenso, that:

H　" (1) Where a person is charged with an offence under any provision of this Act other than s. 42, and it is not proved that he committed that offence but is proved that he committed any other such offence, . . . he may be found . . . guilty of the said other offence. (2) Where a person is charged with a civil offence under s. 42 of this Act and it is not proved that he committed that offence but is proved that he committed any other civil offence . . . he may be convicted of an offence under the said s. 42 in respect of the commission of that other civil offence."

I　That all seems to be consistent with the construction of s. 42 as creating an offence against s. 42 consisting of the commission of conduct which amounted to a civil offence against English law, and the particulars of the charge, even if none had been given, would have had to be added by way of supplement subsequently, amounting to charging as the breach of, or offence against, s. 42, gross indecency with another man. That being so, in the opinion of the court, the

(8) Rule 4 of the Indictment Rules, 1915, is set out in 5 HALSBURY'S STATUTES (2nd Edn.) 998.

provision of s. 8 applies and it was not competent for the court-martial to convict   A
in the absence of the consent of the Director of Public Prosecutions. The result
is that the proceedings (and I deliberately say " proceedings ") which the court-
martial constituted were a nullity.   The decision in *R.* v. *Bates* (9) applies.
There is no question of allowing the appeal in the strictest sense of the term.
The order of the court is that the conviction be quashed on the ground that it
was a nullity for the reasons that I have attempted to indicate.   B

There is nothing really more to be said except to mention, since it was helpfully
brought to the attention of the court, *R.* v. *Bryant* (10). It is unnecessary to
refer to it in detail. The substance of the matter is that the sergeant who appealed
to this court in that case was convicted by court-martial in Egypt of stealing
money, the property of the regimental institute. He had been charged under s. 41
of the Army Act, 1881, as re-enacted, with committing the civil offence of larceny   C
contrary to s. 2 of the Larceny Act, 1916. The court said that those words (11)
were surplusage since really he had been convicted of an offence against s. 41
consisting of larceny, and larceny existed at common law and it was not necessary
to refer to the Larceny Act, 1916. He was properly to be regarded as having
been charged and convicted under the Army Act, which was favourable to him,
since there was a limitation on the sentence to which he could be subject.   D

There is a point about limitation of time for bringing up proceedings, which the
court mentions to show that it has not been overlooked. It is provided in the
Naval Discipline Act, 1957, s. 52, that a person shall not be tried under this part
of this Act for any offence unless the trial is begun within three years after the
commission of the offence, disregarding any time during which he was a prisoner
of war or was illegally absent. Attention was drawn to the fact that there might   E
on the face of it be some conflict between that provision already mentioned in s. 7
(2) of the Sexual Offences Act 1967, which provides that with regard to any offence
under s. 13 of the Act of 1956, gross indecency between men, no proceedings for
an offence shall be commenced after the expiration of twelve months from the day
on which the offence was committed. The court does not think that there is any
difficulty in reconciling those two provisions since the specific provision in the   F
Act of 1967 applies to charges which are brought under s. 13 of the Sexual Offences
Act, 1956. These charges, as has been said perhaps too often already, are brought
under s. 42 of the Naval Discipline Act, 1957. They are charges of having committed offences against that section, but of having committed offences against
that section by being guilty of conduct which is a civil offence constituting
indecency between men. The convictions are quashed.   G

*Appeal allowed. The court certified under s. 1 of the Administration of Justice
Act, 1960, that a point of law of general public importance was involved, viz.,
" Whether the leave of the Director of Public Prosecutions is necessary to institute
proceedings for gross indecency contrary to s. 42 of the Naval Discipline Act, 1957,
and s. 13 of the Sexual Offences Act, 1956, at the trial by court-martial where one of
the men was at the time of the commission of the offence under the age of twenty-one ",*   H
and granted leave to appeal to the House of Lords.

Solicitors: *Registrar of Courts-Martial Appeal Court* (for the appellant);
Treasury Solicitor.

[*Reported by* N. P. METCALFE, ESQ., *Barrister-at-Law.*]

  I

---

(9) [1911] 1 K.B. 964.
(10) [1955] 2 All E.R. 406.
(11) I.e., the words " contrary to s. 2 of the Larceny Act, 1916 ", which were in
the charge sheet of the accused (see [1955] 2 All E.R. at p. 407, letter E).

ALDRICH *v.* ATTORNEY-GENERAL (ROGERS intervening).

[PROBATE, DIVORCE AND ADMIRALTY DIVISION (Ormrod, J.), April 10, October 9 10, 11, November 24, 1967.]

Legitimacy—Jurisdiction—Declaration—Whether court has jurisdiction to make a declaration of the legitimacy of some person other than the petitioner— Whether a declaration on a bare claim for it should be made, assuming that there were jurisdiction—Supreme Court of Judicature (Consolidation) Act, 1925 (15 & 16 Geo. 5 c. 49), s. 21 (b)—Matrimonial Causes Act 1965 (c. 72) s. 39 (1)—R.S.C., Ord. 15, r. 16.

By a petition, which in effect invoked jurisdiction under R.S.C., Ord. 15, r. 16 (which replaced the former Ord. 25, r. 5), the petitioner sought two declarations, viz., first a declaration that he was validly married in 1923 to E. and, second, that N. who was born in 1930 and died in 1965, was the legitimate child of the petitioner and E. N. left no assets within the jurisdiction. E. had died in 1954.

Held: (i) there was no jurisdiction to make the second declaration, that of the legitimacy of N., because—

(a) even if, underlying the second declaration, there were a claim for relief within R.S.C., Ord. 15, r. 16 (see p. 349, letter F, post), yet

(b) by s. 21 (b)* of the Supreme Court of Judicature (Consolidation) Act, 1925, the jurisdiction of the High Court to grant declarations of legitimacy was limited to cases falling within s. 39 of the Matrimonial Causes Act 1965, which did not confer jurisdiction to make declarations of the legitimacy of persons other than the petitioner (see p. 350, letters F, G and I, post).

Dicta of BANKES, L.J., in *Guaranty Trust Co. of New York* v. *Hannay & Co.* ([1914-15] All E.R. Rep. at pp. 39, 40) applied.

Dicta of WILLMER, J., in *Knowles* v. *A.-G.* ([1950] 2 All E.R. at p. 10) followed.

(ii) a declaration that the petitioner's marriage was a valid marriage at the date of celebration would be granted (see p. 351, letter H, post).

Per CURIAM: (i) where nothing was claimed but a bare declaration (as here, where there were no assets within the jurisdiction) the claim ought not to be entertained if the evidence in support of it could not be properly investigated and verified, as seemed to be the case here owing to the death of E. (see p. 351, letters B and C, post).

(ii) nor would it be proper to make use of the power to grant administration conferred by s. 2 of the Administration of Justice Act, 1932, so as to enable the petitioner to establish paternity by seeking a grant (see p. 351, letters D and E, post).

[As to petitions for declarations of legitimacy, see 3 HALSBURY'S LAWS (3rd Edn.) 100, 101, para. 156.

For the Supreme Court of Judicature (Consolidation) Act, 1925, s. 21, see 5 HALSBURY'S STATUTES (2nd Edn.) 350; and for the Administration of Justice Act, 1932, s. 2, see 9 ibid., 791.

For the Matrimonial Causes Act 1965 s. 39, see 45 HALSBURY'S STATUTES (2nd Edn.) 497.]

Cases referred to:
  Collett (otherwise Sakazova) v. *Collett,* [1967] 2 All E.R. 426; [1967] 3 W.L.R. 280.
  Garthwaite v. *Garthwaite,* [1964] 2 All E.R. 233; [1964] P. 356; [1964] 2 W.L.R. 1108; Digest (Cont. Vol. B) 123, *25a.*

---

* Section 21, so far as material, is set out at p. 349, letter I, to p. 350, letter A, post.

Guaranty Trust Co. of New York v. *Hannay & Co.*, [1914-15] All E.R. Rep. 24; **A**
  [1915] 2 K.B. 536; 84 L.J.K.B. 1465; 113 L.T. 98; 30 Digest (Repl.)
  174, *239*.

Har-Shefi v. *Har-Shefi*, [1953] 1 All E.R. 783; [1953] P. 161; [1953] 2 W.L.R.
  690; Digest (Cont. Vol. A) 243, *1071*.

Knowles v. *A.-G.*, [1950] 2 All E.R. 6; [1951] P. 54; Digest (Cont. Vol. A)
  974, *281a*.   **B**

Russian Commercial and Industrial Bank v. *British Bank for Foreign Trade*,
  [1921] All E.R. Rep. 329; [1921] 2 A.C. 438; 90 L.J.K.B. 1089; 126 L.T.
  35; *subsequent proceedings*, sub nom. *British Bank for Foreign Trade, Ltd.*
  v. *Russian Commercial and Industrial Bank*, 38 T.L.R. 65; 35 Digest
  (Repl.) 422, *1149*.

Warter v. *Warter*, (1890), 15 P.D. 35; 59 L.J.P. 45; 62 L.T. 328; 3 Digest **C**
  (Repl.) 419, *171*.

Wayland, In the Estate of, [1951] 2 All E.R. 1041; 48 Dige (Repl.) 166, *1452*.

Petition.

This was a petition by William Stanley Aldrich dated June 29, 1966, praying
for declarations (i) that he was validly married to Elsie Edith Aldrich, then
Elsie Edith Rogers, on June 8, 1923, at the register office in the district of West **D**
Ham; (ii) that one Nina Sheila Dyer, who was born to Elsie Edith Aldrich on
Feb. 15, 1930, and who died on July 3, 1965, was the legitimate child of the
petitioner and Elsie Edith Aldrich.

The petitioner was born on July 15, 1899. By his petition he alleged that
Elsie Edith Aldrich (whom he married in 1923) died on May 13, 1954; that
their marriage was subsisting until her death; that after their marriage the **E**
petitioner and Elsie Edith Aldrich cohabited and lived together, and that at all
times they were domiciled in England. The petitioner further alleged that
Nina Sheila Dyer was the child of Elsie Edith Aldrich, the child's birth being
registered by Stanley Hartop Dyer, who registered the mother's name as Elsie
Dyer, the child being domiciled in England at her birth. Stanley Hartop Dyer
died in 1945. The petitioner alleged that the child was in fact the child of the **F**
petitioner and Elsie Edith Aldrich.

Joseph Jackson, Q.C., and *Margaret Booth* for the petitioner.

J. L. Arnold, Q.C., and *A. B. Ewbank* for the Attorney-General.

J. C. Mortimer, Q.C., and *A. L. J. Lincoln* for Miss Esteves.

S. L. Newcombe and *S. J. Ladak* for the Swiss administrators.

                                                              G
                                              Cur. adv. vult.

Nov. 24. **ORMROD, J.**, read the following judgment: The question for
decision in this case, at this stage, is whether the court has jurisdiction to entertain
the present petition by Mr. William Stanley Aldrich. By his petition, Mr.
Aldrich prays for two declarations, namely, (i) that he was validly married to
Elsie Edith Aldrich (now dead) on June 8, 1923, at the register office in the **H**
district of West Ham; (ii) that one Nina Sheila Dyer who was born to Elsie
Edith Aldrich on Feb. 15, 1930, and who died on July 3, 1965, was the legitimate
child of the petitioner and Elsie Edith Aldrich. This petition in its original
form was brought under the provisions of R.S.C., Ord. 15, r. 16 (1), which was
formerly R.S.C., Ord. 25, r. 5. This is clear from its form and the earlier
interlocutory proceedings. Procedurally, the case has had a chequered career **I**
and is, on its facts, unique in my experience. In these circumstances it is
necessary to set out the salient facts which have given rise to this petition and to
summarise the procedural steps which have led up to this hearing.

The late Miss Nina Dyer died on July 3, 1965, in France but domiciled in

_____

(1) R.S.C., Ord. 15, r. 16, provides: " No action or other proceeding shall be open to
objection on the ground that a merely declaratory judgment or order is sought thereby,
and the court may make binding declarations of right whether or not any consequential
relief is or could be claimed."

A Switzerland, leaving a very large estate indeed, presumably derived from one or both of her former husbands, the Baron von Thyssen whom she married in 1954 and Prince Sadruddin Aga Khan whom she married in 1957 after a divorce from her first husband. Her marriage to Prince Sadruddin Khan was dissolved in 1960. At the time of her marriage to Baron von Thyssen, Miss Dyer acquired Swiss nationality which she subsequently retained. Her estate is being adminis-

B tered under Swiss law. The assets are mainly in Switzerland but there is, I understand, land in Jamaica to the value of roughly £50,000. There are no assets at all in this country. In an affidavit sworn on Oct. 13, 1966, exhibiting various documents including an earlier affidavit sworn by him on Apr. 21, 1966, and a copy of an entry in the register of births for the district of Kensington, recording the birth on Feb. 15, 1930, of a child named Nina Sheila to one Elsie

C Dyer, the petitioner asserts that the child referred to in that entry is identical with the Nina Dyer who died on July 3, 1965, and that the mother, Elsie Dyer, was in fact his wife, Elsie Edith Aldrich, to whom he remained married until her death in 1954. From his affidavit it appears that in 1929 Mrs. Aldrich left him, having formed a liaison with a Mr. Stanley Dyer with whom she lived until his death in 1945. Mr. Dyer was the informant who registered the birth of the

D child Nina in February, 1930. The petitioner, however, alleges that, in spite of her association with Mr. Dyer, sexual intercourse continued to take place between his wife and himself up to and including the period when this child was conceived, and that, although he and his wife never lived together after the birth of the child, she, on various occasions, made remarks acknowledging that he was the father of the child. The petitioner, on this evidence and in reliance on

E the presumption of legitimacy, claims that the child Nina was the legitimate child of his wife and himself.

The importance to him of establishing this fact arises from the provisions of Swiss law under which the lawful father has substantial rights in the estate of a deceased child whether or not the child left a will. In the present case, Miss Dyer left two informal holograph testamentary papers, which purport to be

F wills, by both of which she simply expressed the wish that the whole of her estate might be used for animals and directed that her friend Miss Betty Esteves of the U.S.A. should decide how it was to be used. Copies of these documents are exhibited to the petitioner's affidavit. It is not, I think, in dispute that in Swiss law these documents are valid wills, but there is an issue between the Swiss lawyers whether effect can be given to them. In accordance with Swiss law,

G steps have been taken to appoint three persons to protect the assets of the estate but they are not administrators in the English sense of legal personal representatives, a concept which does not exist in Switzerland. In these circumstances, it is difficult at first sight, to understand the purpose of the present proceedings in this court which has no jurisdiction over the estate of the deceased Miss Dyer, and why the petitioner has not taken the appropriate proceedings in the Swiss

H court to establish his claim to the assets which lie within the jurisdiction of that court. I understand, however, from counsel, and there has been some evidence about it from Maître Vernet who has sworn an affidavit and who gave evidence before me, that, under Swiss law, the issue of the true paternity of Miss Dyer is to be determined according to the principles of English law. Moreover, the existence of the birth certificate showing that Miss Dyer was the daughter of

I Mr. Dyer presents peculiar difficulties to the Swiss courts which are accustomed to regard the particulars in the register of births as binding until the register has been corrected. Moreover, the praetor in charge of this estate has indicated that he would be assisted by a ruling of this court. As I understand it, however, it would not be right to say that in Swiss law the only forum in which the issue of paternity could be decided is the English court.

This is the background to the present proceedings which have given rise to some formidable procedural difficulties which in themselves cast doubt on the jurisdictional aspect of the matter. In the first instance, there was difficulty

in finding a respondent since there is no legal personal representative in Swiss law, **A**
the so-called curators having no locus standi in this respect, and no identifiable
beneficiary under the presumed wills. In these circumstances, the matter
came before LLOYD-JONES, J., on Oct. 13, 1966, on a summons for directions. On
that summons, the learned judge ordered that there be no respondent to the
cause; that copies of the petition and of s. 44 of the Matrimonial Causes Act 1965
(i.e., the section which deals with the rights of persons charged with adultery **B**
to apply for leave to intervene in the proceedings), should be served on two
persons, Clarence Rogers and Stanley Rogers who are brothers of the late Mrs.
Aldrich; and that service of notice of the petition on the Attorney-General be
dispensed with. Clarence Rogers and Stanley Rogers have been served in
accordance with this order and have decided to take no part in these proceedings.
I am told that in Switzerland, as maternal uncles, they might have some interest **C**
in the estate even if Miss Dyer proved to be the illegitimate child of their sister,
Mrs. Aldrich. The fact that it was thought necessary to invoke a section dealing
with intervention by alleged adulterers illustrates the difficulties with which
proceedings such as the present are beset in this division.

Pursuant to these directions, this cause came on for hearing before me for the
first time on Apr. 10, 1967. There was no respondent and no intervener, but **D**
counsel for the Swiss curators and counsel for Miss Esteves, the lady charged in
the wills with the distribution of the estate among animal charities, were in court.
Counsel for the Swiss curators was present mainly to give such assistance as he
could, which was considerable, and counsel for Miss Esteves to obtain leave to
intervene to oppose the petition. His application was opposed by counsel for
the petitioner who argued that Miss Esteves had no locus standi in the matter **E**
at all. It was impossible to deal with counsel for Miss Esteves' application
without evidence from Swiss lawyers as to his client's rights, if any, in Swiss law.
Counsel for the Swiss curators, on the other hand, accepted the position that his
clients, as mere curators, had no interest in the present suit. Meanwhile, between
the order for directions and the hearing on Apr. 10, 1967, a decision of my own
in *Collett* (*otherwise Sakazova*) v. *Collett* (2), had been reported in which I held, **F**
rightly or wrongly, that a petitioner seeking a declaration of validity of his
marriage who had the qualifications set out in s. 39 of the Matrimonial Causes
Act 1965 (i.e., the legitimacy declaration section), must proceed in accordance
with that section and the rules made under it and could not adopt the less formal
procedure of asking for a declaration under R.S.C., Ord. 15, r. 16.

The first declaration for which the petitioner is praying in these proceedings is **G**
a declaration that his own marriage was valid and that he is within the terms
of s. 39. Accordingly, counsel for the petitioner accepted the position that the
Attorney-General ought to have been made a respondent to that prayer. In
the event I adjourned the hearing, directing that the Attorney-General be made
the respondent and asking for his assistance as amicus curiae on all other aspects
of the case, including counsel for Miss Esteves' application to be allowed to **H**
intervene in the proceedings. At the resumed hearing the differences between
counsel for the petitioner and counsel for Miss Esteves had vanished; not only
was there no objection to Miss Esteves intervening, but counsel for Miss Esteves
joined counsel for the petitioner in submitting that there was jurisdiction in
this court to grant both declarations sought by the petitioner. Counsel for the
Attorney-General did not oppose the first declaration but, as amicus curiae, **I**
submitted that there was no jurisdiction to grant a declaration that the late
Nina Sheila Dyer was the legitimate child of the petitioner and his late wife.
I am deeply indebted to counsel for the Attorney-General for his careful and
lucid argument and for the new and not altogether comforting light which his
fresh mind has been able to throw on this fast-growing side-shoot to the normal

(2) [1967] 2 All E.R. 426.

A work of this division, created by the decision of the Court of Appeal in *Har-Shefi v. Har-Shefi* (3). In that case, it was held for the first time that this division could entertain suits for declarations under R.S.C., Ord. 25, r. 5, as it then was.

The question which I have to decide in this case is whether there is jurisdiction under the Rules of the Supreme Court to grant a declaration that a person is or was the legitimate child of the petitioner. This depends on the proper con-

B struction to be placed on R.S.C., Ord. 15, r. 16, a question which has given rise to much difficulty and to many reported decisions. It was considered at length by the Court of Appeal (PICKFORD and BANKES, L.JJ., BUCKLEY, L.J., dissenting) in *Guaranty Trust Co. of New York v. Hannay & Co.* (4). The history of the rule is fully set out in the judgments and it is unnecessary to repeat it. It is not an easy task, however, to extract the ratio decidendi of that case, or to determine

C the limits of this rule, since there are differences in the reasoning adopted in the two majority judgments. Since BANKES, L.J.'s, criteria are probably wider than those suggested by PICKFORD, L.J., I propose to test this case by the former. BANKES, L.J., said (5):

" It is the person, therefore, who is seeking relief, or in whom a right to relief is alleged to exist, whose application to the court is not to be defeated

D because he merely applies for a declaratory judgment, or order, and whose application for a declaration of his right is not to be refused merely because he cannot establish a legal cause of action. It is essential, however, that a person who seeks to take advantage of this rule must be claiming relief. What is meant by this word ' relief? ' When once it is established . . . that relief is not confined to relief in respect of a cause of action, it seems to

E follow that the word itself must be given its fullest meaning."

Later, BANKES, L.J., said (6):

" The claim for a declaration is not in itself a claim for relief and no circumstances are shown from which an inference can be drawn that, underlying the claim, though not apparent on the face of it, there is a claim to relief which the court can entertain."

F In the present case, I doubt very much whether the petitioner has a claim for relief in this sense, and I am inclined to think that the petition is what BANKES, L.J., described as (7) ". . . merely a request to the court to supply them with evidence in a convenient form for use in the American action . . ." If this is right, then the court would have no jurisdiction to entertain the petitioner's

G suit. I do not think that this conclusion is affected by the words in the judgment which follow, to the effect that the respondents were attempting to obtain such evidence against the will of the defendants and possibly at their expense. The matter, however, does not rest there because, BANKES, L.J., laid down one absolute limitation, namely, that (5)

". . . the relief claimed must be something which it would not be unlawful

H or unconstitutional or inequitable for the court to grant . . ."

This brings me to counsel for the Attorney-General's principal point which, I am ashamed to say, is quite new to me. He has drawn attention to the provisions of s. 21 of the Supreme Court of Judicature (Consolidation) Act, 1925, which is in the following terms:

" The High Court shall have such jurisdiction—(a) in relation to matri-

I monial causes and matters, as was immediately before the commencement of the Matrimonial Causes Act, 1857, vested in or exercisable by any ecclesiastical court or person in England in respect of divorce à mensâ et thoro, nullity of marriage, jactitation of marriage, or restitution of conjugal rights, and in

---

(3) [1953] 1 All E.R. 783; [1953] P. 161.
(4) [1914-15] All E.R. Rep. 24; [1915] 2 K.B. 536.
(5) [1914-15] All E.R. Rep. at p. 39; [1915] 2 K.B. at p. 572.
(6) [1914-15] All E.R. Rep. at p. 40; [1915] 2 K.B. at p. 574.
(7) [1914-15] All E.R. Rep. at pp. 40, 41; [1915] 2 K.B. at p. 575.

respect of any matrimonial cause or matter except marriage licences; and
(b) with respect to declarations of legitimacy and of validity of marriage,
as is hereinafter in this Act provided . . .''

It is, of course, para. (b) of this section which is directly in point in this case.
Most unfortunately, this section was not brought to the attention of the Court of
Appeal in Har-Shefi v. Har-Shefi (8) or in Garthwaite v. Garthwaite (9), and I
myself overlooked it in both Garthwaite v. Garthwaite (9) and in Collett v. Collett
(10). I do not think that this omission affects the reasoning in Har-Shefi v.
Har-Shefi (8), but it might have affected the reasoning in Garthwaite v. Garthwaite
(9), in which a petitioner who lacked the necessary qualifications to enable her
to proceed under s. 17 of the Matrimonial Causes Act, 1950 (now s. 39 of the Act
of 1965), was praying for a declaration of the validity of her own marriage. It
may be, however, that a distinction can be drawn between a declaration that
a marriage is still subsisting and a declaration that it was valid ab initio. Had I
remembered this section in Collett v. Collett (10), my conclusion would have been
the same, but it would have been reached more directly.

The effect of this section on the present case is clearly of the greatest importance. Paragraph (b) lays down in express terms that the court shall have such
jurisdiction with respect to declarations of legitimacy '' as is hereinafter in this
Act provided ''. This is, of course, a reference to s. 188 of the Act of 1925 which
became, with minor amendments, s. 17 of the Matrimonial Causes Act, 1950,
and s. 39 of the Act of 1965. I find it quite impossible to construe this section
as meaning that the court has also a jurisdiction to grant declarations of
legitimacy under the Rules of the Supreme Court. If this were the effect of the
rule it would be inconsistent with the section. Moreover, the section itself is
subsequent in date to the rule, and it is not a mere re-enactment of a provision
in an earlier Act. In my judgment, the principle '' expressio unius est exclusio
alterius '' must apply, with the result that the jurisdiction of the court in this
connexion is limited to cases falling within the provisions of s. 39 of the Act of
1965. This section, by sub-s. (1), applies only to declarations of legitimacy of
the petitioner himself and of the validity of the marriage of his father and mother
or of his grandparents or of his own marriage. Subsection (2) provides for
declarations that the petitioner or his parent or remoter ancestor became legitimated under the Legitimacy Act, 1926. There is, therefore, no provision
for making declarations of the legitimacy of persons other than the petitioner.
This conclusion is in accordance with the decision of WILLMER, J., in Knowles
v. A.-G. (11), in which he said (12):

   '' In those circumstances I think I am precluded by a decision now
   sixty years old from making a declaration of legitimacy otherwise than in
   pursuance of the powers conferred by the Act.''

The reference is to Warter v. Warter (13), and the conclusion follows immediately
after a discussion of the effect of R.S.C., Ord. 25, r. 5. The learned judge also
pointed out (14) that, if the court had the jurisdiction claimed for it under the
rule, it would have been unnecessary to include s. 2 in the Legitimacy Act, 1926,
in order to extend the powers of the court to enable it to grant declarations to
legitimated persons.

For these reasons, I am obliged to conclude that there is no jurisdiction to
grant declarations of legitimacy otherwise than in accordance with the provisions
of s. 39 of the Act of 1965, and that, accordingly, the court cannot entertain the
second paragraph of the prayer to this petition.

(8) [1953] 1 All E.R. 783; [1953] P. 161.
(9) [1964] 2 All E.R. 233; [1964] P. 356.
(10) [1967] 2 All E.R. 426.
(11) [1950] 2 All E.R. 6; [1951] P. 54.
(12) [1950] 2 All E.R. at p. 10; [1951] P. at p. 64.
(13) (1890), 15 P.D. 35.
(14) [1950] 2 All E.R. at p. 10; [1951] P. at p. 63.

A   Had I come to the opposite conclusion, I should have had to consider very carefully whether this was a proper case in which to make such a declaration, notwithstanding the natural desire of this court to give every assistance to the Swiss court, because the court would have had to make findings of fact in a potentially highly contentious situation on the evidence of one side alone.   The death of the late Mrs. Aldrich, the only other person who could have given

B evidence on the vital issues, has, or may have, deprived the court of the material necessary to make an adjudication and left it without what LORD DUNEDIN in *Russian Commercial and Industrial Bank* v. *British Bank for Foreign Trade* (15) regarded as an important, if not essential, ingredient in proceedings of this kind, namely " a proper contradictor ".   I should make it clear, however, that, if this court had to decide this issue, i.e., whether the petitioner was the father of

C the late Miss Dyer, in proceedings relating to a claim which had to be adjudicated on in this court, the court would do so on such evidence as was available, e.g., in a suit by the petitioner claiming assets in this country.   Where, however, nothing can be claimed in this court but a bare declaration, the court, in my judgment, ought not to entertain such a claim if the evidence in support of it cannot be properly investigated and verified.

D   Finally, I must deal with counsel for the petitioner's suggestion that I might make use of the power given by the Administration of Justice Act, 1932, s. 2, to make a grant of representation notwithstanding that there is no estate.   In *In the Estate of Wayland* (16), it was held by PEARCE, J., that this meant no estate in this country disposed of by the will that proposed to be admitted to probate. Counsel for the petitioner suggested that, in such proceedings, the petitioner

E could establish the fact of his paternity in order to lead to a grant in this country to him as next-of-kin.   I do not think that, in any event, I could properly make such a grant in these proceedings which are entirely different in character. It would, at the least, be necessary to notify the Swiss court of any such application.   Moreover, I have the gravest doubts whether the section has any application to the present case.   Apart from *In the Estate of Wayland* (17), there is no

F authority on it, and it appears to me to be contrary to principle for this court to make a grant of representation in the estate of a person domiciled in some other country who died leaving no assets within the jurisdiction of this court. Such a grant in a case such as this would be nothing more than a piece of paper.

      In those circumstances, I hold that I have no jurisdiction to entertain the second paragraph of the prayer to the petition.

G   *Joseph Jackson, Q.C.*: In regard to the first prayer of the petition, the declaration of the validity of marriage, I submit that it is open to the court, both in jurisdiction and on the admitted facts, to declare that this was a valid marriage on two dates: first, on the date of its celebration, and second, on Feb. 15, 1930, which is the date of the birth of Miss Dyer.

H   **ORMROD, J.:** I am not prepared to go beyond the precise wording of s. 39 of the Matrimonial Causes Act 1965.   I am saying that the words " was a valid marriage " at the end of s. 39 (1) mean at the date of celebration.   I will make a declaration that the petitioner was validly married to Elsie Edith Aldrich, since deceased, on June 8, 1923.   The second prayer of the petition is dismissed for want of jurisdiction.

Order accordingly.

I
      Solicitors: *Coward, Chance & Co.* (for the petitioner); *Treasury Solicitor* (for the Attorney-General); *Herbert Smith & Co.* (for Miss Esteves); *Prentice Kirkwood & Co.* (for the Swiss administrators).

[*Reported by* ALICE BLOOMFIELD, *Barrister-at-Law.*]

---

(15) [1921] All E.R. Rep. 329 at p. 332; [1921] 2 A.C. 438 at p. 448.
(16) [1951] 2 All E.R. 1041; see at p. 1044.
(17) [1951] 2 All E.R. 1041.

A

NOTE.

ABBEYFIELD (HARPENDEN) SOCIETY, LTD. *v.* WOODS.

[COURT OF APPEAL, CIVIL DIVISION (Lord Denning, M.R., Diplock and Edmund
    Davies, L.JJ.), October 23, 1967.]

B

*Licence—Licence to occupy premises—Charity—Old people's home run by a society
    —Unfurnished room—Agreement for occupation of room on weekly payment—
    Society reserved right to take possession of room at discretion on one month's
    notice—Possession to be taken only if society considered it essential in the
    interests of residents—Bona fide decision by society to take possession—
    Occupier a licensee, not a tenant—Society entitled to possession.*

C

[As to the principles determining whether an agreement creates a lease or a
licence, see 23 HALSBURY'S LAWS (3rd Edn.) 427, 428, para. 1022; and for cases
on the subject, see 30 DIGEST (Repl.) 527-536, *1649-1711* and DIGEST (Cont. Vol.
A) 990-994, *1649b-1743a.*]

Appeal.

D

The plaintiff society, Abbeyfield (Harpenden) Society, Ltd., brought an action
by plaint dated Sept. 4, 1967, in St. Albans county court against the defendant,
Mr. Woods, claiming possession of premises at Laporte House, Milton Road,
Harpenden, Hertfordshire. By its particulars of claim the society pleaded
by an oral agreement in September, 1965, Mr. Woods was permitted to occupy
a bed-sitting room at Laporte House, the society providing food, heating and
light, and a residential housekeeper to cook meals and run the house: that Mr.
Woods agreed to pay £9 weekly for the accommodation and services, and it
was an express term that the society reserved the right to take possession of the
room on giving one month's notice to Mr. Woods. Such a notice was given by
the society to Mr. Woods on Nov. 25, 1966. The net annual value for rating
of Laporte House was £722. By his defence Mr. Woods admitted the agreement,
but pleaded that the right to take possession was subject to a proviso that it would
be exercised only when it was absolutely essential in Mr. Wood's interest. Mr.
Woods pleaded that the agreement constituted a tenancy agreement for a weekly
tenancy of the room, and denied that the society was entitled to possession.
On Sept. 29, 1967, His Honour JUDGE GRANVILLE-SMITH adjudged that the
defendant should give possession of the room to the plaintiff society within
twenty-eight days. Mr. Woods gave notice of appeal, dated Oct. 10, 1967.
The grounds of appeal were as follows: (i) that the judge was wrong in law
in finding that Mr. Woods was a licensee for reward and not a tenant; (ii) that
the judge misdirected himself in law in holding that the provisions of the Rent
Acts did not apply; (iii) that the judge was wrong in his construction of the
terms of a letter dated Sept. 9, 1965, written on behalf of the executive committee
of the society and containing the terms of the alleged agreement, and in particular
in the construction of the passage set out at p. 353, letter C, post; and (iv) that
the judge was wrong in finding that the plaintiff society had an unfettered
discretion in ordering Mr. Woods to deliver up possession.

E

F

G

H

J. Mulcahy for the appellant, Mr. Woods.
G. H. Crispin, Q.C., and *D. R. Stuckey* for the respondent society.

I

LORD DENNING, M.R.: This is a sad case. The Abbeyfield (Harpenden)
Society, Ltd. (" the society ") is a charitable organisation, a company limited by
guarantee. It has opened a home for old people called Laporte House at Harpenden in which it takes about a dozen old people in order to accommodate them.
In September, 1965, the society allowed Mr. Woods, who was, I think, then aged
eighty-five, to have one of the rooms. The society wrote him a letter, the
important terms of which I will read:

A   " You are at liberty to take possession of room No. 9 at the Abbeyfield
House as from Sept. 13 next. The amount you will be required to pay to
the society for this room will be £9 a week . . . The payments will allow you
sole occupation of your room and will entitle you to receive two main meals
each day . . . The cost of running the house, including heating, lighting,
fire insurance and repairs will be the responsibility of the society and the
B   society will also ensure that there will be a resident housekeeper at all times to
take care of the day-to-day running of the house and provide the daily
meals."

Then followed this important paragraph:

      " I hope you will understand that in order to make the Abbeyfield House
C   run properly, the society must reserve the right to take possession of your
room should it at its discretion think fit. You will, however, be given at
least one month's notice of the society's desire to take possession, and I do
assure you that this right will only be exercised in the event of the society
considering it absolutely essential in the interests of yourself and the other
residents of the house."

D The room was not furnished. Mr. Woods himself provided the furniture for the
room.
       A point has arisen whether Mr. Woods went in as a tenant or as a licensee. If
he were a tenant, he would be protected by the rent restrictions legislation. If a
licensee, he would not. I am quite clearly of opinion that he was there only as a
licensee. The modern cases show that a man may be a licensee even though he has
E exclusive possession, even though the word " rent " is used, and even though the
word " tenancy " is used. The court must look at the agreement as a whole and
see whether a tenancy really was intended. In this case there is, besides the one
room, the provision of services, meals, a resident housekeeper, and such like. The
whole arrangement was so personal in nature that the proper inference is, as the
judge found, that he was a licensee on the terms stated in the letter, namely,
F that the society would give him one month's notice and would only exercise that
right in the event of the society considering it absolutely essential in the interests
of himself and the other residents of the house.
       After the agreement was made, Mr. Woods went into the house. Everyone
liked him. He was apparently a dear old man. But he was blind. He got muddled
and could not look after himself properly. The committee very carefully con-
G sidered his case. They came to the conclusion, most regretfully, that he was a
danger there to himself and to the other residents, particularly in case of fire.
They communicated with his friends and with his solicitor. They had special
meetings to consider his case. They made arrangements for him to go into a
nursing home. They offered to help themselves. But to no avail. So, in the last
resort, they felt they had to act. On Nov. 25, 1966, the society served on him a
H notice to leave one month later. It was an unfortunate day to choose—Christmas
Day—but it was not acted on. He did not go. The Society took proceedings in
the county court. Old Mr. Woods himself came to court, now aged eighty-eight.
He said that he did not want to move: he was very comfortable.
       On the terms of this agreement the society has to " consider " whether it is
" absolutely essential " in the interests of himself and the other residents that he
I should go. That is a decision which is for the society. The society must exercise
it in good faith and honestly, not arbitrarily or capriciously. So long as the society
does so, the court will not interfere with its decision.
       I must say that the committee themselves seem to have considered this case
most sympathetically. Evidence was given by one of the committee, Mr. Ackroyd.
He produced the resolution of the committee. He said that Mr. Woods was a
danger to himself and the other residents: that everybody was fond of him, but
it was not safe for him or the home. It seems to me the committee acted very
properly and reasonably. No exception can be taken whatever to what they have

done. I think that the licence has been validly determined. Mr. Woods must go. A
This appeal must be dismissed.

DIPLOCK, L.J.: I agree. This is necessarily a sad case and the only thing
that I have to add is that I have taken the opportunity of reading a large number
of the letters which passed between the society and Mr. Woods' advisers; and it is
quite apparent from those that the society has done its very best to find for Mr. B
Woods accommodation either in a private home or in a county home where his
needs could be looked after, as they cannot be in the home which this society runs.
  I agree this appeal must be dismissed.

EDMUND DAVIES, L.J.: I agree, and have nothing to add.

Appeal dismissed.
C
  Solicitors: *Prentice, Kirkwood & Co.* (for the appellant); *Gillhams,* agents for
Tuckey and Rylatt, Harpenden (for the respondent society).

[*Reported by* Brian Pocock, Esq., *Barrister-at-Law.*]

D

METROPOLITAN PROPERTIES CO. (F.G.C.), LTD.
v. LANNON AND OTHERS.

[Queen's Bench Division (Lord Parker, C.J., Widgery and Chapman, JJ.),
November 20, 21, 22, 23, 1967.]
E
*Rent Restriction—Rent—Determination of fair rent—Evidence—Whether rent
   assessment committee bound to accept expert opinion.*
*Rent Restriction—Rent—Determination of fair rent—Rent assessment committee
   —Bias—Chairman living in other property of which associate company
   of landlords was landlord—Chairman's firm acting for other tenants in that
   property on similar matters in dispute—Whether sufficient interest to dis-   F
   qualify him on account of bias.*
*Rent Restriction—Rent—Determination of fair rent—Rent determined and
   registered to be single figure in respect of premises affected—Rent assessment
   committee to take into account future trends in assessing cost of services—
   Statement of principle on which committee acted with regard to services to be
   given—Rent Act 1965 (c. 95), s. 28 (1).*
G
  Three tenants in a block of flats in Oakwood Court, Kensington Gardens,
London, held under leases in each of which the rent reserved was apportioned
in two parts, one attributable to the occupation of the property with the
benefit of the landlords' general covenants, and the other attributable to
the cost of services which were to be rendered by the landlords to the tenants.
Each tenancy was a regulated tenancy for the purposes of the Rent Act 1965.   H
The tenants applied for a fair rent for each of the flats to be determined and,
pursuant to objection by the landlords to the rent officer's determination,
the matter was referred to the rent assessment committee. There was an
oral hearing before the committee at which expert evidence was called on
both sides to assist the committee in fixing the rent and in assessing the
value of the services to the tenants, and the committeee inspected the flats
at Oakwood Court but not a flat at Melbury Court, which was referred to
as a comparable property. The committee fixed as the fair rent in respect
of each flat an amount that was not only below the amounts put forward
by the experts called at the hearing on behalf of the landlords and the
tenants but also below those put forward by the rent officer. The committee
computed the amount of the rent for services on a basis that involved
deducting £10,000 p.a. from the landlords' schedule of charges shown in
respect of engineers' and caretakers' wages. The committee stated that

A   they had disallowed, among other expenses, management expenses. The chairman of the committee was a solicitor; he lived with his father, who was a tenant at Regency Lodge, the landlord of which was an associate company belonging to the same group as the landlords of Oakwood Court. The chairman's firm had from time to time acted for other tenants in Regency Lodge who were in dispute with their landlord on matters similar to those of

B   the present case. The flats at Oakwood Court were similar to those at Regency Lodge, while the rateable value and accommodation of the chairman's father's flat at Regency Lodge and of the flat of one of the tenants in the present proceedings was virtually the same. On appeal by the landlords under s. 9 of the Tribunals and Enquiries Act, 1958, they raised a question of bias (viz., the contention that the chairman had such an interest in the

C   proceedings in which the committee was adjudicating as to give an impression that he could not act in an unbiased fashion and thus to prevent justice from being seen to be done), and four complaints against the substance of the committee's determination. The first of the four grounds of complaint was that the committee erred in law in fixing the rent at less than the rent of the flat at Melbury Court when there was no evidence to support

D   an inference that the circumstances of the Melbury Court flat were superior to those of the comparable Oakwood Court flat; and the other three grounds of complaint, which related to the assessment of the element of rent attributable to services, were error in law in that (a) there was no evidence to support the deduction of £10,000, (b) failure to have regard to the likely cost of services over the whole period during which registration was to have effect

E   and (c) failure to take into account management charges.

     Held: (i) there was no sufficient connexion between the determination of fair rent for the Oakwood Court flats and any future determination concerning fair rent at Regency Lodge flats to give the solicitor-chairman that kind of interest in the Oakwood Court determination which would disqualify him on account of bias (see p. 362, letter C, p. 368, letter I, and p. 369,

F   letter A, post).

     (ii) the committee were able in law to act on their own impressions and on their own knowledge, and the complaint that they erred in determining a lower rent than that of the flat at Melbury Court when there was no evidence from which to infer that the Melbury Court flat was superior was misconceived (see p. 364, letter B, p. 366, letter G, p. 368, letter I, and p. 369,

G   letter A, post).

     Dicta of LORD GODDARD, C.J., in R. v. Brighton and Area Rent Tribunal, Ex p. Marine Parade Estates (1936), Ltd., ([1950] 2 K.B. at pp. 416, 419, 420) and of LORD PARKER, C.J., in Crofton Investment Trust, Ltd. v. Greater London Rent Assessment Committee ([1967] 2 All E.R. at pp. 1108, 1109) applied.

H   (iii) (a) similarly, in regard to the reduction of £10,000 p.a. in relation to services, the committee, taking the view that they did not wholly accept the evidence on behalf of the landlords and having no further evidence before them, were entitled to adjust the figures as they thought appropriate (see p. 367, letter G, p. 368, letter I, and p. 369, letter A, post).

I   (b) the assessment in regard to the calculating of the service element in the rent should be made as at the date on which it was to take effect and, therefore, it was proper to make the calculations on the footing that what was sought to be achieved was a fair rent as at the date of the application on which registration was to be effected; when, however, the assessment was necessarily made at a later date, it was right to take into account such future trends, e.g., of inflation, as were apparent, and in the present case there was nothing in the material before the court to suggest that the committee made their assessment on any other basis (see p. 368, letters A to D and I, and p. 369, letter A, post).

A

(c) although management expenses were not an inadmissible factor in assessing fair rent, the committee's decision was in truth that as management expenses had already been reflected in another part of the schedule before them (as wages) the particular item of management charge should not be admitted (see p. 368, letters F and I, and p. 369, letter A, post).

B

Per CURIAM: when a rent is determined and registered under s. 28 (1)* of the Rent Act 1965, it must be a single figure in respect of the premises affected, not apportioned between the part attributable to occupation of the premises and the part attributable to services; and when a rent is concerned with the provision of services, the rent assessment committee should endeavour to give in brief form a statement of the principle on which they have acted (see p. 364, letters G and I, p. 365, letter A, p. 368, letter I, and p. 369, letter A, post).

C

Appeal dismissed.

[**Editorial Note.** The letters of guidance to legal professional panel members regarding the effect of membership on their and their partners' professional practices are set out in the footnote at p. 359, letter F, post.

D

As to determinations by rent assessment committees, see SUPPLEMENT to 23 HALSBURY'S LAWS (3rd Edn.), para. 1571B, 5; and for a case on the subject, see 31 DIGEST (Repl.) 676, 7702.

For the Rent Act 1965, s. 28 and Sch. 3, paras. 3, 13, see 45 HALSBURY'S STATUTES (2nd Edn.) 844, 864, 866.

For the Tribunals and Inquiries Act, 1958, s. 9, see 38 HALSBURY'S STATUTES (2nd Edn.) 207.]

E

Cases referred to:

Crofton Investment Trust, Ltd. v. *Greater London Rent Assessment Committee*, [1967] 2 All E.R. 1103; [1967] 3 W.L.R. 256.

R. v. *Brighton and Area Rent Tribunal, Ex p. Marine Parade Estates*, *(1936)*, *Ltd.*, [1950] 1 All E.R. 946; [1950] 2 K.B. 410; 114 J.P. 242; 31 Digest (Repl.) 676, *7702*.

R. v. *Camborne Justices, Ex p. Pearce*, [1954] 2 All E.R. 850; [1955] 1 Q.B. 41; [1954] 3 W.L.R. 415; 118 J.P. 488; 33 Digest (Repl.) 157, *106*.

R. v. *Essex Justices, Ex p. Perkins*, [1927] All E.R. Rep. 393; [1927] 2 K.B. 475; 96 L.J.K.B. 530; 137 L.T. 455; 91 J.P. 94; 33 Digest (Repl.) 157, *105*.

R. v. *Great Yarmouth Justices*, (1882), 8 Q.B.D. 525; 51 L.J.M.C. 39; 46 J.P. 518; 33 Digest (Repl.) 154, *85*.

R. v. *Rand*, (1866), L.R. 1 Q.B. 230; 35 L.J.M.C. 157; 30 J.P. 293; 33 Digest (Repl.) 155, *89*.

R. v. *Sussex Justices, Ex p. McCarthy*, [1923] All E.R. Rep. 233; [1924] 1 K.B. 256; 93 L.J.K.B. 129; 88 J.P. 3; sub nom. *R.* v. *Hurst, Ex p. McCarthy*, 138 L.T. 510; 33 Digest (Repl.) 156, *104*.

Appeals.

These were three appeals by the landlords, Metropolitan Properties Co. (F.G.C.), Ltd., under s. 9 of the Tribunals and Inquiries Act, 1958, and the Tribunals and Inquiries (Rent Assessment Committees) Order 1965† for orders that decisions of the committee of the London Rent Assessment Panel given on Apr. 26,1967, in respect of the rents of three flats should be set aside, and that such other orders as the case might require should be made or that the matters should be remitted with the opinion of the court for re-hearing and determination by a committee of the panel. The grounds of the applications were—(i) that the committee erred in point of law in determining a rent (e.g., in respect of the flat 61 Oakwood Court) less than that determined for another flat, 48 Melbury Court, when there was no evidence to support the inference that the

---
* Section 28 (1) is set out at p. 364, letter E, post.
† S.I. 1965 No. 2151.

A circumstances of 48 Melbury Court were superior to those of 61 Oakwood Court; (ii) that in assessing the element of rent attributable to sums payable in respect of services the committee erred in point of law (a) in that there was no evidence to support their reduction of £10,000 from the landlords' schedule of wages, (b) in that they failed to have regard to a material consideration, namely, the likely cost of those services over the whole period during which the registration

B was to have effect and (c) in that they failed to take into account a material consideration, namely, management charges. The original notice of appeal was dated May 23, 1967, and by a supplementary notice, dated July 25,1967, the landlords gave notice that they would rely on the following additional grounds, viz., that the chairman of the committee making the decision (Mr. Lannon) was disqualified from hearing the cause on the ground that there were reasonable

C grounds for the landlords to believe that he could not give them an unbiased hearing.

Sir Derek Walker-Smith, Q.C., and M. S. Rich for the landlords.
E. A. Bramall for the tenant Mr. Zenker.
Nigel Bridge as amicus curiae.

The respondent Mr. Lannon did not appear and was not represented.

D Two respondent tenants did not appear and were not represented; the third Mr. Kitzinger (tenant of No. 31), appeared in person.

WIDGERY, J., delivered the first judgment at the invitation of LORD PARKER, C.J.: These are three appeals brought under s. 9 of the Tribunals and Inquiries Act, 1958, against a decision of a rent assessment committee formed from the London Rent Assessment Panel, who fixed three rents purporting

E to be fair rents under the Rent Act 1965, in respect of three flats in Kensington known as Nos. 31, 60A and 61 Oakwood Court. The appellants are the owners of Oakwood Court and, consequently, the landlords in respect of each appeal, and the three appeals, which raise identical issues, were heard together before the rent assessment committee, and by consent have been heard together in

F this court.

The three tenants hold under formal leases; the rent reserved under each lease is apportioned in two parts, one part being attributable, as it were, to occupation of the property, with the benefit of the landlords' general covenants, and the other being attributable to the cost of services which were to be rendered by the landlords to the tenants. The court has not had to go into the nature of

G the services in detail, but they include such obvious things as lifts, central heating, hot water and the like. The rateable value of each of the flats is a little under £400, and they were, as I understand it, not within the ambit of the former Rent Restriction Acts, but, by virtue of their rateable value, each tenancy is a regulated tenancy for the purposes of the Rent Act 1965. Accordingly, each tenant was entitled to, and did, apply to the rent officer asking him

H to determine a fair rent in respect of his respective flat. The rent officer made the determination as required under the statute, but the landlords objecting to the rent officer's decision, the matter was automatically referred to the rent assessment committee for determination. Thereupon the procedure to be followed is that set out in Sch. 3 to the Rent Act 1965:

I " 10. The rent assessment committee to whom a matter is referred under para. 9 of this Schedule may by notice in the prescribed form served on the landlord or the tenant require him to give to the committee, within such period, not less than fourteen days from the service of the notice, as may be specified in the notice, such further information, in addition to any given to the rent officer in pursuance of para. 4 of this Schedule, as they may reasonably require and shall serve on the landlord and on the tenant a notice specifying a period, not less than fourteen days from the service of the notice, during which either representations in writing or a request to make oral representations may be made by him to the committee.

A

" 11. Where within the period specified under the preceding paragraph, or such further period as the committee may allow, the landlord or the tenant requests to make oral representations the committee shall give him an opportunity to be heard either in person or by a person authorised by him in that behalf, whether or not that person is of counsel or a solicitor.

" 12. The committee shall make such inquiry, if any, as they think fit and consider any information supplied or representation made to them in pursuance of para. 10 or para. 11 of this Schedule and—(a) if it appears to them that the rent registered or confirmed by the rent officer is a fair rent, they shall confirm the rent; (b) if it does not appear to them that that rent is a fair rent, they shall determine a fair rent for the dwelling-house; . . ."

B

All that was properly done so far as the procedural steps are concerned; the parties desired an oral hearing before the committee, and had one. Indeed, the hearing lasted four days we have been told. The landlords and at least one tenant were represented by counsel, and a considerable volume of expert evidence was called on both sides directed to assisting the committee in the fixing of the rent, and in assessing the value to the tenants of the services rendered to them. In due course the committee gave their decision, and in some respects it was a startling decision, because the amount fixed as the fair rent in the case of each flat was not only substantially below that spoken for by the landlords' expert, not only below that spoken for by the rent officer himself, but also substantially below that spoken for by the expert called on behalf of the tenants. I do not wish it to be thought that that result in itself in any way invalidates the decision of the committee, but it is a decision which the landlords understandably regarded as somewhat unusual, and one which required the closest possible investigation. Whether or not in the end this court can give assistance to the landlords in their present complaints depends, of course, on whether the matter falls within the court's power under s. 9 of the Tribunals and Inquiries Act, 1958, and that section permits an appeal to this court only by an applicant who is dissatisfied on a point of law.

C

D

E

The first matter raised by counsel for the landlords in his submissions to this court has been that the decision of the committee is invalidated by reason of bias in the chairman of the committee, the respondent Mr. Lannon, which deprived the committee of jurisdiction. The matter is put in a supplementary notice of motion in this form:

F

" That the chairman of the committee making the decision was disqualified from hearing the cause on the ground that there were reasonable grounds for [the landlords] to believe that he could not give them an unbiased hearing."

G

For my part, I have the gravest doubts whether a complaint of that kind, which can no doubt be raised in an application for an order of certiorari, is a matter properly to be raised in this court in an appeal under s. 9 of the Tribunal and Inquiries Act, 1958. Nevertheless, by consent of all the parties, counsel for the landlords was allowed to deploy his argument on that point and to tender his evidence on the footing that, if appropriate, steps could be taken later to allow the landlords to move for an order of certiorari. I can, therefore, consider the arguments as to bias without reference to any defect in the proceedings.

H

The first affidavit dealing with this aspect to the matter was made by a Mr. Stern, who is joint managing director of the parent company of which the landlords are subsidiaries. He deposed to the fact that the respondent, Mr. Lannon, the chairman of the committee adjudicating in this case, resides with his parents in a flat at 55 Regency Lodge in Hampstead of which flat his father is the tenant, and of which flat an associated company belonging to the same group as the landlords is the landlord. Further, Mr. Stern deposed to the fact that the respondent Mr. Lannon, a solicitor, and his partner, have from time to time acted for other tenants in Regency Lodge who are in dispute with their landlord

A on matters similar to those which arose in the present case. He deposed to the fact that the respondent Mr. Lannon has personally been concerned in advising tenants of Regency Lodge in this connexion. In a further affidavit, he points out that physically the flats at Oakwood Court are very similar to those at Regency Lodge, and, indeed, he makes a comparison between 55 Regency Lodge where the respondent Mr. Lannon's father is the tenant, with 31 Oakwood

B Court, and shows that their rateable values are virtually the same, their accommodation is virtually the same, and that the determinations by the rent officer are such as to suggest that they are fairly comparable properties.

The respondent Mr. Lannon has himself put in two affidavits. He accepted the primary facts spoken to by Mr. Stern to which I have referred; he draws our attention to certain instructions which have been issued to members of the

C rent assessment panel who may be in professional practice in the same field in other parts of London, and it is quite clear that he has not infringed those directions (1). Furthermore, he says that it never occurred to him when sitting as chairman of this committee that he would in any way be putting his position as chairman in conflict with his interest in the flats in Regency Lodge. We have been told that in practice the rent assessment committees, in London, at any

D rate, do contain one solicitor and one valuer, and that, in order to ensure that these gentlemen shall be of the highest experience and quality, it is the practice to employ professional men who are themselves in private practice, and that, no doubt, is how it came about that the respondent Mr. Lannon has got this dual interest, if interest is the word, in these matters. Before I turn to the law on the subject, I think it is only fair to the respondent Mr. Lannon to make it

E quite clear that no actual bias on his part is here alleged. What is said is that he had such an interest in the proceedings on which he was adjudicating as to give an impression that he could not act in an unbiased fashion and thus to prevent justice from being seen to be done.

F (1) Two letters of the President of the London Rent Assessment Panel gave guidance in regard to professional practice by panel members before rent assessment committees. His letter of Apr. 7, 1966, read—" As a result of discussions I have had with the Lord Chancellor's Office, I am able to tell you that the Lord Chancellor agrees that while panel members who are professionally qualified may not practise before rent assessment committees drawn from the panel, of which they are members, partners may practice before any rent assessment committee drawn from that panel provided that the partner,

G who is a member of the panel, is not sitting on that particular rent assessment committee." A second letter of May 16, 1966, to panel members read—" In my letter of Apr. 7 I told you that the Lord Chancellor had ruled that rent assessment panel members could not appear before rent assessment committees in their own panel areas. Since then the question has been raised whether a rent assessment panel member can appear either as an advocate or a professional witness before a rent officer in his own panel area. I have been informed that in the view of the Lord Chancellor's department the arguments against a panel member appearing before a rent assessment committee

H apply with equal if not extra force to a member appearing before a rent officer in his own area. You will, therefore, shortly be receiving an amendment to the conditions of service of panel members which will make it clear that a panel member cannot appear professionally in his own panel area, although he may do so in another panel area. There is no objection to his partner appearing before a rent officer or a rent assessment committee on which he himself does not sit. I hope you will be able to make suitable arrangements in your practice."

I In relation to the present appeal, the chairman of the rent assessment committee deposed that his firm had acted for two tenants at Regency Lodge in connexion with the landlords' applications to the rent officer for determinations under the Rent Act 1965; that the firm acted for other tenants at Regency Lodge who, in direct negotiations with the landlords, agreed new rents without resort to the rent officer. The chairman deposed that he had not appeared before a rent assessment committee or rent officer in any case arising in London; further that Oakwood Court and Regency Lodge were in different registration areas under s. 22 of the Act of 1965, were totally different in character and situation, and that in adjudicating on the Oakwood Court objections he was wholly uninfluenced by any considerations relating to Regency Lodge.

Turning to the authorities, one goes chronologically first, I think, to *R.* v. **A**
Sussex Justices, Ex p. McCarthy (2), where LORD HEWART, C.J., gave the classic
dictum on this subject. The *Sussex Justices* case (2) concerned an acting clerk
to justices who retired with the justices and advised them in a criminal prosecution against a driver in a motoring offence. It so happened that, arising out
of the same accident, there was a civil claim, and the clerk to the justices himself
was a member of the firm of solicitors acting in that civil claim. On the occasion **B**
of the criminal hearing, the clerk himself did not attend, but sent his partner.
It was nevertheless held that the conviction of the accused must be quashed,
it being improper for the acting clerk, having regard to his firm's relation to
the case, to be present with the justices when they considered their decision.
LORD HEWART said (3):

C

"There is no doubt, as has been said in a long line of cases, that it is
not merely of some importance, but of fundamental importance, that justice
should both be done and be manifestly seen to be done. The question is
not whether in this case this gentleman, when with the justices, made any
observation or offered any criticism which he could not properly make or
offer; the question is whether he was so related to the case by reason of the
civil action as to be unfit to act for the justices in the criminal proceedings. **D**
The answer to that question depends not on what actually was done, but on
what might appear to be done. The rule is that nothing is to be done which
creates even a suspicion that there has been an improper interference with
the course of justice "

Shortly afterwards, a somewhat similar case of *R.* v. *Essex Justices, Ex p.* **E**
Perkins (4), confirmed this principle. It was another case of a clerk to justices
who had a professional interest in the proceedings, and I need cite it only for a
further expression of the principle, given by AVORY, J. He said (5):

"We have here to determine, however, whether or not there might
appear to be a reasonable likelihood of his being biased. If there might, then
justice would not seem to the applicant to be done, and he would have a right **F**
to object to the clerk acting as such."

LORD HEWART'S reference to "suspicion" is somewhat narrowed by a later
decision of this court, *R.* v. *Camborne Justices, Ex p. Pearce* (6). This was again
a case in which a clerk to justices had another interest which might conflict with
his position as clerk. Indeed, in that case he was a member of the county council
which was the prosecuting body in the case with which the bench were concerned. **G**
The facts need not be referred to in greater detail; I refer to the case primarily
for the question posed by SLADE, J., in giving the judgment of the court, and the
answer which the court later gave. SLADE, J., said (7):

". . . the question which this court has to decide is: what interest in a
judicial or quasi-judicial proceeding does the law regard as sufficient to
incapacitate a person from adjudicating or assisting in adjudicating on it **H**
on the ground of bias or appearance of bias?"

Then, having gone through the authorities in some detail, the learned judge
answered that question in this way (8):

"In the judgment of this court the right test is that prescribed by
BLACKBURN, J., in *R.* v. *Rand* (9), namely, that to disqualify a person from

---

(2) [1923] All E.R. Rep. 233; [1924] 1 K.B. 256.
(3) [1923] All E.R. Rep. at p. 234; [1924] 1 K.B. at p. 259.
(4) [1927] All E.R. Rep. 393; [1927] 2 K.B. 475.
(5) [1927] 2 K.B. at pp. 488, 489.
(6) [1954] 2 All E.R. 850; [1955] 1 Q.B. 41.
(7) [1954] 2 All E.R. at pp. 852, 853; [1955] 1 Q.B. at p. 47.
(8) [1954] 2 All E.R. at p. 855; [1955] 1 Q.B. at p. 51.
(9) (1866), L.R. 1 Q.B. 230 at p. 233.

A   acting in a judicial or quasi-judicial capacity on the ground of interest (other than pecuniary or proprietary) in the subject-matter of the proceeding, a real likelihood of bias must be shown. This court is, further, of opinion that a real likelihood of bias must be made to appear not only from the materials in fact ascertained by the party complaining, but from such further facts as he might readily have ascertained and easily verified in the course

B   of his inquiries."

Counsel for the landlords in his address to this court has invited us to say that the phrase employed by Slade, J., in the *Camborne Justices* case (10), namely, that there must be a real likelihood of bias, is, perhaps, putting the matter a little too high having regard to the authorities as a whole. He invites us to say that a safer test is to ask whether the litigant appearing before the adjudicator com-

C   plained of would have a reasonable impression that that adjudicator would be unable to bring an unbiased mind to bear on the problem. As counsel put it in a vivid phrase, the question here is whether the respondent Mr. Lannon's interest in Regency Lodge and all that goes with it would be such as to put him in a position of instinctive opposition to the landlords in the present case.

As I have said, no suggestion of actual bias is made; no suggestion is made

D   that the respondent Mr. Lannon would be likely to have any feelings of spite or malice towards the landlords merely because his father was in a perfectly respectable and well-conducted difference with them in regard to the rent of the flat at Regency Lodge. Nor is it sought to be said that the respondent Mr. Lannon has shown himself to be a " tenants' man " in the sense of having a predisposition towards tenants which would give him bias. What is said is that he had an

E   interest in this very case and an interest of the kind which would disqualify him on the authorities to which I have referred. What is the interest? As I understand it, it is simply this that, when the appeals with which we are now concerned had been heard and when fair rents had been determined and registered in respect of these three flats, those rents would form precedents for subsequent issues affecting Regency Lodge and the rents payable there. It is, of course, well known

F   that, in matters of this kind, valuers do lean heavily on what they are pleased to call " comparable properties ". They tend to support their opinion by reference to suppposedly reliable rents for other places, and the argument is that, when the rents in Regency Lodge came to be considered by a committee, if that ever happened, the committee would be influenced by the decision of the present committee in the Oakwood Court flats. That influence would be such, and would

G   be seen to be such by the landlords, that they would regard the respondent Mr. Lannon, and reasonably regard him, as someone who would, in counsel for the landlords' phrase, be instinctively opposed to their interests. The argument is that the connexion between the flats and Regency Lodge is so close that the decision in regard to these flats would have such a powerful effect on Regency Lodge that this supposition of bias would inevitably arise.

Reference was made to what counsel appearing as amicus curiae calls the somewhat colourful case of *R. v. Great Yarmouth Justices* (11), when something of that kind occurred. That was a case of six ratepayers who appealed against the poor rate under the procedure then in force, and one of the ratepayers was the mayor of the borough who in those days ex officio enjoyed the privilege of presiding over the court. The first five cases were disposed of, the mayor adjudicating, and when the sixth, his own case, arose he left the bench and left the decision to his brethren, but the report shows that the connexion between the mayor's case and the other five was so close that, once a decision had been made in one direction and one sense on the first five cases, the decision in the mayor's case was really a foregone conclusion. That, of course, is not this case. One must, I think, consider what the link or connexion between the case adjudicated on and the case in which

(10) [1954] 2 All E.R. at pp. 855; [1955] 1 Q.B. at p. 51.
(11) (1882), 8 Q.B.D. 525.

the respondent chairman is said to have a personal interest really amounts to. It **A**
may be a matter of difficulty, but for my part I am quite satisfied that the
connexion between the Oakwood Court decision and any future decision on
Regency Lodge is far too remote to justify the inference of bias on which the
landlords rely. I would not go so far as to say that no valuer concerned in the
Regency Lodge case would ever cite Oakwood Court as a comparable but, if he
were driven to rely on Oakwood Court as a primary comparable, he would be **B**
making a grave confession of the weakness of his own case. The two properties
are widely separated geographically and, although they may have physical
similarities, no valuer would, I feel, ever regard Oakwood Court as more than a
second line support for any case which he was making out in regard to Regency
Lodge. Accordingly, I for my part am satisfied as a matter of degree that there is
no sufficient connexion between the two cases to give the respondent Mr. Lannon **C**
that kind of interest in the Oakwood Court appeals which would disqualify him
on account of bias. The court has already given its decision (12) on that point,
and those are for my part the reasons on which that decision is to be supported.

One turns, therefore, to the substantial complaints against the decision itself,
which are to be found in the original notice of motion. Two of these complain
that the committee reached a conclusion which there was no evidence to support. **D**
In the remaining two, criticism is made that the committee failed to take into
account a material consideration which they should have taken into account in
their decision. Before looking at the detail of those four matters of complaint,
it is, I think, helpful to see how far a committee of this kind is required to act on
evidence in the way in which the court of law is undoubtedly required so to act.

The matter first arose shortly after the setting up of the furnished houses rent **E**
tribunals, and came to this court in *R. v. Brighton and Area Rent Tribunal,
Ex p. Marine Parade Estates (1936), Ltd.* (13). In that case, the tenants of premises
applied to a rent tribunal to determine what, in the language of the Act then relevant (14), was called a " reasonable rent " in respect of their premises. The
landlords opposed the application and called, one gathers, a volume of professional
evidence to support the figure which the landlords contended was a reasonable **F**
rent. The rent tribunal did not even look at the figures submitted by the landlords
but reached a decision of their own and determined a rent accordingly. In those
days there was no appeal from such a tribunal, and the matter came before the
court on an application for an order of certiorari. LORD GODDARD, C.J., in giving
the first judgment, referred to these matters and said (15):

> " When the matter came before the tribunal, the tenants called no **G**
> evidence, but counsel who appeared for them made certain statements.
> [Counsel for the landlords] has submitted that it was wrong procedure on
> the part of the tribunal to allow counsel to make those statements; but in
> point of fact no statement made was inaccurate, and the statements were
> afterwards accepted as accurate. Several witnesses called on behalf of the
> landlords gave evidence at length and do not seem to have been cross- **H**
> examined. It is true that at any rate one of them proffered to the tribunal
> certain schedules showing figures which the tribunal seem not to have
> examined: perhaps they would not have understood them if they had.
> That must be a matter entirely for the discretion of the tribunal."

Then he goes on to consider the regulations (16) which governed procedure
before such a tribunal, regulations which are strikingly similar to the provisions
of Sch. 3 to the Rent Act 1965 which I have read. Then LORD GODDARD said (17):

---

(12) At the conclusion of the argument.
(13) [1950] 1 All E.R. 946; [1950] 2 K.B. 410.
(14) The Landlord and Tenant (Rent Control) Act, 1949, s. 1 (1).
(15) [1950] 2 K.B. at p. 416; [1950] 1 All E.R. at p. 947.
(16) The Landlord and Tenant (Rent Control) Regulations, 1949 (S.I. 1949 No. 1096).
(17) [1950] 2 K.B. at p. 419; [1950] 1 All E.R. at p. 949.

A

"It is obvious, therefore, that Parliament intended that the procedure of these tribunals should be of the most informal nature that it is possible to conceive. No court of law can ever proceed to hear a case without having some evidence before it. No court of law can proceed to give judgments affecting people's rights of property unless those people not only are before it but have an opportunity of cross-examining the other side. It is quite obvious

B

here that Parliament has said that the ordinary procedure to which lawyers are accustomed shall not apply to these cases. The probable reason is, as the Attorney-General has stated, that it was supposed that the great majority of cases which would come up for determination under this Act would concern small properties—working-class properties—and unfurnished lodgings, though it may be that 'lodgings' is not the right word—but separate rooms

C

in houses."

Later, he said (18):

"Obviously, therefore, the intention of Parliament was that the procedure of these tribunals should be as informal as possible. Mr. and Mrs. Smith or Mr. and Mrs. Brown, when they want their rent reduced, cannot be

D

expected to have the services of expert witnesses at their disposal: if they go before a tribunal, all that they can say is that they think that they are paying too much—probably they will say that Mrs. Sykes round the corner is paying rather less than they are. That is the sort of thing which it was intended that these tribunals should have before them. The landlord may very likely appear with expert witnesses whom Mrs. Smith and Mrs.

E

Brown would be quite incapable of cross-examining; and it is not intended that there should be a hearing in anything like the way in which courts of law conduct their business or the way in which public inquiries under other statutes and other regulations are meant, but very often fail, to be conducted, so that they are the subject of many cases from the House of Lords downwards. Therefore, it seems to me, the tribunal must be able to act on their

F

own impression and on their own knowledge; otherwise the thing would come to a standstill altogether."

That is a decision affecting the furnished houses rent tribunal's jurisdiction, but it has been applied to proceedings before a rent assessment committee under the Rent Act 1965, by another decision of this court, *Crofton Investment Trust, Ltd.*

G

v. *Greater London Rent Assessment Committee* (19). That was a case which concerned the special provisions of the Act of 1965 in relation to scarcity, and the question was whether the committee had adequate evidence of scarcity before them. LORD PARKER, C.J., in giving the leading judgment of the court, referred to these matters and, dealing with the argument of counsel then appearing for the landlord, he said (20):

H

"His first point is that there was no specific evidence, oral or written, before the committee that there was a substantially greater number of persons willing to become tenants in this locality than there were premises to let available. He said there was no evidence of that, yet in para. (iv) of the decision which I have read they found that there was. For my part I am quite satisfied that this committee, that is to say a committee of this sort under a procedure which is clearly to be intended to be informal and not to be carried through with the precision of a court of justice, is fully entitled to act, as it has been said, on their own impression and on their own knowledge. It is idle in my view to think of gentlemen manning this committee and sitting may be day after day without acquiring experience and knowledge of conditions in the locality, and to say that they should shut their eyes to what they know

---

(18) [1950] 2 K.B. at p. 420.
(19) [1967] 2 All E.R. 1103.
(20) [1967] 2 All E.R. at p. 1108.

of their own knowledge, and act only on such evidence as may or may not A
be put before them, seems to me to reduce the matter to absurdity."

Then, following a reference to the *Brighton* case (21) which I have already read,
LORD PARKER said (22):

"It seems to me that every word of LORD GODDARD in that case is equally
applicable to proceedings before a rent assessment committee."

B

The point then is that the rent assessment committee are entitled, and indeed
in many circumstances bound, to use their own knowledge and impression. They
are, of course, bound as LORD GODDARD pointed out, to hear any evidence which
is tendered, but are not bound by expert opinion, and if, in the last analysis, they
find the expert opinion unsatisfactory, then they must use their own knowledge
and impression. Indeed, as LORD GODDARD pointed out, any other approach C
would render the procedure wholly ineffective in many cases. A judge in civil
litigation, who finds all the evidence unacceptable, can retire behind the onus
of proof and dismiss the plaintiff's claim; but the rent assessment committee,
once they embark on their enquiry, must produce a fair rent at the end of it all,
and if the evidence tendered to them proves unacceptable or unreliable what else
can they do but draw on their wisdom, experience and judgment and do the best I
that they can in the circumstances?

Another matter to which I ought to refer before I turn to the four points on
which this appeal depends is the provision in the Act of 1965 dealing with services.
This is material because much of the argument in this case turned on the portion
of rent attributable to services rendered by the landlord. Section 28 (1) reads:

"The amount to be registered as the rent of any dwelling-house shall
include any sums payable by the tenant to the landlord for the use of
furniture or for services, whether or not those sums are separate from the sums
payable for the occupation of the dwelling-house or are payable under separate
agreements."

Subsection (3) contains a provision for the variation of service charges in the
event of a fluctuation in the cost of providing services. I do not find the meaning
of s. 28 (1) particularly clear. It is, however, I think beyond doubt that, when
a rent is determined and registered, it must be a single figure in respect of the
premises affected, not condescending to apportionment between that part
attributable to occupation of the premises and that part attributable to services.
Indeed, I can find no obligation in the Act itself on the rent assessment committee
to make any specific assessment of the part of the rent attributable to services,
but we are told that in practice this is done, and I would not seek to discourage
what seems to be a desirable practice. Further, I think that it is worth while at
this stage in the development of the Act to point out to rent assessment committees that an undue insistence on the strict letter of the law on this point
may be unwise, because they are, independently of the Act, required to give reasons
for their decision, and, unless such reasons are given coherently, the right of appeal
to this court on a point of law may become ineffectual, or at least the proceedings
may become extremely lengthy, complicated and difficult. Accordingly, I would
put it as a very strong recommendation to rent assessment committees, if no
higher, that, when the rent is concerned with the provision of services, they
should endeavour always to give in brief form a statement of the principle on
which they have acted. If the landlord, as he usually does, calls evidence of the
cost of providing the services, the committee need not adopt that approach, but
they must listen to the evidence, and, if they choose not to adopt that approach,
it is of the greatest possible value in considering the correctness of their decision
if they say why they have not adopted that approach and what approach they
have in fact chosen. They should, in my view, always endeavour to show in a few

(21) [1950] 1 All E.R. 946; [1950] 2 K.B. 410.
(22) [1967] 2 All E.R. at p. 1109.

A lines and without condescending to detailed calculations how they have approached the question of services; have they used costs and, if so, how have they used costs, and if they have not used costs, what is their approach, and why have they adopted it? In saying that, I would not wish for a moment to restrict rent assessment committees in the wide discretion which Parliament has given them, but I think it desirable that they should act in this way if only to achieve

B the other intention of Parliament that their decisions shall be capable of effective review on matters of law by this court.

The decision itself in this case is a lengthy one, and I need not read it in full. The first six or seven pages of typescript review the evidence which was given before the committee, and then they come to deal with their inspections of the physical properties. They say that they made an inspection of Oakwood Court

C which, from the evidence adduced on behalf of the landlords, they expected to be a block of flats far superior to that which they actually found.

" We found flat 31 to be extremely dark, and formed the opinion that electric light would be required in the hall, kitchen and one bedroom during most of the day. In particular we found the rear aspect unsavoury, there being a stack of rain sodden rotting timber close to the walls of the flat in a

D dirty area into which water was dripping and flooding. This certainly detracted from the amenity of the flat as a whole."

That, I think, is an important finding of the committee, because it may well have a very strong bearing on the conclusion to which I earlier referred, namely, a conclusion to fix the rent lower than that spoken to by all those who had given evidence before them. Then they deal with the comparable properties to which

E they were referred.   They say that:

" The only flat in the exact same locality is 48 Melbury Court and whilst we could not inspect the interior, the general appearance of the block and the entrance halls were of a far higher standard than that of Oakwood Court. The size of the flat was similar to that of 31 Oakwood Court and provided

F a basis for comparison . . ."

They then give the areas to show that they are comparable. The committee go on:

" The fair rent of Melbury Court has been determined by the rent officer at £600, and the committee is of the opinion that this figure should serve to guide us."

G I must come back to Melbury Court in a moment. Meanwhile, continuing with the decision, the committee refer to an argument about institutional rents which I can omit. Then their final conclusions are expressed:

" The amount for services has been computed on the basis of a deduction of £10,000 p.a. from the landlords' schedule of charges of the amount shown in

H respect of engineers' and caretakers' wages, so that the figure is now approximately the same as placed before the rent officer as being the figure at that time. To clarify the point, the landlords stated that the figure given to the rent officer was based on the vendors' figures for the year ended Dec. 31, 1964, as computed to reflect subsequent material changes. In addition, we have totally disallowed charges made for insurance, estate office expenses,

I fire extinguisher rental, estate office telephone and management charges, as we do not accept that any of these are services supplied to or for the benefit of the tenants, nor is any provision made for the payment of the same by the lessees in their leases as is normal if the lessors intend their lessees to contribute. Indeed under the leases the landlords' covenant is limited to the supply of hot water, central heating and to the cleaning and maintenance of lifts, staircases and passages. The committee accept however that other services, including porterage, are supplied and that there is a reasonable expectation on the tenants' part that the same will continue. The committee

have therefore reduced the service charge in each case by one third of the
amount put forward by Mr. Weaver (23)."

In the last paragraph, having made a reference to s. 28 (3) of the Act of 1965,
which I need not read, they say:

" Accordingly, we find the amount to be registered as the rent of flat 31 is
£575 of which the sum of £167 is attributable to services, flat 60A £515 in
respect of which £150 is for services, flat 61 £550 in respect of which £135 is
in respect of services . . ."

It is to be observed that, although in those passages which I have read the
committee deal with a number of aspects affecting the proper charge for services,
there is nowhere any statement at all how they arrived at their basic figure
for that part of the rent which is attributable to the occupation of the premises.
We have only the fact that Melbury Court provides a guide, and the conclusions
which I have read.

Turning to the four points raised in the notice of motion, the first is in these
terms:

" That the committee erred in point of law in determining a rent in
respect of the flat less than that determined for 48 Melbury Court when there
was no evidence to support the inference that the circumstances of 48
Melbury Court were superior to those of No. 61 Oakwood Court."

The history of the intervention of 48 Melbury Court into these proceedings was
that it was first referred to by the rent officer as one of the factors affecting his
decision, and then at the hearing before the committee each party referred to it,
no doubt endeavouring to interpret its circumstances in a way favourable to his
own case. There is, as we have been shown, some evidence to suggest that some
valuers thought that Melbury Court was superior to Oakwood Court, and there
is other evidence of at least one valuer who took the opposite view. The committee, as I have said, assessed figures for Oakwood Court which are considerably
below, in total terms, those fixed by the rent officer for 48 Melbury Court, but,
in my judgment, the complaint in this case in the terms which I have read is
wholly misconceived, because there can in no circumstances be any question of a
rent assessment committee being required to treat a particular comparable as
being a determining factor in the absence of some evidence to the contrary. For
the reasons which I hope that I have already adequately given, the argument of
no evidence is one which has little or no place in this kind of proceeding, and
certainly the complaint as stated in the notice is, in my judgment, misconceived.

At one time in the course of argument it seemed that Melbury Court was
assuming a rather more significant position in this case, because at one time it
seemed possible that the committee here had taken Melbury Court, as it were,
as the linchpin of their calculations, and had fixed the rent in the instant cases
merely by appropriate adjustment on the Melbury Court rent. That theory was
given support by the absence of any other reasons being given in the decision
in this case to show how the assessed rents were arrived at by the committee.
If the committee had regarded Melbury Court as being of that predominant
importance they would, in my judgment, have been exceedingly unwise. They
never went into the flat to see what it was like inside; they never enquired what
services were provided for in the total rent which the rent officer had fixed, and
although they were, I accept, perfectly entitled to regard Melbury Court as a
guide, check or comparison, it would, in my judgment, have been exceedingly
unwise to have attached the kind of importance to the Melbury Court rent
which at one time it seemed to have assumed in the argument. For myself,
having considered this case with care, and having read the whole of the decision

---

(23) The assistant controller of the landlords' company.

A and the evidence to which we have been referred, I feel satisfied that it cannot be said here that the committee attached this overwhelming importance to Melbury Court, and accordingly, as it seems to me, they did no more, or at any rate we should not assume that they did more, than make their assessment of the Oakwood Court rents on their own knowledge and experience, taking such guid- ance as they thought proper from the expert evidence and using the rent of B 48 Melbury Court, as they themselves say, as a guide only.

The next complaint is that there was no evidence to support the deduction of £10,000 from the landlords' schedule of wages, to which I have already briefly referred in reading the decision of the committee. What happened here was that the landlords called a Mr. Weaver to give evidence of the cost which the landlords had suffered in the provision of services at Oakwood Court. Mr. Weaver's schedule C sets out a detailed cost totalling some £54,000. It seems that, when Mr. Weaver was subjected to an effective cross-examination by counsel for Mr. Zenker (24), a serious weakness in these figures was detected. In particular, the opening figure of some £27,000 for engineering and caretakers' wages was shown not to be related, as originally was thought, to wages paid over the whole of the year 1966, but to a limited period at the beginning of 1967. In an endeavour to perform a D rescue operation on that point the landlords then called a Mr. Mendelsohn (25), who gave evidence relating to the costs of services during the year 1966, and the effect of his evidence was that Mr. Weaver's figures were some £6,000 overstated. A deduction of £6,000 would, therefore, clearly have been in order on the part of the committee, but complaint is made that they went further and deducted £10,000. The committee reinforced themselves in making a deduction of £10,000 E by referring to yet earlier figures which had been submitted to the rent officer. We have a schedule of these and they total £45,000, or approximately £10,000 less than Mr. Weaver's total. It was quite true, as counsel for the landlords demonstrated to us, that the weaknesses in Mr. Weaver's schedule as disclosed in cross-examination could not in themselves have justified a deduction of £10,000, but, in my judgment, what the committee have done here is to reject Mr. F Weaver's evidence for reasons which clearly were considered by them adequate, and to be not entirely content to accept on their face value the figures given by Mr. Mendelsohn. For reasons which I have already given, it was open to the committee to take that view of that evidence if they thought right, and, if they were unable to base themselves on Mr. Weaver or Mr. Mendelsohn, I repeat the question which I posed to myself earlier: what could they do except do their best in the circumstances? This is a case in which, using no doubt a very blunt instrument, they have endeavoured to adjust the figures to those which they think appropriate. They could not have used a precision instrument because they had no reliable precise information on which to work and, taking that view of what the committee has done, there is no remaining ground for objection on this point.

The third complaint is that the committee failed to have regard to a material consideration, namely, the likely cost of those services over the whole period during which the registration was to have effect. This raises a point which con- cerns the provisions of the Schedule to the Rent Act 1965, for reconsideration and re-assessment of registered rents. Under para. 3 of Sch. 3, there is a provision which in broad terms prevents any review of a registered rent for a period of three years, and in para. 13 of the same Schedule there is a provision that the registra- tion of any rent when entered shall take effect as from the date of the application for the registration. Applied to this case, that means that the rent when registered would be deemed to have been so registered ever since the date of the initial application, which was February, 1966. Accordingly, the question arises what is

---

(24) The tenant of No. 61 Oakwood Court.
(25) Service charge accountant with the landlords' company.

the date on which an assessment in regard to the cost of services should be made, **A**
if that is the course chosen by the committee for calculating the service element
in the rent. For my part, I think that the principle is clear, namely, that the
assessment should be made as at the date on which it is to take effect and that,
therefore, it is proper to make one's calculations on the footing that what is
sought to be achieved is a fair rent as at the date of the application on which
registration will be effected. Nevertheless, I fully accede to counsel for the **B**
landlords' argument that, when the assessment is necessarily made at a later
date, and when at that later date trends of inflation, or whatever there may be,
are apparent, it is right and proper for the committee to take advantage of that
information, because, even when assessing at the date of application, they should
try and forecast future trends, and, if in fact they have direct information as to
what those trends may be it is proper to take those into account. However, **C**
in this case, I find it quite impossible to determine precisely on what basis these
calculations were made. Mr. Mendelsohn's evidence gave the committee all the
material which they required for an assessment on what I have described as the
correct basis, and I can find nothing in any of the material before us to suggest
that they made their assessment on anything other than that basis. Accordingly,
I would reject the third point. **D**

Finally, it is said that they failed to take into account a material consideration,
namely, management charges. To understand this point, one must again go back
to Mr. Weaver's original schedule of the cost of services, which included among
other items " ten per cent. for management of services, and administration
£4,627". It will be remembered that the committee, when dealing with this **E**
point, had dismissed management charges in a somewhat summary way, including
them with such things as fire extinguisher rental and saying: ". . . we do not
accept that any of these are services supplied to or for the benefit of the
tenants . . .". If that meant that the committee were saying to themselves—
" We direct ourselves as a matter of law that management charges are an inadmissible factor when assessing the cost of services,"—I would have thought
that they were clearly wrong, because there is plenty of authority for the propo- **F**
sition that management costs, and indeed in appropriate circumstances management profit, may properly be admitted. The question here is whether the
committee did make that mistake, or whether the decision is justified in another
way. Counsel for the tenant Zenker, who had the advantage of having been
before the committee, has indicated to us what I think is the real explanation, **G**
and it is to be found in brief in the committee's decision. This is a reference by
the committee to Mr. Weaver's evidence in these terms:

> " He gave evidence with regard to the estate office and the ten per cent.
> management charge. He thought this amount was reasonable for if the
> resident engineer and supervisor who carried the brunt of the work were **H**
> not there, the landlords might well have to engage additional office staff."

That phrase, under the guidance of counsel for the tenant Zenker, means that the
work of management, the brunt of the effort, as the committee put it, was
undertaken by a gentleman called the resident engineer and supervisor, who was
at the premises and whose wages were already included in the general item for
wages to which I have already referred. Accordingly, I think that the committee
were not saying that the admission of a management charge was something which
they could not accept as a matter of law, but rather that in this case any management costs had already been reflected in another part of the schedule. If that
simple explanation be adopted, as I think that it ought to be in this case, that is
an end of the landlords' complaint on their final point, and for those reasons I
would dismiss this appeal.

    CHAPMAN, J.: I agree with the judgment which has just been given.

A   **LORD PARKER, C.J.:**   I so entirely agree with what has fallen from WIDGERY, J., that there is nothing which I can usefully add.

Appeal dismissed. Leave to appeal to the Court of Appeal on the points other than that concerning bias, on which leave was not necessary.

Solicitors: *Grangewood, Allen & Co.* (for the landlords);   *Kenneth Brown,*
B   *Baker, Baker* (for the tenant Mr. Zenker);   *Solicitor, Ministry of Housing and Local Government.*

[*Reported by* S. A. HATTEEA, ESQ., *Barrister-at-Law.*]

C   # KELLY *v.* W.R.N. CONTRACTING, LTD., AND ANOTHER (BURKE, Third Party).

[MANCHESTER AUTUMN ASSIZES (Ashworth, J.), October 20, 1967.]

Road Traffic—Traffic sign—Road markings—Cause of action for contravention of
D   *regulation—Vehicle parked in contravention of regulation having causative effect on accident—No negligence at common law—Traffic Signs Regulations and General Directions* 1964 (*S.I.* 1964 *No.* 1857), *reg.* 23 (2) (*a*).

The third party parked his car by a bend of the road, partly on the pavement and partly on the road, but in such a position and manner as involved no negligence on his part in parking the car there. The second defendant
E   drove a lorry owned by his employers, the first defendants, too fast downhill towards the bend; the presence of the parked car caused the second defendant to brake, the lorry skidded after passing the parked car on the lorry's nearside and went through a wall and down an embankment. The plaintiff, who was a passenger in the lorry, was seriously injured. Liability of the first and second defendants to the plaintiff was admitted. On a claim by the
F   defendants for contribution from the third party on the ground of alleged liability for breach of statutory duty in that his car was parked opposite a set of road markings in contravention of reg. 23 (2) (*a*)* of the Traffic Signs Regulations and General Directions 1964, which provided that " no vehicle shall stay on any length of road along which markings have been placed ",

Held: a civil cause of action for breach of statutory duty under reg. 23
G   lay where, as on the evidence in the present case, the contravention had causative effect on the occurrence of the accident and accordingly the third party was liable to make contribution to the compensation payable to the plaintiff, the proportion attributable by the third party being ten per cent. and that attributable to the defendants being ninety per cent. (see p. 371, letters B, E, G and H, post).

H   [As to the elements of the cause of action for breach of statutory duty, see 36 HALSBURY'S LAWS (3rd Edn.) 449, 450, para. 684, and pp. 452, 453, para. 688; and for cases on the subject, see 44 DIGEST (Repl.) 320, *1510, 1511.*

As to road markings as traffic signs, see 33 HALSBURY'S LAWS (3rd Edn.) 561, 562, para. 951, text and note (*p*) and SUPPLEMENT thereto.

For the Road Traffic Act, 1960, s. 52, and s. 51 of Sch. 4 to the Road Traffic
I   Act, 1962, see 40 HALSBURY'S STATUTES (2nd Edn.) 758 and 42 ibid., 922, 935.]

Case referred to:

London Passenger Transport Board v. *Upson,* [1949] 1 All E.R. 60; [1949] A.C. 155; [1949] L.J.R. 238; 45 Digest (Repl.) 21, *58.*

---

* Reg. 23 (2) provides: " The requirements conveyed by the road marking mentioned in the last preceding paragraph shall be that—(*a*) . . . no vehicle shall stop on any length of road along which the marking has been placed at any point between the two ends of the marking; . . .

P

Explained and distinguished in CHOP SENG HENG v THEVANNASAN [1975] 3 All ER 572

Action. A

This was an action commenced by writ issued on July 27, 1966, by Patrick Christopher Kelly against W.R.N. Contracting, Ltd. and Michael O'Connor, claiming damages for personal injuries. On Apr. 28, 1965, the plaintiff was a passenger in a motor lorry owned by the first defendants and driven by their servant, the second defendant. The lorry left the road, collided with a wall, and ran down an embankment where it overturned, thereby causing very serious B injuries to the plaintiff. The defendants by para. 3 of their defence alleged that the accident had been caused by the negligence and/or breach of statutory duty of one Edward Burke, who had left his car on a bend in the road at a point opposite double white lines in the centre of the road (contrary to reg. 23 of the Traffic Signs Regulations and General Directions 1964) at a time when the road surface was greasy thereby presenting the second defendant with an unexpected C obstruction causing him to leave the road. By a third party notice the defendants claimed against Edward Burke an indemnity or contribution on the ground that the accident was caused by his negligence and/or breach of statutory duty. At the trial the defendants admitted liability to the plaintiff, and the question was whether the third party was under any liability to indemnify the defendants against their liability to the plaintiff or to make contribution. HIS LORDSHIP D found that the defendants' lorry was being driven downhill approaching what was admitted by all parties to be a notorious bend and which was marked by a warning sign; that the third party had parked his car (a Ford Anglia, five feet wide) deliberately at a point where it was visible to traffic coming down the hill, and that it was in fact visible for at least one hundred yards; that the nearside wheels of the car were on the pavement and that there was little more than three E feet of the vehicle at the most in the road; that the car was parked opposite to a set of white lines in the centre of the road, and that the carriageway was thirty-one feet wide at that point; that there was abundant room for a vehicle carefully driven to pass the car with safety. It was admitted that the first defendants' lorry was being driven too fast, and in the circumstances HIS LORDSHIP held that there was no ground whatever on which the third party could be found to F have been negligent at common law. The case is reported on the question whether contravention by the third party of reg. 23 (2) (a) of the Traffic Signs Regulations and General Directions 1964 rendered him civilly liable to the defendants. There was a road marking at the bend of the road. It was a continuous double white line. At the point where the third party parked his car the road marking may have ceased to be a double white line and become a single G white line with a dotted line on one side. The trial judge intimated that the marking referred to in reg. 23 (1), (2) (a), was a continuous white line, whether double or single. It was not disputed that the third party's car ought not to have been parked where it was parked, if the requirements of reg. 23 (2) (a) were to be observed.

A. M. Prestt for the plaintiff. H

B. A. Hytner for the defendants.

E. Sanderson Temple for the third party.

ASHWORTH, J., after stating the facts, considering the medical evidence, and assessing the damages (1), continued as follows: I have to ask myself, is it established that the second defendant applied his brakes, and went into a skid I because of the parked car of the third party, or did he do it for some wholly different reason?

I have come to the conclusion it is so established. I think that he did apply his brakes because of the parked car. He was driving terribly carelessly. He applied them very late, maybe because he had not seen the car when he ought to have done, or maybe he was going too fast. At any rate, I think that the presence

---

(1) The damages were assessed at £2,572 0s. 6d., which included the sum of £322 0s. 6d. for special damage.

A of the car, and his sudden realisation of its existence there, caused him to brake, and because of his speed and lack of control over this vehicle, which he had only driven for two days, he failed to control it. It veered to his offside, he tried to correct it, but it ended up through the wall.

Had the presence of the third party's car on the side of the road any causative effect or influence on this accident at all? My answer as a finding of fact is
B " yes, it had ". That takes counsel for the defendants half way. He then says to me that these regulations were made to protect road users in general. The contrary argument is that breach of statutory duty such as is involved here only gives rise to civil liability if the claimant is someone within a particular class for whose protection or benefit the regulations apply, and naturally enough reference is made to the House of Lords decision in *London Passenger Transport Board* v.
C *Upson* (2). That case was concerned with the Pedestrian Crossing Places (Traffic) Regulations, 1941 (3) and the House of Lords held that a breach of those regulations did give rise to civil liability to a person who was, in fact, knocked down in the road in circumstances involving a breach of those regulations.

Counsel for the third party says with force that the Pedestrian Crossing Places (Traffic) Regulations, 1941, were in the nature of things designed to protect
D pedestrians, whereas the Traffic Signs Regulations and General Directions 1964 (4) are of general application, and their breach cannot give rise to civil liability at all. If there is to be a claim, so he submits, it must be a claim at common law and not for breach of statutory duty, though in respect of an act which contravened the statutory instrument. There is no relevant decision on this particular point so far as counsel have been able to ascertain. In my view
E these regulations were designed in the first place to avoid accidents. The marking of roads with double white lines or single lines with dots on one side was a measure which Parliament sanctioned in order to try and stop the toll on the roads by accidents. They were regulations which, because they were designed to prevent accidents, were designed also to prevent injury. Persons who are in breach of the regulations must in the nature of things, in my view, be adding
F to the probabilities that accidents will follow.

Having established here a breach, albeit a very small one, of the regulations I think that the defendants are entitled to say that the third party has contributed to this accident. If he had not broken the regulations the second defendant might not, or would not, have put his brakes on when he did, and might have gone sailing down that hill at a grotesquely fast speed, but it was the third party's
G presence and breach of the regulations which caused the second defendant to take the action which resulted in the plaintiff's injuries.

It is agreed by counsel that the division of responsibility between the second defendant and the third party must be measured by regard to their real responsibility, and I assess the third party's responsibility at a very, very low figure indeed. I hope I shall not be misunderstood by saying I have reached this
H decision with a measure of reluctance, but I am constrained to do it, and I have arrived at the proportion of the sum I have already mentioned as between the defendants and the third party in the ratio of ninety per cent. and ten per cent.

Judgments for the defendants against the third party.

Solicitors: *George Clough, Willis & Co.,* Bury (for the plaintiff); *David Blank,*
I *Alexander & Co.,* Manchester (for the defendants); *H. Smith,* Manchester (for the third party).

[*Reported by* M. DENISE CHORLTON, *Barrister-at-Law.*]

---

(2) [1949] 1 All E.R. 60; [1949] A.C. 155.
(3) S.R. & O. 1941 No. 397.
(4) S.I. 1964 No. 1857.

A

LONDON PERMANENT BENEFIT BUILDING SOCIETY
v. DE BAER.

[CHANCERY DIVISION (Plowman, J.), November 14, 15, 28, 1967.]

Mortgage—Possession of mortgaged property—Stay of execution on an order for possession—Legal mortgagees obtained order for possession—Mortgagor sought stay of execution—Nothing had occurred since making of order which if it had occurred before order was made would have prevented its being made—Whether court had power to grant stay of execution on an order for possession—R.S.C., Ord. 45, r. 11.

Practice—Chambers—Chancery Division—Adjournment to the judge—Plaintiffs' solicitor declined master's invitation to adjourn matter to judge—Before order passed and entered plaintiffs applied for adjournment—Master then adjourned matter to judge—Whether plaintiffs had lost their right to such adjournment.

B

C

Mortgagees under a charge by way of legal mortgage obtained, on application in the Chancery Division by originating summons, an order for possession of the mortgaged premises. Subsequently the defendant applied for a stay of execution. The master granted a stay, and at the hearing before him the mortgagees' solicitor declined his invitation to adjourn the matter to the judge. On the following day, however, the mortgagees asked for the matter to be adjourned to the judge, and it was adjourned without prejudice to the question whether they had lost the right to such an adjournment.

Held: (i) as the order for the stay of proceedings had not been passed or entered, the master had jurisdiction to adjourn the matter to the judge, the present case being within para. 3 of the Practice Direction of September, 1965 (see p. 377, letter I, post).

Practice Direction ([1965] 3 All E.R. 306) applied.

Re Thomas ([1911] 2 Ch. 389) considered.

(ii) nothing having occurred since the order for possession was made which, if it had occurred before then, would have prevented the order being made, the court had no jurisdiction under R.S.C., Ord. 45, r. 11*, in the present case to grant a stay of execution at the instance of the mortgagor against the plaintiff mortgagees, this being in accordance with the principle that a court of equity never interfered to prevent a mortgagee from assuming possession (see p. 379, letter E, and p. 382, letters D and E, post).

Birmingham Citizens Permanent Building Society v. *Caunt* ([1962] 1 All E.R. 163) applied.

D

E

F

G

[As to the stay of execution, see 16 HALSBURY'S LAWS (3rd Edn.) 34, paras. 49, 50; and for cases on the subject, see 21 DIGEST (Repl.) 531-532, *296-307*.

As to the right of a mortgagee by way of legal mortgage to possession of the mortgaged property, see 27 HALSBURY'S LAWS (3rd Edn.) 277, para. 511.

As to the rights of parties to proceedings in chambers in the Chancery Division to have the matter adjourned to the judge, see 30 HALSBURY'S LAWS (3rd Edn.) 337, para. 611.]

H

Cases referred to:

Birmingham Citizens Permanent Building Society v. *Caunt*, [1962] 1 All E.R. 163; [1962] Ch. 883; [1962] 2 W.L.R. 323; Digest (Cont. Vol. A) 77, *187a*.

Booth v. *Walkden Spinning and Manufacturing Co., Ltd.*, [1909] 2 K.B. 368; 78 L.J.K.B. 764; 51 Digest (Repl.) 768, *3421*.

British South Africa Co. v. *Companhia de Moçambique*, [1891-94] All E.R. Rep. 640; [1893] A.C. 602; 63 L.J.Q.B. 70; 69 L.T. 604; 16 Digest (Repl.) 198, *881*.

Brook v. *Emerson*, (1906), 95 L.T. 821; 21 Digest (Repl.) 532, *307*.

---

* R.S.C., Ord. 45, r. 11, so far as material, is printed at p. 374, letter A, post.

A   *Butts* v. *Bilke and Havelock*, (1817), 4 Price, 291; 146 E.R. 468; 21 Digest (Repl.) 531, *304*.

     Carr v. *Royal Exchange Assurance Corpn.*, (1864), 5 B. & S. 941; 122 E.R. 1080; 34 L.J.Q.B. 21; 11 L.T. 595; 21 Digest (Repl.) 539, *386*.

     Cholmondeley (Marquis) v. *Lord Clinton*, (1817), 2 Mer. 171; 35 E.R. 905; 21 Digest (Repl.) 356, *1014*.

B   *Emberson* v. *Fisher*, [1944] 2 D.L.R. 803; [1944] O.W.N. 375; 21 Digest (Repl.) 532, **185*.

     Four-Maids, Ltd. v. *Dudley Marshall (Properties), Ltd.*, [1957] 2 All E.R. 35; [1957] Ch. 317; [1957] 2 W.L.R. 931; 35 Digest (Repl.) 455, *1467*.

     Harrington v. *Ramage*, [1907] W.N. 137; 51 Digest (Repl.) 626, *2387*.

     Hinckley and South Leicestershire Permanent Benefit Building Society v. *Freeman*,
C   [1940] 4 All E.R. 212; [1941] Ch. 32; 111 L.J.Ch. 36; 164 L.T. 399; 51 Digest (Repl.) 671, *2755*.

     Jaffa v. *Weinbaum*, [1925] W.N. 85; 51 Digest (Repl.) 627, *2401*.

     James Westoll, The, [1905] P. 47; 74 L.J.P. 9; 92 L.T. 150; 10 Asp. M.L.C. 29; 20 Digest (Repl.) 309, *494*.

     Kelly v. *White*, [1920] W.N. 220; 13 Digest (Repl.) 452, *758*.

D   *Leonard* v. *Wharton*, (1921), 64 D.L.R. 609; 50 O.L.R. 609; 21 Digest (Repl.) 532, **184*.

     Marine and General Mutual Life Assurance Society v. *Feltwell Fen Second District Drainage Board*, [1945] K.B. 394; 114 L.J.K.B. 94; 172 L.T. 100; 109 J.P. 114; 21 Digest (Repl.) 535, *346*.

     Polini v. *Gray, Sturla* v. *Freccia*, (1879), 12 Ch.D. 438; 41 L.T. 173; 21 Digest
E   (Repl.) 536, *363*.

     Practice Direction, [1965] 3 All E.R. 306; [1965] 1 W.L.R. 1259; 51 Digest (Repl.) 627, *2402*.

     Practice Note, [1884] W.N. 218; 19 L.J.N.C. 147; 51 Digest (Repl.) 640, *2509*.

     Thomas, Re, Bartley v. *Thomas*, [1911] 2 Ch. 389; 105 L.T. 59; 51 Digest (Repl.) 626, *2388*.

F   *Worral Waterworks Co.* v. *Lloyd*, (1866), L.R. 1 C.P. 719; 21 Digest (Repl.) 658, *1476*.

Procedure Summons.

This was an application by Philip Rudston de Baer, the defendant mortgagor, by summons dated Feb. 20, 1967, for a stay of execution on an order for possession of 119, Mortlake High Street, in the London Borough of Richmond, made by
G Master DINWIDDY on Dec. 14, 1966, in favour of the London Permanent Benefit Building Society, the plaintiff mortgagees.

On June 14, 1967, the matter came before Master BALL who ordered a general stay of execution on certain terms. At that hearing the plaintiffs' solicitor declined the master's invitation to ask that the matter should be adjourned to the judge, but on the next day, the plaintiffs applied for adjournment and the
H master accordingly adjourned the matter to PLOWMAN, J., without prejudice to the question whether the plaintiffs had lost their right to an adjournment. The facts are set out in the judgment.

The cases noted below* were cited during the argument in addition to those referred to in the judgment.

I   *R. R. F. Scott* for the plaintiffs.

     M. Essayan for the defendant.

                                   Cur. adv. vult.

     Nov. 28. PLOWMAN, J., read the following judgment: This is a summons by the defendant mortgagor asking for a stay of execution on an order for possession obtained by the plaintiff mortgagees on Dec. 14, 1966. The application is made under R.S.C., Ord. 45, r. 11, which is as follows:

---

* *Flahavan* v. *Gamble* (1817), 1 Newf. L.R. 36; *Clifton Securities, Ltd.* v. *Huntley*, [1948] 2 All E.R. 283; *Re Harrison's Settlement Trust,s* [1965] 3 All E.R. 795.

A

"Without prejudice to Ord. 47, r. 1, a party against whom a judgment has been given or an order made may apply to the court for a stay of execution of the judgment or order or other relief on the ground of matters which have occurred since the date of the judgment or order, and the court may by order grant such relief, and on such terms, as it thinks just."

B

Master BALL, before whom the matter came on June 14, 1967, felt constrained to grant a stay on terms, but the plaintiffs, who at first declined the master's invitation to adjourn the matter to the judge, changed their mind the next day and the master has accordingly adjourned the matter to me without prejudice to the question whether the plaintiffs have lost their right to an adjournment.

The first question which I have to decide is, therefore, whether in the circumstances the plaintiffs have lost that right. If the answer is that they have not, a second question arises, namely, whether there is jurisdiction to grant a stay of execution on a possession order obtained by a legal mortgagee or a chargee by way of legal mortgage. If the answer to that question is in the affirmative, a third question arises, namely whether and on what terms the court should, in the exercise of its discretion, grant a stay. These are questions of some general importance and I should like to express my indebtedness to counsel for their arguments and to Master BALL for the very full and helpful statement of his findings.

C

D

The facts of this case, so far as material to the questions which I have to decide, are as follows. By a charge by way of legal mortgage dated Dec. 29, 1965, the defendant charged the freehold property known as 119 Mortlake High Street, S.W. 14, with the repayment to the plaintiffs of the sum of £7,000 with interest at eight per cent., payable by monthly instalments of £59 8s. 5d. over a period of twenty years. The mortgage, which was in a usual building society form, contained, in cl. 5, a provision that the plaintiffs might at any time during the continuance of the security enter into possession, but that they should not enforce that right unless and until (inter alia) default should have been made by the defendant for three months in the payment of some instalment, and that on the plaintiffs' right to enter into possession becoming enforceable, the whole of the principal money then remaining unpaid should forthwith become due and payable. No. 119 Mortlake High Street is a property in part of which the defendant lives. I gather that he lives there alone, as he is a divorced man whose former wife has the care and control of their two children. The remainder of the property is let off into flats, the tenants of which have not been brought into these proceedings and it may be that the plaintiffs' order for possession is not enforceable against them.

E

F

G

On June 8, 1966, the plaintiffs issued an originating summons for payment and possession. At that date the defendant had made no payment at all under the mortgage. An appointment before the master was taken for Oct. 13, 1966, but on Oct. 11, the plaintiffs and the defendant reached an agreement whereby the defendant was to pay the plaintiffs £300 forthwith followed by fortnightly (in lieu of monthly) instalments of £59 8s. 5d. until all arrears had been discharged. At that time the arrears amounted to £475 7s. 4d. In view of this agreement the case was stood over generally when it came on before the master on Oct. 13.

H

The defendant paid the £300 but he again fell into arrear with his instalments and the plaintiffs therefore restored the originating summons for Dec. 14, 1966, and on that day obtained an order for possession within twenty-eight days after service of the order.

The defendant did not appear before the master on that occasion. He says that he did not receive notice of the appointment. On Dec. 16, he went to France to visit a brother who was ill. The first that he knew of the order for possession was when it was served on him on Jan. 24, 1967, after his return from France. At that time he thought that he had paid off the arrears owing to the plaintiffs, because he had sent them a cheque for £178 5s. 3d. on Dec. 10 and another cheque

A for a similar amount on Dec. 20. Unknown to him, however, the earlier cheque had
been dishonoured owing to a larger cheque paid to him by one of his tenants itself
being dishonoured. The cheque of Dec. 20 was duly paid, but a further cheque
for four instalments which the defendants sent to the plaintiffs on Jan. 30, 1967,
was refused and returned. The defendant then consulted solicitors and on their
advice paid into court the sum of £270 1s. 1d. which they calculated to be the
B amount of the arrears outstanding. On Feb. 20, 1967, the defendant's summons
for a stay of execution on the order for possession was issued.

The defendant says that he has now put his affairs in order and made arrangements to pay off arrears and to comply with his obligations under the mortgage
duly and promptly. He offers to pay his instalments one month in advance and to
provide a guarantor. He says that, if the order for possession were enforced, not
C only would he lose his home, but also he would be unlikely ever to buy another
because no other building society, insurance company or finance house would
accept him as a borrower after learning his record as a borrower from the plaintiffs.
The defendant's summons for a stay came before Master Ball on June 14, 1967,
and I have already stated what happened on that occasion.

I must now deal with the question whether the plaintiffs lost their right to
D have the matter adjourned to the judge by informing the master, through their
solicitor, that they did not wish for an adjournment. There are two aspects of
the matter, one of principle, the other of practice. Both are dealt with by
Warrington, J., in *Re Thomas, Bartley* v. *Thomas* (1), where he said this:

" It is the everyday practice that, until an order is passed and entered,
the matter can be brought before the judge, and if a mistake has been made it
E can be put right. But the matter does not rest there. This was an order made
by the judge in chambers, that is to say, in this particular case made by
the master as the deputy of the judge. It is the right of any party interested
to adjourn a question from the judge's deputy to the judge himself. It is
undoubtedly the practice, as a general rule, that, if a party wishes to obtain
the opinion of the judge in person, he must ask for an adjournment for
F that purpose at the time the master proposes to make the order, or, at all
events, ask for time to consider whether he will ask for an adjournment. That,
undoubtedly, is the usual practice in chambers, and it is a very convenient
practice. But, although that is the practice, it seems to me that the judge has
power, or the master has power, to direct an adjournment at any time before
the order becomes finally binding by being passed and entered; and what I
G propose to do, in order to remove any technical difficulty, is now to direct
that this matter shall be treated as adjourned to me, and to deal with it as if
I had the application for confirmation of the contract now before me. I think
that is the correct way of dealing with the matter for the reason that, until
the order is finally passed and entered, it leaves open an opportunity of
reviewing and reconsidering what has been done."

H Master Ball's order granting a stay on terms has not been passed and entered
and accordingly there was, in my judgment, jurisdiction for him, at the plaintiffs'
request, to adjourn the application to me or for me to adjourn it to myself.

As regards the practice, the matter was formerly regulated by a *Practice Note* (2),
which is as follows:

I " There being apparently some misapprehension as to the practice in
chambers relating to the adjournment of summonses to be heard by the judge
Pearson, J., stated that the settled practice is this, that an adjournment to
the judge will not be granted unless an application is made to the chief clerk,
at the time when the summons is heard by him, either for an adjournment
or for time to consider whether an adjournment shall be asked for. If no
application is made to the chief clerk at the time, the order can only be altered

(1) [1911] 2 Ch. 389 at p. 396.
(2) [1884] W.N. 218.

A

by means of a motion in court to discharge it. If an order is made against a
party properly served in his absence, the result is the same as if, being present,
he does not ask for an adjournment. Time to consider whether an adjournment shall be asked for will be granted, if an application for it is made at the
hearing in a proper case—as if only a clerk who is not fully instructed is
present, or in a country case when reference to the country solicitor is
necessary. This practice is absolutely necessary in order that the business in
chambers may be regularly conducted."

B

It follows from that, that unless an application, either for an adjournment to the
judge or for time to consider the question of an adjournment to the judge was
asked for on the hearing of the summons before the master, the master's order
could only be challenged on a motion to discharge it. It seems however, that in
the course of time some variation in the practice took place, as appears from
Jaffa v. *Weinbaum* (3). The facts of that case were as follows, and I read from the
report:

C

" This was a specific performance action by a purchaser against the vendor
and his assignee. The action was commenced in May, 1924, and the replies
and defences to counterclaims delivered in November. On Feb. 24, 1925,
the plaintiff not having given notice of trial, the defendants obtained a
master's order dismissing the action for want of prosecution. The order
was not to be drawn up before Mar. 4, and not then if in the meantime notice
of trial was given. No adjournment to the judge was asked. On Mar. 2
the managing clerk of the plaintiff's solicitors was instructed to set the action
down for trial on Mar. 3, but by inadvertence, which he explained, he did not
give notice of trial till Mar. 4.   The defendant's solicitor declined to accept
the notice, and drew up the order which was passed and entered on Mar. 11.
The action was consequently not set down for trial. In the meantime, viz.,
on Mar. 10, i.e., within fourteen days after the order was pronounced, the
plaintiff issued and served a notice of motion to discharge the order and for
liberty to give notice of trial and set down."

D

E

F

It is to be noticed that the motion to discharge the master's order was launched
before that order had been passed and entered. I now refer to the arguments and
the judgment (3).

" Counsel for the plaintiff relied on the Judicature Act, 1873, ... and
PEARSON, J.'s *Practice Note* (4) to the effect that unless an adjournment
to the judge is asked for at the time the order is made, or time for consideration given, the order can only be discharged by motion. Counsel
for the vendor relied on *Harrington* v. *Ramage* (5), and contended that the
motion was irregular, the proper course being an adjournment to the judge.
Counsel for the plaintiff, in reply suggested that if necessary the motion could
be treated as an application for adjournment to the judge: *Re Thomas* (6),
where the practice is fully stated. ASTBURY, J., said that the plaintiff had not
asked for an adjournment on Feb. 24 because he intended to give notice
of trial before Mar. 4, and apart from the clerk's inadvertence, which had
been fully explained, this would have been done and the order never drawn
up. The decisions showed that the practice differed in different chambers,
but in his lordships' chambers a master's order could always be adjourned
to the judge on an application made at any time before it was passed and
entered. The plaintiff, thinking he was too late to ask for an adjournment,
moved to discharge the order under the Judicature Act, 1873, s. 50, and
Practice Note (4).   That he was entitled to do according to that practice

G

H

I

(3) [1925] W.N. 85.
(4) [1884] W.N. 218.
(5) [1907] W.N. 137.
(6) [1911] 2 Ch. at p. 396.

A   note, but if necessary he would have leave to treat the notice of motion as an application for adjourning the master's order to the judge.   The plaintiff, having bona fide attempted to act on the master's allowance of time to Mar. 4, ought not to be penalised.   He must, however, pay for the court's indulgence.   In other words, he must pay the costs of and incidental to the motion.   The order would be discharged."

B   The position at this time may perhaps be stated as follows.   (i) Any interested party had the right to adjourn a question from the master to the judge; (ii) the proper time to ask for an adjournment or for time to consider the matter was when the summons was before the master; (iii) even so, a judge or master had power to direct an adjournment at any time before the master's order was passed and entered; (iv) once the master's order had been passed and entered it could

C   only be challenged on a motion to discharge it, and (v) it was perhaps doubtful whether a motion was an appropriate procedure in a case where no application had been made to the master for an adjournment or for time to consider an adjournment at the hearing of the summons and the master's order had not yet been perfected.

In September, 1965, a new *Practice Direction* (7) was issued.   It is as follows:

D   " 1. Any party to proceedings in chambers in the Chancery Division who may wish to exercise his right to have any matter adjourned to the judge in person should apply to the master at the time when the application is heard by him either (a) to have that application adjourned to the judge or (b) for time to consider whether he wishes to ask for such an adjournment.   2. If a master's order is drawn up and perfected, no party can thereafter require

E   that matter to be adjourned to the judge. Any dissatisfied party must then proceed by motion to apply for the order to be discharged or varied.   3. If no such application as is mentioned in para. 1 has been made to the master at the time when he made an order, but nevertheless before such order has been perfected a party wishes the matter to be adjourned to the judge, that party should forthwith and at his own expense restore the summons or application

F   before the master."

The plaintiffs submit that the present case falls within the wording of para. 3 of that direction, and I agree.   That paragraph assumes that the party wishing the matter to be adjourned to the judge has not complied with the proper procedure stated in para. 1, but counsel for the defendant argued that para. 3 applies only where nothing was said about an adjournment at the hearing before the master and does not apply to a case where the right to an adjournment has been expressly disclaimed. This argument was based purely on grounds of convenience. It was said that if the plaintiffs were entitled to change their minds, the usual direction giving a party a specified time within which to request an adjournment would be valueless and nobody would know until the order had been perfected whether it was valid or not.

In my judgment, however, administrative inconvenience is not of itself enough to deprive a party of the right or the court of the jurisdiction which were held to exist in *Re Thomas* (8) and as a practical matter orders such as I am concerned with are, I am told by the chief registrar, normally perfected within a week or ten days of being made, and can be expedited where necessary.   The present case is, in my judgment, covered by para. 3 of the *Practice Direction* (7) and I therefore hold that the matter has been effectively adjourned to me.

I turn now to the question whether the court has jurisdiction under R.S.C., Ord. 45, r. 11, to grant a stay of execution on an order for possession obtained by a legal mortgagee.

Counsel for the defendant submitted that all that R.S.C., Ord. 45, r. 11 does is to enshrine the inherent jurisdiction of the court to stay execution on judgments

(7) [1965] 3 All E.R. 306.
(8) [1911] 2 Ch. 389.

and orders. To support the proposition that such an inherent jurisdiction exists, **A** counsel referred me to the statement in 16 HALSBURY'S LAWS OF ENGLAND (3rd Edn.) p. 34, para. 49, that the court

". . . has an inherent jurisdiction over all judgments or orders which it has made, under which it can stay execution in all cases either for a definite or unlimited period."

B

In my judgment that proposition is too widely stated and is not supported by the two cases which are cited in the footnotes in support of it.

The first is *Polini* v. *Gray, Sturla* v. *Freccia* (9). That case concerned a stay pending an appeal. COTTON, L.J., said this (10):

" The only question we have to consider is, whether or no the court has jurisdiction in a proper case to stay all dealings with a fund pending an appeal to the House of Lords although the court has decided against the title of the plaintiff and dismissed the action. I see no difference in principle between staying the distribution of a fund to which the court has held the plaintiff not to be entitled, and staying the execution of an order by which the court has decided that a plaintiff is entitled to a fund. In that case, as in this case, the court, pending an appeal to the House of Lords, suspends what it has declared to be the right of one of the litigant parties. On what principle does it do so? It does so on this ground, that when there is an appeal about to be prosecuted the litigation is to be considered as not at an end, and that being so, if there is a reasonable ground of appeal, and if not making the order to stay the execution of the decree or the distribution of the fund would make the appeal nugatory, that is to say, would deprive the appellant, if successful, of the results of the appeal, then it is the duty of the court to interfere and suspend the right of the party who, so far as the litigation has gone, has established his rights. That applies, in my opinion, just as much to the case where the action has been dismissed, as to the case where a decree has been made establishing the plaintiff's title."

C

I

That case does not, therefore, in my judgment, justify a statement as wide as that in HALSBURY.

The other case referred to in the footnotes is *Marine and General Mutual Life Assurance Society* v. *Feltwell Fen Second District Drainage Board* (11). That was a case in which the plaintiffs recovered judgment against the defendants for a sum of £1,490, and the defendants applied for a stay of execution. EVERSHED, J., refused to grant a stay, but he said this (12):

" It has been submitted by counsel for the plaintiffs that there is no jurisdiction to grant a stay such as is here suggested, because the discretion contained in R.S.C., Ord. 42, r. 17, is merely to grant a stay for some limited time. In my judgment, reading that order and s. 41 of the Judicature Act, 1925, it would be open to the court, if the circumstances justified it, to grant a stay of execution by a judgment creditor against a body of this character."

R.S.C., Ord. 42, r. 17, was in the following terms, so far as material:

" Every person to whom any sum of money or any costs shall be payable under a judgment or order shall, so soon as the money or costs shall be payable, be entitled to sue out one or more writ or writs of fieri facias or one or more writ or writs of elegit to enforce payment thereof, subject nevertheless as follows: . . . (b) The court or a judge may, at or after the time of giving judgment or making an order, stay execution until such time as they or he shall think fit."

---

(9) (1879), 12 Ch.D. 438.
(10) (1879), 12 Ch.D. at p. 446.
(11) [1945] K.B. 394.
(12) [1945] K.B. at p. 398.

A The rule is therefore one which applied only to money judgments and did not, in my judgment, support the much wider statement in HALSBURY.   Section 41 of the Supreme Court of Judicature (Consolidation) Act, 1925, to which EVER-SHED, J., also referred states that nothing in the Act of 1925 shall disable the court, if it thinks fit to do so, from directing a stay of proceedings in any cause or matter pending before it, but that portion of the section merely preserves existing

B jurisdiction and does not confer any new jurisdiction on the court (see *The James Westoll* (13)).

Counsel for the plaintiffs submitted that if there is an inherent jurisdiction to stay execution above and beyond the jurisdiction conferred by certain statutes (such as s. 62 of the Execution Act, 1844), or by the Rules of the Supreme Court, such inherent jurisdiction is much more limited than the statement in HALSBURY

C suggests, and he cited a number of authorities in support of his argument.   These, in chronological order, were *Butts* v. *Bilke and Havelock* (14);   *Carr* v. *Royal Exchange Assurance Corpn.* (15);   *Worral Waterworks Co.* v. *Lloyd* (16);   *Brook* v. *Emerson* (17);   *Booth* v. *Walkden Spinning and Manufacturing Co., Ltd.* (18); *Kelly* v. *White* (19);   and two Canadian cases, *Leonard* v. *Wharton* (20) and *Emberson* v. *Fisher* (21).   He also cited the statement of LORD HERSCHELL, L.C.,

D in *British South Africa Co.* v. *Companhia de Moçambique* (22) that the Rules of the Supreme Court are limited to matters of procedure and cannot confer new jurisdiction or alter substantative rights.

In my judgment, however, it is unnecessary for me to decide the question of inherent jurisdiction in the present case, because I have reached the conclusion that R.S.C., Ord. 45, r. 11, under which the present application is made, does not,

E on its true construction, confer any power to grant a stay of execution on an order for possession made in favour of a legal mortgagee or a chargee by way of legal mortgage.

The power conferred by that rule to grant relief is a power to do so, and I quote, " on the ground of matters which have occurred since the date of the judgment or order ".   It is, in my judgment, implicit in the rule that the matters

F referred to are matters which would or might have prevented the order being made or would or might have led to a stay of execution if they had already occurred at the date of the order.

In my judgment, however, nothing has occurred in this case since the order of Dec. 14, 1966, which, if it had occurred before that date, could have prevented the order being made or could have entitled the defendant to a stay of execution.

G This, in my judgment, follows from the decision of RUSSELL, J., in *Birmingham Citizens Permanent Building Society* v. *Caunt* (23);   the headnote of that case is partly as follows (24):

" Where the legal mortgagee under an instalment mortgage under which, by reason of default, the whole money has become payable, is entitled to possession, the court has no jurisdiction under the Practice Direction made

H under R.S.C., Ord. 55, r. 5A, or otherwise to decline the order or to adjourn the hearing whether on terms of keeping up payments or paying arrears, if the mortgagee cannot be persuaded to agree to such a course.   To this the sole exception (apart from adjournments which in the ordinary course of procedure may be desirable in circumstances such as temporary inability of a party to attend) is that the application may be adjourned for a short time to afford to the mortgagor a chance of paying off the mortgagee in full

---

(13) [1905] P. 47.   (14) (1817), 4 Price, 291.
(15) (1864), 5 B. & S. 941.   (16) (1866), L.R. 1 C.P. 719.
(17) (1906), 95 L.T. 821.   (18) [1909] 2 K.B. 368.
(19) [1920] W.N. 220.   (20) (1921), 64 D.L.R. 609.
(21) [1944] 2 D.L.R. 803.
(22) [1891-94] All E.R. Rep. 640 at pp. 649, 650;   [1893] A.C. 602 at p. 628.
(23) [1962] 1 All E.R. 163;   [1962] Ch. 883.
(24) [1962] Ch. at p. 883.

or otherwise satisfying him; but this should not be done if there is no
reasonable prospect of this occurring.   A mortgagee applied by summons
to the court for an order for possession of the mortgaged property on the
ground that payment of the instalments was in arrear to the extent of some
£71.   The mortgagors invoking the Practice Direction under R.S.C., Ord. 55,
r. 5A, made an application to the district registrar for the case to stand over
generally.   The district registrar adjourned the summons sine die on terms
that the defendants should make minimum weekly payments of 30s. in order
to overtake the arrears."

So far as relevant the practice direction referred to in that part of the headnote
was as follows:

" When possession is sought and the defendant is in arrear with any
instalments due under the mortgage . . . and the master is of opinion that the
defendant ought to be given an opportunity to pay off the arrears, the
master may adjourn the summons on such terms as he thinks fit . . ."

and then the headnote goes on (25):

" Held . . . (2) That in the circumstances there was no jurisdiction to
decline an order for possession, and that, accordingly, an order for possession
of the mortgaged property within twenty-eight days after service thereof
must be made."

RUSSELL, J., in his judgment said this (26):

" This case raises an important question concerning the rights of a legal
mortgagee of land, entitled according to the terms of the mortgage to possession of the mortgaged property, to insist on an order for possession being
made when he applies for it by originating summons under R.S.C., Ord. 55,
r. 5A, and establishes his right to possession."

And a little later on he said (27):

" Now an order such as that made by the registrar is obviously designed
to achieve this result: that if the borrower complies with its requirements
as to payment off of arrears, the order for possession asked for by the mortgagee will never be made, notwithstanding that by the terms of the contract
of mortgage the default has entitled the mortgagee to possession, and has
made the mortgage moneys presently payable as a lump sum and not by
instalments.   Moreover, default in the new instalment terms ' imposed '
on the occasion of the adjournment by no means necessarily leads to an order
for possession: a fresh default may lead only to fresh terms and a fresh
adjournment.   Is there any power in the court (and, therefore, in a master
or district registrar) in such circumstances to adjourn the application for
possession in that manner and deprive the mortgagee of his right to
possession? "

RUSSELL, J., then dealt with the law.   He stated that it was clear that a legal
mortgagee or a chargee by way of legal mortgage had a prima facie right to
possession.   Among other cases which he cited on this point were *Four-Maids*,
Ltd. v. *Dudley Marshall* (*Properties*), *Ltd.* (28), where HARMAN, J., said this (29),

" . . . the right of the mortgagee to possession in the absence of some
specific contract has nothing to do with default on the part of the mortgagor.
The mortgagee may go into possession before the ink is dry on the mortgage
unless, by a term expressed or necessarily implied in the contract, he has
contracted himself out of that right.   He has the right because he has a

(25) [1962] Ch. at p. 884.
(26) [1962] 1 All E.R. at p. 165; [1962] Ch. at p. 886.
(27) [1962] 1 All E.R. at p. 166; [1962] Ch. at p. 887.
(28) [1957] 2 All E.R. 35; [1957] Ch. 317.
(29) [1957] 2 All E.R. at p. 36; [1957] Ch. at p. 320.

A   legal term of years in the property. If there is an attornment clause, he must give notice. If there is a provision expressed or to be implied, that, so long as certain payments are made, he will not go into possession, then he has contracted himself out of his rights. Apart from that, possession is a matter of course."

B   Russell, J., also cited *Marquis of Cholmondeley* v. *Lord Clinton* (30) where Sir William Grant, M.R., commented (31) ". . . a court of equity never interferes to prevent the mortgagee from assuming the possession". Then Russell, J., said this (32):

C   " There appears no trace, prior to 1936, of any right in any court to deny to a mortgagee asserting or claiming his right to possession, the appropriate order—subject, however, to the qualification that a court in the exercise of its inherent jurisdiction for proper reason to postpone or adjourn a hearing might by adjournment for a short time afford the mortgagor a limited opportunity to find means to pay off the mortgagee or otherwise satisfy him if there was a reasonable prospect of either of those events occurring. Indeed, it would be surprising if there had been such a trace, having regard to the fact that a legal mortgagee does not necessarily require any assistance

D   from the court to assert his right to possession. Moreover, a mortgagee once rightfully in possession could never be ousted by the mortgagor except on paying off in full."

He then referred to the change of the rules in 1936 and to the **Practice Direction** (33), to which I have already referred, and he said this (34),

E   " It was plainly the view of the district registrar, and I have ascertained that it is the general view of the Chancery masters—at least since the decision of Farwell, J., in 1940 in *Hinckley and South Leicestershire Permanent Benefit Building Society* v. *Freeman* (35), which I mention later, that this direction confers on the master or registrar a discretion to adjourn against the wishes of the mortgagee a legal mortgagee's application for possession in order to

F   enable the mortgagor to catch up on instalment arrears and (inferentially) a right, if he does so, to continue to deny the mortgagee possession notwithstanding that on the default the whole money becomes and remains presently payable. Really there are two questions, whether the direction purports to do this: and whether, if it does, it reflects a jurisdiction which existed in the court. The second is, of course, the crucial question, for a practice

G   direction cannot confer on the master a jurisdiction which is lacking in the judge. Before turning to the authorities which have touched on this point, I repeat that I can find no trace of such a jurisdiction, or of any jurisdiction in any court (prior to the practice direction) in relation to a legal mortgagee's established right to possession which goes further than to adjourn for a short time in order that the mortgagor should have an opportunity to

H   displace the mortgagee from his position by payment, or to compound with him, and also, of course, to order possession not immediately but normally on or before the expiry of twenty-eight days from service of the order with the safeguards (which are indeed expository of the law) to be found in the latter part of the common form order in R.S.C., Appendix L, Form 39."

Finally, after considering the arguments of counsel, the construction of the

I   practice direction and a number of authorities, Russell, J., stated his conclusion as follows (36):

    " Accordingly, in my judgment, where, as here, the legal mortgagee

---

(30) (1817), 2 Mer. 171.   (31) (1817) 2 Mer. at p. 359.
(32) [1962] 1 All E.R. at pp. 168, 169; [1962] Ch. at p. 891.
(33) Viz., the Practice Direction set out in the notes in the Annual Practice to R.S.C., Ord. 55, r. 5A, e.g., in the Annual Practice, 1962, pp. 1504-1509.
(34) [1962] 1 All E.R. at pp. 170, 171; [1962] Ch. at p. 894.
(35) [1940] 4 All E.R. 212; [1941] Ch. 32.
(36) [1962] 1 All E.R. at p. 182; [1962] Ch. at p. 912.

under an instalment mortgage under which, by reason of default, the whole   A
money has become payable, is entitled to possession, the court has no
jurisdiction to decline the order or to adjourn the hearing, whether on terms
of keeping up payments or paying arrears, if the mortgagee cannot be
persuaded to agree to this course. The sole exception to this is that the
application may be adjourned for a short time to afford to the mortgagor
a chance of paying off the mortgagee in full or otherwise satisfying him;   B
but this should not be done if there is no reasonable prospect of this occurring.
When I say the sole exception, I do not, of course, intend to exclude adjournments which in the ordinary course of procedure may be desirable in circumstances such as temporary inability of a party to attend, and so forth. The
practice direction on which the district registrar, very understandably, relied
does not assume such a jurisdiction, and if it had it would have been an   C
erroneous assumption."

It is, in my judgment, plain from that case that no matter which has occurred
in this case since the order for possession was made could have prevented that
order being made if it had already occurred at that time. Moreover, it is, I
think, equally plain that the principle that " a court of equity never interferes
to prevent the mortgagee from assuming possession " (which is one way of   D
stating the ratio decidendi of *Caunt's* case (37)) is just as applicable to an application for a stay of execution as it is to an application to adjourn a summons
for possession.

It follows, in my judgment, that R.S.C., Ord. 45, r. 11, does not enable the
court to grant a stay of execution in this case, but if I am wrong about that,
I should feel bound to exercise my discretion by refusing a stay for the same   E
reason as that which leads me to believe that I have no discretion, namely that
to grant a stay would be an unwarranted interference with the rights of the
plaintiffs under their legal charge.

I wish to add a few words about the more general aspects of this matter.
Before Oct. 1, 1966, when the present Rules of the Supreme Court came into
force, R.S.C. Ord. 42, r. 27 provided,   F

" No proceedings by audita querela shall hereafter be used; but any
party against whom judgment has been given may apply to the court or a
judge for a stay of execution or other relief against such judgment, upon the
ground of facts which have arisen too late to be pleaded; and the court or
judge may give such relief and upon such terms as may be just."

That rule has now been replaced by R.S.C. Ord. 45, r. 11. Master BALL, who   G
has great experience of mortgagees' applications states that no mortgagor as
far as he is aware ever sought to obtain a stay of execution in reliance on the
old R.S.C., Ord. 42, r. 27, and that it was generally supposed that once a mortgagee's order for possession had been passed and entered the court had no power
to suspend its operation. He says, however, that the new rule has stimulated   H
a considerable flow of applications such as the present.

The reason, no doubt, is that before the decision of RUSSELL, J., in *Caunt's*
case (37), mortgagors were content to rely on the practice direction in an
endeavour to avoid an order for possession.

However that may be, there is, in my opinion, no justification for the view that
R.S.C., Ord. 45, r. 11 enables defaulting mortgagors to drive a coach and horses
through the decision in that case so as to deprive legal mortgagees of their funda-   I
mental rights and remedies. I therefore dismiss the summons.

Summons dismissed.

Solicitors: *Lewin, Gregory, Mead & Sons* (for the plaintiffs); *Loxdales* (for the
defendant).

[*Reported by* JACQUELINE METCALFE, *Barrister-at-Law.*]

---

(37) [1962] 1 All E.R. 163; [1962] Ch. 883.

A   COSH v. ISHERWOOD.

[QUEEN'S BENCH DIVISION (Salmon, L.J., Fenton Atkinson and Widgery, JJ.),
November 3, 1967.]

*Criminal Law—Loitering—Suspected persons—Loitering antecedent to act the
subject of the charge—Separation of prior similar acts rendering person a*
B   *suspected person—Vagrancy Act, 1824 (5 Geo. 4 c. 83), s. 4.*

On appeal to quarter sessions by the respondent against conviction of
being a suspected person unlawfully loitering with intent to commit a
felony contrary to s. 4 of the Vagrancy Act, 1824. The recorder held that
there was no case to answer. The evidence accepted showed that on
Sept. 9, the two young men who were sitting in a car saw the respondent
C   try the handles of a Humber car parked in front of them. They then saw
the respondent try the handles of two or three other cars. This made them
suspicious. They got out of their car and kept observation on the respondent
and saw him try the handles of a number of other motor cars. The respondent then tried the handles of a white " Mini ", walked away and returned
to try the handle of the " Mini " again. The period of observation of this
D   conduct was five or ten minutes. The respondent was then seen to get into
a motor car (subsequently proved to be his own) in another street.

Held: the respondent's conduct before the young men got out of their
car having aroused suspicion, he was thereafter a suspected person for the
purposes of s. 4 of the Vagrancy Act, 1824, and, in view of the evidence of
his subsequent conduct in loitering by the " Mini " car, which would
E   constitute sufficiently separate acts of loitering when a suspected person,
there was a case to answer (see p. 385, letter G, post).

Dictum of LORD GODDARD, C.J., in *Pyburn* v. *Hudson* ([1950] 1 All E.R. at
p. 1007) applied.

Appeal allowed.

[As to the offence of loitering by suspected persons, see 10 HALSBURY'S LAWS
F   (3rd Edn.) 700, 701, para. 1337; and for cases on the subject, see 15 DIGEST
(Repl.) 926-928, *8871-8893.*

For the Vagrancy Act, 1824, s. 4, see 18 HALSBURY'S STATUTES (2nd Edn.)
203.]

Cases referred to:
G   *Ledwith* v. *Roberts*, [1936] 3 All E.R. 570; [1937] 1 K.B. 232; 106 L.J.K.B. 20;
155 L.T. 602; 101 J.P. 23; 14 Digest (Repl.) 203, *1686.*
Pyburn v. *Hudson*, [1950] 1 All E.R. 1006; 114 J.P. 287; 15 Digest (Repl.)
927, *8882.*

Case Stated.

This was a Case Stated by the Recorder of the City of Oxford in respect of his
H   adjudication on Jan. 9, 1967, on an appeal by the present respondent, Peter
Cosh (in this summary called " the accused "), against conviction under s. 4
of the Vagrancy Act, 1824, by the Oxford City Magistrates' Court on a charge
that he on Sept. 9, 1966, being a suspected person did unlawfully loiter about in
a certain place, Ship Street, with intent to commit a felony. At the conclusion
of the case for the prosecution (the appeal to quarter sessions being by way of
I   re-hearing) it was submitted to quarter sessions there was no case to answer on
the following grounds. (i) That the accused was charged with being a suspected
person, loitering with intent to commit a felony in Ship Street, Oxford.
(ii) That before he could be convicted of that offence there must be evidence,
(a) that he loitered with intent in Ship Street, Oxford; (b) that he was then
a suspected person, and that in order for him then to be a suspected person he
must have committed some antecedent act which made him a suspected person.
(iii) That the evidence adduced by the prosecution, if accepted by the court,
might have made the respondent a suspected person so that he would have been

guilty of an offence if he had loitered with intent in [another street] but was not A
sufficient to make him guilty of being a suspected person loitering with intent in
Ship Street.   It was contended on behalf of the prosecution before quarter
sessions that what the respondent did in Ship Street could be divided up and
that the prosecution could rely on evidence that the accused tried some car
doors in Ship Street to make him a suspected person; and could rely on evidence
that he tried other car doors in Ship Street to make him guilty of loitering there B
with intent.

The recorder upheld the submission of no case for the following reasons.
(i) Before the respondent could be convicted it must be proved (a) that he had
loitered with intent, and (b) that before the act or acts which constituted the
loitering with intent, he had committed some act or acts which made him a
suspected person.   (ii) That " loitering " in itself did not mean a single act, C
but involved conduct over a certain period of time.   (iii) That the antecedent
conduct which was relied on to make the respondent a suspected person must be
distinguishable from the conduct which constituted the alleged loitering though
the various acts need not necessarily be committed at different places or interrupted or separated by time.   (iv) That on the evidence the accused tried the
handle of a " Mini " car in Ship Street, then of a car in front of it, after which D
he again tried the handle of the " Mini " car, and it was impossible to draw any
sensible dividing line between the acts relied on for antecedent conduct and the
acts relied on for loitering, since the evidence was really of one course of conduct
over a very short period of time.   The question for the opinion of the High
Court was whether or not there was on the evidence a case for the accused to
answer.   E

S. Tumnin for the appellant.
Leo Clark for the respondent.

SALMON, L.J., stated the nature of the appeal, summarised the facts,
and continued: It is quite plain that before anyone can be convicted under
s. 4 of the Vagrancy Act, 1824, any acts relied on to show that he was a suspected F
person must be separate from the acts which are relied on to show that he was
loitering with intent to commit a felony.   The acts must be separate acts, but
they need not be different in kind.   The problem which arises in this case has
been considered on a number of occasions by the courts, and I hope that I have
shortly, but accurately, summarised the law in relation to it.   I do not propose
to refer to any of the authorities save to a passage in the judgment of LORD G
GODDARD, C.J., in *Pyburn* v. *Hudson* (1).   This passage seems to me to be
most apposite to the facts of the present case.   LORD GODDARD, C.J., said,
referring to the authority of *Ledwith* v. *Roberts* (2):

" That case laid down that to come within s. 4 of the Act a person must
be within the category of suspected persons before he does the act which
immediately causes his arrest.   I should be sorry to attempt to lay down that H
the acts which cause him to be a suspected person and the act which causes
him to be arrested must be separated by any particular length of time.
There have been many cases in which police have watched men who have
gone round visiting car parks or cars left unattended in the street with the
object either of driving away a car without the consent of the owner or of
helping themselves to property in the cars.   If they have acted thus for I
a length of time, or in such a way that the court thinks that they have by
their conduct brought themselves within the category of suspected persons,
it matters not whether their acts have been done a quarter of an hour,
or half an hour, or, I would say, even five minutes before another act takes
place which causes the constable to arrest them."

(1) [1950] 1 All E.R. 1006 at p. 1007.
(2) [1936] 3 All E.R. 570; [1937] 1 K.B. 232.

A I think that there LORD GODDARD, C.J., plainly was referring to another similar act.

For my part it seems to me quite plain that on the evidence before the recorder, the respondent did acts before the two young men got out of the motor car in which they were sitting which caused them, and very naturally caused them, to suspect either that he was intending to drive a car away without the owner's
B consent, or to help himself to anything of value which he could find in the car. From the moment that they got out of that car to follow him it seems to me that, on the evidence as it stands, the conclusion is inescapable that he was then a suspected person. What he subsequently did was to commit other acts, true they were of a like nature, but they were certainly other acts. He went to a number of other cars and particularly to a white " Mini ", testing the doors
C apparently without success. There was thus clearly evidence that the respondent was loitering with intent to commit a felony, i.e., with an intent to steal. The recorder in giving his reasons for quashing the conviction and not calling on the respondent for any evidence in defence said this:

D   " On the evidence adduced by the [appellant] (which I accepted) the [respondent] tried the handle of a ' Mini ' car in Ship Street, then of a car in front of it, after which he again tried the handle of the ' Mini ' car, and I found it impossible to draw any sensible dividing line between the acts relied upon for loitering since the evidence was really of one course of conduct over a very short period of time."

The error into which the recorder fell was that he took into account only the
E evidence which related to what the respondent was doing when he tried the " Mini " door and then the door of the car in front of it, and then tried the door of the " Mini " again. I would agree that if one looked at that evidence by itself there would be no evidence here to support the charge. It seems to me from what the recorder said, that he did not, as he should have done, consider the antecedent conduct of the respondent. Had he done so, it is impossible
F to see how he could have concluded that there was no sensible dividing line between that antecedent conduct and what the respondent did when he approached the " Mini " and immediately afterwards. The obvious dividing line is to be found at the moment when the two young men got out of their motor car. That divides the conduct of what the respondent did beforehand, namely his conduct in approaching a considerable number of motor cars and
G trying the doors, from the conduct which, according to the evidence, he did later when he went up to other cars including the " Mini " and then came back to the " Mini ". He had done acts which clearly aroused suspicion before those two young men got out of their car, and on the uncontradicted evidence he was thereafter a suspected person who was loitering by the " Mini " with intent to commit a felony. I would allow this appeal and direct that the Case be sent
H back to the recorder to continue the hearing.

Before parting with this case I would like to say this. It may be that if and when the respondent gives evidence the recorder may think that the evidence given by the two young men does not carry conviction to his mind that they accurately observed what the respondent was doing. It may be that, if the respondent gives evidence, he will have some innocent and credible explanation of what he did, even if he did what these young men say that he was doing. I for my part am not expressing any opinion of any kind whether or not in the final result the recorder will come to the conclusion that the conviction before the magistrates should be upheld. I do, however, firmly come to the conclusion that on the evidence which so far has been accepted by the recorder, there was a case to answer, and he erred in law in leaving out of account what I have referred to as the antecedent conduct of the respondent. This was an important, and indeed a vital matter, and his failure to consider it vitiates the decision.

FENTON ATKINSON, J.: I agree, and there is nothing I wish to add.   A

WIDGERY, J.: I also agree.

Appeal allowed.   Case remitted.

Solicitors: *Sharpe, Pritchard & Co.*, agents for *Cyril L. Teal & Son*, Oxford (for the appellant); *Darby & Son* (for the respondent).   B

[*Reported by* PATRICIA JOHNSTON, *Barrister-at-Law.*]

R. *v.* COX (MAURICE).

[COURT OF APPEAL, CRIMINAL DIVISION (Winn, L.J., Fenton Atkinson and Browne, JJ.), November 30, 1967.]

Criminal Law—Murder—Diminished responsibility—When proper to accept plea of guilty to manslaughter.

Criminal Law—Sentence—Hospital order—Order restricting discharge—Accused charged with murder but convicted of manslaughter on ground of diminished responsibility—Punishment not merited owing to mental disorder—Secure hospital available—Whether proper to make hospital order coupled with order restricting discharge—Mental Health Act, 1959 (7 & 8 Eliz. 2 c. 72), s. 60, s. 65.

On an indictment for murder it is perfectly proper, where the medical evidence shows plainly that a plea of diminished responsibility can properly be accepted, to accept a plea of guilty to manslaughter, if such plea is tendered, and thus to avoid a trial for murder (see p. 387, letter F, post).

The appellant was indicted for murder, the victim being his wife, and, pursuant to the direction of the trial judge on the ground of the appellant's diminished responsibility, the appellant was convicted of manslaughter. Owing to mental disorder the appellant did not, so the trial judge said, merit punishment. There was medical evidence justifying the imposing of an order restricting his discharge under s. 65 of the Mental Health Act, 1959, and a vacancy in a secure hospital was available. On appeal against the sentence of life imprisonment, imposed in order to put the appellant in the hands of the Home Secretary, who would have power under s. 72 to order him to be removed to and detained in the specified hospital,

Held: a hospital order and an order restricting discharge without limitation of time would be made in relation to the appellant under s. 60 and s. 65 respectively of the Mental Health Act, 1959 (see p. 388, letter H, post).

R. v. *Morris* ([1961] 2 All E.R. 672) distinguished.

Appeal allowed.

[Editorial Note. Before making a hospital order coupled with an order restricting discharge, the court ascertains, as in the present case, which hospital can receive the patient, so as to be sure that there are facilities for safe custody: cf., the instance stated in *R.* v. *Higginbotham* [1961] 3 All E.R. at p. 620, letters E-G.

As to diminished responsibility, see SUPPLEMENT to 10 HALSBURY'S LAWS (3rd Edn.) para. 534A.

As to the powers of the court to order hospital admissions, see 29 HALSBURY'S LAWS (3rd Edn.) 524, 525, para. 985, and as to orders restricting discharge, see ibid., 527, 528, para. 990.

For the Mental Health Act, 1959, s. 60, s. 65, s. 72, see 39 HALSBURY'S STATUTES (2nd Edn.) 1013, 1019, 1027.]

A Cases referred to:

  R v. *Gunnell,* (1966), 110 Sol. Jo. 706; 50 Cr. App. Rep. 242; Digest (Cont.
      Vol. B) 178, *5364 fa.*

  R. v. *Morris,* [1961] 2 All E.R. 672; [1961] 2 Q.B. 237; [1961] 2 W.L.R. 986;
      45 Cr. App. Rep. 185; Digest (Cont. Vol. A) 381, *5634d.*

B **Appeal.**

  This was an appeal by Maurice George Cox against a sentence of life imprisonment imposed on him at Sussex Assizes on Mar. 20, 1967. He had been indicted
before BLAIN, J. and a jury for murder, the victim being his own wife, whose death
occurred on Jan. 20, 1967. He was convicted, of manslaughter, on the judge's
direction on the ground of diminished responsibility (s. 2 (1)* of the Homicide
C Act, 1957). Leave to appeal was granted by MacKenna, J., in order that it might
be considered whether the case was not distinguishable from R. v. *Morris†,* and
and whether the proper sentence was not an order under s. 60 and s. 65 of the
Mental Health Act, 1959. The facts are set out in the judgment of the court.

  D. Kelly for the appellant.
  The Crown was not represented.

D

  WINN, L.J. delivered the following judgment of the court: From the very
outset of the trial it was quite clear not only that the appellant was prepared to
plead guilty to manslaughter on the grounds of diminished responsibility but also
that the medical evidence available, in the possession of the prosecution as well as
of the defence, showed perfectly plainly that that plea was a plea which it would
E have been proper to accept. However, the matter proceeded to be tried by the
jury, as a result of which time and money were spent and the appellant was no
doubt kept in some anxiety and uncertainty whilst the trial went on. The court
desires to say yet again, not at all for the first time in the experience of every
member of the court, that there are cases where, on an indictment for murder, it is
  perfectly proper, where the medical evidence is plainly to this effect, to treat
F the case as one of substantially diminished responsibility, to accept a plea to
manslaughter on that ground, if the plea be tendered, and to avoid a trial for
murder.

  When sentencing the appellant (and I deliberately do not dwell on any of the
* circumstances of the offence since plainly the appellant was, to put it at the
lowest, not fully responsible at the time when his wife died) the trial judge referred
G to the Mental Health Act, 1959, and said that there was a section (1) in it which
enabled the Home Secretary to transfer any person who was serving a sentence
of imprisonment, if satisfied by reports from at least two medical practitioners,
to be detained in a hospital for medical treatment, if he thought it fit in the public
interest and in all the circumstances expedient. He said, indeed (though I am not
sure what the effect would be) that he would require that the Home Secretary
I should apply his mind to that section. He went on to refer to the well-known case
in 1961 of *R.* v. *Morris* (2); but it seems probable that he looked at the summary
of *R.* v. *Morris* (3) contained in ARCHBOLD'S CRIMINAL PLEADING EVIDENCE AND
PRACTICE (36th Edn.) at para. 718, which does not bring out the particular feature
of the case of *R.* v. *Morris* (2) that there was, at the time when sentence was passed
in that case by JONES, J., no evidence of a vacancy being available in a " secure "

---

  * Section 2 (1), so far as material, provides: " (1) Where a person kills . . . another,
he shall not be convicted of murder if he was suffering from such abnormality of mind
(whether arising from a condition of arrested or retarded development of mind or any
inherent causes or induced by disease or injury) as substantially impaired his mental
responsibility for his acts and omissions in doing . . . the killing."
    † [1961] 2 All E.R. 672.
    (1) Mental Health Act, 1959, s. 72; 39 HALSBURY'S STATUTES (2nd Edn.) 1027.
    (2) [1961] 2 All E.R. 672; [1961] 2 Q.B. 237.
    (3) See [1961] 2 All E.R. 672, letters E, F, p. 675, letter F; [1961] 2 Q.B. 237.

hospital to which he could have sent the accused.   The trial judge in the instant   A
case, having referred to *R.* v. *Morris* (4) said—and in using these words he was
quoting from *R.* v. *Morris* (5):

> " You are not a man whom I regard as meriting punishment as such, but
> in the public interest I am not prepared to put you anywhere near a place
> where you could be at liberty.   And I therefore pass a sentence of life   B
> imprisonment, which will put you in the hands of the Secretary of State
> for Home Affairs in the future.   The Secretary of State will be informed of
> course, of your history, including your mental history."

At the trial and before that sentence was passed, the trial judge had before him
reports from two duly qualified medical officers and he heard the oral evidence of
one of them.   There was, in this case, a safe hospital available since arrangements   C
had been made for the admission of the appellant should the court take the course
of using the powers which the court had under the Act of 1959, at Broadmoor in
Berkshire.   It is quite clear that there was ample ground on which the medical
men could think that that was a course in the interest of the appellant as well as
of the public.   It follows that the requirement of s. 65 (2) was complied with since
that provides that an order under s. 65 of the Act of 1959, referred to as an order   D
restricting discharge, shall not be made in the case of any person unless at least
one of the medical practitioners whose evidence is taken into account by the
court has given evidence orally before the court.   It is unnecessary to refer to
the provisions of s. 60 itself.   In fact, since that sentence was passed, the Home
Secretary has seen fit, by a warrant dated July 1, 1967, to effect the transfer,
pursuant to his powers under s. 72 of the Act of 1959, of the appellant to Broad-   E
moor Hospital, and in the warrant he further directed that the appellant should
be subject to the special restrictions set out in s. 65 of the Act of 1959, until the
direction restricting discharge ceases by virtue of s. 75 to have effect.   In a sense,
today the issue involved is capable of being described as academic since it will
make no difference to the appellant so far as his treatment is concerned, nor, one
supposes, the place where he will be detained, whether he is subject to s. 72 of   F
the Act of 1959, to or s. 60 and s. 65, but the court can well understand that he,
feeling himself no criminal guilt for the death of his wife, though no doubt he
bitterly regrets it, and having heard the trial judge say that he did not think that
he merited punishment, would naturally think it an injustice that he should be
subject to a sentence of life imprisonment, from which it follows that hitherto
at Broadmoor he has been detained as a criminal lunatic.   He attaches a distinc-   G
tion, and the court sees that there is a real distinction between being in Broadmoor under s. 60 and being in Broadmoor under s. 72.   This court thinks, having
regard to the principles enunciated in *R.* v. *Morris* (4) and having also had the
assistance of re-reading the judgment of this court in the case of *R.* v. *Gunnell*, (6)
that in principle the right sentence here was not the sentence passed, but a
hospital order under s. 60 with a restriction order under s. 65 of the Mental   H
Health Act, 1959, without limitation of time.   The appeal is allowed to that extent
and the sentence is varied accordingly.

Appeal allowed.   Sentence varied.

Solicitors: *Registrar of Criminal Appeals* (for the appellant).

[*Reported by* N. P. Metcalfe, Esq., *Barrister-at-Law.*]

---

(4) [1961] 2 All E.R. 672; [1961] 2 Q.B. 237.
(5) [1961] 2 All E.R. at p. 674, letter E; [1961] 2 Q.B. at p. 242.
(6) (1966), 50 Cr. App. Rep. 242.

A

BALL v. RICHARD THOMAS & BALDWINS, LTD.

[COURT OF APPEAL, CIVIL DIVISION (Willmer, Davies and Edmund Davies, L.JJ.),
November 23, 27, 28, 1967.]

B *Factory—Lifting tackle—Hook—Use for purpose of raising materials—Hook*
attached to overhead crane—Use to lift slightly edge of metal scab adhering to
floor—Intention was to facilitate loosening of scab for removal—Hook not of
adequate strength for the use to which it was being put—Flew off when strain
taken by crane and injured workman who was standing too close—Strain
involved was incalculable, so that adequacy of strength could not be computed—
C *Whether operation " raising material "—Contributory negligence—Factories*
Act, 1961 (9 & 10 Eliz. 2 c. 34), s. 26 (1).

At the employers' steel works molten metal tapped from a furnace was
conducted by a trough or launder down an incline to a ladle. In the process
there was inevitably some overspill of molten metal on the landing floor
across which the launder ran, and the overspill as it cooled and hardened
attached itself as " scab " to the brick flooring, the interstices between
D the bricks and the surrounding steel framework. The scab had to be removed
before the furnace could be used again and one of the two methods of removing
it was by using an overhead crane (it was conceded to be one of its contemplated uses)* to lift the edge of the scab slightly, so that the operator could
place a brick under it to enable him to loosen the scab with an oxyacetylene
burner so that the crane could lift it away after chains had been placed round
E it. The workman responsible had been engaged solely on the same task for
much of his fifteen years' service with the employers and was fully aware of
the process and its potential dangers. On being instructed to clear away the
scab, he removed a brick from under the edge of it, hammered a hook under
the edge and signalled to the overhead crane driver to take the strain. It
was conceded† that the hook was not of " adequate strength " within
F s. 26 (1) (a)‡ of the Factories Act, 1961. As the crane started to lift the scab,
the hook, as it was known to be liable to do, straightened or opened, lost all
purchase on the scab, flew out and hit the plaintiff in the face, injuring him.
He was standing within nine feet of the place where the hook had been
inserted at the time, which was less than the safe distance away, as he
knew. The trial judge absolved the employers of negligence at common law
G in the system of work but found them in breach of their statutory duty
under s. 26 (1) (a) to use only lifting tackle (i.e., the hook, s. 26 (3)) which was
of adequate strength " for the purpose of raising . . . materials ", although
they had given evidence to show that the strain involved was incalculable so
that it was impossible to calculate what strength would be adequate strength.
The judge apportioned to the plaintiff twenty-five per cent. of the responsi-
H bility for the accident. On appeal,

Held: (i) the operation was one of " raising " materials within the meaning
of s. 26 (1), notwithstanding that the scab was not a free load of calculable
weight involving a calculable strain on the lifting tackle; accordingly, in
view of the admission that the hook was not of adequate strength for the
use to which it was being put, the employers were in breach of statutory
I duty under s. 26 (1) for which, as it causally contributed to the accident,
they were liable in damages (see p. 394, letter E, p. 395, letter B, p. 397,
letter G, and p. 398, letter D, post).

Milne v. *C. F. Wilson & Co. (1932), Ltd.* ([1960] S.L.T. 162) applied.

---

* See p. 393, letter H, post.
† See p. 397, letter G, post.
‡ Section 26 (1) (a) is set out at p. 392, letter F, post.

A

(ii) the finding that the accident was partly caused by the plaintiff's negligence in standing too near and the trial judge's apportionment of responsibility for the damage should stand (see p. 395, letters E and I, p. 397, letter H, and p. 398, letters F and I, post).

Appeal dismissed.

B

[For the statutory requirements as to lifting tackle in factories, see 17 HALSBURY'S LAWS (3rd Edn.) 82, para. 138, and for cases on the subject, see 24 DIGEST (Repl.) 1061, *248, 249*.

For the apportionment of liability for accidents to servants, see 28 HALSBURY'S LAWS (3rd Edn.) 94, 95, para. 99; and for cases on the subject, see 36 DIGEST (Repl.) 184-192, *983-1018*.

For the Factories Act, 1961, s. 26, see 41 HALSBURY'S STATUTES (2nd Edn.) 267.]

C

Cases referred to:

Beadsley v. *United Steel Cos., Ltd.*, [1950] 2 All E.R. 872; [1951] 1 K.B. 408; 114 J.P. 565; 24 Digest (Repl.) *1061, 249*.

Caswell v. *Powell Duffryn Associated Collieries, Ltd.*, [1939] 3 All E.R. 722; [1940] A.C. 152; 108 L.J.K.B. 779; 161 L.T. 374; 33 Digest (Repl.) 906, *1352*.

D

Gledhill v. *Liverpool Abbattoir Utility Co., Ltd.*, [1957] 3 All E.R. 117; [1957] 1 W.L.R. 1028; Digest (Cont. Vol. A) 590, *249a*.

Milne v. *C. F. Wilson & Co. (1932), Ltd.*, [1960] S.L.T. 162.

Reilly v. *William Beardmore & Co., Ltd.*, 1947 S.C. 275; [1947] S.L.T. 147; 24 Digest (Repl.) 1061, **114*.

E

Appeal.

This was an appeal by the defendants against an order of SWANWICK, J., made at Newport Assizes on Mar. 7, 1967, adjudging that the defendants should pay the plaintiff £4,856 5s. damages. The grounds of appeal were as follows: (i) that the judge was wrong in law and on the facts in holding that the defendants were in breach of their duty under s. 26 (1) of the Factories Act, 1961; (ii) that the

F

judge ought to have held that the defendants were not in breach of their duty under the section; (iii) that the judge was wrong in holding that the plaintiff was only twenty-five per cent. to blame; and (iv) that the judge ought to have held that the plaintiff was guilty of a higher degree of contributory negligence. The plaintiff served a cross-notice that he intended to contend at the hearing of the appeal that the judgment of SWANWICK, J. should be varied by reversing his

G

finding that the plaintiff was one quarter to blame for his accident and that judgment should be entered for the plaintiff for £6,475 damages; and further that the finding that the defendants were liable to the plaintiff for his accident should be affirmed on the additional ground that the defendants, their servants or agents were negligent. The grounds of the cross-notice were as follows: (a) that there was no evidence on which the judge could find the plaintiff guilty of contributory

H

negligence, or alternatively he so found contrary to the weight of the evidence; (b) the facts found by the judge, or alternatively the evidence given at the trial, established that the defendants, their servants or agents were negligent in the respect alleged in the statement of claim; and (c) the judge found and the evidence called at the trial established that the hook used by the plaintiff was not suitable and safe for its purpose, and the defendants failed to take any steps to

I

ensure that the hook was suitable and safe for the purpose for which the plaintiff used it.

T. Watkins, Q.C., and *Piers Ashworth* for the defendants.
J. M. Davies, Q.C., and *Esyr Lewis* for the plaintiff.

DAVIES, L.J., delivered the first judgment at the request of WILLMER, L.J.: On June 11, 1963, when the plaintiff was in the employ of the defendants at their steel works at Ebbw Vale, he sustained a serious accident while at work. The

A seriousness of the accident may be judged by the fact that the judge assessed the damages on the basis of total liability at the figure of £6,475, including an agreed sum of £1,225 for special damage. The judge held, however, that the plaintiff himself was twenty-five per cent. to blame for his accident and, therefore, the sum for which judgment was given was the sum of £4,856 5s.

The judge based his finding of liability on a breach of s. 26 (1) of the Factories

B Act, 1961, to the provisions of which I shall, of course, have to turn. He found that there was no common law negligence on the part of the defendants; but, as I have said, he found that the plaintiff was twenty-five per cent. to blame. From that judgment the defendants appeal to this court. They submit that the judge was wrong in finding that s. 26 (1) applied at all, and they also contend that the judge ought to have found a larger responsibility on the part of the plaintiff

C than twenty-five per cent. The plaintiff resists the appeal with regard to the breach of statutory duty, and cross-appeals, submitting, first, that the judge ought to have made a finding of common law negligence and, secondly, that he was wrong in attributing any proportion of blame to the plaintiff. Those then are the issues before this court.

The plaintiff, Mr. Ball, had been in the employment of the defendants for some

D fifteen years or so, and for a great deal of that time he had been engaged solely on the task on which he was engaged on the day of his accident. The technical description of his occupation was that of oxyacetylene burner. The locus in quo can be seen from a series of photographs which were put in evidence. On the left of photographs (1) and (2) there is a series of furnaces. In the foreground there is in particular to be seen a trough, known as a launder, leading from one of the

E furnaces. This launder, when the furnace is tapped, conducts the hot molten metal from the furnace down the incline into a ladle, which is out of sight on the right of the photograph. It is apparently inevitable that in the course of that process there should be some degree of overspill from the launder of the hot molten metal as it flows down. The floor of the landing across which the launder runs, and on which the plaintiff was working, some twenty feet above the floor

F of the works, is constructed of bricks in a steel framework. The overspill, when it cools and hardens, is appropriately enough known as "scab". For it attaches itself, in the kind of form to be seen in the photographs, to the brick floor and in the interstices between the bricks and also to the steel framework, and actually welds itself to the launder and other metal work.

Before the furnace can be used again it is necessary for all this scab to be

G cleared away. It is essential that the launder should be broken open on its pivot, as shown in photograph (2), so that the slag may be cleared out of the furnace; and this, of course, cannot be done if the scab is holding the launder in the closed position. According to the plaintiff, there are two methods of removing the scab. The first is by cutting up the scab into pieces by means of the oxyacetylene cutter, and then having those pieces carried away by the crane. This is a somewhat

H lengthy process and may take upwards of three hours. The second, and more rapid, method is to use the overhead crane, to which I shall refer in a moment, to lift slightly the edge of the scab in order that the operator may place a brick under the edge and so enable him with his burner sufficiently to loosen the scab to enable the crane to lift it away when chains are placed underneath and around it.

The crane in question was on rails some twenty feet above the landing on which

I the plaintiff was working. The driver's cab was about sixty feet away. It was an auxiliary hoist of twenty-five tons lifting capacity. The main crane, of 160 tons capacity, does not come into this story. The auxiliary hoist was, according to the evidence, regularly used for three purposes: (a) for tipping the contents of the ladles, which are supported by the main crane, into the moulds; (b) for holding the scrap boxes when the furnaces are being charged; and (c) for the purpose of dealing with the scab, as in the present case. Beneath the block of the auxiliary chain there is suspended a heavy chain, as shown in the drawing that was put in during the hearing of the appeal, weighing some two tons, and variously called the

tipping chain or jib chain. At the foot of the chain there were rings from which A
were suspended lighter chains, each terminating in a hook. On the drawing to
which I have just referred four such chains are to be seen, but on the day of the
plaintiff's accident there were only three.

On that day the plaintiff was instructed by the second furnaceman to clear away
the scab as quickly as possible. He therefore decided not to use the slow burning
process, to which I have referred, but instead to use the more speedy process of B
using the crane to enable him to insert something under the scab in order to
facilitate its removal. He therefore removed a brick from under the edge of the
scab, hammered in with a sledgehammer a hook under the edge of the scab, and
signalled to the crane driver to take the strain. Quite obviously it was necessary
at this stage for the plaintiff to have put himself in a place of safety and security,
since it is clear that in such an operation the hook is likely, as it is said, to " fly ". C
What happened, however, on this occasion was that, when the crane started to
lift the scab, the hook straightened or opened, lost all purchase on the scab, flew
out and hit the plaintiff in the face. Hence the injuries.

There are apparently three ways in which the hook can be caused to fly in the
course of this operation. First, the edge of the scab under which the hook is
placed can break, and then, of course, the hook would fly. Secondly, as the hook D
has a small plain level face at its tip, it cannot penetrate the scab at all and so may
lose its purchase, and again will fly. Thirdly, as on this occasion, if the hook is not
strong enough to raise the scab, it will straighten and come out in that way. From
the evidence of Mr. Hewitt, the defendant's expert, it is plain that in the sort of
circumstances that I have described, this particular sort of incident is something
that does happen from time to time. That, I think, is all I need say about the E
accident, save to add this, that the judge found as a fact that when the accident
happened the plaintiff was standing within nine feet of the place where the hook
had been inserted.

Section 26 (1) of the Factories Act, 1961, provides as follows:

> "*Chains, ropes and lifting tackle.* (1) The following provisions shall be F
> complied with as respects every chain, rope or lifting tackle used for the
> purpose of raising or lowering persons, goods or materials: (*a*) no chain,
> rope or lifting tackle shall be used unless it is of good construction, sound
> material, adequate strength and free from patent defect; . . ."

For the present purpose the only other provision to which I need refer is the
definition contained in sub-s. (3), which states: " In this section ' lifting tackle ' G
means chain slings, rope slings, rings, hooks, shackles and swivels ". So we see
that a hook comes within the expression " lifting tackle ". What is said on behalf
of the plaintiff in this case is that this operation was an operation for the purpose
of raising materials, to wit, the scab, and that the facts demonstrate that the
hook was not, and could not have been, in the circumstances, of " adequate
strength ". It is an interesting point, and there is really no authority on it at all. H
The submission made by counsel for the defendants in this court (not perhaps
entirely the same submission as was made to the judge in the court below) is that
this is not an operation of raising. " Raising ", it is said, connotes the lifting from
the ground of a free unattached article or goods; and it is submitted that his
operation was not an operation of raising, albeit it is conceded that the lift which
was being used was a directly vertical lift. It is said that this was ripping fixed I
material, and that therefore the section has no application whatsoever, since
ripping is not raising.

I think it is right that in this connexion I should refer to the passage in the
judge's judgment where he deals with the contention made before him. Having
referred to a Scottish authority, *Milne* v. *C. F. Wilson & Co. (1932), Ltd.* (1), the
judge says this:

(1) [1960] S.L.T. 162.

A   " I would take the view that that section means that no lifting tackle shall
be used unless it is of adequate strength for the purpose of raising the materials
for which it is being used at the time at which the section falls to be considered; and applying that to this case it is a requirement that this hook
should have been of adequate strength for the purpose of raising any material
which was being raised. Counsel for the defendants has contended that that

B   section is not applicable to the task which was being performed by the crane
at the time of this case. He says that ' for the purpose of raising or lowering ',
first of all, he said, meant lifting off the ground, and as the object of the exercise here was not to lift the scab wholly off the ground, but simply to raise it
sufficiently to enable chains to be put around it so that it could be transported
away, it did not come within the application of the section. Moreover he

C   submitted that the section contemplated that the hook or lifting tackle used
must be of adequate strength, which only meant that it must be of adequate
strength when it was being used in the manner and for the purpose for which
it was designed to be used; and that, applying that to the hook, it did not
apply when the tip of the hook was being used for raising. He also submitted to me that the overload in this case was being caused, as he put it,

D   by the pull of the superstructure which was not the object to be raised, and
that the section was not of application.

   " I am afraid that I cannot accede to these propositions. It seems to me
that the word used in the section is for the purpose of ' raising ', not for the
purpose of ' lifting '. In my judgment the section requires that the hook
of that lifting tackle should be of adequate strength for performing any

E   raising purpose or material raising purpose which is being conducted at the
time. In my judgment the purpose for which this hook was being used was
for the purpose of raising the scab, albeit it might not have been lifting it
completely off the ground; it was for the purpose of raising it, and the
evidence was that it was a vertical lift. Counsel for the defendants says that
the same accident could easily have happened if the crane had been used to

F   drag sideways. That situation can be dealt with in a case in which it arises.
In the present case the evidence is that the lift was vertical, and that it was
being used for the purpose of raising this material, and I so find. I do not
think the section, which is designed for the protection of workmen, means that
the hook shall only be of adequate strength when it is being used in the way
in which it is perhaps most normally used. It follows, I think, from what

G   I have said about my construction of the section that I hold that it must be of
adequate strength when it is being used for the raising purposes for which it is
being used at the time and in the manner in which it is being used, and indeed
in which it is contemplated that it shall be used for this, being a normal
procedure, the employers must have appreciated and realised that it would be
used in this way."

H   In this court the issue on this point has, I think, been considerably narrowed.
For it is admitted on behalf of the defendants that the particular user of the crane
was a user that was one of the three clearly contemplated users of it. That
disposed of one matter in issue. Secondly, it is conceded that on the facts the
hook was not of adequate strength for the task on which it was engaged.

I   The issue really boils down to the question whether this operation was " raising ". One ancillary point which has been taken (which I understand has given
EDMUND DAVIES, L.J., some little doubt) was that it was pointed out by counsel
for the defendants that s. 26 (1) (*b*) refers to tables showing

   " the safe working loads of every kind of chain, rope or lifting
tackle in use and, in the case of a multiple sling, the safe working load at different angles of the legs, shall be posted in the store in which the chains, ropes
or lifting tackle are kept, and in prominent positions on the premises, and
no chain, rope or lifting tackle not shown in the table shall be used."

In the present case the evidence of Mr. Hewitt, the expert, was, as one might   A
expect, that when the hook is being used for this operation, whether it is called
raising or lifting or tearing away, the strain is quite incalculable, since it depends
on so many factors, for example, the strength of the scab, the strength of the weld,
and so on, and that it is quite impossible to make any calculation as to what would
or would not be of adequate strength. It seems to me, however, that the defendants really find themselves in this position, that, if it is not possible to calculate   B
what sort of hook will be of adequate strength, as may well be the case, then the
hook should not be used for this purpose at all.

It is perhaps not without interest and not without relevance to the construction
of the section, which uses the words " lifting tackle " and " raising ", that in
common parlance anyone would refer to the operation on which the plaintiff was
engaged as raising or lifting. It was not only raising or only lifting or only   C
hoisting, of course. There was going to be only a slight lift in order to enable the
plaintiff to get something underneath the scab.   Though I do not place too much
reliance on this, it is not uninteresting to observe that counsel for the defendants,
in the course of his cross-examination of the plaintiff, in many instances used the
word " lifting ", and Mr. Edmunds, the crane driver, in describing what he was
doing on the instructions of the plaintiff, uses both " raise " and " lift ". Moreover   D
in the pleaded defence of the defendants, they use, what is perhaps another
synonym, the word " hoisted ".

It is, as I have said, a point within a very small compass; but I have come to
the conclusion without any sort of doubt whatever that this was an operation
of raising. If I might put it perhaps in a frivolous way for a moment, it seems
to me that in effect what the defendants are saying here is that: " It is a raising   E
or a lifting: but it is only a little one." But the operation appears to me to fall
four square within the term " raising ". That being so, I do not myself find it
necessary to go in any detail into the small number of authorities that have been
cited to us, of which two are *Beadsley* v. *United Steel Cos., Ltd.* (2), and *Gledhill*
v. *Liverpool Abattoir Utility Co., Ltd.* (3). Neither of those was a case in which
there was really in issue the question of the strength or adequacy of the chains   F
or lifting tackle; they were cases where, in the first case a mould and in the
second case a dead pig, fell out of the chains or slings.

I think, however, that it is useful to refer to one or two passages in the interesting judgment of LORD CAMERON in the Outer House of the Court of Session in
Milne v. *C. F. Wilson & Co. (1932), Ltd.* (4). LORD CAMERON said this:

    G

" If this matter was free from authority, I should be inclined to say that
' adequate strength ' is to be construed in its ordinary and natural meaning
and that so construed, the adjective ' adequate ' is not limited to adequacy
in respect of the statutory safe working load but that it must necessarily have
regard to the load which in a particular case it is called on to bear. Apart
from authority, I should not be prepared to exclude this test of adequacy or to   H
limit it to the certified safe working load of the particular ropes."

Then LORD CAMERON quoted (5) a passage from the judgment of LORD MONCRIEFF
in *Reilly* v. *William Beardmore & Co., Ltd.* (6) as follows:

" I agree that in discharging that onus it is entirely idle to refer to the
supplementary paragraphs which prescribe the certifying and recording of
' safe working loads '; the requirements of these paragraphs are clearly
supplementary to, and not exegetic of the primary requirement of ' adequate
strength '."

Finally LORD CAMERON said (5):

" In my opinion, the case of *Reilly* (7) is authority for the proposition that

(2) [1950] 2 All E.R. 872; [1951] 1 K.B. 408.   (3) [1957] 3 All E.R. 117.
(4) [1960] S.L.T. at p. 164.   (5) [1960] S.L.T. at p. 165.
(6) [1947] S.L.T. 147 at p. 150.   (7) [1947] S.L.T. 147.

A   adequacy of strength may relevantly be judged by reference to the use to which the chain, rope or lifting tackle is being put on the particular occasion and that in these circumstances the main contention of the defenders is ill-founded."

So that on the question of the construction of the section, it being, I think, established beyond question that the use to which the crane was being put was a

B   normal and anticipated use, the facts demonstrate that the hook was not of adequate strength, and there was clearly a breach of the section in view of the fact that in my judgment the hook was being used for the purpose of raising this scab to the small extent that was necessary.

[HIS LORDSHIP referred to the issue of common law liability, summarised the submissions of the parties, held that it was unnecessary to come to any final

C   decision on the matter and continued:] Liability, in my view, is determined by the section of the Factories Act, 1961. There remains the question of contributory negligence.   [HIS LORDSHIP cited a passage from the trial judge's judgment on where the plaintiff was standing at the time of the accident and from the plaintiff's cross-examination and continued:] The judge, having seen the plaintiff in the witness-box and having heard his evidence, came to the conclusion, as I have

D   indicated, that he was less than nine feet away. How close he had to be to be hit, it is not easy to calculate. For, of course, it depends very largely on whether it was only the sling chain that swung, or whether the tipping chain also swung; whether, as it were, the two chains made an angle, or whether the two chains combined swung together in line.

In my view it is quite impossible to dissent from the judge's finding that this

E   accident was partly caused by the plaintiff's negligence in standing too near. He was, as I have said, a very experienced man who had been doing this job for years and years, and he must have known that the only safe thing to do was to stand so far away that, whatever happened (unless, of course, the chain itself broke and flew off in pieces) he would be out of range. This he plainly did not do, otherwise he would not have been hit. Counsel for the plaintiff's submission to us was that

F   the act of the plaintiff in standing where he did was a mere act of inadvertence done in the furtherance of his job and in his employers' interest. He referred us to the well known authority of *Caswell* v. *Powell Duffryn Associated Collieries, Ltd.* (8) and he asked this court to say that in these circumstances, even though the accident could not have happened without the action that the plaintiff took, it should not be ascribed to him as being an act of negligence.

G   I cannot accept this submission. It is plain that the plaintiff knew that there was a risk. It is plain that he knew that it was dangerous to stand within range, and it is also plain on the evidence that the accident was easily avoidable. There was plenty of room where he was working for him to retreat to a completely safe distance. In those circumstances I am quite sure that the judge was right in coming to the conclusion that the plaintiff was guilty of negligence. There remains

H   only the question of apportionment. It is well known that this court does not readily interfere with an apportionment of liability made in such circumstances by a judge at first instance. I think that the judge was perfectly right in saying that, when a breach of statutory duty has been found on the part of the employers, as is the fact here, it would be wrong to attribute to the injured workman too large a share of responsibility for his own injury. Not only do I think that this court

I   ought not to interfere, but in my view the apportionment made in the circumstances of the present case by the judge was quite right. Accordingly, for my part, I would dismiss the appeal and cross-appeal.

EDMUND DAVIES, L.J.: In the light of the evidence and the manner in which this trial proceeded in the court below, I think that we should here approach the issue of the employers' liability solely on the basis of whether it is established that the workman's injuries were caused, at least in part, by the employers'

(8) [1939] 3 All E.R. 722; [1940] A.C. 152.

breach of s. 26 (1) of the Factories Act, 1961. I say this because I confess that my   A
first reaction was one of surprise that, in the words of the judge, ". . . very little
real attempt has been made to found this case in common law negligence ".
There are features about the general lay-out and method of working which, with
all respect, strike me as positively primitive. Be that as it may, it is to be observed
that no expert evidence was called on the plaintiff's behalf to establish the only
relevant allegation of negligence pleaded, viz., that: B

> " The use of a crane hook to raise such scabs sufficiently to enable chains
> to be placed round them was unsafe in that the hook was liable to come free
> of the scab and fly when it was lifted."

The absence of expert evidence does not, of course, exclude a finding nevertheless
that an unsafe system was adopted, but, as it appears that that allegation was   C
by no means fully canvassed, I think it preferable to base my judgment solely
on the breach of statutory duty charged.

Section 26 (1) of the Factories Act, 1961, applies inter alia to " lifting tackle ",
a term which embraces " hooks "; but to come within the subsection it must be
" lifting tackle used for the purpose of raising or lowering persons, goods or
material ". That means not merely such tackle as is capable of being so used, or   D
even such tackle as may be specifically designed so to be used, but lifting tackle
which at the material time is in fact being used for " raising or lowering persons,
goods or material ". In this particular case it was therefore incumbent on the
plaintiff workman to establish that at the time of the accident the hook which
proved inadequate to the strain placed on it was, or formed part of, lifting tackle
which was being used for " *raising* " the scab of metal which had escaped over the   E
side of the launder.

For the defendants, counsel has persuasively argued that the plaintiff established
nothing of the sort. He accepts that, but for the accident, the time would have
come when the hook would indeed have been used to raise the scab. But he contends that there were two stages in the operation of clearing the platform:
first, to detach the congealed scab from the platform to which it had become   F
adherent, and, secondly, to raise and remove from the platform the scab thus
detached. To this he adds that it was only during the first (or detaching) stage
that the accident occurred, that the stage of " raising " the detached scab was
never reached, and accordingly that no operation falling within s. 26 (1) was being
performed at the time of the accident.

It is perfectly true that the defendants can point to several passages in the   G
evidence which, at first sight, appear to support such a dichotomy. Thus, the
plaintiff himself described the work being done at the time the hook swung and
struck him as " this *ripping* business ", and the crane driver as " *ripping* this
metal ". Again, counsel for the plaintiff himself put to the crane driver: " At
this time you were just trying to *free* the spillage, were you not, *not* lift it up and
take it away? ", and a little later: " So all this time all you were trying to do was   H
to *free* it? ". In other passages, however, the plaintiff asserted that: " The strain
is a partial lift ", and that at the moment of the accident what was being performed was " a vertical lift ", while the crane driver said: " I started lifting
quietly . . . As soon as I started to take any lift at all, the hook opened . . .
I had lifted no distance at all. "

The various phrases employed to describe the operation thus afford an unreliable guide to the applicability of the statutory provision. As always, the only
safe method is to look at the realities of the situation. The defendants are perfectly correct in submitting that the second stage of slinging and raising the
detached scrap had not been reached when the accident occurred. But notwithstanding that counsel for the plaintiff himself put it to the defendants'
expert witness that he was " pulling off " the adherent scab by " an application
of brute force ", a distinction has to be drawn between the *object* sought to be
attained and the *method* adopted for its attainment. The ripping away, pulling

A off, detachment of the adherent scab was the *object* of the exercise. Despite the evidence of the defendants' expert, I think that object might conceivably have been attained in a variety of ways—by burning or by levering and breaking off piece after piece of the scab, if time permitted, or possibly by so positioning and working the crane that, when the chain was made taut and hauled in, the scab would be pulled or dragged off in a horizontal (or non-raising) direction. Whether

B or not, however, all or any of these suggested means of detaching the scab were practicable, the fact remains that the *method* actually selected was that of raising the scab, and thereby tearing it away from the subjacent platform.

    But that is not the end of the matter. One still has to consider whether the operation being performed was one falling within the absolute and penal duty imposed by s. 26 (1), and that is a consideration which, to my way of thinking,

C involves greater difficulty than the point just dealt with. Counsel for the defendants observed that s. 26 (1) clearly contemplates that a *free* load is being dealt with, a load the weight of which is capable of estimation, a load the raising of which would impose on the lifting tackle a known or calculable strain. That strain being ascertained, it can be compared with the table of safe working loads which s. 26 (1) (b) requires shall be kept in a prominent position, and which s. 26 (1) (c)

D enjoins shall be observed in the selection and use of lifting tackle. But (so the submission proceeds) nothing of that kind could be done in the performance of the operation under review. The evidence repeatedly makes it clear that, owing to the adherence of the scab to the platform, the task of tearing it away places on the tackle a strain which is wholly incalculable, and which indeed frequently proves so excessive that the tackle itself gives way. Can s. 26 (1) therefore be held

E to apply to such an operation? I have found this a difficult question, and I remain in some doubt as to the correct answer. On the whole I have come to the conclusion that an affirmative answer is called for. I respectfully agree with LORD MONCRIEFF's observation in *Reilly* v. *William Beardmore & Co., Ltd.* (9), quoted with approval by LORD CAMERON in *Milne* v. *C. F. Wilson & Co. (1932), Ltd.* (10) that, in considering whether the workman has established a breach of s. 26 (1),

F

      " It is entirely idle to refer to the supplementary paragraphs which prescribe the certifying and recording of ' safe working loads '; the requirements of these paragraphs are clearly supplementary to, and not exegetic of, the primary requirement of ' adequate strength '."

    Granted that the operation was one of " raising ", as I think that it was, it is conceded that the hook was not of " adequate strength " within the meaning of the section. That being so, I find the statutory breach established and, further, that it causally contributed to the accident. I would therefore dismiss the defendants' appeal on the issue of liability. On the issues of contributory negligence and apportionment of blame, I agree with, and do not desire to add to, the observations of DAVIES, L.J. I, therefore, would also dismiss the appeal and the

I cross-appeals on these issues.

    WILLMER, L.J.: I agree. Much of the argument for the defendants rested on the proposition that, when the crane and tackle were used for the purpose of ripping off the scab, the load on the tackle was incapable of calculation. Indeed, the argument for the defendants came near to saying that, wherever tackle is used for an operation in respect of which the load is incalculable, s. 26 of the Factories Act, 1961, can have no application. If the argument for the defendants were to prevail, it would mean that this operation of tearing the scab by the use of a crane, which is admittedly a regular and recognised method of procedure, and which is also admittedly a procedure fraught with some degree of danger, would be completely outside the scope of the Factories Act, 1961, and any regulations made thereunder.

---

  (9) [1947] S.L.T. at p. 150.
  (10) [1960] S.L.T. at p. 165.

That, of course, is a possible view to take, but it seems to me that it would be a   A
curious casus omissus if we were to hold that Parliament had failed altogether to
legislate for an operation such as that with which we are concerned in the present
case. I do not think, however, that Parliament did fail to legislate for this operation. I think that s. 26 of the Act of 1961 is plainly applicable. It has been said
many times (and I will say it again) that the Factories Act, 1961, and the regulations made thereunder are directed to the ordinary employer and the ordinary   B
working man, and have to be construed accordingly. The proper approach to
s. 26 (1) of the Act of 1961, therefore, is that of the ordinary employer or ordinary
workman. I try to put myself in that position and ask myself the two crucial
questions which arise in this case. First, was the tackle in this case being used for
the purpose of raising material? I apprehend that any ordinary man would
answer, Yes. That is the common sense view of what was taking place. Secondly,   C
was the hook which opened of adequate strength? In the course of the argument
before us it was conceded, in accordance with the view expressed by LORD
CAMERON in *Milne* v. *C. F. Wilson & Co. (1932), Ltd.* (11) to which we were
referred, that the adequacy of the hook's strength must be related to the work
which was in fact being performed at the time. If that be right, the second question which I have asked answers itself. Plainly the hook which was in use in this   D
case was of inadequate strength for the purpose for which it was being used. In
those circumstances I entertain no doubt that s. 26 of the Act of 1961 applied,
and that there was a breach of it on the part of the employers.

I have felt rather more difficulty on the second aspect of this case, viz., that of
contributory negligence and apportionment as between the two parties. Let me
say straight away that I wholly reject the submission put forward on behalf of the   E
plaintiff that all that he was guilty of was an act of mere inadvertence. In this case
the plaintiff knew exactly what he was doing. He was an experienced man and
he chose to stand in this particular place. There is no question of his being
absent-minded about it. On the contrary, it seems to me that the considerations
relating to the issue of contributory negligence point rather the other way. It
is not difficult to make out a case that the main and substantial cause of this acci-   F
dent was the act of the plaintiff himself in standing in a place where he was liable
to be hit if, for any reason, the hook did fly, as it did. He was perfectly well aware
of the danger. He was carrying out an operation with which he was thoroughly
familiar, and it is demonstrable that he had to move only a few feet away to be
in a position of absolute safety where he could not possibly be hit however the
hook might fly.   G

In those circumstances I was disposed at one time to think that there was a
good deal of force in the contention put forward on behalf of the defendants that
twenty-five per cent. was too small a proportion of blame to be put on the plaintiff.
Proportions of blame, however, are matters very much for the trial judge, who has
the advantage, denied to this court, of seeing the actual parties and witnesses
himself, and of hearing the way in which they give their evidence. This court   H
is notoriously (and I think rightly) reluctant to interfere with the view of the trial
judge who has had that advantage on a mere question of apportionment of
liability. Having said what I have said, I come in the end to the conclusion that
in the circumstances of this case there is no sufficient ground for interfering
with the way in which the judge in his discretion did apportion the liability. I
therefore agree that the appeal and the cross-appeal must be dismissed.

Appeal and cross-appeal dismissed. Leave to appeal to the House of Lords refused.

Solicitors: *Abbott, Baldwin & Co.*, agents for *Francis Ryan & Co.*, Cardiff
(for the defendants); *Evill & Coleman* (for the plaintiff).

[*Reported by* F. A. AMIES, ESQ., *Barrister-at-Law.*]

---

(11) [1960] S.L.T. 162.

A

PRACTICE NOTE.

[QUEEN'S BENCH DIVISION (Donaldson, J.), November 6, 1967.]

Commercial Court—Practice—Date for hearing—Waiting list—Vacated dates—
B   *Setting down for trial—Summonses—Estimated duration—Commercial*
Court Users Liaison Committee.

Nov. 6. **DONALDSON, J.,** read the following statement:

Introduction of a waiting list. Applications to fix a date for hearing are often
made at an early stage in proceedings in the commercial list. This practice
has much to commend it. In particular it gives the parties an opportunity of
C so arranging their affairs as to minimise the disruption to their businesses which
is inevitably attendant on any court hearing. However the practice is not
without disadvantage. Experience shows that at least half of the causes for
which a date has been fixed are settled before, and often long before, that date
is reached. Yet the court has no means of knowing which causes will be settled
and must perforce treat every matter as effective unless and until the contrary
D appears. As a result it is often unable to fix early dates for a hearing unless
there are circumstances of exceptional urgency.

This problem has been discussed with representatives of the Commercial
Court Users Liaison Committee and it has been decided to introduce a waiting
list as an experimental measure. Parties will apply for, and be given, a date
for trial in the usual way. If all parties are agreed that the cause might be
E ready for hearing at an earlier date, it will also be entered on a waiting list.
As any date for hearing is vacated, whether because the matter has been settled
or for any other reason, an opportunity for a hearing on that date will be offered
to causes on the waiting list. Priority will be given to those estimated to last
approximately the same time as that which has become ineffective, and as
between causes of similar estimated length to that which was first entered on the
F waiting list.

The success or failure of this experimental scheme will lie almost entirely in
the hands of the users of the commercial court. The usefulness of a vacated
date is in direct proportion to the notice which can be given of its availability.
Prompt notification of intention to vacate a date is therefore an essential prerequisite of success and the court must, and will, rely on solicitors and counsel
G to keep it fully informed. Acceptance of an unexpectedly early date for hearing
by parties to causes on the waiting list and by their solicitors and counsel will
inevitably involve inconvenience, but it is hoped that all concerned will strive
to make acceptance possible. In no other way can the limited judicial time
available for the hearing of commercial causes be used to the fullest extent.

No monetary advantage is likely to be achieved by refusing an earlier date
H for hearing, since the consequences of delay can usually be, and where appropriate
will be, fully compensated by an award of interest. Nevertheless it must be
emphasised that no party will be compelled to accept a date for hearing which
is offered consequent on the cause being entered in the waiting list.

Setting down for trial. Timely setting down of cases for trial is essential if
court records are to be properly maintained. In recent months there have been
several instances of causes not being set down or being set down immediately
before the hearing. It may assist practitioners to know that in future the
order fixing the date of hearing will normally also provide that

" The cause shall be set down forthwith or not later than one month
before the date fixed for the hearing, whichever be the later."

Summonses for directions should be amended accordingly.

Summonses. Every effort is made to avoid inconvenience to those concerned
in a cause being heard on a day when summonses are heard, usually Tuesday

and Friday, by marking it as not to be heard before a specified time.   This can **A**
only be done if the court can form a reliable estimate of the time which should be
allocated to the hearing of summonses.   To this end it is essential that solicitors
should mark each summons with an estimate of the time which is expected to
be required for its hearing and should notify the court promptly of any revision
of this estimate.   In particular the court should be given the earliest possible
notification should any summons be unlikely to be effective.   The court would **B**
be further assisted if solicitors would prepare an extra copy of each summons for
delivery to or attention by the judge's clerk.

Suggestions concerning the Commercial Court.   The commercial court was
established at the end of the last century in order to meet the special problems
of the commercial community.   Since then it has sought periodically to adapt **C**
its procedures to the continually changing needs of that community.   The
success of this process depends in part on a steady flow of information and
constructive suggestions between the court and those who appear there either
as litigants or as their professional advisers.

The formation of the Commerical Court Users Liaison Committee (1) will
greatly assist this process and it is hoped that all concerned will make the fullest **D**
use of this additional channel of communication.

PRACTICE DIRECTION.

PROBATE, DIVORCE AND ADMIRALTY DIVISION (PROBATE).

*Divorce—Foreign decree—Recognition by English Court—Practice—Oath as to
    domicil or full statement of facts to be submitted, as case requires.*
*Nullity—Foreign decree—Recognition—Practice—Oath as to domicil or full
    statement of facts to be submitted, as case requires.*

A decree of divorce or nullity pronounced by a foreign court will be recognised **C**
if the oath shows that the parties were domiciled in the territory of the foreign
court at the date of commencement of proceedings which gave rise to the decree.

In all other cases a full statement of the facts should be submitted to a registrar
of the principal probate registry or to a district probate registrar for a decision.
The registrar, after consideration of the facts, will decide whether he requires an
affidavit of law or other evidence in addition to the facts which will be sworn to **H**
in the oath, and give any other directions necessary (2).

COMPTON MILLER,
Jan. 1, 1968.   Senior Registrar.

---

(1) Any communication to the committee may be addressed to:—Mr. Seton Pollock,
Secretary, Contentious Business Dept., The Law Society, Chancery Lane, W.C.2.
(2) Registrar's direction dated Oct. 14, 1957, is now obsolete.

A

KINGSTON-UPON-THAMES CORPORATION *v.*
F. W. WOOLWORTH & CO., LTD.
SAME *v.* BLOXIDGE BROTHERS, LTD.

B

[QUEEN'S BENCH DIVISION (Lord Parker, C.J., Widgery and Chapman, JJ.),
December 4, 1967.]

Trade Mark—False trade description—Description recognised by trade—Rolled
gold cuff-links—Front only of links rolled gold—Description equivocal, but
not false bearing in mind cost of article and usages of trade—Description
not likely to mislead public—Whether a false trade description for purposes
of Merchandise Marks Act, 1887 (50 & 51 Vict. c. 28), s. 2 (2) *as substituted*

C

by Merchandise Marks Act, 1953 (1 & 2 Eliz. 2 c. 48), s. 4.

A pair of cuff-links, displayed on a card so as to show only the outer surfaces of the links, were sold in the first respondents' shop. The card bore
the words " Rolled Gold—Lion Brand ", and the price was 4s. The backs
of the links and their connecting chain were not rolled gold. On a charge
of having sold the links by a false trade description, contrary to s. 2 (2)* of

D

the Merchandise Marks Act, 1887, as substituted by the Merchandise Marks
Act, 1953, evidence was given that it was usual in the trade to describe an
article as rolled gold when only the front was rolled gold. On appeal from
dismissal of the charge,

Held: regarding the justices' findings of fact as a determination that the
description, although equivocal, was unlikely, bearing in mind the trade

E

practice and the price, to deceive anyone, there was no error in law in the
justices' conclusion that the description was not false, and accordingly their
dismissal of the charge should stand (see p. 404, letter I, to p. 405, letter A,
post).

Kat v. *Diment* ([1950] 2 All E.R. 657) explained and distinguished.

Per CURIAM: if a trade description is plainly and unequivocally false,

F

then a trade practice cannot be invoked to cure that falsity (see p. 404,
letter H, post).

Appeal dismissed.

[As to the offence of applying a false trade description, see 10 HALSBURY'S
LAWS (3rd Edn.) 685, 686, para. 1314; and as to the meaning of false trade
description, see ibid., p. 689, para. 1317; and for cases on the subject, see

G

46 DIGEST (Repl.) 163-167, *1089-1114.*

For the Merchandise Marks Act, 1887, s. 2, s. 3, see 25 HALSBURY'S STATUTES
(2nd Edn.) 1114, 1116.

For the Merchandise Marks Act, 1953, s. 1, s. 4, see 33 HALSBURY'S STATUTES
(2nd Edn.) 916, 920.]

H

Case referred to:

Kat v. *Diment,* [1950] 2 All E.R. 657; [1951] 1 K.B. 34; 114 J.P. 472; 46
Digest (Repl.) 165, *1098.*

Case Stated.

This was a Case Stated by justices for the county of South West London
acting in and for the petty sessional division of Kingston-upon-Thames in

I

respect of their adjudication as a magistrates' court sitting at Guildhall, Kingston-
upon-Thames, on Mar. 21, 1967.

On Jan. 13, 1967 (i) an information was preferred by the Corporation of
Kingston-upon-Thames, the appellants, against the first respondents, F. W. Woolworth & Co., Ltd., charging that on Oct. 17, 1966, at 10/13, Market Place, Kingston-upon-Thames, the first respondents sold to one John Charles Brookes a
pair of cuff-links with fronts of rolled gold and backs and chains of a base metal
with no gold covering to which was applied by a card inset a false trade description

---

* Section 2 (2), as substituted, is set out at p. 403, letter E, post.

as to the material of which the goods were composed, namely the words " rolled   A
gold ", contrary to s. 2 (2) of the Merchandise Marks Act, 1887, as amended by
s. 4 of the Merchandise Marks Act, 1953; and (ii) an information was preferred
by the appellants against the second respondents, Bloxidge Bros., Ltd., charging
that the second respondents did counsel and procure the first respondents,
F. W. Woolworth & Co., Ltd., to commit the above-mentioned offence, contrary
to s. 35 of the Magistrates' Courts Act, 1952.   B

The following facts were found: (a) On Oct. 17, 1966, John Charles Brookes
purchased a pair of cuff-links for the price of 4s. from the first respondents, F. W.
Woolworth & Co., Ltd., at their premises at 10/13, Market Place, Kingston-upon-
Thames; (b) the cuff-links were displayed for sale in a box containing a card
inset bearing the words " Rolled Gold—Lion Brand ". The cuff-links were
secured on the card inset in such a way that only the two outer surfaces of each   C
link were visible. Other sets of cuff-links were similarly displayed; (c) each of
the cuff-links comprised an oval shaped part joined by a short length of chain to
a torpedo shaped part. Both the oval shaped and torpedo shaped parts consisted
of two separate pieces; a front piece of rolled gold and a back plate of copper
based alloy. Although of similar colour to the fronts neither the back plate nor
the chain was of rolled gold; (d) rolled gold is a thin coating of fairly poor quality   D
gold on a base metal, applied by mechanical means. " Rolled gold " means that
the article is not wholly gold. It is possible to obtain rolled gold chain; (e) rolled
gold was patented in 1855 and has been in common use for one hundred years;
(f) it is a very general practice to describe cuff-links and other articles as " rolled
gold " when only the front or outside surfaces are of rolled gold; (g) this practice
is of very long standing, going back certainly to 1912 and very probably   E
before 1887; (h) the expression " rolled gold " is used loosely throughout the
trade although both nationally and internationally efforts have been made to
formulate a recognised definition of the expression; (i) the buyer of rolled gold
cuff-links costing 4s. would not expect to buy very much gold; (j) there was no
commercial advantage in calling these cuff-links " rolled gold " as opposed to
using some expression such as " rolled gold fronts "; (k) the cuff-links had been   F
purchased, in their display box with card inset, by the first respondents, F. W.
Woolworth & Co., Ltd., from the second respondents, Bloxidge Bros., Ltd., who
had bought the stock of another supplier, which had manufactured such links
for many years but which had recently gone out of business; (l) the first respondents, F. W. Woolworth & Co., Ltd. had purchased cuff-links of similar
composition from the supplier referred to for more than twelve years and probably   G
for as long as twenty-five years; (m) the description " rolled gold " in this case
was not likely to mislead the public or the purchasers; (n) the use of the description "rolled gold " in this case was a recognised use of the term as applied to
inexpensive cuff-links and the trade description was not false.

It was contended by the present appellants before the justices that the meaning
attributed to " rolled gold " in the trade was not material to the issue before the   H
court and that the defence provided by s. 18 of the Merchandise Marks Act, 1887,
had not been made out. It was contended by the present respondents before
the justices: that the trade description " rolled gold " as applied to these
cuff-links was not false or misleading; that if the trade description " rolled
gold " as applied to these cuff-links was false or misleading it was not false or
misleading in a material respect; that the trade description " rolled gold "
was lawfully and generally applied to the goods of this class before the passing
of the Merchandise Marks Act, 1887.

The justices were of opinion that no false trade description had been applied
and that, taking all the facts into consideration, members of the public would
not have been misled by the description and accordingly dismissed the
informations.

G. C. Ryan for the appellants, the corporation.

W. A. B. Forbes for the respondent companies.

A   **LORD PARKER, C.J.:** The short facts giving rise to this case are as follows: On Oct. 17, 1966, a Mr. Brooks purchased a pair of cuff-links for the price of 4s. from the first respondents at their premises at Kingston-upon-Thames. Each of the cuff-links comprised an oval shaped part joined by a short length of chain to a torpedo shaped part. The cuff-links were displayed for sale inset in a card which bore the words " Rolled Gold—Lion Brand ".

B They were secured to that card in such a way that only the two outer surfaces, that is the outer surface of the oval and the outer surface of the torpedo, were visible. The chain was not visible, nor was the back of the oval or the back of the torpedo. Rolled gold is a thin coating of fairly poor quality gold on base metal applied by mechanical means. In this case both the oval shaped and the torpedo shaped parts consisted of two separate pieces, a front piece of rolled

C gold and a back plate of copper based alloy. Although of similar colour to the fronts, neither the back plate nor the chain were of rolled gold. Those cuff-links had in turn been purchased in their display box with card inset by the first respondents, from the second respondents, who had bought the stock off another supplier, which had manufactured such links for many years but which had recently gone out of business.

D   It was in those circumstances that the first respondents were charged with having sold to Mr. Brooks a pair of cuff-links with fronts of rolled gold and backs and chain of base metal with no gold covering to which was applied by the card a false trade description as to the material of which the goods were composed, namely the words " rolled gold " contrary to s. 2 (2) of the Merchandise Marks Act, 1887, as amended. That section as amended, which appears in s. 4 of the

E Merchandise Marks Act, 1953, provides as follows:

> " Every person who sells . . . any goods or things to which any . . . false trade description is applied . . . shall, unless he proves either—(*a*) . . . or (*b*) [which are immaterial to these proceedings] . . . be guilty of an offence against this Act."

F " False trade description " is defined in s. 3 of the Merchandise Marks Act, 1887, as amended by s. 1 (2) of the Act of 1953, to read so far as is material as follows:

> " The expression ' false trade description ' means a trade description which is false or misleading in a material respect as regards the goods to which it is applied . . ."

It was in those circumstances that the justices reached the conclusion expressed
G in the Case Stated:

> " We were of opinion that no false trade description had been applied, and that taking all the facts into consideration, members of the public would not have been misled by the description and accordingly dismissed the informations."

I In arriving at their conclusion they made certain further findings. In paras. (f) to (h) of the Case they found:

> " (f) It is a very general practice to describe cuff-links and other articles as ' rolled gold ' when only the front or outside surfaces are of rolled gold. (g) This practice is of very long standing, going back certainly to 1912 and very probably before 1887. (h) The expression ' rolled gold ' is used loosely throughout the trade although both nationally and internationally efforts have been made to formulate a recognised definition of the expression."

Those findings are clearly based on the evidence given by a Mr. Gaventa, managing director of a company acting as agent for the fancy jeweller who had held that position for nearly fifty years and had been in the trade since 1912. He said:

> " It was quite usual to describe an article as ' rolled gold ' when only the front was rolled gold. It was common with cuff-links. The parts showed

A

were rolled gold and not the parts that did not.   The practice was widespread. Similar articles could be found all over the country.   It was not a new practice when he started in 1912 but has been the practice long before his time. Rolled gold was originally patented in 1855.   It had been common for one hundred years."

In answer to the bench he said:

B

" The words ' rolled gold ' were used loosely throughout the trade. Many meetings had been held trying to find a recognised definition of rolled gold.   In his opinion the cuff-links in question were rolled gold taking into consideration two factors, first the price and secondly the custom of the trade.   He had sold millions of cuff-links made in this way all over the world without any complaint."

C

Finally in paras. (m) and (n) of the Case the justices find the following:

" The description ' rolled gold ' in this case was not likely to mislead the public or the purchasers.   (n) the use of the description ' rolled gold ' in this case was a recognised use of the term as applied to inexpensive cuff-links and the trade description was not false."

D

Before this court counsel for the appellants contends that the description " rolled gold " in this case was plainly false.   Just as a description of cuff-links as solid gold would be false if the whole article was not of gold, so here he submits that the description is false if the whole article, front, back and chain, was not coated with rolled gold.   The justices, it is said, have only negatived falsity by invoking a trade practice, and that in so doing they have misdirected themselves. He relies strongly on *Kat* v. *Diment* (1).   That was a case in which bottled liquids were sold labelled as non-brewed vinegar.   The magistrate had held on the evidence that vinegar could only consist of a product of double fermentation, and the liquor sold as non-brewed vinegar was not vinegar.   In his judgment LORD GODDARD, C.J., said (2):

E

F

" There was clearly evidence on which the magistrate could come to that conclusion, and we cannot review his findings of fact, nor do I wish to throw any doubt on his finding.   In view of that finding, which there was evidence to support, it is impossible to say that the magistrate was wrong in holding that a false trade description had been applied to the goods.   The fact that this description may be known to the trade and be commonly used by them or may be known to the Ministry of Food is, in my opinion, quite immaterial. If the description is false, it matters not whether other people use it or how generally it may be used, unless it is proved that this description was lawfully and generally applied to those goods at the date of the passing of the Merchandise Marks Act, 1887, which was Aug. 23, 1887."

G

Pausing there, that is a reference to s. 18 of the Act of 1887.   In my judgment, if the true view here is that the justices did use this trade practice to negative a plainly false description, they did misdirect themselves.   If a description is plainly and unequivocally false, as it was in the case of *Kat* v. *Diment* (1) then a trade practice cannot be invoked to cure that falsity.   In my judgment, however, it cannot be said here that the description was unequivocally false.   All that was visible was coated with gold, moreover when the description applies to a thin coating on the surface of base metal, it does not necessarily indicate that the coating is on both sides or on all sides of the base metal and on the chain.   What in my judgment the justices have done here is to find that the description, though equivocal was not, bearing in mind the trade practice and the price of 4s., likely to mislead anyone and therefore was not false.   If, as I think from what they say

H

(1) [1950] 2 All E.R. 657; [1951] 1 K.B. 34.
(2) [1950] 2 All E.R. at pp. 658, 659; [1951] 1 K.B. at p. 39.

A in the Case that was their reason, I can see no error in law and there was undoubtedly evidence to support their findings. I would dismiss this appeal.

WIDGERY, J.: I entirely agree.

CHAPMAN, J.: I agree too.

Appeal dismissed.

B Solicitors: *J. Noel Martin, Town Clerk,* Kingston-upon-Thames (for the appellants); *Lovell, White & King* (for the respondent companies).

[*Reported by* N. P. Metcalfe, Esq., *Barrister-at-Law.*]

C

ROSE & CO. (WALLPAPER & PAINTS), LTD.
v. CAMPBELL (Inspector of Taxes).

[Chancery Division (Pennycuick, J.), November 22, 23, 1967.]

D *Income Tax—Allowance—Investment allowance—" Plant "—Capital or revenue expenditure—Pattern books of paint and wallpaper retailer—Effective life of pattern books was two years—No value as separate asset and scrap when discarded—Finance Act,* 1954 (2 & 3 Eliz. 2 c. 44), *s.* 16 (3) *as amended.*

The taxpayer company, a paint and wallpaper retailer, incurred expenditure on wallpaper pattern books, comprising patterns manufactured by another firm selected and purchased by the taxpayer company and printed and bound for it by a third firm. The preparation and useful existence of each book extended into four calendar years, being in process of compilation and manufacture from the middle of the first, in full use in the second and third and replaced by a new pattern book at the beginning of the fourth, in January and February of which sales were held in which the remaining stocks were disposed of. Some six thousand books were prepared for each such period at a cost of about £3 a book, the total cost in 1962 being £15,703. The books remained the property of the taxpayer company and were partly issued without charge to decorating contractors throughout the country, and partly kept for daily use at the taxpayer's company's wholesale and retail branches and depots. The books were essential to the success of its business, about half of its profits being attributable to their distribution. It claimed an investment allowance in its income tax assessment in respect of the expenditure.

Held: no investment allowance could be made in respect of the expenditure on pattern books because it was not capital expenditure on new plant within the meaning of s. 16 (3)* of the Finance Act, 1954, but was revenue expenditure being an outlay incurred in selling the company's papers comparable to expenditure on sale catalogues or advertising material; for the pattern books had a life of only two years, had no value as a separate asset, and had lost their function and were scrapped at the end of that period (see p. 408, letter I, and p. 409, letter A, post).

Semble: the pattern books did not constitute plant for the purposes of s. 16 of the Act of 1954 (see p. 409, letter G, post).

Appeal dismissed.

[As to relief from income tax for capital expenditure, see 20 Halsbury's Laws (3rd Edn.) 491, para. 936; and for cases on the subject, see 28 Digest (Repl.) 115-124, *431-480.*

For the Finance Act, 1954, s. 16, see 34 Halsbury's Statutes (2nd Edn.) 291; and as regards amendments and repeal, see footnote (1), post.]

---

* Section 16 (3), so far as material, is set out at p. 408, letter A, post.

Cases referred to:

Hinton (*Inspector of Taxes*) v. *Maden & Ireland, Ltd.*, [1959] 3 All E.R. 396;
    [1959] 1 W.L.R. 875; 38 Tax Cas. 391; Digest (Cont. Vol. A) 874, *480a*.
Yarmouth v. *France*, (1887), 19 Q.B.D. 647; 57 L.J.Q.B. 7; *on appeal*, (1888),
    4 T.L.R. 561; 34 Digest (Repl.) 299, *2159*.

Case Stated.

The taxpayer company appealed to the General Commissioners of Income
Tax for the city of York against the following assessments to income tax made on
it under Case 1 of Sch. D to the Income Tax Act, 1952, in respect of its trading
profits as a paint and wallpaper retailer: year 1963-64, £171,000 less capital
allowances of £12,000; year 1964-65, £115,000 less capital allowances of £15,000.
The general ground of the appeal notified to the commissioners was that the
taxpayer company claimed investment allowances under s. 16 (1) (3) of the
Finance Act, 1954 (as amended), in respect of its expenditure on certain of
its wallpaper pattern books. The commissioners held that the expenditure
on pattern books was not capital expenditure and that the pattern books could
not themselves be regarded as plant, and they determined the assessments
accordingly as follows: 1963-64 £112,702 less capital allowances £15,459,
balancing charge £596; 1964-65 £120,417 less capital allowances £23,642, balancing charge £1,452. The taxpayer company appealed by way of Case Stated* to
the High Court.

D. C. Potter for the taxpayer company.
C. N. Beattie, Q.C., and *J. R. Phillips* for the Crown.

PENNYCUICK, J.: This is an appeal by the taxpayer company, Rose and
Co. (Wallpaper and Paints), Ltd., against a decision of the General Commissioners
for the York Division given on July 6, 1965. By that decision the General Commissioners disallowed an appeal by the taxpayer company against assessments to
income tax under Sch. D in respect of its profits as a paint and wallpaper retailer
for the years 1963-64 and 1964-65. The point at issue was whether the taxpayer
company was entitled to investment allowances under s. 16 (3) of the Finance
Act, 1954, in respect of its expenditure on certain wallpaper pattern books.

It appears from the Case that the only evidence before the commissioners was
that of Mr. Rosen, a director of the taxpayer company, which they accepted.
I will read the commissioners' findings of fact which are quite short. They are
contained in para. 4 of the Case Stated.

"(a) The wallpaper pattern books contained samples of wallpaper
manufactured by the Wallpaper Manufacturers, Ltd. The [taxpayer company]
selected and purchased these samples, and they incurred further expenditure
in having these printed and bound by Cheapside (Productions), Ltd., of
Bristol.

"(b) The preparation and useful existence of a pattern book spread into four
separate calendar years. From the middle of the first calendar year the
pattern book was in the process of being compiled and manufactured. In the
second and third calendar years the pattern book was in full use, and in the
fourth calendar year it was the custom to have sales in the January and
February at which any remaining stocks were disposed of. At the beginning
of the fourth calendar year the pattern book was replaced by a new pattern
book. A pattern book was, therefore, planned to have a minimum useful life
of two years. For each such period some six thousand of the pattern books
in question were prepared at a cost of about £3 a book, and the [taxpayer
company's] expenditure on these pattern books in 1962, for example, had
been £15,703."

---

* The facts in the Case Stated and the contentions of the parties are reproduced
verbatim in the judgment at p. 406, letter G, to p. 407, letter F, post.

A The statement in para. (b) is rather compressed. It must, I think, mean that the stocks which were not included in the new pattern book were disposed of in the year in which the new pattern book came into operation. To resume—

"(c) The [taxpayer company's] practice in compiling its accounts was to write off three-fifths of the expenditure on pattern books after the first year of full use and the remaining two-fifths after the second year of full use. The **B** [taxpayer company] had not claimed an investment allowance in respect of its expenditure on pattern books for any year previous to 1963-64.

"(d) The pattern books were not sold by the [taxpayer company] but some were issued free of charge through the [taxpayer company's] representatives to decorating contractors throughout the country and others were kept for daily use at all branches and depots of the [taxpayer company] (wholesale **C** and retail) by staff and customers. They remained the property of the [taxpayer company] which reserved the right to withdraw the books. The pattern books were generally accepted and known as containing the [taxpayer company's] particular selection, under the [taxpayer company's] trade name ' Academy '.

"(e) The pattern books were essential to the success of the [taxpayer **D** company's] business, and about half of the [taxpayer company's] sales of wallpaper were attributable to the distribution of the pattern books. The [taxpayer company] was insured against the contingency of the pattern books being lost in the course of transit from the manufacturers; the cover extended only to loss of profit caused by the pattern books not being available for delivery to the [taxpayer company's] customers at the appropriate time, **E** and it did not extend to any loss occurring after the pattern books had been received by the [taxpayer company] from the manufacturers. However, the [taxpayer company's] comprehensive insurance in respect of its business premises covered all books in the [taxpayer company's] custody. The only risk not insured was loss or damage to a book in the custody of a customer."

The contentions are set out in paras. (5) and (6) as follows:
F
"(5) It was contended on behalf of the [taxpayer company] that the pattern books were plant used by the [taxpayer company] in its business, and that it was consequently entitled to an investment allowance in respect of the capital expenditure involved.

"(6) It was contended by [inspector of taxes] that:— (i) The expenditure **G** on the pattern books was not capital expenditure, but was expenditure properly chargeable to revenue account. (ii) The pattern books were not plant."

The third contention has been very properly jettisoned by counsel for the respondent inspector of taxes on this appeal, and the fourth contention is accepted by counsel to be irrelevant.

Paragraph (7) sets out four authorities which were cited.

I "(8) We the commissioners who heard the appeal, having considered the evidence adduced before us and the arguments addressed and authorities cited to us, decided that the expenditure on pattern books was not capital expenditure and that the pattern books themselves could not be regarded as plant."

It will be convenient at this stage to read the section under which the claim for investment allowance is made. Section 16 of the Finance Act, 1954, contains the following provisions (1), so far as now material:

"(1) In the cases provided for by this section, an allowance (in this Act referred to as an ' investment allowance ') shall be made in respect of capital expenditure on new assets incurred after Apr. 6, 1954.

(1) Section 16 is repealed, but not so as to affect allowances in respect of expenditure incurred before Jan. 17, 1966, and in certain other respects (Finance Act 1966, s. 35). Section 16 (3) is printed as amended by Finance Act 1963, s. 33, and Finance Act, 1959, s. 21 (2); see also Finance Act 1967, s. 21 (3).

" (3) An investment allowance equal to [three-tenths] of the expenditure shall be made [in addition to an initial allowance] under chapter 2 of the said Part 10 in respect of expenditure on the provision of new machinery or plant and any provision of the Income Tax Acts applicable to initial allowances under that chapter, so far as it is applicable in relation to allowances for new assets, shall apply also to investment allowances under this subsection . . ."

There follow certain qualifications, to one of which I will briefly refer at a later stage. The question whether the expenditure on the pattern books is capital expenditure is one of accountancy principles and practice. The construction of the word " plant " is a matter of law. The facts are not in dispute. The only matter therefore on which the finding of the commissioners is of weight is the application of the word " plant " on its proper construction to the admitted facts. In the absence of any elaboration of their reasons the weight to be attached to the finding of the commissioners is not very great. I will, however, say at once that I have reached the same conclusion as the commissioners did.

There has been one decision in the House of Lords on these provisions which is of the greatest importance in the present case; i.e., *Hinton (Inspector of Taxes)* v. *Maden & Ireland, Ltd.* (2). As appears from the speeches in the House of Lords in that case, a trader must establish two distinct matters in order to qualify for an allowance under s. 16 (1) and (3) of the Act of 1954, viz., (i) that the expenditure is capital expenditure, and (ii) so far as now in point, that the article on the provision of which the expenditure has been made is plant. I mention at this stage that those are separate considerations because in one of his contentions counsel for the taxpayer company in effect said that there was only one consideration. He put it in this way: " A finding that the expenditure was not capital expediture to the extent that it is a finding of fact is repugnant to the true finding that the books are plant." If the matter were free from authority I should have thought that on the construction of the section that was an arguable point; i.e., that, once one had established that the article in question was plant, that was the end of the matter. However, the House of Lords unequivocally treated the two questions as being distinct and, of course, I must proceed on that basis.

The issues are however closely related, as was pointed out by, for example, LORD JENKINS in these words (3):

" The second question (viz., whether the expenditure on the provision of the lasts and knives was capital expenditure) presents more difficulty, but broadly speaking, I think that subject to the requisite degree of permanence, an appliance which satisfied LINDLEY, L.J.'s definition (4) of plant is well on its way to attaining the status of a capital asset . . ."

The converse must I think be equally true that, if expenditure on a chattel is capital expenditure, that chattel is well on its way to being plant. I propose to approach the present question from that angle as did LORD REID in *Hinton (Inspector of Taxes)* v. *Maden & Ireland, Ltd.* (2), i.e., I will consider first whether the expenditure is to be regarded as capital expenditure.

I am clearly of the opinion that this expenditure did not represent capital expenditure. The life of each set of pattern books is a little more than two years. The sole function of the pattern book is to supply prospective customers during that period with patterns of papers currently in stock. The books have from the very start no value at all as a separate asset. At the end of each period the function of the books is spent. Then the books are scrapped and a new cycle begins. On these facts the cost of the books is, I think, simply an outlay incurred in selling the company's papers. It is comparable to expenditure on sale catalogues or indeed any other advertising material. There was no expert evidence before the

---

(2) [1959] 3 All E.R. 356; 38 Tax Cas. 391.
(3) [1959] 3 All E.R. 369; 38 Tax Cas. at p. 424.
(4) In *Yarmouth* v. *France* (1887), 19 Q.B.D. 647 at p. 658.

A commissioners as to accountancy principles and practice, but it seems to me that, on the ordinary principles and practice of accountancy as I understand them, such expenditure would be regarded as properly attributable to revenue. It would not, I think, be normal practice to bring in this intrinsically valueless article as a capital asset at the cost of manufacture and write it off during the period of its life. I should mention that, by an arrangement with the Revenue which appears in

B para. 4 (c) of the Case Stated, the expenditure on the pattern books was in practice spread over the two years of their life. Nothing, I think, turns on this point in the present case one way or the other. Clearly being spread over two years is no indication that the expenditure ought properly to be treated as capital and, on the other hand, counsel for the Crown accepts that s. 16 (3) (c) operates to prevent the expenditure from being excluded from the category of capital expenditure merely

C on this ground.

On the view which I have expressed as to capital expenditure, the question whether the pattern books are plant does not arise. I will only make certain brief observations on this point. It is now well established that the word " plant " has a very wide meaning. In *Yarmouth* v. *France* (5), LINDLEY, L.J., said this:

D " There is no definition of plant in the Act (6): but, in its ordinary sense, it includes whatever apparatus is used by a business man for carrying on his business,—not his stock-in-trade which he buys or makes for sale; but all goods and chattels, fixed or moveable, live or dead, which he keeps for permanent employment in his business . . ."

The chattel was in that case a horse. LINDLEY, L.J.'s words have been repeatedly

E approved in later cases of the highest authority and were specifically so approved by LORD REID and LORD JENKINS in *Hinton* (*Inspector of Taxes*) v. *Maden & Ireland, Ltd.* (7). The only qualification, which widened LINDLEY, L.J.'s words, is that the word " permanent " must be regarded as denoting no more than some degree of durability; see LORD REID (8) and LORD JENKINS (9). It must be a question of degree in each case whether a given chattel does possess the

F requisite durability. Obviously the life or expectation of life of a chattel is the primary ingredient of durability, but I doubt whether one can take some conventional period of time, e.g., one year, and say that a chattel having that life or expectation of life possesses the necessary degree of durability. One must, I think, for this purpose take into account all the circumstances including the character and the function of the chattel. It would not be useful to elaborate

G that at this point in the present case. I will content myself with saying that I see no reason to doubt that the commissioners attributed the right meaning to the word " plant ". They had been referred to *Hinton* (*Inspector of Taxes*) v. *Maden & Ireland, Ltd.* (7) and a number of other cases. On the facts of this case their conclusion that these pattern books did not constitute plant was a reasonable one. I propose accordingly to dismiss this appeal.

H   *Appeal dismissed.*

Solicitors: *Doyle, Devonshire & Co.*, agents for *Rees T. C. Jones*, Hanley, Staffs. (for the taxpayer company); *Solicitor of Inland Revenue.*

[*Reported by* F. A. AMIES, ESQ., *Barrister-at-Law.*]

---

(5) (1887), 19 Q.B.D. at p. 658.
(6) The Employers' Liability Act, 1880.
(7) [1959] 3 All E.R. 356; 38 Tax Cas. 391.
(8) [1959] 3 All E.R. at pp. 362. 363   38 Tax Cas- at p. 417.
(9) [1959] 3 All E.R. at p. 369; 38 Tax Cas. at p. 424.

R. *v.* COX (PETER).

[COURT OF APPEAL, CRIMINAL DIVISION (Winn, L.J., Fenton Atkinson and Browne, JJ.), November 30, 1967.]

Criminal Law—Conspiracy—Conspiracy to commit crime abroad—Goods fraudulently obtained abroad—No agreement to commit any criminal act in England—Allegation that goods to be sold in England but nothing to show that sale of such goods was criminal offence in England—Whether indictment for conspiracy lay.

Twenty unused cheques on an English bank were made available to the applicant who used some of the cheques in France for the purpose of obtaining fraudulently jewellery from shopkeepers. The applicant was charged in England on an indictment which included a count (count 1) of conspiracy to defraud, and on arraignment the indictment was amended so as to charge also conspiracy to sell the goods so obtained. The indictment as amended, however, contained nothing to indicate that the conspirators agreed to do in England any act that was a crime by English law. On appeal against conviction on count 1,

Held: there being no evidence of any criminal conduct within the scope of the agreement constituting the alleged conspiracy that was agreed to be or was committed in England, the conviction on count 1 would be quashed, for an agreement to commit abroad such a criminal offence as obtaining by false pretences (as distinct from murder or treason) could not be validly made the subject of an indictment in England (see p. 412, letter G, p. 413, letter F, and p. 414, letter A, post).

R. v. *Kohn* ((1864), 4 F. & F. 68) and dictum of LORD GODDARD, C.J., in *R.* v. *Owen* ([1956] 3 All E.R. at p. 438) distinguished.

Per CURIAM: if the crime that conspirators agreed to commit might be committed inside the United Kingdom, then their conspiracy would be indictable in England; but the amendment of the indictment by adding words charging conspiracy to sell in England goods obtained by false pretences abroad was of no significance, for the amended count did not charge conspiracy to commit any criminal offence by disposing of the goods in England (see p. 413, letter A, and p. 411, letter I, post).

[As to the limits of criminal jurisdiction, see 10 HALSBURY'S LAWS (3rd Edn.) 316-319, paras. 577, 579, 581; and for a case on the subject, see 14 DIGEST (Repl.) 126, *877*; as to offence of conspiracy, see 10 HALSBURY'S LAWS (3rd Edn.) 312-314, para. 570.]

Cases referred to:
Board of Trade v. *Owen*, [1957] 1 All E.R. 411; [1957] A.C. 602; [1957] 2 W.L.R. 351; 121 J.P. 177; *affg.* sub nom. *R.* v. *Owen*, [1956] 3 All E.R. 432; [1957] 1 Q.B. 174; [1956] 3 W.L.R. 739; 120 J.P. 553; Digest (Cont. Vol. A) 341, *1100a.*
R. v. *Kohn*, (1864), 4 F. & F. 68; 176 E.R. 470; 14 Digest (Repl.) 126, *877*.

Application.
The applicant Peter Stanley Cox had pleaded guilty at his trial on Apr. 12, 1967, to a count (count 1) of conspiracy to defraud, for which he was indicted jointly with one Dowthwaite. He was sentenced to three years' imprisonment on that count and to six months' concurrent on another count (count 5) of possessing a document so closely resembling a driving licence as to be calculated to deceive, contrary to s. 232 (2) (*b*) of the Road Traffic Act, 1960. The applicant applied for leave to appeal against sentence. On this application coming before the Court of Appeal (LORD PARKER, C.J., WINN, L.J., and COOKE, J.) on Oct. 5, 1967, it was adjourned, the court granting legal aid so that counsel might apply for leave for the applicant to appeal out of time against conviction

Applied in R. *v.* BRIXTON PRISON GOV., *Ex p.* RUSH. [1969] 1 All E.R. 316.

A   notwithstanding his plea of guilty. The Court of Appeal intimated that there was an important matter to be considered on full argument, viz., whether a conspiracy in England to obtain goods abroad by false pretences, and thereafter to bring them back to England and sell them there, was indictable in England. The matter came before the court again on Nov. 17, when it was adjourned, different counsel being instructed for the applicant and further information **B**   being required.

The authority noted below* was cited during the argument in addition to the cases referred to in the judgment.

J. B. R. Hazan for the applicant.
A. E. Holdsworth for the Crown.

C   **WINN, L.J.,** delivered the following judgment of the court: The applicant was arraigned at Essex Assizes on Apr. 12 on a count which, as originally framed, charged him with conspiracy in Essex with a man called Dowthwaite, for that on divers days between Sept. 1, 1966, and Oct. 26, 1966, in the county of Essex they had conspired together to defraud such persons as should thereafter be induced to part with goods to them by falsely representing that they or one of **D**   them had an account at Lloyds Bank, Ltd., Rayleigh in Essex. That was the original count.   On the arraignment, counsel for the Crown, who was prosecuting, applied for leave to amend that count.   Counsel who was then defending, not counsel who has appeared on this application, stated that he did not oppose that amendment.   The amendment so sought and granted was to add the words " and to sell such goods " at the end of the indictment so that it amounted to a **E**   charge that they had also conspired together to sell in Essex such goods as they might obtain by those misrepresentations.   It appears that both counsel thought that that amendment made a material difference to the effect of the count. That is quite plain from what was said in mitigation by counsel then defending the applicant.   He said that the difficulty which he had felt was one of law and not of fact.

F   ". . . it is quite clear that they did come back to this country with the
      goods and that those goods had been disposed of subsequently though it
      is not clear exactly by whom.   In view of that it is right to say that [the
      applicant] then accepted my advice with respect to that point."

He had said a little earlier that he had had in mind a certain reported case, no doubt that of *Board of Trade* v. *Owen* (1), and had at one time thought that, **G**   on his instructions, it was doubtful whether at any initial stage there was an agreement to carry out the fraudulent transaction in France before they actually left England, and then he referred to the effect of their statements to the police. Notwithstanding that, it seems that counsel then appearing for the applicant thought—and it is quite plain from what counsel for the Crown has said to the court today that he thought—that it made this conspiracy indictable, or **I**   strengthened, as counsel for the Crown put it, the argument that the conspiracy was indictable, in England to say that part of the objects contemplated and intended by the conspiracy was that they would sell in England any goods which they obtained by false pretences abroad.   In the opinion of the court, that addition was of no significance; as it seemed to the court counsel for the Crown was ultimately constrained in argument—it is fair to him to say that he has **I**   been pressed hard in argument in this court—to admit that, as framed after amendment, the count did not charge a conspiracy to commit any criminal offence by disposing of the goods in Essex after obtaining them abroad.   What counsel for the Crown has said to this court is that the count in the indictment read literally, read as a count descriptive of the offence charged, is capable of

---

    * ARCHBOLD'S CRIMINAL PLEADING, EVIDENCE AND PRACTICE (36th Edn.) paras.
4059, 4071.
    (1) [1957] 1 All E.R. 411; [1957] A.C. 602.

comprising a conspiracy not only to use in France fraudulently those blank A
cheques which were used there; but also after returning to the United Kingdom
to use here the residue of the cheques which might then be available.   Stated
as a proposition of interpretation of the wording of the count, that submission
is undoubtedly accurate, but when applied to the substance and reality of this
case it seems to the court that it is quite unreal, and quite beside the point so far
as any relevant point is concerned.   On the depositions to which this court has B
been referred, belatedly, there is no evidence of any use of any of the remaining
cheques after the men concerned returned to the United Kingdom.   As the
court understands the facts, an individual, who no doubt was just as fraudulent
as the two accused who were brought before the Essex Assizes (that is to say,
Dowthwaite and the present applicant) made available to them, with criminal
foresight as to how it would be used, a cheque-book which contained a number C
of unused cheques, probably twenty, and of those twenty about five were used
in France in order to obtain fraudulently various jewellery from shopkeepers.
How it comes about that shopkeepers of that hardworking nation were prepared
to part with valuable jewellery against cheques of an English bank filled in
with quite substantial sums in French francs and signed in their presence by a
man who chose to keep his gloves on, so that his companion had to fill in the D
substance of the cheques, really passes the understanding of this court, but it
happened.

Now one turns to what was said, not on the return of Dowthwaite and the
applicant, which must have taken place before Nov. 1, 1967, but on Dec. 22
when the applicant was interviewed by the police.   I do not propose to cause
myself again the annoyance of reading, and certainly not of reading aloud, the E
impudent, arrogant and quite outrageous language used by the applicant on that
occasion.   In substance it came to this:

" You cannot get me for the criminal offences which I admittedly committed in France.   I know better than that.   You cannot charge me here
in England.   It is only in France that I can be charged for those offences."

Whether or not he knew about his liability to be extradited is not clear.   How
much of the law he has read, one does not know.   He probably will find himself
in very grave trouble indeed if he goes on in the future relying on his very partial
grasp of the law of this country.   Unfortunately, however, he was right in this
case to this extent; that it is the law of this country as it now stands (fortunately it is receiving attention by one of the law reform committees) that there G
cannot be an indictment laid in this country for the commission of criminal
offences abroad with the exception of murder and, I think, probably treason.

What, of course, was being said by the prosecution at the trial and has been
said by counsel for the Crown very helpfully and clearly to this court today, is
that that rule of law presents no impediment to indicting persons for conspiracy
in the United Kingdom to commit offences abroad if there are going to be certain H
consequences in this country, which consequences themselves will—though
counsel for the Crown did not add this qualification—constitute offences which
are criminal by the law of this country.   A simple example one could imagine:
men conspiring in Essex to go to the continent and there obtain by false pretences,
such as these dud cheques, firearms with the object of bringing those firearms
back to England and put them illegally into circulation to uncertificated
holders, by sale.   Another indictable offence which would be a conspiracy in
this country, would be agreeing together to go to the continent and obtain by
unlawful means (theft, false pretences or other unlawful means) dangerous
drugs within the Schedule to the Dangerous Drugs Act 1965, and bring them
back to England and putting them into distribution in this country.   The
distinction, however, between those hypothetical cases and this one is that there
is nothing in the wording of the indictment in the instant case, alleging that it
was any part of the intention of the conspirators to commit inside this country

A any criminal offence. The scope of the conspiracy is determined by the agreement of the conspirators. It is quite right that if the terms of their agreement
are such as to comprise the possibility that the crime that they agree to commit
may be committed inside the United Kingdom, then their conspiracy will be
indictable in this country.

   Reference has been made to *R.* v. *Kohn* (2). The conspiracy there was to
B cast away and destroy a certain Prussian merchant ship to the prejudice of
underwriters. In fact the ship was sunk far out of English territorial waters;
but WILLES, J., directed the jury that conspiracy in this country to commit an
offence was criminal and unless the conspiracy was limited to a criminal offence
to be committed abroad the indictment would lie in this country, for it might
have been within the contemplation of the conspirators that the ship might be
C scuttled or otherwise destroyed off the bar close in territorial waters; that is
quite clearly a case where the possibility existed, albeit it may not have been
expressly the intention of the conspirators, to carry out in pursuance of their
conspiracy, and as an overt act of the conspiracy, a crime within the United
Kingdom. When LORD GODDARD, C.J., was giving judgment in the Court of
Criminal Appeal in *Board of Trade* v. *Owen* (3), he referred to count 5 and indeed
D count 6 of the indictment in that case. Those counts never fell to be considered
by the House of Lords. The rest of the case was appealed to that House (4).
Count 5 charged the appellants with conspiracy with various persons to utter
forged documents purporting to be end-user certificates from a department of the
Republic of Ireland. Count 6 charged one of them with uttering such a
certificate. As LORD GODDARD, C.J., said (5), it was clear that even if certain
E evidence had not been tendered, the alleged object of the conspiracy might have
been carried out in this country, for example by personal delivery of the forged
documents to various persons who might be in London. In such circumstances
it was clear from *R.* v. *Kohn* (6) that the appellants could properly be indicted
in this country. In that case there was evidence that that object was carried
out in London. In the present case, as I have said, there is no evidence that any
F criminal conduct within the scope as to which the conspirators came to an
agreement was committed within the United Kingdom. All the evidence as to
intention available from the remarks and conduct of the accused men, and
particularly that of the applicant, was that it was only in France or on the
continent that they intended and agreed with one another that these false
pretence obtainings should be carried out. The very day that they got possession
G of the cheque-book they left the same evening for France. They were back
within either twenty-four or forty-eight hours. Various alterations were made
in passports in order to endeavour to cover up this visit to the continent and,
as I have already said, boastfully, truculently, the applicant repeatedly said,
" You cannot touch me for any of the offences I committed over there ". He
said that more than once in one form or another.

H   There are still areas in which the criminal law of this country is capable of
improvement. There is no doubt at all, as indeed the House of Lords contemplated in *Board of Trade* v. *Owen* (4), that even as the law stands it might be
possible to indict persons here for conspiracy if the conspiracy consisted of committing crimes abroad, provided it could be shown that the performance of the
conspiracy would cause a public mischief in this country or injure a person
I here by causing him damage abroad. Neither of those possibilities referred to in
the speech of LORD TUCKER (7) comprises the situation with which this court

---

   (2) (1864), 4 F. & F. 68.
   (3) [1956] 3 All E.R. 432 at pp. 437-438; [1957] 1 Q.B. 174 at pp. 192-194.
   (4) [1957] 1 All E.R. 411; [1957] A.C. 602.
   (5) [1956] 3 All E.R. at p. 438; [1957] 1 Q.B. at p. 193.
   (6) (1864), 4 F. & F. at p. 472.
   (7) [1957] 1 All E.R. at pp. 412-422; [1957] A.C. at pp. 621-634.

has to deal today.   Improvement, let us hope, there will soon be.   Let us hope **A**
that this loophole will be stopped up before many other criminals such as the
applicant see fit to risk using it.   As the law stands, unfortunately, and with
very bitter regret, this court is bound to say that so far as the conviction of the
applicant on count 1 of the conspiracy is concerned, it must be quashed.   It
follows that so far as this matter is concerned, the applicant is free to go.

Application for leave to appeal against conviction granted.   Conviction quashed. **B**

Solicitors: *Registrar of Criminal Appeals* (for the applicant); *Director of
Public Prosecutions* (for the Crown).

[*Reported by* N. P. METCALFE, ESQ., *Barrister-at-Law.*]

C

KENMIR, LTD. *v.* FRIZZELL AND OTHERS.

[QUEEN'S BENCH DIVISION (Lord Parker, C.J., Widgery and Chapman, JJ.),
November 27, 28, December 13, 1967.]

Employment—Redundancy—Period of continuous employmemt—Change of **D**
*employers consequent on sale of factory premises—When transaction amounts
to transfer of business for the purposes of Contracts of Employment Act*
1963 (*c.* 49), *Sch.* 1, *para.* 10 (2) *and Redundancy Payments Act* 1965
(*c.* 62) *s.* 1.

The respondents were formerly employed by a firm that owned a factory
and manufactured furniture. The firm sold the factory premises to a **E**
company, the appellants, who manufactured the furniture but sold all
their products to another company in the group of which the appellants
were members.   By the same agreement the vendor firm agreed not to
compete in business with the appellants within a certain radius, and to
continue their business until completion in such a manner as would safeguard the interests of the appellants, including the management of employees **F**
of the vendor firm.   There was no agreement to assign goodwill.   The
appellants took possession of the factory and carried on business there.
The respondent employees of the firm then entered the appellants' service.
Subsequently the appellants dismissed the respondents in circumstances
in which the respondents became entitled to redundancy payments.   On
appeal from a decision that, pursuant to para. 10 (2) of Sch. 1* to the Con- **G**
tracts of Employment Act 1963, the respondents' periods of service with
the vendor firm should be aggregated with their periods of service with
the appellants, for the purposes of computing their redundancy payments,
on the ground that there had been a transfer of the firm's trade or business,

Held: in determining whether there was a transfer of a business within
para. 10 (2) of Sch. 1 to the Contracts of Employment Act 1963 the vital **H**
consideration was whether the effect of the transaction was to put the
transferee in possession of a going concern, the activities of which he could
carry on without interruption; and in the circumstances of the present
case the decision that there had been a transfer within para. 10 (2) should
stand (see p. 418, letters E and H, post).

Per CURIAM: an express assignment of goodwill is strong evidence of the **I**
transfer of a business, but the absence of such an assignment is not conclusive if the transferee has effectively deprived himself of the power to

---

* Schedule 1, para. 10, so far as material, is set out at p. 415, letter I, post.   Paragraph
1 (1) of Sch. 1 to the Redundancy Payments Act 1965 provides, so far as material, that
the amount of a redundancy payment . . . shall . . . be calculated by reference
to the period . . . during which [the employee] has been continuously employed; and
. . . that period shall be computed in accordance with Sch. 1 to the Contracts of
Employment Act 1963 . . ."

A compete; similarly the absence of an assignment of premises, stock-in-trade
or outstanding contracts will not be conclusive if the particular circumstances of the transferee nevertheless enable him to carry on substantially
the same business as before (see p. 418, letter G, post).

H. A. Rencoule (*Joiners and Shopfitters*), *Ltd.* v. *Hunt* ((1967), I.T.R. 475
and G. D. Ault (*Isle of Wight*), *Ltd.* v. *Gregory* ((Mar. 2, 1967), unreported)
B applied.

[As to redundancy payments after a change of ownership of a business, see
SUPPLEMENT to 25 HALSBURY'S LAWS (3rd Edn.), para. 945A, 7.

For the Contracts of Employment Act 1963, Sch. 1, para. 10, see 43 HALSBURY'S
STATUTES (2nd Edn.) 286.]

C Cases referred to:

Ault (*G. D.*) (*Isle of Wight*), *Ltd.* v. *Gregory*, (Mar. 2, 1967), unreported.
Rencoule (*H. A.*) (*Joiners and Shopfitters*), *Ltd.* v. *Hunt*, (1967), I.T.R. 475;
[1967] S.L.T. 218.

Appeals.

These were four consolidated appeals by the appellants Kenmir, Ltd., from
D a decision of the Industrial Tribunal given on May 31, 1967, whereby the tribunal
determined a preliminary point arising in applications by each of the respondents,
Peter Atherton Frizzell, Henry Eagle, Thomas Ray Heale and Robert Bellis,
against the appellants for a redundancy payment under s. 1 of the Redundancy
Payments Act 1965 that there had been a transfer of a business from Kenmir
Brothers (a firm) to the appellants, such that the respondents' periods of employ-
E ment with Kenmir Brothers would count as periods of employment with the
appellants, by virtue of para. 10 (2) of Sch. 1 to the Contracts of Employment
Act 1963, for the purposes of computing redundancy payments payable to the
respondents.

P. R. Pain, Q.C., and G. H. Hodgson for the appellants.
R. P. Smith, Q.C., and L. B. Stephen for the respondents.

F
Cur. adv. vult.

Dec. 13. **WIDGERY, J.,** read the following judgment of the court at
the invitation of LORD PARKER, C.J.: For some years the respondents had been
employed by a firm called Kenmir Brothers, but as from June 5, 1964, they
were employed by the appellants. On Dec. 3, 1966, the appellants dismissed
G the respondents, and it was not disputed that such dismissal was by reason
of redundancy within the meaning of s. 1 of the Act of 1965, and that each of
the respondents was entitled to a redundancy payment. The amount of the
payment, however, was dependent on the length of continuous service which
could be claimed by each respondent, and for this purpose they sought to aggregate their period of employment by the appellants with their period of employ-
H ment with Kenmir Brothers. By s. 1 of, and para. 1 of Sch. 1 to, the Act of
1965, the provisions of Sch. 1 to the Contracts of Employment Act 1963, have
effect for determining the period for which an employee has been continuously
employed for the purpose of such a claim. Schedule 1 to the Act of 1963 contains
the following provisions under the cross-heading " Change of employer ":

I " 10 (1) Subject to this paragraph, the foregoing provisions of this schedule
relate only to employment by the one employer. (2) If a trade or business
or an undertaking . . . is transferred from one person to another, the period
of employment of an employee in the trade or business or undertaking at
the time of the transfer shall count as a period of employment with the
transferee and the transfer shall not break the continuity of the period of
employment."

The sole question in these appeals is whether the tribunal erred in law in holding
that there had been the transfer of a business from Kenmir Brothers to the

appellants, so as to enable the respondents to take advantage of this last-   A
mentioned provision.

The relevant facts found by the tribunal are as follows. Kenmir Brothers
were manufacturers of furniture and the respondents were employed in this
business.   Much of the furniture was designed for use in schools and institutions
and was sold direct to the user, but bedroom and dining room furniture was also
made and was sold through the trade.   The appellants also manufacture furniture   B
but their product consists mainly of chair and settee frames.   The appellants
are one of a group of companies known as the Duport Group, and all their production is sold to another company in the same group called Vono, Ltd.   On
June 5, 1964, the partners in Kenmir Brothers entered into an agreement with
the appellants (by their then name of Daintymaid Kitchen Equipment, Ltd.)
for the sale of the factory premises at which the respondents were employed,   C
and the respondents thereupon entered the employment of the appellants.
Apart from terms normally found in a contract for the sale of real property, the
agreement of June 5, 1964, contained the following:

" 10. On completion the purchasers [viz., the appellants, Kenmir, Ltd.]
shall in addition to the balance of the purchase moneys pay to the vendors
[viz., Kenmir Brothers] the sum of £346 for fixtures and fittings and the   D
sum of £3,318 for plant and machinery.

" 11. The purchasers shall be entitled to the benefit of any trade agreements licences or official permits and shall be entitled to use the word ' Kenmir ' in all forms and the trade mark ' Lifetime ' and all necessary documents
to transfer these items will be forwarded on completion.

" 12. The vendors hereby jointly and severally undertake that they will   E
not set up or be in any way interested in or in any way assist others in a
business competing with or similar to that carried on by the purchasers for
a period of five years within a radius of twenty-five miles as the crow flies
from the property hereby agreed to be sold.

" 13. The vendors agree to pay off all creditors of the firm of Kenmir
Brothers and to indemnify the purchasers in respect of any incurred between   F
the date of the contract and completion.

" 14. The vendors declare that there is no contract in existence in connexion with their business arising other than in the usual course of the
business which has not already been disclosed and further that if any such
contract is entered into between the date of this contract and completion
they will disclose the same to the purchasers.   G

" 15.   The vendors hereby undertake that they will carry on their business
as furniture manufacturers between the date of this contract and the date
of completion in such a manner as to safeguard the interests of the purchasers
to the fullest possible extent including for this purpose:— ... (c) the
management of the employees of the vendors."
                                                                          H
The terms of this agreement were duly carried out.   The appellants took
possession of the factory and carried on business there, having adopted the
name of Kenmir, Ltd.   They issued a form of particulars of contract of service
to the respondents, and in each case showed therein the date of commencement
of employment as being the date of the respondents original employment by
Kenmir Brothers.

The case for the appellants before the tribunal was that this transaction was
not the transfer of a business within the meaning of para. 10 (2) of Sch. 1 to the
Act of 1963, but a sale of real property together with fixtures and plant.   It
was pointed out that there was no transfer of stock-in-trade or goodwill, and the
appellants explained the inclusion of cl. 12 and cl. 15 in the agreement by saying
that they had been very anxious to take over the trained labour force employed
by Kenmir Brothers and did not want employees to drift away, or be persuaded
to join any other business which might be set up by the vendors.   The tribunal

A considered the terms of the agreement and all the surrounding circumstances, and held that a transfer of the business had occurred.

In this court, counsel for the appellants contends that there can be no transfer of a business unless the transaction includes an assignment of the goodwill. An assignment of goodwill may be ineffective in itself, and is normally accompanied by a sale of the business premises, stock-in-trade and the like, but it is

B contended that a transaction which excludes a transfer of goodwill is deficient in the vital element which can make the subject-matter of the transfer a " business ". If this argument is correct, it might provide a very simple solution to the problem in this case, but we think that it would be surprising in the context of this legislation if the presence or absence of a transfer of goodwill were conclusive. Schedule 1 to the Act of 1963 is concerned with continuity of employ-

C ment, and uses the phrase " transfer of a business " to describe a situation in which a change of employer should not be regarded as a break in the continuity of the employees' engagements. If a business has no goodwill because it is at a low ebb, or because it sells all its production to an associated company, the factory premises might be sold and all the activities of production transferred to the new owner without interruption; yet, if counsel's argument is right, the

D employees' accrued rights under the Acts of 1963 and 1965 would be lost unless the transfer included a formal and empty phrase purporting to include goodwill.

A similar question arose in the Court of Session in *H. A. Rencoule (Joiners and Shopfitters), Ltd.* v. *Hunt* (1). In that case, the lessee of a factory sold the stock-in-trade of his business, with the fixtures and fittings in the factory, to a purchaser who obtained a new lease of the factory premises. The purchaser took

E over the vendors' former employees and work in progress, and the vendor agreed to introduce the purchaser to the former customers of the business. The agreement expressly provided, however, that the purchaser was not purchasing the business and should have no right to use the old firm name. It was, nevertheless, held that this was a transfer of the vendors' business for the purpose of Sch. 1 to the Act of 1963. LORD CLYDE said (2):

F " The result of this transaction in my opinion, was to transfer to Messrs. Rencoule, Ltd. everything in Mr. Fraser's business except the name and the debts outstanding due to or by Mr. Fraser at the date of the transfer. In particular the transfer of the work in progress coupled with the obligation to introduce the purchaser to customers of Mr. Fraser involved a transfer of the goodwill of his business. The whole operation necessarily meant a smooth

G and unbroken continuity between what was happening before and after the transfer. Whatever the declaration in the missives may have been intended to mean—and it may have been meant only to prevent the purchasers trading under the name of Fraser—it cannot derogate from the plain and unequivocal effect of what was in fact transferred as set out in the missives."

H LORD CAMERON took the same view. He said (3):

" The question to be determined by the tribunal was at large and was not pre-determined by the terms of a contract to which the [workman] was not a party. Upon this view of the matter, I think it is plain that there was a transfer of the business of Fraser to the appellants, a business which continued in the same premises and on the same basis as before and of which the

I goodwill was by clear stipulation acquired by the appellants."

On the same point, LORD MIGDALE said (4):

" What passed to the appellants was more than the stock-in-trade and equipment. The goodwill and current contracts were also transferred. This can be weighed against the declaration that the appellants were not purchasing the business."

---

(1) (1967), I.T.R. 475.   (2) (1967), I.T.R. at p. 478.
(3) (1967), I.T.R. at p. 479.   (4) (1967), I.T.R. at p. 481.

LORD GUTHRIE, after a review of the circumstances of the transaction, observed **A**
(5) that they inferred " that there was a continuity in the business ", and said
that evidence from the purchasers that the main purpose of the transaction was
to obtain a tenancy of the premises was of no avail if " to achieve that purpose
they took over the business conducted in the desired premises ". There is no
reported English case on this point, but it arose in this court in *G. D. Ault (Isle
of Wight), Ltd.* v. *Gregory* (6). In that case, a written agreement provided for the **B**
sale by a firm of: (a) all its stock-in-trade and materials as a builder and contractor; (b) all the vendors plant and equipment; (c) the business premises
together with fixtures and fittings; (d) the benefit of contracts in or relating to
work to be performed by the vendors in the Isle of Wight in connexion with the
business. There was no express assignment of goodwill, but the vendors agreed
not thereafter to be concerned or interested in the business of a builder or **C**
contractor in the Urban District of Sandown/Shanklin, Isle of Wight. Holding
that this agreement amounted to the transfer of the business, DIPLOCK, L.J., said:

> " The agreement which I have read is in my view as plain an example of
> an agreement for the sale of a business as one could find. It sells the whole
> of the stock-in-trade; it sells the plant and equipment; it purports to assign
> the benefit of all contracts and in effect [the vendors] part with the goodwill **D**
> of their business in the Isle of Wight by entering into a covenant not to carry
> on that business any further."

We think that the principles applied in these two cases govern the present case
also. In deciding whether a transaction amounted to the transfer of a business,
regard must be had to its substance rather than its form, and consideration **E**
must be given to the whole of the circumstances, weighing the factors which
point in one direction against those which point in another. In the end, the
vital consideration is whether the effect of the transaction was to put the transferee in possession of a going concern, the activities of which he could carry on
without interruption. Many factors may be relevant to this decision though
few will be conclusive in themselves. Thus, if the new employer carries on **F**
business in the same manner as before, this will point to the existence of a
transfer, but the converse is not necessarily true, because a transfer may be
complete even though the transferee does not choose to avail himself of all the
rights which he acquires thereunder. Similarly, an express assignment of goodwill
is strong evidence of a transfer of the business, but the absence of such an
assignment is not conclusive if the transferee has effectively deprived himself
of the power to compete. The absence of an assignment of premises, stock-in- **G**
trade or outstanding contracts will likewise not be conclusive, if the particular
circumstances of the transferee nevertheless enable him to carry on substantially
the same business as before.

In the present case, the tribunal reached its decision on a broad view of the
circumstances as a whole. This was the proper approach, and there was ample **H**
evidence to support the tribunal's finding. These appeals are, accordingly,
dismissed.

Appeals dismissed. Leave to appeal to the Court of Appeal.

Solicitors: *Vizard, Oldham, Crowder & Cash* and *Robertson, Martin & Co.,*
agents for *T. G. Dickinson,* Tipton (for the appellants); *Hay & Kilner,* Newcastle-
upon-Tyne (for the repondents). **I**

[*Reported by* N. P. METCALFE, ESQ., *Barrister-at-Law.*]

---

(5) (1967), I.T.R. at pp. 482-484.
(6) (Mar. 2, 1967), unreported.

A

PUBLIC PROSECUTOR *v.* KOI.
[AND ASSOCIATED APPEALS.]

[PRIVY COUNCIL (Lord Hodson, Lord Guest, Lord Wilberforce, Sir Douglas Menzies and Sir Garfield Barwick), July 17, 18, 19, 20, 24, December 4, 1967.]

B

Privy Council—Malaysia—War—Prisoners of war—Burden of proof whether prisoner entitled to privileges of protected prisoner of war within Geneva Convention—Effect of raising doubt at trial—Proceedings at trial not sustainable in the absence of notice—Geneva Conventions Act, 1962 (No. 5 of 1962), s. 4 (1), Sch. 3, art. 4, art. 5.

C

Privy Council—Malaysia—Internal security—Consorting in a security area with persons who carried arms—Accused consorted with Indonesian soldiers only—Whether offence under Internal Security Act, 1960 (No. 18 of 1960), s. 57, s. 58.

War—Prisoners of war—Nationals of detaining power not entitled to privileges of Geneva Convention as prisoners of war—Persons owing allegiance to detaining power, though not such nationals, also not so entitled—Geneva Conventions Act, 1962 (No. 5 of 1962), s. 4 (1).

D

Fourteen Chinese Malays, whose nationality was undetermined, were dropped in Johore as part of a party of paratroopers under the command of Indonesian Air Force officers, at a time when the two countries, Malaysia and Indonesia, were in armed conflict. Each man carried a fire-arm, ammunition, two hand grenades, food rations and other military equipment. The Chinese Malays were all captured. Twelve were accused of offences under s. 57 and s. 58 of the Internal Security Act, 1960. At the trial of one of the accused, Chai, it was submitted that, since he was neither a Malaysian nor an Indonesian citizen, he should be treated as a prisoner of war under the Malaysian Geneva Conventions Act, 1962. None of the other accused raised a contention of being a protected prisoner of war nor was any doubt raised as to the status of any of these other accused at the time. Notices pursuant to s. 4 (1)* of the Act of 1962 were not given. All accused were convicted and sentenced to death. On appeal the convictions of two of the accused were quashed on the point being taken that they were entitled to the protection of the Act of 1962 as prisoners of war, and that the trial had not been maintainable by virtue of s. 4 (1) in the absence of notices. The appeals of the remaining ten were dismissed. Among the charges on which the accused were convicted was a charge under s. 58 of the Act of 1960 of consorting with persons having or having possession of arms, etc., in contravention of s. 57.

Held: (i) except in the case of the appellant Chai there had been no mistrial (see p. 427, letter F, post) for the following reasons—

(a) on the hearing of an appeal of an accused who had raised no doubt (for the purposes of art. 5 of the Convention) at his trial whether he was entitled to be treated as a protected prisoner of war, no burden lay on the prosecution, but the onus was on the accused (see p. 429, letter I, post) to prove that he was not so entitled; and in the cases of all the accused save that of the appellant Chai, no such doubt had been raised (see p. 424, letters H and I, post).

R. v. *Guiseppe* ([1943] S.A.L.R. (T.P.D.) 139) distinguished.

(b) a national of a detaining power, being a person who owed a duty of allegiance but had gone over to the enemy, was not entitled to the privileges accorded by the Convention to protected prisoners of war; neither was a person who, though not such a national, owed a duty of allegiance to the detaining power (see p. 426, letter G, post).

---

* The relevant terms of s. 4 (1) are set out at p. 422, letter G, post.

In re Territo ((1946), 156 Fed. Rep. (2d.) 142) not applied.

Joyce v. *Director of Public Prosecutions* ([1946] 1 All E.R. 186) applied.

(ii) (LORD GUEST and SIR GARFIELD BARWICK dissenting) there had been a mistrial in the case of the appellant Chai, because, he having claimed at his trial the protection of the Convention, a doubt within art. 5 was raised in the circumstances, and, no notice having been given pursuant to s. 4 (1) of the Act of 1962, his conviction would be quashed (see p. 427, letter F, post).

(iii) (LORD GUEST and SIR GARFIELD BARWICK dissenting) convictions under s. 58 of the Internal Security Act, 1960, of consorting with persons carrying arms, etc. in contravention of s. 57 were bad and would be quashed, because Indonesian soldiers, with whom alone the accused were charged with consorting, were not persons to whom s. 57 applied (see p. 427, letter D, post).

[As to the privileges of protected prisoners of war, see 39 HALSBURY'S LAWS (3rd Edn.) 49, para. 44.

For the corresponding provisions of the Geneva Conventions Act, 1957, s. 2 (1), s. 7 (1), see 37 HALSBURY'S STATUTES (2nd Edn.) 69, 75.]

Cases referred to:

Joyce v. *Director of Public Prosecutions,* [1946] 1 All E.R. 186; [1946] A.C. 347; 115 L.J.K.B. 146; 174 L.T. 206; 31 Cr. App. Rep. 57; 2 Digest (Repl.) 199, *192.*

R. v. *Guiseppe,* [1943] S.A.L.R. (T.P.D.) 139.

R. v. *Neumann Transport,* [1946] S.A.L.R. (T.P.D.) 1238.

Territo, *In re,* (1946), 156 Fed. Rep. (2d.) 142.

Yamashita, *In re,* (1946), 327 U.S. 1.

Appeals.

These were eleven associated appeals (Nos. 9-17 of 1967 and Nos. 16 and 36 of 1966) from judgments of the Federal Court of Malaysia, whereby the appeals of two of the accused, Oie Hee Koi and Ooi Wan Yui (alias Wong Kam Chin), were allowed in respect of convictions under s. 57 and s. 58 of the Internal Security Act, 1960 (No. 18 of 1960), and whereby the appeals of the remaining ten accused relating to similar convictions were dismissed. All the accused were sentenced to death on conviction by the High Court in Malaya. The appellant in the first two appeals (those of Koi and Yui) was the public prosecutor. The main issue was whether the accused were protected prisoners of war under the Geneva Conventions Act, 1962 (No. 5 of 1962). The appeal of the respondents Koi, allowed by the Federal Court, was allowed on the ground that he was a prisoner of war within the Act of 1962. The principal grounds of the prosecutor's appeal in the case of Koi were—(a) that the Federal Court was in error in holding that the respondent was a prisoner of war within the meaning of the Geneva Convention Act, 1962, and as each was entitled to protection, and that in so holding the Federal Court ran counter to its own previous decisions on broadly similar facts in two other of the appeals (viz., those of Teo Boon Chai and Lee Hoo Boon); (b) that the Federal Court was in error in holding that in the circumstances a burden lay on the prosecution to prove that the accused was disentitled to be treated as a prisoner of war under the Act of 1962. The facts are set out in the opinion of LORD HODSON.

H. A. P. Fisher, Q.C., and *M. P. Solomon* for the Public Prosecutor.

E. F. N. Gratiaen, Q.C., and *L. J. Blom-Cooper* for the respondents Koi and Yui.

E. F. N. Gratiaen, Q.C., M. Carlisle and *Mark Fernando* (of the Ceylon Bar) for the appellant Chai.

S. N. Bernstein and *C. G. Allen* for the appellants Lang, Huat, Sai, Boon and Ho Ming Siang.

A
L. J. Blom-Cooper and *A. P. Lester* for the appellant Boon.

L. J. Blom-Cooper for the appellant Lee Siang.

K. M. McHale for the appellants Lum and Baa.

LORD HODSON: In these associated appeals the main question is whether the accused were entitled to be treated as protected prisoners of war by virtue of the Geneva Conventions Act, 1962, to which the Geneva Conventions of 1949
B are scheduled.

The accused are so-called Chinese Malays either born or settled in Malaysia but in no case was it shown whether or not they were of Malaysian nationality. Most carried blue identity cards issued pursuant to the National Registration Regulation which by reg. 5 (2) (*a*) provide for the issue of "blue bordered cards with blue printing to citizens of the Federation of Malaya". One carried a
C red card appropriate to a non-citizen.

They were captured during the Indonesian confrontation campaign. All but two were dropped in Malaysia by parachute as members of an armed force of paratroopers under the command of Indonesian Air Force officers. The main party was dropped in Johore wearing camouflage uniform. Each man carried a fire-arm, ammunition, two hand grenades, food rations and other
D military equipment. Of the main party thirty-four out of forty-eight were Indonesian soldiers and fourteen Chinese Malays which included twelve of the accused. One was dropped from a different plane similarly equipped. The remaining two accused landed later by sea and were captured and tried. One of these likewise claimed the protection of the Geneva Convention.

All the accused were convicted of offences under the Internal Security Act,
E 1960 of the Federation of Malaya and sentenced to death. Section 57 deals with offences relating to fire-arms, ammunition and explosives and so far as material reads as follows:

" 57. (1) Any person who without lawful excuse, the onus of proving which shall be on such person, in any security area carries or has in his possession or under his control—(*a*) any fire-arm without lawful authority
F therefor; or (*b*) any ammunition or explosive without lawful authority therefor, shall be guilty of an offence against this part and shall be punished with death.

. . .

" (3) A person shall be deemed to have lawful excuse for the purposes of this section only if he proves—(*a*) that he acquired such fire-arm, ammunition
G or explosive in a lawful manner and for a lawful purpose; and (*b*) that he has not at any time while carrying or having in his possession or under his control such fire-arms, ammunition or explosive, acted in a manner prejudicial to public security or the maintenance of public order.

. . .

" 58. (1) Any person who in any security area consorts with or is found
H in the company of another person who is carrying or has in his possession or under his control any fire-arm, ammunition or explosive in contravention of the provisions of s. 57, in circumstances which raise a reasonable presumption that he intends, or is about, to act, or has recently acted, with such other person in a manner prejudicial to public security or the maintenance of public order shall be guilty of an offence against this Part and shall be
I punished with death, or with imprisonment for life."

Proclamation of security areas is dealt with in s. 47 (1) which so far as material reads as follows:

" If in the opinion of the Yang di-Pertuan Agong public security in any area in the Federation is seriously disturbed or threatened by reason of any action taken or threatened by any substantial body of persons, whether inside or outside the Federation, to cause or to cause a substantial number of citizens to fear organised violence against persons or property, he may,

if he considers it to be necessary for the purpose of suppressing such organised   A
violence, proclaim such area as a security area for the purposes of this Part.

. . .

"(3) A proclamation made under sub-s. (1) shall be published in such
manner as the Minister thinks necessary for bringing it to the notice of all
persons who in his opinion ought to have notice thereof and shall have effect
as soon as such notice has been given, without publication in the Gazette.   B
. . ."

All the accused appealed against their convictions on charges laid under s. 57
and s. 58 of the Act of 1960 and their appeals were dismissed by the Federal
Court of Malaysia save in two cases namely that of Oie Hee Koi (Appeal No. 16
of 1967) and that of Ooi Wan Yui (Appeal No. 17 of 1967) in both of which the
appeals were allowed on the ground that the accused were prisoners of war   C
within the meaning of the Geneva Conventions Act, 1962, of the Federation of
Malaya (herein referred to as "the Act of 1962") and as such were entitled
to protection under the Geneva Convention relative to the treatment of prisoners
of war (Sch. 3 to the Act of 1962).

In these two cases the public prosecutor appeals by special leave from the
decision of the Federal Court. In the remaining cases the accused appeal   D
by special leave against the decisions of the Federal Court upholding their
convictions.

The Act of 1962 itself provides as far as material as follows (1):

"2. In this Act, unless the context otherwise requires— . . . ' protected
prisoner of war ' means a person protected by the convention set out in
Sch. 3;   E

" ' the protecting power ', in relation to a protected prisoner of war or a
protected internee, means the power or organisation which is carrying out,
in the interests of the power of which he is a national, or of whose forces he
is, or was at any material time, a member, the duties assigned to protecting
powers under the convention set out in Sch. 3 or, as the case may be, Sch. 4;   F
. . .

"4 (1) The court before which—(a) a protected prisoner of war is brought
up for trial for any offence; or (b) . . . shall not proceed with the trial until
it is proved to the satisfaction of the court that a notice containing the
particulars mentioned in sub-s. (2), so far as they are known to the prosecutor, has been served not less than three weeks previously on the protecting
power and, if the accused is a protected prisoner of war, on the accused and   G
the prisoners' representative."

Section 4 (2) sets out the particulars required which include the name and full
description of the accused, the offence with which he is charged and the court
time and place appointed for trial.

Their lordships observe first that the offences with which the accused were   H
charged were all committed within the territorial jurisdiction of the court of
trial. The direction not to proceed with the trial which is to be given in the
case of a protected prisoner of war is mandatory, that is to say, imperative
in character. It seems that enactments regulating the procedure to be followed
in courts are usually imperative and not merely directory. See MAXWELL on
INTERPRETATION OF STATUTES (11th Edn.) p. 367. The direction is one which   I
is given to the court of trial itself, that is to say to the court of first instance.
It does not purport to be an ouster of jurisdiction but is a direction not to proceed
until etc.

Their lordships observe in the second place that the Act of 1962 does not
indicate directly whether or not a protected prisoner of war includes nationals of,

(1) These definitions in the Act of 1962 correspond with those in s. 7 of the United
Kingdom Geneva Conventions Act, 1957, and the extract from s. 4 (1) corresponds with
s. 2 (1) of the United Kingdom Act.

A or persons owing allegiance to, the captor state. Reference to the protecting power does indicate indirectly that the prisoner of war whose interest is to be protected is a national of some state other than the captor state, or a member of the forces of a party to the conflict but this leaves open the question whether prisoner of war status can be claimed by persons in the latter category who are nationals of or owe allegiance to the captor state. Where there is no protecting

B power designated by parties to the conflict and protection cannot be arranged accordingly, it is provided by art. 10 of the Convention (2) that the protecting power shall accept the services of a humanitarian organisation such as the International Committee of the Red Cross to assume the humanitarian functions performed by the protecting power under the Convention.

It is necessary to refer to the Convention (Sch. 3 to the Act of 1962) in order

C to ascertain the extent of the protection. Article 4 of the Convention is general in its terms and on its face is capable of including the nationals of the detaining power who are captured by that power. Article 4 (A) commences:

"Prisoners of war, in the sense of the present Convention, are persons belonging to one of the following categories, who have fallen into the power of the enemy; "

D There follows a list of categories:

"(1) Members of the armed forces of a party to the conflict as well as members of militias or volunteer corps forming part of such armed forces; (2) Members of other militias and members of other volunteer corps, including those of organised resistance movements, belonging to a party to the conflict

E and operating in or outside their own territory, even if this territory is occupied provided that such militias or volunteer corps, including such organised resistance movements, fulfil the following conditions: (*a*) that of being commanded by a person responsible for his subordinates; (*b*) that of having a fixed distinctive sign recognisable at a distance; (*c*) that of carrying arms openly; (*d*) that of conducting their operations in accordance

F with the laws and customs of war; . . ."

Article 5 so far as material provides:

". . . Should any doubt arise as to whether persons, having committed a belligerent act and having fallen into the hands of the enemy, belong to any of the categories enumerated in art. 4, such persons shall enjoy the

G protection of the present Convention until such time as their status has been determined by a competent tribunal."

The trials of the accused were conducted on the assumption, which their lordships do not call in question, that there was an armed conflict between Malaysia and Indonesia bringing the Convention into operation. Article 2 applies the Convention not only to cases of declared war but to "any other

H armed conflict " which may arise between two or more of the High Contracting Parties, even if the state of war is not recognised by one of them. The existence of such a state of armed conflict was something of which the courts in Malaysia could properly take judicial notice, or if in doubt (which does not appear to have been the case) on which they could obtain a statement from the executive. It was also assumed that both Malaysia and Indonesia are parties to the Conven-

I tion and their lordships were informed that this assumption is in accordance with the facts. Thus, whether any individual accused was entitled, under the Act of 1962, to be treated as a protected prisoner of war, would depend on the following: (i) whether as a matter of fact he was a member of the armed forces of Indonesia or of a volunteer corps forming part of such armed forces and, if so; (ii) whether as a matter of law, the Convention, and consequently the Act of 1962,

---

(2) The Convention is set out in Sch. 3 to the United Kingdom Geneva Conventions Act, 1957.

applies to persons of Malaysian nationality or owing allegiance to Malaysia; **A**
(iii) whether, as a matter of fact, he was a national of Malaysia or a person
owing allegiance to Malaysia.

Article 5 of the Convention is directed to a person of the kind described in
art. 4 about whom " a doubt arises " whether he belongs to any of the categories
enumerated in art. 4.   By virtue of art. 5 such a person is given the protection
of the Convention for the time being, i.e., until such time as his " status has been **B**
determined by a competent tribunal ".   The question then arises whether
the description " protected prisoner of war " in s. 2 of the Act of 1962 includes
persons entitled to provisional protection under art. 5 of the Convention, as
well as persons falling within art. 4 of the Convention.   Their lordships are of
opinion that this is the case.   Thus a person to whom art. 5 applies is a protected
prisoner of war within s. 2 of the Act of 1962 so long as that protection lasts. **C**
If the determination is positive, then he is protected because he falls within one
of the categories in art. 4, and the provision for notice in s. 4 of the Act of 1962
must be complied with.   If the determination is negative, the protection of the
Convention ceases so far as the individual is concerned, and his trial can proceed
free from any further restriction arising under s. 4 of the Act of 1962.

When it is established that an accused person is within one of the categories **D**
in art. 4 of the Convention, s. 4 of the Act of 1962 can be complied with only by
giving the requisite notice; where it is doubtful whether a person is within one
of the categories of art. 4 of the Convention then, so long as that position remains,
all that is required is that the trial shall not proceed unless the notices have
been given.   An enquiry into status could be directed without such a notice, as
s. 4 of the Act of 1962 does not apply to such an enquiry.   Section 4 of the Act **E**
of 1962 relates to all protected prisoners of war whether the protection arises
under the terms of art. 5 of the Convention or because it is established that an
accused is within the terms of art. 4 of the Convention.   Where the doubt arises
under art. 5 of the Convention two courses are open (i) to give the notices as
required by s. 4 of the Act of 1962 or (ii) to obtain a determination whether or
not the accused is a protected person.   If the second course is followed and the **F**
result is negative, then the prosecution can proceed without giving the notices
required by s. 4 of the Act of 1962.   In only one of the cases did any " doubt
arise " at or before their trial whether the accused persons belonged to any of
the categories enumerated in art. 4 of the Convention.   This single case will be
dealt with separately hereafter.

In the two cases in which the public prosecutor is appellant, that is to say **G**
that of Oie Hee Koi and that of Ooi Wan Yui, already mentioned, the Federal
Court, on the point being taken on appeal from the trial judge, held that the
accused were entitled to protection.   By decisions of the Federal Court in the
other cases where the convictions were upheld, the contention that the accused
were entitled to the protection of the Convention was rejected.   In these cases
with the single exception referred to above no point had been raised at the trial, **H**
and therefore no " doubt arose " so as to bring s. 4 into operation.

Their lordships are of opinion that on the hearing of their appeals by the
Federal Court no burden lay on the prosecution to prove that those of the accused
who had raised no doubt at their trials as to the correctness of the procedure
followed were not entitled to be treated as protected prisoners of war.   Although
the burden of proof of guilt is always on the prosecution, this does not mean that **I**
a further burden is laid on it to prove that an accused person has no right to
apply for postponement of his trial until certain procedural steps have been
taken.   Until " a doubt arises " art. 5 does not operate, and the court is not
required to be satisfied whether or not this safeguard should be applied.   Accordingly where the accused did not raise a doubt no question of mistrial arises.

The only authority to which their lordships' attention was drawn which
supports the view that the Geneva Convention, or rather its predecessor which
used similar language, applied so to speak automatically without the question

A of protection or no protection being raised is the case of *R.* v. *Guiseppe* (3). Twelve Italian prisoners of war were tried by a magistrate and convicted on a charge of theft, no notice having been given to the representative of the protecting power as required by the Convention. It was held on an application for review at the special request of the Crown that the conviction and sentences should be set aside. Thus it appears that the Crown asked for review in a case where

B the prisoners of war were nationals of the opposing forces and plainly entitled to the protection of the Convention. Their lordships do not regard this decision as good authority for the proposition that there was a mistrial in the cases under review.

The position of the accused was covered prima facie by customary international law as stated in the passage which appears on p. 268 of 2 Oppenheim's Inter-

C national Law (7th Edn.) edited by the late Professor Lauterpacht concerning the armed forces of belligerents. This passage cited by Thomson, L.P., in the Federal Court in Lee Hoo Boon's case reads as follows:

" The privileges of members of armed forces cannot be claimed by members of the armed forces of a belligerent who go over to the forces of the enemy and are afterwards captured by the former. They may be, and always are,

D treated as criminals. The same applies to traitorous subjects of a belligerent who, without having been members of his armed forces, fight in the armed forces of the enemy. Even if they appear under the protection of a flag of truce, deserters and traitors may be seized and punished."

This edition was published in 1951 after Aug. 12, 1949, the date of the Geneva Conventions, and in their lordships' opinion correctly states the relevant law.

E
A study of the Convention relative to the treatment of prisoners of war leads to a strong inference that it is an agreement between states primarily for the protection of the members of the national forces of each against the other. Many of the articles of the Convention lead to this conclusion, but there are two which point convincingly in this direction namely art. 87 and art. 100. The former deals with penalties to which prisoners of war may be sentenced by the detaining

F power and contains this language:

" When fixing the penalty, the courts or authorities of the detaining power shall take into consideration, to the widest extent possible, the fact that the accused, *not being a national of the detaining power*, is not bound to it by *any duty of allegiance*, and that he is in its power as the result of circumstances

G independent of his own will."

Article 100 deals with death sentences and contains these words:

" The death sentence cannot be pronounced against a prisoner of war unless the attention of the court has, in accordance with art. 87, para. 2 (supra), been particularly called to the fact that *since the accused is not a national of the detaining power*, he is not bound to it by any *duty of allegiance*, and that he

H is in its power as the result of circumstances independent of his own will."

Each of these articles appears to rest on the assumption that a " prisoner of war " is not a " national of the detaining power ". Moreover the reference to the duty of allegiance might fairly suggest the further inference that a person who owes this duty to a detaining power is not entitled to prisoner of war treatment. If

I the matter rested on inference from these articles alone, the argument might not be conclusive, but as has been shown, the inference so to be drawn coincides, as regards nationals of the detaining power, with commonly accepted international law.

On behalf of four of the accused Lee Hoo Boon (No. 13 of 1967), Lee Siang (No. 14 of 1967), Lee Fook Lum (No. 16 of 1966) and Lee A. Ba (No. 36 of 1966) an argument was addressed to their lordships that even nationals of the detaining power are entitled to the benefit of the Geneva Convention.

(3) [1943] S.A.L.R. (T.P.D.) 139.

Reliance was placed on art. 82 and art. 85 of the Convention as dealing with **A**
prisoners of war generally. These persons are said to be subject to the laws in
force in the armed forces of that detaining power (art. 82), and when prosecuted
under the laws of the detaining power for acts committed prior to capture they
are said to retain even if convicted the benefits of the present Convention (art. 85).
Thus it is argued that the customary international law set out in the passage
from OPPENHEIM quoted above has been in effect abrogated. Their lordships do **B**
not accept this submission and have already given reasons for reading the Convention as concerned with the protection of the subjects of opposing states and the
nationals of other powers in the service of either of them, and not directed to
protect all those whoever they may be who are engaged in conflict and captured.
It appears, on examination, that art. 85 was inserted in the Convention to deal
with a limited and particular case of persons accused of violations of the articles **C**
of war or of war crimes (see *In re Yamashita* (4)) and that no general change in
customary international law was intended.

The principal authority relied on for the argument that all captured persons are
to be treated alike is *In re Territo* (5), a decision of the Circuit Court of Appeal
(Ninth Circuit) dated June 8, 1946. The question there under appeal was whether
the petitioner's restraint by the authorities as a prisoner of war was justified or **D**
whether he was entitled to a writ of habeas corpus. The citizenship of the
petitioner was immaterial to the decision. His detention did not depend on
whether or not he was a citizen of the United States of America. The passage
relied on reads as follows (6):

> " we have reviewed the authorities with care and we have found none
> supporting the contention of the petitioner that citizenship in the country   **E**
> of either army in collision necessarily affects the status of one captured on the
> field of battle."

The following passage refers expressly to various authorities which do not support
the contention that the particular protection relied on by the majority of the
appellants extends to nationals of the detaining power who fall into that power's
hands. Notwithstanding the words used by the court their lordships do not, **F**
therefore, find this decision assists the argument for the appellants.

Having reached the conclusion that the Convention does not extend the protection given to prisoners of war to nationals of the detaining power, their
lordships are of opinion that the same principle must apply as regards persons
who, though not nationals of, owe a duty of allegiance to, the detaining power.
It may indeed be said that allegiance is the governing principle whether based on **G**
citizenship or not. Whether the duty of allegiance exists or not is a question of
fact in which a number of elements may be involved. In this connexion it is
convenient to refer to the case of *Joyce* v. *Director of Public Prosecutions* (7)
which concerned an American citizen who resided in British territory for about
twenty-four years and had obtained a British passport. The question was asked
in the speech of LORD JOWITT, L.C., (8) whether there was not in that case such **H**
protection still afforded by the sovereign as to require of him the continuance of
his allegiance.

The continuance of allegiance may be shown in a variety of ways, and it is
unnecessary in the circumstances of these cases to give illustrations, but it is
useful to refer to a decision of the Special Criminal Court Transvaal delivered
later in the same year as *Joyce's* case (7) namely *R.* v. *Neumann Transport* (9). **I**
It was there held that an alien who had taken the oath of allegiance to His Majesty
King George VI, even after his departure from the Union, might still have enjoyed

---

(4) (1946), 327 U.S. 1.
(5) (1946), 156 Fed. Rep. (2d.) 142.
(6) (1946), 156 Fed. Rep. (2d.) at p. 145.
(7) [1946] 1 All E.R. 186; [1946] A.C. 347.
(8) [1946] 1 All E.R. at p. 190, letter G; [1946] A.C. at p. 368.
(9) [1946] S.A.L.R. (T.P.D.) 1238.

A its protection and owed a consequent debt of allegiance, and that the circumstances of his residence within the union and notwithstanding his departure were matters to be determined by evidence in order to decide whether the accused owed allegiance to the state and whether his departure terminated it.

It was not proved that the accused were citizens of Malaysia nor that they owed allegiance to Malaysia, though in many cases there was evidence which, B if the issue had directly arisen, might have suggested that they did; but further findings of fact would have been required to decide either question. Except in the one case where the accused claimed the protection of the Convention at the trial there was no mistrial in proceedings without the notices required by s. 4 having been given. There was nothing to show that the accused were protected prisoners of war or to raise a doubt whether they were or were not. The mere C fact that they landed as part of the Indonesian armed forces did not raise a doubt and no claim was made to provide any basis for the court, before whom the accused were brought for trial, applying s. 4 of the Act except in the one case.

In this single case, that of *Teo Boon Chai* v. *The Public Prosecutor* (No. 15 of 1967), it appears from the record that the accused's counsel claimed that his client was not a Malaysian citizen, and not an Indonesian citizen either, and that D he should therefore be treated as a prisoner of war under the Geneva Convention. The claim was brushed aside on the wrong basis, videlicet that jurisdiction was in question. In the Federal Court the point was taken that it was for the accused to prove that he was entitled to protection and that he did not do so. The claim, having been made to the court before whom the accused was brought up for trial in the circumstances already stated, was in their lordships' opinion sufficient to E raise a doubt whether he was a prisoner of war protected by the Convention. The court should have treated him as a prisoner of war for the time being and either proceeded with the determination whether he was or was not protected, or refrained from continuing the trial in the absence of notices. In this case only their lordships consider that there was a mistrial and that justice requires that the appeal be allowed and the convictions quashed and the case remitted for retrial.

F In the remaining cases there was no mistrial by reason of the absence of the notices required by s. 4. It is unnecessary to decide whether, if the accused were otherwise entitled to the protection of the Convention, the Convention did not attach since by abandoning their uniforms they were liable to be treated as spies to whom art. 4 has no application. Further findings of fact would be necessary before a decision could be reached on this matter.

G Returning to the charges made against the accused under the Internal Security Act, 1960, the point has been taken or adopted during the course of the hearing before their lordships on behalf of all those of the accused who were convicted, under s. 58 of that Act, of consorting with persons carrying or having possession of arms or explosives in contravention of s. 57, that the convictions were bad since the only persons with whom they were alleged to have consorted were Indonesian H soldiers who were not persons to whom s. 57 applied.

Their lordships are of the opinion that this submission is well-founded and that these convictions ought not to be allowed to stand. True the language of s. 57 covers " any person ", but on its proper construction s. 57 cannot be read so widely as to cover members of the regular Indonesian armed forces fighting as such in Malaysia in the course of what, it has been assumed, was an armed I conflict between Malaysia and Indonesia. The Act is an internal security measure part of the domestic law and not directed at the military forces of a hostile power attacking Malaysia. It would be an illegitimate extension of established practice to read s. 58 as referring to members of regular forces fighting in enemy country. Members of such forces are not subject to domestic criminal law. If they were so subject, they would be committing crimes from murder downwards in fighting against their enemy in the ordinary course of carrying out their recognised military duties. It should be added that it was never argued that s. 57 itself had no application to the accused as being irregular or volunteer Indonesian soldiers.

Save in two cases to which their lordships will now turn no other points were A
argued in support of the accused.

These two cases may be dealt with briefly.

In the case of *Lee Fook Lum* v. *The Public Prosecutor* (No. 16 of 1966) the accused
was charged that:

> " between dawn on Aug. 17, 1964 and 9.10 a.m. Aug. 18, 1964, in the
> security area as proclaimed by the Yang Di-Pertuan Agong vide Federal   B
> Legal Notification 245 of Aug. 17, 1964, namely Kampong Parit Jawa, in the
> district of Pontian, in the State of Johore, without lawful excuse, carried
> ammunition to wit, one hand grenade, without lawful authority, and that
> you thereby committed an offence punishable under s. 57 (1) of the Internal
> Security Act, 1960."
                                                                            C
Reliance was placed on the Geneva Convention which has already been discussed.
It was further argued that under s. 80 of the Act of 1960 the consent of the
public prosecutor to the prosection should have been and was not obtained.
The answer to this objection is that the public prosecutor was himself the
prosecutor and his consent is implicit in his action. The provision in s. 80 requiring
consent is applicable where prosecution take place, e.g., before a sessions court   D
and the public prosecutor is not the actual prosecutor.

Next it was argued that under s. 47 of the Internal Security Act 1960, proclamation of a security area was a prerequisite for the commission of the offence
charged, and that there was no evidence that such proclamation had been
published otherwise than in the Gazette dated Sept. 17, 1964, the day of the
alleged commission of the offence. This argument falls to the ground since the
proclamation takes effect from the beginning of the day of publication.   E

The main argument for the accused was that he had established that he had
lawful excuse for carrying the hand grenade the subject of the charge and that
the courts had misapprehended the evidence. The gist of the defence, which
was never established by the evidence, was that he had at all material times
lawful excuse within the meaning of s. 57 (3) of the Internal Security Act, 1960,
in that he intended all along to surrender. The trial judge did use the words   F
" all along ", but in its context it did not extend to the time when the accused
acquired the grenade but only to a later time when he did, according to his
evidence, form the intention of surrendering. This argument also fails.

The last case is that of *Lee A Ba* v. *Public Prosecutor* (No. 36 of 1966). The
identity card of the accused describes him as a Malayan citizen and he was
charged with having in his possession in a security area without lawful excuse   G
ammunition to wit, two hand grenade detonators without lawful authority
contrary to s. 57 (1) (b) of the Internal Security Act, 1960. The accused relied
on the Geneva Convention and in addition argued that the detonators did not
come within the definition of ammunition in s. 2 of the Act of 1960. Section 2
so far as material reads as follows:
                                                                            H
> " ' ammunition ' means ammunition for any fire-arm as hereafter defined
> and includes grenades, bombs and other like missiles whether capable of use
> with such a fire-arm or not . . .
> " ' explosive '—means . . . (b) includes . . . detonators . . ."

Their lordships accept the submission that the detonators were explosives
according to definition and not ammunition, but are of opinion that the error   I
in nomenclature is of no significance. The Criminal Procedure Code provides by
s. 152 (1) that any charge under this code shall state the offence with which the
accused is charged. Section 153 (1) provides for sufficient notice to be given to
the accused of the matter with which he is charged.

These provisions were complied with. Section 156 provides that no error in
stating either the offence or the particulars required to be stated in the charge
and no omission to state the offence or these particulars shall be regarded, at any
stage of the case, as material unless the accused was in fact misled by such error

A or omission. It was not contended that the accused was in fact misled, and their lordships are of opinion that error in stating the offence was immaterial and that there is no substance in the defence based on the misdescription of detonators as " ammunition " instead of " explosives ".

This accused also relied on the absence of consent by the public prosecutor. The answer to this is the same as in the previous case.

B   Their lordships accordingly reported to the Head of Malaysia that the appeals in Nos. 16 and 17 of 1967 be allowed so as to restore the convictions on the first and second charges in No. 16 and the second and third charges of No. 17, and to quash the convictions on the third charge in No. 16 and the first charge in No. 17; that the appeal in case No. 15 be allowed, all the convictions therein be quashed and the case remitted for re-trial on the first and second charges; that the

C   appeals in all the remaining cases be dismissed save and except that the convictions on the charges based on s. 58 of the Internal Security Act, 1960 be quashed in every case.

Their lordships also reported that the costs of the respondents in appeals Nos. 16 and 17 should be paid by the appellant as agreed between the parties. The costs of the appellants in the remaining appeals are to be taxed on the

D   pauper scale.

LORD GUEST and **SIR GARFIELD BARWICK** delivered the following dissenting judgment: These appeals arise out of what has been described as the Indonesian confrontation of Malaysia. The charges against the accused were breaches of various provisions of the Internal Security Act No. 18/1960. The

E   main question raised in all the appeals was whether the accused were entitled as prisoners of war to the protection of the Geneva Convention, dated Aug. 12, 1949, as applied to Malaya by the Geneva Conventions Act, 1962. In all cases the twelve accused were convicted by the trial judge and sentenced to death. In two cases, No. 16 of 1967 Oie Hee Koi and No. 17 of 1967 Ooi Wan Yui, alias Wong Kam Chin, the convictions and sentences were quashed by the Federal

F   Court of Malaysia. In the remaining cases the appeals of the accused were dismissed and the convictions sustained. Appeals have been taken by the prosecutor in case Nos. 16 and 17 and in the remaining cases the accused have appealed to the Board.

On the main question the members of the Board are unanimous that in all the cases except No. 15 of 1967 Teo Boon Chai, alias Tey Ah Sin, the accused were

G   not entitled to the protection of the Geneva Convention. In order to appreciate the point on which our dissent is entered, it is necessary to describe more fully the arguments on the question of the applicability of the Geneva Convention. In reply to the claim that the accused were entitled to the protection of the Geneva Convention the prosecution argued that the Convention did not apply to Malaysian nationals or persons owing allegiance to Malaysia. This argument was

H   countered by the accused saying that it was irrelevant whether they were Malaysian nationals or persons owing allegiance to Malaysia as both classes of persons were protected by the Convention. The argument for the prosecution has been sustained by the unanimous judgment of the Board for the reasons there given. An incidental question was raised in the course of this argument as to whether the onus was on the prosecution to prove that the accused were Malay-

I   sian nationals or persons owing allegiance to Malaysia or whether the onus was on the accused to bring themselves within the protection of the Convention. Again the unanimous advice of the Board, as we understand it, is that when the point was raised as to prisoner of war status the onus was on the accused to prove that they were within the Convention. We find ourselves in complete agreement with the Board's advice on these matters and with the relevant reasons given. We are also in agreement with the Board's advice in connexion with the additional matters raised in Lee Fook Lum (No. 16 of 1966) and Lee A Ba (No. 36 of 1966).

It is on the case of No. 15 of 1967 Teo Boon Chai, alias Tey Ah Sin, that we

find ourselves in disagreement with the advice of the majority of the Board. **A**
They have advised the quashing of the conviction in this case and that the case
should be sent back for retrial. The reasons are that although in the remaining
cases no question of prisoner of war status was raised at the trial, in this case
such a question did arise when the accused pleaded to the charges and the
following took place as recorded at the trial:

> " *Chan*: Accused is not a Malaysian citizen and not an Indonesian citizen **B**
> either. He should therefore be treated as a prisoner of war under the
> Geneva Convention. *Ajaib Singh*: Court has jurisdiction as accused was
> born and bred in this country. Unless there is proof of his being a national of
> any country other than Malaya he cannot take advantage of any
> Conventional Treaty. *Court*: I rule that the court has jurisdiction to try
> accused."   **C**

Mr. Chan was the advocate appearing for the accused. No further reference was
made to the matter and no evidence was led for the accused to justify this
purported challenge of the jurisdiction, nor was any other objection taken to
the trial proceeding.

Section 4 (1) of the Geneva Conventions Act, No. 5 of 1962, provides as **D**
follows:

> " The court before which—(*a*) a protected prisoner of war is brought up for
> trial for any offence; or (*b*) a protected internee is brought up for trial for
> an offence for which that court has power to sentence him to death or to
> imprisonment for a term of two years or more, shall not proceed with the trial
> until it is proved to the satisfaction of the court that a notice containing the
> particulars mentioned in sub-s. (2), so far as they are known to the prose- **E**
> cutor, has been served not less than three weeks previously on the protecting
> power and, if the accused is a protected prisoner of war, on the accused and
> the prisoners' representative."

By s. 2 a protected prisoner of war is a person protected by the Convention,
i.e., The Geneva Convention set out in Sch. 3. Article 4 (A) of the Convention **F**
defines the various categories of prisoners of war and art. 5 is in the following
terms:

> " The present Convention shall apply to the persons referred to in art. 4
> from the time they fall into the power of the enemy and until their final
> release and repatriation. Should any doubt arise as to whether persons,
> having committed a belligerent act and having fallen into the hands of the **G**
> enemy, belong to any of the categories enumerated in art. 4, such persons
> shall enjoy the protection of the present Convention until such time as their
> status has been determined by a competent tribunal."

It is said that when the accused claimed through his advocate the protection
of the Convention, there arose a doubt within the meaning of art. 5 as to his
status and that the court should then have adjourned the trial until a notice had **H**
been served on the protecting power under s. 4 (1) of the Act of 1962, and that the
subsequent trial was a nullity. With respect to the opinion of the majority,
we cannot follow this argument. Although the draftsman of s. 4 of the Geneva
Conventions Act, 1962, probably contemplated, as the language of the section
suggests, that the status of the accused in relation to the Convention will have
been determined by some competent tribunal before he is brought up for trial,
s. 4 must, in our opinion, be construed as apt to include the case where an accused
is brought to trial before that status is determined and to empower the court to
determine that status. Thus, although by definition " protected prisoner of war "
means a person protected by the Convention and art. 5 requires that captured
enemies enjoy the protection of the Convention until their status is determined,
in our opinion, the obligation on the court under s. 4 to adjourn the proceedings
does not arise until that status is determined; and, if not already determined by
some other tribunal, it does not arise until it is determined by the court itself.

A The accused, in our opinion, will be given the protection of the Convention for
which art. 5 provides, if having claimed and evidenced his status before the
court, the question whether or not he is a protected prisoner of war is determined
by the court before any other step is taken in his trial. Here, the accused in reality
did not raise the appropriate claim. In any case he did not press the claim he
did make and certainly did not evidence his status as a prisoner of war. The
B " doubt " which would have to arise under art. 5 would be whether the person
belonged to the categories mentioned in art. 4 (A). Having regard to all that
took place at the time, the point taken by the accused at the trial in substance
was that because he was not a Malaysian citizen nor an Indonesian citizen the
court had no jurisdiction to try him. This was really an assertion that the
Convention applied to those within Malaysian allegiance, though not to Malaysian
C national (citizens). This had nothing to do with the question whether the accused
was a prisoner of war within one of the categories of art. 4. The point taken by
the accused's advocate was really the contrary of what the Board has unanimously
decided, namely that the Convention applied to all prisoners of war who being
Malaysian nationals merely owed allegiance to Malaysia. Moreover, the point
taken by the accused's advocate was in our view misconceived. There was no
D question as to the jurisdiction of the court; the only available plea was whether
the court should adjourn under s. 4 (1) of the Act of 1962. This point was never
taken by the accused at the trial. For these reasons it seems to us that the accused
was in precisely the same position as the other accused and the same reasons
would apply for dismissing his appeal as in these cases. The real point in this case
case on the Geneva Convention was not taken till the hearing before the Federal
E Court.

In substance our disagreement with the majority judgment is that Case No. 15
of 1967 is on all fours with the remaining cases. The Federal Court in our judgment
arrived at a correct conclusion. We would have advised that the appeal be
dismissed and the conviction affirmed.

The other point on which we respectfully differ from the majority judgment
F is of more significant importance as affecting the interpretation of the Internal
Security Act, 1960. All the accused except No. 10 of 1967 were charged with a
breach of s. 58 of the Internal Security Act, 1960, the change being in the
following terms:

"That you between 2.00 a.m. on Sept. 2, and 11.00 a.m. on Sept. 15, 1964,
in a security area, as proclaimed by the Yang Di-Pertuan Agong vide F.L.N.
G 246 dated Aug. 17, 1964, namely at Kampong Tenang, Labis, in the District
of Segamat, in the State of Johore, consorted with members of the Indonesian
Armed Forces who carried fire-arms and ammunitions in contravention of
the provisions of s. 57 (1) of the Internal Security Act, 1960, in circumstances
which raised a reasonable presumption that you intended to act with such
members of the Indonesian armed forces in a manner prejudicial to public
I security and that you have thereby committed an offence punishable under
s. 58 (1) of the Internal Security Act No. 18 of 1960."

Section 57 (1) of the Internal Security Act, 1960, is in the following terms:

"Any person who without lawful excuse, the onus of proving which shall
be on such person, in any security area carries or has in his possession or under
I his control—(a) any fire-arm without lawful authority therefor; or (b) any
ammunition or explosive without lawful authority therefor, shall be guilty
of an offence against this Part and shall be punished with death."

Provisions follow for the establishment of " lawful excuse " and " lawful
authority ". The argument which has found favour with the majority of the
Board is that the Indonesian armed forces are not amenable to the provisions
of s. 57 (1). We may be permitted to ask the rhetorical question—" Why?"
The language of the section is universal and intractable; in terms it is applicable
to all persons, including belligerents. It is not suggested that the defence of

A " lawful excuse " or " lawful authority " is open to the members of the Indonesian
armed forces. The accused are and were at material times subject to the territorial
jurisdiction of the court and so, subject to the Geneva Convention, were the
members of the Indonesian armed forces. Of course, if the language of the
statute is tractable, it should be construed so as to conform to international
obligations, but apart from the fact that the express language of the statute is
in truth intractable, we know of no rule of international law which suggests that
B the national laws may not be applied to the armed forces of an enemy which
invade the national territory. Many political reasons may exist for not attempting to apply some laws to armed invaders in wartime but these are at present
irrelevant. Not only do we not find any rule of international law to which the
national law ought in comity to conform but it seems to us that the very convention with which these appeals are concerned itself set the only limitation
C on the operation of the national law in relation to captured enemies. That they
may be tried for breaches of the national law is basic to the structure of the
Convention: it merely seeks to have procedural limitations placed on their
trial. There is nothing in the Convention to suggest that the offences for which the
prisoners may be tried are limited to offences committed after capture. We can
see no reason therefore why a member of the Indonesian armed forces could not
D be prosecuted for an offence under s. 57 (1). To hold that the Indonesian armed
forces were not amenable to the provisions of s. 57 (1) would, in our view, amount
to an unwarrantable limitation on the power of the Malaysian government to
legislate for the security of the area.

The point that the charge was bad in law was taken for the first time in the
appellants' case. Neither the trial judge nor the Federal Court had the opportunity
E of adjudicating on it. In our view, the point was a bad one; but in any case it
would not in our opinion be in accordance with the practice of the Board to sustain
a point never taken in the courts below, unless the accused has been deprived
of a fair trial and there has been a manifest injustice. If the point had been taken
before the trial judge, the charge might have been amended or different evidence
might have been led to show that the consorting had been also with persons other
F that the Indonesian armed forces or there may have been more explicit evidence
as to the operations on which those forces were engaged. The Board is really
left in the dark as to what the factual position was in Malaysia at the critical
time. Lieutenant Sutikno the Indonesian officer in charge of the party of
Indonesian soldiers and others including the accused said that the purpose of
coming to Malaya was to liberate the people of Malaya from British imperialism
G and to do sabotage work in order to crush the economy of Malaya. Although
apparently there had been on this occasion an armed conflict between the
Indonesian armed forces and Malaysian soldiers, centering about their attempted
capture, it is not known whether a state of war existed between the two states.
If any exception from the generality of s. 57 (1) is permissible, these considerations
might have had an important bearing on the question whether the section applied
H to the Indonesian forces at the time the accused were collaborating in Johore
with them. Owing to the failure of the accused to take the point on the relevancy
of the charge at the trial the matter has been left in doubt, but it is in our view
too late to raise it before the Board.

We would have advised that the appeals in these cases also be wholly dismissed.

*Appeals Nos. 15, 16, 17, allowed to the extent stated (see p. 429, letter B, ante);
other appeals dismissed, save that convictions under s. 58 of Act of 1960 quashed.*

Solicitors: *Stephenson, Harwood & Tatham* (for the Public Prosecutor): *Graham
Page & Co.* (for the appellant Chai); *Garber, Vowles & Co.* (for all other parties).

[*Reported by* KATHLEEN J. H. O'BRIEN, *Barrister-at-Law.*]

A READY MIXED CONCRETE (SOUTH EAST), LTD. *v.* MINISTER
OF PENSIONS AND NATIONAL INSURANCE.

MINISTER OF SOCIAL SECURITY *v.* GREENHAM
READY MIXED CONCRETE, LTD. AND ANOTHER.

B MINISTER OF SOCIAL SECURITY *v.* READY MIXED
CONCRETE (SOUTH EAST), LTD. AND ANOTHER.

[QUEEN'S BENCH DIVISION (MacKenna, J.), October 3, 4, 5, 6, 9, 10, 11, December
8, 1967.]

National Insurance—" Employed person "—Owner drivers employed by manu-
C   *facturers of concrete to deliver concrete—Whether contracts of carriage with*
independent contractors or contracts of service.

L. had been employed by the applicant company as a yardman batcher
in and after 1958. In 1959 the company, which made and sold concrete,
introduced a system of delivery by owner drivers. It was the company's
policy that the making and selling of concrete should be carried on separately
from that of delivering it. A purpose of the owner driver scheme was
D that it would stimulate efficient cartage and care of the vehicle. In May,
1965, L. entered into a new contract with the company for the carriage of
concrete. He also entered into a hire-purchase agreement for a lorry with
an associated hire-purchase company. The lorry was painted in the concrete
company's colours and was adapted to carry their mixing unit. L. was to
procure an " A " carriers' licence, was to make the lorry available at all
E times to the company, and was to use it for no other purpose. He was
entitled to employ competent substitute drivers, but if the company were
dissatisfied he was to provide another substitute; the company was entitled
to require L. himself to drive the lorry for the maximum hours permitted
by law, save for holiday periods. L. was to wear the company's uniform
and to carry out all reasonable orders from competent servants of the com-
F pany, " as if he were an employee of the company ". L. was to maintain
both the lorry and the mixing unit, including the making of fair wear and
tear renewals at his own expense. He was to pay all running costs, and not
to charge the vehicle or mixing unit, which were to be insured by the company. Payment to the owner driver was to be at fixed rates per cubic
G yard for each radial mile, with provision for minimum annual earnings.
L., with other owner drivers, employed and paid a relief driver with the
company's consent. Either party could determine the contract by notice,
the company having the right to acquire the vehicle. The company gave
no instructions to L. about the method of driving the trucks from the plant
to the place of delivery. The contract contained a declaration that L. was
an independent contractor. The company in busy seasons also employed
H employee-drivers at different remuneration. On the question whether
L. was an " employed person ", viz., employed under a contract of service
for the purposes of s. 1 (2) (*a*)* of the National Insurance Act 1965,

---

* Section 1 (2) of the National Insurance Act 1965 provides: " For the purposes of
this Act, insured persons shall be divided into the following three classes, namely—
(*a*) employed persons, that is to say, persons gainfully occupied in employment in
I Great Britain, being employment under a contract of service; (*b*) self-employed
persons, that is to say, persons gainfully occupied in employment in Great Britain
who are not employed persons; . . ." In s. 114 (1) of the Act of 1965 " contract of
service " is defined to mean " any contract of service or apprenticeship, whether written
or oral and whether express or implied "; and " employment " is defined to include
" any trade, business, profession, office or vocation " and " employed " is to be construed accordingly except in the expression " employed persons ". By s. 3 (1) of the
Act of 1965—" subject to the provisions of this Act— . . . (*b*) every employer of an
employed person of any description set out in column 1 of Part 2 of Sch. 1 to this Act . . .
shall be liable to pay weekly contributions in respect of that person at the rate set out
in relation to that description . . ."

Held: a contract of service existed if three conditions were fulfilled (for A
which see p. 440, letter A, post), and, though one of these was that the
servant should be subject to the control of the master to a sufficient degree,
yet for present purposes the important condition was the third, viz., that
the provisions of the contract should not be inconsistent with its being
a contract of service; in the present case the rights conferred and the
duties imposed by L.'s contract with the company were not such as to make B
the contract one of service, and his contract was one of carriage, with the
consequence that L. was not included within the class of employed persons
for the purposes of s. 1 (2) (*a*) of the National Insurance Act 1965 (see
p. 440, letter F, and p. 446, letter G, post).

Quantity... *Queensland Stations Pty., Ltd.* v. *Federal Comr. of Taxation* ((1945), 70
C.L.R. 539) and opinion of LORD WRIGHT in *Montreal Locomotive Works* C
Ltd. v. *Montreal and A.-G. for Canada* ([1947] 1 D.L.R. 161) applied.

[As to employed persons for the purposes of national insurance, see 27 HALS-
BURY'S LAWS (3rd Edn.) 711, 712, para. 1295.

As to contracts of service, see 25 HALSBURY'S LAWS (3rd Edn.) 448, 449,
para. 872, s. 1 (2), s. 3; and for cases on the factors giving rise to the relationship
of master and servant, see 34 DIGEST (Repl.) 17, 18, *8-20*, and 30, 31, *82-91*. D

For the National Insurance Act 1965, see 45 HALSBURY'S STATUTES (2nd Edn.)
952, 954.]

Cases referred to:

Amalgamated Engineering Union v. *Minister of Pensions and National
    Insurance*, [1963] 1 All E.R. 864; [1963] 1 W.L.R. 441; Digest (Cont. E
    Vol. A) 1133, *2632a*.
Bank Voor Handel en Scheepvaart, N.V. v. *Slatford*, [1952] 2 All E.R. 956;
    [1953] 1 Q.B. 248; [1954] 2 W.L.R. 867; *revsd.* sub nom. *Bank Voor
    Handel en Scheepvaart, N.V.* v. *Administrator of Hungarian Property*,
    [1954] 1 All E.R. 969; [1954] A.C. 584; [1954] 2 W.L.R. 867; 2 Digest
    (Repl.) 269, *614*.
Clarke v. *Bailieborough Co-operative Agricultural and Dairy Society, Ltd.*, F
    (1913), 47 I.L.T. 113.
Doggett v. *Waterloo Taxi-Cab Co., Ltd.*, [1910] 2 K.B. 336; 79 L.J.K.B. 1085;
    102 L.T. 876; 34 Digest (Repl.) 37, *127*.
Hardaker v. *Idle District Council*, [1895-99] All E.R. Rep. 311; [1896] 1 Q.B.
    335; 65 L.J.Q.B. 363; 74 L.T. 69; 60 J.P. 196; 34 Digest (Repl.) G
    201, *1416*.
Humberstone v. *Northern Timber Mills*, [1949] A.L.R. 985; 79 C.L.R. 389;
    34 Digest (Repl.) 31, **53*.
Montreal Locomotive Works, Ltd. v. *Montreal and A.-G. for Canada*, [1947]
    1 D.L.R. 161.
Mooney v. *Sheehan*, (1903), 37 I.L.T. 166.
National Labour Relations Board v. *Nu-Car Carriers*, (1951), 189 Fed. 2nd 756. H
O'Donnell v. *Clare County Council*, (1912), 47 I.L.T. 41; 6 B.W.C.C. 457;
    34 Digest (Repl.) 358, **1480*.
Park v. *Wilsons & Clyde Coal Co., Haggerty* v. *Wilsons & Clyde Coal Co.*,
    1928 S.C. 121; *affd.*, 1929 S.C. 38; 34 Digest (Repl.) 33, **63*.
Queensland Stations Pty., Ltd. v. *Federal Comr. of Taxation*, (1945), 70 C.L.R.
    539.
Short v. *Henderson, Ltd.*, (1946), 115 L.J.P.C. 41; 174 L.T. 417; 34 Digest
    (Repl.) 343, *2635*.
U.S. v. *Silk*, (1946), 331 U.S. 704.
Zuijus v. *Wirth Brothers Pty., Ltd.*, (1955), 93 C.L.R. 561.

Cases Stated.

These were three appeals by cases stated from determinations whether each
of three owner drivers were employed under a contract of service for the purposes

A of the National Insurance Act 1965, s. 1 (2). The decisions on two of these appeals were to follow from that on the appeal of Mr. Latimer, and accordingly the matter relevant to that appeal alone is set out here. On Nov. 15, 1965, Ready Mixed Concrete (South East), Ltd. (" the company ") applied to the Minister of Social Security under s. 64 of the National Insurance Act 1965 (the Case Stated being brought under s. 65 of the Act of 1965 and R.S.C. Ord. 111) to determine the

B question whether Mr. Latimer was, by virtue of the contract between himself and the company dated May 15, 1965, an employed or self-employed person for the purposes of the Act of 1965 during the week beginning Nov. 8, 1965, and also whether the company were liable for payment of flat rate contributions in respect of him for the purposes of s. 3 of the Act of 1965 during that week.

   The Minister accepted evidence at an inquiry held on Jan. 11 and Jan. 12,

C 1966, at which both Mr. Latimer and the company were represented, as establishing the following facts among others. Ready Mixed Concrete (United Kingdom), Ltd. carried on the business of making and selling ready mixed concrete and similar materials, and operated through a number of wholly or partly owned subsidiary companies, one of which was the company. The company was incorporated in 1963 and operated at eight plants at various places in the south east

D of England. It was and always had been the policy of the group of companies of which the company was one, that the business of making and selling concrete should be carried on as far as possible separately from the business of delivering the concrete to customers, and formerly delivery of concrete had been effected by an independent company of haulage contractors. In 1959 that contract had been determined, and there had been introduced in the group a scheme of delivery

E by owner drivers working under contracts similar to a form of agreement annexed to the Case Stated*. It was considered that not only would the scheme further the policy of keeping and making and selling of concrete separate from its delivery, but also that the scheme would benefit the group by stimulating speedy and efficient cartage, the maintenance of trucks in good condition, and the careful driving thereof, and would benefit the owner driver by giving him an

F incentive to work for a higher return without abusing the vehicle in a way which often happened if an employee were given a bonus scheme related to the use of his employer's vehicle. It was, and always had been since the introduction of the owner driver scheme in 1959, the intention of the group and of the owner drivers that the latter should be treated as independent contractors and not as servants of member companies of the group†. Some owner drivers had, in

G addition to delivering concrete in pursuance of a contract with a member of the group, carried on other remunerative occupations. A few owner drivers had an interest in more than one truck, themselves employing drivers to work for them, and the company was willing to allow suitable owner drivers to own more than one truck. Notices under the Contracts of Employment Act 1963 had not been issued to owner drivers. Income tax was paid by owner drivers under

H Sch. D of the Income Tax Act, 1952. Contributions were paid by owner drivers as self-employed persons under the National Insurance Act, 1946, until March, 1965, when the Ministry of Pensions and National Insurance requested the payment of contributions by and in respect of them as employed persons.

   Mr. Latimer became employed under a contract of service by a member of the group in 1958 as a yardman batcher at Northfleet. In 1960 he was trans-

I ferred to the plant at Crayford (where the company later operated) as a batcher. In 1963 he entered into a contract with the company whereby he agreed to collect, carry and deliver concrete as an owner driver for two years. At the same time he entered into a hire-purchase agreement‡ relating to a Leyland lorry.

---

* See the summary which states relevant terms of the contract, p. 437, letter B, to p. 439, letter A, post.
   † As to the irrelevance in law of these considerations, see p. 439, letter H, post.
   ‡ His LORDSHIP intimated that there was nothing unusual in the provisions of the hire-purchase contract, mentioning that Mr. Latimer was described in the contract as a " contractor self-employed ".

He finished paying for this in about one year, and the vehicle then became his A property. On May 15, 1965, he entered into a new contract with the company whereby he agreed to collect, carry and deliver concrete as an owner driver for a further period of five years. On June 17, 1965, he entered into a hire-purchase agreement with Readymix Finance, Ltd., whereby in place of his former vehicle which he sold, he agreed to purchase a Leyland vehicle by means of forty-eight consecutive monthly instalments of £62 19s. 6d. the first instalments being pay- B able on July 1, 1965. Since May 15, 1965, Mr. Latimer had collected, carried and delivered concrete at and from the company's plant at Crayford, and had been paid an allowance in accordance with the contract (cl. 20 prescribed the rate of remuneration). Such payments were estimated to amount to approxi- mately £4,500 yearly. For the years ending June, 1964, June 30, 1965, Mr. Latimer received £4,200 and £4,512 respectively from the company under the C contract between them then in force. After the payment of all expenses the net amount of remuneration remaining in Mr. Latimer's hands for the two years was £3,327 and £2,004 respectively. In November, 1965, as many as 709 persons were employed as owner drivers under contracts with members of the group, forty-eight persons were so employed by the company and eight persons, in addition to Mr. Latimer, were so employed at the company's Crayford plant. D

Further facts found in the Case Stated were summarised by His Lordship (MACKENNA, J.) as follows. Loading at the plant began at a time fixed by the plant manager. The nine owner drivers had established a system under which the truck first loaded on one day would be last loaded on the next day and so on in rotation. The owner driver waited in a mess room until a loudspeaker called him for loading. When he had delivered his load he returned to collect E another, and so on through the day. He did not work set hours and had no fixed meal break. While on the plant premises he was expected to comply with directions given on the company's behalf to secure an orderly and safe system of loading, parking and driving, and he complied with them. The company gave no instructions to owner drivers about the method of driving the trucks from the plant to the place of delivery or of discharging the concrete, and did F not tell them what routes to take. While on the delivery site they followed the site foreman's instructions about discharge. The nine owner-drivers arranged the dates of their holidays so as to ensure as far as possible that no more than one driver was on holiday at any one time. With the knowledge and approval of the company they employed between them a single relief driver, contributing equally to his weekly wage of £25. He took over the operation of any vehicle G whose regular owner driver was absent through sickness, or because he was on holiday, or for any other reason. During the busy season the company employed three or four additional drivers under contracts of service. These men worked fixed hours and were paid at the hourly rate of 5s. 11d. Their wages (with overtime at a higher rate) averaged between £18 and £20 a week. They were not responsible for the maintenance or running costs of the trucks they drove. H When not engaged in delivering concrete, they, unlike the owner drivers, did other jobs. They were told what routes to take. The owner drivers could, if they wished, buy their petrol from a pump on the plant premises. Mr. Latimer did not. The additional drivers in the busy season mentioned had to take their supplies from the pump. Owner drivers were allowed to use the company's maintenance facilities, but they were charged for all work done to their vehicles. I The company had made no rules, regulations or requirements under cl. 14 (b), which clause of Mr. Latimer's contract with the company required him to observe such rules, regulations and requirements, except for securing orderly and safe working at the plant. If anyone acting for the company were to seek to instruct Mr. Latimer how to deliver concrete or how to drive his truck, he would (so it was found in the Case Stated) have told that person to mind his own business*.

---

* As to the irrelevance in law of this consideration, see p. 439, letter G, post.

A Nobody had sought to instruct him. The accounts prepared for him by his accountant in accordance with the requirements of the contract were headed " T. H. Latimer, Esq., haulage contractor, Ready Mixed Concrete, 13 Morgan Drive, Stone, Kent ". Mr. Latimer held an " A " licence. The cost of the mixing unit was £2,000. Mr. Latimer had not been required to deliver materials for other group companies.

B The contract between the company and Mr. Latimer was set out in a schedule to the Case Stated. The following summary of relevant provisions is taken from the judgment. The commencement date was June 1, 1965, and the termination date was Apr. 30, 1970. The company were to procure that the hire-purchase company would offer to sell the Leyland lorry to Mr. Latimer on credit terms, painted in colours and with distinguishing signs selected by the company, and

C adapted to carry the company's concrete mixing unit, fleet number 52140, which the company would fix to the lorry, and he was to buy the lorry from the hire-purchase company. The contract referred to the Leyland lorry as " the vehicle ", and to the Leyland lorry with the mixing unit attached as " the truck "; these descriptions are used in the summary. If required to do so Mr. Latimer had at his expense to instal radio equipment on the vehicle. He was to procure an

D " A " carriers' licence under the Road Traffic Act, 1960, covering the use of the truck. Clause 5 provided—

> " The owner driver shall at all times of the day or night during the term of this agreement (excepting only in accordance with the terms hereof) make available the truck to the company for the purpose of collecting carrying and
E delivering the material used for or in connexion with the business of the company (not being a business of carrying or arranging for the carriage of goods) whenever and wherever so required by the company whether such requirement is notified to the owner driver or to his servants or agents and shall duly and promptly collect carry and deliver such quantity or quantities of the materials as and when required in the manner at the time and to the
F destination directed by the company and it is further provided that the truck shall be used exclusively for the purposes set out in this agreement and for no other purpose. In furtherance of the terms of this clause the owner driver shall if so required by the company at his own expense ensure that the company is able to contact him by telephone at his usual residence or residences."

G The company could call on Mr. Latimer to make the truck available for delivering the materials of any other group company, subject to his obtaining a " B " licence, which he must in that case try to get. He had to comply with the conditions of his licences and obey any other rules or regulations, parliamentary, local or parochial. Under cl. 10 he might, with the company's consent and subject to cl. 12, appoint a competent driver to operate the truck in his place.

I He must pay this driver National Joint Council wages or better, and if the company were dissatisfied with the driver he must provide another. Clause 12 was in these terms:

> " 12. Notwithstanding the provisions of cl. 10 of this schedule the company shall be entitled to require the owner driver himself to operate the
J truck on every or any day doing up to the maximum number of hours permitted under the provisions of s. 73 of the Road Traffic Act, 1960, or any statutory amendment or re-enactment thereof and the owner driver shall comply with such requirement unless he shall have a reason for not so doing which would have been valid had he been the employed driver of the company and shall have notified the company in advance of such reason and shall be able to produce and upon the request of the company in fact produce evidence to substantiate the same. The owner driver shall not himself be obliged to operate the truck during such holiday times and

A

periods (not extending for more than two weeks in any calendar year) as have been agreed by the company in writing."

His Lordship intimated that he read cl. 10 and cl. 12 to mean that Mr. Latimer must drive himself if required to do so by the company, unless he had an excuse which would be valid in the case of a servant. Mr. Latimer was further bound by the contract as follows. He was not to operate as a haulier or carrier of goods except under the contract. If he failed to operate the truck himself or to cause another driver to do so, the company might appoint a driver on his behalf, and Mr. Latimer had to pay this driver's wages, and this driver should be deemed to be in his employment. Mr. Latimer had to wear the company's uniform, complying with all the company's rules, regulations or requirements (cl. 14 (b) of the contract), carry out all reasonable orders from any competent servant of the company " as if he were an employee of the company ", and by his conduct and appearance " including the speed and manner in which he operates the truck " use his best endeavours to further the good name of the company. He must not alter the truck without the company's consent. He must keep it freshly painted in the colours and with the signs directed by the company. He must keep it washed, cleansed, oiled, greased, maintained and in good and substantial repair. This obligation extended to the company's mixing unit, whose worn parts he must, with certain exceptions, renew if the need for renewal was due to fair wear and tear. All these things were to be done at his expense. Where the repairs would cost more than £50 or take more than a day to execute, the company might require the work to be done by a named group company or by someone else of the company's choice. The company might specify any repair work which the company thought should be done, and Mr. Latimer had to do it. For all these services Mr. Latimer was to be paid 8s. 6d. per cubic yard for the first radial mile and 1s. 1d. per cubic yard for each mile thereafter.

Provision was made for minimum annual earnings: $£1500 \times \dfrac{280 - Y}{280}$ where Y

represented the number of days in excess of eighty-four when the truck and a driver were not available for at least four hours. Those rates were to be revised at the request of either party if there were any alteration in the National Joint Council's rates of wages or in the cost of fuel, or at his request " in the event of any substantial reduction in the profitability of the agreement to the owner driver by reason of any levy or tax imposed by Parliament on carriers of goods by road transport generally ". Mr. Latimer was to pay all the running costs. He might not charge the vehicle or the mixing unit or make them subject to any lien except under the hire-purchase contract. The company, if the company wished, might pay the hire-purchase instalments direct, and debit them to him. If Mr. Latimer did not pay his bills, the company might pay them for him. He must have his accounts prepared in a form and by an accountant approved by the company. If any provision was made in the account, he must set it aside in a manner approved by the company. The company were to insure the vehicle in his name and the mixing unit in his or theirs, in each case in such form and for such amounts as they thought fit but at his expense, debiting his account with the charges which he authorised them to pay. He was to spend any money which he received under these policies in repairing or replacing the insured property. He had, if required to do so, to assign to the company any rights he might have under the policies. The company were given the right to acquire the vehicle on the expiration or determination of the contract. Either party might determine the contract by notice after Apr. 30, 1970. Before that date the company might determine it by twenty-eight days' notice if Mr. Latimer had been incapacitated for sixty days, and summarily if " (i) Mr. [Latimer] committed a breach of any term of contract, or (ii) was guilty of conduct tending to bring the company into disrepute, or (iii) committed an act of bankruptcy,

A etc., or (iv) if he, having been warned by the company of any ground for dissatisfaction it might have in respect of the operation of the truck should not
within a reasonable time have removed the cause of such dissatisfaction ".
Clause 30 of the contract declared him to be an independent contractor.

The Minister decided that—(a) Mr. Latimer was included in the class of
employed persons for the purposes of the National Insurance Act 1965 during
B the week commencing Monday, Nov. 8, 1965, and (b) the company as his employer
was liable to pay a flat rate contribution in respect of him under s. 3 (b) of the
Act of 1965 for that week.

In the second and third cases, the facts being similar, the owner drivers were
Mr. John King and Mr. Arthur William Bezer.

The cases noted below* were cited during the argument in addition to those
C referred to in the judgment.

R. J. Parker, Q.C., and *G. Slynn* for Ready Mixed Concrete (South East), Ltd.,
Mr. Latimer and Mr. Bezer.

H. A. P. Fisher, Q.C., and *Adrian Hamilton* for Greenham Ready Mixed
Concrete, Ltd. and Mr. King.

Nigel Bridge for the Minister of Social Security, formerly the Minister of
D Pensions and National Insurance.

Cur. adv. vult.

Dec. 8.   **MACKENNA, J.,** read the following judgment, in which he stated
the question which arose for determination, reviewed the facts and summarised
the provisions of Mr. Latimer's contract with the company, Ready Mixed Concrete
(South East), Ltd., as hereinbefore set out.   In relation to cl. 30 of the contract,
E which declared that Mr. Latimer was an independent contractor, His Lordship
observed that the question whether the relation between parties to a contract
was that of master and servant or otherwise was a conclusion of law dependent
on the rights conferred and the duties imposed by the contract; and that if
these were such that the relation is that of master and servant, it was irrelevant
that the parties had declared it to be something else.   Such a declaration was
F not necessarily ineffective, for if it were doubtful for what rights and duties the
parties wished to provide, such a declaration might help in resolving the doubt
and in fixing them in the sense required give effect to the expressed intention.
His Lordship further intimated that the Minister in reaching her conclusion
had been right to disregard the following matters—(i) the finding that if anybody
acting for the company had sought to instruct Mr. Latimer how to deliver con-
G crete or how to drive his truck, Mr. Latimer would have told that person to
mind his own business and that nobody had sought to instruct him (see p. 436,
letter I, ante);   (ii) that in 1962 the Ministry of Pensions and National Insurance had expressed the opinion that the form of contract then used by the
company (which omitted provisions present in the later form of contract) was
H not one of service; and (iii) that it had been the intention of the group and of
the owner drivers that the latter should be treated as independent contractors
and not as servants of member companies of the group (see p. 435, letter G, ante).
His Lordship continued:—

I must now consider what is meant by a contract of service.   A contract
of service exists if the following three conditions are fulfilled: (i) The servant

◄ * *Simmon* v. *Heath Laundry Co.*, [1910] 1 K.B. 543;   *Braddell* v. *Baker*, (1911),
104 L.T. 673;   *Watcham* v. *A.-G. of East Africa Protectorate*, [1918-19] All E.R. Rep.
455;   [1919] A.C. 533;   *Binding* v. *Great Yarmouth Port and Haven Comrs.*, (1923),
128 L.T. 743;   *Century Insurance Co., Ltd.* v. *Northern Ireland Road Transport Board*,
[1942] 1 All E.R. 491;   *Mersey Docks & Harbour Board* v. *Coggins & Griffiths (Liverpool),
Ltd., and McFarlane*, [1946] 2 All E.R. 345;   [1947] A.C. 11;   *Gould* v. *Minister of
National Insurance*, [1951] 1 All E.R. 368;   [1951] 1 K.B. 731;   *Stevenson, Jordan &
Harrison, Ltd.* v. *Macdonald & Evans*, [1952] 1 T.L.R. 101;   *Denham* v. *Midland
Employers' Mutual Assurance, Ltd.*, [1955] 2 All E.R. 561;   [1955] 2 Q.B. 437;   *O'Reilly*
v. *Imperial Chemical Industries, Ltd.*, [1955] 2 All E.R. 567;   *Re C. W. & A. L. Hughes,
Ltd.*, [1966] 2 All E.R. 702;   *Whittaker* v. *Minister of Pensions and National Insurance*,
[1966] 3 All E.R. 531;   [1967] 1 Q.B. 156;   *Rolls Razor, Ltd.* v. *Cox*, [1967] 1 All E.R. 397;
[1967] 1 Q.B. 552.

agrees that in consideration of a wage or other remuneration he will provide **A**
his own work and skill in the performance of some service for his master. (ii) He
agrees, expressly or impliedly, that in the performance of that service he will
be subject to the other's control in a sufficient degree to make that other master.
(iii) The other provisions of the contract are consistent with its being a contract
of service. I need say little about (i) and (ii).

As to (i). There must be a wage or other remuneration. Otherwise there **B**
will be no consideration, and without consideration no contract of any kind.
The servant must be obliged to provide his own work and skill. Freedom to do
a job either by one's own hands, or by another's is inconsistent with a contract
of service, though a limited or occasional power of delegation may not be:
see MR. ATIYAH'S VICARIOUS LIABILITY IN THE LAW OF TORTS (1967), pp. 59-61,
and the cases cited by him. **C**

As to (ii). Control includes the power of deciding the thing to be done, the
way in which it shall be done, the means to be employed in doing it, the time
when, and the place where it shall be done. All these aspects of control must be
considered in deciding whether the right exists in a sufficient degree to make one
party the master and the other his servant. The right need not be unrestricted.
 D

" What matters is lawful authority to command, so far as there is scope
for it. And there must always be some room for it, if only in incidental or
collateral matters."

Zuijus v. *Wirth Brothers Pty., Ltd.* (1). To find where the right resides one must
look first to the express terms of the contract, and if they deal fully with the
matter one may look no further. If the contract does not expressly provide **E**
which party shall have the right, the question must be answered in the ordinary
way by implication.

The third and negative condition is for my purpose the important one, and I
shall try with the help of five examples to explain what I mean by provisions
inconsistent with the nature of a contract of service.

(i) A contract obliges one party to build for the other, providing at his own **F**
expense the necessary plant and materials. This is not a contract of service,
even though the builder may be obliged to use his own labour only and to accept
a high degree of control: it is a building contract. It is not a contract to serve
another for a wage, but a contract to produce a thing (or a result) for a price.

(ii) A contract obliges one party to carry another's goods, providing at his
own expense everything needed for performance. This is not a contract of **G**
service, even though the carrier may be obliged to drive the vehicle himself and
to accept the other's control over his performance: it is a contract of carriage.

(iii) A contract obliges a labourer to work for a builder, providing some simple
tools, and to accept the builder's control. Notwithstanding the obligation to
provide the tools, the contract is one of service. That obligation is not inconsistent with the nature of a contract of service. It is not a sufficiently important **H**
matter to affect the substance of the contract.

(iv) A contract obliges one party to work for the other, accepting his control,
and to provide his own transport. This is still a contract of service. The
obligation to provide his own transport does not affect the substance. Transport
in this example is incidental to the main purpose of the contract. Transport
in the second example was the essential part of the performance.

(v) The same instrument provides that one party shall work for the other subject
to the other's control, and also that he shall sell him his land. The first part of
the instrument is no less a contract of service because the second part imposes
obligations of a different kind (*Amalgamated Engineering Union* v. *Minister of
Pensions and National Insurance* (2)).

I can put the point which I am making in other words. An obligation to do

---

(1) (1955), 93 C.L.R. 561 at p. 571.
(2) [1963] 1 All E.R. 864 at pp. 869, 870.

A work subject to the other party's control is a necessary, though not always a sufficient, condition of a contract of service. If the provisions of the contract as a whole are inconsistent with its being a contract of service, it will be some other kind of contract, and the person doing the work will not be a servant. The judge's task is to classify the contract (a task like that of distinguishing a contract of sale from one of work and labour). He may, in performing it, take into account
B other matters besides control.

I find authority for this way of dealing with the case in the judgment of DIXON, J., in *Queensland Stations Pty., Ltd.* v. *Federal Comr. of Taxation* (3). There the question was whether a payment made by the company to a drover was " wages " within the meaning of a Pay-roll Tax Assessment Act, which depended on whether the relation between the company and the drover was that
C of master and servant. The drover was employed under a written contract to drive 317 cattle to a destination. The contract provided that he should obey and carry out all lawful instructions and use the whole of his time, energy and ability in the careful driving of the stock, that he should provide at his own expense all men, plant, horses and rations required for the operation, and that he should be paid at a rate per head for each of the cattle safely delivered at the
D destination. He was held to be an independent contractor. This passage comes from the judgment of DIXON, J. (4):

" There is, of course, nothing to prevent a drover and his client forming the relation of employee and employer . . . But whether they do so must depend on the facts. In considering the facts it is a mistake to treat as decisive a reservation of control over the manner in which the droving is
E performed and the cattle are handled. For instance, in the present case the circumstance that the drover agrees to obey and carry out all lawful instructions cannot outweigh the countervailing considerations which are found in the employment by him of servants of his own, the provision of horses, equipment, plant, rations, and a remuneration at a rate per head delivered. That a reservation of a right to direct or superintend the per-
F formance of the task cannot transform into a contract of service what in essence is an independent contract appears from . . ."

There follows the citation of a number of English cases, including *Hardaker* v. *Idle District Council* (5), the building contractor's case.

If the independent contractor need not be free from the other party's control " in the performance of the task ", what freedom must he possess if he is to be
G called " independent "? Must he be free to choose the plant, equipment and materials as he wishes, or can he submit to some control in these respects too without affecting the substance of his independent contract? I do not see why not. In practice there will always be some scope for independent action by the man who undertakes to provide the means of performance and to accomplish the result for which he is to be paid.

H I compare, and to some extent contrast, with this judgment of DIXON, J.'s another judgment of the same judge in *Humberstone* v. *Northern Timber Mills* (6). There the question was whether the owner driver of a truck was a servant under a contract of service so as to be covered by a Workmen's Compensation Act. For a number of years the owner had taken his truck at about the same time each day to the respondents' factory where he had been given goods to deliver
I to their customers. He carried on delivering goods until about the same time each evening when he knocked off. He maintained the truck and supplied the fuel at his own expense, and was paid for goods carried at a rate per car-mile. From these facts it was inferred that there was a continuing contract between the respondents and the owner which was not a contract of service. For this last conclusion DIXON, J., gave these reasons (7):

(3) (1945), 70 C.L.R. 539.
(5) [1895-99] All E.R. Rep. 311; [1896] 1 Q.B. 335.
(6) (1949), 79 C.L.R. 389.
(4) (1945), 70 C.L.R. at p. 552.
(7) (1949), 79 C.L.R. at p. 404.

A

" *The question is* not whether in practice the work was in fact done subject to a direction and control exercised by an actual supervision or whether
an actual supervision was possible but *whether ultimate authority over the
man in the performance of his work resided in the employer so that he was
subject to the latter's order and directions.*   In the present case the contract
by the deceased was to provide not merely his own labour but the use of
heavy mechanised transport, driven by power, which he maintained and
fuelled for the purpose.   The most important part of the work to be performed by his own labour consisted in the operation of his own motor truck
and the essential part of the service for which the respondents contracted
was the transportation of their goods by the mechanical means he thus
supplied.   The essence of a contract of service is the supply of the work
and skill of a man.   But the emphasis in the case of the present contract is
on mechanical traction.   This was to be done by his own property in his own
possession and control.   *There is no ground for imputing to the parties a
common intention that in all the management and control of his own vehicle,
in all the ways in which he used it for the purpose of carrying their goods, he
should be subject to the commands of the respondents.*

" In essence it appears to me to have been an independent contract and
I do not think that it was open to the board to find otherwise.

" The subject has recently been dealt with in this court in *Queensland
Stations Pty., Ltd.* v. *Federal Comr. of Taxation* (8).   As in that case the
contract is one for the performance of a service for one party by another
who is to employ plant for the purpose and to be paid by the results."

B

C

D

Were it not for the words which I have italicised I would have said that the
reasoning here was the same as in the earlier case.   Because of the driver's obligation to provide the truck, to maintain and fuel it, and to accept payment by
results, it was a contract for the transportation of goods and not a contract of
service.   But the italicised words seem to make the consignor's right of control
(if it exists) a sufficient condition of a contract of service, and to treat the owner
driver's obligation to provide the truck, etc., merely as evidence, making difficult,
or precluding, the imputation of an intention to the parties that he should be
subject to control.   If the obligation to provide the truck, etc., were relevant
only as evidence of intention in the matter of control, it would cease to be
relevant where the parties had expressed their intention in that matter, and if,
as in the *Queensland* case (8), the contract expressly provided that the driver
should be subject to the other party's control, he would be a servant.   But the
Queensland case (8) decided that the drover's was an " independent contract ":
his obligation to provide the men, the horses, etc., determined its nature and made
it, notwithstanding his submission to control, something other than a contract
of service.   If there is in this respect a difference between the two judgments,
I prefer the earlier.

E

F

G

The opinion of LORD WRIGHT in *Montreal Locomotive Works, Ltd.* v. *Montreal
and A.-G. for Canada* (9), forgotten by at least one of the counsel who argued the
case, and discovered by MR. ATIYAH, must be mentioned here.   There were two
questions in that case, whether a corporation was the occupant of an armaments
factory so as to be liable to pay an occupation tax, and whether it was carrying on
a business in the factory so as to be liable to pay a business tax.   The answer to
both questions depended on whether the corporation was acting as the government's agent in the manufacture of the armaments or as an independent contractor.   All the funds necessary for the enterprise were provided by the government
which bore all the financial risks.   The corporation was subject to the government's control in making the armaments and received a fee for each unit of
production.   It was held on these facts that the corporation was not liable to

H

---

(8) (1945), 70 C.L.R. 539.
(9) [1947] 1 D.L.R. 161.

A pay the taxes.   Mr. Atiyah cites (p. 38) the following passage from Lord Wright's opinion (10):

" In earlier cases a single test, such as the presence or absence of control, was often relied on to determine whether the case was one of master and servant, mostly in order to decide issues of tortious liability on the part of the master or superior. In the more complex conditions of modern industry,

B more complicated tests have often to be applied. It has been suggested that a fourfold test would in some cases be more appropriate, a complex involving (1) control; (2) ownership of the tools; (3) chance of profit; (4) risk of loss. Control in itself is not always conclusive. Thus the master of a chartered vessel is generally the employee of the shipowner though the charterer can direct the employment of the vessel. Again the law often limits the employer's

C right to interfere with the employee's conduct, as also do trade union regulations. In many cases the question can only be settled by examining the whole of the various elements which constitute the relationship between the parties. In this way it is in some cases possible to decide the issue by raising as the crucial question whose business is it, or in other words by asking whether the party is carrying on the business, in the sense of carrying it on for

D himself or on his own behalf and not merely for a superior."

In Lord Wright's first illustration of the shipowner, the charterer and the shipmaster, control is shown in two ways not to be conclusive. Though the shipowner had delegated to the charterer his right to give directions to the shipmaster, and in that limited sense no longer had control, he was still the master.

E Again, though the charterer had the power of giving directions, and in that sense had control, he was not the master. The second illustration shows that a right of control limited by law or by trade union regulations may be sufficient for the relation of master and servant. This does not take us very far in the direction of a fourfold test. It is easier to relate Lord Wright's (2), (3) and (4) to the case mentioned in the last sentence of the quotation. If a man's activities have the

F character of a business, and if the question is whether he is carrying on that business for himself or for another, it must be relevant to consider which of the two owns the assets (" the ownership of the tools ") and which bears the financial risk (" the chance of profit ", " the risk of loss "). He who owns the assets and bears the risk is unlikely to be acting as an agent or a servant. If the man performing the service must provide the means of performance at his own expense and accept payment by results, he will own the assets, bear the risk,

G and be to that extent unlike a servant. I should add that there is nothing in the Canadian case to support the view that the ownership of the assets is relevant only to the question of control. Lord Wright treats his three other tests as having a value independent of control in determining the nature of the contract.

U.S. v. *Silk* (11) was the most important of the American cases cited to me. The case disposed of two suits raising the question whether men working for the plaintiffs, Silk and Greyvan, were " employees " within the meaning of that word in the Social Security Act of 1935. The judges of the Supreme Court agreed on the test to be applied, though not in every instance on its application to the facts. It was not to be what they described as " the common law test ", viz., " power of control, whether exercised or not, over the manner of performing

I service to the undertaking ". The test was whether the men were employees " as a matter of economic reality ". Important factors were said to be " the degrees of control, opportunities of profit or loss, investment in facilities, permanency of relation and skill required in the claimed independent operation."

Silk sold coal by retail, using the services of two classes of workers, unloaders and truck drivers. The unloaders moved the coal from railway vans into bins. They came to the yard when they wished and were given a wagon to unload and

(10) [1947] 1 D.L.R. at p. 169.
(11) (1946), 331 U.S. 704.

a place to put the coal. They provided their own tools and were paid so much A
per ton for the coal they shifted. All the nine judges held that these men were
employees (12):

> " Giving full consideration to the concurrence of the two lower courts in a
> contrary result, we cannot agree that the unloaders in the *Silk* case were
> independent contractors. They provided only picks and shovels. They B
> had no opportunity to gain or lose except from the work of their hands and
> these simple tools. That the unloaders did not work regularly is not signifi-
> cant. They did work in the course of the employer's trade or business. This
> brings them under the coverage of the Act. They are of the group that the
> Social Security Act was intended to aid. Silk was in a position to exercise
> all necessary supervision over their simple tasks. Unloaders have often been C
> held to be employees in tort cases."

Silk's drivers owned the trucks in which they delivered coal to Silk's customers.
They paid all the expenses of operating their trucks including the wages of any
extra help they needed or chose to employ. They came to the yard when they
pleased and were free to haul goods for other people. They were paid for their
deliveries at a rate per ton. Greyvan carried on a road haulier's business. Their D
drivers too owned their trucks and were required to pay all the costs of operation.
They were not allowed to work for anyone else but Greyvan, and had to drive the
trucks themselves or, if they employed a relief driver, to be present when he drove.
They had to follow all the rules, regulations and instructions of Greyvan. They
were paid a percentage of the tariff which Greyvan charged the customers. By
a majority of the court both sets of drivers were held to be independent E
contractors (13):

> " . . . where the arrangements leave the driver-owners so much respon-
> sibility for investment and management as here, they must be held to be
> independent contractors. These driver-owners are small businessmen. They
> own their own trucks. They hire their own helpers. In one instance they
> haul for a single business, in the other for any customer. The distinction, F
> though important, is not controlling. It is the total situation, including the
> risk undertaken, the control exercised, the opportunity for profit from
> sound management, that marks these driver-owners as independent
> contractors."

This reasoning apparently requires that there should be some power of control
vested in the driver if he is to qualify as an independent contractor. That the G
power need not be very extensive appears from the facts in *Greyvan's* case.
The driver's investment, and the risk undertaken by him, seem to be the
important things.

The authorities which I have already cited (the judgment of DIXON, J., in the
Queensland case (14) and LORD WRIGHT'S in the *Montreal* case (15)) show that
the common law test is not to be restricted to the power of control " over the H
manner of performing service ", but is wide enough to take account of
investment and risk.

Section 220 (2) of the American Restatement, Agency 2nd, includes among
the relevant factors:

> " (e) whether the employer or the workman supplies the instrumentalities,
> tools, and the place of work for the person doing the work."

The comment on the first part of this paragraph is in these words:

> " *Ownership of instrumentalities*. The ownership of the instrumentalities
> and tools used in the work is of importance. The fact that a worker supplies
> his own tools is some evidence that he is not a servant. On the other hand,

---

(12) (1946), 331 U.S. at p. 716.
(13) (1946), 331 U.S. at p. 719.
(14) (1945), 70 C.L.R. 539.
(15) [1947] 1 D.L.R. 161.

A   if the worker is using his employer's tools or instrumentalities, especially if they are of substantial value, it is normally understood that he will follow the directions of the owner in their use, and this indicates that the owner is a master. This fact is, however, only of evidential value."

This says in effect that the employer's ownership of the instrumentalities is relevant only because of a rebuttable presumption that the parties meant him to
B   control the use of his own property. It also says that the worker's ownership is evidence that he is not a servant, but it does not say why. If the reason is the same in both cases, and the worker's ownership is evidence only because of its bearing on control, it is plain from what I have already said that I do not agree. The point is discussed by MR. ATIYAH op. cit. at p. 65. I quote these three sentences:
C

" It seems, therefore, that the importance of the provision of equipment lies in the simple fact that, in most circumstances, where a person hires out a piece of work to an independent contractor he expects the contractor to provide all the necessary tools and equipment . . . Indeed it may well be that little weight can today be put on the provision of tools of a minor
D   character, as opposed to the provision of plant and equipment on a large scale. In the latter case the real object of the contract is often the hiring of the plant, and the services of a workman to operate the plant are purely incidental."

I have had these sentences in mind when framing my five examples.

I note a United States decision later than Silk's in which a Federal Court of
E   Appeal held that an owner driver was a servant, stating that his ownership of a trailer merely raised an inference about control which was rebutted by the express terms of the contract: *National Labour Relations Board* v. *Nu-Car Carriers* (16).

I have almost completed my review of the authorities. There is, as well, the dictum of DENNING, L.J., in *Bank voor Handel en Scheepvaart N.V.* v. *Slatford* (17),
F   repeated in his Hamlyn Lectures:

" In this connexion I would observe the test of being a servant does not rest nowadays on submission to orders. It depends on whether the person is part and parcel of the organisation."

This raises more questions than I know how to answer. What is meant by being " part and parcel of an organisation "? Are all persons who answer this
G   description servants? If only some are servants, what distinguishes them from the others if it is not their submission to orders? Though I cannot answer these questions I can at least invoke the dictum to support my opinion that control is not everything.

Then there are " the four indicia " of a contract of service, first mentioned in *Park* v. *Wilsons & Clyde Coal Co., Ltd.* (18) and repeated by LORD THANKERTON
H   in *Short* v. *Henderson, Ltd.* (19):

" (a) the master's power of selection of his servant; (b) the payment of wages or other remuneration; (c) the master's right to control the method of doing the work, and (d) the master's right of suspension or dismissal."

It seems to me that (a) and (d) are chiefly relevant in determining whether there
I   is a contract of any kind between the supposed master and servant, and that they are of little use in determining whether the contract is one of service. The same is true of (b), unless one distingushes between different methods of payment, payment by results tending to prove independence and payment by time the relation of master and servant. Reference to the facts in *Park's* case (18) shows

---

(16) (1951), 189 Fed. 2nd 756.
(17) [1952] 2 All E.R. 956 at p. 971; [1953] 1 Q.B. 248 at p. 290.
(18) 1928 S.C. 121.
(19) (1946), 174 L.T. 417 at p. 421.

A

the use for which these three tests were devised. Park had contracted with the company to drive a stonemine at a money rate per fathom, and he had engaged Haggerty to help him. Park and Haggerty had been injured by the negligence of other men admittedly in the company's service. The question was whether Park and Haggerty were fellow servants of those whose negligence had injured them, so as to be caught by the doctrine of common employment. In deciding whether Haggerty was a servant of the company or of Park, it was obviously relevant to inquire who had selected him, who paid his wages and who had the right of suspending or dismissing him, and if Park did (or could do) these things otherwise than as the company's agent, he himself was unlikely to be their servant.

B

Three workmen's compensation cases in Ireland raised the question whether men, whose work was carrying goods and materials, were employed under contracts of service. *Mooney* v. *Sheehan* (20), *O'Donnell* v. *Clare County Council* (21), and *Clarke* v. *Bailieborough Co-operative Agricultural and Dairy Society, Ltd.* (22). It appears from the statement of facts in each case that the workman had his own horse and cart, but this is not referred to either in the arguments or in the judgments which held that the men were employed under contracts of service. *Doggett* v. *Waterloo Taxi-Cab Co., Ltd.* (23), is an English case under the same Act in which it was held that the owners of a taxi-cab, hired by them to a driver in consideration of a share in the takings, were not his employers under a contract of service. I mention these cases to show that they have not been overlooked.

C

D

I mention also, and for the same reason, an argument addressed to me by counsel for the company, on the provisions of the Road Traffic Act, 1960. The argument, founded on s. 164 (1) and (3), was to the effect that when Latimer was driving his truck a licence was needed under this part of the Act only if he was carrying on his own business. If he was merely the company's servant employed by them to drive his own vehicle on their business, no licence was needed. This cannot have been intended. The draftsman must have considered that a man in Mr. Latimer's position would always be an independent contractor, and if he did so he was probably right. That was the argument. But one cannot be sure than he considered the point, and if one is not sure of that the argument proves nothing.

E

F

It is now time to state my conclusion, which is that the rights conferred and the duties imposed by the contract between Mr. Latimer and the company are not such as to make it one of service. It is a contract of carriage.

G

I have shown earlier that Mr. Latimer must make the vehicle available throughout the contract period. He must maintain it (and also the mixing unit) in working order, repairing and replacing worn parts when necessary. He must hire a competent driver to take his place if he should be for any reason unable to drive at any time when the company requires the services of the vehicle. He must do whatever is needed to make the vehicle (with a driver) available throughout the contract period. He must do all this, at his own expense, being paid a rate per mile for the quantity which he delivers. These are obligations more consistent, I think, with a contract of carriage than with one of service. The ownership of the assets, the chance of profit and the risk of loss in the business of carriage are his and not the company's.

H

If (as I assume) it must be shown that he has freedom enough in the performance of those obligations to qualify as an independent contractor, I would say that he has enough. He is free to decide whether he will maintain the vehicle by his own labour or that of another, and, if he decides to use another's, he is free to choose whom he will employ and on what terms. He is free to use

(20) (1903), 37 I.L.T. 166.
(21) (1912), 47 I.L.T. 41.
(22) (1913), 47 I.L.T. 113.
(23) [1910] 2 K.B. 336.

A another's services to drive the vehicle when he is away because of sickness or holidays, or indeed at any other time when he has not been directed to drive himself. He is free again in his choice of a competent driver to take his place at these times, and whoever he appoints will be his servant and not the company's. He is free to choose where he will buy his fuel or any other of his requirements, subject to the company's control in the case of major repairs. This is enough.

B It is true that the company are given special powers to ensure that he runs his business efficiently, keeps proper accounts and pays his bills. I find nothing in these or any other provisions of the contract inconsistent with the company's contention that he is running a business of his own. A man does not cease to run a business on his own account because he agrees to run it efficiently or to accept another's superintendence.

C A comparison of Mr. Latimer's profits with the wages earned by men who are admittedly the company's servants confirms my conclusion that his status is different, that he is, in the words of the judgment in *Silk's* case (24), a " small businessman ", and not a servant.

That is all I need to say about Mr. Latimer's case.

Happily I need say less about the two other cases, Mr. King's and Mr. Bezer's.
D In each of these the question is whether the man's contract is one of service. The parties are agreed that if Mr. Latimer's contract is not one of service, neither is Mr. King's nor Mr. Bezer's. I agree, and these two cases will be decided accordingly.

Judgments accordingly.

E Solicitors: *Linklaters & Paines* (for Ready Mixed Concrete (South East), Ltd., Thomas Henry Latimer and Arthur William Bezer); *McKenna & Co.* (for Greenham Ready Mixed Concrete, Ltd., and John King); *Solicitor, Ministry of Social Security.*

[*Reported by* Mary Colton, *Barrister-at-Law.*]

F

PRACTICE DIRECTION.

G

Probate, Divorce and Admiralty Division (Admiralty).

Admiralty—Practice—Evidence—Expert evidence—Statement of proposed evidence to be produced to other party.

Where a party intends to adduce expert evidence, he should produce to the
H other party his expert's statement of proposed evidence, together with any reports, plans, models, calculations, etc., relevant to it, for agreement if possible. Failing such agreement, the other party should deliver to the first party a written statement setting out particulars of the matters not agreed. Where both parties intend to adduce expert evidence, each should follow this procedure. Failure by any party to follow this procedure may result in a special order as to costs.

I Jan. 22, 1968.

Sir Jocelyn Simon,
President.

---

(24) (1946), **331**, U.S. 704.

NOTE.

SOLDIERS', SAILORS' AND AIRMEN'S FAMILIES ASSOCIATION *v.* ATTORNEY-GENERAL.

[CHANCERY DIVISION (Cross, J.), November 17, 1967.]

Charity—Chartered corporation—Investments—Construction of charter and rules —On their true construction charity could not take power to make investments outside the ordinary trustee range of investments.

[As to the investment of funds in the hands of charities, see 4 HALSBURY'S LAWS (3rd Edn.) 355, para. 742.]

Case referred to:

> *Jewish Orphanage Endowments Trusts, Re, Sebag-Montefiore* v. *Rothschild Executor & Trustee Co.,* [1960] 1 All E.R. 764; [1960] 1 W.L.R. 344; Digest (Cont. Vol. A) 110, *1586b.*

Adjourned summons.

The plaintiff, the Soldiers', Sailors' and Airmen's Families Association ("the Association "), applied by originating summons, dated Dec. 1, 1966, for the determination of the following question, among others, viz., whether on the true construction of the charter, rules and regulations of the Association it had power to invest its funds (a) in such investments without restriction as its Council might from time to time determine, or (b) only in such investments as were authorised by law for the investment of trust funds.   The plaintiff Association was incorporated in 1885, and was granted a charter in January, 1926.

The charter included the following:

" 1.   The persons now members of the said voluntary association or society known as ' The Soldiers', Sailors' and Airmen's Families Association ' and all such persons as may hereafter become members of the body corporate hereby constituted shall be and are hereby created one body politic and corporate by the name of ' The Soldiers', Sailors' and Airmen's Families Association ' (hereinafter called ' the Association ') . . .

" 4.   The objects for which the Association is established and incorporated are as follows: . . . (c) As and for the primary purpose of the Association to aid the wives families widows and other dependants of all ranks (other than commissioned officers) of all branches of our Imperial Land Sea and Air Forces and in particular but without restricting the generality of this paragraph to carry out such primary purpose by any lawful means heretofore adopted by the said voluntary association or society . . . (h) Generally to do all things necessary or expedient for the proper and effective carrying out of any of the objects aforesaid.

" 5.   The income and property of the Association whencesoever derived shall be applied solely towards the promotion of the objects for the time being of the Association and no portion thereof shall be paid or transferred directly or indirectly by way of dividend or bonus, or otherwise howsoever by way of profit, to the members of the Association . . .'

" 6.   The members of the Association shall consist of (a) members of Council and (b) ordinary members.

" 7.   There shall be a Council of Management (hereinafter called ' the Council ') which shall consist of . . .

" 13*.   Subject to the provisions of this Our Charter all the powers of the Association shall be vested in and exercisable by the Council, Provided always that the affairs of the Association shall be managed and regulated in accordance with the rules set forth in the schedule hereto or with such other

---

* His Lordship (CROSS, J.) intimated that para. 13 was the most important in the present case.

Considered in LIVERPOOL AND DISTRIC
v A-G [1981] 1 All ER 994

A rules as may for the time being be in force under or by virtue of the succeeding provisions of this clause. Any of the rules for the time being in force
may from time to time be altered added to or repealed by the Association
in general meeting and any new rules may from time to time be made in
like manner but so that no resolution proposing any alteration or addition
to or repeal of the rules shall be brought forward unless a copy thereof shall

B have been furnished to the Secretary of the Association at least one calendar
month before the meeting to which the same is to be submitted and no
new rule shall have any force or effect unless and until it shall have been
approved by the lords of Our Council of which approval a certificate under
the hand of the clerk to Our Council shall be conclusive evidence.

"16. It shall be lawful for Us Our Heirs and Successors by supplemental

C charter to add to amend or repeal the provisions of this Our charter or any
of them provided that an extraordinary resolution (which expression where-
ever herein used shall mean a resolution submitted to the Council and
carried by a majority of not less than two-thirds of such members of the
Council as are present at a meeting of the Council specially summoned for
the purpose) to accept and approve such supplemental charter shall have

D been passed by the Council.

"18. And lastly we do by these presents for Us and Our Successors
grant and declare that these Our letters patent shall be in all things valid
and effectual in law according to the true intent and meaning thereof and
shall be taken and construed and adjudged in the most favourable and beneficial sense for the best advantage of the Association as well in Our courts of

E record as elsewhere by all judges justices officers ministers and other subjects
of Us and Our Successors any non-recital mis-recital or other omission defect
or thing to the contrary notwithstanding."

The rules were scheduled to the charter. The first rule related to the appointment and dismissal of staff by the Council. The second rule provided for
meetings of the Council; the third was as to the secretary and summoning

F meetings, and the fourth to the quorum. The fifth rule, as amended in 1953,
provided for the appointment of committees and the delegation by the Council
to the committees " such of their powers or functions as they may think fit ".

Rule 11, to which His Lordship (CROSS, J.) particularly referred, is set out at
p. 450, letter F, post. Rule 12 provided that any of the rules might from time
to time be altered added to or repealed as provided by the charter, viz., with the

G approval of the Privy Council.

The Council of the Association had made regulations under the power given
them by r. 11. HIS LORDSHIP read the following of the regulations:

"25. The Council and all branch committees shall open an account at a
bank, which account must stand in the name of the Association, subject to

H the signature of the honorary treasurer for the time being, or such other
officer or officers as the Council or committee may determine.

"27. Any surplus funds not likely to be required for local use within a
period of twelve months should be remitted periodically in the case of a
division to the honorary county treasurer; and in the case of a county
branch to the head office (through the combined branch committee where

I applicable).

"28. Sums remitted to the head office under reg. 27 will ordinarily
be invested by the Council on behalf of the branch to which they belong.
The Council undertake to realise and repay the investment (or any part of
it) in case of need, and meanwhile to pay the gross interest to the branch
concerned. The Council earnestly request branch committees to make
unconditional gifts to the head office whose guaranteed income is limited and
is heavily committed.

"31. All funds of the Association, other than those required for its

current outgoings or other objects or for the acquisition of any real or **A**
personal property considered by the Council to be suitable for any of its
purposes, shall be invested by the Council in such securities as shall be
determined from time to time by the Council. *All investments shall be held
in the name of the Association, and shall only be made by the Council.*"

The cases noted below* were cited during the argument in addition to the
case referred to in the judgment. **B**

Sir Milner Holland, Q.C., and *J. Bradburn* for the plaintiffs.
N. C. H. Browne-Wilkinson for the Attorney-General.

CROSS, J., having referred to the originating summons and having read
relevant provisions of the charter and rules of the plaintiff Association, continued:
I propose to deal first with the question whether the Council of the Association **C**
could validly give itself power to make investments outside the ordinary trustee
range. One starts with this, that the plaintiff, Soldiers', Sailors' and Airmen's
Families Association, which is a chartered corporation, is a charitable corporation, and accordingly is in the position of a trustee with regard to its funds.
That was submitted by counsel for the Attorney-General and conceded by the
Association. Prima facie, therefore, the funds of the Association can only **D**
be invested as trust funds can be invested under the Trustee Acts (1). Of
course the charter incorporating the Association, just like a trust deed setting
up a trust might have empowered the Association to invest its funds outside
the ordinary range, or have given an unlimited power of investment. Plainly
this charter does not do that. But as I said in *Re Jewish Orphanage, Charity
Endowments Trusts, Sebag-Montefiore* v. *Rothschild Executor & Trustee Co.* (2), **E**
the charter might have empowered the Association to give itself power to extend
the authorised range of investments. Counsel for the Attorney-General accepted
that. The real question in this case is, do this charter and the rules scheduled
to it on their fair construction empower the Council to give itself what the
charter itself does not give it, viz., a wider range of investments than the trustee
range? The Association contends that it does, by virtue of r. 11, which provides: **F**

" The Council subject to the provisions of the charter and of the rules for
the time being in force may make regulations with respect to the carrying
into effect of all or any of the purposes or provisions of the charter."

It is said that those are very wide words and that they enable the Council, if it
thinks fit, to make a regulation extending the range of investments authorised
for the investments of the funds of the Association. In my judgment the **G**
Association's contention is wrong. Paragraph 13 of the charter provides:

" Subject to the provisions of this our charter all the powers of the Association shall be vested in and exercisable by the Council . . . Provided always
that the affairs of the Association shall be managed and regulated in
accordance with the rules set forth in the schedule hereto."

In my judgment it is not possible to extend the powers of the Association either **H**
by rules or by regulations. The power of investment of this Association is therefore limited to trustee investments and can be extended only by an alteration of
the charter under para. 16 of the charter (3). That, therefore, is the declaration
that I propose to make.

Declaration accordingly. **I**

Solicitors: *Riders* (for the plaintiffs); *Treasury Solicitor.*

[*Reported by* JACQUELINE METCALFE, *Barrister-at-Law.*]

---

* *R.* v. *Weymouth Corpn.*, (1741), 7 Mod. Rep. 373; *Re Harari's Settlement Trusts*,
[1949] 1 All E.R. 430; *Re Tobacco Trade Benevolent Association*, [1958] 3 All E.R. 353;
Re Peczenik's Settlement, [1964] 2 All E.R. 339.
(1) See the Trustee Investments Act, 1961; 41 HALSBURY'S STATUTES (2nd Edn.) 1078;
and the Trustee Act, 1925; 26 ibid., 50.
(2) [1960] 1 All E.R. 764. (3) Paragraph 16 is printed at p. 449, letter C, ante.

A   Re CLARKE (*deceased*). CLARKE *v.* ROBERTS AND OTHERS.

[CHANCERY DIVISION (Plowman, J.), January 17, 18, 1968.]

Family Provision—Widow—Able to support herself and in fact supporting
herself—Married in middle age—Arrangement that spouses should live
temporarily only in home of husband's mother, then aged seventy-six—Wife
B   *left after seven months—Husband did not respond to her suggestion that*
they should set up a separate home—By his will husband gave as reason
for not making fuller provision for his wife that she had not kept arrangement
that their matrimonial home should be in his mother's home—Failure of
husband to make reasonable provision for widow—Inheritance (Family
Provision) Act, 1938 (1 & 2 *Geo.* 6 *c.* 45), *s.* 1, *as amended by Intestates'*
C   *Estates Act,* 1952 (15 & 16 *Geo.* 6 & 1 *Eliz.* 2 *c.* 64), *s.* 7, *Sch.* 3.

The plaintiff married the testator in December, 1961, when she was
thirty-six years of age and the testator was forty-nine years of age and was
a bachelor living with his mother, who was then some seventy-six years of
age. The plaintiff was a school teacher when she married the testator; she
was earning over £1,000 a year and continued working after marriage. She
D   went to live with the testator at his mother's house, it being agreed between
her husband and herself that this was a temporary measure only to give
the mother time to get used to the testator's marriage. The testator's
mother, however, was resentful of the plaintiff, and made her feel unwanted,
as a result of which the plaintiff became ill and in July, 1962, some seven
months after her marriage, she left the house. Shortly afterwards she
E   wrote to the testator, saying that they ought to have their own home,
sufficiently far away for his mother to be unable to interfere in their lives
but near enough for him to visit her. He did not reply, but not long afterwards
he made his will in which he left the plaintiff a legacy of £1,000 free of duty,
and gave his residuary estate to his mother absolutely. By cl. 4 of the will
he declared that the reason why he had not made further provision for
F   the plaintiff in his will was that, " having before our marriage after due
consideration agreed the matrimonial home should be in the home of
my mother who is a partial invalid she has seen fit to leave me and set up
a home by herself ". The testator died on Oct. 28, 1964, and his mother
died on Jan. 10, 1965. The testator's net estate for the purposes of the
Inheritance (Family Provision) Act, 1938, as amended, was about £23,000;
G   the mother's estate, apart from her inheritance from her son the testator,
amounted to about £8,000. The mother's estate would pass as on intestacy
to cousins and their issue.

Held: (i) in all the circumstances the testator had failed to make reasonable provision for the maintenance of the plaintiff for the following reasons—

(a) the plaintiff was the only person who had a moral claim on the testator's
H   bounty apart from his mother (see p. 454, letter G, post), and, although
the fact that the plaintiff could and did support herself was a factor to
be taken into account, the testator had not ceased for that reason to be
under moral obligation to provide for her (see p. 454, letter I, to p. 455,
letter A, post).

(b) on the evidence it was the testator who broke the bargain made with
I   the plaintiff when she went to live with him in his mother's home, and the
reasons given by the testator in cl. 4 of his will completely mis-stated that
bargain (see p. 455, letter H, post).

(ii) in all the circumstances, having regard to the fact that the marriage
lasted for less than three years and that the plaintiff was supporting herself
and had a good income, which there was no reason to suppose would diminish,
she would be granted entitlement to one half of the income of the testator's
net estate for the rest of her life or until remarriage (see p. 456, letter C, post).

A
[As to the ordering of reasonable provision for maintenance and the effect
of circumstances and reasons given by the deceased, see 16 HALSBURY'S LAWS
(3rd Edn.) 460-462, paras. 920, 921; and for cases on the subject, see 24 DIGEST
(Repl.) 967-984, *9753-9810*.

For the Inheritance (Family Provision) Act, 1938, s. 1, as amended, see 32
HALSBURY'S STATUTES (2nd Edn.) 139.]

Adjourned Summons.

B

This was an application by originating summons dated May 5, 1965, as amended
on Feb. 22, 1966, by the plaintiff, Peggy Jean Clarke, the widow of Tom Stanley
Clarke, deceased (the testator), and a dependant within the meaning of the
Inheritance (Family Provision) Act, 1938, as amended for an order under the Act of
1938 that such reasonable provision as the court might think fit might be made out
of the net estate of the testator for her maintenance. The testator died on Oct. 28,
1964, having bequeathed by his will dated Sept. 13, 1962, a legacy of £1,000 to
the plaintiff free of duty, and having devised and bequeathed his residuary
estate to his mother, Elizabeth Evelyn Clarke, absolutely. She died on Jan. 10,
1965, and her estate passed, as events happened, as on her intestacy to cousins
and their issue. The testator's net estate for the purposes of the Act of 1938
was about £23,000. The defendants were (i) Geoffrey Ashton Roberts, and
(ii) John Robert King, the executors and trustees of the will of the testator,
and (iii) Roland Frank Charles Jackson, the administrator with will annexed
of the estate of the testator's mother. The facts are set out in the judgment.

C

D

The cases noted below* were cited during the argument.

W. J. C. Tonge for the plaintiff.
Robin Webb for the first and second defendants.
Gavin Lightman for the third defendant.

E

PLOWMAN, J.: This is an application under the Inheritance (Family
Provision) Act, 1938, as amended, by Mrs. Peggy Jean Clarke, widow of the late
Tom Stanley Clarke. The plaintiff is forty-two years of age and she is the only
dependant of the testator within the meaning of the Act of 1938. There were
no children of the marriage between herself and the testator. That marriage
took place on Dec. 30, 1961. At that time the plaintiff was thirty-six years of
age and a spinster, and the testator was forty-nine years of age and a bachelor.
He was a bachelor living with his mother, who was then some seventy-six years
of age and the testator was her only child. He was by profession a chartered
surveyor employed by the Great Ouse Catchment Board and although the
amount of his salary is not in evidence I am told, and I do not think that it is
questioned, that it was £2,000 a year. The plaintiff was a schoolteacher and
at the time when she married the testator she was earning over £1,000 a year,
and she went on working after the marriage and is still working.

F

G

On the marriage the plaintiff went to live with her husband at the house of
his mother. That looks like courting disaster, but what the plaintiff says about
it in her statement is this:

H

" [The testator] was devoted to his mother, who was a very dominating
personality; and it was agreed that as a temporary measure only we should
live with her in her house. It was never however envisaged that this
should continue permanently, and it was only to give her time to get used

---

* *Millichamp* v. *Millichamp*, [1931] All E.R. Rep. 477; 146 L.T. 96; *Re Joslin*,
[1941] 1 All E.R. 302; [1941] Ch. 200; *Re Inns*, [1947] 2 All E.R. 308; [1947] Ch. 576;
Re Franks, [1947] 2 All E.R. 638; [1948] Ch. 62; *Dunn* v. *Dunn*, [1948] 2 All E.R. 822;
[1949] P. 98; *Re Borthwick* (*decd.*), [1949] 1 All E.R. 472; [1949] Ch. 395; *Rose* v.
Rose, [1950] 2 All E.R. 311; [1951] P. 29; *Re Howell* (*decd.*), [1953] 2 All E.R. 604;
Re Doring (*decd.*), [1955] 3 All E.R. 389; *Hutchinson* v. *Hutchinson*, [1963] 1 All E.R. 1;
Re Ducksbury (*decd.*), [1966] 2 All E.R. 375; *Re Clayton* (*decd.*), [1966] 2 All E.R. 370;
Re E. (*decd.*), [1966] 2 All E.R. 44; *In the Estate of Gale*, (*decd.*), [1966] 1 All E.R. 945;
[1966] 2 Ch. 236.

A   to the fact that [the testator] was now married.   [The testator] had promised
me that should this arrangement prove unsatisfactory he would at once
leave his mother in her own house, and make a home for me elsewhere;
and it was agreed that I should take my place as his wife and run the house,
which was to be put in order and redecorated, with our furniture replacing
the existing furniture in the communal living rooms.   It was always our
B   intention to establish a home of our own as soon as this could conveniently
be arranged.   [The testator's] mother was getting on in years (in fact she
was seventy-six when we went to live with her), and it was hoped that after
an interval an amicable arrangement could be come to for us to move out
in circumstances which would not be too upsetting for her."

C No part of the plaintiff's statement is challenged and no application has been
made to cross-examine her, and I accept her statement as being a statement
of truth.

    The arrangement did not work.   According to the plaintiff's evidence, her
mother-in-law was resentful of her, she was jealous of her, she was interfering,
she was mean, she was irritable.   She made the plaintiff feel unwanted and
the plaintiff in a very short while felt herself in an impossible and intolerable
D   position.   Her health was affected; she became ill; she was on the verge of a
nervous breakdown; and on July 28, 1962, some seven months after her marriage,
she left the house where she was living with the testator and his mother.   Shortly
after that, on Aug. 12, 1962, she wrote to the testator, what I can, perhaps,
describe as a very decent letter, in which although I do not propose to read it
in any length, she said this to him:
E

    " I'm afraid that we both have to face the fact that to save our marriage
it is essential that we have our *own* home, not on your mother's doorstep,
but at a distance where it will be possible for you to go and see her, but
sufficiently far away for her to be unable to interfere in our lives.   I am fully
aware that this is a very difficult position for you to be in but don't you
F   think that, left to reign supreme in her own house, to be able to keep it in
the same state as she has known it and with a paid companion to help her
and live with her would be kinder to her; she would be happier than she is
now, resenting daily the changes she sees owing to your marriage.   I do not
feel we are in any way shirking our responsibilities or being selfish to want
to lead our own lives *before* her death."

G That long letter, of which that is only one short extract, was not answered by
the testator, so a fortnight later, on Aug. 26, the plaintiff wrote to him again,
saying:

    " I am very hurt not to have heard from you at all since I came here and
especially not to have received a reply to my letter of Aug. 12.   In that
H   I explained that I thought we ought to have our own home in order to be
able to lead our own lives free from your mother's domination and interference.   Seven months of attempting to live with her have proved to me
beyond doubt that her resentment and jealousy of me as your wife were
increasing daily and her interference was deliberate and calculated to break
up our marriage."

I And so on.   And again she asks him to state what his position is and what he has
decided to do, and again there is no reply to that letter.

    Instead, within two or three weeks after the second letter had been written,
the testator made his will.   It is dated Sept. 13, 1962, and by that will he appoints
the first two defendants to the present application, Mr. Roberts and Mr. King,
to be his executors and trustees.   He leaves the plaintiff, his wife, a legacy of
£1,000 free of duty, and then, subject to that and to the payment of his just
debts, funeral and testamentary expenses, he gives the residue of his estate
to his mother absolutely, and in para. 4 of his will he makes this declaration:

"I hereby declare that the reason why I have not made further provision   A
in this my will for [the plaintiff] is that having before our marriage after
due consideration agreed the matrimonial home should be in the home of
my mother who is a partial invalid she has seen fit to leave me and set up a
home by herself."

The testator died on Oct. 28, 1964, survived by his mother; but on Jan. 10, 1965,
she died, having by her will left the whole of her estate to the testator, so in the   B
event that disposition lapsed and consequently the whole of the testator's
mother's estate, which included the whole of his estate except for the £1,000
left to the plaintiff, passed on the mother's intestacy and descends on a large
number of—I am told, I think, over forty of them—cousins and their issue.
On Feb. 18, 1965, the testator's will was proved by the defendant executors.
On Mar. 19, 1965, letters of administration to his mother's estate were granted;   C
and on May 5, 1965, the present originating summons was issued.

The testator's net estate for the purposes of the Act of 1938 is about £23,000
and the income of that estate is likely to be £1,000 or a little more, perhaps
£1,150.   The testator's mother had an estate of her own, that is to say apart
from what she inherited from the testator's estate, of some £8,000. I should
say something about the plaintiff's resources.   She is a teacher, as I understand,   D
earning a gross salary of some £1,950 which leaves her some £1,300 to £1,350 a
year net.   In addition to that she has a gross income from investments of about
£100 a year, and she has a bungalow of her own which she bought in October,
1966, for £3,850.   In due course, when she retires from teaching, she can expect
the appropriate retirement benefits, although the precise amount of them will
depend on how long she goes on teaching.   E

Now, the first question which I have to consider under the Act of 1938 is this:
is the disposition of the testator's estate effected by his will such as to make
reasonable provision for the maintenance of the plaintiff?   As I have already
indicated, the will does not make any provision at all for her maintenance except
that she is given the legacy of £1,000, and one of the questions that I have to
consider in reaching a conclusion on the question whether the will is unreasonable   F
in not providing further for the plaintiff, is to consider what were the claims on
the testator's bounty at the time of his death.

Counsel for the third defendant (1) has pointed out that the testator's mother,
although not, of course, a dependant within the meaning of the Act of 1938, was a
person who had moral claims on his bounty.   He lived with her, as far as I know,
all his life, and she was old, and although she had £8,000 of her own that included   G
the house in which she lived.   I am prepared to accept that she was a person
with a moral claim on the testator's bounty.   The only other person who had
a moral claim to the testator's bounty was his wife, the plaintiff herself.

Now, it is said by counsel for the third defendant, that it was not unreasonable
for the testator to omit to make any provision for the plaintiff having regard
to her own financial position, the fact that she was earning a substantial salary,   H
the fact that she elected to go on working after she was married to the testator,
and is still working and in a position to support herself.   If the suggestion is
that merely because a wife can support herself adequately a husband has no
moral obligation to provide for her, I do not agree; but I am not sure that this
is the suggestion.   The fact that the wife can support herself is one of the matters
to be taken into account, certainly, but one must have regard to all the circumstances of the case, including that fact and the fact that the wife has supported
herself.

Similarly, it was submitted by counsel that where, as happened here, the
husband and wife had separated during the subsistence of the marriage, and
during that separation the wife had supported herself without making any

_____

(1) I.e., for the administrator with the will annexed of the mother's estate, interested
to support the bequest by the testator to his mother.

A financial claim on the husband, she thereby ceased to be a dependant for the purposes of the Act of 1938, and that her husband ceased to have any moral obligation to provide for her. Again, I do not agree. That that is a factor to be taken into account I readily accept: but that it in itself is sufficient, irrespective of other factors, to destroy any claim that the wife might otherwise have, I am not prepared to accept. As I say, the matter depends on all the relevant
B circumstances of the case and the matters which are stated in the Act of 1938 as being matters to which the court shall pay attention.

One other matter which I have to consider, because s. 1 (7) of the Act of 1938 requires me to consider it, are the testator's reasons,

C   ". . . so far as ascertainable, for making the dispositions made by his will (if any), or for refraining from disposing by will of his estate or part of his estate, or for not making any provision, or any further provision, as the case may be, for a dependant . . ."

Now, I have already read cl. 4 of the testator's will in which he sets out such reason. I will read it again:

D   " I hereby declare that the reason why I have not made further provision in this my will for [the plaintiff] is that having before our marriage after due consideration agreed the matrimonial home should be in the home of my mother who is a partial invalid she has seen fit to leave me and set up a home by herself."

In the context of the submissions of counsel for the third defendant it is to
E be noticed that the testator is not saying that " I do not make any further provision for [the plaintiff] because she is perfectly capable of providing for herself "; and, equally, the testator does not say " the reason that I am not making any further provision for [the plaintiff] is that I must provide for my mother who is an old lady and may need medical and nursing attention ". What he is saying is " the reason that I am not providing for [the plaintiff] is
F that although she got what she bargained for in coming to live with my mother she broke her part of the bargain and left me ".

In saying that, in my judgment, the testator has completely mis-stated what the bargain between himself and the plaintiff was. I have already read the paragraph in the plaintiff's statement which makes it quite clear that her going to live with the testator at the house of his mother was purely a temporary
G measure intended to endure only long enough to get the mother used to the idea that her forty-nine year old bachelor son had got married, and was not intended to be anything in the nature of a permanent arrangement, and I take the view on the evidence before me that, far from its being the plaintiff who broke the bargain, it was the testator himself who broke the bargain which he had made with the plaintiff by putting his mother before the plaintiff, his wife.
H He ought to have left that home long before the plaintiff herself was forced by circumstances to do so, and if this had been a matrimonial dispute and I had to decide the question who had deserted whom then, I should not have had much difficulty, I think, in reaching the conclusion for which counsel for the plaintiff contended, namely, that it was the testator who deserted the plaintiff and not the plaintiff who deserted the testator.

I   Now, in these circumstances, taking all these matters into account, I do not feel any difficulty in reaching the conclusion that this will failed to make reasonable provision for the maintenance of the plaintiff, and it is now my duty to consider what provision ought to be made. Counsel for the plaintiff submits, and counsel for the third defendant accepts, the proposition that in having regard to what is reasonable I must view the circumstances as they stand today, and one of those circumstances, as counsel for the plaintiff points out, is the fact that in the events which have happened the whole of the testator's estate passed on the death of his mother to these distant relatives, none of whom have been shown to have any claim to the bounty of the testator at all, and in those A circumstances counsel submits that the right thing to do would be to give the plaintiff the whole of the net estate.

For myself I think that that would be too much. As counsel for the third defendant points out, I have got to take into account the fact that this marriage lasted for less than three years—only seven months, in fact, spent under the same roof; but the parties remained husband and wife until the testator died. B I have also got to take into account the fact that the plaintiff is supporting herself, that she has a good income and that there is no reason for thinking that it is going to suffer any diminution. To give her the whole of income of the residuary estate would, I think, fail to take properly into account those two matters.

It is always difficult in these cases to know precisely what the right sum is, C but doing the best I can, I think that justice would be done if I say that for the rest of her life, or until remarriage, the plaintiff should be entitled to one half of the income of the testator's net estate, and that is what I propose to order.

Order accordingly.

Solicitors: *Collyer-Bristow & Co.*, agents for *Birketts*, Ipswich (for the plaintiff); D *Robbins, Olivey & Lake*, agents for *Bendall & Sons*, Mildenhall (for the defendants).

[*Reported by* JACQUELINE METCALFE, *Barrister-at-Law.*]

PRACTICE DIRECTION.

PROBATE, DIVORCE AND ADMIRALTY DIVISION (DIVORCE).

Divorce—Matrimonial home—Land charge—Cost of registration allowed—Legal aid taxation—Matrimonial Homes Act 1967 (c. 75) *s.* 2 (6), (7).

Where, during the pendency of a legal aid certificate to take part in proceedings in the Divorce Division, a party registers a Class F land charge or registers a notice or caution in the circumstances envisaged by s. 2 (6) and (7) of the Matrimonial Homes Act 1967, the costs of the registration will be allowed in the costs H taxed under the certificate in accordance with the Legal Aid and Advice Act.

COMPTON MILLER,
Jan. 30, 1968.   Senior Registrar.

Re WEMBLEY PARK ESTATE CO., LTD.'S TRANSFER.
LONDON SEPHARDI TRUST v. BAKER AND OTHERS.

[CHANCERY DIVISION (Goff, J.), November 16, 17, 1967.]

Restrictive Covenant—Restrictive covenant affecting land—Application to High Court—Costs—Incidence of costs—Declaration that land not affected by restrictions—No prior application to Lands Tribunal for modification or discharge—Defendants' costs to date of adjournment to judge to be paid by the plaintiffs on common fund basis—Law of Property Act, 1925 (15 & 16 Geo. 5 c. 20), s. 84 (2).

Restrictive Covenant—Restrictive covenant affecting land—Building scheme— Defined area—Reservation of right to vendor to sell unsold land free from restrictions—Existence of defined area a matter of conjecture—Whether building scheme would be implied.

The plan on a transfer of land in July, 1929, showed a number of blocks or lots on the north side of a named road, but they appeared, so far as the plan showed, to be undeveloped. In fact houses had already been built on some sites shown on the plan. In the transfer the purchaser covenanted for himself and his successors in title, so as to bind the land transferred, to observe restrictions set out in the schedule. There was no annexation of the benefit of the restrictions and, by a provision in the schedule, the vendor reserved the right to dispose of land remaining unsold " either subject to or not subject to " the restrictions or any of them. Many transfers of plots were in evidence, all of which contained like covenants. The vendor, a company, had owned and developed land in the area from about 1918 until 1931, when it went into liquidation and was dissolved. The trial judge found that on the evidence it was a matter of conjecture what area should be taken to be defined as the area subject to the alleged building scheme, and within which area it was contended that the covenants and restrictions should be operative. Moreover there was no evidence of the laying out of a defined area of land in lots. It was submitted that an area, edged green on a plan put in evidence was a natural area to which the building scheme should apply.

Held: (i) reservation to the vendor of freedom to sell land free from restrictions was of little force either for or against the existence of a building scheme (see p. 461, letter A, post).

Dicta of SIR HERBERT COZENS-HARDY, M.R., in *Elliston* v. *Reacher* ([1908-10] All E.R. Rep. at pp. 614, 615) and of FARWELL, J., in *Osborne* v. *Bradley* ([1900-03] All E.R. Rep. at p. 547) followed.

(ii) the existence of a defined area to which any building scheme should apply being a matter of conjecture only, no building scheme was established (see p. 463, letter F, and p. 464, letter C, post).

Principles stated by PARKER, J., in *Elliston* v. *Reacher* ([1908] 2 Ch. at p. 384) applied.

(iii) the defendants would be awarded costs on the common fund basis (see p. 466, letter C, post).

Re Jeffkins' Indentures ([1965] 1 All E.R. 608) followed.

[As to the essentials of a building scheme, and the necessity of there being a defined area of land, see 14 HALSBURY'S LAWS (3rd Edn.) 565, 566, para. 1053; and for cases on the subject, see 40 DIGEST (Repl.) 333-337, *2728-2750.*

As to the jurisdiction of the court to declare whether freehold land is affected by restrictive covenants, see 14 HALSBURY'S LAWS (3rd Edn.) 571, 572, para. 1062; and for cases, see 40 DIGEST (Repl.) 364-367, *2925-2936.*

For the Law of Property Act, 1925, s. 84 (2), see 20 HALSBURY'S STATUTES (2nd Edn.) 607.]

Cases referred to:

Ballard's Conveyance, Re, [1937] 2 All E.R. 691; [1937] Ch. 473; 106 L.J.Ch. 273; 157 L.T. 281; 40 Digest (Repl.) 343, 2783.

Baxter v. Four Oaks Properties, Ltd., [1965] 1 All E.R. 906; [1965] Ch. 816; [1965] 2 W.L.R. 1115; Digest (Cont. Vol. B) 641, 2728a.

Elliston v. Reacher, [1908] 2 Ch. 374; 77 L.J.Ch. 617; 99 L.T. 346; affd. C.A., [1908-10] All E.R. Rep. 612; [1908] 2 Ch. 665; 78 L.J.Ch. 87; 99 L.T. 701; 40 Digest (Repl.) 337, 2749.

Jeffkins' Indentures, Re, [1965] 1 All E.R. 608, n.; [1965] 1 W.L.R. 375; Digest (Cont. Vol. B) 645, 2936d.

Jeffs' Transfer, Re, Rogers v. Astley, [1965] 2 All E.R. 798, n.; [1965] 1 W.L.R. 972; Digest (Cont. Vol. B) 645, 2936b.

Jeffs' Transfer, Re, Rogers v. Astley (No. 2), [1966] 1 All E.R. 937; [1966] 1 W.L.R. 841; Digest (Cont. Vol. B) 642, 2783b.

Nottingham Patent Brick and Tile Co. v. Butler, (1885), 15 Q.B.D. 261; on appeal, [1886-90] All E.R. Rep. 1075; (1886), 16 Q.B.D. 778; 55 L.J.Q.B. 280; 54 L.T. 444; 40 Digest (Repl.) 323, 2781.

Osborne v. Bradley, [1900-03] All E.R. Rep. 541; [1903] 2 Ch. 446; 73 L.J.Ch. 49; 89 L.T. 11; 40 Digest (Repl.) 362, 2897.

Pinewood Estate, Farnborough, Re, New Ideal Homesteads, Ltd. v. Levack, [1957] 2 All E.R. 517; [1958] Ch. 280; [1957] 3 W.L.R. 256; 40 Digest (Repl.) 366, 2936.

Reid v. Bickerstaff, [1908-10] All E.R. Rep. 298; [1909] 2 Ch. 305; 78 L.J.Ch. 753; 100 L.T. 952; 40 Digest (Repl.) 341, 2770.

Renals v. Cowlishaw, [1874-80] All E.R. Rep. 359; (1878), 9 Ch.D. 125; (1879), 11 Ch.D. 866; 48 L.J.Ch. 830; 41 L.T. 116; 40 Digest (Repl.) 346, 2796.

Soothill v. King's Parade Property West Bognor, Ltd., (1967), unreported.

Spicer v. Martin, [1886-90] All E.R. Rep. 461; (1888), 14 App. Cas. 12; 58 L.J.Ch. 309; 60 L.T. 546; 53 J.P. 516; 40 Digest (Repl.) 336, 2744.

Sunnyfield, Re, [1931] All E.R. Rep. 837; [1932] 1 Ch. 79; 101 L.J.Ch. 55; 146 L.T. 206; 40 Digest (Repl.) 365, 2929.

Webb v. Fagotti Brothers, (1898), 79 L.T. 683; 40 Digest (Repl.) 357, 2864.

Adjourned Summons.

This was an application by the London Sephardi Trust, the plaintiffs, by originating summons dated June 29, 1966, for a declaration under the Law of Property Act, 1925, s. 84 (2) (a) that freehold properties consisting of a large piece of back land to the south-west of Wealdstone Brook and a plot on the north-east giving access to Brook Avenue at Wembley Park, registered in the Land Registry under title numbers P.49074 and P.64422 were not affected by restrictive covenants contained in a registered transfer dated July 25, 1929. The plaintiffs' property was this large piece of back land. They had circularised all owners who would be affected in the relevant area, which was edged green on an exhibited plan. Fifty-six persons objected. Fifty of them entered appearance and were represented by counsel. A number of others did not wish to oppose and some did not reply.

There had been no prior application to the Lands Tribunal for the discharge or modification of the restrictions. The plaintiffs had applied for permission for the development of the back land by building a synagogue, and planning permission had been refused; but it appeared that there was left open some prospect that application for permission might be able to be renewed successfully as part of a comprehensive plan for dealing with the back land.

In the course of proceedings prior to the adjournment of the originating summons to the judge evidence was filed on behalf of the defendants. After the summons had been adjourned to the judge, His Lordship (GOFF, J.) gave the defendants leave to file further evidence, and additional evidence, consisting

A   of affidavits by the defendants' solicitor and including exhibits of transfers of land, was filed on behalf of the defendants.

George Newson, Q.C., and J. M. Henty for the plaintiffs.
E. 1. Goulding, Q.C., and John A. Baker for the defendants.

B   **GOFF, J.,** having referred to the nature of the application and having stated that the plaintiffs had circularised owners in order to comply with the court's directions in Re Sunnyfield (1), said that the transfer to the plaintiffs was in evidence and continued: The transfer dated July 25, 1929, was made between the Wembley Park Estate Co., Ltd., as vendors of the first part and Ernest George Mulley, the purchaser, of the other part. It has a plan which shows a number of blocks or lots on the north-east side of Oakington Avenue, but so far C   as the plan goes they all appear to be undeveloped. In that regard the plan was inadequate, as it is clear that by July 25, 1929, a number of houses had already been built on the sites in Oakington Avenue. The plan did not show at all a cul-de-sac known as Forty Close or another cul-de-sac known as Elmside Road, and it finished abruptly, omitting the western portion of the land edged green on the exhibited plan. The transfer contained a grant of a right of way and D   the purchaser, with the consent of the vendors, applied for entry on the register. Then followed two exceptions and reservations, of which the second is material and I will read it. It is as follows:

" Full and free right and liberty for the vendors and their assigns at all times to build upon develop convey and demise all or any part of the remaining property of the vendors in such manner (notwithstanding that by building E   or otherwise the vendors may interfere with any right of light air or support to which the purchaser or his successors in title may be or become entitled) and upon and subject to such terms provisions and stipulations as the vendors may think fit ",

and the vendors, with the consent of the purchaser, applied for registration. F   Then followed a covenant in these terms:

" The purchaser for himself and his successors in title to the intent and so as to bind the land hereby transferred or any part thereof into whosesoever hands the same may come (but not so as to be personally liable for the breach of any of the stipulations after he has parted with the said land) hereby covenants with the vendors and their assigns at all times hereafter G   to observe and perform all and every of the stipulations set forth in the schedule hereto."

Then, it is to be observed, the vendors and the purchaser applied for registration of the covenant. It is also to be observed that that form of covenant did not effect any annexation of the covenant to any land of the vendors nor in this case has it been suggested that there have been any express assignments. The H   schedule set out a number of covenants consistent with a general building scheme and contained, in effect, the second reservation split into two separate provisions:

" (J) The purchaser shall not become entitled to any right of light or air which would restrict or interfere with the free use of any adjoining or neighbouring land or premises for building or other purposes.
I   " (K) The vendors reserve the right to sell dispose of or otherwise deal with any land for the time being remaining unsold, either subject or not subject to the above stipulations contained, or any of them."

The defendants have produced a considerable number of transfers, and it is admitted that they all contain similar covenants, sufficiently similar to be virtually identical, and not exceeding in divergence the limits which one would expect according to the situation, size and purpose of the lots.

---

(1) [1931] All E.R. Rep. 837 at pp. 838, 839; [1932] 1 Ch. 79 at p. 83.

The company owned land in this area which it developed from about the time A
of the first world war down to 1931 or thereabouts. In that year it went into
voluntary liquidation and was dissolved. The company's documents (if they still
exist) have not been traced and no estate plan, particulars of sale, model form
of contract or covenants, or anything of that kind has been produced.

In these circumstances, the first question which arises is: what is the effect
of the freedom reserved to the vendors to sell retained land free from the B
restrictions?

Counsel for the plaintiffs, says that it is conclusive against the existence of a
building scheme in the technical sense, or very nearly so. Counsel for the
defendants on the other hand, says that it is at worst neutral and at best some
indication at any rate in favour of a building scheme. He relies on the fact—
which I have already noticed in passing—that in the transfer of July 25, 1929, C
with respect of the right of way the purchaser, with the consent of the vendors,
applied for registration and as to the reservations the vendor applied with the
consent of the purchaser; but when one came to the covenant the vendor and
purchaser both applied.

In *Elliston* v. *Reacher* (2) there was a limited provision in the covenant itself
not to use the premises as a tavern and so forth without consent and a general D
power for the vendor to deal with the land without reference to and independently of the restrictions, as appears in the report in the Court of Appeal (3).
SIR HERBERT COZENS-HARDY, M.R., said (4) that such a general provision was
of no real importance, and FARWELL, J. (5) said that in *Osborne* v. *Bradley* (6) he
did not intend to say more than that it was an element to consider, not that it
was fatal. E

Counsel for the plaintiffs says that one must draw a distinction between two
kinds of provision. First one may have a power to consent to a particular
purchaser not performing the covenants, which was the matter with which
VAUGHAN WILLIAMS, L.J., was dealing in *Webb* v. *Fagotti Brothers* (7). In that
case VAUGHAN WILLIAMS, L.J., said that it was undesirable, and from that it
follows that its inclusion may be some evidence against a building scheme. F
Secondly, however, there may be a general power to release part of the estate
such as was the case in *Osborne* v. *Bradley* (6), and counsel for the plaintiffs
admits that such a provision is neutral. I am not sure that he need have gone
quite as far as that, because in *Osborne* v. *Bradley* (8) FARWELL, J., said this:

"It is inconceivable to my mind that he should have been willing to
enter into a contract which, expressed in terms, would be with such persons G
as shall have already bought from the vendor under similar conditions and
covenants, and such other persons as shall hereafter buy from him under
similar conditions, the vendor being at liberty, as regards the lots that
remain, to dispose of them in any way that he thinks fit. I think such a
contract as that would be too far-fetched."

True it is that that same judge resiled from his proposition to a considerable H
extent when he came to consider *Elliston* v. *Reacher* (2), but he did say it was a
circumstance to be considered. SIR HERBERT COZENS-HARDY, M.R, gave such
a provision much less significance, but even he said that it was an element to
consider. In any case, however, in my judgment such a general provision has
very little weight and, indeed, one may use it to found an argument either way.
Be that as it may, counsel for the plaintiffs says that here it is an indication, and
not only so but a conclusive, or nearly conclusive, indication because it is made

(2) [1908-10] All E.R. Rep. 612; [1908] 2 Ch. 665.
(3) [1908] 2 Ch. at p. 667.
(4) [1908-10] All E.R. Rep. at p. 615; [1908] 2 Ch. at p. 672.
(5) [1908-10] All E.R. Rep. at p. 615; [1908] 2 Ch. at p. 674.
(6) [1900-03] All E.R. Rep. 541; [1903] 2 Ch. 446.
(7) (1898), 79 L.T. 683.
(8) [1900-03] All E.R. Rep. at p. 547; [1903] 2 Ch. at p. 455.

A   an exception out of the grant.   I cannot myself regard that as conclusive nor do
I think that it adds very much to the ordinary weight of such a provision.

Counsel for the defendants, on the other hand, says that the change in the
form of application to the registrar is a positive indication in his favour; but
he described it as a straw and I think that it is little more.   In my judgment,
the truth is that this particular point tells very little either way.

B   Apart from this, what are the features of a building scheme?   I am content, as
I was in *Soothill* v. *King's Parade Property West Bognor, Ltd.* (9) to take PARKER,
J.'s analysis in *Elliston* v. *Reacher* (10) as a general statement of the effect of
the cases.   PARKER, J., there said (10):

C   " In my judgment, in order to bring the principles of *Renals* v. *Cowlishaw*
(11) and *Spicer* v. *Martin* (12) into operation it must be proved (1) that both
the plaintiffs and defendants derive title under a common vendor;   (2) that
previously to selling the lands to which the plaintiffs and defendants are
respectively entitled the vendor laid out his estate, or a defined portion
thereof (including the lands purchased by the plaintiffs and defendants
respectively), for sale in lots subject to restrictions intended to be imposed on
all the lots, and which, though varying in details as to particular lots,
D   are consistent and consistent only with some general scheme of development;
(3) that these restrictions were intended by the common vendor to be and
were for the benefit of all the lots intended to be sold, whether or not they
were also intended to be and were for the benefit of other land retained by
the vendor;   and (4) that both the plaintiffs and the defendants, or their
predecessors in title, purchased their lots from the common vendor upon the
E   footing that the restrictions subject to which the purchases were made
were to enure for the benefit of the other lots included in the general scheme
whether or not they were also to enure for the benefit of other lands retained
by the vendors."

Counsel for the defendants relied on two earlier cases.   The first was *Nottingham
Patent Brick and Tile Co.* v. *Butler* (13), but he can deduce no more from that
F   than that the question of the common vendor's intention is one of fact on the
evidence and the inferences to be drawn from the evidence, which I accept.
There is nothing in that case which cuts across *Elliston* v. *Reacher* (14).

The second case was *Spicer* v. *Martin* (15), where LORD MACNAGHTEN approved
of this passage from the judgment of SIR CHARLES HALL, V.-C., in *Renals* v.
Cowlishaw (16):

G   ". . . it may I think be considered as determined that anyone who has
acquired land, being one of several lots laid out for sale as building plots,
where the court is satisfied that it was the intention that each one of the
several purchasers should be bound by and should, as against the others,
have the benefit of the covenants entered into by each of the purchasers, is
H   entitled to the benefit of the covenant;   and that this right, that is, the
benefit of the covenant, enures to the assign of the first purchaser, in other
words, runs with the land of such purchaser.   This right exists not only
where the several parties execute a mutual deed of covenant, but wherever
a mutual contract can be sufficiently established."

That, again, is all embodied in *Elliston* v. *Reacher* (14).

---

(9) (1967), unreported.
(10) [1908] 2 Ch. 374 at p. 384.
(11) [1874-80] All E.R. Rep. 359;   [1878] 9 Ch.D. 125;   (1879), 11 Ch.D. 866.
(12) [1886-90] All E.R. Rep. 461;   (1888), 14 App. Cas. 12.
(13) (1885), 15 Q.B.D. 261;   on appeal, [1886-90] All E.R. Rep. 1075;   (1866), 16
Q.B.D.   778.
(14) [1908-10] All E.R. Rep. 612;   [1908] 2 Ch. 665.
(15) [1886-90] All E.R. Rep. at p. 468;   (1888), 14 App. Cas. at p. 23.
(16) [1874-80] All E.R. Rep. at p. 361;   (1878), 9 Ch.D at p. 129.

Counsel for the defendants also relied on *Baxter* v. *Four Oaks Properties,* **A**
Ltd. (17), but in that case there was strong internal evidence of the intention to
create a building scheme.   What CROSS, J., said (18) was:

> " It is, however, to be observed that *Elliston* v. *Reacher* (19) was not a
> case in which there was direct evidence, afforded by the execution of the
> deed of mutul covenant, that the parties in fact intended a building scheme.
> The question was whether one could properly infer that intention in all the   **B**
> circumstances.   In such a case, no doubt the fact that the common vendor
> did not divide his estate into lots before beginning to sell it is an agrument
> against there having been an intention on his part and on the part of the
> various purchasers that there should be a building scheme, because it is,
> perhaps, prima facie unlikely that a purchaser of a plot intends to enter into   **C**
> obligations to an unknown number of subsequent purchasers."

That case is clearly distinguishable and does not cast any doubt on the general
test proposed by PARKER, J., in *Elliston* v. *Reacher* (20);   indeeed, it emphasises
the evidential value of the absence of lotting where there is no express intention.
   There is a further passage (21) which is material for present purposes and which
refers to the necessity of a defined area.   CROSS, J., said: **D**

> " The view taken by the courts has been rather that the common vendor
> imposed a common law on a defined area of land and that whenever he sold
> a piece of it to a purchaser who knew of the common law, that piece of land
> automatically became entitled to the benefit of, and subject to the burden of,
> the common law."

The reference to a defined area comes in part from *Elliston* v. *Reacher* (19) itself   **E**
but more particularly from *Reid* v. *Bickerstaff* (22) where this passage appears
in the judgment of SIR HERBERT COZENS-HARDY, M.R. (23):

> " What are some of the essentials of a building scheme?   In my opinion
> there must be a defined area within which the scheme is operative.   Recipro-
> city is the foundation of the idea of a scheme.   A purchaser of one parcel
> cannot be subject to an implied obligation to purchasers of an undefined   **F**
> and unknown area.   He must know both the extent of his burden and the
> extent of his benefit.   Not only must the area be defined, but the obligations
> to be imposed within that area must be defined."

Counsel for the defendants points to the admitted similarity of the covenants
which are by their nature calculated to benefit purchasers generally.   He says that
the area edged green on the exhibited plan is a natural area and in the absence   **G**
through lapse of time of direct evidence, he submits that I ought to infer that
that was the area of a building scheme.   He says that there was a scheme of
development there with an open space in the middle, and he prays in aid some
rather shadowy evidence that the covenants were regarded as live in recent times.
There was a letter from a Miss Coleman Mills who at one time lived on this estate,   **H**
whatever it was.   She says:

> " First, both my mother (now aged eighty-one but with a very clear
> mind) and myself are quite certain that restrictive covenants did and
> probably do still exist over the land referred to, for the benefit of properties
> in Brook Avenue (formerly known as Station Road) and possibly also those
> in Oakington Avenue . . . I distinctly remember his (24) insistence on the
> fact that the adjoining land (to the west) could never be developed save

(17) [1965] 1 All E.R. 906; [1965] Ch. 816.
(18) [1965] 1 All E.R. at pp. 914, 915; [1965] Ch. at p. 828.
(19) [1908-10] All E.R. Rep. 612; [1908] 2 Ch. 665.
(20) [1908] 2 Ch. at p. 384.
(21) [1965] 1 All E.R. at p. 913; [1965] Ch. at p. 826.
(22) [1908-10] All E.R. Rep. 298; [1909] 2 Ch. 305.
(23) " His " refers to the solicitor who acted for the family on the purchase.
(24) [1909] 2 Ch. at p. 319; [1908-10] All E.R. Rep. at p. 300.

A   for playing fields and must remain as an open space.   He is dead, but his widow might possibly still live there ",

and she said that she remembers the vicar saying that the land would always be an open space.

Again in 1959 there was a planning appeal with regard to land at the rear of
B   No. 54, Forty Avenue at which the question of restrictive covenants was raised, and a number of local residents about that corner of the land supported the local – authority's objection. I was referred to a letter giving the Minister's decision and also to the inspector's report. They were not strictly in evidence, but counsel for the plaintiffs very properly admitted them. The highest point for the defendants in those documents is to be found in a passage in the inspector's
C   report headed " The case for other interested persons ", and in respect of No. 31 it is recorded that a Mrs. Gill stated

" that her husband bought a house in Wembley in 1919 which was subsequently hemmed in with houses, when he bought their present house they understood it would not happen again."

Counsel for the defendants further relied on the dissolution of the company in
D   1931. The plaintiffs' transfer shows that by 1929 development in this area was fairly well advanced and he suggests that it was completed in the next two years and thereupon the company was wound up.

However, I cannot see that the area edged green is necessarily a natural area or the only reasonably possible area. It excludes houses on one side of Oakington Avenue itself. The building scheme, if there were one, may well have included
E   those or have included houses on one or other side of Beechroft Gardens or gone on down to Wembly Park Drive. I simply do not know. No single plan showing any complete area is available. The plan on the plaintiffs' transfer itself is inaccurate in that it does not show the houses in Oakington Avenue and incomplete notably on the west side. To say there was here a defined area seems to me to be no more than conjecture, and I will refer to what KENNEDY, L.J.,
F   said in *Reid* v. *Bickerstaff* (25):

" But we are bound to deal with the case upon the evidence as it stands and to shun conjecture, however plausible and attractive . . ."

In my judgment this objection is fatal.

Even apart from this, there is no positive evidence of intention except the
G   shadowy point on the form of the plaintiff's transfer, and I have no evidence of laying out in lots. I do find, however, a development biting deep into the supposed open space area at both ends, and I have absolutely no evidence what, if anything, the purchasers were informed about the area, the plots already sold or to be sold, or the fact that existing sales had been made subject to like covenants. If I were to decide this case in favour of the defendants it would come down, as counsel for the plaintiffs said—or, at any rate, very nearly—to implying a building scheme from no more than a common vendor and the existence of common covenants. No case goes anything like so far as that, and I think that to imply a building scheme would be going much too far.

Finally counsel for the defendants submitted that, as the plaintiffs have failed to get planning permission and may not be able to do so for a long time, if at all, I should not make an order on the present summons. Further evidence, he said, might come to light particularly if the old company's papers were discovered (26). However, the plaintiffs have made enquiries to that end, and I see no real reason to suppose that they will appear. All persons immediately affected have been notified. Many have objected and their case has been

---

(25) [1908–10] All E.R. Rep. at p. 304; [1909] 2 Ch. at p. 327.
(26) The old company owned land which it developed down to 1931 or thereabouts, when it went into voluntary liquidation and was dissolved. The company's documents had not been traced.

fully argued before the court by eminent leading counsel. In those circum- A
stances, in my judgment, it would be wrong, in the exercise of the discretion
which I have under the statute, to refuse to decide the case on the evidence
before me and leave matters where they are, so that one day the plaintiffs
would have either to start this kind of application all over again—if, indeed,
they could—or to start developing, and to leave the defendants either to let the
matter go by default, when they would be no worse off than if I now decided B
against them, or to bring a witness action. The matter has been fully argued
and in this case, in my judgment, I ought to reach a conclusion on the evidence
before me and make an order, which I do. Accordingly, for the reasons which I
have given, I will declare as asked that the property comprised in the plaintiffs' registered titles is not affected by any of the restrictions contained in the
transfer of July 25, 1929.   C

Declaration accordingly.

[On the question of costs.]

Newsom, Q.C.: The plaintiffs are a charity. I ask that they should have at
least some costs, and preferably all of them, as between party and party. The
history of the practice begins with *Re Ballard's Conveyance* (27); the subsequent D
cases are *Re Jeffkins' Indentures* (28) and *Re Jeff's Transfer, Rogers v. Astley* (29),
to which I refer.

Goulding, Q.C.: I submit that the present case is within the scope of *Re Jeffkins'
Indentures* (28). I ask for the costs of the defendants down to and including the
last appointment before the master, and also the costs of the additional evidence
which was filed after the summons was adjourned to the judge (30). The defen- E
dants could not really decide whether the opposition should succeed until they had
obtained a representative collection of transfers. Costs in *Re Pinewood Estate,
Farnborough, New Ideal Homesteads, Ltd.* v. *Levack* (31) were given as between
solicitor and client, and the defendants' costs should, in my submission, be on
the common fund basis.

GOFF, J.: It appears that from 1939 or thereabouts there has been an
established practice in these matters that where a party applies under the Law
of Property Act, 1925, s. 84, to clear his title he must pay his own costs and he
must also pay the costs of the defendants down to the point in the proceedings
at which they have had a full opportunity of considering the matter and deciding
whether or not to oppose the application, but the defendants get no costs there- G
after. That practice is embodied in a practice note under the authority of
CROSS, J., in *Re Jeffkins' Indentures* (28).

Had the matter rested there, there would, apart from matters of detail, have
been no doubt what order I ought to make, but in 1965 another case (32) came
before BUCKLEY, J. It had started in the Lands Tribunal, but there were a
number of objectors whose title the applicant did not admit and the matter was, H
therefore, transferred to this court for decision. BUCKLEY, J., had to deal with
the costs of a number of objectors who withdrew their opposition and he said
that they relied on *Re Ballard's Conveyance* (27), where the practice was first
established, *Re Pinewood Estate, Farnborough, New Ideal Homesteads, Ltd.* v.
Levack (31) and *Re Jeffkins' Indentures* (28). Those were cases, BUCKLEY, J.,
said (33):

"... in which no application had been made to the Lands Tribunal and in

---

(27) [1937] 2 All E.R. 691; [1937] Ch. 473.
(28) [1965] 1 All E.R. 608.
(29) [1965] 3 All E.R. 798; the second stage is reported [1966] 1 All E.R. 937.
(30) Cf. p. 458, letter I, to p. 459, letter A, ante.
(31) [1957] 2 All E.R. 517; [1958] Ch. 280.
(32) *Re Jeffs' Transfer, Rogers* v. *Astley*, [1965] 2 All E.R. 798, n.
(33) [1965] 2 All E.R. at p. 799.

A which the plaintiff was applying to the High Court under s. 84 (2) of the
Law of Property Act, 1925 with a view to clearing his title."

Then BUCKLEY, J., noted (34) that on behalf of the eleven defendants it was said

" that they were in precisely the same position, notwithstanding that the
plaintiff went to the Lands Tribunal in the first instance. BUCKLEY, J.,
continued:—' In my view, a case which has followed this case's history is
B to be distinguished from cases originating under s. 84 (2). A person who
makes an application under s. 84 (2) to clear his title can reasonably be made
to pay the costs of defendants who withdrew at an early stage after they
have had a chance of seeing the evidence. In the present case there are
different considerations. The plaintiff would never have brought proceedings in the Chancery Division had it not been for the action of the objectors
C at the Lands Tribunal. If persons object at the Lands Tribunal and in
consequence proceedings in the High Court become necessary, and then the
objectors throw in their hand, there is no reason why they should not at least
pay their own costs in the High Court.' "

The matter came before the court again (35) because it was necessary to deal
D with those objectors who did not throw in their hands but who in the result
proved unsuccessful. On that occasion STAMP, J., had to consider it. He cited
the practice note from *Re Jeffkins' Indentures* (36) and said (37):

" It seems to me that the position in this case is quite different from that
with which CROSS, J., was concerned. Here, before ever the plaintiff
even communicated with the defendants, they had intervened on an applica-
E tion that he had made to the Lands Tribunal in order to assert a title which
they, the objectors, claim and they did so in order to prevent him from
building his cottage and to obtain compensation if, in the event, the Lands
Tribunal thought fit to modify the restrictive covenant. I can see no
ground for not making the usual order in a case of hostile litigation between
two parties, one of whom is wholly unsuccessful."

F Counsel for the plaintiffs has argued that there is really no distinction between
the two types of case, and that if one stands on any such distinction, the result
would simply be that people will make a formal application to the Lands Tribunal
in order to bring out the objectors and will then have the matter transferred
to this court so as, on the question of costs, to be in the more favourable position
established by BUCKLEY, J. (38) and STAMP, J. (39) in the two *Re Jeffs' Transfer*
G cases.

I am not at all satisfied that that result will ensue, and if it does the matter
can be further considered when such a case comes before the court. As matters
stand at present it is quite clear that STAMP, J., and BUCKLEY, J., did not intend
to throw any doubt on the practice which has subsisted since as long ago as
1939, and I think that I ought to apply that practice and make an order
H accordingly in the *Re Jeffkins' Indentures* form (36), which I do.

Certain matters of detail have to be considered, however. First, it would
appear that under such an order the defendants have their costs, unless
there were some special circumstances, down to the final appointment before
the master under which the case is adjourned to the judge. I wondered whether
since the defendants had filed a great deal of evidence the order giving them
I their costs ought to have stopped, perhaps, at some earlier stage, but it was
necessary for them to investigate the position and obtain the large number of
transfers which they put in evidence, and the actual increase in the costs already

(34) [1965] 2 All E.R. at p. 799.
(35) *Re Jeffs' Transfer, Rogers* v. *Astley (No. 2)*, [1966] 1 All E.R. 937.
(36) [1965] 1 All E.R. 608.
(37) [1966] 1 All E.R. at p. 944.
(38) [1965] 2 All E.R. 798.
(39) [1966] 1 All E.R. 937.

involved in finding that evidence cannot be substantial. It is difficult to see where **A** one would draw the line if one sought to make a special order, and I will, therefore, follow the ordinary rule.

At the hearing, counsel for the defendants obtained leave to file a further affidavit and he argues that the costs of that ought to be included. I see no reason why I should accede to that request. That was something done after the adjournment for the purpose of further supporting his case. **B**

The last point is whether the costs of the defendants should be on a party and party or common fund basis. It seems to me in principle that they ought to be on a common fund basis since the obtaining of the order is something in the nature of a luxury to the plaintiffs for which they ought to pay. In any event counsel for the plaintiffs concedes, at any rate for the purposes of this case, that if I follow *Re Jeffkins' Indentures* (40) (as I have done) the order ought **C** to be on the common fund basis. So with the addition of this detail, I will make an order in the *Re Jeffkins'* (40) form.

Order accordingly.

Solicitors: *Freke Palmer, Romain & Gassman* (for the plaintiffs); *Perry, Stone & Co. Wembley* (for the defendants).

D

[*Reported by* R. W. FARRIN, ESQ., *Barrister-at-Law.*]

R. *v.* COCKBURN.

[COURT OF APPEAL, CRIMINAL DIVISION (Lord Parker, C.J., Winn, L.J., and Widgery, J.), December 19, 1967.] **E**

Applied in HALSTEAD v PATEL
[1972] 2 All ER 147

Dictum of WINN LJ at 468, 469 disapproved in R v FEELY [1973] 1
All ER 341

Criminal Law—Larceny—Defence—Intention to replace money taken—Ground of mitigation but not defence—Larceny Act, 1916 (6 & 7 Geo. 5 c. 50), s. 17* (1) (a).

A manager of a shop took money from the till on Saturday, Apr. 15, 1967, intending, it seemed, to replace the money by means of a cheque of his **F** daughter's, with which she had supplied him. The manager was in receipt of an allowance from his wife's estate, but had no bank account of his own, and his daughter furnished him with a number of signed blank cheques to fill in; such cheques had been used by the manager in the past and all had been met. The manager was dismissed on Monday, Apr. 17, on other grounds than that the money was taken from the till. At his trial on a charge of larceny as a servant the jury were not directed that it would be a **G** good defence to the charge if the accused were to satisfy them that he intended to replace the money with its currency equivalent, or were to raise a reasonable doubt in the minds of the jury that he so intended.

Held: an intention on the part of accused who had taken money of his employers in circumstances amounting to larceny to replace the currency equivalent of that money was no defence to a charge of larceny of the **H** money taken, though, according to the circumstances, it might amount to strong mitigation (see p. 469, letters A and G, post).

R. v. Williams† ([1953] 1 Q.B. 660; [1953] 2 W.L.R. 937) explained and applied.

Appeal dismissed.

[As to fraudulent taking of property with intention to deprive the owner thereof permanently, see 10 HALSBURY'S LAWS (3rd Edn.) 766, 767, para. **1483**; and for cases on the subject, see 15 DIGEST (Repl.) 1058, *10426-10429.*

---

(40) [1965] 1 All E.R. 608.

* Section 17, so far as material, provides : " Every person who—(1) being a clerk or servant or person employed in the capacity of a clerk or servant—(a) steals any chattels, or money or valuable security belonging to or in the possession or power of his master or employer . . . shall be guilty of felony . . ."

† (1953), 37 Cr. App. Rep. 71; [1953] 1 All E.R. 1068.

A   For the Larceny Act, 1916, s. 17, see 5 HALSBURY'S STATUTES (2nd Edn.)
1021.]

Case referred to:
    R. v. *Williams*, [1953] 1 All E.R. 1068; [1953] 1 Q.B. 660; [1953] 2 W.L.R.
        937; 37 Cr. App. Rep. 71; 117 J.P. 251; 15 Digest (Repl.) 1058,
        10429.
B

Appeal.

This was an appeal by John James Cockburn against his conviction on Oct. 2,
1967, at Huddersfield quarter sessions of larceny as a servant in respect of £50;
he was then sentenced to six months' imprisonment. The appeal against conviction was by virtue of a certificate granted on a point of law. The appellant
C also applied for leave to appeal against his sentence of six months' imprisonment.

The appellant admitted at his trial that he had taken £50 from the till of his
employers' shop on Saturday, Apr. 15, 1967. He said that this was the first
time that he had taken money from the till without putting a chit in the till;
and that the reason why he had not put a chit in the till was that the cashier
was on holiday and he was in charge of the till. He said that he had intended
D to repay the £50 with a cheque from his daughter on Monday, Apr. 17. He
was dismissed on Monday, Apr. 17, as a consequence of an earlier stock-taking
check, which revealed a deficiency in gross profits. On Apr. 18 the area manager
checked the cash at the shop; £106 19s. 11d. was missing. On being telephoned
the appellant replied that as far as he was concerned the cash was correct. The
appellant, after an interview with a director, himself went to the police. He
E made a statement, which the prosecution submitted at his trial amounted to an
admission of stealing the £106 19s. 11d. The appellant denied at his trial that
he had taken the £106 19s. 11d. He said in evidence that his daughter gave
him blank cheques, signed by her, which he was at liberty to fill in when he
required money. When he had not had a cheque handy, he had previously
taken money from the till and had replaced it by a chit. The jury were directed
F that, even on the occasions when a chit was put in the till, the money was
borrowed without authority and was, therefore, stolen; and that it really did
not matter that the money was repaid. Nine cheques were produced by the
defendants, signed by the appellant's daughter, some of which were payable
to the appellant and endorsed by him to his employers, Peter Dominic, Ltd.,
and the rest of which were in payment of his daughter's account. The jury were
G directed that if they thought that the appellant might be telling the truth when
he said that he only took £50, they should convict him of stealing only £50;
and that, if they thought that he intended to replace the money later, that did
not amount to a defence. By his grounds of appeal the appellant complained
of misdirection, the first ground being that the recorder was wrong in law in
directing the jury that intention to repay money borrowed without authority
H was no defence.

    S. Levine for the appellant.
    A. F. B. Scrivener for the Crown.

    WINN, L.J., delivered the following judgment of the court: The appellant
was employed as manager of a shop of Peter Dominic, Ltd., wine merchants in
I Halifax. He was dismissed on Apr. 17, not for any matter connected with this
charge. The next day the area manager carried out a check of the cash at the
shop, and found that about £107 was missing. The appellant then and subsequently maintained that he certainly knew nothing about any shortage to the
extent of £107; he had not taken any such amount at all, but he somewhat
belatedly admitted that he did take £50 from the till on the previous Saturday.
He said that he had intended to cover that £50 withdrawal by a cheque, but it
was discovered on the Monday before he had time to put the cheque in. It
appears that the appellant was helped by his own daughter in a most remarkably

loose and rash fashion in as much as she gave him from time to time bunches of   A
blank cheques which she had signed on her own bank account with authority
from her to fill them in with any amount that he might require, and to put
those cheques into his employers' till against money that he took from the till.
He said that his practice was to put a note into the till when he did not immediately put a cheque, but as and when he found himself with a cheque and at the
till he would put one of his daughter's cheques in the till.   It is right to say that   B
all his daughter's cheques had been met up to the relevant date, a total of nine
of them, some given in payment of her account and some with the daughter's
authority in the manner that I have indicated.   He apparently was receiving
an allowance of about £10 a week from a trust fund left by his late wife, but he
was not operating any bank account of his own at the material time.

The point raised by counsel for the appellant is that it is a good defence in   C
law to a charge of larceny of a sum of money if the defendant is able to satisfy
the jury, or if it remains open in the minds of the jury as a reasonable possibility,
that he intended to replace the money taken with its currency equivalent and
had resources available to him which would enable him to make that replacement.   The court is quite satisfied that that submission of counsel is founded
on, and very ill-founded on, a passage in a report of *R.* v. *Williams* (1) which   D
was before the Court of Criminal Appeal in 1953, when the court was presided
over by LORD GODDARD, C.J., and PARKER and BYRNE, JJ., were the other two
members of the court.   There is in the Weekly Law Reports a passage (2) which
this court sincerely hopes will for the future be disregarded entirely by the Bar
and all others who have occasion from time to time to refer to *R.* v. *Williams* (1).
There is no corresponding passage in the Law Reports (3), or in the Criminal   E
Appeal Reports (4), and I venture to think that beyond peradventure LORD
GODDARD himself must have checked those reports, the Law Reports and the
Criminal Appeal Reports, and taken good care to see that the passage which I
am about to read did not appear in those official reports.   The passage reads
as follows (2):

" It is one thing if a person with good credit and plenty of money uses   F
somebody else's money which may be in his possession and which may
have been entrusted to him or which he may have had the opportunity of
taking, merely intending to use those coins instead of some of his own
which he has only to go to his room or to his bank to obtain.   No jury
would then say that there was any intent to defraud or any fraudulent
taking, it is quite another matter if the person who takes the money is not   G
in a position to replace it at the time but only has a hope or expectation
that he will be able to do so in the future . . ."

I venture to think that quite probably, LORD GODDARD, C.J., felt about that
passage what I myself not only feel but now say: that it is an extremely
dangerous and misleading statement.   It does not appear in the other reports   H
that I have mentioned.

The fact of the matter, however, is this: that whereas larceny may vary
very greatly indeed to the extent, one might say, of the whole heavens between
grave theft and a taking which, whilst technically larcenous, reveals no moral
obloquy and does no harm at all, it is nevertheless quite essential always to
remember what are the elements of larceny and what are the complete and total   I
elements of larceny, that is to say, taking the property of another person against
the will of that other person without any claim of right so to do, and with the
intent at the time of taking it permanently to deprive the owner of it.   If coins,
half a crown, a 10s. note, a £5 note, whatever it may be, are taken in all the

(1) [1953] 1 All E.R. 1068; [1953] 1 Q.B. 660.
(2) [1953] 2 W.L.R. 937 at p. 942.
(3) [1953] 1 Q.B. 660.
(4) (1953), 37 Cr. App. Rep. 71.

A circumstances which I have already indicated with the intention of spending or putting away somewhere those particular coins or notes, albeit not only hoping but intending and expecting reasonably to be able to replace them with their equivalent, nevertheless larceny has been committed because with full appreciation of what is being done, the larcenous person, the person who commits the offence, has taken something which he was not entitled to take, had no claim of

B right to take, without the consent of the owner, and is in effect trying to force on the owner a substitution to which the owner has not consented.

In *R.* v. *Williams* (5), LORD GODDARD, C.J., giving the judgment of the court, said this:

C "... it seems to the court in this case that, by taking the coins and notes and using them for their own purposes, the appellants intended to deprive the Postmaster-General of the property in those notes and coins, and in so doing they acted without a claim of right and they acted fraudulently because they knew what they were doing. They knew they had no right to take the money which they knew was not their money. The fact that they may have had a hope or expectation in the future of repaying that money is a matter which at most can go to mitigation. It does not amount to a

D defence."

It may be very good mitigation indeed. Circumstances vary enormously. *R.* v. *Williams* (6) was a case in which those who were endeavouring to run a sub-post office, a husband and wife, found that their own business, which they were conducting in the same premises, was not prospering. Mrs. Williams—and her

E husband bore her out in this—said in evidence that she thought that when she took some money from the postmaster's side of the business, from the funds held on his behalf, she would be able to repay the money out of her salary and from sales in her own business. The reason why she took the post office money was because the business was in difficulties and had not the necessary funds to carry on. The more reasonable the ground for expecting and feeling confident

F that the money can with certainty and promptitude be repaid, the more substantial are the grounds of mitigation, and the better is the justification for regarding the case as one approaching, though never actually to be equated with, a technicality.

In this case there is a great deal to be said in mitigation and the court can fully appreciate the realities of the situation. The appellant might very well

G have had good grounds for feeling sure that on the Monday there would be a cheque of his daughter's which he could use to replenish the till on which he had made this depredation on the Saturday, and it looks as though that was what his intention may well have been. The fact remains that he was properly found guilty of larceny, and the question is what in the circumstances is the appropriate sentence. This court is prepared to treat the application for leave to appeal

H against sentence as the appeal, and to vary the sentence by substituting such a sentence as will allow this man to be released tomorrow.

Appeal against conviction dismissed. Sentence varied.

Solicitors: *Registrar of Criminal Appeals* (for the appellant); *Sharpe, Pritchard & Co.*, agents for *F. E. Smith*, Halifax (for the Crown).

I   [*Reported by* S. A. HATTEEA, ESQ., *Barrister-at-Law.*]

---

(5) (1953), 37 Cr. App. Rep. at p. 81; cf. [1953] 1 All E.R. at p. 1071; [1953] 1 Q.B. at p. 668.
(6) [1953] 1 All E.R. 1068, [1953] 1 Q.B. 660.

A

Re HOLT'S SETTLEMENT.

wILSON *v.* HOLT AND OTHERS.

[CHANCERY DIVISION (Megarry, J.), December 4, 5, 1967.]

*Trust and Trustee—Variation of trust by the court—Arrangement, deriving force
from consent of adults and approval of court, and thus effecting variation—
Arrangement, when approved, an instrument to which Perpetuities etc. Act
1964 would apply—Life tenant proposing to surrender half of income of trust
fund—Trust for accumulation of that income and deferment of vesting of children's interest until age thirty—Whether court will approve arrangement
involving element of risk in its application to unborn persons—Variation of
Trusts Act, 1958 (6 & 7 Eliz. 2 c. 53), s. 1—Perpetuities and Accumulations
Act 1964 (c. 55) s. 15 (5).*

B

C

By a settlement dated Dec. 22, 1959, the income of a trust fund was to be
paid to the plaintiff, the settlor's daughter, for life and subject thereto, the
trust fund was to be held on trusts for her children who should attain the
age of twenty-one years and, if more than one, in equal shares. The plaintiff   D
was now aged thirty-five years, and had three children aged about ten, seven
and six respectively. The arrangement, for which the court's approval was
sought on behalf of infants and unborn persons under the Variation of Trusts
Act, 1958, was that the plaintiff should surrender her life interest in one half
of the income of the trust fund (which had greatly increased in value since the
date of the settlement), that the income of that half should be accumulated,   E
and that the vesting of the interests of children in that half fund should be
deferred until they respectively reached the age of thirty years. The arrangement took the form of a proposed revocation of existing trusts and the establishment of new trusts, many of which would be similar to the former trusts;
and it was proposed that advantage should be taken in the arrangement of
the provisions of the Perpetuities and Accumulations Act 1964, which, by   F
s. 15 (5), applied only, so far as material to this case, to instruments taking
effect after the commencement of the Act.

Held: (i) where the court made an order under s. 1 of the Variation of
Trusts Act, 1958, approving an arrangement, it was the arrangement, made
binding on infants and unborn persons by the court's approval, that varied
the trusts, not the order of the court itself (see p. 476, letters A, D and I,   G
post).

Practice established by *Re Viscount Hambleden's Will Trusts* ([1960] 1 All
E.R. 353) accepted, but dicta at p. 355, letters D, G, not adopted.

Re Joseph's Will Trusts ([1959] 3 All E.R. 474) considered.

(ii) although the arrangement, when approved, would revoke all prior
trusts and establish new trusts, yet the new trusts would be in many respects   H
similar to the old trusts, and accordingly the arrangement in the present case
would be a " variation " of the former trusts for the purposes of s. 1 of the
Act of 1958 (see p. 477, letters B, D and H, post).

(iii) the arrangement coupled with the court's order constituted an instrument for the purposes of s. 15 (5) of the Perpetuities and Accumlations Act
1964, with the consequence that provisions deriving their validity from the   I
the Act of 1964 might properly be included in the arrangement (see p. 479,
letter A, post).

(iv) as regards unborn persons on whose behalf approval was sought the
court should be prepared to take the sort of risk that an adult would be
prepared to take and, on the merits, the proposed arrangement would be
approved (see p. 480, letters D and F, post).

Re Cohen's Will Trusts ([1959] 3 All E.R. 523) applied.

Re Cohen's Settlement Trusts ([1965] 3 All E.R. 139) distinguished.

A   [**Editorial Note.** The view that the force of an arrangement approved by
    the court under the Variation of Trusts Act, 1958, derives from the consent of
    beneficiaries to the arrangement, the court's order merely making good the want
    of capacity of those persons on whose behalf the court's approval is given, has
    the approval of two, perhaps of a majority, of the House of Lords in *Re Holmden's
    Settlement Trusts* (see p. 149, letter A, ante). The opinions of the law lords in
B   that appeal had not been delivered at the date of the decision of the present case.

    As to the jurisdiction of the court to vary trusts under the Act of 1958, see 38
    HALSBURY'S LAWS (3rd Edn.) 1029, 1030, para. 1772; and for cases on the
    subject, see 47 DIGEST (Repl.) 332-338, *2993-3018*.

    For the Variation of Trusts Act, 1958, s. 1, see 38 HALSBURY'S STATUTES
    (2nd Edn.) 1130.

C   For the Perpetuities and Accumulations Act 1964, see 44 HALSBURY'S STATUTES
    (2nd Edn.) 870.]

Cases referred to:

   Chapman v. *Chapman*, [1954] 1 All E.R. 798; [1954] A.C. 429; [1954] 2 W.L.R.
        723; 47 Digest (Repl.) 329, *2973*.
   Cohen's Settlement Trusts, Re, Eliot-Cohen v. *Cohen*, [1965] 3 All E.R. 139;
D   [1965] 1 W.L.R. 1229; 47 Digest (Repl.) 335, *3001*.
   Cohen's Will Trusts, Re, Cohen's Settlement Trusts, Re, [1959] 3 All E.R. 523;
        [1959] 1 W.L.R. 865; 47 Digest (Repl.) 336, *3011*.
   Grey v. *Inland Revenue Comrs.,* [1959] 3 All E.R. 603; [1960] A.C. 1; [1959]
        3 W.L.R. 759; 47 Digest (Repl.) 17, *49*
   Hambleden's (Viscount) Will Trusts, Re, [1960] 1 All E.R. 353, n.; [1960] 1
E   W.L.R. 82; 47 Digest (Repl.) 339, *3033*.
   Joseph's Will Trusts, Re, [1959] 3 All E.R. 474, n.; [1959] 1 W.L.R. 1019;
        47 Digest (Repl.) 339, *3032*.
   Lloyd's Settlement, Re, [1967] 2 All E.R. 314; [1967] 2 W.L.R. 1078.
   Oughtred v. *Inland Revenue Comrs.,* [1959] 3 All E.R. 623; [1960] A.C. 206;
        [1959] 3 W.L.R. 898; 47 Digest (Repl.) 17, *47*.
F   *Pilkington* v. *Inland Revenue Comrs.,* [1962] 3 All E.R. 622; [1964] A.C. 612;
        [1962] 3 W.L.R. 1051; Digest (Cont. Vol. A) 922, *1132a*.
   Saunders v. *Vautier,* [1835-42] All E.R. Rep. 58; (1841), 4 Beav. 115; 10 L.J.
        Ch. 354; 41 E.R. 482; 49 Digest (Repl.) 1024, *9581*.
   Towler's Settlement Trusts, Re, [1963] 3 All E.R. 759; sub nom. *Re T.'s Settlement
        Trusts,* [1964] Ch. 158; [1963] 3 W.L.R. 987; 47 Digest (Repl.) 337,
G   *3014*.

Adjourned Summons.

    This was an application by originating summons under s. 1 of the Variation
of Trusts Act, 1958, for the approval of a proposed arrangement involving a
variation of trusts established by virtue of a settlement of personalty by deed
H   dated Dec. 22, 1959, on behalf of children or persons unborn incapable of assenting
of themselves to the arrangement.

   P. J. Millett for the plaintiff.
   G. M. Godfrey for the first defendant, the settlor.
   J. P. Brookes for the second, third and fourth defendants, the trustees.
   D. Gidley Scott for the fifth, sixth and seventh defendants.
I

   MEGARRY, J.: This is an originating summons under the Variation of
Trusts Act, 1958. It concerns a settlement of pure personalty which was made
inter vivos on Dec. 22, 1959. The trusts are simple. They consist of a life interest
for Mrs. Wilson (the settlor's daughter), and subject thereto trusts for all her
children who attain the age of twenty-one years and if more than one in equal
shares. The settlement makes no disposition of the ultimate interest if there is no
such child, and so there would be a resulting trust to the settlor. Mrs. Wilson is
now about thirty-five years old and has three children aged some ten, seven and

six years respectively. The sum settled in 1959 was £15,000, but the capital is **A**
now worth something like £320,000, so that its value has increased by more
than twenty times.

In broad terms the arrangement proposed is that Mrs. Wilson should surrender
her life interest in one half of the income of the trust fund. This surrender would
reduce the impact of income tax and surtax on her and her husband, and increase
the value of the children's interests under the trusts. It is also proposed that the **B**
children should have the vesting of their interests deferred until they are aged
thirty years respectively and that half the income of their respective shares
should be accumulated until the age of thirty. The reason given for this is that
if Mrs. Wilson surrendered her life interest in half, the present children (assuming
no more to be born) would, under the trusts as they stand, each become entitled at
the age of twenty-one to capital worth some £75,000 and enjoy an income of **C**
some £3,750 a year. Not surprisingly, Mrs. Wilson says in her affidavit

> " I would be strongly opposed to this. Nor is it only a question of capital,
> for I would consider it equally undesirable for my children to receive an
> income of, say, £3,750 per annum at that stage. I believe it to be most import-
> ant that young people should be reasonably advanced in a career and settled
> in life before they are in receipt of an income sufficient to make them **D**
> independent of the need to work."

Two main questions have been debated before me. I propose to consider these
now, and deal separately with certain details of the proposed arrangement. These
questions are: first, does an order under the Act of 1958 ipso facto vary the
terms of the trust without the execution of the arrangement or any other document by or on behalf of any beneficiary, apart from those on whose behalf s. 1 (1) **E**
of the Act of 1958 empowers the court to approve the arrangement? Secondly, if
after the commencement of the Perpetuities and Accumulations Act 1964 a
variation is made in trusts constituted before the commencement of the Act of
1964, can that variation take advantage of the changes in the rules against
perpetuities and accumulations which that Act has made?

Under the first head, the basic issue is whether an order under the Act of 1958 **F**
by itself varies the terms of the trust. Put rather differently, the question is
whether the Act of 1958 does no more than empower the court to supply on
behalf of the infants, unborn persons and others mentioned in s. 1 (1), that
binding approval which they cannot give, leaving the other beneficiaries to
provide their own approvals in some other document which will bind them. **G**
In the present case the arrangement was drafted on the assumption that the
order of the court will ipso facto vary the terms of the trusts, for the " operative
date " is defined as being the date of the order approving this arrangement, and
the perpetuity period and the accumulation period (which are made use of in the
terms of the trusts) each commence on the operative date.

The only authority directly on the point which has been cited to me is the **H**
decision in *Re Viscount Hambleden's Will Trusts* (1). I do not think I need read
the provisions of the trusts in that case. It was a summons under the Act of 1958
and the judgment of WYNN-PARRY, J., as reported, is very short. The report does,
however, include certain interlocutory observations. WYNN-PARRY, J., made it
clear that his view was that the order of the court ipso facto varied the trusts.
He had had cited to him the decision of VAISEY, J., in *Re Joseph's Will Trusts*, (2),
where that learned judge had inserted words in the order of the court which **I**
authorised and directed the trustees to carry the arrangement into effect. WYNN-
PARRY, J., said (3):

> " I do not agree with that decision. I take the view that I have no
> jurisdiction to make an order including words directing the trustees to carry

---

(1) [1960] 1 All E.R. 353, n.
(2) [1959] 3 All E.R. 474, n.
(3) [1960] 1 All E.R. at pp. 354, 355.

A the arrangement into effect, and those words should be deleted from the draft minutes. Nothing is required except the approval of the court to the arrangement. If that approval is given, the trusts are ipso facto altered, and the trustees are bound thereafter to give effect to the arrangement."

B Later in the course of the argument he said (4): "If I approve an arrangement, I alter the trusts. Res ipsa loquitur." Again, a little later he said (4): "If I approve an arrangement, I vary the trusts." His judgment I may recite in its entirety. It consists of these words (4):

"Very well. I hold that the effect of my approval is effective for all purposes to vary the trusts. Thereafter, the trusts are the trusts as varied. I approve the minutes of order, with the slight alterations which have been referred to, and the arrangement in the schedule."

C If that were a decision of the Court of Appeal I could venerate and obey, even without fully comprehending. But the decision is at first instance, and so is of persuasive and not binding authority. It is my misfortune not to be persuaded by such assertions, even though fourfold, when made without explanation. I bear in mind that in Re Joseph's Will Trusts (5), to which I have already referred,

D was a decision of a very experienced judge of the same division. In his judgment VAISEY, J., referred to two decisions (6) of LORD JENKINS, when sitting as a judge of the Chancery Division, in one of which LORD JENKINS had directed an addition to be made to his order of the same nature as that made by VAISEY, J., in Re Joseph's Will Trusts (5), whereas in the other case LORD JENKINS had not directed any such addition, but, as VAISEY, J., pointed out, we do not

E know the facts in either of those cases.

In that state of the authorities I must go back to the words of the Act of 1958. The Variation of Trusts Act, 1958, s. 1 (1) provides:

"Where property, whether real or personal, is held on trusts arising, whether before or after the passing of this Act, under any will, settlement or other disposition, the court may if it thinks fit by order approve on

F behalf of—. . . ."

At that point I pause; for there is then set out in para. (a) to (d) a number of persons who, being infants or unborn or unascertained, are not in a position to provide their own binding assents to any arrangement. In relation to the Act of 1958 I shall use the term "infants" as a compendious expression to embrace all those who are specified in s. 1 (1) paras. (a) to (d); and by parity of reasoning

G I shall use the word "adults" for all other beneficiaries. Returning, then, to the subsection it continues:

". . . [the infants] any arrangement . . . varying or revoking all or any of the trusts, or enlarging the powers of the trustees of managing or administering any of the property subject to the trusts: . . . "

H Then there is an important proviso requiring that no arrangement shall be approved on behalf of any person (apart from the persons mentioned in para. (d)) unless the carrying out thereof would be for the benefit of that person.

I have been much assisted in this case by the arguments of counsel. I will not attempt to ascribe to each the precise portions of the various arguments as they have emerged: I will simply express my gratitude collectively to all four. The

I argument against the doctrine of ipso facto variation as laid down in the Hambleden case (7) (an argument for which counsel do not bear the sole responsibility) is somewhat as follows. It starts with the well-known mischief which the Act of 1958 was designed to meet, a mischief confirmed by the House of Lords decision in Chapman v. Chapman (8). If under a trust every possible beneficiary

---

(4) [1960] 1 All E.R. at p. 355.   (5) [1959] 3 All E.R. 474, n.
(6) Re Derby's Settlement, (1959), unreported and Re Saville's Will Trusts, (1959), unreported.
(7) [1960] 1 All E.R. 353, n.   (8) [1954] 1 All E.R. 798; [1954] A.C. 429.

was under no disability and concurred in the re-arrangement or termination of **A**
the trusts then under the doctrine of *Saunders* v. *Vautier* (9), those beneficiaries
could dispose of the trust property as they thought fit; for in equity the property
was theirs. Yet if any beneficiary was an infant, or an unborn or unascertained
person, it was held that the court had no general inherent or other jurisdiction to concur in any such arrangement on behalf of that beneficiary.
Accordingly, some while after the decision of the House of Lords to this effect the **B**
Act of 1958 conferred on the court the power contained in s. 1. But, proceeds the
argument, that Act did no more than allow the court to provide the binding
assent which the infant himself could not provide; and the wording of the Act of
1958, shows this to be so. The Act merely provides that "... the court may if it
thinks fit by order approve on behalf of [the infants] any arrangement . . .
varying or revoking all or any of the trusts . . ."; so that all Parliament has **C**
done is to empower the court to provide the binding approval of an arrangement
which the infants themselves could not give.

The argument continues by pointing a contrast between the wording of s. 1 (1)
and two other statutory provisions which may fairly be said to have been present
in the draftsman's mind; for they are mentioned in s. 1 (6). These provisions are
s. 64 of the Settled Land Act, 1925, and s. 57 of the Trustee Act, 1925. Section 64 **D**
of Settled Land Act, 1925, the provides:

> " Any transaction affecting or concerning the settled land . . . which in the
> opinion of the court would be for the benefit of the settled land . . . may, under
> an order of the court, be effected by a tenant for life . . ."

Section 57 of the Trustee Act, 1925 provides that in certain circumstances where **E**
the court considers it expedient " . . . the court may by order confer upon the
trustees . . . the necessary power for the purpose . . . " that is, the purpose
previously set out in the section. In each of these cases the statute authorises the
court to make an order conferring a power to do something which otherwise could
not be done. This, it is pointed out, is very different from a provision which in
terms confers no power but merely authorises the court to approve an arrangement **F**
on behalf of infants.

It is said that there is no escape from this conclusion merely by saying that
when an arrangement is approved under the Act of 1958, the adults provide the
necessary concurrence in assenting by their counsel to the arrangement; for
s. 53 (1) (c) of the Law of Property Act, 1925, stands in the way. This provides
that **G**

> " a disposition of an equitable interest or trust subsisting at the time of the
> disposition, must be in writing signed by the person disposing of the same,
> or by his agent thereunto lawfully authorised in writing or by will."

Where the arrangement is put into effect there is a disposition of an equitable
interest, so that unless there is some document signed by the adult beneficiaries, **H**
or by some agent authorised by them in writing, the requirements of s. 53 (1) (c)
are not satisfied. This contention is supported by a reference to the decision by
the House of Lords in *Grey* v. *Inland Revenue Comrs.* (10) that an oral direction
by a beneficiary to his trustees to hold property on certain trusts is a disposition,
and that " disposition " must be given its ordinary wide meaning. It is further
said that as there is here a transaction under which a moiety of a life interest
will pass from Mrs. Wilson to her children, this is a fortiori a "disposition". **I**
I may add that there is the minor point that the common form of order under
the Act does not normally recite that all the adults have consented to the transaction, though where the insertion of such a recital is required by the parties,
the registrars insert it.

Let me say at once that there would seem to be no great difficulty in inserting

(9) [1835-42] All E.R. Rep. 58; (1841), 4 Beav. 115.
(10 [1959] 3 All E.R. 603; [1960] A.C. 1.

A the consequences of this argument for the future. The adults could either execute the arrangement or, perhaps more conveniently, give written authority to their solicitors or counsel to execute it on their behalf. The latter course would usually be the more convenient because not infrequently changes (often minor) have to be made to the arrangement put before the court. It is, however, a fact that many thousands of orders must have been made in the past on the footing of

B *Re Viscount Hambleden's Will Trusts* (11). If the argument is right there is the very real difficulty that these orders will, perhaps in most cases, perhaps only in some, have effected no variation of the trusts. This is a consideration which is particularly awkward in that a question of jurisdiction is involved; for if the court has no jurisdiction to make an order which itself varies the trusts, and orders have been made on the footing that the orders do ipso facto vary the trusts, then

C it seems at least arguable that such orders were made without jurisdiction. It has also been pointed out that the Inland Revenue has for some while acted on the decision, and that orders of the court have been stamped on the footing that they ipso facto vary the terms of the trusts. Yet again, it is plain that the present practice is convenient. It avoids the burden which usually, perhaps, would not be very great, but in individual cases might be substantial, of getting the necessary

D signatures of the adults either to the document itself or to written authorities. I bear all those considerations in mind; but nevertheless, it seems to me that there is very considerable force in the argument that has been advanced. The decision in *Re Viscount Hambleden's Will Trusts* (11) provides authority to the contrary but no explanation of the grounds for the decision. Accordingly a substantial part of the argument in this case has been directed to the discovery

E of some basis on which the convenient practice of *Re Viscount Hambleden's Will Trusts* (11) can be rested.

In attempting to summarise the argument of counsel for the settlor I am sure I shall fail to do it justice. As I understood it, he submitted that the decision in *Re Viscount Hambleden's Will Trusts* (11) was quite wrong, but that in effect this did not matter. All that the court had to do, he said, was to approve the arrange-

F ment (i.e., the proposal made), and there was no question of the court approving anything which in law amounted to a disposition. The arrangement was not a disposition but merely a bargain or proposal, which was not within the ambit of s. 53 (1) (c) of the Law of Property Act, 1925. The court, he urged, was not concerned to see that the adults consented and certainly not that they executed any disposition. There might thus be no disposition at all; but the persons

G specified by s. 1 (1) of the Act of 1958 would be bound by the order of the court approving the arrangement and the other beneficiaries could not in practice go back on what their counsel had assented to, at any rate so far as it had been acted on. The result would be that, although there would be no new equitable interests actually created under the arrangement, all the beneficiaries would by a species of estoppel be treated as if they had those interests. I hope that counsel

H for the settlor will forgive me if I say that I find this argument somewhat un-attractive. In particular, I find it very hard to believe that Parliament intended the court to approve on behalf of infants arrangements which depended for their efficacy on the uncertainties of estoppel. I bear in mind, too, the wide meaning which *Grey* v. *Inland Revenue Comrs.* (12) gave to the word " disposition " in s. 53 (1) (c).

I Counsel for the trustees, boldly asserted that, when correctly read, the Act of 1958 indirectly did what *Re Viscount Hambleden's Will Trusts* (11) said it did. He went back to the words of s. 1 (1) and emphasised that the power of the court was a power exercisable " by order " and that that power was a power to approve an arrangement " varying or revoking " all or any of the trusts. In emphasising those phrases, he said that the right way to read the section was to say that the

(11) [1960] 1 All E.R. 353, n.
(12) [1959] 3 All E.R. 603; [1960] A.C. 1.

power of the court was merely a power to make an order approving an arrangement A
which in fact varied or revoked the trusts, and not an arrangement which failed
to do any such thing. When the adults by their counsel assented to the arrangement and the court on behalf of the infants by order approved the arrangement,
then there was an arrangement which varied or revoked the trusts. So the order
of the court both conferred jurisdiction and exercised it. His escape from s. 53
(1) (c) had a similar dexterity about it: by conferring an express power on the B
court to do something by order, Parliament in the Act of 1958, had provided by
necessary implication an exception from s. 53 (1) (c). He buttressed his contention by a reference to *Re Joseph's Will Trusts* (13). VAISEY, J., there accepted
that the order which he made directing the trustees to carry the order of the court
into effect was neither contemplated by the Act of 1958 nor expressly authorised
by it. Rather than read into the Act of 1958 words that are not there, said counsel, C
one should construe the Act of 1958 as authorising an order which is efficacious to
achieve its avowed object. He pointed to the long title of the Act of 1958 which
reads

> " An Act to extend the jurisdiction of courts of law to vary trusts in the
> interests of beneficiaries and sanction dealings with trust property."
> D

I hope that counsel for the trustees, too, will pardon me if I say that I did not
find his argument compelling. Indeed, at times I think it tended to circularity.
But I find it tempting; and I yield. It is not a construction which I think the
most natural. But it is not an impossible construction; it accords with the long
title; it accords with the practice which has been relied on for many years in some
thousands of cases; and it accords with considerations of convenience. The point E
is technical, and I do not think that I am doing more than straining a little at the
wording in the interests of legislative efficacy.

However, that is not all. Counsel for the plaintiff, the tenant for life, provided
another means of escape from s. 53 (1) (c) in his helpful reply. Where, as here, the
arrangement consists of an agreement made for valuable consideration, and that
agreement is specifically enforceable, then the beneficial interests pass to the F
respective purchasers on the making of the agreement. Those interests pass by
virtue of the species of constructive trust made familiar by contracts for the sale
of land, whereunder the vendor becomes a constructive trustee for the purchaser as
soon as the contract is made, albeit the constructive trust has special features
about it. Section 53 (2), he continued, provides that " This section does not
affect the creation or operation of resulting, implied or constructive trusts". G
Accordingly, because the trust was constructive, s. 53 (1) (c) was excluded. He
supported this contention by the decision of the House of Lords in *Oughtred* v.
Inland Revenue Comrs. (14). He relied in particular on passages in the speeches
of LORD RADCLIFFE and LORD COHEN, albeit that they were dissenting on the
main point for decision. He pointed out that, although LORD JENKINS (with
whom LORD KEITH OF AVONHOLM concurred) had not decided the point, he had H
assumed for the purposes of his speech that it was correct, and that the rejection
of the contention by LORD DENNING was in a very brief passage. Counsel for the
plaintiff accepts that if there were to be some subsequent deed of family arrangement which would carry out the bargain then this deed might well be caught by
s. 53 (1) (c); but that, he said, cannot affect the " arrangement, " and the parties
might well be willing to let matters rest on that. It seems to me that there is I
considerable force in this argument in cases where the agreement is specifically
enforceable, and in its essentials I accept it. At all events it supports the conclusion that in such cases the practice established by *Re Viscount Hambleden's
Will Trusts* (15) is right. For this and the other reasons that I have given, though
with some hesitation, I accordingly hold this to be the case.

(13) [1959] 3 All E.R. 474, n.
(14) [1959] 3 All E.R. 623; [1960] A.C. 206.
(15) [1960] 1 All E.R. 353, n.

A   Finally, before turning to the second main point, I should mention that in this case the arrangement carries out its purpose by revoking all the existing trusts and establishing a new set of trusts. That being so, it is said that some difficulty arises on the wording of s. 1 (1) of the Act of 1958. This merely empowers the court to approve an arrangement " varying or revoking all or any of the trusts ", and so, it is said, the court cannot approve an arrangement which, instead of merely

B   " revoking " or merely " varying ", proceeds to revoke and then to set up new trusts, thereby producing an effect equivalent to the process of settlement and resettlement. The section, it is argued, says nothing of establishing new trusts for old. As a matter of principle, however, I do not really think that there is anything in this point, at all events in this case. Here the new trusts are in many respects similar to the old. In my judgment, the old trusts may fairly be said to have

C   been varied by the arrangement whether the variation is effected directly by leaving some of the old words standing and altering others, or indirectly, by revoking all the old words and then setting up new trusts partly, though not wholly, in the likeness of the old. One must not confuse machinery with substance; and it is the substance that matters. Comparing the position before and after the arrangement takes effect, I am satisfied that the result is a variation of the old

D   trusts, even though effected by the machinery of revocation and resettlement.

     Counsel for the trustees pressed me with the decision in *Re Towler's Settlement Trusts* (16). He accepts that the point is not a mere matter of form, that is, whether in form there is a mere series of variations of the existing trusts, or whether in form there is a revocation and declaration of new trusts, but he says that the form gives some indications as to whether there is a mere variation or not.

E   For myself, I cannot see much force in this; for so much depends on the individual draftsman who prepares the arrangement. One draftsman may choose to effect the arrangement by a series of variations of the existing trusts. Another may prefer to effect precisely the same variations by the formally more radical process of revocation and new declaration. In any event *Re Towler's Settlement Trusts* (16) seems to me to be an entirely different case. There the infant was

F   within eighteen days of attaining her majority and obtaining an absolute interest in the trust property. The existing trusts were at their very end, and what in substance was proposed was to make a new settlement of what was on the point of becoming an absolute unfettered interest. Further, although WILBERFORCE, J., rejected the wider proposal put before him, he did in fact make some variation in the trusts; and I cannot read the case as going so far as I think that counsel

G   would take it. It is not, of course, for the court to draw the line in any particular place between what is a variation and what on the other hand is a completely new settlement. A line may, perhaps, one day emerge from a sufficiently ample series of reported decisions, but for the present all that is necessary for me to say is whether the particular case before me is on the right side or the wrong side of any reasonable line that could be drawn. In this case I am satisfied that the

H   arrangement proposed falls on the side of the line which bears the device " variation ".

     I can now turn to the second main point, namely, that under the Perpetuities and Accumulations Act 1964. The settlement in this case was made prior to the commencement of that Act, and any variation will be 'made after that commencement. Section 15 (5) provides that

I
     " The foregoing sections of this Act shall apply . . . [and there is then an exception with which I am not concerned] . . . only in relation to instruments taking effect after the commencement of this Act . . . "

     There follows a reference to instruments made in the exercise of a special power of appointment. The Act of 1964 received the royal assent on July 16, 1964, so this is the date of its commencement.

     _____

     (16) [1963] 3 All E.R. 759; [1964] Ch. 158.

The kind of question that arises is this. Suppose an instrument taking effect **A** in 1959, as the original trusts did in this case, and a variation made under the Act of 1958 which merely alters a few words: will such a variation allow the Act of 1964 to apply to the trusts in their revised form? Again, suppose that as here, there is a revocation of the old trusts and a declaration of new trusts, so that in form there is a new start, although in substance merely a variation, does this alter the position? Could something be done by the second method which can- **B** not be done by a method which in form as well as in substance is a mere variation? Is it possible to have a variation under the Act of 1958 once every generation, and then with each variation start afresh with a relaxed perpetuity rule and a new accumulation period bounteously provided by the Act of 1964?

Counsel for the plaintiff boldly answered " Yes " to this last question, and harked back to those spacious days when strict settlements of land were common **C** and once a generation there was a process of settlement and resettlement, with all the old entails securely barred and new entails established. He pointed out that on each resettlement the settlors in effect changed, and that often there would be a similar result on a variation under the Act of 1958. When the settlement was first made the original settlor was the settlor; but when the first variation came to be made, then if there was any alteration in the beneficial interests **D** (as distinct from the mere conferring of additional administrative powers quoad those beneficial interests) the beneficiaries concerned would be the settlors, transferring their interests to be held on new trusts. Thus in effect there would be a new start each time. Counsel for the plaintiff drew my attention to the decision of PLOWMAN, J., in *Re Lloyd's Settlement*, (17), where he said this in effect was done. In that case a settlement inter vivos was made on Mar. 21, 1958. **E** The settlement directed an accumulation, and in the result the only appropriate accumulation period was that of the settlor's life. The effect was to expose the trust property to estate duty risks in respect of an interest which would pass on the settlor's death, and accordingly in 1966 a variation of the trusts was sought under the Act of 1958. By then the Act of 1964 had come into effect. Under the trusts as varied by the arrangement, accumulation was directed for a period of **F** twenty-one years from the date of the settlement; and this period is one which was made available for the first time by the Act of 1964. Accordingly, under the Act of 1958 a settlement made prior to the Act of 1964 was varied after that Act in a way which took advantage of the provisions of that Act. The case is shortly reported, setting out the facts at some length, the cases cited in the argument and the order made; but unfortunately there is no statement of the reasons of **G** the learned judge. Nevertheless it seems to me that the variation in fact there made supports counsel for the plaintiff's contention.

Counsel for the plaintiff also referred me to LEWIN ON TRUSTS (16th Edn., 1964) pp. 741, 742, where an argument which is in accord with counsel's submission is advanced by the learned editor (the passage cannot have been the work of the late Mr. Lewin). I would only observe that there appears on p. 742 to have **H** been a slip in the statement of *Pilkington* v. *Inland Revenue Comrs.* (18); for the reference in the text should, it seems, be to a power of advancement rather than to a power of appointment, and the citation of the case is also erroneous. For myself, I find any analogy with powers of appointment and powers of advancement unsatisfactory. The mischief attacked by the rule against per- petuities in the case of powers of appointment, and now, since the *Pilkington* **I** case, (18) in the case of powers of advancement, is that the property is tied up ab initio. The power is conferred by the settlement, and the person exercising the power can do so only within pre-ordained limits. The power indeed " belongs " to the old settlement, if I may respectfully adopt the language of VISCOUNT RADCLIFFE in the *Pilkington* case (19). Under the Act of 1958, there are no

(17) [1967] 2 All E.R. 314.
(18) [1962] 3 All E.R. 622; [1964] A.C. 612.
(19) [1962] 3 All E.R. at p. 632; [1964] A.C. at p. 642.

A such limits. The property, as it seems to me, is freely disposable. Under an arrangement approved by the court the trusts may be brought wholly to an end. On the other hand they may be varied, and there is no limit, other than the discretion of the court and the agreement of the parties, to the variation which may be made. Any variation owes its authority not to anything in the initial settlement but to the statute and the consent of the adults coming, as it were, ab extra.

B This certainly seems to be so in any case not within the Act where a variation or resettlement is made under the doctrine of *Saunders* v. *Vautier* (20) by all the adults joining together, and I cannot see any real difference in principle in a case where the court exercises its jurisdiction on behalf of the infants under the Act of 1958. It seems to me that the arrangement, coupled with the order of the court, constitutes an " instrument ", or, since the singular includes the plural, "instru-

C ments," which take effect after July 15, 1964. Whether the documents are regarded as separate instruments or as together constituting one composite instrument, the effect is produced by the complex of documents; and what takes effect after July 15, 1964 is the result of this complex of documents. In my judgment, therefore, it is permissible to insert provisions deriving their validity from the Act of 1964 into an arrangement approved under the Act of 1958.

D   That, I think, suffices to dispose of the two substantial points; and I should perhaps say that I have been astute to do so without resort to the Fourth and Sixth Reports of the Law Reform Committee or the discussions which led to these reports, despite their relationship to the Acts of 1964 and 1958 respectively.

I can deal with the merits of this application quite shortly. It seems to me that, subject to one reservation the arrangement proposed is for the benefit of each of

E the beneficiaries contemplated by the Variation of Trusts Act, 1958, s. 1 (1). The financial detriment to the children is that the absolute vesting of their interests will be postponed from age twenty-one to age thirty. As against that, they will obtain very substantial financial benefits, both in the acceleration of their interests in a moiety of the trust fund and in the savings of estate duty to be expected in a case such as this. Where the advantages of the scheme are over-

F whelming, any detailed evaluation, or " balance sheet " of advantages and disadvantages, seems to me to be unnecessary; but I can imagine cases under the Act where it may be important that an attempt should be made to put in evidence a detailed evaluation of the financial and other consequences of the changes proposed to be made, so that it may be seen whether on balance there is a sufficient advantage to satisfy the proviso to s. 1 (1) of the Act of 1958. But

G this is not such a case, and I say no more about it. I should, however, state that I fully concur in the view taken by Mrs. Wilson that, speaking in general terms, it is most important that young children " should be reasonably advanced in a career and settled in life before they are in receipt of an income sufficient to make them independent of the need to work ". The word " benefit " in the proviso to s. 1 (1) of the Act of 1958 is, I think, plainly not confined to financial benefit,

H but may extend to moral or social benefit, as is shown by *Re Towler's Settlement Trusts* (21).

The point that at one stage troubled me concerns the unborn issue. Counsel for the trustees, as in duty bound, put before me a contention that it was possible to conceive of an unborn infant who would be so circumstanced that the proposed rearrangement would be entirely to his disadvantage. He postulated the

I case of a child born to Mrs. Wilson next year, and of Mrs. Wilson dying in childbirth, or shortly after the child's birth. In such a case, he said the benefit of the acceleration of interest resulting from Mrs. Wilson surrendering the moiety of her life interest would be minimal, and there would be no saving of estate duty. All that would happen in regard to such an infant would be that the vesting of his interest would be postponed from age twenty-one to age thirty, and the only

---

(20) [1835-42] All E.R. Rep. 58; (1841), 4 Beav. 115.
(21) [1963] 3 All E.R. 759; [1964] Ch. 158.

possible advantage in that would be the non-financial moral or social advantage   A
to which I have just referred. In support of this contention he referred me to the
decision of STAMP, J., in *Re Cohen's Settlement Trusts, Eliot-Cohen* v. *Cohen* (22).
There, the scheme originally proposed was not approved by the court because there
was a possibility of there being a beneficiary who would get no advantage
whatsoever from the proposed arrangement;   it would merely be to his
detriment.   B

Counsel for the plaintiff, however, points out that there is an essential distinction between that case and this; for there, whatever the surrounding circumstances, the unborn person contemplated could not benefit from the arrangement.
In the present case, he says, all that counsel for the trustees has done is to put
forward the case of an infant who might be born next year; and it would be a
result of the surrounding circumstances, and not of the time of birth or the   C
characteristics of the infant, that that infant might derive no benefit from the
arrangement proposed. Counsel for the plaintiff referred me to *Re Cohen's Will
Trusts, Re Cohen's Settlement Trusts* (23), where DANCKWERTS, J., held that in
exercising the jurisdiction under the Act of 1958 the court must, on behalf of
those persons for whom it was approving the arrangement, take the sort of risk
which an adult would be prepared to take. Accordingly, says counsel for the plain- D
tiff, counsel for the trustees' special infant to be born next year was in the position
that although there was the chance that its mother would die immediately afterwards, there was also the alternative chance that its mother would survive his birth
for a substantial period of time.   In the latter event, which was the more probable,
the advantages of the arrangement would accrue to the infant.   In short, he
distinguished the decision of STAMP, J., in *Re Cohen's Settlement Trusts* (22) on E
the footing that that was the case of an unborn person whose prospects were
hopeless, whatever the events, whereas in the present case the hypothetical unborn
person has the normal prospects of events occurring which will either improve
or not improve his position. Such an unborn person falls, he says, into the category
of unborn persons on whose behalf the court should be prepared to take a risk if
the arrangement appears on the whole to be for their benefit.   F

It seems to me that this is a proper distinction to make, and I accept it.
Accordingly, I hold that the arrangement is for the benefit of the classes of
persons specified in s. 1 (1) of the Act of 1958, and I approve it.

Order accordingly.

Solicitors: *Charles Caplin & Co.* (for all parties).   G

[*Reported by* R. W. FARRIN, ESQ., *Barrister-at-Law.*]

H

I

---

(22) [1965] 3 All E.R. 139.
(23) [1959] 3 All E.R. 523.

A

NOTE.

ADAIR v. GENERAL MOTORS, LTD.

[QUEEN'S BENCH DIVISION (Phillimore, J.), December 7, 8, 1967.]

B *Damages—Personal injury—Amount of damages—Asthma—Plaintiff capable of working though unfit for heavy work ever again.*

[As to damages for personal injury, see 11 HALSBURY'S LAWS (3rd Edn.) 255, 256, para. 427; and for cases on the subject, see 17 DIGEST (Repl.) 101, 164, 165.

C   For the Factories Act, 1961, s. 4, s. 29 (1) and s. 30 (3), see 41 HALSBURY'S STATUTES (2nd Edn.) 248, 272, 274.]

Action.

This was an action commenced by writ issued on Mar. 17, 1966, by David Henry Adair against General Motors, Ltd., claiming damages for personal injuries, the causes of action pleaded being negligence or breach of statutory

D duty under s. 4, s. 29 (1) and s. 30 (3) of the Factories Act, 1961. At all material times the plaintiff was employed as a driver and labourer by the defendants at Stag Lane, Kingsbury, London, N.W.9, where they were engaged in the manufacture of refrigerators. Part of the manufacturing process involved the use of a foam plant where the defendants mixed resin with tolylene diisocyanate (hereinafter referred to as " T.D.I.") to produce an insulating material. T.D.I. was

E a dangerous substance, giving off noxious fumes which could affect the eyes or respiratory organs, and the defendants were aware of this and of the necessity for anyone dealing with the substance to wear a mask. On Oct. 6, 1964, the plaintiff was instructed by his foreman to clean out the foam plant as the result of a spillage. He was provided with a paint scraper, and on instruction entered the plant wearing his ordinary working clothes. After the plaintiff had been

F working for about twenty to twenty-five minutes without protection the foreman returned, provided the plaintiff with a very old ill-fitting mask, and told him that he should wear a mask; the plaintiff then continued working for nearly an hour. About two days later the plaintiff began coughing and suffering from tightness of the chest and breathlessness. In January, 1965, the plaintiff was sent to hospital, where his condition was diagnosed as asthma, the result of exposure

G to T.D.I. By the middle of March, 1965, he was able to return to work where he was employed by the defendants on lighter duties. At the trial the defendants admitted liability to the plaintiff. HIS LORDSHIP found that the plaintiff's condition had not completely improved and that he still suffered from the effect of exposure to the noxious fumes. The plaintiff had had, throughout 1965 a good deal of time off due to asthma and bronchitis; but since 1965 he had

H not lost much time although urged by his doctor to take more. He was not fit for heavy work and never would be, and he was subject to a good deal of discomfort, particularly at night, though not every night; his condition was likely to improve a little, but would probably deteriorate again when he became older; he was unable to earn the hour's overtime pay and "grade money" which he had previously earned, and which amounted to £2 per week;

I he was, however, still earning £23 gross weekly, and he was not likely to be dismissed, but he would be at a substantial discount in the labour market if he did lose his job.

Hugh Griffiths, Q.C., and *C. Fawcett* for the plaintiff.
A. R. A. Beldam for the defendants.

     PHILLIMORE, J., after stating the facts and considering the medical evidence, continued: The liability for this disease from which the plaintiff now suffers is no longer disputed, and all that I have to do is to assess the proper

compensation. This man, who is now forty, was undoubtedly a very fit man at A
the time of this incident. He had been something of an athlete, in the sense
that he played a lot of football and basketball, and was a good swimmer and a
good boxer; although I think, by 1964, his chief recreation was football at the
week-ends. There is no doubt, however, that he was a very fit man, and there
was no reason to anticipate that he would have suffered from bronchitis or
asthma unless, perhaps, as a result of smoking, because he did smoke about B
twenty-five cigarettes a day.

Now he has this breathlessness: he is handicapped in his ordinary life: he
cannot play football: when it comes to decorating his home he has to have
fairly frequent rests: and he has this trouble at night and in the morning, and
that is something which, in possibly a slightly increased degree, he is always
going to suffer. Of course, one has to bear in mind the possibility that he C
might, as he got older, have got bronchitis or asthma. On the other hand, he
might not have done so.

I have got to compensate him for all that he has suffered and will suffer;
I have to compensate him for his loss of wages at the rate of £2 a week net, bearing
in mind that some deduction must be made for the receipt of a lump sum. There
is also a small amount of £188 3s. 11d., agreed special damages. D

I have come to the conclusion that the proper figure for general damage in
this case is £4,000, to which I add the special damage figure of £188 3s. 11d.

Judgment for the plaintiff.

Solicitors: *W. H. Thomson* (for the plaintiff); *E. P. Rugg & Co.* (for the
defendants).
E
[*Reported by* BRIAN POCOCK, ESQ., *Barrister-at-Law.*]

Re SEAFORD (*deceased*). SEAFORD *v.* SEIFERT.
F
[COURT OF APPEAL, CIVIL DIVISION (Willmer, Davies and Russell, L.JJ.), October
27, 30, 31, November 1, 2, 24, 1967.]

Divorce—Decree absolute—Notice of application to make decree nisi absolute—
Filing of notice by registrar on day of receipt—Death of respondent spouse
on day when notice received by registrar but before its receipt—Whether decree
could be made absolute—Matrimonial Causes Rules, 1957 (S.I. 1957 No. G
619), r. 40 (2).

Time—Judicial acts—Relation back to earliest moment of day on which done—
Divorce proceedings—Notice of application to make decree nisi absolute
received by registrar on same day as, but after, respondent spouse's death—
Purported filing of notice on that day—Whether doctrine of relation back had
application to give effect to decree absolute as from the earliest moment of the H
day on which notice was filed.

In March, 1965, a wife obtained a decree nisi of divorce on the ground
of her husband's cruelty, and the husband's appeal was dismissed in June of
the same year. At 11.30 a.m. on July 6, 1965, the husband was found dead
in bed, and medical evidence established that he could not have died later
than 4 a.m. on July 6, but it was impossible to say whether death occurred
before the end of July 5, 1965. At 8.30 a.m. on July 6, 1965, the district
registry received a notice of application for the decree nisi to be made
absolute, which had been posted by the wife's solicitors on the previous
afternoon; this constituted lodgment of the notice for the purposes of
r. 40 (2) of the Matrimonial Causes Rules, 1957, which provided that on the
filing of such a notice the decree nisi should become absolute. At 10 a.m.
the district registrar filed the notice of application and endorsed the court
minutes with a note that the decree had been made absolute at that time.

A   In proceedings by the wife for grant of letters of administration to the
deceased husband's estate as his lawful widow,

Held: no decree could be made absolute before a notice of application had
been lodged and, as in the present case the husband had died before the
lodgment of the notice of application, with the consequence that by then
the substratum of the divorce suit had been destroyed, the lodgment of the

B   notice was a nullity and no decree could thereafter be made absolute,
the doctrine of the relation back of a judicial act to the earliest moment of the
day on which it was made being inapplicable in the circumstances; accordingly the plaintiff, being wife of the husband at his death, was entitled to
letters of administration to his estate (see p. 488, letter I, p. 490, letters
D, E and G, and p. 491, letters A and F, post).

C   *Stanhope* v. *Stanhope* ((1886), 11 P.D. 103) applied.

Kruhlak v. *Kruhlak* (*No. 2*) ([1958] 2 All E.R. 294) doubted.

Decision of CAIRNS, J. ([1967] 2 All E.R. 458) reversed.

[As to an innocent spouse's application to make absolute a decree nisi, see
12 HALSBURY'S LAWS (3rd Edn.) 406, 407, para. 902; and for cases on the

D   subject, see 27 DIGEST (Repl.) 592, *5541*; 689, *6594*.

As to the relation back of judicial acts, see 37 HALSBURY'S LAWS (3rd Edn.)
102, para. 180; and for cases on the subject, see 45 DIGEST (Repl.) 271, 272,
404-412.

For the Matrimonial Causes Rules, 1957, r. 40, see 10 HALSBURY'S STATUTORY
INSTRUMENTS (Second Re-Issue) 250.]

E
Cases referred to:

Chick v. *Smith*, (1840), 8 Dowl. 337; 45 Digest (Repl.) 270, *392*.

Clarke v. *Bradlaugh*, [1881-85] All E.R. Rep. 1002; (1881), 8 Q.B.D. 63;
51 L.J.Q.B. 1; 46 L.T. 49; 46 J.P. 278; 45 Digest (Repl.) 272, *411*.

Edwards v. *Reginam*, (1854), 9 Exch. 628; 23 L.J.Ex. 165; 23 L.T.O.S. 39;

F   156 E.R. 268; 45 Digest (Repl.) 271, *403*.

Harvey v. *Lovekin* (*otherwise Harvey*), (1884), 10 P.D. 122; 54 L.J.P. 1; 27
Digest (Repl.) 512, *4542*.

Kruhlak v. *Kruhlak* (*No. 2*), [1958] 2 All E.R. 294; [1958] 1 W.L.R. 606;
122 J.P. 360; 45 Digest (Repl.) 272, *409*.

Lilley v. *Lilley*, [1959] 3 All E.R. 283; [1960] P. 158; [1959] 3 W.L.R. 306;

G   123 J.P. 525; Digest (Cont. Vol. A) 667, *619ba*.

Lyttleton v. *Cross*, (1824), 3 B. & C. 317; 3 L.J.O.S.K.B. 2; 107 E.R. 751;
23 Digest (Repl.) 369, *4390*.

North, Re, Ex p. Hasluck, [1895] 2 Q.B. 264; 64 L.J.Q.B. 694; 72 L.T. 854;
59 J.P. 724; 45 Digest (Repl.) 252, *197*.

Porchester (*Lord*) v. *Petrie*, (1783), 3 Doug. K.B. 261; 99 E.R. 644; 45 Digest

H   (Repl.) 271, *404*.

Stanhope v. *Stanhope*, (1886), 11 P.D. 103; 55 L.J.P. 36; 54 L.T. 906; 50 J.P.
276; 27 Digest (Repl.) 535, *4818*.

Swann v. *Broome*, (1764), 3 Burr. 1595; 97 E.R. 999; *affd.* H.L., sub nom.
Broome v. *Swan*, (1766), 6 Bro. Parl. Cas. 333; 2 E.R. 1115; 45 Digest
(Repl.) 247, *149*.

I
Tabernacle Permanent Building Society v. *Knight*, [1892] A.C. 298; 62 L.J.Q.B.
50; 67 L.T. 483; 45 Digest (Repl.) 271, *399*.

Warren, Re, Wheeler v. *Mills*, [1938] 2 All E.R. 331; [1938] Ch. 725; 107
L.J.Ch. 409; 159 L.T. 17; 45 Digest (Repl.) 272, *412*.

Whitaker v. *Wisbey*, (1852), 12 C.B. 44; 21 L.J.C.P. 116; 19 L.T.O.S. 156;
16 J.P. 344; 45 Digest (Repl.) 237, *71*.

Wright v. *Mills*, [1843-60] All E.R. Rep. 842; (1859), 4 H. & N. 488; 28
L.J.Ex. 223; 33 L.T.O.S. 152; 157 E.R. 931; 45 Digest (Repl.) 272,
408.

Appeal.   A

The plaintiff appealed against a decree of CAIRNS, J., made on Mar. 20, 1967, and reported [1967] 2 All E.R. 458; whereby he pronounced that the defendant, as the lawful mother of the deceased John Seaford, was the only person entitled to the estate of the deceased and was entitled to a grant of letters of administration of his estate.   The plaintiff sought an order that the decree should be discharged, and that for it should be substituted a decree that the plaintiff was   B the lawful widow of the deceased, and entitled as such to the estate of the deceased and to grant of letters of administration of the estate.   The grounds of appeal were as follows: (i) That the judge was wrong in holding that the onus was on the plaintiff to show that her marriage to the deceased had not been dissolved before the death of the deceased.   (ii) That, if the judge had held, as he ought to have done, that the onus was on the defendant to show that the plaintiff's   C marriage to the deceased had been dissolved, that onus on the facts found by the judge would not have been discharged, and the plaintiff would therefore have been entitled to the relief prayed.   (iii) That, even if the onus of proof was on the plaintiff, the judge ought to have held that she had discharged that onus. (iv) That the judge ought to have held that he was entitled to take note of the actual time, as recorded in the court minutes of the divorce proceedings, when the   D notice of application for decree absolute, referred to in the amended statement of claim in the current proceedings was filed in the Bournemouth district registry and to treat the notice as having been filed at that time.   (v) That in holding that he was not so entitled, the judge was wrong in applying the alleged rule that a judicial act is deemed to relate back to the earliest possible moment of the day on which it was done.   (vi) (a) That that rule, in so far as it was a   E rule of procedure, was not applicable when the court was exercising its probate jurisdiction;   (b) that it was not applicable to a divorce decree, or at any rate not to a decree made under r. 40 of the Matrimonial Causes Rules, 1957;   (c) that the rule was not applicable where the act alleged to be a judicial act was done without jurisdiction, and (d) that it was not applicable where the time of the act appeared from the record.   (vii) That in so far as the judge was obliged to   F hold as he did by the decision of the Divisional Court in *Kruhlak* v. *Kruhlak* (*No. 2*)* that case was wrongly decided and ought to be overruled.   (viii) That the judge ought in any event to have held that he was entitled to take note of the actual time, as proved by the admissions on the part of the defendant, when the notice of application was lodged in the registry and to treat the notice as having been lodged at that time.   (ix) That, if the judge had taken note of the actual   G times either of lodging or of filing the notice of application, it would have been apparent, having regard to the facts found by the judge as to the time of the deceased's death, that both the lodging and the filing were done after the death. (x) That the judge ought to have held on those facts that both the lodging and the filing were done without jurisdiction and were of no effect.   (xi) That the judge ought to have held that, whether or not the lodging and filing being done   H after the death were of any effect, the plaintiff was at the actual time of the death the surviving spouse of the deceased for the purposes of the law relating to the grant of letters of administration of and to the distribution of the estate of an intestate.   (xii) That the plaintiff was, therefore, the widow of the deceased and was entitled as such to the relief prayed.

D. J. M. Campion for the plaintiff.
J. C. Mortimer, Q.C., and *Dawn Freedman* for the defendant.

                                                                          Cur adv. vult.

Nov. 24.   The following judgments were read.

WILLMER, L.J.: This is an appeal against a judgment given by CAIRNS, J. (1) on Mar. 20, 1967, whereby he dismissed the plaintiff's claim for a grant

---

* [1958] 2 All E.R. 294.
(1) [1967] 2 All E.R. 458; [1967] P. 325.

A of letters of administration of the estate of her former husband. The claim
was resisted by the mother of the deceased, who contended that the plaintiff's
marriage to the deceased had been dissolved before he died, and who herself
claimed a grant as his next-of-kin and the only person entitled to his estate.
It is common ground that the deceased died intestate.

B The relevant facts, so far as they are known, can be shortly stated. The
plaintiff was married to the deceased on Nov. 23, 1959. On Mar. 3, 1965, the
plaintiff obtained a decree nisi of divorce on the ground of the deceased's cruelty.
The deceased appealed, but his appeal was dismissed on June 30, 1965. About
11.30 a.m. on July 6, 1965, the deceased was found dead in bed, having apparently
died as a result of an overdose of sleeping tablets. He had last been seen alive
about 9 p.m. on July 5. It was not possible to establish at what time the deceased
C died, but medical evidence, which the judge accepted (2), satisfied him that the
time of death could not be later than 4 a.m. on July 6. Whether or not death
occurred before midnight it was impossible to say. In the meantime the plaintiff's solicitors had on the afternoon of July 5 posted to the district registry a
notice of application for the decree to be made absolute. This was delivered
at the district registry at 8.30 a.m. on July 6. At 10 a.m. on that day the
D district registrar filed the notice of application and endorsed the court minutes
with a note that the decree had been made absolute at that time. In doing so
he followed the practice laid down in a registrar's circular issued by the principal
registry on Apr. 4, 1949.

Rule 40 (1) of the Matrimonial Causes Rules, 1957 (3), provides that an application by a spouse to make absolute a decree nisi pronounced in his favour shall
E be made by lodging in the registry where the cause is proceeding a notice of
application in the prescribed form, and that, if the registrar is satisfied, after
searching the court minutes, that the application is in order, the notice shall be
filed. Rule 40 (2) provides that, on the filing of the notice, the decree nisi shall
become absolute. It is accepted that in the present case the notice of application
was " lodged " when it was delivered at the district registry at 8.30 a.m. on
July 6.

It is plain that on the judge's finding the deceased was already dead at the
time when the district registrar purported to make the decree absolute by filing
the notice of application. The judge, however, held (4) that the making of the
decree absolute, being a judicial act, related back to the earliest moment of the
day on which it was made, i.e., immediately after midnight of July 5/6. He
ruled that the burden of proof was on the plaintiff to prove that the deceased
was already dead before this moment of time, and that she had failed to discharge
that burden. This ruling has not been challenged on appeal. The case must
accordingly be considered on the basis that the deceased was not proved not
to have been alive during some period on July 6.

We have had the benefit, as did the judge, of listening to an interesting and
learned argument, in the course of which the origin and development of the
doctrine of relation back has been traced for us, and we have had cited to us a
number of decisions of considerable antiquity, most of which are referred to in
the judgment of the judge (5). In its original form, the doctrine, which was
established by the old courts of common law, was that a judicial act related back
to the first day of the term; see 2 TIDD'S PRACTICE (1828), p. 935. In 1834,
however, by reg. 3 of what are described as the " Hilary Rules ", made by the
judges in the exercise of their rule-making powers, it was provided that:

" All judgments, whether interlocutory or final, shall be entered of record
of the day of the month and year, whether in term or vacation, when signed,
and shall not have relation to any other day: Provided that it shall be

---

(2) [1967] 2 All E.R. at p. 460; [1967] P. at p. 330.
(3) S.I. 1957 No. 619.
(4) [1967] 2 All E.R. at pp. 460, 461; [1967] P. at p. 330.
(5) [1967] 2 All E.R. 458; [1967] P. 325.

competent for the court, or a judge, to order a judgment to be entered
nunc pro tunc ";

see TIDD'S NEW PRACTICE (1837) p. 548. Since then the rule has been that a
judgment relates back only to the earliest moment of the day on which it is
entered. The rule has been stated to be a rule of law; see *Edwards* v. *Reginam*
(6) and *Wright* v. *Mills* (7). In the former case it was said by COLERIDGE, J. (8):

> " The doctrine that judicial acts are to be taken always to date from
> the earliest minute of the day in which they are done, stands upon ancient
> and clear authority."

Later he said (9):

> ". . . although the court will inquire at what time a party does an act, as
> filing a bill, or delivering his declaration, and for that purpose will take
> notice of the usual hours for sitting, it is otherwise with regard to a judicial
> proceeding."

It is plain, however, that the rule of relation back was not always regarded with
favour by the judges who had to apply it. In *Wright* v. *Mills* (7) the judge
of first instance refused to apply the rule, but followed an earlier decision in
Chick v. *Smith* (10), in which it had been held that the court would take notice
of a fraction of a day where a fieri facias had issued after the death of the defendant, but on the same day. On appeal, however, it was held that this was
wrong, and that the court was bound by the authority of *Edwards* v. *Reginam* (6)
to apply the rule of relation back, even though it was known that the defendant
had in fact died before the time when the judgment was entered. POLLOCK, C.B.,
referring to *Chick* v. *Smith* (10), said (11):

> " We consider that case to be more in accordance with the rules of common
> sense than the rule I have stated relative to judgments being supposed to be
> signed at the earliest hour of the day when they are signed; but although
> it is exceedingly desirable that all decisions of the courts should, as far
> as possible, be in accordance with the decisions of common sense, it is
> impossible to overrule the established practice, which is, indeed the law of
> the land and the right of the suitors."

In *Clarke* v. *Bradlaugh* (12) the existence of the rule of relation back was recognised by this court, but two members of the court expressed the view that the
rule was not to be regarded as of universal application; see per LORD COLERIDGE,
C.J. (13), and BAGGALLAY, L.J. (14). Indeed, from the earliest times it appears
that the rule was hedged about with exceptions, three of which have been relied
on in argument in the present case. Thus: (i) It has been held that the rule
would not be applied where the precise time of signing a judgment, or of doing any
other act of record was made material by statute; *Lord Porchester* v. *Petrie* (15),
per LORD MANSFIELD. (ii) The rule would not be applied where it appeared on
the face of the record that the judgment could not relate back to the first day
of the term, again the same case, and see also *Swann* v. *Broome* (16), per LORD
MANSFIELD. (iii) A third exception was said to arise where it could be shown
that the application of the rule would result in an injustice; see *Lord Porchester*
v. *Petrie* (17); also *Lyttleton* v. *Cross* (18); *Whitaker* v. *Wisbey* (19). In *Lyttleton*
v. *Cross* (20) BAYLEY, J., said:

---

(6) (1854), 9 Exch. 628.   (7) [1843-60] All E.R. Rep. 842; (1859), 4 H. & N. 488.
(8) (1854), 9 Exch. at p. 631.   (9) (1854), 9 Exch. at p. 632.
(10) (1840), 8 Dowl. 337.
(11) (1859), 4 H. & N. at pp. 492, 493; [1843-60] All E.R. Rep. at p. 843.
(12) [1881-85] All E.R. Rep. 1002; (1881), 8 Q.B.D. 63.
(13) [1881-85] All E.R. Rep. at p. 1004; (1881), 8 Q.B.D. at p. 66.
(14) [1881-85] All E.R. Rep. at p. 1005; (1881), 8 Q.B.D. at p. 67.
(15) (1783), 3 Doug. K.B. 261 at p. 274.   (16) (1764), 3 Burr. 1595.
(17) (1783), 3 Doug. K.B. at p. 278.   (18) (1824), 3 B. & C. 317.
(19) (1852), 21 L.J.C.P. 116.   (20) (1824), 3 B. & C. at pp. 325.

" Wherever, therefore, a fiction of law works injustice, and the facts which by fiction are supposed to exist are inconsistent with the real facts, a court of law ought to look at the real facts,"

and HOLROYD, J., said (21):

". . . in all cases where for the purposes of justice it becomes necessary that the true time when any legal proceedings took place should be ascertained, the fiction of law is not to prevail against the fact."

It has been argued that all three of these exceptions apply in the circumstances of the present case. Thus: (i) It is said that by the combined effect of r. 21 of the Non-contentious Probate Rules, 1954 (22) and s. 46 of the Administration of Estates Act, 1925, the plaintiff is entitled to a grant of administration if she is a surviving spouse. It is, therefore, necessary in pursuance of statute to ascertain the precise time of the purported decree absolute in order to determine whether she was still a spouse at the moment when the deceased died. (ii) It is said that to relate the purported decree absolute back to the first moment of the day would be to contradict what appears on the face of the record, i.e., that the notice was in fact filed only at 10 a.m. (iii) It is said that the rule of relation back would result in an injustice, because at the moment of the deceased's death the plaintiff acquired a vested right as his surviving spouse, and it would be wrong to divest her of this right by the application of any fiction of law.

I do not find it necessary to express any concluded view on the question whether the present case should properly be regarded as falling within any of these exceptions to the rule of relation back. For I have come to the conclusion on other grounds (to which I will presently refer) that the rule of relation back ought not to be applied at all in relation to the circumstances of the present case. One question much canvassed before us has been whether the doctrine of relation back (which in its origin was a purely common law doctrine) has ever been applicable in proceedings before the High Court in its divorce jurisdiction. So far as the authorities cited to us go, there have been only two cases where the doctrine has been applied in any but common law proceedings. One is *Re Warren, Wheeler* v. *Mills* (23) where it was held obiter by a Divisional Court to be applicable to bankruptcy proceedings. The other is *Kruhlak* v. *Kruhlak* (*No. 2*) (24) where it was held by a Divisional Court of the Queen's Bench Division in affiliation proceedings to be applicable in relation to the time of making absolute a decree of divorce. Neither of these decisions is binding on us, but it has to be recognised that *Kruhlak's* case (24) is of high persuasive authority, since it did relate to the very matter in question here, viz., the time of making absolute a decree of divorce. It is, of course, open to us to say that that case is distinguishable, seeing that there was there no question of the death of the husband to whom the decree related. For reasons, however, which will appear hereafter, I think that there is room for doubt whether *Kruhlak* v. *Kruhlak* (*No. 2*) (24) was rightly decided.

No authority has been cited to us to show that the doctrine of relation back was ever applied by the old ecclesiastical courts in the exercise of their matrimonial jurisdiction. The remedy of divorce was introduced only in 1857, when the court for divorce and matrimonial causes was set up and the jurisdiction formerly exercised by the ecclesiastical courts was transferred to it. Moreover, it was only in 1860, pursuant to the Matrimonial Causes Act of that year, that the procedure of decree nisi followed by decree absolute was introduced. No case can be found in which the doctrine of relation back was applied in matrimonial proceedings between 1857 and the passing of the Supreme Court of Judicature Act, 1873. It has been argued, however, that as a result of that

(21) (1824), 3 B. & C. at pp. 329, 330.
(22) S.I. 1954 No. 796.
(23) [1938] 2 All E.R. 331; [1938] Ch. 725.
(24) [1958] 2 All E.R. 294.

Act, particularly s. 16 and s. 23 thereof, any judge of the High Court, exercising
any kind of jurisdiction, has been clothed with power to apply any rule which
before the Act could have been applied in any proceedings before any of the
courts whose jurisdiction was transferred to the High Court. Some support
for that view is to be derived from the decision of this court in *Harvey* v. *Lovekin*
(*otherwise Harvey*) (25) where it was held that the High Court, in the exercise
of its matrimonial jurisdiction, had acquired the power previously exercised by
the courts of common law and by the Court of Chancery to administer
interrogatories. In that case SIR BALIOL BRETT, M.R., went so far as to
say (26):

> " Pursuant to these enactments, where there is no provision in the statutes,
> or where there are no rules to the contrary, every Division of the High
> Court may exercise the same procedure as was exercised by any of the
> courts, whether of common law or of equity, which were absorbed into the
> High Court."

I certainly feel the force of this submission: but in spite of it I remain uncon-
vinced that the common law doctrine of relation back, already viewed with
disfavour by the common law judges at the time when the remedy of divorce
was first introduced, was as a result of the Supreme Court of Judicature Act,
1873, made applicable, as it were by a side wind, in matrimonial proceedings
before the newly constituted High Court. The doctrine, after all, is a highly
artificial doctrine, resting as it does on a legal fiction; and I think it is fair to
ask the question why, in reason, it should be regarded as applicable to what was
then a new jurisdiction, more particularly in a case like the present where all the
essential facts are known.

In this connexion it is not inapt to quote some words of LORD ESHER, M.R.,
spoken, it is true, in a slightly different context, but highly relevant to the
question of time. In *Re North, Ex p. Hasluck* (27), he said:

> " No general rule exists for the computation of time either under the
> Bankruptcy Act or any other statute, or, indeed, where time is mentioned
> in a contract, and the rational mode of computation is to have regard in
> each case to the purpose for which the computation is to be made. . . . A
> great deal of difficulty has been caused in the administration of the law, . . .
> by decisions in which technical rules have been formulated which were not
> true—that is, were not in accordance with the facts of the case. To say that
> by the common law a part of a day is the whole of a day is to say something
> which is contrary to the truth; it is a technical rule which was imposed upon
> the law with the result of bringing the law into disrepute. It is immaterial
> whether these older decisions were right in the particular cases; if they, or
> any of them, laid down any general rule as to the mode of computing time,
> that rule has been departed from in recent times, and no longer exists."

It seems to me that where, as here, we are dealing with the question at what
moment of time a marriage is to be regarded as having been dissolved, it is well
to remember the purpose for which the computation is to be made, and that we
should not be bound by any technical rule to find a fictional answer where the
actual facts are known.

In my judgment this case falls to be decided on the short ground that at the
moment of time when the district registrar purported to make the decree absolute,
i.e., 10 a.m. on July 6, he had no jurisdiction to do any such thing, for at that
moment the husband was already dead. The death of the husband not only
caused the suit to abate; it destroyed the cause of action, and there was no
longer any subject-matter to which the purported decree absolute could apply.
In *Stanhope* v. *Stanhope* (28), it was held that, where one of the parties to a

---

(25) (1884), 10 P.D. 122.   (26) (1884), 10 P.D. at p. 128.
(27) [1895] 2 Q.B. 264 at pp. 269, 270.   (28) (1886), 11 P.D. 103.

marriage had died after the decree nisi, it was not competent for the legal personal representative of that party to revive the suit for the purpose of applying to make the decree absolute. For the court has jurisdiction only to dissolve a marriage, and not to declare that the marriage was dissolved at some earlier time. BOWEN, L.J., said (29):

"A man can no more be divorced after his death than he can after his death be married or sentenced to death. Marriage is a union of husband and wife for their joint lives unless it be dissolved sooner, and the court cannot dissolve a union which has already been determined."

Later he said (30):

"It is contrary to the idea of a divorce that it should be sought after the death of one of the parties."

FRY, L.J., added the pungent observation that (31) ". . . no power can dissolve a marriage which has been already dissolved by the act of God". Having regard to this decision, it appears to me that the act of the district registrar in purporting to make the decree absolute at 10 a.m. on July 6 was a complete nullity in the light of the fact, now known, that the husband was then already dead. If it was a nullity, it cannot be re-vitalised by any fiction of law, so as to make it effective from some earlier moment of time when, if it had then been made, it would have been effective.

I think that support for the view that the district registrar had no jurisdiction to act at the time when he purported to act is to be found in the observations of LORD WATSON in *Tabernacle Permanent Building Society* v. *Knight* (32). One of the questions raised in that case was whether the court had jurisdiction to make an order nisi calling on arbitrators to show cause why they should not be required to state a special case for the opinion of the court when on the same day, but without notice of the order nisi, the arbitrators in fact made and signed their award. The case was in the event determined on the facts, it being found that the order nisi was in fact made before the arbitrators had made and signed their award. The point was argued, however, that the order nisi, being a judicial act, must be supposed to have been made at the earliest possible moment of the day, and therefore must in any event be treated as prior to the making of the award. LORD WATSON dealt with that argument as follows (33):

"If there had been any evidence to show that an award was published on the same day as the order but before the latter was applied for, I should not, as at present advised, have been prepared to hold that this case was governed by the decision of the Court of Exchequer in *Wright* v. *Mills* (34). There the court had undoubted jurisdiction, and was moreover seized of the case at the time when, fictione juris, its order was held to have been made. Here the court had no process before it until the initial order was applied for; and it had no jurisdiction to grant the order if at the time of the application there was a completed award."

In my judgment this reasoning can be applied to the circumstances of the present case. It is true that at the time of the purported decree absolute the court was seized of the case, in the sense that the suit as a whole was before it; but there was no jurisdiction to make the decree absolute unless and until the notice of application was lodged. The judge (35) considered, but rejected this reasoning, holding that the notice of application and the making of the decree absolute

---

(29) (1886), 11 P.D. at p. 108.
(30) (1886), 11 P.D. at p. 110.
(31) (1886), 11 P.D. at p. 111.
(32) [1892] A.C. 298.
(33) [1892] A.C. at p. 304.
(34) [1843-60] All E.R. Rep. 842; (1859), 4 H. & N. 488.
(35) [1967] 2 All E.R. at pp. 466, 467; [1967] P. at p. 340.

together constituted a single judicial act. Otherwise, he thought (36) the doctrine of relation back could never be applied in any circumstances, since every
judicial act must be preceded by some form of application for it. In this I think
that the judge (37) fell into error, in that he failed to have regard to the special
and peculiar procedure laid down for making absolute a decree of divorce. The
decree can be made absolute only by filing the notice of application. It is *the*
notice of application which has to be filed. If there is no notice of application,
there can be no decree. It is, therefore, not only permissible but necessary to
look at the position as it was at the moment when the notice of application was
lodged, for, until the notice was lodged, there could be no jurisdiction to make the
decree absolute. Had the notice of application in this case been lodged on or
before July 5, it may be that the district registrar would have had jurisdiction
to file it and make the decree absolute at the time when he purported to do so,
and in that event it could well be said that the decree would relate back to the
earliest possible moment of the day of July 6. Here, however, the notice of
application was not in fact lodged until 8.30 a.m. on July 6, by which time, as
we now know, the deceased was already dead. The situation, therefore, was
that the decree could not be made absolute before 8.30 a.m. because up to that
time no notice of application had been lodged; and it could not be made absolute
at any time after 8.30 a.m. because by then the court no longer had jurisdiction
owing to the death of the deceased and the consequent destruction of the subject-
matter of the suit. Once the peculiar nature of the procedure for making
absolute a decree of divorce is appreciated, I can see no answer to this dilemma.

For these reasons I think that the judge came to a wrong conclusion when he
rejected the claim of the plaintiff for a grant of letters of administration. In my
judgment, on the facts found by the judge, the plaintiff succeeded in proving
that she was still the wife of the deceased at the time of his death. The subsequent purported decree absolute was in my view a nullity, and as such was
incapable of being related back to the first moment of the day. I would
accordingly allow the appeal and make an order for a grant to the plaintiff.

DAVIES, L.J.: The court has had the advantage in this case of hearing
the most learned and far-reaching arguments based on much diligent research
and fortified by the citation of many authorities, both ancient and modern.
These have been discussed and analysed in the judgment which WILLMER, L.J.,
has just delivered and with which I agree in its entirety. Essentially, however,
this case, in my view, falls to be decided on one short point, viz., that if a marriage
has been ended by the death of one of the parties, no application can be made
to the court to dissolve it and no decree of dissolution can be made (*Stanhope* v.
Stanhope (38)).

Whatever be the merits or demerits of the often criticised rule of relation back,
no case has been found, with the exception of *Kruhlak* v. *Kruhlak (No. 2)* (39),
in which it has been applied to the making of a decree absolute of divorce. *Kruhlak*
v. *Kruhlak (No. 2)* (39) is, of course, clearly distinguishable from the present
case. For there the notice of application had been lodged on the day previous
to that on which it was filed and the decree became absolute, both spouses were
alive at all material times and there was undoubted jurisdiction to make the
decree absolute. In any event, however, I should not be prepared to treat the
decision in *Kruhlak's* case (39) as authoritative. For the point appears not to
have been argued at all, and the appellant seems actually to have wished to lose
her appeal.

Even if the rule of relation back can apply to the making of a decree absolute,
however, it cannot possibly do so in the circumstances of the present case. For

---

(36) [1967] 2 All E.R. at p. 467; [1967] P. at pp. 340, 341.
(37) [1967] 2 All E.R. at p. 467; [1967] P. at p. 341.
(38) (1886), 11 P.D. 103.
(39) [1958] 2 All E.R. 294.

at the time when the notice of application was lodged, viz., 8.30 a.m., the husband was already dead. The whole substratum of the petition, viz., the marriage, had gone, and the notice was therefore a nullity. Consequently the act of the registrar in filing the notice at 10 a.m. was also a nullity and could have no effect whatsoever either at 10 a.m. or at the earliest moment of the day.

Cases such as *Wright* v. *Mills* (40) are in an entirely different field. For a judgment against a dead man will be effective against his estate. That fact is illustrated by R.S.C., Ord. 35, r. 9, which provides that

" Where a party to any action dies after the verdict or finding of the issues of fact and before judgment is given, the judgment may be given notwithstanding the death, . . ."

As was pointed out in the argument, manifest absurdities could result from the application of the rule of relation back to cases such as the present. Suppose the registrar actually had personal knowledge that the respondent, or indeed the petitioner, had died before the notice was lodged, how could it be said that he would have had jurisdiction to file the notice and so make absolute the decree dissolving the non-existent marriage? Presumptions and fictions, in my judgment, should have no effect when there is evidence as to the real facts; see the recent decision of this court in *Lilley* v. *Lilley* (41). As we now know, on the judge's findings (42), the real facts, my view of this case could be summarised by altering a well-known Latin phrase to " lex non permittit impossibilia ". I agree that the appeal succeeds.

RUSSELL, L.J.: I am content to decide this case on one short ground without discussing other grounds which have been advanced in favour of allowing the appeal. We have been referred to a number of authorities on the matter of this fiction of the law that a judicial act is performed at a particular time, when everyone knows that it was not then performed. None of these authorities decides that the fiction is applicable to a judicial act purported to be performed at a time when the court was entirely without jurisdiction to perform it, and which was therefore necessarily an absolute nullity. Without authority binding me to do so I should decline to import into the law of England the equation nullity plus fiction equals reality. At 10 a.m. when the judicial act was purported to be performed of filing the lodged application so as to determine the marriage by decree absolute, the marriage had ceased to exist, and the ability of the court to determine it was equally non-existent, whether the court knew or was ignorant of that situation. Whom God had put asunder no man could join together, even for the purpose of putting them asunder again. I too would allow the appeal.

Appeal allowed. Order below discharged and in substitution thereof decree that plaintiff was the lawful widow of deceased and entitled to letters of administration.

Solicitors: *Peacock & Goddard*, agents for *Luff, Raymond & Williams*, Wimborne Minster, Dorset (for the plaintiff); *Wilkinson, Kimbers & Staddon*, agents for *Humphries, Kirk & Miller*, Swanage (for the defendant).

[*Reported by* F. A. AMIES, ESQ., *Barrister-at-Law.*]

---

(40) [1843-60] All E.R. Rep. 842; (1859), 4 H. & N. 488.
(41) [1959] 3 All E.R. 283; [1960] P. 158.
(42) [1967] 2 All E.R. 458; [1967] P. 325.

Re DE LISLE'S WILL TRUSTS.

WHITE v. DE LISLE.

[CHANCERY DIVISION (Pennycuick, J.), December 5, 1967.]

Will—Devise—Valuation—Direction to executors to transfer land at " valuation agreed for probate "—Whether this meant valuation initially made of property to lead to grant of probate or value ultimately agreed with estate duty office for estate duty purposes.

By virtue of cl. 4 of the testatrix' will her nephew became entitled to have transferred to him by her executors certain real property " at the valuation agreed for probate . . .". The question arose whether the words " valuation agreed for probate " in cl. 4 meant (a) the valuation entered by the executors in the inland revenue affidavit and accepted by the probate registry for the purpose of obtaining a grant of probate of the will, namely, £4,750, or (b) the valuation ultimately agreed between the executors and the estate duty office for estate duty purposes, namely £6,000.

Held: on the true construction of cl. 4 the words therein " the valuation agreed for probate " meant the valuation agreed ultimately with the estate duty office, viz., £6,000 (see p. 496, letters C and D, post).

Re Eumorfopoulos ([1943] 2 All E.R. 719) distinguished.

[As to the meaning of some particular phrases used in wills, see 39 HALSBURY'S LAWS (3rd Edn.) 988, para. 1497.

As to the inland revenue affidavit leading to grant of probate, see 16 HALSBURY'S LAWS (3rd Edn.) 187, para. 315; as to the machinery of valuation for estate duty, see 15 ibid., p. 80, para. 167, and as to appeal, see p. 157, para. 325.]

Case referred to:

Eumorfopoulos, Re, Ralli v. *Eumorfopoulos*, [1943] 2 All E.R. 719; [1944] Ch. 133; 113 L.J.Ch. 30; 170 L.T. 21; 48 Digest (Repl.) 591, *5623.*

Adjourned Summons.

This was an application by originating summons amended on Oct. 31, 1967, by the plaintiff Noel Blanco White, D.S.O., M.C., for the determination of questions arising on the will of Flora Mary de Lisle, deceased (dated Sept. 16, 1963), with a codicil (dated May 16, 1965) and in the events which had happened. The questions were (a) whether the trustees were bound by cl. 4 of the will to transfer the premises known as No. 9, Denmark Avenue, Wimbledon, to the first defendant, William Godfray de Lisle, in satisfaction of the pecuniary legacy of £3,000 therein bequeathed to him without requiring him first to pay or account to them for a sum being the difference between £3,000 and the higher value of the premises agreed for probate; and (b) whether the valuation of the premises agreed for probate within the meaning of cl. 4 was either (i) the valuation entered by the executors in the inland revenue affidavit and accepted by the probate registry for the purpose of obtaining a grant of probate of the will, viz., £4,750, or (ii) the valuation ultimately agreed between the executors and the estate duty office for estate duty purposes, viz., £6,000, or (iii) some other, and if so, what, figure. The plaintiff and the first defendant were executors of the will and codicil. The second defendant was Godfray Michael Secretan de Lisle and both he and the first defendant were beneficially interested under the trusts of the will. The facts are set out in the judgment.

R. A. R. Evans for the plaintiff.

D. J. M. Campion for the first defendant.

E. F. R. Whitehead for the second defendant.

A　　**PENNYCUICK, J.**: The second question raised by this summons is in these terms:

" Whether the valuation of the said premises agreed for probate, within the meaning of cl. 4 [of the testator's will] is (i) the valuation entered by the executors in the inland revenue affidavit and accepted by the probate registry for the purpose of obtaining a grant of probate of the said will,

B　　namely, £4,750, or (ii) the valuation ultimately agreed between the executors and the estate duty office for estate duty purposes, namely, £6,000, or (iii) some other, and if so, what, figure."

No other figure was suggested in argument. I will read again the relevant provisions of cl. 4 of the will:

C　　" I bequeath to [the first defendant] the sum of £3,000, and I direct that should he express his desire in writing not later than two calendar months after my death my trustees shall transfer to him in part satisfaction of this my legacy my premises No. 9, Denmark Avenue, Wimbledon, at the valuation agreed for probate . . ."

D　　I decided on the first question on the summons, and in the events that have happened, that the valuation being, on any basis, more than £3,000 and the nephew Godfray, i.e., the first defendant, having exercised the option contained in cl. 4, he must pay for the property the excess over £3,000 of the value of the property. I mention that again in order to record that it is now accepted by counsel for the second defendant, Godfray Michael Secretan de Lisle, that the first defendant is entitled to have the property at whatever is the proper figure under the clause, less

E　　the sum of £3,000. In the events that have happened, counsel for the second defendant now concedes that it would not be right to assert that cl. 4 has wholly misfired and that the first defendant is only entitled to payment of £3,000. The question which I have now to determine is what is meant by the words in the will " valuation agreed for probate ". My first reaction to the words was

F　　that they plainly meant the value as agreed for estate duty purposes with the district valuer; but, after hearing argument on the matter from both counsel, I recognise that they require a much more careful analysis.

The facts with regard to the valuation of the property are set out fully in an affidavit sworn by the plaintiff, Noel Blanco White, who is one of the executors named in the will. Paragraph 3 of his affidavit reads as follows:—

G　　" (a) Immediately after the testatrix' death the executors instructed a firm of estate agents, surveyors and valuers, Messrs. Jackson Rose & Co., of 296A, King's Road, London, S.W.3, to value the said premises (which constituted the only real property owned by the testatrix) for the purposes of estate duty. They valued them at £4,750, as appears by their report dated Jan. 11, 1966, a copy of which is now produced and shown to me. As appears from the letter of Jan. 7, 1966, from the said valuers to me, this deponent, which is now produced and shown to me, the said valuers in putting forward the figure of £4,750, endeavoured to keep it on the low side and expected their valuation to be contested by the district valuer. (b) The executors swore the inland revenue affidavit (in Form A–6) on Feb. 7, 1966, and the said premises were valued therein at £4,750, it being stated in the said affidavit that estate duty was not to be paid on the said premises on the delivery of the said affidavit. (c) Later in February, 1966, the estate duty office assessed estate duty on the testatrix' personal estate which the executors paid prior to the grant of probate to them. No estate duty was assessed or paid on the said premises prior to the grant of probate, but the duty on the personal estate was provisionally assessed by the estate duty office by reference to the values shown in the said affidavit, including the said figure of £4,750. The inland revenue affidavit containing the said valuation of the premises at £4,750, was accepted by the principal probate registry

for the purpose of making a grant of probate to the executors on Mar. 3, 1966.
(d) On Mar. 14, 1966, the estate duty office called for an account of the
testatrix's real property and the executors swore an affidavit (in Form C–1)
as to this on Apr. 23, 1966, showing the value of the said premises as £4,750.
(e) On June 23, 1966, the estate duty office informed the executors that the
valuation office had valued the said premises at £6,500.   The executors
then instructed Messrs. Jackson Rose & Co., to negotiate with the district
valuer as they considered the valuation of the valuation office to be too high.
(f) On Sept. 8, 1966, agreement was reached between Messrs. Jackson Rose &
Co. (acting as agents for the executors) and the district valuer that the value
of the said premises at the testatrix' death on which estate duty should be
paid should be £6,000.   The executors have since paid the estate duty in
respect of the said premises valued at £6,000."

The rival contentions are these.   Counsel for the first defendant, contends that
the expression " valuation agreed for probate " means the value put on the
property by Messrs. Jackson Rose & Co. and accepted by the principal probate
registry for the purposes of making a grant of probate.   Counsel for the second
defendant contends, on the other hand, that the expression " valuation agreed
for probate " means the value ultimately agreed between the executors, acting
through their agents, Messrs. Jackson Rose & Co., and the district valuer.

Reference was made in argument to the decision of SIMONDS, J., in *Re Eumorfopoulos, Ralli* v. *Eumorfopoulos* (1).   In that case a testator who died in December,
1939, possessing a collection of works of art, plate and other valuable articles,
bequeathed by will to his wife such of the contents of his house as she might
select up to the value of £10,000, " taken at the probate valuation ".   The
contents of the house were valued as at the testator's death for the purposes of
the affidavit leading to probate at £9,783, and the widow selected the whole of
them.   Later, an application was made to the revenue authorities, under s. 40
of the Finance Act, 1930, for exemption of part of the contents from estate
duty, on the ground that they were of national, historic or artistic interest, and
exemption was granted as to works of art and other articles valued at £6,258.
In June and July, 1940, the widow sold the bulk of the contents, and, after deduction of expenses, they realised more than £20,000 in excess of the valuation made
for probate.   The revenue authorities claimed estate duty on the proceeds, and
by agreement duty was paid on the value of the net proceeds, less 33⅓ per cent.
The residuary legatees claimed that the widow was only entitled to select articles
to the value of £10,000 as realised at the sale.   It was held that " probate
valuation " meant the valuation made by valuers for the purposes of obtaining
a grant of probate, and, therefore, the widow's claim to retain all the articles,
whether exempted from duty or not, selected by her, succeeded.

The expression which the judge had there to construe was " taken at the
probate valuation ".   On the facts of that particular case, in my view, the judge
came to the only possible conclusion, because the greater part of the chattels
were entitled to exemption as objects of national, historic or artistic interest.
No question of any valuation other than the valuation for probate arose in
regard to the exempted articles.   The judgment was based in the first place
on this ground, but SIMONDS, J., continued (2), as follows:

" But in regard to these articles I think I should come to exactly the
same conclusion even if I did not have the assistance of the conjunction of
unexempted and exempted articles; for there, too, it appears to me that,
what the testator was doing was providing a convenient method as between
the several recipients of his bounty of deciding how the benefit given to the
widow should be measured.   He assumes . . . that a fair and proper valuation would be made, as it was made, by valuers who were called in.   It may

(1) [1943] 2 All E.R. 719; [1944] Ch. 133.
(2) [1943] 2 All E.R. at p. 721; [1944] Ch. at p. 137.

A   be there would be a contest upon that valuation or upon some particular items of it, for the purpose of duty, as between the executors and the revenue authorities; but, as a fair method of ascertaining the value as between the different beneficiaries under the will it is reasonable to assume that he would take the measure of the probate valuation in the sense of the valuation made by the expert valuers."

B   If the present will had contained the same expression, namely, " taken at the probate valuation " or words indistinguishable from those, I should without hesitation have followed what was said by SIMONDS, J. (3). The words used in the present will are, however, different in a vital respect. The testatrix uses the expression " valuation agreed for probate ". The word " agreed " does not occur in the expression used in *Re Eumorfopoulos* (3).

C   In order to determine what the testatrix meant by the expression " valuation agreed for probate " it is necessary to consider what are the steps which are normally taken in the ordinary course to obtain a grant of probate. In relation to land the normal procedure is as follows:—The executors first obtain a professional valuation, which, it is fair to say, is normally on the low side, as

D   appears in the present case from the plaintiff's affidavit. The executors then proceed to lodge with the estate duty office their inland revenue affidavit, which contains particulars as to the assets of the testator's estate and the value put on them by the executors. There is a duty on the executors under s. 8 (3) of the Finance Act, 1894, to specify to the best of their knowledge and belief in an appropriate account annexed to the inland revenue affidavit all property in

E   respect of which estate duty is payable on the death of the deceased. At that stage the estate duty office assesses the duty payable on the property. Apart from very exceptional cases the estate duty office makes its assessment on the basis of the figures in the inland revenue affidavit. It has to put a value on the land whether estate duty is paid on delivery of the affidavit or later, in order to determine the rate of estate duty on the entire estate. At that stage there

F   is no agreement between the estate duty office and the executors as to the proper value of the land for the purposes of duty.

The next stage is for the executors to apply for probate of the will. They make an affidavit setting out inter alia the value of the assets of the estate, and lodge it at the probate registry together with a copy of the inland revenue affidavit and a receipt for duty. Thereupon probate is granted, and, as appears from

G   the probate in the present case, it is certified that an inland revenue affidavit has been delivered showing the gross and net values of the estate, and it is further certified that, as appears by a receipt signed by an inland revenue officer, a specified sum has been paid on account of estate duty and interest on such duty. There is not at that stage or at any stage any agreement between the executors and the probate registry.

The last stage is for the executors or their agents to reach agreement with the district valuer as to the value to be placed on the land. In the vast majority of cases agreement is reached and where necessary an alteration is made in the charge of estate duty. In the case where the parties fail to agree there is an appeal to the Lands Tribunal and in the last resort the duty is payable on the value determined by the Lands Tribunal.

It will be seen from the foregoing account that there is nothing which could be described as an agreement until the final stage when there is an agreement between the executors and the district valuer. There is no agreement between the executors and their own estate agents, nor is there agreement between the executors and the estate duty office at the time the inland revenue affidavit is lodged, and never any agreement between the executors and the probate registry.

To return to the present case, counsel, for the first defendant, contends that

(3) [1943] 2 All E.R. at p. 721; [1944] Ch. at p. 137.

the expression " valuation agreed for probate " means the valuation made by   A
the executors' agents, Messrs. Jackson Rose & Co. and included in the inland
revenue affidavit which, in turn, is the basis used by the estate duty office and
probate registry.   That contention wholly fails to give effect to the vital word
" agreed ".   It is really impossible to treat what happened between the executors
and either the estate duty office or the probate registry as representing an
agreement.   B

Counsel for the second defendant contends that the " valuation agreed for
probate " means the valuation ultimately agreed with the district valuer.   That
construction gives proper effect to the word " agreed ".   It involves placing a
very loose construction on the words " for probate " because the agreement
with the district valuer takes place after probate has been granted.   Counsel
for the second defendant, however, says—and I agree with this—that the words   C
" for probate " can be read as meaning, in rather loose terms, " in connexion
with obtaining probate "; that is to say, there is a valuation agreed with the
district valuer representing the value which ought to have been stated in the
affidavit which has to be produced in order to obtain probate.

The expression which the testatrix used was an inapt one on either view, but
it seems to me that the construction put on it on behalf of the second defendant   D
does much less violence to it than does the construction put on it on behalf of
the first defendant.   I have come, in to the end, to the same conclusion as my
first impression.

Counsel for the first defendant has pointed out that under cl. 4 the first defendant must exercise his option within two calendar months of the death of the
testatrix by which time, in the ordinary course, the valuation of the property   E
will not have been agreed.   He says that one would not expect the testatrix
to have required the first defendant to make up his mind how to exercise the
option until he knew the amount of the valuation.   I do not think there is a
great deal in this point.   The testatrix contemplated that the valuation of the
property would be less than £3,000, so by exercising his option on that view the
first defendant could not, in any circumstances, have let himself in for paying a   F
larger sum for the property than £3,000.

For the reasons I have given, I propose to answer the second question in the
summons in accordance with the second alternative.

Declaration accordingly.

Solicitors: *Noel Blanco White* (for the plaintiff); *Peacock & Goddard* (for the   G
first defendant); *Coward, Chance & Co.* (for the second defendant).

[*Reported by* JENIFER SANDELL, *Barrister-at-Law.*]

A

SLIM AND OTHERS v. DAILY TELEGRAPH, LTD.
AND ANOTHER.

[COURT OF APPEAL, CIVIL DIVISION (Lord Denning, M.R., Diplock and Salmon, L.JJ.), November 27, 28, 29, 30, 1967; January 17, 1968.]

Libel—Fair comment—Defence available against personal imputation—Test is
B *whether an honest expression of genuine opinion.*

Libel—Innuendo—Natural and ordinary meaning complained of—Defamatory inferences from words in their natural and ordinary meaning pleaded— Effect of pleading particular inferences—Whether plaintiffs entitled to select particular imputations—Whether plaintiffs confined to particular inferences pleaded.

C   The second plaintiff, a company, used a narrow path by the river Thames in Hammersmith for access with cars to its factory. The public had a right of way over the path on foot, but the existence of a right of way over it with vehicles was not accepted locally. The local authority had put up a notice some years before saying " No cycling ". The town clerk, who signed the notice, was a solicitor; and, after he had retired in 1958, he
D became legal adviser to the company. The defendant newspaper published in 1964 two letters written by the second defendant about the danger of the path becoming a thoroughfare for vehicles. The first letter said, among other things, that the council's notice forbidding cycling had been removed; that if this made local residents a little cynical they must be forgiven, and that the notice was signed by the former town clerk, who was the same person as the present legal adviser to the company that claimed the right to
E drive lorries along the path. The first plaintiff alleged that the letter libelled him. The third plaintiff, chairman of the company, wrote a letter in reply, which was published, associating the company and himself with general sentiments expressed in correspondence, and denying that the company intended to use the path for the purposes of lorry access. The
F second defendant's second letter, which was the subject of a claim in libel by the company and the third plaintiff, pointed out that the reply did not deny an intention to use the path for cars as distinct from lorries and stated that the cars of the company's employees used the path; the letter said that the third defendant's protestations of injured innocence would be more convicing if his company were really acting in the spirit of his letter,
G and it asked how he could pretend to associate himself with the sentiments of those who wished to preserve the character of the way, when he countenanced such action. The company and the third plaintiff alleged that this letter libelled them. By their statement of claim the plaintiffs alleged defamatory inferences to be borne by the words contained in the letters in their natural and ordinary meaning (e.g., that the first plaintiff had behaved
I with professional impropriety and in a dishonourable manner, and that the plaintiff's wishes to improve riverside facilities and to extend the riverside walk were insincere and hypocritical); and the defendants pleaded fair comment and justification. At the trial the plaintiffs sought to limit the issues as to the natural and ordinary meaning of the words used to the question whether the words had the defamatory meaning alleged in the state-
I ment of claim. On appeal from a judgment awarding damages to the plaintiffs,

Held: the action did not lie for the following reasons—

(i) (per LORD DENNING, M.R.) because, when a plaintiff complained of words in their natural and ordinary meaning he must accept that meaning and all its derogatory imputations and could not select some of the imputations and reject others; in the present case, even if the words had conveyed an imputation that the plaintiffs' conduct was dishonest, insincere or hypocritical, the defence of fair comment was still open and, the defendants not

having been actuated by malice and the matter being one of public interest   A
on which the writer of the letter was expressing a sincere view, the defence of
fair comment succeeded (see p. 502, letters G and I, and p. 503, letters C and
H, post).

     Lewis v. *Daily Telegraph, Ltd.* ([1963] 2 All E.R. 151) considered.

     Silkin v. *Beaverbrook Newspapers, Ltd.* ([1958] 2 All E.R. 516) applied.

     (ii) (per DIPLOCK, L.J.) because, even if the views expressed in the letter   B
were defamatory views in relation to the plaintiffs, they were fair comment
on a matter of public interest (see p. 508, letters D and F, post).

     (iii) (per SALMON, L.J.) because the words complained of did not bear the
meaning or give rise to the inferences attributed to them by the plaintiffs in
the statement of claim (see p. 508, letter I, p. 509, letter H, p. 510, letter B,
and p. 511, letter B, post), and, in any event, the defence of fair comment,   C
if not also of justification, was made out (see p. 510, letter I, and p. 513,
letter C, post).

     Per DIPLOCK, L.J., where a plaintiff chose to set out in his statement of
claim the particular defamatory meaning which he contended was the natural
and ordinary meaning of the words used, the defamatory meaning so averred
was to be treated as the most injurious meaning which the words were   D
capable of bearing, but did not prevent the plaintiff from contending at the
trial that the words bore a meaning that was less injurious to, but still
defamatory of, him (see p. 506, letters F to G, post).

     Per SALMON, L.J.: the plaintiffs were probably confined to the indirect
meanings or inferences that they had chosen to allege in their statement of
claim (see p. 512, letter D, and p. 513, letter B, post).   E

     Dictum of LORD DEVLIN in *Lewis* v. *Daily Telegraph, Ltd.* ([1963] 2 All E.R.
at p. 172) considered.

     Appeal allowed.

     [As to the pleading and proof of an innuendo, see 24 HALSBURY'S LAWS
(3rd Edn.) 86, 87, paras. 154, 157; and for cases on the subject, see 32 DIGEST   F
(Repl.) 78-82, *1007-1048.*

     As to fair comment as a defence, see 24 HALSBURY'S LAWS (3rd Edn.) 70, 71,
para. 123, pp. 74, 75, para. 127; and as a defence where there is personal imputation, see ibid., p. 77, para. 134; and for cases on these subjects, see 32 DIGEST
(Repl.) 172, *1851-1858,* 177, 178, *1906-1913,* 179, 180, *1923-1935.*]

Cases referred to: G

     Capital and Counties Bank, Ltd. v. *Henty & Son,* [1881-85] All E.R. Rep. 86;
         (1882), 7 App. Cas. 741; 52 L.J.Q.B. 232; 47 L.T. 662; 47 J.P. 214;
         32 Digest (Repl.) 23, *135.*

     Hopwood v. *Muirson,* [1945] 1 All E.R. 453; [1945] K.B. 313; 114 L.J.K.B.
         267; 172 L.T. 231; 32 Digest (Repl.) 43, *357.*

     Hough v. *London Express Newspaper, Ltd.,* [1940] 3 All E.R. 31; [1940] 2 K.B.   H
         507; 109 L.J.K.B. 524; 163 L.T. 162; 32 Digest (Repl.) 69, *921.*

     Lewis v. *Daily Telegraph, Ltd.*; *Same* v. *Associated Newspapers, Ltd.,* [1963]
         2 All E.R. 151; sub nom. *Rubber Improvements, Ltd.* v. *Daily Telegraph,*
         Ltd.; *Same* v. *Associated Newspapers, Ltd.,* [1964] A.C. 234; [1963]
         2 W.L.R. 1063; 32 Digest (Repl.) 85, *1073.*

     McCarey v. *Associated Newspapers, Ltd.,* [1964] 3 All E.R. 947; [1965] 2 Q.B.
         86; [1965] 2 W.L.R. 45; Digest (Cont. Vol. B) 492, *1769a.*

     Rookes v. *Barnard,* [1964] 1 All E.R. 367; [1964] A.C. 1129; [1964] 2 W.L.R.
         269; 45 Digest (Repl.) 309, *227.*

     Silkin v. *Beaverbrook Newspapers, Ltd.,* [1958] 2 All E.R. 516; [1958] 1 W.L.R.
         743; 32 Digest (Repl.) 170, *1843.*

     Sim v. *Stretch,* [1936] 2 All E.R. 1237; 32 Digest (Repl.) 32, *192.*

     Turner (otherwise Robertson) v. *Metro-Goldwyn-Mayer Pictures, Ltd.,* [1950]
         1 All E.R. 449; 32 Digest (Repl.) 31, *186.*

A   **Appeal.**

By writ issued on June 24, 1964, the first plaintiff, Horace Cornelius Slim, claimed against the defendants, the Daily Telegraph, Ltd. and John Herbert, and each of them, damages for libel published in the correspondence columns of the issue of the Daily Telegraph and Morning Post newspaper, dated Mar. 30, 1964, under the heading " Double Think "; and the second and third plaintiffs,

B   Vitamins Ltd. and H. C. Graves, and each of them, claimed against the defendants and each of them damages for libel published in the correspondence columns of the issue of the newspaper dated Apr. 23, 1964, under the heading " Right of Way Risks on the Riverside ". The first plaintiff was a solicitor, and had been. since Jan. 1, 1959, legal adviser to the plaintiff company. Between 1928 and 1948 the plaintiff had been deputy town clerk of Hammersmith, and between

C   1948 and 1958 he had been town clerk of Hammersmith. The plaintiff company carried on business as food manufacturers and had occupied, since 1929, and still occupied, factory premises at the western end of Upper Mall, Hammersmith. The third plaintiff, Mr. Graves, was at all material times managing director of the plaintiff company. The first defendants were the proprietors and publishers of the Daily Telegraph and Morning Post newspaper, and the second defendant,

D   Mr. Herbert, resided at 13 Hammersmith Terrace, Hammersmith. The letters alleged to constitute libels and the facts are stated in the judgment of Lord Denning, M.R. On Apr. 28, 1967, Paull, J., gave judgment in the action, awarding to the first plaintiff £3,500 damages, to the third plaintiff, Mr. Graves, £1,500 damages, and to the plaintiff company £500 damages. The defendants appealed by notice dated June 22, 1967.

E
Sir Peter Rawlinson, Q.C., and *H. M. Davidson* for the defendants.
David Hirst, Q.C., and *L. Brittan* for the plaintiffs.

Cur. adv. vult.

January 17. The following judgments were read.

LORD DENNING, M.R.: Mr. Slim, the first plaintiff, is a solicitor. For

F   many years he was town clerk of Hammersmith, but he retired in 1958. On Jan. 1, 1959, he became legal adviser to the second plaintiffs, Vitamins, Ltd., who have a factory in Hammersmith. Mr. Graves, the third plaintiff, is the chairman of Vitamins, Ltd.

Upper Mall is a narrow way in Hammersmith by the River Thames. It has several private houses alongside it, but at one point it passes the factory of Vitamins, Ltd. Its width along this stretch is only nine to ten feet. The public have a right of way along it on foot, but not with vehicles. Some years ago the Hammersmith Council put up a notice forbidding people to cycle along it. It was signed by Mr. Slim as town clerk. Later on it was replaced by a simple notice: " No cycling ". Vitamins, Ltd. assert that they have used this stretch of Upper Mall as an access for their vehicles to their factory. Mr. Slim, as their

I   legal adviser, has been trying to establish that they have a legal right of way for vehicles along it. Many of the local residents deny that they have any such right. One of the local papers saw a spokesman for the firm and published this report: " He would not say whether his firm intended to use the road for heavy vehicles to and from the factory."

At this point Mr. John Herbert, who has lived nearby in Hammersmith for many years, wrote to the Daily Telegraph a letter which they published on Mar. 30, 1964. Mr. Slim complains that it is a libel on him:

" Double Think

" Sir, Rotherhithe is not the only part of London's riverside which is in danger of losing some of its most pleasant features.

" Upstream at Hammersmith the peace of Upper Mall is threatened by a claim of Vitamins, Ltd., a factory nearby, to the vehicular right of way. If this is approved, this narrow stretch of the riverside with its period

A

houses may become a thoroughfare for heavy lorries and a dangerous place for a walk.

"This is not a parochial matter, for the charm of Upper Mall is enjoyed by people from all over London. Its special character is already recognised. Section 30 of the London County Council (General Powers) Act 1953, prohibits the driving and parking of cars on Upper Mall, but this it seems is not sufficient protection.

B

"The local council are still pondering on the firm's claim, but what gives cause for concern is that already at the western end of Upper Mall a council notice forbidding even cycling has been removed. If this has made local residents a little cynical, they must be forgiven.

"For many years this notice was signed by one Horace Slim, the reigning town clerk. Is is now the same Mr. Slim, as legal adviser to Vitamins, Ltd., who claims the right to drive lorries along this very path.

C

Yours faithfully,

London, W.6.   John Herbert."

Following that letter, other residents wrote to the Daily Telegraph objecting to the use of this walk by lorries and commercial vehicles. In reply, Mr. Graves, the chairman of Vitamins, Ltd., wrote a letter to the Daily Telegraph which they published on Apr. 14, 1964:

D

" DOUBLE THINK

"Sir, In recent weeks my company has been accused of an intention to use its right of way to the south of Linden House in Upper Mall, Hammersmith, for purposes of lorry access.

E

"My company has never had such an intention, nor has this ever been its practice, as all those inquiring of it have been informed.

"We therefore associate ourselves with the general sentiments expressed in recent correspondence; but we regret that we should have been wrongfully and recklessly implicated by, inter alia, neighbours who have not had the courtesy to discover our intentions before rushing into print.

F

"I would further point out that the only lorries using its right of way are:

"1. Those of the Hammersmith Borough Council engaged in construction work; and

"2. Those regularly delivering beer, and no doubt other supplies, to the Corinthian Yacht Club.

"At no time during the past thirty odd years has my company in any way abused its privileges of right of way at the point concerned. On the contrary through repeated efforts to obtain planning permission to rebuild on its freehold site, it has sought vastly to improve riverside facilities and appearance, and has offered all facilities for extension of the riverside walk.

G

Yours faithfully,
H. C. H. Graves,

London, W.6.   Chairman, Vitamins, Ltd."

H

It is to be noticed that in that letter Mr. Graves disclaims any intention to use lorries, but he does not mention other commercial vehicles. This provoked Mr. Herbert to reply in a letter which they published on Apr. 23, 1964. Mr. Graves and Vitamins, Ltd. complain that it is a libel on them:

"RIGHT OF WAY RISKS ON THE RIVERSIDE ATTITUDE OF COMPANY

"Sir, Residents of Upper Mall, Hammersmith, and others who use it as a riverside walk, will be pleased to hear Mr. H. C. H. Graves's news that Vitamins, Ltd. do not intend to use it as a right of way for their lorries. His protestations of injured innocence would be more convincing, however, if his company was really acting in the spirit of his letter.

"Cars belonging to his employees are already being driven along the western end of Upper Mall, and in particular that part which has been

A
for pedestrians only for fifty years—there is still in fact a council ' No cycling ' notice.   Residents of Upper Mall who have protested have been told by the drivers that the land belongs to Vitamins, Ltd., and that they must move their cars from in front of their houses if those belonging to the company's employees cannot get past.

B
" It is not surprising, therefore, that no one has asked what the intentions of the company were because they were obvious: to establish the vehicular right of way in front of the London Corinthian Sailing Club willy-nilly, without even waiting for a decision from Hammersmith Borough Council.

" It need hardly be said that the use of cars on this narrow pathway is just as much to be deplored as that of lorries.   How can Mr. Graves pretend to associate himself with the sentiments of those who wish to preserve

C
the character of Upper Mall, let alone keep it safe as a riverside walk, when he countenances such action?

" All he has to do to put everyone's mind at rest is to tell his employees to desist from using Upper Mall as a thoroughfare.

Yours faithfully,

D
London, W.6.   John Herbert."

On June 24, 1964, Mr. Slim, Vitamins, Ltd. and Mr. Graves brought an action for libel against the Daily Telegraph and Mr. Herbert.   To my mind the issue should have been a simple one.   The letters were undoubtedly defamatory, but the matter was clearly one of public interest.   The defendants were protected if the letters were fair comment.   Otherwise they were liable.

E
So the simple issue should have been—fair comment or not?   It became submerged, however in pleadings which covered eighty-three pages, in correspondence which filled three hundred pages, in evidence which covered six days, in argument which covered two or three days, and a judgment which filled thirty-five pages. Eventually the judge tried to cut his way through it.   He thought that the sole question was whether the words bore the meanings put on them by the plaintiffs;

F
and he held that they did.   He held that the letter of Mar. 30, 1964, bore the imputation that Mr. Slim had brought improper pressure to bear on the council employees and was not fit to remain a solicitor.   The judge awarded him £3,500. He held that the letter of Apr. 23, 1964, bore the imputation that Mr. Graves, and, through him, Vitamins, Ltd., were insincere and hypocritical; and also the the company had been guilty of improper conduct by seeking to establish this right of way " willy-nilly ".   He awarded Mr. Graves £1,500 and the company £500.

The reasoning by which the judge reached this conclusion can be best understood if I set it out in the form of a dialogue between the judge and counsel, greatly shortened.

Plaintiffs' counsel: The letter of Mar. 30, 1964, in its natural and ordinary meaning, conveys two derogatory imputations against Mr. Slim.   The first is that he was *inconsistent* (he is a man who runs with the hare and hunts with the hounds).   The second is that he was *dishonest* (he is a man who went behind the scenes and used " back-door influence " with the employees of the Hammersmith council).   I do not complain, says counsel of the first imputation of *inconsistency*; that is a fair comment to make on a matter which I agree is of public interest.   But I do complain, says counsel, of the imputation of *dishonesty*; that was not true and it was not a fair comment.

The judge (to plaintiffs' counsel): I think that you are entitled to limit your complaint to the imputation of dishonesty.   Then he turns to defendants' counsel.

The judge (to defendants' counsel): Do you suggest that Mr. Slim was in any way *dishonest*, such as using back-door influence or the like?

Defendants' counsel: We do not suggest that Mr. Slim was guilty of any such conduct.

The judge: In those circumstances I think that the defences of justification **A** and fair comment cannot arise. The sole question is whether the words bore the imputation of *dishonesty*. I ask myself as a lawyer: were the words capable of bearing that imputation? My answer is: yes. I ask myself as an ordinary reader of the Daily Telegraph: did they in fact bear that imputation? My answer is: yes. They imputed that he acted from dishonest motives, was insincere and acted in bad faith towards his former employers, the Hammersmith **B** Corporation. I give judgment, therefore, for the plaintiff.

The judge applied like reasoning in the case of Mr. Graves and Vitamins, Ltd. He held that the letter of Apr. 23, 1964, imputed that Mr. Graves and the company were guilty of insincerity and hypocrisy: and that, as counsel for the defendants did not suggest they were guilty of such conduct, there was no defence to their claim for damages for that imputation. As to the word " willy-nilly ", that **C** imputed that the company was guilty of arrogant conduct which was not justified; but this only called for quite small damages.

I find myself unable to agree with the judge's reasoning.

In the first place, I think that when a plaintiff complains of the words in their natural and ordinary meaning, he must accept that meaning as it is with all the derogatory imputations that it conveys. He cannot select some of the imputa- **D** tions and reject others as he pleases. The reason is because, when he complains of libel, he complains of the injury which the words do to his reputation in the minds of the ordinary reader. Now the ordinary reader takes the imputations as a whole. He does not divide them up into bits. Nor should the plaintiff be able to do so. It is not a case where he is relying on any other defamatory sense, such as to require particulars under R.S.C., Ord. 19, r. 6 (2), now R.S.C., Ord. 82, **E** r. 3 (1). He is relying on the natural and ordinary meaning of the words. In such case the customary form of pleading has been for the pleader to say: " the said words meant and were understood to mean" so and so, setting out all the derogatory imputations that he can think of. Such has always been the practice to my certain knowledge. The pleader in my time at the Bar never tried to select some of the imputations and reject others: and I do not think that he should **F** be allowed to do so now. I find nothing in *Lewis* v. *Daily Telegraph, Ltd.* (1) to warrant it. When the defendant comes to plead his defence, he cannot select some of the imputations and reject others. If he justifies, he pleads in the customary form: " the said words in their natural and ordinary meaning were true in substance and in fact " without specifying any particular imputations. So we see that, in the customary form of pleading, neither plaintiff nor defendant is **G** allowed to make selections of some of the derogatory imputations. Each must accept the words as conveying all such imputations as the jury think they bear: and make his claim or defence accordingly. Only in this way can we avoid the complications which have disfigured this case.

In the second place, I think that the judge placed too much weight on his question to the defendants' counsel: " do you suggest that the plaintiffs were **H** dishonest, insincere or hypocritical? " and counsel's answer: " No, we do not suggest it." That answer showed only that the defendants were not attempting to *justify* any such imputations, but it did not destroy the defence of *fair comment.* Even if the words did convey the imputation, by way of comment, that the plaintiffs' conduct was dishonest, insincere or hypocritical, the defence of fair comment was still available.

I think that the correct approach is simply this: were these letters fair comment on a matter of public interest? The company, Vitamins, Ltd., claimed that they had a right of way for vehicles along Upper Mall. That was a matter of public interest. So also was the conduct of their officers in regard thereto. That is conceded. The defendants were, therefore, entitled to make any fair comment on it. The letters contained a recital of facts which were virtually undisputed.

(1) [1963] 2 All E.R. 151; [1964] A.C. 234.

A   At any rate, no serious complaint was made about the facts. The complaints which counsel for the plaintiffs made were about the comments. In particular, he complained about the comments " Double Think " and " cynical " in the letter of Mar. 30, 1964: and of the comments " protestations of injured innocence " and " How can Mr. Graves pretend to associate himself " in the letter of Apr. 23, 1964. These comments are capable of various meanings. They may
B   strike some readers in one way and others in another way. One person may read into them imputations of dishonesty, insincerity and hypocrisy (as the judge did). Another person may only read into them imputations of inconsistency and want of candour (as I would). In considering a plea of fair comment, it is not correct to canvass all the various imputations which different readers may put on the words. The important thing is to determine whether or not the writer was
C   actuated by malice. If he was an honest man expressing his genuine opinion on a subject of public interest, then no matter that his words conveyed derogatory imputations: no matter that his opinion was wrong or exaggerated or prejudiced; and no matter that it was badly expressed so that other people read all sorts of innuendoes into it; nevertheless, he has a good defence of fair comment. His honesty is the cardinal test. He must honestly express his real view. So long as
D   he does this, he has nothing to fear, even though other people may read more into it, see *Turner (otherwise Robertson)* v. *Metro-Goldwyn-Mayer Pictures, Ltd.* (2), per Lord Porter and *Silkin* v. *Beaverbrook Newspapers, Ltd.* (3), per Diplock, J. I stress this because the right of fair comment is one of the essential elements which go to make up our freedom of speech. We must ever maintain this right intact. It must not be whittled down by legal refinements. When a
E   citizen is troubled by things going wrong, he should be free to " write to the newspaper ": and the newspaper should be free to publish his letter. It is often the only way to get things put right. The matter must, of course, be one of public interest. The writer must get his facts right: and he must honestly state his real opinion. But that being done, both he and the newspaper should be clear of any liability. They should not be deterred by fear of libel actions.

F   When I said to counsel for the plaintiffs that I thought that the real defence here was fair comment, he suggested that it was not based on true facts and it was actuated by malice. But he did not obtain any such finding from the judge: and in the absence of it, I am not prepared to accept the suggestion. Looking at the published correspondence, it seems to me that these were hard-hitting comments by both protagonists, of which neither can complain in a court of law.
G   On the face of these letters, I think that the comments made by Mr. Herbert and the Daily Telegraph were fair comments on a matter of public interest. They honestly said what they thought. Even if the words did impute dishonesty, insincerity and hypocrisy (which I do not think that they did), nevertheless the writers were expressing their honest opinion; and that is enough to clear them of any liability.

H   As to the word " willy-nilly ", it only means that the company intended to establish their right of way, whether other people were willing or unwilling. If that was a statement of fact, it was perfectly true. If it was a comment, it was perfectly fair. The company cannot complain of it.

I would allow the appeal and enter judgment for the defendants.

I   **DIPLOCK, L.J.:** In the spring of 1964 two short letters appeared in the correspondence columns of the Daily Telegraph. Written by Mr. Herbert, they formed part of a robust though desultory controversy about the prospective use by motor vehicles of a public footpath forming part of Upper Mall in Hammersmith. Neither letter can have taken a literate reader of that newspaper more than sixty seconds to read before passing on to some other, and perhaps more interesting, item. Any unfavourable inference about the plaintiffs' characters

(2) [1950] 1 All E.R. 449 at pp. 460, 461.
(3) [1958] 2 All E.R. 516.

or conduct which he might have drawn from what he read would have been one **A**
of first impression. Yet in this court three lords justices and four counsel have
spent the best part of three days on a minute linguistic analysis of every phrase
used in each of the letters. If this protracted exercise in logical positivism has
resulted in our reaching a conclusion as to the meaning of either letter different
from the first impression which we formed on reading it, the conclusion reached
is unlikely to reflect the impression of the plaintiffs' character or conduct which **B**
was actually formed by those who read the letters in their morning newspaper
in 1964.

Nevertheless, the artificial and archaic character of the tort of libel makes the
exercise necessary in this appeal, even though in the end we return to the first
impression with which we began. Libel is concerned with the meaning of words.
Everyone outside a court of law recognises that words are imprecise instruments **C**
for communicating the thoughts of one man to another. The same words may
be understood by one man in a different meaning from that in which they are
understood by another and both meanings may be different from that which the
author of the words intended to convey; but the notion that the same words
should bear different meanings to different men, and that more than one meaning
should be " right ", conflicts with the whole training of a lawyer. Words are the **D**
tools of his trade. He uses them to define legal rights and duties. They do not
achieve that purpose unless there can be attributed to them a single meaning as
the " right " meaning. And so the argument between lawyers as to the meaning
of words starts with the unexpressed major premise that any particular combination of words has one meaning, which is not necessarily the same as that intended
by him who published them or understood by any of those who read them, but **E**
is capable of ascertainment as being the " right " meaning by the adjudicator
to whom the law confides the responsibility of determining it.

That is what makes the meaning ascribed to words for the purposes of the tort
of libel so artificial. In the present appeal, although legal innuendoes (see *Lewis*
v. *Daily Telegraph, Ltd.* (4)) have been pleaded, no reliance has been placed in
the argument on them. The whole discussion has been about the " natural and **F**
ordinary meaning " of the words used in the letters. What is the " natural and
ordinary meaning " of words for the purposes of the law of libel? One can start
by saying that the meaning intended to be conveyed by the publisher of the words
is irrelevant. However evil the imputation on the plaintiff's character or conduct
he intended to communicate, it does not matter if, in the opinion of the adjudi-
tor on the meaning of the words, they did not bear any defamatory meaning. **G**
However innocent an impression of the plaintiff's character or conduct the publisher of the words intended to communicate, it does not matter if, in the opinion
of the adjudicator on the meaning of words, they did bear a defamatory meaning.
This would be rational enough if the purpose of the law of libel were to afford
compensation to the citizen for the unjustifiable injury to his reputation actually
caused by the publication of the words to those to whom they were communi- **H**
cated. But although in assessing damages the courts now accept this as the
purpose of the civil action (see *Rookes* v. *Barnard* (5) and *McCarey* v. *Associated
Newspapers, Ltd.* (6)), we refuse to accept its logical corrollary that the relevant
question in determining liability for libel is : " What did those to whom the words
were published actually understand them to mean? " The best evidence of that
would be the evidence of the persons to whom the words were actually published.
Yet, save in exceptional cases where a " legal " innuendo is relied on, it is not
even permitted to ask a witness to whom the words were published. " What did
you understand them to mean? " What he did actually understand them to
mean does not matter. This too might be rationalised on the ground that the
publisher of the words ought to be responsible in law only for the injury caused

---

(4) [1963] 2 All E.R. 151; [1964] A.C. 234.
(5) [1964] 1 All E.R. 367; [1964] A.C. 1129.
(6) [1964] 3 All E.R. 947; [1965] 2 Q.B. 86.

A to the plaintiff's reputation by those defamatory inferences which a reasonable man might draw from the words published, and the witness to whom the words were published may not have been reasonable in drawing the defamatory inferences which he in fact drew. This rationalisation, however, breaks down once it is conceded, as it has been by the House of Lords in *Lewis* v. *Daily Telegraph, Ltd.* (7), that one man might be reasonable in drawing one defamatory inference B from the words and another man might be reasonable in drawing another defamatory inference. Where, as in the present case, words are published to the millions of readers of a popular newspaper, the chances are that if the words are reasonably capable of being understood as bearing more than one meaning, some readers will have understood them as bearing one of those meanings and some will have understood them as bearing others of those meanings. But none of this matters. C What does matter is what the adjudicator at the trial thinks is the one and only meaning that the readers as reasonable men should have collectively understood the words to bear. That is " the natural and ordinary meaning " of words in an action for libel.

    The adjudicator, whose opinion as to the meaning of words is decisive for the purposes of libel, used to be the judge; and he was accustomed to the techniques D of construction which lawyers employ to ascertain the " right " meaning of words; but Fox's Libel Act, 1792 (8) was to alter that. The Act of 1792 itself dealt only with criminal libels in which the issue as to the meaning of words was less complex than in civil actions. In a criminal prosecution all that was necessary to determine was whether the words bore *any* meaning defamatory of the persons to whom they referred. It was not necessary to distinguish between E one defamatory meaning and another; and so the effect of Fox's Act, which made the jury the adjudicators as to the meaning of words, could be accurately described as: " Libel or no libel is a question for the jury." A consequence of Fox's Act, however, was that the courts in course of time transferred from judge to jury the function of acting as adjudicator as to the meaning of words in civil actions for libel as well as in criminal prosecutions. In this as in other forms of civil actions, F however, the jury as adjudicators were subject to judicial control. If the jury's decision as to the meaning of words could be demonstrated to be perverse, as for instance where the court was of opinion that no twelve reasonable mean could have ascribed any defamatory meaning to the words, the court could set aside the verdict; or if a particular defamatory meaning submitted to the jury by the plaintiff as being the " right " meaning was one which, in the judge's opinion, G it would be perverse of the jury to accept, he could rule that the words were not capable of bearing that meaning and direct the jury to reject it (*Lewis* v. *Daily Telegraph, Ltd.* (9)).

    The exercise of this kind of control over juries in libel actions involved acknowledging that different men would not be unreasonable in ascribing different meanings to the same words. Hence the distinction between defamatory meanings which words are capable of bearing and *the* particular defamatory meaning which, for the purposes of the tort of libel, they bear. The decision as to defamatory meanings which words are capable of bearing is reserved to the judge, and for this reason, and no other, is called a question of law. The decision as to *the* particular defamatory meaning within that category which the words do bear is reserved to the jury, and for this reason, and no other, is called a question of fact. The recognition, however, that there may be more than one meaning which reasonable men might understand words to bear does not absolve the jury from the duty of deciding on one of those meanings as being the only " natural and ordinary meaning " of the words. Juries, in theory, must be unanimous on every issue on which they have to adjudicate; and, since the damages that they award must depend on the defamatory meaning that they attribute to the

---

(7) [1963] 2 All E.R. 151; [1964] A.C. 234.
(8) 32 Geo. 3 c. 60; 13 HALSBURY'S STATUTES (2nd Edn.) 1120.
(9) [1963] 2 All E.R. 151; [1964] A.C. 234.

words, they must all agree on a single meaning as being the "right" meaning. **A**
So the unexpressed major premise that any particular combination of words
can bear but a single "natural and ordinary meaning" which is "right", survived the transfer from judge to jury of the function of adjudicating on the
meaning of words in civil actions for libel.

Where, an action for libel is tried by a judge alone without a jury, it is he
who has to arrive at a single "right" meaning as "the natural and ordinary **B**
meaning" of the words complained of; and with the concentration of functions
in a single adjudicator, the need for his distinguishing between meanings which
words are capable of bearing and the choice of the one "right" meaning which
they do bear disappears. It would be carrying artificiality too far, even for the
law of libel, to suggest that a judge sitting alone must approach the issue as to
the natural and ordinary meaning of the words complained of by asking himself **C**
not only the question: "What is the natural and ordinary meaning in which the
words would be understood by reasonable men to whom they were published?",
but also the further question—" Could reasonable men understand them as bearing that meaning?" Nevertheless PAULL, J., in the present case did ask himself
both questions and, not surprisingly, answered the second question: "Yes".
It has been submitted that in this court, although we can examine his answer to **I**
the second question, we are bound by his answer to the first question because that
would have been a question for the jury in a jury trial.

That the judge could plausibly pose himself the second and supererogatory
question at all resulted from a further technicality in the law of libel and the
curious course which this particular case took at the trial. Any defamatory
imputation on the plaintiffs' characters or conduct conveyed by the words was **F**
mainly, at any rate, dependent on inferences which the readers would themselves draw from them. The plaintiffs, as they were entitled to do, chose to
set out in their statement of claim the particular defamatory meaning which they
contended was the natural and ordinary meaning of the words. Where this manner
of pleading is adopted, the defamatory meaning so averred is treated at the trial
as the most injurious meaning which the words are capable of bearing, and the
plaintiff is, in effect, estopped from contending that the words do bear a *more*
injurious meaning and claiming damages on that basis. The averment does not
of itself prevent the plaintiff from contending at the trial that, even if the words
do not bear the defamatory meaning alleged in the statement of claim to be the
natural and ordinary meaning of the words, they nevertheless bear some other
meaning *less* injurious to the plaintiff's reputation but still defamatory of him, **•**
nor does it relieve the adjudicator of the duty of determining what is the right
natural and ordinary meaning of the words, though nice questions may arise
whether one meaning is more or less injurious than another. C'est pire qu'un
crime, c'est une faute.

Where an action for libel is tried by judge and jury, it is for the parties to submit to the jury their respective contentions as to what is the natural and ordinary
meaning of the words complained of, whether or not the plaintiff's contention
as to the most injurious meaning has been stated in advance in his statement of
claim. It is for the judge to rule whether or not any particular defamatory
meaning for which the plaintiff contends is one which the words are capable of
bearing. The only effect of an allegation in the statement of claim as to the
natural and ordinary meaning of the words is that the judge must direct the jury
that it is not open to them to award damages on the basis that the natural and
ordinary meaning of the words is more injurious to the plaintiff's reputation than
the meaning alleged, although if they think that the words bear a meaning
defamatory of the plaintiff which is either that alleged or is less injurious to the
plaintiff's reputation, they must assess damages on the basis of that natural
and ordinary meaning which they think is the right one. Where, however, a
judge is sitting alone to try a libel action without a jury, the only questions he
has to ask himself are, "Is the natural and ordinary meaning of the words that

A which is alleged in the statement of claim? " and, " If not, what, if any, less injurious defamatory meaning do they bear? "

In the present case, no doubt with the best of motives, the plaintiffs sought at the trial to limit the issues as to the natural and ordinary meaning of the words complained of to the single question of whether or not they bore the defamatory meaning alleged in the statement of claim. On the pleadings as they
B stood, the only way in which they could do this was by waiving any claim to damages for any less injurious meaning which the words bore, if they did not bear the meaning so alleged. The defendants did not dissent from this course being taken and I will assume that this was what was intended to be done; but the effect, however well-intentioned, was to add a further artificiality to the trial. The natural and ordinary meaning which the plaintiffs alleged the words
C bore was stated with great precision in the statement of claim. The defendants conceded that they could not justify the defamatory meaning so alleged, but did seek to justify the actual words complained of in what they, the defendants, contended was the natural and ordinary meaning of those words—a meaning which, incidentally, the rules of pleading prohibit the defendants from stating in their defence. So far so good if (which I must not be taken to accept) an action
D for libel can be converted into a game of skill in which the contestants choose their own rules and the court is content to apply those rules as umpire; but at least the umpire must be quite clear what the chosen rules are and must apply them consistently. As I read his judgment, the judge did not succeed in doing that. In the important passage of his judgment in which he says that " no question of justification can arise ", he accepts that the only issue left to him
E (apart from damages) in this particular game of skill was whether the words in their natural and ordinary meaning bear the precise defamatory meaning alleged in the statement of claim, but he nevertheless goes on to consider what is a different issue, viz., whether the words bear a defamatory meaning which he expresses in a number of different phrases, all of them less precise than those used in the statement of claim, but which he apparently regarded as paraphrases of
F the relevant paragraphs of the statement of claim. To do so introduces into the proceedings a new complication about the meaning of words—this time not about the meaning of the words used in the alleged libel but about the meaning of the words used in the paragraph of the statement of claim to plead the defamatory meaning which the plaintiffs alleged was the natural and ordinary meaning of the words used in the alleged libel. Any paraphrase of that paragraph which
G was less precise than the actual words used in the paragraph could not bear the same meaning as the words themselves, and if the judge was going to depart in any way from what, on the true construction of the relevant paragraph of the statement of claim, was the precise meaning therein alleged to be that which the libel bore, he should also have gone on to consider whether the defence of justification or fair comment was made out in respect of the words of the alleged
H libel in the meaning which he ultimately decided was their natural and ordinary meaning. This, however, he never did.

What then is this court to do? I do not think that we need send it back for a retrial. No oral evidence given at the trial throws any light on the natural and ordinary meaning of the words to readers of the correspondence columns in the Daily Telegraph. This court is in as good a position as the judge to determine
I what is the natural and ordinary meaning of the words, and in so far as any action for libel can be a simple case, I think that this one is.

What is said in the first letter about Mr. Slim is that when his client or employer was the Hammersmith Borough Council, he took action on their behalf to prevent vehicles, even bicycles, from using Upper Mall and that, now his client is Vitamins, Ltd., he is taking action on their behalf to enable Upper Mall to be used by their vehicles. Well, so he was. There is nothing in that conduct which would lower him in the esteem of right-thinking lawyers. The professional duty of a lawyer is to express the views of his client, not his own personal views. That is one of

the reasons why lawyers as a class have through the centuries been distrusted **A**
by laymen (cf., The Peasants' Revolt 1381: *Hopwood* v. *Muirson* (10)). It makes
laymen, to use Mr. Herbert's mild phrase, " cynical " about lawyers, if indeed
the cynicism expressed in his letter was directed to Mr. Slim's conduct and not,
as I think, to the borough council. The judge took the view that a reader of the
letter would infer that Mr. Slim had used " backdoor influence " with the
borough council to persuade them not to press their opposition to his clients' **B**
intended use of Upper Mall. I do not find it easy to construe that phrase which
was the judge's not the plaintiffs'. Of course Mr. Slim had the advantage derived
from his previous employment of knowing the officials of the council with whom
he was talking or corresponding on behalf of his clients, and maybe the previous
policy of the committees by whom the decisions would be recommended. He
was no doubt in a better position than other solicitors might be to marshal **C**
the arguments for his client in a form most likely to persuade those to whom they
were addressed: but there is nothing professionally improper in this. Indeed,
it was Mr. Slim's duty to his client to do so. I cannot read the letter as implying
that Mr. Slim had done anything more than this. The worst that I can read
into the letter is an expression of Mr. Herbert's view, no doubt shared by many
non-lawyers, that this is an undesirable practice. Even if to express that view **D**
could be defamatory of a lawyer, it is a perfectly fair comment on what was
admittedly a matter of public interest.

As respects the second letter, there has been much discussion about the adverb
" willy-nilly " and the verb " pretend ". For my part I cannot read the former
expression in the context of the letter as meaning anything more than that the
company were persisting in their policy despite opposition by the borough **E**
council and residents in Hammersmith; and so they were. As regards the verb
" pretend ", it was used in reference to the claim made by Mr. Graves in a
previous letter that his company was in general sympathy with the views which
had been expressed by those who wanted to preserve Upper Mall exclusively for
pedestrians. All that Mr. Herbert did in his reply was to draw attention, force- **F**
fully perhaps, to the inconsistency between this claim and the attempts that
Mr. Graves and the company were admittedly making to secure and to enlarge
the right of use of Upper Mall by cars belonging to their employers. Again this
was fair comment.

It would be an evil day for free speech in this country if this kind of controversy on a matter of public though local interest were discouraged by the fear **G**
that every word written to be read in haste should be subjected to minute
linguistic analysis in a court of law of the kind to which these letters have been
subjected on this appeal. As the law of libel now stands, it is not easy to avoid
it. In the result, in the present case I think that we can decide this case in
accordance with common sense and first impression by allowing the appeal.
I venture to recommend once more the law of defamation as a fit topic for the **H**
attention of the Law Commission. It has passed beyond redemption by the
courts.

SALMON, L.J.: Any attempt to rationalise the law of libel would have
proved a daunting task even before 1964. Happily it is unnecessary to attempt
it in the present case. The task would not, perhaps, have been made any easier
by *Lewis* v. *Daily Telegraph, Ltd.* (11), nor by *Rookes* v. *Barnard* (12), or *McCarey*
v. *Associated Newspapers, Ltd.* (13). These cases may one day raise a number
of intransigent problems to which it will then be necessary to try and find a
solution; but the time is not yet. It seems to me that the principal question in
the present case is whether or not the words complained of bear the meanings
attributed to them by the plaintiffs.

(10) [1945] 1 All E.R. 453; [1945] K.B. 313.
(11) [1963] 2 All E.R. 151; [1964] A.C. 234.
(12) [1964] 1 All E.R. 367; [1964] A.C. 1129.
(13) [1964] 3 All E.R. 947; [1965] 2 Q.B. 86.

A　　The words complained of by Mr. Slim appeared in a letter from Mr. John Herbert in the issue of the Daily Telegraph for Mar. 30, 1964. The words complained of by Vitamins, Ltd., and by their chairman and managing director, Mr. Graves, appeared in another letter from Mr. John Herbert in the issue of the Daily Telegraph for Apr. 23, 1964. These letters formed part of a spirited correspondence in that newspaper and in the local press concerning the use of a river-

B　side walk called Upper Mall in Hammersmith. The peace and quiet charm of this place had been preserved and jealously guarded for many years by the borough council, the local residents and those members of the general public who resorted to it. According to them, the narrow part of Upper Mall had always been closed to vehicular traffic and even to bicycles. Vitamins, Ltd., whilst professing their concern to preserve the amenities of the place, claimed the right to drive their

C　vehicles, other than heavy lorries, along the whole of the walk and proceeded to do so. Their premises are adjacent to Upper Mall. Mr. Slim had been deputy town clerk of the Hammersmith Borough Council from 1928 to 1948, and town clerk from 1948 until his retirement in 1958. Thereafter he was engaged by Vitamins, Ltd., as their legal adviser, chiefly in relation to their property interests in Hammersmith and the conduct of negotiations on their behalf with the borough

D　council. In his letter of Mar. 30, 1964, which appeared under the title " Double Think ", Mr. Herbert wrote:

> " The local council are still pondering on the firm's claim, but what gives cause for concern is that already at the western end of Upper Mall a council notice forbidding even cycling has been removed. If this has made local residents a little cynical, they may be forgiven. For many years this notice

E　> was signed by one Horace Slim, the reigning town clerk. It is now the same Mr. Slim, as legal adviser to Vitamins, Ltd., who claims the right to drive lorries along this very path."

The statement of claim alleged in effect that these words in their ordinary and natural meaning inferred that Mr. Slim had behaved with professional impropriety and in a dishonourable manner. Before the judge and in this court,

F　counsel for the plaintiffs, has conceded that unless the words do bear such a meaning, Mr. Slim must lose. He made it plain, to quote from the judge's judgment, that

> " there was and is no question of his asking for damages if all that is established is that the letter meant that while acting honourably and in good faith, he has done something which could be criticised."

G

It is, therefore, unnecessary for me to pause to consider whether Mr. Slim, in spite of his pleading, might have sought to rely on some other and less objectionable defamatory meaning. I am afraid that I cannot agree with the judge that the words complained of do bear the meaning which Mr. Slim attributes to them. I think that the ordinary reader of the Daily Telegraph would consider the words

H　meant that when Mr. Slim was town clerk, he was the champion of one view about Upper Mall, and that when he became legal advisor to Vitamins, Ltd., he became the champion of the opposite view. This, however, does not mean that he has been guilty of what anyone would regard as unprofessional or dishonourable behaviour. It is generally recognised that to do as he did is part of a lawyer's normal duties—although no doubt it is regarded by some laymen with a certain

I　degree of cynicism. Again the ordinary man on reading Mr. Herbert's letter might conclude that Mr. Slim, through the many years he had served the borough council, would have gained great experience of the kind of arguments and considerations likely to·appeal to them, that he would be persona grata with the council's officers, and generally more favourably placed than a comparative stranger in negotiating with them. There would be no question of his applying any improper pressure or deviating by one iota from the path of strict rectitude, but merely because he was who he was, he would have the best chance of persuading the council that his cause was just. No doubt this was as obvious to

Vitamins, Ltd., as it would have been to the ordinary reader of the Daily Tele-   **A**
graph—and may even have been a reason for their retaining him The ordinary
reader may have thought that in doing so, Vitamins, Ltd. were seeking to obtain
an unfair advantage over any other ratepayers with whom they might be in
conflict.   Indeed, the fact that Vitamins, Ltd. did retain the ex-town clerk to
advise them in their dealings with the borough council and to negotiate with
the borough council on their behalf, may well have caused local residents to be a   **B**
little cynical, and even left a strange flavour in their mouths. But this does not
raise a question of honour or professional propriety—only a question of taste.
In my view, Mr. Herbert's letter does not mean that Mr. Slim behaved unpro-
fessionally or in any way dishonourably, and I would accordingly allow the
appeal and enter judgment for the defendants in respect of that letter.

Mr. Herbert's other letter, of which Vitamins, Ltd. and Mr. Graves complain,   **C**
was written in reply to a letter of Mr. Graves appearing in the issue of the Daily
Telegraph for Apr. 14, 1964. In that letter Mr. Graves denied that his company
had any intention of using Upper Mall for the purpose of lorry access. He associated himself and his company with the sentiments of those anxious to preserve
the peace and quiet and general amenities of Upper Mall; he also pointed out
that his company had sought planning permission to rebuild and improve the   **D**
riverside appearance and facilities, including an extension of the riverside walk.
He expressed himself in fairly strong terms about having been, as he put it,
" wrongfully and recklessly implicated by neighbours who have not had the
courtesy to consult us before rushing into print ". In his letter in reply appearing
in the issue of the Daily Telegraph for Apr. 23, 1964, Mr. Herbert wrote: " (Mr.
Graves's) protestations of injured innocence would be more convincing . . . if his   **E**
company was really acting in the spirit of his letter." Mr. Herbert then went on
to point out that cars belonging to the company or its employees were using
Upper Mall as a thoroughfare including the narrow part which had been kept for
pedestrians only for fifty years, and that cars on this narrow pathway were just
as objectionable as lorries. The letter also contained the following passage to
which Mr. Graves and his company took exception: **F**

> " It is not surprising therefore that no one has asked what the intentions
> of the company were because they were obvious: to establish the vehicular
> right of way in front of the the London Corinthian Sailing Club willy-nilly
> without even waiting for a decision from the Hammersmith Borough
> Council . . . How can Mr. Graves pretend to associate himself with the senti-
> ments of those who wish to preserve the character of Upper Mall, let alone   **G**
> keep it safe as a riverside walk, when he countenances such action? "

It seems to me that the words " willy-nilly " mean no more than that Vitamins,
Ltd.'s intention was to establish a vehicular right of way along Upper Mall
whether the local residents or the borough council liked it or not.   The local
residents had made it very plain that they did not like it.   So had the borough   **H**
council by their town clerk's letter to Mr. Slim of Mar. 18, 1964, in which the
town clerk wrote:

> " Whilst your clients' claim is still being investigated, it is not agreed
> that your clients have a right of way for vehicles over the passageway in
> front of Linden House. So far (apart from your client company) I have yet
> to find anyone who believes that this passageway is a carriageway as well   **I**
> as a footpath."

The company's internal correspondence makes it very plain that in spite of the
opposition, they were using the way for their vehicles at least once a day and
considered it important to continue to do so and to log the journeys in order to
establish what they alleged were their existing rights. To my mind, the passage
in Mr. Herbert's letter stating that the company's intention was to establish
a vehicular right of way willy nilly was fully justified and in any event was
fair comment.

A   In the statement of claim, however, it is further alleged that Mr. Herbert's second letter in its ordinary and natural meaning inferred that Mr. Graves in his letter written as chairman of Vitamins, Ltd., to which I have already referred, was insincere and hypocritical in his statements concerning (a) his company's intentions in relation to the use of Upper Mall by the company's vehicles, and (b) the company's wishes to improve the riverside facilities and appearance and

B   to extend the riverside walk. In my view no such inferences can properly be drawn from Mr. Herbert's letter. Indeed he impliedly accepts Mr. Graves' expression of intention not to use Upper Mall for lorries, but points out that its use as a thoroughfare for other motor vehicles (which Mr. Graves admittedly intended) is just as objectionable. Nor does Mr. Herbert cast any doubt on the statement in Mr. Graves' letter to the effect that his company's intention, if

C   planning permission could be obtained, was to rebuild on their freehold site and thereby improve the riverside facilities and appearance and enable the riverside walk to be extended.

    Counsel for the plaintiffs, however, seeks to rely on another inference from Mr. Herbert's letter which has not been pleaded, namely, the inference that Mr. Graves was insincere and hypocritical in pretending to associate himself

D   with the sentiments of those who wished to preserve the peace and quiet of the riverside walk, whilst he was at the same time seeking to use it as a thoroughfare for vehicular traffic. This raises the question as to whether counsel is entitled to rely on such an inference having regard to the terms of his pleading. Words may be defamatory in their ordinary and natural meaning. They may also, or in the alternative, bear a defamatory innuendo. A " true " or " legal " innuendo

E   is a meaning which is different from the ordinary and natural meaning of the words, and defamatory because of special facts and circumstances known to those to whom the words are published. The ordinary meaning and the innuendo give rise to different causes of action, and, accordingly, must be separately pleaded— *Sim* v. *Stretch* (14). Words in their ordinary and natural meaning may be defamatory because of what they say expressly, e.g., " A is a thief "; or because of

F   what they imply to the ordinary sensible man without knowledge of any special circumstances. For many years prior to 1949 it was most unusual to see a statement of claim which did not purport to plead an innuendo. This would either be a " true " innuendo or the ordinary meaning to be naturally inferred from the words, or both a " true " innuendo and a natural inference jumbled up together in the same paragraph. Innuendos were also commonly pleaded even when the

G   words complained of were as plain as could be, e.g.: " X is a fraudulent scoundrel ", or: " Y is a prostitute "; in such cases an innuendo was, of course, unnecessary and indeed absurd. This practice, however, although untidy and sometimes ridiculous, did little harm. It, at any rate, helped the defendant by forewarning him of the meaning which the plaintiff would seek to attribute to the words at the trial. Then in 1949 came a new rule, R.S.C., Ord. 19, r. 6 (2) (now Ord. 82,

H   r. 3 (1)) which provided that:

> " . . . if the plaintiff alleges that the words . . . complained of were used in a defamatory sense other than their ordinary meaning, he shall give particulars of the facts and matters on which he relies in support of such sense."

I   Although to some extent the old practice lingered on, between 1949 and 1964 there were many cases in which plaintiffs, who relied alone on the natural meaning of the words complained of, did not in their statement of claims set out the inferences which at the trial they intended to allege that the words bore. Thus defendants were sometimes left in the dark and the administration of justice was somewhat impeded.

    It was, I think, in order to overcome this difficulty that Lord Devlin stated

(14) [1936] 2 All E.R. 1237.

in *Lewis* v. *Daily Telegraph, Ltd.* (15) that it would be desirable for the statement **A**
of claim to contain a separate paragraph setting out

> " . . . those . . . indirect meanings that go beyond the literal meaning
> of the words but which the pleader claims to be inherent in them."

The whole House agreed that it was permissible for the statement of claim to
contain such a paragraph but forbore to rule whether it was necessary for it to
do so. That point, as I understand LORD DEVLIN'S speech (16) was left open. **B**
LORD DEVLIN'S observations may have been obiter but they carry very great
weight and are of the highest persuasive authority. It is not surprising that
counsel for the plaintiffs accepted them in drawing the statement of claim in the
present case. Indeed, he could hardly have done otherwise having regard to the
warning that the House of Lords might rule that it was necessary for him to do
so. If it should turn out to be necessary, presumably the plaintiff would be **C**
precluded from seeking to set up at the trial any indirect meaning or inference
which he had failed to plead. Supposing, however, that it is not necessary for
the indirect meanings or inferences to be alleged in the statement of claim but
that nevertheless the plaintiff (as here) has chosen to allege them, is he to be
confined to those meanings or may he rely on some entirely different meaning at
the trial? Without committing myself to any concluded-view, I am inclined to **D**
think that the plaintiff is bound by his pleading—otherwise it may prove to be
nothing but a snare for the defendant. I do not mean, of course, that the plaintiff
is strictly confined to the very shade or nuance of meaning which he has pleaded
—but what he sets up at the trial must come broadly within the meaning he has
pleaded. Nor do I think that without any amendment of his statement of claim,
it would be permissible for him to set up any entirely different meaning, even if **E**
it were less injurious to the plaintiff than the meaning pleaded. It is often
difficult to decide which of two defamatory meanings is the more injurious.
If there were a jury, how and by whom would the question be decided? Moreover,
even if one meaning were somewhat less injurious than another, it might still
be very injurious indeed, and the defendant might have had no real chance of
preparing his defence to meet it. After all, there may be many opinions as to **F**
what inference words bear. It would be unfair to expect the defendant to guess
which meaning or meanings the plaintiff intends to attribute to them. He might
guess wrong and thus not only waste a great deal of time and money in raising
a defence of justification or fair comment which would prove to be wholly irrelevant at the trial but he might also come to court wholly unprepared to meet the
actual case sought to be made against him. Moreover, if the plaintiff relies on **G**
two different defamatory meanings, the defendant might wish to justify the
one but not the other, and this, in my view, he is entitled to do.

It has been suggested in argument that this view of the pleading point might in
some way prejudice the defendants because it would preclude them from justifying a meaning on which the plaintiff has not relied in his pleading. If, however,
the plaintiff cannot recover damages in respect of such a meaning, no plea of **H**
justification in respect of it could be relevant. I can imagine a case in which the
words bore two indirect defamatory meanings and the plaintiff chose to confine
himself to the one because he was afraid of justification in respect of the other.
But this manoeuvre could do him no good. The defendants may always invite
the court to consider the words complained of in their context and can also
serve a notice in diminution of damage. If the matters which could have been
pleaded by way of justification of meaning B are not relevant by way of diminution of damage in respect of meaning A, then the fact that the plaintiff does not
seek to recover damages in respect of meaning B, and that accordingly there has
been no plea of justification in relation to it, cannot prejudice the defendant in
respect of the claim founded on meaning A. If the matters which might have

---

(15) [1963] 2 All E.R. at p. 171, letter B; [1964] A.C. at p. 280.
(16) [1963] 2 All E.R. at p. 172; [1964] A.C. at p. 282.

A   been relied on in justification of meaning B (had it been pleaded) are relevant in diminution of damages in respect of meaning A, then those matters can be set out in the appropriate notice.

Accordingly, I incline to the view that on principle Mr. Graves and his company should be confined to the indirect meanings which in their statement of claim they attribute to Mr. Herbert's second letter; and, as I have already
B   indicated, I do not consider that it bears any of these meanings.

I do not think it necessary to reach any final view on the pleading point because even if the view I have provisionally formed is incorrect, Mr. Graves and his company would still fail. If they were entitled to rely on the unpleaded indirect meaning to the effect that it is humbug for Mr. Graves to pretend or
C   claim that he shares the sentiments of those who wish to preserve the peace of Upper Mall, whilst he asserts and purports to exercise the right to use it as a thoroughfare for his company's vehicles, fair comment, if not justification, would on the evidence clearly be a complete answer to the claim. I would, therefore, also allow the appeal in respect of Mr. Herbert's second letter.

There is one last point to which I must refer before parting with this case.
D   It applies equally to the plaintiffs' claim on both Mr. Herbert's letters. Counsel for the plaintiffs contends that if the words of which the plaintiffs complain are capable of the defamatory meaning attributed to them, then this court has no more power to interfere with the judge's findings as to the meaning of those words than it would have had to interfere with the findings of a jury. I cannot accept this argument. It is unsupported by any direct authority,
E   although it is lent some colour by implication from the dicta of GODDARD, L.J., in *Hough* v. *London Express Newspaper, Ltd.* (17). No doubt, even when a libel action has been tried by a judge alone an appellate tribunal may sometimes approach the case by considering, as a matter of law, whether the words complained of are capable of the defamatory meaning which they have been found to bear. If they are, the appellate tribunal will not lightly interfere with the
F   judge's finding of fact. If, however, the appellate tribunal is satisfied that the judge's finding of fact is wrong, it is its duty to reverse him. There is no sensible reason why a judge's finding of fact in a libel action should be more sacrosanct than in any other action. For the reasons I have indicated, I am as satisfied as I can be that the judge's decision was wrong. I say "as I can be", because I am very conscious of the difficulty which a judge faces in trying to
G   ascertain the meaning which the ordinary layman would attribute to words which he reads in his newspaper. Much of a judge's time is spent in construing statutes and legal documents—an apparently similar task to the one which now confronts us, but a task which, in reality, requires a different technique. There have been many differences of judicial opinion even on the question of what words are capable of meaning to the ordinary layman, see e.g., *Lewis* v. *Daily Telegraph,*
H   *Ltd.* (18). The principles are easy to formulate but difficult to apply. They were never better formulated than they were in *Capital and Counties Bank, Ltd.* v. *Henty & Son* (19)—nor perhaps ever worse applied. It was there held that the words complained of were incapable of meaning to ordinary men that the bank was in financial difficulties, yet they caused a run on the bank whose customers, presumably, were ordinary men. If it is difficult to decide whether words are
I   capable of a defamatory meaning, it is still more difficult to decide what they in fact are likely to mean to the ordinary layman. Conscious as I am of the difficulties involved and much as I respect the judge's opinion, I have formed the clear view that Mr. Herbert's letters do not bear the meanings which the plaintiffs attribute to them.

---

(17) [1946] 3 All E.R. 31 at p. 35; [1940] 2 K.B. 507 at p. 516.
(18) [1963] 2 All E.R. 151; [1964] A.C. 234.
(19) [1881-85] All E.R. Rep. 86; (1882), 7 App. Cas. 741.

Accordingly, as I have already indicated, I would allow the appeal and order **A**
judgment to be entered for the defendants.

Appeal allowed; action dismissed. Leave to appeal to the House of Lords refused.

Solicitors: *Simmons & Simmons* (for the defendants); *Lovell, White & King*
(for the plaintiffs).

[*Reported by* F. GUTTMAN, ESQ., *Barrister-at-Law.*] **B**

McCOLLOM *v.* WRIGHTSON.

[HOUSE OF LORDS (Lord Reid, Lord Morris of Borth-y-Gest, Lord Hodson, Lord
   Pearce and Lord Upjohn), December 13, 1967, February 6, 1968.] **C**

*Licensing—Offences—Gaming on licensed premises—Bingo—Free bingo played
   on licensed premises—Prizes other than intoxicating liquor provided—No
   chance of losing—Whether gaming—Betting, Gaming and Lotteries Act 1963
   (c. 2), s. 34 (1), s. 55 (1)—Licensing Act 1964 (c. 26), s. 177.*

The respondent held a justices' on-licence. On three Sundays in April
and May, 1966, free bingo with free prizes was provided on the premises. **D**
Bingo is a game of pure chance. No stakes were hazarded by those taking
part and the prizes were of articles other than intoxicating liquor. No charge
was made for entering the building or playing the game; nor was playing the
game in any way related to purchasing drinks. The prosecutor appealed
from a decision upholding dismissal of informations charging the respondent
(a) with suffering bingo to be played on licensed premises in such circum- **E**
stances that an offence under Part 2 of the Betting, Gaming and Lotteries
Act 1963 was committed, contrary to s. 177* of the Licensing Act 1964, and
(b) with taking part in gaming in a place to which the public had access,
contrary to s. 34 (1)† of the Betting, Gaming and Lotteries Act 1963.
" Gaming " was defined in s. 55 (1) of the Act of 1963 to mean " playing . . .
a game of chance for winnings in money or money's worth ". **F**

Held: (i) the respondent had not committed any offence, because gaming
took place only where there was a chance not only of winning but also
of losing, and accordingly it had not been established that the respondent
had taken part in gaming for the purposes of the Act of 1963 (see p. 516,
letter I, to p. 517, letter A, post).

Principle stated by LORD ALVERSTONE, C.J., in *Lockwood* v. *Cooper* ([1903] **G**
2 K.B. at p. 431) applied.

(ii) moreover, even if the participants in the free bingo bought drinks in the
premises, that did not establish that a stake was hazarded, for an indirect
benefit to the donor of a prize was not equivalent to a stake unless it involved
a contribution being offered before the gaming began, and the playing of the
game in the present case was not in fact related to the purchase of drinks **H**
(see p. 517, letter F, post).

Willis v. *Young & Stembridge* ([1907] 1 K.B. 448) and *Minty* v. *Sylvester*
((1915), 84 L.J.K.B. 1982) considered.

Decision of the DIVISIONAL COURT ([1967] 3 All E.R. 257) affirmed.

[As to what is gaming, see 18 HALSBURY'S LAWS (3rd Edn.) 168, para. 336;
and for cases on the subject, see 25 DIGEST (Repl.) 446, 447, *275-282*; 493-495, **I**
511, 522-527.

For the Betting, Gaming and Lotteries Act 1963, s. 34, s. 55, see 43 HALSBURY'S
STATUTES (2nd Edn.) 346, 366.

---

* Section 177 (1), so far as material, provides: " If the holder of a justices' licence
suffers any game to be played in the premises in such circumstances that an offence
under Part 2 of the Betting, Gaming and Lotteries Act 1963 is committed . . . he shall
be liable . . . to a fine . . .".

† Section 34 (1), so far as material, is set out at p. 516, letter E, post.

A   For the Licensing Act 1964, s. 177, see 44 HALSBURY'S STATUTES (2nd Edn.) 629.]

Cases referred to:

   Lockwood v. Cooper, [1903] 2 K.B. 428; 72 L.J.K.B. 690; 89 L.T. 306; 67 J.P. 307; 25 Digest (Repl.) 446, 280.

B   Minty v. Sylvester, (1915), 84 L.J.K.B. 1982; 114 L.T. 164; 79 J.P. 543; 25 Digest (Repl.) 494, 526.

   R. v. Ashton, (1852), 1 E. & B. 286; 22 L.J.M.C. 1; 20 L.T.O.S. 110; 118 E.R. 444; sub nom. Ex p. Ashton, 16 J.P. 790; 25 Digest (Repl.) 446, 275.

   Willis v. Young & Stembridge, [1907] 1 K.B. 448; 76 L.J.K.B. 390; 96 L.T. 155; 71 J.P. 6; 25 Digest (Repl.) 493, 511.
C

   Appeal.

   This was an appeal by Reginald Whitton McCollom, a police inspector, from the judgment of the Divisional Court of the Queen's Bench Division (LORD PARKER, C.J., WIDGERY and WALLER, JJ.), dated July 12, 1967, and reported [1967] 3 All E.R. 257, dismissing the appeal of the appellant from a decision of
D   the justices for the West Riding of Yorkshire sitting at Knaresborough who dismissed six informations preferred by the appellant against the respondent Brian Melbourne Wrightson. Three of the informations alleged that on Apr. 10, 1966, May 15, 1966 and May 29, 1966, the respondent, being a holder of a justices' on-licence for his premises at Boroughbridge, known as Hotel Cottages, suffered bingo to be played on those premises in such circumstances that an offence under
E   Part 2 of the Betting, Gaming and Lotteries Act 1963 was committed, contrary to s. 177 of the Licensing Act 1964. The last three informations referred to the same three days and charged the respondent with taking part in gaming in a place to which the public had access, viz., Hotel Cottages, contrary to s. 34 (1) of the Betting, Gaming and Lotteries Act 1963. The facts are set out in the opinion of LORD HODSON.

F   R. A. R. Stroyan for the appellant.
   S. S. Gill for the respondent.

   Their Lordships took time for consideration.

   Feb. 6. The following opinions were delivered.

G   **LORD REID:** My Lords, for the reasons given by my noble and learned friend LORD HODSON I would dismiss this appeal.

      LORD MORRIS OF BORTH-Y-GEST: My Lords, for the reasons given by my noble and learned friend LORD HODSON I would dismiss this appeal.

      LORD HODSON: My Lords, this is an appeal from the Divisional Court of
H   the Queen's Bench Division (1) dismissing an appeal by the appellant, who is a police inspector, from a decision of the justices for the West Riding of Yorkshire sitting at Knaresborough. The justices dismissed six informations preferred against the respondent, who is the holder of a justices' on-licence for premises known as Hotel Cottages. The informations related to the playing of bingo on three separate days, the respondent being charged in the first place with suffering
I   bingo to be played on the premises in such circumstances that an offence under Part 2 of the Betting, Gaming and Lotteries Act 1963 was committed, contrary to s. 177 of the Licensing Act 1964. In the second place the respondent was charged on the same occasions with taking part in gaming in a place to which the public had access contrary to s. 34 (1) of the Betting, Gaming and Lotteries Act 1963. No separate question has been discussed as to whether the respondent was " taking part " in gaming as alleged in the No. 4 information. The sole question certified

   (1) [1967] 3 All E.R. 257.

by the Divisional Court as a point of law of general public importance involved **A**
in the decision of these cases is (2)

" whether the playing of a game of chance for winnings in money or
money's worth imports the element of the player hazarding a stake and thus
standing to lose as well as to win."

The facts as they appear from the Case Stated (3) were that on Apr. 2, 9 and 16, **B**
1966, advertisements appeared in local newspapers at the instance of the respondent advertising " Eyes down. Free prizes every Sunday ". This meant that free
games of bingo would take place on the premises on those days for prizes provided
by the management. Police officers in plain clothes visited the premises and took
part in games of bingo in the lounge of the hotel with other members of the
public. The games were conducted by or on behalf of the respondent. No stakes **C**
were hazarded by those taking part in the game of bingo, which is a game of pure
chance, and no charge was made for entering the building or for taking part
in the game nor was the playing of the game dependent on or in any way related
to the purchase of drinks. The prizes provided by the management consisted
of such articles as a rose bowl, a pewter mug, a travelling clock and a wristlet
watch, but did not include intoxicating liquor. No player could lose anything **D**
by taking part in the game.

Contravention of s. 177 of the Licensing Act 1964 comes about if gaming on
licensed premises is suffered by the holder of the licence so that an offence is
committed under Part 2 of the Betting, Gaming and Lotteries Act 1963. The
relevant section of the Act of 1963 is s. 34 (1), which provides:

" Subject to the provisions of this Act, if any person takes part in gaming **E**
in any street or in any other place to which, whether on payment or otherwise,
the public have access, he shall be liable on summary conviction to a fine . . ."

The only issue in this appeal is whether any person was on those days taking
part in " gaming ". There is a statutory definition of " gaming " in s. 55 (1) of
the Act of 1963 (repeated from the Betting and Gaming Act 1960) which reads:
" ' gaming ' means the playing of a game of chance for winnings in money or **F**
money's worth ".

Before the passing of the Act of 1960 the common law authorities were consistent at least in this, that so far as gaming was concerned they held that the
staking of money was essential to it (see *R.* v. *Ashton* (4)). That was an appeal
against a conviction for suffering the playing of dominoes contrary to the Licensing Act then in force. LORD CAMPBELL, C.J., with whom COLERIDGE, WIGHTMAN **G**
and ERLE, JJ., concurred, held (5) that the conviction must be quashed, saying
that the object of the statute was to prevent the contracting of bad habits by
the practice of games where money was staked in public houses and that, if
money were staked, that would be gaming and then there might be a lawful conviction. The information did not charge the allowing of gaming. Later authorities
to which your lordships' attention has been drawn are to the same effect, e.g., **H**
Lockwood v. *Cooper* (6), a decision under the Licensing Act, 1872. LORD
ALVERSTONE, C.J., with whom WILLS and CHANNELL, JJ., concurred said (7):

" To amount to gaming the game played must involve the element of
wagering—that is to say, each of the players must have a chance of losing
as well as of winning."

I am in entire agreement with LORD PARKER, C.J., and with WIDGERY and **I**
WALLER, JJ., the other members of the Divisional Court (8), that the introduction

---

(2) [1967] 3 All E.R. at p. 260, letter I.
(3) See [1967] 3 All E.R. at pp. 257, 258.
(4) (1852), 1 E. & B. 286.
(5) (1852), 1 E. & B. at p. 289.
(6) [1903] 2 K.B. 428.
(7) [1903] 2 K.B. at p. 431.
(8) [1967] 3 All E.R. 257.

A of the word " winnings " first in the Act of 1960 and then in the Act of 1963 has done nothing directly or by inference to alter the law as it previously existed namely that " gaming " only takes place where there is the chance not only of, winning but also of losing, in other words where some stake has been hazarded.

A subsidiary argument was advanced by the appellant, that an indirect benefit to the donor of a prize was equivalent to a stake in the game. This argu-

B ment was based on two cases, one *Willis* v. *Young & Stembridge* (9), and the other *Minty* v. *Sylvester* (10). In the former case, which concerned a lottery as contemplated by the Gaming Act, 1802, medals were distributed free to members of the public. Each medal bore a number and the legend " Keep this, it may be worth £100. See the ' Weekly Telegraph ' to-day ". The winning numbers selected by the newspaper proprietors were unknown to the distributors, and there was no

C need for the holder of a medal to buy a paper in order to get a prize. The object of the scheme was, of course, to increase the circulation of the newspaper. The decision against the respondents, holding that there was a lottery, was reached on the basis that the purchasers of the paper contributed towards the prize fund, although the individual purchaser might not be paying for his chance.

It is unnecessary to consider whether the case was rightly decided for in no

D sense can it properly be said here that by buying drinks or in some other way those who attended the parties purchased anything so as to be indirectly putting up any stake in connexion with the bingo playing. By being attracted to the hotel no doubt they were induced to buy drinks, but in no sense were they contributing to the prizes even if they bought drinks before play began. Moreover, there was, as WIDGERY, J., pointed out (11), an express finding by the justices in the Case

E Stated that the distribution of tickets in the alleged gaming was not dependent on or in any way related to the purchase of drink or anything else. *Minty* v. *Sylvester* (10), also a decision on a lottery which bears some resemblance to *Willis* v. *Young & Stembridge* (12), does not add any further assistance to the appellant's subsidiary argument. It would be necessary in order to make an indirect benefit to the donor of a prize equivalent to a stake in the game that a

F contribution should be made or proffered before gaming begins. After the prize is won, money spent which finds its way into the pockets of the donor of the prize does not automatically become equivalent to a stake.

I would dismiss the appeal.

LORD PEARCE: My Lords, I agree with the opinion of my noble and learned friend LORD HODSON.

G

LORD UPJOHN: My Lords, I concur.

Appeal dismissed.

Solicitors: *Cummings, Marchant & Ashton*, agents for *M. D. Shaffner*, Wakefield (for the appellant); *Eland Hore Patersons*, agents for *Powell, Eddison, Freeman & Wilks*, Harrogate (for the respondent).

H

[*Reported by* S. A. HATTEEA, ESQ., *Barrister-at-Law.*]

I

---

(9) [1907] 1 K.B. 448.
(10) (1915), 84 L.J.K.B. 1982.
(11) [1967] 3 All E.R. at p. 260.
(12) [1907] 1 K.B. 448.

A

GOODBURN (Widow and Executrix of the Estate of JOHN WILLIAM GOODBURN *deceased*) v. THOMAS COTTON, LTD.

[COURT OF APPEAL, CIVIL DIVISION (Willmer, Davies and Edmund Davies, L.JJ.), November 30, December 1, 1967.]

Fatal Accident—Damages—Assessment—Deductions in computing damages—Remarriage—Possibility of deceased's widow remarrying—Whether a factor to be taken into account and what weight to be attributed to it—Apportionment of damages to young children.

B

The plaintiff widow claimed damages against the defendants (who admitted liability) under the Fatal Accidents Acts, 1846 to 1959, and the Law Reform (Miscellaneous Provisions) Act, 1934, in respect of the death of her husband in a road accident. She had married at the age of nineteen in December, 1960. There were two young children of the marriage, who were aged one and two and a half at the time of the accident. The plaintiff was an attractive young woman, and in the course of her evidence she admitted that she had been going out with a young man who was twenty-one years old, that he had asked her to marry him and she had seriously thought of doing so, that she had met his parents and he had spent a night with her at what had been the matrimonial home, that there had been a discussion at the house of her parents-in-law of the effects of such a marriage on her two children, and that, although there was no longer any question of her marrying him owing to frequent arguments, she would remarry if the right person came along. In assessing the damages the trial judge rejected the plaintiff widow's submission that the possibility of her remarrying ought to be wholly disregarded, but applied a multiplier of eleven to an income of £728 a year (i.e., £14 a week), representing her degree of dependency on her deceased husband (whose weekly income had been £20) and awarded £8,050 8s. damages, which included £50 8s. funeral expenses, and apportioned £500 to each child. On appeal on the ground that the damages were excessive having regard to the very real probability of the plaintiff's remarrying,

C

D

E

F

Held: (i) in assessing the damages to be paid under the Fatal Accidents Acts, 1846 to 1959, all the circumstances of the case and chances of life should be taken into account, including the likelihood of the widow remarrying and so terminating her dependency, and including also the possibility of its having an adverse effect on the children's financial future (see p. 520, letter D, p. 521, letter H, p. 522, letter G, and p. 523, letter C, post).

G

(ii) on the facts there was a strong probability that the widow would have remarried by the time that she was thirty years old, viz., within six years after the date of the accident, and a multiplier of eleven was therefore unreal (see p. 522, letter A, p. 522, letter I, to p. 523, letter A, and p. 523, letter I, post).

H

(iii) a proper figure to be taken for each of the children was £1 10s. a week, continuing up to the age of sixteen, which would leave £11 a week balance of dependency available to the widow, viz., £572 per annum; the award of damages would accordingly be reduced to £5,500 (plus £50 8s. funeral expenses) apportioned as to £3,300 to the widow and as to £1,000 and £1,200 respectively to the two children (see p. 521, letter I, p. 522, letter C, p. 522, letter I, to p. 523, letter A, and p. 523, letter I, post).

I

Dicta of PHILLIMORE, J., in *Buckley* v. *John Allen & Ford (Oxford), Ltd.* ([1967] 1 All E.R. at p. 542) disapproved.

Appeal allowed.

[**Editorial Note.** A deduction from damages under the Fatal Accidents Acts was made by the Court of Appeal in a case where a widow remarried before expiry of the time for serving notice of appeal (*Curwen* v. *James*, [1963] 2 All E.R. 619).

A   As to the reduction of damages under the Fatal Accidents Acts on account
of possible remarrriage of the widow, see 28 HALSBURY'S LAWS (3rd Edn.) 102,
para. 111, text and note (*o*); and for cases on the subject, see 36 DIGEST (Repl.)
221-224, *1176-1194*.]

Cases referred to:
 Buckley v. *John Allen & Ford (Oxford), Ltd.*, [1967] 1 All E.R. 539; [1967]
B   2 Q.B. 637; [1967] 2 W.L.R. 759.
 Woodroff v. *National Coal Board*, (1954), unreported.

Appeal.
This was an appeal by the defendants from an order of WILLIS, J., made
at Lincoln on May 12, 1967, whereby it was adjudged that the defendants
should pay to the plaintiff the sum of £8,050 8s., of which £50 8s. was special
C damages, the £8,000 being apportioned as to £500 under the Law Reform
(Miscellaneous Provisions) Act, 1934, and as to £7,500 under the Fatal Accidents
Acts, 1846 to 1959. They sought an order that the judgment be varied and judgment be entered for such lesser amount as the court might consider just and
equitable. The ground of appeal was that the amount awarded by the judge as
damages under the Fatal Accidents Acts, 1846 to 1959, was too high in the
D circumstances.

 A. R. A. Beldam for the defendants.
 S. Brown, Q.C., and *Piers Ashworth* for the plaintiff.

 WILLMER, L.J.: The plaintiff in this case sued as the widow and admini-
E stratrix of the estate of her late husband. She brought this action against the
defendants under the Fatal Accidents Acts, 1846-1959, and the Law Reform
(Miscellaneous Provisions) Act, 1934, claiming damages for herself and her two
infant children in respect of the death of her late husband. Her husband was
unhappily killed in a road accident while riding in a van belonging to the defendants on Mar. 12, 1966. The defendants admitted their liability, and the only
F issue remaining to be determined was the quantum of damages which ought to
be recovered by the plaintiff. That issue was tried by WILLIS, J., on May 11 and
12, 1967. He awarded the sum of £8,050 8s., of which the odd £50 8s. represented
the funeral expenses. As to the balance of the £8,000, he allotted £500 to the
claim under the Law Reform (Miscellaneous Provisions) Act, 1934, and £7,500 to
that under the Fatal Accidents Acts, 1846-1959; and he also apportioned out of
G the total £500 to each of the two children, the balance going to the plaintiff. The
defendants have now appealed to this court, contending that the overall sum so
awarded was too high, and so much too high that this court ought to interfere.
 The plaintiff was married in December, 1960, when she was a girl just nineteen years of age. That means that she is now rising twenty-six. There are
two children of the marriage, a girl called Sonia, born on Dec. 13, 1962, and
H a boy called John William, born on June 5, 1965. The deceased husband was
employed as a painter, and was earning somewhere around £20 per week net.
The judge, having heard the evidence, assessed the degree of dependency at £14
per week, which is equivalent to £728 per annum. On this appeal no objection
has been taken to that finding. The figure at which the judge ultimately arrived
indicates as a matter of arithmetic that he must have been applying a multiplier
I of eleven.
 The one ground of appeal is that the award is excessive having regard to the
very real probability of the plaintiff remarrying. In the court below the judge
was referred to the recent decision of PHILLIMORE, J., in *Buckley* v. *John Allen
& Ford (Oxford), Ltd.* (1). In reliance on that decision it was contended on behalf
of the plaintiff that the possibility of this plaintiff remarrying ought to be wholly
disregarded. The judge declined to take that view, having regard to the fact

_____
(1) [1967] 1 All E.R. 539; [1967] 2 Q.B. 637.

that in this case there was direct evidence as to the prospect of the plaintiff **A**
remarrying. That was evidence of a type which was conspicuously absent in
Buckley v. *John Allen & Ford (Oxford), Ltd.* (2). I have no doubt that it was for
this reason that the judge in fact applied a multiplier of eleven, instead of the
larger multiplier that he might otherwise have applied. What has been contended
on this appeal is that, in the light of all the evidence in this case, even a multiplier
of eleven is still much too high.   **B**

In *Buckley's* case (2) no evidence whatsoever was tendered as to the possibility
of the widow remarrying, and it was in that context that PHILLIMORE, J., refused
to make any deduction on that ground. On the facts which were proved in that
case, I do not think that I would seek to quarrel with the actual decision at which
the judge arrived; but PHILLIMORE, J., in the course of his judgment, went a
good way beyond what was necessary for the decision of that case, and expressed **C**
a strong view that a judge trying a case of this character is ill-equipped to assess
the chances of a widow remarrying. He went so far as to suggest that judges
ought to be relieved of the need to enter into what he described as " this guessing
game ".

I am afraid that I find myself unable to agree with PHILLIMORE, J.'s approach
to this matter. It may, it is perfectly true, be distasteful for a judge to have to **D**
assess and to put a money value on a widow's prospect of remarriage; but it
seems to me that, in assessing the damages to be paid under the Fatal Accidents
Acts, 1846-1959, it is necessary to take into account all the circumstances of the
case, and there can be no doubt that one of the most important circumstances
is the likelihood or otherwise of the widow remarrying. Distasteful though it
may be, the task must be faced of assessing that likelihood. I venture to think **E**
that, difficult as the problem is, it is really no different in principle from the
problem facing any judge where, in a personal injuries action, he must necessarily
gaze into the future and assess the probabilities as to the injured person's chances
of recovery, and as to the injured person's future earning prospects.

In the present case WILLIS, J., described the plaintiff as an attractive young
woman, and, since she is yet barely twenty-six years of age, prima facie it is **F**
permissible to think that her prospects of remarriage should be rated as fairly
favourable. The matter, however, does not stop there, for in this case, as I have
said, there was quite a lot of evidence from the plaintiff directed to this very
subject. That evidence came out in a very curious way, and I think that I should
refer (I hope not in too much detail) to the way in which the matter did develop
at the trial. In examination-in-chief all that the plaintiff said about it was this. **G**
She was asked:

" Are you contemplating getting married again? A.—No. Q.—Have you
been out with any men since your husband has died? A.—Yes. Q.—Were
they relatives or not? A.—With relatives. Q.—Who have you been with?
A.—My brother and his girl-friend. Q.—Have you been out with anyone who
is not a relative? A.—No, they were all relatives, [and then she added] Just **H**
one. Q.—Do you think of marrying him? A.—No. Q.—How many times
have you been out with him? A.—Three times to the dog track."

There the matter was left so far as examination-in-chief was concerned. In
cross-examination, however, the truth was gradually dragged out of the plaintiff
in a series of questions and answers to which I must refer. The man in question **I**
was in due course named. He was a Mr. Walker, who was described as being
a man twenty-one years of age, employed as a carpet fitter. The plaintiff stated
that they started going out together in September, 1966, i.e., approximately
six months after the death of the husband, when she said that they went to the
dog track. They also had something to drink, and she agreed to the proposition
that they spent an enjoyable evening together. She then went on to agree that

(2) [1967] 1 All E.R. 539; [1967] 2 Q.B. 637.

A   she had got to know Mr. Walker's sister, and together with the sister she went to see the parents of her late husband. During the course of that visit there was a discussion, first in relation to the question of the guardianship of the children, and secondly as to the desirability or otherwise of the children's name being changed to Walker in the event of the plaintiff marrying Mr. Walker. Following that the plaintiff said that there was now no question of her marrying Mr. Walker

B   because they were now having frequent arguments; but she admitted that up to Christmas time of 1966 she was thinking seriously of marrying Mr. Walker. She admitted having met Mr. Walker's parents, and she further admitted that on one occasion Mr. Walker had been to spend the night with her in what had been her matrimonial home. Then I think it right to read a few further questions and answers from the transcript.

C   " Q.—So really speaking it is not a question of there not being any question of your remarrying. It is a question really of your being willing to remarry if the right person came along? A.—I suppose I would. Q.—This young man, you say, appeared to be the right person until you had this question of disagreements? A.—Yes. Q.—I suppose that from time to time you must have had some disagreements with your husband? A.—Yes, I did. Q.—The

D   mere fact that you have had disagreements does not necessarily mean that it is all over, does it? A.—It is just how I feel. Q.—Of course, you might feel differently? A.—I do not know. Q.—Has he asked you to marry him? A.—Yes. Q.—Was it in fact at one time your intention to marry him? A.—I thought about it."

E   It will be seen, therefore, that Mr. Walker had got as far as proposing marriage to the plaintiff; and she further went on to admit that since then his feelings towards her did not appear to have changed.

Reading the transcript of that evidence, which I have attempted to summarise, one cannot, I think, fail to receive the impression that the plaintiff was being somewhat less than candid in the evidence which she was giving. I think that it is evident that the judge who heard the evidence formed the same impression,

F   although it is fair to say that he did not actually say so in terms; but the way in which he did state his conclusion was significant when he said this

" *Even if* she does not in the event marry Mr. Walker, it is clear that she has no mind to remain unmarried if she meets the right man."

That being the judge's view of the evidence, if is submitted to us on behalf of

G   the defendants that to take a multiplier of eleven in the circumstances of this case was really quite unreal.

The matter, however, is perhaps a little more complicated than that, for, while it is true to say that, if the plaintiff remarried, her remarriage would in all probability for practical purposes terminate her dependency, the same result would not necessarily follow in the case of the children. On the contrary, one

H   can conceive of circumstances in which the plaintiff's remarriage might actually have an adverse effect on the children's financial future. Counsel for the defendants recognised this, and went out of his way to suggest to us that on any view the amount apportioned to the children should actually be increased so as to allow for the possibility of the plaintiff herself remarrying. He suggested that an allowance of £1 10s. a week in respect of each child should be made and

I   continue up to the age of sixteen. That would mean something like twelve and a half years for Sonia, and fifteen years for John William. If my arithmetic is not sadly adrift, that would involve, instead of £500 for each child, something like £1000, for Sonia and £1,200 for John William. If that were done, the effect would be (subject to the limit of £1 10s. per week) that the children's future would be secured notwithstanding any remarriage on the part of the plaintiff.

As to the plaintiff (and this is really the crux of the case) I feel compelled on the evidence, and having regard to the way in which the evidence came out, to come to the conclusion that there is in this case a strong probability of the

plaintiff remarrying. I go further and say that it would not be in the least **A**
surprising if a remarriage took place in the quite near future. In those circumstances I for my part accept the submission put forward on behalf of the defendants that a multiplier of eleven in the case of this widow is quite unreal in the
light of the evidence which has actually been given. I would approach the case
in this way. To my mind, viewing the probabilities, it would be a matter for
surprise if the plaintiff has not remarried by the time she is thirty years old. **B**
That would involve a period of something like four years from now, or approximately six years from the date of the accident. If it is right to take £1 10s. a
week for each of the children (and for my part I think that that is a perfectly
proper figure to take), then the balance of the dependency available for the
widow is £11 per week, or £572 per annum.

I think that I have now sufficiently disclosed the way in which I have arrived **C**
at my conclusion. In the result I think that this appeal should be allowed,
the overall total of £8,000 reduced to £5,500, of which I would apportion £3,300
to the plaintiff widow, £1,000 for Sonia, and £1,200 for John William. To that
total, of course, must be added the odd figure of £50 8s.

DAVIES, L.J.: I agree. I confess that I have some sympathy with the **D**
difficulties expressed by PHILLIMORE, J., in *Buckley* v. *John Allen & Ford (Oxford),
Ltd.* (3) to which WILLMER, L.J., has referred. It is indeed a most difficult and
invidious task for a judge in any case to embark on the inquiry as to the possibility
or probability of remarriage by a plaintiff widow; but in compliance with the
duty imposed by the statute, it is a task which the judge must undertake in
appropriate cases. In *Buckley's* case, (3), I think, it is very likely that the judge **E**
was completely right in the circumstances of that case. For, although counsel for
the defendants submitted to the judge that some discount should be made in
this regard from the damages which he would otherwise have awarded, it appears
plain that the question was not canvassed for a single moment in the evidence;
no questions were addressed to the widow about it and there was really no
evidence on the matter at all. It is also the fact that the widow in that case was **F**
a good deal older than the plaintiff here; she was thirty-eight. Despite the
difficulties, however, I think that it is a task which must be performed. It involves
the consideration of many imponderable matters. It does not necessarily follow
that, if a widow remarries, so far as dependency is concerned her right to financial
support from those who killed her deceased husband necessarily comes to an
end. Matters like the means of the new husband, or the potential husband, have **G**
to be considered; the question whether the marriage will last has to be considered.
All the manifold chances and changes of life have to be considered. It is indeed
a task which many judges have disliked, and which many people have said that
judges ought not to be called on to perform. But, as the law stands, that is the
position.

In the present case WILLMER, L.J., has summarised the evidence given by **H**
the plaintiff. There can be no doubt whatsoever to my mind that here there is
a real prospect of remarriage, either to this Mr. Walker or to someone else.
Speaking personally, it would not surprise me in the least if the plaintiff got
married, after all, to Mr. Walker, whom she was at one time contemplating
marrying and with regard to whom she says that her ideas have now changed.
Her evidence, as summarised by WILLMER, L.J., and the way in which it was
dragged out of her to my mind is most suspect. Even putting Mr. Walker out
of the picture, it is plain on her evidence that she is marriage-minded. She is a
young woman. The judge described her as an attractive young woman; and I
should have thought it could be said that it is almost certain, as WILLMER, L.J.,
has said, that within a very few years she will remarry.

In those circumstances I entirely agree that the damages awarded by the
judge were too high, and hence I think that this court is bound to interfere.

(3) [1967] 1 All E.R. 539; [1967] 2 Q.B. 637.

A With regard to the figures and apportionment of the damages, I agree in every respect with what has fallen from WILLMER, L.J.

EDMUND DAVIES, L.J.: In the unreported case of *Woodroff* v. *National Coal Board,* (4) decided by this court in 1954, LORD GODDARD, C.J., said that on remarriage a widow

B   " . . . would then cease to be the dependant of her late husband; she would then be the dependant of her new husband."

That, however, is by no means the same as saying that, if remarriage eventuates, the widow must be regarded perforce as restored to the same financial position as she was during her first marriage. To assert that would be to go much too far. The widow may marry a man earning substantially less than her first husband
C did. She may marry a shirker, or a man with more extravagant personal tastes, or perhaps a man who subsequently walks out on her. If she remarries at all, it may be to a man whose expectation of life (either by reason of his greater age or poorer health) is not equal to that of her deceased husband. Somehow all these chances of life must be borne in mind, and real injustice may be done
D to the widow by applying to this complex problem the over-simplified approach that, if there seems a real prospect of remarriage, she must ipso facto be treated as likely to be in exactly the same financial position as she was during her first marriage. Just, however, as all these possibilities must be borne in mind in justice to the widow, so also justice to the defendants demands that regard must be had in all cases to the possibility of remarriage; and for myself I do not
E with respect subscribe to the view expressed in *Buckley* v. *John Allen & Ford (Oxford), Ltd.,* (5) that, if no evidence is led on this topic, the prospect of remarriage can properly be ignored. What effect, however, consideration of that possibility will have on the ultimate assessment of damages is another matter. In this respect the prosect of remarriage is exactly the same as all the other contingencies of life. As MR. MUNKMAN says in his excellent primer on DAMAGES
F FOR PERSONAL INJURIES AND DEATH (3rd Edn.) p. 122:

      " In the circumstances of a given case, a judge (or even a jury) might well feel justified in saying that for all practical purposes the adverse contingencies were negligible, and no reduction should be made. The law is that the contingencies must be *taken into account,* not that a deduction is obligatory."

G The task is frequently perplexing, and its performance cannot be regarded as affording one of the most impressive examples of the exercise of the judicial function. Certainly it is one of the most difficult. Nevertheless, it must be attempted (and indeed performed) no matter how exiguous the evidence which forms its basis. Assumptions are to be avoided. What PHILLIMORE, J., described
H as (6) " the conventional argument that *any* woman with the sum [this widow] is likely to receive is likely to remarry " is indefensibly superficial. On the other hand, it would be wrong to assume that, in the absence of positive evidence as to matrimonial prospects, the possibility of remarriage can be ruled out.

In applying those general principles to the facts of this case I can be very brief. The evidence has already been elaborately analysed by WILLMER, L.J.,
I and it would be supererogation to attempt to add thereto. It is sufficient for me to observe that speculation as to the widow's matrimonial prospects can here proceed on far firmer ground than is usually available in claims under the Fatal Accidents Acts, 1846-1959. The evidence indeed impels me to the same conclusion as my lords, and I concur in holding that this appeal must be allowed, and the sums of £3,300, £1,000 and £1,200 substituted for those awarded at the trial.

(4) (1954), unreported.
(5) [1967] 1 All E.R. 539; [1967] 2 Q.B. 637.
(6) [1967] 1 All E.R. at p. 542, letter D; [1967] 2 Q.B. at p. 644.

Appeal allowed. Total damages reduced from £8,000 to £5,500 apportioned as to A
£3,300 to the plaintiff, £1,000 to Sonia and £1,200 to John William, plus £50 8s.
special damage.

Solicitors: *Barlow, Lyde & Gilbert* (for the defendants); *T. D. Jones & Co.,*
agents for *Riley, Sutcliffe & Co.,* Blackburn (for the plaintiff).

[*Reported by* F. A. AMIES, ESQ., *Barrister-at-Law.*] B

STEPHENSON (Inspector of Taxes) *v.* PAYNE,
STONE, FRASER & CO. (a firm).   C

[CHANCERY DIVISION (Pennycuick, J.), November 28, 29, 1967.]

Income Tax—Deduction in computing profits—Attribution of outgoings to period
of account—Secretarial service charge—Charge by service company wholly
owned by taxpayer firm—Arrangement that service company should make D
only nominal profit—Debit of large charge in excess of normal rate in first
year of partnership business—Arrangement for adjustment in future years
—Charge in first year affecting firm's liability for three years—Whether
part of charge in excess of normal rate allowable as deduction in computing
profits of firm.

A firm of chartered accountants, which owing to death of a partner con- E
stituted a new firm for income tax purposes as from Oct. 30, 1960, formed a
private company, of which the partners owned the shares and were the
directors, for the purpose of providing secretarial and similar services for
the partnership. The company's first period of account ran from Dec. 1,
1960, to May 31, 1962. It was always contemplated that the company
would charge for its services to the partnership. In the summer of 1962 it F
was agreed that the basis of the charge of the company for its services over
the whole period of rendering them should be such as to earn only a nominal
profit. However, for the firm's year ending Nov. 30, 1961, the charge agreed
was to be £47,000, which was £15,000 in excess of the actual cost of the
services (£32,000) in the partnership's period of account ending on Nov. 30,
1961, on the understanding that the charge in later years should be so G
adjusted as to secure for the company over the long term a nominal profit
only. The charge for the following year ending on Nov. 30, 1962, was
subsequently agreed at £21,000 regard being had to the excess of the £47,000
over the actual cost in the previous year. The effect of the charge of the
£47,000 was to reduce the profits of the firm in what was, for income tax
purposes, its first year of business; from this would follow consequential H
reductions in the assessments to income tax for each of the firm's first three
tax years, which would be computed by reference to the profits of the first
year. The taxpayer firm having been disallowed £15,000 part of the £47,000,
the General Commissioners on appeal to them found that £47,000 was a
commercially reasonable price for the company to charge for services costing
£32,000, and that the taxpayer firm got value for it in the long term; they I
also found that no part of the £47,000 constituted a pre-payment.
On further appeal,

Held: the £15,000 was rightly disallowed as an outgoing in computing
the taxpayer firm's profits in its first year of business, because the £15,000
was a misattribution, contrary to ordinary principles of commercial accountancy, in that it attributed the cost of services appropriate to subsequent
periods of account to the taxpayer firm's first period of account (see p. 528,
letters G and I, and p. 529, letter F, post).

A   Dictum of VISCOUNT SIMON in *Gardner, Mountain and D'Ambrumenil, Ltd.*
v. *Inland Revenue Comrs.* ([1947] 1 All E.R. at pp. 653, 654) applied.

Appeal allowed.

[As to computation of profits and gains for income tax purposes, see 20 HALS-
BURY'S LAWS (3rd Edn.) 139, 140, para. 247; and for cases on the subject, see
28 DIGEST (Repl.) 71-75, *268-286*.]

B   Cases referred to:

Gardner, Mountain and D'Ambrumenil, Ltd. v. *Inland Revenue Comrs.*, [1947]
    1 All E.R. 650; 177 L.T. 16; 29 Tax Cas. 69; 28 Digest (Repl.) 377,
    1847.

Strong & Co., Ltd. v. *Woodifield*, [1904-07] All E.R. Rep. 953; [1906] A.C. 448;
    75 L.J.K.B. 864; 95 L.T. 241; 5 Tax Cas. 215; 28 Digest (Repl.)
C   79, *298.*

Vallambrosa Rubber Co., Ltd. v. *Farmer (Surveyor of Taxes)*, (1910), 5 Tax Cas.
    529; 28 Digest (Repl.) 105, *281.*

Case Stated.

The taxpayer firm appealed to the General Commissioners of Income Tax for
D   Holborn in the London Borough of Camden against the following assessments
made on it under Case I of Sch. D to the Income Tax Act, 1952, in respect of
profits arising from the profession of chartered accountants: 1960-61 £2,000;
1961-62 £12,000; 1962-63 £12,000. The point for the commissioners to decide
was whether a service charge of £47,000 debited in the taxpayer firm's accounts
for the year ended Nov. 30, 1961, was wholly admissible in computing for
E   income tax purposes the profits of the firm for that accounting year. The
relevant parts of the Case Stated were as follows:

" 4. (a) Mr. John Frank Butlin, chartered accountant, a partner in the
[taxpayer] firm and Mr. Keith Stanley Carmichael, chartered accountant,
a partner in Messrs. Wilson, Bigg & Co., chartered accountants, of 4, Chiswell
Street, E.C.1, and a director of Foulkes, Lynch and Co., Ltd., accountancy
F   tutors, gave evidence before us on behalf of the firm.

" (b) The evidence given by Mr. K. S. Carmichael was that it was proper
for the firm to charge in its accounts whatever sum was payable in respect
of a service charge for a particular period, under a legally binding agreement,
under which the services were to be rendered; and that in such case the
actual cost of providing the services would be irrelevant; but that, if the
G   services were not rendered under a legally binding agreement which laid
down the price to be paid for the services, the cost of providing the services
would be relevant.

" (c) We accepted their evidence on matters of fact, and, so far as it was
an expression of opinion, we accepted it as given bona fide.

" 5. The following facts were admitted or proved before us:—(i) On the
H   death of a partner, on Oct. 29, 1960, the [taxpayer] firm fell, by virtue of
s. 19 (i) of the Finance Act, 1953 to be treated immediately thereafter as
though a new profession had been set up and commenced. (ii) Assessments
made on the [taxpayer] firm in respect of its profits for the period of one
month to Nov. 30, 1960, and for the year ended Nov. 30, 1961, were dependent upon the application of s. 128 of the Income Tax Act, 1952. (iii)
I   Profits earned by the [taxpayer] firm up to Apr. 5, 1961, formed the measure
of the income tax assessment on the firm for the fiscal year 1960-61 and the
quantum of these profits fell to be determined (under the provisions of
s. 155 of the Income Tax Act, 1952) by a simple time apportionment.

" (iv) The income tax assessment on the [taxpayer] firm for the fiscal
year 1961-62 was required, under the provisions of s. 128 (2) of the Income
Tax Act, 1952 to be ascertained by reference to the profits earned over the
first twelve-month period following the setting up of the new profession,
viz., the twelve month period ending on Oct. 29, 1961. The quantum of

those profits similarly fell to be determined by a simple time apportionment.
(v) The amount of the profits of the [taxpayer] firm to be assessed in the
third year, namely 1962-63, was governed by s. 127 of the Income Tax
Act, 1952 and, in these particular circumstances, the provisions of s. 127
(2) (*b*) of the Income Tax Act, 1952 applied. Hence it was mandatory that
the Commissioners of Inland Revenue should determine which period of
twelve months should be adopted as the measure of the said assessment.
This determination had yet to be effected.

" (vi) Following the said death and consequent change in partnership
a service company, called Bedford Row Nominees, Ltd., of 17, Bedford
Row, W.C. 1 (referred to as ' the service company '), was utilised for the
convenience of the [taxpayer] firm, for the purpose of providing staff, light,
heat, water, fixtures and fittings, etc. and for acting, for administrative
purposes, as secretaries, registrars and executors on behalf of the firm's
clients. (vii) The directors and shareholders of the service company were
the same individuals as the partners in the [taxpayer] firm.

" (viii) The service company was to make a charge to the [taxpayer]
firm once a year and its policy was that it would not make undue profit
at the expense of the firm. (ix) It was not until the summer of 1962 that an
oral agreement was entered into between the partners in the [taxpayer]
firm and the directors of the service company, whereby a service charge
of £47,000 was to be paid to the service company for the year to Nov. 30,
1961. (x) The said figure was reached on the understanding that the
service charge for later years would be so adjusted as to secure for the
service company, over the long term, a nominal profit only. No part of
the figure of £47,000 constituted a pre-payment.

" (xi) The cost of the said services rendered to the [taxpayer] firm for the
year to Nov. 30, 1961, was known to have amounted to some £32,000 so
that the payment of £47,000 resulted in a gross profit for the service company
of £15,000. (xii) In due course the service charge for the subsequent year,
namely to Nov. 30, 1962, was agreed at £21,000. In arriving at that amount
regard was had to the fact that the previous payment of £47,000 was in
excess of the cost of the services to Nov. 30, 1961. (xiii) The accounts of
the service company, contained for the eighteen months period ended May
31, 1962, a credit for a service charge of £48,000 of which £47,000 was
debited in the accounts of the [taxpayer] firm for the year ended Nov. 30,
1961. The balance of £1,000 formed part of the service charge of £21,000
agreed for the year ended Nov. 30, 1962, and referred to in para. 5 (xii)
above. It represented far less than the value of the services provided in
the period from Dec. 1, 1961, to May 31, 1962. (xiv) From the point of
view of the company £47,000 was a commercially reasonable price for the
company to charge anybody for services costing £32,000. The [taxpayer]
firm got value for the £47,000 in the long term.

" 6. It was contended on behalf of the [taxpayer] firm before the commissioners that—(a) the evidence of Mr. Butlin that the payment of £47,000
was made pursuant to a contract between the [taxpayer] firm and the
service company, was unchallenged and ought to be accepted; (b) the
evidence of Mr. Carmichael that no part of the sum of £47,000 constituted
a pre-payment and that the accounts of the [taxpayer] firm for the year to
Nov. 30, 1961, were drawn up on proper accountancy principles, was unchallenged and ought to be accepted; (c) the evidence of Mr. Butlin and Mr.
Carmichael that £47,000 was a sum which it was commercially reasonable
for the [taxpayer] firm to pay for the services made available to it by the
service company was unchallenged and ought to be accepted; (d) the
expenditure of £47,000 for the facilities provided by the service company
was wholly and exclusively incurred for the purposes of the profession
carried on by the [taxpayer] firm and accordingly was wholly deductible

A   in computing the profits of the firm for the accounting year to Nov. 30, 1961.

" 7. It was contended by H.M. inspector of taxes before the commissioners that—(a) The decision to pay the said sum of £47,000 in respect of the year to Nov. 30, 1961, which was not made until 1962, was not made on either a commercial basis or a contractual basis; (b) £32,000 part of the said £47,000, and no more, was the proper charge to be deducted in computing

B   the profits of the [taxpayer] firm for the accounting year to Nov. 30, 1961, in respect of services rendered by the service company in that year.

" 8. We, the commissioners who heard the appeal, having carefully considered the evidence adduced before us accepted the oral agreement referred to in para. 5 (ix) above as bona fide, and we decided that the amount of £47,000 paid by the [taxpayer] firm as a service charge relating to the year

C   ended Nov. 30, 1961, was a sum wholly and exclusively expended for the purposes of the profession in that year and we left the figures for 1960-61 and 1961-62 to be agreed between the parties in accordance with this our decision in principle."

The Solicitor of Inland Revenue gave notice of a new contention in these terms:

" It will be contended on behalf of the Crown that the sum of £47,000

D   was paid by the [taxpayer firm] partly in consideration of the services supplied to it in the period ended Nov. 30, 1961, and partly in consideration of the undertaking by Bedford Row Nominees, Ltd. [the service company] to supply services to the [taxpayer firm] in subsequent periods for a sum of £15,000 less than the sum which would enable that company to earn a nominal profit on the supply of such services, and accordingly (i) of the sum of

E   £47,000 part thereof, namely £15,000 was not a proper charge for the purpose of arriving at a true and fair view of the profits of the [taxpayer firm] for the year ended Nov. 30, 1961; (ii) the sum of £15,000 was not deductible by the [taxpayer firm] in computing its profits for the purpose of its assessment to tax under Case I of Sch. D for the year 1960-61 or 1961-62; (iii) if the sum of £15,000 or alternatively the whole amount of £47,000 was deductible, the

F   relevant accounts of the [taxpayer firm] should be credited with £15,000 or thereabouts, being the value of the [taxpayer firm's] right to future discount on services rendered to it by Bedford Row Nominees, Ltd. [the service company]."

The decision of the commissioners as regards the £47,000 has been set out at letter C, above; they allowed the appeal accordingly. The commissioners reduced the assessments of two years as follows: 1960-61 to £1,432; 1961-62 to £2,696 (both agreed figures). They adjourned the appeal relating to 1962-63 pending a decision of the Commissioners of Inland Revenue under s. 127 (2) (*b*) of the Income Tax Act, 1952.

Desmond C. Miller, Q.C., and *J. R. Phillips* for the Crown.

J. M. Grundy for the taxpayer firm.

PENNYCUICK, J.: This is an appeal by the inspector of taxes against a decision of the General Commissioners for the Holborn Division whereby they allowed an appeal by the respondent taxpayer firm, Payne, Stone, Fraser and Co. against assessments under Case I of Sch. D to the Income Tax Act, 1952 for the years 1960-61, 1961-62 and 1962-63. It is common ground that the assessments should have been made under Case II of Sch. D but nothing turns on this point. In order that the issue may be intelligible it is necessary to bear in mind the provisions as to the basis of computation of the profits of a trade or profession, particularly in regard to the opening years of the trade or profession. These will be found in s. 127 and s. 128 of the Income Tax Act, 1952. I need not read these provisions. It will be sufficient to say that for the first three fiscal years the profit is normally computed by reference to the actual profit of the first yearly period of account. It is therefore much to the interests of the taxpayers to keep the profits of the first yearly period as low as possible.

In the present case the taxpayer firm are in practice as chartered accountants. They have been in practice for a number of years and have made regular profits of substantial amounts. One member of the firm died on Oct. 29, 1960, and thereupon the taxpayer firm fell to be treated as though the surviving partners had set up a new profession. The taxpayer firm's period of account runs to Nov. 30 in each year. Towards the end of 1960 the taxpayer firm caused to be incorporated a company by the name of Bedford Row Nominees, Ltd. (described as " the service company "), for the purpose of providing services to the taxpayer firm. The service company's first period of account began on Dec. 1, 1960, and ran until May 31, 1962. The partners in the taxpayer firm are the sole shareholders in the service company and are also the directors of the service company. It was arranged from the start that the service company should make a charge for its services to the taxpayer firm, but the basis of the charge was not agreed until the summer of 1962, i.e., after the end of the taxpayer firm's period of account ended on Nov. 30, 1961. It was then arranged that the service company's charge should be adjusted to secure what is described as a nominal profit only; but as part of the arrangement the charge for the period of account ended Nov. 30, 1961, was fixed at a figure in excess by £15,000 of the actual cost of the services which had been rendered during that period, and there was to be a corresponding reduction in the charge thereafter. On this basis the profit for the all-important first period of account of the taxpayer firm was diminished by £15,000. The Crown contends that this sum of £15,000 is not admissible as an outgoing for that period.

[His LORDSHIP read the relevant parts of the Case Stated as hereinbefore set out (see p. 525, letter E, to p. 527, letter C, ante), and the notice of a new contention by the Crown and continued:] With all respect to the commissioners, I do not think that their decision can be supported. The attribution of any given outgoing to one or other period of account for the purpose of striking a true balance of profit or loss is a matter to be determined on the ordinary principles of commercial accountancy. Here the basis of charge agreed on in the summer of 1962 by the partners in their dual capacity as such and as directors of the service company was a nominal profit, i.e., the actual cost to the service company of the services which it rendered with or without a very small addition which could be described as nominal profit. It is accepted by counsel for the taxpayer firm, that this basis was to be applicable overall to the whole period for which services had been or were to be rendered, including the period of account already ended on Nov. 30, 1961 (see Case Stated, para. 5 (x) and (xii) p. 526, letters E and F, ante). The partners, however, arranged that in calculating the amount of its service charge the service company should add £15,000 to the actual cost of the services rendered in the year of account ended Nov. 30, 1961, and make a corresponding deduction in making its service charges in the subsequent year or years of account. This was in fact done. It seems to me that this misattribution is manifestly contrary to the ordinary principles of commercial accountancy and distorts the true balance of profit of the taxpayer firm's profession. The point hardly admits of elaboration.

It is clear enough on the findings of the commissioners that, during the period of account ended on Nov. 30, 1961, the service company rendered its services on the footing that it would make a charge for them (see Case Stated, para. 5 (viii), p. 526, letter D, ante). Mr. Carmichael gave evidence in the Case Stated, para. 4 (b)—" that in such case the actual cost of providing the services would be irrelevant ". The commissioners, while only going so far as to accept Mr. Carmichael's evidence as given bona fide, found that the £47,000 was a commercially reasonable price for the service company to charge anybody for services costing £32,000. I am not concerned to question this finding of the commissioners and I do not do so, but neither Mr. Carmichael's evidence nor the commissioners' findings get over the difficulty in the way of the taxpayer firm, viz., that overall the £15,000 was not in truth a profit charge at all, but an allocation of part of the actual cost of the services for the subsequent period of account.

I fully recognise that the service company is a different person in law from the

A   taxpayer firm and that the provision as to the £15,000 was part of the contractual arrangement between them.   On analysis, however, this provision represents no more than a term that each party shall deal with the £15,000 in its own accounts in a particular manner.   It does not touch either the amount payable by the taxpayer firm to the service company or the times at which payments are to be actually made.   I observe the finding in para. 5 (x) of the Case Stated (see p. 526,

B   letter E, ante) that " no part of the figure of £47,000 constituted a pre-payment ". This is literally true.   What took place was a misattribution.

I agree with the commissioners that the whole sum of £47,000 was wholly and exclusively expended for the purposes of the taxpayer firm's profession.   The vice in their finding lies in the words " in that year ".   The expenditure made in the second year could only as to £32,000 properly be attributed to the first year.

C   I was referred to a number of authorities on the attribution of profits to one or another year.   I shall only quote one paragraph from the speech of VISCOUNT SIMON in *Gardner, Mountain and D'Ambrumenil, Ltd.* v. *Inland Revenue Comrs.* (1):

" In calculating the taxable profit of a business on income tax principles . . . services completely rendered or goods supplied which are not to be paid for till a subsequent year cannot, generally, speaking, be dealt with by treating

D   the taxpayer's outlay as pure loss in the year in which it was incurred and bringing in the remuneration as pure profit in the subsequent year in which it is paid or is due to be paid.   In making an assessment to income tax under Sch. D, the net result of the transaction, setting expense on the one side and a figure for remuneration on the other side, ought to appear (as it would appear in a proper system of accountancy) in the same year's profit and loss

E   account, and that year will be the year when the service was rendered or the goods delivered."

So here, there is no doubt that the taxpayer firm was entitled to bring in as an outgoing for the period of account ended Nov. 30, 1961, an amount owing to the service company in respect of the services rendered during that period of account.

F   Again, no doubt, at the end of the period the amount so owing was still a matter for computation.   What was not legitimate was to attribute to the period a disproportionate part of the charge subsequently agreed at a uniform rate.

To avoid misunderstanding I should say in conclusion that the observations in this judgment are addressed, and only addressed, to the particular transaction with which this appeal is concerned.   I propose to allow the appeal accordingly.

G

Appeal allowed.

Solicitors: *Solicitor of Inland Revenue; Callingham, Tucker & Co.* (for the taxpayer firm).

[*Reported by* F. A. AMIES, ESQ., *Barrister-at-Law.*]

H

I

(1) [1947] 1 All E.R. 650 at pp. 653, 654;   29 Tax Cas. 69 at p. 93.   Before the commissioners the taxpayer relied on *Vallambrosa Rubber Co., Ltd.* v. *Farmer (Surveyor of Taxes)* ((1910), 5 Tax Cas. 529);   and the Inspector of Taxes relied on *Strong & Co., Ltd.* v. *Woodifield*, ([1904-07] All E.R. Rep. 953;   [1906] A.C. 448;   5 Tax Cas. 215).

A

PARADISE BEACH AND TRANSPORTATION CO., LTD. AND OTHERS *v.* PRICE-ROBINSON AND OTHERS.

[PRIVY COUNCIL (Lord Pearce, Lord Upjohn and Lord Pearson), October 19, 23, 24, 1967, January 22, 1968.]

B

Privy Council—Bahama Islands—Limitation of action—Land—Adverse posses-sion—Co-tenants—Devise of land in undivided shares—Co-tenants entitled to some only of the undivided shares were in exclusive possession of the whole land for over twenty years for their own benefit—Whether right of entry and right of action accrued on death of testator—Whether time ran notwithstanding possession of co-tenants was not wrongful—Real Property Limitation (No. 1) Act, 1833 (c. 124), s. 3—Real Property Limitation (1874) Act (c. 216), s. 1.

C

A testator devised land in the Bahamas to named children and grand-children in undivided shares as tenants in common. The testator died in 1913. Two of his daughters, themselves entitled to some undivided shares, and their successors in title continued and were in exclusive possession of the land in question thereafter until the commencement of proceedings. The possession of the daughters was for their own use and benefit*, and as tenants in common they were rightfully in possession of the whole land*. The appellants established a paper title to certain other undivided shares in the land, and contended that, as the possession of the daughters and their successors in title was not wrongful, the appellants' title was not statute-barred under the statutes of limitation of 1833 and 1874†.

D

Held: a right of entry and a right to bring an action had accrued, for the purposes of the statutes of limitation, in 1913, and, whatever the nature of the daughters' possession as co-tenants, twenty years' possession before action brought extinguished the title of the appellants (see p. 535, letters D and F, post).

Appeal dismissed.

Dictum of LORD DENMAN, C.J., in *Nepean* v. *Doe d. Knight* ((1837), 2 M. & W. at p. 911) approved.

Appeal dismissed.

F

[As to adverse possession for the purpose of limitation of actions, see 24 HALS-BURY'S LAWS (3rd Edn.) 251, 252, paras. 481, 482; and for cases on the subject, see 32 DIGEST (Repl.) 505, 506, *1115-1122.*

G

As to limitation of actions in regard to land in England where the proceeds of sale are held on trust for tenants in common, see 24 HALSBURY'S LAWS (3rd Edn.) 256, para. 495.]

Cases referred to:

Culley v. *Doe d. Taylerson,* (1840), 11 Ad. & El. 1008; 9 L.J.Q.B. 288; 113 E.R. 697; 32 Digest (Repl.) 496, *1066.*

Doe d. Fishar and Taylor v. *Prosser,* (1774), 1 Cowp. 217; 98 E.R. 1052; 32 Digest (Repl.) 531, *1291.*

H

Doe d. Jones v. *Williams,* (1836), 5 Ad. & El. 291; 5 L.J.K.B. 231; 111 E.R. 1175; 32 Digest (Repl.) 474, *888.*

Henderson v. *Eason,* (1851), 17 Q.B. 701; 21 L.J.Q.B. 82; 18 L.T.O.S. 142; 117 E.R. 1451; 20 Digest (Repl.) 288, *304.*

I

Hobbs, Re, Hobbs v. *Wade,* (1887), 36 Ch.D. 553; 57 L.J.Ch. 184; 58 L.T. 9; 32 Digest (Repl.) 536, *1333.*

Jacobs v. *Seward,* (1872), L.R. 5 H.L. 464; 41 L.J.C.P. 221; 27 L.T. 185; 36 J.P. 771; 38 Digest (Repl.) 829, *416.*

---

* See p. 535, letters A and H, post.

† The relevant s. 1 of the Act of 1833 and s. 3 of the Act of 1874 are set out at p. 533, letters C to I, post.

A   *James* v. *Salter,* (1837), 3 Bing. N.C. 544; 6 L.J.C.P. 171; 132 E.R. 520;
32 Digest (Repl.) 517, *1188.*

Landi, Re, Georgi (or Giorgi) v. *Navani,* [1939] 3 All E.R. 569; [1939] Ch. 828;
108 L.J.Ch. 401; 161 L.T. 131; 32 Digest (Repl.) 532, *1310.*

Magdalen Hospital (Governors) v. *Knotts,* (1878), 8 Ch.D. 709; 47 L.J.Ch. 726;
38 L.T. 624; *affd.* H.L., (1879), 4 App. Cas. 324; 48 L.J.Ch. 579;

B   40 L.T. 466; 43 J.P. 460; 32 Digest (Repl.) 512, *1157.*

Manchester Gas Act, Re, Ex p. Hasell, (1839), 3 Y. & C. Ex. 617; 160 E.R. 848;
32 Digest (Repl.) 531, *1298.*

Nepean v. *Doe d. Knight,* (1837), 2 M. & W. 894; 7 L.J.Ex. 355; 150 E.R. 1021;
32 Digest (Repl.) 496, *1065.*

Pugh v. *Heath,* (1882), 7 App. Cas. 235; 51 L.J.Q.B. 267; 46 L.T. 321; 32

C   Digest (Repl.) 550, *1446.*

Appeal.

This was an appeal by leave by Paradise Beach and Transportation Co., Ltd.,
Beach Head, Ltd., Eleanor Parroti, Jocelyn Moxey, Mizpah Burrows and
Frederick Burrows against a decision of Scarr, J., of the Supreme Court of the
Bahama Islands, Equity side, dated Dec. 19, 1963, dismissing the petition of the
D   appellants presented under the Quieting Titles Act, 1959, for a declaration of
their title in respect of an undivided 17/21 (85/105) shares in land of about
32.15 acres in Paradise Island, Bahamas. By an amended statement of facts
dated Oct. 30, 1963, the appellants abandoned their claim to 9/105th shares,
admitting that these had escheated to the Crown; the appellants claimed to
be the owners of the remainder, viz., 76/105ths shares. The facts are set out
E   in the opinion of Lord Upjohn.

J. A. R. Finlay for the first, third, fourth, fifth and sixth appellants.
S. G. Davies for the second appellant.
K. W. Rubin for the respondents.

LORD UPJOHN: This is an appeal from the judgment delivered on
F   Dec. 19, 1963 of Scarr, J., sitting in the Supreme Court of the Bahamas on the
Equity Side whereby he dismissed the appellants' claim under the Quieting
Titles Act, 1959, to be entitled to seventeen twenty-first undivided shares in a
strip of land known as lot No. 8 running from sea to sea across Hog Island
(recently renamed Paradise) and containing about thirty-two acres. Until the
island was developed recently the land in question was very poor, as the judge
G   said in the course of his judgment " it was mostly coral rock with only pockets
of soil and from the monetary point of view it was, prior to the last war, practically
worthless ". Their lordships have been informed that it is now very valuable.
The appellants claim undivided shares in the land under the will of one John
Alexander Burrows (who will be referred to as the testator) who died on Oct. 23,
1913, having by his will dated Nov. 22, 1912, devised some land including lot
H   No. 8 to certain named children and grandchildren as tenants in common subject
to a life interest in an undivided one-third part-in favour of his widow, who died
in 1918 without ever having entered into possession, so that her interest may for
the purposes of this appeal be ignored. The learned judge in his judgment
traced the complicated devolution of the undivided shares claimed by the appellants and held that their claim so far as the paper title was concerned was estab-
I   lished subject only to the fact that 23/105 shares part of the 17/21 (or 85/105)
shares of the appellants had escheated to the Crown, as one of their predecessors
(Clarence Azgin mentioned in the testator's will) had not only died intestate
without issue but also was illegitimate.

There has been no appeal from those findings, nor has there been any dispute
that the respondents, who are the successors in title of Roseliza Price (who will
be referred to as Roseliza) and her sister Victoria Hanna (who will be referred to
as Victoria), both original takers under the testator's will were each entitled to
10/105 undivided shares in the land. The respondents however claim that

Roseliza and Victoria and their successors have been in exclusive possession of   A
the land since the death of the testator or for more than twenty years before
action brought and that the title of the appellants is barred by the relevant
statutes of limitation. That is the sole question before their lordships, but it is
divided into issues of fact and law; counsel for the second appellant in the main
developed the challenge to the correctness of the findings of fact of the judge on
the question of possession as well as his conclusions on the relevant law, while   B
counsel for the remaining appellants developed his argument on the footing that
the judge erred only in law.

Their lordships must logically deal with the issues of fact first. It is common
ground that during the lifetime of their father the testator Roseliza and Victoria
farmed the land on their father's behalf, so that their possession was his possession,
but after his death they remained there carrying on the farming, not living there,   C
for until the early 1920s there was not even a house on the land which was then
erected by Roseliza, but visiting and farming the land by day. So there is no doubt
that they were in possession throughout but, quite rightly, the judge before
deciding whether this possession was exclusive, recognised that he must examine
the evidence tendered on behalf of the appellants supporting the view that some
of their predecessors had in fact entered into possession. After careful examination   D
of the facts he reached the clearest conclusion that apart from the possible
exception of the testator's eldest son Nehemiah until his death in 1917 and his
(Nehemiah's) son, referred to in the judgment as cousin John (for John not only
succeeded to his father's undivided share but as heir-at-law of certain other
original takers to some other undivided shares as well), until the latter's death
in 1939, none of them ever took possession of any part of the land. The judge   E
reviewed the evidence in relation to cousin John's share in great detail. He heard
and saw the witnesses and had as he expressed it " no hesitation in rejecting the
bulk of the evidence given on behalf of cousin John ". He dealt with the evidence
that cousin John did visit the land on occasions and that he may have received
occasional gifts of vegetables from his aunts Roseliza and Victoria, but he reached
the conclusion that " on the evidence these sporadic acts fall far short of possession,   F
even though one must take a most favourable view of a documentary owner ".
It was argued that these findings were wrong, that all the appellants entered into
possession in or after 1913, alternatively that cousin John did or that two other
of the original takers (Miriam Stuart and Veronica Murray) did so, and the
evidence was reviewed before their lordships. It was said that having regard to
the nature of the land these visits and receipt of presents and so on established   G
possession. Their lordships are quite unable to accept this argument; the matter
is one of fact and they can feel no doubt but that the judge reached the correct
conclusion that none of the appellants' predecessors including cousin John ever
entered into possession of the land. The fact that the learned judge occasionally
expressed the view in his judgment that cousin John was a possible exception
from his general finding of non possession makes no inroad on his clear conclusion   H
as to cousin John's non entry into possession.

Having dealt with the evidence on behalf of the appellants' predecessor
the judge returned to a consideration of the nature of the possession of Roseliza
and Victoria, and after a detailed review of the evidence reached this conclusion :

" it is clear beyond any doubt that Roseliza and Victoria entered into
exclusive possession of this land and the evidence substantiates such   I
possession from 1913 until their deaths and since then by their successors
in title."

Their lordships see no reason to doubt the correctness of that finding and must
turn to the argument addressed to them on that footing by counsel for the
appellants.

The essence of the argument was that, although the respondents and their
predecessors had been in exclusive possession since 1913, yet for the purposes of

A   the relevant statutes of limitation time has not yet started to run in favour of the respondents. The relevant enactments are to be found in the Real Property Limitation (No. 1) Act, 1833 (which will be referred to as the "Act of 1833") and the Real Property Limitation (1874) Act (which will be referred to as the "Act of 1874") and are for all relevant purposes in the same terms as the Real Property Limitation Acts, 1833 and 1874 formerly applicable to this country.

B   The first relevant section was s. 2 of the Act of 1833, but that was repealed and re-enacted by s. 1 of the Act of 1874, and their lordships propose to set out that section first in its logical place.

"1. After the commencement of this Act no person shall make an entry or distress or bring an action or suit, to recover any land or rent, but within twenty years next after the time at which the right to make such entry or C   distress, or to bring such action or suit, shall have first accrued to some person through whom he claims; or if such right shall not have accrued to any person through whom he claims, then within twenty years next after the time at which the right to make such entry or distress, or to bring such action or suit, shall have first accrued to the person making or bringing the same."

D   The following sections are all in the Act of 1833:

"3. In the construction of this Act the right to make an entry or distress or bring an action to recover any land or rent shall be deemed to have first accrued at such time as hereinafter is mentioned; (that is to say), when the person claiming such land or rent, or some person through whom he claims, shall, in respect of the estate or interest claimed, have been in possession or E   in receipt of the profits of such land, or in receipt of such rent, and shall while entitled thereto have been dispossessed, or have discontinued such possession or receipt, then such right shall be deemed to have first accrued at the time of such dispossession or discontinuance of possession, or at the last time at which any such profits or rent were or was so received; and when the person claiming such land or rent shall claim the estate or interest of some deceased F   person who shall have continued in such possession or receipt in respect of the same estate or interest until the time of his death, and shall have been the last person entitled to such estate or interest who shall have been in such possession or receipt, then such right shall be deemed to have first accrued at the time of such death; and when the person claiming such land or rent shall claim in respect of an estate or interest in possession granted, appointed, or G   otherwise assured by any instrument (other than a will) to him, or some person through whom he claims, by a person being in respect of the same estate or interest in the possession or receipt of the profits of the land, or in the receipt of the rent, and no person entitled under such instrument shall have been in such possession or receipt, then such right shall be deemed to have first accrued at the time at which the person claiming as aforesaid, or H   the person through whom he claims, became entitled to such possession or receipt by virtue of such instrument; and when the estate or interest claimed shall have been an estate or interest in reversion or remainder, or other future estate or interest, and no person shall have obtained the possession or receipt of the profits of such land or the receipt of such rent in respect of such estate or interest, then such right shall be deemed to have first accrued at the time I   at which such estate or interest became an estate or interest in possession; and when the person claiming such land or rent, or the person through whom he claims, shall have become entitled by reason of any forfeiture or breach of condition, then such right shall be deemed to have first accrued when such forfeiture was incurred or such condition was broken.

"12. When any one or more of several persons entitled to any land or rent as coparceners, joint tenants, or tenants in common, shall have been in possession or receipt of the entirety, or more than his or their undivided share or shares of such land or of the profits thereof, or of such rent, for his or their

own benefit, or for the benefit of any person or persons other than the person
or persons entitled to the other share or shares of the same land or rent, such
possession or receipt shall not be deemed to have been the possession or
receipt of or by such last-mentioned person or persons or any of them.

" 34. At the determination of the period limited by this Act to any person
for making an entry or distress, or bringing any writ of quare impedit or
other action or suit, the right and title of such person to the land, rent, or
advowson for the recovery whereof such entry, distress, action, or suit
respectively might have been made or brought within such period shall be
extinguished."

Before those enactments it was common ground that the relevant law was the
same as in this country. The reason for this substantial alteration to the previously
existing law is well known.

Onto the Statute of James the common law engrafted the doctrine of " non
adverse " possession, that is to say, that the title of the true owner was not
endangered until there was a possession clearly inconsistent with its due recognition, namely " adverse possession " so that there had to be something in the
nature of ouster. In practice, however, it was very difficult to discover what was
sufficient to constitute adverse possession; thus the possession of one co-tenant
was the possession of the rest though undisputed sole possession for a very long
time might be evidence from which a jury could properly presume ouster. (See
Doe d. Fishar and Taylor v. *Prosser* (1).) All this was swept away by the Act of
1833 as was explained in an illuminating judgment of LORD DENMAN, C.J., in
Culley v. *Doe d. Taylerson* (2). After pointing out that at common law the possession of one tenant in common was possession of all and that there must be an
ouster, he continued (2):

" The effect of this section [s. 2] is to put an end to all questions and
discussions, whether the possession of the lands, be adverse or not; and, if
one party has been in the actual possession for twenty years, whether
adversely or not, the claimant, whose original right of entry accrued above
twenty years before bringing the ejectment is barred by this section."

He then went on to point out that this section standing alone would not have
affected the possession of co-tenants, for at common law the possession of one
was possession of the other and the position would have remained to be determined
by the rules of the common law. He then quoted s. 12 and held that the effect of
the section was to make the possession of co-tenants separate possessions from
the time when they first became tenants in common and that time ran for the
purposes of s. 2 from that time. In the earlier case of *Nepean* v. *Doe d. Knight* (3),
LORD DENMAN, C.J., had said:

" We are all clearly of opinion that the second and third sections of that
Act . . . have done away with the doctrine of non-adverse possession, and . . .
the question is whether twenty years have elapsed *since the right accrued*,
whatever be the nature of the possession."

And then the learned editor of DARBY AND BOSANQUET ON LIMITATION OF
ACTIONS (2nd Edn.) p. 337, when discussing this case, adds:

" so that without an actual ouster the one tenant in common could bring
his ejectment and the other could defend his possession under the statute."

All this is well settled law and there is a number of authorities to the like effect
(see for example *Re Manchester Gas Act, Ex p. Hasell* (4) and *Doe d. Jones* v.
Williams (5)).

---

(1) (1774), 1 Cowp. 217.
(2) (1840), 11 Ad. & El. 1008 at p. 1015.
(3) (1837), 2 M. & W. 894 at p. 911.
(4) (1839), 3 Y. & C. Ex. 617.
(5) (1836), 5 Ad. & El. 291.

A   Counsel for the appellants however has argued that, though this may represent the law where a third party (an intruder) is in possession, that does not apply where no one is in wrongful possession. He points out truly that Roseliza and Victoria were rightfully in possession of the whole land and were committing no wrong by farming all of it. (See *Henderson* v. *Eason* (6), *Jacobs* v. *Seward* (7).) So he submits that time has not yet started to run because the appellants could
B   not sue them as no wrong has been committed by those in possession; put in another way it was argued that time cannot run in favour of the co-tenants in possession until they commit a wrong. Furthermore, it was argued, that while a right to enter arose in 1913 that was not a right " to make an entry " for the purposes of s. 1 of the Act of 1874 for such a right did not arise until an intruder was in possession or until there was some wrongful act by the co-tenants in
C   possession. These arguments necessarily led to the submission that where a co-tenant was lawfully in possession of the whole there must be some wrongful act showing a possession inconsistent with the co-tenants' right to re-enter; something which counsel could not attempt to define, but which was short of adverse possession under the pre-1833 law.

Their lordships have no hesitation in rejecting this argument; to adopt it
D   would defeat the whole object of the Act of 1833. It seems to their lordships clear from the language of the Act and the authorities already referred to that, subject to the qualification mentioned below, where the right of entry has accrued more than twenty years before action brought the co-tenants are barred and their title is extinguished whatever the nature of the co-tenants' possession. That right of entry (ignoring immaterial facts as to the widow and Nehemiah) accrued
E   in 1913.

Counsel for the respondents was inclined to agree with the view that, in contrast to the right of entry, the time for bringing an action or suit had not yet started to run. Their lordships cannot agree; it seems to them clear that for the purposes of s. 1 of the Act of 1874 the right to make an entry and the right to bring an action both accrued at the same time in 1913. The qualification mentioned above arises
F   on s. 12 of the Act of 1833. The " separate possessions " (to adopt the phrase of Lord Denman, C.J. (8)) obviously only start when the occupation is " for his or their own benefit ". That is the crucial question as Sir Wilfrid Greene, M.R., pointed out in *Re Landi, Georgi* v. *Navani* (9). That is primarily a question of fact though the law may sometimes imply that one co-tenant is in possession for another co-tenant, e.g., a father for his infant but not adult son (see *Re Hobbs,*
G   *Hobbs* v. *Wade* (10)), otherwise it is a question of proving some agency or trusteeship or acknowledgment of title on the part of those in possession. These matters were canvassed by counsel for the second appellants, but there were no facts on which he could base any useful argument. The judge reviewed the facts fully and reached the conclusion that the possession of both Roseliza and Victoria was for their own use and benefit and their lordships agree with that conclusion.

H   There was some argument before their lordships whether the commencement of the time for making an entry or bringing an action was to be determined by reference to s. 1 of the Act of 1874 or s. 3 of the Act of 1833. It is however clearly settled, and was not in dispute before their lordships, that s. 3 does not limit the generality of s. 1 but is only explanatory of that section and designed to settle cases where under s. 1 there might be a doubt when time started to run (see *James*
I   v. *Salter* (11), *Governors of Magdalen Hospital* v. *Knotts* (12), *Pugh* v. *Heath* (13)). In *James* v. *Salter* (11) it was assumed that a devisee could not take under any

(6) (1851), 17 Q.B. 701.
(7) (1872), L.R. 5 H.L. 464.
(8) In *Culley* v. *Doe d. Taylerson,* (1840), 11 Ad. & El. at p. 1017.
(9) [1939] 3 All E.R. 569 at p. 572; [1939] Ch. 828 at p. 834.
(10) (1887), 36 Ch.D. 553.
(11) (1837), 3 Bing. N.C. 544.
(12) (1878), 8 Ch.D. 709 at p. 727.
(13) (1882), 7 App. Cas. 235 at p. 238.

branch of the s. 3 and that s. 1 of the Act of 1874 applied. The opinions of text- A
book writers, including LORD ST. LEONARDS, have doubted the correctness of this
assumption (see DARBY AND BOSANQUET, pp. 306-308) but as, whichever section
is applicable, time started to run more than twenty years before action brought
their lordships do not think it necessary to express any opinion on this question.
As the learned judge held it is clear that the appellants' claim is barred by the
Acts of 1833 and of 1874 and their title is thereby extinguished by s. 34 of the Act B
of 1833.   Their lordships would like to express their thanks to SCARR, J., for
his most admirable judgment, full and lucid in relation to the facts and clear
and accurate as to the law.

Their lordships will humbly advise Her Majesty that the appeal should be
dismissed. The appellants must pay the respondents' costs of the appeal.

Appeal dismissed.   C

Solicitors: *Lovell, White & King* (for the first, third, fourth, fifth and sixth
appellants); *Charles Russell & Co.* (for the second appellant); *Bulcraig & Davis*
(for the respondents).

[*Reported by* S. A. HATTEEA, ESQ., *Barrister-at-Law.*]

D

METROPOLITAN PROPERTIES CO. (F.G.C.), LTD. *v.* BARDER.

[COURT OF APPEAL, CIVIL DIVISION (Willmer, Davies and Edmund Davies, L.JJ.),
November 28, 29, 1967.]   E

*Rent Restriction—Separate dwelling—Part of a separate dwelling-house—Flat
let as residence, a separate dwelling-house—Additional room let to tenant
of flat as servant's room—Distinct contracts of letting and different dates,
terms and conditions—Single room not part of the dwelling-house that the
flat constituted for the purposes of the Rent Acts.*

In 1951 a tenant took a twelve years' lease of a flat, and in 1955 he took a F
quarterly tenancy from the same landlord of a single servant's room, opposite
to and across a corridor from his flat, at a separate rent of £52 a year inclusive
of rates payable quarterly in advance. The agreement provided that he
should not assign, underlet or part with possession of the single room and
would use it only for occupation by a servant. It was furnished as a bedroom
only (furniture including a wash-basin) but there was no lavatory; the door of G
the single room was usually kept open and the au pair girls who used the room
had ready access to and from it into the flat. The two rents were in practice
paid by one cheque. In 1963 the tenant entered into a fresh lease of the
flat for fourteen years, with elaborate covenants. The flat came within
the Rent Acts in 1965 by virtue of its annual value. On appeal in an action by
the landlords for possession of the single room,   H

Held: the tenant was not entitled to the protection of the Rent Acts in
respect of the single room for the following reasons—

(i) the single room, which was in the occupation of the tenant through the
au pair girls who used it, was incapable of being separately let as a separate
dwelling by itself and was not, therefore, a dwelling-house* within the
meaning of the Rent Acts (see p. 538, letter G, p. 540, letters D and E, and I
p. 542, letter E, post).

(ii) the single room was not let to the tenant as part of his existing accommodation in the flat, and so was not part of a dwelling-house subject to
the Rent Acts, because the two premises were held under different contracts

* The term " dwelling-house " means, for the purposes of the Rent Acts, " a house
let as a separate dwelling or part of a house being a part so let " (Rent and Mortgage
Interest (Restrictions) Act, 1933, s. 16 (1); 13 HALSBURY'S STATUTES (2nd Edn.)
1057).

A   of tenancy made at different dates, for different terms (one quarterly terminable by notice the other for a fixed term of fourteen years) and subject to
different conditions, and to hold that there was, in effect, one tenancy of
the two would involve the consequence that the tenancy of the single
room could not be determined by either party until expiry of the lease of
the flat (see p. 540, letter C, p. 541, letter I, and p. 542, letters B and D,
B   post).

    Wimbush v. *Cibulia* ([1949] 2 All E.R. 432) considered.

    Appeal allowed.

    [As to what premises constitute a dwelling and a separate dwelling for the
purposes of the Rent Acts, see 23 HALSBURY'S LAWS (3rd Edn.) 743-744, paras.
1497, 1498; and for cases on the subject see 31 DIGEST (Repl.) 640-650, *7473-7536*.]
C
Cases referred to:

    Curl v. *Angelo*, [1948] 2 All E.R. 189; [1948] L.J.R. 1756; 31 Digest (Repl.)
        648, *7524*.

    Dando (S.L.), Ltd. v. *Hitchcock*, [1954] 2 All E.R. 335; [1954] 2 Q.B. 317;
        [1954] 3 W.L.R. 76; Digest (Cont. Vol. A) 1075, *7626a*.

D   *Geller* v. *Highbloom*, [1950] Estates Gazette Digest 258.

    Hiller v. *United Dairies (London), Ltd.*, [1933] All E.R. Rep. 667; [1934]
        1 K.B. 57; 103 L.J.K.B. 5; 150 L.T. 74; 31 Digest (Repl.) 660, *7618*.

    Wimbush v. *Cibulia, Same* v. *Levinski*, [1949] 2 All E.R. 432; [1949] 2 K.B.
        564; 31 Digest (Repl.) 641, *7481*.

Appeal.

E   This was an appeal by the landlords against an order of His Honour JUDGE
MACINTYRE, made on May 11, 1967, in favour of the tenant. They sought an
order for possession of the servant's room No. 3 in Princes Gate Court, Exhibition
Road, London, S.W.7, which was let to the tenant and was the subject of the
action, within twenty-eight days, on the ground that the judge misdirected
himself and was wrong in law: (i) in holding that servant's room No. 3 and flat
F   24a, Princes Gate Court were let to the tenant under a single tenancy of a dwelling-
house; (ii) in not holding that servant's room No. 3 was let to the tenant on a
tenancy which was not a tenancy of a dwelling-house; (iii) in holding that there
was evidence on which he could find that the room could not be let as one room;
(iv) in holding that the onus was on the landlords to prove that the Rent Acts
did not apply to the room; (v) in finding or holding that the Rent Acts did apply
G   to the room; and (vi) alternatively to (i), in not holding that, if servant's room
No. 3 and flat 24a were let to the tenant under a single tenancy of a dwelling-
house, then (a) servant's room No. 3 was also let to him under the same tenancy
and (b) the dwelling-house consisting of the flat and two servant's rooms, having
a combined rateable value of £401, was not subject to the Rent Acts.

    M. Singh for the landlords.
H   *David Keene* for the tenant.

    WILLMER, L.J.:   In this case the appellants, who were the plaintiffs
below, are the landlords, and the respondent (the defendant below) is the tenant,
of residential accommodation at Princes Gate Court in Exhibition Road, London,
S.W.7. The landlords brought the present action in the West London County
I   Court seeking to obtain possession of what is described as "servant's room No. 3",
which had been let to the tenant in addition to the flat in which he lived, viz.,
No. 24a. The question which arose for decision, and which was determined by
the county court judge in favour of the tenant, was whether the tenant was
entitled to claim the protection of the Rent Acts in respect of that servant's
room No. 3.

    The facts of the case are as follows. The tenant has been occupying flat No.
24a ever since 1951. He took a lease of it which was due to expire in 1963. When
1963 came, he entered into a fresh lease, dated June 7, 1963, but operative from

Christmas, 1962, for a further period of fourteen years. He is therefore in **A**
occupation of flat No. 24a for a term which will not come to an end until Christmas,
1976. In 1955 (i.e., four years after he originally went into occupation of flat
No. 24a) he desired to obtain further accommodation for the benefit of an au
pair girl. In those circumstances he took a tenancy on a quarterly basis of this
additional servant's room No. 3. The agreement for that tenancy is evidenced by
the letter which he wrote to the landlords on Aug. 10, 1955. It was expressed **B**
to be a quarterly tenancy at a rent of £52 per annum inclusive of rates, payable
quarterly in advance. By his letter the tenant undertook to use the servant's
room for occupation by a servant only, and not to assign, underlet or part with
possession of it. The servant's room No. 3, as I understand it, is in fact on the
same corridor as the tenant's flat; indeed, the entrance to it is practically
opposite the entrance to his flat. We were informed that the door is usually **C**
kept open, and that the successive au pair girls have always been in the habit
of passing freely from the room into the flat. The room is of course used only as
sleeping accommodation. The evidence shows that it is furnished only as a
bedroom. It is furnished with a bed, a dressing table, an upright chair, a carpet,
a wash-basin and a bed-table.

It is clear that questions arising out of the Rent Acts are not at present very **D**
relevant in relation to the tenant's occupation of flat No. 24a. Until 1976, as I
have pointed out, he holds the flat as a contractual tenant under the fourteen
years' lease of 1963. It is the fact, however, that, having regard to the annual
value of that flat, it is brought within the purview of the Rent Acts by s. 1 of
the Rent Act 1965. The question which now arises for decision is how the letting
of the servant's room No. 3 is to be regarded. The judge thought that in **E**
the absence of authority (and he expressed the view that there was no authority
directly in point) the question should be dealt with on a common sense basis.
He thought that the real effect of what had happened was that for years the
defendant had been using, and therefore occupying, the servant's room No. 3
as part of his residential accommodation. Reliance was placed on the fact that
he habitually paid the rent in respect of both properties by one cheque, and that **F**
the landlords acquiesced in the habit. In those circumstances the judge came to
the conclusions that room No. 3 was occupied by the tenant, and that it came
within the Rent Acts so as to make it impossible for the landlords by notice to
quit to turn the defendant out. The landlords now appeal to this court and
contend that the letting of room No. 3 does not come within the Rent Acts.

Let me first get out of the way two subsidiary points. I do not think that it **G**
can be contended (nor did the judge think that it could be contended) that room
No. 3 is capable of being let as a separate dwelling on its own. In order to come
within the Rent Acts, therefore, it must, I think, be shown that room No. 3 is
in effect let with flat No. 24a so as to form part of the accommodation
comprised within that flat. The other subsidiary point about which I feel no
difficulty at all is that of occupation. I entertain no doubt (and I think that this **H**
is well supported by abundant authority) that the defendant is in occupation of
room No. 3 through the au pair girls who from time to time have actually and
physically occupied that room.

The question which remains to be decided (and I do not pretend that I find it
an easy one) is whether it can be said that room No. 3 is let to the tenant as
part of the existing accommodation comprised within flat No. 24a. Only so, as it **I**
seems to me, is it possible to say that it is brought within the protection of the
Rent Acts. The county court judge was not, I think, quite correct in remarking
that the question was devoid of authority, for we have had certain authorities
cited to us which are no doubt relevant to the question which has to be decided
in this case. The main point put forward in support of this appeal (and the point
on which in the event I think that the landlords are entitled to succeed) is that
the letting of flat No. 24a and the letting of bedroom No. 3 are competely distinct and separate. Whereas the flat is held by the tenant under the lease of

A   1963 for a period of fourteen years, the servant's room No. 3 is held only on a quarterly tenancy. The tenure of the two properties, therefore, is completely different. The rights to determine the respective tenancies are completely different. Subject to the Rent Acts, it is open to the landlords to evict the tenant from the servant's room No. 3 on three months' notice at the end of any quarter; and so far as the tenant is concerned there is, as far as I can see, nothing to prevent

B   his determining his tenancy of the servant's room No. 3 at any time if, for instance, he ceases to have any need to accommodate an au pair girl. This to my mind makes it very difficult to regard the letting of the servant's room No. 3 as part of a single letting with flat No. 24a.

However, as I have said, the matter, is not entirely free from authority, for we have had cited to us a decision of this court in *Wimbush* v. *Cibulia,*

C   *Same* v. *Levinski* (1), and also a decision of HILBERY, J., in *Geller* v. *Highbloom*, (2). The facts in the latter case more nearly approximate to those in the present case; but on the other hand the decision of the Court of Appeal in *Wimbush* v. *Cibulia* (1), if only because it is a decision of this court, is obviously of more compelling authority. That was a case in which two parts of the same house had been let to the same tenant under different agreements, both of them, however,

D   being weekly tenancy agreements. The question was whether they were to be regarded as a single letting or not. The county court judge apparently thought not. This court, on the other hand, thought that they might be regarded as constituting a single letting, and remitted the case to the county court judge in order to determine the necessary facts which would enable him to say one way or the other whether they amounted to a single letting. That decision is of some

E   assistance to the tenant in this case, because it does show that in circumstances similar to those of the present case it is not impossible for additional accommodation acquired under a separate tenancy agreement to be regarded as embraced in one letting with the other accommodation occupied by the tenant. I venture to emphasise, however, the distinction between that case and this, in that there the court was dealing with agreements both of which were for weekly tenancies,

F   and there was no possible difficulty arising from the different methods or times for determining the respective tenancies.

Geller v. *Highbloom* (2), on the other hand, was a case in which part of the premises was being occupied under a long lease, and part, which may be described as the purely residential part, was being occupied by the tenant on a weekly tenancy. The report of the case is extremely brief, and in some respects rather

G   obscure. HILBERY, J., said that he regarded the case as a difficult one. He said (3):

"The question was whether there were separate lettings or one whole letting at the time the matter was brought before the court."

He went on (3):

"The proper inference from the facts was that from and after the

H   time when Mr. Highbloom went into occupation of that part of the premises available for living accommodation, he intended to, and, in fact did, occupy the whole as one letting. He paid a total rent of £6 4s. weekly and as on one letting."

The judge then said that (3):

"... although he felt considerable doubt about the matter, he did not

I   think that these considerations were outweighed by the fact that the tenancy of one could have been determined before expiration of the lease of the other."

In other words, the judge in that case appears to have been presented with the very same problem as we have here, viz., two tenancies of different types determinable at different times and in different ways. The decision is not of

(1) [1949] 2 All E.R. 432; [1949] 2 K.B. 564.
(2) [1950] Estates Gazette Digest 258.
(3) [1950] Estates Gazette Digest at p. 259.

course binding on this court; nor do I find it possible to derive very much   A
assistance from it, having regard to the brevity and obscurity of the report.
It does not persuade me that, in the circumstances of this case, we ought to
dismiss as of no consequence and effect the fact that we are here dealing with
two entirely different contracts, one a fourteen years' lease, and the other a
quarterly tenancy. The mere fact that the tenant did, as a matter of convenience, pay the rent for both premises by means of a single cheque, and that   B
the landlords acquiesced in that, does not seem to me to be of any significance
at all. It would indeed be a matter for some surprise if the parties did not
behave in that way.

In my judgment the fact which outweighs all the other facts in the present
case is that to which I have already referred, viz., that the flat and the servant's
room are held by the tenant under two entirely different contracts. In those   C
circumstances, for my part, I find myself unable to agree with the view of the
county court judge that they were in effect being treated as part of a single
letting. I think that the judge came to a wrong conclusion, and that the
landlords are entitled to succeed on their appeal.

DAVIES, L.J.: I agree, and can state my views about the matter very   D
shortly in view of what WILLMER, L.J., has said. I agree first that contrary to
the allegation made in the particulars of claim, this servant's room No. 3 was
occupied by the tenant since it was occupied as the sleeping quarters of a
servant or au pair girl whom he might be employing from time to time, and it
is not to be supposed for one moment that ever since 1955 until the present
day it was the same au pair girl who was there throughout. I also agree, however,   E
that the tenancy of that room was not within the ambit, or entitled to the
protection, of the Rent Acts, since it was not let as a separate dwelling or let
together with or as part of a separate dwelling. There can be no doubt that this
tiny room opposite the defendant's flat could not possibly be said to be a separate
dwelling. There was apparently a wash-basin in the room, but there were no
lavatory facilities, and it was used only as the au pair girl's bedroom. The whole   F
question really, which has been well argued in this case, is whether this room was
let together with or as part of a separate dwelling.

WILLMER, L.J., has referred to the decision of this court in *Wimbush* v.
Cibulia, (4).   Although the quotation is a somewhat lengthy one, I do think
that one gets some assistance from that case as to the principles to be applied
in approaching this case. I quote from the judgment of JENKINS, L.J., who   G
delivered the judgment of the court in that case (5). Before I quote it, one has
to bear in mind, of course, that the tenancies with which that case was concerned were entered into at different times and were both weekly tenancies.
JENKINS, L.J., said this (6):

"... we find it impossible to hold that the ground floor and basement
of No. 6, Newburgh Street by themselves ever in point of user constituted   H
the separate dwelling of the tenant apart from the first floor rooms
originally let to him since at all times after the letting of the ground floor
and basement to the tenant in 1933 one of the essential operations of
living, namely sleeping, was carried on in the two first floor rooms. The
circumstances in which and purposes for which the additional tenancy
was granted do, however, seem to us to provide a fairly strong indication   I
that, although the additional letting was in form a separate transaction,
the true intention of the parties may well have been that the two tenancies
should be treated as one ' letting ', or at all events should be interdependent,
so that the later in date was supplemental to the earlier, and the one could
not be determined without the other. If that was the true position, in

---

(4) [1949] 2 All E.R. 432; [1949] 2 K.B. 564.
(5) [1949] 2 All E.R. at p. 433; [1949] 2 K.B. at p. 566.
(6) [1949] 2 All E.R. at pp. 434, 435; [1949] 2 K.B. at pp. 569, 570.

A   fact, then we think the result would be that the tenant could claim protection in respect of the whole of the premises consisting of first floor,
ground floor, and back basement room in the same way as if they had all
been comprised in a single tenancy agreement.

    " On the facts so far found, we would not feel justified in dismissing the
appeal on this ground, while, on the other hand, in all the circumstances of
B   the case we are not content without further investigation to accept at its
face value the formally separate character of the two tenancies, with consequences fatal, as it seems to us, to the tenant's case. We are loath to put
the parties to the trouble and expense of a further hearing in the county
court, but matters of evidence and fact under the Rent Acts are pre-
eminently matters for the county court, and we think, therefore, that the
C   proper course in the circumstances will be to remit the case to the county
court for a further hearing directed to the question whether the additional
letting was truly separate and distinct from the original letting, or the
real agreement to be imputed to the parties (conformably with the
actual facts as to user) involved such a consolidation of or interdependence
between the two lettings as to make them in effect equivalent to a single
D   tenancy agreement extending to the whole of the premises."

    Those being the principles, what are the facts here? In the first place, of course,
as WILLMER, L.J., has stated in setting out the history of this matter, the dates
of the two tenancies (and I use the term for the moment without purporting to
decide by the use of that word the issue in this case) were entirely different.
E   The first lease of flat No. 24a was in 1951, and it would appear that from 1951
until 1955 the tenant carried on in No. 24a without having any user of or interest
in room No. 3. In August, 1955, however, he takes this quarterly tenancy of
the servant's room, No. 3. Then, when the lease ran out in 1962 he takes in
1963 a fresh fourteen years' lease of the flat No. 24a. So we see that the terms
of these two tenancies are entirely different. The mode of termination is com-
F   pletely different in that the one is a tenancy for a fixed term whereas the other
is determinable on a quarter's notice on either side; and, as EDMUND DAVIES,
L.J., pointed out in the course of the argument, there are most elaborate covenants in the fourteen years' lease, whereas in the letter of Aug. 10 the only
covenant is:

G   " I undertake to use the servant's room for occupation by a domestic
servant only and will not assign, underlet or part with possession thereof.
I further agree to keep and leave the interior of the room in good and
tenantable repair and condition."

So in all those respects the tenures are entirely different.

    I am bound to say that one consequence of the argument of counsel for the
H   tenant I have found a little difficult. As things stand on paper, neither the
landlords nor the tenant (subject, of course, to forfeiture) can terminate this
lease of the flat No. 24a until 1976. Equally as things stand on paper, either
the landlords or the tenant can terminate the tenancy of room No. 3 by a quarter's
notice. If, as is contended on behalf of the tenant, these two tenancies have,
as it were, formed one, and therefore, I suppose, fall within the word used by
I   JENKINS, L.J., viz., " interdependent ", so that the one could not be determined
without the other, that would mean that the tenant would not be entitled until
1976, however much he wished to do so, to give notice terminating his tenancy
of the servant's room No. 3. Counsel for the tenant, I think, in his argument
was driven to agree that his submission did lead to that conclusion.

    I find that extremely difficult to accept. It might well be that either the
tenant with regard to this ancillary room (and perhaps " ancillary " is particularly apt in this connexion as I believe it is derived from the Latin ancilla, a maid-
servant) might want to give it up at any time if he no longer had domestic

assistance or an au pair girl; and similarly the landlords, wishing to let a servant's   A
room and wishing to receive more than the tenant was paying for it, might on
their side want to get the tenant out of room No. 3. It seems to me quite feasible
and practicable in those circumstances that in 1963 the parties did not wish to
enter into a long lease of room No. 3, and so not only omitted to deal with it,
but deliberately omitted to deal with it for the very good reason that they wanted
to keep these two tenancies separate and distinct.   B

Like WILLMER, J., I cannot find any assistance in this case from the mere
fact that the rent for these two premises was paid by one cheque; it would
obviously be stupid, I should have thought, to pay with two cheques. For
these reasons, in addition to those given by WILLMER, L.J., I, therefore, agree
that the appeal should be allowed.

  C

EDMUND DAVIES, L.J.: I also agree that this appeal should be allowed.
The landlords have rightly not sought to make anything of the fact that
the room occupied by the servant and the flat occupied by the tenant and his
family were physically separated by a landing. We are accordingly not concerned with such decisions as *Hiller* v. *United Dairies (London), Ltd.* (7) and
S. L. Dando, Ltd. v. *Hitchcock* (8).   For the reasons already given by my lords,   D
and notwithstanding the considerations adverted to in *Wimbush* v. *Cibulia* (9),
I find it impossible to regard room No. 3 as let as part of flat No. 24a. On the
other hand, if room No. 3 and flat No. 24a were let as two dwellings, it follows
that they were not let as a separate dwelling-house within the meaning of the
Rent Acts.

The real question here is whether room No. 3 was let as " a dwelling-house ".   E
In my judgment, it clearly was not.   The size of the room, its furnishing and the
use to which it was being put (i.e., as the au pair girl's bedroom) establish that
its user was an annexe or overflow of the flat, and its entirely distinct letting on
a quarterly basis was not the letting of a dwelling-house.

I would stress that the present decision has no application to a case where a
single room is let as the occupier's place of habitation for all purposes; to adopt   F
the words of LORD GREENE, M.R., in *Curl* v. *Angelo* (10) the present case is
totally different:

> ". . . from the case where the only premises demised consist of one room
> and that is the only place where the tenant moves and has his being."

For these reasons I agree with my lords in holding that this appeal must be
allowed.   G

Appeal allowed.   Order for possession of room No. 3 not later than Jan 27, 1968.

Solicitors: *Grangewood, Allan & Co.* (for the landlords); *Donald A. Kershaw &
Co.* (for the tenant).

[*Reported by* F. A. AMIES, ESQ., *Barrister-at-Law.*]

  H

  I

---

(7) [1933] All E.R. Rep. 667; [1934] 1 K.B. 57.
(8) [1954] 2 All E.R. 335; [1954] 2 Q.B. 317.
(9) [1949] 2 All E.R. 432; [1949] 2 K.B. 564.
(10) [1948] 2 All E.R. 189 at p. 191, letter B.

A

ALLEN v. SIR ALFRED McALPINE & SONS, LTD.
BOSTIC v. BERMONDSEY AND SOUTHWARK GROUP HOSPITAL MANAGEMENT COMMITTEE.
STERNBERG AND ANOTHER v. HAMMOND AND ANOTHER.

B

[COURT OF APPEAL, CIVIL DIVISION (Lord Denning, M.R., Diplock and Salmon, L.JJ.), December 13, 14, 15, 18, 1967, January 11, 1968.]

Practice—Want of prosecution—Dismissal of action—Delay—Inordinate delay without excuse—Grave injustice to one party or to both—Discretion to dismiss action without affording opportunity for default to be remedied—Plaintiff left to remedy against his solicitors for negligence—Factors for consideration in exercise of court's discretion.

C

When delay in the conduct of an action is prolonged or inordinate and is inexcusable (as is, per SALMON, L.J., the natural inference in the absence of a credible excuse), and there is substantial risk by reason of the delay that a fair trial of the issues will no longer be possible or that grave injustice will be done to one party or the other or to both parties, the court may in its discretion dismiss the action straight away, without

D

giving the plaintiff opportunity to remedy the default, but leaving him to his remedy against his solicitors for negligence (see p. 547, letters D and E, p. 556, letter B, p. 561, letters F and G, and p. 562, letter D, post). In order to exercise this discretion justly the court will consider the circumstances of the particular case, and, among other factors, whether the blame is really the defendant's (in which case dismissal of the action may be

E

withheld), or, if the blame is the plaintiff's solicitors', whether the plaintiff has effective remedy against them as, e.g., by reason of their being insured against liability for negligence, and, if remedy against the solicitors seems likely to prove ineffective, the degree of serious prejudice to the defendant by the delay (see p. 556, letters D, H and I, p. 561, letters H and I, and p. 562, letter A, post; cf. pp. 550, 552, letters B, A, post).

F

Eaton v. *Storer* ((1882), 22 Ch.D. 91) considered and explained.

Per DIPLOCK, L.J.: (i) an action will be dismissed where the delay or default is intentional and contumelious, as where there is disobedience to a peremptory order of the court (see p. 556, letters A and B, and p. 562, letter E, post).

G

(ii) there is no rule that a plaintiff's solicitor should be given prior warning of the defendant's intention to apply to dismiss an action for want of prosecution, and, if there is any tacit understanding to that effect, the sooner that is abandoned, the better (see p. 555, letter I, post).

Per SALMON, L.J.: where an action is dismissed for want of prosecution and the fault is attributable to the plaintiff's solicitor, the court should take steps to ensure that the plaintiff is personally informed of the decision

H

and briefly of the reasons for which it was made (see p. 562, letter G, post).

The principles stated at letter C, above were applied in three appeals as follows. The first appeal was in an action where a widow was claiming damages against her husband's employers in respect of his death in an accident at work, the causes of action alleged being negligence and breach of statutory duty. The widow had two children. The accident occurred

I

in February, 1959. The plaintiff consulted solicitors within a few days of the accident. The writ was issued and the statement of claim was delivered in July, 1960. In January, 1961, the defendants delivered a defence, which was a simple denial. The defendants, however, had a claim against sub-contractors for contribution or indemnity. No summons for directions was ever issued. In February, 1964, the plaintiff's solicitors tried to find the witnesses, but could trace only four out of six of them. In February, 1965, and February, 1966, they instructed experts to examine pieces of a wooden cover through which the deceased had fallen at the time of the accident, and to examine the site of the accident. In April, 1967, the defendants

applied for an order to dismiss the action for want of prosecution. There A
had thus been delay for over six years in issuing a summons for directions.
The plaintiff's solicitors were insured against liability for negligence.

The third appeal was in an action begun by writ issued on June 14, 1960,
by plaintiffs who claimed indemnity against an executrix in a sum of £32,689
6s. 3d., and claimed also against a firm of solicitors and, for costs, against
a company. The causes of action alleged included fraud and conspiracy B
by the deceased, who died in 1959, the conspiracy alleged being in 1954,
and one of the conspirators being the defendant company. The allegations
against the solicitors included fraud and negligence. Defences were delivered
in the autumn of 1960; all included pleas of the Limitation Act, 1939.
There was a reply in December, 1960, alleging concealed fraud. Pleadings
closed in January, 1961, discovery was completed in December, 1963. The C
cause of action for fraud against the defendant solicitors was withdrawn in
1963, but the cause of action for professional negligence remained. In or
about 1965 the defendant company was dissolved. Between April, 1965,
and March, 1966, letters were written on behalf of the executrix complaining
of the delay which was holding up administration of the estate. In April,
1966, the plaintiff's solicitors delivered an amended statement of claim. In D
October, 1967, application was made for dismissal of the action for want
of prosecution. Thus the allegation of fraud and conspiracy against the
deceased related to matters which had taken place fourteen years ago and
in regard to which the other alleged conspirator, the company, had been
dissolved. The solicitors for the plaintiff were a substantial firm and were
insured against liability for negligence. E

The second appeal was in an action for damages brought by a nurse for
personal injuries sustained by her during her employment in a hospital for
which the defendant hospital authority were responsible. The accident
occurred in September, 1958. The plaintiff instructed solicitors in November, 1958, and on Feb. 21, 1961, they issued a writ. In July, 1961, a statement of claim was delivered. The hospital authority at no time delivered F
a defence. They asked for further and better particulars and for the time
for the defence to be extended. In July, 1962, the plaintiff's solicitor having
been convicted of a criminal offence, the Law Society circularised his clients,
including the plaintiff, advising them to consult another solicitor. The
plaintiff stated that she never received this letter, but eventually discovered
that the clerk to the solicitor who had been dealing with her case was in G
prison. New solicitors having been instructed, the defendants, in August,
1966, repeated the request for particulars, which were delivered in November,
1966. After a request for delivery of the defence in March, 1967, the
plaintiff's then solicitors received a summons to dismiss the action for
want of prosecution. Nine years had then passed since the accident. So
far, however, as the defendants' defence was concerned, they would have the H
hospital records and medical notes from which to refresh their memories
in regard to facts, and thus should not be prejudiced by delay. The solicitors
originally acting for the plaintiff were uninsured and apparently without means.

Held: (i) in the first and third appeals there had been inexcusable delay
due to the negligence of the plaintiffs' solicitors, and it was not possible to
have a fair trial after so long a time; accordingly the actions should stand I
dismissed (see p. 548, letter I, to p. 549, letter A, p. 552, letter D, p. 557,
letters E and I, p. 559, letter I, p. 563, letter G, p. 565, letter E, and p. 566,
letter A, post).

(ii) in the second appeal there would be hardship to the plaintiff if her
action were dismissed, for she had no prospect of recovery from her former
solicitors whose negligence was responsible for her plight; hardship to the
defendants by the long delay was mitigated by the existence of contemporaneous records of the plaintiff's medical condition, the defendants' own

A   delay barred them from obtaining dismissal, and in the circumstances justice would best be done by allowing the action to proceed to trial (see p. 550, letter D, p. 558, letter H, and p. 564, letter I, post).

    First and third appeals dismissed. Second appeal allowed.

[As to the dismissal of actions for want of prosecution, see 30 HALSBURY'S LAWS (3rd Edn.) 410, 411, para. 771; and for cases on the extension of time,
B   see DIGEST (PRACTICE) (Repl.) 256-259, *87-116.*

    For Magna Carta*, see 4 HALSBURY'S STATUTES (2nd Edn.) 26.]

Cases referred to:

    Armory v. *Delamirie,* (1722), 1 Stra. 505;   93 E.R. 664;   3 Digest (Repl.) 67, *83.*

C   *Eaton* v. *Storer,* (1882), 22 Ch.D. 91; 48 L.T. 204; 50 Digest (Repl.) 216, *1792.*

    Fitzpatrick v. *Batger & Co., Ltd.,* [1967] 2 All E.R. 657; [1967] 1 W.L.R. 706.

    Reggentin v. *Beecholme Bakeries, Ltd.,* (1967), 111 Sol. Jo. 216; noted at p. 566, post.

Interlocutory Appeals.

    The first appeal was an appeal by the plaintiff from an order of CHAPMAN, J.,
D   dated Oct. 9, 1967, dismissing her appeal from the decision of Master ELTON, dated May 23, 1967, whereby it was ordered that her action be dismissed for want of prosecution.

    The second appeal was by the plaintiff from an order of MOCATTA, J., dated Oct. 30, 1967, dismissing her appeal from Master DIAMOND who ordered that the action be dismissed for want of prosecution.

E   In the third appeal there was an appeal by the plaintiffs from an order dated Nov. 9, 1967, of MOCATTA, J., dismissing the action and allowing the defendants' appeal from Master LAWRENCE dated Oct. 17, 1967, who allowed the action to proceed provided that the plaintiffs paid £1,500 into court as security for the defendants' costs. The Court of Appeal dismissed the first and third appeals but allowed the second appeal. After judgments were delivered, counsel for
F   the defendants in the first and third appeals asked that an order to pay their costs should be made against the solicitors of the respective plaintiffs under R.S.C., Ord. 62, r. 8 (1). The court adjourned the hearing of that application in order to give the solicitors an opportunity to be represented. The application was heard on Jan. 17, 1968, when no order was made against the solicitors personally, because in the first appeal the solicitors gave certain undertakings to
G   indemnify the plaintiff, and in the third appeal the application was not pressed by the defendants.

Counsel, in the first appeal:

    F. B. Purchas, Q.C., and *D. A. Barker* for the plaintiff.

    Tudor Evans, Q.C., and *R. G. Rougier* for the defendants.

In the second appeal:

H   *J. W. Miskin,* Q.C., and *K. M. McHale* for the plaintiff.

    T. H. Bingham for the defendants.

In the third appeal:

    E. W. Eveleigh, Q.C., and *M. D. Sherrard* for the plaintiffs.

    T. M. Eastham, Q.C., and *N. R. King* for the first defendants.

    R. J. Parker, Q.C., and *W. A. B. Forbes* for the third defendants.

I   *John Wilmers,* Q.C., and *G. W. Ogden,* amici curiae, on instructions of the Law Society.

Cur. adv. vult.

January 11.   The following judgments were read.

---

    * The text in HALSBURY'S STATUTES, as in STATUTES REVISED, accords with that of the STATUTES OF THE REALM prepared under the authority of the Record Commission. This is dated 1297 (25 Edw. 1); the Quotation, at p. 546, letter I, post, which is in fact taken from a recent American translation, follows an earlier text (cf. Ch. 40 as numbered in translations of the Cotton manuscripts deposited in the British Museum). The passage is part of Ch. 29 in the translation adopted by the Record Commissioners.

LORD DENNING, M.R.: In these three cases the law's delays have A
been intolerable. They have lasted so long as to turn justice sour. I will give
details later, but in outline they stand thus. In the first case a widow lost her
husband nearly *nine* years ago. He was killed at work. She had a good claim to
compensation from his employers for herself and her two small children. Her
case has not yet been set down for trial. In the second case, a nurse complained
that she strained her back over *nine* years ago whilst lifting a patient. It meant B
a year off work. If her story is true, she was entitled to compensation from the
hospital authorities. They have not even yet put in a defence to the claim.
In the third case, a man of business bought shares nearly *fourteen* years ago
for £20,000. He brought an action complaining that he was deceived in the
deal, and that his company was let down by the solicitors. The man who
sold the shares has since died. His estate cannot be administered whilst this C
suit is hanging over it. His widow cannot receive the money he bequeathed
to her. Yet the suit has not yet been entered for trial.

In none of the three cases has the party himself been at fault. The widow,
the nurse and the man of business, each one of them wanted to get on. The
fault, I regret to say, has been with the legal advisers. It is not that they
wilfully neglected the cases; but they have put them on one side, sometimes D
for months, and even for years, because of the pressure of other work or of other
claims on their time. Hence these ills. And these are not the only examples.
A few months ago we had a couple of cases of like sort. One was on Mar. 9, 1967,
called *Reggentin* v. *Beecholme Bakeries, Ltd.* (1). The other was on Mar. 17, 1967,
called *Fitzpatrick* v. *Batger & Co., Ltd.* (2). We said (1):

> "Delay in these cases is much to be deplored. It is the duty of the E
> plaintiff's advisers to get on with the case. Every year that passes prejudices
> the fair trial."

We struck out those cases for want of prosecution. This meant that the injured
plaintiffs could not recover their compensation from the defendants; but they
could recover it from their own negligent solicitors. These cases have brought F
home to lawyers that they must get on. A note in the SUPREME COURT PRACTICE
1967 says that (3):

> "These emphatic decisions of the Court of Appeal, which lay down a more
> stringent practice than was formerly followed, have injected a new element
> of expedition in the conduct and preparation of cases before trial, especially
> in relation to ' accident ' cases. Plaintiffs' solicitors who do not ' get on ' G
> with their cases will be at risk of having the plaintiff's action dismissed for
> want of prosecution and themselves rendered liable for negligence to the
> plaintiff as their own former client."

Following those decisions, several other cases have been struck out for delay.
These three are among them. The plaintiffs appeal to this court. I say " the
plaintiffs " appeal, but we cannot shut our eyes to the fact that the plaintiffs' H
solicitors and their insurers are very much concerned in the appeals lest they be
held liable for negligence. The Law Society too are concerned, for counsel
appeared for them and asked to be heard. We permitted him as amicus curiae
to address us on the issues of public policy involved.

It was urged that we ought not to strike out a man's action without trial
because it meant depriving him of his right to come to the Queen's Courts.
Magna Carta was invoked against us, as if we were in some way breaking its
provisions. To this there is a short answer. The delay of justice is a denial of
justice. Magna Carta will have none of it. "... To no one will we deny or
delay right or justice " (Magna Carta: Ch. 40). All through the years men

(1) (1967), 111 Sol. Jo. 216; noted at p. 566, letters F to I, post.
(2) [1967] 2 All E.R. 657.
(3) See SECOND CUMULATIVE SUPPLEMENT, para. 25/1/3.

A have protested at the law's delay and counted it as a grievous wrong, hard to bear. Shakespeare ranks it among the whips and scorns of time* (Hamlet, Act 3, Sc. 1). Dickens tells how it exhausts finances, patience, courage, hope† (Bleak House, c. 1). To put right this wrong, we will in this court do all in our power to enforce expedition: and, if need be, we will strike out actions when there has been excessive delay. This is a stern measure; but it is within the

B inherent jurisdiction of the court, and the rules of court expressly permit it. It is the only effective sanction that they contain. If a plaintiff fails within the specified time to deliver a statement of claim, or to take out a summons for directions, or to set down the action for trial, the defendant can apply for the action to be dismissed (R.S.C., Ord. 19, r. 1; Ord. 25, r. 1; Ord. 34, r. 2). It was argued before us that the court should never, on the first application, dismiss

C the action. Even if there was long delay, the court should always give the dilatory solicitor one more chance. The order should be that the action should be dismissed " unless " he takes the next step within a stated time. Such has been the practice, it was said, for a great many years. It was confirmed by SIR GEORGE JESSEL, M.R., in *Eaton* v. *Storer* (4): and it should not be changed without prior notice. I cannot accept this suggestion. If there were such a

D practice, there would be no sanction whatever against delay. The plaintiff's solicitor could put a case on one side as long as he pleased without fear of the consequences.

 If you read *Eaton* v. *Storer* (5) carefully, it will be seen that the practice described by SIR GEORGE JESSEL, M.R., applies only to moderate delays of two or three months. It does not apply when " there is some special circumstance such

E as excessive delay ". The principle on which we go is clear: when the delay is prolonged and inexcusable, and is such as to do grave injustice to one side or the other, or to both, the court may in its discretion dismiss the action straight away, leaving the plaintiff to his remedy against his own solicitor who has brought him to this plight. Whenever a solicitor, by his inexcusable delay, deprives a client of his cause of action, the client can claim damages against him; as, for instance,

F when a solicitor does not issue a writ in time, or serve it in time, or does not renew it properly. We have seen, I regret to say, several such cases lately. Not a few are legally aided. In all of them the solicitors have, I believe, been quick to compensate the suffering client; or at least their insurers have. So the wrong done by the delay has been remedied as much as can be. I hope that this will always be done.

G I turn to consider the three cases in detail.

1. *As to the first appeal.*

 The accident took place nearly nine years ago. On Feb. 1, 1959, the defendants were building a power station at High Marnham near Newark. One of their workmen was James Allen, aged forty. He was crossing a floor which was high above the ground. There was a hole in the floor with a wooden cover over it.

H As he went across, the wooden cover gave way. He fell thirty-four feet to his death. He left a widow and two small children, a daughter of four years and a son of eight months. Two days later she consulted a firm of solicitors. They represented her at the inquest which was held five days after the accident. Six workmen were called to give evidence. Pieces of the wooden cover were produced. No-one suggested that the dead man was to blame.

I Such was the sad and simple story. The plaintiff had undoubtedly a good claim against the defendants for breach of statutory duty. But they said that

---

* " For who would bear the whips and scorns of time
  " The oppressor's wrong, the proud man's contumely
  " The pangs of dispriz'd love, the law's delay
  " The insolence of office and the spurns
  " That patient merit of the unworthy takes, . . . ".
 † The chapter headed " In Chancery ". The passage runs—" This is the Court of Chancery . . . which so exhausts finances, patience, courage, hope; . . . ".
 (4) (1882), 22 Ch.D. 91 at p. 92.   (5) (1882), 22 Ch.D. 91.

the condition of the floor was due to comething done by other contractors called A International Construction, Ltd.: and they wished to claim contribution or indemnity from them.

The plaintiff's solicitors at first pressed her claim with urgency. They said that she was finding it very difficult to make ends meet with her two children. On July 13, 1960, they issued a writ against the defendants. On July 22, 1960, they delivered a statement of claim. On Jan. 18, 1961, the defendants delivered B their defence. It was a simple denial. The pleadings were then closed. Under the Rules of Court the plaintiff's solicitors ought to have taken out, within one month, a summons for directions, see R.S.C., Ord. 25, r. 1 (1). If they had done so, an order would have been made determining the place and mode of trial and also directing the time for setting down. It would probably have been at the Lincoln Assizes and could have been tried in the summer of 1961. Such should C have been done. But over six years passed and the plaintiff's solicitors have never taken out a summons for directions as required by the rules. In consequence the defendants on Apr. 19, 1967, applied for an order to dismiss the action, as the rules entitled them to do (see R.S.C., Ord. 25, r. 1 (4)).

This delay of over six years was prolonged and inexcusable. There was a gap of two and a half years from August, 1961, to February, 1964, when the D plaintiff's solicitors did nothing, save that on two occasions they saw her about legal aid and got a legal aid certificate. The solicitor handling it said:

" My court commitments were substantial and the day-to-day pressure of them and of the very large volume of my conveyancing and probate work were such that this action did not, regrettably, receive attention."

After that big gap, the plaintiff's solicitors seem to have done a little at long intervals. In February, 1964, they tried to find the witnesses; but it was then five years after the accident. They had great difficulty in tracing them. Then they only found four of them. They never succeeded in finding the other two. In February, 1965, they instructed an expert to examine the pieces of the wooden cover. It was then six years after the accident. Later that year they had some correspondence about documents and copies. In February, 1966, they instructed an expert to examine the site of the accident. That was seven years after the accident. Not much use then. Then they did nothing for another year. Again the reason is given " pressure of work ". The solicitor said:

" It was unfortunately not possible for me to delegate this action or indeed any other matter as my firm is stretched to the utmost."

Then in February, 1967, they wrote and said that they were in a position to proceed further with the action and asked for particulars of the deceased's pre-accident earnings, and one or two other things. That was eight years after the accident. It could have been done one month after the accident. On Apr. 13, 1967, the defendants' solicitors gave these particulars without commenting on the delay; but a few days later they took out a summons to dismiss the action. I do not think that this last incident should be regarded as an acquiescence in the long delay. It was too short-lived to have any impact on the cause.

In all the circumstances I think that the delay was so great as to amount to a denial of justice. It is a matter for great concern that a widow, who had a good claim for compensation, should have been kept out of it for so long, especially at a time when it would have been of the most use to her. She suffered a grievous wrong by the death of her husband. She has now suffered another grievous wrong by the delays of her own solicitor. The defendants too have been gravely prejudiced by the delay. They had a claim for contribution or indemnity from the third party. That claim depended on an investigation of facts which took place nearly nine years ago. The delay has been so great that two out of six witnesses cannot now be traced: and the memory of the other four must be

A greatly impaired. It is impossible to have a fair trial after so long a time. The judge struck out the action. I would not disturb his decision.

2. *As to the second appeal.*

Miss Bostic, the plaintiff, comes from the West Indies. In 1958 she was a nurse at the New Cross General Hospital. On Sept. 25, 1958, she reported sick, complaining of pain in the back. She was sent to the sick bay where she was

B for two months. Then she was transferred to Guy's Hospital, afterwards to the Whittington Hospital, and eventually to the Medical Rehabilitation Centre. She was not discharged till July, 1959. She attributed her pain to a strain whilst lifting a patient; but some of the doctors thought her illness was largely hysterical and that she might be malingering.

C She instructed solicitors as early as November, 1958. They wrote for medical reports, but did little else. Eventually in September, 1960, she was granted a civil aid certificate and instructed a firm of solicitors called Dunphy & Co. of 250, Brixton Road, S.W.9. Mr. Dunphy was a solicitor who had an office at that address, but it was run by a clerk called Gravesande, who had come from British Guiana. He took the profits of the Brixton office and paid Mr. Dunphy

D a weekly rent.

On Feb. 21, 1961, Dunphy & Co. issued a writ on behalf of the plaintiff against the defendants. Nearly five months later, on July 11, 1961, they delivered a statement of claim. It alleged that on Sept. 23, 1958, whilst the plaintiff, together with another nurse, was lifting a patient, the other nurse released her grip of the patient and this threw an increased strain on the plaintiff. Her back

E was jerked and strained and that caused all her subsequent illness and disability. On receipt of the statement of claim, the defendants ought within fourteen days to have delivered a defence. But they never did so. And they have never done so to this day. It would, I should have thought, have been a simple defence denying the accident, the injury and the damages. But instead of delivering a defence, they asked for further and better particulars of the statement of claim.

F They took three and a half months to get out this request. Their solicitors made the request on Nov. 3, 1961, and asked for their time for defence to be extended. Dunphy & Co. replied that they would consult counsel and write again. They never did write again.

The reason why Dunphy & Co. never wrote again became obvious later. On Oct. 15, 1962, Mr. Dunphy was convicted of false pretences, uttering forged

G documents and fraudulent conversion and sentenced to three years' imprisonment. Both he and his clerk Mr. Gravesande were brought up before the Disciplinary Committee of the Law Society. Mr. Dunphy was struck off the roll of solicitors. Mr. Gravesande was prohibited from being employed by any solicitor without the permission of the Law Society.

Pending those proceedings against Mr. Dunphy, the Law Society took steps

H to safeguard the clients. In July, 1962, they sent out a circular letter to every client saying that Mr. Dunphy was no longer in practice and advising them to consult another solicitor. The plaintiff says that she never received this letter. She says that she telephoned every month to Mr. Dunphy's office, but received no reply. She found out eventually that Mr. Gravesande was in prison. In August, 1965, she went to see him there and he told her to instruct a solicitor.

I In the circumstances she went to the Law Society. They gave her a list of solicitors and she consulted her present solicitor, Mr. Smalley. She was granted a civil aid certificate, and Mr. Smalley took up the case on her behalf. When Mr. Smalley looked into the matter, he found that the defendants had never put in a defence. He wrote to them about it and pressed for it. Their solicitors thereupon in August, 1966, repeated the request for particulars which they had made five years before. Mr. Smalley on Nov. 17, 1966, delivered these particulars and pressed the defendants again for the defence. In reply the defendants' solicitors asked for their time for defence to be extended. Mr. Smalley granted it. Again and again they asked for their time to be extended. Again and **A** again Mr. Smalley extended it. Eventually, after giving them nearly four months, on Mar. 7, 1967, Mr. Smalley wrote saying: "We would appreciate receiving your defence as quickly as possible." He never did receive it. Instead he received a summons that the action be dismissed for want of prosecution.

In this case, like the widow's case, there has been prolonged delay. But, unlike the widow's case, it was not the plaintiff's solicitors who were in breach of **B** the rules. It was the defendants' solicitors. They ought to have delivered their defence and never did so. Later on they asked for extensions of time and received them. Now they turn round and ask for the case to be dismissed for want of prosecution. The summons asks for it to be done under the inherent jurisdiction of the court. Counsel for the defendant said that it would be an abuse of the process of the court for the case to proceed. Justice, he said, could **C** not be done after all these years.

True it is that nine years have passed since the accident; but I think that the plaintiff's claim should be allowed to proceed to trial. It was her misfortune that her former solicitor was a rogue and went to prison and that his clerk went also. She has no prospect of compensation from them. At the trial itself, the lapse of time will tell more heavily against her than against the defendants. **D** She has only her recollection to go by, whereas they have the hospital records from the very beginning, with full and complete notes at every stage. I do not see that they are prejudiced by the delay. Justice can be done by them if the case is permitted to go to trial. But if it is struck out, the plaintiff loses all remedy without a trial. I would, therefore, allow the appeal. The defendants must deliver their defence within ten days. The plaintiff's solicitors will **E** then take out the summons for directions and set the case down for trial. Let it all be done as quickly as possible.

3. *As to the third appeal.*

This case goes back for twenty years. In 1949 a Mr. Hammond, started to build a block of flats called Petersham House in South Kensington. He did it through two companies which he controlled, a property company which **F** owned the place, and a building company which contracted to erect the building. Those two companies employed outside sub-contractors to do the work. The building was finished in September, 1950. Afterwards the sub-contractors claimed that nearly £30,000 was owing to them by the two companies. In 1953 this claim was submitted to arbitration. Mr. Hammond's solicitors, Messrs. J. H. Millner & Sons, acted for the two companies, as well as for Mr. **G** Hammond himself.

In 1953, over fourteen years ago, Mr. Hammond entered into negotiations to sell all his shares in the property company to Mr. Sternberg, the plaintiff. The plaintiff saw the balance sheet of the property company as at June 30, 1953. There was a note on it to the effect that there was a contingent liability to the sub-contractors in approximately £15,000, but the property company had been **H** indemnified by the building company and Mr. Hammond personally against any liability. On Feb. 24, 1954, the plaintiff bought Mr. Hammond's shares in the property company for £20,000 and thus became, through the company, the owner of the block of flats.

Mr. Hammond's solicitors, J. H. Milner & Sons, continued to act in the arbitration for the two companies. On Jan. 12, 1959, Mr. Hammond died. The arbitration was still proceeding. Mr. Hammond's solicitors handed over all the papers and the conduct of the arbitration to the plaintiff's solicitors. The arbitration was heard for twenty-nine days. On Feb. 22, 1960, the arbitrator awarded to the sub-contractors the sum of £13,281 18s. 3d. together with interest and costs. The plaintiff and the property company (which he controlled) then sought to recover the whole of this sum from the Hammond side. On June 14, 1960, they brought this action against Mrs. Hammond (the widow and executrix

A of Mr. Hammond), together with the building company and Mr. Hammond's solicitors, J. H. Milner & Sons. The statement of claim was delivered on July 12, 1960. It alleged that in 1953 the building company and Mr. Hammond had in fact agreed to indemnify the property company against the claim by the sub-contractors. It also alleged that in 1954 Mr. Hammond had conspired with his solicitors and the building company to defraud the plaintiff and the property
B company and had in fact defrauded them: and that the solicitors were guilty of misconduct and negligence as solicitors of the property company. The defences were delivered in October and November, 1960. Mrs. Hammond, the executrix, knew nothing of the matter and put the plaintiffs to proof of their charges. The others put in a plain denial. All pleaded the statute of limitations. On Dec. 20, 1960, the plaintiffs replied alleging concealed fraud on the part of Mr.
C Hammond, the building company and the solicitors.

The pleadings were closed on Jan. 4, 1961. A summons for directions was heard on June 15, 1961. The master ordered discovery of documents but made no order as to mode of trial or as to setting down. This was left over. For the next two and a half years the solicitors were engaged in discovery and this was completed by the end of December, 1963. In addition, on Dec. 13, 1963, the
D managing clerk of J. H. Milner & Sons was examined on commission as he was old and in poor health. In consequence the plaintiffs decided to withdraw the charge of fraud and of conspiracy against J. H. Milner & Sons but left the charge standing against Mr. Hammond. Discovery being completed, it is clear that at that time, the end of December, 1963, the plaintiffs' solicitors ought to have restored the summons for directions and set the case down for trial; but they
E did not do so. Nearly three and a half years passed with little being done at long intervals.

Take the first period of delay. It was sixteen months. From December, 1963, to April, 1965, the plaintiffs' advisers did nothing: or, at any rate, nothing to come to the notice of the defendants. Then on Apr. 15, 1965, they submitted a few amendments which they proposed to make to the statement of claim. The
F proposed amendments were quite simple: just striking out the charges of fraud and conspiracy against the solicitors.

Then comes the second period of delay. It was eleven months. From April, 1965, to March, 1966, the plaintiffs were engaged in considering the effect of the dissolution of the building company. (It had been dissolved in January, 1965). It involved another amendment of the statement of claim so as to add
G one short sentence; but they did not obtain leave for the amendments till March, 1966. During this period the solicitors for Mrs. Hammond wrote five letters complaining of the delay. They said that the widow could not finally administer the estate of her husband until the action was disposed of. One of the letters on Nov. 19, 1965, said:

H " Our client has been in touch with us during this week complaining most bitterly of the delay in this matter and she has given us peremptory instructions to take such steps as may be necessary without delay."

On Apr. 29, 1966, the plaintiffs' solicitors delivered their amended statement of claim. It did not affect the defence of Mrs. Hammond, so she did not amend her defence. It involved very minor amendments to the defence of J. H. Milner
I & Sons. They were done and delivered on June 8, 1966.

Now comes the third period of delay. It was for fourteen months from June 8, 1966, to July 3, 1967. In this period the plaintiffs' solicitors did nothing: or, at any rate, nothing to come to the notice of the defendants: save for the taxation of some costs in August, 1966 which did not affect the trial at all. The plaintiffs' solicitor says that he was organising the case so as to set it down for trial. Then on Mar. 3, 1967, his managing clerk was badly injured in a motor car accident and did not return until July 31, 1967. He then wrote asking for

consent to set the matter down for trial. Both defendants retorted by taking **A**
out a summons to dismiss for want of prosecution.

In this case the delay was the fault of the plaintiffs' solicitors. Even allowing for the accident to the managing clerk (6), the rest of the delay was prolonged and inexcusable. The amendments to the statement of claim should
have been done in six weeks. They took over two years. Even after they were
made, there was another year lost. These delays have been such as to cause **B**
grave injustice to the defendants.

Just consider the position of the widow, Mrs. Hammond. Her husband is
charged with fraud and conspiracy, which is said to have taken place fourteen
years ago. He is not here to defend himself. She has to do it for him. She has
been unable to administer the estate whilst this claim is hanging over it. Two
years ago she protested about the delay and her solicitors warned the plaintiffs' **C**
solicitors of the consequences. Since that warning there has been another year's
delay. If this case is allowed to drag on indefinitely, she may herself be dead
before it comes to trial, as well as her husband. The other alleged conspirator,
the building company, is already dead. It was dissolved nearly three years
ago. So it is an action for fraud and conspiracy fourteen years ago in which
both the conspirators are dead. A fine state of affairs !   **D**

Now consider the position of the solicitors, J. H. Milner & Sons. The action
charged them also with fraud and conspiracy fourteen years ago. That
charge was kept hanging over their heads for four or five years. Then it was
dropped. The property company still charges them with misconduct as solicitors
and negligence. It is, I think, a grave injustice to professional men to have
a charge of this kind outstanding for so long. It is impossible to have a fair **E**
trial after all this time.

I think that the judge was entitled in his discretion to strike out this action.
I would dismiss this appeal.

DIPLOCK, L.J.: The procedure of the English courts is based on the
adversary system. The underlying principle of civil litigation is that the **F**
court takes no action in it of its own motion but only on the application of one
or other of the parties to the litigation, the assumption being that each will be
regardful of his own interest and take whatever procedural steps are necessary
to advance his cause. But most litigants are laymen. They cannot effectively
avail themselves of the remedies provided by the courts except with the
professional assistance of lawyers: hence the creation twenty years ago of the **G**
comprehensive scheme for legal aid designed to enable every citizen, whatever
his means, to obtain the skilled assistance of solicitors and counsel in the
enforcement or defence of his legal rights through the machinery of the courts.
Thus, except in the rare cases where a party litigates in person, every step
which a litigant takes in civil proceedings in the courts it taken through the
agency of a solicitor acting on his behalf. So long as the solicitor is diligent in **H**
his duty to his client, the assumption that there will be taken timeously
whatever procedural steps are necessary to advance the party's cause is valid,
and the adversary system works. The assumption is falsified, however, and
our system for administering justice is in danger of breaking down, if the
solicitor either deliberately or through forgetfulness puts his own convenience
before the interests of his client in a particular action.   **I**

This does not happen often. Where it does, it generally takes the form of
unnecessary delay by the solicitor for a plaintiff in taking one or other of the
steps needed to bring an action on for trial. That unfortunately is what has
happened in the three cases in which the present appeals are brought. Where,
as in these three cases, a plaintiff is engaged in civil litigation in which he is
advised he has a reasonable prospect of success, any avoidable delay in bringing it on for trial is likely to be contrary to his interests. There are three

---

(6) He was involved in a motor accident on Mar. 3, 1967.

A   stages between cause of action and trial: the first from cause of action to service of writ, which may include application for legal aid; the second from service of writ to setting down for trial; the third from setting down to the trial itself. Each of these stages inevitably takes time. The plaintiff's solicitor has no control over the time taken before he is consulted or after the action has been set down for trial. The former depends on the client: the latter on the

B   state of business of the courts. What the plaintiff's solicitor can control and should avoid is any delay between being first consulted and setting the action down for trial which is not reasonably necessary for the proper preparation of his client's case. Even if the plaintiff ultimately wins the action, he is kept waiting longer than he need be for the compensation to which he is entitled, and in practice the amount eventually awarded to him is unlikely to be assessed

C   at an increased figure adequate to compensate him for delay caused by the dilatoriness of his own advisers. Moreover, where the case is one in which at the trial disputed facts will have to be ascertained from oral testimony of witnesses recounting what they then recall of events which happened in the past, memories grow dim, witnesses may die or diappear. The chances of the court's being able to find out what really happened are progressively reduced as time

D   goes on. This puts justice to the hazard. If the trial is allowed to proceed, this is more likely to operate to the prejudice of the plaintiff on whom the onus of satisfying the court as to what happened generally lies. There may come a time, however, when the interval between the events alleged to constitute the cause of action and the trial of the action is so prolonged that there is a substantial risk that a fair trial of the issues will be no longer possible. When

E   this stage has been reached, the public interest in the administration of justice demands that the action should not be allowed to proceed.

   It is the contention of the respective defendants that in each of the three cases which are the subject of these appeals that stage has now been reached. They applied to have the actions dismissed. The judges in chambers, following the decisions of this court in *Reggentin* v. *Beecholme Bakeries, Ltd.*, (7) and

F   *Fitzpatrick* v. *Batger & Co., Ltd.*, (8), agreed with the defendants' contention and exercised the discretion conferred on them under the rules of court by dismissing the three actions for want of prosecution.

   Before turning to the particular facts of the three cases, I should refer to three general lines of argument which have been addressed to us on behalf of the plaintiffs and by counsel instructed by the Law Society who appeared as

G   amicus curiae.

   The first line of argument is that it would be unjust to penalise the plaintiff personally for a default which was exclusively that of his solicitors. To dismiss the action is to deprive him of his remedy against the defendant for a wrong which he alleges the defendant has committed; for it is now too late under the limitation statutes for him to bring a fresh action against the defendant.

H   The second line of argument is that the defendant could, if he wished, have taken steps to bring the action expeditiously to trial. Instead he too sat back and allowed so much time to elapse as to make a fair trial of the action impossible, and now seeks to profit from this by escaping liability to the plaintiff.

   The third line of argument relies on what is said to have been a long-established understanding in the solicitors' profession that those acting for defendants do not apply to dismiss an action for want of prosecution without giving sufficient prior warning to enable the plaintiff's solicitor to put matters right by taking the next step in the procedure.

   As regards the position of the plaintiff, it is of course unfortunate that he, though personally blameless, should suffer for the default of his agent; but if he does, he is not without a remedy, for unless he himself has caused or consented to the delay which has resulted in his action being dismissed for want

(7) (1967), 111 Sol. Jo. 216; noted at p. 566, letters F to I, post.
(8) [1967] 2 All E.R. 657.

of prosecution, he will have a right of action against his solicitor for negligence. **A** Liability for professional negligence is a risk against which most solicitors insure. Delay which justifies dismissal of an action for want of prosecution, as distinct from dismissal for disobedience to a peremptory order of the court, is ex hypothesi so prolonged that it involves a serious risk that there will not be a fair trial of the issues. If the action nevertheless proceeds to trial, injustice may be done to the plaintiff as a result of his solicitor's default, but there will **B** be no practicable remedy available to him. On the other hand, if the action is dismissed, the plaintiff in a subsequent action for negligence against his solicitor can recover, in addition to the costs of the action which has been dismissed, compensation for the loss of his chances of recovering damages against the defendant in the dismissed action had it been properly conducted on his behalf by the solicitor. It is true that if the action for professional negligence **C** were fought, the court which tried it would have to assess what those chances were. On this issue, however, the plaintiff would be in a much more advantageous position than if he had sought, despite the inordinate delay, to establish liability against the defendant in the action which had been dismissed. Not only would there be available to him any advice or material which had been given or obtained by his solicitor in support of his case in the dismissed action, but the **D** principle of *Armory* v. *Delamirie* (9) would apply and would impose on the solicitor the onus of satisfying the court that the plaintiff's claim in the dismissed action would not have succeeded had it been prosecuted with diligence. This would be a heavy onus to sustain after so great a lapse of time. The probabilities are that in any case in which the plaintiff had been advised to bring the action which had been dismissed and had never been advised to discontinue it, his **E** subsequent action against his solicitor for negligence would be settled. One would hope that, for the good name of the profession, it would be settled promptly. In the result the blameless plaintiff is not penalised unless his negligent solicitor is not financially able, by his insurers or otherwise, to satisfy the plaintiff's claim against him.

As regards the position of the defendant, the Rules of the Supreme Court **F** give to the plaintiff the initiative in bringing his action on for trial. The pace at which it proceeds through the various steps of issue and service of writ, or pleadings and discovery, of order for directions and setting down for trial is in the first instance within his control. The rules also provide machinery whereby the plaintiff can compel the defendant to take promptly those steps preparatory to the trial which call for positive action on his part and provide an effective **G** sanction against unreasonable delay by the defendant. They enable the plaintiff to sign judgment against the defendant in default and so obtain forthwith the remedy for which the action was brought. The times within which these successive steps should be taken are laid down by the rules, though subject to extension by agreement of the parties or order of the court; but under the adversary system the only sanction for their observance by either party is dependent on the other party's choosing to make an application to the court. **H** Where the delay is on the part of the plaintiff, there are some steps, such as obtaining an order for directions or setting down the action for trial, which the defendant may take himself; but it is seldom in the defendant's interest to press on with the trial of the action, whatever view he takes of the plaintiff's chances of success. He has in any event the use during the period of delay of **I** any money which he might ultimately have to pay in damages. Where the plaintiff's chances of success seem good, there is the possibility that he himself will grow impatient of the law's delay and be willing to settle for a lesser sum than he would be likely to recover if the action were tried expeditiously. Although delay may make a fair trial of the issues more difficult and no-one can be certain who will be the loser by this, it is likely at first to operate more to

(9) (1722), 1 Str. 505.

A the prejudice of the plaintiff on whom the onus of proof lies than to that of the
defendant. Although in exceptional cases there may be reasons why it is to the
defendant's advantage to have an action against him disposed of speedily,
it would be unrealistic to expect him in an ordinary action for damages, particularly in " accident cases ", to take steps to hasten on for trial an action in
which the plaintiff's prospects of success appear at the outset to be good.

B Equally where the plaintiff's prospects of success seem doubtful, the costs
system and the legal aid system operate so as to make it contrary to the
defendant's interest to incur any further costs which will result in bringing
the action on for trial. Even if the plaintiff is in a financial position to meet
them, the defendant will not recover them in full as party and party costs if
the trial goes in his favour. Where, as is so frequently the case today, the

C plaintiff is legally aided, he will recover at best little, and more likely nothing,
of the costs which he incurs.

It is thus inherent in an adversary system which relies exclusively on the parties
to an action to take whatever procedural steps appear to them to be expedient to advance their own case, that the defendant, instead of spurring the
plaintiff to proceed to trial, can with propriety wait until he can successfully

D apply to the court to dismiss the plaintiff's action for want of prosecution on the
ground that so long a time has elapsed since the events alleged to constitute
the cause of action that there is a substantial risk that a fair trial of the issues
will not be possible.

This brings me to the third line of argument based on what is said by counsel
instructed by the Law Society to be the long-established understanding in the

E solicitors' profession. The only purpose of giving to the plaintiff's solicitor
prior warning of the defendant's intention to apply to dismiss the action for
want of prosecution is to give the plaintiff's solicitor an opportunity of bringing
it on for trial before it is too late to do so. Ex hypothesi this is not in the
defendant's interest whether the plaintiff's chances of success are good or bad.
It would be wrong of this court to countenance an understanding in the pro-

F fession that a defendant's solicitor would act against his clients' interest in order
to protect a brother solicitor from a possible liability for negligence. It is said,
however, that in many cases this understanding was in the common interest
of defendants as well as plaintiffs. It operated this way. Where after action
had been brought it became apparent to the plaintiff's solicitor that the action
had little prospect of success, he took no further step in the action and it was

G allowed to remain dormant ever after on the tacit understanding that the
defendant would not seek an order for his costs by applying to have the action
dismissed. It was contended that if the defendant wished to depart from this
understanding, the plaintff should receive warning in time to enable him to
do likewise and to revive the action. If this were in reality a freely negotiated,
albeit tacit, agreement between the parties for a " settlement " of the action

H —and counsel who appeared as amicus curiae so described it—the proper way
of carrying it out would be for the action to be discontinued or dismissed by
consent without any order for costs. But this court should not wear blinkers.
If there is such an understanding, there is implicit in it the threat that if the
defendant seeks to obtain an order for the costs that he has already incurred
in defending an action which ex hypothesi he can defend successfully, he will

I be put to the additional trouble and expense of taking further steps in the
action with little prospect of being able to recover the costs of doing so from
an impecunious or legally-aided plaintiff. Let us not mince words. This tacit
understanding, if it exists, is based at best on bluff, at worst on blackmail.
The sooner it is abandoned the better. To misuse the rules of court for such
a purpose is an abuse of its process.

What then are the principles which the court should apply in exercising
its discretion to dismiss an action for want of prosecution on a defendant's
application? The application is not usually made until the period of limitation

for the plaintiff's cause of action has expired. It is then a Draconian order A and will not be lightly made. It should not in any event be exercised without giving the plaintiff an opportunity to remedy his default, unless the court is satisfied either that the default has been intentional and contumelious, or that the inexcusable delay for which the plaintiff or his lawyers have been responsible has been such as to give rise to a substantial risk that a fair trial of the issues in the litigation will not be possible at the earliest date at which, as a B result of the delay, the action would come to trial if it were allowed to continue. It is for the defendant to satisfy the court that one or other of these two conditions is fulfilled. Disobedience to a peremptory order of the court would be sufficient to satisfy the first condition. Whether the second alternative condition is satisfied will depend on the circumstances of the particular case; but the length of the delay may of itself suffice to satisfy this condition if the C relevant issues would depend on the recollection of witnesses of events which happened long ago.

Since the power to dismiss an action for want of prosecution is only exercisable on the application of the defendant his previous conduct in the action is always relevant. So far as he himself has been responsible for any unnecessary delay, he obviously cannot rely on it. Moreover, if after the plaintiff has been D guilty of unreasonable delay the defendant so conducts himself as to induce the plaintiff to incur further costs in the reasonable belief that the defendant intends to exercise his right to proceed to trial notwithstanding the plaintiff's delay, he cannot obtain dismissal of the action unless the plaintiff has thereafter been guilty of further unreasonable delay. For the reasons already mentioned, however, mere non-activity on the part of the defendant where no procedural E step on his part is called for by the rules of court is not to be regarded as conduct capable of inducing the plaintiff reasonably to believe that the defendant intends to exercise his right to proceed to trial. It must be remembered, however, that the evils of delay are cumulative, and even where there is active conduct by the defendant which would debar him from obtaining dismissal of the action for excessive delay by the plaintiff anterior to that conduct, the F anterior delay will not be irrelevant if the plaintiff is subsequently guilty of further unreasonable delay. The question will then be whether as a result of the whole of the unnecessary delay on the part of the plaintiff since the issue of the writ, there is a substantial risk that a fair trial of the issues in the litigation will not be possible.

Next as to the personal position of the plaintiff. He may, of course, have been G personally to blame for the delay; but generally the ordinary litigant, once he has consulted his solicitor, is helpless before the mysterious arcana of the law. Delay, when it occurs from this stage onwards, is usually not his own fault but that of his solicitor. If, as a result of his solicitor's default, he has a remedy in an action for negligence against his solicitor; and, as already pointed out, if the solicitor is financially able to meet the damages, this remedy is an ade- H quate one. If, however, the solicitor would be unable to meet the damages, the hardship to the plaintiff, whose action against the defendant is dismissed for want of prosecution, is grave indeed. In strict logic, the impecuniosity of the plaintiff's solicitor would not affect the defendant's right to have the action dismissed; but in exercising a discretion, even a judicial one, the courts can temper logic with humanity and the prospect that an innocent plaintiff will be left without any effective remedy for the loss of his cause of action against the defendant is a factor to be taken into consideration in weighing, on the one hand, the hardship to the plaintiff if the action is dismissed, and, on the other hand, the hardship to the defendant and the prejudice to the due administration of justice if it is allowed to proceed.

How do these principles affect the three cases under appeal? I need not repeat their facts which have already been fully stated by LORD DENNING, M.R.

1. *As to the first appeal.*

The plaintiff's claim against the defendants was simple. We cannot try it, but it would seem that she had excellent prospects of success and that the real issue was whether the defendants could recover an indemnity or contribution from third parties—an issue which had to await the trial of the plaintiff's claim. There was no unreasonable delay before issue of the writ and what delay there was before the pleadings were closed in January, 1961, some two years after the accident, was due to the defendants; but thereafter the plaintiff's solicitors proceeded with inexcusable dilatoriness. Four years were wasted before discovery was sought in March, 1965. Lists of documents were given by the defendants and inspection given by June, 1965. Then another twenty months were allowed to pass before in February, 1967 the plaintiff's solicitor wrote the letter to which LORD DENNING, M.R. has referred; and still, six years after the pleadings in this simple claim had been closed, there had not even been a summons for directions which under the rules should have been taken out in February, 1961. On May 21, 1967, Master ELTON on the defendants' application dismissed the action for want of prosecution. His order was upheld by the judge in chambers. By then the accident was more than eight years old. The evidence discloses that as long ago as September, 1961, counsel for the plaintiff advised that proofs should be obtained from six witnesses. Two have disappeared without a trace. No attempt was made to trace the others until February, 1964, and two of these were not found until May and June, 1965— more than six years after the accident they were invited to recall. It may well be that even at this late stage the plaintiff could prove her case against the defendants, but it is as clear as can be that if the action is allowed to proceed, there is a substantial risk that a fair trial will not be possible of the issues between the defendants and the third parties in the third party proceedings which are dependent on the plaintiff's claim. The condition precedent to the defendants' right to have the action dismissed is thus fulfilled.

Next, has the defendants' conduct debarred them from this remedy? This action, in proceeding with discovery in 1965 which involved the plaintiff in incurring costs, would have prevented them from obtaining dismissal of the action at that time despite what was already an inordinate delay; but it was followed by a further twenty months of equally inexcusable delay on the plaintiff's part. The only other positive act by the defendants thereafter was to provide details of the earnings of the deceased and these were followed within a week by the application to dismiss the action. I do not think that this debars them from their remedy.

Finally, as to the plaintiff's personal situtation. Her solicitor, in his affidavit and through counsel whom he has instructed on her behalf, has put the facts before the court with commendable candour. He has not sought to evade such blame as attaches to him personally. He admits his dilatoriness which he frankly ascribes to pressure of other work. He is most anxious that his client should not suffer for it. Fortunately, this is a case where he is insured against liability for negligence. The plaintiff, a widow with two small children, has already been deprived for nine years of a sum of money which in all probability she would have been entitled to recover from the defendants even though they might in turn have been able to recover all or part of it from the third parties. The dismissal of her action, however, will not prevent her from recovering it, together with interest from the date on which that action should with reasonable diligence have been tried, from her solicitor in settlement of his liability to her for his negligence.

For my part I would not interfere with the judge's exercise of his discretion.

2. *As to the second appeal.*

The plaintiff's cause of action, if she has one, arose in September, 1958. The writ was not issued until February, 1961; but notice of the claim was promptly given and the solicitors for the defendants obtained as early as 1958 and 1959 detailed statements from the doctors who treated the plaintiff, who would be the principal witnesses on the issues in the action, and the copies of the relevant medical records. Even if the action had been brought on for trial with reasonable expedition after the issue of the writ, these witnesses would have had to rely largely on their contemporaneous records to refresh their memories. Some of the witnesses, however, who could have spoken as to whether the accident occurred at all in the way the plaintiff said it did, are no longer available.

After delivery of the statement of claim in July, 1961, instead of delivering a defence, as they should have done, the defendants asked for further and better particulars of the statement of claim. They were clearly not entitled to these before defence but the plaintiff's then solicitor did not take this point. Nothing more was done in the action for five years until March, 1966. The plaintiff's present solicitors are not to blame for this. It was the fault of her previous solicitor and his managing clerk, both of whom were convicted and imprisoned at some time during this period, but according to the plaintiff's uncontradicted evidence, she did not learn of this until August, 1965.

Clearly the inexcusable lapse of time for which the plaintiff's former solicitor was responsible has given rise to a substantial risk that the issue whether the accident occurred in the way alleged by the plaintiff cannot now be fairly tried, although the trial of the issues as to her medical condition will not be similarly prejudiced. In this case, however, the defendants' own conduct appears to me to be such as to debar them from the remedy of dismissal of the action. They have at all times themselves been in default in delivering their defence. They still were when, in March, 1967, they applied to have the action dismissed for want of prosecution. In August, 1966, in tardy response to the plaintiff's new solicitor's attempt to revive the action, they demanded delivery of the particulars which they had, quite wrongly, asked for five years before. As a result the plaintiff was induced to incur costs in supplying these, which were delivered in November, 1966. Thereafter the defendants' solicitors again and again asked for and were granted by the plaintiff's solicitor extensions of time to deliver their defence.

This is a case too where the personal hardship to the plaintiff will be very grave if her action is dismissed. She has no prospect of recovering a penny from her former solicitors whose negligence is responsible for her plight. The hardship to the defendants in allowing the action to proceed to trial despite the inordinate delay is mitigated in the present case by the fact that the contemporaneous records of the plaintiff's medical condition and what she said about the cause of that condition to the doctors who treated her still exist, as do the detailed statements obtained by the defendants' solicitors from potential witnesses as early as 1958 and 1959 which, even if the witnesses are unavailable, would be admissible under the Evidence Act, 1938. Her prospects of success may now be far from rosy but, having regard to the defendants' own conduct in the action and the absence of any effective remedy for the plaintiff against her former solicitor, I think that the interests of justice are better served by allowing this action to proceed.

In exercising his discretion to dismiss the action, the only guidance which the judge had from this court was that contained in the two decisions which I have already mentioned. Occasion was not taken in those two appeals, as it has been in these, to analyse the principles by which judges should be guided when applications are made to dismiss actions for want of prosecution. It is, therefore, no criticism of the judge to say that in the light of the principles which have only now been stated, I would reverse his decision in this case and allow the appeal.

A 3. *As to the third appeal.*

This is a much more complicated action and the events out of which it arises took place between ten and fourteen years ago. Preparation for trial was inevitably onerous and no complaint can legitimately be made that discovery was not completed until December, 1963. One defendant was an executrix against whose deceased husband a claim on an indemnity and charges of

B fraud and conspiracy were made. She cannot distribute the estate until the claim is disposed of. The other defendants are a firm of solicitors against whom a charge of fraud was also made, though this had so little substance that the plaintiffs decided to withdraw it as long ago as December, 1963. A charge of professional negligence against them, however, was persisted in.

LORD DENNING, M.R., has described the three successive periods of in-

C excusable delay after December, 1963. They total more than two-and-a-half years, and this in an action where charges of fraud and conspiracy and of professional negligence are still made. So far as it depends on documents, the fair trial of the issue on the alleged indemnity may not have been greatly prejudiced by the delay, although the executrix has been thereby prevented from winding-up the estate; but on the issues of fraud, conspiracy and pro-

D fessional negligence, the lapse of time cannot fail to give rise to a substantial risk that a fair trial of these issues will be no longer possible.

The conduct of both of the defendants requires to be considered. So far as the defendant executrix was concerned, her solicitors were pressing as long ago as 1965 that the action should be brought to trial as quickly as possible so that she could distribute the estate. No heed was paid to these warnings. So

E far as the solicitor defendants were concerned, although an undertaking had been given to them that the charges of fraud would be withdrawn, the simple amendment to give effect to this was not delivered until April, 1966. It is understandable that they should not have sought to dismiss the action for want of prosecution while that charge still remained on the pleadings, but their action thereafter in making a small consequential amendment to their defence

F on June 8, 1966, would in my view have debarred them, though not the defendant executrix, from having the action dismissed for want of prosecution had the plaintiffs thereafter promptly restored the summons for directions in order to have the action set down for trial. The plaintiffs' solicitors, however, merely persisted in their policy of delay. Eight months were allowed to pass before Mar. 3, when their managing clerk sustained a motor accident. The

G defendants would in my view have been entitled to apply to have the action dismissed for want of prosecution by that date. They were not the less entitled to do so five months later when, on the managing clerk's return, the plaintiffs' solicitors finally evinced an intention to set down the action for trial. I can see nothing in the conduct of either defendant to debar them from their right to have the action dismissed for want of prosecution.

In exercising his discretion to do so, the judge was influenced as respects the defendant executrix by the fact that her solicitors had pressed the plaintiffs for expedition as long ago as 1965 and by the prejudice she suffered in being unable to complete the administration of the estate. Both these are in my view relevant considerations and he was right to attach importance to them. As respects the solicitor defendants, he took the view that the nature of the allegations against them, first of fraud and conspiracy and then of professional negligence, were of a character which common fairness required should not be kept hanging over their heads a moment longer than was necessary. I agree. If such damaging charges are to be made, justice particularly requires that they should be disposed of with the minimum of delay.

As regards the personal hardship to the plaintiffs, there is nothing to suggest that if, in truth, they have a genuine claim against either of the defendants which has been lost by their solicitors' negligence, they will not have an effective remedy against them.

In this case I see no grounds for interfering with the judge's discretion. I would dismiss this appeal.

It would not be right to end without one further general observation. The fact that these three appeals have been heard together and this court has been invited to lay down some general guidance as to the principles on which the discretion to dismiss an action for want of prosecution should be exercised, may perhaps lead to the impression that it is common for solicitors to be dilatory in the conduct of litigation for their clients. This would be a wholly unjustifiable slur on a profession which, though undermanned and often today working under great pressure, provides, save in the rarest cases a conscientious, skilled and diligent public service to litigants in the courts of justice. For my part I would not like to leave the unhappy topic of these three appeals without recording a tribute to the way in which the overwhelming majority of the profession conduct litigation in our courts. They fulfil an onerous and essential function in the administration of justice; and they do it well.

SALMON, L.J.: The seven parties to these three appeals have been most ably represented by all the counsel appearing on their behalf. There were thirteen of them. Apparently, however, for fear lest we might be in need of still further help from the Bar in doing justice between the parties, the Law Society has thoughtfully provided us with the services of an amicus curiae. I had always understood that the role of an amicus curiae was to help the court by expounding the law impartially, or if one of the parties were unrepresented, by advancing the legal arguments on his behalf. As I listened to the cogent and forceful argument of counsel who appeared as amicus curiae, I gained the impression— although no doubt it was an illusion—that in reality he held a watching or indeed a speaking brief on behalf of hardly impartial third parties who feared that their interests, or rather those of their members, might be prejudiced should these appeals be dismissed. I do not think that these fears, if they exist, are justified. It is as much in the interests of solicitors as a whole as it is of everyone else that the grossly inordinate and inexcusable delays which sometimes disfigure litigation should cease. The overwhelming majority of solicitors conduct litigation with high efficiency and all reasonable speed. A very small, but alas by no means insignificant, number of cases, particularly accident cases, are, however, conducted with an altogether intolerable dilatoriness. Thus the action, or rather inaction, of a minute minority of solicitors tends, most unfairly, to cast a reflection on the general body of solicitors which it certainly does not deserve.

Delay is not by any means always inexcusable. For example, in some cases the prognosis as to the effect of the plaintiff's injuries is quite uncertain, but the doctors think that it may reveal itself with the passage of time. In such cases there may undoubtedly be good reason for delaying the whole trial. It should be remembered, however, that even there there is procedural machinery for adopting a preferable course—namely, disposing of the issue of liability and leaving over the issue of damages to be decided later, if necessary. The real evil, however, lies in those cases which, for no reason at all, save sheer dilatoriness on the part of the plaintiff's solicitor, do not come on for trial until many years, sometimes five, six or even ten years after the accident out of which they arose. Such dilatoriness undoubtedly amounts to negligence. Once it is generally recognised, as I have no doubt it now will be, that inordinate and inexcusable delay may and probably will result in the action being dismissed for want of prosecution and the liability to pay damages being transferred on to the shoulders of those responsible for the delay, there will, I am confident, be a remarkable improvement—an improvement which it has apparently been impossible to achieve by any other means. I would repeat what was said in this court in *Fitzpatrick* v. *Batger & Co., Ltd.*, (10).

---

(10) [1967] 2 All E.R. at p. 659.

A   " It is of the greatest importance in the interests of justice that . . . actions should be brought to trial with reasonable expedition. It is not only in the interests of defendants that this should be done, but it is perhaps even more in the interest of plaintiffs themselves."

B   After all, the risk that witnesses may die or disappear and that the recollection of those that remain may have grown dim is common to plaintiffs and defendants alike.   In some cases it may bear more hardly on defendants; in others on plaintiffs. But a plaintiff with a good cause of action suffers a real hardship by being kept out of his money for years, whilst a defendant who is liable to pay damages enjoys the use of his money for all the time during which the action is allowed to hang fire.

C   We have rightly been reminded that in these courts what is called the adversary system prevails, and that accordingly, with certain irrelevant exceptions, the courts cannot act of their own motion but only on the application of one or other of the parties. Moreover, it has been emphasised that in deciding any issue, the courts must decide it in accordance with the rights of the particular plaintiff and the particular defendant irrespective of the repercussions of the decision on others. Accordingly, it would be wrong to give the present defendants an advantage to which they are not entitled or to inflict a deprivation on the present plaintiffs to which they are not liable for the purpose of benefiting the general body of plaintiffs or defendants. With all this I entirely agree.

D   A defendant may apply to have an action dismissed for want of prosecution either (a) because of the plaintiff's failure to comply with the Rules of the Supreme Court or (b) under the court's inherent jurisdiction. In my view it matters not whether the application comes under limb (a) or (b), the same principles apply. They are as follows: In order for such an application to succeed, the defendant must show:

E   (i) that there has been inordinate delay. It would be highly undesirable and indeed impossible to attempt to lay down a tariff—so many years or more on one side of the line and a lesser period on the other. What is or is not inordinate delay must depend on the facts of each particular case.   These vary infinitely from case to case, but it should not be too difficult to recognise inordinate delay when it occurs.

F   (ii) that this inordinate delay is inexcusable. As a rule, until a credible excuse is made out, the natural inference would be that it is inexcusable.

(iii) that the defendants are likely to be seriously prejudiced by the delay. This may be prejudice at the trial of issues between themselves and the plaintiff, or between each other, or between themselves and the third parties. In addition to any inference that may properly be drawn from the delay itself, prejudice can sometimes be directly proved. As a rule, the longer the delay, the greater the likelihood of serious prejudice at the trial.

G   If the defendant establishes the three factors to which I have referred, the court, in exercising its discretion, must take into consideration the position of the plaintiff himself and strike a balance. If he is personally to blame for the delay, no difficulty arises.   There can be no injustice in his bearing the consequences of his own fault.   If, however, the delay is entirely due to the negligence of the plaintiff's solicitor and the plaintiff himself is blameless, it might be unjust to deprive him of the chance of recovering the damages to which he could otherwise be entitled. When, however, the solicitor or his insurers are good for the damages, the plaintiff is unlikely to be seriously prejudiced by dismissal of the action.   He will probably recover from his solicitor in an action for negligence all the costs thrown away, in addition to the damages he would have recovered against the defendant. It is true that he may be involved in some further delay, and that in some circumstances it may be more difficult to prove against the solicitor the cause of action which the plaintiff

had against the defendant. As a rule, however, if the plaintiff has a sound cause   A
of action against the defendant, the solicitor's insurers will be anxious to settle
the claim. It is chiefly when the solicitor is uninsured or impecunious that the
necessity to strike a balance arises. The court must then consider the degree
of likelihood of serious prejudice and the degree of serious prejudice likely to
be caused to the defendant by the delay. It must consider also the prejudice
which the plaintiff may suffer in having his action dismissed, bearing in mind   B
the apparent merits of his case, and not forgetting the fact that it was his agent
and not the defendant who caused the delay. In the end, the court must decide
whether or not on balance justice demands that the action should be dismissed.

I do not accept the argument that these principles are in any way unjust to
solicitors. I have every sympathy with the difficulties which sometimes confront
them and with which most of them cope so well—pressure of work, staff short-   C
ages and the like. Solicitors, however, should not, and normally do not, accept
work which they cannot carry out except with years and years of delay. They
hand it on to other firms less busy or better equipped than themselves. As I
have already indicated, it is by no means every delay which constitutes
negligence; there are, of course, ordinary delays inseparable from litigation.
On the rare occasions, however, when there is inordinate and inexcusable delay   D
likely to cause the defendant serious prejudice, the action should normally be
dismissed and the loss attributable to the dismissal borne by those whose negligence has caused it. It would be a serious reflection on the administration of
justice if such gross delays as those to which I have referred should be countenanced by the courts out of tenderness for the legal profession. Nor can I
accept the argument that an application to dismiss an action for want of   E
prosecution should not succeed unless the plaintiff's solicitor has first been warned
by the defendant and continued the delay after the warning. To accede to this
argument would be an encouragement to the careless and lethargic. It would
mean that they could neglect with impunity their client's interests for years
and do so at no risk to themselves until such time, if ever, as a warning shot
was fired. On this point I cannot usefully add anything further to what has   F
fallen from my lords or to what I have said about it in *Fitzpatrick's* case (11).
Plaintiffs are sometimes completely unsophisticated. They accept with resigna-
tion the passage of years with nothing happening. They vaguely attribute all
this to what they have heard called " the law's delays ". They have no idea
that it is usually the fault of their own solicitor that their case has not been tried
or settled long ago. Whenever such cases are dismissed for want of prosecution,   G
the court should, in my view, take steps to ensure that the plaintiff is personally
informed of the decision and briefly of the reasons for which it was made.

It has been argued that in *Reggentin* v. *Beecholme Bakeries & Co.* (12) and in
Fitzpatrick's case (13) this court altered the settled practice and that the new
practice should not be put into effect in respect of delays arising before the
date of those decisions. I do not, however, consider that those decisions did   H
effect any real alterations in the practice or the law. They merely drew timely
attention to what has long been recognised in the courts, namely, that really
serious and inexcusable delay may, and probably will, result in an action being
dismissed for want of prosecution. This court has never said anything to cast
any doubt on this doctrine. If, as we have been told, the practice has in recent
years been somewhat relaxed in chambers, it certainly has not been abrogated.
DIPLOCK, L.J., points out, a stricter view may now be taken of delays occurring
after the recent decisions than of delays occurring before them. The worst of
these latter delays, however, will not escape even now. I am not attracted by
the argument of those responsible for such delays to the effect that they have
been lulled into a false sense of security; that although they have been grossly

(11) [1967] 2 All E.R. at p. 659.
(12) (1967), 111 Sol. Jo. 216; noted at p. 566, letters F to I, post.
(13) [1967] 2 All E.R. 657.

A negligent, they had some reason to believe that they might safely be so and therefore ought not to be held responsible for the harm which their negligence has caused.

I will now briefly consider, without repeating in any detail the facts fully stated by LORD DENNING, M.R., of these three appeals in the light of the principles I have attempted to formulate.

B 1. *As to the first appeal.*

Nearly nine years ago the plaintiff's husband, then aged forty, fell to his death in circumstances which make it plain that he was blameless and that the accident was due to negligence or breach of statutory duty on the part of his employers, the defendants. They had no real answer to the plaintiff's claim. Her damages
C would amount to the financial loss she and her young children suffered through the death of her husband, the family wage-earner. On the facts now before us, I estimate that these damages would have been in the region of £7,000. The widow, no doubt, was in dire need of the money. It is difficult to think of a case which better deserved to be handled with expedition.

The plaintiff consulted her solicitor within a few days of the accident. I have
D no doubt that a little resolution on his part would have secured an early settlement on the basis of full liability. Instead the solicitor has allowed the case to drag on for nearly nine years and still the plaintiff and her children have not received one penny. If the solicitor was too busy to deal properly with the case, he should have sent the plaintiff to someone else who was able to do so. It may be said that since the defendants had no answer to the claim, they cannot
E have been prejudiced by the delay. This no doubt is true so far as their defence to the action is concerned; but there were third party proceedings in which the defendants were seeking an indemnity or contribution from their subcontractors. It would appear that there would have been a reasonable chance of these third party proceedings succeeding if they had been brought on within a reasonable time: but this could not be done until the plaintiff's claim was
F disposed of. The plaintiff's solicitor, of course, knew of the third party proceedings and must have recognised that if he allowed the action to drag on for years, the defendants were likely to be seriously prejudiced in their claim against the third parties. After nine years there would be little chance of proving that the third parties were to blame. The solicitor, however, who was apparently unmoved by the pitiful plight of his own client, was hardly likely to be stirred
G into action by such considerations as these. This case seems to me to be a glaring example of inordinate and inexcusable delay which has seriously prejudiced the defendants. Moreover, there is no real possibility of prejudice to the plaintiff by dismissing the action. Indeed, to some extent she may be better off than if the action were allowed to continue. Her solicitor is insured and has no vestige of a defence to an action for negligence. The damages will
H be all the costs thrown away, together with the sum which the plaintiff would have recovered by way of damages against the defendants. Interest on that sum from the date when it should have been obtained, after allowing for any part of it which the plaintiff might reasonably be expected to have spent between that date and the date of the settlement of her claim against the solicitor, may also be included in the damages recoverable from him. Nothing could be recovered
I against the defendants in respect of this interest element.

The only point that has caused me any hesitation on this appeal arises out of the argument that the defendants have waived or aquiesced in the delay on which they found their application. Clearly no defendant can successfully apply for an action to be dismissed for want of prosecution if he has waived or acquiesced in the delay.

Mere inaction on the part of the defendant cannot in my view amount to waiver or acquiescence. Positive action, however, by which he intimates that he agrees that the action may proceed, is a different matter. If, for example,

he intimates that he is willing for the action to proceed and thereby induces **A**
the plaintiff's solicitors to do further work and incur further expense in the
prosecution of the action, he will be precluded from relying on the previous
delay by itself as a ground for dismissing the action. Should there, however,
be further serious delays on the part of the plaintiff after the defendant's acquiescence in or waiver of the earlier delay, the whole history of the case may be taken
into account in deciding whether or not the action ought to be dismissed. It is **B**
arguable from the correspondence to which reference has been made that the
defendants acquiesced in or waived the plaintiff's delay; and there was certainly
no further delay after this correspondence. On the whole, however, I agree
that in all the circumstances the letters relied on by the defendants did not
amount to acquiescence or waiver, and I would accordingly dismiss this appeal.

In my view, the plaintiff would be wise to take immediate steps to obtain legal **C**
aid in respect of her claim against her present solicitor. No doubt it may be
settled by the insurers, but the plaintiff should have legal assistance in arriving
at a settlement. It is clearly the duty of the plaintiff's present solicitor to
communicate to her in writing the substance of these judgments in so far as
they affect her; and I am sure that he will do so.

2.   *As to the second appeal.* **D**

Counsel for the plaintiff has persuaded me by his most attractive argument
that this appeal should be allowed. There was undoubtedly inordinate and
inexcusable delay on the part of the plaintiff's original solicitor. He was struck
off the roll of solicitors and has been sent to prison. He is uninsured and
apparently without means. His managing clerk also has been sent to prison
and is disqualified by the Law Society from ever again being employed by a **E**
solicitor. The facts disclosed, however, tend to show that there is little real
likelihood of the defendants being seriously prejudiced by the delay. The delay,
indeed, has chiefly prejudiced the plaintiff herself. The statements of the
principal medical witnesses who attended her (some of them on the defendants'
staff) show that they still have clear recollections of her case and there are
detailed medical notes and records in existence which give a vivid picture of **F**
her condition at the material time. It would seem that she may well have a
real claim but one which has been considerably exaggerated. Moreover, in
this case there has been the clearest acquiescence or waiver on the part of the
defendants. In November, 1961, the defendants asked for further and better
particulars of the statement of claim before delivering their defence. Plainly,
in my view, they were not entitled to any of these particulars before pleading. **G**
On Nov. 8, 1961, the plaintiff's original solicitors, however, replied by stating
that they were consulting counsel and after having his advice would write again
concerning the request for particulars. Nothing further transpired until 1966
when the plaintiff's present solicitors came on the scene. No possible criticism
can be made of them. They expressed the view that the defence should immediately be filed before any further and better particulars of the statement of **H**
claim were delivered and that otherwise a summons for judgment might be
issued. The defendants' solicitors replied by requesting the further and better
particulars to be delivered in advance of defence. They thereby clearly intimated
that the defendants were prepared for the action to proceed, and that the plaintiff
should accordingly go to the expense of preparing and delivering the particulars.
This the plaintiff duly did, and the defendants accepted service of the particulars
by post. Thereafter, on no fewer than three different occasions, the defendants
asked for and obtained an extension of time for delivery of the defence. There
certainly was no further fault on the part of the plaintiff, save possibly in failing
to take advantage of the defendants' delay. Ultimately, instead of delivering
their defence, the defendants applied, with surprising success, for the action to
be dismissed for want of prosecution. There was here about as clear a case of
waiver or acquiescence on the part of the defendants as it is possible to imagine.

For all these reasons I agree that this appeal should be allowed.

A 3. *As to the third appeal.*

This relates to events which took place as long ago as 1954. It has been said that the causes of action did not arise until 1959 or 1960 and I am prepared to assume that this is so. The writ was issued in June, 1960, and the action has been allowed to meander along ever since. Even making full allowance for such complexities as the case involves, the judge came to the conclusion that

B there had been altogether inordinate delay on the part of the plaintiff's solicitor —and I am not disposed to disagree. There were minor periods of delay for which there were no doubt excuses, namely, a few months in 1963 after junior counsel originally instructed on behalf of the plaintiffs took silk, and a few months in 1967 when the managing clerk in charge of litigation on behalf of the plaintiff was away ill. The judge, however, took the view that the period of delay

C as a whole was quite inexcusable. Again, I do not disagree with him. I also agree with the judge that the delay is likely to cause serious prejudice to the defendants. Mrs. Hammond is sued as her late husband's executrix. The action against his estate is based on his alleged fraud and conspiracy as well as on an indemnity. It certainly seems very unfair that charges of this kind should be left hanging in the air indefinitely. Moreover, until the matter is resolved, the defendant is

D unable to distribute the estate. She has complained bitterly to the plaintiff's solicitors about the delay and given the clearest warnings of its possible consequences for them and their clients; but they took no notice, and still they allowed the action to drag on inordinately. The other defendants, who are solicitors, have had a charge of professional misconduct and negligence hanging over their heads for more than seven years, and this cannot be other than seriously

E prejudicial to any professional man.

I do not think that the plaintiff will be prejudiced by the dismissal of the action. On the facts before us, he would appear to have a clear claim in negligence against his solicitors. They are a substantial firm; moreover, they are insured against such liability. The damages to which he would be entitled would be equal to the sum he would be likely to have recovered in the action

F which is dismissed. It may be that he will have difficulty in proving against his present solicitors that he would have succeeded in the original action on those parts of his case based on fraud and conspiracy against the one defendant and professional misconduct and negligence against the other, but I do not think that this difficulty would be appreciably greater than that which he would have experienced against the original defendants themselves. He may well be lucky in

G that he will be put to no further expense in pursuing these matters against those defendants, and he may now be able to recover the costs already incurred in respect of those issues. The claim against the Hammond estate based on the indemnity alleged to have been given by the late Mr. Hammond is, however, quite simple. No doubt there may have been good reason for not confining the action to this claim in the first place. I can see no reason to

H suppose that the plaintiff should have any greater difficulty in proving against his present solicitors that this claim would probably have succeeded than he would have had in establishing it against the estate.

Counsel for the plaintiffs sought to rely on the fact that in this case the writ was issued shortly after the causes of action are supposed to have arisen, whereas the period of limitation is six years. He says that the writ might not have been issued until sometime in 1965 or 1966 and presumably that it need not have been served for one year thereafter. Accordingly, so the argument runs, the defendants are no worse off now than they would have been then, and, therefore, the action should not be dismissed for want of prosecution. I hope that I am doing the argument no injustice when I say that it appears to come to this— providing a writ is issued promptly, the plaintiff and his advisers should be allowed to carry on the action as dilatorily as they like, or at any rate in a case such as the present, the first five or six years delay should not count for the purpose of considering whether it is inordinate or inexcusable. This argument does not attract me.

In my judgment, it is quite impossible to come to the conclusion that the   A
judge was wrong when, weighing up all the facts, he decided in his discretion that
justice demanded that the action should be dismissed.

I would accordingly dismiss this appeal.

LORD DENNING, M.R.: The result of the appeals will be as follows:
In the first appeal, the appeal will be dismissed and an order for costs will be   B
made either against the plaintiff or against the solicitors, but we think that
before deciding on that matter, the solicitors ought to be given a reasonable
opportunity to appear, according to Ord. 62, r. 8 (2). We would, therefore,
on that point propose adjourning the case until next Wednesday (14).

On the second appeal, the appeal is allowed with costs here and below and
the order of Master DIAMOND restored.   C

As to the third appeal, again that appeal is dismissed and an order for costs
will be made in the same way as I indicated in the first appeal—either against
the plaintiff or against the solicitor personally. But before any such order is
made, we think reasonable opportunity should be given to the solicitor to appear
before the court, and in the circumstances we will adjourn that matter until
next Wednesday for hearing (14).   D

Solicitors: In the first appeal: *Hair & Co.*, agents for *Burton & Co.*, Lincoln
(for the plaintiff); *Barlow, Lyde & Gilbert* (for the defendants). In the second
appeal: *Donovan J. Smalley* (for the plaintiff); *Hempsons* (for the defendants).
In the third appeal: *Israel, Joslin & Co.* (for the plaintiff); *Kingsley Napley &
Co.* (for the first defendants); *Chamberlain & Co.* (for the third defendants); *The
Law Society.*   E

[*Reported by* F. GUTTMAN, ESQ., *Barrister-at-Law.*]

NOTE.

In *Reggentin* v. *Beecholme Bakeries, Ltd.*, an appeal against the decision of JAMES, J.,
that the action be dismissed for want of prosecution was heard by the Court of Appeal   F
(LORD DENNING, M.R., HARMAN, SALMON, L.JJ.) on Mar. 9, 1967, and the appeal
was dismissed. On Oct. 7, 1961, the appellant's husband fell at the premises of the
respondents (his employers) and injured his back. He remained at work for two or
three months, and a year or so later his solicitors wrote to the respondents claiming
damages for negligence and breach of statutory duty. In March, 1963, he died from
coronary thrombosis which was quite unconnected with the accident. On Jan. 7,
1964, the appellant, his administratrix, issued a writ claiming damages against the   G
respondents. Pleadings were delivered, and on June 29, 1964, an order was made for
directions, including the answering of interrogatories, the delivery of lists of documents
and the inspection of the premises. It was also ordered that the action be set down for
trial within forty-nine days. In November, 1964, the interrogatories were answered,
and the premises were inspected in August, 1965. The next step was a request by the
appellant in November, 1966, for further interrogatories to be answered, whereupon
the respondents applied to have the action dismissed for want of prosecution. JAMES, J.
(overruling Master JACOB) ordered that the action be dismissed. The appellant's argu-   H
ment was that the judge had taken too much notice of the early events in the conduct
of the action. LORD DENNING, M.R., stated that, where an action had been dormant
for some thirteen months or more, defendants were entitled to take out a summons to
dismiss the action, and it could be dismissed if no sufficient reason were shown for
reviving it: that this was a borderline case, but that the decision was in the first place
for the judge in his discretion, and that the court would not interfere unless they were
satisfied that the judge was wrong. In this instance His Lordship was not satisfied
that the judge had been wrong. His Lordship intimated that the appellant's solicitors
were at fault and were liable to her for negligence. HARMAN, L.J., said that, there
being no irreparable injustice involved, the discretion of the trial judge was not lightly
to be interfered with; that the judge was not manifestly wrong and that his decision
should be supported. SALMON, L.J., concurring, stated that, having regard to the
inordinate delay on the part of the appellant's advisers, it was impossible to say that
the judge had been wrong in making the order to dismiss the action; there was every
justification for making the order. The appeal was accordingly dismissed with costs.

---

(14) See p. 545, letter F, ante.

A

NOTE.

SELANGOR UNITED RUBBER ESTATES, LTD. *v.* CRADOCK AND OTHERS (No. 2).

B [CHANCERY DIVISION (Ungoed-Thomas, J.), January 22, 23, 1968.]

Company—Investigation by Board of Trade—Evidence of officer of company before inspector—Whether admissible in subsequent civil proceedings although evidence taken before Companies Act 1967 (c. 81) s. 50—Companies Act, 1948 (11 & 12 Geo. 6 c. 38), s. 167 (2).

C *Statute—Retrospective operation—Procedural provision—Evidence taken at investigation before enactment passed—Whether evidence admissible, by virtue of enactment, in action against a witness after enactment passed—Companies Act 1967 (c. 81) s. 50.*

[As to depositions admissible in evidence at common law and by statute, see 15 HALSBURY'S LAWS (3rd Edn.) 398-401, paras. 713, 715, and compare, as regards statements made by a debtor at his public examination, 2 ibid., 334,
D para. 645 text and notes (*t*), (*u*); and for cases on the subject, see 22 DIGEST (Repl.) 280-288, *2830-2933.*

As to the admissibility or otherwise of notes of evidence on examinations under the companies legislation, see 6 HALSBURY'S LAWS (3rd Edn.) 620, 621, para. 1221, and pp. 627, 628, para. 1236.

For the Companies Act, 1948, s. 167, see 3 HALSBURY'S STATUTES (2nd Edn.)
E 591.]

Case referred to:

McClelland, Pope and Langley, Ltd. v. Howard, (1966), p. 569, post.

Action.

This was an action commenced by writ issued on Apr. 21, 1964.   The plaintiff
F was The Selangor United Rubber Estates, Ltd., a company in liquidation, and the action was brought in the name of the company by the Board of Trade pursuant to s. 169 (4) of the Companies Act, 1948, and by and with the authority of the official receiver as the liquidator (for the report of the application in the action for security for costs, see [1967] 2 All E.R. 1255).   By the re-amended statement of claim re-served on Jan. 16, 1968, the plaintiff claimed (i) a declaration that the first nine defendants were jointly and severally liable to replace moneys of the plaintiff misapplied as alleged in the statement of claim (a) as to the first, seventh, eighth and ninth defendants to the extent of the sum of £249,500; (b) as to the second defendants to the extent of the sum of £195,322 5s. 2d.;   (c) as to the third, fourth, fifth and sixth defendants to the extent of the sum of £232,500 which said sums of £195,322 5s. 2d. and £232,500 were included in the said sum of £249,500; (ii) an order on the first nine defendants and each of them to pay to the official receiver in companies liquidation as liquidator of the plaintiff such sum or sums as the defendants or any one or more of them should be declared liable to replace as aforesaid with interest thereon at the rate of five per cent. per annum;   (iii) against each of the first nine defendants damages for breach of duty; (iv) further, or in the alternative, against the third and seventh defendants damages for negligence; and (v) an order on the first nine defendants jointly and severally to pay to the Board of Trade, or alternatively to the official receiver as aforesaid, the amount of the expenses of and incidental to an investigation of the affairs of the plaintiff defrayed by the Board.

The defendants were (1) Francis Richard Cradock (a bankrupt), (2) Contanglo Banking and Trading Co., Ltd., (3) District Bank, Ltd., (4) Woodstock Trust, Ltd., (5) Francis Evelyn Barlow-Lawson, (6) Francis Arthur Jacob, (7) The Bank of Nova Scotia, (8) John Leonard Burden, (9) William Vernon Squire

Sinclair, and (10) the trustee of the property of Francis Richard Cradock (a **A** bankrupt).

By para. 4 of the statement of claim the plaintiff company pleaded that on Aug. 3, 1960, the Board of Trade in pursuance of powers conferred by s. 165 (b) of the Companies Act, 1948, appointed inspectors to investigate the affairs of the plaintiff company and to report thereon.   On July 31, 1961, the inspectors made their final report pursuant to s. 168 of the Act of 1948.   By order of the **B** Chancery Division made on June 5, 1961, it was ordered that the plaintiff company should be wound up by the court, and the official receiver became the liquidator of the company.   By paras. 3, 4 of the defence of the eighth defendant, Mr. Burden, he admitted the allegations pleaded in para. 4 of the statement of claim, in so far as hereinbefore set out, and did not deny the making of the winding-up order and the appointment of the liquidator.   During the hearing **C** of the action before UNGOED-THOMAS, J., the question arose whether transcripts of evidence of the eighth defendant, Mr. Burden, who was one of the defendant directors, taken on oath pursuant to s. 167 (2)* of the Companies Act, 1948, before the inspector investigating the affairs of the plaintiff company were admissible in evidence against him in the present proceedings by virtue of s. 50 of the Companies Act 1967.   The case is reported on this preliminary point only.   **D**

The cases noted below† were cited during the argument in addition to the case referred to in the judgment.

Arthur Bagnall, Q.C., *J. P. Warner*, *Richard Sykes* and *R. A. Morritt* for the plaintiff company.

A. J. Balcombe for the second defendants.

R. H. W. Dunn, Q.C., and *K. B. Suenson-Taylor* for the third defendants.   **E**

G. B. H. Dillon, Q.C., and *D. J. Nicholls* for the fourth defendants.

J. L. Arnold, Q.C., and *R. B. S. Instone* for the seventh defendants.

The fifth, sixth, eighth and ninth defendants appeared in person.

The first and tenth defendants did not appear and were not represented.

UNGOED-THOMAS, J.: A question has arisen whether transcripts of **F** evidence given before the inspectors investigating the affairs of the plaintiff company are admissible in evidence against the defendant, Mr. Burden, who gave that evidence before the inspectors.   Section 167 (2) of the Companies Act, 1948, provides that:

" An inspector may examine on oath the officers and agents of the company . . . in relation to its business and may administer an oath accordingly."   **G**

It was under that power that Mr. Burden was examined by the inspectors.

When it was sought to put these transcripts in evidence in criminal proceedings before the magistrate, the magistrate decided that the transcripts should not be relied on in those proceedings.   His decision was based, largely at any rate, on the provisions of s. 167 (4) of the Act of 1948 which provides that where other persons (that is, persons other than officers or agents of the company) are examined **H** under an order of the court, then the evidence of such persons when reduced to writing and signed by such persons may be used in evidence against them. He considered that, by reason of that express provision for admitting evidence in sub-s. (4), a transcript of evidence under sub-s. (2), which did not make any express provision about the admissibility in evidence of answers given under that subsection, was not admissible as evidence.

---

* Section 167 (2) is set out at letter G, supra.

† *Collett* v. *Lord Keith*, (1802), 4 Esp. 212; *Smith* v. *Beadnell*, (1807), 1 Camp. 30; *R.* v. *Scott*, (1856), Dears. & B. 47; *R.* v. *Cherry*, (1871), 12 Cox, C.C. 32; *R.* v. *Hillam*, (1872), 12 Cox, C.C. 174; *R.* v. *Coote*, (1873), L.R. 4 P.C. 599; *R.* v. *Erdheim*, [1895-99] All E.R. Rep. 610; [1896] 2 Q.B. 260; *Re Grosvenor & West End Railway Terminus Hotel Co., Ltd.*, (1897), 76 L.T. 337; *Re A.B.C. Coupler & Engineering Co., Ltd. (No. 2)*, [1962] 3 All E.R. 68; *Re Travel & Holiday Clubs, Ltd.*, [1967] 2 All E.R. 606; *Re S.B.A. Properties, Ltd.*, [1967] 2 All E.R. 615; *Re Allied Produce Co., Ltd.*, [1967] 3 All E.R. 399.

A   The magistrate's decision was made before s. 50 of the Companies Act 19 6 came into operation. That section provides that an answer given by a person to a question put to him in exercise of powers conferred by s. 167 of the Act of 1948 (which includes, of course, sub-s. (2) which I have just mentioned) may be used in evidence against him. So the absence of the express provision relied on by the magistrate was cured by the passing of that section in 1967.

B   Section 50 is a procedural provision providing for the admissibility of evidence before a court when it comes to hear a case and deal with the evidence. It applies to future hearings after the Act of 1967 comes into operation; but it then applies even though the hearing be in respect of matters which arose before that section was passed. It is a procedural provision dealing with future procedure, and is not a provision of substantive law dealing with future sub-

C stantive rights. So this section of the Act of 1967 applies to these proceedings now before me, in which I now have to decide whether evidence is admissible or not, even though the evidence relates to matters which occurred before the Act of 1967 was passed.

    There was another matter which at one stage gave me more trouble, and that was the suggestion that Mr. Burden was obliged to answer questions open to

D the objection that the answers might tend to incriminate him. Section 167 (3) of the Act of 1948 provides that in the case of a company officer, such as Mr. Burden, refusing to answer any question put to him, the inspectors might take the matter to the court and the court could then decide whether the refusal amounted to a contempt of court or not. It appears from the House of Lords' observations in *McClelland, Pope and Langley, Ltd.* v. *Howard* (1) that an objection

E to answering a question on the ground that it might tend to incriminate the witness, might thus be brought before the court and decided by it. It is unnecessay, however, for me to pursue this matter, at any rate at this stage, as I now understand that the specific difficulty alluded to by Mr. Burden refers to part of the evidence on which the plaintiffs do not wish to rely, but which they would merely read in the event of Mr. Burden wishing it to be read. If he objects to

F that part being read, then the plaintiffs do not seek to put that part in evidence.

    The position therefore is that in my view the transcript is admissible as evidence (subject to the one agreed exception, on which I express no view) in accordance with the provisions of the Act of 1967.

Ruling accordingly.

G   Solicitors: *Solicitor to the Board of Trade* (for the plaintiff company); *Gouldens* (for the second defendants); *Bower, Cotton & Bower*, agents for *Slater, Heelis & Co.*, Manchester (for the third defendants); *Beer & Co.* (for the fourth defendants); *Simmons & Simmons* (for the seventh defendants).

[*Reported by* JACQUELINE METCALFE, *Barrister-at-Law.*]

H

NOTE.

    In *McClelland, Pope & Langley, Ltd. and Another* v. *Howard and Another* in the House of Lords (LORD REID, LORD HODSON, LORD GUEST, LORD UPJOHN and LORD WILBERFORCE, Mar. 30, 1966), the appellants, viz., the company and Nicholas Langley Pope,

I a director of the company, appealed against an order of the Court of Appeal dismissing their appeal from refusal of an order of certiorari or an order of prohibition against the respondents. The respondents had been appointed inspectors under s. 165 (*b*) of the Companies Act, 1948, to enquire into the affairs of Fiesta Tours, Ltd. and Travel and Holiday Clubs, Ltd. Mr. Pope and another director attended the inspectors in relation to dealings by the appellant company with the companies under investigation, and gave evidence on oath. On Mar. 17, 1965, Mr. Pope, attending to produce books, was again examined on oath by the inspectors, his legal adviser being present at that

---

(1) (1966), see letter I, above.

A time.   To some of the questions put to him Mr. Pope objected that the answers would
tend to incriminate him; the inspectors stated to Mr. Pope that he was not entitled
to refuse to answer questions on that ground.   Further questions were asked which
Mr. Pope answered.   The appellants now sought only an order of prohibition to prevent
the inspectors from including in their report any evidence given by Mr. Pope on Mar. 17
which might incriminate him.   The appellants objected that they were not agents of
either of the companies under investigation, and thus were not within s. 167 of the Act
of 1948 as agents of either of those companies.   The House of Lords held that this
B objection failed as, apart from the factual position, it was too late to rely on such an
objection when applying for a discretionary remedy such as an order of prohibition.
LORD UPJOHN, with whose opinion the other law lords concurred, said in regard to the
other ground of objection, which was the objection which was in fact taken first: " As
to the first ground of complaint, namely, that the taking of the evidence of Mr. Pope
in March, 1965, was contrary to natural justice, it is unfortunate that the inspectors
insisted that he was not entitled to refuse to answer questions on the ground that the
answers would incriminate him.   Section 167 (3) makes it plain that a witness may
C refuse to answer questions, and, if he does so, the question whether he did so properly
is a matter for the court, if the inspectors so refer the matter, and not for the inspectors.
The wrongful assumption of power by the inspectors, however, does not necessarily
entitle the appellants to an order of prohibition.   The questions were in fact answered,
though under protest.   But they were not obtained by trickery or under duress; Mr.
Pope's legal adviser was present throughout and intervened in the cross-examination.
As was pointed out in the Divisional Court, it is difficult to see how in those circum-
D stances an order of prohibition can lie to stop the use of such answers once given.   My
lords, these matters were carefully considered both in the Divisional Court and in the
Court of Appeal, and both courts refused leave to apply for an order of prohibition.
For my part I agree with them, but in any event I can see no possible ground for saying
that both courts have wrongly exercised their discretion in refusing leave.   I would
dismiss this appeal.''

E

SEABRIDGE v. H. COX & SONS (PLANT HIRE), LTD. AND ANOTHER. BARCLAY v. SAME.

[COURT OF APPEAL, CIVIL DIVISION (Lord Denning, M.R., Diplock and Salmon,   F
L.JJ.), December 19, 20, 1967.]

*Practice—Parties—Adding persons as parties—Defendants—Writ amended at
central office on day with which limitation period expired—Service on added
defendants effected subsequently—Action not statute-barred—Amendment
effective on day when writ stamped as amended—R.S.C., Ord. 15, r. 6 (2) (b),*   G
r. 8 (2), (4).

On the day with which the period of limitation for an action for personal
injuries would expire, the plaintiff, having previously obtained an order
under R.S.C., Ord. 15, r. 6 (2) (b)*, that third parties be added as defendants,
took the writ to the central office where it was resealed and stamped as
amended on that day.   It was not served on the added defendants until
two or three days later.   On application to set aside service,   H

Held: the amendment took effect under R.S.C., Ord. 15, r. 8 (4)† on the
date on which it was stamped as amended; accordingly the action against
the added defendants was not statute-barred and service would not be
set aside (see p. 572, letter G, and p. 573, letter A, post).

Per CURIAM: the former position (as under the revoked R.S.C., Ord. 16,
r. 11) may still prevail in the county court (see p. 572, letter I, and p. 573,
letter A, post; and cf. C.C.R., Ord. 15, r. 2).

[As to when a limitation period begins to run, see 24 HALSBURY'S LAWS
(3rd Edn.) 193-196, paras. 347, 348; and for cases on the subject, where the
action is for negligence, see 32 DIGEST (Repl.) 402-404, *268-277.*

------

* R.S.C., Ord. 15, r. 6 (2) (b), so far as relevant, is printed at p. 571, letter H, post.
† R.S.C., Ord. 15, r. 8 (4), so far as material, is set out at p. 572, letter D, post.

A   As to the time when the amendment of a writ against an added defendant took effect under the old R.S.C., see 30 HALSBURY'S LAWS (3rd Edn.) 395, para. 735, note (K).]

Case referred to:

    Marren v. *Dawson Bentley & Co., Ltd.*, [1961] 2 All E.R. 270; [1961] 2 Q.B. 135; [1961] 2 W.L.R. 679; 45 Digest (Repl.) 252, *196.*

B   **Interlocutory Appeals.**

These were four consolidated actions in which appeals were brought; one appeal is referred to here as an example. By notice of appeal dated Nov. 10, 1967, the plaintiff, Barbara June Seabridge, appealed from an order of MOCATTA, J., dated Oct. 31, 1967, dismissing the plaintiff's appeal from an order of Master

C   ELTON, dated Oct. 19, 1967, whereby it was ordered that the service on the second defendants of the amended writ be set aside on the ground that the plaintiff's right of action was statute barred by virtue of the Limitation Act, 1939, s. 2. The second defendants served a respondents' notice dated Nov. 28, 1967, that the order of the judge should be affirmed on the ground that in any event an amendment on the anniversary of the accident was out of time, as

D   would be a writ thus issued. The facts are set out in the judgment of LORD DENNING, M.R.

    A. de Piro, Q.C., and *G. F. B. Laughland* for the plaintiffs.

    R. I. Kidwell for the second defendants.

LORD DENNING, M.R.: On Sept. 18, 1964, the plaintiff, Mr. Barclay,

E   and his family in their car were in collision with a lorry owned by Cox & Sons, the first defendants. The plaintiff's wife and son were killed. The plaintiff himself was injured. So was his son's fiancée, Miss Seabridge. Cox's lorry was on its wrong side of the road. It looked as though there was a clear claim for damages against Cox's.

On Nov. 11, 1965, four writs were issued against Cox's, the owners of the lorry.

F   In their defence, Cox's said that it was an inevitable accident. They had on the lorry remould tyres. One of them burst and threw the lorry off course. They said it was all the fault of the company which supplied the remould tyres, India Tyres, Ltd. On May 18, 1967, Cox's brought in India Tyres, Ltd. as third parties.

When the plaintiffs and their advisers saw the defence of Cox's, they realised

G   there was a risk in going on against Cox's alone: because Cox's might escape liability altogether. So they sought to add India Tyres, Ltd. as defendants. They applied under the modern rule, R.S.C., Ord. 15, r. 6 (2) (*b*). It enables the court to order a party to be added if his

    "... presence before the court is necessary to ensure that all matters in dispute in the cause or matter may be effectually and completely determined

H   and adjudicated upon ..."

The master made an order that India Tyres, Ltd. be added and that the plaintiff be at liberty to amend the writ accordingly. The order was made on Sept. 15, 1967, which was a Friday. Note the date, because the accident was on Sept. 18, 1964, which was nearly three years before. The period of limitation would expire on Sept. 18, 1967, but the plaintiffs would have the whole of that day in

I   which to bring the action (see *Marren* v. *Dawson Bentley & Co., Ltd.* (1)).

On Sept. 18, 1967 (which was the three years' anniversary of the accident), the writ was amended in accordance with R.S.C., Ord. 15, r. 8. On that day an amended writ was taken to the central office. It had on it the name of India Tyres, Ltd. added as defendants in red ink. It was resealed by the central office and a copy was attached to the file. A note was made of the date. A

----

(1) [1961] 2 All E.R. 270; [1961] 2 Q.B. 135. In effect this approves the decision in *Marren* v. *Dawson Bentley & Co., Ltd.*

stamp was put on the writ on that day to show it was amended. There is a   **A**
record at the top of the writ: " Amended on Sept. 18, 1967."   One would have
thought that, as against the defendants, India Tyres, Ltd., the action was
brought just in time; but the amended writ was not served on India Tyres, Ltd.
until two or three days later by post.   India Tyres, Ltd. entered a conditional
appearance.   They said that the amendment was too late.   It only took effect,
they said, on the date of service.   That was Sept. 21.   By that time the three   **B**
years had run and they were entitled to the benefit of the Statute of Limitations.
They sought to set aside the amendment on the ground of irregularity.

The old rule, R.S.C., Ord. 16, r. 11 said that when a party is added, the proceedings against such party should " be deemed to have begun only on the
service of such writ ".   If that rule had been the rule in existence today, I feel
that the words would have compelled the court to hold that, as against India   **C**
Tyres, Ltd., the proceedings only began on Sept. 21, 1967, that is, more than
three years after the date of the accident and they would be entitled to the benefit
of the Statute of Limitations; but that rule has been altered.   In 1962 the
wording of it was changed.   Again in 1964 it was changed once more.   We have
to construe the new rule, R.S.C., Ord. 15, r. 8 (4).   That provides:

  D

" Where by an order under r. 6 . . . a person is to be added as a party . . .
that person shall not become a party until—(a) the writ has been amended
in relation to him under this rule, and (if he is a defendant) has been served
on him."

Counsel for India Tyres, Ltd. argued that this new rule has the same effect as the
old rule.   It means, he said, that the proceedings are not brought against the   **E**
added defendant until he is served.   That argument convinced the master and
the judge.   They set aside the service; but I am unable to accept the argument.
We must read the new rules as a whole.   It seems to me that when the amendment is made in the prescribed manner, namely, by the amendment being taken
to the central office and filed and the amended writ stamped, then at that moment
the amended writ takes effect as against the added defendant.   That procedure   **F**
is equivalent to the issue of a writ against an original defendant.   Once the
amendment is made, the rules as to service apply as against the added defendant,
just as they do to an original defendant on the issue of a writ, see R.S.C., Ord. 15,
r. 8 (2).   The result is that the plaintiff has to serve the added defendant within
twelve months from the date when the amendment is made.

  G

I am prepared to hold, therefore, that when an amendment is made adding a
defendant, the amendment takes effect when it is stamped in the central office.
It takes effect at that moment against that defendant equivalent to the issue
of the writ against him.   If the amendment is so made within the three years,
it is in time, even though it is served later.   In this particular case the amendment
was just in time.   It was on the very last day of the three years.   This still   **H**
leaves ample scope for R.S.C., Ord. 15, r. 8 (4) when it says " that person shall
not become a party until " he has been served.   That only means that he is not
affected by notices, and he cannot enter an appearance until he is served.

We were referred to the County Court Rules, which are the same as the old
R.S.C., Ord. 16, r. 11.   That has not been amended.   In the county court,
therefore, the old position may prevail; but in the High Court, I think, a better   **I**
rule now prevails.   The amendment takes effect when it is stamped in the
central office.

Counsel was forced to concede that, if the plaintiffs had issued another writ on
Sept. 18 on India Tyres, Ltd., it would undoubtedly be in time, even though it
was served later.   I think it should be the same when they add them as defendants by amendment on that day.   In good sense there ought to be no difference.
On a broad and liberal interpretation of the rules, there is no difference.

A   I, therefore, would allow this appeal and hold that the amendment and the service is regular and it is not to be set aside as being statute-barred.

DIPLOCK, L.J.: I agree.

SALMON, L.J.: With some hesitation, I also agree.

B
Appeal allowed.   Leave to appeal to the House of Lords refused.

Solicitors: *J. D. Langton & Passmore*, agents for *Wilkins & Son*, Aylesbury (for the plaintiffs); *Clifford-Turner & Co.* (for the second defendants).

[*Reported by* F. GUTTMAN, ESQ., *Barrister-at-Law.*]

C

CAPITAL FINANCE CO., LTD. v. STOKES AND ANOTHER.

[CHANCERY DIVISION (Pennycuick, J.), December 7, 8, 14, 1967.]

D   *Company—Charge—Creation—Before or after acquisition by company of property comprised in charge—Purchase of land by company, part of purchase price being left on mortgage by the vendor—Particulars not registered —Companies Act, 1948 (10 & 11 Geo. 6 c. 38), s. 95, s. 97.*

Sale of Land—Vendor's lien—Agreement by vendor to leave part of purchase price on mortgage—Equitable charge created forthwith—Exclusion of vendor's lien—Sequence of execution of conveyance and mortgage.

E   By an agreement in writing made on July 27, 1965, the first defendant agreed to sell to the second defendant, a company, a plot of land for the sum of £37,900 on the terms therein set out which included a provision that the vendor would leave seventy-five per cent. of the purchase money with the purchaser to be secured by a first mortgage of the property to be repayable with interest as therein mentioned. By a conveyance made on Feb. 23,
F   1966, the first defendant conveyed the property to the defendant company which paid him £9,475. By a legal charge made also on Feb. 23, 1966, the defendant company charged the property with the payment to the first defendant of the principal money, etc., thereby covenanted to be paid. Particulars of the legal charge were never delivered to the registrar of companies for registration under s. 95* of the Companies Act, 1948. By a debenture made
G   on Oct. 27, 1966, the defendant company charged the property, among other assets, with payment to the plaintiff of the sums therein mentioned. The plaintiff appointed a receiver of the property charged by the debenture. On Oct. 3, 1967 an order for the compulsory winding-up of the defendant company was made on the ground of insolvency. The first defendant had, at all material times, retained possession of the property and of the title
H   deeds. It was admitted that if the first defendant were entitled to an unpaid vendor's lien on the property, the lien would have priority over any charge created by the debenture. In an action by the plaintiff for a declaration that its charge under the debenture had priority over the legal charge and any lien of the first defendant on the defendant company's plot of land,

Held: (i) since by the sale agreement the first defendant had agreed to
I   leave seventy-five per cent. of the purchase price on the security of a legal charge on the property sold, the legal charge was what the first defendant had stipulated to obtain and, being a higher interest than a lien, excluded the creation of a vendor's lien in addition, with the consequence, as the contract to create the legal charge gave rise immediately to an equitable charge, that the first defendant as vendor obtained no lien (see p. 576, letter I, to p. 577, letter A, and p. 577, letter C, post).

---

* Section 95, so far as material, is set out at p. 577, letters F and G, post.

(ii) the property having been first conveyed in the normal way to the **A**
defendant company as purchaser and having been charged by it in favour
of the first defendant as vendor, the charge was created after the defendant
company's acquisition of the land and thus fell within s. 95, not s. 97, of the
Companies Act, 1948, with the consequence that, as particulars were not
registered pursuant to s. 95, the legal charge was void as against the
liquidator (see p. 578, letters B and G, post).   **B**

Church of England Building Society v. *Piskor* ([1954] 2 All E.R. 85) applied.

Re Connolly Brothers, Ltd. (No. 2) ([1912] 2 Ch. 25) distinguished.

[As to a vendor's lien, see 34 HALSBURY's LAWS (3rd Edn.) 296, 297, para. 494.
As to the registration of particulars of charges created by companies, see
6 HALSBURY's LAWS (3rd Edn.) 493, 494, para. 953; and as to registration of **C**
charges created before the acquisition by the company of the property charged,
see ibid., p. 497, para. 961.

As to the sequence of execution of a conveyance and mortgage of premises, see
27 HALSBURY's LAWS (3rd Edn.) 256, para. 465.

For the Companies Act, 1948, s. 95, s. 97, s. 322, see 3 HALSBURY's STATUTES
(2nd Edn.) 533, 536, 704.]   **D**

Cases referred to:

Church of England Building Society v. *Piskor*, [1954] 2 All E.R. 85; [1954]
    Ch. 553; [1954] 2 W.L.R. 952; 35 Digest (Repl.) 454, *1458*.

Connolly Brothers, Ltd. (No. 2), Re, Wood v. *The Co.*, [1912] 2 Ch. 25; 81 L.J.Ch.
    517; 106 L.T. 738; 10 Digest (Repl.) 793, *5150*.

Wilson v. *Kelland*, [1910] 2 Ch. 306; 79 L.J.Ch. 580; 103 L.T. 17; 17 Mans **E**
    233; 10 Digest (Repl.) 780, *5066*.

Action.

This was an action commenced by writ issued on Feb. 2, 1967, by the plaintiff,
Capital Finance Co., Ltd., claiming (i) a declaration that the charge created in
favour of the plaintiff by a debenture made on Oct. 27, 1966, between Belmont
Finance Corpn., Ltd. of the first part and the second defendant (Cityfield Pro- **F**
perties, Ltd.) and others of the second part and the plaintiff of the third part in
respect of the property known an Laurel Nursery, Silver Street, Nailsea in the
country of Somerset had priority over (a) legal charge in respect of the property
made Feb. 23, 1966, between the second defendant of the first part, James Peter
Grosscurth and another of the second part and the first defendant (Joseph
William Stokes) of the third part to secure the payment of the sum of £28,425 **G**
and interest thereon or (b) any lien of the first defendant in respect of the said
sum as an unpaid vendor or otherwise. The plaintiff claimed, secondly, an order
on the first defendant to hand over all the documents of title to the said property
in his possession or power to the plaintiff or as it should direct and thirdly, an
injunction to restrain the first defendant from selling or attempting to sell or
otherwise disposing of the said property without the consent of the plaintiff. **H**
The facts are set out in the judgment.

The cases noted below* were cited during the argument in addition to those
referred to in the judgment.

G. T. Hesketh for the plaintiff.
Gavin Lightman for the first defendant.
The second defendant did not appear and was not represented.   **I**

Cur. adv. vult.

Dec. 14. **PENNYCUICK, J.:** By the writ and statement of claim in this
action the plaintiff company, Capital Finance Co., Ltd. seeks a declaration that

---

* *Re Emery, Ex p. Harvey*, (1839), 1 Most. & Ch. 261; *Teed* v. *Carruthers*, (1892), 2
Y. & C. Ch. Cas. 31; *Vibart* v. *Coles*, (1890), 24 Q.B.D. 364; *Re Molton Finance, Ltd.*,
[1967] 3 All E.R. 843.

A the charge in its favour under a debenture dated Oct. 27, 1966, on the undertaking of the second defendant, Cityfield Properties, Ltd., has priority over
(i) a legal charge dated Feb. 23, 1966, in favour of the first defendant, Joseph
William Stokes, on certain property known as Laurel Nursery, Nailsea, Somerset;
and (ii) any lien of the first defendant on the stated property as vendor together
with an order on the first defendant for delivery of the title deeds of the property.

B No relief is claimed against the second defendant.

By his defence the first defendant relies on his vendor's lien. The second
defendant has not delivered any defence. A petition for the winding-up of the
second defendant was presented on Feb. 14, 1967, and an order for compulsory
winding-up was made on Oct. 3, 1967. By an order dated Nov. 24, in the winding-
up, the plaintiff was given liberty to proceed with this action on its under-

C taking to argue against the claim of the first defendant to have a right to the title
deeds of the property.

The action has been brought on for hearing on a statement of facts agreed
between the plaintiff and the first defendant. The second defendant was not
represented at the hearing.

I will now read the statement of facts.

D
" 1. By an agreement in writing made July 27, 1965, between the first
defendant of the one part and the second defendant of the other part the
first defendant agreed to sell to the second defendant the property known
as Laurel Nursery, Silver Street in the Parish of Nailsea in the county of
Somerset therein particularly described and hereinafter referred to as ' the

E said property ' for the sum of £37,900 on the terms therein set out which
included a provision that the vendor would leave seventy-five per cent. of
the purchase money with the purchaser to be secured by a first mortgage of
the said property and to be repayable with interest as therein mentioned.

" 2. By a conveyance made Feb. 23, 1966, between the first defendant
of the one part and the second defendant of the other part the said property

F was conveyed to the second defendant in fee simple in consideration of the
sum of £37,900, of which the sum of £9,475 only was paid by the second
defendant to the first defendant, subject as therein mentioned.

" 3. By a legal charge made Feb. 23, 1966, by the second defendant of
the first part James Peter Grosscurth and John Sinclair Copeland of the
second part and the first defendant of the third part the second defendant

G (inter alia) charged the said property by way of legal mortgage with the payment to the first defendant of the principal money interest and other money
thereby covenanted to be paid.

" 4. Particulars of the said legal charge have never been delivered to
the registrar of companies for registration in accordance with s. 95 of the
Companies Act, 1948.

H " 5. By a debenture made Oct. 27, 1966, by Belmont Finance Corpn.,
Ltd., of the first part the second defendant and other companies of the
second part and the plaintiff of the third part (inter alia) the second defendant
charged in favour of the plaintiff by way of collateral security its undertaking and goodwill and all its property assets and rights whatsoever and
wheresoever both present and future including uncalled capital and the

I said property with the payment to the plaintiff of the sums therein
mentioned.

" 6. The plaintiff duly appointed Richard Alfred Coleman Mordant to be
receiver and manager of the undertaking of the second defendant and all its
other property which was charged by the said debenture to the plaintiff.

" 7. The said receiver has requested the first defendant to hand over to
him the documents of title to the said property.

" 8. A petition was filed on Feb. 14, 1967, compulsorily to wind up the
second defendant on the ground of insolvency.

"9. The said petition is opposed and has not yet been determined.   A
[I interpose to say that the petition has now been determined by the winding-up order dated Oct. 3.]
"10. The first defendant has at all material times retained possession of the said property and of the title deeds of the said property.
"11. It is admitted that, if the first defendant is entitled to an unpaid vendor's lien on the said property, such lien would have priority over any   B charge created by the said debenture."

It is worthwhile to read in full cl. 14 (ii) of the agreement dated July 27, 1965.

"The vendor will leave with the purchaser seventy-five per cent. of the purchase money to be secured on a first mortgage of the premises and to carry interest at the rate of $7\frac{1}{2}$ per cent. per annum and to be repayable by   C instalments of £600 with interest on the sale of each plot by the purchaser, and it will be a term of the said mortgage that the whole of the moneys secured thereby will be paid to the vendor within two years of completion hereof and two of the directors of the purchaser will join in as sureties."

The conveyance, dated Feb. 23, 1966, was expressed to be made in consideration of the sum of £37,900, the receipt of which the vendor acknowledged, but only   D one-quarter of this sum, that is, £9,475, was actually paid, the remaining three-quarters, that is £28,425, being left on mortgage. The legal charge of the same date is expressed as made in consideration of £28,425, paid to the company, but this sum merely represents the remainder of the purchase price.

The issue between the plaintiff and the first defendant is whether or not the first defendant, on execution of the sale agreement dated July 27, 1965, obtained   E a vendor's lien on the property at Nailsea. Counsel for the plaintiff contends that the first defendant did not obtain a vendor's lien and that on this footing the first defendant has no charge which is not void against the plaintiff under s. 95 of the Companies Act, 1948, for want of registration. Counsel for the first defendant contends that the first defendant did obtain a vendor's lien and, on this footing, it is admitted that the lien has priority over the plaintiff's charge.   F Counsel for the first defendant contends, in the alternative, that the charge falls to be registered under s. 97 of the Companies Act, 1948, and not under s. 95, in which case it would not be void as against creditors. To avoid misunderstanding, I should mention at this stage that in this court at any rate it is not disputed that a valid equitable lien would not be merged in a legal charge which is void against the liquidator and creditors of the company.   G

The first matter to be determined is the nature of the interest held by the first defendant. The law is conveniently summarised in SNELL'S PRINCIPLES OF EQUITY (26th Edn.), pp. 490, 491:

"When a specifically enforceable contract for sale has been made, the beneficial ownership of the property passes at once to the purchaser. Thereafter the vendor, in whom the legal estate is still vested, is to some extent   H a trustee for the purchaser . . .

"As soon as a binding contract of sale is made, the vendor has a lien on the property for the purchase-money and a right to retain the property until the money is paid . . .

"Occasionally, however, the vendor will have no lien. If he receives all that he bargained for . . . [there follow two or three instances] there will be   I no lien on the property sold . . ."

In the present case it was a term of the sale agreement that the first defendant should leave with the second defendant seventy-five per cent. of the purchase money to be secured on a first mortgage of the property. So counsel for the plaintiff says that a legal charge was what the first defendant bargained for, and, a legal charge being a higher interest than a lien, the lower interest is excluded. I think that that is right, provided that it can be shown that the

A first defendant was protected during the period between contract and completion. If that were not so, I can see no reason why a lien should be excluded. On analysis it seems to me that the first defendant was indeed protected during this period.

Immediately on the execution of the sale agreement, the first defendant must have taken an equitable mortgage on the property by virtue of the agreement for

B the creation of the legal charge. See 27 HALSBURY'S LAWS OF ENGLAND (3rd Edn.), p. 171, para. 271:

> " In equity a mortgage is created by a contract evidenced in writing for valuable consideration to execute, when required, a legal mortgage . . ."

This immediate equitable interest of the vendor as mortgagee is a necessary corollary of the immediate equitable interest of the purchaser as owner. Both

C stem from the maxim that equity looks on that as done which ought to be done. The first defendant having thus obtained ab initio an equitable mortgage to secure seventy-five per cent. of the purchase money, there can be no room for a vendor's lien to arise side by side with it as regards that seventy-five per cent.

An equitable mortgage, unlike a vendor's lien, is capable of registration under

D s. 95 and is avoided by the section as against the liquidator and creditors of the company if not registered. The equitable mortgage is, therefore, of no more value to the first defendant in the present case than is the subsequent legal charge.

This is a highly artificial point, but so is the first defendant's claim. The equitable maxim and its operation on a contract of sale are established beyond challenge, but it does give rise to some remarkable refinements.

E The second contention of counsel for the first defendant is that the charge taken by the first defendant represents, not a charge created by the company within s. 95 of the Companies Act, 1948, but a charge subject to which the second defendant acquired the property within s. 97 of the Act. I will read the relevant parts of the two sections.

F " 95. (1) Subject to the provisions of this Part of this Act, every charge created after the fixed date by a company registered in England and being a charge to which this section applies shall, so far as any security on the company's property or undertaking is conferred thereby, be void against the liquidator and any creditor of the company, unless the prescribed particulars of the charge together with the instrument, if any, by which the charge is

G created or evidenced, are delivered to or received by the registrar of companies for registration in manner required by this Act within twenty-one days after the date of its creation, but without prejudice to any contract or obligation for repayment of the money thereby secured, and when a charge becomes void under this section the money secured threby shall immediately become payable.

I " (2) This section applies to the following charges:— . . . (d) a charge on land, wherever situate, or any interest therein . . .

" 97. (1) Where a company registered in England acquires any property which is subject to a charge of any such kind as would, if it had been created by the company after the acquisition of the property, have been required to be registered under this Part of this Act, the company shall cause the

◄ prescribed particulars of the charge, together with a copy (certified in the prescribed manner to be a correct copy) of the instrument, if any, by which the charge was created or is evidenced, to be delivered to the registrar of companies for registration in manner required by this Act within twenty-one days after the date on which the acquisition is completed . . ."

There is a penalty for default under sub-s. (2). The two categories of charge appear to be mutually exclusive. In broad terms, the language of s. 95 contemplates a charge subsequent to the acquisition of the property, that of s. 97 a charge antecedent to the acquisition of the property.

I will consider this point first apart from authority. Where part of the   **A**
purchase price of property is left on mortgage the normal conveyancing procedure
is for the vendor to convey the property to the purchaser, that is, the property
as a whole, and for the purchaser immediately afterwards to charge the property,
that is, the property as a whole, in favour of the vendor. That was the procedure followed in the present case. It seems to me clear that on such a transaction the vendor creates a charge on the property, that is, the property as a   **B**
whole, after its acquisition, so that s. 95 applies.

I was referred to two authorities on the position where part of the purchase price
is advanced by a third party in whose favour the purchaser charges the property
immediately after the conveyance. In *Re Connolly Brothers, Ltd. (No. 2),
Wood* v. *The Co.* (1) it was held by the Court of Appeal that, for the purpose of
equitable priorities, the purchaser, which was a company, acquired only the   **C**
equity of redemption in the property. See per SIR HERBERT COZENS-HARDY,
M.R. (2):

> " Now, what was the effect of that? Did the company as between them-
> selves and Mrs. O'Reilly ever become the absolute owners of the property?
> Or was not the bargain that Mrs. O'Reilly was to have a first charge, and
> the company was only to get the property subject thereto? In my opinion   **D**
> we should be shutting our eyes to the real transaction if we were to hold that
> the unincumbered fee simple in the property was ever in the company
> so that it became subject to the charge of the debenture-holders."

and per BUCKLEY, L.J. (2):

> " If . . . the company acquired the unincumbered fee simple in the property,   **E**
> then the debenture-holders are right. If on the other hand on that date
> the company obtained the property subject to a contractual obligation to
> give a first charge on it to Mrs. O'Reilly, then the debenture-holders can get
> no more."

That decision would be of the greatest weight here if it stood alone. In the more   **F**
recent case of *Church of England Building Society* v. *Piskor* (3) it was held, however, by the Court of Appeal that for the purpose of feeding an estoppel in favour
of a tenant the purchaser must be treated as having acquired the property as a
whole. SIR RAYMOND EVERSHED, M.R., and ROMER, L.J., held that the rights
of the parties must be determined according to the normal conveyancing procedure which was adopted in that case and distinguished *Re Connolly Brothers,
Ltd. (No. 2)* (1) as involving only a conflict of equities. It seems to me that I   **G**
am entitled to treat the analysis made by SIR RAYMOND EVERSHED, M.R., and
ROMER, L.J., as applicable here with regard to the two sections of the Companies
Act, 1948. There can, I think, be no difference in principle where, as here, the
charge is made, not in favour of a third party, but in favour of the vendor himself.

I was referred to the decision of EVE, J., in *Wilson* v. *Kelland* (4). That case,   **H**
however, turned on a different matter and does not, I think, throw any further
light on the present question. It is, perhaps, worthwhile to point out that
EVE, J. (5), uses the neutral expression " the paramount equity of the unpaid
vendors ".

The position as between the two sections of the Companies Act, 1948, must
be the same whether one looks at the position resulting from the sale agreement
or at the position resulting from the conveyance and legal charge.

Counsel for the first defendant contended that in any event the plaintiff's
debenture is void under s. 322 of the Companies Act, 1948 as having been created
within twelve months of the winding-up. This point is taken by the first defendant in his defence and would, I think, if established, be a good defence to the

---

(1) [1912] 2 Ch. 25.   (2) [1912] 2 Ch. at p. 31.
(3) [1954] 2 All E.R. 85; [1954] Ch. 553.
(4) [1910] 2 Ch. 306.   (5) [1910] 2 Ch. at p. 312.

A plaintiff's claim for a declaration of priority. Clearly, however, the point raises issues of fact, e.g., the plaintiff may seek to establish that the company was solvent immediately after the creation of the debenture. The agreed statement of facts contains no material on this point and it seems clear that the parties must be regarded as having excluded this point from the issues which I am asked to determine. On the other hand, I must take care not to make an order which

B would operate as res judicata on this excluded point.

Action dismissed.

Declaration that the first defendant's charge was void against the liquidator and creditors and that he had no lien as unpaid vendor but the finding was without prejudice to any question whether the plaintiff's debenture was invalid as having been created within twelve months of the winding-up of the company.

C

Solicitors: *Sidney Pearlman* (for the plaintiff); *Nye & Donne*, agents for *Perham & Sons*, Bristol (for the first defendant).

[*Reported by* JENIFER SANDELL, *Barrister-at-Law.*]

D

R. *v.* LAWRENCE.

[COURT OF APPEAL, CRIMINAL DIVISION (Diplock, L.J., Phillimore and Blain, JJ.), January 22, 1968.]

E *Criminal Law—Practice—Evidence—Retirement of jury—No further evidence to be adduced.*

The appellant and another man were charged with shopbreaking and larceny, having been found by police officers outside a public house after a shop nearby had been broken into and two safes stolen. They were both wearing gloves. They were taken by the police officers in a car belonging to

F one of the police officers to the police station and, when they had left the car, the two pairs of gloves had disappeared. Under the seat of the car which the appellant had occupied was found a box of cigarettes, by the near-side door (where the appellant had been sitting) was found a pair of gloves and under the off-side seat another pair of gloves. After the jury had retired for some time, they asked to see the car, which had not been identified

G otherwise than as being a two-door car of a certain make. A two-door car of that make was then brought outside the court and the trial judge, counsel and the jury inspected it, but it was not identified by the police officer as being his car. On appeal against conviction,

Held: the conviction must be quashed, because it was a strict rule of procedure that no further evidence should be adduced in a trial after the

H jury had retired to consider their verdict; and it made no difference that the jury were invited to look at the car without identifying it (see p. 581, letter B, post).

R. v. *Gearing* (p. 581, post) applied.

[As to retirement of jury to consider their verdict, see 10 HALSBURY'S LAWS (3rd Edn.) 427, 428, para. 789.]

Case referred to:

R. v. *Gearing*, p. 581, post; (1965), 50 Cr. App. Rep. 18; Digest (Cont. Vol. B) 169, *3561b.*

Appeal.

This was an appeal by Alan Lawrence against his conviction on June 29, 1967, at Liverpool Crown Court before JUDGE TROTTER and a jury of shopbreaking and larceny, for which he was sentenced to eighteen months' imprisonment.

The facts are set out in the judgment of the court.

Distinguished in R. *v.* NIXON.
[1968] 2 All E.R. 33.

The case noted below* was cited during the argument in addition to that   A
referred to in the judgment of the court.

G. H. Wright for the appellant.
R. Z. H. Montgomery for the Crown.

DIPLOCK, L.J., delivered the following judgment of the court: This
appeal raises a short and slightly unusual point of law. The appellant was   B
convicted at the Liverpool Crown Court on June 29, 1967, of shopbreaking and
larceny and was sentenced to eighteen months' imprisonment. The case against
him was a very simple one. He had the misfortune to be in Liverpool outside
a public house and close to the back of a shop, and unknown to him two police
officers, off-duty I think, were in the public house. Someone who was in their
party saw two men in a passage by the public house and they told the police   C
officers. The police officers came out, and there they found the appellant and
his co-accused together, both of them wearing gloves. A grocer's shop nearby
had been broken into, two safes had been taken out, and one of the safes was
found on some waste ground behind the grocer's shop and close to the public
house. The appellant and his co-accused were taken into the car of one of the
police officers, which was a Vauxhall Viva two-door car. When they had left   D
the car, having been taken to the police station, the two pairs of gloves which
they were said to be wearing when they had been first taken to the car had
disappeared, and under the seat of the car which, on the evidence, had been
occupied by the appellant was found a box of cigarettes, being part of the
property stolen. By the near-side door was found a pair of gloves—it was on
the near-side that the appellant was said to have been sitting—and under the   E
off-side seat was found another pair of gloves. The appellant's case was that
he had had nothing to do with the breaking and entering or the larceny, but by
mere chance his co-accused, whom he knew as a frequenter of another public house,
happened to be with him and close to him at the moment when the police officers
came out.

This seems a pretty simple case, but the jury found it more difficult than, on   F
the face of it, it appeared. After retiring for some time, they sent a message
to the commissioner saying that they would like to see the car. The car had
not been identified otherwise than as being a Vauxhall Viva two-door car. Its
number had not been given nor anything to identify it from any other car of the
same make and the same number of doors. An argument took place before the
learned commissioner in the absence of the jury in which counsel for the appellant   G
said that he thought that it would probably be to the appellant's advantage if
the jury could see the car, but he very properly pointed out to the learned commissioner that, on the fairly recent decision of the Court of Criminal Appeal in
R. v. *Gearing* (1), that could not be done because (and I quote the headnote):

" The strict rule of procedure that no further evidence shall be introduced
in a trial after the jury have retired to consider their verdict must be adhered   H
to, and if any further evidence is adduced at that stage, the conviction will
be quashed."

The learned commissioner, with the best of motives no doubt, took the view
that, if the jury were to look at the car, this would not be the introduction of
further evidence but would be a mere inspection of the locus in quo. In the
result—and I must be careful of my words—a Vauxhall Viva two-door car was   I
brought out onto the plateau outside Liverpool Crown Court and the jury,
counsel and the commissioner went out and looked at it. The appellant also
came out rather later, because he had had a dispute with the prison officer
whether or not he should be handcuffed; and we have before us a statement by the
prison officer that, when he got out, he got out too late to see really what was

---

* *R.* v. *Wilson*, (1957), 41 Cr. App. Rep. 226.
(1) p. 581, post.

A   going on. The car which was inspected was not identified by the police constable
as being his car. Precautions, indeed, were taken to ensure that he did not
identify it so that the case would not come within the decision of this court in
R. v. Gearing (2).

In the view of this court, it really does not improve the matter to invite the
jury to look at the car without identifying it, and this court cannot distinguish
B   this case from *R. v. Gearing* (2). In the result, we must apply the rule laid down
in *R. v. Gearing* (2) and quash this conviction. I should, perhaps, add that the
jury after their inspection without requiring to go back to their retiring room
found that the appellant was guilty. Nevertheless, this is not a case in which this
court could apply the proviso (3), for it is difficult to say that the jury must
have convicted whether they saw the car or not, since they expressed a wish to
C   see the car before they could make up their minds whether the appellant was
guilty or not. With some regret, therefore, we quash the conviction.

Appeal allowed. Conviction quashed.

Solicitors: *Mace & Jones*, Liverpool (for the appellant); *Stanley Holmes*,
Liverpool (for the Crown).

D

[*Reported by* N. P. Metcalfe, Esq., *Barrister-at-Law.*]

E

F   (2) In *R. v. Gearing*, the appellant was convicted in July, 1965, at Inner London
Sessions of housebreaking and larceny. A school had been broken into and a number
of articles had been stolen. A police constable found a car belonging to the appellant
in the same road as the school. In the car was the appellant's wife who said that two
other men had been in the car with her. The constable saw a man hiding in a garden
in the road. He chased him without success, but claimed that he was able to see the
man's face, and that he was wearing a light grey suit and had dark hair. Some of
the stolen property was found in the appellant's car and some in the garden. When the
G   appellant was seen, the police constable claimed that he recognised him as being the
man that he had chased. The appellant's case was that he had been asleep at the time
of the housebreaking, but that earlier in the evening he had been out walking with his
wife, two other men and a man named Watson who, he said, was wearing a grey suit.
After the jury had retired to consider their verdict, they came back after a short period
to say that they were unable to agree. Having tried twice more to agree, the foreman
told the trial judge, that there was a question over the identification of the appellant.
There was another man present who had pleaded guilty and the jury wanted to know
H   what was the colour of his hair. In fact, Watson had been arraigned with the appellant
but had pleaded guilty, and the jury had been told that they need not be troubled
with him. The trial judge told the dock-officer to bring him up and thereupon a man
was brought up into court who appeared to have not dark hair but light brown hair. There
was no evidence before the jury that the man who was brought up was Watson. The
foreman of the jury then said that they believed that there were two men and, on the
trial judge asking if the other man was there, he was told that he was not.

I   Lord Parker, C.J., in delivering the judgment of the court quashing the conviction
said: " It has always been a very strict rule of this court that no evidence whatever
must be introduced after the jury have retired. In the last case which dealt with this
matter, *R. v. Wilson* ((1957), 41 Cr. App. Rep. 226), this principle was emphasised. It
was ' the principle that, once the summing-up is concluded, no further evidence ought
to be given, must be maintained in every case '. It went on ' and if further evidence
is allowed at that stage, even on a matter which appears to the Court of Criminal
Appeal irrelevant, the conviction will be quashed '. That is a principle which this court
feels must be adhered to."

(3) I.e., the proviso to s. 4 (1) of the Criminal Appeal Act, 1907, as amended by the
Criminal Appeal Act 1966, s. 4 (1) (c), s. 10 (2) and Sch. 3.

NOTE.

A

R. v. MALIK.

[COURT OF APPEAL, CRIMINAL DIVISION (Lord Parker, C.J., Winn, L.J. and James, J.), December 21, 1967.]

Criminal Law—Evidence—Prison—Charge of using words with intent to stir up   B
*racial hatred—Witness giving evidence of words used by accused at public
meeting—Reference by accused in addressing meeting to the fact that he had
been in prison—Evidence of this given by witness at trial—Accused, who
conducted his own defence, addressed the jury at his trial in some detail on
the matter of his having been in prison—Whether conviction should stand.*

Criminal Law—Trial—Prejudice—Newspaper publishing matter likely to pre-   C
*judice fair trial—Contempt of court—Accused at the time had been charged
before quarter sessions with an offence against s. 6 (1) of the Race Relations
Act 1965 (c. 73) and was awaiting a fresh trial—At the fresh trial accused
admitted using words of the character described in s. 6 (1)—No issue as to
credibility of accused as witness to be balanced against credibility of prosecution witnesses—Accused convicted—Jury could not have come to any*   D
other conclusion—Conviction should stand.

[As to when evidence of previous convictions may be admissible, see 10
HALSBURY'S LAWS (3rd Edn.) 447, para. 823 and as to appeal on the ground of
wrongful admission of evidence, see ibid., 537, para. 987; and for cases on the
subject, see 14 DIGEST (Repl.) 636-640, *6441-6508.*

As to appeal on the ground of there having been a miscarriage of justice, see   E
10 HALSBURY'S LAWS (3rd Edn.) 538, 539, para. 988; and for cases on the
subject see 14 DIGEST (Repl.) 667-670, *6737-6787.*

For the Race Relations Act 1965 s. 6, see 45 HALSBURY'S STATUTES (2nd
Edn.) 35.]

Appeal.

F

This was an appeal by Michael Abdul Malik against conviction and sentence.
The appellant was convicted at Reading Quarter Sessions on Nov. 9, 1967, of an
offence against s. 6 (1)* of the Race Relations Act 1965. The particulars of the
offence had alleged that on July 24, 1967, he, within intent to stir up hatred
against a section of the public of Great Britain distinguished by colour, used at a
public meeting, viz., the Rainbow Hall at Reading, words that were threatening   G
or abusive or insulting, being words that were likely to stir up hatred against
that section of the public on the grounds of colour. He was sentenced to twelve
months in prison.

P. R. Pain, Q.C. and *Lord Gifford* for the appellant.
Kenneth Jones, Q.C. and *J. E. M. Irvine*, for the Crown.

LORD PARKER, C.J., delivered the following judgment of the court: H
On July 24, 1967, there was a meeting at the Rainbow Hall, Reading. There
were some seventy to eighty people present, the majority coloured. The appellant addressed the meeting for about an hour. The prosecution case depended
on the evidence of three journalists, three police officers and two members of
the audience, including one who was a coloured man. Their recollection differed
as to what had been said but differed largely quantitatively rather than qualita-
tively, in that some remembered certain passages of the speech and others
remembered others, and so far as the three police officers are concerned, it was

---

* Section 6 (1) of the Race Relations Act 1965 provides, so far as material: " A
person shall be guilty of an offence under this section if, with intent to stir up hatred
against any section of the public in Great Britain distinguished by colour, race, or
ethnic or national origins— . . . (*b*) he uses in any public place or at any public meeting
words which are threatening, abusive or insulting, being matter or words likely to stir
up hatred against that section on grounds of colour, race or ethnic or national origins."

A agreed that they had, perfectly properly, put their heads together afterwards to make a note as full as they could of what had transpired.

The appellant chose to conduct the proceedings himself. He was perfectly entitled to do so, but it did have the result that none of the prosecution witnesses was cross-examined. He himself gave evidence in which he complained of a number of contradictions in the evidence of the prosecution witnesses, and

B he in effect made a number of points by way of defence. In connexion with the contradictions he denied that he had said many of the things that had been attributed to him. He also said that the meaning of the words that he had used meant something different to him as a West Indian than it would have meant to somebody in this country. Finally he said that he had no intent to stir up hatred within the meaning of the subsection (1). In the course of his evidence,

C however, it was perfectly clear (and indeed this is admitted, and has to be admitted, by counsel for the appellant in this court) that he did use words which, at any rate if taken in isolation, were fully of the character described in the subsection (1). The court refrains from referring in any detail, or at all if possible, to the actual words used.

One of the points taken in this appeal by counsel for the appellant is that the

D recorder failed to direct the jury properly in regard to the matters raised by way of defence. Particularly it is said that he did not sufficiently direct the jury that they must be satisfied that the appellant, as a West Indian, was using the words in the sense that we in England would understand them. In fact, as it seems to this court, the recorder, as one would expect in a case of this sort (which, happily, is rare) went out of his way to introduce and put before the

E jury everything that could be said in this man's favour by way of defence. The matters of which counsel for the appellant has complained were indeed put specifically at the very outset before the consideration of the evidence in the summing-up. He pointed out that the first question was whether words of the kind were used at all and he then went on:

F " As I understand it the other part of his defence is, ' Well, even when you are satisfied that I used certain words, I, a West Indian, was not using those words in the way that you white people, Englishmen, would use them, and therefore you are not to say that the prosecution have proved that those words were likely to stir up hatred in my mind. I had no intent to stir up hatred.' "

G Not only did the recorder say that, but he also went on to say that the jury must be quite satisfied that the appellant was intelligent enough to understand, and had understanding of, the words which he used; finally, the recorder dealt with intent. In other words, the position as left to the jury was, that they must not convict unless they were satisfied (i) that words of that character were used, (ii) that the appellant understood what he was saying, and (iii) that, notwith-

H standing that the appellant was a West Indian, he used those words, which he understood, in the sense that we should understand them. Finally, there was left to the jury the question of intent. This court has carefully considered the summing-up. It was a long one. We are quite satisfied that no valid criticism can be made of it and, therefore, that on that ground there is no reason to interfere with the verdict.

I Another point taken by counsel for the appellant concerns the fact that more than one witness—and it is sufficient for this purpose to refer only to one, viz., a Mr. Dixon—in the course of describing what he remembered of the words used brought out the fact that the appellant had been to prison. Thus he described this appellant at the meeting saying:

" I want to tell you about souls. The black man has soul. The white man has no soul. He is a soulless person."

_____

(1) Section 6 (1) of the Race Relations Act 1965.

Mr. Dixon then went on: " He then went on to talk about prison and the **A**
effect on people." He was asked, " What did he say about prison? " and he
answered:

> " He said, ' Don't let the thought of prison terrify you. I have been to
> prison. At first I was terrified but it is a coloured man's job to go to prison.
> You get to know a lot in prison, a lot that can terrify the white man."

This court is quite satisfied that where the matter at issue is what a man said, **B**
it would be only proper to allow the witness to say what he understood was
said, albeit the speaker had referred to the fact that he had been in prison.
Indeed, if that were not allowed, a prisoner might well complain (as, incidentally,
this appellant did) that only extracts were given and not the full statement that
he had made. Secondly, as it seems to this court, even if one was minded to cut **C**
out the reference to the fact that he had been to prison, it would involve in this
case not merely deleting the five words " I have been to prison " but deleting
and not referring to a considerable amount of the speech, the words of which fell
to be considered. Moreover this prisoner would, in any event, as he in fact did,
address the jury in some detail on this matter of prison and his having been to
prison. The court can see no ground for complaint in regard to that.

Finally, in regard to conviction, there remains the really substantial point **D**
in this case; the point being that having regard to something that had been
published in a newspaper, there was a real danger that this man would not have a
fair trial before the jury. What happened was this; that he was originally up
for trial on Oct. 17 and 18. Indeed he was tried for two days, when the jury
were discharged and a fresh trial was ordered. On Oct. 29, as is well known, **E**
the Sunday Times in an article in the paper of that date on race relations published
a photograph of the appellant and underneath, the words,

> " Michael Abdul Malik, 34, West Indian, came to U.K. 1950, took to
> politics after unedifying career as brothel-keeper, procurer and property
> racketeer. Muddled thinker but natural flair for self-advertisement."

That was, as this court held on Nov. 27, a serious contempt (2), likely to prejudice **F**
the fair trial. The article was on Oct. 29 and the fresh trial, the trial with which
we are concerned, took place on Nov. 8 and 9. Counsel for the appellant says
with some force that in those circumstances it was almost certain that that
article would be seen by some members of the jury. The fact of the abortive
trial would be known locally and no doubt was news locally. The Sunday Times
has a large circulation and particularly as being a responsible newspaper, people **G**
in the locality in Reading who read it would be ready to accept what was there
stated as true and would discuss it amongst themselves, and in those circumstances counsel for the appellant says that there was a real danger, to put it no
higher, that the jury would be prejudiced. This court has considered this matter
with some anxiety because, if the court felt that there was any danger that this
man had not had a fair trial, they would without hesitation set aside this convic- **H**
tion. One has to consider, however, what was said in relation to the facts of
the case, and here no question of credibility was involved because the prisoner
himself admitted, when he went into the box, the use of words of this character.
It was not, therefore, a question of the jury weighing up his credibility against
the credibility of the prosecution witnesses.

The way, however, counsel for the appellant puts it is that it is highly relevant
to what the jury considered to be the man's mental state at the time as regards
intent; and that it is the matter which the court has to consider. It is clear,
as I have already said, that the jury here must have accepted that the words,
which he at any rate admitted in cross-examination, were spoken. They must
have found that he understood the meaning of those words. They must have
found that he used them in the sense in which we understand them, and having

---

(2) R. v. *Thomson Newspapers, Ltd.*, p. 268, ante.

A got to that point, there could be no other conclusion but that he used them
with the intent referred to in s. 6 (1) of the Race Relations Act 1965. It was
quite inevitable, as it seems to this court, that the jury must come to that conclusion; and in those circumstances there could be no possible prejudice affecting
the result of the trial. In those circumstances, the court dismisses the appeal
against conviction.

B As regards sentence, counsel for the appellant has invited us to lay down
principles in regard to offences of this sort and as to how they should be dealt
with. The court has no intention of doing that, if only because each case must
be looked at independently according to the circumstances; no doubt one of the
most important matters to consider being the violence of the words used. This
is an offence which carries on indictment the sentence of two years' imprisonment
C plus a fine of £1,000, and in all the circumstances of the case, it was a serious
offence, and having heard all that counsel for the appellant has said in mitigation,
this court can see no reason whatever to interfere with that sentence. In saying
that, the court has thought it right to put out of its mind this man's previous
convictions. They are mainly of a quite different character, albeit that there
was one in 1958 which involved race relations, but it would be only right to treat
D that as too remote for this purpose, and accordingly the court, in saying that there
is no ground to interfere with the sentence, has put out of its mind the prisoner's
previous convictions. The appeal against sentence is likewise dismissed.

Appeal dismissed.

Solicitors: *B. M. Birnberg & Co.* (for the appellant); *Director of Public
E Prosecutions* (for the Crown).

[*Reported by* N. P. METCALFE, ESQ., *Barrister-at-Law.*]

TEHERAN-EUROPE CO., LTD. *v.* S. T. BELTON
F # (TRACTORS), LTD.

[QUEEN'S BENCH DIVISION (Donaldson, J.), December 11, 19, 1967.]

*Agent—Contract—Foreign undisclosed principal—Principal instructing English
merchants to negotiate purchase of machines from English suppliers—
Machines invoiced to English merchants by English suppliers—Whether*
G *privity of contract between English suppliers and foreign principal—Implied
condition of fitness—Purpose of resale made known to English suppliers—
One such machine seen by representative of foreign principal before contract
—Sale of Goods Act,* 1893 (56 & 57 Vict. c. 71), *s.* 14 (1).

London correspondents acting on behalf of a Persian company negotiated
the purchase of twelve air compressor units from an English company,
H disclosing the fact that they were acting for clients but not identifying
them. The English company's catalogue description of the machines,
which the representative of the Persian company saw, described the machines
as " new and unused ". One such machine was in fact inspected by the
representative of the Persian company in London. It was made known to
the English company that the machines were to be exported to Persia. In a
I letter of Aug. 19, 1957, on which agreement for the sale of the machines
was reached, the correspondents wrote that their clients were asking for a
liberal supply of literature for advertising purposes in Persia. The goods
were in due course invoiced to the English correspondents. The contract
was for the sale of goods by description, being goods which it was in the
English company's course of business to supply. On a preliminary issue in an
action by the Persian company against the English company for damages
for breach of contract on the ground that the machines did not accord with
description and were not fit for the purpose for which they were supplied,

Held: (i) the former trade usage that where a foreign customer had A
instructed English merchants to act for him in obtaining goods from an
English supplier, a resulting contract of sale by the English supplier did not
create responsibility between the foreign principal and the English supplier,
no longer existed, but the fact that the principal was foreign was a factor to be
taken into account in determining whether there was privity of contract
between the principal and the supplier, although its weight might be minimal B
(see p. 591, letter C, post).

Elbinger Act. für Fabrication von Eisenbahn Materiel v. *Claye* ((1873),
L.R. 8 Q.B. 313) not applied.

(ii) having regard to the request for forty copies of illustrated matter
in relation to twelve machines, there had been disclosure to the sellers that
the goods were required for the purpose of resale in Persia as new and C
unused machines, and in the circumstances an inference of reliance on the
sellers' skill or judgment should be drawn; accordingly there was an implied
term of the contract, in accordance with s. 14 (1) of the Sale of Goods Act,
1893, that the goods should be reasonably fit for the purpose for which they
were required (see p. 592, letters E and F, post).

Manchester Liners, Ltd. v. *Rea, Ltd.* ([1922] All E.R. Rep. 605) considered. D

[As to the presumption of absence of privity of contract with foreign principals,
see 1 HALSBURY'S LAWS (3rd Edn.) 218, para. 496; and for cases on the subject,
see 1 DIGEST (Repl.) 752, *2912*, et seq.

As to the impermanence of trade usages, see 11 HALSBURY'S LAWS (3rd Edn.)
203, para. 377.

For the Sale of Goods Act, 1893, s. 14 (1), see 22 HALSBURY'S STATUTES (2nd E
Edn.) 993.]

Cases referred to:

Brandt (H. O.) & Co. v. *Morris (H. N.) & Co., Ltd.*, [1916-17] All E.R. Rep.
925; [1917] 2 K.B. 784; 87 L.J.K.B. 101; 117 L.T. 196; 1 Digest
(Repl.) 729, *2742*. F

Clarkson, Booker, Ltd. v. *Andjel*, [1964] 3 All E.R. 260; [1964] 2 Q.B. 775;
[1964] 3 W.L.R. 466; Digest (Cont. Vol. B) 11, *2368a*.

Elbinger Act. für Fabrication von Eisenbahn Materiel v. *Claye*, (1873), L.R. 8
Q.B. 313; 42 L.J.Q.B. 151; 28 L.T. 405; 1 Digest (Repl.) 752, *2912*.

Holt (J. S.) & Moseley (London), Ltd. v. *Sir Charles Cunningham & Partners*,
(1950), 83 Lloyd L.R. 141. G

Manchester Liners, Ltd. v. *Rea, Ltd.*, [1922] All E.R. Rep. 605; [1922] 2 A.C.
74; 91 L.J.K.B. 504; 127 L.T. 405; 39 Digest (Repl.) 547, *804*.

Miller, Gibb & Co. v. *Smith & Tyrer, Ltd.*, [1917] 2 K.B. 141; 86 L.J.K.B.
1259; 116 L.T. 753; 1 Digest (Repl.) 670, *2355*.

Rushdowne and Bolton and Roberts Hadfield, Ltd. v. *S. F. Read & Co. (London),
Ltd.*, [1955] 1 All E.R. 180; [1955] 1 W.L.R. 146; 1 Digest (Repl.) H
721, *2673*.

Preliminary Issues.

By writ dated Aug. 17, 1959, the plaintiffs, a limited company incorporated
under the laws of Persia, claimed damages for breach of a contract for the sale
of machines. By their statement of claim the plaintiffs alleged that they agreed
to buy and the defendants agreed to sell twelve diesel engines coupled to air
pump compressors with removable tyred trailers at a price of £340 each delivered
to London packers; and further that it was an express term of the contract that
each engine and compressor should be new and unused. The plaintiffs further
alleged that at all material times the defendants well knew that the machines
were required for delivery to Persia and for resale there; alternatively that the
machines were machines which it was in the usual course of the defendants'
business to supply, that the defendants at all material times knew the purpose
for which the machines were required, and that it was an implied term of the

A contract that the machines should be reasonably fit for resale in Persia as new and unused machines. The plaintiffs alleged alternatively that the sale of the machines was a sale by description, the description being contained in the defendants' catalogue of goods; and that it was an implied term of the contract that the machines should correspond with their description and be of merchantable quality. The plaintiffs pleaded that in breach of the alleged terms none of the **B** engines or compressors was either new or unused, and that none of the machines was reasonably fit for the purpose for which it was supplied and that none complied with the description or was of merchantable quality. They alleged loss and damage, and claimed damages. The defendants, by their defence denied the alleged terms of sale and that the sale was a sale by description. The defendants pleaded that they did not enter into the alleged or any agreement with the **C** plaintiffs and they denied the alleged loss and damage. Finally, the defendants pleaded that—

> " Further or in the alternative the plaintiffs were at all material times an undisclosed foreign principal in respect of the agreement now sued upon, and there has at no time been any privity of contract between the plaintiffs **D** and the defendants and the plaintiffs are not entitled to sue the defendants in respect of their alleged cause of action herein (if any, which is denied)."

By order dated July 6, 1961, it was ordered that there be tried as preliminary issues of law and fact (a) the contention set out in the words quoted at letter D, above from the defence, and (b) the issue between the plaintiffs and the defendants as to what were the precise terms of the contract sued on by the plaintiffs. By **E** order dated Apr. 27, 1966, it was ordered that the preliminary issues to re-set down for trial within seven days.

B. Finlay, Q.C., and *W. A. B. Forbes* for the plaintiffs.
E. W. Eveleigh, Q.C., and *P. H. Otton* for the defendants.

Cur. adv. vult.

F
Dec. 19.   **DONALDSON, J.,** read the following judgment: The plaintiffs are a Persian company carrying on business in Teheran as importers of machinery and other goods. Their managing director is a Mr. Rahmena. The defendants are an English company who deal in government surplus goods. In this action the plaintiffs claim damages from the defendants for breach of a **G** contract for the sale by the defendants of air compressor units, it being alleged that the goods when delivered did not accord with the contract description, were not of merchantable quality, and were not fit for the purpose for which they were supplied.

The contract of sale was made in the late summer of 1957 and the writ was issued in 1959. Manifestly this action should have been determined long since, **H** but more than eight years later I am in fact only concerned with preliminary issues. This appalling delay is not the fault of the courts or of either of the parties, but is attributable to an employee of the plaintiffs' solicitors who betrayed their trust and confidence in him to such an extent as ultimately to lead to criminal proceedings, and to his being sentenced to a term of imprisonment. Fortunately very little turns on the recollections of witnesses, and the **I** preliminary issues can be dealt with almost entirely on the basis of contemporary correspondence.

In the course of their importing business the plaintiffs employed London " correspondents ", to use a neutral expression. These correspondents were Richards Marketing, Ltd., to whom I will refer as " Richards ".

In July, 1957, Mr. Rahmena came to London and was shown the defendants' catalogue by Mr. Richards, a director of Richards. Mr. Rahmena was interested in the machinery shown on p. 13 of the catalogue which was illustrated and described thus:

A

" Air compressors mobile. New and unused. Rating 156 cubic feet per minute at 100 lb. per square inch. General specification: Dorman diesel engine air pumps compressor. 4 cylinder 4 D.W.D. V Twin Type T.S. 20. This is a new and unused engine and compressor, assembled as a complete unit by ourselves, on a low loading trailer, which can easily be removed and the trailer used as a low-loader. This trailer will carry five to six tons and has a six foot clearance between the rear wheels. Painted in customer's colours. Fully guaranteed. Price £350 f.o.r. "

B

On July 5, 1957, Mr. Richards in the presence of Mr. Rahmena telephoned to the defendants and told them that he had a client who was interested in purchasing such compressors, but he did not then or at any material time thereafter reveal the name of the client. The purpose of the telephone call was to find out whether a similar machine could be seen in London. Such a machine was in fact to be seen in Whitechapel and Mr. Rahmena and Mr. Richards inspected it.

C

On July 10, 1957, Mr. Rahmena instructed Mr. Richards to negotiate with the defendants for the sale of twelve machines at a price of £300 f.o.r. as compared with the £350 mentioned in the catalogue, but authorised him to agree to £350 if necessary. At the same time he wrote out order No. 20 dated July 10, 1957, which on its face appeared to be an order addressed to Richards by the plaintiffs for twelve such machines at a price of £350 partly packed f.a.s. London. This order was confirmed by order No. 2221 dated July 21, 1957, which emanated from the plaintiffs' office in Teheran. Negotiations between Richards and the defendants were continued by correspondence and on Aug. 10, 1957, Richards wrote a letter which included this paragraph:

D

E

" We have been in communication with our clients and have been instructed to put forward an offer to purchase twelve units at £300 each delivered London packers exclusive of any form of packing and to proceed immediately with shipment of the first two units."

F

This offer was not accepted, but by a letter dated Aug. 19, 1957, from Richards to the defendants and by a letter in reply dated Aug. 22, 1957, agreement was reached for the sale of six machines at a price of £340 each delivered London packers. In the letter Aug. 19, 1957, Richards wrote:

" Our clients are asking for a liberal supply of descriptive literature for advertising purposes in Iran and we shall be obliged for say forty copies illustrated matter."

G

In the letter of Aug. 22, 1957, the defendants wrote:

" As these compressors are for export, we must ask for cash payment before delivery as it is customary for us to have irrevocable credit on the equipment which we export."

H

The machines were in due course invoiced by the defendants to Richards and not to the plaintiffs, whose identity was unknown to them.

The financial agreement between the plaintiffs and Richards was that Richards would pay the cost of the machines, insurance, packing and freight, and that the plaintiffs would accept a ninety-day sight draft for the aggregate of their disbursements plus commission at ten per cent. and interest.

The preliminary issues which I have to determine are as follows:

(a) " The contention raised by para. 12 of the defence ", which may be restated as, " whether there was privity of contract between the plaintiffs and the defendants so that the plaintiffs are entitled to sue the defendants in respect of the cause of action alleged ". This might be called " the agency issue ".

(b) The issue between the plaintiffs and the defendants as to what are or were the precise terms of the contract sued on by the plaintiffs—" the contractual terms issue ".

A   *The agency issue.* Counsel's first submission for the defendants was that the transaction, properly analysed, involved a purchase of the machines by Richards and a re-sale by them to the plaintiffs. Some support for this proposition is to be derived from the plaintiffs' order No. 20 and the confirmatory order No. 2221 of July 21, 1957, but it is not sustainable in the light of the evidence of Mr. Richards and Mr. Rahmena. Neither the plaintiffs nor Richards

B   ever contemplated a sale by Richards at £350 f.a.s. London or any other price, and if there had been a sale it would have been at a price of about £590 c.i.f. Teheran. These orders, although in a form appropriate to a sale, were intended both by the plaintiffs and by Richards as a written confirmation of the latter's authority to negotiate on the plaintiffs' behalf for the purchase of twelve machines at a price not exceeding £350 f.a.s. London. In the circumstances I have no doubt

C   whatsoever that as between the plaintiffs and Richards, Richards acted throughout as the plaintiffs' agents and not as principals.

This finding does not by any means conclude the matter against the defendants, and their counsel's second submission was that even if Richards were the plaintiffs' agents, they did not so conduct themselves as to create privity of contract between the plaintiffs and the defendants.

D   An agent can conclude a contract on behalf of his principal in one of three ways:

(a) *By creating privity of contract between the third party and his principal without himself becoming a party to the contract.* The principal need not be named but the contract must show clearly that the agent was acting as such. Familiar examples are contracts made by X as agents and signed by X, the

E   signature being claused " as agents only ". The consequence of such an arrangement is that the third party can only sue, and be sued by, the principal.

(b) *By creating privity of contract between the third party and his principal, whilst also himself becoming a party to the contract.* The consequence of this arrangement is that the third party has an option whether to sue the agent or the principal, although this is of little practical value if he does not know

F   of the principal's existence. Equally the third party is liable to be sued either by the agent or by the principal. Where both agent and principal are privy to the contract, questions of election can arise (see *Clarkson, Booker, Ltd.* v. *Andjel,* (1)) but no such question arises in this case.

(c) *By creating privity of contract between himself and the third party, but no such privity between the third party and his principal.* In other words, in relation

G   to the third party he is a principal, but in relation to his principal he is an agent. The consequence of this arrangement is that the only person who can sue the third party or be sued by him is the agent.

In the present case it is not suggested that Richards so acted as to exclude their own liability or right to sue—category (a) above. The issue is whether the transaction falls into category (b) or category (c). Nor does counsel for the

H   defendants suggest that this case falls into the category of cases in which the terms of the contract itself negative the existence of any principal other than the ostensibly contracting party. (See BOWSTEAD ON AGENCY (12th Edn.) art. 90.) His submission is that this was a contract made by an agent for a foreign undisclosed principal and that in such circumstances the foreign principal acquires neither rights nor liabilities under the contract.

I   For present purposes I am prepared to accept that Richards contracted on behalf of an undisclosed principal. In doing so I treat the numerous references to " our clients " as being equally capable of being interpreted as a reference to " our principals " or to " our customers ", but the proper view may well be that Richards contracted on behalf of disclosed, but unnamed, principals. However, that may be, I have no doubt that the remainder of the submission is overstated.

---

(1) [1964] 3 All E.R. 260; [1964] 2 Q.B. 775.

The submission by counsel for the defendants rests on an alleged usage of trade that the foreign principal of an English agent does not authorise the agent to establish privity of contract between him and the third party. Counsel for the plaintiff objected that this, being a usage, should have been pleaded and proved, but this is not right, for the courts will take judicial notice of those usages which have been judicially ascertained and established as part of the law merchant (see 11 HALSBURY'S LAWS OF ENGLAND (3rd Edn.) 201, para. 374). The defendants in the present case are able to rely on the decision of in *Elbinger Act. für Fabrication von Eisenbahn Materiel* v. *Claye* (2), as establishing the usage. In that case BLACKBURN, J., said (3):

"I quite agree that a man may, as agent, make a contract on such terms as not only to bind himself but also so as to bind the principal; in other words, so that the principal shall be party to the contract, and may then either sue or be sued. I must say I think that the two things are correlative. A man cannot make a contract in such a way as to take the benefit, unless also he take the responsibility of it. But although such a contract may be where the principals are English; yet where a foreigner has instructed English merchants to act for him, I take it that the usage of trade, established for many years, has been that it is understood that the foreign constituent has authorised the merchants to pledge his credit to the contract, to establish privity between him and the home supplier. On the other hand, the home supplier, knowing that to be the usage, unless there is something in the bargain showing the intention to be otherwise, does not trust the foreigner, and and so does not make the foreigner responsible to him, and does not make himself responsible to the foreigner."

However, the law merchant is far from immutable, and it is, I think, open to any court to find on the basis of evidence that it has changed or, if a change has previously been judicially ascertained and established in other proceedings, to take judicial notice of that change.

Accordingly I was referred to *Miller, Gibb & Co.* v. *Smith & Tyrer, Ltd.*, (4) where SWINFEN EADY, L.J., assumed the continued existence of the usage without deciding the point, and to *H. O. Brandt & Co.* v. *H. N. Morris & Co., Ltd.* (5), in which SCRUTTON, L.J., said:

". . . while I think that one cannot attach at the present day the importance that used to be attached forty or fifty years ago to the fact that the supposed principal was a foreigner, I think it is still a matter to be taken into account in deciding whether the person said to be an English agent has or has not made himself personally liable."

It will be noticed that SCRUTTON, L.J., was considering whether the English agent was liable, which is not in dispute in the present case, and not, at all events expressly, whether the foreign principal was liable. SCRUTTON, L.J.'s view of the law has been echoed in *J. S. Holt & Moseley (London), Ltd.*, v. *Sir Charles Cunningham & Partners* (6). In *Rushdowne and Bolton and Roberts Hadfield, Ltd.* v. *S. F. Read & Co. (London), Ltd.* (7) PEARCE, J., said that SCRUTTON, L.J., had correctly stated the law in *Brandt* v. *Morris* (8) but perhaps came nearer to the decision in *Elbinger's* case (2) when he held that (7)

"where [the agent] contracts on behalf of a foreign principal there is a presumption that he is incurring a personal liability unless a contrary intention appears."

(2) (1873), L.R. 8 Q.B. 313.
(3) (1873), L.R. 8 Q.B. at p. 317.
(4) [1917] 2 K.B. 141 at pp. 150, 151.
(5) [1916-17] All E.R. Rep. 925 at p. 929; [1917] 2 K.B. 784 at p. 797.
(6) (1950), 83 Lloyd L.R. 141 at p. 145.
(7) [1955] 1 All E.R. 180 at p. 183.
(8) [1916-17] All E.R. Rep. 925; [1917] 2 K.B. 784.

A It never emerged very clearly why the defendants in the present case should be showing such marked enthusiasm for being sued by Richards, and such marked reluctance to being sued by the present plaintiffs, but the explanation is probably that (a) a claim by Richards is statute-barred, and (b) they hope that the loss in respect of which Richards could sue would be more restricted than that which forms the basis of the claim by the plaintiffs. If this latter consideration

B has any substance—and it may have none—it provides a very good reason for looking somewhat closely at an alleged usage which, in our present state of dependence on export trade, prevents the foreign customer from suing the English supplier.

I am satisfied that the general trade usage recorded in *Elbinger's* case (9) no longer exists, and that the most that can now be said is that in deciding whether

C privity of contract exists between an English supplier and the foreign principal of an English agent, the fact that the principal is foreign is a factor to be taken into account although its weight may be minimal. The foreign character of the principal is also to be taken into account when deciding whether the English agent has made himself personally liable in addition to any liability of his principal, but in that case the foreign element may be of greater importance.

D In the present case I have no doubt that the plaintiffs authorised Richards to create privity of contract between them and the defendants and that Richards did so. I am also satisfied that the defendants had no reason to believe that Richards were necessarily acting as principals. In this connexion it may not be without significance that the defendants required payment in advance. Accordingly I hold that the contention raised by the defendants in para. 12 of

E the defence fails.

The contractual terms issue. It was agreed before me that the contract was for the sale of goods by description, the description being that contained in Richards' letter to the defendants dated Aug. 19, 1957, and that it was a term of that contract, to be implied by s. 14 (2) of the Sale of Goods Act, 1893, that the goods should be of merchantable quality.

F The only issue between the parties was whether the contract contained the implied term alleged in para. 7 of the statement of claim. That paragraph is as follows:

" Further or alternatively, the said machines were machines which it was in the usual course of the defendants' business to supply and the defendants at all material times knew the purpose for which the said machines were required. In the premises it was an implied term of the said contract that the said machines should be reasonably fit for the purpose for which they were supplied, namely for resale in Persia as new and unused machines."

This issue may not be of great importance since it is difficult to see how there could be a breach of the term alleged without there also being a breach of the

I term implied by s. 13 (1) of the Sale of Goods Act, 1893, that the goods would correspond with the contract description. However, it has been raised and it should therefore be decided.

The implication of this term arises out of the provision of s. 14 (1) of the Sale of Goods Act, 1893, that

"Where the buyer, expressly or by implication, makes known to the seller the particular purpose for which the goods are required, so as to show that the buyer relies on the seller's skill or judgment, and the goods are of a description which it is in the course of the seller's business to supply (whether he be the manufacturer or not) there is an implied condition that the goods shall be reasonably fit for such purpose . . ."

Counsel for the plaintiffs submitted that if he could prove that the plaintiffs, or Richards on their behalf, made known to the defendants the fact that the

(9) (1873), L.R. 8 Q.B. 313.

machines were required for resale in Persia as new and unused machines, he   **A**
did not have to prove anything in relation to reliance on the defendants' skill
or judgment, and he referred me to the speech of LORD BUCKMASTER in *Manchester
Liners, Ltd.* v. *Rea, Ltd.* (10). Whilst this may often be correct from a practical
point of view, I do not think that this decision entitles me to ignore the words
in the section " so as to show that the buyer relies on the seller's skill or judgment ".
That case decides, as I read it, no more and no less than that if a buyer expressly or   **B**
by implication makes known to the seller the particular purpose for which
the goods are required, and if the goods are of a description which it is in the
course of that seller's business to supply, then there is an inference (per LORD
DUNEDIN (11) LORD SUMNER (12)) or prima facie evidence (per LORD ATKINSON
(13)) that the buyer relied on the seller's skill or judgment sufficiently to satisfy
the provisions of the subsection. I have therefore to decide whether the plaintiffs   **C**
by their agents made known to the defendants that the machines were required
for resale in Persia as new and unused machines and, if so, whether there
is anything which rebuts the inference or prima facie case of reliance on the
defendants' skill or judgment.

It is quite clear that the goods were of a description which it was in the course
of the defendants' business to supply, and I think that it was made clear to the   **D**
defendants by Richards' letter of July 5, (14) that the machines were to be exported to Persia. This leaves open the question whether the machines were required
by the plaintiffs for use or for resale in Persia and if the latter whether for resale
as " new and unused machines ". Bearing in mind that only twelve machines
were ever the subject matter of any offer, I think that the request for forty copies
of illustrated matter contained in Richards' letter of Aug. 19, 1957, makes it   **E**
clear that the machines were required for resale in Persia, and I infer that they
were to be re-sold under the same description as that under which they were
bought, namely, " new and unused ". The only fact which can be relied on
in rebuttal of the inference of reliance on the defendants' skill or judgment is
the fact that Mr. Rahmena went to look at one of the machines working in London.
This is quite insufficient,   **F**

Accordingly I find that the contract was one for the sale of goods by description, namely the description set out in the letter of Aug. 19, 1957, that it
was an implied term of that contract that the goods would be merchantable
and in accordance with the contract description and fit for the purpose of being
re-sold in Persia as " new and unused " machine.

Preliminary issues decided in favour of the plaintiffs.   **G**

Solicitors: *Eric G. L. Temple*, Ilford (for the plaintiffs); *Lee, Bolton & Lee*
(for the defendants).

[*Reported by* MARY COLTON, *Barrister-at-Law.*]

  H

---

(10) [1922] All E.R. Rep. 605 at p. 607; [1922] 2 A.C. 74 at p. 79.
(11) [1922] All E.R. Rep. at p. 608; [1922] 2 A.C. at p. 81.
(12) [1922] All E.R. Rep. at p. 613; [1922] 2 A.C. at p. 90.
(13) [1922] All E.R. Rep. at p. 610; [1922] 2 A.C. at p. 85.
(14) This letter was addressed to the defendants and signed on behalf of Richards
Marketing, Ltd. It referred to " our conversation today " (cf., p. 588, letter B, ante)
and after asking about measurement, as freight would depend on measurement, and
intimating that the clients would probably take twelve units in shipments of two at a
time, concluded " we also indicated to you that we would value the opportunity of having
sole distribution of this equipment for Iran on terms which perhaps we can discuss at
a later date."

A

CRONIN *v.* GRIERSON AND ANOTHER.

[HOUSE OF LORDS (Lord Reid, Lord Morris of Borth-y-Gest, Lord Hodson, Lord Pearce and Lord Upjohn), December 11, 12, February 7, 1968.]

B

Gaming—Amusements with prizes—Gaming machine installed in public house with local authority's permit—Machine operated by pulling lever after insertion of sixpence or disc token purchased for money—Winning jackpot of tokens gave advantage of better odds of receiving further jackpots in four more games—Whether a further opportunity to win money or money's worth within Betting, Gaming and Lotteries Act 1963 (c. 2) *s.* 49 (3) (d)—*Whether a "benefit" for the purposes of Betting, Gaming and Lotteries Act* 1964 (c. 78) *s.* 2 (3).

C

The respondents installed an amusement machine in the public bar of their premises under a permit granted by the local authority under Sch. 6 to the Betting, Gaming and Lotteries Act 1963. The machine was operated by the player inserting either a sixpence, which allowed two games, or tokens, each of which had a value of threepence. The tokens could be obtained

D

from the machine. The player played a game by pulling a lever on the side of the machine after having inserted the sixpence or the token. If the player were successful he would receive tokens from the machine, each token being exchangeable for merchandise to the value of threepence. The most that a successful player could receive was twenty tokens. If he received the jackpot, that is, the twenty tokens, a " Jolly Joker " panel lit up and remained alight to allow up to four games. While the " Jolly Joker " was

E

alight, there were better odds of the player receiving further jackpots by continuing to play further games, although there was no certainty of his winning a jackpot. On appeal against the upholding of the dismissal of information preferred against the respondents, charging them in effect with an offence under s. 49 (2) of the Act of 1963 by reason of contravention of conditions imposed by s. 49 (3)* of that Act and s. 2 (1) and (3)† of the Betting, Gaming and Lotteries Act 1964,

F

Held: the advantage, viz., the preferred terms for future playing, which a successful player obtained by winning the jackpot was a benefit within s. 2 (3) of the Act of 1964, with the consequence that the entitlement to this benefit contravened s. 49 (3) (d) of the Betting, Gaming and Lotteries Act 1963, and an offence against s. 49 (2) of the Act of 1963 was established (see p. 598, letters F, H and I, and p. 599, letter I, post).

Per LORD MORRIS OF BORTH-Y-GEST (LORD PEARCE concurring): it is to be doubted whether the winning of the jackpot gave entitlement to a " further opportunity " for the purpose of s. 49 (3) (d) of the Betting, Gaming and Lotteries Act 1963 (see p. 598, letters C and I, post).

I

Decision of the DIVISIONAL COURT ([1967] 3 All E.R. 153) reversed.

[**Editorial Note.** The decision of the House of Lords negatives only the second ratio decidendi of the decision of the Divisional Court (i.e., [1967] 3 All E.R. 153 holding (ii) at letter I on that page). The decision of the Divisional Court concerning the words " further opportunity " in s. 49 (3) (d) of the Act of 1963 remains authoritative.

As to provision of certain amusements with prizes at commercial entertainments, see SUPPLEMENT to 18 HALSBURY'S LAWS (3rd Edn.) para. 469B.

For the Betting, Gaming and Lotteries Act 1963 s. 49, see 43 HALSBURY'S STATUTES (2nd Edn.) 361.

For the Betting, Gaming and Lotteries Act 1964 s. 2, see 44 HALSBURY'S STATUTES (2nd Edn.) 296.]

---

* Section 49, so far as material, is set out at p. 595, letters F and H, post.
† Section 2 is set out at p. 596, letters H to I, and p. 597, letters A to C, post.

Appeal. A

This was an appeal by Michael Charles Cronin, an inspector of police, from a judgment of the Divisional Court of the Queen's Bench Division (LORD PARKER, C.J., WIDGERY and GEOFFREY LANE, JJ.), dated June 28, 1967 and reported [1967] 3 All E.R. 153 dismissing the appellant's appeal on a Case Stated by justices for the county of Oxford, who on Nov. 9, 1966, dismissed an information laid on Oct. 31, 1966, by the appellant against the respondents Francis John B Grierson and Henry James Agguter. The information alleged that the respondents, at premises called the Swan Hotel at Tetsworth, Oxford, to which a permit for the provision of amusements with prizes had been granted by the local authority, were concerned with providing a game played by means of a machine " made playable by the insertion into the machine of one or more coins or tokens in relation to which the conditions of s. 49 of the Betting, Gaming and C Lotteries Act 1963 and of s. 2 of the Betting, Gaming and Lotteries Act 1964 were contravened ". The sole question on appeal was whether in providing such a machine the respondents complied with s. 49 (3) (d) of the Betting, Gaming and Lotteries Act 1963 and with s. 2 (2), (3) of the Betting, Gaming and Lotteries Act 1964. The facts are set out in the opinion of LORD MORRIS OF BORTH-Y-GEST.

Sir Peter Rawlinson, Q.C., and *J. B. R. Hazan* for the appellant. D
Sir Dingle Foot, Q.C., and *R. J. S. Harvey* for the respondents.

Their lordships took time for consideration.

Feb. 7. The following opinions were delivered.

LORD REID: My Lords, I agree with your lordships that this appeal should be allowed. E

LORD MORRIS OF BORTH-Y-GEST: My Lords, the question which arises in this appeal is whether it was shown that there was contravention of any statutory condition which applied to what was called the playing of a game by means of a certain machine. If that was shown then on the facts as found the respondents were guilty of the offence with which they were charged. The F machine in question was installed in and was in use in the public bar of a hotel known as the Swan Hotel at Tetsworth. Its features are carefully described in the Case Stated (1). It is operated by the insertion either of a 6d. (which allowed for two " games ") or of a token. Tokens are discharged from the machine if a player has " success at the game ". A token has a value of 3d. It may be exchanged for merchandise to the value of 3d. Playing the game is simplicity G itself. After inserting a coin or a token all that the player has to do is to pull a lever on the side of the machine. This causes three drums to revolve. Each drum has twenty symbols on it. A player will only achieve success at the game if, when the drums come to rest, some of the symbols appear on a centre line in the particular way or sequence designated and illustrated on the front of the machine. Varying measures of " success " will have the result that the machine, which H operates at random, will disgorge tokens: in some circumstances they will be two in number: in other circumstances five or ten, or fourteen or eighteen or twenty may be yielded. The appearance of three similar symbols (of some of the varieties of symbols) on the centre line which crosses the three drums will yield twenty tokens. That is the " jackpot ". Success could never result in the acquisition of more than twenty tokens by the playing of one game. But the most engaging feature of the machine is revealed at any such moments of triumph as occur when a successful player receives " the jackpot " of twenty tokens. When such a moment comes a " Jolly Joker " panel lights up on the front panel of the machine. It stays alight during and up to the four next games. If, while playing those four next games (in each case played after the insertion of a token) a Jolly Joker symbol appears on the centre line even on any one only of

---

(1) See [1967] 3 All E.R. 153 at pp. 154, 155.

A   the three drums, then the player receives a further jackpot. The machine will
then each time disgorge a further twenty tokens (exchangeable for merchandise
of the total value of 5s.).   When it is appreciated that of the twenty symbols on
a drum six are Jolly Joker symbols it becomes apparent that during the playing
of the four games while the " Jolly Joker " is alight the prospects of a player are
dramatically improved.   If in ordinary play it may be a rare event for anyone

B   to receive the jackpot, success in receiving it is followed by the further and special
bounty that is likely to accrue during the next four games.   The Case Stated
finds that during those games " the odds were in favour of the player receiving
a further jackpot or jackpots each of twenty tokens ", although there was no
certainty of that occurring.   He might therefore receive up to four further
jackpots of twenty tokens each time, though in no one of the four further games

C   would he receive more than twenty tokens.   In regard to this period of benevo-
lence the Case Stated further finds that "the chances of a joker being on the
centre line were eighteen out of twenty". The finding does not lose its significance
even though the accuracy of the mathematical assessment of the state of the
odds may be regarded as open to question.

   If a player found himself in the position of receiving a jackpot yielding him

D   the maximum accretion of twenty tokens, and found himself also with the prospect
of receiving all that might come to him by playing four further games under the
specially favourable conditions then made available for him, he would in my
view most certainly conclude that he had become entitled to a " benefit "
other than and in addition to the twenty tokens which his success in getting the
jackpot had yielded him.   If this conclusion is correct, then in my view it should

E   have been held that the respondents were guilty of the offence with which they
were charged; but, before this result can be demonstrated, it becomes necessary
to study a number of statutory provisions.   They lack the simplicity of the
amusement which they are designed to regulate.

   Section 49 (1) (*a*) of the Betting, Gaming and Lotteries Act 1963 provides
as follows:

F
   " (1) The provisions of this section shall have effect for the purpose
of permitting the provision of amusements with prizes—
   " (*a*) on any premises in respect of which a permit for the provision thereon
of such amusements has been granted by the local authority, and is for the
time being in force, under Sch. 6 to this Act, . . ."

G   In respect of the Swan Hotel there was a permit which was in force which had
been granted by the local authority for the installation of the amusement machine
in accordance with the requirements of Sch. 6 to the Betting, Gaming and
Lotteries Act 1963.   Section 49 (2) is as follows:

   " (2) Nothing in ss. 32, 33, 34, 41 or 42 of this Act shall apply in relation

H   to amusements with prizes provided on such premises as are mentioned in
sub-s. (1) (*a*) or at such a pleasure fair as is mentioned in sub-s. (1) (*b*) of this
section; but, in relation to any such amusement to which any of those
sections would apply but for this subsection, the conditions set out in sub-s. (3)
of this section shall be observed, and if any of those conditions is contravened
every person concerned in the provision or conduct of that amusement shall

I   be guilty of an offence unless he proves that the contravention occurred
without his consent or connivance and that he exercised all due diligence
to prevent it."

   The information which was preferred against each respondent alleged that each
was

   " concerned in the provision of an amusement with prizes taking the form
of a game played by means of a machine, being a game which was made
playable by the insertion into the machine of one or more coins or tokens."

It was found as a fact that the machine was provided and installed by the res- **A**
pondents. The information alleged that in relation to the machine " the conditions of s. 49 of the said Act " [the Act of 1963] " and of s. 2 of the Betting,
Gaming and Lotteries Act 1964 were contravened ". The information did not
further specify which were the conditions that had been contravened, but before
the magistrates they were identified as being those in s. 49 (3) (*d*) of the Act of
1963 and s. 2 (3) of the Act of 1964. Section 49 (3), (4) of the Act of 1963 is **B**
as follows :

" (3) The conditions referred to in the last foregoing subsection are—
" (*a*) that the amount paid by any person for any one chance to win a
prize does not exceed 1s. ;

" (*b*) that the aggregate amount taken by way of the sale of chances in any **C**
one determination of winners, if any, of prizes does not exceed 50s., and that
the sale of those chances and the declaration of the result take place on the
same day and on the premises on which, and during the time when, the
amusement is provided ;

" (*c*) that no money prize is distributed or offered which exceeds 1s. ;

" (*d*) that the winning of, or the purchase of a chance to win, a prize does **D**
not entitle any person, whether or not subject to a further payment by him,
to any further opportunity to win money or money's worth by taking part
in any amusement with prizes or in any gaming or lottery ;

" (*e*) in the case of such a pleasure fair as is mentioned in sub-s. (1) (*b*) of
this section, that the opportunity to win prizes at amusements to which this
subsection applies is not the only, or the only substantial, inducement to **E**
persons to attend the fair.

" (4) Where any amusement with prizes takes the form of a game played
by means of a machine, being a game which is made playable by the insertion
of a coin or coins into the machine, then, notwithstanding that, in addition
to a money prize, a successful player receives the opportunity to play the
game again without the insertion of another coin, the condition set out in **F**
sub-s. (3) (*d*) of this section shall not be deemed to be contravened if the
aggregate amount which can be won by the player without inserting another
coin does not exceed 1s."

It is to be observed that sub-s. (4) refers to a game which is made playable by
the insertion into the machine of a coin or coins. No mention is made of a
token. This cannot have been because the use of tokens was unknown : there **G**
is a reference to tokens in the Act of 1963 (see s. 32 (1)).

Section 2 (1) of the Betting, Gaming and Lotteries Act 1964 is as follows :

"(1) Where any amusement with prizes provided under s. 49 of the Betting,
Gaming and Lotteries Act 1963 (which relates to the provision of amusements
with prizes at certain commercial entertainments) takes the form of a game
played by means of a machine, being a game which is made playable by the **H**
insertion into the machine of one or more coins or tokens, then, in addition
to the conditions set out in sub-s. (3) of that section, the conditions set out
in sub-ss. (2) and (3) of this section shall be observed."

It is to be observed that, though the effect of s. 2 (1) is to add certain conditions
to those contained in s. 49 of the Act of 1963, the subsection refers to a game
which is made playable by the insertion in the machine of one or more coins or
tokens. The subsection applied to the machine now being considered.

The conditions set out in s. 2 (2), (3) are as follows :

" (2) In respect of any one playing of the game a successful player shall
not receive any article other than one, and one only, of the following, namely :
" (*a*) a money prize not exceeding 1s. ;
" (*b*) a prize other than money of a value not exceeding 5s. ;
" (*c*) one or more tokens of a nominal value exchangeable (so far as not

A   used for further playing of the game) for prizes other than money on the
basis of a prize or prizes of a value or aggregate value not exceeding 5s. for
a number of tokens equal to the maximum number of tokens which can be
won at any one playing of the game.

" (3) A player's success at the game shall not entitle any person to, or to
exchange any prize or token for, any benefit other than those provided for
B   by sub-s. (2) of this section."

Further interlocking of the provisions of the two Acts is effected by s. 2 (4) which
is as follows:

" (4) In sub-s. (2) of the said s. 49, the reference to the conditions set out
in sub-s. (3) of that section shall be construed as including a reference to
C   the conditions set out in sub-s. (1) to (3) of this section; and in sub-s. (4)
of that section the reference to the condition set out in sub-s. (3) (*d*) of that
section shall be construed as including a reference to the condition set out
in sub-s. (3) of this section."

Before the magistrates it was contended by the prosecution that there had
been contravention of the condition imposed by s. 49 (3) (*d*) of the Act of 1963
D   in that the winning of or the purchase of the chance to win, a prize, entitled the
player to a " further opportunity " to win money's worth by operating the
machine again.   The contrary contention of the respondents was that the success
of a player at the game, and the receipt by him of a token or tokens, was not the
winning of a prize; and further that the purchase of a chance to win did not
entitle the player to a " further opportunity " to win money's worth by operating
E   the machine again.   The view of the magistrates (who dismissed the informations)
was that the operation of the machine by a player did not create a " further
opportunity to win " as expressed in s. 49 (3) (*d*) of the Act of 1963.   They
held that a player who felt encouraged to play another game because he had
been successful still played it as a game of chance which might be or might not
result in his having a further success which, in any event, would not exceed the
F   legally prescribed limit.   In the Divisional Court (2) the conclusion of the magistrates was upheld.   It was held that a successful player was not presented with
a " further opportunity " to win money or money's worth; that Parliament had
not regulated the use of machines by reference to the odds that they offered;
and that, though with the " Jolly Joker " sign illuminated a player had the
opportunity of better odds, he was not given a " further " opportunity to win
G   inasmuch as the nature of the game and the machine itself remained the same
and the stake and the maximum winnings in a separate game remained the same.

The second contention advanced by the prosecution before the magistrates
was that there had been a contravention of the condition imposed by s. 2 (3)
of the Act of 1964 in that a player's success in winning a jackpot entitled him to a
" benefit " other than those provided for by sub-s. (2) of that section, namely the
H   benefit of enjoying extremely favourable odds, leading to the prospect amounting
to a virtual certainty, of winning at least one further jackpot.   The respondents
contended that a player's success in receiving a jackpot entitled him only to one
of the benefits provided for by s. 2 (2) of the Act of 1964.   This view was upheld
by the magistrates and, in turn, by the Divisional Court (2).   WIDGERY, J.,
referred (3) to the use of the words " article " and " prize " and " tokens " in
I   sub-s. (2) and held that any advantage resulting from gaining a jackpot was not
to be regarded as a "benefit", because that word only denoted something tangible
in the nature of a prize or token or article, and because no one playing on the
machine could in respect of a separate game win a prize greater than that contemplated by s. 2 (2).   GEOFFREY LANE, J., held (4), with the concurrence of
LORD PARKER, C.J., that the word " benefit " should be construed by reference
to the provisions contained in s. 2 (2) and that the advantage resulting from

(2) [1967] 3 All E.R. 153.   (3) [1967] 3 All E.R. at p. 157.
(4) [1967] 3 All E.R. at p. 158.

winning the jackpot would be too intangible and vague an advantage to come **A** within the word " benefit " in sub-s. (3).

In your lordships' House argument was mainly concentrated on the second of the two above recorded contentions. It was common ground that the prosecution should have succeeded if it was shown that in respect of the machine there was a contravention of any one applicable statutory condition. As the first contention was not strongly pressed I do not propose to say more than that I was **B** not persuaded by the appellant that the view of the magistrates and of the Divisional Court (5) was erroneous. We are considering a penal enactment; it must be construed strictly; if there is doubt as to meaning, such doubt must be resolved in favour of the subject. The Case Stated does not precisely raise the issue whether the winning of a token is the equivalent of winning a prize; but, leaving this matter aside, I doubt whether it could be said that the winning of the jackpot **C** gave entitlement to a " further " opportunity to win money or money's worth. Whether a player won the jackpot or not, he could go on playing; he could play again by operating the machine. The further opportunity to play was there whether a player won the jackpot or not; but if he did win the jackpot, then for the next four games the player had new and unique advantages. Here I turn to the second contention. In the Act of 1964 it is recognised by s. 2 (1) **D** that an amusement with prizes provided under s. 49 of the Act of 1963 can take the form of a game played by means of a machine into which one or more coins or tokens are inserted. It followed that the conditions both of sub-s. (2) and of sub-s. (3) of s. 2 of the Act of 1964 had to be observed. In sub-s. (2) are references to a money prize, to a prize other than money of a value not exceeding 5s. and to tokens exchangeable (unless used for further playing) for a prize or **E** prizes not exceeding in aggregate 5s. Then in sub-s. (3) comes the positive prohibition against entitlement to any benefit other than those provided for by sub-s. (2). In my view this provision is both wide and clear. It seems to me to be precisely applicable to the advantage which accrues to one who wins the jackpot. He gets something other than or more than and additional to the maximum which was permitted, and which maximum he receives by his winning the **F** jackpot. His advantage or benefit is a real one. It was designed to be bountiful. He is placed in the position of being able to play further games at overwhelmingly favourable odds. It was submitted by counsel for the respondents that the subsection only contemplated some benefit of an extraneous nature which was unrelated to any further playing of the game or use of the machine. As illustrations counsel suggested that the giving of a free ticket for some outside enter- **G** tainment or privilege would be prohibited. I can see no justification for any such limitation. The subsection refers to " any " benefit. Section 2 (2) of the Act of 1964 had referred to certain specific corporeal limitations of benefit. It seems to me that sub-s. (3) was designed to ensure that those limitations (as defined in sub-s. (2)) would not be evaded. In the present case they were. A successful player who won the jackpot was given preferred terms for further **H** playing and as a result was most likely or almost certain to have further gain. That was a benefit. It was a benefit other than those provided for by sub-s. (2). I consider, therefore, that there was a contravention of a statutory condition. On the facts as found it follows that the prosecution should have succeeded. I would therefore allow the appeal with the result that the cause should be remitted to the Divisional Court with a direction to that court to give directions to the magistrates' court to convict.

LORD HODSON: My Lords, I agree with your lordships that this appeal should be allowed.

LORD PEARCE: My Lords, I have had the opportunity of reading the opinion of my noble and learned friend LORD MORRIS OF BORTH-Y-GEST, with which I agree.

_____

(5) [1967] 3 All E.R. 153.

A   **LORD UPJOHN:** My Lords, this appeal raises a very short point as to the legality of an amusement machine of the type usually referred to as " a one-armed bandit " which is called the " Jolly Joker ". For the purposes of the appeal it is not necessary to do more than mention two of its characteristics:— (a) While the machine may be operated by inserting 6d. which permits two games or pulls at the operating lever, it could also be operated by inserting a token

B   obtainable from the respondents which entitled the player to play one game. Whether 6d. or a token is inserted if the player is successful only tokens are discharged from the machine and they may be exchanged with the respondents for merchandise to the value of 3d. per token, or used for further games.   (b) The machine is of the three band type and will return none or some odds (up to twenty tokens) according to the symbols which come to rest on the centre line.

C   The peculiarity of this machine is that if the player obtains the jackpot not only does he receive twenty tokens but a " Jolly Joker " panel lights up (flashing intermittently) and this permits him, while the panel remains alight, to play four more games (by inserting one token for each game) and it is common ground that during this period the odds on the player receiving the equivalent (in tokens) of one or more further jackpots (that is twenty tokens of a value in merchandise no more than 5s. per game as is allowed by law) are greatly enhanced

D   This is because the machine so operates as to return twenty tokens to the player if a " Jolly Joker " appears in any band in the centre line.   After these four games the Jolly Joker panel light goes off and the machine returns to normal. The justices estimated that during the " Jolly Joker " period, while there is no certainty of the player obtaining the equivalent of another jackpot, for a Jolly

E   Joker might not appear on the centre line, the chances of his doing so were eighteen out of twenty.   Whether their calculations were mathematically correct may be doubted, but it matters not for the respondents concede the principle that his chances of winning twenty tokens during one or some of these four games are greatly increased.

The sole question is whether in such a machine the respondents comply with

F   s. 49 (3) (*d*) of the Betting, Gaming and Lotteries Act 1963 and with s. 2 (2) and 2 (3) of the Betting, Gaming and Lotteries Act 1964.

My lords, I do not think that it is necessary to deal with the Act of 1963 apart from the Act of 1964 for two reasons.   First, without finally deciding the point, I think that the respondents may well be right in submitting that s. 49 of the Act of 1963 taken alone was not concerned with token operated machines;

G   secondly, s. 2 (1)-(3) of the Act of 1964 is by sub-s. (4) of that section to be read into s. 49 of the Act of 1963 so that I find it necessary only to consider that section as so, in effect, amended.   The relevant provision is s. 2 (3) of the Act of 1964 which provides:

" A player's success at the game shall not entitle any person to, or to exchange any prize or token for, any benefit other than those provided by

I   sub-s. (2) of this section."

I need not set out sub-s. (2).

With all respect to the judgment of the Divisional Court (6) it seems to me clear that during the " Jolly Joker " period the player does obtain a benefit beyond those provided by sub-s. (2) for during this period of four games he has an artifi-

I   cially increased chance of gaining a number of tokens much beyond the normal chances or odds during ordinary play.   How has he reached that position? Simply because he has been successful in obtaining a jackpot on one game. That jackpot game gave him tokens to the value of 5s.   That is the most in terms of articles that he is lawfully entitled to under s. 2 (2); but the machine gave him this further benefit of four very advantageous games which goes beyond what he is entitled to under s. 2 (2).   That seems to me to be directly aimed at by s. 2 (3).   " Benefit " is a word of wide import, it means in this context

---

(6) [1967] 3 All E.R. 153.

no more than "advantage". I cannot construe it as being limited to a tangible, **A** corporeal advantage in the sense of a prize token or article as WIDGERY, J., thought (7); indeed the contrast between " article " in s. 2 (2) and " any benefit " in s. 2 (3) points to a wide and not a narrow interpretation of " benefit ". Nor do I think this plain benefit conferred by the operation of the machine during the "Jolly Joker" period is an intangible benefit in the sense of being too vague to be a failure to comply with the subsection as LORD PARKER, C.J. (8) and **B** GEOFFREY LANE, J. (8) thought.

I would allow this appeal.

Appeal allowed.

Solicitors: *Director of Public Prosecutions* (for the appellant); *Norman Slater & Co.* (for the respondents).

[*Reported by* S. A. HATTEEA, ESQ., *Barrister-at-Law.*] **C**

SNELL (Inspector of Taxes) *v.* ROSSER, THOMAS & CO., LTD. **D**

[CHANCERY DIVISION (Ungoed-Thomas, J.), July 5, 6, 7, 1967.]

Income Tax—Profits—Computation of profits—Capital or income receipt— Building contractors—Receipts from sale of land—Land bought in order to enable builders to acquire adjoining house—House alone required for conversion to flats—House constituting stock-in-trade—Land not used or let— Whether profit from land on subsequent sale taxable as income. **E**

In order to acquire a house, Lisvane House, for conversion into flats and resale, this being the first occasion on which the company had extended its ordinary building business to the purchase and conversion of premises, the company had to buy $5\frac{3}{4}$ acres of land with the house, because the house and land were offered for sale together. The company did not use the $5\frac{3}{4}$ **F** acres for development but left them as they were, deriving no income from them. Two years later the company sold the $5\frac{3}{4}$ acres at a profit, that being the first favourable opportunity.

Held: the $5\frac{3}{4}$ acres of land were something incidental to the purchase of the stock-in-trade, viz., Lisvane House, and, never having been treated as an investment or fixed asset of the company, should be regarded as if they **G** were part of the stock-in-trade of the company with the consequence that the proceeds of sale of the $5\frac{3}{4}$ acres were a trading receipt and the profit was taxable income (see p. 607, letter G, post).

Hobson & Sons, Ltd. v. *Newall (Inspector of Taxes)* ((1957), 37 Tax Cas. 609) applied.

Dictum of LORD GREENE, M.R., in *Imperial Tobacco Co. (of Great Britain and Ireland), Ltd.* v. *Kelly* ([1943] 2 All E.R. at p. 121) considered. **H**

[As to whether receipts from the sale of an asset constitute capital or income receipts, see 20 HALSBURY'S LAWS (3rd Edn.) 117-119, paras. 211, 212; 149-152, paras. 263-265; 153, para. 267; and for cases on the subject, see 28 DIGEST (Repl.) 20-38, *78-173*; 50-58, *191-225*.]

Cases referred to: **I**

Californian Copper Syndicate, Ltd. v. *Harris (Surveyor of Taxes)*, (1905), 5 Tax Cas. 159; 28 Digest (Repl.) 60, **171*.

Edwards (Inspector of Taxes) v. *Bairstow*, [1955] 3 All E.R. 48; [1956] A.C. 14; 36 Tax Cas. 207; 28 Digest (Repl.) 397, *1753*.

Hobson & Sons, Ltd. v. *Newall (Inspector of Taxes)*, (1957), 37 Tax Cas. 609; 28 Digest (Repl.) 52, *197*.

---

(7) [1967] 3 All E.R. at pp. 157, 158.   (8) [1967] 3 All E.R. at p. 158.

A   *Imperial Tobacco Co. (of Great Britain and Ireland), Ltd.* v. *Kelly, Imperial Tobacco Co. (of Great Britain and Ireland), Ltd.* v. *Inland Revenue Comrs.*, [1943] 2 All E.R. 119; 169 L.T. 133; 25 Tax Cas. 292; 28 Digest (Repl.) 36, *160.*

McKinlay v. *H. T. Jenkins & Son, Ltd.*, (1926), 10 Tax Cas. 372; 28 Digest (Repl.) 22, *86.*

B   *Thompson (George) & Co., Ltd.* v. *Inland Revenue Comrs., Inland Revenue Comrs.* v. *George Thompson & Co., Ltd.*, (1927), 12 Tax Cas. 1091; 28 Digest (Repl.) 418, *1853.*

Case Stated.

C   The taxpayer company appealed to the General Commissioners of Income Tax for Cardiff against an assessment to income tax made on it under Case 1 of Sch. D to the Income Tax Act, 1952, in respect of profits as builders for 1961-62 in the sum of £5,000. The question for determination was whether a profit of approximately £6,884 made by the taxpayer company on the purchase and sale of 5¾ acres of land adjoining Lisvane House, Lisvane, near Cardiff in the county of Glamorgan, was a profit of the taxpayer company's trade and assessable to

D   tax accordingly. The taxpayer company was incorporated on Jan. 12, 1954, to take over an existing business of building contractors carried on by Mr. Rosser and Mr. Thomas in partnership from 1947 to 1954. No purchase or sale of land, save its business premises, had been made between 1947 and 1954 and none had been made subsequently by the taxpayer company until the purchase of Lisvane House and the 5¾ acres that were offered for sale as one property with it in 1958.

E   The taxpayer company contended before the General Commissioners as follows: (i) that consideration of the taxpayer company's memorandum of association showed that dealing in land was not included in the main objects clause and that the primary purpose of the company was to earn profits as building contractors not as dealers in land; (ii) that consideration of the past activities of the taxpayer company, and of the partnership which it superseded, showed that there had

F   been no dealing in land at all, and to treat the transaction involved as a dealing in land was to run contrary to the company's activities; (iii) that the taxpayer company would not normally have bought the land, but had been obliged to do so in the particular case in order to obtain Lisvane House for conversion into flats; (iv) that the true interpretation of the transaction was that the 5¾ acres of land had been purchased and treated as an investment; (v) that it was consistent

G   with the taxpayer company's view of the matter that it took no steps whatsoever to develop the land and in particular made no application for planning permission; (vi) that it was also consistent to treat the acquisition of land as an investment having regard to the fact that the taxpayer company did not offer or advertise the land for sale and only sold it when pressed to do so by a large public company developing land at the rear; and (vii) that it was illogical to treat as build-

H   ing land land which had been bought in those circumstances and even at the date of hearing had not in fact been used as building land but only for access purposes. The Crown contended before the General Commissioners as follows: (i) that whilst the main objects clause of the taxpayer company's memorandum of association did not include dealing in land, nevertheless the company had power to purchase and sell land under its memorandum; (ii) that the buying of land was

I   a normal activity of builders and the particular land had been bought in the normal course of the taxpayer company's trade; (iii) that the suggestion that the adjoining land had been bought as an investment was not convincing, particularly as there was no investment income or letting or other character of an investment property; (iv) that the true interpretation was that, if the land had not been purchased as an investment, then as a capital item expenditure it could only be treated as a purchase in the course of trade; and (v) that the true interpretation was that the transaction was indeed a transaction in the course of the taxpayer company's trade and the profit accruing was taxable as a receipt arising in the normal course of trading activities—alternatively the receipt **A** arose as an ancillary to trade.

R. E. Borneman, Q.C., and *J. R. Phillips* for the Crown.

M. P. Nolan for the taxpayer company.

UNGOED-THOMAS, J.: This is the Crown's appeal against a decision of the General Commissioners of Income Tax for Cardiff. It raises the question **B** whether the purchase and sale of some land by the taxpayer company, Rosser, Thomas & Co., Ltd., occasioned profit of an income nature which is assessable to tax and which has to be brought in for the purposes of tax assessment under Case I of Sch. D to the Income Tax Act, 1952. The commissioners decided in favour of the taxpayer company on the ground that the purchase and resale of the land was not a trading activity or venture in the nature of their trade. Their **C** conclusion is merely stated as a conclusion, without giving reasons, and without the precise method by which they arrived at that conclusion being traced. It is in these circumstances that the Crown contends that the commissioners wrongly applied the principles established by the authorities to the facts of this case, and that, in so far as the decision is a question of fact, the decision is unreasonable within the very well-known observations of LORD RADCLIFFE in *Edwards* **D** (*Inspector of Taxes*) v. *Bairstow* (1).

There, LORD RADCLIFFE considered the relationship of an error in law to an inference of fact; and I trust I may be forgiven for concluding crudely that, where an inference of fact is drawn which cannot reasonably be sustained, then perhaps the more tactful way of putting it is that it must be due to a mis-application of principles of law or otherwise amount to an error in law. The less **E** tactful but more direct way of putting it would be the way which certainly appeared to receive some degree of favour from LORD RADCLIFFE: that the finding of fact was a finding which the only reasonable conclusion contra-dicts. Whatever the true view be on this rather recherché dissection of lawyers' approaches towards our trying to achieve a just result within the properly preserved framework of the law, the simple question that has to be decided is **F** whether the conclusion reached in this case can be reasonably sustained in view of the primary facts which have been found or are clearly agreed.

Counsel for the Crown, in making the contentions which I have indicated, was careful to make his references to the cases cited in this case references to the principles established by the cases. The principles established by the cases may again be considered as principles of law, or perhaps less tactfully and more directly **G** (and, I must confess, more in accordance with my own personal predilection), as the principles which the courts have established as governing inference of fact from primary findings of fact. I think that that, perhaps, is why counsel for the Crown insisted on framing his submission as carefully as he did and in the form that he did.

With those preliminary observations I shall come now to the Case Stated, and **H** first of all to the facts to which it refers. It says:

"The question for our determination was whether a profit of approxi-mately £6,884 made by the [taxpayer] company on the purchase and sale of 5¾ acres of land adjoining Lisvane House was a profit of the [taxpayer] company's trade aforesaid and assessable to tax accordingly."

In its objects, apart from the common provision of acquiring a business already **I** in existence and the object of carrying on business as builders and contractors, and so on, the taxpayer company included, although not in the forefront of its objects, the purchase, disposal or sale of an interest in any lands, and so on, and the object:

"To sell, . . . dispose of, turn to account or otherwise deal with all or any of the property . . . of the company."

---

(1) [1955] 3 All E.R. 48; 36 Tax Cas. 207.

A So its power to buy, sell and to deal with any of the property of the company were objects of the taxpayer company, but not objects in the forefront of the company's memorandum.

For some time the taxpayer company made no purchase or sale of land other than its registered offices, but in 1958 it found that Lisvane House, a large house on the outskirts of Cardiff, was for sale and was suitable for conversion into
B flats. This was the first occasion on which the taxpayer company had extended its ordinary building business into conversion and sale—and, as I now understand, speculative conversion and sale, not conversion and sale on account. The difficulty was that the purchase of Lisvane House, with its building suitable for conversion into flats, necessarily involved the purchase of the adjoining land because Lisvane House and its adjoining land were put up for sale together.
C In view of the course which the argument has taken, I should like to make it perfectly clear at this stage that the profit on the purchase and sale of this property, in so far as it consisted of the house itself, which was converted into flats and resold, constituted a profit which indubitably was profit subject to taxation. Thus, nothing at all in this case turns on the conversion of Lisvane House being a departure in the conduct of the taxpayer company's operations
D from its previous, purely building, operations. Therefore, for our purposes, the purchase, conversion and sale of Lisvane House—and I am limiting myself at the moment to the building part of the purchase—was a purchase, treatment and sale of stock-in-trade.

As I have said, the taxpayer company also bought the adjoining land. This consisted of 5¾ acres, and the company ascribed £5,000 of the purchase price
E to this land and some £3,800 of the purchase price to the purchase of the house. However that may be, it is clear that the purchase of the land was a substantial part of the purchase, as, indeed, was the purchase of the house. This does not affect the clear position that the land was bought simply because it was necessarily involved in the purchase of the house itself, which was what was required for the taxpayer company's stock-in-trade. Two years later, in September,
F 1960, the taxpayer company sold the 5¾ acres at a substantial profit. The land, in the meanwhile, had simply remained in the condition in which it was at the time of the purchase. Nothing had been done about it. No steps were taken to develop it; nothing was done to advertise it for any purposes; there was no letting of it; no income was derived from it, as there would be from an investment—it was simply still there. It was not in any sense converted into an
G investment; it was not in any sense made a fixed asset of the taxpayer company. If it were from its origin an investment or a fixed asset, then there is nothing that I can see to suggest that it did not remain as such. The question therefore becomes a comparatively narrow one: whether something which is necessarily bought together with what is admittedly bought as stock-in-trade is, when sold off as surplus, the sale of something forming part of the income-making stock of
H the taxpayer company or whether it is sale of capital.

I have been referred to a number of authorities which have considered similar, though not perhaps completely identical, situations. Before coming to these cases I should first mention the test which was laid down by the Lord Justice Clerk in *Californian Copper Syndicate, Ltd.* v. *Harris* (*Surveyor of Taxes*) (2). There he propounds the test:

I " Is the sum of gain that has been made a mere enhancement of value by realising a security, or is it a gain made in an operation of business in carrying out a scheme for profit-making? "

That is the general principle, and it is in accordance with that principle that later cases, worked out on their facts, help to an understanding of this case.

In *George Thompson & Co., Ltd.* v. *Inland Revenue Comrs.* (3) coal was bought

---

(2) (1905), 5 Tax Cas. 159 at p. 166.
(3) (1927), 12 Tax Cas. 1091.

for consumption in the trade; it then turned out that some of the coal was   **A**
surplus, and it was therefore sold.   It was held that that did not make it a capital
asset or the profit on that sale a capital profit.

In *McKinlay* v. *H. T. Jenkins & Son, Ltd.* (4), a company bought lire, and it
seems to me clear on reading the facts of that case that the lire were acquired in
order to buy marble as stock-in-trade in the course of the company's trade.
What happened, however, was that the lire appreciated, and the company or its   **B**
agent (which makes no difference for this purpose) decided to take advantage of
the appreciation and to sell the lire with a view to buying lire again on an anticipated fall in their value, then using the repurchased lire for the purpose of
acquiring marble.   For my part, it seems to me perfectly clear that, as the company sold its lire for the purpose of making a profit on the sale and repurchase
of lire, it was entering on an independent transaction for the purpose of making a   **C**
quick profit and not at all for the purpose of acquiring any stock-in-trade by way
of marble.   In fact, what it was doing was putting the lire out of its control for
the purpose of acquiring marble and using it exclusively for the purpose of an
exchange speculation.   I should therefore have thought that it was clear that
this was an isolated capital transaction, completely divorced from marble
acquisition transactions and constituting, as I have said, a separate operation   **D**
altogether.   For this reason, I find the *McKinlay* case (4) of no assistance in
this case.

That case was, however, the subject of observations later by LORD GREENE,
M.R., in *Imperial Tobacco Co. (of Great Britain and Ireland), Ltd.* v. *Kelly* (5).
In that case, a company had acquired dollars for the purpose of purchasing
tobacco leaf in the United States of America.   The war came, the dollars were   **E**
impounded, and they were paid for at a price which resulted in a substantial
profit to the company.   The question was whether that receipt had to be brought
in for the purposes of tax assessment.   In that case, LORD GREENE, M.R., pointed
out that, in the case of an English company, dollars were not money in the way
in which sterling is money, but that dollars were a commodity like any other
commodity.   So what we have is a company buying a commodity for the purpose   **F**
of its being converted into another commodity for the purpose of that other commodity being sold as stock-in-trade to make a profit for the company in the
ordinary course of trade.   The dollars were merely a stock-in-trade commodity
at one place removed, if I may very roughly so describe it.   That, of course
distinguishes it from the facts in the present case, where the land itself was never
used and was never, as far as I can see, intended to be used for the purpose of   **G**
development.   LORD GREENE, M.R., in the course of his judgment, made some
valuable observations.   He said (6):

"We have here a finding of fact as to the purpose for which the dollars
were bought.   The purchase of the dollars was the first step in carrying out
an intended commercial transaction, namely, the purchase of tobacco leaf.
The dollars were bought in contemplation of that and nothing else.   The   **H**
purchase, on the facts found, was, as I say, a first step in the carrying out of
a commercial transaction, which would be completed by the purchase and
delivery of the leaf and payment of the dollar purchase price for it.   We must
decide this case having regard to the facts as found.   In the light of those
facts, the acquisition of these dollars cannot be regarded as colourless.
They were an essential part of a contemplated commercial operation."

I shall come back to those words.   LORD GREENE later said (6):

"They then realised the commodity which had become surplus to their
requirements.   When I say ' surplus to their requirements ', I mean surplus

(4) (1926), 10 Tax Cas. 372.
(5) [1943] 2 All E.R. 119; 25 Tax Cas. 292.
(6) [1943] 2 All E.R. at p. 121; 25 Tax Cas. at p. 300.

A   to their requirements for the purpose and the only purpose for which the
dollars were acquired."

There I may interpose that they became surplus to requirements because the
Treasury had required them to stop further purchase of tobacco leaf.   In these
observations, the words, " They were an essential part of a contemplated com-

B   mercial operation " have got to be understood in the sense that in the *Imperial
Tobacco Co.* case (7) the commodity itself—viz., dollars—was part of the train
of treatment of stock-in-trade which resulted in the ultimate commodity which
the company sold in the course of trade.   They may, however, have a wider significance.   If these words are taken on their own, it could then be said that here
the purchase of the land was an essential part of the " contemplated commercial

C   operation " of developing Lisvane House by conversion into flats and then
selling them, thereby producing receipts in the course of the company's trade.
It is with this possibility in mind that I shall come later to the case of *Hobson and
Sons, Ltd.* v. *Newall* (*Inspector of Taxes*) (8), which came before HARMAN, J.
Having, however, made that reference to this part of LORD GREENE's judgment,
I shall come now to the observations which he made with regard to *McKinlay*

D   v. *Jenkins* (9).

After stating the facts LORD GREENE, M.R., said (10):

" The view of ROWLATT, J. himself on his decision in that case [it was
ROWLATT, J., who decided the *McKinlay* case (9)] and the grounds of it,
are referred to by him in *Thompson's* case (11).   In *Thompson's* case (11)
ROWLATT, J., said that *McKinlay's* case (9) was decided by him on the

E   footing that the original purchase of the lire had been ' a speculation '."

LORD GREENE went on (10):

" It is, perhaps, fair to say that the Case Stated in *McKinlay's* case (9),
does not appear to contain any basis for a finding that the original purchase
was a speculation."

F   Then, later (10):

" In *McKinlay's* case (9), the company took the opportunity to use
its lire as a speculation.   Even if that had not been their intention in the
first instance, what they did was this.   They took advantage of the turn
in the exchange market to make a quick profit on the exchange, intending
to provide the lire that they would ultimately need at a later date in the hope

G   and on the speculation that in the meanwhile the price of lire would go down,
as in fact it did."

Whatever the true explanation in fact be of the *McKinlay* case (9), it seems to
me that, whether it should truly be regarded as part of a speculation right from
the start, when the lire were purchased, or as having developed into a speculation

H   at a later stage, when the lire came to be sold, in either case it was clearly a
separate operation which affords no assistance, in my view, to the decision which
I have made in this case.

I come now to *Hobson & Sons, Ltd.* v. *Newall* (*Inspector of Taxes*) (8), which
is the case of HARMAN, J., that I have just mentioned.   In that case the facts
were in some respects extremely similar to the facts in this case.   The company

I   had to buy two houses to get land for a garage which it wanted to build.   In
due course it used this land for the garage and built a garage on it, and that
garage was undoubtedly a fixed capital asset of the company.   The houses were
let at the time they were bought.   When vacant possession was obtained, the

---

(7) [1943] 2 All E.R. 119; 25 Tax Cas. 292.
(8) (1957), 37 Tax Cas. 609.
(9) (1926), 10 Tax Cas. 372.
(10) [1943] 2 All E.R. at p. 122; 25 Tax Cas. at p. 301.
(11) (1927), 12 Tax Cas. 1091.

houses were sold, but that was some twenty years later. In the meantime, of **A**
course, rents were received from the letting. These houses were shown in the
company's accounts as stock-in-trade, but that is in no way decisive. The
company was however a property dealer, and it was said with great force for the
taxpayer in the case before me that that distinguishes it from the present case
because the company there could buy and sell the land in the course of its trading.
It nevertheless remains significant that the houses in that case were bought in **B**
order, and merely in order, to get land for the garage, and it was held that the
receipt on the sale of those houses should be brought in as an income receipt in
the course of trade. This is what HARMAN, J., said about these houses (12):

> " It appears that in 1927 the company was in want of a bit of land on which
> to build a garage for its trading purposes, and the only bit of land they
> could get at the time, on which they had room to build a garage, had also   **C**
> two houses upon it. The two houses therefore were purchased . . ."

Pausing there, it is quite clear that the houses in that case, just as with the land
in this case, were bought only because, without the houses in that case and the
land in this case, the property that was required could not be obtained at all.
HARMAN, J., continued (12):
                                                                               D
> " The two houses therefore were purchased not as an investment but
> because the company could not get hold of land for the garage without
> buying them. It is said that those houses, which were sold twenty years
> later, in 1950 or so, were not part of the trading stock of the company and
> the profit so derived was not trading profit. But it was not suggested that
> those houses were bought as an investment even in the sense in which the   **E**
> governing director used that word. They were bought as a business matter.
> The memorandum in cl. (j), says that land may be purchased ' for business
> purposes '. They did not become, as the garage no doubt did, part of the
> fixed assets of the company, used in its trade. They were apparently let
> when they were bought, and they were vacant when they were sold. It
> may well be that the company took the first opportunity of selling, namely, **F**
> when it could first get vacant possession of them. No differentiation between
> them and the other two categories of houses is suggested anywhere in the
> Case. Though there is the obvious difference that these were houses
> bought by the company and not built by the company, yet as they were
> not bought as an investment but were bought ' for business purposes '
> and were sold when they could be sold, it seems to me they were no less   **G**
> part of the stock-in-trade of the company than the rest of the houses with
> which I have been dealing. Therefore, although they are in a somewhat
> different category, I think the commissioners came to a correct view about
> them also."

It appears to me, on a fair reading of this passage, that the judge treated them
as part of the trading stock, because he said that there was no differentiation **H**
between them and the other houses which the company had built and which
were part of the trading stock. They were not acquired as, and they were not
made, investments or fixed assets. What we have there is something which
was bought as a purchase which was, in business terms, forced on the company
in order to get other property which it required. Then, it did not treat the
two houses as, or make them, an investment or a fixed asset of the company, **I**
but disposed of them when a suitable opportunity arose. In the meantime,
although receiving rent from them, the company just left them there, in the
same way as, in this case, the land was left there without any income being
obtained from it at all.

Whilst I appreciate that the company in the *Hobson* case (13) was a property
dealer, whereas the company in this case is not, it nevertheless seems to me that,

(12) (1957), 37 Tax Cas. at p. 618.
(13) (1957), 37 Tax Cas. 609.

A   having regard to the way in which the houses were acquired, not per se as stock-in-trade, for the purpose of being used as stock-in-trade at all, any more than the land in the case we are considering, but as incidental to what was otherwise required for the company's purposes, then, when we find that it is neither a fixed asset nor an investment, but is treated as surplus which has to be disposed of, it comes within the principle of *George Thompson & Co., Ltd.* (14), and perhaps

B   the somewhat wider statement of the principle to which I have drawn attention, made by Lord Greene (15), as something acquired as " an essential part of a contemplated commercial operation ".   To this extent the case before me is stronger than the *Hobson* case (16), because what was wanted by the company in the *Hobson* case (16) and was used by it for its purpose was wanted for capital purposes, and became a fixed asset; whereas in this case what was wanted—

C   viz., Lisvane House, the building itself—was clearly stock-in-trade, and was used as such.

Have the commissioners in this case adequately borne in mind the principles which emerge from the cases which I have quoted; and, if they have done so, should they have come to a different conclusion?   There is no dispute about the primary facts; it is a question of inference from those facts in the light of the

D   principles that have been laid down.   The land did, of course, become an asset of the taxpayer company, as the commissioners said in their Case Stated; but that leaves wide open the question what kind of asset it was.

Here, it has been suggested that this land, as contrasted with Lisvane House itself, must be treated as a separate entity, as subject to separate considerations and, indeed—and I hope I am not doing an injustice to the argument—as though

E   it were acquired and dealt with altogether independently, having nothing to do with the stock-in-trade, which Lisvane House was.   That is not the real situation.   The real situation here is clearly, to my mind, that it was bought because, and only because, Lisvane House could not be bought without it. It was in that sense incidental to the purchase of Lisvane House.   It was never used by the taxpayer company at all, and was disposed of by the company at

F   the first favourable opportunity.   As I read it, therefore, it was simply something incidental to the stock-in-trade, which was disposed of at an early favourable opportunity without being used by the taxpayer company at all.   It was an asset of the taxpayer company which was never treated as an investment by the company.   It never became a fixed asset of the company.   It seems to me that, in accordance with the principles in the cases from which I have quoted, it was

G   part of the stock-in-trade of the taxpayer company, and that on its sale the receipt should properly be treated as an income receipt of the company.   The commissioners, if they had properly applied the principles which I have mentioned, must have come to a different conclusion.   In those circumstances I consider that the Crown is entitled to succeed.

Appeal allowed.

H
Solicitors: *Solicitor of Inland Revenue*; *Rowe & Maw* (for the taxpayer company).

[*Reported by* F. A. Amies, Esq., *Barrister-at-Law.*]

I

---

(14) (1927), 12 Tax Cas. 1091.
(15) [1943] 2 All E.R. at p. 121;   25 Tax Cas. at p. 300.
(16) (1957), 37 Tax Cas. 609.

A

RAYBOULD *v.* RAYBOULD.

[PROBATE, DIVORCE AND ADMIRALTY DIVISION (Baker, J.), November 13, December 20, 1967.]

B

Divorce—Costs—Taxation—Party and party taxation—Counsel's brief fee— Solicitor's fee for attending the hearing—Undefended divorce suit brought by wife, legally aided with nil contribution—Suit heard at Chester—Petitioner's counsel a member of the circuit, travelled from London to Chester—Thirteen members of local bar—Two guineas taxed off counsel's fee as between party and party and added in legal aid column—Petitioner's solicitor's fee of £8 reduced by £3—Both fees restored to party and party column of bill.

C

Counsel, who was a member of the Wales and Chester circuit, came from London to Chester and represented the wife petitioner in an undefended divorce suit. The petitioner was legally aided with a nil contribution. The respondent husband was condemned in costs. Two guineas were taxed off counsel's brief fee of twelve guineas on party and party taxation and were transferred to the common fund column of the bill. The petitioner's solicitor attended the hearing, which lasted nine minutes. He travelled to Chester, was away from his office for at least three hours, and he charged £8, apart from cost of locomotion. The charge was reduced on taxation between party and party to £5.

D

Held: (i) a litigant was entitled to be served by the circuit Bar, the allowable brief fee for the petitioner in an undefended divorce suit being ten to twelve guineas; accordingly the two guineas was chargeable as between party and party against the respondent husband and would be restored to the party and party column of the bill (see p. 612, letter B, post).

E

(ii) in the circumstances a fee of £5 to the petitioner's solicitor for attending the hearing (R.S.C., Ord. 62, App. 2 item 33 (*b*) (ii)) was not reasonable and the fee of £8 would be restored in the party and party column of the bill (see p. 612, letter G, post).

F

[As to the principles of taxation in divorce suits, and as to taxation on a common fund basis where a party is receiving legal aid, see 12 HALSBURY'S LAWS (3rd Edn.) 463, 464, paras. 1037, 1038; and for cases on the allowance of costs, see 27 DIGEST (Repl.) 672, 673, *6387-6414*.

As to taxation on the common fund basis, see 50 DIGEST (Repl.) 495-500, *1755-1779*.]

G

Cases referred to:

Eaves v. *Eaves and Powell*, [1955] 3 All E.R. 849; [1956] P. 154; [1955] 3 W.L.R. 984; Digest (Cont. Vol. A) 779, *5364d*.

Self v. *Self*, [1954] 2 All E.R. 550; [1954] P. 480; [1954] 3 W.L.R. 119; 50 Digest (Repl.) 497, *1768*.

H

Williams v. *Williams*, (1966), unreported.

Young v. *Young and Kohler*, [1955] 1 All E.R. 796; [1955] 1 W.L.R. 395; 50 Digest (Repl.) 499, *1773*.

Summons for review of taxation.

I

By summons dated Aug. 9, 1967, the petitioner, Betty Raybould applied for the respondent to show cause why the taxation of the petitioner's bill of costs should not be reviewed so far as it related to the disallowance of part of the brief fee and to counsel and clerk on the hearing of the petition on a party and party basis, and that a sum of £13 2s. should be allowed in respect of this item on that basis; and also to show cause why the petitioner's solicitors' fee for attending on the hearing of the petition should not be allowed at the sum of £8. The facts are stated in the judgment.

A   *Esyr Lewis* for the wife.

J. D. Haslam, solicitor, intervened on behalf of the Lord Chancellor.

Cur. adv. vult.

Dec. 20. **BAKER, J.**, read the following judgment: This was an application under R.S.C., Ord. 62, r. 35, in chambers for an order to review the taxation
B   by Mr. District Registrar CUNLIFFE at Chester of the wife's bill of costs, following
her undefended divorce suit in which she was legally aided with a nil contribution.
The husband was condemned in the costs to be taxed as between party and party,
and there was the usual further order that the wife's costs be taxed on a common
fund basis in accordance with the provisions of Sch. 3 to the Legal Aid and Advice
Act, 1949. I have been asked to give judgment in open court and I agreed. I
C   am concerned with only two items in the bill: (i) counsel's brief fee, and (ii) the
solicitor's fee for attending the trial.

1. *Counsel's brief fee.* The district registrar taxed two guineas off the item,
" Brief fee to counsel and clerk ", of £13 2s. in the party and party column of the
bill and transferred the two guineas to the common fund column of the bill.
(The " Conference fee and clerk " is, of course, a separate item of £2 7s., in the
D   party and party column and is not in dispute.) The result is that the two guineas
has to be paid by the legal aid fund and not by the husband. If, however, the
wife had made a substantial contribution in excess of the total of the party and
party bill, the two guineas would have had to be paid by her. Likewise, an
unassisted person would have to bear the two guineas, which would be
irrecoverable from the husband.

E   In answer to objections before the district registrar, that this sum is a proper
charge in the party and party costs, the district registrar has said that he has
already held that a decision of this court does not apply to a party and party bill,
and he states that he has set out his reasons in a considered judgment in previous
taxations in the Chester district registry, a copy of which has been supplied to me.
It reads:

" *Chester District Registry.*
Weedall v. *Weedall*	1965. D. No. 202.
Burkall v. *Burkall*	1966. D. No. 82.
Hughes v. *Hughes*	1966. D. No. 212.

" So far as concerns a legal aid taxation, I am clearly bound by the
decision of BAKER, J., in *Williams* v. *Williams* (1), a note of which decision,
authenticated by a learned judge, I have had an opportunity of reading.
The question which I now have to decide is first—is that decision binding
on me on a party and party taxation and if not are the reasons for the
decision so cogent that I should follow them on such a taxation?

" *Williams* v. *Williams* (1) was a party and party and a legal aid taxation
in an undefended divorce case. A fee on brief of twelve guineas was claimed
in the party and party bill and I had reduced it to ten guineas. BAKER, J.,
on appeal 'restored' the fee to twelve guineas but did not say whether or not
the ' restored ' fee was to be allowed against the other party. It has been
argued before me that in this context to ' restore ' necessarily means to
put back to the column from which the amount had been taxed. I agree that
such would be the usual meaning and ought to prevail, unless there is good
reason for saying that the learned judge must have been speaking of restoring
to the bill as opposed to any particular column thereof. I think that there
exist such good reasons.

" First, BAKER, J., decided the point on the provisions of the Legal Aid
and Advice Act, 1949, which give the assisted litigant a right of selection of
counsel but which of course have no bearing whatsoever on a party and party

(1) (1966), unreported.

taxation. Secondly, BAKER, J., said that the question which he had to decide was ' whether a counsel who goes from London to Chester should be allowed on taxation whether a legal aid, a party and party, or a common fund taxation, twelve guineas as opposed to *ten guineas which would be the normal fee for a member of the local Bar in Chester* '. He was clearly there thinking of what counsel should be allowed rather than what one party should recover from the other, although it is true that the learned judge said that the question was whether or not the fee should be allowed to counsel on a legal aid, a party and party or a common fund taxation. Thirdly, although by no means least forceful, *Williams* v. *Williams* (2) was an undefended case. The unsuccessful respondent was not represented before BAKER, J., and the latter's decision therefore, so far as it might be said to bear on the considerations necessary to take into account on a party and party taxation, lacks the cogency of a decision reached after a full argument.

" I think therefore that it is clear that BAKER, J.'s decision is to be regarded as limited to a legal aid taxation, the learned judge not having specifically directed, as was done in the Reading and Bournemouth cases to which the learned judge was referred, that the larger fee was to be allowed as against the other side as well as against the fund (the point did not arise in *Self* v. *Self* (3) to which I shall refer in one moment) which was purely a legal aid taxation).

" Ought I to apply BAKER, J.'s reasoning to a party and party taxation? With great respect to the learned judge I think not; completely different considerations arise. On such a taxation the question is not what is a proper fee for a particular counsel or for counsel from London, but what is a proper sum to allow for counsel as against the other side having regard to the facts of of the particular case, including of course the place of trial. I conceive that this means what was the case worth and not what was counsel himself worth. As I see it, this is and always has been the very essence of party and party taxations. One particular case can never on a party and party basis stand one brief fee if one counsel is employed and a different fee—either larger or smaller—if a different counsel is employed. One does not decide what counsel shall receive but whether his fee as charged shall be allowed against the other side and, if not, how much shall be so allowed.

" Again, with due respect to the learned judge, *Self* v. *Self* (3) which, as I say, was purely a legal aid taxation and on which BAKER, J., founded himself, was concerned with a place—Brighton—where there are three barristers according to the 1966 Law List. (I, for one, am amazed that anyone thought that the lower fee was proper in such a case.) I am concerned with a place which is one of the two chief cities of the circuit (indeed, the circuit is called ' the Wales & Chester Circuit ') and which has a thriving Bar, if not very large in numbers. No case concerning a place in anyway comparable with Chester has been quoted to me. Indeed, the only cases, other than *Self* v. *Self* (3), concerned Reading, where there is no local Bar at all, and Bournemouth, where there are two barristers according to the 1966 Law List and where again I am amazed to hear that the lower fee only had been allowed.

" If it is clear that a ' market rate ' exists for a particular type of work, then I think that it is equally clear that such market rate is the fee allowable as between party and party unless, by reason of the facts of any particular case, a larger—or a smaller—fee is justified.

" There are in Chester fourteen counsel (in three sets of chambers) who are on the panel for divorce work and in almost every case (and there are no less than 570 cases per annum) one of those counsel is briefed. Whilst I

(2) (1966), unreported.
(3) [1954] 2 All E.R. 550; [1954] P. 480.

A　　have, as a result of Baker, J.'s decision, to accept that the Legal Aid and Advice Act, 1949, gives the assisted person the right to choose from a panel of sixty-eight comprising the whole circuit and not out of the fourteen of those sixty-eight who practice in Chester, I have no hesitation in saying that, free from that decision, I consider, as do the great preponderance of litigants in Chester, that the choice of one counsel out of fourteen is ample for an

B　　undefended divorce cause.

"Baker, J., was impressed by the fact that fourteen out of sixty-eight is only one out of five, but I would point out that, although I am speaking without precise figures, the choice at say Liverpool is only about one out of three whilst at a large centre like Newcastle-upon-Tyne the choice is from something like one out of seven and nobody has ever suggested that ten guineas is not a proper fee to allow in either of those places on any taxation of an ordinary undefended divorce bill, whether on a party and party or on a legal aid basis where counsel not having chambers in the place of trial is briefed.

" The market rate for Chester is ten guineas, which is the fee paid in at least ninety-five per cent. of the cases whether legal aid or not, and I conceive that in the ordinary case such is the fee which it is proper to allow on a party and party basis. I cannot think that Parliament ever intended that the legal aid fund should have to pay higher fees than the market rate, and I would respectfully draw the attention of the Lord Chancellor to what seems to me to be an anomaly.

" As the result I tax two guineas off the brief fee in the party and party bill, but I allow that sum in the common fund bill."

That is signed and dated Feb. 9, 1967.

The question in *Williams* v. *Williams* (4) was whether a counsel who goes from London to Chester should be allowed twelve guineas as a brief fee rather than ten guineas, which would be the normal fee for a member of the local bar in Chester. Mr. District Registrar Cunliffe had taxed two guineas off the item in the party and party costs. This court restored it. If it was subsequently taken from the party and party column and made a charge against the legal aid fund only, that was done without authority. In *Young* v. *Young and Kohler* (5), two guineas had been taxed off the fee of counsel who appeared in an undefended divorce petition at Reading. Wallington, J., reinstated the sum of two guineas both in the bill of costs as between solicitor and client and in the party and party bill. Sachs, J., took the same course in *Eaves* v. *Eaves and Powell* (6) (the Bournemouth case). I agree that neither decision entirely covers the present circumstances, but I have had exhaustive enquiries made of the taxing officers in the principal probate registry. The extra two guineas for counsel coming from London to a provincial divorce town has never been disallowed as against the respondent but allowed on the legal aid bill. The practice is not, of course, conclusive. On a taxation on the party and party basis such costs are allowed

". . . as were necessary or proper for the attainment of justice or for enforcing or defending the rights of the party whose costs are being taxed "

(R.S.C., Ord. 62, r. 28 (2)). A common fund taxation is on a more generous basis, and " there shall be allowed a reasonable amount in respect of all costs reasonably incurred " (ibid., r. 28 (4)). There are to be no luxuries on the party and party taxation. The practical problem is therefore whether it is necessary or proper to select counsel from outside Chester. I was informed in *Williams* v. *Williams* (4) that there were fourteen counsel in Chester. I am told that there are now thirteen on the panel for divorce, of whom one is primarily a chancery practitioner and one

---

(4) (1966), unreported
(5) [1955] 1 All E.R. 796.
(6) [1955] 3 All E.R. 849; [1956] P. 154.

is semi-retired, but I see no reason to depart from what I said in *Williams* v. *Williams* (7). It is rarely possible when counsel is first instructed to be certain whether a suit will be defended or undefended, and it does not seem to me to be in any way a luxury or other than proper for solicitors to instruct a London counsel rather than a Chester counsel. Moreover it would be a strange result if the assisted person with a small or nil contribution is to be in a better position and able to have a wider choice than anyone else. I think that the proper approach is that submitted by counsel for the wife and in the end, if not accepted, at least not seriously challenged by Mr. Haslam, that there is no market rate of ten guineas for counsel in Chester. A litigant, whoever he be, is entitled to be served by the circuit Bar, the allowable brief fee being ten to twelve guineas, and it is immaterial whether the petitioner is an assisted person or not. Twelve guineas is chargeable in the party and party column and against the respondent, and I restore that sum in that column.

2. *The solicitor's fee.* The wife's solicitor's office is in Northwich. He travelled to Chester, leaving at 9.15 a.m. to allow for traffic and to have time available, as would be necessary, for the hearing, listed for 10.30 a.m. For this and attending the hearing he charged £8 in the party and party column and £1 5s. for locomotion. Five shillings has been taxed off the locomotion (this is not in dispute although I notice that the wife was allowed twenty-five shillings) and £3 was disallowed from the £8. This is a small matter in which I would not normally interfere, but it is represented that a client is entitled to have the solicitor of his or her choice, particularly when they are both in a place some distance from the divorce town, and that the allowance of £5 is almost derisory and would leave the solicitor out of pocket. There was an unfortunate disagreement about the time of hearing, but I think I am bound, and indeed counsel concedes that I must, accept the time on the court record, which is that the case was called at 10.52 a.m. and concluded at 11.1 a.m. R.S.C., Ord. 62, App. 2, item 33 (*b*) (2) lays down a scale of £3 to £15 for solicitors attending court for the purpose of trial or hearing. The note to item 33 permits travelling and out of pocket expenses, unless the court is situated in the town in which the solicitor practices. It follows that consideration must also be given to the time which is occupied in travelling as well as at the hearing, and this will be reflected in the amount allowed within the scale. This solicitor was away from his office for at least three hours. It is in the public interest that a petitioner, on what may well be the most important day of his or her life, should have present at court the solicitor who has been consulted and it is equally important that the solicitor should be reasonably remunerated. I agree with the submissions made to me that £5 is not reasonable remuneration in the circumstances and I restore the sum of £8 in the party and party column.

Order accordingly.

Solicitors: *Moss & Haselhurst*, Northwich (for the wife); *J. D. Haslam* (for the Lord Chancellor).

[*Reported by* ALICE BLOOMFIELD, *Barrister-at-Law.*]

---

(7) (1966), unreported.

QUISTCLOSE INVESTMENTS, LTD. *v.* ROLLS RAZOR, LTD.
(in voluntary liquidation) AND OTHERS.

[COURT OF APPEAL, CIVIL DIVISION (Harman, Russell and Sachs, L.JJ.), November 20, 21, 22, 23, 24, 27, 28, December 15, 1967.]

Affirmed. H.L. [1968] 3 All E.R. 651.

Bank—Account—Separate account—Trust—Money lent to company for specific purpose, viz., to pay a declared dividend—Loan applicable only for such purpose and to be repaid if not so applied—Bank's knowledge of condition of loan—Money paid into separate account—Voluntary winding-up supervening before dividend paid—Company indebted to bank in sum exceeding loan—Bank setting off amount credited to separate account against company's indebtedness to bank—Lender seeking to recover money lent as being money subject to a trust for repayment—Whether trust created and co-existed with contractual obligation of company under the loan.

R., Ltd., which had in a previous year made large profits, contemplated paying a dividend* amounting to some £200,000. Subsequently there had been a catastrophic change in fortunes and in June and July, 1964, R., Ltd. had a large overdraft with the defendant bank and no liquid assets out of which to pay the dividend, which would have been payable on July 24. The plaintiff company agreed to lend £209,719 8s. 6d. to R., Ltd. subject to two conditions, one of which was that the loan was to be used to pay the forthcoming dividend. R., Ltd. accepted this condition†. In the event of the condition not being fulfilled by July 24, the money was to be repaid to the plaintiff company. Following a meeting between a director of R., Ltd. and a representative of the defendant bank, the plaintiff company's cheque for the amount was sent on July 15, 1964, to the defendant bank with a letter from the director, saying " we would like to confirm the agreement reached with you this morning that this amount will only be used to meet the dividend due on July 24, 1964 ". A separate account, No. 4 ordinary dividend share account, was opened in R., Ltd.'s name by the defendant bank and the proceeds of the cheque were paid into it. At all material times the indebtedness of R., Ltd. to the defendant bank exceeded the sum credited to the No. 4 account. A copy of a letter of the plaintiff company to R., Ltd., dated July 15, 1964, stating the conditions of the loan, was sent to the defendant bank, but was not proved to have been received by the defendant bank until after the money was accepted for the No. 4 account. The dividend had not been paid by the time when R., Ltd. went into voluntary liquidation‡.

Held: the plaintiff company was entitled to repayment of the £209,719 8s. 6d. under a trust in its favour for the following reasons—

(i) (a) the fact that the money was lent did not necessarily negative the existence of a trust, binding R., Ltd., for repayment of the money when the purpose for which it was lent could no longer be fulfilled, as a trust and a loan could co-exist (see p. 620, letter D, p. 622, letters D and E, p. 629, letter D, and p. 630, letter G, post).

(b) in the present case, the money being lent for a specific purpose, a trust had arisen that the money lent should be applied only in payment of the dividend and also for repayment of the money lent if it were not so used, and the non-fulfilment of the primary purpose of the loan did not free the money from the trust for repayment; accordingly the money in No. 4 account had not belonged beneficially to R., Ltd. and had not vested in the

---

* This was a final dividend of 120 per cent. approved at an annual general meeting on July 2, 1964.

† See p. 617, letter I, post, the resolution of July 20, 1964.

‡ The winding-up began on Aug. 27, 1964, but the board of R., Ltd. resolved on a voluntary winding-up on July 17, and to issue an immediate notice to the press.

liquidator of R., Ltd. (see p. 620, letter H, p. 624, letter F, and p. 628,   A
letters C and H, post).

Toovey v. Milne ((1819), 2 B. & Ald. 683), Edwards v. Glyn ((1859), 2 E. &
E. 29) and Re Rogers, Ex p. Holland ((1891), 8 Morr. 243) followed.

(ii) on the facts the defendant bank had knowledge that the terms of the
loan amounted to a condition, and thus had notice of the trust, by which
accordingly the defendant bank was bound (see p. 621, letter D, p. 626, letters   B
B and C, and p. 630, letters F and G, post).

Per HARMAN, L.J.: the plaintiff company could not rely, for the purpose
of establishing the defendant bank's knowledge, on the copy letter from the
plaintiff company to R., Ltd., as the copy was not shown to have been
received by the defendant bank until after the money was accepted for   C
No. 4 account (see p. 621, letter A, post).

Decision of PLOWMAN, J. ([1967] 1 All E.R. 864) reversed.

[As to a bank being bound by notice of a trust, see 2 HALSBURY's LAWS
(3rd Edn.) 168, 169, para. 314; and for cases on trust accounts with banks,
see 3 DIGEST (Repl.) 195-201, 385-413.

As to a banker's lien or set-off, see 2 HALSBURY's LAWS (3rd Edn.) 213, para.   D
395. As to property in possession of a bankrupt for a specific purpose, see
ibid., p. 437, para. 862; and for cases on this subject, see 5 DIGEST (Repl.)
756-762, 6493-6533.

As to a resulting trust on the failure of the purpose of a gift ostensibly beneficial,
see 38 HALSBURY's LAWS (3rd Edn.) 865, para. 1459.]

Cases referred to:

A   **Appeal.**

The plaintiff company appealed against an order of Plowman, J., made on Feb. 17, 1967, and reported at [1967] 1 All E.R. 864, dismissing the plaintiff company's action.   The grounds of appeal were as follows: (i) that the judge was right in assuming and ought to have held that the first defendant company, Rolls Razor, Ltd. (in liquidation), received the sum of £209,719 8s. 6d. lent to

B   it by the plaintiff company, subject to a fiduciary obligation or trust to pay the final dividend declared by the first defendant company on July 2, 1964; (ii) that the judge was wrong in holding that, the purpose for which that sum was paid having failed, there was no obligation on the first defendant company other than the ordinary contractual obligation of a borrower to repay his lender; (iii) that the judge was wrong in holding that the purpose of the loan having

C   failed, there was not an equitable obligation on the first defendant company to hold the sum in trust for the plaintiff company in addition to the contractual obligation to repay the sum; (iv) that the judge was wrong in holding that where there was a primary trust which failed, there did not automatically arise a resulting trust for the person providing the trust moneys and that the doctrine of resulting trust was founded on the unexpressed but presumed inten-

D   tion of the settlor; (v) that at the time when the defendant bank, Barclays Bank, Ltd., received the sum of £209,719 8s. 6d., the defendant bank had express notice that that sum had been provided by a third party for the express purpose of paying the first defendant company's dividend, and accordingly the defendant bank had been at all material times, and was, bound in equity to account for the sum as constructive trustee for the plaintiff company.

E   The first defendant company served a cross-notice that it intended on the hearing of the appeal to contend that the order of Plowman, J., should be affirmed on the following grounds additional to the grounds relied on by the court below: (i) that there was no evidence on which the judge was entitled or required to found the assumption that the first defendant company received the sum of £209,719 8s. 6d. subject to a fiduciary obligation or trust to pay the

F   final dividend; alternatively that such an assumption was unnecessary or alternatively was erroneous, and that accordingly no question of a resulting trust could arise; and (ii) alternatively, in the premises and on the evidence before the judge no resulting trust arose, and or alternatively no equitable obliga- tion was imposed on the first defendant company in relation to the sum.   The defendant bank served a cross-notice that it intended to contend that the order

G   of Plowman, J., should be affirmed on the following grounds additional to those relied on in the court below: (i) the additional grounds contained in the notice served by the first defendant company; (ii) that there was no evidence before the judge on which he could have found that, at the time when the defendant bank received the sum of £209,719 8s. 6d. the defendant bank had notice that the sum was impressed with such a trust as was relied on in the notice of appeal

H   or any trust, and (iii) that in the absence of such notice the defendant bank was not accountable to the plaintiff company as alleged in the notice of appeal or at all.   The third defendant company, Investors Inter-Continental Fund, Ltd., a company whose address was in Canada, was added by amendment of the writ on Mar. 16, 1965.

Arthur Bagnall, Q.C., and *M. D. Sherrard* for the plaintiff company.
Muir Hunter, Q.C., and *David Graham* for the first defendant company.
J. L. Arnold, Q.C., and *Allan Heyman* for the defendant bank.
The third defendant company was not represented.

Cur. adv. vult.

Dec. 15.   The following judgments were read.

HARMAN, L.J.: This appeal arises out of a loan of a sum of over £200,000 made by the plaintiff (appellant) company to the first defendant company (Rolls Razor, Ltd.) to enable that company to pay a dividend declared in June,

1964, and intended to be paid on July 24 following. The money was deposited   A
with the defendant bank and accepted on the footing that it should only be used
for payment of the dividend. That purpose was, however, frustrated by the
liquidation of the first defendant company on the following Aug. 27 before
the dividend had been paid, thus making its payment illegal. It is the bank's
claim in this case, and it succeeded in the court below (1), that this event released
it from its promise not to allow the money to be used for any purpose but   B
payment of the dividend, and entitled the bank to retain the money by way of
set-off against the first defendant company's indebtedness to itself.

If this be right it is a surprising result. The last thing contemplated by either
the plaintiff company or the first defendant company when the loan was made
was that the money should pass into the hands of the defendant bank, and the
latter has in effect acquired a windfall which it can never have expected. It is,   C
however, I think, to be taken that, if this money was at the relevant time the
beneficial property of the first defendant company, the bank is justified, having
regard to the decision of this court in *Rolls Razor, Ltd.* v. *Cox* (2); but it is otherwise if the money was not at that time the beneficial property of the first defendant company, but was to the knowledge of the defendant bank money impressed
with a trust; for it is trite law that only that part of the property of the bankrupt   D
passes to his assignee in which he has both the legal and the beneficial interest
at the time of the bankruptcy. See PARKE, B.'s observation in *Mogg* v. *Baker* (3).

The facts of the case are as follows. In the spring of 1964 the first defendant
company was in queer street. It had achieved a very large trading profit in
the year 1963 and was contemplating the payment for that period of a dividend
amounting with an interim already paid of two hundred per cent.; but it had   E
no liquid assets out of which to pay the dividend. Since the beginning of 1964
there had been a catastrophic change in the fortunes of the first defendant
company. Its business, chiefly in washing machines on hire-purchase, had lost
the favour of the market and it was being outsold by competitors. By June 4,
1964, it appears from a letter sent by the defendant bank to the first defendant
company that its overdraft was £484,000, against a limit of £250,000, and one at   F
least of its subsidiaries, Bylock Electric, Ltd., was in as parlous a state. The
defendant bank threatened to refuse to continue business unless there was an
amendment by the end of the month, or to increase the overdraft. This meant
that the defendant bank would not agree to the payment of the dividend which
the directors had recommended at a meeting on the previous May 14. This
had already been intimated to Mr. Bloom, the chairman, on the previous day.   G

At a general meeting of the first defendant company held on July 2 the recommended dividend was approved and it was to be payable on July 24; but at a
board meeting on the next day, July 3, Mr. Bloom told the board that a permanent
advance of £1½ million was required to make the company financially secure
and that he had so far failed to make arrangements to underwrite an issue of
such a size. Liquidation was at that meeting suggested as a possibility. Mr.   H
Bloom was at this time in negotiation with a well-known financier, and it appears
from a memorandum of the defendant bank dated July 9 that the suggestion
then was that Mr. X should provide £1 million on certain conditions, one of
which was that Mr. Bloom would put in £200,000 and " find the money " for the
proposed dividend.

Mr. Bloom did succeed in finding this money in the shape of a loan from the
plaintiff company which it seems itself borrowed the sum; the source is immaterial. On July 15 there was a board meeting of the plaintiff company at which
it resolved that a loan of £209,719 8s. 6d. (the net amount required to pay the
dividend) should be lent to the first defendant company " for the purpose of
that company paying the final dividend due on July 24 next ", and to draw a

---

(1) [1967] 1 All E.R. 864; [1967] Ch. 910.
(2) [1967] 1 All E.R. 397; [1967] 1 Q.B. 552.
(3) (1838), 3 M. & W. 195 at p. 197.

A   cheque for that sum payable to the first defendant company, and send it to the defendant bank with a covering letter to both confirming that the loan be made on the following conditions: (i) that it be used to pay the forthcoming dividend; (ii) that this dividend should be paid subject to the further finance required by the first defendant company being forthcoming. The resolution added that the letter should further state that in the event of the conditions not being fulfilled
B   by July 24 (the day when the dividend was due to be paid), then the money was to be repaid to the plaintiff company.

On the same day a cheque was drawn in favour of the first defendant company, which sent it to the defendant bank with a covering letter. This followed a meeting between Mr. Goldbart, a director of the first defendant company, and a representative of the defendant bank. The letter, dated July 15, 1964, is
C   headed " Rolls Razor, Ltd.", and is addressed to " G. H. Parker, Esq., Barclays Bank, Ltd., City office ". It reads:

" Dear Mr. Parker,
" Confirming our telephone conversation of today's date, will you please open a No. 4 ordinary dividend share account. I enclose herewith a cheque valued £209,719 8s. 6d. being the total amount of dividend due on July 24,
D   1964. Will you please credit this to the above mentioned account. We would like to confirm the agreement reached with you this morning that this amount will only be used to meet the dividend due on June 24, 1964.
Yours sincerely,
L. Goldbart, director."

Another letter was sent bearing the same date [July 15, 1964] by the plaintiff
E   company to the first defendant company, and a copy to the defendant bank, but it does not appear that this latter letter reached either party until two days later. This letter is addressed to " The Secretary, Rolls Razor, Ltd." It is in these terms:

" Dear Sir,
F   " We are today forwarding a cheque for £209,719 8s. 6d. to Barclays Bank Ltd., City office, for the credit of a special dividend account No. 5 (*sic*).
" This loan is being made to [the first defendant company] on the following conditions:
" (i) That it is used to pay the forthcoming dividend due on July 24 next.
" (ii) That this dividend will be paid subject to the further finance required by [the first defendant company] being forthcoming by that time.
" In the event of these conditions not being fulfilled on or before July 24 the amount of £209,719 8s. 6d. is immediately returnable to us.
Yours faithfully,
M. G. Cass, director."

The second condition there made and the last stipulation were not agreed by the first defendant company as appears by a minute on July 17. At the same meeting the first defendant company's board resolved that the company should petition for winding up. It appears from the minutes of a meeting of the board on July 20 that the board agreed that the money on deposit was paid on these terms. The minute reads:

" . . . in particular with regard to the statement that condition (2) and the last paragraph of the letter dated July 15, 1964, from Quistclose Investments Ltd. had not been agreed by the board. There was considerable discussion as to the basis upon which the sum of £209,719 8s. 6d. had been made available.
" Mr. Wright stated that the board at its meeting on Friday was clear that the sum was to be used only for the purpose of paying the dividend but was not clear as to the other terms and had, therefore, reserved the matter in the minutes.

A "It was, however, accepted by the board that this payment to the company was made as part of a continuing negotiation with no intention that the company should retain the moneys if the relevant conditions were not satisfied and the negotiations did not fructify."

A special No. 4 dividend account had already been opened on July 8 and the cheque was specially cleared and the proceeds lodged in this account. On July 20 the defendant bank informed the board that it was exercising its statutory right to combine all the company's accounts "except for the time being the No. 4 ordinary dividend share account". The reason for this no doubt was that the defendant bank recognised its obligation to retain the money until the first defendant company went into liquidation, and it appears from a bank memorandum on July 24 that the defendant bank anticipated that its right to amalgamate the No. 4 account would arise on liquidation. On Aug. 5 the plaintiff company's solicitors wrote to the first defendant company demanding repayment of the money, but this was never done.

The first defendant company went into liquidation on Aug. 27 and the defendant bank next day, in exercise of its claim, set off the sum on the No. 4 dividend account against other indebtedness of the first defendant company. The writ was issued on Oct. 1 following, claiming a declaration that the plaintiff company was the absolute beneficial owner of the sum standing to the credit of the No. 4 account and that the defendants were trustees either express or constructive of that sum.

The statement of claim set out the facts and by para. 6 stated as follows:

"The terms and conditions on which the said sum was paid and credited as aforesaid were:—(i) that the said sum should be used to pay the said final dividend; (ii) that the said final dividend would be paid subject to the further finance required by the [first defendant company] being forthcoming by July 24, 1964; (iii) that in the event of these conditions not being fulfilled on or before July 24, 1964, the said sum would be immediately returnable to the [plaintiff company]."

The statement of claim further alleged that the defendant bank knew of these conditions and that accordingly both the bank and the liquidator were aware that the money was trust money held on trust for the plaintiff company. The liquidator's defence was that the only term on which the loan was made was that it should be repayable when the first defendant company could afford it and that the terms and conditions set forth in the statement of claim were not applicable. The defendant bank did not admit that any terms were attached to the loan or that the money or any part of it was trust money or that the bank had notice; and these are the issues in the action.

It seems to me tolerably clear, having regard to the statement in the minute of the meeting of July 20 which I have read, that the first defendant company not having used the money for the purpose of paying the dividend for which purpose alone it was lent, could not properly use it for any other purpose than to repay the loan. The judge below acknowledged this (4), saying that the money was subject to a trust in the hands of the first defendant company; but he went on to say that, when that purpose failed by reason of the liquidation, no further trust arose and that the relationship between the plaintiff company and the first defendant company became merely one of debtor and creditor. If this be right the defendant bank will succeed. The first defendant company being hopelessly insolvent, it will make no difference to the shareholders whether this money is applied by the defendant bank against an overdraft due to it or whether it be assets available for the general creditors.

That a loan of money on a specific condition does create a trust attaching to the money in the hands of the borrower, and that this trust subsists in favour of the

(4) [1967] 1 All E.R. at p. 869; [1967] Ch. at p. 931.

A lender if the condition fails seems to me to be settled by authority binding on this court contained in a series of bankruptcy cases. This is a branch of the law of trusts created by the common lawyers, but it is after all none the worse for that. The first case is that of *Toovey* v. *Milne* (5) which I will read:

B ". . . At the trial Abbott, C.J., at the sittings after last Easter Term, at Westminster, it appeared that the circumstances of the case were these. The act of bankruptcy was a lying in prison two months. During the continuance of the imprisonment, the bankrupt being desirous of settling with his creditors, sent his wife to borrow of the defendant, his brother-in-law, £120 for that purpose. The money was accordingly lent, but the purpose failing, £95 was afterwards repaid to the defendant by the bankrupt, who still remained in prison. It did not appear that the individual notes

C composing the £95 were any part of the notes originally advanced by the defendant, nor was there at the time of the advance any express stipulation, that if the object was not attained the money should be restored. Abbott, C.J., thought that this was money advanced for a special purpose, and that it did not pass to the assignee, and that therefore the repayment was protected, and nonsuited the plaintiff. And now

D " *Gurney* moved for a new trial. If these had been the identical notes which had been before advanced by the defendant, or if at the time of the advance there had been any express stipulation to restore the money, in case the object should not be attained, the case might have been different. But neither of these circumstances exist here. Then this is the ordinary case of money in the bankrupt's hands lent to him by the defendant, which is the

E property of his assignee, and consequently the repayment to the defendant cannot be protected. The defendant must claim like the other creditors, and receive his proportionate dividend.

"Abbott, C.J.: I thought at the trial, and still think, that the fair inference from the facts proved was that this money was advanced for a special purpose, and that, being clothed with a specific trust, no property in it

F passed to the assignee of the bankrupt. Then the purpose having failed, there is an implied stipulation, that the money shall be repaid. That has been done in the present case; and I am of opinion that the repayment was lawful, and that the nonsuit was right."

There is a difference between that case and this in that the lent money had been

G repaid to the lender before the assignee made his claim; but that seems to me to be no distinction, for when the purpose of paying the creditors failed, the trust was held not to fail but to continue in favour of the lender and that is why the assignee's claim did not succeed. The money, it was held, was never the beneficial property of the bankrupt.

There is one other case which seems parallel, viz., *Edwards* v. *Glyn* (6). There

H also the money had been returned to the lender and two of the judges decided the case on the footing that *Toovey* v. *Milne* (5) applied, and that the purpose having failed the repayment was protected against the assignee by the trust which brought it about, that the property in the money had never passed to the bankrupt but remained clothed throughout with the specific trust. Lord Campbell, C.J., a third of the judges, did not dissent from this view, though his decision and that of the two remaining members of the court was on another ground, viz., that there had been no fraudulent preference of the lenders. This latter was, of course, on an inconsistent footing, viz., that the money lent was the beneficial property of the debtor.

There are other cases in which *Toovey* v. *Milne* (7) is approved, but in them the money had been paid to creditors before the primary purpose failed, and

---

(5) (1819), 2 B. & Ald. 683, 684.
(6) (1859), 2 E. & E. 29.
(7) (1819), 2 B. & Ald. 683.

they are thus distinguishable. See *Re Rogers, Ex p. Holland and Hannen* (8), A
Re Drucker (No. 1), Ex p. Basden (9) and *Re Hooley, Ex p. The Trustee* (10).
Re Rogers (8) was a decision of the Court of Appeal which approved *Toovey* v.
Milne (11) and *Edwards* v. *Glyn* (12). I must explain that a man named Mozley
lent the money for the special purpose of paying pressing creditors. LINDLEY,
L.J., said (13):

> " The trustee is endeavouring to affirm the transaction in part and to B
> repudiate it in part. He wants to claim the money as the bankrupt's
> because it came to his hands and at the same time to reject the terms and
> conditions on which alone the bankrupt procured it. This is manifestly
> unjust and contrary to principle. If authority be wanted in support of this
> view, it will be found in *Toovey* v. *Milne* (11) and *Edwards* v. *Glyn* (12) and
> other cases of the same class. I entertain no doubt that Mozley [i.e., the C
> lender] could have obtained an injunction to restrain the bankrupt from
> using that money for any purpose except that of paying his pressing creditors.
> If this be so, the money never was the bankrupt's in any proper sense so as
> to vest in his trustee as part of his general assets."

I do not see why this needs to be called a resulting trust: the bankruptcy cases
never so suggest. It is a trust always attaching to the money involved in the D
conditions of the loan. I reject the notion that such a trust can only be implied
on a gift. If it is true that, if the money had been used to pay the dividend, the
obligation to repay would survive and it did exist throughout whether the
dividend were paid or no; I do not see why loan and trust cannot co-exist.
The observation of LINDLEY, L.J., in *Rogers'* case (8) shows that he thought
that a trust existed, and BOWEN, L.J., was of the same opinion. The judge felt E
no difficulty in assuming that the primary obligation (to pay the dividend)
co-existed with the loan, but he declined to go further, on the footing, I think,
that this was to make an implication which was not a *necessary* one because the
contractual obligation to repay was enough. I cannot accept this: the second
trust did not arise on failure of the first: it was present throughout.

The first argument for the defendant bank was that in a case of loan that F
relationship subsisted throughout and that there was a mere contract to use the
money to pay the dividend, which, being frustrated by the liquidation, disappeared, leaving the debtor and creditor position intact. This is the argument
which failed in *Toovey* v. *Milne* (11). A loan it was said involves the result that
the borrower becomes the owner of the borrowed money which it was throughout,
with the result that this sum was a part of the borrower's assets and could be G
set off by the defendant bank against other debts. The judge did not altogether
accept this, but assumed that the promise to use the money only for dividend
purposes did impose a trust, but he declined to imply a further trust for the
lender, holding that the obligation to repay was already present in the loan
transaction and that to imply a trust in addition was unjustified. For myself I
do not see why, if a primary trust to pay the dividend was created, the further H
trust to repay the lender had not always been present, and I cannot see why the
failure of the first trust should destroy the second. However that may be, I
think that we are bound so to hold by the cases I have mentioned.

The defendant bank stands, however, in the position of an assignee for value,
the consideration being the promise to repay: it is therefore not bound by the
trust unless it had notice of it, and that is the remaining question. The defendant
bank admits knowledge of the *purpose* for which the loan was made, but denies
knowledge that this amounted to a *condition* of the loan. What did the defendant

(8) (1891), 8 Morr. 243.
(9) [1902] 2 K.B. 237.
(10) (1915), 84 L.J.K.B. 1415.
(11) (1819), 2 B. & Ald. 683.
(12) (1859), 2 E. & E. 29.
(13) (1891), 8 Morr. at p. 248.

A bank know at the time it accepted the money? For this purpose the plaintiff
company cannot rely on the letter from the plaintiff company to the first defendant company on July 15, which would have put the issue beyond question.
The defendant bank did receive a copy of that letter, but it was never proved that
the receipt was not some days later than the acceptance of the money.

B   The defendant bank, however, did receive with the cheque the covering letter
from Mr. Goldbart, a director of the first defendant company, dated July 15,
which refers to a conversation earlier that day dealing with the opening of a
special dividend account to which the proceeds were to be credited; and that
letter ends with these words:

> " We would like to confirm the agreement reached with you this morning
> that this amount will only be used to meet the dividend due on July 24,
> 1964."

The defendant bank did not answer this letter, but acted on it by clearing the
cheque and crediting the proceeds to the special account. It accepted the money
on the agreed condition that it was *only* to be used for the one purpose. The
defendant bank knew that this was borrowed money (see the answer to
D interrogatory 3 and the bank memorandum of July 9) and the cheque itself
showed the borrower's identity. What then does " only " mean? Clearly
" and for no other purpose ". This implies to my mind that if the dividend be
not paid it must go back to the lender and that, subject to the performance of
the only purpose agreed, it remained the lender's money. I would hold accordingly that the bank accepted the money with knowledge of the facts which made
E it trust money, not the free assets of the first defendant company, and that it
cannot therefore retain it against the plaintiff company's claim. In my judgment,
therefore, the appeal should be allowed.

   RUSSELL, L.J.: The facts of this case so far as not set out in this judgment
are to be found in the report of the case below (14). There are here three
F questions for solution. First: whether the arrangement between the plaintiff
company and the first defendant company was such as to impose on the first
defendant company the character of trustee in respect of the money advanced
by the plaintiff company to the first defendant company. Second: if so, whether
that arrangement was such that the character of trustee would be shed by the
first defendant company on its becoming impossible that the dividend should
be paid, the money being in that event free assets of the first defendant company
and the first defendant company being merely a debtor to the plaintiff company
for an equivalent amount. Third: if the arrangement between the plaintiff
company and the first defendant company was such that such character was
imposed and would not in the stated event be shed, whether the defendant bank
should be held to have been aware, when it received the money from the first
G defendant company on the special account, of those elements of the arrangement
between the plaintiff company and the first defendant company which in law
imposed and would continue the trusteeship, so as to fix the defendant bank
in law with notice of a trust, which would prohibit set-off by the defendant bank
of the credit of the special account against the overdraft of the first defendant
company on its other account.   PLOWMAN, J. (14), was prepared to assume
the first point in favour of the plaintiff company; held the second point against
the plaintiff company; and did not deal with the third point.
   On the first question: the arrangement between the plaintiff company and
H the first defendant company may, I consider, be summarised thus. The money
was advanced by the plaintiff company to the first defendant company on the
condition that the first defendant company should make no use of it other than
in payment of the dividend that had been recently declared. This appears from
the letter dated July 15, from the plaintiff company to the first defendant

---

(14) [1967] 1 All E.R. 864; [1967] Ch. 910.

company saying: "This loan is being made to [the first defendant company]
on the following conditions: (i) That it is used to pay the forthcoming dividend
. . ."; from the letter dated July 17, from the first defendant company to the
plaintiff company confirming that that condition was in accordance with what
had been arranged; from the first defendant company board minutes of July 20
where it was stated to be clear that the sum was to be used only for the purpose
of paying the dividend. And to these could be added, if it were necessary,
the last paragraph of the letter dated July 15, from the first defendant company
to the defendant bank which was sent unsealed to the plaintiff company so
that the plaintiff company could put the plaintiff company cheque in favour
of the first defendant company in the envelope with that letter, and, of course,
was intended to read that letter. That said:

> " We would like to confirm the agreement reached with you this morning
> that this amount will only be used to meet the dividend due on July 24,
> 1964."

Does this impose on the first defendant company the character of trustee of
the money? I do not see why it does not. The arrangement says quite plainly
that the first defendant company is not at liberty to treat the money advanced
as the beneficial property of the first defendant company except for the limited
activity of paying a particular class of its creditors, viz., the shareholders entitled
to the declared dividend. It is argued that the fact that the money was lent
displaces the notion of a trust imposed on the borrower affecting the money.
I do not see why the two conceptions are inconsistent one with the other, the
relationship of creditor and debtor being, of course, necessary if and when the
first defendant company should in fact use the money in the only manner permitted, by paying the dividend. Moreover, there appears to be ample recognition
in the authorities, including those of this court, for the existence of a trusteeship
in a debtor in respect of the money lent. These cases I refer to in connexion
with the second question. Accordingly, in my judgment, PLOWMAN, J. made
a correct assumption on the first question.

Granted that the arrangement referred to above imposed on the first defendant
company the character of a trustee of the money advanced, the trust that was
reposed in the first defendant company was that the first defendant company
would not use the money for any purpose of the first defendant company other
than the payment of the dividend. How then can it be said that, on that one
purpose ceasing to be feasible, the first defendant company shed its character
of trustee in relation to the money and became vis-à-vis the plaintiff company
at liberty to treat the money as beneficially property of the first defendant
company? The arrangement remains that the first defendant company was
not entitled to do this.   PLOWMAN, J. noted (15), that, since in those circumstances the contractual obligation to repay a loan remained, there was no need
to find a trust. With respect, I think this very case demonstrates the need.
He further found no authority for finding more than a contractual obligation
to repay. I am not sure that authority is required; rather I enquire where is the
authority by which in circumstances such as this, money being lent on condition
that no use of it as the borrower's beneficial property save one was open to the
borrower, the borrower can assert that the money lent ever becomes beneficially
the property of the borrower for any other purpose? But I think there is
authority to show the continuing trusteeship of the borrower, the sole permissible
use by the borrower of the money having ceased to be feasible, a trusteeship
necessarily for the lender.

Toovey v. *Milne* (16) concerned the repayment by the bankrupt, during the
period covered by the relation back of the title to the assignee in bankruptcy,
of an amount *lent* for the specific purpose of his settling with his creditors;

---

(15) [1967] 1 All E.R. at p. 869; [1967] Ch. at p. 931.
(16) (1819), 2 B. & Ald. 683.

the whole basis of the decision that the amount paid back could not be claimed from the repaid lender by the assignee was that it was never, either originally or after the settling with the creditors was no longer possible, beneficially the property of the bankrupt. It was remarked in argument that ABBOTT, C.J., in terms based his decision on an " implied stipulation to repay " on failure of the purpose. By this, however, he cannot have meant a mere contract to repay; that already existed by virtue of the fact of a loan; and, if the repayment was merely fulfilment of a contractual obligation to repay, out of the bankrupt's beneficially owned assets, an equivalent amount, the decision must have been the other way.   Rather do I think that ABBOTT, C.J., was using this formula to indicate that the arrangement forbade the use by the bankrupt of the money lent for any purpose other than that of settling with creditors, and *therefore* the money was not beneficially the property of the bankrupt to be caught by the relation back of the assignee's title.

The other case in bankruptcy concerned with a repayment to a lender—as distinct from a user by the bankrupt of money lent pursuant to the purpose for which the loan was made—is *Edwards* v. *Glyn* (17).   The decision in favour of the lending bank, which had been repaid by the bankrupt, was based on two alternative grounds. One was that, assuming the money repaid to be the beneficial property of the bankrupt, there was no fraudulent preference, because of pressure. The other was that, on the basis of *Toovey's* case (18), the money lent was at no time the beneficial property of the bankrupt. It will be observed that the two grounds are inconsistent, for fraudulent preference cannot be relevant for discussion unless the payment is assumed to have been made out of assets belonging beneficially to the bankrupt. Nevertheless the situation was that three of the four judges clearly accepted the trust principle in the *Toovey* case (18) as correct. ERLE, J., considered it to be a specific advance for a specific purpose on the understanding that the money if not used for that purpose should be returned; that there had been a promise that it would be used only for that purpose; and that the case was entirely within the principle of the *Toovey* case (18). CROMPTON, J., remarked that the *Toovey* case (18) laid down a very useful and proper rule of law; that the advance was made for a specific purpose only, and on the understanding that it should be used only for that purpose; the advance being clothed with a specific trust, the bankrupt had not an equitable right to use the money for any other purpose; and the assignee could only take property in which the bankrupt had an equitable right. LORD CAMPBELL, C.J., whose judgment had rested on the point of fraudulent preference only, because the understanding was not with the bank but with guarantors, added that he by no means differed from the others as to the legal, effect on the rights of the assignee, of an advance made to the bankrupt for a specific purpose and clothed with a specific trust.

In this court in 1891 we have the case of *Re Rogers, Ex p. Holland and Hannen* (19), which was a case of a claim by the trustee in bankruptcy against a creditor who had been paid by the bankrupt with money borrowed by him for that purpose on security. In reserved judgments this court rejected the claim. LINDLEY, L.J., after arriving at a conclusion on the facts, referred to the *Toovey* case (18) and *Edwards* v. *Glyn* (17) as authority for the proposition that on the facts the money

" never was the bankrupt's in any proper sense so as to vest in his trustee as part of his general assets."

BOWEN, L.J., considered that the money came to the bankrupt's hands impressed with a trust, and until paid over (i.e., to the defendant creditor) remained impressed with that trust; and that it did not become the property of the bankrupt

---

(17) (1859), 2 E. & E. 29.
(18) (1819), 2 B. & Ald. 683.
(19) (1891), 8 Morr. 243.

divisible among his creditors. He made no specific reference to *Toovey* v. *Milne* A
(20) or *Edwards* v. *Glyn* (21), but his phrase " until paid over " is entirely consistent with the view that a trust remained if circumstances prevented the
payment over.

KAY, L.J., in finding a trust for the special purpose and none other, considered
that this brought the case within the decision in *Toovey's* case (20) which (he
said) was adopted and followed in *Edwards* v. *Glyn* (21) on the trust point. In B
Re Rogers, Ex p. Holland and Hannen (22), therefore, this court approved
Toovey's case (20) and *Edwards* v. *Glyn* (21), and it never occurred to anyone that
there could be any distinction—in point of trust or beneficial ownership—between
a case in which the special and sole purpose of the advance was carried out and
one in which there was repayment because the special and sole purpose could
not be carried out. In *Re Drucker* (*No. 1*), *Ex p. Basden* (23) in 1902 this court C
followed *Re Rogers* (22); it was again a case where the money lent on security
to the bankrupt had been applied in the manner intended. ROMER, L.J., said (24),
that there

". . . never was a moment of time at which this money could have been
used for any other purpose than that of paying . . ."

D

the creditor in question. The principle of these two cases was again applied by
this court in *Re Watson, Ex p. Schipper* (25). PLOWMAN, J., described (26)
the first four of those cases as being cases of fraudulent preference; but fraudulent
preference only arose for discussion in *Edwards* v. *Glyn* (21). He also pointed
out (27) that in none of them was the money lent still in the hands of the bankrupt; but that which kept the money out of the grasp of the title of the trustee E
in bankruptcy by relation back, the lack of beneficial interest in the bankrupt,
must equally protect it from that grasp if it is still in the hands of the bankrupt
at adjudication, and indeed must allow the lender to claim it back from the
trustee if necessary.

Accordingly, on the second of the three questions stated above I am of the
opinion that the payment of the dividend, the sole use of the borrowed money
permitted by the arrangement, having ceased to be feasible, this event did not F
permit the first defendant company to treat the money lent as its free property
or confer on the first defendant company the beneficial entitlement to the money
or change the character of the first defendant company from trustee of that
money to mere debtor of an equivalent sum. Nor am I at all persuaded to the
contrary by the decision of SIR WILLIAM PAGE WOOD, V.C., in *Moseley* v. *Cressey's*
Co. (28). G

The third question is whether the proper conclusion on the facts of the case is
that, when the defendant bank collected the money lent and credited it to the
first defendant company dividend account, the defendant bank was aware of
those elements of the arrangement between the first defendant company and the
plaintiff company which I have said in law made the first defendant company not
the beneficial owner of the money lent but a trustee. That is to say, is the proper H
conclusion that at that time the defendant bank was aware that the arrangement
was that the first defendant company was to take the money lent for the specific
and sole purpose of paying the dividend already declared, being therefore not
entitled vis-à-vis the provider, the plaintiff company, to treat the money as its
own property for any other purpose whatever? If the defendant bank was then
aware of that, the bank was fixed with notice that the moneys in the dividend

(20) (1819), 2 B. & Ald. 683.
(21) (1859), 2 E. & E. 29.
(22) (1891), 8 Morr. 243.
(23) [1902] 2 K.B. 237.
(24) [1902] 2 K.B. at pp. 238, 239.
(25) (1912), 107 L.T. 783.
(26) [1967] 1 All E.R. at p. 866; [1967] Ch. at p. 927.
(27) [1967] 1 All E.R. at p. 867; [1967] Ch. at p. 928.
(28) (1865), L.R. 1 Eq. 405.

A account were in law trust moneys—though the bank may not have appreciated that legal consequence—and of course could not effectively set off the credit to that account against the greater debit on the other account of the first defendant company.

B Before being approached the defendant bank was well aware that the financial situation of the first defendant company was unhealthy and was calling on the first defendant company to reduce its overdraft by a very large sum: see the memorandum of June 3 and letter of June 4. The memorandum of July 9 shows that the defendant bank was told by the first defendant company chairman that losses had been sustained in 1964 estimated at £180,000 at the end of May and rising to £300,000 to the end of June. The memorandum continues with a note of a mooted rescue operation as follows: Mr. X, as HARMAN, L.J., has referred to

C him,

"is prepared to make £1 million available to the company provided that (a) Mr. Bloom puts in £200,000 and finds the dividend. (b) [Mr. X] and Bloom are jointly secured with a debenture over the current assets. (c) Barclays Bank also support the company for a period of two years at a figure of £500,000 against the security of the deeds, which we are now informed have

D been professionally valued at £420,000."

Then the final paragraph:

"One's first reaction is that there is no incentive for the bank to accept [Mr. X's] suggestions, but there is a very real liability for the outstanding documentary credits. Mr. Parker is to furnish the figures of the precise commitments outstanding."

E The next event is the discussion between the defendant bank (Mr. Parker) and the first defendant company (Mr. Goldbart) on July 15, as appears from answers to interrogatories by the defendant bank (Mr. Parker). They had a conversation relating to the provision of funds *to be applied* in payment of a dividend by the first defendant company. Mr. Goldbart said words to the effect that arrange-

F ments had been made with an unnamed person or company to lend or otherwise provide money to the first defendant company *for the purpose of paying the dividend* due to be paid on July 14. Mr. Parker agreed to open a special account to which the monies to be provided for the payment of the dividend were to be credited. (The special account was to be and was entitled "No. 4 Ordinary dividend account".) The letter from the first defendant company to the defendant

G bank of July 15 (enclosing the plaintiff company's cheque for the net amount of the dividend) shows that it was also agreed between the first defendant company and the defendant bank that the account "will only be used to meet the dividend due July 24, 1964".

Now, at this time there is nothing to suggest to the defendant bank that the mooted rescue operation was going ahead. According to the memorandum of

H July 9 it was conditional on extended credit facilities by the defendant bank, and no suggestion is made that the defendant bank was prepared to give these to the first defendant company. The first defendant company was in trouble with the defendant bank, and the defendant bank's latest news of the trading situation of the first defendant company was of very grave and rapidly accelerating losses by the first defendant company in the current year. Here was Mr. Goldbart

I in those circumstances proposing to pay a particular class of creditors (the shareholders in respect of the declared dividend). I cannot bring myself to believe that Mr. Parker can have thought that the plaintiff company was providing the first defendant company with these moneys with no strings attached or otherwise than on *condition* that it should be used to pay the dividend; otherwise he would surely have mentioned the dangers inherent in the course proposed of so applying the free property of the first defendant company. Nor can I bring myself to believe that Mr. Parker can have thought that the money was provided except on the condition that this was the *sole* use to which the first defendant

z

company was entitled to put those moneys. Even if there was a possibility   **A**
of a floating charge in favour of the plaintiff company (adumbrated as part
of the rescue operation already mentioned), for Mr. Parker to believe that the
plaintiff company failed to impose a condition that no other use was to be made
by the first defendant company of the money provided would surely be for Mr.
Parker to place the plaintiff company in the lunatic fringe of the business world.
The defendant bank did not call Mr. Parker or any other witness.   **B**

I consider the right conclusion in the circumstances is that the defendant
bank was aware at the relevant time of the relevant nature of the arrangement
between the first defendant company and the plaintiff company. The fact that
the defendant bank purported to set off on the winding-up only means that the
defendant bank erred in law in thinking that that arrangement did not make
the first defendant company a trustee. As a consequence, in my judgment the   **C**
moneys in the special dividend account could not be set off against the overdraft
of the first defendant company and must be accounted for by the defendant
bank to the plaintiff company. I would add only that this imposes no hardship
on the defendant bank, to whom a decision the other way would have given a
complete windfall of £209,000 odd; for except in the technical sense of undertaking an obligation to repay that sum by crediting it to the first defendant   **D**
company in the special account, the defendant bank gave no consideration for the
receipt of the money: it gave no extension of credit to the first defendant company on the faith of the payment; it did not credit any interest on the sum; it
simply held the sum and maintained the credit on that account until, at the
moment of winding-up, its promise not to set off (included in its promise that the
money should only be used to pay the dividend) was, as it thought, vacated by   **E**
statute as decided in this court in *Rolls Razor, Ltd.* v. *Cox* (29). The defendant
bank officials can scarcely have believed their good fortune when that date
arrived without the money being withdrawn from the dividend account; but
in my judgment it was not good fortune. I therefore also would allow the appeal.

SACHS, L.J.: The essential facts of this case, taking the primary facts and   **F**
the inferences to be drawn from them as a whole, lie in a very narrow compass
and at all material times were all known to the defendant bank. The first defendant company, who had accounts with the defendant bank, were in considerable
financial difficulties; were heavily overdrawn beyond the limits arranged with
the defendant bank; had been pressed to take their accounts elsewhere if they
did not reduce their overdraft within the limit agreed by the defendant bank;
were engaged in negotiations with a view to obtaining massive financial assistance   **G**
from a well-known man of substance; but were anxious to pay, and on July 2,
1964, resolved to pay a dividend of 120 per cent. on their ordinary shares at a
cost of £209,719, a sum which the defendant bank was not prepared to advance
having regard to the above overdraft position. The plaintiff company then on
July 15, by a cheque to be credited to a special dividend account of the first
defendant company, lent that company the £209,719 for the sole purpose of   **H**
paying that dividend: that cheque was sent to the defendant bank to be paid into
a separate account styled " ordinary dividend No. 4 " account, the defendant
bank receiving the cheque for that account being aware that this sum had
been advanced by the plaintiff company solely for the purpose of paying that
dividend and having agreed with the plaintiff company that it was only to be
used for that purpose. The cheque, having been thus received by the defendant
bank about 3.10 p.m. on July 15, was specially cleared, and was duly credited to
the No. 4 dividend account on July 17 at some unascertained time.

Those being the circumstances in which the £209,719 was received by the
defendant bank, I now turn to the subsequent sequence of events. Some time after
1 p.m. on July 17 the board of the first defendant company resolved to present
a petition for a voluntary winding-up and to issue forthwith a notice to that effect

---

(29) [1967] 1 All E.R. 397; [1967] 1 Q.B. 552.

A to the press (30).   In fact, the winding-up commenced on a resolution being passed by the first defendant company at an extraordinary general meeting on Aug. 27.

Between July 17 and the last mentioned date no payment was made to any shareholder, though at the time the cheque was paid into the No. 4 dividend account it was intended that payments be made on July 24, and the defendant

B bank had by that date printed the required dividend warrants drawn on that account bearing that date and also the usual 2d. Revenue stamps. At no time between the two above dates did the defendant bank combine the No. 4 dividend account with either of the other accounts that the first defendant company had with them: indeed, when looking at the internal memoranda of the defendant bank, it is apparent that it considered during this period that it had no right so

C to combine the accounts. On Aug. 28, however, the day after the passing of the winding-up resolution, the defendant bank purported to exercise a right of set-off and transferred the whole of the relevant sum out of the No. 4 dividend account so as to reduce the balance owing to it on the other accounts. The practical effect if it succeeds in this litigation was stated at the Bar to be that its unsecured claim in the liquidation would be some figure between £119,000 and

D £165,000, whereas if it fails it will be between £326,000 and £374,000. In short, it and it alone will get the benefit of the payment made by the plaintiff company.

The defendant bank now claims that this appropriation of the £209,719 to reduce the first defendant company's indebtedness to it is permissible in law despite the fact that it had agreed that this money should not be used for any purpose except the payment of the dividends; despite the fact that it was aware

E that the money had been provided by the plaintiff company to the first defendant company solely for that purpose; and despite the fact (to put it in different words) that the last thing that any party to the transactions intended when the money went into No. 4 dividend account was that it would or could be utilized by the defendant bank to reduce the first defendant company's overdraft. The mere statement of these facts would indicate that there would be something seriously

F wrong with the law of this country if the bank was entitled to pursue such a course in knowing defiance of what had been agreed before it received the money.

Despite the intricate and carefully marshalled submissions made over several days on the narrow issues before this court, the law on these matters seems to me to be adverse to the defendant bank's contentions. There is a consistent line of cases over the last 140 years according to which money advanced by A to B for a

G definite purpose can be impressed with a trust. The first of the line was *Toovey* v. *Milne* (31), which related to £120 lent for settling with certain creditors. ABBOTT, C.J., stated (32) that:

"... the fair inference from the facts proved was that this money was advanced for a special purpose, and that being clothed with a specific trust,

H no property passed to the assignee of the bankrupt."

In *Edwards* v. *Glyn* (33), where £3,000 was lent on the basis that it would be sufficient to stave off a run on a bank—but was returned on its becoming apparent that the run would prove to be too great—ERLE, J., and CROMPTON, J., approved and applied the principle laid down in *Toovey* v. *Milne* (31), and LORD CAMPBELL, C.J., approved the principle but decided the case on another ground.

I Then in 1891 LINDLEY, L.J., (34) and KAY, L.J. (35), in *Re Rogers, Ex p. Holland and Hannen* (36) (where £270 was lent for paying a creditor) similarly

---

(30) The minutes of the meeting recorded a resolution that the company should petition for a voluntary winding-up and that the necessary steps should be taken, but the notice issued to the press was that the directors resolved that the company and its subsidiaries be voluntarily wound up.

(31) (1819), 2 B. & Ald. 683.   (32) (1819), 2 B. & Ald. at p. 684.
(33) (1859), 2 E. & E. 29.   (34) (1891), 8 Morr. at p. 248.
(35) (1891), 8 Morr. at p. 249.   (36) (1891), 8 Morr. 242.

specifically referred to *Toovey* v. *Milne* (37) with approval, whilst BOWEN, L.J., A
in his short judgment said (38):

> " I think the true inference is that the money came to the bankrupt's hands
> impressed with a trust, and until it was paid over it remained impressed with
> that trust. It did not become the property of the bankrupt divisible amongst
> his creditors."
                                                                                      B

So far as can be ascertained from the cases cited to this court in the course of a
very full and helpful argument, the principle laid down in *Toovey* v. *Milne* (37)
has never in any reported case been criticised or even attacked in submissions
by counsel, though in some cases such as *Mosley* v. *Cressey's Co.* (39) the facts
have been such that it was not applied. For my part I see no reason for acceding
to the submission by counsel for the defendant bank that the principle attributed C
to the *Toovey* case (37) is wrong in law: on the contrary, I accept that principle as
correct and regard it as applicable to the present case.

Applying that principle to the facts which I have stated, the proper inference
is that the £209,719 was lent to the first defendant company for a specific purpose
and was impressed with a trust. The primary object of the trust (of which the
defendant bank was on the above facts at all material times fully aware) was   D
the specific purpose of paying dividend No. 4. What then was the position when
that dividend not having been paid the winding-up resolution was passed? If
(contrary to my view) there was still any chance of the shareholders being paid
the dividends from the money in the account, then, of course, the primary
trust remained in being, and the defendant bank could not use the money for
any other purpose. If, however, there was not the slightest chance of the money E
being thus applied, then either because there was throughout a further trust in
favour of the plaintiff company as stated by HARMAN, L.J., or because (as was
pressed by counsel for the plaintiff company) on the well-recognised principle
that what a settlor does not give is retained by him on a resulting trust, the
money was after the winding-up commenced held on trust in favour of the
plaintiff company. Thus in either case the sum in the No. 4 dividend account was F
never the beneficial property of the first defendant company; and the defendant
bank was well aware that whosoever was the person to whom the beneficial
property passed, it never vested in the first defendant company.

In deference to the sustained arguments addressed to the court for and against
the proposition that there was a resulting trust, I would add—at the risk of stating
the obvious—that for the principle that what a settlor does not give is retained G
I have in mind cases such as *Comr. for Stamp Duties of New South Wales* v.
Perpetual Trustee Co., Ltd. (40), where *Re Cochrane* (41) was approved, and also
the speech of LORD HERSCHELL in *Smith* v. *Cooke* (42). It follows that on either
basis the beneficial property in the sums in dividend account No. 4 never at any
material time vested in the first defendant company or the liquidator in any
sense which could entitle the defendant bank to use it (either before or after H
the provisions of s. 31 of the Bankruptcy Act, 1914 became applicable) for a
purpose which was entirely contrary to the terms on which the defendant bank
knew it had been paid into that account.

In this behalf I note that counsel for the defendant bank rightly conceded
(cf., *Foxton* v. *Manchester and Liverpool District Banking Co., Ltd.* (43)) that once
it is shown that the defendant bank was aware that the money was affected by a
trust it does not matter whether they were aware of the detailed terms of the

---

(37) (1819), 2 B. & Ald. 683.
(38) (1891), 8 Morr. at pp. 248, 249.
(39) (1865), L.R. 1 Eq. 405.
(40) [1943] 1 All E.R. 525; [1943] A.C. 425.
(41) [1905] 2 I.R. 626.
(42) [1891] A.C. 297 at p. 300.
(43) (1881), 44 L.T. 406.

A   trust. The defendant bank's action was thus one which they were not entitled to
take.

There is one relevant point to which I would advert with more particularity.
It stems from a passage in the judgment of the trial judge which was so much
canvassed by counsel and which may be no less canvassed should this case go
further. Plowman, J., said (44):

B   " The doctrine of resulting trusts is founded upon the unexpressed but
      presumed intention of the settlor and I see no reason for imputing the
      intention that there shall be some additional or other obligation to refund
      money in a case where a legal obligation to do so already exists.   More
      specifically, I see no reason why if a lender pays money to a borrower for a
      specific purpose which fails, the borrower's contractual obligation to repay
C   the money should have engrafted upon it some additional equitable obliga-
      tion. If there had been no contract of loan in this case the position might
      have been different, but it is with the lending and borrowing of money that
      I am primarily concerned."

On the principle inherent in this passage counsel for the defendant bank
D   strongly relied. If by that observation it was intended to convey—as was submitted by counsel for the plaintiff company to be its meaning—that whenever in
respect of some specific sum of money a common law obligation in indebitatus
assumpsit arises from an express term in contract, there cannot in any case
co-exist such rights as a cestui que trust may in equity have in respect of trusts
existing in relation to that sum, it would not be an accurate statement of the law.
E   It would be equally wrong if it was intended to say that such co-existence cannot
derive from the implied terms of a contract.

It may be in point to remind oneself first of the statement in Bullen & Leake
(3rd Edn.) at p. 44 in relation to one of the common counts in indebitatus, that of
" money had and received ":

      " This is the most comprehensive of all the common counts. It is applic-
F   able wherever the defendant has received money which in justice and equity
      belongs to the plaintiff, under circumstances which render the receipt of it a
      receipt by the defendant to the use of the plaintiff."

And also of the celebrated analysis of the origin of that form of action in the speech
of Lord Sumner in *Sinclair* v. *Brougham* (45). It would then be strange indeed
if today the mere existence of a common law right and remedy in respect of the
G   subject matter of a contract should of itself exclude equitable rights or remedies
in respect thereof. Moreover, it is common place to find actions proceeding in
which both sets of remedies are claimed and enforced. One instance of such
co-existence of the two sets of rights and remedies can be found in *Reading* v.
A.-G. (46). See the speech of Lord Porter (47) made with the concurrence of
Viscount Jowitt, L.C., and the speech of Lord Radcliffe (48), who specifically
H   adopted the judgment of the Court of Appeal as delivered by Asquith, L.J. (49).

It seems to me nothing in point that there was in that case no expressed as
opposed to an implied term of a contract under which there could be founded a
common law claim: nor did counsel for the defendant bank seek so to contend
any more than counsel for the plaintiff company could or did argue that every
contractual transaction which provides a party with a common law cause of
I   action (e.g., for money lent or for money had and received) results in that party
having some equitable remedy in relation to the moneys involved. For my part,
however, I doubt whether the judge's observations were meant to be of such wide

---

(44) [1967] 1 All E.R. at pp. 868, 869; [1967] Ch. at p. 930.
(45) [1914-15] All E.R. Rep. 622 at pp. 648, 649; [1914] A.C. 398 at pp. 453, 454.
(46) [1951] 1 All E.R. 617; [1951] A.C. 507.
(47) [1951] 1 All E.R. at p. 618; [1951] A.C. at p. 513.
(48) [1951] 1 All E.R. at p. 622; [1951] A.C. at p. 518.
(49) [1949] 2 All E.R. 68 at p. 69; [1949] 2 K.B. 233 at p. 234.

effect as counsel for the plaintiff company submitted: it seems rather that he   A
was expressing his view of this particular transaction. None the less I respectfully
differ from his view. One must, to make a trite observation, look at the facts as a
whole and draw such inferences as to what were the terms of the relevant transaction bearing in mind that it was of a commercial category. It is on that basis,
of course, that I have stated the facts at the outset of this judgment, and it is on
that basis that I have reached the conclusions already stated.   B

It is perhaps as well in conclusion to say something more as to the inferences
that were to my mind to be drawn from the primary facts. My endeavour naturally was to adopt the viewpoints respectively of a reasonable man of business or a
reasonable bank official (if there be any difference between those two views)
when entering into the transactions now under consideration. It was on this
footing that I looked inter alia at the answers to interrogatory No. 3 (1) and (2),   C
letter No. 26 of July 15 (50), the background of negotiation as shown to be known
to the parties (but without reference to letter No. 28 of July 15 (51) and the letters
sent by the defendant bank to the first defendant company), and, of course, as
regards the defendant bank, to their internal memoranda. When examining
these it seemed right to take the matter as a whole without seeking to place
phrases in the documents into watertight compartments and then to construe   D
them as if they were contained in a pleading rather than in commercial
correspondence or memoranda.

On that footing it seemed an irresistible inference that, when the plaintiff
company in all the circumstances of the case spoke of the £209,719 as being lent
for the purpose of paying a dividend, that meant on contractual terms for the
purpose of paying that dividend and for no other purpose; and it was thus that   E
in the earlier part of this judgment the phrase occurs to the effect that the moneys
were advanced " solely for the purpose of paying that dividend ". That inference
seems to me to apply equally to the transaction between the plaintiff company
and the first defendant company, and to the transaction between the first defendant company and the defendant bank in so far as the latter's knowledge of the
former transaction has to be examined. Indeed I cannot conceive that had a bank   F
official been called into the witness box he would have expressed any different
view.

It was on looking thus at the transaction that one finds that its terms, be they
express or implied, are, contrary to the much pressed submission of counsel for
the defendant bank, such as to entitle the parties to the loan transaction both to
common law rights with their attendant remedies and also to the other rights   G
for which remedies before 1873 would have required resort to a court of equity.
For the reasons stated I would allow the appeal.

Appeal allowed. Leave to appeal to the House of Lords granted.

Solicitors: *D. J. Freeman & Co.* (for the plaintiff company); *Ashurst, Morris,
Crisp & Co.* (for the first defendant company); *Durrant, Cooper & Hambling*   H
(for the defendant bank).

[*Reported by* F. A. AMIES, ESQ., *Barrister-at-Law.*]

---

(50) This was the letter from the director of the first defendant company to the
defendant bank ; see p. 617, letters C and D, ante.
(51) This was the letter from the director of the plaintiff company to the first defendant
company; see p. 617, letters F and G, ante.

A

Re ST. MARY'S, WESTWELL.

[CANTERBURY COMMISSARY COURT (Commissary-General Lord Dunboyne), November 15, December 1, 1967.]

Ecclesiastical Law—Faculty—Jurisdiction—Sale of chattel—Communion vessel —Vessels too valuable for use and money needed for repair of church—
B
Whether sale on open market would be authorised—Terms of order granting faculty.

Ecclesiastical Law—Faculty—Practice—Submission to archdeacon—Faculty Jurisdiction Measure 1964 (No. 5), s. 9.

The rector and churchwardens petitioned for a faculty authorising sale on the open market of two late Elizabethan silver-gilt livery pots. The vessels
C
belonged to the church, but were no longer used and were deposited at the bank; they were too valuable for use and, even when deposited at the bank, they had to be insured. The object of the sale was to raise funds for the necessary, and in part urgent, repair of the church; on the evidence sale of the vessels should realise sufficient to meet the expected cost of repair.

Held: (i) a faculty would be granted for the sale of the Communion
D
vessels; and the sale permitted would be a sale on the open market, without restriction of the buyers to any limited category, both because such a restriction would not necessarily safeguard the vessels from improper use and because it would reduce the price (see p. 634, letters B, C, F and G, post).

(ii) terms would be imposed as to reserve price and application of the pro-
E
ceeds of sale (see p. 635, letters E to G, post).

Re St. Mary's, Gilston ([1966] 2 All E.R. 408) and *St. Mary, Northolt (Parishioners)* ([1920] P. 97) considered.

Per CURIAM: faculty petitions in the Diocese of Canterbury should be submitted to the appropriate archdeacon for counter-signature (see p. 632, letter D, post).

F
[As to the scope of faculty jurisdiction, see 13 HALSBURY'S LAWS (3rd Edn.) 414-416, para. 922; and for cases on the subject, see 19 DIGEST (Repl.) 491, 492, *3198-3204.*

As to the considerations affecting the court, see 13 HALSBURY'S LAWS (3rd Edn.) 417, 418, para. 924; and for cases on the subject, see 19 DIGEST (Repl.) 492, 493, *3205-3224.*

G
For the Faculty Jurisdiction Measure 1964, s. 9, see 44 HALSBURY'S STATUTES (2nd Edn.) 232.]

Cases referred to:

Exeter (Bishop) v. *Marshall*, (1868), L.R. 3 H.L. 17; 37 L.J.C.P. 331; 18 L.T. 376; 32 J.P. 419; 19 Digest (Repl.) 246, *45.*

St. John's, Margate (Churchwardens) v. *St. John's, Margate (Parishioners, etc.)*, (1794), 1 Hag. Con. 198; 161 E.R. 524; 19 Digest (Repl.) 379, *1774.*

H
St. Mary's, Gilston, Re, [1966] 2 All E.R. 408; [1967] P. 125; [1966] 2 W.L.R. 697; Digest (Cont. Vol. B) 233, *1766a.*

St. Mary, Northolt (Vicar and Churchwardens) v. *St. Mary, Northolt (Parishioners) and St. George-in-the-East (Rector and Churchwardens)* v. *St. George-in-the-East (Parishioners)*, [1920] P. 97; 19 Digest (Repl.) 536, *3717.*

I
Petition for faculty.

By a petition dated June 20, 1967, the rector and churchwardens of St. Mary's, Westwell, with the unanimous approval of the parochial church council, signified by resolution at meetings held on June 1, 1966, and May 1, 1967, petitioned for a faculty authorising the sale of two Elizabeth I silver-gilt livery pots, belonging to the Church of Westwell St. Mary, either by auction with a reserve price or on an unrestricted private market at a price to be fixed by the court. A quin- quennial survey for the parish under the Inspection of Churches Measure, 1955,

3 All ER 269   Applied in Re ST GREGORY'S [1971]

THORNHAUGH [1976] 1 All ER 154   Distinguished in Re ST ANDREW'S,

had revealed that works of repair to the church, some of them being of a very A
urgent nature, the cost of which would be in the region of £27,000, were needed.
The total funds in hand, as shown by the 1966 accounts of the parochial church
council, were in the region of £560; and the population of the parish was about
one thousand persons: the population in effective touch with, and reasonable
physical proximity to, the church, being about 280 persons. The livery pots
were held at the bank for security, and had long since become wholly disused. B

B. T. Buckle for the petitioners.

D. A. L. Smout as amicus curiae.

Cur. adv. vult.

Dec. 1. **THE COMMISSARY-GENERAL:** The incumbent and churchwardens of St. Mary's, Westwell, in the diocese of Canterbury, have applied for C
a faculty to permit them to sell two livery pots on the open market. The petition
is technically unopposed and commends itself to the parochial church council,
to the diocesan advisory committee, and to the archdeacon, although he has
not endorsed it. The omission does not matter in the particular circumstances
of the present case; but every petition of any consequence destined for me should,
before reaching me, be submitted to the appropriate archdeacon for counter- D
signature, on behalf of both himself as archdeacon and the diocesan advisory
committee of which he is a member. Otherwise there is a risk that a faculty
may be granted without the archdeacon having had sufficient notice to exercise
the right that he has under s. 9 of the Faculty Jurisdiction Measure 1964 (1) to
intervene in the proceeding.

The council for the care of churches, which I feel bound to consult whenever E
the sale of church plate is proposed, was in this case unable to agree with the
diocesan advisory committee. I am naturally grateful for the considered,
though conflicting advice on both bodies, and am now further indebted for the
assistance of two experienced counsel and the eleven witnesses called.

The vessels under consideration must, in my view, be treated as Communion
plate. Called " livery pots " they could equally well be described as " flagons ". F
Further particulars of them are to be found in *Archaeologia Cantiana*, (1882) Vol.
xiv, 344 and 378-9, and (1902) Vol. xxv, 133 (published after the latest inventory of
church plate in Kent was compiled at the end of the nineteenth century). Together
the flagons form a superb pair which should not be put asunder. They are unin-
scribed except for " Westwell " in small lettering on the underside of each.
The first bears a London hallmark of 1594 and the second, that of 1597. Presum- G
ably of secular origin, both flagons were subsequently given to the church by a
parishioner, as evidenced by the following extract from the parish register for
1630 (when the donor's brother is believed to have died):

" Gregory Baker, born at Ripple, parish of Westwell, in the county of
Kent, seeing all went into the city, and none into the temple where because
he had found great consolation, he desired to make some poor oblation), H
gave to the church of Westwell two gilt flagons and a gilt Communion
cuppe with a cover, weighing in all 103 ounces. Mr. John Viney being at
that time vicar thereat."

In evidence the Dean of Gloucester made the interesting suggestion that the
above text may allude to George Herbert's religious poems, entitled " The
Temple ", which do not seem to have been published before 1633. Be that as it I
may, both flagons were presented at the same time as the " Communion cuppe "
(which regrettably has not been traced) so that the donor may well have intended
them to be used with the cup. Indeed the liturgical usages of the seventeenth
century were such as to raise a rebuttable presumption in my opinion that any
flagon or pair of flagons which then belonged to an English parish church was
in fact used for the consecration of wine. In all probability both these flagons

(1) See 44 HALSBURY'S STATUTES (2nd Edn.) 232.

A   were habitually so used before they were deposited in the bank where they now
are.   But they are most unlikely to be brought into church again; the cost of
insurance alone would be prohibitive.

The evidence of Mr. Cane, a director of Sotheby's, estimating that they could
be auctioned together at around £32,000, was given before the pound sterling
devaluation by 14.3 per cent. ($2.80 to $2.40 to the £); irrespective of their mone-

B   tary value, vessels which have contained the consecrated elements are precious
in consequence of such sacred service; and to safeguard them from improper
use has long been an imperative of the spirit of certain devout Christians.   It
is seldom easy to decide whether such vessels should be sold at all; it would tax
the wisdom of Solomon to determine whether, in the event of their sale, it is
worth trying to protect them from improper use by restricting the market to, say,

C   another church or a museum.   On that point, the evidence before me has revealed
that, however pardonably, the mind of the church is as schizophrenic as that of
the law.

As to the law, it is clear that church plate may not be removed or alienated
from the church to which it belongs, without diocesan permission.   It is equally
clear that, unless expressly forbidden by such provisions as s. 21 (1) of the Union

D   of Benefices Measure, 1923 (2), or s. 29 (c) of the Reorganisation Areas Measure,
1944 (3), the diocesan chancellor has a discretion to authorise the sale of church
plate, even if it be Communion plate.   But is that discretion fettered by a
principle that Communion plate should not be sold on the open market?   Counsel
for the petitioners had referred me to three unreported cases and to the two
reported cases, Re St. Mary, Northolt (Vicar and Churchwardens) v. St. Mary,

E   Northolt (Parishioners) and St. George-in-the-East (Rector and Churchwardens)
v. St. George-in-the-East (Parishioners) (4) and Re St. Mary's, Gilston (5).   In
the former, Chancellor Kempe, could see no justification for permitting the
sale of Communion plate on the open market.   In the latter, Chancellor
Newsom, Q.C., declined to follow Chancellor Kempe.   Both learned chan-
cellors command respect, not least, Chancellor Kempe, who had been a member

F   of the Archbishop's Ancient Monuments (Churches) Committee just after the
passing of the Ancient Monuments Consolidation and Amendment Act, 1913 (6),
when the supposed inadequacy of control over the disposal of church plate had
attracted the attention of Parliament.

In the St. Mary, Northolt, case (7), Chancellor Kempe sought support for
his views from the so-called Constitution of 1236 of Archbishop Edmund Rich

G   which contained the words: ". . . ornamenta ecclesiae quae pontificalem accipiunt
benedictionem nullo modo in prophanos usus depulentur ".   That directive was
probably not of provincial application (vide, English Historical Review, (July, 1935)
Vol. L, 400), but it echoed certain other thirteenth century diocesan statutes, notably that of Archbishop Stephen of about 1225 insofar as Canterbury Diocese was
concerned.   Having had the advantage of the evidence of the Rev. B. Wigan, a

H   member of the Archbishop's Liturgical Commission, I cannot accept that Chancellor Kempe misconstrued the above Latin to the extent that Chancellor
Newsom, Q.C., supposed in Re St. Mary's, Gilston (8); but neither am I persuaded
that any such directive was concerned with, or is applicable to, a proposal to sell
Communion plate on the open market; nor in any event would this court be
bound by it.   The line of cases culminating in Bishop of Exeter v. Marshall (9)

I   seems to confirm that no directive, rule or usage of pre-reformation canon law

---

(2) See 7 Halsbury's Statutes (2nd Edn.) 517.
(3) See 7 Halsbury's Statutes (2nd Edn.) 917.
(4) [1920] P. 97.
(5) [1966] 2 All E.R. 408; [1967] P. 125.
(6) 17 Halsbury's Statutes (2nd Edn.) 374.
(7) [1920] P. at p. 99; in that passage the word " depulentur " is a misprint and
should read " deputentur ".
(8) [1966] 2 All E.R. at p. 411; [1967] P. at p. 130.
(9) (1868), L.R. 3 H.L. 17.

is any longer binding on this court unless pleaded and proved to have been recog- **A** nised, continued and acted on in England since the reformation, and even if any prohibition of the sale of Communion plate on the open market did ever exist, its recognition certainly has not continued to the present day.

There are two reasons for not restricting the market. First, the restriction will not necessarily achieve its object of safeguarding the article from improper use. As CHANCELLOR NEWSOM, Q.C., observed in *Re St. Mary's, Gilston* (10), **B** the burden of a restrictive covenant cannot be made to run with a chattel; on its sale the vendor loses control on its destination. Secondly, the restriction will usually reduce the obtainable price. Mr. Came said in evidence that the difference in the present case might be £10,000. I cannot believe it would accord with the wishes of the donor, or the interests of the church which he cherished, to rob its funds of so much, for the sake of a restriction of such dubious **C** effect. I am therefore driven to the conclusion that if these flagons must be sold, the sale should be on the open market. It should be added that some effort has been made, in commendably tactful terms, to invite the Episcopal Church of the United States to buy these vessels at a fair price; but the invitation was courteously declined.

The discretion to permit or disallow a sale of church plate in Canterbury **D** diocese has been exercised on principles which were outlined in 1949 by the then Archbishop of Canterbury as follows:

" (i) I always deeply regret it when a church parts with such a possession, alienating it from the House of God to which it was given.

" (ii) Sometimes such alienation is reasonable, however unwelcome, **E** especially if the piece of plate is in effect already alienated by the fact that it cannot be used and is kept permanently in a bank's strong room or a church safe.

" (iii) If it must be sold, one would wish that it either should go to another church were it can be used or should go to a national collection so that it is free from all risk of coming into private hands."

F

The petitioners have satisfied me that the proposed sale is reasonable. The flagons are not only too valuable to use, but also have become a positive burden, because they have to be insured even while in the csutody of the bank; and SIR WILLIAM SCOTT remarked in the case of *St. John's, Margate (Churchwardens)* v. *St. John's, Margate (Parishioners)* (11) that if the ornament were found to be a burthen it might be removed by another faculty. Moreover I am persuaded that **G** nothing but the sale of the flagons will save the church from deteriorating beyond repair. Westwell may remain untouched by development plans. It is a parish of rustic charm with a population of not much more than a thousand. Its church is an early English edifice of some interest and, in the opinion of Mr. Caroe, the architect in charge, is not sufficiently dilapidated to warrant abandoning. Recently, at considerable cost to the parishioners, the shingled spire has been **H** restored. Further necessary repairs would, however, in Mr. Caroe's estimation, cost some £27,000, apart from much-needed improvements to the heating and the desirability of recasting a cracked bell, if not the whole peal. The small congregation of no more than three hundred parishioners obviously cannot be expected to afford expenditure of such magnitude.

In these circumstances the faculty will be granted as requested. There is no **I** demand or need for a declaration to be made that the flagons shall no longer be set apart for the ministrations of the church; but I trust that the petitioners will obtain, and exhibit in the church, electro-type copies of the flagons, or at least a good photograph suitably framed with an explanatory note, to remind posterity of Mr. Baker's munificence.

(10) [1966] 2 All E.R. at p. 412; [1967] P. at p. 132.
(11) (1794), 1 Hag. Con. 198 at p. 202.

A   This case strikes me as illustrative of the mounting urgency of the whole problem of disposal of church plate.   In the *St. Mary, Northolt,* case (12), CHANCELLOR KEMPE recommended the creation of cathedral museums where treasure of a diocese could be deposited on loan.   Some forty years later, thanks to the generosity of the Goldsmiths' Company, Lincoln Cathedral blazed the way, as the expert, Mr. C. C. Oman, has described in evidence.   The project seems

B   admirable as far as it goes; but times have changed since CHANCELLOR KEMPE made his recommendation in 1920.   The Inspection of Churches Measure, 1955, (13) has necessitated surveys which, like Mr. Caroe's at Westwell, reveal the wear and tear of centuries.   The repairs needed may be, as they are at Westwell, far too extensive for the present tax-ridden generation of parishioners to afford. The sale of a redundant church treasure has the attraction of a sound business

C   proposition.   So it is not surprising that pressure to sell unused church plate is increasing noticeably.   I venture to suggest that those who are anxious too prevent the imminent dispersal of the treasures of English churches would do well to establish a central fund, on a national or diocesan basis, which could gradually buy such treasures at a reasonable price and keep them as a national heritage, preferably in cathedral museums.   Meanwhile those tempted to sell

D   church treasures may feel well-advised to await the creation of some such fund. The evidence has satisfied me, however, that at Westwell to delay the sale would destroy the church.

The order of the court is therefore as follows: (i) Provided the vendors instruct the auctioneers to pay the whole of the proceeds of sale direct to the Canterbury diocesan board of finance and provided the registrar approves the reserve price

E   and all other terms and conditions of the auction, this pair of flagons may be sold on the open market.   (ii) From the proceeds of sale shall be paid the expenses of the sale, including the auctioneers' commission, and the taxed costs of the petitioners and of the court, including the expenses of all the judge's witnesses except for Mr. Moule, most of whose evidence was not really admissible.   (iii) Until further order, the income of half the proceeds of sale shall, then and when-

F   ever the capital of the whole fund stands at less than was its original value prior to the payment of such expenses, be accumulated and invested, with a view to restoring the capital of the fund to its original value and at all times preserving at least half of it intact.   (iv) Subject to any further directions and as aforesaid, the fund shall be invested by the board and the income shall be paid to the parochial church council for its general purposes.   (v) The Archdeacon

G   of Maidstone, the parochial church council and the diocesan board of finance are hereby joined as parties and, together with the petitioners and their respective successors in office, given liberty to apply in the proceeding from time to time, generally and, in particular, for further directions to ensure the best use of the capital and income of the fund and the due execution of the order.

Faculty granted.

H   Solicitors: *Trollope and Winckworth* (for the petitioners).

[*Reported by* BRIAN POCOCK, ESQ., *Barrister-at-Law.*]

I

---

(12) [1920] P. at p. 100.
(13) See 35 HALSBURY'S STATUTES (2nd Edn.) 57.

A

R. *v.* GOVERNOR OF BRIXTON PRISON, *Ex parte* GARDNER.

[QUEEN'S BENCH DIVISION (Lord Parker, C.J., Edmund Davies, L.J., and
Widgery, J.), December 13, 14, 1967.]

Extradition—Habeas corpus—Fugitive—Offence of false pretences alleged—   B
Warrants of arrest issued in New Zealand for false pretences, particulars
alleging false pretences as to future event—Not, therefore, offence of false
pretences according to law of England—Whether relevant offence for which
fugitive liable to be returned—Fugitive Offenders Act 1967 (c. 68), s. 3 (1) (c).

Warrants for the arrest of the applicant were issued in New Zealand,
mainly in each instance in respect of an alleged obtaining of a particular   C
sum of money with intent to defraud by means of false pretences, the particulars of the false pretences being that the applicant falsely represented
that a company with which he was concerned would supply certain named
distributors with cosmetics to a named value. The applicant was arrested
in England; the Secretary of State, pursuant to s. 5* of the Fugitive
Offenders Act 1967, issued an authority to proceed, and the applicant was   D
committed to prison pending his extradition to New Zealand. By s. 1† of
the Act of 1967, a person found in the United Kingdom who was accused
of a relevant offence in a Commonwealth country might be arrested and
returned to that country. By s. 3 (1) (a)‡ of, and para. 18 of Sch. 1 to, the
Act of 1967, the offence of obtaining money by false pretences was a
"relevant offence", but by s. 3 (1) (c)‡, the act or omission constituting the   E
offence must be one which would constitute an offence against the law of
the United Kingdom if it took place within the United Kingdom. On an
application for habeas corpus, a preliminary point of law was taken that
the charges disclosed on the warrants did not disclose an offence known to
English law, in that the particulars of the offence alleged described the
false pretences as a representation of a future event, viz., a false pretence   F
that the company would supply the distributor with cosmetics.

Held: the authority to proceed, albeit in general terms, must be taken as
relating to the offences of which the applicant was accused in New Zealand,
viz., in the absence of any indication to the contrary, those which were
set out in the warrants which accompanied the request to the Secretary of
State; and, as it was clear that the acts complained of in those warrants   G
would not constitute offences under the law of England, a writ of habeas
corpus should issue (see p. 641, letters G, H and I, and p. 642, letter E, post).

[**Editorial Note.** The Fugitive Offenders Act 1967, came into operation on
Sept. 1, 1967. It repealed the Fugitive Offenders Act, 1881.

For the position as to offences to which the Act of 1881 applied, and as to
extradition crimes, see 16 HALSBURY'S LAWS (3rd Edn.) 585, para. 1217, and   H
pp. 565, 566, para. 1158.

For the Fugitive Offenders Act 1967 (c. 68) s. 3, s. 5, see HALSBURY'S STATUTES
(2nd Edn.) Interim Service.]

Motion for writ of habeas corpus.

This was an application by way of motion by Robert John Gardner, now
detained in H.M. Prison, Brixton, for a writ of habeas corpus directed to the
Governor of Brixton Prison to bring the applicant before the Divisional Court of
the Queen's Bench Division, and quash a warrant of committal issued on Nov.
13, 1967, by the chief magistrate (FRANK MILTON, ESQ.) at Bow Street Metropolitan Magistrates' Court, pending his return to New Zealand under the Fugitive

---

* Section 5, so far as material, is set out at p. 639, letters F to H, post.
† Section 1, so far as material, is set out at p. 638, letter G, post.
‡ Section 3 (1), so far as material, is set out at p. 638, letter I, post.

<table>
<tr><td>Distinguished and doubted in R v
GOVERNOR OF PENTONVILLE PRISON
[1980] 1 All ER 701</td><td>Considered in GOVERNMENT OF CANADA
v ARONSON [1989] 2 All ER 1025</td></tr>
</table>

A Offenders Act 1967, in respect of offences alleged to have been committed there, contrary to s. 246 (2)* of the New Zealand Crimes Act, 1961 (No. 43). The facts are set out in the judgment of Lord Parker, C.J.

The authorities and cases noted below† were cited during the argument.

Paul Wrightson, Q.C., and *J. W. Harkess* for the applicant.
B *R. H. W. Dunn*, Q.C., and *J. M. Cope* for the New Zealand Government.
J. H. Buzzard and *C. P. C. Whelon* for the Governor of Brixton Prison.

LORD PARKER, C.J.: For reasons which I will state in a moment, it is unnecessary to go in detail through the history of the matter leading up to the charges in which the applicant was committed, but it is, I think, necessafy to give a brief, but general, resumé of the matter giving rise to these proceedings. It
C appears that on Jan. 28, 1966, a company was incorporated in New Zealand by the name of Leidrum and Hartnell, Ltd. It is said that the parent company is an Australian company of a similar name. That company had as its object the sale of cosmetics in New Zealand, and the idea was that in New Zealand both islands would be divided into zones, some forty-five zones in all, and that in each zone there would be an agency, a distributor, who would have exclusive
D rights of sale in the zone, and who would buy the cosmetics from the company and sell them. The idea was to display them in dairies and sell them there. To this end the company issued brochures explaining what they intneded to do, and inviting persons to apply for the agency. They were told in general terms that under this system, the cosmetics would be supplied to them, and that they, the distributors, had to pay in advance. It is said that, over the period since the
E incorporation of the company up to June 17, 1966, when the company ceased to trade, it obtained from distributors, and this is only a general figure, something like £36,000, in respect of which the distributors have received no repayment and no cosmetics for sale. The prosecution case was that this was a gigantic fraud, that this company was not carrying on a genuine business at all, and strong reliance is placed on the fact that, in about the last week before the
F company ceased to trade, virtually the whole of the monies standing to the company's account were withdrawn. The totals went from something like £24,000 down to a matter of £2,000 in a matter of days. Those associated with the company included a Mr. Chaplin, who was a director and had taken over the directorship from the applicant, albeit on the evidence the applicant remained interested in the company. There was a Miss Keane who was assistant vice-
G president, and who in the last few days of the company became secretary as well, and a Mr. McGurgan, who throughout was described as the national marketing manager. When the company ceased to trade, it was found that the applicant and Mr. Chaplin had gone to Australia, and that Miss Keane and Mr. McGurgan were still in Auckland, New Zealand, though it was thought that they were about to leave. It was in those circumstances that warrants for arrest were issued
H against all those associated with the company, and proceedings were started in New Zealand against Miss Keane and Mr. McGurgan in the course of which considerable evidence was taken. So far as the applicant was concerned, thirty-seven warrants were issued, mainly in the form of obtaining from a named distributor a particular sum of money with intent to defraud by means of certain false pretences. In each case the particulars of the false pretences were given as
I

---

* Section 246, so far as material, provides: " (2) Every one who, with intent to defraud by any false pretence, either directly or through the medium of any contract obtained by the false pretence, obtains possession of or title to anything capable of being stolen . . . is liable—(*a*) to imprisonment for a term not exceeding seven years . . ."
† 16 Halsbury's Laws (3rd Edn.) 597; 9 Halsbury's Statutes (2nd Edn.) 886, 887; Archbold's Criminal Pleading, Evidence and Practice (36th Edn.), paras. 1948, 1949, 1950; *Ex p. Plot*, (1883), 48 L.T. 120; *Re Bellencontre*, [1891] 2 Q.B. 122; *R. v. Grubb*, [1914-15] All E.R. Rep. 667; [1915] 2 K.B. 683; *R. v. Dent*, [1955] 2 All E.R. 806; [1955] 2 Q.B. 590; *Re Mourat Mehmet*, [1962] 1 All E.R. 463.

" . . . namely by falsely representing that Leidrum and Hartnell, Ltd.   A
would supply [the distributor in question] with cosmetics to the value of
[the sum in question]."

Some of these warrants alleged attempts, and two dealt with conspiracy in
regard to the company's documents. The matter came before the chief magistrate
at Bow Street, who held that the evidence in the form of these depositions taken
in New Zealand was sufficient to justify committals on thirty-five of the charges,   B
and in due course, as I have said, he committed the applicant to Brixton Prison
pending his return to New Zealand.

The point quite shortly taken by counsel for the applicant, really by way of
preliminary point, without going into the merits, was that the charges disclosed
on these warrants, the thirty-five on which he was committed, did not disclose
an offence known to English law, in that, as I have said, the particulars described   C
the false pretence as a representation of a future event, namely, by falsely pretend-
ing that the company would supply a distributor with goods. Under the Fugitive
Offenders Act, 1881, there is no doubt that this point could not possibly be taken,
because s. 9 of that Act provided that the Act should apply to an offence

" . . . notwithstanding that by the law of the part of Her Majesty's
dominions, in or on his way to which the fugitive is or is suspected of being   D
it is not an offence . . ."

On Sept. 1, 1967, however, the new Fugitive Offenders Act 1967, came into force,
and under that Act the position has been changed in many very material respects.
The really material change so far as this case is concerned is that the position
is equated with the position under the Extradition Act, 1870, under which an   E
" extradition crime " is defined in s. 26 as:

" . . . a crime which, if committed in England or within English
jurisdiction, would be one of the crimes described in Sch. 1 to this Act ",

and, accordingly, English law now becomes a very material matter. Indeed, as
I will show in a moment, it seems to me that the Fugitive Offenders Act 1967,
has gone even further in this regard than the Extradition Act, 1870.   F

Bearing the point in mind that counsel takes on behalf of the applicant, it is,
I think, necessary to look briefly at the provisions of the Act of 1967. Section 1
provides that:

" Subject to the provisions of this Act, a person found in the United
Kingdom who is accused of a relevant offence in any other country being—
(a) a Commonwealth country . . . may be arrested and returned to that   G
country as provided by this Act."

That is s. 1, and it is fundamental to all the provisions of this Act accordingly
that the fugitive offender or the alleged fugitive offender is a person accused
in the country requesting his return, and he must be accused of a relevant
offence. " Relevant offence " is dealt with in s. 3 (1), which provides: H

" For the purposes of this Act an offence of which a person is accused or
has been convicted in a designated Commonwealth country . . . is a
relevant offence if—(a) in the case of an offence against the law of a
designated Commonwealth country, it is an offence which, however described
in that law, falls within any of the descriptions set out in Sch. 1 to this Act,
and is punishable under that law with imprisonment for a term of twelve   I
months or any greater punishment . . ."

Paragraph 18 of Sch. 1 includes, among other offences, obtaining property by
false pretences. Accordingly, pausing there, it is quite clear that the first hurdle,
as it were, would be overcome in this case, namely, that the general description
of this offence, obtaining money by false pretences, falls fairly and squarely within
the provisions of Sch. 1. The second hurdle concerns the terms of imprisonment,
and there is no doubt that that hurdle in this case is also surmounted.

Then s. 3 (1) (c) provides:

A
  " in any case, the act or omission constituting the offence, or the equivalent act or omission, would constitute an offence against the law of the
United Kingdom if it took place within the United Kingdom . . ."

In other words, as it seems to me, this provision is going further than the similar
provisions in the Extradition Act, 1870, and is providing that to be a relevant
offence not only must the offence fall within the general description of the words
B
within Sch. 1, but also the act or omission constituting the offence must
constitute an offence against the law of the United Kingdom.
  Section 4 (3) then goes on to provide that, before anything can be done in this
country, there must be an arrangement made with the country concerned providing that, if the offender is restored, he shall not be charged and tried with
C
any offence other than that in respect of which his return is requested. It
provides:

  " A person shall not be returned under this Act to any country, or
committed to or kept in custody for the purposes of such return, unless
provision is made by the law of that country, or by an arrangement made
with that country, for securing that he will not, unless he has first been
D
restored or had an opportunity of returning to the United Kingdom,
be dealt with in that country for or in respect of any offence committed
before his return under this Act other than—(*a*) [para. (*a*) is alone material
here] the offence in respect of which his return under this Act is requested
. . ."

Again, there is no doubt that that was complied with in the present case, in that
E
the Home Secretary has given a certificate, pursuant to s. 4 (4), that an arrangement has been made with the Government of New Zealand in the case of the
applicant in the terms of s. 4 (3) of the Act (1). Section 5 provides another
step that has to be taken before proceedings take place in this country:

  " (1) Subject to the provisions of this Act relating to provisional warrants,
F
a person shall not be dealt with thereunder except in pursuance of an order
of the Secretary of State (in this Act referred to as an authority to proceed),
issued in pursuance of a request made to the Secretary of State by or on
behalf of the Government of the designated Commonwealth country, or the
Governor of the United Kingdom dependency, in which the person to be
returned is accused or was convicted.
G
  " (2) There shall be furnished with any request made for the purposes of
this section on behalf of any country—(*a*) in the case of a person accused
of an offence, a warrant for his arrest issued in that country; . . . together
. . . with particulars of the person whose return is requested and of the
facts upon which and the law under which he is accused . . . and evidence
sufficient to justify the issue of a warrant for his arrest under s. 6 of this Act.
H
  " (3) On receipt of such a request the Secretary of State may issue an
authority to proceed unless it appears to him that an order for the return
of the person concerned could not lawfully be made, or would not in fact be
made, in accordance with the new provisions of this Act."

Again that step was surmounted in the present case, because the Secretary of
State, on Oct. 20, 1967, issued an authority to proceed. It was in these terms,
I
to the chief metropolitan stipendiary magistrate:

---

 (1) The certificate was dated Oct. 20, 1967, and was in the following terms: " The
New Zealand government undertake that, should [the applicant] be returned to their
jurisdiction under the provisions of the Fugitive Offenders Act 1967, he will not, unless
he has first been restored or had an opportunity of returning to the United Kingdom,
be dealt with for any offence committed before his return other than: (a) the offences
in respect of which his return is requested; (b) any lesser offence proved by the facts
proved before the court of committal; or (c) any other offence being a relevant offence
in respect of which the Secretary of State may consent to his being dealt with."

" A request having been made to the Secretary of State by or on behalf
of the Government of New Zealand for the return to that country of [the
applicant] who is accused of the offences of obtaining money by false pretences; attempting to obtain money by false pretences . . . [and I leave out
the next words, because the magistrate did not commit in regard to the
offences thereafter set out] the Secretary of State hereby orders that a
metropolitan stipendiary magistrate proceed with the case in accordance
with the provisions of the Fugitive Offenders Act 1967."

That authority to proceed having been issued, a warrant for the arrest of the
applicant was made pursuant to s. 6 of the Act of 1967, and he was in due course
arrested. Section 7 goes on to deal with the proceedings before the magistrate
before whom he was brought after his arrest in this country. The material
provision is sub-s. (5), and that provides:

" Where an authority to proceed has been issued in respect of the person
arrested and the court of committal is satisfied, after hearing any evidence
tendered in support of the request for the return of that person or on behalf
of that person, that the offence to which the authority relates is a relevant
offence and is further satisfied—(a) where that person is accused of the
offence, that the evidence would be sufficient to warrant his trial for that
offence if it had been committed within the jurisdiction of the court; (b)
where that person is alleged to be unlawfully at large after conviction of
the offence, that he has been so convicted and appears to be so at large,
the court shall, unless his committal is prohibited by any other provision
of this Act, commit him to custody to await his return thereunder; but if
the court is not so satisfied or if the committal of that person is so prohibited,
the court shall discharge him from custody."

It was under that provision that the applicant was committed on thirty-five
out of the thirty-seven charges. The magistrate, as I understand it, looked quite
rightly at the authority to proceed. He found that the offences to which the
authority related were offences of obtaining money by false pretences and
offences of attempting to obtain money by false pretences, and, having read the
depositions, decided that those offences were relevant offences within s. 3 of the
Act of 1967 to which I have already referred.

Counsel for the applicant's submission is that that approach gives no effect
whatever to s. 3 (1) (c) of the Act of 1967. He submits, and I should add that he
is supported in this by counsel on behalf of the Governor of Brixton Prison,
that s. 3 (1) (c), when it refers to " the offence ", is clearly referring to the offence
with which the person is accused in the Commonwealth country. The provisions
of the Act of 1967 apply only when a man is accused in a Commonwealth
country of an offence. Further, the opening words of s. 3 (1) refer to an offence
of which a person is accused, and, accordingly, when one comes to para. (c), the
words " the act or omission constituting the offence . . ." must be read here as
meaning an act or omission constituting the offence of which the person has
been accused in New Zealand. Counsel for the applicant goes on to say that
the only matters of which it is suggested that the applicant has been accused
in New Zealand are to be found in the warrants for his arrest in New Zealand.
He says that whereas the representations there alleged, namely, representations
as to the future, are offences under the law of New Zealand, they are not offences
under English law. Accordingly, he says that these were not on a true reading of
the statute relevant offences.

Counsel for the New Zealand government in his argument says what is, I think,
quite true, that the warrant of arrest issued in the foreign country is not given
at any rate such prominence as in the other Act, the Act of 1881 and the Act of
1870. Under s. 5 of the Fugitive Offenders Act 1881, clear provision is made
that the endorsed warrant for the apprehension of the fugitive issued in the
foreign country should be before the magistrate and considered by him. Under

A   s. 10 of the Extradition Act, 1870, it is similarly contemplated that the foreign
warrant authorising the arrest should be before the magistrate. By contrast,
under the Act of 1967 no provision is made in s. 7 for that warrant being before
the magistrate, and, indeed, the only reference throughout the whole Act to the
foreign warrant is to be found in s. 5 (2) (*a*), as being a document which must
accompany the request which is sent to the Secretary of State in this country.

B   Counsel also in connexion with that points to the fact that, under s. 7 (5) itself,
not only is no reference made to the warrant; but that what the magistrate's
mind is being directed to is the authority to proceed, and he has to be satisfied
that the offence to which the authority relates is a relevant offence. Accordingly, counsel submits that the offences to which the authority to proceed in
the present case relates are those set out in the authority to proceed itself, namely,

C   the perfectly general description of the offences of obtaining money by false
pretences and offences of attempting to obtain money by false pretences, and,
accordingly, he would say, looking at the authority to proceed and then looking
at the depositions, that there clearly was evidence of obtaining and attempting
to obtain money by false pretences which could be framed as an offence under
English law. Accordingly, the magistrate was right in holding that this was

D   a relevant offence.

   In my judgment, counsel for the New Zealand government's argument gives
really no effect to the provisions of s. 3 (1) (*c*). It seems to me that what is clearly
contemplated here is that a request coming forward to the Secretary of State
must set out in some form, and no doubt the most usual form is the warrant or
warrants of arrest, the offence or offences of which the fugitive is accused, in this

E   case in New Zealand. Not only must it supply a general description which will
fufil the provisions of s. 3 (1) (*a*), but it must condescend to sufficient detail to
enable the matter to be considered under s. 3 (1) (*c*). Similarly, as it seems to
me, it is contemplated that the Secretary of State, in giving his authority to
proceed under s. 5 (1), should again set out the offences to which his authority
is to relate in sufficient detail for the matter to be considered again not only under

F   para. (*a*) but also under para. (*c*) of s. 3 (1). So far as this case is concerned, as
I have said, the authority to proceed was in perfectly general terms, and this
court naturally has not seen and could not look at the request from the Commonwealth power. It seems to me, however, perfectly plain that this authority
to proceed, albeit in general terms, must be taken as relating to the offences of
which the applicant was accused in New Zealand, and on which the request was

G   made for his return.

   That being so, one asks oneself: what were the offences of which the applicant
was accused in New Zealand? In the absence of any indication in the authority
to proceed, it seems to me that one must assume what is only natural in these
cases, that the offences of which he was accused in New Zealand were those
set out in the warrants which accompanied the request to the Secretary of State.

H   If one then looks at the offences set out and considers them in the light of s. 3
(1) (*c*), it seems to me perfectly clear that the acts complained of in the offences
with which the applicant was charged would not constitute offences under the
law of this country. Accordingly, for those reasons, which I have endeavoured
to state shortly, I think that the applicant succeeds on what I may call the
preliminary point, and I find it unnecessary to go into the details of the case

I   with a view to seeing whether the evidence was sufficient to justify the magistrate
in committing on those charges. I would allow this application.

   EDMUND DAVIES, L.J.: I agree, and in the light of LORD PARKER,
C.J.'s observations it is, I think, sufficient for me to say that, in my judgment,
it has not been shown that the applicant has been accused in New Zealand of
any relevant offence within the meaning of the opening words of s. 3 (1) of the
Fugitive Offenders Act 1967. In this context, I have particularly in mind s. 3
(1) (*c*), with its requirements that,

A

" . . . the act or omission constituting the offence, or the equivalent act or omission, would constitute an offence against the law of the United Kingdom if it took place within the United Kingdom . . ."

" The offence " there referred to must mean the offence charged in New Zealand, and " the act or omission " refers to the manner or means whereby the offence so charged in New Zealand was committed. This involves examination of the particulars of the offence charged in New Zealand, and in the present case that examination in turn necessitates consideration of the New Zealand warrants. It is conceded that those warrants particularise the offences in words which, were they incorporated in an information or indictment in this country, would allege no contravention of our criminal law. Section 7 (5) requires to be demonstrated that the offence to which the authority to proceed relates is a relevant offence, and it is true that, for that purpose, the court of committal has to consider " any evidence tendered in support of the request for the return " of the arrested person. As at present advised, however, I do not accept the submission of counsel for the New Zealand government that this obliges the committing magistrate in every case to consider the contents of the depositions. Such a task may, indeed, be necessary for the removal of doubts whether the offence to which the authority relates is a relevant offence. If, however, as in the present case, the other " evidence tendered in support of the request " makes it clear that that offence is not a relevant offence, nothing contained in the depositions can cure that fatal flaw, and their consideration, therefore, becomes otiose.

B

C

D

WIDGERY, J.: I also agree with the order proposed, and in so doing I accept counsel for the New Zealand government's argument that the primary question for determination by the magistrate is whether the offence to which the authority relates is a relevant offence, and that it would be a mistake to say that his primary duty is to see whether the offence charged in the warrants is a relevant offence. However, in this case, having regard to the terms of the authority which LORD PARKER, C.J., has read, and having regard to the fact that the warrants were sent to the magistrate by the Secretary of State with that authority, it seems to me quite clear that the offences to which the authority related were identical with those charged in the warrants.

E

F

Habeas corpus granted. Leave given to appeal to the House of Lords.

Solicitors: *Sampson & Co.* (for the applicant); *Mackrell & Co.* (for the New Zealand Government); *Director of Public Prosecutions* (for the Governor of Brixton Prison).

G

[*Reported by* N. P. METCALFE, ESQ., *Barrister-at-Law.*]

A

MAPP (Inspector of Taxes) *v.* ORAM.

[CHANCERY DIVISION (Ungoed-Thomas, J.), July 11, 12, 13, 24, 1967.]

Reversed, C.A. [1968] 3 All E.R. 1.

Income Tax—Relief—Children's allowance—Son over sixteen full-time under-
graduate—Earnings in France as teacher exceeding amount of child's income
entitlement allowed by s. 212 (4)*—Son's earnings spent wholly in France on*
B   *lodging and incidental outgoings—Whether father's child allowance reducible*
by excess of son's earnings in France over entitlement permitted—Income
Tax Act, 1952 (15 & 16 *Geo.* 6 & 1 *Eliz.* 2 *c.* 10), *s.* 212 (4).

The taxpayer's son, a boy over sixteen who was a full-time undergraduate,
taught in a French school for 2½ months earning £150 which fell into the year
of assessment 1965-66. The £150 was spent in France on lodgings and
C   incidental outgoings, with the result that nothing remained to be brought
into the United Kingdom when he returned. By s. 212 (4)* of the Income Tax
Act, 1952, as amended, in the case of a child entitled in his own right to an
income exceeding £115 a year, the appropriate child allowance for the
taxpayer was to be reduced by the amount of the excess. It was contended
by the Crown that "an income" in s. 212 (4) must be computed in accord-
D   ance with Sch. 9, rules applicable to Sch. E, r. 7†, as equivalent to
"emoluments to be assessed" in that paragraph. On the question whether
the taxpayer's child allowance for 1965-66 should be restricted by reference
to the amount of the son's earnings in France,

Held: the words "an income" in s. 212 (4) of the Income Tax Act, 1952,
meant income that was chargeable to income tax and, as the son's earnings
E   had not been brought into this country and thus were not so chargeable, they
were not required to be taken into account as the son's income for the
purposes of s. 212 (4), with the consequence that the taxpayer's child
allowance was not reducible by the excess of the son's earnings over £115
(see p. 649, letter F, and p. 650, letters D and F, post); moreover the phrase
"emoluments to be assessed" in r. 7 of Sch. 9 to the Act of 1952 was not
F   declaratory of what was "an income" for the purposes of s. 212 (4) of that
Act (see p. 646, letters H and I, post).

Dicta of LORD DUNEDIN in *Whitney* v. *Inland Revenue Comrs.* ([1926]
A.C. at p. 51) and of BUCKLEY, J., in *Prince* v. *Phillips* ((1961), 39 Tax Cas.
at p. 479) applied.

Appeal dismissed.

[As to entitlement to child relief, see 20 HALSBURY'S LAWS (3rd Edn.) 441,
442, para. 824; and for cases on the subject, see 28 DIGEST (Repl.) 301, 302,
1310-1315.

For the Income Tax Act, 1952, s. 156, s. 212, Sch. 9, r. 7, as amended, see
SUPPLEMENT to 31 HALSBURY'S STATUTES (2nd Edn.), AMENDED TEXTS, paras.
[158], [214], [571].]

Cases referred to:

Astor v. *Perry (Inspector of Taxes), Duncan* v. *Adamson (Inspector of Taxes),*
    [1935] All E. R. Rep. 713; [1935] A.C. 398; 104 L.J.K.B. 423; 153
    L.T. 1; 19 Tax Cas. 255; 28 Digest (Repl.) 285, *1260.*

Durbridge v. *Sanderson (Inspector of Taxes),* [1955] 3 All E.R. 154; [1955]
    1 W.L.R. 1087; 36 Tax Cas. 239; 28 Digest (Repl.) 244, *1072.*

Martin v. *Lowry, Martin* v. *Income Tax Comrs.,* [1927] A.C. 312; 96 L.J.K.B.
    379; 136 L.T. 580; 11 Tax Cas. 297; 28 Digest (Repl.) 22, *90.*

Prince v. *Phillips (Inspector of Taxes)* (1961), 39 Tax Cas. 477; Digest (Cont.
    Vol. A) 897, *1311a.*

Ricketts v. *Colquhoun,* [1926] A.C. 1; 95 L.J.K.B. 82; 134 L.T. 106; 90
    J.P. 9; 10 Tax Cas. 118; 28 Digest (Repl.) 242, *1059.*

---

* Section 212, so far as material, is set out at p. 645, letters C to F, post.
† Rule 7 is set out at p. 646, letter C, post.

Scottish Shire Line, Ltd. v. *Lethem (Surveyor of Taxes)*, (1912), 6 Tax Cas. 91; A
28 Digest (Repl.) 69, *198.*

Whitney v. *Inland Revenue Comrs.*, [1926] A.C. 37; 95 L.J.K.B. 165; 134
L.T. 98; 10 Tax Cas. 88; 28 Digest (Repl.) 357, *1578.*

Case Stated.

This was a Case Stated by the Commissioners for the General Purposes of the B
Income Tax Acts for the Division of West Coscote, Leicestershire. On May 9,
1966, the taxpayer, Leonard Murray Oram, appealed against the refusal of the
inspector of taxes to allow a claim to child allowance for the year ended Apr. 5,
1966, in the full amount of £165. The following facts were proved or admitted:
The taxpayer had a son who, being over the age of sixteen years, was, at the
commencement of and during the year of assessment 1965-66 an undergraduate C
at the University of St. Andrews where he was reading modern languages. The
son had been advised and encouraged by his tutor to reside in France and work
there as a temporary teacher at a lycée in order to perfect his knowledge of
French. The son obtained such an appointment which he held from October,
1964, until June, 1965 (the French academic year), and in October, 1965, he
returned to St. Andrew's University to resume his degree course. During the D
year of assessment 1965-66, the son carried out the duties of such appointment for a period of $2\frac{1}{2}$ months, receiving therefore in France a gross emolument
equivalent to £150. During the son's period of residence in France, board was not
provided, and he was required to provide temporary board and travelling and
necessary incidental expenses at his own sole charge. Hence, the son spent in
France all that he had earned, and none of the emoluments of £150 was remitted E
to, or enjoyed in, the United Kingdom.

It was contended for the taxpayer before the commissioners that the words
" income in his own right " within the terms of s. 212 (4) of the Income Tax Act,
1952, meant income computed in accordance with the Income Tax Acts; that was to
say, income for income tax purposes. The French emoluments were not chargeable to income tax under Cases I, II or III of Sch. E. Though the son was resident F
in the United Kingdom his duties had been carried out entirely abroad and no
part of the emoluments had been remitted to or received in the United Kingdom.
The emolument was not, therefore, chargeable to income tax at all. In the
alternative if (which the taxpayer did not admit) " income in his own right "
did not mean " chargeable income " but meant income in some other and more
popular sense, it still fell to be reduced by the amount of such expenditure as was G
essential to enable the emolument to be earned, which expenditure, on the facts
of the present case, manifestly exceeded £35. It was contended by the Crown
before the commissioners that " income " was nowhere defined in the Income
Tax Acts and the words " entitled in his own right to an income " in s. 212 (4)
of the Act of 1952 referred to an income actually received by the son which was
his own. The expression was not confined to income for income tax purposes, H
but must be read in its common sense or everyday meaning. This contention
was abandoned on the appeal (see p. 646, letter A, post). If " income " meant
" chargeable income " there would have been no need in s. 212 specifically to
exclude income from scholarships and bursaries, since such income was already
exempt from charge by virtue of s. 458 of the Act of 1952. Though the gross
emoluments of £150 were not assessable to income tax under Sch. E or at all,
they had been received by the son as income to which he was " entitled in his
own right ", so that the taxpayer's child allowance should be reduced from £165
by deducting therefrom £35 (being the excess of the gross emolument of £150
over the statutory limit of £115). The commissioners should determine that
the taxpayer was entitled to child allowance in respect of the son for the year
of assessment 1965-66 in the sum of £130 (being £165 less £35).

The commissioners found that the son's emoluments were not assessable to
income tax under Sch. E or at all and allowed the appeal. The Crown appealed.

A   *Heyworth Talbot*, Q.C., and *J. R. Phillips* for the Crown.
     Hubert H. Monroe, Q.C., and *S. T. Bates* for the taxpayer.

Cur. adv. vult.

     July 24, 1967. **UNGOED-THOMAS, J.,** read the following judgment:
This appeal raises the question whether the child allowance for 1965-66, to
B   which the taxpayer is entitled in respect of his son, a boy of over sixteen, who
     is a full-time undergraduate at St. Andrew's University, should be restricted by
     reference to the amount of the son's earnings for 2½ months as a teacher in a
     French school. This question turns on the Income Tax Act, 1952, s. 212, as
     amended (1) which provides:

          " (1) If the claimant proves that he has living at any time within the
C ·   year of assessment any child who is either under the age of sixteen years
          or who, if over the age of sixteen years at the commencement of that
          year, is receiving full-time instruction at any university, college, school
          or other educational establishment, he shall, subject to the provisions of
          this and the next following section, be entitled in respect of each such
          child to a deduction from the amount of income tax with which he is charge-
D   able equal to tax at the standard rate on [the appropriate amount for the
          child] . . .
          " [(1A) The appropriate amount for the child shall vary according to the
          age of the child . . . and [subject to sub-s. (4) of this section] (*a*) for a child
          shown by the claimant to have been then over the age of sixteen, shall be
          [£165]; . . .]
E   " [(4) In the case of a child who is entitled in his own right to an income
          exceeding £115 a year the appropriate amount for the child shall be reduced
          by the amount of the excess, and accordingly no relief shall be allowed
          under this section where the excess is equal to or greater than the amount
          which apart from this subsection would be the appropriate amount for the
          child:] Provided that in calculating the income of the child for the purpose
F   of this subsection no account shall be taken of any income to which the child
          is entitled as the holder of a scholarship, bursary, or other similar educational
          endowment."

     It is common ground that the earnings of the child are prima facie income to
     which he is entitled in his own right within the meaning of sub-s. (4). The
G   difficulty in this cases arises over the two words in sub-s. (4), " an income ". The
     son was advised by his tutor to seek an appointment as a temporary teacher
     at a lycée to improve his French, and he obtained such a post. In 1965-66,
     he earned the equivalent of £150 in the 2½ months that fell into that year of
     assessment. That £150 was spent in France on lodgings and incidental outgoings,
     with the result that nothing remained to be brought into this country when he
H   returned here. The inspector took the view, that, in 1965-66, the son had
     been entitled in his own right to an income exceeding £115, from which it
     followed that the £165 mentioned in s. 212 (1A) (*a*), on which deduction at the
     standard rate of tax would prima facie be calculated, would be reduced under
     sub-s. (4) by the amount by which £150 exceeded £115—that is, £35—making
     £130.
I   The taxpayer's contention before me was the same as before the commissioners,
     namely, that " an income " in s. 212 (4) meant income chargeable to income tax;
     or, as he said, in other words, income for income tax purposes. This was identi-
     fied as the net income chargeable to tax after deduction of expenses but before
     deduction of allowances. As the son's foreign income was not brought into
     this country, it is common ground that it was not chargeable to tax, and, there-
     fore, if the taxpayer's contention is correct, it was not an income of the child

     ───────────────────────────────
     (1) So far as relevant, amended by Finance Act, 1957, s. 12 (3) and Finance Act 1963
     s. 12, s. 13.

limiting his parent's child allowance. The Crown's contention before the com- **A** missioners was that " entitled in his own right to an income " in s. 212 (4), " was not confined to income for income tax purposes, but must be read in its common-sense or everyday meaning ". This contention was abandoned before me, and, in the course of argument, the Crown instead identified " an income " in s. 212 (4) as income computed in accordance with the Income Tax Act, 1952, Sch. 9, rules applicable to Sch. E, r. 7; that is, as equivalent to " emoluments **B** to be assessed ", mentioned in that paragraph, after deduction of the narrowly specified expenses to which the paragraph refers. Rule 7 provides:

> " If the holder of an office or employment of profit is necessarily obliged to incur and defray out of the emoluments thereof the expenses of travelling in the performance of the duties of the office or employment, or of keeping **C** and maintaining a horse to enable him to perform the same, or otherwise to expend money wholly, exclusively and necessarily in the performance of the said duties, there may be deducted from the emoluments to be assessed the expenses so necessarily incurred and defrayed."

It was suggested that r. 7 was not directed to charge to tax, but to calculation of emoluments and, therefore, defined the son's emoluments, although they were **D** not subject to charge to tax. It is true that r. 7 does not itself charge tax, but it does not exist except as a cog in the machinery which produces charge to tax. Section 1 provides for tax being charged in respect of profits and gains described in, inter alia, Sch. E, and in accordance with the provision of the Act applicable to that schedule. Paragraph 1 of Sch. E, provides (2) that tax shall be charged in respect of any office or employment on emoluments therefrom falling under **E** one or more of the cases which are set out. It is for the purpose of ascertaining the tax to be charged on these emoluments that we have the " Rules Applicable to Sch. E " in Sch. 9 to the Income Tax Act, 1952, including r. 7. So r. 7 has no raison d'être or existence except to calculate the charge to tax on emoluments. It is not concerned with emoluments which are not subject to a charge to tax; and it is common ground that the son's French emoluments in this case are not **F** subject to a charge to tax. So r. 7 does not directly define the son's emoluments or income. It is then submitted that r. 7 is merely declaratory of what " income " would be apart from the paragraph. Assuming that " income " must mean net income, I for my part am at a complete loss to understand why net income must necessarily (and, of course, on the hypothesis that r. 7 never existed) be income from which the only permissible deductions are the extremely limited expenses **G** specified in r. 7. The narrowness of those expenses has been the subject of so much criticism that I trust that there is no need to elaborate this.

So it seems to me that " emoluments to be assessed " mentioned in r. 7, after deduction of the expenses therein specified, (i) has no place in the Act of 1952 except to ascertain emoluments on which tax is to be charged, and (ii) is not declaratory of what income or even net income would be apart from r. 7. If, **H** however, r. 7 does not apply directly to the calculation of the son's income in this case, nor indirectly as being truly declaratory of what income is apart from r. 7, then it seems to me that the Crown's definition of " an income " by reference to the r. 7 emoluments collapses. Even if it were sought to define " an income " as net income independently of r. 7, there would be the formidable difficulty of identifying what deductions from gross income should be made in arriving at net income—which, very understandably, may well be why no attempt was made to do so and the Crown's case was rested exclusively on r. 7.

I have now dealt with what appears to me to be the nub of the case, but I will consider what other matters canvassed in the very able arguments addressed to me affect this conclusion. It was conceded by the Crown that the Income

---

(2) Schedule E, para. 1, is substituted in s. 156 of the Income Tax Act, 1952, by s. 10 of the Finance Act 1956.

A Tax Act, 1952, has references to " income " where income means income chargeable to tax. Thus, LORD MACMILLAN in *Astor* v. *Perry* (*Inspector of Taxes*) (3),
referred to " any income " in the Income Tax Act, 1918, as being reasonably
construed to mean any income chargeable with tax. The Crown, however,
pointed out by reference to s. 458, s. 412 and s. 227 that " income " was also
used to refer to income not chargeable to tax; but in those cases the character
B of the income was clearly identified by the statute. It was suggested that the
reference in the proviso to s. 212 (4) to " any income to which the child is entitled
as the holder of a scholarship ", etc., shows that "an income " in the paragraph
preceding the proviso must include income not chargeable to tax on the ground
that scholarships are not chargeable to tax. This suggestion fails, however, as
it appears that all scholarships are not free of charge to tax. Reference was made
C to *Martin* v. *Lowry, Martin* v. *Inland Revenue Comrs.* (4), where it is pointed out
that, particularly in the Income Tax Acts, words do not always have the same
meaning, and that in construing them regard must be had to their context, and
to the statement of LORD SALVESEN, in *Scottish Shire Line, Ltd.* v. *Lethem*
(*Surveyor of Taxes*) (5) that

D " Even in a taxing statute it is legitimate to consider which of two
possible constructions is most in accordance with the spirit and intention
of the Act."

LORD MACMILLAN thus states the law in *Astor* v. *Perry* (6):

" So far as the intention of an enactment may be gathered from its own
terms it is permissible to have regard to that intention in interpreting it,
E and if more than one interpretation is possible that interpretation should be
adopted which is most consonant with and is best calculated to give effect
to the intention of the enactment as so ascertained. More especially, where
two sections forming part of a single statutory code are found, when read
literally, to conflict, a court or construction may properly so read their terms
as, if possible, to effect their reconciliation."

F The second sentence which I have quoted from LORD MACMILLAN'S speech
states a principle of construction that is very familiar and regularly applied
in these courts. The first sentence makes it clear that the court is to regard the
intention of the Act in so far as it is established by the terms of the Act interpreted in accordance with the well-established principles of construction. The
intention is itself ascertained by construction. It is, as any judicial conclusion
must be, ascertained by an objective process of reasoning which can be tested,
and not established by guesswork or some mystique of determination which
would make legislators of judges.

The suggestion which is persuasively made here is that the spirit and intention
of s. 212 is to alleviate the burden of taxation on a parent who has to pay for
the maintenance of a child, and to recognise that, if a child has money of his own
the need to lessen the burden is correspondingly diminished, and, therefore,
that " an income " in s. 212 (4) should be construed as including income of the
child not brought into the United Kingdom at all and not chargeable to tax;
but the conclusion does not follow from the premises. If the spirit and intention
were to reduce the relief where the child has money of his own, not only a child's
income but his capital also should fall within it. Why should a child's money
which he has earned and worked for be counted, but not a windfall? The answer
which would immediately occur would be, " because the Act is an Income
Tax Act ". If, however, the child's money is thus to be limited to his income,
this is a qualification to the suggested spirit and intention; and, if there is that

(3) [1935] All E.R. Rep. 713 at p. 724; 19 Tax Cas. 255 at p. 290.
(4) [1927] A.C. 312 at p. 315; 11 Tax Cas. 297 at p. 315.
(5) (1912), 6 Tax Cas. 91 at p. 99.
(6) [1935] All E.R. Rep. at p. 723; 19 Tax Cas. at p. 288.

qualification because the Act is an Income Tax Act, why should not the quali- A
fication go to the income which such Acts tax and not to the income which
they do not tax? An interpretation so governed, as the Crown suggests, by the
spirit of the Act might in some respects, at any rate, as pointed out by the
taxpayer, be reasonably considered to defeat that very spirit. Thus, if the son
in this case were, in his second year in France, to send home earnings of his
first year, the son would be chargeable to tax in that second year on earnings B
in respect of which his father would have suffered deduction from allowance in
the first year. As so often, particularly in tax statutes, the spirit and intention
of the Act in this case is subject to such uncertainty, at any rate in its application
to this particular provision, that it may provide a misleading rather than a
reliable guide, and in any case affords a less certain guide than the construction
of the words without resort to conceptions of spirit and intention.   C

It was said that, throughout the Income Tax Acts, income had some clearly
defined characteristics; but the difference between the parties arose not so much
over some characteristics of income as in identifying and defining the particular
income within s. 212 (4). Even so, however, the taxpayer countered the Crown's
contention that income in the Acts did not include fortuitous payments by
reference to s. 376, under which fortuitous payments are deemed to be income D
for income tax purposes. This emphasised the difficulty of treating as income
within the Act income which the Act itself does not provide the means of defining.
This brings us back, of course, to the wisdom of the Crown in basing its case on
the definition provided by para. 7, and to the danger of attempting to base it
on some conception of income which the Act of 1952 does not make precise.

The history of the category of reliefs which includes s. 212 (4) is of assistance. E
Child allowance goes back to s. 68 of the Finance (1909-10) Act, 1910, where it
depended not in any way on the income of the child but on the total income
of the parents. Section 9 of the Income Tax Act, 1918, similarly made relief
of various kinds, including relief in respect of children, dependent on the amount
of the parents' income; namely, " his total income from all sources for the year
of assessment, estimated in accordance with the provisions of this Act ". This F
total income clearly means the net income chargeable to tax in respect of which
relief to the extent specified is given; and the references in later sections in which
the relief is given to " the income " limits of the taxpayer clearly referred to the
" total income " mentioned in s. 9. However, in the case of relief in respect of
dependent relatives the relief was, by s. 13 (1) of the Act of 1918, limited in
respect of those " whose income from all sources does not exceed £25 a year ". G
So, in the case of these relations, the relief was limited, not only by reference to
the taxpayer's income but also by reference to the income of the person in respect
of whom relief was given; by reference, in the case of the taxpayer, to " his total
income from all sources for the year of assessment ", and, in the case of the person
in respect of whom relief was given, to his " income from all sources ". This
appears clearly to echo " total income from all sources for the year of assessment ", H
and to have the same meaning, that is, income chargeable to tax.

When this section was replaced by s. 22 (1) of the Finance Act, 1920, that later
section referred to the dependent relative's income as, " total income from all
sources ". " Total income from all sources " was a term of art before these Acts,
and was first defined by statute in the Finance Act, 1927, s. 38 (2), replaced with
immaterial modification by s. 524 (1) of the Income Tax Act, 1952. Section 524 (1) I
provides:

" In this Act ' total income ', in relation to any person, means the total
income of that person from all sources estimated, as the case may be, either
in accordance with the provisions of this Act as they apply to income tax
chargeable at the standard rate or in accordance with those provisions
as they apply to surtax."

The Finance Act, 1920, s. 21 and Sch. 4, replaced the relief provisions in s. 9 to

A s. 13 of the Income Tax Act, 1918, by the provisions of s. 17 and of the following
sections of the Act of 1920. In s. 21 (3) of that Act, there first appeared the provision corresponding to s. 212 (4) in this case. It reads: " No deduction shall be
allowed under this section in respect of any child who is entitled in his own right
to an income exceeding £40 a year." So we have in s. 21 (3) of the Finance Act,
1920, the extension to relief in respect of children of the principle of limitation,
B by reference to the income of the dependant in respect of whom relief is given
contained in s. 13 (1) of the Income Tax Act, 1918, and s. 22 (1) of the Act of 1920.
This limitation on the relief in respect of the dependent relative is by reference to
his chargeable income, so it would be strange if the limitation on the relief in
respect of a child by reference to the child's income were by reference to some
other income than chargeable income. Section 17 (1) of the Finance Act, 1920,
C which introduces the relief sections, is in these terms:

> " An individual who, in the manner prescribed by the Income Tax Acts,
> makes a claim in that behalf and who makes a return in the prescribed form
> of his total income shall be entitled for the purpose of ascertaining the
> amount of the income on which he is to be charged to income tax . . . to have
> such deductions as are specified in the five sections of this Act next following
D made from his assessable income."

" Assessable income " is defined by s. 33 of the Act of 1920 as follows:

> " The expression ' assessable income ' in the case of any income other than
> earned income means the amount of that income as estimated in accordance
> with the provisions of the Income Tax Acts."

E And " taxable income " means income after deduction for relief.

The Crown recognises that, if " an income " in s. 212 (4) of the Income Tax
Act, 1952, replacing s. 21 (3) of the Finance Act, 1920, was either such income,
the taxpayer would be entitled to succeed. It is suggested, however, that the
omission in s. 21 (3) to refer to any such income instead of to " an income " indicates that " an income " does not bear either of these two meanings. Even so,
F this would still leave open the question what meaning it does bear; and, for the
reasons which I have given, it seems to me that the history of this relief legislation
supports the conclusion to which I would have come even apart from it—that
" an income " means chargeable income. Reference was made to *Astor* v. *Perry* (7),
and *Whitney* v. *Inland Revenue Comrs.* (8), and particularly to the observations
of Lord Dunedin in the latter case that (9):

> " income of a non-resident in the United Kingdom accruing out of the
> United Kingdom and not brought within the United Kingdom does not fall
> to be estimated according to the provisions of this Act."

It seems, for reasons already given, that that observation would be as applicable
to the income of a person in respect of whom relief is claimed as to the income of
the person claiming the relief. There is no provision in the Act of 1952 for
estimating any such income which is not chargeable for tax.

The latest case which bears on this issue is *Prince* v. *Phillips (Inspector of Taxes)*
(10). In that case, claim for relief was made by a parent in respect of a child
who earned wages, and the parent claimed to deduct from those wages the cost
of the child travelling to and from work, and of his midday meal. Buckley, J.,
observed (11):

> " It has been submitted on behalf of the Crown that ' income ' in sub-s. (4)
> must mean income in the same sense that it means elsewhere in the Act, that
> is to say, income for income tax purposes; and my attention has been drawn

(7) [1935] All E.R. Rep. 713; 19 Tax Cas. 255.
(8) [1926] A.C. 37; 10 Tax Cas. 88.
(9) [1926] A.C. at p. 51; 10 Tax Cas. at p. 109.
(10) (1961), 39 Tax Cas. 477.
(11) (1961), 39 Tax Cas. at p. 480.

A

to two cases, *Ricketts* v. *Colquhoun* (12) and *Durbridge* v. *Sanderson* (*Inspector of Taxes*) (13), which establish that for the purpose of tax under Sch. E the taxpayer is not entitled to deduct from his income expenses which do not arise actually in the performance of his office or employment, such as the cost of travelling to and from his work or the cost of providing himself with food during that part of the day when he is at work. I think that that submission is sound. Indeed, if it were not so, it seems to me that it would be exceedingly difficult ever to arrive at the amount of income which the child is said to be entitled to in his own right, because it would be extremely difficult to determine precisely what expenditure really was so essential as to be a proper deduction. I think travelling expenses and the cost of providing himself with a midday meal is something which the child has to provide out of his income, not something which has to be deducted before ascertaining his income."

B

C

In that case, the child's income was chargeable to tax and fell within Sch. E, r. 7; and in the circumstances of that case there was no occasion for considering whether r. 7 provided for the calculation of income not chargeable to tax. BUCKLEY, J., however, did hold that " income " in s. 212 (4) meant income for income tax purposes. That income for income tax purposes was income from which, as stated by BUCKLEY, J. (14), the Crown admitted national insurance contributions to be a legitimate deduction. Section 377 (2) of the Income Tax Act, 1952, provides that

I

". . . the total income of that person [namely, the taxpayer who pays the contribution] for that year of assessment shall be calculated accordingly for all the purposes of this Act; . . ."

I

So it seems to me that BUCKLEY, J., was treating " income for income tax purposes " as income chargeable to tax. Further, he emphasised that, unless the Act of 1952 provided for the calculation of an income, it would be extremely difficult to determine it; and in the view which I have expressed, the Act of 1952 does not provide for the calculation of income not made chargeable to tax.

So my conclusion is that the taxpayer is entitled to succeed on this appeal.

Appeal dismissed.

Solicitors: *Solicitor of Inland Revenue; Collyer-Bristow & Co.*, agents for *Ingram & Co.*, Leicester (for the taxpayer).

[*Reported by* F. A. AMIES, ESQ., *Barrister-at-Law.*]

---

(12) [1926] A.C. 1; 10 Tax Cas. 118.
(13) [1955] 3 All E.R. 154; 36 Tax Cas. 239.
(14) (1961), 39 Tax Cas. at p. 479.

A

MEERUPPE SUMANATISSA TERUNNANSE *v.* WARAKAPITIYE PANGNANANDA TERUNNANSE.

[PRIVY COUNCIL (Viscount Dilhorne, Lord Guest, Lord Devlin, Lord Wilberforce and Lord Pearson), November 21, 23, 1967, January 23, 1968.]

B   *Ceylon—Estoppel—Licensor and licensee—Licence granted by deputy Viharadhi-pathi—Implied renewal of licence after death of Viharadhipathi—Implied resumption of possession—Payment of dues by licensee—Whether licensee estopped by his conduct from denying title of licensor—Ceylon Evidence Ordinance, 1896 (c. 14), s. 100, s. 116.*

By s. 116* of the Evidence Ordinance of Ceylon no person who came upon
C   any immovable property by the licence of the person in possession thereof was to be permitted to deny that such person had a title to such possession at a time when the licence was given. In 1928 G. became lawful Viharadhipathi of a temple. In 1930 he executed a deed, which he and the appellant both thought was effective to pass the title Viharadhipathi to the appellant. The true effect of the deed, however, so the Supreme Court of Ceylon later held,
D   was to appoint the appellant to manage the temple as G.'s deputy. In 1942 the appellant permitted the respondent to live on a piece of land belonging to the temple, and shortly afterwards the respondent built a residence on it. The land was about eighteen acres in area and was in cultivation. It was assumed that dues (the landlord's share of the produce of the land) which were paid by the respondent to the appellant at this time were paid to him
E   as deputy of G. G. died in 1944, and the appellant's authority to act as deputy then determined. After G.'s death the respondent continued to pay dues as before. Later, however, the respondent withheld dues and the appellant, styling himself as Viharadhipathi, prosecuted the respondent, who then paid the value of the dues and was discharged, without challenging the appellant's title. In an action by the appellant the trial judge made an
F   order for the ejectment of the respondent, but this was reversed on appeal. On further appeal,

Held: (i) for the purposes of estoppel it was not necessary to consider what the appellant's title truly was, for estoppel depended on what title the appellant was apparently claiming and whether, by conduct, the respondent acknowledged it (see p. 655, letters A and E, post).

G   (ii) the licence granted to the respondent in 1942 was revocable, and, if not granted by the appellant in his own right in 1942, the granting of a new licence after the death of G. should be implied; on such renewal of the original licence there was in law a resumption of possession and the respondent was accordingly estopped from challenging the appellant's title as Viharadhipathi (see p. 656, letters E and F, post).

Dictum of SIR RAYMOND EVERSHED, M.R., in *Foster* v. *Robinson* ([1950] 2 All E.R. at pp. 348, 349) applied.

H   [As to estoppel between licensor and licensee, see 15 HALSBURY'S LAWS (3rd Edn.) 249, para. 458.

As to estoppel by the tenant from denying the title of the landlord, see 23 HALSBURY'S LAWS (3rd Edn.) 409, para. 988; and for cases on the subject, see 30 DIGEST (Repl.) 367, 368, *63-100.*]

Cases referred to:

I   *Collins* v. *Claughton,* [1959] 1 All E.R. 95; [1959] 1 W.L.R. 145; Digest (Cont. Vol. A) 1097, *7888b.*

Cornish v. *Searell,* (1828), 8 B. & C. 471; 6 L.J.O.S.K.B. 254; 108 E.R. 1118; 31 Digest (Repl.) 566, *6871.*

---

* Section 116 is set out at p. 653, letter I, post.

Doe d. Johnson v. *Baytup*, (1835), 3 Ad. & El. 188; 4 L.J.K.B. 263; 111 E.R. A
384; 30 Digest (Repl.) 373, *156.*

Doe d. Harvey v. *Francis* (1837), 2 Mood. & R. 57; 174 E.R. 213; *subsequent
proceedings*, sub nom. *Francis* v. *Doe d. Harvey*, (1838), 4 M. & W. 331;
31 Digest (Repl.) 51, *2092.*

Foster v. *Robinson*, [1950] 2 All E.R. 342; 31 Digest (Repl.) 697, *7888.*

Jones v. *Stone*, [1894] A.C. 122; 63 L.J.P.C. 68; 70 L.T. 174; 30 Digest B
(Repl.) 375, *175.*

Oastler v. *Henderson*, (1877), 2 Q.B.D. 575; 46 L.J.Q.B. 607; 37 L.T. 22;
31 Digest (Repl.) 582, *7020.*

Appeal.

This was an appeal, by leave, from the judgment and order of the Supreme C
Court of Ceylon (SANSONI and HERAT, JJ.) dated May 15, 1963, allowing an
appeal by the respondent from the judgment and decree of the district court of
Matara declaring the appellant to be the controlling Viharadhipathi and chief
incumbent of the Sudassanarama temple in Welihinda and as such entitled
to the land in dispute, and ordering ejectment of the respondent and payment
of agreed damages and costs. The respondent by his third amended answer, D
dated Feb. 21, 1957, denied that the appellant was rightful incumbent of the
temple and the appellant's right to maintain the action. The facts are set out
in the opinion of LORD DEVLIN.

E. F. N. Gratiaen, Q.C., H. Wanigatunga (of the Ceylon Bar) and *Mark Fernando*
(of the Ceylon Bar) for the appellant.

H. A. Koattigode and *M. L. S. Jayasekera* (of the Ceylon Bar) for the respondent. E

LORD DEVLIN: The respondent, who was the defendant in the original
proceedings in the district court of Matara is a bikku, that is a monk or priest,
belonging to a temple in Welihinda. In 1942 he was permitted by the appellant,
who was or who claimed to be the Viharadhipathi, that is, the chief priest or
chief incumbent of the temple, to live on a piece of land of about eighteen acres F
in extent situated at Warakapitiya, about a mile away from the temple but part
of its property. The land had previously been leased for cultivation. Shortly
after 1942 the respondent built on this land an avasa, or residence, in which
he lived with dayakas attached to him. It was the respondent's obligation to
hand over to the chief incumbent the paraveni share, that is, the landowner's
share of the produce of the land. This the respondent did until 1953. It is G
his refusal or failure to do so after that year that has led to the present dispute,
the claim with which the Board is concerned being a claim by the appellant to
eject the respondent from the land.

In the courts below the principal matter in issue was whether the appellant
was the rightful Viharadhipathi of the Welihinda Temple. It is common
ground that, if he was, he was entitled to possession of the land and to eject the H
respondent. Proceedings were begun on Sept. 20, 1954, the appellant in his
amended plaint asking for a declaration that he was entitled to the land and for
an order of ejectment. The respondent in his amended answer denied that the
appellant was the rightful chief incumbent and entitled to the land. The respondent claimed also that, if he was elected, he ought to be compensated for
the cost of the avasa and other improvements made to the land. He claimed
further that in any event he was as a bikku entitled to reside in the temple or
on land belonging to it and to be maintained out of the revenues of the temple.
It is not disputed that this is his right as a bikku, unless he has forfeited it by
his contumacy.

The trial began in September, 1957, and after a number of adjournments was
concluded in December, 1960. The district judge by a judgment delivered on
Dec. 21, 1960, decided that the appellant was the lawful Viharadhipathi and so
declared. The judge made an order for the ejectment of the respondent. He

A   refused him any compensation, finding that the buildings had been paid for
out of the income from the land; and this claim for compensation has not been
further pursued.   The learned judge also held that the respondent had by his
contumacy forfeited his right to residence.   On May 15, 1963, the whole of this
judgment was reversed in the Supreme Court which held that the appellant's
action failed because he could not establish his title as Viharadhipathi.

B   The course which the argument has taken before the Board makes it unnecessary for their lordships to do more than indicate the nature of the dispute as to
title.   It is agreed that in 1928 the Rev. Gunananda became the lawful Viharadhipathi of the Welhinda Temple and of three other temples as well.   On Dec. 26,
1930, the Rev. Gunananda, who was residing in one of his other temples and
found it difficult to manage the Welihinda Temple, executed an Adhikari deed
C   which conferred certain rights and duties on the appellant.   In the opinion of
the district judge the Rev. Gunananda by this deed renounced his rights as
Viharadhipathi of the Welihinda Temple in favour of the appellant.   The Supreme
Court on the contrary held that the deed was not a renunciation and that even
if it were the Rev. Gunananda could not lawfully appoint the appellant as his
successor.   The court held that under the rule of sisyanu sisya paramparawa,
D   which governed the succession, the Viharadhipathi must choose his successor
from among his pupils.   The appellant was not one of the Rev. Gunananda's
pupils; the two men were in fact co-pupils of the previous chief incumbent.
The respondent is the Rev. Gunananda's senior pupil.   The court held that the
true effect of the deed was to appoint the appellant to act for the Rev. Gunananda
as the de facto Viharadhipathi of the Welihinda Temple, so that he could manage
E   that temple on the Rev. Gunananda's behalf.   The Rev. Gunananda died in 1944
and therefore any authority to act merely as his deputy would have come to an
end in that year.   Indeed, the respondent contends that on the Rev. Gunananda's
death, he as the senior pupil and in default of any valid appointment succeeded
him as Viharadhipathi; but he concedes that he is now barred under the
Prescription Ordinance (1) from asserting his claim.

F   In the argument before the Board counsel for the appellant invited their
lordships to decide the appeal in his favour on the simple ground that, whether
or not the appellant was the lawful Viharadhipathi, the respondent was estopped
from challenging his title to possession of the land in dispute.   This contention
was not considered in either of the judgments in the courts below.   The plea
was introduced while the appellant was giving evidence.   It was then accepted
G   as an additional issue and the point was put in argument by the appellant's
counsel, but the district judge did not decide it.   There is no note of the argument
before the Supreme Court, but it has not been suggested that the point was there
abandoned.   It was clearly raised in the appellant's case in this appeal and has
not been objected to before the Board.   Their lordships are obviously at a
disadvantage in considering a point which was left undecided by the courts of
H   Ceylon.   The disadvantage is to some extent diminished by the fact that, as
will appear, the point is governed by English law.   The appellant relies on s. 116
of the Evidence Ordinance which reads as follows:

>   "No tenant of immovable property, or person claiming through such
>   tenant, shall during the continuance of the tenancy, be permitted to deny
>   that the landlord of such tenant had, at the beginning of the tenancy, a title
>   to such immovable property; and
>   "no person who came upon any immovable property by the licence of
>   the person in possession thereof shall be permitted to deny that such person
>   had a title to such possession at the time when such licence was given."

The respondent concedes that he was a licensee of the land in dispute.   His
argument against the estoppel rests, as it will appear, on a narrow interpretation
of the Ordinance.   Section 116 is one of three sections that compose Ch. X of the

---

(1) Ceylon Prescription Ordinance (Nos. 22 of 1871 and 2 of 1889 (c. 68).

Ordinance, which is headed Estoppel.   This chapter is a very condensed version   A
of the English common law on estoppel in pais.   Their lordships consider that
it must be interpreted, and if necessary expanded, in the light of the common law.
The Ordinance is one of a number which follow the Indian Evidence Act, 1872.
This Act, as is well known, was drawn up by Sir James Stephen.   In 1876 he
reproduced it in substance for English lawyers in his DIGEST OF THE LAW OF
EVIDENCE.   The object of the DIGEST was to supply a concise code and not an   B
elaborate treatise, and so principles are briefly stated; but in his introduction to
the first edition STEPHEN said that it was " intended to represent the existing law
exactly as it stands ".   Section 116 of the Ordinance corresponds with art. 112
of the DIGEST.   It is therefore in their lordships opinion legitimate, when applying s. 116, to consult and give effect to the English cases, even if they appear to
go further than the language of the section; and specific authority for so doing   C
is given by s. 100 of the Ordinance which provides that

> " Whenever in a judicial proceeding a question of evidence arises not
> provided for by the Ordinance or by any other law in force in Ceylon, such
> question shall be determined in accordance with the English Law of Evidence
> for the time being."

The authorities which settle the English law are conveniently collected in SPENCER
BOWER AND TURNER ON " ESTOPPEL BY REPRESENTATION " (2nd Edn.) p. 170.
This form of estoppel, although it has since the decision in *Doe d. Johnson* v.
Baytup (2) been extended to licensor and licensee and other similar relationships,
originated out of the relationship of landlord and tenant.   The basis for it is the
acknowledgment or recognition of the landlord's title.   The acknowledgment
may be formal as by the execution of a lease or of a deed of attornment; an
attornment has been defined by HOLROYD, J., in *Cornish* v. *Searell* (3) as " the
act of the tenant's putting one person in the place of another as his landlord ".
Estoppel can also rise informally from any act of recognition, the most common
being the payment of rent after entry or after attornment; but then it is
always open to the tenant to explain that the act relied on was not intended or
understood as a recognition.   In *Doe d. Harvey* v. *Francis* (4), PATTESON, J.,
held:

> " . . . that where a tenancy was attempted to be established by mere
> evidence of payment of rent, without any proof of an actual demise, or of
> the tenant's having been let into possession by the person to whom the
> payment was made, evidence is always admissible on the part of the tenant
> to explain the payment of rent, and to show on whose behalf such rent was
> received."

(See also *Jones* v. *Stone* (5)).

It will be observed that s. 116 does not in terms embrace the situation in which
there has been a change of landlords during the tenancy, nor does it deal with
the effect of payment of rent.   It is on this sparseness of language that the
respondent relies.   He concedes, as their lordships have said, that he is the
licensee of the land in dispute; he admits also that he was let into possession
of it by the appellant as licensor, and it was found against him that until 1953
he paid his dues to the appellant in the form of crops or cash.   He points, however, to the words in the second paragraph of s. 116 " at the time when such
licence was given ", which correspond to the words " at the beginning of the
tenancy " in the first paragraphs.   He says that he does not deny that the appellant had as de facto Viharadhipathi at the time when the licence was given in
1942 the title to possession of the land.   He says, however, the situation changed in
1944 when the death of the Rev. Gunananda deprived the appellant of his de facto

(2) (1835), 3 Ad. & El. 188.
(3) (1828), 8 B. & C. 471 at p. 476.
(4) (1837), 2 Mood. & R. 57 at p. 58.
(5) [1894] A.C. 122.

A title; and he contends that there is nothing in the Ordinance to prevent him from challenging the de jure title which after 1944 the appellant assumed.   For the purposes of the argument on estoppel it is unnecessary, and indeed irrelevant, to consider what the appellant's title truly was.   The question is what was the title which the respondent was apparently recognising, and this depends on the title which the appellant was apparently claiming.   There is clear evidence to

B show that the appellant and the Rev. Gunananda both considered that the deed of Dec. 26, 1930, was effective to pass the full title of Viharadhipathi to the appellant and not merely the power of management.   In 1933 the appellant's title was challenged by another bikku of the Welihinda Temple.   On July 16, 1933, the appellant filed a plaint in the district court of Matara seeking against this bikku a declaration that he, the appellant, was the chief incumbent of the

C Welihinda Temple.   The issue was fought and went to the Supreme Court which on June 7, 1937, granted the appellant the declaration for which he asked. The meaning and effect of the deed of Dec. 26, 1930, was not directly in issue, since the defendant based his claim on a title which he sought to derive from an earlier chief incumbent   The Rev. Gunananda gave evidence, however, in support of the appellant's claim to be Viharadhipathi; and, referring to the

D deed, said he gave it " not temporarily ".

   If the appellant was to the knowledge of the respondent claiming his dues as Viharadhipathi de jure and they were paid to him as such, it would be no answer to an estoppel to say that he could have claimed them in some other capacity or as agent for the Rev. Gunananda, when undoubtedly they would have been payable.   The question is whether acknowledgment or recognition of title is to

E be inferred from the transactions between the parties and the inference depends on what the nature of the transactions was and not on what it might have been. In a case where the bare fact of payment is consistent with an inference either way, the transactions would have to be closely investigated before the correct inference could be drawn.   The payments of the paraveni share made before the death of the Rev. Gunananda covered only a short period and occurred a

F long time before the trial took place.   There is no satisfactory evidence of the terms on which they were demanded and made and, though there may be suspicion, there is no proof that the respondent then knew exactly what the plaintiff was claiming his position to be.   Their lordships will therefore assume in favour of the respondent that he intended to pay his dues to the appellant only as agent for the Rev. Gunananda and will treat the case as if it was not until after the

G Rev. Gunananda's death that the appellant claimed the dues in his own right.

   After this there was no room for misunderstanding.   The respondent knew himself to be the senior pupil of the Rev. Gunananda and knew therefore that if the appointment of the appellant was invalid, it was he himself who was the lawful Viharadhipathi.   Yet the payment of dues continued as before.   From 1948 onwards there is documentary evidence of accounts rendered and payments

H made.   In 1953 when payment was first withheld by the respondent, the appellant prosecuted him for criminal misappropriation and on the complaint form the appellant was styled as Viharadhipathi of the Welihinda Temple.   The record shows that the value of the produce appropriated was thereafter paid to the complainant and the respondent was discharged.   Neither formally then nor later in a letter which he wrote to the appellant in September, 1953, did the respondent challenge his title.   The envelope in which this letter was sent was addressed to the appellant under his title of Viharadhipathi in the respondent's own handwriting and it expresses only distress at the bringing of criminal proceedings.

   The construction which the respondent puts on s. 116 is that under it the estoppel operates only in favour of the first landlord of a tenancy or the original grantor of the licence; and that it cannot operate in favour of their successors in title.   This truncates the English doctrine.   Until attornments were virtually abolished by the Law of Property Act, 1925, s. 151, it was customary, if not

necessary, when a reversion was assigned, for the tenant to attorn to the new   A
assignee.   Many of the cases of estoppel in the books relate to tenants who are
prevented by their attornment from denying the title of the assignee.   Their
lordships need not pause to consider whether the language of the first paragraph
of s. 116 would, if literally construed in its application to a term of years, ignore
an attornment and confine the estoppel to the landlord in possession at the
beginning of the tenancy.   If it does, the scope of the paragraph must by virtue   B
of s. 100 be expanded to give full effect to the English law of estoppel.   The same
considerations apply to the second paragraph which, since the present case is
concerned with a licence, is the one on which the appellant relies.

Their lordships must however add that in their opinion not even the most
limited construction of the second paragraph would on the facts of the present
case avail the respondent.   The licence which was granted to him in 1942 was   C
clearly a revocable one.   A revocable licence is automatically determined by the
death of the licensor or by the assignment of the land over which the licence is
exercised.   Thus if the licence was not originally granted in 1942 by the appellant
in his own right, after the death of the Rev. Gunananda the grant of a new
licence must be implied.   The respondent argues nevertheless that he did not
" come upon " the land by virtue of the new licence but by virtue of that which   D
had expired.   In their lordships' opinion the reference in the paragraph to the
licensee coming on the land does not mean only, or even primarily, a physical
entry; it imports a taking of possession under the licence.   When a lease or
licence is renewed, there is no moment at which the tenant or licensee physically
leaves the land and re-enters it.   There is none the less a new taking of possession
in law.   In *Foster* v. *Robinson* (6) Sir Raymond Evershed, M.R., said: E

> " . . . the determination of the former tenancy was equivalent to delivery
> up of possession under that tenancy and then a resumption of possession
> under a new transaction immediately afterwards.   I think, to use the
> language of Sir Alexander Cockburn, C.J., in *Oastler* v. *Henderson* (7)
> there was a virtual taking of possession."

The principle was applied again by the Court of Appeal in *Collins* v. *Claughton* (8)
where Sir Raymond Evershed's dictum was cited.

Their lordships conclude that the plea of estoppel succeeds.   It applies only
to the respondent's interest as a licensee and does not affect his rights as a
bikku.   Counsel for the appellant said that he would not contest these rights.
Their lordships will therefore humbly advise Her Majesty to allow the appeal
and to restore the order and decree of ejectment made in the district court,
subject to the right of the respondent to continue to reside in the avasa on the
land in suit and to be maintained out of the income of that land or of other
temporalities belonging to the Welihinda Temple.   The respondent must pay
the costs of this appeal.   As to the costs in the courts below their lordships
consider that a large part of them must have been incurred on the issue of title
on which the respondent succeeded in the Supreme Court and which the appellant
has not asked the Board to resolve.   Moreover the final result of the proceedings
is to restore to the respondent his rights of residence and maintenance of which he
was deprived by the judgment of the district court.   Their lordships consider
that in these circumstances each party should pay its own costs of the proceedings
in the court below and they will humbly advise Her Majesty to vary accordingly
the order of the Supreme Court.

Appeal allowed.

Solicitors: *Hatchett Jones & Co.* (for the appellant); *A. L. Bryden & Williams*
(for the respondent).

[*Reported by* S. A. Hatteea, Esq., *Barrister-at-Law.*]

---

(6) [1950] 2 All E.R. 342 at pp. 348, 349.   (7) (1877), 2 Q.B.D. 575 at p. 578.
(8) [1959] 1 All E.R. 95 at p. 98.

THE ANNIE HAY.

COLDWELL-HORSFALL v. WEST COUNTRY YACHT CHARTERS, LTD., AND OTHERS.

[Probate, Divorce and Admiralty Division (Brandon, J.), November 20, 21, 1967.]

Shipping—Limitation of liability—Collision—Actual fault or privity of owner who was also master—Whether entitled to limit liability—Merchant Shipping Act, 1894 (57 & 58 Vict. c. 60), s. 503 (1), as amended—Merchant Shipping (Liability of Shipowners and Others) Act, 1958 (6 & 7 Eliz. 2 c. 62), s. 3 (2).

The motor vessel Annie Hay was involved in a collision with the motor vessel Rosewarne in Falmouth Harbour. At all material times the plaintiff was the owner of the Annie Hay as well as being her master and navigator at the time of the collision, and it was agreed that the collision was caused mainly, at any rate, by his negligence while navigating the Annie Hay. The plaintiff claimed to limit his liability to the defendants under s. 503 (1)* of the Merchant Shipping Act, 1894, as amended, and under s. 3† of the Merchant Shipping (Liability of Shipowners and Others) Act, 1958 (which was designed to give effect to art. (2) and (3)‡ of the International Convention relating to the Limitation of the Liability of Owners of Sea-going Ships made at Brussels on Oct. 10, 1957) for damage to property caused by the collision when he was not only the master but also the owner.

Held: (i) the plaintiff was entitled to limit his liability because the expression " any person in his capacity as master " in s. 3 (2) of the Act of 1958 was wide enough, in its ordinary interpretation, to include the plaintiff (see p. 662, letter C, post); but

(ii) if there was a doubt whether that was the correct interpretation, there were two reasons for adopting it—(a) Parliament had repealed s. 508§ of the Act of 1954 by the Act of 1958 and there was no reason to repeal s. 508 (which, if still in force, would have prevented the plaintiff limiting liability) unless something inconsistent with it, viz., s. 3 (2) of the Act of 1958, was being enacted at the same time (see p. 662, letter E, post); and (b) the doubt should be resolved on the basis that this country had fulfilled its international obligations under the convention rather than disregarded them (see p. 664, letter B, post).

Salomon v. *Comrs. of Customs and Excise* ([1966] 3 All E.R. 871) and *Post Office* v. *Estuary Radio, Ltd.* ([1967] 3 All E.R. 679) applied.

[As to limitation of liability of shipowners and others, see 35 Halsbury's Laws (3rd Edn.) 766-768, para. 1181, 770, 771, para. 1184; and for cases on the subject, see 42 Digest (Repl.) 1066-1068, *8826-8843*; 1070-1071, *8857-8866*.

As to international agreements as aids to construction of statutes, see 36 Halsbury's Laws (3rd Edn.) 411, para. 623.

For the Merchant Shipping Act, 1894, s. 503, see 23 Halsbury's Statutes (2nd Edn.) 656.

For the Merchant Shipping (Liability of Shipowners and Others) Act, 1958, s. 3, see 38 Halsbury's Statutes (2nd Edn.) 1095.]

Cases referred to:

Bramley Moore, The, [1964] 1 All E.R. 105; [1964] P. 200; [1964] 2 W.L.R. 259; [1963] 2 Lloyd's Rep. 429; 42 Digest (Repl.) 1076, *8905.*

Gloucester (No. 26), The, [1964] 2 Lloyd's Rep. 554.

Post Office v. *Estuary Radio, Ltd.,* [1967] 3 All E.R. 679; [1967] 1 W.L.R. 1396.

---

* Section 503 (1), so far as material, is set out at p. 658, letter I, to p. 659, letter C, post.
† Section 3 is set out at p. 659, letters D to F, post.
‡ Article 6 (2) and (3) is set out at p. 662, letter I, to p. 663, letter B, post.
§ Section 508 is set out at p. 660, letter C, post.

Dictum of Brandon, J., *applied in* The Abadesa. [1968] 2 All E.R. 726.

Ran, The, Graygarth, The, [1922] P. 80; 91 L.J.P. 113; 126 L.T. 675; 15 Asp.   A
M.L.C. 517; 42 Digest (Repl.) 925, *7180.*

Salomon v. *Comrs. of Customs and Excise*, [1966] 3 All E.R. 871; [1967] 2 Q.B.
116; [1966] 3 W.L.R. 1223; Digest (Cont. Vol. B) 621, *77a.*

Scruttons, Ltd. v. *Midland Silicones, Ltd.*, [1962] 1 All E.R. 1; [1962] A.C. 446;
[1962] 2 W.L.R. 186; [1961] 2 Lloyd's Rep. 365; Digest (Cont. Vol. A)
271, *261a.*   B

Action.

This was an action by the plaintiff claiming to limit his liability for damage to
property caused by a collision between his motor vessel, the Annie Hay, and the
motor vessel Rosewarne in Falmouth Harbour on Aug. 7, 1966. The facts are
set out in the judgment.

The statutes and cases noted below* were cited during the argument in addition   C
to those referred to in the judgment.

Michael Thomas for the plaintiff.
J. Franklin Willmer, Q.C., for the defendants.

BRANDON, J.: In this action begun by writ dated Apr. 6, 1967, the
plaintiff, Mr. Coldwell-Horsfall, claims to limit his liability for damage to   D
property caused by a collision between his boat, the Annie Hay, and another
boat, the Rosewarne, which took place in Falmouth Harbour on Aug. 7, 1966.
The right of the plaintiff to limit his liability is disputed by certain defendants
who have appeared to the action. Those defendants are, first, West Country
Yacht Charters, Ltd., who were named as defendants and who appeared on
Apr. 14, 1967; and, secondly, four members of the Scarfield family, and Annie   E
Roman and Raymond Sharp, who appeared on May 24, 1967. Certain matters
have been agreed between the parties. First of all, it has been agreed that, if
the plaintiff is entitled to limit his liability, then the amount of the limit is
£188 11s. 8d. Secondly, it has been agreed that the collision was caused mainly,
at any rate, by the negligence of the plaintiff while navigating the Annie Hay.
There is a suggestion on the part of the plaintiff that there was also some fault   F
in the navigation of the other boat, the Rosewarne, and his right to contend
that hereafter has been reserved. The plaintiff was at all material times the
owner of the Annie Hay as well as being her master and navigator at the time
of the collision, and the question which arises for decision is whether, on the
true construction of the relevant Acts of Parliament, he is entitled to limit his
liability when he was not only the master but also the owner. As I have said,   G
the relevant facts have been agreed and they are set out in much greater detail
in an agreed statement of facts, but beyond saying that the defendants who have
appeared are persons who have claims for loss of property against the plaintiff
which are put in the aggregate at £2,716 8s. 9d., I do not think that it is necessary
to go into details.

The relevant provisions governing the right of the plaintiff to limit, if he has   H
such a right, are contained in the Merchant Shipping Acts, and more particularly
in s. 503 (1) of the Merchant Shipping Act, 1894, as amended, and in s. 3 of the
Merchant Shipping (Liability of Ship Owners and Others) Act, 1958. The
Merchant Shipping Act, 1894, s. 503 (1), as amended by s. 2 (1) of the Act of
1958, provides as follows:

" The owners of a ship, British or foreign, shall not, where all or any of
the following occurrences take place without their actual fault or privity;

---

* 7 Geo. 2, c. 14; 26 Geo. 3, c. 86; 53 Geo. 3, c. 159; Merchant Shipping
Act, 1854, Merchant Shipping Act, 1906, s. 71; Merchant Shipping Act, 1921, s. 1;
Crown Proceedings Act, 1947, s. 5; Merchant Shipping (Liability of Shipowners and
Others) Act, 1958, s. 8; *Wilson* v. *Dickson,* (1818), 2 B. & Ald. 2; *The Volant,* (1842),
1 Wm. Rob. 383; *The Northumbria,* (1869), L.R. 3 A. & E. 6; *Pyrene Co., Ltd.* v. *Scindia
Navigation Co.,* [1954] 2 All E.R. 158; [1954] 2 Q.B. 420; *A.-G.* v. *Prince Ernest Augustus
of Hanover,* [1957] 1 All E.R. 49; [1957] A.C. 436.

A   (that is to say) (*a*) Where any loss of life or personal injury is caused to
any person being carried in the ship; (*b*) Where any damage or loss is
caused to any goods, merchandise or other things whatsoever on board the
ship; (*c*) where any loss of life or personal injury is caused to any person
not carried in the ship through the act or omission of any person (whether
on board the ship or not) in the navigation or management of the ship or in
B   the loading, carriage or discharge of its cargo or in the embarkation, carriage
or disembarkation of its passengers, or through any other act or omission
of any person on board the ship; (*d*) where any loss or damage is caused to
any property (other than any property mentioned in para. (*b*) of this subsection) or any rights are infringed through the act or omission of any person
(whether on board the ship or not) in the navigation or management of the
C   ship, or in the loading, carriage or discharge of its cargo or in the embarkation,
carriage or disembarkation of its passengers, or through any other act or
omission of any person on board the ship; be liable to damages beyond the
following amounts: . . . ."

and then there are specified amounts calculated on a basis which, so far as
damage to property in this case is concerned, produces the agreed figure which
D   I have mentioned.   Section 3 of the Act of 1958 provides as follows:

" (1) The persons whose liability in connexion with a ship is excluded or
limited by Part 8 of the Merchant Shipping Act, 1894, shall include any
charterer and any person interested in or in possession of the ship, and, in
particular, any manager or operator of the ship.   (2) In relation to a claim
arising from the act or omission of any person in his capacity as master or
E   member of the crew or (otherwise than in that capacity) in the course of his
employment as a servant of the owners or of any such person as is mentioned
in sub-s. (1) of this section—(*a*) the persons whose liability is excluded or
limited as aforesaid shall also include the master, member of the crew or
servant, and, in a case where the master or member of the crew is the servant
of a person whose liability would not be excluded or limited apart from
F   this paragraph, the person whose servant he is; and (*b*) the liability of the
master, member of the crew or servant himself shall be excluded or limited
as aforesaid notwithstanding his actual fault or privity in that capacity,
except in the cases mentioned in para. (ii) of s. 502 of the said Act of 1894."

The references in s. 3 of the Act of 1958 to exclusion of liability as distinct from
limitation of liability are references to rights given by s. 502 of the Act of 1894.
I am not in this case concerned with such rights, and I need not, therefore,
trouble with the reference to exclusion of liability in s. 3 nor with the exception
in s. 3 (2) (*b*) which relates to s. 502.

Counsel for the plaintiff contends that this case comes within s. 3 (2) of
the Act of 1958.   He says that the claims which the defendants have against the
plaintiff are claims arising from the act or omission of a person, namely, the
plaintiff, in his capacity as master of the Annie Hay, and he says, that being so,
that the persons whose liability is limited include the plaintiff as such master
by virtue of s. 3 (2) (*a*).   He goes on further to say that, by virtue of s. 3 (2) (*b*),
the plaintiff is entitled to limit his liability notwithstanding his actual fault or
privity in his capacity as master, that is to say, the fact that he was at fault
personally in the navigation of the Annie Hay does not prevent him from limiting.

Counsel for the defendants contends that the expression " master " in s. 3 (2),
wherever it occurs, should be construed as meaning, and meaning only, a master
who is a servant of the owner or what I may call quasi-owner, by which I mean
such persons as are included in s. 3 (1), namely, managers, operators, etc.   He
says that it should not be construed as including a master who is himself also
an owner or a quasi-owner in the sense in which I have just used that expression.

In support of his argument, counsel for the plaintiff relied on three main
points.   First of all, he said, that the construction which he invited the court

to adopt was in accordance with the ordinary and natural meaning of the words
used.   In that connexion, he said that the expression " any person in his capacity
as master " was capable, in its ordinary and natural interpretation, of including
a person who was also an owner or quasi-owner and, if it was capable of that
meaning in its ordinary and natural interpretation, then that was the meaning
which should be given to it.   He went on to say that, if he were wrong about
that and the meaning of the words was not plain but obscure, then such obscurity
as existed could be dispersed by a consideration of two matters, and these two
matters constituted his second and third arguments in support of his construction.
He said, first, that one should look at the fact that s. 508 of the Act of 1894 had
been repealed by the Act of 1958, which is indeed the case.   Section 508 of the
Act of 1894 provided as follows:

> " Nothing in this Part of this Act shall be construed to lessen or take
> away any liability to which any master or seaman, being also owner or part
> owner of the ship to which he belongs, is subject in his capacity of master
> or seaman, or to extend to any British ship which is not registered as a
> British ship within the meaning of this Act."

The last part of that section is not relevant to the argument, but the point made
by counsel for the plaintiff is that there was a deliberate repeal of a section which
made it clear under the old law that a master who was also owner could not
limit his liability in a case where he had been negligent as master, and counsel
for the plaintiff asked the question rhetorically: " Why should Parliament have
repealed that provision unless it intended to allow a master who was also owner
to limit his liability? "   The other matter on which counsel for the plaintiff
relied was that the Act of 1958 was intended to give effect by domestic legislation
to the adherence of this country to an international convention (1) relating to
limitation of liability, and his argument was that, by that convention, it was
clearly intended that a person in the position of the plaintiff in this case should
be entitled to limit his liability.   He, therefore, argued that the Act of 1958
ought to be interpreted in such a way as to bring it into line with what had been
agreed in the convention.   I shall later look at the relevant provisions of the
convention in order to see how much importance ought to be attached to that
argument.

Counsel for the defendants also relied on three points.   He said, first of all,
that, while the words relied on by counsel for the plaintiff were capable of having
the wider meaning which counsel for the plaintiff invited me to give them,
nevertheless in their context they should be given a narrower interpretation, and
by their context, as I understood him, he meant two things: first of all, their
immediate context in s. 3 (2) of the Act of 1958 and, secondly, their larger context
in the scheme of limitation legislation as a whole.   As regards the immediate
context, he pointed out that, in s. 3 (2), three persons are mentioned: first, a
master;   second, a member of the crew;   and third, a person employed by an
owner or quasi-owner, and he said that, since the third of these persons was
clearly a servant, one should treat the first and second persons as being servants
also.   Secondly, dealing with the larger context, he said that the scheme of the
Acts as they now existed was that there were two categories of persons who could
limit;   on the one hand there were persons in the category of employers who
were entitled to limit in respect of vicarious liability provided that they were not
guilty of personal fault;   and, secondly, there were persons in the category of
employees who could limit their liability, and in their case they could limit
notwithstanding personal fault.   He said that the first category was covered by
the old Acts as extended by s. 3 (1) of the Act of 1958, and that the second

---

(1) International Convention relating to the Limitation of the Liability of Owners
of Sea-going Ships (Cmnd. 353) signed at Brussels on Oct. 10, 1957.

A category was covered by s. 3 (2), and that it would be wrong to create or recognise
a hybrid character who was a cross between the persons in the first category and
persons in the second category. In this connexion, he further suggested that
the only object of including people in the second category, namely, employees,
within the sphere of persons entitled to limit their liability, was to prevent

B persons with claims in effect defeating the right of owners to limit by suing
servants and hoping or trusting that the employers of those servants would stand
behind them and pay any judgment given against them. He referred in that
connexion to the dissenting speech of LORD DENNING in *Scruttons, Ltd.* v. *Midland
Silicones, Ltd.* (2). The third argument relied on by counsel for the defendants,
which he stressed at every point, was that the Acts of Parliament which give

C persons the right to limit their liability are Acts which take away common law
rights; they deprive people who would otherwise be entitled to recover damages
on the basis of restitutio in integrum from doing so, and he said that, because
of that, if any provision in any such Act was capable of either a wide construction
or a narrow construction, then the narrow construction should be preferred as
being the construction which operated less to take away ordinary common law

D rights.

These being the arguments on either side, the first matter to consider is whether
there is any authority to guide the court on the matter. The Act of 1958 is
comparatively recent and there has been no English decision on the point, but
I was referred to a Canadian decision on an analogous point, *The Gloucester*

E (*No. 26*) (3). That was a decision of ANGLIN, D.J.A., sitting in the Exchequer
Court of the New Brunswick Admiralty District. The question which he had
to determine was a similar question arising on a Canadian Act (4) which was
also, as I understand it, intended to give effect to the international convention
mentioned earlier. The decision was that a person in the situation of the plaintiff
could not limit his liability under the Canadian Act. I do not, however, find

F that I can derive very much assistance from that decision for two reasons. In
the first place, it is a decision under a Canadian Act the terms of which are
different from the terms of the Act which I have to construe. I have not investigated the question whether the differences are such as to justify a different result
under the one Act from the result which would be arrived at under the other,
but one has to recognise that this is a decision under a different Act. The second

G reason is, perhaps, the more important reason why I do not think that I can
derive any assistance from the decision; because it seems to me to be based on
the form of the proceedings in which the question arose. The judge appears
to have decided the case mainly on the ground that the defendant, who was
seeking to limit his liability, had been sued as owner, and he indicated that, had
he been sued as master, the position might have been different.

H I do not think that the question whether a person is entitled to limit his
liability or not ought to depend in any way on the form of the proceedings in
which the question is raised. I do not think that it ought to make any difference
whether he is the plaintiff or the defendant; or whether the action is in rem or
in personam. It seems to me that his rights must be the same whatever the
form of the proceedings. I am confirmed in that view by a certain observation
made by LORD DENNING, M.R., in *The Bramley Moore* (5). Referring to an
earlier decision of the Court of Appeal in *The Ran, The Graygarth* (6), which

---

(2) [1962] 1 All E.R. 1; [1962] A.C. 446.
(3) [1964] 2 Lloyd's Rep. 554.
(4) Canada Shipping Act, s. 657; as amended by 9 & 10 Eliz. 2 c. 32, s. 32 of Statutes
of Canada.
(5) [1964] 1 All E.R. 105; [1964] P. 200.
(6) [1922] P. 80.

LORD DENNING evidently found it difficult to understand, he said (7): "... I cannot see why the form of the collision action should be the determining factor in the limitation action."

Since I cannot, for the reasons which I have given, derive assistance from the Canadian case cited to me, it is necessary for me to approach the matter entirely on the basis of my own view as to the true construction of the statute. In my judgment, the construction put forward by counsel for the plaintiff is the correct one, and I have reached that conclusion for three reasons, which are substantially those on which he relied.   First of all, in my judgment, the construction urged by counsel for the plaintiff is in accordance with the ordinary and natural meaning of the words used in s. 3 (2) of the Act of 1958.   The expression " any person in his capacity as master " is wide enough in its ordinary interpretation to include the plaintiff, and it seems to me that what I am being asked to do by counsel for the defendants is to cut down the ordinary and natural meaning of those words.   I am not satisfied that there is anything in either the immediate context or the larger context which makes it necessary to cut down the meaning of those words so as to put a narrower interpretation on them than they would ordinarily bear.   But if I am wrong about that and it can fairly be said that both meanings are plausible and there is a doubt which should be adopted, then it seems to me that there are two powerful reasons for adopting the meaning urged on me by counsel for the plaintiff.

The first of those reasons is the repeal of s. 508 of the Act of 1894 which, if not repealed, would clearly by its terms prevent the plaintiff from limiting his liability in the present case.   I cannot see any reason why Parliament should have seen fit to repeal s. 508 of the Act of 1894 unlesss it was because it was at the same time enacting something inconsistent with it.   No other reason has been suggested for such repeal and I can think of none.   It was vaguely suggested that it was a tidying-up repeal made on the footing that the law would have been the same whether such action had ever been enacted or not.   It may be— I do not know—that the law would have been the same whether that section had been enacted or not, but the fact is that it was enacted and it was enacted in 1894, not for the first time but after being enacted in a number of earlier Acts in that or similar form.   The inference which I draw from this repeal is that there was something else in the Act of 1958 which was inconsistent with the provision repealed.   Then as to the convention, it has not been seriously disputed that the bulk, at any rate, of the Act of 1958 was designed to give effect by domestic legislation to the International Convention relating to the Limitation of the Liability of Owners of Sea-going Ships made at Brussels on Oct. 10, 1957. That convention provides, so far as material, as follows:

" The High Contracting Parties, having recognised the desirability of determining by agreement certain uniform rules relating to the limitation of the liability of owners of sea-going ships, have decided to conclude a convention for this purpose, and thereto have agreed as follows ...",

and there then follow a number of articles of which, I think, I need only read parts of art. 6 and art. 7.   Article 6 provides:

" (2) Subject to para. (3) of this article, the provisions of this convention shall apply to the charterer, manager and operator of the ship, and to the master, members of the crew and other servants of the owner, charterer, manager or operator acting in the course of their employment, in the same way as they apply to an owner himself: Provided that the total limits of the liability of the owner and all such other persons in respect of personal claims and property claims arising on a distinct occasion shall not exceed the amounts determined in accordance with art. 3 of this convention.

" (3) When actions are brought against the master or against members of the crew such persons may limit their liability even if the occurrence which

(7) [1964] 1 All E.R. at p. 108;   [1964] P. at p. 208.

gives rise to the claims resulted from the actual fault or privity of one or more of such persons. If, however, the master or member of the crew is at the same time the owner, co-owner, charterer, manager or operator of the ship, the provisions of this paragraph shall only apply where the act, neglect or default in question is an act, neglect or default committed by the person in question in his capacity as master or as member of the crew of the ship."

Article 7 provides:

" This convention shall apply whenever the owner of a ship, or any other person having by virtue of the provisions of art. 6 hereof the same rights as an owner of a ship, limits or seeks to limit his liability before the court of a contracting state or seeks to procure the release of a ship or other property arrested or the bail or other security given within the jurisdiction of any such state. Nevertheless, each contracting state shall have the right to exclude, wholly or partially, from the benefits of this convention any non-contracting state . . .",

and I need not read the rest of that art. 7. The protocol of signature to the convention provided that a state could adhere to the convention while making certain reservations, but the reservations were limited to three kinds. When this country adhered to the convention, reservations were made in respect of these matters, but an adhering state could not, by the terms of the convention, make reservations about other matters, and this country did not purport to do so. It seems to me clear, from the terms of art. 6 (2) and (3) of the convention, that it was intended by the convention that a person in the situation of the plaintiff should be entitled to limit his liability. If, therefore, Parliament has been successful in giving effect to the convention, then the same result ought to follow from the Act of 1958.

There are two recent decisions of the Court of Appeal which show that, where domestic legislation is passed to give effect to an international convention, there is a presumption that Parliament intended to fulfil its international obligations. If domestic legislation, apparently intended to give effect to an international convention, plainly did not, then I do not think that it would be possible to override the plain language of the statute by applying the presumption which I have mentioned. The authorities show, however, that, if there is any doubt as to the meaning of such an Act, then the court is entitled to look at the convention and, in a proper case, to apply that presumption. The cases to which I refer are *Salomon* v. *Comrs. of Customs and Excise* (8), and *Post Office* v. *Estuary Radio, Ltd.* (9). Diplock, L.J., giving the judgment of the Court of Appeal in the latter case, said (10):

" There is a presumption, however, that the Crown did not intend to break an international treaty (see *Salomon* v. *Comrs. of Customs and Excise* (8), and if there is any ambiguity in the Order in Council it should be resolved so as to accord with the provisions of the convention in so far as that is a plausible meaning of the express words of the Order. Furthermore, the fact that the Order in Council uses different words from the convention does not of itself give rise to any inference that a different meaning was intended. International conventions which are intended to be given effect by States with differing systems of municipal law do not employ the terms of art of the municipal law of any single country, but seek to express, usually at greater length than would be needed if the terms of art of the municipal law of any one country were used, a general concept which can be translated into the terms of art of the municipal law of each country which becomes a party to the Convention."

---

(8) [1966] 3 All E.R. 871; [1967] 2 Q.B. 116.   (9) [1967] 3 All E.R. 679.
             (10) [1967] 3 All E.R. at p. 682.

I agree with counsel for the defendants that it would have made the task of the
court easier if Parliament had chosen to enact the convention in words more
closely approximating to the words of the convention itself; in particular, if
art. 6 of that convention had been transferred bodily into the Act of Parliament
instead of being transferred, as I think it has been, by a more devious method.
On the footing, however, that there is any doubt about the proper meaning to
be ascribed to s. 3 (2) (b), it seems to me to be clear, on the authorities to which
I have referred, that I should resolve that doubt on the basis that this country
has fulfilled its international obligations rather than disregarded them.

For those reasons, I am of the opinion that this action succeeds, and I hold that
the plaintiff is entitled to limit his liability to the sum which has been agreed.

There are certain observations which I should like to make about the form of
the writ and the form of the agreed statement in this case.   I do not make these
observations with any desire to criticise anybody, but in a desire to indicate what
I think is the most useful practice to follow in certain matters.   As regards the
writ, I observe that, in para. 3 of the prayer, there is relief asked for which it
seems to me doubtful whether the court has power to grant.   The court is
asked to stay " all further proceedings in any action or arbitration arising out of
the said collision . . ."   It does not seem to me that that is relief which this court
has power to give, anyhow, in this action.   If there were any actions pending in
this division which ought not to be allowed to continue because of a decree of
limitation, the proper way to get them stayed would be by an application in
those actions.   The same would apply to any actions proceeding in any other
division of the High Court; the proper way to get them stayed would be to make
an application to a judge in that division in that action.   I have no power to
stay actions in other divisions of the High Court, and I do not think that I have
any power, except perhaps by consent, to stay an action in this division unless an
application is made in that action.   The other matter relates to the agreed
statement of facts.   I am grateful to the legal advisers of both parties for making
the trial of this action easier by agreeing the facts.   As I indicated in the course
of the argument, however, I consider that it is desirable that, where there is an
agreed statement of facts, it should consist only of statements of fact and not
recite matters as to which there are conflicting contentions between the parties
and as to which there is no agreement.   This agreed statement of facts, if I may
say so, tends to mix up the two, that is to say, to mix up information as to facts
which are not agreed with information as to facts which are agreed.   It may be
that, in many cases, it will be convenient for the court to know that there are
matters as to which there is no agreement and as to which each side is reserving
its rights.   It may be in the interest of the parties in such cases to put on record
that rights are being reserved in respect of non-agreed matters; but if it is
necessary or desirable to do that, I think that it should be done either in a separate
document or in a separate part of the document rather than having the two
matters mixed up together.   I am not suggesting that such mixing up as occurred
in this case has caused the court any inconvenience.   The statement is plain
and there is no difficulty in extracting from it what are the agreed facts, but,
so far as the general practice is concerned, I think that it is desirable that an
agreed statement of facts should state only agreeed facts.

Decree accordingly.

Solicitors: *Ingledew, Brown, Bennison & Garrett* (for the plaintiff); *Coward,
Chance & Co.* (for the defendants).

[*Reported by* N. P. METCALFE, ESQ., *Barrister-at-Law.*]

A   HOLDER v. HOLDER AND OTHERS.

[COURT OF APPEAL, CIVIL DIVISION (Harman, Danckwerts and Sachs, L.JJ.),
   November 13, 14, 15, 16, 17, December 8, 1967.]

*Acquiescence—Equitable defence—Knowledge—Rescission of sale sought by
   plaintiff beneficiary on ground that purchaser's renunciation of executorship*
B *was invalidated by prior acts of administration—Plaintiff received payment
   on account of his share of proceeds of sale—Whether knowledge of right to
   avoid sale should in the circumstances be imputed to plaintiff.*

*Agriculture—Agricultural holding—Tenancy—Evidence of contractual tenancy
   from owner allowing occupation for an annual payment—Agricultural
   Holdings Act, 1948 (11 & 12 Geo. 6 c. 63), s. 2 (1).*

C *Executor and Administrator—Purchase by executor of asset of estate—No conflict
   of duty and interest—Farms sold by proving executors to son of testator who
   had purported to renounce probate—Son had acted in administration of estate
   before renouncing—Beneficiary claimed to have sale rescinded—Tenancy of
   farms in favour of son disputed by plaintiff—Beneficiaries knowing that son
   was would be purchaser—Sale by auction with reserve price on valuer's*
D *advice—Valuers not instructed by son—Whether rule of equity that purchase
   of trust property by trustee was applicable.*

The testator owned two farms, Glebe Farm (157 acres) and Lower Farm
(259 acres). By his will, made in July, 1956, he appointed his wife, a
daughter, and a son, V., to be executors and trustees and, subject to a legacy
to his widow, gave all his estate to his trustees to sell and divide the pro-
E ceeds between his widow and his ten children (eight daughters and two sons).
The plaintiff, a son of the testator, occupied the farm house on Glebe Farm,
but the testator farmed the land. In 1952 the testator granted V., and one
D., a tenancy of part (153 acres) of Lower Farm at a rent of £250 per annum.
V. also helped his father with Glebe Farm and the untenanted part of Lower
Farm. In 1957, the testator, who was then seventy-two years of age,
F arranged orally with V. that V. should take over the responsibility for farming
Glebe Farm and the untenanted part of Lower Farm and should pay the
testator £504 per annum in all (roughly £2 per acre) for this as from Michaelmas, 1957. The testator continued to live at Lower Farm, as he had done
before, and he paid the rates. On Aug. 7, 1959, the testator died. In
October, 1959, an executors' bank account was opened in the names of the
executors, moneys were paid into it, cheques for sums totalling £600 signed
by all three executors, were drawn on and paid out of the account, and all
three executors endorsed some insurance policies, and instructed solicitors to
act for the estate. Apart from this V. took no part in the administration of
the estate, but he continued to manage the farms. It was conceded at the
trial that by these acts V. acted in the administration of the estate and that
his renunciation of the executorship, subsequently stated, was invalid*. The
testator's widow instructed valuers to value the farms on the basis that
V. and D. (as to 153 acres) and V. (as to the rest) were entitled to tenancies.
The plaintiff disputed V.'s claim to tenancies. At a meeting of beneficiaries
in March, 1960, agreement was not reached. Thereafter V. was separately
represented. On Aug. 22, 1960, V. executed a renunciation of the executorship; and thereafter took no part in it. The execution of the renunciation
was explained at a meeting of beneficiaries in September, 1960, at which
the plaintiff was present. On Nov. 10, 1960, probate was granted to the
testator's widow and the daughter. In July, 1961, the farms were offered
by the proving executors for sale by auction subject to the tenancies in
favour of V. and D. (153 acres) and V. (the rest), reserve prices of £17,000
for Lower Farm and £14,000 for Glebe Farm being fixed on valuer's advice

* The correctness of this admission was questioned (see, e.g., p. 672, letter B, p. 677,
letter A, and p. 680, letter A, post.

given on the basis of the rents being increased as from Michaelmas, 1962, since higher rents than those being paid could be obtained at that time. V. took no part in instructing the valuer. At the auction sale on July 12, 1961, V. bought Lower Farm for £18,250 and Glebe Farm for £14,000. Notices to increase rent were subsequently served on V. He was unable to complete punctually owing to difficulty in obtaining a mortgage. In February, 1962, the plaintiff through his solicitors pressed the executors to forfeit the deposit that V. had paid and to resell. Later the plaintiff issued a writ againt the executors for an account of their dealings with the estate. In June, 1962, V. completed the purchase, having obtained a mortgage for a sufficient sum bearing interest at 7½ per cent. per annum. In June, 1962, a sum of £2,000 was paid to the plaintiff's solicitors on account of his share of the proceeds of sale. He did not know at this time of the acts of V. in relation to cheques and the executors' bank account. The plaintiff, having changed his solicitors, claimed in February, 1963, that the executors had not been entitled to sell to V., and by writ issued in January, 1964, claimed rescision of the sale and a declaration that the farms should be sold with vacant possession. At the trial the tenancy of V. and D. of 153 acres of Lower Farm was not in issue. The trial judge found that V. was an honest witness, that rents paid for the farms in 1961 were substantially lower than the level prevailing in the district, but this did not affect the prices realised as a purchaser would know that the rents could be increased, and that the prices fetched at the auction sale were, on the footing that V. was entitled to a tenancy of Glebe Farm and part of Lower Farm, good prices.

Held: (i) on the evidence† it had been established, notwithstanding that a claim against the estate of a deceased person was to be jealously scrutinised, that as from Michaelmas, 1957, V. had been granted by the testator an agricultural tenancy (coming within s. 2 (1) of the Agricultural Holdings Act, 1948) of Glebe Farm and of all that was then unlet of Lower Farm at an aggregate annual rent of £504 (see p. 671, letter A, p. 674, letter G, and p. 679, letter H, post).

(ii) in the special circumstances of this case the rule of equity by which a trustee's purchase of the trust property might be avoided did not apply, although V. was appointed an executor by the testator's will and it had been conceded that in view of his having joined in some acts of administration of the estate his renunciation of the executorship had been invalid; the special circumstances in the present case included (a) that V. had never interfered in the administration of the estate, (b) that there was no conflict of duty and interest, for the beneficiaries knew that V. was a would-be purchaser and did not look to him to protect their interests, (c) that V. had taken no part in instructing the valuers or in the preparations for the auction sale, and was not in the position of being both vendor and purchaser, and (d) that any special knowledge which V. had was acquired by him as tenant of the farms not as executor (see p. 671, letters E and F, p. 672, letters B, C and D, p. 677, letter F, and p. 680, letter D, post).

Ex p. Lacey ((1802), 6 Ves. 625) and *Ex p. James* ([1803-13] All E.R. Rep. 78) distinguished.

(iii) even if the sale to V. had been voidable at the instance of the plaintiff, the circumstances were such that it would be inequitable to allow the plaintiff to assert any right in equity which he might have, on that assumption, to have the auction sale set aside, because at the time when he received the £2,000 on account of the proceeds of sale he had full knowledge of the sale and stood by, making no attempt to stop completion, and restitutio in integrum was not possible; accordingly, equitable relief by way of rescission

---

† For a brief summary of the evidence, see p. 670, letter I, to p. 671, letter A, post.

A should not be granted, even though the plaintiff did not know until later of
any right to avoid the sale by reason of V.'s renunciation of executorship
being invalid, and (per DANCKWERTS, L.J.) the plaintiff must be taken to
have acquiesced in V.'s purchase (see p. 673, letter G, p. 678, letters E and
G, p. 679, letter B, and p. 682, letter I, to p. 683, letter A, post).

Dictum of WILBERFORCE, J., in *Re Pauling's Settlement Trusts* ([1961]
B 3 All E.R. at p. 730) approved and applied.

Decision of CROSS, J. ([1966] 2 All E.R. 116) affirmed on different grounds
as to holding (i) in the headnote to that report, and reversed on holding (ii),
with the consequence that holding (iii) would not be applicable.

[As to disqualification of trustees for acquiring trust property and the setting
aside of such purchases, see 38 HALSBURY'S LAWS (3rd Edn.) 961-964, paras.
C 1664-1669; and for cases on these subjects, see 43 DIGEST 778-784, *2189-2245*.

As to renunciation of office of executor, see 16 HALSBURY'S LAWS (3rd Edn.)
131-132, paras. 197-199; and as to the elements of estoppel by acquiescence, see
14 HALSBURY'S LAWS (3rd Edn.) 639, para. 1179.

For s. 2 of the Agricultural Holdings Act, 1948, see 28 HALSBURY'S STATUTES
D (2nd Edn.) 29.]

Cases referred to:

Armstrong v. *Jackson*, [1916-17] All E.R. Rep. 1117; [1917] 2 K.B. 822; 86
  L.J.K.B. 1375; 117 L.T. 479; 44 Digest (Repl.) 413, *196*.

Boles and British Land Co.'s Contract, Re, [1902] 1 Ch. 244; 71 L.J.Ch. 130;
  85 L.T. 607; 47 Digest (Repl.) 260, *2290*.

Bulmer, Re, The Trustee and Inland Revenue Comrs. v. *National Provincial
  Bank, Ltd.*, [1936] 3 All E.R. 366; [1937] Ch. 499; 4 Digest (Repl.)
  574, *5103*.

Clark v. *Clark*, (1884), 9 App. Cas. 733; 53 L.J.P.C. 99; 51 L.T. 750; 36
  Digest (Repl.) 573, *1309*.

Cockerell v. *Cholmeley*, (1830), 1 Russ. & M. 418; 39 E.R. 161; 35 Digest
  (Repl.) 97, *20*.

Holt v. *Markham*, [1922] All E.R. Rep. 134; [1923] 1 K.B. 504; 92 L.J.K.B.
  406; 128 L.T. 719; 35 Digest (Repl.) 170, *559*.

Howlett (decd.), Re Howlett v. *Howlett*, [1949] 2 All E.R. 490; [1949] Ch. 767;
  [1949] L.J.R. 1632; 32 Digest (Repl.) 570, *1605*.

James, Ex p., [1803-13] All E.R. Rep. 78; (1803), 8 Ves. 337; 32 E.R. 385;
  47 Digest (Repl.) 258, *2269*.

Lacey, Ex p., (1802), 6 Ves. 625; 31 E.R. 1228; 47 Digest (Repl.) 259, *2278*.

Pauling's Settlement Trusts, Re, Younghusband v. *Coutts & Co.*, [1961] 3 All E.R.
  713; [1962] 1 W.L.R. 86; *revsd.* C.A., [1963] 3 All E.R. 1; [1964] Ch.
  303; [1963] 3 W.L.R. 742; 47 Digest (Repl.) 513, *4656*.

Seddon v. *North Eastern Salt Co., Ltd.*, [1904-07] All E.R. Rep. 817; [1905]
  1 Ch. 326; 74 L.J.Ch. 199; 91 L.T. 793; 35 Digest (Repl.) 20, *119*.

Stafford v. *Stafford*, (1857), 1 De G. & J. 193; 29 L.T.O.S. 368; 44 E.R. 697;
  20 Digest (Repl.) 560, *2636*.

Tennant v. *Trenchard*, (1869), 4 Ch. App. 537; 38 L.J.Ch. 661; 47 Digest
  (Repl.) 260, *2289*.

Willmott v. *Barber*, (1880), 15 Ch.D. 96; 49 L.J.Ch. 792; 43 L.T. 95; *on appeal*,
  (1881), 17 Ch.D. 772; 44 Digest (Repl.) 55, *409*.

Appeal.

The action was brought by the plaintiff, Frank William Holder, the elder son
of the testator, Frank Holder, by writ issued on Jan. 29, 1964, against three
defendants, Emily Louisa Holder (the testator's widow), Barbara Mary Campbell
(a daughter of the testator) and Victor James Holder (the testator's younger son).
The first and second defendants were executors and trustees of the will of the
testator, who died on Aug. 7, 1959; probate of the testator's will dated July 11,
1956, was granted to them on Nov. 10, 1960. The third defendant was also

appointed an executor and trustee of the testator's will, but he renounced probate A by writing dated Aug. 22, 1960. It was conceded that prior to that purported renunciation he had acted in the administration of the testator's estate. The testator owned two farms, Lower Farm and Glebe Farm. The plaintiff disputed a tenancy of Glebe Farm and part of Lower Farm, which the third defendant maintained that the testator had granted to him. On July 12, 1961, the farms were offered for sale by auction by the first and second defendants, subject to the B tenancy in dispute and another tenancy, and were bought by the third defendant for £32,250. The plaintiff by his statement of claim dated Apr. 16, 1964, after alleging among other matters that the third defendant continued to be an executor notwithstanding his renunciation and that he was not entitled to the tenancy of Glebe Farm and part of Lower Farm claimed (i) a declaration that the sales of the two farms ought to be rescinded and set aside with all necessary C accounts and enquiries and a declaration that the farms ought to be sold with vacant possession; (ii) alternatively, as against the first and second defendants, an account of the farms and rents and profits and the proceeds of sale thereof on the footing of wilful default. The first two defendants denied by their defence that the third defendant's renunciation was ineffective and alleged that his tenancy in fact existed, or alternatively that they had reasonable grounds for D thinking that he was tenant and alleged that the plaintiff had acquiesced in the sale of the farms. The third defendant, in addition to pleading like defences, counterclaimed possession of the farm house on Glebe Farm.

On the trial of the action, reported [1966] 2 All E.R. 116, CROSS, J., held that the third defendant's tenancy existed, but set aside the sale to him conditionally on a reserve price, to be calculated as CROSS, J., directed, being reached on a E resale by auction, and ordered that the third defendant should not be entitled to bid at the resale. The plaintiff appealed against the decision that the tenancy existed; and the third defendant cross-appealed against the order* setting aside the sale.

H. E. Francis, Q.C., and Paul V. Baker for the plaintiff.

J. Maurice Price for the first and second defendants.

S. W. Templeman, Q.C., and Martin Nourse for the third defendant.

Cur. adv. vult.

Dec. 8, 1967. The following judgments were read:

HARMAN, L.J.: The plaintiff in the action out of which this appeal arises is the elder son and a beneficiary under the will of the testator Frank Holder. He brought this action against the first two defendants, his mother and sister, the proving executors of the testator's will and also beneficially interested under it, and against the third defendant, the testator's younger son, a beneficiary under the will and named as executor, but who has not proved. The plaintiff's claim was to set aside the sale to the third defendant of two farms the property of the testator, first on the footing that the auction particulars had wrongly stated that G these farms were subject to tenancies in favour of the third defendant and another, whereas they should have been sold with vacant possession. By way of alternative the plaintiff sought to set aside the sales on the ground that the third defendant was an executor of the will and as such disentitled to purchase at the auction. There were also claims against the proving executors for an account on the footing of wilful default, but that was abandoned at the Bar and I need say no more about it. The judge rejected the plaintiff's main claim, holding that the conditions of sale were correct and that the tenancies alleged did exist, but he acceded to the plaintiff's alternative claim and made a very complicated order (1) conditionally setting aside the sale, the condition being that if the reserve price on the resale (to be calculated as a result of enquiries embodied

_____

* As to the form of order, see above and top of p. 669, post.

(1) This order is set out in [1966] 2 All E.R. 116 at pp. 131-133.

A in the order) exceeded the former price, the sales should be set aside and otherwise they should stand.   This is no doubt the right form of order where a resale is ordered, because the purchaser is disqualified as being a trustee.   He is held to his bargain if the new reserve price be not reached, but loses if it be exceeded. The learned judge also held that the third defendant was not entitled to bid at the new auction.

B   The facts are fully stated in the judgment of the judge below (2) and I need not repeat them except in outline.   The testator owned two farms in Gloucester, one called Lower Farm, where he lived with his wife and daughter, the first and second defendants, and his younger son the third defendant, and the other known as Glebe Farm, where the plaintiff has lived since 1952 rent-free as licensee of the farmhouse thereon; he has been ordered by the judge to give up possession

C to the third defendant on that footing.

       In 1952, as was admitted at the Bar though denied in the pleadings, an oral agricultural tenancy was created by the testator in favour of the third defendant and one Denley, who had married one of the third defendant's eight sisters, at a rent of £250 a year, of a part of Lower Farm extending to 153 acres out of 259. There was no written document connected with the transaction.   This left the

D testator farming the remaining 106 acres of Lower Farm and the 157 acres comprising Glebe Farm.   In this he was helped by the third defendant, who lived with his parents both before and after his marriage in 1953 at Lower Farm.   The third defendant also began about the same time to deal in stock on his own account and he kept them with his father's consent on one or other of the farms. By 1955 he owned half the stock on the farms, and by 1957, when he bought

E two hundred ewes from the testator, the whole of it.   By this time the testator was ill and minded to give up farming, and he had a conversation with his son in which he said he could let the farms at £2 an acre.   The third defendant expressed his willingness to take them over at that rent, and to this proposal the testator assented; and thenceforth the third defendant was in control of both farms, so far as not let to him and Denley, at a rent of £504 per annum.   It ap-

F pears that in April, 1957, the third defendant felt that he owed something to the testator for the keep of his stock and he paid him £250, but disclaimed any idea that this was intended to create a tenancy.   In October, 1958, the third defendant paid the testator a cheque for £700, of which, according to the testator's statement to his widow, Mrs. Holder, £500 represented rent from Michaelmas, 1957.

       The testator died on Aug. 7, 1959, having by a will made in 1950 appointed the defendants to be executors and creating a trust for sale with an equal division of the proceeds among his ten children.   He was the owner, besides the two farms, of some £4,000 on deposit at the bank and some personal chattels.   The widow instructed solicitors on behalf of the executors, and the solicitors caused an executors' account to be opened on which during the period between October 1959, and August, 1960, the third defendant joined in signing nine cheques in

I payment of the testator's debts.   The third defendant also signed some documents sent him by an insurance company endorsing over policies on the house and farm machinery.

       The plaintiff took legal advice in August, 1959, and preferred a number of claims of no substance against the executors, as for instance that he was a partner and that he had wages owing to him.   The third defendant continued to live in the house at Lower Farm and carried on the two farms.   As might have been expected, the members of the family could not agree on the disposal of the testator's farms, and there were various abortive meetings in 1960 in an attempt to arrive at a settlement.   At one such meeting in April, 1960, when it became obvious that the third defendant desired to buy the farms and that the plaintiff objected, the third defendant was advised to seek separate advice and in August, 1960, he did instruct solicitors on his own behalf.   They appear to have advised

(2) [1966] 2 All E.R. at pp. 119–125.

him at once that if he wished to buy the properties he must renounce the executor-   A
ship and this he did by an instrument made in August, 1960, which recited that
he had not intermeddled with the estate.   A person in that position is not
debarred from purchasing the trust property: see *Clark* v. *Clark* (3).   In
September, 1960, he offered £30,000 for the farms, but the family thought this
not enough.   Probate was granted to the first and second defendants in November,
1960, on the footing that the third defendant had renounced.   The first defendant,   B
Mrs. Holder, then instructed the valuer, Mr. Hone, who had already valued for
probate at her request, to revise his valuation with a view to fixing reserves for
an auction of the properties.   The probate values, which of course relate to
August, 1959, were agreed with the district valuer at £14,000 for Lower Farm
and £8,000 for Glebe Farm.   The reserves fixed for the purposes of the auction
were £17,000 for Lower Farm and £14,000 for Glebe Farm.   These reserves were   C
fixed on the footing that agricultural tenancies existed first in favour of the
third defendant and his brother-in-law, and secondly of the third defendant
himself.   No attempt had been made to raise the rents since the testator's
death and they were admittedly too low, but any purchaser could increase them
as from Michaelmas, 1962, and the reserves took that fact into account.   The
auction was held in July, 1961, and was attended by all the members of the   D
family in England and some outsiders.   The plaintiff through his solicitor
objected that the sale should be with vacant possession except for a tenancy in
his favour of Glebe Farm house, but the executors' solicitor refused to accede to
this.   The plaintiff raised no further objection.   The third defendant bid
through his solicitor and purchased the properties at an aggregate price of £32,500.
This, as the judge found, was a good price if the alleged agricultural tenancies   E
did in fact exist, but considerably less than a full price if vacant possession could
be given.

The judge held that the agricultural tenancies in question did exist and that
the conditions of sale were rightly drawn, and it is against that decision that
the plaintiff appeals.

This is an issue of fact.   The judge decided it in favour of the third defendant   F
on what he called the absence of evidence that there were no such tenancies.
He said this (4):

"What I have to consider is whether, in the absence of any positive
evidence that they did not intend to create legal rights, there are any circumstances in the case which would, or might, prevent the law from drawing
the inference that a legally binding relationship was created.   After all, if   G
one man allows another to occupy his land in return for an annual payment
the inference, in the absence of evidence to the contrary, must be made that
he is granting a tenancy or a contractual licence."

I pause to say that a contractual licence is enough having regard to the Agricultural Holdings Act (5) to create an agricultural yearly tenancy.

I agree with the judge on his conclusion, but I should have said that it was   H
not necessary to rely on a mere absence of evidence to the contrary but that
there was strong positive evidence of the existence of the tenancies.   The tenancy
in favour of the third defendant and his brother-in-law, although entirely oral,
was admitted at the Bar, and the absence of written evidence altogether fails
to convince me that there was no intention to create a binding arrangement as to
the rent in 1957 in view of the testimony first of the third defendant himself,   I
whose honesty was favourably rated by the judge, secondly the evidence of
the widow to the effect that the testator had told her both in 1957 and in 1958
that rent was payable, thirdly the evidence of Mr. Parker, the testator's accountant, who communicated to the tax inspector when settling the testator's liabilities
that these lettings had been made in 1957.   This was based on information

---

(3) (1884), 9 App. Cas. 733.   (4) [1966] 2 All E.R. at p. 125.
(5) See the Agricultural Holdings Act, 1948, s. 2 (1).

A supplied to him by the testator. I do not see why these pieces of evidence
should be rejected even though it be true that claims against the estate of a dead
man must be scrutinised with a jealous eye. Moreover, it seems to me inherently
improbable that the testator and the third defendant did not intend by
their arrangement to create legal rights and obligations between them. I am
therefore of opinion that the plaintiff's appeal fails and must be dismissed.

B   The cross-appeal raises far more difficult questions, and they are broadly three.
First, whether the actions of the third defendant before probate made his renunciation ineffective. Second, whether on that footing he was disentitled from
bidding at the sale. Third, whether the plaintiff is disentitled from taking this
point because of his acquiescence.

It was admitted at the Bar in the court below that the acts of the third defen-
C dant were enough to constitute intermeddling with the estate and that his
renunciation was ineffective. On this footing he remained a personal representative even after probate had been granted to his co-executors and could have been
obliged by a creditor or a beneficiary to re-assume the duties of an executor.
The judge decided in favour of the plaintiff on this point because the third
defendant at the time of the sale was himself still in a fiduciary position and,
D like any other trustee, could not purchase the trust property. I feel the force of
this argument, but doubt its validity in the very special circumstances of this
case. The reason for the rule is that a man may not be both vendor and purchaser; but the third defendant was never in that position here. He took no
part in instructing the valuer who fixed the reserves or in the preparations for
the auction. Everyone in the family knew that he was not a seller but a buyer.
E In this case the third defendant never assumed the duties of an executor. It is
true that he concurred in signing a few cheques for trivial sums and endorsing a
few insurance policies, but he never so far as appears interfered in any way with
the administration of the estate. It is true he managed the farms, but he did that
as tenant and not as executor. He acquired no special knowledge as executor.
What he knew he knew as tenant of the farms.

F   Another reason lying behind the rule is that there must never be a conflict of
duty and interest, but in fact there was none here in the case of the third defendant, who made no secret throughout that he intended to buy. There is of
course ample authority that a trustee cannot purchase. The leading cases are
decisions of LORD ELDON, L.C.—*Ex p. Lacey* (6) and *Ex p. James* (7). In the
former case LORD ELDON, L.C., expressed himself thus (8):

G   " The rule I take to be this: not, that a trustee cannot buy from his cestui
que trust, but, that he shall not buy from himself. If a trustee will so deal
with his cestui que trust, that the amount of the transaction shakes off the
obligation, that attaches upon him as trustee, then he may buy. If that case
is rightly understood, it cannot lead to much mistake. The true interpretation of what is there reported does not break in upon the law as to trustees.
H The rule is this. A trustee, who is entrusted to sell and manage for others,
undertakes in the same moment, in which he becomes a trustee, not to
manage for the benefit and advantage of himself."

In *Ex p. James* LORD ELDON, L.C., said this (9):

      " This doctrine as to purchases by trustees, assignees, and persons having
I   a confidential character, stands much more upon general principle than
upon the circumstances of any individual case. It rests upon this, that the
purchase is not permitted in any case, however honest the circumstances,
the general interests of justice requiring it to be destroyed in every instance."

These are no doubt strong words, but it is to be observed that LORD ELDON
was dealing with cases where the purchaser was at the time of sale acting for the

(6) (1802), 6 Ves. 625.   (7) [1803-13] All E.R. Rep. 78; (1803), 8 Ves. 337.
(8) (1802), 6 Ves. at p. 626.
(9) [1803-13] All E.R. Rep. at pp. 81, 82; (1803), 8 Ves. at p. 344.

vendors. In this case the third defendant was not so acting: his interference   A
with the administration of the estate was of a minimal character, and the last
cheque that he signed was in August before he executed the deed of renunciation.
He took no part in the instructions for probate, nor in the valuations or fixing
of the reserves. Everyone concerned knew of the renunciation and of the reason
for it, namely that he wished to be a purchaser. Equally, everyone including the
three firms of solicitors engaged assumed that the renunciation was effective and   B
entitled the third defendant to bid. I feel great doubt whether the admission
made at the Bar was correct, as did the judge, but assuming that it was right,
the acts were only technically acts of intermeddling and I find no case where the
circumstances are parallel. Of course, I feel the force of the judge's reasoning
that if the third defendant remained an executor he is within the rule, but in a
case where the reasons behind the rule do not exist I do not feel bound to apply it.   C
My reasons are that the beneficiaries never looked to the third defendant to
protect their interests. They all knew he was in the market as purchaser;
that the price paid was a good one and probably higher than anyone not a sitting
tenant would give. Further, the first two defendants alone acted as executors
and sellers: they alone could convey: they were not influenced by the third
defendant in connexion with the sales.   D

I hold, therefore, that the rule does not apply in order to disentitle the third
defendant to bid at the auction, as he did. If I be wrong on this point and the
rule applies so as to disentitle the third defendant to purchase, there arises
a further defence, namely, that of acquiescence, and this requires some further
recital of the facts.

Completion of the sale was due for Michaelmas, 1961, but by that time the   E
third defendant was not in a position to find the purchase money. The proving
executors served a notice to complete in October, 1961, and, the validity of this
notice being questioned, served a further notice in December. In February,
1962, the plaintiff's solicitor pressed the defendants to forfeit the third defendant's deposit and this was a right given by the contract of sale and is an affirmation of it. Further, in May, 1962, the plaintiff issued a writ for a common   F
decree of administration against the proving executors, seeking thus to press
them to complete the contract and wind up the estate. The contract was in
fact completed in June, 1962, and in the same month £2,000 on account was paid
to and accepted by the plaintiff as his share and he thereupon took no further
steps with his action. In order to complete, the third defendant borrowed
£21,000 from the Agricultural Mortgage Corporation with interest at 7½ per cent.   G
He also borrowed £3,000 from his mother with interest at 6½ per cent., and a like
sum from his sister at a similar rate of interest. In November, 1962, the third
defendant demanded possession of Glebe Farm house from the plaintiff, who at
that time changed his solicitors, and it was suggested by the new solicitors in
February, 1963, that the third defendant was disqualified from bidding at the
auction. This was the first time any such suggestion had been made by anyone   H
The writ was not issued till a year later.

I have found this question a difficult one. The plaintiff knew all the relevant
facts but he did not realise nor was he advised till 1963 that the legal result might
be that he could object to his brother's purchase because he continued to be a
personal representative. There is no doubt strong authority for the proposition
that a man is not bound by acquiescence until he knows his legal rights. In   I
Cockerell v. *Cholmeley* (10) SIR JOHN LEACH, M.R., said this:

"It has been argued that the defendant, being aware of the facts of the
case in the lifetime of Sir Henry Englefield, has, by his silence, and by being
a party to the application to Parliament, confirmed the title of the plaintiffs.
In equity it is considered, as good sense requires it should be, that no man
can be held by any act of his to confirm a title, unless he was fully aware at

(10) (1830), 1 Russ. & M. 418 at p. 425.

A   the time, not only of the fact upon which the defect of title depends, but of the consequence in point of law; and here there is no proof that the defendant, at the time of the acts referred to, was aware of the law on the subject . . .''

There, however, the judge was asked to set aside a legal right. In *Willmott* v. *Barber* (11) Fry, J., said this:

B

"A man is not to be deprived of his legal rights unless he has acted in such a way as would make it fraudulent for him to set up those rights. What, then, are the elements or requisites necessary to constitute fraud of that description? In the first place the plaintiff must have made a mistake as to his legal rights. Secondly, the plaintiff must have expended some money or must have done some act (not necessarily upon the defendant's land) on the faith of his mistaken belief. Thirdly, the defendant, the possessor of the legal right, must know of the existence of his own right which is inconsistent with the right claimed by the plaintiff. If he does not know of it he is in the same position as the plaintiff, and the doctrine of acquiescence is founded upon conduct with a knowledge of your legal rights."

C

D   On the other hand, in *Stafford* v. *Stafford* (12) Knight Bruce, L.J., said this:

"Generally, when the facts are known from which a right arises, the right is presumed to be known . . .''

Like the judge, I should desire to follow the conclusion of Wilberforce, J., who reviewed the authorities, in *Re Pauling's Settlement Trusts, Younghusband* v. *Coutts & Co.* (13); and this passage was mentioned without dissent in the same case in the Court of Appeal (14):

E

"The result of these authorities appears to me to be that the court has to consider all the circumstances in which the concurrence of the cestui que trust was given with a view to seeing whether it is fair and equitable that, having given his concurrence, he should afterwards turn round and sue the trustees: that, subject to this, it is not necessary that he should know that what he is concurring in is a breach of trust, provided that he fully understands what he is concurring in, and that it is not necessary that he should himself have directly benefited by the breach of trust."

F

There is, therefore, no hard and fast rule that ignorance of a legal right is a bar, but the whole of the circumstances must be looked at to see whether it is just that the complaining beneficiary should succeed against the trustee.

G

On the whole I am of opinion that in the circumstances of this case it would not be right to allow the plaintiff to assert his right (assuming he has one) because with full knowledge of the facts he affirmed the sale. He has had £2,000 as a result. He has caused the third defendant to embark on liabilities which he cannot recoup. There can in fact be no restitutio in integrum which is a necessary element in rescission.

H

The plaintiff is asserting an equitable and not a legal remedy. He has by his conduct disentitled himself to it. It is extremely doubtful whether the order if worked out would benefit anyone. I think we should not assent to it, on general equitable principles.

DANCKWERTS, L.J.: This appeal raises two points. The first of these is whether at the date of the testator's death on Aug. 7, 1959, the younger son, Victor, the third defendant, was entitled to a tenancy of and occupied the otherwise unlet portions of the farm as a tenant of the testator. It is quite clear that from 1952 153 acres of Lower Farm, Oxenton, has been let to the third defendant and his brother-in-law, Denley, by the testator at a rent of £250 a year.

---

(11) (1880), 15 Ch.D. 96 at p. 105.   (12) (1857), 1 De G. & J. 193 at p. 202.
(13) [1961] 3 All E.R. 713 at p. 730.   (14) [1963] 3 All E.R. 1; [1964] Ch. 303.

The testator made his will on July 11, 1956, when he was still carrying on his **A** farming business on the rest of Lower Farm and on Glebe Farm. By that will he gave a legacy of £1,000 to his widow and gave his estate to his trustees on trust to sell and divide the proceeds between his widow and his ten children (two sons and eight daughters) in equal shares. He named as executors the third defendant and the widow, the first defendant, and one daughter, Mrs. Barbara Campbell, the second defendant, but in 1957 the testator (who was **B** seventy-two and in bad health) had decided to retire and hand over his farms to his younger son, the third defendant. The third defendant was accepted by the judge to be a trustworthy witness and, if his evidence is accepted, it is clear that the testator (who said that he could let his farms at £2 per acre) intended to let Glebe Farm to the third defendant on an agricultural tenancy at a rent of £504 a year, and to let to him the unlet portion of Lower Farm at a rent annually **C** of £190.

It is said that the terms of the testator's will showed a desire for equality among his children and the testator could not have intended to give the third defendant a special position; but there was every reason why the testator should prefer the third defendant. The third defendant, who was born in 1931, not only farmed the 153 acres of part of Lower Farm but helped his father in his **D** farming business, and with his father's consent built up a farming business of his own and by 1957 there was very little of his father's stock left on the land. There was also another compelling reason for letting the land to the third defendant at a rent, in that the testator, no longer having the profits of a farming business, would need an income for his support. As in the stories of Hans Andersen and Grimm, the younger son was the hardworking and enterprising **E** son, and he was on very good terms with his father. Not so the eldest son, the plaintiff in this action. He was allowed to live rent-free in the small farm-house on Glebe Farm, so that he could look after his father's stock, but the evidence is that he did very little work and was content to live on £2 10s. a week pocket money from his father, and the earnings of his wife as a personnel officer. His wife is now dead. **F**

The third defendant's evidence is supported to some extent by his mother's evidence and by various other incidents, but it is unnecessary to set these out. In my view, it is plain that the third defendant was a tenant of the farms. In accordance with the testator's practice, in none of these matters were there any documents. The lettings were entirely oral agreements. The plaintiff was only a licensee. Accordingly, I would dismiss the appeal on this point. **G**

The other point arises on a claim in the action by the plaintiff, that a purchase by the third defendant from the proving executors, the first and second defendants, Mrs. Holder and Mrs. Barbara Campbell, of the two farms at a price of £32,500 on July 12, 1961, should be set aside on the ground of a conflict between the third defendant's personal interest and his position as one of the executors appointed by the will. **H**

It is necessary to state the events which occurred. After the testator's death on Aug. 7, 1959, nothing was done until the beginning of October, 1959, when the widow, Mrs. Holder, who throughout took charge in respect of the affairs of the estate, gave instructions to Messrs. Griffiths & Lewis, solicitors of Cheltenham, to act for the executors. These solicitors then obtained the signatures of all three of the executors named in the will for the purpose of opening an executors' account at the Cheltenham branch of Lloyds Bank, and on Oct. 22, 1959, £758 14s. was paid in, being almost entirely made up of rent from the third defendant and from the third defendant and Denley for the year 1958-59.

Between Oct. 29, 1959, and August, 1960, nine cheques totalling nearly £600, were drawn, signed by all three of the executors named in the will, for the purpose of paying the funeral expenses, redemption of land tax and some liabilities of the estate. Several insurance policies standing in the testator's name in regard to fire and other similar matters were endorsed with the names of the executors.

A Mrs. Holder instructed Mr. Hone, the local estate agent, to value the farms on the basis that the third defendant, as well as the third defendant and Denley, had tenancies in respect of the farms. Mr. Hone valued on this basis Lower Farm at £14,000 and Glebe Farm at £8,000 (making a total of £22,000) for the purpose of probate, and these values were agreed by the district valuer.

B When the plaintiff heard of the third defendant's claims to tenancies in the middle of November, 1959, he instructed Messrs. Ivens, Thompson & Green, solicitors of Cheltenham, to act for him. In March, 1960, a meeting was held at the offices of Messrs. Griffiths & Lewis, which was attended by Mr. White (of the firm of Griffiths & Lewis) and the three executors, Mr. Brook, of Messrs. Ivens, Thompson & Green, and the plaintiff, and all the other members of the family except three daughters who lived in America. Mr. White put before the

C meeting all the evidence that he had as to the tenancies, and Mr. Hone's valuations were also produced and discussed. No agreement was reached and Mr. White suggested to the third defendant that he had better be separately represented. In April, 1960, a further family meeting was held at Lower Farm, but again no agreement was reached. Soon after this, the third defendant instructed Messrs. T. Weldon, Thompson & Co., of Tewkesbury, to act for him. On Aug. 22,

D 1960, the third defendant executed a deed of renunciation, which recited that he had not intermeddled in the estate. On Sept. 8, 1960, a further meeting (the third) was held in the offices of Messrs. Griffiths & Lewis, which was attended by the same members of the family (including the executors), and four solicitors: Mr. White for the widow and Mrs. Campbell; Col. Hattrell of T. Weldon, Thompson & Co., for the third defendant; Mr. Bazeley for the plaintiff; and another

E solicitor for Mr. Denley. The plaintiff was, of course, among those present. Mr. White explained that the third defendant had executed the deed of renunciation and that only Mrs. Holder and Mrs. Campbell were applying for a grant of probate. The question of the tenancies was again discussed but no agreement was reached.

It was plain that the third defendant had executed the deed of renunciation
F with a view to purchasing the farms. He made an offer of £30,000, which, of course, was well above the probate value, but this was not accepted. It was left on the footing that if the third defendant could not make a better offer the proving executors would offer the farms for sale by auction. It was clear that the third defendant intended to bid at the auction.

From the plaintiff's evidence at the trial, it appeared that the plaintiff objected
G to the third defendant (with whom he was on bad terms) buying the farms at any price or on any terms, but not on the ground of the third defendant's appointment by the will as one of the executors. When the question of ordering resale arose at the hearing of the action, the plaintiff added the additional ground that he would like to buy one of the farms, though he is in receipt of legal aid and it was not apparent how he would be able to produce the price. He was clearly
H actuated by spite.

On Nov. 10, 1960, Mrs. Holder and Mrs. Campbell obtained a grant of probate without the third defendant. On July 12, 1961, the farms were put up for sale by auction. The third defendant took no part in the instructions for sale. A few days before the auction, the executors, Mrs. Holder and Mrs. Campbell, and Mr. White arranged the reserves at Mr. Hone's office. The rents of £250 and £504
I payable in respect of the tenancies in 1961 were lower than could be obtained after notice and, if necessary, arbitration. No notices had been served by the executors, but a purchaser could obtain the higher rents by serving notice himself, and such rents would become payable from Michaelmas, 1962. On this basis the reserves fixed were £17,000 for Lower Farm and £14,000 for Glebe Farm, making a total of £31,000.

The auction took place on July 12, 1961, and was attended by most of the members of the family and a fair number of other persons. The particulars of sale

stated that the farms were subject to tenancies, and that the plaintiff was occupy- **A**
ing Glebe Farm. The date for completion was Sept. 22, 1961. Before the properties
were put up for sale, Mr. Green, of Ivens, Thompson & Green, who was present
with hs client, the plaintiff, claimed that his client had a tenancy of Glebe Farm
House, and was not merely a licensee. Mr. Lewis, for the proving executors,
replied that they were satisfied that the position was as stated in the particulars
and the sale must proceed on that basis. After some brisk bidding both farms **B**
were knocked down to Col. Hattrell, who was bidding on behalf of the third defendant; Lower Farm at £18,250 and Glebe Farm at £14,000, making a total of
£32,250. The third defendant paid a deposit of £3,250, but he was unable to
complete on Sept. 22, because the credit squeeze interfered with his arrangements
to raise the rest of the price on mortgage. On Sept. 26, 1961, the executors
served on the third defendant a notice to increase the rents, and on Oct. 10 they **C**
served on him a notice to complete within twenty-one days, but the third defendant's solicitors contended that this notice was bad, and on Dec. 13, 1961, the
executors served another twenty-one days' notice.

On Feb. 23, 1962, the plaintiffs' solicitors wrote to the executors' solicitors
pressing them to forfeit the third defendant's deposit and to put the farms up for
sale again. The executors took no notice of this and on May 21, 1962, the plaintiff **D**
issued a writ against the proving executors (the first and second defendants)
only, for an account of their dealings with the estate. By this time the third
defendant had been able to make arrangements for payment of the balance of the
purchase price, and the sale was completed by conveyance on June 5, 1962.
The third defendant had obtained £21,000 on mortgage at $7\frac{1}{2}$ per cent. from the
Agricultural Mortgage Corporation (repayable over sixty years) and loans of **E**
£3,000 each from his mother and a sister at $6\frac{1}{2}$ per cent. on second charges, so
that the further amount that the third defendant had to pay was quite small.

On June 27, 1962, £2,000 was sent to Messrs. Ivens, Thompson & Green on
account of the plaintiff's one-eleventh share, and it was calculated that the balance
of his share would be about £1,000. On Nov. 14, 1962, the third defendant's
solicitors gave notice determining the plaintiff's licence to occupy Glebe Farm **F**
House and claiming possession on Nov. 30.

At some time in the latter part of 1962, the plaintiff changed his solicitors and
his new solicitors, Messrs. Rowberry, Morris & Co., of Gloucester, suggested that
the third defendant might not have been entitled to purchase the farms. There
had been four firms of solicitors acting in these matters, but apparently none of
them had raised this point before. After some correspondence between the plain- **G**
tiff's solicitors and the solicitors of the proving executors, on Jan. 29, 1964,
the writ in this action was issued, claiming that the third defendant remained
an executor and the renunciation was invalid, and asking for rescission of the
sale of the farms to the third defendant and a resale, and alternatively against
the proving executors accounts on the footing of wilful default. In his defence
and counterclaim the third defendant claimed that he was a tenant of the farms **H**
and that he was entitled to purchase them, and that the plaintiff consented to or
acquiesced in the sale to the third defendant and could not complain of it. The
third defendant also counterclaimed for possession of the Glebe Farm House.

The attack on the validity of the deed of renunciation was based on five alleged
acts of administration or intermeddling in the estate by the third defendant:
(i) by joining in the opening of an executors' account at Lloyds Bank, Ltd., at **I**
Cheltenham, and in the operation of it by signing nine cheques; (ii) by allowing
the endorsement of insurance policies in the names of all three of the persons
named as executors; (iii) by joining with the other two persons named as executors
in instructing solicitors to act for the executors in the administration of the
estate and continuing to retain them until August, 1960. There were two other
grounds mentioned in the statement of claim, one relating to a Dutch barn and
the other to the testator's stock at the farm, but these were not relied on at the
hearing of the action.

A   The three grounds that were relied on are so technical and trivial and not really the acts of the third defendant, who really simply complied with the directions of Mrs. Holder, that in my opinion they should not have the effect of preventing a renunciation of probate by an executor. However, it was conceded at the hearing that the renunciation was invalid and, accordingly, we must act on that admission and the effect that it has in regard to the position of an executor. In my view this

B   was a mistake. The position thus created appears to be that the third defendant remained technically an executor and could be compelled by a beneficiary or a creditor to take probate, but under the former law and the provisions of the Administration of Estates Act, 1925, the proving executors could convey property forming part of the estate without the third defendant's concurence and could act generally as the executors of the testator.

C   However, even if the third defendant, after the date of the purported deed of renunciation, remained an executor, the questions remain: (i) was the third defendant's position saved by acquiescence or confirmation and (ii) should, in the particular circumstances of this case, the court grant the equitable relief of rescission after completion of the transaction? Further, was the third defendant entitled to bid at the auction?

D   There is no allegation of fraud in the present case. The third defendant acted in complete innocence and did not know that he was regarded as debarred from purchasing the farms. He bought them at a public auction, in respect of which he took no part in regard to the arrangements for the auction, and the judge found (15) that the prices that he paid were good prices. They were well above the reserve prices. The third defendant and the two proving executors were at arm's-

E   length. There was no question of knowledge which the third defendant might have acquired as an executor. He had a great amount of knowledge of the farms acquired by him, while he was a tenant or when he helped his father in the carrying on of the farms, and he was the obvious person to purchase these farms and likely to offer the best price. I agree with HARMAN, L.J., that there was no reason why he should not bid at the auction and purchase the farms.

F   As regards the authorities, no case is at all near to the facts of this case. The principle that a trustee cannot purchase part of the trust estate goes back to the statement of it by LORD ELDON, L.C., in 1802 in *Ex p. Lacey* (16). LORD ELDON stated the principle in the most severe form. The reason given by LORD ELDON, that it is impossible to ascertain what knowledge the trustee may have, seems less persuasive in the light of BOWEN, L.J.'s famous dictum (17) that " the state of a

G   man's mind is as much a fact as the state of his digestion ", and the almost daily experience of any judge engaged in ascertaining the knowledge and intentions of a party to proceedings. The principle is repeated in *Ex p. James* (18). The subject is dealt with in SNELL'S EQUITY (26th Edn.) at p. 259, where it is pointed out that the true rule is not that a trustee may not purchase trust property; it is that a purchase of trust property by a trustee is voidable within a reasonable time

H   at the instance of any beneficiary (citing *Ex p. James* (18), and *Re Bulmer, The Trustee and Inland Revenue Comrs.* v. *National Provincial Bank, Ltd.* (19)).

It is said that it makes no difference, even though the sale may be fair and honest and may be made at a public auction (see SNELL'S EQUITY, p. 260); but the court may sanction such a purchase and, if the court can do that (see SNELL, p. 219), there can be no more than a practice that the court should not allow a

I   trustee to bid. In my view it is a matter for the discretion of the judge.

It has always been accepted that a trustee cannot retire for the purpose of purchasing the trust estate (see *Re Boles and British Land Co.'s Contract* (20)). If that is right, the third defendant would not have benefited much if the deed of

---

(15) [1966] 2 All E.R. at p. 123.   (16) (1802), 6 Ves. at p. 626.
(17) In *Edgington* v. *Fitzmaurice*, [1881-85] All E.R. Rep. 856 at p. 861; (1885), 29 Ch.D. 459 at p. 483.
(18) [1803-13] All E.R. Rep. 78; (1803), 8 Ves. 337.
(19) [1936] 3 All E.R. 366; [1937] Ch. 499.   (20) [1902] 1 Ch. 244.

renunciation had been valid; but the plaintiff's right of action may be barred **A** by acquiescence or confirmation. The cases on this subject are rather confusing in regard to the knowledge that a beneficiary must have in order to prevent his knowledge barring him in a subsequent attempt to set the transaction aside, and how far the beneficiary must know the legal result of the facts of which he was aware.

The matter of the purchase of the farms was discussed fully and at length at **B** the family meetings and I find it impossible to believe that the plaintiff did not know the facts. No one seems to have objected to the third defendant buying on the ground that he was an executor. The plaintiff treated him as not being an executor when he brought his action against the proving executors alone. He accepted the benefits of the sale when he received £2,000. None of the four solicitors involved in the discussions which took place questioned the third **C** defendant's right to purchase. The plaintiff had his own solicitor at his elbow, and that solicitor should have advised him on the legal position. Instead he apparently said nothing, stood by with the plaintiff, and allowed the sale to be completed by conveyance of the farms to the third defendant by the proving executors and the payment of the purchase price by the third defendant, who has altered his position by mortgaging the farms and carrying on the farming business **D** on the farms

As to the cases, *Cockerell* v. *Cholmeley* (21) and *Stafford* v. *Stafford* (22), show different views on the point whether appreciation of the situation in law is necessary. My decision in *Re Howlett (decd.)*, *Howlett* v. *Howlett* (23) did not really deal with the matter. Like HARMAN, L.J., I prefer the view expressed by WILBER-FORCE, J., in *Re Pauling's Settlement Trusts*, *Younghusband* v. *Coutts & Co.* (24), **E** that all the circumstances must be considered and there is no hard and fast rule.

In my opinion the plaintiff has acted in such a way in the present case in regard to the third defendant's purchase of the farms that he must be taken to have acquiesced in or to have confirmed the sale and cannot now claim to have the sale set aside.

There is authority for the general rule that, in the absence of fraud, a trans- **F** action which has been completed will not be set aside: *Seddon* v. *North Eastern Salt Co., Ltd.* (25) and other cases; but there are dicta of McCARDIE, J., in *Armstrong* v. *Jackson* (26) (where a broker sold his own shares to his principal) that the rule does not apply where there is a fiduciary position. In that case, however, there seems to have been fraud.

Whether that be the case or not, on general equitable grounds I am of opinion **G** that in the present case the transaction should not be set aside. The transaction is not void. It is one which is voidable and is liable to be set aside if a proper case is made out for that relief.

As has been pointed out by HARMAN, L.J., the plaintiff is claiming equitable relief against the third defendant, who is the legal owner of the farms and is in occupation of them. He has paid what was a good price at the time of the sale. **H** Much hardship would be caused to the third defendant if the transaction was set aside now. He purchased the farms in good faith, believing that there was no bar to that course. The plaintiff stood by and benefited along with the other beneficiaries by the sale. He had legal advice to hand and made no attempt to stop the completion of the sale. Now, after competition, he is attacking the sale for purely selfish reasons. He cares nothing for the effect that setting aside will **I** have on the estate of the testator and the other beneficiaries under the will. The costs of the sale (some £875) will all be thrown away.

The order made by the judge (27) will cause some unfairness to the third

---

(21) (1830), 1 Russ. & M. 418.   (22) (1857), 1 De G. & J. 193.
(23) [1949] 2 All E.R. 490; [1949] Ch. 767.   (24) [1961] 3 All E.R. at p. 730.
(25) [1904-07] All E.R. Rep. 817; [1905] 1 Ch. 326.
(26) [1916-17] All E.R. Rep. 1117 at p. 1121; [1917] 2 K.B. 822 at pp. 826, 827.
               (27) [1966] 2 All E.R. at pp. 131-133.

A defendant and is so complicated that it will be difficult and expensive to work
out. In fact, it is not really possible in the circumstances to carry out restitution, which is a condition of the equitable relief which the plaintiff seeks. The
plaintiff's position would have been expressed in former times by the words " he
has no equity ".

B For all these reasons, in my opinion the court should not grant the equitable
relief of setting aside or rescission in the present case.

Accordingly, I would, on this part of the case, allow the appeal, discharge the
order made by Cross, J., and dismiss the plaintiff's action with costs. As I have
already indicated, I would dismiss the plaintiff's appeal as regards the counterclaim, with costs.

C   SACHS, L.J.: So far as the plaintiff's appeal is concerned, once the trial
judge had come to the conclusion (28) that the third defendant was an honest
witness (a matter incidentally borne out by intrinsic material in his testimony) it
seems to me that there was a considerable amount of positive evidence tending to
show that the arrangement between the testator and the third defendant was
intended to create legal rights—and having regard to s. 2 (1) of the Agricultural
D Holdings Act, 1948, it matters not whether it was intended to create a tenancy or a
contractual licence.

It became clear that the testator owing to his ill-health intended to make over
the land in question to the third defendant. It was, of course, equally clear that
he did not intend to make a gift of the freehold in the farms, but that he was
making it over by way of an arrangement giving the third defendant the right to
E farm the land and the testator the right to receive rent. It is to be noted that
the third defendant in his evidence, which it is not open to this court to doubt
even if it so wished, distinguished clearly between the £250 which he paid in
April, 1957, before the relevant arrangement was made and the sums he later
arranged to pay: the former was not, and the latter was, termed rent. Rent is,
after all, a periodic payment, and in this case the period was clearly intended to be
F annual: so counsel for the plaintiff was driven to the untenable submission that
nonetheless the testator was entitled in law to evict the third defendant at any
given moment without notice, whatever be the state of the season or of any crops,
whilst the third defendant in his turn was equally entitled to abandon the land
at any given moment.

Even without turning to the evidence of Mrs. Holder and the accountant, Mr.
G Parker, it seems to me that the only proper inference to be drawn was that a
contractual occupation was intended to be effected. The evidence, however, of
Mrs. Holder and Mr. Parker both point clearly in the same direction, and to my
mind the letter written by the latter on the testator's instructions on June 30,
1959, would have been conclusive had the third defendant's evidence left the
issue in doubt. Once Mr. Parker's letter was admitted into evidence it was for the
H court to assess its weight and it seems to me to have the considerable cogency
which I have indicated.

It thus does not seem useful to add anything further to the judgments delivered
by my lords, with each of which I agree, dismissing the plaintiff's appeal.

As regards the cross-appeal, a number of issues have been raised and fully
argued by both parties in a way which has afforded very considerable assistance.
I All these issues were argued on the basis of a concession made on behalf of the
third defendant before the trial judge to the effect that his actions as pleaded
in para. 4 (a), (b) and (c) of the statement of claim constituted an intermeddling
which were of such a character that no deed of renunciation could be effectively
executed by him. Both on the face of the pleadings and on the evidence as adduced
at trial, these acts were of a most minor character and, as already stated by my
lords, were even in aggregate by no means clearly an intermeddling: (b) on its

───
(28) [1966] 2 All E.R. at p. 124.

own clearly was not. That point, however, being thus not open for further argu- **A** ment this judgment proceeds on the basis that the renunciation was invalid.

On that basis the first issue is whether in the circumstances of this unusual case the third defendant remained after executing the deed of purported renunciation under that disability which normally attaches to an executor in relation to purchasing part of the estate or whether he was, as counsel for the third defendant submitted, so "moribund" qua executor that the disability did not attach to him. **B**

The court having been informed that there was no authority touching anyone who had been in a position precisely parallel to that of the third defendant, reliance was placed by counsel for the plaintiff on the rule that no trustee and accordingly no executor could bid for or purchase property vested in him qua trustee or executor. This is the rule as enunciated by LORD ELDON, L.C., in 1802 and 1803 in the leading cases, *Ex p. Lacey* (29) and *Ex p. James* (30), from which **C** HARMAN, L.J., has already cited the relevant passages. These cases related to men who had been acting as assignees of a bankrupt's estate and who had thus gained considerable special knowledge of which they could make use at an auction or otherwise when purchasing that property: indeed at any rate one of them (*Ex p. James* (30)) related to a professional man advising the assignees as such. For the reasons given by HARMAN, L.J., in his judgment after citing those **D** passages I, too, consider that the rule is not applicable in the present case, where the plaintiff was in practice "moribund" qua executor, and was affirmatively established to have gained no helpful knowledge from his position as executor before he executed the deed which was intended to effect a renunciation.

It is moreover a matter which may well be open to argument whether the above rule is, in any event, nowadays quite as rigid as was postulated by counsel for the **E** plaintiff. It is clear that the court has jurisdiction to allow a trustee to bid for trust property (*Tennant* v. *Trenchard* (31)), and in addition it was conceded at the Bar that procedure exists by which a trustee or an executor can obtain the leave of the court in appropriate circumstances to purchase such property: and I understand that such leave has been given even where a beneficiary has objected.

Moreover I agree with DANCKWERTS, L.J., in his comments on that part of the **F** foundation of the rule which stems from the alleged inability of a court to ascertain the state of mind of a trustee: and am inclined to the view that an irrebuttable presumption as to the state of his knowledge may no longer accord with the way in which the courts have now come to regard matters of this type. Thus the rigidity of the shackles imposed by the rule on the discretion of the court may perhaps before long be reconsidered as the courts tend to lean more and more **G** against such rigidity of rules as can cause patent injustice—such as was done in *Cockerell* v. *Chomeley* (32). The rule, after all, appears on analysis to be one of practice as opposed to one going to the jurisdiction of the court.

Next I turn to two further issues: the first is whether the plaintiff acquiesced in the third defendant's purchase of the property; the second is whether, even if there was no acquiescence, he ought to be given that equitable relief which was **H** granted by the trial judge. These two issues have naturally to be considered separately, though many of the factors relevant to the second are also relevant to the first.

The plea of acquiescence in this particular case seems to me to have a close resemblance to one of estoppel: and it is to be noted that in 14 HALSBURY's LAWS OF ENGLAND (3rd Edn.) it is stated, p. 438, para. 1178: **I**

"Acquiescence operates by way of estoppel. It is quiescence in such circumstances that assent may reasonably be inferred and is an instance of of estoppel by words or conduct."

---

(29) (1802), 6 Ves. 625.
(30) [1803-13] All E.R. Rep. 78; (1803) 8 Ves. 337.
(31) (1869), 4 Ch. App. 537.
(32) (1830), 1 Russ. & M. 418.

A   Whilst recognising that these two pleas are not necessarily coterminous it yet seems to me that in the present case if the facts are sufficient to create an estoppel then a fortiori a plea of acquiescence must succeed.

In relation to this plea the first question to be considered is what facts were known to the plaintiff (and for that matter to his solicitor) before the auction took place and before the sale to the third defendant was completed. First, the

B   plaintiff knew that the third defendant was an executor under the will; secondly, turning to the allegation in para. 4 (c) of the statement of claim,

> "In October, 1959, joining with the first and second defendants and instructing solicitors to act on his and their behalf in administering the estate of the testator and continuing to retain the same solicitor until August, 1960,"

C   it is clear from the primary evidence and from the inferences to be drawn from it that the plaintiff knew solicitors had been employed by the executors in the administration of the estate, and that the third defendant was one of those responsible for that employment. (It is not in point that it was his mother who had spoken to the solicitor on behalf of all three executors when they had in fact

D   ratified her so doing.) He also knew that the executors personally or by their solicitors had employed one Hone to effect a valuation.

Next, turning to the allegation in para. 4 (a) (which relates to the executors' account and the cheques drawn on it), the plaintiff at all material times realised, as must be the case also as regards his solicitors, that the executors were in the normal course of events thus discharging liabilities that had fallen on them:

E   indeed he admitted as much under cross-examination in regard to the funeral expenses. Here again the fact that he did not know precisely what cheques had been drawn is not in point. The plaintiff thus knew, as did his solicitor, facts now relied on as constituting intermeddling and but for which no court could have held that there was an intermeddling. So his conduct falls to be assessed on the basis of that knowledge unless he can successfully provide himself with an escape

F   route on asserting that he was not aware of the legal effect of matters within his knowledge. With that last point I will deal separately later.

Next there falls to be considered his conduct in relation to the sale to the third defendant. In the first place it is to be noted that he himself by his solicitor suggested that he and the third defendant should join in purchasing the property: a direct encouragement of the view that the third defendant could purchase

G   property from the estate. Thereafter, during the preparations for an auction the plaintiff did nothing which could in any way be construed as an objection to the third defendant bidding and indeed it is obvious that all concerned assumed that he would. At the auction itself the plaintiff by his solicitor raised an objection to the plaintiff being regarded as a licensee (as opposed to a tenant) of part of the property and perhaps also objected to the third defendant being regarded as

H   anything but a licensee: but not a word was raised against the third defendant bidding at the auction where such bidding would almost certainly enure to the benefit of the estate. Thus by his conduct he expressly and impliedly represented that the third defendant could properly do the very act to which he now objects—purchase the property.

Moreover, after the auction the plaintiff pressed for the rigour of the contract

I   to be enforced and for the third defendant's deposit to be forfeited: indeed he went so far as to issue a writ against the executors, the ostensible object of which was to compel them to enforce the contract in the above way. Then, when the contract had been completed, he duly received a cheque for £2,000 from the proceeds and must have disposed of most of those proceeds in a way which has rendered him eligible for legal aid.

It was in these circumstances that the third defendant made his bid at the auction, completed the sale having paid full value for the property, and involved himself in all the expenses such operations entail. Later—still in the absence of

any indication from the plaintiff that he desired to upset the sale—he expended **A**
money on improving the property.

To my mind (subject to the escape route point) this is a case of the plaintiff
being estopped from now saying that the third defendant should never have bid or
completed. Incidentally it is also a case of approbation by subsequent conduct
from which the plaintiff cannot now resile. A fortiori it is a case of acquiescence.

Next comes the point whether ignorance of the effect in law of facts which **B**
constitute an intermeddling can avail the plaintiff. This is a case where the plaintiff and the defendant were on a completely equal footing. Both were laymen
whose occupation had been on the land, and each was at all material times armed
with professional advice in the shape of a solicitor. In this behalf I would as a
preliminary matter venture to differ from the view taken by the trial judge (33)
that the plaintiff's solicitors' retainer was so limited as not include advising him **C**
generally in all matters touching the third defendant's desire to bid for and
purchase the property. In the absence of any evidence to the contrary from the
solicitor himself it seems to me a clear inference that he was retained to advise
generally on the matters in issue; and if any confirmation were needed of that
view, it can be derived from the answer given by the plaintiff himself at the trial.
Nor am I disposed to draw the inference that the plaintiff's solicitor was wholly **D**
unaware of the law with regard to intermeddling: it seems to me highly unlikely
that he did not turn his mind at some stage to this question in relation to the
facts which he knew. As the plaintiff refrained from calling him into the witness-
box I see no reason why inferences in favour of the plaintiff should be drawn on this
point contrary to those which would normally result from the evidence as a whole
before the trial judge. To my mind, on that evidence it is at any rate open to the **E**
court to draw the following inferences as regards the solicitor. First, that he knew
the facts above stated; secondly, that he had in accordance with his duties considered whether they constituted an intermeddling; next, that he may well have
come to a definite, tenable and perhaps correct conclusion that they did not; and
finally, that he shaped his course on that basis.

Once one comes to the conclusion that the plaintiff and the third defendant were **F**
indeed on an equal footing, each with professional advisers, there seems to me to
be no reason why one should not apply the normal rule that the effect in law of a
person's conduct should be assessed by having regard to his actions in a common-
sense way. In all commonsense the plaintiff did in fact assent to the third
defendant bidding and did so with knowledge of the relevant facts. To provide
him with an escape route of the type propounded by counsel for the plaintiff **G**
would seem to work injustice, and to open the way in a great many cases to
suggesting that a man with appropriate professional advisers should be allowed
to say that he was personally ignorant of the law when he wished to reopen a
concluded transaction. It would also open the way in a great many cases where
the law might be doubtful for a man to come in at almost any stage after a
transaction had been completed and say: " Well, the law is now shown to be **H**
different from what I thought at the time and I object to what has happened
although I had full opportunity to object earlier ". Accordingly, I reject the
" escape route " submissions of counsel for the plaintiff.

It may well be that ignorance of the legal effect of facts may in certain circumstances afford an answer to a plea of acquiescence where conduct does not amount
to an estoppel. But I know of no authority for such a proposition in relation to
estoppel: indeed having regard to the judgments in *Holt* v. *Markham* (34) (a
case in which both parties were ignorant of the legal effect of certain regulations)
I doubt if there is any warrant for it in estoppel in pais.

In so far as there may be cases of acquiescence to which the normal rules of
estoppel do not apply I too agree that the judgment of WILBERFORCE, J., in

(33) [1966] 2 All E.R. at p. 128.
(34) [1922] All E.R. Rep. 134; [1923] 1 K.B. 504.

A *Re Pauling's Settlement Trusts, Younghusband* v. *Coutts & Co.* (35), provides the correct guide and that on that basis too the plaintiff would fail.

As regards the further issue—whether this is a case in which the court should grant equitable relief if it was open to it so to do, I fully agree with what has been said by my Lords and have nothing to add.

I too would allow the cross-appeal.

B *Appeal dismissed. Cross-appeal allowed. Leave to appeal to the House of Lords refused.*

Solicitors: *Nutt & Oliver*, agents for *Rowberry, Morris & Co.*, Gloucester (for the plaintiff); *Field, Roscoe & Co.*, agents for *Griffiths & Lewis*, Cheltenham (for the first and second defendants, the proving executors); *Balderston, Warren &*
C *Co.*, agents for *T. Weldon Thompson & Co.*, Tewkesbury (for the third defendant).

[*Reported by* Henry Summerfield, Esq., *Barrister-at-Law.*]

D   R. *v.* LANFEAR.

[Court of Appeal, criminal division (Diplock, L.J., Lyell and Blain, JJ.), January 30, 1968.]

Criminal Law—Evidence—Medical evidence—Position of doctor giving medical evidence at criminal trial—Weight to be attached to such evidence—Wrong to
E *direct jury that doctor's evidence ought to be accepted in the absence of reasons for rejecting it—Road traffic offence—Driving while unfit to drive through drink.*

The evidence of a doctor giving medical testimony at a criminal trial should be treated, as regards admissibility and other matters of that kind, like that of any other independent witness, but, though a doctor may be
F regarded as giving independent expert evidence to assist the court, the jury should not be directed that his evidence ought, therefore, to be accepted by the jury in the absence of reasons for rejecting it (see p. 685, letters A and F, post).

R. v. *Nowell* ([1948] 1 All E.R. 794) explained.

[Editorial Note. For a statement of the proper view of the position of doctors
G giving medical evidence at criminal trials, see also *R.* v. *Russell* ([1963] 3 All E.R. at p. 605, letter A).

As to the weight to be attributed to expert evidence, see 15 Halsbury's Laws (3rd Edn.) 278, para. 507, and cf., 10 ibid., p. 436, para. 806.

As to driving a motor car while under the influence of drink, see 33 Halsbury's Laws (3rd Edn.) 626-628, paras. 1057-1059; and for cases on the subject,
I see 45 Digest (Repl.) 93, 94, *314-317.*

For the Road Traffic Act, 1960, s. 2, s. 6, see 40 Halsbury's Statutes (2nd Edn.) 712, 717.]

Cases referred to:

 R. v. *Nowell*, [1948] 1 All E.R. 794; 112 J.P. 255; 32 Cr. App. Rep. 173; 45 Digest (Repl.) 94, *315.*

 Reid v. *Nixon, Dumigan* v. *Brown*, 1948 S.C. (J.) 68; 45 Digest (Repl.) 100, **1007.*

Appeal.

This was an appeal by the appellant, Colin Lanfear, against his conviction at the Swansea Borough quarter sessions on July 26, 1967 on two counts (i) of driving whilst unfit through drink, and (ii) of dangerous driving. He was fined

---

(35) [1961] 3 All E.R. 713.

A £30 on count (i) and £15 on count (ii), and he was disqualified for driving for two
years on count (i).

The facts are set out in the judgment of the court.

L. Griffiths for the appellant
G. W. Williams for the Crown.

B **DIPLOCK, L.J.**, delivered the following judgment of the court: This is an
appeal against conviction at Swansea Borough quarter sessions when the appellant
was convicted on one count of driving whilst unfit through drink and another
count of dangerous driving. He was fined £30 on count one and £15 on count two
and he was disqualified from driving for two years on count one. The facts were
simple and an illustration of the classic drunken driver syndrome. At about
C 12.30 in the morning of June 2, 1966, the appellant, driving his car down a well
lit road going out of Swansea on a fine night with a clear view of one hundred
yards, ran slap into the back of a parked motor car with a parking light. The
brake was on, the car was in gear, and he drove it along the road about sixty feet
onto a grass verge.   When he got out of his own car to confront the indignant
owner who had heard the noise and had come down, he swayed, his eyes were
glazed and his speech was slurred. The appellant was taken to the police station
D where he manifested the same symptoms. He was examined by a doctor who put
him through all the familiar tests, the great majority of which he failed, and a
sample of urine disclosed that his blood contained the equivalent of 213 milli-
grammes of alcohol, something over $2\frac{1}{2}$ times the maximum amount under the new
law.   He did not give the second sample required for reasons which it is not easy
to follow—I think because he found it impossible to urinate into the bottle—and
E when he got into the cell he urinated against the wall. The defence which was put
forward in cross-examination of the doctor was that these symptoms, though not
including the alcohol content of the blood, might have been due to concussion.
He did not complain at the time to the doctor that he had struck his head. Next
morning he said that he found that he had got a bump on his head, but he never
consulted a doctor about it. It was about as clear a case as one could find.

F In his notice of appeal the appellant makes a number of complaints about the
summing-up by the learned deputy recorder. As regards all of the complaints
but one, I need say no more than that there is, in the view of this court, no
substance in them. He did complain, however, with justification, about the terms
in which the learned deputy recorder instructed the jury about the attitude which
they should adopt towards the medical evidence. There is considerable excuse
G for the deputy recorder, because he read out to them a passage which appears
in the current volume of ARCHBOLD'S CRIMINAL PLEADING, EVIDENCE & PRACTICE
IN CRIMINAL CASES (36th Edn.), under the heading " Medical Witness ", which is
in the following terms:

" The evidence of any doctor, whether a police surgeon or not, should be
accepted as the evidence of a professional man giving independent expert
H evidence with the sole desire of assisting the court, unless the doctor himself
shows that his evidence ought not to be accepted."

The learned deputy recorder paraphrased that slightly. He said this:

" Let me say immediately about medical evidence in general—this again,
members of the jury, is a matter of law. The evidence of any doctor, whether
a police surgeon or not, is to be accepted as the evidence of a professional man
giving independent evidence with the sole desire of assisting the court unless
the doctor by his own conduct shows that his evidence ought not to be
accepted."

I think that the only difference is that, instead of " himself ", he has substituted
the words " by his own conduct ". Then he goes on subsequently to say this:

". . . his evidence is to be accepted as the evidence of a professional man
giving independent expert evidence with the sole desire of helping the court."

A   This, then, puts him into a position in which, in the absence of reasons for
     rejecting his evidence, his evidence ought to be accepted."

     In the view of this court that is an incorrect statement of the law and the passage
     which is cited in ARCHBOLD, which comes from the case of *R.* v. *Nowell* (1), is
     taken out of its context. In that case the argument before the court was that a
     doctor who had examined a defendant had explained to the appellant that it
B   might be in his own interests to allow the doctor to examine him. The appellant
     eventually agreed to be examined, and was examined, by the doctor, who certified
     that owing to his consumption of alcohol the appellant was unfit to drive a car.
     The argument was that the doctor should be treated as if he were an arm of the
     police, and that there was an inducement held out to the appellant which made
     the evidence of the doctor as to the result of his examination inadmissible. That
C   argument was sought to be supported by a decision of the Scots Court, *Reid* v.
     Nixon, *Dumigan* v. *Brown* (2), and the passage now incorporated in ARCHBOLD
     appeared at the end of the judgment in the Court of Criminal Appeal, where they
     were dealing with that. After referring to the Scots case, the court said (3):

         " It is not necessary to read the judgment of the court which was given by
D   the Lord Justice-General, who made a number of general observations with
         regard to the principles on which he suggested police officers and doctors
         should act in examining persons who are charged with such an offence as
         this. The Lord Advocate, according to the judgment of the Lord Justice-
         General, had stated that in all such cases the police surgeon or other doctor
         summoned by the police to conduct an examination was acting as the hand
E   of the police and not as an independent medical referee. This court can only
         say that it does not agree that that state of affairs, whether it exists in
         Scotland or not, exists in this country. Our view is that the evidence of a
         doctor, whether he be a police surgeon or anyone else, should be accepted,
         unless the doctor himself shows that it ought not to be, as the evidence of a
         professional man giving independent expert evidence with the sole desire of
F   assisting the court."

     What that passage meant in that context was that the evidence should be treated,
     as regards admissibility and other matters of that kind, like that of any other
     independent witness; but taken out of its context, the use of the word " accepted "
     may well, we think, give to the jury a false impression of the weight to be given to
     that evidence. It is therefore desirable that in subsequent editions of ARCHBOLD
G   that passage, which was read by the learned deputy recorder in this case,
     should be corrected. Having said that, however, this, in the view of this court, is
     the clearest possible case in which to apply the proviso. On the evidence before the
     jury no jury properly directed could have possibly found the appellant otherwise
     than guilty of the offence. The appeal is accordingly dismissed.

                                                                  Appeal dismissed.

H   Solicitors: *Registrar of Criminal Appeals* (for the appellant); *Ivor G. Morgan*,
     Swansea (for the Crown).

                         [*Reported by* S. A. HATTEEA, ESQ., *Barrister-at-Law.*]

I

_____

(1) [1948] 1 All E.R. 794; 32 Cr. App. Rep. 173.
(2) 1948 S.C. (J.) 68.
(3) (1948), 32 Cr. App. Rep. at p. 180; [1948] 1 All E.R. at p. 795.

Re ZERNY'S WILL TRUSTS.

SYMONS AND ANOTHER *v.* ZERNY AND OTHERS.

[COURT OF APPEAL, CIVIL DIVISION (Harman, Danckwerts and Winn, L.JJ.), November 9, 10, 1967.]

Will—Option—Purchase—Freehold—Business premises—Business carried on by tenant company in which testator and son had shares—Testator had sold business to company, but had retained freehold properties where business carried on—Son worked with testator in business—Testator bequeathed his share to son and gave him a right of pre-emption, after widow's death, over the freehold premises at a price that was realistic at the date of the will—Son died in widow's lifetime—Whether option personal to son or passed to son's personal representatives.

The testator started a small business in 1909, which he carried on at two freehold properties. His son joined him in the business on leaving school in 1921, and they carried on business together until the testator's death in 1941. The testator formed the business in 1934 into a limited company, in which he held 1,500 shares and his son held five hundred; but the testator retained the ownership of the two freeholds, granting the company short tenancies of them. By his will made on Aug. 26, 1937, the testator gave the son his 1,500 shares in the company, gave a number of legacies and gave the residue of his estate (which included the two properties) to his trustees on trust for sale, with power to postpone the sale, and on trust to invest the proceeds of sale and to pay £10 weekly to the testator's widow during her life; if there were any surplus, it was to be divided equally between his two daughters. The will directed that on the widow's death the residuary estate should be realised, and should be divided as to three-sevenths to one daughter, two-sevenths to the other, and two-sevenths to the son. The testator directed that on any sale of the freeholds his son should have the option of purchasing each freehold at the price stated in the will. The two prices were fairly realistic estimates of the values of the properties at the date of the will. The son carried on the business at the properties until his death in 1963. Thereafter the business came to an end, but the properties were not sold before the widow died in 1967, by which time the properties were worth three times the fixed prices or more. The question arose whether the benefit of the option passed to the son's executors.

Held: the gift of the option was, on the true construction of the will in the light of the circumstances, made in the anticipation that the son would be carrying on the family business when the option became exercisable, and was personal to the son; accordingly his executors were not entitled to the benefit of the option, and the freehold properties passed as part of the testator's residuary estate (see p. 689, letter I, and p. 690, letters E and F, post).

Principle in *Skelton* v. *Younghouse* ([1942] 1 All E.R. 650) applied.

Appeal allowed.

[As to when an option to purchase given by a will is personal to the donee, see 39 HALSBURY'S LAWS (3rd Edn.) 912, para. 1383, text and note (*k*); and for cases on options conferred by wills, see 48 DIGEST (Repl.) 56-58, *404-417*.]

Case referred to:

Skelton v. *Younghouse*, [1942] 1 All E.R. 650; [1942] A.C. 571; 111 L.J.Ch. 185; 167 L.T. 325; 48 Digest (Repl.) 57, *408*.

Appeal.

This was an appeal by Mrs. Betty Wade, the third defendant, a daughter of the testator Bruno Zerny and one of the residuary legatees under his will dated Aug. 26, 1937, against the decision of PLOWMAN, J., dated Feb. 23, 1967, on a

A summons by the plaintiffs Edward Symons and Bernard Sackman, the trustees of the testator's will, that the fourth defendants, Barclays Bank, Ltd., the executors of the testator's deceased son, Walter Marcus Zerny, were entitled to exercise an option to purchase two freehold properties given to the son by the will. The facts are set out in the judgment of HARMAN, L.J.

B A. J. Balcombe for the third defendant, a residuary legatee.
    G. T. Hesketh for the plaintiff trustees.
    D. S. Chetwood for the fourth defendants, the executors of the donee of the option.

C HARMAN, L.J.: This is an appeal from a decision of PLOWMAN, J., dated Feb. 23, 1967, construing the will of a man called Bruno Zerny, who was a dyer and cleaner carrying on business in Holloway. The judge said that his mind had fluctuated considerably in the course of the hearing and I am not at all surprised at that because mine has too—and, I think, those of my brethren. It is a puzzling little case; but in the end I have come down on the side of thinking that the judge was wrong and that the option with which we are concerned was an option meant to be personal to the testator's son.

D The facts are very simple. The testator started his business of a dyer and cleaner in about the year 1909. He had two freehold properties connected with it: one in Wedmore Street, Holloway, which he used as a factory, and the other a property under the Archway there, which he used as a shop. In 1921, the son, Walter Marcus Zerny, leaving school, joined him in the business—one does not know in what capacity, but I suppose he just helped his father. In 1934 the testator

E converted the business into a limited company and he sold the company, the goodwill of the business but not the two properties, which he retained in his own hands and which he let to the company on short tenancies. The consideration for the sale was two thousand shares, of which he caused 1,500 to be registered in his own name and five hundred to be registered in the name of his son, apparently beneficially. The business was carried on by the company as tenant

F of the testator so far as the premiums were concerned, and the tenancies were of short duration, apparently three years or thereabouts. Three years later he came to make his will. It is of course under that document that the question arises; but I shall complete the facts first. The testator died in December, 1941; his will was proved in 1942; and his son died in September, 1963. Last of all, the testator's widow died in April, 1967.

G Now the business had been apparently failing for some time and finally folded up after the son died. There was no goodwill to sell, the business simply shut its doors. The two properties were thereafter let by the executors to other persons. That was only during the last year or so, because the business was not closed until 1965. Therefore one may suppose that events have not turned out as the testator supposed that they would. Testators hardly ever do contemplate that

H their sons will die before their widows, and it is very often the cause of difficulty in construing wills that legatees will not die in the right order: they insist on dying out of order and in events which the testator has not contemplated; and that is the trouble here, so it seems to me.

I The will in this case starts by giving the son the residue of the shares in the business, 1,500 shares, which the testator had. The son, therefore, became the owner of the entirety of the goodwill of the business. No doubt that was a beneficial gift to him at that time. After a number of legacies there comes a residuary gift on trust for sale, with power to postpone, and on trust to invest the proceeds (which would include the assets if not sold) and pay £10 a week to his widow. If there was anything over after that, his two daughters, Bettye Zerny (the second defendant) and Freda Brass (the third defendant), were to have that shared between them. The widow was to have some short occupation of the testator's dwelling-house, and that, under a deed of arrangement between the children and her, was continued during the remainder of her life. She also had

during the same period the use of the furniture, which was not to be sold as long **A**
as she was alive. There was an express power of postponement during the lifetime
of the widow, and the testator then provided that on her death " I direct that my
residuary estate shall be realised and divided . . ." That means that there must
be an immediate winding-up on that event happening. The proceeds of that
operation were to be divided in sevenths, three-sevenths going to Mrs. Brass,
two-sevenths going to Bettye Zerny and the remaining two-sevenths to his son **B**
Walter. Then come the words which cause the trouble.

> " And I further direct that on any sale after the death of my wife of my
> freehold premises 36-38 and 40 Wedmore Street and 42 Archway Road my
> son the said Walter Marcus Zerny shall have the option of purchasing the
> said freehold premises as to 36-38 and 40 Wedmore Street for £4,000
> and as to Archway Road for £2,000;"

C

That is the entire will. During the widow's lifetime all went according to plan
until the death of the son. The widow had her £10 a week, which was in large
part provided by the rents which the company paid for the properties. That
seems to have lasted throughout her life, although the business had been closed
two years before she died, and the son was by then dead four years.

The question which arises is whether, the son not having survived his mother, **D**
his personal representatives are to succeed to the benefit of the option conferred
on him. It is to be observed that the option only arises " on any sale after the
death of my wife ". So that, if the executors had, for administrative reasons, as
they were entitled to do, sold the properties in the widow's lifetime, no option
would ever have arisen and the residue would have been divided in the way which
the will indicates—three-sevenths to one daughter, two-sevenths to the other, and **E**
two-sevenths to the son.

The next thing to remember is that, according to the evidence before us, at
the time when the testator made his will the prices that he put on these two
properties were not so far out from being a realistic estimate of the value.   It
did not look from the will that the testator had any idea of giving his son any
special benefit; but with the enormous rise that there has been in property **F**
values, if the son's estate is entitled to exercise this option in the events which
have happened the son's estate will have, as against his sisters, a very large
benefit. The Wedmore Street premises have been sold for £12,000, and the
Archway property for £6,750, and, if that is to go to the son's estate, his estate
will benefit very much at the expense of his sisters, who otherwise would take
five-sevenths of that money between them. **G**

I start with this, that the authority of the House of Lords constrains me to
say that there is no prima facie view in a case like this.   There used to be thought
to be a rule of construction, though not a rule of law, that an option was prima
facie a personal gift to the donee of the option.   That idea was eschewed in
Skelton v. *Younghouse* (1), where the headnote reads (2): **H**

> " There is no rule of law that an option given by will to a named person
> is prima facie personal to the donee only, and the statement to that effect
> in JARMAN ON WILLS (7th Edn.) p. 73, is incorrect. The question whether
> such an option to purchase is exercisable only by the donee personally or is
> transmissible to his executors or assignees depends on the true construction
> of the will in the light of any circumstances properly admissible in evidence
> . . ."

It was held that, on the circumstances which there existed, the option there
given was an option personal to the donee and did not survive him. Having
regard to that decision I am not entitled to go round adding up the various
considerations which, on the will in that case, influenced the judges who decided

---

(1) [1942] 1 All E.R. 650; [1942] A.C. 571.
(2) [1942] A.C. at p. 571.

A   the case.   The reasons which drove them to the conclusions that they reached
were not quite the same, but they all reached the same conclusion, namely, that
in that case it was a personal option, and that it was a pure matter of construing
the gift in the light of the surrounding circumstances

It appears to be the law also that the fact that the words " executors administrators and assigns " are not explicit in the words granting the option is nihil
B   ad rem.   So, on the contrary, I suppose, is it true to say that the absence of the
words " if living " does not point the other way.   One still simply starts (as
LORD WRIGHT says (3)) " on a razor's edge ", and one must add up the circumstances and see which way they point.   It is largely thus a matter of impression
and, therefore, I have the less hesitation in disagreeing with the judge below.

Now what was the position here?   Here were father and son carrying on this
C   business.   They were the sole owners of it: but the premises in which it was
carried on belonged to the father and not to the company which carried on the
business.   The father seems to have assumed, no doubt naturally, that his
widow's interest should come first.   She was to have £10 a week, and there is
power to sell any part of the estate in order to produce that sum of money.   The
testator gave the whole of the shares carrying the rest of the goodwill to his son,
D   and obviously assumed—as indeed he justifiably assumed—that the son would
be carrying on the business.   In that capacity it was in fact essential for the
company, of which the son was to be the sole owner, to control the premises in
which the business was carried on, and although the widow's interest was considered in the testator's mind to prevail during her lifetime, so that if necessary
the properties might be mortgaged or sold to produce her £10, yet he obviously
E   assumed, first that his son would survive his widow and secondly that he would
be then carrying on the business.   Neither of those things happened.   What is
the proper assumption from that ?   Is it that the son was to have these properties,
whether or no he survived his mother, by way of part of his share in the estate,
or is it that the son was merely to have the opportunity of acquiring these properties because they were an essential adjunct to the business which his father
F   supposed that he would be carrying on?

The inference to my mind is irresistible—that it was in his capacity as owner
of the business that the son must have the option of acquiring the properties,
and that when he ceased to be that owner by his death in 1963, the reason for
giving him that advantage as against his sisters was not any more applicable.
It is quite true that the testator's mind (as far as one can tell) did not conceive
G   that the son was to have the properties at any kind of value which would give
him a great advantage over his sisters, but the fact that he was to have the properties, or the right to have them, seems to me to be entirely conditioned by the
anticipation that he would be carrying on the family business, and these properties were essential for that purpose.   That condition of things ceasing, it seems
to me that the reason why the option should go to him ceased, and the inference
H   from that is that the option was an option personal to him.   It is quite true that
the son might have ceased to carry on the business before the widow's death,
and if he survived his mother he would still have been entitled to the option;
but that is obviously an event not contemplated by the testator, who did contemplate that so long as his son lived he would carry on the business, as indeed
he did.

I   I have come, therefore, to the conclusion purely as a matter of construction
and without looking at the various considerations which in other cases have
induced other judges to come to one view or the other, that this was intended
as a personal gift to the son, and that as it did not arise till after his mother's
death and as he was not there to exercise it himself it is not exercisable.   The
properties, therefore, fall into the residue of the estate, and I would so hold and
allow the appeal accordingly.

---

(3) [1942] 1 All E.R. at p. 656; [1942] A.C. at p. 583.

There was another point, namely whether, if the option were not personal, it **A** was void for some other reason; but that does not arise and I do not propose to say anything about it.

DANCKWERTS, L.J.: The principle is plainly stated in the House of Lords in *Skelton* v. *Younghouse* (4): it is simply that in a case of this kind, on the issue whether the option is personal or assignable or transmissible, there is no **B** presumption either way in favour of the one or the other: it is a matter of construction in the light of the circumstances which affect the case. It is quite true that the particular factor in the House of Lords case which influenced at least several of the learned lords is not present in the instant case; but there are other indications which give some lead to the testator's intention. None of them are clearly and completely conclusive, because it is the situation in cases **C** of this kind that the testator has not made his meaning absolutely clear, and if he had done so we should probably not be troubled with the matter of his will; but there are indications which in my mind, as in the mind of HARMAN, L.J., lead me to the conclusion that the option is intended to be personal to the son.

The son already had 500 shares in the capital of the company and he was given the remaining 1,500 shares by the testator—the testator, therefore, **D** obviously intended the son to be the owner of the business; and I am satisfied that he intended the son to have a personal option to acquire the properties in which the business was being carried on and which he anticipated that the son would carry on, so that the son should be master of the situation and should not be subject to the vicissitudes of the properties being sold over his head. There are other factors, some one way and some the other, but in my view that factor is **E** really the deciding one in this case. I agree that the option was personal to the son, and I also would allow the appeal.

I need not deal with the other point, which does not arise now.

WINN, L.J.: Approaching this interesting and, if I may be allowed to say so, extremely well argued point, conformably with the principles enunciated by my lords I, too, agree that this option is to be construed as an option personal **F** to the son.

In a very few words I will state, somewhat crudely, my own summary of the issue here. The testator having quite plainly demonstrated a wish that his son should continue to run the business which he had created and which his son had joined him in nursing for twenty years, did he by this will leave the son this option because he was his son, or because he was the proprietor of the business? **G** I think that it should be stated in these words: as a matter of construction the testator's gift of this option was to his son personally, because he expected that the son would continue to run the business, rather than to the proprietor of the business, whoever that might be at the time when the option became exercisable, because the testator expected that the proprietor would be his son. In my own mind, those are the two perpendicular planes of the sharp knife on which (as **H** it was said in their lordships' house (5)) a point like this may often be found to rest.

I would allow the appeal.

Appeal allowed. Leave to appeal to the House of Lords refused.

Solicitors: *A. Kramer & Co.* (for the third defendant, a residuary legatee); *Scadding & Bodkin* (for the plaintiffs, the testator's trustees); *H. B. Wedlake, Saint & Co.* (for the defendants, the executors of the donee of the option).

[*Reported by* HENRY SUMMERFIELD, ESQ., *Barrister-at-Law.*]

---

(4) [1942] 1 All E.R. 650; [1942] A.C. 571.
(5) I.e., in *Skelton* v. *Younghouse*, [1942] 1 All E.R. at p. 656; [1942] A.C. at p. 583, per LORD WRIGHT.

A

NOTE.

Re R. (P. M.) (an infant).

[CHANCERY DIVISION (Goff, J.), December 20, 21, 1967.]

B
*Ward of Court—Care and control—Interim care and control—Access—Official
Solicitor as guardian ad litem, seeking control of question of access by parents
—Order made that parents should have access at such times as they should
agree or as, in default of agreement, the Official Solicitor should direct.*

*Ward of Court—Care and control—Interim care and control—Application
adjourned by master for mother to consider whether she wished matter adjourned
to judge—Mother submitted ward to psychiatrist for examination without
the consent of the court or of the Official Solicitor as guardian ad litem of the
ward—Impropriety of this course.*

C

[As to the court's control over the residence of wards of court, see 21 HALS-
BURY'S LAWS (3rd Edn.) 218, para. 481; and for cases on the subject, see 28
DIGEST (Repl.) 709-711, *2175-2199*.]

D
Case referred to:

S. *(infants), Re,* [1967] 1 All E.R. 202; [1967] 1 W.L.R. 396.

Application.

This was an application in wardship proceedings begun by originating summons.
Much evidence had been filed, but the case would not be ready to be heard on
the merits for a considerable time, and divorce proceedings were pending. A
E question of the immediate care and control of the infant ward, a boy who was
a little under seven years old, had arisen. As consequence of medical evidence
it was common ground that, as an interim measure, the ward should not continue
to live with his parents in the matrimonial home, or with either of them separately. The ward was made a defendant, and the Official Solicitor was appointed
F to be his guardian ad litem. The parents and the ward were interviewed,
pursuant to arrangements made by the Official Solicitor, by Dr. Holman at a
child guidance centre. Dr. Holman reported against the father's proposition
for placing the ward with a Mr. G., a friend of the father, and Mrs. G.'s wife,
and suggested that the ward might be placed in a small children's home. The
Official Solicitor, having carefully considered all the evidence, decided against
G Dr. Holman's suggestion and recommended that the father's proposition should
be accepted. The master made the following note consequent on the matter
being before him on Dec. 8, 1967:

" The Official Solicitor does not feel he can really make a long-term plan
for a considerable period . . . On the question of immediate care and control
the Official Solicitor is adamant that the ward must be moved from the
H matrimonial home and the sooner the better. He was firmly opposed to a
suggestion that the ward might go to a home and attend his old school;
' this would be quite intolerable for him '. I agree. The only other home
seriously urged at the moment is that of the G.'s. He is a witness against
the mother and is regarded by her as being strongly partisan. He and his
wife have said that they would endeavour to give the ward respite and
I would avoid all discussions. This choice was opposed by the mother as G.
was a witness for the father and she felt that he would be prejudiced. Her
choice was the father's elder brother, who is a doctor living [at an address
in Surrey] . . . and who has a grown-up family. This does not seem a good
idea to me as the ward has not seen him for a long time. The ward should
go to the G.'s until further order. There will be no access to either party, but
one letter per person per week, Christmas and birthday cards and presents
may be sent as well. The parties will let me know by 1 p.m. on Monday if
an adjournment is wanted. If not (i) Mrs. G. will collect the ward's luggage

from the house, (ii) pick up the ward from school and take him back to the   A
G.'s home in . . . This should be possible on Tuesday, Dec. 12, 1967."

P. J. Millett for the father.
M. H. Jackson-Lipkin for the mother.
John K. Wood for the Official Solicitor.

GOFF, J., having stated the nature of the question for determination and   B
having read the master's note as hereinbefore set out continued: At the request
of counsel for the mother, the master, as appears in the note that I have read,
allowed time to consider whether she wished to have an adjournment to the judge.
Then a most unfortunate incident occurred, which is why I am giving judgment
in open court. Counsel for the mother acting, as I am satisfied, in all good
faith considered it his duty, in order to enable him to advise the mother whether   C
she should ask for an adjournment, and if she did to enable him to give the court
proper reasons for asking it to reverse or vary the master's proposed order, to
advise that the ward should be examined by a psychiatrist. He therefore caused
his instructing solicitors to make an appointment with a well-known consultant,
Dr. Shribman, and the child was taken there by the mother and examined at
length by that doctor. In my view, and whilst as I have said counsel acted in   D
all good faith and in what he conceived to be his duty to the court and to the
ward, the course taken was a serious error of judgment and was improper, and
such a step ought not to be taken in these cases.

The impropriety consisted in this, that the ward was examined without even
the knowledge, and still less the consent of the Official Solicitor or of the court,
and it was particularly wrong as the ward was already a party to the pro-   E
ceedings and the Official Solicitor was his guardian ad litem. He is not only an
officer of the court and the ward's guardian, but he is a solicitor and the ward is
his client. I wish to say with respect that I entirely agree with what was said
by CROSS, J., in *Re S. (infants)* (1). His words were (2):

"Though they are not strictly necessary for my decision in this case I
venture to add a few further observations on this topic. When a child is   F
made a ward no important step in the child's life can be taken without the
court's consent. To my mind the examination of the ward by a psychiatrist
with a view to the report being put in evidence in the case is such a step. If
both sides agree that an examination is necessary and agree on the person
or persons to conduct it, then normally no doubt there would be no reason
for the court to refuse to follow their wishes. But if they disagree then it   G
would seem right that the Official Solicitor should be appointed guardian
ad litem of the ward—as was done in this case—and that he should decide,
subject to the views of the judge, whether or not an examination is needed.
Further, if he decides that it is needed, then, as it seems to me, he should
instruct the psychiatrist or psychiatrists in question so as to ensure that he
or they have all the relevant material and can see both parents. I have no   F
doubt that the psychiatrists who give evidence in wardship cases are persons
of the highest integrity, but if they are instructed on behalf of one party
their views are bound to be coloured to some extent by that party's views.
Further, if they are ordinary human beings, as I hope and believe that they
are, they can hardly help having some faint desire that their side should win
just because it is their side. I am not, of course, suggesting that there
should be anything in the nature of a panel of court experts whose views
would be in any sense sacrosanct. Any psychiatrist instructed by the
Official Solicitor can be cross-examined. Further the Official Solicitor
himself is in no way committed to accepting the views which he expressed
or precluded from obtaining a second and possibly contrary opinion. My
suggestion is simply directed to ensuring that psychiatrists who give evidence
in wardship cases should receive unbiased instructions, and I repeat that the

---

(1) [1967] 1 All E.R. 202.   (2) [1967] 1 All E.R. at p. 209.

A   views which I am expressing are merely tentative. I fully realise that others as qualified, or better qualified, to judge may dissent from them."

CROSS, J., there said that his views were "tentative" and that others might disagree. For my part I entirely agree and would say that this is a practice which should be observed and followed in all these cases.

B   Every effort was made to give the instructions to Dr. Shribman in a neutral way and to be fair, but it was a wrong approach. In my judgment it could not be satisfactory, and in this particular case it resulted in the psychiatrist not being fully instructed, because he was not told of the vital feature that all parties were agreed that the child could not, for the time being at any rate, stay in the home with its parents. Also in my view such a step was bound to jeopardise the successful launching of any plan for removing the ward from the home of its

C parents. I have had the advantage of seeing the psychiatrist, who endeavoured in every way to be impartial and to assist the court, and he is strongly averse to the ward being separated from his mother; but that does not help me a great deal in view of the fact that both parents agree that as an interim measure at least it is imperative that he should be, and the Official Solicitor also agrees.

D   [HIS LORDSHIP turned to consider what choice should be made between the alternative possibilities. Having reviewed relevant factors, HIS LORDSHIP intimated that, in his judgment, the proposition of sending the ward to Mr. and Mrs. G. was the one which had most prospect of success, and would be most for the benefit of the ward. He would accordingly order that the ward should be sent to live with Mr. and Mrs. G. until further order. HIS LORDSHIP turned to the question of access:] The father suggested no access for one month, the mother

E fourteen days. The Official Solicitor approached the matter from a different angle altogether. He feels, and has submitted, that he ought to control this question of access, which should therefore only be at times agreed by the parents with his consent, or in default of agreement determined by him. Whilst he invited me to indicate that it was desirable if possible that the first access should be not later than one month, there should be no guarantee about that

F and it should be left to his discretion. I fully appreciate the reasons which have prompted him to make that suggestion, but I think that it is really going too far. The parents are after all the ward's parents, and, if they can show reason and agree, then I think that they ought to be trusted to try that. If the Official Solicitor feels that they are in any way abusing it or that their access is harmful then, of course, he can bring the matter back to the court. I therefore propose

G to direct that the parents shall have access either jointly or separately at such times as they agree, or in default of agreement as the Official Solicitor directs, but that there shall be no access, save in emergency, during the first three weeks. Until the Thursday or Friday, Dec. 28 or Dec. 29, however, any order or direction or agreements limiting access are suspended, and the parties shall have an equal and unlimited right of access to the ward.

No issue appears to have been made about correspondence, and I will, therefore, follow the same line as the master proposed, viz., that each parent may write to the ward one letter a week in addition to birthday cards and presents. There are, however, to be no letters or telephone calls between the G.'s and either parent with this exception, that in the event of emergency due to illness or accident the G.'s are to be at liberty to communicate direct with both parents and as far as practicable they should do that at the same time. Apart from that, the Official Solicitor himself will keep in touch with the G.'s, who will be at liberty to communicate with him about the ward as freely as they please.

Order accordingly.

Solicitors: *T. D. Jones & Co.* (for the father); *Isadore Goldman & Son* (for the mother); *Official Solicitor.*

[*Reported by* R. W. FARRIN, *Barrister-at-Law.*]

PADFIELD AND OTHERS *v.* MINISTER OF AGRICULTURE, FISHERIES AND FOOD AND OTHERS.

[HOUSE OF LORDS (Lord Reid, Lord Morris of Borth-y-Gest, Lord Hodson, Lord Pearce and Lord Upjohn), July 18, 19, 20, December 18, 19, 20, 1967, February 14, 1968.]

Public Authority—Statutory powers—Duty of Minister—Judicial control of executive discretion—Complaint by milk producers asking for reference to committee of investigation—Discretion of Minister not expressly limited by enactment—Minister declining to refer complaint—Previous applications by producers to Milk Marketing Board unavailing—Producers in a minority on board—Whether mandamus would lie—Agricultural Marketing Act, 1958 (6 & 7 Eliz. 2 c. 47), s. 19 (3).

The appellants, members of the south east regional committee of the Milk Marketing Board, made a complaint to the Minister of Agriculture, Fisheries and Food, pursuant to s. 19 (3) (*b*)* of the Agricultural Marketing Act, 1958, asking that the complaint be referred to the committee of investigation established under that enactment. The complaint was that the board's terms and prices for the sale of milk to the board did not take fully into account variations between producers and the cost of bringing milk to a liquid market. In effect the complaint was that the price differential worked unfairly against the producers in the popular south east region, where milk was more valuable, the cost of transport was less and the price of land was higher. There had been many previous requests to the board, but these had failed to get the board, in which the south east producers were in a minority, to do anything about the matter. The Minister declined to refer the matter to the committee. By letters of May 1, 1964†, and Mar. 23, 1965‡, he gave reasons which included that (in effect) his main duty had been to decide the suitability of the complaint for such investigation, but that it was one which raised wide issues and which he did not consider suitable for such investigation, as it could be settled through arrangements available to producers and the board within the milk marketing scheme; that he had unfettered discretion, and that, if the complaint were upheld by the committee, he might be expected to make a statutory order to give effect to the committee's recommendations.

Held: (LORD MORRIS OF BORTH-Y-GEST dissenting): (i) the matter would be remitted to the Queen's Bench Division with a direction to require the Minister to consider the appellants' complaint according to law, for the following reasons—

(i) (a) (per LORD REID; cf., per LORD PEARCE) where a statute conferring a discretion on a Minister to exercise or not to exercise a power did not expressly limit or define the extent of his discretion and did not require him to give reasons for declining to exercise the power, his discretion might nevertheless be limited to the extent that it must not be so used, whether by reason of misconstruction of the statute or other reason, as to frustrate the objects of the statute which conferred it (see p. 699, letter D, p. 702, letter C, and p. 714, letter H, post).

(b) (per LORD HODSON and LORD UPJOHN) although the Minister had full or unfettered discretion under s. 19 (3) of the Agricultural Marketing Act, 1958, he was bound to exercise it lawfully, viz., not to misdirect himself in law, nor to take into account irrelevant matters, nor to omit relevant matters from consideration (see p. 710, letters A and D, and p. 717, letters D and F, post).

---

* Section 19 (3) (*b*) is set out at p. 697, letter B, post.
† See p. 700, letters A to G, post.   ‡ See p. 698, letter D, post.

A (c) the complaint in the present case was a substantial and genuine complaint, neither frivolous, repetitive nor vexatious; the reasons of the Minister for not referring the matter to the committee of investigation (viz., that the complaint raised wide issues, that his discretion was unfettered so that, in effect, it was sufficient that he should bona fide have considered the matter) were not good reasons in law, and indeed left out of account

B the merits of the complaint and showed that he was not exercising his discretion in accordance with the intention of s. 19 of the Act of 1958 (see p. 701, letter E, p. 702, letter D, p. 712, letters A and E, p. 714, letter I, p. 715, letters G and H, p. 718, letter G, and p. 719, letter D, post).

Dictum of EARL CAIRNS, L.C. in *Julius* v. *Lord Bishop of Oxford* ([1874-80] All E.R. Rep. at p. 49) considered and applied.

C (ii) the fact that a Minister gave no reasons for his decision, whether or not to exercise a discretionary power conferred on him by statute, would not prevent the court from reaching a conclusion in a proper case that a prerogative order should issue (see p. 701, letter F, p. 712, letter C, p. 714, letter H, and p. 719, letter H, post).

D Per LORD UPJOHN: there may be good policy reasons for refusing an investigation [under s. 19 (3) of the Act of 1958], but policy must not be based on political considerations, which are pre-eminently extraneous (see p. 717, letter H, post).

Dictum of FARWELL, L.J., in *R.* v. *Board of Education* ([1910] 2 K.B. at p. 181), adopted.

Appeal allowed.

E [As to the extent of judicial control over the exercise of discretionary statutory powers by public authorities, see 30 HALSBURY'S LAWS (3rd Edn.) 687, 688, para. 1326; and for cases on the subject, see 28 DIGEST (Repl.) 11-13, *38-48.*

As to the Milk Marketing Board and its powers, see 1 HALSBURY'S LAWS (3rd Edn.), 429-431, paras. 838-841.

For the Agricultural Marketing Act, 1958, s. 19, s. 20, see 38 HALSBURY'S STATUTES (2nd Edn.) 26, 29.]

Cases referred to:

Associated Provincial Picture Houses, Ltd. v. *Wednesbury Corpn.,* [1947] 2 All E.R. 680; [1948] 1 K.B. 223; [1948] L.J.R. 190; 177 L.T. 641; 112 J.P. 55; 45 Digest (Repl.) 215, *189.*

Julius v. *Oxford* (*Lord Bishop*), [1874-80] All E.R. Rep. 43; (1880), 5 App. Cas. 214; 49 L.J.Q.B. 577; 42 L.T. 546; 44 J.P. 600; 44 Digest (Repl.) 310, *1415.*

R. v. *Board of Education,* [1910] 2 K.B. 165; 102 L.T. 578; *affd.* H.L. sub nom. *Board of Education* v. *Rice,* [1911-13] All E.R. Rep. 36; [1911] A.C. 179; 80 L.J.K.B. 796; 104 L.T. 689; 75 J.P. 393; 19 Digest (Repl.) 630, *206.*

R. v. *Mitchell, Ex p. Livesey,* [1913] 1 K.B. 561; 82 L.J.K.B. 153; 108 L.T. 76; 77 J.P. 148; 44 Digest (Repl.) 311, *1423.*

R. v. *Steward of Havering Atte Bower,* (1822), 5 B. & Ald. 691; 106 E.R. 1343; 16 Digest (Repl.) 144, *269.*

Appeal.

This was an appeal by the appellants, George Padfield, Geoffrey Loveys Brock and Henry Steven, from a judgment of the Court of Appeal (DIPLOCK and RUSSELL, L.JJ., LORD DENNING, M.R., dissenting) dated July 27, 1966, setting aside the order of the Divisional Court (LORD PARKER, C.J., SACHS and NIELD, JJ.) dated Feb. 3, 1966, granting an order of mandamus directed to the Minister of Agriculture, Fisheries and Food requiring him to refer to the committee of investigation appointed under s. 19 of the Agricultural Marketing Act, 1958, for their consideration and report the complaint of the appellants dated Jan. 4, 1965. By supplemental case, presented pursuant to adjournment of the appeal on July 20, 1967, the appellants raised for decision the question whether on the true construction of s. 19 of the Act of 1958 the Minister was under a duty to

refer the appellants' complaint to the committee of investigation appointed under
s. 19. The facts are set out in the opinion of LORD REID.

T. M. Eastham, Q.C., and *A. B. Dawson* for the appellants.
Sir Dingle Foot, Q.C., and *P. G. Langdon-Davies* for the Minister.

Their lordships took time for consideration.

Feb. 14. The following opinions were delivered.

LORD REID: My Lords, since 1933 there has been in operation a milk
marketing scheme for England and Wales made under statutory provisions now
contained in the consolidating Agricultural Marketing Act, 1958. Under that
scheme producers are bound to sell their milk to the Milk Marketing Board, and
that board periodically fixes the prices to be paid to the producers. England
and Wales are divided into eleven regions. In each region producers receive the
same price, but there is a different price for each region. One reason for this is
that the cost to the board of transporting milk from the producers' farms to
centres of consumption is considerably greater for some regions than for others.
The lowest price is paid to producers in the far western region and the highest
is paid to producers in the south eastern region; prices paid in the other nine
regions vary, but fall between these two extremes. The present differentials
between the regions were fixed many years ago when costs of transport were
much lower. For the last ten years or so south eastern producers have been
urging the board to increase these differentials but without success. It appears
that the present differential between the south east and the far west is 1·19
pence per gallon. South eastern producers contend that the figure should be in
the region of 3½ pence per gallon. As the total sum available to the board to
pay for the milk which they buy in all the regions is fixed each year, giving effect
to the contention of the south eastern producers would mean that they and perhaps
the producers in some other regions would get higher prices, but producers in the
far west and several other regions would get less. This matter has been considered by two independent committees and their recommendations would, at
least to some extent, favour the contention of the south eastern producers.
I mention this fact only because it shows that their contention cannot be
dismissed as wholly unreasonable or inconsistent with the general scheme.

The Milk Marketing Board is composed of twelve members from the regions,
three elected by all producers in the country and three appointed by the Minister.
The board, of course, acts by a majority of its members. It is said that members
each have in mind, quite properly, the interests of their constituents, that the
adoption of the proposals of the south eastern producers would be against
the financial interests of the constituents of most of the members, and that the
experience of the last ten years shows that the south eastern producers cannot
hope to get a majority on the board for their proposals.

The Act of 1958 provides two methods by which persons aggrieved by the
board's actions can seek a remedy. The first is arbitration. The south eastern
producers attempted to invoke that remedy but it is now common ground that
arbitration would be inappropriate. To give effect to their contention would
require a readjustment of the price structure all over the country and this could
not be achieved by arbitration. The other possible remedy is that provided by
s. 19 of the Act of 1958 which is in these terms:

"(1) The Minister shall appoint two committees (hereinafter in this Act
referred to as a ' consumers' committee ' and a ' committee of investigation ')
for Great Britain, for England and Wales and for Scotland respectively.

"(2) A consumers' committee shall—(a) consist of a chairman and of not
less than six other members, who shall be such persons as appear to the
Minister, after consultation as to one member with the Co-operative Union,
to represent the interests of the consumers of all the products the marketing

A of which is for the time being regulated by schemes approved by the Minister; and (b) be charged with the duty of considering and reporting to the Minister on—(i) the effect of any scheme approved by the Minister, which is for the time being in force, on consumers of the regulated product; and (ii) any complaints made to the committee as to the effect of any such scheme on consumers of the regulated product.

B " (3) A committee of investigation shall—(a) consist of a chairman and either four or five other members; and (b) be charged with the duty, if the Minister in any case so directs, of considering, and reporting to the Minister on, any report made by a consumers' committee and any complaint made to the Minister as to the operation of any scheme which, in the opinion of the Minister, could not be considered by a consumers' committee under the last foregoing subsection.

" (4) On receiving the report of a committee of investigation under this section the Minister shall forthwith publish the conclusions of the committee in such manner as he thinks fit.

" (5) For the purpose of enabling any committee appointed under this section to consider any matter which it is their duty under this section to consider, the board administering the scheme to which the matter relates shall furnish the committee with such accounts and other information relating to the affairs of the board as the committee may reasonably require, and shall be entitled to make representations to the committee with respect to the matter in such manner as may be prescribed by regulations made by the Minister under this Part of this Act with respect to the procedure of the committee.

" (6) If a committee of investigation report to the Minister that any provision of a scheme or any act or omission of a board administering a scheme is contrary to the interests of consumers of the regulated product, or is contrary to the interests of any persons affected by the scheme and is not in the public interest, the Minister, if he thinks fit so to do after considering the report—(a) may by order make such amendments in the scheme as he considers necessary or expedient for the purpose of rectifying the matter; (b) may by order revoke the scheme; (c) in the event of the matter being one which it is within the power of the board to rectify, may by order direct the board to take such steps to rectify the matter as may be specified in the order, and thereupon it shall be the duty of the board forthwith to comply with the order.

" Before taking any action under this subsection the Minister shall give the board notice of the action which he proposes to take and shall consider any representations made by the board within fourteen days after the date of the notice.

" (8) Any order made under para. (a) of sub-s. (6) of this section, under para. (c) of that subsection or under the last foregoing subsection shall be subject to annulment in pursuance of a resolution of either House of Parliament, and any order made under para. (b) of the said sub-s. (6) shall not take effect unless it has been approved by a resolution of each House of Parliament . . ."

With a view to getting the Minister to take action under this section the present appellants, who are office bearers of the south eastern regional committee of the board, approached the Minister and met officials of the Ministry on Apr. 30, 1964. The outcome of that meeting was unsatisfactory to them and on Jan. 4, 1965, their solicitors wrote to the Minister making a formal complaint and asking that the complaint be referred to the committee of investigation. The nature of the complaint was stated thus:

" 4. These acts and/or omissions of the board (a) are contrary to the proper and reasonable interests of producers in the south-eastern region

and of other producers near large liquid markets, all of whom are persons
affected by the scheme, and (b) are not in the public interest.

" 6. *As to* (a) *in para.* 4 *above*

" It is contrary to the reasonable and proper interests of the producers
referred to in para. 4 above that (in addition to the other contributions they
properly made under the scheme) they should make a contribution to the
marketing costs of reaching the liquid markets from the more distant parts
of the country which are properly attributable to producers in those more
distant parts and which should be borne by such producers.

" 7. *As to* (b) *in para.* 4 *above*

"(i) the cross-subsidy set out above has caused or contributed to and will
cause or contribute to an unreasonable alteration in the balance of production, reducing growth in the nearer areas and increasing it in the more distant.
This has tended and will tend to increase the total marketing costs to the
public detriment.

" (ii) it is not in the public interest to continue a system of pricing which
unduly favours one set of producers as against others."

To this letter the Minister's private secretary replied on Mar. 23, 1965:

" The Minister has asked me to reply to your letter of Jan. 4 in which you
made a complaint on behalf of [the appellants], against the Milk Marketing
Board, and requested that the complaint should be referred to the committee
of investigation. The Minister's main duty in considering this complaint has
been to decide its suitability for investigation by means of a particular
procedure. He has come to the conclusion that it would not be suitable.
The complaint is, of course, one that raises wide issues going beyond the
immediate concern of your clients, which is presumably the prices they
themselves receive. It would also affect the interests of other regions and
involve the regional price structure as a whole. In any event the Minister
considers that the issue is of a kind which properly falls to be resolved
through the arrangements available to producers and the board within the
framework of the scheme itself. Accordingly he has instructed me to inform
you that he is unable to accede to your clients' request that this complaint
be referred to the committee of investigation under s. 19 of the Act."

Then in reply to a further letter an official of the Minister replied on May 3, 1965:

" I am directed to reply to your letter of Apr. 9 addressed to the Minister's
private secretary. You will appreciate that under the Agricultural Marketing
Act, 1958, the Minister has unfettered discretion to decide whether or not
to refer a particular complaint to the committee of investigation. In
reaching his decision he has had in mind the normal democratic machinery
of the milk marketing scheme, in which all registered producers participate
and which governs the operations of the board."

Thereafter the appellants applied to the court for an order of mandamus commanding the Minister to refer this complaint to the committee of investigation.
On Feb. 3, 1966 a Divisional Court (LORD PARKER, C.J., SACHS and NIELD, JJ.)
made an order against the Minister, but on July 27, 1966 this order was set aside
by the Court of Appeal by a majority (DIPLOCK and RUSSELL, L.JJ., LORD
DENNING, M.R., dissenting).

The question at issue in this appeal is the nature and extent of the Minister's
duty under s. 19 (3) (*b*) of the Act of 1958 in deciding whether to refer to the
committee of investigation a complaint as to the operation of any scheme made
by persons adversely affected by the scheme. The Minister contends that his
only duty is to consider a complaint fairly, and that he is given an unfettered
discretion with regard to every complaint either to refer it or not to refer it to
the committee as he may think fit. The appellants contend that it is his duty to
refer every genuine and substantial complaint, or alternatively that his discretion

A is not unfettered, and that in this case he failed to exercise his discretion according to law because his refusal was caused or influenced by his having misdirected himself in law, or by his having taken into account extraneous or irrelevant considerations. In my view the appellants' first contention goes too far. There are a number of reasons which would justify the Minister in refusing to refer a complaint. For example he might consider it more suitable for arbitration, or

B he might consider that in an earlier case the committee of investigation had already rejected a substantially similar complaint, or he might think the complaint to be frivolous or vexatious. So he must have at least some measure of discretion. But is it unfettered?

    It is implicit in the argument for the Minister that there are only two possible interpretations of this provision—either he must refer every complaint or he

C has an unfettered discretion to refuse to refer in any case. I do not think that that is right. Parliament must have conferred the discretion with the intention that it should be used to promote the policy and objects of the Act; the policy and objects of the Act must be determined by construing the Act as a whole, and construction is always a matter of law for the court. In a matter of this kind it is not possible to draw a hard and fast line, but if the Minister, by reason

D of his having misconstrued the Act or for any other reason, so uses his discretion as to thwart or run counter to the policy and objects of the Act, then our law would be very defective if persons aggrieved were not entitled to the protection of the court. So it is necessary first to construe the Act. When these provisions were first enacted in 1931 it was unusual for Parliament to compel people to sell their commodities in a way to which they objected, and it was easily foreseeable

E that any such scheme would cause loss to some producers. Moreover, if the operation of the scheme was put in the hands of the majority of the producers, it was obvious that they might use their power to the detriment of consumers, distributors or a minority of the producers. So it is not surprising that Parliament enacted safeguards.

    The approval of Parliament shows that this scheme was thought to be in

F the public interest, and in so far as it necessarily involved detriment to some persons, it must have been thought to be in the public interest that they should suffer it; but in s. 19 and s. 20 Parliament drew a line. They provide machinery for investigating and determining whether the scheme is operating or the board is acting in a manner contrary to the public interest. The effect of these sections is that if, but only if, the Minister and the committee of investigation concur in

G the view that something is being done contrary to the public interest the Minister can step in. Section 20 enables the Minister to take the initiative. Section 19 deals with complaints by individuals who are aggrieved. I need not deal with the provisions which apply to consumers. We are concerned with other persons who may be distributors or producers. If the Minister directs that a complaint by any of them shall be referred to the committee of investigation

H that committee will make a report which must be published. If they report that any provision of this scheme or any act or omission of the board is contrary to the interests of the complainers *and* is not in the public interest, then the Minister is empowered to take action, but not otherwise. He may disagree with the view of the committee as to public interest, and, if he thinks that there are other public interests which outweigh the public interest that justice should be

I done to the complainers, he would be not only entitled but bound to refuse to take action. Whether he takes action or not, he may be criticised and held accountable in Parliament, but the court cannot interfere.

    I must now examine the Minister's reasons for refusing to refer the appellants' complaint to the committee. I have already set out the letters of Mar. 23 and May 3, 1965. I think that it is right also to refer to a letter sent from the ministry on May 1, 1964, because in his affidavit the Minister says that he has read this letter, and there is no indication that he disagrees with any part of it. It is as follows:

A

" My colleague Mr. Jones-Parry and I had the opportunity of discussing with you a day or two ago a matter which you first raised with the ministry at the end of January, namely, what means the ministry could suggest for investigating and remedying the grievance felt by your committee concerning the regional price of milk in the south-east.

" 2. We explained that, as it seemed to us, the only procedure available would be for a group of producers in the south-east to formulate a complaint within the terms of s. 19 of the Agricultural Marketing Act, 1958 and request the Minister to refer this to the committee of investigation. We made it clear, however, that the Minister is not bound so to refer any complaint and has discretion to decide whether to do so.

B

" 3. In considering how to exercise his discretion the Minister would, amongst other things, address his mind to the possibility that if a complaint were so referred and the committee were to uphold it, he in turn would be expected to make a statutory order to give effect to the committee's recommendations. It is this consideration, rather than the formal eligibility of the complaint as a subject for investigation, that the Minister would have in mind in determining whether your particular complaint is a suitable one for reference to the committee. We were unable to hold out any prospect that the Minister would be prepared to regard it as suitable.

C

D

" 4. The reasons which led us to this conclusion were explained to you as follows: (a) the guarantee given to milk producers under the Agriculture Acts is a guarantee given to the board on behalf of all producers. The Minister owes no duty to producers in any particular region, and this is a principle that would be seriously called into question by the making of an order concerned with a regional price; (b) such action would also bring into question the status of the milk marketing scheme as an instrument for the self-government of the industry and such doubt would also, by extension, affect the other marketing schemes as well; and (c) it is by no means clear that the Minister could make an order pertaining to the price of milk in the south-east without determining at least one of the major factors governing prices in the other regions, and he would therefore be assuming an in-appropriate degree of responsibility for determining the structure of regional prices throughout England and Wales.

E

F

" 5. I wish to point out that the statement of these reasons is not intended to imply an assessment of the merits of your complaint considered as an issue of equity among regions."

C

The first reason which the Minister gave in his letter of Mar. 23, 1965, was that this complaint was unsuitable for investigation because it raised wide issues. Here it appears to me that the Minister has clearly misdirected himself. Section 19 (6) contemplates the raising of issues so wide that it may be necessary for the Minister to amend a scheme or even to revoke it. Narrower issues may be suitable for arbitration, but s. 19 affords the only method of investigating wide issues. In my view it is plainly the intention of the Act of 1958 that even the widest issues should be investigated if the complaint is genuine and substantial, as this complaint certainly is.

H

Then it is said that this issue should be " resolved through the arrangements available to producers and the board within the framework of the scheme itself ". This re-states in a condensed form the reasons given in para. 4 of the letter of May 1, 1964 where it is said " the Minister owes no duty to producers in any particular region ", and reference is made to the " status of the milk marketing scheme as an instrument for the self-government of the industry" and to the Minister " assuming an inappropriate degree of responsibility ". As I have already pointed out, however, the Act of 1958 imposes on the Minister a respon-sibility whenever there is a relevant and substantial complaint that the board is acting in a manner inconsistent with the public interest, and that has been

A relevantly alleged in this case. I can find nothing in the Act of 1958 to limit this responsibility or to justify the statement that the Minister owes no duty to producers in a particular region. The Minister is, I think, correct in saying that the board is an instrument for the self-government of the industry. So long as it does not act contrary to the public interest the Minister cannot interfere; but if it does act contrary to what both the committee of investigation and the

B Minister hold to be the public interest, the Minister has a duty to act. And if a complaint relevantly alleges that the board has so acted, as this complaint does, then it appears to me that the Act of 1958 does impose a duty on the Minister to have it investigated. If he does not do that, he is rendering nugatory a safeguard provided by the Act of 1958 and depriving complainers of a remedy which I am satisfied that Parliament intended them to have.

C Paragraph 3 of the letter of May 1, 1964 refers to the possibility that if the complaint were referred and the committee were to uphold it, the Minister " would be expected to make a statutory order to give effect to the committee's recommendations ". If this means that he is entitled to refuse to refer a complaint because if he did so he might later find himself in an embarrassing situation, that would plainly be a bad reason. I can see an argument to the effect that if,

D on receipt of a complaint, the Minister can satisfy himself from information in his possession as to the merits of the complaint, and he then chooses to say that, whatever the committee might recommend, he would hold it to be contrary to the public interest to take any action, it would be a waste of time and money to refer the complaint to the committee. I do not intend to express any opinion about that because that is not this case. In the first place it appears that the

E Minister has come to no decision as to the merits of the appellants' case, and secondly, the Minister has carefully avoided saying what he would do if the committee were to uphold the complaint.

It was argued that the Minister is not bound to give any reasons for refusing to refer a complaint to the committee, that if he gives no reasons his decision cannot be questioned, and that it would be very unfortunate if giving reasons

F were to put him in a worse position. I do not agree, however, that a decision cannot be questioned if no reasons are given. If it is the Minister's duty not to act so as to frustrate the policy and objects of the Act of 1958, and if it were to appear from all the circumstances of the case that that has been the effect of the Minister's refusal, then it appears to me that the court must be entitled to act.

G A number of authorities was cited in the course of the argument, but none appears to me to be at all close to the present case. I must however notice *Julius* v. *Lord Bishop of Oxford* (1), because it was largely relied on. There the statute enacted that with regard to certain charges against any clerk in Holy Orders it " shall be lawful " for the bishop of the diocese " on the application of any party complaining thereof " to issue a commission for enquiry. It was

H held that the words " it shall be lawful " merely conferred a power. EARL CAIRNS, L.C., said (2):

" But there may be something in the nature of the thing empowered to be done, something in the object for which it is to be done, something in the conditions under which it is to be done, something in the title of the person or persons for whose benefit the power is to be exercised, which may couple

I the power with a duty, and make it the duty of the person on whom the power is reposed to exercise that power when called upon to do so."

LORD PENZANCE said that the true question was (3)

" whether regard being had to the person enabled, to the subject matter, to the general objects of the statute, and to the person, or class of persons,

---

(1) [1874-80] All E.R. Rep. 43; (1880), 5 App. Cas. 214.
(2) [1874-80] All E.R. Rep. at p. 47; (1880), 5 App. Cas. at pp. 222, 223.
(3) [1874-80] All E.R. Rep. at p. 51; (1880), 5 App. Cas. at pp. 229. 230.

for whose benefit the power may be intended to have been conferred, [the   **A**
words] do or do not create a duty . . ."

and LORD SELBORNE said (4) that the question was whether it could be shown
from any particular words in the Act or from the general scope and objects of
the statute that there was a duty. So there is ample authority for going behind
the words which confer the power to the general scope and objects of the Act
in order to find what was intended. In *Julius'* case (5) no question was raised   **B**
whether there could be a discretion but a discretion so limited that it must not
be used to frustrate the object of the Act which conferred it; and I have found no
authority to support the unreasonable proposition that it must be all or nothing
—either no discretion at all or an unfettered discretion. Here the words " if the
Minister in any case so directs " are sufficient to show that he has some discretion,
but they give no guide as to its nature or extent. That must be inferred from a   **C**
construction of the Act of 1958 read as a whole, and for the reasons which I have
given I would infer that the discretion is not unlimited, and that it has been
used by the Minister in a manner which is not in accord with the intention of
the statute which conferred it. As the Minister's discretion has never been
properly exercised according to law, I would allow this appeal. It appears to
me that the case should now be remitted to the Queen's Bench Division with a   **D**
direction to require the Minister to consider the complaint of the appellants
according to law. The order for costs in the Divisional Court should stand.
The appellants should have their costs in the Court of Appeal, but as extra
expense was caused in this House by an adjournment of the hearing at their
motion they should only have two-thirds of their costs in this House.

E

LORD MORRIS OF BORTH-Y-GEST: My Lords, pursuant to decisions
of policy which have been the basis of Agricultural Marketing Acts since 1931
there have been various marketing schemes. The producers of an agricultural
product are themselves entitled to submit a scheme to the Minister of Agriculture
for the regulation and marketing of a product. There may be a board to administer
the scheme. Subject to compliance with certain conditions the Minister may   **F**
approve such a scheme. A scheme is to be one for regulating the marketing of a
product " by the producers thereof ". The present case concerns one such
scheme, namely the milk marketing scheme. There has been a scheme in operation since 1933. It was then approved by the Minister and has since from time
to time been amended. It is manifest that a scheme will be more acceptable to
some producers of milk than to others. The advantage of having a buyer for all   **G**
the milk which a producer produces will appeal to those who otherwise would
have produced more than they could sell. There will be no such advantage for
those so placed that they could have a sure and ready market for all that they
could produce. If prices are fixed regionally, and are fixed having regard to the
average of transport and marketing costs within the region, there will be some
within the region who could assert that their costs, if they had been left to them-   **H**
selves, would have been less than those of others. If in fixing prices regionally
it is not deemed advisable fully to reflect the variations as between regions of
transport and marketing costs, then it follows that encouragement to production
is being given to certain regions at the expense of others. Within the regions,
therefore, as well as within the industry, the interests of some producers are
being advantaged at the expense of other producers. The less fortunate are   **I**
being helped by the more fortunate. The latter may not welcome the policy
which brings about such a result. They may see no reason why they should not
have more and others less. They may object to a system under which they are
in substance contributing to a subsidy to others. Yet all this may be one of the
results of having a scheme.

---

(4) [1874-80] All E.R. Rep. at p. 54; (1880), 5 App. Cas. at p. 235.
(5) [1874-80] All E.R. Rep. 43; (1880), 5 App. Cas. 214.

A   The milk marketing scheme is administered by a board. It has twelve regional representatives (one for each of ten regions and two for the eleventh region). Those regional members of the board are elected by the registered producers (para. 16 of the scheme). In addition there are three special members elected by all registered producers and not less than two and not more than three persons appointed by the Minister. The scheme provides (by para. 24) that questions

B   arising at any meeting of the board are to be decided by a majority of the votes of members present. There are regional committees whose duty it is to report to or to make representations to the board on the operation of the scheme in relation to the producers in the region—(para. 31). On the coming into force of the scheme a poll of registered producers had to be taken on the question whether the scheme was to remain in force—(para. 44). Under the statutory

C   provisions (s. 1 (8) of the Agricultural Marketing Act, 1931 now s. 2 (7) of the Agricultural Marketing Act, 1958) the scheme had to be laid before Parliament. The board has wide powers to regulate marketing (para. 60). If the board requires registered producers to sell any milk only to the board then

>   " the board shall from time to time prescribe the terms on which and the
>   price at which such milk shall be sold to the board and may also prescribe

D   the form in which contracts for the sale of such milk to the board shall be
>   made."

(See para. 64). The board may prescribe different terms, prices and forms of contract for different classes of producers or classes of sale or descriptions of milk. Two things are apparent. One is that the scheme provides for government of the industry by the industry. The second is that no machinery is provided

E   whereby the work of the board can be over-ruled by some reviewing body in regard to such matters as terms of sale and price fixation.

The appellants are three producers in one region (the south eastern region). They have the support of most, or nearly all, of the other producers in that region. In substance they say that the price being paid to them should be higher. They complain of the operation of the scheme. They asked (by a letter of

F   Jan. 4, 1965) that their complaint should be referred to the committee of investigation which has been appointed under the Act of 1958. It is important to note their complaint. It was

>   " of certain acts and/or omissions in prescribing (under para. 64 of the
>   scheme) the terms on which and the price at which milk shall be sold to the
>   board, in that the board should, but do not, take fully into account variations

G   as between producers in the costs of bringing their milk to a liquid market
>   whether such costs are incurred or not."

They set out figures showing that the range of variation (between regions) of producers' net prices is 1·19 pence per gallon, whereas the range of variation (between regions) of true marketing costs is considerably higher (3·37 pence

H   per gallon in 1961-62 and probably 3·66 pence per gallon in 1963-64). The costs in the south eastern region are the lowest. The cost of transporting milk is naturally at its lowest in regions where the producers are near to centres of population and the milk marketing board pays a higher price at the farm gate to producers in those regions than to producers in other regions. This is known as a differential. Producers in the south eastern region receive a higher regional

I   differential than do producers in any of the other regions.

The complaint as formulated would imply that there should be varying differentials as between all producers, but the case proceeded on the basis that there should be no variation in the differential as between the producers in a particular region. It would seem probable that the essential facts and figures relating to the complaint are either well known or are readily ascertainable. It is quite clear that in the fixing of prices it must have been decided by the board that they would not take regional variations of transport costs " fully " into account. That decision, if taken in good faith, must have been a policy decision.

It must also be the case that the members of the board who fixed the prices must A
have been fully aware of the contentions of the appellants. Every member of
the board must have heard the competing contentions for and against the board's
policy advanced and recited over and over again. They have been canvassed
over the years. It has been for the board to decide as a matter of policy whether
regional prices should or should not " take fully into account variations as
between producers in the costs of bringing their milk to a liquid market." Wider B
issues of policy are, in turn, involved. The appellants in their letter to the Minister
have suggested that the price fixations of the board will have the result of
" reducing growth in the nearer areas and increasing it in the more distant",
and they suggest that this will tend to increase the total marketing costs to the
public detriment. It may or it may not be a good thing to increase production
in the more distant areas. It may or it may not be in the public interest to C
encourage such production. It is no part of our province to attempt to assess
the weight of the competing public interests which are involved, or to consider
whether the policy decisions of the board will or will not in the long run enure
to the public advantage. The board may or may not have reached the widest
decision. It is, however, manifest that the board's decisions have been deliberate.
There is no suggestion that the board has not acted in entire good faith. Nor is D
it said that it has exceeded its powers under the scheme as approved. When in
1964 the appellants made a suggestion to the board that there should be an
arbitration the board, through its solicitors in a letter (dated June 18, 1964) to
the appellants' solicitors, stated:

> " While your clients contend that they ought to have a bigger proportion
> of the available money, there are other producers elsewhere who contend that E
> your clients ought to have a smaller proportion. The proportions actually
> determined by the board are the result of collective decisions of the board
> and do not necessarily represent the view of any one producer or of the
> producers in any one county or region."

In recording the view that the case was not one for arbitration it was said:

> " The board has the duty of determining prices and has done so to the best F
> of its ability. The board considers that as it has acted within its powers and
> in good faith, an arbitrator appointed under para. 93 of the scheme has no
> power to substitute his view (if it differs from the board's) of what those
> prices should be."

On behalf of the board it was further said:

> " Your clients cannot receive more unless some others receive less, and G
> what is really involved is the whole determination of prices throughout the
> country. Paragraph 93 of the scheme is not intended to transfer the board's
> duty of determining prices to an arbitrator at the instance of a particular
> group of producers."

The appellants do not now suggest that arbitration would be appropriate, but H
in asking that their complaint should be referred to the committee of investigation appointed under the Act of 1958 they are in effect asking for an arbitration
in another form. They are asking that the determination of prices should be
made by the committee. The committee could only recommend that the appellants
should receive a higher price on the basis that other producers should receive a
lower price. The position of all those others would be affected. The committee I
would be acting as an appellate body from the decision of the board. It may
have to be decided as a matter of policy and judgment whether the committee
of investigation (which could be concerned with any one of the marketing
schemes coming into existence under the Act of 1958 and was not appointed
to be concerned with any particular scheme such as the milk marketing scheme)
would be the appropriate body to perform the function. The committee of investigation is, however, in existence and it certainly would be open to the Minister if
he deemed it desirable to refer a complaint of the present kind to the committee.

A   Before your lordships it was in the first place submitted that the appellants had a right to have their complaint referred to the committee, and that accordingly an order of mandamus should be directed to the Minister positively commanding him to refer the complaint. This contention was rejected by the Divisional Court and was not even advanced in the Court of Appeal. I, also, would reject it. In my view the Minister is endowed with a discretion. It is for

B him to decide whether to ask the committee to report on any complaint made as to the operation of any scheme made under the Act of 1958. A duty will only devolve on the committee " if the Minister in any case so directs ". These words are in sharp contrast to those which are employed in the Act of 1958 when a positive duty is imposed on the Minister. Thus in s. 2 (3) are the words " shall direct a public enquiry to be held ". In s. 19 (4) are the words

C " the Minister shall forthwith publish ". In s. 20 (3) are the words " the Minister shall refer ". If Parliament had intended to impose a duty on the Minister to refer any and every complaint, or even any and every complaint of a particular nature, it would have been so easy to impose such a duty in plain terms. I cannot read the words in s. 19 (3) as imposing a positive duty on the Minister to refer every complaint as to the operation of every scheme. Such was the appellants'

D contention, though they modified it by suggesting that the duty would not exist in the case of trivial or frivolous or repetitive complaints. In support of their revived contention the appellants submitted that in some circumstances a duty exists to exercise a power. So in the present case it was argued that a power was deposited in the Minister, that the power was given for the benefit of particular persons, that in the Act of 1958 they were specifically designated (e.g., persons

E complaining as to the operation of a scheme) and that in the Act of 1958 the circumstances in which there is entitlement to the exercise of the power are defined (i.e. that there should be a complaint to the Minister as to the operation of the scheme being a complaint which could not be considered by a consumers' committee). Reliance was placed on a passage in the speech of EARL CAIRNS, L.C., in *Julius* v. *Lord Bishop of Oxford* (6). LORD CAIRNS said that the cases

F decided (7):

>   " . . . that where a power is deposited with a public officer for the purpose of being used for the benefit of persons who are specifically pointed out, and with regard to whom a definition is supplied by the legislature of the conditions upon which they are entitled to call for its exercise, that power ought to be exercised, and the court will require it to be exercised."

In my view this passage does not avail the appellants. I can see no provision in the Act of 1958 showing that the appellants or others who might make a complaint similar to theirs were " entitled " to call on the Minister to exercise the power given to him. At most their entitlement was that the Minister should consider and should decide whether or not in the exercise of his discretion he would refer a complaint. It would have to be shown that the Act of 1958 gave the appellants a " right " to have their complaint sent to the committee before the power in the Minister could be held to be one that he was bound to exercise. Thus in his speech in *Julius* v. *Lord Bishop of Oxford* (6) LORD BLACKBURN said (8) that:

>   " . . . if the object for which the power is conferred be for the purpose of enforcing a right, there may be a duty cast on the donee of the power to exercise it for the benefit of those who have that right when required on their behalf."

So also LORD BLACKBURN said (9): " The enabling words are construed as compulsory whenever the object of the power is to effectuate a legal right."

---

(6) [1874-80] All E.R. Rep. 43; (1880), 5 App. Cas. 214.
(7) [1874-80] All E.R. Rep. at p. 49; (1880), 5 App. Cas. at p. 225
(8) [1874-80] All E.R. Rep. at p. 57; (1880), 5 App. Cas. at p. 241.
(9) [1874-80] All E.R. Rep. at p. 59; (1880), 5 App. Cas. at p. 244.

Where some legal right or entitlement is conferred or enjoyed, and for the purpose of effectuating such right or entitlement a power is conferred on someone, then words which are permissive in character will sometimes be construed as involving a duty to exercise the power. The purpose and the language of any particular enactment must be considered. Thus in *R.* v. *Mitchell, Ex p. Livesey* (10) consideration was given to the words of s. 9 of the Conspiracy and Protection of Property Act, 1875, viz:

" Where a person is accused before a court of summary jurisdiction of any offence made punishable by the Act, and for which a penalty amounting to £20, or imprisonment, is imposed, the accused may, on appearing before the court of summary jurisdiction, declare that he objects to being tried for such offence by a court of summary jurisdiction, and thereupon the court of summary jurisdiction may deal with the case in all respects as if the accused were charged with an indictable offence and not an offence punishable on summary conviction, and the offence may be prosecuted on indictment accordingly."

A declaration of objection to being tried by a court of summary jurisdiction was duly made by a person accused of an offence made punishable by the Act who was entitled to object. It was held that accordingly he had a right to trial by jury and that the justices were bound to give effect to his claim and had no jurisdiction to try the case.

On the principles laid down in *Julius'* case (11) it becomes necessary to consider the language used in the Agricultural Marketing Act, 1958 and the purposes of the Act. A consumers' committee under s. 19 (2) is charged with the duty of considering and reporting to the Minister on the effect of a scheme on consumers, and also on " any complaints made to the committee as to the effect of any such scheme on consumers of the regulated product ". The words in s. 19 (3) are in marked contrast. A committee of investigation is only charged with the duty of considering and reporting " if the Minister in any case so directs ". The Minister may refer to them a report of a consumers' committee. He may refer to them a complaint which has been made to him and which in his view could not have gone to a consumers' committee. The language here is in my view purely permissive. The Minister is endowed with discretionary powers. If he did decide to refer a complaint he is endowed with further discretionary powers after receiving a report (see s. 19 (6)). I cannot, therefore, accept the contention of the appellants that they had a right to have their complaint referred to the committee and that the Minister had a positive duty to refer it. The Minister, in my view, had a discretion. It was urged on behalf of the Minister that his discretion was in one sense an unfettered one, though it was not said that he could disregard the complaint. The case proceeded on an acceptance by the Minister that he was bound to consider the complaint and then, in the exercise of his judgment, to decide whether or not to refer it to the committee.

If the Minister proceeded properly to exercise his judgment then, in my view, it is no part of the duty of any court to act as a court of appeal from his decision or to express any opinion as to whether it was wise or unwise. The Minister was given an executive discretion. In speaking of a power given by statute to a local authority to grant certain licences LORD GREENE, M.R. said in his judgment in *Associated Provincial Picture Houses, Ltd.* v. *Wednesbury Corpn.* (12):

The law recognises certain principles upon which that discretion must be exercised, but within the four corners of those principles the discretion is an absolute one and cannot be questioned in any court of law."

I think it follows that an order of mandamus could only be made against the Minister if it is shown that in some way he acted unlawfully. A court could

---

(10) [1913] 1 K.B. 561.
(11) [1874-80] All E.R. Rep. 43; (1880), 5 App. Cas. 214.
(12) [1947] 2 All E.R. 680 at p. 682; [1948] 1 K.B. 223 at p. 228.

A make an order if it were shown (a) that the Minister failed or refused to apply his mind to or to consider the question whether to refer a complaint, or (b) that he misinterpreted the law or proceeded on an erroneous view of the law, or (c) that he based his decision on some wholly extraneous consideration or (d) that he failed to have regard to matters which he should have taken into account.

I propose to consider whether any one of these is established. The order
B that was made by the Divisional Court commanded the Minister

" to consider the said complaint of the applicants according to law and upon relevant consideration to the exclusion of irrelevant considerations."

As to (a) it cannot be asserted that the Minister failed to consider the appellants' complaint. In his affirmation the Minister states that he considered the complaint and all the matters put before him by the appellants. He states that he
C came to his decision for the reasons indicated in the letters of Mar. 23 and May 3, 1965, namely that he " considered that the issue raised by the applicants' complaint was one which in all the circumstances should be dealt with by the board rather than the committee of investigation ". As to (b) I do not consider that the Minister is shown to have misinterpreted the law unless it could be said that any of the considerations recorded in the letters from the ministry were so
D inadmissible as to involve that the Minister took a wrong view of the law or misdirected himself in law. I turn therefore to consider the letters. They formed the foundation for the submission that on the basis of (c) and (d) above the order of the Divisional Court was appropriately made.

As the Minister states in his affirmation that he came to his decision for the reasons indicated in the two letters, it is primarily those letters that are to be
E studied. As, however, he states that in deciding as to the application he had read a letter dated May 1, 1964 written by a ministry representative, and as he has not stated that he excluded from his mind the considerations therein recorded, I think that it is a reasonable inference that they had, or may have had, some influence. It is fair, I think, to regard all three letters as revealing what was in the mind of the Minister. His decision was that the complaint was not one that
F in his view was suitable for investigation by means of the particular procedure of a reference to the committee of investigation. That decision was essentially a policy decision. It concerned a situation that was known and understood in the industry. The main facts in regard to it were known. The differential, or the range between producers' net prices, stands at 1·19 pence per gallon. It has stood at that figure for some years. It was a figure that was first fixed during
G the war. That fact was known to all concerned. So also must it have been known to all concerned that if true marketing costs were taken " fully " into account the range would be much higher. The question whether the differential should be varied must therefore have been a perennial one. If it were, then producers in some regions would get more and producers in other regions would get less. A constant major policy problem must have been whether it is desir-
H able to encourage production in those regions where, if there were no scheme, producers would not fare very well. So also it must have been widely known that two committees had made suggestions relating to this long-standing problem. One of them (the Cutforth committee) had reported as far back as 1936. Another (the Davis committee) had in 1963 suggested that the country should be divided into five price zones each with a different differential and that the total range
I of the prices at the farm gate should be the figure of 2·4 pence per gallon instead of the figure of 1·19 pence per gallon. All these facts and considerations must have been well known.

I know of no reason to assume or to suggest that the members of the board in the discharge of their duties have acted irresponsibly. Because a policy decision under a national scheme results in a measure of advantage to some and a measure of disadvantage to others it does not follow that the members of the board have been guided, not by considerations of the national interest or of the general interest of their industry, but solely by considerations as to how the pockets of

their colleagues would be affected. At any time during the sequence of the **A**
past years it would have been open to a Minister, had he considered it desirable
and politic, to take the initiative under s. 20 (2) of the Act of 1958 and to give
directions to the board concerning prices. It was at all times a question of policy
for successive Ministers, whether or not they should take such action. For any
decision or for any inaction a Minister would be answerable in Parliament. It
was against all this background that the Minister had to consider the appellants' **B**
request in the early part of 1965. In agreement with DIPLOCK and RUSSELL,
L.JJ., I do not consider that it has been shown that he failed to exercise his
discretion; nor has it been shown that he was guided by irrelevant considerations
or that he failed to consider relevant matters. A study of the letters leads me to
the view that the Minister considered it desirable that the milk industry should,
in accordance with its own scheme, be self-governing and that it would not be **C**
good policy for him to over-rule decisions of the Milk Marketing Board which
fixed the price to be paid in a particular region or to particular persons. I do
not find in the letters any statement that the Minister considered that he had
no power to refer the appellants' complaint to the committee: nor any statement
that the Minister considered that he was compelled to leave price fixing to the
Milk Marketing Board. Rightly or wrongly he considered it best to do so. **D**

As a result of the meticulous scrutiny to which the three letters have been
subjected the appellants contend that irrelevant or inadmissible considerations
were taken into account by the Minister.

1. Criticism is made of the passage in the letter of Mar. 23 to the effect that
the complaint of the appellants was " one that raises wide issues going beyond
the immediate concern of your clients which is presumably the prices they **E**
themselves receive ". In the following sentence it is pointed out that the complaint would also affect the interests of other regions and involve the regional
price structure as a whole. I do not read that passage as involving that the
complaint ought not to go to the committee merely because it raised wide issues.
What I think was being pointed out was that the appellants' complaint would
necessarily involve a complete review of the prices in all the regions as fixed **F**
by the board. I see no reason to think that the Minister was unaware of his
powers as, for example, under s. 20 (2). What I think is revealed is that the
Minister as a matter of policy considered it undesirable or inappropriate for him
to over-rule the board in regard to price fixation. This is shown by the letter
of May 1, 1964 where it is said:

" It is by no means clear that the Minister could make an order pertaining **G**
to the price of milk in the south-east without determining at least one of the
major factors governing prices in the other regions, and he would therefore be
assuming an inappropriate degree of responsibility for determining the
structure of regional prices throughout England and Wales."

2. Criticism is made of the passage in which it is said that the Minister con- **H**
sidered that the issue was of a kind which properly fell to be resolved within
the framework of the scheme. It is said that he was mistaking his powers and was
being unmindful of the courses of action open to him either under s. 20 (2) or
after a report from a committee under s. 19 (6) (c). I see no reason to deduce that
the Minister was oblivious of his powers: nor that he was not appreciating that
under the machinery of the scheme a majority vote could result in disadvantages for some districts. If the Minister nevertheless decided that the self-
governing machinery should operate, his decision could be attacked as being
impolitic, but I do not think it could be attacked as being made on inadmissible
considerations.

3. Criticism is further made of the sentence in the letter of May 1, 1964, which
reads:

" In considering how to exercise his discretion the Minister would,
amongst other things, address his mind to the possibility that if a complaint

A were so referred and the committee were to uphold it, he in turn would be expected to make a statutory order to give effect to the committee's recommendations."

This sentence may be obscure and imprecise, but I doubt whether we ought to put the most unfavourable construction on it. If there was a reference to the committee and if the committee reported that some act of the board was
B contrary to the interests of consumers or " of any persons affected by the scheme " and was not in the public interest, then the Minister would himself have a discretion whether or not to take any course of action designated in s. 19 (6). There may be cases where, from a knowledge of the problem and all its aspects and because of his own firm view of what course the public interest demands, a Minister could see that a reference could lead to no useful result. A Minister
C might conclude that whatever report a committee might make a reference to them would only produce needless confusion and disappointment, and would not prompt him to follow a course of action that he considered undesirable. Though the 1964 letter is not very explicit it is for the appellants to show that the Minister was guided by irrelevant considerations. In agreement with DIPLOCK and RUSSELL, L.JJ., I consider that the appellants have failed to show
D this.

For the reasons which I have set out I would dismiss the appeal.

LORD HODSON: My Lords, the appellants say in the first place that this is a case which satisfies the test, propounded in *Julius* v. *Lord Bishop of Oxford* (13) drawing the distinction between a power coupled with a duty
E and a complete discretion. In the former case enabling words are said to be compulsory when they are words to effectuate a legal right. It is argued that the Minister is subject to mandamus here, for he is given a power to be exercised in favour of persons who are defined and accordingly, are given a right to have their claim submitted to a committee of investigation under the provisions of s. 19 of the Agricultural Marketing Act, 1958. This argument was abandoned
F before the Divisional Court, not put forward in the Court of Appeal, but was resurrected before your lordships by way of supplemental case. Section 19 (3), so far as material, reads:

"   . . . (*b*) be charged with the duty, if the Minister in any case so directs, of considering and reporting to the Minister on, any report made by a consumers' committee and any complaint made to the Minister as to the opera-
G tion of any scheme which, in the opinion of the Minister, could not be considered by a consumers' committee under the last foregoing section."

Schemes for regulating the marketing of agricultural products were introduced by the Agricultural Marketing Act, 1931, and are compulsory in their operation on consumers, who are protected as to price and supply, on distributors and on producers, who get the advantage of having no milk left on their hands unsold.
H The discretion must be exercised by the Minister in accordance with the intention of the Act of 1958, but there is nothing in the language used in the subsection introduced by the words " If the Minister in any case so directs " nor in the context of the Act of 1958 and earlier legislation to support the view that an absolute right to an enquiry is given to an aggrieved person. The argument of the appellants is undermined, in my opinion, by their concession that trivial,
I frivolous or vexatious complaints can be shut out as, for example, where a complaint has been recently dealt with in a parallel case. True that the scheme is of a compulsory nature and s. 19 is designed for the redress of grievances, but this is not to exclude the Minister's discretion to reject a complaint if he exercises his discretion according to law. The succeeding section, s. 20 of the Act of 1958, indicates the position of the Minister as responsible for giving directions to a board as to its acts or omissions as he considers necessary or expedient

---

(13) [1874-80] All E.R. Rep. 43; (1880), 5 App. Cas. 214.

in the public interest, and his directions have to be complied with so far as the **A**
board is not required to do anything which it has no power to do.

If the Minister has a complete discretion under the Act of 1958, as in my opinion
he has, the only question remaining is whether he has exercised it lawfully. It is
on this issue that much difference of judicial opinion has emerged, although there
is no divergence of opinion on the relevant law. As LORD DENNING, M.R.,
said, citing LORD GREENE, M.R., in *Associated Provincial Picture Houses, Ltd.* v. **B**
Wednesbury Corpn. (14):

> " a person entrusted with a discretion must direct himself properly in
> law. He must call his own attention to the matters which he is bound to
> consider. He must exclude from his consideration matters which are
> irrelevant to the matter that he has to consider."

In another part of this judgment LORD GREENE drew attention (15) to that **C**
which I have mentioned above, namely, the necessity to have regard to matters
to which the statute conferring the discretion shows that the authority exercising the discretion ought to have regard. The authority must not, as it has been
said, allow itself to be influenced by something extraneous and extra-judicial
which ought not to have affected its decision.

I come now to the facts of the present case. In 1933 the milk marketing **D**
scheme (amended in 1955) came into operation. The members of the board
consist of twelve regional members elected for the several regions by the registered producers, and three special members elected by all registered producers
and not less than two and not more than three persons appointed by the Minister
(see Part II of the scheme, para. 9). Questions arising at a meeting of board are
decided by a majority of the votes of the members present (see Part II para. 24). **E**
The price of milk is fixed by the board for milk delivered at the farm gate.

The south eastern farmers, being much nearer to the great population of
London, are paid what is called a differential to compensate them for the loss
of the advantage they would otherwise have over most other districts in consequence of their proximity to a large market. The differential was fixed many
years ago at 1·19d. per gallon, and the south eastern farmers have long com- **F**
plained that it is too low and sought without success to obtain redress of their
grievance from the board. They have been outvoted since, in the interests of
their own pockets, so it is said, a majority of the other regions opposed them.
This decision has been reached notwithstanding the recommendations of two
committees set up at different times, who have recognised the justice of their
claim. On the Davis committee, set up in 1963, making its report without any **G**
benefit to the south eastern farmers ensuing, and the board having rejected their
claim, the first named appellant approached the Minister at the end of January,
1964, asking what means the Ministry could suggest for investigating and remedying the grievance felt by his committee concerning the regional price of milk
in the south east. Correspondence ensued to which it will be necessary to refer
and the decision of the Minister refusing to refer the complaint to the investigat- **H**
ing committee was contained in a letter of Mar. 23, 1965. The letter reads, so
far as material:

> " The Minister's main duty in considering the complaint has been to
> decide its suitability for investigation by means of a particular procedure.
> He has come to the conclusion that it would not be suitable. The complaint
> is of course one that raises wide issues going beyond the immediate concern
> of your clients, which is presumably the prices they themselves receive.
> It would also affect the interests of other regions and involve the regional
> price structure as a whole.

> " In any event the Minister considers that the issue is of a kind which
> properly falls to be resolved through the arrangements available to

---

(14) [1947] 2 All E.R. at pp. 682, 683; [1948] 1 K.B. at p. 229.
(15) [1947] 2 All E.R. at p. 682; [1948] 1 K.B. at p. 228.

A   producers and the board within the framework of the scheme itself. Accordingly he has instructed me to inform you that he is unable to accede to your clients' request that this complaint be referred to the committee of investigation under s. 19 of the Act."

In response to a further letter from the appellants' solicitors a letter dated May 3, 1965, was received referring to the Minister's unfettered discretion, and

B   adding that in reaching his decision he had had in mind the normal democratic machinery of the milk marketing scheme in which all registered producers participated and which governs the operations of the board.

On the appellants' solicitors enquiring whether it would be asserted that the letters of 1965 were the only matters present to the Minister's mind at the time of his decision, to the exclusion of the considerations set out in the letters which

C   had passed in the year 1964, the Minister affirmed on Nov. 4, 1965, he having been appointed on Oct. 19, 1964 (after the 1964 letters had passed):

"In considering the applicants' application I read among other papers the letter signed by Mr. J. H. Kirk and dated May 1, 1964 . . .

"Before reaching my decision not to refer the applicants' complaint to the committee of investigation I considered all the matters put before me on

D   behalf of the applicants in support of their application. I came to my decision for the reasons indicated in the letters dated Mar. 23, 1965, and May 3, 1965, . . . namely that I considered that the issue raised by the applicants' complaint was one which in all the circumstances should be dealt with by the board rather than the committee of investigation."

E   If the letter of May 1, 1964 be looked at, and it was not disowned by the Minister in his affirmation or at all, it throws further light on the refusal of the Minister to exercise his discretion by referring the complaint to the investigating committee. This letter contains the following:

"3. In considering how to exercise his discretion the Minister would, amongst other things, address his mind to the possibility that if a complaint

F   were so referred and the committee were to uphold it, he in turn would be expected to make a statutory order to give effect to the committee's recommendations. It is this consideration, rather than the formal eligibility of the complaint as a subject for investigation, that the Minister would have in mind in determining whether your particular complaint is a suitable one for reference to the committee. We were unable to hold out any prospect

G   that the Minister would be prepared to regard it as suitable.

"4. The reasons which led us to this conclusion were explained to you as follows: (a) the guarantee given to milk producers under the Agriculture Acts is a guarantee given to the board on behalf of all producers. The Minister owes no duty to producers in any particular region, and this is a principle that would be seriously called into question by the making of an order

H   concerned with a regional price;

"(b) such action would also bring into question the status of the milk marketing scheme as an instrument for the self-government of the industry and such doubt would also, by extension, affect the other marketing schemes as well; and

"(c) it is by no means clear that the Minister could make an order per-

I   taining to the price of milk in the south-east without determining at least one of the major factors governing prices in the other regions, and he would therefore be assuming an inappropriate degree of responsibility for determining the structure of regional prices throughout England and Wales.

"5. I wish to point out that the statement of these reasons is not intended to imply an assessment of the merits of your complaint considered as an issue of equity among regions."

The reasons disclosed are not, in my opinion, good reasons for refusing to refer the complaint, seeing that they leave out of account altogether the merits of the complaint itself. The complaint is, as LORD PARKER, C.J., pointed out, **A** made by persons affected by the scheme and is not one for the consumer committee as opposed to the committee of investigation, and it was eligible for reference to the latter. It has never been suggested that the complaint was not a genuine one. It is no objection, to the exercise of the discretion to refer, that wide issues will be raised and the interests of other regions and the regional price structure as a whole would be affected. It is likely that the removal of a **B** grievance will in any event have a wide effect and the Minister cannot lawfully say in advance that he will not refer the matter to the committee to ascertain the facts because, as he says in effect, although not in so many words, " I would not regard it as right to give effect to the report if it were favourable to the appellants." It has been suggested that the reasons given by the Minister need not and should not be examined closely, for he need give no reason at all in the **C** exercise of his discretion. True it is that the Minister is not bound to give his reasons for refusing to exercise his discretion in a particular manner, but when, as here, the circumstances indicate genuine complaint for which the appropriate remedy is provided, if the Minister in the case in question so directs, he would not escape from the possibility of control by mandamus through adopting a negative attitude without explanation. As the guardian of the public interest **D** he has a duty to protect the interests of those who claim to have been treated contrary to the public interest.

I would allow the appeal accordingly and remit the matter to the Queen's Bench Division so as to require the Minister to consider the complaint of the appellants according to law. I agree with the order for costs proposed by my noble and learned friend LORD REID.   **E**

LORD PEARCE: My Lords, prima facie the appellants have a complaint of substance. They are " persons affected by the scheme ". The " act or omission of the board " in not paying them a higher price differential is " contrary to their interests "; and apparently reasonable prima facie arguments have been advanced to show that this " is not in the public interest ". The **F** appellants' complaint is therefore prima facie suitable to be considered by the committee of investigation. The outline of their complaint is simple. They farm in the more populous south east region. In a more populous region milk is more valuable. The consumer is near at hand. The cost of transport is less; and milk which is drunk fetches higher prices than that which is used for manufacture. As against this the overheads of production are, generally speaking, somewhat **G** higher than in some more rural regions. For instance, the land in the more populous region is almost inevitably more expensive. It seems to follow that if the producer of milk in a populous region is paid precisely the same price as the producer in a sparsely populated rural region, the former is not being fairly treated. Some acknowledgment of this fact is made in a differential of 1·19 pence per gallon which was, we are told, fixed by the Minister during the war. Of this **H** figure ·71 of a penny related to the cost of transport. With rising prices the present differential cost in respect of transport has risen to over 3d. No acknowledgment of this increase in cost has ever been made in the price paid to the farmers in the south east region. Yet, unless the figure fixed by the Minister in the war was too large, which has not been suggested, it would seem that in view of increased costs it must now be too small. Prima facie this would seem unfair.   **I** Two committees, one in 1956 and one in 1963 have, on investigation, lent weight to the appellants' contention; but the gain of the south east would mean some loss in some regions elsewhere. The south east region is in a minority on the board. They have been unable, in spite of fifteen attempts, to persuade the majority to do anything about it. The appellants contend not only that the present situation is unfair to them but also that it is not in the public interest. They argue, for instance, that the present situation discourages the production of milk in the region where it is most valuable. Against, this may be set the

A benefit of encouraging milk production in more sparsely populated regions. Any final conclusion on this matter obviously needs close consideration of all the relevant details. One may sum it up superficially by saying that there is prima facie a complaint of some substance, that it has had support from two committees, and that there seems little likelihood of the majority of the board doing anything to remedy it.

B   This is not a criticism of the majority. Most of them are elected to represent their own regions. One can hardly expect them to vote in favour of something that will injure their own regions. Nor would it be very conducive to the success of the scheme if a region felt that its representative was pursuing altruistic policies in favour of other regions at the expense of those whom he is elected to represent. If justice to a minority is to be imposed at the expense of a majority, **C** it is probably more convenient that it should be imposed aliunde.

This fact was in my opinion recognised by Parliament. It was obvious that the scheme and the Agricultural Marketing Act, 1958, created a monopoly and imposed severe restrictions on individuals' liberty of action. With the aim of general betterment Parliament was interfering with the individual farmer's method of earning a livelihood and subjecting him to the mercies of the majority **D** rule of the board; but (no doubt with these considerations in mind) Parliament deliberately imposed certain safeguards. Two independent committees must be appointed (s. 19). First, there is the " consumers' committee " to deal with consumers' complaints. The findings of this committee do not however produce any effective result, unless and until they have been considered by the more important committee of investigation. That committee is

E   " charged with the duty, if the Minister in any case so directs, of considering and reporting to the Minister on, any report made by a consumers' committee and any complaint made to the Minister as to the operation of any scheme which, in the opinion of the Minister, could not be considered by a consumers' committee " (see s. 19 (3) (*b*)).

F The Minister is bound to publish that report.

" If a committee of investigation report to the Minister that any provision of a scheme or any act or omission of a board . . . is contrary to the interests of consumers of the regulated product, or is contrary to the interests of any persons affected by the scheme and is not in the public interest, the Minister, if he thinks fit so to do after considering the report may "

G amend the scheme so as to rectify the matter, or revoke the whole scheme, or direct the board to take steps to rectify the matter, after hearing any representations from the board (see s. 19 (6)). By s. 20 the Minister has a right of his own motion, independently of the investigation committee, to impose his will on the board; but in that case the board can ask to have the matter heard by the committee of investigation, and, if the committee's report is in the board's **H** favour, the Minister cannot impose his will on the board.

Thus the independent committee of investigation was a corner stone in the structure of the Act of 1958. It was a deliberate safeguard against injustices that might arise from the operation of the scheme. There is provision for arbitration between individual producers and the board; but this is clearly not intended to deal with a case such as the present, and the board has rightly refused **I** arbitration on this matter.

The appellants have therefore no avenue for their complaint except through s. 19, and that section makes access to the committee of investigation dependent on a direction of the Minister to the committee of investigation. There is no provision as to what are the duties of a Minister in this respect. Has he a duty to further complaints of substance which have no other outlet? Or can he refuse them any outlet at all if he so chooses? Need he have any valid reason for doing so? Or if he refuses without any apparent justification, is he exempt from any interference by the courts provided that he either gives no reasons which are demonstrably bad or gives no reasons at all? No express answer to these questions **A** is given in the Act of 1958. The intention of Parliament, therefore, must be implied from its provisions and its structure. Both sides placed some reliance on the case of *Julius* v. *Lord Bishop of Oxford* (16). This dealt with a somewhat analogous problem under an Act (17) which said "it shall be lawful" for the bishop to issue a commission. It was held that the words gave the bishop a complete discretion to issue or decline to issue a commission. That decision rested on the **B** construction of the particular Act, and it made clear that in the context of an Act is to be found the answer to the question how a power given by it is to be exercised. EARL CAIRNS, L.C., said (18):

"The cases to which I have referred appear to decide nothing more than that where a power is deposited with a public officer for the purpose of being used for the benefit of persons who are specifically pointed out, and with **C** regard to whom a definition is supplied by the legislature of the conditions upon which they are entitled to call for its exercise, that power ought to be exercised, and the court will require it to be exercised."

LORD PENZANCE said (19):

"The words ' it shall be lawful ' are distinctly words of permission only **D** —they are enabling and empowering words. They confer a legislative right and power on the individual named to do a particular thing; and the true question is, not whether they mean something different, but whether, regard being had to the person so enabled, to the subject-matter, to the general objects of the statute, and to the person, or class of persons, for whose benefit the power may be intended to have been conferred, they do **E** or do not create a duty in the person on whom it is conferred, to exercise it."

LORD SELBORNE said (20):

"The question whether a judge or a public officer to whom power is given by such words is bound to use it upon any particular occasion, or in any particular manner, must be solved aliunde, and in general it is to be solved from the context, from the particular provisions, or from the general **F** scope and objects of the enactment conferring the power."

It is quite clear from the Act of 1958 in question that the Minister is intended to have *some* duty in the matter. It is conceded that he must properly consider the complaint. He cannot throw it unread into the waste paper basket. He cannot simply say (albeit honestly) " I think that in general the investigation of complaints has a disruptive effect on the scheme and leads to more trouble than **G** (on balance) it is worth; I shall therefore never refer anything to the committee of investigation ". To allow him to do so would be to give him power to set aside for his period as Minister the obvious intention of Parliament, namely that an independent committee set up for the purpose should investigate grievances and that their report should be available to Parliament. This was clearly never intended by the Act of 1958. Nor was it intended that he could silently thwart **H** its intention by failing to carry out its purposes. I do not regard a Minister's failure or refusal to give any reasons as a sufficient exclusion of the court's surveillance. If all the prima facie reasons seem to point in favour of his taking a certain course to carry out the intentions of Parliament in respect of a power which it has given him in that regard, and he gives no reason whatever for taking a contrary course, the court may infer that he has no good reason and that he **I** is not using the power given by Parliament to carry out its intentions. In the present case however the Minister has given reasons which show that he was not exercising his discretion in accordance with the intentions of the Act of 1958.

(16) [1874-80] All E.R. Rep. 43; (1880), 5 App. Cas. 214.
(17) The Church Discipline Act, 1840.
(18) [1874-80] All E.R. Rep. at p. 49; (1880), 5 App. Cas. at p. 225.
(19) [1874-80] All E.R. Rep. at p. 51; (1880), 5 App. Cas. at p. 229.
(20) [1874-80] All E.R. Rep. at p. 54; (1880), 5 App. Cas. at p. 235.

A   In the present case it is clear that Parliament attached considerable importance to the independent committee of investigation as a means to ensure that injustices were not caused by the operation of a compulsory scheme. It provided no other means by which an injustice could be ventilated. It was not content to leave the matter wholly in the power of a majority of the board. Nor was it content that the removal of injustice should be left to the power of the Minister. It wished

B to have the published views of an independent committee of investigation (with wide power to explore the matter fully). It also wished that committee to consider and weigh the public interest—a fact that makes it clear that the question of public interest was not at that stage being left to the Minister. When the report is published then the Minister may and must make up his own mind on the subject. He has power to do what he thinks best and decide whether

C or not to implement the report. He is then answerable only to Parliament, which will have the advantage of being able to understand the pros and cons of the matter from the published report of an independent committee. Until that is published nobody can effectively criticise his action, since nobody will have a balanced view of the strength of the grievance and its impact on the public interest.

D   It is clear, however, as a matter of common sense, that Parliament did not intend that frivolous or repetitive or insubstantial complaints or those which were more apt for arbitration should be examined by the committee of investigation, and no doubt the Minister was intended to use his discretion not to direct the committee to investigate those. It is argued that if he has a discretion to *that* extent, he must also have an unfettered discretion to suppress a complaint

E of substance involving the public interest which has no other outlet. I cannot see why this should be so. Parliament intended that certain substantial complaints (involving the public interest) under the compulsory scheme should be considered by the investigation committee. It was for the Minister to use his discretion to promote Parliament's intention. If the court had doubt as to whether the appellants' complaint was frivolous or repetitive, or not genuine,

F or not substantial, or unsuitable for investigation or more apt for arbitration, it would not interfere. Nothing which has been said in this case, however, leads one to doubt that it is a complaint of some substance which should properly be investigated by the independent committee with a view to pronouncing on the weight of the complaint and the public interest involved.

     The fact that the complaint raises wide issues and affects other regions was

G not a good ground for denying it an investigation by the committee. It is a matter which makes it very suitable for the committee of investigation, with its duty to report on the public interest, and its capacity to hear representatives of all the regions. Moreover the Minister was mistaken in thinking that " normal democratic machinery of the milk marketing scheme " was a ground for refusal to have the complaint investigated. It is alleged that the normal democratic

H machinery of the board is acting contrary to the public interest. The investigation under s. 19 and the Minister's powers under s. 20 were intended to correct, where necessary, the normal democratic machinery of the scheme. Parliament has put into the hands of the Minister and those of the committee of investigation the power and duty where necessary to intervene. A general abdication of that power and duty would not be in accord with Parliament's intentions.

I   I would allow the appeal.

     LORD UPJOHN: My Lords, this appeal is of great importance to the milk producing industry and therefore to the country in general, for it is concerned with the refusal of the respondent Minister to order an inquiry into the complaint of the appellants representing the milk producing farmers of the south east region. In 1931 Parliament, in order to produce better conditions within the agricultural industry and more efficient and economical methods of production and distribution, enacted the Agricultural Marketing Act, 1931,

which provided for schemes to be prepared for the control of various sections of A
the industry. In 1933 pursuant to the provisions of the Act the Milk Marketing
Scheme 1933 for England and Wales was prepared and approved by Parliament
and is, subject to many subsequent amendments, still in force; I shall refer to it
as " the scheme ". Many other schemes relating to the control of other sections
of the industry have been prepared and approved, and the Act now controlling
these schemes is the Agricultural Marketing Act, 1958, an Act consolidating the B
Act of 1931 and later amending Acts. For all relevant purposes schemes have
statutory force.

As was intended by Parliament the scheme was prepared by the industry
itself, a circumstance much relied on in argument on behalf of the Minister;
but that does not mean that it received the unanimous approval of all milk
producers; that would be impossible to expect of any scheme. The scheme pro- C
vided for a board to administer it consisting of members elected by the eleven
regions into which the country was for the purposes of the scheme divided, one
of them being the south east region. It provided for the registration of producers of milk and in those days when compulsory powers were less familiar
than today, went so far as to provide that no unregistered producer should sell
any milk. Furthermore, the scheme empowered the board (a power quickly D
exercised and still in force) to resolve that registered producers should sell only
to the board and then only at the price and on the terms prescribed by the board.
No one doubts that these provisions were greatly to the advantage of the industry as a whole but a scheme which put the milk industry into such a straight
jacket may produce anomalies and individual discontent. In my opinion it was
with this (inter alia) in view and in the realisation that such matters should receive E
review at ministerial level that Parliament enacted the provision now to be found
in s. 19 of the Act of 1958. That section provided that the Minister should
appoint two committees, a consumers' committee and a committee of investigation. The former committee is bound to consider and report to the Minister
upon any approved scheme and any complaints made to them as to the effect
of the scheme on consumers, a matter with which this appeal is not concerned. F
The committee of investigation is by s. 19 (3) (b):

" . . . charged with the duty, if the Minister in any case so directs, of
considering, and reporting to the Minister on . . . any complaint made to
the Minister as to the operation of any scheme which . . . could not be
considered by a consumers' committee . . ."
G
These committees are by the Act of 1958 permanent committees and have been
set up by the Minister to receive and deal with, from time to time, matters
referred to them; another indication that Parliament realised that schemes
might require inquiry and review in operation as time went on and circumstances changed.

The south east region contend that for many years they have received too H
low a price for their products for reasons which I shall not discuss, for they
are set out fully in the speech of my noble and learned friend LORD REID.
Further, it is perfectly clear on the facts that this question, having been considered by two independent committees (with results on the whole favourable
to the south east region) and having been raised on no less than fifteen occasions
at board meetings by the south east regional representative since 1958, cannot I
be dismissed as frivolous, vexatious or trivial. In fairness to the Minister and
his advisers let it be said that this has never been suggested. At first sight,
therefore, I should suppose that this was precisely the type of matter which
Parliament had envisaged would be fit for investigation by the committee of
investigation and report to the Minister, but the Minister has declined either to
investigate the complaint himself, as of course he was perfectly entitled to do,
or to refer it to the committee of investigation.

Section 19 (3) as a matter of language confers a discretion on the Minister

A whether any complaint made to him should be referred to the committee of investigation, the relevant words being " if the Minister in any case so directs " plainly words of discretion and not of duty. It was argued, however, before your lordships, perhaps more strenuously at the first hearing than at the second after supplemental cases had been delivered, that the case was governed by the principle established by the well known case of *Julius* v. *Bishop of Oxford* (21)

B where it was held that words of permission such as " it shall be lawful " might in some cases in fact call for its exercise and create a duty on the donee of the power or permission to exercise it. It was held not to do so in that case where Parliament had conferred on the bishop a power to issue a commission, but like so many cases in our law where it was held that the principle did not apply it is the leading authority for the proposition that there may be, as it is so often said,

C " a power coupled with a duty ". In other words, as was so succinctly stated by the court in *R.* v. *Steward of Havering Atte Bower* (22) " The words of permission . . . are obligatory "; briefly they create a duty not a power. In my opinion, however, that principle can have no application to the present where it is clear that Parliament would have used different words if it had intended that the Minister was under a duty to refer every complaint to the committee

D of investigation; in fact Parliament would have adopted precisely the same language as in s. 19 (2) where consumers are empowered to make their complaints direct to the consumers' committee without any intermediate reference to the Minister. So it is clear that the Minister has a discretion and the real question for this House to consider is how far that discretion is subject to judicial control.

My lords, on the basic principles of law to be applied there was no real difference

E of opinion, the great question being how they should be applied to this case. The Minister in exercising his powers and duties conferred on him by statute can only be controlled by a prerogative order which will only issue if he acts unlawfully. Unlawful behaviour by the Minister may be stated with sufficient accuracy for the purposes of the present appeal (and here I adopt the classification of LORD PARKER, C.J., in the divisional court): (a) by an outright refusal to con-

F sider the relevant matter, or (b) by misdirecting himself in point of law, or (c) by taking into account some wholly irrelevant or extraneous consideration, or (d) by wholly omitting to take into account a relevant consideration. There is ample authority for these propositions which were not challenged in argument. In practice they merge into one another and ultimately it becomes a question whether for one reason or another the Minister has acted unlawfully in the sense

G of misdirecting himself in law, that is, not merely in respect of some point of law but by failing to observe the other headings which I have mentioned.

In the circumstances of this case which I have sufficiently detailed for this purpose it seems to me quite clear that prima facie there seems a case for investigation by the committee of investigation. As I have said already it seems just the type of situation for which the machinery of s. 19 was set up,

H but that is a matter for the Minister. He may have good reasons for refusing an investigation, he may have indeed good policy reasons for refusing it though that policy must not be based on political considerations which as FARWELL, L.J. said in *R.* v. *Board of Education* (23) are pre-eminently extraneous. So I must examine the reasons given by the Minister, including any policy on which they may be based, to see whether he has acted unlawfully and thereby overstepped the true limits of his discretion, or as it has been frequently said in the prerogative writ cases, exceeded his jurisdiction. Unless he has done so the court has no jurisdiction to interfere. It is not a court of appeal and has no jurisdiction to correct the decision of the Minister acting lawfully within his discretion, however much the court may disagree with its exercise.

In his affidavit filed in opposition to the appellants' application for the order

---

(21) [1874-80] All E.R. Rep. 43; (1880), 5 App. Cas. 214.
(22) (1822), 5 B. & Ald. 691 at p. 692.
(23) [1910] 2 K.B. 165 at p. 181.

of mandamus the Minister, after referring to the fact that he had read the letter
dated May 1, 1964, of Mr. Kirk, an under secretary of the ministry, stated that
he reached his decision for refusing a reference to the investigating committee
for the reasons given in his private secretary's letters of Mar. 23 and May 3, 1965,
all addressed to the appellants or their solicitors. So to these letters I must
turn to see whether his reasons are open to challenge on the ground of being
unlawful. The first letter, that of Mar. 23, 1965, in which the Minister gave
his reasons was, so far as relevant, in these terms:

> " The Minister's main duty in considering this complaint has been to
> decide its suitability for investigation by means of a particular procedure.
> He has come to the conclusion that it would not be suitable. The complaint
> is of course one that raises wide issues going beyond the immediate concern
> of your clients, which is presumably the prices they themselves receive.
> It would also affect the interests of other regions and involve the regional
> price structure as a whole.
>
> " In any event the Minister considers that the issue is of a kind which
> properly falls to be resolved through the arrangements available to producers
> and the board within the framework of the scheme itself. Accordingly he
> has instructed me to inform you that he is unable to accede to your clients'
> request that his complaint be referred to the committee of investigation
> under s. 19 of the Act."

This letter seems to me to show an entirely wrong approach to the complaint.
The Minister's main duty is not to consider its suitability for investigation;
he is putting the cart before the horse. He might reach that conclusion after
weighing all the facts, but not until he has done so; but perhaps this is the least
of the criticisms (arising out of his letter) to be directed at the Minister. I have
dealt with it, however, as in argument it was seriously pressed on your lordships
as a conclusive consideration in answer to any challenge to his powers.

His next statement—that it raises wide issues etc.—shows a complete misapprehension of his duties, for it indicates quite clearly that he has completely
misunderstood the scope and object of s. 19. It is when wide issues are raised
and when the complaint of one region raises the matters which may affect other
regions and the regional price structure as a whole, that the Minister should
consider it as a most powerful (though not conclusive) element in favour of
referring the complaint instead of the reverse. Then, again, in his final paragraph
of this letter the Minister reveals the same misconception. It was just because
it was realised that the board structure might produce within its framework
matters for complaint by those vitally affected that the machinery of s. 19 was
set up. This letter shows that the Minister was entirely misdirecting himself
in law based on a misunderstanding of the basic reasons for the conferment on
him of the powers of s. 19. I turn to his second letter, that of May 3, 1965,
which so far as relevant was in these terms:

> " You will appreciate that under the Agricultural Marketing Act, 1958
> the Minister has unfettered discretion to decide whether or not to refer a
> particular complaint to the committee of investigation. In reaching his
> decision he has had in mind the normal democratic machinery of the milk
> marketing scheme, in which all registered producers participate and which
> governs the operations of the board."

This introduces the idea, much pressed on your lordships in argument, that he
had an " unfettered " discretion in this matter; this, it was argued, means that
provided the Minister considered the complaint bona fide that was an end to
the matter. Here let it be said at once, he and his advisers have obviously given
a bona fide and painstaking consideration to the complaints addressed to him;
the question is whether the consideration given was sufficient in law.

My lords, I believe that the introduction of the adjective " unfettered " and
its reliance thereon as an answer to the appellants' claim is one of the fundamental

A matters confounding the Minister's attitude, bona fide though it be. First, the adjective nowhere appears in s. 19, it is an unauthorised gloss by the Minister. Secondly, even if the section did contain that adjective, I doubt if it would make any difference in law to his powers, save to emphasise what he has already, namely that acting lawfully he has a power of decision which cannot be controlled by the courts; it is unfettered. But the use of that adjective, even in an Act

B of Parliament, can do nothing to unfetter the control which the judiciary have over the executive, namely that in exercising their powers the latter must act lawfully, and that is a matter to be determined by looking at the Act and its scope and object in conferring a discretion on the Minister rather than by the use of adjectives.

The second sentence of this letter again only shows what I have earlier pointed

C out, that the Minister has failed to understand that it may be his duty to intervene where there is a serious complaint that the " democratic machinery " of the board is producing unfairness among its members.

Those are the reasons relied on by the Minister for refusing a reference. Summing up the matter shortly, in my opinion every reason given shows that the Minister has failed to understand the object and scope of s. 19 and of his functions

D and duties thereunder, which he has misinterpreted and so misdirected himself in law.

The matter, however, does not end there for in his affidavit the Minister referred, as I have already mentioned, to Mr. Kirk's letter of May 1, 1964, without disapproval. That letter contained this paragraph:

E " 3. In considering how to exercise his discretion, the Minister would, amongst other things, address his mind to the possibility that if a complaint were so referred and the committee were to uphold it, he in turn would be expected to make a statutory order to give effect to the committee's recommendations. It is this consideration, rather than the formal eligibility of the complaint as a subject for investigation, that the Minister would have in mind in determining whether your particular complaint is a suitable one for reference to the committee. We were unable to hold out any prospect that the Minister would be prepared to regard it as suitable."

F This fear of parliamentary trouble (for in my opinion this must be the scarcely veiled meaning of this letter) if an inquiry were ordered and its possible results is alone sufficient to vitiate the Minister's decision which, as I have stated earlier, can never validly turn on purely political considerations; he must be prepared to face the music in Parliament if statute has cast on him an obligation in the proper exercise of a discretion conferred on him to order a reference to the committee of investigation.

G My Lords, I would add only this: that without throwing any doubt on what are well known as the club expulsion cases, where the absence of reasons has not proved fatal to the decision of expulsion by a club committee, a decision of the Minister stands on quite a different basis; he is a public officer charged by Parliament with the discharge of a public discretion affecting Her Majesty's subjects; if he does not give any reason for his decision it may be, if circumstances warrant it, that a court may be at liberty to come to the conclusion that he had no good reason for reaching that conclusion and directing a prerogative order to issue accordingly. The Minister in my opinion has not given a single valid reason for refusing to order an inquiry into the legitimate complaint (be it well founded or not) of the south east region; all his disclosed reasons for refusing to do so are bad in law. I would allow this appeal in the terms proposed by my noble and learned friend LORD REID.

Appeal allowed.   Case remitted.

Solicitors: *Biddle & Co.* (for the appellants); *Solicitor, Ministry of Agriculture, Fisheries and Food.*

[*Reported by* S. A. HATTEEA, ESQ., *Barrister-at-Law.*]

Re WESTON'S SETTLEMENTS.

[CHANCERY DIVISION (Stamp, J.), January 29, 30, 1968.]

Trust and Trustee—Variation of trusts by the court—Jurisdiction—Discretion
—English settlements to be so varied that they could be superseded ultimately
by trusts established in Jersey—Fiscal advantages only—Beneficial trusts
not substantially to be varied—New trustees of English settlements to be
appointed resident in Jersey and out of the jurisdiction—Settlor and family
having moved to Jersey only recently—Whether court should approve variation
and should appoint new trustees resident in Jersey—Trustee Act, 1925
(15 & 16 Geo. 5 c. 19), s. 41—Variation of Trusts Act, 1958 (6 & 7 Eliz. 2
c. 53), s. 1.

In 1964 the plaintiff made two settlements, a voluntary settlement in
favour of his younger son Alan, born in January, 1949, and a marriage
settlement on the marriage of his elder son, Robert, who, at the time of
the hearing, was twenty-five and had an infant son. There were three
trustees of each settlement, two of whom were individuals resident in England
and the third was the plaintiff's wife. Under each settlement the principal
beneficiary had a life interest, a general power of appointment over a quarter
of the trust fund at age thirty, and a similar power over a further quarter
at age forty-five, subject to which and other provisions the trust fund was
to be held on trust for the issue of the principal beneficiary as he should
appoint and subject thereto for his children in equal shares. The plaintiff,
the settlor, was the son of a Russian who came to England in 1894. The
plaintiff was born in 1916 at Sheffield, and changed his name to Weston in
1942. He was the retired chairman of the Stanley Weston Group, Ltd.
Each settlement comprised shares in that company, which were of great
value. The plaintiff lived in England until 1967. Towards the end of
1966 he bought a house in Jersey. He spent four days in Jersey in January,
1967, four days in February, five days at Easter and six days in May. Since
August, 1967, he, his wife and Alan had lived in Jersey. He claimed to be
domiciled and permanently resident in Jersey. The plaintiff was not
wholly retiring from business and considered engaging in business activities
in Europe based on Jersey. In May, 1967, the elder son, Robert, acquired
the lease of a flat in Jersey, the term being due to expire in September, 1969;
but the lease contained an option to renew for three years. He deposed
that in August, 1967, he left the United Kingdom for good, having sold his
house in Sheffield, and went with his family to live in Jersey, where he
intended to make his permanent home. The plaintiff sought (a) an order
under s. 41 of the Trustee Act, 1925, appointing two trustees, resident
in Jersey, of the settlements in place of the present trustees, and (b) approval,
on behalf of Alan and Robert's infant son and persons unborn who might
become interested under the settlements, in respect of a proposed variation
by inserting a power in each settlement for the new trustees after three months
to discharge the trust property from the trusts of the English settlement,
and to subject it to the trusts of a new Jersey settlement containing substantially the same beneficial trusts as the English settlement. The settled
funds would thus be freed of potential liability to capital gains tax (in the
region of £163,000) and to estate duty on the death of Alan or Robert.

Held: in all the circumstances it was not established to the satisfaction of
the court that the living beneficiaries intended to continue to live in Jersey,
with which they had no ties, and, the advantages to be gained from the
orders sought being fiscal advantages only, the court should decline, in the
exercise of its discretion, to make orders which would allow the trust funds
to be removed from the jurisdiction of the court and to be vested in trustees
outside the jurisdiction and subjected to new settlements over which the

A   court would have no control; nor should the court countenance a tax
avoidance of the character proposed (see p. 725, letters B, F and H, post).
Re Seale's Marriage Settlement ([1961] 3 All E.R. 136) distinguished.

[As to the appointment of a person resident outside the jurisdiction as
trustee, see 38 Halsbury's Laws (3rd Edn.) 930, para. 1596; and for cases on
the subject, see 47 Digest (Repl.) 161, *1229-1235.*

B   As to the variation of trusts by the court, see 38 Halsbury's Laws (3rd Edn.)
1029, 1030, para. 1772; and for cases on the subject, see 47 Digest (Repl.)
332-338, *2993-3018.*

For the Trustee Act, 1925, s. 41, see 26 Halsbury's Statutes (2nd Edn.)
118; and for the Variation of Trusts Act, 1958, s. 1, see 38 ibid., 1130.]

C   Case referred to:

Seale's Marriage Settlement, Re, [1961] 3 All E.R. 136; [1961] Ch. 574;
[1961] 3 W.L.R. 262; 47 Digest (Repl.) 333, *2995.*

Adjourned Summons.

This was an application by the plaintiff, Stanley Weston under s. 41 of the
Trustee Act, 1925 and s. 1 of the Variation of Trusts Act, 1958, by originating
D   summons dated Nov. 7, 1967.   He, as settlor, was party to two settlements
dated June 18, 1964, and July 2, 1964.   He sought the following relief (i) that
Terence Cubitt Sowden and Peter Gilroy Blampied, both of Jersey, or some
other fit and proper persons might be appointed trustees of the trusts of the two
settlements in the place of the fourth, fifth and sixth defendants, Ena Weston,
Raphael Howard Boyers and Peter Anthony Smith, who were the then trustees
E   of the two settlements; (ii) that those three defendants might execute such
deed or deeds and further documents or document and take such other steps as
might be necessary according to the law of Jersey to effectuate the appointment
of Mr. Sowden and Mr. Blampied as trustees of the settlements and to transfer
the trust property to or otherwise vest it in Mr. Sowden and Mr. Blampied;
(iii) that the court might approve on behalf of (a) the infant defendants and
F   (b) all persons unborn or unascertained who might thereafter become entitled
to a beneficial interest in the trust funds comprised in the settlements, an arrangement proposed by the plaintiff varying the trusts of the settlements.   The first
defendant was Robert Lawrence Weston, who was a son of the settlor and
claimed to be interested as tenant for life of the settlement dated July 2, 1964,
and in the capital of the settlement of June 18, 1964.   The second defendant
was Nigel James Weston who was the son of Robert Lawrence Weston and
claimed to be interested in the capital of the settlement of June 18, 1964, and
the third defendant was Alan Clive Weston, who was a son of the settlor and
claimed to be interested in the capital of both settlements; both the second and
third defendants were infants.   The facts are set out in the judgment.

I   *J. B. Morcom* for the plaintiff.
M. G. Johnston for the first defendant.
C. I. Howells for the infant second and third defendants.
D. J. M. Campion for the trustees of the settlements.

STAMP, J.: This is an application made by Mr. Stanley Weston who
describes himself as of " Chantal ", 22, Magnolia Gardens, Bel Royal, St. Lawrence, Jersey, retired chairman of the Stanley Weston Group, Limited. He is
the son of one Abrum Wosskow, a Russian, who came to England in 1894,
where he remained till his death on Aug. 5, 1946. Mr. Stanley Weston was
born in England at Sheffield in 1916. He changed his name to Weston in May,
1942. He now has a very considerable fortune. He has two sons, Robert
Lawrence Weston who was born on Nov. 12, 1942, and was married in 1964
and now has one child born in 1966, and Alan Clive Weston who was born on
Jan. 22, 1949, so that he is now nineteen years of age.

In 1964 Mr. Stanley Weston made two settlements. He made a voluntary **A**
settlement under which Alan Clive Weston is the principal beneficiary, and
another settlement on the marriage of Robert Lawrence Weston under which
the latter is the principal beneficiary. It is, I think, sufficient for present purposes to say that under these settlements the principal beneficiary takes a life
interest, has a general power of appointment over a quarter of the trust fund
subject to his attaining the age of thirty, and a similar power over a further **B**
quarter if he attains the age of forty-five, and, subject to those and certain other
powers to which I need not refer, the trust fund is in substance to be held on trust
for the issue of the principal beneficiary as he shall appoint and subject to any such
appointment on trust for his children in equal shares. The assets of the voluntary settlement, consisting almost exclusively of shares in Stanley Weston
Group, Ltd., are of a present value of about £400,000 and I am told that the **C**
assets of the marriage settlement funds, consisting exclusively of such shares,
are of a value of some £320,000.

Mr. Stanley Weston, having lived in England with his family until 1967 and
having purchased the house " Chantal " shortly before the beginning of that
year, spent four days in Jersey in January, 1967, in a hotel; and four days in
February, five days at Easter and six days in May, 1967, at the house which he **D**
had purchased. Since August, 1967, he and his wife and younger son have, as
he says, " lived "—and I use his words—" permanently at that house ".

Mr. Stanley Weston claims to be domiciled and ordinarily resident in Jersey.
Conscious of the tax and duty advantages of so doing, he proposes to transfer
such of his assets as may be in this country to Jersey. He does not contemplate
retirement from business altogether and states that he is considering purchasing **E**
a hotel in Jersey and that his younger son will be employed in the venture. I
have no evidence of the wishes of Mr. Alan Clive Weston in the matter, or that
he is likely to remain domiciled, if such he already is, in Jersey when he is older.
Mr. Stanley Weston is also considering engaging himself in business activities
in Europe based on Jersey.

Mr. Robert Lawrence Weston, after living for a remarkably short time in **F**
that island, also claims to be, or is advised that he is probably, domiciled in
Jersey. I must read what he says in his affidavit which, it is to be remarked,
was sworn on Dec. 5, 1967, the originating summons in this matter having been
issued on Nov. 7, 1967. He says this:

" In May, 1967, I took an assignment of the lease of a flat in Jersey, namely
10, Bel Royal Court, St. Lawrence. This lease is due to expire on Sept. 29, **G**
1969, but it contains an option for the tenant to renew for a further three
years. On Aug. 29, 1967, I left the United Kingdom for good, having
previously sold my house in Sheffield with vacant possession, and went,
with my wife and son, to live in Jersey. We stayed at a hotel in St. Helier
until I got vacant possession of our new flat on Sept. 29, 1967. On that date **H**
we moved into the flat, where we have lived ever since."

" Ever since " was the period from Sept. 29, 1967, until Nov. 7, 1967.

" I leased a flat rather than purchased a house, because I understand
that there are difficulties about selling a house in Jersey within five years
of purchasing it, and I wanted to have time to look round before committing
myself to a house."

I pause there to observe that the deponent apparently did not want to look
round before committing himself to living in Jersey for the rest of his life.

" I have not returned to the United Kingdom since leaving it last August,
and I intend to make Jersey my permanent and only home. I own certain
lands in Sheffield with my brother, but we are in course of selling it. When
it has been sold, I shall (subject to obtaining any necessary permission)
have my share of the proceeds remitted to Jersey. I shall then have no

A   property of any kind in the United Kingdom. My only income is from my marriage settlement, which is one of the subject matters of this application, and the income arising on my holdings . . .",

and the deponent then mentions two holdings of ordinary shares in two other companies.

B   The immediate purpose of this application is to produce a result under which the whole of the assets of the two English settlements will be removed from the jurisdiction of this court and from the clutches of the Commissioners of Inland Revenue and made subject to a Jersey settlement or settlements, such settlements being framed to produce or to reproduce the trusts of the two English settlements which they will respectively replace. As a result of the transaction, the English settlements will no longer comprise any property at all, and this

C   result is to be achieved by a somewhat delicate operation, the immediate result of which, it is said, will avoid a liability or potential liability for a very large sum of capital gains tax. First, this court is asked, in exercise of its jurisdiction under s. 41 of the Trustee Act, 1925, to appoint two professional gentlemen of the highest reputation resident in Jersey to be trustees of the English settlements in place of the three existing individual trustees, two of whom are resident in

D   England, and the third of whom is the wife of Mr. Stanley Weston. The court is then asked to exercise its jurisdiction under the Variation of Trusts Act, 1958, by approving, on behalf of Mr. Alan Clive Weston and the infant son of Mr. Robert Lawrence Weston, and all persons unborn or unascertained who may hereafter become beneficially interested under the settlements, a variation of both settlements by inserting in each of them a power for the two new Jersey

E   trustees, after the expiration of three months, to discharge the trust property from the trusts of that English settlement and to subject it to the trusts of a new Jersey settlement containing, as I have indicated, almost precisely the same or precisely the same beneficial trusts as are at present contained in the two English settlements.

F   It is submitted, on the authority of *Re Seale's Marriage Settlement* (1), a decision of Buckley, J., that I have jurisdiction to do what I am asked to do in this case, and I am told that in another case another judge adopted a similar course. I have no particulars of the facts of that other case. The effect of the order or orders which I am asked to make would be that if the Jersey trustees, having been duly appointed trustees of the English settlements, do in fact exercise the power, as no doubt they will, which I am asked to insert in the English settle-

G   ments, the beneficiaries will in future have to enforce their rights not under the law of England against English trustees before this court, but under the law of Jersey against gentlemen resident in Jersey and before the court in Jersey. I will assume, following the decisions to which I have referred, that I have the necessary jurisdiction to take this course.

H   This, however, leaves open the serious question whether, on the facts of this case, the court ought, in the exercise of its jurisdiction, to countenance the proposals which are put before it. The benefits sought to be achieved by the orders I am invited to make are, to all intents and purposes, entirely of a fiscal character. The fiscal advantages which are envisaged are, as I understand them, these. First of all, as to capital gains tax, s. 25 (1) of the Finance Act

I   1965 provides as follows:

> " In relation to settled property, the trustees of the settlement shall for the purposes of this Part of this Act be treated as being a single and continuing body of persons (distinct from the persons who may from time to time be the trustees), and that body shall be treated as being resident and ordinarily resident in the United Kingdom unless the general administration of the trusts is ordinarily carried on outside the United Kingdom and the

---

(1) [1961] 3 All E.R. 136; [1961] Ch. 574.

trustees or a majority of them for the time being are not resident or not ordinarily resident in the United Kingdom.''

What is anticipated is that after an appropriate period which, as I have already mentioned, is three months, the trustees will be able to claim that within the meaning of the subsection which I have just read the general administration of the trusts is ordinarily carried on outside the United Kingdom, and unquestionably the trustees will then not be resident or ordinarily resident in the United Kingdom. If the shares in the company, Stanley Weston Group, Ltd. were sold today and in existing circumstances, a liability to capital gains tax amounting to no less than £163,000 would be attracted. If I approved the proposals which are put before me, the effect would be, so it is said, that if the shares were disposed of after the interval to which I have referred, the trustees will not be accountable for that sum. Furthermore, provided that the beneficiaries are, as I understand it, neither resident nor ordinarily resident in the United Kingdom during the year of assessment in which the shares are disposed of, none of them will be personally liable for capital gains tax.

Estate duty on the deaths of the two principal beneficiaries will also be avoided if the proposals are sanctioned, or so, at any rate, it is submitted. Under s. 28 of the Finance Act, 1949, exemption is conferred from estate duty in respect of property passing on death if the property is not situate in the United Kingdom and it is shown that the proper law regulating the devolution of property, or the disposition under or by reason of which it passes, is the law neither of England nor of Scotland, and one of the following conditions is satisfied. Among those conditions is the condition that the property passes under or by reason of a disposition made by a person who, at the date at which the disposition took effect, was domiciled elsewhere than in some part of Great Britain. What is said is that once these transactions have been carried out, the proper law regulating the devolution of the property will be that of Jersey and that, provided the property is not brought back to the United Kingdom—there is no difficulty there because a small company can be formed in Jersey for the purpose of holding the trusts' funds—the new settlements will have been made by a person who, at the date at which the disposition took effect, was domiciled elsewhere than in some part of Great Britain. What is said is that these new Jersey settlements will have been made by the existing tenants for life and the infant child of Robert Lawrence Weston all of whom, it is said, are now domiciled outside the United Kingdom, and by the persons unascertained and unborn who are, one would think, at least not domiciled in the United Kingdom.

It is to be noted, in connexion with the avoidance of estate duty, that by the effect of the contemplated transaction the large claims for duty which, it is thought, will ultimately be avoided on the respective deaths of the principal beneficiaries will be achieved in the case of Mr. Robert Lawrence Weston, now aged twenty-five, even if he at the end of a further twelve weeks in Jersey should come to the conclusion that that island is a less desirable place than the first two months led him to believe, and should change his declared intention of living out the rest of his life there and dying there, and should again return to the United Kingdom. Similarly, if Mr. Alan Clive Weston, when he is a little older were to find that life as an employee in one of his father's hotels in Jersey was less satisfactory than a life, however penurious, in this country, and determined to come and live in this country, he would have the happy advantage that when, in the course of nature, he died, the fund—subject to the trusts of the voluntary settlement—would pass to his children unravaged by claims for duty.

This court is not the watchdog of the Commissioners of Inland Revenue, and day after day variations of trusts are sanctioned which will on the one hand provide a tenant for life with capital instead of income, and, on the other, mitigate the burden of duty which would otherwise be payable on his death and would fall on his children. But there must, in my judgment, be some limit to the

A devices which this court ought to countenance in order to defeat the fiscal inten-
tions of the legislature. In my judgment, these proposals overstep that limit.
The facts of this case are: in my view, wholly different from the facts with which
BUCKLEY, J., had to deal in *Re Seale's Marriage Settlement* (2). There BUCKLEY,
J., said this (3): " The evidence establishes to my satisfaction that the husband
and wife intend to continue to live in Canada ..." As regards the present case

B I am by no means satisfied that any of the beneficiaries intend to continue to
live in the Channel Islands. He went on: " .... that their children who are
living in Canada and have been brought up as Canadians are likely to continue
to live in Canada ..." That, of course, does not apply in this case, but none
of the beneficiaries have any ties whatsoever with the island of Jersey. BUCKLEY,
J., goes on:

C
" ... and that it will be for the general advantage of all the beneficiaries
that the administrative difficulties and the difficulties of other kinds ...
which result from the fact that it is an English settlement and the beneficiaries all reside in Canada, should be brought to an end; ..."

I am not satisfied that any administrative difficulties or difficulties other than
D the fiscal difficulties with which all Her Majesty's subjects are confronted, exist
in this case. In the present case the family have only just moved to Jersey and
I draw the inference from the facts that the purpose of this family exodus, or
its principal purpose, is the avoidance of taxation. The family are perfectly
entitled to make their permanent home in Jersey for the purpose of avoiding
taxation, and if this family had settled there I might well think it right to accede

E to the application, though I would remark in passing that there are certain
difficulties in connexion with the law of Jersey in relation to trusts which leave
me in some doubt whether the courts of that island are so well adapted as the
courts in this country to administer such trusts as are found in English settlements. But the family has not been in Jersey for more than a few months and
I do not on the evidence accept that any member of it could possibly establish

F that he is now domiciled in Jersey.

To vest all the assets subject to a settlement in trustees outside the jurisdiction
is, I think, a strong thing to do. To allow those assets to be made subject to a
settlement over which the court has no control is a stronger thing. Where the
beneficiaries have only been in that other country a few short months and one
of the purposes of the transaction is to obtain an exemption from estate duty

G which the legislature has thought fit to grant in respect of foreign settlements, I
am not persuaded that I ought, in the exercise of the discretion of the court, to
countenance the proposals. The objection to so doing would be made apparent
if, in fact, Mr. Robert Lawrence Weston did, so soon as the capital gains tax
liability had been avoided by a disposal of the assets, in fact abandon his home
in Jersey and return to this country. I am not persuaded that this application

H represents more than a cheap exercise in tax avoidance which I ought not to
sanction, as distinct from a legitimate avoidance of liability to taxation.

I should like to add two things. I think that in relation to variation of settlements where enormous sums of money are involved, it is quite wrong that the
court and junior counsel should not have the assistance of leading counsel as
well for the plaintiff as for the trustees. This has been said more than once

I by judges dealing with these matters, and I would like again to repeat it. I
have had great assistance from counsel for the plaintiff, and it is no disrespect
to him to say that I think he has been, perhaps, unfairly treated. Those words
may not be the right ones, but the sense of my remarks is clear. I would also
like to express the hope that this case may be taken to the Court of Appeal
so that judges of this division may have the advantage of the views of that court

(2) [1961] 3 All E.R. 136; [1961] Ch. 574.
(3) [1961] 3 All E.R. at p. 139; [1961] Ch. at p. 579.

A

as to the duties of this court in the kind of circumstances which arise in this case. I can only dismiss the applications.

Applications dismissed.

Solicitors: *Paisner & Co.*, agents for *Boyers, Howson & Whitehead*, Sheffield (for all parties).

[*Reported by* JENIFER SANDELL, *Barrister-at-Law.*]

B

FLETCHER *v.* AUTOCAR & TRANSPORTERS, LTD.

[COURT OF APPEAL, CIVIL DIVISION (Lord Denning, M.R., Diplock and Salmon, L.JJ.), December 11, 12, 13, 1967, January 17, 1968.]

C

Damages—Personal injury—Assessment—General damages—Single compre-
hensive sum on basis of fair compensation—Elements of fair compensation
where injured person deprived of enjoyment for the rest of his life—Duplica-
tion of damages for loss of future earnings and loss of amenities to be avoided.

Damages—Measure of damages—Loss of future earnings—Assessment on
actuarial basis not conclusive.

D

The plaintiff was severely injured in a motor accident for which the defendants admitted liability. He was fifty-six years of age, was the senior partner in a firm of quantity surveyors, and was earning between £3,000 to £4,000 yearly net after tax. He was married and had an adult son who was not dependent on him. The plaintiff lived an active and a full life; he spent all that he earned and saved nothing. His expectation of life

E

was sixteen years and the prospect was that he would have continued working at any rate until sixty-nine years of age, when he would have become entitled under an insurance policy to a pension of £600* per annum. His wife was active in local affairs and was a justice of the peace. The plaintiff's brain was injured in the accident and, for the rest of his life, his mind was gone; he would be able to do nothing, could feel little, would forget every-

F

thing and would be completely dependent. His wife would be able to look after him for about three years, and then he would have to go into an infirmary. The fees payable to the infirmary would be about £1,419 per annum. The trial judge assessed damages, apart from special damages (£10,447 9s. 6d.), under three heads—(a) (the first head of damage) loss of future earnings (£32,000, which included £29,600 for loss of salary of £4,000

G

per annum for ten years actuarily computed, and a sum of £2,400, not actuarily computed, in respect of earnings after retirement); (b) (second head of damage) additional expenses of looking after the plaintiff, including fees to the infirmary (£14,000), and (c) (third head of damage), pain, suffering and loss of amenities (£10,000). Accordingly the trial judge awarded in the aggregate £66,447 9s. 6d. damages, being the sum of the amounts estimated

H

under the three heads of damage together with the special damages. In awarding the amount assessed under (b) for additional expenses, £300 per annum was deducted from the fees of the infirmary in respect of an estimated saving on food and laundry. On appeal as to damages the award of special damages and the amount under the third head of damages were not disputed.

Held (SALMON, L.J., dissenting): the amount of damages awarded should be reduced to £51,447 9s. 6d. for the following reasons—

(i) (a) the damages should be assessed so as to give the plaintiff an amount which was fair compensation in all the circumstances, but it was wrong to attempt to give perfect compensation, as there were personal injuries for which no amount of money would fully compensate (see p. 733, letters B and G, and p. 735, letter I, to p. 736, letters A and B, post).

---

* See p. 746, letter A, post; the contractual amount of the pension was £632, but apparently in all the circumstances the realised pension would be approximately £600.

A *Phillips* v. *London & South Western Ry. Co.* ((1879), 4 Q.B.D. 406) applied.

 (b) fair compensation would be such a sum as would provide for the plaintiff's maintenance in such circumstances as would best ameliorate the discomfort and deprivations that he was bound to suffer, as would provide for his wife so that she should be able to live for the rest of her life in the comfort that the plaintiff would have provided for her, and as would provide

B in addition (per LORD DENNING, M.R.) that any savings which the plaintiff would have made if uninjured would be available for his family, or (per DIPLOCK, L.J.) the proper conventional sum which the courts describe as compensation for loss of the amenities of life (see p. 733, letter H, and p. 743, letter G, post).

 (c) damages were an award of a single sum, and, though heads of com-

C pensation might be regarded separately as aids to reaching a just amount, yet merely to assess amounts under three heads and to award the aggregate of the items so assessed might, in such cases as the present, lead to error; and if deprivation of amenities was assessed under a separate head (as in the third head of damage in the present case) there must be deducted, before awarding the total, an amount in respect of the amount that the matters

D of which the plaintiff was deprived would have cost, for the amount of the cost would have been included in the assessment under the first head of damage in respect of loss of future earnings (see p. 733, letter I, to p. 734, letters A and D, and p. 737, letters B and H, post).

 Shearman v. *Folland* ([1950] 1 All E.R. 976) distinguished.

 (ii) in regard to the amounts estimated by the trial judge under the first

E and second heads of damage—

 (a) the actuarily computed £29,600 in respect of loss of earnings made no allowance for the chances and changes of life, but was based on assumed certainty of amount of the plaintiff's share of profits; in the circumstances an amount based on a median of an income of £3,500 per annum at five or six years' purchase would be appropriate, and the speculative item for earnings

F after retirement at sixty-nine would be reduced, making the estimate in respect of loss of earnings £22,000 instead of £32,000 (see p. 739, letter I, to p. 740, letter A, p. 741, letter H, and p. 735, letter B, post).

 (b) in assessing additional expenses all economies consequent on the action taken that involved the expenses claim should be brought into con-

G sideration; in the present case a smaller establishment would be needed if the plaintiff went into an infirmary, and the amount estimated under the second head of damage in respect of additional expenses should be reduced from £14,000 to £9,000 (see p. 742, letters E and G, and p. 735, letter B, post).

 Appeal allowed.

I [As to the measure of general damages for personal injury, see 11 HALSBURY'S LAWS (3rd Edn.) 255, para. 427; and for cases on the subject, see 17 DIGEST (Repl.) 101, 102, *155-173.*]

Cases referred to:

 British-Transport Commission v. *Gourley,* [1955] 3 All E.R. 796; [1956] A.C. 185; [1956] 2 W.L.R. 41; Digest (Cont. Vol. A) 462, *28a.*

I *Davies* v. *Powell Duffryn Associated Collieries, Ltd. (No. 2),* [1942] 1 All E.R. 657; [1942] A.C. 601; 111 L.J.K.B. 418; 167 L.T. 74; 36 Digest (Repl.) 231, *1229.*

 Phillips v. *London & South Western Ry. Co.,* (1879), 4 Q.B.D. 406; 40 L.T. 813; *on appeal,* 5 Q.B.D. 78; 41 L.T. 121; 43 J.P. 749; *subsequent proceedings,* [1874-80] All E.R. Rep. 1176; 5 C.P.D. 280; 49 L.J.Q.B. 223; 42 L.T. 6; 44 J.P. 217; 17 Digest (Repl.) 190, *860.*

 Rookes v. *Barnard,* [1964] 1 All E.R. 367; [1964] A.C. 1129; [1964] 2 W.L.R. 269; Digest (Cont. Vol. B) 217, *13a.*

Rowley v. *London & North Western Ry. Co.*, [1861-73] All E.R. Rep. 823; A
    (1873), L.R. 8 Exch. 221; 42 L.J.Ex. 153; 29 L.T. 180; 36 Digest
    (Repl.) 223, *1189.*

Shearman v. *Folland*, [1950] 1 All E.R. 976; [1950] 2 K.B. 43; 36 Digest
    (Repl.) 205, *1072.*

Ward v. *James*, [1965] 1 All E.R. 563; [1966] 1 Q.B. 273; [1965] 2 W.L.R.
    455; Digest (Cont. Vol. B) 219, *783a.*   B

Watson v. *Powles*, [1967] 3 All E.R. 721; [1967] 3 W.L.R. 1364.

West (H.) & Son, Ltd. v. *Shephard*, [1963] 2 All E.R. 625; [1964] A.C. 326;
    [1963] 2 W.L.R. 1359; Digest (Cont. Vol. A) 1191, *1053c.*

Wise v. *Kaye*, [1962] 1 All E.R. 257; [1962] 1 Q.B. 638; [1962] 2 W.L.R. 96;
    Digest (Cont. Vol. A) 1191, *1053b.*

Appeal.   C

In an action for damages for personal injuries suffered in a road traffic accident
on July 4, 1964, liability in negligence being admitted by the defendants for the
purposes of the action only, an issue as to damages was tried on June 12, 13, 14
and 15, 1967, by CANTLEY, J., at Liverpool. HIS LORDSHIP directed judgment to
be entered for the plaintiff for £66,447 9s. 6d. The defendants gave notice of
appeal, dated July 6, 1967, on the ground that the damages were too high. The D
facts are stated in the judgment of LORD DENNING, M.R. An actuarial valuation
was before the trial judge and the actuary, Mr. Oldham, gave evidence. The
following account shows the nature of the valuation and the weight given to it
at the trial.

The plaintiff had recently attained fifty-six years of age at the time of the
accident. At the trial of the issue an agreed statement of his income as senior E
partner in a firm of quantity surveyors was before the court. This showed his
share of profits for the years 1961, 1962, and 1963 to be (gross) £6,038, £5,756
and £5,825, and, after deducting income tax and surtax, to be £4,274, £4,104
and £4,204 net; the average was £4,194 net. The trial judge found that the
probability was that the plaintiff would have earned about £4,000 during 1966.
He found that the plaintiff had no savings.   F

An actuarial valuation was made on behalf of the plaintiff for the purposes
of assessing the claim for damages. The purpose of the actuary's report was stated
to be—

    " To advise what value an actuary acting absolutely impartially would
    place on the loss of income to [the plaintiff] and the additional expenses
    incurred on his behalf as a result of the accident, as from June 12, 1967." G

Certain assumptions were made and stated in the report. These were—(a) that
the plaintiff's income after deduction of tax and surtax, had he remained an
active member of the partnership, would have continued at a level of not less than
£4,000 per annum; (b) on the understanding that the partnership articles contained no retirement provisions, and that the only action taken by the plaintiff H
towards providing for his retirement was to effect a retirement annuity policy
producing an income of £632 per annum commencing in December, 1977, when he
would be aged 69½, the actuary assumed that the plaintiff would not have retired
before the age of 65 (in six years' time) and would probably have continued as a full
partner until aged sixty-nine approximately (in ten years' time) when he would
have accepted a reduced share in the partnership for several more years; and
(c) that when the plaintiff's wife ceased to be capable of tending her husband the
additional cost of caring for the plaintiff would increase to £1,500 per annum at
least. The actuary estimated that the plaintiff's expectation of life on June 12,
1967, was 16.8 years; and that the plaintiff's expectation of " active life ", that is,
ceasing not only on death but also in the event of total incapacity due to either
sickness or accident, might be taken as 16.1 years on June 12, 1967. In the
actuary's opinion the value of the lost net earnings or the additional nursing cost
might fairly be taken as either (i) the cost of an immediate annuity from a

A reputable insurance company of an amount which, after deduction of tax on the interest content thereof, would be equal to the lost net earnings or the additional nursing costs incurred, as the case might be (referred to as the " equivalent annuity cost ") or (ii) an amount which, if suitably invested on the Stock Exchange or otherwise, would reproduce, resorting to capital as necessary and allowing for tax on the investment income the lost net earnings or the additional nursing

B costs incurred, as the case might be (referred to as the " equivalent capital sum "). Basing himself on these the actuary was of the opinion that the lost net earnings of the plaintiff, if they were assumed to be initially at a level of £4,000 per annum for six years (age sixty-five) or ten years (age sixty-nine) and reducing by a third thereafter was—

Reducing by a third after	Equivalent Annuity Cost	Equivalent Capital Sum
6 years	£39,700	£37,800
10 years	£42,900	£41,000

Several other computations based on different reductions, etc., were included in the report. The actuary assessed the value of the additional nursing costs incurred, assuming this cost to be £750 per annum and that it increased to £1,500

D per annum after two, five or ten years or remained constant at £750 per annum, as—

Cost increasing to £1,500 p.a. after	Equivalent Annuity Cost	Equivalent Capital Sum
2 years	£16,900	£16,100
5 years	£14,900	£14,300
10 years	£12,400	£12,000
Cost remaining level	£9,100	£8,800

A further alternative on a different hypothesis was also stated in the report.

In regard to the actuarial valuation the trial judge, CANTLEY, J., said that he had had the unusual privilege of hearing the evidence of an expert actuary, Mr. Oldham, who made the report which was exhibited and explained it. Mr.

F Oldham had used the 1920 table of Mortality of Annuitants compiled by the Institute of Actuaries. He, the trial judge, regarded it as sufficient for practical purposes to take a figure of expectation of life for the plaintiff as sixteen years. The trial judge found that the probability was that the plaintiff would have continued to work for the firm until sixty-nine, which was a period of ten years, and that it was possible that the plaintiff would have continued as a partner for

G a year or two after that, drawing his smaller share of profits. In regard to the actuary's computation the trial judge said

" Mr. Oldham considered two matters: one, the cost of an immediate annuity from a reputable insurer of an amount which, after deduction of tax on the interest content, would be equal to the lost net earnings. Alternatively, he has considered the amount which, if suitably invested on the Stock

H Exchange or otherwise, would reproduce, resorting to capital as necessary, and allowing for tax on the investment income, the last net earnings, so with that income and the use of capital the annual net earnings concerned would be replaced and the capital wholly exhausted at the end of the period.

" It is interesting to note that the second method of calculation in every case produces a smaller sum than the first, and as each of those two methods

I would be of equal benefit to the recipient I obviously ought, in fairness to the defendants, to accept the cheaper. Mr. Oldham says, though this is not in his report but was given in evidence in the witness box, that the equivalent capital sum to produce, by what I have called the second method, £4,000 per annum for ten years—that is to say, to the age of sixty-nine—would be £29,600. There are other calculations which he has made and I have considered them all, as well as I can. I note that the equivalent capital sum for £4,000 per annum for six years and then for the rest of the working life, one-third of £4,000, is £29,000. The equivalent capital sum to reproduce

A

£4,000 for ten years, that is to say until sixty-nine, and then one-third of
£4,000 thereafter and the rest of the expectation of working life is £35,000.

" Counsel for the plaintiff says that I should have regard also to inflation,
and Mr. Oldham has produced calculations for the purpose of my inflating
this sum to provide for that contingency. I take it into account, but I also
take into account that the prudent investing of the capital sum largely itself
provides for inflation, and I therefore do not accede to the whole of counsel's
request.

B

" I think on the balance of probabilities that the plaintiff would have
worked as a senior partner and drawn at least £4,000 per annum up to the age
of sixty-nine. I think that thereafter there was a very good chance that for a
year or two he would be given some smaller share in return for such work. I
take all those matters into account and, doing the best that I can from them
and with the assistance supplied to me, I assess this head of damage at
£32,000."

C

The head of damage referred to was loss of future earnings. The trial judge then
turned to the head of damage described as additional expenses. In the course of
his consideration he intimated that he took the view that after three years from
the time of judgment the plaintiff would have to go into the infirmary, that the
fees, unless they went up, would thereafter be £1,419 per annum, and that it would
be right to deduct £300 per annum from the infirmary fees on account of the facts
that the plaintiff's food and laundry would no longer have to be provided at
home. HIS LORDSHIP (CANTLEY, J.) continued—

D

" I should point out that if the plaintiff had been a bachelor living alone
and had transferred his residence to the infirmary, one would have had to have
allowed for the whole saved household expenses, but the plaintiff is not a
bachelor nor did he live alone. He has a wife, a justice of the peace for
Liverpool, who lives in his house with him, and it is perfectly right for him to
continue to maintain his wife in the matrimonial home. Indeed, it is his
obligation to do so, nor is he in my view required—acting reasonably in
mitigation of damage, to drive his wife into an institution or other economical
residence. He is acting reasonably if he continues to maintain his wife in the
way that the wife of a responsible and respectable man, earning over £4,000
per annum is maintained.

E

F

" I have taken a little time in explaining that, because that is why I am
deducting from the infirmary expenses only the actual economies which I
estimate that the plaintiff will make by not being fed and not having his
laundry done at home. Unfortunately Mr. Oldham (the actuary), who has
made the same kind of calculation in respect of future expenditure, has taken
as his basic figures £750 for the household assistance at present and £1,500
for the fees of the infirmary. Both these are in excess of what I find to be the
right figures. This alternative basis gives £500 per annum while the plaintiff
is at home, which is less than I find to be the right figure, coupled with £1,500
per annum for the infirmary, which I find to be more than the right figure.

G

H

" I therefore find myself in a little difficulty in applying Mr. Oldham's
calculations, and I regret now that I did not ask him to do some more. The
one part of Mr. Oldham's calculations which I accept at this point, as opposed
to the earlier part of the claim, is that I am now dealing with the full expectation of life of the plaintiff. I am no longer concerned with how long he would
have been working and earning, but how long he will live and where he will
live, and how much it will cost him.

I

" I have done my best to arrive at what I think to be a proper figure under
this head. Allowing for the variations which I have indicated; allowing also
for the possibility, which I think might be understated as a possibility, that
the fees at the infirmary will go up; allowing also for inflation, my estimate
under this head is £14,000."

A   The trial judge then assessed damages for loss of amenities at £10,000 and concluded—

B   " When I add all those up I reach what I have called earlier a truly daunting figure, because, if I add them up correctly, the total amount is £66,447 9s. 6d., and because I find it a daunting figure I reconsider and look again at the various items. It seems to me that every one of the items replacing money-loss by money has to stand, and, as I said earlier, I cannot see why merely because restitution is made of what has been lost in money, there should be no attempt to compensate for what has been lost in life, so although I am conscious of the high figure that I have reached . . . I propose to adhere to the total which I have already announced."

C   HIS LORDSHIP (CANTLEY, J.) ordered that a trust deed should be drawn up, appointing individual trustees and to be approved by the district registrar, that a sum of £61,447 should be paid into court pending its becoming subject to the trust deed, and that the sum of £5,000 should be paid immediately to the plaintiff's wife, his next friend in the action, the £61,447 being invested. Payment of the 9s. 6d. was waived.

D   *R. M. Bingham*, Q.C., and *T. H. Pigot*, Q.C., for the defendants.
    W. D. T. Hodgson, Q,C., and *R. R. Leech* for the plaintiff.

Cur. adv. vult.

Jan. 27. The following judgments were read.

E   **LORD DENNING, M.R.:** On July 4, 1964, the plaintiff, Mr. William Henry Fletcher, was driving his car along the A.6 road from Preston to Lancaster. The defendants' lorry came round a bend on the wrong side of the road and ran into him. He had a severe head injury and broken shoulder and four broken ribs. He was unconscious for four or five days. He was in hospital for a long time. The broken ribs mended. The broken shoulder left him disabled. His head did not mend. His brain has been gravely affected. The defendants **F** admit liability. The question is what damages should be awarded. The judge has awarded him £66,447 9s. 6d. The defendants appeal, saying that it is too much.

The plaintiff was born in May, 1908. So he was just over fifty-six at the time of the accident. He was a chartered quantity surveyor and a senior partner of a long-established firm in Liverpool. He worked hard and played hard. **G** His life was a full one which he lived with energy and zest. He earned £3,000 or £4,000 a year net after paying his tax. He spent all he earned and saved nothing. His wife was active in local affairs and a magistrate. They have a son, grown up, who lives in New Zealand.

The accident was a catastrophe for the plaintiff. His mind has gone but his body is still there. He is likely to live his normal span of another sixteen years, **H** sitting in a chair all day long, doing nothing, feeling little, forgetting everything. No happiness. No sadness. Just existing. He is utterly dependent on his wife. He has to be dressed in the morning. He takes little interest in food. He tends to stuff his mouth full of food and then has difficulty in swallowing it. When he stands, he does so very slowly. When asked to walk, he shuffles across the room with very short stiff steps. The doctor says of him:

I   " He has apparently become more or less stablised at a very low level of intellectual and emotional capacity and still suffers from a semi-paralysis of the right side. He is in need of constant care and attention and I am afraid he will always be so."

He is at present at home being looked after by his wife; but the strain on her is so great that she will only be able to do it for about three years. Then he will have to go into a mental home for the rest of his days. It will be the Cheadle Royal Infirmary, which is an institution of high standing.

The judge considered the case with the greatest care and assessed compensation   A
for various items separately. He reached these figures:

		£	s.	d.
1. Special damages				
Nursing home and hospital fees from July 4, 1964, to date, travelling expenses of wife and son, telephone calls and all incidental expenses—agreed at		2,747	9	6
Additional help in the house from Nov. 26, 1966, to June 12, 1967 (date of trial)...		200	0	0
		£2,947	9	6
Loss of earnings from date of accident to June 12, 1967 (date of trial)		7,500	0	0
		£10,447	9	6

B

C

2. Loss of future earnings

	£
Loss of future earnings as senior partner from date of trial (June 12, 1967) for ten years to retirement at age of sixty-nine from position of senior partner (May, 1977). During those ten years estimated net earnings (after payment of tax) would be £4,000 a year ... . (say)	£29,600
After retirement he would have continued for a year or two (1977 to 1979) doing some work for the firm with a smaller share ... . (say)	2,400
	£32,000

D

E

3. Additional expenses
Mrs. Fletcher will be able to look after him at home for three
years from June, 1967, to June, 1970, but thereafter she will be
unable to do so. He will then have to go into the Cheadle Royal
Infirmary for the rest of his days. His expectation of life at
date of trial was sixteen years. So he would be at Cheadle
Royal from 1970 to death in 1983.

Extra cost of keeping him at home for three years (£9 a week), plus cost of short stays at Cheadle Royal to give Mrs. Fletcher a break. In all £650 a year for three years—1967-70 ... (say)	£1,750
Cost of keeping the plaintiff from June, 1970, for the rest of his days (thirteen years) at Cheadle Royal. Fees £1,419, a year, less saving on food and laundry at home of £300 a year, making extra expense of £1,119 a year for thirteen years; but the fees may go up in the future ... ... (say)	£12,250
	£14,000

F

G

H

4. Pain and suffering and loss of amenities	
The judge recognised the difficulty of assessing this item in money. "Money is not an equivalent to enjoyment of life, and damages at this point become conventional and artificial "...	£10,000

I

The total of those items comes to £66,447 9s. 6d. The judge said: "I find it
a daunting figure." He also recorded this argument against it:

"Counsel for the defendants has argued that, while it is right that I should
take each of these four matters into account, if adding them together results
in an exceptionally high or daunting figure, common sense requires that
I should then revise the total figure. I do not think this can be right."

A So he gave judgment for the full figure, saying:

"Although I am conscious of the high figure I have reached—suspicious perhaps that I have overlooked something I ought to have taken into account—I propose to adhere to the total which I have already announced."

Whilst I acknowledge the care which the judge devoted to this case, I think that
B his conclusion was erroneous. In the first place, I think that he has attempted to give a perfect compensation in money, whereas the law says that he should not make that attempt. It is an impossible task. He should give a fair compensation. That was settled ninety years ago by the case of *Phillips* v. *London & South Western Ry. Co.* (1). Dr. Phillips was an eminent physician making £6,000 or £7,000 a year. He was so severely injured in a railway accident that
C he was reduced to utter helplessness with every enjoyment of life destroyed. Field, J., in summing up to the jury said (2):

". . . in actions for personal injuries of this kind . . . and it is wrong to attempt to give an equivalent for the injury sustained. I do not mean to say that you must not do it, because you are the masters and are to decide; but I mean that it would operate unjustly, and in saying so I am using the
D language of the great Parke, B., whose opinion was quoted with approval in *Rowley's* case (3). Perfect compensation is hardly possible, and would be unjust. You cannot put the plaintiff back again into his original position."

This direction was approved by Sir Alexander Cockburn, C.J., who added another reason (4):
E
". . . the compensation should be commensurate to the injury sustained. But there are personal injuries for which no amount of pecuniary damages would afford adequate compensation, while, on the other hand, the attempt to award full compensation in damages might be attended with ruinous consequences to defendants. . . . Generally speaking, we agree with the
F rule as laid down by Brett, J., in *Rowley* v. *London & North Western Ry. Co.* (3) . . . that a jury in these cases 'must not attempt to give damages to the full amount of a perfect compensation for the pecuniary injury, but must take a reasonable view of the case, and give what they consider under all the circumstances a fair compensation.'"

Those passages were quoted with approval by Lord Devlin in *H. West &
G Son, Ltd.* v. *Shephard* (5), and undoubtedly represent the law. It is true that in these days most defendants are insured and heavy awards do not ruin them; but small insurance companies can be ruined. Some have been. And large companies have to cover the claims by their premiums. If awards reach figures which are " daunting " in their immensity, premiums must be increased all the way round. The impact spreads through the body politic. Consider
H also the position of the plaintiff. He is the one person entitled to be compensated. What good does all this money do for the poor plaintiff. He cannot use it all by any means. Halve it. Still he cannot use it in his lifetime. In order to give him fair compensation, I should have thought that he should be given a sum which would ensure that he would not, within reason, want for anything that money could buy; and that his wife should be able to live for the rest of
I her life in the comfort that he would have provided for her; and that any savings that he would have made if uninjured would be available for his family.

In the second place, I think that the judge was wrong to take each of the items separately and then just add them up at the end. The items are not separate heads of compensation. They are only aids to arriving at a fair and reasonable

---

(1) (1879), 4 Q.B.D. 406; 5 Q.B.D. 78. (2) (1879), 5 Q.B.D. at p. 79.
(3) [1861-73] All E.R. Rep. 823; (1873), L.R. 8 Exch. 221.
(4) (1879), 4 Q.B.D. at p. 407.
(5) [1963] 2 All E.R. 625 at p. 639; [1964] A.C. 326 at p. 356.

compensation. That was made clear by the decision of this court in *Watson* **A**
v. *Powles* (6), given after the judge had given his judgment (6):

" There is only one cause of action for personal injuries, not several causes
of action for the several items. The award of damages is therefore an award
of one figure only, a composite figure made up of several parts . . . At the
end all parts must be brought together to give fair compensation for the
injuries." **B**

There is, to my mind, a considerable risk of error in just adding up the items.
It is the risk of overlapping. I can best explain this by supposing that the
plaintiff instead of being a married man was a bachelor, aged fifty-six, unlikely
to marry, who earned £4,000 a year and spent it all on the pleasures of living in
hotels and clubs and in recreations such as golf, fishing and shooting, without
saving anything: but then suffered this accident and was taken into Cheadle **C**
Royal Infirmary for the rest of his days. In such a case: (i) it would be perfectly
fair to give him the full costs of accommodation in Cheadle Royal, deducting a
small proportion of it for board and lodging, as was done in *Shearman* v. *Folland*
(7); (ii) it would be fair also to compensate him for the loss of " amenities "
because he could no longer enjoy the pleasures of living in hotels and clubs,
and the recreations of golf, fishing and shooting; (iii) I do not think that **D**
it would be fair, over and above those items, to give him in addition his future
salary in full with no deductions. I look at it in this way. If he had not been
injured, he could not have enjoyed those pleasures and recreations without paying
for them out of his salary. It follows that he should not be given compensation
for being deprived of those pleasures and recreations unless account is taken
of the fact that he would have had to pay for them. If no deduction were made **E**
from his salary, it would mean that he was being given compensation for his
pleasures and recreations as if they were *free*, and as if he was able to *save* all his
salary except for his bare food and lodging, which is contrary to the fact. It
would mean that he was being compensated on the basis that he was a man who
would have saved every penny which he earned and have died leaving a fortune.
Whereas in point of fact he would have saved nothing and left nothing. He **F**
should not, therefore, be given his full loss of earnings. The case of *Shearman*
v. *Folland* (7) contains nothing to the contrary. There was there no loss of
future earnings. The plaintiff there had her own private means, like the millionaire
in the example (8). So the point did not arise. Another way of looking at it is
to say that he should not be given both the full cost of accommodation at Cheadle
Royal and also his full salary; for that again would mean that he would be **G**
saving his full salary and spending nothing. In any way there is an overlap
if he is given his full salary without deductions.

I have taken the example of a bachelor. The plaintiff was not a bachelor.
He was a happily married man with a wife to support. But like principles
apply. He should be compensated not only for his special damage to the date
of trial, but also for all the expenses to which he will be put by reason of the **H**
accident, including the cost of extra help in the house (while he is at home)
and the cost of his accommodation in Cheadle Royal Infirmary (for the rest of
his days), subject to a small deduction for food and lodging, as in *Shearman* v.
Folland (8). He should be compensated for his loss of future earnings to the
extent that he would have used them for supporting his wife in comfort for the
rest of her life, including any savings that he would have made out of his earnings **I**
if uninjured. He should also be compensated for pain and suffering and for the
loss of " amenities ", as they are called, that is the enjoyment of life which he
has now lost. There must, of course be an allowance made for the fact that,
even if he had not been injured, there would be many contingencies which might
upset his future prospects, such as illness, accident, bad trade, and so forth.

(6) [1967] 3 All E.R. 721 at pp. 722, 723.
(7) [1950] 1 All E.R. 976; [1950] 2 K.B. 43.
(8) [1950] 1 All E.R. at p. 978; [1950] 2 K.B. at p. 47.

A Allowance must also be made for the fact that compensation is paid at once in a lump sum (so that it can be invested and interest used at once), whereas his earnings would have been spread over many years. Then at the end we must look at the overall figure to see that it is fair compensation.

Diplock, L.J., has analysed the actuarial calculations and reached a figure with which I agree; but I would place them under these headings:

B

	£	s.	d.
Special damages, as found by the judge (not challenged) ..	10,447	9	6
Loss of amenities, as found by the judge (not challenged) ..	10,000	0	0
Expenses by reason of the accident for the rest of his life (extra help in house and accommodation at Cheadle Royal) ..	9,000	0	0
Loss of future earnings. These should only be allowed to the extent of supporting his wife in comfort for the rest of her life, plus any savings he would have made if uninjured	22,000	0	0
Total	£51,447	9	6

C

D Having reached that figure, I think it proper to look at it again as an overall figure and see whether it is a fair compensation, and reduce or increase it accordingly. I think it is fair. It is more than fair. The interest on it at six per cent. will be over £3,000 a year. Properly invested, it will keep pace with inflation. The income alone should go far to keep the plaintiff and his wife in comfort for the rest of their days, and they should at the end be still able to leave a substantial sum of capital to their family—far more than they would have been able to do **E** if there had been no accident.

I would, therefore, allow the appeal and reduce the judge's figure by £15,000, leaving an award in all of £51,447 9s. 6d.

DIPLOCK, L.J.: This is another of that growing number of cases in which the physical and mental injuries caused by another's negligence have trans- **F** formed the victim into a different man. One kind of life, active, full, and useful came to an end on the day of the accident. Another kind of existence, passive, empty, useless began. The plaintiff, who led that life and must now endure that existence is mercifully incapable of realising the transformation that has taken place. I will not seek to add to the account Lord Denning, M.R., has already given of it.

G Cantley, J., had the task of assessing the monetary compensation to which the law entitles the plaintiff for the disaster which has befallen him. The figures the judge awarded was £66,447 6s. 9d. He described it as " a truly daunting figure "—and so it is. Is it the " right " figure for consequences of this cataclysmic kind?

The judge arrived at it by a method commonly adopted in assessing compensa- **H** tion for physical injuries of a lesser kind, which, though they may be severe indeed, leave the victim the same kind of rational being that he was before. He assessed the compensation under three separate heads of damages: (i) loss of earnings, (ii) additional expenses incurred as a result of the injuries, and (iii) pain and suffering and the loss of the amenities of life. In accordance with the practice of pleading " special damage ", he assessed separately the loss and **I** expenses incurred under heads (i) and (ii) up to the date of trial as special damage. This came to the sum of £10,447 6s. 9d. The balance under head (i) he assessed at £32,000, and under head (ii) at £14,000. Under head (iii), which forms no part of " special damage ", he awarded a total of £10,000. He then added these four items together to reach the total of £66,447 6s. 9d.

In this court the defendants have challenged some of the hypotheses which underlay the judge's calculations of £32,000 under head (i) and £14,000 under head (ii); but a controversy has also developed about the propriety, in a case of this kind at any rate, of assessing the damages for what in law is a single *injuria* as

if it were the sum of the losses sustained under three separate heads unrelated **A**
to one another.

It is a platitude that the purpose of compensatory damages in an action for
personal injuries is to put the victim in the same position as he would have been
if he had not sustained those injuries, *so far as money can do this*. But money
never can do this. The effect of any physical injury is to make the life of the
person who sustains it different from what it would otherwise have been. The **B**
change may be temporary or permanent; it may be slight or fundamental;
but his position can never be the same as it would have been but for the injuries.
Even where a consequence of his injuries is to destroy or reduce his ability to
earn money, to restore to him by way of damages the money which he would
have been able to earn can put him in the same position as before the injuries
only to the extent that he would have spent those earnings otherwise than on **C**
himself—as, for instance, in maintaining his wife and dependants or giving it
away during his life or on his decease. To the extent that he would have spent
on himself, to restore to him the money he would have earned will not put him
in a position to indulge in any of his former activities for which he now is incapacitated by his injuries. So, except to the extent that I have mentioned, the
platitude gives little guide to the scale of values to be applied in assessing the **D**
compensation in money for the change in the life of the victim which results from
the personal injuries he has sustained. The law assumes that any physical
injury to a man's body, wrongfully inflicted by another, involves a change for the
worse and entitles him to some damage. To assess the degree of worsening,
however, involved in one kind of injury as compared with that involved in
another calls for the application of some common standard of comparison: and **E**
to convert the degree of worsening so assessed into money values for the purposes
of compensation calls for the application of some arbitrary conversion table. In *Wise*
v. *Kaye* (9) I suggested that the common standard of comparison for assessing the
degree of worsening was based on the effect of the injuries on the happiness of
the victim. But I was wrong. (See the majority judgments in that case and
the majority speeches in *H. West & Son, Ltd.* v. *Shephard* (10).) I think that **F**
the result of the decisions in these cases is that the standard of comparison which
the law applies, if it is not wholly instinctive and incommunicable, is based,
apart from pain and suffering, on the degree of deprivation—that is, the extent
to which the victim is unable to do those things which, but for the injury, he
would have been able to do.

This is a case in which the plaintiff's deprivation must rank high in the standard **G**
of comparison. If, however, one excludes for the moment his inability to maintain his wife financially, it is not at the maximum, for his physical disabilities
are much less severe than those of the quadriplegics in *Wise* v. *Kaye* (9), *West* v.
Shephard (10) and, alas, other cases, and his intellectual deprivations are accompanied by unawareness of what he has lost. High though his deprivation ranks,
I cannot think that it ranks any higher because the plaintiff before the accident **H**
was a rich man. Had an ordinary working man, who like the plaintiff had led
before the accident a full, active and useful life in his own sphere, sustained the
same injuries with the same physical and mental results, he would in my view
have been entitled to monetary compensation of the same order as the plaintiff
for the transformation of his life into a passive, empty and useless existence.

That does not mean that the total award would be the same, for the plaintiff **I**
would have been deprived in addition of the ability to maintain his wife on a
financial scale higher than that of the wife of an ordinary working man, and the
expenses of suitable arrangements for maintaining the plaintiff in circumstances
which will minimise the personal deprivations that he will suffer may be greater.
It does mean, however, that if deductions for these two elements in the compensation were made in the respective awards to the plaintiff and to an ordinary

(9) [1962] 1 All E.R. 257; [1962] 1 Q.B. 638.
(10) [1963] 2 All E.R. 625; [1964] A.C. 326.

A working man who sustained similar injuries, the balance of both awards ought
to be approximately the same and of the order suggested by the awards in *Wise*
v. *Kaye* (11) and *West* v. *Shephard* (12)—the most recent and authoritative
examples of the current arbitrary conversion scale.

I agree with Lord Denning, M.R., that, in a case of personal injuries which
have transformed the plaintiff's life, to adopt the common method of assessing

B damages separately under the three heads of (i) loss of earnings, (ii) additional
expenses incurred as a result of the injuries, and (iii) loss of the amenities of
life and adding them together, as the judge has done, may lead to error and tends
to result in awarding to the earner of a larger income greater compensation for
his actual physical and mental deprivations than would be awarded to a victim
who earned a smaller income.

C In the ordinary case where the victim after the accident, though deprived of
some activities, is able to live what is broadly the same kind of life as he did
before, this method is convenient provided that it is borne in mind that all three
heads are directed to deprivation and are inter-related. To assess under the
first head the extent to which a man has been deprived of the ability to earn
money may not be easy, but it needs no arbitrary conversion table to measure

D it in money. And since to deprive a man of the ability to earn money is to
deprive him of whatever the possession of it would enable him to do and the
lack of it prevents him from doing, to restore to him by way of damages the
earnings lost as a result of his injuries is to put it in his power to remedy these
deprivations to the extent that he is capable of activities similar to those on which
he would have spent it had he been able to earn. To the extent, however, that

E he is not so capable and cannot spend part of the earnings which have been so
restored to him on the particular activities of which he has been deprived, that
part of the earnings goes to compensate him in part for his deprivation of those
activities, for it is available for other purposes. Of course it does not compensate
him in whole. It may be only a small part of the appropriate compensation,
but unless it is taken into account in the assessment under head (iii) of compensation for loss of the amenities of life, there will be some duplication in the damages
awarded to him for deprivation of those activities.

In the exceptionally severe cases where the life of the victim has been transformed by his physical injuries so that the only activities of which he is now
capable are wholly different from his previous activities, the duplication may be
considerable. If, for instance, he chose before the accident to spend the whole
of his earnings on expensive food and drink and hospitality and expensive
pastimes outside his home and is reduced by his injuries to the life of an invalid
recluse, to restore to him the earnings which he formerly spent in these ways
will not compensate him for the deprivation of his ability to enjoy good food
and drink and hospitality or his former pastimes, although the amount he spent
on them affords an indication of the minimum value which he placed on the
activities of which he has been deprived. He is entitled to more than that, but
if one assesses these deprivations under the separate head of loss of the amenities
of life, one must bear in mind that what these amenities would have cost him
must be deducted in converting into money the loss sustained under this head,
for he will have already been awarded that sum under the head of loss of earnings.

So too with the second head of additional expenses incurred as a result of the
injuries. The need to spend money on nursing and medical treatment deprives
the victim of the ability to do whatever the availability of the money for some
other purpose would have enabled him to do. To the extent, however, that
this expenditure relieves him from expenses of maintaining himself which he
would have incurred but for his injuries, there is a similar duplication with the
assessment under head (iii) for loss of the amenity of enjoying the style of living
which he was able to enjoy before the accident.

(11) [1962] 1 All E.R. 257; [1962] 1 Q.B. 638.
(12) [1963] 2 All E.R. 625; [1964] A.C. 326.

Let me take two contrasted cases by way of example, A and B are bachelors A
of similar age who have always spent the whole of their earnings on their own
living expenses and recreations. A earns £1,000 a year. He leads a full but
scholarly and ascetic life: his main recreations, reading and bird-watching,
cost him nothing. B earns £3,000 a year. He leads a full but sociable and sybaritic
life; his main recreations, shooting and fishing, cost him £1,000 a year. Both suffer
injuries comparable to those which the plaintiff suffered. The cost of maintaining
each of them for the rest of their lives in the greatest ease and comfort which
they are capable of enjoying will be £1,500 a year; and but for their injuries,
the expectation of earning life of each would have been such that a judge would
assess the loss of income of each at ten years' purchase. Here it seems to me
that the injuria suffered by A and B are comparable. Each has suffered a similar
cataclysmic transformation of his life. The compensation to which each is
entitled, though not the same, ought to be at least of the same order; but if that
compensation is assessed separately under the three heads, B will be awarded
under the head of loss of earnings £20,000 more than A; and unless in assessing
compensation under the head of loss of the amenities of life a deduction is made
for the difference in the cost to A and B respectively of the amenities which they
have lost, the total award to B for a comparable injuria would be £20,000 more
than the award to A. That there should be some difference in the two awards
may well be right—but not one of this order. It might be that B had he not been
injured might at some later date have saved part of his income to provide for
greater amenities on his retirement, and it may be that some allowance should
be made for this additional future deprivation.

Finally, let me take the case of C. His age is the same as that of A and B. His
income is £3,000 a year. He spends it all but he is married and £2,000 a year is
devoted to the maintenance of his wife and family. His personal tastes and
recreations are comparable to those of A. He suffers the same deprivations as
A and B; but he also suffers the additional deprivation of being unable to support
his wife and family. The compensation for this additional deprivation is covered
under the head of loss of earnings; and since ex hypothesi the personal amenities
of life which he has lost cost him £2,000 a year less than they cost B, there is no
similar deduction to that required in B's case in assessing the compensation to
which he is entitled under that head.

In discussing the need to bear in mind the inter-relation between the three
conventional heads under which damages for personal injuries are commonly
assessed, I have drawn no distinction between losses and additional expenses
which have been sustained or incurred before the date of trial and those which
will be sustained or incurred thereafter. The only real distinction between pre-
trial and post-trial losses of earnings and additional expenses is that the assessment of the former is less liable to error, for it is based in part on ascertainable
facts; whereas the assessment of the latter is based exclusively on assumptions
to be made by the assessor. The assessment of pre-trial loss of earnings or
additional expenses involves ascertaining what has in fact happened and making
assumptions as to what would have been likely to happen if the victim had not
sustained the personal injuries. The assessment of post-trial loss of earnings
or additional expenses, on the other hand, is dependent on assumptions both as
to what will happen in the future to the victim in the state to which he has been
reduced, as well as to what would have been likely to happen to him if he had not
sustained the personal injuries. There is, however, the technical requirement
under the practice of the courts that the plaintiff is required to specify in his
statement of claim the pre-trial losses and expenses which he claims under these
two heads, and the amount so claimed is called " special damages ". Except
in comparative ease of assessment, however, it is just as much inter-related with
the claim under the head of loss of the amenities of life as post-trial losses and
expenses.

Let me take as an illustration the victim whose leisure activity is shooting which costs him £1,000 a year and whose income is £4,000. He sustains injuries which result in no permanent disability but make him incapable of earning and of shooting for one year which has elapsed by the time of the trial. In assessing the total compensation for the deprivations which he has suffered as a result of the physical injuries, allowance must be made for the saving of £1,000 consequent on his inability to shoot. But for the rule about pleading " special damage ", it would not matter whether the £1,000 was deducted from his loss of earnings and full allowance made for his deprivation of the activity of shooting under the head of loss of amenities of life, or the loss of earnings was awarded in full and the £1,000 deducted in assessing the money value of the loss of the amenities of life. The rule of pleading which confines " special damage " to loss of earnings and additional expenses, however, makes the former course inconvenient, if not impermissible: and it is never followed in practice.

Shearman v. *Folland* (13), a case relied on by counsel for the plaintiffs, is I think no more than an illustration of this. The victim in that case was an elderly lady of independent means who normally lived in hotels. Because of her injuries she was compelled for a time to live in a nursing home. The nursing home fees, of which she claimed the full amount as special damage, were greater than the sums she would have had to pay at the hotel, and in addition she was deprived of the amenities available to an injured person living in a hotel which were not available to her in her injured state in the nursing home. The Court of Appeal held that in assessing " special damage ", the only permissible deduction from the nursing home fees actually paid was that proportion of them which could be properly ascribed to food and accommodation provided in the nursing home, and that the remainder was additional expenses incurred as a result of her injuries. No point was taken on the amount of general damages. The case, which was decided before *British Transport Commission* v. *Gourley* (14), is no authority for the proposition that in the assessment of compensation for deprivation of amenities, no deduction is to be made for expenses which would necessarily have been incurred in order to enjoy them.

I turn now to the assessment in the present case under these three heads:

Loss of earnings :

In the present case CANTLEY, J., has awarded under the head of loss of earnings from Dec. 1, 1964, when the plaintiff's earnings from the partnership ceased, a total sum of £39,500 on the following basis:

(i) £7,500 is the judge's estimate of what the plaintiff would have earned up to the date of trial in June, 1967, and this is included in his award of special damage.

(ii) £29,600 is the present value calculated on an actuarial basis of an income of £4,000 per annum net of tax until June, 1977, when the plaintiff would have reached the age of $69\frac{1}{2}$ years.

(iii) £2,400 is the judge's non-actuarial estimate of the present value of the lesser amount of fees, less tax, which the plaintiff would have earned for a year or two after he reached the age of $69\frac{1}{2}$ years.

The estimate of £7,500 is based on what was actually earned by the partnership, of which the plaintiff was a member, in the $2\frac{1}{2}$ years from December, 1964, to June, 1967. It has been accepted by the defendants as a reasonable estimate and I agree. But it is significant that earnings at the same rate over the next ten years would amount to £30,000, without any discount for acceleration or for the chances that between the age of $59\frac{1}{2}$ and $69\frac{1}{2}$ some illness or accident might have made it necessary for the plaintiff to retire. The judge nevertheless awarded £29,600 for this period.

How did that come about? I think that it was because of the use made of the actuarial calculations. These provide useful arithmetical data which a judge should have in mind, but do not allow for all the chances and changes of this

---

(13) [1950] 1 All E.R. 976; [1950] 2 K.B. 43.
(14) [1955] 3 All E.R. 796; [1956] A.C. 185.

mortal life. The judge assumed that the net income of the plaintiff from the
partnership would rise to and remain at £4,000 a year for the next ten years. He
awarded a capital sum which, invested at interest at current rates, would produce
£4,000 a year free of tax for ten years and be exhausted at the end of that period.
As calculated by the actuary called for the plaintiff, this amounts to £29,600. Put
in the more familiar terms of years' purchase of the assumed income of £4,000
per annum, this represents 7.4 years' purchase. This is substantially more than
the number of years' purchase which a judge would normally apply to the
prospective loss of earnings of a professional man already in his sixtieth year.
Is this because judges do not normally make enough use of actuarial calculations
or because the actuarial calculation in the present case has been misunderstood?

There is no magic about the actuarial calculation. It is based on the following
assumptions, each of which is treated as a *certainty*:

(a) That the plaintiff would have continued to engage in full practice in
partnership as a quantity surveyor until June, 1977, when he would have
attained the age of 69½ years.

(b) That his share in the profits of the partnership, after deduction of tax,
would be £4,000 per annum in each of those ten years.

(c) That in order to earn those profits, he would be put to no expense not
deductible for tax purposes from the profits of the partnership.

(d) That interest rates, tax rates and structure, and the value of money
would remain unaltered throughout the ten years.

With these assumptions as data, the rest is pure arithmetic. The first three
assumptions are special to the plaintiff; the fourth is general. The reliability
of each as a basis for the calculation depends on the degree of probability of its
being right. On this the actuary can throw but little light.

Taking the first assumption, the actuary can say that experience shows that a
person in an executive position of the plaintiff's age who retires on pension at an
age between sixty and sixty-five, has an expectation of life of 16.8 years. He gets
this figure from the life table used by insurance companies for the purpose of
" top hat " pension schemes. But this throws no light on the probabilities of the
plaintiff's remaining fit and able, as well as willing, to continue in full practice
until his seventieth year. That the only provision that he had made for his
retirement was an endowment policy for an annuity maturing at the age of
sixty-nine, makes it likely that he would have continued to work until that
age, or even longer, if he were fit and able to do so. But the risk of some disabling
illness or accident and the inevitable disabilities of age, which make sixty to
sixty-five the common retiring age in most occupations, must be considerable to
any man in his sixties and increasing as the years go by. Even allowing something
for the possibility that he might have carried on in full practice after his seventieth
year, to treat as a *certainty* that he would not be compelled to give up full practice
before ten years cannot in my view be right.

The £4,000 per annum after deduction of tax, which is the second assumed
certainty, does not represent a fixed salary but the estimated share of the plaintiff
in the profits of a partnership under an agreement which would have been subject
to revision. The profits of the partnership had fluctuated considerably in the
2½ years before the trial, although the judge accepted on the evidence that they
had improved by that date. Nevertheless, £4,000 per annum represents an increase
of 33⅓ per cent. on the judge's estimate of £7,500, included in his award of special
damages as being the plaintiff's loss of earnings in the 2½ years immediately
preceding the trial. Again I cannot think that it is right to treat this figure of
£4,000 as a *certainty* throughout the whole period of ten years.

Taking next the third assumption, the evidence disclosed that much of the
success of the partnership in the past had been due to the plaintiff's activities in
bringing business to the firm. This must have involved him in entertainment and
other social activities in excess of the £100 per annum he was permitted to deduct

A for tax purposes. In addition there was the cost of travel to the office, midday meals, and all the other inescapable expenses of a man with a high professional position to maintain.

The fourth assumption, which is not special to the plaintiff, is a purely conventional one adopted for the purpose of calculating the present capital value of an annuity for ten years, disregarding any profit to the grantor, or, put another B way, the discount for accelerated payment of annual sums payable over the next ten years. On the present calculation the discount is twenty-six per cent.— the difference between ten years and 7.4 years' purchase of the annual sum. No-one suggests that the plaintiff could or would invest the capital sum received by him as compensation for loss of earnings in the way assumed for the purposes of the calculation. The calculation is an arithmetical one made on the basis that C the social and economic structure of the country and the value of money will remain unchanged throughout the period of ten years. Plainly this will not be so, and it is often suggested, as it has been in the present appeal, that sums awarded for loss of future earnings should be increased to allow for future inflation. One cannot, however, isolate the factor of inflation from national incomes policy, tax rates and structure, and interest rates. All are inter-related. Nationalisation, D equalisation of incomes, other social and economic changes—all are on the cards. All of these may affect—and not in the same way—an invalid in his sixties possessed of capital and a quantity surveyor in private practice without any savings. I do not think it practicable for the courts to base awards of compensation on speculation about general future or economic trends or about any single factor, such as inflation, which may or may not form part of them. We cannot E know the way the world is going; we are no more likely to be wrong by treating it as standing still—which is what the fourth assumption does.

Having discussed the assumptions special to the plaintiff, it may be helpful to see what effect changes in them would have on the calculation:

F (i) If it were assumed that the plaintiff would have retired in six years (i.e., at the age of 65½ years) instead of ten years, the capital sum of £29,600 would be reduced to £21,000.

(ii) If it were assumed that the plaintiff's earnings for ten years would average £3,000 instead of £4,000, the capital sum of £29,600 would be reduced to £22,200.

(iii) If it were assumed that the plaintiff would retire in six years and that his income during those years would have averaged £3,000, the capital G sum of £29,600 would be reduced to £15,900.

These figures can be usefully compared with the more conventional calculation of years' purchase of the income. For this purpose I think that a judge would have been likely to have taken the median income of £3,500 at five or six years' purchase and so reach a figure in the range of £17,500 to £21,000, instead of the £29,600 which the judge in fact awarded.

To the £29,600, however, the judge added another £2,400. This figure was the judge's estimate of the amounts which the plaintiff would earn after retirement from full practice in 1977 at the age of 69½ years discounted for accelerated payment in 1967. It is not based on any actuarial calculation. It is a highly speculative item relating to the plaintiff's possible earnings in his seventies. If, however, one reduces the number of years' purchase of his income before retirement and thus treats him as retiring at the age of sixty-five or sixty-six, as I have done, some addition must be made for the possibility of subsequent earnings.

In my view a fair way of dealing with the possibility is to award the total sum of £22,000 as compensation for loss of earnings before and after retirement instead of the total of £32,000 at which the judge has arrived.

Additional expenses

Under this head the judge's estimate of the additional expenses to be incurred for nursing and other assistance for the plaintiff during the 16.8 years, which was

his expectation of life at the date of the trial, was the sum of £14,000. He assumed **A**
that the plaintiff would be cared for at home by his wife for three years and that
thereafter he would require institutional care. These assumptions have not been
attacked in this court, although the judge's figure of £650 per annum for the first
three years and £1,119 per annum for the remaining 13.8 years have. The actuary
in his calculations of the present value of the annual sums required for additional
expenses had not adopted either of these monetary figures, nor had he taken the **B**
period of three years as that during which home nursing would be practicable.
Nevertheless, it is possible to ascertain from his calculations that after making
allowance for tax, the appropriate discount for accelerated payment of an
annuity over 16.8 years is about thirty per cent. This means that the judge's
award of £14,000 is the equivalent of a total sum of £20,000 paid in equal annual
instalments over that period. The amount intended to be provided for by the **C**
judge amounted to £1,950 during the first three years and about £15,500 for the
last 13.8 years, giving a total of £17,250. To produce this total an award of £12,000
instead of £14,000 would have been actuarially correct.

There are, however, other criticisms of this part of the judge's award.
It assumes that the plaintiff will in 1970 be removed to Cheadle Royal Infirmary,
an institution outside the national health scheme, and remain there until he dies **D**
in 1984. The judge has said that he has made some allowance for increase of fees
owing to inflation; but whether such institutions will continue to exist until
the 1980's and how they will be financed can be no more than a matter of speculation. Again, in arriving at the annual cost of £1,119 the judge has deducted
from the current fees charged by the institution the sum of £300 which he estimates as the cost of the plaintiff's food and laundry while nursed at home. If, for **E**
the purpose of estimating general damages, damages for loss of amenities of life
and for additional expenses are to be assessed under separate heads, it seems to me
that all economies, consequent on the action taken which involves the additional
expenses claim, must be brought into the estimate made under the latter head.
If he goes permanently into an institution, the plaintiff will have no further need
of his present home. Of course, it is right that he should provide suitable accommodation and establishment for his wife, who is in her middle fifties, which will
ensure her creature comforts comparable with those which she would have
enjoyed had he not been injured. But she will be living alone and it seems to me
neither reasonable not likely that the expense of maintaining a large house suitable
for them both to live in will continue to be incurred once Mr. Fletcher is accommo-
dated permanently in the Cheadle Royal Infirmary or some other institution. I **F**
think that had I adopted the judge's method of calculation, I should have about
doubled his deduction and assumed the net additional expenses in Cheadle
Royal Infirmary at £800 per annum. This would reduce the total sum to be provided for over 16.8 years from £17,250 to £13,000. To produce this total, an
award of around £9,000 would have been actuarily correct.

I would accordingly have reduced the judge's estimate under this head from
£14,000 to £9,000.

Pain, suffering and loss of amenities.

There remains the last head of damages; compensation for pain and suffering
and loss of amenities of life for which the judge awarded £10,000. It has not been
criticised by counsel in this appeal, but I must deal with it, for SALMON, L.J.,
thinks that it is too low. The plaintiff endures some pain in his right arm and hand,
and physical disabilities of a distressing character due to partial paralysis on his
right side, although his total physical disabilities are very much less than those
by which the quadriplegics in *Wise* v. *Kaye* (15) and *H. West & Son, Ltd.* v.
Shephard (16) were affected. He was older than either of the victims in those cases
and was approaching an age at which physical prowess may be expected to

(15) [1962] 1 All E.R. 257;   [1962] 1 Q.B. 638.
(16) [1963] 2 All E.R. 625;   [1964] A.C. 326.

A deteriorate. His brain injury too is much less than theirs but mercifully he, like them, does not appreciate the state to which he has been reduced. He is not conscious of the deprivations of the pleasures and anxieties of ordinary life which he has sustained. Before the accident he led a full and active social and leisure life and spent his substantial income to the full on his living expenses and those of his wife and on his pleasures. None of these amenities is he now able to enjoy,

B but it is to be borne in mind that to the extent that the value which he placed on them was in part reflected in the money that he spent on them, this has already been provided for in compensating him for his loss of earnings. To this extent he has already been awarded money in place of the amenities he would have spent it on. Of course, there is a large balance over to be compensated under this general head of loss of the amenities of life, but it is a balance, not the full value of his

C deprivation. For my part I cannot but attach importance to the fact that he is spared the distress of realising what he has lost. This mitigating factor was there to an even greater extent in the victim in *Wise* v. *Kaye* (15) and was also there in *West* v. *Shephard* (16), but regarded as purely physical deprivations, what they sustained were much worse than those of this plaintiff. If the awards of £15,000 and £17,500 respectively were right in those two cases, as on the authority of

D the majority of his court and the majority of the House of Lords I must accept that they were, I do not find it possible to say that the additional sum of £10,000 awarded to the plaintiff under this general head was wrong if the full amount of loss of earnings is to be awarded without any deduction for what he would have had to spend in order to enjoy the amenities of which he has been deprived.

Adopting the method of assessing damages under the three inter-related heads

E of loss of earnings, additional expenses and compensation for pain and suffering and the loss of amenities of life, as I have felt compelled to do because the evidence was directed to this method of assessment, the total sum that I should award amounts to £51,447 9s. 6d. This is still a very large sum but it is less by £15,000 than that awarded by the judge.

Although there was no evidence specifically directed towards this, for it is not

F a conventional way of assessing damages, it is, I think, possible to check very roughly whether a total award of the order of £51,500 accords with what, in agreement with LORD DENNING, M.R., I think that social justice requires in a case where physical injuries are of a kind which transform an active sentient human being into a mental and physical wreck capable of little more than mere existence. The sum awarded ought to be sufficient: first, to provide for the plaintiff's

G own maintenance in such circumstances as will best ameliorate the discomfort and deprivations he is bound to suffer; secondly, to provide for Mrs. Fletcher, his only dependant, enough to support her in the same standard of material comfort, living apart from him, as she would have enjoyed had he not been injured; and, thirdly, to provide in addition the proper conventional sum to which the courts apply the label of " compensation for loss of the amenities of

H life ". As regards provision for Mrs. Fletcher's maintenance, the plaintiff had made no savings. Had he not been injured, he and Mrs. Fletcher would in any event have been compelled to reduce their standard of living considerably on his retirement and would have been wise to do so earlier so as to save something from his income during his last years of full practice. If one were to make provision for the sum of £2,000 a year free of tax for Mrs. Fletcher for some ten years after the accident and £1,000 free of tax for the remainder of the plaintiff's expectation of life, this would in my view not be ungenerous. It is possible from the actuarial calculations to assess the cost of providing this income as of the order of £20,000 to £21,000. Together these two provisions call for a sum of the order of £36,000. Deducting this from £51,500, there is left a balance of £15,500 as compensation for the plaintiff's loss of the amenities of life.

Is this a proper conventional sum to add to the full provision which has already been made for the plaintiff's future maintenance and that of his dependants?

(15) (16) See p. 742, ante.

He himself can make no use of it. If the other calculations are correct, it will A
accumulate until his death and provide a windfall for his heirs and for the Inland
Revenue. The award of damages should serve some social purpose, but I am
uncertain as to the social purpose which the award of an additional sum is intended
to serve. It cannot be intended as the modern substitute for blood-money, for
that in case of death is fixed at a figure of the order of £500. (See the latest
case in the House of Lords (17).) It cannot be to penalise the wrongdoer, for the B
penalty will fall directly on his employer's insurer and indirectly on the general
body of motorists in the form of increased premiums. I suspect that its social
purpose is to relieve the horror and anguish which ordinary human beings who
constitute society cannot but feel when contemplating the state to which the
victim has been reduced. Death comes to all men; but to reduce a living man to
the condition of a crippled animal shocks the imagination. Perhaps it is because C
there are infinite gradations of physical injuries that the courts have instinctively
felt that the conventional sum, unlike that awarded where injuries cause death,
should bear some relation to the sums awarded for severe though lesser injuries
where the money can be used to ameliorate the victim's lot. Or it may be, and
this I find a more satisfactory rationalisation, that in a case where the victim is
not dead but still exists, one ought to provide a large margin to ensure that what- D
ever contingency may occur for which allowance was not made in assessing the
provision needed for the victim and his dependants, there will be funds to meet
it. However this may be, all I can do is to look at the sums awarded under this
head in comparable cases where the victim could make no use of the moneys
awarded. If £15,000 in *Wise* v. *Kaye* (18) and £17,500 in *West* v. *Shephard* (19),
where there was no substantial overlap with loss of earnings, were right, I cannot E
think that £15,000 in the present case would be wrong.

This method of approach does not involve distinguishing between special
damages and general damages or calculating the financial equivalent of what the
plaintiff has lost. It is simply an attempt to check whether the damages which I
have already sought to re-assess on the same conventional method as that adopted
by the judge are sufficient to provide whatever mitigation money can provide for F
the plaintiff and his dependants together with an additional sum of the order that
the highest court in this country has approved.

I agree that the appeal be allowed and the damages reduced to £51,447 9s. 6d.

SALMON, L.J.: In July, 1964, the plaintiff was fifty-six years of age. He
was senior partner in one of the most reputable and successful firms of chartered
quantity surveyors in the North of England. Of the six highly competent partners G
in that firm, the plaintiff was generally recognised as easily the most efficient
both in getting business and carrying it out. His work, to which he brought
zest and enthusiasm, clearly meant much more to him than merely making money;
but its financial rewards were considerable. His average annual net earnings,
i.e., after payment of income tax and surtax, were appreciably in excess of £4,000.
In addition he had many varied interests. He was prominently connected with H
a number of professional bodies; he was chairman of his local political association;
he enjoyed recreations such as tennis and fishing, and he and his wife, who is a
justice of the peace, took part in many social activities. In short, he led a very full,
interesting, happy and useful life. These facts are all undisputed.

On July 4, 1964, whilst driving his motor car, he met with an accident which was
caused wholly by the defendants' negligence. As a result he suffered the gravest
injuries which have had the most appalling consequences. The vault of his skull
was fractured, causing very severe damage to the brain. Of serious but comparatively minor importance was a bad comminuted fracture of the upper part of
the right arm which has resulted in permanent limitation of movement of the right

(17) See *Dietz.* v. *Lennig Chemicals, Ltd.*, [1967] 2 All E.R. 282.
(18) [1962] 1 All E.R. 257; [1962] 1 Q.B. 638.
(19) [1963] 2 All E.R. 625; [1964] A.C. 326.

A shoulder. The brain injury, in addition to causing partial paralysis of the right arm and leg, has reduced him to a very low level of intellectual and emotional activity. He appears capable of taking very little, if any, interest in anything. He complains bitterly of continual pain in his right arm and hand. He is irritable and very difficult to live with. He is unable to dress or undress himself or even fend for himself in the lavatory. There is, of course, no question of his ever again

B being able to follow his profession or of his condition improving. The judge summed up the matter thus:

> " I saw him shuffle into the witness box and I watched him shuffle out of the witness box and . . . out of the court with assistance. He was a pathetic figure. He is not devoid of intelligence but he has no expression of face or voice to show any interest in his surroundings. He looked—and I am afraid

C he is—a useless, shuffling, senile-looking man, dependant on constant care and attention from others for ever, and incapable of normal social or intellectual activity."

His expectation of life has, however, not been diminished.

The judge awarded him in all damages amounting in round figures to some

D £66,400. The defendants appeal on the ground that this sum is so excessive as to be a " wholly erroneous estimate of damage ". The plaintiff was 59½ years of age at the date of the judgment. The judge took the view that this was a case in which it was appropriate to consider damages under separate heads and so to deal with them in his judgment. I agree with him. No doubt there are many essentially simple cases which are sometimes unnecessarily complicated by too

E detailed an examination and quantification of the items of damage, and in which it is neither necessary nor desirable to mention more than a global figure in the judgment. This was not such a case.

The judge, rightly in my view, considered the question of damages under four heads: (i) financial loss suffered prior to the judgment, i.e., June 12, 1967; (ii) probable loss of earnings subsequent to the judgment; (iii) expenses likely to

F be incurred subsequent to the judgment, and (iv) pain and suffering and loss of amenities from the date of the accident.

Under the first head, he awarded in round figures £10,000—and this figure is not challenged by the defendants.

Under the second head, he awarded £32,000. This figure has been strongly criticised by the defendants in this court. The judge assessed the plaintiff's

G average annual loss of net income at £4,000. This in my view is certainly not unfair to the defendants. Serious questions arise as to the number of years during which, but for the accident, the plaintiff would have continued to earn this income, and the present capital value of its loss. On both these questions the plaintiff called the evidence of an eminent actuary. In some cases the courts have doubted the value of actuarial evidence and rightly criticised the nature of

H the actuarial evidence adduced. This seems to me to be a matter about which it is impossible to generalise. No doubt there are cases in which either because of their nature or of the kind of actuarial evidence tendered, such evidence is of no real help and only adds unnecessarily to the expense and time involved in the trial. On the other hand, there are cases, and I agree with the judge that this is one of them, in which the actuarial evidence is of great value. This evidence in the present case showed that anyone in the plaintiff's position, i.e., a man occupying the position of a high executive would at the age of 59½ have an expectation of life of 16.8 years and might be expected to live in unimpaired health for 16.1 years. No doubt the data on which this evidence was based included cases in which men retire at sixty or sixty-five and also cases in which they retire in their early seventies or later, as they sometimes do. It may be that if men retire at sixty or sixty-five, rather than later, their chances of living are increased, although one has heard the contrary view expressed. Even if the former view be correct, I cannot think that this plaintiff, who admittedly was a healthy man

prior to the accident, would have had less than a ten years' expectation of useful A
life at the age of 59½. The plaintiff had saved no money, in spite of the fact
that his only child was twenty-three and no longer imposed any financial burden
on him. All he had was an insurance policy which would have given him a
pension of £600 a year gross at the age of sixty-nine. The judge rightly concluded that the plaintiff, who loved his work, obviously had no intention of
retiring before he was sixty-nine and might well have continued to work thereafter. B

I do not agree that the judge approached his task on the assumption that it
was certain that the plaintiff would have earned an average of £4,000 a year in
the future. I am sure that he thoroughly appreciated that nothing is certain.
It is not certain that the plaintiff might not have earned on average as little
as £2,000 a year or even less. Nor is it certain that he might not have earned on
average as much as £5,000 or £6,000 a year or even more. The judge concluded   C
that in all probability the plaintiff would have earned an average of £4,000
a year; and in my view this conclusion was amply supported by the uncontradicted evidence. Indeed, on the evidence, the judge might well have
assessed the probable future earnings at somewhat more than £4,000 a year. It
is true that the period between the date of the accident and the date of the trial
included one exceptionally bad year in which the plaintiff earned considerably   D
less than £4,000, but according to the uncontradicted evidence, this was due to
altogether exceptional circumstances. Of course, there might have been another
exceptionally bad year in the future, but there might equally well have been an
exceptionally good one. Having properly fixed £4,000 a year as the plaintiff's
probable average future earnings, the judge, not unnaturally, used this
basis for the purpose of the actuarial calculations.   E

The actuary's evidence showed that in order to produce £4,000 net a year for
ten years so that the whole of the capital and interest would be consumed at the
end of that period, it would be necessary to invest £29,000 at the comparatively
high yield produced by fixed interest bearing securities. These securities, of course,
provide no protection against inflation. To produce the same income from an
investment in equities, which show a lower yield but which do provide protection   F
against inflation, a larger capital sum would be necessary. The purchase of an
annuity would cost even more. The judge accepted the lowest of these three bases.
This can hardly be complained of by the defendants. Nor do I think that he can
be justly criticised for assessing the loss of earning on the assumption that the
plaintiff would probably have gone on earning £4,000 a year net for another ten
years, i.e., until he was sixty-nine and would probably have earned £2,400 in all   G
thereafter. I do not agree that the judge assumed that this was certain,
but only that it was probable. Such an assumption is, in my view, fully justified
by the evidence. This assessment produced the figure of £32,000, which in my
judgment is by no means too generous to the plaintiff, nor in any way unfair to
the defendants who caused the loss.

Even if I were to approach the problem in the more usual but less precise and   H
rational way than the judge was enabled to do by the actuarial evidence called
before him, I do not think that I would arrive at a substantially different figure.
After all, the normal method is nothing else than a rough and ready way of
producing the actuarial result. Obviously the plaintiff did not intend to retire,
at the earliest, until he was sixty-nine. He was a healthy, vigorous man. He might,
of course, through misfortune, have ceased work sooner or he might have continued in full possession of his faculties as a most useful member of his firm and
gone on earning an average of £4,000 a year for a number of years longer. I
think that it is a fair assumption that in all probability he would have gone on
until he was sixty-nine. Ten years at £4,000 a year would produce a figure of
£40,000. This figure, of course, must be discounted on account of his receiving
the money at fifty-nine and perhaps for contingencies. I think, however, that on
the basis of a period of ten years, the discount for contingencies should be small
and is practically cancelled out by the chances of the plaintiff working after the

A age of sixty-nine. In all the circumstances I would scale the figure of £40,000 down to not less than £30,000. I am certainly not prepared to say that £32,000 is too high.

It has sometimes been said when the calculation of compensation for financial loss works out at a high figure that a plaintiff with a capital sum may be able to do better for himself by setting up in business than by investing the damages,

B in a more conventional fashion. This seems to me to be a most dubious proposition particularly with a plaintiff innocent of any commercial experience. At any rate, it can have no application in the present case.

The third head of damages related to the expense to which the plaintiff was likely to be put in the future. The learned judge concluded that the plaintiff was likely to remain at home for three years but that the strain on his wife, who was

C only a few years his junior, would be too great for him to be kept at home any longer. He would then go to the Cheadle Royal Infirmary. The additional expense of keeping him at home for three years would be £650 a year—£450 for extra help in the house and £200 for two three weeks' stay in the Cheadle Royal Infirmary to give his wife a rest and for him to have a check up. The total outlay during the first three years would accordingly be £1,950. He would then spend the rest of his

D life, estimated at thirteen years, in the infirmary at a cost of £1,419 per year. From this figure the judge deducted £300 a year for food and laundry which would otherwise have been incurred at home. None of these facts could be, and none indeed was, seriously attacked, for each was abundantly supported by the evidence. Thirteen years at £,1119 is, in round figures, £14,500. Accordingly, the total expenses over the next sixteen years on the basis of present fees will

E amount to £16,450. The actuary had made no calculation on the basis of these figures but only on the basis of figures which the learned judge rejected, namely, £350 a year for expenses at home and £1,500 for expenses at the infirmary. Accordingly, under this head the judge had to do the best he could without actuarial assistance. I think that having regard to present trends and common experience of constantly rising fees over the last thirteen years, the judge con-

F sidered that there was a strong probability of substantial increases in fees over the next thirteen years. Taking this factor into account and scaling down for receipt of the money now and for contingencies he awarded £14,000 under this head. In my view this figure is high—certainly higher than I should have awarded. I recognise the difficulty in all the circumstances of making any accurate estimate, but I do not think that I would have awarded more than about £10,000 in respect

G of expenses at the infirmary.

It was argued on behalf of the defendants that heads (i) and (iii) overlapped, and that the plaintiff could not recover under head (iii) as well as under head (i), or at any rate that the damages which might otherwise have been recovered under the one should be substantially reduced because of what the plaintiff had re-covered under the other. I am afraid that I have had the greatest difficulty in

H understanding this argument. Under head (ii) the plaintiff is compensated for what he loses by reason of the defendants' negligence, namely earnings. Under head (iii), he is compensated for what he has to pay out by reason of the defen-dants' negligence, namely expenses. The one thing has nothing to do with the other. If the plaintiff had had a service contract under which, work or not, he received £4,000 a year net for life, or instead of being a professional man had spent all his

I time doing public or charitable work with a private income of £4,000 a year net, it was conceded in argument that the defendants would not be excused from compensating him for the expenses to which their negligence had put him. I do not understand how the fact that they have destroyed his income, for which they must pay him compensation, can make any difference to their liability to compensate him for the expenses incurred by reason of their negligence. It is suggested that the income of £4,000 a year which he formerly earned was spent largely in entertaining, amusements and other activities which he can no longer enjoy, and that accordingly that income which is now replaced by the damages

will be exempt from those expenses and should instead be used partly to pay for   A
the expense of the infirmary. The argument really comes to this, that the defendants' negligence has saved the plaintiff from his former extravagances and
that the defendants should therefore be credited with this saving of expense before
being debited with the expense of the infirmary. Pushed to its logical conclusion,
there might in cases such as these be a credit balance in favour of the defendants.
To my mind this argument is entirely misconceived. How the plaintiff spent his   B
income before the accident or how he might, but for his injuries, have spent it
afterwards, has nothing to do with the defendants. If by their negligence the
defendants deprive a plaintiff of his income, the extent of their liability cannot
depend in any way on the frugality or liberality with which he formerly spent
it. If their negligence involves a plaintiff in an expense which he would not
otherwise have incurred, they must compensate him for it notwithstanding the   C
fact that by maiming him they may have curtailed some of his former extravagances. This much seems to me to be plain, both on principle and authority.
Shearman v. *Folland* (20). ASQUITH, L.J., in delivering the judgment of the court
said (21):

> " Strange results might certainly follow if it were possible in every case
> for the defendant to mitigate damages by proving what course of conduct   D
> the plaintiff would probably have followed, or what his expenses would
> probably have been, if the act complained of had never been committed.
> A millionaire accustomed to live at a palatial hotel, where his weekly
> expenses far exceed the charges of the nursing home to which, after being
> injured by the defendant's negligence, he is transplanted, would recover
> nothing by way of special damage. Could it really lie in the mouth of the   E
> wrongdoer in such a case to say: ' I am entitled to go scot-free. I have, by
> my negligent act, not merely inflicted no loss, but conferred a net financial
> benefit on the plaintiff by saving him from the consequences of his habitual
> extravagance '?"

I confess that I consider that instinct is an uncertain guide and should play
only a very small, if any, part in assessing financial loss. I substantially agree
with the learned judge's assessment, save that I would substitute a figure of
£10,000 for £14,000 under the third head and possibly £30,000 instead of £32,000
under the second head. This gives a total of £52,000 or perhaps £50,000 for
financial loss—undoubtedly an obstrusively high figure but not in my view any
higher than justice in the circumstances demands. The judge said that

> " if having added up the various items . . . the total is dauntingly high, I   F
> agree I ought to reconsider the matter but only to see whether I have over-
> valued any of the items, not for the purpose of compressing and bringing them
> into a smaller and more unobtrusive sum."

I entirely agree with that approach. For the purpose of computing financial loss,
it is, in my view, not only permissible but also necessary to assess the value of   G
each head of loss and to add up the sums thus ascertained in order to arrive at
the true amount of the total financial loss. I agree that in order to arrive at a true
net figure under the head " loss of earnings ", one must take into account such
expenses as may have been incurred in achieving them, but I am not satisfied
that the learned judge failed to do so. The necessity to deduct such expenses
is fundamentally different from the proposition, with which I cannot agree,
namely, that in assessing what the plaintiff may recover in respect of expenses
to which he has been put by reason of his injuries, the defendant is entitled to a
discount on the ground that by maiming him he has made it impossible for the
plaintiff to incur, and has therefore " saved " him, certain other expenses. For
my part, I am not prepared to speculate on the social purposes of awarding a
plaintiff damages for financial loss. I think that it is irrelevant. I take the, no

---

(20) [1950] 1 All E.R. 976; [1950] 2 K.B. 43.
(21) [1950] 1 All E.R. at p. 978; [1950] 2 K.B. at p. 47.

doubt, prosaic view that if a plaintiff is likely to be prevented by the defendant's negligence from earning £X a year for Y years, he is entitled to be compensated for the whole amount of that financial loss. To my mind it makes no difference whether he is a miser or a spendthrift, married or single, whether he has chosen to lead a spartan or a sybaritic existence, nor whether he has heavy financial responsibilities or none at all. In my view, it has a hollow ring for the defendant to say: " Quite true I have prevented him by my negligence from earning this sum of money. But, poor man, because of his circumstances and what I have done to him, he could never now enjoy or use all of it. If I pay him what he cannot spend, it will only accumulate as a windfall for this heirs and the estate duty office. Much better, from a social point of view, that I should keep it for myself."

Under the fourth head of damage the judge awarded £10,000 for pain and suffering and loss of amenities. It has been argued on behalf of the plaintiff (and it is, as I understand it, conceded that the point is open to him) that this award is far too low and that accordingly the damages under this head may be increased to offset any reduction which may be made in the damages awarded for financial loss. I will first of all, however, consider what should be the result of this appeal on my assessment of the financial loss, if I agreed with the figure of £10,000 for pain and suffering and loss of amenities. This would mean that my total assessment would be £62,400 or £60,400. Could the judge's assessment of £66,400 be regarded as a " wholly erroneous estimate of damage "? This time-honoured catch phrase means no more than: " Is the award so wrong that the court ought to interfere with it? ". The difference between us is only about six per cent., or, at the most, about nine per cent. It has often been assumed that an appellate court ought not to interfere if the difference is not more than ten per cent. I am not sure, however, that these questions should depend on percentages. Of course, no court, except on a point of law, would reduce an assessment of £2,000 to £1,800, still less to £1,880, but to reduce an award of £1,000,000 by £60,000 or £90,000 might be quite a different matter. In *Davies* v. *Powell Duffryn* (*No. 2*) (22), Lord Wright said:

> " The scale must go down heavily against the figure attacked if the appellate court is to interfere whether on the ground of excess or insufficiency."

On the whole, I think that £6,000 or even £4,000 is sufficiently weighty to depress the scale heavily enough, even when considering an award of £66,400. Accordingly, if I agreed with the assessment of £10,000 for pain and suffering and loss of amenities, I should be inclined to allow the appeal and reduce the total sum awarded by £6,000 or £4,000.

I cannot, however, agree with the damages awarded for pain and suffering and loss of amenities. In my view these damages are inadequate. I quite agree that in considering damages under this head, one is entitled to take into account the damages awarded for financial loss. Exactly how one should do so and to what extent is very difficult to define, and I shall not attempt to do so. Perhaps this is where instinct may play its uncertain role. Certainly, in my view, the assessment of damages should have nothing to do with the financial position or conduct of the defendant, still less with its possible impact on insurance premiums. It has recently been stressed that damages for tort are, with certain irrelevant exceptions, purely compensatory, *Rookes* v. *Barnard* (23). The sole duty of the court is to award a plaintiff that to which he is entitled, namely, fair and reasonable compensation for the loss he has suffered, irrespective of the repercussions of such an award. A plaintiff's loss cannot depend in any way on whether the defendants or their insurers have assets worth many millions or are on the verge of insolvency, nor on whether the defendant's negligence was grossly culpable or amounted merely to inadvertence. I have not lost sight of the oft-quoted citations from Brett, J.'s dissenting judgment in *Rowley* v. *London & North Western*

---

(22) [1942] 1 All E.R. 657 at pp. 664, 665; [1942] A.C. 601 at p. 617.
(23) [1964] 1 All E.R. 367 at p. 407; [1964] A.C. 1129 at p. 1221.

Ry. Co. (24), to the effect that damages should not be to the full amount of perfect compensation but must be reasonable and not exceed what, under all the circumstances, is fair compensation. Much the same was said in *Phillips* v. *London & South Western Ry. Co.* (25). I, of course, accept the dicta in those cases. They are particularly applicable in relation to damages for pain and suffering and loss of amenities. In considering their implications today, the following factors should be kept in mind. Although both the defendants were railway companies, the courts were considering the impact of awards of damages against the general body of defendants in accident cases towards the end of last century. A substantial proportion of such defendants were then uninsured. Moreover, the view was still current that damages for tort were, at any rate in part, a punishment for wrongdoing; and it would be an unjust punishment to make awards large enough to ruin men of reasonable means. Today, however, virtually all defendants in accident cases are insured. This certainly does not mean that compensation should be extravagant, but there is no reason why it should not be realistic. If the current conventional scale of compensation is somewhat too low, as I think it is, to raise it to its proper level would be no more than just to plaintiffs and would ruin no-one. It might result in some moderate increase in premium rates, which no-one would relish, but of which no-one, in my view, could justly complain. It would be monstrous to keep down premiums by depressing damages below their proper level, i.e., a level which ordinary men would regard as fair—unprejudiced by its impact on their own pockets.

I find it difficult, in relation to pecuniary loss, to appreciate the precise difference between the full amount of perfect compensation and fair and reasonable compensation. It is perhaps illustrated in the present case by the difference between the three methods suggested by the actuary of replacing the lost income and the selection of the method which is cheapest for the defendants but the least perfect for the plaintiff.

On the other hand, the full amount of perfect compensation manifestly cannot be given for pain and suffering or loss of amenities for the simple reason that, in the nature of things, there can be no perfect compensation in relation to such matters. The damages awarded under these heads are necessarily conventional. How can you measure in money the loss of an arm, let alone the catastrophic injuries which the present plaintiff has sustained? It may be and sometimes is said that for any particular injury one sum would do as well as another, and that, as long as the conventional scale of damages distinguishes consistently between the various kinds of injuries, the scale should be kept very low. I do not agree. To my mind the damages awarded should be such that the ordinary sensible man would not instinctively regard them as either mean or extravagant, but would consider them to be sensible and fair in all the circumstances. With the fall in value of money, present day awards of damages for really serious injuries tend, in my opinion, to be too low. In assessing damages for pain and suffering and loss of amenities, it is not, I agree, appropriate to separate each item, as I think one should do, in assessing damages for financial loss. If a plaintiff loses an arm and an eye and suffers injury to the brain, it would not be appropriate to assess a sum for damages in respect of each injury and then add up these sums in order to arrive at a total figure of damages for pain and suffering and loss of amenities. This method (which was not adopted by the judge in the present case) might be a guide, but it would usually produce too high a total figure. One has to regard as a whole the plaintiff's general physical and mental state resulting from the accident and give him fair compensation for that.

This court has recently stressed that there should be what is necessarily to some extent a conventional scale of damages in accident cases—(within certain limits) so much for the loss of a leg, so much for the loss of an arm, and so on (see *Ward* v. *James* (26)). This is in order that justice may be done not only between plaintiffs

---

(24) [1861-73] All E.R. Rep. at p. 830; (1873), L.R. 8 Exch. at p. 231.
(25) (1879), 4 Q.B.D. 406.   (26) [1964] 1 All E.R. 563; [1966] 1 Q.B. 273.

and defendants but also between plaintiffs and plaintiffs and between defendants and defendants. The plaintiff's economic and social position is irrelevant. The normal compensation for the loss of an arm as such is the same for a rich man as it is for a poor one. In my judgment it is only if the court were proposing to add something to the normal compensation for the loss of an arm, e.g., on the basis that it has deprived the plaintiff of the special joy that he formerly had from, say, shooting or fishing, that it would be permissible to take into account the expense of these pastimes—otherwise the fact that the injury has saved him what he formerly spent for a rod on a trout stream or a gun in a shoot is wholly immaterial. Were it not so, the most unjust and ridiculous results would follow. A man with a gun in a good shoot and a rod on a good trout stream or salmon river could easily spend £1,500 a year on these sports. On the not unreasonable assumption, if the plaintiff were fairly young, that but for the accident he would have gone on doing so for the next fifteen years, the loss of his arm would have saved him from spending £22,500—a figure very greatly in excess of any amount likely to be recovered for the loss of an arm as such, even if the somewhat inadequate sums currently awarded were raised to a more realistic level. I do not think that in such cases the defendant could argue with much prospect of success that the plaintiff should recover no damages for pain or suffering and loss of amenities in respect of his arm because by depriving him of it they had saved him a sum of money more than double that which 'he could have recovered under the conventional scale. The keen shot or fisherman would always receive the conventional sum for his loss of an arm, no less but nothing more, unless it could be shown that proper compensation for the loss of the pleasure of shooting or fishing exceeded what he would probably have had to pay for it. This might be difficult, save possibly in the case of a plaintiff who relied mainly on the hospitality of his friends for his sport.

In the present case the plaintiff, when he was fifty-six years of age, in excellent health, at the height of his powers, popular and successful, leading a full, interesting and happy life, was suddenly turned into a shambling, useless, pathetic wreck, listless, helpless, irritable, in pain and incapable of taking any interest in or enjoying anything. I do not regard £10,000 as reasonably adequate compensation for all this, even after taking fully into account the very substantial compensation which he is to receive for the financial loss which he has also suffered. In *Wise* v. *Kaye* (27), the plaintiff, who as a result of brain injury was completely unconscious and would remain so for the rest of her life, was awarded £15,000 for loss of the amenities of life in addition to substantial damages for loss of earnings. This court by a majority upheld that award. In *H. West & Son, Ltd.* v. *Shephard* (28), again as the result of brain injury, the plaintiff suffered paralysis of all her limbs. She was unable to speak; such communications as she could make were limited to the movement of eyes, face and hand; she showed her likes and dislikes in relation to food by facial expression. She may to some extent at least have appreciated the position she was in. Her expectation of life had been reduced to five years. The House of Lords by a majority upheld an award of £17,500 damages in her favour in addition to damages for financial loss. The trial judge had added £2,500 to the figure of £15,000 assessed in *Wise* v. *Kaye* (27). He made this addition to compensate the plaintiff for the chance that she might, to some slight extent, have appreciated her plight. These decisions have been criticised in certain quarters, and indeed the High Court of Australia has refused to follow them. But they still represent the law of England. The present plaintiff is obviously in a worse position that the plaintiff in *Wise* v. *Kaye* (27) who never recovered consciousness. In my judgment, he is in no better position than the plaintiff in *West* v. *Shephard* (28). He is in pain and leads a miserable existence. The judge who saw him said that he was not devoid of intelligence. There is no reason to suppose

(27) [1962] 1 All E.R. 257; [1962] 1 Q.B. 638.
(28) [1963] 2 All E.R. 625; [1964] A.C. 326.

that he has any less appreciation of his tragic circumstances than had Mrs.
Shephard. Moreover, he is likely to endure his tragedy not for five but for sixteen
years. Taking fully into account the high sums awarded as reasonable compensation for his financial loss, I would have awarded him a sum of not less than
£17,000 for the total destruction of all those amenities of life which alone are
supposed to make it worth living.

In his dissenting speech in *West* v. *Shephard* (29), LORD REID said that he would
substitute a figure in the region of £10,000 for the figure of £17,500. LORD DEVLIN
in his dissenting speech did not vouchsafe the figure to which he would have
reduced the award of £17,500. He clearly indicated (30), however, that in his
view the longer the expectation of life, the higher the award should be. In the
present case the plaintiff's expectation of life is much greater than that of
the plaintiff in *West* v. *Shephard* (31). It seems to me to follow that even if the
minority view had prevailed in *West* v. *Shephard* (31), an award in the present
case of £17,000 under heading 4 could not be regarded as other than moderate.

Although I differ to some extent from the judge on some items, in the end I
should not have reached any lower global figure than that at which he arrived. I
would accordingly dismiss the appeal.

*Appeal allowed. Damages reduced by £15,000. Leave to appeal to the House of
Lords granted.*

Solicitors: *Wm. Easton & Sons*, agents for *Percy Hughes & Roberts*, Liverpool
(for the defendants); *Weightman, Pedder & Co.*, Liverpool (for the plaintiff).

[*Reported by* F. GUTTMAN, ESQ., *Barrister-at-Law.*]

PRACTICE DIRECTION.

CHANCERY DIVISION.

*Mortgage—Possession of mortgaged property—Second mortgagee—Subsequent
encumbrancers—Enquiry of prior mortgagees before applying for possession.*

A second mortgagee who is intending to apply for an order for possession should
write to the first mortgagee asking whether he has already obtained an order
for possession himself and whether he has any observations to make on the
proposed application. A copy of the letter and any reply thereto should be
produced to the Master on the first hearing. If there are two or more prior
encumbrancers, letters on the same lines should be sent to them all.

By direction of CROSS, J.

W. F. S. HAWKINS,
Chief Master,
Feb. 20, 1968.   Chancery Division.

---

(29) [1963] 2 All E.R. at p. 630; [1964] A.C. at p. 343.
(30) [1963] 2 All E.R. at p. 638; [1964] A.C. at p. 357.
(31) [1963] 2 All E.R. 625; [1964] A.C. 326.

THE NORMAR.

Owners of Motor Vessel Normar v. British Transport Docks Board and Others.

[Probate, Divorce and Admiralty Division (Cairns, J.), December 18, 21, 1967.]

Practice—Third-party procedure—Counterclaim by third party, a defendant in the action—Third-party notice served by second defendants on third defendants claiming indemnity or contribution—Third-party notice treated as statement of claim—Defence and counterclaim by third defendants—Whether court had jurisdiction to entertain counterclaim—Counterclaim including claim for payment and set-off of alleged indebtedness for work done in relation to matters, some of which were not the subject of the plaintiffs' action—Exercise of court's discretion to strike out counterclaim or to direct separate trials—R.S.C., Ord. 15, r. 2, r. 5 (2), Ord. 16, r. 1 (3), r. 8 (3).

In an action against dock owners for damages caused to the plaintiffs' ship by the collapse of a crane at the docks, the dock owners denied negligence and alleged negligence on the part of the manufacturers of the crane or of the manufacturers' sub-contractors who erected the crane. The plaintiffs then added the manufacturers and the crane erectors as second and third defendants respectively. The manufacturers served a third party notice on the crane erectors claiming indemnity under a clause in the sub-contract for contribution under the Law Reform (Married Women and Tortfeasors) Act, 1935, s. 6. The crane erectors counterclaimed against the manufacturers (a) (by para. 5 of their counterclaim) for indemnity or contribution, and (b) (by para. 4 and para. 6 of their counterclaim) for a sum of £4,444 11s. 5d. on account of work done under the sub-contract and for set-off in respect of this sum. The sum of £4,444 11s. 5d. was in respect of the erection of sixteen cranes and not merely of the erection of the one crane that collapsed. On appeal by the manufacturers from refusal of their application to strike out the crane erectors' counterclaim, for which relief they had applied on the ground that a third party could not counterclaim, and from refusal of an order for separate trials of the issues (a) and (b) above if the counterclaim were not struck out,

Held: (i) there was jurisdiction to entertain a counterclaim made by a third party, that jurisdiction deriving from R.S.C., Ord. 16, r. 1 (3)* and, in particular, from the word "defence" therein (see p. 757, letters G and H, post).

Renton Gibbs & Co., Ltd. v. *Neville & Co.* ([1900] 2 Q.B. 181) considered.

(ii) by virtue of the present R.S.C., Ord. 15, r. 2† there was jurisdiction for a defendant claiming against a third party to counterclaim against the counterclaim made by the third party; accordingly the manufacturers could counterclaim in answer to the crane erectors' counterclaim (see p. 759, letter I, to p. 760, letter A, post).

(iii) there was discretion under R.S.C., Ord. 15, r. 5 (2)‡ to strike out the counterclaim or to order separate trials (see p. 758, letter B, post), but, as the manufacturers would be entitled, in accordance with (ii) above, to counterclaim against the crane erectors' counterclaim and thereby the area of the dispute might be enlarged (since the crane erectors' money payment claim related to sixteen cranes), such a counterclaim by the manufacturers might lead to delay in the trial of the plaintiffs' action; in the circumstances, as the plaintiffs were clearly entitled to damages from one or more of the defendants, and as there would be no advantage in directing separate trials, para. 4 and para. 6 of the crane erectors' counterclaim to the third party

---

* R.S.C., Ord. 16, r. 1 (3), is set out at p. 757, letter B, post.

† R.S.C., Ord. 15, r. 2, so far as material, is set out at p. 759, letter G, post.

‡ R.S.C., Ord. 15, r. 5 (2), is set out at p. 757, letter I, post.

notice would be struck out (see p. 760, letters B and I, and p. 762, letter B, post).

Dictum of SCRUTTON, L.J., in *Barclay's Bank* v. *Tom* ([1922] All E.R. Rep. at pp. 279, 280) applied.

Appeal allowed.

[As to third party procedure and co-defendants, see 30 HALSBURY'S LAWS (3rd Edn.) 448, para. 848; and for cases on the subject, see 50 DIGEST (Repl.) 510-511, *1834-1845*, 521. *1912-1919*.

As to counterclaims and third party notice, see 34 HALSBURY'S LAWS (3rd Edn.) 414, 415, paras. 729, 730; and for cases on the subject, see 40 DIGEST (Repl.) 453, 454, *390-394*.]

Cases referred to:

Barclay's Bank v. *Tom*, [1922] All E.R. Rep. 279; [1923] 1 K.B. 221; 92 L.J.K.B. 346; 128 L.T. 558; 50 Digest (Repl.) 511, *1839*.

Eden v. *Weardale Iron and Coal Co.*, (1884), 28 Ch.D. 333; 54 L.J.Ch. 384; 51 L.T. 726; 50 Digest (Repl.) 521, *1915*.

James v. *Page*, (1888), 85 L.T.Jo. 157; 40 Digest (Repl.) 454, *391*.

McCheane v. *Gyles*, [1902] 1 Ch. 287; 71 L.J.Ch. 183; 86 L.T. 1; *subsequent proceedings*, [1902] 1 Ch. 911; 50 Digest (Repl.) 511, *1842*.

Renton, Gibbs & Co., Ltd. v. *Neville & Co.*, [1900] 2 Q.B. 181; 69 L.J.Q.B. 514; 82 L.T. 446; 40 Digest (Repl.) 454, *392*.

Toke v. *Andrews*, (1882), 8 Q.B.D. 428; 51 L.J.Q.B. 281; 40 Digest (Repl.) 453, *390*.

Appeal.

This was an appeal by the second defendants, Morris & Butters, Ltd., against a decision of the Admiralty registrar refusing to strike out parts of a third party defence and counterclaim by the third defendants, Cozens & Sutcliffe, Ltd.

The plaintiffs were the owners of the motor vessel Normar which suffered damage on Feb. 25, 1966, when a crane collapsed on to the ship at Alexandra Dock, Hull. They sued the first defendants, British Transport Docks Board, as owners and occupiers of the dock for damages for negligence. The first defendants by their defence denied negligence and claimed that the fall of the crane was due to the negligence of the manufacturers of the crane or of the sub-contractors who had erected the crane under sub-contract with the manufacturers, or of both the manufacturers and the sub-contractors. The plaintiffs thereupon amended their writ and statement of claim to add the manufacturers as second defendants and the crane erectors as third defendants, alleging negligence against each of them. The second defendants by their defence admitted that they had manufactured the crane under contract with the first defendants and had sub-contracted the erection of it to the third defendants, but they denied negligence and alleged that the fall of the crane was due to the negligence of the first defendants (the dock owners) or of the third defendants (the erectors of the crane). The third defendants admitted by their defence that they had erected the crane in pursuance of such a sub-contract, but they denied neligence and alleged that the fall was due to the negligence of the first defendants (the dock owners) or of the second defendants (the manufacturers). After discovery in the action, the second defendants (the manufacturers) served a third party notice on the third defendants (the crane erectors) claiming indemnity under an indemnity clause in the sub-contract, alternatively, contribution under the Law Reform (Married Women and Tortfeasors) Act, 1935. An order for directions was made, ordering that the third party notice should be treated as the second defendants' (manufacturers') statement of claim, and providing for the third defendants' (crane erectors') defence thereto, for discovery and for trial of the third party claim at or immediately after the trial of the action. The third defendants' defence to the second defendants' claim against them admitted the sub-contract but denied the right to indemnity or contribution. By para. 4 of their defence the third defendants

A (crane erectors) claimed to set-off the sum counterclaimed in para. 6. By para. 5, they counterclaimed indemnity or contribution under the Act of 1935. By para. 6, they counterclaimed £4,444 11s. 5d., alleged to be due for work done under the sub-contract. The second defendants (the manufacturers) applied to the Admiralty registrar to strike out para. 4, para. 5 and para. 6 of the third defendants' (the crane erectors') defence and counterclaim. The registrar made no order on the

B application save as to costs. The second defendants (the manufacturers) appealed and asked that either all three paragraphs be struck out or else that the issues raised by para. 5 and para. 6 be tried separately from the other issues. The appeal was heard in chambers but judgment was given in open court.

    J. C. Tylor for the plaintiffs.

    R. E. Hopkins for the first defendants, the dock owners.

C   *A. P. Clarke* for the second defendants, the manufacturers.

    J. P. M. Phillips for the third defendants, the crane erectors.

Cur. adv. vult.

    Dec. 21. **CAIRNS, J.,** read the following judgment: This is an appeal from a decision of the Admiralty registrar refusing to strike out parts of a third

D party defence and counterclaim. [HIS LORDSHIPS stated the facts, and continued:] The second defendants first contend that, as a matter of law, a defendant on whom a third party notice is served by another defendant cannot counterclaim. There is no authority directly in point, but there are two decisions of the Court of Appeal dealing with the right of an ordinary third party, not a defendant in the action, to counterclaim. The first of these cases is *Eden*

E v. *Weardale Iron and Coal Co.* (1), where it was decided that a third party could not counterclaim against a plaintiff; but BOWEN, L.J., expressed uncertainty (2) whether a third party could counterclaim against the defendant who had brought him in. The second case is *Barclays Bank* v. *Tom* (3). In that case it was decided that a counterclaim would lie by the third party against the defendant who had brought him in, and I shall read a passage from the judgment of

F SCRUTTON, L.J., where he said (4):

> " The question whether a third party can counterclaim against the defendant requires careful consideration, because BOWEN, L.J., when deciding, in *Eden* v. *Weardale Iron and Coal Co.* (1), that a third party could not counterclaim against the original plaintiff, said (2): ' If the application had been for leave to the third party to counterclaim against the defendant, I should have desired to consider the question. It appears to me an open question whether the court could have given leave.' It is important to keep clearly in mind what the third-party procedure is. A plaintiff has a claim against a defendant. The defendant thinks that if he is liable, he has a claim over against a third party. With that matter between the defendant and the third party the plaintiff has clearly nothing to do, not being concerned with the question whether the defendant has a remedy against somebody else. His remedy is against the defendant. But the defendant is much interested in getting the third party bound by the result of the trial between the plaintiff and himself, for otherwise he might be at a great disadvantage if, having fought the case against the plaintiff and lost, he had then to fight the case against the third party possibly on different materials, with the risk that a different result might be arrived at. The object of the third-party procedure is therefore, in the first place, to get the third party bound by the decision given between the plaintiff and the defendant. In the next place, it is directed to getting the question between the defendant and the third party decided as soon as possible after the decision between the plaintiff

(1) (1884), 28 Ch.D. 333.   (2) (1884), 28 Ch.D. at p. 338.
(3) [1922] All E.R. Rep. 279; [1923] 1 K.B. 221.
(4) [1922] All E.R. Rep. at pp. 279, 280; [1923] 1 K.B. at pp. 223-225.

and the defendant, so that the defendant may not be in a position of having
to wait a considerable time before he establishes his right of indemnity against
the third party while all the time the plaintiff is enforcing his judgment
against the defendant. And, thirdly, it is directed to saving the extra expense
which would be involved by two independent actions. With these objects in
view the third-party order usually provides that the third party may appear
at the trial between the plaintiff and the defendant. When the third party
has so appeared, as party to the proceedings, various questions arise as to
what he can do. Can he counterclaim against the plaintiff? The answer
is ' No ', for such a counterclaim would have nothing to do with the issue
in the action to which he is admitted as a party—*Eden* v. *Weardale Iron
and Coal Co.* (5). Can he interrogate the plaintiff? The answer is ' Yes ', if
the object of the interrogatories is to show that the plaintiff's claim against
the defendant cannot be supported—*Eden* v. *Weardale Iron and Coal Co.* (5).
I remember in one case in which I was counsel the third party was, on the
same principle, allowed to raise a defence on behalf of the defendant which
the defendant would not raise on his own behalf. When it has been ascertained that the defendant is liable to the plaintiff the next step is to try, in
such manner as the judge may direct, the question between the defendant and
third party. The defendant says, ' You owe me so much by way of contribution or indemnity '. How may the third party defend himself? Of course
he may deny that he is under any such liability at all. But he may admit
his liability and say that he has a cross-claim against the defendant which
prevents any effective judgment being given against him. He may say, ' Your
right to contribution will result in £100 being due from me to you, but I have
a set-off in another matter in respect of which £100 will be due from you to
me '. Or, again, he may, while admitting his liability to contribution, say
that he has a claim against the defendant which cannot be made the subject
of a set-off but will result in the defendant having to pay him so many pounds.
It seems to me that the proper view to take on this part of the third-party
procedure is that taken by COZENS-HARDY, L.J., in *McCheane* v. *Gyles* (6)—
namely, that 'The Act, therefore, treats the third party procedure as
analogous to a cause instituted by the defendant as plaintiff against the
third party ', with the result that the defendant may defend himself in any
way in which any defendant in an action at the suit of a plaintiff may
defend himself, among which modes of defence is included the making of a
counterclaim. For these reasons it appears to me that GREER, J., came to a
right decision, and that the appeal must be dismissed."

The other member of the court was EVE, J. He gave a short judgment, saying (7):

" I agree. I respectfully agree with the view expressed in *McCheane* v.
Gyles (8) that the Judicature Act, by which the third-party procedure was
created, treats that procedure ' as analogous to a cause instituted by the
defendant as plaintiff against the third party '. It is clear that the service
of the third-party notice does not make the person on whom it is served a
defendant to the action, but it seems to me that it does make him a defendant
quoad the person serving the notice. That seems to be the reasonable view
to take, because the main object of the procedure was to obviate the need
for two actions. In the main action the rights of the plaintiff and the defendant are determined without reference to the defendant's claims over against
the third party, but when those rights have been ascertained it is then open to
the person brought in by the third-party notice to have all relevant disputes
determined between him and the person serving the notice. I think that a

(5) (1884), 28 Ch.D. 333.
(6) [1902] 1 Ch. 287 at p. 301.
(7) [1922] All E.R. Rep. at pp. 280, 281; [1923] 1 K.B. at pp. 225, 226.
(8) [1902] 1 Ch. 287.

A   third party being in the position of a defendant in relation to the person who served the notice, is entitled to counterclaim against him."

On behalf of the second defendants it was contended that this ruling has no application where the third-party is already a defendant. No reason was suggested why the law should so distinguish. It is said to follow from the wording of R.S.C., Ord. 16, r. 8 (3), as contrasted with r. 1 (3) of the same order. Rule 1 (3) is the

B   rule which provides for the service of a third-party notice on a person who is not already a party to the action, and provides:

"Where a third party notice is served on the person against whom it is issued, he shall as from the time of service be a party to the action (in this order referred to as a third party) with the same rights in respect of his

C   defence against any claim made against him in the notice and otherwise as if he had been duly sued in the ordinary way by the defendant by whom the notice is issued."

Rule 8 is the rule which enables a similar notice to be served on a person who is already a party to the proceedings, and r. 8 (3) provides as follows, and I shall omit the references to " appearances " which form part of the sub-rule. The relevant

D   part is this:

". . . the same procedure shall be adopted for the determination between the defendant by whom, and the person on whom, such a notice is served of the claim, question or issue stated in the notice as would be appropriate under this order if the person served with the notice were a third party . . ."

E   What is pointed out on behalf of the second defendants is that, whereas under r. 1 (3) there are conferred on the third party the same rights "in respect of his defence . . . and otherwise " as if he had been sued in the ordinary way, all that is provided by r. 8 (3) is the procedure for determination of " the question or issue stated in the notice "—and it is suggested that the latter sub-rule does not give the person on whom the third-party notice is served all the rights which an ordinary defendant would have, including the right of counterclaim, but gives strictly

F   only rights of defence in respect of the particular claim made on him. It is argued that the right to counterclaim in the case of the ordinary third party is derived from the words " and otherwise " in the sub-rule relating to him. I cannot believe that it was intended by the use of those words " and otherwise " to make a wholly meaningless difference between the two kinds of third party. In my view, the right to counterclaim does not arise under the word " otherwise " in r. 1 (3),

G   but under the word " defence ". It will be clear from the passage that I read from the judgment of Scrutton, L.J., in the *Barclays Bank* case (9) that he based his decision on the view that the counterclaim was a manner of defending the claim made against the third party.

For these reasons, I hold that there is jurisdiction to entertain the counterclaim.

Counsel for the second defendants goes on to say that, in the event of my

H   holding that there is jurisdiction in the court to entertain a counterclaim, nevertheless there is clearly jurisdiction to strike out the counterclaim if it would be convenient to do so, and reliance is placed here on R.S.C., Ord. 15, r. 5 (2), which provides that

"If it appears on the application of any party against whom a counter-

I   claim is made that the subject-matter of the counterclaim ought for any reason to be disposed of by a separate action, the court may order the counterclaim to be struck out or may order it to be tried separately or make such other order as may be expedient."

Counsel for the second defendants invites me to say that, under that rule, there is a discretion to strike out the counterclaim, or to order separate trials, and I ought to exercise my discretion in one or other of those ways in relation to para.

(9) [1922] All E.R. Rep. at pp. 279, 280; [1923] 1 K.B. at pp. 223-225.

4 and para. 6, but not para. 5, of the counterclaim. Counsel for the second defen- **A**
dants concedes that, once it is held that there is jurisdiction for the third defendants to counterclaim against the second defendants, it is convenient that the issue
raised by their para. 5 should be tried along with the other issues in this case. But
in relation to the claim for the £4,444 odd, it is contended that it would be inconvenient and unjust that that should be allowed to stand and be tried along
with or immediately after the main action. I am satisfied there is a discretion **B**
in the court in the matter under the rule that I have just read, and, therefore, the
question is, how should my discretion be exercised?

The £4,444 odd is the balance of account not merely for one crane which was
involved in this accident, but for sixteen cranes which were erected by the third
defendants under their contract with the second defendants. There is, on the
face of it, no connexion between this claim and the issues raised in the action or by **C**
the third-party notice, and, consequently, it is not, to use EVE, J.'s language (10),
a " relevant " counterclaim. The third defendants say, however, that the only
possible answer that they know of for recovering this money is by way of a cross-
claim for defective workmanship and that this forms a link with the action.
This raises the question whether, if the third defendants' counterclaim is allowed
to stand, the second defendants can counterclaim against them for damages. If **D**
not, it would clearly be inequitable that the present counterclaim should be
allowed to stand. It is clear that, when a defendant counterclaims against a
plaintiff, there is a right for the plaintiff to counterclaim against the defendant's
counterclaim. In this connexion, it is convenient to look first at a case which was
decided under the old Rules of the Supreme Court, namely, *Renton Gibbs & Co.,
Ltd.* v. *Neville & Co.* (11). In that case, a counterclaim against a counterclaim was **E**
allowed. The leading judgment was given by COLLINS, L.J., who said (12):

" It has been argued that a counterclaim cannot be set up by a plaintiff
in his reply, and that the rules do not contemplate such a case. In support
of that view reference is made to *James* v. *Page* (13), a case only noticed
in the Law Times. An incidental observation on that case is that what was
there set up was a counter-claim properly so called—a counterclaim used **F**
not as a shield but as a sword. It is contended on behalf of the defendants
that the plaintiffs must submit to have their counterclaim struck out, and that
their proper course is to introduce the subject-matter of their counterclaim
into the statement of claim as an alternative original cause of action. It is
clear that it would be inequitable to allow the defendants to have the benefit
of their counterclaim free altogether from the matters raised in the reply. **G**
The question is whether the rules are so framed as to necessitate the putting
of the parties to the unnecessary expense of beginning the pleadings de novo.
What would be the result if they had to do this? The plaintiffs do not want to
rely on the contract upon which the defendants base their counterclaim,
and indeed they deny that it is binding on them. If they are bound to deal
with the contract in their statement of claim, they would be embarrassed by **H**
having to set up a cause of action, whose existence they deny, inconsistent
with and hampering their real cause of action. In that state of circumstances
it would be an obvious injustice to the plaintiffs to oblige them to introduce
this question under the contract into the statement of claim by an amendment. The natural place for it is in the reply in which it is now found. In this
way the plaintiffs, in dealing with the counterclaim under the contract, can **I**
deny their liability on the ground that the contract is not binding on them,
and can add that, if they are liable, then and only then do they claim to
shield themselves from the result of that liability by claiming unliquidated
damages from the defendants arising out of an alleged breach of the contract
by them. I do not think that we are prevented from allowing the plaintiffs so

(10) [1922] All E.R. Rep. at p. 281; [1923] 1 K.B. at p. 225.
(11) [1900] 2 Q.B. 181.   (12) [1900] 2 Q.B. at pp. 185-187.
              (13) (1888), 85 L.T.Jo. 157.

A   to shape their case. *Toke* v. *Andrews* (14) establishes a principle which abundantly justifies us in affirming the decision of the learned judge. In that case the action was brought for rent in arrear. Before delivery of a statement of defence the tenancy was determined, and thereupon a claim arose to the defendant as outgoing tenant, and another quarter's rent became due to the plaintiff. In answer to the claim in the action the defendant set up a counter-

B   claim on an outgoing valuation to a larger amount than the rent claimed. To that counterclaim the plaintiff in his reply set up a counterclaim for the further quarter's rent accrued since the action commenced. There was no machinery in that case any more than there is in this for effecting that under the rules; but FIELD, J., and HUDDLESTON, B., held that it would be an injustice to the plaintiff if he were obliged to submit to the counterclaim

C   overtopping the amount claimed in his statement of claim. It was held that, looking at the wide language of sub-s. (3), s. 24, of the Judicature Act, 1873, and sub-s. (7) of the same section, it was impossible to say that a matter upon which, if well founded, the plaintiff was clearly entitled to relief as against the defendant's counterclaim was not within the words and the spirit of the enactment, or to hold that such a matter was not properly

D   brought forward at the only stage and in the only manner in which it could be raised. That is practically the state of affairs in the case before us, because it would be unjust to the plaintiffs to make them set up as a claim that which they only want as a defence and a shield to the counterclaim. In my opinion the order of PHILLIMORE, J., was right, and the appeal must be dismissed;"

E   and ROMER, L.J. (15) gave judgment to the same effect. So at that time it is clear that a counterclaim against a counterclaim could be allowed, but, on the basis as indicated by COLLINS, L.J., that it was permissible as a shield rather than as a sword, that is to say, that it could be used only to such extent as might be necessary to defeat the counterclaim of the defendant, but not by way of claiming something against the defendant over and above the amount for which he was counterclaiming.

F   It would, however, appear that this limitation has now disappeared in relation, at any rate, to a counterclaim and cross-counterclaim as between plaintiff and defendant. This emerges from R.S.C., Ord. 15, r. 2, which provides:

" (1) Subject to r. 5 (2), a defendant in any action who alleges that he has any claim or is entitled to any relief or remedy against a plaintiff in the

G   action in respect of any matter (whenever and however arising) may, instead of bringing a separate action, make a counterclaim in respect of that matter; and where he does so he must add the counterclaim to his defence.

" (2) Rule 1 shall apply in relation to a counterclaim as if the counterclaim were a separate action and as if the person making the counterclaim were the plaintiff and the person against whom it is made a defendant."

H   So the effect of that is clearly to give an express right to a plaintiff to counterclaim against a counterclaim, and a note in THE SUPREME COURT PRACTICE 1967, p. 145, with the side note " 15/2/5 ", interprets the rule in that way, because it reads:

" Counterclaim to a counterclaim. Paragraph (2), supra, adopts and prob-ably extends the previous law, and enables the plaintiff to raise a counterclaim to the counterclaim raised by the defendant against him, even though the

I   plaintiff's counterclaim may be more than a mere protection against the defendant's counterclaim . . ."

and then it mentions a separate point. Does this apply to third party proceedings of the type with which I am concerned? I think that it does. In my view, the effect of R.S.C., Ord. 16, r. 8 (3), which I have already read, is to throw one back to look at r. 1 (3) of the same order, and that, in turn, throws one back to R.S.C., Ord. 15, r. 2, and, therefore, in my view, the second defendants would be

---

(14) (1882), 8 Q.B.D. 428.   (15) [1900] 2 Q.B. at p. 187.

entitled to counterclaim against the third defendants' counterclaim, and to **A**
counterclaim not merely so much as was necessary to defeat the third defendants' counterclaim, but to counterclaim the whole of their damages. That is
a view about which, I may say, I have had some doubt. I was very much inclined
at one stage to the contrary opinion, but, in the end, I have reached the
conclusion that that is the true view of the law.

I must, therefore, envisage that, if the present counterclaim is allowed to stand, **B**
there will be a counterclaim against it by the second defendants which has some
connexion with the original action. However, the area of dispute between the
second and third defendants would be greatly enlarged, expensive discovery ranging over the whole of the business between those two parties relating to all the
sixteen cranes would be needed, and inevitably there would be delay, and it may
well be substantial delay, in bringing the action to trial. This particularly affects **C**
the plaintiffs, who support this appeal. They point out that it is nearly two years
since the accident in which their ship was damaged. They issued their writ
promptly, they have proceeded with their steps in the action with reasonable
expedition, discovery is nearly complete, and they will shortly be asking for a
date for the action to be tried. They are clearly entitled to damages against
somebody, and why should they suffer delay while matters which have no **D**
connexion with that claim are investigated? I think that this is an important
objection to allowing the counterclaim to stand. Other inconveniences were
suggested which made less impression on me. One was that the length of the
hearing would be much increased if the counterclaim were allowed to stand. This
could, perhaps, be avoided if the third party issues were tried immediately after
the trial of the action instead of along with it, a course which would be in accord- **E**
ance with the existing order for directions. Another point made is that the second
defendants' solicitors are instructed by insurers under a policy which covers their
liability to the plaintiffs, but not any liability to the third defendants. I do not
attach much importance to this. It is a situation which arises whenever a defendant is insured in respect of a plaintiff's claim but has a counterclaim in which
the insurers are not interested. A point made by counsel on behalf of the first **F**
defendants was that there are other claims, or possible claims, between these
various parties. If the third defendants are allowed to counterclaim against the
second defendants for the balance of their account, and if the second defendants
can then counterclaim against the third defendants for damages for negligent
performance of the whole contract, what of the first defendants' claim for their
damaged crane against the second and third defendants? Then, the crane driver **G**
was injured and may sue the first defendants as his employers. Ought they to be
allowed to make a claim over in these proceedings against the second and third
defendants? Further enlargement of the scope of the proceedings in these various
ways is clearly undesirable.

However, I think that the present issue should be decided without speculating
as to what course other defendants might take hereafter. It does seem to me, for **H**
the reasons which I have indicated, that the prospect of delay, with its inconvenience to the plaintiffs, and the prospect of making these proceedings very complicated, are good reasons for removing para. 4 and para. 6 of this defence and
counterclaim unless there is some really good reason why they should be allowed
to stand. I cannot see that there would be any injustice or inconvenience to the
third defendants in removing this part of their present counterclaim. Their claim
can perfectly well be tried in a separate action, and I look at what was said by
SCRUTTON, L.J., in the *Barclays Bank* case (16) about the objects of third party
procedure, which seem to me to be equally applicable to the case of a counterclaim
arising in third party proceedings, and he mentioned three objects. The first of
them was to get the third party bound by the decision between the plaintiff
and the defendant. That does not arise here. All these defendants are already

---

(16) [1922] All E.R. Rep. at pp. 279, 280; [1923] 1 K.B. at pp. 223-225.

A parties to the plaintiffs' suit, and, on the basis of the existing pleadings, including the third-party notice and para. 5 of the third defendants' counterclaim, the issues will be decided in a way which will be binding on all those concerned. The next object referred to by SCRUTTON, L.J., was to get the question between the defendant and the third party decided as soon as possible after the decision between the plaintiff and the defendant so that the defendant may not be in a position

B of having to wait a considerable time before he establishes his right to indemnity. That is a point which arises only when it is a question of indemnity or, of course, of contribution, and that is already covered by the third party notice itself and the counterclaim in para. 5. Thirdly, says SCRUTTON, L.J., there is the question of saving extra expense which would be involved by two independent actions. It seems to me highly improbable that any great expense would be caused by

C separate actions here. There will be the trivial expense of issuing a fresh writ, but I should have thought that, if anything, expense will be saved by having a comparatively simple form of action running alongside, or subsequent to, the existing action rather than complicating the existing action with the addition of this part of the counterclaim. The only conceivable injustice which I can see that could arise in relation to the third defendants would be if judgment were given

D against them in favour of the second defendants for contribution and if that judgment were enforced before the third defendants had had an opportunity of having tried their claim for balance of account. That matter can easily be dealt with by means of a stay of execution if it does happen that the second defendants get judgment against them for some contribution, and I have no doubt that any court would grant such a stay if informed that the action on the balance of

E account was pending.

The third defendants contend that a good reason for allowing the counterclaim to stand is that there is one main question in these proceedings, namely, whose fault was it that certain defects in the crane which caused the accident were there and were allowed to continue to be there? They say that, once this question is determined, there will be no real dispute about anything else except the quantum

F of damages. That may or may not be so. I do not yet know whether the second defendants accept the third defendants' claim for balance of account, subject to the counterclaim, and I do not know whether, if it is once established who was responsible for the defects in this particular crane, this will determine whether the third defendants were guilty of defective workmanship in regard to the other cranes. Counsel for the third defendants says: " Let the counterclaim stand. Let

G the second defendants plead to it and then at that stage, or after discovery, let somebody apply under R.S.C., Ord. 15, r. 5 (2), if necessary for a separate trial." I do not accede to this proposal for several reasons. First, if I am wrong in my view that the second defendants can counterclaim their damages in full against the third defendants, then it would follow that it would be wrong for the third defendants' counterclaim to stand. It would be most unfortunate if I allowed it to

H stand and at a later stage some other court were to hold the second defendants' right to counterclaim was limited to using it as a shield against the third defendants' claim for balance of account.

Next, if the question enunciated by counsel for the third defendants is really the only question of substance in this litigation, it will be determined as between the second and third defendants on the existing pleadings; it will then be res

I judicata and there will be no danger of two courts coming to different conclusions on the same issue. Next, I cannot see any practical disadvantage to the third defendants in proceeding by separate action. They can issue their writ tomorrow with their claim specially endorsed on it, and, if they serve it at once, the second defendants' time for defence will expire almost as soon as if I gave them twenty-one days from today. I cannot accept that proceedings by way of counterclaim would produce any acceleration of the hearing of the issue raised by them; and delay in bringing on the plaintiffs' action for trial would probably be caused if it was left uncertain today whether the wider issues were to be

tried along with or immediately after it, or were at some later stage to be given A
a separate trial or struck out. Finally, again because of the doubt which remains
in my mind about the scope of a counterclaim on a counterclaim, and because
I see little or no advantage in directing separate trials over striking out the
paragraphs in question, I think that the better course is to strike them out.

I, therefore, allow the appeal and direct that para. 4 and para. 6 of the third
defendants' counterclaim to the second defendants' third party notice be struck B
out.

Appeal allowed.

Solicitors: *Bentleys, Stokes & Lowless* (for the plaintiffs); *John Rigby, British
Transport Docks Board* (for the first defendants); *Clyde & Co.* (for the second
defendants); *Beddington, Hughes & Hobart* (for the third defendants).

C

[*Reported by* N. P. METCALFE, ESQ., *Barrister-at-Law.*]

PRACTICE DIRECTION.

D

CHANCERY DIVISION.

*Adoption—Practice—Directions—Production of records and giving of evidence by
adoption society or local authority—Contested applications—Adoption
Agencies Regulations, 1959 (S.I. 1959 No. 639), reg. 7, as amended by
Adoption Agencies Regulations 1965 (S.I. 1965 No. 2054).*

In contested proceedings under (a) Adoption Act, 1958, (b) Law Reform E
(Miscellaneous Provisions) Act, 1949 and (c) Guardianship of Infants Acts, 1886
and 1925, any adoption society or department of a local authority which has
been concerned with the placing for adoption of the infant or with its care or
supervision may be faced with a request by a party to the proceedings to produce
its records or give evidence.   So far as applications under the Adoption Act,
1958, are concerned, reg. 7 of the Adoption Agencies Regulations, 1959 (1) F
provides that information obtained by any member, officer or representative of a
registered adoption society or local authority shall be treated as confidential and
shall not be disclosed except for the purpose of proceedings under the Adoption
Act, 1958, or for the proper execution of his duty (2).   Regulation 7 of the
Adoption Agencies Regulations, 1959, does not extend to applications for wardship or guardianship of infants, but notwithstanding that, in such applications G
societies and local authorities may be in possession of information which they
would normally consider should be treated as confidential.

In any such case a society or authority which is a party to proceedings may
(in default of agreement between all the parties) apply in the proceedings to the
court for directions as to what records and information should be made available
to the court.   Where it is not a party it may require the person seeking pro- H
duction to make application on its behalf.   If the court is of opinion that disclosure of records or information to the parties would be harmful to the infant
concerned, then directions may be given for such records or information to be
made available to the court in the form of a confidential report.

The practice in adoption cases with regard to the provision of information to
the Official Solicitor as guardian ad litem for the purpose of his report is unaffected.

By direction of CROSS, J.

W. F. S. HAWKINS,
Feb. 8, 1968.   Chief Master, Chancery Division.

---

(1) See 11 HALSBURY'S STATUTORY INSTRUMENTS (First Re-Issue) 210.
(2) Amended by reg. 1 of the Adoption Agencies Regulations 1965.

R. *v.* METROPOLITAN POLICE COMMISSIONER,
Ex parte BLACKBURN.

[COURT OF APPEAL, CIVIL DIVISION (Lord Denning, M.R., Salmon and Edmund Davies, L.JJ.), January 24, 25, 26, 29, 1968.]

Mandamus—Chief officer of police—Enforcement of law—Gaming—Unlawful gaming in clubs—Policy decision reversed—Whether mandamus would lie to Commissioner of Police of the Metropolis—Whether applicant had sufficient interest to maintain proceedings for mandamus—Whether criminal cause or matter so as to exclude appeal to Court of Appeal—Supreme Court of Judicature (Consolidation) Act, 1925 (15 & 16 Geo. 5 c. 49), s. 31 (1) (a).

Under s. 32 of the Betting, Gaming and Lotteries Act 1963 gaming where the chances were not equally favourable to all players was unlawful. Various devices for avoiding the application of the statute law were tried and difficulties of interpretation of the enactment arose; in March, 1967, one device was upheld by the divisional court* but was overruled by a decision† in the House of Lords in December, 1967. In April, 1966, a confidential instruction‡ was issued to senior officers of the Metropolitan police. Underlying this instruction was a policy decision not to take proceedings against clubs for breach of the gaming laws unless there were complaints of cheating or they had become the haunts of criminals. The applicant, being concerned at gaming in London clubs, had an interview with a representative of the commissioner, at which the applicant was given to understand that action in regard to gaming clubs would be taken. Nothing apparently having been done, the applicant wrote to the commissioner in March, 1967, asking him to assist in prosecuting several London clubs. On Dec. 30, 1967, following the decision of the House of Lords previously mentioned, the commissioner issued a statement that it was the intention of the Metropolitan police to enforce the law as it had been interpreted. On appeal in proceedings by the applicant for mandamus directed to the commissioner for three heads of relief, the applicant withdrew two and pursued only his appeal in respect of the third, viz., to reverse the policy decision embodied in the confidential instruction; in the course of the hearing the commissioner gave an undertaking that the confidential instruction would be revoked.

Held: (i) it was the duty of the commissioner, as also of chief constables, to enforce the law, and, though chief officers of police had discretions (e.g., whether to prosecute in a particular case, or over administrative matters), yet the court would interfere in respect of a policy decision amounting to a failure of duty to enforce the law of the land; the present instance was one in which the court would have interfered in appropriate proceedings but for the fact that the applicant had obtained, by reason of the undertaking given to the court, the substance of the relief that he sought (see p. 769, letters E and H, p. 770, letter G, p. 771, letters B and C, p. 774, letter H, p. 776, letter C, and p. 777, letters D and H, post).

(ii) the appeal, after the withdrawal of the two heads of relief, was not in a criminal cause or matter within s. 31 (1) (a) of the Supreme Court of Judicature (Consolidation) Act, 1925, with the consequence that appeal lay to the Court of Appeal (see p. 768, letter E, p. 774, letter I, p. 775, letter A, and p. 776, letters F and I, post).

(iii) the fact that a private prosecutor could have started prosecutions would not have disentitled the applicant to an order of mandamus on the ground that there was available to him as equally effective and convenient remedy (see p. 774, letter I, and p. 777, letter G, post); but (per LORD DENNING, M.R., and SALMON, L.J.) it was questionable whether the applicant

---

* *Kursaal Casino, Ltd.* v. *Crickitt (No. 2)*, [1967] 3 All E.R. 360.
† *Crickitt* v. *Kursaal Casino, Ltd. (No. 2)*, ante p. 139.
‡ The terms of the instruction are at p. 768, letter H. post.

had been so affected by the policy decision as to give him an interest enabling   **A**
him to maintain proceedings for a prerogative order of mandamus (see
p. 770, letter C, and p. 775, letter A, post; cf. p. 777, letter D, post).

Quaere whether the decision in *Mills* v. *MacKinnon* ([1964] 1 All E.R. 155)
was correct (see p. 767, letter A, and p. 775, letter B, post).

Per LORD DENNING, M.R.: the Commissioner of Police of the Metropolis,
like every constable in the land, is independent of the executive; his legal   **B**
status is that he is a justice of the peace as well as a constable; the machinery
by which the duty of a chief officer of the police to enforce the law can itself
be enforced is either by action at the suit of the Attorney-General, or by
prerogative order of mandamus (see p. 769, letters D and I, and p. 770,
letter B, post).

Appeal dismissed.   **C**

[**Editorial Note.** This decision is of general importance in regard to the
duty, discretion and responsibility to the public, of chief officers of police in
relation to enforcement of law. In 1958 the view of the government was stated
in a debate on provincial police forces, in the House of Lords to be that " . . .
no police authority or anyone else has any authority to interfere in relation to
the enforcement of the law by the police . . . full responsibility for enforcement   **D**
is a matter which is reserved entirely to the chief officer of police; in the exercise
of this responsibility he is answerable to the law alone and not to any police
authority; that is the position both in the counties and in the boroughs " (see
HANSARD, Vol. 213, col. 47, Dec. 8, 1958, and compare the observations at p. 769,
letters D to I, post). Perhaps it may fairly be said that the discretion of chief
officers of police over prosecution and enforcement of the statutory criminal   **E**
law must be so exercised as to give effect to the true intention of Parliament
appearing in, and from the circumstances of, the relevant statutes.

As to mandamus against public officers to enforce statutory duties, see 11
HALSBURY'S LAWS (3rd Edn.) 91-93, para. 172; and for cases on the subject,
see 16 DIGEST (Repl.) 358-360, *1351-1370*.

As to the Commissioner of Police of the Metropolis, see 30 HALSBURY'S LAWS   **F**
(3rd Edn.) 63, 64, para. 102.

As to lawful and unlawful gaming see SUPPLEMENT to 18 HALSBURY'S LAWS
(3rd Edn.) title, GAMING AND WAGERING, para. 369A, 2; and for cases on the
subject, see DIGEST (Cont. Vol. B) 317-319.

For the Supreme Court of Judicature (Consolidation) Act, 1925 s. 31 see
5 HALSBURY'S STATUTES (2nd Edn.) 357.]   **G**

Cases referred to:

Allan (J. M.) (Merchandising), Ltd. v. *Cloke*, [1963] 2 All E.R. 258; [1963]
    2 Q.B. 340; [1963] 2 W.L.R. 899; Digest (Cont. Vol. A) 621, *2916*.

Amand v. *Secretary of State for Home Affairs*, [1942] 2 All E.R. 381; sub nom.
    Amand v. *Home Secretary & Minister of Defence of Royal Netherlands*   **H**
    Govt., [1943] A.C. 147; sub nom. *R.* v. *Secretary of State for Home
    Affairs & Minister of Defence of the Royal Netherlands Govt., Ex. p.
    Amand*, 111 L.J.K.B. 657; 167 L.T. 177; 16 Digest (Repl.) 308, *843*.

A.-G. for New South Wales v. *Perpetual Trustee Co.*, *(Ltd.)*, [1955] 1 All E.R.
    846; [1955] A.C. 457; [1955] 2 W.L.R. 707; 119 J.P. 312; 34 Digest
    (Repl.) 224, *1631*.

Casino Club (Bolton), Ltd. v. *Parr*, (1966), 64 L.G.R. 155; Digest (Cont. Vol.
    B) 318, *287c*.

Fisher v. *Oldham Corpn.*, [1930] All E.R. Rep. 96; [1930] 2 K.B. 364; 90
    L.J.K.B. 569; 143 L.T. 281; 94 J.P. 132; 38 Digest (Repl.) 45, *231*.

Jenks v. *Turpin*, (1884), 13 Q.B.D. 505; 53 L.J.M.C. 161; 50 L.T. 808; 49
    J.P. 20; 125 Digest (Repl.) 448, *292*.

Kelland v. *Raymond*, [1964] 1 All E.R. 564; [1964] 2 Q.B. 108; [1964] 2
    W.L.R. 662; 128 J.P. 254; Digest (Cont. Vol. B) 319, *291d*.

A   *Kursaal Casino, Ltd.* v. *Crickitt* (*No. 1*), [1966] 2 All E.R. 639; [1966] 1 W.L.R.
      960; 130 J.P. 301; Digest (Cont. Vol. B), 318, *287d.*

   Kursaal Casino, Ltd. v. *Crickitt* (*No. 2*), [1967] 3 All E.R. 360; [1967] 1 W.L.R.
      1237; *revsd.* H.L., sub nom. *Crickitt* v. *Kursaal Casino, Ltd.* (*No. 2*),
      ante p. 139; [1968] 1 W.L.R. 513.

   Mills v. *Mackinnon,* [1964] 1 All E.R. 155; [1964] 2 Q.B. 96; [1964] 2 W.L.R.
B   363; 128 J.P. 185; Digest (Cont. Vol. B) 318, *291c.*

   Provincial Cinematograph Theatres, Ltd. v. *Newcastle-upon-Tyne Profiteering
      Committee,* (1921), 27 Cox, C.C. 63; 90 L.J.K.B. 1064; 125 L.T. 651;
      85 J.P. 211; 14 Digest (Repl.) 609, *6032.*

   Quinn v. *MacKinnon,* [1963] 1 All E.R. 570; [1963] 1 Q.B. 874; [1963] 2
      W.L.R. 391; 127 J.P. 222; Digest (Cont. Vol. A) 621, *291a.*

C   *R.* v. *Governor of Brixton Prison, Ex p. Savarkar,* [1908-10] All E.R. Rep. 603;
     [1910] 2 K.B. 1056; 80 L.J.K.B. 57; 103 L.T. 473; 24 Digest (Repl.)
     1014, *174.*

   Woodhall, Ex p., (1888), 28 Q.B.D. 832; 57 L.J.M.C. 71; 59 L.T. 841; 52
     J.P. 581; 16 Digest (Repl.) 307, *839.*

Appeal.

D   This was an appeal by the applicant, Albert Raymond Blackburn, from a
decision of the Divisional Court of the Queen's Bench Division dated July 11, 1967,
dismissing his motion for an order of mandamus directed to the Commissioner
of Police of the Metropolis, requiring him (i) to assist the applicant and such other
persons as might have good grounds for requesting his assistance in the prosecution of gaming clubs in the metropolitan police area which contravened the
E   provisions of the Betting, Gaming and Lotteries Act 1963; (ii) in particular to
assist the applicant in respect of the complaint lodged by him with the commissioner on Mar. 21, 1967, concerning the Golden Nugget Club, Piccadilly, and
(iii) to reverse or procure the reversal of a policy decision taken by him or his
superiors that the time of police officers would not be spent on enforcing the
provisions of the Betting, Gaming and Lotteries Act 1963. The commissioner
F   served a respondent's notice that the decision should be affirmed on the following
further grounds: (i) that as a matter of law an order of mandamus will not issue
against a chief officer of police in respect of any of the matters set out in the
applicant's motion and statement because (a) the respondent has no legal duty to
the applicant in regard to any of those matters, and (b) each of the said matters is
a matter lying only within the discretion of the respondent; (ii) that the order
G   sought by the applicant would amount either directly or indirectly to an order to
prosecute certain persons both specified or unspecified, but that as a matter of
law an order of mandamus would not issue for such purposes, and (iii) that there
were alternative remedies available to the applicant in that he might himself
(a) lay informations or (b) apply for voluntary bills of indictment.

H   The applicant appeared in person.
M. D. L. Worsley for the commissioner of Police of the Metropolis.

                                    Cur. adv. vult.
Jan. 29. The following judgments were read.

    LORD DENNING, M.R.: The applicant, Mr. Blackburn moves for a man-
damus against the Commissioner of Police of the Metropolis. He says that
I   it was the commissioner's duty to enforce the law against gaming houses: and
that he has not done it. The applicant seeks an order to compel the commissioner to do it. This motion, thus made, raises questions of constitutional
significance. I will deal with them separately.

1. The law as to gaming houses.

    The common law of England has always condemned gaming houses. This is
not because gambling is wicked in itself, but because of the evils attendant on it.
Hawkins in his Pleas of the Crown (Book I, Ch. 75, sect. 6) writes that:

" All common gaming houses are nuisances in the eye of the law; not only **A**
because they are great temptations to idleness, but because they are apt
to draw together great numbers of disorderly persons, which cannot but be
very inconvenient to the neighbourhood."

The statute law of England has likewise condemned gaming houses. As early as
1541 in the time of Henry VIII Parliament enacted (1) that no person should
for his gain keep a gaming house. The reason then was because gambling disturbed **B**
the military training. It distracted the young men from practising archery
which was needed for the defence of the country. Several statutes have been
passed since. All of them condemned gaming houses because of the mischiefs
attendant on them. When roulette was first introduced over two hundred years
ago, Parliament tried to stop it. A statute of 1744 (2) recited that the " per-
nicious " game called roulette or roly-poly was practised. It prohibited any **C**
person from keeping any house for playing it.

All these statutes, however, proved of no avail to prevent the mischief.
BLACKSTONE said that the legislature had been careful to pass laws to prevent
" this destructive vice ", but these laws had failed to achieve their object. The
reason for the failure was because the gamblers were too quick-witted for the law
to catch them. He said that: **D**

" The invention of sharpers being swifter than the punishment of the
law which only hunts them from one device to another . . ."

See his COMMENTARIES, Book IV, Ch. 13, p. 173. So much so that by the beginning
of the nineteenth century gaming houses were a scandal. The Victorian legislation, aided by the Victorian judges in *Jenks* v. *Turpin* (3) reduced the evil but **E**
did not exterminate it.

History has repeated itself in our own time. Parliament made an attempt
in 1960 to put the law on a sound footing. It had before it the Report of the Royal
Commission* on the subject. The report drew a clear distinction between promoters
who organised gaming for their own profit (which was an evil) and those who
arranged gaming for the enjoyment of others without making a profit out of it **F**
themselves (such as gaming in a members' club which was innocent). The Royal
Commission thought that

" the main object of the criminal law should be to prevent persons being
induced to play for high stakes for the profit of the promoter."

They recommended legislation to achieve this object. The draftsmen set to work
and produced the bill which became the Betting and Gaming Act, 1960, since **G**
re-enacted in the Betting, Gaming and Lotteries Act 1963. The old common
law was abolished. The old statutes were repealed. New sections were enacted
with the intention of ensuring that promoters did not make high profits out of
gaming, either in clubs or elsewhere.

These sections have lamentably failed to achieve their object. Just as in BLACK-
STONE's time, so in ours. The casino companies have set up gaming houses and **H**
made large profits out of them. They always seem to be one device ahead of the
law. The first device they used after the Act of 1960 was to levy a toll on the stakes.
They used to promote roulette without a zero and demand sixpence for themselves
on every stake. That device was declared unlawful in *Quinn* v. *Mackinnon* (4).
Next, they claimed that they could take sixpence from every player on every spin
of the wheel. That device too was held to be unlawful by this court in *J. M. Allan* **I**
(*Merchandising*), *Ltd.* v. *Cloke* (5). Then they claimed that they could charge
every player 10s. for every twenty minutes. That too was found to be unlawful
in *Kelland* v. *Raymond* (6).

---

(1) The Unlawful Games Act, 1541.   (2) The Gaming Act, 1744.
(3) (1884), 13 Q.B.D. 505.   (4) [1963] 1 All E.R. 570; [1963] 1 Q.B. 874.
* Royal Commission on Betting, Lotteries and Gaming, 1949–51 (Cmnd. 8190).
(5) [1963] 2 All E.R. 258; [1963] 2 Q.B. 340.
(6) [1964] 1 All E.R. 564; [1964] 2 Q.B. 108.

A One of their devices at this time, however, succeeded. It was in chemin-de-fer. The promoters charged every player £5 for every "shoe" which took about thirty-five minutes. This was held to be lawful in *Mills* v. *Mackinnon* (7). I must say I doubt that decision. I should have thought that £5 for every thirty-five minutes was worse than ten shillings every twenty minutes. At any rate, it is more profitable.

B After those cases, the casino companies thought out a new device which proved to be far more profitable. They promoted roulette with a zero. This is a game in which the chances over a long period mightily favour the holder of the bank. Under this new device, the organisers so arranged things that they themselves nearly always held the bank; but they claimed it was lawful because the croupier every half hour "offered the bank" to the players. Very rarely, if ever, C was the offer accepted: for the simple reason that it may be ruinous to hold the bank for only a few spins of the wheel. It is only worth holding if you can hold it for a long time, such as a week or a month. Nevertheless the organisers claimed that this "offer of the bank" rendered the gaming lawful. They were supported, we were told, by the opinion of some lawyers in the Temple, but there were conflicting views. At any rate, this device was highly profitable. For a time it was D surprisingly successful, provided it was skilfully worked. It was not worked very skilfully in the first two cases: and the casino companies were convicted, one in Blackpool, the *Casino Club (Bolton), Ltd.* v. *Parr* (8), and the other in Southend, see *Kursaal Casino, Ltd.* v. *Crickitt (No. 1)* (9). This device was, however, worked skilfully in the third case, and the casino company was acquitted in the divisional court in *Kursaal Casino, Ltd.* v. *Crickitt (No. 2)* (10). That case has, however, E recently been overruled by the House of Lords (11). The device of "offering the bank" will no longer work.

The casino companies, however, do not seem to be unduly worried. They have not stopped their gaming. They have put on their thinking-caps and brought out another device. They do not trouble now to "offer the bank" to a player. They give a winner two kinds of chips, ordinary chips on which he collects his F winnings, and special chips which he throws back. No doubt they hope that the same will happen with this device as with the others. It will have to be tested in the courts. Meanwhile they expect to carry on with their gaming. If this is then held to be unlawful, they will try to think of another device: and so on ad infinitum: at least they may think so.

What are the consequences? They were stated with striking clarity by the
G Home Secretary, Mr. Roy Jenkins, in "The Times" of Sept. 13, 1966. He is reported as saying:

"The Betting and Gaming Act, 1960, has led to abuses, particularly in the field of gaming clubs, which were not foreseen by its promoters. This country has become a gambler's paradise, more wide open in this respect than any comparable country. This has led to a close and growing connexion between H gaming clubs and organised crime, often violent crime, in London and other big cities. The fat profits made by proprietors (often out of the play itself and quite contrary to the intention of the Gaming Act of 1960) made them sitting targets for protection rackets. In addition, gaming on credit, with gaming debts unenforceable at law, means that strong-arm methods are sometimes used to extort payment from those who have gambled beyond I their means."

The applicant says that this state of affairs is due to the failure of the police to enforce the law and seeks to compel them to do it.

2. The steps taken by the applicant:
In 1966 the applicant was concerned about the way in which the big **London**

---

(7) [1964] 1 All E.R. 155; [1964] 2 Q.B. 96. (8) (1966), 64 L.G.R. 155.
(9) [1966] 2 All E.R. 639. (10) [1967] 3 All E.R. 360.
(11) Ante p. 139.

clubs were being run. He went to see a representative of the Commissioner of **A**
Police and told him that illegal gaming was taking place in virtually all London
casinos. He was given to understand, he says, that action would be taken; but
nothing appeared to be done. On Mar. 15, 1967, the applicant wrote a letter to
the commissioner in which he again stated that illegal gaming was taking place.
He asked the commissioner to assist him in prosecuting several London clubs.
Following that letter he was seen by Mr. Bearman on behalf of the commissioner. **B**
Mr. Bearman explained to him that there were difficulties in enforcing the provisions of the Act of 1963. He added that the way in which police manpower
was used was a matter for the discretion of the commissioner; and that it was
felt that, as the gaming law stood, there were higher priorities for the deployment
of police manpower. He also stated that it would be contrary to a policy decision
for him to promote or assist in the promotion of a prosecution for breach of s. 32 **C**
of the Act of 1963.

The applicant was dissatisfied and made application to the divisional court for
a mandamus directed to the commissioner requiring three things: (i) to assist
him and others to prosecute gaming clubs; (ii) to assist him in a particular
complaint against a named club; and (iii) to reverse the policy decision. The
divisional court rejected his application. He appeals in person to this court. **D**

Counsel for the commissioner, took an objection to the jurisdiction of this
court. He argued that this was an appeal from a judgment of the High Court
" in a criminal cause or matter ", and that an appeal did not lie to the Court of
Appeal, see s. 31 (1) (a) of the Supreme Court of Judicature (Consolidation)
Act, 1925. He referred us to several cases on the subject, particularly *Provincial
Cinematograph Theatres, Ltd.* v. *Newcastle-upon-Tyne Profiteering Committee* (12) **E**
in the House of Lords. I think that there might perhaps have been something
in this objection if the applicant had persisted in his first two requests. They
might be said to be steps in a criminal matter; but the applicant withdrew
those two and confined himself to the third, i.e., requiring the commissioner to
reverse his policy decision. It seems to me that this is not a step in any " criminal
cause or matter ". The applicant can appeal, I think, to this court on the matter. **F**
So I turn to it.

3. The policy decision:

The policy decision was a confidential instruction issued to senior officers of
the metropolitan police. Mr. Bearman exhibited it in his affidavit in these proceedings. It was dated Apr. 22, 1966, and was in effect an instruction to take no
proceedings against clubs for breach of the gaming laws unless there were com- **G**
plaints of cheating or they had become haunts of criminals. The actual terms of
the instruction were as follows:

" Confidential instruction. Gaming in registered or licensed clubs. For the
time being all applications for authority for an inside observation in licensed
or registered clubs for the purpose of detecting gaming are to be submitted
to A.1 branch for my covering approval." **H**

Mr. Bearman explained in his affidavit that the reason for the instruction was
this:

"In view of the uncertainty of the law, the expense and manpower
involved in keeping gaming observations in such clubs were not justified
unless there were complaints of cheating or reason to suppose that a
particular club had become a haunt of criminals."

It appeared in evidence before us that this policy decision was made under a
misapprehension. It was thought that the first case from Southend (13) was
going to the House of Lords, in which event the law would be settled about the
" offer of the bank ". In point of fact that case was not going there, and the

---

(12) (1921), 27 Cox, C.C. 63; 125 L.T. 651.
(13) *Kursaal Casino, Ltd.* v. *Crickitt (No. 1)*, [1966] 2 All E.R. 639.

A commissioner's officers do not seem to have known of it. I do not know that that misapprehension would have made much difference. The commissioner got to know later that that case was not going there, and he did not revoke the policy decision even then. It was the Southend police who took action, as they had done before. The Metropolitan police did not take action: it was the enterprising Superintendent Crickitt of Southend.

B At any rate, the result of the policy decision of Apr. 22, 1966, was that thenceforward, in this great metropolis, the big gaming clubs were allowed to carry on without any interference by the police. We were told that in one or two cases observations had previously been started: but after this policy decision they were discontinued. No prosecutions were instituted in the metropolis against these clubs. That is what the applicant complains of. He says that the policy
C decision was erroneous and that it was the duty of the commissioner to prosecute. To this I now turn.

4. The duty of the Commissioner of Police:
 The office of Commissioner of Police within the metropolis dates back to 1829 when SIR ROBERT PEEL introduced his disciplined Force. The commissioner was a justice of the peace specially appointed to administer the police force in the
D metropolis. His constitutional status has never been defined either by statute or by the courts. It was considered by the Royal Commission on the Police in their report in 1962 (Cmnd. 1728). I have no hesitation, however, in holding that, like every constable in the land, he should be, and is, independent of the executive. He is not subject to the orders of the Secretary of State, save that under the Police Act 1964 the Secretary of State can call on him to give a report,
E or to retire in the interests of efficiency. I hold it to be the duty of the Commissioner of Police, as it is of every chief constable, to enforce the law of the land. He must take steps so to post his men that crimes may be detected; and that honest citizens may go about their affairs in peace. He must decide whether or no suspected persons are to be prosecuted; and, if need be, bring the prosecution or see that it is brought; but in all these things he is not the servant of
F anyone, save of the law itself. No Minister of the Crown can tell him that he must, or must not, keep observation on this place or that; or that he must, or must not, prosecute this man or that one. Nor can any police authority tell him so. The responsibility for law enforcement lies on him. He is answerable to the law and to the law alone. That appears sufficiently from *Fisher* v. *Oldham Corpn.* (14), the Privy Council case of *A.-G. for New South Wales* v. *Perpetual*
G *Trustee Co. (Ltd.)* (15).
 Although the chief officers of police are answerable to the law, there are many fields in which they have a discretion with which the law will not interfere. For instance, it is for the Commissioner of Police, or the chief constable, as the case may be, to decide in any particular case whether enquiries should be pursued, or whether an arrest should be made, or a prosecution brought. It must
H be for him to decide on the disposition of his force and the concentration of his resources on any particular crime or area. No court can or should give him direction on such a matter. He can also make policy decisions and give effect to them, as, for instance, was often done when prosecutions were not brought for attempted suicide; but there are some policy decisions with which, I think, the courts in a case can, if necessary, interfere. Suppose a chief constable were to
I issue a directive to his men that no person should be prosecuted for stealing any goods less than £100 in value. I should have thought that the court could countermand it. He would be failing in his duty to enforce the law.
 A question may be raised as to the machinery by which he could be compelled to do his duty. On principle, it seems to me that once a duty exists, there should be a means of enforcing it. This duty can be enforced, I think, either by action at the suit of the Attorney-General: or by the prerogative order of mandamus.

(14) [1930] All E.R. Rep. 96; [1930] 2 K.B. 364.
(15) [1955] 1 All E.R. 846; [1955] A.C. 457.

I am mindful of the cases cited by counsel for the commissioner which he said A limited the scope of mandamus; but I would reply that mandamus is a very wide remedy which has always been available against public officers to see that they do their public duty. It went in the old days against justices of the peace both in their judicial and in their administrative functions. The legal status of the Commissioner of Police is still that he is a justice of the peace, as well as a constable. No doubt the party who applies for mandamus must show that he B has sufficient interest to be protected and that there is no other equally convenient remedy; but once this is shown, the remedy of mandamus is available, in case of need, even against the Commissioner of Police of the Metropolis.

Can the applicant invoke the remedy of mandamus here? It is I think an open question whether he has a sufficient interest to be protected. No doubt any person who was adversely affected by the action of the commissioner in C making a mistaken policy decision would have such an interest. The difficulty is to see how the applicant himself has been affected. Without deciding that question, however, I turn to see whether it is shown that the Commissioner of Police has failed in his duty. I have no doubt that some of the difficulties have been due to the lawyers and the courts. Refined arguments have been put forward on the wording of the statute which have gained acceptance by some for D a time. I can well understand that the Commissioner of Police might hesitate for a time until those difficulties were resolved; but, on the other hand, it does seem to me that his policy decision was unfortunate. People might well think that the law was not being enforced, especially when the gaming clubs were openly and flagrantly being conducted as they were in this great city. People might even go further and suspect that the police themselves turned a blind eye to E it. I do not myself think that that was so. I do not think that the suggestion should even be made; but nevertheless the policy decision was, I think, most unfortunate.

The matter has, I trust, been cleared up now. On Dec. 19, 1967, the House of Lords (16) made it quite clear that roulette with a zero was not rendered lawful simply by the " offer of the bank ". Following that decision, on Dec. 30, 1967, F the commissioner issued a statement in which he said:

" It is the intention of the metropolitan police to enforce the law as it has been interpreted."

That implicitly revoked the policy decision of Apr. 22, 1966; and the commissioner by his counsel gave an undertaking to the court that that policy decision G would be officially revoked. We were also told that immediate steps are being taken to consider the " goings-on " in the big London clubs with a view to prosecution if there is anything unlawful. That is all that Mr. Blackburn or anyone else can reasonably expect.

5. *Conclusions*:

This case has shown a deplorable state of affairs. The law has not been enforced H as it should. The lawyers themselves are at least partly responsible. The niceties of drafting and the refinements of interpretation have led to uncertainties in the law itself. This has discouraged the police from keeping observation and taking action; but it does not, I think, exempt them also from their share of the responsibility. The proprietors of gaming houses have taken advantage of the situation. By one device after another they have kept ahead of the law. As soon as one device has been held unlawful, they have started another; but the day of reckoning is at hand. No longer will we tolerate these devices. The law must be sensibly interpreted so as to give effect to the intentions of Parliament; and the police must see that it is enforced. The rule of law must prevail.

SALMON, L.J.: The chief function of the police is to enforce the law. The divisional court left open the point whether an order of mandamus could

(16) See *Crickitt* v. *Kursaal Casino, Ltd. (No. 2)*, ante p. 139.

A   issue against a chief police officer should he refuse to carry out that function. Constitutionally it is clearly impermissible for the Home Secretary to issue any order to the police in respect of law enforcement. In this court it has been argued on behalf of the commissioner that the police are under no legal duty to anyone in regard to law enforcement. If this argument were correct, it would mean that insofar as their most important function is concerned, the police are
B   above the law and therefore immune from any control by the court. I reject that argument. In my judgment the police owe the public a clear legal duty to enforce the law—a duty which I have no doubt they recognise and which generally they perform most conscientiously and efficiently. In the extremely unlikely event, however, of the police failing or refusing to carry out their duty, the court would not be powerless to intervene. For example, if, as is quite
C   unthinkable, the chief police officer in any district were to issue an instruction that as a matter of policy the police would take no steps to prosecute any house-breaker, I have little doubt but that any householder in that district would be able to obtain an order of mandamus for the instruction to be withdrawn. Of course, the police have a wide discretion whether or not they will prosecute in any particular case. In my judgment, however, the action which I have postu-
D   lated would be a clear breach of duty. It would be so improper that it could not amount to an exercise of discretion.

Counsel for the commissioner has argued that the discretion is absolute and can in no circumstances be challenged in the courts. He instances the policy decision not to prosecute, save in exceptional circumstances, young teenage boys who have had sexual intercourse with girls just under the age of sixteen; but
E   this, in my view, is an entirely different and perfectly proper exercise of discretion. The object of the Criminal Law Amendment Act, 1885, which made it a criminal offence to have sexual intercourse with girls under sixteen, was passed in order to protect young girls against seduction. Unfortunately, in many of the cases today in which teenage boys are concerned, it is they rather than the girls who are in need of protection. These are not the sort of cases which the legis
F   lature had in mind when the Criminal Law Amendment Act, 1885, was passed. Moreover, experience has shown that if young boys are prosecuted in such circumstances, the courts usually take the humane and sensible course of imposing no penalty. The object of the statute which made housebreaking a crime was quite simply to prevent housebreaking in the interests of society. Similarly, the object of s. 32 to s. 40 of the Betting, Gaming and Lotteries Act 1963, and
G   the corresponding provisions of the Betting and Gaming Act, 1960, which the Act of 1963 replaced, was quite simply to protect society against the evils which would necessarily follow were it possible to build up large fortunes by the exploitation of gaming. The Acts of 1960 and 1963 were designed to prevent such exploitation and would have been entirely effective to do so had they been enforced. Regrettably they have not been properly enforced. As a result, and
H   entirely contrary to the intention or contemplation of Parliament, an immense gaming industry, particularly in London, has been allowed to grow up during the last seven years. This has inevitably brought grave social evils in its train —protection rackets, crimes of violence and widespread corruption. There are no doubt a few large establishments which are respectably run and from which these evils are excluded; but for every one of these, there are scores of others. As long as it remains possible for large fortunes to be made by the private exploitation of gaming, the evils to which I have referred will grow and flourish until they threaten the whole fabric of society. Since large fortunes can be made out of the exploitation of gaming, naturally a great deal of ingenuity has been exercised to devise schemes for the purpose of evading the law. With a little more resolution and efficiency, these schemes could and should have been frustrated.

In the present case we are concerned chiefly with the game of roulette played with a zero. For the reasons which appear in the evidence before us, so long as the odds offered against any one number are no more than thirty-five to one **A** the chances favour the bank by three to ten per cent., according to the way the bets are laid. If the house holds the bank, the house in the long run is bound to win. It follows that this contravenes s. 32 (1) (*a*) and (*b*) of the Act of 1963, for the " chances in the game are [not] equally favourable to all the players, of whom the bank is one" (cf., sub-s. (1) (*a*)), and the " gaming is so conducted that the chances therein are [not] equally favourable to all the players " (cf., sub-s. **B** (1) (*b*)). We have all heard of the very old song, " The Man that Broke the Bank at Monte Carlo ". The bank could, of course, have a very bad run of luck during one evening and lose heavily. It could perhaps have a very bad run of luck for days and even for weeks, but month in and month out, it is bound to win. This, amongst other reasons, is why the house which holds the bank month in and month out is bound to be more favourably placed than any player who may **C** hold it sporadically for comparatively short periods of time.

In *Kursaal Casino, Ltd.* v. *Crickitt* (*No. 1*) (17) which was decided in the divisional court on Mar. 23, 1966, the justices had held that for the house to hold the bank contravened the law. The point taken by the prosecution, which to my mind was manifestly a good point, was that whoever held the bank was ex hypothesi a player and accordingly the game could not be equally favour- **D** able to all players and was therefore illegal. It would, therefore, make no differ- ence that the house went through the motions of offering the bank to the players and that very occasionally the offer was accepted for short periods of time. The defence had argued that as the bank was offered at regular intervals to all the players, the chances were equal for all. The justices convicted. Incidentally, they also held that as there must be very many players who could not afford to **E** take the bank, the offer, therefore, was in any event neither genuine nor realistic. The divisional court upheld the conviction and concluded that there was ample evidence to support the finding that the offer of the bank was neither genuine nor realistic. It is perhaps a pity, if this was regarded as a test case, that the prosecution were not advised to call evidence, which could easily have been supplied by any actuary or anyone conversant with the game, that whatever **F** the means of the players or however their liability might be limited, it would be quite impossible to offer the bank on any conceivable terms which could possibly result in the gaming being so conducted that the chances therein would be " equally favourable to all the players ". This does not depend on questions of fact or degree or the circumstances of any particular case. It is something which is inherently impossible—as the House of Lords in *Crickitt* v. *Kursaal* **G** *Casino, Ltd.* (*No. 2*) (18) subsequently decided. The divisional court certified (19) a point of law of general public importance, but refused leave to appeal to the House of Lords.

On Apr. 22, 1966, after the time for applying for leave to appeal to the House of Lords had expired, the then assistant commissioner issued the following written confidential instruction: **H**

" For the time being all applications for authority for an inside observa- tion in licensed or registered clubs for the purposes of detecting gaming are to be submitted to A.1 branch for my covering approval."

According to the affidavit of Mr. Bearman, the assistant secretary of the A.1 branch, the then commissioner

" considered that, in view of the uncertainty of the law, the expense and manpower involved in keeping gaming observations in such clubs were not justified unless there were complaints of cheating or reason to suppose that a particular club had become a haunt of criminals."

This, I think, can only mean that, save in the circumstances postulated, no steps were to be taken to bring any prosecution in respect of roulette or other

---

(17) [1966] 2 All E.R. 639.   (18) Ante p. 139.
(19) [1966] 2 All E.R. at p. 643, letter H.

A games in which the bank held an advantage; that is to say, there should be no prosecution in respect of games contravening s. 32 as such. The affidavit continues as follows:

B " At the time when this decision was taken, the *Kursaal* case (20) was believed to be going to the House of Lords on the point certified by the divisional court. Had this been decided in favour of the prosecution, it was felt that roulette and other games where the bank had an advantage would have been clearly illegal and would therefore have come to an end in any reputable club [mark these words] or have been very easy to detect and prosecute."

C This can only mean that if the decision of the divisional court stood, there would have been no difficulty in the way of prosecution, but that the law was thought to be still uncertain because the *Kursaal* (*No. 1*) case (20) was believed to be going to the House of Lords and therefore no step should be taken meanwhile. No one has or could possibly impugn the good faith of the assistant commissioner. It is, however, a very great pity that he apparently did not even take the trouble to discover that the time for asking the House of Lords for leave to appeal

D (which had been refused by the divisional court) had already expired by the date of his confidential instruction of Apr. 22, 1966, and that therefore there was no possibility of any appeal to the House of Lords. Every month which went by added tens or perhaps hundreds of thousands of pounds to the profits made from illegal gaming, and, as the Home Secretary said on Sept. 13, 1966, the connexion between gaming clubs and organised crimes continued to grow.

E In the meantime the Kursaal Casino devised a scheme under which the bank was offered to the players in circumstances supposed to ensure that they could limit their liability to any sum they liked to name. The Kursaal continued playing roulette under this new scheme. They were prosecuted again by the vigilant Superintendent Crickitt of Southend and duly convicted on Dec. 2, 1966: that is to say, more than seven months after the confidential instruction. During this

F period nothing had been done to enforce the law in London because of the belief, apparently, that there was to be an appeal to the House of Lords in *Kursaal* (*No. 1*) (20). This is the appeal that never was and which the slightest enquiry would have revealed never could have been at any time after Apr. 20, 1966.

The inactivity after the conviction in *Kursaal* (*No. 2*) on Dec. 2, 1966, is sought to be excused in Mr. Bearman's affidavit by the fact that it was known that that

G conviction was to be tested in the divisional court. No steps, however, were taken (since no inside observations were kept) to see whether the London gaming houses offered the bank to the players under conditions which allowed the players to limit their liability. There was thus no reason to suppose that the London gaming houses had even the defence open to them which had failed before the magistrates in *Kursaal* (*No. 2*). Another seven months went by before *Kursaal*

H (*No. 2*) (21) was decided in the divisional court on July 10, 1967, in favour of the defence. Apparently still no steps were taken to ascertain on what terms, if any, the bank was being offered to players in London and still the gambling empires were left undisturbed. Then on Dec. 19, 1967, the decision of the divisional court in *Kursaal* (*No. 2*) (22) was reversed by the House of Lords (22).

I We have been told that that decision and its implications are being carefully studied. The study should not take long. LORD PEARSON'S speech, in which all the other law lords concurred, made the law pellucidly clear. In no circumstances can roulette be legal when played with a zero and when the odds are thirty-five to one or less against any one number turning up. The correct odds are, of course, thirty-six to one, since including zero there are thirty-seven numbers on the roulette wheel.

---

(20) [1966] 2 All E.R. 639.   (21) [1967] 3 All E.R. 360.
(22) Ante p. 139.

According to the evidence before this court, however, most of the gaming A
houses in London, in direct defiance of the law as laid down by the House of
Lords, are still playing roulette, unmolested, in exactly the same way (save for
one immaterial variation to which I will refer) as they were doing prior to Dec.
19, 1967. The variation is as follows: If the number backed by a player for,
say, one chip turns up, he receives thirty-five ordinary chips and one special
chip of a different colour. He is not allowed to play with this chip or to exchange B
it for an ordinary chip. The normal practice is for the players to toss the special
chips back to the croupier. Clearly the players are under no illusion. They
realise that these special chips are but a hollow sham devised to deceive the
exceptionally gullible into thinking that the odds being paid out are thirty-six
to one when in reality they are thirty-five to one. If anyone with a special chip
chooses (and very few of them do) to take it to the cash desk to be cashed, it is C
duly cashed but the player concerned has to pay a fee, for example, of £10 in
the Golden Nugget Casino Club and £50 in the Victoria Sporting Club. It may be
that gamblers are reluctant to cash the chips because they do not like paying
the fee or because, rightly or wrongly, they fear that they may be barred—
and most gamblers would rather sacrifice a shade of odds than lose the chance
of gambling.   D
However that may be, it is obvious that in reality the odds on the overwhelming number of bets remain at the rate of thirty-five to one against a single
number turning up. What otherwise could be the object of having a different
coloured chip to make the odds up to thirty-six to one and charging a fee for
cashing it? At most it amounts to giving a player an option either to pay a fee
or to play in a game in which the chances are not equally favourable to all E
players. There is certainly nothing here for a test case. This could only serve
to give the gaming houses a further breathing space for another long spell, at
the end of which no doubt an equally transparent ruse would be devised. What
is now urgently needed is that energetic steps should immediately be taken to
prosecute a substantial number of major London gaming houses in which the
law is being defied. It may be that even when very heavy fines are imposed, F
they will be ineffective, in which event the Attorney-General would no doubt
consider the advisability of bringing relator actions to restrain the present abuses
by injunction.
The applicant has abandoned the first two parts of his application: only the
third part remains which asks for an order of mandamus requiring the commissioner to reverse the policy decision that the time of police officers will not be G
spent in enforcing the provisions of the Betting, Gaming and Lotteries Act 1963.
Counsel for the commissioner, has given an undertaking to this court that the
confidential instruction of Apr. 22, 1966, will be immediately withdrawn and
the whole matter referred to the Director of Public Prosecutions. Moreover,
he has given an assurance that since Dec. 19 last, the policy decision referred to
in Mr. Bearman's affidavit has been reversed and that observation has been H
kept on many of the principal gaming houses in London, including those referred
to in the affidavits filed by the applicant. Had it not been for this undertaking
and assurance, I should, I think, have been in favour of making an order.
I am not impressed by the argument that the applicant has an equally effective
and equally convenient remedy open to him and that, therefore, the order of
mandamus, should in any event be refused in the court's discretion. It seems to
me fantastically unrealistic for the police to suggest, as they have done, that
their policy decision was unimportant because the applicant was free to start
private prosecutions of his own and fight the gambling empires, possibly up to
the House of Lords, single-handed. Nor, as at present advised, do I accept the
argument that this is a " criminal cause or matter " and that therefore, by
reason of the Supreme Court of Judicature (Consolidation) Act, 1925, s. 31 (1) (a),
no appeal lies to this court from the divisional court. No doubt the words
" criminal cause or matter " must be given a very wide construction, but I am

A not convinced that they relate to proceedings in which neither party is at risk
of being prosecuted as a result of the order sought or made (see *Amand* v.
Secretary of State for Home Affairs (23)). I would prefer to keep that point open
as it does not directly arise for decision. The only doubt which I should have
had would have been whether the applicant had a sufficient personal interest
in order to obtain an order of mandamus. As it is, no order is necessary and
B I agree that, accordingly, none should be made.

Before parting with the case, I would, however, like to say that I entirely
agree with the observations made by Lord Denning, M.R., in regard to *Mills*
v. *Mackinnon* (24). That was a decision which rested on some very special
facts found in that case. Should there be another prosecution in relation to
chemin-de-fer and the prosecution were to call a number of respectable people
C who thoroughly understood the game, I should be surprised if the decision were
the same.

EDMUND DAVIES, L.J.: It would be difficult to exaggerate the importance of these proceedings. If there are grounds for suspecting that a grave social
evil is being allowed to flourish unchecked because of a set policy of inaction
decided on by a pusillanimous police force, public confidence must inevitably
D be gravely underminded. We have ranged far and wide in this case—both
choronologically (from Anglo-Saxon times to the present day) and geographically
(from Las Vegas to the Edgware Road)—but we have not travelled an inch
beyond that made necessary by the urgency and importance of the issues raised.

It is, to say the least, singularly unfortunate that, the conviction in *Kursaal
Casino, Ltd.* v. *Crickitt (No. 1)* (25) having been upheld by the divisional court
E on Mar. 23, 1966, and the time for applying to the House of Lords for leave to
appeal having expired, the assistant commissioner issued on Apr. 22 the
" confidential instruction " regarding " gaming in registered or licensed clubs ",
to which my lords have already referred. What prompted it has been one of the
disturbing questions raised by these proceedings. This court was given no
answer to that question directly emanating from its author, the assistant com-
F missioner, but it appears from the affidavit of Mr. Bearman of the administration
department of New Scotland Yard that the assistant commissioner

" . . . considered that, in view of the uncertainty of the law, the expense
and manpower involved in keeping gaming observations in such clubs were
not justified unless there were complaints of cheating or reason to suppose
G that a particular club had become a haunt of criminals."

In other words, no steps were to be taken to investigate whether breaches of
the Betting, Gaming and Lotteries Act 1963, as such were being perpetrated,
and it is conceded by counsel for the commissioner that in consequence observation in some of the biggest gambling clubs in the West End was immediately
stopped. Small wonder, then, that on Jan. 2, 1967, The Times newspaper boldly
H asserted that,

" It is now clear that the Act has failed to achieve its purpose not so
much because it could not be enforced as because the police failed to do so."

The timing of this directive was as maladroit as the reasons given to this court
for its publication.   It prevailed for nearly two years after *Kursaal (No. 1)* (25)
I notwithstanding that Mr. Bearman in his affidavit stated in effect that, as long
as that decision remained undisturbed, it rendered " roulette and other games
where the bank had the advantage . . . clearly illegal ". As long as the directive
remained operative, it has understandably created perturbation in the minds of
many, and the fact that it apparently continued in force even after *Crickitt* v.
Kursaal Casino, Ltd. (No. 2) (26), was decided on Dec. 19, 1967, served to

(23) [1942] 2 All E.R. 381; [1943] A.C. 147.
(24) [1964] 1 All E.R. 155; [1964] 2 Q.B. 96.
(25) [1966] 2 All E.R. 639.   (26) Ante p. 139.

perpetuate that anxiety. Indeed, it was only on the penultimate day of this hear- **A**
ing that counsel for the commissioner, in answer to a direct question by a member
of the court, intimated that oral instructions have been spread around that the
directive no longer remains operative.

A more satisfactory stage was reached, however, when, in the concluding
stages of his address, counsel undertood on behalf of the commissioner that the
criticised directive will be expressly and immediately withdrawn and replaced **B**
by a new directive emphasising the intention of the Metropolitan police to enforce
the law against " roulette with zero and all other forms of gaming where the
bank has an inherent advantage over players . . ." The *main* object sought to be
attained by the applicant in these proceedings was that by mandamus the
commissioner be required " to reverse or procure the reverse of the policy
decision . . . that the time of police officers will not be spent on enforcing the **C**
provisions of the Gaming Act 1963 ". The undertaking now given to this court
has for all practical purposes secured for the applicant the relief that he sought,
and accordingly no grounds remain in respect of which it would any longer be
proper to consider granting mandamus.

That is the practical outcome of these proceedings, and from the public
standpoint a very useful outcome it is. But how stands the law? My lords **D**
have already dealt with it in extenso, and I propose to deal quite briefly with
but some of the points raised by the commissioner. I deal first with jurisdiction. It is urged that these proceedings relate to " a criminal cause or
matter " and that accordingly an appeal from the divisional court lies directly
to the House of Lords and not to this court—see s. 31 (1) (*a*) of the Supreme
Court of Judicature (Consolidation) Act, 1925. I need not again go through the **E**
long line of cases relied on in this connexion by the commissioner, beginning
with *Ex p. Woodhall* (27). In my judgment they have no bearing on the quite
general application now made that the commissioner be compelled to reverse
a policy directive regarding the enforcing of a statute. Such an application
has no reference to any particular criminal cause or matter, and is not even a
remote step in relation to a criminal cause or matter, but is designed simply **F**
and solely to ensure that the police do not abdicate, in consequence of a policy
decision, their functions as law enforcement officers. I, therefore, agree with my
lords in holding that this court has jurisdiction to hear and determine the present
appeal. It is necessary to add, however, that I am persuaded so to hold by reason
of the abandonment of all but the last portion of the motion, for the earlier parts
(and particularly that which related to the prosecution of a specific, named **G**
club) seem to me truly open to the objection as to jurisdiction raised by the
commissioner. In this context, I am not for the present prepared, with respect,
to adopt the view expressed by FLETCHER-MOULTON, L.J. (28) in *R.* v. *Governor
of Brixton Prison, Ex p. Savarkar* (29) that

> " . . . if *any* portion of an application or order involves the consideration **H**
> of a criminal cause or matter, it arises out of it, and in such a case this
> court is not competent to entertain an appeal."

Be that as it may, nothing there said can, in my judgment, apply to a case
(such as the present) where the applicant for relief abandons those parts of his
motion which offend, or may offend, against the rule, and I see no reason why
this court should thereafter be prevented from adjudicating on the validity of
that which remains.

So far, so good, from the applicant's point of view; but even so it is said that
he could not in any event have succeeded in these proceedings. In this context
counsel for the commissioner has addressed to the court an elaborate and learned

(27) (1888), 28 Q.B.D. 832.
(28) [1910] 2 K.B. 1056 at p. 1065.
(29) [1908-10] All E.R. Rep. 603; [1910] 2 K.B. 1056.

A argument in support of the bald and startling proposition that the law enforcement officers of this country owe no duty to the public to enforce the law.
Carried to its logical limit, such a submission would mean that, however brazen
the failure of the police to enforce the law, the public would be wholly without
a remedy and would simply have to await some practical expression of the
court's displeasure. In particular, it would follow that the commissioner would
B be under no duty to prosecute anyone for breaches of the Gaming Acts, no matter
now flagrantly and persistently they were defied. Can that be right? Is our
much-vaunted legal system in truth so anaemic that, in the last resort, it would
be powerless against those who, having been appointed to enforce it, merely
cocked a snook at it? The very idea is as repugnant as it is startling, and I
consider it regrettable that it was ever advanced. How ill it affords with the
C seventeenth century assertion of Thomas Fuller that, " Be you never so high,
the law is above you ". The applicant is right in his assertion that its effect
would be to place the police above the law. I should indeed regret to have to
assent to the proposition thus advanced on behalf of the commissioner, and, for
the reasons already given by my lords, I do not regard it as well-founded. On
the contrary, I agree with them in holding that the law enforcement officers
D of this country certainly owe a legal duty to the public to perform those functions
which are the raison d'être of their existence. How and by whom that duty can
be enforced is another matter, and it may be that a private citizen, such as the
applicant, having no special or peculiar interest in the due discharge of the duty
under consideration, has himself no legal right to enforce it. That is widely different, however, from holding that no duty exists, enforceable either by a relator
E action or in some other manner which may hereafter have to be determined.

It was further urged that, assuming jurisdiction in this court and even assuming that the commissioner is under the duty which this court now unanimously
holds that he does owe, nevertheless the applicant, should be denied the relief
sought inasmuch as it is open to him to lay an information or apply for a voluntary
bill of indictment. The law is, as I believe, that relief by way of a prerogative
F order will not be granted if there is available any other legal remedy, equally
convenient, beneficial and appropriate. Having regard to the course which
these proceedings have taken, no final consideration of this submission is called
for, and I content myself with the simple observation that only the most sardonic
could regard the launching of a private prosecution (a process which, incidentally,
is becoming regarded with increasing disfavour in this country) as being equally
G convenient, beneficial and appropriate as the procedure in fact adopted by the
applicant.

I began by saying that these are important proceedings. They have served
useful public purposes (a) in highlighting the very real anxiety which many
responsible citizens manifestly entertain as to the adequacy of the steps hitherto
taken to exterminate a shocking and growing cancer in the body politic; and
H (b) in clarifying the duty of the police in relation to law enforcement generally.
Accordingly, while, for the reasons given by my lords, there must be a formal
dismissal of this appeal, it may well be that the applicant and his supporters
will nevertheless feel as they leave this court today that in truth theirs has been
the victory.

Appeal dismissed

I Solicitors: *Solicitor, Metropolitan Police.*

[*Reported by* F. GUTTMAN, ESQ., *Barrister-at-Law.*]

PRACTICE DIRECTION.

[COURT OF APPEAL, CRIMINAL DIVISION (Lord Parker, C.J., Winn, L.J., and Ashworth, J.), February 16, 1968.]

Criminal Law—Costs—Acquittal—Quantum—Principle—No discretion to award a proportion only—By whom amount to be ascertained—Costs in Criminal Cases Act, 1952 (15 & 16 Geo. 6 & 1 Eliz. 2 c. 48), s. 1 (1) (b), (2), (5).

[**Editorial Note.** Guidance as to the exercise of discretion over awarding costs to an acquitted person was given in PRACTICE DIRECTION, [1959] 3 All E.R. 471 and *R.* v. *Sansbury*, [1959] 3 All E.R. 472, n.; see also [1961] 3 All E.R. at p. 75, letter D.

As to costs in criminal cases, see 10 HALSBURY'S LAWS (3rd Edn.) 546-548, paras. 1005, 1007, 1008; and for cases on the subject, see 14 DIGEST (Repl.) 683, 6972-6975.

For the Costs in Criminal Cases Act, 1952, s. 1, see 32 HALSBURY'S STATUTES (2nd Edn.) 62.]

Case referred to:

Francis v. *Francis and Dickerson*, [1955] 3 All E.R. 836; [1956] P. 87; [1955] 3 W.L.R. 973; Digest (Cont. Vol. A) 778, *5364c.*

LORD PARKER, C.J., at the sitting of the court read the following direction. The court's attention has been drawn to several recent cases in which on an application being made on behalf of an acquitted person for costs under s. 1 of the Costs in Criminal Cases Act, 1952 (1) the judge, recorder or chairman of quarter sessions (hereinafter referred to as " the judge ") has awarded less than the sum put forward as representing the costs of the defence. Once, however, the judge has exercised his discretion in favour of making an award of costs there is no further discretion to limit the amount awarded to a contribution, such as a percentage of the amount asked for because the section (2) refers to payment of " the expenses properly incurred " in carrying on the defence. At the same time the acquitted person is not entitled to anything more than the costs properly incurred. The proper approach is to assume the defendant to be of adequate but not abundant means and to ask oneself whether the expenses were such as a sensible solicitor in the light of his then knowledge would consider reasonable to incur in the interests of his client, the defendant (see *Francis* v. *Francis and Dickerson* (3)).

Section 1 (5) of the Act of 1952 provides specifically that the amount of costs is to be ascertained by the proper officer of the court and, accordingly, the judge should in general refer the question of amount to the proper officer. Should however the judge have no reason to think that the sum asked for is in any way excessive there is no reason why he should not, in the interests of expedition, award that sum without referring the matter to the proper officer.

[*Reported by* N. P. METCALFE, ESQ., *Barrister-at-Law.*]

---

(1) Section 1, so far as material, provides: "(1) Subject to the provisions of this section, a court of assize or quarter sessions before which any person is prosecuted or tried on indictment or inquisition . . . (b) may, if the accused is acquitted, order the payment out of local funds of the costs of the defence. (2) The costs payable out of local funds under the preceding subsection shall be such sums as appear to the court reasonably sufficient to compensate . . . the accused for the expenses properly incurred by him in carrying on . . . the defence . . . (5) The amount of costs ordered to be paid under this section shall be ascertained as soon as practicable by the proper officer of the court."

(2) Viz., s. 1 (2).

(3) [1955] 3 All E.R. 836; [1956] P. 87.

A

CHENEY *v.* CONN (Inspector of Taxes).
SAME *v.* INLAND REVENUE COMMISSIONERS.

[CHANCERY DIVISION (Ungoed-Thomas, J.), July 3, 1967.]

Income Tax—Charge to tax—Application of proceeds in part for purposes allegedly
B   *contrary to convention ratified by the United Kingdom government—Whether*
assessment to tax invalidated—Allocation of proceeds of taxes to construction
of nuclear weapon—Geneva Conventions Act, 1957 (5 & 6 Eliz. 2 c. 52),
preamble.

International Law—Convention—Ratification by the executive—Implementation
by statute—Conflict between convention and statute—Statute law prevailing—
C   *Geneva Conventions Act, 1957 (5 & 6 Eliz. 2 c. 52), preamble.*

The appellant was assessed to income tax under Sch. D for the year
1964-65 and to surtax for 1963-64. Substantial parts of the receipts from
the taxes for those years were allocated to the construction of nuclear
weapons with the intention of using the weapons, should occasion arise. On
the question whether the assessments on the appellant were invalidated by
D   the proposed use of part of the taxes for a purpose allegedly in conflict with a
Geneva Convention scheduled to the Geneva Conventions Act, 1957,

Held: the charge to tax, effected by virtue of s. 12* and s. 13 of the
Finance Act 1964, and thus also the assessments to such tax, were not
invalid for the following reasons—

(i) the long title of†, and the preamble to†, the Act of 1957 did not make
E   the conventions scheduled to that Act part of the statute law of England,
for the preamble showed that the Act of 1957 was passed with a view to
subsequent ratification of the conventions by the executive, which had, there-
force, such force as was derived from such ratification; accordingly, even if
there were a conflict between a convention and s. 12 or s. 13 of the Finance
Act 1964, the provisions of the Act of 1964, being unambiguous in terms,
F   would prevail (see p. 782, letters E and F, post).

(ii) if the purposes for which the enactments of the Act of 1964 might be
used included an unlawful purpose, the enactments were not thereby vitiated
but any remedy must be directed to the invalidation of use for the unlawful
purposes (see p. 782, letter G, post).

G   [As to international conventions requiring to be implemented by legislation
to become law, see 7 HALSBURY'S LAWS (3rd Edn.) 5, para. 2; as to the Geneva
Conventions, see 39 ibid., p. 42, para. 36.

As to the general charge to income tax, see 20 HALSBURY'S LAWS (3rd Edn.)
11, para. 4.

For the long title and preamble to the Geneva Conventions Act, 1957, see 37
HALSBURY'S STATUTES (2nd Edn.) 68; and for s. 12 and s. 13 of the Finance Act
1964, see 44 ibid., 450.]

Case referred to:

Collco Dealings, Ltd. v. *Inland Revenue Comrs.,* [1961] 1 All E.R. 762; [1962]
A.C. 1; [1961] 2 W.L.R. 401; 39 Tax Cas. 509; 44 Digest (Repl.) 261,
867.

Case Stated.

The taxpayer, Howard William Cheney, appealed to the Commissioners for
the Special Purposes of the Income Tax Acts on July 20, 1965, against the
following assessments: assessments to income tax made on him under Sch. D,
s. 122 of the Income Tax Act, 1952, for the year 1964-65, in the sum of £3,375
less capital allowances of £2,500, and also against an assessment to surtax for
the year 1963-64 in the sum of £9,859. The main contention on behalf of the

---

* Section 12 is set out at p. 780, letter G, post.
† The long title and preamble are set out at p. 782, letter A, post.

taxpayer before the commissioners was that the assessments were invalid in **A**
that a substantial part of the tax revenue (including the sums assessed on the
taxpayer) was allocated to the construction of nuclear weapons, that it was
the policy of Her Majesty's government that nuclear weapons might be used
for retaliation, and that the use of nuclear weapons was contrary to international
law, a substantial part of the relevant international law having been incorporated
in the law of England by the Geneva Conventions Act, 1957. The Crown con- **B**
tended before the commissioners that the validity of the taxing Acts would not
be affected by the use to which money representing tax charged was to be put.

The commissioners decided that it was not relevant to the validity of the assessments to have regard to the purposes for which money representing the tax
charged under the assessments was to be used. They determined the assessments on the basis of the figures agreed by the parties as follows: (i) as to income **C**
tax for the year 1964-65, at the sum of £3,662 less capital allowances of £2,786;
and (ii) as to surtax for the year 1963-64, at £16,359. The taxpayer appealed by
way of Case Stated to the High Court.

P. R. Pain, Q.C., and *I. Brownlie* for the taxpayer.
J. R. Phillips for the Crown.

D

UNGOED-THOMAS, J.: This is an appeal against an assessment under
Sch. D for 1964-65, and also an assessment to surtax for 1963-64. Both these
cases raise the same point. The submission is that the assessments are invalid
because it is to be taken that what is collected will be, in part, applied in expenditure on the armed forces and devoted to the construction of nuclear weapons with
the intention of using those weapons if certain circumstances should arise. It is **F**
conceded for the purposes of this case that a substantial part of the taxes for the
years that I have mentioned was allocated to the construction of nuclear weapons.
The issue therefore becomes whether the use of income tax and surtax for the
construction of nuclear weapons, with the intention of using them should certain
circumstances arise, invalidates the assessments.

The assessments were made under statute, and the relevant statute is the **F**
Finance Act 1964 s. 12—the Finance Act being based on the provisions of
the Income Tax Act, 1952. Section 12 of the Act of 1964 provides:

" Income tax for the year 1964-65 shall be charged at the standard rate of
7s. 9d. in the pound, and in the case of an individual whose total income
exceeds £2,000 at such higher rates in respect of the excess as Parliament
may hereafter determine." **C**

It is accepted that the corresponding provision with regard to surtax (1) is,
mutatis mutandis, to the same effect. The provision which I have just read is
the provision under which the assessment to income tax in question was made.
The provision is, first, of force statutorily; secondly, unambiguous; and, thirdly,
limited to the raising of taxation and not to the purposes for which that taxation **F**
has to be applied or any such policy matters at all.

The ground on which it was argued that the use of this money for the construction of nuclear weapons is illegal is that such use conflicts primarily with Conventions incorporated in an Act of Parliament—and, so it was suggested, impliedly
ratified by them—and also ratified by the Crown in the usual way; and also
because, according to the Case Stated, it was contrary to international law. But
the case as presented before me was rested primarily, at any rate, on a conflict
between two statutes—namely, the statute which refers to the Geneva Conventions (viz., the Geneva Conventions Act, 1957) and the Finance Act 1964.
Before coming to the Act of 1957 I shall deal first with the relationship of statute
law to international law and international conventions.

First, international law is part of the law of the land, but it yields to statute.

---

(1) Viz., s. 13 of the Finance Act 1964.

A   That is made clear by the case of *Collco Dealings, Ltd.* v. *Inland Revenue Comrs.*
(2), where VISCOUNT SIMONDS (3) quoted with approval, and in accordance
with the decision of the House of Lords in that case, MAXWELL ON THE INTERPRET-
ATION OF STATUTES (10th Edn.) p. 148. I quote: " But if the statute is unambiguous, its provisions must be followed even if they are contrary to international
law." It is therefore very understandable why the taxpayer in this case relies
B   primarily, at any rate, not on a conflict between international law in general and
the statute, but on the conflict between the Act of 1957, and its reference to
ratification, and another statute, the Finance Act 1964. Secondly, conventions
which are ratified by an Act of Parliament are part of the law of the land; and,
thirdly, conventions which are ratified, but not by an Act of Parliament, which
would thereby give them statutory force, cannot prevail against a statute in
C   unambiguous terms. The law is thus stated in OPPENHEIM'S INTERNATIONAL
LAW (8th Edn.) at p. 924:

> " The binding force of a treaty concerns in principle the contracting
> States only, and not their subjects. As international law is primarily a law
> between States only and exclusively, treaties can normally have effect upon
> States only. This rule can, as has been pointed out by the Permanent
D   > Court of International Justice, be altered by the express or implied terms
> of the treaty, in which case its provisions become self-executory. Otherwise,
> if treaties contain provisions with regard to rights and duties of the subjects
> of the contracting States, their courts, officials, and the like, these States
> must take such steps as are necessary, according to their Municipal Law, to
> make these provisions binding upon their subjects, courts, officials and the
E   > like."

At p. 40 the law is stated thus:

> " Such treaties as affect the private rights and, generally, as require for
> their enforcement by English courts a modification of common law or of a
> statute must receive parliamentary assent through an enabling Act of
F   > Parliament. To that extent binding treaties which are part of international
> law do not form part of the law of the land unless expressly made so by the
> legislature. That departure from the traditional common law rule is largely
> due to the fact that, according to British constitutional law, the conclusion
> and ratification of treaties are within the prerogative of the Crown, which
> would otherwise be in a position to legislate for the subject without obtaining
G   > parliamentary assent."

It is, I may add, the Queen in Parliament and not the Queen independently of
Parliament, acting as the executive through the cabinet, who makes what is law
in this land.

In WADE AND PHILLIPS' CONSTITUTIONAL LAW (7th Edn.), at p. 274, after a
passage in which it is pointed out that the term " convention " is used of multi-
H   lateral law-making treaties—and, of course, the Geneva Convention, ratified by
the Act of 1957, comes within that description—there is this passage:

> " At first sight the treaty-making power appears to conflict with the
> constitutional principle that the Queen by prerogative cannot alter the law
> of the land, but the provisions of a treaty duly ratified do not by virtue
> of the treaty alone have the force of municipal law. The assent of Parlia-
I   > ment must be obtained and the necessary legislation passed before a court of
> law can enforce the treaty, should it conflict with the existing law."

Then, more particularly, it is pointed out on p. 275 that: " treaties which, for
their execution and application in the United Kingdom, require some addition
to, or alteration of, the existing law " are treaties which involve legislation.

---

(2) [1961] 1 All E.R. 762; [1962] A.C. 1.
(3) [1961] 1 All E.R. at p. 765; [1962] A.C. at p. 19.

Here, the legislation so relied on is, as I have indicated, the Geneva Conventions A
Act, 1957. The title and preamble of the Act of 1957 are as follows:

" An Act to enable effect to be given to certain international conventions
done at Geneva on Aug. 12, 1949, and for purposes connected therewith.
Whereas, with a view to the ratification by Her Majesty of the conventions
set out in the schedules to this Act, it is expedient to make certain   B
amendments in the law."

What the Act of 1957 then does is to make certain specific amendments in the law
by reference to particular provisions in the Geneva Conventions. There is no
conflict whatsoever between the particular provisions included in those specific
amendments and the Finance Act, 1964; nor have any of those specific
amendments been relied on for that purpose.   C
What has been relied on has been the combination of the title and the preamble,
which I have read. It is said that the whole object of the Act of 1957 was, first,
with a view to ratification by the Crown; and, secondly, with a view to giving
effect to the Geneva Conventions. The ratification by the Crown might or might
not have been made. If the ratification were made (as in fact, subsequently, it
was made in this case), then, of course, the ratification would take effect, not by   D
reason of this Act of Parliament at all, but by reason of ratification by the executive. It would then have the consequences in law which ratification by the
executive has, as contrasted with the effect it would have in law if it were ratified
by law, embodied in statute and made by Parliament part of the law of this land.
The title and the preamble relied on do not make the Geneva Conventions statute;
and, therefore, except to the extent of the specific amendments to the law made   E
by the Act of 1957 itself, which I have mentioned and which have not been relied
on for the purposes of this case—and which, indeed, appear hardly applicable to
it at all—the Act of 1957 does not provide material which can be relied on as being
in conflict with the Finance Act 1964 at all. It is conceded by the Crown for the
purposes of this case, though not otherwise, that the ratification in fact took place;
but it is clear that in so far as the ratification has taken place by executive action   F
and not by parliamentary action, it yields to statute. So even if there were a
conflict between what is contained in the conventions ratified and the Finance
Act 1964, the Finance Act 1964, unambiguous as it is, would prevail. Therefore,
on this ground, apart from any other, the taxpayer's case, in my judgment, fails.
I shall mention another limb to the taxpayer's argument; namely, that any
unlawful purpose for which a statutory enactment may be made vitiates the   G
enforcement of that statute. As was pointed out for the Crown, if that argument
were correct it would mean that the supremacy of Parliament would, in effect, be
overruled. If the purpose for which a statute may be used is an invalid purpose,
then such remedy as there may be must be directed to dealing with that purpose
and not to invalidating the statute itself. What the statute itself enacts cannot be
unlawful, because what the statute says and provides is itself the law, and the   H
highest form of law that is known to this country. It is the law which prevails over
every other form of law, and it is not for the court to say that a parliamentary
enactment, the highest law in this country, is illegal. The result therefore is that
on this ground, also, the taxpayer's case fails.
I would merely add this: that references were made in the course of the attractive arguments that were put forward for the taxpayer to the fact that the
intention that taxation was to be applied to nuclear weapons had been amply
demonstrated by parliamentary papers and other reliable means within Parliament itself. This, of course, is quite clear, and I have no hesitation in accepting it;
but either that is part of statute, or otherwise part of the law of the land, or it is
not. If it is part of a statute it is statute law and it has to be applied by this
court. If it is not, then it has no statutory effect and does not affect what is done
by statute, including the provisions of the Finance Act 1964 itself. But the true
situation is that such declarations of policy do not have statutory effect, have not

A   the force of law at all, and therefore cannot affect a statute. The terms of
the statute in this case are perfectly clear and are binding on the courts of this
country.

Appeal dismissed.

Solicitors: *B. M. Birnberg & Co.* (for the taxpayer); *Solicitor of Inland Revenue.*

B   [*Reported by* F. A. AMIES, ESQ., *Barrister-at-Law.*]

C   BILLYACK *v.* LEYLAND CONSTRUCTION CO., LTD.

[QUEEN'S BENCH DIVISION (Edmund Davies, L.J., sitting as an additional judge),
January 29, 30, 31, February 1, 2, 6, 1968.]

Building Contract—Certificate—Local authority's certificate of habitation—
    Contract provided that certificate should be conclusive evidence of completion
D   *of house—Whether certificate conclusive against liability for structural defects.*
Building Contract—Construction—Ambiguity—Building to be built in workman-
    like manner and in accordance with specification—Specification provided that
    excavation should be carried out in accordance with bye-laws and to satisfaction
    of local authority—Certificate given by local authority—Subsequent discovery
    of structural defects due to insufficient excavation for foundations—Whether
E   *liability of contractors in damages excluded by reason of certificate.*

By a contract in writing dated Nov. 21, 1958, and made between the
plaintiff and the defendant building contractors, the defendants agreed to
build a dwelling-house for the plaintiff and " to build and complete [it]
in a workmanlike manner and in accordance with the specification hereto
annexed ". The specification provided that " the excavation, concreting . . .
F   will be carried out in accordance with the bye-laws of the local authority
and to their satisfaction ". Paragraph 19 of the bye-laws provided that
" the foundation of every building should be so designed and constructed
as to sustain the combined dead load of the building and imposed vertical
and lateral loads . . .". Clause 2 of the contract provided that the plaintiff
should pay the defendants half the price when the roof tiles were on " and the
G   balance . . . on the issue of the certificate of habitation by the local authority
which certificate shall be conclusive evidence of the completion of the said
dwelling-house ". On Feb. 3, 1960, the local authority issued a certificate
pursuant to cl. 2 to the effect that the certifier had examined the dwelling-
house and " that the same has been constructed to the best of [his] knowledge
and belief in accordance with (the deposited) plans and the bye-laws of the
council and is fit for human habitation ". Structural defects developed
H   later. These were caused, so the court found, by failure to carry the foundations of the house on the northwest side to a sufficient depth. In an action
for damages the defendants contended, among other contentions, that the
certificate was made conclusive evidence of the completion of the house in
accordance with the contract and that thereafter no complaint could be
maintained by the plaintiff.

Held: the plaintiff was entitled to recover damages because—
(i) cl. 2 of the contract did not bar the plaintiff's claim since the certificate
thereunder was conclusive only that the house was completed and was not
conclusive against complaints, such as complaints of defects in construction,
otherwise open to the plaintiff (see p. 787, letter H, post).
(ii) there was some ambiguity in cl. 1 of the contract whether, having
regard to the words quoted above from the specification, particularly " *and*
to [the local authority's] satisfaction ", the approval of the local authority

provided an effective answer to the plaintiff's claim for alleged breach of
the obligation to build in a workmanlike manner; in view of the ambiguity
the primary obligation to build in a workmanlike manner was not so limited,
the defendant's obligation under the contract remained an obligation to
build in a workmanlike manner a house fit for human habitation, and the
defendants were in breach of that obligation (see p. 788, letters E and I, and
p. 789, letter F, post).

    Newton Abbott Development Co., Ltd. v. *Stockman Brothers* ((1931), 47 T.L.R.
616) followed.   Dictum of LORD WRIGHT, M.R., in *Petrofina S.A. of Brussels*
v. *Compagnia Italiana Transporto Olii Minerali of Genoa* ((1937), 53 T.L.R.
at p. 653) applied.

[As to the obligations of a building contractor in respect of workmanship and
materials, see 3 HALSBURY'S LAWS (3rd Edn.) 435, para. 818, and as to the
obligation that the work shall be fit for its intended purpose, see ibid., 442, para.
837; and for cases on the subject, see 7 DIGEST (Repl.) 346, 347, *38-47.*

As to the conclusiveness of certificates under a building contract, see 3 HALS-
BURY'S LAWS (3rd Edn.) 465, para. 893; and for cases on the subject, see 7 DIGEST
(Repl.) 371, *130, 131.*

As to a building contractor's liability for defects, see 3 HALSBURY'S LAWS
486, paras. 952, 953; and for cases on the subject, see 7 DIGEST (Repl.) 403, 404,
255-262.]

Cases referred to:
    Ator Ul Haq v. *City Council of Nairobi,* (1959), (P.C. Appeal No. 48) (un-
       reported).
    Bateman (Lord) v. *Thompson,* (1875), 2 Hudson's Building Contracts (8th
       Edn.) 191; 7 Digest (Repl.) 371, *130.*
    Hancock v. *B. W. Brazier (Anerley), Ltd.,* [1966] 2 All E.R. 901; [1966] 1
       W.L.R. 1317; Digest (Cont. Vol. B) 64, *41a.*
    Harvey v. *Lawrence,* (1867), 15 L.T. 571; 7 Digest (Repl.) 367, *117.*
    Lynch v. *Thorne,* [1956] 1 All E.R. 744; [1956] 1 W.L.R. 303; 7 Digest (Repl.)
       347, *44.*
    Miller v. *Cannon Hill Estates, Ltd.,* [1931] All E.R. Rep. 93; [1931] 2 K.B.
       113; 100 L.J.K.B. 740; 144 L.T. 567; 7 Digest (Repl.) 346, *39.*
    Newton Abbott Development Co., Ltd. v. *Stockman Brothers,* (1931), 47 T.L.R.
       616; 7 Digest (Repl.) 402, *253.*
    Petrofina S.A. of Brussels v. *Compania Italiana Transporto Olii Minerali of
       Genoa,* (1937), 53 T.L.R. 650; 57 Lloyd L.R. 247; 41 Digest (Repl.)
       371, *1642.*

Action.

This was an action by the plaintiff Henry Billyack against the defendants,
Leyland Construction Co., Ltd., for damages for breach of a contract to build
and complete a dwelling-house for the plaintiff, known as 9, Shortgate, Woodside
Park, London. By his statement of claim served on Feb. 9, 1966, the plaintiff
alleged the contract, that the house was completed on Feb. 2, 1960, and that it
was an express term of the contract that the house should be built and completed in a workmanlike manner; further that it was an implied term of the
contract that the house would be skilfully and carefully designed so as to be fit
for the purpose for which it was required, namely as a dwelling-house, and that
in breach of the express term or implied term of the contract the house was not
built or completed in a workmanlike manner nor skilfully nor carefully designed
so as to be fit for use as a dwelling-house. The particulars given in the statement
of claim showed that the defect principally relied on related to drainage and
subsoil at the northwest corner of the site and alleged failure to take foundations
sufficiently deep. By their defence the defendants alleged, among other matters,
that they had contracted to build the house in accordance with the specification

A annexed to the contract, and that by the specification the excavation and concreting would be carried out in accordance with the bye-laws of the local authority (the Barnet Urban District Council) and to their satisfaction; further that by cl. 2 the certificate of habitation issued by the local authority should be conclusive evidence of the completion of the house. They pleaded that they complied with the express provisions of the contract relating to the foundations, they denied

B that there was any implied term as alleged in the statement of claim, and they alleged that on Feb. 3, 1960, the local authority issued a certificate of habitation, which they would contend was conclusive evidence, binding the plaintiff, of the completion of the dwelling-house in accordance with the contract.

An employee of the defendant contractors had surveyed the field at Totteridge on which the dwelling-house in question was later built, in or about 1956. A

C drain, leading into a pond, was shown on the 1956 ordnance survey of the field, and the proposed site of the house was in the middle of the pond so shown. The pond had, it seemed, been bull-dozed in by a local farmer in 1957. Work on the foundations of the house began in June, 1958. The local authority's normal requirement for foundations was that they should be taken down to a minimum depth of three feet into virgin clay. Excavation by the defendants having revealed a seam of soft black earth a Mr. Townsend, the chief building inspector of the local authority, was called in. He gave instructions that the trench must be cut deeper. His evidence was that on June 17, he found that it had been deepened and that the bottom was in firm yellow clay below the earth; and that he then gave instructions for concreting to proceed and on June 19 again inspected and described himself as completely satisfied that the concrete foundations were correctly

E laid. Accordingly on Feb. 3, 1960, the certificate of habitation, or certificate of completion, was issued by the local authority. This was to the effect that the certifier had examined No. 9, Shortgate and continued—

    ". . . and that the same has been constructed to the best of my knowledge and belief in accordance with (the deposited) plans and the bye-laws of [the local authority] and is fit for human habitation."

Defects in the house, which had an estimated life of not less than fifty years, subsequently appeared, and the court found that by November, 1965, it was in imminent danger of disintegration. Ultimately underpinning experts were consulted, and the evidence of one of their directors, who had visited the site at a time when the excavations for underpinning had exposed the true conditions at foundation level, satisfied the court that although the foundations had gone down to the bottom, approximately, of the earth, they nevertheless rested at material points on ground that was " disturbed ground ". The local authority's inspector had no contemporaneous note of his visits and the only records to which he could refer gave simply the dates of the visits to the building site. Accordingly, on the evidence, the trial judge (Edmund Davies, L.J.) found that, notwithstanding that at the northwest corner of the site of the dwelling-house the foundations were carried down to a depth of four to five feet, they were not then laid in a firm clay which afforded a suitable foundation.

  R. M. Yorke for the plaintiff.
  H. J. Lloyd for the defendants.

Cur. adv. vult.

    Feb. 6. **EDMUND DAVIES, L.J.,** read the following judgment: This case is about a five-year-old house that threatened to fall down. Its owner now seeks compensation from the builders who erected it. The parties entered into an agreement under seal on Nov. 21, 1958. The defendants, who have been in business for some years as building contractors, thereby undertook to build for the plaintiff for the sum of £5,150 the dwelling-house subsequently known as No. 9, Shortgate, Woodside Park, Totteridge. At that time the house was already in the course of erection, it was completed in January, 1960, and on

EE

Feb. 3 of that year the plaintiff entered into occupation. On that day a certificate **A**
was issued to the defendants by the Barnet U.D.C. to the effect that the certifier
had examined No. 9, Shortgate, ". . . and that the same has been constructed
to the best of my knowledge and belief in accordance with (the deposited) plans
and the bye-laws of the council and is fit for human habitation ". Trouble
developed and, although denied until late in the hearing, it was eventually
conceded that at some stage *structural* defects became manifest. As will presently **B**
appear, the defendants were given ample opportunity to inspect the premises
before any remedial works were embarked on, but they ignored the invitation.
At the beginning of 1966 underpinning of the structure was executed at a cost of
£1,801. Although the parties have agreed that, in the event of my finding for the
plaintiff, the assessment of damages be referred, it is necessary for me to make clear
at this stage that, contrary to the somewhat faint-hearted suggestion by the **C**
defence that underpinning was not called for, I am satisfied that it was essential.
Indeed, had it not been carried out, the plaintiff would have failed properly to
mitigate his loss, for without underpinning the house was in real danger of
disintegration.

The two issues arising for determination are: (i) Were these structural defects
caused by the defendants' acts or omissions? (ii) If they were, is the plaintiff **D**
nevertheless precluded by the terms of the contract from recovering compensation
from the defendants?

[HIS LORDSHIP stated that the first question was one of fact and, having
reviewed the evidence and found that the cause of the structural defects which
arose was the failure of the defendants to carry down the foundations on the north
west of the site to a sufficient depth, in accordance with the brief summary at **E**
p. 785, letters C to H, ante, continued:] In my judgment, the cause of the
structural defects which undoubtedly arose was the failure of the defendants
to lay suitable foundations. The defendants submit that, however, even in the
eventuality of my holding as I have done, the plaintiff is without a remedy. I
accordingly proceed to consider question No. 2, namely, do the terms of the
building contract relieve the defendants from legal liability? **F**

Let me turn immediately to the contract itself. By cl. 1 the defendants agreed
to " build and complete in a workmanlike manner *and* in accordance with the
specification hereto annexed the house under consideration." The only material
part of the annexed specification reads in this way: " The excavation, concreting
. . . will be carried out in accordance with byelaws of the local authority *and* to
their satisfaction." **G**

The relevant portions of the bye-laws are the following:

" 19 (1) The foundations of every building shall be—(a) so designed and
constructed as to sustain the combined dead load of the building and
imposed vertical and lateral loads and to transmit these loads to the ground
in such a manner that the pressure on the ground shall not cause such
settlement as may impair the stability of the building, or of any part of **H**
the building, or of adjoining works or structures; and (b) taken down to
such a depth, or be so designed and constructed, as to safeguard the building
against damage by swelling or shrinkage of the subsoil.

" 20 (1) The foundations for the load-bearing structure of a domestic
building where constructed as strip foundations of plain concrete situated
centrally under the walls or piers, shall be deemed to satisfy the requirements
of sub-para. (a) of the last preceding bye-law if—(a) there is no wide variation in the type of subsoil over the loaded area, and no weaker type of soil
exists below that on which the foundations rest within such a depth as may
impair the stability of the structure . . ."

Then by sub-para. (b) of bye-law 20 there is a provision governing the width of
the foundations. Clause 2 of the building contract provided that the owner must
pay to the defendants

A
" one half of the said sum of £5,150 when the roof tiles are on, and the balance of the purchase money on the issue of the certificate of habitation by the local authority which certificate shall be conclusive evidence of the completion of the said dwelling-house."

The relevant portion of the certificate of completion issued by the Barnet Urban District Council on Feb. 3, 1960, has been set out (1).

B
On the basis of these provisions, the submissions advanced on the defendants' behalf may be summarised in this way: (i) While it is conceded that, were the contract silent, there would be an implied term that the foundations must be designed and laid with reasonable skill and care, there were here express stipulations: (a) that the defendants would build and complete in a workmanlike manner; *and* (b) in accordance with the annexed specification, which in turn

C
required that the work be carried out in accordance with the bye-laws of the local authority *and* to their satisfaction.

(ii) These express stipulations negatived the possibility of implying in the contract any such term as that relied on by the plaintiff, namely that " the house would be skilfully and carefully designed so as to be fit for the purpose for which it was required, namely as a dwelling-house ".

D
(iii) Even assuming that, by not carrying the foundations deep enough and so causing the structural defects which admittedly developed, the defendants had failed to comply with their express undertaking to " build and complete in a workmanlike manner ", nevertheless as the local authority had expressed their satisfaction that the bye-laws had been complied with, the plaintiff has no right of action.

E
(iv) Furthermore, the issuing by the local authority of their certificate of completion was, by the concluding words of cl. 2 of the contract, made "conclusive evidence of the completion of the said dwelling-house " in accordance with the contract, and thereafter no complaints of any kind could be made by the purchaser.

F
I deal first with the final submission. It requires very clear words to debar a building owner from exercising his ordinary rights of suing if the work done is not in accordance with the contract—see the observations of LORD DENNING, M.R., in *B. W. Hancock* v. *Brazier (Anerley), Ltd.* (2). The decision in *Lynch* v. *Thorne* (3) may be regarded as turning on the fact that the contract there contained a provision sufficiently explicit to debar the owner notwithstanding the defective nature of the work done. In my judgment, however, no such debarring arises in

G
the present case from the simple provision that the issuing of the certificate of habitation is to be " conclusive evidence of the *completion* of the said dwelling house ". Clause 2 is dealing with the obligation of the building owner to pay and simply fixes the times when payments are to be due from him. It provides that one half of the £5,150 becomes due " when the roof tiles are on " and the balance when the local authority's certificate is issued. To obviate any dispute whether

H
the house is completed, the clause goes on to provide that the certificate is itself to constitute " conclusive evidence thereof "; but the fact of its issue is, in my judgment, conclusive of nothing else and of itself affects in no way any grounds of complaint otherwise open to the building owner. Had the defendants wanted the certificate to have that effect, it was open to them to have inserted in the contract words similar to those employed in cl. 30 (7) of the R.I.B.A. Form of Contract (1963 Edn.) which provides that, in the absence of a written request to appoint an arbitrator,

" the final certificate . . . shall be *conclusive evidence* in any proceedings arising out of this contract . . . that the works have been properly carried out and completed in accordance with the terms of this contract . . ."

(1) See p. 786, letter A, ante.
(2) [1966] 2 All E.R. 901 at p. 904.
(3) [1956] 1 All E.R. 744.

No such words, however, were employed here and the defendants accordingly **A** fail on this part of the case.

The main submission advanced on behalf of the defendants is. in the light of the authorities, rather more difficult. Can the plaintiff succeed on the ground that, as I have found, the defendants were in breach of their express undertaking to " build and complete in a workmanlike manner ", or are the defendants covered by the fact that, as Mr. Townsend testified, they had completed in **B** accordance with the bye-laws and to his satisfaction? The conjunction " and " joins the two parts of cl. 1 of the contract, and there were cited to me a number of authorities to the effect that, where such a conjunction is used, it may well be that in the result the builder is protected if the designated third party expresses his satisfaction with the work done, no matter how badly it was in fact executed. *Lord Bateman* v. *Thompson* (4) is said to have been such a case, but there, as in **C** many of the other cases cited, the architect or other party whose satisfaction was required was himself appointed by the building owner, who could scarcely be heard to complain once his own appointee had in fact expressed satisfaction with the work. The basic facts of the earlier case of *Harvey* v. *Lawrence* (5) appear to be similar in that respect, and this also appears true of several of the cases collected in HUDSON'S BUILDING AND ENGINEERING CONTRACTS (9th Edn.), **D** pp. 310-12. As to the Privy Council decision in *Ator Ul Haq* v. *City Council of Nairobi* (6), I would respectfully adopt the criticism thereof appearing at p. 314 of that same work.

If there be any ambiguity in the building contract drawn up by the defendants in the present case it must, of course, be interpreted contra proferentem. Putting the plaintiff's case at its lowest, I think that the contract can be said to contain **E** some degree of ambiguity if (as is urged by the defendants here) their primary express undertaking to build and complete in a workmanlike manner was intended by them to be limited and controlled by the words next following. Viewed in that light, the expression of satisfaction by the local authority does not, in my judgment, prevent the plaintiff from recovering.

There is, however, another line of cases where a duality or conjunction of **F** undertakings has been held not to have the result contended for by the present defendants. Counsel for the defendant, for whose careful argument the court is indebted, conceded that the facts of *Newton Abbott Development Co., Ltd.* v. *Stockman Brothers* (7) were almost indistinguishable from those of the present case, but nevertheless contended that the decision was irreconcilable with earlier authorities and ought not to be followed. There the defendants agreed to build **G** for the plaintiffs a number of houses in accordance with certain plans and specifications, and the work was also required to be done to the satisfaction of the local surveyor and sanitary inspector. Those officials indicated their satisfaction, but in fact the houses were not properly built. Holding that the plaintiffs could recover the difference between the value of the houses as actually completed and their value had they been properly built, ROCHE, J., said (8) that it was contended **H** that as the surveyor and the sanitary inspector had expressed satisfaction there was nothing more to be said; but, pointing out that there was nothing in the contract to say that their approval was to be final and conclusive, the learned judge accordingly held that that provision in the contract was merely an added protection to the plaintiffs. Clause 1 of the present contract similarly contains no provision making an expression of satisfaction by the local authority conclusive evidence that the builders had discharged their express undertaking to build and complete in workmanlike manner.

---

(4) (1875), 2 HUDSON's B.C. (8th Edn.) 191.
(5) (1867), 15 L.T. 571.
(6) (1959), unreported.
(7) (1931), 47 T.L.R. 616.
(8) (1931), 47 T.L.R. at p. 617.

A   *Petrofina S.A. of Brussels* v. *Compagnia Italiana Transporto Olii Minerali of Genoa* (9) dealt with a contract of affreightment, but is nevertheless helpful in arriving at a proper conclusion in the present case. There the charterparty contained one clause that the ship was to be in every way fit for the voyage, another that the captain was bound to keep the tanks clean, while cl. 27 provided that the ship was to be clean for the specified cargo to the satisfaction of the

B charterers' inspector. The inspector in due course expressed himself as satisfied, but in fact the tanks were not clean and in consequence the cargo was damaged. In an action against the shipowners, their counsel contended that cl. 27 had the effect of excluding the fundamental obligation to provide a ship fit to carry the specified cargo and substituted therefor an obligation merely to clean to the satisfaction of the charterers' inspector. Rejecting this argument and holding

C that the charterers were entitled to recover, LORD WRIGHT, M.R., said (10):

> ". . . If it is sought to effect a limitation of the overriding obligation to provide a seaworthy ship (whether that is express or implied for this purpose does not matter) by other express terms . . . that result can only be achieved if perfectly clear, effective and precise words are used expressly stating that
>
D > limitation . . . without express words, the satisfaction of the inspector cannot be relied on by the owners as a discharge and fulfilment of their obligations."

I apply the ratio decidendi of that case to the present one in this way. In every building contract there are to be implied (in the absence of express words to the contrary) a three-fold undertaking by the builder: (a) that he will do his work in a good and workmanlike manner; (b) that he will supply good and proper

E materials; and (c) that the house will be reasonably fit for human habitation— see *Miller* v. *Cannon Hill Estates, Ltd.* (11), and *B. W. Hancock* v. *Brazier (Anerley), Ltd.* (12). Is there anything expressed in the present contract to exclude any of those terms? Certainly not the undertaking to " complete and build in a workman-like manner", which in fact expresses one of the terms which would otherwise be implied. Then do the added words serve to exclude them or limit the operation

F of the express undertaking? In my judgment, they do not. On the contrary, the obligation of the defendants to build in a good and workmanlike manner a house fit for human habitation remained unaffected by the satisfaction ultimately expressed by the local authority regarding the fitness of the house which in due course was built.

    For the reasons which I have already given, the defendants failed to fulfil

G that obligation, and for that breach I hold the plaintiff entitled to recover such damages as, failing agreement between the parties, may hereafter be assessed.

Judgment for the plaintiff; damages to be assessed.

Solicitors: *Anthony Leader & Co.* (for the plaintiff); *Gilmore, Tilee & Naylor,* agents for *John Whitehead, Marsden & Huck,* Preston (for the defendants).

H   [*Reported by* F. GUTTMAN, ESQ., *Barrister-at-Law.*]

R. v. MOORE.

[COURT OF APPEAL, CRIMINAL DIVISION (Lord Parker, C.J., Sachs, L.J., and
Ashworth, J.), January 30, 1968.]

*Magistrates—Committal to quarter sessions for sentence—Practice—Option to
commit under s. 28 or s. 29—Normally commit under s. 29—Magistrates'
Courts Act, 1952 (15 & 16 Geo. 6 & 1 Eliz. 2 c. 55), s. 28 (1), s. 29.*

*Quarter Sessions—Committal of offender to—Appeal against sentence—Consecutive
terms of detention at a detention centre for two offences—Sentence to such
detention inappropriate after previous sentence to such detention—Sentence
to one day's imprisonment and disqualification for driving ordered for third
offence—Whether appeal lies since Act of 1967—Magistrates' Courts Act,
1952 (15 & 16 Geo. 6 & 1 Eliz. 2 c. 55), s. 28 (1)—Criminal Justice Act
1967 (c. 80) s. 97 (3) (a), (c) (ii), (6), (7).*

The applicant, aged nineteen, pleaded guilty at a magistrates' court to
three offences, viz., (i) larceny, (ii) taking and driving away a motor cycle,
and (iii) driving a motor cycle whilst he was uninsured. He was committed
under s. 28 (1)* of the Magistrates' Courts Act, 1952, to quarter sessions for
sentence, where consecutive terms of three months' detention were imposed
in respect of offences (i) and (ii); the sentence imposed in respect of offence
(iii) was one day's imprisonment concurrent and twelve months' disqualification for driving. Having regard to the applicant's past record and reports
on him before the court, sentence of borstal training would probably have been
appropriate. He had been sentenced to detention at a detention centre in
August, 1966. On application for leave to appeal against sentence,

Held: (i) a right of appeal against the sentences of detention at a detention
centre in respect of the first two offences was not conferred by s. 97† of the
Criminal Justice Act 1967 in view of sub-s. (3), although s. 97 did confer
a right of appeal (cf., sub-s. (3) (c) (ii)) against the sentence of imprisonment
and order for disqualification; nor did sub-ss. (6) or (7) of s. 97 confer any
right of appeal in relation to the sentences for the first two offences in the
present case (see p. 792, letters A, B and G, post).

(ii) only very rarely should a sentence of detention at a detention centre be
imposed when an accused had already served one such sentence (see p. 792,
letter I, post).

Per CURIAM: where there is an option to commit an offender to quarter
sessions for sentence either under s. 28 or under s. 29 of the Magistrates'
Courts Act, 1952, it is normally appropriate to commit under s. 29 (see p. 791,
letter E, post).

[As to appeal against sentence passed at quarter sessions after summary
conviction, see CURRENT SERVICE to HALSBURY'S LAWS (3rd Edn.) para. 958A.

As to committal to quarter sessions for sentence, see 25 HALSBURY'S LAWS
(3rd Edn.) 226, 227, para. 421, and as to the power of sentencing on such committal, see ibid., p. 229, para. 423; and for cases on the punishment of youthful
offenders, see 14 DIGEST (Repl.) 588-592, 5852-5899.]

Application.

On Oct. 19, 1967, the applicant, Brian Moore, pleaded guilty at Coventry
Magistrates' Court to three offences, viz., larceny of lead and fixtures from a

---

* Section 28 (1) of the Magistrates' Courts Act, 1952, provides: Where a person is
convicted by a magistrates' court of an offence punishable on summary conviction with
imprisonment, then, if on the day of conviction he is not less than sixteen but under
twenty-one years old and the court is satisfied having regard to the offender's character
and previous conduct and the circumstances of the offence that it is expedient for his
reformation and the prevention of crime that he should undergo a period of training
in a borstal institution, the court may commit him in custody to quarter sessions for
sentence in accordance with the provisions of s. 20 of the Criminal Justice Act, 1948.

† Section 97, so far as material, is set out at p. 791, letter H, and p. 792, letters A, C
and F, post.

A house that was being demolished, (ii) taking and driving away a motor cycle without the owner's consent, and (iii) driving while uninsured. He was committed under s. 28 of the Magistrates' Courts Act, 1952, to Coventry Quarter Sessions for sentence, where on Nov. 14, 1967, he was sentenced by the recorder (Bernard Caulfield, Esq., Q.C.) to three months' detention consecutive in respect of offences (i) and (ii), and to one day's imprisonment concurrent and disqualifica-

B tion for twelve months in respect of offence (iii). His application for leave to appeal against sentence was referred by Fenton Atkinson, J., to the court, on the question whether the disqualification and day's imprisonment for the third offence conferred a right of appeal against the sentences imposed for the other two offences under s. 97 (3) (c) (ii) of the Criminal Justice Act 1967. The facts appear in the judgment of the court.

C *J. B. R. Hazan* for the applicant*.

SACHS, L.J., delivered the following judgment of the court: On Oct. 19, 1967, at Coventry magistrates' court the applicant, aged nineteen, pleaded guilty to three offences. The first was a larceny on Oct. 6, the second was a taking and driving away of a motor cycle on Oct. 10 whilst he was on bail, and the

D third was using that same motor cycle on Oct. 10 without being covered by insurance. On Nov. 2 the applicant was committed under s. 29 of the Magistrates' Courts Act, 1952, and here the court would pause to mention that this was one of those cases in which it has had to refer only recently, in which there is an option (here as regards the first and second offences) of committing the applicant under s. 28 or s. 29, and in which it is thus normally appropriate to commit

E under s. 29 so that the court of quarter sessions can have all the further powers that then exist. When the matter came before Coventry quarter sessions, the learned recorder imposed the following sentences: for the first offence three months at a detention centre; for the second offence three months at a detention centre consecutive, and, finally, as regards the third offence, one day's imprisonment and disqualification for twelve months, the licence to be endorsed.

F The matter then came on application for leave to appeal before the single judge, and he remitted the case to the full court in order that it might be tested whether the sentences for the first and second offences could be the subject of appeal having regard to the provisions of s. 97 of the Criminal Justice Act 1967, bearing in mind the fact that the sentence of one day's imprisonment and disqualification for twelve months for the third offence was one in respect of which that section

G did specifically confer a right to appeal. As is well known, prior to s. 97 of the Criminal Justice Act 1967 coming into force on Oct. 1, 1967, there was, as regards sentences passed under s. 28 of the Act of 1952, no appeal unless the sentence was one of borstal training. Now when the matter comes before this court, counsel for the applicant has with frankness and clarity put before the court the points for consideration when reviewing the relevant subsections of s. 97 in the

H light of the fact that before the passing of the Act of 1967 there had been no right of appeal in respect of any of the three sentences. First of all s. 97 (1) provides:

"This section has effect for providing rights of appeal against sentence when a person is dealt with by a court of assize or quarter sessions (otherwise than on appeal from a magistrates' court) for an offence of which he was not convicted on indictment."

I Then sub-s. (2) refers to proceedings

". . . where an offender convicted of an offence by a magistrates' court— (a) is committed . . . to be dealt with for his offence at . . . quarter sessions; . . ."

and within this the first two sentences fall. When one comes, however, to sub-s. (3) one finds that it limits the right of appeal to offenders of three categories.

---

* Counsel appearing for the applicant on the application for leave to appeal did not appear on his behalf at the magistrates' court or quarter sessions.

Only the first of those categories is relevant (the second category refers to none A
of the three sentences whilst the third category refers only to the third sentence):
it provides as follows:

"... (a) where, either for that offence alone or for that offence and other
offences for which sentence is passed in the same proceeding, he is sentenced
to imprisonment for a term of six months or more ..."

B

The sentences for the first two offences were not sentences of imprisonment but
sentences to a detention centre; so at this point of the review the sentences under
consideration cease to fall within the ambit of s. 97 unless they can be brought
in by some of its later provisions. Counsel for the applicant accordingly referred
us to sub-s. (6) and sub-s. (7), with a view to the court examining whether the
sentence for the third offence enabled an appeal to be made as regards the other C
two. Subsection (6) provides:

"Where a court of assize or quarter sessions, in dealing with an offender
either on his conviction on indictment or in a proceeding to which sub-s. (2)
of this section applies, has passed on him two or more sentences in the same
proceeding, being sentences against which an appeal lies under s. 3 of the
Criminal Appeal Act, 1907 ..."

D

Pausing there for a moment, it is to be observed that provision is being made
only for cases in which there were passed two or more sentences in the same
proceedings against each of which an appeal lies under s. 3 of the Criminal Appeal
Act, 1907—and so far as the first and second offences are concerned no appeal
lies against either under that section. The subsection then proceeds in so far as
is material:

E

"... an appeal or application for leave to appeal against any one of those
sentences shall be treated as an appeal or application in respect of both or all
of them ..."

There is nothing in those last recited words which assists in overcoming the difficulty that neither of the first two offences was one against which an appeal lay F
under s. 3 of the Criminal Appeal Act, 1907. Then one passes to sub-s. (7). This
commences: "On an appeal against sentence under this section or s. 3 of the
Criminal Appeal Act, 1907 ..." It, accordingly, follows that nothing in sub-s. (7)
can bring the sentences for the first two offences into the ambit of s. 97—unless
there is some later part of that section which has such an effect. There is, however, nothing in the remainder either of sub-s. (7) or of any of the subsequent sub- G
sections which can have that effect. It follows that this court has no jurisdiction
to entertain any appeal relating to the sentences passed for offences (1) and (2).

There is, however, something which should be said with regard to those sentences. They relate to offences committed by a young man who had a record in
that in 1962 he had been sent to an approved school for taking and driving away
and three offences of larceny with four other offences taken into consideration; H
in March, 1966, he was fined for larceny in the form of shopbreaking and in
August, 1966, he had been sent to a detention centre for three months for taking
and driving away. The court of quarter sessions had before it, as this court
has before it, reports which are highly adverse and indicate that the appropriate
sentence should be borstal training. Indeed, it is to be noted that, in the course
of the submissions made by counsel for the applicant in the court below, counsel
was putting forward quite clearly that there were only two alternatives to be
considered in practice, viz., borstal training or probation. In the end, however,
despite all these matters the applicant was sentenced to two consecutive periods
of detention at a detention centre.

This court has said on more than one occasion that it is only in very rare cases
that a sentence to a detention centre should be imposed when the accused has
already served one such sentence. The reason for that lies in the nature of the
discipline at those centres, and the way in which it is expected to have an

A   immediate impact on those serving the sentence. The court feels it right to make perfectly clear that although the learned recorder may well have been disposed to endeavour to avoid sending the applicant to a period of borstal training, he in fact has imposed a sentence which was, in the view of this court, hardly appropriate to the case. The application is refused.

Application refused.

B   Solicitors: *Registrar of Criminal Appeals* (for the applicant).

[*Reported by* N. P. Metcalfe, Esq., *Barrister-at-Law.*]

C

Re LEEK (*deceased*). DARWEN *v.* LEEK AND OTHERS.

[Court of Appeal, civil division (Harman, Russell and Sachs, L.JJ.), December 6, 7, 8, 11, 20, 1967.]

Perpetuities—Rule against perpetuities—Power—Discretion to select beneficiaries
D   *—Single decision—Implication that decision to be reached within reasonable time—Pension provision for managing director of company.*
Trust and Trustee—Uncertainty—Discretionary trust—Power coupled with a trust
     —Class of beneficiaries including persons whom trustee should consider to have a moral claim on the deceased—Impossibility of all persons within class being known to trustee—Second trust " failing them "—Some persons within
E   *class of objects of first trust known to be living—Second trust, therefore, not arising—Both first and second trust ineffective—Pension provision for managing director of company.*

L., the managing director of a company, arranged with it to effect an endowment assurance policy on his life providing for payment of £18,807 on his death before attaining the age of sixty-five, the company meeting the
F   cost but the annual premium being met by a deduction of £1,000 from L.'s salary. The policy was expressed as being effected by the company as trustee for L., and held in trust subject to conditions set out in a letter, dated Dec. 1, 1956, from the company to L., under which the policy moneys on the death of L. were to be held on trust (referred to as " the first trust ") " for the benefit of such one or more of the following persons as the company in its
G   absolute discretion shall decide namely [L.'s] wife, children or other issue or such other persons that the company may consider to have a moral claim upon [L.] " or on trust (referred to as " the second trust ") " failing them upon trust for the benefit of such one or more of the statutory next-of-kin in both cases in such shares and in such manner as the company in its absolute discretion shall decide ". L. subsequently made a will leaving his
H   entire estate to his widow, and two years later, in 1959, he died leaving his widow and three unmarried children. If the trusts stated in the letter of Dec. 1, 1956, were invalid, the policy moneys, which had been paid to · the personal representative of L., would pass to L.'s widow and estate duty would be exigible at about forty-five per cent.; but if trusts were not invalid estate duty would not be so payable,

I   **Held:** (i) the trusts declared in the letter of Dec. 1, 1956, were ineffective and the policy moneys passed to the widow under L.'s will for the following reasons—

(a) the first trust gave rise to a power coupled with a duty, not merely to a bare power, and was void for uncertainty as it was not possible to predicate that the donee (the company) was in a position to know of all persons who might be objects of the power, as such objects included any person whom the company might consider to have a moral claim on L. (see p. 797, letter F, p. 798, letter I, to p. 799, letter A, and p. 800, letters G and I, post).

Re Ogden ([1933] All E.R. Rep. 720) applied.

Re Gestetner ([1953] 1 All E.R. 1150) distinguished.

(b) the second trust did not come into operation, because there were persons who were within the class of objects of the first trust, with the consequence that there was no such failure as would satisfy the words " failing them " which introduced the second trust (see p. 797, letter I, p. 799, letter B, and p. 801, letter C, post).

(ii) neither the first trust nor the second trust infringed the rule against perpetuities, for the decision of the company envisaged by the letter of Dec. 1, 1956, was a single decision, not decisions taken from time to time, and (per HARMAN, L.J., SACHS, L.J., concurring), must be taken within a reasonable time (see p. 797, letter G, p. 798, letters B and F, and p. 800, letter I, post).

Decision of BUCKLEY, J. ([1967] 2 All E.R. 1160) affirmed on (i), but on different grounds, and disapproved on (ii) above.

[As to the certainty of objects to be benefited by a trust and to discretion being given to trustees as to what objects are to be benefited, see 38 HALSBURY'S LAWS (3rd Edn.) 835, 836, paras. 1399-1401; and for cases on the subject see 47 DIGEST (Repl.) 58, 59, *419-423.*

As to the rule against perpetuities, see 29 HALSBURY'S LAWS (3rd Edn.) 281-283, paras. 567-571; and for cases on the subject see 37 DIGEST (Repl.) 55, 56, *1-13.*]

Cases referred to:

Abbott, Re, Peacock v. *Frigout*, [1893] 1 Ch. 54; 62 L.J.Ch. 46; 67 L.T. 794; 37 Digest (Repl.) 113, *437.*

Attwood v. *Lamont*, [1920] All E.R. Rep. 55; [1920] 3 K.B. 571; 90 L.J.K.B. 121; 124 L.T. 108; 45 Digest (Repl.) 442, *263.*

Canning's Will Trusts, Re, Skues v. *Lyon*, [1936] Ch. 309; 105 L.J.Ch. 241; 154 L.T. 693; 37 Digest (Repl.) 125, *521.*

De Sommery, Re, Coelenbier v. *De Sommery*, [1912] 2 Ch. 622; 82 L.J.Ch. 17; 107 L.T. 253, 823; 37 Digest (Repl.) 113, *436.*

Gestetner (decd.), Re, Barnett v. *Blumka*, [1953] 1 All E.R. 1150; [1953] Ch. 672; [1953] 2 W.L.R. 1033; 37 Digest (Repl.) 411, *1400.*

Goldsoll v. *Goldman*, [1914-15] All E.R. Rep. 257; [1915] 1 Ch. 292; 84 L.J.Ch. 228; 112 L.T. 494; 45 Digest (Repl.) 306, *209.*

Gulbenkian's Settlement Trusts, Re, Hacobian v. *Maun*, [1967] 3 All E.R. 15; [1967] 3 W.L.R. 1112.

Hillas & Co., Ltd. v. *Arcos, Ltd.*, [1932] All E.R. Rep. 494; 147 L.T. 503; 39 Digest (Repl.) 448, *34.*

Lassence v. *Tierney*, [1843-60] All E.R. Rep. 47; (1849), 1 Mac. & G. 551; 15 L.T.O.S. 557; 41 E.R. 1379; 47 Digest (Repl.) 115, *821.*

Ogden, Re, Brydon v. *Samuel*, [1933] All E.R. Rep. 720; [1933] Ch. 678; 102 L.J.Ch. 226; 149 L.T. 162; 48 Digest (Repl.) 479, *4339.*

Appeal.

The appellant, the first defendant, was the widow of Lieut-Col. Ivan George Elmer Leek, the former managing director of the fifth defendant, Dosco Overseas Engineering, Ltd. Col. Leek, having become aware of the tax relief allowed in respect of approved penions schemes under s. 388 of the Income Tax Act, 1952, negotiated an assurance policy with the North British and Mercantile Insurance Co., Ltd., and secured the approval of the board of directors of the defendant company to an arrangement recorded in a letter dated Dec. 1, 1956, from the defendant company to himself. Under that arrangement the defendant company was at its own cost to effect with the insurance company a non-profit endowment assurance on Col. Leek's life in a sum of £18,807 payable in the event of his dying before his sixty-fifth birthday, with provision for a payment of £1,880 4s. per annum on his retirement on survival beyond that date. The

A policy was to be expressed as being effected by the company as trustee for Col.
Leek and was to be held by the company in trust for conditions set out in the
letter. The conditions included death benefit provisions*. On Sept. 25, 1957,
the defendant company effected a policy on Col. Leek's life in accordance with
the arrangement. The company was described in the policy as the assured " as
trustee for the person whose life is assured ", i.e., for Col. Leek, and the policy

B was expressed to be issued in accordance with the terms of the letter of Dec. 1,
1956. The arrangement was initiated on the footing that as from Dec. 1, 1956,
Col. Leek's salary as managing director of the defendant company should be
reduced by £1,000 per annum, the amount of the yearly premium on the policy.
It was also subject to the formal approval of the inland revenue being obtained.
Col. Leek's salary was so reduced, and the inland revenue approved the scheme

C on Oct. 18, 1957. Col. Leek died on Dec. 18, 1959, aged forty-nine, while still
managing director of the defendant company. By his will he appointed the
plaintiff, the Right Hon. Cedric Percival, Baron Darwen, to be his executor and
left all his property to his widow, the first defendant. He left three children, the
second, third and fourth defendants, who were all unmarried. Both his parents
and a brother and two sisters also survived him. In due course the insurance

D company paid the defendant company a net sum of £17,890 6s. 8d., being the sum
of £18,807 assured by the policy less £916 13s. 4d. the balance of the current
year's premium from Jan. 1, 1960 to Nov. 1, 1960. On Mar. 1, 1960, the directors
of the defendant company resolved that the whole of the policy moneys should
be applied to the benefit of the first defendant, and on Mar. 16, 1960, it paid
the sum of £17,890 6s. 8d. to the plaintiff who held the fund. The plaintiff

E applied by originating summons for determination of the question whether
he held the fund

" Upon trust for the benefit of such one or more of [the first, second, third
and fourth defendants] and such other persons as [the defendant company]
may consider to have had a moral claim upon [Col. Leek] in such shares
and in such manner as [the defendant company] shall in its absolute discre-

F tion decide; or (b) upon trust for the benefit of such one or more of [the first
four defendants as the statutory next-of-kin of Col. Leek] in such shares
and in such manner as [the defendant company] shall in its absolute discretion decide; or (c) upon trust for himself as the personal representative of
[Col. Leek]; or (d) upon trust for [the defendant company] beneficially; or
(e) upon some other and if so what trusts."

G The Commissioners of Inland Revenue were joined as the sixth defendants
because, if the fund formed part of Col. Leek's estate, duty would be payable
in respect of it on his death.

On Apr. 28, 1967, as reported at [1967] 2 All E.R. 1160, BUCKLEY, J., held that
the first trust expressed in the letter was not void for uncertainty but was void

H on the ground of perpetuity, and the second trust, being dependent on it also
failed on the ground of perpetuity. The fund therefore resulted to the estate of
Col. Leek, and the plaintiff held the sum of £17,890 6s. 8d. on trust for himself
as personal representative of Col. Leek. The first defendant (Col. Leek's widow)
appealed to the Court of Appeal. She sought an order declaring that the plaintiff
held the sum of £17,890 6s. 8d. on trust for the benefit for such one or more of the

I first, second, third and fourth defendants as the statutory next-of-kin of Col. Leek,
in such shares and in such manner as the defendant company should in its absolute
discretion decide. The grounds of appeal were as follows: (i) that the judge having
held that the provision contained in the letter of the defendant company dated
Dec. 1, 1956, in favour of the widow, children or other issue of Col. Leek, or such
other persons as the defendant company might consider to have a moral claim
on Col. Leek, was a provision conferring on the company a power of selection not
coupled with a duty, but which was void for perpetuity, was wrong in law in

---

* The relevant provisions are set out at p. 796, letter F, post.

holding that the trust thereafter declared in the letter in favour of the statutory   A
next-of-kin of Col. Leek was dependent on the first provision, and had therefore
also to fail in consequence of the failure of the previous provision on the ground
of perpetuity; and (ii) that the judge ought to have held that the validity of
the further provision (being a trust) could not have been affected by the invalidity
of the earlier provision (being a bare power), and ought consequently to have
upheld the validity of the further provision.   B

J. W. Mills, Q.C., and *G. M. Godfrey* for the first defendant, the widow.
A. J. Balcombe for the plaintiff executor.
H. E. Francis, Q.C., and *J. P. Warner* for the Crown.

Cur. adv. vult.

Dec. 20. The following judgments were read.   C

HARMAN, L.J.: There are no disputed facts in this case; they are set
out in the affidavit in support of the originating summons and repeated so far as
relevant in the judgment of the judge below (1). The question raised by the
summons and by the appeal is whether a sum of £17,890 6s. 8d. at present in the
hands of the plaintiff is held by him on trust for the assured's widow, the first
defendant, by reason of a decision in her favour by the fifth defendant company, D
Dosco Overseas Engineering, Ltd., which it was empowered to make by the policy
of assurance on the life of her husband, Col. Leek, who died on Sept. 25, 1957,
and left his estate to her. The terms of the policy are stated by reference to a
letter dated Dec. 1, 1956, written by the defendant company to Col. Leek. If,
on the true construction of that letter, the trusts declared were valid, then no
estate duty is payable on the policy moneys on Col. Leek's death. If, on the other E
hand, the trusts fail or are void, as the judge below has held (2) them to be, the
moneys pass to the first defendant, the widow, as the universal legatee of her
husband, and, being part of his estate, must bear duty at the appropriate rate,
which I understand to be some forty-five per cent.

The whole question turns on one paragraph in the letter in question, which is
a letter addressed to Col. Leek and is in these terms: F

" All sums arising out of (a), (b) and (c) above shall be held by the [defen-
dant company] upon trust for the benefit of such one or more of the following
persons as the [defendant company] in its absolute discretion shall decide
namely your wife, children or other issue or such other persons as the
[defendant company] may consider to have a moral claim upon you or failing
them upon trust for the benefit of such one or more of the statutory next-of-
kin in both cases in such shares and in such manner as the [defendant
company] in its absolute discretion shall decide."

Sub-paragraphs (a), (b) and (c) referred to in the paragraph appear in para. 6
of the letter, and the relevant event is the death of the assured while in the
defendant company's service and before the normal retirement date, for this is G
the event which happened.

The first question which the judge decided was whether the first trust was an
imperative trust for all the objects mentioned, that is to say, the wife, children or
other issue of Col. Leek or such other persons as the defendant company might
consider to have a moral claim on him. The judge held (2) that this imposed no
obligation on the defendant company to make a distribution; it was enough
for the defendant company to consider the question whether it should do so,
and they were perfectly at liberty to come to the conclusion that they should
not. The other view is that the trust is a trust to distribute the whole fund, the
power of decision being merely a power to decide what objects of the trust
should receive benefit and when and how.

There is all the difference in the world in law between these two views. If the

A trust be on its true construction a mere power imposing no obligation beyond consideration, then the trust is good from this point of view (see *Re Gestetner (decd.), Barnett* v. *Blumka* (3)), a decision of my own at first instance which has I think received the approval of the higher courts. It is not necessary in a trust so framed to be able to say with certainty that the whole field can be surveyed. It is enough if the donee of the power can say of any particular person making a

B claim that he or she is or is not an object of it.

It was argued that even on this footing the trust was too vague, because the question whether A has a moral claim on B is not a question of fact but of mere opinion depending on so many imponderables, and the personal views of the donee of the power, that it is impossible to say of any given claimant whether he or she has such a claim. If the trust were for such persons as *have* moral claims, I

C would agree with this view, but this is not the trust. The trustees are made the arbiters and the objects are such persons as they may *consider* to have a moral claim; and I do not see why they should not be able on this footing to make up their minds and arrive at a decision.

On the other view the law is, as shown by the leading case of *Re Ogden, Brydon* v. *Samuel* (4), a decision of TOMLIN, J., and recited in *Re Gestetner* (3), that the

D donee of the power must be in a position to know all the objects of it. This in my judgment they could not do in this case with sufficient certainty; and on that footing the trust would be bad.

The judge below held (5) that this was a mere power not coupled with a trust to distribute and, therefore, so far good. He founded himself I think on the words "shall decide". My mind has wavered on this subject and I thought at one time

E that this was right, because it seemed unlikely that, if there were no wife, children or issue, and the trustees could only find one person whom they considered to have a moral claim, one person should be entitled to take the whole fund. It was, however, argued against this that, in those circumstances there might well be other relations, not wife, children or issue, who might be considered to have moral claims on the testator; and on the whole I am of opinion that the first

F trust is a trust coupled with a duty and as such is bad for that reason, as I have explained. It is not possible for the donee of the power to be able to say that all possible objects are before it.

The judge, while holding that the first trust passed the test of uncertainty, held (6) it bad for perpetuity on the footing that the decision might be deferred from time to time beyond the permitted range (see per PARKER, J., in *Re De*

G *Sommery, Coelenbier* v. *De Sommery* (7)). I do not share this view. In my judgment, on the true construction of this clause the decision could not be deferred indefinitely but must be taken within a reasonable time, far less than twenty-one years. Successive interests may indeed be decided on, but the decision must be taken once and for all. If, therefore, I had thought that the trust passed the first test of uncertainty, I should have held that it passed the second test of perpetuity.

H As it is, I must come to the next relevant words, which are "failing them". These words seem to me in their natural meaning to signify failing any objects of the first trust, and indeed I think that it is admitted that that must be their meaning if the first provision be an imperative one. The alternative view is that "failing them" means in effect in default of appointment or failing persons among whom a selection is made, and I should have been inclined to take this view if I

I had held the power to be a mere power. As it is, however, I am of opinion that it cannot be said that there has been a failure, because the testator has been survived by a wife, children and issue. On this view the second provision does not arise and the gift fails altogether, with the result that under the well-known

---

(3) [1953] 1 All E.R. 1150; [1953] Ch. 672.
(4) [1933] All E.R. Rep. 720; [1933] Ch. 678.
(5) [1956] 2 All E.R. at p. 1165, letter G; [1967] Ch. at pp. 1076, 1077.
(6) [1967] 2 All E.R. 1160, holding (ii).
(7) [1912] 2 Ch. 622 at p. 632.

rule in *Lassence* v. *Tierney* (8) the original trust for the assured on whose life the   A
policy depended would survive under cl. 2 of the letter, which states that the
" policy will be expressed as being effected by the [defendant company] as trustee
for you ".   The schedule to the policy itself shows that the defendant company
is the assured as trustee for the person whose life is assured, viz., the testator.

If I had held the trust to be in effect a mere power so that the first provision was
good, I should have held that the words " failing them " meant in default of   B
appointment, and should have held that the second provision arose, viz., such one
or more of the statutory next-of-kin as the company should decide.   Here again
I think that the decision must be made within a reasonable time, and this provision would therefore on that footing be good.   The judge held (9) that the second
trust was bad for perpetuity as being dependent on the first, but if it had arisen
I should not have taken this view (see *Re Abbott, Peacock* v. *Frigout* (10) and   C
Re Canning's Will Trusts, Skues v. *Lyon* (11)).   In the event, therefore, I hold
that the whole trust fails and that the money passes to the widow under the
testator's will and will be subject to duty accordingly.   I would dismiss the
appeal, but not for the reasons given by the judge (12).

     RUSSELL, L.J.:   The arrangement was in these terms, rewritten.   The sum   D
payable on Col. Leek's death before retirement age under the policy shall be held
by the defendant company: (A) upon trust for the benefit of such one or more of
the following persons as the defendant company in its absolute discretion shall
decide (and in such shares and in such manner as the defendant company in its
absolute discretion shall decide) viz., (i) Col. Leek's wife; (ii) Col. Leek's children;
(iii) Col. Leek's other issue; (iv) such other persons as the defendant company   E
may consider to have a moral claim on Col. Leek; or failing them (B) upon trust
for such one or more of the statutory next-of-kin of Col. Leek and in such shares
and in such manner, as the defendant company in its absolute discretion shall
decide.

I consider first the suggestion that either under (A) or (B) or both the rule
against perpetuities is infringed.   BUCKLEY, J., thought so (13), but, with respect   F
to his view, I do not.   The question admittedly turns on whether the defendant
company is empowered to make decisions from time to time, and in my judgment
the language of the provision, in the context of the subject matter, fairly construed, points, whether under (A) or (B), to a single decision on the part of the
defendant company.

Perpetuity being out of the way, there remains the question of certainty, which   G
I find one of some difficulty.   The first, and I think proper, approach is simply to
see what the language apparently means.   It seems to me that it assumes that
the defendant company *will* arrive at a decision and that Col. Leek was relying
on it to do so.   The words " or failing them " seem to me to refer naturally to
the non-existence of persons in class (A) at the death and to assume that the
decision in respct of class (A) will be made if that class exists.   It would be a   H
quite extraordinary use of language to provide in alternative terms a class (B)
of statutory next-of-kin when, if either wife or issue survive, they or he or she
must embrace the whole of that class (B).   It is true that, if class (A) were to consist
of only one old retainer, it is unlikely that it was intended that that person
should take the whole £18,000 to the exclusion of parents or cousins of Col. Leek;
but the force of the language persuades me that this possible outcome was over-   I
looked; or it may have been thought that in such circumstances parents and
cousins might be considered to have a moral claim.   Accordingly I consider that

    (8) [1843-60] All E.R. Rep. 47.
    (9) [1967] 2 All E.R. at p. 1166; [1967] 2 Ch. at p. 1078.
    (10) [1893] 1 Ch. 54.
    (11) [1936] Ch. 309.
    (12) [1967] 2 All E.R. 1160; [1967] Ch. 1061.
    (13) [1967] 2 All E.R. 1160, holding (ii); [1967] Ch. at p. 1077.

A in respect of class (A) as well as the alternative class (B) there is here more than a mere power.

In that case in the present state of authority the inclusion of the fourth head in class (A) vitiates the trust power conferred on the defendant company in respect of class (A), on the ground of uncertainty; and there being in existence persons in class (A), then, on my construction of " or failing them ", the power in respect

B of class (B) never came into existence. Therefore, on different grounds from those which found favour with BUCKLEY, J. (14) I would uphold the decision and dismiss the appeal.

SACHS, L.J.: This case concerns the effect of one short sub-paragraph in a contractual document passing between a commercial company and its managing

C director, one Lieut.-Col. Leek. That sub-paragraph dealt in a compact and businesslike way with the trusts on which the company was to hold any sum payable under an insurance policy if Col. Leek died whilst in their employ and before reaching the age of sixty-five. Had that sub-paragraph been sent by Col. Leek to a member of the legal profession to serve as instructions for the preparation of a formal deed, a document of considerable length might well have resulted,

D after there had been asked of Col. Leek some questions, to which the answers with which this court might have been concerned would have been obvious. Then due and simple precautions would have been taken to see the deed contained nothing which could render its provisions void. This was not done, and to my mind the court should now proceed to construe this sub-paragraph in a businesslike way and with an approach that may differ somewhat from that with which

E there should be examined a deed prepared by a semantically trained professional man familiar with the law as to trusts and the decisions of the courts on the effect of particular sets of words.

There are two questions of principle which, trite though they may be, seem relevant to be raised at the outset. First, is there any reason why there should not apply to this case the principle that, where a phrase in a particular document is capable of more than one reasonable interpretation, that should be preferred

F which produces validity rather than invalidity, just as that which produces legality of object should be preferred to that which produces illegality of object? This maxim is set out in the well-known words of LORD WRIGHT (15):

" It is accordingly, the duty of the court to construe such documents fairly and broadly, without being too astute or subtle in finding defects; but, on the

G contrary, the court should seek to apply the old maxim of English law, verba ita sunt intelligenda ut res magis valeat quam pereat."

On the first day of the hearing I diffidently threw out the suggestion that one of the well-known axioms might have some bearing on the problems in this case. Thereupon I at once felt somewhat as one condemned shortly to go to a colony of outcast heretics. However, when on the third day the judgments in *Re*

H *Gulbenkian's Settlement Trusts, Hacobian* v. *Maun* (16) were read, I found that after all at any rate there was a chance that LORD DENNING, M.R., and WINN, L.J., might be my companions there. Secondly, the question arose as to what terms ought necessarily to be implied in this document. When MACKINNON, L.J.'s officious bystander (16a) and his questions were mentioned, it appeared to be conceded that the test could be applied to some of the questions in issue, provided,

I however, that his lips were tightly sealed if any thought of the rule against perpetuities came into his head.

Suffice it to say at this point that both principles should if possible be applied when one is trying to expand into full form the effect of this compact sub-paragraph. It is otherwise only too easy to find oneself having to adopt a construction which does not allow for the factor that phrases in such a document

(14) [1967] 2 All E.R. 1160; [1967] Ch. 1066.
(15) In *Hillas & Co., Ltd.* v. *Arcos, Ltd.*, [1932] All E.R. Rep. 494 at p. 503; 147 L.T. 503 at p. 514.   (16) [1967] 3 All E.R. 15.   (16a) See [1939] 2 All E.R. at p. 124.

written by a lay writer may have to that writer a reasonable meaning which is   A
not necessarily the one which appeals most to the trained legal mind. The
importance of these principles is not diminished by the suggestion made on
behalf of the Crown that there may be large numbers of documents in existence
today couched in parallel language to the one under consideration.

I now turn to the series of questions raised in the course of this case. When
doing so I will refer to the words   B

> " upon trust for the benefit of such one or more of the following persons as
> the [defendant company] in its absolute discretion shall decide namely
> your wife, children or other issue or such other persons as the [defendant
> company] may consider to have a moral claim upon you "

as the first trust, and the words " or failing them upon trust for the benefit   C
of such one or more of the statutory next-of-kin " as the second trust. The
first issue is whether the first trust imposes on the trustees powers coupled with a
duty of a type which would, if necessary, be exercised by the court, or whether,
on the other hand, they merely entrust the trustees with bare powers. On this
issue I am attracted by the reasoning of Buckley, J., in coming to his conclusion.
He has said (17):   D

> " It is true that in one sense at least it is mandatory. It provides that the
> fund shall be held in trust for certain objects; but for what objects? For
> such one or more of a specified class of potential beneficiaries as the com-
> pany in its absolute discretion shall select. I can find in this language no
> express imposition of a duty to make a selection, but merely of a duty to
> hold the fund in trust for such objects of the power, if any, as the company   E
> may select. The words ' shall decide ', as a matter of grammar and of the
> natural meaning of the English language, do not, in my judgment, have
> any mandatory force."

I would, however, add one further point. Any other construction of the relevant
words could produce a result that could not (as counsel for the Crown conceded)
have been intended by Col. Leek. For if neither wife, children or other issue sur-   F
vived, the whole £18,000 would have perhaps to go to the only person with a
moral claim, even if that moral claim was only for £100 for money due in circumstances for which the law gave no cause of action (e.g., money paid for a past
consideration). This I will call the "£100 claim" point. Having, however, had the
advantage of reading the judgment, of my lords, I am impelled by the narrowest
of margins to adopt their reasoning as being that which a legally trained court   G
on construction should prefer.

The balance being so even, can one then apply the ut res magis valeat principle?
No one could say that a construction adopted by an experienced judge of the
High Court at first instance is not a reasonable construction, and that view is
reinforced by the fact that one of my lords wavered before coming to the opposite
conclusion. Bereft of authority, I would have applied the ut res magis valeat rule,   H
saved the trusts, and thus prevented there being thwarted the wishes of Col.
Leek, the trustees, and all who in practice were intended to benefit under this
compact business document; but in this court I do not, having regard to authority, find myself able to take this course and must suppress any tendencies of
mine to heresy. Accordingly I reluctantly concur in the views expressed by my
lords and hope that what is heresy here may not necessarily be heresy hereafter.

As regards the issues relating to uncertainty and perpetuities, I agree with the
views expressed by my lords, realising that in so doing I respectfully differ from
Buckley, J. (18), finding myself unable to agree with him on the second point.
Here again if the reasoning which I have adopted were wrong, I would for myself
have wished, had I been free so to do, to apply the ut res magis valeat rule. Moreover, as regards the perpetuities point, I find it extremely difficult to see the

(17) [1967] 2 All E.R. at p. 1165; [1967] Ch. at p. 1075.
(18) [1967] 2 All E.R. 1160; [1967] Ch. 1061.

A reason why the presumption of legality in favour of a contract is not here available
when the question arises—does it offend against public policy?—for it is on public
policy that the rule against perpetuities is founded. I gather that my difficulties
on this matter were shared to some extent by the learned author of GRAY ON
PERPETUITIES; see p. 601, para. 633, where he states:

B   " But there is a legitimate use of the rule against perpetuities in matters of
    construction. When the expression which a testator uses is really ambiguous,
    and is fairly capable of two constructions, one of which would produce a legal
    result, and the other a result that would be bad for remoteness, it is a fair
    presumption that the testator meant to create a legal rather than a illegal
    interest."

C   As regards the correct interpretation of " failing this ", I concur with what has
been said by my lords. Again I observe that the ut res magis valeat principle
might have saved the day.   For, taking the matter commercially as a whole, it
seems to me it would have been a reasonable interpretation of this part of the
sub-paragraph to read it as stating as follows: " If for any reason the trustee did
not or could not decide that all the policy money was to be expended on the
D persons named in the first trusts, then the trustees should proceed to implement
the second trusts."   The " £100 claim " point could be prayed in aid in this
behalf; but that note cannot in the event affect my above-stated concurrence.

There is, however, a further matter to which I would advert with the natural
diffidence of one who has for the first time entered the hallowed fields of trusts
and powers, of uncertainties, and of perpetuities, and has incidentally found
roaming there one no less than the Attorney-General seeking to achieve on the
E construction of a short document the one result which could be manifestly
contrary to the legitimate intentions of the dead man and also contrary to the
interests and wishes of each and every one of all others concerned. In the present
case, as in other similar cases which an executor feels impelled of his own volition
to bring before the courts, substantial justice could on occasion easily be done if a
single severable phrase (here " or such other persons as the [defendant company]
F may consider to have a moral claim upon you ") in the relevant document were
excised and the rest were left intact. On the ascertained facts of the present
case to excise the phrase " or such other persons as the [defendant company]
may consider to have a moral claim upon you " could do no possible injustice to
anybody.

In other fields the courts have found their inherent jurisdiction armed them
G with powers to strike out in suitable cases words which created an invalidity and
leave the rest of the material parts of the document standing with good effect.
That is the practice as regards contracts, where, for instance, the blue pencil
can after careful scrutiny (*Attwood* v. *Lamont* (19)) be used to strike out words (cf.,
Goldsoll v. *Goldman* (20)), or clauses operating in invalid restraint of trade, and
similar steps have been taken in other categories of contract. Similarly there are
H powers, albeit limited, to exclude or ignore words in testamentary documents,
leaving the will otherwise intact. In the fields relevant to the present case the
court seems not to have any such powers and indeed counsel for the first defendant
made no submission that such powers existed. Perhaps the Law Commission, in
the interests of avoiding much potential injustice, might consider whether a single
short curative clause in the Bill might be useful. I agree that this appeal has to be
I dismissed by this court.

Appeal dismissed. Leave to appeal to the House of Lords granted.

Solicitors: *Beale & Co.* (for the first defendant and the plaintiff); *Solicitor of
Inland Revenue.*

[*Reported by* F. A. AMIES, ESQ., *Barrister-at-Law.*]

---

(19) [1920] All E.R. Rep. 55; [1920] 3 K.B. 396.
(20) [1914-15] All E.R. Rep. 257; [1915] 1 Ch. 292.

A

CLIXBY v. POUNTNEY (Inspector of Taxes).

[CHANCERY DIVISION (Cross, J.), December 8, 11, 1967.]

Income Tax—Assessment—Additional assessment—Fraud or wilful default—
Default committed on behalf of any person—False returns by taxpayer's
accountant—Taxpayer not personally in default—Power to make additional
assessment at any time—Income Tax Act, 1952 (15 & 16 Geo. 6 & 1 Eliz. 2
c. 10), s. 47 (1).

B

The taxpayer carried on business as a haulage contractor from 1943-44 to
1948-49 inclusive. He employed an accountant to prepare his accounts and
make the necessary returns for income tax purposes. He let the accountant
have his books and vouchers for the purpose, opened certain undisclosed
bank accounts on the accountant's advice and let him have the relevant   C
bank books. The taxpayer said he had complete confidence in the accountant,
accepted his figures without question believing them to show his correct
profits and taxable income, and signed the income tax returns without
checking or examining them. The returns understated the profits of the
business to a substantial extent and sums of untaxed bank interest received
by the taxpayer were not disclosed. In 1963 the Crown made additional   D
assessments on the taxpayer in respect of the undisclosed profits and interest
on the ground that fraud or wilful default had been committed by or on behalf
of the taxpayer in connexion with his income tax under s. 47 of the Income
Tax Act, 1952, authorising such assessments at any time in such circumstances. The accountant had since died. The General Commissioners of
Income Tax were not satisfied that the taxpayer personally had been guilty   E
of wilful default, but were satisfied that the accountant had been guilty of
wilful default committed on behalf of the taxpayer, and they confirmed
the assessments. On appeal by the taxpayer,

Held: the additional assessments must be confirmed because the words
wilful default committed " on behalf of any person " in the proviso to s. 47
(1) of the Act of 1952, on their natural construction, included wilful default   F
by the taxpayer's agent, and they were not given a meaning restricted to
employees by any narrower application of the words in s. 501 (2), a provision
historically related to the proviso to s. 47 (1) (see p. 807, letters A and C, and
p. 806, letter E, post).

Appeal dismissed.

[As to fraud or wilful default committed by a taxpayer in connexion with   G
income tax, see 20 HALSBURY'S LAWS (3rd Edn.) 672, para. 1318; and for a case
on the subject, see 28 DIGEST (Repl.) 386, *1685*.

For the Income Tax Act, 1952, s. 47, see 31 HALSBURY'S STATUTES (2nd Edn.)
53.]

Case referred to: H

Wellington v. *Reynolds (Inspector of Taxes)*, (1962), 40 Tax Cas. 209; Digest
(Cont. Vol. A) 912, *1685b*.

Case Stated.

The taxpayer appealed to the General Commissioners of Income Tax for
Carringham in the county of Lincoln against the following: (i) additional assessments made on him under Case I of Sch. D to the Income Tax Act, 1952, for the
years 1943-44 (subject to the question of wilful default, amount agreed at nil),
1944-45 (£746), 1945-46 (£957), 1946-47 (£1,565), 1947-48 (£2,418) and 1948-49
(nil), in respect of profits arising from the trade of a haulage contractor; (ii)
additional assessments under Case III of Sch. D for the same years (£10, £11,
£20, £21, £15 and £16 respectively) and for the year 1949-50 (£15) in respect of
untaxed interest; (iii) a first assessment under Case I of Sch. D for 1949-50 in
respect of profits from the trades of a haulage contractor and a farmer (£127 and
£88 respectively); and (iv) an additional assessment under Case I of Sch. D in

A　respect of a balancing charge for the year 1949-50 (nil). The additional assessments under headings (i) and (ii) having been first made on Nov. 23, 1963, for the purpose of making good to the Crown a loss of tax attributable to fraud or wilful default, the question for the commissioners' determination in respect of those assessments was whether fraud or wilful default had been committed by or on behalf of the taxpayer in connexion with or in relation to income tax assess-

B　ments for those years so that the proviso to s. 47 (1) of the Income Tax Act, 1952, applied. The commissioners* were not satisfied that the taxpayer personally had been guilty of wilful default, but found that his accountant had been guilty of wilful default committed on his behalf and they therefore confirmed all the assessments appealed against in the agreed amounts. The taxpayer appealed by way of Case Stated to the High Court.

C　　*M. C. Flesch* for the taxpayer.
　　J. R. Phillips for the Crown.

　　CROSS, J.: This is a back duty case. On Nov. 23, 1963, additional assessments were made on the appellant taxpayer, Arthur Raymond Clixby, under Case I of Sch. D to the Income Tax Act, 1952 in respect of profits arising from the

D　trade of a haulage contractor for the years 1943-44 to 1948-49 inclusive and under Case III for the same years, and also the year 1949-1950 in respect of untaxed interest. It is not in dispute that the profits of the taxpayer's business were understated in his returns for the years in question to a substantial extent or that sums of untaxed bank interest received by him in the years in question were not disclosed in his returns. Having regard to the terms of s. 47 of the Income Tax

E　Act, 1952, the additional assessments in question cannot stand unless the Crown can establish that fraud or wilful default was committed by or on behalf of the taxpayer in connexion with or in relation to his income tax. The taxpayer gave evidence and the effect of his evidence is summarised by the General Commissioners of Income Tax in para. 6 of the Case, which I will read.

F　　" The [taxpayer's] evidence was that from the start of his business in 1923 he employed John James Stokes (now deceased) an accountant to prepare the accounts relating to his business and to make all necessary returns for tax purposes. Once in every year John James Stokes called upon the [taxpayer] and collected his books receipts and vouchers and prepared accounts and returns of income which were sent to the [taxpayer], who signed the returns without checking them or examining them, because he had complete faith in John James Stokes and accepted his figures without question believing them to show his correct profits and taxable income. The undisclosed bank accounts had been opened by the [taxpayer] upon the advice of John James Stokes and John James Stokes had the relevant bank books every year and nothing was suppressed from him.

　　" The [taxpayer] admitted that untaxed interest from the bank deposit account had never been shown on any of his returns, and that the word ' none ' had been entered in the appropriate spaces. The [taxpayer] admitted that he had been in business since 1927 and had signed income tax returns since that year. When asked whether he had ever read the returns, he said that he might have read one at some time, but he had had complete faith in his accountant. The [taxpayer] admitted that he had received and read copies of the accounts, but not until after the profits or losses had been agreed. He had read the accounts in the normal course of events. He agreed that outstanding debts would be a material factor and when asked to explain how, if he had looked at the accounts, he had failed to notice the under-stated debtors, he replied that he had had complete faith in Mr. Stokes. When referred to a stock of spares valued at £1,100 in the 1944 accounts, which

---

* The facts of the case, the contentions of the Crown, the findings of the commissioners and the issues for determination by the court are set out at letter F, above to p. 804, lette F, post.

eventually turned out to be worth some £3,000, he said he could not explain the difference in the stock valuations."

Next I will read para. 8:

" It was clear to us from the statements prepared by the [taxpayer's] present accountants (namely exhibits: B, C1, C2, C3 and C4 and D1 and D2) from the working papers of John James Stokes who died in 1954 that John James Stokes had in his possession information relating to the bank accounts and profits sufficient to enable him to make correct returns and prepare accurate accounts on behalf of the [taxpayer]."

The inspector of taxes contended that the additional assessments were valid because (i) the taxpayer himself had been guilty of wilful default in relation to income tax and (ii) wilful default had in any case been committed on his behalf by his accountant, Mr. John James Stokes. The General Commissioners stated their conclusions in para. 9 of the Case as follows:

" We were not satisfied that the [taxpayer] personally was guilty of wilful default, but we were satisfied and we found that the said John James Stokes was guilty of wilful default committed on behalf of the [taxpayer] and accordingly we confirmed all the assessments appealed against."

The taxpayer having expressed dissatisfaction, the commissioners stated a Case for the opinion of the court in the following terms:

" The questions of law for the opinion of the court are: (i) whether we were wrong in finding on the evidence that the said John James Stokes was guilty of wilful default committed on behalf of the [taxpayer]. (ii) whether we were wrong in holding that the additional assessments made upon the [taxpayer] on Nov. 23, 1963, for the years 1943-44 to 1948-49 inclusive were valid because of wilful default committed on behalf of the [taxpayer] by the said John James Stokes."

It would have been strictly more correct to have said that they found that the taxpayer was guilty of wilful default committed not by him personally but on his behalf by Mr. Stokes.

Counsel for the Crown does not seek to challenge the finding of the General Commissioners that the taxpayer was not personally guilty of any fraud or wilful default. On the other hand, counsel for the taxpayer has not sought to challenge the finding that the late Mr. Stokes was guilty of wilful default in connexion with the preparation of the taxpayer's income tax returns in the years in question. The debate before me has been confined to the question of the meaning of the words " committed by or on behalf of " the taxpayer in the proviso to s. 47 (1). I confess that the situation which, on these two unchallenged findings of fact, I must assume to have existed strikes me as somewhat curious, for " wilful default " connotes more than negligence—even great negligence. It involves a deliberate and intentional failure to do what the man in question ought to have done knowing that the omission was wrongful. There was, it is true, no positive decision not to do his duty; but there was conscious carelessness whether or not he was doing his duty (see *Wellington* v. *Reynolds (Inspector of Taxes)* (1)). It is easy enough to envisage a case in which the taxpayer is completely innocent but his or her agent is guilty of fraud or wilful default in preparing the returns. An elderly mother, for example, might entrust the preparation of her returns to her son, who will himself benefit indirectly by the reduction of her income tax liability and who places before his mother for her signature returns which he knows to be false but she does not. It is less easy, however, to see why a professional accountant should prepare returns for a client which he knows to be false or in respect of the preparation of which he is recklessly careless whether they are true or false while the client has no suspicion of inaccuracy. One would have

(1) (1962), 40 Tax Cas. 209 at p. 215.

A   thought that in such a relationship the position would be that either the accountant was only guilty of negligence, or that if he was guilty of fraud or wilful
default his client was privy to it. However, I must take the facts as they are
found.

Counsel for the taxpayer submitted that the proviso to s. 47 (1) only applied
if the taxpayer had himself been guilty of fraud or wilful default or had expressly
B   or impliedly authorised his agent to commit fraud or wilful default or had subsequently ratified it. The unauthorised and unratified fraud or wilful default of
an agent does not, so counsel submitted, entitle the Crown to invoke the proviso.
Counsel relied in support of this construction of the words " on behalf of " in
the history of the legislation dealing with the reopening of assessments and the
exaction of penalties for the making of false returns and other fraudulent conduct
C   in relation to income tax. The Income Tax Act, 1918, contained in s. 125 a power
to the surveyor on discovering the relevant facts to make additional assessments
within three years after the expiration of the year of assessment. Section 132,
which was headed " Provisions against fraudulent practices " ran, so far as
necessary to be stated, as follows:

D   " (1) Where a person who ought to be charged with tax, as directed by
this Act, is not duly assessed and charged by reason that he has—(a) fraudulently changed his place of residence or fraudulently converted, or fraudulently
released, assigned, or conveyed any of his property; or (b) made and
delivered any statement or schedule which is false or fraudulent; or (c)
fraudulently converted any of his property, which was chargeable, by
altering any security relating thereto or by fraudulently rendering it
E   temporarily unproductive, in order not to be charged for the same or any
part thereof; or (d) been guilty of any falsehood, wilful neglect, fraud, covin,
art or contrivance whatsoever, such person shall, on proof thereof to the
General Commissioners for the division in which he has been charged, or if
he has not been charged, then for any division in which he is chargeable, be
assessed and charged treble the amount of the charge which ought to have
F   been made upon him:
" Provided that, if any charge has been made, but that charge is less
than the charge which ought to have been made, such person shall be
assessed and charged, over and above the former charge, treble the amount
of the difference between the charge which was made and the charge which
ought to have been made, such amount to be added to the assessment."
G
Finally, s. 221 (3) provided:

" Proceedings in the High Court for the recovery of any fine or penalty,
and proceedings in England, before the General Commissioners, and in
Scotland either before the General Commissioners or before the sheriff
for the recovery of any penalty which is not recoverable in the High Court,
H   may be commenced within three years next after the fine or penalty was
was incurred."

The position under the Act of 1918 was, therefore, that there was no power to
reopen assessments regardless of lapse of time for fraud or wilful default and,
further, that proceedings to recover penalties or fines for fraudulent practices
had to be started within three years, which was also the period for reopening
I   assessments. Further, counsel submitted, and this was cardinal to his argument,
that it was clear that s. 132 (1) of the Act of 1918 applied only to the acts of the
taxpayer himself and could not possibly apply to a case where the taxpayer
was innocent but some fraud had been committed by his agent which he had
never authorised or ratified. The next Act to which counsel referred was s. 33 of
the Finance Act, 1942 which, so far as relevant, provided as follows:

" (1) Where any form of fraud or wilful default has been committed by or
on behalf of any person in connexion with or in relation to income tax

for the year 1936-37 or any subsequent year of assessment, assessments,   A
additional assessments and sur-charges on that person to income tax for that
year may, for the purpose of making good to the Crown any loss of tax
attributable to the fraud or wilful default, be amended or made at any
time, notwithstanding that, apart from this section, the time limited by
the relevant enactments for the amendment or making of the assessment,
additional assessment or sur-charge has expired.   B

" (2) The time limited by the Income Tax Acts for commencing proceedings
for the recovery of any fine or penalty from any person in connexion with or
in relation to any income tax covered by any assessment (being income
tax for the year 1936-37 or any subsequent year of assessment), shall, where
any form of fraud or wilful default has been committed by him or on his
behalf in connexion with or in relation to that tax, be extended so as to   C
authorise the commencement of such proceedings at any time within three
years from the final determination of the amount of tax covered by the
assessment.

" For the purposes of this subsection the amount of the tax covered by any
assessment shall not be deemed to be finally determined until that assessment
can no longer be varied, whether by any commissioners on appeal or by the   D
order of any court."

Here for the first time one finds provisions enabling assessments to be reopened
and penalties to be exacted at any distance of time in cases of fraud or wilful
default. Here also one finds for the first time in both connexions the words "or
on his behalf". Section 33 (1) of the Act of 1942 is now, of course, the proviso to
s. 47 of the Income Tax Act, 1952, while s. 33 (2) has become s. 501 (2) of the Act   E
of 1952.

Now, says counsel, as it is clear that s. 132 (1) of the Act of 1918 did not apply
to fraud or wilful default of agents committed without authority from or ratification by their principals, it must follow that the words " or on his behalf " in s. 33
(2) of the Act of 1942 cannot extend to such unauthorised or unratified fraud or
wilful default. They must have some narrower meaning and so in consequence   F
must the same words in s. 33 (1), because it would be incredible that the same
words could mean two different things in two successive subsections. Counsel
suggested that the reason for inserting the words in the two subsections may
have been to ensure that they could catch frauds committed by officers or employees of corporations on behalf of the corporation. In further support of his
contention he relied on what was said by the judge (WILBERFORCE, J.) in *Wellington*   G
v. *Reynolds* (2)), to which I have already referred. But to my mind *Wellington* v.
Reynolds (3) was an entirely different sort of case from this. There, as the facts
were found, a wife who was carrying on a business on her own account had
wrongfully concealed from her husband some of the receipts which accordingly
were not included in the returns he prepared and signed. She was not acting
as his agent and it would be absurd to say that her failure to disclose the whole of   H
her profits to him was an omission committed by her on his behalf. I am not
surprised that the Crown did not seek to suggest that it was and that the judge
approved of their attitude; but I do not think that anything which he said can
be taken as covering such a case as this. Further, I do not find it in the least
surprising that Parliament, when it decided in 1942 to allow assessments to be
reopened and penalties claimed at any distance of time if fraud or wilful default   I
was proved, should have wished the provisions which it was enacting to extend to
cases where the fraud or wilful default was committed by an agent and it could
not be proved that the taxpayer was privy to it. After all, by 1942 the preparation
of tax returns had become a complicated matter in which many taxpayers
employed agents of one sort or another, and it would be unfortunate if a taxpayer

(2) (1962), 40 Tax Cas. at p. 216.
(3) (1962), 40 Tax Cas. 209.

A could escape liability by saying: " It is true that you have proved that my agent committed fraud on my behalf; but you have failed to prove that I was privy to it and as you did not discover it until after six years had expired I can take— and propose to take—advantage of it ". On their natural construction the words " on his behalf " are perfectly clear, and I see no justification for reading them in the restricted sense suggested by counsel for the taxpayer. I think that

B Parliament in 1942 assumed that s. 132 of the Act of 1918 applied, in some cases at least, to frauds committed by agents. That assumption may have been wrong, and if it was wrong the further question arises whether the re-enactment of s. 132 of the Act of 1918 and s. 33 (2) of the Act of 1942 in the Act of 1952 has had the effect of extending the penalty provisions to cases of fraud by agents. Assuming however that counsel is right in saying that it has not, the result is simply that the

C words " on his behalf " in s. 33 (2) of the Act of 1942 and s. 501 (2) of the Act of 1952 have never had any effect. That, however, does not entail the consequence that they had no effect in s. 33 (1) of the Act of 1942 or the proviso to s. 47 (1) of the Act of 1952. For these reasons I hold that the appeal fails.

Taxpayer's appeal in respect of 1946-47 allowed and assessments discharged for
D *arithmetical reasons; in other respects appeal dismissed.*

Solicitors: *Sharpe, Prichard & Co.*, agents for *Burton & Dyson*, Gainsborough (for the taxpayer); *Solicitor of Inland Revenue.*

[*Reported by* F. A. AMIES, ESQ., *Barrister-at-Law.*]

E
WRIGHT *v.* TYNE IMPROVEMENT COMMISSIONERS
(OSBECK & CO., LTD., Third Party).

[COURT OF APPEAL, CIVIL DIVISION (Sellers and Danckwerts, L.JJ., and Baker, J.), November 20, 21, December 4, 1967.]

F *Indemnity—Hiring—Indemnity of crane owners against all damage injury or loss " howsoever caused " arising directly or indirectly out of or in connexion with the hiring or use of a crane—Hirers' employee injured when wagon that he was loading was negligently moved forward by crane owners' servant—No negligence by hirers, their employee, or the crane driver—Whether crane owners entitled to indemnity from hirers.*

G The owners of a crane hired it to hirers under a written contract whereby the hirers agreed " to bear the risk of and be responsible for all damage injury or loss whatsoever howsoever and whensoever caused arising directly or indirectly out of or in connexion with the hiring or use of the said crane ". While a docker employed by the hirers was in a wagon into which timber was being lowered by the crane using a sling, the wagon being controlled by a

H capstan driven by a servant of the crane owners, the capstan driver negligently moved the wagon forward causing the docker to collide with the timber. The docker made efforts to avoid the timber and the crane driver made an attempt to lift the timber out of the way, but the forward movement of the wagon and the upward movement of the sling resulted in the docker being knocked off the wagon and injured. The capstan driver and the crane

I owners were wholly to blame for the accident.

Held: (i) notwithstanding the words " howsoever caused " in the indemnity clause, the indemnity extended only to damage, injury or loss arising directly or indirectly out of or in connexion with the hiring or use of the crane (see p. 810, letter F, post).

(ii) the accident arose directly, or at least indirectly, out of or in connexion with the use of the crane, and, therefore, although the use to which the crane was being put was not a blameworthy cause of the accident, the indemnity clause entitled the crane owners to indemnity (see p. 810, letter H, post).

London and North-Eastern Ry. Co. v. *Furness Shipbuilding Co.* ([1934]   **A**
All E.R. Rep. 54) and *Great Western Ry. Co.* v. *James Durnford & Sons, Ltd.*
([1928] All E.R. Rep. 89) considered.

Appeal allowed.

[As to extent of liability under indemnity, see 18 HALSBURY'S LAWS (3rd
Edn.) 534, 535, para. 980; and for cases on the subject, see 26 DIGEST (Repl.)
243-245, *1860-1872.*]   **B**

Cases referred to:

Great Western Ry. Co. v. *James Durnford & Sons, Ltd.*, [1928] All E.R. Rep. 89;
        139 L.T. 145; 26 Digest (Repl.) 244, *1866.*
London and North-Eastern Ry. Co. v. *Furness Shipbuilding Co.*, [1934] All E.R.
        Rep. 54; 103 L.J.K.B. 180; 150 L.T. 382; 26 Digest (Repl.) 245, *1868.*   **C**

Appeal.

In an action tried at Newcastle-upon-Tyne Assizes, WALLER, J., on Apr. 17,
1967, awarded the plaintiff docker, Richard Wright, damages and costs against
the first defendants, Tyne Improvement Commissioners, the owners of a crane,
and dismissed the plaintiff's claim against his employers, Osbeck & Co., Ltd.,
the hirers of the crane. There was no appeal against this part of WALLER, J.'s   **D**
decision. He had however also dismissed a claim by the first defendants, the
crane owners, against the second defendants, the hirers, in third party proceedings
for indemnity against the plaintiff's claim by virtue of a clause in the requisition
for hiring and thus in the contract of hiring. The crane owners now appealed against
the dismissal of this claim for indemnity. The facts are set out in the judgment
of the court.   **E**

T. Watkins, Q.C., and *J. R. Johnson* for the crane owners.
R. P. Smith, Q.C., and *L. D. Lawton* for the hirers.

                                                        Cur. adv. vult.

Dec. 4.   **SELLERS, L.J.,** read the following judgment of the court:
This appeal from a decision of WALLER, J., arises solely on the first defendants' **F**
claim against the second defendants in third party proceedings for a complete
indemnity for the liability imposed on them by the judge's judgment against them
in favour of the plaintiff. The facts are undisputed and their precise nature is
important. On July 16, 1963, the second defendants were engaged in the discharge
of the S.S. Fourteen Ramadhan at the Albert Edward Dock, North Shields. For
this purpose the second defendants (hereafter called " the hirers ") had hired   **G**
from the first defendants (hereafter called " the crane-owners ") four cranes. The
plaintiff was a docker employed by the hirers, and he and others were engaged in
discharging timber by one of the hired cranes from one of the holds. The timber
was being loaded into wagons which had come alongside in a train and then had
been divided between the holds. The wagons were under the control of the crane
owners and were moved by a capstan worked by their servant.   **H**

The plaintiff and a colleague had climbed into an empty wagon. The plaintiff
was at the rear of the wagon when the first sling of timber was lowered into it.
The timber was canted at an angle and it was being held by the crane to enable
the plaintiff and his mate to place " kickers " underneath the load before it was
completely lowered so as to enable the sling to be removed when the load had
settled. Before this could be done the capstan driver operated the capstan and   **I**
moved the wagon so that the plaintiff was brought forward and struck the
suspended load. The plaintiff on his part tried to escape the timber by leaning
on the side and pulling his legs up, and the driver of the crane, seeing what was
happening, sought in vain to raise the sling out of the way, but the wagon continued to move forward and its momentum and the upward movement of the sling
knocked the plaintiff off the wagon. The plaintiff's injuries were caused by the fall
to the ground and this, it would appear, was caused by the combined movement
of the wagon and the upward movement of the sling due to the crane driver's

A praiseworthy attempt to hoist the load clear in an endeavour to avoid the accident. In these circumstances the judge had no difficulty in finding that the accident was caused by the negligence of the capstan driver, and there is no appeal from that. The wagon on which the plaintiff was working ought not to have been moved. No signal had been given by the plaintiff or his mate and no responsibility rested on them or on the hirers. Judgment for the damages of £2,985 10s. 10d. was given

B solely against the crane owners. It is this sum which the first defendants seek to recover against the second defendants.

The crane in use at the time was one of the four hired on July 15, 1963, for this particular discharge on the terms of a written document entitled " Requisition for Crane Power ". It is addressed to the Tyne Improvement Commissioners, the crane owners, who provide the form, and it provides:

C " In consideration of the [crane owners] supplying crane power . . . we agree to pay the [crane owners'] charges therefor at the rate for the time being in force and to observe and be bound by the terms and conditions hereunder written. [It stipulates that] Where the [crane owners'] slings are used the second alternative of cl. 2 should be struck out and where the requisitioner

D [viz., the hirers] is supplying slings the first alternative of cl. 2 should be struck out."

The slings were provided by the hirers, and the applicable clause is as follows:

" We hereby agree to bear the risk of and be responsible for all damage injury or loss whatsoever howsoever and whensoever caused arising directly or indirectly out of or in connexion with the hiring or use of the said crane or

E cranes. We declare that the slings to be supplied by us and used in connexion with the [crane owners'] cranes have been tested and comply with all the requirements of the Docks Regulations, 1934, and any amendment thereof for the time being in force and we hereby agree to keep the [crane owners] their servants and workmen freed from and indemnified against all liabilities costs and demands whatsoever in respect of any such damage injury or loss

F as aforesaid and in respect of any failure on our part to have the slings so tested as aforesaid or in respect of the said slings being in any way defective."

It may be that, as it was stipulated that one alternative had to be struck out as the circumstances required, the agreement ought to be construed without regard to the inappropriate alternative. However, the only substantial difference between

G the two versions refers to the requirement that the slings supplied and used by the hirers with the crane owners' cranes must have been tested and must comply with the requirements of the Docks Regulations, 1934, and the liability of the hirers to indemnify the crane owners was to include liability in respect of damage, injury or loss in respect of the hirers' failure to have the slings so tested or in respect of defective slings. The judge uses the insertion of the provisions with

H regard to slings to assist the interpretation of the remainder of the provisions which are substantially those applicable when the crane owners' slings are used. The only difference (of no moment) is that the word " claims " appears in the first alternative and not in the second. The argument is that the provisions with regard to slings would be unnecessary if the other provisions were to be construed as wide enough to cover the liability without them.

I It was perhaps an inappropriate place to put the obligation to have the slings tested, etc., but once it was inserted it was not out of place expressly to place liability for failure to comply with the requirements on the requisitioner, although we agree with the judge that

" there cannot be any circumstances in which the defective nature of the slings could cause damage, loss or injury which would not arise indirectly in connection with the hiring or use of the said crane."

We do not think, however, that this can serve to cut down the express words of

the remainder of the clause. The words are wide enough, as the judgment holds, **A**
to cover an indemnity against damage, injury or loss due to negligence of the
crane-owners' servant. " Whatsoever, howsoever and whensoever caused " are
sufficient for that.

The question in this case is whether the accident was one " arising directly
or indirectly out of or in connection with the hiring or use of the crane".
The difference of view between the parties has been whether or not these words **B**
require that the damage, injury or loss should have been caused by the hiring or
use of the crane before liability to indemnity arises.

Reference was made to *London & North-Eastern Ry. Co.* v. *Furness Shipbuilding
Co.* (1), and in particular to the speech of LORD ATKIN, where the House of Lords
had to consider the words "in connection with the works" and held that the loss
there claimed was a loss " in connection with the works " of reconstruction of a **C**
bridge although due to the negligence of a porter in failing to close a carriage
door of a train when it left Fenchurch Street Station some miles away. In contrast to that decision *Great Western Ry. Co.* v. *James Durnford & Sons, Ltd.* (2)
was cited. VISCOUNT SUMNER said (3):

> " Again, the liability may arise out of it or it may arise in connexion with—
> but it must still arise, and for legal purposes that must mean arise causally, **D**
> and since the matter dealt with is a legal liability, that must mean in such
> causal connexion as is required to make somebody liable, who has to be
> answerable for the apparatus."

LORD ATKIN was a party to both decisions, and in the *Furness* case (1) he said (4)
that he found the *Durnford* case (2) of no value at all in coming to a conclusion in
the *Furness* case (1). It was a different contract in entirely different circumstances. **E**
LORD ATKIN added that he found on all occasions a difficulty in deriving any value
on a question of construction of one contract from the construction put on a
different contract made in different circumstances by either the House of Lords
or any other tribunal.

The indemnity clause now before the court contains the words " howsoever
caused ", but, of course, the damage, injury or loss claimed must arise directly **F**
or indirectly out of or in connexion with the hiring or use of the crane. It will
depend on the facts whether this requirement has been established or not. " The
hiring of the crane " seems to cover a very wide area but it does not call for
consideration here.

In the present case the process of discharge was actively taking place with the
use of the crane. A load had been slung from the ship and was in the process of **G**
being lowered into the wagon which was to receive it. As the load was being raised
(in an attempt to clear the plaintiff who was being moved towards it in the
moving wagon) it struck the plaintiff and played some part in overbalancing
him out of the wagon. There was no blameworthy cause as far as the use of the
crane was concerned, but we think it must be said that the accident causing the
loss to the crane owners arose directly, or at least indirectly, out of or in connexion **H**
with the use of the crane. If the crane had been out of use and idle there would
have been no accident to the plaintiff.

In our view liability to indemnify the first defendants therefore has been
established and we allow the appeal.

Appeal allowed. Leave to appeal to the House of Lords refused.

Solicitors: *Hyde, Mahon and Pascall*, agents for *Clayton & Gibson*, Newcastle-
upon-Tyne (for the crane owners); *John H. Sinton & Co.*, Newcastle-upon-Tyne
(for the hirers).

[*Reported by* HENRY SUMMERFIELD, ESQ., *Barrister-at-Law.*]

---

(1) [1934] All E.R. Rep. 54; 150 L.T. 382.
(2) [1928] All E.R. Rep. 89; 139 L.T. 145.
(3) [1928] All E.R. Rep. at p. 92; 139 L.T. at p. 147.
(4) [1934] All E.R. Rep. at p. 57; 150 L.T. at p. 384.

A

BRITISH ROAD SERVICES, LTD. *v.* ARTHUR V. CRUTCHLEY & CO., LTD. (FACTORY GUARDS, LTD., Third Parties).

[COURT OF APPEAL, CIVIL DIVISION (Lord Pearson, Danckwerts and Sachs, L.JJ.),
October 10, 11, 12, 13, December 15, 1967.]

B

Bailment—Bailment for reward—Implied term of contract—Obligation to take proper care of goods bailed—Independent contractor of bailee vicariously responsible for his servant's negligence—Whether bailee also liable by reason of such negligence.

C *Independent Contractor—Negligence—Liability of employer for negligence of independent contractor—Bailment—Warehouseman—Security patrols for guarding warehouse provided by independent contractor—Negligence by patrolman employed by independent contractor—Whether warehouseman liable for such negligence.*

Under a long-established course of business between the plaintiff carriers
D and the defendants, delivery notes for goods transported by the plaintiffs and delivered at the defendants' warehouse in the course of transhipment at Liverpool would be handed back to the plaintiffs' lorry drivers, on the defendants' receiving the goods, stamped " Received on A.V.C. [i.e., the defendants'] conditions ". These conditions included a term limiting liability to £800 per ton. A lorry load of whisky, worth £9,126, was delivered by the
E plaintiffs to the defendants' transhipment warehouse in the Liverpool dock area; the whisky was to be delivered by the defendants to the ship (or " locker ") on the following day. The district where this warehouse and other warehouses were was a very vulnerable stretch of property, about seven miles long and stretching five hundred yards from the main dock road, and there was a good deal of criminal activity in the district. The defendants'
F warehouse usually contained many thousand pounds' worth of goods. It was a strongly built building with metal doors that were locked and bolted at night, and had no windows; but it had a skylight made of reinforced glass. The whisky was delivered at the warehouse at about 7.30 a.m. on July 29, 1963. It was unloaded from a lorry and loaded on to a trailer in the warehouse, where it stood for some hours uncovered. At about 4 p.m. the driver of the
G tractor came and covered the load, making the tractor and trailer ready to be driven off at 6.30 a.m. on July 30, 1963. The warehouse was guarded at night by security patrol, for which the defendants contracted with the third parties. Normally the patrolman visited the premises four times nightly, but on this night he visited the warehouse three times only, his last visit
H finishing at 2.18 a.m. The fourth visit, if he had made it, would have been at about 5 a.m. During the night at a time which, so the court of trial inferred, would have been not long after the patrolman's third visit, thieves broke into the warehouse through the skylight, cut the stout bolts on the door, opened it from inside and drove off the vehicle loaded with whisky. The trial judge found that the patrolman was negligent in not making a fourth visit,
I and that his negligence, for which the third parties were vicariously responsible, was to be attributed also to the defendants, but that it did not cause the loss. On appeal by the plaintiffs,

Held: (i) the defendants were liable to the plaintiffs in negligence for the following reasons—

(a) the defendants' system of protection was not adequate in relation to the special risks involved and, accordingly, the defendants had failed to discharge the burden of proving that the loss was not due to any negligence

on their part; their liability in damages would be assessed at £6,135* (see
p. 819, letter I, to p. 820, letter A, p. 821, letter F, p. 823, letter H, and
p. 824, letter G, post).

(b) it was an implied term of the contract of bailment that the defendants
would themselves, or through their servants or agents, take proper care of the
goods bailed, and accordingly, though it was unnecessary to decide this in
view of (a) above, the defendants would be liable for any negligence of the third
parties, who were independent contractors (see p. 820, letter F, p. 821, letter
F, and p. 824, letter H, post).

Dictum of FENTON ATKINSON, Q.C., in *Adams (Durham), Ltd. and Day* v.
Trust Houses, Ltd. ([1960] 1 Lloyd's Rep. at p. 386) applied.

(ii) the decision of the trial judge that the third parties were negligent,
but that their negligence did not cause the loss, should stand (see p. 820, letter
G, p. 821, letters E and F, and p. 825, letter B, post).

(iii) in the circumstances the defendants' conditions of carriage were
incorporated in their contract with the plaintiffs and accordingly the liability
of the defendants was limited to £800 per ton (see p. 817, letter B, p. 821,
letter F, and p. 825, letter F, post).

Decision of CAIRNS, J. ([1967] 2 All E.R. 785) reversed on holding (i) above.

[As to the degree of diligence required by a bailee of goods, see 2 HALSBURY'S
LAWS (3rd Edn.) 114-118, paras. 225-227; and for cases on the subject, see
3 DIGEST (Repl.) 76-79, *147-168* and (warehousemen) 81-85, *169-198*.

As to the onus of proof where goods entrusted to a bailee are lost, see 2 HALS-
BURY'S LAWS (3rd Edn.) 117, 118, para. 227; and for cases on the subject, see
3 DIGEST (Repl.) 78, 79, *161-168*.

As to liability for the negligence of independent contractors, see 28 HALSBURY'S
LAWS (3rd Edn.) 23, 24, para. 21.]

Cases referred to:

Adams (Durham), Ltd. and Day v. *Trust Houses, Ltd.*, [1960] 1 Lloyd's Rep.
380; Digest (Cont. Vol. B) 451, *187a*.

Coldman v. *Hill*, [1918-19] All E.R. Rep. 434; [1919] 1 K.B. 443; 88 L.J.K.B.
491; 120 L.T. 412; 22 Digest (Repl.) 176, *1609*.

Davis v. *Garrett*, [1824-34] All E.R. Rep. 286; (1830), 6 Bing. 716;
8 L.J.O.S.C.P. 253; 120 E.R. 1456; 8 Digest (Repl.) 17, *65*.

Edwards v. *Newland (E. Burchett, Ltd., Third Parties)*, [1950] 1 All E.R. 1072;
[1950] 2 K.B. 534; 3 Digest (Repl.) 84, *193*.

---

* £6,135 was the total amount of the defendants' liability to the plaintiffs on the
footing that the defendants were entitled to limit liability by their conditions of carriage
to £800 per ton, and crediting any whisky recovered. The relevant condition provided
that " the liability of the [defendants] in respect of any loss of the said goods (for which
the defendants should be liable) should be limited (i) to the amount of the liability of
the plaintiffs to the owner and (ii) to the sum of £800 per ton ". The condition was
contained in the 1961 revision of the Conditions of Carriage of Road Haulage Association, Ltd. The particulars delivered by the defendants of the circumstances rendering
the conditions of carriage of Road Haulage Association, Ltd., applicable to the contract
under which they received goods transported by the plaintiffs were as follows:—
" Shortly after the nationalisation of road haulage the plaintiffs commenced to employ
the defendants as carriers (not as sub-contractors) particularly for the transhipment of
goods carried by the plaintiffs' trunk vehicles to the Merseyside area and then transferred
to the defendants' vehicles for delivery to local consignees. Such employment has
since continued regularly. The defendants are now unable to specify any particular
discussions or identify any correspondence (if any) but every receipt for goods so transferred issued by the defendants to the plaintiffs amounting over the years to many
hundreds of receipts bore the stamp " Received under A.V.C. Conditions " and every
invoice rendered by the defendants to the plaintiffs in respect of such employment (of
which again there have been hundreds) has had printed on it the words ' All goods are
handled subject to Conditions of Carriage, copies of which can be obtained on application" or words to the like effect the said Conditions of Carriage being the [conditions of
carriage of Road Haulage Association, Ltd.] or earlier prints or revisions of the same. The
plaintiffs have at no time purported to repudiate such conditions as the conditions on
which the defendants were employed and received such goods ". Cf., p. 817, letter B, post.

A   *Gibaud* v. *Great Eastern Ry. Co.*, [1921] All E.R. Rep. 35; [1921] 2 K.B. 426;
         90 L.J.K.B. 535; 125 L.T. 76; 3 Digest (Repl.) 91, *217.*
     Houghland v. *R. R. Low* (*Luxury Coaches*), *Ltd.*, [1962] 2 All E.R. 159; [1962]
         1 Q.B. 694; [1962] 2 W.L.R. 1015; Digest (Cont. Vol. A) 46, *71a.*
     Lilley v. *Doubleday*, [1881-85] All E.R. Rep. 406; (1881), 7 Q.B.D. 510; 51
         L.J.Q.B. 310; 44 L.T. 814; 46 J.P. 708; 3 Digest (Repl.) 82, *183.*
B   *Shaw & Co.* v. *Symmons & Sons*, [1916-17] All E.R. Rep. 1093; [1917] 1 K.B.
         799; 86 L.J.K.B. 549; 117 L.T. 91; 3 Digest (Repl.) 101, *280.*

Appeal.

This was an appeal by the plaintiffs against an order of CAIRNS, J., made on
Feb. 20, 1967, and reported at [1967] 2 All E.R. 785, in favour of the defendants.
The plaintiff sought an order that the judgment be set aside and that judgment
C be entered for the plaintiffs for damages in the sum of £9,004 19s. 7d. The grounds
of appeal were as follows: (i) that the judge was wrong in holding that the
defendants had proved that their negligence in advertising the presence of the
plaintiffs' whisky in their warehouse, by allowing it to stand for a number of
hours where passers-by could see it, did not cause or contribute to the loss of the
whisky; (ii) that the judge was wrong in holding that the defendants had proved
D that the negligence of the third parties in failing to make the proper number of
visits to the defendants' warehouse during the night of the theft did not cause or
contribute to the loss of the plaintiffs' whisky; (iii) that the judge ought to have
held that the defendants, having negligently advertised the presence in their
warehouse of the plaintiffs' whisky, were further negligent in leaving the whisky
overnight in the warehouse loaded on a trailer which was already hitched to a
E tractor unit, and which was placed in the most convenient position for driving it
away once the doors of the warehouse had been opened; (iv) that the judge
ought to have held that the defendants, having negligently advertised the
presence in their warehouse of the plaintiffs' whisky, and having decided to leave
the whisky overnight laden on a trailer, were further negligent in failing to employ
a nightwatchman or patrolman who would be present throughout the night,
F or to arrange for additional visits to be made to the premises by mobile patrolmen;
(v) that the judge ought to have held that the plaintiffs and the defendants were
never ad idem as to any special terms of contract between them, and ought to have
held accordingly that the plaintiffs, as bailees of the whisky from the consignors
thereof, were entitled to recover from the defendants the full value of the lost
whisky, viz., the sum of £9,004 19s. 7d.

     R. H. Forrest, *Q.C.*, and *R. R. Leech* for the plaintiffs.
     D. B. McNeill, *Q.C.*, and *F. D. Paterson* for the defendants.
     A. Rankin for the third parties.

                                                              Cur. adv. vult.

     Dec. 15. The following judgments were read:

H   **LORD PEARSON:** This case has arisen from the theft of a lorry load of
whiskey, worth £9,126, from a warehouse of the defendants, A. V. Crutchley &
Co., Ltd., in the Liverpool dock area. The theft occurred in the early hours of
July 30, 1963. The action was brought by the plaintiffs, British Road Services,
Ltd., as bailors, against the defendants as bailees, for the loss of the goods. The
defendants brought in Factory Guards, Ltd., as third parties, claiming that, if
I the defendants were held liable to the plaintiffs, they should recover an indemnity
or contribution from the third parties by reason of the third parties' negligent
performance of their contract with the defendants to provide a mobile patrol
service for the protection of the warehouse and its contents.

The main question on this appeal is whether the judge was right in deciding
that the defendants, on whom the burden of proof on this issue rested (*Coldman*
v. *Hill* (1)) had proved that the loss of the goods was not caused by any negligence

(1) [1918-19] All E.R. Rep. 434 at p. 442; [1919] 1 K.B. 443 at p. 458.

or breach of duty on their part or for which they were responsible. He found (2) **A**
that there was some negligence by the defendants themselves in unduly exposing,
the valuable goods in their warehouse to the view of passers-by, and he held that
they would be also responsible to the plaintiffs for the inadequacy of the protection
of the goods as a result of the third parties' negligent performance of their contract
with the defendants. He also found that the loss of the goods was not caused by
that negligence of the defendants or by that negligence of the third parties. **B**
In my opinion, however, a broader approach is appropriate. It is necessary to
consider whether, on the evidence as to the nature and volume of the defendants'
business at this warehouse and the way in which it was conducted, there was not
an inadequate system of protection and, if so, whether this was not a likely cause
of the theft and consequent loss of the goods. I think that that is really the main
point in the case.   **C**

There is a comparatively minor issue—whether the amount of the liability is
under the contract between the plaintiffs and the defendants subject to a limitation of £800 per ton. The issues arising between the defendants and the third
parties depend on the position as between the plaintiffs and the defendants and
cannot conveniently be summarised in advance.

The plaintiffs have a Scottish district and its base is in Edinburgh. An import- **D**
ant part of the business, though of course only a part, is the cartage of whisky
from distilleries to bonded warehouses in the United Kingdom or to ships for
export. If the load of whisky or other goods is for delivery to a ship in Liverpool,
it is sent by lorry on what is called the plaintiffs' " trunk service " to their Liverpool depot and then it is taken over by the plaintiffs' " shunt service ". Sometimes
the shunt service delivers the goods in the same lorry to the ship or to a " locker ", **E**
which apparently resembles a cage and is kept on or in the vicinity of the wharf
for customs or excise purposes. If, however, through congestion of traffic at the
docks or lack of space in a locker, or a need to wait for loading facilities at the
ship or for any other reason, it may not be possible to effect delivery to the ship
or locker on the day of their arrival in Liverpool, the goods may be delivered by
the plaintiffs' shunt service to the defendants' transhipment depot at their **F**
warehouse in Cotton Street. The defendants have special arrangements for
keeping themselves informed as to the conditions on the docks and they effect
delivery of the goods to the ship or locker on the same day, if possible, but if
that is not possible, they have to keep the goods overnight in their warehouse
for delivery on the next day.

Mr. Pugh, the detective officer who had been in charge of the theft case, gave **G**
evidence for the defendants. He said that the main dock road at Liverpool
is about seven miles long, and warehouse premises and similar businesses extend
for practically the full length of it and back from it into the city for about five
hundred yards. He said:

> " It is a vast stretch of very vulnerable property—warehouses containing
> a vast amount of valuable property. In this one little district alone there are **H**
> millions of pounds' worth."

He also said that within half a mile of the defendants' Cotton Street warehouse
there were seven or eight bonded warehouses, and there were dozens and dozens
of other warehouses in the immediate vicinity, and there was a good deal of
criminal activity in the district. There was ample evidence from Mr. Pugh and
other witnesses of whisky being a highly " vulnerable " commodity; i.e., attractive
to thieves because it is valuable and easily disposed of.

The defendants' Cotton Street warehouse, used for their transhipment business,
was built in 1961. It forms part of premises occupied by the defendants and
including, in addition to the warehouses, offices, a joiner's shop, a paint store and a
yard. Some packing of goods for export is carried on. The premises have a
frontage on the main dock road, but the warehouse is a short distance back from

(2) [1967] 2 All E.R. 785 at p. 791.

A the main dock road and extends from Cotton Street at one end to Carlton Street at the other end. The warehouse is strongly built and has large, strong, double roller doors at each end for the entry and departure of vehicles. The doors when shut and fastened for the night have bolts going into the ground and are padlocked and a crossbar is also padlocked. There are no windows of any ordinary kind, but in the roof there is a skylight made of reinforced glass, i.e., glass incorporating

B wire mesh. The height from the floor to the eaves is about twenty-four feet and the furthest distance to the ridge of the roof is according to the plan about ten feet, though a witness said it was about sixteen feet. There is an overhead travelling crane with its gantry. The defendants considered this warehouse to be a " little fortress " and virtually impregnable. Its weak point, however, was the skylight, which could be reached by an enterprising climber, though somewhat perilously,

C over asbestos roofing. On either side of the warehouse there were adjoining premises, and a thief could climb up them and make his way over the intervening roofs to the skylight.

It appears from the plan that the width of the warehouse is about seventy-eight feet, and its length is about 130 feet on one side and about 145 feet on the other side. Along one side there is a platform. On the other side there is a space in which

D there may be trailers, loaded or waiting to be loaded, and motor units (the mechanical horses) hitched on, or waiting to be hitched on, to the trailers. With the doors at both ends open, a passer-by can see right through the warehouse and can see what is in it. He can see goods being unloaded from a visiting lorry on to the platform or on to one of the trailers, and if the goods remain uncovered he can see them standing on the platform or the trailer.

E The defendants' transhipment business carried on at this warehouse and other warehouses is very substantial. Mr. J. V. Crutchley said in evidence that this warehouse is normally fairly full and they have to turn traffic away from time to time. They have many other customers besides the plaintiffs. There was evidence that they had five thousand transhipment customers. They insure the transhipment goods up to £100,000 for one consignment. This load of whisky, worth about

F £9,000, was a load of average value or something above, but by no means the top. Mr. Crutchley was asked: " Is it fair to say you have £25,000 worth of goods in any one warehouse? "; and he said " That is the way we look at it ". Mr. Henry Crutchley said in evidence: " It is not an uncommon thing for us to have a load of whisky." Another witness for the defendants, who had been assistant foreman at the warehouse, said: " There is more than one vehicle stationed

G overnight in the warehouse "; and he mentioned, by way of example, six trailers and their motor units. In a letter of Nov. 10, 1961, from the defendants to the plaintiffs, the defendants referred to

" the numerous consignments of whisky and other spirits we deliver on your behalf to loading steamers at Liverpool and Birkenhead and other local warehouses."

H Mr. Green, the third parties' superintendent, in his evidence said that some weeks before the theft they found the defendants' gates open on a Saturday afternoon and there were three—or perhaps it was two—loads of whisky on the premises. Thus the evidence shows that quite frequently there would be a load of whisky kept in the Cotton Street warehouse overnight—that was not an exceptional

I occurrence.

At one time the defendants had " static watchmen ", i.e., watchmen remaining on the premises throughout the night. According to the evidence, those who could be recruited for this purpose were elderly men and tended to go to sleep on duty. In 1956 the third parties were extending their business into Liverpool, and the defendants made with them a contract for mobile patrolling. This was to take the place of the static watchmen. The contract initially applied to other warehouses of the defendants, and was afterwards applied to their Cotton Street warehouse. The contract provided for the patrolman to do four

rounds between the hours of 6 p.m. and 6 a.m. on each night, and one round   A
between the hours of 12 noon and 6 p.m. on each Saturday, and three rounds
between the hours of 6 a.m. and 6 p.m. on each Sunday and Bank Holiday.
The charge for this in 1956 was £11 4s. 6d. per month.   There were afterwards
increases in the charge, but in 1963 it was still only about £15 per month.   By
their conditions of service attached to the contract the third parties undertook
(inter alia) that: B

"(1) All patrolmen employed in the performance of the duties under this
agreement have been subject to investigation and are reliable, trustworthy
and medically fit.   (2) All patrolmen and personnel employed will be super-
vised by an inspector or senior patrolman who will make periodic check
visits.   (3) If through sudden emergency, injury or illness of the patrolman
or for any other cause outside the control of the [third parties their] servants   C
or agents a patrolman is unable to complete the full number of rounds on any
one night or to perform any other duties then the [third parties] shall direct
the patrolman to increase his number of rounds on a subsequent night or
nights in order to make up any loss in the number of rounds that the
subscriber may have sustained . . .   (6) At the end of each completed month
of the said period of service a record will be delivered to the subscriber giving   D
details of the times the patrolmen have visited the subscriber's premises
during the past month."

Each patrolman had instructions to visit the premises on his round at irregular
intervals and in each set of premises to go to a number of "clocking points".
At each of these points he was to check that everything was in order, and he would
find a key hanging up or otherwise attached, and he was to insert the key in a   E
clock which he carried round with him, and to turn the key, whereupon the
clock would record the time of his visit to that point.   The patrolmen engaged by
the third parties were young and athletic men and had training especially for
dealing with electrical faults, as they had to protect the premises against fire and
water risks as well as risk of theft.
    A feature of the system was that visits to premises were made at irregular   F
intervals.   This was evidently intended to make it more difficult for a gang of
thieves to plan their break-in for a time when the patrolman would be absent.   It
would, however, be desirable, especially for guarding against the fire and water
risks, that the visits should reasonably cover the whole night period from 6 p.m.
to 6 a.m.   The monthly record for June, 1963, is available and shows that in
that month most of the intervals between visits to this warehouse in the night   G
period were of more than two hours, but there was one interval of only one hour
and eight minutes and one of only one hour and six minutes.
    Now I come to the terms of the contract between the plaintiffs and the defen-
dants.   It was not proved that the plaintiffs' conditions of sub-contracting were
ever sent to the defendants, and the defendants in evidence denied that they were
sub-contractors to the plaintiffs.   The plaintiffs' form of delivery note contained   H
the words:

"All goods are carried on the [plaintiffs'] conditions of carriage, copies of
which can be obtained upon application to any office of the [plaintiffs]."

Under the long-established course of business between the parties, however, the
plaintiffs' driver brought his delivery note into the defendants' office at the Cotton
Street warehouse and asked in effect if he could bring his load into the warehouse.   I
If there were room in the warehouse, the permission would be given, and the
delivery note would be rubber-stamped by the defendants with the words
"Received under A.V.C. conditions", followed by the date and the address of
the warehouse.   The delivery note, thus converted into a receipt note, would be
handed back to the plaintiffs' driver and he would bring his load into the warehouse as instructed by the warehouse foreman.   If this had only happened once,
there would have been a doubt whether the plaintiffs' driver was their agent to

A accept the defendants' special contractual terms. This, however, happened frequently and regularly over many years at this and other warehouses of the defendants. Also the defendants' invoices contained the words: " All goods are handled subject to conditions of carriage copies of which can be obtained on application." It may perhaps be material to add that the defendants' conditions of carriage were not peculiar to them, but were the conditions of carriage of Road

B Haulage Association, Ltd. At any rate, I agree with the decision of the judge (3) that the plaintiffs' conditions were not, and the defendants' conditions were, incorporated into the contract between these parties. The effect was that, while the nature of the defendants' liability as bailees to the plaintiffs was unaffected, the liability was limited in amount to £800 per ton, which, when credit is given for sixty bottles of whisky recovered after the theft, produces a total in this case

C of £6,135. Also I would agree with the judge's formulation of the defendants' duty. He said (3):

> " In my judgment the duty of the defendants was the duty to exercise reasonable care of the goods according to all the circumstances of the case: see *Houghland* v. *R. R. Low* (*Luxury Coaches*), *Ltd.* (4)."

D In the present case the load of whisky, which had arrived from Scotland, was received into the defendants' Cotton Street warehouse at about 7.30 a.m. on Monday, July 29, 1963. Owing to congestion at the docks, it could not be delivered to the ship or locker on that day, and it had to be kept in the warehouse. After the lorry had driven in, the whisky was transferred to a waiting trailer. It was left there uncovered for many hours until it was decided that a certain driver of

E the defendants could take it to the docks as soon as the warehouse opened on the following day. The driver came at about 4 p.m., and covered up and fastened the load with his own sheet and ropes. It was correct for him to do this, because he would be responsible for the roadworthiness of his vehicle and its load. A motor unit was hitched on to the trailer, and the complete vehicle was left in a forward position in the warehouse, all ready to be driven out of the warehouse

F on the way to the docks at 6.30 a.m. on the next morning, which would be July 30, 1963. In my opinion it was not negligent of the defendants to transfer the goods directly from the incoming lorry of the plaintiffs to the waiting trailer, or to leave the complete vehicle overnight all ready and conveniently placed to be driven out of the warehouse as quickly as possible. They had to consider many other aspects of their business besides the security aspects, and what they did on this

G occasion, and no doubt equally on other occasions, was proper and convenient for expeditious working.

The defendants are, however, open to some criticism for their omission to cover up the cases of whisky during the many hours which elapsed after the load had been transferred to the trailer early in the morning and before the driver came with his sheet and ropes in the mid-afternoon. The judge decided (5) that this

H omission was negligent, but in all probability did not cause the loss, because the gang of thieves were likely to have been keeping watch on the warehouse and to have seen the whisky going in and being unloaded. I would agree with his decision subject to some doubt whether it was negligence to omit a minor precaution of this kind which was not likely to do much good. I think that the important factor is the general situation. Here was a highly vulnerable load, £9,000 worth of whisky,

I all in position on a vehicle, sheeted and roped and standing just by the doors ready to be driven out and taken away. Any passer-by could have seen the load exposed at an earlier stage and could have taken note of it, and made a plan to steal it, if he was so minded. To any gang of thieves which included a " climber " or " cat burglar " this would be a very tempting proposition. Moreover, as I understand the evidence and the findings, this situation was not exceptional, but one likely

---

(3) [1967] 2 All E.R. at p. 787.
(4) [1962] 2 All E.R. 159; [1962] 1 Q.B. 694.
(5) [1967] 2 All E.R. at p. 791.

to recur from time to time in the ordinary course of business. There was a striking **A**
passage in Mr. Pugh's evidence in cross-examination:

" Q.—And if one leaves a lorry load of whisky in full view of an open gate
all day long? A.—It is an open invitation. Q.—It is an open invitation to
come and do something about it? A.—Yes."

The judge accepted (6) the expert evidence of Mr. Pugh as to the manner and
probable time of the theft. The " climber " climbed up a drainpipe of the neigh- **B**
bouring premises of a co-operative society and over the roofs to the skylight. He
broke through the skylight and descended on to the crane and then to the gantry
and down an " upright " or pillar of the gantry to the floor. Then, with a powerful
cutting tool he broke the padlocks of the doors and opened the doors. Then the
" wheelman " came in and drove the vehicle out of the warehouse and to a disused
warehouse about three hundred yards away. The whisky was there transferred to **C**
another vehicle, and the other vehicle took it to London, where it was disposed
of. Only sixty bottles of the whisky were recovered. The estimated duration
times for these operations were eight minutes from the climbing of the drainpipe
to driving the vehicle out of the Cotton Street warehouse, and a total of not more
than forty-five minutes from the climbing of the drainpipe to the departure of **D**
the other vehicle from the other warehouse. Mr. Pugh considered that the theft
must have been committed between 3 a.m. and 6 a.m., and probably between
3 and 4 a.m., because then the police patrols would be depleted by refreshment
hours and this would be known to the thieves. The judge said (6):

" The natural time to choose to break in would be as soon as possible after
the patrolman's visit and if for some reason it was impracticable for the **E**
thieves to break in before three o'clock, one would expect them to do so at the
earliest possible moment thereafter. Certainly they would wish to have the
operation completed before half past three, for thereafter the patrolman
might arrive at any moment."

On the issue as to the adequacy of the defendants' system of protection, the
principal factor in my estimation is that, although the defendants habitually had **F**
thousands of pounds worth of goods in their warehouse and often had loads of
whisky or other vulnerable goods, and these might be exposed to the view of
passers-by for many hours, so that there was an " open invitation " for thieves
" to come and do something about it ", yet the defendants were content with the
mobile patrol service visiting four times in the twelve-hour night period, and did
not adopt any other precautions either regularly or on some occasions. **G**

There were several other precautions which could have been taken, e.g., more
frequent visits by the mobile patrolmen, static watchmen not of the elderly type
but young men provided by the third parties or a similar organisation, guard dogs,
an audible alarm or a silent alarm. These might have been a static watch on some
nights but not always on the same night in the week, and mobile patrolmen on the
other nights. It appears from the evidence of Mr. Pugh that none of these precau- **H**
tions could be relied on with certainty to prevent a theft by a determined and
ingenious gang of thieves. A watchman can be overcome, a guard dog can be
killed, an audible alarm can be silenced, and a silent alarm can be circumvented
in some way. Also there would be some substantial intervals even between more
frequent visits; but it does not follow that one must adopt a defeatist attitude
of saying that such precautions are not worth taking. Additional precautions
present the thieves with additional problems to be dealt with, so that they have
more things to do, more things that may go wrong, greater expenditure of time,
more risk of detection and more risk of pursuit and capture. In my opinion the
deterrent effect of additional precautions was not sufficiently taken into account
in this case.

It appeared from Mr. Pugh's evidence that the system of mobile patrolling is
better than having elderly static watchmen, and is widely used. Other evidence

(6) [1967] 2 All E.R. at p. 791.

A showed that it has the advantage of cheapness; but Mr. Pugh also gave evidence in cross-examination as to the value of other precautions. I will quote some passages:

" (1) Q.—With regard to the gaps between visits by whatever the organisa-tion may be, if you have four a night there is plenty of time between visits to carry out a burglary like this? A.—Yes, indeed. Q.—The remark that

B you made about night watchmen was that very often it is an old gentleman well past it? A.—Yes, indeed. They were the only men who would do the job for the wages they were offered by the firms. Q.—Would you agree that if you have a man of the character and calibre of these people who work for the security organisations, if one employed one as night watchman to stay all night, that would be an entirely different situation? A.—Oh, indeed, yes.

C " (2) Q.—It must depend upon the number of times when a costly cargo is in the warehouse, but if one is merely going to have four visits during the night, another elementary precaution would be to fit a burglar alarm of some sort? A.—Yes, we advise at least an audible alarm. That means just the bell outside the premises which rings immediately any of the entrance windows, doors or guards are removed. This only frightens off the thief

D if he is so inclined, but it does not always stop the thief committing the offence. It gives the police a good chance of arriving in time to prevent the consummation of the theft. The silent alarm is recommended, but the business people are reluctant to install it because of the cost. It would depend largely on how often you have really valuable commodities. It would have to be in the region of thousands of pounds' worth of property being on the

E premises regularly for it to be profitable to the concern. Q.—With men who work at this speed, the only way of making certain that they were detected at their work would be a night watchman—I do not mean an old age pen-sioner—a watchman all night? A.—Yes, an athletic man to be there continually.

" (3) Q.—It would be very difficult to open these doors from outside?

F A.—These doors are the finest class of doors for such warehouses. Q.—Being of that view, do you consider that it would be desirable then to have some kind of warning system restricted to the skylight area? A.—Yes, that would make the thief's problem even greater."

There was evidence that the third parties would not charge much more for a static watchman than for a mobile patrolman. There was no evidence as to the

G cost of any alarm system, except Mr. Pugh's evidence quoted above that there would have to be in the region of thousands of pounds' worth of property on the premises regularly for it to be profitable to the concern to have a silent alarm. If that is the criterion, the defendants' Cotton Street warehouse seems on the evidence to fall within it.

There was evidence that if an alarm system were fitted to the skylight and

H operated by means of an electric ray, it would be possible for the alarm to be actuated by a pigeon flying through the ray or by a piece of plaster falling from the roof, so that false alarms would cause serious inconvenience to the police. The evidence also showed, however, that an alarm system is not necessarily actuated by an electric ray; it may be actuated by the breaking of glass or the opening of a window.

I I have been reluctant to differ from the judge (7) on the question whether the defendants' system of protection was in all the circumstances adequate. It is not, however, a question of primary fact, but of the inference to be drawn from the accepted evidence. On a careful consideration of the evidence, I feel bound to conclude that the defendants' system of protection, though useful so far as it went, was not proved to be adequate in relation to the special risks involved in the nature and conduct of the defendants' business at their Cotton Street warehouse. Nor was it proved that the inadequacy of the system was not a cause of the theft.

(7) [1967] 2 All E.R. at p. 789.

It is not unlikely, indeed I think it probable, that if the system of protection had   A
been adequate the thieves would not have chosen this warehouse for their attack.
The defendants failed to discharge their burden of proving that the loss was not
caused by any negligence on their part. I would reverse the judge's decision on
this point and hold the defendants liable to the plaintiffs for damages amounting
to £6,135.

In the end I find it unnecessary to decide whether, if the third parties were   B
negligent in performing their contract with the defendants and thereby caused
the loss of the goods, there would be a resulting liability of the defendants to the
plaintiffs. As the question was fully argued, however, I will express my concurrence with the decision of the judge and his reasons. He cited from the
judgment of MR. FENTON ATKINSON, Q.C., as commissioner of assize in *Adams
(Durham), Ltd. and Day* v. *Trust Houses, Ltd.* (8), the following passage: C

" It seems to me that the duty to take reasonable care to keep that car
safe rested on the defendants and they delegated that duty to Atkinson, and
they are responsible to the plaintiffs, not so much as being vicariously
responsible for the torts of Atkinson driving about the streets, but on the
basis that they had entrusted to him the fulfilment of their own contractual
duty, and that duty was not performed, and for that breach of contract,   D
apart from any special condition, in my view they are liable to the plaintiffs."

I think that that is right and applies in the case of an independent contractor,
though in that particular case Atkinson was a servant of the defendants. Although
there can be a bailment without a contract, there usually is and was in this case a
contract, and the obligation of the bailee can be formulated as an implied term of
the contract. This may help to bring out clearly the nature of the obligation. The   E
bailor could not reasonably be expected to be content with a contractual promise
of the bailee to take proper care of the goods or engage a competent contractor
to do so. If that were the contractual promise, then in the event of default by a
competent contractor duly selected by the bailee, the bailor would have no remedy
against the bailee and would have to rely on the possibility of an action of tort
against the contractor. To give business efficacy to the contract, the bailee's   F
implied promise should be that he will himself or through his servants or agents
take proper care of the goods.

There remains for consideration the position as between the defendants and
the third parties. First, the judge was plainly right in deciding (9) that the third
parties were negligent and committed a breach of their contract by failing to pay   G
a fourth visit to the Cotton Street warehouse on the night in question. There was
no valid excuse. Mr. Collins was the mobile patrolman whose duty it was to
make the four visits. He paid his first visit at about 8 p.m. His motor cycle
broke down before he had completed his second round, but he completed it on
foot, making the second visit to this warehouse at 11.50 p.m. He had informed
the office of his mishap, and by arrangement he was picked up by another patrolman, Mr. Knowles, who had a van. They went first to Mr. Collins' district and   H
made his third round, including the third visit to this warehouse at about 2.16
a.m. Then they went off in the van to Mr. Knowles' district and visited premises
there. They returned to the office at 5.20 a.m. Mr. Collins omitted to make
his fourth round, though he could have made it on foot, if not otherwise. He could
either have stayed behind when Mr. Knowles went off to his own district, or he
could have asked Mr. Knowles on the return journey to set him down in his
(Mr. Collins') district so that he could make his round on foot. Indeed Mr. Knowles
might have taken Mr. Collins on the return journey to some of the premises to be
visited and left him to complete the round on foot.

The second question is more difficult. If the fourth visit had been made, would
it or might it have prevented the loss? It would not have been likely to interrupt
the thieves in the act of theft from the warehouse, which only took a few minutes;

---

(8) [1960] 1 Lloyd's Rep. 380 at p. 386.   (9) [1967] 2 All E.R. at p. 791.

A but would it or might it have been in time to enable the police to intercept the thieves' lorry carrying the whisky on its way out from Liverpool? On the findings of the judge, the fourth visit would have made no difference. He said (10):

B " In my judgment it is a strong probability that the theft was completed by that hour [half-past three] and accordingly that the goods were on the thieves' own vehicle and setting out on the next stage of their journey by a quarter-past four. Since the next visit, if it had been paid at all, would probably have been paid at about five, and since there was certainly no breach of duty in failing to visit before that hour, I am satisfied that the breach of duty did not cause or contribute to the loss. The raising of the alarm at or shortly after five o'clock would have been far too late to put a police cordon round the district or to offer any substantial prospect of

C recovering the goods."

The only point which seems doubtful here is the timing of the hypothetical fourth visit, which was not in fact made. Mr. Collins was asked in his examination-in-chief: " If your motor cycle had not broken down about this time, would you have anticipated returning to the Crutchleys' premises? "; and his answer was:

D " Another between five o'clock and six o'clock." This piece of evidence was not challenged in cross-examination. It does not necessarily follow that, after the motor cycle had broken down, a conscientious patrolman duly instructed and assisted by his superintendent would have made the visit at the time originally projected. Nevertheless, it is reasonable to suppose that the original programme would have been carried out as nearly as was practicable, and therefore that the final visit (which in any case should not be too far away from the end of the period)

E would have been made at or about five o'clock. At any rate, on a question of this kind, which is very much a question of fact, I do not think it would be right to depart from the finding of the judge.

Then, as the third parties' breach of contract made no difference to the result, it did not cause any damage to the defendants, and the defendants' claim to recover indemnity or contribution from the third parties fails. I would allow the

F plaintiffs' appeal, directing judgment to be entered for them against the defendants for £6,135. The judgment for the third parties against the defendants stands unaltered, subject to any question there may be as to costs. DANCKWERTS, L.J., who is engaged in another court, has asked me to say on his behalf that he concurs in my judgment and also in that just about to be delivered by SACHS, L.J.

G SACHS, L.J.: The defendants are the proprietors of a warehouse situated in an area of Liverpool which has for long been known as one attracting the attention of gangs of thieves seeking to break into such premises and abstract from them goods which may command a ready sale. The skill and determination with which some of the gangs operate is also common knowledge. In the normal course of business the defendants' warehouse holds over one or more nights what are

H termed " transhipment " goods, i.e., consignments intended for outward shipment which it has not as yet been practicable to load on the ship of which it is to form part of the cargo. Such transhipment goods not uncommonly include what can conveniently be called vulnerable loads, i.e., loads of goods particularly attractive to gangs of thieves because of their high value and the ease with which they can be disposed of.

I This warehouse was on working week-days normally closed up from 6 p.m. till 6 a.m. (Over weekends it was closed up over the whole of Sunday and part of Saturday.) On July 29, 1963, there arrived at the warehouse a vulnerable load consisting of whisky worth some £9,000 which was to be held overnight on common law bailment terms. During the night a gang of thieves broke into the warehouse and stole the load by driving it away on the vehicle (a trailer linked to a mechanical horse) on which it was standing ready to be taken to the docks.

---

(10) [1967] 2 All E.R. at p. 791.

In those circumstances the onus of proof lay on the defendants to prove that at **A** the time of the theft they were taking proper care of the load having regard to all the circumstances, or, if they failed so to prove, then to show that their lack of care was not the cause of the theft. In the present case the first and most important issue to be determined is whether the defendants proved that their system of looking after the goods was one which was proper in all the circumstances.

The common law has always been vigilant in the interests of bailors whose goods **B** are not returned to them by the bailee for a number of reasons: in so far as that viligance relates to the onus of proof, one of the reasons stems from the fact that normally it is only the bailee who knows what care was being taken of the goods, and another from the number of temptations to which a bailee may succumb. Those temptations may vary in each generation according to the nature of the transaction and in these days of rising costs include that of the bailee wishing to **C** pay as little for security as he can " get away with ", and the complacency that can arise from the feeling " after all, we are insured ". The present case provides a good example of the need to scrutinise closely the claim of a bailee that he has discharged the onus of proof to which reference has been made.

In relation to that onus it is to be noted that, because it is the defendant bailee who has the knowledge of his own system and why he has adopted it, a plaintiff's **D** attack on it can often only develop as the defendant unfolds his case. Counsel for the defendants pressed a complaint that some of the points taken against the defendants only emerged relatively late in the case; but that often occurs in this class of case. Moreover, that tendency was in the present instance accentuated by the failure of the two directors of the defendant company, when examined in chief, to deal with matters on which later witnesses for the defendants gave rele- **E** vant evidence, both in chief and in cross-examination. The complaint does not seem to me to be well founded, any more than one that seemed to propound the view that if there are gaps in the bailee's evidence, the bailor should proceed so to cross-examine as to fill them.

With these preliminary observations, I now turn to the facts. Up to 1953 the defendants employed a night watchman, but in that year decided to put **F** night security into the hands of the third parties, Factory Guards, Ltd., a reputable firm operating in Liverpool. Of the alternative systems available the defendants chose to rely solely on the cheapest, known as a " beat " system entailing four visits by a patrolman at irregular intervals over twelve hours. In 1956 this cost only £11 4s. 6d. a month (about £2 10s. a week), a minute figure in relation to a business the nature and extent of which have been related by LORD PEARSON **G** and which insured individual consignments of up to £100,000 each. By 1963 the charge was £15 a month (about £3 7s. a week), and even at that figure must have been a very considerable saving over the cost of a night watchman, old or young. It left the premises unwatched for periods of up to four hours at a stretch save for any police patrols.

The question is whether that beat system, instituted in 1953 and not reinforced **H** in any way, was reasonable in 1963, when the scale of thieving and the scale of the defendants' transhipment business had increased, and by which time (if not earlier) the types of alarm available included silent alarms of types which apparently were commonplace in bonded warehouses in Liverpool, and by which time also there could be hired " static patrols " who could either remain in the premises on every night or else could be there on irregular nights which would not be known to the criminal gangs. Whether it was reasonable for the defendants not to provide such reinforcement naturally depended on a number of facts, such as the frequency with which valuable vulnerable loads came to the warehouse, the cost of the reinforcement, and the turnover of business which would have to bear that cost. On none of those three points did the defendants choose to adduce any reasonable amount of evidence. Thus, for instance, no figures were put in evidence (with supporting books) as to the monthly totals of the value of goods handled or the income derived therefrom; nor any monthly totals of loads of a vulnerable

A nature. The court was left to deal with this aspect of the case on the type of answers to which my lord has referred, much of which was obtained under cross-examination. Nothing was placed before the court on which one could assess whether the cost of any particular precaution would be commercially too heavy. No evidence was adduced as to what were the type or types of silent alarms available, or their costs, or the impediments (if any) to their installation. All that the

B evidence on analysis showed was that reinforcement of one sort or another was available and was in use in Liverpool.

In so far as the defendants sought in argument to rely on the recommendations of the third parties, it is enough to say that the defendants appear to have refrained from telling that firm originally about their vulnerable loads, and clearly did not consult them on this point as conditions varied and the extent

C of their business increased. Indeed the evidence indicates that they misled the third parties on this point, and that evidence stands uncontradicted.

In so far as the defendants sought to rely on the practice of those owning similar warehouses, it is to be observed that in the passage most relied on the witness simply referred to hauliers, and there is nothing to indicate whether he was referring to firms that dealt in transhipment business, and still less as to the

D quantities (if any) of vulnerable goods which those firms were likely to have on their premises; nor was any witness from any such firm called. On this point it is perhaps as well to put in a word of caution with regard to the approach: " Others do it, so it is reasonable for me to do it." Obviously much weight should be given in certain cases to the practice of other firms, but the mere fact that a number of firms continue to follow a practice which common sense shows to be

E inadvisable may not necessarily suffice to satisfy the onus of proof that lies on a bailee.

The upshot of the evidence taken as a whole was that both the police officer (Detective Officer Pugh) and the third parties' witness Mr. Green made it clear that some reinforcement of the best system was advisable when vulnerable loads were not uncommonly on the relevant premises, though the detective officer

F hedged his reply with the following comment:

" The silent alarm is recommended, but the business people are reluctant to install it because of the cost. It would depend largely on how often you have really valuable commodities. It would have to be in the region of thousands of pounds' worth of property being on the premises regularly for it to be profitable to the concern."

G In this way one returns to the points on which the defendants refrained from adducing evidence, e.g., the volume and value of turnover, the number of vulnerable consignments, and the cost of alarms. In those circumstances, after taking into account all the various factors, including the nature of building, which the judge related in his compact and lucid judgment (11), I find myself with regret unable to agree with him that the defendants discharged the burden of proof laid

H on them by the onus of proof, and it follows that accordingly they should be held to be negligent in having failed to provide a reasonable system of safeguarding their warehouses at night. An unreinforced beat watch of four visits in twelve hours was not shown to be of itself enough, and whether the additional safeguards should have taken the form of an alarm of one sort or another or of additional watchmen services matters not.

I In relation to that breach of their obligations, it is to be noted that their duty must be assessed in relation not merely to the risks of a particular " outside job " such as the one under consideration, but also as regards other risks including those of an " inside job ", e.g., where a day employee facilitates the entry of others through some small door—a matter to which no evidence was directed. One must look at the situation as a whole, for often safeguards primarily directed against one form of attack in practice assist when a different form is being used.

(11) [1967] 2 All E.R. 785.

Taking an overall view, some special alarm on the big doors operating by direct **A**
line to a police station or a security organisation normally merits consideration.

In coming to the above conclusions I have not put into the scales the finding
of the trial judge that they were negligent in " advertising " the presence of the
goods. In that respect, however, the defendants seem to me to be in somewhat
of a dilemma; if they are right in their contention that the finding of the trial
judge was not warranted, then they can only maintain their contention by the **B**
assertion, made in this court by their counsel, that in any event their premises
were such that any gang of thieves could easily observe what valuable load was
coming into their warehouse and was being retained there. Accordingly, the
need for proper security must in any event be assessed in the light of the ability
of thieves to know when there was on the premises a vulnerable load which was
worth attacking. **C**

On the basis that the defendants were negligent, the next issue is whether they
discharged the onus of showing that the theft would have occurred even if they
had not been negligent. On facts of the present type a defendant is necessarily
and rightly in a considerable difficulty unless he can establish both the exact time
the theft took place, and also the way in which the thieves at that time would
have put out of action the watchman or defeated the alarm. In the present case it **D**
seems to me that the defendants could neither pinpoint the time with sufficient
exactitude nor could they explain why a night watchman, if available, could
not have been able to call for help, or how if there had been an alarm (bell or
silent) it would have been put out of action if well sited. In argument before this
court, and perhaps also in the judgment of the trial judge, undue weight was
placed on behalf of the defendants on the suggestion that no precautions can **E**
guarantee protection against determined gangs of thieves, a defeatist idea which
pursued to its logical conclusion could lead to hardly any precautions being taken
at all. Anti-thief precautions are intended to have and do have a deterrent effect,
and can well result in a gang preferring to attack some different target where those
precautions do not exist. Moreover, the court can only in the matter of causation
deal with the particular method adopted by the gang, and it is rarely in point **F**
for a defendant to say: " Well, the gang might well have developed some different
line of attack ". In the present case there is no evidence that the skylight attack
could not have been frustrated or alternatively that the getaway would not have
been impeded had there been additional watch of some type kept or an alarm
bell located high on the outer wall, or a silent alarm fixed in the skylight area or
alternatively to the big doors. Whatever be the degree of the onus which a **G**
negligent bailee must discharge when seeking to establish that his negligence did
not cause the relevant loss—a point to which I will return when dealing with
the default of Mr. Collins and the third parties—it is to my mind clear that it
has not been here discharged by the defendants as against the plaintiffs.

Turning now to the failure of the third parties, Factory Guards, Ltd., to keep
a reasonable watch on the night in question, I am in full agreement with the view **H**
expressed by LORD PEARSON and by the trial judge (12), that the defendants
must accept responsibility for the negligence of the third parties in the same way
as if the patrolmen had been the defendants' own employees. The bailee is
responsible for proper care being taken of the goods and to my mind he cannot
escape from that liability merely by employing sub-contractors for that purpose,
however reasonable may be his confidence in them. Any contrary decision would
make a serious and unjustifiable inroad on the rights of bailors, and for this
inroad there does not appear to me to be any authority.

As regards the issue whether the defendants established that the theft would
have taken place even if the patrolman Collins had not been negligent, I have
found it more difficult than the trial judge to reach a conclusion of fact favourable
to the defendants. It is not easy to see why a diligent patrolman properly guided

---

(12) [1967] 2 All E.R. at p. 790.

A   by his superiors should not on that particular night have done his work with the
aid of taking a taxi if his own means of transport failed: nor do I see why his
statement that he would probably have visited the premises at about 5 a.m.
should have been accepted, when his reliability as a witness appears to have been
discredited and in fact he made no visit at all; nor why it should be inferred that
if diligent he would not have made a visit between 3 a.m. and 4 a.m., which would

B   have accorded with the pattern of some of the patrols on previous nights, as shown
on the relevant exhibit; nor why, if he had made that visit between 3 a.m. and
4 a.m., it might not, at any rate, have caused the police to be alerted at a time
when they had a better opportunity to deal with the matter. But in the end I
am, for the same reason as my lord, not prepared to dissent from the finding of
fact that the patrolman would not in any event after his 2.16 a.m. visit have

C   attended at the defendants' premises again until about 5 a.m.

      That conclusion seems to me to be clear whatever be the standard of proof to
be attained by a negligent bailee who desires to establish that his negligence did
not cause the loss. It is certainly clear if the " balance of probabilities " test
adopted by the trial judge (13) is correct. It is no less clear, however, even if the
correct test is " Has the bailee shown that there was no reasonable chance that

D   the loss would not have been incurred had he taken reasonable care? "—which is
probably the modern equivalent of the formula of not being entitled to set up
" the bare possibility of a loss, if his wrongful act had never been done ", as
propounded by Tindal, C.J., in *Davis* v. *Garrett* (14). Which of these two tests
is current remains open for consideration, at any rate, if a further case arises.

      In this court the point was not fully argued, and there was, therefore, no

E   opportunity to consider the line of authorities and dicta relating to the degree
of the onus that lies on bailees who seek to prove that a breach of their obligations
has not caused the loss complained of by the bailor. That line, which concerns
obligations of varying types, commences with *Lilley* v. *Doubleday* (15), and includes *Shaw & Co.* v. *Symmons & Sons* (16), *Gibaud* v. *Great Eastern Ry. Co.* (17),
and *Edwards* v. *Newland (E. Burchett, Ltd., Third Parties)* (18), also does not

F   appear to have been cited to the trial judge. Accordingly, it is perhaps best not
to say more on this issue, which does not arise on the facts as they have been
found.

      On the issue of contractual limitation of liability as between the plaintiffs and
the defendants, I am in agreement with what has been said by Lord Pearson and
have nothing to add.

G   As regards the contractual position between the defendants and the third
parties, I am also in agreement with the judgment of Lord Pearson and only
wish to add that, if the plaintiffs had succeeded against the defendants, then the
latter would have had a remedy over against the third parties to an extent which
it is not necessary to discuss. It seems proper, however, to refer to one of the
points raised in this court by counsel for the third parties. He submitted that the

I   onus of proof on the issue of causation lay on the defendants as against the third
parties, and thus that on the facts of the case the defendants could not affirmatively establish that the relevant negligence had caused the loss even if the plaintiffs had succeeded in showing that the defendants had not discharged the onus
of showing that the negligence did not cause the loss. On first impression this
submission had its attractions, but on further consideration it seems of doubtful

I   avail, for the following reasons. At the time the contract was made between the
defendants and third parties the latter were aware that the former normally held
goods in the warehouse as bailees: that any lack of diligence by the third parties

---

(13) [1967] 2 All E.R. at p. 791.
(14) [1824-34] All E.R. Rep. 286 at p. 288; (1830), 6 Bing. 716 at p. 724.
(15) [1881-85] All E.R. Rep. 406; (1881), 7 Q.B.D. 510.
(16) [1916-17] All E.R. Rep. 1093 at p. 1095; [1917] 1 K.B. 799 at p. 801.
(17) [1921] All E.R. Rep. 35 at p. 39; [1921] 2 K.B. 426 at p. 435.
(18) [1950] 1 All E.R. 1072 at p. 1081; [1950] 2 K.B. 534 at p. 542.

could well result in the defendants becoming liable to the bailor in damages: **A**
and that such liability would be on the basis of the defendants having to discharge
that onus of proof which lies on bailees. Indeed one principal objective of the
contract between the defendants and the third parties was to prevent the loss of
bailed goods. In these circumstances I would have been inclined not to accede
to the above submission. I would allow the plaintiffs' appeal and I agree with the
order proposed by LORD PEARSON.   **B**

*Appeal allowed; judgment for plaintiffs against defendants for £6,135. Leave to
appeal to the House of Lords refused.*

Solicitors: *Herbert J. Davis, Berthen & Munro*, Liverpool (for the plaintiffs);
Herbert Smith & Co. (for the defendants); *Peace & Darlington*, Liverpool (for the
third parties).   **C**

[*Reported by* F. A. AMIES, ESQ., *Barrister-at-Law.*]

                                                                                     D

ALLAM & CO., LTD. *v.* EUROPA POSTER SERVICES, LTD.

[CHANCERY DIVISION (Buckley, J.), January 11, 12, 15, 1968.]

*Licence—Notice to terminate occupation—Date—Earliest date that agreement
can lawfully be terminated—Advertising hoardings—Agreements between* **E**
*contractors and site owners giving licences to maintain display hoardings—
Site owners authorising another advertising contractor, a company, to determine existing licence agreements—Notice to terminate occupation given by
letter signed by solicitors—Letter addressed to parent company and associated
companies, but not separately sent or addressed to associated companies by
name—Sufficiency of notice.*   **F**

The plaintiff companies (a parent company and two wholly owned subsidiaries) had agreements with site owners under which one or other of the
plaintiff companies had erected and maintained on the sites display boards
or other display equipment for advertising purposes. These agreements
were for fixed terms, but were subject to termination by twelve months'
notice on either side, and in a number of cases continued after the expiry **C**
of the terms. The defendant company, a competitor in advertising,
approached many of the site owners and obtained agreements with them.
These provided, among other matters, for the site owner to terminate any
other advertising licence agreement; and the defendant company obtained,
either by a separate document or as a term of their agreements, authority from
site owners to determine such other licence agreements so soon as lawfully **F**
possible. On May 7, 1965, the defendant company's solicitors wrote a letter
addressed to the parent plaintiff company "and associated companies",
enclosing a list of some 218 sites, giving formal notice "to cease occupation
of the sites referred to at the earliest date after the service of this notice that
such agreement" (i.e., each of the plaintiff companies' agreements with site
owners) ". . . can lawfully be terminated". On May 14, 1965, each of the
plaintiff companies wrote a letter to each of the site owners referred to in
the list enquiring whether the defendant company had the site owner's
authority. On Aug. 18, 1965, the defendant company gave similar notice
in respect of 243 sites, including the 218 comprised in the notice of May 7,
the letter being addressed in this instance to each plaintiff company and
signed by a director of the defendant company. On the question whether the
notices of May 7 and Aug. 18 were effectual to bring to an end the pre-existing
agreements between the plaintiff companies and owners of various sites,

A   **Held:** the notices of May 7, 1965, and of Aug. 18, 1965, were valid and effective notices in respect of the properties to which they referred* for the following reasons—

(i) there should be no difficulty in relation to each of the various properties to which either composite notice referred in ascertaining the date for termination, although the day and month were not specified in respect of any

B   particular property; and accordingly the notices were sufficiently certain (see p. 839, letter I, and p. 833, letter A, post).

Addis v. *Burrows* ([1948] 1 All E.R. 177) and *May* v. *Borup* ([1915] 1 K.B. 830) applied.

P. Phipps & Co. (Northampton and Towcester Breweries), Ltd. v. *Rogers* ([1924] All E.R. Rep. 208) distinguished.

C   (ii) as an incorporated company must act through agents, the defendant company, though deriving its authority from the site owners and being their agent for the purpose, could validly give notice of termination by a letter or notice signed by its solicitors, as distinct from one of its directors, since the solicitors were clearly acting in the present case on the instructions of the defendant company and were performing a purely ministerial act in

D   communicating the notice (see p. 832, letter G, post).

(iii) the notice of May 7, 1965, must, on the facts, have reached the subsidiary plaintiff companies and thus was sufficiently given to them, though addressed to the parent plaintiff company " and associated companies " (see p. 832, letter I, to p. 833, letter A, post).

E   [As to notices determining licences, see 23 HALSBURY'S LAWS (3rd Edn.) 431, para. 1026.

As to form of a notice to quit, see 23 HALSBURY'S LAWS (3rd Edn.) 521, 522, para. 1172; and for cases on the necessity for statement of date of expiration, see 31 DIGEST (Repl.) 496, 497, *6212-6224.*]

Cases referred to:

F   *Addis* v. *Burrows*, [1948] 1 All E.R. 177; [1948] 1 K.B. 444; [1948] L.J.R. 1033; 31 Digest (Repl.) 497, *6222.*

Doe d. Rhodes v. *Robinson*, (1837), 3 Bing. N.C. 677; 6 L.J.C.P. 235; 132 E.R. 571; 1 Digest (Repl.) 379, *461.*

May v. *Borup*, [1915] 1 K.B. 830; 84 L.J.K.B. 823; 113 L.T. 694; 31 Digest (Repl.) 494, *6199.*

G   *Phipps (P.) & Co. (Northampton and Towcester Breweries), Ltd.* v. *Rogers*, [1924] 2 K.B. 45; *affd.* C.A., [1924] All E.R. Rep. 208; [1925] 1 K.B. 14; 93 L.J.K.B. 1009; 132 L.T. 240; 89 J.P. 1; 31 Digest (Repl.) 496, *6221.*

Action.

This was an action begun by writ issued on Sept. 16, 1966. In it the plaintiff

H   companies, Allam & Co., Ltd., Advertising Sites, Ltd., and National Solus Sites, Ltd., claimed an injunction to restrain the defendant company, Europa Poster Services, Ltd., from removing or otherwise interfering with any advertising board or hoarding belonging to any of the plaintiff companies, and claiming damages. The second and third plaintiffs were wholly owned subsidiaries of the first plaintiff. The plaintiffs in their statement of claim alleged that each of them carried on

I   business as outdoor advertising contractors and, as a means of carrying on such business, acquired licences from landowners for the use of exterior walls and buildings and other suitable sites for the purposes of affixing thereto or erecting thereon boards or hoardings suitable for the display of advertisements, and granted sub-licences of the boards or hoardings to advertisers. The following statement of facts is summarised from the judgment.

---

* The qualification in respect of possible new agreements, which is stated at p. 839, letter I, post, is not reflected in the statement above, which endeavours to state only the legal decision and the reasons for it.

For the purposes of their businesses the plaintiff companies used two forms of **A** agreement. An example of the earlier form of agreement so used was one in respect of 349, Blackburn Road, Accrington. It was headed with the name of the site owner concerned and was addressed in this instance to the first plaintiff company Allam & Co., Ltd. It provided, among other matters—

> " In consideration of your paying me the sum of £4 (four) per annum, I **B** agree to allow you to fix and maintain a board measuring about seven feet by ten feet on the premises situate at 349, Blackburn Road, Accrington, such rent to be paid half yearly and in advance. The board is to be fixed . . . (1) subject as is hereinafter mentioned this agreement is to remain in force for three years certain commencing from the date when the board is fixed, and shall be terminable thereafter at any time provided twelve months' previous notice in writing has been given by either party to the other." **C**

The date when the board was fixed was identified as having been Jan. 1, 1961. The agreement was signed by a Mr. Conroy, who was apparently the owner of 349, Blackburn Road, Accrington. More recently the plaintiff companies had adopted another form of agreement, which was again a document addressed to one or other of the plaintiff companies. The names of all three plaintiff com- **D** panies were printed at the head of the form, the intention being that those names that were inappropriate to a particular agreement should be deleted. This form of agreement read, so far as material:

> " In consideration of your agreeing to pay me/us a rental at the rate of £ per annum I/we agree to allow you to fix and thereafter maintain and (if you so wish) to illuminate in such manner as you shall think fit . . . **E** advertisement board(s) measuring . . . on the property known as . . . The above rental is payable half yearly in advance on Jan. 1 and July 1 in each year (hereinafter referred to as ' payment dates ') the first payment of rental being a proportionate payment from the date the board(s) is/are fixed to the next payment date to be made within thirty days of the date of fixing. It is understood that you will be solely responsible for any rates **F** which may be assessed on me/us in respect of the board(s). Subject as is hereinafter mentioned this agreement is to remain in force for five years certain commencing from the first payment date after the board(s) is/are fixed and shall continue thereafter unless and until determined by either party giving to the other not less than twelve months' previous notice in writing such notice to expire at any time after the said period of five years." **G**

The date when the board was to be fixed was specified on the face of the agreement.

In January, 1965, the defendant company, Europa Poster Services, Ltd. was incorporated to carry on a business similar to that carried on by the plaintiff companies. A commercial war developed between the defendant company and the plaintiff companies. In the course of it the defendant company approached **H** a large number of site owners with whom the plaintiff companies had agreements and obtained from them agreements in favour of the defendant company in one or other of two forms. The first of these forms was an agreement between the site owner of the one part and the defendant company of the other part. An example was the agreement with Mr. Conroy relating to 349, Blackburn Road, Accrington. It was in these terms, so far as material:

> " An agreement made on Apr. 6, 1965, between Mr. P. J. Conroy, 349, Blackburn Road, Accrington (hereinafter called ' the owner ') of the one part and Europa Poster Services, Ltd. . . . . (hereinafter called the ' the advertiser ') of the other part whereby it is mutually agreed that the owner

---

(1) HIS LORDSHIP intimated that there was a space left blank in the form as printed, which was to be filled in, and that the words " as now fixed " had been written in the space in the particular agreement that he was reading.

A will let and the advertiser will take the exclusive right of posting advertisements upon the gable wall of the owner's premises situate and numbered 349, Blackburn Road, Accrington, and upon any board panel or hoarding now being or hereinafter to be fixed on the said wall and also the exclusive right to fix advertising boards panels or hoardings to such wall upon the terms and conditions following that is to say: 1. Subject as hereinafter mentioned

B this agreement shall remain in force for a period of twelve months from the date when the advertiser shall first display a poster upon the said wall or upon any board panel or hoarding thereon and if on a date at least one month before the expiration of the said period of twelve months the advertiser serves notice in writing on the owner so requiring it the said period shall be extended for a further period of fourteen years or in the case of an owner

C who is a tenant and whose interest in the said premises whether by contract or by statute is less than the said further period of fourteen years for a further period equivalent to the remainder of the duration of his interest in the said premises . . . (2) . . . 3. The owner shall immediately take all steps necessary to determine any other licence agreement or lease (if any) now existing and in force in regard to the said premises at the earliest possible

D date.''

Where an agreement in that form was used the defendant company also obtained from the owner of the property in question written authority. That relating to Mr. Conroy's premises at 349, Blackburn Road, Accrington, was so headed and provided, so far as material:

E " Europa Poster Services, Ltd. In consideration of the sum of 2s. now paid by you to me (the receipt whereof I hereby acknowledge) I hereby (i) Authorise you so soon as may be legally possible to give notice on my behalf terminating any licence agreement or lease giving to any other person advertising rights over or in respect of gable wall 349, Blackburn Road, Accrington.''

F An authority in that form was obtained from all site owners from whom agreements were obtained in the form already referred to. The other form of agreement used by the defendant company avoided the necessity for a separate authority. That form was an agreement between the site owner on the one part and the defendant company, called the advertiser, on the other part, whereby in consideration of the sum of 1s. paid by the advertiser to the owner, the receipt

G of which was acknowledged, the owner agreed to let to the advertiser, and the advertiser agreed to take, the exclusive right of fixing advertising boards panels or hoardings to some specified part of specified premises of the owner—

" and also the exclusive right to post advertisements upon such wall and upon such boards panels or hoardings upon the terms and conditions following that is to say: 1. The owner shall forthwith give notice in writing to any

H other person firm or company having any advertising rights over or in respect of the said wall (hereinafter called ' subsisting advertising rights ') terminating the subsisting advertising rights so soon as may be legally possible. 2. The owner hereby irrevocably appoints the advertiser his agent for the purpose of so terminating subsisting advertising rights and in particular but without prejudice to the generality of the foregoing words for the purpose

I of serving any notices that may be necessary to terminate any subsisting advertising rights. 3. The licence hereby agreed to be granted shall commence to run immediately upon the termination of all subsisting advertising rights or if there be no subsisting advertising rights upon the execution hereof and subject as hereinafter mentioned such licence shall thereafter remain in force until the expiration of twelve months from the date when the advertiser shall first display or cause or permit to be displayed under this licence a

(2) There followed a clause fixing the rent, which HIS LORDSHIP said need not be read.

poster upon the said wall and if on a date at least one month before the   A
expiration of the said twelve months the advertiser serves notice in writing
on the owner so requiring him the said licence shall be extended for a further
period of fourteen years or in the case of an owner who is a tenant and whose
interest in the said premises whether by contract or by statute is less than the
said period of fourteen years for a further period equivalent to the unexpired
residue of his interest in the said premises."   B

Having secured a considerable number of agreements of these natures, the
defendant company, through its solicitors, wrote a letter of May 7, 1965, addressed
to " Messrs. Allam & Co., Ltd. and associated companies, 56/60 Strand, London".
It read:

" We enclose herewith a list of sites wherein our clients, Messrs. Europa   C
Poster Services, Ltd., have entered into agreements, such agreements
giving our clients the right of advertising on the sites referred to after the
expiration of the notices to the existing advertiser. We understand that
you are in occupation of the sites set out in such attached list, and our clients
have the written authority of the site owner to terminate your agreement with
them where such agreement can be lawfully terminated.   D
" Kindly treat this letter as formal notice to cease occupation of the sites
referred to at the earliest date after the service of this notice that such
agreement that you hold can be lawfully terminated. We would be obliged
if you would kindly inform us in the event of there being agreements which
you suggest cannot be lawfully terminated."

That letter was signed by the defendant company's solicitors and was written E
on their stationery. The letter of May 7 was accompanied by a schedule of
properties consisting merely of a list of addresses, 218 in number, and they included
sixty of the sixty-two premises in respect of which the present action was brought.
On May 10 the plaintiff companies' solicitors wrote to the defendant company's
solicitors acknowledging receipt of that letter and requesting a copy of the
relevant agreement or authority in each case; and on May 14 each of the plaintiff F
companies wrote a letter to each of the site owners owning properties listed in the
schedule attached to the defendant company's solicitors' letter of May 7, 1965.
The letter was in common form, whether it came from the first plaintiff company,
the second plaintiff company or the third plaintiff company, and was written by
those companies respectively to those site owners with whom they were
respectively in contractual relationship.   The letter was in these terms: G

"We have received a letter dated May 7, 1965, from Messrs. Kuit, Steinart
Levy & Co., a firm of solicitors in Manchester acting on behalf of Europa
Poster Services, Ltd., purporting to terminate our agreement with you relating to our advertisement on your property. Would you please confirm to us
whether Europa Poster Services, Ltd. have authority from you to terminate   H
this agreement."

They enclosed a stamped addressed envelope for reply.   His Lordship (BUCKLEY,
J.) said that those letters were of significance in this way, that they made it
plain that although the letter of May 7 was addressed to Allam & Co., Ltd. and
associated companies, it was in fact brought to the notice of the second and third
plaintiffs.
On June 2, 1965, the solicitors for the plaintiffs wrote informing the defendant
company's solicitors that they had advised the plaintiffs that the letter of May 7,
1965, was not a valid notice of determination. The defendant company, on Aug.
18, 1965, despatched further notices terminating, or purporting to terminate,
agreements between site owners and the plaintiff companies. These notices of
August, 1965, covered 243 premises and embraced, it seems, all of the 218 premises
which were affected by the compendious notice of May 7, 1965, or, at any rate,
the notices included all the sixty-two premises with which the court was concerned.

A   On this occasion a separate letter was written in respect of each address at which there were premises in respect of which the defendant company believed that one or other of the plaintiff companies had an agreement authorising them to display advertisements. The letter in respect of those premises at that address was sent separately to each of the three plaintiff companies; indeed, it seemed that these letters were addressed to five separate companies, but those five companies in-
B   cluded the three plaintiff companies, so that each plaintiff company received a notice in respect of every one of the 243 sites. The form of letter, which was common to every case, was written on the defendant company's notepaper. It was headed with a subject heading giving the particular address of the site to which the notice was to relate. It read as follows:

C   " We hereby give you notice terminating any right licence lease or agree-
ment you may have to affix to or display boards and/or advertisements of any nature on the above mentioned premises or any part thereof. Such termination shall take effect on the earliest possible date, after the service of this notice, which is permissible under the terms of your licence, lease or agreement (as the case may be), or at law.

D   " We give you this notice on behalf of and with the written authority of the person or persons hereunder designated as the site owners (being the person or persons having the sole right to grant and determine advertising rights licences leases or agreements in respect of the above mentioned premises) and without prejudice to the validity of the notice or notices previously served on you in this behalf by Messrs. Kuit, Steinart Levy & Co. solicitors of Manchester."

E   The letter was signed by a director of the defendant company on behalf of the site owner, and then the appropriate name was inserted of the site owner or person whom the defendant company believed to be the site owner in respect of particular premises to which the notice related.

The cases noted below* were cited during the argument in addition to those
F   referred to in the judgment.

P. R. Oliver, Q.C., and *J. Bradburn* for the plaintiff companies.
S. W. Templeman, Q.C., and *Ian McCulloch* for the defendant company.

BUCKLEY, J., having stated the nature of the action, having reviewed the facts and having read the agreements and letters as hereinbefore set out, con-
G   tinued: Consequent on the notices of May 7, 1965, and Aug. 18, 1965, being served, disputes have arisen, which this action is to determine. It is to be determined, first of all, whether the notices given by or on behalf of the defendant company on May 7, 1965, and Aug. 18, 1965, were valid and effectual to bring to an end the pre-existing agreements between the plaintiff companies and the owners of the various sites. I am invited to decide that general question as a preliminary point,
H   although it may leave some subsidiary matters to be debated hereafter should I decide the question in a particular way.

It is said on behalf of the plaintiff companies that the compendious notice of May 7, 1965, given in respect of 218 sites by one letter is bad for a number of reasons. Counsel for the plaintiffs has submitted that for a notice of this nature determining a contractual relationship between two parties first, the notice must
I   be given by the right person, and he says the notice of May 7, 1965, was not given by the right person. Secondly, he says that it must be given to the right person, and he draws attention to the fact that the letter of May 7, 1965, was addressed to " Allam & Co., Ltd. and associated companies ", which he says is not a sufficient identification to the person to whom the notice was intended to be given. Thirdly,

* *Hirst* v. *Horn*, (1840), 6 M. & W. 393; *Wilson* v. *Taverner*, [1901] 1 Ch. 578; *Hankey* v. *Clavering*, [1942] 2 All E.R. 311; [1942] 2 K.B. 326; *Lemon* v. *Lardeur*, [1946] 2 All E.R. 329; [1946] K.B. 613; *Winter Garden Theatre (London), Ltd.* v. *Millenium Productions, Ltd.*, [1947] 2 All E.R. 331; [1943] A.C. 173; *W. Davis (Spitalfields). Ltd.* v. *Huntley*, [1947] 2 All E.R. 371; *Sunrose, Ltd.* v. *Gould*, [1961] 3 All E.R. 1142.

A   he says that it must be certain in its terms, which he contends this notice was not.

The first of those points depends on the fact that the notice of May 7, 1965, was not given by any of the persons with whom the plaintiff companies were in contractual relationship; was not given by the defendant company as being the authorised agent of any of those persons, but was given by an agent of the defendant company, namely, their solicitors. Counsel for the plaintiffs contends

B   that that is a delegation which it was not open to the defendant company to make. He relies in that connexion on *Doe d. Rhodes* v. *Robinson* (3). The relation of an agent to his principal is normally at least one which is of a confidential character and the application of the maxim delegatus non potest delegare to such relationships is founded on the confidential nature of the relationship. Where the principal reposes no personal confidence in the agent the maxim has no application,

C   but where the principal does place confidence in the agent that in respect of which the principal does so must be done by the agent personally unless either expressly or inferentially he is authorised to employ a sub-agent or to delegate the function to another. If the agent personally performs all that part of his function which involves any confidence conferred on him or reposed in him by the principal it is, in my judgment, immaterial that he employs another person to carry out some purely ministerial act on his behalf in completing the transaction. The defendant

D   company, being an incorporated company, could not in its own person serve notices determining any of these agreements. Any incorporated company must always act through some agent or other and, therefore, this may be one of those cases in which by inference the agent is authorised by the principal to act through an agent in performance of his agency. It seems to me to be of no particular significance if the agent employed is not, for instance, the secretary of the com-

E   pany or one of its directors but is its solicitor. The important consideration is whether, in doing what it did, the defendant company exercised the will-power and made the decisions and did all in respect of its agency under its authority from the various site owners in respect of which those site owners reposed any confidence in the defendant company. The letter of May 7 is, I think, quite clearly written by the solicitors on the instructions of the defendant company, and

F   nothing has been said to suggest that they were doing otherwise than merely acting on instructions to write this letter. I must proceed on the basis that the list of addresses which accompanied the letter, and the substance of the letter itself, were matters that had been determined by the defendant company and that the firm of solicitors were in truth no more than an amanuensis of the defendant company in transmitting the notice in written form to the first plaintiff

G   and whatever is properly embraced within the term " and associated companies ".

Accordingly, in my judgment, there is no substance in the first point taken by counsel for the plaintiffs that the comprehensive notice of May 7, 1965, was bad on the ground that it constituted an unauthorised delegation of the defendant company's authority to give notice determining the agreement.

H   Counsel for the plaintiffs then says that the term " associated companies " is meaningless and that this is not a notice effectively given, at any rate, to the second and third plaintiff companies because it is not addressed to them, and because they cannot be identified as persons to whom the letter was intended to be addressed as " associated companies ". The second and third plaintiff companies are wholly owned subsidiaries of the first plaintiff company and they clearly fall within the descriptive term " associated companies " of the first plaintiff company. However, in my judgment, any difficulty that might otherwise have arisen as a result of the use of this method of address is really disposed of by the letters of May 14, which I have mentioned, which make it plain that the second and third plaintiff companies in fact received full notice of this letter of Messrs. Kuit, Steinart Levy & Co., and that in so far as it was a notice intended to

---

(3) (1837), 3 Bing N.C. 677.

A be addressed to them it reached them. Consequently, I feel no difficulty in that respect.

We come now to what is perhaps the most difficult part of the case. This is an aspect of the case which affects not only the notice of May 7, 1965, but also those of Aug. 18, 1965. This relates to the question whether these notices were sufficiently certain in their terms to be valid notices. In *Addis* v. *Burrows* (4),
B which was a case in the Court of Appeal, where the court was dealing with a notice determining a tenancy given under a tenancy agreement, EVERSHED, L.J., after discussing *P. Phipps & Co. (Northampton and Towcester Breweries), Ltd.* v. *Rogers* (5), said this (6):

C
" Nothing that I say should be taken as qualifying in any way the general duty of landlords to give notices in terms which are sufficiently clear and unambiguous in that the right date is either stated or can be ascertained by the tenant by reference to his tenancy agreement with the terms of which he must be taken to be familiar . . ."

The reference there to the right date is a reference to the date from which the notice to quit was intended to operate. By analogous reasoning a notice given
D by or on behalf of one party to a contract intending to bring that contract to an end, whether it be a contract of tenancy or a contract of some other kind, must be sufficiently clear and unambiguous to convey to the party to whom it is given precisely how it is intended to operate, and when it is intended to operate. It is on grounds of this kind that these notices are attacked.

It will be remembered that the notice of May 7 was expressed to be formal notice

E
" to cease occupation of the sites referred to at the earliest date after the service of this notice that such agreement that you hold can be lawfully terminated."

The letter is not written in very artistic language because it fluctuates from the plural to the singular in a rather unfortunate way. In the second paragraph it
F states that the defendant company " have the written authority of the site owner " —in the singular—" to terminate your agreement with them "—in the plural— " where such agreement can be lawfully terminated ". In the passage that I have just read it contains a reference to " formal notice ". There is a reference to " the sites referred to " and to "the earliest date after the service of this notice that such agreement that you hold can be lawfully terminated ". I do not think the true
G meaning of the letter is really in any doubt. This letter was intended to be a notice to be read in respect of each of the 218 sites listed in the schedule and to be read as a separate notice in respect of each of those 218 sites, terminating the agreement in respect of that site at the earliest date at which it could lawfully be terminated. It is a notice which purports to be given on behalf of the site owner of each of those sites.

H
One point that counsel for the plaintiffs has taken is that a compendious notice of this kind in respect of 218 properties, where the circumstances in respect of the various properties may vary, is itself not a permissible form of notice of termination, because of the multiplicity of problems it may give rise to on account of the different considerations affecting different sites. I do not feel able to accept that argument. This letter must be read in just the same way as it would
I have been read if 218 letters to the like effect had been written, one in respect of each of the 218 sites. If that had been the machinery adopted, it would have been quite impossible to say that any one of the 218 notices were bad merely because 218 notices were served on the same day. I do not accept the argument that by compressing that process into this form, one letter with a schedule of 218 addresses, the validity of the notice is in any way affected. There were differences

(4) [1948] 1 All E.R. 177; [1948] 1 K.B. 444.
(5) [1924] All E.R. Rep. 208; [1925] 1 K.B. 14.
(6) [1948] 1 All E.R. at p. 182; [1948] 1 K.B. at p. 455.

between the circumstances affecting the sites, for at the time when this notice A
was served thirty-four of the 218 sites were the subject of agreements in respect
of which the initial fixed term had not yet expired. The remainder were cases
in which the fixed term had expired and the agreement was continuing from year
to year subject to determination in accordance with its terms. There may
also have been other differences, for it would seem that from time to time some
of the site owners had obtained increases in the annual payments that the plaintiff B
companies were to pay them. Where and whenever such an increase was
obtained the legal poisition would seem to have been that the site owner obtained
a new agreement and very possibly a new agreement with a new fixed term
to run from the date of the increase of the annual payment. So there may
have been different problems arising in respect of different sites but that, in
my judgment, does not vitiate this notice. C

It is then said that the formula which has been adopted for identifying the date
on which the notice is to operate is one which lacks the necessary quality of clarity
and definition, that is to say, that the reference to " the earliest date after the
service of this notice that such agreement that you hold can lawfully be terminated " is too uncertain, particularly when it is borne in mind that the notice
refers not to one property but to 218 properties. D

There are three cases to which I should refer shortly, which have been brought
to my attention in this connexion. The first is *May* v. *Borup* (7). The headnote
reads:

" An agreement for a yearly tenancy provided that the tenancy might be
determined by six months' notice to be given on Mar. 1 and Sept. 1 in any
year. On Dec. 23, 1913, the tenants wrote to the landlord giving notice to E
quit the premises ' at the earliest possible moment ', and stating that if,
as the tenants hoped, a satisfactory reorganisation of their business was
effected, the notice would be ' cancelled '.

" Held, that the fact that the tenants claimed by the notice to exercise
in a certain event a right which they did not possess, namely, to cancel the
notice, did not render the notice bad as being conditional, and that the F
letter constituted a valid notice determining the tenancy at the expiration
of six months from Mar. 1, 1914."

A. T. LAWRENCE, J., said (8):

" First, it is said that it [the notice to quit] is too vague, because the notice
is to quit ' at the earliest possible moment '. No doubt a notice to quit must G
be clear and certain, but I do not think that there is anything vague or uncertain about this notice. The earliest possible moment at which the tenancy
could determine could only be six months after the date on which notice
had to be given. As this notice was given on Dec. 23 and the agreement
required six months' notice from Mar. 1, the earliest possible moment for
the determination of the tenancy could be no other date than Aug. 31." H

On this part of the case SANKEY, J., the other member of the court, said (9):

" A notice to quit must be clear and unambiguous. This notice consists
of two paragraphs, the first of which is in my opinion a clear and unambiguous
notice to quit at the earliest possible moment, that was, in the circumstances,
Aug. 31." I

That case, if it is good law, makes it clear that it is not necessary in a notice of this
nature to specify the date on which the notice is to take effect provided some
formula is used which makes it possible for the recipient of the notice to discover
precisely at what date the notice is intended to take effect.

The next case, that of *Phipps & Co.* v. *Rogers* (10), which went to the Court of

(7) [1915] 1 K.B. 830.   (8) [1915] 1 K.B. at pp. 831, 832
(9) [1915] 1 K.B. at p. 832.   (10) [1924] All E.R. Rep. 208; [1925] 1 K.B. 14.

A Appeal, was heard at first instance by Lush, J. (11). There a hotel was the subject of a tenancy agreement under which the tenancy was determinable by a three months' notice to quit to expire

> " on any one of the days appointed as special transfer sessions by the justices . . . after the expiration of six months from the date when the licence was or is transferred to the tenant."

B
The landlords gave a notice to the tenant to quit the premises

> " on the earliest day your tenancy can legally be terminated by valid notice to quit given to you by us at the date of the service hereof."

Lush, J., held that, as the notice to quit did not state the date when possession was required or indicate it with reasonable clearness so that the tenant could
C know definitely when he had to vacate the premises, it was not a good notice. He distinguished *May* v. *Borup* (12).

At the date of this decision the Law of Property Act, 1925, had not yet been enacted and there was no statutory rule as to the interpretation of the word " month ", which might, therefore, mean either a lunar month or a calendar month. Lush, J., said (13):

D
> " A notice to quit, though it need not actually name the date, must indicate with reasonable clearness when possession will be demanded or given, so that the other party may know what is required of him, and the time must be the proper time as provided by the lease."

Considering the facts of the case he came to the conclusion that the form of
E notice to quit there adopted was not sufficiently explanatory of the date at which the tenant was required to give up possession.

In the Court of Appeal (14) Bankes, L.J., said (15):

> " A much more difficult question, to my mind, is the question whether the notice to quit offends against the rule that a notice to be a good notice must be clear and unambiguous. It is not necessary that a notice should be
F clear and unambiguous in its expressed terms provided it can be rendered clear and unambiguous by the application of the maxim Id certum est quod certum reddi potest."

Then he went on to refer to *May* v. *Borup* (12) and said that he thought that decision must be considered as a decision on the particular facts of the case and
G could not be regarded as an authority that a notice to quit at the earliest possible moment is under ordinary circumstances a good notice. He said (16): " Each case must depend upon its own facts and circumstances . . .". He went on to comment on the particular facts of the case before him. He said (16):

> " In the present case, had the notice been for the first date fixed for the holding of special transfer sessions next ensuing after the expiration of
H three lunar months from the date of this notice, I should be of opinion that the notice was a good notice, having regard to the knowledge which must, I think, be imputed to the particular tenant of the dates fixed for the holding of these sessions. Had the notice omitted any reference to lunar months, I should have hesitated before holding that any of the decided cases went so far as to compel me to impute to the tenant such a knowledge
I of the law as would enable him to decide without doubt a question of construction upon which judges may differ, as they do in the present case. When, as here, the landlord is not content with placing the tenant under the necessity of solving one difficult question of law before he can know the date when he is required to give up possession, but puts him in the position of having to

---

(11) [1924] 2 K.B. 45.   (12) [1915] 1 K.B. 830.
(13) [1924] 2 K.B. at p. 49.   (14) [1924] All E.R. Rep. 208; [1925] 1 K.B. 14.
(15) [1924] All E.R. Rep. at p. 211; [1925] 1 K.B. at p. 20.
(16) [1924] All E.R. Rep. at p. 212; [1925] 1 K.B. at p. 21.

decide not only the earliest day when the tenancy can legally be determined, **A**
but also whether the notice to quit is a valid one, the time has come, in my
opinion, when the court must say that such a notice is certainly not clear
and unambiguous in its expressed terms, and that it requires a degree of
knowledge on the part of the tenant to make it clear and unambiguous which
the court will not impute to him."

SCRUTTON, L.J., dissented from the other members of the court on the question **B**
of validity of the notice. ATKIN, L.J., held the notice to be bad and (17) expressed
a view that *May* v. *Borup* (18) could be wrongly decided.

ATKIN, L.J., said (17):

" In the present case the tenant is left to determine for himself whether
three months means lunar or calendar months, and a lawyer of LUSH, J.'s
great reputation might have advised him calendar months. He might then **C**
have to determine whether the annual licensing meeting could or could
not be a special transfer session, and then he has to find out when the
special transfer session in fact are going to be held. That the law should
impute to every person knowledge of its provisions is one thing, but that a
notice between landlord and tenant which presumes such knowledge is certain
and unambiguous seems to me to be quite a different proposition. The value **D**
of the presumption so far as it bears on certainty is illustrated by the fact
that the landlords themselves took an erroneous view of the meaning of
special transfer sessions. It appears to me that this notice fails in the first
essential of a notice—' certainty '—and is invalid."

That case affords some foundation for the view that where, in order to interpret **E**
the formula used in a notice to quit, or any other notice determining a contractual
relationship, it is necessary to consider some question of law arising, it may be,
on the construction of the agreement sought to be determed that may render
the notice invalid because it is a notice lacking the necessary quality of certainty.

I now come to a later decision of the Court of Appeal in *Addis* v. *Burrows* (19).
There premises were let from Jan. 1, 1944, to June 30, 1945, **F**

" for the term of one year and so on from year to year until the tenancy
be determined at the end of the first or any subsequent year by one of the
parties giving to the other of them six calendar months previous notice in
writing."

On the face of the tenancy agreement there was an ambiguity because the period
from Jan. 1, 1944, to June 30, 1945, was not a term of one year. The agreement **G**
was on a printed form and the words " from Jan. 1, 1944, to June 30, 1945 "
had been typed in. On June 28, 1945, the plaintiffs, the lessors, gave the defendant notice to quit " at the expiration of the year of your tenancy, which will
expire next after the end of one half year from the service of this notice ". The
defendant did not give up possession at the due date and the plaintiff brought
an action. The Court of Appeal held, reversing OLIVER, J., first, that on its **H**
true construction the tenancy granted was for eighteen months certain and
thereafter a yearly tenancy; secondly, the notice to quit was not invalid as
being too vague (they distinguished *Phipps & Co.* v. *Rogers* (20)); thirdly that
the tenancy came to an end on June 30, 1946.

The judgment was delivered by EVERSHED, L.J., who considered the question
of whether the notice was valid or ineffectual. He set out the terms of the
notice and drew attention (21) to the fact that the formula used in it is one of long
standing and that according to WOODFALL ON LANDLORD AND TENANT (24th
Edn.) p. 973:

---

(17) [1924] All E.R. Rep. at p. 215; [1925] 1 K.B. at p. 28.
(18) [1915] 1 K.B. 830.
(19) [1948] 1 All E.R. 177; [1948] 1 K.B. 444.
(20) [1924] All E.R. Rep. 208; [1925] 1 K.B. 14.
(21) [1948] 1 All E.R. at p. 180; [1948] 1 K.B. at p. 452.

A   " The notice need not mention the particular day on which the tenant is required to quit. Thus a notice to quit ' at the expiration of the current year of the tenancy which shall expire next after the end of one half-year from the date hereof ' is sufficient."

Evershed, L.J., went on to say (22):

B   ". . . a notice in that form puts plainly on the tenant the obligation to consider what is the date that is meant by that form of words. Prima facie, the problem is not very difficult. As [Lord Greene, M.R.] observed in the argument, assuming that the tenant can read and write, he requires two things only, namely, a modern calendar and his document of tenancy. Armed with those two instruments he asks himself first: when was this notice served on me? This notice was dated June 28, and I will assume it arrived on the next day. The answer to that question, therefore, is June 29. Having regard to the form, he is next required to find out when one half year ends after the service of the notice.   With the aid of his calendar he will discover that the answer to that question is Dec. 29, 1945. There then only remains the question: when does the year of his tenancy current on Dec. 29, 1945, come to an end?   It is true that involves, or may involve, an interpretation of the tenancy agreement, but, if I am right in the view which I have expressed, he should have no great difficulty in answering that question as: June 30, 1946."

C

D

Later Evershed, L.J., said (23):

E   " In many cases . . . the document is so clear that no problem in any true sense of the word arises at all. On other occasions there may be a doubt or difficulty in the language of the instrument which, however, is the tenant's instrument as well as the landlord's instrument. As has been pointed out by my lord in the course of the argument, when the question of the validity of a notice to quit comes before the courts, judges may differ on the question whether the notice was or was not valid. The tenant is none the less bound, even though in the highest tribunal there may be a divergence of judicial opinion. Without pursuing the matter further, however, the whole object of this formula, as pointed out in the authorities, is to get over the difficulty a landlord might find himself in if he, the landlord, wrongly interpreted the agreement or gave a wrong date. . . . it is intended to cast the duty on the tenant to satisfy himself by looking at the instrument, what is the correct date upon which he ought to go out. The fact that he is involved in that problem is no objection of itself to the form of words which has been used."

F

G

Evershed, L.J., referred to *Phipps & Co.* v. *Rogers* (24) and said (25) that in that case there was

H   ". . . an accumulation of difficulties provided by the joint effect of the language of the tenancy agreement and the very general and unusual form of the notice to quit."

Having commented on *Phipps & Co.* v. *Rogers* (24) he said (25):

". . . in my judgment, the present case falls far short, as regards difficulties imposed on the tenant of *Phipps & Co.* v. *Rogers* (24) which ought not to be regarded as an authority conclusive against the landlords in this case or such as should make us say that the present notice is bad . . . the present notice is one which is very familiar in form and sanctioned by very long usage. If there were no problem of construction on the tenancy agreement, it is plain, . . . that no possible objection could have been taken to this notice. The objection arose because it is said that there was an ambiguity in the

I

---

(22) [1948] 1 All E.R. at p. 181; [1948] 1 K.B. at p. 453.
(23) [1948] 1 All E.R. at p. 181; [1948] 1 K.B. at pp. 453, 454.
(24) [1924] All E.R. Rep. 208; [1925] 1 K.B. 14.
(25) [1948] 1 All E.R. at p. 182; [1948] 1 K.B. at p. 455.

tenancy agreement. That ambiguity I have ventured to answer, and, to my A mind, it is capable of a clear answer. In those circumstances, it seems to me that any difficulty which otherwise there might be in the wording of the notice is got rid of."

LORD GREENE, M.R., in his judgment also commented on *Phipps & Co.* v. *Rogers* (26), and in particular ATKIN, L.J.'s judgment. He said (27):

B

" ATKIN, L.J., then went on to say (28): ' But it appears to defeat the whole object of notice, to leave the date to be ascertained by the tenant as a problem not of fact but of law.' In other words, he is distinguishing the case where the tenant ascertains the date by looking at the agreement from the case where some problem of law has to be settled. A problem of law may arise, on that very point in the agreement, namely, the date, and so C it is suggested here, but I cannot take those observations as meaning that it is sufficient to find ' difficult questions of construction ' (whatever the word ' difficult ' may mean), in the tenancy agreement, to invalidate a notice expressed in this particular way."

A little later he said (29):

D

" If I were wrong as to that, I should say that the question of law on the construction of this particular tenancy agreement was not difficult."

Therefore, that case, in my judgment, clearly establishes that where a formula is used in a notice of this kind which involves reference to some other document, in order to ascertain the date at which the notice is intended to operate, and some question of law arises on the interpretation of that other document relevant to E ascertaining the date, that fact is not necessarily fatal to the validity of the notice.

If I go back to the case of Mr. Conroy as an example, he, in the year 1961, entered into an agreement with the first plaintiff for a fixed period of three years, which had therefore expired by the time when the relevant notice was given, and it was to be determinable thereafter at any time provided twelve months F previous notice had been given in writing by either party to the other. I ask myself: is there any difficulty about Allam & Co., Ltd. discovering the earliest date after May 7, 1965, or, perhaps I should say, after May 8, 1965, which, I suppose, is the date on which I should treat Allam & Co., Ltd. as having received the letter of May 7, 1965, on which their agreement with Mr. Conroy could lawfully be determined? There seems to me to be no difficulty whatever. There G has to be twelve months' notice and, therefore, the notice must be taken as being a twelve months' notice to terminate Mr. Conroy's agreement. There may be other site owners whose fixed period under their agreements with the plaintiff companies had not yet expired at the time when the notice of May 7, 1965, was given.

Let us suppose, by way of example, that Mr. Conroy's agreement had been entered into not in 1961 but in 1963, so that the term of three years under it would H not have expired by May 7, 1965. The earliest date on which his agreement could have been determined would have been either immediately after the end of the fixed period or the expiration of twelve months from the service of the notice, whichever date was later. There seems to me to be no difficulty whatever in the way of the plaintiff companies ascertaining the date on which this notice, read in relation to any one particular property, was intended to take effect and, as I have I already said, I am not impressed by the argument which has been presented, that the fact that the notices were given in respect of 218 properties and not merely in respect of one property, complicates the matter. The fact that notices are given in respect of 218 properties merely means that the process of finding out

---

(26) [1924] All E.R. Rep. 208; [1925] 1 K.B. 14.
(27) [1948] 1 All E.R. at p. 184; [1948] 1 K.B. at p. 458.
(28) [1924] All E.R. Rep. at p. 215; [1925] 1 K.B. at p. 28.
(29) [1948] 1 All E.R. at p. 184; [1948] 1 K.B. at p. 459.

A the appropriate date has got to be gone through 218 times. That is what would have had to have been done, if 218 separate notices had been served.

As regards the notices of Aug. 18, 1965, two points have been relied on by counsel for the plaintiffs. The first is that the notice is expressed

B " to take effect at the earliest possible date after service of the notice which is permissible under the terms of your licence, lease or agreement, as the case may be, or at law."

Counsel for the plaintiffs says that the introduction of the words " or at law " raises a question of law which it would be unfair to require the recipient of the notice to answer for himself in ascertaining the date on which the notice was intended to take place, because it would suggest there might be some other date C than that ascertained by reference to the terms of the agreement at which the notice would take effect. Why the words " or at law " were added I am not quite sure, but they do not seem to me to create any substantial doubt or, in fact, any doubt at all as to when these notices would take effect, and, if the recipient of the notice in any case was in any doubt as to precisely what the legal position was, the doubt is one which could have been resolved with the greatest simplicity D by consulting anyone expert in the law. I do not feel that the introduction of those words creates any complexity which would have the effect of making this notice one which was uncertain or so uncertain, in effect, as to make it unfair to treat it as a valid notice against a recipient.

It is then said that because at the end of the notice there are the words " without prejudice to the validity of the notice or notices previously served on you in E this behalf by Messrs. Kuit, Steinart Levy & Co.", that raises a complexity for the recipient, because he has to scratch his head and say, " I have now received two notices which suggest that my agreement with a particular site owner may determine on one or other of two dates according to whether notice A or notice B is to be treated as valid or effective ". It is well established that where a landlord, having given notice to quit, feels it desirable to give a second notice, perhaps F because of some doubt as to the validity of the first notice, and gives a second notice, that that notice does not amount to a waiver of the earlier notice and is in fact without prejudice to the validity of the earlier notice, and to put into a second notice of that kind words which expressly state that the second notice is without prejudice to the validity of the earlier notice is merely to state a fact. I do not think these words create any such complexity as to bring this case within *Phipps* G *& Co.* v. *Rogers* (30) rather than within *Addis* v. *Burrows* (31).

No doubt if those cases are both good law, as I must assume that they are, the question of the validity of a notice, the interpretation of which involves some question of law, must become a question of degree. There must be cases which, because of the difficulty or complexity of the case, fall within the principle of *Phipps & Co.* v. *Rogers* (30). There must be others which, notwithstanding that H some question of law arises, because of the simplicity or comparative simplicity of the problem fall within *Addis* v. *Burrows* (31). I think that this is a case which falls within the latter principle.

For these reasons I reach the conclusion that both the notices of May 7, 1965 and Aug. 18, 1965, were valid and effective notices in respect of the properties contained in them respectively, except possibly so far as those properties may I have been the subject of a new agreement entered into between the plaintiff companies, or any of them, and the site owner after the date on which the defendant company obtained authority from the site owner to determine his agreement with one of the plaintiff companies. The point was taken, that the notice of May 7, 1965, was not given specifically on behalf of a site owner concerned with the various premises, the addresses of which were contained in the schedule

---

(30) [1924] All E.R. Rep. 208; [1925] 1 K.B. 14.
(31) [1948] 1 All E.R. 177; [1948] 1 K.B. 444.

to the letter.   It seems to me that where an agent gives a notice of this nature   A
on behalf of a principal it is not necessary for him to name his principal by
name.   It is sufficient if he identifies him in any manner which truly amounts
to an indentification.

In the present case I do not feel that there is really any doubt about what is
meant by the term " site owner " in the letter of May 7, 1965. Counsel for the
plaintiffs did, in the course of his argument, say that it might mean, for instance,   B
the freeholder of property which was under lease, but I feel no doubt that on the
true interpretation of the letter " site owner " means the person who is in a position
to grant the right to put advertisements on the particular advertising site and
the " site owner " must, in the terms of this letter, be somebody with whom it was
thought that the plaintiff company had an agreement for that purpose.

The persons who were the site owners in respect of each of the 218 addresses   C
set out in the schedule to the letter can be identified by enquiry based on those
criteria. One has to consider, in respect of each address, who was the person who
was owner of the premises in such a sense that he was able to confer contractual
rights or to permit the plaintiff companies to put advertisements on the building
or whatever other structure there may be on the site.

For that reason I am of opinion that the letter makes it perfectly clear on whose   D
behalf it purports to be written as principal, for it says that

" Europa Poster Services have the written authority of the site owner to
terminate the plaintiff companies' agreement,"

and then proceeds to give notice.

[*Counsel then addressed* HIS LORDSHIP *in relation to sites nos. 7, 8, 43, 44 and 45.*]   E

BUCKLEY, J.: I now have to deal with the case of five properties which
stand in a rather exceptional position. The point with regard to them all is the
same. We will take one as an example, that is to say, serial 7 in the schedule to the
statement of claim, 404, Bolton Road, Blackburn. The original agreement in   F
respect of that property was entered into in 1921 between the then owner of the
property and a company called Van Houten, Ltd.   One of the plaintiff companies
in due course became entitled to the benefit of that agreement as successor in
title to Van Houton, Ltd. and the present owner and occupier of the premises,
Mr. F. King is successor in title of the original party who entered into the
agreement with Van Houten, Ltd.   G

On Apr. 5, 1965, the defendant company entered into an agreement with Mr.
King in the form accompanied by a separate written authority referred to
in my earlier judgment. At the risk of repeating some of the material I set
out in the earlier judgment I will state what the effect of that earlier agreement was. Paragraph 1 provides that the agreement should remain in force for a
period of twelve months from the date when the advertiser should display posters   H
on the wall, which was the subject matter of the agreement, " or upon any board
panel or hoarding thereon ". That was followed by a right for the defendant company to extend the period of licence for a further fourteen years on giving due
notice.

Clause 3 required that the owner

" shall immediately take all steps necessary to determine any other licence
agreement or lease (if any) now existing and in force in regard to the said
premises at the earliest possible date."

Clause 9, to which I did not refer earlier, provided that

" all hoardings boards or panels now upon the said wall shall remain the
property of the owner who shall permit the advertiser [the defendant
company] to have the use thereof for advertising purposes subject to the

A   advertiser at its own expense maintaining them in the same condition as they are now in."

The supporting written authority in this case was given on Apr. 14, 1965, and by that authority, as I mentioned earlier, the defendant company was authorised to give notice on behalf of Mr. King to terminate any licence agreement or lease giving to any other person, that is to say, in these circumstances to one of the plaintiff companies, advertising rights on the property. Clause 2 was in this form:

"I hereby confirm and agree that you shall have the licence mentioned in the agreement between us dated 5/4/65 such licence to commence on the date of the termination of the present licence agreement or lease giving advertising rights over the premises comprised in such licence and to be on the terms and conditions contained in such agreement save in so far as the same are hereby varied."

There were two agreed variations, the first of which provides that the annual payment payable under agreement shall be paid quarterly, the first payment to be made on the first quarter day following the commencement of the period referred to in cl. 1 of the agreement which is the period from the date when the advertiser shall first display a poster on the wall. The second variation was to this effect:

"All hoardings at present on the wall shall notwithstanding the provisions of cl. 9 of the said agreement be removable by the owner thereof and you shall have no right to the use of them unless the present owner shall elect not to remove them from the wall at the termination of his agreement."

Between the dates of the agreement and the written authority one of the plaintiffs obtained from Mr. King a new agreement on Apr. 8, 1965, and that agreement was one which gave them, or purported to give them, permission to affix notice boards to Mr. King's premises and provided that the agreement could remain in force for five years certain commencing from July 1, 1965, and should

"continue thereafter unless and until determined by the party giving to the other not less than twelve months previous notice in writing such notice to expire at any time after the said period of five years."

The sequence of events in respect of the other four properties with which I am now dealing is in substance identical with the case I have taken. It is not disputed, in the light of the judgment I have already delivered, that the new agreement obtained by one of the plaintiff companies from Mr. King on Apr. 8, 1965, if valid was duly determined by one or other of the two notices given by or on behalf of the defendant company, at the end of the fixed period of five years limited by the plaintiff company's new agreement of Apr. 8, 1965; but the defendant company says that the plaintiff companies cannot rely on any new agreement which they have obtained in that way because it is inconsistent with rights already given by the site owners by earlier agreement with the defendant company.

I find some difficulty in seeing how questions affecting the validity of the contracts of the plaintiff companies on the one hand and the defendant company on the other hand with the site owners can be determined in the absence of the site owners who are parties to those contracts. In the outcome counsel for the defendant company asked me to make a declaration to this, or like effect, that in respect of these five properties the plaintiff companies are not entitled to act on their new agreements with the site owners so long as the defendant company's agreements with those site owners remain in operation.

It seems to me that unwittingly (because I suspect that at the time when the written authorities of Apr. 14, 1965, were obtained by the defendant company

they were unaware of the existence of the plaintiff companies' new agreements) **A**
by the terms of those written authorities the defendant company have put it
beyond their power to insist on this, for by the terms of those written authorities
the licence which they obtained under their earlier agreements with the site
owners, which initially were expressed to take effect " from the date when the
advertiser shall first display the poster on the said wall ", are by the terms of
the written authorities to commence on the date of the termination of the **B**
" present licence agreement or lease " giving advertising rights over the premises
comprised in such licence.

Although the new agreements obtained by the plaintiff companies may very
probably have been unknown to the defendant company, they were present
licence agreements at a time when the written authorities were given.   It is
quite true that the licence agreements obtained by the plaintiff on Apr. 8, 1965, **C**
with respect to these five properties are expressed to be for periods commencing
on July 1, 1965, but nevertheless the agreements came into operation as contracts
upon their execution and I think they were " present licence agreements ".
Accordingly, it seems to me that the effect of the written authority on the face
of it, whether it was appreciated by the parties or not, I do not know, was to
make the licence which was granted to the defendant company one which could **D**
only take effect when all existing licence agreements in favour of the parties
had been brought to an end and that, in the case of the new agreements entered
into on Apr. 8, 1965, could not be until five years after July 1, 1965.

For that reason I reach the conclusion that on the true construction of these
documents the defendant company will not be entitled to insist on licence rights in
respect of these five sites until those new agreements have expired.   The notices **E**
which have been given are, in my judgment, effective to bring these agreements
to an end at the termination of the fixed period agreed in those new agreements
which in every case is five years from July 1, 1965, but not effective to bring them
to an end before that date.

It seems to me on that ground that until the expiry of that period the plaintiff
companies are entitled to remain in possession of their rights in those sites.   **F**

Declaration accordingly.

Solicitors: *McKenna & Co.* (for the plaintiffs); *Anthony Edward & Hoffman*,
agents for *Kuit, Steinart, Levy & Co.*, Manchester (for the defendants).

[*Reported by* JENIFER SANDELL, *Barrister-at-Law.*]

TAYLOR *v.* TAYLOR.

[COURT OF APPEAL, CIVIL DIVISION (Willmer, Danckwerts and Russell, L.JJ.), January 23, 24, 1968.]

Land Charge—Vacation of entry in register—Pending action—Summons under s. 17 of the Married Women's Property Act, 1882—Wife, respondent in divorce suit, claiming declaration of entitlement to half share in proceeds of sale of the matrimonial home, and asking for sale, etc.—Property in name of husband who had contracted to sell it—Registration vacated—Land Charges Act, 1925 (15 & 16 Geo. 5 c. 22), s. 2 (1), (6), s. 20 (6).

In May, 1967, while a divorce suit was pending, the respondent wife took out a summons under s. 17 of the Married Women's Property Act, 1882, asking, in effect, for a declaration that she and the husband were beneficial owners in equal shares of the property that had been the matrimonial home (which was in Kent and was vested at law in the husband), and for an order for sale of the property. The wife left the matrimonial home in July, 1967. In September, 1967, the husband entered into a contract to sell the property. The husband admitted that the wife was beneficial owner of some part of the proceeds of sale of the property, but the amount of her share was in dispute. The wife registered a lis pendens under the Land Charges Act, 1925, in respect of her summons under s. 17 of the Act of 1882. The definition* of " land " in s. 20 (6) of the Land Charges Act, 1925, excluded an undivided share in land. On application to vacate the registration,

Held: the registration of the lis pendens should be vacated for the following reasons—

(i) because, as the wife had no interest in the legal estate in the property but had only an undivided share of disputed amounts in the proceeds of sale of the property, which was held by the husband on the statutory trusts for sale, the summons under s. 17 of the Act of 1882 was not a proceeding relating to " land " as defined in s. 20 (6) of the Land Charges Act, 1925 (see p. 847, letter G, and p. 848, letters B, D and I, post), and

(ii) because the summons sought an order for sale, but the purpose of registering a lis pendens was to prevent the effective disposition of the property pendente lite (see p. 848, letters A, F and I, post).

Appeal allowed.

[**Editorial Note.** The Matrimonial Homes Act 1967 (see s. 2) came into operation on Jan. 1, 1968, by virtue of the Matrimonial Homes Act 1967 (Commencement) Order 1967, S.I. 1967 No. 1790.

As to the registration of pending actions, see 23 HALSBURY'S LAWS (3rd Edn.) 63, para. 117, and as to vacation of such entries, see ibid., pp. 64, 65, para. 121; and for cases on the subject, see 38 DIGEST (Repl.) 882, *926* and DIGEST (Cont. Vol. B) 548, *285a.*

For the Land Charges Act, 1925, s. 2, s. 20, see 20 HALSBURY'S STATUTES (2nd Edn.) 1066, 1096; and for s. 17 of the Married Women's Property Act, 1882, see 11 ibid., 804.]

Case referred to:

  Heywood v. *B.D.C. Properties, Ltd. (No. 2),* [1964] 2 All E.R. 702; [1964] 1 W.L.R. 971; Digest (Cont. Vol. B) 548, *285a.*

Interlocutory Appeal.

By petition dated Sept. 27, 1966, the husband, Harold Edward Taylor, sought dissolution of his marriage, which was solemnised on Mar. 24, 1951, with the respondent, Carol Elaine Taylor, on the ground of alleged cruelty, which she denied. There were two children of the marriage, a boy and a girl, born in 1956 and 1958. The husband sought custody of them. By summons dated May 16,

---

* The definition is set out at p. 845, letter B, post.

1967, entitled in the matter of the Married Women's Property Act, 1882, the wife   A
called on the husband to show cause why (i) it should not be declared that they
were the beneficial owners in equal shares of premises known as No. 21, Bradenham
Avenue, Welling, Kent, and (ii) the premises should not be sold and the net
proceeds, after repayment of a mortgage, should not be divided equally between
them. On July 3, 1967, the wife caused a lis pendens to be registered in the register
of pending actions under the Lands Charges Act, 1925, in respect of the summons.   B
On Nov. 8, 1967, an order was made by WRANGHAM, J., dismissing a summons
by the husband to vacate the entry in the register of pending actions. The
husband gave notice, dated Nov. 22, 1967, of appeal from that order on the
grounds—(i) that the lis pendens should never have been registered or, if registered, should have been vacated by the wife; (ii) the lis pendens was wrongfully
on the register and the wife wrongfully refused to remove it; (iii) if and so far as   C
the proceedings in the lis pendens related to land as defined in the Land Charges
Act, 1925, they are not being prosecuted in good faith or at all and (iv) on the
evidence before the trial judge he ought to have ordered the registration to be
vacated.

    M. Browne and *A. B. Ewbank* for the husband.
    J. W. A. Sloss for the wife.   D

    DANCKWERTS, L.J., delivered the first judgment at the request of
WILLMER, L.J.: This is an appeal from an order of WRANGHAM, J., made on Nov.
8, 1967. The matter arises in respect of proceedings between husband and wife, and
the only point with which we have to deal is whether the lis pendens which has
been registered under the Land Charges Act, 1925, should be vacated. The lis   E
pendens has been registered by the wife, the respondent in the divorce proceedings, the husband being the petitioner, under s. 2 of the Land Charges Act, 1925.
It is necessary to refer only quite briefly to the provisions of the Act. Section 2 (1)
provides for a register of pending actions, and it is claimed by the wife in the
present case that the proceedings under s. 17 of the Married Women's Property
Act, 1882, in the circumstances of this case are proceedings relating to land and   F
capable of registration under s. 2 of the Act of 1925. As I have said, sub-s. (2)
simply provides for the particulars which are to be entered on the register, and
they are really extremely meagre:

    ". . . (*a*) the name, address, and description of the estate owner or other
    persons whose estate or interest is intended to be affected thereby; and   G
    (*b*) the court in which the action, information or proceeding was commenced
    or filed; and (*c*) the title of the action, information or proceedings; and
    (*d*) the day when the action, information or proceeding was commenced or
    filed."

The form which has been produced for such registration provides for such
particulars, and I think no more.   H
    The effect of registration is to give notice to an intending purchaser of the
existence of the lis pendens, and the mere particulars stated on the register will
not help him very much to appreciate what the effect of the proceedings is, and
what effect they may have on the purchaser who has already entered into a
contract. Section 2 (6) of the Act of 1925, is the provision which deals with the
vacation of an entry. It provides:

    " The court, if it thinks fit, may, upon the determination of the proceedings,
    or during the pendency thereof if satisfied that the proceedings are not
    prosecuted in good faith, make an order vacating the registration of the
    pending action, and direct the party on whose behalf the registration was
    made to pay all or any of the costs and expenses occasioned by the
    registration and vacating thereof."

The provisions of that subsection are somewhat limited, but there is a decision of

A this court in *Hayward* v. *B.D.C. Properties, Ltd.* *(No. 2)*, (1). The effect of that decision for our purposes is simply to say that the court is not limited to the provisions of s. 2 (6) of the Act of 1925, but that the court has an inherent jurisdiction to remove from the register entries which in the circumstances ought not to to be there at all.

B There is one other provision to which I must refer. The Act of 1925 deals only with charges relating to land; and so it is material to refer to the definition of " land " to be found in s. 20 (6) which has some importance in the circumstances of the present case. The subsection provides as follows:

C " ' Land ' includes land of any tenure, and mines and minerals, whether or not severed from the surface, buildings or parts of buildings (whether the division is horizontal, vertical or made in any other way) and other corporeal hereditaments, also a manor, an advowson and a rent and other incorporeal hereditaments, and an easement, right, privilege or benefit in, over or derived from land, but not an undivided share in land . . ."

The words " but not an undivided share in land " are an important part of the definition for our purposes.

D The case has taken a great deal of time and ranged over very many matters, but in my view the issue is a comparatively narrow one and quite straightforward. There are certain events which I must relate in order to appreciate the situation. The property in question is No. 21, Bradenham Avenue, Welling, and was the matrimonial home of the husband and wife. They have two children, a boy and a girl, aged eleven and nine years respectively. The husband and wife

E became on bad terms shortly before the matters with which we are concerned, and there were disputes, and possibly violence (I do not know), but anyhow apparently the atmosphere was bad for the children as appears presently from a report made by the Official Solicitor. On Sept. 27, 1966, the husband presented a petition in the divorce division for divorce on the ground of cruelty. On Dec. 23, 1966, the wife put in an answer and a cross-petition also on the ground of cruelty.

F On Feb. 14, 1967, there was a supplemental petition by the husband, and on Apr. 5, 1967, there was an answer. On May 16, 1967, the wife took out a summons under s. 17 of the Married Women's Property Act, 1882, and she also took out (I think at the same time) a summons in the divorce division relating to custody of the children.

The form of the summons is of considerable importance, and I will refer to it.

G It is rather misleading to read because it was expressed in a somewhat inverted way, asking that the husband should show cause why certain things should not happen. Putting it, I hope, more clearly, the wife asked for a declaration that she and her husband were the beneficial owners in equal shares of the premises known as No. 21, Bradenham Avenue, Welling, in the county of Kent. That is the first relief which is sought. In the second paragraph what she asks for is, in effect,

H that the premises should be sold, and that the net proceeds of sale, after repayment of a mortgage which was for £700, or something of that sort, in favour of the Planet Building Society, should be divided equally between the wife and the husband. The third paragraph asks alternatively that the husband should pay to the wife the sum of £1,750 in respect of her said interest. Then follow paragraphs dealing with furniture, chattels, and matters of that sort with which we are

I really not concerned.

The question which we have to decide, as I understand it, is whether that form of summons was a proceeding which could be properly registered as a lis pendens relating to land for the purposes of the Land Charges Act, 1925.

There are a few other events which I will mention before I consider the actual question which we have to decide. The summons apparently under the Married Women's Property Act, 1882, was issued on May 16, 1967. On June 28, 1967, there was an application to LLOYD-JONES, J., to direct the Official Solicitor to

(1) [1964] 2 All E.R. 702.

make a report. On July 3, 1967, the lis pendens was registered under s. 2 of the **A**
Land Charges Act, 1925. On July 11, 1967, the Official Solicitor made his report,
and an important part of it at any rate was that it was very bad for the children
to be residing with both parents in the house at No. 21, Bradenham Avenue,
Welling, and he recommended that one of the parents should leave the house
and that only one parent should be residing there, and as the result of that the
wife did leave the property. On July 20, 1967, the summons for custody was **B**
served, and an interim order was made by BAKER, J., which gave the interim
custody of the two children to the husband, and made provision for access by the
wife at Welling, and also in regard to access by her at Trowbridge in the county
of Wiltshire, and that part of the order needs a little explanation. The husband
had been in employment in which he unfortunately became redundant just about
the time of these proceedings, and it was impossible for him to carry on in the **C**
occupation that he had carried on previous to that at Welling. He then proposed
to purchase a business at Trowbridge, and for that purpose, of course, he would
have to buy the business and be resident also at Trowbridge in order to take
advantage of the opportunities which the business provided. That meant that
he must sell the family home because he had apparently only a small amount of
capital in the sum of about £15; and unless he could complete the sale of the **D**
house and use the proceeds, or some part for the purchase, he could not complete
the purchase at Trowbridge. In any case it is obvious that the husband could
not afford to have two houses.

   The next event was that in August, 1967, an application was made to BRANDON,
J. (as vacation judge, I suppose) for directions in regard to a holiday for the
children, it being intended that the children should spend their holiday in Wilt- **E**
shire, and an order was made for that purpose. In September the husband moved
with the children to Wiltshire. On Sept. 28, 1967, the husband entered into a
contract to sell No. 21, Bradenham Avenue to a man named Blake at a price of
£4,800, and completion was provided to be on Oct. 28, 1967. Prior to this there
had been various negotiations and talks between the parties which suggested
that one or other of the husband and wife might assign the interest (whatever it was) **F**
in the family home. The wife was anxious to buy, I think principally because she
thought that she could turn the property into a home for the children, as it had
been, of course, when the marriage was going on all right, and that that would
give her a greater claim to have custody of the children. At this time she was
trying to buy the husband's share out, and he was refusing to sell it; but he made
various offers to her for her interest, and in the end he raised it as far as £2,000, **G**
I think. The value put on the house by the wife in the course of those talks was,
I think, £3,500, of which she claimed that her half share was £1,750; and they got
so far that the husband was prepared to offer to put that sum into the joint
names of the solicitors for each of the parties. Mr. Blake went into possession
the day after the date fixed for completion under the terms of the contract, and
he is in possession now. The position is that the house is in the husband's name, **H**
and there is no dispute that the husband is entitled beneficially to at least a half
share of the proceeds of sale of the house. The wife's interest may be a half share
or, according to the husband, it may be less, or nothing at all. Obviously on the
figures which I have mentioned, the sale to Mr. Blake for £4,800 is a good sale,
being far in advance of the value which the wife had put on the property when the
parties were talking about buying each other out. The husband now admits that
his wife is the beneficial owner of part of the proceeds of sale of the house in some
share, but he does not admit the amount of her claim.

   Assuming that the position is that the wife has also a beneficial interest in the
proceeds of sale of the house, which is in accordance with her claim, as well as
the husband, the result in law, because of the legislation in 1925, is that they
cannot be tenants in common of the premises at law; the husband is the owner in
law of the property. The effect is that there is a trust for sale, and that the
husband can sell as trustee for sale; and indeed the only thing existing in his way

A   in completing the sale (apart from such force, if any, as the registration of the lis pendens may have) is that he will require to appoint a second trustee, so that the two trustees can receive the purchase money and give a good discharge to the purchaser; and the fact that it is in the hands of two trustees is a safeguard to the wife against the husband putting the whole of the proceeds of sale in the bank, or something of that sort, and not giving the wife her share. So in addition

B   to the offer which the husband has made about putting money in the joint names of the solicitors, there is this further protection which arises under the legislation of 1925. One thing which emerges quite clearly is that, whatever else may be said, the husband has entered into a contract to sell the land to Mr. Blake, and if the sale cannot be carried through to completion, the husband will plainly be liable for damages, or relief of some sort, at the instance of proceedings by Mr. Blake.

C   One other fact should be mentioned, and that is that when the solicitor for the wife registered the lis pendens, he gave no notice of it to the husband. He was not legally bound to give him any notice, but it is a courtesy and the usual course to pursue to give the owner of the property notice when a land charge is registered against him. It is rather remarkable that in the present case no notice was given to the husband, and I say no more about the morality of it; but the result was

D   that the husband had no knowledge of the registration of the lis pendens until the purchaser's, Mr. Blake's, solicitors, made the usual searches and discovered the existence of the lis pendens; and that, according to the ordinary practice, was made only in the last ten days or fortnight before the date for completion, when, of course, this registration came to light.

   An application was made before WRANGHAM, J., to vacate the registration of

E   the lis pendens, and he refused to vacate it, taking the view that this did not come within the provisions of s. 2 of the Act of 1925. He also came to the conclusion that it did not quite amount to bad faith or an abuse of the provisions of the law, and that he would not be justified in vacating the entry; but to my mind the learned judge reached a wrong conclusion, and I think that the reason for that is quite clear. The position created by the position of the parties in regard

F   to the property and the effect of the Act of 1925 was never brought clearly before the learned judge or explained to him. If they had been explained to him, he would have appreciated that the wife's interest at the most was a share in the proceeds of sale of the property, and that there was, therefore, no interest which she possessed in the land at all, but merely in the proceeds of sale, and that to my mind is decisive and makes the entry of the lis pendens not a proper entry in the

G   situation in which the matter stands. There is a reference to the land in the summons, but there is not any interest in land which is affected by the proceedings under the Married Women's Property Act, 1882. It has been argued that under s. 17, which gives such wide powers to the registrar or the court dealing with the matter, there is no limit to the order which can be made by the court, and therefore conceivably the court might award the house to the wife, and consequently

H   she would have an interest in the land. Amendments (it is said) may be made to the summons to raise questions of that sort, but no amendment has been put forward in spite of the long period of time which has elapsed since the summons was first taken out.

   In my view s. 17 of the Married Women's Property Act, 1882, does not confer any powers on any court to do the kind of thing which has been suggested by

I   counsel for the wife. There are many cases about this, and there may be some doubts still to be resolved in regard to the matter; but to my mind s. 17 is purely procedural and is intended to enable disputes with regard to matrimonial property to be brought before the court in a summary and cheap manner; it is not intended to alter the rights of the parties in the property in question. There is, also, more to it in the present case than that. The wife in her summons has never suggested that she has any proprietary interest in the land. The very form in which she puts her summons in the first paragraph is that she is the beneficial owner of an equal half share, something which can be given effect to only in

the proceeds of sale of the property when it is sold, and to make the matter more   **A**
difficult for her, she is not opposing a sale (in form at any rate) in the summons;
she is actually asking for sale of the property; and therefore the only way in
which effect can be given to her rights is by the husband selling, as he is the
legal owner, and completing the sale in the manner required by law, which
involves the appointment of a second trustee. But none of that creates an interest
in land in the wife within the meaning of the Land Charges Act, 1925.   **B**

Accordingly, in my view, the lis pendens was never properly capable of being
registered under the Land Charges Act, 1925, which deals with land only, and not
with other property. Consequently, in my view the registration of this lis pendens
should not be allowed to stand, an order should be made by this court for its
vacation, and the appeal allowed.

   C

     RUSSELL, L.J.: In my view, this is a short point: was the wife's summons
registrable as a lis pendens under the Land Charges Act, 1925? Was it a proceeding pending in a court relating to land having regard to the definition which has
been referred to?

The only reference in this summons to land is that the summons demands that
the husband show cause why the property should not be sold; the summons   **D**
demands that it should be sold. The lis, the dispute, is not about any land, but
about what is the entitlement to the beneficial interest in the land, and therefore
the proceeds of such sale. The purpose of registration of a lis pendens is to prevent
effective disposition of the land pendente lite. How can a suit which demands
that the land be disposed of be properly registrable? Before the system of registration was adopted, a purchaser of land with express notice of the lis took subject   **E**
to the lis, and this is still so if one looks at s. 3 (1) of the Land Charges Act, 1925,
even if it is not registered. How could it be said in such a case that a purchaser
with notice of a lis, in which there was no reference to the land except a demand
that it should be sold by the defendant, could get a defective title? This, it seems
to me, shows that a summons in this form cannot be a lis relevant to, or capable
of, valid registration. If the wife's claim which is made in this summons had been   **F**
made in a writ and statement of claim, the lis could not possibly have been
properly registrable. It is said that because the procedure was by summons, and
was entitled in a matter of s. 17 of the Married Women's Property Act, 1882,
the claim is to be regarded as a lis relevantly affecting the land because the
registrar or judge under that section might make an order inconsistent with the
demand for sale. I do not propose to dwell on the scope of s. 17 of the Act of 1882;   **G**
I have said more than enough about it in the past. I find nothing in that point.
If one is going to find out what the lis is, one can look only at the formal document
which contains the contention or claim of the claimant.

Then it is said that the wife now opts not for sale, but to acquire possession or to
buy the property herself, and that she might (or will in due course) alter her claims
on the summons. All I can say is that she has not done this. The lis in question   **H**
was not in my judgment properly registrable initially, and it is not now in a form
capable properly of registration, and the registration should now be ordered to be
vacated.

     WILLMER, L.J.: I agree with both the judgments which have been
delivered, and I do not think that I can usefully add anything further.

                     Appeal allowed; registration of lis pendens to be vacated.

     Solicitors: *H. A. Crowe & Co.* (for the husband); *Thomas Boyd Whyte,*
Bexleyheath (for the wife).

                         [*Reported by* F. A. AMIES, ESQ., *Barrister-at-Law.*]

A

R. *v.* GOULD.

[COURT OF APPEAL, CRIMINAL DIVISION (Diplock, L.J., Widgery and Blain, JJ.),
January 16, 18, 1968.]

B
*Criminal Law—Bigamy—Whether honest belief on reasonable grounds that at
the date of the second marriage the former marriage had been dissolved a good
defence—Offences against the Person Act, 1861 (24 & 25 Vict. c. 100), s. 57.*
*Judgment—Judicial decision as authority—Court of Appeal, criminal division
—Doctrine of stare decisis not applied with same rigidity as in civil division
of Court of Appeal.*

C
The appellant, at the time of his second marriage, honestly believed that
his first marriage had been dissolved and had reasonable grounds for that
belief. His belief was that a decree absolute dissolving his first marriage
had been granted. His first wife was still living, and his first marriage had
not been dissolved at the time of his second marriage. On appeal against
conviction of bigamy under s. 57* of the Offences against the Person Act,
1861,

D
Held: honest and reasonable belief of a fact which, if true, would make
an accused's second marriage innocent was a good defence to a charge of
bigamy, whether the consequence of the belief being true would be that the
case would not be within the words of s. 57 enacting the offence or that
it would be excluded from being an offence by the proviso to s. 57; accordingly the conviction would be quashed (see p. 856, letters B and F, post).

E
Thomas v. *Regem* ((1937), 59 C.L.R. 279) applied.

R. v. *Tolson* ([1886-90] All E.R. Rep. 26) considered.

Reasoning in *R.* v. *King* ([1963] 3 All E.R. 561) not applied, but decision
followed.

R. v. *Wheat, R.* v. *Stocks* ([1921] All E.R. Rep. 602) disproved.

F
Per CURIAM: in its criminal jurisdiction, inherited from the Court of
Criminal Appeal, the Court of Appeal does not apply the doctrine of stare
decisis with the same rigidity as in its civil jurisdiction; thus, if the court
be of opinion that the law has either been misapplied or misunderstood in
a previous decision of the court or its predecessors, the court is entitled to
depart from the view previously expressed notwithstanding that the case
could not be brought within any of the exceptions laid down in *Young* v.

G
Bristol Aeroplane Co., Ltd.†, as justifying the Court of Appeal in refusing to
follow one of its own decisions in a civil case. A fortiori the court is bound
to give effect to the law as the court thinks it is, if the previous decision
to the contrary effect is one of which the ratio decidendi conflicts with that
of other decisions of this court or its predecessors of co-ordinate jurisdiction
(see p. 851, letters D and E, post).

R. v. *Taylor* ([1950] 2 All E.R. 170, holding (ii)) applied.

Appeal allowed.

[As to disproof of mens rea, see 10 HALSBURY'S LAWS (3rd Edn.) 283, para.
524; 284, para. 525, text and note (c); and for cases on the subject, see 14
DIGEST (Repl.) 31, 32, *34-40.*

As to bigamy and bona fide defence on ground first marriage dissolved, see
10 HALSBURY'S LAWS (3rd Edn.) 663, 664, paras. 1265, 1269, text and note (h);
and for cases on the subject, see 15 DIGEST (Repl.) 888, *8558,* 890, 891, *8578-8591.*

As to judicial decisions in the Court of Appeal and Court of Criminal Appeal
as authority binding the court subsequently, see 22 HALSBURY'S LAWS (3rd
Edn.) 799-801, paras. 1687, 1688; and for cases on the subject, see 30 DIGEST
(Repl.) 225-227, *689-715.*

---

* Section 57 is set out at p. 851, letters F to I, post.
† [1944] 2 All E.R. 293; [1944] K.B. 718.

GG

For the Offences against the Person Act, 1861, s. 57, see 5 HALSBURY'S STATUTES A (2nd Edn.) 809.]

Cases referred to:

R. v. *King*, [1963] 3 All E.R. 561; [1964] 1 Q.B. 285; [1963] 3 W.L.R. 892; 48 Cr. App. Rep. 17; Digest (Cont. Vol. A) 418, *8582a*.

R. v. *Prince*, [1874-80] All E.R. Rep. 881; (1875), L.R. 2 C.C.R. 154; 44 L.J.M.C. 122; 32 L.T. 700; 30 J.P. 676; 15 Digest (Repl.) 1032, B *10,142*.

R. v. *Taylor*, [1950] 2 All E.R. 170; [1950] 2 K.B. 368; 34 Cr. App. Rep. 138; 15 Digest (Repl.) 888, *8558*.

R. v. *Thomson*, (1905), 70 J.P. 6; 15 Digest (Repl.) 890, *8579*.

R. v. *Tolson*, [1886-90] All E.R. Rep. 26; (1889), 23 Q.B.D. 168; 58 L.J.M.C. 97; 60 L.T. 899; 54 J.P. 4, 20; 15 Digest (Repl.) 890, *8578*. C

R. v. *Wheat*, R. v. *Stocks*, [1921] All E.R. Rep. 602; [1921] 2 K.B. 119; 90 L.J.K.B. 583; 124 L.T. 830; 85 J.P. 203; 15 Cr. App. Rep. 134; 15 Digest (Repl.) 891, *8591*.

Thomas v. *Regem* (1937), 59 C.L.R. 279.

Young v. *Bristol Aeroplane Co.*, [1944] 2 All E.R. 293; [1944] K.B. 718; 113 L.J.K.B. 513; 171 L.T. 113; *affd.* H.L., [1946] 1 All E.R. 98; D [1946] A.C. 163; 30 Digest (Repl.) 225, *691*.

Appeal.

On Mar. 22, 1967, at Inner London Quarter Sessions the appellant, John Arthur Charles Gould, pleaded guilty on arraignment, in the absence of his counsel, to bigamy. He was sentenced by the deputy chairman (O. S. MACLEAY, E Esq.) to be conditionally discharged for a period of twelve months. His counsel subsequently applied for leave to have the plea of guilty withdrawn on the ground that the appellant had a good defence to the charge in that he had a reasonable and bona fide belief that he had been divorced. After hearing legal argument in which R. v. *Wheat*, R. v. *Stocks** and R. v. *King*† were cited, the deputy chairman ruled that such belief was no defence and declined to allow the plea of guilty to be withdrawn. He drew attention to the fact that it would be F open to the accused to appeal on a point of law, and granted a certificate under s. 3 (*b*) of the Criminal Appeal Act, 1907, that the case was fit for appeal. The facts, briefly summarised, were that the appellant married on Dec. 21, 1959, and there were three children of the marriage. The divorce suit was entered in the undefended list, but on the day before the hearing, the appellant's solicitors gave notice to defend, and the case was transferred to the defended list. Before G it was heard the appellant was sentenced to twelve months' imprisonment. He was released in March, 1966. He then returned to his wife, whom the prison authorities had persuaded to give him another chance, but he left her soon afterwards. In November, 1966, he married again. He stated, when interviewed by the police on the matter, that he had been told by his wife in April, H 1966, that their marriage was finished, and that he left when he was told that; he stated further that he had agreed to marry a second time because he thought that he was divorced.

The authority and case noted below‡ were cited during the argument in addition to the cases referred to in the judgment of the court.

M. G. Walker for the appellant.
E. J. R. Crowther for the Crown.

Cur. adv. vult.

Jan. 18. **DIPLOCK, L.J.**, read the following judgment of the court: On Mar. 22, 1967, the appellant was arraigned at Inner London Sessions on a

---

* [1921] All E.R. Rep. 602; [1921] 2 K.B. 119.
† [1963] 3 All E.R. 561; [1964] 1 Q.B. 285.
‡ ARCHBOLD'S CRIMINAL PLEADING, EVIDENCE AND PRACTICE (36th Edn.), paras. 915, 3802, 3803; R. v. *Connatty*, (1919), 83 J.P. 292.

A   charge of bigamy, and in the absence of his counsel, who was late in arriving at the court, he pleaded guilty to that offence. His counsel when he arrived sought leave of the deputy chairman to withdraw that plea, because he wished to advance the defence that at the time of his second marriage he held honestly and reasonably the mistaken belief that a decree absolute dissolving his previous marriage had been granted. The learned deputy chairman, taking the view

B   that even if that were established it would not amount to a defence, refused to allow the plea of guilty to be withdrawn and, accordingly, the appellant was convicted and sentenced to a conditional discharge.

The question of law in this appeal is whether on a charge of bigamy under s. 57 of the Offences against the Person Act, 1861, an accused's honest belief on reasonable grounds that at the time of his second marriage his former marriage

C   had been dissolved is a good defence to the charge. In *R.* v. *Wheat, R.* v. *Stocks* (1) the Court of Criminal Appeal decided that it was not. The learned deputy chairman rightly regarded himself as bound by that decision; but we are not. In its criminal jurisdiction, which it has inherited from the Court of Criminal Appeal, the Court of Appeal does not apply the doctrine of stare decisis with the same rigidity as in its civil jurisdiction. If on due consideration we were to be

D   of opinion that the law had been either misapplied or misunderstood in an earlier decision of this court, or its predecessor the Court of Criminal Appeal, we should be entitled to depart from the view as to the law expressed in the earlier decision notwithstanding that the case could not be brought within any of the exceptions laid down in *Young* v. *Bristol Aeroplane Co., Ltd.* (2) as justifying the Court of Appeal in refusing to follow one of its own decisions in a civil case (*R.* v. *Taylor*

E   (3)). A fortiori we are bound to give effect to the law as we think it is if the previous decision to the contrary effect is one of which the ratio decidendi conflicts with that of other decisions of this court or its predecessors of co-ordinate jurisdiction.

The offence of bigamy is a statutory offence. Our task is, therefore, to construe s. 57 of the Act of 1861 which is in the following terms (4):

F   " Whosoever, being married, shall marry any other person during the life of the former husband or wife, whether the second marriage shall have taken place in England or Ireland or elsewhere, shall be guilty of felony, and, being convicted thereof, shall be liable, at the discretion of the court, to be kept in penal servitude for any term not exceeding seven years; and any such offence may be dealt with, inquired of, tried, determined, and punished in any county or place in *England or* Ireland where the offender shall be apprehended or be in custody, in the same manner in all respects as if the offence had been actually committed in that county or place: Provided, that nothing in this section contained shall extend to any second marriage contracted elsewhere than in England or Ireland by any other than a subject of Her Majesty, or to any person marrying a second time

I   whose husband or wife shall have been continually absent from such person for the space of seven years then last past, and shall not have been known by such person to be living within that time, or shall extend to any person who, at the time of such second marriage, shall have been divorced from the bond of the first marriage, or to any person whose former marriage shall have been declared void by the sentence of any court of competent jurisdiction."

The enacting words, which are absolute in their terms, set out the three elements in the offence: *(a)* a married person; *(b)* going through the form or ceremony

---

(1) [1921] All E.R. Rep. 602; [1921] 2 K.B. 119.
(2) [1944] 2 All E.R. 293; [1944] K.B. 718.
(3) [1950] 2 All E.R. 170; [1950] 2 K.B. 368.
(4) The section is printed as amended by S.L.R. 3892; the two words in italics were repealed as to England by the Criminal Justice Act, 1925, s. 49 (4), (5) and Sch. 3.

of marriage with another person; (c) during the life of his or her spouse. The A circumstances referred to in the first two parts of the proviso relate to element (b) and element (c) respectively and are true exceptions, that is to say, but for the proviso they would fall within the enacting words which precede it, but the second two parts which refer to cases where the former marriage has been dissolved or declared void at the time of the second marriage are not exceptions. They subtract nothing from and add nothing to the enacting words, for a person whose B former marriage has been dissolved or avoided is no longer a married person and element (a) in the offence is absent. As a matter of legislative history they are survivals from somewhat similar provisions in the original Act of James I (1 Jac. I c. 11) which first made bigamy a felony. What is now the third part of the proviso applied them to divorce a mensa et thoro and was a true exception, for that kind of divorce pronounced by the ecclesiastical court did not dissolve a C marriage; but what is now the fourth even at that date was not an exception from the enacting words, for a person whose former marriage has been declared absolutely void by the ecclesiastical courts was no longer married. In 1603, however, when the jurisdiction of the ecclesiastical courts was still in the realm of political controversy and statutory draftsmanship in its infancy, it may well have been prudent to state expressly what the consequences of decrees of D the ecclesiastical courts should be as respects the newly created felony. In 1861, which was four years after the transfer to the court for matrimonial causes of the former matrimonial jurisdiction of the ecclesiastical courts and the grant to that court of what was then a novel jurisdiction to grant divorce a vinculo, the draftsman of the Offences against the Person Act, 1861, may have thought it prudent to include in the proviso provisions corresponding to those in the Act E of James I and its successor, 9 Geo. IV c. 31, s. 22, lest their omission might give rise to the suggestion that the words " being married " in the enacting part of the section were intended to cover cases where the former marriage had been dissolved or declared void by a decree of the court for matrimonial causes. At any rate, we cannot find any other plausible reason for the inclusion of these two provisions in the proviso. The present case, however, does not fall within F the proviso. The appellant's former marriage had not been dissolved or declared void at the time of the ceremony of his second marriage. The only relevance of the proviso is the light (if any) which it throws on the preceding enacting words. They are, as we have already pointed out, absolute in their terms. If they are to be construed literally, a mistaken but honest and reasonable belief by the defendant in a fact which would make his act of going through the second G form or ceremony of marriage lawful and innocent, would be no defence. The question, therefore, is: are they to be construed literally or as subject to the presumption, which is usually applied to statutes creating new criminal offences, that a crime is not committed if the mind of the person doing the act in question is innocent?

This question came before a court of fourteen judges of the Queen's Bench H Division as a Crown Case Reserved in 1889 (R. v. Tolson (5)). By a majority nine to five they held that the presumption did apply, that the offence created by the enacting words was not an absolute offence, but mens rea was an essential ingredient. In R. v. Tolson (5) the fact which the accused believed, which, had it been true would have made her second marriage lawful and innocent, was that her husband by the former marriage was dead, although seven years had not elapsed since last she saw him. She could not bring herself within the first exception of the proviso. She relied on a mistaken though honest and reasonable belief that element (c) in the enacting words—viz., the continuing life of the first spouse—was absent. It is significant, in view of what was said about this decision in R. v. Wheat, R. v. Stocks (6) that the majority reached their decision

(5) [1886-90] All E.R. Rep. 26; (1889), 23 Q.B.D. 168.
(6) [1921] All E.R. Rep. 602; [1921] 2 K.B. 119.

A in spite of and not because of the first exception in the proviso, and the minority were largely influenced in their dissent by its presence there. It is made very clear by Lord Coleridge, C.J. (7), who was at first inclined to dissent, that their decision was based squarely on the enacting words themselves and was that these, _despite the proviso_, were to be construed as subject to the general rule applicable to statutes creating serious criminal offences that mens rea is a

B necessary ingredient in the offence.

In _R._ v. _Wheat, R._ v. _Stocks_ (8) the accused's mistaken belief related to element (_a_). He claimed to have had at the time of his second marriage ceremony an honest and reasonable belief that his former marriage had been dissolved. The Court of Criminal Appeal, consisting of five judges, held that this belief, had it been proved, would have been no defence. They sought to distinguish _R._ v.

C _Tolson_ (9) on the ground that that decision turned on the presence of the exception relating to seven years absence as indicating that an honest belief in the death of the former spouse before the seven years had elapsed was a defence, which, but for the exception, it would not have been. This, however, is almost exactly the converse of the reasoning of the judges in _R._ v. _Tolson_ (9). The court in _R._ v. _Wheat, R._ v. _Stocks_ (8) also accepted the argument of the Attorney-

D General that (10)

"... this exception creates or involves a presumption of death, which, unless rebutted by the prosecution, entitles the accused to an acquittal— in other words, the accused is presumed to believe in such circumstances that the former wife or husband is dead at the time of the second marriage, and therefore has no intention of doing the act forbidden by the statute."

E This reasoning, however, with great respect, does not bear analysis. The accused has no need to rely on any presumption of death; it is for the prosecution to prove in every case of bigamy that the former spouse was alive at the time of the second marriage. Nor does the proviso depend on the accused's belief in the death of the former spouse but on his lack of knowledge that the former

F spouse was alive. In the case of a young and healthy spouse who goes abroad there may be no reason whatever for believing that he or she is dead. An honest accused may freely admit that he believed his former spouse to be alive at the time of the second marriage, as long as he did not _know_ her to be so at any time within the previous seven years. This was pointed out in terms by Cave, J., in _R._ v. _Tolson_ (11) and was the very reasoning which persuaded Lord Coleridge,

G C.J. (12), that the first exception did not qualify the application to the enacting words of the general presumption that mens rea is a necessary ingredient in the offence. On this reasoning which, with great respect, not only misinterprets the judgments in _R._ v. _Tolson_ (9) but also is in itself fallacious, the court in _R._ v. _Wheat, R._ v. _Stocks_ (13) expressed their opinion that

"... this decision is not in conflict with the decision of the majority of the

H judges in _R._ v. _Tolson_ (9), but is in accord with the principle of the judgment in _R._ v. _Prince_ (14)."

We, however, agree with Latham, C.J., in the Australian case (15) which we are about to cite that these two English decisions of courts of co-ordinate jurisdiction are in conflict. _R._ v. _Tolson_ (9) decides that mens rea is a necessary ingredient of the felony described in the enacting words despite their absolute terms. _R._ v.

I _Wheat, R._ v. _Stocks_ (8) decides the contrary. _R._ v. _Prince_ (14), which was

---

(7) [1886-90] All E.R. Rep. at p. 45; (1889), 23 Q.B.D. at pp. 201, 202.
(8) [1921] All E.R. Rep. 602; [1921] 2 K.B. 119.
(9) [1886-90] All E.R. Rep. 26; (1889), 23 Q.B.D. 168.
(10) [1921] All E.R. Rep. at pp. 603-604; [1921] 2 K.B. at p. 125.
(11) [1886-90] All E.R. Rep. at p. 35; (1889), 23 Q.B.D. at p. 183.
(12) [1886-90] All E.R. Rep. at p. 45; (1889), 23 Q.B.D. at p. 202.
(13) [1921] All E.R. Rep. at p. 604; [1921] 2 K.B. at p. 125.
(14) [1874-80] All E.R. Rep. 881; (1875), L.R. 2 C.C.R. 154.
(15) _Thomas_ v. _Regem_, (1937), 59 C.L.R. 279.

discussed at length in *R.* v. *Tolson* (16) was decided on another statute which the   A
court held was intended to punish abduction of a girl without her father's consent
—an act which the court regarded as mala in se; whereas the legislature in
1861 cannot be thought to have regarded the act of marrying for a second time
as mala in se after a previous marriage had ceased to subsist.

In 1937 the matter came before a High Court of Australia which included
LATHAM, C.J., and DIXON, J., who has earned a world-wide reputation as a   B
common lawyer which is outstanding in the twentieth century.   The decisions
of the High Court of Australia even when so constituted may be persuasive
only—but how persuasive they are.   In *Thomas* v. *Regem* (17) the deceased's
mistake of fact related to element (*a*).   His former marriage was to a woman
who had herself been previously married.   At the time of his second marriage
he believed honestly and on reasonable grounds that his first wife's decree   C
nisi had not been made absolute at the date when he married her.   Had his
belief been correct, his first marriage would have been void ab initio not merely
voidable; but what is important is that his mistake of fact was whether or not
the court had made a decree dissolving the previous marriage of his first wife.
All members of the High Court regarded the case as indistinguishable in principle
from *R.* v. *Wheat, R.* v. *Stocks* (18).   The majority (LATHAM, C.J., and DIXON, J.,   D
with whom RICH, J., agreed) considered *R.* v. *Wheat, R.* v. *Stocks* (18) to be
inconsistent with *R.* v. *Tolson* (16).   LATHAM, C.J., said so in terms (19).   DIXON,
J., after discussing two suggested grounds of distinction says this (20):

> " The truth appears to be that a reluctance on the part of courts has
> repeatedly appeared to allow a prisoner to avail himself of a defence depend-
> ing on his own state of knowledge and belief.   The reluctance is due in   E
> great measure, if not entirely, to a mistrust of the tribunal of fact—the jury.
> Through a feeling that, if the law allows such a defence to be submitted to
> the jury, prisoners may too readily escape by deposing to conditions of
> mind and describing sources of information, matters upon which their
> evidence cannot be adequately tested and contradicted, judges have been
> misled into a failure steadily to adhere to principle.   It is not difficult   F
> to understand such tendencies, but a lack of confidence in the ability of a
> tribunal correctly to estimate evidence of states of mind and the like can
> never be sufficient ground for excluding from inquiry the most fundamental
> element in a rational and humane criminal code."

STARKE, J., dissented (21) on the ground that he ought to follow *R.* v. *Wheat,
R.* v. *Stocks* (18) and that a mistake whether a marriage has been dissolved was   G
a mistake of law and not of fact.   This formed no part of the ratio decidendi
in *R.* v. *Wheat, R.* v. *Stocks* (18) and was disposed of, as we think unanswerably,
by DIXON, J. (22).   EVATT, J., also dissented (23), but on the broader ground
that public policy required that a person who married again during the lifetime
of another person who had been his wife did so at his own risk.   He did not
seek to support this by consideration of the wording of the Victorian Act which   H
was in similar terms to the English one.   No member of the court suggested
that there was any relevant distinction between a mistaken belief in a fact
which if true would have the legal consequence of making the former marriage
void ab initio, and one which would have the legal consequence of avoiding a
voidable marriage or of dissolving a valid one.   The decision of the majority
was that a mistaken belief, held honestly and on reasonable grounds, in a fact

---

(16) [1886-90] All E.R. Rep. 26; (1889), 23 Q.B.D. 168.
(17) (1937), 59 C.L.R. 279.
(18) [1921] All E.R. Rep. 602 ; [1921] 2 K.B. 119.
(19) (1937), 59 C.L.R. at p. 292.
(20) (1937), 59 C.L.R. at p. 309.
(21) (1937), 59 C.L.R. at pp. 294-296.
(22) (1937), 59 C.L.R. at pp. 306-308.
(23) (1937), 59 C.L.R. at pp. 311-321.

A which if true would have had the legal consequence that the defendant was not married at the time of the second marriage ceremony (i.e., that element (*a*) in the offence was lacking) was a good defence.

In *R.* v. *King* (24) the Court of Criminal Appeal in England followed the decision of the High Court of Australia. The mistake of fact there was that at the time of his former marriage the defendant's own previous marriage to

B another person had not been dissolved. Had this been so the former marriage would have been void ab initio and his second marriage, in respect of which he was charged with bigamy, would not have been bigamous. In this respect the case was on all fours with *Thomas* v. *Regem* (25). The Court of Appeal, however, expressed the view not only that their own decision did not conflict with the decision in *R.* v *Wheat*, *R.* v. *Stocks* (26), but that the Australian High Court

C themselves felt that *Thomas* v. *Regem* (25) was clearly distinguishable from *R.* v. *Wheat*, *R.* v. *Stocks* (26). With great respect, this latter view must have been formed per incuriam. We have already referred to the passsages in the judgments of LATHAM, C.J., and DIXON, J., which show the contrary.

If there is a distinction in principle between *R.* v. *Wheat*, *R.* v. *Stocks* (26) and *R.* v. *King* (24) wherein does that distinction lie and how is it to be extracted from

D the wording of the section? In *R.* v. *King* (24) the court approved and followed the direction of the Common Serjeant in *R.* v. *Thomson* (27) of which AVORY, J., had said in *R.* v. *Wheat*, *R.* v. *Stocks* (28): ". . . . we doubt if it can be supported consistently with our present decision." This, as the court pointed out in *R.* v. *King* (29) was obiter, but where does the distinction lie? The mistake in both cases was of the same kind: whether or not a court of competent jurisdiction

E had made a decree dissolving a marriage. No one, apart from STARKE, J., has ever suggested that this is not a mistake of fact. In both cases the fact mistakenly believed to have been true would, if true, have had the legal consequence that at the relevant time for seeing whether element (*b*) of the offence existed, i.e., the date of the second marriage ceremony, element (*a*) was absent—i.e., the defendant was not married. The legal consequences differ in one respect only,

F that in *R.* v. *King* (24) the defendant would never have been married to his former reputed wife, whereas in *R.* v. *Wheat*, *R.* v. *Stocks* (26) he would at some time previous to the relevant time have been married to his former wife.

What construction, however, could be placed on the words of the section which would result in this distinction between the legal consequences of the supposed fact being relevant to the guilt or innocence of the honest and reasonable

G believer of the fact? There might perhaps be a plausible argument based on the second part of the proviso, that the expression " being married " in the enacting words should be construed as " having been married ". This would have the effect of making the provisions of the proviso relating to dissolution and declarations of nullity of the previous marriage true exceptions to the enacting words instead of surplusage as they are if " being married " is construed in the present

H tense, in which grammatically it is. We doubt if in any event it would be permissible to let the tail in the proviso wag the dog in the enacting words. But even if it were, the only effect would be that the fact mistakenly believed to have been true in *R.* v. *King* (24) would, if true, have made the second marriage innocent because the defendant did not come within the expression " having been married " in the enacting words, whereas the corresponding fact in *R.* v.

I *Wheat*, *R.* v. *Stocks* (26) would, if true, have made the second marriage innocent because the defendant did come within the exception in the proviso as being a

---

(24) [1963] 3 All E.R. 561; [1964] 1 Q.B. 285.
(25) (1937), 59 C.L.R. 279.
(26) [1921] All E.R. Rep. 602; [1921] 2 K.B. 119.
(27) (1905), 70 J.P. 6.
(28) [1921] All E.R. Rep. at p. 605; [1921] 2 K.B. at p. 127.
(29) [1963] 3 All E.R. at p. 565; [1964] 1 Q.B. at p. 292.

" person who at the time of such second marriage shall have been divorced from A
the bond of the first marriage ".

Once it is accepted, as it has been in *R.* v. *King* (30), that the offence is not
an absolute one and that honest and reasonable belief in a fact affecting the
matrimonial status of the defendant which, if true, would make his second
marriage lawful and innocent can constitute a defence, there can in our view
be no possible ground in justice or in reason for drawing a distinction between B
facts the result of which would be that he was innocent because he did not come
within the enacting words at all, and facts the result of which would be that he
was excluded from the enacting words by the proviso. Given that the belief
is formed honestly and on reasonable grounds, there can be no difference on
grounds of moral blameworthiness or of public policy between a mistaken belief
that a decree absolute has been granted, as in *R.* v. *Wheat, R.* v. *Stocks* (31) C
and one that it has not, as in *R.* v. *King* (30).   Indeed, it needs little ingenuity
to postulate circumstances in which the existence of a decree absolute would
make the defendant's first purported marriage void ab initio as the absence of a
decree absolute would have done in *R.* v. *King,* (30) and *Thomas* v. *Regem* (32).
To draw such fine distinctions would we think, in the words of DIXON, J. (33):
                                                                                 D
  ". . . lead to consequences which would not only be contrary to principle
  but which would be discreditable to our system of criminal law."

We think that *R.* v. *Wheat, R.* v. *Stocks* (31) was wrongly decided.   We agree
with the High Court of Australia that it conflicts with *R.* v. *Tolson* (34).   In
this respect we respectfully differ from the opinion expressed by the Court of
Criminal Appeal in *R.* v. *King* (30), but our decision is in conformity with the E
result arrived at in *R.* v. *King* (30) and those parts of the reasoning which led
to that result.   The prosecution accept that the appellant at the time of the
second marriage did honestly believe that his former marriage had been dissolved
and that he had reasonable grounds for that belief.   This appeal is, accordingly,
allowed and the conviction quashed.   I should like to say how much we are
indebted to both counsel for the argument in this case, it was of great assistance F
to us.

Appeal allowed.   Conviction quashed.

Solicitors: *Geo. Vaughan & Co.* (for the appellant); *Solicitor, Metropolitan
Police* (for the Crown).

[*Reported by* N. P. METCALFE, ESQ., *Barrister-at-Law.*] G

(30) [1963] 3 All E.R. 561; [1964] 1 Q.B. 285.
(31) [1921] All E.R. Rep. 602; [1921] 2 K.B. 119.
(32) (1937), 59 C.L.R. 279.
(33) (1937), 59 C.L.R. at p. 311.
(34) [1886-90] All E.R. Rep. 26; (1889), 23 Q.B.D. 168.

A

HEATON (Inspector of Taxes) v. BELL.

[CHANCERY DIVISION (Ungoed-Thomas, J.), July 7, 10, 11, 1967.]

Reversed in part. C.A. [1968] 2 All E.R. 1156.

B

Income Tax—Income—Perquisites or profits of office or employment—Car loan scheme for employees—Subtraction from employee's weekly wage to meet costs of scheme—Scheme terminable by either party on fourteen days' notice— Whether net wage after subtraction of weekly amount was the employee's wage for purposes of income tax—Whether car loan was a perquisite of employment—Valuation of such perquisite—Income Tax Act, 1952 (15 & 16 Geo. 6 & 1 Eliz. 2 c. 10), s. 156 (Sch. E), as amended by Finance Act, 1956 (4 & 5 Eliz. 2 c. 54), s. 10—Ibid., Sch. 2, para. 1.

C
The taxpayer was employed by a company which ran a car loan scheme. Under this scheme the company bought a car of which the employee had the use, he paying the maintenance and running costs. He was under an obligation not to let the car be driven by anyone other than himself. Each party could terminate the scheme as between themselves by fourteen days' notice. After the taxpayer joined the scheme £2 10s. or more weekly was D subtracted from his wages in consideration of the costs of the scheme. The conditions of joining the scheme provided for an "amended wage basis". Other documents relating to the scheme referred to wage reduction. On the question of the amount of the taxpayer's emoluments for the purposes of Sch. E* to the Income Tax Act, 1952,

Held: (i) there was one contract for payment of a weekly wage less a E subtraction to be made in calculating the amount of the weekly wage, but there were not two contracts, one for the payment of a gross wage and the other for deduction after the amount of the wage had been calculated; accordingly the amount of the subtraction was not part of the wage of the taxpayer for the purposes of Sch. E to the Income Tax Act, 1952 (see p. 860, letter I, and p. 866, letter D, post).

F   *Machon* v. *McLoughlin* ((1926), 11 Tax Cas. 83) distinguished.

(ii) the car loan to the taxpayer under the scheme was, however, a perquisite of money's worth, for it could be turned to pecuniary account by the taxpayer's giving notice and reverting to receiving the weekly sum which was deducted during membership of the scheme (see p. 867, letter C, post).

(iii) the value of the perquisite, as part of the emoluments of a year of assessment, was fifty times the weekly sum of £2 10s. or so, that being the aggregate amount for a year which the taxpayer could obtain by giving fourteen days' notice terminating his membership of the scheme; and any value for the fourteen days would be disregarded, as there was no evidence of value to the taxpayer of the car loan during the fourteen days before the car could be returned to his employers on termination of his membership of the scheme (see p. 867, letters G and I, post).

Appeal allowed.

[As to the character of emoluments chargeable to income tax under Sch. E, see 20 HALSBURY'S LAWS (3rd Edn.) 312, 313, para. 574, and as to deductions from such emoluments, see ibid., p. 326, para. 598; for cases on taxation of salaries, perquisites and profits of employment, see 28 DIGEST (Repl.) 225-237, *971-1040,* and on deductions for the purposes of Sch. E, see ibid., 242-247, *1059-1099.*

For Sch. E as amended, see 36 HALSBURY'S STATUTES (2nd Edn.) 408, 409, 448, 449, and 31 ibid., 149, 150.]

---

* Tax under Sch. E, now s. 10 of the Finance Act, 1956, as amended, is charged, so far as relevant to this report, on the "emoluments" of the employment "for the year of assessment". "Emoluments" are defined in para. 1 (1) of Sch. 2 to the Act of 1956 as including "all salaries, fees, wages, perquisites and profits whatsoever."

Cases referred to:

Bell v. *Gribble*, [1903] 1 K.B. 517; 4 Tax Cas. 522; 72 L.J.K.B. 242; 88 L.T. 186; 67 J.P. 85; 28 Digest (Repl.) 246, *1088*.

Cordy v. *Gordon*, [1925] 2 K.B. 276; 9 Tax Cas. 304; 94 L.J.K.B. 670; 133 L.T. 184; 28 Digest (Repl.) 234, *1024*.

Machon v. *McLoughlin*, (1926), 11 Tax Cas. 83; 28 Digest (Repl.) 234, *1025*.

Smyth v. *Stretton*, (1904), 5 Tax Cas. 36; 90 L.T. 756; 28 Digest (Repl.) 233, *1021*.

Case Stated.

This was an appeal by the Crown from the decision of the Special Commissioners by way of Case Stated and the following is summarised therefrom.

At a meeting of the Commissioners for the Special Purposes of the Income Tax Acts held on Mar. 1, 1966, the taxpayer, Ralph Garland Bell, appealed against an assessment to income tax made on him under the provisions of Sch. E to the Income Tax Act, 1952, for the year 1963-64 in the sum of £1,532 (less agreed expenses of £11 and superannuation payments of £7). The issue for the determination of the commissioners was whether or not the sums of £2 10s. for weeks up to May 31, 1963, and £2 18s. thereafter (the amount of car loan scheme adjustments) were correctly included in computing the amount of the emoluments of the taxpayer from his employment within the meaning of para. 1 of Sch. E of the Income Tax Act, 1952.

The following facts were found. The taxpayer was at all material times employed by John Waddington, Ltd. (hereinafter called " the company ") as a machine minder. In 1954 the company decided to introduce a voluntary car loan scheme for the benefit of certain employees who earned less than £2,000 a year and who were not directors of the company. The managing director of the company wrote to each employee who was eligible to join in the scheme stating the nature and objects of the scheme. Enclosed with the letter was a document headed " Waddingtons Craftsmen's Car Loan Service Conditions ", a memorandum of terms of service and an application form which were to be signed by an employee who wished to join the scheme. The relevant " conditions " were as follows:

" 1. [the company] will loan a new car (Ford Popular—Austin A30—Ford Anglia—Morris 8) selected by the proposed user.

" 2. [the company] will pay full comprehensive insurance for each year of the service (£15 per annum).

"3. [The company] will pay the road tax for each year of the service £12 10s. per annum).

" 4. [The company] will arrange for the decarbonizing of the car during the second year.

" 5. The user will sign a single agreement.

" 6. An amended wage basis will come into operation if the application is accepted.

" 7. The user will provide his own petrol, oil, grease and other incidentals.

" 8. The user will provide for cleaning and running maintenance.

" 9. If the car is under repair for maintenance or following an accident the amended wage basis will still apply.

"10. Completion of application form does not mean acceptance by the company. They reserve full discretion on each application."

On Feb. 10, 1961, the taxpayer signed an application form to join the scheme. He selected an Austin A40 De Luxe car, and on Mar. 3, 1961, signed a " memorandum of terms of service ". The terms of the memorandum were as follows:

" During my service with you as Lithographer . . . and the carrying out of the various duties you properly assign to me, I am to make use of Motor Car No. 3248 RO for the more efficient discharge of my duties. I am not to permit anyone other than myself to drive or use the car except in an

A emergency. I am to pay for maintenance and running. I agree to keep the car clean and in good condition and to hold it ready for inspection at any time. You have generously agreed to licence and insure the car and to pay for decarbonisation when necessary. Either of us may cancel my obligation and authority to use the car on fourteen days' notice."

B On May 30, 1961, the company secretary gave instructions for the " necessary weekly wage reduction " to be made in respect of the taxpayer's car; this was a reduction of £2 9s. to be applied as from June 2, 1961. The Austin car was handed over to the taxpayer on May 30, 1961. From Apr. 1, 1962, the taxpayer's weekly wage reduction was increased to £2 14s. 6d. as the result of increased costs in running the scheme; but on June 1, 1962, the wage reduction was amended to £2 10s. as the car was then one year old. At the end of May, 1963

C the taxpayer exchanged his car for a Morris 1100 De Luxe and signed an amendment to his memorandum. The taxpayer's wage reduction was amended to £2 18s. The taxpayer's payslip for the week ending June 5, 1964, taken as an example of the manner in which the company calculated the wages of its employees was as follows:

			£	s.	d.
D 1.	Flat rate	43 hours	22	6	7
2.	Overtime premium	2.0625 hours	1	5	7
3.	Cost of living bonus			11	8
4.	Shift premium		4	9	4
5.	Bonus		4	12	8
6.	Spray or hair money			3	4
E 7.	Holiday pay				
8.			£2	13	6

Taxable gross wage			£30	15	8
Standard deductions	£1 17 0				
Graduated pension contribution	7 8				
F P.A.Y.E.	£2 3 0				
			£4	7	8

Net wage			£26	8	0

Item No. 8 was the weekly wage reduction (as amended at the relevant date) under the scheme, which was the only deduction made in arriving at the taxable gross wage. Wherever an employee was absent through sickness and received no wage, no deduction was made for the use of the car because the agreement between the company and the employee under the scheme was that the employee should accept a reduced wage.

In evidence before the commissioners the taxpayer stated that if he had ever been asked whether the company supplied him with a car at a rent deducted from his wage he would have said that he had accepted instead a lower wage and a car free. He did not agree that in order to check his wages he would have to calculate the wage he would have received if he had not joined the scheme and then make a deduction for the car. As the figures were all set out on the payslip all he had to do was to check the arithmetic. The taxpayer understood the memorandum of terms of service to mean that the agreement could be cancelled by either party giving fourteen days' notice and, he would then receive his former wage without any deduction.

It was contended on behalf of the taxpayer before the commissioners: (i) that the company had given him the choice between receiving his wages in money only or wages in money of a reduced amount and the use of the car; (ii) that he was not an employee within the provisions of s. 163 of the Income Tax Act, 1952; (iii) that under the terms of the scheme he was precluded from allowing anyone else to make use of the car except in an emergency, so that while he

remained in the scheme the use of the car could not be turned into money; **A**
(iv) that even if the use of the car had a monetary value then the amount chargeable to tax was what he, an employee, could get for it, which was nil, and not
the cost of the scheme to the company; (v) that the appeal should succeed and
the assessment be reduced to the agreed figure of £1,385.

It was contended on behalf of the Crown before the commissioners: (i) that,
as the deduction in arriving at the net wage paid to the taxpayer was variable, **B**
and the net wage could not be arrived at until the gross wage had been determined,
the taxpayer's emoluments were the gross wages before any deduction for the
use of the car; (ii) that in any event the taxpayer's emoluments were to be
arrived at before taking into account the deduction for the use of the car; (iii)
that, in the alternative, if the true wage was a net wage plus the use of the car,
then the use of the car was money's worth because the taxpayer could surrender **C**
his rights under the contract and by this revert to his former wages and turn the
benefit into pecuniary account; (iv) that the appeal should be dismissed and the
assessment confirmed.

The Special Commissioners decided (a) that the wage was what it was said
to be on the payslip dated June 5, 1964, viz., the sum of items to 1 to 6, less
item 8.   (b) That as, under the memorandum of terms of service the taxpayer **D**
was not to permit anyone but himself to drive or use the car except in an emergency, the use of the car was not money's worth.   Accordingly, the commissioners held that the appeal succeeded in principle and, as the figures had been
agreed between the parties, the assessment for the year 1963-64 should be reduced
to £1,385.   The Crown appealed to the High Court.

Desmond C. Miller, Q.C., and *J. R. Phillips* for the Crown.   **F**
G. B. Graham, Q.C., and *T. H. Walton* for the taxpayer.

UNGOED-THOMAS, J.: This is an appeal to determine the " perquisites
and profits " of the respondent taxpayer, Mr. Bell, within the Sch. E meaning of
" emoluments ".   The assessment is for the year 1963-64, and during the whole **I**
of that period he held the same job as an employee of John Waddington, Ltd.,
with whom he worked as a machine minder.   He was entitled to a weekly wage
assessed on the basic rate with various additions, in the way which is usual
amongst wage-earners in this country.

In 1954 the company introduced what was referred to as a voluntary car loan
scheme.   It is a scheme which may not commend itself to taxpayers who are not **C**
in a position to have the tax advantages which it is claimed that this scheme
produces.   Under this scheme the company bought a car which it thereafter owned.
It treated it as a business asset, and by doing so obtained the tax advantage of a
capital allowance applicable to business assets.   The company paid for the licence
and comprehensive insurance for the car, but the taxpayer was responsible for
paying the maintenance and running costs.   He was under an obligation to drive **I**
the car himself only, and not to let anyone else drive it.   Because of his having
the advantage of this car loan scheme which he joined, a subtraction was made in
respect of his wages.   In the early days, the subtraction was £2 10s. a week, but it
varied thereafter, partly because he substituted a better car in place of the original
car which he had under the scheme, and partly because of the increased costs, to
which the company in some of their documents refer, of running the car loan
scheme.

Two questions arise in this case.   The first is: is this subtraction of £2 10s.
or so a reduction in computing the gross wage, before arriving at the gross wage;
or is it a deduction from the gross wage after arriving at the gross wage?   If it is a
reduction in calculating the gross wage, then it is not part of the emoluments;
but if it is a deduction from the gross wage it is part of it and therefore of the
emoluments.   The second question arises in the alternative, on the assumption
that this £2 10s. was not part of the gross wage.   It is: is the car arrangement a

A benefit included in " perquisites and profits " within the definition of " emoluments " for the purposes of Sch. E as defined in para. 1 (1) of Sch. 2 to the Finance Act, 1956? Then, as a subsidiary to that, there is the further question whether the proper valuation, if it is a benefit capable of being valued, is £2 10s. (or the increased amount substituted thereafter as I have indicated). The commissioners decided both questions against the Crown.

B Before coming to a consideration of the facts of this case, I shall first refer briefly to a couple of cases from amongst those to which I was referred in the course of argument. It will be convenient to take the extracts I propose to quote from these cases irrespective of whether they are concerned exclusively with one or both of these two questions, as they are, to a considerable extent, intertwined. The first quotation comes from *Smyth* v. *Stretton* (1), a decision of Channell, J.:

C " Now, that case is quite clear, a case where a man has a salary from his office, which is what the lord justice puts, and by agreement with somebody else, I presume his father-in-law, has bound himself to set apart a certain portion of that salary year by year and save it and invest it for the benefit of his wife and children, that case is quite clear; it still is income, and he has contracted with somebody else to apply it in a particular way . . ."

D So that an agreement between an employee and an employer that his salary should be applied in a particular way does not preclude its being salary. Channell, J. said (2):

" I agree with what Mr. Danckwerts [counsel for the respondent taxpayer] says, you must look at the substance of it and not the words; but at the same time, I do not say that you must disregard the words . . .,"

E In *Machon* v. *McLoughlin* (3) Rowlatt, J., said:

" I have to find out whether the true way of looking at it is that he is paid a gross wage and has to pay something back or that he is only paid a net wage. That was Vaughan Williams, L.J.'s test in *Bell* v. *Gribble* (4), and that is the test I have to apply. As I pointed out before, it may be a question of words. In every case you have to see whether it is a question of words. I do not think there is very much to show that it is not a question of words."

Taken out of context, I found those quotations confusing. However, when they are read in context the meaning is perfectly clear. What has to be found out is whether the true way of looking at it is that the employee is paid a gross wage and, having become entitled to that gross wage, has then to pay something back. Then Rowlatt, J., adds, " or that he is only paid a net wage ", meaning by that that the figure which is subtracted enters into the calculation of what he is obtaining as a wage, which is the same as appears in the documents of this case, not under the description " net wage " but under the description " taxable gross wage ".

H With regard to the phrase, " it may be a question of words ", this is a matter which has to be approached with caution and with an understanding of the background against which Rowlatt, J., made his observation. It is true that in a sense it may be a matter of words. To take the illustration which Rowlatt, J., gave, where the question was whether the wage earner was paid £200 gross wage and then had £50 deducted from it, or whether the £50 was subtracted before arriving at the gross wage, in each case what would be received is the figure of £150. If one puts oneself in mathematical blinkers and excludes all other considerations, then the answer is mathematically the same in the end—namely, £150; but the rights of the parties are fundamentally different in the two cases. In the latter case there is a contract for a gross wage from which the £50 has been subtracted before arriving at the gross wage, whereas in the former case there

---

(1) (1904), 5 Tax Cas. 36 at p. 43.
(2) (1904), 5 Tax Cas. at p. 42.
(3) (1926), 11 Tax Cas. 83 at p. 90.
(4) [1903] 1 K.B. 517; 4 Tax Cas. 522.

is a contract for a gross wage from which the £50 has not been deducted, and **A**
there is a second, separate contract for the deduction of £50 from that gross
wage. In one case there is one contract varied, in the other case there are two
contracts. Separate rights and liabilities and separate relationships between the
parties arise in the case of both contracts by reason of the words used. Do not
let us underestimate the importance of words. Words are the means by which
we communicate; by which, to a very large extent, we govern our relationships; **B**
by which contracts are made and rights and liabilities are governed. Words
used in one way may have an entirely separate operation from different words
differently used, although the mathematical result at the end of the day may be
the same. Words are themselves matters of substance, because they themselves
form the contractual rights and liabilities which can arise by reason of them.

In *Machon* v. *McLoughlin* (5) ROWLATT, J., said (6):   **C**

" If a person is paid a wage with some advantage thrown in, you cannot
add the advantage to the wage for the purpose of taxation unless that
advantage can be turned into money. That is one proposition. But when
you have a person paid a wage with the necessity—the contractual necessity
if you like—to expend that wage in a particular way, then he must pay tax
upon the gross wage, and no question of alienability or inalienability arises."   **D**

The first sentence of this quotation bears on the second alternative question
which I indicated as arising in this case, and the third sentence in the quotation
bears on the first question that I indicated. That passage was approved by
WARRINGTON, L.J., in the Court of Appeal, who, speaking of the facts in that case,
said (7) that the resolution which changed the method of calculating the gross **E**
wage in that case (8)

" was intended to make the change in substance the difference between an
allowance in kind and remunerating the staff on a cash basis, and that there
is, both from the point of view of the employer and of the employee, a very
substantial difference between the two systems."

F

In this case, the £2 10s. was, as appears from what I have already said, an extraneous item introduced into the calculation of the amount paid to the taxpayer
—and, in the method by which the calculation was made, introduced so that, on
the face of the documents and on the face of the case, it would be clear that it
was before arriving at the taxable gross wage. The other items in the calculation,
apart from the basic wage, are items calculated on the basis of the basic wage **G**
or additional payments which quite clearly and properly come within the calculation of the gross wage. But the £2 10s. in this case is a subtraction of an entirely
different nature, which is sui generis in relation to the rest of the wage calculation.
The question has arisen whether an item of this kind must in its nature be something that cannot be regarded as entering into the calculation of the wage at all,
and must therefore of necessity be a deduction after arriving at the gross wage **H**
and not a reduction in the process of calculating its amount. This, it seems to me,
is one of the elements that has to be taken into consideration in deciding whether
or not what the parties did, on a true construction of the documents and a true
understanding of the arrangements that they made, was the creation of one
contract varied so as to provide for the £2 10s. entering into the calculation of
the gross wage, or whether it was two contracts giving rise to two separate sets **I**
of rights and liabilities and two separate sets of remedies, in which there was one
contract for the wage and a separate contract to provide the car on loan for a
payment to be deducted from the wage earned. It cannot of itself, so it seems to
me, by its nature, exclude this question. It seems to me to be an element to be
considered in answering that question.

---

(5) (1926), 11 Tax Cas. 83.   (6) (1926), 11 Tax Cas. at p. 89.
(7) (1926), 11 Tax Cas. at p. 95.   (8) (1926), 11 Tax Cas. at p. 96.

A   I come now from these rather general considerations to the more detailed provisions of this case. It is pointed out very forcibly that the emoluments which the taxpayer had before he joined the scheme were perfectly clear, and amounted to a sum from which there was no subtraction of £2 10s. or any other figure in respect of the car. It was also pointed out with force that the emoluments would be calculated in precisely the same way the moment he ceased to belong

B   to the scheme, and that his colleagues, whose wages were calculated in the same way as his, had their wages without the subtraction of the £2 10s. for the car. Even over and above that, by fourteen days' notice he could, under the scheme, terminate his membership of the scheme and again receive his wage without any subtraction in respect of it. Those are what I might almost call circumstantial considertions, and they do not go directly to answering the

C   question whether in this case there was this subtraction before or after arriving at what was included in the gross wage.

It is said for the taxpayer that, as he, under his service contract with the company, received a remuneration without subtraction for the car, then it must be shown that there was some variation in this remuneration and in the contract for service and this remuneration, to provide for this subtraction before arriving

D   at the gross wage. That submission appears to me to be correct. It is then said that the evidence in this case does not show that there was such a variation— and we are now at the nub of the case on the first issue.

The company sent to its employees a letter outlining the car loan scheme. It there referred to it as " a scheme whereby a craftsman may run a car, if he so desires, at most reasonable terms ". It refers to it as a scheme which may be

E   taken advantage of " when the pocket permits ". It was suggested that those phrases, " at most reasonable terms " and, " when the pocket permits " were more consonant with an agreement to pay out of the gross wage after it had been calculated than before it had been calculated, but for my part I cannot attach any substantial weight to these phrases. Enclosed with that letter was a document headed " Conditions ". Condition 5 provided: " The user will sign a simple agree-

F   ment." In fact, there was no inter-party agreement consisting of one document between two parties to which there were signatures, but there was an application form, so headed, signed by the taxpayer. Nothing in that application form throws any light on either of the questions that have to be decided in this case. It was simply a straightforward application to join the scheme without reference to the wage at all. Condition 6 reads: " An amended wage basis will come into operation

G   if the application is accepted." The commissioners said (and rightly so in my view) that this reference " in itself does not help us much in determining what was the true wage ", but it does contain the reference to " An amended wage basis " coming into operation. So it contemplates that somehow or other the wage basis is going to be affected, and the wage basis—and I emphasise the word " basis "—could hardly have been affected without affecting the calculation of

H   the gross wage itself; but in itself this condition does not establish that the wage basis was affected. In due course this condition will have to be read in conjunction with what was actually done, and what was actually done will have to be considered in the light of this forecasting observation in condition 6, which I have just read. Condition 9 provides that: " If the car is under repair for maintenance or following an accident the amended wage basis will still apply."

I   Again we have a reference to " amended wage basis ". On the other hand, the car, when it is under repair for maintenance or following an accident, is not available for the wage earner's use, and to that extent may be thought to be rather more consonant with a deduction from the gross wage than with a reduction in the process of calculating it.

There was a further letter to the employees some time later, which is referred to in para. 7 of the Case Stated, when the management wrote to the employees saying that because of high costs it was imperative to raise the amount paid in respect of the cars loaned to the employees, and saying, " This is a very steep rise." Those phrases, again, have been relied on to indicate a deduction rather than **A** a reduction. There is also a reference to " the present wage adjustments " in the same letter, which is certainly more consonant with a wage reduction rather than a wage deduction. Then there was a memorandum of terms of service, which was signed by the taxpayer. That makes no reference at all to the wage position, but provides: " Either of us may cancel my obligation and authority to use the car on fourteen days' notice." That becomes relevant on the second question **B** which I shall have to consider but, with regard to the first question, which I am now considering, it makes no reference whatsoever to wages.

There are, in addition, three documents which refer to " wage reductions ". The first is headed " Craftsmen's Car Scheme " followed by the name of the tax-payer. That gives the substance of the arrangements between himself and the company at the time, and their history. It there refers to the £2 10s., and so on, **C** which I have mentioned, as " wage reductions ". Then there is another document headed " Motor Cars ", which gives the history of the motor cars which the tax-payer had from time to time. Again, that refers to the " reduction ", followed by the amount of £2 10s., and so on, which I have mentioned in this case. There was also a letter written to an employee in the company's wages office by the secretary of the company, asking her: " Will you please arrange the necessary weekly **D** reduction " in the case of the taxpayer and another man. These three documents are internal company documents, and cannot properly be relied on as establishing any wage variation as between the taxpayer and the company, and I leave them out of consideration in arriving at my conclusion.

This leaves the pay slip, which is exhibited to the Case Stated. The pay slip is headed by the taxpayer's name. Then, underneath, there are the calculations **E** of the taxpayer's wage. This was a weekly pay slip, the first column of which is headed " Calculations ", and opposite that there appears in another column the corresponding figures. Under the heading " Calculations ", the first item is " Flat Rate ", and the figures £22 6s. 7d. The second is " Overtime Premium ", the third " Cost of Living Bonus ", and so on. These items, when added up, amount in this particular week to £33 9s. 2d. Then, still under the heading **F** " Calculations ", and not distinguished from the rest of the calculations in any way, is Item No. 8. There, there is no entry of what this calculation is in respect of, but opposite it appears the figure of £2 13s. 6d., which was the current figure in respect of the car loan. There is nothing to distinguish that item or that figure from the earlier items and the earlier figures. Underneath that is " Taxable Gross Wage " and opposite is what would appear at a casual glance in the ordinary way **G** to be an addition of all the previous figures. However, when they are worked out it is found that the £2 13s. 6d., which looks as though it should be an addition with all the others, is, in fact, a deduction, because the taxable gross wage is £30 15s. 8d. The figures, excluding the figure of £2 13s. 6d., total £33 9s. 2d., showing that the £2 13s. 6d. is a deduction. Then, underneath the taxable gross wage there are the following items: " Standard Deductions ", " Graduated Pension Contri- **H** bution " and " P.A.Y.E.", with figures appearing opposite them. When the figures for these items are added up, they amount to £4 7s. 8d., which is then deducted from the £30 15s. 8d., arriving at a net wage of £26 8s.

It is said for the taxpayer that this document shows that the £2 13s. 6d. is a figure which enters into the computation of the taxable gross wage, £30 15s. 8d. Although entering into it by way of subtraction, it nevertheless does enter into **I** it; and, therefore, it is a reduction in arriving at the taxable gross wage and not a deduction from the taxable gross wage after it has been arrived at. The Crown points out, with considerable force, that what provided this £2 13s. 6d. was the taxpayer's services to the company, because it is made by way of subtraction for what he was paid for those services; but that, of course, is not decisive against the taxpayer. Then it says that there is no variation of the structure of the basic wage; that the items based on it—that is, all the other items except the £2 13s. 6d. —are unaffected by the £2 13s. 6d., so there is no variation in the wage structure.

A But, again, this is not a decisive consideration.

In para. 10 of the Case Stated the commissioners say:

> "Whenever an employee was absent through sickness and received no
> wage, no deduction was made for the use of the car because the agreement
> between the company and the employee under the scheme was that the
> employee should accept a reduced wage."

B So there was no deduction and there was no subtraction. There were no means
at all by which the taxpayer was made in any way liable in respect of the car
loan except by way of subtraction when he earned sufficient to cover the amount
subtracted. This, to my mind, is a strong consideration, because there was no
liability at all here apart from a liability involving subtraction from the wage.

C In other words, here is a strong indication that what we have is not two contracts
—one contract with regard to the wage and a separate independent contract
giving rise to separate rights and liabilities but resulting in a deduction from that
wage. Then it was suggested that it may be that the company did not press for
payment in any week in which nothing was earned; but for my part I do not see
why, if that were the explanation, they should not have recouped themselves, in

D weeks where money was earned, in respect of payments for the car loan scheme
not made in weeks where wages were not earned. The commissioners say in
para. 11:

> "In his evidence the [taxpayer] stated that if he had ever been asked
> whether the company supplied him with a car at a rent deducted from his
> wage he would have said that he had accepted instead a lower wage and a

E car free."

So that, as far as the taxpayer is concerned, at any rate, for what it is worth, he
obviously did not consider himself liable for payment in respect of the car in a
week where a wage was not earned. This is at least consistent with the prima
facie impression which is given by the fact that subtraction in respect of the car
was only made in weeks where wages were earned to the extent to which those

F wages could cover the subtraction.

The Crown, however, brought forward another material consideration. They
rightly and forcibly pointed out that the car payments fluctuated, and that if
these were to be included as deductions in arriving at the gross wage we would
be faced with the situation in which the gross wage fluctuated in accordance with
the fluctuation for the car payment; and they submit that this is not a realistic

G situation to be expected in respect of wages.

The case of *Machon* v. *McLoughlin* (9), from which I have already quoted,
was a case in which payments for lodging and dinners were subtracted in respect
of the employee's wage. ROWLATT, J., said (10):

> "I think you have the element here that I had in *Cordy* v. *Gordon* (11).
> One element was that he had to bear, out of the advantage he got, the varying

H cost of living. I have here the consideration that if the man sleeps out, as he
> may have permission to do, either permanently or, I suppose, temporarily,
> he does not suffer a deduction for board. He can certainly have meals out;
> then he deducts a value, upon a scale, of those odd meals from the counter
> amount which he has to allow in reduction of his pay. Therefore if the
> respondent [the taxpayer] is right and if the commissioners are right in a

I case like this, this man's salary varies according to whether he sleeps in
> or whether he sleeps out, whether he dines in or whether he dines out. I
> think that is a very unreasonable view. If he dines in, according to the
> respondent he dines free of income tax; if he dines out he dines subject to
> income tax. I do not think that is the right view."

---

(9) (1926), 11 Tax Cas. 83.
(10) (1926), 11 Tax Cas. at p. 90.
(11) [1925] 2 K.B. 276; 9 Tax Cas. 304.

Here, however, the variation was a variation made by a further contract, and not   **A**
a variation provided for within the terms of the original contract. Where a
variation is provided for within the terms of a contract, it is a proper matter to
be taken into consideration in construing the contract within whose terms the
variation operates. The variation in the amount of £2 10s. was made by a new
contract, and as long as that variation by agreement held that sum remained the
same. For instance, in the memorandum of terms of service it is provided, in   **B**
words endorsed on it, that, instead of the motor car which he was to have under
the original memorandum, " I am to make use of motor car " number so-and-so,
" instead of motor car " number so-and-so, " as from May 31, 1963 ". As long
as that memorandum continued as so varied, and therefore constituted the contract between the parties, the price remained precisely the same. So, I am not
myself impressed by this argument, and consider the situation in *Machon* v.   **C**
McLoughlin (12) distinguishable from the situation in this case. In particular the
reference in the condition, originally mentioned in the letter introducing the
scheme to the employees, to " an amended wage basis " coming into operation,
and the fact that, in the inter-party pay slip, the only provision for payment was
accordingly made by way of subtraction from wages without any provision for
payment even in respect of a week when no wage was earned, seem to me, despite   **D**
the impressive considerations which have been urged on behalf of the Crown,
to establish that the true view of this transaction is that there was one contract
for payment of the wage less an amount to be calculated in arriving at that wage,
and not two contracts, one for the payment of the wage and an entirely separate
contract for the deduction of an amount from that wage after it had been
calculated.   **E**

That brings me to the second alternative: is the car loan a benefit included in
the " perquisites and profits " within the definition of " emoluments ", and what
is the valuation of that benefit if it can be properly valued? Two objections
were raised by the taxpayer to the Crown's claim under this second question.
The Crown accepts that for a profit or perquisite to be subject to taxation as an
emolument it must be a profit or perquisite which is money or money's worth: **F**
it must either be money or something which can be converted into money. It
is said, further, that in this case, on fourteen days' notice this advantage could
be converted into money by the employee at any time by his simply giving notice
under the scheme ending it, thus having his wage restored to its original amount
instead of having the subtraction of £2 10s. or so in respect of the car. Section 156
of the Income Tax Act, 1952, provides: " Tax . . . shall be charged " under Case I,   **G**
on " emoluments for the year of assessment "; and the Finance Act, 1956,
Sch. 2, para. 1, provides, inter alia: " . . . the expression ' emoluments ' shall
include all salaries, fees, wages, perquisites and profits whatsoever." The
contention put forward before me by the Crown was a contention which was
put forward before the commissioners (para. 13 (c) of the Case Stated):

> " that . . . if the true wage was a net wage plus the use of the car, then   **H**
> the use of the car was money's worth because the [taxpayer] could surrender
> his rights under the contract and by this revert to his former wage and turn
> the benefit into pecuniary account."

The commissioners' observations were:

> " From the Memorandum of Terms of Service . . . the [taxpayer] was not to
> permit anyone else but himself to drive or use the car except in an emergency.
> In these circumstances the use of the car is not in our view money's worth."

That was not directed to the contention put forward by the Crown. The commissioners arrived at their conclusion, without dealing with the Crown's contention, on a basis which, as I understand it, was not put before them by the Crown,
nor put before me by the Crown; but the basis on which they arrived at their

(12) (1926), 11 Tax Cas. 83.

A conclusion in that appeal has been relied on in argument by the taxpayer before me.

I come now to this contention, on which there is no express decision, at any rate directed specifically to it. The taxpayer, whilst accepting that, to be taxable, the perquisite must be money or money's worth convertible into money, puts his case in two ways. It is said, first, that the documents with which we are dealing,
B particularly the Case Stated, show that the employee was paid weekly, that the car could not be turned into money in any one week, and that, therefore, in any one week there was here no money's worth because the car loan could not be turned into money in that week. The short answer to that is that the assessment is made on " emoluments . . . for the year of assessment ". The relevance of the perquisite is that it is contained in the definition of " emoluments ", so we are
C dealing with " perquisites for the year of assessment ". Therefore, the taxpayer could, after fourteen days' notice in the year, turn it into money, if it could be turned into money at all.

So I come to the second contention, and here there was a rather interesting, recondite submission. It was that to give notice terminating the car loan scheme would not be to convert the perquisite of the car loan into money, but would
D be to abolish or terminate the scheme altogether and to substitute for it the payment of a wage and restore the pre-scheme position. But what we are concerned with is the valuation of the perquisite, and only the valuation (and I emphasise the word " valuation ") of the perquisite; and the need to value the perquisite is only to ascertain that it could be converted into money's worth. What is the money's worth into which it can be converted is merely for the purpose of valuing
E the perquisite. If it cannot be converted into money's worth, it does not cease to be a perquisite, but it ceases to be a perquisite on which a money value can be put, and therefore cannot be a perquisite in respect of which a poundage can be added for income tax purposes. Therefore, on this analysis, if all we are concerned about is the valuation of the perquisite, it presupposes the existence of the perquisite, and it is no answer to say that getting rid of the car and the car loan
F scheme gets rid of the perquisite altogether. So, indeed, in the Burton Tailor scheme (13), the value of the suit and of the advantage that it gave was assessed on the value which it would fetch in the market, although, of course, disposing of it in the market would be getting rid of the perquisite which it constituted.

Thus, the only question here is what is the valuation of this perquisite, presupposing the existence of the perquisite? We find that on fourteen days' notice
G the employee can obtain at least the sum which is subtracted in his wage slip in respect of the car loan scheme. He cannot do that for the first fourteen days, and therefore for fourteen days in the year he cannot achieve this valuation. But in principle, subject to that observation with regard to the fourteen days, it seems perfectly clear to me that this is convertible into money's worth, and the money's worth into which it is certainly convertible is the amount which is subtracted in
H respect of the gross wage for the car loan. With regard to the fourteen days, it has been canvassed whether this is a matter which should go back to the commissioners or whether I should decide here and now what course should be taken. However, the parties have wisely agreed, having regard to the amount involved, that it would be utterly unjustifiable to refer this back to the commissioners. The only valuation which I have before me is the amount which has been subtracted in the pay slip. I have no indication whatsoever of what the value might be in respect of the fourteen days when the car cannot be returned to the employers' and therefore I consider the fourteen days should be completely omitted in making the appropriate calculation in respect of the emoluments in this year. In respect of the other fifty weeks of the year, it seems to me that the amount to be taken into consideration as the value of the car would be the weekly amount deducted in respect of the car, as appearing in the taxpayer's pay slip.

(13) See *Wilkins* v. *Rogerson*, [1961] 1 All E.R. 358.

The result, in that event, is that the Crown succeeds on the second issue to the
extent I have indicated, whilst failing on the first issue.

Appeal allowed.

Solicitors: *Solicitor of Inland Revenue* (for the Crown); *Biddle & Co.*, agents for
Hepworth & Chadwick, Leeds (for the taxpayer).

[*Reported by* F. A. AMIES, ESQ., *Barrister-at-Law.*]

Affirmed. C.A. [1968] 2 All E.R. 936.

BOWATER PAPER CORPORATION, LTD. *v.* MURGATROYD
(Inspector of Taxes).

[CHANCERY DIVISION (Cross, J.), December 6, 7, 13, 1967.]

Income Tax—Double taxation—Relief—Credit of foreign tax against income tax—
Computation—Tax borne by the body corporate—Attributable to proportion of
" relevant profits " represented by dividends—Meaning of relevant profits—
Profits in accounts of foreign body corporate or as assessed by foreign taxing
authorities—Income Tax Act, 1952 (15 & 16 Geo. 6 & 1 Eliz. 2 c. 10), s. 347,
Sch. 16, para. (9).

The taxpayer company had a subsidiary company (the North America
company) which was resident in Canada and which derived its income from
the dividends of other subsidiaries, some of which suffered Canadian tax
and some United States tax on their respective profits. Under the double
taxation conventions between the United Kingdom and Canada and the
United States, having effect under the Income Tax Act, 1952, s. 347 and
Sch. 16, the taxpayer company was entitled to credit against United
Kingdom income tax in respect of Canadian and United States taxes
paid on the profits of subsidiaries in those countries. The relevant foreign
tax taken into account for this purpose was " that borne by the body
corporate paying the dividend upon the relevant profits in so far as it is
properly attributable to the proportion of the relevant profits which is
represented by the dividend " (para. 9* of Sch. 16). Stated as a fraction,
the proportion of the foreign tax attributable to the relevant profits was a
fraction of which the numerator was the amount of the dividend and the
denominator was the amount of the relevant profits less tax. The depreciation allowed by the taxing authorities abroad was larger than was the
provision for depreciation made by the companies concerned in their accounts.
Thus, if the " relevant profits " element in the denominator was the taxable
profits as computed by the taxing authorities abroad, the denominator
would be smaller than if the " relevant profits " were the amount shown
in the companies' accounts, with the further consequence that the fraction
of the foreign tax to be taken into account against United Kingdom income
tax would be larger. Accordingly there arose the question whether " relevant
profits " in the context of para. 9 of Sch. 16 to the Act of 1952 meant profits
as shown in the accounts of the subsidiaries of the North America company
or the profits as assessed by the taxing authorities abroad.

Held: the " relevant profits " in para. 9 of Sch. 16 to the Income Tax
Act, 1952, meant profits available for distribution as dividend, which were
the profits shown in the accounts; and accordingly it was the amount of
profits computed with the smaller element of depreciation, viz., the depreciation allowed to the particular subsidiary company abroad, which was
to be taken as the relevant profits element in calculating the denominator
in the fraction of foreign tax that could be credited against United Kingdom

---

* Schedule 16, para. 9, is printed at p. 870, letter H, to p. 871, letter D, post.

A   income tax for the purposes of s. 347 double taxation relief (see p. 873, letter A, and p. 874, letter B, post).

Appeal dismissed.

[As to the computation of credits for foreign tax against income tax under double taxation conventions, see 20 HALSBURY'S LAWS (3rd Edn.) 456-458, paras. 857-860; and for cases on the subject see 28 DIGEST (Repl.) 305-308,
B   *1335-1350*.

For the Income Tax Act, 1952, s. 347, Sch. 16, para. 9, see 31 HALSBURY'S STATUTES (2nd Edn.) 333, 541.

For the Double Taxation Relief (Taxes on Income) (U.S.A.) Order, 1946, Schedule, art. XIII, see 11 HALSBURY'S STATUTORY INSTRUMENTS (First Reissue) 108; and for the Double Taxation Relief (Taxes on Income) (Canada)
C   Order, 1946, Schedule, art. XIII, see ibid., p. 120.]

Case referred to:

Inland Revenue Comrs. v. Sterling Trust, Ltd., Sterling Trust, Ltd. v. Inland
   Revenue Comrs., (1925), 12 Tax Cas. 868; 28 Digest (Repl.) 452, *1947*.

Case Stated.

D   The taxpayer company appealed to the Special Commissioners of Income Tax against an objection to its claim for an allowance by way of credit for foreign tax against United Kingdom income tax for the years of assessment 1958-59 to 1961-62, under para. 13 of Sch. 16 to the Income Tax Act, 1952, and also against the following assessments to income tax: 1958-59 £1,880,000 less £617,427 16s. 2d. tax credit relief; 1959-60 £2,400,000 less £880,000 tax credit relief; 1960-61
E   £3,000,000 less £931,000 tax credit relief; and 1961-62 £2,041,000 less £510,000 tax credit relief.   The claim arose under the double taxation conventions with the United States of America and Canada, although no question arose of the interpretation of those conventions.   The relevant provisions were as follows: Double Taxation Relief (Taxes on Income) (U.S.A.) Order, 1946*, Schedule, art. XIII (2):

F   " Subject to such provisions (which shall not affect the general principle hereof) as may be enacted in the United Kingdom, United States tax payable in respect of income from sources within the United States shall be allowed as a credit against any United Kingdom tax payable in respect of that income.   Where such income is an ordinary dividend paid by an United States corporation, such credit shall take into account (in addition
G   to any United States income tax deducted from or imposed on such dividend) the United States income tax imposed on such corporation in respect of its profits, and where it is a dividend paid on participating preference shares and representing both a dividend at the fixed rate to which the shares are entitled and an additional participation in profits, such tax on profits shall likewise be taken into account in so far as the dividend exceeds such fixed
H   rate."

Double Taxation Relief (Taxes on Income) (Canada) Order, 1946†, Schedule, art. XIII (1):

" Subject to the provisions of the law of the United Kingdom regarding the allowance as a credit against United Kingdom tax of tax payable in a territory outside the United Kingdom, Canadian tax payable in respect
I   of income from sources within Canada shall be allowed as a credit against any United Kingdom tax payable in respect of that income.   Where such income is an ordinary dividend paid by a Canadian debtor, the credit shall take into account (in addition to any Canadian income tax chargeable directly or by deduction in respect of the dividend) the Canadian income tax payable in respect of its profits by the company paying the dividend . . ."

---

* S.R. & O. 1946 No. 1327.
† S.R. & O. 1946 No. 1885.

The relevant legislation was contained in the Income Tax Act, 1952, s. 347   A
and Sch. 16, paras. 1-3, 7, 8 and 9.

It was common ground (being so stated in para. 7 of the Case Stated) that in
computing the credit which might be claimed against United Kingdom income
tax under art. XIII (1) of the Double Taxation Agreement between the United
Kingdom and Canada, the Canadian and United States taxes paid on the profits
or income of subsidiary companies (viz., of the North America company) in   B
Canada and the United States of America, from which the North America
company received dividends, might be taken into account in addition to the tax
suffered by the North America company by direct assessment or as result of the
withholding tax deducted from the dividends received from United States
subsidiaries. The North America company itself suffered tax only to a small
extent as it was primarily a holding company. Paragraphs 8-10 of the Case   C
Stated are set out at p. 871, letter F, to p. 872, letter A, post.

The commissioners rejected* the contentions of the taxpayer company and
dismissed its appeal. They determined the appeals on agreed figures as follows:
1958-59 assessment reduced to £1,700,104 (agreed tax credit relief £425,032 5s.);
1959-60 assessment reduced to £1,821,804 (agreed tax credit relief £391,500 7s.
8d.); 1960-61 assessment increased to £3,815,522 (agreed tax credit   D
£1,043,291 3s.); 1961-62 assessment reduced to £1,991,064 (agreed tax credit
relief £660,575 9s. 6d.).

Heyworth Talbot, Q.C., *H. Major Allen*, Q.C., and *Peter Rees* for the taxpayer
company.

Hubert H. Monroe, Q.C., and *J. R. Phillips* for the Crown.

Cur. adv. vult.   E

Dec. 13. **CROSS, J.:** the appellant taxpayer company, Bowater Paper
Corpn., Ltd., which is resident in the United Kingdom, is the parent of a group
of companies, some of which are resident abroad. One of its subsidiaries is
Bowater Corpn. of North America, Ltd., which is a resident of Canada and
which holds, either directly or indirectly, the equity shares of all the Bowater   F
subsidiaries in the United States and Canada. The income of the North America
company is mainly derived from dividends received by it from its subsidiaries,
some of which pay or suffer Canadian tax and others United States tax on their
respective profits or income. In its turn the North America company pays
dividends to the taxpayer company. Under the double taxation conventions
between this country and the United States and Canada to which effect is given   G
by the Income Tax Act, 1952, s. 347 and Sch. 16, the taxpayer company is
entitled to credit against United Kingdom income tax in respect of the United
States and Canadian taxes paid on the profits or income of subsidiaries in the
United States and Canada, from which profits the North America company
itself receives dividends. A dispute has arisen as to the manner in which such
credit should be computed. The question turns on the true construction of para.   H
9 of Sch. 16 which is in the following terms:

" Where, in the case of any dividend, foreign tax not chargeable directly
or by deduction in respect of the dividend is, under the arrangements, to be
taken into account in considering whether any, and if so what, credit is
to be allowed against the United Kingdom taxes in respect of the dividend,
the foreign tax not so chargeable which is to be taken into account shall   I
be that borne by the body corporate paying the dividend upon the relevant
profits in so far as it is properly attributable to the proportion of the
relevant profits which is represented by the dividend.

" The relevant profits are—(a) if the dividend is paid for a specified
period, the profits of that period; (b) if the dividend is not paid for a specified

---

* The material contentions of the taxpayer company and the full decision of the
commissioners are set out at p. 872, letter D, to p. 873, letter D, post.

A   period, but is paid out of specified profits, those profits; (*c*) if the dividend
is paid neither for a specified period nor out of specified profits, the profits
of the last period for which accounts of the body corporate were made up
which ended before the dividend became payable:

"Provided that if, in a case falling under sub-para. (*a*) or sub-para. (*c*)
of this paragraph, the total dividend exceeds the profits available for distri-
B   bution of the period mentioned in the said sub-para. (*a*) or the said sub-
para. (*c*), as the case may be, the relevant profits shall be the profits of that
period plus so much of the profits available for distribution of preceding
periods (other than profits previously distributed or previously treated as
relevant for the purposes of this paragraph) as is equal to the excess; and for
the purposes of this proviso the profits of the most recent preceding period
C   shall first be taken into account, then the profits of the next most recent
preceding period, and so on.

"Profits which have been treated as relevant for the purposes of para. 9
of Sch. 7 to the Finance (No. 2) Act, 1945, as well as profits which have been
treated as relevant for the purposes of para. 9 of Pt. 1 of Sch. 9 to the
Finance Act, 1947, shall be deemed for the purposes of this paragraph to be
D   profits previously treated as relevant for the purposes of this paragraph."

What profits are being referred to? Are they, as the taxpayer company contends, the sums on which the United States and Canadian subsidiaries were
assessed to tax in those countries or, as the Crown contends, the sums of divisible
profits appearing in their respective accounts? For the period in question in
this case it makes a great difference which meaning is put on the word for the
E   reasons which are set out in paras. 8 to 10 of the Case Stated. Of course, the
particular circumstances which give rise to the problem in this case do not
themselves throw any light on its solution; I will, however, read those paragraphs.

"8. In computing their respective profits liable to Canadian or United
States tax there was deducted the depreciation allowance made under the
F   relevant tax legislation to the various subsidiaries. Those depreciation
allowances differed from the provisions which these subsidiaries made
for depreciation in their own books of account. The reasons for this
divergence between tax and book depreciation are explained below.

"9. When the paper mill owned by Bowaters Southern Paper Corpn.
came into operation in 1954, that company elected to amortise the cost
G   of certain plant facilities over a sixty month period for U.S. Federal income
tax purposes, under what is known as a certificate of necessity. The
remaining fixed assets were depreciated for tax purposes on a reducing
balance method. For accounts purposes however, the company has depreciated its fixed assets on a straight-line basis. Under U.S. tax law, a
company which provides for depreciation on the straight-line basis, so as
H   to write off the assets over their useful working life, is entitled to claim,
tax depreciation on the reducing balance basis at twice the rate used in its
accounts; this is known as the 'double declining balance' method. As a
result of claiming this accelerated depreciation, the profit of Bowaters
Southern Paper Corpn. assessable to U.S. tax in the relevant years has
been substantially lower than the profit shown in the company's accounts.
I   In accordance with recognised U.S. accounting practice, the company has
charged the resultant tax saving against its profits and has set aside a
corresponding amount for equalisation of future taxation. Bowaters
Southern Paper Corpn. could not have shown the same rate of depreciation
in its accounts as it was allowed to claim for United States tax purposes
in the years in question, without showing very substantial losses which
would not have been commercially true.

"10. In the case of the Canadian subsidiaries the difference between
accounts and tax depreciation is due to the fact that tax allowances are

computed on a reducing balance basis whereas, for accounts purposes,   A
depreciation is charged on the straight-line method."

One may illustrate the problem by an example given in argument. Suppose:
(a) that the profits, apart from any allowance for depreciation or tax, are $10,000;
(b) that the depreciation allowance given by the tax authorities is $2,000 but
that the allowance made by the company for depreciation in its accounts is
only $1,000; (c) that the rate of tax is fifty per cent. so that the foreign tax   B
is $4,000; and (d) that a dividend of $3,000 is paid. In that case, to find the
proportion of the foreign tax attributable to the dividend one will construct
a fraction of which the numerator will be the dividend of $3,000 and the
denominator the profits, less tax. These, according to the Crown, are $5,000
but the taxpayer company says that they are $4,000. On the Crown's view,
therefore, three-fifths of the tax is attributable to the dividend but on the   C
taxpayer company's view three-quarters.   The contentions of the taxpayer
company before the Special Commissioners are set out as follows in para. 19
of the Case:

" (i) On the true construction of para. 9 of Sch. 16 ' profits ', in the
expression ' relevant profits ' means profits as computed for the purposes   D
of foreign tax. (ii) In the alternative: on the principle of the decision in
Inland Revenue Comrs. v. *Sterling Trust, Ltd.* (1) the taxpayer [company]
was entitled to claim that any dividend paid [by the North America company]
should be deemed to have been paid primarily out of taxed profits, and
not rateably out of taxed and untaxed profits. (iii) In the further alternative:
' profits ' in the expression ' relevant profits ' means profits as computed   E
for the purposes of United Kingdom taxation."

I would say at once that the third contention does not appear to me to be
sustainable and was not relied on by counsel before me.   The Special
Commissioners gave their decision in writing as follows:

" For the purposes of this case the relevant words in para. 9 of Sch. 16
to the Income Tax Act, 1952, are: '. . . the foreign tax not so chargeable   F
which is to be taken into account shall be that borne by the body corporate
paying the dividend upon the relevant profits in so far as it is properly
attributable to the proportion of the relevant profits which is represented
by the dividend '. We have, therefore, to find what foreign tax is properly
attributable to the proportion of the relevant profits which is represented
by the dividend, and to do this it is necessary to construct a fraction and   G
apply it to the foreign tax paid. Both parties are agreed that the numerator
of this fraction is the dividend. Both parties are agreed that the denominator
is ' profits ', to be reduced by the amount of foreign tax, and the dispute
is as to the calculation of these profits. The [taxpayer company's] contention is that they are the profits as computed for the purposes of the foreign
tax. The Crown's contention is that they are ' the gross divisible profits ',   H
this phrase being explained as meaning the profits as shown by the accounts
after deductions, such as depreciation, which are proper to be made in
arriving at profits, but are not appropriations from ascertained profits.

" In our view we have to decide what are ' relevant profits ', for these are
the profits with which para. 9 deals, and they are defined later in the same
paragraph. We do not think we can pay little or no attention to the word   I
' relevant ' where it occurs in the first paragraph of para. 9. We preface
our consideration of the definition of relevant profits by noting that nowhere
in para. 9 is there any qualification, ' as computed for the purposes of the
foreign tax '; and that dividends are in fact paid out of profits available
for distribution and not out of a notional figure of assessment. (a) of the
definition provides that if the dividend is paid for a specified period, the

(1) (1925), 12 Tax Cas. 868.

A   relevant profits are the profits of that period. ' Specified period ' must mean an accounting period, and in many cases such a period will not be an assessment period. There is no provision for apportioning the figure of an assessment to an accounting period. In our view the ' relevant profits ' in this clause must be the profits available for distribution as shown by the accounts. (b) of the definition provides that if a dividend is not paid for

B   a specified period, but out of specified profits, the relevant profits are the specified profits. We think ' the specified profits ' must again be the profits available for distribution as shown by the accounts. (c) provides that if the dividend is paid neither for a specified period nor out of specified profits, the relevant profits are those of the last period for which accounts were made up ended before the dividend became payable. In this case it seems to us

C   inescapable that the relevant profits are those we have described above.

    " The proviso refers to ' profits available for distribution ' for the first time in para. 9. We do not think that the appearance of this phrase in this place creates any difficulty about our views of the definition of ' relevant profits '. For the above-mentioned reasons, we reject the [taxpayer company's] contention. The appeal fails, and we leave the amount of credit in

D   respect of foreign tax to be agreed."

They do not deal expressly with the second contention but they must obviously be taken to have rejected it. Counsel for the taxpayer company placed in the forefront of his argument the contention that " profits " could not possibly mean " profits available for distribution ", as the Special Commissioners held, since a distinction was drawn between them in the proviso, and counsel for the

E   Crown was, as it seemed to me, sufficiently impressed by this argument to feel obliged to attach some other description, such as " gross divisible profits ", to the word. For my part, I think that the proviso shows that " profits " in sub-para. (*a*) and sub-para. (*c*) mean " profits available for distribution ". When it is said that the profits available for distribution of period A are less than the dividend the relevant profits mean the profits of period A plus so much of

F   the profits available for distribution of period B as will equal the dividend, the legislature must have been adding like to like—profits available for distribution in period A to similar profits in period B. If it is asked why, then, did the paragraph not start off by saying that " profits " means " profits available for distribution" the answer surely is that such a definition would be quite inappropriate to sub-para. (*b*). One can only introduce the explanatory description

G   when one comes to the proviso which is dealing only with sub-paras. (*a*) and (*c*).

    This conclusion is not, of course, sufficient to dispose of the argument for the taxpayer company. The question still remains whether in the phrases " profits available for distribution of the period " in sub-para. (*a*) and sub-para. (*c*) and " dividend paid out of specified profits " in sub-para. (*b*) the profits available for distribution or the specified profits mean profits available for

H   distribution, or specified profits as shown by the accounts, or profits available for distribution or specified profits as shown in the tax assessment. To my mind, however, the former meaning is prima facie far more likely to have been meant than the latter. One is dealing with a situation in which a dividend has already been paid and is asking oneself, in effect, what proportion of the profits it represented. The profits shown in the accounts as available for distribution are the

I   funds out of which in reality the dividend was paid. The profits of the relevant period as adjusted for tax purposes might, in theory at least, have been insufficient to cover the dividend, yet it would actually have been paid. The conception of there being two sorts of profits available for distribution in the same period, one the profits shown in the accounts and the other the so-called " taxable profit ", is, I confess, too subtle for me. Further, I have great difficulty in seeing how the profits of some branch of the taxpayer company's activities out of which sub-para. (*b*) contemplates that a dividend may be paid can be anything else than the actual profits of that branch as appearing in the company's accounts.

This way—I dare say an oversimplified way—of looking at the position also, **A**
to my mind, disposes of the alternative contention of the taxpayer company.
There are not, as I see it, two funds of profits here, the accounts profits, only
part of which are taxed, and the assessed profits, all of which bear tax. What
are taxed are, I think, the company's profits for the year, whatever they may be;
but they are taxed according to a yardstick which may compute them at less
or more than they appear in the taxpayer company's accounts. For these **B**
reasons, which do not, I think, differ from those given by the Special Commissioners,
I am of opinion that the Special Commissioners were right and that the
appeal should be dismissed.

Appeal dismissed.

Solicitors: *Allen & Overy* (for the taxpayer company); *Solicitor of Inland*
Revenue. **C**

[*Reported by* F. A. AMIES, ESQ., *Barrister-at-Law.*]

CONWAY v. RIMMER AND ANOTHER.

[HOUSE OF LORDS (Lord Reid, Lord Morris of Borth-y-Gest, Lord Hodson, **D**
Lord Pearce and Lord Upjohn), October 25, 30, November 1, 2, 6, 7, 8, 9,
13, 14, 15, 16, 1967, February 28, 1968.]

Discovery—Production of documents—Privilege—Crown privilege—Disclosure
alleged to be injurious to the public interest—Probationary reports on pro-
bationer police constable—Report of superintendent of police to chief constable
for purpose of obtaining advice of Director of Public Prosecutions—Juris- **E**
diction of court to decide whether, on balance of public interests, document
should be disclosed—Certificate of Home Secretary not conclusive—Docu-
ments to be produced for inspection by the court.

The court has jurisdiction to order the disclosure of documents for which
Crown privilege is claimed, as it is the right and the duty of the court to
hold the balance between the interests of the public in ensuring the proper **F**
administration of justice and the public interest in the withholding of
documents whose disclosure would be contrary to the national interest;
accordingly, a Minister's certificate that disclosure of a class of documents
(or the contents of particular documents) would be injurious to the public
interest is not conclusive against disclosure, particularly where the privilege
is claimed for routine documents within a class of documents, though in a **G**
few instances (e.g., cabinet minutes*) the nature of the class of documents
may suffice to resist application for disclosure (see p. 888, letters C, E and
G, p. 889, letter I, p. 891, letter B, p. 900, letter G, p. 900, letter I, to p. 901,
letter A, p. 905, letter G, p. 910, letter H, p. 910, letter I, to p. 911, letter
A, and p. 914, letter C, E and I, post).

Robinson v. *State of South Australia* (*No. 2*) ([1931] All E.R. Rep. 333) and **H**
Glasgow Corpn. v. *Central Land Board* (1956 S.C. (H.L.) 1) applied.

Smith v. *East India Co.* ((1841), 1 Ph. 50); *Beatson* v. *Skene* ([1843-60]
All E.R. Rep. 882) and *Ankin* v. *L.N.E. Ry. Co.* ([1929] All E.R. Rep. 65)
disapproved.

Duncan v. *Cammell Laird & Co., Ltd.* ([1942] 1 All E.R. 587) not followed. **I**
In reaching a decision whether to order disclosure the court will give
full weight to a Minister's view; and, if the considerations are of such a
character as judicial experience is not competent to weigh, the Minister's
view will prevail, but where the conditions are not of that character, the
court will decide on balance whether the documents shall be disclosed to the
parties; and for this purpose the judge will generally be right to inspect
(per LORD MORRIS OF BORTH-Y-GEST, has power to inspect) the documents,

---

* Compare p. 902, letter C, post.

A   without their being shown to the parties, before reaching his decision (see p. 888, letter I, p. 900, letter H, p. 905, letter G, p. 907, letter E, p. 911, letter F, p. 914, letter G, p. 916, letter A, post; cf., p. 891, letter D, post).

Dictum of MARTIN, B., in *Beatson* v. *Skene* ([1843-60] All E.R. Rep. at p. 885) and of FIELD, J., in *Hennessy* v. *Wright* ((1888), 21 Q.B.D. at p. 512) applied.

B   Observations concerning the Crown's right of appeal (see p. 889, letter B, and p. 916, letter F, post).

In the locker of the appellant, a probationer police constable, another probationer constable found an electric torch. The latter reported to his superiors that this was his torch which he had lost. The respondent, a superintendent in the same constabulary, investigated the matter. In

C   the course of this he stated to the appellant that his probationary reports were adverse and urged him to resign, which the appellant refused to do. The respondent submitted a report to the chief constable with a view to advice being sought from the Director of Public Prosecutions whether to charge the appellant with theft. The respondent later charged* the appellant with theft of the torch. The appellant was tried and acquitted,

D   the jury stopping the case at the close of the prosecution's case. Another probationary report was prepared; it was not known by whom. Soon afterwards the appellant was dismissed from the force as unlikely to become an efficient police officer. He sued the superintendent for malicious prosecution. On discovery in the action the Home Secretary claimed Crown privilege for classes of documents which would include the probationary

E   reports (among which was a report from the Police Training Centre) relating to the appellant and the report leading to his prosecution.

Held: in the present instance it was most improbable that harm would be done by the disclosure of the probationary reports on the appellant, and it had not been suggested that disclosure of the contents of the report to the chief constable would be harmful after the appellant had been acquitted,

F   yet these reports might be of vital importance in the action; accordingly the production of the reports for the inspection of the court would be ordered, and, if it was then found that disclosure would not be prejudicial to the public interest, or that any such possible prejudice would be insufficient to justify non-disclosure, an order for disclosure of the reports should be made (see p. 889, letters F and H, p. 901, letter H, p. 906, letter E, p. 911,

G   letter H, p. 912, letter C, and p. 916, letter G, post).

Per LORD REID: the proper test whether, when privilege is claimed for a document as being one of a class of routine documents which it will be injurious to the public interest to disclose, is whether the withholding of the document is really necessary for the proper functioning of the public service (see p. 888, letter H, post).

H   Test stated by VISCOUNT SIMON, L.C., in *Duncan* v. *Cammell Laird & Co., Ltd.* ([1942] 1 All E.R. at p. 595, letter G.) adopted.

Decision of the COURT OF APPEAL ([1967] 2 All E.R. 1260) reversed.

[**Editorial Note.** The subject of Crown privilege was excluded from the recent report of the Law Reform Committee on Privilege in Civil Proceedings (Cmnd. 3472), the committee stating (para. 7) that it would be the subject of a

I   separate report. Section 28 (2) of the Crown Proceedings Act, 1947 (6 HALSBURY'S STATUTES (2nd Edn.) 66), is not legislative confirmation of the decision in *Duncan's* case (see p. 906, letter D, post).

As to privilege where disclosure of documents is contrary to public interest, see 12 HALSBURY'S LAWS (3rd Edn.) 53-55, para. 73; and for cases on the subject, see 18 DIGEST (Repl.) 139-142, *1256-1282*.]

---

* See the summary of facts in the report of the appeal to the Court of Appeal, [1967] 2 All E.R. at pp. 1263, 1264, particularly p. 1264, letter B.

Applied in D v NSPCC [1977] 1 All ER 589

Dictum of LORD REID at 888 applied in BURMAH OIL CO v BANK OF ENGLAND [1979] 2 All ER 461

Dicta of LORD REID at 880, 8[?] doubted in BURMAH OIL CO v BAN[?] OF ENGLAND [1979] 3 All ER 700

Cases referred to:

A   Queensland Pine Co. v. Commonwealth of Australia, [1920] St. R. Qd. 121;
       22 Digest (Repl.) 387, *2062.
    Robinson v. State of South Australia (No. 2), [1931] All E.R. Rep. 333; [1931]
       A.C. 704; 100 L.J.P.C. 183; 145 L.T. 408; 18 Digest (Repl.) 153, *635.
    Ronnfeldt v. Phillips, (1918), 34 T.L.R. 556; on appeal, C.A., 35 T.L.R. 46;
       17 Digest (Repl.) 420, 22.
B   Sheridan v. Peel, 1907 S.C. 577.
    Smith v. East India Co., (1841), 1 Ph. 50; 11 L.J.Ch. 71; 41 E.R. 550;
       18 Digest (Repl.) 142, 1276.
    Spigelman v. Hocker, Goldblatt v. Hocker, (1933), 50 T.L.R. 87; 150 L.T. 256;
       18 Digest (Repl.) 140, 1263.
    Stace v. Griffith, (1869), L.R. 2 P.C. 420; 6 Moo. P.C.C.N.S. 18; 20 L.T. 197;
C   16 E.R. 633; 32 Digest (Repl.) 133, 1543.
    United States v. Reynolds, [1952] 345 U.S. 1.
    Wadeer v. East India Co., (1856), 8 De G.M. & G. 182; 44 E.R. 360; sub nom.
       Coorg (Rajah) v. East India Co., 25 L.J.Ch. 345; sub nom. Veet Rajunder
       Wadeer (Ex Rajah of Coorg) v. East India Co., 27 L.T.O.S. 30; 18
       Digest (Repl.) 141, 1271.
D   West v. West, (1911), 27 T.L.R. 189, 476; 22 Digest (Repl.) 388, 4167.
    Whitehall v. Whitehall, 1957 S.C. 30; [1957] S.L.T. 96; Digest (Cont. Vol. A)
       492, *579a.
    Williams v. Star Newspaper Co., Ltd., (1908), 24 T.L.R. 297; 72 J.P.Jo. 65;
       22 Digest (Repl.) 386, 4153.
    Wyatt v. Gore, (1816), Holt. N.P. 299; 171 E.R. 250; 22 Digest (Repl.) 387,
E   4159.

Appeal.

   This was an appeal, by leave, by the appellant Michael David Conway, from
the order of the Court of Appeal (DAVIES and RUSSELL, L.JJ., LORD DENNING,
M.R., dissenting) dated June 8, 1967 and reported [1967] 2 All E.R. 1260,
dismissing the appeal of the appellant against the respondent, Thomas Rimmer,
F a former superintendent of police, from an order of BROWNE, J. (in chambers)
dated Feb. 23, 1967, whereby he allowed the appeals of the respondent and of
the Attorney-General from an order of Mr. District Registrar CUNLIFFE, dated
Nov. 24, 1966, that the respondent should produce for inspection five documents
in his list of documents, filed in the action brought by the appellant against the
respondent, for which documents Crown privilege was claimed.   The Attorney-
G General intervened in the litigation in support of the objection to production
of the documents and was second respondent in the appeal to the House of
Lords.   The facts are set out in the opinion of LORD REID.

   P. L. W. Owen, Q.C., and A. J. Price for the appellant.
   The Attorney-General (Sir Elwyn Jones, Q.C.) and Nigel Bridge for the Crown.
   Robin David for the respondent.

H Their lordships took time for consideration.

   Feb. 28.   The following opinions were delivered.

   LORD REID: My Lords, in April, 1963, the appellant became a probationer
police constable in the Cheshire Constabulary for a period of two years.   The
I respondent was a superintendent in that force.   In December, 1964, another
probationer constable lost an electric torch worth about 15s.   He found a torch
in the appellant's locker which he said was his torch and reported this to his
superiors.   The matter was investigated by the respondent.   The appellant
asserted that this torch was his torch.   In the course of the investigation the
respondent stated to the appellant that his probationary reports were adverse
and he urged him to resign.   The appellant refused.   The respondent then
prepared a report, which he submitted to the Chief Constable apparently with a
view to its being sent to the Director of Public Prosecutions for advice whether

Applied in WILLIAMS v HOME OFFICE
[1981] 1 All ER 1151   Dicta of LORD REID, LORD PEARCE
                                 and LORD UPJOHN at 888-889, 911,
                                 915-916 applied in CAMPBELL v   Applied in AIR CANADA v SECRETARY
                                 TAMESIDE MBC [1982] 2 All ER 791   OF STATE (No 2) [1983] 1 All ER 161

the appellant should be charged with theft of the torch.   We do not know what **A**
advice was received from the Director of Public Prosecutions, but after a short
time the respondent was instrumental in bringing a charge of larceny against
the appellant.   He was tried at quarter sessions in Chester and the respondent
gave evidence.   At the close of the prosecution case the jury stopped the case
and returned a verdict of not guilty.   Shortly thereafter another probationary
report was prepared—by whom we do not know—and then the appellant was **B**
dismissed.   He had no right of appeal.

The appellant now sues the respondent for damages for malicious prosecution.
He says that as a result of these events he has found it impossible to obtain
suitable employment.   On discovery of documents being sought the existence
of five documents was disclosed.   Both the appellant and the respondent have
stated to your lordships through their counsel that they wish these documents **C**
to be produced, but production has been withheld on the ground of Crown
privilege.   These documents are (i) and (iii) " probationary reports " on the
appellant dated Jan. 1, and July 21, 1964; (ii) a report on the appellant by a
District Police Training Centre; (iv) a report by the respondent to his chief
constable of Jan. 13, 1965, which admittedly was the report prepared for submission to the Director of Public Prosecutions, and (v) a probationary report **D**
on the appellant dated Apr. 9, 1965.   None of the contents of these documents
has ever been disclosed to the appellant.   These documents may be of crucial
importance in this action.   The appellant has to prove both malice and want of
probable cause.   If the probationary reports were favourable that may tell
strongly in favour of the appellant on the question of malice, if they were unfavourable and were not prepared by the respondent they will tell strongly **E**
against the appellant on this issue.   The respondent's report to the chief constable may well be decisive in the question of want of probable cause.   If the
respondent included in the report all relevant facts known to him and if no
further relevant facts became known to him between the making of the report
and the making of the charge, then advice by the Director of Public Prosecutions
that prosecution would be justified would make it practically impossible to **F**
establish want of probable cause.   If, however, relevant facts known to the
respondent were not included the position would be very different.

Production of these documents has been refused by reason of an affidavit
sworn by the Home Secretary on July 15, 1966, which is as follows:

" I, The Right Honourable Roy Harris Jenkins, one of Her Majesty's
principal secretaries of state, make oath and say as follows: **G**

" 1.   On or about June 3, 1966, my attention was drawn to a copy of a
list of documents delivered in these proceedings on behalf of the [appellant]
and to the documents referred to in the second part of Sch. 1 to the said list
of documents being numbered therein 38; 39; 40; 47 and 48.

" 2. I personally examined and carefully considered all the said documents
and I formed the view that those numbered 38; 39; 40 and 48 fell within **H**
a class of documents comprising confidential reports by police officers to
chief officers of police relating to the conduct, efficiency and fitness for
employment of individual police officers under their command and that the
said document numbered 47 fell within a class of documents comprising
reports by police officers to their superiors concerning investigations into the
commission of crime.   In my opinion the production of documents of each
such class would be injurious to the public interest.

" 3.   Accordingly I gave instructions that Crown privilege was to be
claimed for the said documents and by letter dated June 7, 1966, from the
Treasury Solicitor, the [appellant's] solicitors were so informed.

" 4.   I have been informed of an order made by this honourable court
in these proceedings on June 9, 1966, that the said above-numbered documents should be produced as therein mentioned unless an affidavit sworn
by me should be filed in these proceedings on or before July 21, 1966.

Considered in AIR CANADA v SECRE-
TARY OF STATE (No 2) 1 All ER 910

Dictum of LORD REID at 888 doubted
in AIR CANADA v SECRETARY OF
STATE (No 2) [1983] 1 All ER 910

Dicta of L
PEARCE at 8
CANADA v SE
[1983] 1 All E

A   " 5. I object to the production of each of the said documents on the
grounds set forth in paragraph 2 of this affidavit."

The question whether such a statement by a Minister of the Crown should be
accepted as conclusively preventing any court from ordering production of
any of the documents to which it applies is one of very great importance in the
administration of justice. If the commonly accepted interpretation of the
B   decision of this house in *Duncan* v. *Cammell Laird & Co., Ltd.* (1) is to remain
authoritative the question admits of only one answer—the Minister's statement
is final and conclusive. Normally I would be very slow to question the authority
of a unanimous decision of this House only twenty-five years old which was
carefully considered and obviously intended to lay down a general rule. But
this decision has several abnormal features. VISCOUNT SIMON, L.C., thought
C   that on this matter the law in Scotland was the same as the law in England,
and he clearly intended to lay down a rule applicable to the whole of the United
Kingdom. In *Glasgow Corpn.* v. *Central Land Board* (2), however, this House
held that that was not so, with the result that today on this question the law is
different in the two countries. There are many chapters of the law where for
historical and other reasons it is quite proper that the law should be different in
D   the two countries; but here we are dealing purely with public policy—with
the proper relation between the powers of the executive and the powers of the
courts—and I can see no rational justification for the law on this matter being
different in the two countries. Secondly, events have proved that the rule
supposed to have been laid down in *Duncan's* case (1) is far from satisfactory.
In the large number of cases in England and elsewhere which have been cited
E   in argument much dissatisfaction has been expressed, and I have not observed
even one expression of whole-hearted approval. Moreover, a statement made
by VISCOUNT KILMUIR, L.C., in 1956 on behalf of the government, to which I
shall return later, makes it clear that that government did not regard it as
consonant with public policy to maintain the rule to the full extent which existing
authorities had held to be justifiable.
F   I have no doubt that the case of *Duncan* v. *Cammell Laird & Co., Ltd.* (1)
was rightly decided. The plaintiff sought discovery of documents relating to
the submarine Thetis including a contract for the hull and machinery and plans
and specifications. The First Lord of the Admiralty had stated that " it would
be injurious to the public interest that any of the said documents should be
disclosed to any person ". Any of these documents might well have given
G   valuable information, or at least clues, to the skilled eye of an agent of a foreign
power; but LORD SIMON took the opportunity to deal with the whole question
of the right of the Crown to prevent production of documents in a litigation.
Yet a study of his speech leaves me with the strong impression that throughout
he had primarily in mind cases where discovery or disclosure would involve a
danger of real prejudice to the national interest. I find it difficult to believe
H   that his speech would have been the same if the case had related, as the present
case does, to discovery of routine reports on a probationer constable. Early
in his speech LORD SIMON quoted (3) with approval the view of RIGBY, L.J. (4),
that documents are not to be withheld "... unless there be some plain over-
ruling principle of public interest concerned which cannot be disregarded ".
Summing up towards the end, he said (5):

I   " The rule that the interest of the State must not be put in jeopardy
by producing documents which would injure it is a principle to be observed
in administering justice, quite unconnected with the interests or claims of
the particular parties in litigation ..."

(1) [1942] 1 All E.R. 587; [1942] A.C. 624.   (2) 1956 S.C. (H.L.) 1.
(3) [1942] 1 All E.R. at p. 591; [1942] A.C. at p. 633.
(4) In *A.-G.* v. *Newcastle-upon-Tyne Corpn.*, [1895-99] All E.R. Rep. 747 at p. 750;
[1897] 2 Q.B. 384 at p. 395.
(5) [1942] 1 All E.R. 587 at p. 595, letter C; [1942] A.C. at p. 642.

Surely it would be grotesque to speak of the interest of the State being put in   A
jeopardy by disclosure of a routine report on a probationer. LORD SIMON
did not say very much about objections (6)

> ". . . based upon the view that the public interest requires a particular
> class of communications with, or within, a public department to be pro-
> tected from production on the ground that the candour and completeness
> of such communications might be prejudiced if they were ever liable to be   B
> disclosed in subsequent litigation rather than upon the contents of the
> particular document itself."

At the end he said that a Minister (7)

> ". . . ought not to take the responsibility of withholding production
> except in cases where the public interest would otherwise be damnified,   C
> e.g., where disclosure would be injurious to national defence, or to good
> diplomatic relations, or where the practice of keeping a class of documents
> secret is necessary for the proper functioning of the public service."

I find it difficult to believe that he would have put these three examples on the
same level if he had intended the third to cover such minor matters as a routine
report by a relatively junior officer. My impression is strengthened by the   D
passage at the very end of the speech (8)—

> ". . . the public interest is also the interest of every subject of the realm,
> and while, in these exceptional cases, the private citizen may seem to be
> denied what is to his immediate advantage, he, like the rest of us, would
> suffer if the needs of protecting the interests of the country as a whole were   E
> not ranked as a prior obligation."

Would he have spoken of " these exceptional cases " or of " the needs of protecting the interests of the country as a whole " if he had intended to include all
manner of routine communications? Did he really mean that the protection
of such communications is a " prior obligation " in a case where a man's reputation or fortune is at stake and withholding the document makes it impossible   F
for justice to be done?

It is universally recognised that here there are two kinds of public interest
which may clash. There is the public interest that harm shall not be done to
the nation or the public service by disclosure of certain documents, and there
is the public interest that the administration of justice shall not be frustrated
by the withholding of documents which must be produced if justice is to be done.   G
There are many cases where the nature of the injury which would or might be
done to the nation or the public service is of so grave a character that no other
interest, public or private, can be allowed to prevail over it. With regard to
such cases it would be proper to say, as LORD SIMON did, that to order production
of the document in question would put the interest of the state in jeopardy;
but there are many other cases where the possible injury to the public service   H
is much less and there one would think that it would be proper to balance the
public interests involved. I do not believe that LORD SIMON really meant that
the smallest probability of injury to the public service must always outweigh
the gravest frustration of the administration of justice.

It is to be observed that, in a passage which I have already quoted, LORD
SIMON referred to the practice of keeping a class of documents secret being   I
"*necessary* (my italics) for the proper functioning of the public interest". But
the certificate of the Home Secretary in the present case does not go nearly so
far as that. It merely says that the production of a document of the classes
to which it refers would be " injurious to the public interest ": it does not say
what degree of injury is to be apprehended. It may be advantageous to the

---

(6) [1942] 1 All E.R. at p. 592; [1942] A.C. at p. 635.
(7) [1942] 1 All E.R. at p. 595, letter G; [1942] A.C. at p. 642.
(8) [1942] 1 All E.R. at pp. 595, 596; [1942] A.C. at p. 643.

A functioning of the public service that reports of this kind should be kept secret—
that is the view of the Home Secretary—but I would be very surprised if anyone
said that that was necessary.

There are now many large public bodies, such as British Railways, and the
National Coal Board, the proper and efficient functioning of which is very
necessary for many reasons, including the safety of the public. The Attorney-
B General made it clear that Crown privilege is not and cannot be invoked to
prevent disclosure of similar documents made by them or their servants, even
if it were said that this is required for the proper and efficient functioning of that
public service. I find it difficult to see why it should be *necessary* to withhold
whole classes of routine " communications with or within a public department ",
but quite unnecessary to withhold similar communications with or within a
C public corporation. There the safety of the public may well depend on the
candour and completeness of reports made by subordinates, whose duty it is
to draw attention to defects. So far as I know, however, no one has ever
suggested that public safety has been endangered by the candour or completeness of such reports having been inhibited by the fact that they may have to
be produced if the interests of the due administration of justice should ever
D require production at any time.

I must turn now to a statement made by VISCOUNT KILMUIR, L.C., in this
House on June 6, 1956. When counsel proposed to read this statement your
lordships had doubts, which I shared, as to its admissibility; but we did permit it
to be read, and, as the argument proceeded, its importance emerged. With a
minor amendment made on Mar. 8, 1962, it appears still to operate as a direction
E to, or at least a guide for, Ministers who swear affidavits. So we may assume that
in the present case the Home Secretary acted in accordance with the views
expressed in LORD KILMUIR's statement. The statement sets out the grounds
on which Crown privilege is to be claimed. Having set out the first ground
that disclosure of the contents of the particular document would injure the
public interest, it proceeds:

F   " The second ground is that the document falls within a class which the
      public interest requires to be withheld from production, and LORD SIMON
      particularised this head of public interest as ' the proper functioning of the
      public service '."

There is no reference to LORD SIMON's exhortation, which I have already quoted,
that a Minister ought not to take the responsibility of withholding production of a
G class of documents except where the practice of keeping a class of documents
secret is necessary for the proper functioning of the public service. Then the
statement proceeds:

      " The reason why the law sanctions the claiming of Crown privilege on the
      ' class ' ground is the need to secure freedom and candour of communications
H   with and within the public service, so that government decisions can be
      taken on the best advice and with the fullest information. In order to
      secure this it is necessary that the class of documents to which privilege
      applies should be clearly settled, so that the person giving advice or informa-
      tion should know that he is doing so in confidence. Any system whereby a
      document falling within the class might, as a result of a later decision, be
I   required to be produced in evidence, would destroy that confidence and
      undermine the whole basis of class privilege, because there would be no
      certainty at the time of writing that the document would not be disclosed."

But later in the statement, the position taken is very different. A number of
cases are set out in which Crown privilege should not be claimed. The most
important for present purposes is:

      " We propose that if medical documents, or indeed other documents, are
      relevant to the defence in criminal proceedings, Crown privilege should not
      be claimed."

The only exception specifically mentioned is statements by informers. That is **A** a very wide-ranging exception, for the Attorney-General stated that it applied at least to all manner of routine communications and even to prosecutions for minor offences. Thus it can no longer be said that the writer of such communications has any " certainty at the time of writing that the document would not be disclosed ". So we have the curious result that " freedom and candour of communication " is supposed not to be inhibited by knowledge of the writer **B** that his report may be disclosed in a criminal case, but would still be supposed to be inhibited if he thought that his report might be disclosed in a civil case.

The Attorney-General did not deny that, even where the full contents of a report have already been made public in a criminal case, Crown privilege is still claimed for that report in a later civil case; and he was quite candid about the reason for that. Crown privilege is claimed in the civil case not to protect **C** the document—its contents are already public property—but to protect the writer from civil liability should he be sued for libel or other tort. No doubt the government have weighed the danger that knowledge of such protection might encourage malicious writers against the advantage that honest reporters shall not be subjected to vexatious actions, and have come to the conclusion that it is an advantage to the public service to afford this protection; but it **D** seems very far removed from the original purpose of Crown privilege.

The statement, as it has been explained to us, makes clear another point. The Minister who withholds production of a " class " document has no duty to consider the degree of public interest involved in a particular case by frustrating in that way the due administration of justice. If it is in the public interest in his view to withhold documents of that class, then it matters not whether the **E** result of withholding a document is merely to deprive a litigant of some evidence on a minor issue in a case of little importance, or on the other hand is to make it impossible to do justice at all in a case of the greatest importance. I cannot think that it is satisfactory that there should be no means at all of weighing, in any civil case, the public interest involved in withholding the document against the public interest that it should be produced. So it appears to me that the **F** present position is so unsatisfactory that this House must re-examine the whole question in light of the authorities.

Two questions will arise: first, whether the court is to have any right to question the finality of a Minister's certificate and, secondly, if it has such a right, how and in what circumstances that right is to be exercised and made effective.

A Minister's certificate may be given on one or other of two grounds: either **G** because it would be against the public interest to disclose the contents of the particular document or documents in question, or because the document belongs to a class of documents which ought to be withheld whether or not there is anything in the particular document in question disclosure of which would be against the public interest. It does not appear that any serious difficulties have arisen or are likely to arise with regard to the first class. However wide the power of the **H** court may be held to be, cases would be very rare in which it could be proper to question the view of the responsible Minister that it would be contrary to the public interest to make public the contents of a particular document. A question might arise whether it would be possible to separate those parts of a document of which disclosure would be innocuous from those parts which ought not to be made public, but I need not pursue that question now. In the present case your **I** lordships are directly concerned with the second class of documents.

I shall not deal with the early cases because in most, if not all, of them the documents in question were of a political character or at least of a more important character than ordinary routine reports and communications. I shall deal with such documents later. The first case directly relevant here is *Smith* v. *East India Co.* (9). There the documents related to a claim of a commercial character: they were said to be confidential having passed between the court of directors

(9) (1841), 1 Ph. 50.

A of the company and the British government commissioners for the affairs of India. LORD LYNDHURST, L.C., said (10):

> " Now, it is quite obvious that public policy requires, and, looking to the Act of Parliament, it is quite clear that the legislature intended, that the most unreserved communication should take place between the East India Co. and the Board of Control, that it should be subject to no restraints or limitations; but it is also quite obvious that if, at the suit of a particular individual, those communications should be subject to be produced in a court of justice, the effect of that would be to restrain the freedom of the communications, and to render them more cautious, guarded and reserved. I think, therefore, that these communications come within that class of official communications which are privileged, inasmuch as they cannot be subject to be communicated, without infringing the policy of the Act of Parliament and without injury to the public interests."

The functions of government in India were divided between the company and the Board of Control, so many of the communications between them must have been of a political character and it cannot be right to order production of a document of that character. At first sight it is not obvious why LORD LYNDHURST did not distinguish between documents of that character and others which were of a different character. We now know and LORD LYNDHURST's long political experience must have made him aware, however, that relations between the board and the company were sometimes strained; so it is quite possible that disclosure of non-political documents might have afforded political ammunition to those who criticised this system of government. We do not know what LORD LYNDHURST had in mind but he chose to rely on the reason which I have quoted, and thereby he set a fashion so that in some later cases, where there were in fact much better reasons, this reason alone was relied on.

The next important case is *Beatson* v. *Skene* (11); there the plaintiff, suing for slander arising during operations in the Crimean War, sought production of correspondence with the Secretary for War and of minutes of a court of inquiry. This was refused. POLLOCK, C.B., said (12):

> " We are all of opinion that it cannot be laid down that all public documents of every sort, including treaties with foreign powers, and all the correspondence that may precede or accompany them, and all communications to the heads of departments, are to be produced and made public whenever a suitor in a court of justice thinks that his case requires such production. It is manifest, we think, that there must be a limit to the duty or the power of compelling the production of papers which are connected with acts of State . . . We are of opinion that, if the production of a State paper would be injurious to the public service, the general public interest must be considered paramount to the individual interest of a suitor in a court of justice; and the question then arises, How is this to be determined? It is manifest it must be determined either by the presiding judge or by the responsible servant of the Crown in whose custody the paper is. The judge would be unable to determine it without ascertaining what the document was, and why the publication of it would be injurious to the public service—an inquiry which cannot take place in private, and which taking place in public may do all the mischief which it is proposed to guard against."

Here again disclosure of these documents might well have had political or public repercussions, looking to the intense criticism of the mismanagement of the Crimean War. I do not think that anyone had in mind documents of a routine character. Where public or political consequences of disclosure are apprehended,

---

(10) (1841), 1 Ph. at p. 55.
(11) [1843-60] All E.R. Rep. 882; (1860), 5 H. & N. 838.
(12) [1843-60] All E.R. Rep. at pp. 884, 885; (1860), 5 H. & N. at pp. 852, 853.

POLLOCK, C.B., was obviously right in saying that the Minister is the best judge. A
It does not follow, however, that the same is true if the only objection to publication is apprehension that makers of similar documents will be less candid if they
have to contemplate possible publication of their reports.

In *H.M.S. Bellerophon* (13) there had been a collision between H.M.S. Bellerophon and the plaintiff's vessel. It was the duty of the commanding officer to
report the collision to the Admiralty " with or without remarks as he may think B
fit ". The plaintiff sought discovery of this report. It was objected that this would
be prejudicial to the public service and this objection was upheld on the authority
of *Beatson* v. *Skene* (14). We do not know whether the report contained any such
" remarks ". If it did, it may well have been right to withhold it; but if it was a
purely factual report, I find it difficult to see how the candour of naval officers
in reporting facts could be inhibited by any fear that this report might be C
published.

In *Hennessy* v. *Wright* (15) the documents were state papers passing between
the governor of Mauritius and the Colonial Office; but even so WILLS, J., did not
rule out the possibility that they might be required to be produced at the trial.
About that time there was a number of cases where discovery was refused on the
ground that " the judge could not take it upon himself to say that it was not D
injurious to the public service to order the document to be produced " (per
LORD ESHER, M.R., in *Hughes* v. *Vargas* (16)).

In *Williams* v. *Star Newspaper Co., Ltd.* (17), the Home Office successfully
objected to the production of a report regarding a post mortem examination
by Sir T. Stevenson, but apparently did not object to his giving evidence as to
what he had found; and the same course was taken by the War Office in *Anthony* E
v. *Anthony* (18). No doubt if a report contains more than a statement of the
facts there may be reasons at least for withholding that part which ought not to
be disclosed, but I fail to see what public interest is served by permitting evidence
to be given but withholding the contemporary report of the witness about the
facts. If it is really against the public interest that the facts should be disclosed,
then it may be proper to prevent the witness from giving any evidence about them F
as was done in *West* v. *West* (19), and *Chatterton* v. *Secretary of State for India
in Council* (20).

In *Re Joseph Hargreaves, Ltd.* (21), the Inland Revenue objected to producing
documents submitted to them in connexion with income tax. That seems to me
to have nothing to do with candour. If the State insists on a man disclosing his
private affairs for a particular purpose, it requires a very strong case to justify G
that disclosure being used for other purposes.

In *Ankin* v. *London and North Eastern Ry. Co.* (22), it was a statutory requirement that railway companies should send notice of any accident to the Minister
of Transport. The Minister objected to such a notice being disclosed saying that
such notices

" are furnished for his own information and guidance in the performance H
of his duties, and that their utility in this respect might be prejudiced if they
were compiled by railway companies with the knowledge that any information
contained in them might be used by individual members of the public for the
purpose of prosecuting their private claims against the railway companies
concerned."

SCRUTTON, L.J., said (23):   I

---

(13) (1874), 44 L.J.Adm. 5; 31 L.T. 756.
(14) [1843-60] All E.R. Rep. 882; (1860), 5 H. & N. 838.
(15) (1888), 21 Q.B.D. 509.   (16) (1893), 9 T.L.R. 551.
(17) (1908), 24 T.L.R. 297.   (18) (1919), 35 T.L.R. 559.
(19) (1911), 27 T.L.R. 476.
(20) [1895-99] All E.R. Rep. 1035; [1895] 2 Q.B. 189.
(21) [1900] 1 Ch. 347.
(22) [1929] All E.R. Rep. 65; [1930] 1 K.B. 527.
(23) [1930] 1 K.B. at p. 533; [1929] All E.R. Rep. at p. 67.

A   " It is the practice of the English courts to accept the statement of one
of His Majesty's Ministers that production of a particular document would
be against the public interest, even though the court may doubt whether any
harm would be done by producing it."

Ankin's case (24) is a good example of what happens if the courts abandon all
control of this matter.   It was surely far fetched, and indeed insulting to the
B   managements of railway companies, to suggest that in performing their statutory
duty they might withhold information from the Minister because it might be
disclosed later in legal proceedings.   Moreover, if LORD KILMUIR's statement (25)
means, as I think it does, that Crown privilege is not now claimed for such reports
in criminal cases, that illustrates the flimsiness of this reason.   These reports
relate to accidents, and it is inconceivable that the government would agree to
C   disclose them if that disclosure was really liable to prejudice the public safety
by creating a risk that future reports would not contain full and accurate
information.

The last important case before *Duncan's* case (26) was *Robinson* v. *State of
South Australia (No. 2)* (27).   The state government had assumed the function
of acquiring and marketing all wheat grown in the state and distributing the
D   proceeds to the growers.   A number of actions was brought alleging negligence
in carrying out this function.   The Australian courts had upheld objections by
the state to discovery of a mass of documents in their possession.   For reasons
into which I need not enter, the Privy Council could not finally decide the matter.
What they did was (28):

E   ". . . to remit the case to the Supreme Court of South Australia with a
direction that it is a proper one for the exercise by that court of its power of
itself inspecting the documents for which privilege is set up in order to see
whether the claim is justified.   Their lordships have already given reasons for
their conclusion that the court is possessed of such a power."

This case was of course dealt with in *Duncan's* case (26), but not, I venture to
F   think, in a very satisfactory way.   LORD SIMON said that (29): " Their lordships'
conclusion was partly based on their interpretation of a rule of court . . .".   In
fact it was not.   The passage which I have quoted occurs in the judgment before
there is any reference to the rule of court.   Beyond that LORD SIMON said no more
than (29) " I cannot agree with this view ".   So he thought that, even where
discovery is sought in an action against the State arising out of what was in effect
G   a commercial transaction, the view of the Minister is conclusive.   LORD KILMUIR's
statement, however, promised a considerable relaxation in contract cases.

I shall not examine the earlier Scottish authorities in detail because the position
in Scotland has now been made clear in the *Glasgow Corpn.* case (30), where the
earlier authorities were fully considered.   VISCOUNT SIMONDS said (31):

H   " In the course of the present appeal we have had the advantage of an
exhaustive examination of the relevant law from the earliest times, and it
has left me in no doubt that there always has been and is now in the law of
Scotland an inherent power of the court to override the Crown's objection to
produce documents on the ground that it would injure the public interest
to do so."

I   Now I must examine the English cases since 1942.   In *Ellis* v. *Home Office* (32),

---

(24) [1929] All E.R. Rep. 65; [1930] 1 K.B. 527.
(25) See p. 881, letter I, ante.
(26) [1942] 1 All E.R. 587; [1942] A.C. 624.
(27) [1931] All E.R. Rep. 333; [1931] A.C. 704.
(28) [1931] All E.R. Rep. at p. 341; [1931] A.C. at p. 723.
(29) [1942] 1 All E.R. at p. 595; [1942] A.C. at p. 641.
(30) 1956 S.C. (H.L.) 1.
(31) 1956 S.C. (H.L.) at p. 11.
(32) [1953] 2 All E.R. 149; [1953] 2 Q.B. 135.

Crown privilege had been asserted to such an extent as to cause DEVLIN, J., and the Court of Appeal to express great uneasiness and this led to the making of LORD KILMUIR'S statement in 1956 (33). In *Broome* v. *Broome* (*Edmundson cited*) (34), a wife sought divorce on the ground of cruelty. There had been some investigation by a representative of the Soldiers' Sailors' and Airmen's Families Association. It was sought to recover documents made by that representative. The Secretary of State for War certified:

"I am of opinion that it is not in the public interest that the documents should be produced or the evidence of Mrs. Allsop [the representative of S.S.A.F.A.] given orally."

Admittedly that association and its representatives were neither servants nor agents of the Crown. SACHS, J., said (35):

"In relation to the present case the claim involves the extension or development of Crown privilege in three separate directions, viz., (i) as to the all embracing nature of the evidence privileged [for previous claims in this form have related only to documents], (ii) as to the person affected [the claim referred to all witnesses, as opposed to classes of witnesses], and (iii) as to the heads of public interest [the head here asserted being the maintenance of the morale of the forces]."

Then he said (36):

"It is of obvious importance to ensure generally that claims of Crown privilege are not used unnecessarily to the detriment of the vital need of the courts to have the truth put before them; and the facts of the present case well illustrate how easily it can be sought unnecessarily, albeit in the utmost good faith, to make such a claim."

He allowed Mrs. Allsop to be examined and said (36):

"On all these points her evidence was of assistance to the court; on none of them was there any apparent cause for any intervention in the name of Crown privilege."

The position of the same association was considered in *Whitehall* v. *Whitehall* (37). There the letter which the Minister sought to suppress had already been produced in process. I need not consider the procedural difficulties which emerged. The Lord President (LORD CLYDE) said (38):

"Public interest may in certain circumstances entitle a Minister to prevent the courts seeing documents which are in his department's possession or have emanated from his department, but it would be a quite intolerable extension of this privilege were he able, where no question of national safety is involved, to intervene in litigations between private individuals . . ."

I think it may be too narrow to limit the exception to "national safety". LORD RUSSELL referred (39) to disclosure being injurious to the safety of the realm or affecting diplomatic relations or revealing state secrets or matters of high state policy. LORD SORN said (40):

"The proposition therefore is that the Crown can select any institution which serves the public, or a section of it, and throw a protective veil of secrecy over its internal communings—and even the letters it writes to individuals—by means of a ministerial certificate."

---

(33) See p. 881, letters F, H and I, ante.
(34) [1955] 1 All E.R. 201; [1955] P. 190.
(35) [1955] 1 All E.R. at p. 206; [1955] P. at p. 200.
(36) [1955] 1 All E.R. at p. 207; [1955] P. at p. 201.
(37) 1957 S.C. 30.
(38) 1957 S.C. at p. 39.
(39) 1957 S.C. at p. 40.
(40) 1957 S.C. at p. 43.

A That was a proposition which he was not prepared to accept.

Gain v. *Gain* (41) was a petition for divorce. A surgeon commander was called to give evidence about the husband's condition five years earlier. The husband's solicitor had a copy of a report about this which the witness had made in the course of his duty. The Admiralty claimed Crown privilege for the report. Apparently no objection was made to the witness giving evidence about what he

B had seen and heard when examining the husband, but, on the motion of counsel for the Crown, the witness was prevented from looking at the copy of his report in order to refresh his memory. This was inevitable as the law stood: if a document is protected by Crown privilege the court is powerless and secondary evidence of its contents cannot be given. But the result is little short of being ridiculous. There was no question of requiring the Admiralty to produce any document

C in their possession: the contents were already known; and there was no question of its being against the public interest for the witness to give the facts which he had observed. The only result of the attitude taken up by the Admiralty was to deprive the court of the most reliable account of those facts with no profit to anyone. There must be something wrong with a rule which permits Crown privilege to be asserted in this way.

D These cases open up a new field which must be kept in view when considering whether a Minister's certificate is to be regarded as conclusive. I do not doubt that it is proper to prevent the use of any document, wherever it comes from, if disclosure of its contents would really injure the national interest, and I do not doubt that it is proper to prevent any witness, whoever he may be, from disclosing facts which in the national interest ought not to be disclosed. Moreover, it is the

E duty of the court to do this without the intervention of any Minister if possible serious injury to the national interest is readily apparent. In this field, however, it is more than ever necessary that in a doubtful case the alleged public interest in concealment should be balanced against the public interest that the administration of justice should not be frustrated. If the Minister, who has no duty to balance these conflicting public interests, says no more than that in his opinion the public

F interest requires concealment, and if that is to be accepted as conclusive in this field as well as with regard to documents in his possession, it seems to me not only that very serious injustice may be done to the parties, but also that the due administration of justice may be gravely impaired for quite inadequate reasons.

It cannot be said that there would be any constitutional impropriety in enabling the court to overrule a Minister's objection. That is already the law in

G Scotland. In commonwealth jurisdictions from which there is an appeal to the Privy Council the courts generally follow *Robinson's* case (42), and, where they do not, they follow *Duncan's* case (43) with reluctance; and a limited citation of authority from the United States seems to indicate the same trend. I observe that in *United States* v. *Reynolds* (44), VINSON, C.J., in delivering the opinion of the Supreme Court said:

H " Regardless of how it is articulated, some like formula of compromise must be applied here. Judicial control over the evidence in a case cannot be abdicated to the caprice of executive officers. Yet we will not go so far as to say that the court may automatically require a complete disclosure to the judge before the claim of privilege will be accepted in any case. It may be possible to satisfy the court, from all the circumstances of the case, that there is a reasonable danger that compulsion of the evidence will expose

I military matters which, in the interest of national security, should not be divulged. When this is the case, the occasion for the privilege is appropriate, and the court should not jeopardize the security which the privilege is meant to protect by insisting upon an examintion of the evidence, even by the judge alone in chambers."

---

(41) [1962] 1 All E.R. 63.   (42) [1931] All E.R. Rep. 333; [1931] A.C. 704.
(43) [1942] 1 All E.R. 587; [1942] A.C. 624.   (44) [1952] 345 U.S. 1.

LORD SIMON did not say that courts in England have no power to overrule the A executive. He said in *Duncan's* case (45):

" The decision ruling out such documents is the decision of the judge . . .
It is the judge who is in control of the trial, not the executive, but the proper
ruling for the judge to give is as above expressed."

I.e., to accept the Minister's view in every case. In my judgment, in considering B what it is " proper " for a court to do we must have regard to the need, shown by twenty-five years' experience since *Duncan's* case (46), that the courts should balance the public interest in the proper administration of justice against the public interest in withholding any evidence which a Minister considers ought to be withheld.

I would therefore propose that the House ought now to decide that courts C have and are entitled to exercise a power and duty to hold a balance between the public interest, as expressed by a Minister, to withhold certain documents or other evidence, and the public interest in ensuring the proper administration of justice. That does not mean that a court would reject a Minister's view: full weight must be given to it in every case, and if the Minister's reasons are of a character which judicial experience is not competent to weigh then the Minister's D view must prevail; but experience has shown that reasons given for withholding whole classes of documents are often not of that character. For example a court is perfectly well able to assess the likelihood that, if the writer of a certain class of document knew that there was a chance that his report might be produced in legal proceedings, he would make a less full and candid report than he would otherwise have done.

I do not doubt that there are certain classes of documents which ought not to E be disclosed whatever their content may be. Virtually everyone agrees that cabinet minutes and the like ought not to be disclosed until such time as they are only of historical interest; but I do not think that many people would give as the reason that premature disclosure would prevent candour in the cabinet. To my mind the most important reason is that such disclosure would create or fan ill-informed or captious public or political criticism. The business of government F is difficult enough as it is, and no government could contemplate with equanimity the inner workings of the government machine being exposed to the gaze of those ready to criticise without adequate knowledge of the background and perhaps with some axe to grind. That must in my view also apply to all documents concerned with policy making within departments including it may be minutes and the like by quite junior officials and correspondence with outside bodies. Further, G it may be that deliberations about a particular case require protection as much as deliberations about policy. I do not think that it is possible to limit such documents by any definition; but there seems to me to be a wide difference between such documents and routine reports. There may be special reasons for withholding some kinds of routine documents, but I think that the proper test to be applied is to ask, in the language of LORD SIMON in *Duncan's* case (47), whether the H withholding of a document because it belongs to a particular class is really " necessary for the proper functioning of the public service ".

It appears to me that, if the Minister's reasons are such that a judge can properly weigh them, he must on the other hand consider what is the probable importance in the case before him of the documents or other evidence sought to be withheld. If he decides that on balance the documents probably ought to be produced, I think that it would generally be best that he should see them before ordering production and, if he thinks that the Minister's reasons are not clearly expressed, he will have to see the documents before ordering production. I can see nothing wrong in the judge seeing documents without their being shown to

(45) [1942] 1 All E.R. at p. 595; [1942] A.C. at p. 642.
(46) [1942] 1 All E.R. 587; [1942] A.C. 624.
(47) [1942] 1 All E.R. at p. 595, letter G; [1942] A.C. at p. 642.

A the parties. LORD SIMON said in *Duncan's* case (48) that, where the Crown is a party, this would amount to communicating with one party to the exclusion of the other. I do not agree. The parties see the Minister's reasons. Where a document has not been prepared for the information of the judge, it seems to me a misuse of language to say that the judge " communicates with " the holder of the document by reading it. If on reading the document he still thinks that it
B ought to be produced, he will order its production.

It is important, however, that the Minister should have a right to appeal before the document is produced. This matter was not fully investigated in the argument before your lordships; but it does appear that in one way or another there can be an appeal if the document is in the custody of a servant of the Crown or of a person who is willing to co-operate with the Minister. There may be difficulty
C if it is in the hands of a person who wishes to produce it. That difficulty, however, could occur today if a witness wishes to give some evidence which the Minister unsuccessfully urges the court to prevent from being given. It may be that this is a matter which deserves further investigation by the Crown authorities.

The documents in this case are in the possession of a police force. The position of the police is peculiar. They are not servants of the Crown and they do not take
D orders from the government. But they are carrying out an essential function of government, and various Crown rights, privileges and exemptions have been held to apply to them. Their position was explained in *Coomber* v. *Berkshire Justices* (49) and cases there cited. It has never been denied that they are entitled to Crown privilege with regard to documents, and it is essential that they should have it.

E The police are carrying on an unending war with criminals many of whom are today highly intelligent. So it is essential that there should be no disclosure of anything which might give any useful information to those who organise criminal activities; and it would generally be wrong to require disclosure in a civil case of anything which might be material in a pending prosecution, but after a verdict has been given, or it has been decided to take no proceedings, there is not the
F same need for secrecy. With regard to other documents there seems to be no greater need for protection than in the case of departments of government.

It appears to me to be most improbable that any harm would be done by disclosure of the probationary reports on the appellant or of the report from the Police Training Centre. With regard to the report which the respondent made to his chief constable with a view to the prosecution of the appellant there could be more doubt, although no suggestion was made in argument that disclosure of its contents would be harmful now that the appellant has been acquitted. As I have said, these documents may prove to be of vital importance in this litigation.

In my judgment this appeal should be allowed and these documents ought now to be required to be produced for inspection. If it is then found that disclosure would not, in your lordships' view, be prejudicial to the public interest, or that
I any possibility of such prejudice is, in the case of each of the documents, insufficient to justify its being withheld, then disclosure should be ordered.

LORD MORRIS OF BORTH-Y-GEST: My Lords, stated in its most direct form the question—one of far-reaching importance—which is raised in this case is whether the final decision as to the production in litigation of relevant documents is to rest with the courts or with the executive. I have no doubt that the conclusion should be that the decision rests with the courts. The present case is one between two private litigants. The appellant claims damages for malicious prosecution against the respondent, who was a superintendent in a police force. The defendant has in his possession, custody or power certain documents which, as is admitted, relate to the matters in question in the action. As to five of them the appellant's desire for production is resisted. The Home

(48) [1942] 1 All E.R. at p. 594; [1942] A.C. at p. 640.
(49) (1883), 9 App. Cas. 61.

Secretary swore an affidavit in which he stated that he gave instructions that **A**
" Crown privilege " was to be claimed for those five documents, and in which he
recorded his grounds for objecting to their production.

It is, I think, a principle which commands general acceptance that there are
circumstances in which the public interests must be dominant over the interests
of a private individual. To the safety or the well-being of the community the
claims of a private person may have to be subservient. This principle applies in **B**
litigation. The public interest may require that relevant documents ought not
to be produced. If, for example, national security would be or might be imperilled
by the production and consequent disclosure of certain documents then the
interests of a litigant must give way. There are some documents which can readily
be identified as containing material the secrecy of which it is vital to protect;
but where disclosure is desired and is resisted there is something more than a **C**
conflict between the public interest and some private interest. There are two
aspects of the public interest which pull in contrary directions. It is in the public
interest that full effect should be given to the normal rights of a litigant. It is in
the public interest that in the determination of disputes the courts should have
all relevant material before them. It is, on the other hand, in the public interest
that material should be withheld if, by its production and disclosure, the safety **D**
or the well-being of the community would be adversely affected. There will be
situations in which a decision ought to be made whether the harm that may
result from the production of documents will be greater than the harm that may
result from their non-production. Who, then, is to hold the scales? Who is to
adjudge where the greater weight lies?

We could have a system under which, if a Minister of the Crown gave a certifi- **E**
cate that a document should not be produced, the courts would be obliged to give
full effect to such certificate and, in every case and without exception, to treat it
as binding, final and conclusive. Such a system (though it could be laid down by
some specific statutory enactment) would, in my view, be out of harmony with
the spirit which in this country has guided the ordering of our affairs and in particular the administration of justice. Whether in some cases the law has or has not **F**
veered towards adopting such a system is a matter that has involved the careful
and detailed review of the authorities which was a feature of the helpful addresses
of learned counsel. Though this case requires an answer to be given to the question
whether in the last resort the decision rests with the courts or with a Minister, I see
no reason to envisage friction or tension as between the courts and the executive.
They both operate in the public interest. Some aspects of the public interest are **G**
chiefly within the knowledge of some Minister and can best be assessed by him.
I see no reason to fear that the courts would not in regard to them be fully and
readily receptive to all representations made in appropriate form and with
reasonable sufficiency. If a responsible Minister stated that production of a
document would jeopardise public safety, it is inconceivable that any court
would make an order for its production. The desirability of refusing production **H**
would heavily outweigh the desirability of requiring it. Other examples will
readily come to mind of claims to protection from production which would at
once be fully conceded. But there will be cases where the balance of desirabilities
will not be so clearly evident. Some one will then have to decide. Should it
be the court or should it be the executive?

It was the submission of the Attorney-General (who intervened in the litigation
in support of the objection to production made by the Home Secretary) that the
primary duty to determine whether the public interest requires that a document
be withheld rests with the executive government. The sphere, he contended,
within which the duty falls to be performed embraces all communications (either
in writing or oral) with and between servants of the Crown and persons holding
public office under the Crown whose duties involve the performance of functions
of government on behalf of the Crown. This contention has only to be stated for
its width and range to be appreciated. He further submitted that the court has in

A English law no ad hoc discretion to reject a statement of the executive government (if put forward in appropriate form and in good faith and without mistake or misdirection) recording a determination that the public interest requires that a document be withheld. The court, he submitted, must give conclusive effect to such a statement; it must be regarded as a statement on a matter peculiarly within the knowledge and competence of the executive government; the court

B cannot reject the statement on the ground that the necessities of justice in the particular case outweigh the public interest averred by the executive.

My lords, I am unable to regard these submissions as being acceptable. It is one of the main functions of courts to weigh up competing evidence and considerations. I see no peril in leaving such a process to the courts. They are well qualified to perform it. Their day to day task is to pay heed to evidence and to argument

C and then to consider, to weigh and to decide. It is said that a statement by the executive to the effect that the public interest requires that a document should be withheld is a statement on a matter peculiarly within the knowledge and competence of the executive government and must therefore be accepted by a court. A court would always pay the greatest heed to a statement that production of a document was not in the public interest and in most cases would be likely to

D give effect to it. There are many matters on which the executive will be likely to be best qualified to form a view. It will be easy for a court to recognise this and to give full weight to this consideration. The court, however, will be in a position of independence and will as a result often be better placed than a department to assess the weight of competing aspects of the public interest including those with which a particular department is not immediately concerned.

E It has been clearly laid down that the mere fact that a document is private or is confidential does not necessarily produce the result that its production can be withheld. In many decided cases, however, there have been references to a suggestion that if there were knowledge that certain documents (e.g., reports) might in some circumstances be seen by eyes for which they were never intended the result would be that in the making of similar documents in the future candour

F would be lacking. Here is a suggestion of doubtful validity. Would the knowledge that there was a remote chance of possible enforced production really affect candour? If there was knowledge that it was conceivably possible that some person might himself see a report which was written about him, it might well be that candour on the part of the writer of the report would be encouraged rather than frustrated. The law is ample in its protection of those who are honest in recording

G opinions which they are under a duty to express. Whatever may be the strength or the weakness of the suggestion to which I have referred it seems to me that a court is as well and probably better qualified than any other body to give such significance to it as the circumstances of a particular case may warrant.

It was conceded that objection on behalf of the Crown to production of a document on the ground of injury to the public interest which was shown (a) not

H to have been taken in good faith or (b) to have been actuated by some irrelevant or improper consideration or (c) to have been founded on a false factual premise, would not be final or conclusive and could be overriden by the court. If, as is thus conceded, the court possesses such wide powers of over-ruling an objection to production it would seem only reasonable and natural that it should also have the duty of assessing the weight of competing public interests.

I pass to consider whether there is any obstacle which prevents our arriving at a decision of this case in the direction in which, in my view, the necessities of justice point. Does the decision in *Duncan* v. *Cammell Laird & Co., Ltd.* (50) constitute an obstacle which bars the way? The documents which were being considered in that case included (inter alia) the contract for the hull and machinery of a submarine, letters relating to her trim and many plans and specifications relating to various parts of the vessel. The documents had been acquired or were

(50) [1942] 1 All ER. 587; [1942] A.C. 624.

held by Cammell Laird & Co., Ltd., in their capacity of contractors and agents   A
for the Lords Commissioners of the Admiralty.   Cammell Laird & Co., Ltd., were
directed not to produce the documents and furthermore to object to their
production except under an order of the court.   They were to object on the ground
of Crown privilege.   The First Lord of the Admiralty swore an affidavit saying
that it would be injurious to the public interest if any of the documents were
disclosed to any person.   The master, the judge, the Court of Appeal (51) and   B
this House (52) in turn refused to order inspection.   Even if the litigation had been
in peacetime and not, as was the case, in wartime the correctness of a decision
to refuse inspection would readily be recognised.   The decision, however, was
that the objection to production once made was conclusive.   It was held that a
Minister could make an objection if he considered that the public interest would
be damnified by production (e.g., where disclosure would be injurious to national   C
defence or to good diplomatic relations) or if he considered that the practice of
keeping a class of documents secret " was necessary for the proper functioning
of the public service ".   Furthermore, it was laid down that the court should not
ask to see the documents in order to probe the objection to their production.

My lords, it seems to me that that decision was binding on the Court of
Appeal (53) in the present case.   Your lordships have, however, a freedom   D
which was not possessed by the Court of Appeal (53a).   Though precedent is an
indispensable foundation on which to decide what is the law, there may be times
when a departure from precedent is in the interests of justice and the proper
development of the law.   I have come to the conclusion that it is now right to
depart from the decision in *Duncan's* case (52).

There are many reasons which guide me to the conclusion that I have indicated.   E
Duncan's case (52) proceeded on the basis that the law there being proclaimed
would be in accord with the law in Scotland.   It must now be recognised that
this was erroneous.   In reaching the decision in *Duncan's* case (52) much reliance
was placed on the decisions in two cases, viz., *Admiralty Comrs*. v. *Aberdeen
Steam Trawling and Fishing Co.* (54) and *Earl* v. *Vass* (55).   It appears that it
was only after the hearing that the case of *Earl* v. *Vass* (55) was considered: F
it was not therefore discussed in argument.   These two cases were discussed
in *Glasgow Corpn*. v. *Central Land Board* (56) where an impressive array of citation
was presented in support of the contention that the Scottish courts had always
had an inherent power to disregard a ministerial objection to production taken
on the ground of public interest.   This House in 1956 decided that the Scottish
courts did possess an inherent power to override a ministerial objection (taken   G
on the ground of public interest), if other aspects of the public interest required
this to be done.   LORD NORMAND pointed out that the power had seldom been
exercised and that the courts had emphatically said that it must be used with
the greatest caution and only in very special circumstances.   He added (57):

" It is, indeed, impossible to reconcile in all cases public interest and
justice to individuals, yet the power is not a phantom power and in the   H
last resort it is a real, though imperfect, safeguard of justice."

In reference to the power LORD RADCLIFFE said (58):

" The power reserved to the court is therefore a power to order production
even though the public interest is to some extent affected prejudicially.
This amounts to a recognition that more than one aspect of the public interest
may have to be surveyed in reviewing the question whether a document

(51) [1941] 1 All E.R. 437; [1941] 1 K.B. 640.
(52) [1942] 1 All E.R. 587; [1942] A.C. 624.
(53) See [1967] 2 All E.R. 1260.
(53a) See [1966] 3 All E.R. 77.
(54) 1909 S.C. 335.
(55) (1822), 1 Sh. Sc. App. 229.
(56) 1956 S.C. (H.L.) 1.
(57) 1956 S.C. (H.L.) at p. 16.
(58) 1956 S.C. (H.L.) at pp. 18, 19.

A   which would be available to a party in a civil suit between private parties
      is not to be available to the party engaged in a suit with the Crown. The
      interests of government, for which the Minister should speak with full
      authority do not exhaust the public interest. Another aspect of that interest
      is seen in the need that impartial justice should be done in the courts of law,
      not least between citizen and Crown, and that a litigant who has a case to
B   maintain should not be deprived of the means of its proper presentation by
      anything less than a weighty public reason. It does not seem to me un-
      reasonable to expect that the court would be better qualified than the
      Minister to measure the importance of such principles in application to the
      particular case that is before it.''

C   The two cases of *Earl* v. *Vass* (59) and *Admiralty Comrs.* v. *Aberdeen Steam
      Trawling and Fishing Co.* (60) were examined in the light of the other authorities.
      In regard to the former case VISCOUNT SIMONDS remarked (61) that unfortunately
      in *Duncan's* case (62) there had been reliance—

      ''. . . on a case which, though an appeal from the Court of Session, was
      heard by an English Lord Chancellor who does not appear to have been
D   instructed as to the relevant Scots law but according to his own statement
      communicated with the Lord Chief Justice (ABBOTT, C.J.) and ascertained
      from him what he would have done under the circumstances of the case.
      LORD SIMON was no doubt justified in referring to this case as a decision of
      this House upon the matter in debate but it would not be right to treat
      what he said as an assertion that the decision in *Earl* v. *Vass* (59) was an
E   authoritative exposition of the law of Scotland as it stood in the year 1942.
      That would be to ignore a long chain of authority in the Scottish courts
      in which *Earl* v. *Vass* (59) had been either disregarded or distinguished.''

      On the *Admiralty Comrs.* v. *Aberdeen Steam Trawling and Fishing Co.* (60) case
      VISCOUNT SIMONDS remarked (61)

      ''. . . that to cite this case as authoritative without regard to the earlier
F   case of *Sheridan* v. *Peel* (63) and the later case of *Henderson* v. *M'Gown* (64)
      (the latter a case of particular authority) must give an imperfect view
      of the law of Scotland.''

      In the speeches of LORD NORMAND and of LORD KEITH OF AVONHOLM there
      was further review and analysis of the various authorities. All their lordships
      reached the same conclusion. It was thus expressed by VISCOUNT SIMONDS (65):
G
      '' In the course of the present appeal we have had the advantage of
      an exhaustive examination of the relevant law from the earliest times, and
      it has left me in no doubt that there always has been and is now in the
      law of Scotland an inherent power of the court to override the Crown's
      objection to produce documents on the ground that it would injure the
H   public interest to do so.''

      To such extent as *Duncan's* case (62) proceeded on the view that in Scotland
      a ministerial objection to production had to be treated as conclusive, I think
      that it must now be accepted that such view was a mistaken one. Two of the
      props which were regarded as being support for such a view did not carry the
      weight attributed to them. In a concluding part of his speech in the *Glasgow
I   Corpn.* case (65), after noting the decision in *Duncan's* case (62), VISCOUNT
      SIMONDS remarked:

---

      (59) (1822), 1 Sh. Sc. App. 229.
      (60) 1909 S.C. 335.
      (61) 1956 S.C. (H.L.) at p. 10.
      (62) [1942] 1 All E.R. 587; [1942] A.C. 624.
      (63) 1907 S.C. 577.
      (64) 1916 S.C. 821.
      (65) 1956 S.C. (H.L.) at p. 11.

" It may be that the existence of an inherent power in the court of Scotland   A
provides an ultimate safeguard of justice in that country which is denied
to a litigant in England."

It would, I think, be unfortunate if such a denial must continue for litigants in
England. The law of England ought not to lag behind. At present in regard
to the matter now being considered it is out of accord with the law of most
parts of the Commonwealth.   B

A review of the cases in England prior to *Duncan's* case (66) does not reveal
any entirely consistent line of decision. Many cases merely illustrate the circumstances and situations in which the courts will in fact and in practice recognise
that it is in the public interest that documents should not be produced. Some
cases have, however, proceeded on the basis that the courts are powerless to
over-rule an objection. Some cases, on the other hand have proceeded on the   C
basis that the ultimate decision does rest with the courts and in some there are
statements to that effect. In a case in 1816 (*Anderson* v. *Hamilton* (67)) LORD
ELLENBOROUGH, C.J., refused to admit in evidence the contents of a letter
written by a representative of government in one of the colonies to the Secretary
of State or the answer of the Secretary of State. In *Home* v. *Bentinck* (68) it
was held that the report of an army court of enquiry which the commander in   D
chief had directed was protected from production on a " broad rule of public
policy and convenience ". In *Wyatt* v. *Gore* (69) the defendant was Lieutenant
Governor of Upper Canada. In the course of the case the Attorney-General of
the province was called as a witness and was asked about the nature of some
communications made to him by the defendant relative to the plaintiff's conduct.
The judge ruled (70) that the witness was not bound to answer and that that   E
was so whether the conversations with the Attorney-General were on public
or private business. He said (70):

" The governor consults with a high legal officer on the state of his colony;
what passes between them is confidential: no office of this kind could be
executed with safety if conversations between the governor of a distant
province and his attorney-general, who is the only person upon whom such   F
governor can lean for advice, were suffered to be disclosed."

Whatever view may be taken of this particular decision it is to be noted that
it was conceded that if the communications with the Attorney-General were in
the course of office and related to the internal affairs of the province the witness
would not be required by the court to answer.   G

In an action in 1841, *Smith* v. *East India Co.* (71), the defendants' objection
to produce certain documents was upheld. The defendants set out that the
documents consisted of confidential communications passing between the company and the Commissioners for the affairs of India which had been made in
compliance with legal obligation. LORD LYNDHURST, L.C., pointed out that the
mere fact that the correspondence was confidential and was official did not   H
constitute a sufficient reason for non-production. He held, however, that under
3 & 4 Wm. IV c. 85 the territorial possessions of the company were to be held
by them in trust for the Crown and their assets transferred to the Crown; they
were only to carry on any commercial transactions either for the purposes of
winding-up their affairs or for the purposes of the government of India. He
held that public policy required and the Legislature intended that unreserved   I
communications should take place between the company and the Board of
Control. If those communications had to be produced in court, the effect would

---

(66) [1942] 1 All E.R. 587; [1942] A.C. 624.
(67) (1816), 2 Brod. & Bing. 156, n.
(68) (1820), 2 Brod. & Bing. 130.
(69) (1816), Holt. N.P. 299.
(70) (1816), Holt. N.P. at p. 302.
(71) (1841), 1 Ph. 50.

A be (72) " to restrain the freedom of the communications, and to render them more cautious, guarded and reserved ". He held therefore that they came within (72)

> " that class of official communications which are privileged, inasmuch as they cannot be subject to be communicated, without infringing the policy of the Act of Parliament and without injury to the public interest."

B A somewhat similar result was reached in 1856 in *Wadeer* v. *East India* Co. (73), where Knight Bruce, L.J., said (74):

> ". . . it is clear that the principles on which justice is administered in civil courts, whether between the Sovereign and a subject or between subject and subject, preclude the possibility of the interference of the court for the purpose of the disclosure of State papers, despatches, minutes or documents of any such description which relate to the carrying on of the government, and are connected with the transaction of public affairs."

C The case of *Beatson* v. *Skene* (75) did raise the question which is now being considered. In a slander action in which the jury found for the defendant the plaintiff had subpoenaed the Secretary for War to produce (inter alia) the minutes of a court of inquiry. The Minister had attended and had objected that their production would be prejudicial to the public service. The learned judge had declined to compel their production. A rule nisi for a new trial was obtained. One of the grounds was that the learned judge had been wrong in declining to compel production. The rule nisi was discharged. Pollock, C.B., pointed out (76) in giving the judgment of the court that the minutes of the inquiry would not by themselves have been admissible in evidence and that the person who had made them had not been present at the trial: further, he pointed out that their only relevance was to prove that the defendant had at the inquiry admitted speaking the alleged slanderous words and that the fact that he had spoken them was apparently not contested by the defendant at the trial. Pollock, C.B., nevertheless went on to say that the majority at least of the court agreed with the trial judge in declining to compel production " on the ground that " the Secretary for War had stated that the production would be injurious to the public service. He proceeded to say that (77)

> " if the production of a State paper would be injurious to the public service the general public interest must be considered paramount to the individual interest of a suitor in a court of justice . . ."

G Then he posed the question how the matter was to be determined. Was it to be by the presiding judge or by the responsible servant of the Crown in whose custody was the paper. His answer was (77):

> " It appears to us, therefore, that the question, whether the production of the documents would be injurious to the public service, must be determined, not by the judge but by the head of the department having the custody of the paper; and if he is in attendance and states that in his opinion the production of the document would be injurious to the public service, we think the judge ought not to compel the production of it."

The use of the words " ought not " rather than " cannot " may be significant. Pollock, C.B., further said (78):

> " Martin, B., does not entirely agree with us as to the general view we have taken of this question. He is of opinion that whenever the judge

---

(72) (1841), 1 Ph. at p. 55.
(73) (1856), 8 De G.M. & G. 182.
(74) (1856), 8 De G.M. & G. at p. 187.
(75) [1843-60] All E.R. Rep. 882; (1860), 5 H. & N. 838.
(76) [1843-60] All E.R. Rep. at p. 884; (1860), 5 H. & N. at p. 852.
(77) [1843-60] All E.R. Rep. at p. 885; (1860), 5 H. & N. at p. 853.
(78) [1843-60] All E.R. Rep. at p. 885; (1860), 5 H. & N. at p. 854.

is satisfied that the document may be made public without prejudice to the   A
public service, the judge ought to compel its production, notwithstanding
the reluctance of the head of the department to produce it; and perhaps
cases might arise where the matter would be so clear that the judge might
well ask for it in spite of some official scruples as to producing it; but
this must be considered rather as an extreme case, and extreme cases throw
very little light on the practical rules of life."   B

It appears to me that the court was, therefore, recognising that there is an
inherent power in the court to override an objection to production made by
a Minister. The majority thought that its exercise would only be in extreme
cases; MARTIN, B., thought that its exercise need not be so rare. One consideration which moved the majority was that a judge could not come to a determination (79)   C

"... without ascertaining what the document was, and why the publication of it would be injurious to the public service—an inquiry which cannot
take place in private, and which taking place in public may do all the
mischief which it is proposed to guard against."

I see no reason why in these days there should not be a private examination of a   D
document by a court if such an examination becomes really necessary.

In *Stace* v. *Griffith* (80) the Colonial Secretary of St. Helena had, in a libel
action, objected to produce a letter on account of its official character. LORD
CHELMSFORD in giving judgment in the Privy Council said that the judge at
the trial ought to have expressed an opinion whether the letter was an official
communication which on public grounds ought not to be disclosed. If it were   E
such a letter no evidence of its contents could have been given. The precise
point now being considered was, however, not the subject of any analysis.

In *Dawkins* v. (*Lord*) *Rokeby* (81) the court followed *Home* v. *Bentinck* (82).
I do not derive much assistance from the case nor from *H.M.S. Bellerophon* (83)
which merely followed *Beatson* v. *Skene* (84). In *Kain* v. *Farrer* (85), however,
the question arose as to the sufficiency of an affidavit of the Secretary of the   F
Board of Trade in which he objected " on the ground of public policy to state,
anything further as to the documents in the possession or power of the Board
of Trade ". A further affidavit was ordered. GROVE, J., pointed out (86) that the
affidavit filed said no more than that the documents were official, and was consistent with the meaning that on the ground of public policy no documents
whatever in the possession of the Board of Trade ought to be produced. That   G
said GROVE, J., was not sufficiently precise and did not " bring the documents
referred to within the privilege which is often claimed successfully for documents
of State." Further GROVE, J., said (86):

" A judge should not, in my opinion, consider such an affidavit sufficient;
there should be some ground for him to exercise his discretion on, and
to decide that a high officer of State may, without giving any reason why,   H
state that it is against the public interest that a particular document should
be produced."

The references to the discretion of the judge and the decision of the court are
significant.

In *Hennessy* v. *Wright* (87), there was an application by the defendant for
discovery in an action brought by the governor of Mauritius. As to some

---

(79) [1843-60] All E.R. Rep. at p. 885; (1860), 5 H. & N. at p. 853.
(80) (1869), L.R. 2 P.C. 420.
(81) (1873), L.R. 8 Q.B. 255.
(82) (1820), 2 Brod. & Bing. 130.
(83) (1874), 44 L.J.Adm. 5; 31 L.T. 756.
(84) [1843-60] All E.R. Rep. 882; (1860), 5 H. & N. 838.
(85) (1877), 37 L.T. 469.
(86) (1877), 37 L.T. at p. 470.
(87) (1888), 21 Q.B.D. 509.

A documents in his custody the plaintiff swore an affidavit that they had been acquired and were held by him in his capacity as governor, and that the attention of the Secretary of State had been drawn to the nature and dates of the documents (despatches and reports) which had passed either between the Secretary of State and the plaintiff as governor, or between a royal commissioner and the plaintiff as governor, or between the royal commissioner and the Secretary of State.

B The Secretary of State had directed the plaintiff to object to production on the ground of the interest of the state and the public service. FIELD, J., in his judgment pointed out (88) that the publication of a State document may involve danger to the nation and may be injurious to servants of the Crown as individuals. He refused to order production at that stage of the action, but he left the matter open for decision at the trial. Indeed, not sharing the difficulty felt by the

C majority in *Beatson* v. *Skene* (89) he said (90) that, if he were sitting at nisi prius and if the head of a department took an objection to production on the ground that it would be injurious to the public service, he (FIELD, J.) would consider himself entitled to examine privately the documents to the production of which there was objection, and to endeavour by such means and by means of questions to the head of the department to ascertain whether the fear of injury to the

D public service was the real motive for the objection. WILLS, J., also refused to order production on the interlocutory application. He was (91)

"... reluctant to say anything which could interfere with the discretion of the judge at nisi prius, or to treat it as impossible for circumstances to arise which might justify a judge at the trial in deciding that a particular document of the class under consideration ought to be produced."

E He also said (92):

"The question whether or not in the public interest production of the document should not be allowed is so far a matter of state rather than of legal decision, that it is within the undoubted competence of the responsible Minister of the Crown by taking the proper steps to interfere and raise an

F objection to which every tribunal would be certain, to say the least, to pay respectful attention; and we must be careful in dealing with an interlocutory application like the present to see that a right which has been established for great purposes of public welfare, and which, with one exception presently to be noticed, has been uniformly respected at nisi prius for a great number of years, is not frustrated by an order for discovery."

G In my view, that case also showed that final decision could rest with the court and not with a Minister; it showed that there was an inherent power in the court, if it thought right to override a ministerial objection.

In the case of *Marks* v. *Beyfus* (93) an action was brought against defendants for maliciously and without reasonable and probable cause conspiring to prosecute the plaintiff. The plaintiff called the Director of Public Prosecutions as a witness.

H The judge refused to order him to give answers which would have revealed the names of informants. The Court of Appeal upheld his ruling. The prosecution was a public one and there was a rule that in such a prosecution a witness cannot be asked questions which will disclose the informer. LORD ESHER, M.R., said (94):

"Now this rule as to public prosecutions was founded on grounds of public policy, and if this prosecution was a public prosecution the rule

I attaches; I think it was a public prosecution, and that the rule applies. I do not say that it is a rule which can never be departed from; if upon

(88) (1888), 21 Q.B.D. at p. 512.
(89) [1843-60] All E.R. Rep. 882; (1860), 5 H. & N. 838.
(90) (1888), 21 Q.B.D. at p. 515.
(91) (1888), 21 Q.B.D. at p. 521.
(92) (1888), 21 Q.B.D. at p. 522.
(93) (1890), L.R. 25 Q.B.D. 494.
(94) (1890), L.R. 25 Q.B.D. at p. 498.

the trial of a prisoner the judge should be of opinion that the disclosure of   **A**
the name of the informant is necessary or right in order to show the prisoner's
innocence, then one public policy is in conflict with another public policy,
and that which says that an innocent man is not to be condemned when
his innocence can be proved is the policy that must prevail. But except
in that case, this rule of public policy is not a matter of discretion; it is
a rule of law, and as such should be applied by the judge at the trial, who   **B**
should not treat it as a matter of discretion whether he should tell the
witness to answer or not."

The refusal to order production in *Hughes* v. *Vargas* (95) was on the basis of
the law as laid down in *Beatson* v. *Skene* (96). It was said that if the head of a
public department took an objection that it was contrary to the public interest
to produce a document in court the judge " would not " order its production.   **C**

The decision in *Chatterton* v. *Secretary of State for India in Council* (97) was
considerably concerned with the law of privilege in defamation cases, but in
so far as it related to production in evidence there was no over-ruling of the
cases to which I have referred. In *Re Joseph Hargreaves, Ltd., Re* (98), there
was an objection to production of documents by the Board of Inland Revenue
on the ground that it would be prejudicial and injurious to the public interests   **D**
and service. The refusal of the judge to order production was upheld in the
Court of Appeal. SIR NATHANIEL LINDLEY, M.R., thought that the court ought
not to interfere with the judge's view. He said (99) " I do not intend to say
what is the limit of the power of the court (if there is a limit) to order the production of documents such as these . . ." VAUGHAN WILLIAMS, L.J. (100),
refused to review what he states was the " discretion " of the judge.   **E**

Our attention was called to the case of *A.-G.* v. *Nottingham Corpn.* (101).
The only relevance, however, was that in the report as appearing in 20 T.L.R.,
at p. 258, but not as appearing in the law reports, mention was made of the
fact that a medical inspector of the Local Government Board who was called
as a witness said that he was instructed by the board to say that a report which
he had made on a hospital was privileged and that to reveal its contents would   **F**
be injurious to the public service. The report states that FARWELL, J., expressed
surprise and protested, but said that he could not overrule the president of the
Local Government Board. There is no mention of argument having taken
place and the matter is not discussed in the judgment.

My lords, I have ventured to refer to the decisions in some detail in order to
see whether there is foundation for the view that in the face of ministerial objec-   **G**
tion to production the court is always powerless. It seems to me that the decisions
in the last century yield no such foundation but that, on the contrary, they
tend to show that final decision could rest with the court. Unless there is any
reason to doubt it the court will accept the honesty of a view put forward and
will, therefore, accept the truth of a Minister's assertion that production of a
document will in some measure be detrimental to the public interest. In practice   **H**
this will in the great majority of cases result in a decision that documents should
not be produced; but this does not mean that the court must always and
automatically give effect to every ministerial objection.

In *Williams* v. *Star Newspaper Co., Ltd.* (102), objection on behalf of the
Home Office was made at the trial to the production of a report made after an
exhumation. Counsel submitted that the judge had no option but to decline to   **I**
order production. The judge is reported as saying that he had no means of

(95) (1893), 9 T.L.R. 551.
(96) [1843-60] All E.R. Rep. 882; (1860), 5 H. & N. 838.
(97) [1895-99] All E.R. Rep. 1035; [1895] 2 Q.B. 189.
(98) [1900] 1 Ch. 347.
(99) [1900] 1 Ch. at p. 352.
(100) [1900] 1 Ch. at p. 353.
(101) [1904] 1 Ch. 673.
(102) (1908), 24 T.L.R. 297.

A knowing in what way the publication would be injurious but that he thought that he was bound to rule against production. I cannot regard the report as being very satisfactory. Nor do I find much assistance in the report of *Leigh* v. *Gladstone* (103), where it is recorded that it was ruled that in an action claiming damages for assault reports made by the medical officer of a prison to the governor of a prison following upon operations of forcible feeding were not privileged and

B must be produced. In *West* v. *West* (104), where in a slander action the refusal of the Lord Chamberlain to answer a question was supported, VAUGHAN WILLIAMS, L.J., in speaking of the practice where the head of a public department considered it his duty to refuse to answer a question, is reported as saying that generally the judge assented to the refusal and that the judge had a duty to rule whether he would accept the refusal or not.

C   Of much greater significance is *Asiatic Petroleum Co., Ltd.* v. *Anglo-Persian Oil Co., Ltd.* (105). The plaintiffs wished to have inspection of documents some of which the defendants had been instructed by the Secretary of the Admiralty not to produce or disclose on the ground that production and disclosure would be detrimental to the interests of the State and be of possible assistance to the enemy. Had there been some well-recognised rule of law that a departmental

D objection, provided that it was put forward in suitable and adequate form, must be treated as conclusive and must be upheld, I am sure that SCRUTTON, J., would not have done as he did. He looked at the documents himself and then adjourned the application to the trial: he helpfully added an indorsement that he thought that the government might be right in the view that the documents ought not to be produced to others. An appeal to the Court of Appeal was

E dismissed. SWINFEN EADY, L.J., referred to the rule protecting documents from discovery and said that although instances in which documents have been held to be protected from discovery on the broad principle of State policy and public convenience have usually been cases of public official documents of a political or administrative character yet the rule was not limited to such documents. The test was whether the production of a document would be injurious to the

F general public interest. The court made no criticism of the course followed by SCRUTTON, J. They said that they saw no reason for overruling his exercise of discretion.

    In a case, *Ronnfeldt* v. *Phillips* (106), testing the validity of an order made under defence regulations prohibiting a person from residing in a particular locality a report of a chief constable which had influenced the making of the order

G was called for. There was objection on the ground that its production would be against the public interest. The objection was upheld. The learned judge is reported as having said that once the objection was taken (by responsible officers of government) the court had " no power " to order production, and he said that *Hennessy* v. *Wright* (107) had so decided. I do not think that *Hennessy* v. *Wright* (107) laid down so definite a ruling. In *Anthony* v. *Anthony* (108) the approach

H was somewhat similar to that in *Ronnfeldt* v. *Phillips* (106).

    Whatever view one may form about the decision in *Ankin* v. *London and North Eastern Ry. Co.* (109), the words used by SCRUTTON, L.J., do lend some support to the view that where there is a ministerial objection the court is impotent. It is true that he only speaks (110) of the " practice " of the English courts to accept the statement of a minister, but he goes on to say that they would do so

I " even though the court may doubt whether any harm would be done" by producing a document. This might mean that where the public interest is involved

---

(103) (1909), 26 T.L.R. 139.
(104) (1911), 27 T.L.R. 189, 476.
(105) [1916-17] All E.R. Rep. 637; [1916] 1 K.B. 822.
(106) (1918), 34 T.L.R. 556.
(107) (1888), 21 Q.B.D. 509.
(108) (1919), 35 T.L.R. 559.
(109) [1929] All E.R. Rep. 65; [1930] 1 K.B. 527.
(110) [1929] All E.R. Rep. at p. 67; [1930] 1 K.B. at p. 533.

a court will resolve a doubt on the side of safeguarding the public interest. If so   A
the words of the judgment may refer only to the practice of the courts. There
is, however, some measure of ambiguity.

Though *Robinson* v. *State of South Australia (No. 2)* (111) was not an English
case many of the English and Scottish authorities were considered. A reading
of the judgment of the Board does not lend support to the view that the courts
in England are powerless in the face of a ministerial objection to production.   B
Rather is there a pointer as to the need for the vigilance of the courts. After a
reference to some observations of TURNER, L.J., in *Wadeer* v. *East India Co.* (112)
LORD BLANESBURGH said (113):

> " In view of the increasing extension of State activities into the spheres
> of trading business and commerce, and of the claim of privilege in relation
> to liabilities arising therefrom now apparently freely put forward, his   C
> observations stand on record to remind the courts, that while they must
> duly safeguard genuine public interests they must see to it that the scope
> of the admitted privilege is not, in such litigation, extended."

An illustration of the value of the courts' vigilance is provided by a reading
of the report of *Spigelmann* v. *Hocker* (114.)   Concluding that an objection to the   D
production of a document was not taken in due manner, MACNAGHTEN, J.,
was disposed to order its production, but as a precaution decided himself to
examine the document: he did so, and found nothing in the document that
could conceivably be injurious to the public interest.

My lords, I have embarked on a survey of the decisions prior to *Duncan's*
case (115), because I would have a measure of reluctance in disturbing a decision   E
given in 1942, if it had been a re-statement of clear principles which for long
had been widely accepted. It seems to me, however, that there was much
authority which would have warranted an entirely different statement of principle in *Duncan's* case (115) though doubtless in that particular case without
leading to any different result. This circumstance when coupled with the fact
that it is clear that the law in Scotland differs from that proclaimed in *Duncan's*   F
case (115) affords ample warrant, in my view, to justify a new appraisement of
the position. It can also be said that though courts have since 1942 been obliged
to follow *Duncan's* case (115) they have often expressed disquiet in doing so.
The case of *Ellis* v. *Home Office* (116) may be mentioned as an example of this.
Furthermore, the statements made by VISCOUNT KILMUIR, L.C., in 1956 and 1962
(117), which we were invited to consider, show that the government, being aware   G
of complaints concerning the previous practice, decided to make the modifications
of it which were announced in the two statements. In my view, it should now
be made clear that whenever an objection is made to the production of a relevant
document it is for the court to decide whether or not to uphold the objection.
The inherent power of the court must include a power to ask for a clarification
or an amplification of an objection to production, though the court will be   H
careful not to impose a requirement which could only be met by divulging the
very matters to which the objection related. The power of the court must also
include a power to examine documents privately, a power, I think, which in
practice should be sparingly exercised, but one which could operate as a safeguard
for the executive in cases where a court is inclined to make an order for production though an objection is being pressed. I see no difference in principle between
the consideration of what have been called the contents cases and the class cases.
The principle which the courts will follow is that relevant documents normally

---

(111) [1931] All E.R. Rep. 333; [1931] A.C. 704.
(112) (1856), 8 De G.M. & G. at p. 189.
(113) [1931] All E.R. Rep. at pp. 337, 338; [1931] A.C. at p. 715.
(114) (1933), 50 T.L.R. 87.
(115) [1942] 1 All E.R. 587; [1942] A.C. 624.
(116) [1953] 2 All E.R. 149; [1953] 2 Q.B. 135.
(117) See p. 881, letters F, H and I, ante.

A liable to production will be withheld, if the public interest requires that they should be withheld. In many cases it will be plain that documents are within a class of documents which by their very nature ought not to be disclosed. Indeed, in the majority of cases I apprehend that a decision as to an objection will present no difficulty. The cases of difficulty will be those in which it will appear that, if there is non-disclosure, some injustice may result and that if there is disclosure

B the public interest may to some extent be affected prejudicially. The courts can and will recognise that a view honestly put forward by a Minister as to the public interest will be based on special knowledge and will be put forward by one who is charged with a special responsibility. As LORD RADCLIFFE said in the *Glasgow Corpn.* case (118), the courts will not seek on a matter which is within the sphere and knowledge of a Minister to displace his view by their own; but

C where there is more than one aspect of the public interest to be considered it seems to me that a court, in reference to litigation pending before it, will be in the best position to decide where the weight of public interest predominates. I am convinced that the courts, with the independence which is their strength, can safely be entrusted with the duty of weighing all aspects of public interests and of private interests and of giving protection where it is found to be due.

D   The objection to the production of the probationary reports has been explained as being put forward on the basis that those who make such reports expect them to be confidential, so that they will only be seen by police officers, and that if such reports could ever be subject to production then the future candour of future writers of such reports would be affected, and that this would be disadvantageous to, and therefore injurious to, the public interest.   While

E accepting that the view is held that some measure of prejudice to the public interest would or might result from production, it may be that a greater measure of prejudice to the public interest would result from their non-production. As to the report of the chief constable of Jan. 13, 1965, the matter is put on a somewhat different basis. That was a report of a police officer to his superior in relation to the alleged commission of a crime. Again, it must be accepted

F that the view is held that it would be injurious to the public interest to order its production. The view is put forward that no documents within the class of " reports by police officers to their superiors concerning investigations into the commission of crime " should ever be disclosed. It is submitted that, though the appellant in the present case has been acquitted of the offence with which he was charged, it would be unfortunate ever to make an exception from the practice

G of maintaining the secrecy of such reports. I think that any court must recognise the weight of the consideration that the police in their work of fighting crime, which is work that is so much in the public interest, must in no way be impeded or frustrated. Whether it would be or might be is a matter which it is well within the competence of a court to assess.

    I have come to the conclusion that the appeal should be allowed, and that

H the best procedure to follow for weighing the public and private interests which are involved in this case will be to have an inspection of the five documents which are in question. It can then be decided whether there should or should not be an order for the production of some or all of the documents.

    LORD HODSON: My Lords the privilege of the Crown in respect of the,

I disclosure of documents depends on the public interest. The decision of this House in *Duncan* v. *Cammell Laird & Co., Ltd.* (119), laid down that the Minister's certificate or affidavit must be accepted by the court in any case where the privilege is claimed, whether or not he bases his claim on the contents of the document itself or the class to which the document belongs, irrespective of its contents. The present case raises the question whether the time has come to reconsider that decision. Attention has been drawn to various considerations

---

(118) 1956 S.C. (H.L.) at p. 18.
(119) [1942] 1 All E.R. 587; [1942] A.C. 624.

which have exercised the minds of the court since the decision was given, and **A**
in particular your lordships' attention was drawn to an answer (119a) given by
VISCOUNT KILMUIR, L.C., in answer to a question in this House which showed
the difficulty and, furthermore, the undesirability of maintaining the rule in
its full rigour. It was, inter alia, proposed that in some classes of documents,
such as those concerned with claims for negligence against the Crown, privilege
should in future not be claimed. Likewise, in cases where statements are made by **B**
witnesses to the police in civil cases it was proposed that these should be produced. These proposals have, as your lordships understand, been accepted and
followed.

It is in the case of documents for which protection is claimed on the ground of
their class, irrespective of their contents, on what may be called the " candour "
ground that the principal difficulty arises, for it is not to be disputed that there **C**
are classes of documents which from their very character ought to be withheld
from production if protection is properly claimed on grounds of State. I have in
mind those enumerated by SALMON, L.J., in *Re Grosvenor Hotel London (No. 2)*
(120), such as cabinet minutes, despatches from ambassadors abroad and minutes
of discussions between heads of departments. The expression " class ", however,
covers not only such documents which pass at a high level and which require **D**
absolute protection, but also those communications not readily distinguishable
from those passing in the ordinary course of business conducted by commercial
organisations and carrying only a qualified privilege.

The class of documents with which this appeal is concerned is not on the
highest level from the point of view of the public interest looked at as State
documents, although in another aspect of the public interest looked at as material **E**
on which justice is required to be done they may well be highly significant.
They are documents in the possession or control of the respondent, Thomas
Rimmer, a one-time superintendent of police in the Cheshire constabulary, who
is being sued in an action for malicious prosecution by the appellant, who was at
material times a probationary police constable in the Cheshire constabulary.
The appellant was tried and acquitted at the city of Chester quarter sessions **F**
before a recorder and a jury on an indictment charging him with the larceny of
an electric torch. In the action which he has brought for malicious prosecution
privilege is claimed by the Secretary of State for the Home Department in respect
of certain documents included in the respondent's affidavit of documents as
relevant to the case. These are five in number: four of them are reports on the
appellant and the fifth, dated Jan. 13, 1965, is described as a report by the **G**
respondent to the chief constable. The first four documents are reports on the
appellant while he was a probationer and the Home Secretary has declared
that they fall

> " within a class of documents comprising confidential reports by police
> officers to chief officers of police relating to the conduct, efficiency and
> fitness for employment of individual police officers under their command." **H**

Of the fifth document he has declared that it falls " within a class of documents
comprising reports by police officers to their superiors concerning investigations
into the commission of crime ". He expressed the opinion that the production
of documents of each such class would be injurious to the public interest. These
documents fall into a special category in that the public interest is concerned, **I**
not because the disclosure of the contents may bring serious danger to the State,
but because where government is involved it has been authoritatively stated
that full candour in communications between all those in government service
is necessary and this candour will be endangered if disclosure of such communications is permitted—this, of course, quite irrespective of the contents of the
particular document.

(119a) See p. 881, letters F, H and I, ante.
(120) [1964] 3 All E.R. at p. 370.

A   The documents being police documents are susceptible to the claim of Crown privilege, although the police are not Crown servants, for they are in consimili casu with servants of the Crown, in that they are carrying out functions of the Crown. The authorities are collected in the decision of McCardie, J., in *Fisher* v. *Oldham Corpn.* (121), in which reference is made to *Mackalley's Case* (122), in which constables are described as ministers of the King.

B   The class was referred to by Lord Lyndhurst, L.C., in *Smith* v. *East India Co.* (123). He said (124):

"... it is quite obvious that public policy requires ... that the most unreserved communication should take place ... that it should be subject to no restraints or limitations; but it is also quite obvious that if, at the suit of a particular individual, those communications should be subject to be

C   produced in a court of justice, the effect of that would be to restrain the freedom of the communications, and to render them more cautious, guarded and reserved."

This case concerned correspondence between the East India Co. and the Commissioners for the Affairs of India relating to commercial matters. It may well be wondered why high protective considerations should apply to communications

D   of this class, which must be much more numerous now with the multiplication of state organisations engaged not only in government but in commercial operations; for there is no obvious distinction between governmental and other organisations so far as the necessity of candour is concerned.

Nevertheless, the language used by Lord Lyndhurst has been accepted and followed in a stream of authority which follows, in the main, the same

E   channel and culminates in the case of *Duncan* v. *Cammell Laird & Co., Ltd.* (125). In that case these authorities were fully discussed and it is unnecessary to cover the same ground again for, notwithstanding exceptions to the general rule where individual judges had in the past examined documents before deciding whether production should be ordered, this House laid down the general rule quite categorically as admitting of no exceptions.

F   In every case where Crown privilege has been duly claimed the court was held to be prohibited from examining the claim, whether what are called " contents " or what are called " class " cases are concerned. The opinion of your lordships was given by Viscount Simon, L.C., with whom six other noble and learned lords agreed, having made contributions of their own to the single opinion. The

G   principle to be applied in every case is that documents otherwise relevant and liable to production must not be produced, if the public interest requires that they should be withheld. He said (126):

" This test may be found to be satisfied either (a) by having regard to the contents of the particular document, or (b) by the fact that the document belongs to a class which, on grounds of public interest, must as a class be

H   withheld from production."

Their lordships applied that test to the documents in the case which included the contract for the hull and machinery of the submarine Thetis, letters written before the disaster which befell her, relating to the vessel's trim, reports as to the condition of the Thetis when raised, a large number of plans and specifications relating to various parts of the vessel and a notebook of the foreman painter

I   employed by the respondents. They did not, however, analyse the documents in order to determine under which of the two heads (contents or class) they fell to be included and found it sufficient to lay down the law in the wide terms stated and apply it to the documents as a whole. In those circumstances I agree with

---

(121) [1930] All E.R. Rep. 96; [1930] 2 K.B. 364.
(122) (1611), 9 Co. Rep. 65a.   (123) (1841), 1 Ph. 50.
(124) (1841), 1 Ph. at p. 55.
(125) [1942] 1 All E.R. 587; [1942] A.C. 624.
(126) [1942] 1 All E.R. at p. 592; [1942] A.C. at p. 636.

the majority of the Court of Appeal in holding that the decision in *Duncan* v.   A
Cammell Laird (127) was binding and conclusive.

Nevertheless, your lordships are free to reconsider the matter if it is considered
right so to do. Certainly several cases have arisen in recent years in which the
courts have shown themselves repelled by the idea that all public departments'
communications should be held back at the discretion of the Minister in whose
hand the documents might be. One would have supposed that the qualified   B
privilege which protects non-malicious communications in the ordinary case
should be sufficient just as much where government departments are concerned
as where the affairs of ordinary citizens are concerned under the control of business
which may perhaps employ a vast number of people.

It is, I think, at the present day impossible to justify the maintenance of the
doctrine laid down by LORD LYNDHURST (128) in its widest form. It is strange   C
if civil servants alone are supposed to be unable to be candid in their statements
made in the course of duty without the protection of an absolute privilege denied
other fellow subjects. In this connexion I should refer to the judgment of the
Privy Council in *Robinson* v. *State of South Australia (No. 2)* (129), which held
that the court has always had in reserve the power to enquire into the nature of
the document for which protection is sought and to require some indication of the   D
injury which would result from its production. That case had to do with documents relating to the trading, commercial and contractual activities of a State
where it was held, especially in time of peace, that privilege could rarely be sustained. This ruling was based on observations of TURNER, L.J., in *Wadeer* v.
East India Co. (130), but the Privy Council judgment added that it must not be
assumed from these observations of TURNER, T.J., that documents relating to the   E
trading, commercial and contractual activities of a State can never be protected
under the head of privilege, for it is conceivable that even in connexion with the
production of such documents there may be " some plain overruling principle
of public interest concerned which cannot be disregarded ".

The Board referred to the fact, more obvious today than in 1931, that in view
of the increasing extension of State activities into the spheres of trading, business   F
and commerce, and of the claim of privilege in relation to liabilities arising therefrom now apparently firmly put forward, TURNER, L.J.'s observations (130)
stand on record to remind the courts that, while they must duly safeguard
genuine public interests, they must see to it that the scope of the admitted
privilege is not, in such litigation, extended. The Board adopted the statement
to be found in TAYLOR ON EVIDENCE, s. 939 which reads: " The principle of the   G
rule is concern for public interest, and the rule will be applied no further than the
attainment of that object requires."

In deciding whether *Duncan* v. *Cammell Laird & Co., Ltd.* (127) is open to
reconsideration it is worth remembering that the conclusion was reached under a
misapprehension about the corresponding law of Scotland. The Scottish cases
show that although seldom exercised the residual power of the court to inspect   H
and if necessary order production of documents is claimed. By a misapprehension,
however, in *Duncan's* case (127) the protection in Crown privilege cases in both
countries was held to be absolute. This misapprehension no longer prevails
since the decision of this House in *Glasgow Corpn.* v. *Central Land Board* (131).
The Attorney-General, while seeking to maintain the generality and width
of the rule in *Duncan's* case (127), does, however, concede that objection on   I
behalf of the Crown to production of a document can be overridden if shown
(a) not to have been taken in good faith; (b) to have been actuated by some irrelevant or improper consideration, e.g., the production might expose a want of

(127) [1942] 1 All E.R. 587; [1942] A.C. 624.
(128) (1841), 1 Ph. at p. 55.
(129) [1931] All E.R. Rep. 333; [1931] A.C. 704.
(130) (1856), 8 De G.M. & G. at p. 189.
(131) 1956 S.C. (H.L.) 1.

A efficiency in the administration of a department or lay it open to claims for compensation; or (c) to have proceeded on a false factual premise, e.g., that a document belonged to a class to which it did not in truth belong. Once the concession is made, I find it difficult to see how the court could reach any conclusion on these matters without inspection of the document in question. This, indeed, is conceded by the Crown and goes a long way towards a concession that

B the ultimate control should be with the court.

As I have already indicated the older authorities are not wholly consistent. It is instructive to consider one of the older cases, which was discussed at length in *Duncan's* case (132), and which lends support to the opinion that a residual power remains in the court to order not only inspection but also production in this country, as it does in Scotland. In *Beatson* v. *Skene* (133), POLLOCK, C.B., with

C whom the majority of the Court of Exchequer agreed, concluded (134):

" It appears to us, therefore, that the question whether the production of the document would be injurious to the public service must be determined, not by the judge, but by the head of the department having the custody of the paper; and if he is in attendance and states that in his opinion the pro-

D duction of the document would be injurious to the public service, we think the judge ought not to compel the production of it ... MARTIN, B., does not entirely agree with us as to the general view we have taken of this question. He is of opinion that whenever the judge is satisfied that the document may be made public without prejudice to the public service, the judge ought to compel its production, notwithstanding the reluctance of the head of the department to produce it; and perhaps cases might arise where the matter

E would be so clear that the judge might well ask for it in spite of some official scruples as to producing it; but this must be considered rather as an extreme case, and extreme cases throw very little light upon the practical rules of life."

Robinson's case (135), though disapproved in *Duncan's* case (132), has been

F followed throughout the Commonwealth and there is no indication so far as the researches of counsel have gone that in the United States the courts have acquiesced in the view that the decision rests always with the executive and the courts are excluded from deciding on State privilege. In *Robinson's* case (135) inspection was ordered with a view to production, if the court so ordered. I respectfully agree with the decision in that case and am of opinion that the line

G there taken should be followed. Each case is to be decided by the court. This means private inspection by the court in a proper case before production is ordered. This was thought at the time of the decision in *Beatson* v. *Skene* (133) to have been objectionable, and the same view was taken by this House in *Duncan's* case (132), but I see no objection to it in principle. Indeed, the books contain a number of cases where as a preliminary to the consideration of produc-

H tion to the parties inspection by the court has been ordered. (Compare *Asiatic Petroleum Co., Ltd.* v. *Anglo-Persian Oil Co., Ltd.* (136), a decision of SCRUTTON, J., subsequently upheld by the Court of Appeal.)

I do not regard the classification which places all documents under the heading either of contents or class to be wholly satisfactory. The plans of warships, as in *Duncan's* case (132), and documents exemplified by cabinet minutes are to be

I treated, I think, as cases to which Crown privilege can be properly applied as a class without the necessity of the documents being considered individually. The documents in this case, class documents though they be, are in a different category, seeking protection, not as State documents of political or strategic

---

(132) [1942] 1 All E.R. 587; [1942] A.C. 624.
(133) [1843-60] All E.R. Rep. 882; (1860), 5 H. & N. 838.
(134) [1843-60] All E.R. Rep. at p. 885; (1860), 5 H. & N. at pp. 853, 854.
(135) [1931] All E.R. Rep. 333; [1931] A.C. 704.
(136) [1916-17] All E.R. Rep. at p. 640; [1916] 1 K.B. at p. 830.

importance, but as requiring protection on the ground that " candour " must be   A
ensured.

Finally, I should refer to an argument put forward by the Attorney-General
that by the Crown Proceedings Act, 1947, s. 28, (137), Parliament had confirmed
the decision in *Duncan's* case (138). Section 28 provides:

" (1) Subject to and in accordance with rules of court and county court   B
rules—

" (a) in any civil proceedings in the High Court or a county court to which
the Crown is a party, the Crown may be required to make discovery of
documents and produce documents for inspection; and (b) . . .

" Provided that this section shall be without prejudice to any rule of
law which authorises or requires the withholding of any document or the   C
refusal to answering questions on the ground that the disclosure of the
document or the answering of the questions would be injurious to the public
interest . . .

" (2) Without prejudice to the proviso to the preceding subsection, any
rules made for the purpose of this section shall be such as to secure that the
existence of a document will not be disclosed if, in the opinion of the Minister   D
of the Crown, it would be injurious to the public interest to disclose the
existence thereof."

I do not regard this language as limiting the power of the courts to make declarations as to the law or in any way crystallizing the law as contained in a judicial
decision.

I would allow the appeal and direct that all the documents, that is to say the   E
probation reports and the report made to the chief constable with a view to
prosecution, should be produced but only for inspection in the first place in
order to determine whether the facts discoverable by their production would be
prejudicial or detrimental to the public welfare in any justifiable sense.

LORD PEARCE: My Lords, I agree with the opinion of my noble and   F
learned friend, LORD REID. There is not and never has been any doubt that the
High Court will not order the production of any document where this would
imperil the State or harm the public interest as a whole. It has normally accepted
the Minister's word on such a point. For he is cognisant of the contents of the
document and the background which makes its production harmful. Nevertheless,
the final responsibility lies on the High Court itself with its inherent power to   G
decide what evidence it shall demand in the fulfilment of its public duty to
administer justice. This inherent power has always been remembered and
acknowledged in Scotland, though its use has been very rare and, in the opinion
of some, niggardly. In England it seems at times to have been forgotten; sometimes language has been used which amounts to a denial of its existence and an
abdication of the court's responsibility. Yet at other times there have been   H
expressions, inspections and orders which are only consistent with its existence.

Beatson v. *Skene* (139) which was relied on in *Duncan* v. *Cammell Laird &
Co., Ltd.* (138) reveals the two conflicting points of view. The majority in the
judgment of POLLOCK, C.B., were of the opinion that (140)

" if the production of a State paper would be injurious to the public
service, the general public interest must be considered paramount to the   I
individual interest of a suitor in a court of justice; and the question then
arises, How is this to be determined? "

After pointing out the difficulties of the judge enquiring he concludes that such

---

(137) See 6 HALSBURY'S STATUTES (2nd Edn.) 66.
(138) [1942] 1 All E.R. 587; [1942] A.C. 624.
(139) [1843-60] All E.R. Rep. 882; (1860), 5 H. & N. 838.
(140) [1843-60] All E.R. Rep. at p. 885; (1860), 5 H. & N. at p. 853.

A   an enquiry " cannot take place in private, and [which] taking place in public may do all the mischief which it is proposed to guard against ". It may have been in those days that an enquiry could not be private, but that is not so now. He continues (141):

B   " It appears to us, therefore, that the question, whether the production of the documents would be injurious to the public service must be determined, not by the judge, but by the head of the department having the custody of the paper; and if he is in attendance and states that in his opinion the production of the document would be injurious to the public service, we think the judge ought not to compel the production of it. MARTIN, B., does not entirely agree with us as to the general view we have taken of this
C   question. He is of opinion that whenever the judge is satisfied that the document may be made public without prejudice to the public service, the judge ought to compel its production, notwithstanding the reluctance of the head of the department to produce it; and perhaps cases might arise where the matter would be so clear that the judge might well ask for it in spite of some official scruples as to producing it; but this must be considered rather as an extreme case, and extreme cases throw very little light on the practical
D   rules of life."

It should be noted, first that the word " ought " is used (the language of discretion not compulsion); secondly, that MARTIN, B., disagreed and that the others admitted that there might perhaps be extreme cases where the judge should overrule the executive; thirdly, that the case was dealing with particular docu-
E   ments of some importance; and, fourthly, that the view of the majority was largely founded on the belief that there could not be inspection of the document in private.

Although private inspection may not be desirable as a general rule, when it can be avoided, the court has the power and should clearly use it when necessary. In 1888 FIELD, J. (*Hennessy* v. *Wright* (142)), in 1916 SCRUTTON, J. (*Asiatic Petroleum Co., Ltd.* v. *Anglo-Persian Oil Co., Ltd.* (143)), with the approval of
F   the Court of Appeal), and in 1932 MACNAGHTEN, J. (*Spigelmann* v. *Hocker* (144)), inspected the documents in question; and in *Robinson* v. *State of South Australia* (*No. 2*) (145), the Privy Council ordered inspection and expressly approved *Queensland Pine Co.* v. *Commonwealth of Australia* (146) where in spite of the clear and unambiguous certificate of the Minister there had been inspection by
G   the court.

Such inspections are inconsistent with a denial of ultimate inherent power in the court. It is argued that in some or all of these cases there had been a question whether the objection of the executive had been taken in proper form, and that the judge was merely intervening as the second line of defence, when the Minister, as the first line of defence, had failed to take the objection properly. But in all
H   those cases the court knew well that there was objection. I do not accept that in so important a matter it could properly play about with formalities or regard itself as entering forbidden territory merely because a door had not been formally locked.

There are two expressions of opinion at the highest level which represent the two conflicting lines of thought that run through the earlier cases. *Robinson's*
I   case (147) which was decided in time of peace, and *Duncan's* case (148) which was concerned with the disclosure of plans of a submarine in the middle of a desperate

---

(141) [1843-60] All E.R. Rep. at p. 885; (1860), 5 H. & N. at pp. 853, 854.
(142) (1888), 21 Q.B.D. 509.
(143) [1916-17] All E.R. Rep. at p. 640; [1916] 1 K.B. at p. 830.
(144) (1933), 50 T.L.R. at p. 88.
(145) [1931] All E.R. Rep. at p. 342; [1931] A.C. at p. 725.
(146) [1920] St.R. Qd. 121.
(147) [1931] All E.R. Rep. 333; [1931] A.C. 704.
(148) [1942] 1 All E.R. 587; [1942] A.C. 624.

war. In theory any general legal definition of the balance between individual **A**
justice in one scale and the safety and well-being of the State in the other scale,
should be unaffected by the dangerous times in which it is uttered. In practice,
however, the flame of individual right and justice must burn more palely when
it is ringed by the more dramatic light of bombed buildings; and the human mind
cannot but be affected subconsciously, even in generality of definition, by such a
contrast since it is certainly a matter which ought to influence the particular **B**
decision in the case.

The contrast between peace and war is emphasised by SIR JOHN SIMON, K.C.,
in his argument in 1916 in the *Asiatic Petroleum* case (149):

> " The circumstances here are peculiar because a great war is in progress,
> and the court will be careful before ordering production at such a time.
> There is no case where the privilege has been discussed in time of war." **C**

Again, that contrast was specifically mentioned in *Robinson's* case (150):

> " It must not be assumed from these observations of the lord justice
> [TURNER, L.J., in *Wadeer* v. *East India Co.* (151)] that documents relating to
> the trading, commercial or contractual activities of a State can never be
> claimed to be protected under this head of privilege. It is conceivable that **D**
> even in connexion with the production of such documents there may be
> ' some plain overruling principle of public interest concerned which cannot
> be disregarded '. But the cases in which this is so must, in view of the sole
> object of the privilege, and especially in time of peace, be rare indeed, and the
> distinction drawn by the lord justice remains instructive and illuminating.
> In view of the increasing extension of State activities into spheres of trading **E**
> business and commerce, and of the claim of privilege in relation to liabilities
> arising therefrom now apparently freely put forward, his observations stand
> on record to remind the courts that, while they must duly safeguard public
> interests, they must see to it that the scope of the admitted privilege is not,
> in such litigation, extended."

Robinson's case (152) has been followed in other Commonwealth countries; **F**
but *Duncan's* case (153) has bound the English courts. Thus, there has for a
quarter of a century been a clear and unfortunate dissimilarity between our
courts—and those of Scotland and other Commonwealth countries (and also the
United States). This is in itself a state of affairs which should be avoided if that
be possible consistently with principle. In my view, *Robinson's* case (152) represents the more correct approach. The court has always had an inherent power to **G**
inspect and order the production of a document or classes of document if in its
view the documents, to quote MARTIN, B.'s words, " may be made public without
prejudice to the public service ".

The Crown Proceedings Act, 1947, s. 28 made the ordinary rules of discovery
apply to the Crown when it is a party, subject to any rule of law which authorises
or requires the withholding of any document or the refusal to answer any question **H**
on the ground that the disclosure or the answering of the question could be
injurious to the public interest. " The Crown may therefore be required to authorise the disclosure of official information which would otherwise be an offence
under the Official Secrets Act, 1911 " (PROFESSOR WADE, ADMINISTRATIVE LAW
(2nd Edn.), p. 283). It was argued that the exception as to any rule of law which
authorises or requires the withholding of a document, was a statutory confirma- **I**
tion of *Duncan's* case (153); but it does not create any particular rule of law.
It merely preserves in the operation of the section whatever may from time to
time be the courts' rule of law for the withholding of documents. It affirms

---

(149) [1916] 1 K.B. at p. 828.
(150) [1931] All E.R. Rep. at pp. 337, 338; [1931] A.C. at p. 715.
(151) (1856), 8 De G.M. & G. at p. 189.
(152) [1931] All E.R. Rep. 333; [1931] A.C. 704.
(153) [1942] 1 All E.R. 587; [1942] A.C. 624.

A   nothing as to what that rule of law shall be or how it shall be operated. It is difficult to lay down with precision how far the court should accept the view of the executive on what should be privileged while retaining its inherent power to reject it; and how far it should inspect and form its own views, while giving due weight to the Minister's objection. Certainly the rigidity of approach which crystallised in *Duncan's* case (154) is very undesirable; and it has led to unsatis-

B   factory results.

   So far as concerns particular documents whose disclosure is said to be injurious to the public interest the problem is less acute. If the Crown on the ground of injury to the public objects to the production of the plans of a submarine, as in *Duncan's* case (154), it is obvious that the court would accept the matter without further scrutiny. In a less obvious case the court might require more detailed

C   elaboration by the Crown to show that what on the face of it seems harmless would in fact be harmful. This can as a rule be done without disclosing any secret. In the highest range of security there is provision in the Crown Proceedings Act, 1947, whereby the Crown in really urgent cases of secrecy has a statutory right not to disclose the existence of a document if the disclosure of is existence would be injurious to the public interest, as, for instance, the disclosure of the mere

D   existence of a secret treaty might be. In the lower ranges of importance the judge can, as did SCRUTTON, J., in the *Asiatic Petroleum* case (155), satisfy himself by inspection.

   It is in respect of documents for which privilege is claimed as a class that the real difficulty lies. Even since the date of *Duncan's* case (154) there has been an enormous increase in the extent to which the executive impinges on the private lives

E   of the citizens. New ministries have been created and the old have been enlarged. Inevitably the mass of documentation has proliferated. It now bears little relation to the " State Papers " or other documents of government to which some of the older cases refer. Yet the same privilege has been sought (and given) under the argument that the necessary candour cannot be obtained from civil servants if their documents are to be subjected to an outside chance of production in a court

F   of law. Support for this argument is to be found in *Smith* v. *East India Co.* (156) and *Hennessy* v. *Wright* (157).

   Any department quite naturally and reasonably wishes, as any private business or any semi-State board must also wish, that its documents or correspondence should never be seen by any outside eye. If it can obtain this result by putting forward a general vague claim for protection on the ground of candour it can hardly

G   be blamed for doing so. " It is not surprising " it has been said (PROFESSOR WADE, ADMINISTRATIVE LAW (2nd Edn.) at p. 285) " that the Crown, having been given a blank cheque, yielded to the temptation to overdraw ". Moreover the defect of such an argument is that discrimination and relaxation of the claim could not be acknowledged by the Crown lest it jeopardise the claim of the whole class of documents and of other classes of document. No weighing of the

H   injury done to particular litigants (and thereby to the public at large) by a resulting denial of justice can be made. The ministry puts forward the rigid general claim. The court accepts it. The litigant ruefully leaves the lists, a victim of an injustice, great or small. In some cases this injustice is a necessary evil for the public good, in others it is unnecessary. Yet the court has not weighed the balance or considered whether the public interest in the well-being or routine of the ministry or the public interest in the fair administration of justice should have prevailed in that particular case.

   One may perhaps take police reports of accidents as an extreme example of the malaise that can be produced by a total acceptance of the theory that all documents should be protected whenever the Minister says so on the basis that

(154) [1942] 1 All E.R. 587; [1942] A.C. 624.
(155) [1916-17] All E.R. Rep. 637; [1916] 1 K.B. 822.
(156) (1841), 1 Ph. 50.
(157) (1888), 21 Q.B.D. 509.

candour will be injured if there is production. In *Spigelmann's* case (158) counsel
for the Treasury urgently intervened to prevent production of a policeman's
notebook. Many authorities were cited. Finally the learned judge inspected the
notebook which contained merely the usual account of a road accident. What
policeman *could* be deterred from candour by the thought that a judge might read
his notes? One imagines that he would rather be put on his mettle to make sure
that his observations were sound and accurate, and be stimulated by the thought
that he might prove to be the one impartial recorder on whom justice between
the parties might ultimately turn. When one considers the large public interest
in a just decision of road accident cases, and the absence of any possible corresponding injury to the candour of police reports on accident cases, one realises to
what a complete lack of commonsense a general blanket protection of wide classes
may lead; and it would be an equal departure from commonsense to suppose
that no great public injury could result from disclosure of police reports concerning
their war on really serious crime.

Another unsatisfactory example is the case of *Broome* v. *Broome* (*Edmundson
cited*) (159) where an attempt was made to advance Crown privilege to quite
unreasonable limits. It was relevant in a divorce case to establish whether
a husband, an army sergeant, had been pleasant or unpleasant to his wife when
he met her on her arrival at Singapore, and it was desired to call a representative
of S.A.A.F.A. which had taken a reconciling hand in their matrimonial troubles.
This evidence, like that of a probation officer, might have had privilege as between
the parties, but the Ministry of Defence intervened, in case the parties might
waive the privilege, to object not only to the production of reports made to the
War Office, but also to oral evidence being given by the S.A.A.F.A. representative.
SACHS, J., rightly refused the suggested extension of Crown privilege and innocuous evidence was given by the witness; but the fact that the privilege was
sought shows that it is not easy for the department concerned to make an objective
appraisal of the matter. Again, in the case of *Ellis* v. *Home Office* (160) Crown
privilege claimed on a " class " basis was upheld, but was with reason criticised
at the trial and by the Court of Appeal. In 1956 as a concession to discontent
on this subject VISCOUNT KILMUIR, L.C., announced (161) that privilege would
no longer be claimed in certain matters, e.g., reports on accidents on the road or
accidents on government premises, or involving government employees; for
medical reports on certain employees or when a doctor (or the Crown) is sued for
negligence and for documents needed by the defence on a criminal charge.
These concessions, however, though valuable, left untouched the underlying
defect of the present situation, its inherent rigidity, and, in many cases, its
illogicality.

In my view, it is essential to leave the vague generalities of wide classes and
get down to realities in weighing the respective injuries to the public of a denial
of justice on the one side and, on the other, a revelation of governmental documents which were never intended to be made public and which might be inhibited
by an unlikely possibility of disclosure. Obviously production would never be
ordered of fairly wide classes of documents at a high level. To take an extreme
case, production would never be ordered of cabinet correspondence, letters or
reports on appointments to office of importance and the like; but why should
the same yardstick apply to trivial documents and correspondence with or within
a ministry?

It is conceded that under the existing practice there can be no weighing of
injustice in particular cases against the general public disadvantage of disclosure
and its effect on candour. But it is argued that a judge, who is the only person
who can properly weigh the former, is incapable of properly weighing the latter.

(158) (1933), 50 T.L.R. 87.
(159) [1955] 1 All E.R. 201; [1955] P. 190.
(160) [1953] 2 All E.R. 149; [1953] 2 Q.B. 135.
(161) See p. 881, letter I, ante.

A I do not understand why he cannot do so, especially if the ministry gives some specific details of the type of document in question and some specific reasons why it is undesirable to allow production. It is a judge's constant task to weigh human behaviour and the points that tell for or against candour. He knows full well that in general a report will be less inhibited if it will never see the light of public scrutiny, and that in some cases and on some subjects this may be wholly

B desirable. He also knows that on many subjects this fact has little if any important effect. Against this he can consider whether the documents in question are of much or little weight in the litigation, whether their absence will result in a complete or partial denial of justice to one or other of the parties or perhaps to both, and what is the importance of the particular litigation to the parties and the public. All these are matters which should be considered, if the court is to decide where

C the public interest lies.

Even on the question of candour, the fact that the party who himself made the document wishes for it to be disclosed cannot be quite irrelevant. For it could hardly inhibit a writer's candour to know that it may be disclosed at any time when he himself wishes its disclosure. Moreover, if, as at present, it may be disclosed in criminal proceedings then there is already an outside chance of

D disclosure, and the effect on candour which would be produced by disclosure in *civil* proceedings would thus be an increase in an already existing outside possibility of disclosure. All these matters are not weighed under the practice as it has existed since *Duncan's* case (162). Admittedly, the fact that the maker of a document himself wishes it to be made public is not regarded nor is any consideration given to the importance of a particular document in particular litigation.

E In my opinion, the court should consider whether the document is relevant and important in a reasonable action, so that one may fairly say that the public interest in justice requires its disclosure. It must consider whether the disclosure will cause harm administratively, either because of the undesirability of publishing the particular contents or because of the undesirability of making public a particular class of documents (of which I have given examples above) or for any

F other valid reason. It must give due weight to any representations of the Minister which set out the undesirability of disclosure and explain the reasons. If these do not make the matter clear enough, the court should itself call for and inspect the documents before coming to a decision. If part of a document is innocuous but part is of such a nature that its disclosure would be undesirable, it should seal up the latter part and order discovery of the rest, provided that this will not give a

G distorted or misleading impression. In all these matters it must consider the public interest as a whole, giving due weight both to the administration of the executive and to the administration of justice.

In my opinion, the probation reports on the appellant should be disclosed. In practice they will have considerable influence on the result of the case, although in theory their effect might not be of importance. Both sides hope to get from them support in their respective contentions on the question of malice. However clearly the judge explains their absence, it will be hard to persuade a jury that the reports are not being suppressed for sinister reasons and to prevent its members from harbouring unfair suspicions against the respondent. Their suppression, moreover, will entail a suppression of cross-examination on the point. This would be unfair to both parties. Clearly production is desirable in the interests of justice. Would their production harm the candour of such reports in general, and do a general harm disproportionate to the importance of justice in this particular case? I do not think so. The reports on a probationer are not on a sufficiently high level to do public harm by the disclosure. It is argued that in future if there is any possibility of disclosure such reports will not be written with candid criticism. It is stressed that such a report may have an important effect on a probationer's future service in the force. No doubt the writer

---

(162) [1942] 1 All E.R. 587; [1942] A.C. 624.

of such a report is aware of this, and this in itself, I think, would create a reluc- A
tance to make criticism which might be too harsh, a reluctance that would be
more compelling than any outside possibility of disclosure. There are countless
teachers at schools and universities, countless employers of labour, who write
candid reports, unworried by the outside chance of disclosure, but deeply concerned, as no doubt the police are likewise, lest their criticism may be doing less
than justice to the subject of their report. In my opinion, the balance of public B
good in the circumstances of this particular case tilts in favour of producing the
reports, and their disclosure should therefore be ordered. The report to the chief
constable is of obvious importance. It will probably make or mar the chances
of one or other of the parties. If it is not produced I do not see how there can be
any evidence in chief or cross-examination on a vital point in the case or how the
case can be fairly tried. Nevertheless I see that there might be strong arguments C
against its disclosure. One cannot weigh these considerations on matters of
abstract argument and theory without seeing more of the contents and form of
the document. It is in just such a case as this that a court should inspect the
document. Your lordships should, in my opinion, privately inspect it before
coming to any conclusion.

I would therefore allow the appeal. D

LORD UPJOHN: My Lords, there can be no doubt that the basic principle
to be applied in cases where the Crown claims privilege from production of documents is to be found in the following passage in VISCOUNT SIMON, L.C.'s speech
in *Duncan* v. *Cammell Laird & Co., Ltd.* (163) when he said (164):

"The principle to be applied in every case is that documents otherwise E
relevant and liable to production must not be produced if the public interest
requires that they should be withheld. This test may be found to be satisfied
either (*a*) by having regard to the contents of the particular document, or (*b*)
by the fact that the document belongs to a class which, on grounds of
public interest, must as a class be withheld from production."

This case is concerned only with class documents, for privilege is claimed only F
on that ground in respect of four documents which are no more than reports on
the progress of the appellant, a probationer constable and in respect of one which
is concerned with a report on the appellant for submission to the Director of
Public Prosecutions. The first question is whether the affidavit of the Home
Secretary claiming privilege for these documents is final and conclusive and must
be accepted as such by the courts as the majority of the Court of Appeal G
held (165), following LORD SIMON's view which was summarised in the sentence
(166):

"Although an objection validly taken to production on the ground that
this would be injurious to the public interest is conclusive, it is important
to remember that the decision ruling out such documents is the decision H
of the judge."

He then points out, however, that the judge must so rule.

My lords, apart altogether from our recent liberation from some of the chains
of precedent, which for my part I think should only be exercised rarely and
sparingly, I do not think that the *Duncan* case (163) governs this case for a
number of reasons. First, it is now quite clear that per incuriam the House
misunderstood the law of Scotland as now explained and enunciated in *Glasgow
Corpn.* v. *Central Land Board* (167). While the law of England and that of Scotland may differ in many respects it is really essential, in the interests of justice

(163) [1942] 1 All E.R. 587; [1942] A.C. 624.
(164) [1942] 1 All E.R. at p. 592; [1942] A.C. at p. 636.
(165) [1967] 2 All E.R. 1260.
(166) [1942] 1 All E.R. at p. 595; [1942] A.C. at p. 642.
(167) 1956 S.C. (H.L.) 1.

A to Her Majesty's subjects in both parts of the United Kingdom, that the rules relating to Crown privilege should be the same. This factor alone entitled your lordships to review the matter de novo. Secondly, I do not think that the observations of LORD SIMON were intended to bind or did bind the courts to reach the conclusion that in every case (save where honesty or bona fides were challenged) the affidavit of the Minister claiming privilege is conclusive, and I put this on two

B grounds. In the first place, although it was not so stated in express terms in LORD SIMON's speech I am of opinion that the claim of privilege in that case was based and rightly based on a " contents " basis. The late Mr. A. V. Alexander based his claim at all events in part on the advice of his technical advisers; at a time of total war when the very latest design of submarine founders on her trials the slightest escape to the public of the most innocent details may be a source of

C danger to the State; and it matters not that some details may have been disclosed at an earlier inquiry; the greater publicity of an action may afford enemy agents an opportunity that they missed earlier. So I think LORD SIMON's remarks were, in relation to class documents, strictly obiter. In the second place, whether I am right or wrong in that, I do not think for one moment that LORD SIMON had in mind a type of document, such as routine reports on a probationer constable,

D when he made his general observations on the law. I agree entirely with the cogent arguments advanced by my noble and learned friend, LORD REID, in his speech, for thinking that LORD SIMON never intended that the claim of the Minister should be conclusive in such cases; so on that ground, too, the documents in this case being so different from those in the Duncan case (168), I think that it is open to your lordships to review the matter. Thirdly, I think that there is a

E broader ground on which your lordships can re-examine this matter. The privilege which is claimed is, and I now quote again from the passage in LORD SIMON's speech with which I started, on the ground that documents " liable to production must not be produced if the public interest requires that they should be withheld ". As SWINFEN EADY, L.J., pointed out in Asiatic Petroleum Co., Ltd. v. Anglo-Persian Oil Co., Ltd. (169) the test must be that the information cannot be

F disclosed without injury to the public interest, not that the documents are confidential or official. That is the basic law, and, when descending from that general proposition to an examination of the particular class of document for which privilege is claimed, the court should not be unduly fettered by what has been said by courts in earlier days; and the observations of judges must be read in the light of the general circumstances at the time and the particular type

G of document before the court. Times change; many years ago the claim of Crown privilege was not heard so frequently as to-day, though when made the courts were often, as I think, unduly lenient in interpreting the necessity for withholding production, e.g., H.M.S. Bellerophon (170), and a number of other cases mentioned in your lordships' speeches. The relation between Crown and subject becomes closer every day with the increasing interference, no doubt on sound grounds of

H public policy, of the Crown with the private life of the subject, so that communications within and between government departments relating to the individual subject are of much greater frequency than before. Then for twenty years the subject has been able to sue the Crown, and the increase in crime, motor accidents and the like have all led to a great increase in the number of cases where the Crown is asked to produce documents. So I think that in this field the courts

I are entitled from time to time to make a re-appraisal in relation to particular documents of just what it is that the public interest demands in shielding them from production. This is emphasised by the fact that quite naturally the executive have relied on the Duncan v. Cammell Laird & Co., Ltd. case (168), to claim privilege in class cases on the ground that the public interest requires that the writings of every member of the executive from the highest to the lowest (and

(168) [1942] 1 All E.R. 587; [1942] A.C. 624.
(169) [1916-17] All E.R. Rep. at p. 640; [1916] 1 K.B. at p. 830.
(170) (1874), 44 L.J. Adm. 5; 31 L.T. 756.

in this case we are very near the lowest) must be protected from production for A
the reason that the writer of the document must have a full, free and uninhibited
right to pen his views without fear that they will ever be subject to the public
gaze; in other words, secure in such knowledge he can then and apparently only
then write with the complete candour necessary for the discharge of his functions
as a member of the public service. If, contrary to my view, LORD SIMON meant
to go as far as that I would not hesitate to say that he was misunderstanding B
and misapplying the basic and the only proposition of law by which alone courts
are bound.

My lords, feeling as I do unfettered by any necessity for a strictly textual
adherence to LORD SIMON'S words, I think that the principle to be applied can
be very shortly stated. On the one side there is the public interest to be protected;
on the other side of the scales is the interest of the subject who legitimately C
wants production of some documents, which he believes will support his own or
defeat his adversary's case. Both are matters of public interest, for it is also in
the public interest that justice should be done between litigating parties by
production of all documents which are relevant and for which privilege cannot be
claimed under the ordinary rules. They must be weighed in the balance one against
the other.   D

Your lordships have reviewed the earlier authorities which are many and are
not easy to reconcile and I shall not discuss them again, but it seems to me that
there is sufficient authority to support the view held by all of your lordships
that the claim of privilege by the Crown, while entitled to the greatest weight,
is only a claim, and the decision whether the court should accede to the claim lies
within the discretion of the judge: and it is a real discretion. Thus MARTIN, B., E
(in advance of his colleagues) in *Beatson* v. *Skene* (171); FIELD, J., in *Hennessy*
v. *Wright* (172); VAUGHAN WILLIAMS, L.J., in *West* v. *West* (173); SCRUTTON, J.,
in chambers in *Asiatic Petroleum Co., Ltd.* v. *Anglo-Persian Oil Co., Ltd.* (174) in
1916; MACNAGHTEN, J., in *Spigelmann* v. *Hocker* (175), and the Privy Council in
Robinson v. *State of South Australia* (*No. 2*) (176); finally, of course, the law of
Scotland on this point, seldom though the right to order production seems to F
have been exercised. First, with regard to the " contents " cases there is, I think,
no dispute and it does not strictly arise in this case. A claim made by a Minister
on the basis that the disclosure of the contents would be prejudicial to the public
interest must receive the greatest weight; but even here I am of opinion that the
Minister should go as far as he properly can without prejudicing the public interest
in saying why the contents require protection. In such cases it would be rare G
indeed for the court to overrule the Minister, but it has the legal power to do so,
first inspecting the document itself and then ordering its production. Secondly,
the " class " cases. Here it is to be noted, and I think it is important, that the
emphasis in LORD SIMON'S speech changes, for the public interest is here identified
with " the practice of keeping a class of documents secret is necessary for the
proper functioning of the public service ". These were the words seized on by the H
executive to make good their broad claims that I have already mentioned.

No doubt there are many cases in which documents by their very nature fall
into a class which requires protection such as, only by way of example, cabinet
papers, foreign office despatches, the security of the State, high-level inter-
departmental minutes and correspondence, and documents pertaining to the
general administration of the naval, military and air force services. Nearly
always such documents would be the subject of privilege by reason of their contents but also by their " class ", in any event, they qualify for privilege. So, too,
high-level inter-departmental communications, to take, only as an example on
establishment matters, the promotion or transfer of reasonably high-level personnel
in the service of the Crown; but no catalogue can reasonably be compiled. The

(171) [1843-60] All E.R. Rep. 882; (1860), 5 H. & N. 838.
(172) (1888), 21 Q.B.D. 509.   (173) (1911), 27 T.L.R. 476.
(174) [1916-17] All E.R. Rep. 637; [1916] 1 K.B. 822.
(175) (1933), 50 T.L.R. 87.   (176) [1931] All E.R. Rep. 333; [1931] A.C. 704.

A reason for this privilege is that it would be quite wrong and entirely inimical to the proper functioning of the public service if the public were to learn of these high level communications, however innocent of prejudice to the State the actual contents of any particular document might be; that is obvious. It has nothing whatever to do, however, with candour or uninhibited freedom of expression; I cannot believe that any Minister or any high level military or civil servant would

B feel in the least degree inhibited in expressing his honest views in the course of his duty on some subject, such as even the personal qualifications and delinquencies of some colleague, by the thought that his observations might one day see the light of day. His worst fear might be libel, and there he has the defence of qualified privilege like everyone else in every walk of professional industrial and commercial life, who every day has to express views on topics indistinguish-

C able in substance from those of the servants of the Crown. So this plea of the necessity for the protection of documents written by junior servants of the Crown must depend solely on the necessity for candour and was, in fact, the basis of the argument of the Attorney-General and his learned junior. No one who has been a judge of first instance for some years will have failed to meet this problem occasionally where some really trivial correspondence between some

D ministry and a subject or local authority has been withheld on this ground.

    My lords, this alleged necessity for candour and uninhibited freedom of communication among the executives of government might require some detailed examination were it not for the fact that the executive itself realised after the case of *Ellis* v. *Home Office* (177), that the literal textual interpretation of LORD SIMON'S words simply would not do. So VISCOUNT KILMUIR, L.C., in 1956, (178),

E made a gallant attempt to bring the practice of the Crown based on the *Duncan* v. *Cammell Laird & Co., Ltd.* (179) case into line with modern conditions and the greatly changed relationship since the last war of Crown and subject, by making a statement of principle on which the Crown would act in future; this was later slightly amended in 1962. This attempt, though praiseworthy, produced extraordinary and utterly, not merely illogical but (to me) incomprehensible

F results. My noble and learned friend, LORD REID, has pointed out some of them, and I do not propose to repeat or expatiate on them. That state of affairs cannot be allowed to continue. It is clear, in my opinion, that the judiciary must regain its control over the whole of this field of the law. The tests to be applied to claims for Crown privilege in class cases I think should be as follows:

    There are some documents which, apart altogether with the alleged necessity

G for candour, fall within the claim of protection; and probably at the same time, though not necessarily, within the " contents " class. I have already given some examples and do not repeat them; the judge still has, though I should be surprised if it were ever necessary to exercise it, the rights I have mentioned in the " contents " cases.

    Then within the " class " cases we come to the " candour " cases pure and

H simple. For my part I find it difficult to justify this, when those in other walks of life which give rise to equally important matters of confidence in relation to security and personnel matters as in the public service can claim no such privilege. Here let me turn to police reports which play some part in the last document before your lordships for which privilege is claimed. No one can doubt that a police report, dealing with a suspected crime or with matters which might be

I of conceivable use to the underworld, must be privileged, and for my part I think that privilege should be claimed under the " contents " side if in fact the documents could be of the slightest use to the underworld. No one would want to hamper the police in any way, but I cannot see what harm can be done to them by disclosing a document which either does not assist, or no longer assists in the apprehension of a wrongdoer nor discloses any relevant police information, procedures or activities of interest to the underworld. So I think that if privilege is

---

(177) [1953] 2 All E.R. 149; [1953] 2 Q.B. 135.
(178) See p. 881, letters F, H and I, ante.   (179) [1942] 1 All E.R. 587; [1942] A.C. 624.

claimed for a document on the ground of " class " the judge, if he feels any doubt   A
about the reason for its inclusion as a class document, should not hesitate to call
for its production for this private inspection, and to order and limit its production
if he thinks fit.

There is only one other matter to which I want to refer; it is the question
whether there is any objection to the private inspection by the judge himself
of a document for which privilege is claimed. My lords, in a number of the leading   B
cases, such as *Beatson* v. *Skene* (180) and *Duncan* v. *Cammell Laird Co., Ltd.* (181)
itself, it has been held that there is some objection to the judge looking at the
document in private, as being contrary to the broad rules of justice as we understand it, where all the documents must be open to both sides. I do not understand
this objection. There is a lis between A and B; the Crown may be A or B or, as
in this case, a third party, for both A and B in this case want to see the documents;   C
but when the judge demands to see the documents for which privilege is claimed
he is not considering that lis but quite a different lis, that is whether the public
interest in withholding the document outweighs the public interest that all
relevant documents not otherwise privileged should be disclosed in litigation.
The judge's duty is to decide that lis; if he decides it in favour of disclosure,
cadit quaestio; if he decides it in favour of non-disclosure he banishes its contents   D
from his mind for the purposes of the main lis. There is nothing unusual about
this; judges and juries have to do it every day. So it seems to me to be quite
clear that there is no erosion on our normal ideas of justice inter partes if a judge,
being not satisfied about the Crown's claim to privilege, himself privately inspects
the allegedly privileged documents. But before reaching that stage he may, of
course, require further and better affidavits by the Minister, and may direct the   E
Minister to attend for cross-examination by any party to the litigation before he
inspects the document.

My lords, these procedures are, in my opinion, equally available in the inferior
courts, but if the judge orders disclosure and the Crown intimates its intention
to appeal from that order then, in my opinion, the matter should be adjourned
so that the matter may be tested in the High Court before actual disclosure.   F

On the question of the actual documents in this case I can be very brief. With
regard to the routine reports on this probationer constable I would think quite
clearly they should be disclosed. With regard to the report to the Director of
Public Prosecutions, as one concerning police procedures which might disclose
something of value to the criminal underworld—a point which, under the new
practice which should be adopted after this decision, should be specifically taken   G
in the Minister's affidavit—I agree that your lordships should inspect this document in the first place and in these circumstances purely as a matter of convenience
your lordships should also inspect the routine reports at the same time, before
ordering disclosure.

My lords, I would allow this appeal.

Appeal allowed.   H

LORD REID: I understand that the documents in question are now made
available for inspection by your lordships, so it is unnecessary to make any order
for their production. It will be necessary now to adjourn further consideration
of the cause until the documents have been examined. It will be convenient
to deal with costs when the cause is finally disposed of.

Further consideration adjourned sine die.

Solicitors: *Field, Roscoe & Co.*, agents for *Berkson & Berkson*, Birkenhead (for
the appellant); *Treasury Solicitor*; *Markbys*, agents for *Wayman-Hales*, Chester
(for the respondent).

[*Reported by* S. A. HATTEEA, ESQ., *Barrister-at-Law*.]

---

(180) [1843-60] All E.R. Rep. 882; (1860), 5 H. & N. 838.
(181) [1942] 1 All E.R. 587; [1942] A.C. 624.

A

LINDGREN AND OTHERS *v.* L. & P. ESTATES CO., LTD.

[COURT OF APPEAL, CIVIL DIVISION (Harman, Danckwerts and Winn, L.JJ.),
October 30, 31, November 1, 2, 3, 6, 7, 8, 9 and December 5, 1967.]

B   *Company—Director—Powers—Exercise of independent judgment—Contract to
grant long leases—Company becoming subsidiary of development company—
Director of development company suggesting contract to directors of subsidiary
company—Validity of contract.*

In January, 1959, a development company, which at this time was
substantially controlled by C. and of which L. was also a director, contracted
C   to buy all the shares of the defendant company, which owned many properties,
and obtained an undertaking from the owner of the shares to cause the
defendant company to enter into leases of certain properties to the trustees
of a settlement under which C.'s children were income beneficiaries. Those of
the defendant company's properties that were to be leased were subject to
old tenancies at fairly low rents, which would be unsuitable for inclusion in
D   the portfolio of the development company, but the properties would be
valuable when the leases expired. The scheme was that the defendant
company should grant a lease of these properties to the trustees of the
settlement at a rent substantially exceeding the rents presently receivable
from the properties; this scheme would be acceptable to the income beneficiaries under the settlement, as they were surtax payers, to whom the growth
E   of the trust fund was more attractive than present income. L. was a trustee
of the settlement as well as a director of the development company. C. and L.
suggested to the directors of the defendant company that the defendant
company should agree to lease the properties to the trustees of the settlement.
In March, 1959, the defendant company entered into a written contract with
the trustees of the settlement to lease to them the properties for terms
F   which, as to the great majority of the properties, were for ninety-nine years.
There was no provision for breaking the leases to enable there to be development of the properties when possession was obtainable. The contract was not
implemented by execution of leases, but was acted on for some years. The
control of the development company having passed out of C.'s hands, the
trustees brought an action for specific performance of the contract. On
G   appeal by the defendant company from a decree of specific performance,
the defendant company contended that in making the contract its directors
had acted at the direction of C. and not in the interests of the defendant
company, and that the contract was procured by C. in the interests of
beneficiaries under the settlement and not in the interests of the development
company.

H   **Held:** the contract was not invalid and the plaintiff trustees were entitled
to a decree of specific performance for the following reasons—

(i) no breach of duty by the directors of the defendant company was
established, nor was it proved that they did not exercise independent judgment in deciding that the defendant company should enter into the contract
(see p. 923, letter H, p. 926, letter F, and p. 927, letter G, post); further,
I   (per HARMAN, L.J.), even if it had been the fact that the directors of the
defendant company did not exercise independent judgment, it was not
established that L. knew of it (see p. 921, letter I, post).

(ii) (per HARMAN, L.J.), the directors of the defendant company were
entitled to suppose that the views of C. and L. represented the views of the
board of the development company, or (per WINN, L.J.), C. and L. had the
ostensible authority of the development company for transactions in property,
and the directors of the defendant company could rightly have regard to the

views expressed by C. and L. (see p. 922, letter A, and p. 926, letter A, post;   A
cf., p. 923, letter H, post).

(iii) (per HARMAN, L.J.), L., though a director of the development company,
was not a director of the defendant company and was not bound to protect
the interests of the defendant company as being or about to be a subsidiary
company having an independent board (see p. 922, letter F, post);   and
(per WINN, L.J.), even if there had been a breach of duty of C. or L. to the   B
development company, which was not a party to the action, the breach would
not have entitled the defendant company to relief (see p. 928, letters D and E,
post).

Appeal dismissed;   cross-appeal allowed.

[As to acts ultra vires of directors, see 6 HALSBURY'S LAWS (3rd Edn.) 299,
para. 603, and as to their fiduciary position, see ibid., pp. 299, 300, para. 604;   C
and for cases on directors' powers, duties and liabilities, see 9 DIGEST (Repl.)
497, 498, 3273-3284, 508, 509, 3342-3352, 518, 519, 3420-3426, 529, 3485-3488,
536, 537, 3518-3531.]

Case referred to:
   Regal (Hastings), Ltd. v. Gulliver, [1942] 1 All E.R. 378;   9 Digest (Repl.) 523,   D
      3447.

Appeal.
By writ issued on July 28, 1964, the plaintiffs, Frederick William Lindgren,
William Edward Emms and Isidore Kerman sued the defendant company,
L. & P. Estates, Ltd., claiming specific performance of an agreement dated
Mar. 18, 1959, made between the defendant company of the one part and Ephraim   E
Harris Cotton, Frederick William Lindgren and William Edward Emms of the
other part, and claiming further or in the alternative damages for its breach.

By their statement of claim delivered on Oct. 6, 1964, the plaintiffs alleged that
by the agreement previously mentioned, which recited that the parties thereto
of the other part (referred to as " the lessees ") were then the trustees of a
settlement dated Mar. 15, 1946, and that the agreement provided that the defen-   F
dant company would grant and the lessees would take a lease in a specified form
of the respective properties therein described for a term of ninety-nine years
from Apr. 6, 1958, at the yearly rental of £82,525 reducible to £57,525 from
Oct. 20, 1967.   They further pleaded that cl. 3 (a) of the agreement provided
that either the lessor or the lessees might give not less than one month's notice
to the other, at any time during the period ending with twenty years after the   G
death of the last survivor of the descendants then living of His Late Majesty
King George V, requiring completion of the grant of the lease.   The plaintiffs
further pleaded that, Ephraim Harris Cotton having died, the plaintiffs were
the present trustees of the settlement of 1946 and that by notice dated June 30,
1964, pursuant to cl. 3 (a) of the agreement the plaintiffs had required completion
of the lease on Aug. 3, 1964, but that the defendant company was unwilling to   H
complete the grant of the lease.

These allegations were substantially admitted in the defence of the defendant
company re-served as re-amended on Jan. 24, 1967, but the defendant company
alleged that the written agreement did not contain all the terms on which it
was agreed that the defendant company would grant to the plaintiffs or their
successors the lease referred to.   The defendant company pleaded (among other
matters) that the agreement was entered into at the direction of the plaintiff
Lindgren and one Jack Cotton (alleged to be the two directors of City Centre
Properties, Ltd., called herein " the City company " who managed the affairs of
its subsidiaries, of which the defendant company was one).   The defendant
company pleaded further that the agreement was made with the plaintiffs as
trustees of the settlement of 1946, which was for the benefit of the children of the
said Jack Cotton;   that the agreement was not approved by resolution of dis-
interested directors of the City company, which received no independent advice

A on its terms; and that by virtue of art. 88 for the articles of association of the City company the plaintiff Lindgren and the said Jack Cotton had not power to procure the defendant company to enter into the agreement. The defendant company further pleaded that, if the agreement contained all the agreed terms, then it was improvident and inequitable to the defendant company and detrimental to the interests of the City company, as the owner of all its share capital,

B and that the plaintiff Lindgren and the said Jack Cotton acted in breach of their duty as directors of the City company and " as directors-elect " of the defendant company in procuring the defendant company to enter into the agreement. Alternatively that the said agreement was ultra vires the defendant company and its directors; and that the plaintiffs had express notice thereof and of the said breach of duty by reason of the facts that the plaintiffs Lindgren and Kerman

C were at the date of the agreement directors of the City company and the plaintiff Lindgren was a " director-elect " of the defendant company. The defendant company accordingly alleged that the agreement was not binding on it or, if it were binding, that specific performance of it ought not to be ordered. The defendant company counterclaimed, so far as material to be stated here, for a declaration that the agreement was void and of no effect.

D By order dated Feb. 15, 1967, made by PLOWMAN, J., at the trial of the action it was declared that the agreement dated Mar. 18, 1959, ought to be specifically performed and carried into execution and the same was adjudged accordingly. By notice dated Apr. 10, 1967, the defendant company gave notice of appeal and sought an order in the terms prayed by the counterclaim, varied in a respect not material to this report. Notice of further contentions to be raised on the

E appeal were given by the plaintiffs by notice dated Apr. 26, 1967, and by the defendants by notice dated June 13, 1967.

J. L. Arnold, Q.C., *M. Finer*, Q.C., and *R. B. S. Instone* for the defendant company.

Michael Albery, Q.C., and *Charles Sparrow*, Q.C., for the plaintiffs.

F   *Cur. adv. vult.*

Dec. 5. The following judgments were read.

HARMAN, L.J.: This is an appeal against a decree of PLOWMAN, J., in favour of the plaintiff trustees in a specific performance action in which the
G plaintiff trustees' claim was for specific performance of an agreement for a lease of a group of properties belonging to the defendant company. The plaintiffs are trustees of a settlement made in 1946 by Mr. Ephraim Cotton, who died in 1959. The original trustees were Mr. Ephraim Cotton and the plaintiffs, Mr. Lindgren and Mr. Emms, and the plaintiff Mr. Kerman was appointed trustee in Mr. Ephraim Cotton's place in 1962. The income beneficiaries are four grandchildren of the settlor, all of whom were at all material times of age. The agree-
H ment was made on Mar. 18, 1959, and possession of the subject-matter was handed over immediately to the plaintiffs and the agreement has been operative ever since. The only reason why the matter was not completed in 1959 by deed was the avoidance of stamp duty. The facts are fully stated in the judgment below and I do not repeat them further than necessary to make what follows, I hope, intelligible.

I The agreement on the face of it is perfectly regular and in particular contained a special provision entitling the plaintiffs to give notice at any time to the defendants requiring the grant of the lease of any one or more of the properties comprised in it. This notice has been given and on the face of it there is no defence to the action, which is however defended on two grounds: first, that the written document did not in fact contain the whole of the agreement between the parties, but that there was an extra term not reduced to writing entitling the defendants at any time to put an end to the lease as regards any

or all properties comprised in it. This defence, apart from involving a fraud on   **A**
the Revenue, would have made nonsense of the agreement and the judge rejected
it and there has been no appeal in that respect. There remains, however, a plea
expressed as follows—" The agreemeent is void and of no effect ". What the
pleader meant by this I have never understood. It is quite clear the agreement
was not void, and it has been acted on for years. The case was argued on the
footing that the words meant " is voidable and has been repudiated ", and this   **B**
for reasons which require some recital of the circumstances.

In the year 1959 the whole of the share capital of the defendant company was
owned by a Lady Price. It was a holding company being the owner of various
freehold and leasehold properties which roughly fell into two groups, group (1)
being properties recently let at rack rents which showed a good return on the
value, and group (2) being properties let not so recently and of which rents were   **C**
below the 1958 level and showed a poor return on the value. As and when these
latter leases should fall in, between 1968 and 1985, rents could probably be put
up and the income from the properties very much increased. In 1956 Lady Price
was desirous of realising her property interests, and her advisers, notably a
Mr. Goldsbrough, an accountant, who was a director of the defendant company,
and a Mr. Orchard-Lisle, a surveyor, the other director, both of whom were well   **D**
versed in the property world, approached a company called City Centre Properties,
Ltd. (" the City company "), a public company engaged in property development, and offered the properties to that company. So far as group (1) properties
were concerned this was an attractive proposition as it would provide good
dividends for the City company's shareholders. The group (2) properties, however, would show a very low yield and were not suitable for the portfolio of a   **E**
public company.

The mainspring of the City company was the late Mr. Jack Cotton, a son or
nephew of Mr. Ephraim Cotton and father of the beneficiaries under the settlement, and either he or his friend the plaintiff Mr. Lindgren, who was also a
director of the City company, were desirous of acquiring the former group of
properties without the latter and found a purchaser of the latter in the plaintiff   **F**
trustees of the 1946 settlement. The group (2) properties were thought to be a
suitable investment for the plaintiff trustees because their beneficiaries, the four
children of Mr. Jack Cotton, were all large surtax payers who wanted capital
rather than income profits. Moreover, if a long lease, i.e., one for over fifty
years, were granted, the lessees could deduct tax when paying the rent and could
use for that purpose dividends payable by the City company in which the trustees   **G**
were the largest single shareholders. It was therefore proposed that the City
company should buy the group (1) properties and the trustees the group (2),
but objections were raised to this of a fiscal nature and the plan was changed
to a sale to the City company of the entire share capital of the defendant company.
There was a valuation at arm's length of the defendant company's properties
for this purpose and the purchase price was settled at about £1,750,000, of which   **H**
the group (2) properties represented about £750,000. The arrangement then
made was that the whole transaction should go forward as one, but that the
defendant company should by arrangement with the City company grant a
lease to the trustees, the plaintiffs, of the group (2) properties immediately
before the sale of its shares to the City company. It remained to fix a rent,
and it is perhaps enough to say that for this purpose there was no further valuation, but the value of the group (2) properties was taken as £1,000,000, i.e.,
considerably more than the value agreed for the share transaction, and the rent
was eventually worked out at £82,000 odd a year for the ten freehold properties
in the group and £29,000 for a leasehold in Piccadilly. This would look well in
the defendant company's portfolio and enable a satisfactory dividend to be paid
to the City company, but it would result in a loss to the trustees in the earlier
years of about £40,000 a year, that being the excess of the rent over the existing

A rents from the properties. The agreement, as I say, was signed on Mar. 18, 1959. All went smoothly until the year 1963, when there was some revolution in the Cotton empire with the result that Mr. Jack Cotton ceased to be chairman of the City company and the trustees disposed of their interest in that company, which is now under different management. Mr. Cotton then suggested to the trustees that they should seek the completion of the agreement for a lease;

B this was refused, hence this action.

This defence, so far as I understand it, is to the effect that the agreement for the lease was procured by Mr. Cotton and the plaintiff, Mr. Lindgren, both of whom had interests in conflict with their duties as directors of the City company Mr. Cotton because his children were interested under the settlement and Mr. Lindgren because he was a trustee of it, that this was not the decision of the

C City company but of Mr. Lindgren and Mr. Cotton in breach of their duty to to that company. It was further said that the directors of the defendant company, acted in breach of their duty to it under pressure from Mr. Cotton and Mr. Lindgren and without considering at all whether the bargain was a good one from the point of view of the defendant company. Further, and this was the crux of the defence, it was said that Mr. Lindgren knew of this breach of duty.

D I see no evidence that if there was thus a breach of Mr. Lindgren's and Mr. Cotton's duty to the City company, the directors of the defendant company knew that this was not the decision of the City company board. Indeed both the defendant company's directors were not unfamiliar with the way in which the City company's affairs were conducted and had reason to suppose that the rest of that board did or would concur.

E I altogether reject both these propositions which I have stated. In the first place, the defence and counterclaim contains no allegation of breach of duty by either Mr. Goldsbrough or Mr. Orchard-Lisle, the two directors of the defendant company, and I cannot think that on the pleadings as they stand this point is open. I do not, however, base my decision on this. I do not think that there was

F evidence to justify the finding of a breach of duty by the defendant company's directors. The judge did so find in that he said that Mr. Goldsbrough and Mr. Orchard-Lisle merely " rubber-stamped " the decision made by Mr. Cotton and Mr. Lindgren. In my opinion the evidence does not justify this finding. Mr. Orchard-Lisle was not called at all, and it is clear enough that Mr. Goldsbrough gave a lot of consideration to the subject. The only statement by him that was relied on was that he was " a nominee for " the City company. What he meant

G by this I do not know; possibly that he was looking rather to the interests of the City company than those of the defendant company, but that seems quite irrelevant.

It is true that Mr. Cotton and Mr. Lindgren suggested the agreement to the directors of the defendant company. In my judgment, they did this in what

H they thought were the interests of the City company, which was about to become the holder of all the shares in the defendant company. It is clear enough that for the City company it was essential if the deal was to go through to find someone to take over the group (2) properties, and I am of opinion that Mr. Cotton and Mr. Lindgren, at any rate, thought the bargain an excellent one both for the City company and for the defendant company. After all, it is not easy to find a

I lessee who will for ten years or so face a loss of about £40,000 a year. There is moreover no evidence that Mr. Lindgren knew, even if it were the fact, that Mr. Goldsbrough and Mr. Orchard-Lisle were not exercising an independent judgment. There is a further plea that the agreement was improvident and inequitable to the defendant company, but I do not think that it was when it was made.

Evidence was read of valuers on both sides that in 1959, when the agreement came into operation, though not in 1958, the group (2) properties had a market value much in excess of the capitalised value of the lease, and that therefore

the rent should have been larger and the term shorter, but this is highly specula- A
tive evidence given ten years later, and the losses over that period made the
bargain quite unacceptable to the City company itself. Moreover, the directors
of the defendant company were entitled to suppose that the views of Mr. Cotton
and Mr. Lindgren represented the views of the board of the City company, and
they were entitled to have regard to the views of the company which was acquiring
the whole of the defendant company's shares and to suppose that the City B
company knew its own business. The truth probably is that Mr. Cotton, who
on the evidence never took account of difficulties, relied on being able to get
the group (2) properties back from the plaintiff trustees when they were ready
for development and was not therefore over-careful in fixing the term or the
rent; but that does not justify a repudiation of the agreement now, when it is
about to begin to show the trustees a profit. C

There is no allegation of fraud against the directors of the defendant company.
It is said that they are not even much to be blamed for falling in with Lindgren's
suggestion. Moreover, they are still directors of the defendant company and I
am quite unable to understand how the company so constituted can maintain
this defence. It is quite unlike *Regal (Hastings), Ltd.* v. *Gulliver* (1), where the
directors had made a personal profit out of information acquired as directors D
and had ceased to be directors, and were sued by the company as reconstituted
and made to disgorge their profits; yet this was the nearest that authority
came to the point.

A great number of cases was cited, but I get no benefit from them. It is of
course true that a trustee cannot in general deal with himself or get an advantage
himself in a transaction in which he is on both sides of the table, and authority E
is not needed for so well-known a proposition, but Mr. Lindgren was a director
not of the defendant company but of the City company. He may have been in
breach of his duty to that company but he owed no duty to the defendant
company, although it was about to become a subsidiary of the City company.
To hold that Mr. Lindgren, a director of the City company, was bound to protect
the interests of one of its subsidiaries which had an independent board is to F
stretch the principle altogether beyond reason.

A number of other points is taken for the plaintiffs, as for instance that even
if the contract was voidable it was never avoided, which could only be done by
rescission, and that is not pleaded nor proved. Further, that the contract had
been affirmed in another transaction connected with 104 Piccadilly, already
mentioned. There was also a suggestion of laches, and a point on which the judge G
decided in favour of the plaintiffs that notice to one of the trustees, Mr. Lindgren,
was not notice to all, the other two having no notice. Having regard to the
way the case has been argued in this court, I do not think it necessary to canvass
these matters. I would dismiss the appeal, though not for the reasons given by
the learned judge.

DANCKWERTS, L.J. (read by WINN, L.J.): In this action the plaintiffs, H
who are trustees of a settlement dated Mar. 15, 1946, made by Mr. Ephraim
Cotton, are claiming specific performance of a contract dated Mar. 18, 1959.
The statement of claim, which is simple and straightforward, claims specific
performance of the contract to grant a lease which was acted on for at least
four years.

The defence and counterclaim, which is very ineptly drafted, claims a declaration that the contract is void and of no effect, and repayment of a sum of £100,000
(actually £80,000) which was paid to the plaintiffs for the release of an agreement
dealing with one of the properties which was included in the original transaction.
The defence was originally based on an alleged oral collateral term which the

(1) [1942] 1 All E.R. 378.

A   trial judge has rejected, and from which decision no appeal has been made. The issues which remain are a claim that the agreement was ultra vires the defendant company and its directors.

Whatever else may be the position, it is plain beyond doubt that the agreement was within the powers of the defendant company and of its directors. This is not a very promising start for the defendant company. However, the case put

B   forward is that there was a conflict of interest by reason of the positions of the plaintiffs Mr. Lindgren and Mr. Kerman as directors of another company, City Centre Properties, Ltd. (" the City company "), and the plaintiff Mr. Lindgren as " director-elect " of the defendant company. The position of " director-elect " seems to me to partake more of the atmosphere of comic opera than the sphere of serious legal argument.

C   Further, if Mr. Lindgren was in conflict of interest between his position as a trustee of the settlement and as a director of the City company, that would appear to be a matter between the City company and the trustees of the settlement. The City company is not a party to this action, though it is true that that company now holds all the shares of the defendant company.

A statement of these facts, in my view, is sufficient to dispose of the defence

D   and counterclaim in this action. But this is not all. The defence and counterclaim on behalf of the defendant company is put forward by the two directors of the defendant company who entered into the contract on behalf of the defendant company, and whose conduct is now claimed by the defendant company to have rendered the contract voidable as regards the defendant company. This seems to me to be a very strange situation. Much reliance was placed on

E   behalf of the defendant company on the case of *Regal (Hastings), Ltd.* v. *Gulliver* (2); but the situation in that case was very different. The defendant directors against whom the action succeeded had made a profit from their position and the action was brought against them, when they had ceased to be directors, on behalf of the company by a new board.

The case contended for in the end on behalf of the defendant company was that

F   Mr. Goldsbrough and Mr. Orchard-Lisle, who were at the material times the only directors of that company, had been directed or persuaded or requested by Mr. Jack Cotton and Mr. Lindgren, or at any rate by Mr. Lindgren, to approve the contract between the trustees and the company, and that the two directors had never effectively considered the merits of the contract as their duty to the company required, or (alternatively) that by reason of a mistake of the directors

G   as to the authority of Mr. Cotton and Mr. Lindgren to act on behalf of the City company they were not exercising their powers as directors of the defendant company at all. The City company was not the contracting party with the defendant company, and I find this argument unconvincing. It may well be that the directors of the defendant company paid attention to the advice of Mr. Cotton and Mr. Lindgren, who were experienced and expert property dealers,

H   but, in my opinion, the evidence shows that Mr. Goldsbrough did take an interest in the matter, discussed it with Mr. Lindgren, and applied his mind to it. Mr. Orchard-Lisle was not even called as a witness. The learned judge said that these two directors merely " rubber-stamped " the decisions of Mr. Jack Cotton and Mr. Lindgren. I think that this conclusion is entirely contrary to the evidence, and I must reject it.

The learned judge, however, found that the other trustees of the settlement were not affected by notice of the alleged deficiencies of the directors (or anyone else) by reason of the knowledge of the facts possessed by Mr. Lindgren, and gave judgment for the plaintiffs. I do not find it necessary to consider this question of notice. Nor do I find it necessary to deal with counsel for the plaintiffs' argument that there can only be one judgment in a case involving joint parties.

There are two other matters which I must mention.

There are certainly some grounds for the argument that the defendant company had affirmed the contract by acting on it and treating it as effective for some years, and by the somewhat equivocal letters written on behalf of the defendant company after the dispute had arisen; but I do not propose to base my judgment on that point.

I also wish to state that I do not accept the proposition that the contract was really unfair to the defendant company. This was a commercial transaction, and there were other considerations which entered into the matter besides purely arithmetical calculations (made after the events by " experts "). The simple course of the purchase of the properties by the City company or the defendant company was abandoned for fiscal resaons, and this was the reason for adopting the method of a lease. The City company was ready enough to acquire group (1), producing a good income, but that company did not want to be burdened with group (2), which consisted of properties which were producing a low income return, but in respect of which there were prospects of profitable development as leases fell in.

That, of course, was a speculative matter. The transaction as carried out involved the lessees from the defendant company in a heavy burden for some nine years while the rents receivable showed a deficiency in regard to the rent payable to the defendant company. There must have been few bodies ready to undertake such a liability for such a period of years. The trustees of the Cotton settlement were ready to enter into the transaction because the four adult beneficiaries under the settlement were surtax payers, to whom the prospect of capital accretion in the future would appeal more than increases of current income. Moreover, the trustees were not equipped to be property developers, and consequently it was a reasonable expectation that they would be ready to give back possession of the properties to the defendant company on reasonable terms when underleases fell in and the time came for redevelopment. For this reason a stipulation to this effect was unnecessary, and a term which enabled the defendant company to determine the rights of the trustees at the will of the defendant company at any time (as claimed), when the trustees would lose the benefit of more profitable periods, would seem to be unfair to them and unreasonable.

I am, therefore, of opinion that the plaintiffs are entitled to succeed, though not for the reasons which appealed to the learned judge, and I would dismiss the appeal.

About forty cases and text-books were cited to us, and though the documents were beautifully got up in most convenient files the bulk was very considerable. I am relieved to find that I need not deal with those in detail, though I have not ignored them in my consideration for the purposes of this judgment.

WINN, L.J.: On Mar. 18, 1959, in the presence and by the direction of two directors of the defendant company, the seal of the company was affixed to the agreement of which specific performance is sought by the plaintiffs in this action: that agreement was exchanged with the plaintiffs two days later. Any contention that a plea of non est factum could be sustained in relation to the execution and delivery of the agreement was expressly disclaimed during the hearing of the appeal. Of the pleading delivered by the defendants in this action, which was in many respects obscure, one thing can be said with certainty: it did not allege fraud against any person; fraud in any form was expressly disclaimed as a ground for resisting the plaintiffs' claim in the course of the hearing of the appeal. In the closing stage of a most cogent argument, pertinaciously sustained over a prolonged period by counsel for the defendant company despite many interruptions and requests for clarification of which I was guilty, it was ultimately accepted by the defendant company that its case, in the final analysis, stood or fell within the extremely narrow confines of a plea raised with excessive economy of language by a single sentence in para. 6 of the defence—" the said agreement

A was ultra vires the defendant and its directors ". Manifestly, as counsel conceded, this plea, in so far as it alleged an excess of the vires of the company, was quite unsustainable: it was therefore relied on only in so far as it alleged that the directors had exceeded their powers as directors, without exceeding the corporate powers of the defendant company.

B In some text-books a form of expression is adopted, which is not altogether without judicial authority, for describing such an excess of powers: use is made of a non-capital u/v rather than a capital U/V. The starting point of this residual submission is plainly that where directors of a company purport to do something on its behalf without conforming to the company's internal directives in the articles of association designed to control the conduct of the directors, and the relevant defect of procedure or failure to conform with the articles is known to

C an outside party to the transaction, the company is not bound by it, in the absence, at any rate, of subsequent ratification by the shareholders of the company.

In the instant case, although counsel for the defendant company was loth, I think, to accept this, what was alleged to constitute conduct ultra vires the directors of the defendant company was not any abuse of their powers nor any

D non-compliance with the conditions, formalities or other domestic requirements prescribed by the articles of association, but what may be more accurately connoted by the unattractive but useful modern expression " non-use ".

In a phrase which I adopt, although it may seem unduly succinct and simple, as the summary of a seven-day argument, the defendant company contended that the two directors in question, Mr. Goldsbrough and Mr. Orchard-Lisle,

E failed to use their powers as directors of the defendant company on behalf of the defendant company when they decided to make the agreement in question. It is said that they so failed to use their powers in a way which was " not reprehensible "; counsel for the defendant company expressly so stated: in so failing to use their powers they were not guilty of any " grave dereliction of duty to the defendant company " nor of any " crass negligence "; counsel for the

F defendant company expressly so stated. They were acting in a way which was readily understandable and in the circumstances quite natural; this was common ground between the parties. According to the defendant company's contention the directors agreed to the transaction because they were misled about a material consideration or factor which made it seem to them acceptable for the defendant company, when if they had known the true position they would not and could

G not sensibly have formed that view. It is further said—and this counsel for the defendant company accepted was an essential part of his case—that Mr. Lindgren knew that they had been so misled.

For my part I do not accept any of the three essential constituents of this contention, which are:

(a) that Mr. Goldsbrough and Mr. Orchard-Lisle were misled about a factor

H of dominant importance in the situation which it was their duty to consider, videlicet that the reality was substantially different from what it appeared to them to be;

(b) that because so misled they failed to act for the defendant company, videlicet that despite appearances they really took no decision about the agreement;

I (c) that Mr. Lindgren knew at the material time what is set out in (a) and (b) above.

In case the formulation which I have set out may seem to anyone to do less than complete justice to the summary of the defendant company's case which counsel for the defendant company helpfully gave the court in the course of his reply, I proceed to set out the first six of the seven heads of that summary in the words which I myself used in making a note of them:

1. In March, 1959, the City company were owners in equity of all the shares of the defendant company.

2. A direction or request was given to the defendant company purportedly **A** by the City company to enter into the agreements, videlicet the agreements for the grant of leases to the trustees.

3. This direction or request was not in fact duly given by or on behalf of the City company, but merely by two of the seven directors of that company, both of whom had an interest conflicting with that of the company.

4. Had no such direction or request been given, the board of the defendant **B** company, it is to be inferred, would not have decided to make the contracts: the direction or request was the causa causans of the decision.

5. All the foregoing was well known to Mr. Lindgren.

6. For these reasons the purported decision of the board of the defendant company was not duly taken by that board because an incorrect supposition was the basis of it; Mr. Lindgren well knew that this was so. For my part I **C** accept the first three only of those propositions: I would accept the fourth if " causa sine qua non " were substituted for " causa causans ". The fact that the City company had in January contracted to buy from Lady Price all the shares of the defendant company and had obtained from her an undertaking to cause the defendant company to enter into the leases to the trustees meant that the City company, invoking so far as might have been necessary the aid of **D** Lady Price, was in a position to procure the board of the defendant company to make the agreements. I think that the trial judge went too far in finding that the defendant company was " procured " to enter into those agreements. The judge said in the same passage of his judgment that the City company acting by Mr. Jack Cotton and Mr. Lindgren so "procured" this decision of the defendant company. With respect to him I think myself that it would have been more **E** accurate an expression of his meaning to say that the " procuring " was effected by Mr. Cotton and Mr. Lindgren, but doubt whether the distinction was material to the persons concerned. I am not convinced that the decision was not considered with independent minds by the directors: they were not " procured " as distinct from being persuaded.

The terms of the agreements were not known to the board of the City company **F** before they were made, nor did that board as distinct from Mr. Cotton and Mr. Lindgren, who were members of it, know that the leases so agreed to be granted were for any such period as ninety-nine years (sixty-six in the case of one property) or that there was no enforceable contractual right thereby reserved to secure an earlier opportunity to develop any of the properties.

What is perhaps more important is that the board of the defendant company, **G** consisting at the material time only of Mr. Goldsbrough and Mr. Orchard-Lisle, must, in my judgment, have been greatly influenced in coming to their decision to make the agreements by the belief, which they must naturally have entertained, that the City company, of which their own company was about to become a wholly-owned subsidiary, had approved the making of the contracts and the granting of the leases and had expressed that approval to them through **H** Mr. Lindgren. I would again emphasise that there is no suggestion that Mr. Lindgren fraudulently misrepresented to the directors of the defendant company that the board of the City company had given such approval, or that he was duly authorised by that board to make the request or give the direction in question.

The reality of the matter seems to me to have been this: that those who had **I** occasion in 1959 and earlier to deal with the City company to an extent acquainting them with the way in which the business of that company was conducted, and even more particularly those who played an active part in the affairs of the City company within its organisation, were fully accustomed at the material time to accept the position that the decisions and the policies of Mr. Jack Cotton were the equivalent of decisions and policies of the City company: they had the ostensible authority of the City company for transactions within the course of the company's dealings in property.

A   The court has had occasion to study a great deal of evidence which has left on my own mind the clear impression that it would have mattered little, if anything, to Mr. Goldsbrough and Mr. Orchard-Lisle if they had been told in so many words that the request or direction had emanated from Mr. Jack Cotton and not from any resolution of the duly constituted board of the City company, and that at the time when it was made no director other than Mr. Cotton and

B   Mr. Lindgren knew, at any rate with any precision, what transaction the defendant company were to enter into in respect of properties in which the City company itself would have some interest.

It is, of course, a very speculative question what would have happened on the hypothesis of such a full disclosure having been made, but for my part I think that there would have been a marked balance of probability that Mr.

C   Goldsbrough and Mr. Orchard-Lisle, who were by no means unsophisticated in matters of finance and property values, would have regarded the transaction as one which was so favourable to the City company that its board would after careful consideration have formally approved, apart altogether from the likely effect on such a decision of the influence of Mr. Jack Cotton.

It is germane to this point to state, though I do not propose to elaborate the

D   matter, that in my opinion the transaction was a favourable one for the City company, even though the agreements drawn up contained no term enabling the defendant company to recover the properties before the termination of the leasehold terms: had they contained such a term they would have been extremely advantageous to the City company, and adverse in their effect to the interests of the trustees. The advantage which the City company gained from the trans-

E   action as a whole, including the acquisition of the shares of the defendant company was twofold: First, the City company secured the revenue from the properties which were currently yielding good profit rentals; second, the other group of properties would as a result of the agreements produce for a number of years over £50,000 each year in excess of the rents reserved by the pre-existing leases.

F   Again it must be borne in mind that it was not due to fraud on anybody's part that any person mistakenly believed that the trustees would be compellable to release any of the properties before the expiration of the leasehold terms.

As I see the matter, the high point of the defendant company's attack on the validity of the contracts is that they were entered into by the directors of the defendant company in a mistaken belief, the nature of which has been sufficiently

G   indicated which cogently influenced their decision: the evidence falls far short, in my judgment, of establishing that the directors took no decision or purported to take a decision only because they regarded it as a foregone conclusion that their decision must be to make the agreements, or that they did not consider at all the interests of the defendant company before taking the decision

H   I do not propose to examine the evidence of Mr. Goldsbrough, which has been constantly read and closely scrutinised; I have it well in mind when I say that in my judgment it negatives the suggestion—which is a grave one to make against a chartered accountant, particularly when no hint of it was contained in the pleaded defence—that he just shut his eyes to the implications for his own company of the transaction and blindly entered into the agreements.

I   I do not find myself able to concur in the finding of the judge, which does not seem to me to be a finding of primary fact, but a finding by inference from primary facts not stated in the judgment, that " Mr. Goldsbrough and Mr. Orchard-Lisle were really only rubber-stamping decisions which had been reached by others . . . neither exercised any independent judgment as to the desirability from the point of view of the defendant company of the commercial terms of the lease ". I think this seriously overvalues the weight of a criticism so belatedly made that it should be very strictly judged. It is to be observed that Mr. Orchard-Lisle was not called by the defendant company as a witness: whether he would have

been willing to give evidence once it was revealed to him by the questions put
on behalf of the defendant company to Mr. Goldsbrough that he too might
be the intended object of denigration is, of course, a matter on which it would
not be proper to speculate.

The defendant company further pleaded that Mr. Cotton and Mr. Lindgren
were guilty of breach of duty:—(a) to the defendant company as " directors-
elect ", a resolution of the board of that company having appointed them
directors with effect from the moment when the leases were completed: no
attempt was made to sustain this plea by argument; it does not merit comment.
(b) to the City company as directors of that company, but persons with a conflicting interest inasmuch as they knowingly acted without prior authority
from its board in procuring, ostensibly on behalf of the City company, the
making of the agreements between the defendant company and the trustees and
failed properly to protect the interests of the City company, as holder of the
shares of the defendant company, against the adverse effect of granting long
terms in the group (2) properties without securing any enforceable right of earlier
determination. This contention was advanced from time to time in argument,
but for my own part I was never able to appreciate that it could found any
claim for relief in the present action in which the City company are not parties,
unless it stood up to a test of principle which I put, arguendo, and which counsel
for the defendant company was constrained—I think it is fair to say—to accept
as properly applicable, videlicet, where a transaction effected by A constituted
a breach of an equitable duty which he owed to B, and C is consequentially
harmed, do these facts entitle C to relief in respect of that transaction? For
my part I am not aware that an affirmative answer to that question is afforded
by principle or authority, nor do I think, after having been referred to a number
of cases in which the court has rightly " looked "—as counsel put it—" through
the corporate personality to the realities ", that the test posed is any more
readily satisfied where B and C are related to one another as respectively
parent company and subsidiary and A is a director of B.

The instant case is one in which it has been essential and not always easy to
distinguish between points of prejudice which might have swayed some juries
and matters of substance in law and equity. I do not, however, myself think
that a well-instructed jury would have thought, even on the highly theoretical
valuation evidence, that the City company were overreached by or on behalf of
the trustees: in reality Mr. Cotton and Mr. Lindgren intended to make, but
failed effectively to make, a bargain very favourable to the City company.

I would only add that on any view the agreements were not void but only
voidable and I construe the letter dated July 30, 1964, as an affirmation. In
my view it amounts to asserting that the agreements are maintained, unless
and until the court holds that the " extra term " is not included; at the least
this must constitute affirmation for a period of time as contrasted with avoidance.
Further, the declared attitude of the defendant company, was by that letter
demonstrated then to be, not that equity required avoidance of the transaction,
but that commercial equity could only be observed by performance of the contracts according to the version of their terms asserted by the defendant company.

It is unnecessary to say anything on the complex topic of joint contractors
suing or being sued.

I would dismiss the appeal, and allow, so far as it may be material so to do,
the cross-appeal against the " rubber-stamping " finding.

Appeal dismissed; cross-appeal allowed.

Solicitors: *Titmuss, Sainer & Webb* (for the defendant company); *Simmons &
Simmons* (for the plaintiffs).

[*Reported by* F. A. AMIES, ESQ., *Barrister-at-Law.*]

A

ADCOCK AND OTHERS v. WILSON.

[HOUSE OF LORDS (Lord Reid, Lord Morris of Borth-y-Gest, Lord Guest, Lord Pearce and Lord Wilberforce), February 8, 11, 29, 1968.]

B
Gaming—Lawful and unlawful gaming—Clubs—Bingo—Golden Scoop—1s. stake purchased at first game of each session—Half stake used for ordinary club game and balance retained by club as a contribution to national Golden Scoop game in which five hundred affiliated clubs participated—No communication between players of different affiliated clubs—Whether individuals playing a local bingo game were at relevant time playing in a second game, a national Golden Scoop game—Betting, Gaming and Lotteries Act 1963 (c. 2)
C
s. 32 (1) (b), (4).

The proprietors of a local bingo club had a contract with Golden Scoop, Ltd., the local club being affiliated to the National Golden Scoop Club. Golden Scoop, Ltd., had no premises at which bingo was played. The Golden Scoop was operated at local bingo clubs, of which about five hundred were affiliated. At the local club each player bought a bingo ticket for 1s. at the first game
D
of each session. Of this 6d. was paid by way of stake on the house game, which was conducted in the local club, and 6d. was retained by the local club as a contribution to prizes in the National Golden Scoop Club game. A player was entitled to limit the payment for his bingo ticket to 6d. for the National Golden Scoop Club game only, but, on the evidence, no player had done so. The house game proceeded in the ordinary way. When the winner
E
was ascertained he received the stake money referable to that game. The stake money in the National Golden Scoop Club game was sent by the local club to Golden Scoop, Ltd., together with the name of the winner of the house game and some other information. The money received by Golden Scoop, Ltd. was paid as prize money to certain of the winners of the house games. The prizes were allocated in accordance with rules, and some of them
F
could be of considerable value. In playing bingo at any local club the players were not in communication with players at any other local club. On the evening in question no player of the house game at the local bingo club won a prize in the Golden Scoop, but a sum of £17 5s. in all was paid by the players of the house game as stake money for the National Golden Scoop Club game.
G
Held: on the facts there was not any such game as was called the " National Golden Scoop Club game ", and the players at local clubs were taking part only in the house games there; accordingly, on the night in question, the amount of the stakes paid at the local club for the National Golden Scoop Club game was disposed of otherwise than by payment to a player in the game at the local club, with the consequence that the condition laid
H
down in s. 32 (1) (b)* of the Betting, Gaming and Lotteries Act 1963 was not fulfilled and the gaming at the local club was unlawful (see p. 931, letter I, and p. 933, letter A, post).

Decision of the DIVISIONAL COURT ([1967] 1 All E.R. 1028) affirmed.

[As to lawful and unlawful gaming, see SUPPLEMENT to 18 HALSBURY'S LAWS
I
(3rd Edn.) title GAMING AND WAGERING, para. 369A.

For the Betting, Gaming and Lotteries Act 1963 s. 32, see 43 HALSBURY'S STATUTES (2nd Edn. 343.]

Appeal.

This was an appeal by the appellants from the judgment of the Divisional Court (WINN, L.J., ASHWORTH and WIDGERY, JJ.), dated Feb. 10, 1967, and reported

---

* The relevant terms of s. 32 (1) (b) are set out at p. 930, letter F, post.

[1967] 1 All E.R. 1028 upholding the conviction of the appellants by D. N.   A
O'SULLIVAN, Esq., stipendiary magistrate for the city and county of Kingston-
upon-Hull on June 17, 1966, for being concerned in the organisation of gaming,
viz. the Golden Scoop, contrary to s. 32 (4)* of the Betting, Gaming and Lotteries
Act 1963. The facts are set out in the opinion of LORD MORRIS OF BORTH-Y-GEST.

J. C. G. Burge, Q.C., and G. Gray for the appellants.
Ian Percival, Q.C., and R. H. Hutchinson for the respondent.   B

LORD REID: My Lords, for the reasons given by my noble and learned
friend, LORD MORRIS OF BORTH-Y-GEST, I would dismiss this appeal.

LORD MORRIS OF BORTH-Y-GEST: My Lords, by the provisions of
s. 32 of the Betting, Gaming and Lotteries Act 1963, gaming is lawful if, but only   C
if, it is conducted in accordance with the conditions laid down in the section.
Gaming means the playing of a game of chance for winnings in money or money's
worth. The expression " game of chance " includes a game of chance and skill
combined and a pretended game of chance or of chance and skill combined: it
does not include any athletic game or sport (see s. 55). The appellants were all
charged with being concerned in the organisation of gaming which was unlawful.   D
The charge was that they

" were concerned in the organisation of gaming, namely the Golden Scoop,
which took place at premises known as the Waterloo Bingo Club, 80, Waterloo
Street "

in the city and county of Kingston-upon-Hull. The allegation was that the gaming was unlawful in that money which players put down as stakes was disposed   E
of otherwise than by payment to a player as winnings. The offence was charged
under s. 32 (4). The prosecution alleged that the gaming was unlawful by virtue
of s. 32 (1) in that it was not conducted in accordance with the condition

" that no money or money's worth which any of the players puts down as
stakes, or pays by way of losses, or exchanges for tokens used in playing the   F
game, is disposed of otherwise than by payment to a player as winnings "

(see s. 32 (1) (b)). The meaning of " player " in relation to a game of chance, includes any person taking part in the game against whom other persons taking
part in the game stake, play or bet. Players must, therefore, be persons who
take part in one and the same game.

The date of the offence with which the appellants were charged was Sept. 16,   G
1965, but the issues might well have been raised by reference to any other evening
when bingo was played at the Waterloo Bingo Club. It was in fact played nightly.
The case is concerned, however, with the arrangements which were organised
under the name of the Golden Scoop. The Case Stated sets out the facts as found
by the learned magistrate and I do not propose to recite them fully here. At the
nightly sessions at the Waterloo Bingo Club several rounds or hands or games of   H
bingo were played. The Golden Scoop arrangements applied to the first bingo
game of a session. The Case proceeds to describe the arrangements. One of the
appellants, Golden Scoop, Ltd., is described in the case as " a company which
organised bingo on a national scale and operated through administrative sub-
controls in various parts of the country ". It was found that " The Golden Scoop "
involved participation by a plurality of bingo clubs and that an aim was to increase   I
the attractions of bingo by providing large prizes. At the time relevant to the
charges there were about five hundred bingo clubs throughout the country
participating in the Golden Scoop. The proprietor of each individual bingo club

---

* Section 32 (4), so far as material, reads: " If any gaming takes place on any premises
—(a) which is by virtue of sub-s. (1) of this section ... unlawful gaming ... any person
concerned in the organisation or management of the gaming ... shall be guilty of an
offence ... "

A   made a contract (in a standard form) with Golden Scoop, Ltd. The proprietors
of the Waterloo Bingo Club (two of the appellants) entered into such a contract.
Golden Scoop, Ltd. owns a proprietary club which is called the National Golden
Scoop Club. It runs and organises the Golden Scoop under the terms of certain
Consolidated Rules. It does not, however, have any premises on which bingo
is played, nor does it have any committee. When someone applies to become a

B   member of a club which is affiliated to the National Golden Scoop Club, he applies
at the same time to become a member of the latter club. All the five hundred
clubs operated what has been called " The Golden Scoop " on every night of the
year except Christmas day and, accordingly, it was operated at the bingo sessions
of the Waterloo Bingo Club in respect of the first bingo game played in a session.
Those who so wished bought a ticket for that game at a cost of 1s. On one side

C   was the selection of numbers. On the other side were the words:

> " National Golden Scoop Club Game. The price of this ticket (1s.) consists
> of 6d. by way of stake in the House Game and 6d. by way of stake in the
> National Golden Scoop Club Game."

It was possible for someone to limit his payment to 6d. and to compete only for

D   Golden Scoop prizes. No one at the Waterloo Club ever did so. On Sept. 16,
1965, there were 690 tickets sold (at 1s. each) at the Waterloo Bingo Club for the
first bingo game.

The procedure was that the game proceeded in the ordinary way. The instructions in the rules of the National Golden Scoop Club had to be observed. When the
winner was ascertained he received the stake money referable to what was

E   described on the ticket as the house game. In the Waterloo Club on Sept. 16,
1965, such person would, therefore, be entitled to 690 sixpences (£17 5d.).
In all the other clubs (some 499 in number) there would be a similar procedure
in regard to the first bingo game of a session. The money which was called
the stake money in the " National Golden Scoop Club Game " was all sent by
the Waterloo Bingo Club, and also by all the other clubs, to the head office of

F   Golden Scoop, Ltd. Each club also sent the name of the winner of the club bingo
game and the number of calls which had been made before the game was won. The
money received by Golden Scoop, Ltd. was then paid as prize money to certain
of the winners of the club bingo games. There were six prizes in all. There was
a prize which went to the winner who had the lowest number of calls or alternatively which was divided amongst the winners who each had that lowest number.

G   There was a prize which correspondingly went to the winner or amongst the
winners who had the highest number of calls. There was a prize which went to
the winner, or amongst the winners who " called a full house " in exactly sixty-six
numbers. The various other prizes went in other ways according to the rules.
Some of the prizes could be of considerable value. Thus, on Sept. 16, 1965, two
of the winners from amongst the winners in the five hundred clubs shared between

I   them a sum of £2,148. The appellants were all convicted by the learned magistrate
who stated the question for the opinion of the High Court as being whether he
came to a correct determination and decision in point of law in so convicting the
appellants. The determination of the learned magistrate was affirmed in the
Divisional Court (1).

My lords, it becomes necessary to consider whether the stakes put down by

I   the 690 persons who played the first bingo game at the Waterloo Club on Sept. 16,
1965, were disposed of otherwise than by payment to players as winnings. In
my view, this involves the question whether in fact there was any such thing
as a national " game ". I do not think that there was. In five hundred separate
clubs a large number of people (we were told that the number on the night in
question was probably between 150 to two hundred thousand) were variously taking part in separate games of bingo. Each person was playing

---

(1) [1967] 1 All E.R. 1028; [1967] 2 Q.B. 683.

a game but in no sense were they all playing the same game. It could **A** not rationally be said that they were all playing a game of bingo with each other. In some circumstances arrangements can be made so that people who are geographically separated from each other can play a game with each other; but nothing of the sort was arranged or was happening on the night in question. There were five hundred different games which may well have started at different times and which may well have finished at different times. Once those games were **B** concluded and the various winners were ascertained the distribution of the " National Scoop " money followed by a mere application of the rules. Nothing more remained to be done by those who had been playing the various bingo games. There was nothing more that they could do. As there was nothing further to be done there was nothing further that could be called a game. Could it, then, be said that while those in a particular bingo club were all there taking part in **C** one game of bingo they were also at the same time taking part in some further and different game in which all the persons in all the clubs were taking part? In my view, no such further and different game was taking place. Persons in some bingo clubs might not even have assembled together at a time or at times when players in other bingo clubs were beginning to play. Nothing can be formulated or described which can be recognised as a game or as having the features and normal **D** characteristics of a game. Nothing was taking place beyond the playing of the various separate bingo games. Those in one bingo club were not " players " in relation to those in other bingo clubs. Those playing bingo in one bingo club were not taking part in a game against those playing different games of bingo in all other clubs. It is to be noted that it would have been possible (though it never happened at the Waterloo Club) for someone to play the first bingo game after **E** paying sixpence only for his ticket " by way of stake in the National Golden Scoop Club Game ". Such a person would then play the game of bingo in the ordinary way. It would be the only game that he played. If in his club he was the first in competition with others present to complete the cancelling of his card, he would qualify as the winner whose name, together with the number of calls, would be sent to Golden Scoop, Ltd. As, however, he would not be a competitor **F** for the " winnings " in the club game, that game would have to continue until it could be determined who was entitled to such winnings. All this serves to show that the only activity undertaken by someone who could be eligible to receive one of the national prizes was the activity of playing the local bingo game with all the particular features that might apply to a particular game in a particular place at a particular time. **G**

WINN, L.J., posed the question whether those playing bingo in a club during the first hand of a session became players in any national game. I agree with his answer when he said (2):

" I think not, because that which they were doing was not playing in any game in which all the others or indeed any of the others present, in different clubs were also participating as players." **H**

In my view, the reality of the matter, as ASHWORTH, J., pointed out (3) in his judgment, was that the winner of a local game became eligible for a wider prize not by having taken part in a wider or national game, but by an arrangement made by the proprietors of the National Golden Scoop that those who took part in multiple games might qualify for possible distribution to them of the national prizes. On Sept. 16, 1965, no prize in the Golden Scoop was won by anyone in the Waterloo Bingo Club. The £17 5s. (the total of the so-called stakes in the so-called National Golden Scoop Club game) which represented half of the money paid for the tickets for the first bingo game played that day at the club did not go to persons who could be regarded as " players " vis-à-vis the members of the

---

(2) [1967] 1 All E.R. at pp. 1035, 1036; [1967] 2 Q.B. at p. 700.
(3) [1967] 1 All E.R. at p. 1036; [1967] 2 Q.B. at p. 701.

A   Waterloo Bingo Club. It follows that the gaming which took place at the club was
not conducted in accordance with the condition laid down by s. 32 (1) (*b*) of the
Act of 1963 and was, therefore, unlawful. I find it wholly unnecessary to consider
whether the arrangements could or could not be regarded as amounting to a
lottery. In my view, the learned magistrate was correct in finding the appellants
guilty. I would dismiss the appeal.

B   **LORD GUEST:** My Lords, I concur.

        LORD PEARCE: My Lords, I concur,

        LORD WILBERFORCE: My Lords, I concur.

                                                        Appeal dismissed.

        Solicitors: *Ward, Bowie & Co.,* agents for *David Yablon & Co.,* Bradford (for
C   the appellants); *T. D. Jones & Co.,* agents for *David Morgan,* Kingston-upon-
Hull (for the respondent).

                            [*Reported by* S. A. HATTEEA, ESQ., *Barrister-at-Law.*]

                            ──────────

D   R. *v.* OVENELL
            R. *v.* WALTER A. CARTWRIGHT, LTD.

[COURT OF APPEAL, CRIMINAL DIVISION (Diplock, L.J., Phillimore and Blain, JJ.),
    January 26, 1968.]

E   *Criminal Law—Evidence—Admissibility—Confession—Inducement—Evidence of*
        admission made at interview with investigating officers of customs and excise,
        statement made without caution being administered—Whether statement
        induced by hope of advantage—Judges' Rules, r. 2.
    Criminal Law—Trial—Jury—Direction to jury—Confession—Voluntariness a
        test of admissibility—Jury should not be directed that, unless satisfied of the
        voluntary character of an admission, they should disregard it.

F   In the course of investigating returns made by the applicants for the
purposes of the Purchase Tax Act 1963, investigating officers of the Customs
and Excise interviewed the applicant O. One of the officers, having intimated
in the course of the interview that he could have some sympathy with a
wholesaler who found himself under great pressure from an unregistered
customer to supply goods without charging purchase tax, said to O. soon
G   afterwards, " so that there were in fact off-record sales of chargeable
goods ? ". O. replied " Yes, but I never made a penny out of it . . . " The
admissibility of O.'s reply was challenged, at the trial of the applicants on
charges of making false returns with intent to deceive contrary to s. 33 (2) (*a*)*
of the Act of 1963, on the grounds that it was induced by hope of advantage
to be gained from the sympathy professed by the officers and, alternatively,
H   that it was made in the absence of a caution, contrary to r. 2 of the Judges'
Rules.   Having ruled, in regard to the first ground of objection, that
O.'s answer was admissible, the deputy chairman directed the jury that if
they were not satisfied that the admission was made voluntarily they should
disregard it. On the second ground of objection, it was ruled at the trial
that the officer was not, at the outset of the interview, in possession of
I   evidence which afforded him reasonable grounds for suspecting the commission of an offence, but that after O.'s answer the caution envisaged by
r. 2† of the Judges' Rules ought to have been administered, and, as a matter

────────────

* Section 33 (2) (*a*), so far as material, is set out at p. 935, letter H, post.
    † Rule 2, so far as material, is in the following terms: " As soon as a police officer
has evidence which would afford reasonable grounds for suspecting that a person has
committed an offence, he shall caution that person or cause him to be cautioned before
putting to him any questions, or further questions, relating to that offence . . . "
For the Judges' Rules, see [1964] 1 All E.R. 237.

of discretion, what was said by O. after the quoted admission was ruled   A
to be inadmissible. On application for leave to appeal against conviction,

    Held: the admission had been rightly received in evidence because—

    (i) in deciding in criminal cases on the admissibility of an accused's
admission in evidence, the question of its admissibility, and for this purpose
the question whether it satisfied the test of voluntariness, was a question
for the judge to decide, but the weight to be attached to the evidence, if   B
admitted, was for the jury; accordingly a jury should not be directed,
when considering the weight of the evidence, that unless they were satisfied
that the admission was made voluntarily they should disregard it (see
p. 938, letter D, post).

    Chan Wai-Keung v. *Reginam* ([1967] 1 All E.R. 948) and *Basto* v. *Reginam*
((1954), 91 C.L.R. at p. 640) adopted.   C

    Dictum of BYRNE, J., in *R.* v. *Bass* ([1953] 1 All E.R. at p. 1066) not
followed.

    (ii) where a statement had been made without the caution envisaged by the
Judges' Rules in circumstances in which those rules would have necessitated
a caution, a trial judge had a discretion whether the statement should be
admitted or not; in the present case the discretion had been judicially   D
and properly exercised (see p. 939, letter B, post).

    Per CURIAM: the Judges' Rules are directed to the police and to no one
else, though it is understandable that investigating officers of other services
might be thought to be comparably placed with police officers (see p. 938,
letter I, post).

    Applications refused   E

    [As to the function of the trial judge regarding the admissibility of confession,
see 10 HALSBURY'S LAWS (3rd Edn.) 470, para. 863; and for cases on confessions
made to persons in authority, see 14 DIGEST (Repl.) 488, *4671-4700.*

    As to confessions inadmissible as result of inducement by promises of favour
or advantage, see 10 HALSBURY'S LAWS (3rd Edn.) 473, para. 866 text and   F
note (*d*); and for cases on the subject, see 14 DIGEST (Repl.) 480, 481, *4578-4595.*

    As to the Judges' Rules, see SUPPLEMENT to 10 HALSBURY'S LAWS (3rd Edn.)
para. 865.

    For the Purchase Tax Act 1963, s. 31, s. 33, see 43 HALSBURY'S STATUTES
(2nd Edn.) 1044, 1047.]

Cases referred to: G

    Basto v. *Reginam*, (1954), 91 C.L.R. 628.

    Chan Wai-Keung v. *Reginam*, [1967] 1 All E.R. 948; [1967] 2 A.C. 160;
      [1967] 2 W.L.R. 552; 51 Cr. App. Rep. 257.

    Comrs. of Customs and Excise v. *Harz*, [1967] 1 All E.R. 177; [1967] 1 A.C. 760;
      [1967] 2 W.L.R. 297; 51 Cr. App. Rep. 123.   H

    Ibrahim v. *Regem*, [1914-15] All E.R. Rep. 874; [1914] A.C. 599; 83 L.J.P.C.
      185; 111 L.T. 20; 14 Digest (Repl.) 468, *4513.*

    R. v. *Bass*, [1953] 1 All E.R. 1064; [1953] 1 Q.B. 680; [1953] 2 W.L.R. 825;
      117 J.P. 246; 37 Cr. App. Rep. 51; 14 Digest (Repl.) 476, *4568.*

    R. v. *Murray*, [1950] 2 All E.R. 925; [1951] 1 K.B. 391; 114 J.P. 609; 34
      Cr. App. Rep. 203; 14 Digest (Repl.) 469, *4523.*   I

Applications for leave to appeal.

These were applications by William Ovenell and Walter A. Cartwright, Ltd.,
by notices dated July 17, 1967, for leave to appeal against conviction, and
against sentences imposed, at their trial on June 23, 1967, at Inner London
Quarter Sessions before the Deputy Chairman (RODNEY BAX, ESQ., Q.C.) and
a jury on two counts of furnishing, contrary to s. 33 (2) (*a*) of the Purchase
Tax Act 1963, false purchase tax returns for the periods Apr. 1 to June 30, 1965,

A   and July 1 to Sept. 30, 1965. They were each fined £200 on each count with
nine months to pay, and, in the case of the applicant Ovenell, a sentence of
three months' imprisonment in default of payment was imposed. The facts
are set out in the judgment of the court.

   S. N. Parrish for the applicants.

B   **BLAIN, J.,** delivered the following judgment of the court: On June 23,
1967, these two applicants, the limited company W. A. Cartwright, Ltd. (herein
called " the company ") and one Ovenell, were convicted of furnishing a false
purchase tax return for the period Apr. 1 to June 30, 1965, and convicted also
of a like offence for the period July 1 to Sept. 30, 1965. Each was fined £200 on
each count, with nine months to pay, three months' imprisonment in default
C   in the applicant Ovenell's case, and each was ordered to pay £100 costs. They
now seek leave to appeal against conviction and the notice of application, though
this is not pursued, is against sentence also.

   The company are wholesalers dealing in domestic hardware and kindred commodities. The applicant Ovenell is a director of the company, he controls it,
and to all intents and purposes he owns it. His wife holds one share and he
D   holds the remainder. By virtue of the Purchase Tax Act 1963, and regulations
made thereunder, wholesalers of chargeable goods are required to register with
the Commissioners of Customs and Excise. the company is such a wholesaler
and has been so registered at all material times. It is, therefore, required to
keep proper records of its purchases and sales of what are called chargeable
goods, and when such goods are sold to unregistered persons purchase tax
E   becomes payable to the commissioners, and the records of purchases and sales
are required to show the amount of such tax payable in respect of such sales.
Section 31 of the Purchase Tax Act, 1963, empowers the commissioners to make
regulations for the purpose of giving effect to the provisions of the Act and of
enabling the commissioners to discharge their functions thereunder and, in
particular, for requiring registered persons to keep accounts and to make returns
F   of the amounts for which they are accountable. Under these powers the commissioners made the Purchase Tax Regulations 1965 (1). The regulation in
question here is reg. 7, which requires every registered person in each year to
furnish returns in a prescribed form showing the amount of tax for which he is
accountable in respect of each of the quarterly periods from Jan. 1 to Mar. 31;
Apr. 1 to June 30; July 1 to Sept. 30; and Oct. 1 to Dec. 31, and to pay the
G   amount of tax appearing by such returns to be due. This case is concerned with
the applicants' returns for the second and third periods of 1965.

   Under the provisions of s. 33 (2) (*a*) of the 1963 Act any person who

   " with intent to deceive, for the purposes of this Act or of regulations
   made thereunder, produces, furnishes, sends or otherwise makes use of any
   book, account, estimate, return or other document which is false in a
H   material particular "

shall be liable to a penalty of £500 or to imprisonment for a term not exceeding
two years, or to both. It is under that section that these defendants were charged
and indicted. The return made in respect of the period Apr. 1 to June 30, 1965,
and admittedly signed by the applicant (Mr. Ovenell) was dated July 22, 1965,
I   and indicated the total amount of purchase tax due and payable as £1,125 7s.
The comparable return made in respect of the period July 1 to Sept. 30, 1965,
also admittedly signed by Mr. Ovenell, was dated Oct. 19, 1965, and indicated
the total amount of purchase tax due and payable as £1,068 8s. 7d.

   On Jan. 13, 1966, Mr. Downs, an investigating officer of the commissioners
together with his colleague named Rigby visited the company's premises and
there interviewed Mr. Ovenell, the company's secretary, Mr. Jackson, also being

---

(1) S.I. 1965 No. 1050.

present. There was discussion as to registered customers; as to stock records A
and stock held at the beginning and end of the company's previous financial
year; as to methods of dealing with orders and payment by customers. Then
Mr. Downs asked to see the sales day book, which was produced and which
Mr. Ovenell told him covered all taxable goods transactions. After further
discussion Mr. Downs said to Mr. Ovenell,

B

"Let me say this, I have had some years experience of purchase tax,
and I know that registered wholesalers are sometimes under a certain
amount of pressure; sometimes traders like yourself are faced with demands
from unregistered customers to supply goods without charging purchase
tax, and I know that such pressure on registered wholesalers in this type of
business can be very great indeed. Sometimes such traders succumb to the
pressure."

C

Mr. Ovenell replied, " it doesn't happen now, you fellows cleaned up the trade,
it is much better since that court case ". He was referring to the case of *Comrs.
of Customs and Excise* v. *Harz* (2), which at that time had not reached the Court
of Criminal Appeal. Then came the next statement—it is not in the form of a
question—from Mr. Downs which gives rise to the first ground of the application. D
Mr. Downs said,

"I can have some sympathy for a registered wholesaler who finds himself
under great pressure from an unregistered customer. There seems to me to
be two different types of fraud, one where the registered trader deliberately
defrauds the revenue for his own profit, and another where the registered
trader is faced with the alternative of either making no sale or selling without E
charging tax, and he himself makes no profit from the revenue but has the
advantage of undercutting his competitors by the amount of tax; but a
registered trader does have a duty to account for the tax on all chargeable
sales."

Mr. Ovenell did not say anything, and Mr. Downs went on, " would I be right
in assuming that this is what has happened in this business ? ", and Mr. Ovenell F
said, "something like that, yes ". Mr. Downs then said, "so that there were in
fact off-record sales of chargeable goods? ". Mr. Ovenell said, " Yes, but I never
made a penny out of it . . ." It is not possible to quantify the true liability to
purchase tax in respect of either of the two quarterly periods in question since
the detailed items of goods involved in the off-record sales, as they were called,
are neither recorded nor ascertainable.

G

A submission was made by counsel on behalf of the applicants that that oral
admission of Mr. Ovenell should not be received in evidence on the ground
that it was not truly voluntary within the principle annunciated by LORD
SUMNER in the well-known case of *Ibrahim* v. *The King* (3), the relevant passage
in particular being LORD SUMNER's oft-quoted statement (4),

H

"no statement by an accused is admissible in evidence against him
unless it is shown by the prosecution to have been a voluntary statement
in the sense that it has not been obtained from him either by fear or prejudice
or hope of advantage exercised or held out by a person in authority."

The argument here is concerned only with hope of advantage. In the absence
of the jury, counsel on behalf of the applicants submitted that the words " I can I
have some sympathy for a registered wholesaler who finds himself under great
pressure " spoken by Mr. Downs, and followed by the question " would I be
right in assuming that this is what has happened in this business? " constituted
an inducement to make a statement which, he argues, is therefore not voluntary

(2) [1967] 1 All E.R. 177; [1967] 1 A.C. 760.
(3) [1914-15] All E.R. Rep. 874; [1914] A.C. 599.
(4) [1914-15] All E.R. Rep. at p. 877; [1914] A.C. at p. 609.

A but is obtained by the hope of advantage to be gained apparently from the
sympathy professed by the questioner. He submitted—to use his own phrase
at the trial—that from then on all the conversations came " under the umbrella
of inducement "; and his first ground of appeal is that the deputy chairman
was wrong in rejecting that submission and admitting so much of the evidence
of the conversations as I have read, in particular, the last part of what I have
B read.

What is often called a trial-within-a-trial was held and evidence, still
in the absence of the jury, was called by the prosecution on this question of
inducement or no inducement. A Mr. Griffiths was called from the Greenwich
station of the customs and excise and he described how the company's official
books and records were kept; how he had made a routine check visit to their
C premises in November, 1965, to verify returns and found that the company
appeared to be purchasing substantially more than it was selling. He spoke in
evidence of arithmetical calculations which he had made and said that he had
passed the matter on to Mr. Downs of the investigation branch. Then Mr.
Downs was called, and was cross-examined; it is from his evidence that the
statements and questions and answers that I have quoted are taken. When
D cross-examined he specifically denied that he was seeking to induce Mr. Ovenell
to tell him more or to encourage him to think it might not be too bad for him
if he assented to the questions asked. It thus became a question of fact for
the deputy chairman to say and to rule whether or not the conversations were
voluntary and, therefore, admissible.

The basic reason for the rejection of involuntary statements in our system
E is the greater risk that an induced or involuntary statement may be untrue. Mr.
Ovenell did not in fact challenge the truth of Mr. Downs' evidence or of the
fact that it was said he had made the admissions to Mr. Downs. He did not
give evidence either on the voir dire or, indeed, before the jury later in the trial.
He was perfectly entitled not to do so, the burden being on the prosecution to
satisfy the deputy chairman that the statement was a voluntary one. It would
F have been surprising, to say the least, from what evidence was given if the
deputy chairman had ruled that the statements were involuntary. He did not;
he was satisfied that they were voluntary within the terms of the *Ibrahim* ruling
(5), and he ruled, accordingly, that the answers so far as I have quoted them
were admissible.

In fact, on this aspect of the matter the learned deputy chairman later went
G perhaps too far in favour of the applicants, though understandably so. His
attention had been drawn to the case of *R.* v. *Bass* (6), a case in the Court of
Criminal Appeal; in the judgment of the court in that case there appears a
statement to the effect that whilst it is for the presiding judge to rule whether
a statement is admissible it is for the jury to determine its weight once admitted,
and then the words go on, (7)

H   " and he should further tell them that, if they are not satisfied that it
was made voluntarily, they should give it no weight at all and disregard it."

Doubtless in reliance on that last addendum the deputy chairman in this case so
directed the jury in June, 1967, at the trial; but that addendum seems in fact,
to go further than was intended. The *Bass* case (6) has since been considered
I first of all in *Basto* v. *Reginam* (8), where the High Court of Australia rejected
that addendum, as I have called it, that part of the language in the *R.* v. *Bass* (6)
decision which made it appear that the admissibility of evidence (of which
voluntariness is no more than a test) could ever be a matter for the jury, the

(5) [1914-15] All E.R. Rep. at p. 877; [1914] A.C. at p. 609.
(6) [1953] 1 All E.R. 1064; [1953] 1 Q.B. 680.
(7) [1953] 1 All E.R. at p. 1066; [1953] 1 Q.B. at p. 684.
(8) (1954), 91 C.L.R. 628.

court holding that voluntariness and consequent admissibility are entirely for **A**
the judge—weight to be attached to evidence once admitted being the prerogative of the jury. Since then a case to which DIPLOCK, L.J., has referred, *Chan
Wai-Keung* v. *Reginam* (9) has been decided by the Privy Council case on appeal
from the Court of Appeal of the Supreme Court of Hong Kong. The advice
of the Privy Council in that case is not binding on this court, though greatly
persuasive. The headnote accurately summarises the advice (10):   **B**

   " Voluntariness is a test of admissibility and not an absolute test of the
   truth of a statement. It is a matter for the judge and not for the jury.
   The truth of a confession is not directly relevant when the judge is ruling
   on admissibility, though, if the judge admits the statement, the truth
   of it will be a crucial question for the jury. The judge should not direct the
   C
   jury specifically that they must be satisfied beyond reasonable doubt of the
   voluntariness of the statement before giving it consideration. The only
   question for the jury to consider is the probative value of the statement.
   A confession may be voluntary and yet to act upon it may be quite unsafe,
   and it may have no probative value."

This court accepts the view to be found in *R*. v. *Murray* (11); in the Australian **D**
case of *Basto* v. *Reginam* (12), to which reference has just been made; and in the
Hong Kong appeal to the Privy Council (9) rather than the words which have
been distilled from the language of *R*. v. *Bass* (13). It is right to say that the only
relevance is that it indicates that the deputy chairman's direction to the jury
on the admissions of Mr. Ovenell erred most understandably in the accused's
favour.   **E**

I return to the facts of this case. Following on the conversations on Jan. 13,
1967, at the company's premises, Mr. Ovenell took Mr. Downs to his home and
gave him five bundles of papers which appeared to show details of sales to
customers with dates, delivery note numbers, prices and running totals of balances,
and Mr. Downs took those away. On Jan. 24 he returned with his colleague
to see Mr. Ovenell, and Mr. Ovenell agreed that he did not have the delivery **F**
notes referred to and that few of the sales were invoiced or entered in the sales
day book. No tax was shown on the statutory returns in respect of any of the
transactions not recorded in the sales day book. Analysis of the sales shown in
the papers which Mr. Ovenell gave to Mr. Downs at his house on Jan. 13 seemed
to show a total of nearly £14,000 in the six months covered by the two charges,
but this is no criterion of the amount of purchase tax which should have been **G**
paid because those papers do not show the specific goods involved.

The second ground of appeal is that it is suggested that Mr. Downs was in
breach of the Judges' Rules in failing to caution the appellant at the outset
of the interview on Jan. 13, because it is said he must have been suspicious in
the light of the information he had from Griffiths and, therefore, the time for the
r. 2 caution (14) had arrived. It is then urged that the deputy chairman **H**
should not have admitted the evidence of the conversation because of the lack
of such caution.

Now three things require to be said about the Judges' Rules. First of all,
they are not mandatory on nor even directed to the court at all. They are
rules of conduct directed to the police and no more; indeed, they are directed
to no one but the police, though it is understandable that investigating officers **I**
of other services might be thought to be comparably placed with police officers.
Secondly, where a statement has been made without caution in circumstances

---

(9) [1967] 1 All E.R. 948; [1967] 2 A.C. 160.
(10) (1967), 51 Cr. App. Rep. 257.
(11) [1950] 2 All E.R. 925; [1951] 1 K.B. 391.
(12) (1954), 91 C.L.R. 628.
(13) [1953] 1 All E.R. 1064; [1953] 1 Q.B. 680.
(14) Rule 2, so far as material, is set out in footnote †, at p. 933, ante.

A where compliance with the rules would have necessitated a caution, it is a matter
for the trial judge to exercise his own discretion as to whether the statement
should be admitted or not.   No doubt in exercising that discretion so long as
the statement is not inadmissible he will apply his mind, inter alia, to such
factors and principles as the balance between probative value and potential
prejudice.   Thirdly, in this particular case the deputy chairman did exercise his

B discretion judicially and, in the view of this court, more than fairly to the
applicants. He ruled, as he was perfectly entitled to do having heard the evidence
of Mr. Downs, that Mr. Downs was not at the outset of the Jan. 13 conversation in
possession of evidence that afforded him reasonable grounds for suspecting the
commission of an offence, let alone any particular or definable offence. He went
on to rule that after Mr. Ovenell's admission contained in the words, " Yes,

C but I never made a penny out of it " the r. 2 caution ought then to have been
administered, and as a matter of discretion he did not permit what was said
after that to be given in evidence.   In the opinion of the court there can be no
possible complaint on this ground.

A final point is made that the deputy chairman erred in suggesting to the
jury that the figures of sales unrecorded in the sales day book and computed

D from the papers handed to Mr. Downs at Mr. Ovenell's homes were any indication of the volume of sales attracting purchase tax. That has no relevance here,
even if that inference could be drawn from what the learned deputy chairman
said. The amounts in question were not relevant, because the applicants were
not charged with the evasion of purchase tax or non-payment of purchase tax.
What the applicants were charged with was furnishing false returns with intent

E to deceive. On that the evidence was one-sided and overwhelming.

Thus, in so far as these applications relate to conviction, these appeals are both
dismissed.

It has not been pursued by counsel, but in the notices of application leave to
appeal against sentence was also included, the only ground stated being that
really the company and Mr. Ovenell were one and the same although separate

F penalties were imposed. There is nothing to cause comment in that. If a guilty
man makes himself into two entities and commits a crime in both capacities the
court has to deal with both. These applications in so far as they still subsist for
leave to appeal against sentence are also dismissed.

Applications refused.

G Solicitors: *Muscatt, Nelson & Co.* (for the applicants).

[*Reported by* BRIAN POCOCK, ESQ., *Barrister-at-Law.*]

A

R. v. PEMBROKESHIRE QUARTER SESSIONS, Ex parte BENNELL.

[QUEEN'S BENCH DIVISION (Lord Parker, C.J., Sachs, L.J., and Ashworth, J.), January 23, 1968.]

Licensing—Appeal—Notice of appeal—Service—Time for service—Extension B *of time—Notice of appeal served, within fourteen days allowed by s. 22, on clerk to licensing justices—Notice of appeal served on grantee of licence after expiry of fourteen days—Whether notice had to be served on grantee of licence —Whether quarter sessions could extend time for service—Licensing Act 1964 (c. 26), s. 22.*

On the last day of the fourteen days allowed by s. 22* of the Licensing C Act 1964 for appealing, notice of appeal against the grant of an off-licence to the applicant was given by an opponent to the grant. This notice was served on the clerk to the licensing justices, but was not served on the applicant until two days after the time for giving notice of appeal expired. Quarter sessions decided that there was no obligation to serve the applicant and, if there was, they purported to extend the time for giving notice of D appeal. On application for certiorari,

Held: the order extending time should be quashed for the following reasons—

(i) there was an obligation under s. 22 to serve notice of appeal within fourteen days not only on the clerk to the licensing justices but also on the applicant (see p. 941, letter G, and p. 944, letters C and H, post).   E

(ii) the appeal procedure enacted in s. 21, et seq. of the Licensing Act 1964 was a self-contained code, and the power to extend time provided by s. 84 of the Magistrates' Courts Act, 1952, was inapplicable; therefore, as the self-contained code did not include any enactment enabling time to be extended, and as the right of appeal was purely statutory, quarter sessions had no jurisdiction to extend the time (see p. 944, letters B, G and H, post).   F

Paprika, Ltd. v. *Board of Trade* ([1944] 1 All E.R. 372) applied.

[As to notice of appeal from decisions as to the granting of licences by licensing justices, see 22 HALSBURY'S LAWS (3rd Edn.) 608, para. 1253; and for cases as to notices of appeal, see 30 DIGEST (Repl.) 66, *489-493*.

For the Summary Jurisdiction Act, 1879, s. 31, as substituted, see 14 HALS-BURY'S STATUTES (2nd Edn.) 869.   G

For the Magistrates' Courts Act 1952, s. 84, see 32 HALSBURY'S STATUTES (2nd Edn.) 486.

For the Licensing Act, 1961, s. 12, s. 20, s. 21, and s. 22, see 41 HALSBURY'S STATUTES (2nd Edn.) 584, 593, 594, 596; and for the Licensing Act 1964, s. 21, s. 22, see 44 ibid., 510, 512.]

Cases referred to: H
Ashton, Ex p., (1912), 76 J.P. 383; 30 Digest (Repl.) 117, *864*.
Paprika, Ltd. v. *Board of Trade*, [1944] 1 All E.R. 372; [1944] K.B. 327; 113 L.J.K.B. 209; 170 L.T. 269; 108 J.P. 104; 33 Digest (Repl.) 293, *1194*.
R. v. *East Riding Quarter Sessions, Ex p. Newton*, [1967] 3 All E.R. 118; [1967] 3 W.L.R. 1098.   I
R. v. *Glamorgan Justices, R.* v. *Pontypool Justices*, (1890), 24 Q.B.D. 675; 59 L.J.M.F. 150; 62 L.T. 730; 55 J.P. 39; 33 Digest (Repl.) 305, *1305*.

Motion for prohibition and certiorari.

This was an application by way of motion on behalf of John Allan Bennell for an order of prohibition to prohibit Pembrokeshire quarter sessions from hearing

* Section 22, so far as relevant, is printed at p. 941, letter D, post.

A   an appeal against the grant to the applicant of a justices' off-licence, and an order of certiorari to quash an order made by Pembrokeshire quarter sessions purporting to extend the time for appeal against the grant of the said licence. The facts are set out in the judgment of LORD PARKER, C.J.

D. W. T. Price for the applicant.

B   *T. Watkins,* Q.C., and *T. M. Evans* for the respondents.

    LORD PARKER, C.J.: Before referring to the short facts, it is convenient to look at s. 21 and s. 22 of the Licensing Act 1964 dealing with appeals. Section 21 (1) provides:

C   "... any person aggrieved by any of the following decisions of licensing justices, that is to say—(*a*) a decision granting or refusing to grant a new justices' licence ... may appeal to quarter sessions against that decision."

By s. 22, which provides the procedure for appeals, it is provided that

    " (1) An appeal under s. 21 of this Act shall be commenced by notice of appeal given by the appellant to the clerk to the licensing justices within
D   fourteen days after the decision appealed against.

    " (2) On an appeal against the grant of a justices' licence the applicant for the licence and not the licensing justices shall be respondent and notice of appeal must be given to him as well as to the clerk to the licensing justices ..."

E   The applicant was granted a justices' off-licence by the Milford Haven justices on Nov. 1, but on Nov. 15, which was the last day of the fourteen days within which an appeal could be brought, the Licensed Victuallers Association, who had opposed the grant before the justices, gave notice of appeal to the clerk to the licensing justices. They thus complied with s. 22 (1). They did not, however, on that day serve notice of appeal on the applicant; that they did on Nov. 17, which was two days out of time if there was an obligation to serve notice on the
F   applicant within fourteen days.

    Quarter sessions held that there was no obligation to serve the applicant within the fourteen days and that accordingly the service had been validly effected. They then went on to hold that even if they were wrong, there was jurisdiction in quarter sessions to extend the time for service of the notice under s. 84 (3) of the Magistrates' Courts Act, 1952. It is in those circumstances
G   that the applicant now asks for the relief claimed.

    Counsel for the applicant's first submission is that quarter sessions were wrong, and that there was an obligation under s. 22 to serve not only the clerk to the licensing justices, but also the applicant himself, within fourteen days. In my judgment, counsel is right in that contention. It is true that s. 22 (2) does not specify that the service which has to be made on the applicant as well as on the
H   clerk to the licensing justices, must itself be given within the fourteen days; but, as it seems to me, that is a necessary inference from the terms of the two subsections. Not only as a matter of language is it the natural interpretation, but as it seems to me the consequences would be disastrous if that contention was not right.

    Counsel for the respondents, with his usual frankness, has said that he finds
I   it very difficult to support an argument to the contrary. If this submission were not right, an applicant might be served in a matter of a day or two before the appeal was heard, which would be really nonsense; but more important still is the fact that s. 27 of the Act of 1964 would in effect be completely frustrated. Section 27 provides:

    " (1) The provisions of this section shall have effect where on an application to licensing justices for the grant of a new justices' licence, or for the grant of a licence by way of ordinary removal of a justices' licence, a

person appears before the licensing justices and opposes the grant, but the **A**
justices grant the licence."

That is the case here.   Subsection (2) of s. 27 then provides:

" Until the expiry of the time for bringing an appeal against the grant and,
if such an appeal is brought, until the appeal has been disposed of—(a) the
licence granted shall not come into force . . ."
                                                                            B

Accordingly, if the contrary submission were right, and the service could be
effected after the fourteen days on the person who had been granted a licence,
he might have incurred enormous expense in beginning to operate under the
licence once the fourteen days had expired.   He would then be exposed to the
risk of having incurred all that expense for nothing should the appeal succeed.
In my judgment counsel for the applicant is right in his first contention.   **C**

In those circumstances the only point here is whether quarter sessions had,
as they held that they had, power to extend the time for service of the notice
on the applicant.   It has been held that quarter sessions have no inherent powers
to extend time.   Quarter sessions themselves are creatures of statute, and any
powers they have must be derived from statute.   In *Paprika, Ltd.* v. *Board of
Trade* (1) LAWRENCE, J., said this: **D**

" On the second question, I am of opinion that the committee were right
in holding that they had no power to give leave to appeal against conviction
in the circumstances.   By the Summary Jurisdiction Act, 1879, s. 31 (2)
as amended by the Act of 1933 (2), notice of appeal must be given within
fourteen days of the conviction, and by sub-s. (3) recognisances must be
entered into within twenty-one days; and by the Metropolitan Police   **E**
Courts Act, 1839, s. 50, even more stringent conditions are imposed.   None
of these conditions was complied with, and *Ex p. Ashton* (3) and *R.* v.
Glamorgan Justices (4) show how strict the compliance with these conditions
must be; and the Quarter Sessions Act, 1849, ss. 3 and 9, also support the
view that, in the absence of any express powers to give leave to waive the
conditions, quarter sessions have no power to do so."   **F**

That being so, one has to look to see if there was any statutory power to extend
the time.   The respondents rely on s. 84 (3) of the Magistrates' Courts Act, 1952,
and quarter sessions upheld their contention.   Section 84 (3) provides as follows:

" Where it appears to a court of quarter sessions, on application made
in accordance with the following provisions of this section, that any person **G**
wishing to appeal to that court from a magistrates' court has failed to give
the notice of appeal required by this section within the period of fourteen
days prescribed by sub-s. (1) of this section, the court of quarter sessions
may, if it thinks fit, direct that any such notice of appeal previously given
by the applicant after the expiration of the said period, or any such notice
to be given by him within such further time as may be specified in the   **H**
direction, shall be treated as if given within the said period."

That power, as will be seen from the words I have read, applies in the case of a
notice of appeal required within the period of fourteen days prescribed by sub-s.
(1) of that section which provides that:

" An appeal from a magistrates' court to quarter sessions shall be commenced by the appellant's giving notice of appeal, within fourteen days
after the day on which the decision of the magistrates' court was given, to
the clerk of the magistrates' court and to the other party."

One point I would like to dispose of at once.   There was a time when licensing

---

(1) [1944] 1 All E.R. 372 at p. 374; [1944] K.B. 327 at p. 331.
(2) The Summary Jurisdiction (Appeals) Act, 1933.
(3) (1912), 76 J.P. 383.
(4) (1890), 24 Q.B.D. 675.

A justices could not be said to be a magistrates' court; but the Summary Jurisdiction (Appeals) Act, 1933, s. 1, substituted a new s. 31 in the Summary Jurisdiction Act, 1879. Subsection (1) of the new s. 31 of the Act of 1879 provided:

B " Subject to the provisions of this section, where a person is authorised by or under any Act, including any local Act, to appeal to a court of general or quarter sessions against a conviction, sentence, order, determination or other decision of a court of summary jurisdiction, the following provision shall apply . . ."

That substitution of the new s. 31 (1) added after the word " order " the words " determination or other decision of a court of summary jurisdiction ". In a recent decision of the Court of Appeal in *R. v. East Riding Quarter Sessions,*
C *Ex p. Newton* (5), the Court of Appeal drew attention to the new language to be found in the Act of 1933, and held that having regard to that difference in language, licensing justices were today to be considered as coming within the expression " A magistrates' court " (6) for the purposes of the Act of 1952. Accordingly, the sole question here is whether it can be said that the notice of appeal in question in this case was a notice of appeal required to be given within fourteen days by
D s. 84 (1).

For my part, I find it unnecessary to go into the whole history of the licensing laws and the statutes regarding the powers of the magistrates' court. The real question, as I see it, is whether the group of sections in the Licensing Act 1964 which, as I will show in a moment, are really repeating similar provisions in the Licensing Act, 1961, can be looked on as merely amending pro tanto the
E provisions of s. 84 of the Magistrates' Courts Act, 1952, or whether they form, as it were, a self-contained code regarding appeals.

In the Licensing Act, 1961, a completely new procedure was adopted: whereas previously the grant of a licence required confirmation, s. 12 of the Act of 1961 substituted a new procedure, namely by way of appeal to quarter sessions. Schedule 4 to the Act of 1961 provided the procedure for such appeals. It
F provided, as does the Act of 1964 that no person could appeal against the grant of a licence unless he had resisted the application, and it provided for the time within which the notice must be given and on whom it must be served. Those provisions of the Act of 1961 were provisions made after the Act of 1952 was in full force and effect.

For my part I should have expected, if this was merely a provision for amend-
G ing as it were the ordinary procedure in the Act of 1952, that there would be incorporated in that schedule a power such as is to be found in s. 84 (3) if that were indeed the intention. It would have been so easy to say that the notice prescribed for the purposes of the Licensing Act, 1961, should be treated as a notice required to be given under s. 84 (1). If that had been done, then clearly the power to extend the time under s. 84 (3) would have been incorporated.
H It was those provisions then in the Licensing Act, 1961, which now find their place in the group of sections beginning with s. 21 in the Act of 1964. As it seems to me that is a self-contained code, and the power under s. 84 (3) is not incorporated in it and does not apply to appeals under those sections.

Some confirmation can be found for that interpretation when one considers that the power to extend the time came into being for the first time in the Criminal
I Justice Act, 1948, s. 36, and it is quite clear that the power there given was limited to the case of a person convicted of extension which originally was limited to the case of a person convicted by a court of summary jurisdiction, and the power of extension which originally was limited to cases of conviction by a court of summary jurisdiction is re-enacted by s. 84 (3). I am not suggesting

---

(5) [1967] 3 All E.R. 118.
(6) See Magistrates' Courts Act, 1952, s. 124 (1); 32 Halsbury's Statutes (2nd Edn.) 518.

that the powers in s. 84 (3) are limited to appeals under s. 83, which again is
dealing with appeals by convicted persons; but though not limited in that way,
and though applicable to cases where no self-contained or other provisions
restricting procedure have been laid down, it does seem to me that where one
finds special provisions, their natural reading is that they stand on their own
feet as a self-contained code.

In those circumstances I have come to the conclusion that counsel for the
applicant's submission on this point is right, and that quarter sessions came to a
wrong conclusion in holding that they could extend the time. It follows that the
applicant is entitled to the relief, or at any rate some of the relief claimed and,
subject to any further argument, I think that an order of certiorari should issue
to quash their decision. I cannot see that an order of prohibition is really
required, because it is inconceivable that quarter sessions would then proceed
to hear the case.

    SACHS, L.J.: I agree, and as regards the first point, that service on the
applicant for the licence must be within fourteen days, I have nothing to add.

As regards the second point, there is one matter which powerfully reinforces
the view that s. 22 of the Licensing Act 1964 produces a self-contained code
for appeals to quarter sessions on matters which arise under s. 21. When one
looks at s. 22, it starts with these words:

> " An appeal under s. 21 of this Act shall be commenced by notice of appeal
> given by the appellant to the clerk to the licensing justices within fourteen
> days after the decision appealed against."

Then s. 22 continues for a further six subsections with detailed provisions relating
to such appeals. When one, however, looks at the way in which appeals to
quarter sessions are dealt with in relation to s. 20 (which concerns the consent
required for alterations to on-licensed premises) one finds a complete contrast,
for the whole of the matter of such appeals is dealt with by a brief sub-s. (5) which
provides:

> " A person aggrieved by an order under sub-s. (3) of this section may appeal
> to a court of quarter sessions."

That is the beginning and end of the provisions relating to such appeals.

Nothing to my mind could demonstrate more clearly that whereas appeals
under s. 20 come under the general provisions of s. 84 of the Magistrates' Courts
Act, 1952, appeals under s. 21 are subject to a self-contained code that applies
solely to them.

    ASHWORTH, J.: I agree.

Order of certiorari granted.

Solicitors: *Hextall, Erskine & Co.*, agents for *Cartwright, Taylor & Corpe*,
Bristol (for the applicant); *Peacock & Goddard*, agents for *R. T. P. Williams &
Son*, Haverfordwest (for the respondents).

[*Reported by* JUDITH ASHER, *Barrister-at-Law.*]

A

COLESHILL AND DISTRICT INVESTMENT CO., LTD. *v.* MINISTER OF HOUSING AND LOCAL GOVERNMENT AND ANOTHER.

[COURT OF APPEAL, CIVIL DIVISION (Lord Denning, M.R., Diplock and Salmon, L.JJ.), December 19, 1967.]

Town and Country Planning—Development—" Building, engineering . . . or other operations "—Removal of spoil banked against blast walls of ammunition magazines—Demolition of walls—Alteration of building—External appearance affected—Town and Country Planning Act, 1962 (10 & 11 Eliz. 2 c. 38), s. 12 (1), (2) (a).

A company, having acquired disused ammunition magazines, removed the protective banks of rubble and soil outside their blast walls. The magazines were near a village within a proposed green belt. They were made of concrete; each was seventy feet long, thirty feet wide and ten feet high. From a distance the magazines and blast walls, when covered by the embankment, looked like a large green mound; but when the walls were exposed they looked unsightly. Planning permission to remove the embankment had not been obtained. The local planning authority issued an enforcement notice under the Town and Country Planning Act, 1962, in respect of the removal of the embankment. The company proposed also to demolish the blast walls of the magazines. It had applied for determination whether planning permission was necessary for this. On appeal from a decision of the Divisional Court allowing the company's appeal against the Minister's decisions on both matters, viz., upholding the validity of the enforcement notice and determining that planning permission for removal of the blast walls was necessary,

Held: the removal of the embankment was, and the removal of the blast walls would be, the carrying out of building, engineering or other operations on land within s. 12 (1)* of the Town and Country Planning Act, 1962, and thus constituted, or would constitute, development and accordingly the Minister's decisions would be restored; moreover their removal would not be within the exception provided by s. 12 (2) (a) because, although it would amount to the alteration of a building, the alteration would be one that would materially affect the external appearance of the building (see p. 947, letters A and C, and p. 948, letters B, E and G, post).

Quaere whether the demolishing of a building, as distinct from demolishing a part of it in such a manner as to alter its external appearance, would be development (see p. 947, letter D, p. 948, letter B, and p. 949, letter A, post).

Decision of the DIVISIONAL COURT (ante p. 62) reversed.

[As to what constitutes development, see 37 HALSBURY'S LAWS (3rd Edn.) 259-263, para. 366; and for cases on the subject, see 45 DIGEST (Repl.) 325-327, 6-13.

For the Town and Country Planning Act, 1962, s. 12 (1), s. 43, s. 180 and s. 181, see 42 HALSBURY'S STATUTES (2nd Edn.) 975, 1013, 1147, 1148.]

I Case referred to:

London County Council v. *Marks & Spencer, Ltd.*, [1953] 1 All E.R. 1095; [1953] A.C. 535; [1953] 2 W.L.R. 932; 117 J.P. 261; *affg.* sub nom. *Re 42-48, Paddington Street and 62-72, Chilton Street, St. Marylebone, Marks & Spencer, Ltd.* v. *London County Council*, [1952] 1 All E.R. 1150; 116 J.P. 286; sub nom. *Marks & Spencer, Ltd.* v. *London County Council*, [1952] Ch. 549; 45 Digest (Repl.) 340, *56.*

* Section 12, so far as material, is set out at p. 946, letter I, and p. 947, letter B, post.

KK

Affirmed. H.L. [1969] 2 All E.R. 525

Appeal.   A

This was an application for leave to appeal, and the hearing of the appeal,
by Meriden Rural District Council, acting on behalf of the Warwickshire County
Council, as local planning authority, from a decision of the Divisional Court
(LORD PARKER, C.J., WIDGERY and CHAPMAN, JJ.), given on Nov. 24, 1967,
and reported ante p. 62. The Divisional Court allowed the appeals of Coleshill
and District Investment Co., Ltd., under s. 180 and s. 181 of the Town and   B
Country Planning Act, 1962, against decisions of the Minister of Housing and
Local Government refusing to quash an enforcement notice served in respect
of removing embankments protecting disused ammunition magazines, and
determining that planning permission was required for removing the blast walls
of the magazines. The facts are summarised in the judgment of LORD DENNING,
M.R., and are more fully set out in the judgment of WIDGERY, J., at p. 64, ante. C

A. E. Holdsworth for the local authority.

S. Goldblatt for the company.

The Minister of Housing and Local Government did not appear and was not
represented*.

LORD DENNING, M.R.: The village of Hampton-in-Arden in Warwick- D
shire lies within a proposed green belt. During the war magazines for explosives were built near the village. There were four of them. Each magazine
was made of concrete. Each was seventy feet long, thirty feet wide and ten
feet high. Outside each building there was a blast wall made of concrete.
These blast walls were nine feet high and four feet away from the buildings.
Outside those walls there was an embankment made of earth and rubble all the E
way round. It was eight to ten feet high. In the course of time grass (and
weeds, I suppose) grew on those embankments. From a distance it looked like
a large green mound, not at all unsightly.

After the war the Coleshill & District Investment Co., Ltd. acquired the
property. They determined to use the magazines for storage. They did not
get planning permission, but they proceeded to remove all the embankments. F
They used a mechanical excavator and a lorry for the purpose. Once the
embankments were removed, the magazines and blast walls were exposed. They
were an eyesore in this countryside. The local planning authority issued an
enforcement notice to restore the embankments to the state in which they were
originally. The company appealed to the Minister. The company also wanted
to remove the blast walls. They applied to the Minister to determine whether G
planning permission was required. An inquiry was held. The inspector was

" of the opinion that the exposure of the concrete blast walls and buildings
forming these magazines, by the removal of the grass and vegetation-
covered embankments, had resulted in these ugly structures being much more
prominent in the rural surroundings. The quality of the countryside   H
there, and its effectiveness as part of a proposed green belt, had accordingly
deteriorated to an unacceptable extent."

The Minister upheld the enforcement notice, subject to variations. He also
held that permission was required to remove the blast walls. The company
appealed to the Divisional Court (1), who allowed the appeal. The Divisional
Court (1) held that the removal of the embankment was not, and that the   I
removal of the blast walls would not be " development "; so that permission
was not required.

Section 12 (1) of the Town and Country Planning Act, 1962, provides that

"... ' development ' ... means the carrying out of building, engineering,
 mining or other operations in, on, over or under land ... "

---

* Compare p. 947, letter H, post.
(1) Ante p. 62.

A In my opinion the operations here, first of removing the embankments, and afterwards those of removing the blast walls, are each of them " the carrying out of operations on land ". They involve the use of considerable equipment, such as a mechanical excavator and lorry. They are ejusdem generis with " building and engineering operations ". This view is supported by s. 12 (2) dealing with alterations:

B
" The following operations or uses of land shall not be taken ... to involve development of the land, that is to say:—(a) the carrying out of works for the maintenance, improvement or other alteration of any building, being works which affect only the interior of the building or which do not materially affect the external appearance of the building ... "

C These were alterations to a building. This structure was one composite whole (magazines, blast walls and embankment). The removal of part of it was the alteration of the building. The works affected the external appearance of it. So they were not within the exception in sub-s. (2) (a).

It was argued before us that this was only demolition, and that demolition is not " development ". I can see that, if one entire building is demolished, it D may not be " development "; but it is not necessary to pronounce on that today. Here we have the demolition of a part of a building which amounted to an alteration of it which affected its external appearance. That is, I think, development.

The Divisional Court (2) came to a different view because they considered that the scale of the operation was not such as to make it development. WIDGERY, J., E said (3):

" ... but this little job of shifting a few cubic yards of soil with a digger and a lorry is not, in my judgment, an operation of a kind which could ever be dignified with the title of an engineering operation."

He said that the phrase " other operations " must be (4)

F " ... restricted to operations of the scale, complexity and difficulty which required a builder or an engineer or some mining expert."

As he thought that this case did not come within that scale of " operations ", he held that planning permission was not required either for the removal of the embankment or for the proposed removal of the blast walls. I cannot agree with that view. This was not so small an operation as to be overlooked. I G think that the enforcement notice was valid and should be upheld. The embankments must be restored. The blast walls are not to be removed without permission.

I would allow the appeal and restore the order of the Minister.

DIPLOCK, L.J.: I agree. In the interests of expedition we have heard H this appeal and the application for leave to appeal at the same time, with the consequence that there has not been followed the normal procedure of formal notice of appeal and an opportunity for the company to give a respondent's notice or, indeed, an opportunity for the Minister, who was a party to the proceedings in the Divisional Court (2), to be heard on the appeal. He was, of course, given notice of the application for leave to appeal.

I The argument which has been addressed to us in support of the Divisional Court's decision (2) has been based mainly, not on the grounds on which the Divisional Court (2) based its judgment, but on the propositions that demolition of a building is not development and that no proper distinction can be drawn between demolition of a building and demolition of part of a building.

In Circular No. 67 of Feb. 15, 1949, the Minister said that he was

---

(2) Ante p. 62.   (3) Ante at p. 65, letter I.

(4) Ante p. 66, letter A.

A

" advised that the demolition of a building does not *of itself* involve development, although, of course, it may form part of a building operation, or lead to the making of a material change in the use of the land upon which it stood."

I do not think, in the absence of any argument from the Minister, that it would be right (unless it were necessary) to express a view whether the advice which he received and records in the circular was right or not. I agree with LORD DEN-NING, M.R., however, that to demolish part of a building so as to affect its external appearance is clearly development within the meaning of s. 12 (1) of the Town and Country Planning Act, 1962, as assisted by the definitions in the definition section, s. 221, of " building " and " building operations " respectively.

B

I agree that the appeal should be allowed and the decision of the Minister restored.

C

SALMON, L.J.: I agree, and add a word only because we are differing from the decision of the Divisional Court (5).

This appeal really turns on whether the operations in question were " building, engineering or other operations on land " within the meaning of those words in s. 12 (1) of the Town and Country Planning Act, 1962. It is conceded that " other operations " must be construed ejusdem generis with " building and engineering ". I should have thought that demolition of these nine feet high walls, seventy feet long on two sides of four buildings, and thirty feet long on the other sides of the buildings, and the removal of the embankments resting against those walls for their full length and height, constituted building or engineering operations or other operations sufficiently like them to come within s. 12. This is hardly a job which anyone would undertake to do themselves. Normally one would employ either a building or engineering contractor to do such a job. I am afraid that I cannot accept the view of the Divisional Court (5) that it was such a little job that it cannot be dignified by the name of an " engineering operation".

D

E

I am fortified in the conclusion I have reached by the definition of " building operations " in s. 221 of the Act of 1962 which defines them as including

F

". . . structural alterations of . . . buildings, and other operations normally undertaken by a person carrying on business as a builder."

It is conceded that these walls and the embankments which surrounded the maga-zines were integral parts of the magazine buildings. When these walls and embank-ments are taken away, there would in my judgment be an obvious structural alteration of the whole building.

G

We are asked to give a restrictive meaning to what, in my view, at any rate, is the clear ordinary meaning of words, because it is said, and said very attrac-tively by counsel for the company that in no circumstances can any work of demolition come within the Act of 1962 save in so far as it is part of the pre-liminary work of erecting a new building. I do not see why we should give the wide general words of the Act of 1962 such a restrictive meaning, particularly when one considers that one of the principal objects of the Act of 1962 was to preserve the visual amenities of the countryside. This case illustrates that to do so would be to encourage the mischief against which the Act of 1962 is aimed. Prior to the operations which have been and are proposed to be carried out, there were four magazines and two smaller buildings which were in no way offensive to the view. Now that the embankments have been taken away and when the walls are taken away, the magazines and explosive stores will be revealed in all their naked horror to disfigure the countryside as long as they remain standing. Supposing there were a house of four storeys and the top two were demolished, could any reasonable man say there had been no structural alteration to that building? I am convinced that demolition of part of a building

H

I

(5) Ante p. 62.

A may constitute structural alteration and is therefore a building operation within the meaning of those words in this Act.

It is quite unnecessary to decide whether total demolition of a building by itself amounts to a structural alteration. A possible view is that one could not have any more drastic structural alteration than that. There are, however, dicta in *London County Council* v. *Marks & Spencer, Ltd.* both in the Court of

B Appeal (6) and the House of Lords (7) which may support the contrary view. There is no authority, however, which prevents me from coming to what seems to me to be the sensible conclusion that if you knock down part of a building, and a very important and substantial part of a building, you are thereby structurally altering it. I would allow the appeal.

C *Leave to appeal granted.   Appeal allowed.   Leave to appeal to the House of Lords refused.*

Solicitors: *Sharpe, Pritchard & Co.* (for the local authority); *Tompkins & Co.* (for the company).

[*Reported by* F. Guttman, Esq., *Barrister-at-Law.*]

D

TZORTZIS AND ANOTHER *v.* MONARK LINE, A/B.

E [Court of Appeal, civil division, (Lord Denning, M.R., Salmon and Edmund Davies, L.JJ.), January 23, 24, 1968.]

Conflict of Laws—Contract—Proper law of contract—Sale of ship by Swedish sellers to Greek buyers—Arbitration clause providing for arbitration in London.

F Swedish sellers sold a Swedish vessel to Greek buyers at a price of £38,000 in pounds sterling freely transferable into Swedish kroner. The vessel was to be delivered at, and payment was to be made in, a Swedish port. The contract was in English in a standard form both used in Scandinavia and adopted by the Baltic and International Maritime Conference. The contract did not expressly state what law was to apply, but it provided for an arbitration in the City of London by a single arbitrator, or, if the parties could not agree on a single arbitrator, by three arbitrators, each party appointing one

G arbitrator and the third being appointed by the High Court. On the question whether the contract was governed by Swedish or English Law.

Held: although the transaction had its closest connexion with the law of Sweden, yet by choosing London as the place of arbitration the parties had impliedly chosen English law as the proper law of the contract (see p. 952, letters H and I, p. 953, letter C, and p. 954, letter H, post).

H Dictum of Lord Wright in *Vita Foods Products Inc.* v. *Unus Shipping Co. Ltd.* (*in liquidation*) ([1939] 1 All E.R. at p. 521) applied.

Appeal dismissed.

[As to proper law of contract see 7 Halsbury's Laws (3rd Edn.) 75, para. 140, text and note (*a*); and for cases on the subject, see 11 Digest (Repl.) 420-425, 715-734.]

I Cases referred to:

Hamlyn & Co. v. *Talisker Distillery*, [1891-94] All E.R. Rep. 849; [1894] A.C. 202; 71 L.T.I.; 58 J.P. 540; 11 Digest (Repl.) 423, 724.

N. V. Kwik Hoo Tong Handel Maatschappij v. *James Finlay & Co., Ltd.*, [1927] A.C. 604; 96 L.J.K.B. 902; 137 L.T. 458; 50 Digest (Repl.), 343, 694.

---

(6) [1952] 1 All E.R. 1150; [1952] Ch. 549.
(7) [1953] 1 All E.R. 1095; [1953] A.C. 535.

Distinguished in Compagnie Tunisienne *v.* Compagnie D'Armement Maritime. [1969] 3 All E.R. 589.

Considered in Compagnie D'Armement *v.* Compagnie Tunisienne [1970] 3 All E.R. 71

Naamlooze Vennootschap Handels-En-Transport Maatschappij Vulcaan v. **A**
    A/S, J. Ludwig Mowinckels Rederi, [1938] 2 All E.R. 152; 32 Digest
    (Repl.) 369, 17.

Spurrier v. *La Cloche,* [1900-03] All E.R. Rep. 277; [1902] A.C. 446; 71
    L.J.P.C. 101; 86 L.T. 631; 11 Digest (Repl.) 423, 725.

Vita Foods Products Inc. v. *Unus Shipping Co., Ltd. (in liquidation),* [1939] 1
    All E.R. 513; [1939] A.C. 277; 108 L.J.P.C. 40; 160 L.T. 579; 11 **B**
    Digest (Repl.) 421, 719.

Interlocutory appeal.

This was an appeal by the buyers, George Tzortzis and Constantinas Sykias,
from a decision of DONALDSON, J., given on Nov. 15, 1967, on an interim award
in the form of a special case stated by arbitrators raising the question what was
the proper law of a contract for the sale of a Swedish vessel by the respondent **C**
Swedish sellers to the appellant Greek buyers. The contract for sale was in
the English language. The dispute arose out of an alleged breach of contract
by the sellers in that the vessel was not ready, so it was alleged, for delivery on
Dec. 27, 1963. The buyers alleged that the proper law of the contract was Swedish.
The arbitrators made an interim award in the form of a special case on Aug. 1,
1967. The following extract from the facts found by the arbitrators is taken **D**
from the judgment of DONALDSON, J.:

    " The contract and addendum, each dated ' Stockholm, Nov. 7, 1963 '
were in two parts. The part marked ' Original ' was in fact signed in Stockholm on that date on behalf of the respondents and the part marked ' Copy '
on Piraeus about a fortnight later on behalf of the [buyers]. The contract **E**
and addendum related to the sale by the [sellers] (a Swedish company
carrying on business in Stockholm) to the [buyers] (Greek subjects resident
in Greece) of the respondents' Swedish flag steam ship ' Montrose', therein
described as being classed ' Lloyd's 100 A1 '. The vessel was to be delivered
at a Swedish west coast port after dry docking thereat . . . and was to be
registered by the claimants under the Greek flag. . . . **F**

    " The cash part of the purchase money (£25,000 as per cl. 16) was to be
paid in £ sterling freely transferable to Swedish kroner to the [sellers']
account with the Stockholm Enskilda Bank, Stockholm (hereinafter called
' the Bank ') or as directed by the bank . . . It was conceded by the
[sellers] (before the arbitrators) that the effect of these clauses was that the
money of account was English, the money of payment Swedish. The balance **G**
of the purchase money (£13,000) was to be paid by instalments in freely
transferable £ sterling, secured by a first preferred Greek mortgage of the
vessel in favour of the bank, the wording of the mortgage deed to be approved
by Messrs. Sinclair, Roche & Temperley of London (the [sellers'] London
solicitors) and the mortgage to be registered in London simultaneously with
delivery of the vessel . . . **H**

    " By clause 20 it was provided that the [sellers'] claim on the [buyers] in
connexion with the sale of the vessel had been assigned to the bank and that
the cash amount payable on delivery was to be made to the bank or as
directed by the bank.

    " The form upon which the contract was concluded is a standard form
bearing the code name ' Sale form ' (a) the copyright of which is vested in **I**
the Norwegian Ship Brokers' Association of Oslo, (b) which is printed and
sold by Halvorsen & Larsen A. S. of Oslo, (c) which is approved by the
Norwegian Ship Brokers' Association and adopted by the Baltic & International Maritime Conference, and (d) which is extensively used for ship sale
transactions concluded in London and elsewhere as well as for those
concluded in Norway and other Scandinavian countries.

    " The concept of ' compensation ' (being the expression used in cl. 14)
is a familiar concept in Scandinavian law, particularly in Norway and

A   Sweden. The method provided for appointing a third arbitrator in cl. 15 is a well recognised procedure in Scandinavian countries."

Clause 15 is set out at letter F, infra; it is the arbitration clause. By para. 1 (i) of the interim award the arbitrators declared that the proper law of the contract was English law; and by para. 6 they stated the question of law for the decision of the court, as agreed between counsel for the parties, whether
B   on the facts found and on the true construction of the contract, the proper law thereof was Swedish law or English law. The facts are summarised in the judgment of LORD DENNING, M.R.

Michael Kerr, Q.C., and *R. M. Yorke* for the appellant buyers.
Basil Eckersley for the respondent sellers.

C   **LORD DENNING, M.R.:** On Nov. 7, 1963, there was a contract between Swedish sellers (Monark Line A/B of Stockholm) and Greek buyers (Mr. Tzortzis and Mr. Sykias of Piraeus) whereby the sellers sold the steamship Montrose to the buyers at a price of £38,000 in freely transferable pounds sterling. A deposit was to be made with a Stockholm bank and the cash amount was to be paid in pounds sterling transferable into Swedish kroner. The vessel was to be delivered
D   and taken over at a Swedish west coast port. The memorandum of agreement was in the standard form in use in Scandinavia which had been approved by the Norwegian Shipowners' Association and adopted by the Baltic and International Maritime Conference. Later on disputes arose which were submitted to arbitration. The question now arises: What is the proper law of the contract? Is it Swedish law or English law?

E   If you read the contract apart from the arbitration clause, it is clear that it has its closest and most real connexion with Sweden. Sweden was the place of the contract. It was the place where the contract was to be performed both as to payment and as to delivery, but then comes the arbitration clause (cl. 15) which reads:

F   " If any dispute should arise in connexion with the interpretation and fulfilment of this contract, same shall be decided by arbitration in the city of London and shall be referred to a single arbitrator to be appointed by the parties hereto. If the parties cannot agree upon the appointment of the single arbitrator, the dispute shall be settled by three arbitrators, each party appointing one arbitrator, the third being appointed by the High Court or the corresponding court at the place where the arbitration is to be held."

G
When the dispute arose, each side appointed an arbitrator. The third one was appointed by the High Court in England. There is apparently no provision in the Arbitration Act, 1950, for the court here appointing such a third arbitrator: but it was done by the High Court by consent. The High Court appointed MR. MACCRINDLE as the third arbitrator. Then the question arose as to which
H   was the proper law that they were to apply. Was it English law or Swedish law? The arbitrators held that, in view of the arbitation clause, they were to apply English law. It was taken to the commercial judge, DONALDSON, J., who affirmed their decision.

Now the buyers bring the case to this court. The amount in dispute is comparatively small; but the matter, they say, is of considerable importance.
I   This standard form of agreement is widely used. The buyers contend that, as this contract had its closest and most real connexion with Sweden, Swedish law should be applied, even in a London arbitration. They say that there is no difficulty in London in obtaining evidence as to Swedish law, and that London arbitrators have often to apply foreign law. The sellers answer that, by providing for arbitration in London, the parties have impliedly agreed that English law should be applied.

It is clear that, if there is an express clause in a contract providing what the proper law is to be, that is conclusive in the absence of some public policy to

the contrary; but where there is no express clause, it is a matter of inference   A
from the circumstances of the case. Now there is no express clause here, but
only a clause that arbitration is to be in London. What is the proper inference
in such a case?

The cases on this point start, as counsel for the buyers reminded us, with
Hamlyn & Co. v. *Talisker Distillery*, (1), and *Spurrier* v. *La Cloche*, (2). Those
cases show that where you have the nationals of two countries providing for an   B
arbitration to take place in the country of one of them, that is a very strong indication that the proper law of the contract is the place of the arbitration. Counsel
suggested, however, that it was different when the place of the arbitration was
not the country of one of the two parties of which they were nationals but
another country altogether. There are, however, cases against him, notably
N. V. Kwik Hoo Tong Handel Maatschappij v. *James Finlay & Co., Ltd.*, (3),   C
and *Naamlooze Vennootschap Handels-En-Transport Maatschappij Vulcaan* v.
A/S J. Ludwig Mowinckels Rederi. (4). I see no reason for any such difference.
When Swedish sellers and Greek buyers agree on arbitration in London, it may
fairly be presumed that they mean English Law to be applied. In the *Kwik Hoo
Tong* case (5), LORD PHILLIMORE said:

"... the forum provided for the settlement of disputes is English, and   D
therefore the contract is intended to be governed by English law ..."

In *Vita Foods Products Inc.* v. *Unus Shipping Co., Ltd.* (*in liquidation*) (6), LORD
WRIGHT said:

" The provision in a contract (e.g., of sale) for English arbitration imports
English law as the law governing the transaction ..."   E

If one leaves the cases and turns to the text-books, DICEY AND MORRIS on THE
CONFLICT OF LAWS (8th Edn.), p. 1047 states that—

"... as a rule the parties, by fixing the place of arbitration, implicitly
choose the proper law of their contract in general and that of the arbitration
clause in particular."
   F
PROFESSOR CHESHIRE on PRIVATE INTERNATIONAL LAW (7th Edn.), p. 193
states that an arbitration clause

"... may merely refer possible disputes to the tribunals of the chosen
country or may go further and add that the tribunal shall apply the law
of its own country. This addition, though convenient as a clear indication of
the proper law, is not of vital significance, since for better or for worse   G
English law is committed to the view that qui elegit judicem elegit jus.
An express choice of a tribunal is an implied choice of the proper law."

Both on the cases and the text-books, I am satisfied in this case that, by choosing
the city of London as the place of arbitration, the parties have impliedly chosen
English law as the proper law of the contract.

It was suggested that as the High Court here had no power to appoint the   H
third arbitrator except by consent, there was some difficulty in making this
implication. I, for myself, do not see any difficulty at all.

I would dismiss this appeal.

SALMON, L.J.: I entirely agree with LORD DENNING, M.R., that the
judge and the arbitrator correctly decided that the proper law of this contract   I
is English law.

The law by which the contract is to be governed depends on the intention
of the parties. When that intention is expressed in the contract, rarely does
any difficulty arise. When it is not expressed, difficulties often do arise, for then

---

(1) [1891-94] All E.R. Rep. 849;   [1894] A.C. 202.
(2) [1900-03] All E.R. Rep. 277;   [1902] A.C. 446.   (3) [1927] A.C. 604.
(4) [1938] 2 All E.R. 152.   (5) [1927] A.C. at pp. 609, 610.
     (6) [1939] 1 All E.R. 513 at p. 521; [1939] A.C. 277 at p. 290.

A   the intention has to be inferred. In such circumstances there are many factors
which have to be taken into account—the lex loci contractus, the lex loci,
solutionis, and many others. Sometimes it is said that one has to ask oneself
the question: what is the system of law with which the transaction has its
closest and most real connexion? In this case, if one leaves out of account the
language in which the arbitration clause is framed, there can be no question but

B   that the system of law to be applied would be Swedish law; that clearly is
the system with which the transaction has closest and most real connexion and
all the other factors which usually point to one system of law or another, here
point to the Swedish system of law.

It seems to me, however, that one cannot leave out of account the terms in
which the arbitration clause is framed. I agree with counsel for the sellers that in

C   this case a choice of English law is to be inferred from the parties' express choice of
an English arbitration. This choice raises an irresistible inference which overrides
all the other factors. In the case to which my LORD DENNING, M.R., has referred,
the *Naamlooze Vennootschap Handels-En-Transport Maatschappij Vulcaan* v.
A/S J. Ludwig Mowinckels Rederi (7), LORD MAUGHAM, L.C., said:

D   " In this case, the appellant being a Dutch company and the respondents
Norwegian shipowners, there was a good reason, if not a necessity, for select-
ing the law which should apply to any future disputes, and the submission
of such matters to the arbitration of two persons in London and of an umpire
who in case of difference was to be nominated by the directors of the Baltic
Mercantile and Shipping Exchange showed clearly that English law and
procedure were to be applied."

E   In the following year LORD WRIGHT, who had an unrivalled experience of these
matters, said in *Vita Foods Products Inc.* v. *Unus Shipping Co., Ltd. (in liquidation)*
(8):

" The provision in a contract (e.g., of sale) for English arbitration imports
English law as the law governing the transaction, and those familiar with

F   international business are aware how frequent such a provision is, even
where the parties are not English and the transactions are carried on
completely outside England."

LORD ATKIN, LORD RUSSELL OF KILLOWEN, LORD MACMILLAN and LORD PORTER
all agreed.

It is quite true that what LORD MAUGHAM, L.C., and LORD WRIGHT said

G   was obiter, but it is clearly of the highest persuasive authority, and it seems
also to follow from the decision in *N. V. Kwik Hoo Tong Handel Maatschappij*
v. *James Finlay & Co., Ltd.* (9), decided in the House of Lords in 1927. Moreover, quite apart from authority, it seems to make very good sense. It is
almost incredible that in the circumstances of this case these parties should have
hit on London with English arbitrators if they did not intend English law to be

H   applied. I say " English arbitrators ", although that is not spelt out in the
contract. It is, however, quite obvious that these business men must have known
that the overwhelming probabilities were that, if a dispute arose, they would
first of all try and agree an arbitrator who was resident in or around London.
If they could not agree, they would each appoint an arbitrator who lived in or
around London. If these arbitrators did not agree, then the High Court in

I   England would by consent appoint, as they did in this case, an arbitrator who
was a member of the English Bar and who knows a great deal about English law
and probably very little about Swedish law. This third arbitrator would in fact
decide the case. It is of course theoretically possible that the parties might
have appointed arbitrators from Holland, Spain or Timbuctoo. I suppose that
it is also theoretically possible that the judge who was asked to appoint the third

(7) [1938] 2 All E.R. at p. 156.
(8) [1939] 1 All E.R. at p. 521; [1939] A.C. at p. 290.
(9) [1927] A.C. 604.

arbitrator might have appointed the leader of the Swedish Bar; but looking at the realities of the situation, I have no doubt at all that the parties intended to happen what in fact did happen in the present case.

We know, of course, that often in the commercial court and in other courts it is necessary to apply foreign law to a contract, and that this is certainly not beyond the capacity of English lawyers; but to the ordinary commercial man, entering into a contract of this sort, who goes out of his way to say arbitration in London before English arbitrators, the sensible inference, as was pointed out by LORD MAUGHAM, L.C., and LORD WRIGHT, is that the law of the seat of the arbitration is intended to be the law to be applied to the contract. If the intention had been otherwise, one would have expected the parties to have stated expressly which system of foreign law they intended to apply.

Counsel for the buyers, in the course of his very attractive argument, said it would be insular to hold that English law should be applied. I am afraid I do not agree with him. If this contract instead of inserting " London " had inserted " Paris ", although the case would not have come before me for decision, had I been asked, I should have said that since the parties stipulated arbitration in Paris by French arbitrators, they intended French law to apply. I say the same about an English arbitration in London—English law. After all, English law has certainly not yet been devalued, and there is no reason to suppose that these gentlemen did not desire this contract to be governed by the law of land where they wished it to be held.

Counsel for the buyers has admitted (as he had to in the face of the authorities) that if the choice were between two systems of law, namely the system of country A, in which one of the contracting parties lived, or the system of country B, in which the other contracting party lived, the fact that the arbitration clause provided that the arbitration should take place in country A would be the strongest possible indication that the parties intended the contract to be governed by the system of law of country A. He says it is different where the parties living respectively in countries A and B provide for an English arbitration. As my brother EDMUND DAVIES, L.J., pointed out during the course of the argument, I should have thought this is almost an a fortiori case. I do not think that the Greek shipowners would have very readily consented to the contract being governed by Swedish law and I fancy that the Swedish shipbuilders would have been even slower to agree to the contract being governed by Greek law. I think that it is not at all unnatural, in circumstances such as these, that the parties should agree for the contract to be arbitrated on neutral territory by neutral arbitrators in accordance with a system of law which very often does govern commercial contracts. Indeed, it is not uncommon in the shipping world to find foreign shipowners in their contracts agreeing that any dispute between them shall be decided by the English commercial court according to English law.

I agree that this appeal must be dismissed.

EDMUND DAVIES, L.J.: Despite the attractive and valiant submissions by counsel for the buyers the view expressed by my lords appears to me to be so clearly right, with respect, that I desire to say nothing more than that I entirely agree that this appeal must be dismissed.

Appeal dismissed.

Solicitors: *Hedley, Thompson, Edward & Butler* (for the buyers); *Sinclair, Roche & Temperley* (for the sellers).

A

INLAND REVENUE COMMISSIONERS *v.* LAND
SECURITIES INVESTMENT TRUST, LTD.

[CHANCERY DIVISION (Cross, J.), December 4, 5, 11, 1967.]

B *Profits Tax—Computation of profits—Deduction—Capital payment—Rent charge*
—Rentcharges given as consideration for lessee's purchase of lessor's interest
—Consideration for acquisition of a capital asset—Dissection into capital
and income elements—Deductibility of whole or part of payments—Finance
(No. 2) Act, 1940 (3 & 4 Geo. 6 c. 48), s. 14 (1).

The taxpayer company held leases or sub-leases of six properties for
C periods varying from 71½ to 993¼ years from the Church Commissioners;
and its subsidiary company held leases of five properties from the commissioners for periods of 991¾ or 999½ years. The two companies entered into
an agreement with the commissioners for the purchase from the commissioners of their interests in the six properties and the five properties respectively in consideration in each case of a rentcharge for ten years, the rent-
D charge representing in each case (allowing for the head-lease rent for which
the taxpayer company assumed liability where the commissioners were
leaseholders) a substantial increase on the rent paid to the commissioners.
From the whole of the rentcharge payments made to the commissioners the
companies deducted income tax under s. 177* of the Income Tax Act, 1952,
but the companies were charged to the profits tax on profits computed with-
E out deduction of the rentcharges. On the question whether the rentcharges
were deductible in computing the profits of the companies for profits tax
purposes, the special commissioners found that the rentcharges fell within
s. 177 of the Act of 1952 and therefore held they were so deductible in full.

Held: the right to receive the rents for the remainder of the periods of the
leases or sub-leases, which right the companies acquired by purchasing the
F reversions, was a capital asset, and therefore the rentcharges prima facie
represented, in part, payment for a capital asset; and since, when a capital
asset was acquired in consideration of a rentcharge for ten years, it was
natural to suppose that some part of each instalment of the rentcharge
represented capital, the case would be remitted to the commissioners for
further consideration (see p. 961, letters G and I, and p. 962, letter G, post).

G *Vestey v. Inland Revenue Comrs.* ([1961] 3 All E.R. 978) and *Secretary of*
State in Council of India v. Scoble ([1903] A.C. 299) applied.

Appeal allowed.

[As to deduction of income tax from rentcharges, see 20 HALSBURY'S LAWS
(3rd Edn.) 292, para. 532.

As to deduction of annual payments in computing income for profits tax
H purposes, see ibid., pp. 622, 623, para. 1214; and for cases on the subject, see
28 DIGEST (Repl.) 378, *1648, 1649,* and DIGEST (Cont. Vol. A) 908, *1649a.*

For the Income Tax Act, 1952, s. 177, see 31 HALSBURY'S STATUTES (2nd Edn.)
175; and for the Finance (No. 2) Act, 1940, s. 14 (1), see 12 ibid., p. 507.]

Cases referred to:
Perrin v. Dickson (Inspector of Taxes), [1929] All E.R. Rep. 685; [1930]
I 1 K.B. 107; 98 L.J.K.B. 683; 142 L.T. 29; 14 Tax Cas. 608; 28
Digest (Repl.) 170, *685.*
Secretary of State in Council of India v. Scoble, [1903] A.C. 299; 72 L.J.K.B.
617; 89 L.T. 1; 4 Tax Cas. 618; 28 Digest (Repl.) 167, *672.*
Vestey v. Inland Revenue Comrs., Inland Revenue Comrs. v. Vestey, [1961]
3 All E.R 978; [1962] Ch. 861; [1962] 2 W.L.R. 221; 40 Tax Cas.
112; Digest (Cont. Vol. A) 902, *1548a.*

---

* Section 177, so far as material, is set out at p. 960, letters C to E, post.

Reversed. C.A. [1968] 3 All E.R. 33.

Case Stated.

The taxpayer company appealed to the Special Commissioners of Income Tax against assessments to the profits tax for chargeable accounting periods (year to Mar. 31 in each case) as follows: 1959-60, £30,000 (tax); 1960-1961, £50,000 (tax); 1961-1962, £45,000 (tax); 1962-1963, £24,000 (tax); and 1963-1964, £168,750 (tax).   The question for decision was whether the taxpayer company was entitled, in computing its profits for the purposes of the assessments under appeal, to deduct amounts paid by it in respect of certain rentcharges.   The taxpayer company contended as follows: (i) that the rentcharges reserved in the transfers of properties from the Church Commissioners to the taxpayer company and its wholly-owned subsidiary, Associated London Properties, Ltd., were rentcharges to which s. 177 of the Income Tax Act, 1952, applied, and that (by reference to the statutory provisions concerning the computation of profits for the profits tax) they should be deducted in computing the profits assessed, and the assessments should be reduced accordingly; and (ii) in answer to the Crown's contentions, that the rentcharges were not payments of a capital nature, and no part of them could be regarded as of a capital nature.   The Crown contended as follows: (i) that certain documents which it tendered in evidence were admissible and relevant to the enquiry as to the true nature (capital or income) of the payments made in respect of the rentcharges (the documents were a bundle of letters passing between Sir Harold Samuel, chairman and managing director of the taxpayer company and the Church Commissioners relating to negotiations prior to the agreement under which the rentcharges were payable, and copies of file notes and inter-office memoranda of the commissioners relating to negotiations); (ii) that the reference to " rentcharge " in s. 177 of the Act of 1952 was a reference to a rentcharge of an income nature, and did not extend to a rentcharge of a capital nature; (iii) that on the evidence in the documents tendered by the Crown the rentcharges were part capital and part income, and should be dissected, and that s. 177 applied only to such part as (on dissection) should be found to represent an income payment, and that accordingly the taxpayer company was entitled to deduction, in computing its profits for profits tax purposes, of that part only of the rentcharges and no more; and (iv) that if, contrary to those contentions, the whole of each rentcharge was within s. 177 and the taxpayer company was entitled to deduct income tax therefrom, it was nevertheless not entitled to deduct the payments for profits tax purposes by virtue of s. 14 (1) of the Finance (No. 2) Act, 1940, since on income tax principles they were payments of a capital and not a revenue nature; and that the documents tendered in evidence were relevant and were admissible evidence in relation to that contention.   The Special Commissioners held* that the rentcharges were rentcharges from which s. 177 authorised the taxpayer company to deduct income tax, and the payments made in respect of them were in their nature rents and as such were income payments properly deductible in computing the taxpayer company's profits.   They allowed the taxpayer company's appeal.   The Crown appealed by way of Case Stated to the High Court.

Arthur Bagnall, Q.C., and *J. R. Phillips* for the Crown.
Heyworth Talbot, Q.C., and *M. P. Nolan* for the taxpayer company.

Cur. adv. vult.

Dec. 11.   **CROSS, J.:** The respondent taxpayer company, Land Securities Investment Trust, Ltd., is a large public company carrying on business as a property investment trust company.   Immediately before Jan. 5, 1960, it held leases or under-leases from the Church Commissioners of six properties in London, details of which were as follows: (i) in respect of Marcol House, Regent Street, the freehold of which was vested in the commissioners, the taxpayer company held a lease for 993¼ years from Sept. 29, 1953, at an annual

---

* The decision of the commissioners is set out at p. 960, letter H, and p. 961, letters A to C, post.

A rent of £5,000; (ii) in respect of 158-160, City Road, the freehold of which was vested in the commissioners, the taxpayer company held a lease for 150 years from Dec. 25, 1948, at an annual rent of £2,000; (iii) in respect of 55, 57 and 59, Oxford Street and 2, Soho Square, the freehold of which was vested in the commissioners, the taxpayer company held a lease for 150 years from Dec. 25, 1947, at an annual rent of £2,000; (iv) in respect of King William Street House, of which

B the commissioners held an underlease for $71\frac{1}{2}$ years less two days from June 24, 1949, at a rent of £7,500, the taxpayer company held a sub-underlease for $71\frac{1}{2}$ years less three days from June 24, 1949, at a rent of £17,500; (v) in respect of Granite House, Cannon Street, of which the commissioners held a lease for ninety-nine years from Mar 25, 1935, at a rent of £5,000, the taxpayer company held an underlease for $83\frac{1}{2}$ years less three days from Sept. 29, 1950, at a rent of

C £7,000; (vi) in respect of Regis House, King William Street, of which the commissioners held a lease for ninety-nine years from Mar. 25, 1934, at a rent of £9,500, the taxpayer company held an underlease for $83\frac{1}{4}$ years less three days from Dec. 25, 1949, at a rent of £20,000. Further, (vii) in respect of 112, 113 and 114, Fenchurch Street and 17 and 18 Billiter Street, the freehold of which was vested in the commissioners, Associated London Properties, Ltd., which is a wholly-

D owned subsidiary of the taxpayer company and which is grouped with it for profits tax purposes, held leases of 112 and 113, Fenchurch Street and 18, Billiter Street for $999\frac{1}{2}$ years from June 24, 1954, and of 114, Fenchurch Street and 17, Billiter Street from Mar. 25, 1955, to Dec. 25, 2946, at an aggregate rent of £9,000.

By an agreement made on Jan. 5, 1960, between the Church Commissioners of the first part, the taxpayer company of the second part and its subsidiary

E company of the third part, it was agreed that the commissioners should sell and the taxpayer company should purchase the first six properties before mentioned and that the commissioners should sell and the subsidiary company should purchase the property seventhly mentioned in consideration in each case of a rent-charge for ten years from Apr. 1, 1959, of the following amounts: property 1, £12,000 per annum, property 2, £4,800 per annum, property 3, £4,800 per annum,

F property 4, £23,450 per annum, property 5, £4,700 per annum, property 6, £24,650 per annum, property 7, £21,600 per annum. The agreement was duly completed by seven transfers of which I take that in respect of Marcol House, Regent Street, as an example. That is dated Mar. 25, 1960, and reads:

G " 1.   In consideration of the rentcharge hereinafter reserved and the covenant by [the taxpayer company] hereinafter contained the commissioners being seised in fee simple hereby transfer to [the taxpayer company] (and so that the same covenants shall be implied herein as if the commissioners had been and had been expressed to convey or transfer as beneficial owners) the land comprised in the title above referred to reserving out of the premises to the commissioners a yearly rentcharge of twelve thousand pounds (£12,000) for the period of ten years from Apr. 1, 1959, charged on

H and issuing out of the property hereby transferred and to be paid without any deductions except for property or income tax by equal yearly payments on Mar. 25 in every year the first payment of £12,000 for and in respect of the full year commencing on Apr. 1, 1959, to be made on Mar. 25, 1960, and the last payment to be made on Mar. 25, 1969.

" 2.   [The taxpayer company] hereby covenant[s] with the commissioners

I that [the taxpayer company] will at all times hereafter during the con-tinuance of the term thereof pay the said yearly rentcharge (including the said sum of £12,000 for and in respect of the said full year commencing on Apr. 1, 1959) at the times hereinbefore appointed for payment thereof.

" 3.   For the removal of doubt it is hereby declared that in the event of the exercise in any manner whatsoever by the commissioners of their powers or any of them under s. 121 (4) of the Law of Property Act, 1925, the surplus of all moneys received by or under or by virtue of or arising in consequence

A

of the exercise of the said powers or any of them after satisfaction of all
sums to which the commissioners may be entitled as rentcharge-owners
hereunder shall in all circumstances be held in trust for and payable to [the
taxpayer company].

" 4. It is hereby further declared that the rights of the commissioners
under s. 121 (4) of the Law of Property Act, 1925 shall continue in being for
so long as any part of the rentcharge herein reserved remains unpaid notwithstanding the expiration of the period of ten years hereinbefore
mentioned."

B

Then there are provisions for insurance and against the premises being altered,
which I need not read.

It will be seen that as a result of this transaction the taxpayer company and
its subsidiary company which had previously owned long leases or underleases
at rents totalling £62,500 per annum acquired four freeholds and three leaseholds
(subject, as to the leaseholds, to head rents totalling £22,000 per annum) burdened
with seven rentcharges totalling £96,000 per annum for ten years.

C

The taxpayer company or its subsidiary company have always deducted
income tax at the standard rate on the whole of the rentcharges on the footing
that s. 177 of the Income Tax Act, 1952, entitled it to do so, and the Church
Commissioners have never challenged its right to do so.   The Church Commissioners are, of course, a charity and if income tax has been properly deducted
from the rentcharges it will be repayable by the Revenue to the commissioners;
but the question whether or not it is so deductible and repayable has not yet
been decided as between the Revenue and the commissioners.   The question at
issue in this appeal is how the transaction has affected the profits tax liability
of the taxpayer company.   It is common ground that prior to the transfers the
rents payable by the taxpayer company and its subsidiary were deductible for
profits tax purposes, and it is also common ground that after the transfers the
head rents of £22,000 became deductible for these purposes.   The question is
whether the rentcharges or any part of the rentcharges are deductible.

D

E

I will now set out the statutory provisions which may affect the question.
The Finance Act, 1937, s. 20 (1) provides:

F

" For the purpose of the national defence contribution, the profits arising
from a trade or business in each chargeable accounting period shall be
separately computed, and shall be so computed on income tax principles
as adapted in accordance with the provisions of Sch. 4 to this Act.

" For the purpose of this subsection, the expression 'income tax principles'
in relation to a trade or business means the principles on which the profits
arising from the trade or business are computed for the purpose of income
tax under Case I of Sch. D, or would be so computed if income tax were
chargeable under that Case in respect of the profits so arising."

G

Then, turning to Sch. 4, I will read para. 4:

H

" The principles of the Income Tax Acts under which deductions are not
allowed for interest, annuities or other annual payments payable out of the
profits or for royalties, or (in certain cases) for rent, and under which the
annual value of lands, tenements, hereditaments or heritages occupied for
the purpose of a trade or business is excluded, and under which a deduction
may be allowed in respect of such annual value, shall not be followed:

" Provided that nothing in this paragraph shall authorise any deduction
in respect of—(a) any payment of dividend or distribution of profits; or
(b) any interest, annuity or other annual payment paid to any person carrying
on the trade or business, or any royalty or rent so paid; and, for the purpose
of para. (b) of this proviso, where the trade or business is carried on by a
company the directors whereof have a controlling interest therein, the
directors shall be deemed to be carrying on the trade or business."

I

A The Finance (No. 2) Act, 1940, s. 14 (1) provides:

" No deduction in respect of any interest, annuity or other annual payment shall, by virtue of para. 4 of Part 1 of Sch. 7 to the Finance (No. 2) Act, 1939, or para. 4 of Sch. 4 to the Finance Act, 1937, be allowed in computing the profits of a trade or business for the purposes of excess profits tax or the national defence contribution unless the interest, annuity or other annual

B payment would, on income tax principles, be an allowable deduction in computing profits but for the express provision contained in para. (*l*) of r. 3 of the Rules applicable to Cases I and II of Sch. D that no deduction is to be made in respect of any annual interest or any annuity or other annual payment payable out of the profits or gains.

C " In this subsection, the expression ' income tax principles ' has the same meaning as it has for the purposes of sub-s. (1) of s. 14 of the Finance (No. 2) Act, 1939, and sub-s. (1) of s. 20 of the Finance Act, 1937."

Then, coming to the Income Tax Act 1952, I should briefly refer to s. 122 and s. 123.

" 122.   The schedule referred to in this Act as Sch. D is as follows—,

D Schedule D. 1. Tax under this schedule shall be charged in respect of — (*a*) the annual profits or gains arising or accruing—(i) to any person residing in the United Kingdom from any kind of property whatever, whether situate in the United Kingdom or elsewhere; and (ii) to any person residing in the United Kingdom from any trade, profession, employment or vocation, whether carried on in the United Kingdom or elsewhere; and (iii) to any

E person, whether a British subject or not, although not resident in the United Kingdom, from any property whatever in the United Kingdom, or from any trade, profession, employment or vocation exercised within the United Kingdom . . ."

Section 123, so far as relevant, reads:

F " (1) Tax under Sch. D shall be charged under the following Cases respectively, that is to say—Case I—tax in respect of any trade carried on in the United Kingdom or elsewhere; Case II—tax in respect of any profession or vocation not contained in any other schedule . . ."

Section 137 provides:

G " Subject to the provisions of this Act, in computing the amount of the profits or gains to be charged under Case I or Case II of Sch. D, no sum shall be deducted in respect of— . . . (*f*) any capital withdrawn from, or any sum employed or intended to be employed as capital in, such trade, profession or vocation; . . . (*n*) any rent, royalty or other payment which, under any of the provisions of this Act, is declared to be subject to deduction of tax under Ch. I of Part 7 of this Act as if it were a royalty or other sum

H paid in respect of the user of a patent."

Then s. 169 provides:

" (1) Where any yearly interest of money, annuity or other annual payment is payable wholly out of profits or gains brought into charge to tax— (*a*) no assessment shall be made on the person entitled to the interest, annuity or annual payment; and (*b*) the whole of the profits or gains shall

I be assessed and charged with tax on the person liable to the interest, annuity or annual payment, without distinguishing the interest, annuity or annual payment; and (*c*) the person liable to make the payment, whether out of the profits or gains charged with tax or out of any annual payment liable to deduction, or from which a deduction has been made, shall be entitled, on making the payment , to deduct and retain out of it a sum representing the amount of the tax thereon at the standard rate for the year in which the amount payable becomes due; and (*d*) the person to whom the payment is

A

made shall allow the deduction on receipt of the residue of the payment, and the person making the deduction shall be acquitted, and discharged of so much money as is represented by the deduction, as if that sum had been actually paid." [I need not read sub-s. (2)].

" (3) Where—(a) any royalty or other sum paid in respect of the user of a patent; or (b) any rent, royalty or other payment which, under any of the provisions of this Act is declared to be subject to deduction of tax under this Chapter as if it were a royalty or other sum paid in respect of the user of a patent, is paid wholly out of profits or gains brought into charge to tax, the person making the payment shall be entitled on making the payment to deduct and retain out of it a sum representing the amount of the tax thereon at the standard rate for the year in which the amount payable becomes due."

B

C

Finally s. 177 provides:

" (1) This section applies to the following payments, that is to say— (a) rents under long leases; and (b) any yearly interest, annuity, rent, rentcharge, fee farm rent, rent service, quit rent, feu duty, teind duty, stipend to a licensed curate, or other annual payment reserved or charged upon land, not being rent under a short lease or an annuity within the meaning of the Tith Acts, 1936 and 1951.

" (2) Any payment to which this section applies shall, so far as it does not fall under any other Case of Sch. D, be charged with tax under Case VI of Sch. D and be subject to deduction of tax under Ch. I of this Part of this Act as if it were a royalty or other sum paid in respect of the user of a patent."

D

E

The submissions made to and the decision of the commissioners fell into two parts. First, there was the question whether in applying s. 177 of the Income Tax Act, 1952, to the case one could dissect the rentcharge in question into two portions, one representing capital and the other income. The taxpayer company argued that no dissection was permissible. It was submitted on behalf of the Crown, on the other hand, that s. 177 only applied to so much of the rentcharge as was of an income nature, and for the purpose of ascertaining what that portion was, they tendered in evidence certain correspondence passing between Sir Harold Samuel, the chairman of the taxpayer company, and the Church Commissioners during the negotiations leading up to the agreement, and also a bundle of copies of file notes and inter office memoranda of the Church Commissioners relating to the negotiations. The Special Commissioners dealt with this point as follows (see para. 10 (1) of the Case):

F

G

" We held that the reference in s. 177 to ' any . . . rentcharge ' was an unqualified reference to any rentcharge reserved or charged upon land; that the rentcharges reserved by the deeds of transfer were rentcharges reserved or charged on land; that in determining whether s. 177 applied to such rentcharges, it was irrelevant to enquire whether on -dissection if any dissection be allowable in law, and we thought it was not) they contained a capital and income element; that the said rentcharges were rentcharges from which s. 177 authorised the [taxpayer] company to deduct income tax."

H

In view of this decision it was not necessary for them to decide on the admissibility of or to consider the material which the Revenue wished to put in. It is not annexed to the Case Stated and, although it was available for me to see if I wished, I have not in fact looked at it.

The second question was whether, even if the taxpayer company was entitled to deduct income tax from the whole of each instalment of the rentcharges when it paid them, it nevertheless was not entitled to deduct the payments for profits tax since on income tax principles they were payments of a capital and

I

A not of a revenue character. The Special Commissioners dealt with this contention as follows (see para. 10 (2)):

> " The only other issue before us we understood to be that deduction of
> the rentcharges in computing the assessable profits was prohibited by s. 14
> (1), Finance (No. 2) Act, 1940; the rentcharges being (it was contended)
> payments made to secure capital assets. The only assets which might be
B said to have been acquired by the [taxpayer] company under the transfers
> were the reversions to their leases and underleases. Having regard to the
> length of time unexpired on the latter it seemed to us doubtful whether
> these reversions had any real monetary value. From a commercial point
> of view we thought the reality of the matter was that the [taxpayer] company
> had substituted larger rents for a ten year period for smaller rents for
C varying longer periods. The payments claimed were in their nature rents
> and as such were income payments properly deductible in computing the
> [taxpayer] company's profits. We left figures to be agreed."

The Crown asked for a Case to be stated, which concludes as follows:

> " 12 ... The question of law for the opinion of the court is whether we
D erred in law in holding: (1) that the rentcharges were within s. 177 of the
> Income Tax Act, 1952; (2) that they were not payments of a capital nature;
> and (3) that the said payments were deductible in computing the [taxpayer]
> company's profits for the purpose of the assessments to profits tax under
> appeal."

I must say at once that I find the conclusion of the Special Commissioners that
E the taxpayer company had not acquired any capital assets in consideration of
the rentcharges difficult to follow. No doubt if a man buys a freehold property
subject to a lease which has only a few years to run it is natural for him to regard
himself as buying two things: first, the right to receive the rent for the rest of
the lease, and, second, the right in the not very distant future to come into
possession of the property. In this case, having regard to the length of the
F leases to which the freeholds were subject and the fact that the leaseholds purchased were subject to underleases for their whole duration less a day or so, the
second element was absent; but the right to receive the rents for the remainder
of the leases was itself a capital asset. If the reversions on the taxpayer company's leases had been purchased by a third party who was not a property
dealer, it could hardly have been said that he had not acquired capital assets,
G and the position surely cannot be different because the taxpayer company
purchased the reversions itself and thereby extinguished its liability to go on
paying the rents. No doubt what from a commercial point of view would have
been a similar result might have been achieved by an agreement between the
parties increasing the rents payable under the leases to £96,000 for the ensuing
ten years and reducing them to a nominal figure thereafter; but that is not what
H the parties did. The Church Commissioners sold and the taxpayer company
purchased a capital asset. Of course, a capital asset may be acquired in consideration of payments of a wholly income character. This might have been the
case here if the reversions have been purchased in consideration of perpetual
rentcharges which would have been equivalent to interest on a purchase price
payment of which was indefinitely postponed. When a capital asset is acquired,
I however, in consideration of a rentcharge for ten years, it is natural to suppose
that some part of each instalment will have a capital character, and one would
expect to find an Act which professes to tax income providing that the recipient
of the rentcharge is only to be liable for tax on the income element and the payer
is only to be entitled to deduct tax from the income element.

This brings me to consider s. 177 of the Income Tax Act, 1952. I had to
consider a somewhat analogous question six years ago in *Vestey* v. *Inland Revenue
Comrs.* (1). I wish very much that that case had gone to appeal so that I could

_____
(1) [1961] 3 All E.R. 978; 40 Tax Cas. 112.

have had some guidance other than my own in solving the present problem. **A**
I will not repeat all that I said there. The essence of the matter, as I see it,
is that in *Secretary of State in Council of India* v. *Scoble* (2) the House of Lords
held that one might have an annuity payable under a contract only part of
which was an annuity for the purposes of the Income Tax Acts. The annuity
there in question was of £1,300,000 odd charged on the revenue of India
and payable each year from 1901 to 1948 as the consideration for a railway **B**
and works, the purchase price of which, if the Secretary of State had chosen to
pay a gross sum, would have been £34,850,000. The Secretary of State claimed
to deduct tax on the whole annuity, but the House of Lords decided that he was
only entitled to deduct tax from that part of it which represented interest as
opposed to payment of the capital value. I cannot think that the decision
would have been different if instead of being liable to pay an annuity charged on **C**
the revenue of India the Secretary of State had been liable to pay a rentcharge
charged on lands belonging to the Government of India. It is true that the
provisions in the income tax legislation permitting deduction of tax on payment
of annual sums charged on land have always been separate from those relating
to ordinary annuities, no doubt because tax in respect of property in land was
charged under a separate Schedule; but the principle which applies to annuities **D**
charged on personalty must surely also apply to rentcharges.

That does not, of course, mean that as between the Church Commissioners
and the taxpayer company such part of the rentcharges as may represent capital
stands on a different footing from such part as may represent income. If the
rentcharges fell into arrear, the Church Commissioners would have exactly the
same remedies in respect of every pound owing. The dissection is simply for **E**
the purposes of the Income Tax Acts. It is true that in the *Scoble* case (2) it
was apparent on the face of the contract that part of the annuity represented a
capital repayment. Further, the contract mentioned the rate of interest applicable so that the dissection could be worked out without recourse to outside
evidence. As I said, however, in the *Vestey* case (3), later cases—particularly
Perrin v. *Dickson* (*Inspector of Taxes*) (4)—have shown that if necessary the **F**
courts will have recourse to outside evidence to establish what the true position
is. In this case I have not looked at the documentary evidence which the Crown
wished to adduce, and counsel for the taxpayer company said that if the point
of principle was decided against him he would wish to call Sir Harold Samuel
to give oral evidence. In these circumstances I express no view as to what the
outcome of this case will be. All that I do is to remit it for further consideration **G**
by the Special Commissioners in the light of this judgment.

Appeal allowed.

Case remitted to commissioners for further consideration in the light of the judgment.

Solicitors: *Solicitor of Inland Revenue; Nabarro, Nathanson & Co.* (for the
taxpayer company).
H

[*Reported by* F. A. AMIES, ESQ., *Barrister-at-Law.*]

I

---

(2) [1903] A.C. 299; 4 Tax Cas. 618.
(3) [1961] 3 All E.R. 978; 40 Tax Cas. 112.
(4) [1929] All E.R. Rep. 685; 14 Tax Cas. 608.

A P. A. THOMAS & CO. AND OTHERS *v.* MOULD AND OTHERS.

[QUEEN'S BENCH DIVISION (O'Connor, J.), Dec. 20, 1967.]

Contempt of court—Committal—Breach of injunction—Interim injunction—
Breach of confidence—Injunction not specifying precisely what material was
confidential and of what disclosure was prohibited—Whether alleged disclosure
B   *proved with sufficient certainty for injunction to be enforced by committal.*

The plaintiffs were an associated company specialising in schemes designed
to diminish tax payable by their clients. The defendants had been
employees of the third plaintiffs, working for the first plaintiffs until June,
1967. In an action by the plaintiffs based on alleged acquisition of confidential knowledge of schemes worked out by the plaintiffs, an interim
C   injunction was granted on Oct. 6, 1967, restraining the defendants from
disclosing or using confidential information acquired during their employment by the plaintiffs and relating to schemes for the sale of income, for
splitting endowments or concerned with death in service. The affidavits
filed in support of the motion for the injunction were formal, exhibiting
statements of facts which did not, it seems, fully disclose the details of the
D   schemes alleged to be confidential. The injunction was granted in the
terms asked by the plaintiffs on the basis of a prima facie case of novelty
having been made out. In preparing their defence to the allegation that
the material which the defendants were using was confidential the defendants, after the injunction was granted, wrote to firms competing with the
plaintiffs, in an endeavour to discover whether the plaintiffs' schemes were
E   novel and therefore confidential; these letters, so it was alleged, disclosed
confidential material. On motion to commit the defendants for breach of
the interim injunction the plaintiffs contended that the proper inference
was that the defendants, in communicating their understanding of the
plaintiffs' schemes, must have appreciated that they were at risk of
disclosing confidential information in breach of the injunction.

F   **Held:** when enforcement of an injunction to protect confidential " know-
how " was sought, it was essential to make clear what it was that was to
be protected; the plaintiffs had not done so at this stage of the proceedings,
whatever might be the position at the conclusion of the trial, and relief by
way of committal of the defendants to prison would be refused (see p. 967,
letters C and G, post).

G   [As to the enforcement of an injunction by proceedings for committal, see
21 HALSBURY'S LAWS (3rd Edn.) 432, para. 911, and 8 ibid., pp. 31, 32, para. 57,
and as to proof of default, see 8 ibid., p. 39, para. 65; and for cases on the proof
of breach and remedies for breach, of an injunction, see 28 DIGEST (Repl.) 904-906,
1378-1380, 1389-1401 and 16 DIGEST (Repl.) 47, *487,* et seq.

As to injunctions against the disclosure of confidential information, see 21
H   HALSBURY'S LAWS (3rd Edn.) 395, 396, para. 825; and for cases on the subject,
see 48 DIGEST (Repl.) 854-856, *844-875.*]

Cases referred to:
Suhner & Co. v. *Transradio, Ltd.,* [1967] R.P.C. 329.
Technograph Printed Circuits, Ltd. v. *Chalwyn, Ltd.,* [1967] R.P.C. 339.

I   **Motion for committal.**

The plaintiffs, P. A. Thomas & Co., Life Assurance Advisory Services, Ltd.,
and Austin Thomas, Ltd., brought an action by writ issued on Oct. 3, 1967,
against the defendants, Harold Raymond Mould, Ruthven Barrie Llewellyn
Davies and Rosemary Mansell. The plaintiffs were associated concerns operating
in conjunction with one another. The first-named plaintiffs were a firm of
chartered accountants specialising in giving financial advice with particular
reference to the minimisation of tax and estate duty liabilities; the second-
named plaintiffs were a company specialising in giving of advice as to policies

of life assurance, and the third-named plaintiffs were a service company which **A**
employed the staff of the first and second-named plaintiffs.   By their statement
of claim, served on Dec. 1, 1967, the plaintiffs alleged that the defendants, while
employed by one or other of the plaintiffs became conversant with the affairs
of the first-named plaintiff.   The plaintiffs further alleged that, among other
terms, it was an express or implied term of the employment of each of the defendants that (a) the employee should use his or her best endeavours to promote **B**
the business of the first-named plaintiffs;   (b) should serve the first-named
plaintiff with good faith, and (c) should not during or after his or her term of
employment disclose or divulge or use to the detriment of the plaintiffs or any
of them any secret or confidential knowledge or information acquired during his
or her employment from the plaintiffs or any of them.   The employment of the
defendants by the plaintiffs ceased in June or September, 1967.   The plaintiffs **C**
alleged that each of the defendants in the course of his or her employment
acquired knowledge of certain schemes which he or she well knew or ought to
have known to be confidential.   These schemes, which the plaintiffs alleged
were devised by themselves and their advisers, related to four matters, of which
three only were relevant to these proceedings, viz.—(i) the sale of income; (ii) the
splitting of endowments, and (iii) provision for death in service.   The plaintiffs **D**
alleged breach by the first-named and second-named defendants of the terms
(a) and (b) of their employment previously alleged and as against all defendants,
that each of them had disclosed divulged and used to the detriment of the plaintiffs secret and confidential information acquired by them from the plaintiffs
during their employment relating to the schemes referred to.   The plaintiffs
alleged that the defendants threatened and intended, unless restrained, to **E**
disclose divulge and use to the detriment of the plaintiffs this confidential knowledge and information;   and, among other relief, the plaintiffs claimed against
each defendant an injunction restraining the defendants by themselves their
servants agents or otherwise from disclosing divulging or making use of any
confidential information acquired by them during the course of their employment
by the plaintiffs or from any person who acquired such information in the course **F**
of his employment by the plaintiffs relating to the schemes referred to.   By
notice of motion dated Dec. 5, 1967, the plaintiffs gave notice that the court
would be moved for committal of the two first-named defendants to prison,
or that they be fined, for contempt of court in disclosing and divulging such
confidential information in breach of an interlocutory injunction granted by
SWANWICK, J., in the action on Oct. 6, 1967, the terms of which are set out, so **G**
far as is relevant, at p. 965, letter B, post.

T. H. Bingham for the plaintiffs.
R. H. W. Dunn, Q.C., and *M. E. I. Kempster* for the defendants Mr. Mould
and Mr. Davies.

O'CONNOR, J.: The plaintiffs are associated companies operating in **H**
the held of making detailed financial arrangements the object of which is to
diminish the amount of tax which their clients have to pay.   The defendants
were employees of the third plaintiffs, who were in fact the hiring company,
but working for the first plaintiffs until June, 1967.   The plaintiffs' claim is
that during the course of their employment the defendants learned the " know-
how " of four schemes set out in the statement of claim which were the brain-
children of the plaintiffs, involving very detailed and precise calculations and **I**
formulations of schemes for dealing with four separate types of financial arrangement.   I am concerned with only three of those.   Details of these will be found
fully set out in the reserved judgment given by CHAPMAN, J., when the proceedings
for interlocutory injunctions were before him, the judgment being given on
Nov. 3, 1967.   I can refer to the schemes for the purposes of this motion by a
" shorthand " nomenclature;   the sale of income scheme, the splitting of
endowment scheme, the provision for death in service scheme.

A   The matter first came before the courts on Oct. 3, when an interim injunction was granted by CHAPMAN, J. That was continued by SWANWICK, J., on Oct. 6, but in an altered form to that which had originally been made. The order of which it is said there has been a breach was in the following form. The defendants Mould and Davies were restrained from

B   " disclosing divulging or making use of any confidential information acquired by them during the course of their employment by the plaintiffs or from any person who acquired such information in the course of his employment by the plaintiffs relating to (a) schemes providing for the sale of income; (b) schemes providing for splitting an endowment; (c) schemes concerned with death in service . . . ."

C   There was a fourth one, schemes providing for the use of an annuity written under trust to achieve relief from estate duty, but that forms no part of the present proceedings.

It will be seen that the injunction was in wide terms. The present notice of motion raises a novel point, because what has happened is that in the course of preparing their case to meet the allegation that the material which they were using was confidential, the defendants (and their solicitors in one instance)

D   wrote round to competitors in the field to discover whether that which the plaintiffs were using was indeed novel and, therefore, something which it would be unlawful for ex-employees to use on their own behalf, and, much more important, to disclose to other persons without the consent of the plaintiffs. Quite shortly, it is said that in so doing they have indeed " let the cat out of the bag ", because in making their enquiries they have revealed confidential material, and

E   that therefore they are in breach of the injunction which had been granted on Oct. 6.

It is a matter of history that after a very full hearing on the affidavits before him and after hearing very full argument, CHAPMAN, J., was in no doubt that a prima facie case had been made out that there was novelty in the schemes originated by the plaintiffs and that any disclosure of the details of those schemes

F   which were confidential should be restrained; and he continued the injunction.

It is said by counsel on behalf of the defendants, that before the plaintiffs can invoke the powers of the court to punish for a breach of the court's order, it is for the plaintiffs to prove that there has been a breach, and that in order for them to do that they must first of all establish what it is alleged was confidential and, secondly, show at least prima facie that it was in fact confidential. He

G   argues on behalf of the defendants that this the plaintiffs have failed to do because of the way in which they have mounted these proceeedings.

What was done on the affidavits which were before the court on the previous hearings was to swear purely formal affidavits exhibiting statements of fact. The first affidavit of Mr. Thomas exhibited a statement of fact of which counsel for the plaintiffs, tells me, and I accept, because it is obvious on the face of the

H   document, that it was very carefully drawn in order not to reveal the actual details of the plaintiffs' schemes in respect of these three matters. For example, in dealing with the sale of income scheme Mr. Thomas's statement of fact read in this form:

I   " A scheme which, in varied forms, provides for the assignment of a portion of annual income, whether earned or from assets owned absolutely, in return for a tax-free sum, by means of the creation of a covenant for value, creation of a settlement or creation of a charge on the income, the consideration being received by the client in the form of an endowment, a life annuity or an immediate capital lump sum. This is a scheme which I and my partners have evolved over about the last two years in discussions with Mr. Hemingway, and on it we have received the advice both oral and written of counsel."

That scheme was later enlarged in an affidavit sworn by Mr. Rodgers. It is set out in an exhibit to his affidavit of Oct. 13, where he was dealing with allegations

raised in affidavits sworn on behalf of the defendants that the schemes were   **A**
common in the specialised field in which the plaintiffs were operating and in which
the defendants were seeking to operate.   Mr. Rodgers added to the sale of
income scheme the following information:

> " The plaintiffs' scheme, as defined in [an exhibit to] Mr. Thomas' first
> affidavit, differs from other schemes because it provides for the sale of free
> income and not of a life interest.   The plaintiffs' scheme, which takes three   **B**
> alternative forms, was devised by the plaintiffs, their solicitors and counsel,
> the present variants being worked out only about a year ago.   To the best
> of my knowledge, information and belief, no one else operates a similar
> scheme.   The field in which the plaintiffs operate is a narrow one, and if
> any other concern were operating a similar scheme I would expect hints
> of this to have reached me."   **C**

Then he refers to certain competitors whose schemes had been referred to in the
defendants' affidavits and shows that they may be different.   A similar enlargement of the split endowment scheme and the death in service scheme will be
found in that exhibit.

In October the defendants published to various competitors a memorandum;   **D**
and I can use as an example a letter which was written to Noble Lowndes.   It is
exhibited to Mr. Thomas's affidavit sworn in this motion on Nov. 30.   The
letter, signed by Mr. Mould, was written to a Mr. Foulkard, of Noble Lowndes,
and the material parts read as follows:

> " Our solicitors have now received further affidavits from Peter Thomas
> and his partners.   As I feared they have avoided giving details of the   **E**
> schemes and have simply repeated that they are ' unique ' to their firm.
> I am enclosing a memorandum which sets out my own particular under-
> standing of the various arrangements."

There is then attached to the letter a memorandum.   In dealing with the sale
of income scheme in that memorandum considerable detail is given as to Mr.
Mould's understanding of the plaintiffs' scheme.   It must be remembered that   **F**
Mr. Mould had been employed in a confidential capacity by the plaintiffs from
January, 1966, until he was dismissed in June, 1967.   In addition to the matters
referred to in the statements to which I have already referred, he elaborates his
understanding of the plaintiffs' scheme.   It is unnecessary for the purposes of
this judgment for me to read the full details, but I will read the first paragraph
of his elaboration.   He states: **G**

> " The initial sale or assignment is to a ' captive ' finance company in
> exchange for a tax-free lump sum.   The finance house will then sell or
> assign its right to the income to a captive life assurance company."

Mr. Thomas in his affidavit of Nov. 30, says of this memorandum, in para. 5,

> " The details contained in this memorandum concerning the plaintiffs'   **H**
> sale of income and split endowment schemes are in very material respects
> fuller than those in the affidavits and exhibits filed by the plaintiffs; an
> astute competitor could with these details go a very long way towards
> copying the plaintiffs' schemes.   This memorandum is potentially highly
> damaging to the plaintiffs.   The same is true to a lesser extent of the
> plaintiffs' death in service scheme.   I make no complaint of the details given
> of trust annuities."

It is said by counsel for the plaintiffs that the right inference to be drawn from
the background of this case and the position in which the defendants were in
the middle of October, is that Mr. Mould must have appreciated that in giving
his understanding of what the plaintiffs' scheme was he was running the risk
of making use of material and details which were confidential, which would be a
breach of the injunction.   It is said that Mr. Thomas's affidavit is sufficient,
prima facie, to show that that has been done.

A   This raises, as I have said, a novel point. I take the view, and I take it very strongly, that in this class of case, which it is difficult to handle in court, the correct machinery is in fact available to parties to do this without suffering the damage which the plaintiffs have apprehended. It must be remembered that the application for interlocutory relief is heard in chambers and is therefore not publicised. Any trial of the proceedings subsequently, if they so wish, can be

B   heard in camera under the rules of court. It seems to me that where plaintiffs have got a detailed scheme of this class which is their brain-child and which is complicated and which gives them a lead in the market, until other people think out a similar or better one, they can be protected adequately by the courts, as has been shown in this case. If the plaintiffs, however, seeking to protect their " know-how ", are anxious to enforce any injunction which may be granted

C   to them by seeking the help of the court to punish a breach of it, it seems to me to be quite essential that they should make it absolutely clear what it is they are seeking to protect. It is all very well to say " This is confidential material ". It may well be; but it seems to me that this is a typical example of a case such as those referred to by PLOWMAN, J., in *Suhner & Co.* v. *Transradio, Ltd.* (1) and in *Technograph Printed Circuits, Ltd.* v. *Chalwyn, Ltd.* (1) where the judge

D   pointed out that in considering whether interlocutory relief by way of injunction should be granted, one of the considerations is what is to happen if there is a breach and committal proceedings or punitive proceedings are sought on behalf of the plaintiff.

     In the present case the court has granted the injunction in the terms prayed by the plaintiffs. That is the plaintiffs' own doing. If they wish not to trust the

E   court and its procedure for protecting their legitimate interests by disguising the true nature of their " know-how " in the form which has been done in the present case, they cannot complain if at a later stage they are met with the answer with which they have been met here, of saying: " You are alleging a breach of the injunction: you have done thus and so, thus and so, and thus and so ", and then invite the court to draw the inference that because it is different to

F   that which was set out in statements sworn to by the plaintiffs it must be confidential material—part of the " know-how ", part of the material, on which the injunction bites.

     I am not prepared to say that that has been established here. It may well be so. It may be that these inferences can be drawn on all sorts of balances of probabilities at the end of the day when this case is tried; but where parties

G   seek to invoke the power of the court to commit people to prison and deprive them of their liberty, there has got to be quite clear certainty about it. I see no such certainty in the present case, and I am not prepared to give any relief to the plaintiffs on this motion: it must be dismissed.

[On the question of costs.]

H   *T. H. Bingham*: I ask that the costs be " costs in the cause ", so that whomsoever turns out in the end to be wrong bears the costs.

     O'CONNOR, J.: I do not take that view. The procedure of enforcing this sort of injunction is a matter that requires careful consideration. I shall order the plaintiffs to pay the costs.

Motion dismissed with costs.

I   Solicitors: *Freshfields* (for the plaintiffs); *Nabarro, Nathanson & Co.* (for the defendants Mr. Mould and Mr. Davies).

[*Reported by* MARY COLTON, *Barrister-at-Law.*]

---

(1) [1967] R.P.C. 329.   (2) [1967] R.P.C. 339.

EYRE *v.* EYRE.

[PROBATE, DIVORCE AND ADMIRALTY DIVISION (Lane, J.), November 29, December 20, 1967.]

Divorce—Maintenance of wife—Death of divorced husband—Reasonable provision for former wife out of estate of deceased former husband—Estate bequeathed to deceased's widow, his second wife, and the children of his first marriage—Former wife granted secured provision in deceased husband's lifetime—Former wife given nothing by deceased's will—Substantial estate —Whether failure to make reasonable provision for former wife's maintenance —Matrimonial Causes Act 1965 (c. 72), s. 26.

In regard to an application by a first wife, who divorced the deceased, for maintenance from his estate under s. 26* of the Matrimonial Causes Act 1965, the widow, his second wife, surviving him:—(a) An order for secured maintenance should not properly be treated as a pre-determination of what the former wife is to receive after the death of the deceased, although it is necessarily an important factor to be considered (see p. 973, letter D, post).

(b) There cannot be any general rule that a first wife applying under s. 26 should be accorded financial equality with the widow, though a lack of parity between the financial position of a first and a second wife during the lifetime of the deceased husband should not of itself be treated as a sufficient reason for prolonging this position after his death (see p. 976, letters E and F, post).

(c) The fact that an accretion of wealth to the estate has occurred since the first marriage has ended should not be treated as disentitling the former wife to benefit from that accretion (see p. 977, letter H, post).

The deceased married the applicant in 1925, a son being born in 1927 and a daughter in 1935. In 1946, the applicant divorced the deceased on the ground of his adultery with a woman, whom he then married. They had no issue. In 1947, a consent order for the maintenance of the applicant was made at £1,000 per annum, less tax, to be secured for her life, together with £1,500 per annum, less tax, during the joint lives of herself and the deceased. In 1962 a consent order was made whereunder the deceased by a deed of settlement increased the total secured for the applicant's life from £1,000 to £1,500 per annum, less tax, and the joint lives' payment was increased from £1,500 to £2,000 per annum, less tax. During his lifetime the deceased gave £30,000 to the widow, which was invested. In 1953, when the son married, the deceased gave him £36,000 and in 1961 gave him two-ninths of his own share in an estate and settled a lesser amount on the daughter. The deceased died in 1964. By his will he made no provision for the applicant, but he gave the widow a legacy of £10,000, free of duty, his personal chattels valued for probate at £1,672, his residence, which she later sold for £20,750, and an annuity of £4,000. Under the will the son received two-thirds of the residue of the estate and the daughter one-third under the trusts of her settlement. The net residue of the estate was some £65,000. The applicant, who was sixty-three years old and not in robust health, applied under s. 26 of the Matrimonial Causes Act 1965, for the provision of maintenance out of the net estate of the deceased.

Held: there would be an order for periodical payments to the applicant out of the net estate of the deceased at the rate of £2,000 a year, less tax, from the date of her summons, because—(i) it would have been reasonable

---

* Section 26 (1), so far as relevant, provides: " Where after Dec. 31, 1958, a person dies domiciled in England and is survived by a former spouse . . . (hereafter . . . referred to as 'the survivor') who has not re-married, the survivor may . . . apply to the court for an order . . . on the ground that the deceased has not made reasonable provision for the survivor's maintenance after the deceased's death ".

A for the deceased to have made provision for the applicant's maintenance; (ii) the provision which he in fact made was not reasonable, and (iii) while it would not be appropriate to put the applicant on an equal footing with the widow, a reasonable provision for her would be the amount that she was receiving prior to the death of the deceased, there being a sufficient net estate to enable this to be done without interfering at all with the provision for the

B widow or causing any hardship to the other beneficiaries under the will (see p. 978, letters B and I, post).

[As to provision for a former wife out of the estate of a deceased former husband, see SUPPLEMENT to 16 HALSBURY'S LAWS (3rd Edn.) 462, para. 930A; and for cases on the subject, see DIGEST (Cont. Vol. A) 570, 9774a, 787, 788, 5729b, 5729c, and DIGEST (Cont. Vol. B) 375, 376, 5729da, 5760b, 5760c.

C For the Matrimonial Causes Act 1965, s. 26, see 45 HALSBURY'S STATUTES (2nd Edn.) 483.]

Cases referred to:
> *Bellman (decd.), Re*, [1963] 1 All E.R. 513; [1963] P. 239; [1963] 2 W.L.R. 14; Digest (Cont. Vol. A) 788, *5729c*.

D
> *Minter (decd.), Re, Vasco* v. *Minter*, [1967] 3 All E.R. 412.
> *Roberts* v. *Roberts (executrix)*, [1964] 3 All E.R. 503; [1965] 1 W.L.R. 560; Digest (Cont. Vol. B) 375, *5729da*.
> *Styler, Re, Styler* v. *Griffith*, [1942] 2 All E.R. 201; [1942] Ch. 387; 111 L.J.Ch. 263; 167 L.T. 295; 24 Digest (Repl.) 967, *9755*.
> *Talbot* v. *Talbot*, [1962] 3 All E.R. 174; sub nom. *Re Talbot*, [1962] 1 W.L.R.

E
> 1113; Digest (Cont. Vol. A) 570, *9774a*.

Originating Summons.

The applicant, Mrs. Violet Monica Eyre, applied by originating summons for an order under s. 26 of the Matrimonial Causes Act 1965, requiring provision to be made for her maintenance out of the estate of John Stephen Giles Eyre, deceased, her former husband, who died on Oct. 31, 1964. The summons was

F heard by Mr. Registrar RUSSELL, whose report dated Sept. 22, 1967, was adjourned to LANE, J., in accordance with r. 58A (9A) of the Matrimonial Causes Rules, 1957. The summons was adjourned into open court for judgment. The facts are set out in the judgment.

Joseph Jackson, Q.C., for the applicant.
B. Garland for the first and second respondents, the executors.

G *P. A. Bruce* for the third respondent, the daughter.

Cur. adv. vult.

Dec. 20. **LANE, J.**, read the following judgment: This is an application by Violet Monica Eyre for the provision of maintenance out of the net estate of her former husband, John Stephen Giles Eyre, who died on Oct. 31, 1964. His will was

H dated July 26, 1962, and probate was granted on June 24, 1965. The originating summons was taken out on Oct. 21, 1965, within the time limited, under s. 3 of the Matrimonial Causes (Property and Maintenance) Act, 1958, which has now become s. 26 of the Matrimonial Causes Act 1965. Of the respondents, two are the executors of the estate, namely, Phoebe Sybil Eyre, the widow of the deceased, and Michael Robert Giles Eyre, the son of the deceased and the appli-

I cant. By amendment of the summons on Mar. 23, 1966, a third respondent was added, being Sheila Mary Sybil Laxman, the daughter of the deceased and of the applicant. In accordance with prescribed procedure, the application came first before a registrar of this Division, Mr. Registrar RUSSELL, whose report is dated Sept. 22, 1967. He submitted that it would be proper to order periodical payments to the applicant of £1,000 per annum, less tax, from the date of the death of the deceased. Before me, it is submitted by counsel for the applicant that such an order would be too low. On the other hand, counsel for the executors and counsel for the daughter submit that no order at all should

be made in favour of the applicant, or, if that submission be rejected, that **A**
the periodical payments should not exceed the amount suggested in the registrar's
report.

The deceased and the applicant intermarried on May 12, 1925.   The son was
born in May, 1927, and the daughter was born in May, 1935.   They had no
other children.   In 1946 their marriage was dissolved, the decree being made
absolute on Aug. 27 of that year.   The ground of the divorce was the adultery **B**
of the deceased with the first respondent.   The deceased married her on Sept. 4,
1946.   They had no issue.   At the time of the divorce the son was almost nineteen years old.   The custody of the then eleven-year-old daughter was granted
to the applicant.   The daughter was maintained at boarding school by the
deceased and spent half of her holidays with each parent.   The registrar found
that both children tended to regard their home as being with the deceased rather **C**
than with the applicant and that " they never have had, and have not now, any
particular attachment to [the applicant] ".   The applicant did not re-marry.
After the divorce and an inquiry into means, a consent order was made on
Sept. 15, 1947, for maintenance of the applicant at £1,000 per annum, less tax,
to be secured for her life, together with £1,500 per annum, less tax, during the
joint lives of herself and the deceased.   Later, the applicant sought an increase **D**
in the financial provision thus made for her.   On Feb. 5, 1962, a consent order
was made whereunder the deceased by a deed of settlement increased the total
secured for the applicant's life from £1,000 to £1,500 per annum, less tax, and
the joint lives' payment was increased from £1,500 to £2,000 per annum, less tax.

The registrar found the gross estate to be of a value of about £500,000, of which
about £450,000 derived from an undivided share in what is known as the " Eyre **E**
Estate ", and which consists of real property in the St. John's Wood area.
There was evidence before the registrar that estate duty was expected to be
leviable at the rate of seventy per cent.   Counsel for the executors told me that
it is now anticipated that the rate will be seventy-five per cent.   There was put
before me an affidavit by the son of Nov. 27, 1967, with exhibits setting out the
up-to-date capital and income positions.   Counsel for the applicant did not **F**
receive a copy of this affidavit until the morning of the hearing, and so had little
opportunity of studying it; he did not, however, object to its being put in.   He
points out that the second exhibit to the affidavit shows the gross value of the
estate as being about £30,000 less than the value put on it by the registrar after
prolonged inquiry.   Further, counsel questions the propriety of the exhibit's
showing as liabilities the capitalised value of an annuity to the widow and of the **G**
secured maintenance to the applicant when, as he says, there is, or should be,
enough income from the estate to meet those annual payments.   The registrar,
however, accepted the capitalised values of these annual payments as proper
deductions from the value of the estate for the purpose of arriving at the net
residue.   I do the same.   It may be that the explanation of the discrepancy
between the registrar's valuation of the gross estate and that shown in the **H**
second exhibit is that the former does, and the latter does not, take into account
the value of a house and cottage owned by the deceased.   This is not of much
importance as there can be no question of any lump sum payment to the
applicant; for, while s. 26 of the Matrimonial Causes Act 1965, has now been
amended by s. 7 of the Family Provision Act 1966, so as to enable a court to
order a lump sum payment whatever the value of the net estate, that amendment **I**
is not retrospective.   Thus the only order which the applicant can seek is one
for periodical payments.

During his lifetime, the deceased made substantial gifts to the widow and to
his children.   To the former, who had no money of her own, he gave £30,000
which was invested.   She accumulated the interest thereon and this, together
with other gifts of money and a small allowance from him, amounted to £6,000,
which was on deposit at her bank when the deceased died.   Any estate duty
leviable on the deceased's monetary gifts to her inter vivos is to be borne by the

A estate and I assume that the second exhibit takes account of this. In 1953, when the son married, the deceased gave him £36,000. In 1961 the deceased gave him two-ninths of his own share in the Eyre estate and settled a lesser amount on the daughter. The son and daughter are each personally liable for considerable estate duty on the 1961 gifts, but it was conceded before the registrar that, as he put it, " they are amply provided for and in no sense in need

B financially ".

By his will, the deceased made no provision for the applicant. He gave to the widow a legacy of £10,000, free of duty, his personal chattels, which were valued for probate at £1,672, his residence, which she has since sold for £20,750 net, and an annuity of £4,000. The total capital vlaue of what the widow received inter vivos (ignoring what she accumulated) and what she became entitled to

C on his death was, therefore, about £60,000, apart from the capital value of her annuity. Grossed up for estate duty, this £60,000 would be the equivalent of between £150,000 and £200,000. Under the deceased's will, the son receives two-thirds of the residue of the estate and the daughter receives one-third of the residue under the trusts of her settlement. The will provided for a legacy of £400 to the deceased's gamekeeper, but for no other pecuniary legacies apart

D from the £10,000 to the widow. The registrar estimated the net residue remaining for the son and daughter at £65,000, that is, after deducting estate duty on the gifts inter vivos and by will to the widow, and after deducting the capitalised value of the widow's annuity and the applicant's secured maintenance and all charges on the estate. In the second exhibit to the affidavit of Nov. 27, 1967, which I assume takes into account estate duty at the higher rate of seventy-five

E per cent., the net residue is shown at a higher figure than that found by the registrar, namely, just under £68,000. Owing to the nature of the estate, it is doubtful when, if ever, the son or daughter will receive any capital payment, although the remaining estate will of course be income-producing.

The present position of the widow is this:—She lives in a house in London which she has purchased for £25,000 free from encumbrances. Of her £10,000 legacy,

F she has so far received only £1,600 which she has applied to payments to staff in accordance with the known wishes of the deceased. She has the income on about £31,000 capital invested, the interest at four per cent. on the £8,400 balance of her pecuniary legacy and a state pension. These sources taken together provide an annual income of about £2,000. In addition, there is her annuity of £4,000. Thus, she has a total income of about £6,000 a year. The present

G position of the son and daughter is set out by the registrar in these terms:—

" It is freely conceded on behalf of each that, quite apart from their own positions in life in which they are well established, they have been amply provided for by [the deceased]. From figures with which I have been provided it appears that the deceased made provisions inter vivos which, even after satisfaction of the high claims upon them by the revenue, constitute a net capital worth to the son of not less than £120,000 and to the daughter of not less than £50,000. This is of course quite separate and apart from their interest in the residue of his estate."

I understand that, if periodical payments to the applicant are ordered, these will be paid out of residue and that it is not intended that the widow should

I receive any less than she receives under the will.

Turning to the applicant's position, in the 1950's she inherited about £5,000. This, by judicious investment, had increased by the time of the deceased's death to over £13,000. In 1964 she made an unwise speculative purchase of a cottage for £3,000 which resulted in a bank overdraft of about £4,000. She bought another cottage, in Somerset, in which to live, and also took a lease of a London flat at a rent of £385 per annum, to which her brother contributes in respect of his use of the flat. Further, there was a marriage settlement to which she and the deceased contributed £1,000 many years ago. Each had a life interest in the

income therefrom with remainder to their issue as the applicant may appoint.   A
When the deceased died, her total income was about £4,400 per annum gross,
including her maintenance of £3,500 per annum.   The present position of the
applicant is this:—She has a capital of about £6,000.   She has the cottage
in which she lives most of the time, and which is worth rather less than £4,000,
and the second cottage, which requires much work on it before it could be let
or sold.   The main source of her income is her £1,500 per annum secured main-   B
tenance, but in addition she has the interest on her investments, a retirement
pension, and the whole income of the marriage settlement.   Her total income
is about £2,100 per annum before tax.   She is now sixty-three years of age and
not in robust health.   She has no domestic help.   Her Somerset cottage is
damp and for this reason she lives mainly in the London flat during winter.

Before an order for periodical payments can be made, s. 26 (2) of the Act of   C
1965 requires the court to be satisfied:—

" (a) that it would have been reasonable for the deceased to make provision for the survivor's maintenance; and (b) that the deceased has made
no provision, or has not made reasonable provision for the survivor's
maintenance . . ."

The deceased in fact made provision for the applicant in the form of the secured   D
maintenance to which he agreed and of which the court approved.   I assume,
therefore, that it was reasonable for him to make some provision for her as
survivor; no argument to the contrary was addressed to me.   The question
remains whether the court is satisfied that he has not made reasonable provision.
The burden of proving this must lie on the applicant.   Section 26 (4) requires
the court to have regard to the various matters specified in para. (a), para. (b)   E
and para. (c) and to consider the more general matter referred to in para. (d).
As to para. (a), I have already dealt with the applicant's present capital and
income position.   In the past, although she may have made an unwise investment in the cottage, no question arises of her having squandered capital which
should have been available for her support.   So far as I know she has no prospect
of acquiring further capital or income independently of the deceased's estate.   F
As to para. (b), which relates to the applicant's conduct, dealing with this and
with the conduct of the widow, which is, no doubt, a material matter under
para. (d), the registrar had this to say:—

" It was firmly maintained by all before me that there was nothing to be
said to the matrimonial discredit of either wife, and no evidence was offered   G
as to conduct of either."

Paragraph (c) is concerned with the support which the survivor did or did not
receive from the testator during his lifetime.   All three counsel addressed the
court as to the nature and purpose of secured maintenance and as to its proper
effect on an application under s. 26.   Counsel for the applicant argues that a
secured provision is not intended to cover what a former wife should receive   H
after the death of the husband, but to secure her against his disposing of all his
assets prior to his death; to make sure of at least some maintenance both before
and after his death, and to provide a fund to which recourse can be had if he
fails to comply with any maintenance ordered to be paid during the joint lives.
Counsel points out that s. 16 (1) of the Act of 1965 which contains the relevant
power to order secured maintenance, contains nothing to show that this is   I
intended to last as the sole provision beyond the former husband's death.   Further,
he says that, while there is no fixed rule as to the proportion to be secured, in
practice it is usually about one-third of the total maintenance ordered, and he
relies on this as showing that secured maintenance is not to be taken as the
measure of support for a former wife after the husband's death.   Counsel for
the executors argues to the contrary that the real reason for an order for secured
maintenance is to provide for a former wife after the husband's death; that the
explanation of why, in practice, not more than half the maintenance order is

A secured, even where a husband's income is unearned, is to be found in the incidence
of death duties, and that the object of the inquiry into means made before
maintenance is restored is two-fold: to determine, first what is the right amount
to be paid during the joint lives of the former spouses, and, second, what is to be
paid after the death of the former husband. Further, counsel submits that where,
as in the instant case, secured provision is made shortly before the former hus-
B band's death, and there has been no substantial increase in the estate prior
to his death, the amount secured should be regarded as reasonable provision
thereafter. Counsel for the daughter does not put his argument quite so high
as does counsel for the executors, but stresses the importance of secured maintenance as a factor to be considered under s. 26, particularly in cases like the
present where there has been no increase in the value of the estate since security
C was ordered.

There appears to be no authority laying down any general principle how
secured maintenance should be regarded after the death of a former husband.
This, to my mind, points to the conclusion which I have reached that an order
for secured maintenance should not properly be treated as a pre-determination
of what a survivor is to receive after the death of a former spouse, although it is
D necessarily an important factor to be considered in every application under s. 26.
No doubt in many cases the maintenance secured is all that a former wife can
reasonably hope to receive after the husband's death, if only because either a
joint lives' payment has been derived from earned income which ceases on his
death, or estate duty has reduced the unearned income of the estate. Where,
however, periodical payments under s. 26 are not thus rendered impracticable
E or inappropriate, in my view, the existence of a secured provision should not be
regarded as an obstacle to such payments being ordered.

Two of the main propositions which counsel for the applicant puts forward as
showing a proper prima facie approach to a s. 26 application are, first, that a
former wife ought to be treated as " on a par " with a widow and, second, that
she ought to be awarded at least the amount which the deceased consented to
F pay during his lifetime, plus any appropriate addition in respect of subsequent
increase in the cost of living. As to the first proposition, counsel urges its
applicability in the instant case because there was nothing in the conduct of the
widow or the applicant to put either in a different category from the other, and
because their marriages lasted for approximately the same length of time, that
is to say, twenty-one and eighteen years, respectively. As to the second
G proposition, while submitting that the applicant ought to have at least as much
as she received before the deceased's death, he concedes that any cost of living
increase would be marginal.

There was correspondence commencing on Mar. 21, 1961, between solicitors
for the deceased and for the applicant which led to the increase in the latter's
maintenance in 1962. From this correspondence, to which counsel for the
H daughter attaches importance, it appears that both parties were expecting that,
after the death of the deceased, the applicant would receive only her secured
maintenance. It seems to me, however, that, while this correspondence is
relevant on the issue of whether the deceased failed to make reasonable provision
for the applicant, it cannot fetter the court's power to make an order under s. 26.
That this is so is borne out by the decision of STIRLING, J., in *Re Minter (decd.)*,
I *Vasco* v. *Minter* (1), one of the authorities on which counsel for the applicant
relies. The headnote reads (1):

"On Feb. 10, 1964, the husband having paid the wife £12,000, the court
made by consent an order discharging a previous maintenance order made
in favour of the wife and, she undertaking to make no further claim for
maintenance against the husband or his estate, dismissed her application for
maintenance. The husband died in July 1966, and in 1967 the wife applied

(1) [1967] 3 All E.R. 412.

under s. 26 of the Matrimonial Causes Act 1965 for reasonable provision, basing her application on the ground that the husband fraudulently concealed assets at the time of the compromise negotiated in 1964. On a preliminary issue as to the court's jurisdiction to entertain the wife's application, Held: the order of Feb. 10, 1964, and the wife's undertaking to make no further claim against the husband or his estate for maintenance did not, apart from any question of fraud, constitute a bar to an application by her after her husband's death for reasonable provision out of his estate under s. 26 of the Matrimonial Causes Act 1965; but on such an application the court would have to have regard to the order of Feb. 10, 1964, whether viewed as a positive order or as a dismissal of an application for maintenance.

" Per CURIAM: where a sanctioned agreement expressly excludes the wife's claiming against her husband's estate, that express exclusion does not bar her from subsequently applying under s. 26 for reasonable provision out of his estate."

Counsel for the applicant refers particularly to the following passage (2):

" I have come to the conclusion that she should not be barred. Even if the agreement between the parties includes a covenant to make no claim against the estate, the dismissal of the order for maintenance pursuant to the sanctioning of such agreement is in my view none the less an ' order ' of the court within the wording of s. 26 (4) (c); and if I am right in this, it follows that the court has a statutory obligation to have regard to it. If the dismissal is ' no order ', the court exercising jurisdiction under s. 26 must still consider it. It seems to me that this is decisive not only on the absence of the procedural obstacle, but on the intention of the legislature that the court should not lose ultimate control of a s. 26 application, and that the court should treat ' an order ' or ' no order ' under s. 16 as going to merit but not as affecting jurisdiction."

Counsel for the applicant further relies on *Roberts* v. *Roberts* (*executrix*) (3), a decision of SIR JOCELYN SIMON, P., and in particular on certain passages therein as follows (4):

" It will be apparent from that, that as matters are at present arranged there is little or no prospect of any income from the estate. But, as the learned registrar has put it in his report, when the business is sold the position will be entirely different: there will be a capital sum available, and if it is in the region of £6,000 the income could be £250 to £300 a year, out of which a small weekly sum could be paid to the applicant. If the final figure for the net estate is under £5,000, she could be paid a lump sum."

Then SIR JOCELYN SIMON, P., said (5):

" The first question, therefore, which arises is as follows: is the court satisfied that the deceased failed to make reasonable provision for the maintenance of the applicant after his death? He made no provision at all; was this reasonable? It is argued on behalf of the respondent that the answer to that should be ' Yes ': this is a small estate and it was reasonable for the deceased to devote it exclusively to the maintenance of his second wife, the respondent, with whom he is to be presumed to have found greater happiness than with his first wife, the applicant. I think that it is understandable that the deceased should have made no provision for the applicant and provided exclusively for the respondent; in a sense I think it was natural for him to do so. That, however, is not the question that the section poses, namely: was it reasonable? I have been referred to some of the authorities which have been decided under this Act,

---

(2) [1967] 3 All E.R. at p. 416.
(3) [1964] 3 All E.R. 503.
(4) [1964] 3 All E.R. at pp. 505, 506.
(5) [1964] 3 All E.R. at p. 506.

A　　or under the Inheritance (Family Provisions) Act, 1938. There is a considerable resemblance in the wording of those two Acts but they are not
precisely the same. Therefore, in my view, the decisions under the Act of
1938 are not necessarily authoritative on the Act of 1958; moreover, many
of those cases turned on their particular facts."

B　　There follows a review of some of the authorities and then a further passage (6):

"Adopting the principles and the approach which I find in these authorities, it seems to me that here are two women, the applicant and the respondent, with moral claims on the deceased's bounty. The first wife, the
applicant, devoted twenty-six years of her late youth and early middle age
to the deceased, and nothing is said against her. If the marriage had not
broken up by the deceased's misconduct with the respondent, the applicant
C　　could have expected to continue with his society and support and be the
sole recipient in due course of his bounty. Her moral claim against the
deceased, moreover, was signified by the order for maintenance which the
court made in her favour. The second wife, the respondent, devoted seven
years, when her strength may have been declining, to the service of the
D　　deceased; and in view of the subsistence of that marriage and the terms
of his last will she is to be presumed to have given him greater happiness
than he found in his first marriage. I find little to choose between these
two in trying to weigh their moral claims on the bounty of the deceased.
If anything, I should have thought that the claim of the first wife is the
stronger. It follows that, since the deceased gave no effect at all to the claim
E　　of the applicant, he has failed to make reasonable provision for her maintenance after his death."

In answer to counsel for the applicant's propositions, counsel for the executors
urges that the only relevant test is whether the deceased acted reasonably in
providing no more for the applicant after his death than the secured maintenance.
He suggests that the deceased should properly have felt free to make whatever
F　　disposition of his property he might wish once the 1962 agreed maintenance order
had been made. He further submits that s. 26 does not enable a former wife
to negotiate with the husband's executors or to sue them for maintenance in the
way in which she could have negotiated with or sued the husband during his
lifetime. He points out that the estate has suffered a seventy-five per cent.
reduction in consequence of the duties payable thereon, whereas the reduction in
G　　income suffered by the applicant on the cessation of the joint lives' payment is
much smaller. Although he does not suggest a general rule that each should
suffer a like percentage reduction, he uses the actual proportions of the respective
reductions as an argument against awarding the applicant any more than she
already receives.

Counsel for the daughter relies on *Talbot* v. *Talbot* (7), a decision of BAKER, J.
H　　There the deceased left a widow and three young sons and made no provision
for his first wife. BAKER, J., said (8):

"In the end I have to be satisfied, and I think the onus is on the applicant,
that, quoting s. 3 (2) (*a*) of the Act of 1958, ' it would have been reasonable
for the deceased to make provision for her maintenance '. I respectfully
adopt the test applied by MORTON, J., in *Re Styler*, *Styler* v. *Griffith* (9) when,
I　　considering the Inheritance (Family Provision) Act, 1938, he said: ' I do
not think the court should interfere with a testatrix ' or testator's dispositions
merely because the judge may think that he would have been inclined, if
he were in the position of the testator or testatrix, to make some provision
for a particular person. I think the court has to find that it was unreasonable on the part of the testatrix or the testator to make no provision for

(6) [1964] 3 All E.R. at pp. 507, 508.　　　　　(7) [1962] 3 All E.R. 174.
(8) [1962] 3 All E.R. at p. 177.
(9) [1942] 2 All E.R. 201 at p. 204; [1942] Ch. 387 at p. 389.

the person in question or that it was unreasonable not to make a larger   A
provision.' "

The final sentence of the judgment reads (10):

" I conclude that they must say on the facts of this application that the
widow's claim is paramount and that it is not proved that it would have
been reasonable for this solicitor testator to do other than he did.   This   B
application fails and is dismissed."

Counsel for the daughter underlines counsel for the executors' point that the
proper test under s. 26 is the reasonableness or otherwise of the deceased's
provision for the applicant.   He argues that the court should not look into the
facts de novo, as otherwise all executors would be faced with such an application
and, owing to the availability of legal aid to applicants, the resulting costs   C
would often have to be paid out of small estates.   Next, counsel for the daughter
points to the fact that, during the subsistence of the applicant's marriage to
the deceased, the Eyre estate was not a wealthy one, but became so only after
the divorce in 1946 and in consequence of the post-war property boom.   He
suggests this as a reason for not making any provision for the applicant beyond
her secured maintenance.   Further, he relies on the fact that, during the life-   D
time of the deceased, the applicant was not put in financial parity with the widow
as showing that the applicant ought not to be treated equally with her now.

In my view, there cannot be any general rule that a first wife applying under
s. 26 should be accorded financial equality with a widow.   Even where there is
nothing to choose between them so far as conduct is concerned, there are so
many other factors to be considered in each case, such as age, health, etc., that   E
such a rule, to say the least, would be of no practical value.   The claim of either
a former wife or a widow may be paramount and many estates may be insufficient
to provide adequate maintenance for both (see *Talbot* v. *Talbot* (11) and *Roberts*
v. *Roberts* (12)).   On the other hand, as I see it, a lack of parity between the
financial position of a first and a second wife during the lifetime of the husband
should not of itself be treated as a sufficient reason for prolonging this position   F
after his death.   While he was alive, the standard of life enjoyed by the second
wife was presumably that of the husband.   If, however, there appears to be no
reason in principle for perpetuating such a disparity after his death, neither is
the court concerned to see whether the first and second wives enjoyed, or enjoy,
a like standard of living; its concern under s. 26 is, so far as possible, to ensure
a reasonable provision for the first wife without unreasonably depriving the   G
widow.   If the deceased's provision for the latter is greater than that reasonably
required for his former wife, so be it.

As to the former wife receiving as much after as before the death of the husband,
assuming that her needs and her means apart from the estate remain as they
were before the husband's death, and assuming further that the net estate is
sufficient for the purpose, then, to my mind, it is reasonable that she should   H
continue to receive the same provision as that agreed or found to be appropriate
during the husband's lifetime.   The sufficiency of the estate for this purpose is
to be determined having regard to what is provided for, or needed by, other
claimants on the deceased's bounty (see *Re Bellman* (*decd.*) (13)).   That is a
decision of SCARMAN, J., on which counsel for the daughter relies, particularly
on the following passages, the first of which reads (14):

" Her resources were slender, her earning capacity at the mercy of her
years and her delicate health, her conduct in relation to him had been
admirable, and her immediate financial loss on his death would be considerable.   That their married life had been short and had ended many years
ago, that she had borne him no children, and that she had accepted a joint

(10) [1962] 3 All E.R. at p. 178.   (11) [1962] 3 All E.R. 174.
(12) [1964] 3 All E.R. 503.   (13) [1963] 1 All E.R. 513; [1963] P. 239.
              (14) [1963] 1 All E.R. at p. 517; [1963] P. at p. 245.

A   lives' provision for her maintenance and not a secured provision for her life, which would almost certainly have been at a lower rate, are unchallenged facts, but they do not in the circumstances of this case cause me to doubt my conclusion."

The second passage is as follows (15):

B   " I am satisfied that it would have been reasonable for him to have provided in these circumstances for the maintenance of the applicant. I think her claim had its own merits and, furthermore, could be met without causing any but a merely marginal loss to the two boys. He could not be sure that his estate would show an income as large as £3,000, though there was no reason for him to expect that it would be less. If, however, the income did fall below that figure, the dip into capital, if necessary at all, would not have to be great, even assuming a provision for the applicant. I do not think that on a reasoned appreciation of his resources and of the claims of his two sons on him he could have reached the conclusion that it would be unreasonable to make provision also for the applicant. If one then considers the merits of her claim, one must be satisfied, in my judgment, that it would have been reasonable for him to make provision for her maintenance. As it is clear from the terms of the will that he made none, I think that the applicant has established her entitlement under s. 3 (2) of the Matrimonial Causes (Property and Maintenance) Act, 1958."

C

D

A comparison of the percentage reduction of the estate and of the applicant's income resultant on the deceased's death does not assist me in this case. A

E   comparison between a resultant diminution in the provision for a widow and for a former wife might be of value in some cases, but not in this one because no diminution in the provision for the widow is contemplated.

While it has long been the practice of the courts to give effect, so far as possible, to the wishes of a testator, Sir Jocelyn Simon, P., in one of the passages which I read from his judgment in *Roberts* v. *Roberts* (16), drew attention to the dif-

F   ference between the Inheritance (Family Provision) Act, 1938, and the Act with which we are concerned. It seems to me that s. 26 necessarily envisages and requires in appropriate cases both a limitation on a testator's freedom to dispose of his property as he wishes and, in counsel for the executors' words, a re-writing of the will. Under s. 16 (1) of the Matrimonial Causes Act 1965, the court frequently makes a maintenance order which is much against the will of

G   a living former husband and which may seem to him to be most unreasonable. In my judgment, s. 26 equally enables the court to override the will of a former husband after his death. Under both these sections, the test is whether, in the view of the court, the former wife is reasonably provided for, and it is only if she is not so provided for that the court will interfere. I do not share counsel for the daughter's apprehension as to executors of a former husband being faced with

H   unreasonable claims if his will can be re-written, or if secured maintenance is not to be treated as a final determination of what a former wife is to receive after his death. Legal aid is not granted to everyone who applies for it. The fact that an accretion of wealth to the estate has occurred since the first marriage ended should not, in my view, be treated as disentitling a former wife to benefit from that accretion. Section 16 orders can be adjusted during the lifetime of a

I   former husband appropriately to his changing means, and s. 27 appears to envisage a similar adjustment of periodical payments under s. 26 after his death. It would, therefore, seem illogical to exclude from consideration any accretion of property occurring between the time of the divorce and the former husband's death. There is substance in a point which counsel for the applicant makes to the effect that the applicant, having married a potentially but not actually

(15) [1963] 1 All E.R. at pp. 517, 518; [1963] P. at p. 246.
(16) [1964] 3 All E.R. at p. 506.

wealthy man, should enjoy what should have been hers had the marriage not **A** been dissolved because of the husband's matrimonial misconduct.

Bearing all these matters in mind, and not least the age and state of health of the applicant, the conclusions that I have reached are these:—(i) that it was reasonable for the deceased to have made provision for the applicant's maintenance; (ii) that the provision he in fact made was not reasonable, and (iii) that, while it would not be appropriate in this case to put the applicant on an equal **B** footing with the widow, a reasonable provision for her would be the amount which she was receiving prior to the death of the deceased, there being a sufficient net estate to enable this to be done without interfering at all with the provision for the widow or causing any hardship to the other beneficiaries under the will.

Before effect can be given to these conclusions, it is necessary to consider s. 26 (5), which requires that: **C**

"... the court shall have regard to the nature of the property representing the net estate of the deceased and shall not order any such provision to be made as would necessitate a realisation that would be imprudent having regard to the interests of the dependants of the deceased, of the survivor, and of the persons who apart from the order would be entitled to that property." **D**

In this connexion, I should, perhaps, remark that the third exhibit to the affidavit of Nov. 27, 1967, shows the net income of the estate for the year ending Oct. 31, 1967, to be insufficient to cover all the outgoings which, as that exhibit implies, should be payable out of income. No argument was addressed to me on this exhibit, and I confess that I do not find it of much assistance. More important **E** in my view than the figures it sets out are those which show that, when all estate duty has been paid and the capitalised values of the widow's annuity and the applicant's secured maintenance and all other charges have been deducted, there will still be a residue of £68,000 according to the second exhibit, or of £65,000 according to the registrar. This residue will be income-bearing and the income thereon should be more than £2,000 per annum, that is to say, more than the amount of the unsecured maintenance which the applicant received before the **F** deceased's death. The figure given in the third exhibit as the net amount payable to the widow in respect of her £4,000 annuity is £2,350, from which I assume that periodical payments to the applicant of £2,000 a year less tax would require a net payment of £1,175 per annum. If that be correct, I do not apprehend that any improvident realisation of property would be necessitated by an order for payments of that amount. The principal effect of such an order, as I see it, **G** will be that the son and daughter will together suffer a loss of income commensurate with the amount of those payments until either the order be varied or their mother dies.

Finally, there is another matter to be considered under s. 26 (5), namely, the date from which the periodical payments should commence. This is a difficult estate to administer, and I do not wish to add unnecessarily to the executors' **H** burdens. On the other hand, it would seem unjust to make the payments start from today when most of the delay in reaching finality must have been occasioned by the necessary enquiries concerning the estate. The most appropriate commencement date appears to me to be the date of the applicant's summons.

Accordingly, there will be an order for periodical payments to the applicant out of the net estate of the deceased at the rate of £2,000 a year, less tax, from **I** Oct. 21, 1965.

Order accordingly.

Solicitors: *Theodore Goddard & Co.* (for the applicant); *Lee & Pembertons* (for the executors); *Charles Russell & Co.* (for the daughter).

[*Reported by* ALICE BLOOMFIELD, *Barrister-at-Law.*]

A

FOWLEY MARINE (EMSWORTH), LTD. *v.* GAFFORD.

[COURT OF APPEAL, CIVIL DIVISION (Willmer, Davies and Russell, L.JJ.),
November 6, 7, 8, 9, 10, 13, 14, 15, 16, 1967, January 23, 1968.]

B   *Trespass to Land—Possession—Sea-bed—Title shown by documents vested in*
plaintiff company which had purported to act as owner of tidal creek—Acts
done by plaintiff company having accordingly the quality of assertions of
ownership—Sufficient possession to maintain an action for trespass established.

In 1963 the plaintiff company claimed payment of an annual sum of £5 for
a permanent mooring which the defendant had put down in 1961 in Fowley
Rythe, a tidal creek in Chichester harbour.   The defendant having refused
C   to pay, the plaintiff company claimed in trespass against him for maintaining
the mooring.   On the present appeal the material ground of claim was
possession of the bed and banks of the creek.   The plaintiff company had
alternative grounds based on alleged ownership of the bed and banks.   It
had purchased the creek and part of the foreshore, not immediately adjacent,
in 1963.   There was some evidence that the creek and part of the foreshore
D   had been included in a grant made in 1628 by the Crown, known as the
Wanderford grant, and the plaintiff contended that that coupled with
subsequent conveyances, in particular a conveyance in 1918 which was a
good root of title, showed that the paper title was vested in the plaintiff
company*.   The plaintiff company also alleged a possessory title as against
the Crown by sixty years adverse possession.   The defendant did not claim
E   title to the creek, but denied that the plaintiff company had possession
sufficient to found trespass; he also challenged the plaintiff company's title
to the creek.   A statutory declaration of 1913 by the agent of the then
owner of the creek stated that he had collected rent from a tenant of the
creek and other property for six years prior to 1913.   The creek was used
for navigation by pleasure and fishing craft, and some of the owners of the
F   craft had, it seemed, placed permanent moorings in the creek at varying
dates going back to the first world war.   There was no evidence whether
they had sought permission to do so.   A previous owner of the creek had
himself had a permanent mooring there, and had given a sailing club permission to lay six permanent moorings in return for a rent.   After 1945 the
club had sold the moorings to individual members, and permission had later
G   been given for a further six moorings to be laid by individual members, one
of whom was the defendant, who knew that such permission had been
sought and granted.   In 1963 there were at least twenty-four and probably
thirty or more permanent moorings, and evidence at the trial showed
permission only with regard to about twelve of them.

Held: acts done by the plaintiff company and its predecessors in title,
H   such as the letting of the Rythe from about 1907 to 1913 and the laying
and giving permission to lay moorings, had, when viewed in the light of the
paper title to the Rythe, the quality of assertions of ownership, and, coupled
with the paper title, showed possession by the plaintiff company and its
predecessors in title sufficient to maintain trespass against the defendant;
moreover the acts of others in laying moorings were referable to the pur-
I   suance of an erroneous belief that there was some general right, such as
the right of navigation, which entitled them to lay moorings rather than to an
assertion of possession of the Rythe (see p. 983, letters E, H and I, p. 986,
letter G, p. 987, letter H, p. 988, letters B, G and I, and p. 989, letter D, post).

Per RUSSELL, L.J.: in making title to property such as foreshore, which
must have originally lain in the Crown, it is necessary either to show a
Crown grant to some subject or to show a possessory title acquired against

---

* The title is discussed in the report at [1967] 2 All E.R. pp. 480, et seq.

the Crown; it does not suffice merely to show a good root of title sixty   A
years old (see p. 984, letter D, post).

Decision of MEGAW, J. ([1967] 2 All E.R. 472) reversed (see p. 984, letter
I, post).

[As to possession sufficient to support action for trespass, see 38 HALSBURY'S
LAWS (3rd Edn.) 743, 744, paras. 1212, 1213; and as to trespass being an injury
to a possessory right, see ibid., pp. 744, 745, para. 1214; and for cases on the   B
sufficiency and proof of possession, see 46 DIGEST (Repl.) 362-364, *89-110*,
365, 366, *117-126*.

As to the right to fix moorings in tidal waters, see 39 HALSBURY'S LAWS
(3rd Edn.) 534-536, para. 720; and for cases on the subject, see 47 DIGEST
(Repl.) 741, 742, *827-836*.]
                                                                                   C
Cases referred to:

    Asher v. *Whitlock*, (1865), L.R. 1 Q.B. 1; 35 L.J.Q.B. 17; 13 L.T. 254; 30
        J.P. 6; 31 Digest (Repl.) 44, *2033*.

    A.-G. v. *Parmeter, Re Portsmouth Harbour*, (1811), 10 Price, 378; 147 E.R. 345;
        on appeal, H.L., sub nom. *Parmeter* v. *Gibbs, Re Portsmouth Harbour*,
        (1813), 10 Price 412; 47 Digest (Repl.) 709, *547*.
                                                                                   D
    A.-G. v. *Wright*, [1897] 2 Q.B. 318; 66 L.J.Q.B. 834; 77 L.T. 295; 47 Digest
        (Repl.) 741, *827*.

    Beaufort (Duke) v. *John Aird & Co.*, (1904), 20 T.L.R. 602; 32 Digest (Repl.)
        503, *1109*.

    Lord Advocate v. *Young, North British Ry. Co.* v. *Young*, (1887), 12 App. Cas.
        544; 47 Digest (Repl.) 712, *577*.
                                                                                   E
    Perry v. *Clissold*, [1907] A.C. 73; 76 L.J.P.C. 19; 95 L.T. 890; 38 Digest
        (Repl.) 929, *1198*.

    Wuta-Ofei v. *Danquah*, [1961] 3 All E.R. 596; [1961] 1 W.L.R. 1238; 46
        Digest (Repl.) 366, *126*.

Appeal.

This was an appeal by the plaintiff company by an amended notice of appeal,   F
dated Oct. 7, 1967, from the decision of MEGAW, J., given on Mar. 21, 1967, and
reported [1967] 2 All E.R. 472, seeking an order that that part of the decision
whereby judgment was entered for the defendant on the plaintiff company's
claim be set aside and that the original relief claimed be granted. The grounds
of appeal were as follows: (i) that the judge was wrong in fact and in law in
holding that the plaintiff company was not in possession of Fowley Rythe;   G
(ii) that there was no evidence on which the judge could find proved acts of
possession of Fowley Rythe by persons other than the plaintiff company; (iii) that
in any event the judge had misdirected himself in holding that the defendant
was entitled to assert title of the Crown; (iv) that the judge misdirected himself
in holding that the title in Fowley Rythe passed to the Fowley Oyster Fishery
Co., Ltd., and did not revert to William Henry Baldwin Castle; (v) that on the   H
evidence the judge should have held that the plaintiff company was in possession
of Fowley Rythe and had title thereto.

R. N. Titheridge and *N. Micklem* for the plaintiff company.
C. Lawson, Q.C., and *Joseph Jackson*, Q.C., for the defendant.

                                              Cur. adv. vult.

Jan. 23. The following judgments were read.   I

RUSSELL, L.J., delivered the first judgment at the invitation of WILLMER,
L.J.: In this action the plaintiff company complains of an alleged trespass
by the defendant in maintaining in Fowley Rythe at Emsworth, Hampshire,
a permanent mooring consisting of two anchors with a chain stretched between,
which chain is connected by a further chain or cable with a buoy on the surface
of the water. The plaintiff company's charge of trespass is based on alternative
grounds. First, it is based on mere possession by the plaintiff company of the
bed and banks of the Rythe, sufficient to found an action in trespass. Second,

A   it is said that the title to the Rythe is in the plaintiff company.   This depends on an ancient grant by the Crown to a subject known as " the Wandesford grant ", coupled with conveyances of the Rythe with a good root of title in a conveyance in 1918.   Third, it is said that if the Wandesford grant cannot be relied on to defeat the prima facie title of the Crown to this piece of foreshore (or arm of the sea), a possessory title can be shown to have been acquired against the Crown by

B   sixty years adverse possession, and that this title has come to the plaintiff company.

The defendant does not assert any right against anybody to maintain the mooring in the Rythe.   At the trial he asserted a right to do so as incidental to the public right of navigation, but no longer does so.   The defendant denies possession in the plaintiff company sufficient to found an action in trespass.

C   He challenges the validity of the Wandesford grant, and further says that if originally valid, it was abandoned, or must be deemed to have been surrendered. He challenges the claim to a possessory title against the Crown, and further says that if such title was ever acquired, the title came back to the Crown in 1904 on the dissolution of a limited company, and no new possessory title is shown to have been acquired by the plaintiff or its predecessors in paper title since.

D   The mooring was actually laid by the defendant after permission to do so had on his behalf been asked of, and given by, the plaintiff company's predecessor in paper title in 1961.   The trouble has arisen because, after acquiring the paper title in April, 1963, the plaintiff company in July, 1963, decided to require payment by the defendant of an annual sum for the retention of the mooring, and the defendant declined to pay or to assent to the removal of the mooring.   In

E   September, 1964, the writ was issued.

MEGAW, J., (1) held that the plaintiff company had not shown sufficient possession to found an action in trespass, and that, even if the Wandesford grant were effective, the dissolution of the company above-mentioned put the title back into the Crown.   He dismissed the claim and also the defendant's counterclaim based on an alleged right to maintain the mooring as an incident

F   of the public right of navigation.   The locus in quo was described by MEGAW, J., (2) and I need not again describe it.

It is convenient at this stage to summarise in chronological order the history so far as appears of the site in question.   The Wandesford grant by the Crown to two subjects in 1628 undoubtedly included in its specific parcels an area which embraced the Rythe.   Manorial records of the manor of Emsworth and Warbling-

G   ton show a perambulation of the bounds in 1820 as including in the manor inter alia the Rythe.   In 1838 the Warblington tithe award and map ascribe the ownership of an area of " mud waste and water ", which includes the Rythe, to the lord of the manor.   Further perambulations in the nineteenth century also include the Rythe in the manor.

On July 22, 1870, the trustees of the will of Mr. Ralph Fenwick conveyed to a

H   Mr. Terry three parcels of land.   One was a defined area of foreshore between the north end of the Rythe and the land, another was a defined area that included Fowley Island, and the third was the Rythe.   A conveyance in 1885 of nearby foreshore shows that Ralph Fenwick was at his death lord of the manor.   On Oct. 3, 1870, Mr. Terry conveyed on sale the same three parcels to Mr. T. Jarman. On Jan. 26, 1878, Mr. Jarman's widow conveyed on sale the same three parcels

I   to William Henry Baldwin Castle.   None of those conveyances that include the Rythe was forthcoming.   A completed draft of the Jarman to Castle conveyance was sworn to by Mr. Castle in a statutory declaration in 1913, and the two conveyances of 1870 are therein recited.   On Mar. 31, 1885, by an agreement between Mr. Castle, a Mr. Henderson, and the Fowley Oyster Fishery Co., Ltd. (formed on Mar. 9, 1885) the company ratified and adopted a preformation

_____

(1) [1967] 2 All E.R. 472 at p. 487, letter G; [1967] 2 Q.B. 808 at p. 835, letter C.
(2) [1967] 2 All E.R. at p. 475, letter G, to p. 476, letter A; [1967] 2 Q.B. at p. 815, letter G, to p. 816, letter F.

agreement between Mr. Castle, Mr. Henderson and a trustee for the proposed A
company, the project being to form a company to carry out an oyster fishery
in the relevant area. Among other things Mr. Castle was to convey to the company the three parcels already mentioned, the consideration being the allotment
to him of shares credited as fully paid up. Completion was to be on or before
May 1. The return of shareholdings on the company's file shows that these shares
had been issued before September. In 1889 the name of the company was changed B
from " Fowley " to " Poole ", the registered office being then there. In 1892
the company resolved to wind up because it " cannot by reason of its liabilities
continue its business ". In 1904 the company was dissolved by being struck off
the register under s. 7 (4) of the Companies Act, 1880, and s. 26 of the Companies
Act, 1900, as a defunct company. The information in this paragraph comes from
the official file from the Record Office, and is the sum of relevant available know- C
ledge of the life and death of the company. It is not known whether Mr. Castle
conveyed the three parcels to the company, whether the affairs of the company
were wound up, and how or what has happened to the books and documents of
the company, the 1885 agreement being the only document required by statute
to be filed with the registrar of companies. The 1885 pre-formation agreement
recited that Mr. Henderson had for " some time past " carried on the business of D
oyster breeding, etc., at Emsworth on the properties hereinafter described. It
also recited that Mr. Castle was the freeholder of the oyster grounds and lands
described in the second schedule which had, by arrangement with Mr. Castle,
been worked by Mr. Henderson in his business; the second schedule comprised
the same three parcels already mentioned.

From then on the evidence is silent until the statutory declarations by Mr. E
Castle and a Mr. Fogden in March, 1913, in support of Mr. Castle's title to the three
parcels. These are totally silent on the subject of the Oyster Fishery Co., Ltd.
Mr. Castle says that to the best of his recollection the 1878 and earlier conveyances
were handed over to him in due course in 1878, " but I have never had occasion
to deal with the said lands . . . in any way "; he says that he has searched and
concluded that they must be lost. He goes on to say that from the date of the F
1878 conveyance he had had undisturbed possession of the lands and had used
the same as the absolute owner thereof. Mr. Fogden (a draper of Emsworth)
declared that Mr. Castle had in 1878 purchased Fowley Island, the Rythe, and
the Mudlands (that is, the three parcels), and instructed him to collect the rents
and act as agent in reference thereto; that during the whole of the time from 1878
he (Fogden) had let and managed the said lands; that for some six years past G
Mr. J. R. Mant of Emsworth (a butcher) had been the tenant thereof, and had
paid him the rent therefor during that period. Now it may be that by 1913 the
episode of the oyster company had passed from the minds of Mr. Castle and Mr.
Fogden, and also that Mr. Henderson had, by arrangement with Mr. Castle, for
" some time " before 1885 been including in his oyster business these three parcels.
I would hope so, for the declarations are in important respects quite contrary H
to the facts, and the probable explanation of the absence in 1913 of the documents
of title is that Mr. Castle in 1885 fulfilled his contract with the company, conveyed
these lands to the company, and handed over the title deeds to the custody of the
company, and that all these documents are now either mouldering forgotten in
some box, together with other papers of the company, or have in some way been
destroyed. There is no evidence to suggest that in the liquidation this land was sold. I
On the question of possession I consider, however, that there is no reason to doubt
Mr. Fogden's statement about letting to Mr. Mant in or about the year 1907.

Mr. Castle having died in June, 1918, his executors on Dec. 14, 1918, conveyed
on sale the three parcels to a Mr. Dixon reciting the 1878 conveyance. The
consideration, which in 1878 had been £210, was now £17 10s. To complete the
paper title out of chronological order, Mr. Dixon died in September, 1943; his
executors conveyed on sale the three parcels to G. Andrew, Ltd., in April, 1959,
for £100, and the latter conveyed the same on sale in April, 1963, to the plaintiff

A company for £500. The plaintiff company has since sold the mudlands to the north of the Rythe in plots to frontagers.

The Crown is not party to these proceedings having, we are told, been invited to join, but declined. It is unsatisfactory to decide the question of title to the freehold of the Rythe in the absence of the Crown, though if necessary this must be done. I take, therefore, first the question whether the plaintiff company shows

B at the relevant time sufficient possession of the Rythe to justify an action in trespass in this case. If the answer to this is in the affirmative, it would gain the day for the plaintiff company without decision on freehold title. It is, I think, sufficient for this purpose to take the facts as to acts of possession by the plaintiff company and its predecessors in title as set out in the judgment below, and indeed the plaintiff company relied on such statement of facts. I have already mentioned

C that the defendant (via boatman Dalgleish) in fact sought permission of the plaintiff company's predecessor in title to lay the mooring now in question. The judge sets out his view of the evidence about acts of possession (3), and I take this as incorporated in my judgment.

The judge then reviewed a number of authorities on the subject of possession such as will support an action in trespass. It appears to me that the crux of his

D decision was that persons other than the plaintiff company and its predecessor in title had'done the same thing without evidence of permissions sought or granted, that is to say, laid moorings in the Rythe, and that consequently there could not be said to be exclusive possession; on the contrary there was concurrent possession. It is on this aspect of the case that, I think, the judge was in error. Even if it be assumed (in default of evidence) that others had laid moorings with-

E out permission sought or granted by the plaintiff company or its predecessors, this does not mean that those who did so were " doing the same thing " as the former. The judge found that the paper title was on this aspect of the case irrelevant except to permit the plaintiff company to rely on acts of possession of its predecessors in paper title. I consider that there is a greater significance in the paper title, in that it attaches to the activities of those claiming under it a quality

F of acts of possession of the Rythe, whether the actual laying of moorings, or the granting of permission to others to lay moorings. The plaintiff company's predecessors were doing these things as an assertion of ownership or of the right to possession of the Rythe because they considered themselves so entitled because of the paper title. In so far as others may have laid moorings, they can have done so only because they considered that, whosoever might be in possession of the

G Rythe, they were entitled to lay moorings as incidental to the right of navigation, or pursuant to some other general right, or that whosoever was in possession would not object; their activities were not, therefore, acts of possession or occupation of the Rythe, and they cannot be described as concurrent occupiers or possessors.

It appears to me that there is in this case ample evidence sufficient to show

H possession in the plaintiff and its predecessors, starting with the evidence accepted by the judge (and by me) of a letting from 1907 to at least 1913 of the Rythe to Mr. Mant, the butcher, and continued with evidence of laying, and giving permission to lay, moorings from time to time, without abandonment of the possession to which the paper title would appear to give right, and without those activities by others impinging sufficiently on that possession.

I   I would therefore hold, contrary to the judgment below (4), that the plaintiff company is entitled to succeed in trespass against the defendant.

Should we now deal with the other questions which concern title to the Rythe and which concern only title as between the plaintiff company and the Crown, which is not a party? They would have been relevant in the present case had the plaintiff company needed to rely against the defendant on the possession which the

---

(3) [1967] 2 All E.R. at p. 482, letter E, to p. 484, letter B; [1967] 2 Q.B. at p. 826, letter G to p. 829, letter F.

(4) [1967] 2 All E.R. 472; [1967] 2 Q.B. 808.

law imputes to the owner of the freehold, but it is not necessary for the plaintiff A
company to do so. Put shortly, the questions touching the title are the following.
First, whether the freehold title is shown to have left the Crown under the
Wandesford grant, in which case the plaintiff company can show a good root of
title in the conveyance on sale to Mr. Dixon in 1918. Second, whether, even if the
Wandesford grant cannot be relied on, it is sufficient, to establish title against all
(save the Crown), to show a good root of title sixty years old, by analogy with B
limitation, in which case there are the 1870 and 1878 conveyances available.
Third, whether (on the assumption that I make that Mr. Castle did convey to
the oyster company) the dissolution of the company in 1904 operated to put the
legal estate in the Crown again, or in Mr. Castle the grantor, the former possibility
breaking the title chain since 1878. Fourthly, whether the evidence shows
alternatively a possessory title good against the Crown; and hereunder the C
question of the effect of the dissolution in 1904 might also arise if the possessory
title had been established prior to 1904.

On the second point (which would not by itself avail the plaintiff company
against the Crown) I am prepared to express the view that, in making title to
property such as foreshore, which must have been originally in the Crown, it is
necessary either to show a Crown grant to some subject, or to show a possessory D
title acquired against the Crown; it does not suffice merely to show a good root
of title sixty years old. The third point would not therefore arise.

I do not think that it is either necessary or desirable to decide the first point
whether the Wandesford grant effectively transferred the title from the Crown
to the grantees, or, if so, whether it was abandoned. It is true that we have had
extensive argument on this point, and have considered in considerable detail E
the grant and the decision in *A.-G.* v. *Parmeter* (5) on its scope and validity, and
whether there has been abandonment of the grant. Nevertheless, this matter is
fundamentally outside the scope of decision in this case, and any expression of
conclusion by us would not decide the point for or against the Crown. I am
content to say that, while several of the grounds that moved the Court
of Exchequer to decide that case would decide this case adversely to the plaintiff F
company, I am not satisfied that those grounds were necessarily correct. Moreover there is nothing in the decision of the House of Lords in that case (6) that
would compel this court to decide adversely to the plaintiff company in relation
to the Fowley Rythe either (a) that the grant thereof was ineffective, either as
not including the Rythe, or as for an illegal purpose, or as being on a condition
that was not fulfilled, or (b) that the grant was abandoned. G

Nor do I think that we should express a view whether or not on the evidence
before the court below a possessory title was at any time acquired against the
Crown to Fowley Rythe; nor whether, if such were acquired before the dissolution
in 1904 of the oyster company, that fact should have the effect of making less
valid the claim of the plaintiff company to have succeeded to that possessory title.
All these are questions of considerable difficulty; they are for decision in an action H
between the Crown and the plaintiff company, and are in part dependent on the
evidence adduced in such an action, and not in this. It would, I consider, not
be right, and might be a waste of time, to go into them now, and they are not
necessary to the decision of the immediate problem, which is whether, as against
the plaintiff company, the defendant is entitled to maintain his permanent
mooring in Fowley Rythe. I

In the result I would allow the appeal; declare that the plaintiff company is,
and has at all material times, been in possession of Fowley Rythe; declare that
the defendant is not and has not been entitled, without permission of the plaintiff
company, to maintain his mooring in Fowley Rythe; and give judgment to the
plaintiff company for £10 damages for trespass, a figure which the parties agreed
at the end of the hearing of the appeal was appropriate.

---

(5) (1811), 10 Price 378.   (6) (1813), 10 Price 412.

A   **WILLMER, L.J.:** The plaintiff company in this suit claimed to be the owner in fee simple of the bed of a tidal creek in Chichester Harbour known as Fowley Rythe and in possession thereof. It sought relief against the defendant, who was in occupation of a permanent mooring laid in the Rythe, claiming to treat him as a trespasser because he refused to pay an annual licensing fee of £5. The defendant denied that the plaintiff company was the owner or in possession of

B   Fowley Rythe, and denied that it was entitled to the relief claimed. He in turn counterclaimed for a declaration that he was entitled to moor in the manner complained of without charge. The action was tried by Megaw, J. (7) who by his judgment of Mar. 21, 1967, dismissed both claim and counterclaim. So far as the plaintiff company's claim was concerned, he was not satisfied that the plaintiff company had proved that it was either the owner or in possession of the Rythe.

C   The plaintiff company has now appealed to this court. There is no cross-appeal by the defendant.

The first and, as I think, the decisive question is whether the plaintiff company succeeded in proving sufficient possession of Fowley Rythe to justify its claim to treat the defendant as a trespasser. The defendant has not sought to set up any claim to be himself in possession of the Rythe adverse to the plaintiff company.

D   He sought to justify his retention of a permanent mooring in the Rythe on four alternative grounds, namely, (a) prescription, (b) custom, (c) lost modern grant, and (d) a claim that the maintenance of such a permanent mooring was an ordinary incident of the navigation of tidal navigable waters. Of these four grounds, prescription was expressly abandoned by counsel for the defendant in the court below. The judge found that the evidence given on behalf of the defendant was

E   insufficient to establish any customary right, or to justify the presumption of a lost modern grant, and there had been no appeal against that finding. He also rejected the contention that the laying and maintenance of permanent moorings was an ordinary incident of navigation, and again there has been no appeal on that point. This last contention was based on a dictum of Lord Esher, M.R., in *A.-G.* v. *Wright* (8), which was not only obiter but also in my view did not in

F   any event bear the meaning sought to be put on it.

The sole issue on this part of the case, therefore, is whether the plaintiff company succeeded in making good its claim to be itself in possession of Fowley Rythe. The behaviour of the defendant and of other persons who have sought, and seek, to maintain permanent moorings in the Rythe is relevant only in so far as it tends to cast doubt on the plaintiff company's claim to be in actual possession.

G   The judge, in reaching his conclusion that the plaintiff company had failed to prove actual possession of the whole of the Rythe, was very much influenced by the passage which he quoted from Pollock and Wright on Possession in the Common Law, p. 30, which I think it right to quote again.

"What kind of acts, and how many, can be accepted as proof of exclusive use, must depend to a great extent on the manner in which the particular

H   kind of property is commonly used. When the object is as a whole incapable of manual control, and the question is merely who has de facto possession, all that a claimant can do is to show that he or someone through whom he claims has been dealing with that object as an occupying owner might be expected to deal with it, and that no one else has done so."

I   The judge added the observation (9): "The last eight words are important". As I understand his judgment, it was because he regarded the acts of the defendant and others in maintaining permanent moorings in the Rythe without permission as "equivalent acts of concurrent possession" that he decided against the plaintiff company's claim to be in actual possession.

In these circumstances I think that it is necessary to look first at the evidence adduced on behalf of the plaintiff company in order to see whether it is sufficient

---

(7) [1967] 2 All E.R. 472; [1967] 2 Q.B. 808.   (8) [1897] 2 Q.B. 318 at p. 321.
(9) [1967] 2 All E.R. at p. 485, letter A; [1967] 2 Q.B. at p. 831, letter A.

of itself, in the absence of other evidence, to justify a prima facie claim to posses- A
sion. If it is not, then the plaintiff company must fail in limine; but if it is
sufficient to justify a prima facie claim, it becomes necessary in the second
place to examine the acts of the defendant and other persons in order to see
whether they can fairly be described as " equivalent acts of concurrent
possession ".

I would preface what I have to say on the first of these questions by observing B
that in the course of the lengthy argument before us we have had the benefit
of an abundant citation of authority. But I do not find it necessary to refer to
more than one or two of the cases cited for the propositions on which the
plaintiff company relies are in truth elementary. Thus it is well established
that a person in possession of land has a perfectly good title against all the world
but the rightful owner; see, for instance, *Asher* v. *Whitlock* (10), per SIR C
ALEXANDER COCKBURN, C.J., and *Perry* v. *Clissold* (11), per LORD MACNAGHTEN.
It is equally well established that as against the party in possession a defendant
cannot set up the title of a third party unless he himself claims under it. This the
defendant did not seek to do in the present case. It is true that at the end of
the fifth day of the hearing of the appeal we were faced with an application for
leave to adduce further evidence designed to show, as I understood the applica- D
tion, that the defendant was acting in pursuance of a licence from the local
authority who, it was suggested, held from the Crown. This application, if
granted, could have altered the whole complexion of the case, and we did not
think it right to grant it at such a late stage. There is thus no longer any question
of the defendant claiming under the title of the Crown. It is further well established that, as against a defendant who does not seek to assert any title in himself, E
the slightest evidence of possession is sufficient to establish the plaintiff's claim;
see, for example, *Wuta-Ofei* v. *Danguah* (12), per LORD GUEST.

It is, I think, important to observe that the plaintiff company asserts (and
always has asserted) that it has a good title to the ownership of Fowley Rythe.
It traces its title back, through various successive conveyances, at least to the
year 1913, and probably before. It does not matter for the purposes of this F
part of the case whether it can succeed in proving its title to be good against the
Crown; but at least it is in a position to say that, coupled with even slight acts
of possession, its title is good against anyone who cannot show a better title. It
would, therefore, be wrong in my view to ignore the plaintiff company's paper
title, for its belief in it colours the acts on which it relies as acts of possession
by itself and its predecessors in title. In considering any act relied on as an act of G
possession it must be relevant to have regard to the intention with which the act
is done. It is, therefore, relevant and significant in my judgment to bear in
mind that the plaintiff company and its predecessors were throughout purporting
to act as the owners in whom the title to the soil was vested. Moreover, although
it is perhaps of only marginal significance, I think that it is not altogether irrelevant that, according to the evidence of several witnesses, the plaintiff company H
and its predecessors have for long been reputed owners of the Rythe.

Against this background it is necessary now to examine the facts proved in
evidence and found by the learned judge. These include the following:

(i) In 1913, according to the statutory declarations made by Mr. Castle and
Mr. Fogden, Mr. Castle (the plaintiff company's predecessor) was asserting
possession of Fowley Rythe, and it was stated that for the preceding six years
Mr. Castle's lands, including the Rythe, had been let at a rent to a Mr. Mant of
Emsworth. It does not appear how long thereafter Mr. Mant continued as tenant,
but I think that the inference is that his tenancy probably continued up to the
outbreak of the First War, when it appears that, for reasons of defence, all
permanent moorings laid in the harbour were taken up. With all respect to the

(10) (1865), L.R. 1 Q.B. 1 at p. 5.
(11) [1907] A.C. 73 at p. 79.
(12) [1961] 3 All E.R. 596 at p. 600, letter B.

A contrary argument on behalf of the defendant, I cannot think that the fact that, for the duration of the war, the plaintiff company's predecessor was precluded from exercising possession by laying moorings affected his legal right in any way.

(ii) By a conveyance of Dec. 14, 1918, Mr. Castle's lands, including Fowley Rythe, were acquired by Mr. Dixon, who himself laid a permanent mooring therein for the purpose of mooring his own boats.

B (iii) Between the two world wars, probably about 1933, Mr. Dixon granted permission to the Emsworth Sailing Club to lay six permanent moorings in Fowley Rythe for the use of members of the club who had sea-going boats. It appears from the evidence that during the second war all permanent moorings were again taken up for reasons of defence, but again I cannot think that this fact had any effect, one way or the other, in relation to Mr. Dixon's possession of the Rythe.

C (iv) Mr. Dixon died in 1943, and by a conveyance of Apr. 19, 1950, his executors conveyed his lands, including Fowley Rythe, to G. Andrew, Ltd., the conveyance reciting that at the date of his death, Mr. Dixon was seized in fee simple in possession free from incumbrances.

(v) After the second war about six further permanent moorings were laid by a Mr. Dalgleish, with the permission of Mr. Andrew, for use by members of the D sailing club. One of these moorings, significantly enough, was that of the defendant, the subject-matter of the present dispute.

(vi) By a conveyance of Apr. 2, 1963, G. Andrew, Ltd., conveyed a part of their lands, including Fowley Rythe, to the plaintiff company, the conveyance again reciting that the vendor company was seized of the premises for an estate in fee simple in possession free from incumbrances.

E (vii) The evidence showed that by 1963 at least twenty-four, and perhaps as many as thirty, permanent moorings had been laid in the Rythe, of which about twelve were proved to have been laid with the permission of the plaintiff company's predecessors. As to the remainder, there was no evidence to show whether permission was asked or obtained, except in the case of some six moorings which were laid on the instructions of a Mr. Woodley, manager of the Emsworth Ship-F yard Company, for the use of that company's clients. As to these six moorings, it is not now in dispute that no permission was asked or given, but I do not think that it would be right to assume that the remaining moorings (about which no evidence was given) were all laid without permission.

(viii) Since the date of the conveyance in 1963 the plaintiff company has been actively asserting its right to possession of the Rythe, and has demanded G payment of an annual fee from all those using permanent moorings laid therein. The evidence showed that in 1964 some sixteen of those using permanent moorings paid the fee demanded by the plaintiff company.

The effect of this evidence is that for some sixty years the plaintiff company and its predecessors have in one way or another been asserting possession of the Rythe, and doing so on the basis that they were owners of the soil therein. It H has been argued with some force on behalf of the plaintiff company that there could be no better evidence of possession in relation to a tidal creek than the laying of permanent moorings by the plaintiff company and its predecessors and by others with their permission. In my view, this evidence, if it stood alone, would be amply sufficient to establish a prima facie case of possession in favour of the plaintiff company. I reject the suggestion put forward on behalf of the defen-I dant that in order to establish possession the plaintiff company and its predecessors should have taken further steps, such as the setting up of permanent and visible marks to delineate the area of which they claimed to be in possession. Such marks could well amount to an obstruction to navigation, and I regard the suggestion that they should have been set up in a tidal creek in the middle of Chichester Harbour as quite unrealistic.

It becomes necessary, therefore, to examine the facts relied on by the defendant as constituting " equivalent acts of concurrent possession " sufficient to displace the plaintiff company's prima facie case. What is relied on is, of course, the laying

of moorings in Fowley Rythe by other persons without permission from the plain- A
tiff company or its predecessors. One difficulty in relation to this is that, apart
from the six moorings laid down on the instructions of Mr. Woodley, we do not
know whether any significant number of persons have laid permanent moorings
in the Rythe without permission. Nor, if any significant number did so, do we
know with what animus they did so. The inference which I should be inclined
to draw is that any persons who did lay such moorings without permission B
probably did so in the erroneous belief (as argued on behalf of the defendant)
that they were entitled to do so as an ordinary incident of navigation. There
is no evidence to show that anybody, not even Mr. Woodley, ever laid any such
moorings with any animus possidendi, whether of the Rythe as a whole or of the
particular spot where the moorings were laid.

The question remains whether, assuming the plaintiff company to have C
established a prima facie case of possession, the acts relied on, that is to say, the
laying of moorings without permission by Mr. Woodley, and possibly by others,
can be regarded as sufficient to dispossess the plaintiff company. What is said is
that these acts go to show that the degree of possession enjoyed by the plaintiff
company and its predecessors has never been " exclusive ", which, it is argued, it
would be necessary for the plaintiff company to establish in order to succeed. In D
this connexion, however, it is well to bear in mind the words of LORD WATSON
in *Lord Advocate* v. *Young* (13), where he was considering the question of what
amounts to sufficient proof of possession in the case of foreshore. He said:

" In estimating the character and extent of his possession it must always
be kept in view that possession of the foreshore, in its natural state, can never
be, in the strictest sense of the term, exclusive. The proprietor cannot exclude E
the public from it at any time; and it is practically impossible to prevent
occasional encroachments on his right, because the cost of preventive
measures would be altogether disproportionate to the value of the subject."

It seems to me that what was there said in relation to foreshore must apply a
fortiori to a navigable tidal creek or channel. F

Bearing in mind the absence of any evidence to show that those persons who
laid permanent moorings in the Rythe did so with any animus possidendi, it
seems to me that their acts were wholly different in quality from those of the
plaintiff company and its predecessors, who were acting throughout in virtue of
the right which they always claimed to possession of the Rythe. To revert once
more to the test propounded in the passage which I have already quoted from G
POLLOCK AND WRIGHT (14), while the plaintiff company and its predecessors
have throughout dealt with the Rythe " as an occupying owner might be expected
to deal with it ", I cannot accept that any of the other persons who from time to
time laid moorings therein have been shown to be doing so. In my judgment
the judge fell into error in so far as he treated the acts of these other persons as
" equivalent acts of concurrent possession ". I cannot regard their acts as in any H
way " equivalent " to those of the plaintiff company and its predecessors, nor do
I think that they were acts of possession.

In my judgment the position disclosed by the evidence is analogous to that in
Duke of Beaufort v. *John Aird & Co.* (15), where it was held that the acts of the
defendants and their predecessors in driving piles into the bank of a navigable
river were insufficient to justify a finding of possession so as to affect the rights
of the plaintiffs, in whom the ownership of the soil of the river was vested.

It follows that in my judgment there was no sufficient evidence to displace the
prima facie case of possession established by the plaintiff company. I think that
the plaintiff company's possession was sufficiently " exclusive ", that is, as
exclusive as the nature of the locus in quo would permit. The plaintiff company is

(13) (1887), 12 App. Cas. 544 at p. 553.
(14) Ante, p. 985, letter H.
(15) (1904), 20 T.L.R. 602.

A accordingly entitled, on the defendant refusing to pay the licensing fee demanded, to treat him as a trespasser, and to succeed in its claim for relief. I would allow the appeal on that ground.

This conclusion renders it strictly unnecessary to consider the plaintiff company's wider claim to be the owner in fee simple of Fowley Rythe. This claim raises questions of great difficulty, and, although we have had the advantage of

B hearing a full and learned argument thereon, I agree with the view expressed by RUSSELL, L.J., whose judgment I have had the advantage of studying, that it would not be right or desirable to express any concluded view in the absence of the Crown. Any decision of ours in the present case would not be binding on the Crown. The questions discussed before us may conceivably have to be decided at some time in proceedings between the plaintiff company and the Crown, and

C I would not wish to embarrass the conduct of any such possible future proceedings by any unnecessary expression of opinion in the present case.

I agree with the order proposed by RUSSELL, L.J. (see p. 984, letter I, ante).

DAVIES, L.J., who is unable to be present with us today, has authorised me to say that he agrees with both judgments which have been delivered.

D *Appeal allowed.   Leave to appeal to the House of Lords refused.*

Soicitors: *Waterhouse & Co.*, agents for *Glanvilles*, Portsmouth (for the plaintiff company); *Wilkinson, Kimbers & Stadden*, agents for *Perkins & Harris*, Guildford (for the defendant).

[*Reported by* BRIAN POCOCK, ESQ., *Barrister-at-Law.*]

E

STEAD *v.* STEAD.

F [PROBATE, DIVORCE AND ADMIRALTY DIVISION (Sir Jocelyn Simon, **P., and** Willmer, L.J.), December 13, 1967.]

Magistrates—Husband and wife—Maintenance order—Discharge—Sexual intercourse by former wife, after dissolution of marriage, with man not her former husband—Whether ground for discharge of order—Financial implication of wife's conduct—Matrimonial Proceedings (Magistrates' Courts) Act, 1960

G *(8 & 9 Eliz. 2 c. 48), s. 8 (1).*

On an application under s. 8 (1) of the Matrimonial Proceedings (Magistrates' Courts) Act, 1960, after the parties have been divorced, to revoke or vary a maintenance order in favour of the former wife, there is no distinction in principle between sexual misconduct and any other form of unlawful or immoral behaviour on her part; and the factor with which the court is

H primarily concerned is the financial effects of her conduct (see p. 992, letters F and I, and p. 993, letter G, post).

Dicta of MARSHALL, J., in *Miller* v. *Miller* ([1960] 3 All E.R. at pp. 118, 121) applied.

In 1962 the wife obtained an order in the magistrates' court for, inter alia, maintenance for herself. Later she obtained a decree nisi against

I the husband, which was made absolute in 1963. In 1966 she had intercourse with an unidentified man, in consequence of which she gave birth to a child in 1967. On appeal by her from an order revoking the matrimonial order of 1962 in so far as it awarded maintenance for her on the ground that she had been guilty of an act of sexual intercourse with another man,

Held: there was no good ground on which it would be right in the particular circumstances of the case to deprive the wife of the support which she was deriving from the husband under the order of 1962, merely because years after the divorce she had committed acts of sexual intercourse, for

these bore no relation to the matrimonial relationship and did not affect her   A
financial circumstances (see p. 993, letters F and G, post).

    Appeal allowed.

[As to varying or discharging a maintenance order made by a magistrates'
court, see 12 HALSBURY'S LAWS (3rd Edn.) 491-493, para. 1091; and for cases
on the subject, see 27 DIGEST (Repl.) 722-728, *6901-6950.*

    For the Magistrates' Courts Act, 1952, s. 53, see 32 HALSBURY'S STATUTES   B
(2nd Edn.) 463.

    For the Matrimonial Proceedings (Magistrates' Courts) Act, 1960, s. 8, see 40
HALSBURY'S STATUTES (2nd Edn.) 410.]

Case referred to:

    Miller v. *Miller*, [1960] 3 All E.R. 115; [1961] P. 1; [1960] 3 W.L.R. 658;   C
      124 J.P. 413; Digest (Cont. Vol. A) 791, *5834a.*

Appeal.

This was an appeal by the wife from an order made by the stipendiary magistrate for the city of Leeds on May 4, 1967, revoking a previous matrimonial
order made in favour of the wife. The facts are set out in the judgment of
WILLMER, L.J.   D

    J. M. Collins for the wife.
    J. Crabtree for the husband.

    WILLMER, L.J.: This is an appeal from an order made by the learned
stipendiary magistrate for the city of Leeds on May 4, 1967, whereby he revoked
a previous matrimonial order made in favour of a wife. The marriage between   E
the parties had been dissolved some time before, but I will continue to call her
" the wife ". The ground on which the learned stipendiary revoked the order
was that the wife had been guilty of an act of sexual intercourse with another
man.

    The relevant facts lie within quite a small compass, and I hope can be quite
briefly stated. The parties were married on June 21, 1958, and there is one   F
child of the marriage. On Apr. 12, 1962, the wife obtained an order from the
magistrates in the city of Leeds against the husband on the ground of his persistent cruelty. The order contained a non-cohabitation clause and a provision
for the wife having custody of the child. It also provided for maintenance in
favour of the wife at the rate of £1 15s. per week, and £2 per week in respect of
the child. There was a further hearing in July, 1962, when the only question   G
determined was with regard to the terms on which the husband should have
access to the child. The wife then took proceedings for divorce on the ground
of cruelty, relying on the order which she had obtained from the magistrates.
Those proceedings resulted in her obtaining a decree nisi on Oct. 22, 1962, which
was made absolute on Jan. 23, 1963. There was no claim by the wife in the
High Court proceedings for maintenance. She was content to rely on the order   H
for maintenance which she had already obtained from the magistrates' court.
It will be seen, therefore, that these parties have ceased to be married for a period
of over four years.

    Nothing of significance happened until the year 1966, but about August or
September of that year the wife admittedly had sexual intercourse with an
unidentified young man who, it is said, has since emigrated to South Africa.   I
In consequence of that sexual intercourse she became pregnant, and in fact
gave birth to a child on May 22, 1967. When the husband learned of the wife's
pregnancy, he issued a summons dated Mar. 13, 1967, asking for a revocation
of the magistrates' order in so far as it related to maintenance for the wife herself.
He did not seek to get rid of the order in so far as it provided for the maintenance
of the child. The ground on which the application for revocation was made
was, as I have said, that the wife had been guilty of sexual intercourse with
this unknown young man. At the hearing the husband was represented by a

A solicitor. The wife was not represented and declined the learned stipendiary's offer of an adjournment to enable her to obtain legal representation. The learned stipendiary, in the reasons which he gave for his order, set out the facts to which I have already referred, and then went on:

B "As I understand it, the combined effect of s. 8 of the Matrimonial Proceedings (Magistrates' Courts) Act, 1960, and s. 53 of the Magistrates' Courts Act, 1952, is to give me a discretion by order on complaint to revoke, revive or vary the said matrimonial order. This discretion must be exercised judicially, and having regard to the facts set out above I am of the opinion that it would be inequitable to require [the husband] to continue to pay towards the upkeep of his former wife, and I therefore revoked that part of the order. Had [the husband] been able to prove adultery by his former
C wife, revocation of the order would have been mandatory, and it seemed to me to be unfair to deprive him of his remedy merely because in the particular circumstances of this case he was unable to adduce evidence of adultery. Moreover [the wife] was offered marriage by the said man unknown but declined this offer. She also refused to take any steps to obtain financial assistance from this man in respect of his child."

D With all respect to the learned stipendiary, he fell into error when he said that, had the husband been able to prove adultery, revocation of the order would have been mandatory. The reason why I say that is because s. 8 (2) of the Matrimonial Proceedings (Magistrates' Courts) Act, 1960, provides for a revocation of a matrimonial order being mandatory in the case of adultery only during the subsistence of the marriage. One can well understand that provision and the
E limitation thereby imposed; for clearly an act of adultery by a wife at a time when the marriage relationship subsists is something which is directly relevant to that matrimonial relationship. The same considerations, however, do not follow in the case of a marriage which, like this, has long since ceased to exist at all. In those circumstances, the first ground on which the learned stipendiary based his conclusion was clearly an erroneous ground.
F I am bound to say that the relevant statutory provisions do not provide us with very much guidance as to the matters to be taken into account when an application is made to a magistrates' court for revocation or variation of a matrimonial order. The effect of s. 8 (1) of the Matrimonial Proceedings (Magistrates' Courts) Act, 1960, is merely to apply the provisions of s. 53 of the Magistrates' Courts Act, 1952, to the case of matrimonial proceedings before magis-
G trates. When one turns to s. 53 of the Act of 1952 to see what it is which is being applied to such proceedings, one finds simply this:

"Where a magistrates' court has made an order for the periodical payment of money, the court may, by order on complaint, revoke, revive or vary the order."

H The Act, therefore, gives no guidance at all as to the sort of considerations to be borne in mind by the court when confronted with an application to revoke or vary a matrimonial order.

Some guidance, however, is afforded to us, I think, by a decision of MARSHALL, J., in *Miller* v. *Miller* (1). That was a case in which a wife had obtained a decree of divorce, and an order for maintenance had been made in the High
I Court, which was registered with the local magistrates' court. The wife having subsequently committed adultery, an application to vary was made to the magistrates' court. Appeal from the magistrates' court in that jurisdiction lies to a single judge of the Probate, Divorce and Admiralty Division, and that is how the matter came before MARSHALL, J. The effect of his decision was that a magistrates' court, exercising the power to revoke or vary a High Court order, should act on exactly the same principles as those on which the High Court

(1) [1960] 3 All E.R. 115; [1961] P. 1.

would act in relation to the revocation or variation of an order.   The fact that   A
the original order in that case had been made in the High Court is to be borne
in mind when examining what MARSHALL, J., said.   But it seems to me that it
cannot be wrong to say that a magistrates' court, when called on to vary an
order of its own making, should in substance apply the same principles as would
be applicable in the High Court.   I would venture to refer to two short passages
in MARSHALL, J.'s judgment.   He is reported as saying (2):   B

> " The mere fact that the wife, after obtaining a maintenance order, has
> had sexual intercourse with a single man, or committed adultery with a
> married man, does not of itself entitle a court to vary the order by reducing
> it to a nominal figure.   Such conduct should be taken into account and
> primarily be considered in the light of the difference it makes in the relative
> financial position of the parties.   If a divorced wife, who has re-married   C
> and has acquired from her second husband a right to be maintained, is still
> entitled to some support from her first husband, it follows that a divorced
> wife who lives with another man without going through a second ceremony
> of marriage and who, accordingly, acquires no such right to maintenance
> from that man, is not necessarily disentitled to maintenance from her
> husband without again considering the relative financial position of the   D
> parties."

Then there is a further passage which follows on a quotation by the learned
judge from the magistrates' reasons.   They had decided that it would be morally
indefensible to expect the husband to maintain his ex-wife in the circumstances
of that case.   MARSHALL, J.'s comment on that conclusion was this (3):   E

> " This is coming dangerously close to acting as a court of morals and
> holding that to live in open adultery with another man is by itself a ground
> for varying the payment of maintenance to a nominal amount."

It seems to me, applying the general principles there stated (which, as I have
said, I think can equally be applied to an order made by a magistrates' court),
that what the court is primarily concerned with is the financial implication of the   F
conduct of the wife.   The court is not a court of morals, and, though I do not
think that it would be right to say that in no circumstances should the moral
behaviour of the wife be taken into account, it is the financial repercussion of
her conduct that is the primary consideration.   If it were right to apply purely
moral considerations, it is indeed difficult to see how wide the net must be cast.
If it were right to act as the learned stipendiary has done in this case, and to   G
deprive the wife of her order merely on the ground that she has been guilty of an
act of intercourse—or indeed of any other sexual misconduct—the question
might be asked why it would not be equally right to deprive her of her order
if she were guilty of other immoral conduct, such as an offence of dishonesty.
Counsel for the husband, however, shrank from contending that any such form   H
of misconduct on the part of the wife would entitle the husband to have the
order revoked.   I am bound to say that, in the case of parties who, like these,
have been divorced for a number of years, I can see no distinction in principle
between sexual misconduct and any other form of unlawful or immoral behaviour.
As I have already pointed out, the situation is quite different so long as the
marriage subsists, for then any sexual misconduct on the part of the wife is
directly relevant to the marriage relationship.   Once that relationship has gone,   I
I can see no more relevance in the case of sexual misconduct than in the case of
any other form of misconduct.   That really amounts to saying over again what
I have already said, namely, that what the court is primarily concerned with,
when invited to revoke or vary a previously subsisting matrimonial order, is the
financial effect of the conduct complained of.

(2) [1960] 3 All E.R. at p. 118;   [1961] P. at p. 5.
(3) [1960] 3 All E.R. at p. 121;   [1961] P. at p. 9.

A   I only wish to add two more observations, and they relate to the last two reasons which the learned stipendiary gave for the decision at which he arrived. The first of those was that the unknown man had offered marriage to the wife but that she had declined the offer.   With all respect to the learned stipendiary, I can see no relevance in that fact at all.   If we were to support this view with regard to the relevance of that fact, we should in effect be saying that the court

B   is entitled to put pressure, financial pressure, on a wife to marry a man whom she does not want to marry.   I cannot think that that is a correct view of the policy of the law.   Secondly, the learned stipendiary relied on the fact that the wife refused to take any steps to obtain financial assistance from this other man. Why, I would ask, should she do so?   She had an order against her husband which was brought into being entirely in consequence of the husband's mis-

C   behaviour by being guilty of the matrimonial offence of cruelty.   The fact that years afterwards the wife was guilty of certain immoral conduct with another man goes no distance, I should have thought, towards getting rid of the husband's responsibilities, having regard to the cruelty of which he had been found guilty.   It is not as if the act of sexual intercourse which the wife had with the unknown man made any difference whatsoever to her financial situation.   If it had, if for

D   instance she had accepted his offer to marry her, or if she had accepted an offer from him to support her, then I can see that the situation might well be different. That would be relevant from a financial point of view.   Short of that, I find myself unable to see what relevance there is, in relation to an application to revoke the wife's order, in the fact that she has not chosen to obtain financial assistance from this unknown man.

E   It follows from what I have said that the three reasons which the learned stipendiary gave in support of the conclusion at which he arrived are, in my judgment, all invalid reasons.   For my part, I can see no good ground on which it would be right in the particular circumstances of this case to deprive the wife of the support which she is deriving from the husband under the order of 1962, merely because she has, years later, been guilty of this act, or these acts, of sexual

F   intercourse; acts which bore no relation to the matrimonial relationship, and which did not in any way affect the financial circumstances of the wife.   In those circumstances, although I recognise that this is an appeal from the discretion of the learned stipendiary, I think that it is abundantly clear that he exercised his discretion on wrong grounds, and that it is right and proper for this court to interfere.   I would, accordingly, allow the appeal.

G
        SIR JOCELYN SIMON, P.: I agree.   Although we are differing from the judgment in a matter of discretion of the learned stipendiary magistrate, who, however, did not enjoy the advantage which we have had of a careful argument on behalf of the wife, there is nothing that I feel I can with advantage add to what WILLMER, L.J., has said.   I, therefore, concur in allowing the

H   appeal.

Appeal allowed.

    Solicitors: *Ward, Bowie & Co.*, agents for *Fox, Hayes & Co.*, Leeds (for the wife); *Teeman, Gould & Co.*, Leeds (for the husband).

[*Reported by* ALICE BLOOMFIELD, *Barrister-at-Law.*]

A

FERNANDEZ *v.* WALDING.

[COURT OF APPEAL, CIVIL DIVISION (Sellers, Danckwerts and Winn, L.JJ.),
December 15, 1967.]

Landlord and Tenant—New tenancy—Business premises—Opposition by landlord
—Intention to carry out substantial work of construction on part of premises—
Whether work could reasonably be done without obtaining possession of holding
—Landlord and Tenant Act, 1954 (2 & 3 Eliz. 2. c. 56) s. 30 (1) (f).

B

Landlord and Tenant—New Tenancy—Business premises—Part only of
" holding "—Whether jurisdiction to order tenancy of part of premises
used by tenant for business purposes—Landlord and Tenant Act, 1954, (2 &
3 Eliz. 2 c. 56) s. 23 (3), s. 29 (1), s. 32 (1).

A landlord, the owner of a factory, a single storey building which was
divided physically into three sections, front, middle and rear, had let the
middle section, and two-fifths of the front section, to a tenant. The landlord
retained the remainder of the front section for his own business. The landlord formed the intention to extend his own factory by adding a second
storey over the whole of the front section; this work involved rebuilding
the flank wall between the middle and front sections, and also constructing
a substantial wall and foundations on the tenant's holding to cut off the
tenant's part of the front section from the landlord's. The landlord, having
served notice to determine the tenant's tenancy, opposed an application
for a new tenancy on the ground, under s. 30 (1) (*f*)* of the Landlord and
Tenant Act, 1954, that he intended to carry out substantial work of construction on the holding or part thereof and that he could not reasonably do so
without obtaining possession of the holding. The trial judge found that the
landlord could reasonably carry out the work if he obtained possession of
the whole of the front section and that it was unreasonable to deprive the
tenant of the middle section, and granted the tenant a new tenancy of the
middle section only. On appeal by the landlord and cross-appeal by the
tenant,

C

D

E

F

Held: (i) the court had not jurisdiction in the circumstances to order
the grant, under s. 29 (1)† and s. 32 (1)‡ of the Landlord and Tenant Act,
1954, of a new tenancy of part of " the holding " as defined in s. 23 (3),
that term meaning, when applied to the present case, the part of the factory
which the tenant held and used for business purposes; accordingly there was
no jurisdiction to grant the tenancy of the middle section of the factory
only, excluding the rear two-fifths of the front section (see p. 997, letters
G and I, and p. 998, letters E and F, post).

G

(ii) on the evidence a substantial part (the two-fifths) of the holding was
to be reconstructed and, as the landlord could not reasonably do so without
obtaining possession of the holding, the tenant was not entitled to a new
tenancy of the whole of the holding (see p. 998, letters E, F and H, post).

H

Little Park Service Station, Ltd. v. *Regent Oil Co., Ltd.* ([1967] 2 All E.R.
257) distinguished.

Appeal allowed.

[Editorial Note. The tenant could not make effective request for a new
tenancy, after notice of termination had been served (s. 26 (4) of the Landlord
and Tenant Act, 1954); but, where such a request can be made under s. 26 (3),
it can be made in respect of part of the property comprised in the tenancy (ibid.).

I

---

* Section 30 (1) (f) is printed at p. 995, letter I, to p. 996, letter A, post.

† Section 29 (1), so far as relevant, provides—" Subject to the provisions of this Act,
on an application under s. 24 (1) of this Act for a new tenancy the court shall make
an order for the grant of a tenancy comprising such property . . . as [is] hereinafter
provided."

‡ Section 32 (1), so far as material, is printed at p. 997, letter H, post.

A   As to a landlord's opposition to the grant of a new business tenancy on the ground of proposed demolition or reconstruction; see 23 HALSBURY'S LAWS (3rd Edn.) 893, 894, para. 1717, as to the property to be comprised in the new tenancy see ibid., p. 885, para. 1707 text and notes (*k*), (*l*), p. 893, para. 1723, and for cases on the subject see DIGEST (Cont. Vol. A) 1051-1055, *7417p-7417pkc*.

     For the Landlord and Tenant Act, 1954, s. 23 (3), s. 29, s. 30 (1), s. 32, see 34
B   HALSBURY'S STATUTES (2nd Edn.) 408, 413, 414, 417.]

     Case referred to:
       Little Park Service Station, Ltd. v. *Regent Oil Co., Ltd.* [1967] 2 All E.R. 257; [1967] 2 Q.B. 655; [1967] 2 W.L.R. 1036.

     Appeal.
C   This was an appeal by Edward Joseph Walding, the landlord of a factory building, by notice dated June 29, 1967, against the order of His Honour Deputy Judge PERRETT, made at Ilford county court on June 15, 1967, for the grant of a new tenancy, under the Landlord and Tenant Act, 1954, of part of premises let to the tenant, Eugenio Fernandez, who was the applicant in the county court. The premises let to the tenant were themselves part only of the building. The
D   first ground of appeal stated in the notice of appeal was that the judge erred in law in that his power to order a new tenancy was limited to ordering the grant of a tenancy of the whole holding. By a respondent's notice, dated Dec. 13, 1967, the tenant gave notice of intention to ask that he should be granted a new tenancy of the whole of the holding.

     D. J. Stinson for the landlord.
E   *G. W. Cheyne* for the tenant.

     WINN, L.J. delivered the first judgment at the request of SELLERS, L.J.: It is unnecessary to describe in any detail the premises to which the application related. They are situated near the Southend arterial road in the neighbourhood of Gallows Corner, near Romford. There was a factory, which was the freehold
F   property of the appellant landlord and extended, roughly at right-angles, back from the road. The factory was so constructed that there were in effect (I do not speak of structural details) three sections of the factory. At all material times the landlord was carrying on business himself in the section nearest to the road. As a matter of history, the tenant formerly occupied the section furthest from the road, but in due course (he being until comparatively recently on very
G   good terms with his landlord) was allowed to change from the rear portion into the middle portion; and he was further granted by his landlord a tenancy, the duration of which is somewhat obscure, of an additional part of this whole factory which represented approximately the rear two-fifths of the front section, the landlord himself occupying the rest of the front section. The three sections were separated from one another by roller shutters; when this addition to the
H   middle section was granted to the tenant a breeze-block partition was placed at the end of the portion occupied by the landlord.

     In due course the landlord formed a firm intention, which he implemented to the extent of getting plans and estimates and obtaining planning and by-law permission, to extend his own factory, as he was doing good business in the production of signs—mainly road direction signs. Accordingly in November,
I   1966, he gave notice, pursuant to s. 25 of the Act of 1954, to the tenant by which he required him to give up possession by June 24, 1967, that being ample time. In accordance with the provisions of the Act of 1954, he gave notice that he would oppose any application to the court for the grant of a new tenancy on three grounds. It is convenient to say that the first two were matters which were not supported by evidence and indeed were abandoned at the hearing; but the third ground, the relevant ground, invoked the provisions of s. 30 (1) (*f*) of the Act of 1954:

       " that on the termination of the current tenancy the landlord intends

A

to demolish or reconstruct the premises comprised in the holding or a substantial part of those premises or to carry out substantial work of construction on the holding or part thereof and that he could not reasonably do so without obtaining possession of the holding."

When the judge gave judgment in this matter he made a finding of fact, followed by a finding which purported to be one of fact but which, speaking for myself, I cannot find to be supported by any evidence. The first of those findings was this: " I am satisfied that the landlord wants the premises because he now intends to do that work ". The judge then described the work, which consisted in the main part of adding a second story over the whole of the front section of the three sections and, therefore, over the two-fifths that I have mentioned as being let to the tenant. The judge said:—

" . . . [the landlord] wants the premises because he now intends to do that work and also requires possession to get rid of the tenant he no longer likes."

The landlord and the tenant had quarrelled. The judge continued:—

" I have to be satisfied as to [s. 30 (1) (*f*)]. The landlord intends to rebuild the flank wall, a substantial wall and foundations on the holding between the first and second sections and to cut off part of the first section . . . I am driven to conclude that it is a substantial piece of work."

The flank wall referred to above was the wall between the front section and the middle section of the three sections of the factory premises. The part of the first section, to which the judge referred, was the rear part that was let to the tenant. That finding is well founded on the evidence; but the judge went on to say (and it is not to my own mind very clear precisely what he thought that he was finding at this point):

" But I also have to be satisfied that he needs possession of the holding. I have considered matters. I am satisfied that he can reasonably carry out all the work he wants to do by obtaining possession of the last part of the holding. It is unreasonable to deprive [the tenant] of the rest of the holding to let [the landlord] build a flank end. [The tenant] can conduct his business in the centre section ";

and the judge proceeded to grant a new tenancy to the tenant (the respondent in this court) of that portion only which fell within the second section of this three-section building, not including any part of the two-fifths of the rear of the first section.

In my respectful view, the judge was there considering the wrong issue or question. Paragraph (*f*) of s. 30 (1) does provide (in effect) that the tenant is to have a new tenancy if, inter alia, the landlord fails to establish that he could not reasonably carry out substantial work on the holding or part thereof without obtaining possession of the holding. As I understand that, it is not a question whether, as between landlord and tenant, reasonable men, co-operating one with the other, might well come to an arrangement whereby the tenant, albeit still entitled to possession of the relevant area, might permit, by licence, the landlord to carry out the relevant work on part of the premises. This question, as I see it myself and as I respectfully think that this court has already declared, is one of the reasonable practicability of carrying out the works in question if possession is not in the hands of the landlord but of the tenant by virtue of a new tenancy.

What is invoked here is undoubtedly the carrying out of substantial work of construction on that part of the holding of the tenant which consisted of the rear two-fifths of the front section of this factory premises.

The rights of a tenant and of a landlord under the Act of 1954 require, for the purposes of this judgment, to be briefly examined. By section 23 (3) it is provided that:—

" In the following provisions of this Part of this Act the expression ' the

A   holding ', in relation to a tenancy to which this Part of this Act applies, means the property comprised in the tenancy, there being excluded any part thereof which is occupied neither by the tenant nor by a person employed by the tenant and so employed for the purposes of a business by reason of which the tenancy to which this Part of this Act applies."

B   The reference there to " This Part of this Act " clearly means the whole of Part 2 of the Act; and the words " the property comprised in the tenancy " are the maximum connotation of the term " the holding ", because the definition in s. 23 (3) continues by making an exclusion. I hazard a briefer summary or paraphrase of s. 23 (3) by saying this, that it provides that " the holding " means the business tenancy of the tenant—that part of the property or premises comprised in the tenancy which the tenant holds and uses for business purposes.

C   The Landlord and Tenant Act, 1954, is, as regards Part 2, an Act to afford protection for business premises and goodwill. There may well be, and often are, premises included in a tenancy which do not comply with that definition of " holding ". Then the Act of 1954 provides (1) that no tenancy within the protection of the Act shall come to an end unless terminated in accordance with the Act.

D   Section 25 provides the procedure by which a landlord may terminate a tenancy, as happened here. Section 26 provides that, always assuming that no notice has been given by the landlord under s. 25, a tenant himself, if he has such a tenancy as is referred to in s. 26 (1), but only if he has such a tenancy, may himself initiate steps by which he may become entitled in due course to invoke the jurisdiction of the court to grant him a tenancy. That section, by sub-s. (3),

E   provides that his (the tenant's) notice or request for a new tenancy shall not have effect unless it is made by notice given in the prescribed form to the landlord

> " and sets out the tenant's proposals as to the property to be comprised in the new tenancy (being either the whole or part of the property comprised in the current tenancy). . . .".

F   No such request for a renewed tenancy as to part of the property comprised in the current tenancy was made by this tenant. He was never in a position to make such a request once he had received the s. 25 notice terminating his tenancy.

   However, it is said by counsel for the tenant, in a very helpful and lucid submission, that one may look to s. 26 (3) for guidance in finding what is the meaning of " holding " for the purposes of s. 30 and s. 32. I quite agree with him

G   that it does have relevance there; and, reading together s. 30 (1) (*f*) and s. 26 (3), it is abundantly plain that " holding " cannot mean the same as " part of the holding ", nor can " part of the holding " mean the same as " holding ". It is only " the holding " in respect of which the court has jurisdiction to grant a new tenancy.

   That is expressly provided by s. 32 (1), which provided that subject to s. 32 (2),

H   which has no relevant application—

> " an order under s. 29 of this Act for the grant of a new tenancy shall be an order for the grant of a new tenancy of the holding . . .".

Going back for a moment to s. 23 (3), that means the property comprised in the tenancy apart from any part of such property not used by the tenant as business premises.

I   This county court judge fell into the fundamental error, in my respectful view, of granting, or purporting to grant, a tenancy which he had no jurisdiction to grant. It follows, on any view, that this appeal must be allowed.

   It is said by counsel for the tenant that although the appeal, on the grounds on which it is brought, may properly be allowed, the rights of his client should nevertheless be provided for on the grounds set out in the respondent's notice in this court. This is framed on the footing that the deputy county court judge

---

(1) See s. 24 of the Landlord and Tenant Act, 1954.

ought to have ruled that the tenant was entitled to a new tenancy, not of part   A
of the holding, but of the whole of the holding. This is urged on the ground
that there was no finding by the deputy county court judge that it was impossible
for the landlord reasonably to carry out the substanial work of construction on
the last two-fifths of section No. 1 without obtaining possession of the whole of
the holding.

As I started so I end by saying that it does seem to me that it is not a question   B
of what could be done by reasonable co-operation: it is a matter of what it
is reasonably practicable to do on the assumption that possession of the whole of
the holding remained in this tenant, he having all such rights of exclusion as
his right of possession would give him.

In *Little Park Service Station, Ltd.* v. *Regent Oil Co., Ltd*, (2), a somewhat
similar situation had to be considered by this court. It was there held, with   C
reference to s. 30 (1) (*f*) which I have been discussing, that s. 30 (1) (*f*) required
a landlord to satisfy the court that he could not reasonably carry out the work
of demolition and reconstruction with the tenant in possession and, since the
county court judge had not specifically found that the landlord had proved
that, he had not satisfied the requirements of the section. That was a case
where the premises were open premises, premises which had been used as a   D
petrol filling station. There was a covenant in the lease of the existing tenancy,
which certainly had evidentiary relevance, to permit entry by the landlords
to carry out structural alterations as and when they thought necessary. It was
found as a fact that it would be possible to carry out the work without closing
down the station, and that the tenants were willing to permit the landlords
to enter and carry out the work. The situation in the instant case appears to   E
me to be quite different.

For the reasons which I have endeavoured to give, and mainly because, in my
view, there was no jurisdiction to make the order which this learned judge
purported to make, I would say that this appeal should be allowed.

DANCKWERTS, L.J.: I agree, and I do not want to add anything.   F

SELLERS, L.J.: I agree. I would add only that on the termination of
the current tenancy it was established that the landlord wished to demolish
and reconstruct part of the premises, part of " the holding ", which had been
let to the tenant, who is the respondent to this appeal. It was a " substantial "
part. It was the two-fifths of the end building that my lord has described, and
it was required for demolition and reconstruction, adding a second storey to   G
the premises which was required for the landlord's occupation. In addition to
that, that work involved interference with the end wall of the balance of the
holding was left by digging suitable foundations and erecting a wall to separate
it off from the other premises. The other part of the remaining part of the
premises was required too—and I think this would have been the right finding
of fact by the judge—for the proper carrying out of the work of demolition and   H
reconstruction, because machinery had to be moved out. In any event those
facts established that a substantial part of the holding of the tenant was reasonably required for doing this work and possession was required for that purpose.
In those circumstances the landlord has established all that he had to establish
in order to defeat the tenant's claim for a tenancy on the termination of the
current tenancy.   I

I agree that this appeal must be allowed and judgment entered for the landlord.

Appeal allowed.

Solicitors: *Prestons* (for the landlord); *Sackville Hulkes*, Hornchurch, Essex,
(for the tenant).

[*Reported by* HENRY SUMMERFIELD, ESQ., *Barrister-at-Law.*]

---

(2) [1967] 2 All E.R. 257; [1967] 2 Q.B. 655.

A

Re FIGGIS (deceased). ROBERTS AND ANOTHER
v. MACLAREN AND OTHERS.

[CHANCERY DIVISION (Megarry, J.), January 17, 18, 19, 22, 1968.]

B
Time—Computation—Duration of specified period—Month—Devise of house to wife if she should be living at the expiration of a period of three months from the testator's death—Calendar months—Period reckoned in complete days— Date of testator's death excluded—Law of Property Act, 1925 (15 & 16 Geo. 5 c. 20), s. 61.

A testator devised his freehold house to his wife if she should survive him and " be living at the expiration of a period of three months from my
C death ", free from any charge subsisting on the house " at the date of my death ". He died at about 5 a.m. on Jan. 9, 1966. His wife died at about 11 a.m. on Apr. 9, 1966, viz., six hours later on the day three calendar months after that on which the testator died.

Held: the period of survivorship specified (a) was, in accordance with s. 61* of the Law of Property Act, 1925, one of three calendar months,
D for there was nothing in the context of the devise to require a contrary interpretation, (b) was to be computed in whole days rather than by a more precise measurement from a particular moment on one day to a point of time on the last day, and (c) was to be reckoned excluding the day on which the testator died; accordingly the three months' period began at the end of the day on which the testator died and ended at midnight on Apr. 9, 1966,
E with the consequence that the house did not pass under the devise to the wife (see p. 1002, letter I, and p. 1006, letters E and I, post).

Lester v. *Garland* ([1803-13] All E.R. Rep. 436), *In the Goods of Wilmot* ((1834), 1 Curt. 1) and *Gorst* v. *Lowndes* ((1841), 11 Sim. 434) considered.

Administration of Estates—Estate duty—Direction in testator's will for payment
F *of estate duty out of residue—Duty on any " gifts " made by testator in his lifetime to be so paid—Current and deposit bank accounts in joint names of testator and his wife—Whether credit balances on these accounts at his death were " gifts " to wife within the direction for payment of duty.*

Husband and Wife—Presumption of advancement—Joint bank accounts— Current and deposit accounts—Each spouse having authority to draw on the account, but account operated in fact solely by husband—Wife having
G *separate bank account—Joint accounts kept in credit for many years before husband's death—Whether balances credited to joint accounts belonged to wife on husband's death.*

The husband and wife married in November, 1915. In August, 1917, when he was in the army, he opened a joint current account with a London branch of the Midland Bank in his own and his wife's name. The husband and
H the wife could each draw on the joint account, but the authority which they gave to the bank did not mention survivorship. In June, 1949, the husband opened a joint deposit account at the same branch of the Midland bank. For long prior to his death in 1966 these accounts were substantially in credit. The husband operated them himself, and the wife left them alone. He had no bank account in his sole name. In October, 1929, the wife
I opened a current account in her sole name at another branch of the Midland bank. In 1953 she transferred her sole account to the same branch that held the joint account. Her account was fed from assets of her own and transferred from the joint account. The evidence showed that the husband was meticulous in money matters and controlled all household expenditure. Even when he was ill shortly before he died, and the wife signed a few cheques on the joint account because he could not complete them, she did so only

---

* Section 61, so far as relevant, is printed at p. 1002, letter G, post.

when the bank manager told her that she had authority to draw on   A
the current account. Both joint accounts were very substantially in credit
at the husband's death. By cl. 7 of his will, made in 1953, the husband
directed that any estate duty payable by reason of his death on " any gifts
made by me in my lifetime to my wife " should be paid out of his residuary
estate.

Held: (i) the presumption of advancement in favour of the wife in respect   B
of the sum standing to the credit of the joint accounts had not been rebutted,
moreover, the circumstances that the joint current account was opened in
wartime, and that the husband continued the joint accounts long after any
considerations of convenience had ceased to be effective considerations,
were factors in favour of advancement; accordingly, the moneys standing
to the credit of the joint accounts belonged to the wife on the husband's   C
death (see p. 1010, letter I, and p. 1012, letter C, post).

Re Harrison ((1920), 90 L.J.Ch. 186) and *Re Pattinson* ((1885), 1 T.L.R.
216) followed.

Marshal v. *Crutwell* ((1875), L.R. 20 Eq. 328) distinguished.

(ii) the credit balances on the joint accounts were not within cl. 7 of the
husband's will, since payments into the joint accounts by the husband were   D
not " gifts " in the sense of that word in cl. 7 to the wife at the times of
payment, and the fact that on the husband's death she became entitled to
the credit balances did not bring them within the description " gifts made
by me during my lifetime " in cl. 7; accordingly, estate duty in respect of
the balances was not payable under cl. 7 out of the husband's residuary
estate (see p. 1014, letters E, F and H, post).   E

Young v. *Sealey* ([1949] 1 All E.R. 92) considered.

[As to the computation of periods of time, see 37 HALSBURY'S LAWS (3rd
Edn.) 92, para. 161, and as to the disregard of fractions of a day, see ibid., p. 100,
para. 178; and for cases on the subject, see 45 DIGEST (Repl.) 252-255, *197-231*,
and 269, 270, *360-390*.

As to the presumption of gift by a husband to his wife, see 19 HALSBURY'S   F
LAWS (3rd Edn.) 832, 834, para. 1360; and for cases on the subject, see 27 DIGEST
(Repl.) 150-152, *1093-1112*.

As to the interpretation of provisions in exoneration of death duties, see
16 HALSBURY'S LAWS (3rd Edn.) 386-388, para. 752.

For the Law of Property Act, 1925, s. 61, see 20 HALSBURY'S STATUTES (2nd
Edn.) 558.]   G

Cases referred to:

Cartwright v. *MacCormack*, [1963] 1 All E.R. 11; [1963] 1 W.L.R. 18; 45
    Digest (Repl.) 255, *231*.

Cornfoot v. *Royal Exchange Assurance Corpn.*, [1903] 2 K.B. 363; *affd.* C.A.,
    [1904] 1 K.B. 40; 73 L.J.K.B. 22; 89 L.T. 490; 29 Digest (Repl.)   H
    164, *1015*

Gorst v. *Lowndes*, (1841), 11 Sim. 434; 10 L.J.Ch. 161; 59 E.R. 940; 45 Digest
    (Repl.) 255, *229*.

Harrison, Re, Day v. *Harrison*, (1920), 90 L.J.Ch. 186; 27 Digest (Repl.)
    152, *1110*.

Lester v. *Garland*, [1803-13] All E.R. Rep. 436; (1808), 15 Ves. 248; 33 E.R.   I
    748; 48 Digest (Repl.) 344, *2944*.

Marshal v. *Crutwell*, (1875), L.R. 20 Eq. 328; 44 L.J.Ch. 504; 39 J.P. 775;
    27 Digest (Repl.) 152, *1108*.

North, Re, Ex p. Hasluck, [1895] 2 Q.B. 264; 64 L.J.Q.B. 694; 59 J.P. 724;
    45 Digest (Repl.) 252, *197*.

Owens v. *Green*, [1932] I.R. 225; 25 Digest (Repl.) 569, **87*.

Pattinson, Re, Graham v. *Pattinson*, (1885), 1 T.L.R. 216; 27 Digest (Repl.)
    152, *1109*.

A   *Reid, Re*, (1921), 50 O.L.R. 595; 64 D.L.R. 598; 25 Digest (Repl.) 568, *76.
     Russell v. *Scott*, (1936), 55 C.L.R. 440; 42 Argus L.R. 375; 10 A.L.J. 211;
         25 Digest (Repl.) 568, *74.
     Stewart v. *Chapman*, [1951] 2 All E.R. 613; [1951] 2 K.B. 792; 115 J.P. 473;
         45 Digest (Repl.) 113, *385*.
     Towne v. *Eisner*, (1918), 245 U.S.Rep. 418.
B   *Wilmot, In the Goods of*, (1834), 1 Curt. 1; 163 E.R. 1; 45 Digest (Repl.)
         255, *230*.
     Young v. *Sealey*, [1949] 1 All E.R. 92; [1949] Ch. 278; [1949] L.J.R. 529;
         25 Digest (Repl.) 568, *141*.

Adjourned Summons.

C   This was an application by originating summons dated July 11, 1967, by the
plaintiffs, Albert John Mann Roberts and Alan Peter Humphries who were the
executors and trustees of the wills of Bryan Edward Figgis, deceased, and
Ethel Mary Marshall Figgis, deceased, whereby the plaintiffs asked for the
determination of the following questions. 1. Whether on the true construction
of cl. 4 of the will of the testator, Bryan Edward Figgis (hereinafter called " the
husband ") and in the events which had happened the husband's freehold
D   house Ruthlands was held by the plaintiffs—(a) on the trusts of the will of the
above-named Ethel Mary Marshall Figgis (hereinafter called " the wife ") and as
part of her estate or (b) on the trusts by the will of the husband declared concerning his residuary real and personal estate. 2. Whether the moneys which at
the death of the husband were standing to the credit of (a) the current account
and (b) the deposit account in the joint names of the husband and the wife with
E   Mincing Lane branch of Midland Bank, Ltd., passed by survivorship or otherwise
to the wife and were now held by the plaintiffs (subject to payment of any estate
duty by reference to the death of the husband which might be properly payable
in respect of and out of such moneys) as part of the estate of the wife or were
held by the plaintiffs as part of the estate of the husband. 3. If it should be
determined in answer to question 2 that some or all of such moneys were or
F   became the property of the wife, then whether, on the true construction of cl. 7
of the will of the husband, any estate duty payable by reference to his death in
respect of such moneys ought to be paid out of the husband's residuary estate.
     The first defendant was Athol Hutchinson MacLaren, who was a beneficiary
under the wife's will but not under the husband's will; the second defendant,
Michael John Hope Ryles, was interested in both estates; and the third defen-
G   dant, Mrs. Margaret Lallah Hope Parker, was the adopted daughter of Bryan
Edward Figgis and Ethel Mary Marshall Figgis, and was entitled to a protected
life interest under both wills.
     The cases noted below* were cited during the argument in addition to those
referred to in the judgment.

H   *E. W. Griffiths* for the plaintiffs.
     Raymond Walton, Q.C., and *P. M. H. Mottershead* for the first defendant.
     S. W. Templeman, Q.C., and *T. J. Craven* for the second defendant.
     W. D. Ainger for the third defendant.

     MEGARRY, J.: In this summons three questions arise under the will of
Bryan Edward Figgis, dated Jan. 16, 1953. The first question arises under cl. 4
of the will. This reads:

     " I give my freehold house known as Ruthlands, Waterhouse Lane,
     Kingswood aforesaid or any other house whether freehold or leasehold
     owned and occupied by me at my death to my wife if she shall survive me
     and be living at the expiration of a period of three months from my death

---

     * *Walcot* v. *Botfield*, (1854), Kay 534; *English* v. *Cliff*, [1914] 2 Ch. 376; *Re Aspinal*
(*decd.*), [1961] 2 All E.R. 751; [1961] Ch. 526; *Re Kilpatrick's Policies Trusts*, [1966]
2 All E.R. 149; [1966] Ch. 730; *Re Seaford* (*decd.*), [1967] 2 All E.R. 458; [1967] P. 325;
Trow v. *Ind Coope* (*West Midlands*), *Ltd.*, [1967] 2 All E.R. 900; [1967] 2 Q.B. 899.

free of any mortgage or charge subsisting on such house at the date of my   **A**
death and free also of all estate or other duties payable at my death all of
which I direct shall be paid out of my residuary estate."

The testator (whom I shall also refer to as " the husband ") died at about 5 a.m.
on Jan. 9, 1966. His wife, Ethel Mary Marshall Figgis (whom I shall call " the
wife ") died at about 11 a.m. on Apr. 9, 1966. The wife thus died six hours
later than the husband on the day three calendar months after the day on which   **B**
the husband died.

Questions arise under this clause of the will because, in addition to considerations of the impact of estate duty, the persons entitled under the wife's will are
not identical with those entitled under the husband's will. Each estate, I may
say, is substantial, the husband's being nearly £200,000 net and the wife's over   **C**
£60,000 net. Put shortly, question 1 asks whether or no the requirements of
cl. 4 are satisfied, and so whether the clause carried to the wife the house Ruthlands, which the testator still owned at his death.

Counsel for the first defendant, a beneficiary under the wife's will but not
under the husband's, contends that the wife satisfied the requirements of cl. 4,
in that at the expiration of the period stated the wife was still living. Counsel
for the second defendant, who is interested in both estates, contends the reverse;   **D**
and counsel for the third defendant, Mrs. Parker, who was the adopted daughter
of the couple and takes a protected life interest under both wills, supports
counsel for the second defendant.

Counsel for the first defendant puts his case on three grounds, any one of which
would suffice him: first, that " months " here means lunar months, not calendar
months; second, that if the period of three months means calendar months and   **E**
is to be computed in complete days, the day of the husband's death is to be
included in the period of three months; and third, that if the period of three
months means calendar months, it is to be reckoned from a punctum temporis,
namely, the moment of the husband's death, and reckoned exactly. Each of
these three methods of computation produces the result that the wife survived
the period of three months, though the periods of survival are in a descending   **F**
order of magnitude, being six days, eleven hours and six hours respectively.

I will take the three arguments in turn. First, there is the lunar month argument. The Law of Property Act, 1925, s. 61, provides that

" In all deeds, contracts, wills, orders and other instruments executed,
made or coming into operation after the commencement of this Act, unless   **G**
the context otherwise requires—(a) ' Month ' means calendar month; . . ."

Counsel for the first defendant contends that the husband cannot have contemplated a fluctuating period dependent on calendar months which would vary
in length from twenty-eight to thirty-one days. His difficulty, however, lies
in the phrase in s. 61 " unless the context otherwise requires "; be it observed
that the last word is " requires " and not " admits ". I am quite clear that   **H**
there is nothing in the context in this case which does so require. I do not see
how mere speculation as to what the testator wished to do can properly be treated
as part of the context. Counsel for the second defendant, I think, was quite
right in his submission that even if it was clear that the husband wanted a period
that was certain and not fluctuating, this could not be a context requiring a
contrary construction; for even if it could be called a " context ", irregularity
of duration and thus uncertainty of period is inherent in calendar months, so
that this contention would go far towards nullifying this part of s. 61. In any
case, this is a will made in 1953, and I do not believe that by 1953 " month "
in general usage had come to mean anything other than " calendar month ".
Accordingly, I hold that " months " in cl. 4 of the will means " calendar months ",
and I reject counsel for the first defendant's first contention.

Counsel for the first defendant's second and third contentions may be taken
together. I shall refer to them as the " included day " argument and the

A   "punctum temporis" argument respectively. He very properly conceded first, that a period which is to be calculated "from" a day normally excludes that day; and secondly, that normally the law does not deal in fractions of a day. In each case he stressed the word "normally", and he referred me to 37 HALSBURY'S LAWS OF ENGLAND (3rd Edn.) p. 92, para. 161, p. 100, para. 178. Counsel for the first defendant relied on the leading case of *Lester* v. *Garland* (1).

B   This was a case in which there was a gift in trust for the children of the testator's sister, Mrs. Pointer, if within six calendar months after the testator's death she gave security against intermarrying with A. The testator, Sir John Lester, died between 8 and 9 p.m. on Jan. 12, 1805 and Mrs. Pointer gave security at about 7 p.m. on July 12, 1805 (the headnote seems plainly in error in substituting "9" for "7"). SIR WILLIAM GRANT, M.R., said (2):

C
    "Computing the time de momento in momentum, six calendar months had not elapsed: but it is admitted, that this is not the way, in which the computation is legally to be made. The question is, whether the day of Sir John Lester's death is to be included in the six months, or to be excluded: if the day is included, she did not, if it is excluded, she did, give

D   the required security before the end of the last day of the six months; and therefore did sufficiently comply with the condition."

After discussing the authorities SIR WILLIAM GRANT said (3):

    "It is not necessary to lay down any general rule upon this subject: but upon technical reasoning I rather think, it would be more easy to main-

E   tain, that the day of an act done, or an event happening, ought in all cases to be excluded, than that it should in all cases be included. Our law rejects fractions of a day more generally than the civil law does . . . The effect is to render the day a sort of indivisible point; so that any act, done in the compass of it, is no more referrible (sic) to any one, than to any other portion of it; but the act and the day are co-extensive; and therefore the act cannot properly be said to be passed, until the day is passed."

F   Then he went on (3):

    "In the present case the technical rule forbids us to consider the hour of the testator's death at the time of his death; for that would be making a fraction of a day. The day of the death must therefore be the time of the death; and that time must be past, before the six months can begin to run.

G   The rule, contended for on behalf of the plaintiffs, has the effect of throwing back the event into a day, upon which it did not happen; considering the testator as dead on Jan. 11 instead of Jan. 12; for it is said, the whole of the 12th is to be computed as one of the days subsequent to his death. There seems to be no alternative but either to take, the actual instant, or the entire day, as the time of his death; and not to begin the computation from the

H   preceding day. But it is not necessary to lay down any general rule. Whichever way it should be laid down, cases would occur, the reason of which would require exceptions to be made. Here the reason of the thing requires the exclusion of the day from the period of six months, given to Mrs. Pointer to deliberate upon the choice she would make; and upon the whole my opinion is, that she has entered into the security before the expiration of the

I   six months; in sufficient time therefore to fulfil the condition, on which her children were to take."

Counsel for the first defendant relied on the concluding passage for the proposition that in deciding whether to include or exclude the initial day one must consider which is the more favourable course to the beneficiary. He supported this by a

---

(1) [1803-13] All E.R. Rep. 436; (1808), 15 Ves. 248.
(2) [1803-13] All E.R. Rep. at p. 437; (1808), 15 Ves. at p. 253.
(3) [1803-13] All E.R. Rep. at p. 439; (1808), 15 Ves. at p. 257.

reference to *Re North, Ex p. Hasluck* (4), a case which had nothing to do with   **A**
conditions in wills. The headnote reads (4):

" By the Bankruptcy Act, 1890, s. 1, a debtor commits an act of bankruptcy if execution against him has been levied by seizure of his goods, and
the goods have been held by the sheriff for twenty-one days:—Held, that the
sheriff must hold the goods for twenty-one whole days, in the computation of   **B**
which the day on which the seizure is made is to be excluded."

What counsel for the first defendant mainly relied on was a passage in the judgment of LORD ESHER, M.R., as follows (5):—

" A fair rule of construction seems to be that where the computation is to
be for the benefit of the person affected as much time should be given as
the language admits of, and where it is to his detriment the language should   **C**
be construed as strictly as possible."

RIGBY, L.J., after considering the case of *Lester* v. *Garland* (6), said this (7):—

" In my opinion, although SIR WILLIAM GRANT, M.R., did not put the
proposition in so many words, his judgment leads us to to the conclusion
that the question of whether the day on which the act is done is to be   **D**
included or excluded must depend on whether it is to the benefit or disadvantage of the person primarily interested."

In cases where some voluntary act has to be performed, as in *Lester* v. *Garland*
(6), there may well be merit in allowing the maximum time for the person concerned to do that act; but I am concerned here not with the performance of a
voluntary act but with the occurrence of the involuntary event of death; and I do   **E**
not see the advantage of allowing the maximum time so that the property may
become indefeasibly the property not of the wife (except for a few hours) but
of the wife's estate.   There also may be uncertainties in applying to beneficiaries
under a will the phrase " person primarily interested " used by RIGBY, L.J. (7) in
the case of bankruptcy. If property is to go to either A or B, according to
whether A or B (or for that matter X) survives the testator for a given period,   **F**
it may not always be clear whether A or B is to be regarded as the " person
primarily interested "; for each claims under the will, and the will must be
construed as a whole.   Further, a phrase such as " within three months of my
death " may be used more than once in the same will, and the advantage of the
" person primarily interested " may be served by construing the period long under
one clause and short under another, even though the words defining the period   **G**
are identical in each case. Accordingly, I should be reluctant to adopt the
concept of the " person primarily interested " as a canon for use in the construction of wills unless authority so requires; and I do not think that it does.

Lester v. *Garland* (6) is important, however, in several respects. First, it
freed the courts from fixed rules in the computation of periods;   second, it points
towards a rejection of fractions of days, except where the circumstances other-   **H**
wise require; and third, it illustrates the tendency to exclude the day on which
the initial event occurs (here, the husband's death) before time begins to run.
This tendency is further illustrated in relation to a will by *In the Goods of Wilmot*
(8) which counsel for the second defendant cited, though this is so shortly reported
that it is of little value.   *Gorst* v. *Lowndes* (9), on which counsel for the second
defendant also relied, is much to the same effect.   There, under a direction to
accumulate income for the term of twenty-one years from the testator's death,
the term was construed as excluding the day of the testator's death, so that the
direction embraced a dividend which accrued due on the twenty-first anniversary
of the death. SIR LANCELOT SHADWELL, V.C., held that the day of the testator's

(4) [1895] 2 Q.B. 264.   (5) [1895] 2 Q.B. at p. 270.
(6) [1803-13] All E.R. Rep. 436; (1808), 15 Ves. 248.
(7) [1895] 2 Q.B. at p. 274.
(8) (1834), 1 Curt. 1.   (9) (1841), 11 Sim. 434.

A   death was to be " considered as a point ", and since the term created was a
term " from " that day, that day was excluded.

There is thus a line of authorities on wills in which periods expressed merely
as periods after death, without using the words after the " day of " the death,
have been construed as being periods of complete days which exclude the day
of death.   These authorities point strongly against the included day argument
B   which, in any case, would make the period begin to run from a time anterior to
the death.

As for the punctum temporis argument, no authority has been cited to me
which demonstrates this method of computation under a will.   In *Cornfoot* v.
Royal Exchange Assurance Corpn. (10), however, the headnote reads as follows (10):

C   " In a policy of marine insurance on a ship the insurance was described as
being for a voyage to Algoa Bay ' and for thirty days in port after arrival '
and as continuing ' until the ship with all her ordnance, tackle, apparel, &c.,
shall be arrived at as above upon the said ship, &c., until she hath there
moored at anchor in good safety '.   The ship arrived in Algoa Bay, and was
there moored at anchor in good safety at 11.30 a.m. on Aug. 2, 1902.
D   She remained in Algoa Bay until Sept. 1, 1902, and was there totally lost
through perils insured against at 4.30 p.m. on that day:—Held (affirming
the judgment of BIGHAM, J. (11)), that the expression ' thirty days ' in
the policy meant thirty consecutive periods of twenty-four hours, the first
of which began to run at 11.30 a.m. on Aug. 2; and, therefore, that the
insurance had come to an end before the loss occurred."

E   The words " until she hath there moored at anchor in good safety " were printed
words, and they ran thus because the printed words " twenty-four hours "
which had stood between " anchor " and " in good safety " had been struck out.
In those circumstances the Court of Appeal had little difficulty in reading the
thirty days as meaning thirty periods of twenty-four hours each, running from
the moment of arrival and leaving no uninsured gap between the moment of
F   arrival and the end of the day on which the arrival occurred.   In the present
case there is nothing to turn one's mind to hours rather than days, and no argument based on any gap.

The *Cornfoot* case (10) was distinguished by the Court of Appeal in *Cartwright*
v. *MacCormack* (12).   There the period of insurance was expressed to be " fifteen
days from the commencement date of risk "; and in the context of the policy the
word " date " made the distinction, and showed that the fifteen days was to be
computed from midnight on the day stated in the policy to be the date of commencement.   The case contains a valuable discussion of a number of authorities
on the computation of time, including the decision of the Divisional Court in
Stewart v. *Chapman* (13); and it is helpful as indicating the vitality of the rule
that prima facie fractions of a day will be disregarded.

I   Apart from authority, what do these words mean in this particular will?
Three forms of expression are to be found in it: first, " at my death "; second,
" at the time of my death "; and third, " at the date of my death ".   The
first and second of these occur in cl. 3 (5) and 3 (6).   The first and third
are used in cl. 4.   No-one during the argument has been able to suggest
any rational explanation of the use of one expression rather than another.
I   In particular, in the phrase " at the date of my death " in relation to the mortgage
the words " the date of " seem to have no sensible function: it is difficult to see
why " date " rather than " time " or simply " death " should not have been
used.   This interchangeability of language suggests that all these expressions
are being used as equivalents, and that there is no precise usage in the drafting
of the will as a whole or this clause in particular in relation to the word " death ".
Further, " at the time of my death " or " at my death " are both phrases which

(10) [1904] 1 K.B. 40.   (11) [1903] 2 K.B. 363.
(12) [1963] 1 All E.R. 11.   (13) [1951] 2 All E.R. 613; [1951] 2 K.B. 792.

are capable of meaning either the day of death or the moment of death. Where A
the phrase is " at the date of my death ", on the other hand, it is more difficult
to construe this as a reference to a moment and not to a day. Accordingly, if
all the expressions mean the same, it seems (though the indication is slender)
that the probability is that they all mean " at the date of my death " and not
" at the precise instant of my death ".

There is a further consideration which occurred to me shortly after counsel B
had concluded their submissions; and I mention it with all the diffidence appropriate to a point which has not undergone the purifying ordeal of argument.
It appears to me that there is a different flavour about periods of time expressed
in hours and shorter units, when compared with periods of time expressed in
days and longer units. There seems to be a real difference between " two days ",
on the one hand, and " forty-eight hours " on the other. Yet days and weeks C
comprise an exact number of hours and minutes, and at first it is not easy to
see why a line should be drawn between hours and lesser units, on the one hand,
and days and greater units on the other; and mere subjective impressions are
frail aids to construction. Yet HOLMES, J., has reminded us that

> " A word is not a crystal, transparent and unchanged, it is the skin of a
> living thought and may vary greatly in color and content according to the   D
> circumstances and the time in which it is used: "

Towne v. *Eisner* (14). The explanation, I think, lies in the appropriate instrument of calculation. For the hour or lesser unit one turns to the precision of the
clock or chronometer; for the day or greater unit it is the broader sweep of the
calendar. Accordingly, it seems to me that in the computation of a period of E
time it is relevant to consider the units of measurement in which that period
has been expressed; and if those units are days or greater periods, this provides
some indication that the reckoning is to be in complete days and not de momento
in momentum. I do not say that this indication is compelling or would prevail
against indications to the contrary; but I think that it is entitled to some weight.
Here the period is expressed in months, so that this view supports the argument F
that the period is one of complete days. I bear in mind also that sometimes it
is far from easy to determine the exact moment of death. Quite apart from
medical difficulties in defining the precise instant when life is extinct, some die in
accidents or in solitude, and in circumstances making it impossible to determine
the time of death to within an hour or more. This, too, perhaps gives some small
indication that in computing a period of " three months from my death " the G
testator did not envisage a period which was to begin to run at an exact moment
of time.

As against that, it can be pointed out that the words " survive me and " in
cl. 4 add nothing to the measurement of time, since a wife who is living three
months after the testator's death has of necessity survived him. Yet those
words are there, and as survival is related to a particular point of time, it may be H
said that the insertion of these otherwise unnecessary words manifests an intention
to refer to a point of time rather than to complete days. I do not, however,
think that there can be much weight in this; for if the testator had had any
such intention I find it difficult to believe that he would have entrusted that
intention to so frail and indirect a carrier.

Accordingly, both on authority and on the words of this particular will, I
reach the conclusion that both the included day argument and the punctum
temporis argument should be rejected. The period of three months is a period
to be reckoned in complete days beginning at the end of the day of the husband's
death, and so began to run at midnight on Jan. 9, 1966. It thus ended at
midnight on Apr. 9, 1966, and I accordingly hold that cl. 4 of the will did not
carry the house from the husband to the wife. I therefore answer question 1
of the summons in sense 1 (b).

---

(14) (1918), 245 U.S. Rep. 418 at p. 425.

A   I now turn to the second and third questions; and these are interlinked. When the husband died a sum of £5,705 18s. 10d. stood to the credit of a current account in the joint names of husband and wife in the Mincing Lane branch of the Midland Bank, Ltd.; and a further sum of £10,700 stood to the credit of a deposit account in the joint names of husband and wife at the same branch. The second question is whether these sums form part of the husband's estate

B or part of the wife's. If they form part of the wife's estate (and not otherwise) the third question arises. That is whether cl. 7 of the will requires any estate duty in respect of these moneys to be paid out of the husband's estate. Clause 7 of the will reads as follows:

"I direct that any estate or other duties payable by reason of my death on any gifts made by me in my lifetime to my wife or Margaret shall be

C   paid out of my residuary estate and not by my wife or Margaret."

The reference there to Margaret is to Mrs. Parker. With both the husband and wife dead, there has been an understandable difficulty in ascertaining the full facts relating to these accounts, particularly as the joint current account was opened over fifty years ago. I feel no doubt, however, that the executors, who are the same under each will, have done all that is possible to elicit the facts,

D and I must do the best I can with the material available.

The history of the joint current account is as follows. On July 11, 1912, the husband, who was then a tea and rubber broker, opened a current account in his sole name with the Mincing Lane branch. He married the wife on Nov. 27, 1915, when he was serving in the army. On Aug. 9, 1917, he opened the joint current account here in question in the names of himself and the wife, and transferred

E to it the credit balance in his own current account. Thereafter he had no current account in his sole name anywhere; and for the rest of his life he operated this joint current account as his own. Indeed, apart from a short-lived deposit account, the only sole bank account he had after 1917 was a post office savings bank account which had been dormant for many years before his death. When the current account was opened the husband and wife each signed one of the

F bank's printed forms. It read:

"We request you to open/continue an account or accounts in our joint names and we hereby authorise you from time to time, until we or either of us give you written notice to the contrary, to pay and honour all cheques and orders for payment which may be drawn on any such account, when signed by either of us and to charge the amount of all such cheques and orders to the debit of our said joint account or accounts, whether our said account or accounts is or are in credit or overdrawn at the time such cheques are presented for payment, any loan or overdraft which may from time to time be created on any such account being at our joint and several responsibility, and we also authorise and request you to accept the signature of either of us on orders for the withdrawal of any securities, deeds or articles at any time held by you for us and notices for the withdrawal of and discharges for any moneys held on any deposit account with you in our joint names."

That is signed by both the husband and the wife, and dated Aug. 9, 1917.

As regards the wife, on Oct. 9, 1929, she opened a current account in her sole name with the Beckenham Junction branch of the bank. On Feb. 13, 1953, she transferred this account to the Mincing Lane branch.

I turn to the deposit accounts. The husband seems to have had such an account in his sole name from the end of 1942 until some time in 1944, when it was closed. The joint deposit account was opened on June 22, 1949, by the husband transferring £14,000 from the joint current account. The wife also had a deposit account in her sole name at the Mincing Lane branch, and this was opened on Feb. 13, 1953, by a transfer of £3,000 from the joint deposit account. She also had a dormant post office savings bank account in her sole

name. All the accounts were substantially in credit when the husband died. **A**
Ignoring the post office savings bank accounts, the position was thus that for
over ten years before the husband's death there had been a joint deposit account
and a joint current account. In addition, the wife had a deposit account and a
current account in her sole name. The husband, on the other hand, had no
account in his sole name.

The husband was a man who was clearly meticulous in money matters. There **B**
was put in evidence an account book in his writing which ran from December,
1954, until a little over two months before his death. It records on the left-hand
side cheques and payments by the bank under what I assume to be standing
orders. On the right-hand side there are detailed records of payments which he
had made down to the smallest items such as shillings and pence for fares,
sweets, matches and papers. From entries in this book and the other evidence, **C**
I obtain the impression of a man of settled and detailed financial habits. In the
words of Mrs. Parker, his adopted daughter,

" For as long as I can remember it was the husband's habit to keep control
of all household expenditure. Larger bills he paid himself by cheque.
For smaller items he would give cash to the wife for which she was expected **D**
to account to him."

She also says that the husband did not consider that women were capable of
dealing with business matters, and that soon after his marriage he had unsuccessfully tried to persuade the wife to transfer to him the shares which she then
owned. He seems also, again unsuccessfully, to have attempted to induce
his wife to let him manage her financial affairs. Even during his last **E**
illness he persisted in trying to make out and sign all the necessary cheques;
and he refused to part with his cheque book. To this episode I must return in
due course. Nevertheless, though careful in money matters, he was far from
being mean or ungenerous. In 1960 he gave Mrs. Parker a house and investments costing nearly £20,000; and in 1964 he gave to her and his wife investments
of a total value of over £28,000. His accounts record many other gifts of **F**
relatively small amounts.

I am satisfied from the evidence that, subject to two qualifications, the husband
throughout operated the joint current account and the joint deposit account
as if they were his own, and that the wife left them severely alone. For over
thirty-five years she operated the current account which stood in her sole name;
and this was fed by her investments, by assets from the estates of her father and **G**
mother, and by transfers from the joint current account. In 1929 the husband
gave the bank a standing order to transfer £21 a month from the joint current
account to the wife's current account. This was reduced to £15 in 1931, and to
£10 in 1942, at which figure it remained unchanged until the husband's death.
With two qualifications, the wife never operated either of the joint accounts.
These qualifications were both in respect of the joint current account, and are **H**
as follows. First, while the husband was abroad on active service during the
first world war it seems probable that the wife operated the joint current account,
and that the husband's purpose in opening this account was to enable the wife
to draw money while he was away. After the war the husband was in India
for a while and it is possible that the wife operated the account then; but this is
mere surmise.

Second, during the husband's last illness, the husband, as I have already
mentioned, refused to part with his cheque book. He also refused to permit
Mrs. Parker to make out the cheques so that he need only sign his name. There
were three cheques for household and other expenses which he was unable to
complete. Mrs. Parker took these to the Kingswood branch of the bank, where the
husband had established drawing arrangements on Aug. 16, 1962, and the
manager told her that as the account was a joint account the wife could sign the

A cheques; and the wife then did so. The manager also obtained a new cheque book because, in Mrs. Parker's words,

> ". . . the wife was afraid to try to take and use the husband's cheque book. She would not agree to draw money from her own bank account for household expenses."

B On those facts I turn to the law. Counsel for the first defendant contends that this is a case in which the presumption of advancement applies, so that the wife's estate is entitled to the balances in the two accounts. Counsel for the second defendant, supported by counsel for the third defendant, argues on the other hand that the presumption stands rebutted. The leading case is the decision of SIR GEORGE JESSEL, M.R., in *Marshal* v. *Crutwell* (15). In that case the pre-

C sumption of advancement was held to be applicable to a joint bank account, though on the facts it was decided that the presumption had been rebutted. The headnote reads as follows:

> "The husband of the plaintiff being in failing health transferred his banking account from his own name into the joint names of himself and his wife, and directed the bankers to honour cheques drawn either by

D himself or his wife; and he afterwards paid in considerable sums to this account. All cheques were afterwards drawn by the plaintiff at the direction of her husband, and the proceeds were applied in payment of household and other expenses. The husband never explained to the plaintiff what his intention was in transferring the account, but he was stated by the bank manager to have remarked at the time of the transfer that the balance

E of the account would belong to the survivor of himself and his wife. After the death of her husband (which took place a few months after the transfer) the plaintiff claimed to be entitled to the balance: Held, that the transfer of the account was not intended to be a provision for the plaintiff, but merely a mode of conveniently managing her husband's affairs; and consequently that she was not entitled."

F The concluding passage of the judgment of SIR GEORGE JESSEL, M.R., is as follows (16):

> ". . . . taking into view all the circumstances (as I understand I am bound to do), as a juryman, I think the circumstances show that this was a mere arrangement for convenience, and that it was not intended to be a provision for the wife in the event which might happen, that at the husband's death there might be a fund standing to the credit of the banking account. I take

G into account the circumstance that the wife could draw upon the fund in the husband's lifetime, so that it would not necessarily be a provision for her after his death; and also the circumstance that the amount of the fund at his death must be altogether uncertain; and, having regard to the rule which is now binding on me, that I must infer from the surrounding circum-

H stances what the nature of the transaction was, I come to the conclusion that it was not intended to be a provision for the wife, but simply a mode of conveniently managing the testator's affairs, and that it leaves the money therefore still his property."

That case was distinguished in *Re Harrison, Day* v. *Harrison* (17). The headnote

I reads as follows (17):

> "A husband, in 1908, transferred the money standing to a current account at his bank in his own name into the joint names of himself and his wife. He did not inform his wife of the joint account, and always drew cheques on the account himself. He died in November, 1919. The wife never drew any cheque on the account until shortly before his death, when he was in

---

(15) (1875), L.R. 20 Eq. 328.
(16) (1875), L.R. 20 Eq. at pp. 330, 331.
(17) (1920), 90 L.J.Ch. 186.

failing health and unable to attend to business. The bank manager then   **A**
informed her of the joint account, and advised her to draw a cheque, which she
did. The husband had also from time to time made deposits in the joint
names of himself and his wife, and in August, 1919, consolidated them into
one deposit in the joint names. The wife never knew of this deposit until
after her husband's death. There was then found among his papers an
envelope endorsed with the wife's initials and containing the deposit receipt   **B**
and a document in which he said: ' I would like this paying away at once if
possible as under ', with a list of names with amounts against them: Held,
that the moneys standing to the credit of both the current account and
the deposit account belonged to the wife as survivor, and that the document
did not raise any presumption that the husband regarded the deposit as his
own property."   **C**

In that case RUSSELL, J., carefully compared the facts of *Marshal* v. *Crutwell* (18)
with those of the case before him and said (19):

" None of the circumstances mentioned by SIR GEORGE JESSEL exist in the
present case. Many of those which do exist point in the opposite direction.
There was no motive of convenience here in creating a joint account. One   **D**
cheque only was drawn against the account by the wife, and that was drawn
in very exceptional circumstances which are explained by the bank manager
in his evidence. If I am to infer from the surrounding circumstances what
the motive of the transaction was, I hold that it was intended by the husband
that the moneys standing on current account in the joint names were
intended to belong to the survivor. The case for the defendants as regards   **E**
the deposit account is much more difficult than that as regards the current
account, and I can see nothing to displace the wife's claim. I hold, therefore,
that the moneys standing to the credit of both accounts belong to the wife."

There is also the case of *Re Pattinson, Graham* v. *Pattinson* (20), a decision of
CHITTY, J., which seems to have been somewhat neglected by the text-books.
This case emerged because it was referred to by the High Court of Australia   **F**
in *Russell* v. *Scott* (21), which is a case that could usefully have been cited to
ROMER, J., in *Young* v. *Sealey* (22); for it might have assisted him in his decision
to follow the Court of Appeal of Ontario in *Re Reid* (23), in preference to the
Supreme Court of the Irish Free State in *Owens* v. *Green* (24). But to these cases
I must return later.

Re Pattinson (20) was a case in which a year or two before his death a farmer   **G**
had paid £700 to a bank to the joint account of himself and his wife; and although
he operated this account until his death, he never reduced the balance below
£700. His wife never operated the account at all. There was some evidence that
the husband had said that he had opened the account with the intention of giving
his wife the absolute interest in the balance after his death. In addition to this,
however, CHITTY, J., held that the fact that (25)   **H**

". . . . the wife had during her husband's lifetime never made use of the
account for the purposes of her husband's business, or, in other words, had
not been intrusted with it by him as his agent, went far to show that the
account was opened by the husband as a joint-account in order that his
widow might have the benefit of it on his death. The widow was entitled to
the whole balance of £970 . . ."

The applicability of the presumption of advancement to a joint bank account
seems undoubted; and so the question here is whether that presumption has been
rebutted. Counsel for the second defendant relied on the facts of the case as

(18) (1875), L.R. 20 Eq. 328.   (19) (1920), 90 L.J.Ch. at p. 191.
(20) (1885), 1 T.L.R. 216.   (21) (1936), 55 C.L.R. 440 at p. 452.
(22) [1949] 1 All E.R. 92; [1949] Ch. 278.   (23) (1921), 50 O.L.R. 595.
(24) [1932] I.R. 225.   (25) (1885), 1 T.L.R. at p. 217.

A establishing that the joint current account was opened merely for convenience within the doctrine of *Marshal* v. *Crutwell* (26), and that throughout it was treated by both husband and wife as belonging to the husband alone. The husband opened the account so that the wife could draw on it while he was abroad during the first world war, and this, he said, characterised the account throughout its life. The joint deposit account, which was opened by a transfer from the joint

B current account, had the same origin in convenience, he added. He also put some emphasis on the wife's acquiescence over a long period in the husband treating the joint accounts as his own.

I am not persuaded by these contentions. The difficulties in ascertaining a man's intentions are great enough when there is a plenitude of evidence. Here there is a paucity. Convenience may well have been one reason why the husband

C opened the joint current account in 1917; but after his return from France some fifty years ago until he lay on his deathbed I cannot see any evidence of convenience. The case is very different from *Marshal* v. *Crutwell* (26). There the joint account was opened by the husband less than six months before his death, when he had for some time been in failing health; every cheque on that joint account was drawn by the wife, and not by the husband. Here it cannot be said

D what was in the husband's mind when he opened the joint current account. If convenience was one consideration, as I think that it was, that does not mean that the husband had no thought of the account forming a provision for his wife if he were to be killed. At a time when a bloody war had lasted for over three years, he was leaving a bride of less than two years standing and facing the risks of that war; and although one is in the sphere of inference and speculation, I

E should be slow to hold that an account opened in such circumstances was opened merely for convenience. If the husband had intended to make arrangements for mere convenience, there was indeed no need for him to open a joint account. He could simply have given instructions to the bank to honour cheques drawn on the current account that he had in his sole name. Furthermore, I bear in mind the husband's carefulness in money matters. Once the war was over he might

F have been expected to terminate the joint current account and to resume a current account in his own name, if all that he had intended was to make convenient arrangements. The more careful the man, the more significant the long subsistence of the joint account seems to be.

I regard the joint deposit account as being a fortiori. In any case, the mere fact that it was opened with moneys taken from the joint current account could

G not, I think, suffice to stamp it with the quality of the joint current account, even if that had been opened merely for convenience. Furthermore, in the nature of things a deposit account is far less appropriate than a current account as a provision made for convenience. Certainly in *Marshal* v. *Crutwell* (26) the account seems to have been a current account; and to counsel for the second defendant and counsel for the third defendant I would say, with RUSSELL, J., in *Re Harrison*

H (27):

> "The case for the defendants as regards the deposit account is much more difficult than that as regards the current account, and I can see nothing to displace the wife's claim."

I will add this: even if initially the joint current account was opened merely for

I convenience, I do not think that this character is stamped on the account immutably. Whatever may be the position with an unchanging asset, a current account fluctuates from day to day, and the wife can be advanced only to the extent of what remains after the husband has drawn his last cheque. If after the account is opened the husband changes his intention, I see no reason why effect should not be given to that change. An account initially opened for mere convenience may thus later become an advancement for the wife. Here, as the years slipped by and there was no longer any convenience to serve, I think that

---

(26) (1875), L.R. 20 Eq. 328.   (27) (1920), 90 L.J.Ch. at p. 191.

any considerations of convenience that there were in the initial opening faded A
into insignificance. I attach little weight to the acts of the husband as he lay on
his deathbed, for he was old and ill; but the wife's fear of using his cheque
book, and the fact that it was the bank manager and not the wife who told Mrs.
Parker that the wife could sign cheques on the joint current account, seem to me
to suggest that by 1966 all considerations of convenience had gone. The husband
could hardly have forgotten that the account was a joint account, for the names B
of both husband and wife were printed on the cheques, and doubtless also on the
bank statements. Long before his death, in my judgment, the main or only reason
for the account standing in the joint names of the husband and wife was to benefit
the wife. The fact that the husband had always used the joint current account as
if it were his own seems to me to emphasise rather than detract from the significance of the joint names. Accordingly, I hold that the balance standing to the C
credit of each joint account forms part of the estate of the wife, and I answer
question 2 in that sense.

This decision makes it necessary for me to answer the third question, relating
to the liability of the husband's estate to discharge the estate duty on the balances
in the joint accounts. I have already read cl. 7 of the will. The question is whether
this applies to these balances. D

In the case of an advancement consisting of a certain and unchanging asset
there will usually be no difficulty of this kind. But an active bank account is very
different. Moneys are paid in and moneys are drawn out. Nobody has suggested
anything but that what the wife could take by way of advancement would be the
balance remaining at the husband's death. When, then, is such an advancement
made? Were the gifts of the balances " gifts made by me in my lifetime "? E

Counsel for the first defendant has contended that cl. 7 does apply. In response
to a question from the bench he roundly asserted that as soon as a cheque was
paid into the joint account it thereupon constituted a gift to the wife. True, he
said, it was a gift liable to be diminished by the husband exercising his power to
draw on the account, so that in the end the wife would get only the balance
remaining; but subject to that power, each deposit in the account constituted a F
gift instanter, and so each deposit (or what remained of it) satisfied cl. 7 as being
a gift " made by me in my lifetime ". Counsel for the first defendant supported
his argument by reference to the cases of *Young* v. *Sealey* (28) and *Russell* v.
Scott (29). In *Young* v. *Sealey* (28), the headnote reads as follows (30):

" Money belonging to the deceased intestate was paid by her into joint
banking accounts in the names of herself and her nephew, the defendant, G
but during her lifetime she alone made payments and withdrawals. The
evidence was that she intended the beneficial, as well as the legal interest to
pass on her death to the defendant, whom she had always regarded with
affection. On her death intestate, Held, notwithstanding that the beneficial
interest in the dispositions made by the deceased passed only on her death,
they were not invalid by reason of failure to comply with the requirements H
of the Wills Act, 1837."

Then certain authorities are referred to. Much of the judgment of ROMER, J.,
is occupied with an examination of the conflicting Irish and Canadian decisions
that I have mentioned, *Owens* v. *Green* (31) and *Re Reid* (32). In the end he decided
to follow the Canadian case in preference to the Irish case, although, as appears
from the report, his own views were the reverse. He there said of the intestate, I
Miss Jarman (33):

" I find it difficult to regard Miss Jarman's deposit account transactions as
voluntary settlements by her in the defendant's favour coupled with a

(28) [1949] 1 All E.R. 92; [1949] Ch. 278.   (29) (1936), 55 C.L.R. 440.
(30) [1949] Ch. at p. 278.   (31) [1932] I.R. 225.
(32) (1921), 50 O.L.R. 595.
(33) [1949] 1 All E.R. at p. 108; [1949] Ch. at p. 294.

A power of revocation. I find it equally difficult to regard them as operating as immediately effective gifts of anything, seeing that, as between Miss Jarman and the defendant, the defendant was to have no power of withdrawal so long as Miss Jarman was living, whilst she retained the entire beneficial title to the funds. Further, it is impossible to regard the transactions as donationes mortis causa. There only remains the view, accordingly,

B that the gifts were intended to be postponed until Miss Jarman's death and to operate then so as to pass for the first time to the defendant a beneficial right to assets of Miss Jarman as then ascertained. In my judgment, however, it would not be right for me to defeat the defendant by applying this course of reasoning. In the first place the cases which have come before the courts of this country in which a depositor has put funds in the joint

C names of himself and another, intending to retain control over the funds and to withdraw from them if he thought proper, but with the further intention that the other party (if surviving) should take beneficially whatever might be left of the funds at the death of the depositor, have all, as far as I am aware, resulted in the surviving beneficiary taking free from any trust. It is true that there is no reported case, so far as I know, in which the point now

D raised was presented to the court. That there were cases of this type prior to *Marshall* v. *Crutwell* (34), however, appears from the observations of SIR GEORGE JESSEL, M.R., which he made in that case; and it is impossible to say that the point was not taken in any of them or in any subsequent cases. Secondly, there is the fact that a court whose decisions are entitled to very great respect, namely, the Appellate Division of the Supreme Court of

E Ontario, had the very point before them but did not accept it. In these circumstances, and having regard to the disturbing effect which an acceptance of the argument might well have on titles already acquired, I think it is better that the change in the current of authority which I am invited to make should be made rather by the appellate court than by a court of first instance, assuming that it is to be made at all."

F In *Russell* v. *Scott* (35), the headnote provides little help on the subject with which I am concerned. It reads as follows:

"An elderly lady and her nephew opened a joint account in the Commonwealth Savings Bank by the transfer of a large sum from an account in the lady's name. The nephew, who assisted his aunt in all her matters of business, did not contribute to the account, which was kept in funds by payments from

G the aunt's investments. The account was used solely for the purpose of supplying the aunt's needs. Moneys for this purpose were withdrawn by the nephew as required, the withdrawal slips being signed by both the aunt and the nephew. When the account was opened the aunt told the nephew and others that any balance remaining in the account at her death would belong to the nephew, and it was found as a fact that the aunt intended her nephew

H to take beneficially whatever balance stood to the credit of the account at her death. Upon his aunt's death the nephew claimed the balance of the account. Held that the presumption of a resulting trust in favour of the aunt and her estate was rebutted; the nephew's legal right by survivorship to the balance of the account prevailed and was not the subject of any resulting trust."

I What had happened in that case was that in the court below NICHOLAS, J., had held that the nephew could not take because the provision was testamentary in nature and had not been made in accordance with the statutory requirements for wills; this, of course, was substantially the point raised in *Young* v. *Sealey* (36) a dozen years later. The High Court of Australia reversed that decision. STARKE, J., said (37), citing certain authorities:

(34) (1875), L.R. 20 Eq. 328.   (35) (1936), 55 C.L.R. 440.
(36) [1949] 1 All E.R. 92; [1949] Ch. 278.   (37) (1936), 55 C.L.R. at p. 448.

A

" A person who deposits money in a bank on a joint account vests the right to the debt or the chose in action in the persons in whose names it is deposited, and it carries with it the legal right to title by survivorship . . . The vesting of the right and title to the debt or chose in action takes effect immediately, and is not dependent upon the death of either of the persons in whose names the money has been deposited. In short it is not a testamentary disposition."

B

DIXON, J., and EVATT, J., in a joint judgment, said (38), in commenting on *Owens* v. *Green* (39):

". . . by placing the money in the joint names, the deceased did then and there and by that act give a present right of survivorship."

It appears to me that there is some difficulty in defining the precise way in which the doctrine of advancement operates in the case of bank accounts. It seems quite unreal to regard each deposit in the account as an advancement, subject to diminution by the drawing of subsequent cheques. A husband who over fifty years has paid into a joint account some £10,000 a year, and at his death has drawn out all but £1,000, would on this analysis have made gifts of £500,000 to his wife, only to take back £499,000 of what he has given. This may be the law; it might even be equity; but it is indisputably remarkable. On the other hand, a gift of whatever stands to the credit of the bank account at the husband's death runs the peril of being accounted testamentary in nature, so as to require due execution as a will.

C

D

It may be that the correct analysis is that there is an immediate gift of a fluctuating and defeasible asset consisting of the chose in action for the time being constituting the balance in the bank account. But whether that is right or wrong (and the subject is worthy of academic disputation), I am happy to regard it as a problem that I need not attempt to resolve in this case. For here my duty is but to construe the words of the will. First, there are the words " any gifts ". I take these words to refer to gifts in the ordinary sense of that word. As I have already mentioned, there were ordinary gifts of substantial amounts which the husband made in his lifetime to his wife and Mrs. Parker, and for these the clause was plainly apt. Whatever might have been thought by a learned equity lawyer, had he been the testator, I cannot believe that when the husband paid money into the joint account he regarded himself as making a gift to the wife, any more than he regarded himself as diminishing gifts already made whenever he drew a cheque on that account. Nor do I think that moneys which became indefeasibly the wife's only eo instanti with the husband's death can fairly be said to fall within the phrase " gifts made by me during my lifetime ".

E

F

G

There is also the context in which the phrase appears. Clause 7 of the will is concerned with " any estate or other duties payable by reason of my death on any gifts made by me in my lifetime ". I doubt very much whether the Inland Revenue or anyone else would contemplate that every sum paid into the joint account by the husband within five years of his death ought to be considered for the purposes of a possible liability for estate duty. In short, I hold that cl. 7 is confined in its operation to gifts in the ordinary sense of the word, and does not extend, in counsel for the second defendant's phrase, to amorphous rights in a joint account. Accordingly, I answer " No " to question 3.

H

Declarations accordingly.

Solicitors: *Cartwright, Cunningham* (for the plaintiffs and the third defendant); *Field, Roscoe & Co.* (for the first defendant); *Monier-Williams & Keeling* (for the second defendant).

[*Reported by* R. W. FARRIN, ESQ., *Barrister-at-Law.*]

---

(38) (1936), 55 C.L.R. at p. 455.   (39) [1932] I.R. 225.

WHITE AND OTHERS *v.* TAYLOR AND ANOTHER (No. 2).

[CHANCERY DIVISION (Buckley, J.), Nov. 27, 28, 29, 30, Dec. 1, 4, 5, 6, 7, 8, 11, 12, 13, 14, 18, 19, 20, 21, 1967, February 12, 1968.]

Boundary—Hedge—Presumption of ownership—Close adjoining waste land.

Profit à prendre—Prescription—Lost modern grant—Sheep rights—Right of pasture—Continuity of user—Evidence not showing sufficient continuity of user.

Profit à prendre—Sheep rights—Right of pasture—Grant on sale by auction of lands in single ownership—Former waste land of manor—Construction of grants—Reference to particulars and conditions of sale—Extrinsic evidence where latent ambiguity in particular wording—Apportionment of sheep rights when lot sold at auction no longer held in single ownership—General words in conveyances—Conveyancing Act, 1881 (44 & 45 Vict. c. 41), s. 6.

Profit à prendre—Sheep rights—Access—Watering sheep—Water from well— Right to place troughs for watering sheep on waste land—Necessary access only, but with vehicles where necessary.

An auction sale of an estate in one ownership, which was held in June, 1920, comprised the part of Martin Down in Hampshire that lay to the south of the Blandford-Salisbury Road (lot 38 in the sale) and thirty-seven other lots consisting of neighbouring farm lands (" the C. lands "). The lotting did not in fact coincide with boundaries of pre-existing holdings. Each of the six plaintiffs was a successor in title of a purchaser of one or more of the thirty-seven lots and owned the fee simple of the whole or part of one or more lots. Four of the plaintiffs also owned other land in the neighbourhood of the Down to which they derived title from a different owner (" the S. lands ") or which had been glebe land: neither the S. lands nor the glebe land had been included in the auction sale. The particulars of sale for the auction provided that all lots were sold subject to the right of purchasers of any other lots to use the wells on the first mentioned lots as theretofore accustomed; and stated that practically all the lands carried sheep rights on the Down, the numbers being shown against each lot; and stated that the Down was sold subject to such rights and any other rights thereover as were stated in the conditions of sale. Descriptions of most lots stated that the lot carried a specified number of sheep rights on the Down. The description of the Down stated that it was sold subject to the specified sheep rights and also to all other sheep rights appertaining to lands not included in the sale and to all other rights affecting it and not vested in the vendor. At the auction each sale was recorded in a memorandum of agreement in common form, declaring the lot to have been purchased subject to the conditions of sale. The Down was conveyed to its purchaser by conveyance dated Oct. 21, 1920, which did not mention sheep rights, but conveyed the land subject to easements, quasi-easements and privileges. The defendants were the present owners and occupiers of the Down. Some other conveyances (two being also dated Oct. 21, 1920) of lots used the following wording (" form A ") to grant rights with the lands conveyed—" together with such right of common of pasture for sheep " on the Down as " appertains or belongs " to the land conveyed or any part thereof. Other conveyances used a slightly different wording (" form B ")—" together with the right of common of pasture for sheep " on the Down " to the [land] or some part or parts thereof appertaining or belonging ". Other conveyances of lots contained no reference to sheep rights. In regard to lands conveyed by instruments using forms A or B, no sheep rights could subsist at law at the time of the transactions of sale and purchase owing to the land being in one ownership.

A well had been dug in the Down about a century ago, primarily for watering livestock on the Down. By 1920 it had fallen out of use and was

covered with planks, but in 1925 it was restored to use and was used for   A
drawing water for sheep until the second world war when it again fell into
disuse.

In 1959 when one of the plaintiffs acquired his land, there was (so the
court found) a gap in the hedge bordering the Down. There was no ditch at
this point. After this plaintiff acquired his land, a gate was installed in
the gap, aligned with the side remote from the Down. The defendants   B
counterclaimed in respect of the gap and of the gate alleging trespass by the
plaintiff.

Held: (i) in regard to sheep rights where the conveyance of C. lands
contained form A or form B wording—

(a) although form A wording was unambiguous it referred to rights appertaining or belonging to land in equity as well as to rights appertaining   C
thereto at law, and entitled the court to look to the contracts for sale in
order to see what rights appertained or belonged in equity to each lot
conveyed; the contracts (whether the conveyances included form A or
form B wording) being specifically enforceable conferred sheep rights in
equity as appurtenances to the land bought, and accordingly the purchasers
under conveyances containing such wording became entitled to sheep   D
rights as specified in the particulars of sale, the sequence in which the conveyances were executed being immaterial (see p. 1025, letters D and H, and
p. 1034, letter I, post).

(b) moreover, although the conveyances were not executed all on the same
day, yet as the sales were from the same vendor, were contemporaneous and
were effected on the same conditions of sale, the conveyances should be   E
treated as contemporaneous transactions for the purpose of determining
the rights of the parties and as an exception from the general rule that if a
grantor intends to reserve a right over land conveyed (in this instance over
the Down) he must expressly reserve it in the grant (see p. 1026, letter I,
and p. 1027, letter B, post).

Dictum of SIR GEORGE JESSEL, M.R., in *Allen* v. *Taylor* ((1880), 16   F
Ch.D. at p. 358), and *Beddington* v. *Atlee* ((1887), 35 Ch.D. 317) applied.

(c) further, where the conveyance used the form B wording, extrinsic
evidence would be admissible to resolve the latent ambiguity and to determine to what rights the wording referred, and accordingly it would be
established that the rights granted were the sheep rights specified in respect
of the particular lot (see p. 1027, letters C and H, post).   G

(d) where a lot sold at the 1920 auction was no longer owned intact, but a
plaintiff owned only part of the original lot, his sheep rights in respect of that
part by virtue of form A or form B wording should be ascertained by apportionment on an area basis, viz., by apportioning the original rights in the
proportion that the area of the plaintiff's land bore to the area of the original
lot (see p. 1031, letter H, post).   H

(ii) (in regard to the sheep rights under a conveyance of C. lands which
did not contain form A or form B wording), s. 6 of the Conveyancing Act,
1881, did not avail to transfer the sheep rights, for it was not shown that the
rights in fact appertained or were reputed to appertain to the land, nor was
it established that a definite number of sheep were being repastured on lands
comprised in a purchase; moreover the parties in 1920 had notice, owing to   I
the vendor's unity of ownership, that grazing rights could not be appurtenant
in law to the lots sold and no estoppel arose (see p. 1028, letters E and H,
p. 1029, letter C, p. 1030, letter H, and p. 1034, letter I, post).

White v. *Williams* ([1922] All E.R. Rep. 419) distinguished.

(iii) (in regard to sheep rights in respect of the S. lands and former glebe
lands) although, in order to establish title to a profit à prendre of this
kind by prescription, it was not necessary for a plaintiff to establish continuous exercise of the profit claimed, yet it was necessary to show that the

A   user was of such character, degree and frequency, as indicated an assertion of a continuous right; on the evidence this had not been established, nor should a loss grant be presumed (see p. 1032, letter I, and p. 1034, letter F, post).

(iv) in regard to water rights and access—

(a) on the evidence it had not been established that the use of a well B   was necessary for the enjoyment of sheep rights; and accordingly, a grant of an ancillary right to the use of the well would not be implied (see p. 1035, letter H, post).

Pwllbach Collieries Co., Ltd. v. *Woodman* ([1914-15] All E.R. Rep. 124) applied.

(b) the evidence having established that in 1920 the watering of sheep C   grazing on the Down was necessary for the reasonable enjoyment of the right to graze sheep on the Down, those plaintiffs who had sheep rights on the Down had each an ancillary right to water their sheep on the Down by suitably located troughs supplied by carted water (see p. 1036, letter C, post).

(c) ancillary to the right to depasture sheep on the Down was a right to go D   on the Down, if necessary, with a vehicle to do what was necessary for the maintenance of the depastured sheep (see p. 1036, letter I, post).

(v) (in regard to the gap in the hedge and the gate) when a fenced close adjoined a piece of waste land, there was, in the absence of evidence to the contrary, a presumption that the fence belonged to the owner of the close; accordingly the hedge in question belonged to the plaintiff who owned the E   land neighbouring the Down, and the defendants counterclaim in respect of the gap in the hedge and the gate failed (see p. 1037, letter G, post).

[As to common of pasture appurtenant, see 5 HALSBURY's LAWS (3rd Edn.) 305, para. 706, p. 307 para. 709; and as to the prescription of such rights (being rights in the nature of profits à prendre) see ibid., pp. 331, 332, paras. 765, 766; F   and for cases see 11 DIGEST (Repl.) 32-34, *425-446*. As to presumption of lost modern grant in relation to such rights, see 5 HALSBURY's LAWS (3rd Edn.) 329, para. 761; and for cases see 11 DIGEST (Repl.) 34, *447-455*.

As to the distinction between easements and profits à prendre, see 12 HALS-BURY's LAWS (3rd Edn.) 522, para. 1129; and as to the nature of such profits, see ibid., p. 621, para. 1350.

G   As to the creation of easements by grants, see 12 HALSBURY's LAWS (3rd Edn.) 531, para. 1152; and for cases on the subject, see 19 DIGEST (Repl.) 30, 31, *145-149*, and (on s. 6 of the Conveyancing Act, 1881), see ibid., pp. 35-40, *182-205*. As to the effect of dispositions by a common owner see 12 HALSBURY's LAWS (3rd Edn.) 539, 540, para. 1167, and p. 542, para. 1173; and for cases, see 19 DIGEST (Repl.) 54, 55, *293-303*; and see also, as regards profits à prendre, 12 H   HALSBURY's LAWS (3rd Edn.) 625, para. 1361. As to a grant including ancillary rights, see 12 HALSBURY's LAWS (3rd Edn.) 534, para. 1159; and as to an incorporeal right being attached to an incorporeal hereditament, see ibid., p. 528, para. 1143.

As to the methods of claiming prescriptive title generally, see 12 HALSBURY's LAWS (3rd Edn.) 543, 544, para. 1178; and, as to profits à prendre, see ibid., I   p. 628, paras. 1371, 1372; and for cases on prescription, see 19 DIGEST (Repl.) 57, 58, *313-320*, pp. 72, *408*, et seq. and, as to lost modern grant, see ibid., 66, 67, *364-372*.

As to the rights to take water, see 12 HALSBURY's LAWS (3rd Edn.) 594, 595, para. 1286; and for cases on taking water from a well, see 19 DIGEST (Repl.) 159, *1049, 1050*.

As to presumptions concerning the ownership of hedges, see 3 HALSBURY's LAWS (3rd Edn.) 366, para. 699; and for cases on the subject see 7 DIGEST (Repl.) 283-285, *107-126*.]

Cases referred to: A

Allen v. *Taylor*, (1880), 16 Ch.D. 355; 50 L.J.Ch. 178; 19 Digest (Repl.) 55, *297*.

Beddington v. *Atlee*, (1887), 35 Ch.D. 317; 56 L.J.Ch. 655; 56 L.T. 514; 51 J.P. 484; 19 Digest (Repl.) 35, *182*.

Bunn v. *Channen*, (1813), 5 Taunt. 244: 128 E.R. 683; 11 Digest (Repl.) 38, *530*.

Compton v. *Richards*, (1814), 1 Price, 27; 145 E.R. 1320; 19 Digest (Repl.)   B
54, 294.

David v. *Hanslip*, (1672), 2 Lev. 67, sub nom. *Leniel* v. *Harslop*, 3 Keb. 66; 84 E.R. 597; 11 Digest (Repl.), 38, *523*.

Doe d. Norton v. *Webster*, (1840), 12 Ad. & El. 442; 9 L.J.Q.B. 373; 113 E.R. 879; 17 Digest (Repl.) 348, *1544*.

Drury v. *Kent*, (1603), Cro. Jac. 14; 79 E.R. 13; 11 Digest (Repl.) 38, *524*.   C

Hall v. *Byron*, (1877), 4 Ch.D. 667; 46 L.J. Ch. 297; 36 L.T. 367; 11 Digest (Repl.) 28, *366*.

Hill v. *Grange*, (1556), 1 Plowd. 164; 75 E.R. 253; 31 Digest (Repl.) 253, *3879*.

Hollins v. *Verney*, (1884), 13 Q.B.D. 304; 53 L.J.Q.B. 430; 51 L.T. 753; 48 J.P. 580; 19 Digest (Repl.) 74, *419*.   D

Ives (E.R.) Investments, Ltd. v. *High*, [1967] 1 All E.R. 504; [1967] 2 Q.B. 379; [1967] 2 W.L.R. 789.

Jones v. *Pritchard*, [1908-10] All E.R. Rep. 80; [1908] 1 Ch. 630; 77 L.J.Ch. 405; 98 L.T. 386; 19 Digest (Repl) 45, *241*.

Leggott v. *Barrett*, (1880), 15 Ch.D. 306; 51 L.J.Ch 90; 43 L.T. 691; 36 Digest (Repl.) 601, *1633*.   E

Morse and Webb's Case, (1610), 13 Co. Rep. 65; 2 Brownl. 297; 77 E.R. 1474; 11 Digest (Repl.) 9, *57*.

Pwllbach Colliery Co., Ltd. v. *Woodman*, [1914-15] All E.R. Rep. 124; [1915] A.C. 634; 84 L.J.K.B. 874; 113 L.T. 10; 36 Digest (Repl.) 299, *431*.

Richards v. *Squibb*, (1698), 1 Ld. Raym. 726; 91 E.R. 1384; 11 Digest (Repl.) 9, *66*.   F

Sacheverell v. *Porter*, (1637), W.Jo. 396; Cro. Car. 482; 82 E.R. 208; 11 Digest (Repl.) 38, *542*.

Smith v. *Bensall*, (1597), Gouldsb. 117; 75 E.R. 1034; 11 Digest (Repl.) 38, *533*.

Swansborough v. *Coventry*, (1832), 9 Bing. 305; 2 L.J.C.P. 11; 131 E.R. 629; 19 Digest (Repl.) 54, *295*.   G

Thomas v. *Owen*, [1886-90] All E.R. Rep. 172; (1887), 20 Q.B.D. 225; 57 L.J.Q.B. 198; 58 L.T. 162; 52 J.P. 516; 19 Digest (Repl.) 33, *167*.

Whalley v. *Tompson*, (1799), 1 Bos. & P. 371; 126 E.R. 959; 19 Digest (Repl.) 98, *574*.

Wheeldon v. *Burrows*, [1874-80] All E.R. Rep. 669; (1879), 12 Ch.D. 31; 48 L.J.Ch. 853; 41 L.T. 327; 19 Digest (Repl.) 48. *269*.   H

White v. *Taylor*, [1967] 3 All E.R. 349; [1967] 3 W.L.R. 1246.

White v. *Williams*, [1922] All E.R. Rep. 419; [1922] 1 K.B. 727; 91 L.J.K.B. 721; 127 L.T. 231; 19 Digest (Repl.) 216, *1580*.

Wyat Wild's Case, (1609), 8 Co. Rep. 78b; 77 E.R. 593; 11 Digest (Repl.) 38, *539*.

Action and Counterclaim.   I

This was an action begun by writ issued on Jan. 9, 1963, by the plaintiffs, Reginald Ernest White, John Ashley Densham, Elizabeth Turner, Arthur Edward Singleton, Edward John Hart Baker and Harold Sidney Frampton. Each of the plaintiffs was the owner in fee simple of farm lands in the parish of Martin, Hampshire, described in the statement of claim. The defendants, Reginald Albert Taylor and Martin Down, Ltd., were the owners and occupiers of land which was part of lands compendiously known as Martin Down and was formerly common land of the manor of Martin. The part of Martin Down in respect of

A   which the defendants were sued was the part lying to the south-east of the main Blandford-Salisbury road. The plaintiffs' land, save for the parts of the lands of four of the plaintiffs which were formerly glebe land or had at all material times been ordinary freehold land (see p. 1020, letter I, post), were formerly of copyhold tenure and formed part of the manor of Martin. In respect of the former glebe land and freehold the plaintiff owners claimed rights to depasture sheep

B   on Martin Down as appurtenant to such land, and as respects their lands formerly of copyhold tenure all the plaintiffs claimed to be entitled to sheep rights according to the usage and custom of the manor, alternatively on other grounds, and claimed ancillary rights. The claims made by the plaintiffs in their statement of claim as re-re-amended were—(i) a declaration that they were entitled respectively to the rights of common of pasture for sheep over the defendants' land; (ii) a

C   declaration that the plaintiffs were entitled as part of or incident to the rights of common of pasture to obtain access to and to use a well situate in the defendants' land for the purpose of watering sheep grazed by the plaintiffs in pursuance of their rights; (iii) a declaration that the plaintiffs and their servants or agents were entitled to pass and repass with or without animals or vehicles over and along all or any of certain tracks on the defendants' land shown on the plan

D   annexed to the statement of claim; (iv) an injunction to restrain the defendants and each of them themselves or by their servants or agents or otherwise howsoever from (a) impeding or otherwise interfering with the exercise by the plaintiffs or any of them of their rights of pasture, (b) removing or otherwise interfering with water troughs maintained by the plaintiffs or any of them as incident to the exercise by them of their rights, (c) impeding or interfering with the use by

E   the plaintiffs or any of them or by their servants or agents of the tracks or any of them or of the well, or (d) ploughing, burning, cutting, removing or otherwise damaging or diminishing the grass on the land owned or occupied by the defendants in derogation of the plaintiffs' rights of pasture; (v) an order on the defendants forthwith to restore and make fit for pasture such parts of the defendants' land as had been rendered unfit for pasture by, or by reason of, the acts

F   of the defendants or their servants or agents; (vi) alternatively, an order on the defendants to permit the plaintiffs to enter on the defendants' land for the purpose of restoring and making fit for pasture such parts of the land as had been rendered or become unfit as aforesaid; (vii) if necessary, an inquiry as to the number of sheep which each of the plaintiffs was entitled to depasture on Martin Down and (viii) damages.

G   The defendants delivered a defence and counterclaim, re-served and re-amended on May 23, 1967. Among other pleas, not material to be set out here, the defendants pleaded in para. 21 of their counterclaim that at some date in 1962 the fourth named plaintiff (Mr. Singleton) wrongfully removed or caused to be moved some ten yards of the defendants' boundary hedge at a point marked " T " on the plan annexed to the defence and counterclaim and in place thereof

H   erected a substantial wooden gateway and a paling fence; and they further pleaded (in para. 22) that by reason of all the pleaded acts of trespass on the defendants' land they had suffered damage. By their counterclaim the defendants sought—(i) an order restraining the first, second and fifth named plaintiffs whether by themselves or their servants, workmen or agents from placing or maintaining any water troughs on any part of the defendants' land; (ii) an order

I   restraining the first named plaintiff whether by himself or his servants, workmen or agents from (a) placing or maintaining any drags, harrows, ploughs or other agricultural implements or any other articles on any part of the defendants' land, (b) driving any motor tractor or other vehicles on or over any part of the defendants' land (other than that part over which the public had a right of carriageway), and (c) cutting or in any other manner interfering with any fencing or undergrowth or other vegetation growing on the defendants' land; (iii) an order that the first named plaintiff do remove or cause to be removed the fence erected by him on the defendants' land between the points marked " X " and

"Y" on the plan annexed to the defence and counterclaim; (iv) an order **A**
that the fourth-named plaintiff (Mr. Singleton) do remove the wooden gateway
and paling fence and replace the hedge; (v) a declaration that the defendant
company was entitled to depasture six sheep on the land coloured orange in the
plan annexed to the defence and counterclaim, together with such rights if any,
ancillary thereto as might be established by the plaintiffs or any of them in the
action, and (vi) damages for trespass.   The facts are set out in the judgment.   **B**

P. R. Oliver, Q.C., and *W. H. Goodhart* for the plaintiffs.
H. A. P. Fisher, Q.C., and *Charles Sparrow*, Q.C., for the defendants.

Cur. adv. vult.

Feb. 12. **BUCKLEY, J.,** read the following judgment: This action is about
grazing and other rights over a Down in Hampshire. It has been fought with   **C**
a pertinacity and vigour which says much for the powers of endurance of the
breed of Hampshire sheep farmers to which the plaintiffs belong. The trial has
lasted some eighteen days, apart from four days spent on a preliminary point (1);
and when I say that counsel, who have conducted the case with much skill and
learning, have referred me to no less than eighty-five volumes of reports and
text-books, including a very large number of authorities, ranging in date from   **D**
the last years of the seventeenth century to the present time, it will be appreciated
that the parties have found advisers worthy of their own mettle. I do not,
however, at all complain of the length of the trial, for there are in this case
sufficient distinct causes of action, involving consideration of distinct issues of
fact, to furnish at least half a dozen separate and respectable proceedings.

The Down is called Martin Down. It lies in that corner of Hampshire where   **E**
Dorset, Wiltshire and Hampshire adjoin.   Its total area is just under eight
hundred acres, of which 172 acres lie north of the road from Blandford to
Salisbury and the remainder (with which I am more particularly concerned)
lie south of that road. This Down was formerly the waste, or part of the waste,
of the manor of Martin. It seems that by the year 1920 most of the land which
had formerly been copyhold of the manor had, by surrender or otherwise, become   **F**
ordinary freehold in the hands of the lord of the manor, not subject to any
subsisting copyhold tenure. In 1920 the Down and most of the adjoining and
neighbouring land lying in Hampshire, including most of the village of Martin,
were comprised in a settled estate of which Sir Eyre Coote was tenant for life
in possession. On June 17, 1920, the Down and a number of neighbouring farms
and other properties subject to the settlement were sold by auction.   The   **G**
defendants are together the owners in fee simple of so much of the Down as
lies south of the Blandford to Salisbury road. As such they are successors in
title of the purchaser of the Down at the auction sale.

Four of the original six plaintiffs, namely Mr. Densham, Mrs. Turner, Mr.
Singleton and Mr. Baker, have died since the writ was issued in January, 1963.
Appropriate orders to carry on have been made, bringing in their respective   **H**
personal representatives as plaintiffs. For the sake of simplicity, I shall ignore
the deaths of these four plaintiffs for the purposes of this judgment and speak
of them as if they were still alive.

Each of the six plaintiffs is the owner in fee simple of farm land in the neighbourhood of the Down and as such is the successor in title of a purchaser of such
land at the auction sale. I will call these land "Coote lands". In respect of   **I**
these Coote lands the plaintiffs by their statement of claim in its final amended
form claim the right to depasture on Martin Down—including that part of it
which the defendants now own—the following numbers of sheep respectively—
Mr. White, 648; Mr. Densham, 448; Mrs. Turner, 119; Mr. Singleton, 116;
Mr. Baker, 265, and Mr. Frampton, 141. Four of the plaintiffs, Mr. White,
Mr. Densham, Mr. Singleton and Mr. Frampton, also own other lands in the

---

(1) See *White* v. *Taylor*, [1967] 3 All E.R. 349.

A   neighbourhood of the Down which were formerly either glebe land of the parish of Martin or land of ordinary freehold tenure which belonged to one Street. I will call these lands " Glebe " and " Street " lands. None of these lands was included in the auction sale. In respect of these lands the four plaintiffs claim the right to depasture on the Down the following numbers of sheep respectively:— Mr. White, 46; Mr. Densham, 52; Mr. Singleton, 121, and Mr. Frampton, 42.

B   The plaintiffs' claims to sheep rights in respect of Coote lands are based, first, on the circumstances of the auction sale and on the true construction and effect of the various conveyances by which the several sales then effected were completed; alternatively, on the operation of s. 6 of the Conveyancing Act, 1881, in respect of those conveyances; and in the further alternative on prescription. The claims to sheep rights in respect of Glebe and Street lands are based on

C   prescription alone. The plaintiffs also claim certain rights on the Down connected with watering their sheep and obtaining access to their sheep there, which are claimed as part of or as incidental to their rights of pasture. It will be convenient to leave these for discussion after the major question of the rights of pasture has been dealt with. The plaintiffs also claim that certain public rights of way exist across the defendants' land.

D   The defendants counterclaim for relief in respect of various forms of trespass which they claim that some of the plaintiffs have committed on their land. In particular there is a dispute about whether Mr. White has or has not encroached on the defendants' land by erecting a fence along a line which he, Mr. White, alleges to be the boundary at that point between his land and the Down.

    The properties offered for sale at the auction on June 17, 1920, were divided
E   into thirty-eight lots. Lot 38 consisted of the Down itself. The other thirty-seven lots consisted of various farms, small holdings, cottages, fields and so forth. The plaintiffs are now the owners of the whole or parts of the following lots:—Mr. White, all lot 6 and nearly all of lot 7; Mr. Densham, part of lot 8, all lot 9 and nearly all of lot 11; Mrs. Turner, part of lot 32 and all of lots 33 and 34; Mr. Singleton, part of lot 31; Mr. Baker, part of lot 17, part of lot 25,
F   all lot 30 and the remainder of lot 32; and Mr. Frampton, part of lot 17, part of lot 23, part of lot 28. The lots with which I am particularly concerned are consequently lots 6, 7, 8, 9, 11, 17, 23, 25, 28, 30, 31, 32, 33 and 34. Of these the only lots which remain entirely in the ownership of the plaintiffs are lot 6 (Mr. White), lot 9 (Mr. Densham), lot 30 (Mr. Baker), lots 33 and 34 (Mrs. Turner) and lot 32 (of which Mrs. Turner owns part and Mr. Baker the rest).

G   In the printed particulars of sale the descriptions of the several lots are preceded by general remarks which include this passage:

> " All lots are sold subject to the right of purchasers of any other lot or lots
> to the use of the wells on such first mentioned lots as heretofore accustomed.
> Practically all the land carries sheep rights on Martin Down, the numbers
> being shown against each lot, and Martin Down is sold subject to such
H   > rights and any other rights (if any) thereover as stated in the conditions
> of sale."

    The descriptions of most of the lots include a statement in these terms: " This lot carries X sheep rights on Martin Down ", the number of sheep rights varying from lot to lot. Thus the lots with which I am particularly concerned are
I   respectively stated to carry the numbers of sheep rights following after the lot numbers—lot 6—266 sheep rights; lot 7—390 sheep rights; lot 8—2 sheep rights; lot 9—107 sheep rights; lot 11—354 sheep rights; lot 17—185 sheep rights; lot 23—116 sheep rights; lot 25—117 sheep rights; lot 28—4 sheep rights; lot 30—189 sheep rights; lot 31—155 sheep rights; lot 32—48 sheep rights; lot 33—117 sheep rights, and lot 34—59 sheep rights. The total number of sheep rights so listed in the particulars of sale in respect of all lots described as carrying sheep rights is 2,292. The description of lot 38, that is to say Martin Down, states that

A

" This lot is sold subject to all sheep rights as set forth in these particulars against each lot, also to all other existing sheep rights appertaining
to lands not included in this sale, and to all other rights (if any) affecting
the same and not vested in the vendor."

Some copyhold interests for lives or widowhoods still subsisted at the date of
the sale in certain closes included in some of these lots. Where this was the
case the description of the lot affected contained particulars of the outstanding
copyhold interests. Condition 3 of the special conditions applicable to the sale
contains the following:

B

" In the case of every piece of demesne land which has been granted to
be held by copy of court roll as aforesaid and is now comprised in any lot
what is offered for sale is the right of the lord for the time being of the said
manor to the freehold and inheritance of such demesne land and to all
services and payments due under or by virtue of the grant by copy of court
roll so long as the grant by copy of court roll in each case shall be subsisting
but subject to all existing tenancies of such land and to all rights and
privileges that can be exercised or claimed under or by virtue of the said
grant by copy of court roll or the usage within the said manor in over or
upon the land comprised within such grant or in over or upon any manorial
commons or waste lands whether such rights and privileges shall be referred
to in the Particulars or in any general remarks or stipulations or revision
notes issued by the vendor (which remarks or stipulations or revision notes
are to be deemed as being part of these conditions) or in these conditions of
sale or not so long as the said grant by copy of court roll shall be subsisting."

C

D

E

All these then subsisting copyhold interests have since determined, either by
surrender soon after the Coote sale or on the falling of the relevant lives.
Special condition 4 was in these terms:

" In the case of lot 38 (' Martin Down ') what is offered for sale is the
right of the vendor and his successors in title the lord or lords for the time
being of the said Manor to the soil of the said Down and to all rents or
moneys payable in respect of the use or enjoyment or occupation of the said
soil or any part thereof but subject to such rights of depasturing sheep
thereon or thereover as are included in the particulars of sale of the various
lots or exist independently thereof and to all rights and easements and
privileges in the nature of easements or quasi-easements (if any) in over
upon or affecting the said Down whether existing by grant prescription
custom agreement or license or otherwise howsoever and the vendor shall
not be required to furnish any information or evidence not in his possession
as to the creation thereof or as to the persons entitled thereto."

F

G

It seems to me to be manifest from what I have referred to in the particulars
of sale that the vendor intended that the purchasers of the several lots which
were stated to carry sheep rights should acquire with those lots the right to run
on Martin Down the numbers of sheep specified for those lots respectively for
the purpose of allowing them to graze there, and that he intended that the purchaser of the Down should acquire it subject to such grazing rights. The question
is whether the sales were effected and eventually completed in such a way that
that intention was carried out.

H

I

Each of the sales at the auction was recorded in a memorandum of agreement
in a common form which recorded that a named purchaser was the highest
bidder for a particular lot and was declared the purchaser thereof subject to
the conditions of sale at a specified price. At this stage of the transaction the
conclusion seems to me to be inescapable that the parties intended and agreed
that the vendor should sell and that the several purchasers should buy the lots
as described in the particulars of sale, that is to say that the purchasers of lots
stated to carry sheep rights should acquire those rights and that the purchaser

A of the Down should acquire it subject to all those rights. It is said, however, that the conveyances by which the sales were completed were inappropriate to produce this result.

Before considering the individual conveyances it is convenient at this point to say that in 1953 Mr. White bought that part of the Down containing approximately 172 acres which lies north of the Blandford-Salisbury road. I have **B** already held on a preliminary point in this action (2) that the consequence of this was that he lost all of whatever grazing rights he had over the Down. It is therefore unnecessary for me in this judgment to consider the effect of the conveyances of lots 6 and 7. The Down was conveyed to its purchaser by a conveyance dated Oct. 21, 1920. This contained no reference in express terms to sheep rights. It contains a recital that the vendor had agreed with the **C** purchaser for the sale to him of the hereditaments therein described in fee simple in possession subject as thereinafter mentioned but otherwise free from incumbrances. In the operative part of the deed the Down is conveyed to the purchaser in fee simple

D
"subject to the tenancies affecting the same or any part thereof and to all rights easements and privileges in the nature of easements or quasi-easements and privileges in over upon or affecting the said hereditaments hereby conveyed whether existing by grant prescription custom agreement or license or otherwise howsoever but discharged from all the limitations powers and provisions of the said will and codicil of the testator and from all estates interests and charges subsisting or to arise thereunder."

E A right to graze sheep on the Down would not be properly called an easement, nor a privilege in the nature of an easement, nor a quasi-easement: it would be a profit. As such it would, however, be appropriately described as a right over or upon or affecting the Down. It is the plaintiffs' contention that the effect of the words which I have read was to reserve out of the property conveyed by this conveyance the sheep rights mentioned in the particulars as being rights over, upon or affecting the Down existing by grant, prescription, custom, agreement **F** or otherwise or which as between the vendor and the purchaser must be treated as having then existed.

Two other conveyances with which I am concerned were made on the same date as the conveyance of the Down, Oct. 21, 1920. Lots 8, 20, 23 and 25 were all comprised in one conveyance of that date. By this conveyance these lots

G
"together with such right of common of pasture for sheep on Martin Down as appertains or belongs to the said hereditaments hereby conveyed or any part or parts thereof"

were conveyed to the purchaser in fee simple. For ease of reference I will call the words which I have read from this conveyance "formula A". Lot 11 was **H** conveyed by a conveyance of the same date. The parcels in this conveyance also included formula A. Lots 9 and 33 were together comprised in a conveyance dated Oct. 26, 1920, the parcels in which also included formula A. Lots 1 and 32 were together comprised in a conveyance also dated Oct. 26, 1920. This conveyance did not contain formula A or any other reference to sheep rights. Lot 17 was conveyed by a conveyance also dated Oct. 26, 1920, the parcels in **I** which included formula A. Lot 28 was conveyed on the same date by a conveyance the parcels in which also included formula A. Lot 34 was conveyed by a conveyance dated Nov. 10, 1920, which did not contain formula A or any other reference to sheep rights.

Lot 30 was conveyed by a conveyance dated Nov. 15, 1920, the parcels in which contained a slightly different formula (which I will call "formula B"), namely,

---

(2) See White v. Taylor, [1967] 3 All E.R. 349.

A

"together with the right of common of pasture for sheep on Martin Down to the said hereditaments or some part or parts thereof appertaining or belonging."

Finally, Lot 31 was conveyed by a conveyance dated Nov. 22, 1920, which contained no reference to sheep rights.

The plaintiffs say that on their true construction those conveyances which incorporate either formula A or formula B contain express grants of the grazing rights specified in the particulars of sale in respect of the various lots, whether those rights can with strict accuracy be said to have appertained or belonged to the lots at the dates of the conveyances or not. Moreover, they say that those rights did at the dates of the conveyances appertain or belong at least in equity to the several lots by reason of the terms of the contracts for sale to the predecessors in title of both the plaintiffs and the defendants and by reason of the terms of the conveyance of the Down to the defendants' predecessors in title.

The defendants on the other hand say that the conveyance of the Down contains no words sufficient to amount to a reservation by or regrant to the vendor of any sheep rights over the Down, and that the words "subject to all rights, etc." in the conveyance of the Down are only capable of referring to rights existing at the date of that conveyance. They say no sheep rights could then have existed in relation to the freehold estate in any of the properties sold at the auction because at the time of the auction the freehold estate in all the properties sold was in common ownership and because the lord of the manor, in whom the freehold was vested, could have no right of common over the waste of his own manor. They say that consequently the vendor conveyed the Down to the purchaser without any reservation and therefore could not either contemporaneously or, a fortiori, subsequently grant sheep rights over the Down to anyone else. Of the conveyances incorporating either formula A or formula B the defendants say that these formulae are not apt to create new rights and can properly be read as relating to such rights, if any, as in fact appertained or belonged to the several lots at the dates of the conveyances, of which in consequence of the common ownership, if for no other reason, there were none.

The subject-matter of these sales consisted of either freeholds belonging to the lord of the manor in respect of which no copyhold interests existed, or of freeholds belonging to the lord of the manor subject to existing copyhold interests. In neither case could any rights of common have existed at the date of sale appertaining to the property sold, for the lord of the manor could not have a right of common over the waste of the manor of which he himself was the owner. Consequently, if I am precluded from having regard to the circumstances of the auction sale, there seems to me to be difficulty in saying that the conveyances passed any grazing rights. In *Whalley* v. *Tompson* (3), where a common owner of two adjoining closes. in connexion with one of which a way was used across the other, devised the former with its appurtenances, this was held not to give the devisee a right of way over the other close, since the testator could not at his death have had a right of way over his own property, so that there was then no right of way over the close which was not the subject of the specific devise capable of passing as an appurtenance of the close specifically devised. If in the present case there were sheep rights appertaining by custom to the copyhold interests which still subsisted, these would, it seems to me, be irrelevant to the sale, for such rights would not appertain to the property sold and would, as counsel for the plaintiffs agrees, cease with the termination of the copyhold interests. If the vendor's leasehold tenants enjoyed grazing rights on the Down such rights would again be irrelevant to the sale: they would belong to the tenants under some express or inferred grant and would cease with the termination of their tenancies. Consequently, in my judgment, the plaintiffs can only succeed on this part of the case if according to the proper

(3) (1799), 1 Bos. & P. 371.

A construction of formulae A and B there were rights of grazing appertaining or belonging to the lots in relation to which those formulae were used at the dates of the several conveyances, or if the circumstances were such as to admit of those formulae being construed in some secondary sense.

Counsel for the defendants, contended that the words of formulae A and B are not ambiguous and that they must be construed according to their primary

B meaning. I am willing to accept this submission as regards formula A, from which it follows that I am not entitled to look at the contracts for sale for the purpose of ascertaining whether the parties intended to use that formula in some other sense. Reference to formula A requires the court to enquire whether in fact there was at the date of any conveyance, the parcels in which included that formula, any right of common of pasture for sheep on Martin Down which

C then appertained or belonged to any of the land comprised in the conveyance. As I have already indicated, the circumstances were such that at law no such right could exist by reason of the common ownership of the Down and the land conveyed, but in my judgment the operation of the formula is not confined to rights existing at law. If any such right, as is mentioned in the formula, appertained or belonged to any part of the land conveyed in equity, at the date of

D the conveyance, such right would, in my judgment, fall within the language of the formula. I conceive that I am perfectly entitled to look at the contracts for sale, not, of course, for the purpose of contradicting the conveyances (see *Doe d. Norton* v. *Webster*, (4); *Leggott* v. *Barrett*, (5)) but for the purpose of discovering whether immediately before the several conveyances any such rights as are described in the conveyances appertained or belonged in equity to the properties

E conveyed and were capable of passing under the conveyances. This is not to use the contracts as aids to the construction of the conveyances, but merely to apply the language of the conveyances, construed in accordance with its primary meaning and without any regard to the contracts, to the circumstances existing at the moment of the execution of the conveyances, which included the existence of the contracts. So also I must apply the language of the habendum in the

F conveyance of the Down to the plaintiffs' predecessor in title to the circumstances existing when that conveyance was executed, and ask myself what rights affecting the Down then existed by reason of any agreement. If any such rights existed in consequence of the contracts for sale of the other lots it must, in my judgment, be wrong to ignore them. No question of this kind arose in any of the cases relied on by counsel for the defendants in argument on this part of the

G case. These were all actions at common law except *Hall* v. *Byron* (6), but that case involved no question of equitable rights.

I have already stated my reasons for holding that on the true construction of the contracts for sale of the lots described as carrying sheep rights the purchasers became entitled to grants of those sheep rights. These contracts were of a kind which would have been specifically enforceable in equity, including that part

H relating to sheep rights. It follows, in my judgment, that, when they entered into these contracts, the purchasers thereupon became entitled in equity to the sheep rights in question as appurtenances to the land which they bought, of which the vendor, in accordance with well-established principles, then became a trustee for them subject only to certain limited rights which belong to a vendor in possession pending completion. The order in which the conveyances were

I executed seems to me immaterial. The equities came into being when the contracts were made. All the relevant lots were sold at the auction sale: the contracts were all entered into on one day. Each purchaser must be taken to have known that the vendor was at the same time selling the other lots to the other purchasers on the terms of the conditions of sale.

---

(4) (1840), 12 Ad. & El. 442.
(5) (1880), 15 Ch.D. 306.
(6) (1877), 4 Ch.D. 667.

In *Allen* v. *Taylor* (7) SIR GEORGE JESSEL, M.R., had to deal with a case of   A
contemporaneous sales by common owners of a dwelling house and an adjoining
piece of land. The question was whether the successor of the purchaser of the
land could obstruct the lights of the house. If the vendor had sold the house
but retained the land he could not have obstructed the lights because this would
have been a derogation from his grant. If, on the other hand, he had sold the
land but retained the house, the purchaser of the land could have obstructed   B
the lights. SIR GEORGE JESSEL, M.R., said (8):

"Then there comes a third case. Supposing the owner of the land and
the house sells the house and the land at the same moment, and supposing
he expressly sells the house with the lights; can it be said that the purchaser of the land is entitled to block up the lights—the vendor being
the same in each case, and both purchasers being aware of the simultaneous   C
conveyances? I should have said certainly not. In equity it is one transaction. The purchaser of the land knows that the vendor is at the same
moment selling the house with the lights, and as part of one transaction
he takes the land: he cannot take away the lights from the house. But,
as I said before, it is a question of what is the settled law on the subject.
I see the point is so stated in almost so many words by TINDAL, C.J., in   D
Swansborough v. *Coventry* (9). He says ' In the present case, the sales to
the plaintiff and the defendant being sales by the same vendor, and taking
place at one and the same time, we think the rights of the parties are
brought within the application of this general rule of law ', namely, that a
grantor shall not derogate from his own grant."

SIR GEORGE JESSEL then referred to *Compton* v. *Richards* (10) and *Wheeldon* v.   E
Burrows (11) and said (12):

"In the judgment in *Wheeldon* v. *Burrows* (11) the case is treated as an
exception to the general rule that if a grantor intends to reserve any right
over the tenement granted, it is his duty to reserve it expressly in the
grant. THESIGER, L.J., says this (13): ' It is said that, even supposing   F
the maxims which I have stated to be correct, this case is an exception
which comes within the rule laid down in *Swansborough* v. *Coventry* (14)
and *Compton* v. *Richards* (10), namely, that, although the land and houses
were not in fact conveyed at the same time, they were conveyances made as
part and parcel of one intended sale by auction.' Then he says that that will
not do. Then goes on to say ' In the cases which have been cited the con-   G
veyances were founded upon transactions which in equity were equivalent
to conveyances between the parties at the time when the transactions
were entered into, and those transactions were entered into at the same
moment of time and as part and parcel of one transaction '. So that he
evidently means to say that such a case as that is an exception to the
general rule, and you cannot block up the lights."   H

The reason why the decision in *Wheeldon* v. *Burrows* (11) was not governed
by the two authorities mentioned by THESIGER, L.J., was that in that case
the two sales there under consideration were not contemporaneous.

In the present case, on the other hand, all the sales were contemporaneous,
and they were all on the terms of the conditions of sale of which every purchaser
had notice.   I

In *Beddington* v. *Atlee* (15) an owner of a house and an adjoining plot of land
first contracted to sell the plot of land and subsequently contracted to sell the

---

(7) (1880), 16 Ch.D. 355.   (8) (1880), 16 Ch.D. at p. 358.
(9) (1832), 9 Bing. 305 at p. 309.   (10) (1814), 1 Price, 27.
(11) [1874-80] All E.R. Rep. 669; (1879), 12 Ch.D. 31.
(12) (1880), 16 Ch.D. at p. 359.
(13) [1874-80] All E.R. Rep. at p. 678; (1879), 12 Ch.D. at p. 59.
(14) (1832), 9 Bing. 305.   (15) (1887), 35 Ch.D. 317.

A house. He next conveyed the house to the purchaser of it and later conveyed the plot of land to its purchaser. The question was whether the purchaser of the plot of land could obstruct the lights of the house. It was held that he could not. Putting it shortly, the position was governed by the order of the contracts, not that of the conveyances. Likewise in the present case, in my judgment, the state of affairs on which the language employed in the conveyances operated

B was governed in the relevant aspect by the contracts for sale. The order of the conveyances could not affect this. For these reasons I am of opinion that those conveyances which employed either formula A or formula B were effective to grant sheep rights over the Down consistent with the particulars of sale.

In the case of the conveyance which employed formula B I think that the case can also be put on another and distinct ground. This formula clearly implied that

C at the date of the conveyance in question there was some right of the kind there described or intended to be described to which the parties were referring. There being no such right at law, then if, contrary to my view, the primary meaning of the language is confined to legal rights, extrinsic evidence would be admissible to resolve the resulting uncertainty as to what right the parties had in mind. Evidence of the circumstances of the sale would be admissible for this

D purpose, from which it would be apparent that the right intended to be described was the number of sheep rights mentioned in the description of the particular lot. In *Thomas* v. *Owen* (16), Fry, L.J., said:

"No doubt the word appurtenances is not apt for the creation of a new right; and the word appurtenant is not apt to describe a right which had never previously existed; and, therefore, the mere grant of all appur-

E tenances or of all ways appurtenant to the principal subject of the grant has been held in many cases not to create a new right of way where the right was not pre-existing at the date of the grant. But from as long ago as 1557 (*Hill* v. *Grange* (17)) the word appurtenances has easily admitted of a secondary meaning, and as equivalent in that case to usually occupied."

F In *Pwllbach Colliery Co., Ltd.* v. *Woodman* (18), Lord Parker of Waddington said:

"The second class of cases on which easements may impliedly be created depends not upon the terms of the grant itself, but upon the circumstances under which the grant was made. The law will readily imply the grant or reservation of such easements as may be necessary to give effect to the

G common intention of the parties to a grant of real property, with reference to the manner or purposes in and for which the land granted or some land retained by the grantor is to be used. . . ."

The present case is not one of implied grant, but, in my judgment, the court should be no less ready to seek to give effect to the common intention of the parties in resolving a latent ambiguity in their language than in perfecting their

H transaction by implying what they have omitted to say.

On the view which I have expressed of the construction and effect of the conveyances, the language of the habendum in the conveyance of the Down is appropriate in reference to the sheep rights. The grantee of the Down is to hold it subject to sheep rights already existing in equity in favour of purchasers of other lots. The reference to quasi-easements and to rights and so forth exist-

I ing by agreement make it clear that this language is not intended to be confined to describing rights enforceable at law. It is unnecessary in these circumstances to pursue the question, discussed in argument, whether the qualifying words in this habendum are capable of being read as a reservation accompanied by an implied regrant.

In respect of the conveyances in which neither formula A nor formula B is

(16) [1886-90] All E.R. Rep. 172 at pp. 175, 177; (1887), 20 Q.B.D. 225 at pp. 231, 232.
(17) (1556), 1 Plowd. 164.
(18) [1914-15] All E.R. Rep. 124 at p. 130; [1915] A.C. 634 at p. 646.

used the plaintiffs rely on the Conveyancing Act, 1881, s. 6, which, in the absence **A**
of an express contrary intention, imports general words into any conveyance
of land. They also rely on this section as an alternative argument in the formula A
and formula B cases. They contend that the sheep rights were rights appertaining, or reputed to appertain, to the land conveyed, or, at the time of conveyance, enjoyed with, or reputed, or known as part or parcel of, or appurtenant to,
such land. That a common of pasture may pass under the general words in this **B**
section is established by *White* v. *Williams* (19).

In the year 1846 a tithe apportionment agreement was confirmed for the
parish of Martin, In this agreement rights of common of sheep on the Down are
mentioned and are so referred to as to indicate that rights to depasture specified
numbers of sheep on the Down attached to certain groups or collections of
closes; but it is common ground that this referred to sheep rights attached to **C**
copyhold interests in the land. It cannot therefore afford any ground for discovering a reputation that any sheep rights attached to the freehold. Enjoyment
of grazing facilities on the Down by tenants of the lord of the manor holding
under leases or tenancy agreements could not, in my judgment, establish a
reputation of rights appurtenant to the lands comprised in their holdings. The
implication would be that they so grazed the Down by the consent of the lord **D**
or possibly under contractual rights or grants limited in their operation at the
most to the periods of their tenancies. This could found no reputation of any kind
of right capable of surviving those tenancies.

Consequently, I do not consider that the words " appertaining or reputed to
appertain to the land or any part thereof " in s. 6 avail the plaintiffs in this case.
Can the plaintiffs successfully assert that relevant grazing rights were at the **E**
time of conveyance " enjoyed with " the lands conveyed?   What are claimed
are rights in respect of specified numbers of sheep. To make good such a claim
the claimant must show a grant to him or his predecessors of a right to graze
that number of sheep or possibly a greater number. To establish such a grant
under this part of the general words in s. 6 he must, consequently, show that at
the date of the relevant conveyance the occupier of the land conveyed was in **F**
fact grazing that number of sheep or a greater number on the Down and was
doing so with—that is to say, in respect of—the land conveyed. In this connexion
the fact must be stated that the lotting of the various lots sold at the auction
sale did not coincide with the pre-existing holdings; that is to say, the boundaries
and consequently the areas and identities of the farms were changed to a
significant extent. **G**

Moreover, as is not surprising, in view of the fact that none of the witnesses
was farming any of this land in 1920, none of them is able to state with any
accuracy what the sizes of the flocks of the various farmers were at that time.
The figures which I was given amounted, at the best, to rough estimates and
were sometimes, I think, little better than guesses. In my judgment the plaintiffs
have not successfully discharged the onus of establishing that in 1920 any par- **H**
ticular number of sheep were being depastured on the Down in respect of the
lands now owned by any of the plaintiffs or any part of them. Consequently I
am of opinion that the words " enjoyed with " in s. 6 do not avail the plaintiffs.

That leaves for consideration the words " reputed or known as part or parcel
of or appurtenant to the land or any part thereof ". Counsel for the plaintiffs,
relying on *White* v. *Williams* (19), has contended that in this respect the sale **I**
particulars constitute an admission against the vendor which is binding on the
defendants as his successors, and that the sheep rights mentioned therein were
part and parcel of the land sold. In para. 5B of their amended statement of
claim the plaintiffs plead an estoppel resulting from the purchasers at the auction
having bought on the faith of representations contained in the particulars. The
validity of these arguments depends on the proper interpretation of the references

(19) [1922] All E.R. Rep. 419; [1922] 1 K.B. 727.

A to sheep rights in the particulars. Counsel for the plaintiffs says that these are expressed as being, and were in truth, statement of fact: " This lot carries X sheep rights on Martin Down ". Counsel for the defendants, on the other hand, says that this phrase merely constituted part of the description of what was offered for sale, and so was in the nature of a promissory statement or a state-ment of intention. If the words are to be read as a statement of fact they must

B relate to the legal position existing before the sale and must, I think, amount to representations of mixed fact and law, but they might nevertheless support a plea of estoppel. To construe the particulars I must read them in the light of the surrounding circumstances, or at any rate, those surrounding circumstances which were known to the parties. These included the fact that the vendor was owner in fee simple, not only of the lots described as carrying sheep rights on

C the Down, but also of the Down. It follows that the purchasers must have had notice that in law the rights could not be appurtenant to the lots described as carrying them. If they had not notice of this when they bought, as I think that they had, they must certainly have had actual or constructive notice of it before their purchases were completed by conveyance, in which case I cannot see how they can be heard to say that they were induced by the representation to com-

D plete the purchases. If, on their true interpretation, the words amount to a representation that, notwithstanding the common ownership, the sheep rights were in some way appurtenant at law to the lands conveyed, this would, I am inclined to think, be a representation—and, indeed, a misrepresentation—of pure law which could not found an estoppel. The language of the particulars in this respect, however, is, in my judgment, at least equally as appropriate to counsel

E for the defendants' reading as to that of counsel for the plaintiffs, and the surrounding circumstances, I think, make counsel for the defendants' sense more appropriate. At the least the phrase is ambiguous.

In *White* v. *Williams* (20) a common predecessor in title of the parties owned a farm in Carnarvonshire called Rhwng-y-ddwy-afon (which I will call " R."), another farm in the same district called Tydden Mawr (which I will call " T.M.")

F and what was described in the particulars of sale as a mountain sheep walk. These were all offered for sale by auction at one time. Lot 6 consisted of R. and the particulars of sale stated that the right of pasturage hitherto enjoyed by R. in common with others on the sheepwalk was included in lot 6. Lot 8 consisted of T.M. and the sheepwalk, which was offered for sale subject to and with the benefit of the right of pasturage thereon hitherto attached to T.M. in common

G with other holdings. This, it will be observed, was not really appropriate language if lot 8 included the freehold of both T.M. and the sheepwalk. Lot 6 was, but lot 8 was not, sold at the auction. The purchaser of lot 6 was the predecessor in title of the defendant. The parcels in the conveyance of lot 6 incorporated a reference to the property conveyed having constituted lot 6 at the action. Six years later the property comprised in lot 8 was sold to the predecessor in title

H of the plaintiffs. The plaintiffs disputed the right of the defendants to depasture sheep on the sheepwalk and sued in trespass alleging that they owned the sheep-walk in fee simple in possession. The county court judge held that the right to depasture sheep on the sheepwalk passed to the purchaser of lot 6 by virtue of the Conveyancing Act, 1881, s. 6, without being specifically mentioned on the ground that it always appertained to R., and had always been exercised and

I enjoyed with and reputed and known as appurtenant to R. He also expressed the view that there was no satisfactory proof that the common vendor owned the fee simple in the sheep walk or that he owned more than a right of common or pasturage over it. A right of this kind would not have entitled the plaintiffs to sue in trespass, and was not pleaded. The plaintiffs appealed. The only question argued in the Court of Appeal was whether the right claimed could pass under

(20) [1922] All E.R. Rep. 419; [1922] 1 K.B. 727.

s. 6. The court held that it could and did. On the question as to the title A
ATKIN, L.J., said (21):

> " But the learned county court judge, whose experience gives great weight
> to his opinion, came to the conclusion that the plaintiffs had failed to prove
> that Mr. Huddart was in fact the unrestricted owner in fee simple of the
> land, inasmuch as his acts of ownership were consistent with his merely
> having a right of common or pasturage over it. The particulars and condi- B
> tions of sale, which are obviously admissions against him, and the evidence
> given in the county court confirming those admissions—namely, that
> tenants of other farms had exercised rights of pasturage over this sheep-
> walk—constitute a considerable body of evidence in favour of the learned
> judge's conclusion."

ATKIN, L.J., was, I think, there stating an alternative ground of decision, but C
neither of the other members of the court decided the case on this ground. I am
not altogether clear to what part of the particulars and conditions of sale ATKIN,
L.J., was there referring as containing admissions relevant to the nature of the
plaintiffs' title, unless it was to the circumstance that the sheepwalk was offered
for sale subject to, and with the benefit of, the right of pasturage attached to
T.M. He was not, I think, concerned with the question whether the particulars D
and conditions contained admissions that particular rights of pasturage
appertained to or were enjoyed with R.

White v. *Williams* (22) differed on its facts from the present case in two
significant respects. First, the conveyance of R. referred in terms to the sale
particulars. Secondly, the sales were at different dates. The particulars expressly
included in lot 6 " the right of sheep pasturage hitherto enjoyed by this holding E
... on the sheepwalk ". The reference to the particulars in the parcels in the
conveyance of R. had the effect of rendering the particulars admissible to show
what property was intended to be conveyed. Once the particulars were looked at,
the conclusion that the right of pasturage passed under the general words in s. 6
easily followed, unless, as was contended, those words were inappropriate to pass
a right of this nature, which the court held not to be the case. It does not seem F
to have been suggested that no right of pasturage on the sheepwalk had been
in fact enjoyed in respect of R. The sales having been made at different dates,
the sale and conveyance of T.M. could have no effect on the earlier sale and
conveyance of R. The court had not to consider the interrelation of the two
transactions, as I have to do in the present case, where the sales were synchronal
and where, as I have pointed out, the parties had actual or, at the least, construc- G
tive notice that no grazing rights appertained at law to any of the properties
sold, whatever the particulars of sale might say on the subject. Consequently
in my opinion *White* v. *Williams* (22) is not an authority governing the present
case, as counsel for the plaintiffs submitted.

For these reasons I do not think that the plaintiffs can successfully rely on
the sale particulars as containing admissions or representations as to sheep H
rights which are binding on the defendants either as admissions made by a
predecessor in title or by estoppel. Nor do I think that in the circumstances of
this case the plaintiffs can successfully rely on what is called " proprietory
estoppel " discussed in *E.R. Ives Investments, Ltd.* v. *High* (23), even if this is
open to them on their pleadings, which seems doubtful. There has, I think,
been no such acquiescence on the part of the defendants or of any predecessor I
in title of theirs as to bring that principle into play.

As an alternative way of putting their case the plaintiffs claim prescriptive
rights. They concede, however, that as regards the Coote lands they cannot
make good a prescriptive title at common law because of the common ownership of the Down and the other lots at the date of the auction sale. Their claim

(21) [1922] All E.R. Rep. at pp. 423, 424; [1922] 1 K.B. at p. 738.
(22) [1922] All E.R. Rep. 419; [1922] 1 K.B. 727.
(23) [1967] 1 All E.R. 504; [1967] 2 Q.B. 379.

A in respect of Coote land must consequently be brought within the doctrine of lost modern grant or within the Prescription Act, 1832.

Before I proceed to consider that part of the case I should say something about the effect of those conveyances which incorporated formulae A and B in those cases where the lots sold at the auction are no longer intact, namely, lots 8, 11, 17, 23, 25 and 28. I have been referred to authorities which in my

B judgment clearly establish that where a right of common of pasture is appurtenant to a hereditament the ownership of which is severed, the right of common is severable so that the right of common may appertain partly to one section of the severed hereditament and partly to another: see Wyat Wild's Case (24), Morse and Webb's Case (25), Sacheverell v. Porter (26) and Smith v. Bensall (27).

In the case of a common of pasture for beasts levant and couchant on the

C dominant tenement this is perhaps fairly evident. If A., owning Whiteacre, has such a right over Blackacre and aliens half of Whiteacre, he can no longer have beasts levant and couchant on the whole of Whiteacre but only on the half which he retains. His grantee may have beasts levant and couchant on the alienated half. Together they are entitled against the owner of Blackacre to repasture so many beasts as are levant and couchant on the whole of Whiteacre.

D The owner of Blackacre is unaffected. The relative right of A. and his grantee are determined by the capacity of their respective parts of Whiteacre to carry beasts levant and couchant. But a right to depasture a fixed number of beasts differs significantly from a right for beasts levant and couchant. It is not confined to enjoyment by beasts levant and couchant on the dominant land and may be enjoyed by beasts that do not come from the tenement to which the right is

E appurtenant: Richards v. Squibb (28). It may be aliened so as to become a right in gross, severed from the property of the alienor (Daniel v. Hanslip (29), Leniel v. Harslop (30), Drury v. Kent (31), and see Bunn v. Channen (32) and COOKE ON ENCLOSURES (4th Edn.), p. 21) because its enjoyment is not restricted to cattle on the land of the alienor and severance of the right from the land cannot increase the burden on the servient tenement.

F It must follow that if A., the owner of Whiteacre, has a right to depasture one hundred cows on Blackacre he can alienate half of Whiteacre, retaining the whole of the pasture right for himself, or granting the whole of it to the alienee of the alienated part of Whiteacre, or making any apportionment between himself and the alienee that they may agree.

What, however, if nothing is specifically said about reserving, assigning or

G apportioning the right? The right so far as it was appurtenant to or enjoyed with the alienated half of Whiteacre would pass with it under the statutory general words. How, in these circumstances, should the right be apportioned? In the absence of any peculiar circumstances it should, in by judgment, be apportioned rateably to the area of the alienated part and retained part of Whiteacre. Counsel have been unable to refer me to any authority directly

H bearing on this point, but in my opinion apportionment rateably to area is, in the absence of special circumstances, both equitable and convenient.

Counsel for the defendants contended that apportionment on an area basis was inappropriate in this case for reasons connected with the attribution of sheep rights to particular groups of closes in the tithe apportionment agreement; but as in my view the sheep rights which I am at present considering were

I granted de novo in 1920 the contents of that agreement appear to me to be irrelevant to any apportionment of them.

Apportionments on an area basis, the mathematical accuracy of which is admitted, have been calculated in respect of those lots which are no longer

---

(24) (1609), 8 Co. Rep. 786.   (25) (1610), 13 Co. Rep. 65.
(26) (1637), W.Jo. 396.   (27) (1597), Gouldsb. 117.
(28) (1698), 1 Ld. Raym. 726.   (29) (1672), 2 Lev. 67.
(30) (1672), 3 Keb. 66.   (31) (1603), Cro. Jac. 14.
                    (32) (1813), 5 Taunt. 244.

intact. On the basis of these apportionments Mr. Densham is entitled, in respect **A**
of lots 8, 9 and 11, to 448 sheep rights—i.e., the whole of the rights claimed by
him in respect of Coote land; Mrs. Turner is entitled, in respect of lot 33, to
117 sheep rights; Mr. Baker is entitled, in respect of lots 17, 25 and 30, to 240
sheep rights; and Mr. Frampton is entitled, in respect of lots 17, 23 and 28, to
141 sheep rights. This leaves in issue the following number of sheep rights
claimed in respect of Coote land: Mrs. Turner, 82; Mr. Singleton, 116, and **B**
Mr. Baker, 25. If I am right in my view about the Conveyancing Act, 1881,
s. 6, these claims must be made good, if at all, by prescription. If I am wrong
in my view about the effect of formulae A and B but right in my view about
s. 6, the whole of the claims to sheep rights in respect of Coote land must be
made good, if at all, by prescription.

In addition to these claims in respect of Coote lands the claims in respect of **C**
Street and Glebe lands must be justified, if at all, by prescription.

Before I deal in any detail with the use which has been made of the Down
by the plaintiffs and their respective predecessors, certain other facts should be
stated. As will appear in more detail when I come to deal with the claim to
public rights of way, during the second world war the greater part of the Down
lying south of the Blandford-Salisbury road was requisitioned. Forty-five acres **D**
were in the occupation of the war department, first under requisition and later
under a lease, from September, 1939, until June, 1958, during which period it
was used as a rifle range, and grazing there was impracticable. A further 182
acres were requisitioned at various dates in and between 1941 and 1947 by the
Ministry of Agriculture and Fisheries. This land was in the occupation of a
farmer named Tozer until September, 1959. He ploughed and cultivated it, **E**
but it was put back to grass when he gave up possession. In 1954 the Ministry
acquired the freehold estate in this land and in September, 1959, entered into
an arrangement with a body called the Martin Down Grazing Rights Association
by which the land, or possibly the right to graze it, was let at a rent to the
association. The association, which was an unincorporated body consisting of
persons claiming grazing rights on the Down, let the right to graze this area to **F**
certain of its members for payment. The members who grazed this part of the
Down under this arrangement included four of the plaintiffs, namely, Mr.
Densham, Mr. Baker, Mrs. Turner and Mr. Singleton. This state of affairs continued until May, 1962, when the ministry reconveyed this land to Mr. Golightly,
its former owner, who thereupon sold it to the defendant company. While this
land was occupied by Mr. Tozer there was no grazing there. Grazing by arrange- **G**
ment with the association would clearly not count as enjoyment as of right for
the purposes of any prescriptive claim.

A further 146 acres was requisitioned by the Ministry of Agriculture and
Fisheries in December, 1947, and remained under requisition till October, 1955.
This land was let by the Ministry to the association under some form of licence.
By arrangement with the association the plaintiffs Mr. White, Mr. Densham **H**
and Mr. Baker cultivated it. When the requisition came to an end Mr. Golightly,
the freeholder, continued to permit these three gentleman to cultivate the land
under licence, and they continued to cultivate the 146 acres until about 1959.

To make good a prescriptive claim in this case it is not necessary for the claimant to establish that he and his predecessors have exercised the right claimed
continuously. This is a profit of a kind that, of its nature, would only be used **I**
intermittently. Flocks would not, for instance, be on the Down at lambing time,
or for twenty-four hours of the day, or very possibly on every day of the week
or all round the year. But the user must be shown to have been of such a character, degree and frequency as to indicate an assertion by the claimant of a
continuous right, and of a right of the measure of the right claimed.

Each plaintiff's claim must be considered separately. Mr. Densham acquired
his farm at Martin, in respect of which his claim in this action is made, in
August, 1948. He ran no sheep on the Down until about the years 1954 and 1955,

A when about 170 sheep were run on the Down from his land. There was then an interval of four or five years when again he ran no sheep there. From 1960 or thereabouts until after the issue of the writ on Jan. 9, 1963, he kept a flock of about two hundred to 260 sheep which used at times to run on the Down. Between 1920 and August, 1948, the owners or owner for the time being of Mr. Densham's Coote land ran 250 to three hundred sheep on the Down, but

B from 1938 to 1948 Mr. Main, the then owner, also owned part of Mrs. Turner's Coote land, and from 1920 to 1938 Mr. Bailey, who then owned lot 9, also owned part of Mrs. Turner's Coote land.

The position before 1920 is obscure, for I cannot tell from the evidence how far these lands were from time to time held by copyhold; nor, having regard to the reorganisation of the farms at the time of the Coote sale, can I now discover

C precisely in respect of what land any sheep farmer who then ran sheep on the Down purported to do so.

The position in respect of the Street land is this. William Street, who is the earliest owner or occupier of this land with whom I am concerned, held at the date of the tithe apportionment agreement altogether 204.66 acres, to which 380 sheep rights on the Down were appropriated by that agreement. From before

D 1912 until 1925 or thereabouts successive members of the Street family grazed a flock of about three hundred sheep on the Down, but the evidence does not establish in respect of what land this was done. At times at any rate other land carrying or alleged to carry, sheep rights was tenanted by the Street of the day and farmed by him in addition to the 204 acres. Mr. Densham's property includes 7.83 per cent. by area of the 204 acres, but in the absence of any reliable evidence

E as to the land occupied by the Streets from time to time the plaintiffs have not, in my judgment, established what number of sheep, if any, were run on the Down between 1912 and 1925 in respect of Mr. Densham's Street land.

The Street family continued to own and occupy Mr. Densham's Street land until Mr. Densham bought it in 1948, but there is no evidence of any sheep rights having been exercised in respect of it between 1925 and 1948.

F The Glebe land in the tithe apportionment agreement amounted to twenty-nine acres, to which sixty sheep rights were appropriated. Mr. Densham's property includes thirty-six per cent. by area of this land. There is no evidence of any sheep having been run on the Down in respect of this portion of Glebe land before 1946. From 1946 until 1948 it was owned by Mr. Main, who then owned lots 9 and 11, and as already stated ran 250 to 300 sheep on the Down,

G From 1948 this portion of Glebe land was in the ownership of Mr. Densham. whose use of the Down I have already described.

In these circumstances Mr. Densham cannot, in my judgment make good any prescriptive claim. First, he cannot establish sufficiently continuous user. Between 1948 and the issue of the writ there were two periods, each of five or six years, during which he made no use of the Down. From Jan. 9, 1933, which

H was thirty years before the issue of the writ, to the date of Mr. Densham's purchase in 1948, no sheep rights were exercised in respect of the Street land, nor, it would seem, were any exercised in respect of the Glebe land. During the same period only 250 to three hundred sheep were run on the Down in respect of Mr. Densham's Coote land, and it cannot be said that these were on the Down exclusively under rights attached to Mr. Densham's Coote land.

I In these circumstances it is impossible to conclude that throughout the statutory period of thirty years under the Prescription Act, 1832, s. 1, any sheep rights have been enjoyed as of right and without interruption in respect of any of Mr. Densham's land. The periods of non-enjoyment during Mr. Densham's own ownership, in my judgment, make it impossible to hold that a right to enjoy any such rights has been continuously asserted in respect of his Coote land (as to which see Hollins v. Verney (33)). A fortiori this is impossible in respect of either the Street land or the Glebe land.

(33) (1884), 13 Q.B.D. 304 at p. 315.

The fact that the 182 acres mentioned earlier were under cultivation from A various dates until 1959, and that the 146 acres were under cultivation from 1947 until, perhaps, 1959 cannot, in my judgment, assist Mr. Densham.   On the contrary, these uses of the Down, except so far as the Commons Registration Act 1965 s. 16, applied, amounted to interruptions of the enjoyment of the sheep rights in respect of those areas which were cultivated, at any rate whenever they were under crops.   Section 16 of the Act of 1965 did not apply to any B part of the 182 acres after that land ceased in 1954 to be requisitioned, nor did it apply to any part of the 146 acres after 1955 when that land ceased to be requisitioned.

Secondly, as regards his Coote land Mr. Densham cannot rely on common law prescription because of the united ownership before 1920.

Thirdly, he cannot, in my judgment, make out a case as to his Coote land C under the doctrine of lost modern grant.   Any such grant would, as regards Coote land, have had to have been made since the Coote sale.   Whether such a grant could reasonably be inferred must be considered in the light of all the surrounding circumstances, including the circumstance that a similar inference is, in this action, sought to be drawn in four other cases.   My credulity would, I think, be stretched beyond all reasonable limits were I asked to infer that D five separate grants of sheep rights were made by the defendants' predecessors in title between June, 1920, when the Coote sale took place, and October, 1959, when one of the defendants first bought part of Martin Down, all of which have since been lost and of which nothing is known.   In any case, taking Mr. Densham's Coote land in isolation, the discontinuous nature of the enjoyment of sheep rights in respect of this land is, in my judgment, fatal to any claim E under the doctrine of lost modern grant.

Fourthly, Mr. Densham cannot, in my judgment, successfully claim sheep rights in respect of his Street land or his Glebe land at common law or under lost modern grant (a) because of the discontinuous character of the enjoyment of any such rights in respect of these lands, (b) because no ancient enjoyment is proved in respect of the Glebe land, (c) because the evidence does not establish F whether any enjoyment there was in respect of Street lands before 1925 was in respect of the freehold estate in the land or of a customary right annexed to periodic copyhold interests in the land, (d) because the evidence does not establish in respect of what land the Streets grazed the Down or how many sheep, if any, they ran on the Down in respect of Mr. Densham's Street land, and (e) because Mr. Densham's own grazing on the Down has been quantitatively less than G the rights he asserts and less than the rights he can establish in respect of his Coote land, and consequently no part of it is clearly referable to his Street land or his Glebe land.

Finally, the enjoyment proved in respect of Mr. Densham's Coote land did not at any time exceed three hundred, and could not, in any event, support a prescriptive claim to as many as 448 sheep rights appertaining to that land.   H

[HIS LORDSHIP turned to consider the claims of Mrs. Turner, Mr. Singleton, Mr. Baker and Mr. Frampton, and decided that their claims to prescriptive title to sheep rights failed.   HIS LORDSHIP continued:] I will recapitulate the effect of this part of my judgment.   I hold that the plaintiffs, other than Mr. White and Mr. Singleton, are entitled to the following sheep rights on the Down under express grants contained in conveyances made to purchasers at the Coote I sale: Mr. Densham, 448; Mrs. Turner, 117; Mr. Baker, 240, and Mr. Frampton, 141.   I hold that Mr. White is entitled to no sheep rights for the reasons given in my judgment delivered on the preliminary point, and I hold that, save as aforesaid, the other plaintiffs' claims to sheep rights fail on the grounds, first, that no such passed in respect of any Coote land under the Conveyancing Act, 1881, s. 6, and, secondly, that the circumstances as established by the evidence do not support claims by any of the plaintiffs to sheep rights in respect of any Coote land, Street land or Glebe land under any form of prescription.

A   As an incident of their sheep rights the plaintiffs claim (i) a right to draw water from a well on the Down situate at a point marked Z on the statement of claim plan, (ii) a right to place troughs on the Down for the purpose of watering their sheep there, (iii) a right to cart water to those troughs, (iv) a right to obtain access with vehicles or otherwise to their sheep on the Down and to the well and the troughs, and (v) for all or any of these purposes to use the tracks coloured

B blue and green on the statement of claim plan.

The plaintiffs claim these incidental rights under the doctrine of implied grants discussed in *Pwllbach Colliery Co., Ltd.* v. *Woodman* (34), per LORD PARKER OF WADDINGTON. This is, that where the right claimed is necessary for the enjoyment of some other right expressly granted a grant of the former right will be implied. LORD PARKER gives as an example an express grant of a right to

C draw water from a spring which necessarily involves the right of going to the spring for the purpose. Necessity, for this purpose, means reasonable necessity (*Jones* v. *Pritchard* (35)). The test must be whether the alleged ancillary right is reasonably necessary for the reasonable enjoyment of the principal or primary right. Unless it is so, no basis for implying a grant of the ancillary right exists.

The facts relating to the well are these. It has existed for probably a hundred

D years or thereabouts at least. It must, I think, have been dug for use by persons needing water on the Down, that is to say, primarily, at any rate, to facilitate watering livestock on the Down. It was in use during the first two decades of this century, but by the year 1920 had fallen out of use and was covered with planks or timbers. In about 1925 it was restored to use, when a windlass was installed for drawing water, and it was used for watering sheep from that time

E until some time during the second world war, when it again fell into disuse. No use has been made of its since then. When this well was in use some, but not all, owners of sheep on the Down used it as a source of water for their sheep. They would draw water from the well, fill troughs placed on the Down near to the well. Other owners of sheep on the Down have been accustomed to water their flocks, when on the Down, with water carted from Martin village and put into

F troughs on the Down near the mouth of one or other of the public lanes leading from the village to the Down. All owners of sheep running on the Down have been accustomed to water their sheep in one or other of these ways. No water is naturally available on the Down.

None of the plaintiffs has attempted to establish a prescriptive right to take water from the well. No such right is pleaded.

G   Having regard to the considerable period during which the evidence establishes that no use was made of the well, notwithstanding that sheep were being run on the Down, and to the fact that, when sheep were run on the Down, not all the owners of sheep on the Down used the well, I think that it is clearly impossible to say that the use of the well is necessary for the enjoyment by the plaintiffs of their sheep rights. It would doubtless be convenient for some of them, but

H this is an insufficient ground for implying a grant.

I think, therefore, that the claim in respect of the well fails.

A well-known Dorset sheep breeder called by the defendants gave evidence to the effect that sheep can be grazed on a down where no water is available without being watered during the day. His custom is to put his sheep out on a Dorset down during the summer months at 5 a.m., and he says that they get

I sufficient moisture from the dew on the grass. He expressed the opinion—although he could not say this from direct knowledge—that this was a common practice among Dorset breeders. On the other hand I had evidence from an agricultural consultant, who is also a practical farmer with a large flock of ewes of his own, that sheep in normal circumstances will drink about three times a day and require six to seven litres of water a day, and that without water they

(34) [1914-15] All E.R. Rep. at p. 130; [1915] A.C. at p. 646.
(35) [1908-10] All E.R. Rep. 80 at p. 84; [1908] 1 Ch. 630 at p. 639.

do not survive. The evidence of the numerous witnesses who have been concerned with sheep on Martin Down has been unanimous that the sheep on the Down have been watered and that this is necessary for the welfare of the sheep. I should hardly suppose that the farmers of Martin would have incurred the trouble and expense of drawing and carting water unless they thought this necessary. I reach the conclusion that if, in 1920, anyone concerned with Martin Down had been asked whether sheep grazing there needed to be watered he would have said " Yes ", and that the same would be so today. The object being to discover the presumed intention of the parties to the conveyances in 1920, the earliest date seems to me to be the relevant one. In these circumstances I find that the evidence establishes that in 1920 the watering of sheep grazing Martin Down was regarded as being, and was in fact, necessary for the reasonable enjoyment of the right to graze the Down and, if this be of any significance, I find that the same remains so at the present time.

In my judgment, therefore, the plaintiffs who have established that they have sheep rights on the Down are entitled, as an ancillary right under an implied grant, to water their sheep on the Down be means of suitably located troughs supplied by carted water. I do not think that, as was suggested in argument, this would be a right of too indefinite a kind to be capable of being the subject of a valid grant. In practice these troughs have been situated on the Down near to the well or within about fifty to one hundred yards of the mouth of one or other of the lanes leading on to the Down. The graziers' right must, I think, be to put troughs wherever it is reasonably necessary to do so for the purpose of properly watering the sheep without encroaching on the Down further than is necessary for this purpose. The effect of this will be that the troughs must be located where they can be reached without an unreasonable departure from public or other rights of way or within a reasonable distance of the mouth of one or other of the lanes or of any other necessary access to the Down that any owner of the troughs may have.

Mr. Sparrow for the defendants contended that it could not be necessary for those plaintiffs who are entitled to sheep rights and have land adjoining the Down to have troughs on the Down, because they could instal watering facilities on their own land which would be available to sheep on the Down. I do not accept this argument. It seems to me to place an unreasonable fetter on such plaintiffs' use of their own land. For instance, land where sheep are watered could not be cultivated. Moreover, the right to graze on the Down is a right exercisable anywhere on the Down. Watering facilities at one point on the edge of the Down would be unlikely to be of much, if any, value, when sheep were grazing on a remote part of the Down. Anyone having a right of watering sheep on the Down must have the right of carting water to his trough, provided that in so doing he does not encroach on the Down, or depart from any public or private rights of way available to him more than is necessary for this purpose.

Anyone having a right to depasture sheep on the Down must also incidentally be entitled to go on to the Down, either himself or by his servants or agents—for instance, by his shepherd—to do anything necessary for the proper care and management of his sheep; but this does not mean that an owner of sheep rights can drive anywhere on the Down in a vehicle. There may be occasions when it will be necessary to take a vehicle on to the Down, not on any right of way, for the purpose of doing something necessary in connexion with sheep on the Down; but where the use of a vehicle would not be necessary for purposes connected with the welfare of the sheep and would be merely a convenience for someone in the vehicle, such use would not, in my judgment, be permissible.

[HIS LORDSHIP then dealt with claims to public rights of way and reviewed the physical characteristics of the land and the evidence. On this aspect of the case HIS LORDSHIP held as follows:] (i) Public rights of way with or without vehicles or beasts exist on the following tracks: (a) from the mouth of Sillens

A   Lane to the Blagdon Gap (Q to R on the statement of claim plan); (b) from the
mouth of Sillens Lane to point G on the Blandford-Salisbury road (Q to L to H
to G on the plan); and (c) from the mouth of Sillens Lane to the Pentridge Gap
(Q to L to K on the plan); (ii) a public right of way on foot only exists along
the Postman's Walk (M to J on the plan); (iii) a bridle way exists from the
mouth of Small End Lane to point X (W to V to X on the plan), and from

B   Thornhill Corner to point A (that is, L to M to D to B to A on the plan); but
that no other public rights of way exist over any of the tracks indicated on the
statement of claim plan in blue, green or brown. I say nothing about private
rights of way over any of these tracks. No such private rights are in issue in
this action.

[HIS LORDSHIP turned to the counterclaim which made claims in trespass

C   with which HIS LORDSHIP dealt under six heads. The last of these heads related
to allegations concerning a gap in a hedge at the boundary of Mr. Singleton's
land. HIS LORDSHIP said in regard to this counterclaim:] Finally the defendants
complain that Mr. Singleton has made an opening in the hedge bordering the
Down at its north-east corner between the points marked A and C on the statement of claim plan and has put a gate there. One issue here is whether the hedge

D   in question belongs to the defendants or to Mr. Singleton. I find as a fact that
the gap in this hedge was not made by Mr. Singleton or by anyone acting for
him, or by his authority: it already existed when he acquired his farm in 1959.
After Mr. Singleton became the owner of the farm his son-in-law, Mr. Atter,
who actually farmed and still farms this land, installed a gate in the gap. The
level of the land on the farm side of the hedge is some three feet lower than the

E   level of the Down on the other side of this hedge. The level of the Down at this
point is slightly higher than the level of the ground where the hedge stands.
Mr. Atter said that a ditch exists along the hedge on the Down side, but this
was denied by another witness. I find that there is no ditch or depression of
any significance in this position. Mr. Roe, a director of the defendant company,
asserted that at one time Mr. Atter asked his permission to trim this hedge. I

F   think that Mr. Atter did mention his intention to trim the hedge to Mr. Roe in a
neighbourly way, but he did not, I think, ask permission. The hedge has been
fenced with wire on each side at some time or other. The gate is aligned with that
side of the hedge which is remote from the Down. No assistance is obtainable
from any documents of title.

In my view the solution to the problem of the ownership of this hedge must be

G   found in the presumption which arises, in my judgment, where one finds a
fenced close adjoining a piece of waste land. In such circumstances in the
absence of evidence to the contrary the fence should, I think, be presumed to
belong to the owner of the close. On this ground I reach the conclusion that the
hedge in question belongs to Mr. Singleton. From this, as well as from the
fact that Mr. Singleton did not make the gap, it follows that this claim by the

H   defendants fails.

Order accordingly.

Solicitors: *Stafford Clark & Co.* (for the plaintiffs); *Shaen, Roscoe & Bracewell,*
agents for *R. S. Hawkins & Co.*, Poole (for the defendants).

[*Reported by* JENIFER SANDELL, *Barrister-at-Law.*]

NOTE.

POPPERWELL v. COCKERTON.

[QUEEN'S BENCH DIVISION (Lord Parker, C.J., Diplock, L.J., and Ashworth, J.), February 13, 1968.]

Road Traffic—Excessive speed—Dual-purpose vehicle—Van with transverse seats and with windows fitted on each side—Side windows covered by painted panels of wood screwed into windows—Whether van goods vehicle or dual-purpose vehicle—Road Traffic Act, 1960 (8 & 9 Eliz. 2 c. 16), Sch. 1, para. 14 (2) (b) (ii), as substituted by Motor Vehicles (Variation of Speed Limits) Regulations, 1962 (S.I. 1962 No. 204), reg. 3.

[**Editorial Note.** As from Oct. 27, 1967, Sch. 1 to the Road Traffic Act, 1960, as substituted and amended, was repealed by the Road Traffic Regulation Act 1967 s. 110 (1), s. 113 (2) and Sch. 7, Part 1, and is replaced by Sch. 5 to that Act.

As to speed limits for dual-purpose vehicles, see 33 HALSBURY'S LAWS (3rd Edn.) 499, 500, para. 853; and for cases on the subject, see 45 DIGEST (Repl.) 32, 33, *107-114*.

For the Road Traffic Act, 1960, Sch. 1, as substituted and amended, see SUPPLEMENT to 40 HALSBURY'S STATUTES (2nd Edn.) title " Street Traffic ", para. 1073.]

Case Stated.

This was a Case Stated by justices for the county of Cambridgeshire and Isle of Ely in respect of their adjudication as a magistrates' court sitting at Linton on Mar. 15, 1967.

On Jan. 18, 1967, an information was preferred by the appellant, Malcolm Robert Popperwell, against the respondent, David Malcolm Cockerton, that on Dec. 4, 1966, he unlawfully drove a certain motor vehicle to wit, a motor van, index number 9645 RK on the London to Newmarket road at a speed greater than forty miles per hour, the speed specified in Sch. 1 to the Road Traffic Act, 1960, as the maximum speed in relation to a vehicle of that class or description, contrary to s. 4 and s. 24 of the Road Traffic Act, 1960.

The following were among the facts found. The motor van was an Austin mini van index number 9645 RK. The vehicle was fitted with a rigid roof and had seats fitted, the seats being obviously home made. The seats were transverse and fitted more than one-third of the distance between the rearmost part of the steering wheel and the rearmost part of the floor of the vehicle (cf., Road Traffic Act, 1960, Sch. 1, para. 14 (2) (b) (i), (c)). The findings in regard to the cushioning and attachment of the seats were that, though home-made seats, they were such as to satisfy para. 14 (2) (b) (i) of the Act of 1960. Glass windows were fitted to the sides of the van of an area in excess of two square feet on each side (cf., para. 14 (2) (b) (ii)). Fitted over the off-side side window was a panel completely covering the window. It was secured to the bodywork of the van by screws and was sprayed in the same coloured green paint as the vehicle itself. The near-side panel was not fitted but lay in the van, thus revealing the type of side windows fitted. The rear windows were as fitted by the manufacturers and in excess of 120 square inches. On the day in question the respondent was, according to a speed check made by a police motor cyclist, driving the mini van on the road at a speed varying between sixty-four and sixty-seven miles per hour. The respondent stated, as found in the Case Stated, that he had realised that additional purchase tax was payable by reason of the van becoming a dual-purpose vehicle, and that he had notified the Commissioners of Customs and Excise by letter dated Nov. 28, 1966, and was paying the duty.

A   It was contended by the appellant before the justices (a) that the mini van was travelling in excess of forty miles per hour on the road on that day and that it was then driven by the respondent; and (b) that the respondent's vehicle could not be regarded as a dual-purpose vehicle in accordance with para. 14 of Sch. 1 to the Road Traffic Act, 1960, in that—(i) the vehicle was not permanently fitted with at least one row of transverse seats, because the seat fittings were
B   very loose and inadequate and were therefore not permanent; and (ii) if, on Dec. 4, 1966, the side windows were totally covered by the panels, the vehicle was not lit on each side by windows of glass of an area or aggregate area of not less than two square feet.   Before the justices the respondent conceded that he was driving his vehicle in excess of forty miles per hour on the day and road in question; he contended that the conversion was complete before Dec. 4, 1966,
C   and that, despite minor faults to the seats, they were nevertheless sufficiently permanent; that the requirements of para. 14 (2) (*b*) (ii) of Sch. 1 to the Act of 1960 were satisfied as windows were fitted; that the fact that panels were fitted over them which totally obscured them did not alter the position; and that the vehicle was a dual-purpose vehicle.

The justices found—(a) that the respondent was driving his vehicle in excess
D   of forty miles per hour on the day and road in question; (b) that at the time the vehicle had been converted by the addition of side windows and rear seats and the two side windows were totally obscured by panels; (c) that despite the looseness and inadequacy of the seat fittings they could be properly described as permanent; that para. 14 (2) (*b*) (ii) was satisfied, and that on Dec. 4, 1966, the vehicle was a dual-purpose vehicle and lawfully driven at a speed greater than forty miles
E   per hour.   Accordingly they dismissed the information.   The appellant now appealed.

D. *Macrae* for the appellant.
J. D. *Alliott* for the respondent.

F   **LORD PARKER, C.J.:** The sole question here is whether the respondent's vehicle which he was so driving was a goods vehicle or a dual-purpose vehicle. If it was a goods vehicle, he was going more than forty miles an hour admittedly; if it was a dual-purpose vehicle, he was not restricted to that speed at all.

Schedule 1 to the Road Traffic Act, 1960, deals with dual-purpose vehicles. Paragraph 14 (1) of that schedule, as substituted by the Motor Vehicles (Variation
G   of Speed Limit) Regulations, 1962 (1), reg. 3, provides that:

" In this Schedule ' dual-purpose vehicle ' means a vehicle constructed or adapted for the carriage both of passengers and of goods or burden of any description being a vehicle of which the unladen weight does not exceed two tons and which . . . (*a*) satisfies the conditions as to construction specified in the next following sub-paragraph . . ."

H   The next following sub-paragraph provides:

" (2) The conditions as to construction referred to in the foregoing sub-paragraph are the following:—(*a*) the vehicle must be permanently fitted with a rigid roof, with or without a sliding panel; (*b*) the area of the vehicle to the rear of the driver's seat must—(i) be permanently fitted with at least
I   one row of transverse seats . . ."

The justices have found that this was a vehicle whose unladen weight did not exceed two tons and that it had such a rigid roof; they have also found that there were transverse seats; and there is no appeal against that finding. Sub-paragraph (2) (*b*) of para. 14 then continues:

---

(1) S.I. 1962 No. 204.

A

". . . for two or more passengers and those seats must be properly sprung
or cushioned and provided with upholstered backrests, attached either to
the seats or to a side or the floor of the vehicle, and (ii) be lit on each side
and at the rear by a window or windows of glass or other transparent material
having an area or aggregate area of not less than two square feet on each
side and not less than 120 inches at the rear."

B

The position in regard to that is that the justices found that the respondent
purchased this van in October, 1966, and that in November, 1966, that is in
the month before that which contained the day to which this charge relates,
he had the seats fitted and in addition had windows fitted on each side, and
windows which fitted the conditions as to construction laid down in para. 14
(2) (*b*) (ii).   The point is that, on the day to which the charge relates the respondent, though the evidence is not quite clear, had at least one, if not both, of
those windows on the near and off-side covered by panels of wood screwed into
the windows so as to obscure them entirely, and those panels were painted over
with the same colour as the outside of the van.   The question for the justices
was whether the presence of those panels affected the question whether this was
a dual-purpose vehicle.   The justices were of opinion that the provisions of
para. 14 of Sch. 1 were satisfied if windows were fitted, and the fact that panels
were fitted over them which totally obscured them did not alter this position.
In my judgment, the justices came to a correct decision.   It is true that, on the
day in question, there may not have been light coming into the area behind the
driver's seat, but these conditions are conditions dealing with construction or
adaptation.   As originally constructed, this was a goods vehicle; as adapted,
that is to say by alteration of construction, it became a dual-purpose vehicle.
The fact that these panels were from time to time put up does not, as it seems to
me, in any way alter the construction of the vehicle as it had been altered in
November, 1966, when these windows were put in.

C

D

E

I agree with the justices and would dismiss the appeal.

DIPLOCK, L.J.: I agree.

F

ASHWORTH, J.: I agree.

Appeal dismissed.

Solicitors: *Waterhouse & Co.*, agents for *Few & Kester*, Cambridge (for the
appellant); *Vizard, Oldham, Crowder & Cash* (for the respondent).

G

[*Reported by* N. P. METCALFE, ESQ., *Barrister-at-Law.*]

A

CARFAX WASTE PAPER CO., LTD. *v.* MINISTER OF LABOUR.

[QUEEN'S BENCH DIVISION (Lord Parker, C.J., Diplock, L.J., and Ashworth, J.), February 12, 13, 14, 1968.]

B
Selective Employment Tax—Premium—Waste paper dealers—Activities con-sisted in collecting, cleaning, sorting and separating waste paper, before sale to paper and board mills—Whether activity was part of the manufacture of waste paper—Whether manufacturing—Whether within heading 481 or 499.2 of the Standard Industrial Classification, having regard to heading 832.6, which included dealers in waste paper—Selective Employment Payments Act 1966 (c. 32) s. 1 (2) (a), s. 10 (5).

C
The appellants claimed that the business activities of their establishment satisfied the requirements of s. 1 (2)* of the Selective Employment Payments Act 1966 for entitlement to premium. For this purpose their activities had to fall within Ord. III to Ord. XVI of the Standard Industrial Classifi-cation (viz., within minimum list headings 211-499). The appellants' activities consisted in collecting, cleaning and sorting waste paper and
D separating from it matter deleterious to the manufacture of paper and board. They sold their product to paper mills and board mills for manufacturing purposes. The Industrial Tribunal found that the mills used raw material for their manufacture, one type of raw material being sorted waste paper, but that unsorted waste paper was not such a raw material; and that, accordingly, the appellants' activities were not a part of the process of manufacturing paper or board, and thus did not fall within minimum list
E heading 481† of the Standard Industrial Classification (viz., " Paper or board "). The tribunal further held that the appellants' activities were not within heading 499.2‡ (viz., miscellaneous manufacturing industries), having regard to heading 832.6§ (" Dealing in other industrial materials . . . dealers in waste paper "), as the function of separating and sorting
F was not that of manufacturing, but was one of making existing material available.

Held: (i) the appellants' activities were not those of manufacturing paper or board, but were preliminary thereto, and the court would not interfere with the tribunal's finding that the appellants' activities were not manufacturing activities (see p. 1044, letters D, E and F, p. 1046, letter D,
G and p. 1047, letters C and I, post); moreover it was permissible, in accordance with s. 10 (5)‖ of the Act of 1966, to have regard to minimum list heading 832.6 and, as the appellants' activities were those of waste paper dealers within that heading, any doubt whether headings 481 or 499 extended to the appellants' activities should be resolved against their being within headings 481 or 499 (see p. 1046, letter I, to p. 1047, letter A, and p. 1047, letters
H F and I, post).

Lord Advocate v. *Reliant Tool Co.* (ante p. 162) distinguished.

Samuel McCausland, Ltd. v. *Ministry of Commerce* ([1956] N.I. 36) considered and not applied.

Appeal dismissed.

I
[As to selective employment tax, see SUPPLEMENT to 33 HALSBURY'S LAWS (3rd Edn.) para. 479A.

For the Selective Employment Payments Act 1966 s. 1 (2), s. 10 (5), see 46 HALSBURY'S STATUTES (2nd Edn.) 167, 184.]

---

* Section 1 (2), so far as material, is set out at p. 1042, letter H, post.
† Minimum list heading 481 is set out at p. 1043, letter H, post.
‡ Minimum list heading 499.2 is set out at p. 1045, letter B, post.
§ Minimum list heading 832.6 is set out at p. 1046, letter H, post. This heading is not in Ords. III to XVI, but in a subsequent order.
‖ Section 10 (5), so far as material, is set out at p. 1046, letter F, post.

Cases referred to:

A

Kaye (*Dewsbury Revenue Officer*) v. *Dewsbury Assessment Committee and Burrows*, [1931] All E.R. Rep. 242; [1931] A.C. 446; 100 L.J.K.B. 271; 145 L.T. 73; 95 J.P. 115; 38 Digest (Repl.) 523, *287*.

Lord Advocate v. *Reliant Tool Co.*, ante p. 162; [1968] 1 W.L.R. 205.

McCausland, Ltd. (*Samuel*) v. *Ministry of Commerce*, [1956] N.I. 36.

B

Appeal.

This was an appeal by the appellants, Carfax Waste Paper Co., Ltd., from a decision of the Industrial Tribunal dated Mar. 20, 1967, holding that the appellants had not been engaged in manufacture, either in a preliminary process of manufacturing within minimum list heading 481 of the Standard Industrial Classification, or in any form of manufacture such as might fall within heading 499.2. The tribunal held that the appellants did not qualify, therefore, for repayment of tax and payment of premium in respect of employees at their establishment at Summerstown, S.W. 17, under s. 1 of the Selective Employment Payments Act 1966. The tribunal further found that the appellants' activities fell within heading 832.6. By their notice of appeal, dated Apr. 20, 1967, the appellants stated their grounds to be that they were engaged by way of business wholly or partly in activities falling within headings 481, or 483, or 499.2 or otherwise within Ord. III to Ord. XVI of the classification. By supplementary notice dated May 29, 1967, the appellants stated additional grounds—(i) that the decision was wrong in law in that the tribunal misdirected themselves as to the proper construction of headings 481, 483, 499.2 and 832.6; (ii) that there was no evidence before the tribunal to support their finding that the appellants' activities were within heading 832.6; (iii) that on the evidence and on the construction of headings 481, 483, 499.2 and 832.6 the activities carried on by the appellants at their establishment were activities falling under headings 481, 483 or 499.2, and that the activities satisfied the requirements of s. 1 (2) (*a*) and (*b*) of the Act of 1966. The facts are set out in the judgment of LORD PARKER, C.J.

C

D

E

The authorities and cases noted below* were cited during the argument in addition to those referred to in the judgment of LORD PARKER, C.J.

F

F. B. Purchas, Q.C., and *J. R. V. McAulay* for the appellants.
Sir Dingle Foot, Q.C., and *G. Slynn* for the Minister of Labour.

LORD PARKER, C.J.: This is an appeal by the appellants, Carfax Waste Paper Co., Ltd., from a decision of the Industrial Tribunal given on Mar. 20, 1967, whereby the tribunal held that the appellants did not qualify for repayment of tax and premium in respect of their establishment at Summerstown, S.W.17, under s. 1 of the Selective Employment Payments Act 1966. Section 1 of that Act, as is well known, provides for the repayment of tax paid in respect of an employee and attracts bonus or premium in addition if certain conditions are satisfied. Subsection (2) of that section provides, so far as is material, that:

G

E

"... [this] section applies to any employment in, or carried out from, an establishment where—(*a*) the establishment is engaged by way of business wholly or partly in—(i) activities falling under any of the minimum list headings shown in Ord. III to Ord. XVI of the Standard Industrial Classification ..."

There is a further condition which has to be satisfied before the section operates which concerns the number of persons employed in the establishment and how they are employed. No point, however, arises in this case in regard to that

---

* SHORTER OXFORD DICTIONARY (A—M), definition of " dealer "; " manufacture "; 46 HALSBURY'S STATUTES (2nd Edn.) 167, 184; *Warrington* v. *Furbor*, [1803-13] All E.R. Rep. 292; *McNichol* v. *Pinch*, [1906] 2 K.B. 352; *Hudson Bay Co.* v. *Thompson* (*Valuation Officer*), [1959] 3 All E.R. 150; [1960] A.C. 926; *Ministry of Labour* v. *Genner Iron & Steel Co.* (*Wollescote*), *Ltd.*, [1967] 3 All E.R. 278.

A condition which it is admitted is fully satisfied. The sole question here, accordingly, is whether, contrary to what the tribunal held, the establishment at Summerstown was engaged by way of business wholly or partly in activities falling under any of the minimum list headings shown in Ord. III to Ord. XVI.

The facts are as follows. At this establishment at Summerstown the appellants collect quantities of waste paper. Some of it comes from dealers in waste paper,

B and the remainder from large companies in industry and commerce, such as banks, insurance companies, local authorities, schools and the like. In 1966 some eight thousand tons of waste paper went into this establishment, and there came out from the establishment 7,600 tons of paper which had been cleaned and sorted in the manner which I will shortly describe. When the waste paper arrives at the premises, some of it is in a state in which it can be sent on its

C way without any sorting at all. For the rest, however, it has to be cleaned and sorted through a dusting machine in the first instance, which takes the form of a large revolving drum, and this extracts as it revolves what are called contraries, such things as parts of pens, bits of tin, silver paper and oddments of that sort. After it has gone through the revolving drum, the paper is conveyed along a conveyor belt when hand sorting takes place. The hand sorting will

D extract matters which will interfere with the manufacture of paper and board, such as latex, glue bindings used on cheque books, paper of what is called wet strength, such as tissues, paper with small coloured plastic spots, plastic inks, laminated papers, and in particular bitumen papers which are deleterious in the process of the manufacture of paper and board. In addition large sheets of paper have to be cut down in size and paper separated from bindings by

E tearing out. To assist in the manual sorting of this waste paper, tests have to be applied in certain instances to see what is the nature of the paper or its constituents; acid tests and burning tests are employed. Ultimately the paper so sorted out is baled up into grades, some thirty-two grades, which will go ultimately to paper mills, and some twelve grades which go to board mills, and those bales in their grades are ultimately sold to the paper mills and board mills. It is

F found by the tribunal that although prices have now gone down, in 1962 the price obtained for a bale of clean and sorted paper was about twice the average price of the waste paper bought.

The appellants before the tribunal and before this court sought to bring themselves within either minimum list heading 481 or alternatively minimum list heading 499.2 in the Standard Industrial Classification. Turning first to

G minimum list heading 481, which comes under Ord. XV, Paper, Printing and Publishing, it is headed " Paper and board ", and then the print underneath that, which it is agreed is purely illustrative, provides:

> " Manufacturing all types of paper and board including newsprint, printing and writing paper, wrapping paper, cigarette paper, cardboard and building board; and paper coating. Paper sensitizing is excluded

H and classified in heading 351."

It is, of course, clear, and indeed it is conceded that the activity carried on at Summerstown is not the activity of manufacturing types of paper and board as set out in that minimum list heading. The actual manufacture of the paper or board is done by the paper mills or board mills, to whom the appellants sell these bales. That, however, is not the end of the matter, because an activity may

I fall within the activity of manufacture in the sense of forming an integral part of that activity. Accordingly, the question which one has to ask oneself is whether the activity carried on at Summerstown was a part of the activity of manufacturing paper and board, or whether it was merely an activity carried out preliminary to or ancillary to or in connexion with the activity of the manufacturing process. This case was determined by the tribunal before the case to which the court has been referred, of the *Lord Advocate* v. *Reliant Tool Co.* (1), a decision of the House of

(1) Ante p. 162.

Lords given on Dec. 19, 1967. Notwithstanding that the present case was heard A
before the decision of the House of Lords, it is, I think, clear that the tribunal
did pose to themselves the correct question. In the transcript of the decision
they say:

> " We have no doubt that the [appellants do] not [themselves] manufacture
> paper or board, so as to fall under No. 481. [They] can only fall under that
> if [they are] doing, in a place other than that in which paper or board is   B
> manufactured, some preliminary process of the manufacture."

That is, in my judgment, the correct approach to the matter. Then they conclude
by saying:

> " What the paper or board mills use in the manufacturing process is fibrous
> raw materials. Sorted waste paper is such a material; unsorted waste paper,   C
> in the sense that it has in it elements which cannot be used in the manufacture
> of paper or board, is not."

That is in my judgment a finding of fact which not only accords with common
sense, but it is one arrived at on abundant evidence, and cannot be challenged in
this court unless it can be said that, in arriving at that decision, the tribunal
have in some way misdirected themselves. The difficulty in this case is to deter- D
mine, and it is a question of fact, when the process of manufacture begins. It
ends, of course, with the finished article. It begins in general, I would have
thought, with some working on the raw material. Prima facie anything that takes
place before by way of obtaining the raw material is something preliminary
to or ancillary to the process of manufacture and is not part of it. I say " in
general " because there may be special cases, of which my in judgment the House E
of Lords' case was one, where something takes place before steps are taken to
work on the raw material which can properly be said to be part of a manufacturing
process, the activity in question in the House of Lords' case being the designing
of machine tools, which was of course preliminary to the actual making of the
tools, but which had been held by the tribunal to be part of the manufacturing
process. There are no such special features in the present case.   F

Counsel for the appellants, however, has sought to urge that the tribunal's
finding in this regard is invalidated by certain alleged misdirections. He says in
the first instance that the tribunal's approach to the matter, as is seen from the
passage in their decision (2), has been to decide under which of three headings the
activity in question most properly can be classified. He urges that the minimum
list headings may not be mutually exclusive, and, accordingly, that the approach G
of the tribunal had been wrong. I find it unnecessary to decide in the present case
whether these minimum list headings are mutually exclusive, but even if they are
not, I cannot see for myself that the tribunal's error, if it be an error, in that
approach can in any way invalidate the finding to which I have referred.

Counsel for the appellants also says that the tribunal later on in their decision
have posed the question for themselves: were the appellants in regard to their   H
establishment at Summerstown manufacturers or dealers, the minimum list
heading covering dealers being minimum list heading 832.6? Again, I am far

---

(2) The tribunal's decision contained the following passage: " In deciding whether
the [appellants] in [their] activities satisfy the requirements of s. 1 (2) we are only
concerned with the minimum list heading under which they fall. If that is one within
Ord. III to Ord. XVI the other two conditions of s. 1 (2) are satisfied. There are three   I
headings to be considered. In saying three, we rule out [heading] 483. [Heading] 481
is ' Paper and board ', with detail beginning ' manufacturing all types of paper and
board '; [heading] 483 is ' Manufacture of paper and board not elsewhere specified '.
It would seem that there is no room for anything under [heading] 483 as [heading] 481
speaks of the manufacture of ' all ' types. But the detail of [heading] 483 shows that
it is dealing with the manufacture of things from paper and board, with the possible
exception of ' Wallpaper ', and we consider that, having regard to [heading] 481, [head-
ing] 483 must be read as if it reads ' Manufacture of paper and board goods not elsewhere
specified '. This fits in with detail No. 4 of it. Apart from heading 481, stated above,
the other two are 499.2 . . . and 832.6 . . ."

A from saying that was a misdirection at all, but even if it was, it cannot in my judgment invalidate their finding to which I have referred. Other points were made by counsel, but in my judgment I see no reason whatever to think that the finding to which I have referred, which accords with the evidence and with common sense, is in any way invalidated.

B The other minimum list heading relied on is, as I have said, minimum list heading No. 499.2. Minimum list heading 499 comes under Ord. XVI and is headed: "Miscellaneous manufacturing industries." 1. concerns Musical Instruments; 2. is headed " Other ", and there follows the words: " All other manufacturing industries not elsewhere specified."

C In advancing the argument in favour of the activity coming under minimum list heading 499, counsel for the appellants naturally relies very strongly on the finding made by the tribunal in regard to minimum list heading 481, because the tribunal there say, in the passage to which I have already referred, that while sorted waste is fibrous raw material, unsorted waste is not. The argument is that these appellants were carrying on at Summerstown an activity falling within, which merely means covered by or included in, the activity expressed as " All other manufacturing industries ", namely manufacturing fibrous raw material.

D In regard to that, the tribunal approached the matter as follows. They say:

> " Mere adaptation for sale does not itself show ' manufacture ' under this Act. That the [appellants have] produced waste more valuable, twice as valuable, as that which [they] bought does not show that [they have] manufactured anything. The real question is whether [they have] produced something which [they] did not buy, and something the production of which involves some manufacturing process. The only thing which can have been manufactured, as a preliminary process in the manufacture of paper or board, is fibrous raw material. It is our view that the [appellants] never made that. That was paper, which was in existence in the waste paper. To separate out the usable from the non-usable, or to divide the usable into groups for use for particular purposes, is not to create. The fibrous raw material, paper formerly manufactured, was always there. The [appellants] did not make it; [they] made it available."

The appellants seek to challenge that finding of fact by reference, in the first instance, to some of the cases decided under the Rating and Valuation (Apportionment) Act, 1928, and in particular *Kaye (Dewsbury Revenue Officer)* v. *Dewsbury Assessment Committee and Burrows* (3), one of the cases that were decided by the House of Lords. It was held in those cases that relief from rating could be obtained in regard to a hereditament which was a factory if the process carried on there was a process of adaptation for sale. Those words appeared in the definition of " factory " in the Factory and Workshop Act, 1901. In my judgment, the tribunal were right in saying that they could get no help from those cases, which were based on this definition of " factory " and the use of those express words: " adapting for sale of any article ". The word " manufacture ", it is to be observed, did not appear at all in the definition. Accordingly, the tribunal approached the matter asking themselves whether what took place in the establishment at Summerstown would come within the ordinary and natural meaning of the word " manufacture ". In my judgment, that was a correct approach.

I It is secondly urged that this court, quite apart from the decision in the rating cases, should say that what took place here was in the ordinary sense of the word manufacture, that something was worked up so that the resulting article was different in kind from the waste material with which the appellants started. In that connexion, the court was referred to a decision in Northern Ireland, the case of *Samuel McCausland, Ltd.* v. *Ministry of Commerce* (4). In that case, the court had to say whether what had occurred there was the manufacture of goods. What

---

(3) [1931] All E.R. Rep. 242 at p. 247; [1931] A.C. 446 at p. 454.
(4) [1956] N.I. 36.

had happened was that the company in question bought rye grass seed and pro- **A**
cessed it in the sense of drying the seed, passing it through sieves and mechanical
separators to remove foreign matter and seeds other than rye grass and defective
seeds, and sold the final refined commodity.   LORD MACDERMOTT, C.J., and
PORTER, L.J., held that there had been the manufacture of goods.   LORD
MACDERMOTT, C.J., said this (5):

> " One cannot, as it seems to me, decide this case merely by looking at the   **B**
> goods and giving them a physical description.   One must also consider how
> they came to be what they are and what the company has done to the crop
> in order to obtain the finished product.   The question is, of course, to a large
> extent one of degree, but coming to the best conclusion I can in the light of
> the considerations I have mentioned I am of the opinion that the com-
> pany is, according to the natural meaning of the words ' engaged in the   **C**
> manufacture of goods '."

With that PORTER, L.J., agreed, although, as it seems to me, he relied largely on
the rating cases to which I have referred.   BLACK, L.J., however, in a dissenting
judgment (6) held that no help was to be derived from the rating cases, and that
the question was whether what had happened in this case could in the ordinary
and popular sense be said to be the manufacture of goods.   He agreed with the   **D**
trial judge, CURRAN, J., that it could not.

In my judgment, no help is really to be derived from that case, a case in which
different judges held on the facts that what had taken place was not manufacture
in the ordinary sense of the word.   Here the tribunal have held to the contrary
It seems to me they were fully entitled to do so, and that there can be no grounds   **E**
whatever for challenging the validity of their finding.   Indeed, if I had to, I
would prefer the judgment of BLACK, L.J., and his reasoning to that of the other
two members of the court in the Northern Ireland case.

Finally I would, if necessary, myself rely very strongly on the wording of
minimum list heading 832.6.   Section 10 (5) of the Act provides, and I only read
the relevant words: **F**

> ". . . in determining the activities falling under any particular minimum
> list heading in the Standard Industrial Classification, regard shall be had to
> any express provision of any other such heading."

Accordingly, whether these headings are mutually conclusive or not, it is perfectly
proper to look at other minimum list headings.   When one does look at minimum
list heading 832, one finds that it is headed: " Dealing in Other Industrial   **G**
Materials and Machinery ", and having dealt with ores and metals, timber, hides,
skins and leather and other materials, para. 6 is headed: " Scrap and waste
materials."   Quite clearly the waste paper was scrap and waste material.   Then
there follows the words:

> " Dealers in scrap iron, scrap steel and non-ferrous scrap metals, including
> breaking, sorting, compressing, etc.;   dealers in textile waste, including rug   **H**
> shaking, breaking, and opening of cotton rags;   dealers in waste paper, rags,
> bones, old rope, used bottles, etc. (including marine stores)."

For my part I do not find it necessary to go to 832.6 at all, because I do not
think that the appellants have brought themselves within 481 or 499 looked at
in isolation;   but if I had to turn to heading 832.6, I would come to the conclusion that these appellants' activity falls fairly and squarely under that   **I**
heading.   It is true that the words " breaking ", " sorting " and the like are
only used in connexion with dealers in scrap iron and metal, but it has long been
recognised that the small printed words under the heading are merely illustrative,
and it seems to me quite clear that a man who sorts, grades, separates and the
like, waste material consisting of paper, does not cease thereby to be a dealer.
Accordingly, I would, if it were necessary, unhesitatingly come to the conclusion
that these appellants come within that minimum list heading, and that even

---

(5) [1956] N.I. at p. 43.   (6) [1956] N.I. at pp. 45-52.

A if the headings are not mutually exclusive, this would nevertheless reinforce the view I have taken that they do not come within 481 or 499. The tribunal finally end their decision with these words:

" We consider that the [appellants have] not been engaged in manufacture, either in a preliminary process of manufacture so as to fall under No. 481,
B or in the manufacture of anything, so as to fall under No. 499.2. [They are] we consider, [dealers] in waste paper; waste paper is the merchandise in which [they] deal, and [the fact] that [their] activities make what [they have] bought more valuable does not stop [them] being [dealers]. [Their] activities fall in our view under heading No. 832.6."

For my part I entirely agree with the tribunal's conclusion, and I would only add that as a matter of interest the appellants, until at any rate the passing of the
C Act of 1966, described themselves as " Waste Paper Merchants ". I would dismiss this appeal.

DIPLOCK, L.J.: I agree with the judgment which has been delivered by LORD PARKER, C.J., and in some respects more so. The entitlement to repayment of selective employment tax depends on what people on the premises are
D doing " by way of business ". This in my view makes it relevant to consider not only the physical acts performed on the premises, but the purpose with which they are done. It is also true of the Standard Industrial Classification, where the description of industries or services included in a heading sometimes refers to what is done, it sometimes refers also to who does it, for example, dealers, barristers, consulting engineers and the like. In construing minimum list headings in
E the Standard Industrial Classification which, as the introduction says, was prepared to promote uniformity and comparability in official statistics, one should, in my view, resolve any ambiguities in favour of avoiding overlap, between the industries or services described. The classification may not always have achieved its purpose, but if an activity falls plainly under one heading, and there is a choice between a wide and a narrower construction of another heading which on
F the wide construction is capable of including the activity described in the first heading, and on the narrower construction is not, one should resolve the ambiguity in favour of the narrower construction, and I think that that is what s. 10 (5) of the Selective Employment Payments Act 1966, enjoins us to do.

The ordinary and natural description of the activities of the appellants in this case is dealing in scrap and waste materials, and in particular the activity of
G " dealers in waste paper " in the descriptive words under heading 832.6. No one would in the ordinary way call their activities manufacturing paper and board. The physical acts done are those of collecting and sorting waste materials and separating them into categories in which they will be suitable for use as raw material in a manufacturing process. The purpose is to sell them to those who undertake the manufacturing process. In my view it would not have been open
H to the tribunal in law to hold that in this case the activities amounted to manufacturing paper and board. There may be cases in which the preparation of a raw material for another manufacturing process is itself a manufacturing process. That depends on the nature of the operations undertaken on the premises which constitute the establishment. That is very largely a question of fact for the tribunal. The tribunal here held that the operations which took place in the course
I of the sorting, and the only thing beyond sorting was apparently cutting up some rolls of paper and tearing off non-fibrous materials from other bits of paper, was not a manufacturing process in itself, as they were perfectly entitled to hold, and I agree that the appeal must be dismissed.

ASHWORTH, J.: I agree with both the judgments that have been delivered.
Appeal dismissed. Leave to appeal granted.

Solicitors: *Beddington, Hughes & Hobart* (for the appellants); *Solicitor, Ministry of Labour.* [*Reported by* N. P. METCALFE, ESQ., *Barrister-at-Law.*]

A

PRESTCOLD (CENTRAL), LTD. *v.* MINISTER OF LABOUR.

[QUEEN's BENCH DIVISION (Lord Parker, C.J., Ashworth and Willis, JJ.), February 20, 21, 1968.]

Selective Employment Tax—Premium—Refrigeration of plant—Appellants'
main business activity was to plan cooling installations for abattoirs, super-
markets, hospitals, etc., and to instal cooling equipment—Appellants manu-
factured the coolers, but obtained other components from other manufacturers—
Whether their main activity constituted manufacturing of refrigerators, etc.
within minimum list heading 339.3 and Ord. VI of the Standard Industrial
Classification—Whether appellants establishment satisfied Selective Employ-
ment Payments Act 1966 (c. 32) s. 1 (2) (a) (i).

Although the appellants did some manufacturing of coolers and refrigerators, and of low temperature cabinets, by far the greater part of their
business activities was a third activity, which consisted in providing cooling
rooms at abattoirs, supermarkets, hospitals and other places. They would
survey the site, design the unit, select the machinery, plan the installation,
supply the equipment and assemble and install it. Only the coolers were
actually made by the appellants, the other component parts being made
by manufacturers other than the appellants. The question whether the
appellants' business qualified under s. 1 (2) (a) (i) (b)* of the Selective Employment Payments Act 1966, for the repayment of tax paid and the payment
of premium was referred to the Industrial Tribunal, who dismissed the
appellants' claim. Their claim turned on whether the appellants' third
activity was within minimum list heading 339.3† of the Standard Industrial
Classification (and thus within Ords. III-XVI as required by s. 1 (2) (a) (i)
of the Act of 1966). Heading 500‡ (which was in Ord. XVII—"Construction")
included establishments specialising in sections of construction work such as
installing heating apparatus. On appeal,

Held: although assembly of parts could amount to manufacturing in
appropriate circumstances (see p. 1050, letter F, post), the appellants'
third activity was essentially assembly for installation as part of work of
construction (minimum list heading 500), not assembly for manufacture;
accordingly the appellants' third activity did not fall within Ords. III-XVI
of the classification and their establishment was not within s. 1 (2) of the
Selective Employment Payments Act 1966, with the consequence that the
appellants were not entitled to repayment of tax or payment of premiums
(see p. 1052, letters B, E, G and I, post).

Appeal dismissed.

[As to selective employment tax, see SUPPLEMENT to 33 HALSBURY'S LAWS
(3rd Edn.) para. 479A; see also p. 1041, ante.

For the Selective Employment Payments Act 1966, s. 1, see 46 HALSBURY'S
STATUTES (2nd Edn.) 167.]

Case referred to:

Sedgwick (*Camberwell Revenue Officer*) v. *Camberwell Assessment Ctee. and*
    Watney, Combe, Reid & Co., [1931] All E.R. Rep. 242; [1931] A.C.
    446; 100 L.J.K.B. 271; 145 L.T. 73; 95 J.P. 115; 38 Digest (Repl.)
    523, 288.

---

* Section 1, so far as material, reads: " (2) . . . this section applies to any employment
in, or carried out from, an establishment where—(*a*) the establishment is engaged by
way of business wholly or partly in—(i) activities falling under any of the minimum list
headings shown in Ord. III to Ord. XVI of the Standard Industrial Classification;
and (*b*) more than half of the employed persons employ d in . . . that establishment—
(1) are so employed wholly or mainly in connexion with such activities, . . ."

† Heading 339.3 is set out at p. 1050, letter G, post.

‡ Heading 500, so far as material, is set out at p. 1051, letter C, post.

Reversed. C.A. [1969] 1 All E.R. 69.

A   **Appeal.**

This was an appeal by the appellants, Prestcold (Central), Ltd., by notice dated Aug. 11, 1967, from a decision of the Industrial Tribunal given on July 17, 1967, dismissing the appellants' application. The appellants had applied by originating application in May, 1967, for determination of their claim to be an establishment satisfying the requirements of s. 1 (2) (*a*) and (*b*) of the Selective

B Employment Payments Act 1966 for registration as an establishment in respect of which premium was payable by virtue of s. 1, the establishment in question being the appellants' Amara works at Bromford Lane, Birmingham. The grounds of the appellants' appeal were—(i) that the tribunal misdirected themselves in finding that the appellants' activities could not be brought under any of the minimum list headings shown in Ord. III to Ord. XVI of the Standard Industrial

C Classification; (ii) that the tribunal failed to find and to hold that the appellants were engaged by way of business wholly or partly in activities falling under minimum list heading 339.3, alternatively 339.4, alternatively 474, alternatively 499.2*, and that more than half of the employed persons employed in any employment in, or carried out from, the appellants' establishment were so employed wholly or mainly in connexion with such activities, and were not so employed

D wholly or mainly in non-qualifying activities, and (iii) that the tribunal were wrong in law in holding that the appellants were not engaged in the activities of manufacturing refrigerators and refrigerating machinery.

The cases noted below† were cited during the argument in addition to that referred to in the judgment.

S. C. Silkin, Q.C., and *R. H. Tucker* for the appellants.

E   *G. Slynn* for the Minister of Labour.

LORD PARKER, C.J.: The evidence in regard to the activities carried on at that establishment is to be found partly in the decision itself, partly in the notes of evidence, and partly in an affidavit of a Mr. Dewsnap, a director of the appellants which has been put in with the leave of the court. It appears that at this

F establishment the appellants undoubtedly manufacture coolers and the brackets to suspend them from. In addition they manufacture a cooling blanket for human refrigeration as part of medical treatment. That undoubted manufacture however, is a very small part of their business, accounting for about 12½ per cent., with two men fully employed on it. In addition they make, and I say " make " to use a neutral word, on their premises certain refrigerating plant or refrigerators. The

G affidavit shows that in addition to the coolers, they make special low temperature units, for example, blood-bank refrigerators or low temperature cabinets, and also cabinets for simulating high altitude conditions likely to be found in the operation of the Anglo-French Concorde aircraft, and further plant environment cabinets to simulate plant growth conditions of air flow. Photographs of a blood-bank refrigerator and of the low temperature cabinet for the aircraft industry

H are to be found annexed to the Case. That type of equipment or article is " made " in the sense of being assembled in the works. The coolers incorporated in it are alone the manufacture of these appellants. For the rest they use parts made by associated companies and others, and they are assembled, for example, to produce the blood-bank refrigerator, and similarly with the other articles assembled on the premises.

I   The appellants' third activity, which is really the one on which this case depends, consists in making or providing cooling rooms at abattoirs, butchers' shops, supermarkets, banana storerooms, hospitals and canteens. What the appellants do is to go, let us say, to an abattoir which is either built or in the course of building, they survey the site, they design the unit according to the performance

---

* Heading 499.2 is set out at p. 1051, letter A, post.

† *Minister of Labour* v. *Genner Iron & Steel Co.* (*Wollescote*), *Ltd.*, [1967] 3 All E.R. 278; *Minister of Labour* v. *C. Maurice Co., Ltd.*, (1967), 111 Sol. Jo. 852; *Lord Advocate* v. *Reliant Tool Co.*, ante p. 162; *Carfax Waste Paper Co.* v. *Minister of Labour*, ante p. 1041.

and temperature required and the allied factors, they select the machinery **A**
according to size and type, they plan the installation details and they supply the
equipment. Then they assemble and fabricate the complete equipment, including
fitting together the several components, cutting, bending and flaring the piping,
securing it to bearers and framework individually fabricated to suit the site and
function, connect the piping with control gear and other plant and equipment,
make control circuits, start up, test and set the unit running at the desired **B**
temperature. Again the only part of that equipment that is actually made by
these appellants is the cooler; the other component parts are manufactured
elsewhere and are held in stock at the establishment or are specially obtained.
Finally, the actual electrical wiring and installation is carried out by others.

The tribunal dealt with the matter in this way. They relied on *Sedgwick*
(*Camberwell Revenue Officer*) v. *Camberwell Assessment Ctee. and Watney, Combe,* **C**
Reid & Co. (1), one of the de-rating cases, and from that case they were satisfied
that it was necessary to find that for an article to be manufactured it must undergo
some treatment which changes its quality or character, and they went on:

" In this case we hold that, except as to 12½ per cent. of their activities
[that is the manufacture of the coolers] what the [appellants] did was no **D**
more than assembling parts that were manufactured elsewhere by other
companies."

They also found that 102 employees altogether were employed at the establishment; forty-nine were employed on activities which would not qualify in any
event, and fifty-one others were employed directly on what the tribunal refer to
as the making and installing of refrigerators, that is the third activity to which I **E**
have referred.

In my judgment, the tribunal did misdirect themselves in saying that assembly
of parts could not amount to manufacture, and indeed before this court counsel
for the Minister has very frankly said that assembly may well be a part of manufacture, and he would concede that, for instance, the blood-bank refrigerator
could properly be said to have been manufactured by these appellants, despite **F**
the fact that the only part of it that they had physically made was the cooler,
and the rest consisted of assembling parts to produce the blood-bank refrigerator
shown in the photograph. In my judgment that is right, and that in so far as they
assemble forms of refrigerators on their premises, they can truly be said to be
manufacturing refrigerating machinery, and, therefore, come within minimum
list heading 339.3, which reads: " Manufacturing all types of refrigerators **G**
(including domestic) and refrigerating machinery."

However, pausing there, it is quite clear from the evidence which was put in
that, if one treated that activity as coming within the minimum list heading 339,
it would only add a further nine persons, which clearly is not sufficient to make
the establishment one which qualifies for the repayment of tax and premium.
The whole question is whether the appellants' third activity, the assembling of **H**
parts of refrigerating machinery in these abattoirs, butchers' shops, supermarkets
and the like, comes within minimum list heading 339.3. That as I conceive it
is the real point in this case. I should say that counsel for the appellants would,
in the alternative, rely on minimum list heading 349.3:

" Other Mechanical Engineering. Establishments manufacturing machinery parts not elsewhere specified, or undertaking general sub-contract or **I**
repair work, or whose products are of such a mixed character that they
cannot be allocated elsewhere in Ord. VI."

He tentatively also refers to minimum list heading 474, though I think he would
concede that he cannot bring himself within that; that is a minimum list heading
entitled " Shop and Office Fitting. Manufacturing office, shop, bank, bar and
hotel fittings, show cases, display and exhibition stands " and the like. Finally,

---

(1) [1931] All E.R. Rep. 242; [1931] A.C. 446.

A   if need be, he would rely on the sweeping up provision in minimum list heading
499.2: " All other manufacturing industries not elsewhere specified." I mention
those only because they have been put forward from time to time in the case, but
the real point is whether this third activity of the appellants comes within
minimum list heading 339.3.

The Minister says, that this third activity plainly comes within Ord. XVII,
B   dealing with construction, minimum list heading 500 of which is " Construction ",
and which, after dealing with "Erection and Repairing Buildings of all Types",
and civil engineering work generally, goes on:

" Establishments specialising in demolition work or in sections of construction work such as asphalting, electrical wiring, flooring, glazing, installing heating and ventilating apparatus, painting, plastering, plumbing,
C   roofing. The hiring of contractors' plant and scaffolding is included."

The tribunal made no finding whether the appellants' third activity came within
heading 500. In my judgment the third activity does not come within minimum
list heading 339.3, and does come fairly and squarely within minimum list heading 500. One has only to look at the photographs attached to the Case Stated
D   and compare, for instance, the photograph of the blood bank-refrigerator, which
as I have said is clearly an article of manufacture, with, for instance, two other
photographs which show, quite plainly to the layman, an installation of complicated machinery in a specially constructed room with special installation, pipes
and the like all installed in and attached to the structure. I do not think that
anyone looking at, for instance, the latter of these two other photographs would
E   say that it shows a manufacture; it shows an assembly of component parts
made by a number of different people picked out and chosen as suitable for the
place where the component parts were going to be installed, and then assembled—
in other words the process of manufacture had ended and what was being done
was part of a process of construction in a building. It is true that somebody
must have made walls, others did the installation and others did the wiring, but
F   the matter in my judgment must be looked at as a composite whole, and this
installation of machinery was all part and parcel of providing a cooling room,
and was part of construction.

Counsel for the appellants has put forward some very formidable arguments to
the contrary. He has said that it is quite illogical that, if assembly of component
parts in the appellants' own works is manufacture, the assembly of component
parts in somebody else's premises should not also be manufacture. The answer in
G   my judgment is that one has only to compare some of the photographs, to see
that what is being assembled is quite different in the two instances; in the first
instance there was an assembly as part of manufacture, and in the second instance
there was assembly as a part of installation. Then counsel refers to minimum list
heading 339.4, which is of some interest. That is dealing with space heating,
ventilating and air conditioning equipment, and goes on to refer to the manu-
H   facture of equipment for those purposes, " ventilating and air conditioning
systems and dust extraction systems, including heater batteries, unit heaters,
ventilators, hoods, cowls " and so on: and counsel points out that at the end of
that minimum list heading these words appear: " Establishments specialising in
the installation of equipment are also excluded and classified in heading 500."
I   As I have already indicated, in minimum list heading 500 the installation of
heating and ventilating apparatus is expressly included (2). Counsel for the appellants then refers to the minimum list heading with which we are concerned,
339.3, and points out that no such words of exclusion appear there. It is, of
course, a formidable argument if one were comparing two adjoining sections
or subsections of an Act of Parliament; but I feel quite unable to arrive at the
conclusion which he suggests in comparing the words in two adjoining minimum

(2) Heading 500 is in " Ord. XVII—Construction "; and thus is outside the orders
to which s. 1 (2) (*a*) (i) of the Act of 1966 refers.

list headings of this classification. I do not think that one can interpret this **A**
in the same way as an Act of Parliament, and that one really has to take a broad
view of the matter. It is not without interest that in minimum list heading 474
which was, as I have said, dealing with shop and office fittings, these words
appear: " Installation of these fittings is included when carried out by the
manufacturers ", in other words that is contemplating that installation will not
form part of manufacture unless the installation is carried out by the manufacturer. **B**

In my judgment, the true approach to this matter is to ask oneself whether
what is being done is in an ordinary sense an assembly for manufacture or whether
it is not in essence an assembly for installation as part of construction. In my
judgment, as I have said, it comes within minimum list heading 500.

I had considered at one stage whether this is a case which ought not to go back
to the tribunal, because these matters are largely matters of fact, but it has been **C**
pointed out to us that it is open to this court to draw such inferences as they think
proper from the evidence, and indeed counsel for the appellants has not asked,
nor has counsel for the Minister, that the case should go back to the tribunal. I
am quite satisfied that the only proper inference here is that the assembly that
took place in connexion with the third activity was not an assembly in the process
of or by way of manufacture, and accordingly that it does not come within **D**
minimum list heading 339.3, or indeed in any of the other minimum list headings
relied on by the appellants. Accordingly, though approaching the matter in a
different way to that in which the tribunal did, I have arrived at the conclusion
that the appeal fails and should be dismissed.

ASHWORTH, J.: I agree. I propose only to deal with two points. Minimum list heading 339.3 in its small type provides for: " Manufacturing all **E**
types of refrigerators (including domestic) and refrigerating machinery." So far
as refrigerating machinery is concerned, it cannot be suggested that these
appellants manufacture the machinery that is in issue in this case. What they do
is to buy the machinery and install it in these sites. It is said, however, by counsel
for the appellants that when refrigeration machinery has been bought from other
sources and has then been installed in the form shown in one of the photographs **F**
the result is a refrigerator. That is a step which I find it quite impossible to take.
No one looking at this photograph, nor a stranger coming into that part of the
premises, could possibly say: " Oh, and here is your refrigerator." It just does
not make sense. Therefore, approaching the matter merely on the footing of
minimum list heading 339.3, I take the view that neither of the two headings or
sub-headings which might bring the appellants within them is satisfied. More- **G**
over, if, as I agree with LORD PARKER, C.J., the activities come fairly within
minimum list heading 500, it is not in my judgment for this court or any court to
stretch by elastic the natural meaning of heading 339.3 in order to bring the
appellants' activities within it.

There is one other point which I would venture to deal with. It is quite true
that in minimum list heading 339.4 there is an express exclusion of establishments **H**
specialising in the installation of equipment. For my part I can understand that
from caution it was thought necessary to exclude that particular activity. The
absence of an exclusion in 339.3 is to my mind accounted for by the fact that no
one in their senses would have thought of including it, therefore it was thought
unnecessary to exclude installation of refrigerators or refrigerating machinery from
the precise words of 339.3. For these reasons in addition to those given by LORD **I**
PARKER, C.J., I agree that this appeal fails.

WILLIS, J.: I also agree.

Appeal dismissed. Leave to appeal to the Court of Appeal granted.
Solicitors: *Herbert & Gowers & Co.* (for the appellants); *Solicitor, Ministry of
Labour.*

[*Reported by* N. P. METCALFE, ESQ., *Barrister-at-Law.*]

A

PETTITT *v.* PETTITT.

[COURT OF APPEAL, CIVIL DIVISION (Willmer, Danckwerts and Russell, L.JJ.), January 15, 17, 29, 1968.]

B

Husband and Wife—Property—Matrimonial home—Wife sole legal owner—Improvements to matrimonial home effected by husband—No bargain between husband and wife that he should acquire beneficial interest in matrimonial home in return for his work—Wife left husband and obtained divorce—Whether husband entitled to beneficial interest in matrimonial home in respect of the improvements—Whether husband entitled to payment of the amount thereof—Married Women's Property Act, 1882 (45 & 46 Vict. c. 75), s. 17.

C

Without there being any bargain that he should be reimbursed in respect of his work and materials, the husband did decorative and other work on the matrimonial home, the freehold of which had been purchased entirely out of funds provided by the wife and had been conveyed to her. Subsequently, in 1965, the wife left the husband, and he remained rent free in the former matrimonial home until March, 1967. In divorce proceedings

D

brought by the wife, the husband applied under s. 17* of the Married Women's Property Act, 1882, by summons for a declaration that, as the value of the matrimonial home had been increased as a result of his work, he was beneficially interested in the house and was entitled to be paid accordingly by the wife. At the time of the hearing the husband had left the former matrimonial home and the wife had returned to it. The

E

husband was awarded £300 by the registrar. On appeal,

Held: the registrar's decision would be upheld because the court was bound by the decision of the Court of Appeal on similar facts in *Appleton* v. *Appleton* (see p. 1059, letter G, p. 1067, letter H, and p. 1063, letter H, post), although, if the case were free from authority the court would have decided that the husband was not entitled to any beneficial interest in the proceeds

F

of sale of the former matrimonial home (see p. 1058, letter A, p. 1062, letter C, and p. 1063, letter H, post).

Appleton v. *Appleton* ([1965] 1 All E.R. 44) followed, but criticised as wrongly decided.

Per WILLMER and DANCKWERTS, L.JJ.: s. 17 of the Married Women's Property Act, 1882, does not entitle the court to vary or alter the rights

G

that parties possess in the property that is the subject of the proceedings (see p. 1057, letter A, and p. 1063, letter C, post).

Cobb v. *Cobb* ([1955] 2 All E.R. 696) followed.

Legal Aid—Costs—Assisted person's liability to pay costs—Wife assisted person with nil contribution—Property in issue being matrimonial home vested at law in wife alone—Husband claiming beneficial interest on account of work

H

of improvement done by him—Husband awarded some beneficial interest—Costs awarded against wife—Whether award of costs should stand—Legal Aid and Advice Act, 1949 (12 & 13 Geo. 6 c. 51), s. 2 (2) (e)—Legal Aid (General) Regulations, 1962 (S.I. 1962 No. 148), reg. 18 (2).

A wife, who was the sole legal owner of the former matrimonial home, and was respondent in proceedings by the husband under s. 17 of the Married

I

Women's Property Act, 1882, in which the husband claimed to be entitled to a beneficial interest in the matrimonial home in respect of work done by him on it, was granted a civil aid certificate and assessed to a nil contribution, her property in the home being disregarded by reason of reg. 3 of the Legal Aid (Assessment of Resources) Regulations, 1960†, as the matrimonial home was the subject of the dispute. The value of the matrimonial home

---

* Section 17, so far as material, is set out at p. 1056, letter D, post.
† S.I. 1960 No. 1471.

Reversed. H.L. [1969] 2 All E.R. 385.

was between £6,250 and £6,500, which would be in excess by £3,250 to   A
£3,500 of the figure of £3,000 provided in para. 9 (2) of Sch. 2 to the regulations of 1960, with the consequence that, but for reg. 3, one half of the excess
would have been taken into consideration in assessing the wife's disposable
capital.   The husband was found to be entitled to a small beneficial interest
in the former matrimonial home.   Costs of the s. 17 proceedings were
awarded against the wife.   On appeal,   B

Held: having regard to the substantial asset left to the wife in the form
of her beneficial interest in the former matrimonial home, there was no
ground for interfering with the award of costs against the wife, which
was a reasonable exercise of discretion within s. 2 (2) (e)* of the Legal Aid
and Advice Act, 1949 and reg. 18 (2) of the Legal Aid (General) Regulations,
1962† (see p. 1060, letter G, and p. 1063, letters A and H, post).   C

Appeal dismissed.

[Editorial Note. The decision in this appeal regarding the husband's claim
to an interest in the matrimonial home or the proceeds of its sale should be
considered with *Button* v. *Button*, p. 1064, post.

As to the determination of rights to property as between husband and wife,
see 19 HALSBURY'S LAWS (3rd Edn.) 900, 901, para. 1492; and for cases on   D
beneficial ownership of the matrimonial home, see DIGEST (Cont. Vol. A) 692-695,
2130a-2130f.

As to award of costs against assisted person, see 30 HALSBURY'S LAWS (3rd
Edn.) 502, 503, para. 933.

For the Married Women's Property Act, 1882, s. 17, see 11 HALSBURY'S
STATUTES (2nd Edn.) 804; and for the Legal Aid and Advice Act, 1949, s. 2,   E
see 18 HALSBURY'S STATUTES (2nd Edn.) 535.

For the Legal Aid (Assessment of Resources) Regulations, 1960, reg. 3, Sch. 1,
para. 9 (2), see 5 HALSBURY'S STATUTORY INSTRUMENTS (First Re-Issue) 207,
212; and for the Legal Aid (General) Regulations, 1962, reg. 18 (2), see ibid.,
244.]
                                                                              F
Cases referred to:

Appleton v. *Appleton*, [1965] 1 All E.R. 44; [1965] 1 W.L.R. 25; Digest
  (Cont. Vol. B) 344, *621r.*
Bedson v. *Bedson*, [1965] 3 All E.R. 307; [1965] 2 Q.B. 666; [1965] 3 W.L.R.
  891; Digest (Cont. Vol. B) 349, *2130fa.*
Cobb v. *Cobb*, [1955] 2 All E.R. 696; [1955] 1 W.L.R. 731; Digest (Cont. Vol.
  A) 692, *2130aa.*   G
Hine v. *Hine*, [1962] 3 All E.R. 345; [1962] 1 W.L.R. 1124; Digest (Cont.
  Vol. A) 695, *2130f.*
Jansen v. *Jansen*, [1965] 3 All E.R. 363; [1965] P. 478; [1965] 3 W.L.R. 875;
  Digest (Cont. Vol. B) 344, *621s.*
National Provincial Bank, Ltd. v. *Ainsworth*, [1965] 2 All E.R. 472; [1965]   H
  A.C. 1175; [1965] 3 W.L.R. 1; Digest (Cont. Vol. B) 343, *621l.*
Short v. *Short*, (May 11, 1967), unreported.
Till v. *Till*, (1888), 15 O.R. 133; 27 Digest (Repl.) 132, **485.*
Ulrich v. *Ulrich and Felton*, ante p. 67; [1968] 1 W.L.R. 180.
Wilson v. *Wilson*, [1963] 2 All E.R. 447; [1963] 1 W.L.R. 601; Digest (Cont.
  Vol. A) 671, *621m.*
                                                                              I
Appeal.

This was an appeal by the wife against an order of Mr. Registrar J. D. BEAMISH
GREEN made on Apr. 11, 1967, on a summons by the respondent husband, dated
May 23, 1966, on an application by him under s. 17 of the Married Women's Pro-
perty Act, 1882, for an order the respondent husband had a beneficial interest in the

---

* Section 2 (2), so far as material, is set out at p. 1060, letter A, post.
† S.I. 1962 No. 148.

A proceeds of the sale of Tinker's Cottage, Collington Lane East, Bexhill-on-Sea, Sussex, in the sum of £300 and ordering that the wife pay the husband that sum and the costs of the proceedings. The grounds of the appeal were as follows: (i) that the registrar misdirected himself in law when he found that the husband had an interest in Tinker's Cottage, which property was at all material times the property of the wife; (ii) that the registrar misdirected himself in law when
B he ordered the wife, who was in receipt of legal aid, to pay the costs of the proceedings; and (iii) that the registrar failed to exercise his discretion judicially in ordering the wife to pay the costs. The wife had been issued with a civil aid certificate dated July 28, 1967, to prosecute a divorce suit and to defend proceedings under s. 17 of the Act of 1882.

C *E. A. Machin* for the wife.
   The husband did not appear and was not represented.

Cur. adv. vult.

Jan. 29. The following judgments were read.

WILLMER, L.J.: This case arises out of an application by a husband
D under s. 17 of the Married Women's Property Act, 1882, for a declaration that he is beneficially interested in the proceeds of sale of a house which had been the matrimonial home of the parties. It is not in dispute that the house was purchased with funds provided entirely by the wife, and that she took the conveyance in her own name. It is alleged by the husband, however, that during the period while the parties resided together he carried out certain work
E by way of redecoration and improvement of the property, the result of which was to increase its value to the extent of about £1,000, and he claimed to be beneficially interested to that extent. The matter came before Mr. Registrar J. D. BEAMISH GREEN at Hastings on Mar. 3, 1967, and by his order of Apr. 11, 1967, the registrar ordered that the husband had a beneficial interest in the property to the extent of £300 which sum he directed that the wife should pay
F to the husband. He also made an order for costs against the wife. The wife has now appealed to this court, contending that the husband has not, and never had, any interest in the property in question. There is also a subsidiary appeal against the order for costs, which it is said was wrongly made having regard to the fact that the wife was an assisted person with a nil contribution. We have had the benefit of hearing a full argument from counsel for the wife; but, un-
G happily for us, the husband has not seen fit to take any part in the proceedings before us, or to instruct counsel to present any argument on his behalf. We have, therefore, been deprived of the advantage of hearing argument on both sides.

The facts of the case are simple. The parties were married on Aug. 13, 1952, and there are two children of the marriage, both boys. On their marriage the
H parties took up residence at 12, Chantry Avenue, Bexhill, a house which had been left to the wife by her deceased grandmother. The parties resided at this address till 1960, when the property was sold, the proceeds of the sale amounting to £4,241. Out of the proceeds of sale a plot of land was purchased in Collington Lane East, Bexhill, where a bungalow called Tinker's Cottage was erected, the total cost amounting to £3,813. Here the parties resided until February, 1965,
I when the wife left the husband and went to reside elsewhere, taking the two boys with her. The husband continued to live in Tinker's Cottage, rent free, until shortly before the hearing before the registrar in March, 1967. In 1965 divorce proceedings were commenced, which resulted in the wife obtaining a decree on the ground of cruelty. An order for maintenance was made in respect of the children, but there was no order for maintenance of the wife. The question of custody of the children was adjourned to chambers, and the issue as to property rights in respect of the matrimonial home was left unresolved. Hence the present proceedings.

The husband alleged that during the time when the parties resided at 12,   **A**
Chantry Avenue, he carried out substantial work by way of improvement of
the property as a result of which he said that it was sold for about £750 more
than it would have fetched in its original state. He did not, however, base any
claim on this assertion, the reason being, as I understand it, that in order to
compensate the husband for the work he had done the wife allowed him to use
the balance of the proceeds of sale, which remained after paying for the building   **B**
of Tinker's Cottage in order to discharge his outstanding liability on his car.
The husband's claim was thus based entirely on work which he claimed to have
carried out by way of improvement of Tinker's Cottage. He put the value of
his work (which comprised a certain amount of redecoration, building of cup-
boards and other improvements, and work in laying out the garden) at £723;
but he claimed that the effect of his work was to increase the value of the property   **C**
by £1,000. It is not in dispute that the value of the property at the time of the
hearing was £6,250 to £6,500.

Section 17 of the Married Women's Property Act, 1882, omitting immaterial
words, provides as follows:

" In any question between husband and wife as to the title to or possession
of property, either party . . . may apply by summons or otherwise in a   **D**
summary way to any judge of the High Court of Justice . . . and the judge
. . . may make such order with respect to the property in dispute . . . as he
thinks fit . . ."

By r. 77 of the Matrimonial Causes Rules, 1957, (1) the jurisdiction conferred
by the section may be exercised by a registrar. In the present case no question   **E**
arises with regard to possession of the property in dispute. The husband's
summons contained no claim for possession, and I understand that he has already
vacated the premises. We are concerned only with title and with the husband's
claim to a beneficial interest therein.

In recent years there has been a considerable number of cases in which questions of title in respect of the matrimonial home have been dealt with under s. 17.
This has been due in the main, I think, to two causes. First, social habits have   **F**
changed in that great numbers of married women in these days go out to work
and frequently pool their earnings with those of their husbands, the common pool
being used to defray all the expenses of the home, including mortgage payments
in respect of the purchase of the house. Secondly, owing to the recent increase
in the value of house property, it is not unusual to find that the equity of redemption represents a very considerable sum of money. Many of the reported cases   **G**
have arisen in the context of a house conveyed into the joint names of the spouses,
both spouses having contributed in one way or another to the initial cost of the
purchase and to the payment of mortgage instalments. Except in so far as
they throw light on the true purpose and proper application of s. 17, I do not
find it useful to refer further to these cases. For the situation in the present
case is quite different, having regard to the fact that Tinker's Cottage was   **H**
indubitably acquired with funds wholly provided by the wife, and the conveyance
was taken in her name alone. In *Cobb* v. *Cobb* (2), however, ROMER, L.J.,
said:

". . . I know of no power that the court has under s. 17 to vary agreed
or established titles to property. It has power to ascertain the respective   **I**
rights of husband and wife to disputed property and frequently has to do so
on very little material; but where, as here, the original rights to property
are established by the evidence and those rights have not been varied by
subsequent agreement, the court cannot in my opinion under s. 17 vary those
rights merely because it thinks that, in the light of subsequent events,
the original agreement was unfair."

(1) S.I. 1957 No. 619.
(2) [1955] 2 All E.R. 696 at p. 700.

A This statement of principle has been repeatedly accepted and followed in subsequent cases, and must now, I think, be taken to have been approved by the House of Lords in *National Provincial Bank, Ltd.* v. *Ainsworth* (3); see per LORD HODSON (4), LORD UPJOHN (5) and LORD WILBERFORCE (6). In *Bedson* v. *Bedson* (7), which came before this court shortly afterwards, LORD DENNING, M.R., who had at one time been disposed to favour a somewhat wider view of

B the effect of the section, said:

" I have myself in the past preferred to give it a liberal interpretation in keeping with the width of the words used by Parliament; but those who are wiser than I am have declared that it does not enable the court to vary existing rights. We have always to go back to see what the rights of the parties actually are. I accept this."

C A similar statement of the principle by DIPLOCK, L.J., is to be found in the very recent case of *Ulrich* v. *Ulrich and Felton* (8).

In the present case there can be no room for doubt that, at the time when Tinker's Cottage was acquired in 1960, the wife had an established title to the property, and the husband had none. It has never been suggested that there

D was any subsequent agreement varying the rights of the parties. How then can it be suggested that the husband is now entitled to assert a beneficial interest in the property? The answer put forward on his behalf was that he acquired such a beneficial interest by reason of the work which he carried out with his own hands by way of renovating and improving the property. In the absence of any agreement, this assertion could be justified only on the basis that the court

E ought to impute to the parties some common intention that the husband was to acquire an interest in the property commensurate with the value of the work which he did.

Viewing the matter on general principles, and apart from authority, I see three grave objections in the way of accepting this contention. (i) Ever since 1960 the husband has had the benefit of living rent free in the house provided by

F his wife, and he has further been relieved of what would otherwise have been his duty of providing the wife with a home. Although there is no evidence to show what the rental value of Tinker's Cottage may be, I think it must be obvious that the benefit which the husband derived from living there rent free for a period of seven years, instead of having to provide his wife with a home, must far exceed the value of any work which he did by way of improving the property.

G (ii) I would not regard the work which the husband did as going beyond what any reasonable husband would be expected to do (either with his own hands, or by paying a contractor to do it) if he had the benefit of living rent free in a house provided by his wife. In the same way, a wife who has the benefit of living in a house provided by the husband must be expected to do her part in preserving the property, keeping it clean, and so forth. Or is it to be said that if,

H out of the goodness of her heart, she helps her husband on some occasion to redecorate a room (not an uncommon occupation for a wife in these days), she thereby acquires some beneficial interest in her husband's property? (iii) If it is right to say that, thanks to the work done by the husband, which had the result, as he says, of increasing the value of the property by £1,000, the husband is to be regarded as having acquired a beneficial interest in the property, it must on general principles be equally right to say that work to the value of a few shillings

I would have the same result. If the argument for the husband be sound, the moment he puts up a shelf or touches up a window-sill, it would follow that he has started to acquire a beneficial interest in the property. This would clearly

---

(3) [1965] 2 All E.R. 472; [1965] A.C. 1175.
(4) [1965] 2 All E.R. at p. 477; [1965] A.C. at pp. 1220, 1221.
(5) [1965] 2 All E.R. at pp. 486, 487; [1965] A.C. at pp. 1235, 1236.
(6) [1965] 2 All E.R. at pp. 493, 494; [1965] A.C. at pp. 1246, 1247.
(7) [1965] 3 All E.R. 307 at p. 311; [1965] 2 Q.B. 666 at p. 677.
(8) Ante at pp. 71-73.

be an absurd result, yet it is the logical consequence of the husband's contention.   **A**

In these circumstances, if the question were free from authority, I should for myself have been disposed to take the view that the husband's claim to have acquired some beneficial interest in Tinker's Cottage, or in the proceeds of its sale, was quite without substance. Our attention has, however, been called to the decision of this court in *Appleton* v. *Appleton* (9), a case which is admitted by counsel for the wife to be indistinguishable on its facts from the present case.   **B**
There, as here, a house was purchased by the wife out of funds which had been left to her. Later that house was sold, and with the proceeds another house was purchased in which the parties resided. In that case, as in this, it was alleged by the husband (and not, I think, denied) that he had done substantial work on both houses, which had the effect of considerably enhancing their value. In proceedings under s. 17 of the Married Women's Property Act, 1882, the husband   **C**
claimed to be entitled to a share in the proceeds of sale of the second house. The registrar, although he found that the husband had done substantial work on both houses, decided against the husband's claim. He said (10):

> "It seemed quite clear to me that the [husband] had voluntarily improved his wife's property and such an action in the absence of evidence of any bargain or expressed intention to the contrary gave him no interest in either   **D**
> of the properties or the proceeds of sale."

In this court, however, it was held that the registrar had misdirected himself and had reached an erroneous conclusion. LORD DENNING, M.R., having quoted the words of the registrar as above, said (11):

> "I think that that was an erroneous direction in point of law. As the   **E**
> husband pointed out to us, when he was doing the work in the house, the matrimonial home, it was done for the sake of the family as a whole. None of them had any thought of separation at that time. There could be no occasion for any bargain to be made as to what was to happen in case there was a separation, for it was a thing which no one contemplated at all. In those circumstances, it is not correct to look and see whether there was any   **F**
> bargain in the past, or any expressed intention. A judge can only do what is fair and reasonable in the circumstances. Sometimes the test has been put in the cases: what term is to be implied? What would the parties have stipulated had they thought about it? That is one way of putting it. But, as the parties never did think about it at all, I prefer to take the simple test: what is reasonable and fair in the circumstances as they have developed, seeing that   **G**
> they are circumstances which no one contemplated before? I should have thought that, inasmuch as the registrar found that the husband had done up to about one-half of the work of renovation, the husband should get something. He should be entitled to so much of the enhanced value of both of the properties as was due to his work and materials that he supplied. He should be given credit for a just proportion on any realisation of the house. A   **H**
> percentage of the proceeds ought to go to him commensurate to the enhancement due to his work in improving the property or properties and getting a better price on that account. So I think that the registrar misdirected himself on that point. The husband is entitled to a percentage of the proceeds of sale, if and when the house is sold."

The other two members of the court agreed with LORD DENNING, M.R., and did   **I**
not deliver separate judgments.

The question, and I think the only question, on this appeal is whether that decision is binding on us, or whether, as contended on behalf of the wife, it must be taken to have been overruled by the decision of the House of Lords in *National Provincial Bank, Ltd.* v. *Ainsworth* (12). After careful consideration I do not feel

---

(9) [1965] 1 All E.R. 44.   (10) [1965] 1 All E.R. at p. 45.
(11) [1965] 1 All E.R. at pp. 45, 46.   (12) [1965] 2 All E.R. 472; [1965] A.C. 1175.

A able to take the view that *Appleton* v. *Appleton* (13) has been overruled. It is true that three members of the House expressed views in conflict with the reasoning of LORD DENNING, M.R., in *Appleton* v. *Appleton* (13). It is further true that the other two members of the House expressed their general concurrence. Only LORD UPJOHN, however, made any express reference to *Appleton's* case (13) and said (14) in terms that he regarded it as wrongly decided. The question at

B issue in the *National Provincial Bank* case (15) was an entirely different question from that which arose in *Appelton's* case (13). What was there in dispute was whether a deserted wife, who was still residing in the matrimonial home, had acquired an " equity " which entitled her to resist a claim for possession brought by the bank as mortgagees. The wife was not claiming any title to the property, but was concerned only to protect the right which she asserted to remain in

C occupation until her husband provided her with proper alternative accommodation. There was no issue as to the rights of the spouses under s. 17 of the Act of 1882, and the three members of the House who referred to the Act were careful to point out that the section applied only as between husband and wife; see per LORD HODSON (16), LORD UPJOHN (17), and LORD WILBERFORCE (18). What they said, therefore, with regard to the rights of spouses inter se, though of the highest

D possible persuasive authority, can in my view only be treated as obiter. In my judgment it would be wrong for this court to hold that *Appelton* v. *Appleton* (13) has been overruled. If it was wrongly decided and should be overruled, it is for the House of Lords, and only for them, to say so.

Before I leave this subject, I think it right to refer to one other case which has been before this court since the decision in the *National Provincial Bank* case (15),

E if only to say that I derive no assistance from it. That is *Jansen* v. *Jansen* (19), where the facts were similar to, but by no means identical with, the facts in *Appleton's* case (13). The question was there discussed whether the decision in *Appleton's* case (13) ought to be regarded as overruled, but unhappily the three members of the court reached different conclusions with regard to that point. LORD DENNING, M.R., expressed the view (20) that the decision still stood;

F DAVIES, L.J., concluded (21) that the case then before the court was distinguishable, and expressed no view with regard to the decision in *Appleton's* case (13); RUSSELL, L.J. (22) preferred the view of LORD UPJOHN, though expressing some doubt whether by the rules of precedent he was entitled so to hold. For these reasons I think that we are bound by the decision in *Appleton* v. *Appleton* (13), and it follows that the main part of the appeal in the present case must be

G dismissed.

With regard to the subsidiary appeal against the order for costs, I have already said that the wife was an assisted person with a nil contribution. This assessment was presumably made on the basis that the wife had no sufficient disposable income or disposable capital to justify requiring a contribution. In making their assessment the National Assistance Board no doubt left out of account the value

H of Tinker's Cottage, since this was the subject matter of the dispute between the parties, and therefore had to be excluded from consideration pursuant to reg. 3 of the Legal Aid (Assessment of Resources) Regulations, 1960 (23). On the question whether the wife was properly ordered to pay the husband's costs, the relevant statutory provision is s. 2 (2) (*e*) of the Legal Aid and Advice Act, 1949, which provides that in the case of an assisted person,

I

(13) [1965] 1 All E.R. 44. (14) [1965] 2 All E.R. at p. 487; [1965] A.C. at p. 1236.
(15) [1965] 2 All E.R. 472; [1965] A.C. 1175.
(16) [1965] 2 All E.R. at pp. 477, 478; [1965] A.C. at p. 1221.
(17) [1965] 2 All E.R. at p. 487; [1965] A.C. at p. 1236.
(18) [1965] 2 All E.R. at pp. 492, 493; [1965] A.C. at pp. 1245, 1246.
(19) [1965] 3 All E.R. 363; [1965] P. 478.
(20) [1965] 3 All E.R. at p. 365; [1965] P. at pp. 487, 488.
(21) [1965] 3 All E.R. at p. 367; [1965] P. at p. 490.
(22) [1965] 3 All E.R. at pp. 317, 368-370; [1965] P. at pp. 495-498.
(23) S.I. 1960 No. 1471.

A

" his liability by virtue of an order for costs made against him with respect to the proceedings shall not exceed the amount (if any) which is a reasonable one for him to pay having regard to all the circumstances, including the means of all the parties and their conduct in connexion with the dispute."

This is amplified by reg. 18 (2) of the Legal Aid (General) Regulations, 1962 (24), which provides:

B

" In determining the amount of the assisted person's liability—(a) his dwelling house and household furniture . . . shall be left out of account to the like extent as they are left out of account by the Board in determining his disposable income and disposable capital . . ."

This takes us back to the Legal Aid (Assessment of Resources) Regulations, 1960, Sch. 2 of which, by para. 9, provides as follows:

C

" (1) Except as is provided in the next succeeding paragraph of this rule, in computing the amount of capital of the person concerned, there shall be disregarded, in respect of the value to him of any interest in the dwelling house in which he resides, any sum which might be obtained by him by selling that interest or borrowing money on the security thereof. (2) There shall be taken into account one half of the amount by which the value of the dwelling house, after deducting therefrom the amount of any encumbrance charged thereon, exceeds £3,000."

D

Tinker's Cottage is the dwelling in which the wife, as I understand it, now resides. It is common ground that its value is £6,250-£6,500 and, so far as we have been informed, it is unencumbered. There is thus an excess of £3,250-£3,500, half of which the board, in assessing the wife's disposable capital, could have taken into account but for reg. 3, i.e., if it had not been the subject-matter of the dispute. I see no ground for saying that it would have been inequitable or impracticable for the board to take this excess of value into account.

E

It follows that, in assessing the wife's liability to pay the husband's costs, we must have regard to the fact that, subject to the husband's right to recover £300, she is left with a substantial capital asset half of which, but for reg. 3 of the Legal Aid (Assessment of Resources) Regulations, 1960, it would have been permissible for the board to take into account. This being so, I can see no ground for interfering with the registrar's exercise of his discretion in ordering the wife to pay the husband's costs. In my judgment, therefore, this part of the wife's appeal should also be dismissed. No question of the costs of the appeal arises since the husband has taken no part in it.

F

G

RUSSELL, L.J.: The respondent husband, who describes himself as an estate agent's negotiator, and the appellant wife were married in 1952 and lived until 1961 in a freehold house at 12, Chantry Avenue, Bexhill, the property of the wife, to whom it had been devised by her grandmother. While living there, the husband (obviously a handy man) did a good deal of work mostly in redecorating, and partly in improvements in and around the house. This is set out in his affidavit. The total of the sums set against the various items is £805, which he says he " spent ", but clearly this includes a charge for his labour as well as disbursements. I need not set out the details because his claim was in relation to work done on another house subsequently. He asserted that the work done by him resulted in an increase in the sale price of 12, Chantry Avenue.

H

In 1961 the wife sold 12, Chantry Avenue and invested the greater part of the proceeds of sale in buying a freehold plot in Collington Lane East, Bexhill, and building thereon a bungalow called Tinker's Cottage. There they lived together until March, 1965, when the wife left on account of his cruel treatment of her. In November, 1967, she obtained a decree of divorce on the ground of cruelty. In March, 1967, the husband left Tinker's Cottage and the wife returned to live there. While they were living at Tinker's Cottage the husband (he says) undertook

I

A work thereon which enhanced its value. He submitted for his work done and materials supplied a value of £723 17s., calculated as in an exhibit to his affidavit, and said that the resultant increase in open market value of the property was £1,000. These are the contents of the exhibit:

B " *Bedroom 1.* Redecoration, £40. Building eight-foot double wardrobe in Regency style with filigree plastic bead, etc., and gilt handles to doors hanging rail and shelves to interior, £100. *Hall.* Complete redecoration including Regency style treatment to doors of linen cupboard and cloaks cupboard. Paper to walls, £30. *Kitchen.* Redecoration including alterations to cupboard doors, etc. Fitting of Venetian type blinds, £40. *Dining room.* Redecoration including repapered walls, £30. *Garden.* Complete making with my own hands digging with bulbs building ornamental well, etc., £275 [the

C word " well " may be " wall "]. *Patio.* Making about fifty 2 × 2 paving slabs by hand levelling laying as attractive patio, £50. *Side gate.* Making timber gate with studded effect making frame painting, etc., £15. *Side wall.* Building wall at side nine-inch solid brickwork complete with foundations and tile creasing to top, £100. *Insulation.* Fibre glass insulation to part of roof five rolls Cosywrap @ 21s. and labour, £7 7s. *Concrete coal bunker.*

D Installing same on concrete base and laying concrete path to side of property, £16 10s. *Bathroom and separate w.c.* Redecoration and building cupboard under washbasin, £20. (Total) £723 17s."

In May, 1966, the husband issued a summons in the pending divorce proceedings asking for a declaration that he was beneficially interested in the proceeds of sale

E of Tinker's Cottage in the sum of £1,000, or such other sum as might seem just, and for an order on the wife to pay it to him. I observe that the summons does not mention s. 17 of the Married Women's Property Act, 1882, which accords with the view that the section is merely procedural.

There was a certain amount of expert evidence on both sides on the effect of the husband's work on the value of the property, and in the end the registrar,

F without giving reasons, made an order that the husband had a beneficial interest in the proceeds of sale of Tinker's Cottage in the sum of £300, and that the wife do pay him that sum. The house is not sold, and the wife is now living there. From that order the wife appeals. The husband was not represented, and did not appear on the appeal.

The plot for Tinker's Cottage was bought for a total of £510 in December,

G 1960, and was paid for out of a joint account already overdrawn. The building cost for Tinker's Cottage was similarly met by a cheque for £3,039 10s. 7d. on Jan. 2, 1961, the bank affording short term bridging finance. This totals £3,549, though the husband in his affidavit said that the total was £3,813. The sale of 12, Chantry Avenue was completed in January, 1961, the net proceeds of sale being paid into the joint account in two sums totalling £4,241 11s. 9d. on Jan.

H 14 and 18. The balance was, therefore, some £690, though the effect of the sale and purchase was to put the joint account into credit only some £358. The above information is gleaned from completion statements and the bank account sheets.

The wife's affidavit states that the husband after these transactions said: "I am going to pay off the car, it's due to me because of all the money I've spent on Chantry

I Avenue." The husband's affidavit in reply states that the wife agreed that, because he had worked on Chantry Avenue, the amount due on the car should be paid off. So far as I understand his affidavit, the cheque for £300 was an investment in the Halifax Building Society from which £200 was paid to Larkin, Ltd. I do not know if that was the sum due on the car, or whether this was an extra sum due to the builder. I must at least take it as established that some sum out of the balance of proceeds of sale was, with the wife's assent at the husband's suggestion, used to pay off a hire-purchase debt on the husband's car as a reward for his work and outlay on Chantry Avenue.

Now the sole ground on which it is asserted that the husband is entitled to any A
interest in what is undoubtedly the wife's property, Tinker's Cottage (or in the
proceeds of any sale of it) or to be paid any sum by the wife, is that in fact his
work and expenditure has improved that property. He does not assert that
there was any kind of bargain or understanding between them that he should
ever be to any extent reimbursed or rewarded for it, or that he thought that he
was doing work on property belonging to him. And I do not consider that the B
facts about the payment off of the car hire-purchase debt stated above are
grounds for implying such an agreement or understanding. Quite apart from my
general understanding of the law that prima facie a husband laying out money in
improvement of his wife's property is presumed to be making a gift (see 19
HALSBURY'S LAWS OF ENGLAND (3rd Edn.), p. 832, para. 1360 and p. 840,
para. 1370; and for a Commonwealth case, see *Till* v. *Till* (25)); I should have C
thought it even more reasonable, in the case of the property being the matrimonial
home, that work and expenditure by the husband should not be taken to confer
on him any rights, since he is in the fortunate position of being relieved from the
obligation to spend money on renting a roof for his wife. The registrar based his
decision, however, on the authority of *Appleton* v. *Appleton* (26) in this court,
and the real question for us is whether we think that *Appleton's* case (26) was D
wrongly decided, and whether, if we do so think, we are at liberty to treat it as
no longer authority binding on this court having regard to the views expressed
in the House of Lords in *National Provincial Bank, Ltd.* v. *Ainsworth* (27), both
generally on the scope of s. 17 of the Married Women's Property Act, 1882, and
in particular (by LORD UPJOHN) on the correctness of the decisions of this court
in *Appleton* v. *Appleton* (26) and also in *Hine* v. *Hine* (28), which views I extracted E
in *Jansen* v. *Jansen* (29). My own views on the section and on these decisions are
to be found in more than one reported case; I refer to *Jansen* v. *Jansen* (30),
Wilson v. *Wilson* (31) and *Bedson* v. *Bedson* (32), and it would be tedious to repeat
them here; they accord in particular with the views of LORD UPJOHN referred to
above.

I think that the decision in *Appleton's* case (26) was wrong, and that the F
husband in the present case is not entitled to the order he obtained. I observe
in passing that he also claimed to be entitled to a sum of £215, which was the
amount he got knocked off the builder's bill because he knew him! The registrar
refused to entertain this suggestion because it was not in his " pleading ". If I
thought that it was the general opinion in this court that *Appleton* v. *Appleton* (26)
could not stand since the observations in *National Provincial Bank, Ltd.* v. G
Ainsworth (27), I would find myself able so to treat it and allow the appeal;
but that is not so. In *Jansen* v. *Jansen* (30), LORD DENNING, M.R., reasserted
Appleton v. *Appleton* (26) as authority, and DAVIES, L.J., did not express a view.
In an unreported case of *Short* v. *Short* (33), LORD DENNING, M.R., and DAVIES,
L.J., allowed a sum for the husband's labour. (That was a case of a joint bank
account and work on a plot purchased in joint names out of the proceeds of sale H
of a house in joint names.) I did not agree because the case was not exactly
the same as *Appleton* v. *Appleton* (26). Consequently I think that, though we
consider that the registrar's decision and *Appleton* v. *Appleton* (26) were wrong,
we should obey the rules of precedent and leave it to the House of Lords to say
authoritatively (if they so consider) that *Appleton* v. *Appleton* (26) was wrong.

I therefore reluctantly concur in dismissing the appeal on the main aspect,

---

(25) (1888), 15 O.R. 133.
(26) [1965] 1 All E.R. 44.
(27) [1965] 2 All E.R. 472; [1965] A.C. 1175.
(28) [1962] 3 All E.R. 345.
(29) [1965] 3 All E.R. at p. 370; [1965] P. at pp. 497, 498.
(30) [1965] 3 All E.R. 363; [1965] P. 478.
(31) [1963] 2 All E.R. 447.
(32) [1965] 3 All E.R. 307; [1965] 2 Q.B. 266.
(33) (May 11, 1967), unreported.

A but hope that the House of Lords will have an opportunity to review the various and varying cases that have been decided between husband and wife in respect of property.

On the question of costs, though the wife had a nil contribution, I do not think that the registrar was wrong in ordering costs against the wife, since her house is an asset of sufficiently substantial value, as shown by WILLMER, L.J.

B
DANCKWERTS, L.J. (read by WILLMER, L.J.): I have had the advantage of reading the judgments of WILLMER, L.J., and RUSSELL, L.J., with which I agree. That means that I need not state the facts, and my judgment can be reasonably short. I have never doubted that the jurisdiction conferred by s. 17 of the Married Women's Property Act, 1882, does not entitle the court to alter
C the rights which the parties possess in the property which is the subject of the proceedings. The provisions of s. 17 of the Act of 1882 are in my view procedural. The section was designed to enable questions of ownership to be decided summarily, quickly and cheaply between a husband and wife. The court is empowered to make such order as it thinks fit, but that gives the court a discretion as to the order which the court may make to give effect to the rights of the parties, and
D that is not a power to alter the rights of the parties at the will of the court. The position in my view is stated with admirable correctness by ROMER, L.J., in *Cobb* v. *Cobb* (34). The passage is quoted by WILLMER, L.J., in his judgment, and I need not repeat it. The statement received the approval of at least three of the lords of appeal in *National Provincial Bank, Ltd.* v. *Ainsworth* (35). I agree, therefore, with the opinion of LORD UPJOHN that the case of *Appleton* v. *Appleton* (36)
E was wrongly decided. Counsel for the wife admits, however, that the present case is indistinguishable from *Appleton* v. *Appleton* (36), and so the question arises whether, as *Appleton* v. *Appleton* (36) is a decision of the Court of Appeal, we are at liberty to disregard it. It is, indeed, something of a dilemma, since *Cobb* v. *Cobb* (37) was also a decision of the Court of Appeal, and it is somewhat embarrassing for us to know which view we should accept.

F There is a further point. There seems to me much to be said for the view that, when a husband, living in the matrimonial home, does work which improves the joint home, or increases the amenities of the home for both husband or wife, the services or expenditure provided by the husband are performed by him without expectation of return, in the absence of some different arrangement agreed on by the wife and the husband. As stated in the passages in 19 HALSBURY'S LAWS OF ENGLAND (3rd Edn.), p. 832, para. 1360, p. 840, para. 1370, to which
G RUSSELL, L.J., has referred, the law has, indeed, provided a presumption of advancement in cases of a very similar nature, though the law is slow to imply similar rights in cases in which a husband receives payments from a wife. The law has favoured wives in relation to husbands, and it is too late to reverse this process now in favour of husbands.

H In the result, while I think that the decision of the registrar was not correct, I agree that the uncertainty must be cleared up by the House of Lords, and therefore I too, with reluctance agree that the appeal must be dismissed. In respect of costs, I would not interfere with the decision of the registrar.

Appeal dismissed. Leave to appeal to the House of Lords granted.

Solicitors: *Preston, Lane-Claypon & O'Kelly*, agents for *Perring & Co.*, Hastings
I (for the wife).

[*Reported by* F. A. AMIES, ESQ., *Barrister-at-Law.*]

---

(34) [1955] 2 All E.R. at p. 700.
(35) [1965] 2 All E.R. 472; [1965] A.C. 1175.
(36) [1965] 1 All E.R. 44.
(37) [1955] 2 All E.R. 696.

BUTTON *v.* BUTTON.   A

[COURT OF APPEAL, CIVIL DIVISION (Lord Denning, M.R., Danckwerts and
Widgery, L.JJ.), January 29, 1968.]

*Husband and Wife—Property—Matrimonial home—Husband sole owner at law
—Work done by both spouses on the property—Work done by wife of a kind
that a wife would ordinarily do—Whether wife entitled to beneficial interest*   B
in house or its proceeds of sale—Married Women's Property Act, 1882
(45 & 46 Vict. c. 75), s. 17.

The parties were married in 1955. A year later a cottage which was
empty and out of repair was found by the wife and was bought by the
husband and conveyed into his name alone; it was to be the matrimonial
home. The husband financed the purchase and employed workmen to do some   C
of the necessary work on the cottage; in addition both the husband and the
wife did a lot of work on the cottage, and the wife helped with painting
and decorating and with the garden. In 1958 the cottage was sold and a profit
of £1,000 was made, which was invested in shares in the husband's name.
In 1959 another house was bought and was conveyed to the husband; he
paid the deposit and some other moneys out of the shares, and he paid the   D
mortgage instalments. In 1964 the wife left the husband. In 1965 he was
ordered to pay maintenance at the rate of £7 10s. weekly for the wife and
£2 10s. weekly for each of the two children of the marriage. The marriage
was dissolved on the wife's petition. The husband continued to live in the
matrimonial home. The wife now claimed to be entitled to a half share in it.

Held: the work which the wife had done on the house was the ordinary   E
kind of work which a wife might do in the matrimonial home without
expecting a share or interest in it, and accordingly the wife was not entitled
to a share or interest in the house; moreover the award of maintenance
must have been assessed on the footing that she had no benefit from the house
(see p. 1067, letters E and F, and p. 1068, letter B, post).

Appleton v. *Appleton* ([1965] 1 All E.R. 44) distinguished.   F

Appeal allowed.

[Editorial Note. The principle that work might ordinarily be done by a
spouse on the matrimonial home does not itself lead to entitlement to a beneficial interest in the house applies equally whether the claim to a beneficial
interest is made by a husband or by a wife (see p. 1066, letter I, and p. 1067, letter   G
C, post.) In the absence of any agreement as to entitlement to a beneficial
interest in the house, the distinction lies in the type of work; and if the work
done is the sort of work that a contractor might normally be employed to do, a
claim to entitlement to some beneficial interest in the house by reason of the work
done may be justified.

As to the determination of rights to property as between husband and wife,   H
see 19 HALSBURY'S LAWS (3rd Edn.) 900, 901, para. 1492; and for cases on the
subject see 27 DIGEST (Repl.) 81, *620, 621;* DIGEST (Cont. Vol. A) 667-672;
621a-621n; (Cont. Vol. B) 343-345, *621l-621y.*

For the Married Women's Property Act, 1882, s. 17, see 11 HALSBURY'S
STATUTES (2nd Edn.) 804.]

Cases referred to: I

Appleton v. *Appleton,* [1965] 1 All E.R. 44; [1965] 1 W.L.R. 25; Digest
(Cont. Vol. B) 344, *621r.*

Fribance v. *Fribance,* [1957] 1 All E.R. 357; [1957] 1 W.L.R. 384; Digest
(Cont. Vol. A) 693, *2130ab.*

Jansen v. *Jansen,* [1965] 3 All E.R. 363; [1965] P. 478; [1965] 3 W.L.R. 875;
Digest (Cont. Vol. B) 344, *621s.*

Pettitt v. *Pettitt,* ante p. 1053.

A   *Rimmer* v. *Rimmer*, [1952] 2 All E.R. 863; [1953] 1 Q.B. 63; Digest (Cont.
         Vol. A) 692, *2130a*.
    Tulley v. *Tulley*, (1965) 109 Sol. Jo. 956; Digest (Cont. Vol. B) 344, *621u*.
    Ulrich v. *Ulrich and Felton*, [1968] 1 All E.R. 67; [1968] 1 W.L.R. 180.

Appeal

B   On Mar. 31, 1965, the wife issued a summons under s. 17 of the Married Women's
    Property Act, 1882, claiming against the respondent husband a declaration that
    certain property, 37 Sandalwood Avenue, Chertsey, was owned by the spouses
    in equal shares or that she was entitled to an equal half share of the proceeds
    of sale thereof, and claiming to be sole owner of certain chattels and that other
    chattels were joint property of the spouses. The facts with regard to the two
    houses successively purchased as matrimonial homes are set out in the judgment
C   of Lord Denning, M.R. at letter G, infra, to p. 1066, letter B, post. In regard
    to the application of the profit of about £1,000, which was made on the sale of
    the cottage first bought, the wife's evidence before the district registrar, as regards
    the balance of profit after paying some £700 towards the purchase, was that the
    balance was used to improve the second property acquired. The district registrar
    found that in his view the facts justified the wife's claim to a half share or interest in
D   the house, 37 Sandalwood Avenue. The essence of his finding is set out at p. 1066,
    letter F, post. By notice dated June 26, 1967, the husband, the respondent
    to the summons, gave notice of appeal from the order dated June 16, 1967,
    made by Mr. District Registrar Beamish Green at Hastings District
    Registry; the husband sought an order declaring that he was solely entitled to
E   37 Sandalwood Avenue, or that the district registrar's order be varied by declaring
    that the wife had a lesser share than that declared by him.

    W. E. Barnett for the appellant husband.
    Michael Lewis for the respondent wife.

         LORD DENNING, M.R.: This is another case between husband and wife
    as to the ownership of the matrimonial home. The parties were married on
F   Mar. 26, 1955. The husband was a sales representative and the wife was an
    air hostess. They have two children, a girl born on Jan. 6, 1957, so she is now
    eleven, and a boy born on Sept. 24, 1959, so he is now nine.
         After the marriage the wife was employed for five or six months and brought
    her earnings into the family pool; but they did not have a house of their own
    then. They did not get their own house until April, 1956. They were out looking
G   for one when the wife spotted a cottage called Sendhurst Farm Cottage at Send,
    near Woking, which was empty and out of repair. It needed a lot of money
    spent on it. The building society stipulated that £300 should be spent on im-
    proving it. The cost of it was £2,180. It was conveyed into the husband's name
    alone. He paid the deposit of £380. His employers lent him that money at
    two per cent. interest; but he had to provide his life assurance as collateral
H   security. He borrowed £1,800 on mortgage from a building society. He paid
    the instalments on the mortgage. After getting the house, they both set to work
    improving it. The wife had good ideas and they both did a lot of work in carrying
    them out. He employed bricklayers and carpenters for some of it. Their friends
    helped too. The wife herself helped with the painting and decorating and with
    the garden. The husband worked hard too. They made it very habitable and
I   went into occupation in the autumn of 1956.
         It was submitted to us that the cottage was bought as a joint venture; but
    the registrar did not so find, and, in the absence of any such finding, I think
    that we must take it to have been intended to belong to the husband. After
    all, he provided all the finance and that is the test which folk usually apply. No
    point was taken that it was a post-nuptial settlement such as was discussed in
    Ulrich v. *Ulrich and Felton* (1).

---

    (1) [1968] 1 All E.R. 67.

After being there two years, they decided to sell the cottage. In August, 1958, **A** it was sold for £3,050. So there was a profit of £1,000. That money was put into shares in the husband's name. They went into a flat for a few months. Then in March, 1959, they found a plot of land, 37 Sandalwood Avenue, Chertsey, on which a house was being built. It was bought for £3,485. It was conveyed into the husbands' name. £3,000 was left on mortgage. He paid the deposit and other moneys, in all £700 or £750. He paid them out of the shares. He paid **B** the instalment to the building society of £19 19s. 7d. a month. It was a new house and little work had to be done on it, but they both worked in the garden, and so forth. They lived at 37 Sandalwood Avenue, Chertsey for four or five years; but in the autumn of 1964 the wife left the house, taking the two children with her. In November, 1964, she filed a petition for divorce. She charged her husband with adultery with other women, but she said that she had condoned **C** his adultery by having intercourse with him afterwards up to April, 1964. In addition, she charged him with cruelty. On May 4, 1965, she was granted a decree nisi on the ground of her husband's cruelty. It has since been made absolute.

After leaving her husband, the wife went to live at Hastings. She took a flat there where she lives with her two children. She applied for maintenance. His **D** earnings were £1,400 or £1,500 a year gross. An order was made on him to pay £7 10s. a week for the wife and £2 10s. a week for each child, making £12 10s. a week altogether. That maintenance must, I think, have been assessed on the basis that the wife was in the flat at Hastings and had not got any benefit from the matrimonial home. The husband has continued to live at the house, 37 Sandalwood Avenue, Chertsey paying the instalments to the building society **E** and all outgoings.

The wife took out an application before the district registrar claiming a good deal of the furniture and also a half share in the house itself. No question arises now as to the furniture; but the question is as to the house. The registrar found that the wife was entitled to a half share. He enquired into the case most carefully and set it out clearly. His crucial finding was contained in one sentence: **F**

" I accept the wife's claim that she was economical in her spending and that she spent many hours improving and decorating the house which otherwise would have been costly. It was in part at least due to her efforts that the cottage purchased for £2,000 in 1956 realised £3,050 when it was sold in 1958."

G

The question is whether in point of law and in fact the registrar's finding is justified. We have been throught all the cases once more. In *Appleton* v. *Appleton*, (2), the husband did work on his wife's house. He was a skilled craftsman who did work of an exceptional nature altogether. In *Jansen* v. *Jansen*, (3), the husband converted his wife's house into flats. In both these cases the work done by the husband was of a type which a contractor is normally employed **H** to do, not the odd jobs about the house and not even the painting and decorating which husbands often do. Only yesterday in *Pettitt* v. *Pettitt* (4) another division of this court commented on those cases. In the light of their observations, the position seems to be this. When the matrimonial home belongs to the wife (such as when it is left to her by a legacy or paid for by her own money), the husband does not get a share in the house simply because he puts up a shelf or **I** touches up a window sill or even paints and decorates a room. He has the benefit of living in the house rent free. He does not have to provide a roof over her head. He should not be entitled to a share in the house simply by doing the " do-it-yourself jobs " which husbands often do. He may, however, be entitled

(2) [1965] 1 All E.R. 44.
(3) [1965] 3 All E.R. 363; [1965] P. 478.
(4) Ante p. 1053.

A when the work is of a kind which normally a contractor is employed to do. The reason is because the court may then infer that the parties, if they had thought about it, would have agreed that if they separated, then in adjusting their financial affairs, the husband should be given a share in the proceeds of the house commensurate with the work he had done.

   Now consider the converse position when the wife does work in the husband's
B house. Hitherto the cases have all been concerned with *a wife's financial contribution.* If she puts some of her savings into the purchase of the house or if she goes out to work and earns money which helps, directly or indirectly, to pay the instalments to the building society, then she is usually entitled to a share in the house, and it is often a half share (see *Rimmer* v. *Rimmer* (5); *Fibrance* v. *Fibrance* (6)). She does not, however, get a share if her financial
C contribution is not substantial. That is shown by *Tully* v. *Tully* (7).

   This is the first case, I think, to come before us where the wife has done work on the husband's house but has made no financial contribution. I think that similar principles apply as when it is the other way about. The wife does not get a share in the house simply because she cleans the walls or works in the garden or helps her husband with the painting and decorating. Those are the sort of
D things which a wife does for the benefit of the family without altering the title to, or interests in, the property. Take the present case. The wife was economical in spending on the house keeping, as most wives are. She helped with the decorating and improvements to the house, as many wives do. It no doubt improved the value of the property. I was inclined during the argument to accept that her work was so great as to entitle her at least to a share in the house. But
E after discussion with my brethren, I have come to the conclusion that the proper inference from the evidence is that it was the ordinary kind of work which a husband or wife may do on the matrimonial home without giving the other a share or interest in it.

   One thing which influences me a good deal is the award of maintenance that was made. The wife's maintenance of £7 10s. a week for herself and £2 10s. a
F week for each child must, I think, have been assessed on the footing that the house belonged to the husband, and that as she had no benefit from it, she ought to have enough money to keep her and the children. As I have said on other occasions, I think it would be an advantage if all financial questions between husband and wife could be settled at one and the same time. Maintenance is linked with the property. If the wife stays in the house, her maintenance may
G be reduced on that account. If she gets a substantial capital sum out of the house, it may affect her maintenance. So it would be a good thing if applications as to maintenance and property were heard together. Seeing that the wife and children here have reasonable maintenance, in all the circumstances of the case I do not think it is a case where she has any interest in the house.

   I would allow the appeal accordingly.

H

   DANCKWERTS, L.J.: I am glad to say I am able to agree with the judgment of LORD DENNING, M.R. Yesterday in *Pettitt* v. *Pettitt* (8) I expressed my views on s. 17 of the Married Women's Property Act, 1882, and also on the more controversial cases of *Appleton* v. *Appleton* (9) and others of that kind. The view which I expressed about the section is that it is procedural and does
I not enable the court to alter the existing property rights of the parties.

   As regards the further question whether husband or wife, as the case may be, is entitled to a share in the house which is in the name of the other, the matter is more difficult. I concede that where money contributions have been made

---

(5) [1952] 2 All E.R. 863; [1953] 1 Q.B. 63.
(6) [1957] 1 All E.R. 357.   (7) (1965), 109 Sol. Jo. 956.
(8) Ante p. 1053.   (9) [1965] 1 All E.R. 44.

by both husband and wife, there may well be an intention that there should be **A**
shares in the ownership of the house, in whosesoever name the house may happen
to be; but where the claim is based on work done, it seems to me the matter
is more problematical and it is more difficult to ascertain an intention to give
any particular share. This seems to me to be one of those cases, and it seems
to me that there was not work done in this case which would justify the court
in holding that the wife was entitled to a share in the house which was in the **B**
husband's name.

I, therefore, agree with the judgment of LORD DENNING, M.R.; and I would
allow the appeal.

WIDGERY, L.J.: I agree with the judgment of LORD DENNING, M.R., and
although we are differing from the learned district registrar, there is nothing that I **C**
can usefully add.

Appeal allowed.

Leave to appeal to the house of Lords refused.

Solicitors: *Simmonds, Church Rackham,* (for the husband); *John Lester,*
Hastings (for the wife).   **D**

[*Reported by* F. GUTTMAN, ESQ., *Barrister-at-Law.*]

E

BARNETT *v.* CHELSEA & KENSINGTON HOSPITAL MANAGEMENT COMMITTEE.

[QUEEN'S BENCH DIVISION (Nield, J.), October 25, 26, 27, November 8, 1967.]

F

*Hospital—Negligence—Liability for negligence of members of staff—Casualty
officer—Duty to see and examine patient presenting himself at casualty
department and complaining of illness, when casualty department open—
Arsenical poisoning—Patient's death not caused by the negligence.*

At about 5 a.m. on Jan. 1, 1966, three night watchmen drank some tea.
Soon afterwards all three men started vomiting. At about 8 a.m. the men **G**
walked to the casualty department of the defendants' hospital, which was
open. One of them, the deceased, when he was in the room in the hospital,
lay on some armless chairs. He appeared ill. Another of the men told the
nurse that they had been vomiting after drinking tea. The nurse telephoned
the casualty officer, a doctor, to tell him of the men's complaint. The
casualty officer, who was himself unwell, did not see them, but said that **H**
they should go home and call in their own doctors. The men went away, and
the deceased died some hours later from what was found to be arsenical
poisoning. Cases of arsenical poisoning were rare, and, even if the deceased
had been examined and admitted to the hospital and treated, there was
little or no chance that the only effective antidote would have been administered to him before the time at which he died. In an action against the
defendant hospital management committee for damages for negligence in
that the deceased's condition was not diagnosed nor treated at the hospital, **I**

Held: in failing to see and examine the deceased, and in failing to admit
him to hospital and treat him, the hospital's casualty officer was negligent
and did not discharge the duty of care which in the circumstances was owed
to the deceased by the defendants as hospital authority (see p. 1073, letters G
and H, and p. 1074, letter B, post); but the plaintiff had not discharged the
onus of proving that the deceased's death was caused by the negligence, or,

A   if there were a burden on the defendants of showing that his death was not due
to the negligence, they had discharged that burden, with the consequence
that the plaintiff's claim failed (see p. 1074, letters D and I, post).

[Editorial Note. It should be emphasised that a premise of this decision is
that the casualty department was open for receiving patients (see p. 1072, letter D,
B   post).
As to the liability of hospital authorities for negligence by their medical staff
see 28 HALSBURY'S LAWS (3rd Edn.), 19, 21, para. 17, and for cases on the subject,
see 33 DIGEST (Repl.) 532-535, *100-112.*]

Cases referred to:
Bonnington Castings, Ltd. v. *Wardlaw,* [1956] 1 All E.R. 615; [1956] A.C. 613;
C   [1956] 2 W.L.R. 707; 34 Digest (Repl.) 268, *1899.*
Cassidy v. *Ministry of Health,* [1951] 1 All E.R. 574; [1951] 2 K.B. 343; 33
Digest (Repl.) 534, *112.*
Donoghue (or McAlister) v. *Stevenson,* [1932] 1 All E.R. Rep. 1; [1932] A.C.
562; 101 L.J.P.C. 119; 147 L.T. 281; 36 Digest (Repl.) 85, *458.*
Heaven v. *Pender,* [1881-85] All E.R. Rep. 35; (1883), 11 Q.B.D. 503; 52
D   L.J.Q.B. 702; 49 L.T. 357; 47 J.P. 709; 36 Digest (Repl.) 7, *10.*
Le Lièvre v. *Gold,* [1893] 1 Q.B. 491; 62 L.J.Q.B. 353; 68 L.T. 626; 57 J.P.
481; 36 Digest (Repl.) 9, *27.*

Action.
This was an action for negligence brought by the widow and administratrix
of William Patrick Barnett against the Chelsea and Kensington Hospital
E   Management Committee. The facts are set out in the judgment.
The cases noted below* were cited during the argument in addition to those
referred to in the judgment.

P. R. Pain, *Q.C.,* and *L. S. Shields* for the plaintiff.
John Wilmers, Q.C., and *D. D. H. Sullivan* for the defendants.
F
                                                        Cur. adv. vult.

Nov. 8.   **NIELD, J.:**   At the outset of my judgment in this case I propose
to indicate the general conclusions which I have reached. I do so for two reasons:
the first so that those who are most nearly interested are not required to wait
throughout a lengthy judgment to know what my decision is likely to be; the
second so that counsel may consider whether or no further argument is needed
G   before judgment is finally entered. My conclusions are: that the plaintiff has
failed to establish, on the balance of probabilities, that the deceased's death
resulted from the negligence of the defendants, my view being that, had all care
been taken, the deceased might still have died. My further conclusions, however,
are that Dr. Banerjee was negligent in failing to see and examine the deceased, and
H   that had he done so his duty would have been to admit the deceased to the ward
and to have treated him or caused him to be treated.
The plaintiff is the widow of William Patrick Barnett, who died on Jan. 1,
1966, from arsenical poisoning, and she is also the administratrix of his estate.
She claims damages on behalf of herself and two of her children as dependants
of the deceased and also on behalf of his estate. The defendant committee were
I   at all material times responsible for the management of St. Stephen's Hospital,
Chelsea.
The deceased was employed as a night watchman at a hall of residence at the
Chelsea College of Sciences and Technology. Also employed in a similar capacity

---

* *Armory* v. *Delamirie,* (1722), 1 Stra. 505; *Ratcliffe* v. *Evans,* [1891-94] All E.R.
Rep. 699; [1892] 2 Q.B. 524; *The Ophelia,* [1916] 2 A.C. 206; *Coldman* v. *Hill,* [1918-19]
All E.R. Rep. 434; [1919] 1 K.B. 443; *Bolam* v. *Friern Hospital Management Committee,*
[1957] 2 All E.R. 118.

but in a different part of the college were Frederick Whittall and Herbert Weig- **A**
hall—the latter being the senior watchman. On Dec. 31, 1965, these three watchmen came on duty at about 9.30 p.m. and later had some drinks to celebrate the
coming of the New Year. Shortly before 4 a.m. next morning the watchman
Mr. Whittall was attacked by an intruder and struck on the head with an iron
bar. The police were called and took Mr. Whittall to St. Stephen's Hospital. He
was received by a nurse and was seen by the casualty officer, Dr. Banerjee, who **B**
dressed his injuries and advised him to return at 9.45 a.m. for an x-ray to make
sure that there was no bone injury. The deceased was sent for and drove Mr.
Whittall back from the hospital to the college in his car.

At about 5 a.m. all three watchmen drank some tea. Some of it came from a
flask and some was freshly made in a teapot. After drinking the tea the deceased
complained of the heat in the room and then within twenty minutes of drinking **C**
the tea all three men started to vomit, and the vomiting continued persistently
until about 8 a.m. when the day workers arrived at the college. The three
watchmen then made their way in the deceased's car—which he drove quite
normally—to the casualty department of St. Stephen's Hospital. There was
no-one at the reception desk and, in fact, there is no receptionist on duty there
during the night. In the daytime a receptionist is stationed at the desk and takes **D**
particulars of all who call at the casualty department.

There is some difference between the accounts of the various witnesses as to
what took place in the casualty department and I think that Nurse Corbett's
recollection is at fault on several points. In fact Mr. Weighall met Nurse Corbett
in the middle of the room and asked if they could, as he put it, please see a doctor,
as after drinking some tea at 5 a.m. they had been vomiting continuously. **E**
Mr. Weighall was suffering from cramp and thinks that he may have mentioned
it. On the accident record card someone has written " cramp " but we do not
know who it was. Mr. Whittall told Nurse Corbett, as the fact was, that he had
been at the hospital earlier and had gone back to his work and also said that they
had all been vomiting. The deceased walked quite normally to the far side of the
room and lay not " sat " as Nurse Corbett said—on some armless chairs placed **F**
together with his head on his hand. He did not speak and appeared ill, and
Nurse Corbett could see this. Mr. Weighall went two or three times to the lavatory
thinking that he was about to vomit, although he did not do so, and these visits
too could be seen by Nurse Corbett. Nurse Corbett, it was said, seemed somewhat
hesitant as to what she should do. While in the room Mr. Weighall stood with his
arm on the back of a chair to obtain relief, if he could, from the cramp which he **G**
felt in the area of his stomach and also in his feet. It was obvious to anyone that
he was suffering and, indeed, could not keep still. When Mr. Weighall told Nurse
Corbett that the vomiting followed the drinking of tea, Nurse Corbett said " tea
would not cause that", and it is clear to me that it was at first thought that these
three men had been drinking to excess, although Nurse Corbett did not continue
to have this impression. **H**

At this time Mr. Weighall became angry and speaking abruptly and almost
shouting he said " I didn't come here for nothing. We are ill. Can we or can we
not see a doctor? " Nurse Corbett then spoke on the telephone, not immediately
after speaking to Mr. Weighall as she says, but five or ten minutes later, and said
words to this effect: " Is that Dr. Banerjee? There are three men complaining
of vomiting after drinking tea " and Dr. Banerjee replied: **I**

" Well, I'm vomiting myself and I have not been drinking. Tell them to
go home and go to bed and call in their own doctors—except Mr. Whittall
who should stay because he is due for an x-ray later this morning."

It is thus clear that Mr. Whittall must, as he says, have told the nurse about his
earlier visit and she in turn must have told Dr. Banerjee that Whittall had been
there earlier.

Dr. Banerjee's message was given by the nurse to the three men and they,

A   thinking it was final, all left. Mr. Whittall decided not to stay because no treatment had been suggested. The deceased walked normally from his chair and then
drove his two companions back to the college, and again drove perfectly properly.
At the college the deceased went into the telephone room and lay down on the
floor with a cushion under his head. About 9.10 a.m. Mr. Whittall asked the
deceased how he felt and the deceased said " Leave me alone, I'll be all right ".

B   According to the evidence of a Mr. Waterman given before the coroner at the
inquest he, Mr. Waterman, saw the deceased after 9 a.m. in the hall sitting on a
packing case beside the radiator. It was a cold morning. He then went to sit in
the staff tearoom. " I saw him ", said Mr. Waterman,

> " at 11 a.m. in the staff tearoom. I was the only one on duty. I went in to
C   see him several times. By 11 a.m. he had stopped vomiting and had dry
retches. He had a headache. I offered to get him anything he fancied from
the chemist. I went off duty at 1.50 p.m. I last saw [the deceased] at about
12.15 p.m."

When asked further questions he said:

D   > " He always was rather short of breath and rather pale. He did not seem
unduly distressed when I last saw him."

Mr. Whittall then went home and called in his own doctor, Dr. Sutcliffe. Dr.
Sutcliffe did not advise Mr. Whittall to go to hospital, but saw him again twice
that day at the request of the police.

E   Mr. Weighall appears to have stayed at the college all morning. About 1 p.m.
he went to the deceased who said, when asked if Mr. Whittall could call a doctor,
" Leave me, I'll be all right ", but Mr. Weighall said " Well, I'm sorry, but I
am going to get a doctor ". He then telephoned for the doctor retained by the
college who came and it is clear to me it was too late to do anything for the
deceased and the deceased died about 1.30 p.m.

F   The point was made that these men, the watchmen, might have called in the
college doctor instead of going to the hospital, but I do not think that they can
be in any way blamed for not calling in the college doctor. They would not know
the terms of the college doctor's appointment by the college and might well have
hesitated before disturbing him at an early hour. As I have said, the deceased
died about 1.30 p.m. and the information to the medical superintendent which
is on the form exhibited says, when asked to state the date and hour of arrival,
G   " 2 p.m. Jan. 1, 1966 " and in reply to the question if any known illness state
nature, etc. " Gastritis and nausea and vomiting for some hours previously ".
The inference is that some person with murderous intent had introduced arsenic
into the tea, and the coroner's verdict was one of murder by a person or persons
unknown. I have said something of the course which Mr. Weighall's evidence
took, and it is further to be noted that Mr. Weighall was seen at the hospital and
H   his account on his medical card shows a diagnosis of gastritis.

The plaintiff's case is pleaded in this way:

> " The said death was due to the negligence of the defendants by their
servants or agents in not diagnosing or treating the deceased's condition."

I   It is put on behalf of the plaintiff that the defendants should have inferred that
the deceased was suffering, or might be suffering, from poisoning; that they failed
to investigate or diagnose the deceased's condition when he presented himself at
the hospital; that they failed to treat him for poisoning, and they so failed having
knowledge of the history of vomiting.

I turn to consider the nature of the duty which the law imposes on persons in
the position of the defendants and their servants and agents. The authorities
deal in the main with the duties of doctors, surgeons, consultants, nurses and
staff when a person is treated either by a doctor at his surgery or the patient's

home or when the patient is treated in or at a hospital. In *Cassidy* v. *Ministry* A *of Health* (1), DENNING, L.J., dealt with the duties of hospital authorities and said:

" In my opinion, authorities who run a hospital, be they local authorities, government boards, or any other corporation, are in law under the self-same duty as the humblest doctor. Whenever they accept a patient for treatment, they must use reasonable care and skill to cure him of his ailment. The B hospital authorities cannot, of course, do it by themselves. They have no ears to listen through the stethoscope, and no hands to hold the knife. They must do it by the staff which they employ, and, if their staff are negligent in giving the treatment, they are just as liable for that negligence as is anyone else who employs others to do his duties for him. Is there any possible difference in law, I ask, can there be, between hospital authorities who C accept a patient for treatment and railway or shipping authorities who accept a passenger for carriage? None whatever. Once they undertake the task, they come under a duty to use care in the doing of it, and that is so whether they do it for reward or not."

Here the problem is different and no authority bearing directly on it has been cited to me. It is to determine the duty of those who provide and run a casualty D department when a person presents himself at that department complaining of illness or injury and before he is treated and received into the hospital wards. This is not a case of a casualty department which closes its doors and says that no patients can be received. The three watchmen entered the defendants' hospital without hindrance, they made complaints to the nurse who received them and she in turn passed those complaints on to the medical casualty officer, E and he sent a message through the nurse purporting to advise the three men. Is there, on these facts, shown to be created a relationship between the three watchmen and the hospital staff such as gives rise to a duty of care in the defendants which they owe to the three men?

In *Donoghue* v. *Stevenson* (2), LORD ATKIN, referred to *Le Lièvre* v. *Gold* (3), when A. L. SMITH, L.J., said: F

" ' The decision in *Heaven* v. *Pender* (4) was founded upon the principle that a duty to take care did arise when the person or property of one was in such proximity to the person or property of another that, if due care was not taken, damage might be done by the one to the other.' I think that this sufficiently states the truth if proximity be not confined to mere physical proximity, but be used, as I think it was intended, to extend to such close and G direct relations that the act complained of directly affects a person whom the person alleged to be bound to take care would know would be directly affected by his careless act."

In my judgment, there was here such a close and direct relationship between the hospital and the watchmen that there was imposed on the hospital a duty of H care which they owed to the watchmen. Thus I have no doubt that Nurse Corbett and Dr. Banerjee were under a duty to the deceased to exercise that skill and care which is to be expected of persons in such positions acting reasonably, or, as it is, I think very helpfully, put by the learned author of WINFIELD ON TORTS (7th Edn.) p. 183—

" where anyone is engaged in a transaction in which he holds himself out as I having professional skill, the law expects him to show the average amount of competence associated with the proper discharge of the duties of that profession or trade or calling, and if he falls short of that and injures someone in consequence, he is not behaving reasonably."

Moreover, the author proceeds to give a warning that the rule must be applied

(1) [1951] 1 All E.R. 574 at p. 585; [1951] 2 K.B. 343 at p. 360.
(2) [1932] All E.R. Rep. 1 at pp. 11, 12; [1932] A.C. 562 at p. 581.
(3) [1893] 1 Q.B. 491 at p. 504.   (4) [1881-85] All E.R. Rep. 35; (1883), 11 Q.B.D. 503.

A   with some care to see that too high a degree of skill is not demanded, and he gives as an example " a passer-by who renders emergency first-aid after an accident is not required to show the skill of a qualified surgeon ".

Let me say at this stage that there is no complaint against Nurse Corbett that she failed in her duty.

B   There are two main questions here: Has the plaintiff established, on the balance of probabilities, (i) that Dr. Banerjee was negligent, and, if so, (ii) that such negligence caused the death of the deceased?

The first of these questions can be divided into four other questions—(i) Should Dr. Banerjee have seen the deceased? (ii) Should he have examined the deceased? (iii) Should he have admitted the deceased to the wards? (iv) Should he have treated or caused to be treated the deceased?

C   The first two of those four questions can be answered together. It is not, in my judgment, the case that a casualty officer must always see the caller at his department. Casualty departments are misused from time to time. If the receptionist, for example, discovers that the visitor is already attending his own doctor and merely wants a second opinion, or if the caller has a small cut which the nurse can perfectly well dress herself, then the casualty officer need not be

D   called. However, apart from such things as this, I find the opinion of Dr. Sydney Lockett entirely acceptable. He said—and I give his words as nearly as I can, not having had a shorthand writer—

" In my view, the duty of a casualty officer is in general to see and examine all patients who come to the casualty department of the hospital."

E   He then cited some exceptions such as I have given.

" When a nurse is told that three men have been vomiting, having drunk tea, and have abdominal pains her duty is to report it, and she should report accurately to the doctor. The first step she should take to deal with the matter is to take a history "

F   and the doctor put it most emphatically in this way:

" I cannot conceive that after a history of vomiting for three hours a doctor would leave the matter to a nurse, however experienced the nurse."

Without doubt Dr. Banerjee should have seen and examined the deceased. His failure to do either cannot be described as an excusable error as has been submitted, it was negligence. It is unfortunate that Dr. Banerjee was himself

G   at the time a tired and unwell doctor, but there was no-one else to do that which it was his duty to do. Having examined the deceased I think that the first and provisional diagnosis would have been one of food poisoning.

The third question is should Dr. Banerjee have admitted the deceased to the wards? It is sufficient to say that I accept Dr. Lockett's opinion that, having regard to all the circumstances, it was Dr. Banerjee's duty to have admitted him.

H   The fourth question is should Dr. Banerjee have treated the deceased or caused him to be treated, and it is the case that, once admitted, the deceased's case could have gone to the medical registrar or to others if such was the desire. The immediate purpose of admission would be for observation and diagnosis. No-one who has listened to the evidence can doubt that arsenical poisoning is extremely difficult to diagnose. Professor Camps accepted some figures which were put

I   to him which were these, that out of six thousand deaths between 1955 and 1965 from poisoning only five were due to arsenical poisoning. Again, that three or four million people are admitted to about five thousand hospitals in the course of a year and only sixty are cases of arsenical poisoning or potassium loss.

I conclude that after a period of observation and after taking the patient's blood pressure and subjecting him to other general tests, and on a reconsideration of the history, in particular the fact that vomiting had occurred within twenty minutes of drinking the tea and also finding loss of fluid, the doctor would have rejected the provisional diagnosis of food or staphyloccocal poisoning and have

decided that it might well have been a case of metallic poisoning. In any event, **A**
I am satisfied that the deceased's condition of dehydration and severe malaise
was such that intravenous treatment should have been given. Further, I think
it would have become plain that it was necessary to test a specimen of the
deceased's blood and in the end to send certain other specimens away for analysis
to discover what poison it was which was causing the deceased's condition.

Thus it is that I find that under all four headings the defendants were negligent **B**
and in breach of their duty in that they or their servants or agents did not see and
did not examine and did not admit and did not treat the deceased.

It remains to consider whether it is shown that the deceased's death was caused
by this negligence or whether, as the defendants have said, the deceased must have
died in any event. In his concluding submission counsel for the plaintiff submitted
that Dr. Banerjee should have examined the deceased and, had he done so, he **C**
would have caused tests to be made which would have indicated the treatment
required and that, since the defendants were at fault in these respects, therefore
the onus of proof passed to the defendants to show that the appropriate treatment
would have failed, and authorities were cited to me. I find myself unable to accept
this argument and I am of the view that the onus of proof remains on the plaintiff,
and I have in mind (without quoting it) the decision quoted by counsel for the **D**
defendants in *Bonnington Castings, Ltd.* v. *Wardlaw* (5). However, were it
otherwise and the onus did pass to the defendants, then I would find that they
have discharged it, as I would proceed to show.

There has been put before me a timetable which, I think, is of much importance.
The deceased attended at the casualty department at 8.5 or 8.10 a.m. If Dr.
Banerjee had got up and dressed and come to see the three men and examined **E**
them and decided to admit them, the deceased (and Dr. Lockett agreed with this)
could not have been in bed in a ward before 11 a.m. I accept Dr. Goulding's
evidence that an intravenous drip would not have been set up before 12 noon,
and if potassium loss was suspected it could not have been discovered until 12.30.
Dr. Lockett, dealing with this, said " If [the deceased] had not been treated until
after 12 noon the chances of survival were not good ". **F**

Without going in detail into the considerable volume of technical evidence
which has been put before me, it seems to me to be the case that when death
results from arsenical poisoning it is brought about by two conditions; on the
one hand dehydration and on the other disturbance of the enzyme processes. If
the principal condition is one of enzyme disturbance—as I am of the view that
it was here—then the only method of treatment which is likely to succeed is the **G**
use of the specific or antidote which is commonly called B.A.L. Dr. Goulding said
this in the course of his evidence:

> " The only way to deal with this is to use the specific B.A.L. I see no
> reasonable prospect of the deceased being given B.A.L. before the time
> at which he died,"

and at a later point in his evidence: **H**

> " I feel that even if fluid loss had been discovered death would have been
> caused by the enzyme disturbance. Death might have occurred later."

I regard that evidence as very moderate, and that it might be a true assessment
of the situation to say that there was no chance of B.A.L. being administered
before the death of the deceased. **I**

For these reasons, I find that the plaintiff has failed to establish, on the grounds
of probability, that the defendants' negligence caused the death of the deceased.

Judgment for the defendants.

Solicitors: *W. H. Thompson* (for the plaintiff); *Nigel Ryland* (for the
defendants).   [*Reported by* MARY COLTON, *Barrister-at-Law.*]

---

(5) [1956] 1 All E.R. 615; [1956] A.C. 613.

Affirmed. C.A. [1969] 2 All E.R. 193.

A

LONDON ARTISTS, LTD. *v.* LITTLER

[AND ASSOCIATED ACTIONS].

[QUEEN'S BENCH DIVISION (Cantley, J.), February 12, 13, 14, 15, 16, 19, 20, 21, 22, 23, 26, 27, 1968.]

B *Libel—Fair comment—Public interest—Communication to press—Letter deploring simultaneous termination of engagements privately by four artistes in a play running at a London theatre—Whether simultaneous giving of notices was a matter of public interest.*

Libel—Fair comment—Words defamatory of plaintiffs defended as being fair comment on coincidence of acts of other persons—Whether defence open to defendant.

C

Libel—Privilege—Qualified privilege—Communication to press—Simultaneous termination of their engagements at London theatre by four artistes privately giving contractual month's notice—Unusual happening likely to curtail run of successful play—Coincidence of notice with alleged wish to transfer another play to that theatre—Letter to artistes by employing impressario deploring their simultaneous notice—Communication of letter to national press—Alleged defamation of artistes' theatrical agents and other plaintiffs who were not the artistes—Principles governing qualified privilege.

D

For the purposes of the defence of fair comment on a matter of public interest, matters which may qualify as being of public interest may be broadly divided into two classes:

E
(a) matters in which the public in general have a legitimate interest directly or indirectly, nationally or locally, clear examples being matters connected with national and local government, public services and institutions, and

(b) matters which are expressly or impliedly submitted to public criticism or attention, established examples being productions at public theatres and the performances of theatrical artistes offered for public entertainment,

F
but not including the private lives of public performers (see p. 1086, letter I, to p. 1087, letter A, post).

On June 22, 1965, four theatrical artistes (three of whom were recognised as "stars") through their agents, the first named plaintiffs, each gave privately a month's notice in writing (as permitted in their contracts) to

G
terminate on the same day their engagement in a play which was staged by the defendant at a London theatre, Her Majesty's Theatre. The coincidence of the simultaneous giving of notice was, on the evidence, in the highest degree unusual. Coincidental with it, so the defendant submitted, was the fact that the management was trying to transfer another play to Her Majesty's Theatre. On June 23, 1965, the defendant wrote a letter in

H
closely similar terms to each of the three stars*, deploring their conduct in giving simultaneous notice and referring to all four plaintiffs in these associated actions, all of whom were connected with the entertainments industry, and at a press conference on the same day he made the letter available to the national press in which it received wide publicity. It was alleged by the first plaintiffs that the words of the defendant's letter meant and were

I
intended to mean that they had been parties to a conspiracy to procure the artistes to leave the play at Her Majesty's Theatre in order that the play should close and that possession of the theatre could thereby be obtained for the second and third named plaintiffs, and that the first plaintiffs had not acted as independent agents in the interest of the artistes, as they purported to do, but had been obliged to serve the interests of the second and third named plaintiffs. At the close of the evidence for the plaintiffs

---

* The text of the letter written to Miss Coral Browne is set out at p. 1077, letter H, to p. 1078, letter E, post.

a defence* of justification (viz., the existence in fact of a conspiracy) was **A**
withdrawn; it being conceded, in effect, that there was not in fact such a
conspiracy. For the purposes of ruling on further defences, viz.—(i) a
defence that the occasion of publication of the letter in the national press was
one of qualified privilege, and (ii) a defence that the words in the letter
published to the press were fair comment on a matter of public interest—the
court assumed that the letter was capable of a meaning defamatory of each **B**
of the plaintiffs. The matter of public interest (for the purposes of (ii) above)
was, so the defendant contended, the coincidence of the simultaneous giving
of the notices privately by the four artistes and the alleged desire of the
management of the theatre to transfer another play to that theatre.

Held: (i) the publication of the letter to the public through the press
was not publication on an occasion of qualified privilege, because that **C**
privilege was confined to cases where a defendant had a legal, social or moral
duty to communicate the information to the general public, and in the
present case, although the information might be of general public interest,
it was not a matter on which the public had any legitimate interest in being
informed; nor did the defendant's own legitimate interests require such
publication to be made (see p. 1085, letters A, C and E, post). **D**

Principles stated by BUCKLEY, L.J., in *Adam* v. *Ward* ((1915), 31 T.L.R.
at p. 304) applied.

Webb v. *Times Publishing Co., Ltd.* ([1960] 2 All E.R. 789) distinguished.

(ii) the coincidence (or double coincidence) above referred to did not
render the action of the artistes, in giving simultaneously and privately
notices terminating their engagements, a matter of public interest, even if **E**
taken in conjunction with a desire of the theatre's management to put on
another play, for the action of the artistes, and the desire of the management,
were not matters submitted impliedly to public criticism and attention;
accordingly, the defence of fair comment on a matter of public interest was
not open to the defendant in respect of the publication of the letter to the
public through the press (see p. 1087, letters G and I, post). **F**

Per CURIAM: assuming, contrary to (ii) above, the matter to be one of
public interest, the defendant could not maintain by way of defence to the
allegation of conspiracy a plea that his words were fair comment, because
the uttering of matter defamatory of the plaintiffs could not be defended
as against them on the ground that it was fair comment on the conduct of
others, viz., the artistes (see p. 1088, letter G, post). **G**

[Editorial Note. The publications of the letters to the artistes were each
on a privileged occasion (see p. 1085, letter F, post).

As to what is an occasion of qualified privilege at common law, see 24 HALS-
BURY'S LAWS (3rd Edn.) 56, 57, paras. 100, 101; as to the defence of fair comment, see ibid., pp. 70, 71, paras. 123, 124; and for examples of matters of **H**
public interest, see ibid., pp. 72-74, para. 126. For cases on qualified privilege
and fair comment, see 32 DIGEST (Repl.) 129-133, *1506-1533a*, and 169, 170,
183, *1835-1843*; and as to what matters rank as matters of public interest,
see ibid., 172-176, *1859-1895*.]

Cases referred to:
Adam v. *Ward*, [1916-17] All E.R. Rep. 157; [1917] A.C. 309; 86 L.J.K.B. **I**
    849; 117 L.T. 34; *affg.* (1915), 31 T.L.R. 299; 32 Digest (Repl.) 150,
    1690.
Allbutt v. *General Council of Medical Education & Registration*, (1889), 23
    Q.B.D. 400; 58 L.J.Q.B. 606; 61 L.T. 585; 54 J.P. 36; 32 Digest
    (Repl.) 148, *1678*.

---

* Particulars of the defence are set out in summarised form at p. 1079, letters A
to E, post.

A   *Banks* v. *Globe & Mail, Ltd.,* [1961] S.C.R. 474; 28 D.J.R. (2d) 343; 32 Digest
        (Repl.) 172, *712*.
    Brown v. *Croome,* (1817), 2 Stark. 297; 171 E.R. 652; 32 Digest (Repl.) 157,
        1730.
    Chapman v. *Lord Ellesmere,* [1932] All E.R. Rep. 221; [1932] 2 K.B. 431;
        101 L.J.K.B. 376; 146 L.T. 538; 32 Digest (Repl.) 30, *185*.
B   *Cox* v. *Feeney,* (1863), 4 F. & F. 13; 32 Digest (Repl.) 137, *1901*.
    Mangena v. *Wright,* [1909] 2 K.B. 958; 78 L.J.K.B. 879; 100 L.T. 900;
        32 Digest (Repl.) 167, *1823*.
    Purcell v. *Sowler,* (1877), 2 C.P.D. 215; 46 L.J.Q.B. 308; 36 L.T. 416; 41
        J.P. 789; 32 Digest (Repl.) 174, *1870*.
    Standen v. *South Essex Recorders, Ltd.,* (1934), 50 T.L.R. 365; 32 Digest
C   (Repl.) 156, *1726*.
    Stuart v. *Bell,* [1891] 2 Q.B. 341; 60 L.J.Q.B. 577; 64 L.T. 633; 32 Digest
        (Repl.) 142, *1623*.
    Webb v. *Times Publishing Co., Ltd.* [1960] 2 All E.R. 789; [1960] 2 Q.B. 535;
        [1960] 3 W.L.R. 352; 32 Digest (Repl.) 162, *1769*.

Actions.
D
These were four actions heard together, brought by each of four plaintiffs
connected with the entertainment industry in respect of the publication of a
letter written by the defendant, Emile Littler, to each of three theatrical stars,
and communicated by the defendant to the public through the national press,
in particular by publication in The Daily Telegraph for June 24, 1965. The
second to fourth plaintiffs claimed also damages for slander in respect of words
E   spoken by the defendant at a press conference at which he communicated
the contents of the letter to the press. The plaintiffs in the second action were
the Grade Organisation, Ltd.; the plaintiffs in the third action were Associated
Television, Ltd., and the plaintiff in the fourth action was Mr. Lew Grade. Mr.
Emile Littler was sole defendant in each action. The defences material to this
report were those of qualified privilege and fair comment but the defendant
F   also pleaded justification. The action brought by the first plaintiffs is taken as
example in this narrative. By writ issued on June 25, 1965, the first plaintiffs,
London Artists, Ltd., claimed damages for libel published in a letter dated
June 23, 1965, from the defendant to Miss Coral Browne and re-published
also in an article in the issue of The Daily Telegraph for June 24, 1965. By
their statement of claim the first plaintiffs alleged that they were carrying on
G   the business of theatrical agents and in the course of it acted as agents for
Mr. Anthony Quayle, Miss Coral Browne, Miss Anna Massey and Mr. Corin
Redgrave. They further alleged that by letter dated June 23, 1965, sent to
Miss Browne, the defendant, Mr. Emile Littler, falsely and maliciously wrote
and published of and concerning the first plaintiffs the following words—

H   " We have been friends for years and I am hurt that you did not see me
before being a party to what, on the face of it, appears to be a plan to close
the run of ' The Right Honourable Gentleman ' by joining in and sending
me a month's formal notice from your agent.
    " ' The Right Honourable Gentleman ' has been one of your greatest
hits in London and is still doing better than any play in the West End.
I   In spite of this Her Majesty's Theatre's new directorate are trying to get
our play out of the theatre. Fighting for you all, play, artistes, staff and
author, I have not acceded to their request to move because we have a
valid contract and are paying top rent and faithfully fulfilling all obligations.
Until box office takings drop below £3,500 for two consecutive weeks we can
contractually continue at Her Majesty's Theatre.
    " Her Majesty's Theatre, and a great many other theatres in London, are
now controlled by Associated Television of which Mr. Lew Grade is the
managing director. Mr. Grade's contract for service with Associated

Television, Ltd., is with the Grade Organisation, Ltd.　The Grade Organisa-　**A**
tion, Ltd. owns ' London Artists, Ltd.' (and other theatrical agencies) and
they manage our stars:

> Anthony Quayle
> Coral Browne
> Anna Massey
> and　　　　　　　　　　　　　　　　　　　　　　　　　　　　　　　**B**
> Corin Redgrave.

London Artists, Ltd., on June 22, by identical letters, gave notice to me by
hand for each artiste to terminate their services with the play on the same
identical date of July 24.

" In other words because I do not wish to disturb over a year's established　**C**
success at Her Majesty's Theatre, I am being put into a position by my
landlords, Associated Television, Ltd., whereby, by withdrawing all Grade
Star labour, the play must close down on the date on which these notices
expire.

" A great part of the success of ' The Right Honourable Gentleman '
has been the casting of this show and the combined effect of withdrawing　**D**
suddenly the three Grade stars and another Grade artiste on a given date
must finish our play for everybody at Her Majesty's and give Associated
Television, Ltd., possession of the theatre.　You must all realise this and
know that there has never been such a situation in the history of the theatre.
I feel this is such a serious matter, affecting all branches of the industry,
that I must make this correspondence available to Equity, the Society of　**E**
West End Theatre Managers and the national press."

The letter, as pleaded, bore the signature " Emile Littler ".　The first plaintiffs
further alleged that the defendant communicated copies of the letter to the
national newspapers for the purpose of publication and that it was published,
as previously stated, on June 24, 1965;　they alleged that the defendant sent　**F**
copies to Equity and to the Society of West End Theatre Managers, and caused
a copy thereof to be exhibited on a notice board at Her Majesty's Theatre.
The first plaintiffs pleaded:

" The said words in their natural and ordinary meaning meant and were
understood to mean that the [first plaintiffs] had been party to a conspiracy
to procure the actors to leave the play ' The Right Honourable Gentleman '　**G**
in order that the play would close and possession of the theatre could thereby
be obtained for Associated Television, Ltd. and the Grade Organisation,
Ltd. and that the [first plaintiffs] had not acted as independent agents on
behalf and in the interests of their clients, as they purported to do, but
had been obliged to serve the interests of Associated Television, Ltd. and
the Grade Organisation, Ltd."　　　　　　　　　　　　　　　　　　　　**H**

The first plaintiffs alleged that they had been greatly injured in their credit,
reputation and business, and they claimed damages.

By his defence the defendant, after various pleas and denials, including a
plea that the words complained of were true in substance and in fact, pleaded as
follows:　　　　　　　　　　　　　　　　　　　　　　　　　　　　　　　**I**

" Further or in the alternative, the said words were fair comment made
in good faith and without malice on a matter of public interest, namely
the fate of the play ' The Right Honourable Gentleman ' which was at all
material times enjoying a successful run on the public stage at Her Majesty's
Theatre.　The defendant will rely if necessary on s. 6 of the Defamation
Act, 1952.

" Further or in the alternative, the said words were published on occasions
of qualified privilege."

A Among matters included in particulars of the defence it was alleged* that Associated Television, Ltd., and A.B.C. Pictures, Ltd., financed the production of the play " Robert and Elizabeth " which had at all material times been staged at the Lyric Theatre; that Associated Television, Ltd., held nearly all the ordinary shares of Associated Theatres, Ltd., which by itself or a subsidiary company. was the lessee of the Lyric Theatre, that an agent of the producer of " Robert

B and Elizabeth " orally explained in April, 1965, to the defendant at his office that the money capacity of the Lyric Theatre did not show a weekly surplus adequate to discharge initial production costs and that his principals were interested in transferring the play to Her Majesty's Theatre.   By para. 20A of the defendant's amended particulars of defence, it was alleged as follows—

C " By writing or orally at a place or places and time or times unknown to the defendant or partly orally and partly by writing the [first plaintiffs] by themselves combined and planned with Mr. Lew Grade, Associated Television, Ltd., and the Grade Organisation, Ltd. by themselves their servants or agents to procure the termination of the run of ' The Right Honourable Gentleman ' at Her Majesty's Theatre ... [and certain acts and letters previously referred to] were respectively performed and written

D and delivered pursuant to such agreement, combination and plan; the existence whereof is necessarily to be inferred by reason of the facts and matters hereinbefore set forth.   The defendant will give particulars of any material document after discovery."

The defendant further alleged that he had been associated with the theatre

E for some forty years and had never encountered a situation similar to that disclosed by the facts thereinbefore set forth.

By their reply the first plaintiffs joined issue with the defendant on his defence. They further alleged that the defendant was actuated by express malice in the publication of the words complained of in the statement of claim.   They pleaded that the words were not fair or bona fide comment but assertions of fact and did

F not relate to a matter of public interest; and that, further, the occasion was not an occasion of qualified privilege.

Following on argument and submissions by counsel for the parties at the close of the evidence led for the four plaintiffs, counsel for the defendant stated that the defendant no longer relied on the plea of justification, and he asked for, and was granted, leave to amend the further particulars of defence by deletion

G of para. 20A (see p. 1085, letter I, post).   Thereupon legal argument ensued in the absence of the jury, relating to the defences of qualified privilege and fair comment.   With regard to the plea of fair comment, counsel for the defendant contended that the following passages in the letter previously quoted were comment:

H (In the first paragraph) " what, on the face of it, appears to be a plan to close the run of ' The Right Honourable Gentleman ' by joining in and sending me a month's formal notice from your agent."

(The whole of the fourth paragraph) " In other words, because I do not wish to disturb over a year's established success at Her Majesty's Theatre, I am being put into a position by my landlords, Associated Television, Ltd., whereby, by withdrawing all Grade Star labour, the play must close

I down on the date on which these notices expire."

(In the final paragraph) " I feel this is such a serious matter, affecting all branches of the industry, that I must make this correspondence available to Equity, the Society of West End Theatre Managers and the national press."

The rulings of CANTLEY, J., on the defendant's pleas of qualified privilege and

---

* At the trial the accuracy of certain of these allegations was disputed by the plaintiffs.

fair comment were given (at the invitation of counsel) before evidence was led A
for the defendant.

The cases noted below* were cited during the argument in addition to those
referred to in the judgment.

Desmond Ackner, Q.C., and *A. L. J. Lincoln* for the first plaintiffs.
G. R. F. Morris, Q.C., and *A. T. Hoolahan* for the second plaintiffs.
C. L. Hawser, Q.C., and *Brian T. Neill* for the third and fourth plaintiffs. B
Colin Duncan, Q.C., Peter Bristow, Q.C., and *Michael Kempster* for the defendant.

Cur. adv. vult.

Feb. 27. **CANTLEY, J.**, read the following judgment: These four actions
arise out of the publication by the defendant of a letter written by him to
theatrical artistes (1) and communicated by him to the public by means of the C
national press. In the case of three of the plaintiffs there were also claims for
slander (2) by means of words supplemental to the letter spoken by the defendant
at the press conference at which he published the contents of the letter to the
press. The four theatrical artistes had each by their agents, the first plaintiffs,
London Artists, Ltd., simultaneously given four weeks' notice to the defendant
to terminate their engagement in the play " The Right Honourable Gentleman ", D
which was then running at Her Majesty's Theatre.

For present purposes I am assuming, without any difficulty whatever, that the
letter and the defendant's words were capable of a meaning defamatory of
each of the plaintiffs, and, contrary to the true facts, suggested that the plaintiffs
had each taken part in a plot or manoeuvre to procure the termination of the
run of the play " The Right Honourable Gentleman " at Her Majesty's Theatre, E
by arranging for the four theatrical artistes simultaneously to give identical notice
to leave the cast.

In relation to the publication to which I have referred and also in relation
to the publication of the letter to each of the artistes, the defendant has pleaded
that the occasion was one of qualified privilege. I am invited by all parties to
rule at this stage whether or not the occasions were so privileged. It has not been F
suggested that there is any further evidence which I need to hear before forming
my view on this matter.

In relation to the publication to the general public by means of the press,
counsel for the defendant relies on the decision of PEARSON, J., in *Webb* v. *Times
Publishing Co., Ltd.* (3). In that case the defendants published a report of the
trial in a Swiss Court of a British subject who had formerly been tried in England, G
and the report contained matter which was defamatory of the plaintiff. PEARSON
J., held (4):

" that there was no qualified privilege of a general or ' blanket ' character
attaching to fair and accurate reports of judicial proceedings in foreign

---

* *Campbell* v. *Spottiswoode*, (1863), 3 B. & S. 769; *McQuire* v. *Western Morning News*, H
[1900-03] All E.R. Rep. 673; [1903] 2 K.B. 100; *Thomas* v. *Bradbury Agnew & Co.,
Ltd.*, [1904-07] All E.R. Rep. 220; [1906] 2 K.B. 627; *Peter Walker & Son* v. *Hodgson*,
[1909] 1 K.B. 239; *Aga Khan* v. *Times Publishing Co.*, [1924] 1 K.B. 675; *Sutherland*
v. *Stopes*, (1924), 39 T.L.R. 677; [1924] All E.R. Rep. 19; [1925] A.C. 47; *Burton* v. *Board*,
[1928] All E.R. Rep. 659; [1929] 1 K.B. 301; *Coetzee* v. *Union Periodicals, Ltd.*, [1931]
W.L.D.S. 37; *Caswell* v. *Powell Duffryn Associated Collieries, Ltd.*, [1939] 3 All E.R. 722;
[1940] A.C. 152; *Turner* v. *Metro-Goldwyn-Meyer Pictures, Ltd.*, [1950] 1 All E.R. 449; I
Kemsley v. *Foot*, [1952] 1 All E.R. 501; [1952] A.C. 345; *Truth (N.Z.), Ltd.* v. *Avery*,
[1959] N.Z.L.R. 274; *Jones* v. *Skelton*, [1963] 3 All E.R. 952; *Egger* v. *Lord Chelmsford*,
[1964] 3 All E.R. 406; [1965] 1 Q.B. 248; *Broadway Approvals, Ltd.* v. *Odhams Press,
Ltd.*, [1965] 2 All E.R. 523; *Montereale* v. *Longmans Green & Co., Ltd.*, (Feb. 23, 1965),
The Times.

(1) Mr. Anthony Quayle, Miss Coral Browne, Miss Anna Massey; Mr. Corin Redgrave
also gave notice at the same time as the three first named artistes, but the defendant
did not write a similar letter to him.
(2) These claims were abandoned at the hearing.
(3) [1960] 2 All E.R. 789; [1960] 2 Q.B. 535.   (4) [1960] 2 Q.B. at p. 536.

A   courts, since the reasons for the existence of such privilege attaching to reports of English judicial proceedings, based on the close concern of the whole British public in the administration of the law under which they live, were not readily applicable nor transferable to reports of foreign judicial proceedings."

B   He held, however:

"that qualified privilege attached to this particular report, for its subject-matter was closely connected with the administration of justice in England and was, therefore, of legitimate and proper interest to the English newspaper-reading public. The foundation of all privilege was the public interest in the sense of a legitimate and proper interest as opposed to an interest due to idle curiosity or a desire for gossip. Where such an interest

C   could be shown, there was such privilege for a newspaper report of foreign judicial proceedings."

Counsel for the defendant has submitted that the principle on which Pearson, J., decided *Webb's* case (5) is a principle of general application, namely, that there is a qualified privilege for any publication giving the public information on a

D   subject of proper and legitimate interest to the public, unless it can be shown that the publication was not made bona fide with a view to giving the public such information. If that principle were to be true without further qualification, it would indeed be a charter to persons, including those whom counsel for the first plaintiffs classified as the obstinate, the stupid and the unreasonable, (6) to disseminate untrue defamatory information of apparently legitimate public

E   interest, provided only that they honestly believed it and honestly thought that it was information which the public ought to have. If that were the law, few defendants would ever again need to plead the defence of fair comment or take on themselves the burden of proving that their comment was founded on facts and that the facts were true.

Counsel for the defendant further submitted that even if there is no general

F   right under the protection of privilege to publish information of interest to the public, the defendant in the present case was himself vitally interested in the subject-matter and the public had a corresponding interest in receiving the information which he gave them. Even if the principle be restricted to publication by a person who has himself some legitimate interest in the matter to which the publication relates, it gives him a startling licence to defame and on a grand

G   scale, unless he has further to show that he was under a legal, social or moral duty to give the information to the public, or that such publication was necessary for the proper defence of his own interests, or that the publication was strictly confined to those persons who indeed have a corresponding interest with him. Counsel for the defendant conceded yesterday that so far as communication to the public at large is concerned, the privilege should be confined to cases where,

H   to adopt the neat phrase suggested by counsel for the third and fourth plaintiffs, the publication was *in the* public interest and not merely *of* public interest. That is, I think, another way of saying that it must be the legal, social or moral duty of the publisher to communicate the information to the general public.

In the Court of Appeal in the case of *Adam* v. *Ward* (7), Buckley, L.J., said this:

I   "In *Cox* v. *Feeney* (8), a dictum of Tenterden, C.J., is quoted in the following terms: ' A man has a right to publish, for the purpose of giving the public information, that which it is proper for the public to know.' With great respect, I doubt whether there is contained in those words an

(5) [1960] 2 All E.R. 789; [1960] 2 Q.B. 535.
(6) His Lordship intimated, at the conclusion of his judgment, that this passage was not in any way intended to suggest that the defendant was among the classes specified.
(7) (1915), 31 T.L.R. 299 at p. 304.
(8) (1863), 4 F. & F. 13 at p. 18.

A

accurate statement of the circumstances in which a privileged occasion arises for the publication of matter interesting to the public. I am not prepared to hold that the publication even by a public body of its proceedings or conclusions in a matter of public interest is on that account and without more privileged. *Purcell* v. *Sowler* (9) is, I think, an authority to the contrary. I doubt whether in *Mangena* v. *Wright* (10) PHILLIMORE, J., was right in saying, that, ' where the communication is made by a public servant as to a matter within his province, it may be the subject of privilege in him ' if those words are intended to convey that those facts without more will create a privileged occasion. More, I think, is wanted. But the following proposition, I think, is true—that if the matter is matter of public interest and the party who publishes it owes a duty to communicate it to the public, the publication is privileged, and in this sense duty means not a duty as matter of law, but, to quote LINDLEY, L.J.'s words in *Stuart* v. *Bell* (11) ' a duty recognised by English people of ordinary intelligence and moral principle, but at the same time not a duty enforceable by legal proceedings, whether civil or criminal '."

B

C

In *Purcell* v. *Sowler* (9) which was referred to by BUCKLEY, L.J., in *Adam* v. *Ward* (12), privilege was sought for publication in a Manchester newspaper of the proceedings of a Board of Guardians at which charges of neglect were made against the plaintiff. The defendant set up a defence of privilege. SIR ALEXANDER COCKBURN, C.J., said this (13):

D

" It is not, therefore, because the matter under consideration is one which in its immediate consequences affects only a particular neighbourhood that it is not a matter of public concern. The management of the poor and the administration of the poor law in each local district are matters of public interest. In this management the medical attendance on the poor is matter of infinite moment, and consequently the conduct of a medical officer of the district may be of the greatest importance in that particular district, and so may concern the public in general. I, therefore, cannot concur with the Common Pleas Division in thinking that the matter to which the present libel relates was not a matter of public interest, within the rule as to privileged publications.

E

F

"The true question in the present case is whether, though the subject-matter was of general interest, the occasion on which the words were uttered was privileged, so as to protect the bona fide publication of the report."

G

He went on to hold that the occasion was not so privileged. MELLISH, L.J., said (14):

" The law on the subject of privilege is clearly defined by the authorities. Such a communication as the present ought to be confined in the first instance to those whose duty it is to investigate the charges. If one of the guardians had met a person not a ratepayer or parishioner, and had told him the charge against the plaintiff, surely he would have been liable to an action of slander. I do not mean to say that the matter was not of such public interest as that comments would not be privileged if the facts had been ascertained. If the neglect charged against the plaintiff had been proved, then fair comments on his conduct might have been justified."

H

He went on also to reject the privilege. BRAMWELL, J.A., who may be described as an ordinary judge of the Appeal Court, said (15):

I

" If this had been a discussion on the plaintiff's conduct, the facts not being in controversy, the matter was a subject of such general public

(9) (1877), 2 C.P.D. 215.   (10) [1909] 2 K.B. 958 at p. 978.
(11) [1891] 2 Q.B. 341 at p. 350.   (12) (1915), 31 T.L.R. at p. 304.
(13) (1877), 2 C.P.D. at p. 218.   (14) (1877), 2 C.P.D. at p. 221.
                 (15) (1877), 2 C.P.D. at p. 222, 223.

A   interest as would have given a right to comment upon it; and fair and bona fide comments would have been justified. But that is not this case. This is a case in which the defendants have published a true and bona fide report of a statement of facts charged against the plaintiff, but a statement which shows that the person making it was making it in the absence of the plaintiff and without any knowledge on the part of the person making it. B   There was no duty to report such ex parte proceedings; if the guardians did not exclude strangers, as they might well have done, the reporter ought to have taken care what he was about, and not to have reported libellous matter; and the defendants, having published it, must take the consequences."

C   In *Chapman* v. *Lord Ellesmere* (16) it was sought to establish qualified privilege for a report in " The Times " newspaper of a decision of the stewards of the Jockey Club finding that a horse had been drugged and warning the plaintiff off Newmarket Heath. It was held that such publication was not privileged. It is true that the members of the Court of Appeal gave somewhat differing reasons for their conclusions, but each one of them was against the present contention.

D   LORD HANWORTH, M.R., said this (17):

" There remains the question whether the plea of privilege can afford protection to the defendants in respect of these paragraphs. It is said that it was a matter of public interest, that it was the duty of the news agencies and of ' The Times ' to give to their clients and readers information that was of interest to all racing people, to all the betting public, to all who stand E   outside these two classes, but yet take an interest in the sport of horse-racing, and, in particular, in the maintenance of its honour and freedom from corrupt practices—the practice of drugging horses for races having at that time attracted much attention. These are strong arguments. But, though the vehicle of the public press has been held to be a proper and protected one so as to defeat a claim for libel where it has been used ' as the F   only effective mode ' to answer a charge which had already received as wide a circulation (see *Adam* v. *Ward* (18) and *Brown* v. *Croome* (19)); there is no authority which protects the statement in the newspaper, where it is made, not in answer, but as a fresh item on which a general interest, as distinguished from a particular interest already aroused, prevails. BUCKLEY, L.J., in *Adam* v. *Ward* (20) stated a proposition, which was approved in the G   House of Lords (21) in the following terms: ' If the matter is of public interest and the party who publishes it owes a duty to communicate it to the public, the publication is privileged, and in this sense duty means not a duty as a matter of law, but, to quote LINDLEY, L.J.'s words in *Stuart* v. *Bell* (22) " a duty recognised by English people of ordinary intelligence and moral principle ".' But these words must be taken in relation to the facts H   of the case. It appears to me that the learned judge meant by the words ' matter is of public interest ', has already become of public interest. The duty cannot arise in respect of a matter not yet made public to all."

SLESSER, L.J., said (23):

" As regards the publication to the news agencies and to ' The Times ', for both of which the defendants other than the Times Publishing Co., Ltd., I   are attacked, and as regards the liability of the Times Publishing Co., Ltd., itself, my decision that there is no general interest to the public or

---

(16) [1932] All E.R. Rep. 221; [1932] 2 K.B. 431.
(17) [1932] All E.R. Rep. at pp. 229, 230; [1932] 2 K.B. at p. 456.
(18) (1915), 31 T.L.R. 299.   (19) (1817), 2 Stark 297 at p. 301.
(20) (1915), 31 T.L.R. at p. 304.
(21) [1916-17] All E.R. Rep. 157 at p. 164; [1917] A.C. 309 at p. 322.
(22) [1891] 2 Q.B. at p. 350.
(23) [1932] All E.R. Rep. at p. 236; [1932] 2 K.B. at p. 469.

duty owed to the public to publish matter which concerned a section of   **A**
the public only, which decision I have already indicated in connection with
one of the proposed grounds for privilege in the case of the ' Racing
Calendar ', necessarily deprives all publications other than that of the
' Racing Calendar ' of privilege, and, therefore, apart from the publication in
the ' Racing Calendar ', which is protected for the two peculiar reasons which
I have stated, there is, if the finding of the jury can be supported, no defence   **B**
to the action against any of the defendants in any matter other than the
publication in the ' Racing Calendar '."

SLESSER, L.J., was referring to the decision that there was protection for publication of the same information in a racing calendar which had a circulation limited
to those who were directly and immediately concerned with the events which
were reported. ROMER, L.J., said (24):   **C**

"As regards the publication to and in ' The Times ', and to the Press
agencies, the defence of privilege cannot, I think, prevail. So far as regards
the stewards, such a publication seems to me to go beyond any duty that
they owed to anyone. So far as regards the Times Publishing Co., Ltd., it may
in one sense be true to say that they owe a duty to their readers to publish   **D**
any and every item of news that may interest them. But this is not such
a duty as makes every communication in their paper relating to a matter
of public interest a privileged one. If it were, the power of the press to libel
public men with impunity would in the absence of malice be almost
unlimited."

I have been referred in the course of argument to another unsuccessful attempt   **E**
to claim a general qualified privilege for publication in the press in a case tried
by SWIFT, J., *Standen* v. *South Essex Recorders, Ltd.* (25).

This topic also came before the Supreme Court of Canada in 1961 in the case of
Banks v. *Globe & Mail, Ltd.* (26). Delivering the judgment of the Supreme
Court, CARTWRIGHT, J., said this (27):

"There are of course many cases in which publication of defamatory   **F**
matter in a newspaper may be privileged either by statute or at common
law; examples are to be found in the Libel and Slander Act, R.S.O. 1950,
s. 9 and s. 10, and in such cases as *Adam* v. *Ward* (28) and *Allbutt* v. *General
Council of Medical Education & Registration* (29). In the first of these
it was held that the Army Council owed a duty to publish to the whole
world a letter vindicating a general who had been falsely accused before the   **G**
same audience of discreditable conduct and that publication in the press
was therefore privileged; in the second it was held that publication in the
press of an accurate report of proceedings within the jurisdiction of the
General Medical Council erasing the name of the plaintiff from the medical
register was privileged on the ground, inter alia, that it was the duty of the
council to give the public accurate information as to who is on the register   **H**
and if a person's name is erased accurate information of the cause of its
erasure. The decision of the learned trial judge, in the case at bar, quoted
above, appears to involve the proposition of law, which in my opinion is
untenable, that given proof of the existence of a subject-matter of wide
public interest throughout Canada, without proof of any other special
circumstances any newspaper in Canada (and semble therefore any   **I**
individual) which sees fit to publish to the public at large statements of fact
relevant to that subject-matter is to be held to be doing so on an occasion
of qualified privilege."

---

(24) [1932] All E.R. Rep. at pp. 238, 239; [1932] 2 K.B. at p. 474.
(25) (1934), 50 T.L.R. 365.
(26) [1961] S.C.R. 474; 28 D.J.R. (2d) 343.
(27) [1961] S.C.R. at p. 483; 28 D.J.R. (2d) at p. 351.
(28) [1916-17] All E.R. Rep. 157; [1917] A.C. 309.   (29) (1889), 23 Q.B.D. 400.

A The cases to which I have referred show a uniformity of approach. In my view the privilege for publication in the press of information of general public interest is confined to cases where the defendant has a legal, social or moral duty to communicate it to the general public, or does so in reasonable self-defence to a public charge, or in the special circumstances exemplified by *Adam* v. *Ward* (30). A duty will thus arise where it is in the interests of the public that the

B publication should be made and will not arise simply because the information appears to be of legitimate public interest.

In the present case I am not satisfied that the defendant was under any duty to communicate this information to the public generally. It was merely his own ex parte impression and deduction which, as such things often do, turned out to be sadly wrong. I am not satisfied that the public generally have any

C legitimate interest in receiving this information, although they no doubt found it very interesting. Nor am I satisfied that the defendant's own legitimate interests required this hasty and unfortunate publication to be made. I reject the wide principle which it was originally sought to derive from *Webb* v. *Times Publishing Co.* (31), although I do not, of course, for a moment presume to doubt the correctness of that decision in the circumstances of that case. I do not think

D that on examination of that decision, it has extended the defence of privilege beyond the principles enunciated by Buckley, L.J., in *Adam* v. *Ward* (32) which I have already read.

In my view, before this protection of qualified privilege is extended beyond its existing limits the court should, as it has done in the past, first take into account the extent to which public advantage may be out-weighed by private

E injustice and injury. In the present type of case any public advantage is likely to be heavily so out-weighed. For these reasons I rule that the occasions of publication to the public via the press were not privileged.

The publications by the defendant to the artistes and the letters sent to them stand in a different situation altogether. I think it is too clear to call for the giving of any reasons, and I simply without more ado hold the publication of

F each of these to be publication to the artistes on a privileged occasion.

I have also had the advantage of long, careful and instructive argument (33) on whether the defendant should be allowed to put before the jury the pleaded defence of fair comment on a matter of public interest. I was originally under the impression that I was being asked by all parties to rule on that matter at this stage; but it appeared yesterday afternoon that the defendant wished me to

G reserve my decision at least until all the evidence had been given (34). However, the discussions and argument have ranged very far and occasonally very wide, and it is difficult to suppose that there is anything more which could usefully be said or any further authority which could usefully be cited; and all parties are agreed that it would at least tend to guide and limit the future course of this trial if I now stated the views that I have formed on the information now before

H me. I accordingly proceed to do so, and I may add that I do not at present see any prospect of changing the views which I have formed, nor would I welcome any matter by way of repetition of arguments which I have already heard, or authorities to which I have already been referred.

In relation to the claim of each plaintiff, the defendant pleads fair comment on a matter of public interest. He has given particulars of the facts on which

I he alleges the comment to be based, and these particulars are now amended by deletion (35) of para. 20A. It is at least clear to me on what facts the defendant

---

(30) [1916-17] All E.R. Rep. 157; [1917] A.C. 309.
(31) [1960] 2 All E.R. 789; [1960] 2 Q.B. 535.
(32) (1915), 31 T.L.R. at p. 304; cited at p. 1081, letter I, to p. 1082, letter C, ante.
(33) The cases cited during the argument on the defences of qualified privilege and fair comment are noted in footnote *, p. 1080, ante.
(34) In the event a ruling was finally given, see p. 1088, letter H, post.
(35) Paragraph 20A of the particulars is set out, as far as necessary, at p. 1079, letters C and D, ante.

says his comment is based. So far as the defendant's letter to the artistes is **A**
concerned, the defence of fair comment can apply only to such part of it, if any,
as the jury, if allowed, find to be comment, and that comment must be based
on the facts and must be fair comment having regard to such of the facts as
are proved to be true. If and in so far as the letter contains any statement of
fact which is defamatory, the plaintiff who is thereby defamed is entitled to
damages, for there is now no plea of justification for any statement of fact at all. **B**

Whether the defence of fair comment is allowed to go to the jury depends on
three things which are for me to decide. 1. I have to decide whether the matter
on which the defendant says he was commenting was or was not a matter of
public interest. The onus is on the defendant to satisfy me on the balance of
probability that it was a matter of public interest, and until he does so the
question of fair comment will not arise. 2. I have to determine whether any part **C**
of the letter is capable of being comment, and, in particular, those parts which
counsel for the defendant has clearly and plainly indicated to us are all which he
wishes to invite the jury to consider as comment (36). Where any part of
the letter is reasonably capable of being understood by one ordinary and
sensible reader as comment and by another ordinary and sensible reader
as fact, I do not have to make the choice, for that would be for the jury **D**
to decide. Nor do I have to decide how I would choose to construe the letter
myself. Nor must I be overwhelmed by the importance of my own first impression, for a second look can reveal a possible different construction which might
have been the first impression of somebody else. Unless without arrogance I
decide that the words are not reasonably capable of being comment, I must leave
it to the jury to decide whether they are comment or fact. In comment is **E**
included inference, provided it appears that the writer is offering the inference
as no more that his personal opinion and not as an assertion of fact from his
premises. 3. I believe that in this particular case I have also to decide whether
the plea of fair comment on the matter referred to is available against these
plaintiffs.

I return to the primary task now of deciding whether the matter on which the **F**
defendant says that he was commenting was a matter of public interest. In his
defences the defendant describes it as the fate of the play " The Right Honourable Gentleman " then running at Her Majesty's Theatre. In his submission to
me, counsel for the defendant expanded this as meaning the unprecedented
coincidence of the notices given by the four artistes, which was in date also
coincidental with the desire of the management of " Robert and Elizabeth " to **G**
get into the theatre where they were playing. The overwhelming majority of
the evidence is that the coincidence of the sudden and simultaneous notice of
the four artistes, three of them stars, was in the highest degree unusual and
unknown in all the experience of those witnesses who had experience. One witness, with that combination of inexperience and confidence which is sometimes
the prerogative of youth, stated that it was not an uncommon occurence, but **H**
I pay no attention to him.

Does this coincidence or double coincidence qualify as a matter of public
interest. Although some text-books state that this is a difficult question for a
judge to decide, there is no text-book and no reported case that I have discovered
which offers any working definition for the assistance of the judge in his task.
All that one usually gets is a miscellaneous list of decided examples or groups of **I**
examples, but it is broadly possible to divide them into two classes:—(a) Matters
of public interest in the sense that the public in general have a legitimate interest
in them directly or indirectly, nationally or locally. Clear examples are matters
connected with national and local government, public services and institutions,
and so on. (b) Matters which are expressly or impliedly submitted to public
criticism or attention, performances and productions at public theatres and the

---

(36) The passages indicated are set out at p. 1079, letters H and I, ante.

A performances of theatrical artists offered for public entertainment, are established examples of this class.

On the other hand, the private life of a public performer is not a matter of public interest, however interested or titillated the public might be to read or hear about it.

The conduct of the artistes in the present cases poses a difficult problem. All
B that they had done was to send to the defendant by their agents a private letter, exercising their contractual right to terminate their engagement on due notice. Such an act by an individual artiste could not begin to be a matter of public interest. It was a private act and not done to invite public attention or comment. The public would have no business even to know about it at the time. The unusual feature in the present case was that all four artistes did it together,
C but it was still not done in public or submitted by them to public gaze. It was not a strike of artistes during a performance or even during the run of a play. Until the time when the defendant wrote and published his letter, the public knew nothing whatever about it. If on June 22, 1965, it had been announced that the four artistes would not be appearing in the play after July 24, it would have occasioned no public emotion, except that such members of the public
D as had booked for performances after that date would be disappointed. If it had been announced that the play was being taken off at the end of July, it would similarly have caused no excitement, although those who had booked or who intended to book for later dates would be disappointed. Such things happen and for various reasons. Similarly, the fact that the management was trying to transfer another play to Her Majesty's Theatre would not by itself be of public
E interest, in the sense which the authorities use the term. The public would know nothing about it and would not be entitled to know anything about it.

I have to judge whether the coincidence of conduct, unknown to the public, was a matter of public interest, and I have to decide this unaffected by the method by which the public in fact got to know about it. A plot by actors and persons and organisations in the entertainment industry to force the end of the
F run of the play so that another production could have the use of the theatre would undoubtedly be a matter of public interest, and, indeed, of public concern, but this plot is alleged not as the matter of public interest but as the comment on it. Counsel for the defendant says that this coincidence was something such as is referred to in the collection of examples in para. 748 of Gatley on Libel and Slander (6th Edn.), namely, a matter which may be said to invite
G comment or challenge public attention. It seems to me, however, that the examples given in Gatley under that paragraph are all examples within the second class to which I have already referred, namely, matters which are expressly or impliedly submitted to public criticism and attention. This coincidence was not one of those things.

Counsel for the defendants has submitted that to some extent this question
H has to be decided as a matter of impression, and that it is not possible to derive, from examination of all the authorities, one general guiding principle which will answer all problems. I appreciate that, and I see and indeed feel the force of it and of the difficulty with which it is dealing. It is only fair that I should concede that I find this to be something of a borderline case, but I am not satisfied that the matter which is relied on for this plea was one of public interest.

I It is, therefore, strictly unnecessary for me to decide whether the part of the letter relied on as comment is capable of being so understood. I refer particularly to the paragraph beginning " In other words " (37). Counsel for the defendant contends that this is reasonably capable of being an inference offered as the writer's personal opinion having regard to the opening paragraph of the letter and to what (for lack of a better expression) I will call the whole pattern of the letter. I did not myself originally read this as comment, and I am not saying

---

(37) The paragraph referred to is set out at p. 1078, letter C, ante.

that I do so now, but having had my attention drawn to it as a possible construc- **A**
tion, I have come to the conclusion that I cannot hold that the words are not
reasonably capable of being construed in that way, and if the plea went to
the jury, I would leave them to decide that question.

I think I should also give my views on whether, assuming the matter referred
to to be one of public interest, the defendant can, in relation to these plaintiffs,
assert as a defence that what he said was fair comment on that matter. Putting **B**
the case in the way which seems to me to be most favourable to the defendant,
he is saying, in relation to the artistes, that in his opinion they seem to have combined with the plaintiffs, either as principals, puppets or pawns, in a disreputable
plot to end the run of the play for the advantage of some other production.
It is now conceded there was no plot, although all the indications up to the
present are that the defendant honestly believed that there was one. The situation **C**
may be stated in summary form as follows: A expresses a defamatory opinion
of B as an essential and major part of his comment on the conduct of C, and when
sued by B says that he has a complete defence because what he said was fair
comment on the conduct of C.

The industry and experience of counsel engaged in this case, and my own
endeavours, have failed to disclose a single reported case where a plea of fair **D**
comment of this type has even been asserted. I cannot say that I am surprised,
because if this is the law, it seems to me to be grossly unfair. A man may comment
honestly on the conduct of others, with resulting hardship to them, but in all
cases the victims must have put themselves in a position where they expressly or
impliedly invited public attention, or else comment on them was one of the accepted risks of their activities. It is at least their own acts or omissions or con- **E**
duct which have excited, if not provoked, the comment. In commenting on the
the public performance of an artiste, it is not permissible to make defamatory
statements or comments on his private life. In my view, it is an a fortiori case
that one cannot make defamatory statements or comments about someone else
altogether, unless one is prepared to justify it.

Counsel for the defendant, to whose submission I listened with the respect **F**
which is due to his great learning and experience, has said that I should first
ascertain whether there was a matter of public interest, and then go on to consider whether this was comment on it, and that it does not matter that the
comment defames persons who were not actually involved in the conduct
commented on provided the conduct commented on was a matter of public
interest. I am conscious that I may, in counsel for the defendant's better **G**
judgment, be expounding a heresy, but I cannot believe it right that this plea
can be raised against these plaintiffs. It seems to me that the reality of the
situation is that the conduct which is being commented on is the conduct of the
plaintiffs, and that it is being commented on without any basis of fact to support
it. For these reasons, I would hold that this plea is not available to the
defendant against these plaintiffs. **H**

[After further submissions by counsel for the defendant regarding the stage
at which HIS LORDSHIP would rule on the defence of fair comment, counsel for
the defendant invited HIS LORDSHIP to rule at this stage on the point of law and
HIS LORDSHIP accordingly ruled that the defence of fair comment was not open
to the defendant.]

Rulings accordingly on the defences of qualified privilege and fair comment (38). **I**

Solicitors: *Oswald Hickson, Collier & Co.* (for the first plaintiffs); *Allen &
Overy* (for the second plaintiffs); *Nicholson Graham & Jones* (for the third and
fourth plaintiffs); *M. A. Jacobs & Sons* (for the defendant).

[*Reported by* K. DIANA PHILLIPS, *Barrister-at-Law.*]

_____

(38) On Mar. 5, 1968, judgment was directed to be entered for the four plaintiffs
for £2,250 with costs.

A
EDWARDS (Inspector of Taxes) *v.* WARMSLEY HENSHALL & CO.

[CHANCERY DIVISION (Cross, J.), December 12, 21, 1967.]

Income ~~Tax~~—Deductions in computing profits—Expenses—Disbursements
" wholly and exclusively laid out . . . for the purposes of the . . . profession "—
B   *Accountant—Expenses of attending accountancy conference—Sole reason*
for trip to New York—Income Tax Act, 1952 (15 & 16 Geo. 6 & 1 Eliz. 2
c. 10), s. 137 (a).

The taxpayers were a firm of chartered accountants founded in 1880, which
up to 1945 had mainly developed their business amongst the business life
of Chester, Cheshire and North Wales but had come to have clients in many
C   parts of the world. They received a circular from the Institute of Chartered
Accountants in England and Wales expressing a desire that the institute
should be worthily represented at the eighth international congress of
accountants to be held in New York in September 1962. They selected one
of their partners to attend, considering that the information obtained and
contacts made would be of benefit and assistance to the firm. He travelled
D   to New York and back only for the congress by a chartered flight arranged
by the institute which involved fourteen days' stay, the shortest period
enabling him to attend the congress, and no other method of returning earlier
would have saved expense. Business sessions occupied one and a half of the
six days of the congress, the remaining time being taken up with informal
discussions, visits to other businesses and various sightseeing and other
E   social events. The theme of the congress was auditing and financial reporting
in the world economy, and papers were presented dealing with the three
major subjects from the standpoints of communicating financial information
to investors, banks, government agencies and others, and of internal control
and information for management purposes. It was to assist in the development of professional standards and thought. The partner took part in a
F   syndicate which discussed the Common Market. After the congress the
partner visited American accountants and various business concerns, one
firm of accountants with whom he had dealings in connexion with a client. He
made many useful contacts at the congress and was the better able to advise
clients with intersts in other parts of the world. When visiting accountants
he had seen methods of accounting which he considered would be an advan-
G   tage to his firm, which was considering the introduction of modifications of
them. The prestige of the firm was increased by his attendance. On appeal to
the General Commissioners of Income Tax, they found that the partner went
to America for the sole purpose of attending the congress, and that (in effect)
the object of his going was the earning of profits by, and the enhancing or
maintaining of the profit-earning capacity of, the firm. The commissioners
H   held (in effect) that the part of the partner's expenses directly attributable to
attending the congress* was wholly and exclusively laid out for the purposes
of the profession within s. 137 (a) of the Income Tax Act, 1952, and they
allowed them as a deduction in computing the profits of the firm for income
tax. At the hearing before the judge the Crown did not challenge the finding
that the partner went to America for the sole purpose of attending the congress.
I   **Held:** having regard to the finding of the commissioners last mentioned,
the " duality " point on which the decision in *Bowden* v. *Russell* turned did
not govern the present case (see p. 1094, letter E, post); the finding that the
object of the firm's incurring the expenses was to enhance or maintain its
profit-earning capacity was one with which the court ought not to interfere,
for, on the evidence and argument before the commissioners, it was a finding
which it was open to them to reach, and, therefore, their allowance of the

---

* For particulars of the expenses claimed, see p. 1090, letter I, post.

deduction of the expenses should stand (see p. 1095, letter C, and p. 1095, **A** letter I, to p. 1096, letter A, post).

Bowden (Inspector of Taxes) v. *Russell and Russell* ([1965] 2 All E.R. 258) distinguished.

Appeal dismissed.

[As to disbursements wholly and exclusively laid out for the purposes of a profession for income tax purposes, see 20 HALSBURY'S LAWS (3rd Edn.) 166-170, **B** paras. 286-292; and for cases on the subject, see 28 DIGEST (Repl.) 154-158, *594-623*.

For the Income Tax Act, 1952, s. 137, see 31 HALSBURY'S STATUTES (2nd Edn.) 134.]

Cases referred to:

    Bentleys, Stokes and Lowless v. *Beeson (Inspector of Taxes)*, [1952] 2 All E.R. **C**   82; 33 Tax Cas. 491; 28 Digest (Repl.) 98, *387*.

    Bowden (Inspector of Taxes) v. *Russell and Russell*, [1965] 2 All E.R. 258;   [1965] 1 W.L.R. 711; 42 Tax Cas. 301; Digest (Cont. Vol. B) 408, *618a*.

    Maclean (Inspector of Taxes) v. *Trembarth*, [1956] 2 All E.R. 113; [1956] 1   W.L.R. 437; 36 Tax Cas. 653; 28 Digest (Repl.) 243, *1065*. **D**

    Morgan (Inspector of Taxes) v. *Tate & Lyle, Ltd.*, [1954] 2 All E.R. 413; [1955]   A.C. 21; [1954] 3 W.L.R. 85; 35 Tax Cas. 367; 28 Digest (Repl.) 91,   *345*.

    Strong & Co., Ltd. v. *Woodifield*, [1904-07] All E.R. Rep. 953; [1906] A.C. 448;   75 L.J.K.B. 864; 95 L.T. 241; 5 Tax Cas. 215; 28 Digest (Repl.) 79,   *298*. **E**

    Union Cold Storage Co., Ltd. v. *Jones*, (1923), 8 Tax Cas. 725; 28 Digest (Repl.)   136, *517*.

Case Stated.

The respondent taxpayers, Warmsley Henshall & Co., a firm of chartered accountants whose office was situated at 29, Eastgate Row North in the city of Chester, appealed to the General Commissioners of Income Tax for Chester **F** against an assessment to income tax made on them for 1963-64 under Sch. D, Case II of the Income Tax Act, 1952, in the estimated sum of £14,000. The only question before the commissioners was whether the expense incurred by Mr. James Ellis Evans, one of the partners in the firm, in attending the eighth international congress of accountants held in New York in September, 1962 was an allowable deduction in computing the profits of the taxpayer firm for **G** income tax purposes. The following extracts from the Case Stated, which were read by CROSS, J., show the facts and the contentions before, and findings of, the commissioners:

" 3. Appearing on behalf of the [taxpayers] firm was the said Mr. James Ellis Evans, chartered accountant, of 29, Eastgate Row North, Chester.

" 4. The following facts were admitted or proved: (a) Mr. James Ellis **H** Evans is one of the five partners in the [taxpayers] firm of chartered accountants; (b) Mr. Evans attended the eighth international congress of accountants held in New York from Sept. 23 to Sept. 28, 1962. Business sessions had occupied one and a half of the six days of the congress, while the remaining time was taken up with informal discussions, visits to other businesses and various sightseeing and other social events; (c) the expenses claimed were **I** £160 14s. 8d., which was that part of the total expense incurred by Mr. Evans directly attributable to his attending the congress. That sum was made up as follows: Return air passage, £110 14s. 8d.; conference fee, £20; living expenses for the six days of the conference at £5 per day, £30—£160 14s. 8d.

" (d) In June, 1961, Mr. Evans had received from the Institute of Chartered Accountants in England and Wales a circular giving provisional details of the congress to be held fifteen months later, in which the council of the institute expressed a desire that ' the institute be represented at this

A important event in a manner worthy of the major part which members had taken over the years in the international development of the profession '. A copy of this circular and a copy of the official report of the congress were produced; these are not attached to this Case but are available for the High Court if required; (e) The [taxpayers] firm had been founded in 1880 and had up to 1945 mainly developed its business amongst the business life of Chester,

B Cheshire and North Wales, but it now had clients in many parts of the world, and although they did not aspire to the status of the prominent London firms, they considered that they were more than a small county town practice; (f) Mr. Evans and other partners in the firm had been chairmen of the Chester and North Wales Branch of their institute and he considered that all the subjects discussed were quite definitely relevant to the practice

C of his firm and that these conferences are an essential part of professional life and that he could not and would not have attended this conference if he had not been a chartered accountant in practice; (g) The air passage referred to in sub-para. (c) above was by special chartered flight arranged by the said institute.

"(h) The congress had been attended by 3,728 delegates from all over

D the world of whom 750 came from the United Kingdom and represented the Institute of Chartered Accountants in England and Wales, the Institute of Chartered Accountants in Scotland, the Association of Certified and Corporate Accountants, the Institute of Cost and Works Accountants and the Institute of Municipal Treasurers and Accountants who recognise that the key to progress was organised research by the profession both on a

E national and an international level; (i) the theme of the congress had been 'Auditing and financial reporting in the world economy' and the three major subjects on which papers were presented were each dealt with from the standpoint of communicating financial information to investors, banks, government agencies and others and also from that of internal control and information for management purposes, and was to assist in the development of

F professional standards and thought; (j) for one half day Mr. Evans took part in a syndicate which, amongst other matters, discussed the theory of the Common Market; (k) Mr. Evans visited American accountants and various business concerns after the congress had ended; (l) a number of the accountants who attended this congress were from firms of a similar nature to that of which Mr. Evans was a partner; (m) Mr. Evans quoted

G the case of Maclean (Inspector of Taxes) v. Trembarth (1), which he contended upheld his contention.

"5. On cross-examination by the inspector, Mr. Evans gave evidence, which we accepted, that (a) the chartered flight which he went on was the flight which gave him the shortest period in America which enabled him to attend the congress, and that this flight resulted in his having to

H stay in America for fourteen days and that there was no other method of his returning to this country after the congress had been concluded which would have resulted in his saving any expense, and further that he was not claiming for expenses in America at any other time than when he was attending this congress; (b) the partners of his firm had selected him to attend; (c) until this step had been taken he made no other arrange-

I ments for visiting any other part of the United States; (d) He had made many useful contacts at the congress and was therefore better able to advise clients who had interests in other parts of the world, and that after the congress he had attended one firm of accountants in America with whom he had business dealings from time to time in connexion with one of his own clients; (e) he had seen, when visiting other firms after the congress had ended, methods of accounting which he considered would be an advantage

(1) [1956] 2 All E.R. 113; 36 Tax Cas. 653.

A

to his firm, and some modifications of these systems had been discussed and were being considered for introduction by his firm; (f) It was as quick to fly to New York as to travel to the south coast of England to attend a conference there; (g) he only attended the congress in New York because he had been instructed to do so by his partners, and that if he had not been so instructed he would not have visited the United States at that time; (h) all the partners of the firm considered that the information and contacts made would be of great benefit to and assistance to the firm, and that in actual fact some useful contacts were made and examples of other methods of accounting were seen which may be adopted by the firm, and that the prestige of the firm was increased as a result of a partner attending the congress.

B

" 6. The inspector of taxes contended: (i) that as the congress was held in New York it was so far away that it did not warrant a small firm of the nature of [the taxpayers] sending a delegate to attend and that the subjects of this congress did not warrant the sending of a partner; (ii) that as Mr. Evans had visited other parts of the United States during his visit, the object of his visit had not been only to attend this congress; (iii) that it was not wholly and exclusively for the benefit of his firm; (iv) that the expenditure of £160 14s. 8d. was not an allowable deduction within the Income Tax Act, 1952, s. 137 (a), and (v) that the appeal should be dismissed and the assessment for 1963-64 should be determined in the sum of £17,024.

C

D

" 7. The commissioners considered the facts laid before them and held (a) that distance could not rule out a claim for allowance of expenses; (b) that the subject matters of this congress were of sufficient general interest to members of the accounting profession that they should not be ruled out from attending such congress by reason of the subject matters thereof; (c) that on the evidence given by Mr. Evans, which was not refuted by the inspector in cross-examination, he would not have gone to America except to attend this congress, and that he had not made any arrangements for meeting any persons or visiting any other part of the U.S.A. until he had been instructed to attend the congress, and that he had used the flights which gave him the shortest period which he could stay in America. We held that there was no duality of purpose in Mr. Evans attending the congress and in fact Mr. Evans had only claimed expenses directly attributable to his attending the congress; (d) that it was wholly and exclusively expenses of the profession within the meaning of s. 137 (a) of the Income Tax Act, 1952, by reason of the fact (i) that he had been instructed to attend the congress by his firm; (ii) that the standing of the firm must have been enhanced by a member of that firm attending such congress; (iii) that they are not precluded from attending such congress because it may not have an immediate or direct effect on expanding their business; (iv) that the respondent firm in various ways obtained some benefit from the fact that Mr. Evans attended the congress; (e) that the four cases quoted by [the Crown] were not in line with the facts of this case and therefore this case had to be decided on the facts before them."

E

F

G

H

Then the commissioners referred to the cases cited: *Strong & Co., Ltd.* v. *Woodifield* (2); *Union Cold Storage Co., Ltd.* v. *Jones* (3); *Bentleys, Stokes & Lowless* v. *Beeson* (*Inspector of Taxes*) (4); and *Bowden* (*Inspector of Taxes*) v. *Russell & Russell* (5).

I

" 8. The commissioners unanimously agreed that the expenses of £160 14s. 8d. should be allowed as a deduction in computing the profits of the [taxpayer] firm for 1963-64 and determined the appeal by increasing the assessment to the agreed figure of £16,864."

(2) [1904-07] All E.R. Rep. 953; (1906), 5 Tax Cas. 215.
(3) (1923), 8 Tax Cas. 725.
(4) [1952] 2 All E.R. 82; 33 Tax Cas. 491.
(5) [1965] 2 All E.R. 258; 42 Tax Cas. 301.

A   The Crown appealed by way of Case Stated to the High Court.

  G. B. Graham, Q.C., and *J. R. Phillips* for the Crown.
  Hubert H. Monroe, Q.C., and *M. P. Nolan* for the taxpayers.

Cur. adv. vult.

    Dec. 21. **CROSS, J.:** This is an appeal by the inspector of taxes against
B   a decision of the General Commissioners of Income Tax for the Chester Division,
    given on July 2, 1965, that the respondent taxpayers, Messrs. Warmsley Henshall
    & Co., a firm of chartered accountants practising at 29, Eastgate Row North
    in the city of Chester, were entitled in computing their profits for income tax
    purposes for the year 1963-64 to deduct expenses, amounting to £160 14s. 8d.,
    incurred by James Ellis Evans, one of their partners, in attending the eighth
C   international congress of accountants held in New York in September, 1962.
    [HIS LORDSHIP read the extracts from the Case Stated set out at p. 1090, letter G,
    to p. 1092, letter I, ante, and continued:] To be allowable as deductions, the
    expenses claimed must be, in the words of s. 137 (*a*) of the Income Tax Act, 1952,
    " wholly and exclusively laid out or expended for the purposes of the trade " or
    " profession ". Those words have been considered by the courts again and again
D   in different contexts. In *Strong & Co., Ltd.* v. *Woodifield* (6), LORD DAVEY gave
    a paraphrase of them in words which have frequently been quoted with approval
    as expenses incurred

> " for the purpose of enabling a person to carry on and earn profits in the
> trade."

E   It is, however, well settled that an expense may be allowable even though it is
    not directly related to the earning of profits here and now. It is enough that it
    was incurred for the purpose of maintaining or enhancing the profit-earning
    capacity of the buiness. (See *Morgan (Inspector of Taxes)* v. *Tate & Lyle, Ltd.* (7),
    and in particular the speech of LORD REID (8).) On the other hand, it is clear
    that the expense must be incurred with the single purpose of earning profits
F   in or maintaining or enhancing the profit-earning capacity of the business. If
    those who incurred the expense had some further object in view, the expense
    will not be allowable; though, of course, if there was no purpose beyond the single
    purpose required by the statute, the fact that the expenditure may have other
    effects beyond those aimed at will not prevent it being allowable. (See *Bentleys,
    Stokes & Lowless* v. *Beeson (Inspector of Taxes)* (9).) Finally, it is I think clear that
G   what one has to consider is the purpose in the minds of those who incurred the
    expense. The fact that the expenditure has not in fact achieved the purpose of
    earning profits or maintaining or enhancing the profit-earning capacity of the
    business, or that the commissioners or the court may not think that it was in fact
    well calculated to do so, is irrelevant except in so far as those circumstances may
    cast doubt on the genuineness of the purpose alleged by those who incurred the
H   expense.
    The question whether or not the expenses of attending an international pro-
    fessional congress fall within s. 137 (*a*) was considered by PENNYCUICK, J., in
    Bowden (Inspector of Taxes) v. *Russell & Russell* (10), which was one of the cases
    cited to the commissioners by the inspector. Up to a point, the facts were similar
    to those found in this case, but there was one great difference. Mr. Taylor, who
I   was a solicitor and who had in 1960 attended the annual meeting of the American
    Bar Association in Washington, and the Commonwealth and Empire Law
    Conference in Ottawa, admitted that his object in crossing the Atlantic was not
    exclusively to attend those meetings but partly to have a holiday over there with

---

(6) [1904-07] All E.R. Rep. 953 at p. 956; (1906), 5 Tax Cas. 215 at p. 220.
(7) [1954] 2 All E.R. 413; 35 Tax Cas. 367.
(8) [1954] 2 All E.R. at p. 428; 35 Tax Cas. at p. 421.
(9) [1952] 2 All E.R. at pp. 85; 33 Tax Cas. at pp. 504, 505.
(10) [1965] 2 All E.R. 258; 42 Tax Cas. 301.

his wife, who accompanied him. Counsel for the inspector in that case put his   A
submissions under two heads, which he labelled " Remoteness " and " Duality "
respectively. He argued first that the expense of attending these conferences
in America had only a remote connexion with the profession of a solicitor carrying
on general practice in Lancashire and could not properly be said to be expenses
incurred for the purpose of enabling the taxpayer firm to carry on and earn
profits in that profession; and secondly that the expenses were incurred not only   B
for the purpose of Mr. Taylor attending the conference in America but also for
the purpose of his having a holiday there.

PENNYCUICK, J., decided the case against the taxpayer on the ground of duality
of purpose. With regard to the other contention, he said (11):

> " Having decided the appeal on the issue of duality, I think it is undesirable   C
> for me to express a view on the issue of remoteness. Although each case turns
> on its particular facts, the deductibility or otherwise for the purposes of
> tax of the expense of attending conferences is a matter of wide importance
> which has not yet, I understand, been judicially considered and I do not think
> I ought to make any observations on it which are not necessary for the
> determination of the present appeal. Counsel for the Crown concurs in this   D
> view."

The inspector here evidently had the case of *Bowden* (*Inspector of Taxes*) v. *Russell
and Russell* (12) well in mind. His first contention was directed to the " remoteness " point, and his second contention to the " duality " point. The commissioners dealt with the " duality " point in para. 7 (c) of the Case Stated, where
they held that Mr. Evans went to America with the sole purpose of attending   E
the congress; and the Crown does not seek to challenge this finding. They do,
however, challenge the decision of the commissioners on the " remoteness "
point, which is contained in para. 7 (1), (b) and (d) of the Case.

I will deal first with three minor points. In para. 7 (a) the commissioners
say that distance could not rule out a claim for allowance of expenses. The Crown
did not seek to argue that it could. International conferences must of necessity   F
often be held abroad, and the time taken and expense involved in an English
accountant attending a conference in New York is not much greater than the
time taken or expense involved in an accountant in Penzance attending a conference in, say, Edinburgh. The objection of the Crown before me was not based
on distance but on the nature of the conference and the character of the taxpayer's
firm.   G

The second minor point is that in para. 7 (b) and (d) the commissioners express
the view that members of the accountancy profession should not be " ruled out "
or " precluded " from attending such a congress because of its subject-matter
or because it might not have an immediate or direct effect in expanding their
business. Plainly that language is open to criticism. The success of the Crown
in this appeal would not " rule out " or " preclude " any accountant from attend-   H
ing any international congress of accountants held in any part of the world
provided that he could raise the necessary funds and get the necessary permission
to convert them into foreign currency. The disallowance of such expenses for
tax purposes, however, might deter accountants from attending such conferences,
and that, I think, is all that the commissioners meant, although they expressed
themselves rather badly.   I

The third minor point is that while the opening words of para. 7 (d), which refer
to s. 137 (a) of the Income Tax Act 1952, run:

> " That it was wholly and exclusively expenses of the profession within
> the meaning of s. 137 (a) of the Income Tax Act, 1952 by reason of the fact,"

_____

(11) [1965] 2 All E.R. at p. 264; 42 Tax Cas. at p. 307.
(12) [1965] 2 All E.R. 258; 42 Tax Cas. 301.

A   etc., the words of the section are, " wholly and exclusively laid out . . . for the purposes of the . . . profession ". In *Strong & Co., Ltd.* v. *Woodifield* (13) to which I have already referred, Lord Davey stressed the importance of the actual words used, and said this :

B   " I think that the payment of these damages was not money expended ' for the purpose of the trade ' . . . It is not enough that the disbursement is made in the course of, or arises out of, or is connected with, the trade, or is made out of the profits of the trade. It must be made for the purpose of earning the profits."

It was submitted on behalf of the Crown, in the light of those facts, that the commissioners may not have had clearly in their minds the true problem which
C   they had to decide. I think that that is hypercriticism. I cannot doubt that the commissioners had the words of the section in their minds, although unfortunately they did not quote them accurately at that stage in the Case, and that they asked themselves the right question—viz., whether this expenditure was incurred by the partners in the taxpayers' firm with the sole object of earning profits for or maintaining or enhancing the profit-earning capacity of the business.

D   Was the answer " Yes " which they gave to that question one which could not reasonably be given? At this point the Crown adopted before me a line of argument of which there is no hint in the Case Stated. " The purpose " said counsel for the Crown " of the partners in sending Mr. Evans to this conference was not to enhance the profit-earning capacity of the firm but to advance the supposed interests of the profession of accountants. There may perhaps be some firms of
E   accountants whose links with the American business world are so many and so strong that they might reasonably expect to advance their personal business interests by attending such a conference as this, but this is emphatically not true of such a firm as [the taxpayers]. What they responded to was the desire of their institute expressed in the circular referred to in para. 4 (d) of the Case, but a wish to improve the status or the image of the accountancy profession in this
F   country is not a purpose which falls within s. 137 (*a*) of the Income Tax Act, 1952."

Counsel for the taxpayers reacted to this line of argument in two ways. First he contended that it was not open to the Crown at all. Secondly, he said that, if they were allowed to take the point, the Case must be sent back to the commissioners for them to find out, first, whether the supposed interests of the
G   profession at large did influence the firm in their decision to send Mr. Evans to the conference; and secondly, if they did, to explore in the light of further evidence whether there was in truth any such distinction between the interests of the profession as a whole and the individual business interests of its members, as the argument presupposed. Counsel for the Crown agreed that, if the point was to be properly argued, the Case would have to go back, so that all that I have to
H   decide is whether or not I should give the Crown the chance of developing the point in this case by sending it back.

The conclusion at which I have arrived is that I ought not to send the Case back, though this will rob the decision in this case of any general significance. The Crown, as I see it, must take the consequences of not having raised before the commissioners the question of " duality " of purpose as between the interests
I   of the firm and the interests of the profession. They allowed the commissioners to proceed on the footing that, if they rejected the contention that Mr. Evans had other reasons for going to America beyond that of attending the congress, the only question for them to ask themselves was whether the nature of the congress was such that the partners could not reasonably think that the profit-earning capacity of the firm would be furthered by Mr. Evans attendance at it. In deciding that the partners could reasonably take the view that the interests of the firm would be advanced, the commissioners may possibly have taken into

---

(13) [1904-07] All E.R. Rep. at p. 956; 5 Tax Cas at p. 220.

account considerations which, if the argument of the Crown is correct, they ought **A**
to have disregarded. If and so far, however, as they did so the Crown is itself to
blame. On the evidence put before them and in the light of the submissions made
to them the conclusion at which the commissioners arrived was, as I see it, a
conclusion at which it was open to them to arrive and with which I ought not to
interfere. For those reasons, therefore, I shall dismiss the appeal.

Appeal dismissed. **B**

Solicitors: *Solicitor of Inland Revenue ; Linklaters & Paines*, agents for *Walker,
Smith & Way*, Chester (for the taxpayer).

[*Reported by* F. A. AMIES, ESQ., *Barrister-at-Law.*]

C

Affirmed in part, reversed in part.
C.A. [1968] 2 All E.R. 1252.

INLAND REVENUE COMMISSIONERS *v.* HAGUE
(Married Woman).
HAGUE *v.* INLAND REVENUE COMMISSIONERS.

[CHANCERY DIVISION (Cross, J.), December 15, 21, 1967.]   **D**

*Surtax—Tax advantage—Counteracting—Conclusiveness of finding of main object
by Special Commissioners—Return of capital and capitalisation of profits—
Bona fide commercial transaction—One of main objects found to be tax
advantages to stockholders generally—Not a finding which no reasonable man
could reach—What fraction of payment to stockholder quantified to counteract
tax advantage—Finance Act* 1960 (8 & 9 *Eliz.* 2 *c.* 44), *s.* 28 (1), (3).   **E**

*Surtax—Tax advantage—Counteracting—Married woman not separately assessed
—Return of capital and capitalisation of profits—Notice served on married
woman—Whether she obtained tax advantage—Validity of notice—Finance
Act* 1960 (8 & 9 *Eliz.* 2 *c.* 44), *s.* 28 (1), (3), *s.* 43 (4) (*g*).

Following the sale of two of its four mills under a Government scheme for
the reduction of capacity and modernisation in the cotton spinning industry,   **F**
a cotton spinning company had the right to compensation of £112,976 in
respect of the mills and machinery disposed of, but became liable to a levy of
£58,986. At that time the company's issued share capital consisted of
£284,235 ordinary stock. It had assets, realisable on a liquidation, of £1
million or £3 10s. for each £1 of stock, revenue reserves (in the previous
year) of £594,929, and an excess of cash, tax reserve certificates and a market   **G**
value of investments over current liabilities, including taxation provision
of £228,696. The reduction in its production capacity and increasing use of
man-made fibres (ordered monthly instead of six-monthly with cotton,
resulting in a lower holding of stocks) had reduced the requirement for working capital and the company had money surplus to requirements. It was
decided to repay £284,235 to stockholders (equal to the amount of stock   **H**
issued) as surplus to the company's requirements and by way of reduction
of capital. To enable that to be done, and with that sole purpose in view,
but bearing tax considerations in mind and in particular the surtax liability
which would have fallen on stockholders if the payment were made by way of
dividend, the company resolved in November, 1959, on sub-division of its
shares into 5s. ordinary shares and—(i) to capitalise £189,490 made up of   **I**
£129,490 part of the balance of profits (in the profit and loss account) and
£60,000 (in a capital redemption reserve fund), and (ii) to distribute that
sum as a bonus in the form of 757,960 ordinary shares of 5s. each to
existing stockholders. In the result the issued share capital of the company
became £473,725 ordinary stock.

About a year later the company resolved on reduction and increase of
capital—(a) to reduce the capital from £473,725 ordinary stock to £234,842
10s. by returning 12s. for every £1 of that stock and reducing the nominal

A   amount of every £1 of it to 8s.; and (b) to increase the capital of the company
again to £519,077 10s. by creating 1,136,940 new ordinary shares of 5s. each.
Stockholders received £284,235 under the resolutions. H., a stockholder,
received £24,022 10s. and his wife (not separately assessed to tax) received
£7,500. The Commissioners of Inland Revenue served notices on both
stockholders under s. 28 of the Finance Act, 1960, specifying in the case
B   of the first stockholder certain adjustments of the computation of his
liability to surtax as being requisite for counteracting tax advantages
obtained by him, and in the case of his wife certain adjustments to the
computation of the joint total income of her husband and herself as being
requisite for counteracting tax advantages obtained by her. The Special
Commissioners, on appeal to them, considered that the transaction was
C   made for bona fide commercial reasons, but that one of the main objects
was the obtaining of tax advantages for stockholders generally. They also
found that Mrs. H. was not in a position to obtain, and had not obtained,
a tax advantage. On appeal by H. the Crown contended that in order to
quantify H.'s tax advantage within s. 28 (2) (*c*)* (viz., the consideration
that he " so received that he did not pay tax on it as income "), so as to
D   compute the sum required to counteract that tax advantage, the proportion
of H.'s repayment of capital which was attributable to tax advantage was
that which the amount of undistributed profits capitalised bore to the sum
repaid, viz., that the fraction was £129,490/£284,235. On the other hand
H. contended that the whole £284,235 was pre-existing capital, and that the
£129,490 was capitalised merely to provide capital for the company after the
E   repayment, so that no part of his receipts should be regarded as attributable
for the purposes of s. 28 (2) (*c*) to the undistributed profits capitalised. The
Crown appealed against the finding that Mrs. H. had not obtained a tax
advantage within s. 28.

Held: (i) it could not be predicated of the finding of the Special Commissioners (namely, that one of the main objects of the transaction was to
F   obtain a tax advantage for stockholders) that it was a finding that no reasonable man could possibly reach; accordingly that finding should stand
(see p. 1103, letter C, post).

Inland Revenue Comrs. v. *Brebner* ([1967] 1 All E.R. 779) considered.

(ii) as the repayment of capital made to H. came out of the company's
capital of £473,725, made up as to £284,235 and £60,000 of sums never
G   available for distribution by way of dividend and of £129,490 so available,
the fraction of that repayment to be treated as having been available for
distribution was £129,490/£473,725 (see p. 1104, letter B, post)

(iii) having regard to the obscurity of s. 28 and s. 43 of the Finance Act
1960, the earlier decision of the High Court that a wife not separately
charged to tax was liable to be served with a notice under s. 28 would be
H   followed, notwithstanding doubt as to its correctness (see p. 1104, letters
C to E, post).

Inland Revenue Comrs. v. *Brook* ([1967] 3 All E.R. 620) followed.

H.'s appeal allowed in part; Crown's appeal allowed.

[As to the counteracting of tax advantages, see SUPPLEMENT to 20 HALSBURY'S
I   LAWS (3rd Edn.) para. 276A; and for cases on the subject, see DIGEST (Cont.
Vol. B) 429, *1613b, 1613c.*

For the Finance Act, 1960, s. 28 and s. 43, see 40 HALSBURY'S STATUTES (2nd
Edn.) 447, 465.]

Cases referred to:
Inland Revenue Comrs. v. *Brebner,* [1967] 1 All E.R. 779; [1967] 2 A.C. 18;
        [1967] 2 W.L.R. 1001.

---

* Section 28, so far as material, is set out at p. 1103, letter F, post.

Inland Revenue Comrs. v. *Brook*, [1967] 3 All E.R. 620; [1967] 3 W.L.R. 1320. A

Case Stated.

The first taxpayer, Mr. W. T. Hague, appealed to the Special Commissioners of Income Tax against a notice served on him by the Commissioners of Inland Revenue under s. 28 of the Finance Act, 1960, specifying certain adjustments to the computation of his liability to surtax for 1960-61 as being requisite for counteracting a tax advantage obtained by him. The questions for determination B by the commissioners were: (i) whether certain transactions in securities by the company, Hagues Textiles, Ltd., were carried out for bona fide commercial reasons and whether none of them had as its main object, or one of its main objects, to enable tax advantages to be obtained; and (ii) whether certain distributions by the company represented a return of sums paid by subscribers on the issue of securities within s. 28 (2) (iii). The commissioners found that the C main purpose of the transactions was to pay out surplus money to stockholders, but that enabling tax advantages to be obtained by stockholders was one of their main objects*. They also held that so much of the money paid to stockholders as did not exceed a sum capitalised by resolution of the company in November, 1959, did not represent a return of sums paid by subscribers on the issue of securities. They therefore confirmed the notice. Mr. Hague appealed D by way of Case Stated to the High Court.

The second taxpayer, Mrs. Kathleen Hague, appealed to the Special Commissioners of Income Tax against a similar notice served on her by the Commissioners of Inland Revenue under s. 28 of the Finance Act, 1960, specifying certain adjustments to the computation of the joint total income for surtax purposes of her husband, Mr. Hague, and herself for 1960-61 as being requisite for counteracting E a tax advantage obtained by her. The questions for the commissioners' determination were the same as those raised by the husband's appeal, and in addition a third question: whether Mrs. Hague was in a position to obtain, or had obtained, a tax advantage in consequence of the transaction. The commissioners made findings in substantially the same terms as in the case of the husband, but they held also that Mrs. Hague was not a person who was in a position to obtain F or had obtained a tax advantage, and they therefore cancelled the notice. The Crown appealed by way of Case Stated to the High Court.

Arthur Bagnall, Q.C., and *J. R. Phillips* for the Crown.
H. Major Allen, Q.C., and *B. Pinson* for the taxpayers.

Cur. adv. vult. G

Dec. 21.   **CROSS, J.:**   At a meeting of the Special Commissioners held on July 21 and 22, 1966, the taxpayers, Mr. William T. Hague and his wife Mrs. Kathleen Hague, each appealed against notices served on them respectively by the Commissioners of Inland Revenue under s. 28 of the Finance Act, 1960, specifying, in the case of Mr. Hague, certain adjustments to the H computation of his liability to surtax for the year 1960-61 as being requisite for counteracting tax advantages obtained by him, and, in the case of Mrs. Hague, certain adjustments to the computation of the joint total income for surtax purposes of her husband and herself for the year 1960-61 as being requisite for counteracting tax advantages obtained by her.

The facts found by the Special Commissioners, which were the same in each I appeal, were as follows. Hagues Textiles, Ltd. (which I shall call " the company "), was incorporated in 1945 to purchase and acquire the business of three cotton spinning companies, and it has since carried on business as cotton and artificial fibre spinners. At all material times it was a company, with thirty-two members,

---

* The facts of the case, the contentions of the parties, and the decisions of the commissioners in Mrs. Hague's case (which was in similar terms to that in Mr. Hague's appeal with an additional holding) are set out at p. 1098, letter I, to p. 1100, letter I, p. 1101, letter I, to p. 1102, letter D, and p. 1102, letters E to H, post.

A to which para. (*d*) of s. 28 (2) applied. Originally, the company operated five mills. One, Stockfield Mill, was sold in 1954, leaving the company with Orb Mill, Vale Mill, Hawthorn Mill and Ram Mill. During the 1950s, the company recognised that it needed to modernise and re-equip its mills. The necessary re-equipment would require large resources which the company could not command, and the directors had in contemplation cutting down capacity and
B concentrating on Ram Mill, which was the most modern.

In May 1959 a Government White Paper was published containing proposals for a reduction of capacity in the industry generally, a plan for compensation for machinery scrapped, a subsidy for modernisation and a levy. The directors of the company welcomed this and, despite the opposition of some of the stockholders, Orb Mill and Vale Mill were disposed of, part of their machinery being
C transferred to Ram Mill, which was re-equipped by scrapping mules and substituting ring spindles. Hawthorn Mill was kept in operation, being considered to have some useful years of life left. The company received compensation under the Cotton Industry Act 1959 amounting to £112,976 in respect of the mills and machinery disposed of. It also became liable to levies under the Act of 1959 which, in the event, totalled £58,986. During the discussions concerning the
D reorganisation of the company's business, some of the stockholders were in favour of putting the company into liquidation. It was estimated that the total amount realisable on a liquidation would be about £1 million, which would represent nearly £3 10s. for each £1 of stock. The majority of the directors, however, considered that rationalisation would produce further profits.

Shortly after its incorporation, the issued capital of the company consisted
E of £60,000 redeemable preference stock and £378,980 ordinary stock. In 1950, £94,745 was repaid to the ordinary stockholders consequent on a reduction of capital, whereby 2s. 6d. in each 10s. of stock held by them was repaid, leaving £284,235 ordinary stock in issue. Subsequently, the £60,000 preference stock was redeemed, so that the issued capital came to consist of £284,235 ordinary stock. There was a capital redemption reserve fund of £60,000. The company's
F balance sheet as at Apr. 4, 1959, showed revenue reserves of £594,929. The total of its cash (in hand or at the bank), tax reserve certificates and the market value of its investments exceeded its current liabilities, including taxation provision, by £252,885. The corresponding figure on Apr. 2, 1960, was £228,696. In addition, the company anticipated receiving about £112,000 compensation, against which it would have to set the levies becoming payable. The reduction in capacity,
G together with a gradually increasing use of man-made fibres (which it could order monthly instead of six-monthly as in the case of cotton, resulting in a lower holding of stock), reduced the requirement for working capital. The company thus had money surplus to its requirements.

It was decided that £284,235 should be paid out to stockholders, such money being surplus to the company's requirements. This sum was equal to the amount
H of stock then issued. It was further decided that this payment should be made by a return of money to stockholders in a reduction of capital. To enable this to be done, it was arranged first to capitalise certain funds and issue bonus shares to be converted when issued into stock. At the time when this was arranged, there was no question of the company either requiring further capital or being over-capitalised. The sole purpose of capitalisation and issue of bonus shares
I was to put the company into a position to pay out £284,235 by means of a reduction of capital, and the sole purpose of reducing the capital was to pay over to stockholders money which was considered surplus to the company's requirements. There was no question of paying out the money by way of dividend, because that course would have attracted surtax in the hands of the stockholders, and for that reason it was rejected. It was not disputed that tax considerations were borne in mind when the decision as to how the matter should be arranged was made. The decisions were communicated to the stockholders in two letters by the chairman, exhibited to the Case, which I do not think that I

need read. At an extraordinary general meeting of the company held on Nov. A
25, 1959, the following resolutions were passed:

" (1) That each of the existing unissued ordinary shares of 10s. each in the
capital of the company be subdivided into two shares of 5s. each. (2) That the
£60,000 unclassified capital (resulting from the redemption of £60,000 five
per cent. non-cumulative redeemable preference stock) be classified as
240,000 ordinary shares of 5s. each. (3) That it is desirable to capitalise the
sum of £189,490 being as to £129,490 part of the undivided profits of the
company standing to the credit of the company's profit and loss account
and as to £60,000 the capital redemption reserve fund, and accordingly that
such sum of £189,490 made up as aforesaid be distributed as a bonus
amongst the persons who on Nov. 2, 1959 were the holders of ordinary stock
of the company, and that such bonus be not paid in cash, but be applied on
behalf of such stockholders in payment in full for 757,960 ordinary shares of
the company of 5s. each and that such ordinary shares credited as fully
paid up be accordingly allotted to such stockholders respectively in the
proportion of one of such shares for every 7s. 6d. of ordinary stock then held
by such stockholders respectively, and such distribution shall be accepted
by such stockholders in full satisfaction of their interest in the said capitalised
sum. (4) That the said 757,960 ordinary shares in the capital of the company
when issued fully paid up be converted into ordinary stock."

As a result, the authorised capital of the company was left as £473,725 ordinary
stock, all issued, and £45,352 10s. in 181,410 5s. ordinary shares, none issued.

At an extraordinary general meeting of the company held on Nov. 9, 1960,
the following special resolutions were passed:

" (1) That the capital of the company be reduced from £519,007 10s.
divided into £473,725 ordinary stock and 181,410 ordinary shares of 5s. each
to £234,842 10s. divided into £189,490 ordinary stock and 181,410 ordinary
shares of 5s. each and that such reduction be effected by returning to the
holders of the £473,725 ordinary stock capital paid up on such stock to the
extent of 12s. for every £1 ordinary stock held by them (being capital in
excess of the wants of the company) and by reducing the nominal amount
of every £1 of ordinary stock from £1 to 8s. (2) That immediately and
contingently upon such reduction of capital taking effect, the capital of the
company be increased to its former amount of £519,077 10s. by the creation
of 1,136,940 new ordinary shares of 5s. each."

The reduction of capital was confirmed by the court on Nov. 28, 1960. The
amount returned to stockholders pursuant to this resolution was £284,235.

Prior to the resolution of November, 1959, Mr. Hague held £24,022 10s.
stock, and consequent thereto there was allotted to him 64,060 shares, which
were converted into £16,015 stock, bringing his holding to £40,037 10s. stock.
On the reduction of capital in November, 1960, he received £24,022 10s., being
12s. for every £1 of stock held by him. Mr. Hague was further entitled for an
absolute interest to a share of one-ninth of the estate of Mr. Joseph T. Hague,
deceased. Prior to the resolution of November, 1959, the trustees thereof held
£29,533 17s. 6d. stock, and consequent thereto there was allotted to them 78,757
shares, which were converted into £19,689 5s. stock. On the reduction of capital
in November, 1960, the trustees received £29,533 17s. 6d.

Mrs. Hague was at all relevant times a married woman living with her husband,
and was not separately assessed to surtax. Prior to the resolution of November,
1959, she held £7,500 stock, and consequent thereon there were allotted to her
twenty thousand shares, which were converted into £5,000 stock, bringing
her holding to £12,500 stock. On the reduction of capital in November, 1960,
she received £7,500, being 12s. for every £1 of stock held by her.

Before I read the contentions and the decision of the commissioners, I should
refer to the relevant part of s. 28 of the Finance Act, 1960.

A   " (1) Where—(*a*) in any such circumstances as are mentioned in the next
     following subsection, and (*b*) in consequence of a transaction in securities
     or of the combined effect of two or more such transactions, a person is in a
     position to obtain, or has obtained, a tax advantage, then unless he shows
     that the transaction or transactions were carried out either for bona fide
     commercial reasons or in the ordinary course of making or managing
B   investments, and that none of them had as their main object, or one of their
     main objects, to enable tax advantages to be obtained, this section shall
     apply to him in respect of that transaction or those transactions . . .
        " (2) The circumstances mentioned in the foregoing subsection are that—
     . . . [paras. (*a*) and (*b*) I need not read] (*c*) the person in question receives,
     in consequence of a transaction whereby any other person—(i) subsequently
C   receives, or has received, an abnormal amount by way of dividend; or (ii)
     subsequently becomes entitled, or has become entitled, to a deduction as
     mentioned in para. (*b*) of this subsection, a consideration which either is, or
     represents the value of, assets which are (or apart from anything done
     by the company in question would have been) available for distribution
     by way of dividend, or is received in respect of future receipts of the com-
D   pany or is, or represents the value of, trading stock of the company, and
     the said person so receives the consideration that he does not pay or bear
     tax on it as income; or (*d*) in connection with the distribution of profits of a
     company to which this paragraph applies, the person in question so receives
     as is mentioned in para. (*c*) of this subsection such a consideration as is
     therein mentioned.   In this subsection—(i) references to profits include
E   references to income, reserves or other assets, (ii) references to distribution
     include references to transfer or realisation (including application in discharge
     of liabilities), and (iii) references to the receipt of consideration include
     references to the receipt of any money or money's worth, but the assets
     mentioned in para. (*c*) of this subsection do not include assets which (while
     of a description which under the law of the country in which the company
F   is incorporated is available for distribution by way of dividend) are shown
     to represent a return of sums paid by subscribers on the issue of securities . . .''

There follows a definition of the companies to which para. (*d*) of the subsection
applies; and, as the Case Stated says, there is no doubt that it does apply
to this company.   Subsection (3) provides:

G   " Where this section applies to a person in respect of any transaction
     or transactions, the tax advantage obtained or obtainable by him in con-
     sequence thereof shall be counteracted by such of the following adjustments,
     that is to say an assessment or additional assessment, the nullifying of a
     right to repayment or the requiring of the return of a repayment already
     made (the amount to be returned being chargeable under Case VI of Sch. D
H   and recoverable accordingly), or the computation or recomputation of
     profits or gains, or liability to tax, on such basis as the Commissioners of
     Inland Revenue may specify by notice in writing served on him as being
     requisite for counteracting the tax advantage so obtainable or obtained."

Then, s. 43 (4) (*g*) contains a definition of " tax advantage " which I should
read.

I   " ' tax advantage ' means a relief or increased relief from, or repayment
     or increased repayment of, income tax, or the avoidance or reduction of an
     assessment to income tax or the avoidance of a possible assessment thereto,
     whether the avoidance or reduction is effected by receipts accruing in such
     a way that the recipient does not pay or bear tax on them, or by a deduction
     in computing profits or gains."

It was contended on behalf of Mr. and Mrs. Hague that the sum of £284,235
paid to stockholders pursuant to the resolution of November, 1960, represented

a return of sums paid by subscribers on the issue of securities within s. 28 (2) (iii), **A**
which I have read, inasmuch as prior to the resolution of November, 1959,
£284,235 stock was issued, and that accordingly the notice should be cancelled.
It was further contended that the transactions detailed in the notice were carried
out for bona fide commercial reasons, and that none of them had as its main
object or one of its main objects to enable tax advantages to be obtained, and
that accordingly the notice should be cancelled. It was further contended on **B**
behalf of Mrs. Hague that she had not obtained any tax advantage in consequence
of the transactions in question; that s. 28 accordingly had no application to her,
and that the notice should be cancelled.

Against that, the contentions of the Commissioners of Inland Revenue were,
first, that the transactions were not carried out for bona fide commercial reasons;
secondly, that the main object, or one of the main objects, of the transactions **C**
was to enable tax advantages to be obtained; thirdly, that such part of the
£284,235 paid out to stockholders as did not exceed the sum capitalised pursuant
to the resolution of November, 1959, did not represent a return of sums paid
by subscribers in the issue of securities; and, fourthly, that Mrs. Hague had
obtained a tax advantage in consequence of the transactions.

The Special Commissioners who heard the appeal gave their decision as follows **D**
—and I am reading now from the Case Stated on Mrs. Hague's appeal which is
in similar terms to that on Mr. Hague's appeal with the addition of the last
paragraph:

"We found that the occasion which gave rise to the transactions in question
was the reorganisation of the company's business, which would result in the
company having assets surplus to its requirements; a further consideration **E**
influencing the company's directors was the preference expressed by some
stockholders for a liquidation, it being expected that a payment out would
satisfy them. Looking at the transactions broadly, their main purpose was
to pay out surplus money to stockholders and this was achieved by a bonus
issue followed by a return of capital. Section 28, however, required us (in our
opinion) to ask ourselves whether it had been shown that none of the trans- **F**
actions detailed in the notice had as their main object, or one of their main
objects, to enable tax advantages to be obtained. We concluded that this
had not been shown. We found, on all the evidence, that one of the main
objects of the transactions was the obtaining of tax advantages for stockholders generally. We also found that so much of the money paid to stockholders as did not exceed the sum capitalised pursuant to the resolution of **G**
November, 1959, did not represent a return of sums paid by subscribers on
the issue of securities.

"We held, however, that Mrs. Hague was not a person who was in a
position to obtain or had obtained a tax advantage within the meaning of
s. 28. In our view the reference in the section to a person who ' has obtained '
a tax advantage must, in the context, mean a person who has obtained it **H**
for himself or herself, and Mrs. Hague was not such a person by reason
of a tax advantage having accrued not to her but to her husband. We
accordingly cancelled the notice."

The Commissioners of Inland Revenue expressed dissatisfaction with the decision
in Mrs. Hague's case, and Mr. Hague expressed dissatisfaction with the decision **I**
in his case, and two Cases were stated by the Special Commissioners. Although
they do not say so in terms, the Special Commissioners plainly considered that
the transaction in question was carried out for bona fide commercial reasons,
and the Commissioners of Inland Revenue did not challenge that conclusion
before me.

Turning now to the second hurdle which the taxpayer has to surmount under
s. 28 (1), one must, of course, bear in mind that it does not follow that, because
a tax advantage was obtained in the course of a transaction, therefore the

A obtaining of that tax advantage was the main object, or one of the main objects, of the transaction. As LORD UPJOHN pointed out in *Inland Revenue Comrs.* v. *Brebner* (1), no commercial man in his senses carries out commercial transactions otherwise than in the way which will result in his paying the least possible amount of tax. Nevertheless, looking at the transaction as a whole it may be reasonable to say that the obtaining of the tax advantage was merely incidental

B and not one of its main objects. The question, as the House of Lords stressed in the *Brebner* case (2), is one to which different minds may easily give different answers. In that case, the Special Commissioners had decided that the obtaining of the tax advantages in question was not one of the main objects of the transaction, and the House of Lords refused to disturb that decision; but they pointed out—indeed, it was conceded in argument—that, if the commissioners

C in that case had reached the contrary conclusion, their decision would have been equally unassailable. As I see it, therefore, I cannot interfere with the decision of the Special Commissioners on this point unless I am satisfied that the view that it was one of the main objects of this transaction to obtain a tax advantage was one which no reasonable man could possibly form. I am not able to say that. Indeed, there would seem to me to be rather more to be said for the view that the

D obtaining of a tax advantage was a main object of this transaction than there would have been for a similar conclusion in the *Brebner* case (2)—a conclusion which the House of Lords said, if the commissioners had come to it, would have been unassailable.

On the footing that he failed on the point as to the obtaining of a tax advantage being one of the main objects of this transaction, counsel for the taxpayers did

E not seriously dispute that Mr. Hague was liable to pay some additional tax. He contended, however, that Mr. Hague's liability had been wrongly quantified. The words in s. 28 (2) (*c*) which bear on this point appear to be:

"... receives ... a consideration which either is, or represents the value of, assets which are (or apart from anything done by the company in question would have been) available for distribution by way of dividend ..."

F I do not myself think that the later words:

"... but the assets mentioned in para. (*c*) of this subsection do not include assets which (while of a description which under the law of the country in which the company is incorporated is available for distribution by way of dividend) are shown to represent a return of sums paid by

G subscribers on the issue of securities ..."

really throw much light, or indeed any light, on this problem. Those words were apparently directed to the case where the law of the country in which the company was incorporated provides that the capital of the company can be distributed as income.

Immediatly before the resolution of Nov. 25, 1959, the company's issued

H capital was £284,235. This was increased by the resolution to £473,725 by the capitalisation of, first, the capital redemption reserve fund of £60,000 and, secondly, £129,490 out of the revenue reserves of the company. The problem appears to be to discover how much of the sum received by Mr. Hague, which was obviously " the consideration " referred to in the section, was attributable to the £129,490 which prior to the capitalisation was available for distribution by

I way of dividend. Counsel for Mr. Hague submitted that none of it was so attributable. He pointed out that the company wished to repay the £284,235 cash capital, and only capitalised the capital redemption reserve fund and £129,490 of the undistributed profits in order to have some capital after all the pre-existing capital had been repaid. Consequently, he said, it would be fair to attribute the whole repayment to the pre-existing capital of £284,235. Counsel for the

---

(1) [1967] 1 All E.R. 779 at p. 784; [1967] 2 A.C. 18 at p. 30.
(2) [1967] 1 All E.R. 779; [1967] 2 A.C. 18.

Crown, on the other hand, submitted that, as ex hypothesi one of the main objects **A**
of the transaction was to gain a tax advantage, it was proper to attribute the
repayment to the undistributed profits which were capitalised so far as those
would extend, and that consequently the proportion of the sum received by
Mr. Hague which was attributable to the £129,490 was the fraction 129,490
over 284,235.

For myself, I do not think that either of these contentions is right. The   **B**
payment made to Mr. Hague came out of a capital of £473,725, made up as of
£284,235 and £60,000 of sums never available for distribution by way of dividend,
and of £129,490 which prior to its capitalisation was available for distribution
by way of dividend. Consequently, as I see it, the fraction to apply to the payment
made to Mr. Hague is 129,490 over 473,725.

There remains the question raised by the appeal of the Commissioners of Inland   **C**
Revenue in Mrs. Hague's case. It would certainly be a flaw in the section if a
payment to a married woman not separately assessed to tax escaped the net. I
understand that this loophole, if it existed, was stopped by further legislation
in 1962; but, in fact, in *Inland Revenue Comrs.* v. *Brook* (3), where the year of
assessment was 1960-61 and the facts were, for this purpose, indistinguishable
from those in the present case, UNGOED-THOMAS, J., held that s. 28 itself caught   **D**
a payment to a married woman not separately assessed. That decision, of course,
is not binding on me, and counsel for Mrs. Hague has argued strenuously that
the case was wrongly decided. I appreciate the force of some of his criticisms,
particularly that based on the wording of s. 28 (3), and I am not sure that if the
question was res integra I would have reached the same conclusion as the judge
did. The language of s. 28 and the definition of " tax advantage " in s. 43 of the   **E**
Finance Act, 1960, are, however, singularly obscure and such doubts as I feel
are not great enough to warrant my refusing to follow the decision in *Inland
Revenue Comrs.* v. *Brook* (3).

First taxpayer's appeal allowed in part. Crown's appeal in second case allowed.

Solicitors: *Solicitor of Inland Revenue; Pritchard, Englefield, Leader, Henderson*,
agents for *Knott & Castle*, Manchester (for the taxpayers).   **F**

[*Reported by* F. A. AMIES, ESQ., *Barrister-at-Law.*]

Re C. L.

[COURT OF PROTECTION (Cross, J.), February 7, 14, 1967.]

Mental Health—Patient's property—Variation of trusts—" Benefit " of patient   **G**
*—Form of application to court—Patient's income substantially in excess of her
requirements—Arrangement proposed whereby patient should give up, for the
benefit of adopted children, a protected life interest and a contingent interest
in remainder—Proposed arrangement one that patient would make if she were
capable of managing her affairs—Approval of Chancery judge necessary on
behalf of adult patient—Whether proposed arrangement for benefit of patient,*   **H**
*although financially to her detriment—Variation of Trusts Act, 1958 (6 & 7
Eliz. 2 c. 53), s. 1 (3).*

A patient who owned free investments worth about £44,000 and was
entitled under her husband's will to a protected life interest which produced
an income of some £14,000 per annum gross, was entitled also to an income
of about £7,000 per annum gross from a protected life interest under a   **I**
settlement made by her husband. The trust funds subject to the settlement
would (in effect)* be held on trust after the patient's death in favour of her
two adopted daughters and, in certain events, their children, with an
ultimate trust in favour of the patient. The adopted daughters applied by

---

(3) [1967] 3 All E.R. 620.
* There were in fact two settlements, and the patient's interest in remainder arose
under the second settlement, to which the funds subject to the first settlement were to
pass after her death.

A   summons under the Variation of Trusts Act, 1958, for approval of a pro-
     posed arrangement whereby the patient would give up for no consideration
     her protected life interest under the settlement and her contingent interest
     in remainder in the funds subject to it for the benefit of the adopted daughters.
     By relinquishing her protected life interest under the settlement the patient's
     spendable income would be diminished, having regard to income tax and
B   surtax, by less than £500 p.a.   Application being made to the Court of
     Protection either for the patient's receiver to be authorised, pursuant to
     s. 103 (1) (d)* of the Mental Health Act, 1959, to consent to an application
     for approval of the proposed arrangement or, alternatively, for an order,
     pursuant to s. 1 (3)† of the Act of 1958, that the carrying into effect of the
     proposed arrangement would be for the benefit of the patient.
C   **Held:** (i) no arrangement for variation of trusts affecting an adult
     incapable of consenting to it could take effect unless approved by the
     Chancery judge on behalf of the adult, and accordingly, it would be inappro-
     priate for the Court of Protection to direct the patient's receiver to consent
     to the proposed arrangement (see p. 1108, letter E, post).
         (ii) it was not always necessary for there to be some element of financial
D   advantage to a patient under incapacity before a proposed arrangement
     could be said to be for the patient's benefit; it was for the benefit of the
     patient to do what the patient would have done if of full capacity, and in
     the present case the carrying out of the proposed arrangement would be
     declared under s. 1 (3) of the Variation of Trusts Act, 1958, to be for the
     benefit of the patient (see p. 1110, letters F and I, post.)
E   *Re Tinker's Settlement* ([1960] 3 All E.R. 85, n.) distinguished.

     [**Editorial Note.**   Notes for guidance on the practice under s. 1 (3) of the
     Variation of Trusts Act, 1958, were issued as Practice Note [1959] 3 All E.R. 897.
     The jurisdiction of the High Court over approval of the proposed arrangement
     (s. 1 (1) of the Act of 1958) was exercised in chambers immediately after the
     determination under s. 1 (3).
F   As to applications for variation of trusts where the arrangement affects an
     interest of a mental patient, see 29 HALSBURY's LAWS (3rd Edn.) 591, para. 1079.
         As to the jurisdiction under the Variation of Trusts Act, 1958, see 38 HALS-
     BURY's LAWS (3rd Edn.) 1029-1031, paras. 1772-1773; and for cases on the subject
     see 47 DIGEST (Repl.) 332-338, *2993-3018.*
         For the Variation of Trusts Act, 1958, s. 1, see 38 HALSBURY's STATUTES
G   (2nd Edn.) 1130.
         For the Mental Health Act, 1959, s. 103 (1) (d), see 39 HALSBURY's STATUTES
     (2nd Edn.) 1050.]

     Cases referred to:
         Clore's Settlement Trusts, Re, Sainer v. *Clore,* [1966] 2 All E.R. 272; [1966]
H   1 W.L.R. 955; Digest (Cont. Vol. B) 435, *1132b.*
         Constantinidi v. *Ralli,* [1935] Ch. 427; 104 L.J.Ch. 249; 152 L.T. 489; 40
             Digest (Repl.) 584, *889.*
         Evans, Re, (1882), 21 Ch.D. 297; 46 L.T. 785; 33 Digest (Repl.) 652, *940.*
         Hinde, Re, Ex p. Whitbread, (1816), 2 Mer. 99; 35 E.R. 878; 33 Digest (Repl.)
             652, *938.*
I   *Tinker's Settlement, Re,* [1960] 3 All E.R. 85, n.; [1960] 1 W.L.R. 1011; 47
             Digest (Repl.) 338, *3016.*
         W.A.B., Re, (Mar. 7, 1952), unreported.

     Originating Summons.
     This was an application made initially to the Court of Protection by summons
     dated Oct. 24, 1967, asking that pursuant to s. 103 (1) (d) of the Mental Health
     Act, 1959, or otherwise the receiver be authorised and directed in the name and

     * Section 103 (1) (d) is set out at p. 1109, letter A, post.
     † Section 1 (3) is set out at p. 1107, letter B, post.

on behalf of the patient at the hearing of an originating summons issued in the   **A**
Chancery Division to consent to the arrangement varying the trusts of two
settlements dated Nov. 14, and Nov. 21, 1952; and by amendment made when
before the Court of Protection, alternatively, that pursuant to s. 1 (3) of the
Variation of Trusts Act, 1958, it might be ordered and declared that the carrying
out of the said arrangement, subject to such amendments (if any) as might
thereafter be approved by the Court of Protection would be for the benefit of the   **B**
patient. The application, being adjourned to the nominated judge*, was heard
in chambers and is reported by permission of the judge. By originating summons
dated June 8, 1967, to which the patient was a defendant, the plaintiffs, who
were beneficiaries under the two settlements, applied to the High Court, Chancery
Division, for an order under s. 1 of the Variation of Trusts Act, 1958, approving
an arrangement referred to in the originating summons.   **C**

    Martin Nourse for the applicants.
    J. E. Vinelott for the respondent, the receiver.

                                                      Cur. adv. vult.

    Feb. 14. **CROSS, J.,** read the following judgment: The patient is seventy-
eight years old. After the death of her husband in 1958 her health deteriorated   **D**
and in 1959 she was admitted into a mental home. In 1961 the Official Solicitor
was appointed receiver of her estate. The patient owns investments worth some
£44,000. She has a protected life interest in one half of the estate of her husband,
the gross income of which half share is about £14,000 a year. She has also a
protected life interest in a trust fund settled by her husband on Nov. 21, 1952,
the gross income of which is about £7,000 a year. She has to pay very large   **E**
sums by way of income and surtax; but even so her spending income is substantially in excess of her requirements. After the death of the patient the fund
settled by the settlement of Nov. 21, 1952, will be added to the fund settled by a
settlement made on Nov. 14, 1952, by the patient's husband in favour of their
two adopted daughters and, in certain events, the daughters' children, with an
ultimate trust for the patient which is unlikely ever to take effect. On June 8,   **F**
1967, the two adopted daughters took out a summons under the Variation of
Trusts Act, 1958, in the matter of the two settlements of Nov. 14 and 21, 1952.
to which the patient, their children and the trustees are defendants seeking
the approval of the court to an arrangement by which the patient gives up for
no consideration her protected life interest under the settlement of Nov. 21
and her contingent interest in remainder under the settlement of Nov. 14 and   **G**
at the same time certain alterations are made in the other trusts of the latter
settlement to which I need not refer. If the protected life interest of the patient
in the settlement is got rid of, there will be a great saving in estate duty if she
lives for a few more years and, having regard to the income tax and surtax which
she has to pay, the reduction in her spending income will be trifling—less than
£500 a year. If she were capable of managing her affairs, it is almost certain   **H**
that her legal advisers would advise her to consent to the arrangement for the
benefit of her adopted children and highly probable that she would accept
that advice.
    I must now refer to the provisions of the Variation of Trusts Act, 1958,
which relate to persons in the position of the patient. Section 1 provides:

    " (1) Where property, whether real or personal, is held on trusts arising,   **I**
    whether before or after the passing of this Act, under any will, settlement
    or other disposition, the court may if it thinks fit by order approve on
    behalf of—(*a*) any person having, directly or indirectly, an interest, whether
    vested or contingent, under the trusts who by reason of infancy or other
    incapacity is incapable of assenting . . . [I need not read paras. (*b*), (*c*) or (*d*)]

---

* Viz., one of the judges nominated by the Lord Chancellor under s. 100 of the Mental
Health Act, 1959.

A ... any arrangement (by whomsoever proposed, and whether or not there is any other person beneficially interested who is capable of assenting thereto) varying or revoking all or any of the trusts, or enlarging the powers of the trustees of managing or administering any of the property subject to the trusts; provided that except by virtue of para. (*d*) of this subsection the court shall not approve an arrangement on behalf of any person unless the carrying

B out thereof would be for the benefit of that person.

" (3) subject as hereinafter provided the jurisdiction conferred by sub-s. (1) of this section shall be exercisable by the High Court, except that the question whether the carrying out of any arrangement would be for the benefit of a person falling within para. (*a*) of the said sub-s. (1) shall be determined by order of the judge (1) or master in lunacy if a committee has been appointed

C of that person's estate or a receiver has been appointed of his income.

" (6) Nothing in this section shall be taken to limit the powers conferred by s. 64 of the Settled Land Act, 1925, s. 57 of the Trustee Act, 1925, or s. 171 of the Law of Property Act, 1925, or the powers of the Judge in Lunacy."

D The legal advisers of the patient formed the view that the arrangement, although one to which the patient if she was of sound mind would consent, was not one which could be said to be for her benefit. Accordingly, by an application which they made to the Court of Protection on Oct. 24, 1967, they asked for an order

" that pursuant to s. 103 (1) (*d*) of the Mental Health Act, 1959, or otherwise the receiver be authorised and directed in the name and on behalf of the patient at the hearing before the judge of an originating summons issued

E in the Chancery Division of the High Court of Justice in proceedings the short title and reference to the record whereof are [they then give the relevant title] by counsel to consent to the arrangement varying the trusts of the two settlements dated Nov. 14 and 21, 1952, referred to in the heading of the said originating summons which is exhibited to the affidavit of the applicant [they give her name] sworn in the said proceedings subject to such

F (if any) amendments thereto as may be approved by the Court of Protection.

When the application came before the master he expressed a doubt whether such an order as was being asked for was appropriate having regard to the terms of the Variation of Trusts Act, 1958, and, as he thought that it was at least arguable that the arrangement could be said to be for the benefit of the patient,

G he caused the application to be amended to ask—and this is in red ink on the summons:

" Alternatively, that pursuant to s. 1 (3) of the Variation of Trusts Act, 1958, it may be ordered and declared that the carrying out of the said arrangement subject to such further amendments (if any) as may hereafter

H be approved by the Court of Protection would be for the benefit of the patient."

Normally the master deals with applications under s. 1 (3) of the Act of 1958 himself, but in view of the doubt as to the appropriate procedure in such a case as this he adjourned this application to the judge. When the matter came before me, so that I might have both views properly argued, counsel for the applicants

I submitted that the carrying out of the arrangement was not for the patient's benefit but that I could properly direct the receiver to give his consent to it on her behalf in the variation proceedings, while counsel for the receiver submitted that I could not properly take that course but that I could declare that the carrying out of the arrangement would be for the patient's benefit. Both sides agreed that were I to hold that the arrangement proposed was not for the patient's benefit and also that I could not properly direct the receiver to give his consent

---

(1) Viz., a nominated judge (Mental Health Act, 1959, s. 100 (1)); at the present time all the Chancery judges have been so nominated.

to it, that would not mean that the scheme could not go through. The arrange- **A**
ment proposed could be limited so far as the patient was concerned to the lifting
of the protective trusts to give her an absolute life interest, a change which
would obviously be for her benefit since it would increase her property rights;
then after the arrangement was approved a second application could be made
to the Court of Protection for an order surrendering her life interest. This course
would however entail—for reasons which I need not go into—changes in the **B**
parts of the arrangements which do not affect the patient. It would, therefore,
involve some delay and added expense; so it is better to adopt one or other of
the courses suggested in the summons if either is possible.

I will deal first with the suggestion that I should direct the receiver to consent
to the arrangement on behalf of the patient. The Variation of Trusts Act, 1958,
might well have provided that if an adult not capable of assenting to the arrange- **C**
ment has no receiver, the court shall have power to approve it on his behalf
but that if he has a receiver, the receiver can consent to the scheme on his behalf
if directed to do so by the Court of Protection; but the Act of 1958 does not
take that form. It gives the court power to approve the scheme on behalf of all
incapable adults whether they have receivers or not, but provides that if they
have receivers, the Court of Protection and not the court before which the **D**
arrangement comes for approval shall decide whether it is for the benefit of the
patient. This last provision would be unnecessary—and, indeed, inappropriate
—if the Court of Protection could properly direct the receiver to assent to the
scheme on the patient's behalf as though he were a consenting adult. The Act
of 1958 as I read it requires that no arrangement which affects an adult incapable
of assenting to it can take effect unless the Chancery judge approves it on his **E**
behalf.

I turn next to the question whether the carrying out of this arrangement
would be for the benefit of the patient. Before the passing of the Mental Health
Act, 1959, there was no statutory power to make voluntary payments out of
the income or capital of the patient to members of his family or collateral relative
or friends or charities. Nevertheless, for very many years past the Lord Chan- **F**
cellors and other judges exercising the lunacy jurisdiction had made such payments in what they considered to be appropriate cases by virtue of the Crown's
prerogative to manage the patient's property. The principle on which they
proceeded was that it was in a broad sense of the word for the benefit of the
patient to have done for him what he would in all probability have done himself
if he had been of sound mind (see LORD ELDON, L.C., in *Re Hinde, Ex p. Whit-* **G**
bread (2) and SIR GEORGE JESSEL, M.R., in *Re Evans*, (3)). In the unreported
case of *W.A.B.* (4) which was heard by SIR RAYMOND EVERSHED, M.R., JENKINS,
L.J. and HODSON, L.J., on Mar. 7, 1952, it was suggested by counsel that the
Lunacy Act, 1890, had given statutory authority to make gifts out of the patient's
property to relatives. The court rejected that submission but held that the
Act of 1890 had not cut down their prerogative powers and authorised the **H**
dispositions in question—substantial gifts made with the object of avoiding
estate duty—under the inherent jurisdiction. Section 102 (1) and s. 103 (1) (*d*)
of the Mental Health Act, 1959, give a statutory power to make gifts and have
no doubt to that extent replaced the prerogative jurisdiction. Section 102 is
in the following terms:

" (1) The judge may, with respect to the property and affairs of a patient, **I**
do or secure the doing of all such things as appear necessary or expedient—
(*a*) for the maintenance or other benefit of the patient, (*b*) for the maintenance
of other benefit of members of the patient's family, (*c*) for making provision
for other persons or purposes for whom or which the patient might be
expected to provide if he were not mentally disordered, or (*d*) otherwise
for administering the patient's affairs."

---

(2) (1816), 2 Mer. 99 at p. 103.   (3) (1882), 21 Ch.D. 297 at p. 300.
(4) (1952), unreported.

A Then s. 103 provides:

  " (1) Without prejudice to the generality of the foregoing section, the judge
shall have power to make such orders and give such directions and authorities
as he thinks fit for the purposes of that section, and in particular may for
those purposes make orders or give directions or authorities for . . . (omitting
paras. (a), (b) and (c)] (d) the settlement of any property of the patient, or
B the gift of any property of the patient to any such persons or for any such
purposes as are mentioned in paras. (b) and (c) of sub-s. (1) of the foregoing
section, so however that in such cases as a nominated judge may direct the
powers conferred by this paragraph shall not be exercisable except by the
Lord Chancellor or a nominated judge."

C If the patient's life interest had not been " protected " and an application were
being made for its surrender, the order would not be made under sub-s. 102 (1) (a)
as an application of the patient's property " for her benefit " but under s. 102
(1) (b) as a gift for the benefit of members of her family. It was suggested that this
showed that the carrying out of an arrangement which involved the parting
with the life interest without any corresponding financial benefit to the patient
could not be regarded as being for her benefit. I do not agree. I do not think
D that the Act of 1959 changed the basis of the jurisdiction with regard to gifts,
namely that it is for the benefit of the patient that the court should do what
it is satisfied that he would have done. The fact that the section distinguishes
between gifts to relatives and expenditure which is directly beneficial to the
patient does not entail the consequence that the former cannot be said to be for
his benefit. Viewing the problem therefore from the aspect of the Court of
E Protection, I would have no difficulty in saying that the carrying out of the
arrangement proposed in this case would be for the patient's benefit.

  I am, however, primarily concerned with the meaning of the word " benefit "
in the Variation of Trusts Act, 1958, and it is said that Re Tinker's Settlement (5)
shows that the carrying out of an arrangement cannot be for the benefit of anyone
for the purposes of the Act of 1958 unless it confers some financial benefit on
F him. In that case the headnote read (6) that by a settlement dated Apr. 4,
1951, it was provided that certain funds should be held by the trustees for the
settlor's son and daughter in equal shares. Clause 1 (3) provided that if the son
attained the age of thirty, he should become absolutely entitled to his share,
and cl. 1 (5) that if he should die before attaining that age, then his share was
to accrue to the daughter's share. The settlement provided that if the daughter
G should attain the age of thirty the income of her share should be payable to
her during her life and after her death the capital was to be held on trust for
her children. The settlor applied to the court under s. 1 of the Variation of
Trusts Act, 1958, for approval on behalf of unborn persons interested in the
settled funds of a variation of the trusts of the son's share whereby, should
the son die before attaining the age of thirty, leaving a child or children who
H attained the age of twenty-one one-half of the son's share should be held on
trust for such child or children, and that cl. 1 (5) should be made subject to a
new clause to that effect. At the date of these proceedings, the son and daughter
were both unmarried and under thirty years of age. It was held that the court
could not sanction the proposed variation, which was, in fact, a claim for rectification of the settlement, unless it was satisfied that it would be for the benefit of
I the unborn children of the daughter; that this proposal to give away half of that
to which those children would be entitled if the son died under thirty years of
age could not possibly be said to be for their benefit; and that, therefore, the
variation would not be approved. I will read the part of the judgment of
RUSSELL, J., which relates to this point (7):

  " . . . it is quite clear that, before I sanction this arrangement, which
involves half of the son's share being given, in the event mentioned, to his

---

(5) [1960] 3 All E.R. 85, n.   (6) [1960] 1 W.L.R. 1011.
     (7) [1960] 3 All E.R. at p. 87.

children and not accruing to the daughter's half, I must be satisfied that the   **A**
arrangement is beneficial to the unborn children of the daughter. It seems
to me that it is one of the weakest claims for rectification that I have
seen, perhaps only rivalled by that in *Constantinidi* v. *Ralli*, (8) . . . and
I cannot bring myself to think that I would be benefiting the daughter's
children if I gave away half of that which will come to the daughter's
share, if the son dies under thirty. Counsel for the applicant has argued   **B**
that this is a sensible and fair thing to do because somebody has blundered—
somebody has forgotten about the son's children—and it would seem very
hard that this half of this substantial settlement should go away from
his children to his sister and her children. In a broad sense, . . . it would
be beneficial to the sister's children as members of the family viewed as
a whole that something which was reasonable and fair should be done.   **C**
I cannot apply the jurisdiction under the Variation of Trusts Act, 1958, in
that broad way. Although it may very well be that one can throw that
kind of consideration into the scale beside a financial benefit which has
already been established, yet one cannot regard that sort of consideration
as a benefit in itself. I would myself be only too pleased if I were able to
approve this proposed arrangement, but, having regard to the type of claim   **D**
for rectification which is adumbrated, I do not find myself able to approve
such a compromise or arrangement or variation under the Act of 1958 as
is sought under para. (2) of the summons."

Now with the decision in that case, if I may say so with respect, I agree entirely.
Obviously one could not say that the daughter's children if they had been in
existence and of full age would in all probability have consented to the proposed   **E**
change in the settlement. The most that one could say would be that it would
be the fair thing to do and that one hoped that they would see their way to
doing it. For the court to force this act of generosity on them before their birth
and say that it was for their benefit would be absurd. If and so far, however,
as the judge was saying that there must always be some element of financial
advantage to the infant or otherwise incapable person in question before an   **F**
arrangement can be said to be for his benefit, I think that he went too far.
Suppose a young man of eighteen to be entitled to a great fortune; suppose
some comparatively small part of it to have come to him by reason of some such
blunder in drafting as occurred in the *Tinker* case (9); suppose the persons to
whom that part ought to have come to be in straitened circumstances; and
suppose finally that the young man feels a strong moral obligation to right what   **G**
he considers to be a wrong as soon as possible and says to his trustees " Cannot
something be done for these cousins of mine now? Must I really wait until I
am twenty-one? " In such circumstances, the trustees could properly pay part
of the trust fund to the cousin's as an advancement for the young man's benefit
(see *Re Clore's Settlement Trusts,Sainer* v.*Clore*, (10)) and if it was more convenient
to achieve the desired result by an arrangement under the Variation of Trusts,   **H**
Act, 1958, I see no reason why the carrying out of the arrangement could not
be considered as being for his benefit although it was financially to his detriment.
It would be odd if the word " benefit " had a narrower meaning in the context
of a variation than it has in the context of an advancement. For these reasons
I propose to make an order under s. 1 (3) of the Variation of Trusts Act, 1958
in this case.   **I**

Order accordingly (11).

Solicitors: *Callingham, Tucker & Co.*, (for the applicants). *Official Solicitor.*

[*Reported by* Jacqueline Metcalfe, *Barrister-at-Law.*]

---

(8) [1935] Ch. 427.   (9) [1960] 3 All E.R. 85.   (10) [1966] 2 All E.R. 272.
(11) The judge sitting in the Chancery Division then heard in chambers the application
for the court's approval under s. 1 (1) of the Act of 1958 in respect of the proposed
arrangement.

A

PROTHEROE v. PROTHEROE.

[COURT OF APPEAL, CIVIL DIVISION (Lord Denning, M.R., Danckwerts and Widgery, L.JJ.), February 1, 1968.]

B
Trust and Trustee—Profit from trust—Matrimonial home—Leasehold premises—
Husband held leasehold interest on trust for himself and wife—After wife
had presented petition for divorce husband bought freehold reversion—Freehold
reversion held on same trust as leasehold premises.

A husband and wife acquired a leasehold dwelling-house as their matrimonial home. The leasehold was transferred into the name of the husband alone but it was not in dispute that the lease was held by the husband on trust for

C himself and the wife in equal shares. In March, 1964, the husband left the home; in July the wife presented a petition for divorce, and in October, 1964, the husband purchased the freehold reversion in the matrimonial home for £200, which he borrowed from a building society. The leasehold was worth separately £2,450, but the freehold would fetch £3,950. On the question whether the wife was entitled to a half share in the freehold of the matri-

D monial home,
Held: the wife was entitled equally with the husband to the net proceeds of sale of the freehold of the matrimonial home, since, as the husband had held the leasehold as trustee, the freehold reversion was regarded in equity as having been acquired on the same trusts as the leasehold was held; the husband, however, was entitled to be reimbursed the purchase price of

E the freehold reversion and the expenses in connexion with its acquisition (see p. 1112, letter G, post).

Keech v. *Sandford* ((1726), Sel. Cas. Ch. 61) applied.

Appeal dismissed.

[As to constructive trusts arising from acquisition of a reversion on a lease held on trust, and constructive trusts of profits from trust property, see 38 HALS-

F BURY'S LAWS (3rd Edn.) 857, paras. 1442, 1444; and for cases on the subject, see 47 DIGEST (Repl.) 105, 106, *763-769*, 108, 109, *785-789*. The present decision may be contrasted with that in *Bevan* v. *Webb* ([1905] 1 Ch. 620) and the dictum in *Phipps* v. *Boardman* ([1964] 2 All E.R. at p. 202, letter A) at first instance.]

Case referred to:

G   *Keech* v. *Sandford*, (1726), Sel. Cas. Ch. 61; 2 Eq. Cas. Abr. 741; Cas. *temp.* King 61; 25 E.R. 223; 28 Digest (Repl.) 544, *591*.

Appeal.
By notice dated Sept. 8, 1967, the appellant husband, William Protheroe, appealed, seeking to set aside and discharge or vary an order made by Mr. Registrar CAIRD on July 17, 1967, whereby it was adjudged and declared that the

H respondent wife was entitled equally with the husband in the net proceeds of sale of freehold premises, 151 Faraday Road, Wimbledon, subject to the prior reimbursement of the husband of his payments under the separate mortgage on the freehold and the legal expenses in connexion therewith. The grounds of the appeal were—(i) that the order of the registrar was against the weight of the evidence; (ii) that the registrar was wrong in law to extend the share to which the

I wife was entitled in the leasehold interest in the premises to the freehold interest therein; and that the registrar should have held that the wife's interest was limited to her interest in the leasehold only, with the consequence that her share should have been limited to one-half of the market value of the leasehold interest in the premises at the date on which the husband bought the freehold interest therein.

K. W. Wheeler for the husband.
H. S. Law for the wife.

LORD DENNING, M.R.: The husband and the wife were married on A
Oct. 20, 1954. The wife had a child by a previous marriage. She had two children
by this marriage, one born in 1955, a girl, and the other born in 1961, a boy.
They bought a house, 151 Faraday Road, Wimbledon, as their matrimonial
home. It was a leasehold which at that time had fourty-four years to run and
it cost £1,375. It was taken in the husband's name but the wife paid the deposit
and the husband paid the expenses. He paid also the building society instalments. B
The wife did not go out to work, but the registrar was satisfied that they were
entitled to the leasehold in equal shares. That is not disputed.

In March, 1964, the husband left the house. The wife filed a petition for divorce
on the ground of the husband's cruelty. That petition was presented on July 24,
1964. There was a decree nisi on Mar. 17, 1966, and a decree absolute on Mar. 3,
1967.   C

Here is the important point. After the wife filed her petition, in October, 1964,
the husband purchased the freehold of the house. The owners asked £500, but
he managed to get it down to £200, and eventually he bought the freehold for
£200. He borrowed the money from the building society. He paid an extra sum of
£3 8s. a month in respect of that freehold interest. In point of law the leasehold
merged in the freehold and he was the owner of the whole freehold.   D

The question now arises: what about the wife's half share? It has been contended on behalf of the husband that she only had a half share in the leasehold
and that she had no share in the freehold which it was said was entirely his own
property. He bought the property after she left. He had no intention whatever
of giving this freehold reversion to her. The point is of considerable financial
importance. A valuation has been made of the property. The leasehold would be E
worth separately £2,450, whereas if the whole were sold freehold, it would be
worth £3,950. In other words, £1,500 difference. The husband says that £1,500
difference belongs to him and that he had no intention whatever that it should
belong to the wife.

The short answer to the husband's contention is this. Although the house
was in the husband's name, he was a trustee of it for both. It was a family asset F
which the husband and wife owned in equal shares. Being a trustee, he had an
especial advantage in getting the freehold. There is a long established rule of
equity from *Keech* v. *Sandford* (1), downwards that if a trustee, who owns the
leasehold, gets in the freehold, that freehold belongs to the trust and he cannot
take the property for himself. On that principle when the husband got in the
freehold, it attached to and became part of the trust property. Nevertheless, the G
expense to which he was put in getting it in ought to be allowed him. The registrar held that the wife

" is entitled equally with the husband in the net proceeds of sale of the
freehold premises, 151, Faraday Road, Wimbledon, subject to the prior
and entire reimbursement of the husband of his payments under the separate
mortgage on the freehold and the legal expenses in connection therewith."   H

That seems to me a very proper order in accordance with the well-established
doctrines of equity. It meets the justice of the case. It was pointed out to us
that the maintenance payable to the wife is less, and a good deal less, because
she has the benefit of living in the matrimonial home.

I see no error at all in the way the registrar dealt with this case and I would
dismiss the appeal.   I

DANCKWERTS, L.J.: I agree.

WIDGERY, L.J.: I agree.   *Appeal dismissed.*

Solicitors: *R. W. Platt* (for the husband); *Sowman, Wells, Potter, Coton & Co.*
(for the wife).   [*Reported by* F. GUTTMAN, ESQ., *Barrister-at-Law.*]

---

(1) (1726), Sel. Cas. Ch. 61.

A

PAYNE v. PAYNE.

[COURT OF APPEAL, CIVIL DIVISION (Willmer, Danckwerts and Russell, L.JJ.), January 19, 22, 1968.]

Divorce—Maintenance of wife—Variation of order—Consent order—Whether question of amount of maintenance at large when first contested before the court

B *—Matrimonial Causes Act 1965 (c. 72), s. 31.*

By a consent order made on Oct. 25, 1965, at the time of the hearing of a divorce petition, the husband was ordered to pay to the wife (who was granted a decree) maintenance for herself at the rate of £1,500 annually during their joint lives; this sum was agreed on the basis of the husband's annual income being £5,000. Until August, 1964, the husband had been

C earning at that rate. On his employment then ending he was paid a substantial sum by way of compensation, which was not disclosed to the wife at the time of the decree, and in February, 1966, he obtained employment at the rate of £5,500 annually. The former wife sought variation of the maintenance order. There were two children of the marriage for whom the former wife was providing a home. The husband had re-married and his second

D wife had a substantial income. The husband swore an affidavit on the application for variation; the affidavit included untrue information regarding the amount of the compensation that he had received. The husband had to pay £130 annually under a compulsory superannuation scheme in his new employment, but this was not known to the registrar, who varied the consent order by awarding the former wife £1,800 annually less tax as maintenance.

E On appeal by the husband to the judge this award was reduced to £1,600 on the footing that the husband was receiving a salary larger by £370 annually than when the maintenance was agreed at £1,500 annually. The former wife appealed,

Held: where the original order for maintenance was a consent order and not one which had been reached after judicial inquiry, it was permissible,

F when the amount of maintenance was first contested before the court, to treat the question as one that was at large and for the court to reach its own figure of what was the appropriate amount then to award; in the present case the registrar had not been satisfied that there had been full and frank disclosure by the husband of his resources and the award of £1,800 annually less tax would be restored (see p. 1117, letters B and E, and p. 1118, letters

G A, B and G, post).

Foster v. *Foster* ([1964] 3 All E.R. 541) distinguished.

Per RUSSELL, L.J.: even if it be assumed that the husband's income at the time of the consent order did exceed £5,000 annually, the matter should not be considered wholly de novo but regard should be had to the amount agreed on the basis of his income being £5,000 annually; I should myself

H have been inclined to reduce the figure awarded by a sum to reflect that the husband's true salary was £5,370 not £5,500 annually, but I do not think that in the end injustice is done by the award of £1,800 (see p. 1118, letters C and F, post).

Appeal allowed.

I [As to matters to be considered on an application for variation of an order for maintenance, see 12 HALSBURY'S LAWS (3rd Edn.) 445, 446, paras. 1001, 1002; and for cases on the subject, see 27 DIGEST (Repl.) 622-624, *5803-5840* and DIGEST (Cont. Vol. B) 376, 377, *5822c, 5822d.*

For the Matrimonial Causes Act 1965, s. 31, see 45 HALSBURY'S STATUTES (2nd Edn.) 488.]

Cases referred to:

Ette v. *Ette*, [1965] 1 All E.R. 341; [1964] 1 W.L.R. 1433; Digest (Cont. Vol. B) 345, *636de.*

Distinguished in WALES V WADHAM [1977] 2 All ER 125

Foster v. *Foster*, [1964] 3 All E.R. 541; [1964] 1 W.L.R. 1155, n.; Digest (Cont.   **A**
Vol. B) 376, *5822c*.

J. v. *J.*, [1955] 2 All E.R. 85; *sub nom. J.-P.C.* v. *J.-A.F.*, [1955] P. 215;
[1955] 2 W.L.R. 973; *Varied* C.A., [1955] 2 All E.R. 617; *sub nom.*
J.-P.C. v. *J.-A.F.*, [1955] P. at p. 236; [1955] 3 W.L.R. 72; Digest
(Cont. Vol. A) 790, *5768a*.

Interlocutory appeal.

This was an appeal by the wife by notice dated Nov. 15, 1967, against an order
of WRANGHAM, J., made on July 6, 1967, allowing the husband's appeal against
an order of Mr. Registrar TOWNLEY MILLERS. The registrar, on the application
of the wife, had varied a consent order for maintenance contained in the decree
nisi of divorce made on Oct. 25, 1965, in a suit between the husband and wife on   **C**
Oct. 25, 1965. The consent order in the decree nisi provided that the husband
should pay the wife maintenance for herself at the rate of £1,500 per annum by
monthly instalments during their joint lives on the basis of the husband's annual
income being £5,000. The order of the registrar provided that the husband
should pay to the wife maintenance for herself during their joint lives at the rate
of £1,800 per annum less tax. The order of WRANGHAM, J., provided that the   **D**
amount of maintenance should be £1,600 per annum less tax. The grounds of
appeal were: (i) that the husband did not discharge the burden of proof to show
that the order of the registrar was wrong; (ii) that the judge failed to take any
or sufficient account of a sum of £11,872 1s. 1d. net which the husband received
by way of compensation for loss of office; (iii) that the judge was wrong in the
inference which he drew from the fact that the order embodied in the decree   **E**
nisi was by consent of the parties; and (iv) that the judge was wrong in failing
to take account of the rate of the husband's current personal expenditure.

E. R. Moulton-Barrett for the former wife.
J. C. J. Tatham for the husband.

WILLMER, L.J.: This is an appeal from an order made by WRANGHAM, J.,   **F**
on July 6, 1967, varying a previous order made by Mr. Registrar TOWNLEY
MILLERS on May 30, 1967, with regard to the quantum of maintenance which
ought to be paid by an ex-husband to his ex-wife following divorce proceedings.
The sum which had been awarded by the registrar was £1,800 annually, less tax.
That was reduced by the judge to the sum of £1,600 annually less tax. On this
appeal we have been invited to restore the registrar's figure.   **G**

I have found very considerable difficulty in arriving at a conclusion in this case,
but I have in the end come to the conclusion that the appeal ought to be allowed
and the registrar's figure restored. The main source of my difficulty in the case
(and I will state this at once at the outset of my judgment) has been the fact
that the husband throughout has been anything but frank in the disclosures
which he has made with regard to his available income. I will come back later to   **H**
particular matters of criticism in relation to his non-disclosures.

The matter started with a consent order which was made at the time of the
hearing of the divorce petition on Oct. 25, 1965. As the result of an agreement
which was reached between the parties, the husband elected not to proceed
with his petition, but allowed the wife to obtain a decree of divorce on her answer.
As part of what was agreed, and as part of the order made when the decree nisi   **I**
was pronounced, it was provided that the husband should pay to the wife as from
Oct. 25, 1965, until further order, first, alimony pending suit, and thereafter,
as from decree absolute, maintenance for herself during their joint lives at the
rate of £1,500 a year payable monthly on the basis of the husband's annual
income being £5,000. The husband, as we now know, had been employed for a
number of years by the Sunday Mirror, but his contract of employment with
them was determined in August, 1964. He was out of employment for a matter
of some six months, but in February, 1965, he obtained fresh employment with

A   Tit-Bits. He was in that employment at the time of the decree and at the time
of the consent order. Whilst with the Sunday Mirror he had been receiving
a salary of £5,000 a year, and again during the period while he was working for
Tit-Bits he was receiving a salary of £5,000 a year. That no doubt was the reason
why the consent order was said to have been made on the basis of his income being
£5,000 a year. We now know that, quite apart from the salary which he had been
B   earning, the husband also received a very substantial sum of money as compensation for his loss of employment at the time when he left the Sunday Mirror in
August, 1964. Even now I do not think that we know the exact size of the bonus
which he then received, but it is near enough if I say that, after tax had been
deducted, there remained in his hands something of the order of £11,500.

At the time when the consent order was made, the parties had been living
C   separate and apart for a considerable time, and the wife had no exact knowledge
with regard to this large capital payment which the husband had received. We
are told, however, that she had her suspicions. So far as I understand it, nothing
was disclosed at the time when the consent order was made with regard to the
amount received by way of compensation, nor as to what use the husband had
made of the money so paid to him.

D   To move forward now from October, 1965, the husband obtained fresh employment in February, 1966, when he moved from Tit-Bits to become managing editor
of The People. In that new employment he obtained a salary of £5,500 a year.
The situation, therefore, did alter following the consent order at any rate to this
extent, that the husband's salary increased by an amount of £500 a year. In due
course the wife issued a summons asking for a variation of the consent order.
E   She was then apparently under the impression that the husband's salary as managing editor of The People was a good deal more than it has in fact been found to be.
She filed an affidavit in May, 1966 setting out the effect of the consent order, and
stating (as was the fact) that she had been granted the custody of the younger
child of the marriage, and that she also had an elder daughter making her home
with her. So far as education fees are concerned, I understand that the husband is
F   paying (and always has paid) the fees of the younger child. The elder child has
left school and has been at college. The wife, however, does have the responsibility
of housing these children, and I suppose looking after them and feeding them
during such periods as they are at home. It should also be mentioned that, as
part of the order made at the time of the divorce, the husband made over to the
wife his interest in the house which had been the matrimonial home. The wife
G   has continued to reside there, and has kept a home there for the children of the
marriage; but, as she made clear in the second of her affidavits, she does that at
some considerable cost to herself. For the house is subject to a mortgage of £6,300
on which the interest payments amount to £260 a year. Moreover, the mortgage
is secured by a policy of insurance on the life of the husband on which she has to
pay premiums amounting to £309 8s. a year. This is not a case, therefore, of a
H   husband who has provided his divorced wife with a home in which she can live
rent free. He has, it is true, provided a home, but it is a home which costs the
wife a good deal of money to maintain.

The husband swore his affidavit of means in response to the wife's application
on June 29, 1966, and I think that it is right to say that most of what is stated in
para. 2 of the affidavit, in which he dealt with the capital sum received by way of
I   compensation, has turned out to be false. He said that when he resigned his
position with the Sunday Mirror, the sum that he received by way of compensation, after deduction of tax, amounted to £9,500. That was not true. He said that
at that time he had an overdraft of £800. That was not true, as now appears from
his bank account, which has been produced. He said that he was in debt in the
sum of about £3,500 in respect of arrears of income tax and expenses connected
with the flat in which he was then living. That at best was only a partial truth.
What had happened was that he had been associating for a long time with another
woman whom he has since married, and this other woman had advanced a sum of

£3,500 or more to him, partly to help him pay his income tax, and partly to help A him furnish the flat in which they now live. It appears that, apart from what is mentioned in that paragraph, there was a further £800 which had also been advanced by the husband's present wife. Then he spoke of seven months during which he was unemployed; it was in fact six months. He did not mention the fact that he obtained employment for a year with Tit-Bits. He said that during the period of his unemployment he incurred expenses, including bills in connection B with his former matrimonial home, totalling about £2,800. I do not know how that figure was arrived at. What we do know is that somehow or another, this husband succeeded in getting through the whole of the £11,500 which he received by way of compensation in the course of just over a year after the initial payment was made to him. He put some £4,000 of it temporarily on deposit, but almost at once began drawing on that, and by the time that the consent order came to be made, C that deposit had been completely wiped out. The husband was once again in the red on his current account, and the whole of the amount received by way of compensation had gone. Where it had gone remains obscure. The husband was not called to give oral evidence; he was not asked to attend for cross-examination because, during the preliminary inquiries which were made before the hearing came on, he took up the attitude, through the mouth of his solicitors, that he D simply did not remember and could not answer the questions that were being asked. That also has turned out not to be true. We know that that is so because, when the case reached this court and each of us in turn started asking questions, the truth about a number of the questions was gradually wormed out of the husband through the mouth of his counsel. The plain fact, and I regret to say it, is that the husband simply did not take seriously the request for information E which had been received, and so far as I can see made not the slightest effort to account for the receipts and payments about which he was being questioned in relation to the material period.

When the matter eventually came before the registrar, which it did only in May, 1967, after a prolonged operation in an attempt to obtain some discovery from the husband, the registrar took the view that, on the basis of the husband's F new employment at £5,500 a year, and on the basis of the husband's inability to account for a number of receipts which appeared in his bank statements, it was proper to increase the amount of the consent order to the sum of £1,800. He did not, in arriving at that figure, take into consideration a relatively trivial sum of £130 a year, which it now appears that the husband has to pay under a compulsory superannuation scheme as part of his contract of employment with his present G employers.

When the matter came before the judge on appeal, this latter circumstance was drawn to the attention of the judge, and he quite rightly appreciated that it was a matter which had not been before the registrar, and to that extent the situation was different from what had then been understood. He also took the view, however, which he expressed in a short judgment which he delivered, that H the registrar was not entitled to speculate on the husband having other sources of income in addition to his salary. The judge said:

"I am not satisfied that those speculations are founded with sufficient certainty to take them into account."

The judge then went back to the consent order and, taking the view that the I parties had agreed that £1,500 a year was appropriate on the basis of an income of £5,000 a year, he thought that on the new salary of £5,370 a year (that is, £5,500 less £130), an increase of £100 a year was the most that could be justified for the maintenance of the wife, and he accordingly allowed the appeal to the extent of reducing the wife's maintenance to £1,600 a year. It is in that situation that the matter comes before us.

The first question which I think must be resolved is what is the proper method of approach to the issue which has arisen. I ventured during the course of the

A argument to refer to *Foster* v. *Foster* (1). That was a case which came before this court on appeal from a variation order made by a judge. It was a case in which there had been an original maintenance order, and we took the view that in that situation the jurisdiction of the court was a jurisdiction only to vary the previously existing maintenance order. We thought that it was wrong to say that on varia-tion proceedings the whole question was at large, in the same way as it is on an

B original application for maintenance. I thought it right to draw attention to that case because here again we are faced with a variation order. On reflection, however, I do not think that the principle stated in *Foster* v. *Foster* (1) should be applied in the circumstances of this case. In *Foster* v. *Foster* (1) the original maintenance order had been arrived at after judicial inquiry. Here it was a consent order, arrived at on the basis of that which the husband was at the time

C prepared to disclose about his personal affairs. I am left in the position that I am far from satisfied that at that time he made anything like a full disclosure of the relevant circumstances. Beyond saying, therefore, that the parties at the time thought that £1,500 a year maintenance would be appropriate on the basis of an income of £5,000 a year, I do not think that the original consent order can be regarded as so sacrosanct, as it were, as the original maintenance order was held

D to be in *Foster* v. *Foster* (1).

In all the circumstances of this case it seems to me that when the matter came before the registrar for the first time on a contest with regard to the amount of maintenance which should be paid, it was right for him to treat the matter as one in which the question was at large, and to arrive at his own figure of what was an appropriate sum to award by way of maintenance on the facts as then disclosed

E to him. On the basis of a husband earning a salary of £5,500 a year, and about whom there were at least some grounds for suspicion that he had not by any means put all his cards on the table, I find it difficult to say that £1,800 a year was an unreasonable figure for the learned registrar to arrive at. It is to be remembered that, apart from other considerations, the wife was, as I have said, providing a home for the children of the marriage. It is true that the husband had since

F remarried, but as we are told he had married a woman occupying herself a substantial position in journalism, and enjoying a substantial income. I do not put that forward as any ground for suggesting that it was a source of income for the husband, but it is at least some guarantee that he will not have to support a second wife at the same time that he is supporting his first wife.

That being so, prima facie I would regard the registrar's award of £1,800 a year

G maintenance as being a proper award to make in all the circumstances. In my view the judge fell into error when he interfered. I do not think that the difference caused by £130 worth of superannuation payment was of sufficient importance to justify any interference by the judge. Nor do I think that he was justified in criticising the registrar for "speculating", as the judge described it, on other possible sources of income which the husband might have. I think that it is

H probably wrong to say that the learned registrar did "speculate" about other possi-ble sources of income. The truth of the matter is (and it is abundantly justified) that he was not satisfied that he had had a full and frank disclosure from the husband about what his resources were. As we now know, it is quite plain that he had not. In such circumstances it is well established that the court is entitled to draw inferences adverse to a husband who has not made a proper disclosure of

I his available resources. That was held by SACHS, J., in *J.* v. *J.*, (2) a decision which was subsequently upheld, so far as that point at any rate was concerned, by this court (3). It was also held by LLOYD-JONES, J., in *Ette* v. *Ette* (4), where it was again decided that it was proper to draw inferences adverse to the husband from the fact of his failure to make a proper disclosure. I think that that is right.

(1) [1964] 3 All E.R. 541.
(2) [1955] 2 All E.R. 85; [1955] P. 215.
(3) [1955] 2 All E.R. 617; [1955] P. at p. 236.
(4) [1965] 1 All E.R. 341.

To that extent it seems to me that the judge fell into error in criticising the way **A** in which the registrar behaved on the hearing of the summons.

In all the circumstances, therefore, I have reached the conclusion, as I have said not without difficulty, that the judge fell into error in varying the order made by the registrar. The circumstances were not such as to justify such a variation, and that being so I think that this appeal should be allowed, and the registrar's order restored. **B**

DANCKWERTS, L.J.: My mind has wavered considerably during the hearing of this appeal, but in the end I have come to the same conclusion as WILLMER, L.J., and for the reasons which he has given in his judgment. Accordingly I agree with his judgment. I agree that the appeal should be allowed, and the order of the registrar restored. **C**

RUSSELL, L.J.: In my view, even if it is to be assumed that the annual income of the husband at the time of the consent order was more than £5,000 a year, I do not myself think that the matter should be considered wholly de novo and without regard to the consent. It seems to me that regard must be had to the fact that the parties agreed that there was a relation between the figures of £1,500 and £5,000 in considering a variation and its quantum. If, for example, **D** it was clear that the annual income of the husband was now £5,000 and no more, no variation could properly be made; and if it was clear, as the judge thought, that the annual income was £5,370 and no more, an increase of £300 would not be justified, and the appropriate increase would be about £100, as the judge ordered. The registrar, however, was not prepared to accept that the husband was properly **E** to be regarded as having an annual income of no more than his salary. Having regard to the unreliability of the husband's evidence in many respects, his almost complete failure to assist the court when asked in March, 1967, for particulars of receipts appearing in his bank account, indeed his continual inability to account for certain of them, I think that the registrar was well entitled to draw adverse inferences as to the present faculties of the husband to provide maintenance, and **F** I think that the judge should not have overruled that view of the registrar. I would myself have been inclined to reduce the figure by a sum to reflect the fact that the salary was truly £5,370 and not £5,500, a fact not known to the registrar. On the other hand, it might be said that a notional income should be attributed to the husband to reflect investment in the lease of the flat of part of his " golden handshake ". I do not think in the end that injustice is done by the registrar's **G** order, and I would restore it. I have referred to the parties as " husband " and " wife ", but they are, of course, now no longer married.

Appeal allowed.

Solicitors: *Dixon, Ward & Co.*, Richmond (for the wife); *Frederick Wills & Co.* (for the husband). **H**

[*Reported by* ELLEN B. SOLOMONS, *Barrister-at-Law.*]

A

R. *v.* BOTT AND ANOTHER.

[LEICESTER WINTER ASSIZES (Veale, J.), February 12, 13, 20, 1968.]

Criminal Law—Committal—Evidence—Written statements—Copy to be given to each of the other parties to the proceedings, whether sufficient to give copy to

B *solicitor representing accused—Criminal Justice Act 1967 (c. 80) s. 2 (2) (c).*

For the purpose of fulfilling the condition of admissibility in evidence before examining justices imposed by s. 2 (2) (c)* of the Criminal Justice Act 1967, it is sufficient that a copy of the written statement to be tendered in evidence is given to the solicitor of the other party to the proceedings, rather than to the other party himself; but if a solicitor represents several accused,

C as many copies should be given to the solicitor as there are accused whom he represents (see p. 1122, letters F and H, post).

[As to evidence before examining justices, see 10 HALSBURY'S LAWS (3rd Edn.) 359, para. 656 text and note (*f*).]

Cases referred to:

D   *Nimmo* v. *Alexander Cowan & Sons, Ltd.*, [1967] 3 All E.R. 187; [1967] 3 W.L.R. 1169.

  Quartz Hill, etc. Co., Re, Ex p. Young, (1882), 21 Ch.D. 642; 51 L.J.Ch. 940; 47 L.T. 644; 22 Digest (Repl.) 520, *5786*.

Trial on indictment.

Charles Edward Bott and Barry Robert Baker were jointly charged on indict-

E ment at Lincoln Assizes in February, 1968, with an offence of aggravated robbery; each accused was charged in the alternative with simple robbery, and in the further alternative Bott was charged with receiving stolen property. The accused were represented by the same solicitor, who was retained by them before the committal proceedings before the examining justices took place on Jan. 3, 1968. Section 2 of the Criminal Justice Act 1967 came into force on Jan. 1, 1968, and

F copy statements were given by the prosecution to the solicitor for the accused before the hearing. Two sets of copy statements were given to the solicitor by the prosecution, as he represented two accused. The solicitor, who had already taken general instructions, did not give the statements to the accused. He took further detailed instructions from them after the committal. Counsel moved on behalf of the accused to quash the indictment on the ground that the committal was

G bad. The case was adjourned to Leicester Assizes for legal argument.

F. B. Smedley for the accused: there has not been compliance with s. 2 (2) (c) of the Criminal Justice Act 1967, since copy statements have never been given to each of the other parties to the proceedings themselves, but only to the solicitor who was acting for them.

  W. C. Woodward for the Crown: there has been compliance with s. 2 of the Act

H of 1967, because on the true construction of sub-s. (2) (c) a written statement is not thereby required to be given to the " other parties " personally. If the motion to quash the indictment should succeed, application will be made for a voluntary bill of indictment in the same form as the existing indictment.

  Feb. 20.   **VEALE, J.,** having stated the nature of the charges and referred

I to the giving of the copy statements to the solicitor, and having intimated that the way in which the solicitor dealt with the matter was understandable and probably convenient, continued: The point raised on this motion to quash the indictment is obviously one of importance, and I adjourned the case to these assizes to enable counsel to argue the matter fully. Technical it may be, but if good in law an accused is entitled to take the point. Section 2 of the Criminal Justice Act 1967 so far as is for the moment relevant reads as follows:

---

  * Section 2 (2) (c) is set out at p. 1120, letter A, post.

A

"(1) In committal proceedings a written statement by any person shall, if the conditions mentioned in the next following subsection are satisfied, be admissible as evidence to the like extent as oral evidence to the like effect by that person.

"(2) The said conditions are—. . . . (c) before the statement is tendered in evidence, a copy of the statement is given, by or on behalf of the party proposing to tender it, to each of the other parties to the proceedings."

B

At the outset it can be argued that if one looks no further than sub-s. (2) (c) itself, it draws a distinction between a party and someone acting on behalf of a party, for before the statement is tendered in evidence a copy is to be given "by or on behalf of the party proposing to tender it" to "each of the other parties to the proceedings". It would indeed have been simple to add some such words as "or their solicitor" at the end of the sub-paragraph; but such words are conspicuously absent.

C

It is in my judgment necessary to look at other sections of the Act of 1967 in order to attempt to ascertain the meaning of the "parties to the proceedings" in s. 2 (2) (c), and, indeed, counsel for the accused is entitled to point to several instances where the word "party" is used in a sense clearly indicating the person accused himself, and not his solicitor. Thus in s. 3 (4) certain matters only may be published in a report of the committal proceedings, which cannot now otherwise be reported. These matters include by sub-para. (b) "the names, addresses, and occupations of the parties", as well as by sub-para. (d) "the names of counsel and solicitors engaged in the proceedings". The word "parties" in that sub-paragraph is clearly used in its personal sense. Again, in s. 9, the word "party" is used more than once. Section 9 relates to any criminal proceedings other than committal proceedings. Section 2 is therefore expressly excluded from the operation of s. 9. By s. 9 (8)—

D

E

"a document required by this section to be served on any person, may be served (a) by delivering it to him or to his solicitor; . . ."

This subsection of s. 9 lends point to the absence of any such words in s. 2 (2) (c); but it does not stop there. Section 9 (2) contains both the word "party" and the word "parties". The condition for admissibility of a written statement in s. 9 (2) (c) is similar in its language to s. 2 (2) (c), and s. 9 (8) expressly permits "service" on a solicitor. Further, the condition set out in s. 9 (2) (d) reads:

F

"None of the other parties or their solicitors, within seven days from the service of the copy of the statement, serves a notice on the party so proposing objecting to the statement being tendered in evidence under this section: . . ."

G

Here again "parties" are distinct from "their solicitors". Section 9 (4) (a) also contemplates action "on behalf of" a party. Section 10 (1) refers to an "admission by any party" being conclusive evidence "as against that party". I shall return in a moment to the words "admission by any party", but conclusive evidence "as against that party" would seem to refer to the party himself. It is also, I think, permissible to refer to s. 36 (2) which reads:

H

"Expressions used in any provision of this part of this Act relating to magistrates' courts or proceedings before such courts, and also used in the Magistrates' Courts Act, 1952, have the same meanings in any such provision as they have in that Act."

The words are "used in", not "defined in" the Magistrates' Courts Act, 1952. There is no definition of "party" in the interpretation sections of the Act of 1952, but it is clear that the words "party" and "parties" as used in s. 60 and s. 61 of that Act, relating to domestic proceedings, refer to the party or parties in person. Looking therefore at these other sections of the Act of 1967 to which I have just referred, a formidable case can be made for saying that the words "parties to the proceedings" in s. 2 (2) (c) do not include a solicitor.

I

There are, however, arguments the other way. Again dealing with the Act of 1967 itself, one can look at s. 2 (3) (c). This requires that when an exhibit is

A referred to in a statement, there must be with the copy statement " a copy of
that document ", or " such information as may be necessary in order to enable
the party to whom it is given to inspect that document or a copy thereof ". I
would have thought that this must be contemplating inspection by a solicitor,
who, in many, if not in all cases, would be the person one would expect to inspect.
Again, s. 2 (4) in my view points strongly to " party " meaning " the side in the
B proceedings ", or " the party acting through a solicitor ". By s. 2 (4), notwithstanding the admissibility in committal proceedings of a written statement by
any person, the court " may of its own motion, or on the application of any party
to the proceedings require that person to attend before the court and give
evidence ". Where an accused is legally represented any such application would
be made by the legal representative. " Party " in this subsection must include
C " party acting through his solicitor "; in other words, it must include an application by or on behalf of an accused; and what I have just said refers to the similar
wording of s. 9 (4) (b). Further, the word " parties " in the phrase " if the parties
agree before or during the hearing ", in the proviso to s. 9 (2) must contemplate
an agreement expressed by counsel or solicitor when the accused is represented.
    I have already mentioned s. 10 (1) relating to admission of facts:

D   ". . . the admission by any party of any such fact under this section shall
        as against that party be conclusive evidence . . . of the fact admitted."

But by s. 10 (2) (d), an admission under this section " if made on behalf of a defendant who is an individual, shall be made by his counsel or solicitor ". Therefore,
in the same sentence in s. 10 (1), the word " party " is being used with two shades
of meaning, " party " in the first instance meaning " party acting by his counsel
E or solicitor ", and in the second instance meaning " party in person ". In fact,
of course, the word " party ", if one looks at a dictionary, can bear many quite
different meanings, and many varying shades of meaning. It may mean a portion,
a body of persons, a social gathering, or a single person. There is even some
Gilbertian judicial authority for saying that often a young barrister is an
impecunious party.
F   By the Supreme Court of Judicature (Consolidation) Act, 1925, s. 225, " party "
is defined as including " every person served with notice of or attending any
proceeding, although not named on the record ", but these words are subject to
the general words " unless the context otherwise requires ". Indeed, the word
" party " has in the past been used in different senses in the same statute. In
Re Quartz Hill Co., Ex p. Young (1), SIR GEORGE JESSEL, M.R., said:
G   " The wording of the Chancery Amendment Act, 1852 (15 & 16 Vict. c. 86),
      is open to criticism. The word ' party ' appears to be sometimes used there in
      its proper sense and sometimes in that of ' person '."

In s. 2 (2) (c) of the Criminal Justice Act 1967 the words are, " given . . . to each
of the parties to the proceedings ". Why the word " given " was adopted I do
H not know, unless it was an attempt to instil an air of informality, but the word
" parties " is part of the phrase " parties to the proceedings ". I have to decide
whether in all the circumstances " parties to the proceedings " in s. 2, (2) (c)
means the parties personally, or whether it simply means the parties' side of the
proceedings, thereby including their solicitors.
    In the Criminal Justice Act 1967 the word " party " is in my view used in
I differing senses in different places, and I am unable to compliment the draftsman
on his choice of wording; but in order to ascertain the meaning to be attributed
to s. 2 (2) (c) one must, I think, look to the intention lying behind the words of the
section.
    As recently as the case of Nimmo v. Alexander Cowan & Sons, Ltd. (2), LORD
UPJOHN quoted with approval MAXWELL ON THE INTERPRETATION OF STATUTES
(11th Edn., 1962), p. 183:
      " In determining either the general object of the legislature, or the mean-
      ing of its language in any particular passage, it is obvious that the intention

_____
(1) (1882), 21 Ch.D. 642 at p. 645.   (2) [1967] 3 All E.R. 187 at p. 196.

which appears to be most in accord with convenience, reason, justice and legal   A
principles, should in all cases of doubtful significance be presumed to be the
true one."

Sections 1 and 2 of the Criminal Justice Act 1967 introduced a very substantial
alteration of the law. The use of statements at committal proceedings is hedged
about with conditions designed to protect an accused person, who can, of course,
if he desires, object to the use of any statement. He is not to be taken by surprise   B
at the contents of a statement; hence the words of s. 2 (2) (c). If an accused is
not represented, s. 1 does not apply at all. When an accused is represented,
the person who must know the precise contents of the statements is the solicitor
or counsel representing him, otherwise he could not decide on any plan of action.
In many cases, if an accused had to be given the statements personally they might
never reach the solicitor at all. This, of course, would be the accused's own fault,   C
but so many accused persons are careless and not accustomed to dealing with
documents. I can foresee, if a giving of statements to the accused personally is
required, requests by solicitors for additional copies for themselves, and a solicitor,
only able to get the statements at the last minute from his client, might well
consider it necessary to apply for the attendance of the witness, thereby causing
delay which would have been avoidable, had he had the statements in good time.   D
Again, the solicitor can normally be easily located for the purpose of giving
statements, which by no means applies to all accused persons. Further, an accused
may put in statements as well as the prosecution. I ask myself what would be the
position if the defendant had to serve personally the Director of Public Prosecutions in those cases where he is the prosecutor. Finally, if a solicitor is given the
copies of the statements there can be no prejudice to his client. Indeed, as I   E
see it, it would be in many cases to his advantage.

In these circumstances, convenience, reason and justice compel me to the
conclusion that giving copy statements to a solicitor acting on behalf of an accused
is a sufficient giving to the other party or parties to the proceedings within the
meaning of s. 2 (2) (c), and I so hold, despite what appears in the Magistrates'
Courts Rules. I have come to this conclusion with some hesitation, in view   F
of the argument which has been addressed to me. It would have been so simple
to have made the position quite clear, and I regard the absence of clarity as
unfortunate.

Before concluding this judgment, I desire to mention two other matters.
First, if copy statements given to a solicitor for a client are in turn given, albeit
informally, to the client by the solicitor, I would have had no hesitation in holding   G
that that was a sufficient giving for the purposes of s. 2 (2) (c). Secondly, it
frequently happens that one solicitor represents two accused jointly charged. I
do not think that in such circumstances there is a sufficient compliance with
s. 2 (2) (c) if only one copy of the statements is given to the solicitor. The section
does not put the burden of making copies on the solicitor. The same number of
copy statements must be given as the number of accused represented by the   H
solicitor.

In two cases earlier during the recent Lincoln assizes I quashed the indictments
on the application of the prosecution, no objection being raised by the defence to
that or to the subsequent application for a voluntary bill. The grounds of both
those applications to quash on behalf of the prosecution were that only one copy
of statements was given to a solicitor who had been acting for two accused, and   I
there was agreement that this was not a giving of statements to each of the other
parties to the proceedings. In the result this motion fails.

Motion refused.

Solicitors: *Claytons*, Nottingham (for the accused); *P. N. Vine, Prosecuting
Solicitor*, Nottingham (for the Crown).

[*Reported by* GWYNEDD LEWIS, *Barrister-at-Law*].

A LIPMANS WALLPAPER, LTD. v. MASON & HODGHTON, LTD.
AND ANOTHER.

[CHANCERY DIVISION (Goff, J.), November 23, 24, 29, 30, December 1, 4, 5, 1967.]

Sale of Land—Leasehold interest—Consent to assignment—Vendors' duty—
Sub-lease—Consent refused by immediate landlord—Ground of refusal that
B *assignees' user would contravene covenant in head-lease—Whether vendors*
under a duty to approach freeholders for a licence or to afford purchasers
opportunity to do so.

Sale of Land—Contract—Rescission—Notice—National Conditions of Sale
(17th Edn.) condition 10 (5)—Whether notice of rescission could be given
validly without first giving notice under condition 8 (6).

C
Premises, the subject of a demise for 999 years from Sept. 29, 1918, were
sub-demised to the first defendants in September, 1958. The sub-lease
contained a covenant by the sub-tenants not to assign without the immediate
landlord's consent. By covenant in the head-lease the user was restricted
to use as an estate office and sales room, but the sub-lease did not contain
a similar restriction and, in 1961, the freeholders licensed the use of the
D premises for the first defendants' business. In November, 1965, there was,
so the court found, a contract for sale by the first defendants of the sub-
tenancy to the plaintiffs. This contract was by correspondence incorporating the National Conditions of Sale (17th Edn.). The first defendants
applied to their immediate landlord for licence to assign; but this was
refused on the ground that the proposed user by the assignees contra-
E vened the restriction in the head-lease. The first defendants forthwith
gave notice, under condition 10 (5) of the National Conditions of Sale (17th
Edn.), rescinding the agreement for sale to the plaintiffs, and surrendered
their sub-tenancy to their immediate landlord. In an action by the plaintiffs
for specific performance,

F **Held:** (i) the first defendants were not under obligation to the plaintiffs,
by virtue of the contract for sale, to take steps to endeavour to persuade
their immediate landlord to change its mind and to consent to the proposed
assignment, nor to approach the freeholders for a licence for the proposed
change of use, nor to afford the plaintiffs opportunity themselves to approach
the freeholders; accordingly the first defendants were in a position in
which they could validly exercise a contractual right of rescission (see p. 1129,
G letters E and I, post).

Dictum of PAGE WOOD, L.J., in *Lehmann* v. *McArthur* ((1868), 3 Ch. App.
at p. 501) applied.

(ii) on the true construction of condition 10 (5) of the National Conditions
of Sale (17th Edn.) notice of rescission could be given validly without first
giving a ten days' notice under condition 8 (6) (see p. 1130, letters E and G,
H post); accordingly the first defendants had validly rescinded the contract
for sale (see p. 1131, letter I, post).

[As to the duty to obtain consent to an assignment of a lease, see 23 HALS-
BURY'S LAWS (3rd Edn.) 642, para. 1355; 34 ibid., 325, 326, para. 551; and
for cases on the subject, see 40 DIGEST (Repl.) 311, 312, *2564-2569.*

I As to the exercise of a right of rescission of a contract for the sale of land,
see 34 HALSBURY'S LAWS (3rd Edn.) 248, 249, para. 413; and for cases on vendor's
failure to obtain the landlord's consent to assign, see 40 DIGEST (Repl.) 258,
2161, 2162.]

Cases referred to:

Basma (Abdul Karim) v. *Weekes,* [1950] 2 All E.R. 146; [1950] A.C. 441;
40 Digest (Repl.) 28, *127.*

Lehmann v. *McArthur,* (1868), 3 Ch. App. 496; 37 L.J.Ch. 625; 18 L.T. 806;
32 J.P. 660; 44 Digest (Repl.) 113, *933.*

Marshall and Salt's Contract, Re, [1900] 2 Ch. 202; 69 L.J.Ch. 542; 83 L.T. 147;   **A**
  31 Digest (Repl.) 425, *5524*.
Property and Bloodstock, Ltd. v. *Emerton*, [1967] 2 All E.R. 839; [1967] 3
  W.L.R. 973.
Rutherford v. *Acton-Adams*, [1915] A.C. 866; 84 L.J.P.C. 238; 113 L.T. 931;
  44 Digest (Repl.) 159, *1385*.

Action.   **B**

By writ issued on Mar. 11, 1966, Lipmans Wallpaper, Ltd., the plaintiffs,
brought an action against the defendants in which, by their statement of claim
served on Mar. 15, 1966, they claimed (a) against Mason & Hodghton, Ltd., the
first defendants, specific performance of a contract arising from the exercise of a
right of pre-emption granted on Aug. 7, 1962, and exercised by letter dated Nov.
11, 1965, for assignment of the residue of the term demised by sub-lease, dated   **C**
Sept. 24, 1958, of premises known as 474, Harrow Road, London, and (b) against
A.P.L. Properties, Ltd., the second defendant, a declaration that the sub-lease
was not merged in the leasehold reversion, and an order that the second defendant
should assign the residue of the term comprised in the sub-lease to the plaintiffs;
and claimed, against both defendants, an order vesting the residue of the term
in the plaintiffs and an injunction to restrain the defendants and each of them   **D**
by their respective servants, workmen and agents from interfering with the
plaintiffs' quiet enjoyment of the premises comprised in the sub-lease.

The following statement of fact is summarised from the judgment. By
an indenture dated Apr. 7, 1921, the Ecclesiastical Commissioners for England
demised to James William Flood and Jane Flood certain premises known as
The Estate Office, 474, Harrow Road, Paddington, in the county of London   **E**
for a term of 999 years from Sept. 29, 1918, at a yearly rent of £14. The lease
contained stringent repairing covenants and a covenant which restricted the
use of the premises to those of an estate office and sales room. At all material
times the reversion on that lease was vested in the London County Council or
the Greater London Council. On Sept. 24, 1958, the then lessee granted a sub-
lease to the first defendants, referred to herein as " Masons ". This sub-lease   **F**
was for a term of fourteen years as from Sept. 29, 1958, at a rent during the
first seven years of £275 per annum, and during the last seven years £325 per
annum, with an additional rent to cover the expense of insurance. The sub-lease
also contained repairing covenants (guaranteed by sureties), though not quite so
stringent as those in the head-lease, and a covenant against user of the premises for
illegal or immoral purpose and certain other user; but the sub-lease contained no   **G**
general or specific provision limiting the user to any particular business. The
sub-lease contained a covenant against assignment, which was in these terms—

" And will not assign underlet or in any manner part with the possession
of the said demised premises or any part thereof for the whole or any part of
the term hereby granted without the previous licence and consent in writing
of the landlord first obtained but so that such consent shall not be unreason-   **H**
ably withheld to an assignment or underletting of the whole of the
demised premises to a respectable and responsible person Provided that
the tenant may without first obtaining the landlord's consent let the first
floor for residential purposes at a rack rent if the tenancy or lease . . ."

should be of the kind therein described.   **I**

The first defendants, Masons, carried on their business of glass cutters and
makers of stained glass at 474, Harrow Road for many years (at least since 1948).
Latterly their business was not very successful. As a result they kept repairs
and decorations to a minimum and they became liable for breaches of the repairing
covenant. This liability was put by a witness at a figure of £2,000. Those
who controlled Masons were minded to dispose of the premises and to retire from
business. In July, 1961, a Mr. Kershman on behalf of the second defendant,
A.P.L. Properties, Ltd., negotiated the purchase of the head-lease subject to

A and with the benefit of the sub-lease. He insisted on the first defendants obtaining a licence from the freeholders for carrying on their business; this licence was granted on Dec. 12, 1961.   The plaintiffs carried on business in adjoining premises as wholesalers and retailers of wallpapers, paints and decorators' sundries. They wished to expand their premises.   On Jan. 31, 1962, Masons agreed to assign to the plaintiffs the sub-lease dated Sept. 24, 1958, in consideration of the

B plaintiffs undertaking responsibility for the repairs to the premises.   This assignment was to be subject to, but with the benefit of, a tenancy of the upper part, and, on completion, the plaintiffs were to grant a weekly tenancy to Masons of certain parts of the ground floor.   Mr. Kershman was anxious to get in the sub-lease for the second defendant; he planned, if he could get the consent of the freeholders, to modernise the property for office purposes.   The second

C defendant was not prepared to agree to the sharing of the premises envisaged by the agreement of Jan. 31, 1962.   On Aug. 7, 1962, however, the plaintiffs agreed to rescind the agreement of Jan. 31, 1962, and to substitute a right of pre-emption, which was as follows—

" Re 474, Harrow Road, W.9.

D " In consideration of your agreeing at our request to release us from our liability under the agreement between us dated Jan. 31, 1962, to assign to you the leasehold premises known as 474, Harrow Road, London, W.9 (hereinafter called ' the said premises ') held by us under a lease (hereinafter called ' the lease ') dated Sept. 24, 1958, we [Masons] hereby undertake and agree with you that if at any time hereafter during the residue of the term

E created by the lease, we shall desire either to surrender the lease to the lessor or to sell our estate and interest in the said premises we will before entering into any contract for such surrender or sale give you notice of such desire and full particulars of the proposed terms of such surrender or sale (hereinafter called ' the said terms ') and if within fourteen days thereafter you notify us in writing that you are prepared to purchase our estate and

F interest in the said premises on the said terms then we hereby agree that we will sell our estate and interest to you on the said terms (with such modifications as may be necessary to make them applicable to a sale to you) and we will not proceed with the proposed surrender or sale to any other person. And it is hereby agreed and declared that unless the said terms shall stipulate to the contrary, the sale to [you] shall be completed in accordance with the

G provisions of the National Conditions of Sale (17th Edn.) so far as the same are not varied by the said terms and are applicable to a sale by private treaty."

This document was sealed with the seal of Masons, and signed by a director and the secretary.   It had the following footnote—

H " To Mason & Hodghton, Ltd., 474, Harrow Road, London, W.9.   In consideration of the above, we [the plaintiffs] hereby release you from the agreement dated Jan. 31, 1962 (a copy whereof is attached hereto) and agree to cancel the estate contract registered in H.M. Land Charges Register on Mar. 8, 1962, under No. 26378 forthwith."

That agreement was duly registered as an estate contract in the land charges
I register.

On July 9, 1965, Masons were in treaty for a sale of the sub-lease for £1,000. They gave notice of that to the plaintiffs pursuant to the pre-emption agreement; but the plaintiffs did not exercise their right to purchase.   The sale went off and Masons demanded the vacation of the estate contract, to which the plaintiffs ultimately acceded.   It was vacated on Oct. 7, 1965.   Towards the end of September, 1965, Masons negotiated a surrender of the sub-lease to the second defendant for the consideration of £550 and a complete release of Masons (and their sureties) from liability on the repairing covenants in the sub-lease.   This

came to the knowledge of the plaintiffs. The plaintiffs claimed to be entitled   **A**
to first refusal of the premises at £550. Masons' solicitors by letter notified the
plaintiffs' solicitors that Masons had received an offer for the premises, 474,
Harrow Road, and enclosed an agreement which they said incorporated the
terms of such sale. They enclosed a draft, which, though referring to a vendor
and a purchaser, was in fact a draft surrender. This draft provided that "the
sale" should be subject to the current edition (the 17th) of the National Con-   **B**
ditions of Sale. Clause 8 of the draft was a release of Masons (and their sureties)
from all liability for breaches of covenants from the sub-lease. By letter dated
Nov. 11, 1965, the plaintiffs' solicitors purported to accept an offer of sale so
communicated. The letter of Nov. 11, 1965, was in these terms—

"Re 474, Harrow Road, W.9.

"We acknowledge receipt of your letter of Nov. 2, giving notice pursuant   **C**
to the undertaking dated Aug. 7, 1962, of the offer received by [Masons]
in respect of the above premises. We hereby give you notice that [the
plaintiffs] elect to purchase [Masons'] interest in the above premises on the
terms specified in the said undertaking, and they accordingly call upon
[Masons] to sell their leasehold interest in the above premises to [the plain-
tiffs] with vacant possession at the price of £550. [The plaintiffs] will, in   **D**
the assignment, indemnify [Masons] against all future liability under the
lease of the premises. We note the reference in your letter of Nov. 2 to
cl. 8 of the draft contract sent therewith, but we would draw your attention
to the fact that the undertaking of Aug. 8, 1962, specifically provides that
the property shall be sold to [the plaintiffs] on the same terms as those
contained in the offer received by [Masons] with such modifications as may   **E**
be necessary to make them applicable to a sale to our clients. The indemnity
referred to in the previous paragraph is a necessary modification for the
release referred to in your letter. We enclose our cheque for £55 being
the deposit payable herein to be held by you as stakeholders. We shall be
obliged if you will kindly acknowledge receipt of this letter and the cheque
sent herewith and confirm that [Masons] will comply with their undertaking   **F**
to sell the property to our clients and will not proceed any further with their
proposed sale to A.P.L. Properties, Ltd. [the second defendant] or any other
person. Will you also please confirm that [Masons] are immediately
applying for the necessary licence to assign to [the plaintiffs] whose bankers
are Barclays Bank, Ltd., 101, Commercial Street, Spitalfields, E.1. If
the landlords require further references, please let us know and these will be   **G**
supplied."

The agreement constituted by this correspondence, if any, was registered as
an estate contract on or about Nov. 11, 1965; the entry was on the register
at the time when subsequently the first defendants surrendered the sub-lease
to the second defendant. On Nov. 24, 1965, there was a conference between
all parties concerned, including Mr. Kershman on behalf of the second defendant.   **H**
Thereafter Masons applied to the second defendant for licence to assign. The
application, which was by letter was as follows—

"The solicitors for [the plaintiffs] are still contending that the terms of
the option agreement to which we have previously referred are binding and
are calling for the lease to be assigned to their clients, failing which, we are   **I**
informed, this will leave their clients with no alternative but to institute
proceedings for specific performance thereof. [Masons] wish to cease
trading as soon as possible, and further do not wish to be involved in litigation. We are therefore instructed to apply (and now do so) for licence
to assign the lease dated Sept. 24, 1958, in respect of the above premises to
[the plaintiffs] of 46, Old Castle Street, E.1. The proposed assignee has
given as a reference Barclays Bank, Ltd. of 101, Commercial Street, Spitalfields, E.1, and if further references are required we can no doubt obtain

A   the same.   We shall be pleased to hear from you within the next seven days the result of this application."

Masons also returned the deposit cheque which had been paid by the second defendant.   On Jan. 18, 1966, Mr. Kershman, as director of the second defendant, replied to the request for licence to assign, and in the course of his letter he asked for full details of the proposed user of the premises by the plaintiffs.   Giving
B   evidence at the hearing he said that when he wrote that letter he had already made up his mind to refuse the licence because the user proposed by the plaintiffs was not in accordance with the covenants in the head-lease, but he wanted to have the proposed user placed on record.   Masons, having ascertained the necessary information from the plaintiffs, replied by letter of their solicitors to Mr. Kershman saying that the intended user by the plaintiffs would be a
C   shop room and warehouse for the business of wallpaper, paint and decorators' materials merchants, and asked whether the licence would be forthcoming. In fact general warehouse user was also not a permitted user for town and country planning purposes in relation to the premises, 474, Harrow Road.   On Feb. 3, 1966, Mr. Kershman replied by letter to Masons' solicitors—

D   " You may or may not be aware of the fact that we do not hold the freehold interest in this property.   Under the terms of the lease under which we hold, the use of the property is restricted and would prohibit the user proposed by [the plaintiffs].   After due consideration we do not feel that we can consent to assignment of [Masons'] lease the effect of which would be to jeopardise our own interest in the property.   In the circum-
E   stances licence to assign is refused and we must ask you for an assurance by return of post that [Masons] will not proceed with the proposed assignment to [the plaintiffs].   Failing such assurance by return we regret that we shall have no alternative but to instruct our solicitors to apply for an injunction to restrain [Masons] from assigning their interest to [the plaintiffs]."

F   Whereupon, after taking the advice of counsel, Masons, while maintaining that there was no contract at all between them and the plaintiffs, rescinded such contract, if any, as there might be.   This they did by letter dated Feb. 11, 1966, in which their solicitors wrote—

" It is now clear that the licence to assign cannot be obtained, and we accordingly give you formal notice under condition 10 (5)* of the National
G   Conditions of Sale (17th Edn.) that if (which is denied), any contract exists between our respective clients, it is hereby rescinded."

Masons immediately completed the surrender to the second defendant.   Masons' solicitors reported this surrender to the plaintiffs' solicitors by letter dated Feb. 16, 1966.

H   The cases noted below† were cited during the argument in addition to those referred to in the judgment.

K. W. Rubin for the plaintiffs.
W. J. C. Tonge for the first defendants.
M. Waters for the second defendant.

I   **GOFF, J.,** having reviewed the relevant facts, documents and correspondence, continued: On these facts the first question which I have to determine is whether the letters of Nov. 2, 1965, and Nov. 11, 1965, constituted a contract, for it is clear that if they did not none was made thereafter.   It is conceded that if the letter of Nov. 11 had stopped short in the second paragraph with the words

---

* The terms of condition 10 (5) are at p. 1130, letter A, post.
† *Doe d. Newby* v. *Jackson*, (1823), 1 B. & C. 448;   *Cowen* v. *Truefitt, Ltd.*, [1899] 2 Ch. 309;   *Gooch* v. *Clutterbuck*, [1899] 2 Q.B. 148;   *Re Wallis and Barnard's Contract*, [1899] 2 Ch. 515;   *Milner* v. *Staffordshire Congregational Union (Incorporated)*, [1956] 1 All E.R. 494; [1956] Ch. 275.

" specified in the said undertaking " there would probably have been a concluded A
contract and that the court must then, in default of agreement as to the necessary
modifications, have implied some form of obligation on the plaintiffs' part to
secure by bank or insurance guarantee comparable immunity for the first defendants (" Masons ") and their sureties to that which they would receive under the
proposed surrender.   It is said, however, that if one looks at the letter of
Nov. 11, 1965, as a whole, it shows that the parties were never ad idem because B
they were each interpreting in an entirely different way the undertaking of
Aug. 7, 1962, by reference to which the offer was made and accepted.   Moreover
it is certain that the subsequent correspondence—to which, in my view, one is
entitled to refer, not to prevent that which would otherwise be a concluded
contract from so being, but to assist in deciding whether the earlier letters did
in truth form a contract—makes the difference of view abundantly clear.   C

The plaintiffs, on the other hand, say that there was a concluded contract, in
that the offer was for sale on the terms of the undertaking and that is what they
accepted; and they submit that what followed in their letter of Nov. 11, 1965,
was nothing more than a statement of the manner which the plaintiffs considered
appropriate for working out the provision for the right of pre-emption embodied
in the words " with such modifications as may be necessary to make them D
applicable to a sale to you ".   Therefore, even if, as in my judgment must be so,
the plaintiffs were placing their obligations too low, there was, they say, a contract
binding each party for better or worse to give effect to what are described in the
right of pre-emption as " the same terms " with all necessary modifications,
whatever such modifications might turn out to be.

That is a short question of construction; but not, I think, an easy one.   On E
the whole, I have come to the conclusion that there was a concluded contract.
Masons made their offer of Nov. 2, because they were bound, or conceived themselves to be bound by the right of pre-emption so to do.   They therefore intended
to, and did, offer the premises in accordance with the terms of that agreement.
The plaintiffs for their part, intended to, and as it seems to me did, accept on
the same footing; and therein lies a sufficient consensus.   The parties took F
different views as to the effect of the contract they were making, but I do not
think that is sufficient to vitiate their agreement.

Then, did Masons effectively rescind that contract as they purported to do
by their letter of Feb. 11, 1966?   That question falls into two separate parts,
perhaps overlapping: first, whether they ever became entitled to rescind; and,
secondly, if so, whether they did it effectively.   G

The first part is a question of fact, and the second of construction.   It was
their duty to use their best endeavours to obtain the landlord's consent.   I
take this from PAGE WOOD, L.J., in Lehmann v. McArthur (1):

"... I think McArthur was only bound to try to get the landlord's consent
without going into the question whether the refusal was reasonable or
unreasonable, and without taking the risk of legal proceedings to enforce H
his consent."

It is conceded, and in my view rightly conceded, that Masons could not escape
that duty by rescinding on the ground that consent was not obtainable, without
first using their best endeavours to get it.   However, they applied and were
met with a refusal on grounds not obviously unreasonable; and even if they
were, PAGE WOOD, L.J., said that they were only bound to try without going I
into the question whether the refusal was reasonable or unreasonable.

They did not simply leave it there; but their solicitor, Mr. Cowland, telephoned
Mr. Kershman—he was, of course, the mind of the second defendant, and its
solicitor—and Mr. Cowland met with an entirely uncompromising attitude.
Mr. Kershman said that nothing would make him change his mind.   Prima facie,
therefore, as I see it, Masons had discharged their duty and were entitled to

(1) (1868), 3 Ch. App. 496 at p. 501.

A rescind. The reason given by Mr. Kershman, however, was one which might be capable of remedy. Nevertheless, Masons neither enquired whether the position would or might be changed if a licence or some kind of assurance were forthcoming from the freeholders, nor did they themselves seek to obtain such a thing, or even give the plaintiffs an opportunity of so doing, or inform them how matters stood.

B Therefore, the question becomes this: did they in that commit a breach of their duty? At first I was strongly inclined to feel that they did, but I am persuaded that that would be a wrong view. The mere failure to inquire whether such a step might induce a change of mind could not in itself be a breach of duty—though if they were minded to try to remove the difficulty in that kind of way it would no doubt have been a wise precaution to ask whether the exercise,

C if undertaken, was likely to have any chance of success. The breach of duty, if breach there were lay in not themselves approaching the freeholders, or not informing the plaintiffs so that they might do so. As counsel for the plaintiffs put it in his reply, they served notice without taking any adequate steps either to persuade Mr. Kershman to change his mind, or to find out from the Greater London Council whether that council would be minded to grant a licence for

D the change of user; and, more seriously, they failed to give the plaintiffs any opportunity. Again, the breach of duty, if any, lay in rescinding without giving the plaintiffs reasonable opportunity of laying before Mr. Kershman, or it may be Masons, facts which would give them, Masons, an opportunity of getting a licence.

As it seems to me, Masons were not under any duty themselves to approach

E the freeholders. Their duty to try and obtain the licence of the second defendant to assign could not, I think, involve obtaining a licence or consent to a change of user from somebody else. If that be right, it is difficult to see how Masons could be obliged to allow the plaintiffs an opportunity for so doing. If they were, then the question must arise at once, how long must they wait? One remembers that in 1961, when a licence was sought, it took five months. It

F seems to me that it would be a slippery slope and, instead of the security which the right to rescind would afford, they would at once be exposed to the risk, if they grew impatient at the delay, that it would be said that they had not allowed a reasonable time. It was not their duty to give time, reasonable or otherwise, to enable the plaintiffs so to change the position as to enable them to get a licence to assign which, as things stood, was not obtainable.

G It is said: " but suppose the landlord had asked for an additional reference, surely Masons could not rescind without telling the plaintiffs and asking them to get it ". That seems to me to be an entirely different position, and each case must depend on its own facts. Nearer home, perhaps, counsel for the plaintiffs said that they did not give the plaintiffs a chance of showing that they had permission. If the plaintiffs already had permission and Masons had rescinded

H without approaching the plaintiffs, it is possible that a breach of duty might have been established—I do not know. But that again is not this case. Here, the complaint is that Masons did not give the plaintiffs an opportunity of approaching the freeholders. That, it seems to me, was something that Masons were not bound to do. They might have been willing to do so, and where a vendor is anxious for the sale to go through he may go to considerable lengths to that end.

I They were not, however, bound to do that, and I think that they were entitled to stop at the juncture which had been reached, of a categorical refusal by Mr. Kershman.

In my view, Masons' defence on this point is strengthened by the facts, that there had already been considerable delay for which the plaintiffs were at least partly responsible, and that the premises were by now vacant. Indeed, the plaintiffs, by an amendment, claim damages for deterioration on that very account. I would, however, arrive at my conclusion even without those elements.

I must then turn to the point of construction, which arises on condition 10 (5) **A** of the National Conditions of Sale, which is as follows:

" The sale is subject to the reversioner's licence being obtained, where necessary.   The fee for such licence shall be paid by the vendor, but, if the licence cannot be obtained, the vendor may rescind the contract on the same terms as if the purchaser had persisted in an objection to the title which the vendor was unable to remove."   **B**

Counsel for the plaintiffs said that that was a reference back to condition 8 (6) and (7), and that therefore Masons could not rescind without first serving a ten days' notice under condition 8 (6).   That condition reads:

" If the purchaser shall persist in any objection to the title which the vendor shall be unable or unwilling, on reasonable grounds, to remove, and   **C** shall not withdraw the same within ten days of being required so to do, the vendor may, subject to the purchaser's rights under s. 42 and s. 125 of the Law of Property Act, 1925, by notice in writing to the purchaser or his solicitor, and notwithstanding any intermediate negotiation or litigation, rescind the contract."

Condition 8 (7) reads as follows: **D**

" Upon such rescission the vendor shall return the deposit, but without interest, costs of investigating title or other compensation or payment, and the purchaser shall return the abstract and other papers furnished to him."

In my judgment, that is not the true construction.   There is really no authority on this point.   It is said in the statement of the facts in *Property and Bloodstock,* **E** *Ltd.* v. *Emerton* (2), that condition 10 (5) refers to condition 8 (6) and (7). That is at most only a dictum even if it comes from the judgment at all.   In any case the point was not argued in that particular case, and the passage I read (3): ". . . which results in the purchaser only receiving back the deposit without interest or costs ", which, of course, in itself, is referring only to condition 8 (7).

In a sense, condition 10 (5) does refer both to condition 8 (6) and to 8 (7); but **F** in my judgment, it is only in condition 8 (7) that the terms are to be found.   Condition 10 (5) gives an immediate right to rescind in the event there postulated, of the landlord's consent not being obtainable; and it is unnecessary to refer to condition 8 (6) to found a right to rescind.   Condition 8 (6) is only machinery under which a right of rescission might arise in a different case.   If and when it has arisen its exercise will be on the terms specified in condition 8 (7).   So also **G** when a right to rescind arises under condition 10 (5) its exercise imports the terms in condition 8 (7).   In my judgment, the referential words in condition 10 (5) do not refer to the circumstances in which the right to rescind is to arise, or the manner in which it may be exercised.   If condition 10 (5) did refer to condition 8 (6) so as to require a ten days' notice, it could only be to give the plaintiffs an opportunity of waiving the objection and taking an assignment **H** without a licence, not to give the plaintiffs an opportunity to take steps to enable the first defendants to lay fresh facts before the second defendant.

I cannot think that condition 10 (5) was directed to any such point as that. Indeed, in my judgment it would not fit on that footing, because the plaintiffs could not waive their objection, in my judgment, and insist on an assignment without a licence.   Counsel for the plaintiffs says that they could, because this is **I** a defect of title, as indeed it is—see *Re Marshall and Salt's Contract* (4) and in *Rutherford* v. *Acton-Adams* (5), which is a case in the Privy Council, VISCOUNT HALDANE, dealing with the right to specific performance, stated (6):

(2) [1967] 3 W.L.R. 973 at p. 976; cf. [1967] 2 All E.R. 839 at p. 842.
(3) [1967] 3 W.L.R. at p. 976.
(4) [1900] 2 Ch. 202.
(5) [1915] A.C. 866.
(6) [1915] A.C. at p. 870.

A   " ... the court will decree specific performance with compensation for any small and immaterial deficiency, provided that the vendor has not, by misrepresentation or otherwise, disentitled himself to his remedy.   Another possible case arises where a vendor claims specific performance and where the court refuses it unless the purchaser is willing to consent to a decree on terms that the vendor will make compensation to the purchaser, who

B   agrees to such a decree on condition that he is compensated.   If it is the purchaser who is suing the court holds him to have an even larger right. Subject to considerations of hardship he may elect to take all he can get, and to have a proportionate abatement from the purchase-money."

Counsel for the plaintiffs has referred me also to SNELL'S PRINCIPLES OF EQUITY (26th Edn.) p. 659, where it is said:

C   " Although a substantial misdescription entitles the purchaser to refuse to be bound by the contract, in many cases he may nevertheless insist on the vendor conveying what he has with an abatement of the purchase-money as compensation."

A similar right is described in EMMET'S NOTES ON PERUSING TITLES (14th Edn.)

D   p. 85:

" If it is the purchaser who is suing, the court holds him to have an even larger right.   Subject to considerations of hardship he may elect to take all he can get, and to have a proportionate abatement from the purchase-money."

E   Counsel for the plaintiffs also relied on *Abdul Karim Basma* v. *Weekes* (7), also a Privy Council case; but that is plainly distinguishable.   That was a case in which three tenants in common agreed to sell certain property which agreement could not be enforced against one of them because she was a married woman who had no power to make the contract without the concurrence of her husband, but the purchasers was nevertheless entitled to take the other two-thirds shares from the other two contracting parties.   In the passages first cited and in that

F   case, one is, in my judgment, considering an entirely different position from that which arises where the defect, although it be a defect of title, is that the vendor cannot convey without a breach of a prior contract with a third party; and, whether or not a court of equity would in any case order specific performance which involved the defendant breaking a pre-existing contract, I am sure that the principle cannot be applied to this type of case, and in particular to a case

G   where the vendor has a power of rescission.

It is said that the damages would be only nominal—that is the damages which could be recovered against the vendors, Masons in this case, if they assigned without licence.   I am not sure that that would be right; but even if it were, they would be exposed to liability in costs and to the hazards of litigation.   More-over, the landlord might sue for an injunction.   Counsel for the plaintiffs says

H   that would not be possible because the plaintiffs would have taken an assignment and there would be no scope for an injunction; but the landlord might move before completion.   Indeed, there is something of a dilemma here, for if it be right it affords some justification for what appears to be precipitate haste on the part of Mr. Kershman in his letter of Feb. 3, 1966, in demanding an immediate assurance that Masons would not proceed with the assignment to the plaintiffs

I   and threatening to apply for an injunction in the very letter in which he refused the licence.   Further, the matter is not merely one of title, but of the protection afforded by a condition which is at least for the benefit of the vendors as well as the purchaser, if not exclusively for that of the vendors, and therefore, in my judgment, one which could not be waived by the plaintiffs.

For these reasons, in my judgment Masons were entitled to rescind, and did validly rescind, the contract, and that is sufficient to dispose of the case as

---

(7) [1950] 2 All E.R. 146; [1950] A.C. 441.

against both defendants.   But if they wish me to deal with the independent   A
defence which has been canvassed by the second defendants, which would only
arise had the decision on rescission gone the other way, I will do so.   [At the
request of the parties the court then dealt with that matter on the assumption
that the case had been decided the other way.]

Claim dismissed as against Masons with costs; as against the second defendant
with costs: judgment on the counterclaim of the second defendant with costs; stay   B
of execution on counterclaim pending appeal, for twenty-one days, and on lodging
notice of appeal to continue pending hearing of appeal.

Solicitors: *Asher Fishman & Co.* (for the plaintiffs); *Wright, Son & Pepper*
(for the first defendants); *Kershman & Morris* (for the second defendant).

[*Reported by* R. W. FARRIN, ESQ., *Barrister-at-Law.*]   C

Re SWALEDALE CLEANERS, LTD.

[CHANCERY DIVISION (Pennycuick, J.), January 22, 25, 1968.]   D

Company—Shares—Transfer—Restriction on transfer—Delay—Loss of veto—
Private company—Transfers of deceaseds' shares duly lodged—Number of
directors reduced below minimum—No new director appointed—Unreasonable
delay—Shares freed from restriction and rendered freely transferable—Delay
of four months.

A private company was incorporated in 1946 with an authorised and issued   E
capital of ten thousand shares of £1 each.   The company's articles incorporated, with certain variations, Table A of the Companies Act, 1929.   Article 8
provided that the directors might refuse to register any transfer of shares
and that cl. 19* of Table A should be modified accordingly. Clause 19 contained
the following provision which was not altered by the articles: " If the directors refuse to register a transfer of any shares, they shall within two months   F
after the date on which the transfer was lodged with the company send to the
transferee notice of the refusal."   A corresponding provision was re-enacted
in s. 78 (1)† of the Companies Act, 1948.   Article 14 provided that the number
of directors should be not less than two.   Clause 83‡ of Table A provided that
the continuing directors might act for the purpose of increasing the number
of directors to obtain a quorum.   On Aug. 3, 1967, the shares of the company   G
stood as to four thousand shares in the name of S. and as to five hundred
shares in the name of the applicant; the rest of the shares stood in the names
of two deceased persons, as to five thousand in one name and as to five
hundred in the other.   Two transfers of the shares of the deceased persons had
been executed in favour of the applicant.   S. and the applicant were the
only directors of the company and on Aug. 3, 1967, they held a combined   H
directors' and annual general meeting.   The applicant retired by rotation
from being a director and was not re-appointed; but his appointment as
acting secretary was confirmed.   The transfers of shares were produced and
registration of them was refused.   No step was taken by S. to appoint an
additional director after the number fell below two until Dec. 18.   The
applicant filed a notice of motion on Dec. 11, 1967 (i.e., four months later)   I
asking for an order pursuant to s. 116 of the Act of 1948 that the register
of members of the company be rectified by inserting the applicant's name
as the owner of the deceased's shares.   On Dec. 18, 1967, S. appointed an
additional director; the directors subsequently refused to register the
transfers.

Affirmed. C.A. [1968] 3 All E.R. 619.

---

* Clause 19, so far as material, is set out at p. 1134, letter C, post.
† Section 78 (1) is set out at p. 1134, letter, G, post.
‡ Clause 83 is set out at p. 1134, letter F, post.

A   **Held:** nothing having been done between Aug. 3, 1967, and Dec. 18, 1967,
to appoint an additional director and to bring the transfers, which had been
lodged by Aug. 3, before a duly constituted board meeting, there had been
unnecessary delay; the general principle that a transfer duly lodged should
be brought before the board within a reasonable time after it was lodged
applied where the articles of association contained a restriction on transfers,

B   and rectification of the register by registering the applicant as tranferee of
the deceaseds' shares would be ordered, S. having lost by the delay any
power of veto that art. 8 would otherwise have conferred on him (see p. 1136,
letters D, F and H, post).

        Re Joint Stock Discount Co., Nation's Case ((1866), L.R. 3 Eq. 77) applied.

        [As to exercise of power to refuse registration, see 6 HALSBURY'S LAWS (3rd
C   Edn.) 253, para. 527; and for cases on the subject, see 9 DIGEST (Repl.) 388-390,
2506-2512.

        For the Companies Act, 1948, s. 78, see 3 HALSBURY'S STATUTES (2nd Edn.)
523.]

        Cases referred to:

        Bede Steam Shipping Co., Ltd., Re, [1917] 1 Ch. 123; 86 L.J.Ch. 65; 115 L.T.
D   580; 9 Digest (Repl.) 392, *2524.*

        Hackney Pavilion, Ltd., Re, [1923] All E.R. Rep. 524; [1924] 1 Ch. 276; 93
            L.J.Ch. 193; 130 L.T. 658; 9 Digest (Repl.) 388, *2507.*

        Joint Stock Discount Co., Re, Nation's Case, (1866), L.R. 3 Eq. 77; 36 L.J.Ch.
            112; 15 L.T. 308; 9 Digest (Repl.) 223, *1424.*

E   *Moodie* v. *Shepherd (W. & J.) (Bookbinders), Ltd.,* [1949] 2 All E.R. 1044;
            9 Digest (Repl.) 421, *2728.*

        Motion.

        This was a motion by notice dated Dec. 11, 1967, by Leslie William Smart,
the applicant, for an order pursuant to s. 116 of the Companies Act, 1948, that
the register of members of Swaledale Cleaners, Ltd., might be rectified (i) by
F   striking out the name of Henry Smart therefrom as the holder of five thousand
shares of the company numbered 1 to 5,000 inclusive, and by inserting in lieu
thereof the name of the applicant, as the holder of all the five thousand shares;
(ii) by striking out the name of Agnes Maud Smart therefrom as the holder of
five hundred shares of the company numbered 5,001 to 5,500 inclusive, and by
inserting in lieu thereof the name of the applicant as the holder of all the five
G   hundred shares. The applicant asked, secondly, that he might be authorised
to effect the necessary alterations in the register for carrying such order into
effect. The respondents were the company and Major Leslie Smart, who held
four thousand shares in the company.

        The cases noted below* were cited in argument in addition to those referred
to in the judgment.

H   *T. M. Shelford* for the applicant.
        S. S. Gill for the respondents.

                                                                Cur. adv. vult.

        Jan. 25. **PENNYCUICK, J.:** I have before me a motion under s. 116
of the Companies Act, 1948 for the rectification of the register of Swaledale
I   Cleaners, Ltd., to which I will refer as " the company ". The applicant is Mr.
Leslie William Smart. The respondents are the company and Major Leslie Smart,
who is the only other person interested in the company. I will for convenience
refer to the two individuals as " the applicant " and " Major Smart " respectively.

        The company was incorporated in 1946 to carry on the business of cleaners
and dyers. It is a private company with an authorised and issued capital of ten
thousand shares of £1, each. The articles of the company incorporate, with

---

        * *Re Copal Varnish Co., Ltd.,* [1916-17] All E.R. Rep. 914; [1917] 2 Ch. 349; *Re
Allen-Meyrick's Will Trusts,* [1966] 1 All E.R. 740.

variations, Table A under the Companies Act, 1929. I will refer at the outset **A**
to certain provisions in the company's articles, including the incorporated
provisions:

> " 8. The directors may at any time in their absolute and uncontrolled
> discretion refuse to register any transfer of shares; and cl. 19 of Table A
> shall be modified accordingly.
> " 14. Unless and until the company in general meeting shall otherwise **B**
> determine, the number of directors shall not be less than two nor more than
> seven."

The company in general meeting never has in fact otherwise determined.

Table A under the Companies Act, 1929, contains in clauses 17-22 common
form provisions relating to the transfer and transmission of shares. Clause 19, **C**
which, as I have mentioned is varied by art. 8 of the company's articles, contains
in the concluding sentence, which is not altered, these words:

> " . . . If the directors refuse to register a transfer of any shares, they
> shall within two months after the date on which the transfer was lodged
> with the company send to the transferee notice of the refusal."

Clause 67 provides that the business of the company shall be managed by the **D**
directors. Clauses 73-80 contain provisions for the rotation of directors, including
a power in the directors to appoint any person as an additional director. Clause
82 provides that:

> " The quorum necessary for the transaction of the business of the
> directors may be fixed by the directors, and unless so fixed shall when
> the number of directors exceeds three be three, and when the number of **E**
> directors does not exceed three, be two."

It has not in fact been fixed. Clause 83 provides that:

> " The continuing directors may act notwithstanding any vacancy in their
> body, but, if and so long as their number is reduced below the number fixed
> by or pursuant to the regulations of the company as the necessary quorum **F**
> of directors, the continuing directors may act for the purpose of increasing
> the number of directors to that number, or of summoning a general meeting
> of the company, but for no other purpose."

The Companies Act, 1948, contains in s. 78 (1) a statutory provision corresponding
to the last words of cl. 19 of Table A under the Act of 1929, namely:

> " (1) If a company refuses to register a transfer of any shares or deben- **G**
> tures, the company shall, within two months after the date on which the
> transfer was lodged with the company, send to the transferee notice of
> the refusal."

The shareholding of the company as it stood at Aug. 3, 1967, was as follows:
five thousand shares stood in the name of Henry Smart, who was then deceased; **H**
four thousand shares stood in the name of Major Smart; five hundred shares
stood in the name of Agnes Maude Smart, then deceased; and five hundred
shares stood in the name of the applicant. By that time two transfers of shares
had been executed. One is a transfer of five thousand shares by Sybil Mary
Smart, as administratrix of Henry Smart, to the applicant. The other is by
the applicant and Susan Bramham, administrators of the estate of Agnes Maude **I**
Smart, again to the applicant. Both those transfers are in proper form, duly
executed and stamped.

At Aug. 3, 1967, there were two directors of the company, namely the only
surviving shareholders in the company, Major Smart and the applicant. The
applicant was also the acting secretary. On Aug. 3, 1967, there was held a
combined directors' and annual general meeting of the company. At that meeting
there were present Major Smart and the applicant and three professional men in
attendance: a solicitor representing each of the two individual members of the

A company, and also the company's accountant. A minute of what took place at that meeting has been prepared by Major Smart and, so far as now material, is in these terms, after setting out the persons present and in attendance:

"1. The meeting was declared constituted and the minutes of the last annual general meeting were taken as read. 2. Mr. L. W. Smart not being a permanent director retired by rotation and offered himself for re-election.

B Mr. L. W. Smart was not reappointed . . . 5. There were produced the following transfers of shares:—(a) A transfer of five thousand ordinary shares from Mrs. Sybil Mary Smart to Mr. Leslie William Smart. (b) A transfer of five hundred ordinary shares from Mr. Leslie William Smart and Mrs. Susan Bramham to Mr. Leslie William Smart. The registration of these transfers of shares was formally refused. 6. Mr. L. W. Smart as acting

C secretary of the company was formally confirmed and appointed secretary of the company with effect from Oct. 14, 1966."

There is no substantial difference in the evidence of the two parties as to what happened at that meeting, although the applicant does not accept that para. 5 in the minute represents exactly what took place. I do not think that it is

D necessary to go in detail into this matter because it is common ground first that, as recorded in para. 2 of the minute, the applicant ceased to be a director of the company when he was not reappointed after offering himself for re-election; and second, that from that moment on there was not a quorum of directors capable of passing a board resolution.

It does not appear from the evidence that any formal board resolution refusing

E to register the transfer of shares was proposed, but if it had been so proposed it could not have been validly passed. There is no suggestion that any resolution was ever purported to be passed by the company as such on this matter. Major Smart states in his evidence that Mrs. Eunice Annie Smart was available outside the room for appointment as a director if then so required, but in fact she was not called into the room and no appointment of an additional director was made.

F The present notice of motion was filed on Dec. 11, 1967, i.e., at an interval of more than four months after the meeting of Aug. 3, 1967. The motion seeks an order pursuant to s. 116 of the Act of 1948 that the register of members of the company may be rectified

"(i) By striking out the name of Henry Smart therefrom as the holder of five thousand shares of the said company . . . and by inserting in lieu

G thereof the name of Leslie William Smart as the holder of all the said five thousand shares,"

and correspondingly as regards the five hundred shares registered in the name of Agnes Maude Smart. Evidence on the motion was filed on the one side by the applicant and by Mr. S. N. Walton, who was the solicitor in attendance at the meeting on his side, and on the other part by Major Smart. I do not

H think that there is any real conflict of evidence on relevant matters and I need not go further into what is said in those affidavits. On Dec. 18, 1967, after the notice of motion was launched, Major Smart did appoint Mrs. Eunice Smart an additional director of the company, and he states that at some unspecified date the board thus newly constituted formally refused to register the transfers now in question.

I It is well established that a share in a company is an item of property freely alienable in the absence of express restriction under the articles; see *Re Bede Steam Shipping Co., Ltd.* (1). It is also well established that where the articles of a company contain a power of veto by the board, such as that here, the right of alienation is only displaced by a positive resolution of the board exercising the power; see *Re Hackney Pavilion, Ltd.* (2), where Astbury, J., uses the

---

(1) [1917] 1 Ch. 123.
(2) [1923] All E.R. Rep. 524 at p. 525; [1924], 1 Ch. 276 at p. 280.

expression " an active formal exercise of the right to decline ". That decision A
was approved by the House of Lords in *Moodie* v. *W. & J. Shepherd (Bookbinders),
Ltd.* (3).

The issue on the present motion is whether the power of veto has been lost by
undue delay in bringing the transfers before a meeting of the board. On analysis
this involves two distinct questions, namely (i) has there in fact been undue
delay and (ii) if so, has the delay put an end to the power. B

(i) It has been decided, in a case where articles of a company contained no
restriction on transfers, that the proper time for bringing a transfer before the
board is the first board meeting after the transfer has been lodged at which,
in the ordinary course of business, a transfer would be confirmed, and that if
the transfer is not brought before the board on that occasion there is unnecessary
delay within the statutory predecessor of s. 116; see *Re Joint Stock Discount* C
Co., Nation's Case (4). The issue there was an entirely different one, namely
who was to be treated as a contributory in a winding-up, but the principle is,
I think, of general application. I see no reason why the principle should not
equally apply where the articles do contain a restriction on transfers. It must,
however, habitually happen in the case of a private company that board meetings
are not held regularly, at any rate for the purpose of considering transfers. D
Where this is the position the transfer must, I think, be brought before the
board within a reasonable time after it is lodged. What is a reasonable time must
depend on the particular circumstances, and one cannot lay down any precise
conventional time. Nevertheless the period of two months mentioned in cl. 19 of
Table A under the Act of 1929, and specified in s. 78 of the Act of 1948, may, I
think, safely be taken as the outside limit after which there is unnecessary delay. E

The position is not, I think different in this respect where the board has been
reduced below the quorum capable of acting, but where there is a continuing
director with power to appoint additional directors. I am not concerned here
with the exceptional cases where it is impossible for some reason to constitute a
board. In the present case the transfers were lodged on or before Aug. 3, 1967.
Major Smart has throughout been in a position to appoint an additional director, F
and then to bring the transfers before a properly-constituted board meeting.
Nothing was done between Aug. 3 and Dec. 18, a delay of over four months. I
conclude that in those circumstances there has been unnecessary delay.

(ii) The power of veto is a restriction on the right of alienation and as such
must, I think, be exercised at the proper time for its exercise, if it is to be exercised at all. For this purpose the proper time is the occasion on which the transfers G
are placed before the board for confirmation if—and it seems to me only if—
they are so placed without unnecessary delay. If there is unnecessary delay in
placing the transfers before the board, the power of veto must, I think, be
regarded as lost, so that the right of transfer becomes unrestricted. It cannot
be the law that the board of a company can improperly delay considering a
transfer and then when driven to do so, as for instance here, by the launching H
of a motion, exercise the power of veto. There appears to be no authority on
this point.

I conclude that Major Smart has, by unnecessary delay, lost his chance of
keeping the beneficial owner of the majority of shares in this company off the
register, and I propose to make the order sought by the motion (5).

Order accordingly. I

Solicitors: *Denis Hayes & Co.*, agents for *Stanley W. Walton & Hardy*,
Darlington (for the applicant); *Emsley, Collins & Co.*, Leeds (for the respondents).

[*Reported by* JENIFER SANDELL, *Barrister-at-Law.*]

---

(3) [1949] 2 All E.R. 1044.
(4) (1866), L.R. 3 Eq. 77.
(5) For the terms of the order sought, see p. 1133, letters F and G, ante.

A

MEGGS v. LIVERPOOL CORPORATION.

[LIVERPOOL COURT OF PASSAGE (Richard Forrest, Q.C.), January 27, 1967.]

[COURT OF APPEAL, CIVIL DIVISION (Lord Denning, M.R., Salmon and Winn, L.JJ.), June 27, 1967.]

B *Highway—Non-repair—Sunken flagstone in pavement—Pedestrian injured by tripping and falling—Pavement in continual use and no complaint by local inhabitants—Prima facie case that pavement dangerous to traffic not shown.*

The plaintiff, aged seventy-four, tripped, fell and suffered injury when walking on a flagstone in a pavement sixteen to twenty-two feet wide, which was part of the highway. At the place where the accident occurred a patch
C of six or so flagstones had sunk unevenly, and one of them had a projecting point of a quarter of an inch. On the evidence it was established that although local inhabitants knew of the condition of the pavement, they continued to use it, and no defect had been reported to the defendants, who were the highway authority responsible for maintaining the pavement. Moreover, two members of the highway department passed this stretch of pavement
D regularly, and they had never considered it to be in need of repair. On appeal in an action by the plaintiff for breach of duty to maintain the highway causing personal injuries to her,

Held: users of the highway must take account of the possibility of unevenness in a pavement, and the evidence was not sufficient to establish prima facie that the highway was dangerous to traffic and that there was a
E breach of obligation to keep the pavement in repair, such as it would be necessary for the plaintiff to establish before the defendant highway authority need have recourse to the statutory defence under s. 1 (2) (3) of the Highways (Miscellaneous Provisions) Act, 1961; accordingly the plaintiff's claim failed (see p. 1139, letters F and I, and p. 1140, letter A, post).

Appeal dismissed.

F [As to the principle that highway authorities were not liable to individuals for non-repair, see 19 HALSBURY'S LAWS (3rd Edn.) 149, 150, para. 228; and for cases on the subject, see 26 DIGEST (Repl.) 418-423, *1278-1309.*

As to liability at common law for failure to repair a highway lying in nuisance, see 19 HALSBURY'S LAWS (3rd Edn.) 271, 272, para. 435; as to liability of highway authorities for repairs to highway carried out negligently, see ibid., pp. 150, 151,
G para. 229.

For the Highways (Miscellaneous Provisions) Act, 1961, s. 1, see 41 HALSBURY'S STATUTES (2nd Edn.) 453.]

Action.

This was an action brought in the Court of Passage of the City of Liverpool.
H By writ issued on Feb. 22, 1965, the plaintiff claimed damages for personal injuries, loss and expense caused by the negligence and/or breach of duty of the defendants, the corporation of the city of Liverpool, their servants and/or agents. In her statement of claim the plaintiff alleged that shortly after 10 p.m. on Dec. 4, 1964, she was walking along the footwalk at the point where a number of metal water grids had been built by the defendants, their servants or agents
I into, and which formed part of, the surface of the footwalk when, " due to the negligence or breach of duty of the defendants, their servants or agents, in causing or permitting the grids and their surrounding flagstones to be out of level and forming dangerous projections in the surface of the footwalk ", the plaintiff caught her foot against the projecting edge of a flagstone and she tripped and fell. By their defence the defendants denied negligence and breach of duty. They further pleaded that if any dangerous projections existed they had taken such care as in all the circumstances was reasonably required to secure that the footwalk was not dangerous to pedestrians, and that if the

plaintiff had suffered any injuries loss or damage the same were caused or **A**
contributed to by her own negligence in failing to keep a proper look-out.

J. E. Jones for the plaintiff.
I. H. M. Jones for the defendants.

Jan. 27, 1967. **R. H. FORREST, Q.C., Presiding Judge:** I have the
greatest sympathy for the plaintiff. Unfortunately, in my view, her claim **B**
fails. She is seventy-four years old, but is active enough and still works as a
cleaner in the centre of Liverpool. She lives in Mill Lane. The accident occurred
near her own house close to Wavertree Clock Tower. This is a busy part of the
road, there are shops and it is served by a bus route. There is a shelter near
this place. A large number of pedestrians pass over it daily.

The plaintiff did not exaggerate her accident in any way at all. At 10 p.m. **C**
she went out to get some lemonade for her sick daughter. She had walked
about two paving stones beyond a water hydrant when she fell. She did not,
in fact, specifically say that she tripped but I assume that she did. She certainly
did not trip or slip on the grid. The fact that she did trip is not, however,
enough. She must prove that the defendants failed in their capacity as highway
authority to maintain, which includes to repair, the highway. **D**

I need not dwell on the question of the standard of repair as this is not the first
case of this kind with which I have had to deal. In support of the proposition that
the defendants failed in their duty a great deal of evidence was called from people
living locally who, if there was a defect, knew of it. What puzzles me about their
evidence, if their description is correct, is why they walked over that particular
part. No-one suggests that the defects were bad enough to cover the whole **E**
width of the pavement. The pavement is sixteen to twenty-two feet wide.
This is, in my view, a pointer whether it was dangerous. No-one reported the
defect to the defendants and no-one said that it was so dangerous that he would
not walk over it. As to the actual condition of the footwalk, I accept the
evidence of Mr. Ollerhead. There was a patch of some six flags, which are
shown in the drawing, where the flags had sunk in varying degrees. The biggest **F**
defect that could be found was a tripping point of a quarter of an inch. Since, in
fact, a citizen had been injured, Mr. Ollerhead had the flags lifted and relaid,
but that is no admission that they were a danger beforehand.

Whatever the merits or demerits of the methods of the highway department
of getting information, Mr. Ollerhead passed it twice a day. He had never
seen anything which he thought was in need of repair. Mr. Greenslade, one **G**
of the foremen, bicycles past two or three times a week and keeps a look out
for defects and he saw nothing wrong.

On the totality of the evidence and looking at the reality of the situation that
thousands use the footwalk, and that no-one has avoided it or reported it, I
am not satisfied that there was such a danger present as to indicate a failure on
the part of the highway authority to discharge their duty. This also deals **H**
with the allegations of negligence. It is not necessary for me to decide the
question of the defendants' statutory defence.

Judgment for the defendants.

Appeal.

By notice of appeal dated Mar. 10, 1967, the plaintiff asked for an order that
the judgment of the Presiding Judge of the Court of Passage of the City of **I**
Liverpool be reversed and set aside and that, in lieu thereof, judgment should
be entered for the plaintiff for damages such as the court should consider just or
to be assessed or that a re-trial be had. The grounds of appeal were as follows:
(i) that the judge was wrong in finding that (a) no danger existed in the highway,
(b) there was no failure on the part of the defendants to repair the highway;
(ii) that the judge should have found that (a) there was a danger in the highway, (b) the defendants had not taken reasonable care to ensure the highway was
not dangerous to pedestrians; (iii) that the judge did not pay due or proper

A regard to the fact that the onus of proving that reasonable care to ensure the highway was not dangerous to pedestrians lay on the defendants; and (iv) that the judge's findings were against the weight of the evidence and/or wrong in law.

J. E. Jones for the plaintiff.

I. H. M. Jones for the defendants.

B

June 27, 1967. **LORD DENNING, M.R.:** In this case the plaintiff, a widow of seventy-four years of age, who lives in Mill Lane, Liverpool, at 10 p.m. went to get some lemonade for her daughter. She walked along the High Street which is a busy road. There was a pavement sixteen to twenty-two feet wide. As she went along she tripped. She tripped because the flagstones were **C** uneven. They had sunk in different places: so much so that one of them had sunk about three-quarters of an inch. She tripped and fell and hurt herself. She had some cuts and was shaken up. She went to the doctor that very evening. She reported it to the police. The police reported it to the highway authority, the defendants. A few days later the defendants came and levelled the flagstones and thenceforward the pavement was reasonably level. She **D** brought this action for damages against the defendants complaining of the condition of the pavement.

In the old days there would have been a simple answer to this claim. A highway authority were not liable for the bad state of a highway if it was due to non-feasance, that is, not doing any repairs. A highway authority were only liable for misfeasance, that is, doing things badly. That distinction was **E** criticised for years: and in 1961 it was abolished by s. 1 of the Highways (Miscellaneous Provisions) Act, 1961.

What is the effect of the abolition? It means that the highway authority are under a duty to maintain the highway and keep it in repair. If it is in a dangerous condition so that it is not reasonably safe for people going along it, then prima facie there is a breach of the obligation to maintain and keep it in repair: and **F** any person who suffers particular damage on account of it can bring an action against the highway authority. But the highway authority can escape liability if they prove that they took all reasonable care to see that it was safe, having regard to the various matters set out in s. 1 (2), (3) of the Act of 1961. At the outset, however, in order to make a prima facie case, the plaintiff must show that the highway was not reasonably safe, i.e., that it was dangerous to traffic.

G   The judge in the present case heard the evidence. Witnesses came and said that the pavement was uneven. One lady said that her son had fallen there. Another said that it was difficult to get a wheelchair over it because it wobbled. The judge discounted their evidence, because they still went on using the pavement without reporting it. He summed it up in this way:

" On the totality of the evidence and looking at the reality of the situation, **H**   that thousands use the footwalk, that no-one has avoided it or reported it, I am not satisfied that there was such a danger present as to indicate a failure on the part of the [defendants] to discharge their duty."

That is a finding of fact. Counsel for the plaintiff invites this court to review that finding of fact—to look at reported cases—and to say that this pavement was dangerous or was not reasonably safe. I must say I cannot go with that **I** argument. It seems to me, using ordinary knowledge of pavements, that everyone must take account of the fact that there may be unevenness here and there. There may be a ridge of half an inch or three-quarters of an inch occasionally, but that is not the sort of thing which makes it dangerous or not reasonably safe.

I see no reason for disturbing the finding of the presiding judge of the Court of Passage, and I would dismiss this appeal.

SALMON, L.J.: I entirely agree.

WINN, L.J.: I also agree. I would like to say that I think the first section A
of the Highways (Miscellaneous Provisions) Act, 1961, may on a future occasion
require even fuller argument and consideration than it has received in this
appeal. I am not sure that I yet understand the scope of the section. I agree
that the appeal should be dismissed.

Appeal dismissed.

Solicitors: *Bower, Cotton & Bower*, agents for *S. B. Levin*, Liverpool (for the B
plaintiff); *Thomas Alker*, Town Clerk, Liverpool (for the defendants).

[*Reported by* BRIAN POCOCK, ESQ., *Barrister-at-Law.*]

C

Re CRAVEN INSURANCE CO., LTD.

[CHANCERY DIVISION (Pennycuick, J.), January 15, February 9, 1968.]

*Company—Winding-up—Compulsory winding-up—Insurance company—Mar-
gin of solvency not maintained—Discretion of court—Firm prospect that* D
*statutory margin of solvency will be attained in the near future—Whether
winding-up order should be refused—Relevant factors in deciding on exercise
of discretion—Insurance Companies Act, 1958 (6 & 7 Eliz. 2 c. 72), s. 13 (1)
—Companies Act 1967 (c. 81), s. 79 (1).*

An insurance company, incorporated in January, 1966, had in its financial
year ending Mar. 31, 1967, a substantial premium income. On Dec. 31, 1967, E
the company was solvent; its assets exceeded its liabilities by £167,184,
but it had not at that date a margin of solvency that would satisfy s. 13 (1)*
of the Insurance Companies Act, 1958, as substituted. The margin of solvency required was that the assets should at all times exceed liabilities by
the " relevant amount ". The relevant amount was one-fifth of the general
premium income of the preceding financial year. In the present instance F
the relevant amount for the year current at Dec. 31, 1967, was £355,928.
The company had firm prospects of some £124,000 further capital. This
would reduce the deficit on the required margin of solvency to £64,744.
Forecasts of the general premium income for the company's financial year
ending Mar. 31, 1968, showed that the " relevant amount ", for the purposes
of computing the company's required margin of solvency after March, 1968, G
would be less by £66,053 than for the corresponding relevant amount computed on the general premium income for the financial year ending Mar. 31,
1967. Thus there was good prospect that the company would have the
required margin of solvency as from Mar. 31, 1968. On a winding-up
petition presented by the Board of Trade under s. 15 (2) of the Act of 1958,
as substituted†: H

Held: there being a firm prospect of the statutory margin of solvency
being attained by the company in the near future, the court would, in the
exercise of its discretion, dismiss the petition, the company giving undertakings to supply the Board of Trade with particulars of its general premium
income for the year ending Mar. 31, 1968, and of its assets and liabilities as at
that date, so soon as practicable, and to supply audited accounts for the I
year ended Mar. 31, 1968 (see p. 1143, letter I, and p. 1144, letter E, post).

Per CURIAM: the statutory provisions as to the margin of solvency are
presumably framed for the protection of a company's policy-holders and third
parties having claims against the policy-holders; accordingly, factors such
as the public disadvantage by throwing workers out of employment are

---

* Section 13 (1), as substituted by the Companies Act 1967, s. 79, is set out at p. 1141,
letter I, to p. 1142, letter A, post.

† Section 15 (2) of the Act of 1958 is substituted by s. 81 of the Companies Act 1967.

A   not such as the court can legitimately take into consideration in deciding on the exercise of its discretion whether to make a winding-up order under the joint operation of s. 15 (2) and s. 13 (1), of the Act of 1958 (see p. 1144, letter I, post).

[As to the margin of solvency and an insurance company being deemed to be unable to pay its debts, see 22 HALSBURY'S LAWS (3rd Edn.) 435, 436, para. 875,
B   and SERVICE.

As to inability to pay debts as a ground for winding-up by the court, see 6 HALSBURY'S LAWS (3rd Edn.) 531-533, paras. 1031, 1033; and for cases on the subject, see 10 DIGEST (Repl.) 853-855, *5620-5635.*

For the Insurance Companies Act, 1958, s. 13, see 38 HALSBURY'S STATUTES
C   (2nd Edn.) 139.]

Case referred to:
    South Yorkshire Motor Insurance Co., Ltd., Re, (1967), The Times, July 21; 111 Sol. Jo. 601.

Petition.

This was a petition by the Board of Trade for the winding-up of Craven
D Insurance Co., Ltd.   The petition alleged that the company was incorporated on Jan. 12, 1966, under the Companies Act, 1948; that its nominal capital was £500,000 divided into five hundred thousand ordinary shares of £1 each, and that the amount of the capital issued and paid up or credited as paid up was £152,310; that the company was established to undertake and carry on various kinds of insurance including motor vehicle insurance and generally insurance
E business of every description, and other objects, and that in January, 1966, the company commenced to carry on and had since carried on within Great Britain motor vehicle insurance business (as defined by s. 59 (5) of the Companies Act 1967).   The petition further alleged that the value of the company's assets did not exceed the amount of its liabilities (computed in accordance with s. 13 (2) of the Insurance Companies Act, 1958) by the amount which was relevant
F for the purposes of s. 62 (1) (*a*) of the Companies Act 1967; and that by reason of these circumstances the company was deemed for the purposes of s. 222 of the Companies Act, 1948, to be unable to pay its debts.   The board alleged that in the premises it was just and equitable that the company should be wound-up by the court under the provisions of the Companies Act, 1948, and asked for a winding-up order or that such other order might be made as to the court
G should seem meet.

Ian McCulloch for the company.
P. J. Millett for the Board of Trade, the petitioners.
R. H. W. Marten for the directors and some of the shareholders of the company.

    PENNYCUICK, J.: I have before me a petition by the Board of Trade
H for the compulsory winding-up of Craven Insurance Co., Ltd., to which I will refer as " the company ".   The petition has been presented under the provisions of the Insurance Companies Act, 1958, as amended by the Companies Act 1967. The ground on which the petition is based is that the company's net assets are below the statutory margin of solvency.   I will, at the outset, read some provisions from the two Acts.   Section 79 (1) of the Companies Act, 1967, replacing
I s. 13 (1) of the Insurance Companies Act, 1958, provides as follows:

" (1) For sub-s. (1) of s. 13 (margin of solvency) of the principal Act, there shall be substituted the following subsection:

" ' (1) An insurance company to which this Act applies, being a company which carries on (whether within or outside Great Britain) general business, shall be deemed for the purposes of s. 222 of the Companies Act, 1948 (which authorises the court to wind up a company unable to pay its debts), to be unable to pay its debts if, at any time in its first financial year, the value

of its assets does not exceed the amount of its liabilities by £50,000, or if, **A**
at any time after the expiration of that year, the value of its assets does not
exceed the amount of its liabilities by the amount which is the relevant
amount for the purposes of s. 62 (1) (*a*) of the Companies Act 1967; and the
provisions of this Act as to winding-up shall have effect accordingly '."

Except where the general premium income of a company is under £50,000 or
over £2,500,000, the relevant amount for the purposes of s. 62 (1) (*a*) of the **B**
Companies Act 1967 as prescribed in the Table under sub-s. (2) of the section
is one-fifth of the general premium income of the company in its past preceding
financial year.   That is the relevant amount now material.   Section 13 (2) of the
Act of 1958 defines the general premium income of an insurance company as
meaning
                                                                              C
"... the net amount, after deduction of any premiums paid by the
company for reinsurance, of the premiums received by the company in that
year in respect of all insurance business ... other than long term business."

Power to present a winding-up petition is conferred on the Board of Trade by
s. 15 (2) of the Act of 1958, as amended by s. 81 of the Act of 1967.   It will be
seen that the margin of solvency at any given date involves two factors, namely **D**
(i) the relevant amount, that is, so far as now in point, one-fifth of the general
premium income for the last complete financial year preceding the given date;
and (ii) the excess of assets over liabilities at the given date.   The first factor
remains static throughout the financial year and is adjusted at the conclusion of
the year.   The second factor varies from day to day.

The facts in the present case may be stated as follows.   The company was **E**
incorporated and commenced business on Jan. 12, 1966.   Its paid up capital is
£152,310.   Its period of account ends on Mar. 31 and its first period of account,
that is, approximately, fifteen months, ended on Mar. 31, 1967.   The company
did a large volume of business during this period.   Its general premium income
for the period was over £2m.   After making the necessary adjustments (by
reason that the period exceeded twelve months) one-fifth of the general premium **F**
income for the financial year ended on Mar. 31, 1967, was £355,928.   The company encountered difficulties and there has been dissatisfaction over its management.   I have no detailed evidence as to those matters and am not concerned
to go into them.   It is sufficient to say that the company has throughout continued to carry on active business although certain of its assets have been frozen
as a result of the present petition.   On the latest figures the excess of its assets **G**
over its liabilities is substantial, but is far short of the relevant amount, ascertained by reference to its general premium income for the year ended Mar. 31,
1967.

The Board of Trade after conducting various investigations from about
August, 1967, onwards, presented the present petition on Dec. 12, 1967.   The
petition came on for hearing for the first time on Jan. 15, 1968, and has been **H**
adjourned for the purpose principally of obtaining up-to-date information as
to the company's financial position and also for the purpose of arranging for
the provision of further capital.   An independent firm of accountants, Messrs.
Whinney Murray & Co., has now made a report on the assets and liabilities of
the company as at Dec. 31, 1967.   It has been impossible in the time to produce
audited accounts, but there appears to be no reason to doubt the substantial **I**
accuracy of Messrs. Whinney Murray & Co.'s conclusions.   They put the excess
of assets over liabilities, after making various adjustments and allowances, at
£167,184.   The figures are not in dispute and it would not be useful to go into
details.   This figure shows a deficit of £188,742 against the relevant amount,
namely £355,928.   Firm arrangements have been made by the company to
to raise a further £124,000 by way of subscription for new non-voting convertible
preference shares.   Particulars of this arrangement will be found in the affidavit
sworn by Mr. Stevenson, a solicitor of the company, on Feb. 5, 1968.   It is not

A in dispute that this £124,000 will certainly be forthcoming. The arrangement involves, as I understand it, a provision whereby a certain individual will be excluded from any further share in the management of the company. The new capital will reduce the deficit to £64,744, a still formidable sum.

That however is not the end of this matter. Messrs. Whinney Murray & Co. have computed the general premium income of the company for the calendar
B year ended Dec. 31, 1967, at £1,449,372. One fifth of this sum is just under £289,875. The general premium income for the calendar year is not in itself a relevant factor in the ascertainment of the margin of solvency, but the computation does show that if the general premium income for the current quarter, that is, that to end on Mar. 31, 1968, were the same as that for the quarter ended Mar. 31, 1967, then the relevant amount for the year ended Mar. 31, 1968, would
C be less by £66,053 than the relevant amount for the year ended Mar. 31, 1967. Such a difference would be sufficient to wipe out the deficiency of £64,744, leaving a very small margin. It is impossible to forecast with certainty the general premium income for the current quarter, but in the present state of the company's affairs one would expect the general premium income to diminish rather than increase.

D I must next consider the law. It is accepted on behalf of the Board of Trade that the court has, under the Act of 1958, as amended, a judicial discretion whether it shall make a winding-up order. The discretion must, however, be exercised in accordance with the policy of the Act of 1958, and without seeking to lay down any rigid rule I feel no doubt that an order should be made in the simple case where a company's excess of assets over liabilities is below the
E relevant amount and where there is no firm prospect of redressing the position within a short time. On the other hand, the court must, I think, undoubtedly have power to refuse an order where such a firm prospect does exist. To take two extreme instances: the court would, I think, have such a discretion where the requisite further capital will assuredly be forthcoming within a week; or, again, where the company's financial year will end within a week and it is known with
F certainty that the relevant amount will then fall below the excess of assets over liabilities.

I was referred to one authority only, the decision of BUCKLEY, J., in *Re South Yorkshire Motor Insurance Co., Ltd.* (1). There, the margin of solvency was the fixed sum of £50,000. The company was short by some £5,000 of the margin of solvency and had so far failed to raise the necessary amount. At the last
G moment, however, a possible, but not firm, source of finance had been discovered. BUCKLEY, J., refused an adjournment in these terms (2):

"His lordship did not think that he could ignore the fact that the company had been carrying on business for some eight months, since its attention was drawn to s. 13, with an inadequate margin of solvency. Since the presentation of the petition it had not been underwriting any business. The
H burden was on the company to show that it had the required margin. If Parliament had provided, as it had done, that companies carrying on that kind of business must have a certain measure of solvency and that if they had not got that margin they should be deemed to be unable to pay their debts and so be liable to be wound up, it was not for the court to facilitate them to carry on business even for a short time."

I I am in complete agreement with the broad principle underlying this judgment and I would take the same course without hesitation where there was a deficiency in the margin of solvency and there was no firm prospect of meeting the margin of solvency in the near future. BUCKLEY, J., was not, however, concerned with the position where such a firm prospect existed, and I am sure that he did not intend to say that even in that case the court should in no circumstances allow

(1) (1967), The Times, July 21; 111 Sol. Jo. 601.
(2) (1967), The Times, July 21.

any further grace.   The words " even for a short time " are not, I think, addressed A
to that sort of case.

To return to the present case, it would plainly be wrong to allow the company
to continue its business even for a short time with a deficit of £64,744
in its margin of solvency unless the end of the deficit can be clearly foreseen
in the near future.   Nor is there any suggestion of injecting further capital.
The critical consideration is that in all probability the deficit will be wiped out B
when one-fifth of the general premium income for the year ended Mar. 31, 1968,
takes the place of one-fifth of the general premium income for the year ended
Mar. 31, 1967, as the relevant amount.   It would, I think, be harsh and rather
startling to wind-up a company which carries on a substantial business and is
solvent in the ordinary sense to the amount of over £290,000, including £120,000
in new ready money, where there is every prospect that in less than eight C
weeks the deficit on the margin of solvency will automatically disappear.
The statutory provisions are not punitive.   The past is only significant insofar
as it throws light on the future.   On the best consideration I can give it I do
not feel bound to make a winding-up order.   I do not think it would be right
to do so.

It is clearly impossible to keep this petition in suspense with the resulting D
freezing of the company's business.   I must either make an order today or
dismiss the petition.   I propose to dismiss the petition; but as a term of doing
so I must ask for certain undertakings on behalf of the company.   I will consult
counsel as to the precise terms of those undertakings, but, in general, I think
they should be (a) as soon as practicable after Mar. 31 and, at the latest, within
one month of that date, to supply the Board of Trade with particulars of its E
general premium income for the year ended Mar. 31, 1968, and of its assets and
liabilities as of that date and (b) as soon as practicable after Mar. 31 and, at the
latest, within three months of that date, to supply the Board of Trade with
audited accounts for the year ended Mar. 31, 1968.   There is also, I understand,
to be an undertaking to the effect that the company will not henceforth employ
a named individual in any capacity.   F

I must next add a clear warning that should the company, after Mar. 31, fail
to keep up its margin of solvency and should the Board of Trade present a further
petition, it is most unlikely that the court would give the company any further
shrift.

I must, in conclusion, mention one quite different matter.   An affidavit was
filed on behalf of the company by a Mr. Binns, who is Member of Parliament G
for the division in which the company's offices are situated.   Mr. Binns, at
great personal trouble, has interviewed not only the directors but all the workers
employed by the company, who are some 280 in number; those are all clerical
workers.   They would lose their employment if a winding-up order were made
and are anxious to support the company even to the extent of working for a
month without wages.   Mr. Binns says that it would be greatly to the public H
disadvantage to throw all those workers out of employment.   I appreciate
this factor, but I am more than doubtful whether I could legitimately take it
into account in exercising my discretion.   The statutory provisions as to the
margin of solvency are presumably framed for the protection of the company's
policy-holders and third parties having claims against the policy-holders.   I
do not think it would be right to treat the court as having a wide discretion I
exercisable amongst other things in the interests of employees and of the public
generally.   I have put this consideration entirely out of mind in reaching my
conclusion.   I propose accordingly to dismiss this petition.
                                              Petition dismissed.

Solicitors: *Coles & Stevenson* (for the company); *Solicitor, Board of Trade*;
Thorold, Brodie, Bonham-Carter & Mason (for directors and shareholders).

[*Reported by* JENIFER SANDELL, *Barrister-at-Law.*]

A

BUCKPITT *v.* OATES.

[DEVON ASSIZES (John Stephenson, J.), January 25, 1968.]

Contract—Intention to create legal relationship—Contribution to cost of petrol incurred by friend in driving plaintiff on journey by car—Whether giving rise to legal contract.

B *Negligence—Defence—Volenti non fit injuria—Infant—Infant passenger injured in collision—Driver of car also an infant—Infant passenger knowing that driver not insured.*

The plaintiff and the defendant, both of whom were seventeen years old, were in the habit of riding from time to time in each other's cars. Neither of them had insurance cover against risk of injury to passengers. The

C evidence showed that the plaintiff knew that the defendant was not so insured. A notice affixed to the facia panel of the defendant's car immediately in front of the passenger seat gave warning to passengers that they rode in the car at their own risk, not being covered by insurance and the defendant said that the plaintiff was present when he fixed the notice to the car. Some two or three weeks later, when the defendant was persuaded to

D drive the plaintiff in his, the defendant's car, the plaintiff sitting in the passenger seat, the car struck a wall due to the defendant's negligence and the plaintiff was injured. The plaintiff had paid the defendant 10s. towards the cost of the petrol, which in fact did not cost so much. On the question whether the defence volenti non fit injuria was an answer to the plaintiff's claim for damages,

E **Held:** (i) on the facts the plaintiff agreed to be carried at his own risk and to exempt the defendant from liability for the negligence which caused the accident; the plaintiff, though an infant in law, could not enforce a right which he had voluntarily waived or abandoned, and accordingly the defence of volenti non fit injuria succeeded (see p. 1148, letter F, and p. 1149, letter D, post).

F (ii) there was no legal contract of carriage, the arrangement between the parties to the journey being one not intended to create legal relationship (see p. 1147, letters D and E, post).

[As to consideration for a contract unenforceable at law, see 8 HALSBURY'S LAWS (3rd Edn.) 113, para. 197; and for cases on the subject, see 12 DIGEST

G (Repl.) 230, *1718-1722*.

As to the application of the defence volenti non fit injuria, see 28 HALSBURY'S LAWS (3rd Edn.) 82-84, para. 88; and for cases on the subject, see 36 DIGEST (Repl.) 150-155, *781-818*.]

Cases referred to:

Balfour v. *Balfour*, [1918-19] All E.R. Rep. 860; [1919] 2 K.B. 571; 88 L.J.K.B.

H 1054; 121 L.T. 346; 12 Digest (Repl.) 21, *3*.

Connolly v. *Spikens*, (Dec. 22, 1967), " Daily Express ".

Olson v. *Corry & Gravesend Aviation, Ltd.*, [1936] 3 All E.R. 241; 155 L.T. 512; 34 Digest (Repl.) 46, *216*.

Action.

This was an action by the plaintiff against the defendant for damages for

I personal injuries sustained in a motor car accident on Sept. 10, 1965, when the defendant's Triumph car, which he was driving, and in which the plaintiff was passenger, struck a wall. The following facts are taken from the judgment. The plaintiff, who was just under eighteen years old, drove a Hillman Minx motor car and the defendant, who was seventeen years old, owned and drove a Triumph motor car. It was the practice of each of them to ride from time to time in the other's car. Neither of them was able to obtain insurance cover against risk of injury to passengers. The evidence showed that on one occasion the plaintiff had told the defendant that he, the plaintiff, was not insured against

passenger risk and had said that he was in the same position when riding in **A**
the defendant's car as the defendant was in when riding in his car. Some two
or three weeks before the accident the defendant had a notice affixed to the facia
panel of his car immediately in front of the passenger's seat which said:

> "Warning. Passengers ride in this vehicle at their own risk. Neither
> the owner nor the driver will be liable for loss of life or personal injury
> or other loss or damage howsoever caused. Passengers are not covered   **B**
> by insurance."

The defendant said that the plaintiff saw the notice on the day it was fixed to
the car and the trial judge was satisfied that both the plaintiff and the defendant
fully appreciated that the other was not covered by insurance against passenger
risk. Shortly before the accident, the defendant, who was a motor mechanic,   **C**
carried out some repairs to the plaintiff's car at Paignton, where he lived. On
the evening of Sept. 10, 1965, the plaintiff drove his car from Paignton to
Newton Abbot and back with the defendant in the passenger seat. After they got
back to Paignton, the plaintiff remembered that they had left something behind
in a café at Newton Abbot and persuaded the defendant to drive him back there
in the defendant's Triumph car by offering to contribute to the cost of the petrol. **D**
At some stage the plaintiff paid the defendant 10s. as a contribution towards the
cost of the petrol for the journey. The defendant said in evidence that the cost
of the petrol was not as much as 10s. On the journey back to Paignton, on
which the defendant drove and the plaintiff was passenger, the car collided with a
wall and the plaintiff was injured.

The defendant admitted that the collision was caused by his negligence, and it **E**
was agreed that the damages were quantified by agreement at £750. By para. 4
of the defence the defendant raised the defence that the plaintiff voluntarily
assented to the risk of negligence on the part of the defendant, reliance being
placed on the notice affixed to the facia panel of the defendant's car.

David Keene for the plaintiff.   **F**
T. G. Field-Fisher for the defendant.

JOHN STEPHENSON, J., stated the facts and continued: On those facts,
the question arises: did the plaintiff expressly or impliedly assent or agree to
the risk of being injured by the defendant's negligence in the way in which he
was? Counsel on behalf of the plaintiff has submitted that he did not, and he has **G**
submitted, first of all, that this plea of volenti non fit injuria is not open to the
defendant because the notice on which he relies in support of that plea was a
term of contract, and that contract is void against the plaintiff because it is a
contract which is, on balance, onerous and not for the infant's benefit. Counsel,
on behalf of the defendant has, in my judgment rightly, conceded that, if there
was an enforceable contract between the plaintiff and the defendant to carry **H**
the plaintiff in the defendant's car, and it was a term of that contract that the
plaintiff should be carried at his own risk, the contract would be void and the
defendant would be unable to rely on the notice, and he would have to submit
to judgment. Secondly, counsel for the plaintiff submitted that, even if there
was no contract between the plaintiff and the defendant, the plaintiff, being an
infant, cannot be rendered volens by a bargain of this nature and by such a **I**
notice as this. Thirdly, he has submitted that, even if the plaintiff could be
made volens by such a notice, this plaintiff on these facts was not volens because
he did not consent to bear the risk of any injury to himself caused by the
defendant.

First, was there a contract between the plaintiff and the defendant? Counsel
for the defendant submits that there was not. He says that this was a friendly
arrangement not intended to create a legal relationship between these two parties.
It was part of a wider arrangement that each should be given rides in each

A other's cars and it gave rise to no contractual obligations; the only legal relationship which arose out of these rides was the legal duty imposed by law on a driver to take reasonable care for the safety of his passenger, a duty which is no different from the duty which he owes to every other road user outside his vehicle, to take care not to injure him—the duty that one neighbour, in the legal sense, owes to another. Counsel for the plaintiff, I think, very nearly

B conceded that, if there had been no payment of 10s. in this case, there would have been no legally binding or enforceable contract. He says that payment clearly shows that, even if a gratuitous contract to carry cannot be inferred from the circumstances of this case, on the evidence I have heard there was clearly here a binding contract to carry for consideration, and, in effect, a contract to carry a passenger for reward. He submits that, if the plaintiff had not paid

C the 10s. and had refused to make any contribution towards the petrol used on this journey, the defendant could have sued the plaintiff for it. I find that a hopelessly unreal assessment of the position. I cannot believe that either of these young men regarded himself as entering into a binding contract. They are not lawyers and their view, even if I have assessed it correctly, is not a conclusive test. It seems to me, approaching the matter with as much common sense as I

D retain, that this sum of 10s. was a present from the plaintiff to the defendant for his help in going back to collect these goods—I do not even know what they were, or whether they belonged to the plaintiff or to the defendant, or to both of them—and that there was no question of any binding promise either to carry or to pay. The agreement—and clearly there was an agreement on the part of the defendant to drive the plaintiff back to Newton Abbot, and on the part of

E the plaintiff to be driven back to Newton Abbot by the defendant—was much more like the agreement which is given by Atkin, L.J., as an example of an agreement between the parties which does *not* result in a contract within the meaning of that term in our law, in *Balfour* v. *Balfour* (1). I, therefore, prefer the contention of the defendant to that of the plaintiff, and I find that there was a friendly arrangement, or (I can hardly avoid using the phrase) a " gentlemen's

F agreement " to go on this trip, which gave rise to no legal obligations or rights except those which the general law of the land imposes or implies. That leaves only the question whether those legal rights and duties could be modified or surrendered, and whether in fact they were modified or surrendered on the facts of this case.

I come, therefore, to counsel for the plaintiff's second submission, that the

G plaintiff, because he was an infant, could not as a matter of law surrender his legal right to be compensated for injury, loss or damage arising out of the negligent driving of the defendant. He did not go as far as to submit that an infant could never be volens, that he could never willingly and freely assent to undertake the risk of injury with full knowledge of what he was undertaking. He conceded that an infant might be volens, and might be defeated by a plea of volenti non

H fit injuria in a case where he was the author, in part at any rate, of his own injury. In a case such as this, however, where a plaintiff—an innocent infant passenger— was in no way responsible for the collision which injured him, or for the driving of the vehicle and the way in which it was driven into the wall, he submitted that no such plea could be entertained or could succeed. If it is impossible for an infant to bind himself by agreement to undertake to be driven in a vehicle

I at his own risk, it should be—and he submitted it is so in law—impossible for him to agree to it without binding himself contractually, and he cannot be worse off because he takes a ride in a car under a friendly arrangement than he would be if he took it under a binding and legally enforceable contract of carriage. Both counsel for the defendant and counsel for the plaintiff have been unable in their searches—I confess, somewhat to my surprise—to discover any officially reported case in which a plea of volenti non fit injuria has been raised, successfully

---

(1) [1918-19] All E.R. Rep. 860 at pp. 864, 865; [1919] 2 K.B. 571 at pp. 578, 579.

or unsuccessfully, against an infant plaintiff, with the exception of *Olsen* v. **A**
Corry and Gravesend Aviation, Ltd. (2).   There, an exemption from liability
clause in a deed of apprenticeship was held not to be binding on an infant plaintiff.
A plea of volenti non fit injuria, in which it was alleged that the plaintiff consented to the risk of negligence both by entering into the deed and by working
on the defendant's premises, was rejected by the learned judge on the ground
that the infant plaintiff had not been proved to have the knowledge and **B**
appreciation of the risk necessary to support the plea.

Quite clearly, this plea is one which, like that of contributory negligence,
becomes less likely to succeed on the facts as the age and experience of the infant
diminish; but I can, myself, see no reason why the fact that a man, or a girl,
is under the age of twenty-one years should prevent him or her from knowing
and appreciating the risk of another's negligence and expressly or impliedly **C**
assenting to undertake that risk.

" No act is actionable as a tort at the suit of any person who has expressly
or impliedly assented to it . . . No man can enforce a right which he has
voluntarily waived or abandoned."

That is the view of the law set out, as regards intentional harms as well as **D**
accidental harms, in SALMOND ON TORTS (14th Edn.), p. 47.   As regards
accidental harms, it is said (at p. 48) that the consent means

" a waiver by a plaintiff of an admitted breach of duty, but the better
view is that consent here means the agreement of the plaintiff, express or
implied, to exempt the defendant from the duty of care which he otherwise
would have owed."
                                                                       E
Those wide words " No man can enforce a right which he has voluntarily
abandoned " and

" consent here means the agreement of the plaintiff, express or implied,
to exempt the defendant from the duty of care which he otherwise would
have owed ",
                                                                       F
seem to me to extend to infants.   No man—and it seems to me, no infant—
can enforce a right which he has voluntarily waived or abandoned, and he can
agree, expressly or impliedly, to exempt the defendant from the duty of care
which he otherwise would have owed.   Of course, the court will always consider
with great care whether a particular plaintiff had the means and the knowledge
and experience to appreciate fully and freely the risk and what he was consenting **G**
to.   As I have said, I have no doubt in this case that the terms of the notice
were appreciated by the plaintiff, and that he realised that, when he rode in the
defendant's car, he was riding in it as a passenger at his own risk.   I cannot
see any objection in law to drawing that conclusion in the case of an infant.
It is a question of fact and not of law whether he has assented.

That indicates what I think is the right answer to counsel for the plaintiff's **H**
third submission, which is that, on the facts of this case, the plaintiff did not
assent to be carried on this journey at his own risk.   He frankly concedes that
the plaintiff must be taken to have assented to being carried at his own risk on
any journey that he may have taken in the defendant's car on the day on which
he read the notice for the first time; but that, says counsel, was two or three
weeks before the date of the accident, and why should it be assumed or inferred **I**
that the assent which he had given with regard to that journey was repeated
or continued immediately before and during the journey which he took on
Sept. 10, 1965?   Why should it not?   The latter is the question which must
arise in the mind of anybody who approaches this case as a jury, namely, with
some regard to the reality of the matter.   It seems to me to be a question of

_____

(2) [1936] 3 All E.R. 241.

A fact and degree, and I think that counsel for the plaintiff agrees. If a man were to get into the same friend's same car with the same notice on the facia board a long time after he had first seen and marked the notice, it might be arguable that he was not assenting long afterwards to be carried on the same terms as those on which he had previously assented to be carried. At least, any evidence which he gave to suggest that he had forgotten the terms of the notice, or was

B being carried on some different terms, would certainly be admissible, and might even be credible. Here, however, I have no evidence which would convict the plaintiff of forgetfulness or lack of intelligence, and I find that it is impossible not to draw the inference, bearing in mind the relationship between these two young men and the way in which they were in the habit of riding as passengers in each other's cars, each with the knowledge that he himself was not insured against passenger risks, that each had also got the knowledge throughout the

C time of their association during August and September, 1965, and that throughout that time each impliedly assented to that position. I do not think that the evidence warrants any other inference, and I can draw no other inference.

Therefore, I find that the plaintiff did agree to be carried at his own risk and to exempt the defendant from liability for the negligence which caused his

D accident on this journey. I find that he did surrender his right to be compensated for that negligence, that he was volens, and the defendant's plea of volenti non fit injuria, in the form in which it is raised in para. 4 of the defence, succeeds.

It is to be noticed that the defendant is and was at all material times also an infant. Counsel have not felt able to suggest to me that that makes any difference in law, and I think that it follows from the reasons which I have given in this

E judgment, which I have not had an opportunity of reserving, that this plea might well have succeeded even if the defendant had been over twenty-one years of age. It seems to me, however, that it would be very odd that a defendant who is himself under twenty-one, should not be able to say to a man of equal age, whose own motor car was in the same position as his except that he had not got a warning notice on the dashboard: " You agreed to be carried at your

F own risk in my car, as I agreed to be carried at my own risk in yours." It seems to me that both common sense and justice together point in this case to the conclusion at which I have arrived. There will be judgment in this action for the defendant.

I should have said that I have been referred to the report—not by a barrister —in the " Daily Express " newspaper of Dec. 22, 1967, of Connolly v. Spikens (3).

G There Miss Connolly, the plaintiff, was a pillion passenger who sued, among others, the driver of the motor cycle on which she was riding and proved that she had been injured by his negligence. Mr. Spikens, the defendant, according to this newspaper report, raised the unusual defence that he was immune from a claim by the plaintiff because he told her that he was not insured for pillion passengers and that she could only ride on his motor cycle at her own risk. If

H that plea had been made good, that case would be as near as makes no difference to being on all fours with the present case, because the plaintiff at the time of the accident was 16½ years of age. The learned judge, however, accepted her denials that she ever consented to a condition that she would not sue and added, according to the report, that, even if she had done so, she was a child of 16½ and such an agreement was obviously not to her benefit and could not be enforced

I in law. The decision there was that the defence failed on the facts. Here, counsel for the plaintiff has rightly agreed that he cannot argue that the last sentence quoted in the report was part of the ratio by which the learned judge decided that case. It is of interest to see that the learned judge took that view of the plea in that case, but it was obiter dictum. I do not know what arguments were addressed to the learned judge on the point, and, if the learned judge said that in every case where a defendant driver meets a claim by an infant passenger

---

(3) (Dec. 22, 1967), " Daily Express ".

with this plea it could never succeed, I would respectfully feel unable to follow **A**
him. If this case had to be put on the basis of a legally binding contract, it
was conceded that that observation of the learned judge would apply to defeat
the plaintiff's claim.

Judgment for the defendant.

Solicitors: *Boyce, Hatton & Co.,* Torquay (for the plaintiff); *Gowman,*
Easterbrook & Co., Paignton (for the defendant).   **B**

[*Reported by* DEIRDRE McKINNEY, *Barrister-at-Law.*]

Re MANMAC FARMERS, LTD.   **C**

[CHANCERY DIVISION (Pennycuick, J.), January 29, 30, 1968.]

Company—Winding-up—Compulsory winding-up—Liquidator—No liquidator
appointed at first meeting of creditors in place of official receiver—Majority
of creditors desiring liquidator to be appointed subsequently in place of official   **D**
receiver—Order made on motion to convene meeting to determine whether
liquidator should be appointed—Preliminary meeting of creditors unnecessary
—Companies Act, 1948 (11 & 12 Geo. 6 c. 38), s. 346.

A receiver was appointed by debenture-holders of a company in May,
1967. An order for the compulsory winding-up of the company was made on
July 3, 1967. The first meetings of the creditors and contributories were held   **E**
on Aug. 1, 1967. No liquidator was then proposed in place of the official
receiver. The assets of the company were in the hands of the receiver for the
debenture-holders. As at the date of his appointment the receiver showed
a surplus of assets available for the unsecured creditors amounting to
£161,000 odd. The official receiver made a report on Nov. 3, 1967, in which he
estimated that there would be a surplus of £70,000 available for the unsecured   **F**
trade creditors. The debts owing to unsecured creditors amounted to
£500,429. The applicant company was a creditor for £233,638 12s. 5d., and
the application was supported by six other trade creditors, the aggregate of
the debts of the applicant company and supporting creditors being more than
half the total amount of the debts owing to unsecured creditors. The
applicant company, being dissatisfied with the progress of the liquidation   **G**
(no criticism being made of the deputy official receiver who had carried it
out), applied to the official receiver to re-summon the first meetings of
creditors and contributories under s. 346* of the Companies Act, 1948, with a
view to appointing a liquidator in place of the official receiver. The official
receiver contended that as a preliminary there must be convened a meeting
of creditors to determine whether they wished to apply for the re-summoning   **H**
of the first meetings.

Held: where, as here, the figures were such as to make it virtually certain
that the creditors as a class would support the substantive resolution, a
preliminary meeting would not serve a useful purpose; accordingly, the
court would make an order for the convening of a further first meeting of the
creditors and contributories of the company for the purpose of appointing,   **I**
if thought fit, a liquidator in place of the official receiver, without directing
any preliminary meeting to be convened (see p. 1153, letters C and H,
post).

[As to the first meeting of creditors and contributories, see 6 HALSBURY'S
LAWS (3rd Edn.) 609, para. 1195; and for cases on the subject, see 10 DIGEST
(Repl.) 930, *6359, 6360.*

---

* Section 346, so far as material, is set out at p. 1152, letter C, post.

A   As to the regard had to wishes of creditors, see 6 Halsbury's Laws (3rd Edn.) 553, para. 1064.

    For the Companies Act, 1948, s. 252, s. 346, see 3 Halsbury's Statutes (2nd Edn.) 660, 723.]

Cases referred to:

B   *Heywood* v. *B.D.C. Properties, Ltd. (No. 2)*, [1964] 2 All E.R. 702; [1964] 1 W.L.R. 971; Digest (Cont. Vol. B) 548, *285a*.

    Newman (George) & Co., Re, [1895] 1 Ch. 674; 64 L.J.Ch. 907; 72 L.T. 697; 9 Digest (Repl.) 646, *4298*.

    Radford & Bright, Ltd., Re, [1901] 1 Ch. 272; 70 L.J.Ch. 78; 10 Digest (Repl.) 929, *6356*.

C   *Radford & Bright, Ltd., Re, (No. 2)*, [1901] 1 Ch. 735; 70 L.J.Ch. 352; 84 L.T. 150; 10 Digest (Repl.) 929, *6357*.

    Reynolds (Charles) & Co., Ltd., Re, [1895] W.N. 31; 10 Digest (Repl.) 913, *6229*.

Motion.

    This was a motion by notice dated Jan. 24, 1968, by the plaintiff, Co-operative Wholesale Society, Ltd., which was a creditor of Manmac Farmers, Ltd.,
D in the sum of £233,638 12s. 5d. The plaintiff asked for an order pursuant to s. 346 of the Companies Act, 1948, directing that the official receiver as liquidator of the company should forthwith convene a meeting of creditors of the company for the purpose of considering and, if thought fit, passing resolutions appointing a liquidator in the place of the official receiver and to determine whether an application should be made for the appointment of a committee of inspection and
E who were to be members of any such committee.

    P. J. Millett for the official receiver.

    Jeremiah Harman for the applicants.

    PENNYCUICK, J.: By this motion Co-operative Wholesale Society, Ltd. seeks an order pursuant to s. 346 of the Companies Act, 1948, directing that
F the official receiver as liquidator of Manmac Farmers, Ltd., to which I will refer as " the company ", should convene a meeting of the creditors of the company for the purpose of considering and, if thought fit, passing resolutions appointing a liquidator in the place of the official receiver, and certain other relief.

    The facts of the case are not in dispute. An order for the compulsory winding-up of the company was made on July 3, 1967. The first meetings of the creditors
G and contributories were held on Aug. 1, 1967. No liquidator was then proposed in place of the official receiver. The assets of the company are in the hands of a receiver who was appointed under a debenture on May 22, 1967. A statement of affairs at that date showed a surplus of assets available for the unsecured creditors amounting to £161,000 odd. The official receiver made a report on Nov. 3, 1967, in which he estimated that there would be a surplus of £70,000
H available for the unsecured creditors. The debts owing to unsecured creditors amount in all to £500,429. The applicant company is a creditor for £233,638 12s. 5d. The application is supported by six other trade creditors whose debts amount in the aggregate to £83,400. The result is that the total debts owing to the applicant and the creditors which support it are £316,000 which is considerably more than half the total amount of the debts owing to unsecured
I creditors.

    The liquidation has so far been carried out by the deputy official receiver for the Salford district. No criticism is made against that officer for the manner in which he has conducted the liquidation, but the creditors who appear on this motion are dissatisfied with the progress of the liquidation and the deputy official receiver was only too willing that a liquidator should be appointed in his place. He has not got the staff or facilities at his office for dealing with a liquidation of this magnitude. Accordingly Co-operative Wholesale Society, Ltd., and those companies which support it, made an application to the official receiver

to re-summon the first meetings of the creditors and contributories under s. 346   **A**
of the Companies Act, 1948. The official receiver has no objection in principle to
this course being taken, but he contends that a certain preliminary step must
be taken, namely, the convening of a meeting of the creditors in order to determine
whether they wish to make an application for the re-summoning of the first
meetings of creditors and contributories. In those circumstances the present
motion has been brought.

    Co-operative Wholesale Society, Ltd. and the creditors which support it **B**
contend that no preliminary meeting is necessary and invite the court itself at
this stage to re-convene the first meetings. Section 346 of the Companies Act,
1948, is in these terms:

    " (1) The court may, as to all matters relating to the winding-up of a
company, have regard to the wishes of the creditors or contributories of   **C**
the company, as proved to it by any sufficient evidence, and may, if it thinks
fit, for the purpose of ascertaining those wishes, direct meetings of the
creditors or contributories to be called, held and conducted in such manner
as the court directs, and may appoint a person to act as chairman of any
such meeting and to report the result thereof to the court. (2) In the case of
creditors, regard shall be had to the value of each creditor's debt."   **D**

The note in Buckley on the Companies Acts at p. 695 states:

    " This section may be used for the purpose of re-summoning the statutory
' first meetings ' of creditors and contributories."

See s. 252 of the Act of 1948 and *Re Radford & Bright, Ltd.* (1), and *Re Radford &*
Bright, Ltd. (*No. 2*), (2). In the second of the *Radford & Bright* cases Wright, J.,   **E**
said this (3):

    " I think that under s. 91 of the Companies Act, 1862 [that was the
statutory predecessor of s. 346] the court has an almost unlimited power as to
ordering meetings of creditors or contributories to be summoned. If it were
not so, it is obvious that in the infinite variety of circumstances that can
exist in the winding-up of companies emergencies might easily arise with   **F**
which no one would have any power to deal, with the result that great
injustice might ensue."

On the face of it s. 346 appears clearly to cover the present application, that is
to say the court is asked to direct the re-summoning of meetings of creditors
and contributories—I will come back to the question of contributories at a   **G**
later stage—for the purpose of ascertaining their wishes on the question whether
an independent liquidator shall be appointed in place of the official receiver.
Again, so far as the facts are concerned, it appears perfectly clear that this
is a case in which an independent liquidator should be appointed in place of the
official receiver in order to carry on this important and apparently quite
complicated liquidation.   **H**

    Counsel for the applicant and those supporting it, invited me, therefore, to
make an order as sought on the motion. Counsel for the official receiver
contended that the present application is not in accordance with recognised
practice and, indeed, is contrary to some statutory provision. Counsel for the
official receiver outlined the usual practice and he produced the file in another
case which shows step by step what is the usual practice. The steps may be   **I**
summarised as follows: 1. A creditor who represents more than one-tenth in
value of the whole of the unsecured creditors requests the liquidator to convene
a meeting of creditors for the purpose next mentioned. 2. The liquidator convenes
a meeting of creditors in order to determine whether an application be made to
the court to re-summon the first meetings of creditors and contributories with the
object of nominating a liquidator in place of the official receiver. 3. This preliminary meeting of the creditors is held and the resolution put. 4. If the resolution is

A passed an application is made to the registrar for an order to re-summon the first meetings of the creditors and contributories with the foregoing object. 5. The registrar makes an order to re-summon the first meetings. 6. The re-summoned meetings are held and the resolution is put. 7. If the resolution is passed at any rate at the meeting of creditors an application is made to the registrar to appoint the liquidator nominated. 8.—and last—the registrar makes an order

B appointing a liquidator.

The procedure which I have outlined above is curiously repetitive. It involves an application to the liquidator to convene a meeting to consider a preliminary resolution to apply to the registrar to convene other further meetings to consider the substantive resolution. The object underlying this procedure must, I think, be to ensure that the creditors as a class are likely to support the substantive

C resolution before the first meetings of both the creditors and the contributories are re-convened. This in many cases might be an expensive procedure. Where, as here, however, the figures are such as to make it virtually certain that the creditors as a class will support the substantive resolution, the preliminary meeting appears to serve no useful purpose of any kind.

Counsel for the official receiver says that a decision of a class on any question

D must be either unanimous or expressed at a properly convened meeting. That is, of course, so and he cites the well-known case of *Re George Newman & Co.* (4). So, here, the decision of the creditors as a class on the substantive question will be expressed at a meeting convened to consider that substantive question. The issue is whether a preliminary meeting is necessary at all in the circumstances of this case. The significance of the figures is that they make it clear beyond doubt

E that the preliminary meeting is unnecessary. Counsel for the official receiver says that it would be contrary to the provisions of s. 346 to dispense with a preliminary meeting. I cannot see why this is so. The section no doubt envisages that the creditors on any given question will be ascertained at a properly convened meeting of the creditors as a class. The section nowhere provides or implies that those wishes must be ascertained twice over.

F Section 239 takes the matter no further. That section is concerned with the substantive resolution to be passed at the first meetings, i.e., the nomination of the liquidator and the application to the registrar to appoint him. Counsel for the official receiver referred to *Re Charles Reynolds & Co., Ltd.* (5), but that decision does not, so far as I can see, throw any further light on the question. No other statutory provision was cited which could have the effect of making it

G impossible as a matter of law to by-pass this preliminary meeting of the creditors. Counsel for the official receiver pointed out, truly, that the whole procedure to appoint a liquidator instead of the official receiver is normally carried through in chambers and, he says, a motion is inappropriate procedurally. It is, however, well settled that any matter which can be brought before the court by summons can be brought before the court by motion (see *Heywood* v. *B.D.C.*

H *Properties, Ltd. (No. 2)* (6), per HARMAN, L.J.). In the present case, having regard to the time which has elapsed and the importance of getting the liquidator into the saddle as soon as possible, it seems to me that the procedure by way of motion is appropriate. I must accordingly make an order in the terms of the notice of motion.

I [*The notice of motion only asked for a direction that the official receiver should convene a meeting of creditors; but it was accepted by counsel that a meeting of contributories must also be convened.*]

Order accordingly.

Solicitors: *Solicitor, Board of Trade; Herbert Oppenheimer, Nathan & Vandyk* (for the applicant).

[*Reported by* JENIFER SANDELL, *Barrister-at-Law.*]

---

(4) [1895] 1 Ch. 674.   (5) [1895] W.N. 31.
(6) [1964] 2 All E.R. 702 at pp. 702-704.

A

VAUGHAN *v.* McKENZIE.

[QUEEN'S BENCH DIVISION (Lord Parker, C.J., Winn, L.J., and Ashworth, J.), February 19, 21, 1968.]

County Court—Execution—Bailiff—Entry—Use of force—Respondent, knowing bailiff had come to levy execution, entered her house and tried to shut the door against the bailiff—Bailiff pushed door open to obtain entry—Respondent assaulted him—Whether an assault on the bailiff in the execution of his duty —County Courts Act, 1959 (7 & 8 Eliz. 2 c. 22), s. 30.

B

On May 5, 1967, a warrant of execution against the goods of the respondent was issued by Leeds county court. The appellant, a bailiff of that court, went with another bailiff to the respondent's house on May 22. The house was closed, but the respondent returned to it later and, when outside her front door, was told the reason for the appellant's visit; but the warrant was not shown or read to her. The respondent entered the house and immediately attempted to shut the door, but the other bailiff put his foot in the door and pushed. The appellant assisted the other bailiff and they forced open the door with the object of gaining entry to the house, whereupon the respondent struck the appellant on the head with a milk bottle. On appeal from the dismissal of a charge against the respondent of having assaulted the appellant in the execution of his duty, contrary to s. 30 of the County Courts Act, 1959,

C

D

Held: the bailiffs had no right to force their way into the respondent's house for the purpose of gaining entry to enforce their warrant of execution, and in so doing they were not acting in execution of their duty; accordingly the information had been rightly dismissed (see p. 1156, letter H, and p. 1156, letter I, to p. 1157, letter A, post).

E

Broughton v. *Wilkerson* ((1880), 44 J.P. 781) and *Rossiter* v. *Conway* ((1893), 58 J.P. 350) followed.

PER CURIAM: the mere fact that the warrant was neither shown nor read to the respondent did not have the consequence that the bailiffs were not acting in the execution of their duty, since the respondent knew the purpose for which they had come (see p. 1155, letter I, post).

F

Appeal dismissed.

[As to the right of entry in execution of civil process, see 16 HALSBURY'S LAWS (3rd Edn.) 41, 42, paras. 61, 62; and for cases on the subject, see 21 DIGEST (Repl.) 567, 568, *615-640.*

G

As to the offence of assault on officers of county courts, see 9 HALSBURY'S LAWS (3rd Edn.) 133. para. 260; and for cases on the subject, see 13 DIGEST (Repl.) 377, *66-71.*

For the County Courts Act, 1959, s. 30, see 39 HALSBURY'S STATUTES (2nd Edn.) 122.]

H

Cases referred to:

Broughton v. *Wilkerson,* (1880), 44 J.P. 781; 21 Digest (Repl.) 567, *623.*

Nash v. *Lucas,* (1867), L.R. 2 Q.B. 590; 32 J.P. 23; 18 Digest (Repl.) 324, *698.*

Rossiter v. *Conway,* (1893), 58 J.P. 350; 46 Digest (Repl.) 420, *640.*

Southam v. *Smout,* [1963] 3 All E.R. 104; [1964] 1 Q.B. 308; [1963] 3 W.L.R. 606; Digest (Cont. Vol. A) 317, *57a.*

I

Case Stated.

On May 26, 1967, at a court of summary jurisdiction sitting at Leeds, the appellant preferred an information before JOHN RANDOLPH, Esq., stipendiary magistrate for the City of Leeds against the respondent for that she did assault the appellant, an officer of the Leeds county court, while in the execution of his duty as such officer contrary to s. 30 of the County Courts Act, 1959. The facts found are summarised in the judgment of LORD PARKER, C.J. It was

A contended by the respondent before the magistrate (a) that the appellant and another bailiff who was with him were trespassers and that she had used no more force than was reasonably necessary to evict them; (b) that as the warrant had not been shown or read to her the appellant was not acting in execution of his duty.

B The stipendiary magistrate was of the opinion (a) that the appellant and the other bailiff were not justified in law for the purpose of gaining entry to execute a civil warrant in attempting to push open a door which the respondent was endeavouring to shut and that they were accordingly trespassers; (b) that, in any event the appellant and the other bailiff, not having shown or read the warrant to the respondent, were not acting in execution of their duty. The question for the opinion of the High Court was whether, on the above facts, the

C stipendiary magistrate came to a correct conclusion in point of law.

Nigel Bridge for the appellant.
The respondent did not appear and was not represented.

LORD PARKER, C.J., having stated the nature of the appeal, continued:
On May 5, 1967, a warrant of execution against the goods of the respondent

D was issued by the Leeds county court for some £91 in respect of costs. The appellant, who is a bailiff of the Leeds county court, went with another bailiff on May 22 to the house where the respondent lived. When they got there, the house was closed, the respondent being away. The bailiffs waited, and later the respondent returned with her child. Outside the front door, the appellant and the other bailiff told the respondent that they were bailiffs, and had come

E to levy execution on her goods. It is true that no warrant was produced to her, but it is quite clear that she knew full well who they were, and what they had come about, because she immediately told them that she had written to the county court and the Lord Chancellor regarding these costs, and she said that she would not admit them to the house.

F What happened then, was that she and the child entered the house and immediately attempted to shut the door, but the other bailiff, Mr. Richmond, got his foot in the door and pushed against it, the respondent on her side pushing to keep him out. The appellant came to the assistance of Mr. Richmond, and both of them forced the door open with the object of gaining entry to the house, whereupon the respondent finding a milk bottle handy, picked it up and struck the appellant on the head with the bottle of milk, whereby he sustained

G a one inch long cut requiring three stitches. Those are the short facts of this case. The magistrate stated his opinion in this form:

" (a) That the appellant and Richmond were not justified in law for the purpose of gaining entry to execute a civil warrant, in attempting to push open the door which the respondent was endeavouring to close against

H them and that they were accordingly trespassers; (b) that, in any event, the appellant and Richmond, not having shown or read the warrant to the respondent, were not acting in the execution of their duty."

So far as that latter reason is concerned, I am quite satisfied that the magistrate was wrong. This was a case where she plainly knew that they were bailiffs, and plainly knew the object with which they had come, and the fact that the warrant

I was not produced was not, in the circumstances, fatal to these proceedings.

The real question here is whether the bailiffs were justified in attempting to push open the door by force against the will of the respondent. I confess that in the course of the argument my own feeling was that the magistrate had come to a right conclusion, and it is to be observed that in *Southam* v. *Smout* (1), which was dealing with the mode of entry which is lawful there is a passage in

---

(1) [1963] 3 All E.R. 104; [1964] 1 Q.B. 308.

the judgment of LORD DENNING, M.R., where, after referring to *Nash* v. *Lucas* (2) **A** he said (3):

> " SIR ALEXANDER COCKBURN, C.J., said (4) that the later authorities say you may open a door which is only fastened by a latch. He thought that was going a very long way, further than the American courts had done, but the authorities were limited to the case where the door is shut but can be opened without violence." **B**

I find it difficult to see what the real difference is, for present purposes, between a door which is momentarily opened but which is sought to be closed and can only be opened fully by violence, and a door which is shut and which can only be opened by violence.

However, in the course of the proceedings WINN, L.J., with his usual industry, **C** found the case of *Broughton* v. *Wilkerson* (5). The facts of that case were almost identical with the present; there the bailiff went to the respondent's house, he knocked at the outer front door, which was locked; the respondent came to the door, opened it and held it until they had an altercation; the appellant then took hold of the door, put his foot between it and the doorpost and shoved his shoulder against it to obtain entry; he did not produce the warrant or tell the **D** respondent what his business was, but the respondent knew him well and said: " You, you shan't come in " and shoved him out. SIR ALEXANDER COCKBURN, C.J. said (6):

> " The justices seem to give a wrong reason for their decision, but the decision was right. The officer had no right to force his way into the respondent's house, which was the respondent's castle. Whether the officer **E** was known or not this was illegal, and therefore he was not in the execution of his duty at all when he was assaulted. He seems to have provoked the assault. I think as he was clearly not in the execution of his duty, our judgment must be for the respondent."

LUSH, J., said (6): **F**

> " Every man's house is his castle. That has been settled long ago, and a bailiff cannot force his way inside to lay execution for a debt. It is impossible to read this case and say that the bailiff was in execution of his duty."

Further industry, this time on the part of counsel for the appellant, has found that that case has been approved in *Rossiter* v. *Conway* (7). That case differed **G** in certain immaterial respects; it was a constable executing a warrant of distress; that does not affect the matter, and instead of a foot between the door and the door post it was an arm. The court in that case held that the constable was not acting in the execution of his duty, and relied on and approved the earlier case of *Broughton* v. *Wilkerson* (5). Both those cases are binding on this court, and I have no doubt in those circumstances that this appeal must be **H** dismissed.

WINN, L.J.: I agree. The essential criterion in any such situation as there was in the present case is whether the householder has left a means of entrance available for the bailiff without the employment of any degree of force. As LORD PARKER, C.J., has said, this is a case where a foot was interposed **I** between the door post and the door itself. In the other two cases arms were

---

(2) (1867), L.R. 2 Q.B. 590.
(3) [1963] 3 All E.R. at p. 108; [1964] 1 Q.B. at p. 322.
(4) (1867), L.R. 2 Q.B. at p. 594.
(5) (1880), 44 J.P. 781.
(6) (1880), 44 J.P. at p. 481.
(7) (1893), 58 J.P. 350.

A thrust in, but it is perfectly clear that whilst in those cases some force was used, in neither of them was entrance being sought vi et armis.

ASHWORTH, J.: I agree.

Appeal dismissed. Leave to appeal to the House of Lords granted, the court certify-ing under s. 1 of the Administration of Justice Act, 1960, that a point of law of general
B *public importance was involved, viz., whether an officer executing civil process may lawfully enter the dwellinghouse of the execution debtor through an unfastened door if the execution debtor knowing the officer's business physically resists his entry.*

Solicitors: *Treasury Solicitor* for the appellant.

[*Reported by* PATRICIA JOHNSTON, *Barrister-at-Law.*]

C
———————

BLIGH *v.* MARTIN.

[CHANCERY DIVISION (Pennycuick, J.), February 14, 15, 16, 1968.]

Limitation of Action—Land—Adverse possession—Seasonal tenancy granted
D *by adverse possessor of field to tenant who, unknown to either party, had the documentary title to the freehold—User of field for cattle during winter months, when seasonal tenancy not current, not bringing adverse possession to an end—Mutual mistake—Seasonal tenancy extending also to other lands —Whether tenancy of field void—Whether adverse possessor established title by virtue of Limitation Act, 1939 (2 & 3 Geo. 6 c. 21), s. 10 (3).*

E An arable field of farmland was included in the parcels of a conveyance in 1945 to the defendant, though he did not become aware that this field had been conveyed to him until 1965. The same field was included in the parcels of a conveyance by the same grantor in 1948, and the plaintiff's title rested, so far as deeds were concerned, on this conveyance. A dispute having arisen in 1966 between the plaintiff and the defendant as to the
F ownership of the field, the plaintiff brought an action in which he claimed title by adverse possession, the periods of adverse possession in legal dispute being, as events happened, (i) a period from the end of 1954 to Lady Day, 1960, (ii) a period from then until Sept. 29, 1960 and (iii) the period there-after until Feb. 16, 1961. During the first of these three periods the defen-dant, as contractor under a contractual arrangement made with the plaintiff
G through the plaintiff's agents, did work of ploughing, sowing and harvesting the field; he also turned cattle out on the stubble during the four or five winter months, but the plaintiff's agents did not know of this. During the second period the defendant had a seasonal grazing tenancy or licence from the plaintiff of the estate that included the field, this being for six months of the year at a rent; the defendant continued to put cattle on the field in the winter. The third period was, for legal purposes, on the same
H footing as the winter season immediately preceding that second period. The defendant contended that the field ceased to be in the plaintiff's adverse possession at some time during the three periods.

Held: the plaintiff had established a possessory title by virtue of twelve years adverse possession within s. 10* of the Limitation Act, 1939, for the
I following reasons—

(a) because, as regards the first period the defendant's user of the field by turning cattle on to it did not amount to dispossessing the plaintiff and did not bring to an end the plaintiff's adverse possession (see p. 1161, letter A, post); and during the rest of the year the defendant's user of the land was as contractor to the plaintiff.

Leigh v. *Jack* ((1879), 5 Ex D. 264) and *Williams Brothers Direct Supply Stores, Ltd.* v. *Raftery* ([1957] 3 All E.R. 593) applied.

———————
* Section 10, so far as material, is set out at p. 1160, letters A to C, post.

A

(b) because, as regards the second period, the fact that the plaintiff was in receipt of rent from the defendant under the seasonal grazing tenancy had the consequence, by virtue of s. 10 (3) of the Act of 1939, that the plaintiff had adverse possession of the field, and his adverse possession did not cease in the winter months by reason of the defendant's putting cattle on the field (see p. 1161, letter H, and p. 1162, letter B, post); further, the mistake involved in the purported grant of the seasonal tenancy by the plaintiff, who had not the paper title to grant it, to the defendant, who had the paper title to the field, did not have the consequence that the seasonal tenancy of the field was void, since the purported tenancy extended also to the rest of the plaintiff's estate and the tenancy agreement could not be dissected for mutual mistake so as to be void as to part only of the land therein comprised (see p. 1162, letters E and F, post).

B

C

Bell v. *Lever Brothers, Ltd.* ([1931] All E.R. Rep. 1) distinguished.

[As to how an owner ceases to be in possession of land for the purposes of the limitation of actions, see 24 HALSBURY'S LAWS (3rd Edn.) 251, 252, para. 482; and for cases on the subject, see 32 DIGEST (Repl.) 530, 531, *1273-1283*.

As to the consequences of mistake in relation to contract, see 26 HALSBURY'S LAWS (3rd Edn.) 893, para. 1651, and ibid., pp. 898, 899, 901, paras. 1662, 1667.

D

For the Limitation Act, 1939, s. 4 (3), s. 9 (3), s. 10, see 13 HALSBURY'S STATUTES (2nd Edn.) 1164, 1171.]

Cases referred to:

Allen v. *England*, (1862), 3 F. & F. 49; 176 E.R. 22; 32 Digest (Repl.) 530, *1280*.

E

Bell v. *Lever Bros., Ltd.*, [1931] All E.R. Rep. 1; [1932] A.C. 161; 101 L.J.K.B. 129; 146 L.T. 258; 35 Digest (Repl.) 102, *63*.

Cooper v. *Phibbs*, (1867), L.R. 2 H.L. 149; 16 L.T. 678; 35 Digest (Repl.) 98, *28*.

Doe d. Baker v. *Coombes*, (1850), 9 C.B. 714; 19 L.J.C.P. 306; 15 L.T.O.S. 90; 137 E.R. 1073; 32 Digest (Repl.) 530, *1279*.

F

Leigh v. *Jack*, (1879), 5 Ex. D. 264; 49 L.J.Q.B. 220; 42 L.T. 463; 44 J.P. 488; 32 Digest (Repl.) 503, *1108*.

Williams Brothers Direct Supply Stores, Ltd. v. *Raftery*, [1957] 3 All E.R. 593; [1958] 1 Q.B. 159; [1957] 3 W.L.R. 931; 32 Digest (Repl.) 5081, *1132*.

Action.

G

This was an action brought by the plaintiff, Philip Augustus Bligh, against the defendant, Arthur Martin, by writ issued on Apr. 6, 1966, to establish a possessory title to a piece of land. He claimed (i) a declaration that he was entitled in fee simple to the piece of land consisting of 3,817 acres or thereabouts and being O.S. No. 446 in the parish of Horsham in the county of Sussex; (ii) a declaration that the defendant Arthur Martin, had no right title, estate or interest in or over any part of the land; (iii) an injunction to restrain the defendant by himself his servants, agents or workmen or otherwise, from entering on or otherwise trespassing on any part of the land; (iv) an injunction ordering the defendant to remove the poles which he had erected or caused to be erected on the land; and (v) damages. The facts are set out in the judgment.

H

Raymond Walton, Q.C., and *M. Essayan* for the plaintiff.
H. E. Francis, Q.C., and *I. L. R. Romer* for the defendant.

I

PENNYCUICK, J.: There is virtually no dispute as to the facts. No. 446 together with two other plots Nos. 447 and 447a make up a single large field. There has not at any material time been any division by hedge or otherwise between 446 and its neighbour 447. By a conveyance dated Sept. 24, 1945, Mrs. Katharine Mosse conveyed an estate known as Roffey House to the defendant. The parcels in this conveyance included No. 446, but not No. 447

A or 447a. The defendant did not become aware that this conveyance included No. 446 until 1965.

By a conveyance dated Feb. 10, 1948, Mrs. Mosse conveyed to one Reeder an estate known as Greenfields Farm, adjoining the Roffey House estate on its west side. The parcels in this conveyance likewise included No. 446. They also include Nos. 447 and 447a. Mrs. Mosse had in 1948 no title to No. 446 which

B she had already conveyed to the defendant. By a conveyance dated Feb. 16, 1949, Mr. Reeder conveyed the Greenfields Farm estate, including No. 446, to George Herbert Boxell and Alfred Boxell. By a conveyance dated Dec. 31, 1954, the Boxells conveyed the Greenfields Farm Estate, including No. 446, to Land and Estates Development Co., Ltd. By another conveyance of the same date that company conveyed the Greenfields Farm Estate, including

C No. 446 to the plaintiff.

The defendant admits that during the period from Feb. 16, 1949, the date of the conveyance to the Boxells, until Dec. 31, 1954, the date of the conveyances to the company and then to the plaintiff, he, the defendant, exercised no rights of ownership over No. 446. From Dec. 31, 1954, until the spring of 1960, the plaintiff farmed the Greenfields Farm estate through a firm of local agents,

D Messrs. King & Chasemore, of Horsham. The partner concerned was a Mr. Sherratt. The agents, on behalf of the plaintiff, made an arrangement with the defendant that the defendant should (a) occupy part of the estate as tenant or licensee at a rent for grazing and (b) carry out the usual operations of ploughing, sowing, harvesting and so forth on the other part of the estate as a contractor for reward, the rent due from him under (a) and the payments due to him under

E (b) to be set off against each other. No. 446 was, during this period, arable and was included in part (b).

The defendant's principal occupation is that of the proprietor of an institution at Roffey Place, but he is a practical farmer. During this period, the defendant performed a great deal of work on No. 446 in the capacity of a contractor, this work extending over the greater part (but by no means the whole) of each year.

F There was a variable interval—put by him at an average of four to five months—during which neither he nor anyone else was doing any work on No. 466. During this interval he from time to time put dry heifers on the stubble. They were able to find some fodder round the hedges. He regarded himself as doing this for the mutual benefit of himself and Messrs. King & Chasemore. Mr. Sherratt did not know he was doing it.

G Relations between the defendant and Messrs. King & Chasemore were at all times entirely co-operative and harmonious. In the later years of the period, some attempts were made, by under-sowing, to convert No. 446 to pasture, but these attempts were at first unsuccessful. Then in 1960 Messrs. King & Chasemore, on behalf of the plaintiff on the one hand and the defendant on the other hand, entered into a new arrangement. This consisted of a seasonal grazing

H tenancy or licence of the Greenfields estate as a whole, including No. 446, for a period of six months, running from Mar. 25 to Sept. 29, at a lump sum rent. During the winter, the defendant continued (in his own words) to run cattle through No. 446, where they found some food. This arrangement continued until 1965 inclusive, but was then determined. In 1965 the defendant did discover his paper title. In October, 1966, he placed poles along the boundary

I of No. 446 and has since continued to assert his title to No. 446. The plaintiff claims to have acquired a possessory title; and the present writ was issued on Apr. 6, 1966.

Evidence was given on behalf of the plaintiff by Mr. Sherratt and, on the other side, by the defendant himself. Each of these gentlemen was a demonstrably honest witness, and there is no issue of fact on which it is necessary to make any more detailed findings. The question which I have to determine is one of law.

I will now read some sections from the Limitation Act, 1939.

" 4 (3) No action shall be brought by any other person to recover any land after the expiration of twelve years from the date on which the right of action accrued to him or, if it first accrued to some person through whom he claims, to that person . . .

" 10 (1) No right of action to recover land shall be deemed to accrue unless the land is in the possession of some person in whose favour the period of limitation can run (hereafter in this section referred to as ' adverse possession ') and where under the foregoing provisions of this Act any such right of action is deemed to accrue on a certain date and no person is in adverse possession on that date, the right of action shall not be deemed to accrue unless and until adverse possession is taken of the land.   (2) Where a right of action to recover land has accrued and thereafter, before the right is barred, the land ceases to be in adverse possession, the right of action shall no longer be deemed to have accrued and no fresh right of action shall be deemed to accrue unless and until the land is again taken into adverse possession.   (3) For the purposes of this section . . . (b) receipt of rent under a lease by a person wrongfully claiming, in accordance with sub-s. (3) of the last foregoing section, the land in reversion shall be deemed to be adverse possession of the land."

Turning back to s. 9 (3), the person in question is described in these terms:

"... some person wrongfully claiming to be entitled to the land in reversion immediately expectant on the determination of the lease . . ."

It will be observed that the twelve-year period for the purpose of the statute began on Feb. 16, 1949, and accordingly ran until Feb. 16, 1961.   This brings in the first summer season of the new arrangement, i.e., the season of 1960.

It is not in dispute that the Boxells took and retained adverse possession of plot No. 446 within the meaning of s. 10.   The question is whether, at some time between Dec. 31, 1954, and Feb. 16, 1961, the land ceased to be in adverse possession for the purpose of s. 10 (2).   For this purpose it is necessary to consider separately, first the period from Dec. 31, 1954, to Lady Day in 1960— I pause to observe that it is accepted by counsel for the defendant that no difference can be made between the earlier years of that period and the last two years of the period—second, the period from Mar. 25, 1960, to Sept. 29, 1960, and, third, the period from Sept. 31, 1960, to Feb. 16, 1961.

1. Possession is a matter of fact depending on all the particular circumstances of a case.   In very many cases possession cannot, in the nature of things, be continuous from day to day, and it is well established that possession may continue to subsist notwithstanding that there are intervals, and sometimes long intervals, between the acts of user; see on this point *Leigh* v. *Jack* (1), and in particular per BRAMWELL, L.J., (2)

"... in order to defeat a title by dispossessing the former owner, acts must be done which are inconsistent with his enjoyment of the soil for the purposes for which he intended to use it . . ."

and, for a more recent authority, see *Williams Brothers Direct Supply Stores, Ltd.* v. *Raftery* (3).

In the case of farmland, this must habitually be the position; for example, as regards arable land during the winter months.   In the present case, I feel no doubt that the plaintiff should be regarded as having remained in possession of No. 446 continuously throughout this period.   The defendant was on No. 446 primarily in the capacity of a contractor employed by the plaintiff.   His own use of the land by turning heifers on to it during winter months falls, it seems to me, far short of dispossessing the plaintiff.   Possession is, from its nature, exclusive in this connexion.   There is no question of concurrent possession.   It would, I think, be quite wrong to regard the owner of arable farmland as having

---

(1) (1879), 5 Ex.D. 264.   (2) (1879), 5 Ex.D. at p. 273.
                (3) [1957] 3 All E.R. 593; [1958] 1 Q.B. 139.

A   been dispossessed of that land because during certain winter months he personally
makes no use of it and some other person puts cattle on it.

    Counsel for the defendant, cited *Allen* v. *England* (4). In that case, Erle, C.J.,
gave a short judgment in these terms (5):

B
> " It may be taken that the plaintiff had the beneficial occupation for more
> than twenty years, and if that will give him a title, I will give him leave
> to move. But, in my judgment, every time Cox put his foot on the land
> it was so far in his possession that the statute would begin to run from the
> time when he was last upon it."

    Counsel for the defendant relied on that case as an authority for saying that
whenever the lawful owner puts foot on land in the possession of another, then
C   he is to be treated as having taken possession himself, so that the adverse posses-
sion ceases. I do not think that that case is an authority for such a proposition.
Allen v. *England* (4) is a case of permissive user of a garden where the owner
paid periodical visits to the garden. In those circumstances, the way in which
Erle, C.J., put it was no doubt correct; but the way in which he puts it is not,
I think, in point in the ordinary case of adverse possession. In that ordinary case,
D   one must find that the true owner took possession in the ordinary sense of that
word, to the exclusion of the wrongful occupier. I was referred on this point
to a number of cases. I shall not go through them, but will mention as an instance
that of *Doe d. Baker* v. *Coombes* (6). I conclude, then, that as regards the first
period, the plaintiff remained in adverse possession of No. 446 and that there was
no cessation of that adverse possession.

E   2. The summer period in 1960 presents what seems to me the real difficulty
in this case. The question appears to be entirely novel. During this period, the
position was that the defendant was in physical possession of the plot under a
tenancy agreement granted by the plaintiff, to whom the defendant paid rent.
Counsel for the plaintiff contended that the position is covered by s. 10 (3) (*b*),
of the Limitation Act, 1939, which I have read. That provision is no doubt
F   primarily addressed to the state of affairs in which the land is already in the
possession of a tenant when the adverse possession begins; that is to say, the first
act of adverse possession is the receipt of rent by the wrongful claimant from the
tenant. The provision would have no particular significance in the ordinary case
where the wrongful claimant first takes physical possession himself and then lets
the land to a tenant, since in that case the possession of the tenant is no less
adverse to that of the rightful owner than is the possession of the wrongful
G   claimant. It seems to me, however, that on the plain meaning of the words used,
the provision does cover that position. There is receipt of rent under a lease
by the person who wrongfully claims to be entitled to the land in reversion
immediately expectant on the determination of the lease, and none the less so
by reason that he granted the lease himself. If that is the proper construction of
H   sub-s. (3), then it must cover the altogether exceptional position in which the
tenant who pays the rent to the wrongful claimant is himself the rightful owner.
I do not see any reason in principle why this should not be so. Indeed, as regards
the freehold interest, it appears to be a striking instance of adverse possession.

    Counsel for the defendant conceded that s. 10 (3), applies where the land is
already in the possession of a tenant when the adverse possession begins, but he
I   says the subsection has no application where the wrongful claimant has taken
possession himself before granting a tenancy. On this footing he goes on to contend that the only relevant possession during the six-month summer period was
that of the plaintiff himself; and that, of course, would represent the cessation
of adverse possession within the meaning of sub-s. (2). I do not think that that is
a natural construction to put on sub-s. (3).

---

(4) (1862), 3 F. & F. 49.
(5) (1862), 3 F. & F. at p. 52.
(6) (1850), 9 C.B. 714.

Both counsel pointed out that where land is subject to a tenancy, the landlord **A** and the tenant have each, in correct legal parlance, possession of the land, though in different senses. Counsel then proceeded to draw opposing conclusions from this position. It seems to me that, for the purpose of adverse possession of freehold land under the Limitation Act, 1939, the land must be regarded as in the possession of one or other of the two parties concerned, i.e., the landlord or the tenant; and it seems to me that sub-s. (3) designates the landlord as the relevant **B** party for this purpose. On that footing it follows that the plaintiff, having been in receipt of rent during this summer period, remained throughout the period in adverse possession of the land.

Counsel for the defendant, however, raised one further contention. He pointed out that where one finds a purported grant of a tenancy by a wrongful claimant to the rightful owner, that tenancy is void. He referred on this point to *Bell* v. **C** *Lever Brothers, Ltd.* (7), and in particular to the speech of LORD ATKIN (8). There, LORD ATKIN, after referring to *Cooper* v. *Phibbs* (9), went on to stress that in such a case the agreement for a lease was not merely voidable but void. I have no doubt that this principle would apply here if No. 446 had been the only land comprised in the tenancy granted by the plaintiff to the defendant. In fact, however, the tenancy was of the whole of the Greenfields Farm Estate, and **D** plot No. 446 represents less than one-tenth of the total area of the Greenfields Farm Estate. In those circumstances, counsel for the defendant did not seek to contend that the entire tenancy agreement was void. What he did contend was that the agreement was void as regards No. 446. He did not cite any authority for dissecting the agreement in this way, and I cannot see any principle on which the agreement could be so dissected. The ground of the decision in *Bell* v. *Lever* **E** *Brothers, Ltd.* (7) and *Cooper* v. *Phibbs* (9) was mutual mistake. Mutual mistake may be a ground for setting aside a contract as a whole, or for certain other relief; for example, refusal of specific performance—see generally 26 HALSBURY'S LAWS OF ENGLAND (3rd Edn.), pp. 901 and 905—but there appears to be no ground for saying that, where there is a mistake in the subject matter which is not fundamental, then the contract can in some way be broken up and re-drawn so as to **F** give effect to the true nature of the subject matter. Unless this tenancy agreement can be regarded as void, there can, so far as I can see, be nothing to exclude the operation of s. 10 (3).

3. The position as regards the short period after the summer season of 1960 is the same as that in respect of the winter season immediately preceding that summer season, and no separate argument has been directed to me on it. **G**

For the reasons which I have sought to give, it appears to me that the plaintiff has made out a good possessory title to No. 446, and I propose to make a declaration to that effect.

Declaration accordingly.

Solicitors: *Nabarro, Nathanson & Co.* (for the plaintiff); *Collyer-Bristow & Co.*, agents for *Eager & Sons*, Horsham (for the defendant). **H**

[*Reported by* JENIFER SANDELL, *Barrister-at-Law.*]

I

---

(7) [1931] All E.R. Rep. 1; [1932] A.C. 161.
(8) [1931] All E.R. Rep. at p. 28; [1932] A.C. at p. 218.
(9) (1867), L.R. 2 H.L. 149.

A

THE QUEEN OF THE SOUTH.

CORPS AND ANOTHER (TRADING AS CORPS BROTHERS) *v.* OWNERS
OF PADDLE STEAMER QUEEN OF THE SOUTH. PORT OF LONDON
AUTHORITY (INTERVENERS).

B

[PROBATE, DIVORCE AND ADMIRALTY DIVISION (Brandon, J.), October 3, 16,
20, 23, November 17, 1967.]

*Admiralty—Appraisement and sale—Harbour authority's claims for rates
incurred by ship—Authority given to Admiralty marshal to pay rates and
include expenditure in his expenses of sale—Procedure in future cases—
Port of London (Consolidation) Act, 1920 (10 & 11 Geo. 5 c. clxxiii), s. 75
—R.S.C., Ord. 75, r. 12 (1).*

C

*Admiralty—Jurisdiction—Action in rem—Claim in contract arising out of
agreement to render services to ship by use of motor boats—Arrest of ship—
Whether plaintiffs entitled to proceed in rem—Interpretation Act, 1889
(52 & 53 Vict. c. 63), s. 1 (1)—Administration of Justice Act, 1956 (4 & 5
Eliz. 2 c. 46), s. 1 (1) (h), s. 8 (1).*

D

In June and July, 1967, the plaintiffs, a firm carrying on the business
of motor boat proprietors, licensed lightermen and watermen, rendered
services to the Queen of the South, a paddle steamer owned by the defendants, under an oral contract. The services consisted of mooring and
unmooring the ship and conveying her crew to the ship and the shore,
the plaintiffs providing the necessary motor boats and men. Meanwhile,

E

the ship incurred various port rates payable to the Port of London Authority.
On July 31, 1967, the plaintiffs issued a writ, and on the same day served
it and arrested the ship. Since that arrest, the ship had continued to
incur mooring charges. In September, 1967, the plaintiffs filed notice of
motion, asking for judgment in default on their claim, and for an order
for the appraisement and sale of the ship. Three days later, the Port

F

of London Authority, as interveners, purported to seize the ship by virtue
of their powers under s. 75* of the Port of London (Consolidation) Act,
1920, in order to enforce payment of the rates due to them. The plaintiffs
later filed a statement of claim, and the interveners filed notice of motion
asking for the dismissal of the plaintiffs' claim for want of jurisdiction, or
alternatively for various other orders designed to protect their position in

G

respect of the recovery of their charges. By the Administration of Justice
Act, 1956, s. 1 (1) (h)†, the Admiralty jurisdiction of the High Court included
jurisdiction to hear and determine any claim arising out of any agreement
relating, among other matters, to the use or hire of a ship; and by s. 8 (1)‡
of that Act, the expression " ship " included a motor boat, and by the
Interpretation Act, 1889, s. 1 (1)§, the singular included the plural.

H

Held: (i) as the plaintiffs' services had been rendered by the use of their
motor boats suitably manned for the work to be done, the court had jurisdiction to entertain their claim, such jurisdiction being conferred by s. 1
(1) (h) of the Act of 1956, in conjunction with s. 8 (1) thereof and with s. 1 (1)
of the Interpretation Act, 1889; and in the circumstances the court would
pronounce for the plaintiffs' claim (see p. 1168, letter I, and p. 1169,
letter B, post).

I

(ii) (a) the court had power to authorise the Admiralty marshal to pay a
claim of a dock authority for rates out of the proceeds of sale of the ship,

---

* Section 75 is set out at p. 1169, letters G to I, post.
† Section 1 (1), so far as material, is set out at p. 1167, letters H and I, post.
‡ Section 8 (1), so far as material, is set out at p. 1168, letter C, post.
§ Section 1 (1), so far as material, provides: " In this Act and every Act passed after
the year 1850 . . . unless the contrary intention appears . . . (b) words in the singular
shall include the plural . . ."

where that would be for the benefit of all those interested in the ship in
order that she might be sold advantageously; and, since on the facts in the
present case it would be for the benefit of all persons so interested that the
marshal should be so authorised, in order that the ship might be sold free
from the statutory possessory lien of the interveners and their rights of
detention and sale, the court would authorise the marshal to pay the interveners' rates, the interveners giving a written undertaking to the court
not to exercise their rights of detention and sale (see p. 1174, letter A
post).

The Parita ([1964] 1 Lloyd's Rep. 199) and The Westport (No. 2) ([1965]
2 All E.R. 447) applied.

(b) the authority so conferred on the marshal would extend to paying
the interveners' rates since the arrest of the ship up to the date of delivery
of the ship to the purchasers, but the amount so paid (which the marshal
would treat as expenses payable out of the proceeds of sale) was not to
exceed the net proceeds of sale after deduction of his other expenses (see
p. 1174, letter C, post).

Semble: (i) the interveners' right of detention was of such a character
that it could, with their consent at any rate, be transferred from the ship
herself to a fund in court constituted from the proceeds of sale of the ship
(see p. 1173, letter E, post).

The Sierra Nevada ((1932), 42 Lloyd L.R. at p. 312); The Emilie Millon
([1905] 2 K.B. 817) and The Countess, Mersey Docks & Harbour Board v. Hay,
([1923] A.C. 345, 490) considered.

(ii) the procedure outlined at p. 1174, letter G, post, should be followed
in future cases where similar questions arise.

[As to Admiralty jurisdiction in actions in rem and extent thereof, see SUPPLE-
MENT to 1 HALSBURY'S LAWS (3rd Edn.) paras. 88, 125; and for cases on the
subject, see 1 DIGEST (Repl.) 120-122, 67-78.

As to priority of maritime liens, see 35 HALSBURY'S LAWS (3rd Edn.) 788,
para. 1214; and for cases on the subject, see 42 DIGEST (Repl.) 1102, 9161-9165.

For the Interpretation Act, 1889, s. 1, see 24 HALSBURY'S STATUTES (2nd Edn.)
206.

For the Administration of Justice Act, 1956, s. 1, s. 8, see 36 HALSBURY'S
STATUTES (3rd Edn.) 3, 17.]

Cases referred to:

Acrux, The, [1962] 1 Lloyd's Rep. 405; Digest (Cont. Vol. A) 6, 1644a.
Countess, The, Mersey Docks & Harbour Board v. Hay, [1923] A.C. 345, 490;
    92 L.J.P. 65; 129 L.T. 325; 16 Asp. M.L.C. 161; 42 Digest (Repl.)
    1099, 9141.
Emilie Millon, The, [1905] 2 K.B. 817; 75 L.J.K.B. 31; 93 L.T. 692; 10
    Asp. M.L.C. 162; 42 Digest (Repl.) 1105, 9217.
Ousel, The, [1957] 1 Lloyd's Rep. 151.
Parita, The, [1964] 1 Lloyd's Rep. 199.
Sea Spray, The, [1907] P. 133; 76 L.J.P. 48; 96 L.T. 792; 10 Asp. M.L.C. 462;
    42 Digest (Repl.) 1103, 9187.
Sierra Nevada, The, (1932), 42 Lloyd L.R. 309.
Spermina, The, (1923), 17 Lloyd L.R. 17, 52, 76, 109.
Westport (No. 2), The, British Mexican Petroleum Co., Ltd. v. M/S or Vessel
    Westport, [1965] 2 All E.R. 447; [1965] 1 W.L.R. 871; [1965] 1 Lloyd's
    Rep. 549; Digest (Cont. Vol. B) 6, 915a.

Motions.

These were two motions in an action in rem, the action being brought by the
plaintiffs, Alan James Corps and Rodney Francis Corps, trading as Corps Bros.,
against the defendants, Coastal Steam Packet Co., Ltd., the owners of the paddle
steamer Queen of the South, to recover the costs of services rendered by them

A to that ship. The first motion was by the plaintiffs for judgment in default of appearance and for an order for the appraisement and sale of the ship   The second motion was by the Port of London Authority, as interveners, asking for various orders set out in the judgment at p. 1171, letters A to G post, they having purported to seize the ship under their statutory powers in order to enforce payment of various port rates due to them.   The facts are set out in

B the judgment.

The authorities and cases noted below* were cited during the argument in addition to the cases referred to in the judgment.

D. H. Hene for the plaintiffs.

Michael Thomas and *A. P. Clarke* for the interveners, the Port of London Authority.

C The defendants did not appear and were not represented.

Cur. adv. vult.

Nov. 17. **BRANDON, J.,** read the following judgment: The court has before it two motions in an action in rem brought by watermen against the paddle steamer Queen of the South to recover the costs of services rendered by

D them to that ship. The first motion is by the plaintiffs for judgment in default of appearance and for an order for the appraisement and sale of the ship. The second motion is by the Port of London Authority, who have intervened in the action, asking for various orders the nature of which I shall describe later. Two main questions arise on these motions: first, whether the plaintiffs' claim is of such a kind as to entitle them to bring an action in rem in respect of it; second,

E if so, what, if any, order should be made to avoid any difficulty which might otherwise arise from the fact that the interveners claim a paramount right to detain and sell the vessel under their statutory powers in order to recover rates owing to them.

The facts and circumstances giving rise to these motions are these. The plaintiffs, Alan James Corps and Rodney Francis Corps, trading as Corps Brothers,

F are a firm carrying on the business of motor boat proprietors, licensed lightermen and watermen. The work which they do in this capacity includes among other things ship mooring and boat attendance. Their office is at 21, Clement's Road, Bermondsey, and they do their work mainly on the River Thames. The Queen of the South is a British paddle steamer registered at the Port of Glasgow. She is owned by Coastal Steam Packet Co., Ltd., who were employing her during

G the summer of 1967 as a passenger vessel for day trips from London. For this purpose they appointed as managers A. E. Martin & Co., Ltd., of 52-53, Crutched Friars, in the city of London. In June, 1967, an oral contract was made between Mr. Eldridge, an employee of A. E. Martin & Co., Ltd., and the plaintiffs, by which it was agreed that the plaintiffs should whenever necessary moor and unmoor the ship at her berth in the London river and convey her crew between

H the ship and the shore. It was understood that the plaintiffs would provide for these purposes the necessary motor boats and men. In pursuance of that agreement, on various dates between June 17 and July 24, 1967, the plaintiffs rendered services to the ship. These consisted of mooring and unmooring the ship while she was at Harrison's wharf, Purfleet; mooring and unmooring the

---

I * Roscoe's Admiralty Practice (5th Edn.) 283; 1 British Shipping Laws (Admiralty Practice, 1964 Edn.), paras. 387, 1561, 1570; 35 Halsbury's Laws (3rd Edn. 135, para. 197; 787, para. 1211, note (*p*); 792, para. 1221, note (*l*); *The Harmonie*, (1841), 1 Wm. Rob. 178; *The Constaf*, (1862), Lush. 506; *The Charles Amelia*, (1868), L.R. 2 A. & E. 330; *Castrique v. Imrie*, [1861-73] All E.R. Rep. 508; (1870), L.R. 4 H.L. 414; *The St. Lawrence*, (1880), 5 P.D. 250; *The Heinrich Bjorn*, (1883), 8 P.D. 151; *The Gettysburg*, (1885), 5 Asp. M.L.C. 347; *The Cella*, (1888), 13 P.D. 82; *The Veritas*, [1900-03] All E.R. Rep. 501; [1901] P. 304; *The Tergeste*, [1903] P. 26; *The James W. Elwell*, [1921] P. 351; *The Ile de Ceylan*, [1922] All E.R. Rep. 264, [1922] P. 256, *The Russland*, [1924] P. 55; *The Arantzazu Mendi*, [1939] 1 All E.R. 719; [1939] A.C. 256; *The Mari Chandris*, [1942] P. 94; *The Zafiro*, [1959] 2 All E.R. 537; [1960] P. 1; *The Skylark*, [1965] 3 All E.R. 380; [1965] P. 454; *The Charger*, [1966] 3 All E.R. 117.

ship and conveying ship's crew, catering staff and repairers' men while the ship A
was at Tower buoys; and mooring and unmooring the ship and conveying her
crew while she was at Erith buoys. The total sum which became due to the
plaintiffs from the defendants in respect of those services was £290 3s.

Meanwhile the Queen of the South incurred various port rates payable to
the interveners. These rates up to the end of July, 1967, consisted of the following:—for the period June 10 to July 15, mooring charges £2 7s. 6d.; for the B
period June 24 to July 12, pier tolls £275; and for the period June 27 to July 10,
river tonnage dues, £40 4s., making a total of £317 11s. 6d. An account dated
July 26, 1967, relating to the first and second of these three items and also to
water supplied to the ship, was sent by the interveners to the ship's managers,
and should, in the ordinary course of post, have been received by them about
July 27, 1967. On July 31, 1967, the plaintiffs issued the writ in this action C
and on the same day served the writ and arrested the ship at Erith buoys. Since
that arrest the ship has continued to incur mooring charges at the rate of
£10 0s. 8d. per week. On Sept. 25, 1967, the plaintiffs filed notice of motion, asking
for judgment in default on their claim with costs, and for an order for the appraisement and sale of the ship. On Sept. 28, 1967, the interveners purported to
seize the ship under their statutory powers in order to enforce payment of the D
rates due to them. They gave effect to their intention by placing in a prominent
position on the starboard side of the wheelhouse a notice of seizure reading as
follows:

"To the master and owners of the Paddle Steamer Queen of the South
and all whom it may concern. Take notice that I, Walter Howard Thorburn,
an officer of the Port of London Authority duly authorised in that behalf E
by virtue of the power contained in the Port of London (Consolidation)
Act, 1920, s. 75, have this day seized the Paddle Steamer Queen of the
South and the tackle and furniture aboard now lying at Erith charges
of £289 5s. 1d. due and demanded remaining unpaid and further take notice
that if the said Paddle Steamer Queen of the South and the tackle and
furniture on board be not redeemed by the payment to the Port of London F
Authority of the said sum of £289 5s. 1d. within five days of this day of
seizure, I, Walter Howard Thorburn may sell the same and make of the
proceeds of that sale a sum in reduction of the amount due in respect of the
said rate."

That notice was signed by Mr. Thorburn on behalf of the interveners. G

On Oct. 3, 1967, the plaintiffs' motion came on for hearing before me. It
then appeared that the plaintiffs had not filed a statement of claim as required
by R.S.C., Ord. 75, r. 21 (3). Since the question whether there was jurisdiction
to entertain the plaintiffs' claim in rem was plainly going to arise, I thought that
it was important that a statement of claim setting out clearly the facts relied
on should be filed in accordance with this rule. I also thought that further H
evidence in support of the claim might well be needed. For these reasons, as
well as because I was told of the actual or impending intervention by the Port
of London Authority, I ordered that the motion should be adjourned. The
Port of London Authority in fact appeared as interveners on the same day,
Oct. 3, 1967, after obtaining leave to do so under R.S.C., Ord. 75, r. 17. On
Oct. 11, 1967, the plaintiffs filed a statement of claim, and on the same day the I
interveners filed notice of motion asking for the dismissal of the plaintiffs' claim
for want of jurisdiction, or alternatively for various other orders designed to
protect their position in respect of the recovery of their charges. The plaintiffs'
adjourned motion and the interveners' motion were heard by me together on
Oct. 16, 20 and 23. The plaintiffs' motion was supported by an affidavit
of Mr. Peters sworn on Sept. 25, 1967, proving service of the writ, a certificate of non-appearance dated Oct. 13, 1967, and an affidavit of Mr. Alan
James Corps, one of the plaintiffs, sworn on Oct. 10, 1967, verifying the facts on

A which the claim was founded. Subsequently Mr. Corps' affidavit evidence was at my suggestion amplified by oral evidence from him, so that the court could have before it the precise details of the work done by the plaintiffs. The interveners' motion was supported by three affidavits, one of Mr. Le Mesurier sworn on Oct. 3, 1967, one of Mr. Thorburn on Oct. 13, 1967, and one of Mr. White sworn on Oct. 23, 1967.

B I shall deal first with the question of jurisdiction. The plaintiffs' claim has been put forward in the indorsement of the writ and in the statement of claim as a claim for necessaries. I venture to think that the legal advisers of the plaintiffs, in describing and pleading the claim on this basis, did not have clearly present to their minds the terms of the Administration of Justice Act, 1956, on which the jurisdiction of the court to entertain actions in rem now depends,

C but were rather still living in the era prior to the coming into force of that Act, when the jurisdiction concerned depended on earlier provisions in the Supreme Court of Judicature (Consolidation) Act, 1925.

The history of the matter so far as jurisdiction is concerned is this. By s. 6 of the Admiralty Court Act, 1840, the High Court of Admiralty was given jurisdiction over claims for necessaries supplied to foreign ships,

D whether within the body of a county or on the high seas. By s. 5 of the Admiralty Court Act, 1861, the same court was given further jurisdiction over claims for necessaries supplied to any ship elsewhere than in the port to which she belonged, unless at the time of institution of the cause any owner or part-owner was domiciled in England or Wales. By s. 33 of the Act of 1861, the jurisdiction of the court could be exercised either in rem or in per-

E sonam. By the Supreme Court of Judicature Acts, 1873 and 1875, all the jurisdiction of the High Court of Admiralty, including its jurisdiction over claims for necessaries under the Admiralty Court Acts, 1840 and 1861, was transferred to the High Court, and its exercise assigned to the Probate, Divorce and Admiralty Division. Section 6 of the Admiralty Court Act, 1840, and s. 5 of the Admiralty Court Act, 1861, were repealed by the Supreme Court of

F Judicature (Consolidation) Act, 1925, and their combined effect, so far as jurisdiction over claims for necessaries is concerned, was re-enacted in s. 22 (a) (vii) of that Act. The power to exercise the jurisdiction either in rem or in personam was continued by s. 33 (2) of the Act of 1925. In the result, the Act of 1925 preserved but did not extend the previous Admiralty jurisdiction in respect of necessaries. Section 22 and s. 33 of the Supreme Court of Judicature

G (Consolidation) Act, 1925, were repealed by the Administration of Justice Act, 1956, and the Admiralty jurisdiction of the High Court was re-defined, with various extensions, by s. 1 and s. 3 of that Act. Section 1 of the Act of 1956, so far as material, provides:

"(1) The Admiralty jurisdiction of the High Court shall be as follows, that is to say, jurisdiction to hear and determine any of the following ques-

H tions of claims . . . (h) any claim arising out of any agreement relating to the carriage of goods in a ship or to the use or hire of a ship; . . . (m) any claim in respect of goods or materials supplied to a ship for her operation or maintenance; (n) any claim in respect of the construction, repair or equipment of a ship or dock charges or dues; . . . (p) any claim by a master, shipper, charterer or agent in respect of disbursements made on account of a ship;

I . . ."

Then, after listing other specific claims, the subsection ends with the words

"together with any other jurisdiction which either was vested in the High Court of Admiralty immediately before the date of commencement of the Supreme Court of Judicature Act, 1873 (that is to say, Nov. 1, 1875) or is conferred by or under an Act which came into operation on or after that date on the High Court as being a court with Admiralty jurisdiction . . ."

Section 3 (4) of the Act of 1956, as amended by the County Courts Act, 1959, **A**
s. 204 and Sch. 3, provides:

> "In the case of any such claim as is mentioned in paras. (*d*) to (*r*) of
> sub-s. (1) of s. 1 of this Act, being a claim arising in connection with a ship,
> where the person who would be liable on the claim in an action in personam
> was, when the cause of action arose, the owner or charterer of, or in posses-
> sion or in control of, the ship, the Admiralty jurisdiction of the High Court **B**
> . . . may (whether the claim gives rise to a maritime lien on the ship or not)
> be invoked by an action in rem against—(*a*) that ship, if at the time when
> the action is brought it is beneficially owned as respects all the shares therein
> by that person; . . ."

Section 8 (1) of the Act of 1956, which, with s. 1 to s. 7 forms Part I of the Act,
provides: **C**

> "In this Part of this Act, unless the context otherwise requires,—' ship '
> includes any description of vessel used in navigation; . . ."

It will be observed that claims for necessaries do not figure at all, as such, among
the claims specified in the lettered paragraphs of s. 1 (1) of the Act of 1956.
It appears, however, although I have not heard any argument on the subject **D**
and, therefore, express no concluded opinion on it, that the effect of the sweeping-
up provisions at the end of s. 1 (1) is to preserve to the court, independently of,
and concurrently with, any jurisdiction specifically conferred by para. (*a*) to
para. (*s*), the same jurisdiction over claims for, inter alia, necessaries, as was
formerly conferred by the Acts of 1840, 1861, 1873 and 1875, and 1925.

Assuming this to be correct, the question which arises for decision in the **E**
present case can conveniently be divided into two parts. First, would the court
have had jurisdiction over the plaintiffs' claim under the Act of 1925? If so,
then it appears that it has the same jurisdiction, by virtue of the sweeping-up
provisions of s. 1 (1) under the Act of 1956. Second, has the court such jurisdiction by virtue of any of the lettered paragraphs (*a*) to (*s*) of s. 1 (1) of the
Act of 1956? **F**

So far as the first part of the question is concerned, counsel for the plaintiffs
did not contend that the court would have had jurisdiction under the Act of 1925,
and, therefore, had it by virtue of the sweeping-up provisions of s. 1 (1), under
the Act of 1956. He did not say in terms why he did not so contend. I take it,
however, that at least one reason was because, although there was no direct
evidence that the company which owned the Queen of the South was an English **G**
company, he knew this in fact to be the case, and knew, therefore, that the
proviso relating to English domicil in s. 22 (1) (vii) of the Act of 1925 would, on
any view of the sweeping-up provisions, prevent the court having jurisdiction.
So far as the second part of the question is concerned, counsel for the plaintiffs
contended that there was jurisdiction under one or more of paras. (*h*), (*m*) and (*p*)
of s. 1 (1) of the Act of 1956. This was disputed by counsel for the interveners. **H**
I will deal with para. (*h*) first. Counsel for the plaintiffs argued that the
agreement between the plaintiffs and the ship's managers, under which the
services claimed for were rendered, was "an agreement relating to the use or hire
of a ship" within the meaning of the paragraph. He said that the plaintiffs'
services were rendered by the use of their motor boats suitably manned for the
work to be done; that, by s. 8 (1) of the Act of 1956, the expression "ship" **I**
included a motor boat; and that, by s. 1 of the Interpretation Act, 1889, the
singular included the plural. Therefore, he said, the agreement came within the
paragraph. Counsel for the interveners, in disputing these arguments, sought
to draw a distinction between an agreement relating to the use of a ship, and
an agreement relating to the rendering of services in the course of which a ship
was used. He said that the former was within para. (*h*), but the latter was not.
He further said that the agreement in the present case was in the second category.
I did not think that his argument based on this distinction was convincing.

A I can see that there might be an agreement for services, in the course of which there was only some incidental and minor use of a ship, which it might be inappropriate to describe as an agreement relating to the use of a ship. In the present case, however, it seems to me clear, on the written and oral evidence before me, that the whole of the services rendered by the plaintiffs were based on the use of motor boats owned and operated by them. It is true that in some cases the men

B engaged in mooring and unmooring did their work on a quay or on a buoy; but they were landed on the quay or on the buoy from a motor boat and taken off again by the same means. In these circumstances, I have come to the conclusion that the argument of counsel for the plaintiffs that the claim comes within para. (h) is well founded, and I hold that the court has jurisdiction to entertain it on that ground.

C That conclusion makes it unnecessary to decide whether the claim comes also within para. (m) or para. (p). As at present advised, I cannot see how it could come within para. (p). Further, I see considerable difficulty about holding that it comes within para. (m). On this point, counsel for the interveners argued with force that para. (m) related to contracts of sale or hire, under which the property in, or possession of, the goods or materials supplied passed to the shipowners

D or their servants, and did not extend to contracts for work and labour under which neither property nor possession was transferred. Against that, counsel for the plaintiffs argued that the paragraph covered also contracts for work and labour in connexion with which goods (which for this purpose he said included motor boats) were provided or made available, even though neither the property in nor the possession of such goods was transferred. I was not impressed with the

E latter argument, anyhow in relation to the facts of this case. Since it is not necessary, however, to decide the point, I do not propose to express a concluded opinion on it.

I turn now to the second question raised by these motions. That is, what order, if any, should be made to meet the difficulties arising from the actual or potential assertion by the interveners of their statutory rights to detain or sell

F the vessel in order to enforce payment of rates. The rights concerned are given by the Port of London (Consolidation) Act, 1920. Section 75 provides:

" In case all or any part of any rate in respect of any vessel is not paid on demand to the officer of the Port Authority authorised by them to demand and receive the same then and in every such case the Port Authority may recover such rate or part thereof from the owner or master of such vessel

G summarily or in any court of competent jurisdiction or the officer to whom such rate or part thereof ought to have been paid taking such assistance as he thinks necessary may at any time or at any place within the limits of the Port of London, seize and detain such vessel (whether laden or empty) and the tackle and furniture on board thereof until payment of such rate or part thereof together with reasonable charges for such seizure and detention

H and if such vessel tackle and furniture shall not be redeemed within five days after such seizure such officer may sell the same rendering to the owner thereof on demand the surplus if any of the proceeds of such sale after deducting therefrom the amount of such rate or part thereof so payable as aforesaid and reimbursing himself the expense incurred by him under the provisions of this section. Provided always that no such officer shall be

I answerable for any loss, injury or damage which may happen to such distress while in his custody unless the same shall happen through his wilful or gross negligent act or default."

Section 84 provides:

" Before selling (except in case of emergency) any vessel or goods for the purpose of recovery of rates and expenses or either of them under the powers contained in the foregoing provisions of this Act, the Port Authority shall give to the owner of any vessel or to the owner or consignee of any goods

forty-eight hours' notice of their intention to sell the same by posting a   A
prepaid letter addressed to such owner or consignee at the place (if any)
in the United Kingdom where he carries on business or at his last known
place of abode in the United Kingdom or if such owner or consignee or his
last place of business or abode should not be known to the Port Authority
then before selling any vessel or goods aforesaid a like notice shall be exhibited
by the Port Authority for forty-eight hours at the head office of the Port   B
Authority."

So far the interveners have only taken steps to exercise their right of detention.
They have done this by placing on the ship on Sept. 28, 1967, the notice of
seizure to which I referred earlier.

It has been argued for the plaintiffs, first, that the interveners had no right
to seize the ship at all while she was under the arrest of the court in the plaintiffs'   C
action, and, second, that in any case the placing of a notice on the ship was not
an actual seizure. I do not accept either of these arguments. As to the first
point, I do not see why the interveners should not exercise their statutory
right of detention even while the ship is under arrest provided that they do not
interfere with the marshal's custody, which it is not suggested that they have
done. To hold otherwise would involve implying an unnecessary qualification   D
in s. 75 of the Act of 1920. As to the second point, I think that, having regard
to practical considerations, the placing of the notice was an overt act sufficient
for the purpose for which it was intended. Accepting, however, in favour of the
interveners that there was a lawful and effective seizure of the ship by them on
Sept. 28, 1967, such seizure could only, by the terms of s. 75, be a seizure in
respect of the mooring charges of £2 7s. 6d. and pier tolls of £275 mentioned   E
earlier, which were demanded by letter to the agents dated July 26, 1967. It
could not be a seizure in respect of any other rates then due but not demanded,
or becoming due thereafter. The interveners have not at any time taken any
steps to exercise their right of sale, either in respect of the particular rates just
referred to, or any other rates. The fact that the interveners have not yet taken
steps to exercise certain powers, however, does not mean that they may not do   F
so later. Subject to the making of the necessary demand under s. 75, and the
giving of the necessary notice under s. 84, it seems that the interveners could at
any time in the future take steps to detain and sell the ship in respect of all rates
which are now, or may hereafter become, due to them.

This being the nature of the rights which the interveners have already exercised, or may in the future exercise, against the ship, the purpose of their inter-   G
vention is, so I understand it, two-fold. First, they are concerned that they shall
not, as a result of standing by and doing nothing, while the plaintiffs obtain a
judgment against the ship and an order for her sale, be held to have waived
or abandoned their statutory rights. This concern arises, I was told, from the
decision in *The Acrux* (1). Second, recognising the potential conflict between
the court's power of sale in an action in rem against the ship and their own rights   H
of detention and sale under the Act of 1920, and recognising also the practical
difficulties which such conflict may put in the way of an advantageous sale
either by the court or by them, they seek an order of the court which will avoid
such conflict, while nevertheless ensuring payment of the rates due to them in
priority to other claims against the ship, including that of the plaintiffs.

It might be thought that a solution to this problem would be easy to find;   I
but the difficulties which arise when it is sought to find one are well illustrated
by the variety of alternative orders for which the interveners have felt it necessary
to ask in their notice of motion as originally drawn. In para. 1 of the notice of
motion, the interveners asked that the plaintiffs' claim be dismissed for want
of jurisdiction. I have dealt with that matter earlier and decided it in favour of
the plaintiffs. In para. 2 to para. 5, the interveners asked for a series of different

(1) [1962] 1 Lloyd's Rep. 405.

A orders to deal with the matter of their rates.   In para. 2 they ask for an order, and I quote from the notice of motion,

B

" that the marshal do give to the [interveners] an undertaking to pay to them all their charges which are rates within the meaning of s. 75 of the Port of London (Consolidation) Act, 1920, whether incurred before or after the arrest of the Queen of the South, and that the undertaking be in the terms of the draft undertaking served herewith or in such other terms as to the court may seem just."

I do not think that it is necessary to read the draft undertaking.   In para. 3 they ask,

C

" Alternatively for an order (a) that the Admiralty marshal do withdraw from the Queen of the South in order that the [interveners] may be at liberty to exercise their rights under s. 75 of the Port of London (Consolidation) Act, 1920, and, (b) that the [interveners] be at liberty to exercise their aforesaid rights and thereafter pay into court the surplus of the proceeds of sale of the Queen of the South after deducting therefrom the amount of any rates due and owing to them and after reimbursing themselves the

D expense incurred by them under the provisions of the said s. 75; (c) and for a declaration that the Queen of the South be sold by the [interveners] free from all liens and encumbrances; (d) and for an order prohibiting any further arrest of the Queen of the South."

In para. 4 they ask

E

" In the further alternative for an order (a) that the [interveners] be at liberty hereafter to exercise their rights under the said s. 75 against the proceeds of sale in court of the Queen of the South when sold by the Admiralty marshal, and (b) that the [interveners] be paid the amount of their dues and charges which are rates within the meaning of the said s. 75 in priority to all claims save those for the Admiralty marshal's expenses and the costs of arrest."

F In para. 5 they ask

" In the further alternative for a declaration that the [interveners] are entitled to exercise their powers under the said s. 75 in respect of the Queen of the South when she is in the hands of a purchaser from the Admiralty marshal."

G During the hearing, counsel for the interveners told me that he would not pursue para. 3, para. 4 or para. 5; but later he amended the notice with leave by adding a sixth paragraph asking for yet another form of order.   Paragraph 6 reads,

H

" In the further alternative for an order that on the [interveners] undertaking not to seize, detain or sell the Queen of the South in pursuance of their statutory powers (a) the Admiralty marshal be directed to pay to the [interveners] out of the net proceeds of sale of the Queen of the South the sum of £277 7s. as a first charge thereon after the Admiralty marshal's expenses and the plaintiffs' costs of arrest and (b) the Admiralty marshal be authorised to include in his claim against the proceeds of sale as part of his expenses all charges due and owing to the [interveners] in respect of

I the Queen of the South incurred after the date of her arrest in this action and to pay the same to the [interveners]."

Counsel for the plaintiffs, besides taking the two points against the interveners which I mentioned earlier and said that I did not accept, took the line that he had no authority to agree, and would not agree, to any of the orders asked for by the interveners, or to any other order designed to help them in recovering their dues in priority to the plaintiffs' claim.   In these circumstances, it is necessary for the court to decide the matter on the basis of the legal rights of the parties.

The right of a dock or harbour authority under its private Acts to detain a A ship for rates is a statutory possessory lien: *The Countess, Mersey Docks & Harbour Board* v. *Hay* (2), per LORD BIRKENHEAD, L.C. The right of such an authority to sell a ship in order to reimburse itself for rates out of the proceeds may be compared with a mortgagee's right of sale usually given to him by contract and in any case by s. 35 of the Merchant Shipping Act, 1894. It is well established that, in an action in rem against a ship, the court has power to B sell her free of both a repairer's common law possessory lien and a mortgagee's contractual or statutory right of sale. It does so on the basis that the rights of which the ship is freed by the sale, together with any priority over other rights to which they may be entitled, are transferred to, and preserved against, the proceeds of sale in court.

If the matter were free from authority, I should have thought in principle C that the court should be able to deal with the statutory possessory lien of a dock or harbour authority in the same way as it deals with the common law possessory lien of a repairer; and with the statutory right of sale of such an authority in the same way as it deals with the contractual or statutory right of sale of a mortgagee. That is to say, I should have thought that the court should have power in an action in rem against a ship, to sell her free from both rights, while trans- D ferring equivalent rights with equivalent priority to the proceeds of sale in court; and further should have power to do this whether the dock or harbour authority consents or not. If the court does not have such power it is extremely incon- venient. For it means that, in any case where a dock or harbour authority has a right of detention or sale, the court cannot transfer the ship to a purchaser free of encumbrances, with all the disadvantages arising from such a situation E discussed by HEWSON, J., in *The Acrux* (3). It appears from the decision of the Court of Session in Scotland in *The Sierra Nevada* (4) that, by the law of Scotland, the court does have such power, certainly where the dock or harbour authority consents, and perhaps also where it does not. The actual decision only covers the case where the authority consents, but there are passages in LORD FLEMING'S judgment which seem to indicate that, if necessary, he might have been pre- F pared to go further and hold that the court could exercise the power even without such consent. In particular, the manner in which he equates common law and statutory possessory liens in his discussion (5) of the principles involved seems to me to point in that direction.

While that is the view of the law which I should have taken if the matter were free from authority, it is clear that it is not supported by the English G decisions, to which I must now refer. In *The Emilie Millon* (6) the Court of Appeal, setting aside an order of the Liverpool Court of Passage made in a wages action in rem, held, first, that the court could not, in such an action, make an order for the sale and delivery of a ship to a purchaser which would deprive a dock authority of its statutory right of detention without its consent; and, second, that such a right of detention was not a right capable of being transferred H to, and preserved against, a fund in court representing the ship. That decision was applied, expressly or by implication, directly or indirectly, in *The Sea Spray* (7), *The Spermina* (8) and *The Ousel* (9). If that decision is still in both respects good law, it means not only that the court cannot transfer a dock or harbour authority's rights of detention and sale to a fund in court representing the ship without the consent of the authority; but also that it cannot do so even with I such consent, because there is in law no right capable of being so transferred.

(2) [1923] A.C. 345 at p. 354; 16 Asp. M.L.C. 161 at p. 164.
(3) [1962] 1 Lloyd's Rep. 405.
(4) (1932), 42 Lloyd L.R. 309.
(5) (1932), 42 Lloyd L.R. at pp. 310, 311.
(6) [1905] 2 K.B. 817; 10 Asp. M.L.C. 162.
(7) [1907] P. 133; 10 Asp. M.L.C. 462.
(8) (1923), 17 Lloyd L.R. 17, 52, 76, 109.
(9) [1957] 1 Lloyd's Rep. 151.

A   The question arises, however, whether what I shall for convenience call the second part of the decision in *The Emilie Millon* (10) is still good law.   In *The Sierra Nevada* (11), the Scottish case to which I referred earlier, LORD FLEMING declined to apply it, and held that, on the facts before him, a harbour authority's right of detention had been transferred, with its consent, to the fund in court. He was, of course, not bound by *The Emilie Millon* (10).   But it was relied on

B   against the harbour authority in the argument before him, and he considered it carefully, together with *The Countess* (12), in his judgment.   Having done so, he expressed the views (13) (i) that the second part of the decision in *The Emilie Millon* (10) was not necessary for the determination of the appeal and was, therefore, obiter, and (ii) that it was, in any case, inconsistent with the later decision of the majority of the House of Lords in *The Countess* (12).

C   So far as (i) is concerned, I agree with LORD FLEMING that the second part of the decision in *The Emilie Millon* (10) was not necessary to the determination of the appeal, but I should hesitate to treat it as unauthoritative on that ground. So far as (ii) is concerned, however, it seems to me that there is great force in LORD FLEMING's view.   My reason for saying this is as follows.   In *The Countess* (12), the dock authority's right of detention was, by a consent order made in a

D   detinue action brought against the dock authority by the shipowners, transferred to a fund in court which the majority of the House of Lords treated as representing the ship.   Moreover, although such order was only made by consent in the detinue action to which the shipowners and the dock authority were the sole parties, it was treated by the majority of the House of Lords as binding on third parties, namely, barge-owners with claims against the ship competing with those of the

E   dock authority, who had never consented to the order or even had an opportunity of doing so or not doing so.   This seems to me to indicate, contrary to the second part of the decision in *The Emilie Millon* (10), that the dock authority's right of detention was of such a character that it could, with the consent of the dock authority at any rate, be transferred from the ship herself to a fund in court representing the ship.

F   If that is the right view, the court could in the present case, with the consent of the interveners at any rate, sell the Queen of the South free of the intervener's right of detention, while preserving to them an equivalent right, with equivalent priority over other claims, against the proceeds of sale in court.   On that basis the court could make an order on the lines of para. 4 of the interveners' notice of motion, although some modification of the wording would, I think, be necessary.

G   The court would, in effect, be treating the interveners in the same way as it would treat a repairer who had a common law possessory lien, and the order would be similar to the order made in such a case.   The adoption of this approach would have the advantages of bridging, in part at least, the gulf which has yawned between English and Scottish law on this topic, and of mitigating, in part at least, the practical difficulties arising from a strict application of both

H   grounds of the decision in *The Emilie Millon* (10).   It involves, however, deciding a highly disputable question of law, on which I should prefer not to express a final opinion unless it were essential to do so.   In fact, I do not think that it is essential, for it seems to me that there is another and perhaps simpler solution to the problem.

    Recent decisions of this court show that, where it is for the benefit of all those

I   interested in a ship that the marshal should incur expenditure on her in order to enable him to sell her to advantage, the court may authorise him to incur such expenditure (see *The Parita* (14); *The Westport (No. 2), British Mexican Petroleum Co., Ltd.* v. *M/S or Vessel Westport* (15)).   Applying the principle of

---

(10) [1905] 2 K.B. 817; 10 Asp. M.L.C. 162.
(11) (1932), 42 Lloyd L.R. 309.
(12) [1923] A.C. 345; 16 Asp. M.L.C. 161.
(13) (1932), 42 Lloyd L.R. at p. 312.   (14) [1964] 1 Lloyd's Rep. 199.
            (15) [1965] 1 Lloyd's Rep. 549; [1965] 2 All E.R. 447, n.

those decisions to the present case, it seems to me that the court has power, if **A**
it thinks that it is for the benefit of all those interested in the Queen of the South,
in order that she may be sold to advantage, that the marshal should pay off the
claims of the interveners for rates which had accrued due before the arrest,
to authorise him to do so, and to include the expenditure in his expenses of sale.
It further appears to me that, so far as rates which have accrued due to the
interveners since the arrest are concerned, the court can also authorise the **B**
marshal to include these in his expenses. Indeed it would, I think, be in accordance with the usual practice for him to do this, even without any special authorisation from the court. In my judgment, on the facts of this case, it would be
for the benefit of all those interested in the Queen of the South that the interveners' claims for rates should be paid off, so that the marshal can sell the vessel
free of the interveners' rights of detention and sale, whether already exercised **C**
or capable of being exercised hereafter. If the marshal cannot sell the ship free
of such rights, he may be unable either to find a purchaser at all, or at any rate
to find one willing to pay a proper price. If the interveners are to be paid off
in this way, however, it must be on the basis that they give a written undertaking to the court not to exercise their rights of detention or sale in respect of
the rates concerned. **D**

In the result, I shall: (i) pronounce for the plaintiffs' claim in the sum of
£290 3s.; (ii) order the appraisement and sale of the ship; (iii) direct the marshal
that, subject to a written undertaking by the interveners to the effect stated
earlier, he is to pay to the interveners, and charge in his expenses of sale, all
rates owing to the interveners up to the date of delivery to the purchasers in
respect of which the interveners would have power to exercise rights of detention **E**
or sale under s. 75 and s. 84 of the Act of 1920, provided always that the amount
so paid is not to exceed the net proceeds of sale after deduction of the marshal's
other expenses; (iv) reserve all questions of priority.

I have been asked to indicate how future cases, in which similar questions
arise can most conveniently be dealt with. In my view, the marshal should
ask all interested parties of whom he knows by letter whether they consent, **F**
or at least do not object, to his paying off rates in respect of which a dock or
harbour authority has powers of detention or sale, and including them in his
sale expenses. After a reasonable time for answer has elapsed, he should apply to
the registrar under (16) R.S.C., Ord. 75, r. 12 (1), for authority to pay the rates
If all interested parties have consented, or at least not objected, to such payment,
the registrar should, in general, feel free to give the authority asked for. If one **G**
or more interested parties object, the registrar should either determine the
matter himself, or, if he thinks preferable, refer it to the judge. In either case,
that is to say whether, where there is an objection, the matter is determined
by the registrar, or referred by him to the judge, all interested parties should
be given an opportunity of being heard by service of notice on them in accordance
with the rule. **H**

Order accordingly.

Solicitors: *Keene, Marsland & Co.* (for the plaintiffs); *Ivor Hughes, Port of
London Authority* (for the interveners).

[*Reported by* N. P. METCALFE, ESQ., *Barrister-at-Law.*]

I

---

(16) R.S.C., Ord. 75, r. 12 (1) provides: " The marshal may at any time apply to the
court for directions with respect to property under arrest in an action and may, or,
if the court so directs, shall, give notice of the application to any or all of the parties
to any action against the property."

A

R. *v.* BATHURST.

[COURT OF APPEAL, CRIMINAL DIVISION (Lord Parker, C.J., Winn, L.J., and
Ashworth, J.), March 5, 1968.]

B *Criminal Law—Murder—Diminished responsibility—Summing-up—Comment by
judge on failure of accused to give evidence—Accused's truthfulness in
giving information to medical experts not challenged—Conviction of murder
set aside—Comment on such failure only rarely proper—Form which comment
might take—Homicide Act,* 1957 (5 & 6 *Eliz.* 2 c. 11), *s.* 2 (1).

On the trial of the appellant for murder, a plea of diminished responsibility under s. 2 (1)* of the Homicide Act, 1957 was raised on his behalf.
C Medical evidence was called on his behalf and also on behalf of the prosecution, but the appellant did not give evidence himself. The medical experts
for the prosecution did not question the truthfulness of the appellant in
answering questions and giving information to them. In summing-up the trial
judge made strong comment on the appellant's failure to give evidence, intimating that many symptoms which the doctors described depended entirely
D on their evidence and that, though the appellant was entitled to remain silent,
he had abstained from adding to the material on which the jury could reach
a verdict, and that the jury might ask themselves why. On appeal by the
appellant against conviction for murder,

Held: although there might be cases in which an accused for whom a plea
of diminished responsibility was raised ought to give evidence when the plea
E was in issue, since it was for the defence to lay the foundation of fact on
which medical opinion could be based, yet the occasions when comment on
his failure to give evidence could be proper must be very rare (see p. 1177,
letter H, and p. 1178, letter B, post); in the present case, where there was no
challenge to the appellant's truthfulness when giving information to the
medical experts, it was unfair to comment on his not giving evidence, and
F the conviction of murder would be set aside and a conviction of manslaughter
would be substituted (see p. 1178, letters G and I, and p. 1179, letter C, post).

R. v. *Ahmed Din* ([1962] 2 All E.R. 123) explained.

Per CURIAM: where comment was justified, it might take the form that
the accused was not bound to go into the witness box, but that the burden
was on him (viz., to prove facts forming a foundation for the opinion of
G of medical experts) and if he did not give evidence, he ran the risk of not
being able to prove his case (see p. 1179, letter A, post).

Appeal allowed.

[As to the defence of diminished responsibility, see SUPPLEMENT to 10 HALS-
BURY'S LAWS (3rd Edn.) para. 534A; and for a case on the subject, see DIGEST
(Cont. Vol. B) 151, *239bba.*
H For the Homicide Act, 1957, s. 2, see 37 HALSBURY'S STATUTES (2nd Edn.)
174.]

Case referred to:
  R. v. *Ahmed Din,* [1962] 2 All E.R. 123; [1962] 1 W.L.R. 680; 46 Cr. App.
    Rep. 269; Digest (Cont. Vol. A) 330, *239bc.*

I **Appeal**
This was an appeal by Eric Wilfred Bathurst, by leave granted by the Court
of Appeal (criminal division) on Jan. 30, 1968, against his conviction at Leeds
Assizes on June 13, 1967, before MELFORD STEVENSON, J., and a jury of the

---

* Section 2 (1), so far as material, reads: " Where a person kills . . . another, he
shall not be convicted of murder if he was suffering from such abnormality of mind
(whether arising from a condition of arrested or retarded development of mind or any
inherent causes or induced by disease or injury) as substantially impaired his mental
responsibility for his acts and omissions in doing the . . . killing."

Applied in R v NAUDEER [1984]
3 All ER 1036

murder of Sandra Ann Kathleen Holt. He was sentenced to imprisonment for life. **A**
The facts are set out in the judgment of the court.

Sir David Renton, Q.C., and *V. R. Hurwitz* for the appellant.
J. F. S. Cobb, Q.C., and *E. Lyons* for the Crown.

LORD PARKER, C.J., delivered the following judgment of the court:
May I say at the outset that there is no question, and never was, of the appellant's **B**
being acquitted of everything. The killing was admitted; the sole defence
was diminished responsibility, and the sole question here is whether the verdict
was properly one of murder or should be one of manslaughter. The facts need
not be stated at any length. This is a case of a man who, after being separated
from his wife, became infatuated with a girl almost half his age; she was his
mistress for 3½ years and finally left him, taking up with another man called **C**
Michael Baldwin. There is no doubt that for one reason or another this drove
the appellant to desperation, and on Mar. 11, 1967, he went out and bought a
knife at a shop in Leeds; that same afternoon he went to the house where Michael
Baldwin lived, and where he found that the girl was residing. There was talk
that he would leave her alone completely if only he could have a few words in
private with her. They then went into another room, and shortly afterwards **D**
there was a scream. When Michael Baldwin and his father and mother, who
were there, went into the room, they found the girl leaning against the wall
clutching her left side, a knife was on the floor, and the appellant knelt down by
the side of the girl obviously very distressed, saying " Don't die, Ann ". She did
die, and it was found that she had a stab wound in the heart. Those are the
only facts in connexion with the killing that need to be mentioned. **E**

The defence sought to set up the defence of diminished responsibility. They
called two psychiatrists, a Dr. Milne and a Dr. Dransfield, who both gave evidence
to the effect that the appellant was suffering at the time from reactive depression,
that that was a mental illness, and that his mental responsibilty at the time of the
killing was substantially diminished. The appellant himself gave no evidence,
and the prosecution in rebuttal called Dr. O'Brien and Dr. Fiddian, who gave **F**
evidence that in their view the depression was not of such a degree as to be
described as a mental illness, and accordingly that he was not suffering from
diminished responsibility within the meaning of s. 2 of the Homicide Act, 1957.
It is to be observed that the jury were out for only twenty-five minutes and
returned a verdict of murder.

The reason why the court gave leave to appeal in this case was a comment **G**
that the trial judge made in relation to the fact that the appellant had chosen
to remain silent and not to go into the witness box and give evidence. I will read
the full passage:

> " As someone said earlier in this case this is not a question of insanity,
> this is a question of an intelligent man."

H

I interpose there to say that the appellant, at the time of the killing, was about
forty years of age and was earning nearly £1,500 a year as an area sales manager
of a cash register company. The trial judge continued:

> " I emphasise that for this reason, namely, the accused person is under
> no obligation to give evidence; he has a right to do so if he wishes, but he
> cannot be required to give evidence. That is something that is often **I**
> referred to in criminal cases as the privilege of silence. He is entitled to take
> the attitude ' Well, you the prosecution get on with it, and put before the
> court such facts as you can, and I will say nothing '. That is the right of
> everyone in a criminal case.   [The appellant] has chosen to remain
> silent in this case and remain in the dock, even in relation to a matter where
> there is a burden of proof on him. You will, of course, bear in mind that
> while he is perfectly entitled to remain silent, that is his right, nevertheless
> the fact that he is entitled to give evidence on his own behalf gives him an

A   opportunity of adding to the material at your disposal on which you could
come to a conclusion, and he has not afforded you that opportunity; he
has chosen to remain where he is, and the evidence about him, the evidence
of the symptoms, or many of them, which the doctors describe depends
entirely on what they have said. It may help you to reflect that your task
might well have been easier if he had given evidence. He has not. You

B   see, it would be quite wrong, I think, if you said to yourselves ' Oh well, all
this must be nonsense, because he has not given evidence '. But common-
sense compels you to reflect, does it not, that while he might or might not
have added a great deal to the case he has abstained from making the
contribution that he might have done. You may ask yourselves why.
It is entirely a matter for you. Of course, we have the advantage of knowing

C   that he has enjoyed the guidance of experienced counsel."

That undoubtedly is a strong comment, and the court in granting leave was
concerned to consider the question how far any comment was justified in the
case of an accused who was pleading diminished responsibility, and if justified
in certain circumstances, whether this comment was justified on the facts of

D   this case.
    As the court understands it, the argument in favour of commenting on the
absence of evidence on the part of the accused in a diminished responsibility
case stems from the decision of the Court of Criminal Appeal in *R.* v. *Ahmed
Din* (1). In that case where the defence of diminished responsibility was raised,
all the medical witnesses agreed that the prisoner was suffering from an abnormality of the mind resulting from paranoia due to a belief in his wife's infidelity

E   for which there were no reasonable grounds. The doctors had obtained their
information either from the prisoner himself or from his daughter. No evidence
had been called by the defence to lay a basis for the opinion that the prisoner's
belief was unreasonable, and the prosecution had cross-examined the doctors
only with a view to eliminating the question of insanity. It was held that it
was the duty of the prosecution to probe the question whether the prisoner's

F   beliefs were due to a delusion or not, and to scrutinise the medical reports closely
to see how much of them consisted of purely medical evidence; and that in such
a case there was a burden on the defence to prove facts on which the doctors
could express their opinion as experts. In giving the judgment of the court
I said (2):

G   "As it seems to this court, the prosecution, while not cross-examining
the doctors on medical matters on which they were in full agreement, had
a duty to prove the question whether or not the appellant was suffering
from a delusion. Equally, as it seems to this court, it is for the defence to
prove the facts on which the doctors can express their opinion as experts.
Here they did not attempt to do so, but relied on hearsay evidence given

H   by the doctors."

That case sets out what undoubtedly is the true position, namely that while
questions of diminished responsibility are largely matters of medical opinion,
nevertheless where there is any issue on the matter, it is for the defence to lay
a foundation of fact on which the experts can give their opinion. Having said
that, however, this court is quite clear that the court in *R.* v. *Ahmed Din* (1)

I   never had in mind the idea that the accused himself would have to be called.
Their comment in that case was directed to the fact that the wife was not called
to say that there were no reasonable grounds for his belief that she had been
unfaithful, thus supporting the defence that he was suffering from a delusion;
nor was the daughter called from whom some of the information was obtained.
The court never had in mind the idea that the accused himself would be called,

---

(1) [1962] 2 All E.R. 123.
(2) [1962] 2 All E.R. at pp. 126, 127.

and indeed it is quite obvious when one looks at that case that it would be per- A
fectly ridiculous to suppose that he should be called; if he did he would have to
go into the box and say, " I was suffering from a delusion ", which was the one
thing which he could not possibly prove.

Having said that, this court feels strongly that while it may be there are
cases in which an accused ought to go into the witness box, albeit his plea is one
of diminished responsibility, yet the cases when comment on his failure to do B
so can properly be made must be very rare. One has only to recall one's own
experience at the Bar that almost in every case counsel defending a prisoner
raising this defence would prevent him, if he could, from going into the witness
box; and I think the experience of all practising barristers today would be the
same. The accused may well be suffering from delusions, he may be on the
border of insanity; it would be the last thing that any counsel would do to C
allow his client to go into the witness box, and in those cases at any rate any
comment on his failure to do so would be clearly unfair. The court, is prepared
to concede, however, that there may be cases where an accused ought to go into
the box, and where his failure to do so may be commented on, albeit the plea is
one of diminished responsibility. There might be a case where the prosecution,
by cross-examining the psychiatrist called for the defence, indicate that they D
were challenging some particular point, and a point which could only be spoken
to by the accused as opposed to some relations, friends, or the like, and in such
a case, probably a very rare case, some comment might be justified.

In the present case, the court is quite satisfied that the comment here was
unjustified. Counsel for the Crown very properly, had probed the matter
cross-examining the psychiatrists called for the defence, suggesting to them that E
what they spoke to was only what the appellant himself had said, but never from
beginning to end suggesting that what the appellant had said was lies, that he was
malingering, that he was deceiving the doctor. Indeed, so far as the facts of
this case were concerned, it is to be observed that when psychiatrists were
called in rebuttal, one of them said that he had no reason to believe but that what
he had been told was the truth. It is perfectly true that what the appellant F
had told the medical experts for the defence and what he had told the medical
experts for the prosecution, was different. What had happened was that Dr.
Milne for the defence had questioned the appellant and in answer had obtained
a lot of information which was not given to Dr. O'Brien, the prosecution expert,
for the very good reason that Dr. O'Brien had not questioned him on those
matters. From beginning to end in this case, however, in the opinion of this G
court, there was no real challenge of the truthfulness of the appellant in answering
questions, and giving information to the medical experts. In those circumstances
this court feels that it was unfair to comment, as the learned trial judge did, on
the appellant's failure to give evidence, and in particular by the passage:

> " But common sense compels you to reflect, does it not, that while he
> might or might not have added a great deal to the case he has abstained   H
> from making the contribution that he might have done. You may ask
> yourselves why."

It may be it is a matter of speculation, but it certainly looks as if the learned
trial judge was inviting the answer to that question to be: well, if he did go
into the witness box he would have said what he told the doctors was lies.   I

That is enough to dispose of this case; but the court would like to point out
that the form of the comment, if comment is justified in any particular case on a
plea of diminished responsibility, is a comment which is undoubtedly different
from the comment which is justified when the burden is on the prosecution.
Then, as is well known, the accepted form of comment is to inform the jury
that, of course, the accused is not bound to give evidence, that he can sit back
and see if the prosecution have proved their case, and that, while the jury have
been deprived of the opportunity of hearing his story tested in cross-examination,

A the one thing that they must not do is to assume that he is guilty because he has not gone into the witness box. When one comes to this sort of case, the case where the burden is on the defence and the accused does not go into the witness box, the comment is directed to something quite different; it would more likely take this form, that the accused is not bound to go into the witness box, nobody can force him to go into the witness box, but the burden is on him,

B and if he does not, he runs the risk of not being able to prove his case.

In the opinion of this court the comment made by the learned judge was unjustified on the facts of this case. It may well, as counsel for the appellant suggests, have been the determining factor, the matter which really swayed the jury in the end to return a verdict of murder. In all the circumstances this court feels that the only safe course is to set aside that verdict, and substitute one

C of manslaughter. The court will substitute a sentence of ten years' imprisonment.

Appeal allowed. Verdict of manslaughter substituted.

Solicitors: *Conway, Kremer & Co.*, Leeds (for the appellant); *Director of Public Prosecutions* (for the Crown).

[*Reported by* S. A. HATTEEA, ESQ., *Barrister-at-Law.*]

D

CLOUGH AND OTHERS *v.* CLOUGH AND OTHERS.

[COURT OF APPEAL, CIVIL DIVISION, (Lord Denning, M.R., Danckwerts and

E   Widgery, L.JJ.), February 2, 1968.]

Practice—Want of prosecution—Dismissal of action—Delay—Statement of claim delivered after summons for dismissal of action taken out before hearing of summons—Discretion of court—Inordinate delay without excuse—Action dismissed—R.S.C., Ord. 19 r. 1.

F On October 7, 1961, the three plaintiffs were passengers in a motor car driven by the first defendant; the motor car came into collision at cross roads with a motor coach owned by the second defendant and driven by the third defendant. The plaintiffs were injured. The drivers blamed each other. Nearly three years later, on Oct. 2, 1964, the plaintiffs issued a writ and served it on the defendants. The second and third defendants entered an appearance. No statement of claim was delivered for about three years.

G On Sept. 1, 1967, the second and third defendants took out a summons to dismiss the action for want of prosecution. Before the summons was heard the plaintiffs delivered a statement of claim. On appeal from dismissal of the summons,

Held: (i) under the present R.S.C. Ord. 19, r. 1, differing in this respect from the former R.S.C. Ord. 27, r. 1, where a summons to dismiss an action

H for want of prosecution had been issued for failure to deliver a statement of claim there was a discretion, if the statement of claim were delivered before the hearing of the summons, whether the action should or should not be dismissed for want of prosecution (see p. 1181, letter C, post).

Ernest Lyon, Ltd. v. *Sturges & Co.* ([1918] 1 K.B. 326) no longer applicable.

(ii) the delay in the present case was prolonged and inexcusable, and was

I such as to do grave injustice as between the parties; accordingly the action should be dismissed (see p. 1181, letters E and G, post).

Allen v. *Sir Alfred MacAlpine & Sons, Ltd.* (ante p. 543) applied.

Appeal allowed.

[As to the dismissal of actions for want of prosecution see 30 HALSBURY'S LAWS (3rd Edn.) 410, 411, para. 771; and for cases on the subject see 30 DIGEST (Repl.) 164, 165, *166-173*, and for cases on the extension of time, see DIGEST (PRACTICE) (Repl.) 256-259, *87-116*.]

Cases referred to: A

    Allen v. *Sir Alfred McApline & Sons, Ltd.*, ante p. 543.

    Fitzpatrick v. *Batger & Co., Ltd.*, [1967] 2 All E.R. 657; [1967] 1 W.L.R. 706.

    Lyon (Ernest), Ltd. v. *William Sturges & Co.*, [1918] 1 K.B. 326; 87 L.J.K.B.
        494; 118 L.T. 427; 50 Digest (Repl.) 140, *1229*.

Interlocutory appeal.

    The action leading to this appeal arose out of a traffic accident on Oct. 7,   B
1961, the plaintiffs being passengers in a motor car driven by the first defendant,
which collided with a vehicle owned by the second defendant and driven by
the third defendant.   The appellants in the present appeal were the second
and third defendants. The writ was issued on Oct. 2, 1964. The second and
third defendants entered appearances; the first defendant did not. No statement of claim was delivered. On Sept. 1, 1967, the second and third defendants   C
served a summons to dismiss the action for want of prosecution. A statement
of claim was delivered on Oct. 5, 1967. On Oct. 10, 1967, the summons was
heard before Mr. District Registrar KUSHNER at Manchester district registry,
who refused to dismiss the action. By order dated Oct. 31, 1967, ORR, J., on
appeal from the order of the district registrar, dismissed the appeal. By notice   D
dated Nov. 28, 1967, the second and third defendants appealed from the order
of Oct. 31, 1967, seeking an order that they might be dismissed from the action.

    G. A. Carman for the second and third defendants, the appellants.

    A. A. R. Thompson for the plaintiffs.

    LORD DENNING, M.R.: This is another summons to dismiss for want   E
of prosecution. On Oct. 7, 1961, there was a collision between a motor car, which
was being driven by Mr. Harry Clough with three passengers, his wife and a
Mr. and Mrs. Hardman. The motor car was in collision with a motor coach at
cross roads where there were traffic lights. Each driver accused the other of
" crashing the lights ". The coach was owned by Mr. Higson and driven by Mr.
Birrell. The three passengers in Mr. Clough's car were injured. They had an   F
unanswerable claim for damages against the drivers of the two vehicles. They
instructed solicitors. There were negotiations for a time in 1962, but they seem
to have come to an end in 1963, when the insurers for the motor coach said
the claims had better go to court and be proved. No writ was issued until just
before the three years period of limitation was up.

    On Oct. 2, 1964, a writ was issued. It was duly served on the defendants.   G
The second and third defendants, the owner of the motor coach and its driver,
èntered an appearance on Dec. 10, 1964. The first defendant, Mr. Clough, the
driver of the car, did not enter an appearance at all. Under R.S.C., Ord. 18,
r. 1 the plaintiffs ought to have delivered a statement of claim within fourteen
days after the entry of appearance. It ought to have been delivered by
Dec. 24, 1964; but it was never delivered. Time passed. Nothing was done   H
by the plaintiffs. Then nearly three years later the solicitors for the second and
third defendants read a case in this court of *Fitzpatrick* v. *Batger & Co., Ltd.*,
(1). They saw that the plaintiffs had not delivered a statement of claim. So they
took out a summons to dismiss for want of prosecution. R.S.C., Ord. 19, r. 1
provides that on failure to deliver a statement of claim. ". . . the court may by
order dismiss the action or make such other order on such terms as it thinks   I
just." The summons was due to be heard on Oct. 10, 1967; but a few days
before it came on, the plaintiffs tried to make good their default. On Oct. 5,
1967, they served a statement of claim against the second and third defendants
and also the first defendant. So when the summons came on for hearing, there
was a statement of claim already delivered. This seems to have influenced the
registrar. He refused to dismiss for want of prosecution. The defendants appealed

_____

(1) [1967] 2 All E.R. 657.

A to the judge. He too refused to dismiss for want of prosecution. Now the defendants appeal to this court.

Before the recent revision of the rules, the delivery of the statement of claim pending the summons would have cured the default. That is shown by the case of *Ernest Lyon, Ltd.* v. *William Sturges & Co.*, (2), decided under the old R.S.C., Ord. 27, r. 1. That rule has been changed. Under the new R.S.C., Ord. 19,

B r. 1 the delivery of a statement of claim no longer cures the default; but the editors of the SUPREME COURT PRACTICE 1967, do not seem to have noticed it. In the first place the note in p. 280, para. 19/1/1 is wrong. It says that the new rule made no substantial change, whereas it did so. In the second place, the note on pp. 280, 281, para. 19/1/4 cites *Lyon* v. *Sturges* (2) as if it was still good law. That is incorrect. Under the new rule, if a plaintiff fails to deliver a statement

C of claim within the specified time, there is a discretion to dismiss for want of prosecution. The default is not cured by the delivery of a statement of claim pending a summons.

Once *Lyon* v. *Sturges* (2) is out of the way, we have to consider the nature of the delay. We were told by counsel that there had been negotiations and that that might account for the delay; but no affidavit has been put before us. No

D excuses have been proffered to show why there has been this great delay: first, three years before the issue of the writ, and then three years again and nothing done, until the summons to dismiss for want of prosecution. It is plain to me that the delay here was both prolonged and inexcusable. Next, the question is whether the delay was such as to do grave injustice to one side or the other or both. I think that it was. There was a serious question between the defendants

E where the responsibility lay. The second and third defendants said that they were not to blame at all. That enquiry is seriously prejudiced by the delay of six years that has taken place. It is impossible to do justice between the defendants at this distance of time. I would add too that the three passenger plaintiffs suffer a grave injustice. They had an unanswerable claim for damages for their injuries. Yet all these years have elapsed without anything being done.

F The case falls fairly and squarely within the principles which we stated in the recent case of *Allen* v. *Sir Alfred McAlpine* (3): and we must adopt the stern measure which we adopted there. It is true that dismissal for want of prosecution is a matter for the judge's discretion, but if we are satisfied that his discretion was wrongly exercised, we must interfere. ORR, J. had not before him the latest cases in which the principles have been stated. I feel sure that, if

G he had had them, he would have taken the course which we do now. I would dismiss the action and leave the plaintiffs to their remedy against their own solicitor. I would allow the appeal accordingly.

DANCKWERTS, L.J.: I agree completely with the judgment of LORD DENNING, M.R.

H **WIDGERY, L.J.,:** I also agree.

Appeal allowed. Action dismissed.

Solicitors: *David Blank, Alexander & Co.*, Manchester (for the second and third defendants); *Conn, Goldberg & Co.*, Manchester (for the plaintiffs).

[*Reported by* F. GUTTMAN, ESQ., *Barrister-at-Law.*]

I

---

(2) [1918] 1 K.B. 326.
(3) Ante p. 543.

JELBERT v. DAVIS AND ANOTHER.

[COURT OF APPEAL, CIVIL DIVISION (Lord Denning, M.R., Danckwerts and Edmund Davies, L.JJ.), February 13, 14, 1968.]

Easement—Right of way—Extent—Grant of right of way at all times and for all purposes in common with all other persons having the like right—Change of user of dominant tenement—Agricultural land changed to caravan and camping site—Reasonable use of right of way for changed purpose permissible —Proposed user excessive, being such as would interfere with enjoyment of right of way by other persons entitled to the like right—Excessive use restrainable by injunction.

In 1961 the plaintiff bought some agricultural land, not far from Penzance. It did not adjoin a public highway, and the conveyance granted him a right of way " at all times and for all purposes " over a driveway, retained by the vendor, " in common with all other persons having the like right ". The driveway was 180 yards long. It had a metalled surface. The entrance to it from the public highway was between stone gateposts, ten feet apart. The driveway then widened to fourteen and a half feet. It was flanked by trees throughout its length. In 1966 the plaintiff obtained planning permission to use his land, during the spring and summer, as a tourist caravan site for not more than two hundred caravans or tents. The defendants had the same right of way as the plaintiff. The second defendant lived at a lodge at the end of the driveway, and farmed land further up the driveway. He might need to use it for large agricultural vehicles, e.g., combine harvesters. The first defendant had a cottage close to the driveway and had to use it to get to his cottage. The defendants objected to the driveway being used for caravans or cars of campers; they put up a notice at the entrance—" Private drive. No entry for campers or caravans ". The plaintiff brought an action against the defendants for interfering with his right of way, and the defendants counterclaimed that he was not entitled to use the driveway to enable his land to be used as a camping or caravan site.

Held: (i) the words of the grant of the right of way were wide enough to entitle the plaintiff to use the driveway for access to his land when the land was used for a new and different purpose, viz., as a caravan and camp site (see p. 1184, letters H and I, and p. 1186, letter F, post).

(ii) the plaintiff was not entitled, however, to use the right of way to an extent which exceeded what was contemplated at the time of the grant and so as to interfere unreasonably with the enjoyment of the like right by others entitled to it; in the present case the proposed user in connexion with a camping or caravan site that might include two hundred units would be excessive and beyond anything contemplated at the time of the grant, and a declaration would be made that the plaintiff was not entitled to use the right of way in such manner as to cause substantial interference with its use by the defendants (see p. 1185, letter A, p. 1186, letters A, D and H, and p. 1187, letter A, post).

Dictum of FARWELL, J., in *Todrick* v. *Western National Omnibus Co., Ltd.*, ([1934] 1 Ch. at p. 206) applied.

Appeal allowed.

[As to the extent of a right of way created by express grant, see 12 HALSBURY'S LAWS (3rd Edn.) 572, 573, paras. 1243, 1244; 19 DIGEST (Repl.) 116, 117, *714-723*.]

Cases referred to:

Malden Farms, Ltd. v. *Nicholson*, (1956), 3 D.L.R. (2d) 236; [1956] O.R. 415; 19 Digest (Repl.) 118, *328.*

A *Robinson* v. *Bailey*, [1948] 2 All E.R. 791; 19 Digest (Repl.) 117, *721.*
Todrick v. *Western National Omnibus Co., Ltd.*, [1934] Ch. 190; 103 L.J.Ch.
　　57; 150 L.T. 296; *on appeal*, C.A., [1934] All E.R. Rep. 25; [1934]
　　Ch. 561; 103 L.J.Ch. 224; 151 L.T. 163; 19 Digest (Repl.) 100, *600.*
White v. *Grand Hotel, Eastbourne, Ltd.*, [1913] 1 Ch. 113; 82 L.J.Ch. 57;
　　107 L.T. 695; *affd.*, H.L., sub nom. *Grand Hotel, Eastbourne* v. *White,*
B　　84 L.J.Ch. 938; 110 L.T. 209; 19 Digest (Repl.) 124, *780.*

Appeal.

This was an appeal by the defendants, Ronald Turle Davis and William
Osborne by notice dated Aug. 18, 1967, from a judgment of His Honour JUDGE
CHOPE, given on July 20, 1967, at Penzance county court seeking that the
judgment might be reversed and discharged in so far as it had adjudged that
C the plaintiff, Ronald James Jelbert, was entitled to use a particular right of way
in connexion with the use of his land as a tourist caravan and camping site;
and in so far as it had adjudged that the plaintiff had been at liberty to apply for
an injunction to protect the right of way and that the counterclaims of the
defendants should be dismissed. The defendants sought an order that judgment
should be entered for them and that the plaintiff should be restrained, whether
D by himself his servants agents licensees or otherwise howsoever, from using
the right of way in connexion with user of his land as a tourists' caravan and
camping site. The grounds of appeal specified in the notice included the following—(a) that the county court judge was wrong in holding that the right of way
was capable of accommodating the use of the right of way in connexion with
a tourists' caravan and camping site of two hundred units as proposed by the
E plaintiff; that the county court judge misdirected himself in failing properly
to take into account the extent of the present user and physical limitations of
the right of way and of the increase in user and congestion resulting from the
plaintiff's proposed user of the right of way; that the county court judge was
wrong in law in holding that on the true construction of a conveyance dated
Oct. 5, 1961, granting the right of way to the plaintiff, he was entitled to use it
F in connexion with the proposed use of his land as a caravan and camping site;
and that the county court judge was wrong in law in holding that the plaintiff's
proposed user would not be excessive user to which he was not entitled and that
such user would not cause an actionable nuisance to the defendants or either of
them. The facts are set out in the judgment of LORD DENNING, M.R.

G *M. A. F. Lyndon-Stanford* for the defendants.
J. W. Priest for the plaintiff.

LORD DENNING, M.R.: The plaintiff, Mr. Jelbert is the owner of a
considerable area of land at Kenegie, Gulval near Penzance. He bought it in
1961. It was used as agricultural land at that time. It lies back from the highway
from Penzance to St. Ives. It does not adjoin the highway at any point. In order
H to get from his land to the public highway, the plaintiff has to go along a lane or
driveway which does not belong to him; but his conveyance of Oct. 5, 1961,
gives him a right of way along it. He was granted the land

　　" together with the right of way at all times and for all purposes over
　　the driveway retained by the vendor leading to the main road in common
　　with all other persons having the like right subject to the purchaser or his
I　　successors in title paying a proper proportion of the cost of repairing and
　　maintaining it in repair."

There was another clause (No. 2) which I will read, but I do not think that it
affects the matter which we have to decide. It said that

　　" the property is sold subject to but with the benefit of all rights of way
　　whether public or private and other rights easements and quasi-easements
　　as now used and enjoyed for or against the same whether by the vendor
　　or other persons."

That is only a sweeping-up clause which is put in so as to cover any rights of way   **A** which were not expressly granted. It does not affect the express grant along the driveway which I have read.

At first the plaintiff used his land for agricultural purposes only; and his farm vehicles used the driveway; but in 1964 he was minded to turn a portion of his land into a caravan and camping site. He applied to the planning authority, the Cornwall county council, for permission. He proposed that the campers should   **B** use the lane as a means of access to the highway. At first the county council refused permission. They thought that such use of the lane would give rise to considerable traffic problems; but two years later they changed their minds. On June 23, 1966, the planning authority granted permission to the plaintiff, allowing him to use the land as a tourist caravan and camping site. They attached conditions to the permission. In particular, there were not to be more than two hundred tour-   **C** ing caravans or tents stationed on the land: it was only to be used from Apr. 1 to Oct. 31, in each year: and no caravan was to remain on the site for longer than three weeks. The planning authority must, therefore, have been satisfied that the traffic problems could be overcome.

The planning permission did not affect the legal rights of the owners of the soil. The planning authority could not, and did not, give the plaintiff any right to go   **D** along this lane for himself or for the campers. He had to rely on his conveyance for such a right. The lane was a strip of land about 180 yards long. Some of it was owned by the first defendant Mr. Davis and the rest by the second defendant Mr. Osborne. It was a drive bordered on each side by trees and with a metalled portion in the middle. Those two gentlemen objected to the right of way being used by caravans and cars. They put up notices at the entrance saying: " Private   **E** drive. No entry for campers or caravans." The plaintiff took objection to these notices. He took the two defendants to court. He said that the notices were a nuisance and a slander of his title. The defendants denied the charge. They counterclaimed for an injunction to restrain the plaintiff from using this right of way in connexion with the tourist caravan and camping site. The judge, in a most careful and helpful judgment, decided in favour of the plaintiff. He said: **F**

" I have no doubt that the congestion in the summer months will indeed be considerably worse but the mere fact that there may be congestion of that nature does not enable the defendants to say the plaintiff's right of way, if it otherwise extends to the type of vehicle concerned, is to be cut down."

The defendants appeal to this court.

The issue has been exceptionally well argued before us by counsel on both sides.   **G** It turns eventually on the true construction of the grant contained in the conveyance of Oct. 5, 1961. In particular, of the words " the right of way at all times and for all purposes over the driveway leading to the main road ". What is the extent of that right when the land is changed from agricultural use to a caravan and camping site? The change will mean no doubt that a *different* kind of vehicle   **H** will be used for *different* purposes; but that change is, by itself, quite permissible. It is covered by the words of the grant " at all times and for all purposes ". That is shown by *White* v. *Grand Hotel, Eastbourne, Ltd.* (1). In that case a private dwelling-house was turned into a hotel. That meant a different user. But it was held to be within the grant. That case was applied in *Robinson* v. *Bailey* (2). In that case a plot of land, which was expected to be used as a dwelling-house,   **I** was turned into a place for storing building materials. The different user was held to be within the right of way. In view of those cases counsel for the defendants conceded that he could not complain that the way was to be used for caravans instead of agricultural vehicles, such as carts or tractors. He could not object, for instance, to a user in connexion with ten caravans; but he did object, he said, to excessive user.

---

(1) [1913] 1 Ch. 113.
(2) [1948] 2 All E.R. 791.

A   In my opinion a grant in these terms does not authorise an unlimited use of the way. Although the right is granted " at all times and for all purposes ", nevertheless it is not a sole right. It is a right " in common with all other persons having the like right ". It must not be used so as to interfere unreasonably with the use by those other persons, that is with their use of it as they do now, or as they may do lawfully in the future. The only way in which the rights of all can
B   be reconciled is by holding that none of them must use the way excessively.

More generally, the true proposition is that no one of those entitled to the right of way must use it to an extent which is beyond anything which was contemplated at the time of the grant. The law on this subject was stated by FARWELL, J., in *Todrick* v. *Western National Omnibus Co., Ltd.* (3), which was approved by the Court of Appeal (4). FARWELL, J., said (5):

C   " In considering whether a particular use of a right of this kind is a proper use or not, I am entitled to take into consideration the circumstances of the case, the situation of the parties and the situation of the land at the time when the grant was made . . . a grant of this kind must be construed as a grant for all purposes within the reasonable contemplation of the parties at the time of the grant."

D   In that case FARWELL, J., held (and the Court of Appeal approved it (4)) that a way, which was only seven feet, nine inches wide, could not be used for omnibuses which were seven feet, six inches wide, leaving only 1½ inches clearance on each side between the gateposts. That was obviously not within the contemplation of the parties. We were also referred to a Canadian case, *Malden Farms, Ltd.* v. *Nicholson* (6). There was a right of way alongside a lake which was at the time
E   unspoilt land. The lake-shore was transformed into a camping site and a beach resort. The judges in Canada applied *Todrick's* case (4) and granted an injunction against the way being used for the public bathing beach and picnic ground or otherwise using the way so as to substantially interfere with the other users' user of it.

F   The question thus turns on the facts and circumstances of the particular case. Is the proposed user so extensive as to be outside the reasonable contemplation of the parties at the time the grant was made? This way is 180 yards long. As you enter from the road there are stone gateposts. They are only ten feet apart. Once you are through the gateposts and come into the drive, there is a hard metalled way. It has guttering on its outer fringes which is really part of the
G   metalled way. It widens out from ten feet at the gateposts up to fourteen feet, six inches and fifteen feet inside. The judge by an error put it at sixteen or seventeen feet, that is a couple of feet wider than it was. It is bordered by trees for the whole of the 180 yards of its length. If two hundred units, such as caravans, dormobiles or cars, used this caravan site, there would be six hundred people there. All those people may go out in a car two or three times a day. In the morning to the beach. In the afternoon for an outing; and such like. All of them
H   would be using this driveway.

It seems to me that user on that scale would interfere greatly with the rights of the defendants. The second defendant lives at the lodge at the end of the driveway. He has his grandchildren there in the summer. He farms land further up the lane. If he wishes to bring a combine harvester up the lane, or a cattle lorry, or any other vehicle, he would find it very difficult indeed when there are six
I   hundred people in the camp. His life in the lodge would be far from peaceful. The first defendant has a cottage close to the lane and is interested in the hotel nearby. He has to go up and down the lane to get to his cottage. He could not fail to be much inconvenienced. I must say that, on the evidence, I think that if this caravan site is used to its full intensity for two hundred units, there would

---

(3) [1934] Ch. 190 at pp. 205-207.
(4) [1934] All E.R. Rep. 25; [1934] Ch. 561.
(5) [1934] Ch. at pp. 206, 207.
(6) (1956), 3 D.L.R. (2d) 236.

be such congestion that it would interfere with the reasonable use by the **A** defendants of their own right of way: and it would be a nuisance to them.

In my opinion, therefore, the proposed user for two hundred units would be excessive. It would be far beyond anything contemplated at the time of the grant. I would point out, however, that there is a possible way in which the parties may resolve the difficulty. They are both very reasonable people. It appears that under this deed there is, some distance away, a special ten feet right of way given **B** to the plaintiff whereby he can get access to the main road by another route, not using this lane. Counsel for the defendants acknowledges that the plaintiff can use the alternative route for motor vehicles. That would reduce considerably any nuisance or interference to the defendants. No planning permission has yet been given for this access; but it might be. So far as this lane is concerned, however, the parties must abide by the law as we declare it to be. I am quite **C** clear that two hundred units is excessive. We were asked to state what number is permissible. I am afraid that we cannot give any guidance on this point. It is a matter of fact and degree depending on what happens. Beyond saying that two hundred units are too many, I am afraid we must leave it to the parties themselves to work out what is a reasonable user.

I think, therefore, that the appeal should be allowed. We will not grant an **D** injunction but make a declaration which DANCKWERTS, L.J., has been good enough to draft.

DANCKWERTS, L.J.: I agree. I am satisfied that cl. 2 of the relevant conveyance is merely a general clause which a conveyancer would put in in order to prevent the vendor becoming liable on his covenants for title through some **E** oversight as regards the various rights, which may be complicated in a case of this kind. In my view it has no effect on the proper construction of this grant of a right of way.

On the authorities, it is plain that the easement so granted is in such wide terms that the use by the plaintiff of it for caravans is permissible; but it is an easement which on its terms is a right which is to be used " in common with all other **F** persons having the like right ". That includes the defendants. A use of the right of way which is so excessive that it renders the rights of such other persons practically impossible, therefore, is not justified. The difficulty is to fix the limit in respect of such use. The test must be whether the interference is so substantial as to interfere with the rights of other persons in an unreasonable manner. It cannot be right that the others should be swamped by the traffic created by the **G** plaintiff so as to amount to a legal nuisance. It is impossible to quantify this in figures, particularly as the problem relates to the future. These people are neighbours and share the right of way and there must be give and take and accommodation. Time will show what is practicable, and in the interests of both parties a practical solution must be found or a deadlock will result.

In those circumstances the relief which I suggest is: " An order declaring that **H** the plaintiff is entitled to use the right of way claimed for use with caravans but not in such a manner as to cause substantial interference with the use of the right of way by the defendants or either of them or to cause a nuisance to the defendants or either of them. Liberty to the defendants to apply for an injunction." Then I understand that the defendants are prepared to give an undertaking, which should be incorporated in the order, relating to the notices which were put up at the gates **I** and of which the plaintiff complained.

EDMUND DAVIES, L.J.: The fact that planning permission was, perhaps somewhat surprisingly, granted in 1964 to the plaintiff to use his land for two hundred units does not bear on the nature of the permitted user of the driveway and in no way clothes the plaintiff with any authority to exercise his right of way to an excessive extent. For the reasons already given by LORD DENNING, M.R., that contemplated by the plaintiff would, in my judgment, inevitably involve

A an excessive user and cannot be permitted. I, therefore, agree with my lords that this appeal must be allowed and I concur in the order proposed.

Appeal allowed. Declaration accordingly.

Solicitors: *White & Leonard* and *Corbin Greener*, agents for *Jewill, Hill &*
Bennett, Penzance (for the appellants); *T. J. Chellew & Son*, St. Ives (for the
B respondent).

[*Reported by* F. GUTTMAN, ESQ., *Barrister-at-Law.*]

C

NOTE.

BANDEY v. PENN.

D [QUEEN'S BENCH DIVISION (Lord Parker, C.J., Winn, L.J., and Ashworth, J.),
February 28, 1968.]

Employment—Redundancy—Dismissal by reason of redundancy—Tenant farmer
terminating tenancy on retiring—Employee farm worker dismissed on
termination of tenancy—Offered re-employment by in-coming tenant farmer
refused it—No transfer of ownership of business—Employee dismissed on
E *account of redundancy—Redundancy Payments Act 1965 (c. 62) s. 13 (1),*
(3), (4).

[**Editorial Note.** The present decision may be compared with *Dallow*
Industrial Properties, Ltd. v. *Else* ([1967] 2 All E.R. 30), which decided a not
dissimilar question in relation to the sale of factory premises.

As to the dismissal of an employee by reason of redundancy, see SUPPLEMENT
F to 38 HALSBURY'S LAWS (3rd Edn.) para. 808C.

For the Redundancy Payments Act 1965 s. 2 (3), s. 13, see 45 HALSBURY'S
STATUTES 292, 301.]

Appeal.

This was an appeal by Anthony Leonard Bandey from a decision of the Indus-
G trial Tribunal, given on Oct. 19, 1967, holding that he was not entitled to a
redundancy payment from his former employer, William John Penn, the
respondent. The facts are set out in the judgment of LORD PARKER, C.J.

R. G. Freeman for the appellant.

The respondent was not represented.

H **LORD PARKER, C.J.:** The appellant was employed from October, 1954,
to Oct. 15, 1966, as a stockman and general farm worker by the respondent, Mr.
Penn, at the Manor Farm, Whiston, Northamptonshire. The respondent
was a tenant farmer and on his termination of his lease on Oct. 10 he had given
notice to the appellant terminating his contract of service. In fact the respondent was not going to farm elsewhere, but was going to retire. In due course
I the farm was taken over by another tenant farmer, a Mr. Phipps, who had
approached the appellant and asked him to work for him. For some reason or
another the appellant did not accept that offer, and presumably went off to
other employment. The case for the respondent before the Industrial Tribunal
was that he had transferred the ownership of his business within the meaning
of s. 13 (1) of the Redundancy Payments Act 1965 to Mr. Phipps; that Mr.
Phipps had offered the appellant similar employment; that there had been an
unreasonable refusal by the appellant to accept it; and accordingly that he was
not entitled to any redundancy payment at all.

The sole question on appeal is whether there was a transfer of the ownership **A** of the business from the respondent to Mr. Phipps, because it is conceded that if there were such a transfer the appellant was acting unreasonably in refusing to accept Mr. Phipps' offer. Section 13 (1) of the Redundancy Payments Act 1965 provides that:

" The provisions of this section shall have effect where—(a) a change occurs (whether by virtue of a sale or other disposition or by operation of **B** law) in the ownership of a business for the purposes of which a person is employed, or of a part of such a business, and (b) in connexion with that change the person by whom the employee is employed immediately before the change occurs (in this section referred to as ' the previous owner ') terminates the employee's contract of employment, whether by notice or without notice." **C**

If such a transfer occurs, then the subsequent provisions (1) of s. 13 bring into play s. 2 (3) of the Act of 1965, which, as modified, deals with offers of renewal of employment and re-engagement, and rejection of such offers, by the person to whom the business is transferred. In my judgment it is quite impossible on the facts of this case to say that any business has been transferred within the **D** meaning of s. 13 (1). The respondent was not disposing of the ownership of business; indeed in evidence he said " I was not selling my business "; all that he was doing was to terminate his lease, which was an asset in that business, and all he got was in effect the tenant right, improvements, crops and the like, and payment at an agreed valuation for dead stock.

I refrain from doing more than saying that on the facts of this case it is **E** impossible to say that s. 13 was invoked, because while this is a very important case, nobody has appeared on behalf of the respondent to argue otherwise; and while I have no doubt about the position on the facts of this case, I should hesitate to lay down any general principles which might apply in the future to other cases.

Accordingly the appellant was plainly dismissed on account of redundancy, **F** namely because the respondent had ceased to carry on business at the place where the appellant was employed, and the respondent is unable to invoke the provisions of s. 13. Accordingly I would allow this appeal and send the case back to the tribunal in default of agreement to assess the amount of the redundancy payment.

WINN, L.J.: I agree.   **G**

ASHWORTH, J.: I agree.

Appeal allowed.

Solicitors: *O. H. Parsons* (for the appellant).

[*Reported by* N. P. METCALFE, ESQ., *Barrister-at-Law.*] **H**

 I

---

(1) Subsections (3) and (4) of s. 13 apply sub-ss. (3), (4) of s. 2 subject to modifications appropriate in view of the fact that the offer of employment is made by the transferee of the business.

A

R. *v.* SADDLEWORTH JUSTICES, *Ex parte* STAPLES.

[Queen's Bench Division (Lord Parker, C.J., Winn, L.J., and Ashworth, J.),
February 19, 1968.]

B
*Road Traffic—Driving under age—Heavy motor car—Driver under twenty-one
years of age—Whether prosecution may elect to proceed under s.* 110 *rather
than s.* 5—*Road Traffic Act,* 1960 (8 & 9 *Eliz.* 2 *c.* 16), *s.* 5, *s.* 97 (1), *s.* 110
(*b*), *as amended by Road Traffic Act,* 1962 (10 & 11 *Eliz.* 2 *c.* 59), *s.* 8 *and
Sch.* 1.

Three months before his twenty-first birthday the applicant was found
driving a motor coach, which ranked as a heavy motor car for the purposes
of the Road Traffic Act, 1960*, and consequently could not lawfully be

C
driven by a person under twenty-one years of age†. He pleaded guilty
before a magistrates' court to driving whilst disqualified contrary to s. 110‡
of the Road Traffic Act, 1960. He was fined and disqualified for a period
of twelve months. On a motion for certiorari to quash the conviction on
the ground that he had been wrongly charged under s. 110, which should

D
be applied only where the disqualification was by order of the court,
Held: the prosecution had, in effect, a right to elect to proceed against
the applicant either for an offence of driving under age contrary to s. 5§
of the Road Traffic Act, 1960 (which section carried comparatively minor
penalties and only discretionary disqualification) or to proceed under s. 110
(which carried greater penalties and obligatory disqualification); and accord-

E
ingly, the applicant had been properly charged and convicted, and certiorari
would be refused (see p. 1191, letter B, post).

[As to the minimum age for driving, see 33 Halsbury's Laws (3rd Edn.)
451, 452, para. 769; as to disqualification for driving, see ibid., pp. 638, 639,
para. 1080.

F
For the Road Traffic Act, 1960, s. 5, s. 97, s. 110, see 40 Halsbury's Statutes
(2nd Edn.) 716, 800, 811; and for the Road Traffic Act, 1962, s. 8 and Sch. 1,
paras. 6, 10, see 42 ibid., 895, 923, 924.]

Motion for certiorari.

This was a motion by notice dated Jan. 18, 1968, on behalf of John Staples
for an order of certiorari to remove a conviction of driving while disqualified
contrary to s. 110 of the Road Traffic Act, 1960, and to quash the conviction.

G
The applicant was convicted on Oct. 4, 1967, by the justices for the petty sessional
division of Saddleworth in the West Riding of Yorkshire sitting at Uppermill
after the applicant had pleaded guilty to driving on Apr. 28, 1967, while disqualified under Pt. 2 of the Act of 1960, contrary to s. 110 thereof. The applicant
was fined £5, his driving licence was endorsed and he was disqualified for holding
a driving licence for twelve months. The facts are set out in the judgment of

H Lord Parker, C.J.

The case noted below|| was cited during the argument.

J. Ward for the applicant.
R. A. R. Stroyan for the respondent justices.

LORD PARKER, C.J.: On Apr. 28, 1967, some three months before his
I twenty-first birthday, the applicant, John Staples, was found driving a Leyland

---

* See s. 253 (3) of the Road Traffic Act, 1960; 40 Halsbury's Statutes (2nd Edn.)
922.

† Section 97 (1) provides " A person shall not drive on a road a motor vehicle of a
class or description specified in the first column of the following Table if he is under the
age specified in relation thereto in the second column of that Table . . ." The table
specifies twenty-one as the age for driving a heavy motor car.

‡ Section 110 is set out at p. 1190, letter C, post.
§ Section 5 is set out at p. 1190, letter F, post.
|| *R. v. Campbell, Ex p. Nomikos,* [1956] 2 All E.R. 280.

motor coach, which is classed as a heavy motor car and can lawfully be driven   A
only by somebody over the age of twenty-one.   This resulted in his being brought
before the petty sessional division of Saddleworth in the West Riding of Yorkshire
on Oct. 4, 1967, when he entered a plea of guilty to driving whilst disqualified
contrary to s. 110 of the Road Traffic Act, 1960.   He was fined and his licence
was endorsed and he was ordered to be disqualified for holding a driving licence
for driving a motor vehicle for twelve months.   B

In these proceedings counsel now moves on his behalf for an order of certiorari
to quash that decision, alleging that he was wrongly charged under s. 110, and,
that being so, that his plea of guilty was really a nullity, and asking for the
conviction to be quashed. The position is a little curious. Section 110 provides:

" If a person disqualified for holding or obtaining a licence—(a) applies
for or obtains a licence while he is so disqualified, or (b) while he is do dis-   C
qualified drives on a road a motor vehicle, or if the disqualification is limited
to the driving of a motor vehicle of a particular class or description, a motor
vehicle of that class or description, he shall be liable on summary conviction
to imprisonment for a term not exceeding [twelve months (1)] or, if the
court thinks that having regard to the special circumstances of the case
a fine would be an adequate punishment for the offence, to a fine not exceed-   D
ing [£100 (1)], or to both such imprisonment and such fine."

Finally under s. 5 (1) of the Road Traffic Act, 1962, there is an obligatory
disqualification of twelve months.

What counsel for the appellant says, and I confess that I felt in the first
instance that the law ought to be as he submitted it, is that the offence created   E
by s. 110 only applies to cases where a man has been disqualified by the order
of the court. Counsel refers to the first section in Part 2, s. 97, which provides
the minimum age for driving different forms of vehicles and specifies twenty-one
as the minimum age at which a person may lawfully drive a heavy motor car.
Then counsel takes us back to s. 5 of the Act of 1960, which is clearly dealing
with such a case, because it provides: F

" A person who drives, or causes or permits a person to drive, a motor
vehicle in contravention of the provisions of this Act relating to a minimum
age for driving motor vehicles of different classes and descriptions [that
is clearly a reference to s. 97] shall be liable on summary conviction to
a fine not exceeding [£50 (2)], or in the case of a second or subsequent
conviction . . ."   G

to an increased fine and a term of imprisonment.   There s. 97 and s. 5 clearly
go together and one would think that they would form, as it were, a watertight compartment, whereas s. 110 would be dealing with cases of persons who
were disqualified by orders of the court.   However, as it seems to me, s. 110
is very much wider.   Section 107, which is dealing with s. 97, provides:

" A person who under s. 97 of this Act is prohibited by reason of his   H
age from driving a motor vehicle or a motor vehicle of any class or description
is disqualified for holding or obtaining a licence other than a licence authorising him to drive such motor vehicles, if any, as he is not by the said s. 97
forbidden to drive."

When one comes to s. 110 one finds those very words " If a person disqualified   I
for holding or obtaining a licence ", which are taken from s. 107 and s. 110 then
continues:

" (a) applies for or obtains a licence while he is so disqualified, or (b) while
he is so disqualified drives on a road a motor vehicle, or if the disqualification
is limited to the driving of a motor vehicle of a particular class or description,
a motor vehicle of that class or description . . ."

(1) Section 110 was amended by Road Traffic Act, 1962, s. 8, Sch. 1, Pt. 1, para. 6.
(2) As amended by Road Traffic Act, 1962, s. 8 and Sch. 1, Pt. 2, para. 10.

A The words " a motor vehicle of that class or description " are clearly carrying forward the very words of s. 107, and indeed those are words which could not apply to a disqualification by order of the court because a disqualification by order of the court applies to all vehicles and not vehicles of a particular class. Finally as it seems to me, the matter is conclusively decided against counsel for the appellant when one notices that in s. 10 and in s. 109, and no doubt

B in other places where Parliament intends disqualification to be confined to disqualification by an order of the court, it says so in express language.

The truth of the matter, as I see it, is that this is a case where under the law as it is at present the prosecution can in effect elect to proceed under s. 5 with its comparatively minor penalties, and only discretionary disqualification, or to proceed under s. 110 with its greatly increased penalties and its obligatory

C term of disqualification. In my judgment the applicant was properly convicted on his plea of guilty and I would refuse this application.

WINN, L.J.: I agree.

ASHWORTH, J.: I agree.

Application refused.

D

Solicitors: *Pritchard, Englefield, Leader & Henderson,* agents for *J. Bright, Clegg & Son,* Rochdale (for the applicant); *Cummings, Marchant & Ashton,* agents for *M. D. Shaffner,* Wakefield (for the respondent justices).

[*Reported by* N. P. Metcalfe, Esq., *Barrister-at-Law.*]

E

LAWRENCE *v.* SAME.

F [Queen's Bench Division (Lord Parker, C.J., Winn, L.J., and Ashworth, J.), February 22, 1968.]

Quarter sessions—Appeal to—Appeal against conviction—Jurisdiction—Substitution of conviction of alternative offence—Conviction by justices for malicious wounding—On appeal conviction for common assault substituted—Whether

G *quarter sessions had jurisdiction to substitute a conviction of the lesser offence— Offences against the Person Act,* 1861 (24 & 25 Vict. c. 100), s. 20.

On appeal to quarter sessions against conviction by justices on an information charging the appellant with malicious wounding contrary to s. 20 of the Offences against the Person Act, 1861, quarter sessions quashed the conviction but substituted a conviction for common assault. On further appeal,

H **Held:** since magistrates had long been unable, unless the accused consented, to try at any one time more than one information, alleging one offence, a magistrates' court before which an accused was charged with a more serious offence had no power to convict him of another and lesser offence on that information, even though the ingredients of the lesser offence were elements of the offence charged; accordingly, quarter sessions had had no

I power to substitute a conviction of common assault, but should have merely acquitted the appellant of malicious wounding (see p. 1193, letter H, and p. 1194, letters E and G, post).

Martin v. *Pridgeon* ((1859), 1 E. & E. 778) and *R.* v. *Brickill* ((1864), 4 New Rep. 166) applied.

Per Curiam: there would be no practical difficulties in dealing with charges before the justices, because as soon as they acquitted an accused of the more serious charge, they could ask for a summons to be preferred for the lesser offence (see p. 1194, letter F, post).

[As to the offence of unlawful wounding, see 10 HALSBURY'S LAWS (3rd Edn.) A
735, 736, para. 1411; and for cases on the subject, see 15 DIGEST (Repl.) 999,
1000, *9836-9847.*

As to conviction of offences different from that charged on indictment, see
10 HALSBURY'S LAWS (3rd Edn.) 428-430, para. 791; and as to dismissal of an
information where a different offence is disclosed at the trial, see 25 HALSBURY'S
LAWS (3rd Edn.) 188, para. 340. B

For the Summary Jurisdiction Act, 1848, s. 10, see 14 HALSBURY'S STATUTES
(2nd Edn.) 780.

For the Offences against the Person Act, 1861, s. 20, see 5 HALSBURY'S STATUTES
(2nd Edn.) 795.

For the Magistrates' Courts Rules, 1952, r. 14, see 13 HALSBURY'S STATUTORY
INSTRUMENTS (First Re-Issue) 377.] C

Cases referred to:
> *Brangwynne* v. *Evans*, [1962] 1 All E.R. 446; [1962] 1 W.L.R. 267; 126 J.P.
> 173; 33 Digest (Repl.) 233, *644.*
> *Martin* v. *Pridgeon*, (1859), 1 E. & E. 778; 28 L.J.M.C. 179; 38 L.T.O.S. 119;
> 23 J.P. 630; 120 E.R. 1102; 33 Digest (Repl.) 229, *619.*
> *R.* v. *Brickill*, (1864), 4 New Rep. 166; 33 L.J.M.C. 156; 10 L.T. 385; 28 D
> J.P. 359; 33 Digest (Repl.) 229, *621.*
> *R.* v. *Taylor*, (1869), L.R. 1 C.C.R. 194; 38 L.J.M.C. 106; 20 L.T. 402; 33
> J.P. 358; 14 Digest (Repl.) 359, *3497.*

Case Stated.

This was a Case Stated by the chairman (F. H. CASSELS, ESQ.) and other justices E
of the South West London Quarter Sessions sitting at Kingston-upon-Thames
in the county of Surrey on Dec. 2, 1966. On Oct. 31, 1966, the appellant Dennis
Ernest Lawrence was convicted by the justices of the peace sitting at Kingston-
upon-Thames of malicious wounding contrary to s. 20 of the Offences against
the Person Act, 1861. On Nov. 8, 1966, the appellant lodged notice of appeal
to the South West London Quarter Sessions on the ground that the conviction F
was against the weight of the evidence.

The following facts were found. (i) At about 1.15 p.m. on Sept. 15, 1966, a
fight broke out between the appellant and the respondent Albert Reginald Same,
on board the respondent's boat known as " the Merry Maiden " which was
moored at the rear of 66a, High Street, Kingston-upon-Thames; (ii) the fight
arose as a result of a quarrel over the accidental severing of the respondent's G
mooring chain; (iii) the first blow was struck by the appellant but at no time did
the appellant strike the respondent in the face with one of the respondent's
dumb-bells as alleged by the respondent.

The justices were satisfied that the respondent was wounded, but they were not
satisfied that the wound sustained by the respondent was due to the deliberate
act of the appellant. They, accordingly, allowed the appeal against conviction for H
malicious wounding but substituted a conviction for common assault.

The question for the High Court was whether there was power in a magistrates'
court or at quarter sessions to substitute a conviction for an offence not charged
in the information.

R. D. Grey for the appellant.
L. A. F. Borrett for the respondent. I

LORD PARKER, C.J.: This is an appeal by way of Case Stated from a
decision of justices of the South West London Quarter Sessions who, on an appeal
from the appellant's conviction by justices of the peace sitting at Kingston-upon-
Thames of malicious wounding contrary to s. 20 of the Offences against the Person
Act, 1861, set aside that conviction and substituted a conviction for common
assault. The sole question, and one would think a very simple question, is whether
quarter sessions had power to do that, which in turn depends on whether the

A   magistrates had jurisdiction to do that. The chairman was clearly worried, and in an extract from the transcript it appears that his worry concerned the fact that if quarter sessions did substitute common assault, there could be no appeal. The chairman assumed that the justices would have had power to substitute a conviction for common assault, which is the real question now before this court.

As is well known, it has been decided for long that an accused may be convicted

B   of a lesser felony than that charged or a lesser misdemeanour than that charged, provided that the substituted offence formed an ingredient in the greater offence. Perhaps the leading authority on that, although there were many cases leading up to it, is to be found in *R.* v. *Taylor* (1). In that case the accused had been charged on two counts, one of unlawful and malicious wounding, and the other of unlawfully and maliciously inflicting grievous bodily harm. The question was

C   whether the jury were entitled to return a verdict of common assault. KELLY, C.B., said this (2):

"There is no count in the indictment for an assault, nor is the word 'assault' used in the indictment. Each of the two counts is, however, for an offence which necessarily includes an assault, and the offences charged as well as the offence of which the prisoner has been found guilty are mis-

D   demeanours. If there were an absence of authority, we think on principle that the jury could properly find a verdict of guilty of a common assault on this indictment. It is not necessary that matters of aggravation stated in the indictment should be proved, and if not proved the prisoner may be found guilty of the offence without the circumstances of aggravation."

E   He then goes on to refer to a previous case supporting the principle which he was laying down.

The real question is whether that principle is applicable in a magistrates' court trying a case summarily. The short facts in the present case were that on this charge of malicious wounding the facts found were that a fight broke out between the appellant and the respondent on the respondent's boat moored at High Street,

F   Kingston-upon-Thames. Undoubtedly the appellant struck the first blow, and it was said that he had wounded the respondent with one of the respondent's dumb-bells. Quarter sessions were quite satisfied that the respondent was wounded, but as they put it. "We were not satisfied that the wound sustained by the respondent was due to the deliberate act of the appellant". It was in those circumstances that they substituted the conviction of common assault.

G   Before considering any authorities, it is important as it seems to me to consider whether that principle to which I have referred in regard to the right of a jury on a trial on indictment, is applicable or not to a trial in a magistrates' court. There would at first glance be no reason why in logic and in common sense a magistrates' court should not be in a position to adopt exactly the same course; they are judge and jury combined. The fact remains, however, that so far as at

H   any rate I am concerned, I have not come across cases in which justices have sought to do this. One can see, I think, the reason why. It has always been, or at any rate since s. 10 of the Summary Jurisdiction Act, 1848, was passed, impossible for magistrates to try more than one information alleging one offence at the same time; that of course is apart from the defendant consenting to the trial of more than one offence. That is now to be found in r. 14 of the Magistrates' Courts Rules, 1952, (3) and is supported by abundant authority, of which a recent one is

I   *Brangwynne* v. *Evans* (4). Accordingly, if there had been a second information for common assault, it could not, apart from consent, have been tried at the same time. The position of course is different when one is considering an indictment. An indictment could have an alternative count for common assault, and that

---

(1) (1869), L.R. 1 C.C.R. 194.
(2) (1869), L.R. 1 C.C.R. 195.
(3) S.I. 1952 No. 2190.
(4) [1962] 1 All E.R. 446.

count, without any question of there being consent, could and would be tried with A
the more substantial offence or offences. To that extent there is clearly a difference.
It seems to me that the reason why on a trial on indictment a jury is entitled to
convict of the lesser offence is on the basis that at any rate there is a tacit count
of common assault which can be tried at the same time. That as it seems to me is
the principle lying behind the difference in practice. Coming to the authorities,
counsel for the appellant has referred to two cases, the first in 1859 and the next B
in 1864, which no doubt support this conclusion. The first is *Martin* v. *Pridgeon*
(5). There a man was summoned for being drunk in a street and guilty of riotous
behaviour, it was all one offence, contrary to a section of the Town Police Clauses
Act, 1847. In fact the drunkenness was proved, but not the riotous behaviour,
and thereupon the appellant was convicted of drunkenness only, contrary to
another Act. It was held that the conviction was bad, and that the justices had C
no power to convict of the lesser offence. In the later case of *R.* v. *Brickill* (6),
the defendant had been charged under the Municipal Corporations Act, 1835,
with an assault on a constable in the execution of his duty, and the magistrates
dismissed the summons for assaulting the policeman in the execution of his duty,
but fined the defendant 5s. and costs for a common assault. The court again held
that the justices had no power to do that, and they referred to the case of *Martin* D
v. *Pridgeon* (5) amongst others in support of their judgment.

Those two cases undoubtedly support the conclusion to which I somewhat
reluctantly arrive; but it is only right to say that they do not base their judgments
on what I think is the true principle involved. The basis of the judgments both
in *Martin* v. *Pridgeon* (5) and in *R.* v. *Brickill* (6) was that the lesser and alternative charge was under a different statute to the substantial offence. I myself E
find it difficult to see any reason for that, but be that as it may, they do support
the general conclusion to which I have come, and which seems to be the general
practice in magistrates' courts. There are no practical difficulties when the
matter is dealt with before the magistrates, because as soon as they are minded
to acquit the defendant of the substantial charge, the wounding, they can immediately ask for a summons to be preferred for the lesser offence, common assault, F
and proceed to deal with it at once.

For those reasons, which I have endeavoured to state shortly, I regretfully
come to the conclusion that quarter sessions had no power to substitute a verdict
of common assault, and accordingly I think that the case should go back to them
with a direction merely to acquit of the conviction of malicious wounding.

                                                                 G

     WINN, L.J.: I agree in all respects with the judgment delivered by LORD
PARKER, C.J.

     ASHWORTH, J.: So do I.

                                              Appeal allowed. Case remitted.

     Solicitors: *J. B. Wheatley & Co.* (for the appellant); *Bell & Sherrard*, Kingston-
upon-Thames (for the respondent).   H

                    [*Reported by* OM. P. MIDHA, ESQ., *Barrister-at-Law.*]

(5) (1859), 1 E. & E. 778; 23 J.P. 630.
(6) (1864), 4 New Rep. 166; 28 J.P. 359.

A   LONDON BOROUGH OF NEWHAM v. BENJAMIN.

[COURT OF APPEAL, CIVIL DIVISION (Lord Denning, M.R., Danckwerts and Widgery, L.JJ.), January 30, 31, February 1, 1968.]

Compulsory Purchase—Compensation—Assessment—Time for assessment—Short tenancy, less than a year—Service of notice to treat—Whether tenant entitled
B   *to immediate assessment or only when possession taken—Lands Clauses Consolidation Act, 1845 (8 & 9 Vict. c. 18), s. 18, s. 121.*

Ten days after confirmation by the Minister of Housing and Local Government of a compulsory purchase order made in respect of lands required for re-development, the acquiring authority served notice to treat on, among others, the lessee of property included in the order. The lessee's interest
C   was that of a tenant of business premises whose tenancy was due to expire within a year of the date of service of the notice to treat*. The notice required particulars of the lessee's estates and interests in the property, and of his claim, to be supplied within twenty-eight days. The notice further stated that the acquiring authority was willing to treat for the purchase of the property, and that, if the lessee and the authority did
D   not agree within twenty-eight days, the acquiring authority would require compensation to be settled in the manner directed by the Town and Country Planning Act, 1962, and the Acts incorporated therewith. The lessee supplied particulars of his interest and claimed compensation within the stipulated twenty-eight days, and, as no agreement as to compensation was reached, he referred the assessment of the compensation to the Lands Tribunal. It was
E   not disputed that the lessee had a " short tenancy ", viz., that he was a person with " no greater interest [in the property] than as a tenant for a year or from year to year" within s. 121† of the Lands Clauses Consolidation Act, 1845.

Held: the compensation of a lessee who had a " short tenancy " was, by virtue of s. 121 to be assessed only when the acquiring authority " required [him] to give up possession of the lands ", for s. 18‡ of the Act of 1845 was
F   to be read subject to s. 121, which made exclusive provision for short tenancies and constituted a proviso or exception to s. 18 in respect of them; the lessee was not, therefore, entitled to require compensation to be assessed immediately after service of the notice to treat (see p. 1199, letters A, D and H, and p. 1200, letters F and H, post).

Dicta of BLACKBURN, J., in *R.* v. *London Corpn.* ((1867), L.R. 2 Q.B. at
G   p. 300) and of SIR GEORGE JESSEL, M.R., in *Syers* v. *Metropolitan Board of Works* ((1877), 36 L.T. at p. 278) followed with approval.

Per DANCKWERTS AND WIDGERY, L.JJ.: the practice of serving a notice to treat in the case of short tenancies is not wrong (see p. 1200, letter B, post; cf., p. 1198, letter I, and 1199, letter A, post).

Appeal allowed.

H   [**Editorial Note.** Section 18 and s. 121 of the Lands Clauses Consolidation Act, 1845, are now reproduced in s. 5 (1), (2) and s. 20 (1)-(4) of the Compulsory Purchase Act 1965; 45 HALSBURY'S STATUTES (2nd Edn.) 92, 108.

As to compensation on compulsory purchase to " short tenancies ", see 10 HALSBURY'S LAWS (3rd Edn.) 221, 222, para. 408; and for cases on the subject, see 11 DIGEST (Repl.) 293-295, *1985-2009.*
I   For the Lands Clauses Consolidation Act, 1845, s. 18 and s. 121, see 3 HALSBURY'S STATUTES (2nd Edn.) 902, *949.*]

Cases referred to:
R. v. *London Corpn.*, (1867), L.R. 2 Q.B. 292; 16 L.T. 280; 11 Digest (Repl.) 142, *222.*

---

* See p. 1198, letter F, post, as regards the tenant's interest when he subsequently held over under s. 24 of the Landlord and Tenant Act, 1954.
† Section 121, so far as material, is set out at p. 1198, letter D, post.
‡ Section 18 is set out at pp. 1197, 1198, letters I to A, post.

Rowton Houses, Ltd.'s Leases, Re, Square Grip Reinforcement Co. (London), Ltd. A
     v. *Rowton Houses, Ltd.*, [1966] 3 All E.R. 996; [1967] Ch. 877; [1967]
     2 W.L.R. 160; Digest (Cont. Vol. B) 121, *200a*.
Selborne (Gowns), Ltd. v. *Ilford Corpn.*, [1962] R.V.R. 301.
Syers v. *Metropolitan Board of Works*, (1877), 36 L.T. 277; 11 Digest (Repl.)
     187, *533*.

Case Stated.

B

The acquiring authority, the London Borough of Newham, appealed to the
Court of Appeal, by notice dated June 20, 1967, against a decision of the Lands
Tribunal given on Jan. 23, 1967, on reference to the tribunal of Mr. Benjamin's,
the claimant's claim for compensation in respect of the compulsory purchase
of premises at 367, Queen's Road, West Ham, E.13, of which the claimant was
the lessee with an unexpired term of less than a year. The order was made   C
on May 30, 1963, was confirmed on July 20, 1965, and on July 30, 1965, notice
to treat was served on the claimant, Mr. Benjamin. Mr. Benjamin acquired
in 1937 a leasehold interest due to expire on June 24, 1966. He held this as
nominee for a company which carried on business at the premises.

By consent an order was made by the tribunal on Feb. 17, 1966, that questions   D
be disposed of as a preliminary point of law, viz., (a) as at the time of the service
of the notice to treat, i.e., on July 30, 1965, the claimant had a term expiring
on June 24, 1966, and as the unexpired residue of the term was less than a year,
that compensation payable (if any) would fall to be determined under s. 121
of the Lands Clauses Consolidation Act, 1845, and not as the claimant contended
under s. 63 of that Act; (b) further, as the acquiring authority had not so far   E
required the claimant to give up possession of the lands occupied by him, that
the notice to treat was of no effect and that the claim for compensation was
premature. The tribunal held that the claimant was entitled to proceed under
s. 63 of the Act of 1845, and that the notice to treat was not to be treated as
null and void, nor the claim as premature. The grounds of the acquiring
authority's appeal were as follows—(i) the tribunal was wrong in interpreting the   F
notice to treat as a document which bound the acquiring authority to purchase
the claimant's interest in the lands and to pay compensation; (ii) the tribunal
failed to recognise that the notice to treat required by s. 18 of the Lands Clauses
Consolidation Act, 1845, was in part exploratory in character; (iii) the tribunal
was wrong in viewing the action necessarily or properly taken by the acquiring
authority under s. 18 as being alternative to the action that might be taken (but
had not been taken) under s. 121 of the Act of 1845; (iv) the tribunal failed to   G
hold that in respect of all " short " tenancies s. 121 defined conclusively the
circumstances in which compensation for the taking of land might be payable
under the Act; (v) the tribunal failed to recognise that s. 37 and s. 39 of the
Landlord and Tenant Act, 1954, provided adequate compensation for a " short "
tenant who was in occupation or who remained in occupation after the expiry   H
of his original interest; (vi) the tribunal wrongly disregarded the clear trend
of the authorities cited before it, and (vii) the tribunal should have held that
the claimant was not entitled to claim compensation under s. 63 of the Act of
1845 and that any other claim by him was premature and ill-founded.

Sir Joseph Molony, Q.C., and *J. D. James* for the acquiring authority.
Ronald Bernstein and *M. S. Rich* for the claimant.   I

LORD DENNING, M.R.: This is a test case on compulsory acquisition.
The question is this: when a local authority compulsorily acquire business premises which are held on a " short tenancy ", at what time is the compensation to
be assessed? The facts are these. The claimant, Mr. Benjamin, has for many years
carried on business at 367, Queen's Road, West Ham, E.13. He had a long lease
from the owners which expired on June 24, 1966. He did not go out on that day.
He continued as tenant under s. 24 of the Landlord and Tenant Act, 1954. He

A is still there as tenant under that Act. Some years before the end of the lease, the acquiring authority wished to acquire the land for redevelopment. On May 30, 1963, it made a compulsory purchase order which was confirmed by the Minister of Housing and Local Government on July 20, 1965. Ten days later on July 30, 1965, the acquiring authority served on the owners and on the claimant a notice to treat. It was in the standard form served on " all the parties interested

B in the lands " which were to be compulsorily acquired. The relevant parts of it for present purposes are:

" Town and Country Planning Act, 1962

" The council [i.e., the acquiring authority] demand of you and each of you the *particulars* of your respective estates and interests in the said lands and hereditaments . . . *and of the claim or claims* made by you and each of

C you . . . within twenty-eight days . . . And the council hereby give you and each of you further notice that the council *are willing to treat* with you and each of you for the purchase of the same . . . And the council having given you and each of you further notice that if for twenty-eight days after the service of this notice . . . you or any of you respectively and the council shall not agree . . . the council will forthwith proceed to require the amount of com-

D pensation payable to you and each of you to be settl :d in the manner directed *by the said Act and the Acts incorporated therewith."*

On Apr. 23, 1965, i.e., within the twenty-eight days stated in the notice, the claimant's surveyors sent to the town clerk their reply to it. They gave particulars of the claimant's interest showing it to be a leasehold interest expiring on June 24,

E 1966. They gave particulars of his claim for compensation, viz., £250 for the value of that interest and £5,640 for disturbance and for injurious affection. No agreement was reached. So on Oct. 25, 1965, the claimant referred the assessment of compensation to the Lands Tribunal. The question then arose as to the time at which compensation was to be assessed. The tribunal ordered it to be tried as a preliminary point of law.

F The point is this: is the compensation to be assessed at once by the Lands Tribunal or is it to be deferred until the acquiring authority require the claimant to give up possession? The President of the Lands Tribunal (Sir Michael Rowe, Q.C.), has given a most careful and valuable decision. He analysed the statutes and the cases. He said that " with great hesitation " he had come to the conclusion that the claimant, Mr. Benjamin, was entitled to proceed at once for compensation under the statute and was not bound to wait until possession

G was required. The acquiring authority now appeals to this court.

The enactments are very complicated. The compulsory purchase order was made under the Town and Country Planning Act, 1962, which incorporates the Acquisition of Land (Authorisation Procedure) Act, 1946, which in turn incorporates the Lands Clauses Consolidation Act, 1845. Reading through those

H statutes, the point comes down to this: if the compensation falls to be assessed under the general " notice to treat " provisions contained in s. 18, s. 23, s. 63 and s. 85 of the Act of 1845, then it is to be assessed at once as at the date of the notice to treat (*Re Rowton Houses, Ltd.'s Leases,* see *Square Grip Reinforcement Co. (London), Ltd.* v. *Rowton Houses, Ltd.* (1), per Danckwerts, L.J.). If the compensation falls, however, to be assessed under the special " short tenancy "

I provision contained in s. 121 of the Act of 1845, then it does not fall to be assessed until the acquiring authority requires possession to be given to it. In either case it is to be assessed by the Lands Tribunal (see the Land Compensation Act, 1961). Section 18 of the Act of 1845 provides:

" When the promoters of the undertaking shall require to purchase or take any of the lands which by this or the special Act, or any Act incorporated therewith, they are authorised to purchase or take, they shall give notice

(1) [1966] 3 All E.R. 996; [1967] Ch. 877.

A

thereof to all the parties interested in such lands, or to the parties enabled
by this Act to sell and convey or release the same, or such of the said parties
as shall, after diligent inquiry, be known to the promoters of the undertaking,
and by such notice shall demand from such parties the particulars of their
estate and interest in such lands, and of the claims made by them in respect
thereof; and every such notice shall state the particulars of the lands so
required, and that the promoters of the undertaking are willing to treat for
the purchase thereof, and as to the compensation to be made to all parties
for the damage that may be sustained by them by reason of the execution
of the works."

B

The acquiring authority here on July 30, 1965, gave a notice to treat to the
claimant which complied with that section. His counsel argues that, having given
it, it cannot go back on it. It says that the acquiring authority is willing to treat
for the purchase of the lands. That invitation was accepted. The party to whom
it is addressed, even on a short tenancy, is entitled, says counsel for the claimant
to take advantage of it at once and to say: " I want my compensation assessed
now." Section 121 of the Act of 1845 provides:

C

" If any such lands shall be in the possession of any person having no
greater interest therein than as a tenant for a year or from year to year,
and if such person be required to give up possession of any lands so occupied
by him before the expiration of his term or interest therein, he shall be
entitled to compensation for the value of his unexpired term or interest in
such lands . . ."

D

Counsel for the acquiring authority says that the interest of the claimant here
was a short tenancy. He argues that, even though a notice to treat was given,
the compensation must be assessed under s. 121, and under that section it does
not fall to be assessed until he is required to give up possession.

E

One thing is clear. On July 30, 1965, when the notice to treat was given, the
claimant had a " short tenancy ": for the simple reason that his lease at that
date had less than one year to run. He had " no greater interest therein than as a
tenant for a year or from year to year " within s. 121 of the Lands Clauses Consolidation Act, 1845. His lease expired on June 24, 1966, and he held over under
the Landlord and Tenant Act, 1954. His interest then too was a " short tenancy "
for it was " no greater than as a tenant . . . from year to year ". It was so held,
quite rightly, by the Lands Tribunal in *Selborne (Gowns), Ltd.* v. *Ilford Corpn.* (2).
It is true that, apart from the compulsory acquisition, he would have been entitled
to apply for a new tenancy. Parliament, however, has enacted that his compensation under s. 121 is to be assessed without regard to his right to apply for a new
tenancy (see s. 39 (1) of the Act of 1954). It expressly says that he is to be no worse
off than if his landlord intended to demolish the premises or wanted them for his
own business (see s. 39 (2)), in which case he would have been compensated by
being paid twice the rateable value (see s. 37 (2) of the Act of 1954.)

F

G

H

Counsel for the claimant accepts that the claimant had a " short tenancy "
within s. 121; but he says that, in the case of short tenancies, the acquiring authority has an option open to it. It can, if it pleases, serve a notice to treat, in
which case it is bound by it and compensation is to be assessed straightaway; or,
alternatively, it can wait until it requires possession and then make a simple
demand for possession, in which case compensation is only assessed when it
requires possession. Counsel for the acquiring authority says, however, that
no such option is open to the authority. It is its duty, he says, under s. 18 to
serve notice to treat on " all the parties interested in the land ". At the time of
serving that notice, it may not know the extent of the interests. It must wait
until it gets the particulars of the interests. If it then appears that the tenant in
possession has a " short tenancy ", there is no alterative open to it. The compensation is to be assessed under s. 121, i.e., when it requires possession, and not before.

I

(2) [1962] R.V.R. 301.

A In short, s. 121 is the exclusive provision for "short tenancies". It is not an alternative to s. 18 but an exception to it.

On the authorities, I think that the argument of counsel for the acquiring authority is correct. It seems to me that s. 18 is a general section dealing with every kind of interest. It must be read subject to s. 121, which is a proviso or exception to it. This was stated clearly by BLACKBURN, J., in *R.* v. *London Corpn.* (3):

B

"Section 121 of the Lands Clauses Consolidation Act, 1845, comes by way of proviso, taking out of the previous general enactment providing for everything, a particular branch for which it makes a particular provision."

It was put plainly by SIR GEORGE JESSEL, M.R., in *Syers* v. *Metropolitan Board of Works* (4):

C

"The first question I have to consider is, whether the heading as to leases was intended to provide altogether for compensation in the cases specially provided for [that includes s. 121] because it is not every lease, but only certain leases, which are provided for. It does appear to me that the sections from s. 119 to s. 122 were intended to be specific provisions for those special cases, and to decide what is to be done in those cases, and to decide it once

D for all."

If that be right, as I think that it is, it follows that all "short tenancies" come under s. 121 of the Act of 1845. Compensation is to be assessed when the tenant is required to give up possession. Even if he is given notice to treat, it only means that compensation is to be assessed "in the manner directed by the said

E Act and the Acts incorporated therewith", i.e., in accordance with s. 121 of the Act of 1845.

It seems to me that the whole object of the legislation was to put short tenancies on a special footing of their own because they were short. In most cases the acquiring authority would not pay any compensation to short tenants. The authority would acquire the reversion and give notice to quit or persuade the previous

F owners to give notice to quit. In that case the tenant would not get any compensation. It is only when the tenant is required to go out earlier, before his short tenancy expires, that he gets his compensation, and he then gets it under s. 121.

I ought to add that counsel for the claimant mentioned to us the provisions of the Acquisition of Land (Authorisation Procedure) Act 1946, Sch. 2, para. 3 (1), under which the acquiring authority can obtain possession "after serving notice to treat" and giving fourteen days' notice. That is a convenient procedure for

G getting possession, but it does not seem to me to alter the fact that for "short tenancies" the compensation is assessed in accordance with s. 121 when the tenant is required to give up possession.

I find myself, therefore, taking a different view from SIR MICHAEL ROWE. I hold that the compensation does not fall to be assessed immediately but waits until possession is required by the acquiring authority. I would allow the appeal

H accordingly.

DANCKWERTS, L.J.: I agree with the judgment of LORD DENNING, M.R., and I do not find it necessary to add more than a few words. It seems to me that s. 121 of the Lands Clauses Consolidation Act, 1845, was a special provision dealing with a special kind of tenancy. They were tenancies which stood on a different

I footing from the other tenancies which were liable to last for some time, or at any rate a definite time. They were tenancies which had less than a year to go before they expired or where there was a tenancy from year to year, and those could at any rate before statutory limits were imposed on the matter, be determined by the acquiring authority waiting for the interest of that tenant to expire by operation of time and then no need for compensation would arise. These

(3) (1867), L.R. 2 Q.B. 292 at p. 300.
(4) (1877), 36 L.T. 277 at p. 278.

were all special cases and required different treatment from other interests in land.   A

Therefore, it was a reasonable provision that compensation should only be payable, as it is under s. 121, if the tenant was turned out before the expiration of the period of his tenancy. That provision was one which was intended, it seems to me, to apply to all these " short tenancies ", a term which has been recognised in the Housing Act, 1957, s. 98. I do not consider that the practice   B of serving a notice to treat in these cases is necessarily wrong. I do not think that the notice to treat was a nullity. It seems to me that the notice to treat can well perform a useful function in announcing to persons concerned the desire of the acquiring authority to acquire the interests in the property. It also has the useful effect of demanding particulars of the interests of the various persons concerned, which, as has been pointed out by counsel for the acquiring authority, may well   C not be known to the authority.

Therefore, I see no incongruity between a notice to treat and the procedure under s. 121. It seems to me they are both perfectly compatible and the assessment of compensation in the case of short tenancies properly falls to be settled under the terms of s. 121 when the tenant is turned out. For these reasons I agree that the appeal should be allowed.   D

WIDGERY, L.J.: I agree with the order proposed and add a few words only, in deference to the argument of counsel for the claimant. It seems to me that s. 121 of the Lands Clauses Consolidation Act, 1845, comprises a simple and comprehensive code for dealing with the interests of a short tenant who is in possession of land sought to be taken by the acquiring authority. It is, I think,   E important to recognise that the procedure under s. 121 contemplates the termination of the tenant's interest, which is to be distinguished from the normal procedure under the earlier sections which compensates for the acquisition of a given interest. I think it would be very surprising if the draftsman of the Act of 1845, having by this simple provision provided for tenants to be compensated by the acquiring authority, also intended that the more cumbersome provision for   F acquisition under s. 18 should apply.

I am quite satisfied that this is a situation in which s. 121 operates by way of proviso, and provides the only means by which the acquiring authority can compulsorily remove a short tenant who is in possession. It follows from that that if the acquiring authority wishes to proceed against a short tenant who is in possession, a notice to treat under s. 18 is not a necessary preliminary step. On   G the other hand, for the reasons which have already been given, it seems to me it is perfectly proper for the acquiring authority to give such a notice if it thinks fit, and that beneficial results may flow from it. One thing which cannot flow from a notice to treat given in such circumstances is the right for either side to treat the case as one in which the tenant's interest is to be acquired under s. 18 and the sections which immediately follow s. 18. Therefore, neither side has the   H right to proceed to assess compensation in the manner contemplated by those sections. I would, therefore, allow the appeal.

Appeal allowed. Leave to appeal to the House of Lords refused.

Solicitors: *Town Clerk*, London Borough of Newham (for the acquiring authority); *Davies, Arnold & Cooper* (for the claimant).

[*Reported by* F. A. AMIES, ESQ., *Barrister-at-Law.*]   I

[END OF VOLUME ONE.]